THE
ALL ENGLAND
LAW REPORTS
1984

Volume 1

Editor
PETER HUTCHESSON LL M
Barrister, New Zealand

Assistant Editor
BROOK WATSON
of Lincoln's Inn, Barrister
and of the New South Wales Bar

Consulting Editor
WENDY SHOCKETT
of Gray's Inn, Barrister

London
BUTTERWORTHS

ENGLAND	Butterworth & Co (Publishers) Ltd 88 Kingsway, **London** WC2B 6AB
AUSTRALIA	Butterworths Pty Ltd, **Sydney, Melbourne, Brisbane, Adelaide** and **Perth**
CANADA	Butterworth & Co (Canada) Ltd, **Toronto** Butterworth & Co (Western Canada) Ltd, **Vancouver**
NEW ZEALAND	Butterworths of New Zealand Ltd, **Wellington**
SINGAPORE	Butterworth & Co (Asia) Pte Ltd, **Singapore**
SOUTH AFRICA	Butterworth Publishers (Pty) Ltd, **Durban**
USA	Butterworth Legal Publishers, **Seattle**, Washington, **Boston**, Massachusetts, **Austin**, Texas and **St Paul**, Minnesota D & S Publishers, **Clearwater**, Florida

©

Butterworth & Co (Publishers) Ltd

1984

ISBN 0 406 85150 6

Typeset by CCC, printed and bound in Great Britain by William Clowes Limited, Beccles and London

REPORTERS

House of Lords

Mary Rose Plummer Barrister

Privy Council

Mary Rose Plummer Barrister

Court of Appeal, Civil Division

Mary Rose Plummer Barrister
Frances Rustin Barrister
Diana Procter Barrister
Carolyn Toulmin Barrister

Diana Brahams Barrister
Patricia Hargrove Barrister
Sophie Craven Barrister

Court of Appeal, Criminal Division

N P Metcalfe Esq Barrister
Dilys Tausz Barrister
Martine Kushner Barrister

April Weiss Barrister
Raina Levy Barrister

Chancery Division

Jacqueline Metcalfe Barrister
Evelyn M C Budd Barrister
Hazel Hartman Barrister
Vivian Horvath Barrister

Queen's Bench Division

David Bartlett Esq Barrister
M Denise Chorlton Barrister

J M Collins Esq Barrister
K Mydeen Esq Barrister

Family Division

Bebe Chua Barrister

Admiralty

N P Metcalfe Esq Barrister

Revenue Cases

Rengan Krishnan Esq Barrister
Clare Mainprice Barrister

Courts-Martial Appeals

N P Metcalfe Esq Barrister

SUB-EDITOR

Radhika Edwards Barrister

MANAGER

John W Wilkes Esq

House of Lords

The Lord High Chancellor: Lord Hailsham of St Marylebone

Lords of Appeal in Ordinary

Lord Diplock
Lord Fraser of Tullybelton
Lord Keith of Kinkel
Lord Scarman
Lord Roskill

Lord Bridge of Harwich
Lord Brandon of Oakbrook
Lord Brightman
Lord Templeman

Court of Appeal

The Lord High Chancellor

The Lord Chief Justice of England: Lord Lane
(President of the Criminal Division)

The Master of the Rolls: Sir John Francis Donaldson
(President of the Civil Division)

The President of the Family Division: Sir John Lewis Arnold

The Vice-Chancellor: Sir Robert Edgar Megarry

Lords Justices of Appeal

Sir John Frederick Eustace Stephenson
Sir Frederick Horace Lawton
Sir George Stanley Waller
Sir James Roualeyn Hovell-Thurlow-
  Cumming-Bruce
Sir Edward Walter Eveleigh
Sir Desmond James Conrad Ackner
Sir Robin Horace Walford Dunn
Sir Peter Raymond Oliver
Sir Tasker Watkins VC
Sir Patrick McCarthy O'Connor
Sir William Hugh Griffiths

Sir Michael John Fox
Sir Michael Robert Emanuel Kerr
Sir John Douglas May
Sir Christopher John Slade
Sir Francis Brooks Purchas
Sir Robert Lionel Archibald Goff
Sir George Brian Hugh Dillon
Sir Stephen Brown
Sir Roger Jocelyn Parker
Sir Nicolas Christopher Henry Browne-
  Wilkinson

Chancery Division

The Lord High Chancellor

The Vice-Chancellor

Sir John Norman Keates Whitford
Sir Ernest Irvine Goulding
Sir Raymond Henry Walton
Sir John Evelyn Vinelott
Sir Martin Charles Nourse
Sir Douglas William Falconer

Sir Jean-Pierre Frank Eugene Warner
Sir Peter Leslie Gibson
Sir David Herbert Mervyn Davies
Sir Jeremiah LeRoy Harman
Sir Donald James Nicholls
Sir Richard Rashleigh Folliott Scott

Queen's Bench Division

The Lord Chief Justice of England

Sir Joseph Donaldson Cantley
Sir Hugh Eames Park
Sir Bernard Caulfield
Sir William Lloyd Mars-Jones
Sir Ralph Kilner Brown
Sir Peter Henry Rowley Bristow
Sir Hugh Harry Valentine Forbes
Sir David Powell Croom-Johnson
Sir Leslie Kenneth Edward Boreham
Sir Alfred William Michael Davies
Sir John Dexter Stocker
Sir Kenneth George Illtyd Jones
Sir Haydn Tudor Evans
Sir Peter Richard Pain
Sir Kenneth Graham Jupp
Sir Ralph Brian Gibson
Sir Walter Derek Thornley Hodgson
Sir James Peter Comyn
Sir Anthony John Leslie Lloyd
Sir Frederick Maurice Drake
Sir Brian Thomas Neill
Sir Michael John Mustill
Sir Barry Cross Sheen
Sir David Bruce McNeill
Sir Harry Kenneth Woolf

Sir Christopher James Saunders French
Sir Thomas Patrick Russell
Sir Peter Edlin Webster
Sir Thomas Henry Bingham
Sir Iain Derek Laing Glidewell
Sir Henry Albert Skinner
Sir Peter Murray Taylor
Sir Murray Stuart-Smith
Sir Christopher Stephen Thomas Jonathan
    Thayer Staughton
Sir Donald Henry Farquharson
Sir Anthony James Denys McCowan
Sir Iain Charles Robert McCullough
Sir Hamilton John Leonard
Sir Alexander Roy Asplan Beldam
Sir David Cozens-Hardy Hirst
Sir John Stewart Hobhouse
Sir Michael Mann
Sir Andrew Peter Leggatt
Sir Michael Patrick Nolan
Sir Oliver Bury Popplewell
Sir William Alan Macpherson
Sir Philip Howard Otton
Sir Paul Joseph Morrow Kennedy
Sir Michael Hutchison

Family Division

The President of the Family Division

Sir John Brinsmead Latey
Sir Alfred Kenneth Hollings
Sir Charles Trevor Reeve
Dame Rose Heilbron
Sir Brian Drex Bush
Sir Alfred John Balcombe
Sir John Kember Wood
Sir Ronald Gough Waterhouse

Sir John Gervase Kensington Sheldon
Sir Thomas Michael Eastham
Dame Margaret Myfanwy Wood Booth
Sir Anthony Leslie Julian Lincoln
Dame Ann Elizabeth Oldfield Butler-Sloss
Sir Anthony Bruce Ewbank
Sir John Douglas Waite
Sir Anthony Barnard Hollis

CITATION

These reports are cited thus:

[1984] 1 All ER

REFERENCES

These reports contain references to the following major works of legal reference described in the manner indicated below.

Halsbury's Laws of England

The reference 26 Halsbury's Laws (4th edn) para 577 refers to paragraph 577 on page 296 of volume 26 of the fourth edition of Halsbury's Laws of England and the reference 37 Halsbury's Laws (3rd edn) 135, para 239 refers to paragraph 239 on page 135 of volume 37 of the third edition.

Halsbury's Statutes of England

The reference 5 Halsbury's Statutes (3rd edn) 302 refers to page 302 of volume 5 of the third edition of Halsbury's Statutes of England.

The Digest

References are to the green band reissue volumes and the blue band replacement volumes of The Digest (formerly the English and Empire Digest), and to the continuation volumes.

The reference 36(2) Digest (Reissue) 764, *1398* refers to case number 1398 on page 764 of Digest Green Band Reissue Volume 36(2).

The reference 47 Digest (Repl) 781, *25* refers to case number 25 on page 781 of Digest Blue Band Replacement Volume 47.

The reference Digest (Cont Vol E) 640, *2392a* refers to case number 2392a on page 640 of Digest Continuation Volume E.

Halsbury's Statutory Instruments

The reference 20 Halsbury's Statutory Instruments (4th reissue) 302 refers to page 302 of the fourth reissue of volume 20 of Halsbury's Statutory Instruments; references to other reissues are similar.

Cases reported in volume 1

Digest of cases reported in volume 1

CORRIGENDA

[1983] 1 All ER
p 1097. **Practice Direction.** Paragraph 3 should read: 'The "independent" reporter may not see a report by the court welfare officer. This is confidential to the parties and the court.' and not as printed.

[1983] 3 All ER
p 450. **R v Wilson (Clarence).** Counsel for the respondents E J and R P Jenkins should read '*Anthony Scrivener QC* and *Gregory Stone*'.

[1984] 1 All ER
p 32. **Re J (a minor).** Line *d*4 should read '. . . limited as they are by statute, do *not* extend . . .'
p 344. **R v Governor of Brixton Prison, ex p Walsh.** Lines *j*3 and *j*4 should read '. . . a pre-existing duty in the governor of a prison to bring *up* a lawfully detained person . . .'
p 627. **R v Ayres.** Solicitors for the appellant should read '*Hatchett Jones & Kidgell*, agents for *Wolferstans*, Plymouth'.
p 669. **Hamilton v Martell Securities Ltd.** Line *a*5 should read 'Whereas he *is liable to contribute* part of the cost of repair . . .'

Alcom Ltd v Republic of Colombia
b ## (Barclays Bank plc and another, garnishees)

COURT OF APPEAL, CIVIL DIVISION
SIR JOHN DONALDSON MR, MAY AND DILLON LJJ
21, 24 OCTOBER 1983

c *Constitutional law – Foreign sovereign state – Immunity from suit – Enforcement proceedings – Exceptions – Commercial transactions – Default judgment obtained against foreign sovereign state in respect of claim for sale of goods – Plaintiff obtaining garnishee orders nisi to attach moneys in foreign state's accounts at London banks – Ambassador certifying that accounts used or intended for use in day-to-day running expenses of embassy in London – Whether such running expenses included as commercial transactions – Whether foreign state entitled to claim immunity*
d *from enforcement in respect of accounts – State Immunity Act 1978, ss 3(1)(3), 13(4), 17(1).*

In June 1982 the plaintiffs issued a writ against the defendant, a friendly foreign sovereign state with an accredited diplomatic mission in the United Kingdom, claiming a sum of money in respect of goods sold and delivered. In December the plaintiffs obtained judgment in default of notice of intention to defend, and subsequently sought to levy
e execution against moneys in bank accounts held to the credit of the defendant's embassy in London. In September 1983 the plaintiffs obtained garnishee orders nisi against the respective accounts. The defendant state applied to the High Court to discharge the orders, claiming immunity from execution under the provisions of the State Immunity Act 1978. By s 3(1)(a)ᵈ of the 1978 Act a state was not immune from proceedings relating to 'commercial transactions' entered into by the state, such transactions being defined by
f s 3(3)ᵇ as including 'any contract for the supply of goods or services . . . and any other transaction or activity (whether of a commercial, industrial, financial, professional or other similar character) into which a State enters or in which it engages otherwise than in the exercise of sovereign authority'. Furthermore, by s 13(4)ᶜ a state was not immune from the enforcement of a judgment against property which was used or intended to be used by it for 'commercial purposes', which by s 17(1)ᵈ were defined as the purposes of
g commercial transactions. In claiming immunity, the defendant's ambassador certified that the funds in the bank accounts were not used or intended for use for commercial purposes but to meet the expenditure necessarily incurred in the day-to-day running of the diplomatic mission. Under s 13(5) such a certificate was sufficient evidence that the property against which enforcement was sought was not used for commercial purposes unless the contrary was proved. The judge held, inter alia, that a bank account used for
h an embassy was prima facie non-commercial and he discharged the garnishee orders nisi. The plaintiffs appealed. On the appeal the question arose whether funds in bank accounts used for the day-to-day expenditure of an embassy were used or intended for use for 'commercial transactions' and therefore property against which execution could be levied.

j **Held** – Since the purpose of a bank account for the day-to-day running expenses of an

---

a Section 3(1) is set out at p 3 *b*, post
b Section 3(3) is set out at p 3 *j*, post
c Section 13, so far as material, is set out at p 3 *d* to *f*, post
d Section 17(1), so far as material, is set out at p 3 *h*, post

embassy was to assist the embassy in paying for goods and services and entering into
other transactions which enabled it to function, the purpose of such an account was a   *a*
'commercial purpose' within s 17(1) of the 1978 Act, having regard to the wide
interpretation which was to be given to the terms 'commercial transactions' and
'commercial purposes' in ss 3(3) and 17(1) of that Act and the fact that the Act made no
distinction between consumer payments and commercial activities. The moneys in the
embassy's bank accounts were accordingly property used or intended to be used for
commercial purposes and as such were, under s 13(4) of the 1978 Act, not immune from   *b*
the levying of execution. The appeal would accordingly be allowed and the garnishee
orders nisi restored (see p 5 *f g* and p 6 *d* to *h*, post).

Dictum of Lord Bridge in *I Congreso del Partido* [1981] 2 All ER at 1083 considered.

Notes

For sovereign and diplomatic immunity from suit, see 8 Halsbury's Laws (4th edn) para   *c*
410 and 18 ibid para 1548, and for cases on the subject, see 1(1) Digest (Reissue) 54–59,
358–382.

For the State Immunity Act 1978, ss 3, 13, 17, see 48 Halsbury's Statutes (3rd edn) 90,
96, 99.

Case referred to in judgments   *d*

I Congreso del Partido [1981] 2 All ER 1064, [1983] AC 244, [1981] 3 WLR 328, HL.

Interlocutory appeal

The plaintiffs, Alcom Ltd, appealed with the leave of the judge against the judgment of
Hobhouse J dated 21 October 1983 whereby he ordered to be set aside the garnishee
orders nisi made by Master Topley on 27 September 1983 ordering Barclays Bank plc and   *e*
the First National Bank of Boston to attach such sum standing to the credit of the
defendant, the Republic of Colombia, as would satisfy the judgment of £41,690·56 and
£147·50 costs obtained by the plaintiffs on 10 December 1982. The facts are set out in
the judgment of Sir John Donaldson MR.

Stephen Desch QC and *Richard Slowe* for the plaintiffs.   *f*
Anthony Thompson QC and *Timothy Saloman* for the defendant.

SIR JOHN DONALDSON MR. This appeal raises a novel question: can you garnishee
the London bank accounts of an accredited diplomatic mission? The accounts concerned
are those of the Colombian Embassy. The ambassador has certified that they are used and
are intended to be used only to meet the expenditure necessarily incurred in the day-to-   *g*
day running of the mission. On 21 October 1983 Hobhouse J on this evidence set aside
garnishee orders nisi which had been granted to the plaintiffs, and the plaintiffs now
appeal. For my part, I should very much have preferred to have been able to reserve
judgment, but the matter is one of extreme urgency because, until this appeal is disposed
of, the accounts remain frozen. Accordingly, it seems to me right that, whatever the
imperfections of expression which will flow from taking that course, we should give   *h*
judgment forthwith.

The history of the matter is that the plaintiffs issued a writ against the Republic of
Colombia claiming £41,690·56 in respect of goods sold and delivered together with
interest and costs. In due course they succeeded in signing judgment in default of a
notice of intention to defend. We have been told this morning that the defendant
republic intends to apply to set that judgment aside on the grounds that leave to serve   *j*
out of the jurisdiction should not have been given and that there were irregularities as to
service. In fairness to the defendant, I should add that it has also been indicated that it
will in due course be urging on the court that it has merits in the sense that it will be
contending that there never was a contract for the sale of these goods, that in any event
no prices were agreed and that the prices which have been claimed are excessive. But

a those proceedings have not yet been issued, or, at all events, had not been issued before the short adjournment, and for the purposes of deciding this appeal it therefore has to be assumed that the judgment is regular.

We know very little about the contract for the sale of goods which forms the basis of the judgment, although we were told that it related to some security equipment required for the embassy. It is, of course, accepted that the Republic of Colombia is a friendly foreign sovereign state, but that of itself does not provide the state with immunity from *b* proceedings since s 3(1) of the State Immunity Act 1978 provides:

'A State is not immune as respects proceedings relating to—(a) a commercial transaction entered into by the State; or (b) an obligation of the State which by virtue of a contract (whether a commercial transaction or not) falls to be performed wholly or partly in the United Kingdom.'

c So much is common ground. But, when it comes to levying execution on a bank account, there are special provisions, and the defendant submits that there is no basis for issuing garnishee proceedings against these accounts. Again the issue turns on the provisions of the 1978 Act. The key sections are as follows. Section 13 provides:

'... (2) Subject to subsections (3) and (4) below ... (b) the property of a State shall not be subject to any process for the enforcement of a judgment or arbitration award *d* or, in an action in rem, for its arrest, detention or sale ...

(4) Subsection (2)(b) above does not prevent the issue of any process in respect of property which is for the time being in use or intended for use for commercial purposes; but, in a case not falling within section 10 above, this subsection applies to property of a State party to the European Convention on State Immunity only if [and then two conditions are set out in paras (a) and (b); I need not read them because *e* the Republic of Colombia is necessarily not a party to the European Convention].

(5) The head of a State's diplomatic mission in the United Kingdom, or the person for the time being performing his functions, shall be deemed to have authority to give on behalf of the State any such consent as is mentioned in subsection (3) above and, for the purposes of subsection (4) above, his certificate to the effect that any *f* property is not in use or intended for use by or on behalf of the State for commercial purposes shall be accepted as sufficient evidence of that fact unless the contrary is proved ...'

I next turn to s 14(4), which provides:

'Property of a State's central bank or other monetary authority shall not be regarded for the purposes of subsection (4) of section 13 above as in use or intended *g* for use for commercial purposes; and where any such bank or authority is a separate entity subsections (1) to (3) of that section shall apply to it as if references to a State were references to the bank or authority.'

The credit balances on these accounts were not, of course, the property of the Central Bank of Colombia.

h Section 17(1) is a definition section, and it defines 'commercial purposes' as meaning 'purposes of such transactions or activities as are mentioned in section 3(3) above'. That takes me to s 3(3), which is in the following terms:

'In this section "commercial transaction" means—(a) any contract for the supply of goods or services; (b) any loan or other transaction for the provision of finance and *j* any guarantee or indemnity in respect of any such transaction or of any other financial obligation; and (c) any other transaction or activity (whether of a commercial, industrial, financial, professional or other similar character) into which a State enters or in which it engages otherwise than in the exercise of sovereign authority; but neither paragraph of subsection (1) above applies to a contract of employment between a State and an individual.'

In my judgment, there can be no real doubt that the chose in action constituted by a credit balance on a bank account is 'property' within the meaning of that word in both   *a*
sub-ss (2)(*b*) and (4) of s 13. Were it otherwise there would be no need for s 14(4), the section referring to central banks.

It follows that the issue is whether the plaintiffs can bring themselves within s 13(4). This in its turn depends on whether the credit balances are 'for the time being in use or intended for use for commercial purposes'. Incorporating the relevant definitions derived from ss 17(1) and 3(3), this test can be rewritten as follows: are these credit balances in   *b*
use or intended for use for purposes (a) of any contract for the supply of goods or services, (b) of any loan or other transaction for the provision of finance, (c) of any guarantee or indemnity in respect of any such transaction, (d) of any other financial obligation, or (e) of any other transaction or activity (whether of a commercial, industrial, financial, professional or other similar character) into which a state enters or in which it engages otherwise than in the exercise of sovereign authority?   *c*

Counsel for the defendant does not accept this test because he submits that the words 'otherwise than in the exercise of sovereign authority' govern paras (*a*) and (*b*) as well as para (*c*) of s 3(3). He supports this by reference to the words 'any other transaction', arguing that since the 'other transactions' are those which do not involve the exercise of a sovereign authority, the preceding transactions to which they are 'other' must be subject to a similar restriction. He says that this is an application of the ejusdem generis   *d*
rule.

For my part, I fear that I am quite unable to accept that construction. Had Parliament so intended, it would have cast the section in such a way as to remove the words 'into which a State enters or in which it engages otherwise than in the exercise of sovereign authority' from para (*c*) and put them in the same position as the words 'but neither paragraph of sub-s (1) above applies to a contract of employment between a state and an   *e*
individual' so as to make it clear that they governed all three paragraphs. There would also have been other ways no doubt of achieving the same result as a matter of drafting, but that is the obvious way of doing it. Indeed, at one stage I did seriously wonder whether, acting without authority, the Queen's Printer had wholly altered the sense of the 1978 Act by misplacing the words, but there has been no suggestion that that is the case and, indeed, it is an extremely unlikely hypothesis. I fear that we have to construe   *f*
the section in the way in which it is printed.

I should have added that, in setting out this test in extenso, I have omitted the reference to the contracts of employment which is contained in sub-s (3) since that part of the subsection is relevant only to s 3(1).

The plaintiffs have adduced no evidence to contradict the ambassador's certificate which was, in full, in the following terms: *g*

'The funds deposited by the Colombian Embassy in its bank accounts at [then he names the bank accounts] are not in use nor intended for use for commercial purposes but only to meet the expenditure necessarily incurred in the day to day running of the Diplomatic Mission.'

The plaintiffs submit that they have no need for such evidence, since the certificate   *h*
contradicts itself. In their submission, expenditure incurred in the day-to-day running of a diplomatic mission will always be intended for use for commercial purposes, giving that phrase the very wide meaning attributed to it by the 1978 Act, and bearing in mind that the words 'commercial transaction' are used purely as a term of art in the Act and that accordingly their ordinary meaning is no reliable guide to the meaning which they are intended to bear in context.   *j*

Hobhouse J rejected this submission on the following grounds, and I quote from counsel's note of his judgment. He said under the heading 'My reasons':

'(1) One must construe the Act against the general background of general principles of international law which include [the] well-established distinction between state and trading activities. (2) One must have regard not only to the paragraphs of s 3(3) but also to the phrases "commercial purposes" and "commercial transaction". If the activities are not ordinary commercial purposes but consumer activities one must not strain the language. (3) The examples given by Mr Slowe [counsel for the plaintiffs] are covered by s 3(1)(b) [and I ought to add by way of explanation that the examples to which he is referring were paying people who supply goods and services to the embassy]. (4) In the light of s 13 one must consider the primary not the secondary purposes. The primary purpose of the account is running an embassy. (5) The point made by [the plaintiffs] proves too much because it means nothing short of an act of State would take a transaction outside the section. If one pursues [the plaintiffs'] argument all the way all money is going to be used for commercial purposes and [is] subject to execution. In my opinion a bank account used for an embassy is prima facie non-commercial. If I were wrong and buying services for the embassy is commercial, no one is entitled to assume the account is not used for non-commercial purposes, eg paying the ambassador, paying officials who come over from [Colombia], helping stranded citizens of [Colombia] in [the United Kingdom]. None of those [are] commercial purposes. [Therefore it is] not made out that the account is wholly or predominantly commercial. A [garnishee] order attaches [to] the whole account. The account does not distinguish between the two purposes. [Therefore] even on a construction favourable to the plaintiffs the [garnishee] orders must at least in part offend against the Act and [therefore] must be set aside. If hereafter evidence is placed before the court to show certain moneys are used for commercial purposes it may be possible for a court to make a [garnishee] order nisi.'

I agree that, if the 1978 Act is ambiguous, a court is entitled to have regard to the general principles of international law and to resolve that ambiguity in the way most consistent with those principles. However, those principles appear to require a court to have regard to the transactions under scrutiny rather than to the reasons why the transactions were undertaken. This was pointed out by Lord Bridge in I Congreso del Partido [1981] 2 All ER 1064 at 1083, [1983] AC 244 at 278 where he gave as an example of a commercial, trading or private law transaction the ordering of uniforms for the maintenance of the army, the latter being a sovereign function. In any event, I can detect no ambiguity in the 1978 Act.

The judge's view that regard must be had to the primary purpose of running the embassy rather than the secondary purpose of paying for goods and services seems to me to involve falling into the very error to which Lord Bridge drew attention and to be devoid of justification in fact or on the wording of the Act. The purpose of money in a bank account can never be 'to run an embassy'. It can only be to pay for goods and services or to enter into other transactions which enable the embassy to be run. Again I can find no trace of wording in the Act which could justify the distinction between commercial and consumer activities.

Hobhouse J was clearly concerned with the width of the definition of 'commercial transaction' for which the plaintiffs were arguing and thought that, if accepted, no diplomatic mission's funds would be free from attachment. I think that there are two answers to this comment. The first is that a mission could have drawing powers on a London account which was not that of the state, but of its central bank. That account would then have the protection of s 14(4). The second is that the real protection for missions lies in the jurisdictional provisions of s 3(1). If the state is amenable to the jurisdiction of the English courts in accordance with that subsection, there seems no logical reason why its money should not be attachable in satisfaction of a judgment. Protected property, such as the mission's buildings, is obviously in a different category, but such buildings are not used for commercial purposes.

There remains the alternative basis of the judge's judgment, namely that a garnishee order attaches to the whole of any credit balance and that the court accordingly needs to be satisfied that the whole balance is intended for use for commercial purposes. This seems to me to be correct in principle. Accordingly, all three members of the court pressed counsel for the defendant to give examples of expenditure incurred in the day-to-day running of the embassy which did not fall within the very wide definition of *a* 'commercial transactions' contained in s 3(3).

The examples given by the judge do not seem to me to bear out his thesis. The payment of the salary of the ambassador or other embassy officials might indeed be outside the definition, although I can see an argument to the contrary, but it is conceded that they are not in fact paid out of these accounts. His other example, expenditure designed to help stranded citizens, would be incurred for the purpose of a commercial *b* transaction, as defined, being either expenditure for the purpose of a contract for the supply of services, for example an air ticket, or a loan or, if a gift or grant to the person concerned, a transaction or activity otherwise than in the exercise of sovereign authority. Counsel for the defendant added for our consideration the rebate of duty on hydrocarbon oil. This comes into the argument in this way. It is suggested that, if the first secretary uses his car and buys petrol for it, the embassy can claim a rebate on the fuel duty and on *c* the value added tax. This rebate will be paid into the embassy account and then paid out to the first secretary. For my part I do not understand why this does not fall within para (*c*) of s 3(3) as 'another transaction or activity into which a State enters or in which it engages otherwise than in the exercise of sovereign authority'.

Accordingly, I am quite unable to accept the ambassador's certificate. Let me make it quite clear that, when I say that, I am not in any way impugning either the ambassador's *d* integrity or the certificate itself. I fully accept that it was given in the utmost good faith and no doubt was given on the basis of advice. The ambassador quite clearly took the view that the running of an embassy was a non-commercial activity, and I am bound to say that I entirely agree with him as a matter of common sense and looking at it broadly. However, we are constrained to look at it in terms of the definition contained in the 1978 Act of Parliament, and on that basis I have to reject his conclusion, which appears in the *e* first part of the certificate, because of the reasons which appear in the second part of the certificate.

Both the ambassador, in his affidavit, and counsel for the defendant, in his argument, have stressed the disruptive effect of the garnishee order. We have been told that the telex can no longer be used, because the ambassador cannot be sure when he will be able to pay for the service. Indeed, short of financing the embassy out of his own pocket or *f* persuading the government of Colombia to remit further funds to this country, I can quite see that the embassy may be brought to a standstill. This is a very remarkable result and one which may well not have been intended by Parliament. Unfortunately we are bound to give effect to parliamentary intentions as expressed in the statute, and in my judgment, under the terms of the statute, the embassy's bank accounts are available to satisfy any regular judgment against the State of Colombia. *g*

For those reasons I would allow the appeal and would restore the garnishee orders nisi.

MAY LJ. I too have been considerably concerned about this case. However, in the end I think that the wording of the relevant parts of ss 3, 13 and 17 of the State Immunity Act 1978 is clear and that its application to the facts of the case as they are before us has the result arrived at by Sir John Donaldson MR. *h*

I too would allow the appeal.

DILLON LJ. I agree.

Appeal allowed. Leave to appeal to the House of Lords granted.

Solicitors: *William T Stockler* (for the plaintiffs); *Boodle Hatfield & Co* (for the defendant).

Diana Procter   Barrister.

a

Shove v Downs Surgical plc

QUEEN'S BENCH DIVISION
SHEEN J
11, 12, 20, 21, 22, 29 JULY 1983

b *Contract – Damages for breach – Wrongful dismissal – Income tax – Damages awarded subject to taxation – Whether burden of taxation in hands of plaintiff too remote – Whether court to award sum to compensate actual or net loss.*

Since a plaintiff's liability to pay income tax is not too remote to be taken into account when determining or estimating his actual loss for wrongful dismissal and since the damages to which he is entitled will be taxable in his hands, his liability to pay income
c tax is not to be regarded as too remote when assessing the damages to be awarded to him to compensate him for his actual loss. It follows that in awarding damages the court will estimate the net amount which would have been received by the plaintiff after deduction of income tax from his gross income and will then add an amount equivalent to his estimated income tax so that the net amount represents as realistically as possible the actual loss suffered (see p 9 g to j and p 10 c, post).
d Dicta of Lord Reid in *British Transport Commission v Gourley* [1955] 3 All ER at 808, of Lord Reid in *Taylor v O'Connor* [1970] 1 All ER at 368 and *Stewart v Glentaggart Ltd* 1963 SC 300 followed.

Notes
e For the incidence of tax on damages, see 12 Halsbury's Laws (4th edn) para 1155, and for cases on the subject, see 17 Digest (Reissue) 88–90, *34–36, 45*.

Cases referred to in judgment
Addis v Gramophone Co Ltd [1909] AC 488, [1908–10] All ER Rep 1, HL.
British Transport Commission v Gourley [1955] 3 All ER 796, [1956] AC 185, [1956] 2 WLR
f   41, HL.
Cox v Philips Industries Ltd [1976] 3 All ER 161, [1976] 1 WLR 638.
Radford v De Froberville [1978] 1 All ER 33, [1977] 1 WLR 1262.
Robinson v Harman (1848) 1 Exch 850, [1843–60] All ER Rep 383, 154 ER 363.
Stewart v Glentaggart Ltd 1963 SC 300.
Taylor v O'Connor [1970] 1 All ER 365, [1971] AC 115, [1970] 2 WLR 472, HL.
g

Action
By a writ issued on 12 October 1982 the plaintiff, Norman Granvill Shove, claimed against the defendants, Downs Surgical plc, damages for summary dismissal of the plaintiff as sole managing director of the defendants without giving 30 months' notice in breach of an agreement made under seal on 15 December 1980. The facts are set out in
h the judgment.

Philip Naughton for the plaintiff.
G Caws for the defendants.

j   *Cur adv vult*

29 July. The following judgment was delivered.

SHEEN J. In this action the plaintiff claims damages from the defendants for breach of his contract of employment. The defendants have admitted liability. My task is to assess the damages to which the plaintiff is entitled. That raises a number of questions which have been forcefully contested before me.   *a*

The plaintiff was born in England on 14 April 1920. On 1 July 1937 he commenced training with Down Bros Ltd, a company in the same group as the defendant company. The plaintiff served in the army for six years during the 1939–45 war. Apart from those six years, his whole career has been with companies in the Downs group. The plaintiff served the Downs group of companies in Canada and the United States of America for a number of years but returned to the London office as a director of sales in 1972. He   *b* became chairman of the board and joint managing director in 1977 and was chairman and managing director in 1981–82. In July 1982 the plaintiff became ill. On 29 July he was admitted to hospital in North Cheam where he underwent coronary bypass surgery on 19 August. He was able to return to his home on 27 August. On 25 August 1982, there was a special meeting of the directors of the defendant company in respect of which a note appears in these terms: *c*

'Following discussions with the company's merchant bankers and stockbrokers and after lengthy consideration by the Board, it was agreed unanimously that the Board no longer had any confidence in [the plaintiff], either as Chairman or Managing Director, and that it was in the best interests of shareholders, employees and creditors for him to leave the company.'   *d*

On 7 September 1982 Mr Barnes and Mr Howe called on the plaintiff, who was convalescing at his home, and handed him a letter dated 6 September, which was a repudiation of the contract of employment. By letter dated 24 September 1982 a firm of solicitors, Messrs Rowe & Maw, on behalf of the plaintiff accepted that repudiation subject to his right to damages. He received his salary and other benefits until 30 September 1982.   *e*

At the relevant time the terms of employment of the plaintiff were contained in an agreement made on 15 December 1980, under which the plaintiff was entitled to not less than 30 calendar months' notice in writing of the termination of his employment. There can be no doubt that the plaintiff is entitled to recover such sum as will make good to him the financial loss which he has suffered and will probably suffer as a result of the wrongful termination of his contract of employment.   *f*

No evidence was given on behalf of the defendants. I do not know what was in the minds of the directors of the defendant company who decided to terminate the employment of the plaintiff so abruptly. Any man who has served a company loyally for a period of over 40 years is entitled to be treated with consideration. When he is ill he ought, as a matter of ordinary humanity, to be treated with both sympathy and tolerance. The manner in which the plaintiff's service to the defendant company was terminated   *g* suggests that the remaining directors of the company were unconcerned with such precepts and impervious to the distress which would inevitably be caused to the plaintiff.

In the letter of 6 September 1982, to which I have already referred, Mr Michael Barnes, who had acted as chairman at the board meeting, wrote:

'It would be in the best interests of all concerned if you were prepared to make a   *h* dignified exit on grounds of ill health. If however you decide not to do this the board will take the other route and break your contract. This will probably harm you more than us and is something which we should prefer to avoid.'

The only way in which this court can remedy the wrong which was done to the plaintiff is by an award of damages. I must start by deciding what principles are applicable in the assessment of damages and then apply those principles to the facts of this case. I   *j* can think of no better way of starting than that adopted by Oliver J in *Radford v De Froberville* [1978] 1 All ER 33 at 40, [1977] 1 WLR 1262 at 1268:

'As to principle, I take my starting point from what, I think, is the universal starting point in any enquiry of this nature—that is to say, the well-known statement a of Parke B in *Robinson v Harman* (1848) 1 Exch 850 at 855, [1843–60] All ER Rep 383 at 385, which is in these terms: "The rule of the common law is, that where a party sustains a loss by reason of a breach of contract, he is, so far as money can do it, to be placed in the same situation, with respect to damages, as if the contract had been performed".'

In *British Transport Commission v Gourley* [1955] 3 All ER 796 at 808, [1956] AC 185 at b 212 Lord Reid stated the general principle on which damages are assessed and then said:

> 'But the general principle is subject to one qualification. A loss which the plaintiff has suffered, or will suffer, or a compensatory gain which has come, or will come, to him, following on the accident may be of a kind which the law regards as too remote to be taken into account. In my judgment, the real question in this case is whether the plaintiff's liability to pay taxes is something which the law must regard
c as too remote when determining or estimating what he has lost as a result of the accident. The defendant is only bound to pay damages based on an assessment of the plaintiff's actual and prospective loss taking into account all those factors which are not in law too remote. It has sometimes been said that tax liability should not be taken into account because it is res inter alios. That appears to me to be a wrong approach. Let me take the case of a professional man who is injured so that he can
d no longer earn an income. Before his accident he earned fees and he paid rent and rates for his office, the salaries of clerks, the expenses of running a car and other outgoings, and he would have continued to do so if he had not been injured. Apart from one matter to which I shall refer later, I cannot see why these expenses are any less res inter alios than his payments of income tax in respect of his net earnings. Indeed, he could not avoid liability to pay tax, but he might have been able to
e diminish his outgoings if he had chosen to spend more time and effort himself on his work, or in travelling in the course of his work. Yet no one would suggest that it is improper to take into account expenditure genuinely and reasonably incurred, or that the plaintiff's damages should be assessed on the fees which he would have continued to receive without regard to the outgoings which he would have continued to incur.'

f In the same case Lord Goddard said ([1955] 3 All ER 796 at 806–807, [1956] AC 185 at 210):

> '. . . generally, damages must be decided by the application of reasonable common sense. The principles set out above would be applicable in wrongful dismissal actions, in which the court has to calculate damages for loss of earnings which would
g have been subject to tax had they been earned.'

In *Gourley's* case the damages awarded were not subject to diminution by taxation in the hands of the plaintiff. In the instant case the damages to which the plaintiff is entitled will be taxable in his hands. They will be taxable whether or not I accept all the submissions made on behalf of the defendants. This has given rise to much debate as to
h the correct principle to be applied. On one view of such a case it is said that, because the income of which the plaintiff has been deprived and the damages which he will receive are both taxable, the court should ignore taxation altogether. At the other extreme it was argued that the correct principle is to start by estimating the net amount which would have been received by the plaintiff after the deduction of tax from his gross income. That net amount would represent as realistically as possible his actual loss. Thereafter, in
j assessing the damages, the court should take into account the plaintiff's liability to tax on the damages awarded so that the net amount received should, so far as possible, equal the net or actual loss suffered. This was the approach adopted by the Outer House in *Stewart v Glentaggart Ltd* 1963 SC 300. Payments made on retirement or removal from office or employment are liable to tax, if at all, by virtue of s 187 of the Income and Corporation Taxes Act 1970. The first £25,000 of any such payment is exempt from liability to tax.

This tax-free bracket (up to £25,000) has led to a third and intermediate approach to the question how damages should be assessed in a case such as the instant one. It is argued that, if the award of damages is less than £25,000, then the principle in *Gourley's* case is applicable; but, if the award of damages exceeds £25,000, then some other principle must apply. It seems to me that such an approach must lead to problems bordering on the absurd. The assessment of the income tax which a plaintiff would have had to pay if his employment had not been terminated cannot be made with precision. The facts of this case demonstrate that. Now let it be supposed that, after assessing the probable liability to tax and deducting that sum from the gross income which a man would have received but for the wrongful termination of his employment, the difference is a sum which is a few pounds more than £25,000. On that hypothesis, is the court bound to apply different principles from those which would have been applied if the result had been a few pounds less than £25,000? I do not think that that can be correct.

It seems to me that if, in assessing the plaintiff's actual loss, his liability to pay taxes is something which the law does not regard as too remote then by parity of reasoning, his liability to pay tax should not be regarded as too remote when assessing the sum of money which it is necessary for the court to award to compensate him for his loss. That appears to be the view of Lord Reid. In *Taylor v O'Connor* [1970] 1 All ER 365 at 368, [1971] AC 115 at 129 he said:

'This case is in a sense *British Transport Commission v Gourley* [1955] 3 All ER 796, [1956] AC 185 in reverse, for that case instructs us that we must see what the plaintiff really lost taking account of taxation. There damages had to be reduced if taxation was taken into account. Here they have to be increased.'

Turning now to the question of damages, I will deal first with the claim for damages for distress. It is alleged in the statement of claim that the manner and circumstances of the repudiation of the contract were likely to and did cause the plaintiff distress and injury to his health. I do not doubt that the plaintiff suffered distress. I am not satisfied that he suffered any injury to his health, but it seems to me that this part of the plaintiff's claim must fail on the authority of *Addis v Gramophone Co Ltd* [1909] AC 488 at 491, [1908–10] All ER Rep 1 at 3, where Lord Loreburn LC said:

'If there be a dismissal without notice the employer must pay an indemnity; but that indemnity cannot include compensation either for the injured feelings of the servant, or for the loss he may sustain from the fact that his having been dismissed of itself makes it more difficult for him to obtain fresh employment.'

Counsel for the plaintiff recognised the difficulty which faced him in the light of that decision and sought to argue that the events which occurred in September 1982 were breaches of conduct during the course of the plaintiff's employment, and that, if so, a different principle applies. He relied on the decision of Lawson J in *Cox v Philips Industries Ltd* [1976] 3 All ER 161, [1976] 1 WLR 638.

In my judgment, that decision affords no assistance to the plaintiff, because the award of £500 made in that case was made in respect of the relegation of the plaintiff to a position of lesser responsibility during his employment. In this case, the letter dated 6 September 1982 was a clear repudiatory breach of contract. It was accepted as such by the plaintiff, whose solicitors accepted the repudiation, subject to the right of the plaintiff to recover damages. In my judgment, those damages cannot include any damages for distress.

If the defendant had given the plaintiff 30 months' notice of termination of his employment, he would have enjoyed, for the period between 1 October 1982 and 31 March 1985 the following benefits: (1) a salary of £36,000 per annum subject to the deduction of tax; (2) a subscription to the British United Provident Association (BUPA) for himself and his wife at £350 per annum; (3) the use for his own private motoring of a Daimler motor car, in respect of which the defendants would have borne the entire cost

of servicing, repairing, taxing and insuring; (4) membership of the defendants' pension
a scheme; and (5) membership of the defendants' permanent health insurance scheme.

[His Lordship then considered schedules submitted by counsel for both sides which
showed detailed calculations of the plaintiff's probable tax liability if he had continued
in employment with the defendants until 31 March 1985. His Lordship also considered
the plaintiff's loss of benefits of the defendants' insurance scheme and his loss of the use
of a car provided by the defendants. His Lordship then considered the question of
b mitigation of loss and held that the plaintiff would be able to mitigate his loss to the
extent of £5,000 over the relevant period. His Lordship continued:]

In the result, the compensation to which the plaintiff is entitled is the sum of the
following ingredients: (1) loss of salary: £53,000 net; (2) BUPA subscriptions: £700; (3)
cost of life insurance: £6,600; (4) loss of use of motor car: £10,000. That makes a total of
£70,300 against which must be set off £5,000 for mitigation of loss, leaving a net loss of
c £65,300. It has been agreed between the parties that there should be a deduction of 7%
of such sum as I find due to the plaintiff to reflect the fact that he is receiving early
payment for part of his damages, 7% of £65,300 is £4,571 and; after deduction of that
sum, the net compensation due to the plaintiff is £60,729.

I have been provided with a schedule which sets out the amount of tax which will be
deducted from any sum awarded as damages. It is apparent from that schedule that in
d order to leave the plaintiff with the sum of £60,729 I must award damages in the sum of
£83,477, in addition to which, it is agreed that the plaintiff is entitled to the sum of
£553·84 in respect of accrued holiday pay. That sum is due under his contract of
employment and is not compensation for breach of the contract.

Accordingly, there will be judgment for the plaintiff for the sum of £84,030·84.

e *Judgment for the plaintiff for the sum of £84,030·84.*

Solicitors: *Rowe & Maw* (for the plaintiff); *Travers Smith Braithwaite & Co* (for the
defendants).

K Mydeen Esq   Barrister.

Jelson (Estates) Ltd v Harvey   *a*

CHANCERY DIVISION
GOULDING J
23 MAY 1983

COURT OF APPEAL, CIVIL DIVISION   *b*
CUMMING-BRUCE AND DILLON LJJ
19, 20 SEPTEMBER 1983

Contempt of court – Civil contempt – Committal – Committal for breach of court order – Defence of autrefois acquit – Plaintiff issuing defective notice of motion to secure committal – Judge at outset of hearing dismissing motion because of irregularity and making no order on it – Plaintiff issuing fresh notice complying with rules – Whether defendant entitled to defence of autrefois acquit – RSC Ord 52, r 4.   *c*

The defendant was the occupier of two manufacturing units on an industrial estate, where he carried on the business of processing industrial waste. In January 1983 the plaintiff, the freehold owner of the estate, brought an action against the defendant for breaches of covenant and in February 1983 obtained interlocutory injunctions restraining   *d*
the defendant from blocking or obstructing the land and roadway on the estate and from depositing industrial waste or rubbish in the forecourts of his units so as to cause them to be untidy. By a notice of motion dated 11 April 1983 the plaintiff applied to a judge seeking the defendant's committal for civil contempt on the ground that he had disobeyed the order of February 1983. The notice of motion did not set out on its face   *e*
the grounds of the plaintiff's application as required by RSC Ord 52, r 4[a] and accordingly the judge dismissed the motion for irregularity without hearing any of the evidence or considering the merits. On 28 April the plaintiff issued a fresh motion which complied with Ord 52, r 4. At the hearing of the new motion the defendant contended, inter alia, that, by analogy with criminal proceedings, he was entitled to rely on the defence of autrefois acquit, since by reason of the earlier defective notice of motion he was being   *f*
put in jeopardy twice in respect of the same alleged contempt. The judge held that the defendant had not been put in jeopardy at the hearing of the first motion because on that occasion the judge had not heard the evidence or considered the merits of the alleged contempt and in consequence the defence of autrefois acquit was not open to the defendant. He further held that on the evidence the defendant was in breach of the injunctions and was therefore guilty of contempt, and he fined the defendant £5,000.
The defendant appealed.   *g*

Held – (1) For the purposes of civil contempt proceedings the principle that no one should be tried twice for the same offence applied, so that the criminal rules governing the defence of autrefois acquit or autrefois convict were available to a contemnor where he had previously been in jeopardy for the same contempt. Furthermore (per Dillon LJ), in considering the criteria whether a person had previously been in jeopardy, it was not   *h*
appropriate to look at what might theoretically have happened, but rather at what had in fact happened on the first occasion and whether the person had been acquitted on the merits or by reason of a technicality (see p 18 *a b* and p 19 *j* to p 20 *c* and *e*, post); *Haynes v Davis* [1915] 1 KB 332 considered.

---

a   Rule 4, so far as material, provides: *j*
    '(1) Where an application for an order of committal may be made to a Court other than a Divisional Court, the application must be made by motion and be supported by an affidavit.
    (2) . . . the notice of motion, stating the grounds of the application and accompanied by a copy of the affidavit in support of the application, must be served personally on the person sought to be committed . . .'

a (2) On the facts, the defence of autrefois acquit was not open to the defendant because on the first motion the judge had noticed the irregularity at the outset and had refused to proceed to adjudicate on the merits. Consequently the defendant had never been in any peril of any punishment on the first motion. Furthermore, it was clear that the defendant had never been acquitted on the merits. It followed that on the second motion the judge had been right to hear and determine the matter. In all the circumstances, however, the fine would be reduced to £2,500 and the appeal would be allowed to that
b extent (see p 19 b to h and p 20 d e and g h, post); Haynes v Davis [1915] 1 KB 332 distinguished.

Notes

For applications to commit for civil contempt, see 9 Halsbury's Laws (4th edn) paras 92–93, 101, and for cases on the subject, see 16 Digest (Reissue) 94–95, 927–937.
c   For the plea of autrefois acquit in criminal proceedings, see 11 Halsbury's Laws (4th edn) paras 241–244, and for cases on the subject, see 14(1) Digest (Reissue) 440–458, 3774–3899.

Cases referred to in judgments

Chanel Ltd v FGM Cosmetics [1981] FSR 471.
d *Danchevsky v Danchevsky (No 2)* [1977] CA Transcript 416A.
Grimble & Co v Preston [1914] 1 KB 270, DC.
Haynes v Davis [1915] 1 KB 332, DC.
Henderson v Henderson (1843) Hare 100, [1843–60] All ER Rep 378, 67 ER 313.
Yat Tung Investment Co Ltd v Dao Heng Bank Ltd [1975] AC 581, [1975] 2 WLR 690, PC.

e ### Cases also cited

Comet Products UK Ltd v Hawkex Plastics Ltd [1971] 1 All ER 1141, [1971] 2 QB 67, CA.
Danchevsky v Danchevsky (No 1) [1974] 3 All ER 934, [1975] Fam 17, CA.
Halsted v Clark [1944] 1 All ER 270, [1944] KB 250, DC.
R v Marsham, ex p Pethick Lawrence [1912] 2 KB 362, [1911–13] All ER Rep 639, DC.
Yianni v Yianni [1966] 1 All ER 231, [1966] 1 WLR 120.
f

Motion

By an order made by Warner J on 7 February 1983, the plaintiffs, Jelson (Estates) Ltd, obtained interlocutory injunctions restraining the defendant, Geoffrey James Harvey, from (i) blocking up or obstructing by vehicles or otherwise or permitting the blocking
g up or obstructing of land on Hayhill Industrial Estate, Barrow-upon-Soar, Loughborough, Leicestershire in any manner whatsoever, and (ii) depositing any industrial waste or rubbish on the forecourts of units 11 and 12 of the Hayhill Industrial Estate so as to cause the units to appear untidy or so as to cause nuisance or annoyance to the adjoining or neighbouring units. On 11 April 1983 the plaintiffs issued a notice of motion seeking the defendant's committal for contempt of court in failing to comply with the order of 7
h February and on 22 April Warner J dismissed the notice without hearing evidence and refused to make any order, by reason of the fact that the notice of motion failed to comply with RSC Ord 52, r 4. On 28 April 1983 the plaintiffs issued a second notice of motion. On the hearing of the second motion the defendant contended, inter alia, (i) that the plaintiffs' notice of motion dated 11 April 1983 which was dismissed by Warner J with no order being made on it operated as a bar to the making of any order on the
j plaintiffs' second notice of motion dated 28 April 1983, by reason of the defence autrefois acquit, and (ii) that the second injunction was too vague and ambiguous to be capable of enforcement. The facts are set out in the judgment.

A J Trace for the plaintiffs.
Richard de Lacy for the defendant.

GOULDING J. This is a motion in which the plaintiffs, Jelson (Estates) Ltd, seek committal of the defendant, Mr Harvey, to prison for alleged contempt of court in infringing an order made on 7 February 1983. The material facts can be shortly stated. The order in question of 7 February 1983 was one whereby Warner J restrained the defendant until after judgment in the action or further order in the mean time from, putting it shortly, obstructing certain land on the Hayhill Industrial Estate at Barrow-upon-Soar or depositing any industrial waste or rubbish on certain parts of that industrial estate. The plaintiffs allege that the defendant has broken that order.

On 11 April 1983 the plaintiffs issued a notice of motion returnable on 22 April seeking the committal of the defendant 'for his contempt of this court in failing to refrain whether by himself or his servants or agents or any of them or otherwise howsoever from . . .' and then there was set out the full description of the acts of obstruction or depositing rubbish forbidden by the order of February 1983; but no particulars were given of the matters in respect of which the order of the court was said to have been disobeyed. The notice of motion contained the proper indication that the plaintiffs intended to read and use in support of the application a certain affidavit proving the contempt, a copy of which was served with the notice of motion. That was the affidavit of a solicitor, Mr G H Tew. That motion duly came on before Warner J. He did not read Mr Tew's affidavit on 22 April because the point was taken, and I think it is now common ground that it was properly taken, that the notice of motion did not comply with RSC Ord 52, r 4 as it did not state the grounds of the application. It merely alleged that the court's order had been broken and gave no particulars whatever. Reference should be made not only to r 4 but also to r 6, the third paragraph whereof provides that, except with the leave of the court hearing an application for an order of committal, no grounds shall be relied on at the hearing except those set out in the notice of motion. But the paragraph continues: 'without prejudice to the powers of the Court under Order 20, rule 8', that being the rule that allows the amendment of documents either on application or the court's own motion. So, the irregularity of the notice of motion having been drawn to the attention of the judge, he, as I said, did not read the evidence or go into the merits in any way, but disposed of the motion by declaring that the court did not think fit to make any order thereon and by giving the defendant his costs of the motion in any event.

The judge, as I understand it, was referred, in support of the objection to the notice of motion, to a recent decision of Whitford J in *Chanel Ltd v FGM Cosmetics* [1981] FSR 471, where the judge referred to earlier authorities and emphasised the importance of the notice of motion in committal cases being sufficiently specific. According to the recollection of counsel, there was no application by the plaintiffs for leave to amend their notice of motion, but counsel asked for leave to serve short notice of motion in a proper document according with the rules. That application for leave to serve short notice was declined by the judge, who said No, the plaintiffs must proceed in the normal way; thus, it would seem, contemplating that a further motion might be founded on the same alleged contempt.

However that may be, the plaintiffs in the present case did in fact serve a further notice of motion dated 28 April 1983, which sets out with considerable particularity the alleged infringements of the order of February. The return date for that second notice of motion was 10 May, on which day Vinelott J was moved on behalf of the plaintiffs. He stood the motion over to be heard as a motion by order, and thus it comes before me today. It only needs a comparison of the two notices of motion to see how important the rules are, and how oppressive to the defendant the extremely general form of the first notice was, since one finds that in the second notice a number of different acts on different days are alleged, and each one of them will have to be dealt with by the defendant (if he is called on to resist the application on its merits) in some considerable detail.

Counsel, who has argued the case with much ability on behalf of the defendant, says that the court is unable to, or at any rate clearly should not, entertain a second motion founded on the same contempts. There is no doubt that it is so founded because the a affidavit served with the second notice of motion and referred to therein is the very same affidavit of Mr Tew that was referred to in its predecessor.

There are really, I think, three branches in the argument of counsel for the defendant. First of all, he relies on the maxim nemo debet bis vexari pro una et eadem causa or, as it is sometimes put, the rule against double jeopardy. He says that the defendant, having been charged with contempt of court by the first motion, and having succeeded in the sense that that motion was finally disposed of without any penalty being imposed, has

b been cleared of the alleged offence and is entitled (in the language of the criminal law) to plead autrefois acquit.

That argument requires very careful examination. There was never any reading of the evidence adduced against the defendant. Nor did the judge consider the merits of the alleged case of contempt at all. He disposed of the motion by declining to make any order on it simply because of the irregularity of the notice. One cannot help feeling that

c if a criminal analogy is to be sought, the analogy is rather with a prosecution which fails for an indictment found to be defective before arraignment; or with a case in a court of summary jurisdiction which fails because there is some statutory or other defect in the information. And in those cases, as I understand it, a plea of autrefois acquit would not be available.

But, still arguing by analogy, counsel for the defendant presses the court with a case

d on the Sale of Food and Drugs Act 1899. By s 19 of that Act it was provided that in any prosecution under the Sale of Food and Drugs Acts the summons should state particulars of the offence or offences alleged and there must be served therewith a copy of any analyst's certificate obtained on behalf of the prosecutor. In *Haynes v Davis* [1915] 1 KB 332 an information was preferred against Mr Haynes for having sold deficient milk, and when the case came on for hearing the magistrate was informed that no certificate of

e analysis had been served with the summons as required by the statute. Because of that irregularity he dismissed the summons without hearing any evidence as to the facts. A second summons was then taken out by the prosecuting authority in respect of the same alleged offence, and that second summons was served with a copy of the analyst's certificate. The Divisional Court held by a majority that the appellant had been in peril of being convicted on the first summons and therefore was entitled to plead autrefois

f acquit to the second summons. Ridley and Avery JJ, who formed the majority, thought that the question depended on whether the magistrate on the first occasion had jurisdiction to hear and determine the summons in respect of the offence that was then before him. They held that the magistrate had had jurisdiction in spite of the failure to serve a copy of the analyst's certificate, and therefore Mr Haynes had indeed been in peril and could not be put in peril again.

g Counsel for the plaintiffs has argued here that Warner J, because of the defect in the notice of motion, had no jurisdiction on 22 April to hear the application and that *Haynes v Davis* can be distinguished on that ground. I am loath to accept that, because although the judge was of course perfectly right to refuse to hear the motion, I for my part find it difficult to think that if he had overlooked or waived the irregularity and proceeded to read the evidence he would have acted without jurisdiction.

h However, I have been referred by neither side to any authority showing how far and in what manner the doctrines of the criminal law about previous acquittal are applicable in a case of civil contempt. And although I am quite clear that if a man has been cleared of an alleged civil contempt on a proper investigation of the merits he should not be put in jeopardy a second time, it does not seem to me that one should too readily draw procedural analogies between the contempt process and those either of indictment or

j summary prosecution. I think it is in accordance with the proper nature and application of the rule against double jeopardy that an applicant should not be prevented from renewing a complaint of contempt of court simply because of a procedural defect in his first attempt to do so; and I think it would be generalising the authority of *Haynes v Davis* too much to apply it by analogy to the present case. I am therefore of opinion that this first branch of the submissions of counsel for the defendant must fail.

The second branch was this. He said it is an abuse of the process of the court, generally speaking, to attempt to relitigate facts that could have been brought before the court on a previous occasion. Here, he says, but for the negligence or inadvertence of the plaintiffs' advisers, the facts could have been brought before the court under the first notice of motion, and therefore it is an abuse of process to try to do it again.

That seems to me a misconception of the doctrine put forward in such cases as *Henderson v Henderson* (1843) 3 Hare 100, [1843–60] All ER Rep 378 and *Yat Tung Investment Co Ltd v Dao Heng Bank Ltd* [1975] AC 581. Where there is litigation of a certain question or issue before the court resulting in a final or substantial order which decides it, then it is well established that it is too late (save in exceptional cases) for a party to adduce in subsequent litigation against the same opponent, or one privy to him, a fact that might well have been brought forward on the previous occasion. That doctrine, however, does not apply where there is a mere procedural defect and the court has never gone into the merits, though both parties were before it. Here the judge himself, I think, recognised (if his remarks are correctly reported) that he was not deciding the question of the alleged contempt and that the plaintiffs, if they put their proceedings in order, might try again. Accordingly, the doctrine of res judicata, in its wider or more general form relied on by counsel for the defendant does not in my judgment avail him.

His third point really turned on the power of the court to allow, on application or of its own motion, the amendment of any proceedings. It is submitted that although there was no formal application for amendment, Warner J undoubtedly had power to allow amendment of the first notice of motion, and the fact that he finally disposed of it is at least by implication a decision that the plaintiffs should not be allowed to amend. And if it is not thought right that they should amend the notice of motion, then there is a strong argument for saying that it would be an abuse of the process of the court to get round such a decision by a fresh notice of motion relying on the same grounds and the same evidence. However, I think that is attempting to read into Warner J's order something that is not there. I think that all that he decided was that he would not give relief on the notice of motion dated 11 April, leaving it entirely open to the plaintiffs to serve a proper notice of motion that the court could then consider on its merits.

Thus, although I have been impressed by the majority decision in *Haynes v Davis*, in the end I feel it not to be safely applicable to the present case. I think that the preliminary objection fails and the plaintiffs must be permitted to move as they now seek to do.

Ruling accordingly.

24 May. Goulding J considered the motion and found the defendant to be in breach of both injunctions. His Lordship imposed on the defendant a fine of £5,000.

Evelyn M C Budd   Barrister.

Interlocutory appeal
The defendant appealed.

Richard de Lacy for the defendant.
A J Trace for the plaintiffs.

CUMMING-BRUCE LJ. On 10 January 1983 the plaintiffs issued a writ accompanied by a statement of claim, in an action in which they complain of breaches of covenant, being covenants in the fifth schedule to an instrument of transfer whereby the defendant became the occupier of some property on an industrial estate, the property of the plaintiffs. The remedies sought in the prayer in the statement of claim were injunctions to restrain the defendant, his servants or agents from 'blocking up or obstructing or permitting the blocking up or obstruction' of certain land and a road on the industrial estate, and an injunction to restrain the defendant from parking lorries, trucks, vans and a   trailers on the forecourt of certain units on the estate and from depositing any industrial waste or rubbish on the estate so as to cause the units to appear untidy, and an injunction to stop him burning it. The fifth schedule to the instrument of transfer included a covenant to keep all parts of the property transferred in a proper and tidy condition.

On an application before him, Warner J made an interlocutory injunction in the following terms: the defendant was restrained by himself or his servants or agents from doing any of the following acts:

b

'(1) blocking up or obstructing by vehicles or otherwise or permitting the blocking up or obstructing as aforesaid of the land [described in terms of a plan], (2) depositing any industrial waste or rubbish on the fore courts of Units 11 and 12 the said Hayhill Industrial Estate so as to cause the said units to appear untidy . . .'

That was the order made by the judge on 10 February.

c   It was followed by a notice of motion whereby the plaintiffs sought punishment of the defendant for contempt of court for (1) failing to refrain from blocking up or obstructing by vehicles or otherwise the land the subject matter of the injunction and (2) failing to comply with the injunction prohibiting the defendant from depositing any industrial waste or rubbish on the forecourts. The notice of motion did not set out the grounds on which the plaintiffs were alleging the breaches of the injunction. It was supported by an d   affidavit, but the notice of motion was irregular.

When that notice of motion came before Warner J on 22 April he made the following order:

'UPON MOTION made by Counsel for the Plaintiff for an order that the Defendant do stand committed to prison for his contempt in disobeying the Order dated 7th February 1983 . . . THIS COURT DOES NOT THINK FIT to make any Order on the said e   Motion . . .'

The judge made that order when a point had been taken on behalf of the defendant that the notice of motion was irregular in that it did not comply with the rules by setting out on its face the grounds on which the plaintiffs relied for their submission that there had been contempt of court. The judge said in terms that he refused, after dismissing the f   motion, to allow the motion to be amended, because, having dismissed the motion, there was nothing to amend. The judge clearly contemplated, as was sufficiently clear from what he said, that if the plaintiffs wished to proceed they must get their tackle in order and serve a notice of motion that complied with the rules.

That indeed was done. Notice of motion was then served which complied with the rules. Eventually it came before Goulding J. The first point taken on the part of the g   defendant was that it was not open to the judge on the second notice of motion to proceed to consider the case on the merits and to decide whether to impose any punishment, because by analogy with the process in criminal proceedings the defendant could rely on the defence which is recognised in criminal proceedings under the nomenclature of autrefois acquit, and the submission before the judge was that when Warner J had made no order on the irregular motion brought before him he had exercised jurisdiction and h   dismissed the motion, but though he did so without any inquiry into the merits, on the authorities in criminal cases two propositions apply. First, proceedings for civil contempt, namely for breach of an order of the court by way of breach of an injunction, are quasi-criminal in character, so that the principles that apply in entertaining and proceeding on motions for contempt for a civil contempt should follow the analogy of criminal proceedings with some strictness. Second, relying on *Haynes v Davis* [1915] 1 KB 332, the j   correct approach was as follows. The judge, though he had made no order on the motion and had not considered the motion on its merits, had entertained jurisdiction in the sense or with the effect that the defendant was in jeopardy for punishment for contempt until the judge decided. He dismissed the motion on the grounds of its irregularity. The defendant had in fact been in jeopardy. It was not open to the plaintiffs to commence a second set of proceedings seeking to prove the same contempt as that which it was alleged was the basis of the proceedings on which the defendant had been in jeopardy on the first occasion.

A number of authorities were cited before us in support of the two propositions propounded by the defendant. As to the first proposition that there is an analogy between the criminal process and proceedings for contempt by way of breach of an injunction, the defendant relies on the decision of this court in *Danchevsky v Danchevsky (No 2)* [1977] CA Transcript 416A. That decision established that, for the purposes of proceedings for contempt of a civil court by disobedience of its order, the principle nemo bis vexari applies, so that the criminal rules governing the defences of autrefois convict and autrefois acquit should avail the contemnor if he has previously been in jeopardy of punishment for the contempt for which it is sought to punish him. So the defendant establishes his first proposition.

When, however, I come to the proposition on which the defendant relies and which is collected from the majority judgments in *Haynes v Davis* to which I have already referred, those judgments, in my view, have to be considered extremely carefully. They were judgments of the Divisional Court of the Queen's Bench Division when it was hearing an appeal by case stated from an order made by the stipendiary magistrate for South Staffordshire. Those proceedings were proceedings in a court of summary jurisdiction commenced by information. By s 19(2) of the Sale of Food and Drugs Act 1899 it was provided that in such proceedings when the summons is served it must be accompanied by a certificate of analysis in accordance with the provisions of s 19(2). On the facts before the stipendiary magistrate the information was in proper form, but it had not been served together with the requisite certificate of analysis. When the magistrate realised that, he dismissed the summons. No evidence as to the facts was given. Whereupon a new summons was issued. The information and complaint in that summons were the same and based on the same facts as the first summons which the magistrate had already dismissed. But with the later summons the irregularity was cured and the analyst's certificate was duly served on the appellant in compliance with s 19(2). The magistrate was of the opinion that on the hearing of the first summons the appellant had never been in peril, as the facts were not further gone into after the irregularity of procedure had been disclosed. The question for the opinion of the court was whether the magistrate came to the right decision in point of law.

Ridley and Avory JJ were for allowing the appeal. The grounds by which they were moved were a little different. Ridley J took the view that the magistrate had jurisdiction when he was considering the summons and that during the period before he decided to dismiss the summons for irregularity the defendant had been in jeopardy. Therefore the principle of autrefois acquit applied. Avory J based his judgment on the ground that the defendant had been in peril. He took the view that it was not a condition precedent to the attaching of the jurisdiction that the analyst's certificate should be served with the summons. He went on to say ([1915] 1 KB 332 at 337):

'I cannot believe that a poor man who has no legal assistance and who does not take this objection because he does not know of it is in peril of being convicted, and that the man who has legal assistance and takes the objection never is in peril. The question whether the one or the other is in peril is to be ascertained by inquiring whether the magistrate had jurisdiction to deal with the offence. Apart from any opinion of my own, I think that *Grimble* v. *Preston* ([1914] 1 KB 270) [also a case in the Divisional Court] decides that the magistrate had jurisdiction. That being so, the magistrate was wrong in convicting the appellant on the second summons.'

Lush J in his minority judgment disagreed with the decision of Ridley and Avory JJ, and in his judgment he explained his reasons for holding that in the circumstances that had happened the defendant had never been in jeopardy. He did not agree with the view that Avory J had expressed about the effect of *Grimble & Co v Preston* in the Divisional Court the year before. This court is not of course bound by a decision of the Divisional Court of the Queen's Bench Division, but naturally this court approaches with respect a

decision of the Divisional Court, particularly where it appears to have stood for some 70
years without disapproval. But, for myself, having considered the judgments, I prefer
the view taken in the minority judgment of Lush J, and, if it is necessary, I would hold
that this court should follow the approach of Lush J rather than the approach of the
majority. I take the view, however, that it is not necessary to determine that matter,
because I am not satisfied that these proceedings, civil proceedings for contempt, are so
close to the subject matter which the court was considering in *Haynes v Davis* (bound as
they were to administer the law in accordance with the provisions of the Summary
Jurisdiction Acts) as to make it necessary or even useful in this court to take the view that
it should proceed in exactly the way that the Queen's Bench Divisional Court did when
reviewing the case stated by the magistrate in *Haynes v Davis*.

I would take the broader approach: accepting that these were proceedings for the
punishment of the defendant for breach of an injunction made in civil proceedings,
when the judge observed the irregularity on the notice of motion and decided that it
would be wrong, that is to say unfair, to proceed to adjudicate on the merits when the
grounds had not appeared from the notice of motion so that the defendant had not had
time specifically to consider those grounds, there was, in my view, no room in these
proceedings for contempt for the application of the doctrine of autrefois acquit by
analogy with criminal proceedings. I would take the view that the judge, when making
no order on the motion, never in fact allowed the defendant to be in any peril of any
punishment on that notice of motion, and it seems to me wholly unreal to borrow from
criminal law a doctrine which in the criminal law may properly be applied with greater
strictness than is necessary in these civil proceedings. I can see nothing the least unfair in
the course that Warner J took when he made no order on the summons, clearly with a
view to enabling the plaintiffs to issue a second notice of motion curing the irregularity
by stating the grounds on which the plaintiffs relied.

So I take the view that there is nothing in the case of *Haynes v Davis* which ought to
influence this court to hold that the doctrine of autrefois acquit should have been applied
by analogy by Goulding J. If it was necessary, as I have said, I would prefer the approach
of Lush J in *Haynes v Davis* to the approach of the majority, and it may be that some day
it will be necessary and appropriate for the decision in *Haynes v Davis* to be reconsidered
either in the Divisional Court or in their Lordships' House.

So I would hold that the first ground of appeal against the order of Goulding J fails.
Goulding J was right to proceed to inquire into the merits and to decide whether he
should impose a penalty.

[His Lordship then went on to consider the merits of the plaintiffs' motion for
contempt and concluded that the judge was right in holding that the defendant had been
in contempt of court. His Lordship held, however, that the penalty by way of fine should
be reduced from £5,000 to £2,500 on the ground that the injunctions were restricted to
the deposit of industrial waste or rubbish and did not cover the deposit of the pallets and
skips which made the units untidy. His Lordship concluded:]

To that degree I would allow the appeal and I would move that the fine be reduced to
£2,500.

DILLON LJ. I agree. I will turn in a moment to the point of autrefois acquit, which
counsel has put forward as the main ground of the defendant's appeal, but first I will
make a few comments on the other aspects of the appeal.

[His Lordship then considered the limits of the injunctions and held that the fine
should not be reduced more than to the extent indicated by Cumming-Bruce LJ. His
Lordship continued:]

The main point argued, and, if I may say so, argued with great care and skill by counsel
for the defendant in support of the appeal, was that the second motion to commit was
misconceived and should have been dismissed on the ground of autrefois acquit, because
the first motion to commit, which came before Warner J, was dismissed. It is quite clear,
as it seems to me, from the decision of the Court of Appeal in *Danchevsky v Danchevsky*

(*No 2*) [1977] CA Transcript 416A that the rules of autrefois convict apply to proceedings for civil contempt and prevent a person being punished twice for the same act of contempt. Lawton LJ in *Danchevsky* said that civil contempt of court in the form of a breach of an undertaking or injunction is a common law misdemeanour, and so it would follow that the civil court could not do anything that a criminal court could not have done. In *Danchevsky* the main issue was whether the order was an order of which there was a once and for all breach or an order of which the conduct of the defendant amounted to a continuing breach. That is not directly relevant here, but it seems to follow that if the doctrine of autrefois convict applies, so equally the doctrine of autrefois acquit applies and a person cannot be proceeded against a second time on an allegation of civil contempt if he has already been acquitted of that charge.

Goulding J in his judgment in the present case said: 'I am quite clear that if a man has been cleared of an alleged civil contempt on a proper investigation of the merits he should not be put in jeopardy a second time . . .' With that I entirely agree. I think the question is whether on a true appreciation of the circumstances the defendant here was ever in jeopardy a first time on the first notice of motion to commit him. The rules of court provide in RSC Ord 52, r 4 that the notice of motion by which an application for an order of committal is made must state the grounds of the application and must also be accompanied by a copy of the affidavit in support of the application. The notice of motion which came before Warner J, although it referred to the affidavit, did not state the grounds of the application. Therefore the technical point was taken for the defendant, and was rightly acceded to by Warner J, that the notice of motion failed to comply with the rules and should not be investigated; it should be dismissed out of hand, as it was.

Counsel for the defendant now says, 'Oh, but the defect might have been waived. The court, had the defect been waived, would have had jurisdiction to investigate the merits, and so Mr Harvey [the defendant] was in jeopardy of committal.' It seems to me that he never was in jeopardy, because the point was firmly taken and accepted by the judge at the outset of the hearing. The merits were never gone into. It is not appropriate to look at what might theoretically have happened in a different scenario of the facts. It is necessary to consider in each case where the question is one of autrefois acquit what actually happened. So far as the authorities are concerned, counsel for the defendant has to rely on the decision of the majority of the Divisional Court in *Haynes v Davis* [1915] 1 KB 332, to which Cumming-Bruce LJ has referred. For my part, I prefer the minority judgment of Lush J in that case (see [1915] 1 KB 332 at 339–340). I would regard the criterion as being that put by Lush J and interpreted by him in his judgment. A man who has been once tried and acquitted for a crime may not be tried again for the same offence if he was in jeopardy on the first trial; in considering whether he was in jeopardy, one of the factors is whether the acquittal was on the merits, by verdict at the trial or, in summary cases, by dismissal on the merits. Accepting the further explanation given by Lush J in that judgment as to what is meant by acquittal on the merits, it is quite clear that in the present case the defendant was not acquitted on the merits. Therefore the point of autrefois acquit is not available to him and I reject that ground of appeal.

The appeal should, however, be allowed to the extent of reducing the penalty, as Cumming-Bruce LJ has indicated.

Appeal allowed to the extent that fine reduced to £2,500.

Solicitors: *Cripps Harries Willis & Carter*, agents for *Oldham Marsh & Son*, Melton Mowbray (for the defendant); *Kingsford Dorman*, agents for *Geoffrey Tew & Co*, Leicester (for the plaintiffs).

Diana Procter   Barrister.

Re E (minors) (wardship: jurisdiction)

COURT OF APPEAL, CIVIL DIVISION
EVELEIGH AND DUNN LJJ
19, 20, 24 JANUARY 1983

Child – Care – Local authority – Wardship proceedings – Jurisdiction of court to review decisions of local authority – Wardship proceedings by natural parent – Proceedings by local authority for care order pending – Whether fact care proceedings merely pending and care order not in force affecting exercise of wardship jurisdiction – Whether rule that court will not exercise wardship jurisdiction merely to supervise local authority's discharge of care order duties applicable – Children and Young Persons Act 1969, s 1.

A local authority obtained a place of safety order in respect of three young children and commenced proceedings in the juvenile court for care orders under s 1ᵃ of the Children and Young Persons Act 1969. Before the proceedings were heard, the children's mother, who wanted access with a view to their phased return to her, commenced wardship proceedings in which she applied for care and control of the children under the supervision of the local authority. The local authority objected to the court exercising its wardship jurisdiction. The judge held that, as the welfare of the children did not require them to be wards of court, the case was not an appropriate case for wardship, applying the rule that the wardship jurisdiction should not be exercised as a means of supervising a local authority's discharge of its duties towards a child in its care. The mother appealed.

Held – Applying the principles that the court will not exercise its wardship jurisdiction unless the welfare of the child requires it and that the court will not exercise its wardship jurisdiction merely in order to supervise a local authority's exercise of its discretion under a care order, the mother's appeal would be dismissed notwithstanding that the care proceedings were only pending and a care order was not then in force (see p 25 e to j, p 26 c to p 27 a, p 28 f to j and p 29 a b, post).

A v Liverpool City Council [1981] 2 All ER 385 applied.

Notes

For the care of a child by a local authority, see 24 Halsbury's Laws (4th edn) para 787.

For wardship jurisdiction, see ibid paras 576–583, and for cases on the subject, see 28(2) Digest (Reissue) 911–916, 2220–2247.

For the Children and Young Persons Act 1969, s 1, see 40 Halsbury's Statutes (3rd edn) 849.

Cases referred to in judgment

A v Liverpool City Council [1981] 2 All ER 385, [1982] AC 363, [1981] 2 WLR 948, HL.
B (a minor) (wardship: child in care), Re [1974] 3 All ER 915, [1975] Fam 36, [1975] 2 WLR 302.

---

a Section 1, so far as material, provides:
'(1) Any local authority . . . or authorised person who reasonably believes that there are grounds for making an order under this section in respect of a child or young person may . . . bring him before a juvenile court.
(2) If the court before which a child or young person is brought under this section is of opinion that any of the following conditions is satisfied with respect to him, that is to say—(a) his proper development is being avoidably prevented or neglected or his health is being avoidably impaired or neglected or he is being ill-treated . . . and also that he is in need of care or control which he is unlikely to receive unless the court makes an order under this section in respect of him, then . . . the court may if it thinks fit make such an order.
(3) The order which a court may make under this section in respect of a child or young person is . . . (c) a care order . . .'

H (a minor) (wardship: jurisdiction), Re [1978] 2 All ER 903, [1978] Fam 65, [1978] 2 WLR 608, CA.   *a*
R v Worthing Justices, ex p Stevenson [1976] 2 All ER 194, DC.
W (a minor) (justices' decision: review), Re (1981) 2 FLR 360.
Y (a minor) (child in care: access), Re [1975] 3 All ER 348, [1976] Fam 125, [1975] 3 WLR 342, CA.

Cases also cited   *b*
C (a minor), Re (1982) 12 Fam Law 216.
Hertfordshire CC v Dolling (1982) 3 FLR 423.
M v Humberside CC [1979] 2 All ER 744, [1979] Fam 114.
R v Gravesham Juvenile Court, ex p B (1982) 12 Fam Law 207.
R v Milton Keynes Justices, ex p R [1979] 1 WLR 1062, DC.
R (K) (an infant), Re [1963] 3 All ER 337, [1964] Ch 455.   *c*

Interlocutory appeal
On 19 May 1982 at the instigation of the Hampshire County Council (the local authority) the juvenile court made a place of safety order in respect of three children of the mother. On 28 May the local authority commenced proceedings under s 1 of the Children and Young Persons Act 1969 and sought care orders in respect of the children, which *d* proceedings were set down for hearing by the Gosport Juvenile Court on 9 June. On 8 June the mother initiated wardship proceeding requesting the High Court to make the children wards of court and to give care and control to the mother with supervision to the local authority. On 9 June the local authority withdrew the care proceedings. On 8 July the district registrar ordered the children to be made wards of court and made an interim order that the children remain in the care of the local authority with the mother *e* having access. The wardship proceedings came before Balcombe J at Winchester on 14 December 1982, when the judge made an order discharging the wardship proceedings and ordering that the children cease to be wards of court. The mother appealed. The facts are set out in the judgment of Eveleigh LJ.

William H Webster for the mother.   *f*
Linda Davies for the local authority.

Cur adv vult

24 January. The following judgments were delivered.

    g
EVELEIGH LJ. I take the introduction to the facts of this case from the judgment of Balcombe J almost verbatim. There are three children concerned: twin boys who were born on 27 August 1980 and who are therefore two years old, and a girl who was born on 30 November 1981 who is therefore one year old. On 19 May 1982 the Hampshire County Council, as the appropriate local authority, obtained a place of safety order from the juvenile court and had, on 28 May 1982, initiated proceedings under s 1 of the *h* Children and Young Persons Act 1969 before the juvenile court, applying for a care order in relation to each of those children. They had been placed with foster parents. That application was due to be heard by the Gosport juvenile court on 9 June 1982. However, on 8 June 1982 wardship proceedings were initiated, naming the mother and the father of these children as the first and second plaintiff, and the Hampshire County Council (the local authority) as the defendants, asking for an order that the three children be made *j* wards of court and that care control should be committed to the mother, with supervision to the local authority. On 9 June the care proceedings were withdrawn. The father, in fact, has taken no part in these proceedings, and Balcombe J made an order that he should be made a defendant rather than a plaintiff to the application.

The matter came before the district registrar initially on 8 July 1982 when the solicitor

for the local authority took the point that the decision of the House of Lords in *A v*
a *Liverpool City Council* [1981] 2 All ER 385, [1982] AC 363 meant that the High Court did
not have, or at any rate should not exercise, jurisdiction in wardship in a case of this
nature. What then happened, it seems, was that, as the mother was content, and indeed
accepted, that the children should, for the time being, be where they were, the registrar
took the view that there was nothing to be gained by making a ruling on the question of
jurisdiction, and accordingly made an order, pursuant to s 7(2) of the Family Law Reform
b Act 1969, that the children should remain wards of court and that they should, in the
interim, remain in the care and control of the local authority. He made provision for
access by the mother, which was subsequently varied in a matter of detail in August 1982
to provide for weekly access.

It was argued in the court below and here that the present case is not governed by and
is not affected by *A v Liverpool City Council* [1981] 2 All ER 385, [1982] AC 363 because,
c it is said, in that case an order had been made, whereas in this case there was not an order
in existence committing the children to the care of the local authority, and the argument
took the line of the grounds of appeal that had been argued in this court. Putting those
grounds in what I might call their order of importance, the first, which is (e) of the
grounds of appeal, says:

d 'The learned Judge was wrong in law in holding that he was bound by the
decision of the House of Lords in the above case in that he failed to attach sufficient
weight or give due consideration to any of the following matters . . . (e) The fact
that the procedure under the Children and Young Persons' Act 1969 does not allow
the Juvenile Court (or the Crown Court on appeal) to make provision for, or control,
a phased return to the parent or an experimental period of increasing contact by
way of access.'
e
I need not read out all of that ground, but it concludes with this sentence:

'By reason of the foregoing it is further submitted that the learned Judge failed to
give due consideration to the fear that it would be most unfair that recourse to the
Wardship jurisdiction should, if necessary, be available to the First Defendant, as the
f local authority, (in order to overcome perceived defects in the said legislation) and
not to the Plaintiff, as the children's natural mother, when the result in the latter
may be in the children's best interest in the long term as opposed to long term
fostering or living in a children's home under a care order.'

Then the notice of appeal goes on to say:

g 'In the further premises the learned Judge failed to give due consideration to
whether or not:—(1) The interests of the said minors would be better served by an
order which the High Court can make under Section 7 of the Family Law Reform
Act. In this regard it be further alleged that the learned Judge failed to pay any or
any sufficient regard to the fact that Section 21(2A) of the Children and Young
Persons' Act 1969 (introduced by Section 108(4)(c) of, and paragraph 69 of Schedule
3 to the Children Act 1975) precludes a Juvenile Court from discharging a care order
h unless the Court is satisfied that the relevant child will receive the care and control
which he requires. In expressly restricting the power of the Juvenile Court it may
prevent this tribunal from taking a risk which, in the best interests of the said child
or children, perhaps ought to be taken. In this case the risk would be lessened if the
High Court in Wardship were able to give due consideration to and assist in the
implementation of the Plaintiff's proposals for the children.'
j
There then followed other grounds which are put forward as matters which should affect
the court in the exercise of its discretion: for example, the fact that legal aid is not yet
available to the parents in care proceedings, and reference is made to *R v Worthing Justices,
ex p Stevenson* [1976] 2 All ER 194. Then there is relied on the fact that the first defendant,
who is the local authority, did not raise any objection to the issue of jurisdiction after 8

July 1982 until the date of the hearing in the High Court before Balcombe J; and, finally, the argument that, by submitting to the order of the registrar, the local authority elected *a* to submit to the jurisdiction of the High Court in wardship, and it is said that Balcombe J was wrong in allowing the local authority to reverse its election as the parties were all ready for trial.

The argument then can be divided really into two parts. The first part is that this court's jurisdiction is not ousted or limited by *A v Liverpool City Council* [1981] 2 All ER 385, [1982] AC 363 and that the court should exercise its jurisdiction for the reasons set *b* out in the grounds of appeal and, as I say, argued before the judge. The second part consists of, perhaps, peripheral considerations, namely that legal aid is not available to the parents, that witnesses were at court, as indeed they were, ready to testify in the matter, that affidavits were before the court, and the fact, it is said, that the local authority did not raise any objection to the jurisdiction and, as it is alleged, there was an election. I will return to the second part later but, in passing, would simply say that those matters *c* do not seem to me to be matters that directly affect the welfare of the child but are urged in support of the claim of the parent to intervene.

Balcombe J considered *A v Liverpool City Council* (which I shall return to in a moment) and, while it was, as I understood the argument of counsel for the mother, originally submitted to this court that the judge treated the matter as though he had no jurisdiction, the judge did, as I read his judgment, take the view that he had jurisdiction but would *d* not exercise his discretion as asked. In his judgment he said:

> 'If I had been satisfied that the welfare of the children in this case would be prejudiced by my not hearing the case now I would certainly have continued to hear it. But the position is that I am told that a hearing before the juvenile court could have been heard next week. That is not practicable because one of the leading *e* witnesses for the local authority is about to leave the country for a short time. Indeed, I had arranged, if this case had been proceeded with before me, to hear her evidence first: but a hearing can be arranged for early in January, dates have been put aside for it, by which time that witness will be back in this country . . . I have been told by the local authority that the existing arrangements for access will be maintained, the children will not be prejudiced.' *f*

So it seems clear to me that he considered whether or not to exercise his discretion in the way that he was asked to, and later he said: 'If I had been satisfied that the welfare of the children would be prejudiced by the order I am proposing to make, then it would have been clearly appropriate not to accede to the application.' He, in fact, made an order that the children cease to be wards of court. The proceedings in the juvenile court have been reinstated and we are told that they can be heard very soon indeed, I think this very *g* week.

Now, it is quite clear, and indeed there has been no argument to the contrary in this court, that *A v Liverpool City Council* does not oust the jurisdiction of the High Court in wardship. Lord Wilberforce said ([1981] 2 All ER 385 at 388–389, [1982] AC 363 at 373):

h

> 'This is not to say that the inherent jurisdiction of the High Court is taken away. Any child, whether under care or not, can be made a ward of court by the procedure of s 9(2) of the Law Reform (Miscellaneous Provisions) Act 1949. In cases (and the present is an example) where the court perceives that the action sought of it is within the sphere of discretion of the local authority, it will make no order and the wardship will lapse. But in some instances, there may be an area of concern to which *j* the powers of the local authority, limited as they are by statute, do not extend. Sometimes the local authority itself may invite the supplementary assistance of the court. Then the wardship may be continued with a view to action by the court. The court's general inherent power is always available to fill gaps or to supplement the powers of the local authority; what it will not do (except by way of judicial review

a where appropriate) is to supervise the exercise of discretion within the field committed by statute to the local authority.'

Lord Roskill said ([1981] 2 All ER 385 at 391, [1982] AC 363 at 376):

'My Lords, I do not doubt that the wardship jurisdiction of the court is not extinguished by the existence of the legislation regarding the care and control of deprived children, a phrase I use to include children whose parents have for some reason failed to discharge their parental duties towards them. I am not aware of any decision which suggests otherwise.'

b

But what the Liverpool case does do is to emphasise that Parliament has provided a responsible authority to play the role of a parent and to provide for the welfare of the child, an authority that is well equipped for that purpose and, in this case, it seems to me that the mother is asking the court to take over responsibility for the child from another c on the grounds that the conduct of that other in caring for the child may not be for the child's good in that access may turn out to be desirable to a greater extent than that other will permit. So, it is said, the court must assume immediate responsibility in the matter in case it may be necessary at some future date to compel the local authority to grant access, although we do not know whether or not it will refuse access or refuse it inadvisedly.

d This court would not interfere with a responsible parent on the basis that it is just possible that he may act in a way that could be improved on if he had greater powers or resources. It seems to me that, if the jurisdiction of this court were invoked in that way, absolutely anyone could come before it. The argument on behalf of the mother overlooks the fact that this court is asking itself: 'Is this child in good hands? Is there any reason to think that greater power will be required, greater supervision by the court will be e required to ensure that that responsible authority set up by Parliament will perform its proper duty?' It seems to me quite impossible to conclude that a situation has arisen, or can be envisaged, that requires the intervention of the court at this stage. What we are being asked to do is to put the court immediately in the position to supervise the exercise of the discretion of the local authority, that which A v Liverpool City Council makes it clear the court will not do. Counsel for the mother says that there there was a care order in f force and here there is not one in force. For myself, I cannot see that that makes any difference to the principle to be applied in the case.

In Re W (a minor) (justices' decision: review) (1981) 2 FLR 360 at 361 Sir John Arnold P said:

'There is no challenge to the existence of the jurisdiction, and it is indeed well established that the wardship jurisdiction is not as such ousted by the circumstance g that there is in existence an order or a pending proceeding (for I can see no valid distinction between the two) under either of the juvenile court jurisdictions, either that under s. 1 of the Children and Young Persons Act 1969 or that under s. 2 of the Children Act 1948 [now s 3 of the Child Care Act 1980] where the function of the juvenile court is to quash or sustain a resolution transferring parental rights.'

h I too can see no valid distinction between the two.

In A v Liverpool City Council [1981] 2 All ER 385 at 389, [1982] AC 363 at 374 Lord Roskill, having referred to earlier cases in a long line of authority which the Liverpool case followed, said:

'The effect of those and other decisions is clear and is well summarised by the learned judge in his judgment in the present case: "The court will not, indeed j should not, exercise its wardship jurisdiction when what is sought to be done is to question the manner in which a local authority in whose favour a care order has been made is exercising its statutory jurisdiction".'

I would add 'or in which it might exercise its statutory jurisdiction if a care order were made'.

As to the other part, namely that affidavits had been prepared, that witnesses were at court ready to testify, that the local authority did not persist in taking the jurisdiction point before the registrar, strictly speaking, I regard them as irrelevant. The court was concerned with the welfare of the infant. All other things being equal, it might have been prepared to go more deeply into the case, but I cannot see in an infant case how there is room for any doctrine of election by the local authority. Nor is there room for the argument that the local authority failed to take any particular point. The judge has to approach this matter on the basis that he has been asked to exercise a discretion, and it is for him to do so. Nothing that has happened below in a case of this nature should in any way fetter his approach to that question.

Finally, criticism was made of the fact that the judge did not read, or apparently did not read, the affidavits. He did have before him a welfare report which he read. Now, there was nothing said to the judge and nothing has been said to this court to cause it to think that there is the slightest need to consider the matter further. If the evidence and the affidavits contain in them something to indicate that there was a real risk to the child if this court failed to go more fully into the matter, then counsel would undoubtedly have opened that to the court. But the matter was presented to the judge and has been presented before this court as one of principle, and really it has centred on the argument, with which one can have some sympathy, that the power for the parents to intervene is more restricted and that the local authority's handling of the child is not subject to supervision by the juvenile court. That really has been the grounds of the appeal and the grounds of the application in the wardship proceedings. I have heard nothing on the particular facts of this case to cause the court to inquire deeply into them and, if we had heard in this court of some reason for suspicion that all might not be well, then we too would have asked for more information on that matter. I, therefore, regard it as wrong to criticise the judge if in fact he did not read through all the affidavits in this case.

I would dismiss this appeal.

DUNN LJ. I agree that the judge was right in exercising his discretion to refuse to accept jurisdiction in wardship in the circumstances of this particular case. There is no doubt that the jurisdiction exists and that a series of decisions of long standing binding on this court and culminating in *A v Liverpool City Council* [1981] 2 All ER 385, [1982] AC 363 show that the court will not exercise its wardship jurisdiction unless the welfare of the child requires it. So in *Re H (a minor) (wardship: jurisdiction)* [1978] 2 All ER 903, [1978] Fam 65 this court upheld an order by the judge discharging a care order made in the juvenile court because that was the only way in which the result which was best in the paramount interests of the child could be achieved. In *Re B (a minor) (wardship: child in care)* [1974] 3 All ER 915, [1975] Fam 36 Lane J continued wardship proceedings so that the court could, if necessary, exercise a remedy, namely the grant of an injunction, which was not available to the juvenile court and which it was in the interests of the child should be available.

In this case the only ground on which it is suggested that the court should exercise the wardship jurisdiction is because, if the court in wardship made a care order under s 7(2) of the Family Law Reform Act 1969, the court would have power to grant access to the natural mother with a view to the children being rehabilitated and ultimately returned to her care (see *Re Y (a minor) (child in care: access)* [1975] 3 All ER 348, [1976] Fam 125). If, on the other hand, a care order is made by the juvenile court, then under s 1 of the Children and Young Persons Act 1969 the justices would have no power to order access, and the decision whether or not the children should be rehabilitated with their natural mother would rest with the local authority without supervision from any court except by judicial review, which would almost certainly not be appropriate. The difficulty I find with that argument is, as counsel for the local authority pointed out, that Parliament has set up a statutory scheme which gives wide powers to local authorities to provide for the welfare of children. Under that scheme, once a care order has been made by the juvenile court, the decision whether the child should be rehabilitated with its natural parents, and consequently whether there should be access to that end, is a matter for the discretion of

a the local authority and not for the court. In my view, it is not for the High Court in its wardship jurisdiction to say that it should take over a discretion which has been vested in local authorities by Parliament.

If the argument of counsel for the mother is right, then it would mean that in every case where the natural parent wished to challenge the local authority's decision as to access, the parent could invoke the wardship procedure. This would not only nullify the

b statutory scheme but would also be impracticable. According to Lord Wilberforce in *A v Liverpool City Council* [1981] 2 All ER 385 at 387, [1982] AC 363 at 371, about 90,000 children in England and Wales are in need of some supervision and assistance and there are over 65,000 care orders or parental rights resolutions by local authorities. We were told in this case that in 1982 alone some 246 new care orders were made in juvenile courts in favour of the Hampshire County Council. It would be quite impossible for the

c High Court in its wardship jurisdiction to deal with this additional volume of cases, leaving aside the enormous increase in costs to the legal aid fund. I repeat and adopt the passage of the judgment of Balcombe J which deals with this point:

'Now, it is the experience of anyone who has anything to do with cases concerning the welfare of children, firstly, that as a matter of practice local authorities with children in care normally attempt to rehabilitate the children with their natural

d parents if they consider that that is in the children's interests. That seems to me to be a part of their statutory duty under s 18(1) of the Child Care Act 1980 which provides that in reaching any decision relating to a child in their care the local authority shall give first consideration to the need to safeguard and promote the welfare of the child throughout his childhood. Secondly, that although there may be no statutory power to ensure it, if the local authority has come to the decision

e that the child's welfare does require rehabilitation with its parents, it is in practice able to achieve that result even though the necessary machinery is not present, under the Children and Young Persons Act 1969. If I were to hold that the absence of that machinery were to be a ground for justifying the invocation of the wardship jurisdiction it would be possible to say that was the ground in every single case where a child is in care because, as I have said, the normal aim is to rehabilitate the

f child with its parents. As I say, if the lack of any power in the juvenile court to order phased rehabilitation were to be decisive it would mean that in every case that would be a ground for applying in wardship and not leaving the matter, as the House of Lords has said one should do, to the statutory procedure. I cannot believe that the House of Lords was unaware of this lacuna in the legislation giving power to the juvenile court. The remedy appears to me to be for Parliament, if it thinks it

g appropriate, to provide for the necessary power to the juvenile court. As I understand the decision in *A v Liverpool City Council* [1981] 2 All ER 385, [1982] AC 363 which binds me, it is not appropriate to exercise wardship jurisdiction merely because of that lacuna.'

I venture to suggest that the real reason for the mother's application in this case, and

h the real reason why so many wardship applications involving local authorities have been made in recent years, is partly because parents do not willingly accept the decision of local authorities because they think that they are the decision of the particular social workers in dealing with whom the natural parents have run into personal difficulties. This is, of course, not so. Decisions of local authorities, as those who deal with these cases know, are effectively made by case conferences at which, although, of course, the social

j worker in charge of the case is present and makes his or her report, there are also a number of other qualified persons, including medical practitioners, and it is the decision of the case conference which goes forward and becomes the decision of the local authority. Not infrequently the recommendation of the particular social worker is not accepted by the case conference.

Another reason for these applications arises, in my view, from the unsatisfactory nature of the proceedings in the juvenile court from the point of view of the parents, and the lack of any effective right of appeal by parents. In the course of his submissions, *a* counsel for the mother pointed out to us the limited rights of audience of parents in the juvenile court. He pointed out that the juvenile court has no power to order an independent welfare report and so must rely on a report by a social worker who, as an employee of the local authority, is party to the proceedings, and he pointed out the fact that parents are not eligible for legal aid in the juvenile court and that the only right of appeal from an order under s 1 of the 1969 Act is by the child to the Crown Court. None *b* of these criticisms is new. They have been frequently made by judges of the Family Division and in this court, most recently by Ormrod LJ in *Re W (a minor) (justices' decision: review)* (1981) 2 FLR 360. The basic anomaly, as Ormrod LJ pointed out in that case, is that orders under s 1 may be made in delinquency cases where the child is, in effect, in the dock and the proceedings are essentially criminal, as well as in the neglect or ill-treatment cases where the parents are in the dock, but where the proceedings are *c* not criminal. To split the two types of procedure would not mean that the delinquent child need be dealt with differently by the juvenile court from the way in which it is at present dealt with, and the remedies open to the juvenile court for delinquency could perfectly easily be preserved; but neglect or ill-treatment proceedings could be dealt with by the domestic court, who are well accustomed to deal with problems of children since they already have jurisdiction to deal with custody in matrimonial proceedings, and the *d* considerations relating to care orders on the ground of neglect or ill-treatment are more akin to custody proceedings than to criminal or delinquency proceedings.

If that course were adopted an appeal would lie from the domestic court to the Divisional Court of the Family Division instead of to the Crown Court, which is a wholly inappropriate tribunal for this purpose. In a proper case the Divisional Court could direct that the child should be made a ward of court. The existing procedures undoubtedly give *e* grounds for a sense of grievance by many parents involved in care proceedings in the juvenile court but so far, despite judicial urging, Parliament has done nothing about it. This, I think, is why there are so many applications in wardship, because the parents feel that they have a fairer and more satisfactory trial in the High Court than in the juvenile court. But we have to accept the law as it stands and, looking at the situation as we must, from the point of view of the welfare of the children as opposed to the rights and feelings *f* of parents, I cannot think it right that the High Court should interfere with a statutory scheme which, in effect, places the responsibility for the children's welfare in the hands of local authorities and gives local authorities what Parliament considers to be adequate powers to safeguard the children's welfare.

In reaching this view I do not rest myself on any narrow jurisdictional distinction, for example, that this case is distinguishable from *A v Liverpool City Council* [1981] 2 All ER *g* 385, [1982] AC 363, because no care order has yet been made. There has merely been an application by the local authority. It is, however, noteworthy that in *Re W (a minor) (justices' decision: review)* (1981) 2 FLR 360 at 361 Sir John Arnold P at first instance found no difference in principle between a care order and an application for a care order in considering the question of jurisdiction. In my view, before the court can exercise its jurisdiction in wardship, it must be satisfied that such exercise is in the interests of the *h* child and, in considering that question, the court will, in an appropriate case, consider whether the child's welfare is likely to be adequately safeguarded under the statutory scheme or whether, in the particular circumstances of the case, the welfare of the child requires the exercise of some additional remedy open to the High Court but not available through the statutory scheme. In order to determine this question it is not necessary for the court to hear all the evidence. We were told the judge read the welfare report and *j* had the basic facts of the case opened to him. I think it is unfortunate that the jurisdiction issue in this case was not decided earlier, and before all the evidence; but I am satisfied that there was sufficient material before the judge to enable him to rule on the question of jurisdiction. Having read that material it seems to me that there was nothing special in the circumstances of this case requiring the exercise of the wardship jurisdiction.

a   I say nothing about the merits of the case because a hearing is pending before the juvenile court, and I desire to say nothing to influence their decision whether or not to make a care order. All I will say, however, is that this is typical of the hundreds of cases that are heard by juvenile courts up and down the country and I see no need, in the interests of the children, for the exercise of the wardship jurisdiction. For those reasons and for the reasons given by Eveleigh LJ I would dismiss this appeal.

b   *Appeal dismissed. Leave to appeal to House of Lords refused.*

Solicitors: *Coffin Mew & Co*, Gosport (for the mother); *R A Leyland*, Winchester (for the local authority).

Bebe Chua   Barrister.

c

Re J (a minor) (wardship: jurisdiction)

COURT OF APPEAL, CIVIL DIVISION

CUMMING-BRUCE LJ AND SIR GEORGE BAKER

d   7 JULY 1983

Child – Care – Local authority – Wardship proceedings – Jurisdiction of court to review decisions of local authority – Wardship proceedings by natural parent – Care order – Discharge of care order – Juvenile court lacking power to impose conditions on discharge of care order – Mother applying for discharge of care order – Mother commencing wardship proceedings to enable High Court to supervise return of child to her on discharge of care order by juvenile court – Whether High Court should exercise wardship jurisdiction – Children and Young Persons Act 1969, ss 1, 21(2).

e

In November 1981 the local authority obtained a place of safety order in respect of a child born in April 1981 on whom the mother had inflicted injuries. In December 1981 a juvenile court made a care order under s 1[a] of the Children and Young Persons Act 1969 in respect of the child. The local authority decided that it was not possible to rehabilitate the child with the mother and in March 1982 placed the child in a long-term foster home and terminated the mother's access to the child. In November 1982 the mother married a stable man by whom she was pregnant and in December issued proceedings in the juvenile court for the discharge of the care order. She accepted that because the child had been out of her care for some time a period of gradual reintroduction and rehabilitation of the child with her would be desirable before the child was returned to her but, since the juvenile court only had power, under s 21(2)[b] of the 1969 Act, either to continue the

f

g

---

h

j

care order or discharge it without being able to impose conditions controlling the return of the child to her, the mother issued wardship proceedings in which she sought care and *a* control of the child. The application in the juvenile court was adjourned for directions to be given in the wardship proceedings. The registrar decided to continue the wardship for the restricted purpose of controlling the return of the child to the mother and on appeal by the local authority the judge upheld that decision. The local authority appealed to the Court of Appeal, contending that the wardship should be discharged under the principle that the court would not exercise its wardship jurisdiction merely in order to *b* supervise a local authority in discharging its duties towards a child in its care.

Held – Since the juvenile court lacked power to impose conditions controlling the return of a child to its natural parent when it thought it right to discharge a care order, the High Court was entitled to invoke its wardship jurisdiction for the purpose of supervising the return of a child to the care of its natural parent, thus enabling the juvenile court to *c* exercise its jurisdiction to discharge the care order without being inhibited by its lack of power to attach conditions to the discharging of the order. Since there was a real risk that the juvenile court might feel compelled to refuse to discharge the care order simply because it had no power to impose such conditions it was right that the wardship should be continued for the limited purpose of enabling the court to exercise such control itself. It followed that the judge had been right to continue the wardship, and the local *d* authority's appeal would accordingly be dismissed (see p 34 *b* to *e* and *j* and p 35 *b*, post).

Dictum of Lord Wilberforce in *A v Liverpool City Council* [1981] 2 All ER at 388–389 applied.

Re E (minors) (wardship: jurisdiction) [1984] 1 All ER 21 distinguished.

Notes
e

For the care of a child by a local authority and its duty towards a child in care, see 24 Halsbury's Laws (4th edn) paras 787, 797.

For discharge of a care order, see ibid para 755.

For wardship jurisdiction, see ibid paras 576–583, and for cases on the subject, see 28(2) Digest (Reissue) 911–916, 2220–2247.

For the Children and Young Persons Act 1969, ss 1, 21, see 40 Halsbury's Statutes (3rd *f* edn) 849, 878.

Cases referred to in judgments
A v Liverpool City Council [1981] 2 All ER 385, [1982] AC 363, [1981] 2 WLR 948, HL.
E (minors) (wardship: jurisdiction), Re [1984] 1 All ER 21, [1983] 1 WLR 541, CA.
H (a minor) (wardship: jurisdiction), Re [1978] 2 All ER 903, [1978] Fam 65, [1978] 2 WLR *g* 608, CA.
M v Humberside CC [1979] 2 All ER 744, [1979] Fam 114, [1979] 3 WLR 234.

Interlocutory appeal
Wiltshire County Council (the local authority) appealed, with the leave of Bush J, from an order of Bush J dated 11 May 1983 dismissing the local authority's appeal from an *h* order of Mr Registrar Garland made on 11 April 1983 which directed that the minor in question was a ward of court and that the wardship should continue notwithstanding proceedings in a juvenile court by the mother of the minor applying for discharge of the care order made in respect of the minor. The facts are set out in the judgment of Cumming-Bruce LJ.

j

Margaret Bowron for the local authority.
Jane Hoyal for the mother.

CUMMING-BRUCE LJ. Bush J gave leave to the local authority to appeal to this court against an order that he made in wardship proceedings whereby he ordered that a the wardship should continue subject to limiting the steps to be taken in connection with the filing of evidence in the wardship proceedings, until the conclusion of proceedings in the juvenile court. The local authority seeks from this court a decision that the judge was wrong in continuing the wardship and asks that the wardship be discharged, relying on the application to the facts of this case and the procedural steps that have been taken to principles explained by the House of Lords in the well-known case of *A v Liverpool City Council* [1981] 2 All ER 385, [1982] AC 363, and by applying the

b principles explained by Balcombe J in *Re E (minors) (wardship: jurisdiction)* [1983] 1 WLR 541 and by the Court of Appeal ([1984] 1 All ER 21, [1983] 1 WLR 541) when they affirmed the order and the reasoning of Balcombe J.

The matter arises in this way, and I take the facts shortly. The little girl, the ward with whom the court is concerned, was born in April 1981. The mother was in deep personal trouble at the date of the birth. The father had attacked her violently two days before the

c birth, was arrested and subsequently sentenced to two years' imprisonment for his attack on her. During the earliest period of the child's life, on the evidence in the affidavits, the mother was trying to cope with her new baby in very difficult, personal circumstances. Then there were two occasions when the mother inflicted injuries, not by any means of the most serious kind, but unnecessary injuries, on her baby in circumstances in which the mother herself realised that her behaviour had not been appropriate. The mother on

d both occasions reported to the doctor the fact of her having lost self-control and her anxiety about the consequences on the baby. That was the immediate background to the local authority obtaining in November 1981 a place of safety order which was followed by an interim care order and, on 17 December 1981, a care order was made by the Salisbury juvenile court. On reception into care the child was placed with foster parents and the mother was granted access, but on 1 March 1982 the local authority, in the

e exercise of its statutory powers, moved the child to a long-term foster home having decided that successful rehabilitation was improbable. Having placed the child with long-term foster parents, the local authority decided that access by the mother to the child was not in the child's best interests in all the circumstances.

The mother had a chequered background history which must undoubtedly have been regarded as relevant by the statutory authority when considering the future of the child.

f The local authority, on the evidence, reviewed from time to time relevant questions as to whether access should begin again, or not, and whether there was any material change in its arrangements which should be made, and so the child continued, in spite of strenuous attempts by the mother and the child's grandmother to end the long-term fostering so that the mother could recover the child.

In August 1982 there began a chain of events which dramatically altered the mother's

g situation. In August she met a gentleman four or five years younger than herself, but grown up. By November 1982 the pregnancy of the mother was confirmed, the father being that gentleman of whom I have spoken. In the same month on 15 November the mother married that gentleman and throughout the winter the case was reconsidered by the local authority in the light of a request from the mother and on 8 December the mother issued a complaint to the juvenile court for discharge of the care order. On 3

h February 1983 the case came before the juvenile court and was adjourned on the application of the child's guardian ad litem for preparation of reports. On 3 March the hearing before the juvenile court took place and was adjourned part-heard to 16 March. On 14 March the mother issued a wardship summons seeking directions as to the care and control of the ward. On 16 March the hearing before the juvenile court was resumed but was adjourned on the application of the local authority for directions from the High

j Court. On 11 April directions in the wardship were given by Mr Registrar Garland. At the end of that month the mother gave birth to her second child, whose father was the gentleman whom she had married in November 1982.

The registrar gave his decision. There was an appeal from that decision to the judge. It is that decision of the judge in the wardship that has been brought before this court, the local authority seeking discharge of the wardship.

Of course, it is well established, as a result of the *Liverpool* case, that the court will not use its prerogative powers in such a way as to intervene in the discharge by the local *a* authority of the powers and responsibilities confided to it by Parliament in relation to the care of children. Once a care order has been made the effect of the legislation is that it is the local authority that is reponsible for the decision about how the child should be brought up, who should bring the child up on the ground, whether the natural parents are likely to be suitable for rehabilitation, which is necessarily a continuing responsibility and has to be looked at from time to time, whether the natural parent or parents should *b* have access to the child, and those decisions the local authority must take, being guided by its view as to what is in the best interests of the child.

In the *Liverpool* case [1981] 2 All ER 385 at 388–389, [1982] AC 363 at 373, at the end of his speech, Lord Wilberforce having confirmed that the courts should exercise their prerogative powers, with self.discipline and restraint, went on to say:

> 'In my opinion Parliament has marked out an area in which, subject to the *c* enacted limitations and safeguards, decisions for the child's welfare are removed from the parents and from supervision by the courts. This is not to say that the inherent jurisdiction of the High Court is taken away. Any child, whether under care or not, can be made a ward of court by the procedure of s 9(2) of the Law Reform (Miscellaneous Provisions) Act 1949. In cases (and the present is an example) where the court perceives that the action sought of it is within the sphere of *d* discretion of the local authority, it will make no order and the wardship will lapse. But in some instances, there may be an area of concern to which the powers of the local authority, limited as they are by statute, do not extend. Sometimes the local authority itself may invite the supplementary assistance of the court. Then the wardship may be continued with a view to action by the court. The court's general inherent power is always available to fill gaps or to supplement the powers of the *e* local authority; what it will not do (except by way of judicial review where appropriate) is to supervise the exercise of discretion within the field committed by statute to the local authority.'

In *Re E (minors) (wardship: jurisdiction)* [1984] 1 All ER 21, [1983] 1 WLR 541 this court was considering whether it was appropriate to continue the wardship where the *f* local authority had obtained a place of safety order, and decided that the High Court could not exercise its wardship jurisdiction. It would not supervise the exercise by the local authority of discretion committed to it by statute and that there was no reason for continuing the wardship. This court affirmed the judgment of Balcombe J and held that, on the facts before them, there was no occasion for duplicating the statutory duties of the local authority who had the child on a place of safety order, by continuing the *g* responsibility of the wardship judge after the wardship application had been made.

The court held obiter that there was no distinction between the situation facing the court in a place of safety situation as compared to a care order situation. I agree that for this purpose there is no practical distinction. Dunn LJ, in the course of his judgment, said ([1984] 1 All ER 21 at 28, [1983] 1 WLR 541 at 557):

> '. . . before the court can exercise its jurisdiction in wardship, it must be satisfied *h* that such exercise is in the interests of the child and, in considering that question, the court will, in an appropriate case, consider whether the child's welfare is likely to be adequately safeguarded under the statutory scheme or whether, in the particular circumstances of the case, the welfare of the child requires the exercise of some additional remedy open to the High Court but not available through the statutory scheme.' *j*

His conclusion was that 'there was nothing special in the circumstances of this case requiring the exercise of the wardship jurisdiction'.

After first hearing counsel for the local authority it seemed to me that the instant case was indistinguishable from *Re E (minors) (wardship: jurisdiction)* because the only a   distinction was a distinction without any difference, namely that the instant case arises after a care order has been made as compared to a place of safety order. But counsel for the mother has given me a greater insight into the history of this matter and what it really was that moved the judge to continue the wardship. The answer is this. As is well known, on an application to the juvenile court to discharge a care order there are only two decisions that the juvenile court can make. It can discharge the care order and it can refuse to discharge the care order. If it refuses to discharge the care order, the child stays

b   in care. And the consequences of the two orders which are open to the juvenile court are: if the natural parents succeed the consequence of the order is that the child is returned to the natural parents, in this case the mother; if the mother fails, the care order continues and the local authority continues to exercise its statutory duties and powers. The juvenile court has no power to impose any conditions as the conditions on which it will discharge the care order, and, though in one case there was a suspension of the operation of the

c   justices' order, both counsel before us, after considering that, are of the view that it is extremely doubtful whether there is any power to suspend such an order. The matter has not been argued before us and I do not propose to make any observation about it, save to say that I naturally respect the doubts entertained by industrious counsel.

There has been reference in the cases to a lacuna in the statutory scheme. In my view there is a lacuna in the statutory scheme which can only be filled by the legislator in

d   order to complete the powers available to the local authority and to the juvenile court under the statutory scheme. The difficulty is this. When a child has been in long-term care for year, having left her mother's care on 6 November 1981 and access to the mother having ceased on 16 March 1982, there are manifest practical problems arising if it is decided that in principle the care order should be discharged and the child returned to her mother, because by the time the juvenile court resumes its hearing, this girl, who is

e   just over two years' old, would not have seen her mother for over a year and would not have been in her mother's care for more than 18 months. The child will then only be just over two. Some programme for reintroduction and rehabilitation is essential as a necessary concomitant to discharge of the care order. But the juvenile court has no power to order any such programme and if the mother decides to give an undertaking to the juvenile court not to take the child away from the foster parents until she has got to

f   know her and re-establish the link, there is no sanction to enforce such an undertaking. The justices, when they resume the case, are in this difficulty. Of course, they may decide, on the facts, that the moment has not yet come to discharge the care order for the reasons, for example, that the mother's new home has not persisted for very long, that the marriage to her husband has not had too much time to settle down and that it is as lately as the end of April that the mother was saddled with the responsibility of looking

g   after her second baby. Those might be reasons for the juvenile court to decide that the application for discharge of the care order is premature. Nothing that I say should be taken as giving the slightest indication as to the answer to that question, which I have not considered at all.

Alternatively the justices may on the facts decide that the time has come to discharge the care order and return the child to mother and her new husband but that it is not

h   feasible to do that without a careful programme of phased reintroduction as a condition precedent to the transfer. As the justices may only discharge the care order if they think it is appropriate, having regard to the interests of the child, then, if that is a view that the justices form on the facts, they would almost certainly be compelled to refuse to discharge the care order because of the risk that the mother might go straight from the court and carry the child away. The lacuna in the statute is that the justices cannot impose any

j   conditions as to reintroduction before the transfer takes place.

In these proceedings the mother's legal representative asked the local authority's solicitor if he would give an undertaking to make the child a ward of court if the justices discharged the care order, which shows a very responsible attitude on the part of the mother. The solicitor of the local authority felt unable to commit himself, and I know not and make no observation about the merits of the stance that he took up. That was the background of the mother herself trying to make the child a ward of court because the local authority would not, or at any rate had not given any undertaking to do so. The object of the mother's application to ward the child was to fill the lacuna in the statute because she could not be confident that the local authority was prepared to do so. Had the local authority felt able to commit itself to making the child a ward of court immediately on the contingency of the discharge of the care order, the mother would never have applied at all.

In these circumstances I take the view that had the local authority applied to make the child a ward in order to protect the child during the transitional period by enabling the wardship judge to exercise power which the juvenile court I would think ought to have, but certainly has not got, such an application by the local authority would be exactly the kind of application contemplated by Lord Wilberforce at the end of his speech, to fill a gap in the statutory scheme, not in this case a gap in the powers of the local authority but a gap in the powers of the juvenile court. If the wardship does not continue, there is a real risk that the justices may feel compelled to refuse to discharge the care order simply because they do not know what is going to happen to the child, but are confident that it would be wrong for the child to be transferred before the mother had got to know her. The purpose of the wardship proceedings, as I understand it, is to enable the justices to discharge their jurisdiction without the inhibition, anxiety and uncertainty flowing from the fact that otherwise they cannot know whether the child will be protected on the discharge of the order.

For those reasons, I would hold that Bush J was right in continuing the wardship in the restricted way that he did, having regard to the directions that he gave, and I would move that the appeal be dismissed.

SIR GEORGE BAKER. The hour is late and agreeing, as I do, with all that Cumming-Bruce LJ has said, I will add little.

In M v Humberside CC [1979] 2 All ER 744 at 751, [1979] Fam 114 at 123, I said:

'Now, to summarise, it seems to me that the High Court will assume jurisdiction only in limited circumstances. First, if the powers of the lower court require to be supplemented, that is to say, where its powers are inadequate. Second, if there has been some irregularity or excess in the exercise of the powers of the local authority, and, third, the composite head, if there is something exceptional, something really unusual about the case which necessitates the intervention of the High Court.'

I can see no reason to alter anything I said there having read, as carefully as I can, the speeches of the House of Lords in A v Liverpool City Council [1981] 2 All ER 385, [1982] AC 363, particularly the passage cited by Cumming-Bruce LJ in the speech of Lord Wilberforce, and a passage in the speech of Lord Roskill ([1981] 2 All ER 385 at 393, [1982] AC 363 at 378) (speaking of the decision in Re H (a minor) (wardship: jurisdiction) [1978] 2 All ER 903, [1978] Fam 65 which was cited):

'I venture to think that the decision can perhaps be better supported on the ground that the wardship jurisdiction of the court could properly be invoked in addition to the statutory jurisdiction of the local authority because it was only in this way that the result which was best in the paramount interest of the child could be achieved, the local authority and juvenile court being unable, within the limits of their powers, to achieve that result.'

I have also considered with care, and particularly the passages which Cumming-Bruce LJ has cited, the judgments in Re E (minors) (wardship: jurisdiction) [1984] 1 All ER 21, [1983] 1 WLR 541 in this court. It would, it seems to me, be very unfortunate if the justices decided, or appeared to decide, to dismiss the application to discharge the care order because there was no sure way in which the child could gradually be reintroduced to the mother. Indeed the justices had no power to make such a programme or to lay a down conditions. It would be quite different, may I stress, if they decided, and appeared to decide, to dismiss the application on the true merits of the mother's case.

In saying that I must not be taken to be acceding to the agreement which apparently exists between counsel that there is, in fact, no power in the justices to suspend the handing over of the child and the operation of the order. I suspect the arguments that may have appealed to both counsel are the very same arguments that were used 10 or 15 years ago to support the view, held ultimately to be quite erroneous, that justices had no b power to suspend the operation of a custody order and leave a child in the custody in which it was until, eg the time for appeal had elapsed. However, that is merely by the way and we have not heard any argument on the point. Suffice it to say that I entirely agree with all that Cumming-Bruce LJ has said and in particular the conclusion reached by Bush J.

c *Appeal dismissed.*

Solicitors: *Collyer-Bristow*, agents for *I A Browning*, Trowbridge (for the local authority); *Mary Ryan* (for the mother).

Patricia Hargrove   Barrister.

d

General Accident Fire and Life Assurance Corp Ltd and others v Tanter and others
e
The Zephyr

QUEEN'S BENCH DIVISION (COMMERCIAL COURT)
HOBHOUSE J
30, 31 MAY, 1–3, 6–10, 13–16, 20 JUNE 1983
f

Discovery – Privilege – Waiver – Defendant giving notice before trial to claimant of intention to adduce contemporaneous document as evidence at trial – Document a memorandum from defendant to solicitor – Defendant's counsel producing memorandum at trial and cross-examining claimant's witness as to its veracity – Defendant not obtaining court's leave to admit memorandum g *– Claimant's counsel contending privilege waived in confidentiality of memorandum and consequently in all documents relating to topics in memorandum – Claimant's counsel applying for discovery of all related documents – Whether pre-trial notice amounting to waiver of whole memorandum – Whether cross-examination sufficient to introduce memorandum as evidence – Whether waiver of privilege extending to all documents relating to topics contained in memorandum.*

h
The plaintiffs brought an action against a number of underwriters and a broking company. The underwriters cross-claimed against the brokers and before the trial the brokers' solicitors served a notice on the underwriters' solicitors under the Civil Evidence Act 1968 preparatory to seeking leave from the court to admit in evidence at the trial a memorandum written by A, one of the brokers' directors, to the brokers' solicitors j recounting conversations between two of the brokers' directors and also between B, the other director, and P, one of the underwriting defendants, and/or P's solicitor. At the time of the memorandum it had not been anticipated that the underwriters would claim against the brokers. B had countersigned the memorandum as apparent verification of its contents. The memorandum had not been disclosed on discovery because it was privileged. At the trial and before leave to put the memorandum in evidence had been

sought the underwriters called P to give evidence and the brokers' counsel produced the memorandum and cross-examined him as to its contents after counsel indicated that he would be calling B to give evidence when the brokers' case was presented. Counsel's efforts to have P acknowledge the veracity of the memorandum were unsuccessful and no reference was made to the memorandum on re-examination. Counsel for the underwriters then applied to the court for specific discovery of all documents relating to the topics of conversation mentioned in the memorandum, particularly the relevant proofs of the evidence of the brokers' directors and all relevant pre-trial communications between the brokers and their solicitors and counsel, on the basis that privilege in the memorandum had been waived by the brokers and had thereby been waived in respect of all those documents and conversations. Counsel also claimed the right to cross-examine the brokers' witnesses on all those documents and topics.

Held – The application would be dismissed for the following reasons—

(1) The application was misconceived and premature since at the time it was made leave had not been sought to put the memorandum in evidence pursuant to the 1968 Act and B had not then given evidence. At that stage the memorandum had merely been used as a vehicle for cross-examination and was not part of the evidence before the court. The giving of notice under the 1968 Act before the trial operated as a waiver of privilege in the whole of the memorandum but such waiver did not extend to documents relating to the matters referred to in the memorandum. It was only if and when the memorandum was adduced in evidence at the trial that the issue of potential further waiver could arise and then it would have to be determined according to the underlying principle of fairness in the conduct of the trial (see p 47 d to f and h j, post); *Lyell v Kennedy (No 3)* [1881–5] All ER Rep 814, *Burnell v British Transport Commission* [1955] 3 All ER 822, *Nea Karteria Maritime Co Ltd v Atlantic and Great Lakes Steamship Corp* [1981] Com LR 138 and *Great Atlantic Insurance Co v Home Insurance Co* [1981] 2 All ER 485 applied.

(2) Assuming that the memorandum would later be admitted in evidence, fairness would require that the consequent waiver of privilege be limited to the waiver of confidentiality in the relevant transaction since otherwise there would be a continuing and ever-widening process of discovery. The various conversations recounted in the memorandum were the transaction in respect of which privilege would be waived but since the subject matter of those conversations was not part of the transaction the waiver would not extend to all documents and conversations relating to the topics of conversation recounted in the memorandum. Accordingly, if and when B gave evidence and the memorandum was admitted pursuant to the 1968 Act, fairness would require that he be liable to cross-examination on the totality of the transaction but the waiver of privilege would go no further than that and the underwriters would have no right to disclosure of documents beyond those which were relevant to that transaction (see p 48 a to f and p 49 e f, post); *Nea Karteria Maritime Co Ltd v Atlantic and Great Lakes Steamship Corp* [1981] Com LR 138 applied; *George Doland Ltd v Blackburn Robson Coates & Co (a firm)* [1972] 3 All ER 959 doubted. *Burnell v British Transport Commission* [1955] 3 All ER 822 distinguished.

Notes

For legal professional privilege in respect of communications between legal adviser and client and for waiver of that privilege, see 13 Halsbury's Laws (4th edn) paras 71–76, 84, and for cases on the subject, see 18 Digest (Reissue) 105–115, 163, 774–874, 1303–1308.

For the Civil Evidence Act 1968, see 12 Halsbury's Statutes (3rd edn) 910.

Cases referred to in judgment

Burnell v British Transport Commission [1955] 3 All ER 822, [1956] 1 QB 187, [1956] 2 WLR 61, CA.

Doland (George) Ltd v Blackburn Robson Coates & Co (a firm) [1972] 3 All ER 959, [1972] 1 WLR 1338.

Euroshipping Corp of Monrovia v Minister of Agricultural Economics and Marketing 1979 (1)
a   SA 637, CPD.
Grant v South Western and County Properties Ltd [1974] 2 All ER 465, [1975] Ch 185,
[1974] 3 WLR 221.
Great Atlantic Insurance Co v Home Insurance Co [1981] 2 All ER 485, [1981] 1 WLR 529,
CA.
Lyell v Kennedy (No 3) (1884) 27 Ch D 1, [1881–5] All ER Rep 814, CA.
b   *Nea Karteria Maritime Co Ltd v Atlantic and Great Lakes Steamship Corp* [1981] Com LR
138.
Occidental Worldwide Investment Corp v Skibs A/S Avanti, The Siboen and The Sibotre [1976] 1
Lloyd's Rep 293.
Waugh v British Rlys Board [1979] 2 All ER 1169, [1980] AC 521, [1979] 3 WLR 150, HL.

c ### Application
By a writ issued on 25 June 1981 and amended on 11 and 18 December 1981 the first
plaintiff, General Accident Fire and Life Assurance Corp Ltd, and eight other plaintiffs
who were insurance companies or representatives of various Lloyd's syndicates claimed
against the first defendant, Peter William Tanter, sued on his behalf and on behalf of all
members of Lloyd's syndicate 920, the second defendant, Ian Richard Posgate, sued on
d his behalf and on behalf of all members of Lloyd's syndicate 127, the third defendant,
Mark Edmund Denby, sued on his behalf and on behalf of all member's of Lloyd's
syndicate 700, the fourth defendant, John Albert Reeve Moller, sued on his behalf and
on behalf of all members of Lloyd's syndicates 275 and 645 (collectively called 'the
underwriters') and the fifth defendant, Berisford Mocatta & Co Ltd (the brokers), for
contribution of certain respective percentages of a loss claim which arose out of the loss
e of the mv Zephyr, pursuant to reinsurance underwritten by the underwriters. By notice
dated 25 April 1983 the underwriters applied to the court for an order that the brokers produce to them
documents relating to a memorandum dated 6 October 1981 from a principal of the
brokers to their solicitors. The facts are set out in the judgment.

f *Adrian Hamilton QC* and *John Thomas* for the plaintiffs.
Mark O Saville QC and *Stephen Ruttle* for the underwriters.
Jonathan Mance QC and *Julian Flaux* for the brokers.

HOBHOUSE J. I now have to give my ruling on an application that has been made by
the defendant reinsurance underwriters during the course of this trial. This is the trial of
g an action in which the plaintiffs have been suing the defendant reinsurance underwriters
since 25 June 1981 and by amendment they have also been suing the fifth defendants
Berisford Mocatta & Co Ltd, whom I will call 'the brokers', since 11 December 1981. The
reinsurance underwriters have cross-claimed against the brokers by a notice dated 25
April 1983. A central factual issue in the action between all parties is what was said by a
broker, Mr Baxter, to the reinsurance underwriters at the time of the underwriting of
h the reinsurance slip. The three individuals concerned signed the slip on various dates, Mr
Tanter on 17 December 1980, Mr Posgate on 2 January 1981 and Mr Emms on 5 January
1981.
Before the trial started, the brokers' solicitors purported to serve a notice under the
Civil Evidence Act 1968 on the solicitors for the reinsurance underwriters. It was in a
letter dated 6 March 1983, and read as follows:

j

> 'We enclose a copy of the interoffice memorandum of our clients, Berisford
> Mocatta dated 6 October 1981. We hereby give you notice under the Civil Evidence
> Act 1968 that our clients will seek to give in evidence the statements contained in
> that document at the trial of this action. The circumstances in which the documents
> came into existence are as follows: it is a contemporaneous memorandum from Mr

Reginald Baxter to Mr Francis Mocatta, with a copy to Mr Clive Brown of this firm, recording the terms of a conversation which had taken place that day, 6 October, *a* between Mr Baxter and Mr Ian Posgate, the second defendant in this action. The conversation took place at Mr Posgate's box in Lloyd's, Lime Street, London EC3 during a meeting between Mr Baxter and Mr Posgate called at the behest of the latter.'

Mr Mocatta was one of the two principal directors of the broking firm; Mr Baxter was also a director. Mr Clive Brown was the person concerned at the brokers' solicitors, Messrs *b* Hewitt Woollacott & Chown. The memorandum which was attached is not in all respects accurately described in this letter. It is a memorandum which is dated 6 October 1981 and it is in form, a communication by Mr Mocatta to his firm's solicitor, Mr Brown. The document has been countersigned by Mr Baxter, and clearly therefore Mr Baxter has adopted and verified what is reported in that document. There are a number of matters which are dealt with in that memorandum. The first is a conversation on 6 October *c* between Mr Baxter and Mr Posgate, in the course of which Mr Posgate is alleged to have agreed that no signing indication was given to him in January 1981 and the second a tripartite conversation immediately following the first between Mr Baxter and Mr Posgate and Mr Fick of Messrs Elborne Mitchell & Co, the solicitors acting for the reinsurance underwriters. Third, it deals with a telephone conversation between Mr Baxter and Mr Fick that took place later the same day, and, on my reading of the *d* memorandum, it also, fourth, includes a report of what Mr Baxter told Mr Mocatta about his own practice on that same occasion.

So there are various matters that are dealt with in this memorandum, but it all forms part of one report made by Mr Mocatta to his solicitor, Mr Brown. It may be that the notice under the 1968 Act was intended to be confined to that part of the memorandum which relates to the actual conversation between Mr Baxter and Mr Posgate or between *e* Mr Baxter, Mr Posgate and Mr Fick, solicitor for the underwriters, on the floor of Lloyd's.

I also mention that it would appear from the memorandum and the matters which it describes that at that time, that is 6 October 1981, it was probably not then contemplated that there would be litigation between the brokers and the reinsurance underwriters. If litigation was then contemplated between those parties it would be very odd that *f* solicitors for one party would be having conversations with witnesses of another party, without the solicitors for that other party being present and having given their consent to that meeting. However it is not necessary that I say more than that this is a possible inference from the document.

The trial of this action started on 10 May 1983. On 8 June Mr Posgate was called by the defendant underwriters, and he gave evidence-in-chief not referring to 6 October 1981 at all. He was then cross-examined by the counsel for the brokers. He was first of *g* all, in the relevant sequence, cross-examined about the events of 6 October 1981, and whether he had or had not made an admission on that day. Then he was further cross-examined by counsel, making use of the memorandum of 6 October to which I have referred.

The matter arose in this way. Counsel for the brokers started to refer to the document which had not previously been referred to at all during the trial. Copies were distributed *h* to myself and to the witness, and counsel for the underwriters pointed out that there was a question mark about its status under the 1968 Act. I inquired whether Mr Baxter was going to be called. Counsel for the brokers said: 'I'm certainly calling Mr Baxter, that is why we have given this notice.' I then asked: 'What is the point of putting this to Mr Posgate?' Counsel said: 'It is simply a convenient way of putting what I suggest happened at the meeting.' I said: 'That probably clarifies it.' Counsel for the underwriters then said: *j*

'On the question of waiving privilege, it does seem to me to be a communication from client to solicitor and it may well be that under these circumstances my friend, if he wishes to rely on this document (and I have no objection if he wishes to) is waiving his privilege in relation to allied documents with the consequences that they would have to be produced.'

I said: 'We will deal with that problem when it arises.' Counsel said: 'I am not objecting
a to my friend putting this, but would call for these documents.' I then left that to be
sorted out between counsel, whether they could reach agreement about it. Counsel for
the brokers then proceeded on that afternoon, and again on the following morning, to
cross-examine Mr Posgate, making use of the document. It is right to point out that he
made full use of the document in that he not only used it as a convenient means of
summarising what was going to be Mr Baxter's evidence, but he sought unsuccessfully
b to impress Mr Posgate with the fact that Mr Baxter had signed a memorandum
contemporaneously and therefore urged Mr Posgate to accept what counsel said Mr
Baxter was going to say.

For example, counsel asked:

> 'Q. Have you any explanation why Mr Baxter might have written this
> memorandum or indicated the contents of this memorandum and been prepared to
c > sign it if what it said was not correct? A. It looks as though it was dictated by Mr
> Mocatta.
> Q. Signed by Mr Baxter? A. Dictated by Mr Mocatta.
> Q. Have you any explanation why Mr Baxter would be prepared to put his
> signature to anything not correct in relation to this conversation? A. I have already
> intimated that I am sure he would be prepared to do so, which obviously he would
d > not approve of my saying.'

So counsel for the brokers' efforts to impress Mr Posgate with Mr Baxter's signature were
unsuccessful and they were unsuccessful in any part of his use of that document, whether
it related solely to the conversations on the floor of Lloyd's on 6 October, or what was
said in the document to be Mr Baxter's recollection of what happened at the earlier stage
e when the slip was originally signed. There was no reference to the document or to 6
October in re-examination. The status of the document at that stage of the proceedings
appears to have been this. It was originally a privileged document. Although
contemporaneously prepared, it was specifically a document which was a communication
by a client to his solicitor, and it was furthermore prepared with a view to assisting in
litigation which at that stage was in any event contemplated between the plaintiffs and
f the brokers. I do not treat this document as being on a par with the documents or articles
referred to in *Grant v South Western and County Properties Ltd* [1974] 2 All ER 465, [1975]
Ch 185 on which counsel for the broker relied. It is also right to say that the subject
matter of the document, certainly in so far as it related to communications between Mr
Baxter and Mr Posgate or Mr Fick, does not appear to have been privileged. Anyway, I
can proceed on that assumption. Because the document was privileged, it was not
g disclosed on discovery. When the letter of 6 May 1983 was written, privilege in the
document was clearly waived.

Following the sending of the letter of 6 May 1983, the document could be used by the
other parties to the litigation; they could either use it as an admission, or they could
themselves put it in under the 1968 Act, relying on the notice which had previously
been given by the brokers. But this document could not be adduced in evidence by the
h brokers themselves, except under the provisions of the 1968 Act, and then only with the
leave of the court if Mr Baxter was called. Section 2 of the 1968 Act makes express
provision with regard to the situation where the maker of a statement (and the relevant
statement here is that of Mr Baxter) is called to give evidence at the trial.

First of all, the statement under the 1968 Act may not be given in evidence without
the leave of the court, and second it may not, subject to certain exceptions, be given in
j evidence until after the maker has concluded his evidence in chief.

The position is that leave has not yet been applied for to put it in evidence under the
1968 Act, and such leave has not yet been given and Mr Baxter has not yet given evidence.
In my judgment, although there has been extensive use made of the document by
counsel for the brokers in cross-examination of Mr Posgate, it has so far merely been used
as a vehicle for cross-examination and it is not part of the evidence in the case properly so
called. If, for example, there were a jury in this case, I might, in order to avoid prejudicing

a jury, have required counsel to conduct his cross-examination in a different way, but in any event I would have directed the jury to disregard this document unless and until it was proved in the proper way and the statements made in it were proved properly.

So its present status is that it is not evidence, it is merely a document which, as a matter of convenience has been used as part of a cross-examination and by reason of its signature has been used in an attempt, albeit an unsuccessful attempt, to impress a witness, Mr Posgate, who was not impressed. For the future, we have not yet reached that stage of the trial when the document can be put in under the 1968 Act. Leave may or may not be given for it to be put in. It has that potential and no more. Furthermore, it is clearly a document from which Mr Baxter may refresh his memory when he comes to give evidence.

It will be apparent from what I have already said that we are still in the middle of the trial and the brokers have not yet opened their case. Counsel for the underwriters submits that by reason of the matters to which I have referred, he is entitled to discovery from the brokers and by implication he says that he is entitled to ask the brokers' witnesses about documents and about conversations in cross-examination. But the form of the application and submission that is made is very widely stated, and it is conveniently set out in the letter of 15 June 1983 sent by the defendant underwriters' solicitors, to the brokers' solicitors. It refers to the cross-examination of Mr Posgate and use made of the document and refers to the fact that counsel for the underwriters indicated to the court that the brokers had waived the privilege that attached to this document. It then continues:

'Our clients require specific discovery of all other documents previously privileged that are or have been in the possession, custody or care of your clients and in relation to which privilege has thereby been waived. We are now entitled to specific discovery of all documents that relate to or bear upon a number of topics.'

Those topics have been redefined by counsel for the underwriters, so I will use his redefinition. Then it says:

'In particular, without prejudice to the generality of this request our clients seek discovery of the proofs of evidence of Mr Baxter and Mr Mocatta, all communications between your clients and yourselves and all instructions to counsel and memoranda prepared by you in so far as these documents relate to the above matters. Your clients have not yet given discovery of any of these documents, accordingly we now make a formal request for discovery and we would wish this to take place as soon as possible.'

The redefinition of the relevant matters adopted by counsel is under five heads. They are: (1) the conversation between Mr Posgate and Mr Baxter on 6 October 1981; (2) what was said between Mr Posgate and Mr Baxter in January 1981; (3) what Mr Baxter habitually says or suggests to underwriters when presenting slips to them for signature; (4) what Mr Baxter said to Mr Tanter and Mr Emms in December 1980 and January 1981 respectively; and (5) a conversation that Mr Baxter had with Mr Fick, the solicitor for the underwriters, in October 1981, presumably on the telephone.

Counsel for the underwriters is quite right to say that all those topics are topics which are referred to either directly or indirectly in the conversations which are recorded in the memorandum of 6 October 1981. To put it shortly, they are the subject matter of the various conversations that are recorded in this memorandum.

The application that I have to rule on, therefore, is whether there should be such discovery and what should be the scope of cross-examination that is to be permitted when Mr Baxter or other witnesses are called by the brokers. Counsel for the underwriters refers to, and relies primarily on, *George Doland Ltd v Blackburn Robson Coates & Co (a firm)* [1972] 3 All ER 959, [1972] 1 WLR 1338, and he relies also on the decision of the Court of Appeal in *Great Atlantic Insurance Co v Home Insurance Co* [1981] 2 All ER 485, [1981] 1 WLR 529. The *Doland* case is a case which like the present concerned use of evidence

under the 1968 Act which would otherwise be privileged and the consequences of the
a use of such evidence. It is a decision of Geoffrey Lane J and is not binding on me. It was
reached in the course of a trial and it is recorded that no cases were referred to in the
judgment or were cited in argument. A gentleman, a Mr King, who was the managing
director of the plaintiff company had given evidence about certain matters which were
the basis of his complaint, or his firm's complaint, against the defendant company,
Blackburn & Co. Mr King's evidence was challenged. Mr King in support of his own
b credit had said that he was in the habit over the years of ringing up his solicitor, Mr
Jackson, on the telephone and using him as a sounding board for his ideas. Consequently,
Mr Jackson was also called to give evidence to confirm this and say what Mr King had
said to him on the telephone at the relevant times relating to the transactions that gave
rise to the complaint. In so doing it was sought to use the statements of Mr King made
to Mr Jackson under the 1968 Act, those statements being proved by the calling of Mr
c Jackson as a witness. The judge identified two questions of fact which were referred to in
the conversation and to which that evidence went. They were ([1972] 3 All ER 959 at
961, [1972] 1 WLR 1338 at 1340):

> '. . . did Mr King instruct Mr Bedford to investigate the statement of his partner,
> Mr Clement, that the companies were no longer losing money? and, secondly . . .
> the question of whether Mr Clement had in fact used that expression or something
d > like it.'

That was the relevant subject matter of the conversation between Mr King and Mr
Jackson.
    Counsel for the defendants then sought to cross-examine Mr Jackson and sought
directions as to his freedom of action in conducting that cross-examination. He sought
e to cross-examine the witness as to any document or any oral conversation or instructions
relating to either of those two points in the conversation between the witness and Mr
King which might have come into existence, so far as documents were concerned, or
taken place, so far as conversations were concerned, from that moment in early January
1967 up to the date of trial, including any proofs of witnesses and instructions to counsel
or anything else, providing that they were related to the two points. Counsel for the
f plaintiffs objected, and his objection was overruled in part. It was held that on the
question whether the ambit of the cross-examination should be confined only to matters
relating to the conversations themselves, counsel's submission was wrong. The judge said
([1972] 3 All ER 959 at 962, [1972] 1 WLR 1338 at 1341):

> 'Up to that date, the date of impending litigation, if I may call it that, in my
> judgment the defendants are entitled to ask for and see any documents relating to
g > the facts of the two items contained in the telephone conversation to which I have
> made reference.'

In that short sentence, Geoffrey Lane J was deciding that the scope of cross-examination
was to be defined by reference to the two topics and not to be confined to matters directly
relating to the conversations themselves. The absurd conclusion that all counsel's
h instructions, briefs and proofs should be disclosed was avoided in that case by a further
argument of counsel for the plaintiffs which was accepted by Geoffrey Lane J. The judge
stated ([1972] 3 All ER 959 at 962, [1972] 1 WLR 1338 at 1341):

> 'The mere fact that the plaintiffs may have waived the professional privilege
> which exists between client and solicitor does not, in my judgment, also result in
> the waiver of the further privilege which protects documents brought into existence
j > for the purpose of litigation; and therefore, in my judgment, the privilege which
> counsel for the plaintiff contends for relating to, for instance, brief to counsel and
> proofs taken from witnesses is a good one and stands, despite the waiver relating to
> the initial evidence which I have described.'

The judge therefore made use of a distinction between simple solicitor and client

privilege and the privilege which arises in relation to anticipated litigation. He said, as
regards the latter, that there was no waiver; as regards the former, there was. In so far as
any documents existed regarding the two relevant topics but which were only covered
by solicitor and client privilege, then they were liable to be disclosed and could be the
subject of cross-examination. The same would apply to oral conversations.

Counsel for the underwriters' submission in the present case follows precisely the logic
of that case and that decision. He says that the equivalent of the two points to which
Geoffrey Lane J referred were the five topics which he himself formulated. Furthermore,
he says that in this case there is no problem about the difference between solicitor and
client privilege and privilege which arises from anticipated litigation. Here litigation
was anticipated at the relevant time, and therefore there is no restriction to be placed on
the scope of questioning or, indeed, on the scope of discovery, and that is why, he
submitted, it is proper to have discovery of proofs of evidence, instructions to counsel
and memoranda prepared by the solicitors for the purposes of trial, or, indeed, any other
purpose.

This is a submission of astonishing breadth. If it is to be acceded to, it has very serious
implications, not only for the disclosure of confidential documents that are created or
obtained for the purposes of a trial and its preparation but also for a whole number of
situations that arise almost every day in litigation. For example, statements under the
1968 Act are frequently put in in evidence. They are frequently statements which have
been given to a solicitor and which, in the absence of a notice under the 1968 Act being
served, would be privileged. They are very often not the only statement that a witness
has made to the solicitor. Likewise, the same point arises with regard to affidavits.
Affidavits, until they are served or used in court, are obviously privileged, but affidavits
themselves may be preceded or succeeded by other statements made by the witness or
records of other statements made by the witness to the solicitor.

Again, in re-examination statements may be used to contradict a suggestion by
opposing counsel in cross-examination of recent invention by a witness. That use in re-
examination obviously waives the privilege that previously existed in that statement. It
would be submitted, and indeed counsel for the underwriters does not shrink from that
submission, that the waiver of the privilege of that statement also waived the privilege
for all other statements or comparable documents. Likewise, again, a witness may use a
statement that he has made contemporaneously to refresh his memory. When he goes
into the witness box, he may be invited by his counsel to look at a contemporaneous
record which he has made. That record may be a privileged document. On his being
invited to look at it, obviously privilege is waived in that document and the other parties
are entitled also to see that document. But, as I understand it on the logic of the
submission of counsel, that waiver of that privilege carries with it a waiver of privilege
in other statements made by that witness to his solicitors and other related documents.
Therefore, this point is far-reaching and is potentially very important.

Counsel for the underwriters also was not deterred by the fact that he submits that use
of part of a document makes the whole of the document disclosable, and therefore this
very submission might give rise to an almost infinite regress through the privileged
documents held by a party. One document makes another document disclosable; that
other document will make further documents disclosable, and so on. This is merely one
of the difficulties about his submission. He suggested with complete fairness, but not
wholly logically, that one of the ways in which that sort of problem might be avoided is
by covering up parts of documents which related to different subject matter or by leaving
it to the good faith of the relevant solicitors to select those documents, or those parts of
the documents, which did relate to the topic on which privilege had been waived.

He appears to have support for his main submissions but not for this last suggestion in
Great Atlantic Insurance Co v Home Insurance Co [1981] 2 All ER 485, [1981] 1 WLR 529.
That is a decision of the Court of Appeal, by which I am bound, but in fact the actual
decision in it was relatively limited. It was a decision with regard to the use of part of a
document. Part of a document had been used in opening. It was a document which,

apart from waiver, would have been privileged, but it was thought at the time that it was
a used in opening at the trial that what was in the bundle and read out was the totality of
the document. It subsequently emerged that that was not the case and that there was
more to the document than in fact appeared from the copy used. The argument in that
case was whether, having used part of the document and read it in opening as part of that
party's case, he was entitled not to disclose the remainder of that document. The Court
of Appeal, following a previous similar decision in *Burnell v British Transport Commission*
b [1955] 3 All ER 822, [1956] 1 QB 187, held that the document, unless it was a clearly
separable document dealing with completely different subject matters, so that in effect it
might be treated as two separate documents, must be treated as a whole: if you were
waiving privilege as to part of it, then you waived privilege as to the whole of the
document.

In that case, on the facts, it appears that the document was put in evidence at the trial
c because it was an agreed document and was read in opening by counsel. It may have
been limited evidence, but it nevertheless was evidence in the case. Quite apart from
what happened at the trial, the privilege in the document had of course been waived at
an earlier stage when it was disclosed to the opposite party.

That case was not concerned with any extension of privilege beyond the document
itself; this is quite clear from the report (see [1981] 2 All ER 485 at 490, [1981] 1 WLR
d 529 at 535). So the decision in the case was not concerned with the point that I have to
deal with.

Templeman LJ referred to the *Burnell* case, which was also a case of total or partial user
of a document and which affirmed the principle that fairness required that, where part
of a document was being used, the privilege in respect of the whole of the document
must have been waived (see [1981] 2 All ER 485 at 492, [1981] 1 WLR 529 at 538). That
e was a document which was used in cross-examination. It was a document of which the
maker was the person who was being cross-examined, and it therefore was a document
which had been put in evidence.

Templeman LJ referred very shortly to the *Doland* case. He said ([1981] 2 All ER 485
at 492, [1981] 1 WLR 529 at 538):

f   'In *George Doland Ltd v Blackburn Robson Coates & Co* the deliberate waiver of
privilege of certain communications between solicitor and client relating to two
particular subject matters before litigation became pending or contemplated
involved waiver of any other communications relating to those two subject matters
but did not involve waiver of the further privilege which applied to documents
which were brought into existence after litigation was pending or contemplated.'

g He then referred to a case, *Nea Karteria Maritime Co Ltd v Atlantic and Great Lakes
Steamship Corp* (11 December 1978), which is still, remarkably, not reported by any series
other than the Commercial Law Reports (see [1981] Com LR 138). It was decided by
Mustill J. Templeman LJ said ([1981] 2 All ER 485 at 492, [1981] 1 WLR 529 at 538–
539):

h   '. . . Mustill J . . . succinctly summarised the position as follows: "I believe that the
principle underlying the rule of practice exemplified by *Burnell v British Transport
Commission* is that, where a party is deploying in court material which would
otherwise be privileged, the opposite party and the court must have an opportunity
of satisfying themselves that what the party has chosen to release from privilege
represents the whole of the material relevant to the issue in question. To allow an
j   individual item to be plucked out of context would be to risk injustice through its
real weight or meaning being misunderstood. In my view, the same principle can
be seen at work in *George Doland Ltd v Blackburn Robson Coates & Co* in a rather
different context." [Templeman LJ continued:] I agree and would only add that it
would not be satisfactory for the court to decide that part of a privileged document
can be introduced without waiving privilege with regard to the other part in the

absence of informed argument to the contrary, and there can be no informed argument without the disclosure which would make argument unnecessary. Counsel for the plaintiffs attempted to distinguish the decisions in *Burnell v British Transport Commission* and *George Doland Ltd v Blackburn Robson Coates & Co* on the ground that it was necessary in those cases for the whole statement to be disclosed in order that the consistency of the testimony of a witness could be scrutinised. In my judgment, however, the rule that privilege relating to a document which deals with one subject matter cannot be waived as to part and asserted as to the remainder is based on the possibility that any use of part of a document may be unfair or misleading, that the party who possesses the document is clearly not the person who can decide whether a partial disclosure is misleading or not, nor can the judge decide without hearing argument, nor can he hear argument unless the document is disclosed as a whole to the other side. Once disclosure has taken place by introducing part of the document into evidence or using it in court it cannot be erased.'

Dunn LJ agreed.

The decision in that case, therefore, related to a limited question but the judgment did involve a citation of the *Doland* case without disapproval, and it did involve an approval of the statement of Mustill J. In adopting Mustill J's judgment, Templeman LJ adopts the phrase 'deploying in court' and himself uses the words 'introduced' and 'introduces'.

In the case which Templeman LJ was concerned with, material had been introduced in the sense that it had been adduced in evidence. In *Burnell* it had been adduced in evidence. In *Doland* it was being adduced in evidence, and, as will be seen in *Nea Karteria*, the relevant material which was said to give rise to the waiver had also been adduced in evidence.

Counsel for the brokers submits that the *Doland* case was either wrongly decided or in any event should not be followed in the present context. He submits that it is inconsistent with principles laid down in, for example, the earlier decision of *Lyell v Kennedy (No 3)* (1884) 27 Ch D 1, [1881–5] All ER Rep 814 in the Court of Appeal. He furthermore submits that the submissions made by counsel for the underwriters are absurdly broad and contrary to accepted practice in these courts, as, for example, is illustrated by *Occidental Worldwide Investment Corp v Skibs A/S Avanti, The Siboen and The Sibotre* [1976] 1 Lloyd's Rep 293 at 332. I have already commented on the *Burnell* case and the principle of fairness which in the use of evidence which it is based on and the fact that it related to the attempted use of part of a document which had been adduced in evidence. I now, therefore, pass to Mustill J's decision. It is a decision with regard to a problem which arose in the course of a trial. There were two points. One was whether the cross-examination of a witness, a seaman, about a previous statement that he had made waived privilege in respect of another document that was referred to in that statement. That other document was a statement made by the boatswain. Mustill J held that the privilege in that further document was not waived because the witness had not been cross-examined about that other document; he had only been cross-examined about what he himself had said. The only material which the court had been asked to take into account in that context was the statement made by the seaman, and not the statement made by the boatswain. The other point in the case was a point which arose out of an interview between the seaman and a Greek lawyer. I will read shortly from the facts regarding that ([1981] Com LR 138):

'In November 1978 the seaman was interviewed in Greece by T, a Greek lawyer who had been given a written list of questions by the English solicitors of the Plaintiffs. The seaman's answers were incorporated in a document known at the trial as "P 35". His answers were inconsistent with his evidence and he was taxed with this in cross-examination. In particular he was asked [by Counsel for the Second Defendants] about a passage in P 35 which referred to a part of the boatswain's statement made to the Plaintiff's solicitors in 1975. [The second defendants] then called on the Plaintiffs to produce the boatswain's statement, and *a* the Plaintiffs claimed privilege in respect of it. The seaman claimed in evidence that he had made the statements in P 35 "just to be rid of the lawyers." The Plaintiffs therefore called T, the Greek lawyer, to explain the background to, and nature of, the interview conducted by him in 1978. [The second defendants] submitted that the Plaintiffs should be required to produce the list of questions which had formed the basis of that interview.'

b Mustill J analysed the principles which he considered to be relevant. He had authorities cited to him, including *Lyell v Kennedy*, which is that same authority as counsel for the brokers relies on in the present case. It is convenient that I should just read a quotation from Cotton LJ in *Lyell v Kennedy* 27 Ch D 1 at 24; cf [1881–5] All ER Rep 814 at 924 which Mustill J himself quotes:

c 'There was this contention raised, which I have not forgotten: that the Defendant had waived his privilege, and therefore could not claim it at all. That, in my opinion, was entirely fallacious. He had done this, he had said, "Whether I am entitled to protect them or not I will produce certain of the documents for which I had previously claimed privilege—I will waive that, and I will produce them," but that did not prevent him relying on such protection with regard to others which he did not like to produce. It is not like the case of a man who gives part of a conversation

d and then claims protection for the remainder, and we think there is no ground for the contention that there has been here a waiver of privilege.'

That is the cardinal quotation from Cotton LJ's judgment. Mustill J also referred to the *Burnell* case and to the *Doland* case, including reference to the two topics which Geoffrey Lane J had taken into account.

e Mustill J then said that these cases did not support the argument of the second defendants. He continued ([1981] Com LR 138 at 139):

'... the argument overlooks the distinction between questions addressed to a witness about his own previous inconsistent statement, and those related to a statement made by someone else. Where a witness is cross-examined about a prior statement of his own, he must first be asked whether he admits that he did in fact

f make the statement. Once this admission is obtained, the statement becomes part of the *corpus* of material on the basis of which the court reaches its decision: not because the statement thereby necessarily becomes evidence of the facts to which it speaks, but because the inconsistency is itself a fact which tends to impeach the credibility of the witness.'

g I would add myself that s 3 of the 1968 Act normally does make such statements evidence.

Continuing with Mustill J:

'This is not so with questions of the second type. The fact that counsel puts to a witness that someone else has made a statement out of court which contradicts his oral evidence does not make the statement part of the material either by being assented to by the witness (in which case it becomes part of his own evidence) or by

h admission in evidence by some other procedure (such as tender under the Civil Evidence Act). But until something of that sort happens, it has no status in court at all, and cannot help the court to decide upon the credibility of the witness, or indeed upon anything else.'

That is part of the reasoning of Mustill J with which I respectfully agree. It is of direct

j relevance to the present case. He dealt with the question of the matters with regard to the Greek lawyer by considering the relevance of what the plaintiffs were seeking to do by adducing the Greek lawyer's evidence. I will read that passage ([1981] Com LR 130 at 139):

'As stated in the reasons which I gave for my previous ruling, I believe that in summary and in perhaps not very concise terms one can see a rule of positive law being stated in the interests of justice, that where a party chooses to deploy evidence which would otherwise be privileged the court and the opposition must, in relation to the issue in question, be given the opportunity to satisfy themselves that they have the whole of the material and not merely a fragment. Thus I must start by asking myself what are the issues in relation to which the material has been deployed? Of course, the prime issue is whether and, if so, in what circumstances, the seaman accepted the truth of an account of events different from one which on two other occasions he has put forward. This involves the question whether he did give the answers recorded in document P35, whether that document represents a complete record of what happened and of what might be termed the general atmosphere of the meeting, having regard to the seaman's evidence that he signed the statement to get rid of the lawyers.'

The report continues:

'It was essential, therefore, for the court to see the meeting as a whole, and for that purpose the Judge's view was that the whole of the substance of the meeting was a "legitimate subject for disclosure and for cross-examination".'

Applying these principles the judge held that the list of questions which had been prepared for use at the meeting were so to speak part of the meeting. They were in a sense the agenda for the meeting and formed the basis for one part of the exchange between the lawyer and the seaman. He therefore held that they were legitimately the subject of cross-examination and indeed must be disclosed. He said that that followed the waiver of privilege arising from the giving of evidence on the meeting. He said ([1981] Com LR 138 at 140):

'And I think the interests of justice, which I believe to underlie the authorities on this part of the case, demand that the opposition and the court should have an opportunity to satisfy itself as to the accuracy of the evidence given by the lawyer as to the way in which he conducted the interview.'

He rejected the submission that other matters prior to the meeting should be disclosed. He said:

'By waiving privilege in respect of the conversation the Plaintiffs have, as it seems to me, within degrees which may have to be looked into later, waived privilege as to documents coming into existence after the event but in relation to the conversation. It does not seem to me to follow that the same conclusion applies to documentary or oral material coming into existence beforehand. [He concluded:] I am fortified in the view which I have formed because I believe it to be in accord with the reasoning underlying the decision of Mr Justice Geoffrey Lane in *George Doland Ltd v Blackburn Robson Coates & Co*, but I would in any event have come to the conclusion which I have indicated.'

Looking at the reasoning of Mustill J, it seems to me clear that he is approaching the matter using the words 'deploying in evidence' in a strict sense. In other words, he is looking to see what is in evidence and what is not in evidence; and in applying the principle he repeatedly refers to what was given in evidence. The section in his judgment relating to the boatswain's statement does not in any way detract from that conclusion because what he is looking to see is there, first, what was in evidence, which was solely the statement made by the seaman, and whether that statement made by the seaman inevitably involved what was said by the boatswain, which it did not. Furthermore he applies what for convenience can be called a single transaction test. He looks to see what is the issue in relation to which the material has been deployed. He held that the issue was what was said at the meeting between the lawyer and the Greek seaman, and the correct evaluation of that meeting. But he did not accept that it extended to other matters

which did not form part of that transaction. He did not treat the transaction as being the
a facts of the subject matter of the conversation at the meeting. What he says about
'documents coming into existence after the event *but in relation to the conversation*' (my
emphasis) adopts the same approach. This judgment does not, in my view, support
counsel for the underwriters' submission. It does not support the submission that you do
not have to take into account whether or not the document has been put in evidence as
opposed to whether or not it has merely come before the court, or that privilege has been
b waived without its being put in evidence.

It seems to me clear from the passage that I have read that Mustill J did attach great
importance to that distinction. Furthermore, it is central to Mustill J's judgment that
you must define what is the subject matter with which you are concerned. He did not
treat the subject matter as all the things about which the seaman spoke, but he merely
treated as the subject matter what had been said on that occasion. This may raise some
c conflict between his decision and that of Geoffrey Lane J, because Geoffrey Lane J
certainly seems to have approached the matter on the basis of considering what was the
subject matter of the conversation, namely his two topics, or two points, rather than the
accuracy of evaluating what was or was not said on the relevant occasion or occasions.

Applying those decisions, I have come to the conclusion that counsel for the
underwriters' application is misconceived and premature and that his submissions are
d incorrect. Furthermore, I have come to the conclusion that the decision in *Doland* may
be wrong unless it is to be justified on its own facts. In my judgment the correct
conclusion in the present case is that the document dated 6 October 1981 and the
statements it contains have not yet been adduced in evidence. Therefore the principle on
which counsel for the underwriters relies has not yet come into play; second, that when
and if the document is put in evidence the consequences for the waiver of privilege will
e be solely with regard to what Mr Baxter did or did not say on 6 October. What will have
happened is that the putting into evidence of that document will have opened up the
confidentiality of that transaction. It has not opened up the confidentiality of later
privileged communications; for example, what Mr Baxter has said subsequently and
separately to the solicitors and, for example, later statements that he has made to his
solicitors remain privileged. The confidentiality of them has not been waived and they
f have not ceased to be privileged. The principles on which I am relying in arriving at this
conclusion have been covered by the full arguments of counsel. It is right that I should
summarise them. The first is that under the English adversarial procedure a party can
choose what evidence he does or does not adduce at the trial. Second, under the rules of
legal professional privilege certain categories of communication are protected from
pretrial discovery and from being the subject matter of the investigation at the trial. This
g is essential to the adversarial procedure followed in this country. The reasons underlying
it and its importance have been discussed in many cases, including by Lord Simon in
Waugh v British Rlys Board [1979] 2 All ER 1169 at 1177, [1980] AC 521 at 536–537.
Third, a party is at liberty to decide whether or not to waive privilege and, if so, the
extent to which he does so. This is expressly stated in *Lyell v Kennedy* in the passage to
which I referred. This applies to interrogatories and it applies to the discovery of
h documents. The issue in the present matter is the degree to which it applies in the
proceedings in court. Fourth, the waiver of a part of the document or conversation is a
waiver of the whole of that document or conversation as was stated in *Lyell v Kennedy* and
as was the subject of decision in the *Burnell* case and the *Great Atlantic* case. Fifth, with
regard to waiver before a trial, there can be no question that these principles are correct
and that, for example, the waiver in the present case of the confidentiality and privilege
j in the document dated 6 October 1981 does not of itself waive privilege in anything else.
Sixth, by adducing evidence at a trial one does get involved in potential further waiver.
The underlying principle is one of fairness in the conduct of the trial and does not go
further than that. The fact that this principle does not arise unless you adduce the
evidence at the trial is clearly stated in the judgment of Mustill J and it was clearly raised
by the facts in *Doland* and it was likewise raised by the facts in *Great Atlantic* and *Burnell*.

Further, if the evidence is adduced then the extent of the waiver relates to the transaction to which that evidence goes. The extent of the transaction has to be examined and where it is what somebody said on a particular occasion, then that is the transaction. It is not the subject matter of those conversations. It does not extend to all matters relating to the subject matter of those conversations.

In support of that latter point I would observe that if counsel for the underwriters' submissions were to be accepted in full at face value they would be tantamount to a disruption of legal professional privilege. Any waiver of privilege at all would be liable to have the most wide-ranging consequences and indeed give rise to a reductio ad absurdam. If one follows the approach of looking at the transaction concerned rather than at the subject matter of the communications, that problem does not arise.

Seventh, the necessity that the evidence shall have been adduced also involves that it must be adduced by the party who is waiving the privilege or who is alleged to be waiving the privilege. Once a document has had its privilege waived then of course it is open to be used by any party. Counsel for the underwriters or counsel for the plaintiffs could have used the document in the present case at any time after 6 May 1983. They likewise can use it, if it was used by Mr Baxter to refresh his memory when Mr Baxter comes to give evidence. But it cannot be suggested that any use by an opposite party amounts to a waiver by the original party of anything. Likewise the mere production of the document on discovery, or in some pretrial procedure, cannot in the ordinary course be treated as a waiver of anything beyond the document itself.

Eighth, with regard to the consequences, once evidence is adduced it gives rise to a right to cross-examine freely and fairly with regard to the transaction in respect of which the document is adduced or the evidence is called. The principle applies to the introduction of both documentary and oral evidence. Fairness requires that the opposite party shall be entitled to investigate by cross-examination the transaction and therefore be entitled to ask for and see documents that are relevant to that transaction. But the requirements of fairness do not go beyond that; no conclusion is to be drawn from the use by Mustill J, or indeed by the Court of Appeal, of language such as 'the whole of the material' or 'the whole of the material and not merely a fragment' to extend the principle beyond the actual transaction so as to include the matters which are merely referred to in the relevant communication. That is the essence of the decision of Mustill J and any other conclusion would be a departure from his decision. With regard to the *Doland* case it may well be that the actual decision was correct, but I am clear that the conclusions which have been sought to be drawn from the decision are not correct. It may well be that the explanation of the decision is that the relevant party, by calling a solicitor, and indeed by previously having referred to his relationship and dealings with his solicitor, treated such dealings and relationship as being, as a whole, no longer confidential. Part of the essence of privilege is confidentiality. Confidentiality is a complex concept; its limits have been the subject matter of other cases. But if a party once starts anyway as between the relevant parties before the court, to treat the relationship as not confidential, it may well be that the whole basis of the former privilege ceases to exist. I am slightly confirmed in that conclusion by a South African case which has been cited to me by counsel for the brokers, *Euroshipping Corp of Monrovia v Minister of Agricultural Economics and Marketing* 1979 (1) SA 637. It contains, among other things, an extensive discussion of the connection between privilege and confidentiality and the consequences of ceasing to treat a particular relationship as a confidential relationship. That may well be what happened in *George Doland v Blackburn Robson Coates & Co* [1972] 3 All ER 959, [1972] 1 WLR 1338. If that did happen then it follows that that election had opened up the whole of the relationship between the solicitor and client under that heading. It also explains the distinction between that relationship and the subsequent situation that later arose of anticipated litigation. The report is very brief. It is not possible to evaluate the extent to which what I have said may be a sound analysis of the decision. But if the correct view of the *Doland* case is that the extent of the waiver should be assessed by reference to the

subject matter of the conversation which took place, as opposed to the conversation itself,
then I regard the decision as inconsistent with that of Mustill J and the decision of Mustill
J is to be preferred. Likewise, I am not happy about the distinction that is drawn in the
Doland case between privilege which arises from the solicitor and client relationship and
the privilege which arises from anticipated litigation. Its use in that case assisted in the
avoidance of absurd results and it may do so in other cases, but it does not do so in the
present case. Counsel for the underwriters submitted, with complete logic, that if he was
right in his approach then the privilege had been waived right down to and including
the trial preparation documents (eg briefs to counsel) because litigation was throughout
contemplated. It may be again that the reason for the distinction between litigation
privilege and solicitor and client privilege, and its use in the *Doland* case, lies in what I
have said about the waiver of confidentiality. But in my judgment the distinction is not
one which is valid to apply as a criterion in all cases and it is not one which would be
valid to apply in the present case. It is not a substitute for the correct criterion.

Last, there is the question of discretion. If I were being asked to order discovery under
the rules of court, I would always have a discretion whether or not to do so. But in so far
as it is a matter of allowing questions in cross-examination or requiring a witness to
answer them, or to produce documents, then, on the subject matter of such questions, I
do not have a discretion other than what is involved in the proper conduct of the trial.
Further it may be commented that in any event the discretion under the rules is primarily
directed to disposing fairly of the cause or matter, that is the phrase in RSC Ord 24, rr 8
and 13 and it is of the essence of counsel for the underwriters' submissions that he is
entitled to this further documentation and discovery in order to enable the court to
dispose fairly of this case. So that the criteria really are the same. The discretion element
in so far as it exists in my judgment is merely an assessment of what is fair and what is
necessary for justice and is not a discretion in any broader sense of the word.

My decision is as I have previously indicated that the application for discovery is
premature and that when and if Mr Baxter is called and gives evidence with regard to 6
October 1981, statements under the 1968 Act (if any) being put in with leave, then he
will be liable to be cross-examined with regard to the totality of the transaction of 6
October 1981. I hold that the waiver of privilege does not go further than that.

Application dismissed.

Solicitors: *Ince & Co* (for the plaintiffs); *Elborne Mitchell & Co* (for the underwriters);
Hewitt Woollacott & Chown (for the brokers).

K Mydeen Esq   Barrister.

Re J W Laing Trust

a

Stewards' Co Ltd v Attorney General and another

CHANCERY DIVISION

PETER GIBSON J   b

27, 28 JANUARY, 25 FEBRUARY 1983

Charity – Cy-près doctrine – Occasion for applying property cy-près – Original purposes of charitable gift – Original purposes ceasing to provide suitable and effective method of using property – Original purposes – Conditions attached to gift – Requirement that whole of capital and income of charitable gift be distributed within ten years of donor's death – Gift for charitable c *purposes generally – Inexpedient to distribute capital within ten years of donor's death – Whether court could approve cy-près scheme discharging trustee from obligation to distribute capital within ten years – Whether direction to distribute within ten years an 'original purpose' of gift – Whether court having power under inherent jurisdiction to approve scheme discharging trustee from obligation to distribute – Charities Act 1960, s 13(1)(e)(iii).*

d

In 1922 the settlor set up a charitable trust by transferring some £15,000-worth of shares in a company controlled by him to another company as trustee. The settlor was interested in Christian evangelism and the trustee company had been founded to handle funds for evangelical activities. The memorandum of trust provided that the trust fund was to be devoted to 'charitable purposes', and it was a requirement binding on the trustee that it should wholly distribute both the capital and the income of the fund within ten years of e the settlor's death. The memorandum of trust further provided that the settlor was appointed by the trustee to be its agent in the distribution of the fund. Until 1964 the settlor, acting as the trustee's agent, distributed the income of the fund among various Christian evangelical bodies, who came to depend on the charity. None of the recipients were in a position to handle large sums of capital. After 1964 the trustee distributed the f income but did so according to the settlor's distribution policy. Because of the increase in the value of the fund, in 1932 and 1939 the settlor had indicated to the trustee that it should disregard, as being no longer expedient, the requirement in the memorandum of trust that the trust fund be distributed within ten years of the settlor's death. The settlor died in 1978. By 1982 the value of the shares had increased to the extent that the fund was worth £24m and, having regard to the size of the fund and to the type of body g which benefited from it, it would have been impractical and would have imperilled the causes which the settlor had wished to support if the trustee was required to distribute the fund within ten years of the settlor's death. The trustee applied to the Charity Commissioners to remove that requirement and when they refused the trustee, with the Attorney General's support, applied to the court, pursuant to s 13[a] of the Charities Act 1960, to settle a cy-près scheme for the administration and management of the trust h which discharged the trustee from the obligation to distribute the fund within ten years of the settlor's death. The trustee contended that the direction to distribute was one of the 'original purposes' of the charitable gift and that it had 'ceased . . . to provide a suitable and effective method of using the [trust] property' having regard to the spirit of the gift, and that therefore the court had jurisdiction under s 13(1)(e)(iii) to make a scheme or, alternatively, should exercise its inherent jurisdiction to approve such a scheme for a j charity.

Held – (1) The requirement that the fund be distributed within ten years of the settlor's

---

a   Section 13, so far as material, is set out at p 52 j to p 53 e, post

death was not part of the 'original purposes' of the gift within the meaning of s 13(1) of
a the 1960 Act, because (a) on the true construction of s 13(1) the 'original purposes' of a
charitable gift were the particular charitable purposes to which the gift was to be applied,
and such purposes did not extend to a direction to distribute the gift by a particular date,
since such a direction was merely a matter of administration and did not indicate a
specific method of using the property, and (b) not all provisions attached by a donor to a
charitable gift were to be treated as conditions attached to the gift and thus as part of the
original purposes of the gift and accordingly alterable under a cy-près scheme: although
b some conditions might accurately be described as subsidiary purposes, others were no
more than directions. It could not be said that the unsatisfactory nature of the direction
to distribute meant that the 'original purposes' of the gift had ceased, for the purposes of
s 13(1)(e)(iii), to provide a suitable and effective method of using the trust property. In
any event, a charitable gift, such as that made by the settlor, which had from the date of
c the gift been devoted, as to both capital and income, to general charitable purposes was
not capable of being applied cy-près. Accordingly, the requirement that the fund be
distributed within ten years of the settlor's death, being administrative in character, was
not susceptible to alteration by a cy-près scheme under s 13 (see p 53 *h* to p 54 *a* and *c* to
g, p 55 *a* and p 56 *c* to *f*, post); *Re Robinson* [1923] 2 Ch 332, *Re Dominion Students' Hall
Trust* [1947] Ch 183 and *Re Lysaght (decd)* [1965] 2 All ER 888 considered.
d   (2) However, under its inherent jurisdiction the court could approve a scheme by
which the trustees of the fund would be discharged from the obligation to distribute the
capital of the fund within ten years of the settlor's death, and, taking into account all the
circumstances of the charity, including the altered circumstances of the charity since the
requirement as to distribution was laid down 60 years previously and the nature of the
bodies to which the income of the fund had in the past been distributed, the court would
e approve such a scheme because it was inexpedient that the capital of the fund should be
distributed within ten years of the settlor's death. Accordingly, the application would be
granted under the court's inherent jurisdiction (see p 57 *j* to p 58 *c*, post).

Notes

For the cy-près doctrine, see 5 Halsbury's Laws (4th edn) paras 666–675, and for cases on
f the subject, see 8(1) Digest (Reissue) 399–414, 1343–1472.
      For the Charities Act 1960, s 13, see 3 Halsbury's Statutes (3rd edn) 605.

Cases referred to in judgment

Dominion Students' Hall Trust, Re, Dominion Students' Hall Trust v A-G [1947] Ch 183.
Inglewood (Lord) v IRC [1983] 1 WLR 366, CA.
g *Lepton's Will Trusts, Re, Re Lepton's Charity, Ambler v Thomas* [1971] 1 All ER 799, [1972]
      Ch 276, [1971] 2 WLR 659.
Lysaght (decd), Re, Hill v Royal College of Surgeons of England [1965] 2 All ER 888, [1966]
      Ch 191, [1965] 3 WLR 391.
Pearson v IRC [1980] 2 All ER 479, [1981] AC 753, [1980] 2 WLR 872, HL.
Robinson Re, Wright v Tugwell [1923] 2 Ch 332.

h

Originating summons

By an originating summons dated 10 March 1982 the plaintiff, Stewards' Co Ltd, sought,
inter alia, the following relief: that a scheme be settled by the judge for the administration
and management of the trusts of a memorandum under seal dated 30 August 1922 from
the plaintiff to Mr J W Laing (the settlor) enabling the trustees for the time being of the
j trusts to be discharged from the obligation to distribute the capital subject to the trusts
within ten years of the settlor's death either (a) under the inherent jurisdiction of the
High Court in respect of charities or alternatively (b) under s 13 of the Charities Act 1960
on the footing that the direction as to distribution, in so far as it was a purpose of the
trusts, had ceased to provide a suitable and effective method of using the property subject
to the trusts, regard being had to the spirit of the original gift by the settlor, and that the

property and funds subject to the trusts ought to be applied cy-près. The defendants to the summons were the Attorney General and John Laing plc. The facts are set out in the *a* judgment.

Hubert Picarda for the plaintiff.
Christopher McCall for the Attorney General.

Cur adv vult *b*

25 February. The following judgment was delivered.

PETER GIBSON J. I have already held that the charitable trust set up by the settlor in 1922 was completely constituted on 30 August 1922, the date of a memorandum which was under seal and addressed to the settlor, Sir John Laing (then Mr J W Laing), by which *c* the plaintiff company acknowledged receipt of 15,000 shares in John Laing & Sons Ltd. The memorandum continued thus:

> '. . . the proceeds of which and the dividends thereon from time to time declared and paid are to be devoted to charitable purposes, it being understood that the capital and income is to be wholly distributed within your lifetime or within ten *d* years of your decease. The company appoints you, during your lifetime its agent in the distribution of the income it may receive on the above mentioned shares and of the proceeds of sale thereof, it being understood that such distribution shall be made for charitable purposes alone.'

It is accepted by the plaintiff that the words in the memorandum relating to distribution, although introduced by the words 'it being understood', should be treated *e* as a requirement binding on the plaintiff.

The plaintiff, shortly before the death of the settlor, which occurred on 11 January 1978, and also since that date, applied to the Charity Commissioners to remove the requirement to distribute the capital before the expiration of ten years from the death of the settlor. But the commissioners declined to do so, though, very properly, they have *f* authorised these proceedings to be brought.

The relevant paragraph of the originating summons with which I am now concerned seeks relief in this form:

> 'That a scheme may be settled by the Judge for the administration and management of the trusts of a Memorandum under seal dated the 30th August 1922 from Stewards' Company, Limited to Mr J. W. Laing (hereafter called "the *g* Settlor") enabling the Trustees for the time being of the said trusts to be discharged from the obligation to distribute the capital subject to the said trusts within 10 years of the death of the Settlor (a) under the inherent jurisdiction in respect of charities of Her Majesty's High Court of Justice; or alternatively (b) under section 13 of the Charities Act, 1960 on the footing that the said direction as to distribution (in so far as the same is a purpose of the trusts), has ceased to provide a suitable and effective *h* method of using the property subject to the trusts regard being had to the spirit of the original gift by the Settlor and that the property and funds subject thereto ought to be applied cy-pres.'

However, the first defendant, the Attorney General, has persuaded the plaintiff to seek an order under the Charities Act 1960, s 13 first and, only if that fails, to seek an order under the inherent jurisdiction. Accordingly, I must first determine whether the *j* statutory conditions of s 13 are satisfied. The provisions of s 13, the whole of which I shall read except for sub-s (4), are as follows:

> '(1) Subject to subsection (2) below, the circumstances in which the original purposes of a charitable gift can be altered to allow the property given or part of it

to be applied cy-près shall be as follows:—(a) where the original purposes, in whole or in part,—(i) have been as far as may be fulfilled; or (ii) cannot be carried out, or not according to the directions given and to the spirit of the gift; or (b) where the original purposes provide a use for part only of the property available by virtue of the gift; or (c) where the property available by virtue of the gift and other property applicable for similar purposes can be more effectively used in conjunction, and to that end can suitably, regard being had to the spirit of the gift, be made applicable to common purposes; or (d) where the original purposes were laid down by reference to an area which then was but has since ceased to be a unit for some other purpose, or by reference to a class of persons or to an area which has for any reason ceased to be suitable, regard being had to the spirit of the gift, or to be practical in administering the gift; or (e) where the original purposes, in whole or in part, have, since they were laid down,—(i) been adequately provided for by other means; or (ii) ceased, as being useless or harmful to the community or for other reasons, to be in law charitable; or (iii) ceased in any other way to provide a suitable and effective method of using the property available by virtue of the gift, regard being had to the spirit of the gift.

(2) Subsection (1) above shall not affect the conditions which must be satisfied in order that property given for charitable purposes may be applied cy-près, except in so far as those conditions require a failure of the original purposes.

(3) References in the foregoing subsections to the original purposes of a gift shall be construed, where the application of the property given has been altered or regulated by a scheme or otherwise, as referring to the purposes for which the property is for the time being applicable . . .

(5) It is hereby declared that a trust for charitable purposes places a trustee under a duty, where the case permits and requires the property or some part of it to be applied cy-près, to secure its effective use for charity by taking steps to enable it to be so applied.'

It is common ground between counsel for the plaintiff and counsel for the Attorney General that the purpose of sub-s (2) is to preserve the requirement under the law prior to the 1960 Act that the donor must show a general charitable intent by his gift. This requirement is manifestly satisfied by the gift in this case, expressly devoted, as it is, to charitable purposes. The duty imposed by sub-s (5) is new. The plaintiff considers itself to be under that duty and submits that the present case is a case falling within s 13(1)(e)(iii).

For the court to have jurisdiction to make the order sought by the plaintiff under s 13 two questions must be answered affirmatively. (1) Is the requirement to distribute before the expiration of ten years from the settlor's death included in 'the original purposes' of the charitable gift? (2) If so, have the original purposes, in whole or in part, since they were laid down, ceased to provide a suitable and effective method of using the property available by virtue of the gift?

Both counsel unite in submitting that both questions should be answered in the affirmative, though on the first question counsel for the plaintiff did not disguise his own predilection for the view that the requirement as to distribution was an administrative direction rather than a purpose of the gift.

To answer the first question it is necessary to identify the original purposes of the gift. I venture to suggest that, as a matter of ordinary language, those purposes in the present case should only be identified as general charitable purposes and nothing further. I would regard it as an abuse of language to describe the requirement as to distribution as a purpose of the gift. Of course, that requirement was one of the provisions which the settlor intended to apply to the gift, but it would, on any natural use of language, be wrong to equate all the express provisions of a gift, which ex hypothesi the settlor intended to apply to the gift, with the purposes of a gift. To my mind the purposes of a charitable gift would ordinarily be understood as meaning those charitable objects on

which the property given is to be applied. It is not meaningful to talk of the requirement
as to the distribution being either charitable or non-charitable. The purposes of a   *a*
charitable gift correspond to the beneficiaries in the case of a gift by way of a private
trust.

However, as counsel for the Attorney General rightly submits, the meaning of
'purposes' in s 13 must be construed in its statutory context. He submits that in the 1960
Act a distinction is recognised between the purposes of a gift and its administration.
Thus, in s 46 the word 'trusts' in relation to a charity is defined as meaning the provisions   *b*
establishing it as a charity and regulating its purposes and administration. He also drew
my attention to s 18(1)(a), under which the Charity Commissioners have power to
establish a scheme for the administration of a charity, and submitted that such a scheme
is to be contrasted with s 13, under which the original purposes of a charitable gift can
be altered to allow a cy-près application of property the subject of that gift. I accept,
therefore, that the question I must answer is whether the requirement as to distribution   *c*
is part of the orginal purposes or a provision relating to administration.

The other guidance that I can obtain from the 1960 Act as to the meaning of 'purposes'
is from the references to purposes in s 13. From them it is apparent that the relevant
purposes are those for which the property given is applicable, and that the relevant purposes
include those which provide a use for part only of the property available by virtue of the
gift, those which were laid down by reference to an area or class of person, those which   *d*
have been provided for by other means, those which have ceased to be in law charitable,
and (in s 13(1)(e)(iii)) those which have ceased in some other way to provide a suitable or
effective method of using the property. Save possibly for the last reference, none of those
references seem to me to support a meaning for the word 'purposes' wide enough to
cover the direction as to distribution; rather, they support the view that the purposes in
question are the particular charitable purposes for which the property is to be applied   *e*
and nothing further. Section 13(1)(e)(iii) does, however, contemplate that the purposes
may provide a method of using the property and, in one sense, a requirement to use
capital by a particular date might be said to provide a method of using the property. But,
to my mind, that is an unnatural way of construing s 13(1)(e)(iii), as the requirement as
to distribution is not so much a method of using the property as a direction as to the date
by which the property is to be used. This tells one nothing of that on which the capital is   *f*
to be applied. If the words of that sub-paragraph are given their natural meaning in their
cy-près context, to my mind they refer to a specific mode of application of the property
in respect of which the donor has indicated a general charitable intention. The internal
evidence of s 13 itself does not, therefore, encourage an interpretation of 'purposes'
extending beyond what I have ventured to suggest was that word's natural meaning.

Counsel for the Attorney General submitted that the distinction between 'purposes'   *g*
and 'administration' is akin to that recognised elsewhere in the law between dispositive
and administrative provisions. He drew my attention to *Pearson v IRC* [1980] 2 All ER
479 at 486, [1981] AC 753 at 774, where Viscount Dilhorne, after referring to s 8(1) of
the Perpetuities and Accumulations Act 1964 (which itself distinguished between the
administration and the distribution of property), recognised a distinction in the context
of the capital transfer tax legislation between dispositive and administrative powers of   *h*
trustees. I was also referred to what was said in *Lord Inglewood v IRC* [1983] 1 WLR 366
at 373, where, again in a capital transfer tax context, Fox LJ, giving the judgment of the
Court of Appeal, referred to a similar distinction. But, while I do not question that the
distinction between administrative and dispositive provisions exists and is relevant in
other contexts, it does not seem to me to follow that it is precisely the same distinction
that is being drawn in the Charities Act 1960 when Parliament has simply referred, in   *j*
the context of charitable gifts, to purposes on the one hand and administration on the
other.

Counsel for the Attorney General submitted that the purposes of a gift included not
only the specific charitable purposes but also any provision as to time affecting the gift,
and that 'purposes' could also include the identity of the property given, the identity of

a the trustee and any other provisions affecting distribution, such as, for example, in the present case, the agency of the settlor in making distributions. In effect, that is to equate every provision which may affect how the trust property is to be distributed with the purposes of the gift. That seems to me to be a very strange use of language and, in the context of s 13, an impossible construction. For example, it is clear that the property and the purposes for which the property is applicable are treated as distinct. Counsel for the Attorney General posed the example of a trust to charity A for 20 years followed by a

b trust to charity B, and submitted that the purposes of the gift must include the fact that the interest of charity A is limited to a period of 20 years, and that it is subject to that limited interest that the property is held for charity B. Let me assume (without deciding) that in that case the identification of the purposes must include the time by which charity A's interest is limited. Nevertheless, the present case is readily distinguishable. The interest of charity in the present case is immediate, unlimited and absolute, extending,

c as it does, to both capital and income forthwith.

Both counsel advanced a more subtle argument on the following lines. (1) Section 13 not merely re-enacted the circumstances in which cy-près applications were allowed under the previous law but also extended those circumstances. (2) Prior to the 1960 Act the court had allowed by way of cy-près schemes the removal of impracticable conditions attached to charitable gifts. (3) Such conditions must be regarded as purposes within the

d meaning of s 13. (4) The requirement as to distribution is also to be treated as, or as similar to, a condition and so a purpose within s 13.

I accept the first and second of these propositions. The first is supported by the remarks of Pennycuick V-C in Re Lepton's Will Trusts, Re Lepton's Charity, Ambler v Thomas [1971] 1 All ER 799 at 803, [1972] Ch 276 at 284. The second is illustrated by cases such as Re Robinson, Wright v Tugwell [1923] 2 Ch 332 and Re Dominion Students' Hall Trust, Dominion

e Students' Hall Trust v A-G [1947] Ch 183.

But I have difficulty with the third and fourth propositions. I baulk at the universality of the third. Take Re Robinson, Wright v Tugwell. The testatrix gave money for the endowment of an evangelical church but imposed 'an abiding condition' that a black gown be worn in the pulpit, a condition held by P O Lawrence J to be impracticable as defeating the main evangelical intention of the gift. It is not clear from the report

f whether the money that was given could be used for the provision of black gowns. If it could, then I would accept that the condition might accurately be described as a subsidiary purpose, as indeed the judge appears to describe the condition (at 336). But, if not, to my mind this case is more accurately described as falling within the class of cases where the main charitable purpose is practicable but a subsidiary purpose or direction is impracticable. I was referred by counsel for the plaintiff to Tudor on Charities and

g Mortmain (4th edn, 1906) pp 202ff, where there is a heading 'Subordinate Purpose Impracticable'. But the text goes on to refer to 'subsidiary purpose or direction'. If a purpose is limited, as I think s 13 requires, to that for which the property comprised in the gift is to be applied and the money given could not be applied in providing a black gown, I do not think that the wearing of a black gown would be a purpose within s 13. But I do not see why the circumstances of Re Robinson cannot be fitted within s 13(1)(a)(ii)

h on the footing that the condition stipulated for is a direction and not an original purpose.

On the other hand, the relevant condition in Re Dominion Students' Hall Trust went to defining the class of persons to whom the benefit of the charity was limited, that is to say male students of the overseas dominions of the British Empire of European origin. The requirement that the students be of European origin was removed as tending to defeat the main object of the charity. There is no difficulty in treating that condition as part of

j the original purposes, or alternatively as a direction, and in either event the circumstances of that case would fall within s 13(1)(a)(ii).

In argument reference was also made to Re Lysaght (decd), Hill v Royal College of Surgeons of England [1965] 2 All ER 888, [1966] Ch 191, in which there was a gift by a testatrix to the Royal College of Surgeons to found medical studentships limited those who could qualify for such studentships by excluding persons of the Jewish and Roman Catholic

faith. That excluding condition was removed by Buckley J as tending to defeat the
charitable gift, because it was an essential part of the testatrix's intentions that the Royal
College should be a trustee and it refused to accept the gift with that condition. Again it
seems to me that the condition would in a like case be treated as part of the original
purposes of the gift, alternatively as a direction, and again in either event falling within
s 13(1)(*a*)(ii). I would add that, despite the importance attached by the testatrix to the
identity of the trustees as recognised by Buckley J, it does not seem to me to follow that
for the purposes of s 13 the identity of the trustee in such a case is a purpose rather than
a direction within s 13(1)(*a*)(ii). However, I would observe that, though *Re Lysaght* related
to the case of the will of a testatrix who died after s 13 of the Charities Act 1960 came
into operation, it was not decided under that Act and it is not apparent from the report
that any consideration was given to the statutory provisions.

In my judgment, therefore, it does not follow that all conditions attached to gifts must
be treated as 'purposes' within s 13. Even if I am wrong on that, it still does not seem to
me to follow that the requirement as to distribution should be treated as a condition of a
character similar to those in the pre-1960 cases to which I have referred. Both counsel
have stressed to me, with the assistance of the contemporary documents at the time of
the gift, the lack of importance that the settlor attached to the requirement as to
distribution, and counsel for the Attorney General in particular rightly criticised the
ground on which the Charity Commissioners had refused one of the plaintiff's
applications, that is to say because the requirement as to distribution was, as they put it,
'fundamental'. It cannot be right that any provision, even if only administrative, made
applicable by a donor to his gift should be treated as a condition and hence as a purpose.

I confess that from the outset I have found difficulty in accepting that it is meaningful
to talk of a cy-près application of property that has from the date of the gift been devoted
as to both capital and income to charitable purposes generally, albeit subject to a direction
as to the timing of the capital distributions. No case remotely like the present has been
drawn to my attention.

In the result, despite all the arguments that have been ably advanced, I remain
unpersuaded that such a gift is capable of being applied cy-près and, in particular, I am
not persuaded that the requirement as to distribution is a purpose within the meaning of
s 13. Rather, it seems to me to fall on the administrative side of the line, going, as it does,
to the mechanics of how the property devoted to charitable purposes is to be distributed.
Accordingly, I must refuse the application so far as it is based on s 13.

That conclusion renders it unnecessary for me to answer the second question which
had to be answered affirmatively if s 13 were to apply. Although that question has been
fully argued I think it undesirable to express obiter views on it, the more so as both
counsel have contended for the same answer and I have, therefore, heard no contrary
argument. However, many of the submissions made by counsel on that question are of
direct relevance to my consideration of the next question for me to answer, that is to say
whether the court, under its inherent jurisdiction, should direct the removal of the
requirement as to distribution. To that question I now turn.

On this question both counsel submit, and I accept, that the court is not fettered by
the particular conditions imposed by s 13(1)(*e*)(iii), but can, and should, take into account
all the circumstances of the charity, including how the charity has been distributing its
money, in considering whether it is expedient to regulate the administration of the
charity by removing the requirement as to distribution within ten years of the settlor's
death.

The evidence before me shows that the settlor throughout his life was a man of strong
religious convictions and particularly interested, and personally involved, in the activities
of the religious group known as the Christian (or Open) Brethren. That group has never
had any central organisation of the group's churches or their missionaries. There are
approximately 450 such missionaries. The plaintiff company is now a charity. Although
in 1922 it did not hold its property for exclusively charitable purposes, nevertheless it
was founded to hold property for missionary purposes and for the transmission of funds

for the missionary and other work of the Christian Brethren, and there can be no doubt
a but that it was chosen by the settlor to act as trustee because of its connections with the
Christian Brethren.

When the charity was founded in 1922 the 15,000 shares in John Laing & Sons Ltd
were worth little more than their par value, £15,000. No doubt because of a prudent
failure to diversify the charity's investments, the assets of the charity, which largely
consist of shares and loan stock in Laing companies (which are now public companies),
b had increased by 30 June 1982 to no less than £24m. In August 1922 no one would have
foreseen either that the settlor would live for more than half a century longer and attain
the age of 98 before he died on 11 January 1978, or that the assests of the charity would
increase so astonishingly. The income of the charity in the year to 30 June 1982 exceeded
£1·2m.

The settlor acted as agent of the plaintiff in effecting distributions until the end of
c 1964. He followed an income distribution policy which fostered Christian evangelical
activities, and since then the plaintiff has, in the exercise of its discretion, continued an
active distribution policy, financing home and overseas evangelism and the relief of
poverty. Various Christian causes have come to depend on the charity for their continued
support and, in the view of the plaintiff, they are in need of continued support from the
charity in the manner adopted hitherto. By far the greater part of the distributions have
d been to individuals or bodies not well suited to receive large sums of capital to finance
their future activities. There is a particular difficulty in relation to providing for the
future work of the Christian Brethren because they do not accept any organisation as a
governing or controlling body but operate on an individual basis. There would be severe
practical inconveniences and difficulties in distributing the very large sums of capital
now held by the plaintiff in a way that would ensure continuance of the causes which the
e settlor wished to support by the charity. The court should always be slow to thwart a
donor's wishes, but in this case the settlor himself, as early as 5 October 1932, indicated
to the plaintiff by letter that he wished the plaintiff to be at liberty to disregard the
requirement as to distribution. On 26 January 1939 the settlor wrote again to the
plaintiff, referring to the capital value of his gift as then worth £30,000, and saying
'considering that the capital value is more, and in view of many Christian activities, I
f wish to withdraw the stipulation that the capital should be distributed within 10 years of
my death'. It is clear that even then, after that comparatively modest increase in capital
value in that comparatively short period of the charity's existence, the settlor appreciated
that the requirement as to distribution was inexpedient.

The chairman of the directors of the plaintiff, Mr Andrew Gray, in his first affidavit,
says this of the plaintiff:

g   'The Plaintiff—itself a registered charity in its own right—has broad experience
      in the fields of Christian ministry and (so far as not already covered by that concept)
      the relief of the poor. It considers that this experience makes it sensitive to the ever-
      changing needs of the modern world, and enables it to adapt to such changes by
      shifts in the emphasis of its giving. The Plaintiff would not presume to claim that
      no other body has this capability, but having regard to its long association with the
h   Settlor, who remained a director of the Plaintiff until his death, it considers that it
      may reasonably suggest that it may be better able than most to fulfil his wishes for
      the distribution of the funds he so generously provided.'

The plaintiff has considered causing another charitable body to be set up to carry on
permanently the work now conducted by the charity, but it took the view that it would
j be unacceptable for it to adopt such a device to circumvent the restriction as to
distribution. For my part, I would have thought that the plaintiff could distribute the
capital to any other charitable body or bodies if it thought fit, but that merely serves to
emphasise the unimportance of the requirement as to distribution.

In my judgment, the plaintiff has made out a very powerful case for the removal of
the requirement as to distribution, which seems to me to be inexpedient in the very

altered circumstances of the charity since that requirement was laid down 60 years ago. I
take particular account of the fact that this application is one that has the support of the   *a*
Attorney General. Although the plaintiff is not fettered by the express terms of the gift
as to the charitable purposes for which the charity's funds are to be applied, it is, in my
view, proper for the plaintiff to wish to continue to support the causes which the settlor
himself wished the charity to support from its inception, and which would suffer if that
support was withdrawn as a consequence of the distribution of the charity's assets. I have
no hesitation in reaching the conclusion that the court should, in the exercise of its   *b*
inherent jurisdiction, approve a scheme under which the trustees for the time being of
the charity will be discharged from the obligation to distribute the capital within ten
years of the death of the settlor. I shall discuss with counsel the precise form of order that
is appropriate.

Order that trustees be discharged from obligation to distribute capital of trust within ten years of   *c*
settlor's death.

Solicitors: *Freshfields* (for the plaintiff); *Treasury Solicitor.*

Vivian Horvath   Barrister.

d

R v Huntingdon District Council,
ex parte Cowan and another   *e*

QUEEN'S BENCH DIVISION (CROWN OFFICE LIST)
GLIDEWELL J
19 AUGUST 1983

Entertainment – Public entertainment – Entertainments licence – Application for licence –   *f*
Objections to licence being granted – Duty of authority to inform applicant of objections – Duty to
give applicant opportunity to make representations in reply – Local Government (Miscellaneous
Provisions) Act 1982, Pt I.

Judicial review – Alternative remedy available by way of appeal – Discretion of court to grant
relief – Factors to be taken into account.   *g*

When dealing with an application under Pt I of the Local Government (Miscellaneous
Provisions) Act 1982 for an entertainments licence, a local authority is under a duty to
inform the applicant of the substance of any objection to its being granted, or of any
representation in the nature of an objection, and to give him an opportunity to make
representations in reply (see p 64 *f g*, post).   *h*
    Where an applicant applies to the High Court for a judicial review and there is an
alternative remedy available to him by way of appeal, the court should always ask itself,
when deciding whether to grant the relief sought, which of the two alternative remedies
is the more convenient and effective in the circumstances, not only for the applicant but
in the public interest, and should exercise its discretion accordingly (see p 63 *g h*, post).

j

Notes
For music and dancing licences, see 37 Halsbury's Laws (3rd edn) 38–47, paras 78–90,
and for cases on the subject, see 45 Digest (Repl) 223–227, 221–247.
    For the Local Government (Miscellaneous Provisions) Act 1982, Pt I, see 52 Halsbury's
Statutes (3rd edn) 1805.

Cases referred to in judgment

a   *Comr of Police v Tanos* (1958) 98 CLR 383, Aust HC.
Liverpool Taxi Owners' Association, Re [1972] 2 All ER 589, [1972] 2 QB 299, [1972] 2 WLR 1262, CA.
R v Barnsley Metropolitan Borough Council, ex p Hook [1976] 3 All ER 452, [1976] 1 WLR 1052, CA.
R v Gaming Board for Great Britain, ex p Benaim [1970] 2 All ER 528, [1970] 2 QB 417,
b   [1970] 2 WLR 1009, CA.
Russell v Duke of Norfolk [1949] 1 All ER 109, CA.
Wiseman v Borneman [1969] 3 All ER 275, [1971] AC 297, [1969] 3 WLR 706, HL.

Application for judicial review

Michael Richard Cowan and Graham Stanley Kingwood applied, with the leave of
c   Nolan J granted on 1 August 1983, for (i) an order of certiorari to quash the decision of the Huntingdon District Council, dated 22 June 1983, to refuse to grant the applicants an entertainments licence in respect of the premises known as Cuddles, St Neots, and (ii) an order of mandamus directing the local authority to hear the application according to law. The facts are set out in the judgment.

d   *David Richardson* for the applicants.
John Steel for the local authority.

GLIDEWELL J. This is an application by way of judicial review for an order of certiorari to quash the decision of the Huntingdon District Council refusing to grant a
e   licence for public entertainment for premises known as Cuddles, St Neots, and for mandamus directed to the council requiring them to hear the application according to law.

The facts are derived from the affidavit on behalf of the applicants of Mr Cowan of 9 August 1983 and from that of Mr Few, the solicitor for the district council of 15 August. Quite shortly, they are these. Whitbreads, the well-known brewers, purchased the lease
f   of the premises, which was then known as the Greenacres, on 2 March 1979. At some subsequent date the name was changed to that which it now bears.

Under the legislation formerly in force, there was not merely a liquor licence for the sale of intoxicating liquor on the premises, but also a music and dancing licence. Indeed that was renewed, after Whitbreads purchased the premises, each year. But in fact there was no music or dancing at the premises until, in December 1982, Whitbreads decided
g   to open at the premises a discotheque, that is to say an establishment with dancing to recorded music. Thereafter (and I am not concerned with the detail of this) there is evidence of some complaints from people living in the locality.

On 14 March 1983 the Act which now governs the grant of what are called 'Public Entertainments Licences', that is to say the Local Government (Miscellaneous Provisions) Act 1982 had come into force. On that date Whitbreads applied, through Mr Cowan, for
h   an entertainments licence for these premises. The district council, whose function it now is to consider and make a decision on that application, received observations on it from the chief officer of police and the fire authority, though it seems that the observations from the latter authority were not in the form of objections. They also received a petition from a number of members of the public, presumably in opposition either to the licence being granted or to the hours at which the premises were open for public entertainment,
j   I know not which.

Whitbreads were not informed by the local authority that any objections had been received. They were not informed that there was opposition. It follows that they were not informed of the substance of the observations or of the terms or substance of the petition. They were given no opportunity to comment on what objectors had said either by way of oral hearing or in writing. On 22 June 1983 the application was refused.

With that short résumé of the facts, I turn to the legislation which, as I have said, is contained in the Local Government (Miscellaneous Provisions) Act 1982. From 1 January 1983 this governs licences for public entertainment which include those formerly known as music and dancing licences. It includes others types of entertainment as well, but that is irrelevant.

The licensing authority is now the local authority whereas formerly it was the magistrates' court. The principal section is s 1 of the Act, which provides:

'(1) Subject to subsection (2) below, Schedule 1 to this Act shall have effect with respect to the licensing outside Greater London of the public entertainments referred to in that Schedule . . .'

Schedule 1 contains what is, in effect, a code dealing with 'grant, renewal and transfer of entertainments licences'. By para 1:

'(1) An entertainment to which this paragraph applies shall not be provided in any place except under and in accordance with the terms of a licence granted under this paragraph by the appropriate authority.
(2) Subject to sub-paragraph (3) below, this paragraph applies to public dancing or music or any other public entertainment of a like kind . . .'

Sub-paragraph (3) is irrelevant to the present case. Sub-paragraph (4) is relevant:

'The appropriate authority may grant to any applicant, and from time to time renew, a licence for the use of any place specified in it for all or any of the entertainments to which this paragraph applies on such terms and conditions and subject to such restrictions as may be so specified.'

That was the power which the local authority was exercising in this case. By para 6 of the schedule:

'(1) An applicant for the grant, renewal or transfer of an entertainments licence in respect of any place shall give not less than 28 days' notice of his intention to make the application to—(a) the appropriate authority; (b) the chief officer of police; and (c) the fire authority.'

Then summarising: even if the applicant does not apply (if, for instance, he forgets to apply for a renewal) the authority may, if they think fit, after consulting the chief officer of police and the fire authority, grant the application. The applicant is required by sub-para (3) to 'furnish such particulars and give such other notices as the authority may by regulation prescribe'.

By sub-para (4):

'In considering any application for the grant, renewal or transfer of an entertainments licence, the appropriate authority shall have regard to any observations submitted to them by the chief officer of police and by the fire authority.'

Paragraph 8 provides for a licence to continue in force after the date of its expiry, if an application for renewal has been made before that date but it has not been determined.

Paragraph 17 provides for appeals. Sub-paragraph (1) provides for an appeal by the applicant 'for the grant, renewal or transfer of an entertainments licence' whose application is refused, such appeal to be within 21 days to the magistrates' court for the petty sessions area in which the place is situated, 21 days, that is to say, after he is notified of the refusal of his application. There is a further right of appeal by sub-para (3) against the decision of the magistrates' court to the Crown Court. By sub-para (4):

'On an appeal to the magistrates' court or the Crown Court under this paragraph the court may make such order as it thinks fit.'

It follows from that last provision that the appeal is by way of rehearing and the *a* powers of the magistrates' court to inquire into relevant matters and of the Crown Court on appeal from them are not in any way trammelled.

It is noticeable that para 6 does not contain any reference to objections save as is to be inferred from the reference to seeking and taking account of the observations of the chief officer of police and the fire authority. There is nothing expressly about objections by other persons at all, or about notifying the applicant of objections or of representations or about giving him any opportunity to answer them.

b Counsel for the applicants submits that where an objector has made representations to the local authority, or where the local authority itself has some reason to believe that there is doubt about whether it should grant the application (in other words it has some point in mind of its own) then it is under a duty to give notice to the applicant, either by sending a copy of the representations or objections, or at least giving the substance of them, or if it is its own point, telling the applicant what the point is.

c Then it must, says counsel for the applicants, give the applicant the opportunity to make representations in answer, to seek to deal with the objection or the point, and it may be that this needs to be by way of oral hearing. I should say that, as a precaution, since it had to be done within 21 days, an appeal to the magistrates' court has been entered in this case.

Counsel for the applicants' basic point is that the rules of natural justice require an *d* authority charged with a decision such as this, whether or not to grant a licence, to give to the applicant an opportunity to know of the objections and, if he can, to answer them.

He referred me first to the previous legislation, and indeed the current legislation in Greater London. The previous legislation dealing with this matter outside Greater London was to be found in the Public Health Acts Amendment Act 1890. Under those provisions, the licensing authority, as I have already said, was the magistrates' court. *e* There was no requirement in that Act for the notification of objections nor any specific requirement that the applicant for a public music and dancing licence should have any opportunity to meet objections.

But it is agreed (it was not challenged by counsel on behalf of the local authority) that the universal practice before this year of courts hearing applications for public music and dancing licences was that if there were any objection, or if they themselves were *f* concerned about any particular question, the applicant would be notified of the substance of the matter that was to be dealt with and he would have an opportunity of dealing with it at a hearing.

It follows, submits counsel for the applicants, that when passing the 1982 Act, Parliament must have assumed that this practice would continue to be followed by local authorities and indeed intended that it should.

g In London the matter is dealt with by the London Government Act 1963, in particular s 52 of and Sch 12 to the Act. That Act, similarly, has no specific provision requiring a hearing or laying down any rules for how an application for a music and dancing licence is to be conducted. But the Greater London Council has itself adopted a most detailed code for dealing with this matter. It provides for publicity for the application, for notifying the applicant of objections, for holding a hearing if there are objections and for *h* listening to the applicant's reply.

Counsel for the applicants, of course, says that the fact that in London this is done, though not specifically required by the Act, must also have been well known to Parliament when it passed the 1982 Act. He therefore phrased his major submission in this way. Where an authority is vested by Parliament with the responsibility of exercising the powers of licensing, the authority is under a duty to exercise those powers in *j* accordance with the rules of natural justice unless those rules are clearly and expressly excluded by the relevant statutory provisions.

That last point he bases on the decision of the House of Lords in *Wiseman v Borneman* [1969] 3 All ER 275, [1971] AC 297. That was dealing with very different legislation, the Finance Act 1960. But in it Lord Wilberforce said ([1969] 3 All ER 275 at 285–286, [1971] AC 297 at 318):

'. . . the legislature may certainly exclude or limit the application of the general
rules. But it has always been insisted that this must be done, clearly and expressly: *a*
"Such an intention is not to be assumed nor is it to be spelled out from indirect
references, uncertain inferences or equivocal considerations. The intention must
satisfactorily appear from express words of plain intendment" (*Comr. of Police* v.
Tanos ((1958) 98 CLR 383 at 396), per DIXON, C.J., and WEBB, J.)'

Lord Guest in his speech had earlier said ([1969] 3 All ER 275 at 280, [1971] AC 297 at   *b*
311):

'The true view, in my opinion, is that expressed by TUCKER, L.J., in *Russell* v. *Duke
of Norfolk* ([1949] 1 All ER 109 at 118): "There are, in my view, no words which are
of universal application to every kind of inquiry and every kind of domestic
tribunal. The requirements of natural justice must depend on the circumstances of
the case, the nature of the inquiry, the rules under which the tribunal is acting, the   *c*
subject-matter that is being dealt with, and so forth. Accordingly, I do not derive
much assistance from the definitions of natural justice which have been from time
to time used, but, whatever standard is adopted, one essential is that the person
concerned should have a reasonable opportunity of presenting his case."'

Despite Lord Guest's observation that in effect each natural justice case differs from   *d*
every other one, counsel for the applicants sought to assist me by referring me to a
number of decisions of the Court of Appeal, namely *R v Gaming Board for Great Britain,
ex p Benaim* [1970] 2 All ER 528, [1970] 2 QB 417, *Re Liverpool Taxi Owners' Association*
[1972] 2 All ER 589, [1972] 2 QB 299 and *R v Barnsley Metropolitan Borough Council, ex p
Hook* [1976] 3 All ER 452, [1976] 1 WLR 1052.

R v Gaming Board for Great Britain was a case in which the gaming board had a duty of   *e*
considering whether to grant a certificate of consent enabling an application to be made
for a gaming licence. Although in the particular circumstances of the case it was held
that the board had acted fairly and was not obliged to disclose the sources or details of the
information it had received or objections, nevertheless the court clearly held that the
board was under a duty to give the applicants a sufficient indication of what objections
had been made against them to enable them to meet them.   *f*

In *Re Liverpool Taxi Owners' Association* a committee chairman undertook not to
increase the number of licensed taxi cabs in Liverpool before new legislation was enacted.
However, before that legislation, the committee then resolved to increase the number
and it did so without hearing representations from the taxi operators' association. It was
held that this was in breach of natural justice and the resolution to increase the number
was quashed.   *g*

Finally, in *Ex p Hook*, there was held to be a breach of natural justice in the hearing of
an appeal against the termination of a licence to have a stall in a market when the
applicant had not been given a full indication of what the substance of the complaints
against him was.

Those are all examples of natural justice. I must confess, though I have quoted them,
that they do no more than indicate the general scope of the subject. It does seem to me   *h*
that I have to deal with the matter as Lord Guest said it has to be dealt with, in relation to
its particular facts and the nature of the legislation with which I am dealing.

In reply, counsel for the local authority accepts that the authority have a duty to act
fairly but he does not accept that the duty extends to disclosing the objections or giving
any opportunity for reply. He maintains that the authority are perfectly entitled to act as
they have done. Indeed, as I apprehend it, this is a matter of principle on which the   *j*
authority is interested in being guided. Counsel submits that local authorities have many
administrative or quasi-administrative functions where there is no duty to give
information to applicants or to give applicants any right to make representations.

He also submits that really things have not changed very much as a result of the new
legislation, save that another layer of decision-making has been inserted below the two

existing layers. This, he says, in effect will save time in the magistrates' court because if

a an application is not opposed, and there is no objection to it, then it will be granted normally by the authority and those applications will not have to go to the magistrates' court. I suppose he would also say (though he did not actually say) that if the application is so hopeless that the applicant does not think it worth appealing to the magistrates' court from the decision of the local authority, then that is another one out of the way as well. But that apart, those that are refused but have sufficient merit to persuade the

b applicants to appeal, get to the magistrates' court and will be dealt with in the magistrates' court just as they would have been under the old legislation, the only difference being that this time they get there by way of an appeal against refusal of an application rather than by way of an original application.

What seems to me to be counsel for the local authority's strongest argument, however, is this, that the other parts of the 1982 Act, which are dealing with different sorts of

c licensing, do provide detailed procedures for the making of objections, for the notification of objections to the applicant, for representations to be made by the applicant, and, indeed, for a hearing.

There are two such codes in effect contained in the Act. First, in relation to the control of sex establishments, under s 2 of and Sch 3 to the Act (I was taken through it helpfully but I do not think it necessary for the purposes of this judgment to go into the detail)

d there is no doubt there is a detailed code which lays down expressly how the objections are to be made, that they are to be notified to applicants, that applicants should have the right of reply, and so on and so forth.

Similarly, in relation to what are called 'closing orders' on take-away food shops, which means orders not for their complete closing but as to the hour at night at which they are to close, which are governed by ss 4 and 5 of the Act, s 5 contains a similar detailed and

e comprehensive code dealing with all these matters.

What counsel for the local authority submits, with a great deal of force, is this is one Act and a normal principle of statutory construction is that an Act must be construed as a whole. It follows, he says, that where you have in relation to two similar subjects dealt with by the Act, detailed provisions providing for objections, notification, representations by an applicant and a hearing, and no such provisions in relation to entertainment

f licences, that can only be because Parliament intended that those provisions should not apply to entertainment licences and thus the Act, in effect, is expressly excluding the necessity for those provisions.

Counsel also advanced a secondary argument, that the relief sought by the applicants is discretionary (as it undoubtedly is) and that since there is a right of appeal to the magistrates' court which has been exercised, I should not exercise my discretion to grant

g these applicants any relief. I propose to deal first with the second point because if I find in counsel's favour on that point, that would be an end to the matter.

As I have said, the relief sought is discretionary. Where there is an alternative remedy available but judicial review is sought, then in my judgment the court should always ask itself whether the remedy that is sought in the court, or the alternative remedy which is available to the applicant by way of appeal, is the most effective and convenient, in other

h words, which of them will prove to be the most effective and convenient in all the circumstances, not merely for the applicant, but in the public interest. In exercising discretion whether or not to grant relief, that is a major factor to be taken into account.

Counsel in this case of course, and those engaged in it, are well aware that in the case I heard immediately before this case under the same legislation, from the metropolitan borough of Gateshead, I refused relief on that very ground and on that ground alone.

j There, there was a complaint about bias in the particular case and the complaint that was made was relevant only to that case. That does seem to me to be a material difference between that case and this, because whatever my decision on that case, it affected only that case, whereas in this case, what I am being asked to deal with is a matter which affects the conduct by local authorities throughout the country of their functions under this legislation.

I am told (one is always glad to be told whether one is making law for the first time) that this is a matter which has not hitherto been decided. If I do decide to grant some relief by way of judicial review, it inevitably follows that whether I am right or wrong in the decision I make, at least I will be deciding a question which has not hitherto been decided. It therefore seems to me that in this case I should exercise my discretion to go on to deal with this matter, rather than to say, 'Well, the applicants can go to the magistrates' court and that will deal with their problem in this particular case'.

So I go back to the substantive question. The exercise of a licensing function, in my judgment, by any authority, is one to which the rules of natural justice (including the requirement of giving notice of the substance, at least, of objections, and giving some opportunity for the applicant to respond to those objections) would normally apply.

The question which has exercised my mind is: does the fact that, in the other parts of the Act to which I have referred, specific provision is made for those features, whereas no such provision is made in Sch 1, mean that Parliament intended that that rule of natural justice should not here apply? I have come to the conclusion that I ought not to draw that deduction.

It is true, as counsel for the local authority submitted, that these three parts of the Act are all dealing with licensing functions in one way or another. But from the way in which the various parts have been drafted, it looks very much as though they have been separately drafted, almost as though they were parts of separate statutes, certainly as though they were separate codes without reference one to the other.

For instance, as a matter of interest, in relation to this matter, the procedural passages are contained in Sch 1; in relation to sex establishments, the procedural matters are in Sch 3, whereas, when you come to take-away food shops, all the procedural matters are not in a schedule but are defined in one of the sections of the Act itself, namely s 5, which does mean, to my mind, either that they were drawn up by different draftsmen or, at least, that it did not occur to anybody to deal with the matters as if they were all part and parcel of the same sort of legislation.

I think I am entitled to the view that this part of the Act is a self-contained code, and also entitled to follow counsel for the applicants' submission that Parliament must have been aware of the practice hitherto obtaining in the magistrates' court when dealing with music and dancing licences.

Accordingly, in my judgment, a local authority is under a duty, when dealing with entertainments licences, first, to inform the applicant of the substance of any objection or of any representation in the nature of an objection (not necessarily to give him the whole of it, nor to say necessarily who has made it, but to give him the substance of it); and, second, to give him an opportunity to make representations in reply.

I am not going to lay down, because it does not seem to me necessary to do so, any clear requirement what those representations should be or in what form they should be. I do not think it necessarily follows that an oral hearing should take place; it may well be that in many cases written representations will suffice. I think it is for the local authority to decide if in a particular case hearings are required or to lay down their own procedure in this respect, but that some such opportunity is required I have no doubt. That being so, I am prepared to grant some form of relief as sought.

Certiorari granted. Decision of local authority dated 22 June 1983 quashed.

Solicitors: *Field Fisher & Martineau* (for the applicants); *L B Marks & Co*, agents for *John E Few*, Huntingdon (for the local authority).

Sophie Craven   Barrister

R v Terry

HOUSE OF LORDS
LORD FRASER OF TULLYBELTON, LORD SCARMAN, LORD BRIDGE OF HARWICH, LORD BRANDON OF OAKBROOK AND LORD BRIGHTMAN
28 NOVEMBER, 15 DECEMBER 1983

Road traffic – Excise licence – Fraudulent use of licence – Intention to defraud – Intent – What intent must be proved – Whether necessary to prove intent to avoid paying proper licence fee – Whether sufficient merely to prove intent to deceive person performing public duty – Vehicles (Excise) Act 1971, s 26(1).

It is not necessary, on a charge of fraudulently using an excise licence contrary to s 26(1)[a] of the Vehicles (Excise) Act 1971, for the Crown to establish an intent to avoid paying the proper licence fee; it is sufficient merely for the Crown to prove an intent by deceit to cause a person responsible for a public duty to act, or refrain from acting, in a way in which he otherwise would not have done (see p 66 j, p 67 b c and p 68 b to p 69 a, post).

Welham v DPP [1960] 1 All ER 805 and dicta of Viscount Dilhorne and of Lord Diplock in *Scott v Comr of Police for the Metropolis* [1974] 3 All ER at 1037, 1040 applied.

R v Manners-Astley [1967] 3 All ER 899 overruled.

Notes

For fraudulent use of vehicle licences, see 40 Halsbury's Laws (4th edn) para 179.

For the Vehicles (Excise) Act 1971, s 26, see 41 Halsbury's Statutes (3rd edn) 456.

Cases referred to in opinions

R v Manners-Astley [1967] 3 All ER 899, [1967] 1 WLR 1505, CA.

Scott v Comr of Police for the Metropolis [1974] 3 All ER 1032, [1975] AC 819, [1974] 2 WLR 379, HL.

Welham v DPP [1960] 1 All ER 805, [1961] AC 103, [1960] 2 WLR 669, HL.

Appeal

The Crown appealed with leave of the Court of Appeal, Criminal Division against the decision of that court (Dunn LJ, Balcombe and Leonard JJ) on 5 May 1983 allowing an appeal by the respondent, Neil William Terry, against his conviction on 25 February 1982 in the Crown Court at Warrington before Mr Recorder R E Snape and a jury of fraudulently using an excise licence contrary to s 26(1) of the Vehicles (Excise) Act 1971. The Court of Appeal certified, under s 33(2) of the Criminal Appeal Act 1968, that the following point of law of general public importance was involved in the decision: whether, on a charge of fraudulently using an excise licence contrary to s 26(1) of the 1971 Act, the Crown was required to establish an intent to avoid paying the proper licence fee or whether it was sufficient to prove an intent by deceit to cause a person responsible for a public duty to act, or refrain from acting, in a way in which he otherwise would not have done. The facts are set out in the opinion of Lord Fraser.

John M T Rogers QC and *Thomas Teague* for the appellant.
Rhys Davies QC and *Paul O'Brien* for the respondent.

Their Lordships took time for consideration.

15 December. The following opinions were delivered.

LORD FRASER OF TULLYBELTON. My Lords, on 25 February 1982 the respondent was convicted in the Crown Court at Warrington on two counts, viz (1) theft

---

a   Section 26(1), so far as material, is set out at p 65 c, post

of a vehicle excise licence and (2) fraudulently using an excise licence contrary to s 26(1) of the Vehicles (Excise) Act 1971. He appealed against his conviction on the second *a* count. On 5 May 1983 his appeal was allowed by the Court of Appeal, Criminal Division (Dunn LJ, Balcombe and Leonard JJ) on the ground that a person does not 'fraudulently' use an excise licence within the meaning of that section unless he uses it in an attempt to evade paying the proper licence fee, and that the respondent had not been shown to have used it for that purpose. In reaching that decision the Court of Appeal was, as it recognised, bound by its own decision in *R v Manners-Astley* [1967] 3 All ER 899, [1967] *b* 1 WLR 1505. Accordingly, the present appeal is in substance against the decision in *R v Manners-Astley*.

Section 26(1) of the 1971 Act, so far as relevant, provides:

'If any persons forges or fraudulently alters or uses . . . (a) any mark to be fixed or sign to be exhibited on a mechanically propelled vehicle in accordance with section 19 or 21 of this Act; or . . . (c) any licence or registration document under this Act, *c* he shall be liable on summary conviction to a fine . . . or on conviction on indictment to imprisonment . . .'

The relevant provisions of that section are substantially the same as the provisions of s 17(1) of the Vehicles (Excise) Act 1962, which was the section under consideration in *R v Manners-Astley*. *d*

The facts in this case were as follows. On 18 May 1981 the respondent hired a Ford Escort car from a car-hire firm. When he returned it on 22 May 1981 its excise licence disc was missing. On 1 June 1981 he was driving his own car, a Ford Cortina, which had no licence disc displayed on the windscreen. He was stopped by a police officer, who asked him where his excise licence was. The police officer had been riding a motor cycle and at the time he asked the question he had not seen the licence disc. When he looked *e* into the car he saw an excise licence disc lying on the dashboard of the car. The respondent reached into the car, picked up the licence and handed it to the police officer saying, 'I don't think this is the right one'. The police officer at once noticed that the licence did not relate to the respondent's Cortina car. In fact it related to the Escort car which he had hired some days previously. The Crown case is that the respondent stole the excise licence relating to the Escort and that he fraudulently used it on his own Cortina with the *f* intention that a police officer who saw it would wrongly think that the Cortina was properly licensed. The respondent's case was that the licence had fallen off the Escort while on hire to him, and that he had taken it into his house unintentionally and was about to return it to the hire company. Further, he said that by 1 June he had already applied for a new licence for his own Cortina and that he was not using the licence from the Escort in an attempt to avoid paying the licence fee on the Cortina. The recorder *g* directed the jury that they had only to consider two questions on this count: first, whether the licence relating to the Escort had been exhibited on the dashboard of the Cortina, and, if so, second, whether it had been placed there by the respondent with the intention that it would be accepted as a genuine document applicable to the Cortina. The respondent contends that this was a misdirection because it left it open to the jury to convict him even if they accepted his statement that he had already applied for a licence *h* for the Cortina and was therefore not trying to avoid paying the proper licence fee for that car but was merely trying to avoid being charged with using the car without a licence being exhibited in breach of s 12(4) of the 1971 Act. The issue therefore is whether an attempt to avoid paying the licence fee is an essential element of the offence of using a licence fraudulently.

My Lords, the meaning of the words 'with intent to defraud' was considered by this *j* House in *Welham v DPP* [1960] 1 All ER 805, [1961] AC 103. For the purposes of this appeal there is in my opinion no relevant difference of meaning between 'with intent to defraud' and 'fraudulently'. In *Welham v DPP* the appellant was convicted under s 6 of the Forgery Act 1913 on a charge of having 'within intent to defraud' uttered a forged hire-purchase proposal and a forged hire-purchase agreement. His defence was that he

had no intention of defrauding the finance companies which advanced money and that
the reason for bringing the forged documents into existence was to evade credit
restrictions by misleading the relevant authorities into thinking that the finance
companies were advancing money not as straight loans (which would have been illegal)
but under hire-purchase agreements (which would have been legal). His appeal against
conviction was dismissed by the Court of Criminal Appeal, whose decision was affirmed
by this House. The grounds of decision by this House were that 'with intent to defraud'
was not confined to the idea of depriving a person by deceit of some economic advantage
or inflicting on him some economic loss, but that they applied where a document was
brought into existence for no other purpose than of deceiving a person responsible for a
public duty into doing something that he would not have done but for the deceit, or not
doing something that but for it he would have done. I shall cite two passages from the
speech of Lord Radcliffe (see [1960] 1 All ER 805 at 808, [1961] AC 103 at 123–124),
with whose speech Lord Tucker, Lord Keith and Lord Morris agreed. The first is as
follows:

> 'Now I think that there are one or two things that can be said with confidence
> about the meaning of this word "defraud". It requires a person as its object; that is,
> defrauding involves doing something to someone. Although in the nature of things
> it is almost invariably associated with the obtaining of an advantage for the person
> who commits the fraud, it is the effect on the person who is the object of the fraud
> that ultimately determines its meaning . . . Secondly, popular speech does not give,
> and I do not think ever has given, any sure guide as to the limits of what is meant
> by "to defraud". It may mean to cheat someone. It may mean to practise a fraud on
> someone. It may mean to deprive someone by deceit of something which is regarded
> as belonging to him or, though not belonging to him, as due to him or his right.'

In the second passage, after referring to a dictionary definition and to the writings of
Rudyard Kipling, Lord Radcliffe went on:

> 'There is nothing in any of this that suggests that to defraud is, in ordinary speech,
> confined to the idea of depriving a man by deceit of some economic advantage or
> inflicting on him some economic loss. Has the law ever so confined it? In my
> opinion, there is no warrant for saying that it has. What it has looked for in
> considering the effect of cheating on another person and so in defining the criminal
> intent is the prejudice of that person . . . Of course, as I have said, in ninety-nine
> cases out of a hundred the intent to deceive one person to his prejudice merely
> connotes the deceiver's intention of obtaining an advantage for himself by inflicting
> a corresponding loss on the person deceived. In all such cases, the economic
> explanation is sufficient. But in that special line of cases where the person deceived
> is a public authority or a person holding a public office, deceit may secure an
> advantage for the deceiver without causing anything that can fairly be called either
> a pecuniary or an economic injury to the person deceived. If there could be no
> intent to defraud in the eyes of the law without an intent to inflict a pecuniary or
> economic injury, such cases as these could not have been punished as forgeries at
> common law, in which an intent to defraud is an essential element of the offence,
> yet I am satisfied that they were regularly so treated.'

Lord Denning, with whose speech Lord Radcliffe expressed his agreement, said ([1960]
1 All ER 805 at 816, [1961] AC 103 at 134):

> '. . . it appears that the appellant on his own evidence had an intent to defraud;
> because he uttered the hire-purchase documents for the purpose of fraud and deceit.
> He intended to practise a fraud on whomsoever might be called on to investigate
> the loans made by the finance companies to the motor dealers. Such a person might
> be prejudiced in his investigation by the fraud. That is enough to show an intent to
> defraud.'

Welham v DPP was considered by the Court of Appeal in *R v Manners-Astley*, where the appellant had been convicted of fraudulently using an excise licence contrary to s 17(1) *a* of the 1962 Act by displaying a vehicle licence issued for one vehicle on another vehicle. The Court of Appeal quashed the conviction on two grounds, one of which was that the jury had not been directed to consider whether the appellant had intended to defraud the Excise by avoiding payment of the licence fee. The Court of Appeal distinguished the decision in *Welham* as being one limited to cases under the Forgery Act 1913. In taking that limited view of the decision the court was, in my respectful opinion, wrong. The *b* speeches in *Welham* were directed to the meaning of 'intent to defraud' in general and were not limited to its meaning in the Forgery Act 1913. I agree with the view expressed by Viscount Dilhorne in *Scott v Comr of Police for the Metropolis* [1974] 3 All ER 1032 at 1037, [1975] AC 819 at 838, where he said:

> 'While the meaning to be given to words may be affected by their context and Lord Radcliffe [in *Welham*] was only considering the meaning of intent to defraud *c* in s 4 of the Forgery Act 1913, the passages which I have cited from his speech are, I think, of general application . . .'

(The passages cited by Viscount Dilhorne were those in the first quotation that I have made above.)

Lord Diplock, who also took part in the decision of *Scott v Comr of Police for the d Metropolis*, summarised the law in three propositions, of which the third was as follows ([1974] 3 All ER 1032 at 1040, [1975] AC 819 at 841):

> 'Where the intended victim of a "conspiracy to defraud" is a person performing public duties as distinct from a private individual it is sufficient if the purpose is to cause him to act contrary to his public duty, and the intended means of achieving *e* this purpose are dishonest. The purpose need not involve causing economic loss to anyone.'

In the present case I see nothing in s 26(1) of the Vehicles (Excise) Act 1971 which leads me to think that the word 'fraudulently' ought to be given a more limited meaning than that attributed to the words 'intent to defraud' in *Welham v DPP*. On the contrary the context indicates that they should bear a wide meaning. One of the offences created *f* by s 26(1)(*a*) is fraudulently using any mark (ie a number plate) which is required to be fixed to a vehicle: see s 19(1). It is easy to imagine cases where false number plates might be used by dishonest persons for the purpose of deceiving police officers and causing them to act in the way that they would not otherwise have acted, without any intention of evading payment of the licence fee, and I have no doubt that s 26(1) is applicable to such cases. There is nothing in the section to exclude the application of the general rule *g* stated in *Welham*.

I am accordingly of opinion that the decision in *R v Manners-Astley* was erroneous and should now be overruled. It follows that the decision of the Court of Appeal, Criminal Division in the present appeal was wrong.

For these reasons I would allow the appeal and restore the conviction of the respondent. The first alternative in the certified question should be answered in the negative, and the *h* second alternative in the affirmative.

LORD SCARMAN. My Lords, I agree with the speech of my noble and learned friend Lord Fraser. I would allow the appeal and answer the certified question as he proposes.

LORD BRIDGE OF HARWICH. My Lords, for the reasons given in the speech of *j* my noble and learned friend Lord Fraser, I agree that this appeal should be allowed and the certified question answered in the manner he indicates.

LORD BRANDON OF OAKBROOK. My Lords, I have had the advantage of reading in draft the speech prepared by my noble and learned friend Lord Fraser. I agree *a* with it, and for the reasons which he gives I would allow the appeal, restore the respondent's conviction, and answer the certified question in the manner proposed.

LORD BRIGHTMAN. My Lords, I agree.

Appeal allowed. Conviction restored. First alternative in certified question answered in the negative, second alternative in the affirmative.

b

Solicitors: *Sharpe Pritchard & Co*, agents for *E C Woodcock*, Chester (for the Crown); *Manches & Co*, agents for *Ashalls*, Warrington (for the respondent).

Mary Rose Plummer   Barrister.

c

Practice Direction

FAMILY DIVISION

d

Ward of court – Guardian ad litem – Two parties requiring appointment of guardians ad litem – Appointment of Official Solicitor and of near relative or divorce court welfare officer.

Where in wardship proceedings there are or will be two parties requiring the appointment of guardians ad litem, e g where there is a child whom the court has ordered to be joined and the parent of the child is also a minor or is incapable of managing his or her affairs, *e* consideration should be given to the appointment of the Official Solicitor as guardian ad litem of the child party. This would not normally be suitable if the Official Solicitor has acted for the parent in other proceedings and would of course be impossible if the Official Solicitor is already guardian ad litem of the other minor or incapable party. In such a case the child party's guardian ad litem should normally be a suitable near relative who is *f* willing to act or a divorce court welfare officer from an area outside the area of the court making the order; such a guardian ad litem would also be suitable for the other minor or disabled party if the Official Solicitor is already guardian ad litem of the child party.

Where a divorce court welfare officer is to be appointed, the order should state 'a divorce court welfare officer nominated by the chief probation officer for the area of [*the selected area*]'. The associate should obtain the name and address of the chief probation *g* officer from the local divorce court welfare service.

Issued with the concurrence of the Lord Chancellor.

J L ARNOLD
President.

8 December 1983

Dexter v Courtaulds Ltd

COURT OF APPEAL, CIVIL DIVISION
LAWTON, FOX AND KERR LJJ
8, 9 NOVEMBER 1983

Interest – Damages – Personal injury – Rate of interest – Special damage – Loss of wages – Plaintiff injured in course of his employment – Plaintiff off work for two periods as a result of accident and losing wages – Loss quantified at end of each period – Trial not taking place until four years later – Principles to be applied – Whether interest should be awarded at full or half rate – Whether interest may be awarded at other than half rate when special circumstances exist.

In August 1977 the plaintiff, a fitter, sustained personal injuries in the course of his employment with the defendants and, as a result, was off work for a period of four months during which time he lost his wages. He then returned to work, but as a result of his injuries was off work for another six weeks in 1978 and again lost wages. He brought an action against the defendants claiming damages for personal injuries. At the trial in May 1982 he was awarded, inter alia, special damages of £505·62 and interest thereon from the date of the accident until the date of the trial at half the appropriate rate of interest allowed on the general damages. On appeal the plaintiff, by a cross-notice, contended that since the quantum of loss was known at the end of each period of incapacity interest on the special damages should have been awarded at the full rate from the time at which that incapacity had been calculated.

Held – Since the case was a typical and common type of personal injury case with nothing unusual about it, interest on the special damages should be awarded at half rate from the date of the accident. Accordingly, the judge had not erred in calculating interest and the appeal would therefore be dismissed (see p 73 *e f* and p 74 *d* and *h j*, post).

Jefford v Gee [1970] 1 All ER 1202 applied.

Per curiam. In the generality of personal injury cases the principle enunciated by the Court of Appeal in 1970 with respect to the calculation of interest on special damages should continue to be applied, viz interest should be awarded on the total sum of the special damages from the date of the accident until the date of trial at half the appropriate rate of interest allowed on the general damages. Where there are special circumstances, known to the plaintiff and his advisers but not, perhaps, to the defendant, which make it unfair to apply that principle, the plaintiff should say so when claiming interest and should set out the facts on which the court can adjudge whether there are such special circumstances (see p 74 *d* to *j*, post); *Jefford v Gee* [1970] 1 All ER 1202 applied.

Notes

For award of interest on damages, see 12 Halsbury's Laws (4th edn) para 1204, and for cases on the subject, see 34 Digest (Reissue) 553–554, 4430–4439.

Cases referred to in judgments

Dodd v Rediffusion (West Midlands) Ltd (4 December 1979, unreported), QBD.
Ichard v Frangoulis [1977] 2 All ER 461, [1977] 1 WLR 556.
Jefford v Gee [1970] 1 All ER 1202, [1970] 2 QB 130, [1970] 2 WLR 702, CA.

Appeal

The defendants, Courtaulds Ltd, appealed against the judgment of Bush J given in the Queen's Bench Division at Birmingham on 28 May 1982 whereby he awarded the plaintiff, Paul David Dexter, damages of £2,672·28 and agreed interest thereon of £270·85 (being agreed special damages of £505·62 and agreed interest thereon of £151·68, and general damages of £2,166 and agreed interest thereon) in respect of injuries sustained by the plaintiff in the course of his employment with the defendants

a on 22 August 1977, the judge having assessed liability as to the plaintiff as one-third and as to the defendants two-thirds. By a respondent's notice by way of cross-appeal the plaintiff asked the court to set aside the judgment in so far as the judge found the plaintiff guilty of contributory negligence and awarded him interest on the special damages at half rate from the date of the accident. The case is reported only on the issue of interest raised by the cross-appeal. The facts are set out in the judgment of Lawton LJ.

b
Raymond Walker for the defendants.
Nicholas Worsley for the plaintiff.

LAWTON LJ. This is an appeal by the defendants, Courtaulds Ltd, against a judgment delivered by Bush J on 28 May 1982, whereby he ordered that the defendants should pay

c the plaintiff, Mr Paul David Dexter, a sum of £2,943·13 as damages for personal injuries which he sustained in the course of his employment with the defendants on 22 August 1977. The sum of £2,943·13 was made up in part of agreed special damages of £505·62 and agreed interest (in the sense of rate and period being agreed) at £151·68.

The plaintiff was a fitter employed by the defendants at their Spondon premises. In the course of his work he had to go to various parts of the factory, including a four-storey

d building on the roof of which there was a structure called the 'penthouse'. Inside the penthouse was a largish machine, part of which had to be dismantled at intervals of about two months, cleaned and then put back. In order to accomplish this job the plaintiff had to use at the final stages of his work a piece of wood in order to lever one of the components into its final position. The evidence was not clear as to what size of wood it had to be. There was some evidence that the lever, the piece of wood, would probably

e have to be about 5 or 6 feet long. The plaintiff himself suggested he could do the levering with a shorter piece of wood than that, but common sense says that a fairly substantial piece of wood had to be used.

The plaintiff, in the ordinary course of working as a fitter, would not be carrying around pieces of wood which he could conveniently use on the comparatively rare occasions he would have to use a piece of wood. It follows that, for the purposes of doing

f the job which he was doing on 22 August 1977, he would have to get a piece of wood from somewhere. He said, and the judge accepted his evidence, that there were pieces of wood lying around on the roof of the building where this penthouse was situated, that he decided to look for a piece of wood which would be suitable for the job he wanted it for, and that whilst he was doing so he fell through a fanlight which was on the roof. He himself does not remember falling through the fanlight. He was badly injured about

g both the head and the chest and it is understandable that he would have had a loss of memory after an accident of that kind. [His Lordship then considered the evidence, dismissed the appeal on the question of liability and contributory negligence, and continued:]

There does, however, arise by way of cross-notice an interesting and very important point, so it seems to me, about the way in which interest should be calculated for the

h purpose of personal injury litigation. This point was brought to the attention of the trial judge by counsel for the plaintiff, who has told us that the point is of common occurrence in personal injuries litigation and that judges are differing about the way interest should be calculated. In order to deal with this point, I must call attention to the fact that the plaintiff was off work for four months from 22 August 1977. During that time he lost his wages. Clearly he was entitled, in the circumstances, to be awarded damages which

j would compensate him for his loss of wages. He then returned to work. As a result of his injury he was off work for another six weeks in 1978. Once again he lost wages. The trial did not take place until 25 May 1982. As a consequence he was out of pocket for something like four years. By the time he went back to work after his first period of incapacity the amount of his loss of wages for that period was known. There was no difficulty whatsoever about calculating it. He was deprived, by the course the trial took, of the benefit of that lump sum from the date when his first period of incapacity came to an end to the date of trial. The same can be said about the second period of incapacity. *a*

Counsel for the plaintiff submitted that, on principle, since the quantum of loss was known at the end of each period of incapacity, interest should be paid at the full rate from the time at which that incapacity had been calculated. He invited our attention to two judgments at first instance. The first in order of time is *Ichard v Frangoulis* [1977] 2 All ER 461, [1977] 1 WLR 556. The facts of that case are not very clear from the report. It appears that the plaintiffs, husband and wife, had been on holiday in Yugoslavia and *b* that they had been involved in a collision on a road. As a result of the collision they had been injured. The allegation was that the defendant was responsible for the collision. There is no detail, as far as we can find, how the sum of £2,000 claimed by way of special damage was made up. We do not know, for example, whether it represented any loss of earnings on the part of the plaintiff or his wife. We do not know whether it represented any damage to his motor vehicle or any medical expenses or any costs of bringing the *c* vehicle home from Yugoslavia. That is one of the problems arising about the extent to which this judgment is an apt one for the purposes of deciding the point of principle which has to be decided in this case. But in the course of dealing with interest, Peter Pain J said ([1977] 2 All ER 461 at 462–463, [1977] 1 WLR 556 at 558):

> 'So far as special damage is concerned, it has been agreed that that stands at *d* £2,000, but there has been discussion as to what is the appropriate provision as to interest. Counsel for the plaintiffs, founding himself on *Jefford v Gee* [1970] 1 All ER 1202, [1970] 2 QB 130, has suggested that one should take the lower rate of interest—half the rate which would otherwise be applicable, which we have not as yet determined—on the basis of that case, but I feel quite satisfied that that was done in *Jefford v Gee* because that was a case where there was a continuing loss of earnings. *e* I think the principle is different where the special damages is all, or virtually all, incurred at the date of the accident, and, as a matter of convenience and to allow for the fact that the defendant may not have paid all his bills immediately, and so on, and to take a broad view, I say that interest should run from 1st November 1971 on the special damage, again at the rate which I hope will be agreed to be the appropriate rate.' *f*

Counsel for the defendants has submitted that that decision may very well have been wrong. He does not put it more emphatically than that, because there is not enough information about the nature of the special damage.

Counsel for the plaintiff also invited our attention to an unreported judgment of Forbes J delivered at Birmingham on 4 December 1979 in *Dodd v Rediffusion (West Midlands) Ltd*. It is clear from that part of the judgment which we have been shown (we *g* have only been shown the part relating to interest) that at Birmingham at that time Forbes J on a number of occasions had awarded interest in a way which departed from the principle of *Jefford v Gee*. In that case he gave his reasons in clear language. He said:

> 'If you look at *Jefford v Gee* you will find that was a case in which the loss of wages continued. If you want to take a short cut in the mathematics you can do it by *h* taking the total amount, and you can say that either you take half the interest over the whole period or the whole of the interest over half the period and you get exactly the same answer. It is a nice short cut instead of having to calculate from week to week over the whole period. Lord Denning MR chose to take the whole period and half the rate, and that is utterly appropriate where the thing is continuing, but where the wages were lost years ago it is not the right way of doing it because it is *j* very unfair to the plaintiff. The object of the interest is that he technically ought to have been paid the money at the time it was due, and because he was not he was entitled to interest for it not being paid, so if he lost £100 in wages five years ago then he ought to be entitled to the full interest on that for the five years. That is the way my mind works on it. As long as you take half the period, so that if he lost

a   wages over 20 weeks and you say: I will take the middle of that period, ten weeks, and calculate the full rate to that tenth week, then you are doing fairly by both plaintiff and defendant, and that is the way my mind works on *Jefford v Gee*, and, as I say, I would take the full rate of interest from a date in April, which is approximately midway between the periods when he was technically losing his benefit.'

That way of thinking has its attractions and it may well be that in some cases it is the
b   appropriate way of dealing with special damage. The sort of case in which it may well be a fair way of dealing with interest is the case of a man who sustains injury as a result of somebody else's negligence. He happens to be a high-earning self-employed man. He is off work for something like three or four months, thereby having sustained a very substantial loss of income, but for some reason the trial does not come on for four or five years. It would seem, in circumstances such as those, that he ought to be compensated
c   for the loss which he sustained through being unable to work for some time after the accident. Another kind of case where there might be special circumstances and where the principle enunciated by Forbes J should apply is where a man sustains an injury so serious that it requires an expensive operation, which he pays for out of his own pocket and which is successful, so that he is able to go back to work soon after the accident. Again, for some reason beyond his control, the trial does not come on for four or five
d   years. It does seem unfair in a case like that, he having paid out a substantial sum for medical expenses years before, he cannot get back from the wrongdoer the full rate of interest on those medical expenses.

Counsel for the defendants, however, submitted to us that, although there may be occasional cases where the principles of assessment of interest according to *Jefford v Gee* can be departed from, in the generality of cases they ought not to be departed from, and that this comes within the generality of cases. In my opinion, this is a typical and
e   common type of personal injury case: there is nothing unusual about it at all. If there is nothing unusual about this case, and I am of the opinion that there is not, the submission of counsel for the defendants was that we are bound to apply the principle set out in *Jefford v Gee*.

It is relevant for this purpose to remind oneself of that decision. It was an important
f   case, because the court, consisting of Lord Denning MR, Davies and Salmon LJJ, clearly intended to lay down general principles for application in personal injury cases. On its facts it differs from this case, because the plaintiff was so seriously injured that his special damages were mounting up right until the date of trial; there was a continuing loss of special damage; whereas in this case the last occasion there was a loss of wages was in 1978. But Lord Denning MR, giving judgment, pointed out that in strict logic interest ought to be calculated, certainly in the case of a wage-earner, from week to week, but in
g   most cases that would be a very tiresome way of finding out what was fair compensation for a head of damage like this. He put the matter in this way under the heading 'Loss of wages' ([1970] 1 All ER 1202 at 1208, [1970] 2 QB 130 at 146):

'This occurred week by week. In principle, the interest should be calculated on each week's loss from that week to the date of trial. But that would mean too much
h   detail. Alternatively, it would be possible to add up the loss every six months and allow interest on the total every six months until trial. That would seem fair, especially as the loss for the initial weeks might be for total incapacity, and afterwards only for partial incapacity when he could do light work. More rough and ready, the total loss could be taken from accident to trial: and interest allowed only on half of it, or for half the time, or at half the rate.'

j   Counsel for the plaintiff invited our attention to the phrase 'taken from accident to trial'. He submitted that the court should not be deemed to have been thinking of a case like the present when there had been a known and quantified loss as long ago as 1978.

The riposte of counsel for the defendant to that submission was this. He pointed out that in *Jefford v Gee* the court had been dealing not only with loss of wages, which in that case had continued until trial, but with items of damage which had been known and quantified long before trial. That is clear from the report, because Lord Denning MR went on to say, under a cross-heading of 'Medical expenses': 'In principle interest should run from the date on which they are paid. But they are not usually so large as to warrant separate calculation.' And under a cross-heading 'Damage to scooter and clothing' he said: 'In principle interest should run from the date when the account is paid for repairs or replacements. But, here again, the amounts are not so large as to warrant separate calculation.' In his judgment he summarised all the various heads of damage and, with regard to special damage, he said ([1970] 1 All ER 1202 at 1212, [1970] 2 QB 130 at 151): 'Interest should be awarded from the date of the accident to the date of trial at half the appropriate rate.'

Of course, as a matter of strict law, that was a judgment on the facts of that case, but it is clear, in my judgment, what Lord Denning MR was doing. He appreciated that personal injury claims are very common. There are hundreds of thousands of them every year. It is convenient for everybody that simple straightforward rules should apply to them. In those circumstances, he and his brethren who were sitting with him enunciated broad principles which are to be applicable in the generality of personal injury cases.

If this case is one falling within the broad spectrum of personal injury cases, then it seems to me that *Jefford v Gee* requires this court to apply the *Jefford v Gee* principle. As, in my judgment, this is a straightforward case of personal injuries, the *Jefford v Gee* principle should be applied. That is what the trial judge did. In my judgment, he was right to do so.

One final point does arise. As I have indicated, there may be special circumstances in which it would not be fair to apply the broad principles enunciated in *Jefford v Gee*. If there are special circumstances, which make it unfair to apply those principles, they are circumstances which would be known to the plaintiff and his advisers. They may not be known to the defendant. The defendant in this class of case very often, indeed I would have thought more often than not, has to decide whether a payment into court should be made. In the generality of cases under the provisions of RSC Ord 22, r 1(8), any payment into court has to include interest, not separately itemised. The defendants' advisers when deciding on a payment into court nowadays are able to calculate the interest on special damage on the *Jefford v Gee* principle, and that is clearly convenient. But, if the plaintiff at the trial is going to say, 'There were special circumstances here which make the application of the *Jefford v Gee* principle unfair,' then the payment into court, if the judge finds they were special, may be inadequate because interest has been calculated in the wrong way.

In the course of the argument Kerr LJ suggested that in personal injury cases, when the plaintiff wishes to say that there are special circumstances which exclude the application of the *Jefford v Gee* principle, he should say so when claiming interest and set out the facts on which the court can adjudge whether there were special circumstances. In my judgment, Kerr LJ's suggestion is one which solicitors would do well to bear in mind. Maybe those who are concerned to amend the Rules of the Supreme Court when necessary will have regard to what I have said in this judgment, if my brethren agree.

I would dismiss the appeal.

FOX LJ. I agree and do not wish to add anything.

KERR LJ. I also agree and there is nothing I wish to add.

Appeal dismissed. Leave to appeal to House of Lords refused.

Solicitors: *Browne Jacobson & Roose*, Nottingham (for the defendants); *Robin Thompson & Partners*, Birmingham (for the plaintiff).

Mary Rose Plummer   Barrister.

a

Keen and another v Holland

COURT OF APPEAL, CIVIL DIVISION
DUNN, OLIVER AND FOX LJJ
18, 19 OCTOBER, 8 NOVEMBER 1983

b   *Agricultural holding – Tenancy – Agreement whereby land let for more than one year but less than two years – Tenancy agreement not executed until a few days before expiry of term – Agreement made on basis that protected tenancy would not be granted – Whether agreement creating 'interest less than a tenancy from year to year' – Whether tenancy a protected tenancy – Agricultural Holdings Act 1948, s 2(1).*

c   *Estoppel – Convention – Parties adopting conventional basis for their relations – Parties agreeing that tenancy agreement concluded between them not to have effect which in law it had – Grant of agricultural tenancy on basis that it would not be protected tenancy – Whether tenant estopped from claiming statutory protection – Whether unconscionable for tenant to rely on protection of statute – Agricultural Holdings Act 1948, s 2(1).*

d

The plaintiffs were the freeholders of a farm which in 1966 was let on a yearly tenancy to a tenant who, at some time between 1966 and 1972, sublet it to the defendant. The tenancy was determined by notice to quit from the plaintiffs on 25 March 1974 and the subtenancy on 29 September 1973 by notice to quit from the tenant. On the expiration of the defendant's subtenancy the plaintiffs consented to his remaining in occupation of

e   the farm until he found another farm but only on terms which would not attract the protection of the Agricultural Holdings Act 1948, viz under a letting for a period of more than one year but less than two years. The defendant accepted the arrangement and after considerable prior negotiation two successive tenancies were granted retrospectively on those terms. The second tenancy expired on 1 November 1977 without the defendant having found any alternative accommodation. In October 1977 the second

f   plaintiff had written to the defendant proposing a further tenancy of 13 months up to 1 December 1978 but the matter was not pursued until 4 September 1979, when the second plaintiff wrote to the defendant offering him a tenancy of 13 months from 1 September 1978 to 31 October 1979. The defendant accepted that offer and, without any prior negotiation, the agreement was signed on 19 October 1979, a few days before the agreed term was due to expire. When the term expired the tenant claimed to be a

g   protected tenant on the ground that, because a grant of land could not take effect retrospectively so as to confer an interest in land on the grantee before the execution of the grant, when the defendant signed the agreement the land was let to him for an interest less than a tenancy from year to year and accordingly, by virtue of s 2(1)*[a]* of the 1948 Act, it took effect as a tenancy from year to year which could only be determined in accordance with the provisions of the Agricultural Holdings (Notices to Quit) Act

h   1977. The plaintiffs brought an action in the county court for possession of the farm but the judge dismissed the claim on the ground that what had been created was an interest less than a tenancy from year to year which therefore took effect as a tenancy from year to year and so qualified for the protection of the 1948 Act. The plaintiffs appealed, contending (1) that an 'interest' within s 2(1) of the 1948 Act was not confined to the legal interest created by the particular agreement but was to be construed according to

j   the intention of the parties and what was expressed in the agreement, and (2) that even if the defendant qualified as a person entitled to the protection of the 1948 Act he was estopped from asserting that his interest in the land was other than an interest which did not qualify for such protection.

---

a   Section 2(1), so far as material, is set out at p 78 *j*, post

Held – The appeal would be dismissed for the following reasons—

(1) In deciding whether a tenancy agreement created 'an interest less than a tenancy *a* from year to year' within s 2(1) of the 1948 Act the court had to look at what, as a matter of law, the tenant's interest in the land was under the relevant agreement, and the parties could not take that actual interest out of the ambit of s 2(1) by agreeing to treat it as an interest of some other length or type. Since the third agreement could not, as a matter of law, create a term of years retroactively it had in fact only created a tenancy for less than a year and accordingly it took effect as a tenancy from year to year which attracted the *b* protection of the 1948 Act (see p 79 *d* to *f*, p 80 *g* to *j* and p 82 *h*, post); *Roberts v Church Comrs for England* [1971] 3 All ER 703 applied; *Colton v Becollda Property Investments Ltd* [1950] 1 KB 216 considered.

(2) Although the defendant knew throughout that the plaintiffs were not willing to grant a tenancy that would attract the protection of the 1948 Act and both parties believed that each of the tenancies granted effectively produced that result, the defendant *c* was not estopped from invoking the protection of the Act, because the terms of s 2(1) were mandatory once the factual situation therein described existed and could not be overridden by an estoppel, even if the conditions for an estoppel existed. Moreover, having regard to the purpose of the 1948 Act, it could not be said to be unconscionable for a tenant who was protected by it to rely on the protection which it specifically conferred on him (see p 81 *j* to p 82 *c* and *g h*, post); *Johnson v Moreton* [1978] 3 All ER 37 *d* applied; *Amalgamated Investment and Property Co Ltd (in liq) v Texas Commerce International Bank Ltd* [1981] 3 All ER 577 considered.

Notes

For the creation of an agricultural tenancy, see 1 Halsbury's Laws (4th edn) para 1007, and for cases on the subject, see 2 Digest (Reissue) 8–11, *15–28*. *e*

For estoppel by conduct, see 16 Halsbury's Laws (4th edn) para 1069, and for cases on the subject, see 21 Digest (Reissue) 198–204, *1430–1467*.

For the Agricultural Holdings Act 1948, s 2, see 1 Halsbury's Statutes (3rd edn) 689.

For the Agricultural Holdings (Notices to Quit) Act 1977, see 47 ibid 2.

f

Cases referred to in judgment

Amalgamated Investment and Property Co Ltd (in liq) v Texas Commerce International Bank Ltd [1981] 3 All ER 577, [1982] QB 84, [1981] 3 WLR 565, CA.
Colton v Becollda Property Investments Ltd [1950] 1 KB 216, CA.
Gladstone v Bower [1960] 3 All ER 353, [1960] 2 QB 384, [1960] 3 WLR 575, CA.
Hoveringham Group Ltd v Scholey & Sons Ltd (21 May 1981, unreported), Ch D. *g*
Johnson v Moreton [1978] 3 All ER 37, [1980] AC 37, [1978] 3 WLR 538, HL.
Roberts v Church Comrs for England [1971] 3 All ER 703, [1972] 1 QB 278, [1971] 3 WLR 566, CA.
Welch v Nagy [1949] 2 All ER 868, [1950] 1 KB 455, CA.

Cases also cited *h*

Kok Hoong v Leon Cheong Kweng Mines Ltd [1964] 1 All ER 300, [1964] AC 993, PC.
Reid v Dawson [1954] 3 All ER 498, [1955] 1 QB 214, CA.
Taylor Fashions Ltd v Liverpool Victoria Trustees Co Ltd [1981] 1 All ER 897, [1982] QB 133.

Appeal *j*

The plaintiffs, Ernest David Keen and Robert Graham Hilary Keen, appealed against the judgment of his Honour Judge Smithies in the Bournemouth County Court on 11 November 1982 dismissing the plaintiffs' application for possession of premises known as Lynes Farm, Ringwood, Hampshire, and granting the defendant, David George Holland, a declaration that he was a tenant from year to year of the farm by reason of the *a* provisions of the Agricultural Holdings Act 1948. The facts are set out in the judgment of the court.

Hazel Williamson for the plaintiffs.
Geoffrey Jaques for the defendant.

Cur adv vult

b 8 November. The following judgment of the court was delivered.

OLIVER LJ. This is an appeal from an order made by his Honour Judge Smithies sitting in the Bournemouth County Court on 11 November 1982 whereby he dismissed the plaintiffs' claim for possession of an agricultural holding occupied by the defendant and known as Lynes Farm, Ringwood, Hampshire. The ground on which the judge felt *c* bound to dismiss the plaintiffs' claim was that the defendant was a protected agricultural tenant under the provisions of the Agricultural Holdings Act 1948, and that forms the first ground of the plaintiffs' appeal to this court. There is a second and alternative ground on which the plaintiffs claim that the judge's judgment ought to be reversed, namely that, even if, as a technical matter, the defendant qualifies as a person entitled to the protection of the 1948 Act, he is nevertheless estopped from asserting that his interest in *d* the land was other than an interest which does not qualify for such protection. This latter contention necessitates a rather fuller recital of the background facts than might otherwise be necessary.

The plaintiffs are and were at all material times the freeholders of the land concerned. In fact one of the plaintiffs owns part of the land in severalty and they are joint owners of the balance, but it is unnecessary to differentiate between their separate interests. The *e* land had previously belonged to their mother, Mrs Phyllis Keen, who, in 1966, had let it to a family friend, Mr Jeffery, on a yearly tenancy from 25 March 1966. The land was conveyed to the plaintiffs in April 1966 subject to that tenancy. At some time between 1966 and 1972 Mr Jeffery sublet the land to the defendant. In 1972 the plaintiffs were desirous of resuming possession of the land and served Mr Jeffery with a notice to quit which was limited to expire on 25 March 1974. Mr Jeffery was willing to give up *f* possession. No counter-notice claiming the benefit of the Agricultural Holdings Act 1948 was served. On 28 July 1972 Mr Jeffery served notice to quit on the defendant expiring on 29 September 1973. It is common ground that the defendant was not within the protection of the 1948 Act and that as from the termination of Mr Jeffery's tenancy in March 1974 he would have had no answer to a claim for possession at the suit of the plaintiffs.

g In fact at this time everything was being dealt with in the most friendly and co-operative manner. The defendant was anxious to stay on on the land for the moment while he looked for another farm and the plaintiffs were anxious to accommodate him so far as they could. They were, however, quite adamant that they were not prepared to grant him any interest which would attract the protection of the 1948 Act and negotiations took place between them and Mr Jeffery, who was a chartered surveyor, *h* acting on behalf of the defendant, to find a way out of the difficulty. Originally the possibility of granting a short tenancy with the consent of the Minister of Agriculture, Fisheries and Food under the provisions of s 2(1) of the 1948 Act was considered but this was abandoned in favour of the alternative suggestion of the grant of a tenancy for a term exceeding one year but less than two years, which the decision of this court in *Gladstone v Bower* [1960] 3 All ER 353, [1960] 2 QB 384 had established as being an *j* agricultural tenancy not protected by the 1948 Act. Correspondence ensued from which it is quite clear, as the judge found, first, that the plaintiffs' intention was so to deal with the land as not to attract the protection of the 1948 Act and, second, that the defendant and those advising him clearly understood that the plaintiffs would only grant him a tenancy if it could be done in such a way that the protection of the 1948 Act did not apply to it.

The negotiations in fact turned out to be protracted and the defendant meanwhile held over, but without payment of any rent, while they continued. Provisional terms for **a** the grant of a tenancy for a period of 21 months from 1 November 1974 were arrived at in November 1974 but it was not until March 1975 that a draft tenancy agreement was submitted for approval and by June 1975 the plaintiffs were pressing for the defendant either to agree or to vacate. Further delay occurred, however, while a schedule of condition was prepared and agreed and it was not in fact until 2 January 1976 that a tenancy agreement was finally signed. Under that agreement the defendant was granted **b** a tenancy of the farm retrospectively from 1 November 1974 until 1 October 1976.

No question arose about the defendant's position under this agreement but on its expiry he still had not found anywhere to go and further negotiations took place for the grant of a further tenancy to be likewise for a period of more than one but less than two years. Again the preparation and approval of a formal agreement took some time and no new agreement was executed until 29 June 1977 when a tenancy was granted from **c** 1 October 1976 to 1 November 1977. That tenancy likewise expired without the defendant's having found any alternative accommodation. In October 1977 the second plaintiff wrote proposing yet a further tenancy for 13 months, ie up to 1 December 1978 but this seems not to have been pursued and the suggestion was not in fact taken up again until the summer of 1979. On 4 September of that year the second plaintiff wrote to the defendant in these terms: **d**

'My brother Dr. E. D. Keen and I would be willing to let the above property to you on the same terms as those contained in two several tenancy agreements dated 29th June 1977, the first between my brother and myself of the one part (hereafter referred to as "the first agreement") and the second between myself of the one part and yourself of the other part (hereafter referred to as the second agreement"), except that:—1. The term of your tenancy of the land comprised in the first and **e** second agreements shall be from 1st September 1978 to 31st October 1979. 2. The rent for the before mentioned period in respect of the land comprised in the first agreement shall be £2,520. 3. The rent for the before mentioned period in respect of the land comprised in the second agreement shall be £480. If you agree to take the tenancies of the above property on the before mentioned terms, perhaps you would sign the duplicate of this letter and return it to me, with a remittance for the **f** rents of £3,000.'

This formal letter was accompanied by a personal letter in which the second plaintiff said:

'If your tenders for other farms are unsuccessful, I will ask Mr. Willis to negotiate with you on behalf on my brother and myself for one further term of a year and a **g** month from 1st November next. I really do need possession of the Farm as I am seriously contemplating retiring from my own job and I shall be looking to the farm to provide me with an income.'

The formal letter of agreement was in fact signed by the defendant and returned on 19 October 1979, that is only a few days before the agreed term of the tenancy was due to expire. **h**

Thereafter, in December 1979, the plaintiffs opened further negotiations for the 'one further term' which had been referred to and it then transpired that the defendant was claiming a protected tenancy under s 2(1) of the 1948 Act.

That is, of course, the key section and it provides, for relevant purposes, as follows:

'. . . where under an agreement made on or after the first day of March, nineteen **j** hundred and forty-eight, any land is let to a person for use as agricultural land for an interest less than a tenancy from year to year . . . then, unless the letting . . . was approved by the Minister before the agreement was entered into, the agreement shall take effect, with the necessary modifications, as if it were an agreement for the letting of the land for a tenancy from year to year . . .'

The effect of that is that it then becomes subject to the restrictions on notices to quit
a contained in ss 23 to 25 of the 1948 Act (now ss 1 to 3 of the Agricultural Holdings
(Notices to Quit) Act 1977).

Thus the way in which the legislature has chosen to provide protection for agricultural
tenancies has been to impose restrictions on notices to quit agricultural holdings and to
put agricultural tenancies, whether for less than a year or for two years or more, on the
same footing as tenancies from year to year which, of course, require to be determined
b by notice to quit. Interests for less than a year are, as already noted, equated with tenancies
from year to year by s 2(1) and tenancies for two years or more are, for relevant purposes,
treated in the same way by s 3(1). Parliament appears, however, to have overlooked the
case of a tenancy for fixed term of more than one but less than two years and such a term
was held in *Gladstone v Bower* not to be a protected tenancy. Although the provisions of
ss 23 to 25 of the 1948 Act were re-enacted in 1977, no step was taken to bring such
c tenancies within the Act and it must therefore be assumed that the legislature was
content to permit such tenancies to be created free from the restrictions on termination
applicable to other agricultural tenancies.

It is not, therefore, in dispute that, if the tenancy created as a result of the letter
agreement had taken effect, as a matter of law and as was intended, as a tenancy for a
period of 13 months from 1 September 1978, it would have constituted a tenancy which
d did not require to be terminated by notice to quit and would not have attracted the
protection of the Act.

The defendant's contention that he is a protected tenant is, however, based on the fact
that the agreement which he signed was in fact signed on a date when the term expressed
to be granted by it had only a very few days to run. The decision of this court in *Roberts
v Church Comrs for England* [1971] 3 All ER 703, [1972] 1 QB 278 establishes, or, rather,
e reiterates, that a grant of land cannot take effect retrospectively so as to confer an interest
in land on the grantee before the execution of the grant. Accordingly, on 19 October
1979, when the defendant signed and returned the letter agreement the land (which is
clearly let for agricultural purposes) was let to him for an interest less than a tenancy
from year to year.

Thus, it is argued, the agreement took effect as a tenancy from year to year which can
f only be determined by a notice to quit given in accordance with the provisions of s 1 of
the Agricultural Holdings (Notices to Quit) Act 1977 and enforceable only subject to the
restrictions contained in s 2 of that Act.

This was the argument which found favour with the judge. He held that, however the
interest of the tenant may have been described in the agreement, what in fact it created
was an interest less than a tenancy from year to year which was therefore statutorily
g converted into a tenancy from year to year and so qualified for the protection conferred
by the Act. In so holding, he followed a decision of his Honour Judge Mervyn Davies QC
sitting as a judge of the High Court in *Hoveringham Group Ltd v Scholey & Sons Ltd* (21
May 1981, unreported) on facts substantially indistinguishable from those in the instant
case.

Counsel for the plaintiffs argues that the judge (and, by necessary implication, Judge
h Mervyn Davies) wrongly construed s 2(1). She accepts that as a matter of strict legal
analysis the defendant had no interest in the land prior to 19 October 1979 and that the
agreement concluded on that date could not, as a matter of law, create a term of years
retroactively. She submits, however, that the 'interest' which is referred to in s 2(1) is not
to be confined to the legal interest created by the particular agreement under consideration
but is to be construed according to the intention of the parties and what is expressed in
j the agreement.

As an alternative, although it is, we think, merely a different way of expressing the
same concept, she submits that where (as here) the tenant is already in occupation before
the formal grant of a tenancy, a tenancy agreement for a term commencing from a prior
date is to be treated as clothing him, as between the parties, with the status of tenant
under the agreement as from the agreed commencement date. His 'interest' for the

purposes of the 1948 Act is, therefore, to be determined in accordance with that agreed status. Terms of a tenancy are frequently negotiated well prior to the execution of a formal tenancy and it is commonplace that the tenancy when formally granted is expressed as creating a term commencing on a date prior to the date of the instrument. Whilst it is no doubt true that no estate is created until the instrument is executed, the agreement as to the duration of the term is effective for all other purposes, for instance as regards payment of rent and covenants in the lease. Counsel for the plaintiffs points out that in *Gladstone v Bower* itself the term of 18 months expressed to be created was in fact a term of 13 months only as a result of delay in execution of the agreement, but was nevertheless referred to in the judgment of Pearson LJ as a term of 18 months.

We are, however, unable to attach any significance to this. On any analysis the term there was for more than one and less than two years and no point was taken on the actual length of the term. Counsel for the plaintiffs has, however, drawn the court's attention to *Colton v Becollda Property Investments Ltd* [1950] 1 KB 216 esp at 231 where Denning LJ observed:

> 'It continually happens that the tenant goes into occupation whilst the negotiations are still pending and before the lease is executed, and then, afterwards, when the lease is drawn up, it is expressed to start as from the date the tenant went into occupation. In such cases, in point of law the legal interest of the tenant starts from the date when the lease was executed . . . But as between the parties it may start from the date stated in the lease, because the parties, by their agreement, have related its commencement back to the date when the tenant went into occupation. This relation back is not to be regarded as a nullity; it may often mean that the conditions and covenants of the lease relate back to that time also.'

That case, however, was concerned with a very different problem, the issue being whether the defendants had demanded a premium in contravention of s 8(1) of the Increase of Rent and Mortgage Interest (Restrictions) Act 1920 which prohibited (except in the case of a grant of a tenancy of 14 years or upwards) the landlord from 'requiring' a premium 'as a condition of the grant' of a tenancy. The court accepted that the lease in that case (which was dated some three months after the commencement of the term expressed to be granted) was not a lease for the full period of 14 years, but found in the circumstances that that was not necessarily determinative of the question whether the premium had been 'required as a condition of the grant' of a 14-year term.

The court found that there had been an antecedent agreement, albeit not yet confirmed by the defendants' full board, for the grant of a 14-year term and that the plaintiff's claim for the return of the premium therefore failed. We cannot see that this case is of any assistance to counsel for the plaintiffs in the instant case, where it cannot be claimed that there was, prior to the execution of the tenancy, any agreement between the parties and where the only question is whether, under the agreement in fact concluded, the land was let to the tenant for 'an interest less than a tenancy from year to year'. It seems to us, as a matter of construction of the section, that it is looking simply to the question of what, as a matter of law, the tenant's interest in the land is under the agreement for the relevant tenancy and that the parties cannot take that actual interest, whatever it may be, out of the ambit of s 2(1) by agreeing to treat it as an interest of some other length or type.

In our judgment, therefore, it follows that *Hoveringham Group Ltd v Scholey & Sons Ltd* was rightly decided and that the judge in the instant case came to the right conclusion on the first point.

There remains the issue of estoppel. As to this, counsel for the plaintiffs bases her argument on the decision of this court in *Amalgamated Investment and Property Co Ltd (in liq) v Texas Commerce International Bank Ltd* [1981] 3 All ER 577, [1982] QB 84 and contends that there was what is now known as an estoppel by convention which precludes the defendant from now alleging that the agreement concluded in October 1979 had the effect which, in law, it clearly did have. She relies in particular on the formulation by

Lord Denning MR in the following two passages ([1981] 3 All ER 577 at 584, [1982] QB
84 at 121–122):

> '... when the parties to a contract are both under a common mistake as to the
> meaning or effect of it and thereafter embark on a course of dealing on the footing
> of that mistake, thereby replacing the original terms of the contract by a conventional
> basis on which they both conduct their affairs, then the original contract is replaced
> by the conventional basis.'

He states the 'general principle shorn of limitations' as follows:

> 'When the parties to a transaction proceed on the basis of an underlying
> assumption (either of fact or of law, and whether due to misrepresentation or
> mistake, makes no difference) on which they conducted the dealings between them,
> neither of them will be allowed to go back on that assumption when it would be
> unfair or unjust to allow him to do so.'

It should perhaps be added that Lord Denning MR was alone in expressing the
proposition as broadly as this.

Applying this to the facts of the instant case, counsel for the plaintiffs submits that,
since it was known to the defendant throughout (as the judge found) that the plaintiffs
were not willing to grant a tenancy other than one which did not attract the protection
of the 1948 Act and since both parties believed, at any rate until after the expiry of the
last of the three tenancies in fact granted, that each of them effectively produced that
result, it is unconscionable on the part of the defendant either (i) now to claim that the
tenancy did not as a matter of law create the term of 13 months which both parties
thought that it effectively created or (ii) to rely on a statutory protection which both
parties at the date of the grant of the tenancy intended that he should not have. The
judge rejected the plaintiffs' case on estoppel on two grounds. In the first place, he did
not regard the defendant's reliance on his statutory rights as unconscionable having
regard to what he described as the 'unequal bargaining position' as between landlord and
tenant and having regard to the purpose of the legislation. Second, whatever may have
been the position as regards the first two agreements between the parties, which were
the result of considerable prior negotiation, by the time the September letter was sent
the question of the defendant's position had been left in abeyance for over a year. The
letter was put forward without any prior negotiation and the defendant was asked to
agree to a tenancy for a term which, however expressed in the agreement, was due to
expire in just over a month's time. It could not, therefore, be said that the creation of a
term of more than one year did in fact form the conventional basis on which the parties
were acting.

As regards the first ground, counsel for the plaintiffs submits that there was no
evidence that the plaintiffs had sought to exploit their superior bargaining power as
landlords and that in relying, as he did, on the protective purpose of the 1948 Act, the
judge was unduly influenced by the decision of the House of Lords in *Johnson v Moreton*
[1978] 3 All ER 37, [1980] AC 37, which was directed to a rather different question and
was, she submits, clearly distinguishable. That case established that, although there is no
specific provision in the 1948 Act against contracting out of the provisions of s 24(1) (as
there is in relation to certain other sections), a contract by an agricultural tenant not to
serve a counter-notice under s 24(1) is void as being, by necessary implication, prohibited
by the Act. Here, counsel for the plaintiffs points out, the parties were seeking to enter
into an agreement which, it is clearly established, is not prohibited by the Act. If they
can agree on a term which does not attract the protection of the Act, there is, she submits,
no legal impediment to their being estopped from denying that that is what they have
done and it is no answer to say that the Act is one for the protection of agricultural
tenants for this is to beg the question. The Act is one for the protection only of
agricultural tenants under tenancies to which the Act applies.

Attractively as this argument was put, it is not, in our judgment, sound. Once there is in fact an actual tenancy to which the 1948 Act applies, the protection of the Act follows and we do not see how, consistently with *Johnson v Moreton*, the parties can effectively *a* oust the protective provisions of the Act by agreeing that they shall be treated as inapplicable. If an express agreement to this effect would be avoided, as it plainly would, then it seems to us to follow that the statutory inability to contract out cannot be avoided by appealing to an estoppel. The terms of s 2(1) are mandatory once the factual situation therein described exists, as it does here, and it cannot, as we think, be overriden by an estoppel even assuming that otherwise the conditions for an estoppel exist (see, for *b* instance, the somewhat similar though not wholly analogous position under the Rent Acts: *Welch v Nagy* [1949] 2 All ER 868, [1950] 1 KB 455). We agree with the judge that, having regard to the purpose of the 1948 Act, it cannot be said to be unconscionable for the tenant who is protected by it to rely on the protection which the statute specifically confers on him. Once the protection attaches, the jurisdiction to grant possession is exercisable only subject to the statutory provisions and it is a little difficult to see how the *c* parties can, by estoppel, confer on the court a jurisdiction which they could not confer by express agreement.

That is sufficient to dispose of the argument, but there seem to us to be other insuperable obstacles to a successful plea of estoppel. This is not strictly a case of the parties having established, by their construction of their agreement or their apprehension of its legal effect, a conventional basis on which they have regulated their subsequent *d* dealings as in the *Amalgamated Investment* case. The dealing alleged to give rise to the estoppel is the entry into the agreement itself in the belief that it would produce a particular legal result. In fact, for reasons which had nothing to do with the defendant the plaintiffs got it wrong; and what counsel for the plaintiffs appears to us to be contending for is a much wider conventional estoppel than has yet been established by any authority, namely that, where parties are shown to have had a common view about *e* the legal effect of a contract into which they have entered and it is established that one of them would not to the other's knowledge have entered into it if he had appreciated its true legal effect, they are, without more, estopped from asserting that the effect is otherwise than they originally supposed.

So broad a proposition cannot be deduced from the actual decision in the *Amalgamated Investment* case and although it may be supported on the basis of the very wide proposition *f* of Lord Denning MR referred to above, it cannot, in our judgment, be right. If, for instance, the parties had been negligently advised by a solicitor that a yearly tenancy was not protected by the 1948 Act and had entered into one accordingly, it would, we should have thought, be an impossible contention (quite apart from *Johnson v Moreton*) that the tenant was estopped from invoking the protection which the Act confers on such a tenancy. As the judge pointed out, nobody in the instant case can have been under any *g* illusions about the fact that at the time when the plaintiffs tendered the agreement the term expressed to be granted had all but expired and we share the judge's difficulty in seeing how a mere erroneous belief that the formality of signing this document would result in the defendant's obtaining an unprotected tenancy for a month or so can properly be described as the 'conventional basis' for their dealings so as to give rise to an estoppel.

In our judgment, the judge came to the right conclusion on this point also and we *h* accordingly dismiss the appeal.

Appeal dismissed.

Solicitors: *Arnold Cooper & Tompkins*, Chichester (for the plaintiffs); *Burges Salmon*, Bristol (for the defendant).

Mary Rose Plummer   Barrister.

Simmons v Simmons

a

COURT OF APPEAL, CIVIL DIVISION

EVELEIGH AND PURCHAS LJJ

2, 23 MARCH, 12 APRIL 1983

b
Legal aid – Charge on property recovered for deficiency of costs – Enforcement of charge – Discretion of Law Society – Money recovered in proceedings – Court ordering sale of matrimonial home and division of proceeds between husband and wife – Whether wife's share of proceeds 'property recovered or preserved in proceedings' – Whether property recovered or preserved in proceedings including money recovered in proceedings – Legal Aid Act 1974, s 9(6) – Legal Aid (General) Regulations 1980, reg 97(2).

c
Legal aid – Charge on property recovered for deficiency of costs – Duty of assisted person's solicitor – Enforcement of charge – Exemptions from charge – Discretion of Law Society – Money recovered in proceedings – Assisted person's solicitor under absolute duty to pay money recovered to Law Society forthwith – No question of charge or exemption therefrom arising once payment made – Legal Aid Act 1974, s 9(6) – Legal Aid (General) Regulations 1980, regs 88, 91, 96(d), 97(2).

d

The husband and wife had two young children and a house worth about £49,000 which was the only substantial matrimonial asset. The wife obtained a divorce from the husband in proceedings in which both parties were legally aided. In ancillary proceedings the judge gave the wife custody of the children and ordered that the matrimonial home be sold and that the wife receive £26,750 from the proceeds with the balance going to

e
the husband. In making that order the judge endeavoured to redistribute the family assets to provide adequate accommodation for both parties but in so doing he failed to take into account the charge which would be imposed by s 9(6)[a] of the Legal Aid Act 1974 on any property recovered or preserved for the wife as security for the wife's costs of some £8,000 incurred by the legal aid fund. The Law Society took the view that the costs would be payable immediately out of the £26,750 payable to the wife. Since that

f
would reduce the wife's share of the proceeds of sale to less than the £20,000 required to purchase a home for herself and her children the wife appealed from the judge's order, contending that the matrimonial home should not be sold and that she ought to be allowed to remain in it with the children, in which case the Law Society's charge would thereby attach to the home but would not be immediately enforceable. The husband, who wanted his share of the proceeds of sale to buy another property, contended that

g
'property recovered or preserved for an assisted person' included money and therefore that the discretion which the Law Society had under reg 97(2)[b] of the Legal Aid (General) Regulations 1980 to postpone immediate collection of legal aid costs in favour of taking a charge over 'property recovered or preserved' entitled the Law Society to take a charge over the wife's share of the proceeds. The husband further contended that, since

h
reg 96(d)[c] provided that the Law Society's 'charge' was not to apply to the first £2,500 of any money recovered, some £5,000 (in respect of each party's share of the proceeds) would be excluded from the charge on the proceeds of sale and that would be sufficient to make the judge's order viable.

j
Held – The wife's appeal would be allowed for the following reasons—
    (1) For the purposes of s 9(6) of the 1974 Act money recovered or received by a legally aided party as a result of proceedings was not 'property . . . recovered or preserved' in the

---

a   Section 9(6) is set out at p 87 g, post
b   Regulation 97(2) is set out at p 89 c, post
c   Regulation 96, so far as material, is set out at p 88 h j, post

proceedings, and therefore the Law Society's discretion under reg 97(2) of the 1980 regulations to take a charge over property recovered or preserved was not applicable *a* when money was recovered or preserved (see p 89 *d e*, p 90 *d e* and p 92 *c*, post).

(2) Furthermore, both reg 96(*d*) and reg 97(2) of the 1980 regulations, which respectively provided that the Law Society's charge was not to apply to the first £2,500 of any money recovered and that the Law Society could postpone immediate collection of the legal aid costs in favour of taking a charge over the property recovered, presupposed that the Law Society was in a position to take a charge, whereas such a charge was *b* precluded when reg 91*d* was applicable, namely when money was recovered, since in that case the assisted person's solicitor had an absolute duty to pay forthwith to the Law Society all moneys received by him on behalf of the assisted person and no question of a charge could arise once such a payment had been made (see p 88 *j* to p 89 *b*, p 90 *b d e* and p 92 *a* to *c*, post).

(3) Since the terms of the judge's order required the wife's share of the proceeds of sale *c* to be paid to her, her solicitor would be required under reg 91 of the 1980 regulations to pay her share of the proceeds direct to the Law Society and no question would arise of the Law Society postponing payment and taking a charge on that money or of the parties being entitled to an exemption under reg 96(*d*) of £2,500 from their respective shares of the proceeds from such a charge. Furthermore, since the immediate payment of the legal aid costs would mean that there were insufficient family assets to provide adequate *d* accommodation for both parties, thus destroying the basis of the judge's order, and since the court's primary consideration had to be to preserve a home for the wife and children, the proper order to make was that, conditionally on the wife's consenting to the dismissal of her application for a lump sum and periodic payments, the husband should transfer his interest in the matrimonial home to the wife in return for a charge on the house in his favour for £12,000 (see p 89 *e* to *g*, p 90 *d e*, p 91 *j* and p 92 *c*, post); *Mesher v Mesher* *e* *and Hall* (1973) [1980] 1 All ER 126, *Martin v Martin* [1977] 3 All ER 762 and *Harvey v Harvey* [1982] 1 All ER 693 considered.

Per curiam. Amendments to s 9(6) of the 1974 Act and regs 88*e* and 91 of the 1980 regulations, to exclude the proceeds of sale of the matrimonial home or funds allocated for the purchase of a primary home for either party to a marriage or a child of the marriage, would avoid the hardship caused in certain cases. A mere discretion granted to *f* the Law Society to defer enforcement of the charge would not be sufficient to permit the court to assume that the moneys would not be collected or that the charge would not be enforced (see p 92 *c*, post).

Notes

For money recovered by an assisted person, see 37 Halsbury's Laws (4th edn) paras 933– *g* 934.

For the charge for the benefit of the legal aid fund on property recovered, see ibid paras 938–939.

For the Legal Aid Act 1974, s 9, see 44 Halsbury's Statutes (3rd edn) 1048.

Cases referred to in judgment

Carson v Carson [1983] 1 All ER 478, [1983] 1 WLR 285, CA.   *h*
Hanlon v Hanlon [1978] 2 All ER 889, [1978] 1 WLR 592, CA.
Hanlon v Law Society [1980] 2 All ER 199, [1981] AC 124, [1980] 2 WLR 756, HL.
Harvey v Harvey [1982] 1 All ER 693, [1982] Fam 83, [1982] 2 WLR 283, CA.
Jones v Law Society (1983) Times, 27 January, 127 SJ 105.
Martin v Martin [1977] 3 All ER 762, [1978] Fam 12, [1977] 3 WLR 101, CA.
Mesher v Mesher and Hall (1973) [1980] 1 All ER 126, CA.   *j*

Interlocutory appeal

June Patricia Simmons (the wife) appealed from an order of Sir John Arnold P made on

---

d   Regulation 91 is set out at p 88 *d* to *f*, post
e   Regulation 88, so far as material, is set out at p 90 *a b*, post

a 22 October 1982 on the wife's application for ancillary relief in divorce proceedings, that the former matrimonial home be sold and that Ernest John Simmons (the husband) should pay the wife a lump sum of £26,750 out of the net proceeds of sale and the husband should retain the balance of the net proceeds of sale. The grounds of the appeal were that Sir John Arnold P misdirected himself in making the order in that (1) the purpose of the order was to make adequate provision for the children of the family by providing a home for them and the wife (to whom he had given the custody of the

b children) but (2) the result of the order would be that after payment out of the wife's lump sum of the Law Society's charge in favour of the legal aid fund, in respect of the wife's costs, she would be unable to purchase a home for herself and the children and (3) accordingly, the proper course would be to make an order allowing her and the children to remain in the former matrimonial home bearing in mind the husband's income, assets and all the circumstances and the fact that such an order would enable the costs

c incurred by the legal aid fund to be met by a statutory charge on the home and would avoid the immediate payment to the legal aid fund of the costs incurred by the wife. By a respondent's notice the husband sought to uphold Sir John Arnold P's order on grounds additional to those on which the order was made. The facts are set out in the judgment of Purchas LJ.

d *Peter Archer QC* and *Jennie Horne* for the wife.
Thomas Coningsby and *J A Hodgson* for the husband.

Cur adv vult

23 March. The following judgments were delivered.

e **PURCHAS LJ** (delivering the first judgment at the invitation of Eveleigh LJ). This is an appeal by June Patricia Simmons (the wife) from part of an order made by Sir John Arnold P on 22 October 1982. Leave to appeal against this part of his order was given by the President on 2 February 1983. The order was made after a substantial hearing and resulted from a detailed judgment dealing with many matters in issue between the parties including the custody of two children of the marriage, detailed provisions for

f access to the respondent husband and orders under ss 23 and 24 of the Matrimonial Causes Act 1973.

   This appeal concerns a limited issue as to the proper disposal of the matrimonial home. The short history is as follows. The parties were married on 19 December 1964. The husband is now 41 years of age and the wife 38 years of age. There are two children of the family: Jack Paul, who was born on 27 February 1974 and is, therefore, nine years of

g age; and George John, who was born on 17 October 1977 and who is just under five-and-a-half. There were a series of matrimonial homes. The final one, which was bought in joint names, was in Wanstead. This was a four-bedroomed house of ample proportions with three reception rooms. At the time of the hearing before Sir John Arnold P its value was put at around £49,000. There was a mortgage outstanding of £10,500. The net equity after costs of sale etc was placed at around £37,000. Counsel who appears for the

h wife has suggested that this figure might be a little high in that the costs of sale etc may well have been understated. The outgoings on the house, including capital repayment of the mortgage, are in the region of £2,750 per annum.

   After about 16 years the marriage unhappily broke down. The wife presented a petition dated 23 October 1980 based on the irretrievable breakdown of the marriage and behaviour on the part of the husband falling within s 1(2)(b) of the 1973 Act. By

j consent an order was made which resulted in the husband leaving the matrimonial home on 29 October 1980. He has since then remained away from the home. Decree nisi was pronounced on 18 June 1981. There was an application for maintenance pending suit on 27 February 1981. On the husband's undertaking to continue to pay all the outgoings on the house no order was made for maintenance pending suit. The husband is a senior art teacher earning in the region of £10,000 gross per annum. The wife is in part-time employment earning in the region of £221 per month. Proposals which she has made include taking student lodgers, which would enable her to bring her total monthly income, including child allowance, to about £428. This calculation is exhibited to the wife's affidavit dated 15 February 1983. The husband now resides in a ground-floor flat owned by a Mrs Berry, with whom he lives and whom he plans to marry. This accommodation has only one bedroom and two other rooms. It is adequate for a weekend stay by the children, but not for longer stays. Access on a generous scale was ordered by Sir John Arnold P, including half the school holidays and alternate weekends. It is, therefore, important that the husband should be able to improve his accommodation if for this purpose alone. The wife remains on in the matrimonial home. The accommodation provided by this is more than is absolutely necessary for her and the two children; but, as I have already mentioned, she plans to make proper use of the accommodation by letting one or more of the rooms. This would enable her to be financially self-supporting and to service the mortgage and maintain the family home without having recourse to the husband, apart from a contribution towards the maintenance of the children.

Sir John Arnold P made an order bearing in mind the importance of safeguarding the children, but also doing justice between the parties as it then appeared to him. This involved an order for the sale of the house and a further order that out of the proceeds of the sale the wife should receive £26,750. I quote from his judgment:

'Now, the prime need of this family is proper housing for the children, and I approach the problem on that basis. Certainly the children's present home . . . where they live with their mother [the wife], is ample to provide a proper home; but if, consistently with providing a proper home for them, the [husband's] capital (it is the only capital he has of substance) or a substantial proportion of it can be released to him, it seems to me to be fair, as between [wife] and [husband], that that should be so, provided that it can be done consistently with achieving the prime purpose. There is obviously, as there always is in a matter of this sort, a degree of speculation about exactly what will be available on the market at exactly the appropriate moment. But I am satisfied, on the evidence which I have seen, that for about £32,500 or £33,000 the [wife] can acquire a freehold house with four bedrooms tolerably near to the school. The mortgage and the costs which would necessarily have to be repaid and paid on a realisation of the former matrimonial home will leave something like £37,000 or £37,500 free for division between the two spouses. The [wife's] mortgage ability, I am told, ranks at about £7,000, provided she has a sufficient primary security. The [husband], without consenting to it, has made plain through his counsel that he attaches very considerable importance to having some free capital even at a cost of having to provide for the [wife] substantially more than her share of the proceeds of sale of the matrimonial home, and a figure which has been mentioned in that connection (and it seems to me to be a proper figure) is a figure which on present expectations would be something like three-quarters of the proceeds of sale, a figure of £26,750.'

As Sir John Arnold P remarked in the extract I have cited from his judgment, there must always be a degree of speculation. Speaking for myself, had I been approaching this problem at first instance I would probably not have had the courage to have put into operation such a closely tailor-made scheme as the one proposed. Having said that, however, the President approached the problem on entirely the correct basis, that is achieving, if it was possible, the provision of adequate accommodation for both parties by means of a careful redistribution of the family assets. Certainly such a provision standing unqualified could not be criticised in this court.

The keystone of the scheme proposed by the President was the payment to the wife of the sum of £26,750 from the proceeds of the sale of the matrimonial home. The President had unfortunately left out of account the charge for the benefit of the legal aid fund created by s 9(6) of the Legal Aid Act 1974 (as amended). This charge, making as it would a substantial inroad into the figure available to the wife to rehouse herself, a effectively brought about the collapse of the scheme. The latest estimate of the wife's liability to the legal aid fund is £8,000. According to a calculation produced by counsel for the wife, all that she would have available to buy a new home for the family would be £15,900 plus £7,000 mortgage: a total of £22,900. This would not be sufficient.

Counsel for the husband has attempted skilfully and attractively to support a respondent's notice in order to uphold the order of the President or to place before the court an alternative solution. Counsel for the wife, on the other hand, has argued in

b support of the appeal that a sale of the matrimonial home cannot in the full circumstances be justified and that in order to preserve a home for these young children and their mother she should be entitled to continue to live there, making on her part a contribution by taking in lodgers and achieving her own individual financial viability, but receiving in exchange a transfer of the husband's interest in the property.

Before coming to a consideration of the charge in favour of the legal aid fund it is

c necessary to notice two further events. In *Jones v Law Society* (1983) Times, 27 January, Sir John Arnold P was incorrectly[1] reported to have said:

'Perhaps some way could be found within the regulations so that the discretion of the Law Society could attach its charge to a fund which was intended to purchase a home as well as attaching to an existing home.'

d This comment was made in connection with an application which had been made by a respondent husband for a declaration that the Law Society was not entitled to a charge on moneys retained by his former solicitors as part of a settlement between him and the petitioner wife in regard to the disposal of the matrimonial home. Sir John Arnold P, following *Hanlon v Law Society* [1980] 2 All ER 199, [1981] AC 124, refused the application and in fact said that perhaps by statutory amendment or amendment of the Legal Aid

e (General) Regulations 1980, SI 1980/1894, a way could be found to grant discretionary power to the Law Society enabling it to defer enforcement of a charge over a fund intended to be used in the purchase of a home.

The second matter is the presentation to the court of a letter from the Law Society dated 1 March 1983, stating that, as a result of counsel's opinion which it has obtained, as indicated in its leaflet headed 'Legal Aid—the Statutory Charge' (2nd edn, January 1982),

f the Law Society has been advised that where the only property recovered or preserved is money, it has no power to postpone the operation of the charge. Counsel for the husband has invited us to consider this matter which obviously is one of some general importance.

Section 9(6) of the 1974 Act provides:

'Except so far as regulations otherwise provide, any sums remaining unpaid on account of a person's contribution to the legal aid fund in respect of any proceedings

g and, if the total contribution is less than the net liability of that fund on his account, a sum equal to the deficiency shall be a first charge for the benefit of the legal aid fund on any property (wherever situated) which is recovered or preserved for him in the proceedings.'

Section 4(1) of the 1974 Act provides:

h 'In respect of advice or assistance given to any person (in this section and section 5 below referred to as a "client"), the client shall not, except in accordance with the following provisions of this section, be required to pay any charge or fee.'

Subsection (2) provides for the payment of contributions by the client. Section 5 deals with the payment of charges or fees which would be properly chargeable to a client unless he were protected by s 4(1). Subsection (3) of s 5 provides:

j 'Except in so far as regulations otherwise provide, charges or fees to which this section applies shall constitute a first charge for the benefit of the solicitor . . . (b) on any property (of whatever nature and wherever situated) which is recovered or preserved for the client . . .'

---

1 See correction (1983) Times, 28 January

Subsection (4) provides:

> 'In so far as the charge created by subsection (3) above in respect of any charges or *a* fees to which this section applies is insufficient to meet them, the deficiency shall, subject to subsections (5) and (6) below, be payable to the solicitor out of the legal aid fund.'

Regulations made under powers granted by the 1974 Act have where money is concerned superseded the effect of s 5 by providing for the immediate payment over of *b* moneys recovered. The legal aid fund, therefore, accepts the liability to pay solicitor's fees with a right to recover where the payments made exceed the contribution received from the assisted person under s 9(6) of the Act. The use of the word 'charge' in various parts of the Act creates some difficulty in construction when used in relation to the word 'property'. 'Property' is not defined for the purposes of the Act. In some sections it would appear to be restricted to real property, but in other contexts would appear to extend to *c* include moneys recovered. In s 5(3)(*b*) the use of the word 'charge' in connection with property would appear to extend to the wider interpretation of a first claim on a fund of money as well as a charge capable of registration under the Land Charges Acts.

I now turn to review some of the regulations to which the provisions of the sections of the 1974 Act just cited are specifically made subject. The relevant regulations are the Legal Aid (General) Regulations 1980, SI 1980/1894, as amended by SI 1981/173, SI 1982/ *d* 1892:

> '*Solicitor to pay moneys recovered to The Law Society*
>
>   **91.**—(1) An assisted person's solicitor shall forthwith—(*a*) inform the appropriate area committee of any property recovered or preserved for the assisted person; and (*b*) subject to paragraph (2), pay all moneys received by him by virtue of an order or agreement made in the assisted person's favour to The Law Society.   *e*
>
>   (2) Where the appropriate area committee considers that the rights of the fund will thereby be safeguarded and so directs, the assisted person's solicitor shall—(*a*) pay to The Law Society under paragraph 1(*b*) only such sum as, in the opinion of the appropriate area committee, should be retained by The Law Society in order to safeguard the rights of the fund under any provisions of the Act and these Regulations; and (*b*) pay any other moneys to the assisted person.'   *f*

The relief from the duty created by para (1) of reg 91 to pay 'forthwith' all moneys received is mitigated only where the rights of the fund will be safeguarded by the payment of a portion only of the moneys recovered. In practice, this provision has been operated by requiring an undertaking to be given by the solicitor involved that the costs which will become payable by the legal aid fund shall not exceed the amount of money *g* retained by the Law Society under para (2)(*a*) of reg 91.

Regulation 96 provides some exemptions from what is described as 'the statutory charge'. Again 'statutory charge' is not defined by the regulations. It must, therefore, refer to a charge created by statute and the statute involved must be the 1974 Act. Where the nature of the charge may vary from one section to another it is perhaps unsafe to attempt to assign to the expression 'statutory charge' when used in the regulations a *h* necessarily definitive and universal meaning. It is probably safer to consider each regulation in its own context. Returning to reg 96, this provides:

> 'The charge created by section 9(6) of the Act shall not apply to ... (*d*) the first £2,500 of any money, or the value of any property, recovered or preserved by virtue of—(i) an order made ... under section 23(1)(*c*) or ... [section] 24 ... of the Matrimonial Causes Act 1973 ...'   *j*

This regulation envisages a statutory charge involving lump sums of money as well as real property and reg 96(*d*) excludes from the charge created by s 9(6) of the 1974 Act the first £2,500 of such money or the value of such real property. The regulation, however, must be read in the context of the duty on the solicitor to pay all moneys recovered forthwith to the Law Society under reg 91. Counsel for the husband argued

a that reg 96(*d*) could be used to preserve up to £2,500 of the moneys received by each of the parties from the proceeds of the sale of the matrimonial home. Taking each party, a total of £5,000 could be salved, although it must be remembered that the husband's costs are thought to amount to about £7,000. In view of the absolute provisions of reg 91 I am unable to accede to this submission.

The alternative submission of counsel for the husband was that the provisions of

b reg 97 granted to the Law Society a discretion to postpone collection of the moneys due to the legal aid fund and to transfer a charge to property bought with the proceeds of the sale of the matrimonial home. Regulation 97 provides:

> '(1) Any charge on property recovered or preserved for an assisted person arising under section 9(6) of the Act shall vest in The Law Society.
>
> (2) The Law Society may enforce any such charge in any manner which would

c be available if the charge had been given *inter partes*.

> (3) Any such charge affecting land shall in the case of unregistered land be a land charge of Class B within the meaning of section 2 of the Land Charges Act 1972 and in the case of registered land shall be a registrable substantive charge . . .'

Without para (3) of reg 97, it would, in my judgment, be clear that 'property' in the

d context of reg 97 must mean real property in view of the provisions of reg 91. But para (3) would, in such an event, contain the superfluous words 'affecting land'. The best solution is probably to adopt a broad and not strict approach to construing these regulations. Regulation 91 would appear to pre-empt any cause for a charge to arise where moneys are involved. This would support the argument that where charges are mentioned in the regulations they must refer to property of one sort or another. It is

e possible that 'property recovered' might extend to chattels, choses in action etc.

The wife's costs so far incurred for which she will be liable to reimburse the legal aid fund under the provisions of the scheme were estimated at the time of the notice of appeal dated 18 January 1983 to be in excess of £6,000 (now being put at £8,000). Sir John Arnold P made no order as to costs, therefore there will be a charge on the sum of £26,750 received from the sale of the matrimonial home in the hands of the wife's

f solicitors which will so reduce the sum received by her as to make it impossible for her to implement the scheme designed by the President. The sum will have to be paid over forthwith to the Law Society under reg 91, subject only to the balance of that sum left after the wife's solicitors have given an undertaking that their costs will not exceed a certain sum. Viewing the question realistically, it is unlikely that those solicitors will be able to give an undertaking that the costs will not exceed a figure somewhat in excess of

g £8,000. I have little doubt that the amount released to the wife under the provisions of reg 91(2) will be substantially less than £20,000. I will consider this later in this judgment. For the reasons I have already given, I do not think that there is any relief to be obtained under the provisions of reg 96(*d*) in this context.

I now turn to consider the alternative scheme which is set out in a letter from Barclays Bank addressed to the husband's solicitors dated 8 February 1983. In essence the scheme

h is for the husband to raise a sum of £38,000 by way of a bridging advance secured on the matrimonial home by a first legal charge. The period of time for the advance is envisaged as four months or thereabouts. I quote from the third paragraph of the letter:

> '. . . We are only prepared to consider the proposition on the basis outlined by [the husband] that the funds are used to enable [the wife] to buy the new property so that the matrimonial home is vacated.'

j This envisages a sum of money being transferred into the hands of the wife or her solicitors as a result of her transferring her interest in the matrimonial home to the husband without which he would not be in a position to grant the first legal charge demanded by the bank. If this is the plan envisaged then, in my judgment, that money falls within the provisions of reg 88:

'*Moneys recovered to be paid to solicitor or The Law Society*

88. Subject to regulations 90 and 96, all moneys payable to an assisted person— *a*
(*a*) by virtue of any agreement or order made in connection with the action, cause
or matter to which his certificate relates, whether such agreement was made before
or after the proceedings were taken . . . shall be paid or repaid, as the case may be, to
the solicitor of the assisted person or, if he is no longer represented by a solicitor, to
The Law Society, and only the solicitor, or, as the case may be, The Law Society,
shall be capable of giving a good discharge for moneys so payable.'   *b*

Thus, any sum which became available to the wife as a result of any agreement involving
the bank would eventually be funds in the hands of her solicitor and subject to reg 91.
That disposes of the scheme as disclosed in the bank's letter.

In argument counsel for the husband also developed a suggestion that the husband
should buy a house and transfer it to the wife and so avoid any moneys coming into the
possession of the wife or her solicitor. The detailed mechanics of such an arrangement   *c*
were not fully deployed and certainly would involve considerable concessions and
goodwill on the part of the wife unless she were to be protected by some agreement
which would immediately invoke the provisions of reg 88. Without going into great
lengths, I have come to the conclusion that any such scheme as proposed by counsel
under which the husband placed himself in possession of two alternative houses, one of
which he released to the wife, were not sufficiently secure or practical to justify disposing   *d*
of the family home over the heads of the wife and children. I have, therefore, come to
the conclusion that the operation of the 1974 Act and the regulations effectively prevent
the putting into effect of the scheme proposed by Sir John Arnold P or any other scheme
proposed by counsel for the husband as a substitute and that, therefore, the appeal must
be allowed.

It is necessary to consider what is the appropriate order to make in respect of the   *e*
matrimonial home. Unhappily the impact of the 1974 Act and the regulations have, in
my judgment, moved this family from one whose total assets might in the special
circumstances have been just sufficient, even if marginally so, to provide adequate
accommodation for both husband and wife and children to a family whose total assets
are insufficient to achieve this purpose. One must then revert to first principles in solving   *f*
the problem. As Sir John Arnold P said in his judgment, the first object is to preserve an
adequate home for the wife and the two young children placed in her custody.

Where the only asset of substance is the matrimonial home, the courts have varied
from time to time as to the proper approach in the light of s 25 of the Matrimonial
Causes Act 1973. Where the matrimonial home is the only capital asset, then, had the
marriage continued, neither party would have had access to the asset as a source of
providing either capital or revenue (see *Martin v Martin* [1977] 3 All ER 762, [1978] Fam   *g*
12). The solution proposed in the particular circumstances prevailing in *Mesher v Mesher
and Hall* (1973) [1980] 1 All ER 126, which preserved the matrimonial home until the
children had grown up or ceased full-time education, and thereafter distributed the
proceeds of the sale between the parties has been criticised as a general approach by the
Court of Appeal on a number of occasions, e g in *Hanlon v Hanlon* [1978] 2 All ER 889,
[1978] 1 WLR 592, *Harvey v Harvey* [1982] 1 All ER 693, [1982] Fam 83 and *Carson v*   *h*
Carson [1983] 1 All ER 478, [1983] 1 WLR 285. In the particular circumstances of this
case, in my judgment, the provisions of s 25 of the Matrimonial Causes Act 1973 require
that a home is preserved for the wife and the two young children of the family along the
lines in *Martin v Martin* and *Harvey v Harvey*. Whether in the particular circumstances
of this case an out and out transfer of the husband's interest in the house to the wife
should be made or whether the house should be settled on a trust for sale with provisions   *j*
similar to those adopted in *Harvey v Harvey* requires further consideration. The husband's
position is somewhat worse than that of the respondent in *Martin v Martin* because it is
accepted that he has a need to improve the standard of accommodation, either by
extending the flat where he presently lives or by selling that with the assistance of Mrs
Berry and buying better accommodation.

In view of the animosity and tensions that have arisen in this case, it might be more

a conducive to a settled existence for the children and facilitate the operation of access if there is a definite and immediate disposal of the asset. There is not sufficient capital available to provide the husband with the few thousand pounds he requires in order to improve his accommodation. Sir John Arnold accepted this need in the context of there being sufficient funds available. Now that is no longer the case it is necessary to see what can be omitted without prejudice to the family as a whole. Bearing in mind the husband's

b earnings capacity and the apparent capacity of Mrs Berry to be self-supporting, including servicing her own mortgage on her present property said to be worth £20,000, the probabilities are that the husband will have access to sufficient funds to improve his accommodation position. This ignores what may well be said to be the husband's contribution to the matrimonial home or his right to an interest, albeit postponed, in the equity represented by this asset. It is based on the husband's earning capacity and the fact

c that he is housed in accommodation owned by the lady he intends to marry; and at the moment seems to offer the only way in which both parties and the children can be housed at all. The table exhibited to the wife's affidavit of 15 February 1983 demonstrated that the wife can use the extra accommodation available by renting this to students to supplement her income, so that she can both preserve and enhance the property and be self-sufficient. If the wife was prepared to consent to her application for periodical

d payments to be dismissed, this would relieve the husband of a contingent liability which might continue for a considerable period of time. It would be some compensation for his losing either his interest in the family asset or his interest in the equity being reduced or postponed. These children are nine and five. If a *Mesher*-type order had been made, the sale of the house and the distribution of the assets would not take place for probably another 12 years and maybe longer if either child went for further education. Whether

e an order in the *Mesher* form, the *Martin* form or the *Harvey* form is made, the question arises: who is to pay the mortgage instalments and meet the upkeep and maintenance of the property in the mean while? By the time the sale took place, if these liabilities were shared the interests of the parties would not have been greatly distorted. Experience to date shows that the parties in this case do not find it easy to deal with financial details of this kind. There is an issue before us which we have not decided as to why the electricity

f bills have not been paid etc. This augurs ill in the future for the efficacy of any order providing for shared financial responsibilities.

The wife is able to shoulder the burden at some considerable sacrifice to herself. If she does this for 13 years her equity in the house would have substantially increased in relation to the residual equity in favour of the husband, and the mortgage might well have been eliminated. This, together with his being relieved from the burden of making

g periodical payments, would, in my mind, on a broad basis of what is just between the parties within the terms of s 25 of the 1973 Act, permit the husband's interest in the matrimonial home to be satisfied. I would, therefore, providing the wife is prepared to consent to her claim for periodical payments being dismissed, favour an immediate transfer of the husband's interest in the house to the wife, subject to a charge in favour of the husband rather than the more complicated trusts for sale which were established in

h Martin v Martin and Harvey v Harvey. The amount of the charge should reflect the value of the husband's present interest in the house, reduced to take into account the fact that he is to be relieved of liability to pay periodical payments in the future, or to be responsible in the future for the payment of the mortgage instalments and for maintenance of the matrimonial home. The wife will have to meet all future mortgage repayments and be responsible for all outgoings. The value, as reduced, of the husband's

j interest in the house I would put at £12,000.

I would allow the appeal and, on the wife consenting to an order dismissing her application for periodical payments and lump sum provision, substitute an order transferring the husband's interest in the matrimonial home to her (subject to a charge for £12,000). If she is not prepared to do this, the matter must be sent back for further consideration in the Family Division. If, through some good fortune befalling her, the

wife is able to obtain funds to pay off the husband's charge, then she will be able freely to deal with the property. If the wife decides to leave the property the husband will recover *a*
a sum which will leave him something in hand after meeting his obligation to the legal aid fund.

I revert to the comment made by Sir John Arnold P in *Jones v Law Society*; amendments to s 9(6) of the 1974 Act and regs 88 and 91 to exclude the proceeds of the sale of the matrimonial home or funds allocated for the purchase of a primary home for either of the parties to the marriage or a child of the marriage to whom s 41 of the 1973 Act *b*
applies would avoid the hardship caused in this case. A person's home and the tools of his trade are already excluded from assessment under the 1974 Act. However, a mere discretion granted to the Law Society would not, in my judgment, be sufficient to permit the court to assume that the moneys would not be collected; nor a charge enforced unless the position was secured by direct enactment.

EVELEIGH LJ. The judgment of Purchas LJ has been handed down. I agree with it *c*
entirely, and, although we are differing from Sir John Arnold P, I am quite satisfied that this is because we had more information as to the legal aid situation, that is to say more positive than he had, and therefore, although we are differing from him, I do not propose to add anything to Purchas LJ's judgment.

12 April. At a resumed hearing the wife consented to an order dismissing her application *d*
for periodical payments and a lump sum. The appeal was allowed and an order made transferring the husband's interest in the matrimonial home to the wife subject to a charge for £12,000 in favour of the husband only enforceable on the house being sold, the husband to pay the outgoings up to the date of transfer.

Appeal allowed ; order accordingly. *e*

Solicitors: *Roberta Tish & Co*, Walthamstow (for the wife); *Piper Padfield & Derby*, Ilford (for the husband).

Henrietta Steinberg   Barrister. *f*

R v Law Society, ex parte Sexton

COURT OF APPEAL, CIVIL DIVISION
WALLER, O'CONNOR LJJ AND SIR DAVID CAIRNS
13, 14 JULY 1983 *g*

Legal aid – Charge on property recovered for deficiency of costs – Enforcement of charge – Discretion of Law Society – Money recovered in proceedings – Transfer of charge on money recovered – Wife recovering lump sum in ancillary proceedings – Whether Law Society having discretion to transfer charge from lump sum to home to be acquired instead of requiring payment over of lump sum – Whether assisted person's solicitor's obligation to pay money received over to *h*
Law Society fulfilled if charge transferred to other property – Legal Aid Act 1974, ss 9(6), 17(9) – Legal Aid (General) Regulations 1980, regs 91(1)(b), 97(2).

In ancillary proceedings heard as part of a divorce suit the court ordered, by consent, that the husband pay the wife a lump sum of £15,000. The wife was legally aided and her costs in the ancillary proceedings amounted to some £7,000 more than the lump sum *j*
she would receive under the consent order. It was conceded that the lump sum was 'property . . . recovered . . . for [the wife] in the proceedings' within s 9(6)[a] of the Legal Aid Act 1974 and that the Law Society therefore had a charge on the money as security

---

a   Section 9(6) is set out at p 94j, post

a for the costs incurred by the legal aid fund in the proceedings. The wife asked the Law Society to exercise the discretion conferred on it under reg 97(2)*b* of the Legal Aid (General) Regulations 1980 regarding enforcement of the s 9(6) charge by transferring the charge on the lump sum to a house which she intended buying, instead of requiring immediate payment over of the lump sum to the Law Society under reg 91(b)*c*. When the Law Society refused to transfer the charge on the lump sum the wife sought judicial review of its decision. When judicial review was refused the wife appealed.

b

Held – Where the property recovered or preserved in legally aided proceedings was money rather than other forms of property the Law Society had no discretion to take a charge over the money and transfer the charge to other property, since regs 88*d* and 91(1)(b) of the 1980 regulations required the rights of the legal aid fund to be safeguarded by the payment of money recovered to the assisted person's solicitor and then by him to *c* the Law Society forthwith and no question of a charge could arise once he had paid over the money. The wife's appeal would accordingly be dismissed (see p 96 *a* to *d* and *h*, post).

Simmons v Simmons [1984] 1 All ER 83 followed.

Hanlon v Law Society [1980] 2 All ER 199 considered.

Per Sir David Cairns. Section 17(9)*e* of the 1974 Act which provides that 'payment' is *d* to be interpreted as 'not . . . requiring the making of an actual payment, so as to prevent the obligation to make it being satisfied in whole or in part . . . in any other way' does not cover a charge on money or a house in place of actual payment to the legal aid fund where that is required, since a charge is not equivalent to the handing over of money (see p 97 *a*, post).

e **Notes**

For money recovered by an assisted person, see 37 Halsbury's Laws (4th edn) paras 933, 934.

For the charge for the benefit of the legal aid fund on property recovered or preserved, see ibid paras 938, 939.

For the Legal Aid Act 1974, ss 9, 17, see 44 Halsbury's Statutes (3rd edn) 1048, 1062.

f

Cases referred to in judgment

Hanlon v Law Society [1980] 2 All ER 199, [1981] AC 124, [1980] 2 WLR 756, HL.

Simmons v Simmons [1984] 1 All ER 83, CA.

Cases also cited

g *Catlow v Catlow* (1877) 2 CPD 362.

Law Society v Rushman [1955] 2 All ER 544, [1955] 1 WLR 681, CA.

IRC v National Federation of Self-Employed and Small Businesses Ltd [1981] 2 All ER 93, [1982] AC 617, HL.

Jones v Law Society (1983) Times, 27 January, 127 SJ 105.

h **Appeal**

In divorce proceedings between Ronald Sexton (the husband) as the petitioner, and Elizabeth Marion Jane Sexton (the wife) as the respondent, both parties were legally aided with nil contributions. The wife applied for ancillary relief and by an order dated 5 October 1982 Booth J ordered that the husband pay her a lump sum of £15,000 in return for her transferring her interest in the matrimonial home to the husband absolutely. By *j* virtue of s 9(6) of the Legal Aid Act 1974 the Law Society had a charge on the matrimonial home as security for the costs of the proceedings incurred by the legal aid fund. The wife

---

b Regulation 97(2) is set out at p 95 *b*, post

c Regulation 91 is set out at p 95 *f* to *h*, post

d Regulation 88, so far as material, is set out at p 95 *e*, post

e Section 17(9), so far as material, is set out at p 96 *j*, post

had incurred costs in the region of £22,000 and asked the Law Society to transfer the charge under s 9(6) in respect of her costs from the lump sum she had recovered from *a* the husband to a house which she intended purchasing or to the assets of a business if she were to start one. The Law Society decided that it had no power under s 9(6) and the Legal Aid (General) Regulations 1980, SI 1980/1894, to accept a charge on other property in lieu of requiring immediate payment over of the money received by the wife. The wife applied, with the leave of Forbes J granted on 8 March 1983, for an order of certiorari to quash the Law Society's decision and an order of mandamus requiring the Law Society *b* to reconsider its decision. On 15 April 1983 Woolf J refused the application without hearing argument on the ground that he was bound by Court of Appeal authority to refuse it. The wife appealed to the full Court of Appeal against the refusal to grant the application. The facts are set out in the judgment of Waller LJ.

Nigel Ley for the wife.
Duncan Matheson for the Law Society.   *c*

WALLER LJ. In this case the appellant, Mrs Sexton (the wife), applied to the Divisional Court for an order by way of judicial review that the Law Society were wrong in their construction of s 9 of the Legal Aid Act 1974 and the Legal Aid (General) Regulations 1980, SI 1980/1894, in coming to the conclusion that they had no power to transfer a *d* charge arising under s 9 to other property.

Woolf J, hearing that application, did not hear any argument because the parties agreed that the matter was concluded by the decision of this court in *Simmons v Simmons* [1984] 1 All ER 83. Woolf J refused the application so that the wife could appeal to this court in the hope that a court of three judges would come to a different conclusion from the court in *Simmons v Simmons*, which consisted of only two judges.

The original order of Booth J, out of which this application arises and which was made *e* on 5 October 1982, was as follows:

'By consent it is ordered that (1) the petitioner do pay to the respondent a lump sum of £15,000 by three instalments of £5,000 each at six monthly intervals, the first to be paid [on a particular date, and other dates to be arranged]. (2) the respondent shall forthwith transfer to the petitioner absolutely her legal and *f* beneficial interest in the property.'

So that the effect of the decision, albeit by consent of the parties, was that the share which the wife had in the matrimonial home was to be transferred to the husband, and in return he was to pay her £15,000.

Both parties were legally aided, and the Law Society had a charge on this sum of money as security for the costs incurred by the legal aid fund. The wife asked the Law *g* Society to transfer the charge from the money to a house which she intended purchasing.

It is submitted on her behalf that the money is property, that it can be subject to a charge and that the Law Society in its discretion can transfer the charge from the money to the house. The Law Society says that it has no discretion in the matter and that money recovered, save for £2,500, must, by reg 96(*d*), be paid ultimately to the Law Society.

The matter is primarily governed by s 9(6) of the Legal Aid Act 1974, which is in these *h* terms:

'Except so far as regulations otherwise provide, any sums remaining unpaid on account of a person's contribution to the legal aid fund in respect of any proceedings and, if the total contribution is less than the net liability of that fund on his account, a sum equal to the deficiency shall be a first charge for the benefit of the legal aid *j* fund on any property (wherever situated) which is recovered or preserved for him in the proceedings.'

So this sum of £15,000 is money recovered in the proceedings. It is common ground before us that money is property and, in personal injury actions, the Law Society frequently exercises its charge on the moneys recovered as damages.

I must next refer to the regulations which are contained in the Legal Aid (General)
a Regulations 1980. There are three important regulations to which I wish to refer. First
of all, reg 97 provides for vesting and enforcement of the statutory charge:

'(1) Any charge on property recovered or preserved for an assisted person arising
under section 9(6) of the Act shall vest in The Law Society.

(2) The Law Society may enforce any such charge in any manner which would
be available if the charge had been given *inter partes . . .*'
b

Counsel for the wife submitted that *Hanlon v Law Society* [1980] 2 All ER 199, [1981]
AC 124 was a case where it was held that charges could be transferred from one property
to another and that, in the circumstances of this case, the Law Society could transfer the
charge from money to house. In *Hanlon's* case a number of matters were raised with
which we are not concerned; but their Lordships did decide that where there was a
c house, the subject of a property adjustment order, and a house to which its charge
applied, the Law Society not only had a discretion to postpone the enforcement of that
charge (a discretion which it frequently exercised) but also had a discretion to transfer
the charge on the matrimonial home in a proper case from one property to another.

The submission of counsel for the wife was that that was something which could be
done in this case. But unfortunately there are other regulations in the 1980 regulations
d which deal specifically with money. In this regard I would refer to reg 88, which is
headed, 'Moneys recovered to be paid to solicitor or The Law Society', and which provides,
so far as material:

'Subject to regulations 90 and 96, all moneys payable to an assisted person . . .
shall be paid or repaid, as the case may be, to the solicitor of the assisted person or, if
he is no longer represented by a solicitor, to The Law Society . . .'
e

Regulation 91, which is entitled 'Solicitor to pay moneys recovered to The Law Society',
is the regulation which is critical in this case. That regulation provides:

'(1) An assisted person's solicitor shall forthwith—(a) inform the appropriate area
committee of any property recovered or preserved for the assisted person; and (b)
f subject to paragraph (2) pay all moneys received by him by virtue of an order or
agreement made in the assisted person's favour to The Law Society.'

So, subject to para (2), the money having been paid to the solicitor, he has to pay it
over to the Law Society. Paragraph 91(2) provides:

'Where the appropriate area committee considers that the rights of the fund will
g thereby be safeguarded and so directs, the assisted person's solicitor shall—(a) pay to
The Law Society under paragraph (1)(b) only such sum as, in the opinion of the
appropriate area committee, should be retained by The Law Society in order to
safeguard the rights of the fund under any provision of the Act and these
Regulations; and (b) pay any other moneys to the assisted person.'

h Counsel for the wife has drawn our attention to the earlier regulations which reg 91
replaced (being regulations which dealt with the same problem) in 1950, 1960, 1962 and
1971. He has submitted that certain variations in the wording were intended by the
draftsman to give a more liberal construction to reg 91. It is true that between 1950 and
1960 there was an appreciable change in the form of the regulations, but from 1960
onwards, although there were minor changes, in my opinion the meaning is identical. I
j do not find that there was any change other than a verbal one.

So one has to look at reg 91 and see whether it can be construed so that the provision
which enables the appropriate area committee to express the opinion that the rights of
the fund would be protected can be construed as including protection by transferring the
charge from the money to other property so that the Law Society would then have a
charge on that property and the appropriate area committee would consider that that
was satisfactory.

In my opinion, the words do not permit such a construction. In reg 91(2) the words are:

> 'Where the appropriate area committee considers that the rights of the fund will *thereby* be safeguarded and so directs the assisted person's solicitor *shall*—(*a*) pay to The Law Society . . . (*b*) only *such sum* as, in the opinion of the appropriate area committee . . .'

In my opinion the combination of the words and phrases I have emphasised does not permit of the construction proposed by counsel for the wife. He submits that the words 'if any' should be inserted after 'such sum', but I do not accept that there is any need to insert such words because the meaning is clear. 'Thereby safeguarded' clearly refers to the obligation to 'pay such sum'. An obligation to pay a sum of money is not fulfilled by transferring the charge to other property. The money must be paid.

I have come to the conclusion that regs 88 and 91 make it impossible to avoid paying the money in circumstances such as the present, first of all to the assisted person's solicitor and second, on his part, over to the Law Society.

The decision of the House of Lords in *Hanlon's* case is not inconsistent with this. That case was concerned wholly with property other than money. The charge was on the property. So long as the Law Society is dealing only with property other than money, the Law Society has a discretion. However, in my opinion when it is dealing with money, that is to say money which has been preserved or recovered, the Law Society has no discretion at all.

Although I mentioned at the beginning of this judgment the decision of this court in *Simmons v Simmons*, I have not referred to it in the course of my reasons and have not relied on it for any step in this judgment. However I now return to it and say that, for the reasons which I have expressed, I have arrived at precisely the same conclusion as did this court in *Simmons v Simmons*. So no question arises whether a three-judge court can overrule a two-judge court. What has happened is that a three-judge court has added the weight of its opinion to that of a court which has already given the same opinion.

However, I cannot part with this case without an expression of sympathy for the Law Society on the one hand and with some legally aided litigants on the other. The Law Society has to administer these regulations so as to effect the purpose of the legal aid scheme. It endeavours, by warnings and directions, to reduce the amount of litigation when marriages break up, but this case illustrates that there is no reasonable limit to the total of costs which may be incurred.

On the other hand, the rules are such that those legally aided persons who behave with restraint in their litigation are nevertheless sometimes prevented from arriving at a reasonable settlement by reason of the effect of these regulations. I cannot see any solution that can be produced by decisions of the court. The Law Society does what it can to discourage too much litigation but any solution which would enable a reasonable party to be protected could only be arrived at by amendment to the regulations.

I would dismiss this appeal.

O'CONNOR LJ. I agree.

SIR DAVID CAIRNS. I also agree that the appeal should be dismissed for the reasons given by Waller LJ. I would only add that a second argument was submitted to this court by counsel for the wife, based on s 17(9) of the Legal Aid Act 1974, which provides in effect that the word 'payment' and other corresponding words in that part of the Act are to be interpreted as 'not . . . requiring the making of an actual payment, so as to prevent the obligation to make it being satisfied in whole or in part by an allowance on account or in any other way'.

Counsel has asked us to say that that provision in the Act should be deemed to apply also to the regulations, which I think is not unreasonable. He then submits that 'in any other way' would cover a charge on money or a house in place of actual payment. I a cannot conceive that s 17(9) was intended to be interpreted as widely as that. I think the words 'or in any other way' are to be understood ejusdem generis with the words before them and to mean that which is equivalent to the actual handing over of money, which a charge clearly is not.

Appeal dismissed. Leave to appeal to the House of Lords refused.

b Solicitors: *Ralph Haeems & Co* (for the appellant); *David Edwards*, Secretary, Legal Aid (for the Law Society).

Sophie Craven   Barrister.

c

d

Presho v Insurance Officer

HOUSE OF LORDS

e LORD DIPLOCK, LORD FRASER OF TULLYBELTON, LORD KEITH OF KINKEL, LORD ROSKILL AND LORD BRANDON OF OAKBROOK

22, 23 NOVEMBER, 15 DECEMBER 1983

National insurance – Unemployment benefit – Disqualification for benefit – Loss of employment due to stoppage of work – Stoppage of work due to trade dispute – Person directly interested in trade dispute – Different workers belonging to different unions employed by same employer – f   Claimant belonging to union not participating in dispute – Claimant laid off work because of dispute – Whether claimant 'directly interested in the trade dispute' – Whether claimant disqualified for unemployment benefit – Social Security Act 1975, s 19(1).

Where workers belonging to different unions are employed by the same employer at the same place of work and there is a trade dispute between the employer and one of the unions to which some of the workers belong, the workers belonging to the other unions are 'directly', and not merely indirectly, 'interested in that trade dispute' within s 19(1)[a] of the Social Security Act 1975 as amended by s 111(1)[b] of the Employment Protection Act 1975 (and are therefore disqualified for receiving unemployment benefit during the continuation of any stoppage of work at their place of employment which is caused h   thereby), if, as a result of a collective agreement (whether legally binding or not) or established industrial custom and practice at the place of work concerned, the outocme of the dispute will automatically be applied by the employer to the workers belonging to the other unions. Whether those conditions are satisfied in any particular case is a pure question of fact, which, because of their wide knowledge and experience of industrial relations matters, insurance officers, local tribunals and social security commissioners are j   exceptionally well qualified to answer (see p 98 *f* to *h* and p 101 *e* to p 102 *a*, post).

Dicta of Lord Denning MR and of Bridge LJ in *R v National Insurance Comr, ex p Stratton* [1979] 2 All ER at 282, 286 and *Watt v Lord Advocate* 1979 SC 120 approved.

---

a   Section 19(1), so far as material, is set out at p 99 *g h*, post
b   Section 111(1) is set out at p 99 *h j*, post

Notes

For trade dispute disqualification for receiving unemployment benefit, see 33 Halsbury's   *a*
Laws (4th edn) para 413.

For the Social Security Act 1975, s 19, see 45 Halsbury's Statutes (3rd edn) 1099.

For the Employment Protection Act 1975, s 111, see ibid 377.

Cases referred to in opinions

R v National Insurance Comr, ex p Stratton [1979] 2 All ER 278, [1979] QB 361, [1979] 2   *b*
WLR 389, CA.

Watt v Lord Advocate 1979 SC 120.

Appeal

On 4 December 1978 the local insurance officer refused a claim by Kathleen Presho for
unemployment benefit under the Social Security Act 1975 for the period 18 to 22   *c*
November 1978 on the ground that the stoppage at her place of work was due to a trade
dispute in which she had not proved she was not directly interested within the meaning
of s 19(1) of the 1975 Act. The claimant appealed to the local tribunal for Accrington and
Rossendale, which dismissed her appeal on 22 August 1979. The claimant appealed to a
social security commissioner (Mr M J Goodman), who by decision made on 27 March
1981 dismissed her appeal. The claimant appealed to the Court of Appeal (Stephenson,   *d*
Kerr and Slade LJJ), which allowed the appeal on 28 April 1983, set aside the decision of
the commissioner and ordered payment of benefit to the claimant for the relevant period.
The insurance officer appealed to the House of Lords with the leave of the Court of
Appeal. The facts are set out in the opinion of Lord Brandon.

Simon D Brown and *Stephen Aitchison* for the insurance officer.   *e*
Benet Hytner QC and *John L Hand* for the claimant.

Their Lordships took time for consideration.

15 December. The following opinions were delivered.
   f

LORD DIPLOCK. My Lords, I have had the advantage of reading in draft the speech
of my noble and learned friend Lord Brandon. I agree with it, and for the reasons he
gives I would allow this appeal.

LORD FRASER OF TULLYBELTON. My Lords, I have had the advantage of
reading in draft the speech of my noble and learned friend Lord Brandon. I agree with it   *g*
and for the reasons stated in it I would allow this appeal.

LORD KEITH OF KINKEL. My Lords, I agree that this appeal should be allowed for
the reasons given in the speech of my noble and learned friend Lord Brandon.

LORD ROSKILL. My Lords, I have had the advantage of reading in draft the speech   *h*
to be delivered by my noble and learned friend Lord Brandon. For the reasons he gives I
would allow the appeal and restore the decision of the commissioner.

LORD BRANDON OF OAKBROOK. My Lords, the respondent (the claimant) was
in November 1978 employed by Brooke Bond Oxo Ltd at its food factory at Great
Harwood, Lancashire. During or following a short period when she was laid off work in   *j*
consequence of an industrial dispute in which she was not herself a participant, she
applied to an insurance officer for unemployment benefit for the period 18 to 22
November 1978. The insurance officer refused her claim on the ground that, in the
circumstances of the case, she was disqualified by the relevant legislation from receiving
such benefit. The claimant brought a first appeal to a local tribunal at Accrington, which

by a decision made on 22 August 1979 dismissed her appeal. The claimant brought a
a second appeal to the social security commissioner, Mr Commissioner Goodman, who by
a decision made on 27 March 1981 dismissed that appeal also. By notice of appeal dated
28 January 1982 the claimant brought a third appeal to the Court of Appeal. That court
by an order dated 9 May 1983 unanimously allowed her appeal, set aside the
commissioner's decision and directed that unemployment benefit should be paid to the
claimant for the relevant period. The Court of Appeal further gave leave to the
b commissioner to present a petition of appeal to your Lordships' House.

The material facts are set out in paras 3, 4 and 8 of the commissioner's decision, which
read as follows:

'3. The claimant was at the material time employed as an instructor/machine
operator, that is a production worker, at the food factory in question. She was a
member of the Union of Shop, Distributive and Allied Workers (USDAW). Also
c employed at the factory were 57 maintenance engineers who were members of the
Amalgamated Union of Engineering Workers (AUEW). That Union put in a
demand for the phase 1 and phase 2 increases (under the pay policy then in force) to
be consolidated into their basic wages which demand would, if conceded,
presumably represent a financial improvement for them, in that over-time rates
calculated on basic rates would thereby be increased.
d 4. The management of the factory did not feel able to concede this demand. A
work to rule was imposed by the maintenance engineers. As a result of an alleged
refusal by 2 engineers to do a particular job and their subsequent suspension, work
came to a standstill at the factory. On Monday 20th November 1978 all 417
production workers were laid off, as machines were not being repaired. The stoppage
of work ended on Thursday 23rd November 1978, when work resumed in the
e factory, the terms of settlement being that pay negotiations would be brought
forward to an earlier date in 1979 than had been originally contemplated.
8. Although the claimant was a member of a union (USDAW) which did not at
that time make a claim for a consolidation of the phase 1 and phase 2 increases, it is
in my view incontrovertible on the evidence that the factual situation at the factory
was such that, if the demand by AUEW were conceded it would automatically be
f applied to the USDAW workers as well . . .'

Section 19(1) of the Social Security Act 1975, before its amendment by s 111(1) of the
Employment Protection Act 1975, provided:

'A person who has lost employment as an employed earner by reason of a stoppage
of work which was due to a trade dispute at his place of employment shall be
g disqualified for receiving unemployment benefit so long as the stoppage continues
. . . but this subsection does not apply in the case of a person who proves—(a) that
he is not participating in or financing or directly interested in the trade dispute
which caused the stoppage of work; and (b) that he does not belong to a grade or
class of workers of which, immediately before the commencement of the stoppage,
there were members employed at his place of employment any of whom are
h participating in or financing or directly interested in the dispute.'

Section 111(1) of the Employment Protection Act 1975 provides:

'In section 19(1) of the Social Security Act 1975 (disqualification for unemployment
benefit where stoppage of work due to trade dispute)—(a) in paragraph (a) the words
"or financing" and the word "and", and (b) paragraph (b), are hereby repealed.'

j The result of this amendment is that an employee who is laid off by reason of a
stoppage of work due to a trade dispute at his place of employment is disqualified for
receiving unemployment benefit unless he can prove (and the burden of proof is on him)
two matters: first, that he is not participating in, and, second, that he is not directly
interested in, the trade dispute which caused the stoppage of work.

In the present case it is common ground that the claimant did not participate in the trade dispute between AUEW and the management of the factory. The sole question *a* which has to be decided, therefore (remembering that the burden of proving the negative is on the claimant), is whether she was 'directly interested in the trade dispute' within the meaning of that expression as used in s 19(1) of the Social Security Act 1975 as amended by s 111(1) of the Employment Protection Act 1975. That question has already been considered by the insurance officer, the local tribunal and the commissioner, all of whom decided it adversely to the claimant. It has then been considered by the Court of Appeal, *b* who disagreed with all the decisions below and decided the question favourably to the claimant. It is, I think, right to add that, although the present case involves only a relatively small amount of money in respect of a stoppage of a few days some five years ago, it is being treated as a test case, the final decision of which by your Lordships' House will regulate the way in which a very large number of similar claims, pending or yet to be made, will be dealt with. *c*

My Lords, the decisions of the insurance officer, the local tribunal and the commissioner were all based on the same reasoning. That reasoning was that, since the outcome of the trade dispute between the AUEW and the management of the factory would, in accordance with the industrial custom and practice which existed at the factory, be applied automatically 'across the board' to all the other workers there, including in particular production workers such as the claimant, she was directly interested in such *d* trade dispute for the purposes of s 19(1) of the Social Security Act 1975 as amended.

The reasoning which led the Court of Appeal to reach the opposite conclusion is to be found in the judgments of Kerr and Slade LJJ, with both of which Stephenson LJ agreed. Kerr LJ said:

> 'The proper meaning of "directly", I think . . . is that the circumstances are such that the probable outcome of the dispute will automatically affect the claimant by *e* virtue of some pre-existing agreement whether legally binding or not . . . To put the converse, I think that a claimant is not "directly" interested in the dispute if its outcome, in relation to those who have stopped work, will only affect the claimant after and as the result of further separate and distinct negotiations, even if these are likely to lead to a similar or even to a substantially identical outcome, and whatever the eventual outcome may turn out to be.' *f*

Slade LJ said:

> 'Nevertheless, I think it clear that, in using the word "automatically" in para 8 of his decision, the commissioner can have meant no more than "virtually automatically", which is indeed the phrase used by him at the end of para 9 of his decision. I think it is common ground that in the circumstances of the present *g* case . . . even after the outcome of the relevant trade dispute had been settled, further negotiations would have had to follow before the conditions of pay of the group of workers to which [the claimant] belonged could have been finally determined. It may perhaps be that in practice the outcome of these further negotiations would have followed the outcome of the trade dispute, as the night would have followed the day. Nevertheless, these negotiations were a contingency *h* which would necessarily have had to be interposed between the outcome of the dispute and the occurrence of the change in [the claimant's] terms of employment; and in my opinion they would necessarily have had the effect of breaking the chain of causation linking the dispute and any pay-rise which she might ultimately receive. In these circumstance, applying the test which I regard as the correct one, I do not think that [the claimant] can properly be said to have been "directly" *j* interested in the relevant trade dispute in the instant case.'

The grounds on which the Court of Appeal decided the case were those which were advanced by counsel for the claimant before that court. They can be formulated in this way: that, while the claimant was indirectly interested in the trade dispute between the management of the factory and the AUEW, she was not directly so interested because

a further formal negotiations between the management of the factory and the USDAW might be necessary before the outcome of the management's dispute with the AUEW was applied to members of the USDAW, including the claimant, who were also employed at the same factory.

At the hearing of the appeal in your Lordships' House, counsel for the claimant, with your Lordships' leave, presented an argument which he frankly and fairly admitted it

b had not occurred either to him or to his learned junior to present to the Court of Appeal. This argument consisted in the broad proposition that a worker can only be directly interested in a trade dispute if it is his own pay or conditions of work which form the subject matter of such dispute. In support of this argument counsel for the claimant relied on the fact that s 19(1) of the Social Security Act 1975 as amended refers to a person being interested in the trade dispute itself, and not in the outcome of such dispute.

c If the argument of counsel for the claimant had stopped there it might at least have given your Lordships some fresh food for thought. His argument, however, did not stop there, for he felt obliged, with characteristic realism, to concede an exception to the generality of his broad proposition, which he described as the 'coat-tails' situation. By this expression he meant a situation in which the outcome of a trade dispute, involving only one group of employees belonging to union A, was automatically and immediately

d applied, either in accordance with a collective agreement, whether legally binding or not, or in accordance with established industrial custom and practice at the place of work concerned, to all other groups of employees, even though these belonged to other unions, B, C or D.

In my view, the expression 'directly interested in the trade dispute', as used in s 19(1) of the Social Security Act 1975 as amended, must be given its ordinary and natural

e meaning in the context in which it occurs. That context is that of situations arising out of industrial relations, including among other possible situations that of a trade dispute causing a stoppage of work at some factory or other place of work, at which different groups of workers, belonging to different trade unions, are employed by the same employers.

Approaching the question in that way it seems to me impossible to say that a person

f can only be directly interested in a trade dispute if it is his own pay or conditions of work which form the subject matter of the dispute. Nor can I accept the distinction which was sought to be drawn between a person being interested in a trade dispute and his being interested in the outcome of a trade dispute. The two concepts appear to me, in the relevant context, necessarily to overlap, and indeed to amount to very much the same thing.

g I would accept as a correct statement of the relevant law the exception to the broad proposition of counsel for the claimant which he felt obliged to concede, and which he said was applicable in what he metaphorically described as a 'coat-tails' situation. To put the matter more fully, I would hold that, where different groups of workers, belonging to different unions, are employed by the same employers at the same place of work and there is a trade dispute between the common employers and one of the unions to which

h one of the groups of workers belong, those in the other groups of workers belonging to other unions are directly, and not merely indirectly, interested in that trade dispute provided that two conditions are fulfilled. The first condition is that, whatever may be the outcome of the trade dispute, it will be applied by the common employers not only to the group of workers belonging to the one union participating in the dispute, but also to the other groups of workers belonging to the other unions concerned. The second

j condition is that this application of the outcome of the dispute 'across the board', as it has been aptly described, should come about automatically as a result of one or other of three things: first, a collective agreement which is legally binding; or, second, a collective agreement which is not legally binding; or, third, established industrial custom and practice at the place of work concerned.

My Lords, it is, in my opinion, a pure question of fact whether, in any particular case, the two conditions to which I have just referred are satisfied or not. It is, moreover, a question of fact of a kind which insurance officers, local tribunals and the commissioner are, by reason of their wide knowledge and experience of matters pertaining to industrial relations, exceptionally well qualified to answer. In the present case the commissioner found as a fact that these two conditions were satisfied, in that the employers would, by reason of the factual situation at the factory, by which he clearly meant the established industrial custom and practice there, apply automatically the outcome of their dispute with the AUEW to other groups of workers belonging to other unions at the same factory, including the group of workers belonging to the USDAW, of which the claimant was one. It was not, and could not with any chance of success have been, contended that there was no or insufficient evidence to support that finding of fact by the commissioner. Indeed, having read the notes of the evidence given before the local tribunal, I consider that any finding the other way would have been perverse.

There appear to me to be three important considerations which go to support the approach which I have adopted to the interpretation of the expression 'directly interested in the trade dispute' as used in s 19(1) of the Social Security Act 1975 as amended.

The first consideration is that the approach which I have adopted accords with that which has been adopted since 1926 by a substantial number of social security commissioners (or their earlier equivalents) after the expression concerned had first appeared in this class of legislation in 1911. The observations of the Court of Appeal in *R v National Insurance Comr, ex p Stratton* [1979] 2 All ER 278 at 282, 286, [1979] QB 361 at 369, 374 per Lord Denning MR and Bridge LJ make it clear that, where there has been a consistent line of decisions in this field of national insurance by specialised tribunals over a large number of years, a court should be slow to depart from them. I agree with those expressions of opinion and regard them as applicable in the instant case.

The second consideration is that the approach which I have adopted accords substantially with the ratio decidendi of the majority judgment of the Court of Session (the Lord President (Elmslie) and Lord Johnston, Lord Avonside dissenting) in *Watt v The Lord Advocate* 1979 SC 120. In this connection I would draw particular attention to the passage in the judgment of the Lord President (at 127) in which he deals with the meaning of the same expression 'directly interested in the trade dispute', as used in the same context in s 22(1) of the National Insurance Act 1965.

The third consideration is that, if the expression 'directly interested in the trade dispute' were to be given a narrower and more legalistic interpretation than I think it right to give it, the way would be wide open for deliberate and calculated evasions of the basic provision of s 19(1) of the Social Security Act 1975 as amended, with the result that the effectiveness of the subsection to achieve its manifest object would be much reduced.

It seems to me, with great respect to the members of the Court of Appeal who decided in favour of the claimant, that their decision can only be explained on the basis either that they gave too restricted a meaning to the expression 'directly interested in the trade dispute' in the context in which it appears or that they felt justified in differing from the commissioners on what was to my mind a pure question of fact. Since an appeal from the social security commissioner to the Court of Appeal can only be brought on a question of law, the former explanation appears more likely than the latter. Whatever the basis of the decision, however, I am of opinion that it was erroneous and cannot stand.

My Lords, for the reasons which I have given, I would allow the appeal, set aside the order of the Court of Appeal dated 9 May 1983 and restore the decision of the commissioner made on 27 March 1981.

Appeal allowed.

Solicitors: *Solicitor to the Department of Health and Social Security; Hextall Erskine & Co* (for the claimant).

Mary Rose Plummer   Barrister.

a Tor Line AB v Alltrans Group of Canada Ltd
The TFL Prosperity

HOUSE OF LORDS

LORD DIPLOCK, LORD FRASER OF TULLYBELTON, LORD KEITH OF KINKEL, LORD ROSKILL AND LORD
b BRANDON OF OAKBROOK

21, 22 NOVEMBER, 15 DECEMBER 1983

*Shipping – Time charterparty – Exceptions – Baltime charterparty – Damage – Clause exempting
owners from liability for 'damage . . . whatsoever and howsoever caused' – Whether clause
exempting owners from liability for financial damage caused to charterers.*

c The shipowners chartered a roll-on roll-off ferry to the charterers under a charterparty in
the Baltime form which provided, by cl 13[a], that 'The Owners only to be responsible for
delay in delivery of the Vessel or for delay during the currency of the Charter and for loss
or damage to goods onboard, if such delay or loss has been caused by want of due
diligence on the part of the Owners . . . in making the Vessel seaworthy . . . or any other
personal act or omission or default of the Owners . . .' Clause 13 further provided that
d the owners were 'not to be responsible in any other case nor for damage or delay
whatsoever and howsoever caused even if caused by the neglect or default of their
servants'. The vessel did not conform with the deck heights specified in the charterparty,
with the result that the charterers were unable to load the vessel in the way they intended.
The charterers' claim against the owners for loss of freight was upheld at arbitration and,
on appeal, by the judge, who held that cl 13 did not afford the owners a defence to the
e charterers' claim. On appeal by the owners, the Court of Appeal held that although the
charterers' claim was for financial damage it nevertheless came within the scope of
'damage . . . whatsoever and howsoever caused' and therefore cl 13 afforded the owners a
complete defence. The charterers appealed to the House of Lords.

Held – On the true construction of cl 13 of the charterparty the phrases 'in any other
f case' and 'damage or delay whatsoever and howsoever caused' were not terms of complete
and universal exclusion from liability since they related back to, and therefore restricted
exemption from liability in respect of, those faults or defects referred to earlier in cl 13,
namely delay in delivery or during the currency of the charter and physical damage or
loss to goods on board. Accordingly, cl 13 did not provide exemption from liability in
the case of claims for financial loss. The owners were therefore not protected against
g liability for breach of the warranty as to deck heights in the charterparty. The charterers'
appeal would accordingly be allowed (see p 104 *h j*, p 108 *a* to *j*, p 109 *d f* and *h*, p 110 *e f*
and p 111 *b* to *e* and *j* to p 112 *d*, post).

Burton & Co v English & Co (1883) 12 QBD 218 applied.

Nippon Yusen Kaisha v Acme Shipping Corp [1972] 1 All ER 35 overruled.

Dicta of Walsh J in *Westfal-Larsen & Co A/S v Colonial Sugar Refining Co Ltd* [1960] 2
h Lloyd's Rep at 210–211 and of McNair J in *Gesellschaft Burgerlichen Rechts v Stockholms
Rederiaktiebolag SVEA, The Brabant* [1966] 1 All ER at 967 criticised.

---

a Clause 13 provides (the numbers on the right are the line numbers on the printed form):

13. The Owners only to be responsible for delay in delivery of the Vessel or for delay during   95
the currency of the Charter and for loss or damage to goods onboard, if such delay or loss has been   96
caused by want of due diligence on the part of the Owners or their Manager in making the Vessel sea- 97
j worthy and fitted for the voyage or any other personal act or omission or default of the Owners or   98
their Manager. The Owners not to be responsible in any other case nor for damage or delay whatsoever 99
and howsoever caused even if caused by the neglect or default of their servants. The Owners not   100
to be liable for loss or damage arising or resulting from strikes, lock-outs or stoppage or restraint 101
of labour (including the Master, Officers or Crew) whether partial or general.   102

The Charterers to be responsible for loss or damage caused to the Vessel or to the Owners by goods   103
being loaded contrary to the terms of the Charter or by improper or careless bunkering or loading,   104
stowing or discharging of goods or any other improper or negligent act on their part or that of   105
their servants.   106

Notes

For the construction of exceptions in a charterparty, see 43 Halsbury's Laws (4th edn) *a* para 449.

Cases referred to in opinions

Burton & Co v English & Co (1883) 12 QBD 218, CA.

Cosmos Bulk Transport Inc v China National Foreign Trade Transportation Inc [1978] 1 All ER 322.   *b*

Dreyfus (Louis) & Cie v Parnaso Cia Naviera SA [1960] 1 All ER 759, [1960] 2 QB 49, [1960] 2 WLR 637, CA; *rvsg* [1959] 1 All ER 502, [1959] 1 QB 498, [1959] 2 WLR 405.

Gesellschaft Burgerlichen Rechts v Stockholms Rederiaktiebolag SVEA, The Brabant [1966] 1 All ER 961, [1967] 1 QB 588, [1966] 2 WLR 909.

Helvetia-S, The [1960] 1 Lloyd's Rep 540.

Istros (owner) v F W Dahlstroem & Co [1931] 1 KB 247.   *c*

Nippon Yusen Kaisha v Acme Shipping Corp [1972] 1 All ER 35, [1972] 1 WLR 74, CA.

Photo Production Ltd v Securicor Transport Ltd [1980] 1 All ER 556, [1980] AC 827, [1980] 2 WLR 283, HL.

Suisse Atlantique Société d'Armement Maritime SA v NV Rotterdamsche Kolen Centrale [1966] 2 All ER 61, [1967] 1 AC 361, [1966] 2 WLR 944, HL.

Westfal-Larsen & Co A/S v Colonial Sugar Refining Co Ltd [1960] 2 Lloyd's Rep 206, NSW *d* SC.

Appeal

Tor Line AB (since renamed Investment AB Torman) (the charterers) appealed against the decision of the Court of Appeal (Sir John Donaldson MR, Dillon LJ and Sir Denys Buckley) on 30 March 1983 allowing an appeal by the respondents, Alltrans Group of *e* Canada Ltd (the owners), against the decision of Bingham J on 20 January 1982 giving leave to appeal against the award of the umpire, Mr Alan Kent, in an arbitration between the parties over a dispute arising out of a charterparty in the Baltime form dated 24 April 1979 of the vessel TFL Prosperity. Having granted leave Bingham J held, on the hearing of the appeal, that the owners were not entitled to rely on an exemption clause (cl 13) in the charterparty to avoid liability for breach of warranty of description of the vessel in *f* the charterparty, which breach of warranty prevented the charterers from loading the vessel in the way in which they had intended, namely with two 40-foot long containers one on top of the other and the pair on a trailer. In so holding, Bingham J upheld the award of the umpire. The facts are set out in the opinion of Lord Roskill.

Kenneth Rokison QC and *Stephen Tomlinson* for the charterers.   *g*
Bernard Rix QC and *Michael Tugendhat* for the owners.

Their Lordships took time for consideration.

15 December. The following opinions were delivered.

h

LORD DIPLOCK. My Lords, I have had the advantage of reading in draft the speech of my noble and learned friend Lord Roskill. I agree with it, and for the reasons he gives I would allow this appeal.

LORD FRASER OF TULLYBELTON. My Lords, I have had the advantage of reading in draft the speech of my noble and learned friend Lord Roskill. I agree with it *j* and for the reasons stated in it I would allow this appeal.

LORD KEITH OF KINKEL. My Lords, I have had the benefit of reading in advance the speech to be delivered by my noble and learned friend Lord Roskill. I agree with it, and for the reasons he gives I too would allow the appeal.

LORD ROSKILL. My Lords, in this appeal your Lordships' House is invited for the
first time to construe cl 13 of the well-known and widely used Baltime uniform time
charter. The printed form of this time charter first saw the light of day as long ago as
February 1909. It is thus almost three-quarters of a century old. Its printed provisions
have from time to time since been amended as the list of dates on the top left hand corner
of the present printed form shows. The last amendments were made in 1950. What is
now cl 13 has from time to time itself appeared in somewhat different forms and with a
different number in earlier versions. In what appears to have been the 1920 version, the
predecessor of the present cl 13 was numbered cl 12 and was also expressed in slightly
different language. But only one of the English cases in which the scope of this clause has
been considered has reached the Court of Appeal and the number of decisions at first
instance during the last three-quarters of a century is surprisingly few having regard to
the degree of protection which owners claim that it accords them against claims by
charterers.

The present appeal arises in the following circumstances. The respondents (the owners)
were the demise owners of a vessel named the TFL Prosperity (the vessel). By a time
charter dated 24 April 1979 the respondents in that capacity time chartered the vessel to
the appellants (the charterers) for a period of six months and ten days on the terms of this
charter. The version used was that amended with effect from 1 January 1950. To the 25
clauses of the printed form, some of which were, as is usual, either deleted or amended,
the parties added a massive number of typed clauses, numbered 26 to 60 inclusive.

The vessel was of a type known as 'roll-on roll-off' and the charterers required her for
their roll-on roll-off liner service which they operated between Europe and the Middle
East. It was no doubt for this reason that cl 26, the first of the additional typed clauses,
specified in great detail the description of certain fixed structural attributes of the vessel
together with particulars of her speed and consumption. I need not set out cl 26 in full.
Reference can if necessary be made to the details set out in the decision of Bingham J (see
[1982] 1 Lloyd's Rep 617 at 620). Among the provisions of cl 26 under the heading 'Free
Heights' was 'Main Deck: 6·10 m'. In fact the free height of the main deck at one critical
point was only 6·05 metres. As a result a mafi trailer double stacked with 40-foot
containers could not be loaded into the main deck. The charterers claimed damages from
the owners. The damages claimed, so far as now relevant, were mainly for loss of freight
but there was also a small claim for damages for delay. The owners raised various
defences. One alone remains relevant, that based on cl 13 which bears the rubric
'Responsibility and Exemption'. The charter contained a London arbitration clause and
the dispute was accordingly referred to arbitration, each party appointing an arbitrator.
The arbitrators appointed the late Mr Alan Kent as umpire. The arbitrators disagreed and
accordingly Mr Kent entered on the reference. In due course he made a long and careful
award in favour of the charterers, rejecting the defence based on cl 13 and awarding
them damages both for loss of freight and for delay. Mr Kent also dealt with other
matters no longer relevant.

The owners sought leave to appeal on five matters which had been in issue before Mr
Kent. Bingham J gave leave only on the question whether cl 13 afforded a defence to
these two claims. On 20 January 1982 the judge in a reserved judgment reached the
same conclusion on this issue as had Mr Kent (see [1982] 1 Lloyd's Rep 617). But he gave
the owners leave to appeal, certifying that this issue was one of general public importance,
as indeed, having regard to the extent of the use of this form, it clearly was.

On 30 March 1983 the Court of Appeal (Sir John Donaldson MR, Dillon LJ and Sir
Denys Buckley) allowed the appeal and held that cl 13 did afford a defence to the
charterers' claims for damages (see [1983] 2 Lloyd's Rep 18). The Court of Appeal gave
the charterers leave to appeal to your Lordships' House.

A somewhat similar clause to cl 13 appeared in the Gencon voyage charter which first
came into use in 1922. This clause was considered by Diplock J in *Louis Dreyfus & Cie v
Parnaso Cia Naviera SA* [1959] 1 All ER 502 at 507–508, [1959] 1 QB 498 at 514–515.

But Diplock J's decision on the central issue in that case was subsequently reversed by the Court of Appeal (see [1960] 1 All ER 759, [1960] 2 QB 49). For that reason the effect of the exception clause was not further considered (see [1960] 1 All ER 759 at 762, [1960] 2 QB 49 at 57–58). I doubt whether that case therefore affords any assistance in resolving the present problem.

Counsel for the charterers advanced three main submissions. First, he contended that cl 13 on its true construction did not in any event protect the owners against a claim for financial loss suffered by the charterers by reason of the owners' breaches of charter. This submission could not have been successfully advanced in the courts below by reason of the decision of the Court of Appeal to which I have already referred, namely *Nippon Yusen Kaisha v Acme Shipping Corp* [1972] 1 All ER 35, [1972] 1 WLR 74. The Court of Appeal there held, contrary to counsel's present submissions, that cl 13 did protect the owners against claims for financial loss.

My Lords, let me say at once that I was a party to that decision, together with Lord Denning MR and Cairns LJ. The correctness of the decision was vigorously challenged by counsel for the charterers and equally vigorously supported by counsel for the owners.

Second, counsel for the charterers urged that, even if *Nippon Yusen Kaisha v Acme Shipping Corp* was correctly decided and cl 13 fell to be construed as the Court of Appeal had there held, it did not operate to protect the owners against a claim for damages for breach of the provisions regarding the vessel's description but only in respect of their obligations during the performance of the contractual adventure.

Third, counsel for the charterers contended that cl 26, being in type and specially added, must prevail over cl 13, which was in print. Though this argument appears to have appealed to Bingham J (see [1982] 1 Lloyd's Rep 617 at 627) and to have been used by him to reinforce his conclusion that cl 13 did not in any event protect the owners in the event of non-compliance by them with the provisions regarding the vessel's description, counsel for the charterers did not seriously press this third argument. Your Lordships did not find it necessary to hear counsel for the owners on it. I will only make this observation. In the charter as executed the whole of the printed preamble was struck out and cl 26 with all its details was clearly intended to replace the printed preamble. If physically cl 26 had appeared as a substitute preamble to the charter, that substitute preamble, whether in type or in print, together with all the other clauses of the charter, including cl 13, would have fallen to be construed as a whole and if, contrary to either of the charterers' two principal submissions, cl 13 does protect the owners I am afraid I do not follow why a contrary conclusion should be reached merely because the substitute preamble would appear as a typed clause on the first page of the charter and cl 13 would appear as a printed exception clause on the second page.

My Lords, I propose first to consider the true construction of cl 13 and to do so without reference to any of the decided cases to which your Lordships were referred in argument. Clause 13 reads as follows:

> 'Responsibility and Exemption.
>
> 13. The Owners only to be responsible for delay in delivery of the Vessel or for delay during the currency of the Charter and for loss or damage to goods onboard, if such delay or loss has been caused by want of due diligence on the part of the Owners or their Manager in making the Vessel seaworthy and fitted for the voyage or any other personal act or omission or default of the Owners or their Manager. The Owners not to be responsible in any other case nor for damage or delay whatsoever and howsoever caused even if caused by the neglect or default of their servants. The Owners not to be liable for loss or damage arising or resulting from strikes, lock-outs or stoppage or restraint of labour or vehicles (including the Master, Officers or Crew) whether partial or general. The Charterers to be responsible for loss or damage caused to the Vessel or to the Owners by goods being loaded contrary to the terms of the Charter or by improper or careless bunkering or loading, stowing or discharging of goods or any other improper or negligent act on their part or that of their servants.'

As Lord Denning MR pointed out in his judgment in *Nippon Yusen Kaisha v Acme Shipping Corp* the clause contains four separate sentences. But, while each sentence falls to be analysed in detail, each must also be related to the others so as to construe cl 13 as a whole. To say that the grammar of these four sentences, and indeed the drafting, is in many places sadly defective and that on any view there is surplusage at various points in the clause does not solve the problems of construction but merely adds seriously to their complication. Unhappily bad grammar, bad drafting and verbal surplusage are common features in the drafting of clauses in charters. I should mention that the words 'or vehicles' in the third sentence had been added to the printed form in type, no doubt because of the cargo which it was known that the charterers intended to load and carry, but that addition cannot affect the construction of cl 13 as a whole.

I now turn to consider each of the four sentences in detail and I begin by breaking the first sentence down into its component parts as follows:

'The Owners only to be responsible

    (1) for delay in the delivery of the Vessel or
    (2) for delay during the currency of the Charter and
    (3) for loss or damage to goods onboard,

if such delay or loss has been caused by

    (a) want of due diligence on the part of (i) the Owners or (ii) their Manager in making the Vessel seaworthy and fitted for the voyage or
    (b) any other personal act or omission or default of (i) the Owners or (ii) their Manager.'

Three observations fall to be made on the first sentence which I have broken down in this way. First, it is clear that it is referring to and only to two types of delay and one type of loss or damage, namely loss or damage to goods on board, a type of loss and damage which in the context is plainly intended to be physical. Second, this sentence says that the owners will 'only' be 'responsible', ie 'legally liable', if either of those two types of delay or that single type of loss or damage is due to one or other of the causes specified in (a) or (b) above, namely (a) want of due diligence on the part of either the owners or their manager in making the vessel seaworthy or (b) any other personal act or omission or default of either of them. In short, as is emphasised by the position at the outset of the sentence of the adverb 'only', the first sentence is directed to and only to legal liability for two particular types of delay and one particular type of physical loss or damage due to one or other of those causes. For those matters the owners expressly accept 'responsibility', ie 'legal liability'.

My Lords, it follows that the first sentence only deals with those matters for which liability will be accepted. It does not, expressly at least, deal with those other matters for which liability is to be excluded. If cl 13 finished at the end of the first sentence, in my view the owners would not have protected themselves against 'responsibility', ie 'legal liability', for other types of delay or for other physical loss or damage due to causes other than those to which I have already referred. This further protection is therefore sought in the second sentence.

I turn to break down the second sentence in the same way as I have broken down the first:

'The Owners not to be responsible

    (1) in any other case nor
    (2) for damage or delay whatsoever and howsoever caused even if caused by the neglect or default of their servants.'

It will be seen at once that whereas the first sentence speaks in the same printed line (line 96) of 'loss or damage' in one place and only of 'loss' in another, the second sentence (line 99) does not mention 'loss' at all but only 'damage'. Moreover, the use of the conjunction 'nor' in the second sentence is ungrammatical as a means of linking together the two parts of the second sentence. If one construes the words 'in any other case' literally, the second part of the second sentence and indeed the whole of the third *a* sentence, to which I will refer shortly, become surplusage because on that view there would necessarily be no other 'case' liability for which is not already excluded. Moreover, such a literal construction would mean, as my noble and learned friend Lord Brandon pointed out during the argument, that the owners would be under no liability if they never delivered the vessel at all for service under the charter or delivered a vessel of a totally different description from that stipulated in the preamble. *b*

My Lords, I cannot think that this can be right. Some limitation must be read into the first part of the second sentence. If for the moment one ignores the words beginning with 'nor', the natural construction of the phrase 'in any other case' is 'in any other case of delay in the delivery of the vessel or during the currency of the charter or of loss or damage to goods on board' or, to put the same point more shortly, 'in any other such case'. My noble and learned friend Lord Keith observed during argument that the same *c* point can equally well be made by putting a punctuation mark before the word 'nor', e g a full stop, a colon or a semicolon, without doing any violence to the language used. But what of the words from 'nor' onwards? These ensuing words suggest to my mind that the draftsman feared that if the words 'in any other case' stood alone it might be suggested that they were neither clear nor strong enough to exclude liability for damage or delay or at least when caused by the negligence of the owners' own servants. The introduction *d* of the words 'whatsoever' and 'howsoever caused' makes use of one of the classic methods of ensuring that liability for the relevant damage or delay is intended to be excluded, especially when the words 'howsoever caused' are reinforced by the express reference to the negligence of the owners' own servants.

It is, I think, against this background that the word 'damage' must be construed in the second part of the second sentence. If I am right in thinking that the first part of the *e* second sentence means 'in any such case as has been mentioned in the first sentence', then the second part of the second sentence is also directed to the same type of 'damage' or 'delay' as is referred to in the first sentence, ie delay in delivery or during the currency of the voyage and 'damage' (which must, I think, in the context of these two sentences include 'loss') to goods on board. In short the first two sentences are linked and must be related to the same subject matter of delay and loss or damage to goods on board brought *f* about by one or more of the several causes respectively mentioned in these two sentences. Further, as counsel for the charterers pointed out, if 'damage' includes financial loss or damage there is no need for the apparent dichotomy between 'delay' and 'damage' since all delay must lead to financial loss of some kind.

I turn to the third sentence. This reads:

> 'The Owners not to be liable for loss or damage arising or resulting from strikes, *g* lock-outs or stoppage or restraint of labour or vehicles (including the Master, Officers or Crew) whether partial or general.'

No detailed breakdown of the third sentence is required. Counsel for the owners relied strongly on this sentence and also on the fourth sentence as supporting his construction of 'damage' in the second part of the second sentence. The third sentence is clearly *h* required to give the owners protection in the case of loss or damage arising or resulting from strikes etc, these being risks which have not been excluded by the first two sentences. I unreservedly accept that 'loss or damage' in the third sentence includes financial as well as physical loss or damage. But before considering the significance of this it will be convenient to refer to the fourth sentence, which reads:

> 'The Charterers to be responsible for loss or damage caused to the Vessel or to the *j* Owners by goods being loaded contrary to the terms of the Charter or by improper or careless bunkering or loading, stowing or discharging of goods or any other improper or negligent act on their part or that of their servants.'

While the first three sentences of cl 13 are concerned with stating for what the owners will and will not be liable, the fourth sentence is concerned with the positive assertion of

those matters for which the charterers are to be liable. Having regard to the obligations
a imposed on the charterers by, in particular, cl 4, to which I need not refer in detail but
which requires the charterers to provide and pay for many things including bunkers and
loading and discharging, I doubt whether the fourth sentence of cl 13 imposes greater
liabilities than would in any event fall on the charterers either under the charter or at
common law.

The strength of the argument of counsel for the owners undoubtedly lies in the fact
b that in the third and fourth sentences the phrase 'loss or damage' clearly includes financial
as well as physical loss or damage. Not only is this plain from the context of the third
sentence but in the fourth sentence the phrase 'loss or damage caused to the Vessel *or to
the Owners* (my emphasis)' strongly reinforces this meaning.

Counsel for the owners pointed out that if the construction of the first two sentences
and in particular of the second sentence which I have adumbrated were correct, this
c House would be construing the relevant phrases in a different sense in different parts of
the same clause. It is of course a proper canon of construction that the same words or the
same phrases should where possible be given the same meaning in the same clause, but
that canon must always yield to particular contexts. The crucial question is whether the
words 'damage or delay' in the second part of the second sentence take their colour from
the first or from the third and fourth sentences. On no view can the same meaning be
d given to 'loss or damage' in the third and fourth sentences as in the first sentence, where
the phrase is unquestionably confined to physical loss or damage to goods on board.

If I am right in thinking the second sentence is directed to matters not covered by the
first, it follows that looking at cl 13 as a whole the more natural construction of the
second sentence is to treat it as looking back to the first rather than as looking forward to
the third and fourth sentences. Counsel for the owners is no doubt right in saying that
e the second sentence widens the protection given by the first, since it covers matters not
expressly covered by the first. But he properly conceded that no distinction could be
made between 'loss' in line 96 and 'damage' in line 99. Once it has become clear that on
no view can the critical phrase be given the same meaning in the first as in the third and
fourth sentences and once this concession is made, any argument founded on the need
for consistent construction throughout the whole clause necessarily loses its force.

f My Lords, the principles applicable to the construction of exceptions clauses in charters
have long been established. I need only refer to the well-known judgments of Brett MR
and Bowen LJ almost exactly one hundred years ago in *Burton & Co v English & Co* (1883)
12 QBD 218 at 220, 222. One quotation from Bowen LJ's judgment will suffice:

g 'There is . . . another rule of construction which one would bring to bear upon
this charterparty, and that is, that one must see if this stipulation which we have got
to construe is introduced by way of exception or in favour of one of the parties to
the contract, and if so, we must take care not to give it an extension beyond what is
fairly necessary, because those who wish to introduce words in a contract in order to
shield themselves ought to do so in clear words.'

These are the principles I have applied to the question of construction, and applying
h them, still without regard to any of the decided cases, I find myself unable to construe cl
13 as a whole and in particular the second sentence as protecting the owners against
liability for the breach of cl 26 which in the umpire's and in the judge's views they
undoubtedly committed.

My Lords, against this background I turn to consider the decided cases. Is there
anything in them which should lead to a different conclusion? The first relevant decision
j is *Istros (owner) v F W Dahlstroem & Co* [1931] 1 KB 247, a decision of Wright J. This was
not a case of damage but of delay caused by the master being in breach of his obligation
to prosecute the voyage with 'utmost dispatch' (cf cl 9 of the present form). The charterers
withheld time charter hire. The owners claimed that hire. The umpire held that the
owners were protected by what was then cl 12, now cl 13, of the charter because the
delay was not caused by any personal act, omission or default of the owners or their
managers. Wright J upheld the award. It is to be noted that the charterers did not appear

to attack the award. This decision is, if I may say so with respect, plainly correct. The judge was only concerned with delay during the currency of the charterparty. He was *a* not concerned with anything akin to the present problem. I see nothing in that decision, which has stood unquestioned for half a century, which either is open to criticism or affects the present case.

Chronologically the next case is some thirty years later, *The Helvetia-S* [1960] 1 Lloyd's Rep 540, a decision of Pearson J. The facts of that case are so far removed from the present that I need spend no time on it. It is enough to record that the judge in a brief passage *b* rejected an argument that cl 13 protected the owners (see [1960] 1 Lloyd's Rep 540 at 548–549). I see no reason to doubt the correctness of his view.

By a strange coincidence, some six weeks later *Westfal-Larsen & Co A/S v Colonial Sugar Refining Co Ltd* [1960] 2 Lloyd's Rep 206 was decided by Walsh J in the Supreme Court of New South Wales. The plaintiff shipowners claimed general average contribution from the defendant charterers, who set up the not unusual defence of unseaworthiness, to *c* which the owners riposted by reliance on cl 13. It is to be observed that the claim was not one for loss of or damage to cargo but arose because of the inability of the vessel to maintain proper steam by reason of bunker trouble which it seems was the fault of the chief engineer.

My Lords, the judge upheld the owners' contention. I will not lengthen this speech with full quotations from his careful judgment (the relevant parts of which appear at *d* [1960] 2 Lloyd's Rep 210–211). Suffice it to say that, not without obvious and stated hesitation, he construed the first sentence of cl 13 as exhaustive and as confining the whole area of responsibility to one of personal default. Thus on his view, as he said, the second and third sentences were unnecessary. But in his view the second sentence was designed to emphasise the exhaustive character of the first. He also relied on the word 'only'. *e*

But, my Lords, with profound respect to the judge, in construing the first sentence not only has he misunderstood the significance of the word 'only' in the position in which it appears in the clause but he appears to have treated the words 'or any other personal act' etc as standing on their own instead of as related together with the immediately preceding words to the two cases of delay and the single case of loss or damage to goods on board, brought about by either of the two specified causes to which I have already drawn *f* attention. I fear that the judge misconstrued the clause and that he should have held that it did not protect the owners in the events which had happened.

My Lords, the next decision is that of McNair J in *Gesellschaft Burgerlichen Rechts v Stockholms Rederiaktiebolag SVEA, The Brabant* [1966] 1 All ER 961, [1967] 1 QB 588. It was a complicated case in which the owners sought to rely on cl 13 but failed since the judge held that a special typed clause, cl 28, must be treated as prevailing over cl 13. Mr *g* Michael Kerr QC for the charterers had sought to argue in the alternative that independently of that special clause, cl 13 did not protect the owners and that the *Westfal-Larsen* case was wrongly decided. The judge rejected this argument, stating that the construction put on the clause by Walsh J had been correct (see [1966] 1 All ER 961 at 967, [1967] 1 QB 588 at 604). My Lords, for the reasons which I have already given when venturing to criticise the reasoning of Walsh J, I think, with respect, that McNair J was *h* wrong in what he said, though I am not suggesting that on the construction of that particular charterparty the decision was in any way wrong.

My Lords, in *Cosmos Bulk Transport Inc v China National Foreign Trade Transportation Inc* [1978] 1 All ER 322 the effect of cl 13 again arose in circumstances which made it unnecessary for the judge, Mocatta J, to express a final view on it. He said that he 'willingly' accepted what had been said in the *Westfal-Larsen* case and in *The Brabant* about *j* the clause (see [1978] 1 All ER 322 at 335). Since I have already criticised the former decision and the relevant passage in the latter I do not think it necessary to refer further to this case.

Finally I turn to *Nippon Yusen Kaisha v Acme Shipping Corp* [1972] 1 All ER 35, [1972] 1 WLR 74, to which I have already referred. There the matter came first of all before Mocatta J and then before the Court of Appeal on a motion to set aside an award for error *a* of law on its face on the ground that the umpire had been wrong in holding that the owners were protected by 'the exemption clause in the charterparty'. That exemption clause was not set out in the award though it was admitted to be cl 13. The charterers claimed damages for delay and also for certain expenses caused by the master wrongly refusing to enter a port in Nicaragua. The claim failed because of cl 13. The question was whether the second sentence of cl 13 protected the owners against claims for financial as well as for physical loss and damage. All the members of the Court of Appeal agreed

b with Mocatta J that the clause did so protect the owners (see the rival arguments summarised by Lord Denning MR and by myself at [1972] 1 All ER 38, 40, [1972] 1 WLR 78, 80).

My Lords, it is I hope always proper to admit to judicial error and I must now do so. Having had the benefit of the further detailed consideration of cl 13 in the present case and been able closely to analyse it afresh, and having perhaps for the first time fully

c appreciated the significance of the position of the word 'only' in the first sentence, a point seemingly not made in argument in the Court of Appeal in *Nippon Yusen Kaisha v Acme Shipping Corp*, I accept that I reached the wrong conclusion. Whether if the charterers' argument on 'damage' had been accepted, as it should have been, the owners could have escaped under cl 13 on the ground of 'delay during the currency of the charter' for reasons analagous to those which prevailed in *Istros (owner) v F W Dahlstroem & Co* was a

d matter left undecided by the Court of Appeal and it is not now necessary to express any view on that point.

Having thus considered the authorities in some detail I conclude that there is nothing in any of them which would lead me to a different conclusion from that which I have reached solely on the language of cl 13. It follows that on its true construction cl 13 does not in any event afford the owners a defence to the present claim by the charterers. I

e therefore respectfully agree with the conclusion reached by Mr Kent and by Bingham J and equally respectfully disagree with the conclusions of the Court of Appeal.

But, my Lords, there is a second reason why I would reach the same conclusion. I can deal with this more briefly. Even had I reached a different conclusion on construction and had felt able to accept the submissions of counsel for the owners, I would still have rejected his submissions that there was no relevant limitation on what he contended was

f the natural meaning and scope of cl 13. He submitted that since there was no express limitation in the clause none should be implied, at any rate where the complaint was of a breach of warranty relating to the vessel's description. Pressed to state whether he contended that cl 13 applied even where the owners failed wholly to deliver the vessel, he understandably shrank from carrying his argument to that length. He suggested there were two limitations. The first was where there was personal default by the owners

g or their manager, for which the clause on his construction expressly dealt. He contrasted this with what he called 'misfortune risks', a somewhat strange phrase the ambit of which must be necessarily uncertain but by which I understood him to mean any liability alleged to arise otherwise than by reason of such personal default. The other was repudiatory breach. By this I understood him to mean breach of such a character as would enable the innocent party without more to rescind the charter. So far as the

h submission regarding repudiatory breach is concerned, it is trite law that an innocent party is not obliged to rescind. If the innocent party were to refuse to rescind and if the submission of counsel for the owners on the construction of cl 13 were correct, I find it difficult to see why the innocent party's claim for damages would not be barred by the clause, while if he did rescind and sought in addition to claim damages the former remedy would be available but not the latter.

j My Lords, with all respect I am unable to accept either of these submissions. Though counsel for the owners invited your Lordships' attention to certain passages in the speeches in this House both in *Suisse Atlantique Société d'Armement Maritime SA v NV Rotterdamsche Kolen Centrale* [1966] 2 All ER 61, [1967] 1 AC 361 and in *Photo Production Ltd v Securicor Transport Ltd* [1980] 1 All ER 556, [1980] AC 827, I cannot find in either of those decisions any support for his contentions and I do not think it necessary to discuss those cases further. In truth, if cl 13 were to be construed so as to allow a breach of the warranties as to description in cl 26 to be committed or a failure to deliver the vessel at all to take place without financial redress to the charterers, the charter virtually *a* ceases to be a contract for the letting of the vessel and the performance of services by the owners, their master, officers and crew in consideration of the payment of time charter hire and becomes no more than a statement of intent by the owners in return for which the charterers are obliged to pay large sums by way of hire, though if the owners fail to carry out their promises as to description or delivery they are entitled to nothing in lieu. I find it difficult to believe that this can accord with the true common intention of the *b* parties and I do not think that this conclusion can accord with the true construction of the charter in which the parties in the present case are supposed to have expressed that true common intention in writing.

For all these reasons I would allow this appeal with costs in this House and below and restore the order of Bingham J upholding Mr Kent's original award.

c

LORD BRANDON OF OAKBROOK. My Lords, I have had the advantage of reading in draft the speech prepared by my noble and learned friend Lord Roskill. I agree with it, and for the reasons which he gives I would allow the appeal and make the other orders proposed by him.

Appeal allowed. *d*

Solicitors: *Ingledew Brown Bennison & Garrett* (for the charterers); *Clyde & Co* (for the owners).

Mary Rose Plummer   Barrister.

e

Customs and Excise Commissioners v Viva Gas Appliances Ltd

HOUSE OF LORDS *f*

LORD DIPLOCK, LORD FRASER OF TULLYBELTON, LORD SCARMAN AND LORD BRIDGE OF HARWICH
1, 24 NOVEMBER 1983

Value added tax – Zero-rating – Building works – Alteration of building – What amounts to 'alteration' – Whether any limitation on what work to fabric of building may amount to 'alteration' – Finance Act 1972, Sch 4, Group 8, item 2. *g*

On the true construction of item 2[a] of Group 8 of Sch 4 to the Finance Act 1972 'alteration' of any building covers all work to the fabric of the building which falls short of complete erection or complete demolition except that which is so small or trivial as to be ignored as de minimis (see p 115 *g* and p 116 *d e* and *h* to p 117 *a*, post).

Customs and Excise Comrs v Smitmit Design Centre Ltd [1982] STC 525 disapproved. *h*

Notes

For zero-rating of supplies in connection with the alteration of buildings, see 12 Halsbury's Laws (4th edn) para 912.

For the Finance Act 1972, Sch 4, Group 8, item 2, see 42 Halsbury's Statutes (3rd edn) 219, but note that with effect from 4 September 1978 Sch 4 to the 1972 Act was *j* substituted by the Value Added Tax (Consolidation) Order 1978, SI 1978/1064, art 3 and Sch 1.

As from 26 October 1982 item 2 of Group 8 of Sch 4 to the 1972 Act was replaced by item 2 of Group 8 of Sch 5 to the Value Added Tax Act 1983.

---

a Item 2 is set out at p 113 *f*, post

Cases referred to in opinions

a *ACT Construction Ltd v Customs and Excise Comrs* [1982] 1 All ER 84, [1981] 1 WLR 1542, HL.

Customs and Excise Comrs v Morrison Dunbar Ltd [1979] STC 406.

Customs and Excise Comrs v Smitmit Design Centre Ltd, Customs and Excise Comrs v Sharp's Bedroom Design Ltd [1982] STC 525.

Pearlman v Keepers and Governors of Harrow School [1979] 1 All ER 365, [1979] QB 56,

b   [1978] 3 WLR 736, CA.

Appeal

Viva Gas Appliances Ltd (the taxpayer company) appealed, with the leave of the House of Lords granted on 23 June 1983, against an order of the Court of Appeal (Waller, Dunn and Slade LJJ) ([1983] STC 388) on 22 March 1983 reversing the decision of Forbes J

c ([1982] STC 706) on 16 June 1982 dismissing the Crown's appeal against a decision of a value added tax tribunal sitting at Manchester (chairman Mr F C Shepherd) on 3 November 1981 whereby it was found that works carried out by the taxpayer company qualified for zero-rating as alteration of a building under the Finance Act 1972, Sch 4, Group 8, item 2. The facts are set out in the opinion of Lord Diplock.

d *Philip Lawton QC* and *Stephen J Allcock* for the taxpayer company.
Simon D Brown and *Andrew Collins* for the Crown.

Their Lordships took time for consideration.

24 November. The following opinions were delivered.

e

LORD DIPLOCK. My Lords, this appeal brought by leave of this House provides the second occasion within two years on which your Lordships have had to consider the meaning of some ordinary English words used in Sch 4 to the Finance Act 1972 to describe services, the supply of which is zero-rated under s 12 of that Act.

The words in question are those which I have italicised in the description of item 2 in

f Group 8 in the schedule, a group which bears the heading 'Construction of Buildings etc'. Item 2 reads:

'The supply, *in the course of the construction, alteration or demolition of any building* or of any civil engineering work, of any services other than the services of an architect, surveyor or any person acting as consultant or in a supervisory capacity.'

g In *ACT Construction Ltd v Customs and Excise Comrs* [1982] 1 All ER 84 at 87, [1981] 1 WLR 1542 at 1545–1546 Lord Roskill, with whose speech the other four members of the Appellate Committee expressed their complete agreement, approved the interpretation which had been put on the words by Neill J in the following passage in his judgment in *Customs and Excise Comrs v Morrison Dunbar Ltd* [1979] STC 406 at 413:

'In dealing with a case to which item 2 of Group 8 is said to apply, I consider that

h one should first look to see whether the supply of the services in question is a supply in the course of the construction, alteration or demolition of a building. Each of these words is important and should be given its proper weight. The word "alteration", it is to be noted, is found between "construction" and "demolition" and it follows, in my view, that the alteration to which item 2 applies is an alteration *of the building* and therefore one which involves some structural alteration.' (Neill J's

j emphasis.)

The *ACT Construction* case involved also a question whether the work with which that case was dealing was a 'work of repair or maintenance' and so excluded from item 2 of Group 8 by note (2)(a) even if it would otherwise have fallen within it; but that is not a matter that arises in the instant case.

The work undertaken by the taxpayer company in the instant case which it claims is entitled to be zero-rated consisted of the installation of gas fires in substitution for coal-burning fireplaces in old houses.

The following is a description by the value added tax tribunal of the general nature of the work involved in the provision of the services with which this appeal is concerned, together with that tribunal's decision whether the work fell within Group 8, item 2:

'The works fall into a number of categories.

First, there were cases in which a gas appliance was fitted to a flue which already existed and which had either been used or was designed to be used for the consumption of solid fuel. In such cases it would be necessary to break out the fireclay fireback, which had been built into the fireplace in such a way as to become an integral part of it and had no possibility of being removed otherwise than by its total demolition ... Clearly some degree of structural work or demolition was involved ... We consider that the degree of alteration was sufficient ... to be regarded as an alteration to the building which was the house.

The second group of operations was the fixing of a fire in front of such an opening. This involved the connecting of the fire to the end of a pipe outlet newly connected to the meter or pre-existing. Behind the fire was a plate held to the wall by adhesive tape or alternatively there might be a fire surround in which the necessary opening had been cut, and into either of which the spigot of the fire flue was inserted. Such a fire surround would be held to the wall by up to six fixing plates. We do not consider that either of these operations of itself involved an adequate degree of alteration to a building to satisfy the test, but we do consider that it was nevertheless inseparable from the operation described in the preceding paragraph, in cases to which that paragraph applied.

Thirdly, in some of these installations gas supplies had to be brought by running pipes through walls and under floors from the position of the meter.

The length of the pipe run could not be precisely established from any documentation, but we hold that provided it was substantial in length and not merely minimal extension of an existing supply, it would satisfy the criteria.'

The tribunal's decision, from which these passages are quoted, was delivered shortly before, and thus without the benefit of, the judgment of this House in the *ACT Construction* case.

The Commissioners of Customs and Excise appealed to the High Court from this decision under s 13 of the Tribunals and Inquiries Act 1971 and RSC Ord 55. Such an appeal lies only on a point of law and Ord 55, r 3(2) requires the grounds of appeal to be stated in the originating motion by which the appeal is brought.

In the instant case the identification of the error of law alleged to have been made by the tribunal could hardly have been expressed in terms more Delphic than those appearing in the originating summons. It said:

'... the said Tribunal erred in Law in holding 1. That the works undertaken in the course of the installation of gas fires amounted to a supply of services in the course of an alteration to [sic] the buildings into which the said fires had been installed. 2. That the said supplies were chargeable to tax at the zero rate.'

This left to counsel for the Crown untrammelled scope to argue in favour of whatever glosses he thought fit to place on the statutory words that fall to be construed. It would appear from the judgment of Forbes J, by whom the appeal was heard in the High Court ([1982] STC 706), that the preferred glosses, all three of which were cumulative were: that the alteration of the structure or fabric of the building must (1) be 'substantial in relation to the building as a whole', (2) 'have some degree of permanence' and (3) be 'irreversible'. However, the two latter glosses, whatever additional problems of interpretation they might themselves pose, need not detain your Lordships. They do not appear to have been persisted in on the Crown's appeal to the Court of Appeal, nor do they find any place in the printed case lodged on behalf of the Crown as respondent to the further appeal to this House.

Forbes J rejected all three suggested glosses; and it is instructive to see from his
judgment how the argument addressed to him in favour of gloss (1), with which alone
your Lordships are concerned, was developed. It provides an object lesson in the misuse
of judicial statements made in contexts that are dissimilar.

The adjective 'structural' as qualifying the noun 'alteration' does not itself appear at all
in the statutory words to be construed. It is a qualification that is derived from the
context in which the noun appeared and might equally well have been expressed by
some such words as 'alteration to the fabric' of the building. The expression 'structural
alteration' had, however, been incorporated in an earlier statute passed for a wholly
different purpose, the Leasehold Reform Act 1967, where the context in which the
expression was to be found is 'any improvement made [sc to a dwelling house held on a
long lease] by the execution of works amounting to structural alteration, extension or
addition'. In *Pearlman v Keepers and Governors of Harrow School* [1979] 1 All ER 365 at
373, [1979] QB 56 at 72 Geoffrey Lane LJ had expressed the opinion that, in the context
of that Act, the word 'structural' meant 'something which involves the fabric of the house
as opposed to the provision merely of a piece of equipment'. In fact the relevant alteration
to the fabric of the house in *Pearlman*'s case, which consisted of the installation of a
complete new central heating system, involved major alterations to the walls, floors and
ceilings of the house, so little importance can be attached, even in the context of the
Leasehold Reform Act 1967, to the Lord Justice's inclusion of the adjective 'substantial'
in his subsequent remark: '. . . if there is any substantial alteration, extension or addition
to the fabric of the house the words of the schedule are satisfied.' Neither of the other
members of the court in *Pearlman*'s case (Lord Denning MR and Eveleigh LJ) made any
reference to the need that the alteration, extension or addition should be substantial.

Pearlman's case was cited in argument in *Customs and Excise Comrs v Smitmit Design
Centre Ltd* [1982] STC 525, a decision of Glidewell J reached after the judgment of this
House in the *ACT Construction* case. Glidewell J accepted that the alteration must affect
the structure of the building to some material extent, by which I take it he meant that
the effect on the structure must not be so slight or trivial that the court is obliged to
ignore its very existence under the rule of law expressed in the latin maxim de minimis
non curat lex. Glidewell J, however, went on to lay down a further criterion, borrowed
without acknowledgment from Geoffrey Lane LJ's judgment in *Pearlman*'s case. Secondly,
he said (at 534): '. . . the alteration must be substantial in relation to the building as a
whole.' He gave no reason for this proposition, which was clearly intended to lay down a
test for qualifying for zero-rating under item 2 that was more difficult to satisfy than
that which the de minimis rule itself imports.

Forbes J in the instant case was unable to find any warrant for the imposition of this
second and more severe criterion in the statutory words in item 2. Nor, with respect, can
I. If the alteration to the fabric of the building satisfies the de minimis rule I can see no
reason why it should not fall within the statutory description 'alteration . . . of any
building' whether the extent to which it falls outside that rule be great or small.

From the judgment of Forbes J upholding the tribunal's decision, the Crown appealed
to the Court of Appeal. That court (Waller, Dunn and Slade LJJ) in a unanimous
judgment allowed the appeal (see [1983] STC 388). After noting that in item 2 the phrase
'of the building' is not followed by any words such as 'or any part or parts thereof', the
ratio decidendi of the court was epitomised in the following two sentences (at 392):

'The conjunction of the words "construction" of a building, "demolition" of a
building and "alteration" of a building indicates that the kind of alteration must not
only be structural but not unlike construction or demolition and therefore should
be substantial, i e in relation to a building be more than a minimal alteration of the
building. If the work is to qualify as an "alteration" it must be sufficiently substantial
in relation to the relevant building as a whole that it can properly be described as an
"alteration *of the building*".' (The Court of Appeal's emphasis.)

My Lords, the last sentence in the passage from the court's judgment that I have cited
would appear at first sight to import an element of proportionality between the

magnitude of the piece of work carried out on its fabric that is relied on as an 'alteration' of the building and the size of the building on whose fabric that work has been done. But any such intention is promptly disavowed, because the judgment goes on (at 392):

> 'We do not suggest that a piece of work, which would be alteration of a small building, would not also be alteration of a large building. It is the nature and substance of the work which indicates whether or not it would amount to alteration of a building.'

My Lords, I cannot with great respect follow the logic of the reasoning contained in the passages from the Court of Appeal's judgment that I have cited. The maxim noscitur a sociis may be a useful aid to statutory interpretation, but the contexts in which it is applicable are limited. In the case of a word which is capable of bearing various shades of meaning, the fact that it is included in a list of words of greater precision in which some common characteristic can be discerned may enable one to say that the chameleon word takes it colour from those other words and of its possible meanings bears that which shares the characteristic that is common to the other. But here the socii relied on by the Court of Appeal, 'construction' and 'demolition', have no common colour for 'alteration', which is sandwiched between them, to take. 'Demolition' far from sharing a common characteristic with 'construction' is its antithesis. Once what constitutes the relevant 'building' has been identified, 'construction', as the Court of Appeal had earlier pointed out, in the absence of any reference to 'part of a building', means erecting the building as a whole and 'demolition' means destroying it as a whole, so 'alteration' is left to cover all works to the fabric of the building which fall short of complete erection or complete demolition. I can see no ground on which the meaning of the ordinary English word 'alteration' qualified by the adjectival phrase 'of any building' should be construed as excluding any work on the fabric of the building except that which is so slight or trivial as to attract the application of the de minimis rule.

My Lords, it is evident from the passages that I have already quoted from the decision of the tribunal relating to the first three groups of alterations that the tribunal had firmly in their minds the de minimis rule and had reached the conclusion that it did not apply to the services supplied by the taxpayer company that were the subject of the appeal to them, although it would have had the effect of excluding from item 2 what the tribunal referred to as the second group of operations if these had not formed, in the tribunal's view, an inseparable part of the first category of works undertaken by the taxpayer company. Parenthetically it is worth while pointing out that in the last paragraph of their decision that I have quoted it is plain that the tribunal are using the chameleon word 'substantial' as the antonym of 'merely minimal', ie as something that is not so slight or trivial as to attract the application of the de minimis rule.

It has not been contended before your Lordships that the services supplied by the taxpayer company did not involve *some* alteration to the fabric of the houses in which the work was undertaken; nor, if the only other condition that must be fulfilled to qualify the work for zero-rating is that the de minimis rule should not compel its exclusion from item 2, has it been contended on behalf of the Crown that the conclusion that the de minimis rule did not apply to the services that were the subject of the appeal to the tribunal was one that no reasonable tribunal properly instructed as to the law could have reached. So it was not open to the High Court to hold that the tribunal had erred in point of law.

For these reasons I would allow the appeal and restore the order of Forbes J.

LORD FRASER OF TULLYBELTON. My Lords, I have had the advantage of reading in draft the speech of my noble and learned friend Lord Diplock. I entirely agree with it and, for the reasons stated in it, I would allow this appeal.

LORD SCARMAN. My Lords, I have had the advantage of reading in advance a draft of the speech delivered by my noble and learned friend Lord Diplock. For the reasons he gives I also would allow the appeal and restore the order of Forbes J.

LORD BRIDGE OF HARWICH. My Lords, for the reasons given in the speech of
my noble and learned friend Lord Diplock, I too would allow this appeal.

Appeal allowed.

Solicitors: *Solicitor for the Customs and Excise*; *Speechly Bircham*, agents for *Simpson &
Ashworth*, Accrington (for the taxpayer company).

Mary Rose Plummer   Barrister.

Dimbleby & Sons Ltd v National Union of Journalists

COURT OF APPEAL, CIVIL DIVISION

SIR JOHN DONALDSON MR, GRIFFITHS AND STEPHEN BROWN LJJ

28, 29 NOVEMBER, 1, 6 DECEMBER 1983

*Trade dispute – Acts done in contemplation or furtherance of trade dispute – In contemplation or
furtherance of – Secondary action in furtherance of dispute – Validity of secondary action –
Contract for supply of goods or services between employer who is party to dispute and employer
to whom secondary action relates – Goods or services supplied to subsidiary company of employer
who was party to dispute – Union action aimed at disrupting supply of goods or services to
subsidiary company – Whether secondary action by union immune from action in tort – Trade
Union and Labour Relations Act 1974, s 13(1) – Employment Act 1980, s 17(3).*

In 1979 a newspaper publishing company (TBF Ltd) refused to re-engage a number of
journalists which it had dismissed for taking strike action. The journalists, some of
whom remained unemployed and in dispute with TBF Ltd over its refusal to re-engage
them, were members of the defendant union. Thereafter the union blacked TBF Ltd and
instructed its members to refuse to work for or to supply copy to TBF Ltd, which
nevertheless continued to publish newspapers, which were printed by an associated
company, TBF (Printers) Ltd. The plaintiffs were the sellers and distributors of a number
of local newspapers published by two subsidiary companies. In August 1983 the plaintiffs
entered into a contract with TBF (Printers) Ltd to print their newspapers. Those
journalists employed by the plaintiffs who were members of the defendant union refused
to supply copy to the plaintiffs for printing by TBF (Printers) Ltd on the grounds that
TBF Ltd had been blacked by their union and their refusal to comply with that blacking
would result in their expulsion from the union. The plaintiffs then suspended the
journalists and issued a writ seeking injunctions restraining the union from (i) inducing
its members to breach their contracts of employment with the plaintiffs and (ii)
interfering with the plaintiffs' contract with TBF (Printers) Ltd. The plaintiffs also sought
interlocutory relief in similar terms. The judge granted the interlocutory injunctions
sought and the union appealed, contending, inter alia, that it was immune, under s 13(1)[a]
of the Trade Union and Labour Relations Act 1974, from action in tort by the plaintiffs
because its actions were taken 'in contemplation or furtherance of a trade dispute' in
relation to either the plaintiffs' journalists or the TBF Ltd journalists, since the plaintiffs'
journalists' dispute was a dispute between workers and their employer relating wholly or
mainly to terms and conditions of employment or the workers' suspension or dismissal
or the allocation of work between workers and was therefore a 'trade dispute' as defined
by s 29(1)(a), (b) or (c)[b], while the TBF Ltd journalists' dispute was a 'trade dispute' as

---

a   Section 13(1) is set out at p 123 *d*, post
b   Section 29(1) is set out at p 123 *f g*, post

defined by s 29(1)(*b*) by virtue of being a dispute over the non-engagement of workers by their employer. The plaintiffs contended that any immunity from action which the union might otherwise have enjoyed by virtue of s 13(1) had been removed by s 17^c of the Employment Act 1980 because the union's action amounted to unlawful secondary action since the contract which the union was seeking to disrupt was not a contract for the supply of goods or services 'between an employer who is a party to the dispute [ie TBF Ltd] and the employer under the contract of employment to which the secondary action relates [ie the plaintiffs]'.

Held – (1) On the evidence, it was seriously arguable that the plaintiffs had a cause of action at common law against the union for unlawfully inducing the plaintiffs' journalists to break their contracts of employment, unlawfully interfering with the contract between the plaintiffs and TBF (Printers) Ltd and unlawfully interfering with the contracts between the plaintiffs and their advertisers by hindering the performance of those contracts (see p 122 *b* to *d* and *g* to *j*, p 123 *a* to *c*, p 126 *a* to *c* and *e* to *h* and p 127 *j* to p 128 *b* and *g*, post); dictum of Lord Diplock in *Merkur Island Shipping Corp v Laughton* [1983] 2 All ER at 195 applied.

(2) The dispute between the plaintiffs and their journalists was not a 'trade dispute' within s 29(1) of the 1974 Act because it was concerned neither with the terms and conditions of the journalists' employment, nor with the allocation of work between workers employed by the same employer (since the allocation objected to was the allocation of printing work to the employees of another employer, TBF (Printers) Ltd), nor with the suspension or termination of the workers' employment (since the dispute did not relate wholly or mainly to the suspension or dismissal of the plaintiffs' journalists but to the decision by the plaintiffs to use TBF (Printers) Ltd as their printers). However, the dispute between TBF Ltd and its journalists was a 'trade dispute' for the purposes of s 29(1) since it was a dispute between an employer and its ex-workers concerning the employer's refusal to re-engage them. The union's action had therefore been taken 'in furtherance of a trade dispute' within s 13(1) (see p 123 *h j*, p 127 *b* to *j* and p 128 *g*, post).

(3) However, any immunity which the union might otherwise have had under s 13(1) of the 1974 Act had been removed by s 17 of the 1980 Act and not saved by s 17(3) because s 17(3) only saved secondary action from being actionable in tort where the contract which the union sought to disrupt was between 'an employer who is a party to the dispute' and the employer under the contract of employment to which the secondary action related, whereas on the facts the employer who was a party to the dispute was TBF Ltd (and not TBF (Printers) Ltd) and it was the contract between the plaintiffs and TBF (Printers) Ltd (and not TBF Ltd) for the supply of goods and services (ie journalists' copy) that the union was seeking to disrupt. Accordingly, the plaintiffs' cause of action at common law in respect of the interferences with their contractual rights by the union's unlawful secondary action had been restored by s 17 of the 1980 Act and they were entitled to the interlocutory relief sought. The union's appeal would therefore be dismissed (see p 124 *a* to *g*, p 125 *b* to *h* and p 128 *c* to *g*, post).

Notes
For the legal liability of trade unions, see Supplement to 38 Halsbury's Laws (3rd edn) para 677B.3.

For the Trade Union and Labour Relations Act 1974, s 13, see 44 Halsbury's Statutes (3rd edn) 1769, and for s 13(1) of that Act (as substituted by the Trade Union and Labour Relations (Amendment) Act 1976, s 3(2)), see 46 ibid 1941.

For the Employment Act 1980, s 17, see 50(2) ibid 2635.

Cases referred to in judgments
BBC v Hearn [1978] 1 All ER 111, [1977] 1 WLR 1004, CA.

---

c   Section 17, so far as material, is set out at p 124 *h* to p 125 *b*, post

a   *Hadmor Productions Ltd v Hamilton* [1982] 1 All ER 1042, [1983] 1 AC 191, [1982] 2 WLR
     322, HL.
     Marina Shipping Ltd v Laughton [1982] 1 All ER 481, [1982] QB 1127, [1982] 2 WLR 569,
     CA.
     Merkur Island Shipping Corp v Laughton [1983] 2 All ER 189, [1983] 2 AC 570, [1983] 2
     WLR 778, HL.
     Thomson (D C) & Co Ltd v Deakin [1952] 2 All ER 361, [1952] Ch 646, CA.

b   *Torquay Hotel Co Ltd v Cousins* [1969] 1 All ER 522, [1969] 2 Ch 106, [1969] 2 WLR 289,
     CA.
     Universe Tankships Inc of Monrovia v International Transport Workers' Federation [1982]
     2 All ER 67, [1983] 1 AC 366, [1982] 2 WLR 803, HL.

Interlocutory appeal

c   The defendants, the National Union of Journalists, appealed against the judgment and
     order of Sir Neil Lawson, sitting as a judge of the High Court, on 18 November 1982,
     whereby he granted the plaintiffs, Dimbleby & Sons Ltd, interlocutory injunctions (i)
     restraining the defendants whether by themselves, their officers, servants or agents from
     issuing instructions to or otherwise encouraging journalists employed by the plaintiffs
     from refusing to assist or participate in the production of copy and material for
d   publication in the Richmond and Twickenham Times, the Brentford, Chiswick and
     Isleworth Times, the Barnes, Sheen and Mortlake Times and the Teddington and
     Hampton Times, and (ii) requiring the defendants to withdraw such instructions or
     encouragement already given. The judge granted a temporary stay of execution of the
     order. The facts are set out in the judgment of Griffiths LJ.

e   *John Hendy* (led on 1 December by *J Melville Williams* QC) for the union.
     Stephen Silber for the plaintiffs.

     At the conclusion of the arguments the Court of Appeal announced that for reasons to be
     given later the appeal would be dismissed. The court granted a short stay of execution
     pending hearing from counsel for the defendants as to the steps which the union would
f   take to comply with the order. Following a brief hearing in the matter on 1 December,
     the order took effect.

     GRIFFITHS LJ (giving the first judgment at the invitation of Sir John Donaldson MR).
     In 1978 there was a national strike of journalists working on provincial newspapers.
     After negotiations between the National Union of Journalists (the NUJ) and the employers'
g   organisation, the Newspaper Society, the strike was settled at the beginning of 1979.
     With one exception all the newspaper proprietors reinstated the journalists who had been
     dismissed during the strike.
         The one exception was T Bailey Forman Ltd, a company that published a newspaper
     in Nottingham. This company refused to re-employ 28 journalists that they had dismissed
     for taking part in the strike; the journalists were all members of the NUJ. From the
h   moment the company refused to reinstate the journalists they were involved in a trade
     dispute with those journalists within the meaning of s 29 of the Trade Union and Labour
     Relations Act 1974, as amended by s 18 of the Employment Act 1982.
         The union was outraged by the company's decision. It regarded it as blatant
     victimisation of its members and in breach of a no-victimisation agreement with the
     employers which was one of the terms on which the strike had been settled. The union
j   declared the company to be 'black'; not one of its members should work for it nor should
     they supply copy to it.
         In coming to the support of its members in this fashion there is no dispute that the
     union was protected from any action at common law by the provisions of s 13 of the
     1974 Act as amended by the Trade Union and Labour Relations (Amendment) Act 1976.
         The dispute continues to this day. There are still five of the sacked journalists who

have been unable to find alternative employment and the union continues to support them with dispute pay and, as far as the union is concerned, T Bailey Forman Ltd is still 'black'.

T Bailey Forman Ltd continues to publish its newspaper but it employs no members of the NUJ. The newspaper is printed by another company TBF (Printers) Ltd; this company also employs no union labour and what is of particular significance it does not employ any members of the National Graphical Association (1982) (the NGA).

The plaintiffs carry on business as sellers and distributors of weekly newspapers published on Fridays entitled the Richmond and Twickenham Times, the Brentford, Chiswick and Isleworth Times, the Barnes, Sheen and Mortlake Times and the Teddington and Hampton Times (which I shall call 'the specified newspapers'). They are published by Richmond and Twickenham Times Ltd and Brentford and Chiswick Times Ltd, which companies are wholly-owned subsidiaries of the plaintiffs. These companies have an agreement with the plaintiffs that in consideration for the plaintiffs' providing printing facilities and journalists at the plaintiffs' expense for the specified newspapers the plaintiffs were entitled to and did receive all the advertising and sales revenue of the specified newspapers. Prior to 19 August 1983 the specified newspapers were printed by Dimbleby Printers Ltd (Printers). A dispute arose between Printers and the NGA as a result of which all the employees of Printers who were members of the NGA went on strike after publication of the specified newspapers on 19 August 1983.

All the strikers were dismissed, the printing company is not operating and Printers and the NGA are in dispute. In these circumstances if the papers were to be produced the plaintiffs had to find another printer. The choice was very limited because NGA is a powerful union operating a closed shop in many printing firms and would have blacked any 'Dimbleby' copy.

The plaintiffs therefore entered into negotiations with TBF (Printers) Ltd, who employed no NGA members and were thus not vulnerable to a threat that the NGA would withdraw their members if they printed for the plaintiffs.

On 7 October 1983 the plaintiffs told their journalists, the majority of whom were members of the NUJ, that the papers were no longer to be printed by Printers and would in future be printed by TBF, but that this would have no effect on the working conditions of the journalists, who should continue to hand in their copy to the Richmond office as before.

Miss Joanna Davies, the mother of the chapel, had some anxiety about this decision. She convened a meeting of the NUJ chapel which comprised nine of the journalists employed by the plaintiffs and invited Mr Knowles, one of the NUJ national officers, to address them. This meeting took place on 10 October.

Mr Knowles has sworn an affidavit dated 28 October in which he deals with what he said at that meeting. He says his approach was gentle and reassuring, almost avuncular. He explained the background of the dispute between the union and TBF, his conviction that the union would instruct them to withdraw their labour when the national executive council met later that week, and the consequences if they refused to obey the union's instructions. There is no reason to doubt Mr Knowles's assertion that he was neither bullying nor intimidating, but, however it was delivered, the message he spelt out is to be found in the documents produced immediately after that meeting by those who attended it.

A document published by the Dimbleby chapel of the NUJ entitled 'Why the Times are Changing' contained the following passage:

'While we sympathise with the plight of the Dimbleby printers, all of whom were sacked after a seven-week dispute over redundancies, the NUJ action is a quite separate issue. Having decided some time ago to print out at Nottingham, David Dimbleby forced all the journalists to choose between working for him at the expense of our NUJ membership, or keeping our NUJ membership at the expense of our jobs. The choice was as stark and unacceptable as that. It was an agonising decision for all of us to be faced with. Since the NUJ is still in dispute with T. Bailey Forman, the national organiser had no alternative but to inform us that we would be banned from the NUJ and "blacked" by other NUJ publications if we continued working for Dimbleby. However, we were advised to decide individually what course of action to take, and no pressure was exerted by union officials.'

A letter dated 24 October signed by all the members of the Dimbleby NUJ chapel contains the following passage:

'The National Union of Journalists, of which all 13 are members, has had a long-standing dispute with T. Bailey Forman, and what we were being asked by the company was as stark as this: File copy to be printed by a blacked firm, and to hell with your NUJ cards. Our loyalty to Dimbleby Newspapers and to their aims to be, as you put it, "definitive journals of record, traditional in approach, comprehensive yet modern in style and presentation", has surely never been questioned. But when asked to choose between that loyalty, with very little explanation or assurances, and our NUJ cards, we had no alternative. As career journalists, our first loyalty had to be to ourselves.'

Another letter to the like effect written by Miss Davies on behalf of all members of the Dimbleby chapel was published in the Richmond and Twickenham Guardian of 3 November.

Whatever language Mr Knowles may have used, these documents are very strong evidence that the message was clear, 'If you supply copy you will lose your union card.'

After the meeting Mr Knowles reported by letter of 10 October to Mr Ashton, the general secretary of the NUJ. On 11 October there was a telephone conversation between Mr Dimbleby and Mr Ashton during which Mr Dimbleby told Mr Ashton that he had entered into a printing contract with TBF and that he could not withdraw from it. On 12 October Mr Richards, the editor of the Dimbleby newspapers, sent a memorandum to the journalists warning them that if they went on strike they would not be re-employed in any circumstances. On 13 October the union riposted with a strike notice to take effect on 17 October. On 17 October the journalists met the editor. The editor withdrew the threat of dismissal, but the journalists refused to submit any copy that was to be printed by TBF and they were suspended. There followed some further meeting and correspondence but to no effect and on 25 October the plaintiffs issued their writ and applied for interlocutory injunctions.

The relief sought by the plaintiffs in their writ falls under two main heads: firstly, to stop the union from inducing breaches of the contracts of employment they have with their own journalists and, secondly, to stop the union from procuring breaches of or interfering with their contract with TBF (Printers) Ltd and with a number of contracts to place advertisements in their newspapers.

Before the judge the plaintiffs succeeded in obtaining injunctions in the following terms:

'IT IS ORDERED that the Defendants whether by themselves, their officers servants or agents or howsoever otherwise be restrained from issuing instructions to or otherwise encouraging in any manner whatsoever journalists employed by the Plaintiffs from refusing to assist or participate in the production of copy and material for publication in the Richmond and Twickenham Times, the Brentford, Chiswick and Isleworth Times, the Barnes, Sheen and Mortlake Times and the Teddington and Hampton Times. AND IT IS FURTHER ORDERED that the Defendants do withdraw any instructions or encouragement already given which amounts to a breach of the Order set out above.'

The union challenges the judge's decision on a number of grounds. A court confronted with a dispute of this nature has to proceed painstakingly through a number of stages before it can ultimately decide on the legality or otherwise of the union's actions. The course the court must follow has been charted for it by Lord Brightman and Lord Diplock: see *Marina Shipping Ltd v Laughton* [1982] 1 All ER 481, [1982] QB 1127 and *Merkur Island Shipping Corp v Laughton* [1983] 2 All ER 189, [1983] 2 AC 570.

I must therefore set out on this wearisome and tortuous journey, pausing as I go to deal, at the appropriate places, with the union's submissions and to comment, wherever necessary, on the judge's conclusions. If unions and employers from time to time lose their way in the maze I am about to enter, I can only say that I am not surprised..

The first stage of the inquiry is to consider whether the plaintiffs have a cause of action at common law. Bearing in mind that this is an application for an interlocutory injunction, the question is: does the evidence at this stage reveal that it is at least seriously arguable that they have such a cause of action? There can be only one answer to this question. The union have instructed the journalists not to supply any copy to their employers if it is to be printed at TBF. It is not suggested that there is any term in the journalists' contracts of employment that entitled them to refuse to provide such copy, and such an instruction, backed by the sanction of expulsion from the union if it is disobeyed, constitutes the tort of inducing the journalists to break their contracts of employment with the employer.

Furthermore by giving this unlawful instruction the union is interfering with the plaintiffs' contract with TBF Printers Ltd, and also with contracts between the plaintiffs and a number of their advertisers. The union is thus committing the further torts of wrongful interference with a number of the plaintiffs' contracts: see the speech of Lord Diplock and his citations from *D C Thomson & Co Ltd v Deakin* [1952] 2 All ER 361, [1952] Ch 646 and *Torquay Hotel Co Ltd v Cousins* [1969] 1 All ER 522, [1969] 2 Ch 106 in *Merkur Island Corp v Laughton* [1983] 2 All ER 189 at 195, [1983] 2 AC 570 at 607–608.

At this stage of the inquiry I must consider two submissions made on behalf of the union. Firstly, it was submitted that, even if the union had attempted to induce the journalists to break their contract of employment and had attempted to interfere with the plaintiffs' commercial contracts, the plaintiffs could not succeed in an action against the union because they could not prove that the union's actions caused them any damage.

This submission is founded on assertions contained in the affidavits of the mother of the Dimbleby chapel and one other member of the chapel to the effect that then their reason for refusing to supply copy was the desire to support the members of their union who had been victimised by TBF and not the instruction of their union or the fear of losing their union card. I am afraid I find these statements very difficult to accept when I compare them with what they said in the contemporary documents to which I have already referred. Of course we are only at the interlocutory stage and how things will eventually turn out at trial one cannot say. But for the present I am bound to say that the evidence points very strongly to the conclusion that the union's instructions backed by the sanction of expulsion was a powerful inducement to the journalists to break their contracts of employment.

The judge's findings on this point are not easy to reconcile with one another. In one passage he says:

'I am wholly satisfied that this decision of the chapel members was reached independently of any inducement, instruction or interference, far less any threat held out or made by the defendants.'

I can only say I disagree with him. Later he says:

'It being conceded that the actions of the NUJ in relation to the journalist members of the union employed by the plaintiffs are capable of constituting inducement or interference with the performance of their contracts of employment, is there a serious case for consideration that those actions did in fact amount to such inducement or interference? The plaintiffs also allege threats to the NUJ members employed by them. It is quite wrong, on the evidence, to find that the plaintiffs had a serious case on the ground of threats. As to inducement or interference, however, *a* the evidence is contradictory and it is impossible for me to hold otherwise than that the plaintiffs arguably do have a serious case to put forward.'

At this point in his judgment I agree with him that there is a serious case to put forward based on inducement and interference. This being the case, I find it unnecessary to decide whether the conduct of the union amounts to a threat.

Secondly, it was submitted that, as in fact the plaintiffs had managed to produce newspapers and have them printed by TBF (Printers) Ltd, there can have been no *b* interference with that contract. The sole object of the union's action was to make it as difficult as possible for the plaintiffs to fulfil their printing contract with TBF and if they could to frustrate it altogether. I can think of nothing more calculated to hit at that contract than the withdrawal of all the copy that the plaintiffs expected to send to the printer. The plaintiffs were forced to go to extraordinary shifts to find copy from other sources and the interference with that contract appears to me to be clear beyond *c* argument. There was also ample evidence to support the view that continuing advertising contracts were likely to be adversely affected.

I now move to the second stage of the inquiry, which is to decide whether the provisions of the Trade Union and Labour Relations Act 1974 as amended by the 1976 Act protect the union from these otherwise tortious activities. Section 13(1) of the 1974 Act, as substituted by s 3(2) of the 1976 Act, reads:
d
'An act done by a person in contemplation or furtherance of a trade dispute shall not be actionable in tort on the ground only—(*a*) that it induces another person to break a contract or interferes or induces any other person to interfere with its performance; or (*b*) that it consists in his threatening that a contract (whether one to which he is a party or not) will be broken or its performance interfered with, or that he will induce another person to break a contract or to interfere with its performance.'

e The definition of a trade dispute in s 29(1) of the 1974 Act as amended by s 18 of the Employment Act 1982 now reads:

'(1) In this Act "trade dispute" means a dispute between workers and their employer which relates wholly or mainly to one or more of the following, that is to *f* say—(*a*) terms and conditions of employment, or the physical conditions in which any workers are required to work; (*b*) engagement or non-engagement, or termination or suspension of employment or the duties of employment, of one or more workers; (*c*) allocation of work or the duties of employment as between workers or groups of workers; (*d*) matters of discipline; (*e*) the membership or non-membership of a trade union on the part of a worker; (*f*) facilities for officials of trade unions; and (*g*) machinery for negotiation or consultation, and other *g* procedures, relating to any of the foregoing matters, including the recognition by employers or employers' associations of the right of a trade union to represent workers in any such negotiation or consultation or in the carrying out of such procedures.'

The union will be protected if it can show that its action was taken in furtherance of a *h* trade dispute. The judge held that the union's action was taken in furtherance of trade disputes relating to both the Dimbleby and the TBF journalists. I agree that it was taken in furtherance of the TBF dispute, which was clearly a dispute within the definition contained in s 29(1)(*c*). It was argued by the plaintiffs that the dispute had burned itself out, but the evidence is to the contrary: it is a running battle and the union is still paying dispute pay to five of its members. The union can therefore at this stage successfully *j* claim the protection of s 13(1).

As the union is protected because of the dispute with TBF it does not strictly matter whether or not it can claim protection because the Dimbleby journalists are also involved in a trade dispute. I must however record my view that the Dimbleby journalists are not involved in a trade dispute within the meaning of s 29.

The judge held firstly that they were in dispute over their terms and conditions of employment because they had asked to be excused from obeying an instruction to provide copy for TBF and the plaintiffs had refused to change their orders. This seems to me to be a wholly artificial way of looking at the situation.

The row that had blown up had nothing to do with the Dimbleby journalists' terms and conditions of employment. Neither the union nor the journalists had raised any complaint about their terms and conditions. The refusal to work was not concerned with their terms and conditions: it was to put pressure on the plaintiffs not to deal with TBF. A similar line of argument to this was put forward and rejected by Lord Denning MR in *BBC v Hearn* [1978] 1 All ER 111, [1977] 1 WLR 1004. In that case technicians who were members of a trade union, the Association of Broadcasting Staff (ABS), and employed by the BBC had on the instructions of ABS refused to man satellite transmission equipment for broadcasts to South Africa. It was held that, since there had been no attempt on behalf of ABS to renegotiate the terms and conditions of their members' contracts with the BBC but an attempt at coercive interference with the performance of those contracts, there was no trade dispute as defined by s 29(1) of the 1974 Act.

Even if there had been in this case a request at the last moment to include a term in the contract that the journalists' copy should not be supplied to TBF, I very much doubt if that would have been sufficient to turn the present situation into a trade dispute. Lord Cross said in *Universe Tankships Inc of Monrovia v International Transport Workers' Federation* [1982] 2 All ER 67 at 82, [1983] 1 AC 366 at 392:

'A trade union cannot turn a dispute which in reality has no connection with terms and conditions of employment into a dispute connected with terms and conditions of employment by insisting that the employer inserts appropriate terms into the contracts of employment into which he enters.'

In my view there was no dispute about terms and conditions of employment within the meaning of s 29(1)(a).

The judge also held that there was a dispute relating to the plaintiffs' threat of dismissal of the journalists and their subsequent suspension which fell within s 29(1)(b). Again I am afraid I cannot agree with him. The threat of dismissal was withdrawn before the journalists stopped work, and they were only suspended after they had refused to work. The journalists have not stopped working because they have been dismissed or suspended: they have stopped working because of the dispute between the union and TBF.

The judge rightly rejected the submission that there was a dispute within the meaning of s 29(1)(c) and there is no challenge to his finding in this court. The short point is that there is no dispute over the allocation of work as between employees of the plaintiffs.

For these reasons the plaintiffs and their journalists are not engaged in an industrial dispute within s 29(1).

I have come now to the final stage of the inquiry, which is to decide whether s 17 of the Employment Act 1980 removes the protection which was given by the earlier, 1974 and 1976 Acts arising out of the TBF dispute. Section 17 is designed to stop certain forms of secondary action. We are concerned in this appeal with the first three subsections:

'(1) Nothing in section 13 of the 1974 Act shall prevent an act from being actionable in tort on a ground specified in subsection (1)(a) or (b) of that section in any case where—(a) the contract concerned is not a contract of employment, and (b) one of the facts relied upon for the purpose of establishing liability is that there has been secondary action which is not action satisfying the requirements of subsection (3), (4) or (5) below.

(2) For the purposes of this section there is secondary action in relation to a trade dispute when, and only when, a person—(a) induces another to break a contract of employment or interferes or induces another to interfere with its performance, or (b) threatens that a contract of employment under which he or another is employed will be broken or its performance interfered with, or that he will induce another to break a contract of employment or to interfere with its performance, if the employer under the contract of employment is not a party to the trade dispute.

a
(3) Secondary action satisfies the requirements of this subsection if—(a) the purpose or principal purpose of the secondary action was directly to prevent or disrupt the supply during the dispute of goods or services between an employer who is a party to the dispute and the employer under the contract of employment to which the secondary action relates; and (b) the secondary action (together with any corresponding action relating to other contracts of employment with the same employer) was likely to achieve that purpose.'

b
The 'contract concerned' in sub-s (1)(a) is the contract with TBF Printers Ltd, or the contracts with the advertisers. Counsel on the union's behalf submitted that the contracts with the plaintiffs' journalists were the 'contracts concerned', but such a construction would render the subsection virtually meaningless. The section is dealing with secondary action and it can only be given meaning by construing 'contract concerned' as the contract at which the secondary action is aimed. Subsection (1)(a) is therefore satisfied.

c
In order to see if sub-s (1)(b) is satisfied one has first to look at sub-s (2) to see if the union is taking secondary action within the meaning of the section. The union is inducing the journalists to break their employment with the plaintiffs, it is taking this action because of its trade dispute with TBF, and the plaintiffs are not a party to that dispute. There is therefore secondary action within the meaning of sub-s (2).

d
But not all forms of secondary action are outlawed by sub-s (1)(b): the secondary action may fall within the protection of sub-s (3), (4) or (5).

At first the union very understandably claimed that it was protected by sub-s (3), but this arose out of a misunderstanding of the way in which TBF conducted their business. T Bailey Forman Ltd do not print their newspapers on their own presses: they have them printed by an associated company. Until the plaintiffs' lawyers took the point no one regarded this as of any significance: the companies were run by the same people from
e
the same office and with the same ethos; they did not use union labour. But when one looks closely at sub-s (3) it can be seen to be a matter of vital importance. In order to attract the protection of sub-s (3) the goods and services, in this case the copy, must be supplied to 'an employer who is a party to the dispute'. TBF (Printers) Ltd, to whom the goods and services are supplied, are not a party to the dispute with the NUJ: the union's dispute is with T Bailey Forman Ltd. So one arrives at the end of the journey at what
f
seems a curious result: if T Bailey Forman Ltd had produced their papers on their own presses, the union's action would have been protected, but, because the owner of the business chooses to operate through associated companies, the union is unprotected. I see no escape from this conclusion and agree with the judge that s 17 of the 1980 Act has removed the protection which the union would have enjoyed under the 1974 and 1976 Acts.

g
Mindful of the guidance given to this court by Lord Diplock in *Hadmor Productions Ltd v Hamilton* [1982] 1 All ER 1042 at 1046, [1983] 1 AC 191 at 220, I can see no grounds on which it would be right for this court to interfere with the discretion exercised by the judge in granting this interlocutory injunction. I would therefore dismiss this appeal.

h
SIR JOHN DONALDSON MR. I approach this dispute by the three stages commended by the House of Lords in *Merkur Island Corp v Laughton* [1983] 2 All ER 189, [1983] 2 AC 570.

Stage 1. Have the plaintiffs established that the union's conduct would, if the 1974 Act (as amended) had not been passed, have given them a cause of action in tort?
j
The union has quite clearly instructed its members in the employ of the plaintiffs not to supply copy or other material if it is to be printed by the TBF group of companies. Furthermore it has been established that this was the operative cause of the journalists' action. It was suggested that the journalists would have acted in the same way regardless of whether the union had so instructed them, but this is wholly unconvincing. Mr Knowles, a national officer of the union, addressed the Dimbleby chapel in terms which were 'gentle and reassuring—almost avuncular', to use his own words, but the message

was clear: 'Do as you are told or face disciplinary action.' No doubt some members were more ready than others to comply with the union instruction and scarcely veiled threat   *a* concerning the consequences of non-compliance, but this will usually be the case and does not render the union's conduct any less the cause of the journalists' actions.

This conduct would, if the 1974 Act (as amended) had not been passed, quite clearly have given the plaintiffs more than one cause of action in tort. The first would have been the unlawful inducement of the plaintiffs' journalist employees to break their contracts of employment. The second would have been unlawful interference or the threat of   *b* unlawful interference with the performance by the plaintiffs of their contract with TBF (Printers) Ltd. The third cause of action would have been of a similar nature in relation to various contracts between the plaintiffs and advertisers in their newspapers.

The cause of action based on inducing a breach of the journalists' contracts of employment requires little explanation. It is not suggested that under the terms of those contracts of employment the journalists were entitled to refuse to produce copy simply   *c* because it would provide work for a company in the TBF group. However, the causes of action based on interference with commercial contracts between the plaintiffs and TBF (Printers) Ltd and between the plaintiffs and the advertisers may require a little more explanation. The essential elements of this tort were explained in *Merkur Island Corp v Laughton*. They consist of the following.

(i) *That the person charged with actionable interference knew of the existence of the contract and*   *d* *intended to procure interference with its performance or its breach*
On 11 October 1983 Mr David Dimbleby informed Mr Ken Ashton, the general secretary of the union, that the decision to have printing done by TBF was 'irreversible'. In context this could only mean that the plaintiffs had entered into a firm contract with the printers. The instruction to withdraw labour given on 13 October 1983 was clearly intended to procure a breach of that contract or to interfere with its performance.   *e*

(ii) *That the person so charged did definitely and unequivocally persuade, induce or procure the employees concerned to break their contracts of employment with the intent mentioned in (i) above*
This was clearly established on the evidence.

(iii) *That the employees so persuaded induced or procured did in fact break their contracts of employment*   *f*
This also is clearly established.

(iv) *That the interference with the performance by the plaintiffs of their contract with TBF (Printers) Ltd ensued as a necessary consequence of the breaches by the journalists of their contracts of employment*
It was faintly argued that, because there was in fact no breach of this contract and the   *g* paper continued to be published, there was no interference. This argument cannot be accepted. 'Interference' means hindrance as well as prevention and the loss of the services of staff journalists was quite clearly a hindrance to the performance by the plaintiffs of their contractual obligations towards TBF (Printers) Ltd.

Stage 2. Have the defendants established that, apart from the effect of sub-ss (1) to (7) of s 17 of   *h* *the Employment Act 1980, they are protected from suit by s 13 of the Trade Union and Labour Relations Act 1974 as amended by the 1976 Act and by s 17(8) of the 1980 Act?*
Section 13(1) provides:

'An act done by a person in contemplation or furtherance of a trade dispute shall not be actionable in tort on the ground only—(*a*) that it induces another person to break a contract or interferes or induces any other person to interfere with its   *j* performance; or (*b*) that it consists in his threatening that a contract (whether one to which he is a party or not) will be broken or its performance interfered with, or that he will induce another person to break a contract or to interfere with its performance.'

The defendants submit that their action in instructing the Dimbleby journalists to refuse

a to supply copy and other material which would be printed by TBF (Printers) Ltd was taken in furtherance of two different trade disputes. The first was a dispute between the plaintiffs and their journalists (i) concerning their terms and conditions of employment (s 29(1)(a) of the 1974 Act (s 29(1) being amended by s 18 of the Employment Act 1982)), (ii) concerning the allocation of work as between workers or groups of workers (s 29(1)(c)) and (iii) concerning their suspension or dismissal (s 29(1)(b)). The second dispute was a dispute between TBF Ltd and those of the journalists whom they dismissed in 1978 and
b who still wish to be reinstated.

Disputes between the plaintiffs and their journalists

The judge held that there was a dispute between the plaintiffs and their journalists concerning their terms and conditions of service and, on the evidence at present available, this is clearly wrong. The journalists never suggested that they were entitled to refuse to
c supply the copy and other material merely because it would be printed by TBF (Printers) Ltd. Nor was there any suggestion that their terms and conditions of employment should be altered to make this permissible. Had there been any such suggestion, we would have had to bear in mind the dictum of Lord Cross in *Universe Tankships Inc of Monrovia v International Transport Workers' Federation* [1982] 2 All ER 67 at 82, [1983] AC 366 at 392
d that—

'A trade union cannot turn a dispute which in reality has no connection with terms and conditions of employment into a dispute connected with terms and conditions of employment by insisting that the employer inserts appropriate terms into the contracts of employment into which he enters.'

The judge also, and rightly, held that there was no 'trade dispute' between the plaintiffs
e and their journalists concerning the allocation of work between workers or groups of workers, because, in the light of the amended definition of 'trade dispute', this can only occur when all the workers concerned are employed by the employer who is party to the dispute (in this case the plaintiffs). What was objected to was the allocation of printing work to the employees of TBF (Printers) Ltd.

Finally the judge held that there *was* a trade dispute between the plaintiffs and their
f journalists concerning the threat to suspend them or terminate their employment. In this I consider that the judge erred. Under the amended definition of 'trade dispute', the dispute in order to qualify as such must 'relate wholly or mainly to' one of the specified subject matters. This dispute did not relate wholly or mainly to the suspension or dismissal of the plaintiffs' journalists. It related to the decision by the plaintiffs to have the copy printed by TBF (Printers) Ltd.

g *Dispute between TBF Ltd and its dismissed journalists*

This, as the judge held, was a trade dispute within s 29(1) since it was between an employer (TBF Ltd) and its ex-workers and it concerned the refusal of TBF Ltd to re-engage them. Although it was argued that this dispute had died of old age (it began in 1978) the evidence suggests that some of the journalists are still in receipt of dispute pay
h from the union and I agree with the judge in thinking that the dispute is still alive.

I have no doubt that the action taken by the union was taken in furtherance of the trade dispute between TBF Ltd and its dismissed journalists and it follows that the union emerges successfully from stage 2.

Stage 3. Is the protection afforded by s 13(1) of the 1974 Act removed by s 17 of the 1980 Act?
j Section 17 is set out in *Merkur Island Shipping Corp v Laughton* [1983] 2 All ER 189 at 194, [1983] 2 AC 570 at 606 and I need not repeat the exercise. It will avoid the protective effect of s 13 where (a) 'the contract concerned' is not a contract of employment and (b) one of the facts relied on for the purpose of establishing liability is that there has been secondary action which is not action satisfying the requirements of sub-s (3), (4) or (5). For the reasons which I have already given, the plaintiffs would, but for the effect of

s 13(1), have causes of action (i) for inducing the Dimbleby staff journalists to break their contracts and (ii) for interfering with the performance of the printing contract with TBF *a* (Printers) Ltd and the plaintiffs' contracts with the advertisers. These are the contracts to which the union has to seek to apply s 13(1) and these are therefore 'the contracts concerned'. The contract between the plaintiffs and their staff journalists is a contract of employment and accordingly that cause of action is one to which s 13 continues to apply. However, the 'interference' causes of action relate to contracts which are not contracts of employment. As to these causes of action the union has to rely on (b) above. *b*

The union has to show that one of the facts relied on by the plaintiffs for the purpose of establishing liability is that there has been 'secondary action'. This is defined in sub-s (2) of s 17. It can do this because the plaintiffs must necessarily allege that the union has induced the Dimbleby staff journalists to break their contracts of employment with the plaintiffs and the plaintiffs are not parties to the only trade dispute in furtherance of which the industrial action is being taken. So far so good. However, the union will lose *c* the protection of s 13(1) if the secondary action does not satisfy the requirements of s 17(3), it not being suggested that it satisfies the requirements of sub-s (4) or (5) of s 17.

It is here that the union is confronted with an insuperable difficulty. One of the requirements of s 17(3) is that the purpose or principal purpose of the secondary action was directly to prevent or disrupt the supply during the dispute of goods or services between an employer who is a party to the dispute and the employer under the contract *d* of employment to which the secondary action relates. However, the purpose or principal purpose of the union's secondary action was directly to prevent or disrupt the supply of goods or services (copy and similar materials) not to TBF Ltd, who were parties to the dispute, but to TBF (Printers) Ltd, who were not parties to the dispute. Accordingly the subsection is not satisfied and s 17 removes the protection which the union would otherwise have enjoyed under s 13 of the 1974 Act. *e*

It may strike some people as odd that the liability of the union should depend on what they may reasonably regard as almost being a matter of chance, namely whether the directors of the TBF group decided to arrange that one subsidiary should employ journalists and another undertake printing as contrasted with deciding that one subsidiary should undertake both printing and journalism. Whether or not the union would be right so to regard the position, that appears without doubt to be the law. *f*

I should perhaps make it clear that in this appeal we have been concerned with an interlocutory order and that, although I have stated my conclusions without qualification, they are all subject to the qualification that if and when there is a full trial of the action the evidence may reveal a quite different situation.

For the reasons that I have given, I agree that the appeal should be dismissed.

g

STEPHEN BROWN LJ. I have had the advantage of reading the judgments of Sir John Donaldson MR and of Griffiths LJ and I agree that this appeal should be dismissed for the reasons which they have given.

Appeal dismissed. Leave to appeal to the House of Lords refused.

h

15 December. The Appeal Committee of the House of Lords allowed a petition by the defendants for leave to appeal.

Solicitors: *Bindman & Partners* (for the union); *Cameron Markby* (for the plaintiffs).

Diana Procter   Barrister.

Clea Shipping Corp v Bulk Oil International Ltd
The Alaskan Trader

QUEEN'S BENCH DIVISION (COMMERCIAL COURT)

LLOYD J

18, 19, 20, 29 JULY 1983

Contract – Repudiation – Election whether to accept repudiation – Owners chartering vessel under time charter to charterers for period of two years – After one year of contract vessel off-hire for six months while repairs carried out – Charterers repudiating charterparty on being informed that vessel ready for sail after repairs – Owners refusing to accept repudiation and maintaining vessel with crew ready to sail until expiry of charterparty – Whether owners having unfettered right to elect to refuse to accept repudiation – Whether owners allowed to enforce contractual rights according to strict legal terms – Whether owners' conduct more than merely unreasonable in refusing to accept repudiation – Whether owners having legitimate interest in performing contract rather than claiming damages.

By a time charter dated 19 October 1979 the owners chartered a vessel to the charterers for a period of approximately 24 months. After the vessel had been in service for nearly a year, the vessel suffered a serious engine breakdown and it became apparent that the repairs would take several months. The charterers then indicated that they had no further use for the vessel but the owners nevertheless went ahead with the repairs at a cost of £800,000. The repairs were completed on 7 April 1981. The owners then informed the charterers that the vessel was once again at their disposal, but the charterers declined to give the master of the vessel any orders since they regarded the charterparty as having come to an end. The owners refused to treat the charterers' conduct as a repudiation of the charterparty and maintained the vessel at anchor with a full crew ready to sail until the time charter expired in December 1981. Hire was paid throughout the period from 7 April until December 1981, first under a letter of credit opened in favour of the owners and thereafter by the charterers themselves without prejudice. When the charterparty came to an end the question whether the charterers could recover the hire paid for the period from April to December 1981 was referred to arbitration. The charterers contended that the owners ought to have accepted the charterers' conduct as a repudiation of the charterparty and confined their claim to damages. The owners contended that in the case of repudiation the innocent party had an unfettered right to elect whether to accept or refuse the repudiation and accordingly they were entitled to keep the vessel at the disposal of the charterers throughout the period and to retain the hire. The arbitrator found that the owners had no legitimate interest in pursuing their claim for hire rather than a claim for damages. He held that, the owners ought to have accepted the charterers' repudiation by midnight on 8 April 1981 with a view to mitigating their damage and accordingly that the charterers were entitled to recover the hire, while remaining liable for damages. The owners appealed.

Held – Although an innocent party had, in general, an unfettered right to elect whether to accept a repudiation of a contract, the court would in exceptional cases, in the exercise of its general equitable jurisdiction, refuse to allow an innocent party to enforce his full contractual rights if he had no legitimate interest in performing the contract rather than claiming damages. On the facts the arbitrator had found that the owners had no legitimate interest in continuing to perform the contract, and accordingly had declined to grant the owners the remedy to which they would otherwise have been entitled. There was no error of law in the arbitrator's approach, and the appeal would therefore be dismissed (see p 136 j, p 137 a to e and j to p 138 a and g and p 139 b, post).

Dicta of Lord Reid in *White & Carter (Councils) Ltd v McGregor* [1961] 3 All ER at 1182 and of Lord Denning MR and of Orr LJ in *Attica Sea Carriers Corp v Ferrostaal Poseidon Bulk Reederei GmbH, The Puerto Buitrago* [1976] 1 Lloyd's Rep at 255, 256 applied.

Decro-Wall International SA v Practitioners in Marketing Ltd [1971] 2 All ER 216 and *Gator Shipping Corp v Trans-Asiatic Oil Ltd SA and Occidental Shipping Establishment, The Odenfeld* [1978] 2 Lloyd's Rep 357 considered.

Notes

For effects of repudiation and rights of the innocent party, see 9 Halsbury's Laws (4th edn) paras 546, 551–558, and for cases on the subject, see 12 Digest (Reissue) 411–416, 3032–3049.

Cases referred to in judgment

Attica Sea Carriers Corp v Ferrostaal Poseidon Bulk Reederei GmbH, The Puerto Buitrago [1976] 1 Lloyd's Rep 250, CA.

Decro-Wall International SA v Practitioners in Marketing Ltd [1971] 2 All ER 216, [1971] 1 WLR 361, CA.

Gator Shipping Corp v Trans-Asiatic Oil Ltd SA and Occidental Shipping Establishment, The Odenfeld [1978] 2 Lloyd's Rep 357.

Graham v Kirkaldy Magistrates (1882) 9 R (Ct of Sess) 91, HL.

Hounslow London BC v Twickenham Gardens Developments Ltd [1970] 3 All ER 326, [1971] 1 Ch 233, [1970] 3 WLR 538.

Langford & Co Ltd v Dutch 1952 SC 15.

Scandinavian Trading Tanker Co AB v Flota Petrolera Ecuatoriana, The Scaptrade [1983] 2 All ER 763, [1983] 3 WLR 203, HL.

White & Carter (Councils) Ltd v McGregor [1961] 3 All ER 1178, [1962] AC 413, [1961] 2 WLR 17, HL.

Appeal

Clea Shipping Corp (the owners) appealed with leave of Bingham J granted on 19 November 1982 on questions of law arising out of an award made by Mr Alexander John Kazantzis as sole arbitrator in an arbitration between the owners and the respondents, Bulk Oil International Ltd (the charterers), namely (i) whether on the facts found the charterparty between the owners and the charterers dated 19 October 1979 terminated at midnight on 8 April 1981 by reason of the charterers' repudiation, (ii) whether the owners were obligated to accept the charterers' repudiation of the charterparty if the charterers established that the owners had 'no legitimate interest' in keeping the charterparty in existence, and (iii) if the answer to (ii) was yes, whether on the facts found the owners had 'no legitimate interest' in keeping the charterparty in existence. The facts are set out in the judgment.

Anthony D Colman QC and *R D Jacobs* for the owners.
Julian Cooke and *Christopher C Russell* for the charterers.

Cur adv vult

29 July. The following judgment was delivered.

LLOYD J. This is an appeal under s 1 of the Arbitration Act 1979 from an award of Mr Alexander Kazantzis. The award is dated 15 June 1982. Leave to appeal was granted by Bingham J on 19 November 1982. The facts are startling.

On 19 October 1979 the Alaskan Trader was chartered by the respondents as disponent owners to the claimants for a period of 24 months, 15 days more or less. She was an old vessel, having been built in Sweden in 1954. She was acquired by her head owners in September 1979, only a few weeks before the date of the charter. She was delivered under the charter on 20 December 1979, and thereafter performed services on short Mediterranean voyages carrying gas oil from Haifa. On 19 October 1980, after she had been in service for nearly a year, the vessel suffered a serious engine breakdown. It was clear that the repairs would take many months. The charterers indicated that they had no further use for the vessel. The market had turned against them. At the time of the charter the market rate was $13–$14 per ton. By October 1980 it had declined to $8–$9 per ton. Nevertheless, the owners went ahead with the repairs at a cost of $800,000. Throughout the period of the repairs the vessel was, of course, off-hire. The repairs were completed on 7 April 1981. The owners thereupon informed the charterers that the vessel was again at their disposal. But the charterers declined to give the master any orders. They regarded the charterparty as having come to an end. The owners could have treated the charterers' conduct as a repudiation of the charterparty. But they did not do so. They anchored the vessel off Piraeus, where she remained with a full crew on board, ready to sail, but idle, until the time-charter expired on 5 December 1981. She was then sold for scrap.

Hire was paid throughout the period from 8 April 1981 to 5 December 1981, first under a letter of credit opened in favour of the disponent owners and thereafter by the charterers themselves without prejudice to their right to recover hire. At the expiry of the charterparty there were numerous claims and cross-claims which were brought before Mr Kazantzis as arbitrator. But the principal claim related to the hire for the period from 8 April to 5 December 1981. The owners argued that they were entitled to retain the hire, since they had kept the vessel at the disposal of the charterers throughout the period. They relied on the decision of the House of Lords in *White & Carter (Councils) Ltd v McGregor* [1961] 3 All ER 1178, [1962] AC 413, and the decision of Kerr J in *Gator Shipping Corp v Trans-Asiatic Oil Co Ltd SA and Occidental Shipping Establishment, The Odenfeld* [1978] 2 Lloyd's Rep 357. The charterers on the other hand argued that the owners ought, in all reason, to have accepted the charterers' conduct as a repudiation of the charter, and claimed damages. Even if no alternative employment could be found for the vessel, it would have been a great deal cheaper to lay the vessel up, rather than maintain her with a full crew on board. They relied on the decision of the Court of Appeal in *Attica Sea Carriers Corp v Ferrostaal Poseidon Bulk Reederei GmbH, The Puerto Buitrago* [1976] 1 Lloyd's Rep 250.

The arbitrator, having heard all the arguments which I have heard, and been referred to all the cases, upheld the charterers' contention. He held that the charterers were entitled to recover hire in the sum of $1,853,310, but that they were, of course, liable in damages, which are yet to be assessed. His reasons are set out with enviable clarity if not brevity, though brevity was scarcely possible, in a document of nearly 50 pages. The crucial paragraphs are 30 and 31. Having concluded that the owners were not obliged to accept the charterers' repudiation in October 1980, before the repairs had been carried out, he continued:

'30. The position was very different when the vessel was tendered ready for service after completion of repairs. The Charterers refused to accept the vessel and made it clear they never would. At that stage there was nothing contingent or anticipatory about the Charterers' action. It was clear that the Charter was dead. The Owners however did not accept that the moribund condition of the Charter was equivalent to termination in the legal sense. They contended that all was required of the vessel under the Charter was that she should be at the Charterers' disposal; the hire thereby fell due and it would be unjust to permit the Charterers to avoid a debt by requiring the Owners to accept repudiation and claim damages. There is a superficial logic in this argument but it is apt to lead to absurd situations. In this case the Owners contend that they kept the vessel with a full crew and engine ready for over 7 months, waiting for orders which they well knew would never come. I am satisfied that this commercial absurdity is not justified by a proper interpretation of the decided cases. I consider that the analogy of a contract between master and servant applies more closely to a time charter than the analogy of a simple debt. The Owner supplies the vessel and crew; the Charterer supplies fuel oil, pays a disbursements and gives orders. The Charterers were also able to satisfy me that at that stage the Owners had no legitimate interest in pursuing their claim for hire rather than a claim for damages. In these respects the present case differs materially from the case of *White & Carter* v. *McGregor*, and is more closely analogous to the case of *The Puerto Buitrago* [1976] 1 Lloyd's Rep 250, where the judgments of Lord Denning MR and Orr LJ are particularly in point. I considered that the decision in b *The Odenfeld* [1978] 2 Lloyd's Rep 357 turned on the highly unusual circumstances of that case.

31. I am satisfied on this basis that the Charter was terminated around the time the vessel was finally ready for service. Following the highly repudiatory telex from the Charterers' Solicitors sent on the 6th April, when the vessel was about to be put at the Charterers' disposal, the vessel was ready after successful completion of trials c at 0043 on the 7th April. Thereafter the Master cabled the Charterers for orders at 1600 on 7th April. There was no response save for another repudiatory message from the Charterers' Solicitors. Taking into account the Charterers' clear refusal to accept delivery I am satisfied that by midnight on 8th April the Owners should have accepted the Charterers' repudiation with a view to mitigating their damages.'

When the matter came before Bingham J on the application for leave to appeal, he d ordered the arbitrator to expand his reasons for saying that '... the Owners had no legitimate interest in pursuing their claim for hire rather than a claim for damages'. The explanation for the arbitrator's use of that language becomes evident when one looks at the speech of Lord Reid in *White & Carter v McGregor*. The arbitrator complied with Bingham J's order in a further lengthy document which has been put before me.

Counsel for the owners now seeks to persuade me that the arbitrator was wrong in e law. He submits that in a case of repudiation the innocent party has an unfettered right to elect whether to accept the repudiation or not. Here the owners chose not to accept the repudiation. Provided they continued to keep the vessel at the disposal of the charterers, as they did, they were entitled to their hire. The arbitrator was wrong in law in holding that the owners *ought* to have accepted the charterers' repudiation by midnight on 8 April 1981.

Although the argument ranged far and wide, the appeal can, in my view, be decided f quite simply. But, before stating my decision, I should first refer to the relevant decisions which are binding on me, or of strong persuasive force.

In *White & Carter v McGregor* [1961] 3 All ER 1178, [1962] AC 413 the plaintiffs agreed to display advertisements for the defendant's garage on litter bins in the neighbourhood for a period of three years. The very same day the defendant said he did g not wish to go on with the contract. The plaintiffs declined to accept the repudiation. They went ahead with the contract, and sued for the agreed price in debt. It was held by the House of Lords that they were justified. The minority, while conceding that an unaccepted repudiation does not put an end to the contract, nevertheless held that the plaintiffs' only remedy lay in damages, since it was obviously not a suitable case for specific performance. Lord Hodson, with whom Lord Tucker agreed, drew no distinction h between anticipatory breach and breach at the date of performance. In either case the innocent party has an unfettered right of election. He said ([1961] 3 All ER 1178 at 1193, [1962] AC 413 at 445):

'When the assistance of the court is not required the innocent party can choose whether he will accept repudiation and sue for damages for anticipatory breach or j await the date of performance by the guilty party. Then, if there is failure in performance, his rights are preserved. It may be unfortunate that the appellants have saddled themselves with an unwanted contract causing an apparent waste of time and money. No doubt this aspect impressed the Court of Session but there is no equity which can assist the respondent. It is trite that equity will not rewrite an a improvident contract where there is no disability on either side. There is no duty laid on a party to a subsisting contract to vary it at the behest of the other party so as to deprive himself of the benefit given to him by the contract. To hold otherwise would be to introduce a novel equitable doctrine that a party was not to be held to his contract unless the court in a given instance thought it reasonable so to do. In this case it would make an action for debt a claim for a discretionary remedy. This would introduce an uncertainty into the field of contract which appears to be

b unsupported by authority either in English or Scottish law save for the one case viz *Langford & Co Ltd v Dutch* (1952 SC 15) on which the Court of Session ([1961] SLT 144) founded its opinion and which must, in my judgment, be taken to have been wrongly decided.'

Lord Reid agreed with Lord Hodson and Lord Tucker that on the facts the plaintiffs' claim in debt must succeed. But his speech contains two important observations on the

c law. First, he pointed out that it is only in rare cases that the innocent party will be able to complete performance of his side of the contract, without the assent or co-operation of the party in breach. Obviously, if the innocent party cannot complete performance, he is restricted to his claim for damages. A buyer who refuses to accept delivery of the goods, and thereby prevents property passing, cannot, in the ordinary case, be made liable for the price. The peculiarity of *White & Carter v McGregor* [1961] 3 All ER 1178 at 1182,

d [1962] AC 413 at 429, as Lord Reid pointed out, was that the plaintiffs could completely fulfil their part of the contract without any co-operation from the defendant.

The second observation which Lord Reid made as to the law was that a party might well be unable to enforce his contractual remedy if 'he had no legitimate interest, financial or otherwise, in performing the contract rather than claiming damages'. Lord Reid did not go far in explaining what he meant by legitimate interest except to say that

e the de minimis principle would apply. Obviously it would not be sufficient to establish that the innocent party was acting unreasonably. Otherwise Lord Reid would not have rejected the formulation of the Lord President (Cooper) in *Langford & Co Ltd v Dutch* 1952 SC 15 at 18 that 'the only reasonable and proper course' was for the pursuers to accept the repudiation. As Lord Reid said ([1961] 3 All ER 1178 at 1182, [1962] AC 413 at 430):

f 'It might be, but it never has been, the law that a person is only entitled to enforce his contractual rights in a reasonable way and that a court will not support an attempt to enforce them in an unreasonable way. One reason why that is not the law is no doubt because it was thought that it would create too much uncertainty to require the court to decide whether it is reasonable or equitable to allow a party to enforce his full rights under a contract. The Lord President cannot have meant that.'

g Nor does Lord Reid go far in explaining the juristic basis on which the court can confine the plaintiff's remedy to a claim for damages. All he says is that, in the absence of legitimate interest, 'that might be regarded as a proper case for the exercise of the general equitable jurisdiction of the court' (see [1961] 3 All ER 1178 at 1183, [1962] AC

h 413 at 431). This is presumably a reference back to what had been said by Lord Watson in *Graham v Kirkcaldy Magistrates* (1882) 9 R(Ct of Sess) 91 at 92.

It is clear that, on the facts, no attempt had been made by the defendant to establish absence of legitimate interest. Accordingly, counsel for the owners was right when he submitted that the two observations which I have mentioned were both, strictly speaking, obiter. I further accept that the language used by Lord Reid is tentative. But I do not accept counsel's submission that Lord Reid was merely recording the arguments of

j counsel, a possibility canvassed by Salmon and Buckley LJJ in *Decro-Wall International SA v Practitioners in Marketing Ltd* [1971] 2 All ER 216, [1971] 1 WLR 361.

The next case is *Hounslow London BC v Twickenham Garden Developments Ltd* [1970] 3 All ER 326, [1971] 1 Ch 233, a case relied on strongly by counsel for the charterers. That case concerned a building contract between a firm of contractors and the local borough council. The council sought to terminate the contract, but the contractors refused to accept the repudiation. They relied on *White & Carter v McGregor*. Megarry J analysed the speeches in that case, and drew attention to the two observations, or limitations, in the speech of Lord Reid. He described both limitations as important. As to the first, he held that the building contract in the case before him contemplated the passive, if not active, cooperation of both parties in its performance. Accordingly, the case fell within the first of Lord Reid's limitations, and it was unnecessary for him to consider the second limitation as to legitimate interest. For reasons which will appear later, I need therefore say no more about that case.

Very soon afterwards *Decro-Wall v Marketing* came before the Court of Appeal. That was a case of a sole agency agreement. The plaintiffs, a manufacturing company carrying on business in France, purported to terminate the agreement on the ground of an alleged repudiation by the defendants, an English marketing company. The defendants sought a declaration that the agreement was still subsisting, and an injunction to restrain the plaintiffs from appointing another sole agent. It was argued for the plaintiffs that, if they were wrong in their main submission, then at least the defendants were obliged to accept their purported termination of the agreement as a repudiation. They relied on the first of the two observations of Lord Reid in *White & Carter v McGregor*, namely that the sole agency agreement could not be performed without the co-operation of the plaintiff manufacturers, and that therefore the contract had come to an end without any election by the defendants. The plaintiffs' argument was rejected. Both Salmon and Sachs LJJ made clear that it is not the right to elect which is limited by the first of Lord Reid's observations but the range of remedies. You cannot claim remuneration under a contract if you have not earned it; if you are prevented from earning it, your only remedy is in damages. In the *Decro-Wall* case the defendants were not claiming remuneration. They were claiming a declaration and an injunction. Accordingly, what Lord Reid had said was irrelevant to the case before them. Nothing was said in the *Decro-Wall* case about the second of the two observations of Lord Reid in *White & Carter v McGregor*.

The next case, on which counsel for the charterers relied, is *The Puerto Buitrago* [1976] 1 Lloyd's Rep 250. In that case a vessel suffered an engine breakdown in the course of her service under a demise charter. There was a provision in the charter that the vessel should be dry-docked before redelivery, and any repairs found to be necessary were to be carried out at charterers' expense. The repairs were estimated to cost $2m. The value of the vessel when repaired would only have been $1m. The charterers declined to carry out the repairs. They purported to redeliver the vessel in her unrepaired state. The owners refused to accept redelivery. They argued that the charterers were bound to repair the vessel, and that hire continued to be payable until they had. The Court of Appeal decided in favour of the charterers. They held, on a preliminary question of law, that the obligation to repair was not a condition precedent to the right to redeliver. But they went on to consider three other questions of law which had been agreed between the parties, but which only arose if they were wrong on the first question of law. For the purpose of the fourth question, they assumed that the charterers were in breach by insisting on redelivering the vessel without first repairing her. On that assumption the fourth question was whether the owners were obliged to accept the charterers' conduct as a repudiation. The owners argued that they were not. They relied on *White & Carter v McGregor*. The Court of Appeal rejected the owners' argument. Lord Denning MR said that *White & Carter v McGregor* has—

'no application whatever in a case where the plaintiff ought, in all reason, to accept the repudiation and sue for damages—provided that damages would provide an adequate remedy for any loss suffered by him. The reason is because, by suing for the money, the plaintiff is seeking to enforce specific performance of the contract—and he should not be allowed to do so when damages would be an adequate remedy ... What is the alternative which the shipowners present to the charterers? Either the charterers must pay the charter hire for years to come, whilst the vessel lies idle and useless for want of repair. *Or* the charterers must do repairs which would cost twice as much as the ship would be worth when repaired—after which the *a* shipowners might sell it as scrap, making the repairs a useless waste of money. In short, on either alternative, the shipowners seek to compel specific performance of one or other of the provisions of the charter—with most unjust and unreasonable consequences—when damages would be an adequate remedy. I do not think the law allows them to do this.' (Lord Denning MR's emphasis.)

(See [1976] 1 Lloyd's Rep 250 at 255.)

b Orr LJ confined his judgment to the fourth question. He set out the two passages from Lord Reid's speech which contain the two observations I have mentioned. He then continued (at 256):

c 'The present case differs from that case in that here it cannot be said that the owners could fulfil the contract without any co-operation from the charterers and also because in this case the charterers have set out to prove that the owners have no legitimate interest in claiming the charter hire rather than claiming damages, and the passages above quoted strongly suggest to me that if either or both of these factors had been present in *White & Carter v. McGregor* Lord Reid might well have agreed with Lord Morton and Lord Keith as to the outcome of the appeal, with the result that there would have been a majority in favour of dismissing it. I would add that in *Decro-Wall International S.A. v. Practitioners in Marketing Ltd.*, ([1971] 2 All ER

d 216, [1971] 1 WLR 361) references were made by all the members of the Court to the first of the above passages quoted from Lord Reid's speech but not to the second, which was irrelevant to the facts of that case. I have considered these passages but they do not lead me to doubt the validity of the conclusion I have reached in this very different circumstances of this case.'

In that passage Orr LJ was distinguishing *White & Carter v McGregor* on two separate *e* grounds. First, unlike *White & Carter v McGregor*, the charterparty could not be performed without the co-operation of the charterers. Second, unlike *White and Carter v McGregor*, the charterers had set out to prove (and presumably had proved) that the owners had no legitimate interest in claiming hire rather than damages. Browne LJ specifically agreed with Lord Denning MR and Orr LJ on the fourth question.

f Counsel for the owners argued that what the Court of Appeal said on the fourth question was obiter. Even if I assume that to be so, there is, at the very least, the strong persuasive authority of the majority of the Court of Appeal, Orr and Browne LJJ, in support of what Lord Reid had said in *White & Carter v McGregor* that the absence of a legitimate interest is a ground on which the owners may be compelled to accept damages in lieu of hire.

Lastly, there is *Gator Shipping Corp v Trans-Asiatic Oil Ltd SA and Occidental Shipping*
g *Establishment, The Odenfeld* [1978] 2 Lloyd's Rep 357, on which counsel for the owners relied. That case concerned a 10-year time charter entered into in May 1973. By 1975 the freight market had collapsed. In January 1976, the charterers refused to go on paying any more hire. They treated the charter as having come to an end. The plaintiffs, a shipping finance company to whom the charter hire had been assigned, claimed hire for the period from January to September 1976. The charterers denied liability and counter-
h claimed a declaration that the charterparty had been terminated in January 1976. There were a number of preliminary issues for determination by the court. The third issue was whether, on the assumption that the charterers had repudiated the charterparty, the owners ought to have accepted the repudiation. Kerr J held that they did not. He was invited to consider *White & Carter v McGregor*, *Decro-Wall* and *The Puerto Buitrago*. He took the view that *The Puerto Buitrago* was an extreme case on the facts. Nevertheless he
j accepted the importance of the case as—

'a presently binding authority on the Court in limiting or qualifying the generality of the principle of a virtually unfettered right of election in favour of the innocent party.'

(See [1978] 2 Lloyd's Rep 357 at 373.)

I do not know whether by referring to a *presently* binding authority Kerr J was indicating that in his view the case may have been wrongly decided. For present purposes it does not matter. Kerr J's own formulation of the law, derived from *The Puerto Buitrago* and *Decro-Wall*, was that—

'any fetter on the innocent party's right of election whether or not to accept a repudiation will only be applied in extreme cases, viz. where damages would be an adequate remedy and where an election to keep the contract alive would be wholly unreasonable.'

(See [1978] 2 Lloyd's Rep 357 at 374.)

On the facts Kerr J held, as I have already mentioned, that the owners were not obliged to accept the repudiation at any time up to September 1976, the period with which he was concerned. But he guarded himself against expressing any view as to the future. He said (at 375):

'However, in saying this I must not be thought to be implying that Occidental and the plaintiffs could necessarily have maintained the same position for a further six years. As was pointed out by the Court of Appeal in the *Decro-Wall* case, the reality is that deadlocked situations of this kind are usually resolved by the practicalities. Moreover, the passage of time might in itself alter the legal position of the parties, because an insistence to treat the contract as still in being might in time become quite unrealistic, unreasonable and untenable. I am only saying that in my view on the facts of the present case this had not happened by September, 1976.'

In the light of these authorities, I must return to the facts of the present case. It may be convenient to repeat a few sentences from para 30 of the award:

'I am satisfied that this commercial absurdity is not justified by a proper interpretation of the decided cases. I consider that the analogy of a contract between Master and servant applies more closely to a timecharter than the analogy of a simple debt. The Owner supplies the vessel and crew; the Charterer supplies fuel oil, pays disbursements and gives orders. The Charterers were also able to satisfy me that at that stage the Owners had no legitimate interest in pursuing their claim for hire rather than a claim for damages. In these respects the present case differs materially from the case of *White & Carter v. McGregor*, and is more closely analogous to the case of *The Puerto Buitrago* [1976] 1 Lloyd's Rep 250, where the judgments of Lord Denning MR and Lord Orr are particularly in point.'

It seems to me that the arbitrator is here distinguishing clearly between the two observations or limitations on the general principle to which Lord Reid had drawn attention in his speech. He is saying that a time charter is more analogous to a contract between master and servant than a simple debt, ie that it is a contract which calls for co-operation between both parties. He is also saying ('The charterers were *also* able to satisfy me . . .') that the owners had no legitimate interest in pursuing their claim for hire as distinct from damages. I will take the legitimate interest point first.

In addition to arguing that what Lord Reid had said about legitimate interest was only a quotation from counsel, and in any event obiter, arguments with which I have already dealt, counsel for the owners submitted that Lord Reid was, quite simply, wrong. It seems to me that it would be difficult for me to take that view in the light of what was said by all three members of the Court of Appeal in *The Puerto Buitrago*. Whether one takes Lord Reid's language, which was adopted by Orr and Browne LJJ in *The Puerto Buitrago*, or Lord Denning MR's language in that case ('in all reason'), or Kerr J's language in *The Odenfeld* ('wholly unreasonable . . . quite unrealistic, unreasonable and untenable'), there comes a point at which the court will cease, on general equitable principles, to allow the innocent party to enforce his contract according to its strict legal terms. How

a
one defines that point is obviously a matter of some difficulty, for it involves drawing a line between conduct which is merely unreasonable (see per Lord Reid in *White & Carter v McGregor* [1961] 3 All ER 1178 at 1182, [1962] AC 473 at 429–430, criticising the Lord President in *Langford & Co Ltd v Dutch* 1952 SC 15) and conduct which is *wholly* unreasonable (see per Kerr J in *The Odenfeld* [1978] 2 Lloyd's Rep 357 at 374). But

b
however difficult it may be to define the point, that there *is* such a point seems to me to have been accepted both by the Court of Appeal in *The Puerto Buitrago* and by Kerr J in *The Odenfeld*.

I appreciate that the House of Lords has recently re-emphasised the importance of certainty in commercial contracts, when holding that there is no equitable jurisdiction to relieve against the consequences of the withdrawal clause in a time charter: see *Scandinavian Trading Tanker Co AB v Flota Petrolera Ecuatoriana, The Scaptrade* [1983] 2 All ER 763, [1983] 3 WLR 203. I appreciate, too, that the importance of certainty was

c
one of the main reasons urged by Lord Hodson in *White & Carter v McGregor* in upholding the innocent party's unfettered right to elect. But, for reasons already mentioned, it seems to me that this court is bound to hold that there is *some* fetter, if only in extreme cases; and, for want of a better way of describing that fetter, it is safest for this court to use the language of Lord Reid, which, as I have already said, was adopted by a majority of the Court of Appeal in *The Puerto Buitrago*.

d
I would add only two observations of my own. First, although the point is sometimes put in terms of the innocent party being obliged to accept the repudiation (it is so put by the arbitrator in the last sentence of para 31 of his award), I think it is more accurate to say that it is the court which, on equitable grounds, refuses to allow the innocent party to enforce his full contractual rights. It is, as Sachs LJ said in *Decro-Wall*, the range of remedies which is limited, not the right to elect. The court is not exercising a dispensing power; nor is it rewriting an improvident contract. It is simply refusing a certain kind of

e
relief. In America the courts take the uncomplicated view that whether the repudiation is accepted or not, the innocent party is *always* obliged to mitigate his damages: see *Williston on Contracts* (3rd edn, 1968) vol 11, § 1301, *Corbin on Contracts* (1951) vol 4, § 983 and Professor A L Goodhart 'Measure of damages when a contract is repudiated' (1962) 78 LQR 263 at 267.

f
Second, on the point of uncertainty, it is of course true that the existence of a fetter on the right to claim hire, even if it only be exercised in extreme cases, necessarily introduces an element of uncertainty. Thus it can be said with force that bankers need to know where they are when accepting an assignment of charter hire as security for their loan. On the other hand, absolute certainty can never be attained. Counsel for the charterers gave as an example the doctrine of frustration which may import a degree of uncertainty

g
into commercial contracts of all kinds. So may the Unfair Contract Terms Act 1977 in the case of a consumer contract and also in the case of certain contracts for the sale of goods.

On the facts of *The Odenfeld*, Kerr J held on various grounds that the owners had ample justification for enforcing their claim for hire, at least until September 1976, although he went on to hold that the owners must be taken to have accepted the charterers'

h
repudiation when they laid up the vessel in July 1976. Kerr J did not use the language of 'legitimate interest'. But he must be taken to have found that the charterers had failed to prove absence of legitimate interest on the part of the owners in claiming hire. One of the grounds on which Kerr J so found was the difficulty in calculating damages.

In the present case, by contrast, the arbitrator has found, and found clearly, that the owners had *no* legitimate interest in pursuing their claim for hire. In my view that

j
finding is conclusive of this appeal. Counsel for the owners argued that the finding must be wrong in law. The arbitrator must have misunderstood what was said by Lord Reid, or applied the wrong test. But I could only accept that submission if the conclusion reached by the arbitrator was one which no reasonable arbitrator could have reached applying the right test. I cannot take that view. Indeed I can well understand why the arbitrator reached the conclusion he did. It is of course quite unnecessary for me to say

whether I would have reached the same conclusion on the facts myself; nor by saying
even that, do I mean to imply that I would have reached a different conclusion. It was   *a*
the arbitrator who heard the evidence over many days, not me. It was for him to decide.

Counsel for the owners then turned to the further reasons given by the arbitrator
which I have mentioned earlier in this judgment. But counsel was unable to extract any
error of law or any mistake in approach. The arbitrator analysed in detail the main
grounds on which it could be said that the owners were justified in continuing to claim
hire, rather than damages, namely the requirements of the bank, the difficulty in   *b*
assessing damages and the difficulty in obtaining alternative employment. These are all
matters which were considered by Kerr J in *The Odenfeld*. For example, on the question
of damages the arbitrator said:

> 'I did not accept that the assessment of damages in fact presented any special
> difficulty, or that the poor prospects of obtaining alternative employment would
> preclude the Owners from obtaining substantial damages. It was a matter of   *c*
> evidence.'

On the difficulty of assessing damages therefore, as on the other matters, the arbitrator
reached, as he was entitled, a different view on the facts than did Kerr J in *The Odenfeld*. I
cannot begin to say that he was wrong in law.

The arbitrator also gave thought to another consideration, that the owners, being a   *d*
one-ship company, might have decided to keep the charterparty on foot in order to
protect their parent company from heavy claims under the charter. Counsel for the
owners argued that this showed a wrong approach on the part of the arbitrator. But the
arbitrator specifically stated in para 7 of his further reasons that the consideration which
I have just mentioned could not in any event be regarded as a legitimate interest in
claiming hire rather than damages. So there is nothing in that point.   *e*

Finally, counsel for the owners argued that there is an inconsistency in the arbitrator's
reasoning in so far as he held that the owners were not obliged to accept the charterers'
repudiation in October 1980, but nevertheless *were* so obliged in April 1981. I see no
necessary inconsistency. In October 1980 the vessel was unrepaired. She was not capable
of performing any services under the charterparty. She was not costing the charterers
anything, as she was off-hire and would remain off-hire for many months. In this sense   *f*
the charterers' repudiation in October 1980 was anticipatory. The position was, as the
arbitrator rightly said, very different in April 1981, when the vessel was again capable of
earning hire. In *The Odenfeld* Kerr J accepted that the legal position might change over
time, because of changing circumstances. Even if there were an inconsistency in the
arbitrator's reasoning, which I do not think there was, it would not justify me in
reversing his decision as to the April repudiation.   *g*

I turn last to the alternative ground on which the arbitrator based his decision, that
this was a contract which called for co-operation between the parties, and therefore fell
within Lord Reid's first limitation. Counsel for the charterers argued that a time charter
is a contract for services, to be performed by the owners through the master and crew,
and through the use of their vessel. As a contract for services, it is, as Lord Diplock
pointed out in *The Scaptrade* [1983] 2 All ER 763 at 766, [1983] 3 WLR 203 at 207—   *h*

> 'the very prototype of a contract of which before the fusion of law and equity a
> court would never grant specific performance . . .'

As in any other contract for services the owners earn their remuneration by performing
the services required. If they are wrongfully prevented from performing any services,   *j*
then, as in any other contract for services, the only remedy lies in damages. The fact that
the owners' remuneration in this case, called hire, is payable in advance makes no
difference. Counsel for the owners, on the other hand, argued that the owners earned
their hire simply by holding the vessel and the services of their master and crew at the
charterers' disposal. He concedes that in the case of master and servant, where the master

a has wrongfully dismissed the servant, the servant cannot earn remuneration by holding himself at the disposal of his master. He is confined to his remedy in damages. But counsel for the owners submits that a time charter is different. In view of my decision on the legitimate interest point, it is unnecessary for me to decide between these rival arguments, or to explore the nature of a time charter contract any further. All I will say is that, at first blush, there seemed much to be said for the argument of counsel for the charterers. I say no more, because in *The Odenfeld* Kerr J found a similar argument
b unimpressive.

For the reasons I have given I would dismiss the owners' appeal and uphold the award.

Appeal dismissed. Leave to appeal granted.

Solicitors: *Holman Fenwick & Willan* (for the owners); *Norton Rose Botterell & Roche* (for
c the charterers).

K Mydeen Esq   Barrister.

First National Securities Ltd v Hegerty and another

d
QUEEN'S BENCH DIVISION
BINGHAM J
27 OCTOBER, I NOVEMBER 1982

Equity – Charge – Creation of equitable charge – Joint tenancy – Borrower agreeing to create
e *charge over property as security for loan – Borrower joint tenant of property – Other joint tenant not consenting to creation of charge – Whether equitable charge created over borrower's beneficial interest in the property.*

Execution – Charging order – Land – Discretion – Charging order nisi on land – Discretion of judge to make charging order absolute – Principles governing exercise of judge's discretion –
f *Charging Orders Act 1979, ss 1(5), 2.*

In 1978 the husband and the wife purchased their family home as joint tenants, but in November 1979 the husband separated from his wife. In December 1979 the husband borrowed £3,000 from the lenders and purported to grant them a legal charge over the home. The wife's signature was forged on both the loan application and the legal charge
g and she was unaware of either transaction. The husband fell into arrears in repaying the loan instalments and in February 1981 the lenders obtained, ex parte, a charging order nisi pursuant to s 2[a] of the Charging Orders Act 1979 in respect of the husband's beneficial interest in the home, having previously obtained a default judgment for the arrears. In March 1981 the wife commenced divorce proceedings and in April the husband agreed to transfer any interest he had in the home to the wife. The wife was
h joined as a party to the charging order proceedings and in May 1982 she successfully applied to have the charging order nisi discharged. The lenders appealed.

Held – (1) Since the wife was not a party either to the loan agreement or to the legal charge she could not incur any liability in respect of those transactions. However, the husband's conduct was a sufficient act of alienation to sever the beneficial joint tenancy
j and convert the husband and wife into tenants in common, and the husband's disposition created a valid equitable charge in the lenders' favour over the husband's equitable interest in the home (see p 141 j to p 142 a and h j, post) *Cedar Holdings Ltd v Green* [1979] 3 All ER 117 and *Williams & Glyn's Bank Ltd v Boland* [1980] 2 All ER 408 considered.

---

a Section 2, so far as material, is set out at p 142 c, post

(2) Furthermore, a judgment creditor who as such had a prima facie right to enforce his judgment was entitled to a charging order absolute unless some good reason could be shown why the court should refuse to make the order in the exercise of its discretion under s 1(5)[b] of the 1979 Act after considering all the circumstances of the case. On the facts, the wife had not rebutted the presumption that the lenders were entitled to have the charging order made absolute by showing that her position would thereby be prejudiced since although any later transfer of the home to the wife would be subject to the charging order (which would be an encumbrance on the title) her possession of the house could not be disturbed by the lenders without them making a separate application to the court pursuant to s 30 of the Law of Property Act 1925, at which point the competing equities of the parties would be weighed and considered in full. The appeal would accordingly be allowed (see p 143 *f* to *j*, post).

Notes

For equitable charges and mortgages, see 28 Halsbury's Laws (4th edn) paras 509–512, 515, and for cases on the subject, see 35 Digest (Reissue) 54–57, 355–381.

For severance of joint tenancies, see 39 Halsbury's Laws (4th edn) paras 534–541, and for cases on the subject, see 38 Digest (Reissue) 606–612, 5071–5137.

For the Law of Property Act 1925, s 30, see 27 Halsbury's Statutes (3rd edn) 385.

For the Charging Orders Act 1979, ss 1, 2, see 49 ibid 767, 769.

Cases referred to in judgment

Cedar Holdings Ltd v Green [1979] 3 All ER 117, [1981] Ch 129, [1979] 3 WLR 31, CA.
Holliday (a bankrupt), Re, ex p the trustee of the bankrupt v The bankrupt [1980] 3 All ER 385, [1981] 2 WLR 996, CA.
Irani Finance Ltd v Singh [1970] 3 All ER 199, [1971] Ch 59, [1970] 3 WLR 330, CA.
Lowrie (a bankrupt), Re, ex p the trustee of the bankrupt v The bankrupt [1981] 3 All ER 353.
National Westminster Bank v Stockman [1981] 1 All ER 800, [1981] 1 WLR 67.
Roberts Petroleum Ltd v Bernard Kenny Ltd (in liq) [1982] 1 All ER 685, [1982] 1 WLR 301, CA; *rvsd* [1983] 1 All ER 564, [1983] 2 WLR 305, HL.
Tebbutt v Haynes [1981] 2 All ER 238, CA.
Williams and Glyn's Bank Ltd v Boland [1980] 2 All ER 408, [1981] AC 487, [1980] 3 WLR 138, HL.

Appeal

By a writ dated 31 October 1980 the appellant, First National Securities Ltd (the lenders), claimed against the defendant, John Hegerty (the husband), the sum of £3,730·17, being the balance of moneys and interest due under the terms of a loan agreement made between the parties. On 23 January 1981 the lenders obtained judgment by default against the husband for the sum of £3,966·75. On 17 February 1981, on an ex parte application by the lenders, Master Creightmore granted a charging order nisi over the property at 24 Mill Road, West Mersea, Essex owned jointly by the husband and his wife, Josephine Rosemary Hegarty. The wife was joined as a respondent to the charging order proceedings and applied for the discharge of the charging order nisi. The discharge was granted by Master Topley on 6 May 1982. The lenders appealed. The appeal was heard in chambers but judgment was given by Bingham J in open court. The facts are set out in the judgment.

Peter Cowell for the lenders,
Margaret C Windridge for the wife.
The husband did not appear.

Cur adv vult

---

b   Section 1(5) is set out at p 142 *d e*, post

1 November. The following judgment was delivered.

a   **BINGHAM J.** This is an appeal by the plaintiffs, First National Securities Ltd (the lenders), against the refusal of Master Topley on 6 May 1982, to make absolute a charging order nisi made on 17 February 1981, and against his discharge of that order. There are two defendants, John Hegerty and his wife Josephine Rosemary Hegerty, but it was only the wife who appeared and resisted the appeal. When making his order Master Topley
b   expressed the hope that the judgment on any appeal might be given in open court since there are apparently a number of cases giving rise to similar problems and guidance is sought. The lenders supported this request for the same reason and I accordingly give judgment in open court.

The husband and the wife married in 1960 and have one son, now nearly 18. The husband was a police officer. In anticipation of his leaving the police force they bought
c   for £9,750 a house, 24 Mill Road, West Mersea, Colchester, which is at the centre of this appeal. The house was, on 19 July 1978, conveyed to them both in fee simple as joint tenants. The purchase was financed by a large building society mortgage. The husband and wife were then living in a police house and did not move into the house: indeed, the husband never moved in. In November 1979 he left the wife and went to the Republic of Ireland, where he now lives.

d   Before leaving this country the husband did two things. First, on 10 December 1979, he borrowed £3,000 from the lenders. His successful application for a loan was made on behalf of him and the wife and bore his signature and also the apparent signature of the wife. It is, however, accepted that she did not sign the document and that her signature is forged. She knew nothing of this loan and received no benefit. The loan agreement contained the usual acceleration clause on default in payment of any instalment. Second,
e   the husband, on 12 December 1979, executed a legal charge on the house in favour of the lenders. Again the document purported to be executed on behalf of both husband and wife but again it is common ground that the wife's signature was forged. The wife knew nothing of this transaction either.

The wife moved into the house with the son in January 1980. In March 1981 she filed a divorce petition seeking, among other things, the transfer to her of the husband's
f   interest in the house under s 24 of the Matrimonial Causes Act 1973. No decree or order has yet, as I understand it, been made, but on 1 April 1981, the husband signed a document agreeing to the transfer of any interest he might have in the house into the sole name of the wife. In April 1982 the wife registered her application for a property adjustment order as a pending action.

Meanwhile the husband had fallen into arrears in repaying the loan instalments. The
g   lenders issued a writ in October 1980. Judgment was signed in default on 23 January 1981, for the sum of £3,966·75 and £100 costs. On 17 February 1981 Master Creightmore, on an ex parte application, made a charging order nisi in respect of the husband's beneficial interest in the house. The lenders duly registered this order as a pending action. This is the order which Master Topley refused to make absolute and discharged in May 1982, although he did join the wife as a party so that she could resist
h   the lenders' application, which she did, successfully.

So much for the bare narrative. The legal effect of these various events, so far as relevant for present purposes, was I think as follows. (1) By virtue of the July 1978 conveyance the husband and wife became joint tenants on the statutory trusts of the legal estate in the house. The beneficial interest of the husband and wife in the house was as joint tenants or more probably, since it seems likely that they contributed unequally to
j   the purchase price, as tenants in common. I am not concerned with what their respective shares may have been and am in any event in no position to decide. (2) Since the wife was not a party to the loan agreement with the lenders she incurred no liability in respect of it. The agreement took effect as if it was the husband's alone. (3) Since the wife did not execute the legal charge to the lenders she incurs no liability under that instrument either. It does however seem to me that the instrument may, none the less, have had two effects. If the husband and wife were up to then equitable as well as legal joint owners of

the house I think that this disposition by the husband was a sufficient act of alienation to sever the beneficial joint tenancy and convert the husband and wife into tenants in common. In any case the disposition was in my view effective to create a valid equitable charge in favour of the lenders of the husband's beneficial interest in the house. The second of these propositions is inconsistent with the decision of the Court of Appeal in *Cedar Holdings Ltd v Green* [1979] 3 All ER 117, [1981] Ch 129, but that case was held by the House of Lords in *Williams & Glyn's Bank Ltd v Boland* [1980] 2 All ER 408, [1981] AC 487 to have been wrongly decided and I think the House of Lords would accordingly have accepted both the propositions I have stated as being correct.

Formerly, the court could not have made an order charging the husband's beneficial interest in the house because the relevant statutory provisions related to interests in land and the beneficial interest in the proceeds of sale of land held under a trust for sale was not an interest in land: see *Irani Finance Ltd v Singh* [1970] 3 All ER 199 [1971] Ch 59. A change was made by s 2 of the Charging Orders Act 1979 which provided:

'(1) . . . a charge may be imposed by a charging order only on—(a) any interest held by the debtor beneficially—(i) in any asset of a kind mentioned in subsection (2) below, or (ii) under any trust . . .
(2) The assets referred to in subsection (1) above are—(a) land . . .'

The result is that in such cases orders may be made, and in practice are made (see e g *National Westminster Bank v Stockman* [1981] 1 All ER 800, [1981] 1 WLR 67). It should, however, be noted that under s 1(5) of the 1979 Act—

'In deciding whether to make a charging order the court shall consider all the circumstances of the case and, in particular, any evidence before it as to—(a) the personal circumstances of the debtor, and (b) whether any other creditor of the debtor would be likely to be unduly prejudiced by the making of the order.'

In the present case the husband, and not the wife, is of course the debtor and the wife is not a creditor of the debtor nor is there evidence of any creditor of the debtor other than the lenders. But that does not relieve the court of the duty of considering all the circumstances of the case.

In support of his appeal counsel for the lenders made two main submissions. First, he submitted that as judgment creditors, prima facie entitled to enforce their judgment, the lenders should ordinarily be granted a charging order absolute unless the judgment debtor established some good reason why the order should not be made. Reliance was placed on the helpful summary of the relevant principles given by Lord Brandon in *Roberts Petroleum Ltd v Bernard Kenny Ltd (in liq)* [1982] 1 All ER 685 at 690, [1982] 1 WLR 301 at 307. No such reasons were shown here. Second, counsel for the lenders submitted that the court should not refrain from making the order absolute for fear of prejudicing the wife's position, since even if the order were made absolute the lenders could not sell the house without obtaining an order for sale under s 30 of the Law of Property Act 1925, at which stage the competing equities of the respective parties would be carefully weighed: see e g *Re Holliday* [1980] 3 All ER 385, [1981] Ch 405 and *Re Lowrie* [1981] 3 All ER 353. Counsel added that if the abortive legal charge to the lenders operated as an equitable charge on the husband's beneficial interest a charging order would add nothing (see s 3(4) of the 1979 Act) but the position was not entirely clear and the lenders were entitled to seek every reasonable safeguard.

I have already indicated my view that the abortive legal charge did have the effect of giving the lenders an equitable charge on the husband's share of the proceeds of sale of the house but I think it better to approach this application on the basis that the charging order, if made absolute, would add something to the lender's existing security.

Counsel for the wife asked me to adjourn this appeal since evidence might be forthcoming to show that the husband had made no contribution to the purchase of the house and had no beneficial interest in it. Having considered this request I felt bound to refuse it. The hypothesis seems very unlikely bearing in mind that at the relevant time the husband was working and the wife was not. The wife has, moreover, had 18 months

in which to repair this glaring omission, if it be such, in her affidavit sworn in April
1981. The precise extent of the husband's beneficial interest may have to be the subject
of inquiry hereafter; it seems to me safe to assume that he has some interest.

Counsel for the wife alternatively urged me to transfer the lenders' application to the
Family Division so that all claims and questions relating to the house and the competing
interest in it could be determined by the same judge at the same time. If the present
questions here arose between the husband and wife or either of them and a third party
in a family context I should, without hesitation, conclude that the Family Division was
the appropriate forum (see *Tebbutt v Haynes* [1981] 2 All ER 238). But the present
question arises primarily between creditor and debtor from a transaction having nothing
directly to do with the matrimonial relationship. I see no reason why the lenders should
be obliged to pursue their quest elsewhere. The enforcement of a third party creditor's
Queen's Bench judgment seems a suitable matter for this court to rule on.

So I turn to the main submission of counsel for the wife. This is that the appeal should
be dismissed because the making of a charging order absolute would be unfairly
prejudicial to the wife. It was pointed out that if the wife had pursued her property
adjustment application earlier she might have obtained a transfer of the husband's
beneficial interest to her unencumbered by a charging order. Now the making of an
order would necessarily restrict to some extent the benefit which she could obtain under
such an order. For that reason no order should be made and the options open to the
Family Division judge should not be in any way circumscribed.

I accept that these are matters to be considered among 'all the circumstances of the
case' but I do not think they weigh very heavily against the legitimate claims of the
lenders. The lenders parted with £3,000 to the husband. They took what appeared on its
face to be a valid legal charge on the house. It was suggested that they should have
insisted on some more formal witnessing of the signatures on the charge, both shown as
having been witnessed by the lady with whom the husband is now living in Ireland, but
I do not think they departed from normal practice. The husband has no grounds for
resisting an order and his declaration of willingness to resign his interest to the wife must
be regarded as a piece of self-interested effrontery. Of course, the making of a charging
order absolute to some extent strengthens the hand of the lenders and correspondingly
weakens that of the wife. That is why they have taken up their present positions. I do
not think, however, that the wife can complain very strongly of her inability to acquire
a beneficial interest which the husband was, during the marriage, free to charge and did
his best to convey to the lenders for good consideration. Moreover, I accept that the wife's
possession of the house cannot be disturbed until there has been an application under
s 30 of the 1925 Act and a full hearing at which the wife's personal and family position
can be investigated. That is the stage for finally determining which of the competing
voices is entitled in equity to prevail. Without the benefit of a charging order the lenders
will have no standing to initiate such an investigation. They could in theory seek,
without an order, to sell the husband's beneficial interest in the proceeds of sale but that
would not disturb the wife's possession and such a sale would not be a practical possibility.

As is made clear by authority, and by ss 1 and 2 of the 1979 Act, the question whether
a charging order nisi should be made absolute is one for the discretion of the court. I find
nothing in the circumstances of this case which begins to displace the lenders' prima
facie entitlement to an order. I accordingly differ from the master and allow the appeal.
The lenders do not ask for costs so I make no order save for a legal aid taxation of the
wife's costs. I am grateful to counsel for the lenders for his expert guidance through areas
of the law which I do not habitually frequent.

Appeal allowed. Leave to appeal granted. No order for costs.

Solicitors: *Davis & Co*, Harrow (for the lenders); *Thompson Smith & Puxon*, Colchester (for
the wife).

K Mydeen Esq   Barrister.

Thames Guaranty Ltd v Campbell and others *a*

QUEEN'S BENCH DIVISION
MANN J
9, 10, 12 MAY 1983

Equity – Charge – Creation of equitable charge – Joint tenancy – Borrower agreeing to create charge over property as security for loan – Borrower joint tenant of property – Other joint tenant **b** *not consenting to creation of charge – Lender making advance on assumption that borrower sole proprietor of property – Borrower depositing title documents with lender as security without other joint tenant's consent – Whether equitable charge created over borrower's beneficial interest in the property – Whether other joint tenant entitled to recover title documents from lender.*

In January 1973 the husband and the wife jointly purchased a home but before **c** registration of the transfer to them as joint tenants was complete the plaintiff company agreed with the husband by letter to grant him a loan. The letter stated that 'this facility is to be secured by a first charge on your property'. At that time the company did not know and could not have known that the transfer was to be to the husband and the wife as joint tenants. On 1 June 1973, after registration was completed, the documents of title were sent to the company by the husband's solicitors on his instructions. The wife did **d** not consent either to the charging of the property or to the deposit of the title documents with the company. On two further occasions in 1975 the company agreed to renew the loan and increase the principal sum. On each occasion the letter offering the loan to the husband stated that it would 'continue to be secured by a first charge on the property' and the letters acknowledged that the husband and wife were the joint owners. The husband subsequently became bankrupt and the company claimed against him for **e** unpaid principal and interest, contending that it was a secured creditor by virtue of an equitable charge granted in its favour over the husband's interest in the property. The wife counterclaimed for the return of the title documents and contended that the company did not have a valid charge.

Held – (1) Since the creation of an equitable charge depended on the intention of the **f** parties, either express or implied, what had to be considered was the intention evidenced by the letters and the property, if any, which was intended to be the subject of any such charge. On the facts, the first letter was not intended to be a charge but merely promised to create a charge and the two subsequent letters assumed the prior existence of a charge. Moreover, the husband had promised to create a charge over the whole of the property and at that time the company could not have known that he was a joint tenant. **g** Accordingly, a charge had not been created over the property by the letters. Furthermore, the court would not exercise its discretion by ordering the husband to partly perform his promise by creating an equitable charge over his own beneficial interest, even though that promise had been supported by consideration moving from the company, because to do so would prejudice the wife as a third party by making her vulnerable to an order for the sale of the property on the company's application (see p 149 *j* to p 150 *a* and *c* to *f*, **h** p 151 *g h* and p 152 *j* to p 153 *a*, post); dictum of Lord Langdale MR in *Thomas v Dering* [1835–42] All ER Rep at 718, *Cedar Holdings Ltd v Green* [1979] 3 All ER 117 and dictum of Buckley LJ in *Swiss Bank Corp v Lloyds Bank Ltd* [1980] 2 All ER at 425–426 applied.
(2) The deposit of documents of title with a creditor could only create an equitable charge if the deposit was effective in that the creditor had the right to retain them until the debt was paid. Since joint tenants were jointly entitled to the documents as trustees **j** of the legal estate and since trustees could only act with unanimity, the company could not retain the documents without the wife's consent. Moreover, the husband could not surrender custody of the documents for the purpose of charging his own beneficial interest. Accordingly, there had not been an effective deposit which could give rise to a

charge and the wife therefore was entitled to recover the documents for the joint custody
a of herself and her husband (see p 152 *f* to *h* and p 153 *c*, post).

(3) However, the company had proved its debt as an unsecured creditor of the husband
and was entitled to have judgment against him for the outstanding principal and interest
(see p 148 *e f*, post).

Notes

b For equitable charges and mortgages, see 28 Halsbury's Laws (4th edn) paras 509–512,
515, and for cases on the subject, see 35 Digest (Reissue) 54–57, 355–381.

For severance of joint tenancies, see 39 Halsbury's Laws (4th edn) paras 534–541, and
for cases on the subject, see 38 Digest (Reissue) 606–612, 5071–5137.

For cases on joint tenancies, see 38 Digest (Reissue) 596–606, 4940–5067.

c **Cases referred to in judgment**

Bank of New South Wales v O'Connor (1889) 14 App Cas 273, [1886–90] All ER Rep 672,
PC.

Cedar Holdings Ltd v Green [1979] 3 All ER 117, [1981] Ch 129, [1979] 3 WLR 31, CA.

Devaynes v Noble, Clayton's Case (1816) 1 Mer 572, [1814–23] All ER Rep 1.

James v James (1873) LR 16 Eq 153.

d *Moseley v Cressey's Co* (1865) LR 1 Eq 405.

Nanwa Gold Mines Ltd, Re, Ballantyne v Nanwa Gold Mines Ltd [1955] 3 All ER 219, [1955]
1 WLR 1080.

National Provincial and Union Bank of England v Charnley [1924] 1 KB 431.

Pryce v Bury (1853) 2 Drew 11, 61 ER 622.

Swiss Bank Corp v Lloyds Bank Ltd [1981] 2 All ER 449, [1982] AC 584, [1981] 2 WLR 893,
e HL; *affg* [1980] 2 All ER 419, [1982] AC 584, [1980] 3 WLR 457, CA.

Thomas v Dering (1837) 1 Keen 729, [1835–42] All ER Rep 711.

Wallis & Simmonds (Builders) Ltd, Re [1974] 1 All ER 561, [1974] 1 WLR 391.

Williams & Glyn's Bank v Boland [1980] 2 All ER 408, [1981] AC 487, [1980] 3 WLR 138,
HL.

Action and counterclaim

f By a writ dated 26 October 1976 the plaintiffs, Thames Guaranty Ltd (the company), a
company in liquidation, brought an action against the first defendant, Theophillus Count
Campbell (the husband), claiming repayment of principal and interest amounting to
£10,451·83 on a loan made by the company, which loan was guaranteed by the second
defendant, Likemarts Ltd, on the authority of the third defendant, Michael Jonathan
Gillis, a director of the second defendant. By an order dated 13 April 1981 Laurel May
g Campbell (the wife) was added as fourth defendant and given leave to counterclaim
against the company for delivery up to her of the certificate of title relating to a property
at 10 Holmewood Gardens, London SW2, purchased by the husband and wife and for
cancellation of a charge in favour of the company registered against the title. The second
and third defendants settled the claim against them and took no part in the proceedings.
The facts are set out in the judgment.

h

J G Boggis for the company.
The husband appeared in person.
A V B Bartlett for the wife.

Cur adv vult

j 12 May. The following judgment was delivered.

MANN J. In this action the plaintiff is a company which is in liquidation. Before the
commencement of the winding up on 22 March 1976 the company carried on a business
as bankers. In the course of its business and between 22 August 1972 and 22 March 1976
the company granted four overdraft facilities to Mr T C Campbell (the husband), who is

the first defendant. The husband's indebtedness to the company on 22 March 1976 is said to have been £9,594·54. Nothing having been paid by him the indebtedness is said to have grown by reason of interest charges to £34,362·44 as at 9 May 1983.

The husband was adjudged bankrupt on 13 July 1977. The Official Receiver is his trustee in bankruptcy and is the second third party and fifth defendant in this action. He played no part in the proceedings.

The fourth defendant is the first defendant's wife. The second and third defendants and the first third party have, in consequence of compromises, played no part in the proceedings and I shall not refer to them again.

The matrimonial home of the husband and the wife is at 10 Holmewood Gardens, London SW2. It is a modest terraced house. On 11 October 1972 the husband and the wife purchased a leasehold interest in the house for £4,000, that purchase was completed on 15 November and the transfer was to the husband and the wife jointly. Shortly thereafter the ground landlord was approached with a view to his selling the freehold reversion. He was willing to do so for the sum of £975 and contracts were exchanged on or about 19 December.

The solicitors acting for the husband and the wife were a firm called Osmond Gaunt & Rose who, on 12 January 1973, received a cheque from the husband. On presentation that cheque was not met. On 22 January the solicitors had a telephone conversation with the company. The terms of that conversation are unknown but, in consequence of it, the solicitors wrote to the company, in the following terms, on 23 January:

> 'Dear Sirs,
>
> Re: 10 Holmewood Gardens, S.W.2.
> *Theophillus Count Campbell*
>
> We refer to our telephone conversation of the 22nd January when you informed us that on presentation of Mr. Campbell's cheque for £900, this cheque would be met subject to our confirming that we will hold the Title Deeds of the above property to your order. We confirm that we have instructions from our client to hold the Title Deeds relating to the Freehold and Leasehold interests of the above property to your order, and you may accept this letter as our undertaking so to do.'

A cheque was duly met and the purchase was completed on 2 February.

The transfer was to the husband and the wife as 'Joint tenants in law and equity' and in that transfer they declared that the leasehold interest vested in them should merge and be extinguished in the freehold title. Shortly thereafter the documents of title were sent to the land registry for a first registration. The title number is SGL 157598 and the proprietors are the husband and the wife.

On 3 April 1973 the company wrote to the solicitors in these terms:

> 'Dear Sirs,
>
> Re: 10 Holmewood Gardens, S.W.2.
> *Theophillus Count Campbell*
>
> In a recent discussion with our mutual client we have agreed to provide him with a temporary advance facility secured by a first charge on his property at the above address. Accordingly we would appreciate receiving the Title Deeds relating to this property in order that our interest may be properly registered. Perhaps you would be good enough to contact Mr. Campbell regarding the contents of this letter a copy of which has been sent to him.'

The reply from the solicitors was in these terms:

> 'We are in receipt of your letter of the 3rd April. We are awaiting completion of Registration of the Title by the Land Registry. We are hoping to receive Land Certificate shortly and this will be forwarded to you immediately on receipt.'

On the same day, that is on 9 April 1973, the solicitors wrote to the husband in these terms:

'Dear Mr. Campbell,

Re: 10 Holmewood Gardens, S.W.2.

Further to my telephone conversation with you of the 6th April when you confirmed to me that the Title Deeds of the above property were to be sent to Thames Guaranty Limited, I enclose herewith a copy of a letter which I have today written to them.'

The land certificate and the preregistration deeds were sent to the company by the solicitors on 1 June and they informed the husband of that fact on the same day. Nearly eleven months later, on 29 April 1974, a solicitor acting for the company gave a notice of deposit of land certificate to the land registry and that notice was registered in the charges register on 30 April.

That the husband authorised deposit of the documents of title with the company does not admit of doubt. However, the company concedes that the wife neither consented to the deposit nor even knew of it until some years later. She asked for the documents to be sent to her on 17 April 1976 but that request was refused.

I turn away from the dealings in regard to the property to consider the position concerning the four overdraft facilities granted by the company to the husband. The first facility was dated 24 August 1972, the terms of it are not material. The second was dated 24 May 1973 and is in these terms:

'Dear Mr Campbell,

In order to place your facility at this office on a regular basis this writing indicates the terms of the accommodation granted. Amount: £5,000. Term: Not to exceed 3 months from date of this letter, at which time it is expected that the facility will either be paid up in full or the loan transferred to the new company being formed under your direction on terms to be arranged. Interest Rate: Interest will be charged at the rate of 4% p.a. over base which is at present 8½% p.a. Interest will be calculated on a daily basis, charged and be due and payable monthly. Security: This facility is to be secured by a first charge on your property at 10, Holmewood Gardens, London, S.W.2, registered in favour of Thames Guaranty Limited. To complete our documentation on this transaction I wonder if you would be good enough to sign the attached copy of this letter and return it to me as soon as possible.'

That letter is signed by the husband.

The third facility was dated 13 January 1975 and is in these terms:

'Dear Mr. Campbell,

In order to regularize the facility originally granted on 24th May, 1973 and subsequently renewed, we write to indicate the terms on which we are willing to renew this facility. Amount: £6,062.31. Term: To be repaid in full, together with all interest accrued, by 31st December, 1975. Interest Rate: Interest will be charged at a rate of 4% p.a. over our base rate, which at the date of this letter is 13%, and will be calculated at monthly rests. Security: This facility will continue to be secured by a first charge on the property owned by you and your wife at 10, Holmewood Gardens, London S.W.2, registered in favour of ourselves. Please be good enough to sign and return the attached duplicate of this letter as confirmation of your agreement to the terms contained herein.'

That facility is indorsed 'Accepted' and signed by the husband.

The final facility was dated 27 November 1975 and is in these terms:

'Dear Mr. Campbell,

We set out below the terms and conditions on which we are prepared to renew your overdraft facility to include an increase in the principle sum due, of £3500:—

Amount: £9794.61 *Purpose*: To extend your existing facility and to grant to you an additional advance of £3500. This additional advance is to be applied as to the *a* payment of £1500 to Air Jamaica, £1400 to Messrs Fyffes Limited and the residue of £600 as a further personal advance to yourself. *Term*: To be repaid in full by the 31st May 1976. *Interest Rate*: Interest will be charged at the rate of 6% per annum above our base rate (currently 11% per annum) with a minimum interest rate of 15% per annum, calculated on daily overdrawn balances debited and payable monthly. *Security*: This facility will continue to be secured by the first charge given *b* by yourself on the property at 10 Holmewood Gardens, London SW2, which is owned jointly by your wife and yourself.'

There is then a reference to a guarantee, which I need not refer to, and it continues: 'If the foregoing terms and conditions are acceptable to you, kindly sign and return the duplicate of this letter as your confirmation thereof.' That facility is indorsed 'Agreed' *c* and signed by the husband.

The use of those facilities by the husband together with interest charges produced, according to records of the husband's account kept by the company, an indebtedness, as I have said, of £9,594·54 on 22 March 1976. Those records were discovered amongst the company's papers and were produced to me by Mr R G Lewis, who is the manager engaged in the day-to-day control of the liquidation of the company. He also produced *d* calculations which showed that using the agreed interest rates, albeit with a slight qualification which operates in the husband's favour, the indebtedness as at the commencement of this hearing on 9 May had enlarged to £34,362·44.

On the facts which I have stated there fall to be considered at this stage of the proceedings (1) the company's claim against the husband and (2) the wife's counterclaim against the company. *e*

I deal with the company's claim against the husband which is for the debt to which I have referred. The husband, who appeared in person, told me that he was not and never had been happy with the figures submitted to him by either the company or its liquidator. However, he did not make any specific criticism and I have no reason to doubt the accuracy of the records and calculations which have been put before me. Accordingly, the company is entitled to judgment against the husband for £34,362·44. *f*

The wife's counterclaim against the company and the company's defence to it have caused an argument whether the company has an equitable charge over the husband's beneficial interest in the property. The company asserts that it has and the husband's trustee in bankruptcy, that is to say the Official Receiver, accepts that it has. If the assertion and acceptance are correct then the company could, as a person interested, apply to the court for an order directing the sale of the house: see the Law of Property Act *g* 1925, s 30. If the assertion and acceptance are incorrect, as the wife argues that they are, then any initiative in regard to a sale would seem to lie with the husband's trustee in bankruptcy.

The company does not assert an equitable mortgage nor does it rely on s 66 of the Land Registration Act 1925, which relates to the creation of a lien by deposit of the land certificate, albeit the registration on 30 April 1974 indicates that at that time there was *h* some thought of such a reliance by those then advising the company. The company's case is dependent on the creation of an equitable charge by the husband. That the husband had it in his power to create an equitable charge of his equitable interest is indisputable: the question is, did he exercise that power?

Counsel for the company has argued that a charge was created on the basis of an evinced intention to charge whatever beneficial interest it was the husband had in the *j* property. Alternatively, he argued that the deposit of the documents of title had the same effect.

Counsel for the wife argued that at the most there was a contract to create a charge and that that contract is not one of which specific performance could be ordered. As to the alternative argument, he says the deposit was ineffective and he counterclaims for the

a   return of the documents to the husband and the wife in their capacity as trustees for the
     sale of the legal estate.
     The nature of an equitable charge was considered by Buckley LJ in *Swiss Bank Corp v
     Lloyds Bank Ltd* [1980] 2 All ER 419 at 425–426, [1982] AC 584 at 594 to 596. He said:

> 'An equitable charge may, it is said, take the form either of an equitable mortgage
> or of an equitable charge not by way of mortgage. An equitable mortgage is created
> when the legal owner of the property constituting the security enters into some
b   > instrument or does some act which, though insufficient to confer a legal estate or
> title in the subject matter on the mortgagee, nevertheless demonstrates a binding
> intention to create a security in favour of the mortgagee, or in other words evidences
> a contract to do so (see Fisher and Lightwood's Law of Mortgage, 9th Edn, 1977,
> p 13). An equitable charge which is not an equitable mortgage is said to be created
> when property is expressly or constructively made liable, or specially appropriated,
c   > to the discharge of a debt or some other obligation, and confers on the chargee a
> right of realisation by judicial process, that is to say, by the appointment of a receiver
> or an order for sale (see Fisher and Lightwood, p 14) ... The essence of any
> transaction by way of mortgage is that a debtor confers on his creditor a proprietary
> interest in property of the debtor, or undertakes in a binding manner to do so, by
> the realisation or appropriation of which the creditor can procure the discharge of
d   > the debtor's liability to him, and that the proprietary interest is redeemable, or the
> obligation to create it is defeasible, in the event of the debtor discharging his
> liability. If there has been no legal transfer of a proprietary interest but merely a
> binding undertaking to confer such an interest, that obligation, if specifically
> enforceable, will confer a proprietary interest in the subject matter in equity. The
> obligation will be specifically enforceable if it is an obligation for the breach of
e   > which damages would be an inadequate remedy. A contract to mortgage property,
> real or personal, will, normally at least, be specifically enforceable, for a mere claim
> to damages or repayment is obviously less valuable than a security in the event of
> the debtor's insolvency. If it is specifically enforceable, the obligation to confer the
> proprietary interest will give rise to an equitable charge on the subject matter by
> way of mortgage. It follows that whether a particular transaction gives rise to an
f   > equitable charge of this nature must depend on the intention of the parties
> ascertained from what they have done in the then existing circumstances. The
> intention may be expressed or it may be inferred. If the debtor undertakes to
> segregate a particular fund or asset and to pay the debt out of that fund or asset, the
> inference may be drawn, in the absence of any contra indication, that the parties'
> intention is that the creditor should have such a proprietary interest in the segregated
g   > fund or asset as will enable him to realise out of it the amount owed to him by the
> debtor (compare *Re Nanwa Gold Mines Ltd* [1955] 3 All ER 219, [1955] 1 WLR 1080
> and contrast *Moseley v Cressey's Co* (1865) LR 1 Eq 405 where there was no obligation
> to segregate the deposits). But notwithstanding that the matter depends on the
> intention of the parties, if on the true construction of the relevant documents in the
> light of any admissible evidence as to surrounding circumstances the parties have
h   > entered into a transaction the legal effect of which is to give rise to an equitable
> charge in favour of one of them over property of the other, the fact that they may
> not have realised this consequence will not mean that there is no charge. They must
> be presumed to intend the consequence of their acts.'

     That analysis was, in my judgment, not disturbed by anything said in the House of Lords
j   ([1981] 2 All ER 449, [1982] AC 584). It is also useful to refer to the analyses in *National
     Provincial and Union Bank of England v Charnley* [1924] 1 KB 431 at 449–450 per Atkin LJ,
     Megarry and Wade *The Law of Real Property* (4th edn, 1975) pp 899, 902 and *Snell's
     Principles of Equity* (28th edn, 1982) p 437.
     I consider, in the light of the observations which I have read, the three relevant
     indorsed facility letters and I ask myself two questions. First, what is the intention

evinced by those letters? Second, what is the specific property to which that intention relates?

a

I have read the letters previously but I rehearse again the relevant passages. First, the facility of 24 May 1973 which recites 'Security':

> 'This facility is to be secured by a first charge on your property at 10, Holmewood Gardens, London, S.W.2, registered in favour of Thames Guaranty Limited.'

The second letter of 13 January 1975, said:

b

> 'Security: This facility will continue to be secured by a first charge on the property owned by you and your wife at 10, Holmewood Gardens, London S.W.2, registered in favour of ourselves.'

The final letter, that is the letter of 27 November 1975, said:

> '*Security:* This facility will continue to be secured by the first charge given by *c* yourself on the property at 10 Holmewood Gardens, London SW2, which is owned jointly by your wife and yourself.'

In my judgment the facility of 24 May 1973 contained a promise to create a charge. The words 'is to be' impel that conclusion. In my judgment the meaning of the words 'your property at 10 Holmewood Gardens' is the whole legal and beneficial interest in *d* the property. Those whole interests were not within the husband's power to charge. There is no reason to believe that the company could have known of that inability until they received the land certificate in early June 1973. In my judgment they were innocent of the true position on 24 May 1973.

In my judgment the facility of 13 January 1975 postulated the existence of a charge. The words 'will continue to be' impel that conclusion; they are not words of creation. In *e* my judgment the facility of 27 November 1975 is to the same effect as that of 13 January; it assumes the existence of the charge. Like its immediate predecessor the assumption is in regard to a property owned jointly by the husband and the wife.

I cannot, and do not, find in the three facilities the creation of a charge. There is the promise of a charge and, on two occasions, an assumption that the promise has been fulfilled. The promise was supported by a consideration, an accommodation of £5,000, *f* and if it is specifically enforceable it would have created an equitable charge. There are obstacles in the company's path. The husband promised to charge that which was not his to charge, that is to say the whole legal and beneficial interest in the property. However, the courts will order specific performance of a contract at the instance of an innocent purchaser to the extent of a vendor's actual interest: see *Fry on Specific Performance* (6th edn, 1921) para 1257. There is no reason why an innocent person who gives consideration *g* for the promise of a charge on the whole should not be in a position equivalent to that of a purchaser and thus secure an order for partial performance. In this case any order would be for the creation of a charge on the husband's beneficial interest in the property.

The ability of the purchaser to secure an order for partial performance, and hence that of a person to whom a charge is promised, is subject to a discretion in the court which is of long standing and which is expressed in *Fry* para 1270 as follows: *h*

> 'The principle [ie the principle of partial performance] will not, it seems, be applied where the alienation of the partial interest of the vendor might prejudice the rights of third persons interested in the estate. Thus where a tenant for life without impeachment of waste under a strict settlement had contracted for the sale of the fee, the Court refused to compel him to alienate his life interest, on the ground that a stranger would be likely to use his liberty to commit waste in a *j* manner different from a father, and more prejudicial to the rights of those in remainder.'

And the reference given for that is *Thomas v Dering* (1837) 1 Keen 729, [1835–42] All ER Rep 711.

Counsel for the wife relies on this discretion. He says that if an order was made in favour of the company it would prejudice the right of the wife as a joint tenant to the occupancy of the matrimonial home in that she would be exposed to proceedings under s 30 of the Law of Property Act 1925 at the instance of a secured creditor which would be very likely to result in an order to sell. A sale would be serious for the wife. She told me that, at the age of 61, she resides in the house with her husband, her youngest son aged 22, and on occasion her three grandchildren by her eldest son, they being aged 10, 8 and 2. Neither husband nor wife has any income apart from a state retirement pension and the wife has, apart from a trivial sum in the Post Office Savings Bank, no capital asset other than her share in the house.

Counsel for the wife relied on observations of Goff LJ in *Cedar Holdings Ltd v Green* [1979] 3 All ER 117 at 127–128, [1981] Ch 129 at 147. With those observations Shaw LJ agreed. Goff LJ said:

> 'I think too that counsel's case must fail on another ground, namely that even in the straightforward case where the vendor has some estate or interest in the land, albeit less than he contracted to give, the court will not order specific performance to the extent of his true estate or interest "where the alienation of the partial interest of the vendor might prejudice the rights of third persons interested in the estate" . . .'

Goff LJ then referred to the passage in *Fry* which I have read and to the case of *Thomas v Dering* referred to in the text. He continued by quoting Lord Langdale MR's judgment in *Thomas v Dering* (1837) 1 Keen 729 at 747–748, [1835–42] All ER Rep 711 at 718:

> '". . . I apprehend that, upon the general principle that the Court will not execute a contract, the performance of which is unreasonable, or would be prejudicial to persons interested in the property, but not parties to the contract, the Court, before directing the partial execution of the contract by ordering the limited interest of the vendor to be conveyed, ought to consider how that proceeding may affect the interests of those who are entitled to the estate, subject to the limited interest of the vendor" . . . Such specific performance would, as it seems to me, prejudice the other co-owner, the wife, in two ways . . . In any case whether or not the court would ultimately order a sale under s 30 of the Law of Property Act 1925, such specific performance must be prejudicial to her position in proceedings against her under that section.'

For the purposes of those observations the facts of that case are materially indistinguishable from the present.

The observations of the two members of the Court of Appeal are binding on me and if, as Goff and Shaw LJJ held, that partial specific performance in that case would have been refused as prejudicial to the wife then so must it be here. I should add that, although in *Williams & Glyn's Bank v Boland* [1980] 2 All ER 408 at 415, [1981] AC 487 at 507 Lord Wilberforce, with whom the other Law Lords agreed, said that he considered *Cedar Holdings v Green* to have been wrongly decided, I do not regard that consideration as affecting the remarks on which I have relied, and counsel for the company did not so suggest.

For the above reasons I reject the company's first argument in regard to an equitable charge.

I turn to the alternative argument based on the deposit with the company of the document of title on behalf of the husband. A deposit which the wife neither consented to nor knew of until some years later.

The company relied on a passage in the opinion of the Privy Council given by Lord Macnaghten in *Bank of New South Wales v O'Connor* (1889) 14 App Cas 273 at 282, [1886–90] All ER Rep 672 at 677 where he said:

> 'It is a well established rule of equity that a deposit of a document of title without

either writing or word of mouth will create in equity a charge upon the property to which the document relates to the extent of the interest of the person who makes the deposit.'

I was also referred to *Re Wallis & Simmonds (Builders) Ltd* [1974] 1 All ER 561 at 564, [1974] 1 WLR 391 at 395 where Templeman J quoted from *Coote on Mortgages* (9th edn, 1927) vol 1, p 86, where it was written:

'A deposit of title deeds by the owner of freeholds or leaseholds with his creditor for the purpose of securing either a debt antecedently due, or a sum of money advanced at the time of the deposit, operates as an equitable mortgage or charge, by virtue of which the depositee acquires, not merely the right of holding the deeds until the debt is paid, but also an equitable interest in the land itself. A mere delivery of the deeds will have this operation without any express agreement, whether in writing or oral, as to the conditions or purpose of the delivery, as the Court would infer the intent and agreement to create a security from the relation of debtor and creditor subsisting between the parties, unless the contrary were shown; and the delivery would be sufficient part performance of such agreement to take the case out of the statute [ie out of s 40 of the Law of Property Act 1925].'

The authorities to which I have referred are silent on the question whether one joint tenant can, by depositing the documents of title to the legal estate without the consent of the other joint tenant, thereby charge his beneficial interest in the property which is the subject of the joint tenancy. Counsel have been unable to discover a discussion of the point in any case, work of authority or other text book. I was referred by counsel for the wife to *Pryce v Bury* (1853) 2 Drew 11, 61 ER 622 but I find it impossible to discern from that report, or from the note to *James v James* (1873) LR 16 Eq 153, what actually was the ground of Kindersley V-C's decision. I derive no help from the case.

In my judgment the deposit of title deeds with the creditor does not operate as an equitable charge unless the deposit is an effective one. A deposit is an effective one in my view if the creditor can retain custody until his debt is paid. I do not regard the deposit of title deeds by one joint tenant without the consent of the other as being effective in that sense. My reasons are as follows.

Joint owners of a legal estate are jointly entitled to the custody of the title deeds relating to that estate (see 39 Halsbury's Laws (4th edn) para 388). The two are trustees of the deeds no less than they are of the legal estate. Trustees can act only with unanimity. One cannot part with custody of the deeds without consent of the other. That custody is not a thing which either can by himself effectively surrender for the purpose of dealing with his own beneficial interest. The wife has, in my view, at all times been entitled to request the return of documents of title to the joint custody of herself and the husband. There was thus no effective deposit.

I must add, first, that counsel for the wife addressed arguments to me on the basis that contrary to his contention the deposit did create a charge. Those arguments were to the effect that either the debt for which the charge was given, that is the advance of £900 towards the purchase of the freehold, had been repaid (see *Devaynes v Noble, Clayton's Case* (1816) 1 Mer 572, [1814–23] All ER Rep 1) or that the terms to be implied from the deposit had been superseded by those expressed in the facility letters. I express no view on those arguments. Second, counsel for the company argued that the undertaking to deposit which had been given before 24 May 1973 might be taken as reinforcing the undertaking given by the husband in regard to the facility of that date. It may well be that it does reinforce the promise but I do not regard that undertaking as altering the promissory nature of the undertaking given.

For the reasons which I have given the husband did not create an equitable charge over his beneficial interest in the property. The wife is therefore successful on the issue with *a* the company. The particular method of pleading her counterclaim is at para 10 of a pleading served on 23 June 1981 where it is said:

'10. In the premises the 4th Defendant is entitled (with the 1st Defendant) to an order for delivery up of the said certificate and is entitled under Section 82(1) of the Land Registration Act 1925 to an order for rectification of the register by the cancellation of the said notice of deposit. AND the 4th Defendant counterclaims: (1) *b* An order that the Plaintiffs deliver up to the 4th Defendant the Land Certificate of title no. SGL 157598; (2) An order that the charges register of title No. SGL 157598 be rectified by the cancellation of the notice of deposit of land certificate registered on 30th April 1974.'

The delivery up to the husband and the wife, as trustees, must follow from what I have said. The notice of deposit of the land certificate seems in any event to have been *c* misconceived as the company does not now rely on s 66 of the Land Registration Act 1925.

After hearing submissions from counsel concerning his powers under s 82 of the Land Registration Act 1925, his Lordship entered judgment for the company against the husband in respect of the amount claimed by the company together with interest, *d* granted the relief claimed by the wife in her counterclaim by ordering rectification of the register, and dismissed the company's claim against the wife.

Order accordingly.

Solicitors: *Lieberman Leigh & Co* (for the company); *Howard Thomas & Petrou*, West Norwood (for the wife).

K Mydeen Esq   Barrister.

R v Islington London Borough Council, ex parte Knight

QUEEN'S BENCH DIVISION (CROWN OFFICE LIST)
McCULLOUGH J
19, 20, 23 SEPTEMBER 1983

Compulsory purchase – Compensation – Disturbance – Land acquired by agreement – Land – Council tenancy – Tenant surrendering tenancy to local authority to enable authority to have vacant possession to carry out improvements – Whether surrender of tenancy constituting acquisition of 'land' by local authority – Land Compensation Act 1973, s 37(3)(c).

The applicant was the secure tenant of a dwelling owned by a local authority which wished to obtain vacant possession of the dwelling in order to rehabilitate and improve it. The authority accordingly served notice under s 33 of the Housing Act 1980 that it intended to seek vacant possession and allocated a new house to the applicant, who accepted it and surrendered the tenancy of her existing dwelling. The applicant claimed removal expenses and a home loss payment, both of which were paid by the authority, and also compensation for disturbance, pursuant to s 37[a] of the Land Compensation Act 1973, which was refused by the authority. The applicant applied for judicial review of the authority's refusal, contending that for the purposes of s 37(3)(c) of the 1973 Act 'land' included an interest in land and her secure tenancy was such an interest and that therefore her surrender of her tenancy amounted to a displacement from 'land acquired by agreement', which entitled her to compensation for disturbance.

Held – Construing the 1973 Act in context with other legislation dealing with compulsory acquisition and compensation, the acquisition of land under that Act was to be distinguished from the extinguishment of an interest. Accordingly, even if the applicant's secure tenancy could be said to be 'land' for the purposes of s 37(3)(c), the effect of the applicant's surrender of her tenancy meant merely that her interest was extinguished and not that land was 'acquired' by the local authority by agreement. The applicant was therefore not entitled to judicial review of the authority's refusal to pay her compensation for disturbance (see p 157 e f j, p 158 b to e and p 159 a, post).

Dictum of Widgery LJ in *Newham London BC v Benjamin* [1968] 1 All ER at 1200 applied.

Notes

For payments for disturbance, see 8 Halsbury's Laws (4th edn) paras 341–342.

For the Land Compensation Act 1973, s 37, see 4 Halsbury's Statutes (3rd edn) 203.

For the Housing Act 1980, s 33, see 50(1) ibid 925.

Cases referred to in judgment

Newey v Liverpool City Council (26 March 1982, unreported), QBD.
Newham London BC v Benjamin [1968] 1 All ER 1195, [1968] 1 WLR 694, CA.

Application for judicial review

Ethel Annie Knight applied, with the leave granted by Glidewell J on 11 May 1983, for (i) an order of certiorari quashing the decision of Islington London Borough Council notified by letter dated 7 February 1983 refusing the applicant's claim for a disturbance payment pursuant to s 37 of the Land Compensation Act 1973, and (ii) a declaration that she was entitled to a disturbance payment under s 37(1) consequent on her displacement

---

a   Section 37, so far as material, is set out at p 156 *a* to *h*, post

a from land known as and situated at 12 Gwynne House, Margery Street Estate, Margery Street, London WC1. The facts are set out in the judgment.

Andrew Bano for Mrs Knight.
C J Lockhart-Mummery for the London borough.

b   *Cur adv vult*

23 September. The following judgment was delivered.

c **McCULLOUGH J.** Mrs Knight applies for judicial review of the refusal of Islington London Borough Council to make a disturbance payment to her under s 37 of the Land Compensation Act 1973.

Until 14 October 1982 she was the tenant of a dwelling house at 12 Gwynne House, Margery Street in that borough. Gwynne House is a large building standing on land the freehold of which was acquired by Finsbury Borough Council in 1930. That authority built Gwynne House a few years later. On the reorganisation of local government in *d* 1974 the London Borough of Islington succeeded to the interest of Finsbury Borough Council.

On 12 January 1975 or thereabouts Mrs Knight and her husband began to live in no 12. Her husband was joint tenant with her mother, but after her death on 6 December 1978 Mr Knight became sole tenant, and when he died on 1 March 1982 Mrs Knight took his place. She had a weekly tenancy. By virtue of s 28 of the Housing Act 1980 it *e* was a secure tenancy.

On 9 November 1981 the London borough had served on Mr Knight a notice under s 33 of the Housing Act 1980 stating that a court order for possession of no 12 was being sought on the grounds—

f
> '8—That the landlord intends, within a reasonable time of obtaining possession of the dwelling house—(a) to demolish or reconstruct the building or part of the building comprising the dwelling house; or (b) to carry out work on that building or on land let together with, and thus treated as part of the dwelling house; and cannot reasonably do so without obtaining possession of the dwelling house.'

The notice went on to say:

g
> 'The reasons for taking this action are: The dwelling is in need of rehabilitation and the council plans to carry out this work in Spring/Summer '82. The extent and nature of the improvement are such that they cannot be done if the tenant is in occupation.'

In Mrs Knight's case no court order was required because the London borough allocated a new house to her, to which she was content to move, and accordingly she *h* surrendered her tenancy of no 12.

The council paid her a home loss payment under s 29 of the Land Compensation Act 1973. It was accepted that she was so entitled because she had been displaced from a dwelling on land which had previously been acquired by an authority possessing compulsory purchase powers (namely Finsbury Borough Council), because the dwelling was to be improved and because she had occupied it for more than five years. In addition *j* she received a payment under s 93 of the Housing Finance Act 1972, which empowers a local authority to pay the removal expenses of a tenant who moves from one of the council's dwellings to another dwelling.

Section 37 of the Land Compensation Act 1973 (as amended by the Housing Act 1974, the Housing Rents and Subsidies Act 1975 and the Rent Act 1977), so far as material, reads as follows:

'(1) Where a person is displaced from any land in consequence of—(a) the acquisition of the land by an authority possessing compulsory purchase powers; (b) the making, passing or acceptance of a housing order, resolution or undertaking in respect of a house or building on the land or the service of an improvement notice, within the meaning of Part VIII of the Housing Act 1974, in respect of a house on the land; (c) where the land has been previously acquired by an authority possessing compulsory purchase powers or appropriated by a local authority and is for the time being held by the authority for the purposes for which it was acquired or appropriated, the carrying out of any improvement to a house or building on the land or of redevelopment on the land, (d) the carrying out of any improvement to a house or building on the land or of redevelopment on the land by a housing association which has previously acquired the land and at the date of the displacement either is registered or is specified in an order made by the Secretary of State under section 80 of the Housing Finance Act 1972 or paragraph 23 of Schedule 1 to the Housing Rents and Subsidies Act 1975, he shall, subject to the provisions of this section, be entitled to receive a payment (hereafter referred to as a "disturbance payment") from [and then the different paying authorities are listed] . . .

(2) A person shall not be entitled to a disturbance payment—(a) in any case, unless he is in lawful possession of the land from which he is displaced; (b) in a case within subsection (1)(a) above, unless either—(i) he has no interest in the land for the acquisition or extinguishment of which he is (or if the acquisition or extinguishment were compulsory would be) entitled to compensation under any other enactment; or (ii) he has such an interest as aforesaid but the compensation is subject to a site value provision and he is not (or if the acquisition were compulsory would not be) entitled in respect of that acquisition to an owner-occupier's supplement . . .

(3) For the purposes of subsection (1) above a person shall not be treated as displaced in consequence of any such acquisition, improvement or redevelopment as is mentioned in paragraph (a), (c) or (d) of that subsection unless he was in lawful possession of the land—(a) in the case of land acquired under a compulsory purchase order, at the time when notice was first published of the making of the compulsory purchase order prior to its submission for confirmation or, where the order did not require confirmation, of the preparation of the order in draft; (b) in the case of land acquired under an Act specifying the land as subject to compulsory acquisition, at the time when the provisions of the Bill for that Act specifying the land were first published; (c) in the case of land acquired by agreement, at the time when the agreement was made; and a person shall not be treated as displaced in consequence of any such order, resolution, undertaking or improvement notice, as mentioned in paragraph (b) of that subsection unless he was in lawful possession as aforesaid at the time when the order was made, the resolution was passed, the undertaking was accepted or the notice was served . . .

(5) Where a person is displaced from any land as mentioned in subsection (1) above but is not entitled, as against the authority there mentioned, to a disturbance payment or to compensation for disturbance under any other enactment, the authority may, if they think fit, make a payment to him determined in accordance with section 38(1) to (3) below . . .'

Before summarising the rival contentions of the parties it is useful to state what is agreed. (1) Until 14 October 1982, the date of the surrender, Mrs Knight had an interest in the land in question. (2) She falls within s 37(1)(c), since the land had been previously acquired for housing purposes by an authority possessing compulsory purchase powers and was in 1982 being held by the London borough for the same purposes and her displacement was in consequence of an improvement to her house. (3) Section 37(2) does not disqualify her from receiving a disturbance payment. (4) Her entitlement to such a payment depends on the construction of the words 'land acquired' in s 37(3)(c).

a   For Mrs Knight counsel submits that the London borough 'acquired' the land at the time of the surrender and, as she was then in lawful possession, s 37(3)(c) does not take away her right to a payment.

For the London borough counsel submits that the only acquisition of the land was in 1930, when the freehold was acquired. There was no acquisition at the time of the surrender and, as she was not in possession in 1930, s 37(3)(c) disentitles her to a payment.

b   Counsel for Mrs Knight argues that, although 'land' is not defined in the Land Compensation Act 1973, the same meaning should be attached to the word as in the Land Compensation Act 1961, where, by s 39(1), it is said, inter alia, that 'land' includes any interest in land. Until 14 October 1982 Mrs Knight had such an interest, namely her tenancy, and at that date the London borough 'acquired' her interest. As she was then in possession, and as the surrender was plainly an 'agreement', s 37(3)(c) entitles her to a payment.

c   Counsel for the London borough does not accept this meaning of 'land' in s 37(3)(c), and in support he points, convincingly in my judgment, to the reference to an 'interest in land' in s 37(2)(b). But, and more importantly, he submits that even if 'land' in s 37(3)(c) includes an interest in land, and therefore includes Mrs Knight's tenancy, the London borough did not 'acquire' her tenancy. It is to the meaning to be given to the word 'acquired' that the argument in this case has principally been directed.

d   Counsel for Mrs Knight puts his argument in a number of ways. He says that to acquire the freehold of land by compulsory purchase is not enough. The acquiring authority (or, presumably, the original landlord) has to put an end to all interests which prevent vacant possession. To 'acquire' the land there must be physical, i e vacant, possession of it. Later he submitted that any process by which such adverse interests are brought to an end is 'acquisition'.

e   Counsel for the London borough accepts none of this. He points to what he submits is an essential difference between acquisition and extinguishment. Mrs Knight's tenancy was not 'acquired' at the time of the surrender. Nor was the land 'acquired' when, in consequence of that surrender, the London borough obtained vacant possession. The effect of the surrender was to extinguish her interest. Indeed the same would have followed had the London borough found it necessary to obtain from the court an order under the Housing Act 1980 giving to it possession of her house.

f   Which construction is correct? There is no doubt, and indeed counsel agree, that s 37(3) appears to have been inserted in order to prevent the payment of compensation to those who took possession of land when they knew, or had the means of knowing, that they were liable to be displaced from it. But, if the construction contended for by the London borough is correct, Mrs Knight is excluded, despite the fact that she took possession at a time when she could not have known of her liability to be displaced years hence. She is excluded simply because she happened to take possession after 1930, whereas another tenant, who happened to take possession in 1929, would receive compensation.

g   The object of s 37 (which was a new provision, rather than a re-enactment) would appear to have been to compensate those displaced from land who would not otherwise be entitled to compensation, eg under the Land Compensation Act 1961. Mrs Knight is such a person. Compensation in other branches of the law is given to those who suffer loss. It is strange, to me at least, to determine a loser's entitlement to compensation by reference, not to what he has lost, but to whether or not it can be said that someone else has gained or 'acquired' what he lost.

h   These are not the only considerations. I have no doubt that counsel for the London borough is correct when he says that the Land Compensation Act 1973 should be construed in context with the other statutes in the field of compulsory acquisition and compensation, notably the Land Compensation Act 1961, the Compulsory Purchase Act 1965 and the Acquisition of Land Act 1981, which in broad terms replaced the Acquisition of Land (Authorisation Procedure) Act 1946.

j   By s 87(1) of the 1973 Act the phrase 'acquiring authority' is to have the same meaning as in the Land Compensation Act 1961. The definition which is to be found in s 39(1) of the 1961 Act is not of itself indicative of the meaning to be given to the word 'acquired' (or to any other derivative of 'acquire'), but it would be surprising if Parliament had intended the concept of acquisition to bear a different meaning in the 1973 Act from that which it bore in the 1961 Act.

I recognise that the phrase 'acquiring authority' does not itself appear in s 37 of the 1973 Act, the ambit of which extends beyond situations of compulsory purchase. But s 37 contains a number of references to the acquisition of land by an authority, and I see no reason to think that Parliament intended any difference of meaning for the purposes of s 37.

There is no doubt that in this legislation, and indeed in the wider field of the law of landlord and tenant, there is a vital distinction between the acquisition of an interest and the extinguishment of an interest: see eg Widgery LJ's judgment in *Newham London BC v Benjamin* [1968] 1 All ER 1195 at 1200, [1968] 1 WLR 694 at 701–702. When a landlord is granted a possession order against a tenant the tenant's interest is thereby extinguished. The landlord obtains vacant possession. This process is not described as one of 'acquisition'. Nor is the obtaining of vacant possession a prerequisite of 'acquisition'. Freehold can be 'acquired' though tenants remain in occupation.

The distinction between 'acquisition' and 'extinguishment' is recognised in s 37 itself, where, in s 37(2)(b)(i), the two words appear in contradistinction. I find it impossible to accept, as counsel for Mrs Knight at one time contended, that the single word 'acquisition', where it appears alone in s 37, can do duty for both.

These are the principal reasons why I must accept the submissions made on behalf of the London borough. A further indication that they are correct may perhaps be found in the very existence of s 37(3)(c). On the construction which I think is right the words have a purpose. It may be, and I believe it is, arbitrary to compensate the weekly tenant who went into possession in Gwynne House in 1929 (assuming, for the purpose of this illustration, that it had then existed), but to deny it to her neighbour who went into possession in 1931, but at least the words have a function. If counsel for Mrs Knight were correct they would be surplusage. Someone in lawful possession of the land who agrees to what counsel for Mrs Knight would call the 'acquisition' of his interest will, inevitably, be in lawful possession of the land at the time when the agreement is made. So, on his construction, para (c) adds nothing to the phrase, 'unless he was in lawful possession of the land', which appears near the start of s 37(3).

In reaching my conclusion I am differing from the unreported decision of his Honour Judge Morris-Jones QC, sitting as a judge of the High Court in Liverpool on 26 March 1982, in *Newey v Liverpool City Council* and I must say a word about that case. The plaintiff there sought and obtained against the Liverpool City Council a declaration that she was entitled to a disturbance payment under s 37 of the 1973 Act. The council had bought the freehold of the land in 1866 and had thereafter built on it. The plaintiff held a weekly tenancy of a cottage on the land from 1962 until 1974 when, in anticipation of redevelopment, she was rehoused. The city council argued that she was not entitled to a disturbance payment and relied, inter alia, on s 37(3)(c). The judge held that 'The agreement to which the paragraph refers must in this case be the agreement between the then acquiring authority and the person then in lawful possession'. Counsel for the London borough suggests that the judge may have been led into this, as I believe, erroneous conclusion by a concession apparently made by counsel for the local authority. Earlier in the judgment appears a sentence which reads: 'It is agreed that the property was acquired by the defendants by agreement.' The context in which this sentence appears indicates that by 'the property' the judge meant the plaintiff's tenancy. In other words it was apparently conceded that the local authority 'acquired' the plaintiff's tenancy. For this reason, submits counsel for the London borough, and I think he may well be right, the judge was led into error. Judge Morris-Jones, like me, was exploring an area of the law with which he was not familiar. It may be that he did not have as careful and patient an exposition of the relevant principles as I have had in this case.

a

The application must be refused.

Application dismissed.

Solicitors: *Suzanne Tarlin* (for Mrs Knight); *C Tapp* (for the London borough).

Vivian Horvath   Barrister.

b

Aveyard v Aveyard

COURT OF APPEAL, CIVIL DIVISION
c CUMMING-BRUCE LJ AND REEVE J
8 NOVEMBER 1983

County court – Appeal – Leave – Application for leave – Ex parte application – Application made some weeks after hearing – Advisability that application be dismissed – Application to be adjourned to allow other party to be heard if judge minded to grant leave.

d

Where an application is made ex parte to the judge in the county court for leave to appeal some weeks after the hearing, the judge should, because of the real risk that he may be unable to recall accurately all the facts and circumstances relevant to the grant of leave, follow the practice of the Court of Appeal and confine himself to the power to dismiss the application. If he is minded to grant leave he should adjourn the application to give *e* the other party an opportunity to make submissions (see p 160 g to j, post).

Notes
For obtaining leave to appeal from a county court, see 10 Halsbury's Laws (4th edn) para 656, and for cases on the subject, see 13 Digest (Reissue) 520–521, 4307–4316.

f **Interlocutory appeal**
The mother appealed against the decision of his Honour Judge Hallam in the Leeds County Court on 24 January whereby he dismissed an application for an order defining the reasonable access ordered between the mother and a child of the family on 3 September 1983. The case is reported only on the practice to be followed on applications for leave to appeal from a county court.

g
Louise S Godfrey for the mother.
John M Collins for the father.

CUMMING-BRUCE LJ, after giving his reasons for dismissing the mother's appeal, said: Counsel for the father has raised a procedural point on which he asks for our ruling. *h* We have not heard him on the merits of the appeal but we think it proper to make an observation.

What happened in this case was that there was no application for leave to appeal at the end of the hearing before the judge and there is a matter of dispute (which it is unnecessary for this court to resolve as leave to appeal was, in the end, given by the learned registrar) whether, having regard to the form of the judge's order and the reality of the matter that access was being prevented, leave to appeal was necessary at all. On *j* that we make no observation because it is unnecessary for us to do so. But after some discussion, some weeks after the hearing before the judge, an ex parte application was made before the judge on behalf of the proposed appellant, the mother, asking for leave to appeal. This was quite misconceived because the time for appeal had expired. The judge had no jurisdiction to give leave and the application should have been made to the

Registrar of Civil Appeals, which later took place. However, the judge heard the ex parte application and granted leave.

It is submitted by counsel for the father that, having regard to the passage of time, the advantage that the judge usually has when the judge is asked to give leave to appeal was an advantage that he no longer enjoyed because it might well be that he no longer had clearly in his mind all the relevant facts and circumstances, so that it was unwise to rely on the assistance he got in ex parte proceedings from one side. In fact counsel for the father told us that, had notice been given to the other side, they would have strenuously opposed grant of leave to appeal.

It is important that I should say that counsel for the father has not referred us to any rule dealing with the matter, that is to say dealing with the form of applications for leave to appeal when made to the county court judge. When applications are made to the Court of Appeal there is a clear rule, which is RSC Ord 59, r 14. The effect of that rule is that applications should be made ex parte in the first place and may be refused by the Court of Appeal in ex parte proceedings but may not be granted save on an adjournment and notice to the other side. It may be that the practice is different in the case of the application to the judge who gave judgment and made the order, because he at that time knows all about the case, and really does not need any assistance from either party in order to form in his mind whether to grant leave to appeal. I make no observation on the proper procedure when it is contemplated to make an application to the trial judge for leave to appeal a day or two after the end of the hearing.

The point of counsel for the father is this. When weeks have elapsed, so that it is very unlikely that the judge can clearly recollect all the relevant matters, the common sense of the matter is that, if the application is made to him in ex parte proceedings, he should not grant leave to appeal without an adjournment and giving an opportunity to the other side to make any contrary submissions, that is to say procedure analogous with the procedure under Ord 59, r 14. It has this practical effect, which is why counsel for the father raised it. The application made to the county court judge was out of time. The judge had no jurisdiction. The application was misconceived. The judge did not realise that and granted leave to appeal. That order was void for want of jurisdiction. The matter eventually came before the Registrar of Civil Appeals. The registrar found himself faced with the situation in which the judge had granted leave to appeal and counsel for the father tells us that the registrar attached importance to the fact that the judge had granted leave, which is perfectly natural because, where a judge has granted leave, even without jurisdiction, it is a matter which is likely to carry weight with the Registrar of Civil Appeals.

I would venture to say this, conscious of the fact that we have heard no argument on the rules and we have not had the advantage of anything from the judge. If an application for leave to appeal is made to a judge after some weeks have elapsed since the hearing, there is a real risk that he will be unable to recall accurately all the facts and circumstances relevant to the grant of leave to appeal and in those circumstances it would be wise and safe, as a matter of caution, for the judge to follow the practice of the Court of Appeal by confining himself in the ex parte proceedings to the power to dismiss the application. If he is minded to grant it he should adjourn the proceedings in order that the other party may be served with notice and given the opportunity of making submissions.

REEVE J. I agree. [His Lordship went on to say that he took the view that the judge's decision was plainly right, and that a minimum period of two to three years should elapse before the mother could renew her application.]

Appeal dismissed. No order for costs.

Solicitors: *Barrington Black Austin & Co*, Leeds (for the mother); *Barrie Hill & Co*, Leeds (for the father).

Patricia Hargrove   Barrister.

Re West Anstey Common

CHANCERY DIVISON
WHITFORD J
11, 12 OCTOBER 1983

Commons – Registration – Disputed claims – Reference to commons commissioner – Extent of inquiry by commissioner – Objection taken to registration of part of land – No objection taken to registration of remainder of land – Whether commissioner bound to inquire into validity of registration of whole of land – Commons Registration Act 1965, ss 5, 6(1).

A local authority provisionally registered, under s 4 of the Commons Registration Act 1965, an area of land as common land. N objected, under s 5[a] of the 1965 Act, to part of the land being included in the land provisionally registered, on the ground that he was the owner. His objection was referred, under s 6(1)[b] of the 1965 Act, to a commons commissioner. The commissioner held that N's objection was valid and accordingly he excluded that part of the land from the land provisionally registered as common land. As no objection had been taken to the registration of any other part of the land the commissioner confirmed the registration of the remainder of the land as common land. H, who claimed to be the owner of certain other parts of the land, appealed, under s 18 of the 1965 Act, against the commissioner's decision. He contented that, once an objection had been made to the registration of part of an area of land as common land, the status of the whole of the area of land was put in question, and accordingly that the commissioner had erred in law in not inquiring into the validity of the registration of the whole of the area of land as common land, even though no objection had been taken to such registration.

Held – The extent to which any particular objection to the registration of an area of land as common land put in question the status of the whole of the area depended on the particular circumstances of each individual case. Since, on the facts, the sole question which had been referred to the commissioner was whether that part of the land over which N claimed ownership had been rightly included in the area provisionally registered as common land, there was, in the absence of any objection to the registration of the remainder of the land, no need for him to inquire into anything except the validity of the registration so far as it concerned that part. It followed that the commissioner had not erred in law and the appeal would accordingly be dismissed (see p 167 *c* to *e* and *h*, post).

Re Sutton Common, Wimborne [1982] 2 All ER 376 explained.

Notes
For referral of the registration of common land to a commons commissioner, see 6 Halsbury's Laws (4th edn) para 673, and for the hearing before the commissioner, see ibid paras 695–696.

For the Commons Registration Act 1965, ss 4, 5, 6, 18, see 3 Halsbury's Statutes (3rd edn) 922, 923, 924, 931.

Cases referred to in judgment
Corpus Christi College, Oxford v Gloucestershire CC [1982] 3 All ER 995, [1983] QB 360, [1982] 3 WLR 849, CA.
Ilkley and Burley Moors, Re (1983) Times, 16 February.
R v Commons Comrs, ex p Winnington (1982) Times, 26 November.
Sutton Common, Wimborne, Re [1982] 2 All ER 376, [1982] 1 WLR 647.

---

a   Section 5, so far as material, is set out at p 164 *f* and *j*, post
b   Section 6(1) is set out at p 165 *a b*, post

Cases also cited

Box Parish Council v Lacey [1979] 1 All ER 113, [1980] Ch 109, CA.   *a*
Central Electricity Generating Board v Clwyd CC [1976] 1 All ER 251, [1976] 1 WLR 151.

Case stated

Devon County Council provisionally registered, under s 4 of the Commons Registration
Act 1965, West Anstey Common (including Anstey Rhiney Moor, Guphill Common,
Anstey Money Common, Woodland Common and part of Twitchen Common) as   *b*
common land. Ernest John Nicholls and George Elston Nicholls objected, under s 5 of
the 1965 Act and reg 5 of the Commons Registration (Objections and Maps) Regulations
1968, SI 1968/989, to Woodland Common being included in the land so registered.
Their objection was referred, under s 6 of the 1965 Act, to a commons commissioner, J L
Morris Smith Esq. He held that the Nichollses' objection was valid and he excluded
Woodland Common from the land provisionally registered as common land. As no   *c*
objections had been taken to the registration of any other part of West Anstey Common
as common land, he confirmed the registration of the remainder of the common as
common land. At the request of the appellant, Hugh Michael James Harrison, who
claimed to be the owner of Anstey Rhiney Moor and Guphill Common, the commissioner
stated a case for the opinion of the High Court pursuant to s 18(1) of the 1965 Act on 11
May 1983. By notice of motion dated 26 May 1983 the appellant sought an order,   *d*
pursuant to s 18, that all matters relating to the registration of West Anstey Common as
common land and to rights of common over it be remitted to a commons commissioner
for rehearing. The respondents to the motion were the parish trustees of West Anstey,
Oswald Philip John Weaver, John William James Milton (for himself and as personal
representative of Arthur John Milton deceased), Fred Davey, Colin George Smith, Alan
Thurstan Williams, Albert John Tarr, Margaret Joyce Tarr, Philip J Vesey, Lesley Ann   *e*
Vesey, John Herbert Griffiths, Christopher John Brisley, David Hume Stewart Harrows,
David Francis Bassett, Diana Chrystal Bassett and Somerset County Council. The facts are
set out in the judgment.

Vivian Chapman for the appellant.
Sheila Cameron QC for the respondents.   *f*

WHITFORD J. In January 1982 Mr L J Morris Smith, sitting as a commons
commissioner, gave a decision in a matter concerning West Anstey Common, including
Anstey Rhiney Moor, Guphill Common, Anstey Money Common, Woodland Common
and Twitchen Common, all in North Devon.
    There is before me an appeal by way of case stated brought at the suit of a Mr H M J
Harrison. The dispute referred to the commons commissioner, on which he gave the   *g*
decision to which I have already referred, related to registrations in the lands, rights and
ownership sections of registered unit no CL134 in the register maintained by the Devon
County Council. Although I am not concerned with anything arising out of the disputes
touching the ownership section, I would just briefly refer to two entries in this section,
one being an entry in which ownership of a section 7D on the registry map was claimed
by Mr Edward Michael Harrison, and the other being a claim in respect of land on the   *h*
relevant map made by Ernest John Nicholls and George Elston Nicholls. If one looks at
the map, it can be seen that the land in respect of which the proprietary interest has been
claimed by Mr Harrison, who, I may say, is the father of the appellant, effectively
comprised Anstey Rhiney Moor and Guphill Common. The land in which the Nichollses
claim a proprietary interest is Woodland Common.
    The appellant apparently succeeded to the interest of his father and had done so, I   *j*
think, at about the time when, pursuant to the provision of the Commons Registration
Act 1965, various claims were being registered and a variety of objections were being
taken. He claims to be aggrieved by the decision of the commons commissioner, which
he says is erroneous in point of law, and, as a person aggrieved, it is not disputed that he
is perfectly entitled to appeal pursuant to the provisions of s 18 of the 1965 Act provided
he can satisfy the court that the decision of the commons commissioner was erroneous

in point of law. In the case stated, reference is made to the grounds on which Mr Harrison claims to be aggrieved by the decision in point of law. When the matter came to be heard in court, it was suggested that perhaps these grounds were not as happily put as they might have been and four alternative modes of framing the objection were put forward by counsel for the appellant. The submissions that he has made were directed to issues which can, I hope, be relatively easily understood.

As I have said, there were entries in the rights section and the ownership section, and there were objections. There was only one relevant objection, so far as the land section was concerned; it was no 529. It was made by the Nichollses and their objection was to the entry in the land section, relating to that portion of the land which is shown at F on the map, namely Woodland Common. This, it was said, was and always had been the private property of the objectors or perhaps their predecessor. There had never been any rights of common thereover and consequently they were objecting. Their objection, of course, would, if it succeeded, as in circumstances which I must briefly relate the commons commissioner held it did, effectively dispose of certain claims under the rights section in respect of exercise of rights of common over Woodland Common.

In his decision the commissioner said of this objection that it related only to part of the whole common, the unit of land described generally as 'West Anstey Common'. The ground of objection certainly related only to that south-eastern corner which comprises Woodland Common. Only certain of the rights entries related to Woodland Common and some evidence was given. So far as this objection is concerned, what the commissioner said in his decision was:

> 'There is no need to consider the evidence since ultimately the parties concerned accepted the Objection [ie the objection of the Nichollses]. Ms P J Tuckett, the applicant for registration at Entry No 4 in the Rights Section was not present or represented at the hearing and in the absence of evidence to establish the right I must, I think, regard the Objection as successful in its application to her right. In the result, on this part of the case, I shall exclude Woodland Common from the land registered in the Land Section.'

That brings me to the principal point in the case made by counsel for the appellant, which goes to this, that the commissioner was bound, the objection of the Nichollses no 529 having been taken, to inquire not only into the validity of the objection in so far as it related to the inclusion of Woodland Common but into the validity of the whole of the registration, although there were no objections being taken to the registration in respect of any part of the land other than Woodland Common. There is no doubt about it that no objection was taken, but quite why is irrelevant to anything that I have to consider. It seems strange because quite plainly the appellant's father, at least, was well aware of the fact that rights were being registered and objections were being taken. Ten years ago one might have thought objection would likely to have been taken by the Harrison interest in respect of that part of the land over which they claim to have a proprietary interest, namely Anstey Rhiney Moor and Guphill Common. They might well have claimed this land should never have been admitted to registration. It is quite plain from an affidavit that has been put in by the appellant that they wish to challenge the claims of others to rights of common, which it is said have been exercised over these portions of the land in the past.

It was said, understandably, that it may seem a little hard, so far as the other parties to this matter are concerned, that no objection having originally been taken when it ought to have been taken, there should now be a rehearing in which effectively what is going to be argued is a series of objections which ought to have been taken, which could have been taken, but which were not taken. It was also said that quite plainly the scheme of the 1965 Act and regulations made under it is based on the fact that there was to be a very tight timetable so far as the entry of objections were concerned, with no provision whatsoever for the exercise of any discretion under which a person failing to take an objection within the allotted time should be entitled to enter any such objection after the expiry of the relevant period for the taking of objections. It was not suggested, as I understand it, that there could be any discretion. I think counsel for the appellant is quite right when he says I should not consider the question how hard it may be on others. If *a* in fact there has been an error in law the matter will have to go back, whatever the costs in terms of time and money to everybody concerned may be.

I have spoken very briefly about the one entry in the land section. There were a number of entries in the rights section including entries, I think they were nos 1 and 7, which were concerned with claims of rights of common in respect of what I can perhaps describe as Harrison land, because there was no objection entered to the claims at the *b* time. The appellant wants to challenge the entry in the land section which has been made with the exclusion only of Woodland Common, for if he is successful on this then the rights will fall by the way as well. The point as I see it in the end falls within a relatively small compass, for the question I have got to decide is whether the commissioner was bound on the Nichollses' objection to inquire into the validity of the whole of the registration, which is the submission made by counsel for the appellant, or whether his *c* duty was the rather more limited duty, and this was the submission of counsel for the respondents, of giving a decision in relation only to the objection made by the Nichollses, namely to the inclusion of Woodland Common within the land registration.

I was referred to provisions of the 1965 Act by counsel for the appellant which he suggests established quite plainly that, where objections are made to entries in the land section, they can only be made to the entry in respect of the land section as a whole *d* because there is no express provision under the 1965 Act for an objection in respect of a part only of a land registration. I am bound to say that it does seem to me that this might be thought perhaps by a casual observer to be a rather extraordinary position in an Act which, though it has at times been the subject of a degree of criticism, was, in fact, intended to provide for the making of claims within a relatively short space of time and the entry of objections and the disposal of these objections in as short a time as might be *e* possible without, one might have thought, the incurring of any unnecessary expense.

Section 5 of the 1965 Act deals with notification of objections to registration and it is really concerned with seeing that proper publicity is given to registration and to objection, and sub-s (2), which deals with the period during which objections can be taken, is in these terms:

> 'The period during which objections to any registration under section 4 of this *f* Act may be made shall be such period, ending not less than two years after the date of the registration, as may be prescribed.'

It envisages an objection to 'any' registration and not, says counsel for the appellant, to 'any part' of a registration. It does not seem to me that the language in any way excludes the possibility of making objection to a part of a registration, and I should have thought *g* that common sense would have indicated that if an objection was only going to go to a part of the registration, and the rest of it was not going to be challenged, it would have been absurd to envisage a procedure in which, because there was a challenge to a part only, consideration would have to be given, for this might involve an enormous amount of time and expense and a very large number of people, to the registration as a whole. If nobody was concerned to enter any other objection why should anything else be *h* considered.

I was referred to sub-ss (3) and (7), which use similar language, which to my mind do not in turn exclude the making of an objection to a part of a registration. These provisions too do not in terms, to my mind, make it imperative that any challenge can only be to the whole of the registration. I think, myself, it is not without interest to remember that sub-s (6) is in these terms: *j*

> 'Where such an objection is made, then, unless the objection is withdrawn or the registration cancelled before the end of such period as may be prescribed, the registration authority shall refer the matter to a Commons Commissioner.'

So it is contemplated by this subsection that there will have been some objection which, because it has not been withdrawn or been cancelled, has got to be dealt with. It is to be

dealt with by reference to a commons commissioner. Section 6, which has the sidenote
'Disposal of disputed claims', is in these terms:

'(1) The Commons Commissioner to whom any matter has been referred under
section 5 of this Act shall inquire into it and shall either confirm the registration,
with or without modifications, or refuse to confirm it; and the registration shall, if
it is confirmed, become final, and, if confirmation is refused, become void,—(a) if
no appeal is brought against the confirmation or refusal, at the end of the period
during which such an appeal could have been brought: (b) if such an appeal is
brought, when it is finally disposed of . . .'

Section 6 contemplates confirmation of the registration with or without modifications
and these words, to my mind, give a clear indication that it was within the contemplation
of those responsible for these provisions that there might have to be a modification
because, for example, there might have been objection going to part only of the
registration and not to the registration as a whole. I was referred to some of the
regulations. In 1966 there were some general regulations and counsel for the appellant
suggested that some assistance might be got by reference to the notes which appear on
the specimen forms of objection, but I confess that I do not think anything useful can be
gathered from those notes. I was referred also to the Commons Registration (Objections
and Maps) Regulations 1968, SI 1968/989, to which counsel for the numerous respondents
to these proceedings had, in fact, taken me. Regulation 5 provides that every objection
for registration must be on a form which is numbered as Form 26, and there is a
provision in reg 5(4) relating to objections to registrations relating to part only of the
land comprised in a registered unit. It is also of application to objections to part only of
claims to rights of common and claims to ownership. What para (4) does is to provide
that, if there is an objection to part only of the land comprised in the registered unit, the
objection form must be accompanied by a plan clearly defining, by distinctive colouring,
the land to which the objection relates signed by the person who has signed the form.
There was, so far as the objection to land is concerned, an objection to part only of the
land comprised in a registered unit, being registered as common land, and it was
accompanied by grounds and a map indicating that the objection was only taken in
respect of that part of the plan which I have identified as Woodland Common.

Counsel for the appellant sought to persuade me that a distinction must be drawn to
the objection which under reg 5 is an objection to a registration and the grounds which
relate only to a part of the registration in support of his claim that a commissioner is
bound to inquire into, and presumably a registration authority is bound to refer, the
question of the whole of the registration, notwithstanding the fact that the objection is
to only a part of the registration. Of course, what was in fact referred to the commissioner
in this case was only the objection to a part of the registration to the inclusion of
Woodland Common.

In support of his case counsel for the appellant relies very much on the judgment of
Walton J in *Re Sutton Common, Wimborne* [1982] 2 All ER 376, [1982] 1 WLR 647. This is
a case which has been the subject of comment in subsequent cases. In observations which
were in both cases obiter in *Corpus Christi College, Oxford v Gloucestershire CC* [1982] 3 All
ER 995 at 1000, 1008, [1983] QB 360 at 367, 377, Lord Denning MR expressed some
doubt as to the correctness of the approach of Walton J to the question of burden of
proof. On this aspect of the matter, Oliver LJ thought Walton J had been right, and,
indeed, in *Re Ilkley and Burley Moors* (1983) Times, 16 February Nourse J endorsed the
approach of Walton J to the question of onus. I was referred also to *R v Commons Comrs,
ex p Winnington* (1982) Times, 26 November, and was furnished with a transcript of
Woolf J's judgment.

Let me just deal with the question of onus, because the second of counsel for the
appellant's submissions was that the onus of proving the validity of registration which is
referred to the commissioner lies on the person making the registration. I entirely accept
that, where there is a claim and an objection and the matter is referred to the
commissioner, then the onus must in the first instance, before the commissioner, lie on

the claimant. Where there is an objection therefore it is on the person who has made the claim to which an objection is taken to establish his case. Where no objection is taken, the question of onus simply does not arise. *Re Sutton Common* must be considered in relation to its special facts which are set out in the judgment of Walton J (see [1982] 2 All ER 376 at 380–381 [1982] 1 WLR 647 at 653). This was a case of a tract of land identified as unit CL 141 in the register maintained by the Dorset County Council. It found its way into the register on an application by Mrs Colyer, who was representing the Ramblers' Association for the Wessex area. It is not without interest to note that among other facts it was found that a small part of the area should never have been included. It was part of the garden of a house belonging to some Misses Jackson, and, effectively, Walton J was really only concerned with the rest of the land, 74·3 acres, which was in the ownership of no less than three different proprietors. There was an application made by a Mr Butler in the rights section which was applicable to CL 141 because he claimed rights of grazing and certain other rights of common, and there was a provisional entry in the register. There were objections to the entry in the land register by a company, the Medlycott Trust and the tenth Earl of Shaftesbury, and there was an objection also taken by the appellants before Walton J, Robert Thorne Ltd, to Mr Butler's entry in the rights section. Curiously enough, Robert Thorne Ltd did not object to the registration in the land section because, so Walton J thought, they had not really taken legal advice. None of the objections were withdrawn and the case went before the same commissioner as the commissioner in the present case. Of Mr Butler's claim, Walton J said that that 'disappeared . . . in a puff of smoke', which left, for consideration, the remaining, as Walton J put it in inverted commas, 'matter', I quote his words—

> 'which was, of course, whether the registration of CL 141 should be confirmed in the land section, on the basis, there was obviously none other available once Mr Butler's rights disappeared, that the land was waste land of a manor. So at this stage it would have appeared that the correct course for the commissioner to take, would have been to have called on Mrs Colyer, who appeared on behalf of the Ramblers' Association, to demonstrate (i) what was the manor in question and (ii) what lands comprised waste of that manor.'

(See [1982] 2 All ER 376 at 381, [1982] 1 WLR 647 at 654).

None of that happened. Walton J went on to say:

> 'But the course that the commissioner took was to deal with the matter piecemeal, just as if what was before him was not "the matter", ie the registration of CL 141 as a whole, but simply two quite separate disputes namely, one between the Medlycott Trust and the Ramblers' Association, and one between the Earl of Shaftesbury and the Ramblers' Association. This appears to me to have been altogether a wrong approach.'

Of course the circumstances in *Re Sutton Common* were wholly different from the circumstances in the present case. Nobody stands in the position of Mrs Colyer. No question arises, as it apparently did in that case, of considering the point whether the entry in the land section of West Anstey Common as common land might proceed on the basis that it was waste land and not subject to rights of common. The rights claims were all in respect of rights of common over, initially, the entirety of the land, but at a later date, by agreement between the parties and the non-appearance of one claimant, restricted to the land other than Woodland Common. Having summarised some of the arguments, and coming to deal with question of onus, Walton J said ([1982] 2 All ER 376 at 383, [1982] 1 WLR 647 at 656):

> 'Now it appears to me that basically the matter is a very simple one. Throughout, it appears to me that the onus of proving his case is on the person making the registration, once that registration requires confirmation by a commissioner.'

I think some emphasis must be given to the words 'once that registration requires confirmation by a commissioner'. It was on this aspect of the matter that Walton J was confirmed by Oliver LJ, Nourse and Woolf JJ. Walton J went on to say ([1982] 2 All ER 376 at 383, [1982] 1 WLR 647 at 656–657):

'He must be prepared to establish his case. Of course, in many situations extremely little in the way of proof will be required. To take an example used at the hearing in this case, if there is a large area of land which is registered as a common, and an objection is taken as to a small piece on the fringes of the land, which happens to be somebody's back garden, then although the objection of that person theoretically puts in question the status of the whole of the area, provided that nothing else arises to cast the slightest doubt on the status of the remainder of the land, the commissioner will, I think, be fully entitled to rely on the original statutory declarations made by the registrant pursuant to reg 8(1) of the Commons Registration (General) Regulations 1966, SI 1966/1471, as discharging the necessary burden of proof.'

Here Walton J does say that the objection taken to a small piece on the fringe of the land theoretically puts in question the status of the whole of the area. The extent to which any particular objection may put in question the status of the whole area is going to depend on the particular circumstances of individual cases, but I adopt the view of Walton J that it is only when a question of registration is bound to require confirmation by the commissioners that the question of onus of proof arises. In this case, all that was referred to the commissioner was the question whether or not Woodland Common ought to have been included within the land registration. On that the commissioner was able to come to a conclusion which is amply justified in the reasons given in his decision.

In my judgment I cannot accept, no other objection having been taken to the entry in the land section, that there was any justification, let alone any need, for the commissioner to inquire into the validity of the registration, other than its validity in respect of this small part of the land as a whole. If there had been, then no doubt the onus would have rested on the council who made the original entry.

There are two other matters to which I ought to make brief reference. The first was this, that it was submitted by counsel for the appellant, as a matter of law, that the commissioner must not exclude relevant evidence whether or not it was offered by the person who has lodged an objection. I think it is plain from the judgment of Walton J in *Re Sutton Common* that Walton J took the view that evidence relevant to any question before the commissioner for consideration ought to be taken into account by the commissioner, and I am entirely of the same opinion, but evidence which the appellant in this case is apparently prepared to put forward which might be extremely relevant to an objection entered by the Harrison interest would not be relevant to the only question which was before the commissioner, namely should Woodland Common be included or should it not? And, finally, it was submitted that the commissioner cannot discharge his duty to inquire without making a finding on the evidence relating to the registration which is referred to him. The duty of the commissioner in relation to his decision is governed by the Commons Commissioners Regulations 1971, SI 1971/1727.

So far as any inquiry and the making of a finding on evidence is concerned, there was no need to make any finding on evidence relating to the status of Woodland Common because, as a result of the non-appearance of one claimant and the agreement, apparently, of the others, no evidence was tendered to support the validity of the registrations.

In my judgment this is not a case in which the commissioner has erred in law and the appeal must, accordingly, be dismissed.

Appeal dismissed.

Solicitors: *Robbins Olivey & Blake Lapthorn,* agents for *Barrow & Chapman,* Dulverton (for the appellant); *Crosse-Wyatt & Co,* South Molton (for the respondents other than Somerset County Council); *D J R Clark,* Taunton (for Somerset County Council).

Evelyn M C Budd   Barrister.

Sutton v Sutton

CHANCERY DIVISION

JOHN MOWBRAY QC SITTING AS A DEPUTY JUDGE OF THE HIGH COURT

23, 24, 25, 28 MARCH, 10 JUNE 1983

Divorce – Property – Transfer of property – Agreement between parties – Wife consenting to divorce in return for agreement by husband to transfer property to her – Agreement not made subject to order of court – Refusal by husband to transfer property after divorce obtained – Application by wife for order for specific performance of agreement – Whether agreement ousting court's jurisdiction to make property adjustment order – Whether against public policy to enforce agreement – Whether order for specific performance should be granted.

Divorce – Collusion – Agreements and arrangements – Enforcement – Matrimonial Causes Act 1973, s 1(2)(d).

Contract – Part performance – Contract concerning land – Acts constituting part performance – Transfer of property on divorce – Wife consenting to divorce in return for agreement by husband to transfer matrimonial home to her – Refusal by husband to transfer matrimonial home after divorce obtained – Whether wife's consent to divorce constituting sufficient act of part performance of agreement to transfer matrimonial home – Law of Property Act 1925, s 40.

The parties married in 1954 and in 1961 they bought the matrimonial home with the help of a mortgage for which the husband alone was responsible. The wife contributed to the purchase but the house was conveyed into the husband's name alone. Some years later they separated and the husband sought a divorce. They orally agreed between themselves (i) that the wife would consent to a divorce under s 1(2)(d)[a] of the Matrimonial Causes Act 1973, take over responsibility for the mortgage and not apply for maintenance and (ii) that the husband would let her keep such money as she had saved and would transfer the house to her. The agreement was not made subject to the court's approval. The husband drew up the divorce petition, which was dealt with by post, without the aid of solicitors. The wife gave her consent to the petition by post, paid off the mortgage and did not apply for maintenance. After obtaining the decree absolute of divorce, the husband refused to transfer the house to the wife. The wife brought an action against the husband seeking an order for specific performance of the agreement. The husband contended that the agreement was not legally enforceable because (i) there was no memorandum or note of it within s 40[b] of the Law of Property Act 1925, (ii) there was no mutuality, (iii) the agreement was collusive in that it procured, or provided for the conduct of, the divorce petition, and (iv) the agreement purported to oust the jurisdiction of the court and it would accordingly be contrary to public policy to enforce it.

Held – (1) Although there was no memorandum or note of the agreement within s 40 of the 1925 Act, there had been a sufficient act of part performance on the wife's part

---

a   Section 1(2), so far as material, provides: 'The court hearing a petition for divorce shall not hold the marriage to have broken down irretrievably unless the petitioner satisfies the court of one or more of the following facts, that is to say . . . (*d*) that the parties to the marriage have lived apart for a continuous period of at least two years immediately preceding the presentation of the petition . . . and the respondent consents to a decree being granted . . .'

b   Section 40, so far as material, provides:

'(1) No action may be brought upon any contract for the . . . disposition of land or any interest in land, unless the agreement upon which such action is brought, or some memorandum or note thereof, is in writing, and signed by the party to be charged or by some other person thereunto by him lawfully authorised.

(2) This section . . . does not affect the law relating to part performance . . .'

a because the evidence showed that her consent to the divorce petition had been tied to the agreement about the house and was referable to it (see p 172 *b* to *e*, post); *Steadman v Steadman* [1974] 2 All ER 977 applied.

(2) Although the husband could not enforce the wife's promise not to ask for maintenance and although he could not have compelled her to consent to the divorce, once she had performed what was an appreciable part of the agreement by giving her formal consent to the petition, he could not assert that there was no mutuality (see p 172
b *f g*, post); *Price v Strange* [1977] 3 All ER 371 applied.

(3) The agreement was not void on the ground of collusion because the effect of s 1(2)(*d*) of the 1973 Act was not only that collusion was no longer a bar to a decree but also that the former rule that collusive agreements between parties to divorce proceedings were invalid no longer applied (see p 172 *j* to p 173 *c*, post); *Beales v Beales* [1972] 2 All ER 667 considered; *Hope v Hope* (1857) 8 De GM & G 731 distinguished.

c (4) The court's jurisdiction under ss 23 and 24 of the 1973 Act to order maintenance and make property adjustments could not, however, be ousted by a private agreement between the parties. Since the agreement between the husband and the wife had not been made subject to the court's approval, it purported to oust the court's jurisdiction, and accordingly it would be contrary to public policy to enforce it as a contract and order the husband to transfer the house to the wife. It followed that, although it was open to
d the wife to apply to the court under s 24 of the 1973 Act for an order requiring the husband to transfer the house to her, her application to enforce the agreement as a contract would be dismissed (see p 173 *h* to p 174 *b* and *d e*, p 175 *b* to *e* and p 176 *g h*, post); *Hyman v Hyman* [1929] All ER Rep 245 and dictum of Denning LJ in *Bennett v Bennett* [1952] 1 All ER at 422 applied; *Goodinson v Goodinson* [1954] 2 All ER 255 and *Williams v Williams* [1957] 1 All ER 305 distinguished.

e **Notes**

For the remedy of specific performance, see 44 Halsbury's Statutes (4th edn) para 401.

For collusion as a bar to matrimonial relief, see 13 ibid para 654.

For the Law of Property Act 1925, s 40, see 27 Halsbury's Statutes (3rd edn) 399.

For the Matrimonial Causes Act 1973, ss 1, 23, 24, see 43 ibid 541, 564, 566.

f **Cases referred to in judgment**

Ashley v Ashley [1965] 3 All ER 554, [1968] P 582, [1965] 3 WLR 1194, DC.
Backhouse v Backhouse [1978] 1 All ER 1158, [1978] 1 WLR 243.
Beales v Beales [1972] 2 All ER 667, [1972] Fam 210, [1972] 2 WLR 972.
Bennett v Bennett [1952] 1 All ER 413, [1952] 1 KB 249, CA.
g *Chaterjee v Chaterjee* [1976] 1 All ER 719, [1976] Fam 199, [1976] 2 WLR 397, CA.
Dean v Dean [1978] 3 All ER 758, [1978] Fam 161, [1978] 3 WLR 288.
Edgar v Edgar [1980] 3 All ER 887, [1980] 1 WLR 1410, CA.
Gonin (decd), Re, Gonin v Garmeson [1977] 2 All ER 720, [1979] Ch 16, [1977] 3 WLR 379.
Goodinson v Goodinson [1954] 2 All ER 255, [1954] 2 QB 118, [1954] 2 WLR 1121, CA.
Hope v Hope (1857) 8 De GM & G 731, 44 ER 572, LJJ.
h *Hyman v Hyman* [1929] AC 601, [1929] All ER Rep 245, HL.
Price v Strange [1977] 3 All ER 371, [1978] Ch 337, [1977] 3 WLR 943, CA.
Steadman v Steadman [1974] 2 All ER 977, [1976] AC 536, [1974] 3 WLR 56, HL.
Williams v Williams [1957] 1 All ER 305, [1957] 1 WLR 148, CA.

Action

j The plaintiff, Guiseppina Maria Sutton, brought an action against the defendant, Alan Sutton, seeking (i) an order for specific performance of an oral agreement whereby the defendant agreed to convey to her certain property in Claverley, Shropshire, (ii) damages in lieu of or in addition to an order for specific performance, and (iii) further or other relief. The defendant denied that he had agreed to convey the property to her and counterclaimed (i) for a declaration that, as between the parties, he held the property (a) on trust for sale for the benefit of the parties in equal shares, (b) otherwise howsoever and, if so, how, (ii) for an order that the plaintiff consent to and concur in the defendant selling the property with vacant possession on terms that the defendant pay to the plaintiff, after the sale, a moiety of the net proceeds of sale, (iii) alternatively to (ii), for an order that the property be sold with vacant possession, (iv) if necessary, execution of the trusts declared under (i), (v) if necessary, rescission of the agreement alleged by the plaintiff, and (vi) further or other relief. The facts are set out in the judgment.

Reziya Harrison for Mrs Sutton.
John Randall for Mr Sutton.

Cur adv vult

10 June. The following judgment was delivered.

JOHN MOWBRAY QC. Mr and Mrs Sutton were married in 1954. In 1961 they bought a bungalow to live in in Claverley in Shropshire. It was conveyed into Mr Sutton's name alone, but Mrs Sutton contributed to it and they are agreed that, if it were not for the events I shall be mentioning, each of them would be entitled to a beneficial half share.

The house was bought with the help of a £2,100 mortgage loan from Mr Sutton's employers' pension fund. Mr Sutton alone was liable on the mortgage.

By about 1974 Mr and Mrs Sutton were having frequent rows, mainly about money by their accounts of it, and Mr Sutton left, though he came back occasionally.

In 1977 the two of them agreed, by word of mouth, on an amicable divorce based on two years' separation and Mrs Sutton's consent under s 1(2)(*d*) of the Matrimonial Causes Act 1973. They spoke about it and agreed a financial settlement. Subject to one point, their accounts of what they agreed coincide. They both say that Mrs Sutton agreed that she would consent to the divorce and take over responsibility for the mortgage, and would not apply for maintenance, and that in return Mr Sutton agreed to let her keep her savings and car and let her have the house. But Mrs Sutton says that Mr Sutton agreed to transfer the house to her outright and he says that he only agreed it was to be hers to live in as long as she wanted. I shall return to this shortly.

At the end of December 1977, following the agreement, the mortgage was paid off out of an account at Claverley post office in Mrs Sutton's name. Mr Sutton consulted a solicitor twice, briefly, but Mrs Sutton never did. Mr Sutton drew up his own petition. It is dated 20 February 1978 and is based on s 1(2)(*d*). It was dealt with by the postal procedure, without solicitors; Mrs Sutton consented to the petition by post. She has not made any claim for maintenance. The decree absolute was made on 8 June 1978, but Mr Sutton has not transferred the house to Mrs Sutton. In this action Mrs Sutton is asking for an order for specific performance of Mr Sutton's promise which, she says, was to transfer the house to her outright and damages in lieu or in addition. The first thing I have to decide is whether that is what Mr Sutton promised, or whether he only agreed that Mrs Sutton could live in it.

The agreement

Mrs Sutton's evidence on this point was that she said she would like to have the bungalow and pay for it and would keep the contents, together with her savings and car. She says that Mr Sutton said that he would give her the house, which meant put it in her name and make it legally hers. Mrs Sutton says that she did not understand him to say that he would retain any rights in the house; she says she never thought he would get any share in the house when she sold it. In her evidence at this point she added emphatically: 'Nothing. Finish.' In cross-examination Mrs Sutton said that Mr Sutton never said such words as 'as long as you want to live in it' and that, if he had, he would never have had the money. She meant the money from the Claverley post office account.

In re-examination, Mrs Sutton said: 'I did not want to have any maintenance; just the
a house to live in.' She meant that was the reason she was to have the ownership of the
house, not that she was only to have a right to live in it.

In his evidence-in-chief Mr Sutton said that he told his wife she could stay in the house,
also that on the divorce the law was that the house was split down the middle, but that
he would never throw her out. He admitted he might have said she could have the house
but he said that meant to live in, as he might say to a boy, 'You can have my shed to work
b in' or 'to keep your bike in'.

Mr Sutton's counsel made something of the fact that after the divorce Mr Sutton
repaired and improved the house and the fences. In many cases acts of that kind would
tend to indicate that the person who did them thought he still had a beneficial interest,
but here Mr and Mrs Sutton remained on unusually amicable, even affectionate, terms
after the divorce. He brought her coal, logs, meat and vegetables, mowed the lawn,
c mended her car and electric cooker. In the circumstances, acting as her 'Mr Fix-it', as
counsel for Mr Sutton put it, it carries little or no weight. It is the same with his paying
the fire insurance after the divorce. I think their relationship also explains why Mrs
Sutton did not insist on a formal transfer of the house at the time of the divorce. She said
she asked Mr Sutton for the deeds but he just said, 'Trust me, I will keep them for you
until you need them'. I do not know if that took place but I accept that her not insisting
d on a transfer does not raise any real doubt that she thought that she was entitled to one.

Later on, Mrs Sutton put the house up for sale, without asking Mr Sutton, which, I
consider, shows that she thought that she alone was entitled to it.

Generally, I would prefer Mr Sutton's evidence to that of Mrs Sutton where they
differed. He struck me as a particularly straightforward and honest witness. On this one
question, however, he seemed to be a little on the defensive and I prefer Mrs Sutton's
e recollection of what was said. I think that, as he half admitted, Mr Sutton said something
to the effect that Mrs Sutton could have the house. In the circumstances, a bystander
would take that to mean the ownership of the house. I find that that was the effect of the
agreement between them. This conclusion is supported by the fact that both parties
wanted a clean break; any future rights of Mr Sutton to the house would prevent the
break from being clean, as they both intended.

f Mr Sutton could not explain away what he had written in his divorce petition. The
printed part of para 8 reads:

> 'No agreement or arrangement has been made or is proposed to be made between
> the parties for the support of the petitioner/respondent and any child of the family
> except . . .'

g He completed that like this:

> 'an agreement that the respondent accepts the marital home in lieu of any
> maintenance so waives any rights to maintenance now or in the future. This has
> been agreed upon.'

At para 10 he wrote:

h
> 'The parties have lived apart from a continuous period of at least two years
> immediately preceding the presentation of the petition and the respondent consents
> to a decree being granted.'

And, under 'Particulars' at para 11, after something about their worsening relationship,
he wrote:

j
> 'We have both agreed the marriage is dead and would be better dissolved as soon
> as possible. I have agreed she keeps her savings and the bungalow which is paid for
> and worth approximately £20,000 and she waives all rights to maintenance against
> me to give me the chance to get on my feet again.'

It is not possible to understand those passages in the sense that Mr Sutton suggested in
evidence, for instance, 'The respondent accepts *to live in* the matrimonial home'.

Since the divorce, Mr Sutton has discovered that Mrs Sutton had much bigger savings than he thought (over £3,000 in the Abbey National Building Society at the time of the divorce), he has had an accident at work which has meant that he cannot work again, and he has remarried. Also, Mrs Sutton has inherited a house in Italy from her father. I think these things may have led Mr Sutton to repent of his bargain and convince himself that he did not intend the objective meaning of the words he used in his petition and which I have found he spoke to Mrs Sutton.

So I find proved an agreement by word of mouth between Mr and Mrs Sutton that she would consent to the divorce, take over the mortgage and not ask for maintenance, and he would let her keep her savings and car and make over the house to her outright. The plea in the defence that it was an unconscionable bargain was not persisted in. It is, though, within s 40 of the Law of Property Act 1925. No memorandum of it satisfies the section. Counsel for Mrs Sutton did not contend that the divorce petition, signed by Mr Sutton, was a memorandum within the section, because it does not state the term about Mrs Sutton taking over responsibility for the mortgage as a term of the contract. Then, was there part performance?

Part performance

In my view, Mrs Sutton's consenting to the divorce as agreed was an act of part performance. It is true that she was quite content to be divorced and that in the abstract consenting to a divorce does not indicate any contract, let alone a contract about land. But here the term about the house was in the petition which must have been posted to her when her formal consent was sought under the postal procedure which was followed. That means that her consent to the petition was in itself, in the circumstances, tied to the contract about the house. *Steadman v Steadman* [1974] 2 All ER 977, [1976] AC 536 is authority for that and I do not read Walton J as casting any doubt on it by anything he said in *Re Gonin (decd), Gonin v Garmeson* [1977] 2 All ER 720, [1979] Ch 16.

Mutuality

Counsel for Mr Sutton argued that there was no mutuality, so specific performance should not be granted. He pointed out that Mrs Sutton's promise not to ask for maintenance was not enforceable. That is common ground. I shall come to the reasons later. Mrs Sutton herself said, in cross-examination, that her offer not to ask for maintenance was a big thing to offer. I find that it was an important part of the bargain. If this point had been taken early enough it might well have afforded a defence, but Mrs Sutton's consent to the divorce was at any rate an appreciable part of the agreement. Mr Sutton stood by and let her perform that part of her bargain irretrievably, and that raised an equity which prevents him from asserting this defence: see *Price v Strange* [1977] 3 All ER 371 at 384, [1978] Ch 337 at 358 and *Snell's Principles of Equity* (28th edn, 1982) p 580. For similar reasons, it is no defence to specific performance that Mr Sutton could not have compelled Mrs Sutton to consent to the divorce. Now she has consented and the divorce has been granted, that point comes too late.

Collusion

The agreement between Mr and Mrs Sutton was blatantly collusive, in the sense that it procured the divorce petition, or provided for its conduct, or both. Before 1971 any collusive agreement was not only a bar (absolute to 1966, then discretionary) to any decree; it was also illegal and wholly void as a contract: see *Hope v Hope* (1857) 8 De GM & G 731, 44 ER 572 and *Price v Strange* [1977] 3 All ER 371 at 378, [1978] Ch 337 at 351 per Goff LJ.

Counsel for Mr Sutton argued that, although collusion is no longer any kind of a bar to a decree, a collusive contract is still entirely void. He prayed in aid *Chitty on Contracts* (25th edn, 1983) vol 1, para 1065. It supports his argument, but I do not see how collusion leading to a divorce under s 1(2)(*d*) of the Matrimonial Causes Act 1973 can be illegal, because a divorce can only be decreed under that provision if the respondent consents. In fact, it seems to me that s 1(2)(*d*) completely alters the public policy on this point. The considerations which moved the Court of Appeal in *Hope v Hope* cannot stand with that provision. Turner LJ's judgment is inconsistent with s 1(2)(*d*) (see 8 De GM & G 731 at 744–745, 44 ER 572 at 577).

In my view, since 1 January 1971, when the Divorce Reform Act 1969 took effect, incorporating the predecessor of s 1(2)(*d*) of the 1973 Act, public policy has not invalidated a contract on the ground of collusion, any more than it has barred a collusive divorce. Baker P decided in *Beales v Beales* [1972] 2 All ER 667 at 672, [1972] Fam 210 at 219 that a respondent could consent under the predecessor paragraph conditionally on not having to pay any costs and that, if he did this, the court could not order him to pay costs. If the old rule about collusion had applied to the arrangement, it would have been illegal and the court could not have been bound. So *Beales v Beales* indicates that collusive agreements are no longer void. Paragraph 1065 of *Chitty* is out of date.

Counsel for Mr Sutton also cited *Dean v Dean* [1978] 3 All ER 758 at 763, [1978] Fam 161 at 167, where Bush J said:

'This public policy has, in my view, survived the disappearance of collusion, first as an absolute and then as a discretionary bar to divorce.'

But Bush J was talking about a different rule of public policy. I must turn to it next.

Ousting the jurisdiction

The agreement between Mr and Mrs Sutton was that she would consent to the divorce, take over the mortgage and not ask for maintenance, and he would let her keep her savings and car and make over the house to her. They obviously intended by that agreement to dispose of the whole financial consequences of the divorce. There is a plain implication that he was not to transfer any other property to her and that she was not to make any payment or transfer to him. The agreement was not made subject to the court's approval. If it is enforceable as a contract, it leaves nothing for the court to do under ss 23 and 24 of the 1973 Act, which empower the court to order maintenance and make property adjustments. *Bennett v Bennett* [1952] 1 All ER 413, [1952] 1 KB 249 went on a slightly different argument but Denning LJ said ([1952] 1 All ER 413 at 422, [1952] 1 KB 249 at 262):

'Any private agreement of the parties which purports to make maintenance a debt enforceable at law must of necessity impliedly oust the jurisdiction of the Divorce Court to fix it, vary it or discharge it, and it is, by reason of that implication, invalid . . .'

That applies equally to a private agreement fixing the property adjustment on a divorce, except that there is not the same power to vary property adjustment orders. The agreement between Mr and Mrs Sutton purported to dispose of the whole financial consequences of the divorce, both maintenance and property questions. If it was enforceable as a contract there was nothing left for the court to do under s 23 or s 24 of the 1973 Act because the agreement prejudged and foreclosed all financial questions.

The House of Lords decided in *Hyman v Hyman* [1929] AC 601, [1929] All ER Rep 245 that a wife could not validly contract with her husband not to apply for maintenance on a divorce and that a contract of that kind did not prevent her from applying. Lord Hailsham LC stated the principle like this ([1929] AC 601 at 608, [1929] All ER Rep 245 at 248):

'. . . I am prepared to hold that the parties cannot validly make an agreement either (1.) not to invoke the jurisdiction of the Court, or (2.) to control the powers of the Court when its jurisdiction is invoked.'

That is the rule of public policy which survived the disappearance of the rule against collusion. In my judgment, it applies to the contract here and prevents the financial settlement it contained, including Mr Sutton's promise to transfer the bungalow, from being enforced as a contract. I say 'as a contract' because Mrs Sutton can still apply for an order under s 24 of the 1973 Act, requiring Mr Sutton to transfer the house to her. She does not even need leave to do this because r 68(3) of the Matrimonial Causes Rules 1977, SI 1977/344 applies: see *Chaterjee v Chaterjee* [1976] 1 All ER 719 at 724–725, [1976] Fam 199 at 207–209 per Ormrod LJ. Like Denning LJ in *Bennett v Bennett* [1952] 1 All ER 413 at 420, [1952] 1 KB 249 at 260, I would not subscribe to a decision which left the wife with no remedy in such circumstances, and it is an important part of my reasoning that Mrs Sutton can make an application under s 24. On such an application, the agreement will be a very important factor for the court to take into account as part of the conduct which will have to be considered under the opening words of s 25 of the 1973 Act, but it will not be the only consideration. Mr Sutton will be able to urge his discovery of the amount of Mrs Sutton's savings, his injury at work, his remarriage and her inheritance from her father. The registrar will be bound to consider those and all the things listed in s 25 and take into account the fact that, although Mr Sutton had a little legal advice and some understanding of the legal position, the agreement was not negotiated between solicitors.

I say no more about those things for fear of seeming to indicate how the registrar should decide. Nothing, anywhere in this judgment, is intended to give any indication about that either way. But I hope that my findings of fact, after seeing and hearing the parties give oral evidence, may be helpful. I am making some findings not strictly necessary for my own decision for that reason.

I mount the unruly horse of public policy with trepidation, but two reasons can be given why public policy requires Mrs Sutton to go under s 24, with the safeguards for Mr Sutton that I have mentioned, instead of enforcing his promise as a contract. First, the public at large has an interest in seeing that a husband makes proper provision for his wife on a divorce, with the result that she cannot contract out of her rights: see *Hyman v Hyman* [1929] AC 601 at 608, 629, [1929] All ER Rep 245 at 248, 258–259 per Lord Hailsham LC and Lord Atkin. By the same token, the parties cannot agree to make and accept a particular provision simply because it seems appropriate to them. The court needs to consider it on behalf of the community at large. The precise reasoning of the House of Lords in *Hyman v Hyman* was that there was a public interest in keeping the wife off what is now social security. *Ashley v Ashley* [1965] 3 All ER 554 esp at 559, [1968] P 582 esp at 591 per Simon P shows that there is still a public interest in ensuring that the provision which either of the parties makes or accepts on a divorce is just, not only as between themselves but also as between them on the one hand and, on the other, the general community which provides social security in case of need. That must apply to property adjustment as well as to maintenance, especially where the wife waives her right to maintenance as Mrs Sutton has. At the present day, it cannot make any difference whether it is the husband or the wife who is questioning the agreed financial settlement.

Second, experience in the courts since 1929 has revealed another aspect of the public interest in overseeing these arrangements. It arises because such arrangements are made in the throes of marital breakdown, when emotional pressures on the parties are apt to be high and their judgment clouded. Ormrod LJ referred to this in *Edgar v Edgar* [1980] 3 All ER 887 at 894, [1980] 1 WLR 1410 at 1418 and Balcombe J in *Backhouse v Backhouse* [1978] 1 All ER 1158 at 1165–1166, [1978] 1 WLR 243 at 250–251, where he also gives some examples of the courts' experience of such agreements. Those cases are not direct authority on the point which I have to decide because *Edgar v Edgar* was governed by s 34 of the 1973 Act, to which I shall refer later, and in *Backhouse v Backhouse* Balcombe J only said that such agreements ought not to be encouraged if made without legal advice. But they provide another reason for the public policy against enforcing them. I hasten to add that I am not accusing Mr or Mrs Sutton of taking any kind of unfair advantage or overreaching each other, because they remained on amicable terms before and after the divorce, but the rule of public policy has to cater for the kinds of danger that can usually arise. They require the court to keep its hand on questions of property adjustment as well as maintenance in every divorce and not allow its control to be ousted.

a Counsel for Mrs Sutton stated frankly that Mrs Sutton had brought the present proceedings instead of applying under s 24 because she could see risks in applying under that section. It is important that Mr Sutton should have the protection afforded to him in an application under s 24, rather than simply being sued in contract because, if Mrs Sutton succeeded in this action, he could not apply to the Family Division to get the house back under s 24. The reason is that he made no claim for ancillary relief in his petition and has remarried.

b Where a financial agreement on a divorce is made subject to the court's approval, it obviously does not oust the court's discretion and does not purport to. Such agreements are harmless and ought to be encouraged. They are valid as contracts because the court retains control. The agreement between Mr and Mrs Sutton is different because they impliedly excluded the court's discretion and that makes the whole financial settlement unenforceable as a contract.

c *The contrary arguments*

Counsel for Mrs Sutton argued skilfully and persuasively on this point, as on the others. She urged that, although the court's jurisdiction on divorce could not be fettered or ousted by a private contract between the parties, that did not prevent the agreement from being enforced as a contract. As I read them, though, the authorities I have

d mentioned show that the reason why such an agreement does not oust the jurisdiction in the way it purports to is precisely that it is not enforceable as a contract. If it was enforceable as a contract it would bind the court on the same principle as applied in *Beales v Beales* [1972] 2 All ER 667, [1972] Fam 210, because it binds both of the parties before the court. It cannot be allowed to bind the court, and the rule of public policy prevents this by making it unenforceable between the parties.

e It is true that a wife can enforce as a contract a term in the maintenance agreement by which the husband promises to pay her a specified sum of maintenance. Such agreements are harmless and are to be encouraged so long as they do not purport to exclude the wife from applying for an additional amount. She can sue for what the husband has contracted to pay and still apply to the court for more. As Lord Atkin said in *Hyman v Hyman* [1929] AC 601 at 625, [1929] All ER Rep 245 at 257, there is no caste in contracts. If no divorce

f is in prospect, the agreement cannot be said to purport to fetter the court's powers on the divorce. This, in my view, together with the implied exclusion in the present case of all financial arrangements other than those agreed, distinguishes such cases as *Goodinson v Goodinson* [1954] 2 All ER 255, [1954] 2 QB 118 and *Williams v Williams* [1957] 1 All ER 305, [1957] 1 WLR 148, which counsel for Mrs Sutton cited. It also answers the argument that the rule of public policy that I am applying would prevent any kind of dealing

g between husband and wife at any time. When no divorce was in contemplation, an agreement could not purport to oust the powers which arise on divorce, and of course if property has actually been transferred under an agreement the question of enforcing it no longer arises.

Counsel for Mrs Sutton also argued that a rule of public policy which prevented a wife from enforcing a promise such as Mr Sutton's could operate unfairly, especially where

h she was unable to apply to the court under s 23 or s 24. That could happen, for instance, if her husband had died after the divorce or if, like Mr Sutton here, she was the petitioner, had not applied for ancillary relief and had remarried. The point does not arise here, but I think the answer may be that when no application could be made to the court the agreement could not be said effectively to oust any jurisdiction and, for that reason, no rule of public policy would prevent it from being enforced.

j Under the present heading, I should refer again to *Bennett v Bennett* [1952] 1 All ER 413, [1952] 1 KB 249. It was not decided on quite the same reasoning as I have adopted. It was decided on more roundabout reasoning, if I can use that word without disrespect. The wife there agreed to waive maintenance altogether. The Court of Appeal held that unenforceable as purporting to oust the court's jurisdiction to award maintenance, but the action was brought by her to enforce her husband's covenant to pay her a life annuity

in return. His covenant was not held unenforceable for the same direct reason that it
tended itself to oust the jurisdiction, but for the reason that the consideration for it was
the wife's unlawful waiver. That the Court of Appeal did not apply the direct reasoning
to the husband's covenant might be thought to throw doubt on my applying it to Mr
Sutton's promise to make over the house, especially in view of the statement of Denning
LJ which I have quoted and the words which followed and completed it (see [1952] 1 All
ER 413 at 422, [1952] 1 KB 249 at 258): 'for the ouster goes to the whole consideration.'
I do not consider, though, that the course the Court of Appeal took prevents me from
following the more direct route. I think that the Court of Appeal followed the course
they did because it was specially clear that the wife's outright waiver was an ouster and
its unlawful nature was squarely demonstrated by *Hyman v Hyman* [1929] AC 601, [1929]
All ER Rep 245.

I have taken the more direct route because I doubt whether reasoning similar to the
Court of Appeal's would apply to the present case. It seems to me that a substantial part
of the consideration for Mr Sutton's promise about the house was Mrs Sutton's agreement
to consent to his petition. As I have said under the heading of collusion, I do not think
that was an unlawful consideration. That is why I have had to see whether Mr Sutton's
promise about the house purported itself with the rest of the agreement to oust the
court's jurisdiction. It is a point which could only arise now that collusion no longer
voids contracts. I expect that is why there is no authority directly on the point I have
decided. None the less, a finding of fact about Mrs Sutton's assumption of the mortgage
debt might prove useful. I consider that in equity the £2,100 which was used to pay it
off belonged to Mr and Mrs Sutton jointly or in equal shares. It was in the account at the
Claverley post office, which was in her name alone, but I am satisfied that she could not
have accumulated it except with help of contributions from him as part of their joint
household finances.

Section 34 of the 1973 Act

I mention s 34 of the Matrimonial Causes Act 1973 only to dismiss it. The section
applies to both separation agreements and divorce and property agreements. It provides
that an agreement made at any time containing financial arrangements which purport
to restrict any right to apply to the court for an order containing financial arrangements
is void, though the rest of the agreement may be valid and enforceable. I think financial
arrangements there, defined in s 34(2) to include provisions securing the disposition of
any property, include the kind of arrangements which the court can make under s 24
and would cover Mr Sutton's promise about the house. But the definition of maintenance
agreements in s 34(2) makes it clear that only written agreements are covered. I mean no
disrespect to the valour of the argument of counsel for Mrs Sutton to the contrary if I
simply say it did not convince me. I think s 34 supports the common law rule of public
policy which I have applied.

In the result, for the reasons I have tried to explain, I shall dismiss Mrs Sutton's claims
for specific performance and damages in lieu or in addition. The reasons would also
preclude any award of common law damages. On Mr Sutton's counterclaim, for the
same reasons, I will declare that as between the parties he holds the bungalow in
Claverley, in the county of Shropshire, on the statutory trusts for sale and otherwise and
the net proceeds of sale and the net rents and profits until sale on trust for himself and
Mrs Sutton in equal shares.

I should like to hear counsel on Mr Sutton's counterclaim for an order for sale in the
light of Mrs Sutton's wish to apply for an order under s 24.

[His Lordship then heard submissions from counsel, and continued:] I will make an
order for sale in 56 days and that it is not to be proceeded with in the mean time if Mrs
Sutton diligently prosecutes either an application under s 24 or an appeal. I will dismiss
Mrs Sutton's application with costs.

Order accordingly.

a Solicitors: *Roche Hardcastles*, agents for *R N Williams & Co*, Wolverhampton (for the plaintiff); *Robbins Olivey & Blake Lapthorn*, agents for *Sharpe & Millichip*, West Bromwich (for the defendant).

Hazel Hartman   Barrister.

b
Note
Hoey v Hoey

COURT OF APPEAL, CIVIL DIVISION
c CUMMING-BRUCE LJ AND REEVE J
8 NOVEMBER 1983

County court – Judgment or order – Reasons for decision – Custody cases – Importance of judgment stating findings of fact and reasons for decision – Judgment necessary in event of appeal – Even if no appeal judgment necessary for possibility of future application for variation of
d *custody order – When judge gives no reasons but states at hearing that he will give them on request any request for reasons should be dealt with without delay.*

Notes
For the necessity for a note of the decision of a judge in a county court, see 10 Halsbury's Laws (4th edn) paras 398, 669, and for cases on the subject, see 13 Digest (Reissue) 526–
e 528, 4370–4401.

Interlocutory appeal
The mother appealed against an order made on 30 June by his Honour Judge Smithies in the Southampton County Court whereby the judge (i) committed the custody of the two children of the marriage to the father and directed that the mother have reasonable access
f and (ii) refused an application by the mother for an injunction requiring the father to leave the matrimonial home. The case is reported only with respect to the necessity for a circuit judge to give reasons for his decision.

F R Moat for the mother.
Barrington Myers for the father.

g **CUMMING-BRUCE LJ**, after stating that he agreed with the judgment which had been delivered by Reeve J that the only variation of the judge's order which should be made would be to amend the order committing custody of the children of the marriage to the father to be an order for joint custody in favour of both parties, and after briefly considering some of the judge's findings of fact, said:
h When counsel were addressing the judge, the judge apparently made many observations indicating how his mind was working, though he had not indicated that he did not accept that it was a proper case for joint custody, and at the end of the submissions he announced that he was not intending to give formal judgment but that if the case went further he would state his reasons on request.
I venture, with respect to the judge, to say that on any view that was an inappropriate
j course, because even if there had been no appeal, there may be and frequently are change of circumstances in the lives of the parents and in the lives of the children. One party or another may apply to the court again for a variation of the existing custody order in the light of the change of circumstances. If the judge has failed to give a judgment stating his findings of fact, which form the basis of the order, in subsequent proceedings the parties and the court may find it difficult to judge whether there has been a relevant

change of circumstance which changes the basis of the judge's earlier order. I would go further. Apart from that important and practical reason, in contested custody proceedings *a* it is usual, and was the case here, for both parents to be strongly emotionally involved and extremely anxious to succeed in an application for care and control. In such a situation, however inconvenient it may be, the judge should always state his reasons for judgment so that the parents know reasonably precisely how the judge's mind was working. If there is an appeal it is open to the judge, if he wishes, when a note of his judgment has been brought into existence and sent to him for his approval, to elaborate *b* his reasons because an oral judgment delivered, to use the common phrase, 'off the cuff' is often imperfect and the judge is always entitled to correct it by adding what he would have said if at the time of delivering his judgment he had remembered to cover all the grounds. For that reason the course taken by the judge was unsatisfactory and I would hope it is a course which will not be followed again in a case of disputed issues of care and control. *c*

That is not quite the end of the story. The judge said that if the parties wished to take the matter further he would give reasons for his judgment and on no less than three occasions within days of the making of the judge's order, the mother's solicitors asked the judge to give reasons for his judgment. In the event this court did not receive the notes of judgment until 5 September 1983, the date on which they were received by the mother's solicitors. We are told by counsel for the mother that that gave rise to a feeling *d* of resentment and suspicion on the part of the mother. The reasons contained material which had not sufficiently, or at all, been disclosed by the judge when he made observations during the submissions of counsel. The mother was taken by surprise. The notice of appeal had already been drawn up and issued and, as it turns out, once the reasons for judgment were known the bottom dropped out of all the grounds of appeal as drafted in the original notice. And there was no supplementary notice of appeal and *e* no application for amendment of the grounds of appeal after the reasons for judgment were obtained. That was wrong.

The matter is dealt with very clearly in *Rayden on Divorce* (14th edn, 1983) vol 1, p 627, under the heading 'Amendment of notice of appeal'. If the appeal had not already appeared in the list of forthcoming appeals, a supplementary notice of appeal could have been filed without leave, provided the other party did not object, and, if the appeal had *f* already been listed in the list of forthcoming appeals, an application could and should have been made to the Registrar of Civil Appeals and, if necessary, to a single judge. That was a failure on the part of the legal representatives of the mother. I do not think it made any difference, having regard to the submissions that we have heard from counsel for the mother, save for this: counsel sought to adumbrate the submission that it was wrong in some way for the court to have regard to the judge's reasons because they varied so *g* significantly from the content of the observations that he had made when counsel were before him making their submissions. It was not clear at first whether counsel for the mother was submitting that the judge's reasons were inaccurate, but it then turned out that that was not his submission and that the foundation of his submission was, although there is no ground of appeal to that effect, that perhaps there ought to be a new trial because the mother was resentful and suspicious of the reasons for judgment which had *h* emerged so belatedly and appeared to vary so significantly from the observations that the judge had made at the hearing.

That leads me to say this. If for some reason, which is a good reason, the judge does not give his reasons for judgment at the hearing but announces that on request he will give reasons for judgment if the case is going further, the judge is under a clear obligation to draft and send to the proposed appellant's solicitors those reasons without any delay so *j* that the notice of appeal and the decision whether to appeal can both be dealt with in the light of the judge's reasons.

The hearing before the judge concluded on 30 June 1983. It is a common feature of a circuit judge's life that when he has disposed of a case he finds himself with heavy commitments on the trials, criminal or civil, which thereafter he is engaged on and it may become extremely difficult for him to fit in the time to throw his mind back to the case and draft accurate reasons. It may be that the delay in this case was contributed to by a judge's reasonable wish to have a holiday, because August is a holiday month. We know not the facts, but I would venture to state that, if a judge commits himself by not giving a judgment for some good reason but saying that he will give reasons for judgment if requested, then on receiving the request he should send the parties his reasons for judgment without any delay; and I state that with full appreciation of the practical difficulties of a circuit judge's life.

I thought it right to make these observations on procedure in the hope that it may contribute to avoiding any similar situation in the future. But, for the reasons stated by Reeve J, I agree that the appeal should be dismissed save in so far as it should be varied by varying the judge's custody order and substituting a joint custody order. But that variation will be made on the undertaking of the solicitors for the mother to file a supplementary notice of appeal giving notice of that application for variation, because there is nothing before the court at the moment to that end.

Appeal dismissed. Order varied. No order for costs.

Solicitors: *Woodford & Ackroyd*, Southampton (for the mother); *Reeder & Co*, Southampton (for the father).

Patricia Hargrove   Barrister.

Mercury Communications Ltd v Scott-Garner and another

CHANCERY DIVISION

MERVYN DAVIES J

17, 18, 19, 21 OCTOBER 1983

COURT OF APPEAL, CIVIL DIVISION

SIR JOHN DONALDSON MR, MAY AND DILLON LJJ

31 OCTOBER, 1, 2, 3, 9 NOVEMBER 1983

Trade dispute – Acts done in contemplation or furtherance of trade dispute – Meaning of trade dispute – Dispute relating 'wholly or mainly' to termination of employment – Union campaigning against privatisation of public telecommunications system and licensing of private systems – Plaintiff granted licence to operate private system – Union instructing members not to interconnect plaintiff's system to public system – Whether a 'trade dispute' existing between union's members and their employer – Whether dispute relating wholly or mainly to termination of employees' employment – Trade Union and Labour Relations Act 1974, ss 13(1), 29(1).

The British Telecommunications Act 1981 transferred the operation of the telecommunications system within the United Kingdom to a public corporation, BT, and also empowered the Secretary of State to licence the operation of private telecommunications systems which could compete with BT. In February 1982 the Secretary of State granted such a licence to the plaintiff company. In order to operate its system effectively the plaintiff needed to interconnect its system with the BT system and in November 1982 BT and the plaintiff entered into a formal agreement making provision for interconnection between the two systems. The defendant union, to which many of BT's employees belonged, opposed both the licensing of competing private systems such as that operated by the plaintiff and a proposal by the government, embodied in a Bill which was before

Parliament, to convert BT into a public company and to sell shares in the company to the public. The union accordingly instructed its members not to interconnect the plaintiff's system to BT's system if called on to do so. In June 1983 BT ordered certain union members to interconnect the two systems but they refused to do so. BT's management then suspended certain employees and effected some interconnection themselves. The union then 'blacked' the plaintiff and its shareholders by refusing to carry out maintenance work at their premises. The union also threatened to take industrial action against the plaintiff's customers. The plaintiff issued a writ against the union seeking, inter alia, an injunction restraining the union from inducing or procuring a breach of contract between BT and the plaintiff and from otherwise interfering with the plaintiff's business. The plaintiff also sought interlocutory relief in the same terms, pending the trial of action. The plaintiff contended that the union's actions amounted to an interference with the plaintiff's trade or business by unlawful means. The union contended that its actions were done 'in contemplation or furtherance of a trade dispute' and it was therefore immune, under s 13(1)[a] of the Trade Union and Labour Relations Act 1974, from action in tort by the plaintiff. The plaintiff submitted (i) that, having regard to s 29(1)[b] of the 1974 Act, which restricted the definition of a 'trade dispute', for the purposes of the Act, to 'a dispute between workers and their employer', there was no trade dispute between the union's members and their employer, namely BT, since the union's primary dispute was with the government and the plaintiff over the policy of liberalising the telecommunications system and selling shares in BT, and (ii) that if there was a dispute it was not a 'trade dispute' because it did not 'relate wholly or mainly' to the termination of the employment of workers or to any other matter specified in s 29(1). The union submitted that there was a dispute between its members and BT over prospective job losses and that the refusal to interconnect the systems of BT and the plaintiff was in furtherance of that dispute. The judge held that, although the union had campaigned vigorously against the government's policy as manifested by the licensing of the plaintiff, an actual 'trade dispute' between the union's members and their employer, BT, had crystallised when BT ordered union members to interconnect the two systems and those members refused. The judge further found that the dispute related wholly or mainly to the termination of employment and that therefore the union was immune from action by the plaintiff. The plaintiff appealed, submitting that a job security agreement between BT and the union (which only came to the plaintiff's notice after the judge had given judgment) negated the union's claim that job security was at the root of any dispute.

Held – (1) The judge had been right to conclude that there appeared to be a dispute between BT and members of the union which occurred when those members refused to carry out BT's orders to interconnect the plaintiff's and BT's telecommunications systems. It was thus very likely that there was a dispute between 'workers and their employer' for the purposes of s 29(1) of the 1974 Act (see p 201 *e f*, p 209 *h* to p 210 *c* and p 216 *d* to *f*, post).

(2) Although there was apparently a dispute between BT and members of the union, that dispute was unlikely to be held to be a 'trade dispute' as defined in s 29(1) of the 1974 Act because, on the true construction of s 29(1) and having regard to the general context, namely the wider dispute between the union on the one hand and the government, the plaintiff and BT on the other, the dispute between BT and members of the union was not likely to be held to 'relate wholly or mainly' to the termination of employment in the light of the job security agreement and the evidence showing the union's wider dispute to be political and idealogical in character rather than wholly or mainly concerned with jobs (see p 202 *g* to *j*, p 203 *c* to *e* and *h*, p 204 *g* to *j* p 205 *d*, p 209 *b*, p 210 *a* to *d* and *h j*, p 211 *a d e*, p 212 *f* to p 213 *d*, p 215 *f* to *h*, p 216 *a* and *g* and p 217 *a* and *e* to *g*, post); *General Aviation Services (UK) Ltd v Transport and General Workers' Union* [1975] ICR 276, *BBC v Hearn* [1978] 1 All ER 111, *NWL Ltd v Woods* [1979] 3 All ER 614,

a   Section 13(1) is set out at p 208 *e f*, post
b   Section 29(1), is set out at p 208 *g* to *j*, post

a *Duport Steels Ltd v Sirs* [1980] 1 All ER 529, *Health Computing Ltd v Meek* [1981] ICR 24 and *Hadmor Productions Ltd v Hamilton* [1982] 1 All ER 1042 considered.

(3) Since it was unlikely that the union would be able to establish a defence under s 13(1) of the 1974 Act by showing that its actions were done in contemplation or furtherance of a 'trade dispute' within s 29(1) and in view of the new evidence before the court concerning the job security agreement, the court was required to exercise afresh its discretion whether to grant the plaintiff interlocutory relief according to the balance of

b convenience. Having regard to the fact that the plaintiff had shown that it had a real prospect of succeeding at the trial and that it could not be adequately compensated by damages if the union succeeded at trial whereas the union could, the appeal would be allowed and the interlocutory injunction sought by the plaintiff would be granted (see p 205 *f* to p 206 *b* and *g*, p 208 *d e*, p 210 *c d*, p 211 *e*, p 213 *b* and *f* to *h*, p 214 *e f* and p 217 *e* to *g* and *j* to p 218 *f*, post); *American Cyanamid Co v Ethicon Ltd* [1975] 1 All ER

c 504 applied.

Quaere. Whether for there to be a 'trade dispute' within s 29(1) of the 1974 Act there must be a 'purposive dispute', in the sense that the purpose of the industrial action is to achieve something from the other side and the dispute is capable of being resolved by negotiation, in contrast to merely coercive interference with an employer's business as an appendage to a separate dispute between different parties (see p 201 *c* to *f* and p 209 *g h*,

d post).

Notes

For the legal liability of trade unions, see Supplement to 38 Halsbury's Laws (3rd edn) para 677B.3.

For the Trade Union and Labour Relations Act 1974, ss 13, 29, see 44 Halsbury's Statutes (3rd edn) 1769, 1779, and for s 13(1) of that Act (as substituted by the Trade

e Union and Labour Relations (Amendment) Act 1976, s 3(2)), see 46 ibid 1941.

As from 1 December 1982 s 29(1) of the 1974 Act was amended by the Employment Act 1982, s 18.

Cases referred to in judgments

American Cyanamid Co v Ethicon Ltd [1975] 1 All ER 504, [1975] AC 396, [1975] 2 WLR

f 316, HL.

BBC v Hearn [1978] 1 All ER 111, [1977] 1 WLR 1004, CA.

Duport Steels Ltd v Sirs [1980] 1 All ER 529, [1980] 1 WLR 142, QBD, CA and HL.

Express Newspapers Ltd v MacShane [1980] 1 All ER 65, [1980] AC 672, [1980] 2 WLR 89, HL.

Garland v British Rail Engineering Ltd [1982] 2 All ER 402, [1982] 2 WLR 918, CJEC and

g HL; *rvsg* [1979] 2 All ER 1163, [1979] 1 WLR 754, CA.

General Aviation Services (UK) Ltd v Transport and General Workers' Union [1975] ICR 276, CA.

Hadmor Productions Ltd v Hamilton [1982] 1 All ER 1042, [1983] 1 AC 191, [1982] 2 WLR 322, HL.

Health Computing Ltd v Meek [1981] ICR 24.

h *NWL Ltd v Woods, NWL Ltd v Nelson* [1979] 3 All ER 614, [1979] 1 WLR 1294, HL.

Cases also cited

Acrow (Automation) Ltd v Rex Chainbelt Inc [1971] 3 All ER 1175, [1971] 1 WLR 1676, CA.
Associated Newspapers Group Ltd v Wade [1979] 1 WLR 697, CA.
Corry v National Union of Vintners Grocers and Allied Trades Assistants [1950] IR 315.

j *Gouriet v Union of Post Office Workers* [1977] 3 All ER 70, [1978] AC 435, HL.
Lonrho Ltd v Shell Petroleum Co Ltd [1981] 2 All ER 456, [1982] AC 173, HL.
Stratford (J T) & Son Ltd v Lindley [1964] 3 All ER 102, [1965] AC 269, HL.
Torquay Hotel Co Ltd v Cousins [1969] 1 All ER 522, [1969] 2 Ch 106, CA.

Motion

By a writ dated 5 October 1983 the plaintiffs, Mercury Communications Ltd (Mercury),

sought as against the defendants, Bryan Stanley (sued on his own behalf and as
representing the national executive council of the second defendant, the Post Office
Engineering Union) and the union (1) an injunction restraining the defendants and each
of them whether by themselves, their servants or agents or otherwise howsoever from (a)
inducing and/or procuring and/or threatening to induce and/or procure a breach of the
contractual relations between Mercury and British Telecommunications whether by
inducing and/or procuring and/or threatening to induce and/or procure breaches of
contracts of employment or by any other unlawful means howsoever, so as to cause loss
harm or damage to Mercury, (b) interfering with the business of Mercury whether by
interfering with existing contractual relations or otherwise, and whether by inducing
and/or procuring and/or threatening to induce and/or procure breaches of contracts of
employment or by any other unlawful means howsoever so as to cause loss, harm or
damage to Mercury, (2) an order requiring the defendants to rescind the resolution of the
union's executive council made in or about March 1982 whereby a decision was taken to
instruct union members not to co-operate with Mercury, and to rescind any other
subsequent resolution or resolutions of a like nature relating to Mercury, (3) an order
requiring the defendants to withdraw the restrictions issued in or about May 1982 and
any other such instructions of a like nature whereby the said resolution or resolutions
were implemented, by communicating in writing with their said members that the said
instructions were withdrawn, and (4) damages. By a notice of motion dated the same day
Mercury sought against the defendants interlocutory relief in the same terms as the
injunctions and orders sought in the writ. By an amendment dated 27 October John
Scott-Garner, the president of the union and a member of its national executive council,
was substituted as the first defendant because Bryan Stanley was not a member of the
union's national executive council. The facts are set out in the judgment.

Alexander Irvine QC, Richard Field and *Patrick Elias* for Mercury.
Christopher Carr QC and *Cherie Booth* for the defendants.

Cur adv vult

21 October. The following judgment was delivered.

MERVYN DAVIES J. This is a motion for interlocutory relief in an action by Mercury
Communications Ltd (Mercury) against Mr Bryan Stanley and the Post Office Engineering
Union (the union). Mr Stanley is sued on his own behalf and as representing the members
of the national executive council of the union. Mr Stanley is the general secretary of the
union but it turns out that he is not in fact a member of the national executive council.
This fact emerged at the hearing and by consent of the defendants it was agreed that Mr
Scott-Garner, the union president and a member of the national executive council be
made a defendant in place of Mr Stanley.
    The writ is dated 5 October 1983 and claims:

'(1) An injunction restraining the Defendants and each of them whether by
themselves, their servants or agents or otherwise howsoever from (a) Inducing and/
or procuring and/or threatening to induce and/or procure a breach of the contractual
relations between the Plaintiffs and British Telecommunications whether by
inducing and/or procuring and/or threatening to induce and/or procure breaches of
contract of employment or by any other unlawful means howsoever, so as to cause
loss, harm or damage to the Plaintiffs (b) Interfering with the business of the
Plaintiffs whether by interfering with existing contractual relations or otherwise,
and whether by inducing and/or procuring and/or threatening to induce and/or
procure breaches of contracts of employment or by any other unlawful means
howsoever so as to cause loss, harm or damage to the Plaintiffs.
    (2) An order requiring the Defendants to rescind the Resolution of the Executive
Council in or about March 1982 whereby a decision was taken to instruct union
members not to co-operate with the Plaintiffs, and to rescind any other subsequent
resolution or resolutions of a like nature relating to the Plaintiffs.

(3) An order requiring the Defendants to withdraw the restrictions issued in or
about May 1982 and any other such instructions of a like nature whereby the said
resolution or resolutions were implemented, by communicating in writing with
their said members that the said instructions are withdrawn.

(4) Damages.

(5) Such further or other Order as this Honourable Court deems fit.

(6) Costs.'

The notice of motion bears the same date as the writ and seeks interlocutory orders in
the terms of items (1) to (3) that I have read.

The evidence in support of the motion is an affidavit by Mr Derek Evans sworn on 5
October 1983. There are 13 exhibits to the affidavit. Then there is a second affidavit
sworn by Mr Evans on 17 October 1983 with two exhibits and an affidavit of Mr S A
Bailey sworn on 17 October 1983. These two later affidavits were not made available to
the defendants before the first day of the hearing before me. The evidence filed on behalf
of the defendants consists of three affidavits by Mr Bryan Stanley, the one sworn on 14
October 1983, with three exhibits, the second sworn on the same date showing one
exhibit and the third is an affidavit now sworn which was read to me in draft. Mr
Stanley's first affidavit says that he has been shown Mr Evans's affidavit sworn on 5
October 1983, together with its exhibits.

Mr Evans is the chief executive of Mercury Communications Ltd. Mercury are a
private company incorporated on 28 June 1981. Their capital is now £1m divided into
1,000,000 shares of £1 each. Their shareholders are as to 40% a subsidiary of Cable and
Wireless plc, as to 40% a subsidiary of British Petroleum plc and as to the remaining 20%
a subsidiary of Barclays Merchant Bank Ltd. On 22 February 1982 the Secretary of State
in exercise of powers conferred on him by s 15(1) of the British Telecommunications Act
1981 granted to Cable and Wireless plc a licence to run a telecommunications system in
the United Kingdom on terms that Mercury would act as Cable and Wireless's agents in
running the system. A copy of the relevant parts of the licence was included in the
exhibits before the court.

On 10 September 1982 the Mercury shareholders entered into a joint venture
agreement for the design, construction, operation and commercialisation of a system
called the Mercury Telecommunications System. The system was to be owned by the
shareholders proportionately to their shareholdings in Mercury. By another agreement
also dated 10 September 1982 the shareholders appointed Mercury their managing agents
for the purpose of effecting the realisation of the Mercury Telecommunications System.
This second agreement recites the licence in favour of Cable and Wireless dated 22
February 1982 that I have already mentioned.

So in effect, as I understand, the Mercury shareholders were to own the Mercury
System and the Mercury company were to be agents of the shareholders to operate that
system.

The activities I have mentioned took place against a background of change in the law
relating to telecommunications. Until 1981 the Post Office had a monopoly in the
operation of telecommunications systems within the United Kingdom. By the
Telecommunications Act 1981 the public corporation British Telecommunications (BT)
was established. BT took over from the Post Office its telecommunications functions. By
s 10 there was transferred to BT the property rights and liabilities comprised in that part
of the Post Office's undertaking concerned with the provision of telecommunications
and data processing services. By s 12 BT was given the exclusive privilege of running
telecommunications throughout the British Islands. Then by s 15 of the 1981 Act, a
section I have already referred to, there is provision for the grant of licences for the
running of telecommunication systems. A licence is granted by the Secretary of State or
by BT acting with the consent of the Secretary of State.

Not only has there been this ending of the Post Office monopoly and transfer of
functions to BT, but also there has been before Parliament a Bill called the

Telecommunications Bill 1983. The Bill will be before a standing committee of the House of Commons on 25 October 1983. It is a formidable document of 188 pages. *a* Among other things it is proposed to abolish BT's exclusive privilege of running telecommunications systems, for the transfer of all BT's property rights and liabilities to a successor company. There are financial arrangements respecting the successor company and provision for the sale of its shares: see Part V of the Bill. In other words, there is contemplated 'privatisation', as it is now called, of BT. The Bill also requires that, as a condition of any licence granted to BT and Mercury (the Bill providing for the renewal *b* of the current Mercury licence), both BT and Mercury will be obliged to permit interconnection of each other's telecommunications systems.

Reverting to the 1981 Act and the documents executed pursuant to that Act that I have already mentioned, I am told that Mercury are at liberty to compete fully with BT in providing telecommunications services subject to certain restrictions imposed by the licence dated 22 February 1982. In any event Mercury had embarked on establishing *c* within the United Kingdom a digital communications network. In para 9 of his first affidavit Mr Evans says:

'... The network is primarily intended to offer a choice to business users of telecommunications for whom digital transmission is particularly suitable in facilitating high speed transfer of large volumes of data, for instance between computers, as well as carrying voice and video traffic. For trunk transmission *d* between business centres, the network will be based primarily upon optical fibre cable laid alongside British Rail tracks; for local distribution of Mercury services to and from customers' premises within business centres, a mixture of cable and microwave radio facilities will be used, supplemented by inter-connection with the BT network, details of which I will deal with later in this Affidavit.'

There is an intention as well to provide international connections with use made of *e* communications satellites.

A new Mercury network within the United Kingdom requires a degree of interconnection between the Mercury and BT networks. On 5 November 1982 an agreement was made between BT and Mercury providing for interconnection in various ways. *f*

The position of the defendants in this situation is that they take objection to Mercury being allowed to use the BT network and to the proposals to privatise BT. The defendant union has, I understand, about 130,000 members. The work of interconnection depends on the union members, in the course of their employment by BT, helping or at any rate not obstructing that work. The defendant union is anxious both to prevent further interconnection and to oppose the privatisation proposals. The union has been active in *g* pursuing these objectives.

Mr Evans referred to several documents which illustrate the union's activities. (i) The union journal for December 1982, in the course of an article referring to the interconnection agreement date 5 November 1982 that I have already mentioned sets out a resolution of the national executive council of the union passed in March 1982. It reads: *h*

'The NEC have resolved that it is the Union's intention to instruct [its] members not to connect any of the Project Mercury traffic through the public switched network and the interface of the international network.'

(ii) An extract from Computer Weekly dated 6 May 1982 reports the general secretary of the union, Mr Stanley, saying that the national executive have decided to take any *j* action necessary to oppose the connection of Mercury to BT's network and any further liberalisation of telecommunications. (iii) An extract from the Guardian dated 8 May 1982 indicates that Mr Stanley in April or May 1982 sent a circular to all branches of the union. Therein members were instructed not to make any connections for the time being between the public telephone cable system and the alternative network. Connection

between the Mercury network and the international telecommunications network was
also banned. (iv) In the union journal for October 1982 the deputy secretary of the union
is reported as saying:

> 'We have opposed Mercury from the first time it was suggested and we shall
> oppose it in the future, and any form of alternative network which is set up to
> compete with British Telecom by selling services to third parties.'

(v) On 31 March 1983 Mr Stanley wrote to the Daily Telegraph. He said:

> 'Sir — Your leader of March 28 referred to action being taken by the Post Office
> Engineering Union against the new private business telecommunications company,
> Mercury. I am sure you would agree that it is important for our view to be correctly
> stated in your newspaper. Mercury, on its own admission, is not going to provide
> any new service. It will dilute British Telecom's future profitability by competing
> on the most lucrative business routes currently available. Mercury is, therefore, an
> unnecessary duplication and waste of national resources. Although we remain
> firmly of the view that it will not be for the benefit of the community as a whole,
> competition is an established fact. We believe that British Telecom will compete
> and be effective against its rivals. However, we do object to the fact that British
> Telecom is being forced to give up its own telecommunications network for use by
> these rivals. This is the purpose of our industrial action against connecting Mercury
> to British Telecom's network. Mercury was created to establish an independent
> alternative network to British Telecom. Although we do not support this, we
> acknowledge the fact that it is going to happen. However, we do not intend to see
> Mercury exploiting the network which British Telecom has created over very many
> years, and which is based upon the work of our members, in order to do this. This
> is especially so as this exploitation will reduce British Telecom's business and hence
> the job opportunities for these members. No respectable business should be forced
> to hand over the use of its assets in this way, British Telecom included.'

There is then a paragraph that I need not read and the letter is signed: 'Bryan Stanley,
General Secretary.' (vi) Going back a little in time there is then a document dated 13
October 1982 and headed, 'Campaign Against Privatisation'. This is a newsletter issued,
as I understand, by a committee representing 250,000 BT trade union employees,
including those employees who are members of the union involved in this case. The
newsletter announces a meeting on 15 October 1982 at which the case against privatisation
would be outlined, and a march from Tower Hill on 20 October 1982, 'the Day of
Action'. The day of action was said to be only 'the start of the Campaign Against
Privatisation'. Some demonstrations followed and then on 6 April 1983 a series of
selective strikes was launched in the London area. On 5 April 1983 Mr Stanley wrote to
Sir George Jefferson, who is the chairman of BT. Mr Stanley said:

> 'Further to my letter of 31st March 1983, I now write to let you know that as
> from today Tuesday 5th April 1983, the National Executive Council of the Post
> Office Engineering Union has instructed staff maintaining the Bank of England
> telecommunications installations and the staff employed in Whitehall RSC, to
> withdraw their labour to further demonstrate the Union's total opposition to the
> proposed privatisation of British Telecom. This action is in defence of the future of
> telecommunications in Britain and the jobs of the staff employed by British Telecom.
> The action would cease immediately if the Government were to withdraw their ill
> thought out proposals.'

So one has a withdrawal of labour to show the union's opposition to privatisation. In fact
the action mentioned in this letter dated 5 April 1983 was called off on 12 May 1983.
This was in consequence of the announcement of a general election. It will be
remembered that in the letter dated 31 March 1983 that I have referred to, Mr Stanley
states that the union's industrial action was against interconnection. So it appears that

industrial action was contemplated both against further interconnection and future privatisation. Mr Evans states in para 15 of his affidavit that on 22 June 1983 BT management effected some interconnection between BT's and Mercury's systems. Mr Evans goes on:

'In addition BT suspended certain workers who had refused to obey instructions to effect the connection. Following this action the National Executive Council of the Union decided on a meeting on 23rd June 1983 to take selective strike action in retaliation against BT management because of latter's action in carrying out work which union members had refused to do.'

On 27 July 1983 there was a special meeting of the national executive council of the union. It was decided to escalate industrial action against Mercury by going against the Mercury shareholders, that is, Cable and Wireless, BT and Barclays Bank. Action is apparently determined by a committee of the general purposes committee of the union called the industrial strategy sub-committee. The action then determined is set out in a bulletin dated 15 August 1983. I need not read it all. It includes the statement:

'It is the NEC's intention to carefully monitor and develop the industrial action and to ensure that our policy of no interconnection for Mercury is successful.'

I now come to 18 September 1983. On this date there was a special conference of the union. The purpose was to discuss privatisation. It was resolved to set up opposition to privatisation by steps including selective industrial action. Mr Evans referred to a report in the Financial Times of 4 October 1983 and, as well, in his second affidavit he was able to give some more information about this special conference. He produced a copy of the report which the national executive council presented to the conference. The chairman in the conference agenda states that the subject matter of the conference was privatisation. The report is headed, 'PRIVATISATION'. It is in three sections: 'SECTION A. THE SITUATION FACED BY THE UNION SECTION B. THE UNION'S RESPONSE SECTION C. THE PUBLICITY CAMPAIGN AGAINST PRIVATISATION SECTION D. TELECOMMUNICATIONS BILL . . .' Counsel for Mercury referred me to several paragraphs in this report. First, there is para 23 which sets out proposition 42 passed at the annual conference in June 1982. It reads:

'That in the event of British Telecom being privatised the [union] will continue to oppose the principles of privatisation by the following programme. (a) To continue to use the whole spectrum of opposition, including industrial action against any private company, or individual speculator who attempts to connect to, or hive off any part of British Telecom for financial gain. (b) To continue the fight for the return of British Telecom to public ownership, without compensation to those speculators who use the established resources of British Telecom for their own financial gain. (c) Upon the return of a Labour Government, seek the removal of National management whose connivance with the Tory Government was a betrayal of BT staff and greatly enhanced the chances of the privatisation of BT.'

The report also contains these paragraphs:

'24. In summary, these Propositions instruct the National Executive Council that, in order to safeguard our industry, jobs and working conditions the Union continues to oppose the Government's privatisation policies using a campaign of industrial action against financial and business institutions and any other bodies seeking to make financial gain from the privatisation of British Telecom . . .

31. The National Executive Council will seek to carry through a flexible campaign that will be capable of meeting the developing nature of the opposition to our policies. Having re-examined all the actions undertaken so far by the Union against privatisation, the National Executive Council has set out the following strategy to achieve the objectives above—(i) To re-invigorate and step up the publicity campaign against the privatisation of British Telecom with respect to the members, other BT

Trade Unions, the public and the Labour movement. This is covered in paragraphs
33 to 37 of this Report. (ii) To develop forms of industrial action in pursuit of these
objectives. This is covered in paragraphs 38 to 40 of this Report. (iii) To press for co-
ordination of action of—All BT Unions through the British Telecoms Union
Committee. Other public sector Unions confronting privatisation both directly and
through the TUC. This is covered in paragraphs 34, 35 and 37 of this Report. (iv)
To pursue a vigorous Parliamentary campaign using all means possible to defeat the
proposals contained in the 1983 Telecommunications Bill. This is covered in
paragraphs 41 to 49.'

Then there is para 32;

'Timing 32. The timing of the Union Campaign against privatisation will evolve
over a number of months. It will be related to–(i) Developments surrounding the
Mercury interconnect issue. (ii) The build up to, and the passage of, the
Telecommunications Bill through Parliament. (iii) If the Bill is successful, the
floatation [sic] of BT plc. (iv) No major changes on the strategy of the anti-
privatisation campaign will be taken without reference to Conference.'

Finally, para 38:

'Industrial Action Project Mercury 38 The Union's policy to prevent any
interconnection between Project Mercury and the BT network was endorsed by the
1982 Conference of the Union. Instructions were issued to Branches at the beginning
of 1983 that no member should undertake any work which would entail making a
physical connection between the BT network and Mercury. Prior to Annual
Conference in June, we were warned by the London North Central Area and London
City Branches that an instruction to carry out such connection was imminent. Area
Management eventually issued those instructions in the week commencing 20th
June. The members involved loyally followed the Union's policy and refused to
carry out management's instructions and as a consequence, were suspended from
duty. A few days later it was discovered that senior members of management had
gone into a building in the North Centre Area where the work was being blacked
and had carried out work proper to [union] members in an attempt to undermine
the action. Retaliatory action in the form of withdrawal of key groups of members
in selected locations was therefore taken by the branches in the Area, with the
backing and authority of the National Executive Council, to make plain to
management that we would not allow them to undermine our action. Where such
members of management have been proven to be members of the STE, they have
been subjected to disciplinary action by their organisation. At the time of preparing
this report, the action on Mercury is confined to the central London area, but reports
received from a number of Branches appear to indicate that instructions to provide
connections for Mercury are imminent in a number of other parts of the country
and it now seems almost certain that the dispute will widen in the very near future.'

Counsel for Mercury relied on the report and these paragraphs in particular as showing
that it cannot be said that the union is campaigning merely against the Telecommunications Bill. The union, he says, is opposed both to privatisation and liberalisation, ie
allowing competition. As well, para 32, it is said, makes clear that Mercury are part of
the privatisation issue; so that the union activity is not in furtherance of a dispute with
BT, but rather one campaign embracing both opposition to Mercury and to privatisation.
I am told that the whole of the national executive report was accepted in principle
although section C was subject to some amendment.

In his second affidavit, Mr Evans brings up to date the position as respects the industrial
action taken against the Mercury shareholders. In short, he says that no maintenance
work was carried out at some of the principal premises of British Petroleum, Barclays
Bank and Cable and Wireless from 15 August 1983 to 11 October 1983. Service was
resumed on this latter date, a date subsequent to the issue of the writ.

These events, I understand, have not in any way reassured Mercury. It is feared that the union's intention is to prevent interconnection. The position is in general, so it is said, that on the orders of the union the employees of BT who are members of the union will refuse to co-operate with Mercury either by refusing to touch Mercury installations or by carrying out their duties to BT in so obstructive a fashion that Mercury's activities will be seriously hindered.

Mr Evans gave evidence of the damage that is being done to Mercury by the union action. Potential customers are being deterred not only because they suppose that Mercury may not be able to function, but, even if they do function, that there may be retaliatory action against customers of Mercury. Mr Bailey's affidavit amplifies this aspect of Mercury's case. He is the sales and marketing director of Mercury. In the course of his affidavit Mr Bailey says:

'7. The effect of the [union's] action against Mercury has had the most serious consequences. Actual orders taken so far have fallen several million pounds short of the targets which we realistically believed would have been achieved by this stage; and Mercury can ill afford these consequences given the massive capital investment which has been made. My overall assessment is that, as a result of the [union's] action, Mercury has irretrievably lost orders worth about £·5 million and £1·5 million per annum from customers who have now gone elsewhere and a further £4 million per annum is directly in jeopardy. The longer term loss stands to be much greater because, in the normal course of events, Mercury could reasonably expect substantial further orders from these "lost" customers as new Mercury services are introduced.'

I now turn to Mr Stanley's evidence. Mr Stanley is, of course, the general secretary of the union. He says he is authorised to make his affidavit on behalf of the union and he makes it on his own behalf as a defendant. In para 6 of the affidavit Mr Stanley says he wishes to state 'as clearly and as emphatically as I am able the purpose and object which underlies the industrial action which my Union is taking'. It is then explained (see para 9) that the reason why the union opposes the entry of competing organisations into the market in which BT operates is the risk of redundancy among union members. Mr Stanley goes on, and I will quote him at length:

'9 ... Where, as in this case, the traditional monopoly of British Telecommunications is being broken and the market opened up to competition, it would be nothing less than astonishing if my members were not extremely alarmed about the prospects for their future employment which would result from entry in the market of a rival organisation.

10. I therefore wish to state unequivocally and with all the emphasis at my command that the purpose and object of the industrial action complained of by the Plaintiffs is to prevent the risk of job losses arising from the entry into the market of an unwelcome competitor.

11. I have stated above the reason why my Union and its members do not welcome the opening up of the market to a competitor organisation. However, we recognise that it is not within our power to prevent the enactment of legislation which does precisely this. We may do our best to seek to persuade and to lobby by the normal democratic processes. We may argue that competition would be a bad thing in the national interest. And these are, indeed, steps we have taken. But we recognise that, at the end of the day, if the Government is determined that the traditional monopoly of BT shall be ended and if its policy commands Parliamentary support, we are compelled to accept, with whatever degree of reluctance, the fact that we cannot ensure the maintenance of the monopoly.

12. However, insofar as the entry of a competitor organisation into the market is to be facilitated by the use by this organisation of BT's facilities, my members are in a position to prevent those facilities being made available to such a rival organisation.

a   Of course, if a rival organisation were to start to trade in the field of telecommunications and were to acquire or create its own facilities independently of those owned or operated by BT, we could not prevent this occurring. But so long as any such competitor organisation depends upon being able to draw upon facilities owned by BT and serviced and manned by my Union's members, they are in a position to prevent that organisation from trading in the way it would wish.

b   Similarly, by emphasising and underlining that they will decline to co-operate with any such organisation, my members are in a position to create a disincentive to any potential future rival organisation which might be considering seeking to enter the market in the way the Plaintiffs have done.

    13. The industrial action which is currently taking place and which is directed against BT for agreeing to provide to the Plaintiffs facilities represents an attempt by my Union's members to do what lies within their power to prevent the risk of redundancies to which I referred above from arising. I should add that it is

c   particularly galling to my Union's members to be asked to assist the Plaintiffs in connecting the plaintiffs to BT's network. In effect, they are being asked to undertake duties the fulfilment of which will be the very act which puts their own jobs in jeopardy. This is a dimension of the situation which is plainly likely to be a sensitive one. However, the issue upon which the members of my Union stand firm is that they do not support the creation of rival organisations which may put their own

d   jobs at risk and they are prepared to refuse to inter-connect the BT network which will bring this about. The reason for their action is quite clearly their fear for their jobs.'

    Mr Stanley refers in para 18 of his affidavit to Mr Evans's assertion in para 14 of the Evans affidavit that the union's action is aimed at Mercury and the government because

e   of the union's intransigent opposition to government policy. This assertion, he says, is fanciful. He reiterates the aim of the industrial action is to protect members' jobs.

    There is then a reply to Mr Evans's assertion in para 13(v) of the Evans affidavit that the union is really in dispute with Mercury and the government and not with BT at all. I think I must again quote at length from Mr Stanley's affidavit:

f   '21. The first of the two points made by Mr. Evans to which I referred above was his assertion that the Union are really in dispute with Mercury and the Government and not with BT. This is a complete misconception on his part. The present dispute has certain unusual features. In 1981, both the Union and the management of BT were opposed to liberalisation. The management of BT obviously appreciated that their own position might be deleteriously affected. There is now produced and shown to me marked "BS2" a true copy of two press releases issued by Sir George

g   Jefferson, the chairman of BT dated 15th April and 2nd July 1981. These press releases indicate the nature of apprehensions felt at the senior levels of BT in 1981 concerning the policy of liberalisation. Needless to say, the anxieties of senior management were shared within Union circles. At that stage, therefore, there was a similarity of thought and attitude on the part of management and Union. There is also produced and shown to me marked "BS3" a true copy of a letter dated 22nd July

h   1981 which I sent to the branches of the Union together with the two annexes. In the last paragraph of my letter I drew attention to the need to consider the implications of the government's proposals for the future security of our members' employment. I also drew attention to the final paragraph of annexe B. My union is not opposed to private industry playing a part in telecommunications so long as this does not put at risk the operations of BT and hence the jobs of the Union's members.

j   22. In due course, BT held discussions with the government and entered into the inter-connection agreement with the plaintiffs referred to in the affidavit of Mr. Evans. It is not for me to say with what degree of reluctance on the part of the senior management of BT this might have been done. But the fact is that the criticism of allowing alternative networks manifested by the press releases to which I have referred above and which were issued in 1981 did not win the day. In due course liberalisation became a reality and BT have entered into an inter-connection agreement with the Plaintiffs. It is over this that the Union are in dispute with BT. Whatever might have been the wish or preference of BT they have in fact allowed a rival organisation to inter-connect with its network. It is this fact which puts them at odds with my Union. The fact that many executives of BT may nurture attitudes and opinions not dissimilar from those of my members is beside the point. The action which BT is taking is inconsistent with the desire of my members to retain the traditional monopoly over telecommunications facilities within BT. Once BT embarked upon a course of seeking to facilitate and implement liberalisation, they embarked upon a course which could only lead to a dispute between them and the Union. This is in fact what has occurred. The current position is that my members are being required by the management of BT to carry out certain operations which will involve connecting the Plaintiffs with BT's facilities. My members are not prepared to do that. Accordingly, they are not prepared to carry out the instructions of management in that regard. There is, accordingly, a dispute between my members and BT. The cause of this dispute lies in the fact that BT wish my members to take a step which my members regard as putting their jobs at risk. To suggest that there is no dispute between the Union and BT or that the dispute is "really" with the Government or the Plaintiffs is quite wrong. The industrial action that is being taken is in pursuance of a dispute with BT over whether members of the Union should be required to act in a way which they see as placing their jobs in jeopardy. The subject matter of the dispute is the risk to jobs. The precise form that risk takes is the connection of Mercury to BT's network. The parties to the dispute are BT and their employees, although the action of the employees is, of course, directed and co-ordinated by the Union acting on their behalf.

23. While it is not easy to single out any particular moment in time at which the similarity of posture between BT and the Union was replaced by a state of dispute, a number of significant meetings took place between the senior management of BT and Union representatives. The proceedings of these meetings are confidential and I am extremely reluctant to betray such confidences. Effective industrial relations depend upon management and Unions being able to trust one another in confidential matters. I am anxious to respect that confidence. However, I regard it as perfectly proper for me to disclose the facts that show how the dispute developed. At a meeting on the 14th September 1981 with the Chairman and senior management of BT I warned them that if inter-connection between a private network and BT's network were allowed there would be serious repercussions from the Union. On the 21st December 1981 at another meeting with the Chairman and senior management of BT I made it clear that the Union was totally opposed to inter-connection with Mercury. It was at this meeting that BT estimated that the loss of revenue if Mercury were introduced would be in the range of £150 million to £600 million per annum. On the 19th January 1983 at a meeting with senior management of BT I stated that a state of dispute between BT and their employees was developing. I said at that meeting that although the Union had succeeded in persuading their members to co-operate in providing exchange lines for the Plaintiffs, the inter-connection of Mercury with the BT's public switched network could be the point at which active staff resistance was encountered. This warning proved to be well-founded. The membership of the Union employed by BT have declined to connect Mercury to the BT network.

24. The position between BT and the Union is, therefore, that they have moved from their initial stance of a shared dislike of alternative networks. BT's management is now attempting to effect liberalisation in the form of connecting Mercury to its network. Employees of BT are declining to participate in that work. BT and their employees are, in my respectful submission, therefore in a state of dispute. The basis of the dispute and the circumstance that has brought it about and which pervades it is the fear of job losses if Mercury are connected to the network.'

There ends that long extract from Mr Stanley's affidavit.

a   I asked counsel for the union, whether or not the union had informed BT that the union was in dispute with BT and was told that BT had not been expressly so informed. Mr Stanley's second affidavit merely exhibited 14 letters from branches of the union throughout England and Wales. The letters voiced the greatest anxiety about the effect of the changes and proposed changes that are taking place in the realm of telecommunications law in England.

b   Mr Stanley's third (draft) affidavit did not appear until the second day of the hearing before me, when counsel for Mercury was already engaged on his submissions. In this third affidavit Mr Stanley says that at the special conference on 18 September 1983 the union faced two separate issues, namely (1) the question of the liberalisation of the telecommunications industry and in particular the Mercury competition, and (2) privatisation. As to (1), while recognising that the battle against loss of monopoly was

c   lost the union nevertheless continued to oppose interconnection. That is to say, as I understand, the union would not seek to stop Mercury operating a network that was not dependent on any interconnection with the BT network. Mr Stanley's third affidavit then goes on to deal with the discussion between BT and the union concerning interconnection. It will be remembered that the interconnection agreement is dated 5 November 1982. In para 8 of the affidavit Mr Stanley says that the chairman of BT was

d   warned on 19 January 1983 of industrial action if any attempt was made to order union members to connect Mercury into the BT network. There followed a meeting on 15 February 1983. Mr Stanley states that the attempt at that meeting to find an accommodation between BT and the union with regard to Mercury broke down. The union concluded that a confrontation with BT over Mercury was imminent. I was referred to a letter sent by the strategy committee to members of the national executive

e   council. This letter deals separately with Mercury and privatisation. In the Mercury section of the letter the committee reported to the national executive council that it was agreed that London North Central Area branch be advised that the national executive council instruction not to connect Mercury to the public network be reaffirmed. In the privatisation section of the letter it is requested that the strategy committee give consideration to the timing of the selective industrial action against privatisation already

f   agreed in principle by the national executive council in February. It is recommended that the action should begin on 5 April 1983 in London; that is the day of action that I have referred to. As I have said, the action did not go far because the general election intervened. Mr Stanley goes on to say that it was not until 10 June 1983 that BT ordered interconnection. The union members so ordered refused to do the work and were sent home. It was then that BT management itself effected some interconnection. This is, of

g   course, a cause of complaint for the union. On 22 June 1983, Mr Norman, the assistant general secretary, wrote to Sir George Jefferson as follows:

h   'As you are aware, the [union] remains implacably opposed to any interconnection between the BT network and Project Mercury. It is our view that such interconnection is detrimental to the interests of our members and BT as a whole. We believe that Mercury is unnecessary and is an unfair competitor with no commitment to provide a public service. We see no reason why such an organisation should be allowed to steal our business. Members of the [union] are therefore under instruction not to carry out any work which would lead to such an interconnection. I therefore wish to express, on behalf of my National Executive Council, the strongest possible

j   objection to the use of management staff in the London North Centre Area to carry out work proper to [union] members involving the provision of service to Mercury. Any action of this kind by management, which is clearly designed to undermine our Union's continued opposition to Mercury, can only serve to inflame the situation and strengthen the Union's resolve. Our Executive is therefore left with no alternative but to consider what steps it should take to retaliate in response to what we regard is a total provocative act by management.'

Sir George Jefferson replied on 29 June 1983 as follows:

'Thank you for your letter of 22 June.   *a*

The question of interconnect between BT's Inland network and others, including Mercury, is an integral part of Government policy for the liberalisation of telecommunications which was introduced under the 1981 Telecommunications Act; Mercury has been licensed under that Act. There was no doubt that Government intended to implement that policy and we have taken the view that it was in the best interests of BT to make a proper commercial arrangement with Mercury.   *b*

As you are aware, it is the Government's policy to make arrangements for payments by licensed telecommunications operators, such as Mercury, who connect to BT's network, to contribute appropriately through access charges to the costs, borne by BT, of facilities of a public service nature. Under our present agreement with Mercury preliminary payments of this nature are already provided. It is not, therefore, correct to say that Mercury is an unfair competitor. Should it at any time   *c* appear to be so, we have the right to refer the facts to the Office of Fair Trading, or in due course to OFTEL.

The Board cannot accept that the [union] have any justification for issuing instructions to its members to refuse to comply with the instructions of management in pursuance of a proper commercial contract between BT and Mercury, particularly when that contract actually brings business and work to BT as this does.   *d*

Actions of this sort, already taken by some of your members, will damage the confidence of customers in the reliability of British Telecom as a supplier of telecommunications services, and it is possible as a result that both Government and customers may themselves take action detrimental to BT's ability to maintain employment in its work force.

It is the Board's clear view that this action by the Union is contrary to the interests   *e* of job security for our employees.

I therefore must ask your National Executive Council to withdraw the instruction to your members not to carry out any work which would lead to interconnection with the Mercury system, and to request your members to work normally.'

Mr Stanley's affidavit then states in para 14:   *f*

'In my respectful submission, it is plain beyond argument that by this stage a dispute had arisen between BT and the Union. On the one hand the Union had given instructions to its members that they should not interconnect Mercury. On the other hand, Sir George Jefferson had written to say that this instruction was given without any justification. It is also noteworthy that Sir George Jefferson ended his letter by requesting that the instruction issued by the Union should be   *g* withdrawn. I contend that there was the clearest possible dispute between BT and its employees by that stage.'

Mr Stanley, of course, accepts that the union has campaigned and will campaign against privatisation, but he says that it is a matter of common sense that the union should try to co-ordinate its activities in relation to both disputes, i e, as to interconnection   *h* and as to privatisation, albeit that the two questions raise two separate issues.

I have now mentioned the principal items of evidence before me. I bear in mind that it is not now my task to decide the final rights of the parties to this dispute, but merely to decide whether or not in all the circumstances it is appropriate to make some interlocutory order at the behest of Mercury or to dismiss the motion.

I am to be guided by the principles laid down in *American Cyanamid Co v Ethicon Ltd*   *j* [1975] 1 All ER 504 at 510, [1975] AC 396 at 407, to be applied in the light of s 17(2) of the Trade Union and Labour Relations Act 1974 as inserted by the Employment Protection Act 1975 and amended by the Employment Act 1982. Section 17(2) reads:

'It is hereby declared for the avoidance of doubt that where an application is made to a court, pending the trial of an action, for an interlocutory injunction and the party against whom the injunction is sought claims that he acted in contemplation or furtherance of a trade dispute, the court shall, in exercising its discretion whether or not to grant the injunction, have regard to the likelihood of that party's succeeding at the trial of the action in establishing the matter or matters which would, under any provision of section 13 or 15 above, afford a defence to the action.'

Section 17(2) is material in this case, because the union claim that the acts complained of by Mercury were acts done in contemplation or furtherance of a trade dispute.

The other statutory provisions which I have to have in mind are s 13(1)(a) of the 1974 Act (as substituted by the Trade Union and Labour Relations (Amendment) Act 1976), and s 29(1) and (6) of the 1974 Act as amended by s 18 of the Employment Act 1982. Section 13(1) reads:

'An act done by a person in contemplation or furtherance of a trade dispute shall not be actionable in tort on the ground only—(a) that it induces another person to break a contract or interfer or induces any other person to interfere with its performance...'

Section 29(1) and (6) as amended read:

'(1) In this Act "trade dispute" means a dispute between workers and their employer which relates wholly or mainly to one or more of the following, that is to say—(a) terms and conditions of employment, or the physical conditions in which any workers are required to work; (b) engagement or non-engagement or termination or suspension of employment or the duties of employment, of one or more workers; (c) allocation of work or the duties of employment as between workers or groups of workers; (d) matters of discipline; (e) the membership or non-membership of a trade union on the part of a worker; (f) facilities for officials of trade unions; and (g) machinery for negotiation or consultation, and other procedures, relating to any of the foregoing matters, including the recognition by employers or employers' associations of the right of a trade union to represent workers in any such negotiation or consultation or in the carrying out of such procedures...

(6) In this section—"employment" includes any relationship whereby one person personally does work or performs services for another; "worker", in relation to a dispute with an employer, means—(a) a worker employed by that employer...'

which is a paragraph that I need not read.

The statutory provisions must be read with in mind the cautionary words of Lord Diplock that are in *Duport Steels Ltd v Sirs* [1980] 1 All ER 529 at 541–542, [1980] 1 WLR 142 at 156–158. The case for Mercury begins from the assertion that the union's activities in preventing interconnection between the BT and Mercury networks are tortious at common law. Counsel for the union accepted that assertion. There are, it is said, two torts involved, (1) indirectly inducing a breach of the intercommunication agreement by unlawful means and (2) interference with Mercury's business by unlawful means. What Mercury complain of is that the defendant union is inducing its members to break their contracts of employment. That would be 'unlawful means' at common law for the purposes of the two torts. But s 13(1) of the 1974 Act as amended confers immunity in inducing a breach of contract, including a contract of employment, when done in contemplation or furtherance of a trade dispute. It was common ground between counsel for Mercury and counsel for the union that the effect of the decision in *Hadmor Productions Ltd v Hamilton* [1982] 1 All ER 1042, [1983] 1 AC 191, is that if the inducement is of the character now complained of it is not capable of constituting unlawful means as a necessary ingredient of either of the two torts complained of. So the basic question emerging is whether or not the defendants have acted in contemplation etc of a trade dispute. But, having so far agreed, counsel for the union then parts company with counsel for Mercury. The union's case was in outline this: (a) There is in existence a trade dispute between BT and its employees who are members of the defendant union. (b) The subject matter of the dispute is fear of job losses. (c) The action taken by BT employees in refusing to connect and the union's action in advising this course is action taken in furtherance of that dispute. (d) Accordingly, the union is within the statutory immunity conferred by s 13(1). (e) In any event the court's discretion having regard to s 17(2) ought to be exercised in the union's favour.

In light of counsel's concession I am justified in regarding the union's instructions to its members not to connect up the two networks as being actionable in tort at common law. But there is this possibility of the statutory defence, s 13(1)(a), saying that an act done by a person in contemplation or furtherance of a trade dispute shall not be actionable in tort on the ground only (a) that it induces another person to break a contract or (b) interferes or induces any other person to interfere with its performance.

On this interlocutory application I have to have regard to the likelihood of the union succeeding at the trial in establishing a s 13 defence. That results from s 17(2).

So it comes to this: what is the likelihood of the union at the trial establishing that, in ordering its members not to connect up, it was acting in furtherance of a trade dispute as defined in s 29(1)? This question involves considering (a) whether or not there is in the situation before me a 'trade dispute' within s 29(1), and (b) if so, whether or not the acts as shown in the evidence amount to acts done in contemplation etc of that dispute.

As to (a) the union's case was that, while it was and would continue to campaign against privatisation and liberalisation in the telecommunications industry, it and its members were, as well, in dispute with BT in consequence of BT's orders in June 1983 to its employees to connect up with the Mercury network. BT said, 'Connect,' and the men said, 'We will not.' The reason for the refusal, so it was said, was that to connect to Mercury would lead to Mercury (and later other companies) doing work now done by BT so that connection was the first step towards possible job losses. So there was a dispute over BT's co-operation with Mercury. On this analysis there is, it is said, a trade dispute within s 29(1). The dispute is between the engineers and their employer BT. It relates wholly or mainly to termination of employment. No doubt it relates as well to a dislike of privatisation, but the concern expressed by members as shown in the documents in exhibit BS5 shows that the concern has in great measure been about job losses. The exhibit shows concern in letters from Bishop's Stortford, Leeds, Purley and many other parts of the country. It appears, too, in Mr Stanley's evidence. (See para 10 of this first affidavit, which I have already quoted.)

I had supposed that fear of future job losses could not be prayed in aid at this early stage. One would suppose that some real threat of dismissal would have to be shown before it could be said that a dispute relates to termination of employment. The authorities show that this supposition may be wrong: see *Hadmor Productions Ltd v Hamilton* [1982] 1 All ER 1042 at 1050–1051, [1983] 1 AC 191 at 226 and *Health Computing Ltd v Meek* [1981] ICR 24. So if there is a dispute it may be a dispute relating to termination within s 29(1)(b). The phrase has been 'is connected with' rather than, as now, 'which relates', but I do not see in the circumstances of this case that it matters which phrase is taken.

There is then the consideration that BT was obliged to enter into the interconnection agreement with Mercury, so that BT has now no justification vis-à-vis Mercury for failing to afford the facilities to Mercury. There is then the further consideration that BT is obliged to do its duty under the statute and is powerless to negotiate with the union in any true fashion over the interconnection issue. I read some words of Lord Diplock in *NWL Ltd v Woods* [1979] 3 All ER 614 at 624, [1979] 1 WLR 1294 at 1304:

'My Lords, if a demand on an employer by the union is about terms and conditions of employment the fact that it appears to the court to be unreasonable because compliance with it is so difficult as to be commercially impracticable or will bankrupt the employer or drive him out of business does not prevent its being a dispute connected with terms and conditions of employment. Immunity under s 13 is not forfeited by being stubborn or pig-headed. Neither, in my view, does it matter that the demand is made and the dispute pursued with more than one object in mind and that of those objects the predominant one is not the improvement of the terms and conditions of employment of those workers to whom the demand relates. Even if the predominant object were to bring down the fabric of the present economic system by raising wages to unrealistic levels, or to drive Asian seamen from the seas except when they serve in ships beneficially owned by nationals of their own countries, this would not, in my view, make it any less a dispute connected with terms and conditions of employment and thus a trade dispute, if the actual demand that is resisted by the employer is as to the terms and conditions on which his workers are to be employed. The threat of industrial action if the demand is not met is nonetheless an act done in furtherance of that dispute.'

The words spoken relate to a dispute over conditions of employment, but they may well apply to disputes over possible job losses. (See also per Lord Diplock in *Duport Steels Ltd v Sirs* [1980] 1 All ER 529 at 544, [1980] 1 WLR 142 at 161.)

Counsel for Mercury submitted that there was no trade dispute within s 29(1). He said that the union's and the members' activities in refusing to connect up Mercury was not related to any dispute between BT and its employees. The refusal was part of a single campaign by the union against the government and Mercury. Any suggestion that there was one campaign against privatisation and another against liberalisation was, he said, pedantic and unrealistic. Certainly there are documents in the exhibits which support this view. A reading of the national executive council's report on the special conference, from which I have quoted, suggests that: see paras 32 and 38. The engineers' conduct in refusing to connect was, it was said, 'all of a piece' with action that is part of a single anti-government campaign calculated to cause the government to change its privatisation proposals. I have no doubt that some union members oppose with fervour the government's proposals for changes within the telecommunications industry. But this was largely, if not wholly, a matter of words until BT in June 1983 ordered connection. Opposition then took the form of deeds in the form of disobedience to the orders of BT. It seems to me that a particular dispute then crystallised. It was a dispute with BT whether or not BT installations should be made available to Mercury. It was a dispute which related (according to the authorities I have mentioned) wholly or mainly to termination of employment, ie job losses. Accordingly there is, in my view, in existence a trade dispute within s 29(1).

Mercury referred to *BBC v Hearn* [1978] All ER 111, [1977] 1 WLR 1004. I do not think it assists them. That case shows that, under the industrial law prevailing in 1977, a union acting coercively may be without the protection of s 13(1). I infer that the protection does not extend to a dispute that is not related to anything that is itemised in the current law ie paras (a) to (g) of s 29(1). But, as I have said, the dispute here does seem to be related to s 29(1)(b).

The next question, there being a trade dispute, is whether or not the union, in ordering its members to disobey BT orders, was acting 'in contemplation or furtherance of' the dispute. I was referred in this connection to *Express Newspapers Ltd v MacShane* [1980] 1 All ER 65, [1980] AC 672. On the facts before me I answer this question in the affirmative.

I now turn to s 17(2) of the 1974 Act as amended. I see that in exercising my discretion whether or not to grant an injunction I am to have regard to the likelihood of the union succeeding at the trial in establishing a s 13(1) defence. At the trial when there is oral evidence and cross-examination there may emerge impressions that differ considerably from those arising from the affidavit evidence before me. However that may be, my view on the affidavit evidence is that the union are likely at the trial to establish a s 13(1) defence.

The discretion in the matter of interlocutory orders is governed by the principles of *American Cyanamid Co v Ethicon Ltd* [1975] 1 All ER 504 at 510, [1975] AC 396 at 407. How s 17(2) fits into these principles is explained in *NWL Ltd v Woods* [1979] 3 All ER 614 at 624, 627, 632–633, [1979] 1 WLR 1294 at 1305, 1308, 1314 per Lord Diplock, Lord Fraser and Lord Scarman. See also *Duport Steels Ltd v Sirs* [1980] 1 All ER 529 at

546–547, 549, 553, [1980] 1 WLR 142 at 163, 166, 171. Those cases were decided when unions themselves could not be sued. That is not now the position: see s 15 of the Employment Act 1982. Lord Diplock in the *NWL Ltd* case [1979] 3 All ER 614 at 625, [1979] 1 WLR 1294 at 1306 took into account the character of the individual defendants before him in that case. While that is so the principles laid down are clearly still for guidance. I have to bring into the *Cyanamid* 'balance of convenience' the 'additional element' of s 17(2). I note that the s 17(2) element is not an 'overriding' or 'paramount' factor: see the *NWL Ltd* case [1979] 3 All ER 614 at 626, [1979] 1 WLR 1294 at 1307. I do not now set out any attempt to assess the financial possibilities that Lord Diplock refers to *American Cyanamid Co v Ethicon Ltd* [1975] 1 All ER 504 at 510, [1975] AC 396 at 408. In a case of this kind it is impractical, if not impossible, to assess the financial consequences of making or not making an order. On the other hand, proceeding further with the *Cyanamid* principles, there is something to be said for the submission of counsel for the defendants that the status quo should remain. Counsel for Mercury drew attention to Lord Fraser's words in *Duport Steels Ltd v Sirs* [1980] 1 All ER 529 at 549, [1980] 1 WLR 142 at 166 including the statement:

'If the court considers, on the available evidence, that the threatened act would probably have an immediate and devastating effect on the applicant's person or property e g by ruining plant which could not be replaced without large expenditure and long delay, the court ought to take that into account.'

That consideration has weighed with me, but I do not think its weight goes so far as obliging me to make an order in this case.

Taking all the relevant considerations into account, including my view that the union is likely to succeed at the trial by virtue of s 13(1), I decline to make any order on the motion.

I add that counsel for Mercury before me reserved a point. It was that he desired to contend that union members refusing to carry out BT's instructions to connect are in breach of s 45 of the Telegraph Act 1863, and as such are, despite s 13(1), resorting to 'unlawful means' for the purposes of both the torts he complains of.

Motion dismissed.

Jacqueline Metcalfe Barrister.

Interlocutory appeal
Mercury appealed.

Robert Alexander QC, Alexander Irvine QC, Patrick Elias and *Timothy Charlton* for Mercury.
Christopher Carr QC and *Cherie Booth* for the defendant.

Cur adv vult

9 November. The following judgments were delivered.

SIR JOHN DONALDSON MR. This is an appeal from a decision of Mervyn Davies J refusing to order a halt to certain industrial action by the Post Office Engineering Union (the union). The appeal is both important and urgent. It is important because this is the first occasion on which this court has been called on to consider the changes made in the Trade Union and Labour Relations Act 1974 by the Employment Act 1982. Accordingly, our decision may well affect other industrial disputes. It is urgent since the appellants', Mercury's, claim, and it may well be the fact that as a result of this industrial action they are suffering huge losses which imperil the future of their business.

The role of the court

Disputes of this nature give rise to strong, and indeed passionate, feelings on each side. This is understandable and it makes it all the more important that everyone should know where the courts stand. They are on neither side. They have an independent role, akin to that of a referee. It is for Parliament and not for the courts to make the rules which determine what action is and what is not permissible in the course of an industrial dispute. It is for the courts, and not for Parliament, to interpret those rules and to uphold the freedom of both sides to take whatever action they consider appropriate within those rules, whilst restraining both sides from taking action which, however appropriate it might otherwise be, is outside those rules. In a word, Parliament makes the law and is solely responsible for what the law is. The duty of the courts is neither to make nor to alter nor to pass judgment on the law. Their duty is simply to apply it as they understand it. Mervyn Davies J approached his task on this basis and this court will do the same.

The background to the dispute

For many years the Post Office enjoyed a monopoly in the operation of telecommunications systems within the United Kingdom. Then, in 1981, Parliament passed the British Telecommunications Act. This established British Telecommunications (BT) and transferred to it the telecommunications business of the Post Office. It also empowered the Secretary of State to license rival telecommunications systems. This latter provision met with very strong disapproval from the union and many of its members, the vast majority of whom are employed by BT. It was probably also unwelcome to the management of BT. However, neither the union nor BT were or are in a position to prevent the Secretary of State issuing such licences and on 22 February 1982 he issued a licence the effect of which was to authorise Mercury to establish a telecommunications system within the United Kingdom on the terms set out in the licence.

The process of licensing competitors of BT and thereby eroding its monopoly is known in the industry as 'liberalisation'. This is to be contrasted with the process of altering the nationalised status of BT by converting it into a public limited company and issuing its shares to the public. The latter process is known as 'privatisation'. The machinery for liberalisation already exists in the shape of the British Telecommunications Act 1981. That for privatisation is contained in the Telecommunications Bill at present before Parliament. Whether and when and in what form this Bill will become law must be a matter for speculation by others than the courts, but the existence of the Bill and the union's attitude towards it are part of the background to this appeal.

The effective operation of the Mercury system requires a degree of interconnection with the BT system, if BT subscribers are to be able to communicate with Mercury subscribers and vice versa. It also requires connection with what is described as the 'interface' of the international system, this (United Kingdom) interface being at present part of the BT system. Such a right and duty of interconnection is really inherent in the grant of the licence to Mercury, but was formalised in an interconnection agreement made between BT and Mercury on 5 November 1982. The duration of the agreement is the subject of a somewhat complicated clause, but, unless replaced by another similar agreement, it will last until November 1997.

The union is opposed to liberalisation in general and the grant of a licence to Mercury and the setting up of the Mercury communications system in particular. It is also opposed to privatisation. It has pursued its policy of opposition by argument and by industrial action. The first industrial action took place in March 1982, when the union's national executive committee resolved to instruct the membership not to connect Project Mercury to the BT system. This was followed by a 'day of action' in October 1982 and a series of selective strikes in April 1983. Thus far BT had not in fact required its employees to connect the two systems and this phase, with which we are not directly concerned, ended in May 1983 when the general election campaign began and the strike action was called off.

The second phase, with which we are directly concerned, began on 10 June 1983 when

BT ordered certain employees to interconnect the two systems. The union replied with a call to action in the form of a letter to branches and an 'industrial action bulletin', both dated 20 June 1983. BT management replied by themselves effecting some interconnection. The union thereupon instructed its members to 'black' Mercury shareholders and BT services at Mercury's own premises. This was followed in September by a threat to take industrial action against any customers of Mercury.

The writ in the present proceedings was issued on 5 October 1983 and it appears that the industrial action against the shareholders of Mercury and the threat of action against Mercury subscribers has been lifted, at least pending the outcome of the present interlocutory proceedings.

The issues

It is important to remember that what Mervyn Davies J had to decide, and what this court has to decide, is what orders, if any, should be made pending the trial of the action. Furthermore it appears that, contrary to the usual situation, there will be a full trial of the action and matters will not rest with the grant or refusal of an interlocutory order. It follows from the interim nature of the proceedings that it is no part of our function to reach any definitive decision on the issues between the parties. We have to apply the well-known principles enshrined in *American Cyanamid Co v Ethicon Ltd* [1975] 1 All ER 504, [1975] AC 396, modified to accommodate the special provisions of s 17(2) of the Trade Union and Labour Relations Act 1974 as inserted by the Employment Protection Act 1975 and amended by the Employment Act 1982. Section 17(2) requires the court to—

> 'have regard to the likelihood of [the defendant's] succeeding at the trial of the action in establishing the matter or matters which would, under any provision of section 13 . . . above, afford a defence to the action.'

But I stress that we are concerned with degrees of likelihood, not with whether the defendants will undoubtedly succeed.

Immunity

It is common ground that, for the purposes of these proceedings, we can assume that there is a serious issue to be tried whether the defendants have committed the torts of inducing breach of contract and interference with business by unlawful means. It follows that we can proceed to examine the only defence which is relevant at this stage, namely that under s 13(1) of the 1974 Act, as substituted by the Trade Union and Labour Relations (Amendment) Act 1976. If we were of opinion that that defence was prima facie likely to succeed, we should then have to consider a separate argument by Mercury based on s 45 of the Telegraph Act 1863. This latter point was reserved before Mervyn Davies J and I will return to it hereafter.

Section 13(1) of the 1974 Act, as substituted, is in the following terms:

> '*Acts in contemplation or furtherance of trade disputes.*—(1) An act done by a person in contemplation or furtherance of a trade dispute shall not be actionable in tort on the ground only—(a) that it induces another person to break a contract or interferes or induces any other person to interfere with its performance; or (b) that it consists in his threatening that a contract (whether one to which he is a party or not) will be broken or its performance interfered with, or that he will induce another person to break a contract or to interfere with its performance.'

The essence of this defence is that the acts complained of shall have been done in contemplation or furtherance of a trade dispute. Clearly the first stage in considering this defence is to concentrate on whether the defendants are likely to establish that there was a trade dispute as defined.

'Trade dispute' defined·

'Trade dispute' is defined by s 29(1) of the 1974 Act, as amended by s 18 of the Employment Act 1982. Prior to the amendment it read:

'In this Act "trade dispute" means a dispute between employers and workers, or between workers and workers, which is connected with one or more of the following, that is to say [and then various subject matters of disputes are set out.]'

For present purposes we are only concerned with 'termination of employment'.

As amended, s 29(1) reads:

'In this Act "trade dispute" means a dispute between workers and their employer which relates wholly or mainly to one or more of the following, that is to say . . .'

It will be seen that this revision considerably narrows the scope of 'trade dispute'. Disputes between workers and workers, demarcation disputes, no longer qualify. Nor do disputes between workers and an employer, unless the employer is *their* employer. Finally it is no longer sufficient that the dispute should be 'connected with' one of the specified subject matters. It now has to 'relate wholly or mainly to' that subject matter.

Was there a trade dispute?

This is a mixed question of fact and law, but primarily one of fact. Mervyn Davies J in his very full and careful judgment has set out most of the relevant evidence adduced before him. I see no advantage in reproducing the relevant parts of his judgment and content myself with saying that his judgment and this judgment must be read together. Before us the evidence was supplemented by two further affidavits from Mr Stanley, the general secretary of the union. They were his fourth and fifth affidavits. Mercury also filed an affidavit by their company secretary, Mr R de L Holmes.

In essence Mr Stanley's fourth affidavit states that, at a meeting in February 1983 between BT and the union, it was made clear to BT that if management gave any instruction to interconnect with the Mercury system 'conflict' would result. This is relevant to an inquiry by the judge whether the union had ever informed BT that it was 'in dispute' and the answer which he was given, namely that BT was never expressly so informed. Mr Stanley's answer is that, under the accepted procedures operating in the industry, there was no provision for a formal declaration of 'dispute' and that the equivalent situation had been reached by February 1983. I wholly accept this evidence.

Mr Holmes's evidence was rather more important and startling. Those who have referred to the judgment of Mervyn Davies J will be aware that the union's case, supported by Mr Stanley's evidence, was that, and I quote from para 22 of his first affidavit, which is set out in the judgment:

'. . . In due course liberalisation became a reality and BT have entered into an inter-connection agreement with [Mercury]. It is over this that the Union are in dispute with BT. Whatever might have been the wish or preference of BT they have in fact allowed a rival organisation to inter-connect with its network. It is this fact which puts them at odds with my Union. The fact that many executives of BT may nurture attitudes and opinions not dissimilar from those of my members is beside the point. The action which BT is taking is inconsistent with the desire of my members to retain the traditional monopoly over telecommunications facilities within BT. Once BT embarked upon a course of seeking to facilitate and implement liberalisation, they embarked upon a course which could only lead to a dispute between them and the Union. This is in fact what has occurred. The current position is that my members are being required by the management of BT to carry out certain operations which will involve connecting the plaintiffs with BT's facilities. My members are not prepared to do that. Accordingly, they are not prepared to carry out the instructions of management in that regard. There is, accordingly, a dispute between my members and BT. The cause of this dispute lies in the fact that

BT wish my members to take a step which my members regard as putting their jobs at risk. To suggest that there is no dispute between the Union and BT or that the dispute is "really" with the Government or [Mercury] is quite wrong. The industrial action that is being taken is in pursuance of a dispute with BT over whether members of the Union should be required to act in a way which they see as placing their jobs in jeopardy. The subject matter of the dispute is the risk of jobs. The precise form that risk takes is the connection of Mercury to BT's network. The parties to the dispute are BT and their employees, although the action of the employees is, of course, directed and co-ordinated by the Union acting on their behalf.'

Mr Holmes makes two comments. The first is that it is surprising that the union should be so apprehensive as to the effect of the arrival of Mercury on the job prospects of the union members, when the terms of the licence restrict Mercury to a gross turnover not exceeding 3% of the gross turnover of BT. The second is that, if job security was at the root of any dispute, it is more than a little surprising that no one ever mentioned the existence of a formal job security agreement between BT and the union which was executed in September 1980. This had come to the notice of Mercury on 27 October, nearly a week after judgment had been given by Mervyn Davies J, by the pure chance that they heard the chairman of BT refer to it in the course of a radio interview. That job security agreement, which has now been produced, provides as follows:

'3　The Post Office and the [union] accept the following principles as being central to the operation of this agreement.
3.1　In keeping with the spirit of the agreement and to ensure its full and effective implementation the Union and the Post Office will continue the long standing policy of free and flexible co-operation based on consultation and negotiation at all appropriate levels.
3.2　The parties accept that retraining, and/or reasonable relocation, and/or redeployment should continue and are necessary requirements in order to maintain job security.
3.3　The provisions of this agreement are binding in all negotiations covered by it.
4　Given adherence to the provisions and obligations of this agreement the Post Office undertakes that no one covered by this agreement will be compelled to leave its service on redundancy grounds.
5　In the event of a major manpower problem arising from causes outside the control of the Post Office which after the application of the terms of this agreement would still result in manpower surplus, the Post Office Engineering Union acknowledges that the Post Office reserves the right to withdraw, after consulting the Union, the undertaking given in paragraph 4 above and that there would be immediate national consultation about the further measures to be taken.'

This was no casual agreement which could be forgotten or overlooked. It had been carefully negotiated over a period of months. It appears as a printed booklet, which presumably had a wide circulation, and the agreement with its appendices and notes of guidance runs to 60 pages.

Mr Stanley in his fifth affidavit stated that the issues of liberalisation and privatisation had not emerged when this job security agreement was negotiated and that it contemplated only technological change. Accordingly he had never appreciated its relevance. He had no doubt that there was a—

'strong and widespread belief amongst my members that the JSA will not protect their jobs if Mercury succeeds in creaming off the most profitable parts of BT's business traffic.'

Mr Stanley went on to suggest that if, as a result of the advent of Mercury, BT found itself to be overmanned, it would claim to invoke the right to withdraw from the agreement, which is contained in cl 5, on the grounds that a major manpower problem had arisen from causes outside its control.

a

The evidence proves beyond doubt that there were major disagreements between the union and the government about its policy of liberalisation and privatisation and its action in licensing Mercury, between the union and Mercury about its attempt to set up a competing telecommunications system and between the union and BT about its decision to enter into a long-term interconnection agreement and its instruction to

b employees to interconnect the BT and Mercury systems. However, counsel for Mercury submits that there is no 'dispute' between BT and the union. The importance of this submission lies in the fact that under the amended law only a dispute between BT and its employees can constitute a trade dispute and attract immunity for the industrial action being taken.

On the face of it, this is a somewhat startling proposition. However, on examination,
c there is something to be said for it. The argument goes like this. If you have a true trade dispute between workers and their employers, a common form of industrial action is to picket the entrance of their place of work. If suppliers wish to deliver goods and are turned away, there can fairly be said to be a disagreement between the suppliers and the union about whether the supplies should be delivered, but there is no 'dispute' between them. A dispute, so the argument goes, has to be what might be described as a primary
d disagreement capable of being resolved by negotiation and, if resolved, ending all matters in dispute. Workers or employers have to be seeking action or inaction or a change of action on the part of the other and this must be the purpose of the industrial action. To be a trade dispute there must be a 'purposive dispute'. By contrast, a disagreement which is not a purposive dispute as between the immediate parties, but is purely an appendage to a dispute between different parties, is not itself a separate dispute.

e Whilst I would accept that it may be possible to have what might be described as 'a satellite disagreement' which does not constitute a 'dispute' between the parties to the disagreement, but is part of a dispute between one of those parties and a third party, I do not think that it is in the least likely that this will be held to be the case here. The likelihood, approaching certainty, is that it will be held that there is a dispute between BT and some or all of its employees who are members of the union. Mervyn Davies J so
f held and I agree with him.

Assuming that there is such a dispute, the next question is whether it relates wholly or mainly to one or more of the matters specified in s 29(1) of the 1974 Act. For present purposes the only such matter which is claimed to be relevant is 'termination of employment'.

The judge dealt with this aspect in the following passage in his judgment (see pp 194–
g 195, ante):

'I had supposed that fear of future job losses could not be prayed in aid at this early stage. One would suppose that some real threat of dismissal would have to be shown before it could be said that a dispute relates to termination of employment. The authorities show that this supposition may be wrong: see *Hadmor Productions Ltd v Hamilton* [1982] 1 All ER 1042 at 1050–1051, [1983] 1 AC 191 at 226 and
h *Health Computing Ltd v Meek* [1981] ICR 24. So if there is a dispute it may be a dispute relating to termination within s 29(1)(b). The phrase has been "is connected with" rather than, as now, "which relates", but I do not see in the circumstances of this case that it matters which phrase is taken. There is then the consideration that BT was obliged to enter into the interconnection agreement with Mercury, so that BT has now no justification vis-à-vis Mercury for failing to afford the facilities to
j Mercury. There is then the further consideration that BT is obliged to do its duty under the statute and is powerless to negotiate with the union in any true fashion over the interconnection issue. I read some words of Lord Diplock in *NWL Ltd v Woods* [1979] 3 All ER 614 at 624, [1979] 1 WLR 1294 at 1304: "My Lords, if a demand on an employer by the union is about terms and conditions of employment the fact that it appears to the court to be unreasonable because compliance with it is

so difficult as to be commercially impracticable or will bankrupt the employer or drive him out of business does not prevent its being a dispute connected with terms and conditions of employment. Immunity under s 13 is not forfeited by being stubborn or pig-headed. Neither, in my view, does it matter that the demand is made and the dispute pursued with more than one object in mind and that of those objects the predominant one is not the improvement of the terms and conditions of employment of those workers to whom the demand relates. Even if the predominant object were to bring down the fabric of the present economic system by raising wages to unrealistic levels, or to drive Asian seamen from the seas except when they serve in ships beneficially owned by nationals of their own countries, this would not, in my view, make it any less a dispute connected with terms and conditions of employment and thus a trade dispute, if the actual demand that is resisted by the employer is as to the terms and conditions on which his workers are to be employed. The threat of industrial action if the demand is not met is nonetheless an act done in furtherance of that trade dispute." The words spoken relate to a dispute over conditions of employment, but they may well apply to disputes over possible job losses. (See also per Lord Diplock in *Duport Steels Ltd v Sirs* [1980] 1 All ER 529 at 544, [1980] 1 WLR 142 at 161.) Counsel for Mercury submitted that there was no trade dispute within s 29(1). He said that the union's and the members' activities in refusing to connect up Mercury was not related to any dispute between BT and its employees. The refusal was part of a single campaign by the union against the government and Mercury. Any suggestion that there was one campaign against privatisation and another against liberalisation was, he said, pedantic and unrealistic. Certainly there are documents in the exhibits which support this view. A reading of the national executive council's report on the special conference, from which I have quoted, suggests that: see paras 32 and 38. The engineers' conduct in refusing to connect was, it was said, "all of a piece" with action that is part of a single anti-government campaign calculated to cause the government to change its privatisation proposals. I have no doubt that some union members oppose with fervour the government's proposals for changes within the telecommunications industry. But this was largely, if not wholly, a matter of words until BT in June 1983 ordered connection. Opposition then took the form of deeds in the form of disobedience to the orders of BT. It seems to me that a particular dispute then crystallised. It was a dispute with BT whether or not BT installations should be made available to Mercury. It was a dispute which related (according to the authorities I have mentioned) wholly or mainly to termination of employment, ie job losses. Accordingly there is, in my view, in existence a trade dispute within s 29(1).'

I hope that I do him no injustice when I say that I do not understand how the authorities which he mentioned enabled him to jump from a finding that the dispute was whether BT installations should be made available to Mercury to a finding that it was a dispute which related wholly or mainly to termination of employment. He had mentioned four authorities. *Hadmor Productions Ltd v Hamilton* and *Health Computing Ltd v Meek* both indicate that future termination of employment is as much within s 29(1) as an immediate termination. They do not however assist at all in deciding to what any particular dispute wholly or mainly relates. Still less do they suggest that it is immaterial whether one uses the phrase 'is connected with' or 'which relates'. Indeed the *Hadmor* case decides in terms that the latter phrase, when coupled with 'wholly or mainly', is narrower. *NWL Ltd v Woods* decides that under the old law, where the test was 'in connection with', it did not matter that the dispute was being pursued with more than one object in mind and that the predominant one was outside the section if the other was within it. The position is manifestly different under the amended section. *Duport Steels Ltd v Sirs* is quite immaterial to a determination of whether there is a trade dispute, relating as it does to whether action is taken in furtherance of an established trade dispute and, if there are two such disputes, how one decides which dispute is being furthered.

Thinking, as I do, that the judge misdirected himself, I must now ask myself whether

on the evidence presently available, which is more extensive than that available to the
judge, the dispute between the union and its members on the one hand and BT on the
other is likely to be held to be a trade dispute. In so doing, I have to follow the instructions
given to me by Parliament as expressed by the words used in the statute (see *Duport Steels
Ltd v Sirs* [1980] 1 All ER 529 at 542, [1980] 1 WLR 142 at 158 per Lord Diplock).

The starting point must be the meaning of the phrase 'relates wholly or mainly to' the
matters specified in s 29(1). As I have already mentioned, prior to the coming into force
of the 1982 Act, s 29(1) was wide in that a dispute could be a trade dispute if it was only
'connected with' the specified subject matters and in that trade disputes were not confined
to workers and *their* employer. Consistently with this amendment, the word 'worker' has
also been redefined by s 29(6) as being, in relation to a dispute with an employer—

> '(a) a worker employed by that employer; or (b) a person who has ceased to be
> employed by that employer where—(i) his employment was terminated in
> connection with the dispute; or (ii) the termination of his employment was one of
> the circumstances giving rise to the dispute.'

This latter amendment narrows the specified subject matters wherever the word 'worker'
appears, eg 'allocation of work or the duties of employment as between workers or
groups of workers'. The dispute must therefore not only be between workers and their
employer, but must relate wholly or mainly to matters which are specific to that
employment. Thus there can be no trade dispute between employer A and his workers
relating to the pay and conditions of workers employed by employer B.

In context the phrase 'relates wholly or mainly to' directs attention to what the dispute
is about and, if it is about more than one matter, what it is mainly about. What it does
not direct attention to is the reason why the parties are in dispute about this matter. Thus
a situation can arise in which company A's workers will accept a particular rate of pay
and company B's workers will not, the difference being that those who work for company
B know that for one reason or another they will become redundant within the next year
or so and think, perhaps not unreasonably, that they have little to lose and something to
gain in terms of immediate remuneration and in the rate of redundancy payment by
pressing for higher wages meanwhile. A contributory cause of the dispute and possibly
the main cause is the belief that redundancy ('termination . . . of employment' in the
words of the section) is just round the corner, but the dispute is not about that or, if it be
preferred, it relates wholly or mainly to pay ('terms and conditions of employment').

The view that the words of the statute 'relating to' mean 'about' (in the sense, of course,
of 'concerning' rather than 'approximately') is supported by a decision of this court in
Garland v British Rail Engineering Ltd [1979] 2 All ER 1163, [1979] 1 WLR 754 and by the
decision of the House of Lords ([1982] 2 All ER 402, [1982] 2 WLR 918), although in
that case the words were used in a different context. *Garland's* case also draws attention
to the fact that 'relating to' or 'about' can receive a broader or a narrower application
according to context, ie 'broadly speaking about' or 'actually about' to use popular rather
than legislative language. In the context of an admittedly restrictive amendment to the
statute, I incline to the view that Parliament intended a relatively restrictive meaning to
be given to the phrase, but this probably does not matter since the words 'wholly or
mainly' themselves indicate and provide a degree of restriction.

In this context we were referred to *General Aviation Services (UK) Ltd v Transport and
General Workers' Union* [1975] ICR 276, but I have not been able to derive any assistance
from that decision, since the legislative context was so different. In particular it was
sufficient to establish in an industrial dispute that any employer and any workers should
be in dispute about future job losses and that the respondent to the complaint of unfair
industrial practice should, in furtherance of that dispute, have knowingly induced a
breach of contract.

For Mercury it was submitted that the dispute between BT and its employees was an
example of coercive interference with the performance of the interconnection agreement
between Mercury and BT and so wholly outside s 29 and we were referred to *BBC v Hearn*

[1978] 1 All ER 111, [1977] 1 WLR 1604. There is, it is true some resemblance. Lord Denning MR pictured the union in that case as telling the BBC, 'Stop this televising by the Indian Ocean satellite, stop it yourself. If you don't we will ask our own people to stop it for you' (see [1978] 1 All ER 111 at 117, [1977] 1 WLR 1004 at 1011). This is not so very different, mutatis mutandis, from the present case, where, according to Mr Stanley's fourth affidavit, the union asked BT not to implement the interconnection agreement and told it that if any instruction was given to interconnect there would be conflict, ie the union would instruct its members to disobey the instructions. In neither case has there been the slightest suggestion that the terms and conditions of employment are such that an instruction to televise or to interconnect was not a proper instruction. In neither case has any attempt been made to request an alteration in the terms and conditions of employment which would make such an instruction improper. This is thus a possible conclusion and one which would negative the existence of a trade dispute.

However, I think that the same result is reached by a different route. The most obvious way of finding out what a particular dispute is wholly or mainly about is to inquire what the men concerned, in this case primarily those who refuse to interconnect, said to management at the time. Unfortunately we have no evidence, but it is a fair inference from what we do know that they said that the interconnection was contrary to their union's instructions. This throws one back to what the dispute between the union and BT was wholly or mainly about. That was not, of course, a relevant dispute because the union is neither an employer nor a worker in this context, but the subject matter of the dispute between BT and its employees can legitimately be taken to be the same as that between the union and BT.

What the union's dispute with BT is about is the subject matter of para 22 of Mr Stanley's first affidavit, which I have already quoted:

> '... BT have entered into an inter-connection agreement with [Mercury]. It is over this that the Union are in dispute with BT ... [BT] have ... allowed a rival organisation to inter-connect with its network. It is this fact which puts them at odds with my Union ... The action which BT is taking is inconsistent with the desire of my members to retain the traditional monopoly over telecommunications facilities within BT. Once BT embarked upon a course of seeking to facilitate and implement liberalisation, they embarked upon a course which could only lead to a dispute between them and my Union.'

Mr Stanley goes on to say that the *cause* of the dispute is that BT wished his members to take a step which his members regarded as putting their jobs at risk (my emphasis) and a few sentences later this suffers a further change when he states that the subject matter of the dispute is the risk to jobs.

Well, which is the subject matter: facilitating and implementing liberalisation, agreeing to interconnect, ordering interconnection or the risk to jobs? Only the latter would enable the dispute to qualify as a trade dispute. The evidence has to be looked at as a whole, but I find it impossible to conclude on the evidence at present available that the risk to jobs was a major part of what the dispute was about. I say that because I find it inconceivable that, if the dispute was wholly or mainly about jobs, the union would not have approached BT asking for a guarantee of job security or a strengthening of the job security agreement. Yet nothing of the sort appears to have happened and the union did not even think that this agreement was relevant to the present proceedings. On the other hand there is massive evidence that the union was waging a campaign against the political decisions to liberalise the industry and to privatise BT. In this context one has but to refer to the documentation for the special union conference held in September 1983, from which we learn that—

> 'the National Executive Council has set out the following objectives—(i) To seek the withdrawal of the 1983 Telecommunications Bill and the philosophy behind it. (ii) Our intention is not to bring down the Government but to defend the jobs and job opportunities, protect and enhance the conditions of service, pay and pensions

of our members in both British Telecom and the Post Office. (iii) To maintain the integrity, unity and strength of the Union. (iv) To prevent the breaking up of British Telecom and the Post Office. (v) To protect and enhance the services offered to the public. (vi) To work for the return of a Government committed to restore to public ownership without compensation any public sector industry, or part thereof, privatised by this Government. In addition to restore the public monopoly over telecommunications and the postal service.'

Lest it be thought that all this relates to privatisation rather than liberalisation, it is right to mention that a paragraph under the heading 'Timing' is in the following terms:

'32. The timing of the Union Campaign against privatisation will evolve over a number of months. It will be related to—(i) Developments surrounding the Mercury interconnect issue. (ii) The build up to, and the passage of, the Telecommunications Bill through Parliament. (iii) If the Bill is successful, the floatation [sic] of BT plc . . .'

The liberalisation and privatisation issues were thus interconnected, as is indeed clear from much of the other documentation.

My conclusion on the evidence, provisional though it has to be, is reached without any doubt or hesitation. It is that it is most unlikely that the union will be able to establish that there was at any material time a trade dispute between BT and its employees.

Furtherance

In order to make good the defence under s 13 of the 1974 Act it is, of course, necessary for the industrial action complained of to have been taken in contemplation or furtherance of the trade dispute. This question does not arise if I am correct in concluding that there was no trade dispute.

Conclusion on the likelihood of the s 13 defence prevailing

For the reasons which I have given, I think it highly unlikely that the s 13 defence will prevail when the action is fully heard, but it is always possible that different evidence will by then be available to the court or that, as a result of cross-examination, the existing evidence will take on a different complexion.

Discretion

In considering whether this court should substitute its own view of how the discretion to grant interlocutory relief should be exercised for that of the judge, I have reminded myself of the guidance afforded by the speech of Lord Diplock in *Hadmor Productions Ltd v Hamilton* [1982] 1 All ER 1042 at 1046, [1983] 1 AC 191 at 220. Having concluded that the judge misdirected himself and that additional evidence has been produced which was highly relevant to the issues of fact which he had to determine, it seems to me that this court is bound to exercise that discretion afresh.

I have also reminded myself of the later passage in Lord Diplock's speech (see [1982] 1 All ER 1042 at 1048–1049, [1983] 1 AC 191 at 223) on the interrelationship of s 17(2) of the 1974 Act and the guidance given by the House of Lords in *American Cyanamid Co v Ethicon Ltd* [1975] 1 All ER 504 at 510–511, [1975] AC 396 at 407–408. Proceeding by the appropriate stages, the questions and my answers are as follows.

(i) Q. Has Mercury shown that there is a serious question to be tried? A. Yes.

(ii) Q. Has Mercury shown that it has a real prospect of succeeding in its claim for a permanent injunction at the trial? A. Yes.

(iii) Q. If Mercury succeeded, would it be adequately compensated by damages for the loss which it suffered as the result of the union being free to continue to take industrial action pending the trial? A. No. Mercury is in a relatively frail condition as a newcomer to the field and has very large sums invested in the project. New customers cannot be attracted whilst industrial action is threatened and the losses will vastly exceed the maximum liability which can be imposed on the union, namely £250,000 (see s 16 of the Employment Act 1982).

(iv) *Q*. If the union were to succeed at the trial in establishing its defence under s 13 of the 1974 Act, would it be adequately compensated by an award under the cross-undertaking? *A*. Yes. The union would suffer no loss since, on this hypothesis, the dispute is wholly or mainly about redundancy and there is no suggestion that a temporary cessation in the industrial action would cause or hasten any redundancy.

(v) *Q*. Where does the balance of convenience lie? *A*. It lies in protecting Mercury pending the trial of the action.

Section 45 of the Telegraph Act 1863

I mentioned earlier that Mercury also relies on s 45 of the Telegraph Act 1863. This provides, so far as is material, that—

> 'If any Person in the Employment of the Company . . . by any wilful or negligent Act or Omission prevents or delays the Transmission or Delivery of any Message . . . He shall for every such Offence be liable to a [fine].'

This has been applied to persons in the employment of BT by para 2(1)(a) of Sch 3 to the British Telecommunications Act 1981.

The submission made on behalf of Mercury is that the employees of BT who refuse to maintain the BT installations of Mercury and their shareholders as part of the 'blacking' and who refuse to interconnect the Mercury system with the BT system were guilty of offences against s 45 of the 1863 Act. It is then submitted that the statutory prohibition contained in this section creates a public right which, exceptionally, is enforceable by particular members of the public who suffer damage as a result of the breach of the statutory prohibition.

With the agreement of both parties, we decided to defer hearing the union's answer to this submission. We did so because counsel for the union had had inadequate time in which to study it in detail and because a decision would be unnecessary if, having considered the arguments on the trade dispute defence, we concluded that an interim injunction should be ordered.

If it ever becomes necessary to decide this point, the matter will be of the very greatest importance because, so far as I can see, if Mercury are right, the effect of s 45 is to impose far stricter limits on the industrial action which can be taken by the employees of BT than apply to most other workers. Indeed it might make most industrial action by them unlawful. However, not having heard the counter-arguments of the union, I am in no position to form any view and have formed no view as to the soundness of Mercury's arguments.

For the reasons which I have given, I would allow the appeal.

MAY LJ. The judge below and Sir John Donaldson MR have set out the facts of this case about which there is no dispute and have referred to the relevant parts of the evidence presently before the court about facts which are in dispute. I need not burden this judgment, therefore, with any repetition.

At the start of his judgment Sir John Donaldson MR stated and explained the role of the court in relation to the issues between the parties in this, and indeed in all, litigation. Not only do I respectfully agree with and reiterate what he has said but I also quote certain passages from the speech of Lord Diplock in *Duport Steels Ltd v Sirs* [1980] 1 All ER 529 at 541–542, [1980] 1 WLR 142 at 157–158, to which we were referred by counsel for the defendants in respectful submission about the approach which the court should adopt. Lord Diplock said:

> 'My Lords, at a time when more and more cases involving the application of legislation which gives effect to policies that are the subject of bitter public and parliamentary controversy, it cannot be too strongly emphasised that the British

a Constitution, though largely unwritten, is firmly based on the separation of powers: Parliament makes the laws, the judiciary interpret them. When Parliament legislates ... the role of the judiciary is confined to ascertaining from the words that Parliament has approved as expressing its intention what that intention was, and to giving effect to it. Where the meaning of the statutory words is plain and unambiguous it is not for the judges to invent fancied ambiguities ... In controversial matters such as are involved in industrial relations there is room for

b differences of opinion as to what is expedient, what is just and what is morally justifiable. Under our Constitution it is Parliament's opinion on these matters that is paramount ... So in relation to s 13(1) of the 1974 Act ... The legitimate questions for a judge in his role as interpreter of the enacted law are: "How has Parliament, by the words that it has used in the statute to express its intentions, defined the category of acts that are entitled to the immunity? Do the acts done in

c this particular case fall within that description?"'

It must also be remembered that the present proceedings are interlocutory. Neither this court nor Mervyn Davies J seeks or is able to express final decisions on the issues between the parties. Those will have to wait until the trial, when witnesses will give oral evidence and be subject to cross-examination. Mercury's present applications are merely for interim injunctions to last until trial; whether they are then continued, amended or

d rescinded will be a matter for the trial judge on the evidence that is adduced before him.

I shall have to analyse the nature and substance of the litigation in which this appeal is brought, against the relevant statutory provisions, a little later in this judgment. For the present it is sufficient for me to record that the defendants accept for present purposes that there is a serious issue to be tried whether they have committed the torts of inducing breach of contract and interference with business by unlawful means, within para (*a*) or

e para (*b*) of s 13(1) of the Trade Union and Labour Relations Act 1974, as substituted by the Trade Union and Labour Relations (Amendment) Act 1976. They nevertheless submit that the acts complained of by Mercury and which are alleged to have constituted those torts were acts done in contemplation or furtherance of a trade dispute and that the defendants are therefore immune from liability pursuant to s 13(1) as substituted. Mercury in their turn accept that, if the acts complained of were done in contemplation

f or furtherance of a trade dispute, then the defendants did enjoy statutory immunity by virtue of that section so amended.

The general principles which should govern a court's exercise of its discretion whether or not to grant an interlocutory or interim injunction were of course laid down in *American Cyanamid Co v Ethicon Ltd* [1975] 1 All ER 504, [1975] AC 396, to which also I shall have to return later in this judgment. At this stage, however, it is necessary for me

g to set out the provisions of s 17(2) of the 1974 Act as inserted by the Employment Protection Act 1975 and amended by the Employment Act 1982:

> 'It is hereby declared for the avoidance of doubt that where an application is made to a court, pending the trial of an action, for an interlocutory injunction and the party against whom the injunction is sought claims that he acted in contemplation or furtherance of a trade dispute, the court shall, in exercising its discretion whether

h or not to grant the injunction, have regard to the likelihood of that party's succeeding at the trial of the action in establishing the matter or matters which would, under any provision of section 13, or 15 above, afford a defence to the action.'

It was therefore for the judge below and is now for this court, subject to the question whether in the end we can or should interfere with the exercise of the former's discretion,

j to consider the likelihood of the defendants' succeeding at the trial to establish what I shall hereafter refer to as the 'section 13' or 'trade dispute' defence.

Now this action has been brought by Mercury against Mr Scott-Garner (by amendment) as the president and a member of the national executive council of the Post Office Engineering Union (the union) and the latter itself. The union may be so sued by virtue of s 15(2) of the Employment Act 1982 which, in so far as is material, is in these terms:

'Where proceedings in tort are brought against a trade union—(a) on a ground specified in paragraph (a) or (b) of section 13(1) of the 1974 Act ... then, for the purpose of determining in those proceedings whether the union is liable in respect of the act in question, that act shall be taken to have been done by the union if, but only if, it was authorised or endorsed by a responsible person.'

Whatever else may be in issue in this case, there is no doubt that all the acts of which complaint is made by Mercury were authorised or indorsed by a responsible person, as defined in later subsections of s 15 of the 1982 Act.

Nevertheless it is I think important to bear in mind that it is acts of the union of which Mercury complain. These were instructions from its national executive council to its members, employees of British Telecommunications (BT), not to comply with their employers' instructions to interconnect Mercury and BT equipment and to refuse to comply with their employers' instructions, as and when given, to carry out maintenance and installation work on BT's own telephone equipment and lines at and to Mercury's offices and at and to various buildings belonging to the shareholders of Mercury. The 'blacking' of maintenance and installation work on BT's own services to Mercury and their shareholders was lifted by the union in the middle of October 1983. We were told by counsel for the defendants that he was instructed that the union had no present intention of reimposing this blacking, but he could give no undertaking about it in so far as the future was concerned.

As I have said, it is accepted by the defendants that there is a serious issue to be tried whether these acts of the union were tortious. Without referring to the relevant material in detail, because I think it unnecessary, in my opinion it shows that at the least it is very likely that unless the s 13 defence is made out the acts of the defendants will at the trial be held to have been wrongful.

I turn therefore to consider that defence. Section 13(1) as substituted is in these terms:

'An act done by a person in contemplation or furtherance of a trade dispute shall not be actionable in tort on the ground only—(a) that it induces another person to break a contract or interferes or induces any other person to interfere with its performance; or (b) that it consists in his threatening that a contract (whether one to which he is a party or not) will be broken or its performance interfered with, or that he will induce another person to break a contract or to interfere with its performance.'

Two questions then arise. First, was there in existence at the material time a relevant trade dispute? Second, were the acts of the union of which Mercury complain done by the union in contemplation or furtherance of that trade dispute? For the meaning of 'trade dispute' in the relevant legislation, I turn to s 29 of the 1974 Act as amended by s 18 of the Employment Act 1982. The subsections of s 29 with which we are concerned are sub-s (1) and (6) which are in these terms:

'(1) In this Act "trade dispute" means a dispute between workers and their employer which relates wholly or mainly to one or more of the following, that is to say—(a) terms and conditions of employment, or the physical conditions in which any workers are required to work; (b) engagement or non-engagement or termination or suspension of employment or the duties of employment, of one or more workers; (c) allocation of work or the duties of employment as between workers or groups of workers; (d) matters of discipline; (e) the membership or non-membership of a trade union on the part of a worker; (f) facilities for officials of trade unions; and (g) machinery for negotiation or consultation, and other procedures, relating to any of the foregoing matters, including the recognition by employers or employers' associations of the right of a trade union to represent workers in any such negotiation or consultation or in the carrying out of such procedures ...
(6) ... "worker", in relation to a dispute with an employer, means—(a) a worker employed by that employer; or (b) a person who has ceased to be employed by that

employer where—(i) his employment was terminated in connection with the
dispute; or (ii) the termination of his employment was one of the circumstances
giving rise to the dispute.'

Section 18 of the 1982 Act makes it clear, first, that the amendments of s 29 of the 1974
Act were intended to limit the ambit of what is a 'trade dispute' to disputes only between
workers and their own employer. Second, the words 'relates wholly or mainly to' were
substituted for the words 'is connected with'. In my opinion the words 'trade dispute' in
the relevant legislation now bear a substantially more restricted meaning than they did
before December 1982 when the amending section came into force.

In the instant case the dispute relied on by the union before the judge and before us
was the one which it was contended existed between BT and its engineers when the latter
complied with their union's instructions to black the interconnection of the Mercury
and BT equipment, and the maintenance and installation work at Mercury's offices and
the other shareholders' buildings, thus disobeying the lawful and reasonable instructions
of their employer, BT. Indeed, on the facts of this case there was no other dispute on
which the union could rely.

Counsel for Mercury nevertheless first argued that the disobedience by BT's employees
of their employer's instructions could not properly be described as a 'trade dispute' at all.
In the more usual industrial dispute between an employer and its employees, for instance,
the union of which the employees are members organises pickets on the gates to the
employer's premises and tries to prevent not only employees entering to do their work
but also suppliers of goods or services who seek to deliver to those premises. Whether or
not the pickets successfully deter the supplier's lorry or not, counsel contended that no
one could say that their union was in dispute, or had a dispute, with that supplier. The
present case he suggested was the obverse of this example. Here the union's primary
dispute is with Mercury and in furtherance of that dispute it is doing the equivalent of
stopping suppliers of goods and services to Mercury. Thus there is no dispute, properly
so called, between BT and the union, still less between BT and its employees.

In this connection he referred us to *BBC v Hearn* [1978] 1 All ER 111, [1977] 1 WLR
1004, where the essential facts were that the union in that case threatened to instruct its
members not to work on the transmission of the Cup Final by satellite to South Africa,
to demonstrate its disapproval of apartheid, unless the BBC agreed to its request not to
broadcast the Final to South Africa. It was held that there was no trade dispute because
the difference of view between the BBC and the union was not connected with the latter's
terms and conditions of employment or any other of the matters listed in s 29(1) of the
1974 Act, which fell to be applied in its unamended form in that case. As Lord Denning
MR said at one point in his judgment of the union's activity, 'It was coercive interference
and nothing more' (see [1978] 1 All ER 111 at 118, [1977] 1 WLR 1004 at 1011).

In the context of industrial relations, counsel for Mercury submitted that a 'dispute'
must involve acts done by employees in disagreement with their employer with the
object of achieving something which they want from the employer. Picking up a phrase
which, no doubt unwisely, I preferred in the course of argument, he argued that to have
a dispute there must be 'purposive disagreement, not merely coercive interference'. In
the instant case the blacking undertaken by BT's employees on the instructions of the
union was merely coercive interference with BT's business.

With all respect to the argument of counsel for Mercury, although I do not think that
it can be dismissed outright, on the material before us I think that it is wrong and I do
not think that when all the evidence is before the trial judge it is likely to prove acceptable
to him. In each of the three judgments in *BBC v Hearn* there are one or more references
to the 'dispute' between the union and the BBC. The case is merely authority for the
conclusion that that dispute was not a trade dispute within the legislation then in force.
Almost ex hypothesi there will always be at least an element of coercive interference in
any industrial dispute; in my opinion, if one asked any reasonable man in the street
whether at the material times in the present case there was a 'dispute' between BT and its

employees who were refusing to carry out the former's instructions, his answer would
almost certainly be in the affirmative.

a

The next question that I must consider, therefore, is how likely is it that at the trial of
this action the union will be able to satisfy the judge that the dispute between BT and its
employees at the material times was a 'trade dispute' within the amended provisions of
s 29(1). In my opinion the words 'which relates wholly or mainly to' mean 'is
predominantly about'. Next, of the various subject matters of potential trade disputes
listed in paras (a) to (g) of s 29(1), the only relevant one on the evidence, and the only one

b

relied on by the union, is 'termination of employment of one or more workers'. The
question at this stage thus becomes: how likely is it that at trial the union will be able to
satisfy the judge that the dispute between BT and its employees was predominantly
about possible job losses, or redundancies? In the passage from his judgment which Sir
John Donaldson MR has quoted, the judge below concluded that it was likely that the
union would be able to do so.

c

With all respect to the judge, I find myself driven to the opposite conclusion: partly
because at two points in this part of his judgment I think that he erred in his approach;
and partly because we have had the benefit of having put before us important additional
evidence to that which was before him.

First, as I have already said, I think that the amendments to s 29(1) made by s 18 of the
1982 Act have restricted the scope of the former substantially. Thus, after referring to

d

the two cases of *Hadmor Productions Ltd v Hamilton* [1982] 1 All ER 1042, [1983] 1 AC
191 and *Health Computing Ltd v Meek* [1981] ICR 24, in which the courts had to consider
s 29(1) in its unamended form, I think that the judge erred when he said (see p 194,
ante):

> 'The phrase [was] "is connected with" rather than, as now, "which relates", but I
> do not see in the circumstances of this case that it matters which phrase is taken.'

e

Before considering further the two authorities I have just mentioned, I should deal
with another on the same point to which we were also referred and in which the phrase
under consideration was 'industrial dispute' as defined by s 167(1) of the Industrial
Relations Act 1971 in which the material phrase was 'relates wholly or mainly to', as it is
again now in the amended s 29(1) of the 1974 Act. The authority is *General Aviation

f

Services (UK) Ltd v Transport and General Workers' Union* [1975] ICR 276. There industrial
strife broke out when, without consultation, the British Airports Authority introduced a
Canadian company at London Airport to provide a comprehensive ground-handling
service for any airline that desired it. Not surprisingly those already employed on this
work at the airport took the view that the introduction of the new company posed a
threat to their jobs. In my view the only aspect of the decision in that case which is

g

relevant for our purposes is that this court there held that a dispute can certainly relate
wholly or mainly to 'termination or suspension of employment' even though the cause
of it is merely the fear of future redundancies. This decision was approved by the House
of Lords in *Hadmor Productions Ltd v Hamilton*, to which I shall refer again hereafter.

What then was the dispute between BT and its employees in this case wholly or mainly
about? The judge's finding on this point was that it was a dispute which on the authorities

h

to which he referred related wholly or mainly to termination of employment, that is to
say job losses. However, in each of the three authorities on which the judge relied the
relevant phrase was 'is connected with' rather than 'which relates wholly or mainly to'
and, as I have already said, I think that the judge erred in concluding that in the
circumstances of the case it did not matter which phrase was taken. That this is so is in
my opinion clearly demonstrated by the passage from Lord Diplock's speech in *NWL Ltd

j

v Woods* [1979] 3 All ER 614 at 624, [1979] 1 WLR 1294 at 1304 which the judge quoted.
In that passage Lord Diplock pointed out that it mattered not in that case that the
predominant subject of the dispute was not one of the matters set out in s 29(1) of the
1974 Act provided that one could say that one of the subjects of the dispute, with which
it could be said to be connected, at least in part, was one of such matters. In the instant

case the change in the wording of the statute is clearly of importance: the amended subsection now does require the court to look to the predominant purpose. Of the other authorities on which the judge relied, in my judgment two were not directly relevant to the question of what was the predominant subject of the dispute. On the issue of job losses, that is to say 'termination or suspension of employment . . . of one or more workers', which are the relevant works in para (b) of s 29(1), the ratio of the decision in the House of Lords in *Hadmor Productions Ltd v Hamilton* [1982] 1 All ER 1042, [1983] 1 AC 191 was that a fear of future redundancies was fully within the meaning of the paragraph and that the argument that there could not be a trade dispute based on this ground until redundancy notices had already been issued or threatened by the employer was unsustainable. This was again the basis of the decision in *Health Computing Ltd v Meek* [1981] ICR 24, to which also the judge referred.

Finally, the decision in *Duport Steels Ltd v Sirs* [1980] 1 All ER 529, [1980] 1 WLR 142 was in my judgment one on the meaning of and correct approach to the phrase 'in contemplation or furtherance of a trade dispute'. In the *Duport Steels* case the essential decision of the House of Lords was that a trade union which proposed to call out on strike employees of companies in the private sector of the steel industry to increase pressure on the public authority, the British Steel Corp, whose employees who were members of the union were already on strike, was acting in contemplation or furtherance of that latter dispute. Respectfully, I do not think that the decision in the *Duport Steels* case was relevant to the determination of the different issue before the judge in the instant one.

In the result, therefore, in my opinion the latter's approach to the question whether or not the dispute between BT and its employees referable to Mercury was a trade dispute within s 29(1), and thus more particularly whether the union was likely to succeed on the s 13 defence at trial, cannot be supported. This does not mean that the ultimate exercise of discretion by Mervyn Davies J not to grant interlocutory injunctions was wrong, but it does not only entitle but requires this court to exercise an original discretion in the case itself.

I turn then to consider, on all the evidence now before us, what was the sole or main matter about which the employees of BT were in dispute with the latter when they refused to interconnect Mercury and blacked the work at the premises of Mercury and their shareholders. In my opinion this has to be decided on an ordinary commonsense approach, analogous to that which is adopted when a court has before it a question of causation. A reasonable starting point for the inquiry in the instant case is the fact that the employees of BT disobeyed their employers as they did because they were instructed to do so by the union. There is no question in this case, for instance, of original unofficial action by some employees being taken up and made official for all by the union. Further, although it would be unfair to suggest that BT's employees acted as they did merely because they were told to do so by their union and without applying their own minds at all to the reasons why they were disobeying instructions as they were, when an industrial dispute is created by a trade union's instructions it is surely right to ask why the union gave them when one is attempting to discover what the dispute, which flowed from compliance with those instructions, was wholly or mainly about. I have no doubt that the union gave those instructions because BT attempted to implement the interconnection agreement with Mercury. Nevertheless it would of course be wrong to hold that this was in itself the sole or indeed a main cause of the dispute. The union saw the attempt to interconnect Mercury as the thin end of the wedge which could ultimately lead to the failure of its campaign against liberalisation and then privatisation. If this campaign failed, there was, it was said, a serious risk of redundancies and, amongst other things, the likelihood that BT would become less profitable, which would also reduce the scope for improvement in the terms and conditions of employment of its employees. In the various affidavits sworn by Mr Stanley and filed on the defendants' behalf in these proceedings this is repeated and emphasised, for instance in para 10 of his first affidavit:

'I therefore wish to state unequivocally and with all the emphasis at my command that the purpose and object of the industrial action complained of by [Mercury] is to prevent the risk of job losses arising from the entry into the market of an unwelcome competitor.'

Mercury's claim necessarily involves an attack on the genuineness of these contentions of Mr Stanley. Their case in brief is that the blacking of Mercury and their shareholders was part of the union's relatively long-standing campaign against Mercury and the government and the policies of liberalisation and thereafter privatisation for which it stands. Of course Mr Stanley has to base himself on an alleged risk of redundancies, because under the relevant legislation as now enacted this is the only defence that the union can have in this action, and in particular against the interlocutory injunctions now sought. Be that as it may, I remind myself, on the one hand, that I should not lightly disregard Mr Stanley's sworn evidence, particularly at the interlocutory stage. On the other hand, s 17(2) of the 1974 Act does require me to have regard to the likelihood of the defendants succeeding on this point at trial. Thus, so far as I think legitimate, I must make an attempt to look forward to trial, to use my experience of conducting litigation, to anticipate that the contents of Mr Stanley's present affidavits will perfectly properly be filled out at the hearing and further witnesses called, no doubt amongst them the writers of some of the letters exhibited to Mr Stanley's second affidavit sworn on 14 October 1983. Equally, there is no doubt that Mr Stanley will be cross-examined about his evidence at trial and I have looked in the material presently before us for aspects of the case on which such a cross-examination might be mounted and tried to reach some conclusion, without speculation, about the likelihood that any such cross-examination might weaken the effect of his evidence as he has presently deposed. I remind myself, for instance, of some of the matters to which counsel for Mercury referred in his submissions, of the fact that Mr Stanley did not exhibit the report of the union's special conference of 18 September 1983 until his third affidavit was filed, of the fact that he did not refer to or exhibit the job security agreement between the union and BT until his fifth affidavit, although I also have well in mind the evidence about BT's insistence in negotiations that the job security agreement should contain what was described as the force majeure clause, cl 5, about what is said by Mr Stanley to be the views of his union members about the efficacy of the job security agreement, and about the reference already said to have been made to cl 5 by a senior member of BT's management to two senior officials of the union on 10 August 1983.

On the other hand, there was no evidence before the judge or before us that there had been any discussion between the union and BT about the effect that the arrival of Mercury on the telecommunications scene might or would have on redundancies, or about the effect of the job security agreement in these circumstances.

Further, although I fully appreciate that we live in a time of high unemployment with fears of redundancy prevalent throughout industry, the evidence that we presently have leads me to the conclusion that to the knowledge of the union BT clearly anticipated being able to accommodate any job losses that might result either from competition or from technological advance by natural wastage and retirement.

Finally, in my opinion all these matters have to be considered in the context that there is no doubt that the union is and has for some time been conducting a campaign against liberalisation and privatisation, in which the defence of its members' jobs and conditions of service has only been one of the issues. I think that from the union's own documents which are before us this has been and is in substantial degree a political and ideological campaign seeking to maintain the concept of public monopoly against private competition. I have no doubt that those who strenuously contend for the continuation of a monopoly in the postal and telecommunications fields honestly and fervently believe that this is in the best interests of the jobs and conditions of service of those working in the industry. It does not however follow that industrial action taken to further that campaign amounts to a dispute which is wholly or mainly about fears of redundancies if that monopoly is not maintained. Doing the best I can, I have come to the conclusion

that it is unlikely that the defendants in this case will succeed in satisfying a court at trial
a that the dispute between BT and its employees over the blacking of Mercury and their
shareholders was a 'trade dispute' within the relevant legislation as now enacted. If I were
wrong and the dispute were truly one which was wholly or mainly about the fear of
redundancies, then I would have no doubt that the union, in instructing its members to
take the action that they did, was acting in contemplation or furtherance of the trade
dispute which then ex hypothesi was in being.

b   In the result, however, I think that it is unlikely that the defendants will succeed at the
trial of this action in establishing the s 13(1) defence.

I turn therefore to the general principles on which courts should exercise or decline to
exercise their discretion to grant interlocutory injunctions laid down in the well-known
decision in *American Cyanamid Ltd v Ethicon Ltd* [1975] 1 All ER 504, [1975] AC 396. I do
so having well in mind the passage from Lord Diplock's speech in *NWL Ltd v Woods*
c [1979] 3 All ER 614 at 624, [1979] 1 WLR 1294 at 1305, and in particular the necessity
to consider the practical realities of industrial situations to which Lord Diplock referred.
However in the present case the real dispute, as I think, is not between BT and the union
but between the latter and Mercury and between the union and the government. The
industrial action is no doubt being used as a bargaining counter in the dispute between
the union and the government; it is not in reality being so used in any dispute between
d the union and BT or Mercury. In this particular case there is no good reason why the
industrial action now being taken cannot, if temporarily postponed, be revived if the
union does succeed at trial, and revived effectively. I do not think that the grant or refusal
of an interlocutory injunction will dispose finally of this action; both counsel told us that
there is likely to be a trial and this is my opinion also.

In *American Cyanamid Co v Ethicon Ltd* [1975] 1 All ER 504 at 510, [1975] AC 396 at
e 408 Lord Diplock laid down that a court should first consider whether the plaintiff is
likely to be adequately compensated by damages were he to succeed at trial but not be
protected by an interlocutory injunction in the mean time. If damages would not provide
an adequate remedy for the plaintiff, then mutatis mutandis one must undertake a
similar inquiry in so far as the defendant is concerned. It is only where there is doubt as
to the adequacy of the respective remedies in damages available to either party or both
f that the question of balance of convenience arises, and with it such considerations as the
maintenance of the status quo. In his judgment the judge below expressed the view that
in a case of this kind it is impractical, if not impossible, to assess the financial consequences
of making or not making an order. With respect, I disagree.

On the evidence before us I have no doubt that damages will not be an adequate
alternative remedy to Mercury if interlocutory injunctions are not granted. The evidence
g satisfies me that if the union's blacking continues the loss which Mercury will sustain
will be very substantial, difficult to assess, but certainly in excess of the limit of £250,000
on the union's potential liability imposed by s 16(1) and (3) of the Employment Act
1982. On the other hand, in the particular circumstances of the present case, I think that
such loss, if any, to the union from a postponement for something of the order of three
or four months, which we were told is what the parties contemplate under the order for
h a speedy trial made by the judge below, will be small indeed and well within the capacity
of Mercury to reimburse.

For these reasons I would allow this appeal and grant the interlocutory injunctions
sought.

DILLON LJ. In the judgment under appeal, the judge, after a careful summary of the
j principal items of evidence which he considered to be relevant, examined first the
requirement of s 17(2) of the Trade Union and Labour Relations Act 1974 (as inserted by
the Employment Protection Act 1975 and amended by the Employment Act 1982) that
the court must on an interlocutory application for an injunction such as this consider the
likelihood of the defendants' succeeding at the trial in establishing the matters which
would under s 13 of the 1974 Act afford them a defence to the action. He held on the

affidavit evidence that the defendants were likely at the trial to establish a s 13 defence. He recognised, however, that the s 17(2) element as he called it was not an 'overriding' or 'paramount' factor and he accordingly went on to consider the application of the principles of *American Cyanamid Co v Ethicon Ltd* [1975] 1 All ER 504, [1975] AC 396.

At this stage he commented that it was impossible to assess the financial consequences of making or not making an order, and he thought that there was something to be said for a submission for the defendants that the status quo should remain. Since the preservation of the status quo comes at the very end of an *American Cyanamid* exercise, his comments may be open to the criticism that he has not given sufficient weight to the absence of financial detriment to the defendants or their members if an injunction is granted for the short time until trial or to the fact that on the balance of convenience the non-financial detriment to the defendants if an injunction is granted (in that their members will lose some of the advantage of their industrial muscle) is far outweighed by the loss to the plaintiffs, Mercury, if no injunction is granted. It does appear however that the judge did have in mind the devastating effect on Mercury's business which continuation of the defendants' industrial action will have, and on the whole I take the view that the basis of his decision was that in his view the prospects of the defendants' succeeding at the trial by virtue of s 13(1) were so great as to outweigh all other factors.

We have therefore in this appeal to consider primarily whether the judge was right in his assessment of the defendants' prospects of success by virtue of s 13(1). We have however fresh evidence before us, and so we have additionally to consider whether the fresh evidence invalidates the reasons given by the judge for his conclusion. In relation to the fresh evidence, it is in my judgment pertinent to bear in mind the comment of Lord Diplock in *Hadmor Productions Ltd v Hamilton* [1982] 1 All ER 1042 at 1049, [1983] 1 AC 191 at 224 that the greater the likelihood of a s 13 defence succeeding, the greater the weight to be attached to it. The converse must also apply. If the effect of the fresh evidence is significantly to reduce the defendants' prospects of success by virtue of s 13, then, if I am correct in my interpretation of the basis of the judge's decision, it may be a legitimate conclusion for this court that that reduction in the defendants' prospects of success is sufficient to invalidate the judge's conclusion after his balancing exercise.

I turn to consider the judge's assessment of the defendants' prospects of success under s 13 on the evidence which was before the judge. But it is necessary first to say a little about some of the authorities, *General Aviation Services (UK) Ltd v Transport and General Workers' Union* [1975] ICR 276, a decision of this court, *Hadmor Productions Ltd v Hamilton*, where the House of Lords approved the *General Aviation Services* case, and *Health Computing Ltd v Meek* [1981] ICR 24, a decision of Goulding J.

The present definition of 'trade dispute' is to be found in s 29 of the 1974 Act as amended by s 18 of the Employment Act 1982. One of the amendments made by the 1982 Act was to substitute the words 'which relates wholly or mainly to one or more of the following' for the words 'which is connected with one or more of the following'. The words so substituted were part of the definition of 'industrial dispute' in the Industrial Relations Act 1971 and the *General Aviation Services* case was a decision on that definition in the 1971 Act. In that case baggage handlers at Heathrow had objected, because of fear of job losses, to the introduction by the airport authority at Heathrow of an aircraft handling company to provide ground handling services for airlines using the airport. The dispute was not between the workers and their own employers and so because of a different amendment in the definition of 'trade dispute' would not now be within the definition; that is not for present purposes relevant. An independent inquiry found that the workers' fears of job losses were groundless, but on the evidence in the case there was a clear finding that these fears were genuine and widely entertained: see the judgment of Orr LJ (at 294). In those circumstances the court held that there was an industrial dispute within the definition because the dispute related wholly or mainly to the termination of employment of workers, even though the redundancies feared lay wholly in the uncertain future and there had been no actual threat of a redundancy notice being served.

Hadmor Productions Ltd v Hamilton was a decision on the definition of 'trade dispute' in s 29 of the 1974 Act in its unamended form, ie with the words 'which is connected with one or more of the following'. What had happened was that the union of which the defendants were officers had blacked the showing by a television company of films made by Hadmor Productions, an independent production unit, because they had not been made in the television company's own studios. The reason for the union's action was plainly a fear of job losses among the union's members employed in the television company's own studios. Lord Diplock, who regarded the case as a classic instance of a trade dispute in a period of recession, found significant parallels in the *General Aviation Services* case, although the wording 'which is connected with one or more of the following' was wider than the wording 'which relates wholly or mainly to one or more of the following'. The important point for present purposes is however that, as no other explanation for the union's action but fear of job losses was found and as the words 'wholly or mainly' were not included in the definition of 'trade dispute' which the court had to apply in *Hadmor Productions*, the court did not have to consider those words 'wholly or mainly' at all.

Health Computing Ltd v Meek was another decision on the definition of 'trade dispute' in s 29 of the 1974 Act in its original form, with the words 'which is connected with one or more of the following'. The plaintiffs were endeavouring to sell computer systems and equipment to hospitals and the union of which the defendants were officials had instructed its members employed in the health service to have no dealings with the plaintiffs. The reason put forward was fear of job losses. Goulding J applied the *General Aviation Services* case and dismissed a motion for an interlocutory injunction on the ground that the defendants were likely to succeed at the trial in their defence under s 13. He said ([1981] ICR 24 at 33):

'... I am of opinion that a dispute about job security, a dispute motivated in whole or in part by the fear of redundancy, is a trade dispute.'

That of course, though no doubt correct at the time, would be a misdirection now under the amended definition of 'trade dispute'; to qualify the dispute must now be motivated wholly or mainly by the fear of redundancy.

In the present case the union's members are in dispute with the plaintiffs and BT over the interconnection of Mercury's equipment with the BT exchanges. But, prima facie, that dispute is only an aspect of a wider dispute between the union and its members of the one hand and Mercury, BT and the government on the other hand over the breaking, whether by liberalisation or privatisation, of the telecommunications monopoly hitherto enjoyed by BT, or its predecessor, the Post Office, as a nationalised industry. Other possible reasons have been mentioned in argument, but the main question for the trial is likely to be whether the union's members' actions in refusing interconnection are wholly or mainly due to fear of job losses or, even if partly due to fear of job losses, are mainly due to political objection to the breaking of the monopoly of a nationalised industry. This is a question on which the words 'wholly or mainly' in the statutory definition are of fundamental importance, but it does not seem to me that the judge has addressed his mind to those words at all.

At the start of the relevant passage in his judgment, the judge says (see p 194, ante):

'I had supposed that fear of future job losses could not be prayed in aid at this early stage. One would suppose that some real threat of dismissal would have to be shown before it could be said that a dispute relates to termination of employment. The authorities show that this supposition may be wrong...'

He then refers to *Hadmor Productions Ltd v Hamilton* and *Health Computing Ltd v Meek* and he continues:

'So if there is a dispute it may be a dispute relating to termination within s 29(1)(b). The phrase has been "is connected with" rather than, as now, "which relates", but I do not see in the circumstances of this case that it matters which phrase is taken.'

It seems to me, with all respect, that it does matter very considerably which phrase is taken, because of the words 'wholly or mainly', unless the judge is only concerned with the point that a dispute may relate to termination of employment even though there has been no real threat of dismissal (as in the *General Aviation Services* case and *Hadmor Productions* case). The judge then turned to discuss a different point, and stated a little later in his judgment that when BT in June 1983 ordered connection 'a particular dispute then crystallised'. He concluded (see p 195, ante):

> 'It was a dispute with BT whether or not BT installations should be made available to Mercury. It was a dispute which related (according to the authorities I have mentioned) wholly or mainly to termination of employment, ie job losses. Accordingly there is, in my view, in existence a trade dispute within s 29(1).'

The authorities which the judge had mentioned were not however concerned with the words 'wholly or mainly' at all. They were only concerned to show that a dispute may relate to or be concerned with job losses even though no real threat of dismissal had been made. As I see it, the judge has been so concerned with the question of remoteness, that on the authorities a dispute could be said to relate to fear of job losses even though no threat of dismissal had been made, that he did not address his mind to the difficult and different question whether this dispute did not in truth mainly relate to a political objection to the breaking of the monopoly of a nationalised industry or to some other causes than fear of job losses.

The finding that a particular dispute crystallised when in June 1983 BT ordered connection does not answer that question either way since so far as the finding goes it does not indicate either way whether the particular dispute related to the fear of job losses. Moreover, on the facts of this case the particular dispute which crystallised in June 1983 cannot be looked at in isolation from the wider dispute, mentioned above, which had been going on for many months before. The court has no doubt to consider whether the particular dispute which crystallised is a trade dispute within the statutory definition, but, in considering that, the court is bound to consider what was said earlier in relation to the wider dispute. Mr Stanley in the first of his affidavits invites the court to draw a clear distinction between the reason for the adoption of the union policy and the arguments that are advanced in an attempt to persuade others of the correctness of that policy. That however begs the question; the court has to consider, albeit only provisionally for the purposes of s 17(2), what is the reason for the adoption of the union's policy and on that question the arguments advanced by the union are obviously relevant evidence.

In considering whether a dispute relates wholly or mainly to any of the matters listed in s 29 it is necessary to consider not merely the occasion which caused the dispute to break out but also the reason why there was a dispute. It tells one nothing to say in the *General Aviation Services* case [1975] ICR 276 that the dispute was about the introduction of the aircraft handling company or to say in *BBC v Hearn* [1978] 1 All ER 111, [1977] 1 WLR 1004 that the dispute was about the instruction given by the BBC to transmit film of the Cup Final to South Africa or to say in the present case that the dispute was about the instruction to interconnect. Counsel accepts, for Mercury, that it is necessary to go a stage further and ask why the union's members objected to the instruction to interconnect. He says that the answer to that question is that the members wanted to destroy competition and he submits that it is not permissible to go further and ask why they wanted to destroy competition. I do not agree. In both the *General Aviation Services* case and the *Hadmor Productions* case the answer to the question why the union members objected to some course of action (the introduction of the aircraft handling company or the showing of films made by an independent unit) could have been that the members were afraid of competition; but the court went on to hold that the real reason was fear of job losses. Indeed, rather than asking what the dispute is about, which can produce a variety of answers of different degrees of helpfulness, it is better to turn the question round, and, having isolated 'fear of job losses' as the only factor within s 29 relied on by the union, to ask 'Is this dispute wholly or mainly about fear of job losses?'

a   To be within the definition in s 29 as it now stands the dispute has to be a dispute between the workers, the union's members, and their employer, BT, and not a dispute between the union and BT. It is therefore the state of mind of the members which the court has to consider in assessing for the purposes of s 17(2) whether there is a trade dispute.

b   Mr Stanley asserts in categorical terms in his first affidavit that the purpose and object of the industrial action taken to prevent interconnection and indeed the reason why in the wider dispute the defendants oppose the liberalisation or privatisation of BT is to prevent the risk of job losses arising from the entry into the market of an unwelcome competitor. He says that the reason for the members' action is quite clearly their fear for their jobs. Counsel for the defendants submits, as a general proposition, that workers will not take industrial action unless they are really afraid that their jobs are at risk or their pockets will be affected.

c   Obviously there is a considerable element of truth in counsel's submission. There are many instances where workers have declined to come out on strikes for solely political objectives. There are also, however, instances where workers have taken industrial action because their union had instructed them to do so even though they may themselves have had no desire to do so, or where, as in *BBC v Hearn*, industrial action has been taken where there was no threat to jobs or to the members' pockets.

d   Whether the dispute between the union's members and BT and Mercury is a trade dispute has to be considered objectively. The court has to consider all the evidence and it is not concluded by the ipse dixit of Mr Stanley. Where industrial action has been taken by the members at the behest of the union, the court must very often be entitled to infer that the members are by their action indorsing proclaimed objectives of the union, and that, conversely, the union is by its public statements about the dispute speaking on behalf of the members.

e   In the present case there can be no doubt that the union has for many months opposed with fervour the government's proposals for changes within the telecommunications industry. That is part of the wider dispute already mentioned. The judge seems in his judgment to have dismissed all this as a matter of words only until BT in June 1983 ordered connection. I do not think he was right to do that. The background to the particular dispute, and the attitude of the union which required the workers to take the industrial action and which professes to speak for the workers, must in my judgment be relevant in assessing, as required by s 17(2), whether the dispute between the workers and BT and Mercury relates wholly or mainly to fear of job losses.

f   If the attitude of the union is relevant, then the further evidence adduced in this court is also relevant to the assessment. The judge was never told of the job security agreement. In this court counsel for the defendants has sought to brush it aside because it is not a binding contract in law or on the ground that cl 5 enables BT to withdraw the undertaking about redundancies whenever BT finds the undertaking inconvenient. But that is to ignore the realities of industrial relations. The union pressed for a job security agreement even though the union knew that it would not constitute a binding contract, and the union was overall well content to have the job security agreement with cl 5 in it, rather than nothing, when it became clear that it was not possible to negotiate a formula more favourable to the union than cl 5. In addition the new material put before the court by the defendants themselves in order to explain the context of the job security agreement shows that the defendants were well aware of the prospects of growth and expansion in the telecommunications industry and well aware that natural wastage and the job security agreement would avoid redundancies from technological advances. Mr Stanley's assertions that the particular dispute and the wider dispute are all about jobs have to be set against the fact that the defendants have not, in their campaign against Mercury, liberalisation, privatisation and interconnection, ever mentioned or invoked the job security agreement.

g

h

j   The ultimate decision whether there is a trade dispute will be made at the trial and will be made on evidence, including no doubt the cross-examination of Mr Stanley, which is not before us. Because, however, the judge has in my judgment misdirected

himself in important respects which I have endeavoured to indicate and because of the
relevance and importance of the fresh evidence, I take the view that this court is required   *a*
in this case, exceptionally, to make its own assessment under s 17(2) of the likelihood of
the defendants establishing the matters which under s 13 would afford a defence to the
action, and especially of the likelihood of the defendants establishing that the dispute is a
trade dispute. (If there was a trade dispute, the refusal to connect Mercury was, I do not
doubt, in furtherance of that dispute.)

On the material before us, I would not regard the defendants' prospects of success in   *b*
establishing that there is a trade dispute as overwhelming, as in *Hadmor Productions Ltd v
Hamilton* [1982] 1 All ER 1042, [1983] 1 AC 191 or as the judge may have thought in the
present case. My assessment is that the defendants may succeed at the trial, but if they do
it will have been a close run thing.

It follows, in my judgment, that I am entitled to exercise my own discretion as to the
grant or refusal of an injunction and I am not bound, in this case, by the judge's exercise   *c*
of his discretion. Apart from the defendants' prospects of success under s 13, assessed as
above, the relevant factors on an *American Cyanamid* exercise are, as I see them, on the
one hand that on the evidence Mercury are likely to suffer enormous, irrecoverable and
possibly crippling damage if no injunction is granted, and on the other hand, so far as
the defendants are concerned, that, to put it colloquially, the horse will not have bolted
between now and the trial. The work of interconnection which is in issue over the short   *d*
period until the trial is not, as I understand counsel for Mercury, an immediate, once and
for all connection of Mercury's system to the BT network, but is at this stage merely a
question of connecting up each individual customer of Mercury to the BT network as
and when Mercury have made an appropriate arrangement with that customer and
installed their equipment in his premises. While some customers may be connected up
between now and the date of trial, the connection of future customers thereafter will   *e*
depend on the outcome of the trial, and it seems highly unlikely that such connections
as are are effected in the next few months until the trial takes place will cause any loss of
jobs among the union's members. In the light of these factors I would grant Mercury the
interlocutory injunctions they seek

It is unnecessary to comment in this judgment on the industrial action which the
defendants have taken against Mercury's shareholders, since that action has now happily   *f*
ceased. It is also unnecessary to comment on Mercury's alternative case, on which we
have not heard full argument, under s 45 of the Telegraph Act 1863 as amended.

*Appeal allowed. Injunction in terms of notice of motion. Leave to appeal to the House of Lords
granted provided application made to Judicial Office within 48 hours*[1].

Solicitors: *Bird & Bird* (for Mercury); *Lawford & Co* (for the defendants).

Diana Procter   Barrister.

---

1   No application was made

Edicron Ltd v William Whiteley Ltd

COURT OF APPEAL, CIVIL DIVISION
WALLER, SLADE AND ROBERT GOFF LJJ
6 OCTOBER 1983

Landlord and tenant – Business tenancy – Compensation for refusal of new tenancy – Premises 'being or comprised in the holding' and continuously occupied by tenant for 14 years for business purposes – Premises – Amount of compensation – Entitlement to double compensation – Tenant not entitled to double compensation if change in occupier of 'the premises' and new tenant not the successor of previous occupier's business – Whether 'premises' referring to any premises in holding or particular premises in holding used by tenant for his business – Whether tenant entitled to double compensation if at least part of relevant holding continuously occupied by him for business purposes – Landlord and Tenant Act 1954, s 37(3)(a)(b).

In June 1967 the landlord granted the tenant a lease of the first floor of a building which had three floors. Thereafter the tenant occupied the first floor continuously for the purposes of its business while the second and third floors were occupied by another tenant for the purposes of a different business. In 1976 the tenant surrendered the lease of the first floor in return for a lease of the whole building for the purposes of its business. In doing so the tenant did not succeed to the previous occupier's business when it went into occupation of the second and third floors under the new lease. When in July 1980 the landlord served a notice on the tenant under s 25 of the Landlord and Tenant Act 1954 opposing the grant of a new tenancy of the holding, the tenant gave up possession and became entitled, by virtue of s 37(1) of the 1954 Act, to compensation on quitting the holding. The tenant applied to the court to determine the amount of compensation. Under s 37(3)(a)[a] a tenant was entitled to compensation based on twice the rateable value of the holding if during the 14 years prior to the termination of the tenancy 'premises . . . comprised in the holding' had been occupied by the tenant for the purposes of his business. However, under s 37(3)(b) a tenant was precluded from receiving compensation at the double rate and was restricted to compensation based simply on the rateable value alone if during the previous 14 years there had been a change in the occupier of 'the premises' and the new tenant was not the successor of the previous occupier's business. Since there had been a change of occupier of the second and third floors during the 14 years prior to the termination of the tenancy and since the tenant was not the successor of the previous occupier's business on the second and third floors the question arose whether the tenant was precluded by s 37(3)(b) of the 1954 Act from receiving compensation at the double rate. The judge held that there had been 'a change in the occupier of the premises' for the purposes of s 37(3)(b) because 'premises . . . comprised in the holding' in s 37(3)(a) and 'the premises' in s 37(3)(b) meant any premises comprised in the holding and that therefore 'a change in the occupier of the premises' encompassed the change of occupation of the second and third floors from the previous occupier to the tenant. The judge accordingly held that s 37(3)(b) applied and that the tenant was therefore precluded from receiving compensation at the double rate. The tenant appealed.

Held – On the true construction of s 37(3)(a) and (b) of the 1954 Act the 'premises . . . comprised in the holding' referred to the particular premises which had been occupied by the tenant for the purposes of his business, so that provided that at least part (that part being 'the premises') of the relevant holding was occupied by the tenant for the purposes of his business for a continuous period of 14 years prior to the termination of the tenancy he was entitled to compensation at the double rate. It followed that for the purposes of s 37(3)(b) 'the premises' which were relevant in deciding whether there had been a change

---

a   Section 37(3), so far as material, is set out at p 222 *d e*, post

of occupation were the particular premises in the holding which had been occupied by
the tenant for the purposes of his business and not just any premises in the holding
which had been occupied by him. On that basis, 'the premises' for the purposes of
s 37(3)(a) and (b) were the first floor only, and since the tenant had been in continuous
occupation of the first floor for the purposes of its business throughout the relevant 14-
year period it was entitled under s 37(3)(a) to compensation at the double rate in respect
of the whole building on quitting. The appeal would accordingly be allowed (see p 222 j
to p 223 d and j to p 224 j, post).

Notes
For compensation on quitting business premises, see 27 Halsbury's Laws (4th edn) paras
518–519.
    For the Landlord and Tenant Act 1954, ss 25, 37, see 18 Halsbury's Statutes (3rd edn)
559, 576.

Appeal
Edicron Ltd, the former tenants of premises, appealed against the judgment of his
Honour Judge Thomas sitting as a judge of the High Court given on 10 February 1983,
whereby he adjudged that William Whiteley Ltd (Whiteleys), the former landlords,
should pay Edicron compensation of £22,437 pursuant to s 37 of the Landlord and
Tenant Act 1954 on quitting premises at Redan House, Queensway, London W2. Edicron
sought judgment for compensation in the sum £44,874, ie double compensation,
contending that the judge had erred in law in holding that Edicron was not entitled to
double compensation under s 37(2)(a) for the following reasons: (1) having correctly held
that Edicron fulfilled the first condition for double compensation in para (a) of s 37(3),
namely that premises comprised in Edicron's holding had been occupied for the whole
of the prescribed 14-year period, he wrongly held that Edicron was disentitled to double
compensation by reason of the second condition, in para (b) of s 37(2); (2) the judge erred
in law in failing to hold that the second condition was applicable only where there had
been a change in the occupier of 'the premises' within s 37(2)(b) and that that expression
meant the same as the expression 'premises being or comprised in the holding' in
s 37(3)(a), being shorthand for the latter expression; (3) the judge ought therefore to have
held that the expression 'the premises' in s 37(3)(b) meant the actual premises ascertained
by the court as 'being or comprised in the holding' for the purpose of s 37(3)(a); (4)
accordingly, the judge having correctly held that the premises being or comprised in the
holding for the purpose of s 37(3)(a) were the first floor of Redan House in respect of
which there had been no change in occupier throughout the 14-year period, wrongly
held that because there had been a change in occupier of some other premises comprised
in the holding (namely the second and third floors of Redan House), para (b) of s 37(3)
was applicable and had not been fulfilled; and (5) the judge erred in law in failing to hold
that in all the circumstances para (b) of s 37(3) was not applicable and Edicron, having
fulfilled para (a) of s 37(3), was entitled to double compensation. The facts are set out in
the judgment.

Robert Reid QC and *Simon Berry* for Edicron.
John Furber for Whiteleys.

SLADE LJ (delivering the first judgment at the invitation of Waller LJ). This is an
appeal from part of a judgment of his Honour Judge Thomas, who was sitting as a judge
of the High Court, delivered on 10 February 1983. He decided that the respondents,
William Whiteley Ltd, as former landlords, should pay to the appellants, Edicron Ltd, as
former tenants, a sum of £22,437, with interest, as compensation under s 37 of the
Landlord and Tenant Act 1954, as amended by the Local Government, Planning and
Land Act 1980. I will refer to the respondents as 'Whiteleys' and to the appellants as
'Edicron'.
    Edicron submits that the sum properly payable is twice that which was awarded to it

a   by the judge, namely £44,874, with interest. The appeal in substance raises a short question of construction on two words in s 37(3)(b) of the 1954 Act.

The facts of the case are simple. On 21 June 1967 Whiteleys granted to Edicron a lease of the first floor of Redan House, Queensway, London for a term from 29 September 1966 to 29 September 1980. Edicron went into occupation of the first floor that day and occupied it continuously for the purposes of its business until 24 May 1982. On 6 December 1976 Edicron surrendered the earlier lease of the first floor and was granted, b   by Whiteleys, a new lease of the first, second and third floors of Redan House for a term of 20 years from 6 December 1976. From 6 December 1976 until 24 May 1982 Edicron has been continuously in occupation of the second and part of the third floors, in addition to the first floor.

On 23 December 1976 Edicron granted an underlease of the greater part of the third floor to IVS (UK) Ltd for a term of three years from that date. In the event, the latter company remained in occupation of that part of the third floor until 4 December 1981. c   On 17 July 1980 Whiteleys served on Edicron a notice under s 25 of the 1954 Act, relying on ground in para (f) of s 30(1) of the 1954 Act as its ground of opposition to a new tenancy. This notice expired on 6 December 1981. Before that date, on 21 July 1980, Edicron had served a counter-notice on Whiteleys. On 7 November 1980 Edicron issued an originating summons seeking a new tenancy under s 24 of the 1954 Act. On 4 d   December 1981 IVS (UK) Ltd vacated the part of the third floor which had been let to it. On 7 December 1981 Edicron moved back into that part and occupied it for the purposes of its business. It did not, however, take over the subtenants' previous business. Thenceforward it occupied all three floors.

On 24 February 1982 Edicron discontinued its originating summons proceedings, with leave of the court. Under s 64 of the 1954 Act, the term of Edicron's lease of the first, second and third floors continued for a further three months until 24 May 1982. e   On that date Edicron gave up possession of the whole of the first, second and third floors. On 24 February 1983 Edicron issued these proceedings for the purpose of determining compensation payable to it under s 37 of the 1954 Act.

As at 24 May 1982, s 37(1) of the 1954 Act, as amended by the Law of Property Act 1969, so far as material for present purposes, reads as follows:

f   '... where no other ground is specified in the landlord's notice under section 25 of this Act ... than those specified in the said paragraphs (e), (f) and (g) and either no application under the said section 24 is made or such an application is withdrawn, then, subject to the provisions of this Act, the tenant shall be entitled on quitting the holding to recover from the landlord by way of compensation an amount determined in accordance with the following provisions of this section.'

g   It is common ground that Edicron became entitled to recover a sum by way of compensation from Whiteleys under this subsection on quitting the holding. 'The holding' is defined by s 23(3) of the 1954 Act as meaning—

'the property comprised in the tenancy, there being excluded any part thereof which is occupied neither by the tenant nor by a person employed by the tenant h   and so employed for the purposes of a business by reason of which the tenancy is one to which this Part of this Act applies.'

Before the judge, a question arose whether such compensation fell to be calculated, on the one hand (a) by reference to the holding in its state at the date of quitting by Edicron, that is to say the whole of the first, second and third floors, or, on the other hand (b) by j   reference to the holding as it was when Whiteleys gave its notice under s 25, on 17 July 1980, when the holding consisted of the three floors less the part of the third floor which, at that date, was still sublet. The judge decided that it fell to be calculated in the latter manner. There has been no appeal by Edicron from that part of his decision, so that we have heard no argument on this point and proceed on the footing that his conclusion on it was correct.

Section 37(2) of the 1954 Act, as amended by the 1980 Act, specifies the amount
payable by way of compensation under s 37(1):   **a**

> '... (a) where the conditions specified in the next following subsection are
> satisfied it shall be the product of the appropriate multiplier and twice the rateable
> value of the holding, (b) in any other case it shall be the product of the appropriate
> multiplier and the rateable value of the holding.'

For the purposes of sub-s (2), the phrase 'the rateable value of the holding' is defined by   **b**
sub-s (5). It is common ground that, in accordance with the latter definition, on 17 July
1980 (which is taken as the relevant date) the rateable value of the holding, as it then
stood (that is to say the first, second and third floors, less the sublet part of the third floor)
was £9,972. By virtue of the Landlord and Tenant Act 1954 (Appropriate Multiplier)
Regulations 1981, SI 1981/69, the appropriate multiplier is 2¼.
On this appeal, the dispute between the parties turns solely on the question whether   **c**
the conditions specified in s 37(3) are satisfied. If they are not, as the judge decided, the
compensation payable can only be 2¼ × £9,972 (£22,437) which, with interest, was the
sum which he actually awarded to Edicron. If the conditions are satisfied, then the sum
payable is twice that amount.
The conditions specified in sub-s (3) are as follows:

> '... (a) that, during the whole of the fourteen years immediately preceding the   **d**
> termination of the current tenancy, premises being or comprised in the holding
> have been occupied for the purposes of a business carried on by the occupier or for
> those and other purposes; (b) that, if during those fourteen years there was a change
> in the occupier of the premises, the person who was the occupier immediately after
> the change was the successor to the business carried on by the person who was the
> occupier immediately before the change.'   **e**

There is no dispute that Edicron can bring itself within condition (a). It occupied the first
floor of Redan House for the purposes of its business from 29 September 1966 until the
termination of its tenancy of the three floors. Accordingly, it did occupy 'premises ...
comprised in the holding', albeit not the entirety of the holding, for the purposes of its
business for the whole of the 14 years immediately preceding the termination of its   **f**
tenancy. The judge, however, concluded that condition (b) was relevant and not satisfied.
He considered that the phrase 'the premises' referred to in condition (b) meant the same
as 'premises being or comprised in the holding', referred to in condition (a). He pointed
out that Edicron's occupation of the second and part of the third floors began much less
than 14 years before the termination of its tenancy. There was therefore during those
years a change in the occupation of *some* premises 'being or comprised in the holding'. It   **g**
was common ground (as he pointed out) that when Edicron went into occupation of the
second and third floors, it did not succeed to the business of the previous occupier.
Accordingly, he concluded that Edicron did not satisfy condition (b).
The correctness, or otherwise, of his ultimate decision must turn entirely on the
correctness, or otherwise, of his interpretation of the crucial phrase 'the premises', which
appears in s 37(3)(b). As I have said, he regarded this phrase as bearing the same meaning   **h**
as the phrase 'premises being or comprised in the holding' used in condition (a). He did
not amplify the reasons which led him to this conclusion but counsel on behalf of
Whiteleys has submitted that the judge's construction was not only in accordance with
the intention of Parliament, but was grammatically correct. He pointed out, clearly
correctly, that the phrase 'the premises' in condition (b) must refer back to something.
He submitted that this short phrase is simply a form of shorthand used by the draftsman,   **j**
instead of repeating in condition (b) the longer phrase 'premises being or comprised in
the holding', and that the short phrase bears exactly the same meaning as that longer
phrase.
With all respect to the argument and to the judge's conclusion on this point, I do not
for my part think that this construction of the subsection is sustainable on a fair reading
of the words used. It seems to me that, as counsel has submitted on behalf of Edicron,

para (*a*) of sub-s (3) of s 37 postulates the ascertainment of particular premises as being
a the relevant premises 'being or comprised in the holding' for the purposes of condition
(*a*). As the words 'comprised in' make clear, these relevant premises need not necessarily
constitute the entirety of the holding and, on the facts of the present case, they do not
constitute the entirety. As the judge rightly held, the relevant 'premises being or
comprised in the holding' for the purposes of condition (*a*) in this case were the first floor
of Redan House in respect of which there had been no change of occupier.

b In my judgment, on a fair reading of the relevant wording, counsel for Edicron must
be right in submitting that the brief phrase 'the premises' in condition (*b*) in its context
means those particular premises which have been ascertained under (*a*) as premises 'being
or comprised in the holding' and as having been occupied for the purposes of a business
carried on by the occupier.

The judge seems to have regarded the phrase 'the premises' in (*b*) as meaning '*any*
premises being or comprised in the holding'. But this interpretation seems to me to
c ignore the use of the definite article 'the' in the phrase 'the premises'. This use of the
definite article, coupled with the repetition of the word 'premises', rather than 'holding',
seems to me to make it clear that the premises referred to are those particular premises
which have been referred to in condition (*a*) and ascertained in accordance with that
condition.

d Accordingly, simply looking at the language of the subsection, I feel little doubt that
the interpretation which counsel for Edicron seeks to place on it is the correct
interpretation.

However counsel for Whiteleys, in his attractive argument, sought to submit that his
and the judge's construction was more likely to represent the intention of Parliament in
enacting the relevant legislation. Out of deference to his argument, I think I should
e make some observations on this aspect of the matter.

The result of the judge's construction would be that any change of occupation of any
part of the relevant 'holding' during the 14-year period would be fatal to a claim for
double compensation unless the change had been accompanied by the transfer of a
business conducted on that same part. Counsel for Whiteleys submitted that this would
not be a surprising result. He pointed out that in all cases the basis of compensation is the
f rateable value of the holding, that the extent of a holding as defined by the legislation
can fluctuate and that Parliament has attached crucial importance both to the length and
the fact of occupation for the purposes of a business in the provisions for compensation
contained in sub-ss (2) and (3). He submitted that it is entirely reasonable that, if a tenant
has originally occupied one floor only of a three-floor holding, and, in the course of the
14-year period preceding the termination of his tenancy has gradually moved into the
second and third floors (not taking over the business previously carried on there), he
g should not be entitled to compensation at the double rate for all three floors. He
submitted that the award of compensation at double rate for all three floors in those
circumstances would enable him to reap where he has not sown.

I think that the latter comment has some force. On the other hand, if counsel is right,
the tenant in such a case would be deprived of the ability to reap even where he *has* sown.
h For it is an 'all or nothing' situation. In the present case, if Whiteleys' contentions were
right, then Edicron would not be entitled to compensation at the double rate even in
respect of the first floor in which it has continuously carried on its business for the whole
of the 14-year period.

On the whole I think that the construction which Edicron seeks to place on the
wording of s 37(3)(*b*) is not inconsistent with what one may reasonably suppose to have
j been the intention of the legislature in enacting that subsection. The wording of
condition (*a*) plainly echoes, and is intended to echo, the wording of s 23(1) of the 1954
Act, which provides that Pt II of the Act applies to 'any tenancy where the property
comprised in the tenancy is or includes premises which are occupied by the tenant and
are so occupied for the purposes of a business carried on by him or for those and other
purposes'. The effect of s 23(1) thus is that for the Act to apply to a tenancy it is not in all
cases necessary that the whole of the property comprised in the tenancy should be used

for business purposes. True it is that the tenant's rights, if any, to compensation are to be measured by reference to the rateable value of 'the holding'. But it follows from the *a* definition of 'the holding' in s 23(3), already quoted, that in some circumstances a tenant, on quitting a holding, may be entitled to compensation under s 37(1) in respect of a holding, part of which consists of premises which have never been occupied for the purposes of a business.

The purpose of condition (*a*) in s 37(3), as I read it, is to ensure that a tenant shall not qualify for compensation at the double rate unless *at least part* of the relevant holding has *b* been occupied for the purposes of a business for a continuous period of 14 years immediately preceding the end of his current tenancy, during which period it may fairly be assumed that a substantial goodwill will have become attached to that particular business. Condition (*a*), however, does not by itself render it necessary that the relevant occupation shall have been by the same person for the whole of the 14-year period, to enable the ultimate tenant to qualify for compensation at the double rate.   *c*

What then is to happen if there has been a change in the occupation? Condition (*b*), as I see it, is designed to deal with that situation. Under that condition a change of occupation of the relevant premises during the 14-year period need not disqualify the quitting tenant from receiving compensation at the double rate, *if* the same business has been carried on on those premises throughout the 14-year period. If, however, during this period there has been change of occupation, in respect of the premises identified *d* under condition (*a*), compensation at the double rate is not to be available unless the person who was the occupier of those premises immediately after the change succeeded to the same business as that carried on by the person who was the occupier immediately before the change; in this contingency there must be identity of the relevant business throughout the 14-year period if there is to be a qualification for double compensation.

That, as I read it, is the purpose of s 37(3)(*b*). It is perfectly true that, as counsel for *e* Edicron conceded, the application of the 1954 Act, even on his construction, may lead to many results which may appear anomalous on the facts of particular cases where compensation is claimed. Nevertheless, the construction for which Edicron contends seems to me broadly to make good sense if I am right in regarding the primary purpose of sub-ss (2)(*a*) and (3) of s 37, when read together, as being to provide additional compensation for loss of goodwill in respect of a long-established business.   *f*

To summarise my conclusions, therefore, they are these. The phrase 'the premises' in condition (*b*) means the same particular premises as are referred to in condition (*a*), that is to say, on the facts of the present case, the first floor of Redan House. During the relevant period of 14 years, there was no change in the occupation of that first floor. It was occupied for the purposes of Edicron's business. Accordingly condition (*b*) is, on the particular facts of this case, not in point at all; it does not require to be satisfied because *g* there was no change in the occupier of the relevant 'premises' during the 14-year period. Condition (*a*), as I have already said, is satisfied. Accordingly, in my judgment, Edicron is entitled to compensation at the double rate provided for by sub-s (2) of s 37, since it brings itself within sub-s (3). The rate at which it is entitled to compensation is the product of the appropriate multiplier and twice the rateable value of the holding, namely twice times 2¼ × £9,972, that is to say £44,874, together with interest.   *h*

For the reasons which I have given, I would allow this appeal and order accordingly.

ROBERT GOFF LJ. I agree.

WALLER LJ. I also agree.   *j*

Appeal allowed.

Solicitors: *Pickering Kenyon* (for Edicron); *Thornton Lynne & Lawson* (for Whiteleys).

Sophie Craven   Barrister.

Cayne and another v Global Natural Resources plc

COURT OF APPEAL, CIVIL DIVISION

EVELEIGH, KERR AND MAY LJJ

24, 25 AUGUST 1982

Injunction – Interlocutory – Principle governing grant – Triable issue – Serious question to be tried of which outcome uncertain – Not necessary for parties firmly to establish outcome of case – Whether defendant's deposed positive case necessarily to be preferred to plaintiff's case relying solely on inference.

Injunction – Interlocutory – Principle governing grant – Grant or refusal effectively ending action – Court's approach to grant or refusal – Avoidance of injustice – Grant of injunction having effect of giving judgment for plaintiff and denying defendant right to trial.

For the purposes of an application for an interlocutory injunction there is a triable issue between the parties if there is a serious question to be tried (ie one for which there is some supporting material) of which the outcome is uncertain. Accordingly, where the plaintiff's case relies solely on inference and the defendant has sworn a positive affidavit which, if true and accepted, destroys that inference, the court should not necessarily conclude that the plaintiff has failed to establish a triable issue, because on such an application it is not necessary for the parties to establish firmly the outcome of the case, and the mere fact that a party's case is deposed to does not make it incontrovertible (see p 230 *b* to *e*, p 231 *g h*, p 235 *d e*, p 236 *f* and p 238 *h*, post); dictum of Lord Greene MR in *Re Smith & Fawcett Ltd* [1942] 1 All ER at 545 distinguished.

Where the grant or refusal of an interlocutory injunction will have the practical effect of putting an end to the action, the court should approach the case on the broad principle of what it can do in its best endeavour to avoid injustice, and to balance the risk of doing an injustice to either party. In such a case the court should bear in mind that to grant the injunction sought by the plaintiff would mean giving him judgment in the case against the defendant without permitting the defendant the right of trial. Accordingly, the established guidelines requiring the court to look at the balance of convenience when deciding whether to grant or refuse an interlocutory injunction do not apply in such a case, since, whatever the strengths of either side, the defendant should not be precluded by the grant of an interlocutory injunction from disputing the plaintiff's claim at a trial (see p 232 *g h*, p 233 *c* to *g*, p 234 *e f*, p 236 *b* to *f*, p 237 *j* and p 238 *e* to *h*, post); *NWL Ltd v Woods* [1979] 3 All ER 614 applied; *American Cyanamid Co v Ethicon Ltd* [1975] 1 All ER 504 explained.

Notes

For the principles governing the grant of interlocutory injunctions, see 24 Halsbury's Laws (4th edn) paras 953–956, and for cases on the subject, see 28(2) Digest (Reissue) 968–980, 67–161.

Cases referred to in judgments

American Cyanamid Co v Ethicon Ltd [1975] 1 All ER 504, [1975] AC 396, [1975] 2 WLR 316, HL.

NWL Ltd v Woods [1979] 3 All ER 614, [1979] 1 WLR 1294, HL.

Smith & Fawcett Ltd, Re [1942] 1 All ER 542, [1942] Ch 304, CA.

Interlocutory appeal

The plaintiffs, James Cayne (suing on behalf of himself and all other share warrant holders who had served written requisitions on the defendant, Global Natural Resources plc (Global), dated 30 April 1982 pursuant to s 140 of the Companies Act 1948) and Munro Bank, appealed against the judgment of Sir Robert Megarry V-C given on 12

August 1982 whereby he dismissed the plaintiffs' motion for injunctions restraining Global until trial of the action or until further order from doing certain acts without first obtaining the approval of Global in general meeting. The facts are set out in the judgment of Eveleigh LJ.

Leonard Hoffmann QC and C Aldous for the plaintiffs.
Allan Heyman QC and T Stockdale for Global.

EVELEIGH LJ. My statement of the facts is taken almost verbatim from the judgment of Sir Robert Megarry V-C. This motion is brought by a Mr James Cayne on behalf of certain shareholders in Global Natural Resources plc (which I shall call 'Global') against Global; and a Mr Munro Bank is a co-plaintiff. Under the notice of motion, as amended, the plaintiffs seek injunctions restraining Global until trial of the action or further order from doing two acts without first obtaining the approval of Global in general meeting. The first act is completing or implementing an agreement made between Global, NRC Properties of Texas Inc (a Texas company which I shall call 'NRC Properties') and McFarlane Oil Co Inc dated 21 June 1982. I shall call this 'the June contract'. This provides for the merger of McFarlane Oil Co Inc (which I shall call 'McFarlane') into NRC Properties, which is a wholly-owned subsidiary of Global, in consideration of the shareholders in McFarlane becoming entitled to receive from Global 3·25m common one cent shares in Global, as well as certain other things. It is the issue of these 3·25m shares which is at the heart of the dispute. The second act which the plaintiffs seek to enjoin is the issuing and allotting of any shares in Global to shareholders of McFarlane or anyone else on their behalf or at their direction, or to anyone to whom such a shareholder has assigned his right to such shares. The shareholders on whose behalf Mr Cayne sues are members of what is termed a 'concert party', namely those who have joined in an agreement directed towards obtaining certain changes in the control of Global, whereas the second plaintiff, Mr Munro Bank, is a shareholder in Global who is not included in the concert party.

The case is riddled with complexities of one kind or another. Nevertheless, the central core of the motion can be put quite shortly. The plaintiffs' case, in broad outline, is that the issue of the 3·25m shares is being made in order to maintain the present directors in office. The holders of over 5% of the voting rights have required the company to give notice of resolutions to remove all the existing directors and to appoint others, and these are intended to be moved at the annual general meeting of Global, which is now fixed for 13 September next. If the 3·25m shares in Global are issued in time for the new shareholders to vote at the annual general meeting, they are likely, say the plaintiffs, to vote to support the existing board of Global, being the board which has entered into the June contract with McFarlane under which the shares are to be issued; and the plaintiffs contend that this was the dominant motive for Global entering into that contract. Global, on the other hand, deny this and say that the dominant motive was to strike a bargain which was for the true benefit of Global. The fact that this issue arises on a motion being heard in the long vacation is due to a number of factors, including the fact that the date for completion under the June contract is 17 August, that between 31 August and 4 September next McFarlane has the right, if an injunction is granted, to escape from the contract and that the date of Global's annual general meeting is 13 September next.

The provisions for completion are a little complex. In addition to completion, which the contract calls the 'closing', there is the 'effective time of the merger'. This is the close of business on the date the Secretary of State of Texas issues the relevant statutory certificate of merger, whereupon McFarlane will cease to exist and be merged into NRC Properties. The 'closing date', which as I have said is 17 August, is not immutable, for under section 1.3 of the contract closing is to take place on that date, or at such other time as the parties may mutually agree, or 'if any condition of the Closing has not been fulfilled or waived by such date, as soon as practicable thereafter, subject to the provisions of Section 10'. Section 10 of the contract allows the contract to be 'terminated and abandoned before the effective time of the Merger' by mutual consent, or by written notice. Such a notice may be given in two cases.

First, if the merger has 'not been consummated prior to 31 August 1982 solely by reason of a Legal Restraint' (as defined), McFarlane may give Global on or after 31 August 1982 and prior to 4 September 1982 (a period which in argument was called 'the window') written notice of McFarlane's election to terminate the contract. 'Legal restraint' is defined so as to include an injunction of a court in proceedings based on a claim that the dominant motive of Global's directors in making the contract was to gain an advantage in the dispute at the forthcoming annual general meeting (I summarise the effect of the relevant parts of section 9.2(c) and (d) of the contract). Second, either McFarlane or Global may give notice to the other if either the merger has not been made effective on or before 1 November 1982, or else, before then, 'a final non-appealable judgment' has been given by a court of competent jurisdiction enjoining the merger or the payment of the consideration to the McFarlane shareholders. (This, I think, must be the meaning of the provision; I discard a mysterious (x) and (y) in brackets in the relevant part of section 10 of the contract, which I suspect of being flotsam from an over-retentive memory of a word processor during the turmoil of drafting.)

Global is an unusual company. It was incorporated in England on 15 September 1970, became a public company on 25 June 1971 and in April 1982 it was reregistered under the Companies Act 1980 as a public limited company. Though its registered office is in Brighton, it is resident in Jersey, and its articles of association prevent it from carrying on business in the United Kingdom. Its share capital is $US250,000, divided into 25m common shares of one cent each. Nearly all the shares are bearer shares, transferable by delivery, and so there are special arrangements for shareholders to be able to vote by proxy at meetings by depositing their shares with a bank or certain other bodies. Only seven of the shares are registered, and of course this makes communication with shareholders a difficult matter. No annual general meeting may be held in the United Kingdom, and the company is to be managed by the board outside the United Kingdom; and board meetings may be held anywhere except in the United Kingdom. Notices may be served on the holders of bearer share warrants by advertising in Jersey, in a leading London daily newspaper and such other papers as the board decides.

The reason for these and other provisions lies in the origin of Global. It was formed to acquire certain assets from Fund of Funds Ltd and IOS Growth Fund Ltd (together called 'FOF') which were in liquidation in Canada. The main assets were shares in subsidiary companies owning oil and gas properties in North America, $20m in cash and 47% of the issued capital of a real estate company. For these assets Global issued a little over 20m common shares in Global to FOF in the form of a single share warrant to bearer. This was called the 'balance warrant'. FOF then declared a dividend for FOF shareholders of one Global share for each FOF share. FOF had some 112,000 shareholders in many parts of the world (it is said in some 120 countries, though mainly in Europe and North America), and, as they claimed their Global shares, Global share certificates were issued to them and the balance warrant was correspondingly reduced. The balance warrant was latterly held by a trustee, who traced claimants and had their claims verified.

By 30 June 1980 the balance warrant represented a little over 21% of the issued Global shares (some 4·77m shares), and the trustee was intending to sell all shares remaining after another year or so. The trustee since July 1977, a Mr Carter, was a director of Global, and he voted the shares in the balance warrant in accordance with directions given by the Supreme Court of Ontario. These votes supported the board. He had been appointed by the Ontario court, and when he died on 16 April 1982 that court appointed a Mr John Orr in his place. With the approval of that court, on 30 June 1982 Mr Orr sold 1·2m Global shares, all that then remained in the balance warrant except a few which he retained to meet costs. They were all bought for various clients by the New York firm of Bear Stearns & Co, stockbrokers and financial advisers. The present state of affairs is that out of the 25m Global shares that are authorised, over 21m have been issued, some 600,000 are retained to meet second stock options, 3·25m are to be issued under the June contract and some 3,000 remain unallocated and unissued. The 3·25m shares in dispute thus represent virtually the whole of the shares in Global which are unissued and available. Between them, the directors of Global have only some 67,000 shares in Global, whereas on 22 June last the concert party had over 1·2m shares.

Section 14 of the Companies Act 1980 was referred to by counsel for the plaintiffs at the hearing before Sir Robert Megarry V-C with the object of showing that the contract between Global and McFarlane had been entered into with undue haste. In its application to the present case, s 14 of that Act provides that the directors of Global may not allot shares in Global after 21 June 1982 without the authority of Global in general meeting unless this is done in pursuance of an offer or agreement made before 22 June 1982. The contract in this case, of course, was made on 21 June 1982 and it is admitted by the defendants that that date was deliberately chosen in order that the contract would not be subject to opposition by the shareholders at a general meeting. It was regarded to be in the best interests of the company, say the defendants, for that contract to be implemented as speedily as possible.

In addition, counsel for the plaintiffs referred to s 75 of the Companies Act 1980. That provides for the court to make an order if the affairs of the company are being or have been conducted in a manner which is unfairly prejudicial to the interests of some of the members, including the applicants, or if any act or proposed act or omission of the company is or would be prejudicial in this way.

On the fourth day of the hearing before Sir Robert Megarry V-C counsel for the plaintiffs made an application. A petition under s 75 had been issued on 2 August, although it has not been served, and the application made to the Vice-Chancellor was that he should treat the petition as being before him, sitting as he would have to for that purpose as a Companies Court, and, accepting an undertaking by the plaintiffs to issue and serve a notice of motion in the petition, treat the notice of motion as being before him and treat the evidence in the instant motion as also being evidence in the motion in the petition. This the Vice-Chancellor declined to do, but said that he would listen to argument based on s 75 in support of the subsisting motion on the footing that such argument might have a bearing on the exercise of the discretionary power to grant an injunction under the ordinary Chancery jurisdiction.

The matters relied on (and I state them simply to complete the facts and history of the case) in support of an argument under s 75 were based on an introduction document submitted to the Stock Exchange on behalf of Global in connection with the listing of Global shares on the Stock Exchange. The particular matter relied on was that an assertion was made in that document as follows:

'No issue will be made which would effectively alter the control of Global or the nature of its business without, in either case, the prior approval of the shareholders in general meeting.'

It was submitted, on behalf of the plaintiffs, that the issue contemplated amounted to 13·3% of the equity shareholding in Global, which indeed is correct, and that would be a breach of the provision.

It was accepted, taking the number of shares as a whole, that if every shareholder were to vote then, of course, the effective control would not be altered but the bearer shares were held by so many different people so difficult to contact that the attendance at a previous or previous general meetings had shown that the total votes cast was in the region of six million and in proportion to that kind of voting display the issue of the 3·25m contemplated in this case would effectively alter the control. It is also a fact of the case that those supporting the plaintiffs owned around 10% of the shares. The Stock Exchange did not take the view, apparently, that the effective control had been altered and Sir Robert Megarry V-C himself was not prepared to conclude that it had.

The second matter relied on was under the admission to listing document in connection with the Stock Exchange listing. A provision in that document stated that a transaction which showed a figure of 25% according to certain tests, for example a comparison of the net profits attributable to the assets acquired with the net profits of the acquiring company, should be made conditional on approval by the company in general meeting. The plaintiffs produced certain figures intending to show that the 25% was well exceeded.

This point was put to the Stock Exchange but it did not elicit any ruling. It seems that the Stock Exchange were taking the view that in reality this company, Global, had little connection with this country and that probably accounts for them giving no ruling on that matter.

Sir Robert Megarry V-C, in deciding whether or not the injunction should be granted restraining the company from issuing the shares to the McFarlane interest, came to the conclusion that the case with which he had to deal was not one which called for the application of the *Cyanamid* test of the balance of convenience. He clearly had in mind the passage in that case, *American Cyanamid Co v Ethicon Ltd* [1975] 1 All ER 504 at 510, [1975] AC 396 at 408, where Lord Diplock said:

'So unless the material available to the court at the hearing of the application for an interlocutory injunction fails to disclose that the plaintiff has any real prospect of succeeding in his claim for a permanent injunction at the trial, the court should go on to consider whether the balance of convenience lies in favour of granting or refusing the interlocutory relief that is sought.'

The Vice-Chancellor came to the conclusion that there was no such real prospect of success and, consequently, he had to go no further.

He further said, which is perhaps putting it in a slightly different way, that he could find no triable issue. He arrived at that conclusion on the following basis. He said that the affidavits put in on behalf of the plaintiffs stated facts which were, for the most part anyway, incontrovertible but they were quite unable to advance direct evidence that the intention of the directors in making this issue was for a wrongful purpose, namely to influence the shareholding and to retain their position on the board. That assertion would depend entirely on the inferences to be drawn from the facts as stated in the plaintiffs' affidavits. Whilst reading their affidavits in isolation that inference could clearly be drawn, none the less he had to have regard to the defendants' affidavits which stated, on oath, quite categorically that such was not the motive of the directors and that their motive was to conclude a business deal which they regarded as in the best interest of the company. He said that it would not be right, in his view, to come to a conclusion adverse to the defendants when they had sworn a positive affidavit and the plaintiffs' case relied on inferences.

He referred to a judgment of Lord Greene MR in *Re Smith & Fawcett Ltd* [1942] 1 All ER 542 at 545, [1942] Ch 304 at 308–309 and said:

'In this connection I should say something about *Re Smith & Fawcett Ltd*, on which [counsel for the defendants] placed much reliance. That case concerned the refusal of the directors of a private company to register a transfer of shares. Lord Greene MR said: "It is said that on the evidence before us we ought to infer that the directors here were purporting to exercise their power to refuse a transfer, not *bona fide* in the interests of the company, but for some collateral purpose—namely, the desire of the leading director to acquire part of the shares for himself at an under-value. Speaking for myself, I strongly dislike being asked on affidavit evidence alone to draw inferences as to the *bona fides* or *mala fides* of the actors . . . If it is desired to charge a deponent with having given an account of his motives and his reasons which is not the true account, then the person on whom the burden of proof lies should, in my judgment, take the ordinary and obvious course of requiring the deponent to submit himself to cross-examination."'

The Vice-Chancellor quoted that passage to the end.

In this case counsel for Global did offer to tender his witnesses for cross-examination and counsel for the plaintiffs refused that offer on more than one ground. He said, and rightly so, that he had not the full ammunition that he would wish to have for such cross-examination, that he would be much better prepared when discovery had taken place completely and that he did not regard it as incumbent on him to cross-examine the directors because, he said, on the authority of the *Cyanamid* case that would amount to an attempt to try the issue and *Cyanamid* had made it clear that such a course should not be pursued. It was no part of a party to a motion of this kind to establish firmly the outcome of the case.

Sir Robert Megarry V-C undoubtedly was influenced by the lack of cross-examination and he followed the line indicated by Lord Greene MR. For myself, I am not of the view that Lord Greene MR's words are applicable to an application such as the present case. He was dealing, it seems to me, with a final matter. It was an application for the rectification of the register. It was not an interlocutory application, so the court had to make a final decision on the merits. It was that task which Lord Greene MR found distasteful to have to do on untested affidavits which, in effect, were in conflict.

In the present case, if this is to be approached as one in which a triable issue has to be established, I myself would come to the conclusion that there was here a triable case. The plaintiffs' evidence, as I have said, clearly pointed to the inference which they asked the court to draw. Global's evidence, if true and accepted, of course clearly destroyed that inference. But the great question that has to be determined is whether the defendants' case is accepted or not. The mere fact it is deposed to does not make it incontrovertible. Therefore, when the evidence is not accepted by the plaintiffs, I am left in doubt as to the outcome of the trial on that issue. If I am in doubt and if the issue seems to be one that is not frivolous, in other words is one for which there is supporting material, then I would conclude that there is a triable issue. So on that point I would respectfully disagree with the conclusion arrived at by the Vice-Chancellor.

But that is not the end of it because he then went on to consider the case on the basis that he was wrong in coming to that conclusion. He said that this is a case in which the loss to Global would be difficult to assess. He said it was a case where McFarlane, the other contracting party, might exercise its right to be released from the contract as it would be entitled to do in the event of an injunction being granted. But he said that damages would also be difficult to assess on the plaintiffs' side. He then said:

'It seems to me that the adequacy of the remedy in damages available to the parties is at least doubtful [he was there using the words of Lord Diplock in the *Cyanamid* case] and so I must consider the balance of convenience. The refusal of an interlocutory injunction, said [counsel for the plaintiffs], would inflict two kinds of irreparable loss on the plaintiffs. They would be deprived of their right to elect a new board of directors, and they would see Global, in which they hold shares, carrying out what they contend to be a bad bargain with McFarlane. They would, however, amend their writ and seek to rectify the register so as to set aside the issue of the 3·25m shares, though this might not succeed. Further, nobody at this stage can say what the result of the voting at the annual general meeting will be; various forms of publicity, including publicity about this motion, may materially swell the ranks of those attending the meeting, at least by proxy. If on the other hand an interlocutory injunction were to be granted, this at least would put the completion of the June contract in doubt, and very possibly more than that. There is at least some evidence that McFarlane could exercise their right to withdraw, and there is also much evidence that the transaction is very much in the interests of Global; and that, of course, is a matter for the directors to judge. Apart from any loss of a desirable acquisition, there would be the waste of much time and money spent on arranging the transaction. If one attempts to weigh these and various incidental matters against each other, it is not at all easy to see which way the balance tilts. One is far from comparing like with like. If in ascertaining the balance of convenience one is entitled to put into the scales the plaintiffs' prospects of success or failure, in accordance with the conclusion that I reached in discussing *NWL Ltd v Woods* [1979] 3 All ER 614, [1979] 1 WLR 1294, then I think that this brings the balance down on the side of Global. If this cannot be done, then the *Cyanamid* case states that it is a counsel of prudence to preserve the status quo. The status quo in the present case was little discussed in argument, and it is not easy to determine what it is. In one sense, the status quo is represented by the June contract, made about ten days before the issue of the writ and the notice of motion. In another sense, the status quo is that of the 3·25m shares in Global being unissued and uncommitted, as they were before the June contract was made. The latter seems the preferable view. Yet, if that is so, the grant of an interlocutory injunction does not seem to fall within the *Cyanamid* concept of preserving the status quo; for that is based on the "only effect of the interlocutory injunction" if the defendant succeeds at the trial being "to postpone the date at which he is able to embark on a course of action which he has not previously found it necessary to undertake" (see the *Cyanamid* case [1975] 1 All ER 504 at 511, [1975] AC 396 at 408). With the possibility or probability of McFarlane withdrawing from the contract if an injunction is granted, it does not seem to me that there could be said to be no more than a mere postponement of the merger. I do not think that the maintenance of the status quo provides much assistance in the present case. If that is so, then once more the relative strength of each party's case may be considered.'

He went on to say that he had loyally tried to apply the *Cyanamid* principle to this case. He found it difficult to do so and thought that this was an exceptional kind of case where it ought to be permissible for the judge to take a broad view. He said:

'Where the contention is that inferences from the facts show some wrongdoing on the defendants' part, I hope that *Cyanamid* will not preclude the court from expressing some view on the extent to which those inferences are met by the affidavits. Oath against oath is one thing, a mere inference against an oath is another. At any rate, if I am permitted to view this motion broadly, my view of it, regarded as a whole, is the same, though firmer and clearer, as that to which I have struggled by applying the *Cyanamid* process. Whichever way the matter is regarded, in the exercise of my discretion I would dismiss the motion.'

He had concluded then, first, that this was not a case where there was a triable issue and therefore the application failed in limine. If he was wrong about that, then on the balance of convenience he found it came down in favour of Global. He was influenced in that conclusion by his view of the prospects of success. Finally, he approached it on a broad front and said in the exercise of his discretion this was not an appropriate case for an injunction.

The first ground of appeal as appears from the notice of appeal is to the effect that—

'The Learned Judge was wrong in holding that the Affidavit evidence before him did not show that there was a "serious question to be tried" and that the Plaintiffs "have a real prospect of succeeding" in their claim to an injunction at the trial . . .'

As I have said, I for my part would uphold that ground of appeal, that is to say to the extent of saying I find here that there is a triable issue. I would not go so far on the facts of this case as to say that there was established a real prospect of success if that means something more. As I have said, I simply do not know.

Then the second ground of appeal is that the judge (and this of course will apply to his alternative finding) wrongly concluded that Global could not be adequately compensated in damages for any loss which might result at the trial if it appeared that the plaintiffs were not entitled to the injunction sought. It was alleged, and this court was told, that a guarantee would be obtainable to support a cross-undertaking in damages.

The third ground was that the judge wrongly concluded that the motion fell within *NWL Ltd v Woods* [1979] 3 All ER 614, [1979] 1 WLR 1294.

For myself, I would not regard the cases on either side as being ones where it would be absolutely impossible to arrive at a figure for damages with the court, in the hallowed words of so many judgments, doing the best it could to arrive at a figure. But I do share the view of Sir Robert Megarry V-C and I do not think he put it any higher, that assessment would be extremely difficult on both sides.

I now turn to the third ground, that in the Vice-Chancellor's alternative finding he wrongly concluded that this case fell within the spirit of *NWL Ltd v Woods*. The view that the Vice-Chancellor took on the facts was this. If an injunction was granted to the plaintiffs, that would be an end to the substance of the matter and the injunction would not in effect amount to a holding operation: it would be giving the plaintiffs all that they came to the court to seek, namely their injunction, and when the time came for trial there would be no point in a trial because the object of the plaintiffs would have been achieved seeing that the annual general meeting would have been held. He said:

'In the present case, what really matters to the parties is whether or not the 3·25m shares in Global should be issued; and the possibility of proceeding to trial for damages is but a pale shadow of the real claim.'

With that I agree. If the injunction is granted the general meeting will be the next step. The plaintiffs will succeed or they will not succeed in mustering the support that they seek to remove the directors from the board. If an injunction is refused then the agreement will be implemented and there will be no point in seeking an injunction thereafter. It will not be possible to unscramble the situation, so that whichever way this decision goes it seems highly likely that it will finally determine the issue.

Counsel for the plaintiffs has submitted, however, that *NWL Ltd v Woods* does not govern the present case and we ought not to have regard to it. Largely, as I understand it, he bases that submission on the contention that Global can adequately be compensated in damages and that *NWL Ltd v Woods* was dealing with a case where the loss caused could not be met by an award of damages.

In *NWL Ltd v Woods* [1979] 3 All ER 614 at 626, [1979] 1 WLR 1294 at 1307 Lord Diplock said:

'Where, however, the grant or refusal of the interlocutory injunction will have the practical effect of putting an end to the action because the harm that will have been already caused to the losing party by its grant or its refusal is complete and of a kind for which money cannot constitute any worthwhile recompense, the degree of likelihood that the plaintiff would have succeeded in establishing his right to an injunction if the action had gone to trial is a factor to be brought into the balance by the judge in weighing the risks that injustice may result from his deciding the application one way rather than the other.'

It was that passage which Sir Robert Megarry V-C relied on.

In my view, whether this is a complete *NWL* case or not, it is not one which lends itself to the convenience test. The fact that there may be some further collateral matter to be tried and the fact that there cannot subsequently be a claim by Global for damages arising from the grant of an injunction does not mean that the case must be one which is suitable for the application of the balance of convenience guidelines laid down in the *Cyanamid* case. Having asked myself the various questions referred to in *Cyanamid*, I have reached the conclusion that this case is one that the court has to approach on a broad principle: what can the court do in its best endeavour to avoid injustice?

If one approaches the case in that way, it is necessary to look a little into the background of this application. It is submitted in this court that the plaintiffs are seeking to preserve the voting value of their shares; and indeed that is right, they are. But the voting value of the shares in this particular case, if taken in isolation, is really very little indeed. The shares which are intended to be issued to McFarlane are available for issue at some time or another. They may be legitimately issued, and indeed the directors say that they are being or are intended to be legitimately issued to McFarlane; but they may be legitimately issued to others and then the voting power of the plaintiffs' shares will to that extent be diminished. The importance of the voting power from the plaintiffs' point of view is not its value as voting power generally speaking but its value at the moment in order to enable the plaintiffs to achieve a particular object which they have in mind.

It is not necessary to go into all the evidence that one has seen on this matter. Suffice it
to say that it would appear that shareholders came on the scene introduced by the finance
house of Bear Stearns & Co in America with the view to persuading the company to
adopt a policy of realisation of assets. That policy is one to which the present board is
opposed, and that is what this application is all about. It is in order that the policy of the
board may be changed to accord with the wishes and intentions of the holders of 10% of
the equity. The court in that situation is not simply being asked to preserve the voting
rights or the strength of the plaintiffs (that cannot be done anyway) but to prevent an
issue of shares to McFarlane as part of a financial manoeuvre. The plaintiffs are perfectly
entitled to make such an application to this court and ask the court to enforce the
plaintiffs' rights. However, in an application for an injunction when the court is being
asked to exercise its discretion in enforcing those rights, regard may be had to all of the
circumstances. The real aim of Global is to change the policy of the board. We are not
concerned with the rights and wrongs of that policy. The question, it seems to me, is:
should the court exercise its discretion bearing in mind all the circumstances of the case,
when to decide in favour of the plaintiffs would mean giving them judgment in the case
against Global without permitting Global the right of trial? As stated that way, it seems
to me that that would be doing an injustice to the defendants.

On behalf of the plaintiffs it is submitted that to refuse to make an order will be
depriving the plaintiffs of the right to trial. It may well be that it will deprive the
plaintiffs of the opportunity on 13 September at the annual general meeting of achieving
their ends in the way in which they now might be able to achieve them; that is right,
but the plaintiffs come to this court and ask the court to exercise its discretion; it is not
Global which is making that application. It seems to me that, with the risk that this
decision will produce an injustice on one side or the other, it would be wrong to run the
risk of causing an injustice to a defendant who is being denied the right to trial where
the defence put forward has been substantiated by affidavits and a number of exhibits in
this case.

In saying that I wish to express no view as to the strength of that defence. What I can
safely say is that on the evidence before the court the case for the plaintiffs is not
overwhelming. It does not mean it is not a good one, but counsel for the plaintiffs quite
properly could not contend in this court that he was presenting an overwhelming case.
If that was so, it may be that the court would be entitled to come to a different conclusion,
even though it meant in effect depriving Global of a right to trial. But I do not have to
consider that. It seems to me that the risk of injustice to Global in this case is greater than
is the risk of doing an injustice to the plaintiffs. Should I be wrong in expressing the view
that this injunction should be refused, and if this injunction is indeed refused, then it
may be the matter will, with great difficulty, have to be ironed out in a claim for damages
against someone. I know not. For myself, I would have arrived at the same conclusion as
that arrived at by Sir Robert Megarry V-C, but, as I have said, not on the basis that no
triable issue was disclosed.

Since the matter came before the Vice-Chancellor there have been proceedings in the
United States. An application was made by a Mr Warner, one only of the plaintiffs
represented in this case, although a substantial shareholder, on 23 August (that is to say
three days ago) to a federal circuit judge in Cincinnati asking for the same kind of
injunction or order as has been prayed in the Chancery Division. The grounds put
forward contained those grounds submitted on behalf of the plaintiffs in this case and a
further ground which rested on an alleged violation that this transaction would entail an
infringement of the American Securities Exchange Act 1934. An order was made which
restrained the issue of these shares, and that order (which we are told is being appealed,
if that is the right word, in the United States) as it stands is effective until midnight of 3
September. Counsel for the plaintiffs has asked this court to consider an amended
application, namely that this court should grant an injunction to supplement, as it were,
the American situation and to run from 3 September.

It seems to me that that is something we are quite unable to do and which would be quite improper to do. It is not the role of this court to supplement the decision of the American court. That court is seised of the matter. If a court should come to the conclusion that the order was wrongly made and the injunction is lifted before 3 September, that will be a matter for the American court. It seems to me it would be wholly wrong for this court to say that we ourselves would not have granted the injunction, but because an American court has made an order we will grant a different kind of injunction to take effect if the American court then changes its mind and thinks that there should not be an injunction. It perhaps is a little unfair to counsel for the plaintiffs to express my opinion in that way because his argument ran on the lines that, as the American court has made an order, that affected Global's argument that should this court make an order McFarlane could escape through the window. He said that argument is no longer open to counsel for Global because McFarlane may escape on the strength of the American order.

However, we do not know what is going to happen in the United States in the course of the next few days, and for my part I think that it is right to decide this case without regard to what has happened in America. Counsel for Global has asked us to say that we should use the American application as a factor to be taken into consideration in this case in that it meant that the plaintiffs would not come before this court with clean hands. For myself I would not be prepared to reach such a conclusion, certainly in relation to the majority of the plaintiffs anyway in this case, and I do not find it necessary to deal further with that matter.

For the reasons which I have stated I would support the conclusion arrived at by Sir Robert Megarry V-C and I would dismiss this appeal.

KERR LJ. I agree that this appeal must be dismissed. In the same way as Sir Robert Megarry V-C and Eveleigh LJ, I do not regard this case as one which falls within the mould of the decision of the House of Lords in *American Cyanamid Co v Ethicon Ltd* [1975] 1 All ER 504, [1975] AC 396. Nor do I regard that decision as going further than to lay down guidelines in situations where two prerequisites are present.

The first, as stated by Lord Diplock, is that the question whether to grant or refuse an interlocutory injunction has been placed into a state of balance to the extent that the court can see that the plaintiffs' case raises a serious issue to be tried. If the plaintiffs fail at that point, then clearly there is no case for an injunction, and obviously the *Cyanamid* guidelines cannot come into play.

The second prerequisite, as it seems to me, is that a trial is in fact likely to take place, in the sense that the plaintiffs' case shows that they are genuinely concerned to pursue their claim to trial, and that they are seeking the injunction as a means of a holding operation pending the trial. It is only in such cases, in my view, that the decision is any guide, though undoubtedly a valuable one, to the problem whether or not the plaintiffs should be protected by an injunction; and it is to be noted that this was indeed the position in the *Cyanamid* case itself. It must also be remembered that the grant or refusal of an injunction is ultimately a matter of statutory discretion, and that the powers of the courts in this regard cannot be fettered by decisions in general terms, when the facts of cases will vary infinitely.

It may well be self-evident that the decision in *Cyanamid* cannot be treated as laying down rules of law which are applicable to all cases in which an interlocutory injunction is claimed, but it may be helpful to mention two matters in this regard. First, a literal application of the well-known passage in the speech of Lord Diplock (see [1975] 1 All ER 504 at 510, [1975] AC 396 at 408) would lead to the result that whenever a plaintiff puts forward a serious issue to be tried, and whenever he is also able to show that any inconvenience, let alone injustice, to the defendant by the grant of an injunction is capable of being compensated in damages against the plaintiff's cross-undertaking, the court would be bound to grant an injunction. This was virtually the plaintiffs' submission to this court, but it cannot possibly have been Lord Diplock's intention. The question whether the defendant can be adequately compensated in damages normally only arises

if the case is in fact taken to trial by the plaintiff. True, if the plaintiff does not do so, the
defendant could still claim damages against the plaintiff's cross-undertaking on the
ground that no injunction should ever have been granted. But this is no answer, since it
is for the plaintiff to make out a case for the exercise of the court's discretion in his
favour; and, in any event, defendants rarely proceed to a trial of issues whose investigation
they had not sought, but were concerned to resist. The test for the application of *Cyanamid*
is therefore whether the case is one where the court can see that it is likely to go to trial
at the instance of the plaintiffs, and whether the grant of an injunction is therefore
appropriate or not, as a way of holding the situation in the interim.

The second matter, apart from other cases in which the decision in *Cyanamid* has
already been distinguished, is that it was distinguished by Lord Diplock himself in *NWL
Ltd v Woods* [1979] 3 All ER 614, [1979] 1 WLR 1294, to which Eveleigh LJ has already
referred. Lord Diplock distinguished *Cyanamid* because the contest about the grant or
refusal of an interlocutory injunction was effectively the only contest between the parties,
since it was clear that the action would never proceed to trial. The fact that in that case
the court's approach to the grant or refusal of an interlocutory injunction was prescribed
by statute (see s 17(2) of the Trades Union and Labour Relations Act 1974) does not affect
the matter; nor was it put on that basis by Lord Diplock himself when he placed the
decision in *Cyanamid* in its proper perspective in contrast to situations such as in that case.

In *NWL Ltd v Woods* the outcome on the merits was easily foreseeable, and indeed
Lord Diplock regarded it as a 'virtual certainty' (see [1979] 3 All ER 614 at 626, [1979] 1
WLR 1294 at 1307). In the present case this is not so. The respective contentions of the
parties on the merits are much more evenly balanced. I agree with Eveleigh LJ that there
is clearly a triable issue, and to that extent I respectfully differ from the views expressed
by Sir Robert Megarry V-C. There is a serious question to be tried of which the outcome
is uncertain. To that extent the present case is different from *NWL Ltd v Woods*. But,
nevertheless, it lies much closer to that case than to *Cyanamid*, when one comes to the
question how the court's discretion should be exercised.

The practical realities in this regard are that, if the plaintiffs succeed in obtaining an
injunction, they will never take this case to trial. The reasons are easy to see. This is a
contest which centres on the respective voting power of the plaintiffs on the one hand
and of the present board of directors on the other. This contest will be fought out at the
annual general meeting in Jersey on 13 September next. The plaintiffs want to remove
the present directors and put themselves into their place. The present directors, naturally,
wish to retain their position.

Each side regards the voting power created by the additional 13% of shares proposed
to be issued to McFarlane as potentially decisive in that contest, though nobody knows
for certain whether it will be or not. However, for the purpose of deciding whether or
not to grant an injunction, it seems to me that this court must assume, as do both parties,
that this additional voting power may well prove to be decisive.

On that basis the realities are the following. If an injunction is granted, the plaintiffs
may well become, or become able to control, the new board of directors. They will then
manage and represent the company. At that point it seems to me to be quite inconceivable
that they would continue the present proceedings to trial against the company itself. In
effect, as counsel for the defendant, Global, said, they would then be in the position of
being both plaintiff and defendant, and it could hardly be imagined that they would
consider it to be in the interests of the company, or of the general body of shareholders,
to pursue these proceedings against the company. To do so would be a self-inflicted
blood-letting in public. In that connection it must be remembered that, for reasons
which we do not know, the present directors are not defendants to these proceedings.
The sole defendant is the company itself. What has to be considered in envisaging the
realities of the position if an injunction is granted is therefore whether or not the new
board of directors, ie effectively the plaintiffs on the present prospects of the outcome of
the battle of votes, would then continue this action against the company itself. I cannot
see this happening for one moment.

Of course, the plaintiffs might then sue the former board of directors on one basis or another. But that is irrelevant, because they are not defendants; and it would have to be   *a*
in different proceedings, which might or might not take place. The plaintiffs might also seek to undo the present directors' acts by means of other kinds of proceedings, such as their petition under s 75 of the Companies Act 1980 (though that seems equally unreal), or by means of the petition to rectify the register in order to set aside the issue of 13% of the shares to McFarlane.

I doubt whether any of these things would happen; but, whether they happen or not,   *b*
this action is never likely to be taken to trial if the plaintiffs obtain an injunction. On the other hand, if an injunction is refused, then the plaintiffs may well decide to pursue this action, as well as the other remedies mentioned above, even if they lose the battle at the annual general meeting. But the overriding consideration for present purposes is that, if an injunction is granted, the effective contest between the parties is likely to have been finally decided summarily in favour of the plaintiffs.   *c*

This being the position, the question is then whether, on the material before the court, the plaintiffs can justify such a result at this stage. As was pointed out by Eveleigh LJ during the argument, what the plaintiffs are in effect asking is for summary judgment in their favour. Admittedly, the plaintiffs have strong inferences about the defendants' real motives on their side. There are considerable grounds for suspicion. But Global has strong evidence on oath on its side, and, when this is read together with the exhibits, it is   *d*
quite clear that Global has a fully arguable case, which it is entitled to have tested on its merits at a full trial.

As was pointed out during argument, if this position were viewed as an application for summary judgment under RSC Ord 14, then it would be clear beyond argument that Global must be given unconditional leave to defend, because it would obviously be entitled to a full trial. However, the grant of an injunction would preclude this, so far as   *e*
can be foreseen at present, for the reasons already stated.

In these circumstances it seems to me that it would be wholly wrong for this court, in effect, to decide the entire contest between the parties summarily in the plaintiffs' favour on the untested material before us. This does not present any overwhelming balance on the merits in the plaintiffs' favour, or any other overriding ground for an immediate injunction without a trial. There is only a triable issue whose outcome is doubtful; and   *f*
that issue should be tried and not pre-empted.

The only other matter to be mentioned concerns the new development, since the hearing before Sir Robert Megarry V-C, of the proceedings in the United States District Court in Cincinnati, Ohio. It seems to me that these proceedings cannot be taken into account in one way or another. We do not know whether the present restraint will continue beyond 3 September and be still in force on 13 September. Nor do we know   *g*
whether the American courts, if the matter goes to appeal in some form or another, might not take a similar line to that taken by this court for the reasons explained in our judgments.

In that connection it is obviously not for this court to question the propriety of a plaintiff in these proceedings (as Mr Warner admittedly is, even though his motion in the District Court quite wrongly states that he is not) to institute parallel proceedings   *h*
under legislation in force in the United States, on the basis of allegations and evidential material which largely cover precisely the same ground. However, it is to be noted that the District Court did not have before it any adequate or proper information about the state of the proceedings in this country in so far as that may be relevant. Thus, it seems astonishing, not to use a stronger epithet, that the only reference to these proceedings in Mr Warner's motion should have been that there is an injunction in force here which   *j*
may be lifted today; as indeed it is. The true state of affairs, which has not so far been disclosed in those proceedings, is that this case was fully argued on the merits before Sir Robert Megarry V-C, for six days, on grounds which are virtually identical to those which are now put forward in the American proceedings, but that the decision was clearly against the grant of an injunction in a lengthy and closely reasoned judgment.

That was nowhere mentioned. The Vice-Chancellor then only granted an injunction for
a a few days, as is customary in our courts, in order to give an opportunity to the
unsuccessful plaintiffs to appeal to this court. Yet that was the only reference in the
motion to the position concerning an injunction in the English courts. The plaintiffs'
strictures of the present directors may well be fully justified. On the other hand, it is also
clear from the evidence that Bear Stearns & Co, the moving spirit behind the plaintiffs,
would have found it possible to take a much more charitable view if they had been
b appointed as financial advisers to Global, as they suggested. They said that they would in
that event see their way to cast all their votes in line with the present board. There may
not be much to choose between the parties on the ethical plane. But there is an old adage
about asking for equity with clean hands.

When the American courts are apprised of the full situation, they may take a different
view from that taken by Judge Spiegel; or they may not. It is quite impossible for this
c court to speculate about the likely outcome of the American proceedings, or what may
be the position in that regard on 13 September. We must therefore decide this case quite
independently from the American proceedings. For the reasons which I have stated I am
left in no doubt that in our courts an interlocutory injunction must be refused, and that
accordingly this appeal must be dismissed.

d
MAY LJ. I too agree that this appeal should be dismissed. For my part I wish only to
add a few comments on the well-known decision in *American Cyanamid Co v Ethicon Ltd*
[1975] 1 All ER 504, [1975] AC 396, to which Eveleigh and Kerr LJJ have referred, and
on its application to the present case.

A consideration of that authority formed a substantial part of the judgment of Sir
Robert Megarry V-C. In particular, in the course of that judgment, he considered
e whether the decision in *Cyanamid* 'in its original form' applied or whether this motion
fell to be decided on those principles as further explained and applied to the special
factors of the later case of *NWL Ltd v Woods* [1979] 3 All ER 614, [1979] 1 WLR 1294, to
which Eveleigh and Kerr LJJ have also referred.

Sir Robert Megarry V-C also reminded us once again that words in a judgment ought
f not, however eminent the judge, to be construed as if they were an Act of Parliament.
Respectfully I entirely agree. I think that one must be very careful to apply the relevant
passages from Lord Diplock's familiar speech in the *Cyanamid* case not as rules but only
as guidelines, which is what I am certain Lord Diplock intended them to be.

Further, in the *Cyanamid* case there was a serious question to be tried between the
parties, which could only be resolved by a trial. It was clearly contemplated that there
g would be a trial. The application for the interlocutory injunction was merely a holding
operation pending that contemplated trial. To support that assertion, I need only refer to
the well-known passage in the *Cyanamid* case [1975] 1 All ER 504 at 510, [1975] AC 396
at 408 where, in stating the guidelines based on the adequacy of damages as a remedy,
Lord Diplock specifically directed attention to the possible result of a postulated trial,
first one way and then the other. It is only thereafter, if damages after a trial are thought
h to be inadequate, that one is then enjoined to look at what is described as the 'balance of
convenience'. That is the phrase which, of course, is always used in this type of
application. It is, if I may say so, a useful shorthand, but in truth, and as Lord Diplock
himself made clear in the *NWL* case, the balance that one is seeking to make is more
fundamental, more weighty, than mere 'convenience'. I think that it is quite clear from
both cases that, although the phrase may well be substantially less elegant, the 'balance of
the risk of doing an injustice' better describes the process involved. Again, I need only
j refer to a very brief passage from the speech of Lord Diplock in the *NWL* case [1979] 3
All ER 614 at 625, [1979] 1 WLR 1294 at 1306.

In that latter case such a balancing process necessarily resulted in the court deciding
that no interlocutory injunction should be granted, because when it was done it became
quite clear that there was a substantially greater risk of injustice to the defendant as the

statutory defence available to him was so well founded that there was little question but that he would succeed at the trial.

In the present case before us, we have not concerned ourselves, and it would not be right for us to concern ourselves, with the weight of either side's case. This may indeed have been one of the reasons why Sir Robert Megarry V-C was as troubled about the application of the *Cyanamid* decision as he was. However, for the reasons already given by Eveleigh and Kerr LJJ, not based on the strength of the respective arguments and evidence before us, this instant case is also one in which the grant or refusal of an injunction will in effect dispose of the action in favour of the successful party.

At this juncture I quote another short passage from the speech of Lord Diplock in the *NWL* case [1979] 3 All ER 614 at 625, [1979] 1 WLR 1294 at 1306, where he said:

'. . . when properly understood, there is in my view nothing in the decision of this House in *American Cyanamid v Ethicon Ltd* to suggest that in considering whether or not to grant an interlocutory injunction the judge ought not to give full weight to all the practical realities of the situation to which the injunction will apply. *American Cyanamid Co v Ethicon Ltd*, which enjoins the judge on an application for an interlocutory injunction to direct his attention to the balance of convenience as soon as he has satisfied himself that there is a serious question to be tried, was not dealing with a case in which the grant or refusal of an injunction at that stage would, in effect, dispose of the action finally in favour of whichever party was successful in the application, because there would be nothing left on which it was in the unsuccessful party's interest to proceed to trial.'

With those considerations in mind, I do not think that in cases such as the present, whatever the strengths on either side, where the decision on an interlocutory application for an injunction will effectively dispose of the claim, the court can legitimately, nor is it bound, to apply the *Cyanamid* guidelines, which, as I have already said, I think are based on the proposition that there will be a proper trial at a later stage when the rights of the parties will be determined.

It may well be that it is the same ultimate consideration which the court has in mind, namely the question whether it is likely to do an injustice. Where a plaintiff brings an action for an injunction, I think that it is, in general, an injustice to grant one at an interlocutory stage if this effectively precludes a defendant from the opportunity of having his rights determined in a full trial. There may be cases where the plaintiff's evidence is so strong that to refuse an injunction and to allow the case to go through to trial would be an unnecessary waste of time and expense and indeed do an overwhelming injustice to the plaintiff. But those cases would, in my judgment, be exceptional.

In general, as I say, where a plaintiff brings an action and in it seeks an interlocutory injunction on the basis that the defendant has breached the former's rights, then justice requires that that defendant should be entitled to dispute the plaintiff's claim at a trial, and if the grant of the injunction would preclude this then it should not be granted on an interlocutory basis.

In so far as the supervening litigation in Cincinnati is concerned, I agree entirely with the comments which Kerr LJ has made about and in connection with it, and I do not wish to add anything to what he has said. For those reasons, and for those already adumbrated by Eveleigh and Kerr LJJ, I agree that this appeal should be dismissed.

Appeal dismissed.

Solicitors: *Herbert Smith & Co* (for the plaintiffs); *Theodore Goddard & Co* (for Global).

Mary Rose Plummer   Barrister.

Hart v Aga Khan Foundation (UK)

QUEEN'S BENCH DIVISION

LLOYD J SITTING WITH MASTER CLEWS AND MR J M BRADSHAW AS ASSESSORS

23 JUNE, 7 JULY 1983

Costs – Taxation – Litigant appearing in person – Claim for costs for expenditure of time in appearing in court – Claim for costs for expenditure of time in preparing case – Litigant suffering pecuniary loss – Litigant allowed two-thirds of amount allowed to a solicitor for similar work – High Court proceedings – Whether litigant allowed notional costs of instructing counsel – Whether litigant allowed notional counsel's fees – Whether litigant can claim costs based on amount allowed to a solicitor if part of preparatory done in leisure time – Whether in calculating notional amount allowable to a solicitor taxation should proceed on basis of time a solicitor would spend or time actually spent by litigant – RSC Ord 62, r 28A(1)(2)(3).

The following principles are applicable in taxing the costs of a litigant in person under RSC Ord 62, r 28A[a]—

(1) Where the litigant has suffered pecuniary loss and the costs allowable for time spent in court are, by virtue r 28A(1) and (2), to be taxed on the basis of two-thirds of the amount that would have been allowable if a solicitor had been employed, the notional costs of a solicitor in instructing counsel to appear in the High Court, including counsel's fees, are not allowable on the taxation, because (a) r 28A(1) and (2) refers only to the litigant being notionally represented by 'a solicitor' and not by a solicitor and counsel, and (b) counsel's fees are technically a disbursement made by a solicitor rather than 'work' done by him (see p 241 *f* to p 242 *b*, post).

(2) Where the litigant does part of the preparatory work for his case in his working time (and thereby loses wages or salary) and part of the preparatory work in his leisure time, he is entitled to recover up to two-thirds of what would have been allowed to a solicitor for the preparatory work done in his working time and is restricted, by virtue of r 28A(3), to recovering £2 an hour for the preparatory work done in his leisure time (see p 242 *f g*, post).

(3) In calculating, for the purposes of r 28A(2), two-thirds of the amount that would have been allowable if the litigant had been represented by a solicitor, the taxation should proceed on the basis of the time a solicitor would have spent doing the work rather than on the basis of the time actually spent by the litigant (see p 242 *g h*, post).

Notes

For a litigant in person's costs, see 37 Halsbury's Laws (4th edn) para 750.

Cases referred to in judgment

London Scottish Benefit Society v Chorley (1884) 13 QBD 872, [1881–5] All ER Rep 1111.
Parikh v Midland Bank Ltd [1982] CA Bound Transcript 101.

Summons to review taxation

On 13 June 1981 the plaintiff, Diane Lavinia Macleod-Johnstone Hart, a litigant in person, obtained judgment in her action against the defendants, the Aga Khan Foundation (UK), for £750 damages. The defendants were ordered to pay the plaintiff's costs of the action taxed on the High Court scale. On 24 June 1982 Master Berkeley taxed the plaintiff's bill of costs. On 2 July the plaintiff lodged two objections to the taxation. Her first objection related to item 8 in the bill, namely costs of attending court, for which pursuant to RSC Ord 62, r 28A(2) the master had allowed £83 per day as being two-thirds of what he would have allowed a solicitor on the notional basis that the plaintiff was

---

a   Rule 28A, so far as material, is set out at p 240 *j* to p 241 *b*, post

represented by a solicitor. The plaintiff's objection was that the master should also have
allowed under r 28A(2) two-thirds of a solicitor's notional cost of briefing leading and
junior counsel to appear in court. The second objection related to item 10 in the bill,
namely costs of preparation for the hearing, for which the master had allowed £1,025
pursuant to r 28A(2) and (3). The plaintiff's objection was that the master should have
allowed the plaintiff £4,474 for the costs of the preparatory work. On 15 December 1982
Master Berkeley gave his reasons for overruling the plaintiff's objections. By a summons
dated 23 December 1982 the plaintiff sought an order that her objections be allowed.
The summons was heard in chambers but judgment was given by Lloyd J in open court.
The facts are set out in the judgment.

The plaintiff appeared in person.
Mr T C Little, solicitor's clerk, for the defendants.

Cur adv vult

7 July. The following judgment was delivered.

LLOYD J. This is a summons to review a taxation by Master Berkeley in an action
brought by the plaintiff against the Aga Khan Foundation (UK), the defendants. The
plaintiff was successful in her action. She has at all stages acted as a litigant in person, as
she has on this appeal. Accordingly, the taxation has had to be conducted in accordance
with the special rules applicable in such cases.

Prior to the Litigants in Person (Costs and Expenses) Act 1975, a successful litigant in
person who was awarded his costs could recover his out-of-pocket expenses, but no more.
The purpose of the 1975 Act was to enable him to recover costs on a more generous basis.
The detailed provisions are set out in RSC Ord 62, r 28A. That rule gives rise to a number
of difficult questions of construction, on which I was told that there is no reported case.
Accordingly, at the suggestion of Master Clews, one of my assessors, and with the consent
of the parties, I am giving this judgment in open court.

The facts are briefly as follows. The plaintiff is an actress. She lives at 18 Thurloe Place,
London SW7. Immediately opposite her house there is a building on an island site known
as the Ismaili Centre. The building is not yet complete. It belongs to the defendants. On
21 November 1980 the plaintiff commenced an action against the defendants claiming
damages for nuisance arising out of the defendants' building activities on the site. She
also claimed an injunction.

The action came on before Boreham J in June 1981. It lasted 4½ days. At the end of the
trial, Boreham J gave judgment in favour of the plaintiff. He awarded her £750 damages,
together with her costs on the High Court scale.

In due course, the plaintiff prepared her bill of costs. For her attendance at the trial she
claimed £1,520 for the first day of the hearing, and £520 for the subsequent days making
£4,120 in all. In addition she says she spent a total of 214 hours preparing for the trial,
for which she has charged £4,474. These two items together come to £8,594. The
master has allowed a total of £1,443.

The plaintiff lodged objections, which were answered by the defendants. The
objections were heard on 2 November 1982, and overruled. The master was asked to
give his reasons which he did in a document dated 15 December 1982. The first objection
related to the plaintiff's costs of attending the hearing. The figures of £1,520 and £520
which I have already mentioned, are based on two-thirds of the notional cost of briefing
leading counsel and junior counsel, together with two-thirds of a daily attendance fee for
a solicitor. In his reasons the master says: 'Plainly, it would not be right to allow as a
disbursement counsel's brief fee that had not been incurred.'

RSC Ord 62, r 28A provides as follows:

'(1) On a taxation of the costs of a litigant in person there may, subject to the
provisions of this rule, be allowed such costs as would have been allowed if the work

a and disbursements to which the costs relate had been done by or made by a solicitor on the litigant's behalf.

(2) The amount allowed in respect of any item shall be such sum as the taxing officer thinks fit not exceeding, except in the case of a disbursement, two-thirds of the sum which in the opinion of the taxing officer would have been allowed in respect of that item if the litigant had been represented by a solicitor.

b (3) Where in the opinion of the taxing officer the litigant has not suffered any pecuniary loss in doing any work to which the costs relate, he shall not be allowed in respect of the time reasonably spent by him on the work more than £2 an hour ...'

As I have already said, these provisions give rise to a number of difficulties. Thus I am told that the question raised by the first objection, whether to include a notional brief fee c for counsel in calculating the ceiling under r 28A(2), has been the subject of differing views among taxing officers as well as judges.

On the one hand it is said that a solicitor would not be able to present a case himself in the High Court without briefing counsel, and therefore the cost of briefing counsel (and leading counsel where appropriate) should be included. If it be said that there is no justification for including a fee for counsel which has not in fact been incurred, the d answer would be that neither has the cost of retaining a solicitor been incurred: both are notional. Moreover, as the plaintiff herself emphasised, there is no apparent reason why an unsuccessful defendant should get off more lightly just because the successful plaintiff has conducted his or her own litigation in person.

These are strong arguments, but the arguments the other way are stronger. The whole object of an award for costs is to indemnify the successful party to a greater or lesser e extent against costs which he has in fact incurred. He cannot recover costs which he has not incurred.

To this general principle Parliament has provided a limited exception in the case of a litigant in person. Provided he has suffered pecuniary loss, he can recover for work which he has himself done up to two-thirds of what would have been allowed if that work had been done by a solicitor.

f I accept that the words in r 28A(2) 'if the litigant had been represented by a solicitor' are capable of a wider meaning. I agree that the notional exercise which the taxing officer is required to undertake might have involved an investigation of what would have happened if the litigant in person had retained a solicitor, and if the solicitor had instructed counsel, and so on. But in my judgment that is not the true construction of the rule. Rule 28A(2) must be read in the light of r 28A(1). There is a clear contrast g between work and disbursements. Disbursements are allowed in full, just as they were before the 1975 Act, provided they would have been allowed if incurred by a solicitor, and provided they are actually incurred by the litigant in person. Work, on the other hand, is treated as if it had been done by a solicitor, and is then allowed up to two-thirds of the appropriate rate. What a solicitor would have been allowed is, of course, notional; but there is no room for a notional disbursement. Otherwise one would get the absurd h position that the litigant in person would be allowed 100% of counsel's notional brief fee as a 'disbursement', but only two-thirds of the solicitor's notional fee for attendance. No doubt the reason why the litigant in person is allowed only up to two-thirds of what would have been allowed to a solicitor, is because the balance of one-third represents the solicitor's profit. It cannot have been intended that the litigant in person should recover the notional profit on the barrister's brief fee, but not the notional profit on the solicitor's j fee for attendance.

The plaintiff meets that difficulty by claiming only two-thirds of counsel's fees. But there is no warrant in the language of r 28A(1) or (2) for treating counsel's fees in that way. Under r 28A(1) the work is to be treated as if it had been done by a solicitor, not by solicitor and counsel. By the same token, r 28A(2) provides a ceiling of two-thirds of what would have been allowed if the litigant in person had been represented by a solicitor (and

I emphasise the word 'solicitor'). There is no reference to counsel in r 28A(2); the omission is not accidental.

Accordingly, I agree with Master Berkeley that notional counsel's fees should be excluded from the calculation, as should all other notional disbursements that would or might have been made by a solicitor, unless they are actually incurred by the litigant in person.

The second question of principle arises on r 28A(3). Where the litigant in person suffers no pecuniary loss at all, he cannot recover more than £2 an hour. Where he does all the work during time during which he otherwise would have been remunerated, he can recover up to two-thirds of what would have been allowed to a solicitor for doing that work. But what is the position when he does part of the work during what I will call working time, and part of the work during what I will call leisure time? One view is that if he suffers any pecuniary loss at all, in respect of any item of work, however small, then he should be able to recover in respect of that item up to the two-thirds limit under r 28A(2). That view is based on the double use of the word 'any' in r 28A(3). But I do not agree with that construction. It seems to me to go against the whole object of the rule.

As I have already mentioned, litigants in person were not, before the 1975 Act came into force, allowed anything for their time and trouble: only for their out-of-pocket expenses. The reason was stated by Bowen LJ in *London Scottish Benefit Society v Chorley* (1884) 13 QBD 872 at 877; cf [1881–5] All ER Rep 1111 at 1113. After referring to Coke's Institutes (2 Co Inst 288), Bowen LJ said:

> 'What does Lord Coke mean by these words? His meaning seems to be that only legal costs which the Court can measure are to be allowed, and that such legal costs are to be treated as expenses necessarily arising from the litigation and necessarily caused by the course which it takes. Professional skill and labour are recognised and can be measured by the law; private expenditure of labour and trouble by a layman cannot be measured. It depends on the zeal, the assiduity, or the nervousness of the individual.'

The 1975 Act makes an inroad on that principle. It effects a statutory compromise. So far as his working time is concerned, the litigant in person can now recover up to two-thirds of what would have been allowed to a solicitor, whatever his actual loss of earnings. Sometimes his opponent will gain from that compromise; sometimes he will lose. As for his leisure time, the compromise was that a litigant in person should be able to recover, but only for time reasonably spent, and then only up to the modest limit of £2 an hour. I can see no reason why work on an item done in leisure time should be subject to a different and higher limit just because some part of the work on that item was done in working time.

That leads on to the third and last point of principle, whether the time allowed in calculating the maximum under r 28A(2) is the time actually taken by the litigant in person in doing the work, or the time which would have been taken by a solicitor. The answer must, I think, be the time that would have been taken by a solicitor. This will of course involve an assessment by the taxing officer. But it is the sort of assessment to which taxing officers are well accustomed. Thus, assuming the item of work takes the litigant in person 40 hours of working time, but would have taken a solicitor only 10 hours, or its equivalent, then the overall limit for the item under r 28A(2) is 10 hours multiplied by two-thirds of the appropriate rate plus uplift. If the resulting rate is, for example, £20 per hour the maximum for that item would be £200. If, however, only half the work done by the litigant in person is done in working time and half in leisure time, then the limit under r 28A(2) is five hours at £20 per hour plus 20 hours at £2 per hour, making a total maximum of £140. Theoretically, on that approach, the limit under r 28A(3) might exceed the limit under r 28A(2). But it could not happen in practice, or only very rarely, because of the provision that it is only leisure time reasonably spent that counts towards the limit; apart from which the Court of Appeal has held in an unreported case, that the limit under r 28A(2) is an overall limit, however much time may have been reasonably spent by the litigant in person (see *Parikh v Midland Bank Ltd* [1982] CA Bound Transcript 101).

I can now return to the facts of the present case.

I have already dealt with objection (1). I have held that the master rightly disallowed two-thirds of the notional counsel's fees in arriving at a ceiling for item 8 of the bill of costs. What he did was to allow £83 a day, being two-thirds of what he would have allowed for attendance by a solicitor of partner's status. His approach was correct and there can be no possible criticism of his figure. Objection (2) relates to the time taken in preparation. This has been claimed under item 10 of the bill of costs at £20 an hour for 214 hours, making £4,474. The master allowed £1,025. He took the view that a solicitor would have taken no more than 40 hours for the work in question, giving a total under item 10, including mark-up, of £1,600 at the most. Two-thirds of that figure (which I accept) is the maximum which he could have allowed.

The master recognised that a litigant in person will take appreciably longer than a solicitor. Even so, he regarded 214 hours claimed by the plaintiff as being out of all proportion. Instead, he arrived at a total of 86 hours, of which he allowed 43 hours as working time at £15 an hour and 43 hours as leisure time at £2 an hour, making 725, to which he added £300 'loss of income from property', making £1,025 in all.

The plaintiff in her objections appears to accept the total of 86 hours, but says that the whole of the 86 hours should have been allowed at £15 an hour. At the hearing before me, however, she said that that was a mistake; and she wished to claim the full 214 hours. Having taken the advice of my assessors, I agree with the master's total of 86 hours. For the reasons which I have already given, I consider that the master was right in principle in seeking to divide the 86 hours between working time and leisure time. That division is necessarily somewhat arbitrary, particularly in the present case, where the plaintiff has no working time in the ordinary sense, but says that she lost a 12-week provincial tour, plus three weeks of rehearsals as a result of the impending litigation. I see no reason to disagree with the view the master took on the facts, save that I can see no justification for adding £300 for 'loss of income from property'. However, there is no cross-appeal in regard to that £300 by the defendants.

The total of £1,025 under item 10 seems to me generous, as it also seems to my assessors, and seemed to Master Berkeley. It represents just under two-thirds of £1,600 which would have been allowed if all the work had been done by a solicitor, which is thus the maximum under r 28A(2). The plaintiff has not made out her second objection, any more than she has made out her first. I would uphold the taxation by Master Berkeley, and dismiss the appeal.

Appeal dismissed.

Solicitors: *Masons* (for the defendants).

K Mydeen Esq   Barrister.

Burns v Burns

COURT OF APPEAL, CIVIL DIVISION

WALLER, FOX AND MAY LJJ

19, 25 MAY, 26 JULY 1983

Trust and trustee – Constructive trust – Unmarried couple – Principles applicable in determining beneficial interests in property – Man acquiring house in his sole name – Mistress not directly contributing to purchase price or mortgage instalments – Couple living in house with their children for 17 years – Mistress looking after well-being of family by performing domestic duties and caring for children – Whether mistress entitled to beneficial interest – Whether common intention that mistress was to have beneficial interest.

In 1961 the plaintiff, who was then aged 20, began living with a married man, the defendant, knowing that there was no prospect of his marrying her. Soon afterwards, she gave birth to their first child and gave up her employment, changed her name to the defendant's and was held out to their friends as his wife. In 1963, when she was expecting their second child, the defendant decided to buy a house in place of their rented accommodation, partly because that would be better use of his money. The house was purchased in his sole name and he provided the purchase price out of his own money and by way of a mortgage. The plaintiff made no direct contribution either to the purchase price or to the mortgage instalments. The couple lived in the house with their two children for 17 years. Until 1975 the plaintiff was unable to earn because she was bringing up the children but during that period she performed the domestic duties in the house as well as looking after the children. From 1975 she was able to take employment and to earn. Although the defendant gave her a generous housekeeping allowance and did not ask her to contribute to household expenses, she used her earnings to contribute towards the housekeeping expenses and to buy fixtures and fittings and consumer durables, such as a washing machine, for the house. She also redecorated the interior of the house. In 1980 the plaintiff left the defendant and brought proceedings against him claiming that she was entitled to a beneficial interest in the house by reason of her contributions to the household over the 17 years they had lived there and sought a declaration that the house was held by the defendant on a resulting trust for both parties beneficially in such shares as the court might determine. The judge held that the plaintiff was not entitled to any beneficial interest in the house. The plaintiff appealed.

Held – When an unmarried couple separated, the powers conferred by the Matrimonial Causes Act 1973 in relation to the division of the property of married couples on divorce did not apply, and accordingly the court had no jurisdiction to make an order on the basis of the fair and reasonable division of property. Instead, where property had been purchased in the man's sole name without the woman making any direct contribution to the purchase price or without the parties making an agreement or declaration regarding the beneficial interest in the property, there was a prima facie inference that the man was the sole legal and beneficial owner. That inference could only be displaced if the court could impute, from the conduct of the couple down to the date of their separation, a common intention that the woman was to have a beneficial interest in the property, and that in turn depended on whether the woman had made a substantial financial contribution towards the expenses of the couple's household which could be related to the acquisition of the property, eg where her financial contributions to the household expenses enabled the man to pay the mortgage instalments. The court would not impute a common intention that the plaintiff was to have a beneficial interest in the property merely from the fact that she had lived with the defendant for 19 years, had looked after the family's well-being by performing the domestic duties of the household and had brought up their children, or from the fact that she had bought chattels for the household out of her earnings and had redecorated the house. The plaintiff's appeal would therefore be dismissed (see p 250 *d* to p 251 *d* and *f* to *j*, p 252 *f* to p 253 *b* and *g* to p 254 *j*, p 255 *d* to *f*, p 256 *a b* and *h*, p 257 *c d*, p 258 *b* to *h*, p 263 *e f*, p 264 *h j* and p 265 *c* to *f*, post).

Pettitt v Pettitt [1969] 2 All ER 385, *Gissing v Gissing* [1970] 2 All ER 780, *Falconer v Falconer* [1970] 3 All ER 449, *Hazell v Hazell* [1972] 1 All ER 923 and *Richards v Dove* [1974] 1 All ER 888 applied.

Hall v Hall (1981) 3 FLR 379 and *Bernard v Josephs* [1982] 3 All ER 162 considered.

Notes

For resulting trusts arising out of joint transactions by an unmarried couple, see 38 Halsbury's Laws (3rd edn) 868–873, paras 1462–1469, and for cases on the subject, see 47 Digest (Repl) 127, 925–927.

For the Matrimonial Causes Act 1973, see 43 Halsbury's Statutes (3rd edn) 539.

Cases referred to in judgments

Appleton v Appleton [1965] 1 All ER 44, [1965] 1 WLR 25, CA.
Balfour v Balfour [1919] 2 KB 571, [1918–19] All ER Rep 860, CA.
Bernard v Josephs [1982] 3 All ER 162, [1982] Ch 391, [1982] 2 WLR 1052.
Button v Button [1968] 1 All ER 1064, [1968] 1 WLR 457, CA.
Cooke v Head [1972] 2 All ER 38, [1972] 1 WLR 518, CA.
Crisp v Mullings (1975) 239 EG 119, CA.
Davis Contractors Ltd v Fareham UDC [1956] 2 All ER 145, [1956] AC 696, [1956] 3 WLR 37, HL.
Diwell v Farnes [1959] 2 All ER 379, [1959] 1 WLR 624, CA.
Evers's Trust, Re, Papps v Evers [1980] 3 All ER 399, [1980] 1 WLR 1327, CA.
Eves v Eves [1975] 3 All ER 768, [1975] 1 WLR 1338, CA.
Falconer v Falconer [1970] 3 All ER 449, [1970] 1 WLR 1333, CA.
Gissing v Gissing [1970] 2 All ER 780, [1971] AC 886, [1970] 3 WLR 255, HL; rvsg [1969] 1 All ER 1043, [1969] 2 Ch 85, [1969] 2 WLR 525, CA.
Hall v Hall (1981) 3 FLR 379, CA.
Hazell v Hazell [1972] 1 All ER 923, [1972] 1 WLR 301, CA.
Pettitt v Pettitt [1969] 2 All ER 385, [1970] AC 777, [1969] 2 WLR 966, HL.
Richards v Dove [1974] 1 All ER 888.
Shirlaw v Southern Foundries (1926) *Ltd* [1939] 2 All ER 113, [1939] 2 KB 206, CA.
Tanner v Tanner [1975] 3 All ER 776, [1975] 1 WLR 1346, CA.
Ulrich v Ulrich and Felton [1968] 1 All ER 67, [1968] 1 WLR 180, CA.
Walker v Hall [1983] CA Bound Transcript 300.

Case also cited

Cantliff v Jenkins [1978] 1 All ER 836, [1978] QB 47, CA.

Appeal

By an originating summons dated 14 January 1981 the plaintiff, Valerie Burns, claimed a beneficial interest in the property known as 142 Osidge Lane, Southgate, London, the legal estate in fee simple in which was vested in the defendant, Patrick Burns, with whom the plaintiff had lived as man and wife for 19 years. By a judgment given on 1 March 1982 Dillon J dismissed the originating summons. The plaintiff appealed seeking an order that the property was held by the defendant on trust for the plaintiff and the defendant in such shares as the court might determine. The facts are set out in the judgment of Waller LJ.

Quintin Iwi for the plaintiff.
The defendant appeared in person.

Cur adv vult

29 July. The following judgments were delivered.

WALLER LJ. This is an appeal from a decision of Dillon J given on 1 March 1982 when he found that the plaintiff, Mrs Burns, had no interest in the house in which she and the defendant, Mr Burns, although not married, had lived together as man and wife for 17 years.

The parties started living together in the summer of 1961. At that time the plaintiff was aged 20 earning about £12 a week as a tailor. She left the accommodation of her parents and went to live with the defendant in a rented flat where a boy was born on 29 April 1962. The plaintiff was known as Mrs Burns. In 1963 when she was again pregnant she and the defendant decided to move to a house and the defendant bought the house the subject of these procedings in July 1963. It was in his name and he obtained £4,500 out of the total purchase price of £4,900 by mortgage. The second child was born on 9 October 1963. The plaintiff made a statutory declaration of change of name, her passport was in the name of Burns and their friends and acquaintances believed them to be married. The parties lived together until 1980 when the plaintiff left although relations had deteriorated in the previous two years. She could not earn any money when the children were small and it was not until 1975 that she made any appreciable money. When she did earn money she did not keep a separate account, it went in with her housekeeping allowance from the defendant. She did purchase certain fixtures and fittings for the house and material for sheets and bed covers and so on, and she also did some decorating, including wallpapering the house completely in 1977 or 1978. She also bought certain consumer durable goods such as a dishwasher, washing machine, tumble drier, a bed and some other furniture. The plaintiff submitted that these facts alone produced a resulting trust so that she is entitled to a share in the equity of the house and that the courts should recognise the changes in custom which have taken place over the past 10 or 20 years.

We have had to consider this case in the light of *Pettitt v Pettitt* [1969] 2 All ER 385, [1970] AC 777, a case concerning the interpretation of s 17 of the Married Women's Property Act 1882, and *Gissing v Gissing* [1970] 2 All ER 780, [1971] AC 886, a case concerning the application of s 53 of the Law of Property Act 1925. There have been certain developments since those two cases were decided.

(1) The Matrimonial Proceedings and Property Act 1970, which was passed on 29 May 1970 and came into force on 1 January 1971, empowered the court to make property adjustment orders. This power was re-enacted in the Matrimonial Causes Act 1973, s 24.

(2) There has been an increase in the number of decisions involving a man and woman living together without getting married. In *Cooke v Head* [1972] 2 All ER 38, [1972] 1 WLR 518 the Court of Appeal considered the case of a bungalow built by such a couple and considered what the interests of the woman were as against the man. There is also *Richards v Dove* [1974] 1 All ER 888, a decision of Walton J against the mistress. In *Eves v Eves* [1975] 3 All ER 768, [1975] 1 WLR 1338, where this court held that there was a constructive trust in favour of the mistress, Brightman J, with whom Browne LJ agreed, drew the inference that the plaintiff was entitled to have some beneficial interest in return for her labour towards the reparation of a house and the considerable physical work she had done when the house was being prepared. See also *Tanner v Tanner* [1975] 3 All ER 776, [1975] 1 WLR 1346, where this court held that there was a contractual licence to the woman for so long as the children were of school age and reasonably required the accommodation. See also *Re Evers's Trust* [1980] 3 All ER 399 at 401, [1980] 1 WLR 1327 at 1330, where, dealing with the case of an unmarried couple, Ormrod LJ said:

> 'This is a situation which is occurring much more frequently now than in the past and is a social development of considerable importance with which the courts are now likely to have to deal from time to time.'

There is also *Hall v Hall* (1981) 3 FLR 379 at 381, where Lord Denning MR said:

a
'Then the question arose about the house, 6 Hammonds Close. She [the plaintiff] claimed a share in the equity. She said that they had lived together for 7 years. The judge found—and the man agreed—that they would not have been able to make the moves and buy the house except for the fact that this couple had been living together and they had both been earning. Her contributions paid for a great amount of the furniture, equipment and fittings. She also bought a car. And she contributed her earnings towards the housekeeping. So it is said that she is entitled to a share in
b
the equity of the house: not on the matrimonial law which governs husband and wife, but on the principle of a resulting trust. There have been a number of cases recently in the courts where women in the position of this lady have been given protection to this extent: if a man and a woman have been living together as husband and wife, and the woman has been contributing towards the establishment of the joint household, although the house is in the man's name, there is a resulting
c
trust as a matter of ordinary common justice for her. The two cases in which that principle has been settled are *Cooke v Head* ([1972] 2 All ER 38, [1972] 1 WLR 518) and *Eves v Eves* ([1975] 3 All ER 768, [1975] 1 WLR 1338) to which I would add the case of *Tanner v Tanner* ([1975] 3 All ER 776, [1975] 1 WLR 1346).'

Finally there is *Bernard v Josephs* [1982] 3 All ER 162, [1982] 1 Ch 391.

Although there was a difference of judicial opinion in *Pettitt v Pettitt* that case was
d
mainly concerned with s 17 of the Married Women's Property Act 1882 whereas in the present case we are concerned with two people living together as man and wife for 19 years as if they were married but not legally married. In *Pettitt v Pettitt* Lord Hodson and Lord Upjohn disagreed with the approach of Lord Reid and Lord Diplock, but I do not read the speech of Lord Morris as going quite so far. In the circumstances of this case I find the observations of both Lord Reid and Lord Diplock helpful. Lord Reid said ([1969]
e
2 All ER 385 at 390, [1970] AC 777 at 794–795):

'We must first have in mind or decide how far it is proper for the courts to go in adapting or adding to existing law. Whatever views may have prevailed in the last century, I think that it is now widely recognised that it is proper for the courts in appropriate cases to develop or adapt existing rules of the common law to meet new conditions. I say in appropriate cases because I think we ought to recognise a
f
difference between cases where we are dealing with "lawyer's law" and cases where we are dealing with matters which directly affect the lives and interests of large sections of the community and which raise issues which are the subject of public controversy and on which laymen are as well able to decide as are lawyers. On such matters it is not for the courts to proceed on their view of public policy for that would be to encroach on the province of Parliament. I would therefore refuse to
g
consider whether property belonging to either spouse ought to be regarded as family property for that would be introducing a new conception into English law and not merely developing existing principles. There are systems of law which recognise joint family property or communio bonorum. I am not sure that those principles are very highly regarded in countries where they are in force, but in any case it
h
would be going far beyond the functions of the court to attempt to give effect to them here. But it is, I think, proper to consider whether, without departing from the principles of the common law, we can give effect to the view that, even where there was in fact no agreement, we can ask what the spouses, or reasonable people in their shoes, would have agreed if they had directed their minds to the question of what rights should accrue to the spouse who has contributed to the acquisition or
j
improvement of property owned by the other spouse. There is already a presumption which operates in the absence of evidence as regards money contributed by one spouse towards the acquisition of property by the other spouse. So why should there not be a similar presumption where one spouse has contributed to the improvement of the property of the other? I do not think that it is a very convincing argument to say that, if a stranger makes improvements on the property of another without any

agreement or any request by that other that he should do so, he acquires no right. The improvement is made for the common enjoyment of both spouses during the *a* marriage. It would no doubt be different if the one spouse makes the improvement while the other spouse who owns the property is absent and without his or her knowledge or consent. But if the spouse who owns the property acquiesces in the other making the improvement in circumstances where it is reasonable to suppose that they would have agreed to some right being acquired if they had thought about the legal position I can see nothing contrary to ordinary legal principles in holding *b* that the spouse who makes the improvement has acquired such a right.'

In *Gissing v Gissing* [1970] 2 All ER 780 at 783, [1971] AC 886 at 897 Lord Reid summarised the situation in this way:

> 'Returning to the crucial question there is a wide gulf between inferring from the whole conduct of the parties that there probably was an agreement, and imputing *c* to the parties an intention to agree to share even where the evidence gives no ground for such an inference. If the evidence shows that there was no agreement in fact then that excludes any inference that there was an agreement. But it does not exclude an imputation of a deemed intention if the law permits such an imputation. If the law is to be that the court has power to impute such an intention in proper cases then I am content, although I would prefer to reach the same result in a rather *d* different way. But if it were to be held to be the law that it must at least be possible to infer a contemporary agreement in the sense of holding that it is more probable than not there was in fact some such agreement then I could not contemplate the future results of such a decision with equanimity.'

In *Pettitt v Pettitt* [1969] 2 All ER 385 at 414–415, [1970] AC 777 at 824 Lord Diplock said: *e*

> 'I do not propose to examine in detail the numerous cases decided in the last 20 years and cited in the argument before your Lordships' House in which in the absence of evidence that spouses formed any actual intention as to their respective proprietary rights in a family asset, generally the matrimonial home acquired as a result of their concerted actions, the courts have imputed an intention to them. I *f* adhere to the view which I expressed in *Ulrich v. Ulrich and Felton* ([1968] 1 All ER 67, [1968] 1 WLR 180) in the passage which my noble and learned friend LORD HODSON has already cited at length.'

The passage from *Ulrich v Ulrich and Felton* [1968] 1 All ER 67 at 72, [1968] 1 WLR 180 at 188–189 cited by Lord Hodson reads as follows: *g*

> 'When these young people pool their savings to buy and equip a home or to acquire any other family asset, they do not think of this as an "ante-nuptial" or "post-nuptial" settlement, or give their minds to legalistic technicalities of "advancement" and "resulting trusts". Nor do they normally agree explicitly what their equitable interests in the family asset shall be if death, divorce or separation parts them. Where there is no explicit agreement, the court's first task is to infer from their *h* conduct in relation to the property what their common intention would have been had they put it into words before matrimonial differences arose between them. In the common case today, of which the present is a typical example, neither party to the marriage has inherited capital, both are earning their living before marriage, and the wife intends to continue to do so until they start having children. They pool their savings to buy a house on mortgage in the husband's name or in joint names *j* and to furnish and equip it as the family home. They meet the expenses of its upkeep and improvement and the payments of instalments on the mortgage out of the family income, to which the wife contributes so long as she is earning. In such a case, the prima facie inference from their conduct is that their common intention is that the house, furniture and equipment should be family assets . . .'

And Lord Diplock then went on to say in *Pettitt v Pettitt* [1969] 2 All ER 385 at 415, [1970] AC 777 at 824–825:

'I think it fairly summarises the broad consensus of judicial opinion disclosed by the post-war cases (none of which has reached your Lordships' House), as to the common intentions which, in the absence of evidence of an actual intention to the contrary, are to be imputed to spouses when matrimonial homes are acquired on mortgage as a result of their concerted acts of a kind which are typical of transactions between husband and wife today. And I firmly think that broad consensus of judicial opinion is right. The old presumptions of advancement and resulting trust are inappropriate to these kinds of transactions and the fact that the legal estate is conveyed to the wife or to the husband or to both jointly though it may be significant in indicating their actual common intention is not necessarily decisive since it is often influenced by the requirements of the building society which provides the mortgage. In imputing to them a common intention as to their respective proprietary rights which as fair and reasonable men and women they presumably would have formed had they given their minds to it at the time of the relevant acquisition or improvement of a family asset, the court, it has been suggested, is exercising in another guise a jurisdiction to do what it considers itself to be fair and reasonable in all the circumstances and this does not differ in result from the jurisdiction which LORD DENNING, M.R., in *Appleton* v. *Appleton* ([1965] 1 All ER 44 at 46, [1965] 1 WLR 25 at 28) considered was expressly conferred on the court by s. 17 of the Married Women's Property Act 1882. It is true, as LORD RADCLIFFE pointed out in *Davis Contractors, Ltd.* v. *Fareham Urban District Council* ([1956] 2 All ER 145 at 160, [1956] AC 696 at 728), that when the court imputes to parties an intention on a matter to which they in fact gave no thought "In their [sc. the parties] place there rises the figure of the fair and reasonable man. And the spokesman of the fair and reasonable man, who represents after all no more than the anthropomorphic conception of justice, is and must be the court itself." The officious bystander of MACKINNON, L.J. (see *Shirlaw* v. *Southern Foundries (1926), Ltd. & Federated Foundries, Ltd.* ([1939] 2 All ER 113 at 124, [1939] 2 KB 206 at 227)) may pose the question, but the court, not the parties, gives the answer. Nevertheless, there is a significant difference between applying to transactions between husband and wife the general legal technique for imputing intention to the parties and exercising a discretion such as that which LORD DENNING, M.R., suggested was conferred on the court by s. 17 of the Married Women's Property Act 1882. In applying the general technique the court is directing its attention to what would have been the common intention of the spouses as fair and reasonable husband and wife at the time of the relevant transaction while they were still happily married and not contemplating its break-down. The family asset might cease to be needed for the common use and enjoyment of themselves and their children without the marriage breaking down at all. The circumstances of the subsequent break-down and the conduct of the spouses which contributed to it are irrelevant to this enquiry. If these circumstances are such as to call for an adjustment of the spouses' respective proprietary rights which results from their previous transactions the court has jurisdiction to make such adjustments under the Matrimonial Causes Act 1965 (see *Ulrich* v. *Ulrich and Felton* ([1968] 1 All ER 67, [1968] 1 WLR 180)). It has no such jurisdiction under s. 17 of the Married Women's Property Act 1882.'

While both Lord Reid and Lord Diplock expressed the view that the doctrine of family property was no part of English law I do not read the speeches of either of them as ruling out the possibility of applying what Lord Diplock described as the general legal technique for imputing intention to the parties (see [1969] 2 All ER 385 at 389–390, 415, [1970] AC 777 at 794, 825).

In *Hall v Hall* (1981) 3 FLR 379 this court held that there was a constructive trust. The contributions of the plaintiff in the present case were not as great as they were in *Hall v*

Hall in financial terms but she had given up her work and was bringing up the two children of the association. When she did earn some money some of it went towards the running of the house and she did purchase the various things that I have already mentioned. On the other hand the fact that the couple lived together for 19 years in this case, of which 17 were in the house, is rather stronger than *Hall v Hall* where the total time was seven years. There was, however, a concession made. Dunn LJ said (at 383):

'It was conceded before the judge, and conceded here, that in the events which occurred there was a resulting trust of the third house, 6 Hammonds Close, Totton, in favour of the plaintiff, so that the defendant held that house partly in trust for her. The judge put it in this way: "The defendant says that he would not have been able to make the moves and buy the homes except for the fact that both were living together and both earning. I accept that she should have some contribution . . . It is clear that having lived together for nearly 7 years in many respects as husband and wife, pooling their joint resources and the plaintiff applying substantially all her earnings to the housekeeping and having done a good deal of work for nothing, certainly the plaintiff is entitled to a proportion of the equity." '

Lord Reid in the passage I have quoted above drew attention to those matters on which the courts should not proceed on their view of public policy and those where it is proper to develop or adapt existing rules to meet new conditions. He refused to consider the concept of family property and said that that was for Parliament. Parliament did deal with matrimonial property in the Matrimonial Proceedings and Property Act 1970, which became law in the year following that decision. This case is not covered by matrimonial property legislation nor is it one which could readily be dealt with by legislation. Therefore the facts have to be considered to see whether it is possible to do justice between the parties, and more particularly in the light of *Hall v Hall*. In the passage I have quoted above from *Gissing v Gissing*, Lord Reid considered the possibility of imputing a deemed intention. If the law permits such an imputation, would the facts of the present case justify it? The plaintiff was living with the defendant as man and wife, was known to friends and relatives as a married couple, but she was not married. The consequence was that she had no statutory protection once the boys had grown up. The relationship lasted 19 years, during which time she brought up their two children. She ran the house, even though the contribution to the fabric was minimal. In *Hall v Hall*, although the relationship lasted only seven years and there were no children, there was a concession because of the woman's contribution to the housekeeping. During the first seven years of this relationship the plaintiff was looking after their children and had had to give up her employment to do so. Save for the concession it is not easy to draw a distinction between the two cases at the end of seven years and if this be right, in the present case where the relationship continued for a further 12, the case would be very much stronger.

If the law permits it a deemed intention between the parties would surely include some provision to make up for the statutory rights which marriage would have given in the event of a break up.

I have, however, had the advantage of reading in draft the judgments of Fox LJ and May LJ and, for the reasons they give, am reluctantly persuaded that the law does not permit this court to impute a deemed intention on the facts of this case.

FOX LJ. The house with which we are concerned in this case, 142 Osidge Lane, Southgate, was purchased in the name of the defendant and the freehold was conveyed to him absolutely. That was in 1963. If, therefore, the plaintiff is to establish that she has a beneficial interest in the property she must establish that the defendant holds the legal estate on trust to give effect to that interest. That follows from *Gissing v Gissing* [1970] 2 All ER 780, [1971] AC 886. For present purposes I think that such a trust could only arise (a) by express declaration or agreement *or* (b) by way of a resulting trust where the

a
claimant has directly provided part of the purchase price or (c) from the common
intention of the parties.

In the present case (a) and (b) can be ruled out. There was no express trust of an interest
in the property for the benefit of the plaintiff; and there was no express agreement to
create such an interest. And the plaintiff made no direct contribution to the purchase
price. Her case, therefore, must depend on showing a common intention that she should
have a beneficial interest in the property. Whether the trust which would arise in such

b
circumstances is described as implied, constructive or resulting does not greatly matter.
If the intention is inferred from the fact that some indirect contribution is made to the
purchase price, the term 'resulting trust' is probably not inappropriate. Be that as it may,
the basis of such a claim, in any case, is that it would be inequitable for the holder of the
legal estate to deny the claimant's right to a beneficial interest.

In determining whether such a common intention exists it is, normally, the intention

c
of the parties when the property was purchased that is important. As to that I agree with
the observations of Griffiths LJ in Bernard v Josephs [1982] 3 All ER 162 at 170, [1982] Ch
391 at 404. As I understand it, that does not mean that for the purpose of determining
the ultimate shares in the property one looks simply at the factual position as it was at
the date of acquisition. It is necessary for the court to consider all the evidence, including
the contributions of the parties, down to the date of separation (which in the case of man

d
and mistress will generally, though not always, be the relevant date). Thus the law
proceeds on the basis that there is nothing inherently improbable in the parties acting on
the understanding that the woman—

'should be entitled to a share which was not to be quantified immediately on the
acquisition of the home but should be left to be determined when the mortgage
was repaid or the property disposed of, on the basis of what would be fair having

e
regard to the total contributions, direct or indirect, which each spouse had made by
that date.'

(See Gissing v Gissing [1970] 2 All ER 780 at 793, [1971] AC 887 at 909 per Lord Diplock.)
That approach does not, however, in my view preclude the possibility that while,
initially, there was no intention that the claimant should have any interest in the
property, circumstances may subsequently arise from which the intention to confer an

f
equitable interest on the claimant may arise (eg the discharge of a mortgage or the
effecting of capital improvements to the house at his or her expense). Further, subsequent
events may throw light on the initial intention.

Looking at the position at the time of the acquisition of the house in 1963, I see
nothing at all to indicate any intention by the parties that the plaintiff should have an
interest in it. The price of the house was £4,900. Of that, about £4,500 was raised by the

g
defendant on a mortgage. The mortgage was in his own name; he assumed responsibility
for the debt. The balance of the purchase price and the costs of the purchase were paid
by the defendant out of his own moneys. The plaintiff made no financial contribution;
she had nothing to contribute. As to the reason for buying the house the judge said that
he had no doubt that it was an important factor in the decision that the defendant realised
that it was much better use of money to buy an asset (a house) rather than rent a flat

h
(which was what he was doing previously).

It seems to me that at the time of the acquisition of the house nothing occurred
between the parties to raise an equity which would prevent the defendant denying the
plaintiff's claim. She provided no money for the purchase; she assumed no liability in
respect of the mortgage; there was no understanding or arrangement that the plaintiff
would go out to work to assist with the family finances; the defendant did nothing to

j
lead her to change her position in the belief that she would have an interest in the house.
It is true that she contemplated living with the defendant in the house and, no doubt,
that she would do housekeeping and look after the children. But those facts do not carry
with them any implication of a common intention that the plaintiff should have an
interest in the house. Taken by themselves they are simply not strong enough to bear
such an implication.

I come then to the position in the years after the house was purchased. I will deal with them under three heads, namely financial contributions, work on the house and finally housekeeping. There is some overlapping in these categories.

So far as financial contributions are concerned, the plaintiff's position really did not change during the 1960s. She had no money of her own and could not contribute financially to the household. All the mortgage instalments were paid by the defendant alone. By the end of the 1960s as a result of qualifying as an instructor in flower arrangement she was able to earn a little by giving lessons in flower arrangement. But as I understand the judgment, the amounts were small particularly since the lessons had to be given in the evening with the result that the plaintiff had to have a baby sitter.

Then in 1972 the plaintiff took flying lessons and qualified as a pilot of light aircraft in 1973. But that was simply a pastime and neither produced nor was intended to produce any addition to the family budget; it was, in fact, an expense.

The plaintiff's driving instruction business did produce an income. It started in 1972 and to begin with was on a small scale. The business increased and, after 1975, the plaintiff 'was earning a certain amount' from it according to the judge's finding. By the time she left the defendant in 1980 she was earning, in all, about £60 per week (which we were told during the hearing was net of expenses). It looks as though she was earning at this rate from about 1977 or 1978 onwards.

There was never any question of the plaintiff being asked by the defendant to apply her earnings to household expenses so as to relieve him. She was free to do what she liked with her earnings.

The judge's findings as to expenditure by the plaintiff was as follows. (i) She made gifts of clothing and other things to the defendant and the children. (ii) She paid for the housekeeping. The defendant allowed her, latterly, £60 per week for housekeeping. It seems to be accepted that the defendant was generous with money and the plaintiff was not kept short as regards housekeeping money. (iii) She paid the rates. The housekeeping payments made by the defendant were, however, fixed at an amount which took account of this. (iv) She paid the telephone bills. That was a matter of agreement between her and the defendant because she spent a lot of time on the telephone talking to her friends. (v) She bought a number of chattels for domestic use: a dishwasher, a washing machine, a tumble dryer and either a drawing room suite or three armchairs and a bed for her separate room. The bed, the dishwasher and the chairs she took with her when she left in 1980. (vi) She provided some doorknobs and door furnishings of no great value.

None of this expenditure, in my opinion, indicates the existence of the common intention which the plaintiff has to prove. What is needed, I think, is evidence of a payment or payments by the plaintiff which it can be inferred was referable to the acquisition of the house. Lord Denning MR in *Hazell v Hazell* [1972] 1 All ER 923 at 926, [1972] 1 WLR 301 at 304 thought that expression, which appears in the speech of Lord Diplock in *Gissing v Gissing* [1970] 2 All ER 780 at 793, [1971] AC 886 at 909, was being over used. He said (quoting from *Falconer v Falconer* [1970] 3 All ER 449 at 452, [1970] 1 WLR 1333 at 1336) that if there was a substantial financial contribution towards the family expenses that would raise an inference of a trust. I do not think that formulation alters the essence of the matter for present purposes. If there is a substantial contribution by the woman to the family expenses, and the house was purchased on a mortgage, her contribution is, indirectly, referable to the acquisition of the house since, in one way or another, it enables the family to pay the mortgage instalments. Thus, a payment could be said to be referable to the acquisition of the house if, for example, the payer either (a) pays part of the purchase price or (b) contributes regularly to the mortgage instalments or (c) pays off part of the mortgage or (d) makes a substantial financial contribution to the family expenses so as to enable the mortgage instalments to be paid.

But if a payment cannot be said to be, in a real sense, referable to the acquisition of the house it is difficult to see how, in such a case as the present, it can base a claim for an interest in the house. Looking at the items which I have listed above, and leaving aside, for the present, the housekeeping which I will deal with separately, none of the items a   can be said to be referable to the acquisition of the house. The making of ordinary gifts between members of a family certainly is not. Nor, in the circumstances as found by the judge, are the payments of rates or the telephone bills. The provision of the door knobs etc is of very small consequence. As regards the purchase of chattels for domestic use, the plaintiff must, I think, have regarded at any rate some of these as her own property since she took them away with her when she left. But quite apart from that I do not think that the provision of chattels, by itself, is evidence of any common intention that the plaintiff

b   should have a beneficial interest in the house. In *Gissing v Gissing* [1970] 2 All ER 780 at 786, [1971] AC 986 at 900 Viscount Dilhorne, after referring to the requirement of a common intention that the wife should have an interest in the house, said:

'To establish this intention there must be some evidence which points to its existence. It would not, for instance, suffice if the wife just made a mortgage

c   payment while her husband was abroad. Payment for a lawn and provision of some furniture and equipment does not itself point to the conclusion that there was such an intention.'

Lord Diplock said ([1970] 2 All ER 780 at 794, [1971] AC 886 at 910):

'The court is not entitled to infer a common intention . . . from the mere fact that

d   she provided chattels for joint use in the new matrimonial home.'

It is to be borne in mind that the judge found that if the plaintiff wanted more money at any time from the defendant she could have had it. She was, no doubt, happy to use her own money to buy things for the house, but, against the financial background, such purchases are no indication of a common intention that she was to have an interest in the house.

e   As regards work on the house, in 1971 a fairly substantial improvement was made to the house; the attic was converted into a bedroom with a bathroom en suite. That was paid for wholly by the defendant.

In 1977 or 1978 the plaintiff decorated the house throughout internally because she wished the house to be wallpapered and not painted. I do not think that carries her case any further. Thus in *Pettitt v Pettitt* [1969] 2 All ER 385 at 416, [1970] AC 777 at 826

f   Lord Diplock said:

'If the husband likes to occupy his leisure by laying a new lawn in the garden or building a fitted wardrobe in the bedroom while the wife does the shopping, cooks the family dinner and baths the children, I for my part, find it quite impossible to impute to them as reasonable husband and wife any common intention that these

g   domestic activities or any of them are to have any effect on the existing proprietary rights in the family home . . .'

Accordingly I think that the decoration undertaken by the plaintiff gives no indication of any such common intention as she must assert.

There remains the question of housekeeping and domestic duties. So far as housekeeping expenses are concerned, I do not doubt that (the house being bought in the

h   man's name) if the woman goes out to work in order to provide money for the family expenses, as a result of which she spends her earnings on the housekeeping and the man is thus able to pay the mortgage instalments and other expenses out of his earnings, it can be inferred that there was a common intention that the woman should have an interest in the house, since she will have made an indirect financial contribution to the mortgage instalments. But that is not this case.

j   During the greater part of the period when the plaintiff and the defendant were living together she was not in employment or, if she was, she was not earning amounts of any consequence and provided no money towards the family expenses. Nor is it suggested that the defendant ever asked her to. He provided, and was always ready to provide, all the money that she wanted for housekeeping. The house was not bought in the contemplation that the plaintiff would, at some time, contribute to the cost of its acquisition. She worked to suit herself. And if towards the very end of the relationship she had money to spare she spent it entirely as she chose. It was in no sense 'joint' money. *a* It was her own; she was not expected and was not asked to spend it on the household.

I think it would be quite unreal to say that, overall, she made a substantial financial contribution towards the family expenses. That is not in any way a criticism of her; it is simply the factual position.

But, one asks, can the fact that the plaintiff performed domestic duties in the house and looked after the children be taken into account? I think it is necessary to keep in *b* mind the nature of the right which is being asserted. The court has no jurisdiction to make such order as it might think fair; the powers conferred by the Matrimonial Causes Act 1973 in relation to the property of married persons do not apply to unmarried couples. The house was bought by the defendant in his own name and, prima facie, he is the absolute beneficial owner. If the plaintiff, or anybody else, claims to take it from him, it must be proved the claimant has, by some process of law, acquired an interest in *c* the house. What is asserted here is the creation of a trust arising by common intention of the parties. That common intention may be inferred where there has been a financial contribution, direct or indirect, to the acquisition of the house. But the mere fact that parties live together and do the ordinary domestic tasks is, in my view, no indication at all that they thereby intended to alter the existing property rights of either of them. As to that I refer to the passage from the speech of Lord Diplock in *Pettitt v Pettitt* [1969] 2 *d* All ER 385 at 416, [1970] AC 777 at 826 which I have already mentioned and also to the observations of Lord Hodson and of Lord Reid in the same case (see [1969] 2 All ER 385 at 403, 391, [1970] AC 777 at 811, 796). The undertaking of such work is, I think, what Lord Denning MR in *Button v Button* [1968] 1 All ER 1064 at 1067, [1968] 1 WLR 457 at 462 called the sort of things which are done for the benefit of the family without altering the title to the property. The assertion that they do alter property rights seems to me to *e* be, in substance, reverting to the idea of the 'family asset' which was rejected by the House of Lords in *Pettitt v Pettitt*. The decision in *Gissing v Gissing* itself is really inconsistent with the contrary view since the parties lived together for ten years after the house was bought. In *Hall v Hall* (1981) 3 FLR 379 at 381 Lord Denning MR did say this:

'It depends on all the circumstances and how much she has contributed—not *f* merely in money—but also in keeping up the house; and, if there are children in looking after them.'

With respect I do not find support for that in the other authorities and I do not think that it is consistent with principle. I am not clear to what extent the matter was material in *Hall v Hall*. So far as looking after children is concerned, it appears that there were no *g* children per Dunn LJ (at 382). The case seems to have proceeded on the concession made by the man that the woman was entitled by way of resulting trust to a share in the house. The parties lived together for seven years and it was accepted by the man that they could not have bought the house but for the fact that both were earning per Lord Denning MR (at 381). The parties, in fact, pooled their resources, see the findings of the judge (at 383). Accordingly, it seems to me that the case may well have been one where the woman, *h* through the pooling of their income, made a contribution, direct or indirect, to the mortgage payments.

The result, in my opinion, is that the plaintiff fails to demonstrate the existence of any trust in her favour. The case is no stronger than that put by Lord Diplock in *Gissing v Gissing* [1970] 2 All ER 780 at 793, [1971] AC 886 at 909–910:

'Where the wife has made no initial contribution to the cash deposit and legal *j* charges and no direct contribution to the mortgage instalments nor any adjustment to her contribution to other expenses of the household which it can be inferred was referable to the acquisition of the house, there is in the absence of evidence of an express agreement between the parties, no material to justify the court in inferring that it was the common intention of the parties that she should have any beneficial interest in a matrimonial home conveyed into the sole name of the husband, merely because she continued to contribute out of her own earnings or private income to other expenses of the household. For such conduct is no less consistent with a common intention to share the day-to-day expenses of the household, while each spouse retains a separate interest in capital assets acquired with their own moneys or obtained by inheritance or gift. There is nothing here to rebut the prima facie inference that a purchaser of land who pays the purchase price and takes a conveyance and grants a mortgage in his own name intends to acquire the sole beneficial interest as well as the legal estate; *and the difficult question of the quantum of the wife's share does not arise.*' (Lord Diplock's emphasis.)

I should comment briefly on certain of the authorities to which we were referred by counsel for the plaintiff.

In *Falconer v Falconer* [1970] 3 All ER 449 at 452, [1970] WLR 133 at 1336 Lord Denning MR made it clear that where what is relied on is a financial contribution to family expenses the contribution must be substantial to raise an inference of a trust.

In *Cooke v Head* [1972] 2 All ER 38 at 41, [1972] 1 WLR 518 at 520 the principle is stated by Lord Denning MR, with whom the other members of the court agreed, that—

'It is now held that, whenever two parties by their joint efforts acquire property to be used for their joint benefit, the courts may impose or impute a constructive or resulting trust.'

In the present case, in my opinion, the facts do not justify the conclusion that the property was acquired by the joint efforts of the parties.

Bernard v Joseph [1982] 3 All ER 162, [1982] Ch 391 is a quite different case to the present. It was, it is true, a case of man and mistress, but the property was conveyed into joint names and the parties assumed joint liability in respect of the mortgage. Part of the house was let and the rents 'helped greatly towards the mortgage instalments' (see [1982] 3 All ER 162 at 165, [1982] Ch 391 at 396). In these circumstances, the plaintiff, Miss Bernard, plainly was entitled to a substantial interest in the property. I do not think the case is of assistance in relation to the present problem.

For the reasons which I have given I think that the appeal must be dismissed. I only add this. The plaintiff entered on her relationship with the defendant knowing that there was no prospect of him marrying her. And it is evident that in a number of respects he treated her very well. He was generous to her, in terms of money, while the relationship continued. And, what in the long term is probably more important, he encouraged her to develop her abilities in a number of ways, with the result that she built up the successful driving instruction business. Nevertheless, she lived with him for 19 years as man and wife, and, at the end of it, has no rights against him. But the unfairness of that is not a matter which the courts can control. It is a matter for Parliament.

MAY LJ. This appeal raises a question which arises nowadays with increasing frequency. If a man and a woman marry, acquire a home, live in it together, bring up children, but sadly sooner or later separate and divorce, the courts have a wide discretion to adjust their subsequent respective financial situations under the provisions of the Matrimonial Causes Act 1973. In particular, the court has power to determine the spouses' respective rights to the matrimonial home, which is usually the family's main asset, and by virtue of s 25(1) of the 1973 Act is given a wide discretion to exercise its powers to place the parties, so far as it is practicable and just to do so, in the financial position in which they would have been if the marriage had not broken down and each had properly discharged his or her financial obligations and responsibilities towards the other.

However, it is becoming increasingly frequent that couples live together without being married, but just as if they were so. They acquire a home for themselves and their children, whom they bring up in the same way as the family next door. Nevertheless, it also happens, just like their married friends, that differences do arise between the couple and they separate. In some cases the man and the woman can agree what is to happen in those circumstances, for instance to their erstwhile joint home. But if they do not agree, they come to the courts for the resolution of their dispute. In the case of an unmarried couple in these circumstances there is no statute which gives a court similar power to those which it has as between husband and wife. In these cases the question therefore arises: what principles is the court to apply?

For my part, I agree that the principles which the courts must apply are those laid down in *Pettitt v Pettitt* [1969] 2 All ER 385, [1970] AC 777 and *Gissing v Gissing* [1970] 2 All ER 780, [1971] AC 886. Those two cases concerned disputes between couples who had in fact been married, where the claims were made under s 17 of the Married Women's Property Act 1882 and not under the matrimonial legislation. But it is quite clear that the House of Lords decided that s 17 is merely a procedural section giving the courts no overriding general discretion in such circumstances and that the principles to be applied are in general the same whether the couple have been married or not. I respectfully agree however with the warning expressed by Griffiths LJ in *Bernard v Josephs* [1982] 3 All ER 162 at 169, [1982] Ch 391 at 402, where he said:

'... but the nature of the relationship between the parties is a very important factor when considering what inferences should be drawn from the way they have conducted their affairs. There are many reasons why a man and a woman may decide to live together without marrying, and one of them is that each values his independence and does not wish to make the commitment of marriage; in such a case it will be misleading to make the same assumptions and to draw the same inferences from their behaviour as in the case of a married couple. The judge must look most carefully at the nature of the relationship, and only if satisfied that it was intended to involve the same degree of commitment as marriage will it be legitimate to regard them as no different from a married couple.'

Further, in this particular field different people have very different views about the problems and relationships involved. In my view, as Parliament has not legislated for the unmarried couple as it has for those who have been married, the courts should be slow to attempt in effect to legislate themselves. As Lord Reid said in *Pettitt v Pettitt* [1969] 2 All ER 385 at 390, [1970] AC 777 at 794–795:

'We must first have in mind or decide how far it is proper for the courts to go in adapting or adding to existing law. Whatever views may have prevailed in the last century, I think that it is now widely recognised that it is proper for the courts in appropriate cases to develop or adapt existing rules of the common law to meet new conditions. I say in appropriate cases because I think we ought to recognise a difference between cases where we are dealing with "lawyer's law" and cases where we are dealing with matters which directly affect the lives and interests of large sections of the community and which raise issues which are the subject of public controversy and on which laymen are as well able to decide as are lawyers. On such matters it is not for the courts to proceed on their view of public policy for that would be to encroach on the province of Parliament.'

It follows that in these disputes between unmarried couples who have broken up, the courts do not have a general power to do what they think is fair and reasonable in all the circumstances, as they have under the appropriate provisions of the Matrimonial Causes Act 1973. In *Pettitt v Pettitt* [1969] 2 All ER 385 at 395, [1970] AC 777 at 801 Lord Morris said:

'It follows further, from my view, as I have expressed it above that with respect I do not agree with the statement in *Appleton* v. *Appleton* ([1965] 1 All ER 44 at 46 [1965] 1 WLR 25 at 28) that if after a separation there is an application under s. 17 by a spouse who claims sole ownership of a house the test to be applied by the court is: "What is reasonable and fair in the circumstances as they have developed, seeing that they are circumstances which no one contemplated before?" In such a situation the duty of the court is to decide whether the house was in the sole ownership of the one spouse who claimed such ownership.'

Lord Morris expressed the same view later when he said ([1969] 2 All ER 385 at 398,
a [1970] AC 777 at 805):

'Nor is there power to decide on some general principle of what seems fair and
reasonable how property rights are to be re-allocated.'

In his speech in the same case Lord Diplock also disapproved of the decision in *Appleton
v Appleton* and thus of the suggestion that in circumstances such as those with which we
b have to deal in this case the court has an overriding dispensing power (see [1969] 2 All
ER 385 at 416, [1970] AC 777 at 826).

The speeches in *Pettitt v Pettitt* and *Gissing v Gissing* also make it clear that there is no
general concept in English law of 'family property' or 'family assets': see *Pettitt v Pettitt*
[1969] 2 All ER 385 at 390, 403, 409, [1970] AC 777 at 795, 810, 817 per Lord Reid,
Lord Hodson and Lord Upjohn and *Gissing v Gissing* [1970] 2 All ER 780 at 785, [1971]
c AC 886 at 900 per Viscount Dilhorne. Lord Diplock recognised in his speech in the latter
case that the view which he had expressed to the contrary in *Pettitt v Pettitt* had been
disapproved by the majority.

I think that one therefore reaches the position that the resolution of these disputes
must depend on the ascertainment according to normal principles of the respective
property rights between the man and the woman.
d Further, two similar factors militate against and indeed prevent any application of
general principles of contract law to the problem. First, it is seldom if ever that the man
and the woman in these circumstances in fact come to any agreement between themselves
about what should happen to the matrimonial home if they were to part. As Lord Morris
said in *Pettitt v Pettitt* [1969] 2 All ER 385 at 394, [1970] AC 777 at 799–801:

e 'In the lengthening line of cases in which questions between spouses have called
for adjudication under s. 17, the nature of the difficulties which arise is constantly
and recurringly made manifest. When two people are about to be married and
when they are arranging to have a home in which to live they do not make their
arrangements in the contemplation of future discord or separation. As a married
couple they do not, when a house is being purchased or when the contents of a
f house are being acquired, contemplate that a time might come when [a] decision
would have to be made as to who owned what. It would be unnatural if at the time
of acquisition there was always precise statement or understanding as to where
ownership rested. So, if at a later date questions arise as to the ownership of a house
or of various things in it, though as to some matters no honest difference of view
will arise, as to others there can be such honest differences because previously the
parties might never really have applied their minds to the question as to where
g ownership lay.'

Second, even if it be shown in any particular case that the parties had reached some
agreement between themselves, there is I think real doubt whether this can be said to
have been intended to create enforceable legal relations between them: cf *Balfour v Balfour*
[1919] 2 KB 571, [1918–19] All ER Rep 860. There is in any event a very real evidentiary
h difficulty to which, for instance, Lord Reid referred in *Pettitt v Pettitt* [1969] 2 All ER 385
at 391, [1970] AC 777 at 796, where he said:

'The real difficulty is in inferring from some vague evidence of an arrangement
what in fact the arrangement was. There is often difficulty in determining what
were the terms of a commercial contract because the parties did not apply their
minds to central matters. It has often been pointed out that spouses living happily
j together rarely apply their minds to matters which must be determined if their
arrangement is to be given contractual force. So it is extremely difficult at a later
date to determine what if any contractual effect can be given to some rather
indefinite arrangement which preceded the expenditure of money by one of the
spouses, and it is hardly possible to apply the ordinary rule that the essential terms
of a contract must be sufficiently clearly established before it can be enforced. I do

not think that there is much to be said for a rule of law if one finds the judges are constantly doing their best to circumvent it by spelling out contractual agreements from very dubious material.'

Further, as their Lordships pointed out in the two leading cases, if the only realistic conclusion on the material before the court is that the parties in fact never made any agreement binding at law between them, then it necessarily follows that it is impossible to imply such agreement or, which comes to much the same thing, to imply more precise terms where any existing arrangement is imprecise.

In the result, my opinion is that the correct and general approach to these cases should be that summed up in a passage from Lord Pearson's speech in *Gissing v Gissing* [1970] 2 All ER 780 at 787–788, [1971] AC 886 at 902 where he said:

'I think it must often be artificial to search for an agreement made between husband and wife as to their respective ownership rights in property used by both of them while they are living together. In most cases they are unlikely to enter into negotiations or conclude contracts or even make agreements. The arrangements which they make are likely to be lacking in precision and finality which an agreement would be expected to have. On the other hand, an intention can be imputed; it can be inferred from the evidence of their conduct and the surrounding circumstances. The starting point, in a case where substantial contributions are proved to have been made, is the presumption of a resulting trust, though it may be displaced by rebutting evidence. It may be said that the imputed intent does not differ very much from an implied agreement. Accepting that, I still think it is better to approach the question through the doctrine of resulting trusts rather than through contract law. Of course, if an agreement can be proved it is the best evidence of intention.'

Where the legal estate to the family home had been taken in joint names then generally the beneficial interests will depend on the respective contributions of the parties to the acquisition of the property: see *Crisp v Mullings* (1975) 239 EG 119 and the recent decision of this court in *Walker v Hall* [1983] CA Bound Transcript 300.

Where the legal estate in the family home has, however, been taken in the name of one of the parties only, then prima facie it will carry with it the whole of the beneficial interest. But for the reasons to which I have briefly referred, a claim to a beneficial interest in land made by a person in whom the legal estate is not vested can in certain circumstances be made by resorting to the doctrine of resulting trusts. Where the legal estate to the family home is in one name only, which is usually the male member of the couple, and the parties to the acquisition of the house have not expressed their common intention that the beneficial interest should be shared between them, it may nevertheless be possible to infer that common intention from their conduct and thus give rise to a resulting trust to which the courts will give effect. It may be demonstrably inequitable to permit the legal title holder to retain the whole of the beneficial interest in the property. The inference about the parties' common intention to which the court will give effect in this way is that which objectively a reasonable man would draw from their words and conduct at the relevant time.

At the hearing of this appeal our attention was drawn to a number of authorities, to some of which I shall briefly refer, and thereafter state what I think is the general approach adopted by the courts to these disputes which can be deduced from the two leading cases in 1970 and 1971 and those which have followed them.

In *Falconer v Falconer* [1970] 3 All ER 449, [1970] 1 WLR 1333 the couple were married in 1960. About a year later a building plot was bought in the wife's name as a site for a house. Part of the purchase price was provided by the wife's mother and the balance was borrowed on mortgage in which the husband joined as surety. A house was then built on the plot with money raised by another mortgage of the plot with the partially erected house on it. As the plot was in the wife's name she was the mortgagor. However her husband again stood surety. The husband's father also guaranteed the

repayments under the mortgage. After they moved into the house, the husband paid his
wife a regular sum by way of housekeeping money. The wife herself went out to work
and paid the mortgage instalments out of the total of her own earnings and her
housekeeping money. About 18 months later the marriage began to go wrong and the
husband moved out of the house. From that time and for two years thereafter he paid
one half of the mortgage instalments and the rates on the property. Subsequently the
wife formed an association with another man and the husband stopped his payments.
The marriage was ultimately dissolved. On the husband's summons under s 17 of the
Married Women's Property Act 1882, the county court judge held that the land itself
belonged to the wife but that the husband had a half interest in the house. The wife's
appeal to the Court of Appeal was dismissed and in the course of his judgment Lord
Denning MR referred to the decision in *Gissing v Gissing* and said ([1970] 3 All ER 449 at
452, [1970] 1 WLR 1333 at 1336):

> 'It stated the principles on which a matrimonial home, which stands in the name
> of husband or wife alone, is nevertheless held to belong to them both jointly (in
> equal or unequal shares). It is done, not so much by virtue of an agreement, express
> or implied, but rather by virtue of a trust which is *imposed* by law. The law imputes
> to husband and wife an intention to create a trust, the one for the other. It does so
> by way of an *inference* from their conduct and the surrounding circumstances, even
> though the parties themselves made no agreement on it. This inference of a trust,
> the one for the other, is readily drawn when each has made a financial contribution
> to the purchase price or to the mortgage instalments. The financial contribution
> may be *direct*, as where it is actually stated to be a contribution towards the price or
> the instalments. It may be *indirect*, as where both go out to work, the one pays the
> housekeeping and the other the mortgage instalments. It does not matter which
> way round it is. It does not matter who pays what. So long as there is a substantial
> financial contribution towards the family expenses, it raises the inference of a trust.
> But where it is insubstantial, no such inference can be drawn, see the cases collected
> in the dissenting judgment of Edmund Davies LJ ([1969] 1 All ER 1043 at 1049,
> [1969] 2 Ch 85 at 97), which was upheld by the House. The House did, however,
> sound a note of warning about proportions. It is not in every case that the parties
> hold in equal shares. Regard must be had to their respective contributions. This
> confirms the practice of this court. In quite a few cases we have not given half-and-
> half but something different.' (Lord Denning MR's emphasis.)

Megaw LJ ([1970] 3 All ER 449 at 454, [1970] 1 WLR 1333 at 1338) in his judgment
quoted a passage from Lord Pearson's speech in *Gissing v Gissing* [1970] 2 All ER 780 at
788, [1971] AC 886 at 903 which was to this effect:

> 'I think also that the decision of cases of this kind has been made more difficult
> by excessive application of the maxim "Equality is equity". No doubt it is reasonable
> to apply the maxim in a case where there have been very substantial contributions
> (otherwise than by way of advancement) by one spouse to the purchase of property
> in the name of the other spouse but the proportion borne by the contributions to
> the total price or cost is difficult to fix. But if it is plain that the contributing spouse
> has contributed about one-quarter, I do not think it is helpful or right for the Court
> to feel obliged to award either one-half or nothing.'

In the next case, *Hazell v Hazell* [1972] 1 All ER 923, [1972] 1 WLR 301, the couple
were again husband and wife. They bought a house for the matrimonial home which
was conveyed into the husband's name. The purchase price was obtained in part by a
loan from the husband's parents and the remainder by a mortgage from a building
society. In order to meet the increased expenditure involved it was agreed between the
parties that the wife should go out to work and she used her earnings to supplement the
limited housekeeping moneys which her husband gave her, including clothing for
herself and the children. The top floor of the house was let and the rent was received by

the husband. After 15 years the wife left the husband who stayed on in the house and continued to pay the outgoings. Four years later the parties were divorced. The wife applied under the 1882 Act claiming that she was entitled to a share in the matrimonial home. The deputy county court judge found that she had indeed made substantial contributions to the family expenses but decided that she was not entitled to any share of the house because there was no express or implied agreement to give her one. He went on, however, to hold that if he was wrong in so deciding on that basis, then the wife should have a share amounting to one-fifth. On the wife's appeal, this court held that she was entitled to a share in the ultimate value of the matrimonial home by virtue of the contributions which she made to supplement the housekeeping expenses. On the facts, her earnings had helped her husband to pay the mortgage instalments. In his judgment Lord Denning MR referred to what he had said in *Falconer v Falconer* and his reference there to *indirect* contributions by one member of a couple to the purchase price of the matrimonial home, and a little later said ([1972] 1 All ER 923 at 927, [1972] 1 WLR 301 at 305):

> 'Stephenson LJ suggested that it might be inferred that [the wife's] contributions were referable to the acquisition of the house. That seems to be sufficient ground from which the court could and should impute a trust. It would be inequitable for the husband to take the whole when she has helped him so much to acquire it. So I would reverse the decision of the judge and hold that the wife is entitled to a share in the house.'

Lord Denning MR then upheld the deputy county court judge's assessment of one-fifth. Megaw LJ agreed and in the course of his judgment, dealing with the question of contributions, said ([1972] 1 All ER 923 at 928, [1972] 1 WLR 301 at 306):

> 'In my judgment it is sufficient if as a matter of common sense the wife's contribution ought to be treated as being a contribution towards the expenses of the acquisition of the matrimonial home.'

In *Cooke v Head* [1972] 2 All ER 38, [1972] 1 WLR 518 the couple were not married. They planned to build a bungalow in which they could live after the man's wife had divorced him and they were able to get married. A plot of land was purchased in the man's name and he paid the deposit and arranged the mortgage. Both the man and the woman helped to build the bungalow, the woman's part of the work including demolishing a building, removing hard core and rubble, working a cement-mixer and painting. They both saved each week as much as they could from their earnings. They pooled their savings and used these for mortgage repayments and buying furniture. However, theirs was a relatively short-lived association, for when the bungalow was near completion but not entirely finished they separated and the man alone continued to live in it repaying the mortgage. It seems that the parties lived together for between two and three years. On an application by the woman for a declaration that the bungalow was owned jointly by herself and the man, Plowman J held that she had a one-twelfth interest in the property. She was dissatisfied and appealed. I quote brief passages from the judgment of Lord Denning MR, again with which Karminski and Orr LJJ agreed:

> 'The particular case of man and mistress came before the Court of Appeal in *Diwell v Farnes* [1959] 2 All ER 379, [1959] 1 WLR 624. The court was divided in opinion. The majority thought that a mistress was not in the same position as a wife. She could recover her actual contributions to the purchase price, but could not claim any part of the windfall on resale. Willmer LJ approached the case much as we approach cases between husband and wife. He would have given the mistress one-half. His approach is more in accord with recent development (see [1959] 2 All ER 379 at 389, [1959] 1 WLR 624 at 638) . . . In the light of recent developments, I do not think it is right to approach this case by looking at the money contributions of each and dividing up the beneficial interest according to those contributions. The matter should be looked at more broadly, just as we do in husband and wife cases.

We look to see what the equity is worth at the time when the parties separate. We assess the shares as at that time. If the property has been sold, we look at the amount which it has realised, and say how it is to be divided between them. Lord Diplock in *Gissing v Gissing* [1970] 2 All ER 780 at 793, [1971] AC 886 at 909 intimated that it is quite legitimate to infer that "the wife should be entitled to a share which was not to be quantified immediately on the acquisition of the home but should be left to be determined when the mortgage was repaid or the property disposed of". Likewise with a mistress.'

(See [1972] 2 All ER 38 at 42, [1972] 1 WLR 518 at 520–521.)

Lord Denning MR then considered the various matters which should be taken into account in assessing the parties' share in the family home in these circumstances and ultimately held that the woman plaintiff was entitled to one-third of the net proceeds of sale, instead of the one-twelfth found by the judge at first instance.

Richards v Dove [1974] 1 All ER 888 also concerned an unmarried couple. They first lived as man and mistress in rented accommodation and then in a house which was bought and taken in the man's name. He paid £350 by way of deposit, of which £150 had been lent to him by his mistress. The balance of £3,150 was obtained by a mortgage to the man from the local authority. After the couple moved in, as had been the situation in their earlier rented accommodation, the mistress continued to pay for the household food and gas; the man paid all other bills including the mortgage repayments. Walton J dismissed the woman's application for a declaration that the house was vested in the man on trust for both of them. In his view it did not follow that the application of the relevant principles produced the same result whether the parties were married or not, because it was impossible to leave out of the picture the fact that as between husband and wife the former has certain legal duties relating to the maintenance of his wife, whereas between man and mistress the whole relationship is consensual, with no legal obligations imposed. In his view all that the mistress had done in the case before him was to provide the loan of £150 towards the deposit and then to carry on as they had for a number of years in rented accommodation, with the man paying off the mortgage. In truth, as the judge held, this mistress made no 'real' or 'substantial' contribution to the acquisition of the matrimonial home and accordingly was not entitled to any share of it.

Eves v Eves [1975] 3 All ER 768, [1975] 1 WLR 1338 also concerned an unmarried couple living together. They bought a house in the man's name partly by the sale of his previous house and partly by a mortgage which he obtained. At the time of the purchase the man told his mistress that if she had been 21 years of age he would have had the house put into their joint names as it was to be their joint home. At the subsequent trial he said that he had used the plaintiff's age as an excuse for not having had the house put into joint names. At the outset the house was in a very dirty and dilapidated condition and the couple each worked hard to improve it. Ultimately, some three years later, the man left the house and married another woman. Pennycuick V-C held that the plaintiff woman had not established a claim to be entitled to any share of the property and dismissed her application. She successfully appealed. On my reading of the judgments in this court the basis for Lord Denning MR's view that the woman was entitled to a declaration was that the untrue statement by the man that but for her age he would have put the house into their joint names amounted to a recognition by him that, in all fairness, she was entitled to a share in the house, equivalent in some way to a declaration of trust. He went on to say that the declaration was not for a particular share but for such share as was fair in view of all that she had done and was doing for the man and their children and would thereafter do. In his judgment, however, Brightman J, with whom Browne LJ agreed, referred to *Gissing v Gissing* and expressed his view that the actual decision in that case was that the wife had made no contribution to the acquisition of the title to the matrimonial home from which it could be inferred that the parties intended her to have any beneficial interest in it. He went on to hold that the case then before his court was different: the man clearly led the plaintiff to believe that she was to have some undefined interest in the property. That, of course, he said, was not enough by itself to create a beneficial interest in his favour but if it was part of the bargain between the parties, expressed or to be implied, that the plaintiff should contribute her labour towards the reparation of a house in which she was to have some beneficial interest, then in his view the arrangement became one to which the law could give effect. Although Pennycuick V-C had been unable to find any link in the evidence, Brightman J disagreed and found it in these circumstances ([1975] 3 All ER 768 at 774, [1975] 1 WLR 1338 at 1345):

> 'The house was found by them jointly. It was in poor condition. What needed to be done was plain for all to see, and must have been discussed. The plaintiff was to have some interest in the house, or so she was led to believe, although her name would not be on the deeds. They moved in. They both set to and put the house to rights. I find it difficult to suppose that she would have been wielding the 14-pound sledgehammer, breaking up the large area of concrete, filling the skip and doing other things which were carried out when they moved in, except in pursuance of some expressed or implied arrangement and on the understanding that she was helping to improve a house in which she was to all practical intents and purposes promised that she had an interest.'

In the result the court held that the woman was entitled to a one-quarter share in the family home.

Of all the authorities to which our attention was drawn, I think that the facts of *Hall v Hall* (1981) 3 FLR 379 are the closest to those of the instant case. In *Hall*'s case the couple were unmarried. The woman left her husband and went to live with the man, who was divorced. They bought a flat in the man's name, the woman contributing to the furnishings and the general household expenses. Subsequently a house was bought in the man's name, the purchase money coming partly from the proceeds of the sale of the flat, partly from the man's savings and partly by way of mortgage. Within a year the couple separated. On the woman's application to the county court for a share in the family home, she was awarded one-fifth and her appeal to the Court of Appeal against this award was dismissed. At first sight the decision in *Hall v Hall* might not seem to be in accord with the principles applied in the earlier authorities. However, having read the judgments in the case it is clear that the decision proceeded on a concession by counsel for the man, both before the county court and in the Court of Appeal, that in the events which had occurred there had been a resulting trust of the family house in favour of the woman. In these circumstances, save to the extent that the members of the Court of Appeal in *Hall*'s case did not expressly say that they thought that this concession had been wrongly made, I think that one should be careful about reaching the conclusion that *Hall*'s case extended the basis of the woman's entitlement in man/mistress cases of the type with which we are concerned. With the greatest respect and particularly having regard to the reference to *Falconer v Falconer* in the judgments, I think that the concession in *Hall v Hall* was wrongly made.

Be that as it may, in the course of his judgment Lord Denning MR said (at 381):

> 'So it is said that she is entitled to a share in the equity of the house: not on the matrimonial law which governs husband and wife, but on the principle of a resulting trust. There have been a number of cases recently in the courts where women in the position of this lady have been given protection to this extent: if a man and a woman have been living together as husband and wife, and the woman has been contributing towards the establishment of the joint household, although the house is in the man's name, there is a resulting trust as a matter of ordinary common justice for her. The two cases in which that principle has been settled are *Cooke v Head* ([1972] 2 All ER 38, [1972] 1 WLR 518) and *Eves v Eves* ([1975] 3 All ER 768, [1975] 1 WLR 1338) to which I would add the case of *Tanner v Tanner* ([1975] 3 All ER 776, [1975] 1 WLR 1346). It is quite clear from the authorities that, although a couple are not husband and wife, the woman can—because of her contributions to the joint household—after a time obtain a share in the house by

way of a resulting trust. But what should that share be? That is always the difficulty. It is not always one half. It may be a good deal less. It depends on the circumstances and how much she had contributed—not merely in money—but also in keeping up the house; and, if there are children, in looking after them.'

As will have been apparent, in some of the earlier decisions before *Pettitt* and *Gissing*, Lord Denning MR had held that the court did have power 'to do what is fair and reasonable in all the circumstances'. In both *Pettitt* and *Gissing* the House of Lords made it quite clear, in my view, that no such general power exists. In all the decisions prior to *Hall*'s case in which the wife or woman was held to be entitled to a share in the family home, on the evidence she had made a 'real' or 'substantial' contribution either to the deposit paid for the acquisition of the family home or to the instalments of the mortgage with the assistance of which it was bought. In *Pettitt v Pettitt* [1969] 2 All ER 385 at 416, [1970] AC 777 at 826 Lord Diplock, whose speech was the most favourable to the applicant's case, said:

'It is common enough nowadays for husbands and wives to decorate and make improvements in the family home themselves, with no other intention than to indulge in what is now a popular hobby, and to make the home pleasanter for their common use and enjoyment. If the husband likes to occupy his leisure by laying a new lawn in the garden or building fitted wardrobes in the bedroom while the wife does the shopping, cooks the family dinner or baths the children, I, for my part, find it quite impossible to impute to them as reasonable husband and wife any common intention that these domestic activities or any of them are to have any effect on the existing proprietary rights in the family home on which they are undertaken. It is only in the bitterness engendered by the break-up of the marriage that so bizarre a notion would enter their heads.'

In these circumstances, I respectfully think that the dictum of Lord Denning MR that the woman's contribution to the family well-being by keeping the house and looking after the children can be taken into account in assessing the extent to which a resulting trust has arisen in her favour was wrong.

On the other hand it would appear from a passage from the judgment of the county court judge quoted by Dunn LJ in the Court of Appeal that in *Hall*'s case (1982) 3 FLR 379 at 384 the woman had been working and had been applying substantially all her earnings towards the housekeeping. In these circumstances it may have been argued that the woman had made an actual financial contribution to the acquisition to the family home, in that her pooled earnings had at the least made it easier for the man to pay the mortgage instalments.

Finally, I turn to *Bernard v Josephs* [1982] 3 All ER 162, [1982] Ch 391, to which I have already referred. That was again a case concerning an unmarried couple who lived in a family home which was taken in joint names. The couple assumed joint liability under a local authority mortgage for the whole of the purchase price. Each of them contributed to the initial expenses of the acquisition of the house. While they were living together the man spent some £2,000 on decoration and repairs and then they let off part of the house to tenants. After the relationship had ceased and the parties had separated the woman claimed under s 30 of the Law of Property Act 1925 for an order for the sale of the house and a declaration that she was entitled to a half share. She succeeded both at first instance and in the Court of Appeal. In view of the fact that in *Bernard v Josephs* the family house had been taken in joint names, I do not think that the broad approach referred to by Lord Denning MR in his judgment, in which he also mentioned both the earlier decisions in *Cooke v Head* and *Hall v Hall*, is necessarily equally appropriate where the legal estate to the family home has been taken in the name of only one of the man and woman concerned.

Griffiths LJ in his judgment first referred to s 17 of the 1882 Act and s 30 of the 1925 Act, stressing that both of these are essentially procedural and that neither gives the court a wide discretion to decide the question of ownership of the house in accordance with its idea of what would be 'fair' in all the circumstances. He said ([1982] 3 All ER 162 at 169, [1982] Ch 391 at 402): 'The respective interests of the parties must be determined by the application of the law relating to trusts.' A little later in his judgment he said ([1982] 3 All ER 162 at 170, [1982] Ch 391 at 403): 'The starting point of any inquiry into the beneficial ownership of a house in joint names must be the conveyance.' He then held that in the absence of any express declaration about the beneficial interest at the time of the acquisition of the family house, the court must look to see the respective contributions of the parties towards the purchase price. Griffiths LJ continued ([1982] 3 All ER 162 at 170, [1982] Ch 391 at 404):

> 'In such a case the judge must look at the contributions of each to the "family" finances and determine as best as he may what contribution each was making towards the purchase of the house. This is not to be carried out as a strictly mathematical exercise; for instance, if the man was ill for a time and out of work so that the woman temporarily contributed more, that temporary state of affairs should not increase her share, nor should her share be decreased if she was temporarily unable to work whilst having a baby. The contributions must be viewed broadly by the judge to guide him to the parties' unexpressed and probably unconsidered intentions as to the beneficial ownership of the house. There is of course an air of unreality about the whole exercise, but the judge must do his best and only as a last resort abandon the attempt in favour of applying the presumption of equality, which may so often give an unfair result.'

In my view Griffiths LJ was here clearly referring to the parties' respective *financial* contributions to the acquisition of the matrimonial home, even though these must be looked at in the round.

Kerr LJ in his judgment also considered the respective contributions of the man and woman to the acquisition of the house, on the broad lines indicated by the earlier authorities distinguishing the parties' contributions to the ordinary everyday expenses of living and keeping up the family home. He contrasted the two types of contributions and in relation to the second said ([1982] 3 All ER 162 at 172, [1982] Ch 391 at 406):

> 'They also both contributed to their living expenses during this period. [The woman] paid for their food and household necessities, and [the man] paid the electricity and other bills. I only mention the latter contributions in passing, since the judge rightly took no account of these domestic arrangements, which might apply equally to any people living together in, for instance, rented accommodation, and which throw no light on what should be their shares in the property in which they live.'

In the light of all these cases, I think that the approach which the courts should follow, be the couples married or unmarried, is now clear. What is difficult, however, is to apply it to the facts and circumstances of any given case. Where the family home is taken in the joint names, then unless the facts are very unusual I think that both the man and the woman are entitled to a share in the beneficial interest. Where the house is bought outright and not on mortgage, then the extent of their respective shares will depend on a more or less precise arithmetical calculation of the extent of their contributions to the purchase price. Where, on the other hand, and as is more usual nowadays, the house is bought with the aid of a mortgage, then the court has to assess each of the parties' respective contributions in a broad sense; nevertheless the court is only entitled to look at the financial contributions, or their real or substantial equivalent, to the acquisition of the house; that the husband may spend his weekends redecorating or laying a patio is neither here nor there, nor is the fact that the woman has spent so much of her time looking after the house, doing the cooking and bringing up the family.

The inquiry becomes even more difficult when the home is taken in only one of the two names. For present purposes I will assume that it is the man, although the same approach will be followed if it is taken in the name of the woman. Where a matrimonial or family home is bought in the man's name alone on mortgage by the mechanism of a deposit and instalments, then if the woman pays or contributes to the initial deposit this points to a common intention that she should have *some* beneficial interest in the house. If thereafter she makes direct contributions to the instalments, then the case is a fortiori and her rightful share is likely to be greater. If the woman, having contributed to the deposit, but although not making direct contributions to the instalments, nevertheless uses her own money for other joint household expenses so as to enable the man the more easily to pay the mortgage instalments out of his money, then her position is the same.

b Where a woman has made no contribution to the initial deposit, but makes regular and substantial contributions to the mortgage instalments, it may still be reasonable to infer a common intention that she should share the beneficial interest from the outset or infer a fresh agreement after the original conveyance that she should acquire such a share. It is only when there is no evidence on which a court can reasonably draw an inference about the extent of the share of the contributing woman, that it should fall back on the maxim 'equality is equity'. Finally, when the house is taken in the man's name alone, if the

c woman makes no 'real' or 'substantial' financial contribution towards either the purchase price, deposit or mortgage instalments by means of which the family home was acquired, then she is not entitled to any share in the beneficial interest in that home even though over a very substantial number of years she may have worked just as hard as the man in maintaining the family, in the sense of keeping house, giving birth to and looking after

d and helping to bring up the children of the union.

On the facts of the instant case, which Waller LJ has outlined, I think that it is clear that the plaintiff falls into the last of the categories to which I have just referred and accordingly I too would dismiss this appeal. When one compares this ultimate result with what it would have been had she been married to the defendant and taken appropriate steps under the Matrimonial Causes Act 1973, I think that she can justifiably

e say that fate has not been kind to her. In my opinion, however, the remedy for any inequity she may have sustained is a matter for Parliament and not for this court.

WALLER LJ. This appeal is dismissed, for the reasons which have been handed down.

Appeal dismissed with costs but order for costs not to be enforced without leave. Application for leave to appeal to the House of Lords refused.

f *17 November. The Appeal Committee of the House of Lords (Lord Diplock, Lord Scarman and Lord Brightman) dismissed a petition by the plaintiff for leave to appeal.*

Solicitors: *Boyes Sutton & Perry*, Barnet (for the plaintiff).

Sophie Craven   Barrister.

g

A v B

QUEEN'S BENCH DIVISION (COMMERCIAL COURT)
h LEGGATT J
27, 28 JUNE 1983

Solicitor – Lien – Retaining lien – Solicitor discharging himself in course of action – Non-payment of costs – Solicitor entering default judgment for amount of unpaid costs – Solicitor arresting client's vessel to secure payment of costs – Client applying for order that papers in action be
j *handed over to new solicitor instructed by client – Whether arrest of vessel providing alternative security to lien – Whether solicitor waiving lien – Whether exceptional circumstances existing justifying court in refusing to order solicitor to hand over papers to new solicitor.*

In late 1981 the plaintiffs' vessel was blacked by port labour at the instigation of an international federation of transport workers unions. The plaintiffs instructed a firm of solicitors in the matter, and in due course obtained an injunction against the federation's officials on the ground that the blacking constituted unlawful secondary industrial action. Shortly afterwards the vessel's crew went on strike and were, in consequence, dismissed. *a* The plaintiffs instituted proceedings against the crew and obtained an injunction ordering the crew to leave the vessel. In conducting the litigation to that stage the plaintiffs' solicitors incurred costs and disbursements amounting to some £30,500, and, after setting off certain payments on account and receiving certain costs from parties unsuccessful in the litigation, about £20,000 of the solicitors' original bill remained outstanding. Throughout 1982 the solicitors unsuccessfully pressed for payment of their *b* costs. Meanwhile a claim was made against the plaintiffs for payment of the vessel's crew. The solicitors emphasised to the plaintiffs the importance of defending that claim but they made it plain that they could not assist in doing so unless payment of their costs were made. By October 1982 the crew's claim had progressed to a stage where the solicitors' assistance was required to defend it. The plaintiffs were told by the solicitors that they had until 11 November to serve a defence. On 5 November, however, the *c* solicitors, with a view to securing payment of their costs, procured the arrest of the vessel and issued a summons for an order declaring that they had ceased to act as solicitors for the plaintiffs in order that they might be removed as solicitors from the record. The plaintiffs then instructed other solicitors, who applied to the original solicitors for the papers in the case, but they refused to hand them over, asserting that they had a lien on them. On 26 November the original solicitors applied for a default judgment in the sum *d* then outstanding of about £25,000, and on 13 January 1983 default judgment was entered. The plaintiffs applied for an order that the original solicitors deliver up all papers in the case which they retained by virtue of the lien in respect of their costs, on the plaintiffs' new solicitors undertaking to hold the papers without prejudice to that lien and to return them intact after the action was over. It was common ground that the original solicitors had discharged themselves by the arrest of the vessel and that they had *e* done so in circumstances which made their action reasonable. The plaintiffs contended, however, that by arresting the vessel the solicitors had taken alternative security from the plaintiffs and had waived their lien on the papers. The plaintiffs further contended that there were no exceptional circumstances that would justify the court in departing from its general practice to order a solicitor who discharged himself during litigation to yield up, without prejudice to his lien, papers required for use in the litigation to the *f* solicitor who replaced him against an undertaking by the new solicitor, so long as he retained the papers, to allow the old solicitor access to them and to return them to him as soon as the litigation was completed.

Held – (1) The arrest by the solicitors of the plaintiffs' vessel was merely part of a process of enforcement following the default judgment entered by the solicitors and was to be *g* distinguished from such contractual arrangements as a solicitor might in the ordinary course make for the provision by his client of a security that could properly be regarded as given in substitution for the solicitor's lien on the client's papers. The arrest of the vessel was accordingly not inconsistent with the maintenance of the solicitors' lien and did not lead to any inference of an intention to waive the lien (see p 272 *e f*, post); *Bissill v Bradford and District Tramways Co Ltd* (1893) 9 TLR 337 distinguished; *Re Morris* [1908] *h* 1 KB 473 considered.

(2) Where during litigation a solicitor discharged himself, the usual practice of the court was to order the old solicitor to hand over to the new solicitor the papers which he had on the undertaking of the new solicitor to hold them subject to the old solicitor's lien, even if that rendered the lien useless. However, the court would not exercise its power automatically, the matter being equitable and therefore one of discretion, to be *j* exercised judicially on the facts of the case. In approaching the matter the overriding principle was that the order which would be made would be that which would best serve, or at least not frustrate, the interests of justice, and the principle that a litigant should not be deprived of material relevant to the conduct of the case and so driven from the judgment seat, if that would be the result of permitting the lien to be sustained, was to be weighed against the principle that litigation should be conducted with due regard

a to the interests of the court's own officers, who should not be left without payment for
what was justly due to them. On that basis, and contrasting the conduct of the solicitors,
who had behaved impeccably and of whose conduct there had been no criticism, with
that of the plaintiffs, who, without any excuse, had not paid that which was the subject
of the default judgment against them, the balance of hardship would be far greater on
the solicitors if the lien were not enforced, because they would then probably recover
nothing, whereas it was open to the plaintiffs to preserve their position in the continuing
b litigation simply by paying the solicitors' costs, which they had never themselves directly
disputed. The plaintiffs' application would accordingly be dismissed (see p 274 h j, p 276
c d and f to p 277 b, post); dictum of Templeman LJ in *Gamlen Chemical Co (UK) Ltd v
Rochem Ltd* [1980] 1 All ER at 1058–1059 applied; *Gamlen Chemical Co (UK) Ltd v Rochem
Ltd* [1980] 1 All ER 1049 distinguished; *Heslop v Metcalfe* (1837) 3 My & Cr 183 and *Re
Taylor Stileman & Underwood* [1891–4] All ER Rep 953 considered.

c
Notes
For discharge of a solicitor's retaining lien, see 44 Halsbury's Laws (4th edn) para 235,
and for cases on the subject, see 43 Digest (Repl) 297–300, 3120–3145.

Cases referred to in judgment
d *Bissill v Bradford and District Tramways Co Ltd* (1893) 9 TLR 337, CA.
Gamlen Chemical Co (UK) Ltd v Rochem Ltd [1980] 1 All ER 1049, [1980] 1 WLR 614, CA.
Heslop v Metcalfe (1837) 3 My & Cr 183, 40 ER 894, LC.
Morris, Re [1908] 1 KB 473, CA.
Taylor Stileman & Underwood, Re [1891] 1 Ch 590, [1891–4] All ER Rep 953, CA.

e **Summons**
By a summons dated 17 June 1983 the plaintiffs, who owned and managed a vessel,
applied in the Commercial Court to the judge in chambers for an order that Messrs
Holman Fenwick & Willan (Holmans), a firm of solicitors who had been instructed by
the plaintiffs in connection with certain litigation in which the plaintiffs were engaged,
should forthwith deliver up all papers relating to the litigation, which Holmans retained
f by virtue of a lien in respect of their costs, on an undertaking by other solicitors instructed
by the plaintiffs to hold the papers without prejudice to Holmans' lien and to return the
papers intact after the litigation was ended and to allow Holmans access to them in the
mean time. The summons was heard in chambers but judgment was given by Leggatt J
in open court at the request of the parties. The facts are set out in the judgment.

g *Timothy Saloman* for the plaintiffs.
Christopher S C S Clarke for Holmans.

LEGGATT J. At the instigation of the parties to this application my judgment is
delivered in open court. In so doing I shall attempt to preserve the anonymity of certain
h persons connected with it.
The plaintiffs are respectively the owners and managers of a particular vessel which I
need not name. The defendants, Holman Fenwick & Willan (to whom I shall refer as
'Holmans'), are solicitors well known in this court.
The plaintiffs apply for an order that Holmans do forthwith deliver up all papers
relating to this case, which they retain by virtue of a lien in respect of costs, on the
j plaintiffs' solicitors undertaking to hold the papers without prejudice to Holmans' lien
and to return the papers intact after the action is over and to allow Holmans access to
them in the mean time.
The circumstances in which Holmans at first acted for the plaintiffs, but thereafter
ceased to do so, can be shortly stated. In November and December 1981 the vessel was at
Hull trading under a time charter. She was blacked by port labour at the instigation of
the International Transport Workers Federation (the ITF).

The plaintiffs applied for an injunction against ITF officials on the footing that the blacking constituted unlawful secondary industrial action, and in due course the *a* Commercial Court granted an injunction, ITF's appeal against it being subsequently dismissed by the Court of Appeal. That did not conclude the vessel's troubles, however, because shortly afterwards, according to the plaintiffs, the crew went on strike and were, in consequence, dismissed. Proceedings were accordingly instituted by the plaintiffs against the crew. The plaintiffs were successful in obtaining an injunction ordering the crew to leave the ship.   *b*

In conducting this litigation Holmans incurred costs and disbursements amounting to £30,463·68. That sum was reduced to £24,914·30 by setting off against the total indebtedness the sum of $10,000 paid to them on account. It was further reduced by another £5,000 in costs received from parties unsuccessful in the litigation to which I have referred. The result is that of Holmans' original bill there remains an amount of £19,914·30 outstanding. The litigation, initiated as I have described, still continues and *c* there is for hearing tomorrow a counterclaim under RSC Ord 14 on behalf of crew members, resistance to which, it is said on the plaintiffs' behalf, requires the use of those documents, or some of them, in relation to which Holmans are asserting a lien.

When originally they sought payment early in 1982 Holmans were successful in procuring, as they now acknowledge on affidavit, a so-called guarantee from a representative body to contribute to the amount of their costs in the event of their being *d* unable to obtain payment. By affidavit on Holmans' behalf, it is said that the secretary of the representative body, in course of a telephone call in December 1981, indicated that he would contribute towards Holmans' costs if they were unable to obtain payment from the plaintiffs. That telephone conversation has never been confirmed in writing and the offer was made on what is described as the strict understanding that the existence of it should be kept secret from the plaintiffs, in order, of course, to do all that could be done *e* to ensure that the plaintiffs might discharge the debt without taking up the offer then being made by the representative body. It is right to remark that the deponent describes the offer made as one 'guaranteeing' Holmans' costs; and he expresses the hope that it will not be necessary to call on the representative body for an actual payment.

In the course of 1982 a claim for wages by the crew was advanced on their behalf. Throughout the latter part of 1982 Holmans continued to press for payment of their *f* costs. In so doing they emphasised the importance of defending the claims made by the crew but made it quite plain to the plaintiffs that they could not assist in doing so unless payment of their costs were made.

At the beginning of November 1982 Holmans also made plain to the plaintiffs the risk of judgment being signed against them in default. They had themselves previously investigated the possibility of arresting the plaintiffs' vessel for purposes of enforcing *g* their costs.

In October the counterclaim on behalf of the crew had progressed to a stage where Holmans' assistance was required for purposes of defending it, and the plaintiffs were told on 1 November that they had until 11 November to serve a defence in that matter. On 5 November, when matters in the litigation had reached a critical stage, Holmans took two steps which had the effect of bringing the retainer to an end. First, they *h* procured the arrest of the vessel in Venice and, second, they issued a summons for an order under Ord 67, r 6 declaring that they had ceased to act as solicitors for the plaintiffs in order that they might procure their removal as solicitors from the record.

Soon thereafter the plaintiffs' present solicitors were instructed, and were met, on applying to Holmans for the papers in the case, by the assertion by Holmans of the lien on which they continue to rely. It was the reaction of the plaintiffs' present solicitors that *j* Holmans were not entitled to a lien or, at all events, were not entitled to withhold production of the papers against an appropriate undertaking, on the ground that they had discharged themselves as solicitors for the plaintiffs.

On 26 November 1982 Holmans applied for a default judgment in the sum then outstanding of £24,914·30. On 13 January 1983 they signed a default judgment.

In these circumstances two principal issues arise: first, assuming that Holmans

discharged themselves from their retainer, whether the plaintiffs are entitled to the order
a now sought and, second, whether Holmans' lien on documents was waived by the arrest
of the plaintiffs' vessel in November 1982 for the purpose of securing payment of their
fees.

It is common ground that Holmans did discharge themselves on 5 November 1982, at
the latest, in circumstances which counsel for the plaintiffs characterises as 'unequivocal
and dramatic', by arrest of the vessel. It is right to record that the only reference of any
b kind to any suggestion that Holmans were not entitled to payment of the fees, which are
now the subject of the default judgment, was made in a telex message of 9 November
1982, when the mortgagees, on being invited to assist in procuring the discharge of the
arrest by contributing to the amount of Holmans' outstanding fees, said:

'. . . owners have informed us that in their view your fees are excessive, and are
contrary to your express advance indication of probable fees chargeable.'

c
That assertion was not made in any sense as agents for the plaintiffs and the plaintiffs
have not seen fit themselves or by instruction given to their solicitors to persist in that
allegation, if indeed they made it in the first place. It may be remarked in passing that
the unconventional course of the litigation in which the fees were incurred would
certainly suffice to account for any 'express advance indication' having proved erroneous.

d   Counsel for the plaintiffs stresses that Holmans discharged themselves when they
were, as he puts it, 'in the middle of the crew litigation', but the fact that they discharged
themselves when they did came about only because their costs were not paid. They were
not paid notwithstanding the passage of a considerable period of time in the course of
which not only were reminders sent but clear explanations were given to the client what
the consequences would be if no payment were forthcoming. It is said that there are two
e respects in which the position of Holmans is mitigated: first, by the arrest of the vessel,
which continues to be maintained, and, second, by the so-called guarantee to contribute
to their costs, which they were successful in obtaining in the form I have explained from
a representative body.

The authority most closely in point on an application of this nature is the decision of
the Court of Appeal in *Gamlen Chemical Co (UK) Ltd v Rochem Ltd* [1980] 1 All ER 1049,
f [1980] 1 WLR 614. That was a case in which solicitors asserted a lien for their costs. They
did so in circumstances where the plaintiffs joined one of the defendants' solicitors'
partners as defendant. Thereupon the solicitors informed the defendants of their
difficulties in conducting a defence and requested payment of their fees up to date. Fees
were disputed. On the hearing of a summons for removal from the record the question
was whether the solicitors had discharged themselves, and whether, in the circumstances,
g their possessory lien had been lost. It may save the need to cite from the judgments in
that case at any length if I say that it is common ground that if, while litigation is
continuing for which a solicitor is retained, his retainer is terminated the rights of the
solicitor depend on whether he is discharged by the client or discharges himself. If he is
discharged by the client other than for misconduct, he is entitled to keep his lien and the
court has no power to interfere with the exercise of it. If, on the other hand, he discharges
h himself, he enjoys what has been called a 'qualified lien' and the court will, as a matter of
general practice, order the solicitor, without prejudice to his lien, to yield up papers
required for use in the litigation to the solicitor who replaces him, against an undertaking
by the new solicitor, so long as he retains the papers, to allow the old solicitor to have
access to them and to return them to him as soon as the litigation has been concluded. It
is also common ground in this case that, at least as a matter of form, the solicitors
j discharged themselves and also that they did so in circumstances which made this action
reasonable.

As I have already indicated, two questions arise: first, whether in the exercise of the
court's discretion an exception should be made in the circumstances of this case from
what is the general practice in relation to a solicitor's lien, and, second, whether Holmans
have waived their right in any event to retain the lien.

Since, if I am in the plaintiffs' favour on the issue of waiver, it will resolve the matter

definitively without the need to consider the exercise of discretion, that issue may
conveniently be considered first. Counsel for the plaintiffs argues that a solicitor's lien on   *a*
documents will be waived if he takes alternative security from a client with the intention
of satisfying his claim for fees by this alternative means. In aid of that contention he
relies on *Re Taylor Stileman & Underwood* [1891] 1 Ch 590, [1891–4] All ER Rep 953.
That was a case which was subsequently applied, also by the Court of Appeal, in *Bissill v
Bradford and District Tramways Co Ltd* (1893) 9 TLR 337. In *Bissill's* case Lord Esher MR
referred to *Re Taylor Stileman & Underwood*, saying that it had been argued that the   *b*
security was really of no value. He continued (at 337):

> 'But it clearly might have been of considerable value, and Mr. Justice Stirling
> came to the conclusion that it was of value. These solicitors did take a security from
> the clients, and did not tell them at the time that they intended to insist on their
> lien. In the case of "*In re* Taylor, Stileman, and Underwood" ([1891] 1 Ch 570 at 597,   *c*
> [1891–4] All ER Rep and 953 at 955), Lord Justice Lindley said:—"Whether a lien
> is waived or not by taking a security depends upon the intention expressed or to be
> inferred from the position of the parties and all the circumstances of the case. In this
> particular instance we are dealing with a solicitor and his client. It strikes me that,
> if a solicitor takes from his client such a security as this solicitor took, the *primâ facie*
> inference is that he waives his lien. That appears to me the right and proper   *d*
> conclusion to come to, bearing in mind that it is the solicitor's duty to explain to his
> client the effect of what he is about to do." And Lord Justice Kay said ([1891] 1 Ch
> 590 at 601, [1891–4] All ER Rep 953 at 957):—"A solicitor has a duty to perform
> towards his client to represent to his client all the facts of the case in a clear and
> intelligible manner, and to inform him of his rights and liabilities, and where you
> find a solicitor dealing with his client and taking from him such a security as was   *e*
> given in this case, not expressly reserving his right of lien, I quite agree that the
> inference ought to be against the continuance of the lien." The rule in respect of
> matters of this kind was there laid down, and the Court had to apply that rule in the
> present case. Mr. Justice Stirling had found that these solicitors did take security,
> and security which was of substance and value, and at the time they did not in any
> way intimate to their client that they meant to insist on their lien. Under those   *f*
> circumstances the proper inference was that the lien was done away with.'

In *Bissill v Bradford and District Tramways Co Ltd* the two principal passages relied on
by counsel for the plaintiffs from *Re Taylor Stileman & Underwood* were quoted in the
passage which I have read. I ought also to refer to the passage cited from the judgment of
Lopes LJ in the *Taylor Stileman* case [1891] 1 Ch 590 at 598, [1891–4] All ER Rep 953 at
955–956, where he said: *g*

> 'Another point is raised by the Appellant, that the solicitors have lost their lien by
> taking security. It appears to me that in each case the question whether the lien is
> waived by taking security must be decided according to the particular circumstances.
> I do not mean to say that taking a security necessarily imports an abandonment of
> the lien; but if there are circumstances in the taking of the security which are
> inconsistent with the continuance of the old security, it is to be inferred that the   *h*
> solicitor intended to abandon his lien. In the present case the security given is a
> promissory note payable on demand with interest at £5 per cent. under which the
> amount could be recovered at once. There is also a charge upon a policy. The
> promissory note is not given by the wife alone, but the husband joins as surety.
> Under these circumstances it is only a fair inference to draw that there was an
> intention between the parties to give up the old security of the lien and to rely on   *j*
> the security I have mentioned.'

In the light of these authorities counsel for the plaintiffs submits, first, that whether a
lien is abandoned depends on intention, express or implied, and, second, that if a solicitor
fails to tell his client that he intends to reserve his lien the lien is prima facie abandoned.

He remarked that there was no suggestion here, at any material time, that the lien was
a being reserved.

The other authority on which counsel relies is *Re Morris* [1908] 1 KB 473, in which
the facts are of no special consequence for present purposes. Lord Alverstone CJ said (at
475):

> 'Prima facie a solicitor has a lien for his charges upon the papers of his client. This
> lien may be lost, released, or waived in the same way as the liens which other persons
b > possess. The main difference between the case of a solicitor's lien and those other
> liens is that, where a solicitor takes any security which is in any degree inconsistent
> with the retention of a lien, it is his duty to give express notice to the client if he
> intends to retain the lien, and that, should he not do so, his lien will be taken to be
> abandoned.'

c Buckley LJ undertook a detailed analysis of earlier cases including, in particular, *Re
Taylor Stileman & Underwood*. Of that case he said (at 478):

> 'It will be found that each of the Lords Justices relies, not upon the fact that the
> solicitor had taken security from his client without explaining that he reserved his
> lien, but that he had taken such a security as the solicitor there took.'

d He referred to the nature of it and, having examined references in the judgments of
the earlier case, Buckley LJ concluded (at 479):

> 'I do not think the Court meant to lay down a new or extended rule. In my
> judgment the facts of this case have to be looked at to see whether the solicitor has
> taken a security incompatible with the retention of his lien, or has made with his
> client an arrangement which sufficiently indicates the intention of the parties that
e > the right shall no longer be enforced.'

Counsel for the plaintiffs accepts that for a waiver to be established it is necessary to
show that the taking of the other security was incompatible with the continuance of the
lien. He maintains that in the present case that was the position. By reference to the
documents he stresses, first of all, that when Holmans inquired into the prospect of
f arresting the vessel they had not ascertained the amounts of such mortgages as were
outstanding in respect of her. That might suggest that they expected to be able to recover
the amount of their costs in consequence of the arrest. They referred to the fact, in case
it was not obvious, that the action had been taken against the ship to enforce payment.
They made it plain that they had arrested the vessel for that purpose and they sought to
look to the mortgagees to contribute to their costs for the purpose of procuring the
g release of the vessel.

Counsel for the plaintiffs contends that if one looks at the nature of the security one
may see that it was intended to replace such security as was constituted by the lien. So far
from reserving their lien, he contends that Holmans were attempting to get paid through
the arrest and he observes that they are continuing to use the ship to try to enforce their
judgment. Their prospects of success in so doing must by now be diminishing.

h Counsel for Holmans acknowledges that, if a solicitor takes security for costs generally
and that security is inconsistent with his lien and the solicitor does not in so doing reserve
the lien, then prima facie he will be taken to have abandoned it; but he says that that is a
principle which applies only where the lien will be unaffected by the security taken. Any
attempt to enforce the lien during the operation of the alternative security will be
ineffective, first, because the taking of the alternative security may lead to an assumption
j that that is the only method by which the solicitor seeks to be paid. Second, the solicitor
cannot exercise the lien if he has made a new contract with his client whereby he has
agreed to look for payment to the new security which the client is providing, at any rate
if the circumstances suggest that it is only to the new security that he intends to look.
Third, the solicitor has a duty to explain to his client the significance of what the client is
doing. Counsel for Holmans stresses that it is indeed the client who, in the ordinary

course, is doing something in relation to the alternative security, that is to say he is
providing it in circumstances where it can be contended that it is to be in substitution   *a*
for the lien to which the solicitor would ordinarily be entitled.

Counsel for Holmans contends that considerations of this kind can have no application
to an arrest of a vessel such as occurred here. First, he contends that the arrest of the vessel
did not constitute the taking of security, or alternative security, in the sense in which
that expression may be found used in the cases, because the arrest was part of a process of
execution. Counsel for the plaintiffs argues against this contention observing that   *b*
Holmans have indeed taken security, at least in the sense of arresting the vessel, and have
kept it zealously. Second, counsel for Holmans contends that it is only if the security
taken was inconsistent with the lien asserted that the lien is in peril of being treated as
abandoned. Counsel for the plaintiffs resists this argument saying that I should, in the
circumstances, infer that it was intended to substitute the security afforded by the arrest
of the vessel for the lien hitherto available to be exercised by the solicitors. Third, counsel   *c*
for Holmans contends that no intention to waive the lien can here be inferred. To that
counsel for the plaintiffs remarks that there is no reference to the lien on the
contemporary documents and the courts have stressed the importance in a fiduciary
relationship such as between solicitor and client of the importance of the solicitor
explaining to his client what it is that is involved in the taking of the alternative security.
The essence, therefore, of what lies between the parties on the issue of waiver is that   *d*
counsel for the plaintiff maintains that the arrest of the vessel was in itself incompatible
with the continuance of the lien; and the reason why he contends that it was is that the
arrest was avowedly for the purpose of enforcing payment. He quarrels with the use by
counsel for Holmans of the word 'execution' as a description of the arrest, and it may
well be that such a description when the arrest was first accomplished would have been
premature. But it appears to me that it was indeed part of a process of enforcement and   *e*
is to be distinguished from such contractual arrangement as a solicitor might, in the
ordinary course, make for the provision by his client of a security that can properly be
regarded as given in substitution for the lien. In my judgment, the arrest of the vessel
was in no way inconsistent with the maintenance of Holmans' lien, and my conclusion
is that no intention to waive the lien can be inferred from the fact of the arrest. For these
reasons, I hold that the lien was not waived.   *f*

Let me turn then to consider, in a little more detail, the circumstances in which the
court may refrain from ordering a solicitor who has discharged himself from providing
for use in continuing litigation documents in relation to which he is asserting a lien. In
explaining why, notwithstanding the apparent unfairness of the principle, the court
nevertheless maintains it, except in exceptional circumstances, Goff LJ in *Gamlen Chemical
Co (UK) Ltd v Rochem Ltd* [1980] 1 All ER 1049 at 1056, [1980] 1 WLR 614 at 622 cited a   *g*
passage from the judgment of Lord Cottenham LC in *Heslop v Metcalfe* (1837) 3 My & C
183 at 188–190, 40 ER 894 at 896–897 where he said:

> 'Undoubtedly, that doctrine may expose a solicitor to very great inconvenience
> and hardship, if, after embarking in a cause, he finds that he cannot get the necessary
> funds wherewith to carry it on. But, on the other hand, extreme hardship might   *h*
> arise to the client, if—to take the case which is not uncommon in the smaller
> practice in the country—a solicitor, who finds a poor man having a good claim, and
> having but a small sum of money at his command, may go on until that fund is
> exhausted, and then, refusing to proceed further, may hang up the cause by
> withholding the papers in his hands. That would be great grievance and means of
> oppression to a poor client who, with the clearest right in the world, might still be   *j*
> without the means of employing another solicitor. The rule of the Court must be
> adapted to every case that may occur, and be calculated to protect suitors against
> such conduct . . . I then take the law as laid down by Lord Eldon, and, adopting that
> law, must hold that Mr. Blunt is not to be permitted to impose upon the Plaintiff
> the necessity of carrying on his cause in an expensive, inconvenient and

disadvantageous manner. I think the principle should be, that the solicitor claiming the lien should have every security not inconsistent with the progress of the cause.'

Goff LJ referred finally to the argument of counsel ([1980] 1 All ER 1049 at 1058, [1980] 1 WLR 614 at 623–624)—

'that the conduct of the defendants was repudiatory in refusing to pay the costs, and he says that the original solicitors have accepted that repudiation, but that again can only be right if the defendants are wrong on the points which they have taken, and I do not see how it can affect our judgment at this stage.'

The other judgment in the Court of Appeal was delivered by Templeman LJ, who referred also to *Heslop v Metcalfe* for the citation already given by Goff LJ and stated the law as follows ([1980] 1 All ER 1049 at 1058–1059, [1980] 1 WLR 614 at 624–625):

'Where the solicitor has himself discharged his retainer, the court then will normally make a mandatory order obliging the original solicitor to hand over the client's papers to the new solicitor against an undertaking by the new solicitor to preserve the lien of the original solicitor. I wish to guard myself against possible exceptions to this general rule. The court in fact is asked to make a mandatory order obliging the original solicitor to hand over the papers to the new solicitor. An automatic order is inconsistent with the inherent, albeit judicial, discretion of the court to grant or withhold a remedy which is equitable in character. It may be, therefore, that in exceptional cases the court might impose terms where justice so required. For example, if the papers are valueless after the litigation is ended and if the client accepts that he is indebted to the original solicitor for an agreed sum and has no counterclaim, or accepts that the solicitor has admittedly paid out reasonable and proper disbursements, which must be repaid, the court might make an order which would only compel the original solicitor to hand over the papers to the new solicitor, on the usual terms preserving the lien but providing that in the first place the client pays to the original solicitor a sum, fixed by the court, representing the whole or part of the moneys admittedly due from the client to the original solicitor. Much would depend on the nature of the case, the stage which the litigation had reached, the conduct of the solicitor and the client respectively, and the balance of hardship which might result from the order the court is asked to make.'

Templeman LJ, when he came to apply those matters for the purpose of determining whether exceptional reasons did exist why the court should impose terms on the defendants modifying the usual practice, concluded his judgment by saying ([1980] 1 All ER 1049 at 1060, [1980] 1 WLR 614 at 627):

'Whether the clients this day can lay their hands on the money to pay the original solicitors' demands, I know not, but the clients dispute the original solicitors' right to be paid in principle and in quantum. It would be disastrous for the clients if their new solicitors could not, at this stage, obtain the papers held by the original solicitors.'

Against that background, counsel for the plaintiffs contends first of all that the conclusion as to exceptional reasons was that of Templeman LJ only and he argues that the general principle should be applied for four reasons. First, Holmans have arrested the vessel and so terminated the retainer. He says that they suffered the litigation to come on more quickly than the sum which they had obtained on account would cover and thereafter acted at their peril. Second, he refers to the timing of the discharge, remarking that it occurred six days before a threatened default judgment, although in the result no such judgment was then proceeded with. Third, he says that they took the security constituted by the arrest with the intention of using the ship as the means of enforcing payment. And, fourth, he asserts that Holmans had some form of guarantee, namely that afforded by the representative body.

Counsel for the plaintiffs resists conclusion of the affidavit sworn on behalf of Holmans by one of their partners which gives nine reasons, in para 21 of the affidavit, why the order sought should not be granted. First, it is said there is no dispute that the sum claimed is due. As to that, counsel for the plaintiffs can only refer to the passage which I have read from the telex message from the mortgagees. Second, it is claimed that effectively the plaintiffs discharged Holmans. Counsel for the plaintiffs would have it that that is an argument which did not prevail in *Gamlen v Rochem Ltd*. It seems to me that the reason why it did not was that, both in principle and in quantum, there was shown to be a dispute in that case as to the costs which the solicitors claimed. Third, it is said that there is already a default judgment for the sum due. To that counsel for the plaintiffs replies that it is not surprising that the plaintiffs let the judgment go by default since their vessel, which was their primary, if not their only, asset had been arrested and not released. Fourth, it is said that the papers retained would be valueless if not returned until after the proceedings. In answer to that, counsel for the plaintiffs refers to the passage in *Gamlen v Rochem Ltd* [1980] 1 All ER 1049 at 1058, [1980] 1 WLR 614 at 624 where Templeman LJ alludes to the documents there in question, saying, '. . . for what they are worth', a phrase which carries the implication that they might prove to have little, if any, value at the end of the case. Fifth, the deponent refers to the arrest of the vessel as proving to be inadequate security unless the mortgages are invalid. Counsel for the plaintiffs observes that none the less Holmans are thereby enabled to hold an advantage over the plaintiffs because they are continuing to detain the vessel. Sixth, the deponent remarks that the plaintiffs do not suggest any inability to pay; and boldly, doing the best he can without any relevant material, counsel for the plaintiff bids me infer as being in favour of the plaintiffs that they cannot pay, since they have not, and might have been expected to do so were they able to, if they were conducting themselves and their affairs properly. Seventh, it is said that there is no evidence that the documents are required to defend the proceedings now imminent between the plaintiffs and the former members of their crew. Counsel for the plaintiffs is, however, able to point to advice given by Holmans to their then clients, the plaintiffs, to the effect that they would have valid defences to certain items claimed against them. He says that the plaintiffs will need the documents to show, in particular, that their decision to terminate the contracts of certain of the crew members was justified. Eighth, Holmans maintain that any such difficulty as may arise from the imminence of the RSC Ord 14 proceedings has been caused by the plaintiffs themselves. To that, counsel for the plaintiffs says that such difficulties are inherent in any situation where litigation is continuing and solicitors invited to maintain one side of the litigation are without the requisite papers. Lastly, the affidavit sworn on Holmans' behalf remarks that unless payment is made or security given the firm is unlikely to be able to recover from the plaintiffs the sum which is the subject of the default judgment or any part of it. As to that, counsel for the plaintiffs reminds me that this is a perennial factor in cases of this nature and also that there may be some prospect of recovery from the representative body.

Counsel for Holmans acknowledges that, in the light of the *Gamlen* case, the proper approach is this. First, where during litigation a solicitor discharges himself, the usual practice is to order the old solicitor to hand over to the new solicitor the papers which he has, on the undertaking of the new solicitor to hold them subject to the lien even if the result of that be to render the lien fruitless. Second, the court does not do this automatically. Whether it grants the order is an equitable matter, and therefore one of discretion, with the result that it is to be exercised judicially on the facts of the case. Counsel for Holmans recognises it to be an overriding principle that that order will be made which will best serve, or at least not frustrate, the interests of justice. In making that assessment he says the court should weigh two matters: (a) that a litigant should not be deprived of material relevant to the conduct of his case and so driven from the judgment seat, if that would be the result of permitting the lien to be sustained, and (b) that litigation should be conducted with due regard to the interests of the court's own officers, who should not be left without payment for what is justly due to them. The reason, says counsel, why an order for production is usually made is, quite simply, that usually the interests of justice require it. Examples may be where a litigant has run out of ready money and is unable to pay or secure the claim, so that without the documents he faces the prospect of the success against him of an onerous claim or the failure by him of a valid claim, or the litigant may dispute whether any sum is due and, if some sum, then what sum. Or, the solicitor may have discharged himself wrongfully, with the result that he ought not to be assisted by the court to retain the lien which he does not deserve. He emphasises by reference to the *Gamlen* case and reliance on passages from the judgment of Templeman LJ in particular, which I have read, the fact that in that case there was a dispute, both in principle and quantum, as to the amount of the solicitors' costs. It seems also to have been established in that case that there would be hardship suffered by the party concerned if they were to continue to be deprived of the documents.

When reviewing the relevant factors in this case, counsel for Holmans remarks that here, by contrast, there is no dispute as to the fees, either in principle or as to quantum. In principle there could be none, for the reason that the litigation which was conducted for the plaintiffs was important, expedited and successful. As far as quantum is concerned, having rendered their bill in April 1982, they followed it by frequent reminders and explained by letters and telex messages what the consequence would be of failure to pay. There has been no application by or on behalf of the plaintiffs to tax the amount of the solicitors' costs as there could have been, and in the result those fees are now the subject of a default judgment. Indeed, the time for taxation has expired and it is now only by force of s 70(3) of the Solicitors Act 1974 after the passage of 12 months that in special circumstances the court might allow the party charged to have the amount of the bill taxed. There is, however, no material from which the existence of any such special circumstances could be discerned or inferred.

As being relevant also to the court's consideration of whether an exception to the normal rule of practice should be here permitted, counsel for Holmans relies on the fact that the lien is, in truth, the only effective security against the plaintiffs available to Holmans, because, although the vessel was arrested, there is no equity in her unless the mortgages be invalid.

The documents, counsel for Holmans contends, are valueless in themselves. As for the offer from the representative body, he says it is irrelevant, for a number of reasons. What was given was no more than an oral undertaking, the terms of which are in dispute; there is doubt as to the authority, or extent of the authority, of the person who gave it. It was, in its nature, an oral promise to answer for the debt, default or miscarriage of another, and it was subject to a condition of confidentiality which has necessarily been broken as part of the obligation of Holmans, in aid of their present application, to make full disclosure of the facts which the court would, or might regard, as material. Counsel also contends that there is no reason why the court should cast on the representative body the burden which would be involved in their discharging, or helping to discharge, Holmans' outstanding costs, and should not, for that reason, refuse Holmans the relief to which they would otherwise be entitled.

On the balance of the hardship, counsel for Holmans maintains that Holmans would suffer greater hardship if the order were refused than would their former clients if the order was made. He observes that it is unsatisfactory for the plaintiffs to say that there is no evidence that they cannot pay. They have had all the opportunity in the world, if that were their true position, to have said so on affidavit or to have given instructions to that effect to the solicitors now acting for them. Moreover, they are not put in any position of sudden difficulty, since the situation that Holmans' retainer was terminated has obtained since the beginning of November 1981.

Counsel for the plaintiffs seeks to meet an argument of counsel for Holmans to the effect that there is here seen to have been a fundamental breach by the client of the contract for a retainer by reference to the *Gamlen* case, where, as he says, it was assumed that the solicitors had reasonable cause to discharge the retainer, yet that did not affect the applicability of the general rule. The principle, he says, echoing Lord Cottenham LC, must fit all cases; and what is really being made to the court on this occasion is an invitation to rewrite the law. In principle, a solicitor is not entitled to stop litigation and it is relevant here that the termination was abrupt and dramatic and made at a stage when the client had need of the services of the solicitors. Whether or not the guarantee of the representative body proves to be legally enforceable, it should nevertheless be regarded as having some efficacy, and as constituting, at any rate, a moral commitment of the body concerned to pay, in the event of default by the plaintiffs in the discharge of Holmans' bill of costs.

Counsel for the plaintiffs rightly reminds me that there is outstanding a guarantee to meet the claim of the crew members which will be set at peril in the event that the plaintiffs are unable to resist the counterclaim through lack of documents. Without such documents they may not be able to make good the point commended to them by Holmans that the claim of the crew is an inflated one.

It seems to me that there is force in the argument of counsel for Holmans that, just as a solicitor is prevented from reliance on his lien by his own misconduct, so a client who has repudiated the contract pursuant to which the retainer was originally given need not be surprised if he finds himself unable to rely on the general rule of practice which would enable him to have possession of documents against an undertaking to preserve the lien meanwhile and to return them to the solicitor asserting the lien at the conclusion of the litigation to which the papers relate.

It may well be that Goff LJ was silent on the exceptions which the court may contemplate to the general rule of practice which the court in the *Gamlen* case held to be applicable. But by contrast Templeman LJ undoubtedly was not silent on that topic, nor was anything said to undermine his observations on it, by Goff LJ. I consider that there is a clear analogy between the case where the client admits a sum or sums to be due to his solicitor and the case here where there is a default judgment. As for the considerations referred to by Templeman LJ (see [1980] 1 All ER 1049 at 1059, [1980] 1 WLR 614 at 625), the claim has involved Holmans in a massive amount of work against a payment of no more than $10,000. Whereas the stage of the action at which their retainer was terminated and they discharged themselves might have resulted in considerable hardship to the plaintiffs at the time when it occurred, that contingency has long since passed. When I contrast the conduct of solicitor and client, I have, on the one hand, solicitors who have behaved impeccably and of whose conduct there has been no criticism and, on the other, clients who, quite simply, have not paid that which is now the subject of a default judgment against them, nor have they offered any scintilla of an excuse for not having done so.

I am satisfied that the balance of hardship would be far greater on Holmans if the lien were not enforced because they would probably recover nothing, whereas it is open to the plaintiffs to preserve their position in the continuing litigation simply by paying Holmans' costs which they have never themselves directly disputed.

The plaintiffs have no proven inability to pay. In so far as I should draw any inference from their silence, it must clearly be that they are able to pay, but are, for reasons which seem good to them but which they have not seen fit to impart to the court, not prepared to do so.

The lien now constitutes, so far as the evidence goes, the only security available to Holmans which is worth the name. It would be useless at the end of the action. Whereas the circumstances that it would be does not of itself constitute any ground for creating an exception on the general rule, it appears to me that, unless that would be the result, the court should be slow to create any such exception. There is no evidence that the documents concerned are essential to the plaintiffs' resistance to the counterclaim, though I am prepared to assume that they, or some of them, are at least material. Notwithstanding the comments which I have sought to reproduce, made by counsel for the plaintiffs in answer to the conclusion of the affidavit sworn on behalf of Holmans, the nine reasons there given why the court ought not to grant the order sought constitute a wholly accurate and fair summary of Holmans' position. Accordingly, I accept the submission of counsel for Holmans that, if ever there was a case for departing from the general practice so as to permit the continuance of the lien, this is it, and I do so.

I have considered whether it would be useful to make the discharge of the lien dependent on the giving of a guarantee, or subject to any other such term, but I can see no event which the giving of a guarantee or the imposition of any such term could sensibly abide, because the amount of the client's, that is the plaintiffs', indebtedness has been established by judgment, and no objection has been taken to the amount of it even if the plaintiffs were entitled to take the objection on the present application. Accordingly, it is dismissed.

I would not wish to part from this matter without paying particular tribute to the conduct of this case, on his clients' behalf, of counsel for the plaintiffs. It has appeared to me that his tenacity and moral fibre in the face of adverse, but never, I trust, hostile response on the part of the court is in the highest traditions of the English Bar. So saying cannot but underscore the quality of the argument of counsel for Holmans since it is he who has been the victor.

Plaintiffs' application dismissed.

Solicitors: *Lloyd Denby Neal* (for the plaintiffs); *Holman Fenwick & Willan.*

K Mydeen Esq   Barrister.

Attorney General v Able and others

QUEEN'S BENCH DIVISION
WOOLF J
18, 19, 20, 28 APRIL 1983

Declaration – Jurisdiction – Jurisdiction of civil court to grant declaration regarding criminal law – Declaration regarding criminality of future conduct – When declaration can be granted – Whether court should grant declaration that distribution of booklet on suicide a criminal offence.

Criminal law – Suicide – Liability for complicity in another's suicide – Aiding, abetting etc suicide of another – Distribution of booklet containing advice on committing suicide – Booklet distributed by society believing in voluntary euthanasia – Whether supply of booklet to person who subsequently commits or attempts suicide an offence – Whether distribution of booklet amounting to aiding, abetting, counselling or procuring suicide – Suicide Act 1961, s 2(1).

The executive committee of a society which existed to promote voluntary euthanasia published a booklet entitled 'A Guide to Self-Deliverance' and sold it on request to members of the society aged 25 and over. Some 8,000 copies were distributed in that manner. The booklet's expressed aims were to overcome the fear of dying and to reduce the incidence of unsuccessful suicides. The booklet set out in detail several methods of what it termed 'self-deliverance' but could have deterred some people from committing suicide. The society took the view that the booklet would not encourage suicide and that it was in the public interest to make the advice it contained available to those persons who requested the booklet. The Attorney General, however, took the view that distribution of the booklet constituted an offence under s 2(1)[a] of the Suicide Act 1961, but because he wished to avoid prosecuting members of the society's executive committee, who were respectable persons and had issued the booklet out of genuine and strongly-held beliefs, he applied in civil proceedings for declarations that the future supply of the

---

a   Section 2(1) is set out at p 279 h, post

booklet to persons who were known to be, or were likely to be, considering or intending to commit suicide constituted the offence of aiding, abetting, counselling or procuring the suicide of another, contrary to s 2(1) of the 1961 Act, if after reading the booklet such a person committed or attempted to commit suicide, and constituted an attempt to commit an offence under s 2(1) even where such a person after reading the booklet did not commit or attempt suicide. The respondents, who were members of the society's executive committee, submitted that it was inappropriate to grant the declaratory relief sought.

Held – (1) Although the Attorney General was entitled to seek the assistance of the civil courts in upholding the criminal law, where he sought a declaration regarding the criminality of future conduct the civil court would have regard to the danger of usurping the criminal courts' jurisdiction and the function of the jury in a future criminal trial if the civil court declared whether future conduct would be criminal. Accordingly, a declaration regarding the criminality of future conduct would only be granted if the Attorney General clearly established that there was no risk that such a declaration would treat as criminal conduct which was not clearly in contravention of the criminal law (see p 284 c d and f to j, post); dicta of Lord Fraser in *Gouriet v Union of Post Office Workers* [1977] 3 All ER at 119 and of Viscount Dilhorne in *Imperial Tobacco Ltd v A-G* [1980] 1 All ER at 876 considered.

(2) Whether the distribution of the society's booklet to a person who then committed or attempted suicide constituted the offence under s 2(1) of the 1961 Act of aiding, abetting, counselling or procuring a person's suicide depended on whether the distributor was an accessory before the fact to the suicide or attempted suicide. It followed that to establish that the distributor had committed an offence under s 2(1) it had to be proved that he had distributed the booklet to a person whom at the time of the distribution he knew to be contemplating suicide, with the intention of assisting and encouraging that person to commit suicide by means of the booklet's contents, and further that that person was in fact assisted and encouraged by the booklet to commit or attempt to commit suicide. Where, however, the person requesting the booklet did not make clear to the distributor the purpose for which he required the booklet, so that it might, for example, be required for research or general information rather than to commit suicide, or where the booklet had nothing to do with a person's subsequent suicide or attempted suicide because, for example, the suicide happened a long time after he received the booklet, the distributor would lack the necessary intent to commit the offence under s 2(1) by assisting and encouraging the suicide or attempted suicide. That being so, to grant the declarations sought might result in treating as criminal conduct that which was not criminal, and the application for the declarations would accordingly be refused (see p 285 c d, p 286 c and g to j, p 287 c and j and p 288 b to e g h, post); R v Fretwell (1862) 9 Cox CC 152 considered.

Notes

For complicity in suicide, see 11 Halsbury's Laws (4th edn) para 1168, and for a case on the subject see 15 Digest (Reissue) 1175, 9991.

For declaratory judgments, see 1 Halsbury's Laws (4th edn) paras 185–187, and for cases on the subject, see 30 Digest (Reissue) 187–222, 184–359.

For the Suicide Act 1961, s 2, see 8 Halsbury's Statutes (3rd edn) 519.

Cases referred to in judgment

A-G (ex rel Hornchurch UDC) v Bastow [1957] 1 All ER 497, [1958] 1 QB 514, [1957] 2 WLR 340.

A-G's Reference (No 1 of 1975) [1975] 2 All ER 684, [1975] QB 773, [1975] 3 WLR 11, CA.

Gouriet v Union of Post Office Workers [1977] 3 All ER 70, [1978] AC 435, [1977] 3 WLR 300, HL.

Imperial Tobacco Ltd v A-G [1980] 1 All ER 866, [1981] AC 718, [1980] 2 WLR 466, HL.

National Coal Board v Gamble [1958] 3 All ER 203, [1959] 1 QB 11, [1958] 3 WLR 434, DC.

R v Bainbridge [1959] 3 All ER 200, [1960] 1 QB 129, [1959] 3 WLR 656, CCA.

a   *R v Baker* (1909) 28 NZLR 536.

R v Fretwell (1862) 9 Cox CC 152, CCR.

R v McShane (1977) 66 Cr App R 97, CA.

R v Reed [1982] Crim LR 819.

Royal College of Nursing of the United Kingdom v Department of Health and Social Security [1981] 1 All ER 545; *affd* [1981] 1 All ER 545, [1981] AC 800, [1981] 2 WLR 279, CA;

b   *affd* [1981] 1 All ER 545, [1981] AC 800, [1981] 2 WLR 279, HL.

Originating summons

By a summons dated 9 July 1982 the Attorney General sought as against the respondents, Brenda Able, Celia Fremlin, Harry Ree, Jean Davies and Barbara Smoker, members of the executive committee of the Voluntary Euthanasia Society (the society) (1) a declaration

c   that the supply of a booklet published by the society known as a Guide to Self-Deliverance, to a class of persons known to or likely to include persons intending to commit suicide constituted an offence contrary to s 2 of the Suicide Act 1961 if any such person subsequently committed suicide after reading the advice contained in the booklet, (2) a declaration that the supply of the booklet to a class of persons known to or likely to include persons intending to commit suicide constituted an attempt to commit an

d   offence contrary to s 2 of the 1961 Act if no such person subsequently committed suicide after reading the advice contained in the booklet, (3) a declaration that the supply of the booklet to a class of persons known to or likely include persons considering committing suicide constituted an offence contrary to s 2 of the 1961 Act if any such person subsequently committed suicide after reading the advice contained in the booklet, and (4) a declaration that the supply of the booklet to a class of persons known to or likely to

e   include persons considering committing suicide constituted an attempt to commit an offence contrary to s 2 of the 1961 Act if no such person subsequently committed suicide after reading the advice contained in the booklet. The facts are stated in the judgment.

Simon D Brown and *Stephen Aitchison* for the Attorney General.
Geoffrey Robertson and *Andrew Nicol* for the respondents.

f

Cur adv vult

28 April. The following judgment was delivered.

g   **WOOLF J.** In this case, Her Majesty's Attorney General applies by originating summons for declaratory relief that, in the circumstances specified by him, the distribution of a booklet entitled 'A Guide to Self-Deliverance', which is published by the executive committee of the Voluntary Euthanasia Society (which also used to be known as Exit), is unlawful as being either an offence or an attempted offence contrary to the provisions of s 2(1) of the Suicide Act 1961.

h   That Act, by s 1, abrogated the rule of law whereby it was a crime for a person to commit suicide. Section 2(1) provides:

'A person who aids, abets, counsels or procures the suicide of another, or an attempt by another to commit suicide, shall be liable on conviction on indictment to imprisonment for a term not exceeding fourteen years.'

j   The respondents to the summons, whose names were changed at the outset of the proceedings, are members of the executive committee of the society. The society is an unincorporated association of members. Its amended constitution recites the purposes for which the society was established. These are:

'(2) The Society shall work for the legalisation of voluntary euthanasia and for the enactment and beneficial working of any other measure seeking to establish the right, within properly defined limits, to avoid suffering and to die peacefully. (3)

The Society shall publish and distribute a form of declaration enabling members and others to make known their wishes with regard to terminal and emergency treatment. (4) The Society may take any other steps intended to promote a general acceptance and understanding of the principles of voluntary euthanasia. (5) The Society may consider and evaluate questions relating to the avoidance of suffering and to peaceful death and may provide information and practical and other advice to members of mature years and reasonable length of membership (by, for example, publication and distribution of a pamphlet or booklet) as to how most appropriately a prolonged and painful death can be avoided, and a life can be ended painlessly by someone hopelessly and painfully ill who has decided to embark on self-deliverance. (6) The Society may carry out research in relation to all the above purposes and apply funds accordingly.'

The respondents dispute the claim for relief on two main grounds. First, it is said that this is not a case in which it would be proper for the court to exercise its jurisdiction to grant declaratory relief, since it is for the criminal courts and not this court to apply the criminal law and if the law is unclear, the proper body to clarify the law is Parliament and not the courts. Second, they submit that the distribution of the booklet is not unlawful. The respondents go on to contend that if it is appropriate to grant declaratory relief, then a declaration should be granted that—

'No offence against Section 2 of the Suicide Act is committed by publishing or supplying factual information about methods of committing suicide or arguments about the propriety of so doing, if its publisher or supplier (a) has no knowledge that the recipient has a present intention of committing suicide, or (b) lacks an intention to persuade a particular recipient to commit suicide, or (c) where the information or argument published is by its nature or by the circumstances attending its publication unlikely to precipitate suicidal attempts.'

Before considering the issues between the parties, it is necessary for me to deal with the facts giving rise to the application in so far as they are established before me. The background to the publication of the booklet can be ascertained from a chronology which is set out in the booklet itself.

In July 1979 the then executive committee decided to ask the then 2,000 members whether they would appreciate a booklet describing how to end one's life. There was an overwhelming response in favour. In October 1979 a resolution was passed in favour of producing the booklet and thereafter the membership of the society increased rapidly by 1,000 a month. In June 1980 the committee obtained opinions from two different Queen's Counsel, who gave conflicting views as to the likelihood of prosecution. In July 1980 it was decided not to publish. In August 1980 the Scottish society decided to produce a booklet for its members. That booklet was published in September 1980 under the title 'How to Die with Dignity'. On 18 October 1980, when the membership of the society had increased to 10,000, an annual general meeting appointed a new committee pledged to publish the booklet.

On 22 October 1980 Dr Scott, a retired doctor, brought proceedings in the High Court to restrain publication of the booklet and obtained an undertaking that it would not be published, the grounds of his application being that it was contrary to the constitution of the society to publish the booklet. In February 1981 the constitution was changed and, in March 1981, Dr Scott withdrew his proceedings on the society paying his costs.

In June 1981 the booklet was first distributed. There has since been a considerable demand for the booklet. According to the respondents' evidence, by 25 November 1982 (ie in less than 18 months) 8,300 copies had been sold. This is despite the fact that the society has taken steps to limit the sales by charging £6 for each copy of the booklet and by limiting the sales to members of three months' standing, aged 25 or over.

It is next necessary to consider the booklet itself. Before I do so, I should make the position of the court clear.

I am, of course, aware of the serious debate whether or not voluntary euthanasia should be legalised. However, I am not in any way concerned with the morality of voluntary euthanasia or the morality of publishing and distributing a booklet of this sort. The court's sole concern is with the legal issues between the parties, to which I have already alluded and, in particular, to the lawfulness of distributing the booklet. Although that is the position of the court, justice requires that I should make it clear that there has been no suggestion made on behalf of the Attorney General that, if it is lawful to distribute a booklet of this nature, there is anything objectionable about the form or contents of this particular booklet. Indeed, having read the booklet more than once, it is manifest that no objection of that sort could be made. If it is appropriate to have distributed a booklet dealing with this subject, then this booklet provides a satisfactory treatment which it would not be easy to improve on. As the extracts which I will quote will make clear, it could deter a would-be suicide, but it will, in many cases, assist them to commit suicide when they might not otherwise do so, and this should be apparent to any reasonably intelligent person who has read the booklet.

Since the conclusion of the evidence, I have been supplied with a supplement to the booklet which has not been published by the society. That supplement, supplied by Dr Scott, confirms the views which I have just expressed.

On the inside page of the booklet there appears the statement: '*Before considering Self-Deliverance*; HAVE YOU RUNG THE SAMARITANS? *Their number is in your local phone book.*'

The booklet commences with a preface by the late Arthur Koestler, to which I should refer because it indicates the reasons for publishing it. The preface begins:

'When people talk of "the fear of death", they often fail to distinguish between two types of fear which may be combined in experience but are separate in origin. One is the fear of the *state* of death (or non-existence); the other the fear of the *process* of dying, the agony of the transition to that state. The aim of this booklet—and of the Society which, after much soul-searching, decided to publish it—is to overcome the second of these fears.'

Later, he said:

'If the agnostics among us could be assured of a gentle and easy way of dying, they would be much less afraid of *being* dead. This is not a logical attitude, but fear is not governed by logic.'

There is then an introduction, which commences:

'The reasons for writing this pamphlet are quite simple. Those who join Exit do so because they believe that they have a right to a say in the manner and timing of their death, particularly if it seems likely that the process of dying will be a long one and distressing either to them or to their friends and families. For some the main fear will be of continuing pain, while for others the main fear is of paralysis of body or mind or simply weariness with a life that has deteriorated beyond repair.'

The introduction goes on to say that—

'Exit receives frequent requests from members for advice about how they might most appropriately end their lives themselves if the need should arise. The main objectives of the Society are to secure the enactment of the 1969 Voluntary Euthanasia Bill by Parliament . . . Pending such legislation, we see no alternative to supplying on request the necessary information to bring about their own deliverance. Exit neither advocates nor deplores suicide. It has a neutral stance, and regards such decisions as matters of personal belief and judgment.'

The introduction concludes by stating:

'The Society certainly does not wish to encourage people to commit suicide, and in fact wishes to discourage people from killing themselves merely because of some personal crisis which will look a good deal less serious a few days or even a few hours later.'

The booklet then deals with the question of suicide and Christianity and gives assistance as to the forms of powers of attorney designed to avoid being given life sustaining treatment in circumstances 'where they consider it better for their life to end'. The next two pages of the booklet are entitled 'Why you should think again'. There are then set out, under seven separate headings, reasons why the reader should indeed think again before seeking to take his own life. The next page is entitled 'Before taking a final decision about seeking self-deliverance'. There are then four numbered paragraphs, the first of which advises the reader to 'consider over a substantial period—months if possible, rather than weeks—whether self-deliverance is the best way of dealing with your problems'. The second asks the reader to consider 'whether your problems could be overcome by seeking medical or other help, by changing your way of life', etc. The third paragraph warns that 'no method of suicide is absolutely foolproof' and a failure could result in brain damage or damage to other organs. It points out that failed suicides are often handled unsympathetically. The final paragraph states: 'Of those who survive apparently serious suicide attempts . . . a significant proportion find that they can cope with life after all.'

The booklet then deals with 'Care and distribution of this pamphlet' in these terms:

> 'In writing this pamphlet the readers we have had particularly in mind are those who might have wished to benefit from the provisions of the proposed 1969 Voluntary Euthanasia Bill. It is because we are anxious to discourage people from ending their lives without due thought and consideration of the alternatives that we have decided that this pamplet should be available only to those who have been members of Exit for at least three months. We accept that it may, despite all precautions, occasionally come into the hands of potential impulsive suicides, but we feel that we have to set against that risk the very real misery experienced by a much larger number of people who are currently forced to suffer against their will, sometimes for long periods. Accordingly we urge those who request the pamphlet to consider the wishes of our membership in deciding how it should be stored. We recommend that they keep it in a secure place and that they do not show it to others. If they ever decide to end their lives, before doing so they should either destroy the booklet or, better, send it back to us.'

The booklet then sets out certain general principles, among which are: 'Although this pamphlet is designed to reduce the incidence of unsuccessful attempts, it would be naive to think that it can prevent them entirely'. Then: 'We imagine that those who contemplate using this pamphlet will wish to die in such a way that their discovery will cause the minimum of distress to their families and friends.'

The booklet then turns to 'How not to do it' and sets out five separate methods of 'self-deliverance' in clear, straightforward and reasonably detailed terms. The booklet also contains a guide to sedative drugs, a list of references to other works, a passage dealing with coroners and inquests, a statement of the law and then it deals with the position of life assurance, medical research and transplants. Finally, there is a postscript by a Dr Eliot Slater, which makes it clear that the writer believes it is the absolute right of every human being to choose to live or to choose to die.

I have dealt with the booklet in some detail because its contents are the most important evidence in the case and I consider it right to try and give an indication of the balanced nature of those contents. It is, however, not possible to obtain the full effect of the booklet from the passages cited. This can only be obtained by reading the booklet as a whole.

In his affidavit, filed on behalf of the respondents, Dr Brewer argues that the ordinary reader would find the descriptions as to methods 'off-putting in their nature and subject-matter' and that the booklet, 'by giving details of what it accurately terms "elaborate preparations"', provides facts which dispel the emotion that suicide is an easy matter to accomplish. He disputes that the effect of the publication of the booklet is likely to encourage suicide and expresses the opinion that 'it will not cause a significant increase in suicide or suicidal attempts'. I emphasise the words 'a significant increase in' because they were inserted in longhand, presumably by the doctor before he deposed the affidavit because he appreciated it would cause some increase. In my view, the doctor underestimates the effect of the booklet. He concludes his affidavit by saying:

'I conclude that there is no reason to suspect that receipt of the booklet will have the effect of persuading persons to take their own lives, or "tipping over the brink" those who are contemplating such a course.'

He states that in his opinion, 'it is in the public interest to make it available in a responsible and balanced form to those adults prepared to take steps to obtain it'.

The Attorney General, by the evidence filed on his behalf, takes the opposite view. It is explained how the matter came to the attention of the authorities in consequence of the suicide, at Claridges Hotel, of Robert McLeod, who was only 22. This was on 20 July 1981, only shortly after the first distribution of the booklet, yet a copy was found in his room. There are exhibited various documents which were obtained from the society's London office. These and the other evidence make it clear that this highly intelligent young man was determined on taking his own life and was convinced of his moral right to do so. Further inquiries were then made and it was ascertained from the various police forces that, over the period of approximately 18 months after the first distribution of the booklet, there were 15 cases of suicides linked to the booklet and 19 suicides where documents were found which showed that the deceased was a member of, or had corresponded with, the society. As is pointed out on behalf of the Attorney General, there may be many other cases, particularly as members are invited in the booklet, if they decide to end their lives, before doing so either to destroy the booklet or send it back to the society.

Mr Nursaw, the Attorney General's legal secretary, explains in his affidavit why these proceedings were commenced, in the following manner:

'When Her Majesty's Attorney General's attention was drawn to these cases the view was taken that the distribution of the booklet to Exit's subscribers constituted an offence under Section 2 of the Suicide Act 1961. However, when this opinion was communicated to Exit in an attempt to bring the distribution to an end, the Executive Committee's solicitors disputed its correctness ... It is accepted that the members of that committee are respectable persons who chose to issue the booklet out of genuine and strongly-held beliefs and who would not follow a course of action which they know to be criminal. In view of the existence of a genuine dispute as to the precise ambit of the law it was considered desirable to seek a declaration from this Honourable Court to resolve that dispute quickly and authoritatively without exposing respectable people to prosecution for an offence carrying a maximum penalty of 14 years imprisonment. Although initially it was envisaged that an injunction would be sought as well as a declaration, it has now been decided solely to seek declaratory relief at this stage. This decision has been taken in the light of the letter of 7 May 1982 and in the confident expectation and belief that should this Honourable Court uphold Her Majesty's Attorney General's interpretation of the law all further publication and distribution of the booklet would cease immediately. Her Majesty's Attorney General and the Director have decided that it would not be right to bring criminal proceedings in respect of acts done by the Defendants in distributing the booklet before the decision of this Honourable Court is made known.'

Before I proceed to set out my conclusions as to the legal effect of the evidence, I should deal with the first ground of opposition raised by the respondents, since if it would not be appropriate to grant declaratory relief it would not be right for me to proceed further with my examination of the facts and the issues of law which arise from them.

The House of Lords has recently dealt with the question of the propriety of the civil courts granting declaratory relief in cases involving the criminal law in *Imperial Tobacco Ltd v A-G* [1980] 1 All ER 866, [1981] AC 718. In that case it was the company which sought the declaratory relief and the Attorney General who opposed the grant of it. Before the matter came before the High Court, criminal proceedings had already been

commenced. Giving the leading speech, Viscount Dilhorne said ([1980] 1 All ER 866 at
876, [1981] AC 718 at 742):

a

> 'My Lords, it is not necessary in this case to decide whether a declaration as to the
> criminality or otherwise of future conduct can ever properly be made by a civil
> court. In my opinion it would be a very exceptional case in which it would be right
> to do so. In my opinion it cannot be right to grant a declaration that an accused is
> innocent after a prosecution has started.'

b

That there can be circumstances where it is appropriate to give declaratory relief I
accept. Indeed, in *Royal College of Nursing of the United Kingdom v Department of Health and
Social Security* [1981] 1 All ER 545 I gave such relief, and my decision to do so was not
subject to criticism in either the Court of Appeal or the House of Lords (see [1981] 1 All
ER 545, [1981] AC 800). Furthermore, if it is open to a private individual, in exceptional
circumstances, to obtain such relief, it is certainly open to the Attorney General to do so,
since his right to seek the assistance of the civil courts in upholding the criminal law has
been fully recognised by the courts: see *A-G (ex rel Hornchurch UDC) v Bastow* [1957] 1 All
ER 497, [1957] 1 QB 514.

c

The position of the Attorney General in this respect was also dealt with by the House
of Lords in *Gouriet v Union of Post Office Workers* [1977] 3 All ER 70 at 119, [1978] AC 435
at 523–524, where Lord Fraser said:

d

> 'It seems to me entirely appropriate that responsibility for deciding whether to
> initiate preventive proceedings for injunction or declaration in the public interest
> should be vested in a public officer, and for historical reasons that officer is the
> Attorney-General. It is well established that he is not bound to prosecute in every
> case where there is sufficient evidence, but that when a question of public policy
> may be involved the Attorney-General has the duty of deciding whether prosecution
> would be in the public interest: see the statement by Sir Hartley Shawcross in 1951
> quoted in Edwards's The Law Officers of the Crown (1964, p 223). It seems even
> more necessary that similar consideration should be given to the public interest
> before initiating preventive procedure for injunction or declaration.'

e

There are, however, differences between this case and other cases where declaratory
relief has been granted in aid of the criminal law. Declarations are being sought that
certain conduct is criminal, not that certain conduct is not criminal. The declarations are
addressed to future distributions of the booklet and it is a real possibility that if a
declaration is granted but, despite this, further distributions take place, there could be a
criminal prosecution. This makes it particularly important that this court should bear in
mind the danger of usurping the jurisdiction of the criminal courts.

f

In this connection, I do not accept in full the submission of counsel for the Attorney
General that because the proceedings are brought by the Attorney General, it will only
be appropriate exceptionally to refuse declaratory relief. It is true, as counsel contends,
that in effect the Attorney General is in a position to obtain declarations as to the law
from the Court of Appeal, Criminal Division on an Attorney General's reference.
However, while the court's decision on such references frequently clarifies the law, the
court does so in relation to specific facts which are before it, in exactly the same way as it
would in the case of an ordinary appeal against conviction. Furthermore, if a court
declares what conduct will be criminal, it may be performing exactly the task which the
jury would have to perform at a criminal trial. However, if the court rules that conduct
is not criminal, it is performing a similar function to the judge at a criminal trial who
stops the case on a submission of no case to answer. While of course recognising the
advantages of the application of the law being clear in relation to future conduct, it would
only be proper to grant a declaration if it is clearly established that there is no risk of it
treating conduct as criminal which is not clearly in contravention of the criminal law.

g

h

j

Adopting this standard, I consider it appropriate to proceed to consider whether, on
the evidence which is before me, the Attorney General has established that he is entitled
to the declaratory relief which he seeks. A starting point of such consideration must be

the terms of s 2(1) of the 1961 Act itself. The intent of the subsection is clear. Section 1 of the Act having abrogated the criminal responsibility of the suicide, s 2(1) retains the criminal liability of an accessory at or before the fact. The nature of that liability has, however, changed. From being a participant in an offence of another, the accessory becomes the principal offender. This has the result that to attempt to 'aid, abet, counsel or procure the suicide of another, or an attempt by another to commit suicide' can be an offence even if the person concerned does not attempt to commit suicide: see *R v McShane* (1977) 66 Cr App R 97 and s 3 of the Criminal Attempts Act 1981. This is of significance in relation to the present issues because if the distribution of the booklet amounts to an offence under s 2(1) of the 1961 Act when the person to whom the booklet is distributed commits suicide or attempts to commit suicide, then the distribution to that person, if there is no attempt to commit suicide, could be an attempt to commit an offence under s 2(1) in the appropriate circumstances.

This being the general effect of s 2(1), the issue can be confined to considering whether distributing the booklet to someone who commits suicide or attempts to commit suicide makes the distributor 'an accessory before the fact' to the suicide or attempted suicide, the position so far as the distributor is concerned being exactly the same as it would be if either suicide or attempted suicide was still a criminal offence.

Of the opening words of s 2(1), the words 'aids, abets' are normally regarded as referring to an accessory at the fact, and the words 'counsels or procures' to an accessory before the fact. However, it is not right to ignore the words 'aids, abets' in considering whether a person is an accessory before the fact.

As is pointed out in *Russell on Crime* (12th edn, 1964) vol 1, p 150 the conception of accessories before the fact is one of great antiquity and it cannot properly be understood without consideration of its history. Coke used both the word 'aide' and the word 'abetting' in dealing with accessories before the fact (see 1 Co Inst 182). Hale said (1 PC 615):

'An accessory *before*, is he, that being absent at the time of the felony committed, doth yet procure, counsel, command, or abet another to commit a felony.'

Therefore, in the ordinary case, in deciding whether or not an offence has been committed, it is preferable to consider the phrase 'aids, abets, counsels or procures' as a whole. However, some of the previous decisions of the courts are explained by the fact that in the particular circumstances of that case, the court was considering only one part of the phrase.

The editor of *Russell on Crime* also provides assistance as to what is the 'bare minimum' which is necessary to constitute a person an accessory before the fact. It is stated (p 151):

'... the conduct of an alleged accessory should indicate (a) that he knew that the particular deed was contemplated, and (b) that he approved of or assented to it, and (c) that his attitude in respect of it in fact encouraged the principal offender to perform [and I would here add 'or attempt to perform'] the deed.'

In relation to the first minimum requirement, those responsible for publishing the booklet, because of its terms, would almost certainly know that a significant number of those to whom the booklet was intended to be sent would be contemplating suicide. They would not know precisely when, where or by what means the suicide was to be effected, if it took place, but this does not mean they cannot be shown to be accessories. As Lord Parker CJ said in *R v Bainbridge* [1959] 3 All ER 200 at 202, [1960] 1 QB 129 at 134:

'... if the principal does not totally and substantially vary the advice or the help and does not wilfully and knowingly commit a different form of felony altogether, the man who has advised or helped, aided or abetted, will be guilty as an accessory before the fact.'

As the judge had directed the jury in that case: 'It must be proved he knew the type of crime which was in fact committed was intended.'

In relation to the second requirement, if the recipients of the booklet committed or attempted to commit suicide, the contents of the booklet indicate that the publishers *a* approved or assented to their doing so. To conclude otherwise is inconsistent with the whole object of the booklet, which is to assist those who feel it necessary to resort to self-deliverance.

I turn, therefore, to the final minimum requirement. I have no doubt that, in the case at least of certain recipients of the booklet, its contents would encourage suicide. Ignorance how to commit suicide must by itself be a deterrent. Likewise, the risks *b* inherent in an unsuccessful attempt must be a deterrent. The contents of the booklet provide information as to methods which are less likely to result in an unsuccessful attempt. This assistance must encourage some readers to commit or attempt to commit suicide. This is clearly appreciated by the publishers, thus their care to control the persons to whom the booklet is to be sold and their advice as to the safe keeping of the booklet.

I, therefore, have come clearly to the conclusion that there could be circumstances in *c* which to supply the booklet could amount to an offence.

This conclusion is consistent with the decision of the Court of Appeal in *R v Reed* [1982] Crim LR 819, reported shortly in the Criminal Law Reports and of which case I have a transcript. That case concerned the former secretary of the society. He is now wholly disowned by the society, which disapproves of his conduct, that conduct having come to light as a result of his prosecution. Although he was convicted of offences under *d* s 2 of the 1961 Act and the Court of Appeal did not intervene, the decision of the court is of limited assistance because Reed's conduct went far beyond anything which is here being considered. The case against him was that he put his co-accused in touch with people so that the co-accused could actually assist them in committing suicide. As is stated in the transcript:

'there was no dispute that the conduct of Reed in putting Lyons in touch with *e* would-be suicides . . . constituted taking the appropriate steps to produce a result. The issue and the only issue was what result was intended. Was it the bringing of comfort to the sufferer, as Reed contended, or was it the procuring of suicide, as the Crown contended?

Some assistance is to be obtained from a New Zealand case, *R v Baker* (1909) 28 NZLR *f* 536. In that case it was held:

'Where one person writes a letter to another explaining how a crime of a particular nature may be committed, and the other person subsequently attempts to commit a crime of that nature, the writer of the letter is guilty of an attempt to commit that crime . . . even though when the letter was written no specific crime of that nature *g* was in the contemplation of either of the parties.'

However, that case has to be approached with caution as it has been the subject of considerable criticism by academic writers.

The fact that the supply of the booklet could be an offence does not mean that any particular supply is an offence. It must be remembered that the society is an *h* unincorporated body and there can be no question of the society committing an offence. Before an offence under s 2 can be proved, it must be shown that the individual concerned 'aided, abetted, counselled or procured' a suicide or an attempt at suicide and intended to do so by distributing the booklet. The intention of the individual will normally have to be inferred from facts surrounding the particular supply which he made. If, for example, before sending a copy of the booklet, a member of the society had written a letter, the *j* contents of which were known to the person sending the booklet, which stated that the booklet was required because the member was intending to commit suicide, then, on those facts, I would conclude that an offence had been committed or at least an attempted offence contrary to s 2 of the 1961 Act. However, in the majority of cases, a member requesting the booklet will not make clear his intentions and the supply will be made without knowledge of whether the booklet is required for purposes of research, general

information, or because suicide is contemplated. Is it, therefore, enough that in any
a particular case the person responsible for making the supply would appreciate that there
is a real likelihood that the booklet is required by one of the substantial number of
members of the society who will be contemplating suicide? It is as to this aspect of the
case that there is the greatest difficulty and little assistance from the authorities.

Counsel on behalf of the respondents contends that before a person can be an accessory,
there must be a consensus between the accessory and the principal, and there can be no
b consensus where the alleged accessory does not even know whether the principal is
contemplating (in this case) suicide. As, however, is pointed out in Smith and Hogan
Criminal Law (4th edn, 1978) while counselling implies consensus, procuring and aiding
do not. The authors say (p 116):

> '... the law probably is that: i) "Procuring" implies causation but not consensus,
> ii) "abetting" and "counselling" imply consensus but not causation and iii) "aiding"
c > requires actual assistance but neither consensus nor causation.'

As a matter of principle, it seems to me that, as long as there is the necessary intent to
assist those who are contemplating suicide to commit suicide if they decide to do so, it
does not matter that the supplier does not know the state of mind of the actual recipient.
The requirement for the necessary intent explains why in those cases where, in the
d ordinary course of business, a person is responsible for distributing an article, appreciating
that some individuals might use it for committing suicide, he is not guilty of an offence.
In the ordinary way, such a distributor would have no intention to assist the act of
suicide. An intention to assist need not, however, involve a desire that suicide should be
committed or attempted.

In this connection, I must refer to *R v Fretwell* (1862) 9 Cox CC 152. In that case the
e Court of Criminal Appeal decided that the mere provision of the means of committing a
crime is not sufficient to make the provider guilty as an accessory. In giving the judgment
of the court, Erle CJ said (at 154):

> 'In the present case the prisoner was unwilling that the deceased should take the
> poison; it was at her instigation and under the threat of self-destruction that he
> procured it and supplied it to her; but it was found that he did not administer it to
f > her or cause her to take it. It would be consistent with the facts of the case that he
> hoped she would change her mind; and it might well be that the prisoner hoped
> and expected that she would not resort to it.'

While I accept that this reasoning does not accord with mine, I do not regard the case
as requiring me to come to a different conclusion from that which I have indicated. That
g case is inconsistent with *National Coal Board v Gamble* [1958] 3 All ER 203, [1959] 1 QB
11 and I regard it as confined to its own facts, for the reasons indicated in Smith and
Hogan *Criminal Law* (4th edn, 1978, pp 120, 121).

Counsel for the respondents points out, and this I accept, that in some cases the booklet,
far from precipitating someone to commit suicide, might have the effect of deterring
someone from committing suicide when they might otherwise have done so. In such
h circumstances, he submits, it would be quite nonsensical to regard the supply of the
booklet as being an attempted offence contrary to s 2 of the 1961 Act. I agree, though I
recognise that on one approach the result would be different. The reason why I agree
with the submission is because, in such a case, the booklet has not provided any assistance
with a view to a contemplated suicide. Such assistance is necessary to establish the actus
reus for even the attempted offence.

j There will also be cases where, although the recipient commits or attempts to commit
suicide, the booklet has nothing to do with the suicide or the attempted suicide; for
example, a long period of time may have elapsed between the sending of the booklet and
the attempt. In such a case, again, I would agree with counsel for the respondents that
there would not be a sufficient connection between the attempted suicide and the supply
of the booklet to make the supplier responsible. This does not mean that it has to be
shown that the suicide or attempted suicide would not have occurred but for the booklet.

However, if 'procuring' alone is relied on, this may be the case. As Lord Widgery CJ stated in *A-G's Reference (No 1 of 1975)* [1975] 2 All ER 684 at 686–687, [1975] QB 773 at 779–780:

> 'To procure means to produce by endeavour. You procure a thing by setting out to see that it happens and taking the appropriate steps to produce that happening ... You cannot procure an offence unless there is a causal link between what you do and the commission of the offence ...'

However, you do not need to procure to be an accessory and the same close causal connection is not required when what is being done is the provision of assistance.

I therefore conclude that to distribute the booklet can be an offence. But, before an offence can be established to have been committed, it must at least be proved (a) that the alleged offender had the necessary intent, that is, he intended the booklet to be used by someone contemplating suicide and intended that that person would be assisted by the booklet's contents, or otherwise encouraged to take or to attempt to take his own life; (b) that while he still had that intention he distributed the booklet to such a person who read it; and, (c) in addition, if an offence under s 2 of the 1961 Act is to be proved, that such a person was assisted or encouraged by so reading the booklet to take or to attempt to take his own life, otherwise the alleged offender cannot be guilty of more than an attempt.

If these facts can be proved, then it does not make any difference that the person would have tried to commit suicide anyway. Nor does it make any difference, as the respondents contend, that the information contained in the booklet is already in the public domain. The distinguishing feature between an innocent and guilty distribution is that in the former case the distributor will not have the necessary intent, while in the latter case he will.

However, in each case it will be for a jury to decide whether the necessary facts are proved. If they are, then normally the offence will be made out. Nevertheless, even if they are proved, I am not prepared to say it is not possible for there to be some exceptional circumstance which means that an offence is not established.

The situations with which I have just sought to deal illustrate the problems in this case of granting any form of declaration to Her Majesty's Attorney General. However, as I am clearly of the view that the supply of this booklet can amount to an offence contrary to s 2 of the 1961 Act if the recipient commits or attempts to commit suicide, there can be no question of the respondents being granted a declaration.

Recognising the difficulties created by the sort of situations to which I have referred, in the course of argument counsel for the Attorney General submitted alternative forms of declarations from those set out in the originating summons. However, despite his gallant efforts, he has failed so far to produce a declaration which would not have the effect of indicating that an offence has been committed when, in fact, no offence would be committed. Having examined the facts and the law, I am satisfied that there is no form of declaration that it would be appropriate to grant. That it is desirable for the law to be clarified I accept, but if there is to be any clarification as a result of the proceedings before this court, it must come not as a result of my granting a declaration, but from the limited assistance which I have been able to give in the course of this judgment. One happy consequence of this conclusion is that both parties will be at liberty to appeal and no doubt, as a result of such an appeal, all will be made clear. If it is not, only Parliament can provide the answer.

It remains for me to express my gratitude for the very considerable assistance which I have received from all counsel in this case. I am very grateful for the care and assistance with which they made their submissions.

Application refused.

Solicitors: *Treasury Solicitor*; *Calvert-Smith & Sutcliffe*, Richmond, Surrey (for the respondents).

April Weiss   Barrister.

Re E(SA) (a minor) (wardship)

HOUSE OF LORDS
LORD DIPLOCK, LORD SCARMAN, LORD ROSKILL, LORD BRIDGE OF HARWICH AND LORD BRANDON
OF OAKBROOK
16, 17, 19 JANUARY 1984

Child – Care – Wardship proceedings – Scope of court's jurisdiction – Right to adopt course of action not contemplated by parties.

A court exercising its wardship jurisdiction is not confined to deciding the issues raised by the parties as in a normal adversarial dispute. Accordingly, because its duty is to serve the true interests and welfare of the ward, the court may in exceptional cases decide on a course of action not advocated by any party to the proceedings. However, where the child has been in the care of a local authority for a considerable period of time and has successfully been placed with foster parents the court will pay great attention to the views and proposals of the local authority (see p 289 *h* and p 290 *g* to p 291 *b*, post).

Notes
For jurisdiction of court in wardship proceedings, see 24 Halsbury's Laws (4th edn) paras 576–583, and for cases on the subject, see 28(2) Digest (Reissue) 911–916, 2220–2247.

Interlocutory appeal
The father of a minor who had become a ward of court on 21 September 1982, appealed with leave of the Appeal Committee of the House of Lords granted on 8 December 1983 against the decision of the Court of Appeal (Dunn and May LJJ) on 17 November 1983 allowing an appeal by the respondent local authority, Essex County Council, from an order made by Wood J sitting in chambers in the Family Division of the High Court on 26 August 1983 whereby he continued the wardship of the minor and granted care and control of the minor to the appellant and made a supervision order in favour of Mr Andrew Hatton, the court probation officer. The Court of Appeal substituted an order that the minor be committed to the care of the respondent local authority and granted the authority leave to prepare him for adoption. The facts are set out in the opinion of Lord Scarman.

David Croft QC and *John R Davies* for the appellant.
Margaret Puxon QC and *Margaret Windridge* for the local authority.

Their Lordships took time for consideration.

19 January. The following opinions were delivered.

LORD DIPLOCK. My Lords, I have had the advantage of reading in draft the speech of my noble and learned friend Lord Scarman. I agree with it, and for the reasons he gives I would allow this appeal and make the order proposed by him.

LORD SCARMAN. My Lords, I would allow this appeal. The respondent, the Essex County Council, instituted on 21 September 1982, wardship proceedings in respect of a boy who was then six years eight months old. The boy is now eight years old. His father and mother were made defendants in the proceedings. The mother has taken no part in the case: she left home on Boxing Day 1977, since when she has not concerned herself with the care or upbringing of the boy. The father, who is the appellant in your Lordships' House, has fought the case. Both he and the local authority accept that the boy should remain until his future is settled and secure a ward of court. The local authority seeks an order that the boy be committed to its care and control and that leave be given to prepare him for adoption and to place him in a home with a view to adoption. The father strongly opposes the adoption proposal and seeks an order that care and control be committed to him. In effect, he is asking that after a long period in which the boy has been (with his assent) in the care of the local authority he should be able to resume parental care and control.

The matter came before Wood J in August 1983. Eight days were occupied taking evidence, oral, documentary, and by affidavit. The judge reserved his judgment, which he delivered on 26 August. He examined and analysed the evidence in great detail. He made clear findings of fact in the areas of dispute. He saw and heard the father give evidence over a period of two days and reached an assessment of his character. A report by a court welfare officer, Mr Hatton, was available: it had been made pursuant to an order of the court made by the registrar before whom, in accordance with the usual practice, the matter had first come after issue of the originating summons. Mr Hatton was called as a witness, and it is clear that the judge attached great weight to his evidence. The judge's decision was to reject the adoption proposal, to commit the child to the care and control of his father, to place him under the supervision of Mr Hatton, to give Mr Hatton and the parties liberty to apply, and to retain the matter to himself.

The local authority appealed. The Court of Appeal (Dunn and May LJJ) also went into the case with very great care. They concluded that the risk of breakdown in the care and upbringing of the boy if he were to be entrusted to his father was so great and the need for an immediate decision enabling the boy to enjoy a permanent settled home was so urgent that it was plain that the judge was wrong in rejecting the adoption proposal and in returning the boy to his father.

The father appeals with the leave of this House. At first sight the appeal would seem (and so it appeared to the Appeal Committee who granted leave) to raise the well-known but always difficult question as to the circumstances in which an appellate court is justified in substituting its judgment for that of the trial judge. But when in the course of the hearing of the appeal your Lordships came to study the full history of the case and, in particular, the report and evidence of Mr Hatton, it became clear that neither the trial judge nor the Court of Appeal had considered a third possible course of action in place of the two courses (adoption or father resuming parental control) between which both courts believed they had to make a choice. The third option is that a period of access, including staying access, should be granted to the father at the discretion and under the supervision of Mr Hatton, the court welfare officer, so that an area of uncertainty might be clarified, the uncertainty being whether father and son, whose attachment for each other was a feature of the evidence and the subject of a specific finding by the judge, could develop a sound relationship enabling a stable home situation to be established by the natural parent.

Neither party directed any attention in their submissions to the possibility of a trial period of access before reaching a final decision between the course of adoption or father's resumption of parental control. No doubt in most cases it does suffice for the court to confine its attention to the questions raised by the parties. And no doubt this usually suffices in wardship cases as well. But a court exercising jurisdiction over its ward must never lose sight of a fundamental feature of the jurisdiction that it is exercising, namely, that it is exercising a wardship, not an adversarial, jurisdiction. Its duty is not limited to the dispute between the parties: on the contrary, its duty is to act in the way best suited in its judgment to serve the true interest and welfare of the ward. In exercising wardship jurisdiction, the court is a true family court. Its paramount concern is the welfare of its ward. It will, therefore, sometimes be the duty of the court to look beyond the submissions of the parties in its endeavour to do what it judges to be necessary. When a local authority or a parent persuades the court that it should make a child its ward, the court takes over the ultimate responsibility for the child. No doubt, it will only be in exceptional cases that the court decides on a course not advocated by any party to the proceedings. Moreover, in a case where a child has been in the care of a local authority a   for a considerable period of time and the child has been placed successfully, as in the present case, with excellent and devoted foster-parents, very great attention will be paid to the views and proposals of the local authority. Nevertheless, exceptional cases, however rarely, do arise. For example, mistakes can be made even by experienced social workers. If any be made which in the court's judgment had an important bearing on the case, the court must take the course it thinks best, even if to do so means adopting a course of action not contemplated by the parties.

b   An immediate decision being required of the House in the interests of the ward in order to enable the court within a reasonable period of time to reach a final decision on the ward's future, I think it neither necessary nor prudent to embark on what has already been twice done, namely a recital of the history of the case. All is told, and well told, in the judgment of Wood J and in the Court of Appeal. The error of the judge and of the Court of Appeal was to think that on the evidence available to them they could determine

c   whether the true interests of the child would be best served by adoption or resumption by the father of parental control. A careful examination of Mr Hatton's evidence reveals the existence of a critical area of uncertainty which it was vital in the long-term interests of the child to clarify before a final decision is taken. It was an uncertainty which, had not the local authority mistakenly refused permission to Mr Hatton to observe boy and father together, might not have arisen.

d   In his report filed on 18 May 1983 Mr Hatton wrote, under the heading 'Conclusions':

> 'v) [The father] seems committed and determined to care for [his boy]. It is often difficult for a working single parent to meet the day to day needs of a child and there could be problems for [the father]. He seems prepared if all else failed to give up work but there are good people . . . who are ready and willing and seem able to give him as much help as possible. [The father' mother], despite her advancing
>
e   years, seems at present to have much to contribute to [the boy's] life.
>
> vi) [The father] has not shown to me that he would definitely be able to meet [his son's] emotional needs. He talked about feelings of love, which I am sure he experiences and probably [the boy] does as well but when discussing [the boy's] future care he tended to concentrate on practical issues. If allowed custody it would be important that he encourage [the boy] to develop his own friends and interests.
>
f   vii) I have not been permitted to observe [father and son] together and it is in my opinion uncertain whether they will be able to establish a rapport that will provide [the boy] with the long term consistent care and affection that urgently needs to be provided for him. If the court does consider it appropriate that [the father] should again have responsibility for [his son's] care I believe that it is essential that this should only happen after a successful period of access. One difficulty is that if such
>
g   access was commenced and failed it would delay [the boy] being established in a permanent substitute family. For access to be a success [the father] would need to be prepared to put aside past differences and work constructively at least with the foster parents but ideally also with Mr Lucas, and probably with other social services staff. If the court felt it to be appropriate, the Court Welfare Service would be willing to provide support during this period. In my opinion a period of access should include
>
h   staying access and be long enough to see if the father and son relationship is likely to now stand the test of time. Six months would seem an appropriate period . . .
>
> ix) [The son] does retain attachment to his father who has shown to me a sincere commitment now to provide for his son. The situation is different to when rehabilitation was previously attempted as [the father] has finally severed his attachment to his second wife. Adoptive parents are available but it may just be that
>
j   a final effort to rehabilitate [son] to his father would now be successful.'

When Mr Hatton gave evidence he was cross-examined by counsel for the local authority about the risk of a breakdown in the relationship between the boy and his father if the father was given care and control. He recognised the risk, and stated his belief (surely correct) that there should be a transitional period of access before a final decision to return the boy to his father was taken. He suggested a period of six months and he expected problems. He was then asked by the judge to look at it from the boy's point of view. He said:

'Yes, there is a risk. I would anticipate that there is a risk with adoption, too. There is a risk when one moves any child. This is the first time in all the inquiries which I have carried out for the High Court and the county court where I have not had the opportunity of seeing the respective parties with the child. I must say that I am really not able to comment about Mr E and [his son] together, which places me in a difficult position.'

The gap in the court's knowledge of a vital factor to be assessed in the making of a final decision could not have been revealed more starkly. It was very wrong on the part of the local authority to deny the welfare officer appointed by the court and ordered to report the opportunity to observe father and son together. No doubt, the authority's decision arose from the best of intentions: but it revealed a total and frightening misunderstanding by its social service advisers of the role of the court and of the court's officer in wardship proceedings.

Mr Hatton was, of course, considering in the parts quoted from his report and evidence how best to manage the father's resumption of parental control, if that should be the court's decision. But there emerges enough to make it abundantly clear that if the area of uncertainty could be resolved it might prove to be very wrong to deny the child an upbringing by his natural father to whom he was attached.

It is impossible, in my judgment, in the state of the evidence to make a final decision now as to parental control of the ward without running the risk of making a disastrously wrong irrevocable choice: and it would be wrong to prepare the child for adoption before a decision had been taken to reject care and control by the father. It is always a very serious decision to remove permanently a child from his natural parents, or parent (if only one, as here, be available) and from his natural family. The evidence indicated that a decision might well be possible after a period of access supervised and closely watched by the court's welfare officer. What will be learnt from this period of access it is impossible at this stage to know. Adoption may prove necessary: but, if there is a real prospect of a stable and loving relationship developing between father and son, the delay will have served the true interests of the child. A home with his natural parent, if circumstances are right and a loving relationship exists, must be best. But the material on which to base a decision is not yet available.

For these reasons I would allow the appeal and set aside the order of the Court of Appeal of 17 November 1983. I would propose that the cause be remitted back to the High Court of Justice, Family Division, reserved to Wood J, with the following directions: (1) that the minor, 'E', do remain a ward of the High Court of Justice, Family Division, during his minority or until further order; (2) that the said minor be committed to the care and control of the respondent local authority until further order, the said council undertaking to keep the said minor fostered with Mr and Mrs C (provided always that they are agreeable to fostering him) until further order; (3) that the said minor be placed under the supervision of Mr Hatton, an officer of the Essex Probation and After Care Service; (4) that Mr Hatton do arrange at his discretion and do, to the extent that he considers necessary, supervise access by the appellant to the said minor, such access to include staying access; (5) that Mr Hatton do report to the court upon the success or otherwise of such access as soon as he considers it appropriate to do so but not later than 31 May 1984; (6) that no steps be taken to prepare the said minor for adoption or to place him in a home with a view to adoption unless and until ordered by the court; (7) that Mr Hatton or any party to the proceedings have liberty to apply. I propose there should be no order as to costs save that the costs of the appellant be taxed on a common fund basis in accordance with the provisions of Sch 2 to the Legal Aid Act 1974.

LORD ROSKILL. My Lords, I have had the advantage of reading in draft the speech delivered by my noble and learned friend Lord Scarman. For the reasons he gives I too would allow this appeal and make the order proposed by him.

LORD BRIDGE OF HARWICH. My Lords, I agree that the appeal should be allowed and that the order proposed by my noble and learned friend Lord Scarman be made.

LORD BRANDON OF OAKBROOK. My Lords, I have the advantage of reading in draft the speech prepared by my noble and learned friend Lord Scarman. I agree with it, and for the reasons which he gives would allow the appeal and make the order proposed by him.

Appeal allowed.

Solicitors: *Gepp & Sons*, Chelmsford (for the appellant); *R W Adcock*, Chelmsford (for the local authority).

Mary Rose Plummer   Barrister.

Messenger Newspapers Group Ltd v National Graphical Association

COURT OF APPEAL, CIVIL DIVISION

SIR JOHN DONALDSON MR, GRIFFITHS AND STEPHEN BROWN LJJ

30 NOVEMBER 1983

Contempt of court – Sequestration – Position of third party in relation to writ of sequestration – Third party not holding contemnor's assets – Trade union fined for contempt of court and writ of sequestration issued – Request by sequestrators to union's auditors for information regarding assets – Auditors declining to comply with request – Whether auditors under duty to disclose information to sequestrators.

A trade union was fined for contempt of court and when the union failed to pay the fine a writ of sequestration was issued on the application of the plaintiff. The sequestrators requested the union's auditors to disclose information regarding the union's assets but the auditors refused, on the grounds that the union had not consented to such disclosure and that in any event since the auditors themselves did not hold any property belonging to the union they were not obliged to comply with the request. The sequestrators applied for an order that the auditors disclose the information asked for.

Held – Where a writ of sequestration had been issued and the sequestrators, in the exercise of their duties thereunder, required a third party to take any action, including the disclosing of the contemnor's assets or the divulging of any information concerning them, the third party was under a duty not knowingly to obstruct the sequestrators in the performance of their duties since to do otherwise would amount to obstructing the court. That principle applied regardless of whether the third party held property belonging to the contemnor. Since the sequestrators' request was necessary and proper and had been made in the exercise of their duties under the writ of sequestration, the auditors were obliged to comply with it, and the Court would accordingly make an order that they do so (see p 295 *a* to *f* and p 296 *a b*).

Eckman v Midland Bank Ltd [1973] 1 All ER 609 applied.

Per curiam. The consent of the contemnor has no relevance to whether a third party is required to give information to sequestrators since sequestration would otherwise be impossible to effect (see p 295 *f* and p 296 *a b*, post).

Notes
For the rights and duties of third parties in regard to sequestration, see 17 Halsbury's
Laws (4th edn) paras 508, 512.

Case referred to in judgments
Eckman v Midland Bank Ltd [1973] 1 All ER 609, [1973] QB 519, [1973] 2 WLR 284,
     NIRC.

Application
In sequestration proceedings brought by the plaintiff, Messenger Newspapers Group Ltd,
against the defendant trade union, the National Graphical Association (1982) (sued as the
National Graphical Association), the commissioners of sequestration appointed by the
court pursuant to an order of Eastham J on 25 November 1983 applied, in the course of
an application by the union for leave to withdraw its appeal against the order of Eastham
J, for an order that the union's auditors, Messrs Stoy Hayward & Co of Baker St, London,
comply within 24 hours with the request of the commissioners contained in a letter
dated 28 November 1983 that they disclose to the commissioners information regarding
(i) the names of persons holding property on behalf of the union, (ii) the union's annual
return for the six months to 28 March 1983 and (iii) the names of the union's stockbrokers
or other investment advisers and their bankers. The facts are set out in the judgment of
Sir John Donaldson MR.

Charles Garside for the plaintiff.
Terence Rigby for the union.
Howard Page for the sequestrators.

SIR JOHN DONALDSON MR. I deal first with the position of Messrs Stoy Hayward
& Co, the auditors of the union involved in this case, the National Graphical Association
(1982). They have been asked by the sequestrators to give them such information as they
have concerning the location, nature and other details of the assets of the union. That is
a proper request and a necessary request if they are to give effect to their duties under the
writ of sequestration.

Stoy Hayward & Co's solicitors have replied to this effect:

'We are concerned that this letter [the letter from the sequestrators] seeks
information from our clients about the affairs of their clients, National Graphical
Association (1982). Our clients are not at the present time authorised by their client
to give you the information which you seek, although they have written to them
seeking their consent. We have considered the terms of the Orders sent with Mr
Larkins' letter of 28th November. Our clients hold no property of the National
Graphical Association (1982). In those circumstances our clients are unable to satisfy
themselves that there is any legal basis for the requests made in the letter of 28th
November. If you disagree with this proposition, perhaps you would set out for us
the basis of your contention and we shall consider the matter further.'

That letter is dated 29 November 1983 and, so far as I know, the sequestrators have not
yet had an opportunity of replying to it. But the matter has very properly been brought
to our attention and it is right that we should deal with it.

A somewhat similar problem arose in 1972 with the Midland Bank. The Midland
Bank were called on by sequestrators to pay over money, or to give information as to its
whereabouts, and they said that they were unable to do so without an express order of
the court. The matter came before the court and is reported in *Eckman v Midland Bank
Ltd* [1973] 1 All ER 609, [1973] QB 519. In a judgment of the court which reviewed the
various authorities, I set out the underlying principle ([1973] 1 All ER 609 at 615, [1973]
QB 519 at 527):

'In our judgment, the position of a third party in relation to a writ of sequestration is analogous to that of a third party in relation to an injunction, namely, that he is subject to a duty not knowingly to take any action which will obstruct compliance by the sequestrators with the terms of the writ of sequestration which require them to take possession of the assets.'

In the context of *Eckman v Midland Bank* we were only concerned with a bank which either held moneys or had held moneys. There was no way in which the bank could have information, except in one or other of those contexts. But the principle which was being applied was wider. It was, as I say, that no one should knowingly take any action to obstruct the sequestrators in the execution of their duty and thereby obstruct the court.

Applying that principle to the union's auditors, who must have records of where the union's property is and of what it consists, it is a very clear obstruction of the sequestrators to refuse to divulge that information.

I have no doubt that Messrs Stoy Hayward & Co have acted in a way which they thought was entirely correct and nothing that I say must be considered a criticism of them as professional accountants any more than what I said in *Eckman v Midland Bank Ltd* was a criticism of the Midland Bank. We made it entirely clear in that case that the Midland Bank were wrong in law and technically were in contempt of court, but it was the first time that the matter had been raised and they were entitled to come to the court in order to have the matter clarified. Messrs Stoy Hayward & Co are entitled to think that their case could be considered as being different. We are quite clear that it is not different, that it is covered by exactly the same principle, but that is the reason why, although technically in contempt, we see no reason why the matter should go further than our declaring what their duty is and requiring them to perform it.

We will make an order requiring Messrs Stoy Hayward & Co to disclose the information which the sequestrators have asked for. We will stay the operation of that order for 24 hours to enable Messrs Stoy Hayward & Co to appear before this court if they wish to challenge the ruling which we have given and argue that it is wrong. If they do so, we shall of course listen to what they have to say and review our decision. If we are satisfied that we are wrong, we shall alter it. But, unless they appear within 24 hours to argue to the contrary, our order will take effect and they will be obliged to give the information for which the sequestrators have asked. It is, of course, quite irrelevant whether the officers of the union do, or do not, consent. A sequestration would be quite impossible if it required the consent of, for example, the officers of the company against whom a writ of sequestration is issued.

So much for that aspect of the matter.

We had expected today that there would be an appeal against the amount of the two fines and against the sequestration order. So far as the sequestration order was concerned, we had been giving some thought to ways in which a total sequestration might be modified, on the lines that we modified it under our interim order: some way in which, while fulfilling the needs of the court and its authority, it would nevertheless allow the union to carry on its *lawful* trade union activities. But in view of the fact that the union has decided not to proceed with the appeal, we cannot give effect to that intention. It is entirely a matter for the union and we have indeed invited it to reconsider its decision not to appeal solely in order that we might consider ways in which the sequestration order could be varied or administered, leaving it free to carry on its lawful union activity. However, it is entirely a matter for the union. It has decided not to appeal. The consequence of that will be that the order made by the judge, Eastham J, will remain unaffected; our interim order varying his order allowing the union to carry on will, of course, now expire, and the union and all its assets will be subject to a total sequestration order.

If, on reflection, the union thinks that that is an unsatisfactory situation from the point of view of its members, it will be open to it to apply to Eastham J, asking him to give the sequestrators such instructions as he thinks proper, with a view to ameliorating the effects of the total sequestration order. But that must be entirely a matter for the union.

All that we can say is that the appeal will be dismissed, since it has not been prosecuted, and it will be dismissed with costs.

GRIFFITHS LJ. I agree.

STEPHEN BROWN LJ. I agree.

Appeal dismissed

Solicitors: *Church Adams Tatham & Co*, agents for *Cobbetts*, Manchester (for the plaintiff); *Kershaw Gassman & Matthews* (for the union); *Clifford-Turner* (for the sequestrators).

Diana Procter   Barrister.

Savings and Investment Bank Ltd v Gasco Investments (Netherlands) BV and others

CHANCERY DIVISION

PETER GIBSON J

18, 19, 20, 28 JULY 1983

Company – Inspectors' report – Evidence – Admissibility of report as evidence – Interlocutory proceedings – Whether affidavit evidence founded on information contained in report can be used in interlocutory proceedings – Whether references in affidavit to inspectors' opinions may be struck out – Companies Act 1948, ss 165, 172 – RSC Ord 41, rr 5(2), 6.

Document – Admissibility in evidence – Record as evidence of facts stated therein – Report of Department of Trade inspectors into affairs of company – Whether report a 'record' – Companies Act 1948, ss 165, 172 – Civil Evidence Act 1968, s 4(1).

A report of inspectors appointed under ss 165 and 172 of the Companies Act 1948 to investigate the affairs and ownership of a company contains only opinions and is inadmissible as evidence in court proceedings save for the limited purpose of winding-up proceedings brought by the Secretary of State or by a person for whose protection the inspectors were appointed, in which case the court is permitted to treat the report not as evidence in the ordinary sense but as material on which it can make a winding-up order if that material is not challenged by proper evidence. Furthermore, even if the inspectors' opinions contained in their report are referred to in an affidavit sworn for the purpose of being used in interlocutory proceedings (which may, by virtue of RSC Ord 41, r 5(2)[a], contain statements of information or belief), such references to the inspectors' opinions may be struck out under Ord 41, r 6[b] as being references to evidence which is otherwise inadmissible and therefore 'irrelevant' under r 6 (see p 304 *a* to *e*, p 305 *e f*, p 306 *a* to *d* and p 307 *h*, post); *Re Grosvenor and West-end Railway Terminus Hotel Co Ltd* (1897) 76 LT 337, *Re J L Young Manufacturing Co Ltd* [1900] 2 Ch 753, *Hollington v F Hewthorn & Co Ltd* [1943] 2 All ER 35, *Re SBA Properties Ltd* [1967] 2 All ER 615, *Third Chandris Shipping Corp v Unimarine SA* [1979] 2 All ER 972 and *Re St Piran Ltd* [1981] 3 All ER 270 considered.

---

a   Rule 5(2) provides: 'An affidavit sworn for the purpose of being used in interlocutory proceedings may contain statements of information or belief with the sources and grounds thereof.'

b   Rule 6 provides: 'The Court may order to be struck out of any affidavit any matter which is scandalous, irrelevant or otherwise oppressive.'

a A report of inspectors appointed under ss 165 and 172 of the 1948 Act is not a 'record' for the purposes of s 4(1)ᶜ of the Civil Evidence Act 1968 and accordingly is not admissible under s 4(1) as evidence of the existence of any fact mentioned in it (see p 307 *d* to *f*, post); *H v Schering Chemicals Ltd* [1983] 1 All ER 849 applied.

Notes

b For proceedings arising out of a report of inspectors appointed by the Secretary of State for Trade, see 7 Halsbury's Laws (4th edn) para 975.

For the admissibility of hearsay evidence in relation to winding-up petitions, see ibid para 1023.

For affidavits in support of a petition, see ibid para 1022, and for cases on the subject, see 10 Digest (Reissue) 959–963, 5667–5691.

c For the Companies Act 1948, ss 165, 172, see 5 Halsbury's Statutes (3rd edn) 243, 248.

For the Civil Evidence Act 1968, s 4, see 12 ibid 913.

Cases referred to in judgment

American Cyanamid Co v Ethicon Ltd [1975] 1 All ER 504, [1975] AC 396, [1975] 2 WLR 316, HL.

d *Grosvenor and West-end Railway Terminus Hotel Co Ltd, Re* (1897) 76 LT 337, CA.

H v Schering Chemicals Ltd [1983] 1 All ER 849, [1983] 1 WLR 143.

Hollington v F Hewthorn & Co Ltd [1943] 2 All ER 35, [1943] KB 587, CA.

J (an infant), Re [1960] 1 All ER 603, [1960] 1 WLR 253.

Quilter v Heatly (1883) 23 Ch D 42, CA.

SBA Properties Ltd, Re [1967] 2 All ER 615, [1967] 1 WLR 799.

e *St Piran Ltd, Re* [1981] 3 All ER 270, [1981] 1 WLR 1300.

Third Chandris Shipping Corp v Unimarine SA, The Pythia, The Angelic Wings, The Genie [1979] 2 All ER 972, [1979] QB 645, [1979] 2 WLR 122, CA.

Young (J L) Manufacturing Co Ltd, Re, Young v J L Young Manufacturing Co Ltd [1900] 2 Ch 753, CA.

f ### Interlocutory application

On 16 March 1982 the plaintiff, Savings and Investment Bank Ltd (SIB), brought an action against the defendants, (1) Gasco Investments (Netherlands) BV, (2) H & W Fourteen Ltd, (3) Gasco Investments Ltd and (4) St Piran Ltd, claiming, inter alia, repayment of a debt and interest owed to it by the first and third defendants respectively and seeking an injunction restraining the fourth defendant from disposing of its assets.

g On 18 February 1983 SIB issued a notice of motion seeking injunctive relief against the defendants until the trial of the action. SIB indicated that at the hearing of the motion it intended to use an affidavit sworn by Gerhard Adolf Weiss on behalf of the joint liquidators of SIB. The first, third and fourth defendants, applied to the court (i) for an order under RSC Ord 41, r 6 and the court's inherent jurisdiction to strike out paras 23 and 25 to 41 inclusive of Mr Weiss's affidavit on the ground that the contents thereof

h were scandalous, inadmissible, irrelevant and/or otherwise oppressive, and (ii) for an order under RSC Ord 24, rr 10 and 11 to compel SIB to produce for their inspection two

---

c Section 4(1) provides: 'Without prejudice to section 5 of this Act, in any civil proceedings a statement contained in a document shall, subject to this section and to rules of court, be admissible as evidence of any fact stated therein of which direct oral evidence would be admissible, if the

j document is, or forms part of, a record compiled by a person acting under a duty from information which was supplied by a person (whether acting under a duty or not) who had, or may reasonably be supposed to have had, personal knowledge of the matters dealt with in that information and which, if not supplied by that person to the compiler of the record directly, was supplied by him to the compiler of the record indirectly through one or more intermediaries each acting under a duty.'

documents which they stated were referred to in the affidavit. The facts are set out in the
judgment.   *a*

John Lindsay QC and *Charles Aldous* for the first, third and fourth defendants.
Jonathan Parker QC and *John Trenhaile* for SIB.

Cur adv vult
                                                                                                                   b

28 July. The following judgment was delivered.

PETER GIBSON J. I have before me an application by the first, third and fourth
defendants (to whom I will refer collectively as 'the defendants') in two parts. The first
and major part is to strike out certain passages in an affidavit sworn on behalf of and
intended to be used by the plaintiff when a motion by which it seeks injunctive relief is   *c*
heard. The second part of the application is to compel the production of two documents
for inspection by the defendants, those documents being, so the defendants say, referred
to in that affidavit. Originally included in that second part of the application was a third
document, but the objection to that document's production has now been withdrawn.
    The plaintiff, Savings and Investment Bank Ltd (SIB), is an Isle of Man company which
carried on a banking business in the Isle of Man until its banking licence was revoked in   *d*
June 1982. It was compulsorily wound up by the Isle of Man court on 2 August 1982,
and two chartered accountants, Mr Jordan and Mr Beer, are the joint liquidators thereof.
    The first defendant, Gasco (Netherlands) BV (Netherlands), is a company incorporated
in the Netherlands. It is wholly owned by an Antilles company which is in turn wholly
owned by the third defendant, Gasco Investments Ltd (Gasco), a company incorporated
in Hong Kong.   *e*
    The second defendant has played no part in these proceedings and can be ignored.
    The fourth defendant, St Piran Ltd (St Piran), is an English holding company. On 18
December 1979 the Secretary of State for Trade appointed Mr Gerald Godfrey QC and
Mrs A J Hardcastle (the inspectors) under ss 165(*b*) and 172 of the Companies Act 1948 to
investigate the affairs and ownership of St Piran, then a company listed on the London
Stock Exchange. They produced an interim report on 30 September 1980 on their   *f*
investigations into the ownership of St Piran and a final report dated 31 March 1981 on
their investigations under s 165(*b*). They surveyed the affairs of St Piran from June 1970
until the time of their final report and were critical of certain aspects of the way the
affairs of St Piran had been conducted. However, they made no finding of criminal
conduct but suggested that the Secretary of State might consider that he had the duty to
wind up St Piran under his powers contained in s 35 of the Companies Act 1967, thereby   *g*
enabling the shareholders to express their views to the court and the court to reach its
own conclusion. But by the time their report was made, Netherlands had offered to
acquire and was in the process of acquiring all the shares of St Piran, and the Secretary of
State declined to seek a winding-up order against a company actively trading without
criminality, the shareholders of which had received an offer for their shares. The matters
on which the inspectors reported all precede the events which gave rise to the proceedings   *h*
with which I am concerned. Those events commence in April 1981, by which time
Netherlands owned a substantial holding of shares in St Piran and had offered to acquire
the remaining shares.
    On 9 April 1981 SIB entered into a written agreement with Netherlands and Gasco
whereby SIB agreed to lend Netherlands £3m and to grant an overdraft facility to Gasco
and Gasco guaranteed Netherlands' obligations. At the same time by a memorandum of   *j*
deposit Netherlands agreed to deposit with SIB by way of security the St Piran shares it
then held and any further shares it was to acquire. On 14 October 1981 there was a
further written agreement relating to the loan, then increased to £4·5m, by SIB to
Netherlands and to an increased overdraft facility for Gasco. That agreement provided
for repayment to SIB of the indebtedness on demand but in any case not later than 12

months from 9 April 1981. Also on the same day a second memorandum of deposit
a relating to the St Piran shares was executed. Further, by a side letter on that date SIB
agreed that, before relying on any default by Netherlands or Gasco and seeking
registration of any St Piran shares deposited with SIB, it would give 14 days' notice
specifying the default and requiring it to be remedied.

The defendants allege that there was an oral variation to the second loan agreement.
They say that a meeting at the end of October or the beginning of November 1981 Mr
b Killin, a director of SIB, and Mr Turnbull, the defendants' solicitor, agreed that SIB would
not demand repayment before 30 September 1982. SIB disputes that such a variation was
agreed. In January 1982 SIB demanded repayment of Netherlands' and Gasco's
indebtedness to it and sought registration of the St Piran shares. Netherlands and Gasco
refused to pay, and registration was refused. On 16 March 1982 SIB issued the writ in
the present proceedings, claiming repayment of the debt and interest owed respectively
c by Netherlands and Gasco and injunctions restraining the transfer of St Piran shares as
well as an injunction restraining St Piran itself from disposing of shares in any subsidiary
or of its assets notwithstanding that St Piran was not a party to any agreement with SIB.

Shortly after the issue of the writ, SIB obtained an ex parte injunction against the
defendants from Mervyn Davies J on 17 March 1982, the intention of which was to
preserve its security in the form of the St Piran shares. That injunction was continued at
d an inter partes hearing by Vinelott J on 26 March 1982 until judgment or further order,
but there was no contest on the merits as the defendants had been advised that England
was not the appropriate jurisdiction and they did not wish to lose their ability to take the
jurisdictional point. The defendants took that point when they took out a summons on
8 April 1982 for a stay of the proceedings. On 7 May 1982 SIB issued an RSC Ord 14
summons and three days later it served its statement of claim. There has been a
e preliminary hearing before the master of the defendants' summons for a stay of SIB's Ord
14 summons, but neither has proceeded further. On 18 May SIB petitioned for the
winding up of Netherlands on the basis of the debt SIB claimed was due under the loan
agreements and interest, but that petition was struck out by Vinelott J on 20 February
1983. On 4 June 1982 Netherlands and Gasco launched proceedings in the Isle of Man
against SIB for damages caused by what they alleged were improper and premature
f demands for repayment. Those proceedings are still afoot. On 2 August 1982 SIB was
wound up, its deficiency as regards creditors as shown in its statement of affairs exceeding
£18m. On 13 August 1982 Falconer J allowed a modification of the injunctions granted
by Vinelott J so as to permit the sale by St Peran of shares in a subsidiary against an
undertaking by St Piran to lodge £6·1m out of the proceeds of sale with the defendants'
solicitors. On 15 December 1982 Nourse J with the consent of SIB discharged the
g injunctions ordered by Vinelott J. However on 18 February 1983 SIB issued a further
notice of motion seeking injunctive relief until trial against each of the defendants
similar to the orders to the discharge of which it had consented in December, but it has
not sought relief over until the hearing of that motion. Counsel for the defendants has
informed me that between 15 December 1982 and 14 March 1983, at a time when no
injunction subsisted, the ownership of all the shares in St Piran were transferred to a
h wholly-owned United Kingdom subsidiary of Gasco, Gasco Investments (UK) Ltd.

On 14 March 1983 Walton J discharged the undertaking given by St Piran to Falconer
J relating to the £6·1m against two new undertakings given by St Piran. One was to keep
aggregate assets amounting to at least £6m in value in the ownership of St Piran and/or
its subsidiaries. The other was that St Piran would not cause any registration of St Piran
shares without giving at least three days' notice to SIB. Those undertakings were given
j until after judgment on the motion of 18 February 1983, but counsel for the defendants
before me offered to extend those undertakings until judgment in the action.

A major complication affecting SIB's claim in the present action came to the attention
of Mr Jordan in July 1982. It must have been known to SIB even before then. However,
it was not revealed to any of the courts before whom SIB appeared or to the defendants
until January 1983. There is a document in existence bearing the date 17 February 1982

which on its face is a deed of assignment by SIB to a company called Graylaw Holdings
Ltd (Graylaw). By it SIB is expressed to assign the benefit of the debt owed by Netherlands   *a*
and Gasco to SIB and the security therefor for a consideration of £5m. The deed appears
to have been executed by two officers of SIB and Graylaw respectively, but the copy I
have seen does not show that it was sealed by either company. Another document which
on its face is a board minute of Graylaw dated 8 July 1982 states that there was no such
assignment, but Graylaw's solicitors by a letter dated 30 November 1982 told SIB's
solicitors that the assignment was effective and that the board minute of 8 July was   *b*
prepared at the express request of SIB's directors to save SIB and thereby protect Graylaw's
deposits (in excess of £5m) with SIB.

There is evidence of further purported assignments. Mr Beer in his affidavit on 25
February 1983 refers to a purported assignment by Graylaw to one Nalborough in
September 1982 of the benefit of the debt owed by Netherlands and Gasco and to a
further assignment by Nalborough to Lyntoncroft Ltd in January 1983. By an assignment   *c*
dated 15 October 1982 Graylaw purportedly assigned the benefit of the debt and security
to Barclays Bank Ltd. By a further deed of assignment dated 24 January 1983 Graylaw
purportedly assigned the debt and security to Lyntoncroft Ltd, and by a further deed of
assignment dated 1 February 1983 Lyntoncroft Ltd purportedly made a further
assignment to Aznarar Investment Co SA.

The validity of these various assignments subsequent to 17 February 1982 depends at   *d*
least in part on whether there was an effective assignment to Graylaw. On 16 February
1983 SIB commenced proceedings in the Isle of Man against Graylaw, which is now in
liquidation, Lyntoncroft Ltd, Barclays Bank Ltd and Aznarar Investment Co SA in an
attempt to sort out the position. In the meantime some doubt exists whether SIB is the
proper plaintiff in the present proceedings.

Several affidavits have been filed on each side in respect of SIB's motion of 18 February   *e*
1983. The crucial affidavit in the present case is that of Mr G A Weiss, which he swore
on 21 March 1983 on behalf of the joint liquidators of SIB. That affidavit contains the
material on which both parts of the application by the defendants are based. I shall deal
first with the passages relevant to the application to strike out. Mr Weiss in the first
paragraph says:

'Save as hereinafter expressly appears I make this Affidavit from my own   *f*
knowledge.'

He makes no statement elsewhere in the affidavit as to his belief in the truth of matters
which are not from his own knowledge. Mr Weiss states that the sums then owing by
Netherlands and Gasco amounted to nearly £6m. He stressed that the only security for
the debt consisted of St Piran shares. He said that neither Netherlands nor Gasco had a   *g*
place of business within the United Kingdom or substantial assets within the jurisdiction,
and he said that he was advised that it would be difficult and time consuming to execute
any kind of effective judgment against Netherlands and Gasco in their respective
countries of incorporation.

In para 23 of his affidavit Mr Weiss referred to the inspectors' reports which he
exhibited, and he summarised the principal matters in respect of which SIB relied on the   *h*
final report: (1) the moving spirit behind Berriedale Investments Ltd (described in that
report as the controlling shareholder of Gasco) and the Gasco group is a Mr James Raper;
(2) Mr Raper conducted a long-term strategy of directly taking over St Piran's interests in
the Far East, leading St Piran to diversify within the United Kingdom; (3) the
circumstances and nature of the management agreement with St Piran (Hong Kong) Ltd
(a subsidiary of St Piran); (4) 'certain unsatisfactory aspects of Mr Raper's conduct in   *j*
relation to the companies which he controlled'.

In paras 25 to 41 Mr Weiss dealt in greater detail with the final report, which runs to
228 pages. He said it was difficult to summarise such a lengthy and complex document,
but he sought to extract some of the more important and salient points made by the
inspectors, and he then set out various matters taken from that report, giving references

to 99 specific paragraphs in the report. He explains the reasons why he referred to the report, in para 42 thus:

> 'Against this background the joint liquidators fear that unless appropriate interlocutory relief is granted, there is a very real danger that Mr. Raper will exercise his ultimate control in such a way either as to dispose of the Saint Piran shares, which are relied on by the Plaintiff as its security for the debt, or to dilute the value of those shares by dealing with Saint Piran's assets or those of its subsidiaries, such dealings taking place either within the jurisdiction of this Honourable Court or by transferring such assets outside the jurisdiction.'

The application to strike out those paragraphs in the affidavit which refer to the reports is made under RSC Ord 41, r 6, which is in this form:

> 'The Court may order to be struck out of any affidavit any matter which is scandalous, irrelevant or otherwise oppressive.'

There is a note to RSC Ord 41, r 6, in *The Supreme Court Practice 1982* vol 1, p 704, para 41/6/1 to the effect that the court will only strike out matter which is both scandalous and irrelevant, or is otherwise oppressive; but it is manifest from the present wording of the rule that the words are disjunctive, so that the court may strike out on the grounds of irrelevancy alone.

Counsel for the defendants makes three submissions on the application of the rule in the present case: first, that the passages in the affidavit are irrelevant, because they do not relate to the matters in dispute between the parties on the hearing of the motion; second, that they are irrelevant, because they contain the opinions of the inspectors, and such opinions are not admissible evidence; third, that the passages are oppressive, in that they would allow SIB to make prejudicial use of numerous statements in the report which the defendants could not safely allow to go unchallenged and which could only be countered by producing voluminous evidence in answer.

Counsel for SIB makes five submissions in reply. First, he submits that the passages in question are relevant, because they do relate to a matter in dispute at the hearing of the motion, that is to say whether there is a real risk that SIB's security will be dissipated. Second, he submits that they are relevant, because they contain material admissible by virtue of Ord 41, r 5(2) in interlocutory proceedings. Under r 5(2), an affidavit sworn for the purpose of being used in interlocutory proceedings may contain statements of information and belief with the sources and grounds thereof. Third, he submits that the passages in question are not oppressive, as it is unnecessary on an interlocutory application for the court to make any findings of fact, and it would be inappropriate to have a trial to establish the facts contained in the report. Fourth, he submits that there is statutory authority in s 4 of the Civil Evidence Act 1968 for admitting the statements in the reports. Fifth, he submits that the court in the exercise of its discretion under Ord 41, r 5(2) should not accede to the defendants' application, because he submits that it is inappropriate for me to strike out passages on which SIB wishes to rely at the hearing of the motion. That, he says, is for the judge hearing the motion to determine.

I shall deal with counsel for SIB's last point first, as, if correct, it would absolve me from the task of considering this application further. Counsel for the defendants explained the reasons why he has applied to strike out as twofold. First, the defendants need to know before the effective hearing of the motion whether they should go to the expense and trouble of putting in a large amount of additional evidence to counter what is contained in the report. He points out that a decision on this point may assist SIB as well, since SIB may wish, if the passages are struck out, to put in admissible evidence to prove what it now seeks to show by way of reference to the inspector's reports. Second, for a judge other than the judge hearing the motion to strike out the passages in the affidavit would avoid the motions judge having to perform the mental gymnastics of putting out of mind the lengthy inadmissible passages to which he would have been referred.

In my judgment on both of those grounds it is right for me to deal with this application now. I keep well in mind that I am not hearing the motion, and in the circumstances I think that I should only strike out if satisfied that this is a plain and obvious case for doing so. Judges frequently have to take decisions on evidence in advance of a main hearing to be determined by another judge, and there is a manifest convenience in the course on which the defendants have embarked. It is of course true that judges are accustomed to put out of mind matters which they have seen or heard and judged to be inadmissible, but the greater the amount of such material the more desirable it seems to me to have the question of striking out determined in advance.

I proceed therefore by considering the first ground suggested by the defendants why the passages are irrelevant. What is a matter in issue on the motion may, of course, differ from what is a matter in issue at the trial. The judge hearing the motion will no doubt be looking to see whether SIB's claim to have been entitled to make demands for repayment and for registration of the St Piran shares before 30 September 1982 constitutes a serious question to be tried at the trial. It is common ground that the passages in Mr Weiss's affidavit do not relate to that question, but it is clear that amongst the other matters which the judge will then consider is whether there is a serious risk of the defendants or any of them dissipating SIB's security such as by causing value to pass out of the St Piran shares, and it is on that point that Mr Weiss refers to the passages in the report.

In amplification of the summary made by Mr Weiss of the four principal matters for which he relied on the report, counsel for SIB referred me to passages in the final report relating to five different matters: (1) the reorganisation of St Piran's Far Eastern interests between October 1977 and December 1979, the inspectors referring to certain abortive attempts by Mr Raper to cause those interests to be vested in a company which he would control and expressing concern over a failure to keep the St Piran board and shareholders informed; (2) a management agreement between St Piran (Hong Kong) Ltd, St Piran's Hong Kong subsidiary, and Gasco, whereby Gasco was entitled to certain management fees for services which the inspectors suggested might have been provided more cheaply by other means; (3) the deposit of about £200,000 made with Berriedale for some three months by St Piran's Hong Kong subsidiary, supposedly for a proposed property development by that subsidiary but which the inspectors believed was used for the ultimate benefit of the parent company, Berriedale; (4) an unsuccessful investment made by St Piran in an Australian company and sold in November 1979 at a loss, about which the inspectors say that, if there was an intention that Mr Raper or Berriedale or Gasco should hold a significant interest in the Australian company, St Piran should not have borne the whole of the loss; (5) a potential conflict of interest for Mr Stone, the chairman of St Piran and the managing director of Gasco, of whom the inspectors say there must be some doubt whether in the event of such conflict he would act for the benefit of Gasco or St Piran.

Counsel for the defendants submits that the inspectors' opinions, some of them expressed tentatively and conditionally, on matters some distance in time from the present, relating to a period when St Piran was not wholly owned by a Gasco subsidiary and disclosing no crime, fraud of creditors or evasion of any judgment, are not relevant to the issue of whether there is a danger of the dissipation of SIB's security. He says that the sort of fact that would be relevant is evidence of a defendant having made itself judgment-proof to evade a judgment.

That, I think, is to set an impracticably high standard for the admissibility of evidence, and the court is accustomed to act on rather less. The reports disclosed the opinion, right or wrong, of the inspectors to have been that Mr Raper prior to March 1981 was prepared to manipulate or attempt to manipulate the affairs of St Piran and its subsidiaries, looking to the interests of himself and his companies more than the interests of St Piran, and I can see that this has a relevance, though to my mind it is only slight, in considering whether there is a serious risk to SIB's security pending judgment. However, having reached the conclusion that the passages are not wholly irrelevant, I would not strike

_a_ them out on this ground.

The second ground of irrelevancy relied on by counsel for defendants is that the passages in the inspectors' reports which are referred to by Mr Weiss in his affidavit are statements of the opinions of the inspectors and that as such they are inadmissible. That inadmissible evidence is irrelevant matter within the meaning of RSC Ord 41, r 6 is not disputed by counsel for SIB (and see, for example, Re J (an infant) [1960] 1 All ER 603,

_b_ [1960] 1 WLR 253). Counsel for the defendants relies on the general principle in the law of evidence that evidence of opinion is not admissible. That principle is subject to a number of exceptions, such as the opinion of an expert. It is also subject to the qualification that has been made by the courts that, in proceedings to wind up a company, inspectors' reports may be relied on in certain circumstances. I will deal with that qualification in greater detail a little later.

_c_   The general principle is exemplified by Hollington v F Hewthorn & Co Ltd [1943] 2 All ER 35, [1943] KB 587, to which counsel for the defendants referred me. In that case it was held by the Court of Appeal that the conviction of a defendant for careless driving was inadmissible evidence of his negligence in proceedings for damages on that ground against him and his employer, the main reason being that the conviction merely proved that another court was of opinion that the defendant was guilty of careless driving. The

_d_ admissibility of evidence of a conviction is, of course, now governed by statute, but counsel for the defendants submitted, in my view correctly, that that decision still represents the position at common law. He says that if the judgment of a competent court after a judicial hearing is excluded, a fortiori the reports of inspectors after an investigation neither judicial nor quasi-judicial should be. To the extent that the reports contain hearsay statements as distinct from mere opinion, counsel for the defendants

_e_ submits that such statements are inadmissible in the absence of a statement of information and belief with the sources and grounds thereof in accordance with RSC Ord 41, r 5(2). He referred me to the comments of the Court of Appeal in Re J L Young Manufacturing Co Ltd [1900] 2 Ch 753 to the effect that the court should not look at affidavit evidence founded on information and belief unless the court can ascertain the sources and grounds thereof.

_f_   Every report of inspectors will no doubt report (1) oral statements by witnesses to such inspectors, (2) documentary evidence put before such inspectors and (3) the opinions of such inspectors in respect of both kinds of evidence. The final report contains all three, but it is clear to my mind that it is the opinions of the inspectors that are chiefly relied on by Mr Weiss. For example, the only statement made to the inspectors which is both recorded in the report and which Mr Weiss expressly sets out is the assertion by Mr Stone

_g_ in relation to his potential conflict of interest; but it is clear that the reason why Mr Weiss refers to it is not for Mr Stone's assertion but for the inspectors' comment thereon, expressing their doubts about the correctness of that assertion.

Counsel for the defendants took me through all the reported cases relating to the status of inspectors' reports as evidence in court proceedings, from Re Grosvenor and West-end Railway Terminus Hotel Co Ltd (1897) 76 LT 337 to a case on the very reports of the

_h_ inspectors with which I am concerned, Re St Piran Ltd [1981] 3 All ER 270, [1981] 1 WLR 1300. In the Grosvenor case a writ of prohibition was sought against inspectors appointed by the Board of Trade under the provisions of the Companies Act 1862, which required such inspectors on the conclusion of their investigation of the affairs of a company to report their opinion to the Board of Trade. But it was pointed out by Lord Esher MR (at 338) in refusing relief that the report itself was not evidence of anything

_j_ contained in it but was merely evidence of the opinion of the inspectors. At that time the report could not found any action by the Board of Trade, but the Companies Act 1928 and subsequent Companies Acts have expressly enabled the Crown to take certain action in consequence of inspectors' reports. Thus by s 169(3) of the Companies Act 1948 (now s 35 of the Companies Act 1967) the Board of Trade was empowered to present a petition to wind up a company if it appeared from a report that it was just and equitable so to do.

In the light of that statutory provision the court has held in a series of cases that it can treat the report as material on which, if it is not challenged by proper evidence, the court can proceed to make a winding-up order. Pennycuick J said in *Re SBA Properties Ltd* [1967] 2 All ER 615 at 621, [1967] 1 WLR 799 at 806, after referring to the *Grosvenor* case, that it was still true today that the report of the inspectors was not evidence in a court of law of the existence of any fact mentioned in it, but he said that the court could treat the report not as evidence in the ordinary sense but as material on which, if it was not challenged, the court could proceed to make a winding-up order on the ground that it was just and equitable so to do. He thought that the whole tenor of s 169(3) was to that effect.

In the *St Piran* case Dillon J held that in circumstances where inspectors are appointed under s 165(b) of the Companies Act 1948, since one reason for the appointment might be to protect the interests of minority shareholders, such a shareholder should be able to rely on the inspectors' report to support a contributory's petition to the same extent that it could be used to support a petition by the Secretary of State. Counsel for the defendants accepted for the purposes of this hearing the correctness of that decision, whilst reserving the right to challenge it elsewhere. But he submitted that none of the authorities casts doubt on the proposition for which he contended, that the inspectors' reports contained mere statements of opinion which cannot be used as admissible evidence in court proceedings, save for the limited purpose of winding-up proceedings brought by the Secretary of State or by a person for whose protection the inspectors were appointed to report, and then only when not challenged by proper evidence. In the present case counsel for SIB accepts that SIB, which is not a contributory, is not otherwise within the class of persons for whose protection the inspectors were appointed.

Counsel for SIB's approach is fundamentally different from that of counsel for the defendants. He submits that the authorities to which counsel for the defendants refers, such as *Hollington v F Hewthorn & Co Ltd* [1943] 2 All ER 35, [1943] KB 587 and the cases on inspectors' reports, deal only with the admissibility of evidence at the trial, whereas what is admissible in interlocutory proceedings is governed by RSC Ord 41, r 5(2). He submits, and counsel for the defendants agrees, that the motion of 18 February 1983 is a true interlocutory proceeding in that it will not decide the rights of the parties but will preserve the status quo until trial. He says that a party seeking interlocutory relief must be able to tell the court why he feels apprehensive about what may happen if interlocutory relief is not granted. Such a party cannot, he says, prove that that which he fears will happen will in fact happen, and that RSC Ord 41, r 5(2) reflects this situation in allowing statements of information or belief. He referred me to the remarks of Lord Denning MR in *Third Chandris Shipping Corp v Unimarine SA* [1979] 2 All ER 972 at 985, [1979] QB 645 at 669 where the Master of the Rolls stated in the context of an application for a Mareva injunction that the plaintiff must give some grounds for believing that there is a risk of assets being removed before judgment. But Lord Denning MR then went on to discuss the type of hard fact that constitutes such grounds, and the objective nature of the court's inquiry in such cases was stated by Lawton LJ in the same case ([1979] 2 All ER 972 at 987, [1979] QB 645 at 671):

'There must be facts from which the Commercial Court, like a prudent, sensible commercial man, can properly infer a danger of default if assets are removed from the jurisdiction.'

I do not see that the court is in the least concerned with why subjectively an applicant for interlocutory relief should have cause for concern. What it is concerned with is whether objectively the facts put before the court indicate that a real danger exists.

Counsel for SIB submits that RSC Ord 41, r 5(2) permits the adducing by the deponent of the opinions of others, whether or not they are experts, provided they are identified. He further submits that hearsay, whether firsthand or more remote, is admissible, provided that the immediate supplier of the hearsay to the deponent is identified. Thus in the present case, he submits, it is sufficient that Mr Weiss has identified the inspectors as the source of the information to him, whether that information consists of opinion or hearsay and whether or not the original source of the hearsay statement is identified. He says that all such material is admissible, though it is for the judge hearing the motion to decide whether any and if so what weight should be attached to that material. Counsel for SIB referred me to s 171 of the Companies Act 1948, as amended by s 88(2) of the Companies Act 1981, as being consistent with his submissions. The section provides that a copy of a report by inspectors which is certified by the Secretary of State shall be admissible in any legal proceedings as evidence of the opinion of the inspectors in relation to any matter contained in the report. This section, which prior to its amendment in 1981 required the seal of the company to make the report admissible, goes back to s 61 of the Companies Act 1862, under which Act the inspectors were required to 'report their opinion' to the Board of Trade. That section to my mind deals merely with the formality of how the inspectors' reports are to be proved in legal proceedings. I accept counsel for the defendants' submission that it is not a blanket provision allowing reports to be used in all cases as evidence.

Neither counsel has been able to cite any authority which elucidates the scope of what is or is not permitted by Ord 41, r 5(2). It is obvious from r 5(2) itself that it operates as an exception from the primary rule of evidence stated expressly in Ord 41, r 5(1) that a person may only give evidence as to 'facts', which he 'is able of his own knowledge to prove'. Rule 5(2), by including statements of information or belief, plainly allows the adduction of hearsay. It also allows a statement of belief, that is to say an opinion; but in its context that belief must be that of the deponent, and such statements will have no probative value unless the sources and grounds of the information and belief are revealed.

To my mind the purpose of r 5(2) is to enable a deponent to put before the court in interlocutory proceedings, frequently in circumstances of great urgency, facts which he is not able of his own knowledge to prove but which, the deponent is informed and believes, can be proved by means which the deponent identifies by specifying the sources and grounds of his information and belief. What r 5(2) allows the deponent to state that he has obtained from another must, in my judgment, be limited to what is admissible as evidence. Take, for example, a case where there are unsuccessful without prejudice discussions to settle an action, in the course of which a statement is made by a party which is highly relevant to an issue in interlocutory proceedings. I apprehend that the court would strike out from an affidavit made by another party who heard the statement any reference to such statement having been made, as it would not be admissible as evidence and so would be irrelevant. So too, in my judgment, a statement in an affidavit referring to other forms of inadmissible evidence should be treated as irrelevant. That would include statements of opinion not being within any recognised exception to the general principle to which I have referred.

Further I find it impossible to accept counsel for SIB's submission that it is sufficient in order to comply with r 5(2) that the deponent should identify only the source to him of his information even though it is clear that that source was not the original source. Thus, if the deponent was informed of a fact by A, whom the deponent knows not to have firsthand knowledge of the fact but who had obtained the information from B, I cannot believe that it is sufficient for the deponent to identify A as the source of the information. That, to my mind, would largely defeat the requirement that the sources and grounds should be stated and would make it only too easy to introduce prejudicial material without revealing the original source of hearsay information by the expedient of procuring as the deponent a person who receives information second hand. By having to reveal such original source and not merely the immediate source, the deponent affords a proper opportunity to another party to challenge and counter such evidence, as well as enabling the court to assess the weight to be attributed to such evidence. Even in a period in which the court's practice on interlocutory motions is governed by the rules laid down in *American Cyanamid Co v Ethicon Ltd* [1975] 1 All ER 504, [1975] AC 396 and accordingly the court avoids determination of the facts at that stage, it is still common experience that many cases do not progress beyond and are decided by the outcome of an interlocutory motion.

In my judgment the court ought not to allow in affidavits to be used in interlocutory proceedings material which cannot be proved because it is mere opinion or is otherwise inadmissible. This is the more important in cases like the present when the material sought to be adduced will never be adjudicated on at the trial, because, as is common ground, it is not relevant to the issues at the trial.

In the present case it is not, of course, the opinion of any Tom, Dick or Harry that is in question but the opinion of a statutory fact-finding body which has given its opinion after a lengthy inquiry and after obtaining evidence from those whose duty it was to give that evidence. The inspectors in the present case are an eminent Queen's Counsel and a chartered accountant and they have manifestly been painstaking in the preparation of their reports. I have no reason to think that the inspectors have not done their work carefully and well. I would willingly give the report a special evidential status if I could, but the consistent approach of the courts in the winding-up cases has been to accept that the contents of an inspectors' report are only opinions and inadmissible save for the statutory justification for treating the reports in winding-up proceedings as material on which the court could act if that material was not challenged in a proper way. That is so even though r 30 of the Companies (Winding-up) Rules 1949, SI 1949/330, allows a verifying affidavit for a petition to be sufficient prima facie evidence of the statements in the petition and the statutory form of affidavit allows the deponent to state his belief without stating the source of his information. That approach is inconsistent with affording any wider recognition to the reports as evidence.

I have already recorded counsel for SIB's acknowledgment that SIB cannot claim to be within the scope of the class for whose benefit it may be presumed the inspectors were appointed. Counsel for SIB submitted that if counsel for the defendants were right even a judgment could not be relied on in interlocutory proceedings. If use were sought to be made of a judgment in precisely the same manner as use is sought to be made of the report, I think that would indeed follow, but I am unimpressed by the suggestion that that demonstrates that the argument is incorrect.

Counsel for the defendants also submitted that the passages in question were oppressive. It is not necessary for me to express a conclusion on this in view of the decision I have reached on the question of irrelevancy, but in case I am wrong on that question and in deference to the arguments of counsel I shall express my views on this briefly.

Mr Weiss identified 99 separate paragraphs in the final report in his affidavit. From the way that the matter is put in that affidavit, I accept counsel for SIB's submission that SIB is not confined to those paragraphs but could use other passages in the report. Counsel for SIB in fact referred me to 25 further paragraphs and, given the broad description of the four principal matters identified by Mr Weiss and the possibility of other less than principal matters on which SIB may wish to rely, there is a vast amount of material that SIB may use on the hearing of the motion. A party who chooses not to counter evidence that is put in by his opponent does so at his peril, and counsel for the defendants tells me that there is much in the report that the defendants would wish to dispute.

Counsel for SIB submits that this is not oppressive, because under the rules in *American Cyanamid Co v Ethicon Ltd* [1975] 1 All ER 504, [1975] AC 396, the court will not be concerned to determine the facts on the hearing of the motion. But the defendants are entitled to put in evidence to counter any prejudicial material that they think incorrectly records the facts and indeed unless they put in such evidence they may be harmed, particularly as the trial will not provide an opportunity for ascertaining the facts on this matter. Given what I have described as the slight relevance that this material has to the issue of whether there is a real danger to SIB's security, I have reached the clear conclusion that the passages in Mr Weiss's affidavit are indeed oppressive.

I move on to the alternative ground on which counsel for SIB seeks to adduce the matters contained in the report. He submits that each of the reports is a record compiled

a by a person acting under a duty from information which was supplied by a person, whether acting under a duty or not, who had or may reasonably be supposed to have had personal knowledge of the matters dealt with in that information within the meaning of s 4 of the Civil Evidence Act 1968. He rightly says that the inspectors who formed a statutory fact-finding body were acting under a duty to compile their report, and the information supplied to them was supplied by persons giving evidence under a statutory

b duty.

The crucial question is whether the reports can properly be called records. Counsel for the defendants submits that they cannot, and he relies on the recent statement by Bingham J in *H v Schering Chemicals Ltd* [1983] 1 All ER 849, [1983] 1 WLR 143. In that case the documents in question were summaries of the results of medical research and articles and letters published in medical journals. Bingham J, after reviewing the

c authorities, came to the conclusion that the documents were not records within s 4. He said ([1983] 1 All ER 849 at 852, [1983] 1 WLR 143 at 146):

'The intention of that section was, I believe, to admit in evidence records which a historian would regard as original or primary sources, that is documents which either give effect to a transaction itself or which contain a contemporaneous register of information supplied by those with direct knowledge of the facts.'

d

Counsel for SIB accepts that, judged by that standard, the reports are not records, but he submits, again rightly, that Bingham J was in no way concerned with documents such as a report of inspectors. Nevertheless I respectfully accept as correct the test propounded by Bingham J. To my mind it is obvious that a report by inspectors, containing as it does a selection of the evidence put before the inspectors and their comments and conclusions

e thereon, is not a record in any ordinary sense of the word. It falls short of simply compiling the information supplied to them in the sense that some information will not be included in the report, and it goes beyond such a compilation in that it expresses opinions thereon. In my judgment, therefore, this alternative submission of counsel for SIB must be rejected.

I would add that I am in any event not satisfied that the notice under the Civil Evidence

f Act 1968 served by SIB complied with the requirements of RSC Ord 38, r 23. Those requirements include in relation to each statement in a record particulars of the person who originally supplied the information from which the record was compiled. The notice served by SIB merely states:

'The information from which the said records were compiled was originally supplied by the various witnesses who gave evidence before the said Inspectors and

g was also derived from the various documents considered by the said Inspectors in the course of compiling the said records.'

But I doubt if such particulars adequately identify which of the 55 witnesses (the suppliers of the information) supplied what information for the purposes of the rule.

In my judgment, therefore, the court, if it chooses to exercise its discretion under RSC

h Ord 41, r 6, can strike out the paragraphs in question in Mr Weiss's affidavit. I bear in mind that this is a case where SIB has had ample time to try to obtain more direct evidence of the matters to which the inspectors' opinions relate and that there is no evidence before me of any difficulty in obtaining such evidence. I can see no reason why I should not exercise my discretion, and accordingly I shall strike out paras 23 and 25 to 41 inclusive of that affidavit.

j There are also references to the inspectors' reports in Mr Killin's affidavit of 16 March 1982. If and in so far as those references are incorporated referentially into the evidence to be used on the motion, I am prepared to direct that they too be expunged.

I turn finally to the second part of the application by the defendants by which they seek production of two documents, the minute book of meetings of the board of SIB during February 1982 and SIB's register of seals for the same period. That application is made under RSC Ord 24, rr 10 and 11. Under r 10, if one party refers in pleadings or in an affidavit to any document, any other party is entitled to serve a notice requiring production of that document for inspection. Under r 11, if the party served with the notice objects to the production of the document, then the court on the application of the party serving the notice may make an order for production of the document for inspection. But that is subject to Ord 24, r 13(1), which prohibits the court ordering production unless the court is of opinion that the order is necessary either for disposing fairly of the matter or for saving costs.

Counsel for the defendants relies on two passages in Mr Weiss's affidavit. The first, in para 6, is this:

'There is no record of any Board resolution authorising the fixation of the Plaintiff's seal to the document.'

The second is in para 15(2):

'There is no minute of the Board of the Plaintiff dealing with the execution of the Deed. Mr. Ashton-Hill, another director of the Plaintiff, and Mr. Moroney, a Manx attorney instructed by the Plaintiff, examined the Register of Seals and no entry appears therein with reference to the sealing of the assignment.'

These are references, of course, to the assignment to Graylaw.

Counsel for the defendants submits that there is an express reference to the register of seals and that there are implied references to a minute book. He says that it is apparent that those documents exist, and the defendants wish to verify for themselves whether or not the assignment of the debt to Graylaw was authorised by the board of SIB and SIB's seal was authorised to be affixed. He says that those documents are material on the motion as well as the trial as they go to the question whether or not there was a valid assignment by SIB to Graylaw and thus to the question whether SIB is the proper plaintiff.

I agree that there are references to both documents for the purposes of the rule, so that the onus is on SIB to show just cause why production should not be ordered. Counsel for SIB has told me that there is a file of board minutes as well as a register of seals, but he submits that the rule does not entitle a party who is told that there is no entry of a particular description to search through the other side's documents to verify that negative proposition. I agree with him. This is not a case where a party refers to a document on which he relies in pleadings or in an affidavit. SIB through Mr Weiss is simply stating a negative, and it would seem to me to be wrong to allow the defendants in these circumstances in advance of discovery, which has yet to take place, a roving commission, albeit one limited in time. As *Quilter v Heatley* (1883) 23 Ch D 42 shows, when there is a reference to an entry in a book, inspection under RSC Ord 24, r 11 will be limited to that entry, and the other entries can be covered up.

Carrying that principle to its logical conclusion, it would be possible for SIB to cover up all the documents in the files relating to board minutes and all the other entries in the register of seals on the footing that there is no relevant document or entry, as indeed Mr Weiss has sworn. Counsel for SIB has indicated that there are some pages missing from the register of seals, and he is prepared to reveal to the defendants what are the dates between which those missing pages came.

In all the circumstances I am not satisfied that an order for production of either of the two documents sought is necessary for disposing fairly of the matter or for saving costs, and I shall therefore dismiss this part of the defendants' application.

Application for order to strike out paragraphs in the affidavit granted; application for order for production of documents dismissed.

Solicitors: *Hancock & Willis* (for the first, third and fourth defendants); *D J Freeman & Co* (for SIB).

Vivian Horvath   Barrister.

Re E (mental health patient)

CHANCERY DIVISION

SIR ROBERT MEGARRY V-C

21 OCTOBER, 11 NOVEMBER 1983

Mental health – Legal proceedings brought on behalf of patient – Ownership of papers in legal proceedings – Action brought on behalf of patient by Official Solicitor as next friend – Patient's father wishing to appeal against judgment – Whether papers 'property' of patient – Whether father as new next friend entitled to possession of papers in existence as result of proceedings – Whether displaced next friend entitled to withhold papers – Mental Health Act 1983, ss 95, 96, 112.

Mental health – Legal proceedings brought on behalf of patient – Functions of next friend in legal proceedings – Responsibility for papers in proceedings – Liability for costs of unsuccessful litigation – Indemnity for costs of proceedings.

E suffered a cerebral haemorrhage when she was five months old which left her partially paralysed and with a mental age of three. In 1975 she suffered another haemorrhage and, as a result of not receiving prompt treatment at the hospital to which she was admitted, she became a quadriplegic. In 1978, acting by the Official Solicitor on her behalf, she successfully brought a claim for damages for negligence against the relevant area health authority and the two doctors employed by it who were responsible for the delay in treating her. In February 1981 judgment was given in E's favour and the damages which were awarded were thereafter administered by the Court of Protection under the Mental Health Act 1959, and subsequently under the Mental Health Act 1983. E's parents lodged an appeal against the award, but in December 1981, as a result of counsel's joint opinion that the appeal was very unlikely to succeed, the appeal was abandoned. In 1983 the parents consulted new solicitors with a view to appealing out of time, and in March 1983 those solicitors wrote to the Official Solicitor and the solicitors instructed by him in the claim for damages, requesting the release of all the papers which were in existence as a result of the proceedings, in order to enable them to advise the parents not only on the prospects of the success of an appeal out of time but also on whether proceedings for negligence lay against those who had been advising and acting for E at the time. The Official Solicitor refused to release any papers other than a copy of the judgment and the pleadings. In July 1983 E's father sought an order from the Court of Protection that the papers relating to E's litigation be released to the new solicitors. Under s 95(1)[a] of the 1983 Act the court could, in regard to 'the property and affairs' of a patient, do anything which appeared to be necessary or expedient for the maintenance or other benefit of the patient or for administering the patient's affairs and, under s 96(1)[b], could make orders and give directions and authorities in that regard, in particular for the conduct of legal proceedings in the name of the patient or on his behalf. By s 112[c] property was defined as including 'any thing in action, and any interest in real or personal property'. The master made an order for the production of certain documents on the ground that the papers were the 'property' of the patient and therefore the court was empowered under s 95(1) to order their production. The Official Solicitor appealed.

---

[a] Section 95(1), so far as material, provides: 'The judge may, with respect to the property and affairs of a patient, do or secure the doing of all such things as appear necessary or expedient—(a) for the maintenance or other benefit of the patient . . . or (d) otherwise for administering the patient's affairs.'

[b] Section 96(1), so far as material, provides: 'Without prejudice to section 95 above, the judge shall have power to make such orders and give such directions and authorities as he thinks fit for the purposes of that section and in particular may for those purposes make orders or give directions or authorities for . . . (i) the conduct of legal proceedings in the name of the patient or on his behalf . . .'

[c] Section 112, so far as material, is set out at p 313 h, post

Held – On its true construction 'property' was to be widely construed for the purpose of ss 95, 96 and 112 of the 1983 Act and accordingly included all rights of property even if those rights were conditional or subject to the claims of others or in some way fell short of full and unencumbered ownership. Applying that construction, a patient's rights in papers used by his next friend in litigation on his behalf were part of the patient's 'property' for the purposes of ss 95, 96 and 112, subject to the rights of others, e g solicitors instructed by the next friend who had a claim for costs. Accordingly, the papers used by the Official Solicitor in litigation on E's behalf were E's property, subject to the payment of the costs, if any, of the Official Solicitor and the solicitors instructed by him, and therefore the master had jurisdiction to order the production of the documents. The Official Solicitor's appeal would accordingly be dismissed (see p 313 g to p 314 a and g and p 315 a, post).

Per curiam. Although a next friend is responsible to the court for the propriety and progress of a patient's proceedings, he does not become a litigant himself: his functions are essentially vicarious and even if he is professionally qualified his function as a vicarious litigant is to make informed decisions rather than to exercise his professional skill (see p 312 j to p 313 a and d e, post).

Notes

For parties and proceedings relating to mental disorder and legal incapacity, see 30 Halsbury's Laws (4th edn) paras 1017–1019, and for cases on the subject, see 34 Digest (Reissue) 28–29, 240–249.

For cases on legal proceedings by a next friend, see 28(2) Digest (Reissue) 869–876, 1703–1789.

Cases referred to in judgment

Chantrey Martin & Co v Martin [1953] 2 All ER 691, [1953] 2 QB 286, CA.
Gibbon v Pease [1905] 1 KB 810, [1904–7] All ER Rep 454, CA.
Horsfall, Ex p (1827) 7 B & C 528, 108 ER 820.
Steeden v Walden [1910] 2 Ch 393, [1908–10] All ER Rep 380.

Appeal

By a summons dated 5 July 1983 the father of E, a patient under the Mental Health Act 1959, and subsequently under the Mental Health Act 1983, applied to the Court of Protection for an order that the papers relating to E's claim for damages for negligence brought by the Official Solicitor acting as her next friend against the relevant area health authority and two doctors, be released to the father's solicitors. On 1 August 1983 the Court of Protection master made an order for the production of all the documents sought, requiring them to be produced to the solicitors acting for E's father within 21 days. On 9 August the Official Solicitor appealed against the order, seeking its total discharge or alternatively that he should be directed to produce the documents only if the Queen's Bench Division so ordered. On 18 August a stay of the order of the Court of Protection pending the determination of the appeal was made by consent. The appeal was heard in chambers but judgment was given by Sir Robert Megarry V-C in open court. The facts are set out in the judgment.

Dirik Jackson for the Official Solicitor.
K L May for E's father.

Cur adv vult

11 November. The following judgment was delivered.

SIR ROBERT MEGARRY V-C. This is an appeal in an unusual case. It concerns the position of the next friend of a patient under the Mental Health Act 1959, and latterly under the Mental Health Act 1983. I heard the appeal in chambers, but it was agreed that it was desirable for the judgment to be made available for the public and the profession, and so I am delivering it in open court.

The basic facts may be stated shortly. E is now some 36 years old. Some five months after her birth she suffered a cerebral haemorrhage which left her with an arm that was totally paralysed and a leg which was partially paralysed; and in the event her mental age has not progressed beyond about three years of age. In 1961 she and her parents, who had been born abroad and had lived there, came to England. In 1975, when E was about 28 years old, she suffered another haemorrhage. There was a grave delay of some 20 days before she received the appropriate treatment, and as a result she is now a quadriplegic. In 1978 E, acting by the Official Solicitor as her next friend, sued two doctors and the relevant area health authority for damages for negligence. Negligence was admitted, and on 23 February 1981 Wien J gave judgment for E for £43,912·01. Thereafter the damages were paid into the Court of Protection, and the Official Solicitor was appointed receiver for E, on, I think, 20 November 1981. He continued in this office until the management division of the Court of Protection became receiver in his place on 1 January 1983. The judgment of Wien J, some 20 pages long, was concerned solely with the one question in dispute, that of the quantum of damages. The judge plainly awarded damages on the footing that E would continue to be a patient in a national health service hospital, free of charge. She is and has been at all material times a patient at such a hospital on a voluntary basis.

E's parents were dissatisfied with the amount of damages awarded; and I understand that notice of appeal was duly lodged. On 16 November 1981 a joint opinion was given by an experienced leader and a junior. Their conclusion was that the appeal was very unlikely to succeed. The opinion discussed the general damages, the absence of any award for private nursing care, and certain special damage and future expenditure. The main complaint appears to have been under the second head; for the parents assert that they want to have E at home with them and that the damages ought to have included a sum to enable E to have proper nursing attendance there. In December 1981, in view of the joint opinion, the appeal was abandoned.

At some later stage, probably early in 1983, the parents consulted solicitors. On 10 March 1983 these solicitors wrote to the solicitors who had been instructed by the Official Solicitor in the litigation, asking for the release of all the papers in the case so that they could advise the parents on the prospects of success in seeking to appeal out of time. They wrote similarly to the Official Solicitor. The Official Solicitor offered to provide a copy of the judgment of Wien J and of the pleadings, but the parents' solicitors wanted all the papers, and the Official Solicitor would not agree to releasing any more of them. In due course it emerged that the release of all the papers was sought in order to make it possible to consider not only whether to attempt to appeal out of time but also whether to take proceedings, presumably for negligence, against those who had been advising and acting on behalf of E at the time.

On 5 July 1983 E's father took out a summons in the Court of Protection, asking for an order that the papers relating to E's claim for damages brought by the Official Solicitor as her next friend be released to the father's solicitors. The list of the nine categories of documents sought includes the pleadings, which have already been disclosed, and all correspondence between the Official Solicitor and the Court of Protection, a claim which is no longer being pursued. The other seven categories remain in dispute. These include proofs of evidence, medical reports, instructions to counsel, counsel's advice, solicitors' notes and memoranda (referring not to the Official Solicitor's own documents but to the documents of the solicitors instructed by him to conduct the litigation), and certain other correspondence. On 1 August 1983 the master of the Court of Protection heard the application, and made an order for the production of all the documents except those in the category which is not being pursued, requiring them to be produced to the solicitors for E's father within 21 days. On 9 August 1983 the Official Solicitor appealed against this order, seeking its total discharge, or alternatively that he should be directed to produce the documents if the Queen's Bench Division so ordered. That is a reference to a possible application to the Queen's Bench Division under the Supreme Court Act 1981, s 33(2), and RSC Ord 24, r 7A, which relate to the production of documents in advance of the institution of proceedings in claims for death or personal injuries: I put it very shortly. By consent, a stay of the order of the Court of Protection pending the determination of this appeal was made on 18 August.

In the event, on 21 September 1983 E, acting by her sister as her next friend, issued an originating summons in the Queen's Bench Division under the Supreme Court Act 1981, s 33, seeking disclosure of all nine categories of documents as against the Official Solicitor and the solicitors that he had instructed. The originating summons was supported by an affidavit sworn by a solicitor in the firm advising E's parents. I was told that on 14 October the Queen's Bench master dismissed this application as not being appropriate and as being premature, in view of the present appeal from the order of the Master of the Court of Protection. When I inquired whether the Queen's Bench master had considered adjourning the originating summons before him until the present appeal was decided, I was told that he had not been asked to do this, and that he did not appear to have considered it. The question for me is whether or not the order of the master of the Court of Protection should stand.

In her decision, the master of the Court of Protection rejected the contention that rr 73, 74 and 76 of the Court of Protection Rules 1983 contained anything that assisted the father's claim. She said that these rules conferred powers on the Court of Protection itself, and that the master would refuse to allow them to be used by a solicitor for purposes other than those of that court. I agree; and before me counsel who appeared on behalf of the father placed no weight on these rules. The master's decision was based on property. The papers of E's next friend were the property of E; E was a patient; and under s 102(1) of the Mental Health Act 1959 the master, in exercising the functions of the judge—

'may, with respect to the property and affairs of a patient, do or secure the doing of all such things as appear necessary or expedient—(a) for the maintenance or other benefit of the patient . . . or (d) otherwise for administering the patient's affairs.'

The Mental Health Act 1983 repealed this provision on 30 September 1983, but replaced it by provisions in s 95(1) of that Act which are in identical terms. Before me, counsel who appeared on behalf of the Official Solicitor also referred me to s 96(1)(i) of the 1983 Act, which replaced s 103(1)(h) of the 1959 Act in terms which, so far as material, are identical. This, without prejudice to the generality of the provision that I have just quoted, gives the judge power to make such orders and give such directions and authorities as he thinks fit for the purposes of that provision, and in particular he may for that purpose make orders or give directions or authorities for the conduct of legal proceedings in the name of the patient or on his behalf.

As I have indicated, the foundation of the master's decision was that the next friend's papers were the property of the patient; and this of course led to a discussion of the position of the next friend. Certain authorities were put before me, but they did not carry the matter very far. I have since been able to look into the books, and it seems to me that some assistance is to be found in *Seton's Judgments and Orders* (7th edn, 1912) pp 932–935, *Simpson on Infants* (4th edn, 1926) pp 293–306 and *Daniell's Chancery Practice* (8th edn, 1914) pp 99–121, and in certain of the authorities there cited. Much of the learning relates to infants rather than patients; but there does not seem to me to be any difference between them that is relevant to this case.

The main function of a next friend appears to be to carry on the litigation on behalf of the plaintiff and in his best interests. For this purpose the next friend must make all the decisions that the plaintiff would have made, had he been able. The next friend may, on behalf of the plaintiff, do anything which the Rules of the Supreme Court require or authorise the plaintiff to do, though the next friend must act by a solicitor: see Ord 80, r 2. It is the next friend who is responsible to the court for the propriety and the progress of the proceedings. The next friend does not, however, become a litigant himself: his functions are essentially vicarious. Nevertheless, it is an important part of his functions that by acting he makes himself personally liable to the other party to the litigation for the costs of unsuccessful proceedings, and also for any damages under an undertaking in damages. On the other hand, if it was proper to institute the proceedings, and they have been conducted with propriety, the next friend will be entitled to be indemnified in respect of the costs by the plaintiff, or at least out of the plaintiff's estate: see e g *Steeden v Walden* [1910] 2 Ch 393, [1908–10] All ER Rep 380, and the books that I have already mentioned.

I have found no clear authority on the ownership of papers brought into existence on behalf of a patient. I would have thought that, initially at all events, he who pays owns. Thus a solicitor, on being paid, must deliver up to his client not only any deeds or original document but also the drafts and copies thereof (*Ex p Horsfall* (1827) 7 B & C 528, 108· ER 820); and the property in plans for a completed building passes from the architect to the building owner when the latter pays the architect his fees (*Gibbon v Pease* [1905] 1 KB 810, [1904–7] All ER Rep 454). That, however, is subject to the right of a professional man to retain memoranda, notes and similar documents made by him for his own information in carrying out his work for his client: see *Chantrey Martin & Co v Martin* [1953] 2 All ER 691 at 694–695, [1953] 2 QB 286 at 292–293. This qualification, however, does not seem to me to apply to a next friend as such. Even if the next friend is (as here) professionally qualified, his functions are essentially those of a vicarious litigant throughout. It is for him to decide on behalf of the plaintiff what is to be done in the litigation, having regard to the professional advice that he is given. If he is a lawyer himself, that will doubtless help him to consider that advice and make a proper decision; but his function is to make informed decisions and not to exercise whatever professional skills he has. If, for example, a next friend is replaced by a new next friend (which may be done under an order of the court: see Ord 80, r 3(4)), I can see no ground on which the displaced next friend could properly withhold from the new next friend any papers connected with the litigation, at all events once the displaced next friend has been indemnified for his costs. In this, as in the rest of this judgment, I speak only of cases in which, as here, the next friend instructs solicitors to act in the litigation; I say nothing about cases in which the Official Solicitor, being the next friend, also conducts the litigation himself qua solicitor. I should perhaps add that usually no order is required for the initial appointment of a next friend; on filing the requisite documents he simply commences the proceedings: see Ord 80, r 3(2), (6) and (8).

Now in the present case I infer that the next friend has in fact been reimbursed his costs out of the patient's estate. A letter from the Official Solicitor dated 19 April 1983 refers to the file in his office having been put away after all outstanding matters had been completed last year. On that footing, I think that his papers in the matter have become the property of E, the patient. Even if this is not so, I think that E's rights in those papers are sufficient to fall within the meaning of 'property' in ss 95 and 96 of the 1983 Act, replacing ss 102 and 103 of the 1959 Act. In those sections I consider that the word 'property' should be construed widely so as to include all rights of property, even if they fall short of being absolute ownership. By s 112, replacing s 119(1) of the 1959 Act, '"property" includes any thing in action, and any interest in real or personal property'. When consideration is given to the purpose of the legislation, it seems clear enough that 'property' ought to be treated as including all rights of property, even if those rights are conditional, or if they are subject to the claims of others, or if in some other way they fall short of full and unencumbered ownership. Parliament cannot have intended that rights of property which, though valuable, are imperfect should be excluded from the provisions that were being made for the protection and benefit of patients. Accordingly, even if the costs of the next friend had not been reimbursed out of the patient's estate, I think that E's 'property' includes her rights to the papers in the litigation, even if she can enforce those rights only on indemnifying her next friend, the Official Solicitor.

It therefore appears to me that the master's order is soundly based. The order cannot, of course, adversely affect the rights of others, and so, for example, it must take effect subject to the subsisting right (if any) of the Official Solicitor to his costs out of E's estate, and subject to any rights of the solicitors who were instructed by the Official Solicitor. During the argument there was considerable discussion about the present status of the Official Solicitor. In a letter last April he referred to himself as being functus officio, but this was questioned on the ground that under Ord 80, r 3 he remained the next friend until replaced under an order of the court. I find this proposition improbable: if litigation ended 20 years ago, will it be said that the next friend in that litigation still remains the next friend today? Can there be a next friend in litigation which is dead and not merely dormant? If a person becomes next friend to a patient, is he or she next friend for their joint lives? After all, even when the time for appealing has expired an application for leave to appeal out of time may still be made, as, indeed, is in contemplation in this case. However, I do not think that I need decide anything on this, for whether the Official Solicitor is still E's next friend or whether he has ceased to be her next friend, the papers are hers (subject to any rights of others), and there are no grounds on which the Official Solicitor can or should retain them as against E or someone else properly acting on her behalf, at all events when acting under an order of the Court of Protection.

Let me make it plain that the Official Solicitor has not been obstructive in these matters. His attitude has been one of doubting the jurisdiction of the Court of Protection and also of questioning whether the release of the documents is for the benefit of E. In my judgment the Court of Protection has the requisite jurisdiction. As for the question of the benefit of E, the master said in her judgment that her overall concern was for the patient's benefit; but she did not enlarge on the reasons why she thought that the release of the papers would be for E's benefit. I can see that there might be cases in which the papers would contain matter which could be damaging to a patient's state of mind if the patient recovered from his or her disability and then perused the papers. That, however, cannot arise in the present case, where there is no hope whatever of E ceasing to be under disability. Is it, then, in the interests of E for the papers to be considered by a prospective next friend with a view to obtaining advice on the prospects of success in an appeal out of time, and whether proceedings for negligence ought now to be brought?

If this had to be done at the expense of E's estate, I would be very doubtful whether it could be said to be for her benefit. On the material at present before me (and I emphasise that I have little more than the pleadings, the judgment and the joint opinion), I can see little prospect of success on either head. But an examination of the papers might produce a different view, and if that examination is to be conducted on the footing that none of the cost will fall on E's estate unless, indeed, it is found to be in the interests of E that the claim should be pursued, then it seems to me that it is for the benefit of E that this examination should be made. It may be a long shot, but it is a free long shot. On being assured that the examination will be made on that footing (and I think that it is desirable for this to be made explicit), I propose to dismiss the appeal. I cannot see that there is any possible disadvantage to E in having more money under the administration of her receiver, and there are obvious advantages.

I appreciate that this judgment leaves many matters unresolved. What, said counsel for the Official Solicitor, if the jurisdiction of the Court of Protection had not been invoked? Here, of course, the award of damages brought the Court of Protection into the picture; but if a claim by a penniless patient failed, the Court of Protection would have no part to play, and so the master of that court could not have made the order. Similarly as to infants, where of course the Court of Protection has no jurisdiction. In such cases, how is it to be decided whether the next friend should release the papers to a new prospective next friend? In personal injury cases, the Supreme Court Act 1981, s 33(2) and Ord 24, r 7A may well suffice; but not every case is a personal injury case. I think that the word 'capricious' which counsel for the Official Solicitor used is perhaps a little harsh, though I entirely agree that this, like some other points about next friends, might with advantage receive attention. Be that as it may, it plainly would be wrong in this case to deny jurisdiction to the Court of Protection merely because there are other cases in which that jurisdiction cannot be used to solve similar problems. I do not forget that proceedings in the nature of a bill of discovery may be brought, but those are substantial proceedings which ought not to have to be brought on a relatively short point such as this.

Given the assurance that I have mentioned, I shall dismiss the appeal. I do not know whether there are any details of the master's order which require consideration, but if there are, I shall hear counsel on them. I shall add this. As I have considered a number of authorities that were not discussed in argument, I shall, if either counsel so requests, direct that the order is not to be drawn up for some short period so that they can consider whether they wish to make any further submissions on any point not sufficiently explored in argument. Counsel may not be surprised when I say that although these authorities have obviously affected some of what I have said in this judgment, I do not think that they have in any way altered the conclusion that I would have reached without their aid.

Appeal dismissed.

Solicitors: *Official Solicitor; Evill & Coleman*, Putney (for E's father).

Vivian Horvath   Barrister.

Cairnplace Ltd v CBL (Property Investment) Co Ltd

COURT OF APPEAL, CIVIL DIVISION
CUMMING-BRUCE LJ AND REEVE J
2, 3, 25 NOVEMBER 1983

Landlord and tenant – Business premises – Terms of new tenancy – Inclusion of term that tenant provide guarantor of his obligations under new lease – Whether court having jurisdiction to order inclusion of such term – Landlord and Tenant Act 1954, ss 35, 41A(6).

Landlord and tenant – Business premises – Terms of new tenancy – Inclusion of term that tenant pay landlord's costs in respect of preparation of lease – Whether court should exercise discretion to include such term – Landlord and Tenant Act 1954, s 35 – Costs of Leases Act 1958, s 1.

Where a tenant applies under the Landlord and Tenant Act 1954 for the grant of a new tenancy of business premises the court has jurisdiction under s 35[a] of that Act to include a term in the new lease that the tenant obtain a guarantor of his obligations under the lease (see p 318 f to j and p 319 b, post).

In order to meet the situation which may arise where the landlord's security for the performance of the tenants' obligations under a new business tenancy will not be the same as the security afforded him under the old lease because there has been a cessation of the obligations of one or more of the joint tenants or partners who were parties to the old lease, s 41A(6)[b] of the 1954 Act empowers the court to impose a term in the new lease

---

a   Section 35, so far as material, provides: 'The terms of a tenancy granted under . . . this Act . . . shall be such as may be agreed between the landlord and the tenant or as, in default of such agreement, may be determined by the court . . .'

b   Section 41A(6), so far as material, provides: 'Where the court makes an order under . . . this Act for the grant of a new tenancy on an application made by the business tenants it may order the grant to be made to them or to them jointly with the persons carrying on the business in partnership with them, and may order the grant to be made subject to the satisfaction, within a time specified by the order, of such conditions as to guarantors, sureties or otherwise as appear to the court equitable, having regard to the omission of the other joint tenants from from the persons who will be the tenant under the new tenancy.'

requiring the tenants to obtain guarantors of their obligations, but that power to impose conditions 'as to guarantors, sureties or otherwise' does not affect the court's jurisdiction under s 35 to order, for other reasons, that the tenant obtain a guarantor of his obligations on the grant of a new tenancy (see p 319 *a b*, post).

When exercising its discretion under s 35 of the 1954 Act to determine the terms of a new lease of business premises, the court should not deprive the tenant of the protection afforded to him by s 1^c of the Costs of Leases Act 1958 by including a term requiring him to pay the costs incurred by the landlord in respect of the preparation of the new lease (see p 320 *g h*, post).

Notes

For the terms of a new tenancy of business premises, see 27 Halsbury's Laws (4th edn) paras 511–515, and for cases on the subject, see 31(2) Digest (Reissue) 956–961, 7763–7777.

For the Landlord and Tenant Act 1954, ss 35, 41A, see 18 Halsbury's Statutes (3rd edn) 574, 583.

For the Costs of Leases Act 1958, s 1, see ibid 614.

Cases referred to in judgment

Barclays Bank Ltd v Ascott [1961] 1 All ER 782, [1961] 1 WLR 717.
Kirkwood v Johnson (1979) 38 P & CR 392, CA.
O'May v City of London Real Property Co Ltd [1982] 1 All ER 660, [1983] 2 AC 237, [1982] 2 WLR 407, HL.

Appeal

Cairnplace Ltd (the tenant) appealed against that part of an order made by her Honour Judge Rowland in Westminster County Court on 11 August 1982 whereby it was ordered that its new tenancy of the business premises consisting of the ground floor shop and basement at 21 Noel Street, London W1, should include a term (i) that the tenant should pay the scale costs of the respondent, CBL (Property Investment) Co Ltd (the landlord) in respect of the preparation of the new lease, and (ii) that the tenant should provide two sureties to guarantee the due observance of the tenant's obligations throughout the currency of the new tenancy. The facts are set out in the judgment of the court.

Richard B Ritchie for the tenant.
Peter St J Langan QC for the landlord.

Cur adv vult

25 November. The following judgment of the court was delivered.

CUMMING-BRUCE LJ. This is an appeal against parts of an order made by her Honour Judge Rowland in the Westminster County Court on 11 August 1982 granting to Cairnplace Ltd, the appellant (hereinafter called 'the tenant'), a new tenancy of business premises consisting of the ground floor shop and basement at 21 Noel Street, London W1. The parts of the order with which this appeal is concerned are those that provide (1) that the tenant should pay the scale costs of CBL (Property Investment) Co Ltd, the respondents (hereinafter called 'the landlord'), in respect of the preparation of the new lease, and (2) that the tenant should provide two sureties to guarantee the due observance of its obligations throughout the term of the new tenancy, within six months of the execution of the lease.

By a lease dated 8 May 1972 the landlord granted a tenancy of the premises to Tartan

---

c   Section 1 is set out at p 320 *b c*, post

Textiles Ltd for a term of 10 years from 25 March 1972 at a rent of £3,500 per annum which was increased after five years to £4,500 under the provisions of a rent review clause. Clause 4(15)(a) of the lease contained a covenant by Tartan Textiles Ltd not to assign underlet or part with the possession of the whole of the demised premises for the whole or any part of the term without the licence in writing of the landlord which should not be unreasonably withheld. And there was a proviso that in the case of an assignment to a limited company then, if so demanded by the landlord, two directors of the company should join in as sureties to guarantee the due observance of its obligations during the term assigned.

By cl 4(31) of the lease Tartan Textiles Ltd further covenanted 'to pay the scale costs of the Landlords solicitors in respect of [the] lease and the Stamp Duty on the counterpart thereof'. On 24 February 1981 the landlord granted a licence to Tartan Textiles Ltd to assign the lease to the tenant. The licence included the appropriate guarantees by two directors of the tenant, Messrs Lester and Rifkin. The assignment was executed on 6 March 1981. At that time there was just over one year of the original lease to run. It can, we think, reasonably be inferred that at that time both the tenants and the landlord contemplated that an application would, in due course, be made for a new tenancy under the provisions of the Landlord and Tenant Act 1954. In fact Mr Landau, who was the solicitor to, and a director of, the landlord, gave evidence in terms that he expected that the tenant would wish to renew the lease.

On 4 June 1981, in accordance with s 25(1) of the 1954 Act, the landlord served notice on the tenant terminating the tenancy. On the following day the tenant informed the landlord that it was not willing to give up possession. On 24 September 1981 the tenant issued an application for a new tenancy in the prescribed form. Its proposal was that the new tenancy should be for a term of ten years from 25 March 1982, with a rent review at five years, at an annual rent of £6,000 and otherwise on the same terms as the existing lease. On 13 October the landlord filed an answer, which was later amended on 1 March 1982 stating that it did not oppose the grant of a new tenancy and that the terms of a new lease had been agreed with two exceptions. The two exceptions concerned cll 7 and 4(30) of the draft lease. The landlord required the inclusion of those two clauses; the tenant was unwilling to agree. By cl 7 Messrs Lester and Rifkin (who were to be parties to the lease and therein described as 'the sureties') were required to covenant with the landlord to guarantee the due observance by the tenant of all the obligations under the lease. And by cl 4(30) the tenant was required 'to contribute the sum of £200 plus value added tax towards the costs of the landlord's solicitors in respect of [the] lease'.

The hearing took place before the judge on 11 August 1982. She ordered that a new tenancy be granted on the terms set out in the schedule to her order, which reads as follows:

'(1) The new lease of the premises . . . to include a term requiring the applicants [the tenant] to provide two guarantors with obligations as in the original licence who are directors of the applicants within six months of the execution of the lease to operate for the duration of the new lease. (2) Acceptance by the applicants not to be unreasonably withheld. (3) Costs clause to remain as in the original lease.'

She also ordered the tenant to pay the costs of the proceedings before her on scale 2.

The judge made the following findings in regard to the financial status of the tenant:

'The tenant company was incorporated in September 1980 and started trading about the end of 1980 and the beginning of 1981. It employs outdoor workers for the manufacture of ladies' garments and supplies the cheaper end of the clothing trade as wholesalers. The share capital of the company is £3,000 and there are four directors. As a recent company it was unable to produce accounts which, it appears, are in draft form but Mr Lester gave evidence that the turnover since trading commenced was approximately £767,000 with net profits of approximately £35,000. The company has about 12 main customers including Debenhams, Top

Shop, Dorothy Perkins and C & A. Mr Lester anticipated recovery from the general
recession and an increase of turnover. He agreed that the net profit margin was low,
approximately 4½% of the turnover before corporation tax, but pointed out that
stock-in-hand is allowed against corporation tax if profit is eroded. The present
position of the tenant is that it has a bank overdraft of about £30,000, security for
which is provided by two houses belonging to two directors. The maximum limit
for overdraft facilities is £60,000. The company has been in credit at times during
1981 and the bank account fluctuates almost weekly. Mr Lester is reluctant to join
in the new lease as guarantor, giving as his reason that it is unnecessary and the
company is sufficient in itself.'

The judge also found that the tenant's liability for rent and rates from the inception of
the new tenancy would be increased from £7,000 to £11,000 per annum.

She asked herself whether a requirement to provide guarantors was just, fair and
reasonable in the special circumstances of the case, and answered as follows:

'I have taken all factors into consideration, including the terms on which the lease
was assigned, that the same parties are involved, the recent incorporation of the
tenant company, its financial position, prospects vulnerability, the increased rent
and any hardship to the tenant. In my view such a term should be just, fair and
reasonable provided there is protection for the tenant and that acceptance of the
guarantors proposed should not be unreasonably withheld. The argument that the
landlord is seeking additional insurance and protection to which he is not entitled
does not apply. It can equally be said that a tenant is asking the landlord to take a
risk which its own directors are not prepared to take.'

The judge then proceeded to consider whether she had jurisdiction to include the terms
required by the landlord in the new lease and she decided that she had, and exercised the
discretion in favour of the terms as specified in the first paragraph of the first schedule of
her order. She also made the order sought by the landlord that the tenant should pay the
landlord's costs of preparing the lease.

Jurisdiction

The first question raised by the tenant is whether the judge had jurisdiction under s 35
of the 1954 Act to impose the term set out in the first paragraph of the schedule to her
order. They submit that the whole object of the 1954 Act is to provide the tenant with
security of tenure which in the context means that the tenant must be granted a new
tenancy without any further security for the performance of his obligations other than
his own promise to perform them. They seek to derive support from the provisions of
s 41A(6) because if the court already had jurisdiction to include a term for guarantors the
subsection would be unnecessary. And they contend that some limitation must be put as
a matter of construction on the wide terms of s 35. The 1954 Act deals with the
contractual relationship of landlord and tenant only, and the court has no power over
third parties. Whatever else is negotiable, security of tenure is not. They seek to rely on
the reasoning of the speeches in *O'May v City of London Real Property Co Ltd* [1982] 1 All
ER 660, [1983] 2 AC 237, *Barclays Bank Ltd v Ascott* [1961] 1 All ER 782, [1961] 1 WLR
717, and *Kirkwood v Johnson* (1979) 38 P & CR 392.

We reject these submissions. The words of the section in their ordinary meaning are
clearly wide enough to include all those provisions which will become contractually
binding on the parties when the lease is executed. The term imposed by the judge is not
a condition precedent, and we find nothing in the cases relied on by the tenant to support
the proposition that it was outside the powers conferred by s 35. There are many terms
commonly included in leases which depend for their efficacy on the co-operation of third
parties; an obligation to insure is a ready example. And we do not accept that it is a
relevant distinction that in such common terms there is a market into which the tenant
may go to fulfil his obligation as compared to the difficulty which may face him if
required to obtain guarantors specifically identified as individuals or members of a small

class such as directors of the tenant company. In our view that distinction is relevant to discretion, not to jurisdiction. There is a simple explanation of the inclusion of sub-s (6) in s 41A of the 1954 Act. The subsection contemplates, among other situations, the termination of the obligations of one or more of the joint tenants or partners who were parties to the old lease. The old lease therefore afforded the landlord a different security for the performance of the obligations of the business tenants from that available in the new lease. It was to meet this situation that s 41A(6) of the 1954 Act provided that, although there might be no provision for guarantors in the old lease, the court should have specific power to impose a term requiring them in the new lease between parties who were not identified with the parties in the old lease. We hold that there was jurisdiction to impose the term in the first paragraph of the first schedule to the order.

Discretion

We consider that on the facts, the case for the exercise of discretion in the way in which the judge exercised it could hardly be stronger. Clause 15(h) of the lease made between the landlord and Tartan Textiles Ltd on 8 May 1972 expressly provided for guarantors being directors of satisfactory standing of the limited company seeking assignment of the demised premises for all or part of the term of ten years granted by the lease. When Tartan Textiles Ltd and the tenant and its directors, Messrs Lister and Rifkin, negotiated a licence to assign the tail end of the lease, all parties, including the two directors, agreed that in consideration of the licence to assign granted on 25 February 1981 the two directors, as sureties, would covenant in the terms set out in cll 3 and 4 of the licence. That instrument was signed and sealed by the two guarantors. The assignment followed on 6 March 1981, and included the covenant by the two directors in cl 2 thereof. Six months later, following the landlord's contractual notice to quit at the end of the term, the tenant applied to the court for a new lease for a term of ten years. Obviously that application was contemplated by the tenant when it entered into possession for the purpose of establishing a new business in the parcels assigned for a term expiring at the end of the year. The tenants submit that the term proposed by the landlord is a new term. The lease of 8 May 1972 only required guarantors on assignment of the term assigned. Those guarantees lasting a year were duly given. There was no provision in the lease of 1972 for guarantees to be given extending to the term of any new lease sought by the tenant pursuant to the provisions of Pt II of the Landlord and Tenant Act 1954. But, as we understand the tenant's arguments, even that would not have availed the landlord because the tenant has strenuously argued here and below that the court would have no jurisdiction anyway. Then the tenant's argument proceeds that a term for guarantees for a year odd is a different and much less rigorous obligation than a guarantee for ten years.

This is an unattractive submission. The term of ten years is a term proposed by the tenant. The practical effect of the argument is that if there are greater risks of the tenant's default over a ten year term than over the year for which the assignment was contractually effective, the landlord, not the directors of the company, should bear the risk. As the whole adventure was promoted by the two directors who, we were told, by their voting rights control the company, it is not an argument which might be expected to stimulate sympathy on the part of the judge. In our view there is no ground for disturbing her exercise of discretion.

In the foregoing, we have deliberately confined our reasoning to the facts of the instant case. But the judge's decision on the exercise of discretion is only an illustration of what is fair and reasonable having regard to the existing lease and to all the circumstances. Thus the principle which we have affirmed is wider than the application of the principle to the facts of this case. We only add this observation in case our judgment is interpreted more narrowly than is the case. Each case, as the section makes clear, must be decided on its own facts; there may be many other circumstances differing widely from those in the instant case, in which it would be fair and reasonable for the court to determine that there should be guarantors of the tenant's obligations in the new lease.

The cost of the leases

The tenant also appeals against the term determined by the judge pursuant to s 35 of the 1954 Act, which provided that the costs clause was to remain as in the original lease. Clause 4(31) of the existing lease was a covenant by the tenant 'To pay the scale costs of the Landlord's solicitors in respect of this Lease and the Stamp Duty on the Counterpart thereof'. As there are now no relevant scales, it is common ground on this appeal that if the order is upheld in principle, the obligation on the tenant should be varied to an obligation to pay the landlord's reasonable costs rather than a simple repetition of cl 4(31) of the existing lease.

The point is a short one. The Costs of Leases Act 1958 provides:

'**1.** Notwithstanding any custom to the contrary, a party to a lease shall, unless the parties thereto agree otherwise in writing, be under no obligation to pay the whole or any part of any other party's solicitor's costs of the lease.

2. In this Act—(*a*) "lease" includes an underlease and an agreement for a lease or underlease or for a tenancy or sub-tenancy . . .'

Therefore, if the terms of the new lease had been negotiated between the parties, neither party was under any obligation to pay the other party's solicitor's costs of the lease unless otherwise agreed in writing. The judge dealt concisely with this issue. She gave a summary of the submissions made by counsel for the tenant and for the landlord, and decided that she saw no reason to vary the costs clause and preferred the argument of counsel for the landlord. This argument was to the effect that s 35 of the Act confers on the judge the discretion to determine other terms, which was not supplanted by the 1958 Act.

With respect to the judge we do not accept her decision on this issue. In 1954 there was a custom that the tenant should pay the landlord's costs of preparing a lease which was a practice generally followed by conveyancing solicitors in the absence of express agreement in the agreement for a lease. So when in 1972 the lease between the landlord and Tartan Textiles Ltd (the existing lease) included cl 4(31) the clause was consistent with the general practice, and before the 1958 Act came into operation there is no doubt that the court had the power to embody it as 'another term' in the new lease pursuant to s 35 of the 1954 Act. But in 1958 Parliament relieved the tenant of the usual obligation which conveyancing custom and practice had imposed on tenants. Thereafter it was only if there was express agreement in writing whereby the tenant agreed to pay the landlord's costs of preparation of the lease that the tenant was under an obligation.

Where Parliament has enacted a later Act designed to relieve tenants of a specific obligation, it is not in our view a correct exercise of judicial discretion to use the wide power conferred on the court by the general words of s 35 of the 1954 Act to deprive the tenant of the protection conferred on him by a later Act dealing specifically with this very obligation. It is perfectly correct to say that s 35 deals with the powers of the court and not with the agreement of a term by the parties. But it does not follow that the court when exercising its discretion in determining other terms pursuant to s 35 can fairly and reasonably deprive the tenant of a protection that Parliament conferred on him in 1958.

For those reasons we allow the appeal in respect of the order in regard to the costs of the lease made by the judge and delete that clause from the new lease.

Appeal allowed in part. Leave to appeal to the House of Lords refused. Stay refused.

Solicitors: *Barry Phillips & Co* (for the tenant); *Landau & Co* (for the landlord).

Bebe Chua   Barrister.

Davy-Chiesman v Davy-Chiesman and another

COURT OF APPEAL, CIVIL DIVISION

SIR JOHN DONALDSON MR, MAY AND DILLON LJJ

24, 25, 26 OCTOBER, 18 NOVEMBER 1983

Solicitor – Costs – Payment by solicitor personally – Legal aid – Order that solicitor of legally-aided person pay costs of both parties – Solicitor representing legally-aided husband in claim for financial relief – Legal aid certificate granted on basis of counsel's advice to seek sum of money on trust for child of family and not to seek lump sum because husband was undischarged bankrupt – Counsel reconsidering advice and advising husband to seek only lump sum payment – Solicitor relying completely on counsel's advice although chances of application succeeding very remote – Solicitor failing to inform legal aid committee of change of circumstances in the litigation – Husband's application not granted by court – Court ordering wife's costs to be paid out of legal aid fund – Law Society applying for costs of both husband and wife to be paid by solicitor personally – Whether solicitor having duty independent of counsel's advice to inform legal aid committee of change of circumstances – Whether reliance on advice of properly instructed counsel absolving solicitor from being guilty of dereliction of duty in allowing litigation to continue when chances of success remote – Legal Aid Act 1974, s 13(1) – RSC Ord 62, r 8(1).

In January 1980 the husband, who was an undischarged bankrupt, filed a petition for divorce and also sought financial relief under s 23(1) of the Matrimonial Causes Act 1973. The decree nisi was made absolute in August 1980. In March 1981 the husband applied for legal aid in order to proceed with his claim for ancillary relief. The Law Society issued a legal aid certificate which was limited to the preparation of papers for counsel and obtaining counsel's opinion and conditional on the papers and opinion being referred back to the legal aid committee to enable it to decide whether to amend or discharge the certificate. On 26 February 1982 the husband and his solicitor had a conference with counsel to discuss, inter alia, whether if a lump sum was ordered to be paid to the husband by the wife it would go to the husband's trustee in bankruptcy. In a written opinion dated 2 March 1982 counsel advised (a) that any lump sum ordered to be paid to the husband immediately be appropriated by the husband's trustee in bankruptcy and accordingly no court would make such an order, (b) that there was a possibility that an application for periodic payments for a short period might succeed and (c) that a sum to purchase a house for the husband and provide a home for the child of the family during access visits might be ordered to be settled on trustees, which would not make the sum awarded available to the husband's trustee in bankruptcy. The solicitor forwarded counsel's opinion to the legal aid committee and the limitation on the legal aid certificate was removed. On 19 April the husband and his solicitor attended a further conference with counsel, who advised, contrary to his written opinion, that the husband should apply for a lump sum to be made payable to him direct. At the hearing before the judge counsel made an application for a lump sum and expressly abandoned all other financial claims in the petition. On the second day of the hearing, the husband informed the court in the course of his evidence that he only sought a sum to be settled on the child of the family and to provide a home for himself and the child during access visits, and that he was not asking for a lump sum. The judge adjourned the hearing to allow counsel to consult with the husband and the solicitor. The husband was prepared to abandon the application for a lump sum but counsel strongly advised pursuing the claim. As a result the hearing continued. The judge dismissed the application, holding that it was without merit and should not have been made. The wife obtained an order for costs to be paid by the husband and then applied for her costs to be paid out of the legal aid fund pursuant to s 13(1)[a] of the Legal Aid Act 1974. Following an adjournment, the Law Society contended that the costs of both parties in the lump sum proceedings had been incurred 'improperly or without reasonable cause', within RSC Ord 62, r 8(1)[b], and it applied to the court for it to exercise its jurisdiction to make against the husband's solicitor orders (a) disallowing his own costs as between solicitor and client, (b) directing him personally to pay the costs of the wife in connection with the husband's application and (c) directing him to indemnify the Law Society in respect of any fees properly payable to counsel out of the legal aid fund. The judge dismissed the Law Society's application against the solicitor and ordered that the wife's costs be paid out of the legal aid fund. The Law Society appealed.

Held – A solicitor acting for a legally-aided client owed a duty to the legal aid committee to inform them of any change in the circumstances of the litigation and although the solicitor was entitled to rely on the advice of properly instructed counsel that did not absolve him from his responsibility to exercise his own independent judgment. Thus where it appeared to a solicitor that his legally-aided client no longer had a reasonable chance of success he was under a duty to notify the legal aid committee of that change in circumstances and if he failed to do so he was personally liable to bear the costs of his client and of the other party in the litigation. Since, on the facts, it must have been apparent to the solicitor at or shortly after the conference of 19 April 1982 that the form of relief which counsel then intended to seek would fail because the husband's bankruptcy would mean that any capital sum would not go direct to the husband and furthermore was the one form of relief which counsel had ruled out in his written opinion of 2 March 1982, it followed that in not exercising his own independent judgment and in failing to inform the legal aid committee that the husband's application had become most unlikely to succeed, the solicitor had failed to discharge his duty to the legal aid committee. A fortiori, at the commencement of the hearing of the husband's application and again during the adjournment to enable counsel to consult the husband and the solicitor, the solicitor had failed to discharge that duty. The fact that the solicitor had acted in accordance with counsel's advice was not sufficient to absolve him from being guilty of a serious dereliction of duty. The court was therefore entitled to exercise jurisdiction over the solicitor pursuant to RSC Ord 62, r 8(1) and would order him to bear the costs of the litigation of both the husband and the wife. The Law Society's appeal would accordingly be allowed (see p 332 c to f, p 333 h to p 334 b and d and p 335 a b and h to p 336 f, post).

Dicta of Viscount Maugham and of Lord Wright in *Myers v Elman* [1939] 4 All ER at 488, 508–509, *Edwards v Edwards* [1958] 2 All ER 179, dictum of May J in *Currie & Co v Law Society* [1976] 3 All ER at 839 and *R & T Thew Ltd v Reeves (No 2)* [1982] 3 All ER 1086 considered.

Notes

For the jurisdiction of the court to order costs against a solicitor personally, see 36 Halsbury's Laws (4th edn) 157, 196–199, paras 203, 259–262, and for cases on the subject, see 43 Digest (Repl) 375–389, 3976–4147.

For the Matrimonial Causes Act 1973, s 23, see 43 Halsbury's Laws (3rd edn) 564.

For the Legal Aid Act 1974, s 13, see 44 ibid 1053.

---

a   Section 13(1), so far as material, provides: 'Where a party receives legal aid in connection with any proceedings between him and a party not receiving legal aid (. . . referred to as "the unassisted party") and those proceedings are finally decided in favour of the unassisted party, the court by which the proceedings are so decided may . . . make an order for the payment to the unassisted party out of the legal aid fund of the whole or any part of the costs incurred by him in those proceedings. . .'

b   Rule 8(1) is set out at p 328 *f*, post

Cases referred to in judgments

Currie & Co v Law Society [1976] 3 All ER 832, [1977] QB 990, [1976] 3 WLR 785.

Edwards v Edwards [1958] 2 All ER 179, [1958] P 235, [1958] 2 WLR 956.

Maroux v Sociedade Comercial Abel Pereira da Fonseca SARL [1972] 2 All ER 1085, [1972] 1 WLR 962.

Myers v Elman [1939] 4 All ER 484, [1940] AC 282, HL.

Stephens v Hill (1842) 10 M & W 28, 152 ER 368.

Shaw v Vauxhall Motors Ltd [1974] 2 All ER 1185, [1974] 1 WLR 1035, CA.

Thew (R & T) Ltd v Reeves (No 2) [1982] 3 All ER 1086, [1982] QB 1283, [1982] 3 WLR 869, CA.

Cases also cited

Allen v Sir Alfred McAlpine & Sons Ltd [1968] 1 All ER 543, [1968] 2 QB 229, CA.

Francis v Francis and Dickerson [1955] 3 All ER 836, [1955] P 87.

Kelly v London Transport Executive [1982] 2 All ER 842, [1982] 1 WLR 1055, CA.

Interlocutory appeal

The No 14 (London West) Area Legal Aid Committee appealed against the order of Latey J dated 3 February 1983 whereby he dismissed an application by the legal aid committee for orders that the second respondent, Ralph S Haeems (the solicitor), who acted as solicitor for the petitioner, William Keith Davy-Chiesman (the husband), in the husband's application for ancillary relief (i) should be ordered personally to pay the costs of the respondent, Dawn Yvonne Davy-Chiesman (the wife), of the ancillary relief proceedings, (ii) should be disallowed his own costs of acting for the husband in such proceedings, and (iii) should be ordered to indemnify the Law Society, as administrators of the legal aid fund, against fees properly paid by the fund to counsel in connection with such proceedings. The judge further ordered that the wife's costs of the application for ancillary relief be paid out of the legal aid fund pursuant to s 13 of the Legal Aid Act 1974. The facts are set out in the judgment of May LJ.

Swinton Thomas QC and *Duncan Matheson* for the legal aid committee.
Kenneth Machin QC and *John Caudle* for the solicitor.
Ian Kennedy QC and *Iain Hughes* as amicus curiae.

Cur adv vult

18 November. The following judgments were delivered.

MAY LJ (delivering the first judgment at the invitation of Sir John Donaldson MR). This is an appeal with leave from a judgment of Latey J of 3 February 1983. He then had before him an application by the legal aid committee made pursuant to RSC Ord 62, r 8, in respect of the costs of certain proceedings between a divorced husband and wife. Those proceedings related to financial relief claimed by the husband who was in receipt of legal aid under a legal aid certificate in which a member of the respondent firm of solicitors was the nominated solicitor. The nature of the relief sought by the legal aid committee will appear more clearly after a recital of the relevant facts. For the sake of convenience, although they are now divorced, I shall refer to the two lay parties principally concerned as husband and wife.

In the early 1970s the wife was a very successful business woman. She had created a chain of employment agencies both in England and other countries abroad. Her husband was also a business man. The two of them met in 1974 and began to live together in

December 1974 in a house, Tudor Orchard, which the wife had bought before she and the husband had met. Their only son was born on 4 May 1976. On 29 May 1976 they were married. In the mean time the husband had been involved in serious criminal frauds in respect of which he was convicted in January 1977 and sentenced to six years' imprisonment. In addition he was made the subject of a criminal bankruptcy order originally in the sum of £1,250,000, although I understand that his liability has been reassessed at something of the order of £200,000.

In January 1979 the wife presented a petition for divorce based on 'behaviour', to use the shorthand term. The husband defended the suit which was heard in July 1979 by Dunn J. After a three-day hearing the judge dismissed the petition, holding that although the husband's criminal conduct had been a cause of the breakdown of the marriage, the major cause was the wife's infatuation with another man she had met in 1978, after the husband had gone to prison. That affair had come to an end long since.

In January 1980 the husband in his turn presented a petition based on adultery with the man just mentioned. In addition to the normal prayers for dissolution and custody of the infant child, by his petition the husband also asked for financial relief of all the forms contemplated by s 23(1) of the Matrimonial Causes Act 1973 as well as appropriate property adjustment orders under the provisions of s 24(1) of the 1973 Act. In so far as dissolution was concerned, the husband's petition was uncontested. There was a decree nisi in February 1980, which was made absolute in August 1980.

On 7 January 1981 the husband gave the usual notice of his intention to proceed in the suit for financial relief, referring to his prayer for periodical payments, secured periodic payments, a lump sum and a property adjustment order.

On 7 March 1981 the husband applied for legal aid to be heard on the questions of custody, access and financial relief. He had hitherto been represented by solicitors who are no longer concerned in any way in these proceedings. They withdrew on 20 November 1981. On 1 December 1981 the firm of solicitors, Messrs Ralph Haeems & Co, were instructed on his behalf. A particular partner of that firm has been concerned with this matter throughought.

On 25 February 1982 the legal aid committee issued a legal aid certificate to the husband to enable him to be represented on applications for financial provision and access to the child of the family, but limited to the preparation of papers for counsel and obtaining counsel's opinion. This condition required the papers and that opinion to be referred back to the General Committee when available for decision whether the certificate should be amended or discharged.

On the following day, 26 February, the solicitor with his lay client had a conference with counsel. It is clear from the solicitor's attendance note, which we have seen, that the first question which he raised with counsel was whether any lump sum ordered to be paid by the wife to the husband would go straight to the latter's trustee in bankruptcy. In an affidavit sworn on 31 January 1983 the solicitor agreed with the husband's evidence about what took place at this conference contained in an affidavit sworn by the latter on the same day. The husband said that discussion did take place about whether the trustee in bankruptcy would be able to seize any lump sum ordered to be paid to him, the priority of the statutory charge of the legal aid fund, and whether it was still practicable for him to claim periodic payments from the wife. He went on to say that in this conference counsel had advised that it would not be possible for the husband to obtain an order from the court for a trust to be set up for the child of the marriage. Counsel said that there had been a number of decisions of the court on this topic some three years before. However, although the solicitor said that he agreed with the evidence given by the husband in his affidavit to which I have just referred, he went on to say that the purport of counsel's advice was that the husband was entitled to a lump sum and provided that it was wanted for a genuine need the Official Receiver would not be entitled to seize it. When he was cross-examined at the hearing before Latey J on the application from which this appeal is brought, he effectively told the judge that at this conference of 26 February 1982 counsel had advised that any lump sum which the court saw fit to order should not go to the husband but should go to trustees for the benefit of the child. This was of course contrary to the evidence of the husband in the affidavit to which I have just referred and with which the solicitor agreed in his affidavit: it was also contrary to advice given in an earlier opinion by counsel in February 1979, although this of course had not, at least by then, been seen by the solicitor. It is also to be remembered that according to the latter and the husband in their affidavits of 31 January 1983 at least one thing which counsel had advised was that no court would make an order for a trust in favour of the child. There has clearly been some confusion, at least in the solicitor's mind, about what counsel was advising in this conference, but taking everything into account I think it is clear that the latter was advising that no lump sum should be payable direct to the husband: if it were, then it would be taken immediately by the trustee. For my part, even though the solicitor may not have been very experienced in divorce work, I would have expected that this would have been apparent to any competent solicitor who had the fact of the husband's bankruptcy in mind. That the point was present to the mind of this solicitor is quite clear from the first question in his attendance note on this conference.

In any event, the point was made quite clear in counsel's written opinion on 2 March 1982. It is necessary for me to quote specifically from it. The third paragraph was in these terms:

'The position with regard to the pending application for financial relief is somewhat more complicated. In my opinion, on the face of the affidavits before me, he would be entitled to periodical payments from his former wife. His criminal bankruptcy effects that claim only marginally by reason of the discretionary power of the trustee to appropriate part of the maintenance payments for the benefit of his creditors. With regard to his application for lump sum provision, if he were to obtain an order for lump sum provision the whole of that sum would be appropriated by the trustee for the benefit of his creditors. However, the purpose of Mr. Davy-Chiesman in making this application is to obtain a home for himself and a home in which he could have his child to reside with him. He could, in my opinion, succeed in that application not by obtaining a lump sum order but by obtaining an order that money be settled upon trustees to purchase for his use a house. That, undoubtedly, in my opinion, would be the appropriate course for Mr. Davy-Chiesman to take in this particular matter.'

Counsel then went on to deal with a possible application for periodical payments and returned to the question of any lump sum payment and the position of the trustee in bankruptcy later in his opinion where he wrote:

'With regard to Mr. Chiesman's application for lump sum provision that would undoubtedly constitute after-acquired monies which the trustee would be able to appropriate for the benefit of the creditors and would be bound so to do. However, Mr. Chiesman informs me that the reason for which he seeks such [lump] sum provision is to provide himself with housing and such suitable housing as would enable him to have his son stay with him for periods of staying access. Against a background of the circumstances in which the matrimonial home came to be purchased, I am of the opinion the Court might well consider that his attitude in this respect was reasonable. [If] it was of the opinion it was reasonable for monies to be provided in order to acquire for Mr. Chiesman a home, the manner in which that could be done would be for the Court to order that a suitable sum be settled upon trustees to purchase for the use of Mr. Chiesman a suitable home. That would provide Mr. Chiesman with the home which he desires. Those monies then would not come within the reach of the trustee in bankruptcy. It is in the above circumstances that I do consider that legal aid should be extended to Mr. Davy-Chiesman in order to enable him to pursue his present pending application for ancillary relief as well as his application for access to the child of the family.'

I think that it is quite clear what counsel was advising on 2 March 1982 and also that it ought to have been equally clear to the solicitor. First, that any lump sum ordered in favour of the husband would at once be appropriated by the trustee in bankruptcy and that accordingly no court would make any such order. Second, there was a possibility that an application for periodical payments for a short period would succeed. Third, that the court might also order a sum to be settled on trustees, and thus not be available to the husband's trustee in bankruptcy, to purchase a suitable home for the husband.

The solicitor forwarded counsel's opinion to the legal aid committee and on 16 March 1982 the limitation was removed from his legal aid certificate. The husband was thereafter legally aided in his application against his wife for financial provision. At no material time thereafter did the solicitor communicate with the legal aid committee.

We then move to a procedural application which was made by another counsel acting on behalf of the original counsel who had written the opinion to which I have just referred, which application was made to Latey J on 17 March 1982. The solicitor's attendance note of the following day, if it be correct, and I see no reason to doubt it, shows that counsel then told the judge that the husband wanted a sum of money from his wife for the purpose of having this settled in trust for his child. The relevant passage from the solicitor's affidavit sworn on 31 January 1983 is in these terms:

> 'On the 17th March, 1982 I attended the High Court of Justice with the petitioner and counsel . . . The hearing was for directions and was before Mr. Justice Latey. During the course of the hearing counsel stated, inter alia, that the lump sum sought by the petitioner was for the purpose of the settlement upon trust on the said child Marcus. The learned judge pointed out that the Official Receiver would be able to apply for part of the income of a bankrupt, but went on to express the view that if money were to be for the purchase of a house for the use of the child, then it would not be an attempted defeat of the bankruptcy.'

On the hearing of the application presently appealed from, this passage in the affidavit surprised the judge who looked back at his note of the application for financial provision. When the solicitor came to give evidence he said that he had in fact elided two sentences in his attendance note, that he had consequently misinterpreted it and that the judge had not made this comment. Be that as it may, it is clear that on 17 March counsel was not advancing the claims which the original counsel had specifically advised should be made in his opinion of 2 March 1982. In addition, the claim that was mentioned, namely a lump sum for the purpose of settlement on trust for the child, was one which the solicitor knew perfectly well counsel had previously advised that the court would not grant. In his affidavit the solicitor made it quite clear that counsel had so advised in the conference of 26 February 1982, Yet he did nothing about this; he did not get in touch with the legal aid committee; he did not even raise the point with counsel.

Then on 19 April 1982 the solicitor and client attended a further conference with original counsel. In his affidavit to which I have already referred the solicitor deposed to the fact that—

> 'the purpose of this conference was to enable counsel to enquire into the petitioner's means and to establish the use to which he proposed to put any lump sum that he may be given by this Honourable Court.'

That counsel was then advising that the application should be for a lump sum payable to the husband direct I think is confirmed by the contents of para 5 of an affidavit settled by counsel, which the solicitor arranged for the husband to swear on 20 May 1982. What is inescapable is that this change of front by counsel was wholly irreconcilable with his opinion of 2 March 1982 on which the original limitation on the husband's legal aid certificate had been removed.

Then on 9 June 1982 counsel's brief was delivered by the solicitor. In the instructions counsel was 'instructed to represent the petitioner in his application for a lump sum returnable before a Judge of the High Court on Tuesday the 15th June, 1982'. In the light of what had gone before, these instructions are now capable of a number of interpretations, even if we assume that the solicitor had fully applied his mind at this stage to the nature of the application which it was proposed to make on his client's behalf before Latey J a week later. In these circumstances, I think that the terms in which counsel's brief were drawn do not take this matter any further, one way or the other.

Then we come to the actual hearing of the husband's application which began before Latey J on 15 June and in which judgment was given on 18 June 1982. As the judge said in the first sentence of his judgment on that occasion, and also in the judgment on the application presently appealed from, counsel opened the application as one for a lump sum payment to the husband only. He expressly told the judge that all the other financial claims in the petition were not being pursued and were abandoned. The solicitor's evidence under cross-examination on the later application shows that he appreciated that this was wholly contrary to the advice given by counsel in his opinion of 2 March 1982, but this fundamental change of front caused him no surprise, I believe because he had realised from the time of the conference with counsel of 19 April 1982 that this was just what counsel was indeed proposing to ask for.

However, matters did not rest there. On the second day of the hearing the husband in his evidence said that all he was asking for and indeed all that he had ever asked for was some sort of a settlement for the child and that he thought that the best way of achieving this would be to purchase a flat or house in which he (the husband) could live and have staying access to the child. The husband made it clear that he was not asking for a lump sum for himself. The judge pointed out to counsel that there was no such application before the court and indeed all applications other than one for a lump sum payment to the husband himself had been expressly abandoned. It is quite clear that the judge was fully aware of the fact that the litigation before him was being pursued at perhaps heavy expense to the wife but at no expense to the husband who had the protection of a legal aid certificate. In those circumstances he invited counsel to consider the matter with his clients, both lay and professional. There was a short adjournment to enable counsel to do so. From the solicitor's affidavit to which I have already referred and his evidence on the hearing of the application now appealed from, it is clear that during the short adjournment counsel told the husband that it was obvious that the judge was against him. The husband agreed and said that he was then willing to abandon his application for financial relief. Nevertheless counsel, who both the solicitor and the husband said possessed a strong personality, advised that the application should continue: the grounds on which he did so do not appear from the material before us. Consquently they returned into court and counsel told the judge that the application would go on: a claim for a lump sum for the husband and nothing else.

It did indeed continue for a further two days. It is I think unnecessary to go into the details of the judge's judgment on the substantive application. Suffice it to say that he accepted the wife's evidence; he rejected the husband's evidence, being left with the clear impression that part of his motives was to damage his wife; in the end the judge expressed his conclusion in this way:

'The application, in my judgment, is without any merit, should not have been made and most certainly should not have been pursued to its end. It will be rejected together with the husband's other financial claims which have been abandoned.'

Naturally the question of costs then arose. Knowing that the husband had a legal aid certificate, counsel for the wife first asked for and obtained an order that her client's costs should be paid by the husband, but on terms that that order should not be enforced without leave of the court. Counsel then went on to make an application that the wife's costs should be paid out of the legal aid fund pursuant to the provisions of s 13 of the Legal Aid Act 1974 on the ground that she would suffer severe financial hardship unless such an order were made and that it would be just and equitable in all the circumstances that provision for her costs should be made out of public funds. Following the usual procedure, the judge adjourned that application so that the legal aid fund could consider the matter and make representations if it wished. In the event the Law Society, as the body responsible for the administration of the legal aid fund, issued an application *a* pursuant to RSC Ord 62, r 8 that the solicitor who had acted for the husband and was the solicitor nominated in the husband's legal aid certificate should pay the husband's and wife's costs personally. That application was listed for hearing at the same time as the wife's adjourned application for payment of her costs out of the legal aid fund. They both came before Latey J on 3 February 1983. The Law Society accepted that, if they failed in their application against the solicitor, the wife was entitled to the order against *b* the legal aid fund for which she was asking. On the other hand, if their application that the costs should be paid by the solicitor succeeded, they contended that it would be unjust and inequitable in those circumstances to make any order under s 13 of the 1974. In the result, having heard evidence and argument, the judge dismissed the legal aid committee's application against the solicitor under RSC Ord 62 and consequently ordered that the wife's costs of the proceedings, which culminated in the hearing before him in *c* June 1982, should be paid out of the legal aid fund pursuant to the statutory provision to which I have referred. The instant appeal is by the legal aid committee against the dismissal by the judge of their claim against the solicitor.

I should add that, after he had heard the submissions on costs at the end of the original hearing in June 1982, the judge ordered that a transcript of the proceedings and his judgment should be sent to the Law Society and, in so far as counsel was concerned, that *d* the matter should be referred to the Senate of the Inns of Court and the Bar. During the hearing of this appeal we were told that the disciplinary sub-committee of the latter had considered counsel's position and, having heard his explanation and version of events, decided that the matter should be dealt with informally and took no other action. An abortive attempt was made to add him to the legal aid committee's summons under Ord 62, r 8, but it was soon realised that such an application could not succeed on the wording *e* of the rules and it was not further proceeded with.

Order 62, r 8(1) is in these terms:

> 'Subject to the following provisions of this rule, where in any proceedings costs are incurred improperly or without reasonable cause or are wasted by undue delay or by any other misconduct or default, the Court may make against any solicitor *f* whom it considers to be responsible (whether personally or through a servant or agent) an order—(*a*) disallowing the costs as between the solicitor and his client; and (*b*) directing the solicitor to repay to his client costs which the client has been ordered to pay to other parties to the proceedings; or (*c*) directing the solicitor personally to indemnify such other parties against costs payable by them.'

The rule itself is intended to cover and provide for the inherent jurisdiction of the court *g* over solicitors, particularly in respect of costs, in circumstances in which the court thinks it right to exercise that jurisdiction. The relief which was sought against the solicitor pursuant to the terms of that rule in these proceedings was as follows: (*a*) that he should personally pay or cause to be paid the costs of the parties to the proceedings, and of the application, to the extent that the court might deem just and equitable; (*b*) that he should *h* be disallowed his own costs as between solicitor and client in respect of work done on or after 25 February 1982 under the relevant legal aid certificate; and (*c*) that he should indemnify the Law Society in respect of all sums payable out of the legal aid fund by way of fees payable to counsel again in respect of work done under the legal aid certificate.

The leading case on the nature and extent of this inherent jurisdiction of the court is *Myers v Elman* [1939] 4 All ER 484, [1940] AC 282. It is, I think, unnecessary to detail *j* the facts of that case and I turn immediately to the speech of Viscount Maugham. In discussing the nature of the court's jurisdiction Viscount Maugham distinguished between the court's jurisdiction to strike solicitors off the rolls on the grounds of professional misconduct on the one hand and the jurisdiction to make special orders as to costs on the other. He said ([1939] 4 All ER 484 at 488, [1940] AC 282 at 289):

a
'In my opinion, the jurisdiction as to costs is quite different. Misconduct or default or negligence in the course of the proceedings is in some cases sufficient to justify an order. The primary object of the court is, not to punish the solicitor, but to protect the client who has suffered and to indemnify the party who has been injured. R.S.C., Ord. 65, r. 11, provides the necessary machinery where the person injured is the client of the solicitor. It is a rule supplementary to the summary jurisdiction of the court. It is not limited to misconduct or default, but expressly

b
extends to costs incurred improperly or without reasonable cause, or costs which have proved fruitless by reason of undue delay in proceeding under a judgment or order. The jurisdiction to order the solicitor to pay costs to the opposite party is exercised on similar grounds.'

c
Lord Atkin said that the duty on a solicitor was a 'duty owed to the court to conduct litigation before it with due propriety . . .' (see [1939] 4 All ER 484 at 497, [1940] AC 282 at 302). Lord Russell dissented on the facts of that particular case. Lord Wright again contrasted the two concurrent jurisdictions and put the matter in this way ([1939] 4 All ER 484 at 508–509, [1940] AC 282 at 319):

d
'The underlying principle is that the court has a right and a duty to supervise the conduct of its solicitors, and visit with penalties any conduct of a solicitor which is of such a nature as to tend to defeat justice in the very cause in which he is engaged professionally, as was said by LORD ABINGER, C.B., in *Stephens* v. *Hill* ((1842) 10 M & W 28, 152 ER 368). The matter complained of need not be criminal. It need not involve peculation or dishonesty. A mere mistake or error of judgment is not generally sufficient, but a gross neglect or inaccuracy in a matter which it is a solicitor's duty to ascertain with accuracy may suffice. Thus, a solicitor may be held

e
bound in certain events to satisfy himself that he has a retainer to act, or as to the accuracy of an affidavit which his client swears. It is impossible to enumerate the various contingencies which may call into operation the exercise of this jurisdiction. It need not involve personal obliquity. The term "professional misconduct" has often been used to describe the gound on which the court acts. It would perhaps be more accurate to describe it as conduct which involves a failure on the part of a

f
solicitor to fulfil his duty to the court and to realise his duty to aid in promoting, in his own spehere, the cause of justice. This summary procedure may often be invoked to save the expense of an action. Thus, it may, in proper cases, take the place of an action for negligence, or an action for breach of warranty of authority brought by the person named as defendant in the writ. The jurisdiction is not merely punitive, but compensatory. The order is for payment of costs thrown away

g
or lost because of the conduct complained of. It is frequently, as in this case, exercised in order to compensate the opposite party in the action.'

Lord Porter agreed that there were the two concurrent jurisdictions over solicitors to which the other Law Lords had referred.

In *Edwards* v *Edwards* [1958] 2 All ER 179, [1958] P 235 Sachs J had to consider whether an order should be made against solicitors acting for a wife in matrimonial

h
proceedings to pay the husband's costs under the inherent jurisdiction of the court in a legal aid case where once there had been discovery it should have been obvious that the wife would be unable to establish her case of wilful neglect. The judge referred to the speeches in *Myers* v *Elman*, expressed the view that the jurisdiction is exercised not to punish the solicitor but to protect and compensate the opposite party, commented that the mere fact that an error is of an order which constitutes or is equivalent to negligence

j
is not of itself reason for invoking the jurisdiction, and then continued ([1958] 2 All ER 179 at 186, [1958] P 235 at 248):

'No definition or list of the classes of improper acts which attract the jurisdiction can, of course, be made, but they certainly include anything which can be termed an abuse of the process of the court and oppressive conduct generally. It is from the authorities clear, and no submission to the contrary has been here made, that unreasonably to initiate or continue an action when it has no or substantially no *a* chance of success may constitute conduct attracting an exercise of the above jurisdiction.'

The judge then considered whether the fact that the solicitor in that case was acting under a legal aid certificate affected the position. He held that it did not and drew attention to the possibility, of which in general the courts are now well aware, that unless *b* care is exercised oppressive advantage can be taken in litigation by a party who is legally aided against one who is not. This is particularly so in matrimonial causes.

In *Mauroux v Pereira Sociedade Comercial Abel da Fonseca SARL* [1972] 2 All ER 1085, [1972] 1 WLR 963 a similar application under the principles set out in *Myers v Elman* and Ord 62, r 8 was made to Megarry J. In his judgment he pointed out that the speeches in *Myers v Elman* were not altogether consistent and the thought that the relevant *c* jurisdiction was compensatory, at least primarily. He referred to a passage from Lord Wright's speech and then went on to express his view that, with perhaps an exception for exceptional cases, it was plain that to invoke the jurisdiction it was not enough to establish negligence.

I myself had to consider the nature and extent of this particular jurisdiction in *Currie & Co v Law Society* [1976] 3 All ER 832, [1977] 1 QB 990. I sought to reconcile the *d* speeches in *Myers v Elman* and Lord Wright's dictum which I have already quoted, 'The jurisdiction is not merely punitive but compensatory', in this way ([1976] 3 All ER 832 at 839, [1977] 1 QB 990 at 997):

> '. . . I do not think that the issue is fundamentally one of the extent to which the solicitor in question has been negligent, although the existence or absence of negligence may be relevant. The jurisdiction of the court over solicitors in this *e* respect is, in the words of Lord Wright in his speech in *Myers v Elman* [1939] 4 All ER 484 at 509, [1940] AC 282 at 319, "not merely punitive, but compensatory". The jurisdiction is in my opinion both punitive and compensatory in this sense: where the costs of litigation are unnecessarily increased by the substantial failure on the part of a solicitor to fulfil his duty to the court to promote in his particular sphere the cause and proper administration of justice, then the court will require *f* him to compensate those who have incurred costs which they would not otherwise have incurred but for such failure by that solicitor, or whose costs have been similarly increased thereby; and as those costs have to be paid by the solicitor personally, and not by the party to the litigation who would otherwise have to pay them, the order is in that sense and to that extent punitive.'

g

On the hearing of this appeal counsel for both the legal aid committee and the solicitor were content that we should deal with the case on the basis of this passage from my judgment in *Currie's* case, although counsel for the solicitor stressed the references in the speeches in *Myers v Elman* to the necessity for there to have been serious or gross misconduct or negligence before the court was entitled to exercise this inherent jurisdiction under Ord 62, r 8. *h*

Our attention was also drawn to the decision in *R & T Thew Ltd v Reeves (No 2)* [1982] 3 All ER 1086, [1982] QB 1283. In that case another division of this court had before it a similar application against a firm of solicitors that they should be ordered personally to pay certain costs in certain litigation pursuant to the court's inherent jurisdiction. *Currie's* case does not appear to have been cited to the court in *Thew's* case and it is clear that the court in that case did not make the same reconciliation of the references to the concurrent *j* punitive and compensatory natures of the inherent jurisdiction over costs as I respectfully had in the earlier decision. For present purposes this matters not. The issue in *Thew's* case was whether the conduct of an articled clerk had been sufficiently serious to warrant the exercise of the inherent jurisdiction. The court held that it had not and quoted Viscount Maugham's reference to 'a serious dereliction of duty', Lord Atkin's mention of 'gross negligence' and the passage from Lord Wright's speech in *Myers v Elman* to which I have

a already referred. In his judgment in *Thew's* case Lord Denning MR said that the inherent jurisdiction to order solicitors to pay costs personally 'is only available where the conduct of the solicitor is inexcusable and such as to merit reproof' (see [1982] 3 All ER 1086 at 1089, [1982] QB 1283 at 1286). O'Connor LJ, with whom Dunn LJ agreed, put it in this way ([1982] 3 All ER 1086 at 1090, [1982] QB 1283 at 1288):

b 'The cases show that such an order ought not to be made unless it is shown that the Thews have suffered loss as a result of serious misconduct by the solicitors in the case.'

In my opinion we should approach the facts of the present case and the question of the exercise of the inherent jurisdiction in the same way.

c The contention advanced on behalf of the Law Society as appellant in this court and, in their capacity as the body responsible for the legal aid fund, before the judge below was that, in light of the principles laid down in *Myers v Elman* as subsequently explained and applied as I have mentioned, there was an obligation on solicitors acting for legally-aided clients to inform the Law Society of material and serious changes in the situation of the relevant litigation. In particular in the present case, when it became apparent that counsel was or might be proposing to present the husband's claim in a manner which he

d had advised in his opinion of 2 March 1982 could not succeed, the solicitor should have advised the Law Society of this. Had this been done, the argument proceeded, the husband's legal aid certificate would have been discharged or possibly revoked, the litigation would not have continued and the substantial costs of both husband and wife not incurred.

On the hearing of this appeal we had the benefit of submissions by counsel as amicus

e curiae, instructed on behalf of the contentious business committee of the Law Society, on the overall effect of the Legal Aid Act 1974 and regulations made thereunder. Counsel contended, and I respectfully agree, that subject to any express provisions of the Act or regulations to the contrary, the interrelationship of lay client, solicitor and counsel and the incidents of that interrelationship, for instance relating to privilege, are no different when the client is legally aided from cases when he is not: this is apparent from ss 2(5)

f and 7(6) of the 1974 Act. Just as in a case where the client will be paying for any litigation himself, solicitor or counsel instructed on behalf of a client seeking legal aid should only advise litigation where there is a reasonable chance of success. They have to balance on the one side the extent of the chance of success and the amount that will be recovered if the litigation in fact succeeds, against the extent of the chances of failure on the other side and what the client would have to pay by way of costs, of both parties, if the

g litigation should so fail. Counsel's submission then continued that where such balance changes, where the scales tip in the opposite direction, there was an obligation to advise the lay client not to proceed and, in a legal aid case, if that advice were rejected, then reg 68(1) of the Legal Aid (General) Regulations 1980, SI 1980/1894, require both solicitor and counsel to report the matter to the Law Society. Regulation 68(2) gives a discretion to the legal advisers in doubtful cases. Regulation 71 is in these terms:

h '71. An assisted person's solicitor and his counsel (if any) shall give the general committee such information regarding the progress and disposal of the proceedings to which the certificate relates as the committee may from time to time require for the purpose of performing its functions under the scheme . . .'

and, it was contended, it imposes no duty to communicate with the Law Society unless

j asked. Regulation 74 enables both solicitor and counsel to comply with these obligations without committing any breach of any privilege owed to the client.

In these circumstances it was contended that there was no duty to report to the Law Society in legal aid matters except where specifically required to by the regulations, even if a failure to report could nevertheless bring the solicitor within the principles of *Myers'* case. Further, although the duty to report under reg 68(1) is placed on each of solicitor and counsel, there is nothing in that or the other regulations to suggest that the ordinary rule should not apply, namely that save in exceptional circumstances a solicitor cannot *a* be criticised where he acts on the advice of properly instructed counsel. Nevertheless, counsel acting as amicus accepted that if a time came when a solicitor thought that he should report to the Law Society under reg 68(1) but counsel did not, and the solicitor, notwithstanding counsel's views, remained himself of the opinion that the circumstances contemplated by reg 68(1) did obtain, then, notwithstanding counsel's advice, it remained his duty to report. In reply to these submissions, counsel for the appellant, that is to say *b* the legal aid committee, referred us to regs 78 and 79 which empower a general committee to discharge or revoke a certificate in specified circumstances arising 'as a result of information which has come to its knowledge'. Counsel submitted that these regulations would in truth be empty of substantial meaning if there were no duty on solicitors to report matters to the Law Society in the legal aid litigation apart from the provisions of reg 68.   *c*

For my part I agree, as also I do especially with the view of Sachs J in *Edwards v Edwards* [1958] 2 All ER 179, [1958] P 235, that solicitors are subject to the inherent jurisdiction of the court and also the provisions of Ord 62, r 8 in legal aid cases to precisely the same extent as where a client is paying for himself. Without prejudice to that view, I think that the obligation to report under reg 68(1) is personal to both the solicitor and counsel. I also agree that a solicitor is in general entitled to rely on the advice of counsel *d* properly instructed. However, this does not operate so as to give a solicitor an immunity in every such case. A solicitor is highly trained and rightly expected to be experienced in his particular legal fields. He is under a duty at all times to exercise that degree of care, to both client and the court, that can be expected of a reasonably prudent solicitor. He is not entitled to rely blindly and with no mind of his own on counsel's views. Thus if, despite counsel's advice that the circumstances postulated by reg 68(1) do not obtain, he *e* (the solicitor) remains of the view that they do, then he continues under a duty to report that view. The committee would no doubt in those circumstances then seek the opinion of counsel himself and decide thereafter whether to continue to support the litigant. It should not be thought that a solicitor is under any obligation to keep the legal aid committee informed of the ordinary progress of litigation or of day-to-day fluctuations in estimates of the prospects of success unless it appears to him or should appear to a *f* reasonable solicitor that the legally assisted client, for one reason or another, no longer has any substantial chance of success in litigation in respect of which he is in receipt of legal aid (see per Buckley LJ in *Shaw v Vauxhall Motors Ltd* [1974] 2 All ER 1185 at 1189, [1974] 1 WLR 1035 at 1040).

On the substantive application and appeal, counsel for the legal aid committee submitted that this solicitor clearly was or ought to have been aware of the general *g* principles of bankruptcy law and the probability that if any order for payment of a lump sum in favour of the husband were made this would be immediately appropriated by the husband's trustee in bankruptcy. He no doubt wished to have this view confirmed by counsel and that was why he raised this point in the first question for the latter in his attendance note of 26 February 1982. Further, that this was his view was confirmed by the evidence which he gave before Latey J on the hearing of the application against him *h* under Ord 62, r 8. This solicitor was or ought to have been aware that no court would make an order on the husband's application for financial relief which required a payment of a lump sum to him. To put it another way, he was or ought to have been aware that any application for such an order would be bound to fail. As I have indicated, the evidence of what advice counsel did give in the conference of 26 February 1982 was somewhat confused. I think it probable that counsel advised on the lines I have just *j* mentioned. If he did not, I would have expected the solicitor to be somewhat surprised and to have raised the matter further with him. In any event counsel did make the matter quite clear in his written opinion of 2 March 1982. It was on that opinion that the Law Society removed the original condition that there had been on the husband's legal aid certificate. Thus it was suggested that it should have been clear to the solicitor

from the indication given by counsel making the procedural application on 17 March
and a fortiori from the advice given by the original counsel in the conference of 19 April,
that the proposal had then become one to make an application in a form which counsel
had previously advised could not succeed. It was argued that at least by the 19 April
conference the solicitor should have told the Law Society of the proposed change of
approach, or at the least have raised the question with counsel. In fact the solicitor did
nothing. Let me then leave aside the contents of the brief delivered on 9 June and move
on to the opening of the husband's application before the judge by counsel on 15 June.
When counsel expressly abandoned all but the approach which he had theretofor advised
was bound to fail, it was submitted to the judge below and to us that no reasonable
solicitor could have failed to take the matter up with counsel and indeed report the
situation to the Law Society. If this had not been his duty at any earlier stage, the
solicitor's failure to act at that stage was clearly a breach of his duty to the legal aid fund
and the court of such seriousness that not only did it entitle the court to exercise its
inherent jurisdiction as asked under Ord 62, r 8, but that in all the circumstances the
court should do so.

The legal aid committee's argument continued that the position was a fortiori on the
second day of the trial when the judge granted the short adjournment and invited the
husband's advisers to reconsider the position. The husband realised at that stage that his
application was going to fail. The solicitor must also have so realised. Yet the legal aid
committee were not informed. Once again, even if there had been no earlier sufficiently
clear and serious breach by the solicitor of his obligation, nevertheless the court should
act under Ord 62, r 8, at least in respect of the costs incurred from that short adjournment
onwards. It was submitted that the fact that the application continued on the advice of
counsel afforded this solicitor no defence in the particular circumstances of this case.

Both before the judge and this court, counsel for the respondent solicitor submitted,
first, that his client's conduct was not of such seriousness as to come within the principles
adumbrated in *Myers v Elman* [1939] 4 All ER 484, [1940] AC 282 and the subsequent
cases, and, second, that even if the solicitor's failure to inform the Law Society, or indeed
do anything at all, might otherwise have been so serious as to have come within those
principles, it should not be so held in the circumstances of this case because the solicitor
throughout acted on the advice of counsel.

The judge accepted in particular this last submission. In his judgment he said:

'... it will be unreal to ignore the evidence of the forcefulness of counsel's
personality and the strength and conviction with which he expressed his views.
Counsel for the solicitor in my judgment is right in saying that it must be a
particularly blatant and extraordinary case where, in the absence of advice from
counsel, the solicitor takes it on himself to refer back to the legal aid committee ...
But ... where it is a matter of evaluation and assessment of prospects, of anticipating
the reaction of a court, in a word, of judgment, as in this case, it would, in my view,
be quite wrong to say that the solicitor has erred in accepting the advice of
experienced counsel, properly instructed.'

With all respect, I cannot agree with the judge's conclusion. In my opinion it ought to
have been patent to any reasonable solicitor, and was in fact fully understood by this
solicitor at or shortly after the conference of 19 April 1982, that the form of relief for
which alone counsel was proposing to ask fell foul of the fundamental requirement that
because of the husband's bankruptcy any capital sum would not go direct to him and was
indeed the one form of relief which counsel had in the clearest terms rejected in his
written opinion of 2 March 1982. I do not forget the evidence of the forcefulness of
counsel's personality, nor his experience, which the judge accepted. But making all
allowances for that, I cannot avoid the conclusion, differing respectfully from the judge,
that this solicitor did abdicate responsibility for his proper part and role in the relevant
litigation. I think that he relied blindly and with no mind of his own on counsel's views
on which, it must or ought to have been apparent to him, some question should have

been raised. In my judgment this failure by the solicitor to question counsel's advice, let alone to report the situation on his own to the legal aid committee, as in any event I *a* think that he should have done, was a substantial failure on his part to fulfil his duty to the court to promote in his particular sphere the cause of and proper administration of justice. In the circumstances I think that the court should exercise its inherent jurisdiction over him in respect of all the costs of the litigation after 19 April 1982.

I would therefore allow this appeal and grant the legal aid committee's application in the form sought, subject to the substitution of 19 April 1982 for 25 February 1982 in the *b* relevant part of the originating application.

I feel it right to add one further comment to this judgment. I have mentioned the fact that counsel's part in this matter has been considered by the Senate and I have stated the course taken by that body after hearing counsel's explanation. This explanation we have not heard ourselves and I am very mindful of the care that we should exercise in commenting on the way in which counsel handled the husband's application through to *c* its ultimate dismissal by Latey J on 18 June 1982. In fairness to the solicitor, however, against whom, as I have said, I think that an order under Ord 68, r 2 should be made, I feel that I should say that in my opinion counsel's decision to continue even after the judge had granted the adjournment for him and the solicitor to take stock, and when it was clear that the application as he was then presenting it was bound to fail, is most surprising, to say the least. *d*

Be that as it may, for the reasons I have given I would allow this appeal to the extent indicated.

DILLON LJ. Although the argument in this appeal has ranged fairly widely over matters of principle, the only real issue is whether in the circumstances of this case the solicitor is entitled to be exonerated from liability because he acted throughout under *e* the advice, and indeed under the domination, of experienced counsel properly instructed.

Pace certain of the submissions which counsel as amicus put before us on behalf of the Law Society in its capacity of protector of the interests of practising solicitors engaged in contentious business, certain points are in my judgment clear beyond possibility of serious argument, viz: (i) the court has a jurisdiction, the basis of which was very helpfully examined by May J in his judgment in *Currie & Co v Law Society* [1976] 3 All *f* ER 832, [1977] QB 990, to order the solicitor for a party to litigation to bear personally the costs of his own client or of another party to the litigation; (ii) the circumstances in which that jurisdiction will be exercised have been expressed in slightly different language by different judges in the reported cases such as *Myers v Elman* [1939] 4 All ER 484, [1940] AC 282 and *R & T Thew Ltd v Reeves (No 2)* [1982] 3 All ER 1086, [1982] QB 1283 (which I do not for my part regard as vitiating the analysis of May J in *Currie & Co* *g* *v Law Society*). Broadly, however, what has to be shown is that the solicitor has been guilty of 'a serious dereliction of duty' or 'serious misconduct'; (iii) unreasonably to initiate or continue an action when it has no or substantially no chance of success may constitute conduct attracting an exercise of the above jurisdiction; (iv) in general there is no reason in principle why the fact that a solicitor is acting under a legal aid certificate should preclude the exercise of this jurisdiction; (v) in his judgment in the present case *h* on the husband's application for financial provision against the wife, Latey J found, and was amply justified in finding, that the application was without any merit and should not have been made and most certainly should not have been pursued to its end; and (vi) a solicitor nominated to act for a litigant in receipt of legal aid owes a duty to inform the legal aid committee of any change in circumstances as a result of which it appears to the solicitor, or would appear to a reasonable solicitor, that the assisted person who is his *j* client no longer has any, or any substantial, chance of success in continuing to prosecute or defend the litigation in question: see per Buckley LJ in *Shaw v Vauxhall Motors Ltd* [1974] 2 All ER 1185 at 1189, [1974] 1 WLR 1035 at 1040.

All this is trite law, and I do not need to elaborate it.

Undoubtedly, however, and rightly, the solicitor is in very many circumstances protected from personal liability if he has acted on the advice of experienced counsel properly instructed. This is inherent in the division of the profession into two branches, a division which in my experience is normally highly beneficial to the litigant and to the community at large. But the protection to the solicitor is not automatically total. The solicitor is highly trained and expected to be experienced in his particular fields of law and he does not abdicate all responsibility whatever by instructing counsel.

In the present case, the fact that he was acting on counsel's advice must absolve the solicitor from liability in respect of the grant in March 1982 of legal aid for the prosecution of the husband's claim for financial provision against the wife. I have for my part considerable difficulty in seeing how on the facts of this case anyone could have seriously thought that this husband had after a very short marriage any financial claim against this wife, but on that the solicitor was entitled to rely on the opinion of counsel. Moreover, even if counsel did at the conference, apparently for instructional purposes, on 26 February 1982 express views which were inconsistent with those which he expressed in his written opinion of 2 March 1982, the solicitor was entitled to regard the written opinion as representing counsel's considered view, and to forward that opinion to the legal aid committee without qualification. At this stage there was no dereliction of duty or misconduct on the part of the solicitor.

The matter does not, however, end there. The obvious danger, as the solicitor plainly appreciated, was that the husband was subject to a criminal bankruptcy order in a very large sum. It was therefore of fundamental importance that any capital sum should not go direct to the husband. Any reasonable solicitor would have appreciated this and this solicitor did appreciate it, as his evidence shows. No court would have ordered the payment to the husband out of the wife's resources of a capital sum which was likely to be annexed at once by the husband's trustee in bankruptcy.

When, however, counsel for the husband came to open the husband's application to Latey J in June 1982, counsel asked for payment to the husband of a not insubstantial sum, and on the husband's behalf he abandoned all other claims. The solicitor appreciated, as his evidence under cross-examination shows, that this was irreconcilable with counsel's opinion of 2 March 1982, but the change of front occasioned the solicitor no surprise because the solicitor had realised from the time of the conference which he had with counsel on 19 April 1982, or shortly thereafter, that payment of a lump sum to the husband, with which the husband could buy a house for himself, was what counsel was proposing to ask for.

The point is underlined by para 5 of the affidavit, settled by counsel, which the solicitor arranged for the husband to swear on 29 May 1982.

This solicitor was, on the judge's findings which I would not for a moment dispute, an entirely honest man and a diligent and conscientious solicitor. But he allowed his own skill and ability to be entirely subordinated to the dominant and forceful personality of counsel, counsel admittedly in whom his client had confidence and not of his own choice, and counsel of ample experience and properly instructed.

In my judgment the duty which a solicitor owes to inform the legal aid committee of any change of circumstances as mentioned above is independent of the duty which counsel owes to advise that the legal aid committee be informed. By this I mean that the solicitor's duty is not just to pass on any views expressed by counsel; he has to consider for himself the effect of the change of circumstances, to use his own common sense and to form his own opinion, though obviously in doing that he will take the view expressed by counsel into account.

Obviously also the legal aid committee is not to be bombarded with notifications of every minute fluctuation in the estimate of the percentage prospects of success. We are only concerned with a duty to notify when it appears or should appear to a reasonable solicitor that the assisted person no longer has any reasonable chance of success.

In the present case, however, it must have been glaringly apparent to any reasonable solicitor, at or shortly after the conference of 19 April 1982, and it was, I think, fully understood by this solicitor, that the form of relief for which alone counsel was going to ask fell foul of the fundamental requirement that because of the bankruptcy any capital sum would not go direct to the husband, and was indeed the one form of relief which *a* counsel had in the clearest terms rejected in his opinion of 2 March 1983.

In these circumstances the solicitor was at that stage guilty of 'a serious dereliction of duty' or 'serious misconduct' and I am unable to agree with the judge that it is sufficient to absolve the solicitor that he acted in accordance with the advice of counsel. I would accordingly hold that a case for exercising the court's jurisdiction over solicitors in respect of costs is made out at this stage.   *b*

A fortiori such a case is made out at the later stage when on the second day of the trial and while the husband was giving evidence the judge adjourned for a short time in order that counsel, the solicitor and the husband could take stock of the position. It was then plain to the husband that the application was going to fail. It must have been equally plain to the solicitor. The husband was willing to abandon the application. Yet it was unreasonably continued for a further two days' contested hearing, and the legal aid *c* committee was never informed of what was happening. The continuation was at the insistence of counsel, but since, on the evidence before us, counsel offered no rational explanation of how he was going to get over the difficulty to which the judge had drawn attention, that a capital sum paid to the husband, which was all that was being asked for, would be seized by the trustee in bankruptcy, I cannot see that it can in the circumstances exonerate the solicitor that he acted on the advice of counsel.   *d*

I would allow this appeal to the extent and with the consequences indicated by May LJ.

I should add that counsel is not a party to these proceedings and therefore this court has not heard any explanation from him of his conduct. For that reason I have not named him in this judgment. But the court cannot be prevented, by the fact that there is no explanation from counsel available to the court, from dealing with the case as it appears *e* from the material which is before the court.

SIR JOHN DONALDSON MR. I have had the advantage of reading in draft the judgments of May and Dillon LJJ with which I agree. Accordingly I would allow the appeal and make the order proposed by May LJ.   *f*

Appeal allowed with costs in the Court of Appeal and below. Application for leave to appeal to the House of Lords refused.

Solicitors: *Peter E Putt* (for the legal aid committee); *Ralph Haeems & Co*, Peckham (for the solicitor); *Mark Sennett*, Secretary, Contentious Business (for the Law Society).

Frances Rustin   Barrister.

a # Trustees of the British Museum v Attorney General

CHANCERY DIVISION
SIR ROBERT MEGARRY V-C
27, 29 JULY and 24 OCTOBER 1983

b *Variation of trusts – Variation by the court – Investment clause – Extension of powers of investment – Extension of powers beyond those permitted under Trustee Investments Act 1961 – Factors to be taken into consideration – Whether changes in investment market and practice entitling court to vary investment powers by giving trustees wider powers of investment than those permitted under Trustee Investments Act 1961 – Trustee Investments Act 1961.*

c Having regard to changed conditions in the investment market and prevailing investment practice, the court should be prepared in suitable cases to extend trustees' powers of investment beyond those prescribed in the Trustee Investments Act 1961, taking into account, inter alia, the combined effect of (1) the width of the proposed investment powers, (2) the efficacy of provisions for advising and controlling the trustees in the d exercise of the extended powers, (3) the desirability, where the proposed extended powers of investment are to be very wide, of a scheme dividing the trust fund into two parts, one to be confined to safe investment and the other to be used for investments involving a greater risk, and (4) the standing of the particular trustees. Where the proposed extended powers of investment are to be less wide the only division which is desirable is between investments which the trustees can make only after they have taken advice and e those which they can make without taking advice. The size of the trust fund is also a material consideration, because a very large fund where the investments can be spread may justify wider investment powers than a smaller fund; and the object of the trust may also be material, eg the desirability of the trustees of a museum increasing the capital value of the trust fund so that articles may be purchased for the museum at a time of soaring prices may justify a greater risk being taken in the investment of the fund in f order to achieve capital appreciation (see p 342 e to p343 c, post).

Mason v Farbrother [1983] 2 All ER 1078 considered.

Re Kolb's Will Trusts, Lloyds Bank Ltd v Ullmann [1961] 3 All ER 811 and *Re Cooper's Settlement, Cooper v Cooper* [1961] 3 All ER 636 not followed.

g ## Notes

For trustees' powers to invest, see 38 Halsbury's Laws (3rd edn) 987–1001, paras 1710–1725.

For variation of trusts under the Trustee Act 1925, see ibid 1027–1029, para 1771, and for cases on the subject, see 47 Digest (Repl) 328–332, 2970–2992.

For variation under the Variation of Trusts Act 1958, see 38 Halsbury's Laws (3rd edn) h 1029–1031, paras 1772–1778, and for cases on the subject, see 47 Digest (Repl) 332–338, 2993–3018.

For the Trustee Investments Act 1961, see 38 Halsbury's Statutes (3rd edn) 228.

Cases referred to in judgment

j *Clarke's Will Trusts, Re* [1961] 3 All ER 1133, [1961] 1 WLR 1471.
Cooper's Settlement, Re, Cooper v Cooper [1961] 3 All ER 636, [1962] Ch 826, [1961] 3 WLR 1029.
Kolb's Will Trusts, Re, Lloyds Bank Ltd v Ullmann [1961] 3 All ER 811, [1962] Ch 531, [1961] 3 WLR 1034; on appeal (1962) 106 SJ 669, CA.
Mason v Farbrother [1983] 2 All ER 1078.

Porritt's Will Trusts, Re (1961) 105 SJ 931.
University of London Charitable Trusts, Re [1963] 3 All ER 859, [1964] Ch 282, [1963] 3 *a*
WLR 1081.

Originating summons

By a summons dated 5 June 1983 the trustees of the British Museum (the trustees), the
plaintiffs, sought an order that a scheme for the future management and regulation of
the charitable funds mentioned in the schedule to the summons and held by the trustees
be approved and established in the terms of a draft scheme exhibited to an affidavit to be *b*
sworn on behalf of the trustees, or in such other terms as the court thought fit. The
defendant to the summons was the Attorney General. The summons was heard in
chambers but at the request of counsel for both parties judgment was given by Sir Robert
Megarry V-C in open court. The facts are set out in the judgment.

c

Timothy Lloyd for the trustees.
Christopher McCall for the Attorney General.

Cur adv vult

d

24 October. The following judgment was delivered.

SIR ROBERT MEGARRY V-C. In this case the trustees of the British Museum have
issued an originating summons relating to charitable funds held by them. The defendant
to the summons is the Attorney General. The trustees are an incorporated body; for
convenience I shall call them 'the trustees'. The object of the summons is to obtain the *e*
approval of the court to a scheme that will give the trustees wider powers of investment
than those that they have at present under a scheme approved by Pennycuick J on 18 July
1960. I heard the application in chambers, but at the request of counsel who appeared
for the trustees and the Attorney General respectively, I am delivering judgment in open
court. There are, I was told, a number of other cases which are likely to be affected by the
decision, and it is thought that the Charity Commissioners may be assisted by it in *f*
applications to them to approve schemes for other charities. The main point of
importance is whether the court should continue to apply the principle that was laid
down in cases such as *Re Kolb's Will Trusts* [1961] 3 All ER 811, [1962] Ch 531 (a case in
which an appeal was compromised: see (1962) 106 SJ 669), *Re Cooper's Settlement* [1961]
3 All ER 636, [1962] Ch 826, and *Re Porritt's Will Trusts* (1961) 105 SJ 931, and was
recognised in *Re Clarke's Will Trusts* [1961] 3 All ER 1133, [1961] 1 WLR 1471, and *Re* *g*
University of London Charitable Trusts [1963] 3 All ER 859, [1964] Ch 282.

As is well known, the instrument establishing a trust may prescribe powers of
investment which are either narrower or wider than those laid down by the general law:
see the Trustee Act 1925, s 69(2); Trustee Investments Act 1961, s 1(3). Subject to any
such provision in the instrument, statute has prescribed the range of authorised
investments for trustees. Under Pt I of the Trustee Act 1925, and in particular s 1, the *h*
range of authorised investments was in the main confined to what are generally called
gilt-edged securities, and other securities which carried interest at fixed rates. It did not
extend to industrial equities, no matter how large and prosperous the concerns. However
suitable this was before the 1939–45 war, with a stable pound, it had ceased to be
satisfactory when the post-war inflation began to emerge; and in establishing new trusts
it became increasingly common to insert investment clauses that were markedly wider *j*
than the statutory provisions. That, however, did not help pre-existing trusts, and in
these cases a number of successful applications to the courts to widen the investment
powers were made under the Trustee Act 1925, s 57, under the Variation of Trusts Act
1958, and, in the case of charities, under the Charitable Trusts Acts 1853 to 1925, as was
done in respect of the 1960 scheme in the present case.

In the end, the Trustee Investments Act 1961 was enacted. By this time, the purchasing
a power of the pound was about half what it had been in 1939. The Act laid down an
elaborate code. Under this, a much wider range of investments was authorised if the
trustees first divided the trust fund into two equal parts. One part was confined to
'narrower-range' investments, which very roughly corresponded to the investments
which were authorised under the Trustee Act 1925. The other part extended to 'wider-
range' investments. The most important constituents of these (and I put it very shortly)
b were fully paid-up securities in United Kingdom companies with a paid-up capital of at
least £1m which were quoted on a recognised United Kingdom stock exchange and each
year for the previous five years had paid a dividend on all shares ranking for dividend.
Equities in such companies thus became available for trustee investment; but as with all
investments authorised by the Act, save only certain narrower-range investments, the
trustees were required to obtain proper advice in accordance with the Act before making
c the investment.

The Act was passed on 3 August 1961; and in October of that year the first three cases
that I have cited, *Kolb, Cooper* and *Porritt*, all fell for decision. In each case an application
had been made, doubtless before the Act was passed, for an extension of the powers of
investment. Each case seems to have been decided without either of the others being
cited; but in each the judge (Cross, Buckley and Pennycuick JJ respectively) reached the
d same conclusion. In the words of Cross J in *Re Kolb's Will Trusts* [1961] 3 All ER 811 at
815, [1962] Ch 531 at 540:

> '... the powers given by the [1961] Act must, I think, be taken to be prima facie
> sufficient and ought only to be extended if, on the particular facts, a special case for
> extending them can be made out.'

e Buckley J said in *Re Cooper's Settlement* [1961] 3 All ER 636 at 639, [1962] Ch 826 at 830:

> '... from this time this court will have to be satisfied, whenever applicants under
> s. 1 of the Variation of Trusts Act, 1958, ask for relaxation of trustees' powers of
> investment, that there are special grounds which make it right that trustees should
> have wider powers of investment than the legislature has indicated in the Trustee
f Investments Act, 1961, as the normally appropriate powers.'

Pennycuick J said in *Re Porritt's Will Trusts* (1961) 105 SJ 931:

> 'The court should not, in the absence of special circumstances, enlarge the range
> of investments beyond that prescribed by the Trustee Investments Act, 1961.'

g That was in 1961; and no doubt for some time that doctrine remained soundly based.
However, in recent years the court, usually in chambers, has become ready to authorise
extensions of the power of investment, often by an increased willingness to accept
circumstances as being 'special'. Further, it has become increasingly common for
draftsmen of wills and settlements to insert special investment powers which are far
wider than those conferred by the 1961 Act. Then in October 1982 the Law Reform
h Committee made its 23rd report *The Powers and Duties of Trustees* (Cmnd 8733), this time
on the subject of the powers and duties of trustees; and in this the committee reached
the conclusion that the 1961 Act has proved to be 'tiresome, cumbrous and expensive in
operation', and that 'the present statutory powers are out of date and ought to be revised':
see para 3.17. The committee's proposals for reform rejected any scheme for fixed
proportions of the trust fund which could be invested in one type of investment or
i another, and instead proposed that investments should be divided into those which could
be made without taking advice and those which could be made only on taking advice.
The former category would include all the narrower-range securities, with certain
additions, and the latter would include all other investments quoted on the English Stock
Exchange. Subject to taking advice when necessary, trustees should be free to invest in
such proportions as they choose: see para 3.21, 22. That was the recommendation.

I cite the report not as authority but as showing what the distinguished members of the committee recognised to be the position some 20 years after the 1961 Act was passed. *a* In addition to that, I have before me detailed evidence of changes in the investment market that have occurred since the 1960 scheme was approved. Before I consider that evidence, I must say something about that scheme.

By the scheme, a number of separate funds were consolidated into three pools, pool A, pool B and pool C. Pool A comprised those funds which allowed only the income to be used for general or special purposes connected with the museum. For pool B, the capital *b* and income could both be used, but only for special purposes connected with the museum, while for pool C the capital and income could be used for general purposes connected with the museum. Each pool was to be divided into two parts. One, the 'free part', was, at the date of division, to have twice the value of the other part, the 'restricted part'. The restricted part was confined to investments authorised by s 1 of the Trustee Act 1925, whereas the free part could be invested in a much wider range of investments *c* set out in the scheme. I summarise the categories. First, there was the purchase of land in the United Kingdom if it was freehold or leasehold with at least 200 years to run; but not more than £20,000 could be invested thus. Second, there were investments in securities of (or guaranteed by) the government of the United States of America or any state thereof. Third, there were the securities of local authorities, public utility companies or railways in the United Kingdom, Canada, Australia or New Zealand. Fourth, there *d* were securities of any company incorporated in the United Kingdom, or under the laws of Australia, New Zealand or the United States of America or any state thereof.

These provisions were subject to certain restrictions. No investment under the third or fourth head could be made in any security not dealt in or officially quoted in a recognised stock exchange in London, New York, Toronto, Montreal, Melbourne, Wellington, Zurich or Amsterdam. Further, any investment in a company (except *e* United Kingdom banks or insurance companies) was excluded if the security was liable to calls, with a saving for new issues; and investment in the ordinary or deferred stock or shares of a company was excluded unless the company had a paid-up capital of at least £750,000. Finally, there was an obligation for the trustees to employ a professional adviser of not less than 15 years' standing as a stockbroker, merchant banker or member of a finance house, to keep the trust investments under review and recommend any *f* changes that he considered advisable. Plainly this is a most important obligation.

The trustees are a body of great distinction. There are some two dozen of them. Their powers of investment are exercised by a finance committee and an investment sub-committee, each consisting of the same six trustees. From the positions that they hold and have held it is plain that between them they have a wealth of experience in practical affairs. The professional investments adviser consists of Lazard Securities Ltd; and, in *g* addition, for the last 10 or 12 years the trustees have had the assistance of two unpaid independent advisers of distinction. The investment sub-committee meets quarterly, and more frequently when necessary, and there is a system for consultation between meetings whenever this is necessary. The trust funds have a value of between £5m and £6m. The result of these arrangements has been that until recently it has been possible for the value of the trust funds to keep pace with what is generally (if inaccurately) *h* described as inflation; but it is becoming increasingly difficult to do this within the terms of the 1960 scheme, and in any case the combined effect of reductions in grants from public funds and 'the startling escalation in the price of museum objects' has intensified the need to keep pace with inflation and, if possible, outstrip it.

The evidence before me establishes that over the last 20 years significant changes in investment practice have occurred, especially in the case of large trust funds. The main *j* factors producing these changes may be summarised as follows. First, increased rates of inflation have encouraged a movement from fixed interest investments to equities and property. As I have mentioned, by 1960 the purchasing power of the pound had fallen to about half of what it had been in 1939; and in the next 20 years it lost some five-sixths of that reduced value. Second, differences in rates of inflation between one country and another have from time to time made it wise to replace investments in one country by those in another. Third, the exploitation of oil and other natural resources in certain countries has markedly affected the value of particular currencies. Fourth, in recent years the rate of economic growth has been greater in some countries (not least in Japan) than in the United Kingdom. Fifth, leading companies in the United Kingdom have found it difficult to grow faster than the economy as a whole, whereas some smaller companies with specialist markets have been able to grow faster. There have also been trends away from the manufacture of capital goods towards the service and energy industries, and away from manufacturing 'high volume' goods towards manufacturing which adds a high value to the goods. Sixth, the abolition of exchange controls in October 1979 has greatly facilitated overseas investment. Coupled with these factors has been an increased volatility in prices, with sharp changes taking place within three or four days, and sometimes a day. Seventh, unit trusts and certain forms of unsecured loans such as Eurobonds now offer valuable investment opportunities.

I feel no doubt that it is in the best interests of the trustees and the trusts that there should be relaxation of the terms of the 1960 scheme which will take account of these changes. At the same time, any scheme must have appropriate safeguards. The main features of the scheme put forward in this case, as it stands revised after discussion, may be stated as follows.

1. The proposals continue to preserve the existing arrangements of pools A, B and C, and the division of funds in the pools into one-third for the restricted part and two-thirds for the free part. The proposed scheme thus builds on the foundations of the 1960 scheme.

2. The restricted part may be invested in the narrower-range investments under the 1961 Act, or in such other investments as are authorised trustee investments, without any requirement for the trustees to obtain advice.

3. The free part may be invested in a much wider range of investments than formerly. The categories may be summarised as follows. (a) First, there is the purchase of land in the United Kingdom if it is freehold or leasehold with at least 75 years to run; but not more than 20% of the free part may be thus invested. The 200 years has thus become 75, and the £20,000 is now 20%. (b) Second, there are wider-range investments within the 1961 Act, or any other trustee investments. (c) Third, there are any other investments or property of any nature, wherever situate, including the making or purchase of loans with or without security, as the trustees in their absolute discretion think fit. The great width of this provision is, however, substantially curtailed in a number of respects. (i) It does not include land, nor chattels such as bullion, commodities or works of art. (ii) It is limited to securities listed or regularly dealt in on the Stock Exchange or on any other stock exchange outside the United Kingdom which is a member of the International Federation of Stock Exchanges if the amount to be invested, when added to any loans and any other investments (except land) not so listed or dealt in, would exceed 30% of the value of the free part. (iii) No investment in ordinary or deferred stock or shares may be made unless the company has a paid-up capital of at least £750,000. (iv) No option may be bought if the cost, when added to the cost of all other options held by the trustees, would exceed 5% of the value of the free part. (v) Any investment in a company (except United Kingdom banks or insurance companies) is excluded if the security is liable to calls, with a saving for new issues.

That is the range of investments permitted; and machinery is provided for making the valuations needed for determining the 20%, the 30% and the 5%. The provision requiring the employment of a professional adviser is repeated, and a new power to employ professional investment managers is added. This enables the trustees to employ such managers, and from time to time to delegate to them the exercise of all or any of the trustees' powers of investment and valuation for such period (not exceeding 12 months at a time) and subject to such conditions and restrictions as the trustees think fit. The trustees may at any time alter or revoke the delegation or its terms, and the managers are bound to exercise their powers in accordance with the trustees' instructions as to

investment policy. There is provision for the managers to inform the trustees within 14
days of any exercise of these powers, and the trustees are liable for the acts or defaults of   *a*
the managers as if they were the acts or defaults of the trustees.

I am conscious that such a scheme gives extremely wide powers of investment to the
trustees. At the same time I consider that it is proper and desirable that such powers
should be given, and I have made an order accordingly. There are four factors that I
should mention in particular. First, there is the eminence and responsibility of the
trustees, the machinery for obtaining highly skilled advice, and the success that this   *b*
machinery has achieved over the past 20 years. Second, there are the changed conditions
of investment, conditions which require great liberty of choice if, on skilled advice,
advantage is to be taken of opportunities which often present themselves on short notice
and for short periods; and for this, the provision for delegation is plainly advantageous.
Third, there is obvious advantage in there being freedom to invest in any part of the
world. At the same time, there is due recognition of the prudence of maintaining a solid   *c*
core of relatively safe investments while setting free a substantial part for investments
which, though less 'safe', offer greater opportunities for a substantial enhancement of
value. Opinions may vary about the precise percentages; certainly my views have
fluctuated. However, in the end I have reached the conclusion that the percentages put
forward are reasonable. In reaching my conclusion on this and other points I have been
reassured by the fact that counsel for the Attorney General has whole-heartedly supported   *d*
the scheme after it had undergone careful examination.

Fourth, I bear in mind the large size of the trust fund. From the point of view of
powers of investment, this carries the matter out of the realm of the ordinary private
trust into the field of pension funds and large institutional investors; and for success in
this field a wide flexibility of the powers of investment is plainly desirable, if not essential.

From what I have said it will be seen that much of what I say depends to a greater or   *e*
lesser extent on the special position of the trustees and the trust funds in the case before
me. On the other hand, there is much that is of more general application, and it may be
convenient if I attempt to summarise my views.

1. In my judgment, the principle laid down in the line of cases headed by *Re Kolb's
Will Trusts* [1961] 3 All ER 811, [1962] Ch 531 is one that should no longer be followed,
since conditions have changed so greatly in the last 20 years. Though authoritative, those   *f*
cases were authorities only rebus sic stantibus; and in 1983 they bind no longer. However,
if Parliament acts on the recommendation of the Law Reform Committee and replaces
the 1961 Act with revised powers of investment, the *Kolb* principle may well become
applicable once more. Until then, the court should be ready to grant suitable applications
for the extension of trustees' powers of investment, judging each application on its
merits, and without being constrained by the provisions of the 1961 Act.   *g*

2. In determining what extended powers of investment should be conferred, there
are many matters which will have to be considered. I shall refer to five, without in any
way suggesting that this list is exhaustive, or that anything I say is intended to fetter the
discretion that the court has to exercise in each case.

(i) The court is likely to give great weight to the width and efficacy of any provisions
for advice and control. The wider the powers, the more important these provisions will   *h*
be. An existing system of proven efficacy, as here, is likely to be especially cogent.

(ii) Where the powers are of great width, as in the present case, there is much to be
said for some scheme of fractional division, confining part of the fund to relatively safe
investments, and allowing the other part to be used for investments in which the greater
risks will be offset by substantial prospects of a greater return. On the other hand, when
the powers are appreciably less wide than they are in the present case, I would in general   *j*
respectfully concur with the views expressed by the Law Reform Committee that no
division of the fund into fractions should be required, and that the only division should
be into investments which require advice and those which do not. Nevertheless, although
a division of the fund into fractions should not be essential, there may well be cases
where such a division may be of assistance in obtaining the approval of the court.

a (iii) The width of the powers in the present scheme seems to me to be at or near the extreme limit for charitable funds. Without the fractional division of the fund and the assurance of effective control and advice I very much doubt whether such a scheme could have been approved. What the court has to judge is the combined effect of width, division, advice and control, which all interact, together with the standing of the trustees.

(iv) The size of the fund in question may be very material. A fund that is very large may well justify a latitude of investment that would be denied to a more modest fund;
b for the spread of investments possible for a larger fund may justify the greater risks that wider powers will permit to be taken.

(v) The object of the trust may be very material. In the present case, the desirability of having an increase of capital value which will make possible the purchase of desirable acquisitions for the museum despite soaring prices does something to justify the greater risks whereby capital appreciation may be obtained.

c Since writing this judgment I have been referred to the very recent decision in *Mason v Farbrother* [1983] 2 All ER 1078; and counsel on both sides sent me a helpful joint note on the subject. Much of the judgment is directed to questions of jurisdiction and the details of the revised investment clause there under consideration. Of these matters I need say nothing. However, in considering whether the jurisdiction to approve the revised clause ought to be exercised, his Honour Judge Blackett-Ord, Vice-Chancellor of
d Lancaster, appears to have treated the *Kolb* line of cases as still being binding authorities, saying (as indeed is the case) that the rule was not absolute but applied in the absence of special circumstances. He then said (at 1086–1087) that 'the special circumstances in the present case are manifest: in a word, inflation since 1961'. He added that the trust in question was unusual in that it was not a private or family trust but a trust of a pension fund with perhaps something of a public element in it.

e For my part, I would hesitate to describe inflation since 1961 as amounting to 'special circumstances'; it is, unhappily, a very general circumstance. With all respect, I can see little virtue (judicial comity and humility apart) in seeking to preserve the rule and yet establishing universal special circumstances that will engulf the rule. I do not, of course, know what arguments on this point were addressed to the court, but for the reasons that I have given I would prefer to say that the rule has gone, and with it any question of what
f circumstances are special. However, the ultimate result is much the same, and although the reasoning in the two cases differs, I am happy to think that there is this support for my conclusion in the present case.

Order accordingly.

Solicitors: *Treasury Solicitor* (for both parties).

Vivian Horvath   Barrister.

R v Governor of Brixton Prison
and another, ex parte Walsh

QUEEN'S BENCH DIVISION
KERR LJ AND WEBSTER J
11, 27 OCTOBER 1983

Criminal law – Bail – Magistrates' court – Defendant in prison on remand in custody when due to appear in court to which he had been remanded on bail – Duty of prison governor to produce him to court – Whether governor in breach of duty in failing to produce prisoner to court – Whether Secretary of State under duty to produce or procure production of prisoner in court – Criminal Justice Act 1961, s 29(1) – Magistrates' Courts Act 1980, s 128(1)(b).

Habeas corpus – Writ of habeas corpus ad respondendum – Whether existence of court's power to issue writ to prison governor to bring up prisoner imposing duty on governor to bring up prisoner.

The applicant was remanded on bail by a magistrates' court, pursuant to an order made under s 128(1)(b)[a] of the Magistrates' Courts Act 1980, in connection with certain criminal charges, but before he was due to appear before the court he was remanded in custody by another magistrates' court in connection with other criminal charges. On the day on which he was due to appear before the first magistrates' court to answer to his bail the governor of the prison to which he had been remanded in custody was unable to produce him because staff shortages at the prison prevented the governor from supplying the necessary escort for the applicant. The applicant applied for judicial review of the governor's failure to produce him to the court, submitting that the governor and/or the Home Secretary were under a duty to produce him or procure his production to the court to which he had been remanded to appear on bail. The applicant also sought an order directing the governor to produce him to that court on the date on which he was required to appear and a declaration that the governor and the Home Secretary were under a duty to produce him to that court. The applicant also applied for a writ of habeas corpus ad respondendum directing the governor to bring him before yet another magistrates' court which had remanded him to appear on bail in relation to further criminal charges.

Held – The applications would be refused for the following reasons—
(1) The failure of the governor to produce the applicant to the courts to which he was remanded on bail did not amount to a breach of duty on the part of the governor or the Home Secretary, because (a) although an order made under s 128(1)(b) of the 1980 Act 'directed' the person remanded on bail to appear before the court on the date specified in the order, the order did not, by inference or implication, impose on the governor of a prison where that person was detained a duty to produce him before that court on that date, (b) the power conferred on the Home Secretary by s 29(1)[b] of the Criminal Justice Act 1961 to 'direct that person to be taken to that place' where it was desirable in the interests of justice that a person detained in prison should attend at some other place (being a power which in practice was delegated to the governor of the prison) did not impose on the Home Secretary or the governor any duty to produce that person to a magistrates' court to which he had been remanded on bail, since the power in s 29(1) was merely discretionary and the Home Secretary's only duty was to consider whether to exercise that discretion, and (c) a pre-existing duty in the governor of a prison to bring up a lawfully detained person could not be inferred from the court's discretionary power

---

a   Section 128(1), so far as material, is set out at p 348d, e, post
b   Section 29(1), so far as material, is set out at p 348 h, post

to issue a writ of habeas corpus ad respondendum directing the governor to do so (see p 348 *e* to *g*, p 349 *c f g* and p 350 *j*, post).

(2) Furthermore, in view of the circumstances regarding staff shortages at the prison, it would not be appropriate for the court to issue a writ of habeas corpus ad respondendum to the governor and therefore the court would refuse to issue such a writ (see p 350 *b* and *h j*, post).

Notes

For the production in court of a prisoner, see 37 Halsbury's Laws (4th edn) para 1180.

For the Magistrates Courts' Act 1980, s 128, see 50(2) Halsbury's Statutes (3rd edn) 1554.

For the Criminal Justice Act 1961, s 29, see 25 ibid 868.

Case referred to in judgment

Raymond v Honey [1982] 1 All ER 756, [1982] 2 WLR 465, HL.

Application for judicial review and habeas corpus

Patrick John Walsh applied, with the leave of McCullough J granted on 16 September 1983, for (1) judicial review of the failure or refusal of the Governor of Brixton Prison and/or the Secretary of State for Home Affairs to produce the applicant to the South Western, Horseferry Road and Highbury Corner Magistrates' Courts on the dates he was remanded on bail to appear at those courts, by way of (a) an order directing the governor to bring the applicant before those courts on the dates on which he had been remanded to appear at those courts and (b) a declaration that the governor and the Secretary of State were under a duty to bring the applicant before the courts before whom he had been remanded to appear on bail, and (2) a writ of habeas corpus ad respondendum directed to the Governor of Brixton Prison to bring up the applicant before the South Western Magistrates' Court for trial and examination. The facts are set out in the judgment of the court.

Ian A Macdonald for the applicant.
Simon D Brown for the prison governor and the Secretary of State.

Cur adv vult

27 October. The following judgment of the court was delivered.

WEBSTER J. This is the judgment of the court on an application for habeas corpus ad respondendum to bring up the applicant for trial at the South Western and Highbury Corner Magistrates' Courts on two dates on which he has been remanded to appear at those courts, and an application for judicial review directed to the governor of Brixton Prison and to the Secretary of State for Home Affairs in which the applicant seeks an order directing the governor to bring the applicant before those courts on those dates and a declaration that the governor is under a duty to do so.

The applications arise in the following cirumstances. Arising out of an incident on 18 June 1983 the applicant was summonsed to appear on four charges at Horseferry Road Magistrates' Court. At the first hearing of that summons he was remanded on bail to 9 August 1983. In the meantime, however, he had been summonsed to appear before the South Western Magistrates' Court on 8 August 1983 on a charge of burglary, on which date he was remanded in custody to 15 August 1983. Since that date he has been remanded in custody by that court on that charge on successive dates, the last of such remands being a remand on 19 August 1983 when he was remanded in custody to 11 October 1983 to appear at Highbury Corner Magistrates' Court, to which court the case had been transferred for committal.

When, therefore, he was due to appear at Horseferry Road Magistrates' Court on 9 August 1983 he was already in custody but he was not produced to that court. The case was therefore remanded, and his bail on the four charges on which he appeared at that court was enlarged, to 9 September 1983; but again he was not produced. On 9 September 1983 he was remanded again, and his bail was again enlarged, to 16 September 1983 and on that date, again, he was not produced. On that date the court directed that a bench warrant be issued, but that warrant cannot be executed until the applicant has been released from custody. No date can at present be contemplated, therefore, for his next appearance at Horseferry Road Magistrates' Court on those four charges.

The applicant, however, faces two other charges in addition to the charge of burglary at the South Western Magistrates' Court. The first is a charge of assault. At the first hearing of that charge he was remanded on bail until 2 September 1983 but he was not produced to the court on that date. He was, on that date, remanded on bail to 10 November 1983.

The other charge which the applicant faces at the South Western Magistrates' Court is a charge of attempted theft. On the first hearing of that charge on 30 June 1983, he was remanded in custody but on 7 July 1983 he was remanded on bail. On 21 July 1983 he was remanded to 29 September 1983; on that date, partly because of a listing error, he was not produced to the court until the afternoon with the result that his case could not be heard; and he was, therefore, remanded to 24 October. On this occasion he was remanded in custody.

Before summarising this history we should add that, on the charge of burglary before the South Western Magistrates' Court, having been remanded in custody on 22 August 1983 to 12 September 1983, he was not produced on that date.

There have, therefore, been five occasions when the applicant has not been produced to one court or the other. The first occasion was on 9 August 1983. The explanation given by the prison governor, and accepted by the applicant, for that fact is that the applicant had only been received at Brixton Prison on the day before, 8 August, and that he did not tell the reception board until the morning of 9 August that he was on bail to appear at Horseferry Road Magistrates' Court on that day. No application for his production had been made by the police and it was too late for any action to be taken by the prison; and in these circumstances the applicant makes no complaint now about the failure to produce him on that date.

The second occasion was 2 September 1983 when he was not produced to the South Western Magistrates' Court on the charge of assault. As to that occasion, the prison governor, in his affidavit, states that no application to produce him had been made to the prison although the prison had informed the court that he was in custody, and accordingly the applicant makes no complaint about that occasion.

The third occasion was on 9 September 1983 when he was not produced to the Horseferry Road Magistrates' Court. The prison governor, in his affidavit, says that the prison were unable to produce him to the court on that date because of staff shortages, in that insufficient prison officers were available to act as escorts. He says that to assign other prison officers to perform this escort duty would have resulted either in essential facilities such as workshops and the welfare and legal aid office having to be closed, restrictions having to be placed on visits, the reception of clothing, food parcels and mail, and prisoners having to be confined to their cells, or in the security of the prison being put at risk. Although the applicant accepts that this was the reason for his non-production on that date, he none the less complains that in failing to produce him on that date, the prison governor and the Secretary of State were in breach of duty.

The fourth occasion on which he was not produced to a court was on 12 September 1983 when he was not produced to the South Western Magistrates' Court on the charge of burglary. The prison governor's explanation that that failure was due to an administrative misunderstanding is accepted by the applicant, and no complaint is made about it.

The fifth and final occasion on which he was not produced was on 16 September 1983 at Horseferry Road. The prison governor says that on that occasion, also, the prison were unable to produce the applicant due to staff shortages and, as in the case of his non-production on 9 September to that court, the applicant, though accepting that explanation

as a matter of fact, submits that by failing to produce him to the court on that occasion
a the prison governor and the Secretary of State were in breach of duty.

At the hearing of the applications on 11 October, we were told that the applicant had
been produced to Highbury Corner Magistrates' Court on that day in relation to the
charge of burglary which had been transferred by the South Western Magistrates' Court
to that court. For reasons which will become apparent, the applicant does not apprehend
that he will not be produced to the South Western Magistrates' Court on 24 October,
b since he has been remanded in custody to that court on that date. He is, however,
apprehensive that he will not be produced to the South Western Magistrates' Court on
10 November, in relation to the charge of assault, because on that matter he has been
remanded on bail.

The central point which arises on these applications is whether the governor of a prison
is under a duty to produce a prisoner, remanded either on bail or in custody, to the
c magistrates' court to which he has been remanded and whether the Secretary of State is
under a duty to produce him or to procure his production.

Where a prisoner is remanded in custody counsel who has appeared for the prison
governor and the Secretary of State admits that the prison governor is under such a duty,
which arises from the provisions of s 128(1)(*a*) of the Magistrates' Courts Act 1980 which
provides:

d   '(1) Where a magistrates' court has power to remand any person, then, subject to
        section 4 of the Bail Act 1976 and to any other enactment modifying that power,
        the court may—(*a*) remand him in custody, that is to say, commit him to custody
        to be brought before the court at the end of the period of remand or at such earlier
        time as the court may require . . .'

e When a defendant is remanded in custody pursuant to that provision the justices make
an order directed (in the Inner London area and in the Metropolitan Police District) 'to
each and all the Constables of the Metropolitan Police Force and to the Governor of Her
Majesty's Prison at . . .' in this case Brixton. The order recites the decision to adjourn the
hearing until a certain time on a certain date and to remand the defendant in custody
and contains a direction in these terms:

f   'You, the said Constables, are hereby required to convey the accused to the said
        prison and there deliver the accused to the governor thereof, together with this
        warrant: and you, the governor, to receive the accused into your custody and, unless
        the accused is released on bail or you are otherwise ordered in the meantime, to keep
        the accused until the above date and then convey the accused to the said magistrates'
        court at the above time.'

g Counsel on behalf of the prison governor accepts that this is an order which the
magistrates have power to make and with which it is the duty of the governor to comply.
In his affidavit, Mr Hayzelden, assistant secretary in the Home Office prisons department,
explains how the order is carried into effect. It is the police, and not the governor, who
convey the prisoner to court, the police operating the collection and distribution of
h prisoners to London magistrates' courts from a central point. The Prison Rules 1964, SI
1964/338 provide by r 38(2) that a prisoner required to be taken into custody anywhere
outside a prison shall be kept in the custody of an officer appointed under s 3 of the
Prison Act 1952 or a police officer. An exception to those arrangements arises where a
prisoner is remanded in custody by more than one court, a so-called 'dual custody case'.
In such a case the prisoner is conveyed to court by a prison officer who holds the second
j warrant and can thus retain the prisoner in custody. This is to avoid the situation of a
prisoner appearing before a court which does not impose a custodial sentence being
allowed to go free, notwithstanding that there is an extant custody warrant.

It is not contended by counsel on behalf of the applicant that the governor was in
breach of any duty in the present case to produce the applicant to a court to which he has
been remanded in custody. The only failure to produce him in such circumstances was

the failure to produce him to the South Western Magistrates' Court on the charge of
burglary for the fourth hearing on 12 September 1983, but, as we have already said, no
complaint is made of that failure because it is accepted that it was due to an administrative
misunderstanding.

The central point of dispute which arises, therefore, is whether the governor is under
a duty to produce someone in his custody, or whether the Secretary of State is under a
duty to produce him or to procure his production, to a court to which, in respect of the
proceedings in question, he has been remanded on bail at a time when he is in custody as
a result of some other order. Those were the circumstances which applied to each of the
two occasions when the applicant was not produced to the Horseferry Road Magistrates'
Court, namely on 9 and 16 September 1983, being the two occasions of which the
applicant complains and each of which, it is contended on his behalf, constituted a breach
of duty on the part of the prison governor and the Secretary of State. Counsel on behalf
of those respondents contends that there was no breach of duty on the part of either of
them on those occasions and that there is no duty on either of them to produce, or to
procure the production of, a defendant to the court in question in such circumstances.

Counsel on behalf of the applicant, as we understand him, submits that the duty arises
in one or more of three ways: firstly, by implication from s 128(1)(b) of the Magistrates'
Courts Act 1980; secondly, as a matter of the construction of s 29 of the Criminal Justice
Act 1961; and thirdly, at common law.

Section 128(1)(b) of the 1980 Act is in these terms:

'Where a magistrates' court has power to remand any person, then subject to
section 4 of the Bail Act 1976 and to any other enactment modifying that power,
the court may . . . (b) where it is inquiring into or trying an offence alleged to have
been committed by that person or has convicted him of an offence, remand him on
bail in accordance with the Bail Act 1976, that is to say, by directing him to appear
as provided in subsection (4) below . . .'

At one stage in his argument it seemed that counsel may have been submitting that a
duty to produce the defendant is to be inferred or implied, or that it arises in some way,
from the provisions of that paragraph of that subsection. An order made by the
magistrates under that paragraph is, he submits, a lawful order so that a prison governor
is under a duty to enable a defendant prisoner to comply with it in so far as he is able to
do so because, if he does not enable the prisoner to comply with it, he will be preventing
the order from taking effect. We reject this submission. There is, in our view, nothing
in that paragraph of that subsection which imposes a duty, or which empowers
magistrates to impose a duty, on a prison governor except, possibly, a duty not to be in
contempt of court. It is not alleged, on these applications, that there has been any such
contempt, but we will return to the relevance of contempt later in this judgment.

Section 29(1) of the Criminal Justice Act 1961, on which counsel for the applicant
primarily relies, provides:

'If the responsible Minister is satisfied, in the case of a person detained in any part
of the United Kingdom in a prison . . . that the attendance of that person at any
place in that or any other part of the United Kingdom is desirable in the interests of
justice . . . the responsible Minister may direct that person to be taken to that place.'

The Secretary of State for Home Affairs is the responsible minister within the meaning
of that provision. According to Mr Hayzelden's evidence prison governors are authorised
by the Secretary of State to exercise his discretion under s 29(1), but the devolution of the
power is personal to governors and it will generally be only on the governor's authority
that an inmate may be produced pursuant to the power under that section.

Counsel for the applicant, turning, as it seems to us, a blind eye to the word 'may' in
those provisions, submits that they impose a duty on the prison governor concerned and
the Secretary of State to produce to a magistrates' court persons in the prison governor's
custody who have been remanded to appear at that court on a duly notified date, provided

that the prison governor has been informed of the terms of that remand. He submits
a that the provisions are couched in broad language which, though conferring, as he
concedes, no more than a discretion on the minister in certain cases at least, does so
because the provisions apply to many different situations (other than remands to
magistrates' courts) where such a discretion is clearly necessary, such as the attendance of
a prisoner at an identity parade or his giving evidence in civil proceedings.

Counsel for the prison governor and the Secretary of State, on the other hand, submits
b that it would be very odd if this provision is to be construed as containing any mandatory
element since, ex facie, it imposes a power not a duty, and since it is manifestly intended
to confer a discretion in most of the situations in which it would apply such, for instance,
as the two situations to which we have already referred.

In our view the provisions of s 29(1) of the 1961 Act cannot be construed so as to
impose any duty on the minister save the duty to consider the exercise of his discretion
whenever circumstances arise which impose that duty and, when exercising his discretion,
c to do so properly. In this case, however, it is not contended on behalf of the applicant
that the minister has been in breach of duty in having failed to consider the exercise of
his discretion or in having exercised it improperly: the submission is simply that in this
case there was no discretion but only a duty.

Counsel for the applicant supports his third submission, namely that a duty exists at
d common law, by referring to the undoubted power of the court, in a case such as this, to
issue a writ of habeas corpus ad respondendum at common law or under the Habeas
Corpus Act 1803 and by contending that the mere existence of that power imports or
implies the existence of a pre-existing common law duty to produce the person in
question on the part of anyone against whom in any given case the writ in principle
could be issued. But he concedes that he has no authority to support that submission and
e he also concedes that the power to issue the writ of habeas corpus in any such case is
discretionary. The court has power to issue a writ of habeas corpus ad respondendum to
bring up a prisoner to answer a criminal charge, without being satisfied that the applicant
is being illegally detained. In this respect that writ differs materially from the writ of
habeas corpus ad subjiciendum. Such a writ issues when the applicant is illegally detained
or detained pursuant to an invalid order. But in the present case and, we suspect, in many
f cases in which the writ of habeas corpus ad respondendum is properly issued the applicant
is detained pursuant to a valid order for his detention. In these circumstances it is
impossible to imply or infer the existence of any pre-existing duty to bring up a prisoner
to give evidence from the power to issue a writ of habeas corpus for that purpose, and we
are satisfied that there is no such pre-existing duty and that the submission is
misconceived.

g In our judgment, therefore, neither the prison governor nor the Secretary of State
were in breach of any duty when the applicant was not produced to the court on 9 or 16
September 1983.

It does not necessarily follow from this conclusion that a prison governor is never
under a duty to produce a prisoner to court on such an occasion. It has not been necessary,
for the purpose of these applications, to consider the Prison Act 1952 or the Prison Rules
h 1964, SI 1964/388, but in *Raymond v Honey* [1982] 1 All ER 756 at 758, [1982] 2 WLR
465 at 468 Lord Wilberforce said that the first of the two basic principles from which to
start in considering whether any contempt has been committed is that '. . . any act done
which is calculated to obstruct or interfere with the due course of justice, or the lawful
process of the courts, is a contempt of court'. Subject to the terms of the order committing
a prisoner to custody, and to the provisions of the 1952 Act and the 1964 rules, it might
j be that, in particular circumstances, a governor of a prison could be in contempt of court
by refusing or failing to produce a prisoner to a court if he had the power and ability to
do so.

Even though no breach of duty has been committed, counsel for the applicant would
urge us, none the less, to issue a writ of habeas corpus ad respondendum to ensure the
production of the applicant at the South Western Magistrates' Court on 10 November, to

which, in respect of the charge of assault, he has been remanded on bail. He seeks no such writ to ensure the applicant's production at the same court on 24 October on the charge of attempted theft, because in relation to the hearing of that charge on that date he has been remanded in custody so that the applicant has no apprehension that there will be any failure on the part of the prison governor to produce him.

We do not propose to order the issue of any writ of habeas corpus ad respondendum. Although we accept that we have power to issue such a writ without having to be satisfied that there is any illegal or wrongful detention of the applicant, we do not think that the circumstances disclosed on the present application are such that we should exercise our discretion to do so. We are in no position to know what the circumstances will be on 10 November, we do not know whether, on that date, there will be a shortage of prison escorts nor how many other prisoners will be similarly affected nor, if there are other such prisoners, about the relative effect on each of them, including the applicant, of their non-appearance at court on that date. We might, were we to issue the writ in favour of the applicant, be giving him unfair priority, and this we do not propose to do.

Mr Hayzelden has given evidence about the present difficulties at Brixton prison. He says that that prison, in addition to the manning of the prison itself, provides prison officers for the Crown Court throughout London and is responsible for conveying prisoners from a number of prisons to the Crown Court and for administration of the cells area and custody of prisoners whilst at court. The Crown Court commitment varies according to the number of courts sitting. The prison has insufficient officers to fulfil all the tasks allocated to it, and the shortfall is estimated to vary between 35 and 60 officers per day. In these circumstances the prison is not always able to meet applications for production of prisoners to courts made by the police. The procedure which the prison adopts to cope with the problem is to review the productions requested 24 hours before they are due. If it transpires that there are insufficient officers to act as escorts, the prison attempts to draw up a list of priority cases. The prison endeavours to inform the courts concerned, in those cases where it would be unable to produce the prisoners, and the police are invited to collect the prisoners, together with the warrant of commitment under which they are held.

This gives the police the authority to keep the prisoner in custody and to return him to the prison. The problem which the shortage of prison officers creates has been in existence for approximately the last 18 months but has only recently become acute owing to a significant increase in the number of productions sought. The Home Office recognises that the present situation is unsatisfactory and causes inconvenience and expense to all those involved, not least the accused himself. The Home Office is recruiting up to 800 additional prison officers in the year 1983–84 which it is hoped will lead to an improvement in the situation.

Mr Hayzelden points out, as does counsel for the prison governor and the Secretary of State, that recent legislative provisions allow an accused to be remanded in custody in his absence (see the Criminal Justice Act 1982, s 59) and give a magistrates' court for a county, a London commission area or the City of London jurisdiction to try all summary offences committed within the county, the London commission area or the City of London as the case may be (see the Magistrates' Courts Act 1980, s 2). He concludes that if these provisions were to be taken advantage of more frequently they would serve to ease the problem considerably, as productions could be avoided altogether in some instances, and others could be limited to one court for several different cases. Although counsel on behalf of the Secretary of State told us that the Home Office is not complacent about this problem, we recognise that it does exist and we have taken the problem, and the procedure which Mr Hayzelden describes for drawing up a list of priority cases when there is a shortfall of escorts, into account in deciding not to exercise our discretion to order the issue of a writ of habeas corpus.

Although, for the reasons explained above, we consider that no breach of any statutory or common law duty has been established in this case, and that in the circumstances there is also no sufficient ground for the issue of a writ of habeas corpus, we must

conclude by pointing out that the history of events in this case is highly unsatisfactory,
both from the point of view of the applicant and of the administration of justice.
Defendants to criminal charges are entitled to have their cases dealt with as speedily as
the availability of court time will allow. The courts, for their part, are entitled to expect
that defendants in custody will be produced on the day for which their cases have been
listed. If they are not produced, the court's time is wasted, and other cases may have been
listed unnecessarily for a later date. The present case may well be exceptional due to the
multiplicity of the charges which the applicant faced and the number of his remands
over a short period. We hope that it is exceptional. Nevertheless, it clearly indicates the
need to consider the present system of communication between the courts, the police
and the prisons, at any rate in the Greater London area, in relation to the listing of cases
in the magistrates' courts, quite apart from the problem of prison staffing which is
already under review.

Application dismissed.

Solicitors: *Hallmark Carter & Atkinson*, Brixton (for the applicant); *Treasury Solicitor.*

April Weiss   Barrister.

Note
Bolivinter Oil SA v Chase Manhattan Bank and others

COURT OF APPEAL, CIVIL DIVISION
SIR JOHN DONALDSON MR AND GRIFFITHS LJ
5, 9 DECEMBER 1983

*Injunction – Ex parte injunction – Matters to be considered before granting injunction – Injunction
prohibiting payment of irrevocable letter of credit etc – Injunction not normally to be granted in
absence of substantial challenge to validity of letter of credit etc – Uncorroborated statement of
bank's customer not normally sufficient evidence.*

Notes
For ex parte injunctions generally, see 24 Halsbury's Laws (4th edn) para 1051, and for
cases on the subject, see 28(2) Digest (Reissue) 1115–1118, 1106–1138.
  For letters of credit generally, see 3 Halsbury's Laws (4th edn) paras 131–150, and for
cases on the subject, see 3 Digest (Reissue) 665–673, 4121–4148.

Interlocutory appeal
After a hearing in chambers on 31 October 1983 of an application made ex parte by the
plaintiffs, Bolivinter Oil SA, at which the first defendants, Chase Manhattan Bank, were
represented by counsel Staughton J granted injunctions (1) restraining the first defendants
by themselves their agents or servants or otherwise from making payment to the second
defendants, Commercial Bank of Syria, in respect of a letter of guarantee issued by the
second defendants to the third defendants, General Company of Homs Refinery, a body
corporate of Syria, in June 1982, (2) restraining the second defendants by themselves
their agents or servants or otherwise from requesting payment from the first defendants
in respect of the letter of guarantee, (3) restraining the second defendants by themselves
their agents or servants or otherwise from making payment to the third defendants in
respect of the letter of guarantee and (4) restraining the third defendants by themselves
their agents or servants or otherwise from making any claim under the letter of
guarantee. On 29 November 1983 at a hearing pursuant to a summons of which all three

defendants had notice but at which only the plaintiffs and the first defendants appeared Staughton J continued the injunction against the third defendants until trial or further *a* order and the injunctions against the first and second defendants until after 1 December 1983 or if notice of appeal were served by that date until after the hearing of the appeal. The plaintiffs appealed, seeking the continuation of the injunctions against the first and second defendants until trial or further order. The case is reported only with respect to the approach to be followed by the court in considering ex parte applications for injunctions restraining payment under irrevocable letters of credit, performance bonds *b* or guarantees.

Nicholas Phillips QC and *John Thomas* for the plaintiffs.
Peter Scott QC and *Christopher S C S Clarke* for the first defendants.
The second and third defendants were not represented.

c

Cur adv vult

9 December. **SIR JOHN DONALDSON MR**, giving the judgment of the court dismissing the appeal, said: Before leaving this appeal, we should like to add a word about the circumstances in which an ex parte injunction should be issued which prohibits a bank from paying under an irrevocable letter of credit or a performance bond or *d* guarantee. The unique value of such a letter, bond or guarantee is that the beneficiary can be completely satisfied that, whatever disputes may thereafter arise between him and the bank's customer in relation to the performance or indeed existence of the underlying contract, the bank is personally undertaking to pay him provided that the specified conditions are met. In requesting his bank to issue such a letter, bond or guarantee, the customer is seeking to take advantage of this unique characteristic. If, save in the most *e* exceptional cases, he is to be allowed to derogate from the bank's personal and irrevocable undertaking, given be it again noted at his request, by obtaining an injunction restraining the bank from honouring that undertaking, he will undermine what is the bank's greatest asset, however large and rich it may be, namely its reputation for financial and contractual probity. Furthermore, if this happens at all frequently, the value of all irrevocable letters of credit and performance bonds and guarantees will be undermined. *f*

Judges who are asked, often at short notice and ex parte, to issue an injunction restraining payment by a bank under an irrevocable letter of credit or performance bond or guarantee should ask whether there is any challenge to the validity of the letter, bond or guarantee itself. If there is not or if the challenge is not substantial, prima facie no injunction should be granted and the bank should be left free to honour its contractual obligation, although restrictions may well be imposed on the freedom of the beneficiary *g* to deal with the money after he has received it. The wholly exceptional case where an injunction may be granted is where it is proved that the bank knows that any demand for payment already made or which may thereafter be made will clearly be fraudulent. But the evidence must be clear, both as to the fact of fraud and as to the bank's knowledge. It would certainly not normally be sufficient that this rests on the uncorroborated statement of the customer, for irreparable damage can be done to a bank's credit in the *h* relatively brief time which must elapse between the granting of such an injunction and an application by the bank to have it discharged.

Appeal dismissed.

Solicitors: *Richards Butler & Co* (for the plaintiffs); *Allen & Overy* (for the first defendants).

Frances Rustin   Barrister.

Commission of the European Communities v United Kingdom

(Case 165/82)

COURT OF JUSTICE OF THE EUROPEAN COMMUNITIES

JUDGES MERTENS DE WILMARS (PRESIDENT), KOOPMANS, BAHLMANN, GALMOT (PRESIDENTS OF CHAMBERS), LORD MACKENZIE STUART, O'KEEFFE, BOSCO, DUE AND EVERLING

ADVOCATE-GENERAL S ROZÈS

22 MARCH, 7 JUNE, 8 NOVEMBER 1983

European Economic Community – Equality of treatment of men and women – Failure of member state to fulfil obligations – Failure to declare provisions contrary to principle of equality of treatment in collective agreements, contracts of employment and rules of undertakings, professions and occupations null and void – Exemption in case of employment in private households or where no more than five employed – Restriction for men of access to employment as midwives – Whether United Kingdom legislation fulfilling EEC requirements – Sex Discrimination Act 1975, ss 6(3), 20, 77(1) – EEC Council Directive 76/207, arts 2(2), 3(2)(b), 4(b), 5(2)(b), 9(2).

EEC Council Directive 76/207 of 9 February 1976 provided for the implementation in member states of the EEC of the principle of equal treatment for men and women as regards access to employment, including promotion, access to vocational training and working conditions. By art 4(b)[a] of that directive provisions relating to access to vocational training which were contrary to that principle and which were included in collective agreements, individual contracts of employment, internal rules of undertakings or rules governing independent occupations or professions were to be declared null and void or were to be amended. Articles 3(2)(b) and 5(2)(b) made similar provisions in relation to access to employment and working conditions. The Commission of the European Communities brought an action against the United Kingdom complaining that the United Kingdom had failed fully to implement the directive. The Commission alleged (i) that, although the United Kingdom had, by s 77(1)[b] of the Sex Discrimination Act 1975, conformed to those requirements so far as individual contracts of employment were concerned, no such legal provision existed with regard to collective agreements, internal rules of undertakings or rules governing independent occupations and professions, (ii) that s 6(3)[c] of the 1975 Act, which excluded employment in private households and cases where five or fewer people were employed from the application of the 1975 Act, went beyond the exemption provided for in art 2(2)[d] of the directive where in certain cases the sex of the worker constituted a determining factor, and (iii) that s 20 of the 1975 Act, under which males were granted only very limited access to training, employment and promotion as midwives likewise went beyond the exemption in art 2(2). The United Kingdom contended (i) that legally binding collective agreements were covered by s 77 of the 1975 Act but that collective agreements in the United Kingdom were generally non-binding and that the directive did not apply to such agreements, (ii) that the exclusion from prohibition of discrimination provided for by s 6(3) of the 1975 Act was justified by the exception provided for in art 2(2) of the directive, and (iii) that the limitation in s 20 was, in the light of social developments in the United Kingdom, in conformity with art 2(2) but was being kept under review pursuant to art 9(2)[e] of the directive.

---

a   Article 4(b), so far as material, is set out at p 362 h, post

b   Section 77(1) is set out at p 355 e, post

c   Section 6(3), so far as material, is set out at p 357 g, post

d   Article 2(2) is set out at p 363 c, post

e   Article 9(2) is set out at p 358 a, post

Held – (1) In order to ensure that it was completely effective, EEC Council Directive 76/207 covered all collective agreements whether legally enforceable or not because, even if collective agreements were not legally binding as between the parties who signed them or with regard to the employment relationships which they governed, they nevertheless had important de facto consequences for the employment relationships to which they referred and, in the interests of industrial harmony, gave undertakings some indication of the conditions which employment relationships were or were not required to satisfy. To that extent the United Kingdom had failed to fulfil its obligations under the EEC Treaty and the Commission's first complaint would therefore be upheld (see p 362 e to p 363 a and p 364 b c and e f, post).

(2) Since not all kinds of employment in private households were ones where, by reason of their nature or the context in which they were carried out, the sex of the worker constituted a determining factor, and since it had not been shown that, merely because of its small size, in an undertaking with not more than five employees the sex of the worker would be a determining factor by reason of the nature of his activities or the context in which they were carried out, the exclusion contained in s 6(3) of the 1975 Act went, by reason of its generality, beyond the exception provided for in art 2(2) of the directive itself. To that extent also the United Kingdom had failed to fulfil its obligations under the EEC Treaty and the Commission's second complaint would therefore be upheld (see p 363 d to f and p 364 b c and e f, post).

(3) In the light of social developments in the United Kingdom, where midwifery was not traditionally engaged in by men, and because it was a sphere in which respect for the patient's sensitivities was of particular importance, it could not in the circumstances be said that, for the time being, the United Kingdom had exceeded the limits of the power granted to member states under arts 2(2) and 9(2) of the directive and the Commission's third complaint could not therefore be upheld (see p 363 h to p 364 a c and f, post).

Notes

For equal treatment of men and women in respect of employment under EEC law, see 16 Halsbury's Laws (4th edn) para 521.

For the Sex Discrimination Act 1975, ss 6, 20, 77, see 45 Halsbury's Statutes (3rd edn) 229, 243, 280.

For the EEC Treaty, see 42A ibid passim.

Cases cited

EC Commission v Italian Republic Case 300/81 (1 March 1983, unreported), CJEC.
EC Commission v Italian Republic Case 145/82 [1984] 1 CMLR 148, CJEC.
EC Commission v UK Case 170/78 [1983] 3 CMLR 512, CJEC.
Heron Corp Ltd v Commis [1980] ICR 713, EAT.

Application

By an application dated 28 May 1982 the Commission of the European Communities applied to the Court of Justice of the European Communities for a declaration that the United Kingdom had failed to fulfil its obligations under the EEC Treaty by failing to enact within the prescribed period the provisions needed in order to comply with EEC Council Directive 76/207 of 9 February 1976 on the implementation of the principle of equal treatment for men and women as regards access to employment, vocational training and promotion and working conditions. The language of the case was English. The facts are set out in the opinion of the Advocate-General.

John Forman, agent for the EC Commission, for the Commission.
Ian Glick for the United Kingdom.

7 June. **The Advocate-General (S Rozès)** delivered the following opinion[1]: Mr President, Members of the Court, in this action brought against the United Kingdom the

---

1 Translated from the French

Commission maintains that the incorrect implementation of EEC Council Directive
a 76/207 is fourfold. 1. Contrary to the obligations laid down by the directive, the United
Kingdom legislation does not ensure that provisions contrary to the principle of equal
treatment which are contained in collective agreements, on the one hand, and in the
internal rules of undertakings or the rules governing the independent occupations and
professions, on the other hand, are null and void (at law) or may be declared null and
void or may be amended (by the courts). 2. and 3. By reason of an erroneous interpretation
b of the exception provided for in art 2(2) of the directive, s 6(3) of the Sex Discrimination
Act 1975 excludes from its field of application employment for the purposes of a private
household and cases where five or fewer people are employed. 4. By granting to persons
of the male sex only very limited access to training for the occupation of midwife and to
the occupation itself the United Kingdom is also interpreting art 2(2) of the directive in
an excessively restrictive manner. I shall examine each of these complaints.

c I—1. By virtue of arts 3(2)(*b*), 4(*b*) and 5(2)(*b*) of the directive member states must take
the measures necessary to ensure that any provisions contrary to the principle of equal
treatment regarding access to employment (art 3), access to the various types of vocational
training (art 4) and working conditions (art 5) are null and void or may be amended. It is
of scant importance whether such provisions are contained in individual employment
d contracts, collective agreements, the internal rules of undertakings or the rules governing
the independent occupations and professions.
According to the Commission the legislation in force in the United Kingdom conforms
to those requirements only as far as individual employment contracts are concerned.
Section 77(1) of the 1975 Act provides:

e 'A term of a contract is void where—(*a*) its inclusion renders making of the
contract unlawful by virtue of this Act, or (*b*) it is included in furtherance of an act
rendered unlawful by this Act, or (*c*) it provides for the doing of an act which would
be rendered unlawful by this Act.'

However, no legal provision of the same type exists with regard to collective
agreements, the internal rules of undertakings or the rules governing the independent
f occupations and professions. Therefore, in the Commission's view, the clear and
unequivocal obligation imposed on member states by the above-mentioned articles of
the directive is not fulfilled.
2. The United Kingdom does not share that opinion. Its view is that it is unnecessary
to adopt a rule similar to s 77(1) of the 1975 Act for collective agreements, the internal
rules of undertakings and the rules governing the independent occupations and
g professions. It considers that to do so would in no way help to ensure attainment of the
purpose of arts 3, 4 and 5 of the directive, namely implementation of the principle of
equal treatment in the areas referred to therein.
(a) I shall first consider collective agreements.
In the United Kingdom's view the existing rules on collective agreements adequately
ensure implementation of the directive.
h The United Kingdom states in the first place that, since the entry into force of the
Trade Union and Labour Relations Act 1974, it is not customary for collective agreements
to be legally binding and that it is not aware of there being any legally binding collective
agreements now in force in the United Kingdom.
It goes on to say that by virtue of s 3 of the Equal Pay Act 1970 collective agreements
may be submitted to the Central Arbitration Committee, whose task it is to declare what
j amendments it considers to be necessary in order to remove discrimination in terms and
conditions of employment between men and women. The effect of the declarations
made by the committee is in fact that whenever a discriminatory provision is included
in an individual employment contract that contract is amended as a result.
The United Kingdom consistently adheres to the view that the directive does not
require the annulment or the possibility of annulment or amendment of documents

such as collective agreements which have no legal effect. To impose such a requirement would be rather like 'beating the air'.

Finally, it particularly emphasises the fact that if a collective agreement were legally binding (an extremely unlikely eventuality) and if one of its provisions were contrary to the principle of equal treatment that provision would be void by virtue of s 77 of the 1975 Act. The same applies to provisions of a collective agreement which are contrary to the principle of equal treatment and are incorporated in individual contracts.

(b) As regards the provisions of internal rules and rules governing the independent occupations and professions, the United Kingdom's defence is substantially the same as in the case of collective agreements. By virtue of s 77(1) discriminatory provisions contained in such documents are null and void in those cases where they have binding force or where they are reproduced in individual employment contracts. However, the United Kingdom also refers to other sections of the 1975 Act which assist in combating discrimination. In a case of discrimination regarding employment as a result of the inclusion of a discriminatory provision in the internal rules of an undertaking or in the rules of a body governing an occupation or profession, that discrimination would be caught by s 6 of the 1975 Act. Moreover, if an undertaking whose business object was to find employment offered work, by virtue of its internal rules, only to persons of one sex, that would be prohibited by s 15 of the 1975 Act. Furthermore, if the provision contrary to the principle of equal treatment related to authorisation or qualification for a particular profession or trade, it would be prohibited by s 13(1) of the 1975 Act.

Consequently, the United Kingdom considers that in that case too it is unnecessary to adopt other legislative measures in order to apply the principle of equal treatment to undertakings and the independent occupations and professions, since its present legislation, which comes into operation at the point at which the person discriminated against is prejudiced, already ensures observance of that principle.

3. The Commission is not satisfied with those arguments. It refers to the clear terms of the relevant provisions of the directive by virtue of which the member states are to take the necessary measures to ensure that provisions contrary to the principle of equal treatment appearing in collective agreements, internal rules of undertakings and rules governing the independent occupations and professions are, or may be declared to be, null and void or may be amended. No rule of law applicable in the United Kingdom makes the fulfilment of that obligation possible. In the Commission's opinion, there is a fundamental difference between a legal situation created by the annulment or amendment of a discriminatory provision, which causes that provision to cease to exist, and the situation at issue, where a provision continues to exist even if, at law, it is unenforceable. The Commission also points out that before 1974 collective agreements were in themselves legally binding and that there is no reason for considering that the same may not apply in the future.

4. In my opinion in this purely legal debate the Commission's position appears to be more sound, in particular by reason of the requirements of clarity and legal certainty to which the decisions of the court attach great importance in cases where a state is charged with failing to fulfil its obligations. It is true that to date the case law has related to administrative practices which, the court has held (most recently in *EC Commission v Italian Republic* Case 145/82 [1984] 1 CMLR 148 at 156, para 10), 'cannot be regarded as a valid fulfilment of the obligation imposed by Article 189 of the Treaty on member-States to which the directives are addressed', since those practices 'by their nature may be altered at the whim of the authorities and lack the appropriate publicity'. But it seems to me that because of the general nature of its terms, the following sentence, taken from para 10 of the judgment of the court in *EC Commission v Italian Republic* Case 300/81 (1 March 1983, unreported), also applies to this case: 'It is important . . . for each Member State to implement the directive in question in a manner which fully satisfies the requirements of clarity and legal certainty which the directive is intended to achieve in the interests', in this case, of women and men regarding access to employment, training, advancement and working conditions. The terms of arts 3, 4 and 5 of the directive at issue in this case

a seem to me to leave member states no greater margin of discretion regarding the implementation thereof than those of the directive on credit establishments at issue in Case 300/81.

Moreover, a situation in which possibly discriminatory provisions continue to exist in documents such as collective agreements, the internal rules of undertakings and the rules governing the independent occupations and professions is just as ambiguous, above all for workers who in most cases have no legal training, as the situation created by the

b implementation of a directive merely by means of administrative practices. It should also be noted that workers have easier access to collective agreements, the internal rules of undertakings and the rules governing the independent occupations and professions than to EEC Council Directive 76/207 or to the United Kingdom laws depriving those documents, in general, of legally binding force. Thus, workers may believe that because their contracts of employment reproduce possibly discriminatory provisions from the

c types of document referred to they are legal and may not be challenged at law and the workers may therefore be deprived of the advantages of a directive which was in fact adopted for their benefit. In order to avoid such risks of confusion, the best course is to make it possible for such discriminatory provisions to be removed from those documents, as required by the directive.

That course of action is greatly facilitated by the fact that it has already been followed

d with regard to one of the areas covered by the directive, namely that of working conditions. As has been seen, s 3 of the Equal Pay Act 1970 gives the Central Arbitration Committee the task of declaring what amendments need to be made in order to remove any discrimination in that regard where a collective agreement (or an employer's pay structure) contains provisions specifically applicable only to male workers or only to female workers. What is possible with regard to working conditions must be possible

e with regard to the other matters referred to in the directive.

As regards the specific provisions of the 1975 Act which make possible the annulment of any discriminatory clauses of certain types contained in the internal rules of an undertaking or the rules governing an independent occupation or profession, it is sufficient to note that, regardless of their actual scope, they do not cover the whole area covered by the Community provision.

f In the circumstances, the first complaint made by the Commission seems to me to be well founded.

II—1. The Commission considers, in the second place, that the provisions of s 6(3) of the 1975 Act are contrary to the terms of the directive, in particular arts 3, 4 and 5 thereof. That is the substance of the Commission's second and third complaints.

Section 6(3) of the 1975 Act excepts from the prohibition of discrimination against job

g applicants and employees which is laid down in s 6(1) and (2), (a) 'employment for the purposes of a private household' or (b) cases 'where the number of persons employed by the employer, added to the number employed by any associated employers of his, does not exceed five (disregarding any persons employed for the purposes of a private household)'.

However, as the United Kingdom pointed out during the oral procedure, that

h exception is not unqualified: even in the cases referred to in s 6(3) employers are prohibited by virtue of s 4 of the 1975 Act from victimising any of their employees who seek to avail themselves of the rights granted to them by law regarding equal treatment or who help other people to do so.

In the United Kingdom's view the jobs covered by that exception fall within the field of application of art 2(2) of the directive in conjunction with art 9(2) thereof.

j By virtue of art 2(2), the directive is to be—

'without prejudice to the right of Member States to exclude from its field of application those occupational activities and, where appropriate, the training leading thereto, for which, by reason of their nature or the context in which they are carried out, the sex of the worker constitutes a determining factor.'

Article 9(2) provides for its part that—

'Member States shall periodically assess the occupational activities referred to in *a* Article 2(2) in order to decide, in the light of social developments, whether there is justification for maintaining the exclusions concerned. They shall notify the Commission of the results of this assessment.'

2. The United Kingdom considers that 'employment . . . for the purposes of a private household' and employment in very small undertakings may be excluded from the field *b* of application of the directive because they involve close personal relationships between employees and employers, so that it would not be legally possible to prevent the latter from employing persons of a particular sex.

The United Kingdom thus bases its view on that part of art 2(2) by virtue of which discrimination is lawful with regard to those occupational activities for which, by reason of the context in which they are carried out, the sex of the worker constitutes a *c* determining factor.

In the case of employment for the purposes of a private household, it states that such employment frequently involves very close personal relationships between employer and employee and that the employee often lives in the household, as in the case of resident companions or personal maids. It also contends that, contrary to the Commission's view, the concept of 'private household' is clear. Thus, if a chauffeur is not actually *d* employed in his employer's household but for the purposes of his business, the exception will not apply: see *Heron Corp Ltd v Commis* [1980] ICR 713, a case on analogous provisions of the Race Relations Act 1976. On the contrary, a family cook or gardener will normally come within that exception.

With regard to employment in very small undertakings, the United Kingdom draws attention in the first place to the strictly limited character of the exception. Whilst *e* persons employed for the purposes of a private household are not to be taken into account in the figure of five employees, the exception does not on the other hand extend to cases where associated employers maintain a number of small establishments each of which employs no more than five persons but which together employ more. The United Kingdom also justifies that exception by reason of the close personal relationships that often exist in small undertakings. It mentions by way of example female owners and *f* managers of small shops, in particular those who are elderly, who desire to employ assistants of their own sex.

It considers therefore that at the present time it is justified in not applying EEC Council Directive 76/207 in the United Kingdom to the types of employment referred to in s 6(3) of the 1975 Act, in view of the social developments which have taken place.

3. In my opinion this argument has been effectively refuted by the Commission. *g*

(a) Like the Commission I consider, in general terms, that since art 2(2) of the directive provides for an exception it must be strictly construed. I also consider, for the same reason, that it is for the member states to prove that a particular occupational activity may be excluded from the field of application of the directive because, by reason of the nature thereof or the context in which it is carried out, the sex of the worker constitutes a determining factor. *h*

As regards more specifically the two exceptions contained in s 6(2) of the 1975 Act, the Commission points out in the first place, on the basis of its report to the Council on the implementation of the directive, that there are no such exceptions in any member state other than the United Kingdom. Although it is unnecessary to draw from this any conclusions from the legal point of view, I think it may nevertheless be stated with regard to that situation that it would be quite astonishing if it were only in the United *j* Kingdom that the present stage of social development prevented the application of the directive to employment for the purposes of a private household or in very small undertakings.

(b) The Commission also claims that 'employment for the purposes of a private household' is an extremely imprecise notion. It emphasises in particular that no guidance is given as to what a 'household' is or when it is considered to be 'private'. It wonders in particular whether the expression must be interpreted narrowly or broadly and what categories of workers should be included therein. I am not entirely convinced by the Commission's argument. It is in fact quite possible, as the United Kingdom has indicated, that the content of this concept may be progressively defined by case law, which is the usual manner in which the content of a concept having legal implications is defined.

Likewise, I do not associate myself with the criticism made by the Commission regarding the figure of five employees adopted for the second exception contained in s 6(3) of the 1975 Act. If it is admitted at the outset that an exception is justified for very small undertakings, that figure, which does not appear to be manifestly inappropriate, must also be allowed in view of the fact that every choice necessarily involves a threshold which to some extent, however small, is bound to be arbitrary.

(c) There are other reasons which enable me to adhere to the Commission's view regarding the specific matter of the types of employment referred to in s 6(3) of the 1975 Act. In the first place, the United Kingdom has not furnished proof that in all the cases covered by the exception at issue the conditions in which the work in question is performed make it necessary to allow employers to practise discrimination. It is not true that all occupational and professional activities capable of being covered by the exception contained in that provision involve the close personal relationships which constitute the justification for it.

As the Commission rightly points out, the United Kingdom itself admits this in the words it uses: employment for the purposes of a private household frequently (and therefore not always) involves very close personal relationships; close personal relationships often (here too, not always) exist in small undertakings.

I also consider that the terms of s 6(3) do not satisfy the condition laid down in art 2(2) by virtue of which the exclusion must relate to 'occupational activities'. There is no doubt that it is not necessary, as the United Kingdom rightly points out, for the exclusion of occupational activities pursuant to art 2(2) to be effected by listing them activity by activity; it seems to me to be perfectly permissible for a member state to implement the directive by enacting laws which prohibit discrimination, reiterating the actual wording of that article and, for the rest, leaving the national courts to determine case by case, subject to review by this court under art 177 of the EEC Treaty, what occupational activities are excluded from the general prohibition. But it cannot be considered, without stretching the meaning of the words, that the concepts of employment for the purposes of a private household (and not for example the concept of resident domestic staff) and employment in undertakings with five or fewer employees correspond to occupational activities.

For the foregoing reasons, the second and third complaints made by the Commission also seem to me to be well founded.

III The last complaint made by the Commission against the United Kingdom regarding the fulfilment of its obligations under EEC Council Directive 76/207 also involves the question of the interpretation to be given to art 2(2) thereof. It concerns the exclusion of midwives from the field of application of the 1975 Act.

1. Section 20 of the 1975 Act provides that midwives are excluded from the provisions of s 6(1) and (2)(a) and that s 14 concerning vocational training bodies does not apply to the training of midwives. It should however be added that that provision has also amended the legislation relating to midwives (for England and Wales, the Midwives Act 1951) so as to allow persons of the male sex access to and the right to engage in that occupation. However, on a transitional basis, that access is limited, since men are entitled to follow midwifery training courses only in centres approved by the Secretary of State (see para 3(1) of Sch 4 (transitional provisions) to the 1975 Act). At the present time, two centres have been approved, one in London and the other in the Central Region of Scotland. Similarly, by virtue of para 3(2) of Sch 4 to the 1975 Act, a man may engage in the occupation of midwife only at the places designated by the Secretary of State, namely four hospitals in London and Edinburgh.

I would add that, as the United Kingdom pointed out in response to a question put to it by the court, those restrictions should soon be lifted. Those changes, which are to be *a* made by means of orders which are in course of preparation, should enter into force at the end of August 1983. However, needless to say, that legislative development does not affect the assessment to be made, from the legal point of view, of the United Kingdom rules: only the state of the legislation when these proceedings were commenced is relevant for that purpose (in that regard, see the opinion of Mr Advocate-General VerLoren van Themaat in *EC Commission v UK* Case 170/78 [1983] 3 CMLR 512 at 524 *b* and the references cited therein).

2. In the United Kingdom's view, the discriminatory provisions in force are justified by art 2(2) of the directive by reason of the specific nature of the occupation of midwife and the conditions in which midwives work. The United Kingdom adds that those provisions have been periodically reviewed in the light of social developments, pursuant to art 9(2) of the directive. It was in fact as a result of wide-ranging consultations with *c* the health authorities, the professional and occupational groups concerned and other organisations regarding the report on two studies on male midwives carried out in London and in the Central Region of Scotland that the United Kingdom government recently reached the conclusion that the present restrictions on vocational training and the employment of men as midwives should now be lifted. It should however be noted that the removal of those restrictions has been made subject to two conditions: women *d* must have the possibility of being cared for by a female midwife if they so choose and, if a male midwife is provided, there must be appropriate supervision.

(a) The United Kingdom justifies its position in the first place on the basis of the specific features of the duties of a midwife in the United Kingdom. It emphasises the unique role played by midwives during the pre-natal period and particularly during the post-natal periods as regards care involving intimate personal contact with the woman. *e* It also points out that midwives remain with patients for extended periods and at frequent intervals and that they may have to be on duty alone, particularly at night, in the midwifery ward of a hospital and above all at the patient's home. Disregarding a minority of women who give birth at home aided only by a midwife (8,156 births in 1980), regard must be had to the much more frequent situation where women who have given birth in hospital are cared for at home by midwives for ten days after delivery *f* (586,352 in 1980; in the same year, there were 615,708 births where the mothers remained in hospital for the ten days following delivery).

In that respect, the work of a midwife is distinguished, according to the United Kingdom, from that of gynaecologists (or obstetricians) and from general practitioners who undertake obstetric work. The United Kingdom admits that at the actual moment of birth the difference between the role of midwife, the obstetrician and the general *g* practitioner is less great. Moreover, it observes that the urgent needs of the moment may cause women and their husbands to be less concerned about intimate procedures carried out by a man.

But, for the rest, it states that specialists and general medical practitioners are rarely alone with patients because a female attendant is almost invariably present. It also notes that the care provided by them is usually intermittent and of short duration. *h*

This distinction does not seem to me to be convincing at the present time, when facilities for the provision of care of various kinds at the same place are becoming more and more widespread and no longer raise the same problems.

(b) The United Kingdom placed emphasis on the specific features of the occupation of midwife and expresses the fear that certain women (or their husbands) may refuse the services of male midwives. It fears that, if such women were not permitted to choose a *j* female midwife, they may put themselves and their newborn children at risk by refusing any care. It considers in particular that members of certain ethnic minorities living in the United Kingdom may react in that way. Accordingly, a degree of caution is required; immediate and unrestricted access for men to the occupation of midwife would entail the risk of substantial opposition among those ethnic minorities, and indeed among

other groups. In other words, the gradual introduction of the concept of male midwives
a and of the principle of equal treatment in the occupation of midwife is necessary, in the
opinion of the United Kingdom, in order to take into account, in particular, the
sensitivities and beliefs of people who live in the United Kingdom but whose cultural
background is not in the strict sense British.

3. The Commission, without contesting the truthfulness of those observations, replies
that in practice the reactions apprehended by the United Kingdom should not raise
b difficulties in so far as, on the one hand, account will be taken of the preferences of
women in confinement and, on the other hand, at least for some time to come, male
midwives will no doubt remain the exception rather than the rule. This argument is
considered by the United Kingdom as tending to permit discrimination 'in practice' but
not in law.

I do not consider that the alleged specific nature of the conditions in which the
c occupation of midwife is practised in the United Kingdom is such as to justify, under art
2(2) of the directive, the discriminatory rules against men. I think that the guarantee of
a free choice for patients, which is maintained in the proposed British rules, is a condition
which is necessary and sufficient to allay the fears expressed by the United Kingdom
government.

For all the foregoing reasons, I propose that the court should give judgment as follows:
d (1) by failing to adopt all the provisions needed in order to comply with EEC Council
Directive 76/207 of 9 February 1976 on the implementation of the principle of equal
treatment for men and women as regards access to employment, vocational training and
promotion, and working conditions, the United Kingdom has failed to fulfil its
obligations under the EEC Treaty; (2) the United Kingdom shall pay the costs.

e 8 November. **THE COURT OF JUSTICE** delivered its judgment which, having
summarised the facts, procedure and submissions of the parties, dealt with the law as
follows:

1. By application lodged at the court registry on 3 June 1982 the Commission of the
European Communities brought an action before the court under art 169 of the EEC
Treaty for a declaration that by failing to enact within the prescribed period the provisions
f needed in order to comply with EEC Council Directive 76/207 of 9 February 1976 on
the implementation of the principle of equal treatment for men and women as regards
access to employment, vocational training and promotion, and working conditions, the
United Kingdom has failed to fulfil its obligations under the treaty.

2. The Commission charges the United Kingdom with only partially implementing
the directive in so far as it has failed to amend and supplement the Sex Discrimination
g Act 1975, which, although abolishing discrimination in certain areas of employment,
allows it to continue in other areas in which by virtue of the directive discrimination was
to be abolished by 12 August 1978 at the latest.

3. The Commission's complaints relate to the following points. (a) Neither the 1975
Act nor any other provision of the legislation in force in the United Kingdom provides
that provisions contrary to the principle of equal treatment contained in collective
h agreements, rules of undertakings and rules governing independent occupations and
professions are to be, or may be declared, void or may be amended. (b) Contrary to the
provisions of the directive, s 6(3) of the 1975 Act provides that the prohibition of
discrimination does not apply to employment in a private household or where the
number of persons employed by an employer does not exceed five (disregarding persons
employed in a private household). (c) Finally, by virtue of s 20 of the 1975 Act the
j prohibition of discrimination based on sex does not apply to the employment, promotion
and training of midwives.

The first complaint

4. The government of the United Kingdom considers that this complaint is unfounded.
By virtue of s 18 of the Trades Union and Labour Relations Act 1974, any collective

agreements made before 1 December 1971 or after the entry into force of that Act are to be presumed not to have been intended by the parties to be legally enforceable unless they are in writing and contain a provision in which the parties express their intention that the agreements are to be legally enforceable. In fact, collective agreements are not normally legally binding. The United Kingdom government is not aware of there being any legally binding collective agreements at present in force in the United Kingdom.

5. Even if collective agreements containing provisions contrary to the principle of equality of treatment do exist, those provisions, in so far as they are not capable of amendment under s 3 of the Equal Pay Act 1970, would be rendered void by s 77 of the 1975 Act.

6. The consequences of any provision in the internal rules of an undertaking or in the rules governing an independent occupation or profession which is contrary to the prohibition of discrimination would similarly be rendered void by the same provision. This would apply to any contract between members of a profession or occupation or between them and an undertaking or any occupational or professional body with legal personality. If any discrimination in employment were to result from the existence of such a discriminatory provision in the internal rules of an undertaking or of an occupational or professional body, that discrimination would be caught by s 6 of the 1975 Act. Moreover, if for example an undertaking whose business was to find employment for workers offered work, by virtue of its internal rules, only to persons of one sex, to the exclusion of persons of the other sex, that would be prohibited by s 15 of the 1975 Act.

7. Finally, if a provision contrary to the principle of equal treatment related to authorisation or qualification for a particular profession or occupation, it would be dealt with by s 13(1) of the 1975 Act, which, in substance, makes it unlawful for an authority or body which can confer an authorisation or qualification 'to discriminate against a woman'.

8. These arguments are not sufficient to nullify the complaints made by the Commission. Whilst it may be admitted that the United Kingdom legislation satisfies the obligations imposed by the directive as regards any collective agreements which have legally binding effect, in so far as they are covered by s 77 of the 1975 Act, it is to be noted on the other hand that the United Kingdom legislation contains no corresponding provision regarding either non-binding collective agreements, which the United Kingdom government declares to be the only kind in existence, or the internal rules of undertakings or the rules governing independent occupations or professions.

9. The United Kingdom's argument to the effect that the non-binding character of collective agreements removes them from the field of application of that directive cannot be accepted, even if account is taken of the United Kingdom's observation that individual contracts of employment entered into within the framework of a collective agreement are rendered void by s 77 of the 1975 Act.

10. Article 4(b) of EEC Council Directive 76/207 provides that the application of the principle of equal treatment in the areas to which it relates means that member states must take the necessary measures to ensure that—

'any provisions contrary to the principle of equal treatment which are included in collective agreements, individual contracts of employment, internal rules of undertakings or in rules governing the independent occupations and professions shall be, or may be declared, null and void or may be amended.'

11. The directive thus covers all collective agreements without distinction as to the nature of the legal effects which they do or do not produce. The reason for that generality lies in the fact that, even if they are not legally binding as between the parties who sign them or with regard to the employment relationships which they govern, collective agreements nevertheless have important de facto consequences for the employment relationships to which they refer, particularly in so far as they determine the rights of the workers and, in the interests of industrial harmony, give undertakings some indication

of the conditions which employment relationships must satisfy or need not satisfy. The need to ensure that the directive is completely effective therefore requires that any clauses in such agreements which are incompatible with the obligations imposed by the directive on the member states may be rendered inoperative, eliminated or amended by appropriate means.

The second complaint

12. According to the United Kingdom, the exclusions from the prohibition of discrimination provided for in s 6(3) of the 1975 Act in the case of employment in a private household or in undertakings where the number of persons employed does not exceed five are justified by the exception provided for in art 2(2) of the directive itself, according to which—

> 'This Directive shall be without prejudice to the right of Member States to exclude from its field of application those occupational activities and, where appropriate, the training leading thereto, for which, by reason of their nature or the context in which they are carried out, the sex of the worker constitutes a determining factor.'

13. It must be recognised that the provision of the 1975 Act in question is intended, in so far as it refers to employment in a private household, to reconcile the principle of equality of treatment with the principle of respect for private life, which is also fundamental. Reconciliation of that kind is one of the factors which must be taken into consideration in determining the scope of the exception provided for in art 2(2) of the directive.

14. Whilst it is undeniable that, for certain kinds of employment in private households, that consideration may be decisive, that is not the case for all the kinds of employment in question.

15. As regards small undertakings with not more than five employees, the United Kingdom has not put forward any argument to show that in any undertaking of that size the sex of the worker would be a determining factor by reason of the nature of his activities or the context in which they are carried out.

16. Consequently, by reason of its generality, the exclusion provided for in the contested provision of the 1975 Act goes beyond the objective which may be lawfully pursued within the framework of art 2(2) of the directive.

The third complaint

17. The Commission's third complaint relates to the fact that the 1975 Act ensures access to the occupation of midwife and to training for that occupation only within certain limits. This is said to entail discrimination based on sex.

18. The United Kingdom acknowledges the facts. By virtue of para 3 of Sch 4 to the 1975 Act, until a day to be specified by order of the Secretary of State, men are granted access to the occupation in question and may be trained for that purpose only in certain specific places. This situation is due to the fact that in the United Kingdom the occupation in question is not traditionally engaged in by men. In a sphere in which respect for the patient's sensitivities is of particular importance, it considers that at the present time that limitation is in conformity with art 2(2) of the directive. However, it adds that it intends to proceed by stages and keep the position under review, in accordance with the obligations imposed by art 9(2) of the directive.

19. That provision requires member states periodically to assess the occupational activities referred to in art 2(2) in order to decide, in the light of social developments, whether there is justification for maintaining the permitted exclusions. They are to notify the Commission of the results of that assessment.

20. It is undeniable that in the area in question, as the United Kingdom acknowledges, the member states are under an obligation to implement the principle of equality of treatment. It must however be recognised that at the present time personal sensitivities may play an important role in relations between midwife and patient. In those

circumstances, it may be stated that, by failing fully to apply the principle laid down in the directive, the United Kingdom has not exceeded the limits of the power granted to the member states by arts 9(2) and 2(2) of the directive. The Commission's complaint in that regard cannot therefore be upheld.

21. It is apparent from all the foregoing considerations that, by failing to adopt in accordance with EEC Council Directive 76/207 of 9 February 1976 the measures needed to ensure that any provisions contrary to the principle of equality of treatment contained in collective agreements or in the internal rules of undertakings or in the rules governing the independent professions or occupations are to be, or may be declared, void or may be amended, and by excluding from the application of that principle employment for the purposes of a private household and any case where the number of persons employed does not exceed five, the United Kingdom has failed to fulfil its obligations under the EEC Treaty.

22. In all other respects, the application is dismissed.

Costs

23. Under art 69(2) of the Rules of Procedure, an unsuccessful party is to be ordered to pay the costs if they have been asked for in the successful party's pleadings. However, by virtue of para (3) of the same article, the court may order each party to bear its own costs if either of the parties is unsuccessful in one or more of its submissions.

24. It is appropriate to have recourse to that provision in this case, since the Commission has failed in one of its submissions.

For those reasons the court: (1) declares that, by failing to adopt in accordance with EEC Council Directive 76/207 of 9 February 1976 the measures needed to ensure that any provisions contrary to the principle of equality of treatment contained in collective agreements or in the rules of undertakings or in the rules governing the independent professions and occupations are to be, or may be declared, void or may be amended, and by excluding from the application of that principle employment for the purposes of a private household and any case where the number of persons employed does not exceed five, the United Kingdom has failed to fulfil its obligations under the EEC Treaty; (2) dismisses the application in all other respects; (3) orders each of the parties to bear its own costs.

Agents: *John Forman*, Legal Service of the EC Commission (for the Commission); J D Howes, Treasury Solicitor's Department (for the United Kingdom).

Mary Rose Plummer   Barrister.

Gillick v West Norfolk and Wisbech Area Health Authority and another

QUEEN'S BENCH DIVISION (CROWN OFFICE LIST)

WOOLF J

18, 19, 26 JULY 1983

National health service – Family planning clinics – Contraception – Circular containing guidance to area health authorities – Legality of advice contained in circular – Advice given regarding contraception for girls under 16 – Whether doctor should give advice and treatment on contraception to girl under 16 without parental consent – Whether doctor committing criminal offence or acting unlawfully by giving advice on contraception to girl under 16 – Whether doctor interfering with parental rights – Sexual Offences Act 1956, ss 6(1), 28(1)(3).

Minor – Medical treatment – Consent – Nature of consent which minor can give to medical treatment without obtaining parental consent.

The Department of Health and Social Security, in the exercise of its statutory functions, issued a circular to area health authorities containing guidance on the operation of the family planning service provided as part of the national health service. The departmental circular contained advice to the effect that a doctor consulted at a family planning clinic by a girl under 16 regarding the prescription of contraceptives would not be acting unlawfully if he prescribed contraceptives for the girl, so long as in doing so he was acting in good faith to protect her against the harmful effects of sexual intercourse. The circular further stated that, although a doctor should proceed on the assumption that advice and treatment on contraception should not be given to a girl under 16 without parental consent and that he should try to persuade the girl to involve her parents in the matter, nevertheless, the principle of confidentiality between doctor and patient applied to a girl under 16 seeking contraceptives and therefore in exceptional cases the doctor could prescribe contraceptives without consulting the girl's parents or obtaining their consent if in the doctor's clinical judgment it was desirable to prescribe contraceptives. The plaintiff, who had five daughters under the age of 16, sought an assurance from her local area health authority that her daughters would not be given advice and treatment on contraception without the plaintiff's prior knowledge and consent while they were under 16. When the authority refused to give such an assurance the plaintiff brought an action against the authority and the department seeking (i) as against both defendants a declaration that the advice contained in the circular was unlawful, because it amounted to advice to doctors to commit the offence of causing or encouraging unlawful sexual intercourse with a girl under 16, contrary to s 28[a] of the Sexual Offences Act 1956, or the offence of being an accessory to unlawful sexual intercourse with a girl under 16, contrary to s 6(1)[b] of the 1956 Act, and (ii) as against the authority a declaration that a doctor or other professional person employed by them in their family planning service could not give advice and treatment on contraception to any child of the plaintiff below the age of 16 without the plaintiff's consent, because to do so would be unlawful as being inconsistent with the plaintiff's parental rights. The plaintiff conceded that, in order to be entitled to the first declaration sought, she was required to show that a doctor who followed the advice contained in the circular would necessarily be committing a criminal offence or acting unlawfully.

Held – The plaintiff was not entitled to the declarations sought, and her action would be dismissed, for the following reasons—

---

a   Section 28, so far as material, is set out at p 371 *d e*, post

b   Section 6(1), so far as material, provides: 'It is an offence . . . for a man to have unlawful sexual intercourse with a girl under the age of sixteen.'

(1) A doctor at a family planning clinic who prescribed contraceptives to a girl under 16 in accordance with the advice contained in the department's circular would not *a* thereby be committing the offence of causing or encouraging unlawful sexual intercourse with the girl, contrary to s 28(1) of the 1956 Act, because, regardless of whether the doctor's conduct could be said to amount to encouraging unlawful sexual intercourse with the girl, she would not be in the doctor's 'care' for the purposes of s 28(3)(c) while he was treating her at the clinic and therefore he would not be 'responsible' for her for the purposes of s 28(1). Furthermore, in prescribing contraceptives for a girl under 16 a *b* doctor would not necessarily be committing the offence of being an accessory before the fact to a man's unlawful sexual intercourse with the girl, contrary to s 6(1) of the 1956 Act, because it would have to be proved that the doctor provided the girl with contraceptives with the intention of encouraging her to have sexual intercourse with a man, whereas in the majority of cases the probabilities were that the doctor would be against unlawful sexual intercourse with a girl under 16 and would only prescribe *c* contraceptives to a girl under 16 to protect her from unwanted pregnancy and sexually transmitted disease in circumstances where intercourse with her would take place whether or not the doctor prescribed contraceptives (see p 371 *b c* and *f* to *j*, p 373 *a* to *c* and p 375 *d e*, post); *National Coal Board v Gamble* [1958] 3 All ER 203 and *Lynch v DPP for Northern Ireland* [1975] 1 All ER 913 considered.

(2) A parent's interest in his or her child did not amount to a 'right' but was more *d* accurately described as a responsibility or duty. Accordingly, giving advice to a girl under 16 on contraception without her parents' consent was not unlawful interference with parental 'rights'. Furthermore, the prescribing of contraceptives to a girl under 16 without parental consent in those exceptional cases where such a course was recommended in the department's circular could only be unlawful if it amounted to trespass to the girl, ie a physical act done to her without consent, but a girl under 16 was herself capable of *e* giving consent to minor medical treatment such as the prescription of contraceptives, without the need to obtain parental consent, if she was a normally intelligent girl who was reasonably capable of assessing the advantages and disadvantages of the proposed treatment and giving effective consent to such treatment. It followed that neither the giving of advice on contraception to a girl under 16 without parental consent nor the prescription of contraceptives to a girl under 16 without parental consent if the girl *f* herself properly consented to the treatment would amount to unlawful conduct (see p 373 *e f* and *j* to p 374 *b* and p 375 *c* to *e*, post); *Johnston v Wellesley Hospital* (1970) 17 DLR (3d) 139 applied.

Notes

For causing or encouraging the commission of unlawful sexual intercourse with a girl under 16, see 11 Halsbury's Laws (4th edn) para 1066, and for cases on the subject, see 15 *g* Digest (Reissue) 1228, 10493–10496.

For unlawful sexual intercourse with a girl under 16, see 11 Halsbury's Laws (4th edn) para 1234, and for cases on the subject, see 15 Digest (Reissue) 1222–1224, 10454–10466.

For the Sexual Offences Act 1956, ss 6, 28, see 8 Halsbury's Statutes (3rd edn) 420, 432.

Cases referred to in judgment

A-G v Able [1984] 1 All ER 277, [1983] 3 WLR 845.
Hewer v Bryant [1969] 3 All ER 578, [1970] 1 QB 357, [1969] 3 WLR 425, CA.
Johnston v Wellesley Hospital (1970) 17 DLR (3d) 139, Ont HC.
Lynch v DPP for Northern Ireland [1975] 1 All ER 913, [1975] AC 653, [1975] 2 WLR 641, HL.
National Coal Board v Gamble [1958] 3 All ER 203, [1959] 1 QB 11, [1958] 3 WLR 434, *j* DC.
P (a minor), Re (1981) 80 LGR 301.
R v Bourne (1952) 36 Cr App R 125, CCA.
R v Cooper (1833) 5 C & P 535, 172 ER 1087, NP.
R v Tyrrell [1894] 1 QB 710, [1891–4] All ER Rep 1215, CCR.

Royal College of Nursing of the UK v Dept of Health and Social Security [1981] 1 All ER 545;
affd [1981] 1 All ER 545, [1981] AC 800, [1981] 2 WLR 279, CA; *affd* [1981] 1 All ER
545, [1981] AC 800, [1981] 2 WLR 279, HL.

Cases also cited
Chatterton v Gerson [1981] 1 All ER 257, [1981] QB 432.
D (a minor) (wardship: sterilisation), Re [1976] 1 All ER 326, [1976] Fam 185.
Parry-Jones v Law Society [1968] 1 All ER 177, [1969] 1 Ch 1, CA.
R v Allan [1963] 2 All ER 897, [1965] 1 QB 130, CCA.
R v Broadfoot [1976] 3 All ER 753, CA.
R v Cox (1884) 14 QBD 153, [1881–5] All ER Rep 68, CCR.
Thambiah v R [1965] 3 All ER 661, [1966] AC 37, PC.
Thornton v Mitchell [1940] 1 All ER 339, DC.

Action
By a writ issued on 5 August 1982 the plaintiff, Victoria Gillick, sought (1) as against the
defendants, Norfolk Area Health Authority (subsequently amended to West Norfolk and
Wisbech Area Health Authority) and the Department of Health and Social Security, a
declaration that on its true construction a Health Service notice (HN (80) 46) issued by
the department had no authority in law and gave advice which was unlawful, wrong and
adversely affected or might adversely affect the welfare of the plaintiff's children and/or
the rights of the plaintiff as parent and custodian of the children, and/or the ability of the
plaintiff properly and effectively to discharge her duties as parent and custodian, and (2)
as against the area health authority alone a declaration that no doctor or other professional
person employed by them in the family planning service or otherwise might give any
contraceptive and/or abortion advice and/or treatment to any child of the plaintiff below
the age of 16 without the plaintiff's prior knowledge and consent. Pursuant to the order
of Master Prebble dated 5 February 1983 the action was set down in the Crown Office
list. The facts are set out in the judgment.

Gerard Wright QC and *David Poole* for the plaintiff.
Simon D Brown for the department.
The area health authority were not represented.

Cur adv vult

26 July. The following judgment was delivered.

WOOLF J. The plaintiff, who is the mother of five daughters all below the age of 16,
and who resides in the area of the West Norfolk and Wisbech Area Health Authority,
brings these proceedings seeking two declarations in respect of a Health Service notice
(HN (80) 46) issued by the Department of Health and Social Security in December 1980
which was a revised version of part of an earlier notice (Health Service circular (interim
series) (HSC (IS) 32)) which was first issued in May 1974. The notice outlined the
arrangements to be made for the organisation and development of a comprehensive
family planning service within the national health service and it was accompanied by a
memorandum of guidance which dealt, inter alia, with family planning clinics. The
section of the memorandum which dealt with the young was section G. As it was part of
the plaintiff's case that the true effect of the advice could only be assessed when the
revised version was considered in the light of what it replaced, I should read out both
versions.
The first version was in the following terms:

'40. In 1972 there were 1,490 births and 2,804 induced abortions among resident
girls aged under 16; these figures are vivid reminders of the need for contraceptive

services to be available for and accessible to young people at risk of pregnancy, irrespective of age. It is for the doctor to decide whether to provide contraceptive *a* advice and treatment, and the Department is advised that if he does so for a girl under the age of 16, he is not acting unlawfully provided he acts in good faith in protecting the girl against the potentially harmful effects of intercourse. The Department is also advised that other professional workers who refer, advise or persuade a girl under 16 years of age to go to a doctor in his surgery or at a clinic or elsewhere for the purpose of obtaining contraceptive advice and treatment would *b* not, by such act alone, be acting unlawfully.

41. The Medical Defence Union have advised that the parents of a child, of whatever age, should not be contacted by any staff without his or her permission even though as a matter of clinical judgment the refusal of permission to involve the parents may affect the nature of the advice given to the child. Nevertheless it would always be prudent to seek the patient's consent to tell the parents . . .'   *c*

There is then an extract from the Report of the Committee on the Working of the Abortion Act (the Lane Committee) (Cmnd 5579 (1974)) dealing with contraception, parental consent and confidentiality. I read part of it (para 243):

'. . . If the girl refuses this permission, the doctor has three alternative courses open to him: he may break confidentiality with the girl in order to obtain her *d* parents' consent to the treatment; he may refuse to continue with the treatment in the absence of consent by the parents, and so fail to give the girl the care which he considers medically necessary and leave her at risk of becoming pregnant; or he may continue with the treatment without parental consent. The last course may involve a technical assault if a vaginal examination is undertaken or an intra-uterine device is fitted; but no action has hitherto been taken against a doctor in such circumstances *e* and we express no opinion as to whether legal or disciplinary proceedings would be likely to be successful. The doctor in each individual case has to balance his obligation of confidentiality against the desirability that, unusual circumstances apart, the parents of a child should be informed of, and agree to, the treatment given to her. This is of particular importance where a young girl has already had an abortion. The doctor may also be influenced by the knowledge that other girls may *f* be deterred from seeking necessary medical advice if they feel that their confidence may not be respected.'

With regard to this version, counsel for the plaintiff submits that it amounts to the department openly encouraging the provision of advice and contraceptives to girls under 16, with whom it is illegal to have sexual intercourse, that the advice suggests that it is *g* for the doctor, and not for the parents of the child, to decide whether the girl under 16 should be provided with contraceptive advice and treatment, and that the doctor can be a doctor at a clinic who may not have any previous knowledge of the girl so that he is wholly ill-equipped to deal with the socio-psychological problems involved in deciding whether or not to provide contraceptive advice or treatment. Counsel for the plaintiff also submits that the advice on the law which is given is wrong and that it wholly *h* disregards the legitimate interest of the parents of the girl in question.

The revised version of December 1980 reads as follows:

'There is widespread concern about counselling and treatment for children under 16. Special care is needed not to undermine parental responsibility and family stability. The Department would therefore hope that in any case where a doctor or other professional worker is approached by a person under the age of 16 for advice *j* in these matters, the doctor, or other professional, will always seek to persuade the child to involve the parent or guardian (or other person in loco parentis) at the earliest stage of consultation, and will proceed from the assumption that it would be most unusual to provide advice about contraception without parental consent. It is, however, widely accepted that consultations between doctors and patients are confidential; and the Department recognises the importance which doctors and patients attach to this principle. It is a principle which applies also to the other professions concerned. To abandon this principle for children under 16 might cause some not to seek professional advice at all. They could then be exposed to the immediate risks of pregnancy and of sexually-transmitted disease, as well as other long-term physical, psychological and emotional consequences which are equally a threat to stable family life. This would apply particularly to young people whose parents are, for example, unconcerned, entirely unresponsive, or grossly disturbed. Some of these young people are away from their parents and in the care of local authorities or voluntary organisations standing in loco parentis. The Department realises that in such exceptional cases the nature of any counselling must be a matter for the doctor or other professional worker concerned and that the decision whether or not to prescribe contraception must be for the clinical judgment of a doctor.'

Counsel for the plaintiff, although recognising that the revised section G is an improvement on its predecessor, submits it still has the same defects. It still encourages the giving of advice and treatment to children under 16 without consulting their parents. It still leaves the final decision, whether or not to prescribe contraception to the clinical judgment of the doctor. The legal advice is not changed and, while it expresses the 'hope' that the doctor will seek to persuade the child to involve the parents, it clearly is recommending that advice can be given without parental consent.

Having regard to the contents of the guidance, the plaintiff wrote a series of letters to the area health authority seeking an assurance that—

'in no circumstances whatever will any of my daughters. . . be given contraceptive or abortion treatment whilst they are under sixteen, in any of the Family Planning Clinics under your control, without my prior knowledge, and irrefutable evidence of my consent? Also, should any of them seek advice in them, can I have your assurance that I would be automatically contacted in the interests of my children's safety and welfare.'

In a subsequent letter dated 29 January 1981 the plaintiff again wrote to the area health authority enclosing a copy of an article which indicated that in the Suffolk Area Health Authority, in the event of a parent registering his or her objection to a minor receiving contraceptive advice, this would be honoured.

In their response, and in particular in a letter of 19 February 1981, the area health authority made it clear that they were acting in accordance with the guidance contained in the circular from the department. The authority did go on to say that it was—

'prepared to make your wishes known to the Family Planning Clinic in Wisbech and the two clinics in Kings Lynn because we fully accept that special care is needed not to undermine parental responsibility and family stability. [The letter however went on to say:] what I cannot do is to give you a categorical assurance in the terms you request because we believe it is widely accepted that consultations between doctors and patients are confidential and therefore the final decision must be for the doctor's clinical judgment.'

Not being satisfied with this offer, the plaintiff commenced these proceedings. The statement of claim, in para 7, sets out the particulars of her complaints and the declarations which she seeks in these terms:

'The said Notice, which has no authority in law, gives advice which is unlawful and wrong and which adversely affects or which may adversely affect the welfare of the Plaintiff's said children, and/or the rights of the Plaintiff as parent and custodian of the said children.

PARTICULARS

The said advice: (a) condones and/or encourages and/or recommends and/or directs the giving of contraceptive or abortion advice to a child below the age of 16, thereby contemplating the fact or the possibility of a criminal offence against such child, namely the offence of unlawful sexual intercourse with an infant; further, it contemplates the barring of the parent and/or custodian of such child from access to information necessary for the proper and effective discharge of his or her duties towards such child, and in particular the duties of supervising the physical and moral welfare of such child; (b) permits and/or advises a doctor to conduct a physical examination on a child below the age of 16 and/or to prescribe and/or administer drugs to such child without the prior knowledge or consent of the said child's parent or guardian; (c) condones and/or encourages and/or connives at unlawful conduct on the part of males over the age of 14 against female children below the age of 16, namely the committing of offences of unlawful sexual intercourse with an infant.'

The plaintiff claims:

'(i) a declaration against the First Defendants and the Second Defendants on a true construction of the said Notice and in the events which have happened, including and in particular the publication and the circulation of the said Notice, the said Notice has no authority in law and gives advice which is unlawful and wrong, and which adversely affects or which may adversely affect the welfare of the Plaintiff's said children, and/or the rights of the Plaintiff as parent and custodian of the said children, and/or the ability of the Plaintiff properly and effectively to discharge her duties as such parent and custodian; (ii) a declaration against the First Defendants that no doctor or other professional person employed by the First Defendants either in the Family Planning Service or otherwise may give any contraceptive and/or abortion advice and/or treatment to any child of the Plaintiff below the age of 16 without the prior knowledge and/or consent of the said child's parent or guardian.'

There are two principal limbs to the argument of counsel for the plaintiff. The first is that the guidance advises doctors either to commit offences as principals of causing or encouraging unlawful sexual intercourse with a girl under 16 contrary to s 28 of the Sexual Offences Act 1956, or offences of being an accessory to unlawful sexual intercourse with a girl under the age of 16 contrary to s 6 of the 1956 Act. The second limb is that the guidance authorises doctors to give advice and treatment to children under 16 without their parents' consent, which, if it is not a criminal offence under the foregoing provisions, is inconsistent with the rights of the parents of that child and the ability of the parents properly and effectively to discharge their duties as parents of supervising the physical and moral welfare of their children.

Having regard to the first limb of the argument, counsel for the department raises the general question as to the propriety of the court granting a declaration because of the involvement of the criminal law. He reminded me about what I said on this subject in *A-G v Able* [1984] 1 All ER 277, [1984] 3 WLR 845 (the 'Exit' case). Although I am mindful of the dangers of trespassing on the jurisdiction of the criminal courts, I do not consider that I should be inhibited from dealing with the issues raised in this action. It has not been suggested that the plaintiff was acting inappropriately by commencing these proceedings in the ordinary way by writ rather than by an application for judicial review, and the propriety of considering the issues is indicated by the fact that the declarations which the plaintiff seeks could have been applied for on an application under RSC Ord 53. In issuing the guidance, the department were exercising their statutory functions and, if in the course of so doing they were giving advice which was unlawful or, more accurately, if the advice, if followed, would result in unlawful acts, then their decision to do so could be challenged on the conventional ground that it was wholly unreasonable to exercise their discretion to give advice with this result. Although distinctions can be drawn between this case and *Royal College of Nursing of the UK v Dept of Health and Social Security* [1981] 1 All ER 545, [1981] AC 800, I do not see any real distinction between the department in that case seeking a declaration that the advice *a* which they were giving was lawful and the plaintiff in this case seeking a declaration that the advice would result in acts which were unlawful. It was not contended that the giving of the advice itself amounted to a crime.

Counsel for the department makes a second point with regard to the form of relief which is being sought which I consider has more substance and which was not contested: that, unless the plaintiff can show that the result of following the department's advice is the commission of a criminal offence by a doctor or unlawful conduct by a doctor, the

b plaintiff is not entitled to the declarations which she seeks. In this I regard counsel for the department as being substantially correct. If the doctor could exercise his clinical judgment to give advice and to prescribe contraceptives without committing an offence or otherwise acting unlawfully, then it cannot be said that the department have acted either unlawfully or unreasonably in leaving the ultimate decision, at least in exceptional cases, to the doctor, since the department must be entitled to assume that their advice

c would only be followed in a lawful manner where this is possible and reasonably practical.

I will now deal with the two limbs of the plaintiff's argument. It will be appreciated that in doing so I am only concerned with the legality of the department's guidance. It is not my task to express any view as to the advisability or morality of the department's conduct.

Does the prescribing of contraceptives to a girl under 16 amount to criminal conduct on the part
d *of a doctor?*

Section 28(1) of the Sexual Offences Act 1956 makes it—

> 'an offence for a person to cause or encourage . . . the commission of unlawful sexual intercourse with . . . a girl under the age of sixteen for whom he is responsible.'

e Subsection (3) provides:

> 'The persons who are to be treated for the purposes of this section as responsible for a girl are . . . (c) any other person who has the custody, charge or care of her.'

Putting aside the question of whether or not the doctor's conduct could be said to amount to encouraging unlawful sexual intercourse, I cannot accept the submission of

f counsel for the plaintiff that when a girl goes to a clinic for advice and/or treatment she is in the ad hoc care of the doctor or the clinic. The words should not be narrowly construed but, in my view, they are inappropriate to cover a situation where a girl attends a clinic to seek help.

So far as the offence against s 6 of the 1956 Act is concerned, I accept that a doctor who is misguided enough to provide a girl who is under the age of 16, or a man, with advice

g and assistance with regard to contraceptive measures with the intention thereby of encouraging them to have sexual intercourse is an accessory before the fact to an offence contrary to s 6. I stress the words 'with the intention thereby of encouraging them to have sexual intercourse'. However, this, I assume, will not usually be the attitude of a doctor.

There will certainly be some cases, and I hope the majority of cases, where the doctor

h decides to give the advice and prescribe contraceptives despite the fact he was firmly against unlawful sexual intercourse taking place but felt nevertheless that he had to prescribe the contraceptives because, whether or not he did so, intercourse would in fact take place, and the provision of contraceptives would, in his view, be in the best interests of the girl in protecting her from an unwanted pregnancy and the risk of a sexually transmitted disease. It is whether or not in such a situation the doctor is to be treated as

j being an accessory that I have found the greatest difficulty in applying the law.

Counsel for the plaintiff submits, and I accept that he is right in this submission, that it is necessary to distinguish between motive and intent. Even if your motives are unimpeachable, if you in fact assist in the commission of an offence, counsel submits you are an accessory. He relies on the judgment of Devlin J in *National Coal Board v Gamble* [1958] 3 All ER 203 at 207, [1959] 1 QB 11 at 20. In that case, Devlin J said:

'A person who supplies the instrument for a crime or anything essential to its commission, aids in the commission of it; and if he does so knowingly and with *a* intent to aid, he abets it as well and is therefore guilty of aiding and abetting ... Another way of putting the point is to say that aiding and abetting is a crime that requires proof of mens rea, that is to say, of intention to aid as well as of knowledge of the circumstances, and that proof of the intent involves proof of a positive act of assistance voluntarily done.'

Devlin J's judgment in that case was considered by Lord Simon in *Lynch v DPP for* *b* *Northern Ireland* [1975] 1 All ER 913 at 941–942, [1975] AC 653 at 698–699:

'As regards the actus reus, "aiding" and "abetting" are, as Smith and Hogan note (*Criminal Law* (3rd edn, 1973) p 93), synonymous. But the phrase is not a pleonasm; because "abet" clearly imports mens rea, which "aid" might not. As Devlin J said in *National Coal Board v Gamble* [and he quotes the passage I have just quoted]. The *c* actus reus is the supplying of an instrument for a crime or anything essential for its commission. On Devlin J's analysis the mens rea does not go beyond this. The act of supply must be voluntary (in the sense I tried to define earlier in the speech), and it must be foreseen that the instrument or other object or service supplied will probably be used for the commission of a crime. The definition of the crime does not in itself suggest any ulterior intent; and whether anything further in the way of *d* mens rea was required was precisely the point at issue in *Gamble's* case. Slade J thought the very concept of aiding and abetting imported the concept of motive. But Lord Goddard CJ and Devlin J disagreed with this. So do I. Slade J thought that abetting involved assistance or encouragement, and that both implied motive. So far as assistance is concerned, this is clearly not so. One may lend assistance without any motive, or even with the motive of bringing about a result directly contrary to *e* that in fact assisted by one's effort.'

However in applying those statements of the law, three matters have to be borne in mind. First of all, contraceptives do not in themselves directly assist in the commission of the crime of unlawful sexual intercourse. The analogy of providing the motor car for a burglary or providing poison to the murderer, relied on in argument, are not true *f* comparisons. While, if the man wears a sheath, there may be said to be a physical difference as to the quality of intercourse, the distinction that I am seeking to draw is clearer where the woman takes the pill or is fitted with an internal device, when the unlawful act will not be affected in any way. The only effect of the provision of the means of contraception is that in some cases it is likely to increase the likelihood of a crime being committed by reducing the inhibitions of the persons concerned to having *g* sexual intercourse because of their fear of conception or the contraction of disease. I therefore see a distinction between the assistance or aiding referred to by Lord Simon and Devlin J and the act of the doctor in prescribing contraceptives. I would regard the pill prescribed to the woman as not so much 'the instrument for a crime or anything essential to its commission' but a palliative against the consequences of the crime.

The second factor that has to be borne in mind is that the girl herself commits no *h* offence under s 6 since the section is designed to protect her from herself: see *R v Tyrrell* [1894] 1 QB 710, [1891–4] All ER Rep 1215. This creates problems with regard to relying on any encouragement by the doctor as making him the accessory to the offence where the girl alone attends the clinic. The well-known case of *R v Bourne* (1952) 36 Cr App R 125 has to be distinguished, because there the woman can be said to have committed the offence although she was not criminally responsible because of duress. *j* The doctor, if he is to be an accessory where the woman alone consults him, will only be an accessory if it can be shown that he acted through the innocent agency of the woman, the situation dealt with in *R v Cooper* (1833) 5 C & P 535, 172 ER 1087.

The final point that has to be borne in mind is that there will be situations where long-term contraceptive measures are taken to protect girls who, sadly, will strike up promiscuous relationships whatever the supervision of those who are responsible for a their well-being, the sort of situation that Butler-Sloss J had to deal with in *Re P* (*a minor*) (1981) 80 LGR 301. In such a situation the doctor will prescribe the measures to be taken purely as a safeguard against the risk that at some time in the future the girl will form a casual relationship with a man when sexual intercourse will take place. In order to be an accessory, you normally have to know the material circumstances. In such a situation the doctor would know no more than that there was a risk of sexual intercourse taking place at an unidentified place with an unidentified man on an unidentified date, hardly the

b state of knowledge which is normally associated with an accessory before the fact.

Under this limb of the argument, the conclusion which I have therefore come to is that, while a doctor could, in following the guidance, so encourage unlawful sexual intercourse as to render his conduct criminal, in the majority of situations the probabilities are that a doctor will be able to follow the advice without rendering himself liable to criminal proceedings. Before leaving this limb of the argument, I should make it

c absolutely clear that the absence of consent of the parents makes no difference to the criminal responsibility of the doctor. If his conduct would be criminal without the parents' consent, it would be equally criminal with their consent.

Is the giving of advice or the prescribing of contraceptives without parental consent unlawful?

Turning to the second limb of the argument, this only arises in what is described in the revised section G as 'exceptional cases' which are left to the clinical judgment of a

d doctor. Unlike the first limb of the argument, this argument cannot apply when, in what is assumed in the guidance to be the usual situation, the advice about contraception will take place with parental consent, so there can be no interference with the 'rights' of the parents.

For advice to be given and contraceptives prescribed without their consent, counsel for the plaintiff submitted, would be inconsistent with the fundamental rights of the parents.

e However he cited no authority to establish such 'rights', and the interest of parents, I consider, are more accurately described as responsibilities or duties. The interference in the exceptional case with 'parental rights' could only make the doctor's acts unlawful if his conduct also amounts to a trespass. This limb can only therefore apply where the doctor does some physical act to the child without there being a consent which would amount to a defence for the purpose of the law of trespass.

f It is most surprising that there is no previous authority of the courts in this country whether a child under 16 can consent to medical treatment. So far as minors over the age of 16 are concerned, the Family Law Reform Act 1969 provides in s 8(1):

> 'The consent of a minor who has attained the age of sixteen years to any surgical, medical or dental treatment which, in the absence of consent, would constitute a

g > trespass to his person, shall be as effective as it would be if he were of full age . . .'

However, s 8(3) provides:

> 'Nothing in this section shall be construed as making ineffective any consent which would have been effective if this section had not been enacted.'

h The 1969 Act was passed in consequence of a Report of the Committee on the Age of Majority (the Latey Committee) (Cmnd 3342 (1967)). The relevant parts of that report have been put before me and it is stated (para 479):

> '. . . increasingly at the present time it is becoming customary to accept the consent of minors aged 16 and over. There is no rigid rule of English law which renders a minor incapable of giving his consent to an operation but there seems to

j > be no direct judicial authority establishing that the consent of such a person is valid.'

In the absence of binding authority, the position seems to me to be as follows. The fact that a child is under the age of 16 does not mean automatically that she cannot give consent to any treatment. Whether or not a child is capable of giving the necessary consent will depend on the child's maturity and understanding and the nature of the consent which is required. The child must be capable of making a reasonable assessment of the advantages and disadvantages of the treatment proposed, so the consent if given can be properly and fairly described as a true consent. If the child is not capable of giving consent, then her parents can do so on the child's behalf. If what is involved is some treatment of a minor nature, and the child is of normal intelligence and approaching 16, it will be easier to show that the child is capable of giving the necessary consent; it will be otherwise if the implications of the treatment are long-term. Taking an extreme case, I would have thought it is unlikely that a child under the age of 16 will ever be regarded by the courts as being capable of giving consent to sterilisation.

In so propounding the approach, I respectfully adopt the judgment of Addy J of the Ontario High Court in *Johnston v Wellesley Hospital* (1970) 17 DLR (3d) 139. I would quote from his judgment (at 143–145) and would particularly rely on the passage quoted from Nathan *Medical Negligence* (1957):

'The new question which requires consideration is whether a consent was required from the parents or guardian of the plaintiff previous to the medical procedure being undertaken by the doctor, or, more specifically, whether the plaintiff, being an infant, was capable at law of giving his consent to the treatment, for, if he was capable at law of giving his consent and did in fact give it, there would, of course, be no necessity of obtaining any parental consent. The question of consent, of course, is very relevant to the case because, if there was no legal consent, the treatment administered by the doctor would constitute an actionable assault, the question of negligence would not enter into consideration, and liability, in so far as the doctor at least is concerned, would flow automatically in the circumstances of the present case. There is, of course, no question here of this being an emergency treatment of the kind which would justify a doctor acting without consent in order to preserve life or to prevent a serious impairment of the patient's health. Treatment could easily have been postponed to obtain parental consent, if required. Also, parental consent could easily have been obtained between the time of the original visit and interview and that of the actual treatment. There is no doubt that the plaintiff in fact consented to receiving treatment by the carbon dioxide slush method for, as stated previously, he specifically requested it, although, as pointed out later, the actual technique used by Dr. Williams was somewhat different from the technique previously used. Although the common law imposes very strict limitations on the capacity of persons under 21 years of age to hold, or rather to divest themselves of, property or to enter into contracts concerning matters other than necessities, it would be ridiculous in this day and age, where the voting age is being reduced generally to 18 years, to state that a person of 20 years of age, who is obviously intelligent and as fully capable of understanding the possible consequences of a medical or surgical procedure as an adult, would, at law, be incapable of consenting thereto. But, regardless of modern trend, I can find nothing in any of the old reported cases, except where infants of tender age or young children were involved, where the Courts have found that a person under 21 years of age was legally incapable of consenting to medical treatment. If a person under 21 years were unable to consent to medical treatment, he would also be incapable of consenting to other types of bodily interference. A proposition purporting to establish that any bodily interference acquiesced in by a youth of 20 years would nevertheless constitute an assault would be absurd. If such were the case, sexual intercourse with a girl under 21 years would constitute rape. Until the minimum age of consent to sexual acts was fixed at 14 years by a statute, the Courts often held that infants were capable of consenting at a considerably earlier age than 14 years. I feel that the law on this point is well expressed in the volume on *Medical Negligence* (1957), by Lord Nathan, p. 176: "It is suggested that the most satisfactory solution of the problem is to rule that an infant who is capable of appreciating fully the nature and consequences of a particular operation or of particular treatment can give an effective consent thereto, and in such cases the consent of the guardian is unnecessary; but that where the infant is without that capacity, any apparent consent by him or her will be a nullity, the sole right to consent being vested in the guardian." '

Counsel for the plaintiff submitted that the explanation for the absence of authority is that at least in Victorian times it would never have been suggested that anything but parental consent would suffice for a child under 16. I do not know whether he is justified in making this submission, though I recognise that he could be. However, even assuming that he is right, it does not mean that I am required to ignore the change in attitudes since the Victorian era. I would respectfully rely for support on the vivid language of Lord Denning MR in *Hewer v Bryant* [1969] 3 All ER 578 at 582, [1970] 1 QB 357 at 369 where he said: 'The common law can, and should, keep pace with the times.' (I would add 'where there is no authority to the contrary'.)

The quality of the consent of the child will therefore be critical where the parents have not consented and the conduct of the doctor would otherwise be trespass. This will not apply to the majority of methods of contraception. However, whether it does so or not, it should not be thought, as a result of anything I have said, that I disagree with the clear advice given in the revised circular that in every case it 'would be most unusual to provide advice about or methods of contraception without parental consent'. However, having regard to that advice, I find that there is nothing unlawful in the department recognising that in the exceptional case there remains a discretion for the clinical judgment of a doctor whether or not to prescribe contraception.

This means that, as the law stands at present, the plaintiff is not entitled to either of the declarations which she seeks. I appreciate that my decision will be extremely disturbing not only to the plaintiff, but to many others who are naturally very concerned about the provision of contraceptive advice and treatment to those under 16.

However, to put my decision in context, I would stress the following points. Firstly, if the department's guidance is followed, it should only be in the exceptional cases that parents are not consulted. In the normal case of concerned parents, such as the plaintiff, if the department's guidance is followed, they will be consulted. Secondly, as is indicated in this case, some area health authorities are prepared to register with the local clinics the view of parents. Thirdly, even in the exceptional cases, the doctor, according to the guidance, has to exercise his residual discretion. In many matters concerning our health, we have to rely on doctors to act responsibly and, in this area, it is to be expected that the doctors will exercise their responsibility, which is a heavy one, in a proper manner. In this regard, the plaintiff has in this case obtained confirmation, if confirmation was necessary, that doctors can be guilty of a criminal offence if they intentionally encourage unlawful sexual intercourse, and doctors will no doubt bear this in mind in exercising their responsibility. Finally, if, contrary to my conclusions, the plaintiff had been right in what I regard as being her principal argument, the result would not have been to substitute in those exceptional cases the discretion of the parents for that of the doctor, but to prevent children under 16 being lawfully provided with contraceptives in any circumstances.

The statistics to which I have referred, even in 1972, of pregnancies among the very young indicate to those whose religious beliefs do not dictate the contrary that some of those children, at any rate, were very much in need of assistance in avoiding such pregnancies. The need must be even greater today and, at least as a result of my conclusions, the help will still be available, although, in the exceptional case, it may be provided without parental consent.

Action dismissed.

Solicitors: *Berrymans*, agents for *Ollard & Bentley*, March (for the plaintiff); *Treasury Solicitor*.

Dilys Tausz   Barrister.

Sport International Bussum BV and others v Inter-Footwear Ltd

COURT OF APPEAL, CIVIL DIVISION

ACKNER AND OLIVER LJJ

9, 10, 17 NOVEMBER 1983

Equity – Forfeiture – Relief – Jurisdiction of court – Circumstances in which relief will be granted – Licence granted to defendants to use certain names and trade marks – Licence terminated on failure of defendants to provide guarantee for payment as provided by agreement – Whether court having jurisdiction to grant relief against forfeiture – Whether equitable relief applicable to contract unconnected with interest in land.

By an agreement dated 15 June 1982 the plaintiffs granted licences to the defendants to use certain names and trade marks in consideration for the defendants paying £105,000 in three instalments. It was further agreed that the defendants would provide guarantees for the second and third instalments 'immediately upon payment'. If the defendants failed to pay any instalment on its due date or failed to furnish either guarantee, the whole sum would become due and the licence would terminate forthwith. The defendants failed to provide the second guarantee until a fortnight after the payment of the second instalment. The plaintiffs sought judgment for the whole outstanding balance and a declaration that the licences had been terminated. The judge held (i) that as a matter of construction the stipulation calling for the guarantee to be given 'immediately upon payment' was one in respect of which time was of the essence, and (ii) that there was no jurisdiction in the court to grant relief from the termination of the licence. The defendants appealed, contending (i) that the jurisdiction to relieve against forfeiture was not confined to any particular type of case and was appropriate where the forfeiture provision was one inserted with the object of securing the payment of money or a stated result which could still be effectively attained when the matter was referred to court, and (ii) that the phrase 'immediately upon payment' did not mean simultaneously with payment but meant no more than as soon as possible after payment.

Held – The court would not extend the equitable jurisdiction to grant relief against forfeiture to ordinary commercial contracts unconnected with interests in land, or to contracts creating interests in other property, corporeal or incorporeal, since it was doubtful whether, outside the sphere of landlord and tenant, the jurisdiction could be exercised in a case where the forfeited interest depended on contract only and where relief would in effect involve specifically performing that contract. Furthermore, the phrase 'immediately upon payment' in the agreement contemplated either a minimal or at least a very short time after the fixed date, and on the time construction of the contract time was intended to be of the essence. It followed that the judge had been right to refuse the relief sought by the defendants. The appeal would accordingly be dismissed (see p 379 h j, p 380 a to c, p 382 e and p 384 a b and j to p 385 d and h j, post).

Dictum of Robert Goff LJ in *Scandinavian Trading Tanker Co AB v Flota Petrolera Ecuatoriana, The Scaptrade* [1983] 1 All ER at 307–309 applied.

Shiloh Spinners Ltd v Harding [1973] 1 All ER 90 and *Scandinavian Trading Tanker Co AB v Flota Petrolera Ecuatoriana, The Scaptrade* [1983] 2 All ER 763 considered.

Notes

For relief against forfeiture, see 16 Halsbury's Laws (4th edn) paras 1447–1451, and for cases on the subject, see 20 Digest (Reissue) 898–899, 6695–6703.

Cases referred to in judgments

Afovos Shipping AS v R Pagnan & Flli, The Afovos [1980] 2 Lloyd's Rep 469; *rvsd* [1982] 3 All ER 18, [1982] 1 WLR 848, CA.

Barton Thompson & Co Ltd v Stapling Machines Co [1966] 2 All ER 222, [1966] Ch 499,
a   [1966] 2 WLR 1429.
Coatsworth v Johnson (1886) 55 LJQB 220, [1886–90] All ER Rep 547, CA.
Dendy v Evans [1910] 1 KB 263, [1908–10] All ER Rep 589, CA.
Mardorf Peach & Co Ltd v Attica Sea Carriers Corp of Liberia, The Laconia [1977] 1 All ER
    545, [1977] AC 850, [1977] 2 WLR 286, HL,
Peachy v Duke of Somerset (1721) 1 Stra 447, 93 ER 626.
b   *Scandinavian Trading Tanker Co AB v Flota Petrolera Ecuatoriana, The Scaptrade* [1983] 2
    All ER 763, [1983] 2 AC 694, [1983] 3 WLR 203, HL; *affg* [1983] 1 All ER 301, [1983]
    QB 529, [1983] 2 WLR 248, CA.
Shiloh Spinners Ltd v Harding [1973] 1 All ER 90, [1973] AC 691, [1973] 2 WLR 28, HL.
Starside Properties Ltd v Mustapha [1974] 2 All ER 567, [1974] 1 WLR 816, CA.
Stockloser v Johnson [1954] 1 All ER 630, [1954] 1 QB 476, [1954] 2 WLR 439, CA.
c   *Swain v Ayres* (1888) 21 QBD 289, CA.

Interlocutory appeal

The defendants, Inter-Footwear Ltd, appealed with leave of the judge against the order of
Staughton J made on 12 October 1983 whereby he granted leave to the first plaintiffs,
Sport International Bussum BV, to enter judgment for £35,000 against the defendants
d   and declared that a licence which had been granted by an agreement made between the
defendants on the one hand and the first plaintiffs, the second plaintiffs, Inter-Shoe (Hong
Kong) Ltd, and the third plaintiff, Heleen Margreet Alten-Van Zeggelaar (for and on
behalf of the estate of Frits Alten deceased), on the other hand, which agreement was
contained in the schedule to a consent order made on 18 June 1982, had been terminated.
The facts are set out in the judgment of the court.

e

Leonard Hoffmann QC and *Jonathan Turner* for the defendants.
Colin Ross-Munro QC and *Michael Burton* for the plaintiffs.

Cur adv vult

f   17 November. The following judgment of the court was delivered.

OLIVER LJ. This is an appeal with the leave of the judge from an order of Staughton J
made in the Commercial Court on 12 October 1983 granting leave to the first plaintiff to
enter judgment against the defendants for a sum of £35,000 and declaring that a licence
granted by an agreement contained in the schedule to a consent order made on 18 June
g   1982 had been determined.

The order was made on the application of the first plaintiff under the liberty to apply
contained in the consent order referred to, that order being simply an order in the
Tomlin form staying all further proceedings in the action on scheduled terms save for
the purpose of carrying the terms into effect, for which purpose liberty to apply was
reserved in the order.

h   The action in which this order was made was one of a number of sets of proceedings
between the plaintiffs and the defendants and in it the plaintiffs claimed something in
excess of £120,000 in respect of unpaid commissions together with various other
substantial sums by way of damages. It is evident from the terms contained in the
schedule to the order that they were intended to put an end to the whole of the litigation
between the plaintiffs and the defendants on payment to the plaintiffs of an aggregate
j   sum considerably less than the total claimed in the action.

The schedule begins with a series of definitions, the material ones for present purposes
being that the plaintiffs were defined as 'SI' and the defendants as 'IF'. There was also a
reference to various trade names and trade marks which were compendiously defined as
'the Names and Trademarks'.

The material clauses for present purposes were nos 3, 4, 5, 8, 9, 13 and 17, which were,
respectively, in the following terms:

'3. IF agrees to pay SI the sum of £105,000 in three instalments as follows: (a) £35,000 on the signing hereof ("the First Instalment"); (b) £35,000 on 14 June 1983 ("the Second Instalment"); (c) £35,000 on 14 June 1984 ("the Third Instalment").

4. IF shall pay each instalment by bankers' draft delivered to SI's solicitors on or before the date for its payment.

5. IF shall furnish two guarantees issued by Nedbank Limited in a form approved by SI's Solicitors; (a) The first forthwith (to secure the payment of the Second Instalment); (b) The second immediately upon payment of the Second Instalment (to secure the payment of the Third Instalment): for this purpose, IF shall forthwith irrevocably instruct the said Bank to provide such guarantee on the date the Second Instalment is paid, and to appropriate thereto on such date such of IF's security as the said Bank may hold to secure the payment of the Second Instalment (or such equivalent security as the said Bank may require) . . .

8. SI licenses IF for a period of two years from the date hereof to use the Names and Trademarks for the sale of sports shoes, boots and leisure footwear. [There follows an enumeration of territories in which IF was to have an exclusive licence and an enumeration of other territories in which it was to have a licence concurrently with SI.]

9. SI hereby agrees to IF having concurrent use of the emblem in all jurisdictions of the world as from 15 June 1984 upon condition that:—(a) IF shall have informed SI's solicitors in writing by 4 p.m. on 14 June 1983 of its intention to use the emblem; and (b) IF shall have paid the sum of £5,000 to SI's Solicitors by 4 p.m. on 14 June 1984 . . .

13. If IF fails to pay any instalments on its due date (as provided in Paragraph 3) or duly to furnish either guarantee (as provided in Paragraph 5): (a) the full unpaid balance of the sum of £105,000 shall forthwith become due and payable, and SI may enter judgment and, so far as necessary, execute against IF for such balance, and (b) the licences referred to in Paragraph 8 and the right referred to in Paragraph 12 shall forthwith determine . . .

17. This Agreement is in full and final settlement of all claims, actions, proceedings and demands whatsoever, wheresoever and howsoever arising and whether known or unknown between SI and its Associates and IF which they had, have, or at any future time may have against each other arising out of any dealings prior to the date hereof.'

The first sum of £35,000 was duly paid and the instructions referred to in cl 5(b) were given to the defendants' bankers, Nedbank, which duly issued a guarantee for the instalment due on 14 June 1983.

Thereafter, nothing of any materiality occurred until 13 June 1983 when the defendants, no doubt mindful of the strict time limit imposed by cl 9 of the terms, gave written notice of their intention to use the emblem therein referred to. Although addressed to the plaintiffs' solicitors, it seems in fact to have been sent (with a duplicate) via the defendants' then solicitor, Mr Wood, who, on 14 June, sent it on to the plaintiffs' solicitors under cover of a letter which was delivered by hand and which contained also a banker's draft for the sum of £35,000 due on that day. It does not seem to have occurred to Mr Wood that there might be any difficulty about the provision of the guarantee called for under cl 5(b) and his letter merely asked: 'Kindly acknowledge safe receipt of the above and return the duplicate of our clients' letter duly signed to ourselves.' In the event, nothing further was done about the guarantee, Mr Wood having apparently failed to appreciate that the bank, which had security only to meet the first guarantee given on the conclusion of the settlement terms, would be unlikely to be willing to issue a further guarantee for payment of a like sum on 14 June 1984 until it had received an assurance that its original guarantee had been discharged. Thus, although the second instalment due under cl 3 was duly paid on 14 June 1983, although not via Nedbank, the defendants in fact defaulted in providing the guarantee called for by cl 5(b). That default continued until 27 June. On 20 June the plaintiffs' solicitors wrote drawing attention to the default and announcing that they intended to apply for judgment for the outstanding £35,000, cl 13 having now come into effect, and that they considered the licences granted by cl 8 to have determined. This stimulated a response from Mr Wood to the extent of challenging the assertion that his clients were in default, but it signally failed to produce a guarantee in accordance with para 5, and it was not in fact until 29 June that Mr Wood wrote to the plaintiffs' solicitors informing them that the bank had agreed to accept their letter of 20 June as discharging the initial guarantee and that they were now willing to issue the further guarantee called for by cl 5(b).

There followed various procedural steps which do not now matter: judgment for the outstanding £35,000 had been obtained ex parte and that was set aside, arrangements being made for an inter partes hearing, and on 28 October 1983 the matter was heard inter partes by Staughton J. Two issues were argued before him. (1) As a matter of construction, was the stipulation which called for the guarantee to be given 'immediately upon payment of the Second Instalment' a stipulation which required compliance by a particular time and, if so, was it one in respect of which time was of the essence so that cl 13 had come into operation? (2) If cl 13 had come into operation, was there jurisdiction in the court to grant relief from the termination of the licence thereby effected?

Staughton J answered both questions in a sense contrary to the defendants' contentions and the defendants argue on this appeal that he was wrong on both counts although, of course, if they succeed on question (1), question (2) no longer arises.

As regards the construction of cl 5 counsel for the defendants does not contend that the word 'furnish' means anything other than 'provide', so that he accepts that, whenever it was to take place, the clause contemplates that a guarantee would be put into the hands of the plaintiffs or their advisers. But he says that 'immediately upon payment' does not mean 'simultaneously with payment'; it means no more than 'as soon as is reasonably practicable after payment'. What was reasonably practicable, he suggests, appears from the machinery provided by para (b) because one sees from that that there was to be a roll-over of the security provided by the defendants to back the guarantee and it was, or should have been, obvious from that that the bank could not in practice issue the guarantee until somebody satisfied them that the original guarantee had been discharged.

The irrevocable instructions given to the bank ensured that, if only the plaintiffs had got in touch with them to inform them that they had duly received the second instalment of £35,000, the guarantee was there for the asking. Accordingly, although no guarantee was ever provided in fact, it could not be said that there had been any excessive delay at the time when the plaintiffs purported to operate cl 13 such as would enable the court to say that the provision was not 'immediate'.

There seem to us to be a number of difficulties about this, all of which are, in our judgment, fatal to the submissions of counsel for the defendants, which, we sense, were put forward with rather more hope than confidence. In the first place, the provision of the guarantee was the defendants' responsibility and it is no answer to say that the plaintiffs could, by taking certain steps which they were never asked to take, have secured that which the defendants had undertaken to give them. Secondly, there was no reason whatever why the defendants could not, by taking suitable steps to satisfy the bank, have produced the guarantee virtually contemporaneously with the payment, certainly on the same day. They were not bound to wait until 14 June to make the payment which was called for by the agreement 'on or before' 14 June. Thirdly, an appeal to the machinery of cl 5(b) is, we think, a double-edged weapon for, if one looks at what was contemplated there, it was that the guarantee would be issued on the very day that the payment was effected, and that in itself casts some light on what the parties intended when they used the word 'immediately' in the selfsame clause. Fourthly, and finally, even if that word does not contemplate some interval of time between the payment and the provision of the guarantee, a lapse of six days clearly, in our judgment, goes beyond the bounds of immediacy and a fortiori so does the time which actually elapsed between the payment on 14 June and 29 June when the plaintiffs were told that the bank were able to provide the guarantee.

Before the judge an argument was sought to be based on what was said to be the contrast between the precision with which the time limits specified in cl 9 were expressed and the perhaps rather looser terminology of cl 5, but the judge thought that nothing turned on this and we agree with him. It was not, in any event, an argument on which counsel for the defendants sought to rely in this court.

Once one arrives, as, in our judgment, one inevitably does, at the conclusion that, as a matter of construction, the phrase 'immediately upon payment' contemplates either a minimal or at least a very short lapse of time after the fixed date, the provisions of cl 13 show, we think, beyond doubt that that time, whatever it was, was intended to be of the essence of the contract and, accordingly, it follows that the judge was right in concluding, as he did, that he must give judgment for the sum sought and make the declaration for which he was asked unless he could be satisfied that the case was one where some equitable relief was available to ameliorate the rigours of cl 13.

It is the argument on this latter point which has occupied the major part of the time taken on the hearing of this appeal and, as it is a point of some general interest, we reserved judgment. What the defendants seek to do is to invoke, in relation to this commercial agreement, the equitable jurisdiction to relieve against forfeiture most commonly (although, perhaps, not exclusively) encountered in relation to forfeiture of leasehold interests for non-payment of rent or breach of covenant. The judge expressed the view that, had he been satisfied that the case was one in which such a jurisdiction could properly be invoked, he would have adjourned the matter to give the defendants an opportunity to adduce evidence for the purpose of showing reasons why he should exercise his discretion in favour of granting relief. He concluded, however, that the case was not one where such a jurisdiction could be exercised. Similarly, before this court counsel for the defendants has indicated that, if the court were to be satisfied as a matter of law that relief against the rigours of cl 13 could be granted, he would be asking the court either to receive evidence in order to determine whether it should be granted or to remit the case to the judge for that determination. The latter would, we think, be the appropriate course if the question arose but, for the reasons given below, it does not, in our judgment, arise.

The equitable jurisdiction to grant relief against the forfeiture of leasehold interests is, of course, well established and has received statutory recognition and, indeed, extension in the provisions of s 146 of the Law of Property Act 1925. There is, however, no reported case to which counsel have been able to refer us in which it has ever been applied to a commercial agreement of a character similar to that with which we are concerned on this appeal, although, of course, there is ample authority for the application to such agreements of the closely analogous jurisdiction to relieve against penalties. The defendants argue, therefore, from general principle and their argument rests essentially on four propositions, viz: (1) the jurisdiction to relieve against forfeiture is not confined to any particular type of case; (2) it is appropriate to be applied where the forfeiture provision is one which is inserted with the object of securing the payment of money or a stated result which can still be effectively attained when the matter comes before the court; (3) it may be that it is confined to cases in which the agreement reserving the right of forfeiture is one which creates a proprietary or possessory title; (4) but if so, the agreement in the instant case is one which satisfies conditions (2) and (3) above.

The first of these propositions is not seriously open to doubt. Although commonly found in cases of mortgages and leases, relief has been granted in cases of copyholds or where, as in the case of *Starside Properties Ltd v Mustapha* [1974] 2 All ER 567, [1974] 1 WLR 816, the forfeiture amounts to a penalty, and in *Barton Thompson & Co Ltd v Stapling Machines Co* [1966] 2 All ER 222, [1966] Ch 499 Pennycuick J considered that it was arguably capable of applying to a lease of chattels.

It is propositions (2) and (3) which form the sheet-anchor of the case of counsel for the defendants and they rest on the two most modern authorities in the House of Lords, namely *Shiloh Spinners Ltd v Harding* [1973] 1 All ER 90, [1973] AC 691 and *Scandinavian Trading Tanker Co AB v Flota Petrolera Ecuatoriana, The Scaptrade* [1983] 2 All ER 763, [1983] 2 AC 694. From these cases counsel for the defendants argues that, wherever one finds a coalescence of two conditions, namely that the agreement with which the court is concerned is one which creates a proprietary or possessory right and that a forfeiture clause has been inserted for securing the attainment of a particular result which is still capable of being attained at the date of the hearing, then the equitable doctrine of relief is applicable, in the sense of being capable of being applied as a matter of jurisdiction. Whether the case is or is not an appropriate one for its application must depend on the individual circumstances of the parties, which are a matter of evidence.

Turning first, therefore, to the *Shiloh Spinners* case [1973] 1 All ER 90 at 100, [1973] AC 691 at 722, counsel for the defendants relies on the following passages from the speech of Lord Wilberforce:

'There cannot be any doubt that from the earliest times courts of equity have asserted the right to relieve against the forfeiture of property. The jurisdiction has not been confined to any particular type of case. The commonest instances concerned mortgages, giving rise to the equity of redemption, and leases, which commonly contained re-entry clauses; but other instances are found in relation to copyholds, or where the forfeiture was in the nature of a penalty. Although the principle is well established, there has undoubtedly been some fluctuation of authority as to the self-limitation to be imposed or accepted on this power. There has not been much difficulty as regards two heads of jurisdiction. First, where it is possible to state that the object of the transaction and of the insertion of the right to forfeit is essentially to secure the payment of money, equity has been willing to relieve on terms that the payment is made with interest, if appropriate, and also costs (*Peachey v Duke of Somerset* (1721) 1 Stra 447, 93 ER 626 and cases there cited) . . . Secondly there were the heads of fraud, accident, mistake or surprise [which are] always a ground for equity's intervention, the inclusion of which entailed the exclusion of mere inadvertence and a fortiori of wilful defaults.'

The general proposition, put in the way most helpful to the defendants in the instant case, is to be found where Lord Wilberforce said this ([1973] 1 All ER 90 at 101, [1973] AC 691 at 723):

'. . . it remains true today that equity expects men to carry out their bargains and will not let them buy their way out by uncovenanted payment. But it is consistent with these principles that we should reaffirm the right of courts of equity in appropriate and limited cases to relieve against forfeiture for breach of covenant or condition where the primary object of the bargain is to secure a stated result which can effectively be attained when the matter comes before the court, and where the forfeiture provision is added by way of security for the production of that result.'

The court has also been referred to the speech of Lord Simon in a passage in which he was prepared to go further and to assert an unlimited and unfettered jurisdiction to relieve against forfeitures (see [1973] 1 All ER 90 at 103–104, [1973] AC 691 at 726–727). That was, however, a minority opinion and one which was subsequently disapproved as a 'beguiling heresy' in the *Scandinavian Trading* case.

Now, certainly in the passages quoted, Lord Wilberforce was contemplating that the jurisdiction exists in *some* cases where the primary object of the forefeiture is to secure a stated result, but he cannot, we think, have had it in mind that the jurisdiction was exercisable wherever the stated condition existed. It is inherent in his statement of principle that it applies only in 'appropriate and limited cases' and, while it is true that he went on to consider the conduct of the applicant for relief in order to determine whether the case was an 'appropriate' one, we cannot find in his speech any suggestion that he was treating 'appropriate' and 'limited' as synonyms. Had he intended to do so he and the other members of the House who agreed with him must have accepted Lord Simon's broader proposition, which they plainly did not.

Thus the *Shiloh Spinners* case, in our judgment, establishes as a matter of decision no more than this: that one essential hallmark of the limited cases in which the equitable jurisdiction to relieve will be exercisable is that the forfeiture clause has been inserted with the object mentioned. Indeed, we do not understand counsel for the defendants to put it higher than this.

He submits, and this will require to be examined, that the primary object of cl 13 in the agreement, the subject matter of this appeal, was the object stated by Lord Wilberforce and that at least this qualifies the case as one where relief can be granted if it is, indeed, one of the 'limited' cases.

That brings us to the *Scandinavian Trading* case [1983] 2 All ER 763, [1983] 2 AC 694 where the appellants were seeking to invoke the doctrine in order to obtain relief from a provision enabling shipowners, who had chartered a vessel to the appellants under a time charter, to withdraw the vessel for non-payment of hire on the stipulated date. Before considering Lord Diplock's observations regarding the ambit of the equitable jurisdiction it is, we think, important to appreciate what the appellants' claim in that case involved. The action was one in which the shipowners had simply sought a declaration that they were entitled to withdraw the vessel and the charterers asked for relief against the exercise of that contractual right, the exercise of which could not, as Lord Diplock observed, give rise to any remedy in damages. Effectively therefore, and this may be of importance in the instant case, what the charterers were seeking, albeit perhaps indirectly, was an injunction to restrain the shipowners from withdrawing the vessel, that being in fact the only effective way in which relief could be given. This in effect would amount to an indirect order for specific performance and, since a time charter (not being a charter by demise) is a contract for services, specific performance of the very type of contract in respect of which it is clear that there is no jurisdiction to grant such a decree. We mention this because it does, as it seems to us, illustrate at least one limit on the type of case where relief can be granted. Where that which is forfeited is a right depending solely on a contract and where relief from that forfeiture in effect means that the court would be specifically enforcing the contract, it is difficult to see how relief could be granted where, quite apart from the forfeiture, the court would not, in any event, grant specific performance. We will return to this a little later although, on the view that we take in this case, it is not central to its decision.

Now, taken at its narrowest, the *Scandinavian Trading* case may be said to establish no more than this: that the equitable jurisdiction to relieve against forfeiture does not extend to a time charter not being a charter by demise. There is, however, the more general proposition to be derived from it, that, even where the primary object of the insertion of a forfeiture clause may be said to secure the payment of money or the performance of some other obligation, the equitable jurisdiction does not extend to contracts which do not involve the transfer or creation of proprietary or possessory rights. Lord Diplock refers to the observations of Lord Wilberforce in the *Shiloh Spinners* case which have been quoted above in the context of a discussion of the judgment of Lloyd J in *Afovos Shipping AS v R Pagnan & Flli, The Afovos* [1980] 2 Lloyd's Rep 469 where, at first instance, the question of relief from forfeiture in relation to a withdrawal clause in a charterparty had arisen. In relation to that question Lord Diplock said this ([1983] 2 All ER 763 at 767, [1983] 2 AC 694 at 701–702):

'In dealing with the jurisdiction point in *The Afovos* Lloyd J, in addition to adopting Lord Simon's suggested analogy [in *Mardorf Peach & Co Ltd v Attica Sea Carriers Corp of Liberia, The Laconia* [1977] 1 All ER 545, [1977] AC 850] between re-entry on leasehold premises for non-payment of rent and withdrawal of a ship for non-payment of hire (an anology which I reject for the reasons that I have already given), sought to extract from the speech of Lord Wilberforce in *Shiloh Spinners Ltd v Harding* [1973] 1 All ER 90, [1973] AC 691 a more general proposition that wherever a party to a contract was by its terms given a right to terminate it for a breach which consisted only of non-payment of a sum of money and the purpose of incorporating the right of termination in the contract was to secure the payment of that sum, there was an equitable jurisdiction to grant relief against the exercise of the right of termination. My Lords, *Shiloh Spinners Ltd v Harding* was a case about a right of re-entry on leasehold property for breach of a covenant, not to pay money' but to do things on land. It was in a passage that was tracing the history of the exercise by the Court of Chancery of its jurisdiction to relieve against forfeiture of property that Lord Wilberforce said ([1973] 1 All ER 90 at 100, [1973] AC 691 at 722): "There has not been much difficulty as regards two heads of jurisdiction. First, where it is possible to state that the object of the transaction and of the insertion of the right to forfeit is essentially to secure the payment of money, equity has been willing to relieve on terms that the payment is made with interest, if appopriate, and also costs." That this mainly historical statement was never meant to apply generally to contracts not involving any transfer of proprietary or possessory rights, but providing for a right to determine the contract in default of punctual payment of a sum of money payable under it, is clear enough from Lord Wilberforce's speech in *The Laconia*. Speaking of a time charter he said ([1977] 1 All ER 545 at 550, [1977] AC 850 at 870): "It must be obvious that this is a very different type of creature from a lease of land."'

It is this passage which is the foundation for proposition (3) put forward by counsel for the defendants.

Counsel for the defendants does not put it so high as to say that the equitable jurisdiction is exercisable in this case simply because the contract is one which creates (as he submits it does) a proprietary right, for he recognises that it does not at all follow from the proposition that there is no jurisdiction to grant relief except in cases of contracts creating rights of a proprietary or possessory nature that there is jurisdiction to grant relief in the cases of all contracts where such rights are created.

He claims, however, that there is no substantial difference between the contract between the plaintiffs and the defendants and the ordinary commercial lease. We think that the answer to this is that, historically, the availability of equitable relief from forfeiture has been confined to cases where the subject matter of the forfeiture is an interest in land. As was pointed out by Robert Goff LJ in delivering the judgment of this court in the *Scandinavian Trading* case [1983] 1 All ER 301 at 307, [1983] QB 529 at 538–539, there were sound policy reasons for the application of the jurisdiction to grant relief in such cases, policy reasons which, it may be, cannot now be said to have any real validity in the case of commercial leases. He said:

'We proceed on the basis that the equitable jurisdiction which the charterers invoke should not be regarded as rigidly confined to certain specific circumstances, or to be incapable of development. Even so, we must have regard to the fact that, so far as is relevant to the present case, the principal areas in which courts of equity have been prepared to grant relief in the past are (1) relief against the forfeiture of property, notably in cases concerning mortgages and leases, and (2) relief against penalties. There has in fact been a tendency in recent years (on which we do not feel called on to express any opinion in the present case) to extend the latter form of relief in favour of a purchaser in breach of a contract of sale where instalments of the purchase price already paid have been unconscionably retained by the vendor: see in particular *Stockloser v Johnson* [1954] 1 All ER 630 at 634ff, 637ff, [1954] 1 QB 476 at 483ff, 488ff per Somervell and Denning LJJ; cf [1954] 1 QB 476 at 494ff per Romer LJ. The equitable relief may be available in the context of a transaction which can be described as commercial, for example in the case of leases of commercial premises, and of penalties in contracts which may be described as commercial (though foreign parties to English commercial contracts are sometimes startled to discover that this is so). However, whatever may be the breadth of the application of these principles today, we need not be surprised at the type of case in which equity has thought it right to intervene in the past. No doubt at bottom the equitable jurisdiction "rests upon the idea that it is not fair that a person should use his legal rights to take advantage of another's misfortune, and still less that he should scheme to get legal rights with this object in view": see *Holdsworth's History of English Law* vol 5 (3rd edn, 1945), p 330. However, the cases where equity has intervened are cases where parties were frequently not at arm's length, and frequently also where the relevant contract conferred an interest in land, the loss of which could have serious personal consequences.'

The fact remains that the jurisdiction never was, and never has been up to now, extended to ordinary commercial contracts unconnected with interests in land and, though it may be that there is no logical reason why, by analogy with contracts creating interests in land, the jurisdiction should not be extended to contracts creating interests in other property, corporeal or incorporeal, there is, at the same time, no compelling reason of policy that we can see why it should be. And the fact is that the defendants in this case are seeking an extension by analogy, and an extension not based on any pressing consideration of legal policy but simply on an appeal to sympathy for what is considered to be a hardship arising from strict adherence to a bargain which they concluded with their eyes open.

To quote again from Robert Goff LJ in the *Scandinavian Trading* case [1983] 1 All ER 301 at 308, [1983] QB 529 at 529:

'The question whether it should be so extended must be considered on its merits, as a matter of policy, taking into account the relatively slight assistance available to us from the authorities, though the fact that the jurisdiction has never before been extended to purely commercial transactions must surely cause us to regard the extension, which we are now invited to make, with a considerable degree of caution.'

Counsel for the plaintiffs has submitted that, if one looks at the matter, as, indeed, we think that one should, as a question of whether, as matter of policy, the jurisdiction should be enlarged to bring cases such as the present within the circle of the 'limited' cases to which it is to apply, there are not merely no pressing considerations in favour of such an extension but, on the contrary, very weighty considerations against it. Those considerations, the ability of parties at arm's length to look after their own interests, the importance of certainty in commercial transactions, the necessity for both parties to know where they stand without the delays involved in investigations about whether the court will grant relief, are admirably set out in the judgment of this court in the *Scandinavian Trading* case [1983] 1 All ER 301 at 308–309, [1983] QB 529 at 540–541 in a passage quoted with approval by Lord Diplock in his speech in the same case (see [1983] 2 All ER 763 at 768–769, [1983] 2 AC 694 at 703–704). It would be a work of supererogation to set it out again here.

These considerations, counsel for the plaintiffs submits, are present, par excellence, in the instant case. Here were two commercial concerns, locked in litigation, advised by counsel and solicitors. They could not be more at arm's length. One can hardly conceive of a case in which certainty is more important than in a contract putting an end to litigation. The fact that part of the subject matter was the use of a trade mark underlines the need both for certainty and for the avoidance of delay, for, if a licence is determined, the licensor will wish to know at once, particularly in the case of an exclusive licence, whether he is entitled to preserve or to build up his goodwill by entering on the territory himself or granting licences to others. We find these submissions persuasive and, in our judgment, the judge was right in concluding that the instant case was not one where he had jurisdiction to grant relief from forfeiture.

Additionally, he was not satisfied in any event that the primary purpose of cl 13 was to secure the payment of money. We do not dissent from this conclusion. No doubt one object was to provide a stimulus for performing the defendants' obligations on time, but the revocation of the licence provided no sort of security for the payments which do not appear to have been related in any way to licence fees or royalties and the clause is equally consistent with a simple desire to enable the plaintiffs, if the defendants defaulted, to sign immediate judgment for the outstanding balance and sever all further relations with them.

This is sufficient to dispose of the appeal but, in fact, there appears to us to be another reason why the equitable jurisdiction to grant relief could not apply to a case such as this. The case is one of contract only and, in so far as there were any rights created or transferred which could be described as 'proprietary', they were rights which rested only in contract and to that extent distinguishable from the legal estate created by the grant of a lease or a mortgage. Assuming that relief were capable of being granted, effectively it could be granted only by compelling the plaintiffs to regrant the permission which had been revoked. An exclusive licence to use a trade mark creates no estate, although it enables the licensee to obtain an injunction if the licensor, in breach of contract, seeks to use the mark in competition with him. Thus, effectively, the licensee applying for relief from forfeiture is in exactly the same position as the charterer in the *Scandinavian Trading* case. Now, no doubt the contract creating the licence is one which, unlike the time charter in that case, could have been the subject matter of a decree of specific performance, so that, to that extent, the case is distinguishable; but we find it difficult to see how the court could decree specific performance (and thus grant the only relief of any value), when the party seeking it has to do so on the basis that he himself is in default in performing one of the essential terms of the contract; for it is, in general, the case that the plaintiff in a specific performance action must aver that he is, and has at all material times been, ready, able and willing to perform his part of the contract. Counsel for the defendants sought to dispel the doubts which were raised in the course of the argument by reference to the case of a lessee holding under an agreement for a lease. It would, he submitted, be absurd to suggest that such a lessee could not seek relief against forfeiture for, for instance, non-payment of rent on the ground that, since he was in breach of his obligations, he could no longer seek specific performance and therefore had no interest in respect of which relief could be granted. He referred to what he submitted was the analogous case of the holder of a legal estate who applied for relief after his estate had actually been determined, where a court of equity would formerly have compelled the regrant of the forfeited estate (see *Dendy v Evans* [1910] 1 KB 263 at 266–267, [1908–10] All ER Rep 589 at 591). The difficulty that we feel about this is that, although the position of a person holding under an agreement for a lease and who has once become entitled to have a lease granted is now equated to that of an actual lessee for the purposes of s 146 of the Law of Property Act 1925 (see s 146(5)), the position prior to s 5 of the Conveyancing Act 1892 was, absurdly or not, exactly as we have described, that is to say, because he had debarred himself from specific performance by failing to perform the obligations cast on him by the agreement, he was excluded from the protection conferred by what is now s 146 but was then s 14 of the Conveyancing Act 1881 (see *Coatsworth v Johnson* (1886) 55 LJQB 220, [1886–90] All ER Rep 547; *Swain v Ayres* (1888) 21 QBD 289). It is true that this point does not appear to have been taken in *Starside Properties Ltd v Mustapha* [1974] 2 All ER 567, [1974] 1 WLR 816, where the court appears not only to have granted relief against a penalty but also to have confirmed the defendant in possession, although it does not appear that, having regard to her default in payment, she could have compelled a conveyance of the property. The question at issue there, however, was not whether relief should be granted, there being no appeal against the judge's order to that effect, but whether the court had power to extend the time for performance of the condition on which relief had been granted.

In the light of the view that we take that the instant case is not, in any event, one to which the equitable jurisdiction is applicable, it is unnecessary finally to decide the point but, for the reasons given above, we have considerable doubt whether, outside the sphere of landlord and tenant, the equitable jurisdiction could in any event be exercised in a case where the forfeited interest depends on contract only and where relief, in effect, involves specifically performing that contract. In our judgment, therefore, the appeal should be dismissed.

Appeal dismissed. Leave to appeal to the House of Lords refused.

Solicitors: *Lovell White & King* (for the defendants); *Baker & McKenzie* (for the plaintiffs).

Carolyn Toulmin   Barrister.

Bulk Oil (Zug) AG v Sun International Ltd and another

COURT OF APPEAL, CIVIL DIVISION

ACKNER AND O'CONNOR LJJ

19, 20, 30 SEPTEMBER 1983

Arbitration – Award – Leave to appeal against award – Factors to be considered by court when deciding whether to grant leave – Award involving complex question of EEC law – Arbitration Act 1979, s 1.

In April 1981 the sellers agreed to sell a large quantity of United Kingdom North Sea crude oil to the buyer, the contract providing that the oil's destination was free but always in line with the exporting country's government policy. When the buyer's vessel arrived at the North Sea terminal, those responsible at the terminal refused to load the vessel because the oil's destination was Israel and the export of North Sea crude oil to Israel was said to be contrary to United Kingdom government policy. The buyer's claim that the sellers were in breach of contract was referred to arbitration, in which the buyer contended, inter alia, that the United Kingdom government's policy announced in 1979 which precluded the export of North Sea crude oil to Israel was contrary to a 1975 association agreement between the EEC and Israel which prevented EEC member states from imposing new restrictions on trade with Israel. The arbitrator, in an interim award, held that the export of United Kingdom crude oil to Israel was contrary to United Kingdom government policy, that that policy was not contrary to the EEC–Israel agreement and that there had been no breach of contract when the sellers refused to load the oil. The judge granted the buyer leave to appeal against the arbitrator's award. The sellers appealed to the Court of Appeal, contending that in granting leave to appeal to the High Court the judge had refused to apply the guidelines laid down by the House of Lords on when a court should grant leave under s 1[a] of the Arbitration Act 1979 to appeal against an arbitration award and had wrongly held that the court had to adopt a different approach when dealing with an application for leave to appeal against an arbitration award on a point of EEC law.

Held – The appeal would be dismissed for the following reasons—

(1) Although the control of arbitration proceedings in the member states of the EEC was left to national systems of law, it was the duty of the national courts, in their role of supervisors of arbitration proceedings, to ensure the observance of EEC law. Accordingly, since an arbitrator could not himself refer questions on EEC law to the Court of Justice of the European Communities for a ruling, and because of the advantages enjoyed by the European Court when deciding questions of EEC law and the dangers of an English court applying English canons of statutory construction to the interpretation of EEC legislation, it was appropriate for the judge to grant the buyer leave to appeal to the High Court as a first step towards seeking a reference to the European Court under art 177 of the EEC Treaty (see p 389 *e f*, p 391 *f* to *h* and p 392 *b* and *g*, post); *Amministrazione delle*

---

a   Section 1, so far as material, provides:

'. . . (3) An appeal under this section may be brought by any of the parties to the reference—(*a*) with the consent of all the other parties to the reference; or (*b*) subject to section 3 below, with the leave of the court.

(4) The High Court shall not grant leave under subsection (3)(*b*) above unless it considers that, having regard to all the circumstances, the determination of the question of law concerned could substantially affect the rights of one or more of the parties to the arbitration agreement; and the court may make any leave which it gives conditional upon the applicant complying with such conditions as it considers appropriate . . .'

a *Finanze dello Stato v Simmenthal SpA* Case 106/77 [1978] ECR 629, dictum of Lord Diplock in *R v Henn* [1980] 2 All ER at 196, *Nordsee Deutsche Hochseefischerei GmbH v Reederei Mond Hochseefischerei Nordstern AG & Co KG* Case 102/81 [1982] ECR 1095 and dictum of Bingham J in *Customs and Excise Comrs v ApS Samex (Hanil Synthetic Fiber Industrial Co Ltd, third party)* [1983] 1 All ER at 1055–1056 applied.

b (2) The guidelines laid down by the House of Lords on when a court should grant leave under s 1 of the 1979 Act to appeal against an arbitration award were not applicable in all cases and were not intended to remove the discretion granted to the court hearing a particular application, although great care was to be exercised to ensure that the exceptions did not become so numerous as to destroy the value of the guidelines. In all the circumstances the judge had been right in his assessment of the importance and significance of the issue which had been raised and to conclude that the guidelines did not apply to the case before him, because (a) the point was an entirely new one on which c there was no authority, (b) it was a question of potentially very great importance not only to the parties but to others, (c) it was important that authoritative guidance be given and there would remain none without the grant of leave, (d) the point was capable of serious argument, did not admit of only one possible answer and was not covered by an EEC authority precisely in point, (e) it involved potentially a very large sum of money, (f) it involved a complex question of EEC law on which the view which both the judge and d the arbitrator had formed could well be wrong, and (g) if the point was decided in the buyer's favour, then the sellers would have been in breach of contract in failing to load the vessel with the declared destination in Israel and the buyer would have succeeded in the arbitration (see p 390 *d* to *f*, p 391 *a b* and p 392 *c* to *g*, post); dictum of Sir John Donaldson MR in *Antaios Cia Naviera SA v Salen Rederierna AB, The Antaios* [1983] 3 All ER at 780 applied; *Pioneer Shipping Ltd v BTP Tioxide Ltd, The Nema* [1981] 2 All ER 1030 e explained.

Notes

For appeals to the High Court from an arbitrator's award, see 2 Halsbury's Laws (4th edn) para 627.

For references to the Court of Justice of the European Communities, see 37 ibid paras f 642–648.

For the Arbitration Act 1979, s 1, see 49 Halsbury's Statutes (3rd edn) 59.

For the EEC Treaty, art 177, see 42A ibid 436.

Cases referred to in judgments

Amministrazione delle Finanze dello Stato v Simmenthal SpA Case 106/77 [1978] ECR 629.

g *Antaios Cia Naviera SA v Salen Rederierna AB, The Antaios* [1983] 3 All ER 777, [1983] 1 WLR 1362, CA.

Broekmeulen (C) v Huisarts Registratie Commissie Case 246/80 [1981] ECR 2311.

BVS SA v Kerman Shipping Co SA, The Kerman [1982] 1 All ER 616, [1982] 1 WLR 166.

Customs and Excise Comrs v ApS Samex (Hanil Synthetic Fiber Industrial Co Ltd, third party) [1983] 1 All ER 1042.

h *Halfdan Grieg & Co A/S v Sterling Coal and Navigation Corp, The Lysland* [1973] 2 All ER 1073, [1973] QB 843, [1973] 2 WLR 904, CA.

Italmare Shipping Co v Ocean Tanker Co Inc, The Rio Sun [1982] 1 All ER 517, [1982] 1 WLR 158, CA.

Nordsee Deutsche Hochseefischerei GmbH v Reederei Mond Hochseefischerei Nordstern AG & Co KG Case 102/81 [1982] ECR 1095.

j *Pioneer Shipping Ltd v BTP Tioxide Ltd, The Nema* [1981] 2 All ER 1030, [1982] AC 724, [1981] 3 WLR 292, HL.

R v Henn, R v Darby [1980] 2 All ER 166, [1981] AC 850, [1980] 2 WLR 597, HL.

Cases also cited

CILFIT Srl v Ministro della Sanita Case 283/81 [1983] 1 CMLR 472, CJEC.

Criel (Suzanne), née Donckerwolcke and Henri Schou v Procureur de la République au Tribunal de Grande Instance, Lille and Director General of Customs Case 41/76 [1976] ECR 1921.

EC Commission v UK Case 804/79 [1981] ECR 1045.

Garden Cottage Foods Ltd v Milk Marketing Board [1983] 2 All ER 770, [1983] 3 WLR 143, HL.

Hoffmann-La Roche AG v Centrafarm Vertriebsgesellschaft Pharmazeutischer Erzeugnisse mbH Case 107/76 [1977] ECR 957.

Oxford Shipping Co Ltd v Nippon Yusen Kaisha (5 March 1982, unreported), QBD.

Interlocutory appeal

By notice dated 31 December 1982 Sun International Ltd and Sun Oil Trading Co (Sun) appealed against the order of Bingham J on 21 December 1982 whereby leave was given to Bulk Oil (Zug) AG (Bulk) to appeal against the interim award of the arbitrator (Mr Richard Yorke QC) made on 8 October 1982 in an arbitration between Bulk as applicant and Sun as respondents. By a respondent's notice under RSC Ord 59, r 6(1) dated 11 January 1983 Bulk gave notice that in the event that Bingham J's order was set aside it would contend that in its place an order should be made under art 177 of the EEC Treaty referring to the Court of Justice of the European Communities certain questions concerning the interpretation of EEC legislation. The facts are set out in the judgment of Ackner LJ.

Adrian Hamilton QC, Francis Jacobs and *Peter Brunner* for Sun.
David Vaughan QC and *Michael Mark* for Bulk.

Cur adv vult

30 September. The following judgments were delivered.

ACKNER LJ. Sun International Ltd and Sun Oil Trading Co Ltd (Sun) agreed in April 1981 to sell a large quantity of United Kingdom North Sea crude oil to Bulk Oil (Zug) AG (Bulk). The contract contained a clause which read:

> 'Destination free but always in line with exporting country's government policy. United Kingdom government policy, at present, does not allow delivery to South Africa.'

When a vessel was nominated by Bulk and arrived at the North Sea terminal to load the cargo of North Sea crude, those responsible at the terminal refused to load the cargo. The reason for that refusal was that the declared destination of the oil was Israel and the export of North Sea crude to Israel was said to be contrary to the policy of the United Kingdom government. Because of that refusal there were a number of claims which were referred to arbitration. The arbitrator, Mr Richard Yorke QC, in his interim award held that the export of United Kingdom crude to Israel was contrary to United Kingdom government policy and that therefore there was no breach of contract committed by Sun when it refused to load the oil. He held that there was a breach of contract by Bulk.

On 28 October 1982 Bulk sought leave to appeal against this award on a number of grounds, but when the matter came before Bingham J on 21 December only one ground was selected, the remaining grounds being stood over for subsequent argument, which is apparently to take place in two months' time. The one ground which was selected related to Bulk's contention that, if the United Kingdom government policy precluded the export of North Sea crude oil to Israel, then that policy was itself void under EEC law. Bulk's argument was put largely in a 41-page written submission by counsel on its behalf. Sun submitted an 18-page submission in reply. Both submissions were replete with references to authority. In addition, both sides made short supplementary oral submissions.

The arbitrator in his interim award summarised Bulk's argument in a few sentences.
a The application of the association agreement between the EEC and Israel dated 11 May
1975 (see EEC Council Regulation 1274/75) prevented any member state from imposing
new restrictions on trade with Israel. The Secretary of State for Energy's policy
announcement on 31 January 1979 was a new restriction and, in so far as it purported to
apply to Israel, was void. If it was void then it could not be relied on by Sun as a reason
for refusing to load Israeli-bound vessels under the contract.

b It was apparently common ground that the party adversely affected by the decision
would want a ruling from the Court of Justice of the European Communities in
Luxembourg. As an arbitrator cannot refer any question to Luxembourg, there would
first have to be an appeal from the award. The arbitrator, being of the opinion that the
views of arbitrators at first instance are not likely to carry much weight at Luxembourg,
decided to deal with the submissions quite shortly.

c The point of law on which leave to appeal was sought is set out in the second schedule
to the notice of motion in para 2(D). It is put in this way:

'The United Kingdom Government policy in the period from April to June 1981
relating to the export of North Sea crude oil from the United Kingdom was void or
unlawful under EEC law insofar as it restricted or precluded or sought to restrict or
preclude the export of such oil to Israel in that (contrary to the findings of the
d Arbitrator) (i) Restrictions on exports from the United Kingdom to Israel were
precluded by the Agreement of 11th May 1975 between the European Economic
Community and the State of Israel as enacted into Community Law by Council
Regulation 1274/75. (ii) The export of crude oil was within the then current ambit
of the said Agreement and the EEC Treaty. (iii) The said policy was contrary to the
provisions of the said Treaty and in particular Articles 5, 113 and 228 thereof
e whether or not the export of crude oil was within the then current ambit of the said
Agreement.'

It was plain to Bingham J, as indeed it was to us, that leave to appeal was sought as the
first step towards seeking a reference under art 177 of the EEC Treaty.

Bingham J, in the exercise of his discretion, gave leave to appeal against the arbitrator's
f decision and also gave leave to appeal against his own decision. Bingham J, having read
the award and having heard such brief argument as is appropriate on an application of
this kind, was of the opinion that the arbitrator was right when he concluded that the
export of crude oil was outside the current ambit of both the Treaty and the EEC–Israel
agreement. Bingham J considered a further argument which was not expressly dealt
with by the arbitrator but which he concluded inferentially must have been decided
g against Bulk. The argument was that since the Community has entered the field of
regulating commercial relations between the Community and its members on the one
hand and third countries on the other, and since the Community has enacted various
regulations touching on this matter and in particular touching on relations between the
Community and Israel, member states are precluded from implementing national
measures without notifying and consulting the Commission and seeking their approval.
h Bingham J concluded that, on the materials presented to him, he would have decided
this point adversely to Bulk, as he inferred so had the arbitrator. The reasons given by
Bingham J for his two conclusions referred to above are set out succinctly in his judgment
and there is no need to add to the length of his judgment by setting them out in extenso.

The judge then considered the principles relevant to the grant of leave against the
award of an arbitrator. Although both sides before the arbitrator showed a firm intention
j to seek to appeal against the decision, if it was adverse to them, neither party consented
to an appeal by the other party if the decision was in its favour. Accordingly, it was not a
case falling within s 1(3)(a) of the Arbitration Act 1979. The matter had therefore to be
approached as falling under s 1(3)(b) of the 1979 Act.

He asked himself the first question which arises under s 1(4) of the 1979 Act, namely
whether a question of law arises which could substantially affect the rights of one or

more of the parties, and he understandably concluded that it was plain beyond argument that that requirement was satisfied. He then considered the importance of the question raised and said:

'There has been some discussion before me whether this case should be treated as a one-off question affecting these parties only or as a more general question affecting a wider section of the commercial community. On the one hand, it is apparently the case that the clause in question is not a printed clause to be found in any standard form. On the other hand, I am told that it is a clause which is to be found in North Sea oil contracts, either in this form or in a very similar form. It also appears to me that any British prohibition on the export of crude oil to Israel is likely to affect traders other than Bulk and, given the importance of oil to the economy of any country, it is a question of potentially very great importance to the state of Israel. It is not, moreover, Israel alone which is the subject of the British prohibition, but it extends to any country not falling within the group formed by the International Energy Agency, the member states of the Community and, as I understand, Finland. It therefore appears to me that any doubt about the legality of the British policy is an important matter far transcending the interests of the particular parties to this litigation. If either of the tests in *Pioneer Shipping Ltd v BTP Tioxide Ltd, The Nema* [1981] 2 All ER 1030, [1982] AC 724 is appropriate, it would therefore seem to me that the lower of those tests is what Bulk must satisfy.'

The judge was clearly right in his assessment of the importance and significance of the issue which had been raised.

Bingham J then considered the application of the guidelines laid down in *The Nema*. He said that if either of the *Nema* tests were appropriate then the lower of those tests is what Bulk must satisfy. However, in his view there was ground for saying that these tests may not be applicable in all cases. I agree. This court, in the recent case of *Antaios Cia Naviera SA v Salen Rederierna AB, The Antaios* [1983] 3 All ER 777 has so stated. In the words of Sir John Donaldson MR (at 780), the speeches in *The Nema* were intended to provide guidelines rather than to remove the discretion granted to the judge hearing the application and guidelines by definition permitted exceptions, albeit great care must be exercised to ensure that the exceptions do not become so numerous as to blur the edges of the guidelines or even render them invisible.

Bingham J set out the following passage from the judgment of Parker J in *BVS SA v Kerman Shipping Co SA, The Kerman* [1982] 1 All ER 616 at 622, [1982] 1 WLR 166 at 173:

'What then of other cases which do not directly fall within the categories specifically dealt with? It is, in my judgment, clear that in all cases more is normally required than *The Lysland* criteria [see *Halfdan Greig & Co, A/S v Sterling Coal and Navigation Corp, The Lysland* [1973] 2 All ER 1073, [1973] QB 843] unless there are special circumstances. It is also clear that the more far-reaching the effects of the determination of the point of law involved, the less strict the criteria should be. It therefore appears to me that, if the point is one which will affect not only persons within a particular trade but persons in other trades as well, and, indeed, persons not in commerce or trade at all, it would be proper to grant leave on the basis of very little more than a demonstration that the point was capable of serious argument. Furthermore, if the point was, in addition, an entirely new one on which there was no authority, I would regard this as a special circumstance making it proper to grant leave on no more than *The Lysland* criteria on the ground that it was of importance that authoritative guidance be given at the earliest possible moment. Before reverting to the present case, I should perhaps stress that Lord Diplock repeatedly used the word "normally" when setting out the guidelines, thus recognising that each case must, as Lord Denning MR said in *The Rio Sun* [1982] 1 All ER 517 at 520–521, [1982] 1 WLR 158 at 162, ultimately depend on its own circumstances.'

Immediately following this reference Bingham J observed:

'In my judgment, the present case may well be said to fall within the category that Parker J defined.'

I infer that he expressed this view because (1) the point was an entirely new one on which there was no authority, (2) it was important that authoritative guidance be given at the earliest possible moment and (3) the point was capable of serious argument. Point (3) above seems to me to be of considerable importance to this appeal. Counsel for Sun has forcefully contended that Bingham J, in stating in terms that he was not of the view either that the arbitrator was plainly wrong in the decision he reached or that there was a strong prima facie case that he was wrong, must be taken to have concluded that the point was incapable of serious argument. This was clearly not the view of the arbitrator, who said in terms in the course of the submissions that it would be decided either way. Moreover, it could not have been the view of Bingham J, otherwise there would have been no point in citing *The Kerman* and concluding that the application could well be said to fall within the category that Parker J had defined.

Bingham J then continued:

'But there is an additional reason for not directly following what the House of Lords has laid down as the ordinary rules. On a point of English law, an English judge can reasonably be expected to take a view, on reading an award and hearing summary argument, whether he considers an arbitrator's award to be right or wrong. He may in the event prove to be incorrect in his decision, but it is a test which none the less he can reasonably be expected to undertake. It is a very much harder task for him to undertake on a point of Community law and harder still for him to do with any confidence of being correct. The cases show that, even where English judges have been confident that a point of Community law should be decided in one way, the Court of Justice of the European Communities has not infrequently decided it in the other.'

Only a week previously, Bingham J in *Customs and Excise Comrs v ApS Samex (Hanil Synthetic Fiber Industrial Co Ltd, third party)* [1983] 1 All ER 1042 at 1055–1056 set out in some detail the advantages enjoyed by the Court of Justice when deciding questions of Community law. He no doubt also had in mind the cautionary observations of Lord Diplock in his speech in *R v Henn, R v Darby* [1980] 2 All ER 166 at 196, [1981] AC 850 at 904 as to the dangers of an English court applying English canons of statutory construction to the interpretation of the EEC Treaty or, for that matter, of the regulations or directives.

Bulk, in its written submissions before the arbitrator and in its oral submissions before Bingham J, had heavily relied on the decision of the Court of Justice in *Nordsee Deutsche Hochseefischerei GmbH v Reederei Mond Hochseefischerei Nordstern AG & Co KG* Case 102/81 [1982] ECR 1095. While that case decides that the control of arbitration proceedings is left to national systems of law, it does emphasise the duty of national courts, in their role as supervisors of arbitration proceedings, to ensure the observance of Community law. Bingham J cited in particular a passage from the judgment in which the court said ([1982] ECR 1095 at 1111, paras 14–15):

'As the Court has confirmed in its judgment of 6 October 1981 *Broekmeulen*, Case 246/80 [1981] ECR 2311, Community law must be observed in its entirety throughout the territory of all Member States; parties to a contract are not, therefore, free to create exceptions to it. In that context attention must be drawn to the fact that if questions of Community law are raised in an arbitration resorted to by agreement, the ordinary courts may be called upon to examine them either in the context of their collaboration with arbitration tribunals, in particular in order to assist them in certain procedural matters or to interpret the law applicable, or in the course of a review of an arbitration award—which may be more or less extensive depending on the circumstances—and which they may be required to effect in case of an appeal or objection, in proceedings for leave to issue execution or by any other method of recourse available under the relevant national legislation. It is for those national courts and tribunals to ascertain whether it is necessary for them to make a reference to the Court under Article 177 of the Treaty in order to obtain the interpretation or assessment of the validity of provisions of Community law which they may need to apply when exercising such auxiliary or supervisory functions.'

Further support for the proposition that there is a duty on a national court to apply the provisions of Community law and protect the right conferred on individuals by such law is to be found in *Amministrazione delle Finanze dello Stato v Simmenthal SpA* Case 106/77 [1978] ECR 629 at 643–645, paras 13–27.

Counsel for Bulk has not submitted, nor did Bingham J decide, that whenever a question of Community law arises leave to appeal must be given. Clearly the point which it raises must be capable of serious argument and not admit of only one possible answer or be covered by a Community authority precisely in point.

At the end of the day this appeal comes down to a short point. Counsel for Sun has contended, adopting the language of Sir John Donaldson MR in the *Antaios* case [1983] 3 All ER 777 at 780, that, as Bingham J did not consider that a strong prima facie case had been made out that the arbitrator might well have been wrong in his decision on EEC law, then the application did not come within the *Nema* guidelines and should have been refused. In my judgment, Bingham J was fully entitled to conclude that the guidelines did not cater for a case of this kind. He based his decision to grant leave on the following factors: (1) the point was an entirely new one on which there was no authority; (2) it was a question of potentially very great importance, not only to the state of Israel, but to any country not falling within the group formed by the International Energy Agency, the member states of the Community and Finland; (3) it was accordingly important that authoritative guidance be given and there would remain none without the grant of leave; (4) the point was capable of serious argument; (5) it involved potentially a very large sum of money (the final award has now been made and including interest the total figure awarded is nearly $15m); (6) it involved a question of Community law of complexity on which the view which both he and the arbitrator had formed could well be wrong; (7) if the point was decided in Bulk's favour then, for the reasons given by the arbitrator, Sun would have been in breach of contract in failing to load the vessel with the declared destination in Israel and Bulk would have succeeded in the arbitration.

The above factors were all factors which in my judgment Bingham J was entitled to take into account and which, taken cumulatively, justified his granting leave.

I would accordingly dismiss this appeal.

O'CONNOR LJ. I agree that this appeal should be dismissed, for the reasons given by Ackner LJ.

Appeal dismissed.

Solicitors: *Ince & Co* (for Sun); *Maislish & Co* (for Bulk).

Diana Procter   Barrister.

R v Birmingham Juvenile Court and others, ex parte S and another
R v Birmingham Juvenile Court and others, ex parte P and another

QUEEN'S BENCH DIVISION (CROWN OFFICE LIST)

EWBANK J

11, 14 NOVEMBER 1983

Children and young persons – Care proceedings in juvenile court – Care order – Interim care order – Application for renewal of order – Duty of court – Matters to be considered – Children and Young Persons Act 1969, s 2(10).

Children and young persons – Care proceedings in juvenile court – Care order – Interim care order – Order for 28 days – How period of 28 days is calculated – Children and Young Persons Act 1969, s 20(1)(a).

Children and young persons – Care proceedings in juvenile court – Care order – Interim care order – Duty to deal with care proceedings as expeditiously as possible.

There is no analogy between successive adjournments of care proceedings under the Children and Young Persons Act 1969 and successive applications for bail under the Bail Act 1976, and therefore the test for renewing an interim care order made under s 2(10)[a] of the 1969 Act is not the same as that for granting or refusing a renewed application for bail. When considering whether to renew an interim care order the court has a duty to investigate all the circumstances and to hear evidence relating not only to matters which have occurred since the previous order was made or which were not brought to the attention of the court on that occasion but also to matters which were considered on the previous occasion (see p 396 *b* to *h*, post); *R v Nottingham Justices, ex p Davies* [1980] 2 All ER 775 distinguished.

A 28-day interim care order made by a court under s 2(10) of the 1969 Act is, by virtue of s 20(1)(a)[b] of that Act, effective for 27 whole days after the day on which it is made and expires at the beginning of the twenty-eighth day (see p 395 *j*, post).

Care proceedings ought to be dealt with as expeditiously as possible, since it is usually in the interests of both the child and the parents that a decision about the future be made as soon as possible (see p 395 *b c* and p 396 *f g*, post).

Notes
For interim care orders, see 24 Halsbury's Laws (4th edn) paras 750, 757, and for adjournment of hearings for care orders, see ibid para 766.

For the Children and Young Persons Act 1969, ss 2, 20, see 40 Halsbury's Statutes (3rd edn) 852, 877.

For the Bail Act 1976, see 46 ibid 288.

Cases referred to in judgment
E (minors) (wardship: jurisdiction), Re [1984] 1 All ER 21, [1983] 1 WLR 541, CA.

J (minors), Re [1980] CLY 1828.

---

a Section 2(10), so far as material, is set out at p 395 *c*, post

b Section 20(1), so far as material, provides: '. . . "interim order" means a care order containing provision for the order to expire within the expiration of twenty-eight days, or of a shorter period specified in the order beginning—(a) if the order is made by a court, with the date of the making of the order . . .'

R v Nottingham Justices, ex p Davies [1980] 2 All ER 775, [1981] QB 38, [1980] 3 WLR 15, DC.

Applications for judicial review

R v Birmingham Juvenile Court and ors, ex p S and anor

The parents of S applied, with the leave of Webster J granted on 4 October 1983, for an order of certiorari to quash an order of the Birmingham Juvenile Court renewing an interim care order which had been made in respect of S in care proceedings instituted by the local authority. The facts are set out in the judgment.

R v Birmingham Juvenile Court and ors, ex p P and anor

The parents of two young children, XP and YP, applied, with the leave of Webster J granted on 4 October 1983, for an order of certiorari to quash an order of the Birmingham Juvenile Court renewing an interim care order which had been made in respect of the children in care proceedings instituted by the local authority. The facts are set out in the judgment.

Barbara Calvert QC for the applicants.
R M K Gray QC for the local authority.
The juvenile court was not represented.

Cur adv vult

14 November. The following judgment was delivered.

EWBANK J. I have applications before me in two cases for judicial review. Both cases arise because the clerk to the Birmingham Juvenile Court has been advising his bench of magistrates that there is an analogy between successive adjournments of care proceedings and successive applications for bail and that, accordingly, the court should apply the same test in renewing an interim care order as it does in refusing a renewed application for bail.

The first case is the case of S. That case refers to a baby girl who was born on 29 June 1983. She has older brothers and sisters, and care orders have been made in respect of them. Her father has been guilty of scheduled offences, but these occurred some years ago. Because of those two factors, on the day the child was born a place of safety order was sought and obtained. The ground of the place of safety order was that it was probable that her proper development would be avoidably prevented or neglected. That application was made under the Children and Young Persons Act 1969.

On the same day, that is the day of the child's birth, the parents issued an originating summons in wardship proceedings. Their aim, apparently, was to forestall the local authority. The wardship matter came before his Honour Judge Toyn sitting as a High Court judge on 1 July 1983. He was referred to *Re E (minors) (wardship: jurisdiction)* [1984] 1 All ER 21, [1983] 1 WLR 541. Since a place of safety order had been obtained and since care proceedings were intended, he dismissed the wardship summons.

The care proceedings were first heard on 25 July. The notes of evidence, which were presumably taken by the clerk of the court, are not available to this court because the clerk of the court says that it is not his practice to issue notes of evidence in care proceedings. I have, however, been shown a solicitor's note of the evidence. There appear to have been three witnesses. There was a health visitor, who said that she had no qualms about the baby being with the mother until a final decision was taken. There was an area manager of a social services centre, who said that the social worker concerned with the family was on holiday and he knew nothing about the case. The mother also gave evidence. Her evidence was about her accommodation and was comparatively short. The father's convictions were put in, as were the care orders which had been made in relation to the other children.

The magistrates, having heard this evidence, made an interim care order in favour of the local authority. No reasons were given by them, and that order was returnable on 22 August.

The maximum period for which an interim order can be made, under s 20(1) of the 1969 Act, is 28 days. It is intended, in the ordinary way, that a case should be heard at the adjourned hearing, although provision is made for subsequent adjournments. The reason for the 28-day maximum period is clear: children, particularly young children, put down roots quickly and time is running against the parents. Accordingly, it is important that the local authority, should be ready to proceed with their case when the interim care order has expired.

The power to make an interim care order arises under s 2(10). That subsection provides:

'If the court before which the relevant infant is brought in care proceedings is not in a position to decide what order, if any, ought to be made . . . the court may make an interim order in respect of him.'

That power to make an interim order, therefore, is only exercisable if the court is not in a position to decide what order to make.

Under s 22(4) of the 1969 Act there is provision for an appeal from an interim order. It is an unusual provision to find and it is not, I suspect, designed for this type of case. The subsection provides:

'The High Court may, on the application of a person to whom an interim order relates, discharge the order on such terms as the court thinks fit . . .'

The parents appealed to the High Court under that section. The appeal came before Nolan J on 10 August 1983. He was referred to *Re J (minors)* [1980] CLY 1828. I have been provided with a transcript of the judgment of Waterhouse J in that case, delivered on 28 September 1979. Waterhouse J, in dealing with this type of appeal and having set out the terms of s 2(10), said:

'In other words, if the court has not made up its mind about the s 1 case, the court has a general discretion to make an interim care order. It would not be right for this court [ie the High Court] to interfere with the exercise by justices of a discretion conferred on them by statute unless it was shown that the justices had acted either mistakenly on the facts or on the basis of some wrong principle.'

Speaking for myself, I would extend that to include also that the High Court ought to interfere if the justices were plainly wrong.

Nolan J dismissed the appeal. It is clear that there is no ground on which he could properly have allowed it.

The care proceedings came back before the magistrates on 22 August. As I have pointed out, the maximum period of an interim care order is 28 days. The 22 August was 28 days after the previous hearing, counting days in the ordinary way. My attention has been drawn, however, to s 20(1)(a) of the 1969 Act, which provides that the order begins on the day it was made and not the day after. Accordingly, it is said on behalf of the parents that the order expires 27 days after the order was made and not 28 and that, therefore, the order had already expired before the return date. The true view, however, in my judgment, is that the order remains effective during the twenty-seventh day and expires at the beginning of the twenty-eighth.

Section 22(2) of the 1969 Act provides that the child should be brought before the court on the expiration of the order, which, in my judgment, is the twenty-eighth day. I am, therefore, of the view that there is nothing in this point raised by the parents. I am told that, as a result of this appeal, the magistrates' court have altered their practice and, instead of counting 28 days, they have changed to 27. They can now resume their previous practice. Even if there had been a valid point on time, it would not prevent further interim orders being made under s 2(10) of the 1969 Act.

On 22 August, when the matter came before the magistrates, there was a different bench. I am told (although this has not been confirmed) that they did not have the notes of evidence of the previous hearing, nor did they have the reasons, if any were given, for the previous decision. The clerk of the court advised the bench that the justices did not have to hear evidence unless it could be shown beforehand that new evidence was available to the court, and that the situation was analogous to renewed applications for bail under the Bail Act 1976, following the decision in *R v Nottingham Justices, ex p Davies* [1980] 2 All ER 775, [1981] QB 38.

In that case, the Court of Appeal held that, although the magistrates' court had a duty to consider granting bail on every application that was made, a previous refusal of bail by the court was a finding that the court was satisfied that one or more of the exceptions for the granting of bail existed and as such the matter was res judicata, or analogous thereto, unless that finding was reversed on appeal. Accordingly, it was held that justices considering a renewed application for bail had no duty to consider matters previously considered and should confine themselves to circumstances that had since occurred, or to matters not brought to the attention of the court on the previous occasion.

The parents' solicitor submitted that this advice was wrong, but the magistrates followed the advice of their clerk and made a further interim care order for 28 days. The case was due back to the magistrates' court on 19 September. The advice given by the clerk to the magistrates on this and subsequent occasions when interim care orders were made is the main ground of the present application.

I have come to the conclusion that the advice the clerk gave was wrong. My reasons are as follows. First, merely because the same general principles of law may apply to two different types of proceedings, it does not follow that there is any analogy between those proceedings. Second, care proceedings are not analogous to bail applications, and it is misleading to think of them in that way, even if some of the same principles apply. Third, in care proceedings, as in other cases involving custody and the upbringing of the child, the welfare of the child is of paramount consideration. Magistrates must avoid the application of any rule or practice which prevents their making orders in the best interests of a child. Four, while it is correct for the magistrates to bear in mind, in a case where no new evidence is available, that a previous bench has heard evidence and made an interim care order, nevertheless the court should hear what the parents wish to say and take into account (a) that care proceedings are intended to be dealt with with expedition and, generally, if the parents are ready for them to proceed, the local authority who started the proceedings ought to be ready too, (b) that it is usually in the interests of the child that a decision about the future be made as soon as possible, (c) that time is running against the parents and that delay may prejudice their interests as well as the interests of the child, and (d) that the only decision the previous magistrates' court have made under s 2(10) is that it was not in a position to decide what order, if any, ought to be made. That is the reason, and the only reason, why an interim care order has been made.

It follows, accordingly, in my judgment, that the clerk was wrong in suggesting the bail analogy to the magistrates. That is not to say, however, that the decision of the magistrates to make a further interim care order was necessarily wrong.

I have described how the parents unsuccessfully applied to the High Court for the child to be made a ward of court, and to the High Court on an appeal under s 22(4). Their next step was to apply for a discharge of the interim care order under s 21(2).

That application was made on 23 August 1983, the day after the second interim order was made. The only appeal against an interim order is to the High Court under s 22(4). The parents had tried this and failed. Their plan now was to appeal to the Crown Court under s 22(4) if they failed in this application for a discharge of the interim care order.

The hearing of the application to discharge the order was fixed for 1 September. At the hearing, the solicitor for the local authority submitted that, since no new evidence was available, the court should not consider the application. This submission was rightly and summarily rejected. However, the court heard that evidence was being sought from an independent social worker and accordingly decided that the application should be adjourned until 19 September, when the care proceedings themselves were due to be heard. It is pointed out on behalf of the parents that the parents had a right under the 1969 Act to apply to discharge the interim care order but, since this order would expire the day before the next hearing, they would be deprived of their right to have it discharged on the merits. This submission is correct so far as it goes.

The real complaint is that the parents feel that they have been deprived of a potential appeal to the Crown Court. This too is correct. But, where the 1969 Act only allows adjournments of up to 28 days at a time, it is clear that old orders may be replaced by new orders and that from time to time rights of appeal will be lost.

The care proceedings came back before another bench of magistrates on 19 September. In theory, the parents' application to discharge the previous care order was also before the court. The local authority was still not ready. The solicitors for the parents asked that the case should proceed, but the clerk of the court advised the magistrates that there was no fresh evidence, so another interim care order ought to be made. The magistrates took the view that, if they made any other order, they would be acting as a court of appeal against the first bench.

This is a misunderstanding by the magistrates of their position and duties. They only needed to remind themselves that all the first bench had decided, some two months earlier, was that they were not in a position to decide what order, if any, to make. They would then have realised that the question of being a court of appeal from that bench of magistrates could not arise. By taking this view, they were merely rubber-stamping the first order and depriving themselves of the opportunity and duty to consider the interests of the child and the other matters to which I have already referred.

On 4 October an application was made to Webster J for leave to make this application for judicial review. That leave was granted, this case coming to me pursuant to that leave. Since then, a further interim care order has been made, and the full hearing of the care proceedings is due to take place on 17 November.

It is pointed out with some force by counsel on behalf of the parents that the baby, now some 4½ months old, was taken from the mother at birth and, although the case has been back to the courts five times, the only evidence heard was on the first hearing and then of a sketchy nature. Each court since has refused to hear evidence on successive applications by the local authority for renewal of the interim care order on the so-called analogy with bail applications.

The parents now bring this application for an order of certiorari to quash a selection of the orders that had been made. Their criticisms have substance and their prospects of obtaining care of the child are probably prejudiced. However, since a full hearing has been arranged for this week, there can, in my view, be no point in making the orders sought and I decline to do so.

The second case concerns a girl of 2½ and a boy of 1½ years of age. A place of safety order was taken out on 17 June 1983. Care proceedings were started, the ground for those proceedings being that the proper development of the children was being neglected and that there had been bruising seen on the girl.

There then followed a series of interim care orders along the same pattern as in the case of S. The clerk of the court gave the same advice to the bench of magistrates on each occasion as in the case of S. However, one feature that stands out in this case, which illustrates the restrictive effect of the advice the magistrates were receiving, occurred on 13 October 1983.

The care proceedings were back before the magistrates, and the interim care order had run out. On that occasion, the parents gave instructions that they had noticed bruising on the girl on three successive occasions of access. Their solicitor asked that this evidence be heard. The solicitor for the local authority said that the bruising that had occurred was accidental and that, although allegations were made that bruises had been seen on the girl when she was with her parents and that they were not accidental, that was only a small part of the local authority's case. The magistrates declined to investigate this aspect of the matter, as I understand it, because it was not 'fresh evidence'. In coming to this decision, they were applying the principles that might be applied on an application for a renewal of bail. It is difficult to see how they could come to this conclusion in a case involving the care of a child.

This instance alone shows how wrong decisions can be made by trying to apply a rule in bail applications to decisions about children. The parents, in the case of P, have as much substance in their criticisms as the parents in the case of S. However, in this case a final care order was made on 27 October, and there is no point in considering whether to quash any of the interim care orders. I, therefore, decline to do so.

Applications dismissed. No order for costs.

Solicitors: *Michael T Purcell & Co*, Birmingham (for the applicants); *Sharpe Pritchard & Co*, agents for *G W T Pitt*, Birmingham (for the local authority).

Bebe Chua   Barrister.

Ninemia Maritime Corp v Trave Schiffahrtsgesellschaft mbH & Co KG
The Niedersachsen

QUEEN'S BENCH DIVISION (COMMERCIAL COURT)
MUSTILL J
29, 30 MARCH, 11 APRIL, 10 MAY 1983

COURT OF APPEAL, CIVIL DIVISION
EVELEIGH, KERR AND DILLON LJJ
18, 19, 29 JULY 1983

Injunction – Interlocutory injunction – Danger that defendant may transfer assets out of jurisdiction – Injunction restraining removal of assets out of the jurisdiction – Injunction in advance of judgment on plaintiff's claim – Discretion to grant injunction when just and convenient to do so – Factors to be considered in exercise of discretion – Whether plaintiff required to show he has a good arguable case – Whether plaintiff required to show real risk of prejudice if injunction refused – Supreme Court Act 1981, s 37.

The test to be applied by the court when deciding to exercise its statutory discretion to grant a Mareva injunction to a plaintiff pursuant to s 37[a] of the Supreme Court Act 1981 whenever it appears 'to the court to be just and convenient to do so' is whether, after the plaintiff has shown that he has at least a good arguable case and after considering the whole of the evidence before the court, the refusal of a Mareva injunction would involve a real risk that a judgment or award in the plaintiff's favour would remain unsatisfied because of the defendant's removal of assets from the jurisdiction or dissipation of assets within the jurisdiction (see p 415 *b d e*, p 419 *e* to *j* and p 422 *d* to *f*, post).

A Mareva injunction will not be granted merely for the purpose of providing a plaintiff with security for a claim, even when it appears likely to succeed and even when the granting of the injunction will not cause hardship to the defendant (see p 419 *c d* and p 422 *f g*, post).

---

a   Section 37, so far as material, is set out at p 415 *b* to *d*, post

Notes

a For injunctions restraining the disposition of property, see 24 Halsbury's Laws (4th edn) para 1018, and for cases on the subject, see 28(2) Digest (Reissue) 1091–1094, 918–960.
For the Supreme Court Act 1981, s 37, see 51 Halsbury's Statutes (3rd edn) 632.

Cases referred to in judgments

American Cyanamid Co v Ethicon Ltd [1975] 1 All ER 504, [1975] AC 396, [1975] 2 WLR 316, HL.

b *Barclay-Johnson v Yuill* [1980] 3 All ER 190, [1980] 1 WLR 1259, CA.
Bakarim v Victoria P Shipping Co Ltd, The Tatiangela [1980] 2 Lloyd's Rep 193.
Etablissement Esefka International Anstalt v Central Bank of Nigeria [1979] 1 Lloyd's Rep 445, CA.
Farey-Jones (Insurance) Ltd v IFM Funding GmbH [1979] CA Transcript 223.
Galaxia Maritime SA v Mineralimportexport, The Eleftherios [1982] 1 All ER 796, [1982] 1
c WLR 539, CA.
Garden Cottage Foods Ltd v Milk Marketing Board [1983] 2 All ER 770, [1983] 3 WLR 143, HL.
Hadmor Productions Ltd v Hamilton [1982] 1 All ER 1042, [1983] AC 191, [1982] 2 WLR 322, HL.
Home Insurance Co v Administratia Asigurarilor de Stat (29 July 1983, unreported), QBD.
d *Iraqi Ministry of Defence v Arcepey Shipping Co SA (Gillespie Bros & Co Ltd intervening), The Angel Bell* [1980] 1 All ER 480, [1981] QB 65, [1980] 2 WLR 488.
Mareva Compania Naviera SA v International Bulkcarriers SA, The Mareva (1975) [1980] 1 All ER 213, CA.
Montecchi v Shimco (UK) Ltd [1979] 1 WLR 1180, CA.
Negocios del Mar SA v Doric Shipping Corp SA, The Assios [1979] 1 Lloyd's Rep 331.
e *Piccinini v Partrederiet Trigon II, The Alfred Trigon* [1981] 2 Lloyd's Rep 333.
Rahman (Prince Abdul) Bin Turki Al Sudairy v Abu-Taha [1980] 3 All ER 409, [1980] 1 WLR 1268, CA.
Rasu Maritima SA v Perusahaan Pertambangan Minyak Dan Gas Bumi Negara (Pertamina) and Government of Indonesia (as interveners) [1977] 3 All ER 324, [1978] QB 644, [1977] 3 WLR 518, CA.
f *Third Chandris Shipping Corp v Unimarine SA, The Pythia, The Angelic Wings, The Genie* [1979] 2 All ER 972, [1979] QB 645, [1979] 3 WLR 122, CA.
Vitkovice Horni a Hutni Tezirstvo v Korner [1951] 2 All ER 334, [1951] AC 869, HL.
Z Ltd v A [1982] 1 All ER 556, [1982] QB 558, [1982] 2 WLR 288, CA.

Interlocutory application

g On 8 March 1983 the plaintiffs, Ninemia Maritime Corp (the buyers), successfully applied ex parte to Mustill J for an injunction restraining the defendants, Trave Schiffahrtsgesellschaft mbH & Co KG (the sellers), for a period of 28 days or until further order from removing from the jurisdiction or otherwise disposing of or dealing with any of their assets within the jurisdiction of the court so as to reduce the value thereof below $US787,000 on the buyers undertaking, inter alia, to issue a writ and serve it on the
h sellers forthwith. On 10 March 1983 the buyers issued the writ against the sellers claiming damages for breach of a memorandum of agreement between the parties, dated 24 January 1983, for the sale and purchase of the vessel Niedersachsen. By summons dated 21 March 1983 the sellers made an interlocutory application to set aside or vary the injunction. The application was heard in chambers but judgment was given by Mustill J
j in open court. The facts are set out in the judgment.

Stewart Boyd QC and *Victor Lyon* for the buyers.
Timothy Young for the sellers.

Cur adv vult

10 May. The following judgment was delivered

MUSTILL J[1]. This matter is before the court on an application by Trave Schiffahrtsgesellschaft mbH & Co KG (the sellers) to discharge a Mareva injunction obtained on 8 March 1983 by Ninemia Maritime Corp (the buyers).

The claim which the injunction was intended to protect relates to the sale of the Niedersachsen under a memorandum of agreement dated 24 January 1983. The contract, which was in the Norwegian Sale Form, contained the following terms:

> '18. Delivery of the vessel where presently anchored off Dubai, without dry-docking, safely afloat, charterfree, with steam raised in both boilers and ready to sail . . . present class fully maintained, free of recommendations, free of average damages affecting class . . .
>
> 19. In connection with class requirements sellers to arrange for a divers inspection under class supervision and in accordance with class requirements for the inspection of . . . tail-end shaft . . . Sellers also to arrange for confirmation from class, that there is no leaking to stern simplex gland . . .'

The claim is based on allegations that the vessel was out of conformity with the contract at the time of delivery in two distinct respects. First, there were leaks and other deficiencies in the tubing of the starboard boiler. Second, there were defects in the stern tube and tailshaft. The claim was assessed at a total of $US787,000, consisting of $550,000 for the estimated cost of repairs to the starboard boiler, $147,000 being the running cost of the vessel during 21 days of repairs, and $90,000 relating to the stern tube.

The matter first came before the court on 7 March 1983, when the buyers applied ex parte for an injunction. As it happened, I was the judge to whom the application was made. The application was led by a draft affidavit of Mr T E Nott-Bower, a director of the buyers' United Kingdom agents. This exhibited a long telex which had been sent a few days previously by Mr S E Tsakalotos (who was described as 'the buyers' surveyor' although, as it subsequently appeared, he was also a director of the United Kingdom agents of the buyers' managers) giving details of complaints about the boiler tubing, and about the presence of sea water in fluid drawn from the stern-tube drain. The affidavit went on to disclose that four days previously Germanischer Lloyd, the society in which the ship was classed, had given a telex confirmation that the vessel was in class free of recommendations; but the deponent asserted that the local non-exclusive surveyor representing the society appeared to be operating the rules of the society in a negligent manner and in effect turning a blind eye to defects in the tubing.

Next, the affidavit stated that the sellers were maintaining that the vessel was ready for delivery, and that closing should take place on 8 March. Mr Nott-Bower's affidavit continued:

> 'I verily believe that if the Plaintiffs take delivery of the ship and pay the whole of the price to the sellers they will have no security for legitimate claims and will thus be effectively prevented from pursuing legitimate claims. The vessel is under steam, her class certificates are in order and a notice of readiness has been issued. Accordingly, the Plaintiffs are effectively put in the position of being obliged to take delivery though knowing that the vessel is defective. The Defendants are a West German corporation who are selling both of their only tow vessels. The Defendants have an account with Citibank, London, WC2 i.e. within the jurisdiction of this Honourable Court. The moneys payable under the [memorandum of agreement] are to be paid into such account. I verily believe that on closing such moneys as held in such account will be removed very quickly so that the Defendants will have no

---

1   Judgment in this case was delivered on Mustill J's behalf by Lloyd J, who began by saying: 'In this matter I am giving judgment on behalf of Mustill J, who has asked me to read his judgment. It is quite long. I shall not read the whole of it, but I shall read that part which affects any questions of costs or applications for leave to appeal. Copies of it have been made available.'

assets in this country against which the Plaintiff Buyers would be able to enter any award or judgment. I am pessimistic about the prospects of the Defendants honouring any award or judgment unless they are forced to keep sufficient assets in this country. A request was made by a telex dated 4th March 1983 to the sellers that they should undertake to indemnify the buyers in respect of further leakages when steam was raised but such request was ignored . . . Finally, I should mention that it would be the intention of the Plaintiffs not to disclose the existence of any injunction that the Court may make until immediately after closing and delivery of the ship. If the Defendants are notified of the injunction beforehand, the Plaintiffs fear that the Defendants will sell the vessel elsewhere or may seek to assign the proceeds of sale to a third party.'

When the matter first came before me, I declined to grant an injunction. At the time of the application, the ship had not been tendered for delivery; the price had not been paid; the buyers had no cause of action in respect of the alleged defects. There was at the time no asset to be attached, and no claim for which to attach it. Quite apart from any other ground of objection, this appeared to rule out any question of an injunction.

Undeterred by this reverse, the buyers reappeared on the following day, with a further affidavit to the effect that delivery had now taken place, and the price had been paid. In the changed circumstances, I considered that an injunction could properly be granted, but I limited the sum attached to the figure of $787,000, rather than grant it in an unlimited form, as the buyers had asked.

The sellers now appear on notice to set this order aside.

The proceedings illustrate a further stage in the development of the Mareva jurisdiction. Originally, the relief was reserved for cases where the creditor required protection until the hearing of an RSC Ord 14 summons, founded on a debt which was undisputed or indisputable. In *Rasu Maritima SA v Perusahaan Pertambangan Minyak Dan Gas Bumi Negara (Pertamina) and Government of Indonesia (as interveners)* [1977] 3 All ER 324, [1978] QB 644 the jurisdiction was enlarged, so as to enable security to be granted in respect of claims against foreign defendants which were not appropriate for summary judgment. Subsequently, the procedure has expanded into fields far removed from the commercial world in which it was first developed, and at the same time the principles have been refined, so as to provide certain safeguards for a defendant or other person who might suffer hardship if subjected to an order in the unadorned form which was in use at the outset.

These developments have been accompanied by a rapid and sustained increase in the number of applications for Mareva relief. It is, I think, a fair assumption that most applications are successful. In the early years defendants seem to have been content to put up security in order to obtain the release of the frozen assets, without questioning the propriety of the original order. More recently, defendants have with increasing frequency appeared inter partes, pursuant to the liberty to apply which always forms part of a Mareva order, so as to vary the terms of the order to a less restrictive form. More recently still, defendants have become bolder, and in some cases less willing or able to sustain the very serious damage which can result from an abrupt termination of their liquidity, and have come to the court with applications often supported by copious evidence, to argue that, even if the initial grant of the order was justified in the light of the one-sided material placed before the judge hearing the matter ex parte, it should not now be maintained. Applications of this nature can raise really difficult problems, the more so as there is doubt as to the principles which should be applied. Since I have had the benefit of very full argument on these principles, an argument much more extensive than is usually advanced on the hearing of Mareva proceedings, I thought it useful to adjourn the judgment into open court, so as to point out some of the difficulties with which the court is faced in dealing justly with this radical jurisdiction. On more than one previous occasion, the appellate courts have enunciated guidelines on the grant of Mareva relief which have proved of great practical value to courts of first instance. If

further guidance were to be given, in this or some other case, on the manner in which
applications to discharge Mareva injunctions should be approached, I am confident that
it would prove equally welcome.

It is convenient to deal with the issue of principle in the light of two questions. First,
what probability of success at the ultimate trial is the plaintiff required to demonstrate,
before an injunction can be properly granted or maintained? Second, what type of
prejudice must the plaintiff demonstrate, in the shape of a risk of dissipation of assets,
and with what degree of conviction must it be shown, before the defendant's assets can
properly be detained to await a possible judgment? I will deal with these issues in turn.

PRINCIPLES

The strength of the plaintiff's case

That the judge hearing a Mareva application is not only entitled but bound to make
some assessment of the plaintiff's chance of success at the trial is, I believe, not open to
dispute. Before going on to consider what, in the light of the reported cases, the judge
ought to look for, it is necessary to point out that, although the statements of principle in
the reported cases are expressed so as to apply equally to the grant of an injunction as to
the maintaining in force at an inter partes hearing of an injunction once ex parte, in
practice the judge is faced with a wholly different situation at the two successive stages.
This is well illustrated by the present case. At the initial hearing there was one affidavit
supported by 130 pages of exhibits. This is a great deal more than on most occasions is
brought before the ex parte judge, since where the application is particularly urgent the
evidence is given by counsel speaking on instructions, with an undertaking subsequently
to adduce an affidavit in support. Even so, it was quite impossible to form any real
estimate of the plaintiff's prospects of success at any trial which might take place. In the
special circumstances of the case I refused the application, for reasons already given. A
renewed application, which did succeed, was led by a further affidavit of two paragraphs,
which took the underlying merits of the dispute no further. At the end of the two
hearings, which together must have lasted substantially less than an hour, the only view
which it was possible to form was that, although the plaintiffs faced some fairly obvious
problems, it was a case which, on the evidence and exhibits, they might well win.

The position at the current hearing is quite difficult. Ten affidavits have been adduced,
and the exhibits have been much enlarged. The documentary material has been read and
analysed in considerable detail. The hearing has occupied, with some interruptions, more
than two sitting days. I will concentrate on the problems raised by the application to
discharge the injunction, since it is on this that I have to rule. I must, however, emphasise
that for practical reasons an elaborate examination of this kind is simply impracticable at
the ex parte stage, given the number of applications which have to be dealt with outside
sitting hours. The damage done by the over-hasty grant of an injunction may well be
irretrievable, since an application for the discharge of the injunction may come too late
to save a defendant whose liquidity has been abruptly shut down. The cross-undertaking
in damages is of no consolation to a company which has been ruined. This being so, there
may perhaps be something to be said for imposing stricter requirements at the ex parte
stage than are called for by the current practice, if this useful remedy is not to be a vehicle
for oppression.

On the issue of principle the following cases were cited in argument: *Rasu Maritima
SA v Perusahaan Pertambangan Minyak Dan Gas Bumi Negara (Pertamina) and Government of
Indonesia (as interveners)* [1977] 3 All ER 324, [1978] QB 644; *Z Ltd v A* [1982] 1 All ER
556, [1982] QB 558; *American Cyanamid Co v Ethicon Ltd* [1975] 1 All ER 504, [1975] AC
396; *Vitkovice Horni a Hutni Tezirstvo v Korner* [1951] 2 All ER 334, [1951] AC 869; *Farey-
Jones (Insurance) Ltd v IFM Funding GmbH* [1979] CA Transcript 223; *Bakarim v Victoria P
Shipping Co Ltd, The Tatiangela* [1980] 2 Lloyd's Rep 193. These cases are not easily
reconciled, but to my mind they establish that the strength of the plaintiff's case is
relevant in two distinct respects: (1) the plaintiff must have a case of a certain strength,
before the question of granting Mareva relief can arise at all. I will call this the 'threshold';
(2) even where the plaintiff shows that he has a case which reaches the threshold, the

strength of his case is to be weighed in the balance with other factors relevant to the
exercise of the discretion. It seems to me plain that the second proposition is justified by
common sense and by the authorities. It is the first which raises problems. There are
only two direct authorities on the location of the threshold. The first is the judgment of
Lord Denning MR in the *Pertamina* case, and the second that of Kerr LJ in *Z Ltd v A*. In
the former case Lord Denning MR said ([1977] 3 All ER 324 at 334, [1978] QB 644 at
661):

> 'So I would hold that an order restraining removal of assets can be made whenever
> the plaintiff can show that he has a "good arguable case". That is a test applied for
> service on a defendant out of the jurisdiction: see *Vitkovice Horni a Hutni Tezirstvo v
> Korner*; and it is a good test in this procedure which is appropriate when defendants
> are out of the jurisdiction. It is also in conformity with the test as to the granting of
> injunctions whenever it is just and convenient as laid down by the House of Lords
> in *American Cyanamid Co v Ethicon Ltd*.'

This passage calls up two lines of authority. One relates to the general principles
governing the grant of interlocutory injunctions. With great respect, I see real difficulties
here. In the ordinary way, a plaintiff seeks an interlocutory injunction for the purpose of
holding until trial the substantive relief which he hopes to obtain on final judgment.
The interlocutory injunction is a direct reflection of his cause of action. The relief granted
on a Mareva application is of a quite different character. It bears no relation to the relief
granted at the trial. The plaintiff, however successful at the trial, will not obtain a
perpetual injunction in terms of the interlocutory Mareva injunction. The latter bears
on assets which in the great majority of cases have no connection at all with the cause of
action on which the injunction is founded.

Moreover, even if the analogy with ordinary interlocutory injunctions were accepted,
it would not lead to 'a good arguable case' as the test. The *Cyanamid* case teaches that the
court should not attempt to weigh the merits except to ascertain at the outset that the
plaintiff's case is not derisory, and then to employ it as a factor of last resort if all other
considerations are equal. The standard of 'a good arguable case' seems to have no place
here.

The analogy with proceedings under RSC Ord 11 also seems rather distant. It is true
that the service of a writ out of the jurisdiction commands a foreigner to appear, against
his will. But he need not comply, if he does not choose. The Mareva injunction, by
contrast, bites directly on the defendant's assets; he must come in and defend, or lose
them. Moreoever, it is now the law, which was not so when the *Pertamina* case was
decided, that the Mareva injunction applies to persons resident in the United Kingdom,
so the relationship with Ord 11 seems even more remote.

Nevertheless, the *Pertamina* case is the foundation authority, and the test of a 'good
arguable case' was adopted by the Court of Appeal in *Farey-Jones (Insurance) Ltd v IFM
Funding GmbH* [1979] CA Transcript 223 so it seems appropriate to adopt it here. But
what exactly does the expression mean? The issue before the House of Lords in *Vitkovice
Horni a Mutni Tezirstvo v Korner* [1951] 2 All ER 334, [1951] AC 869 was whether, on the
affidavit evidence, it was 'made sufficiently to appear to the court or judge that the case
is a proper one for service out of the jurisdiction': see Ord 11, r 4. The case is not easy to
analyse, but it appears that the following propositions are justified. (1) The plaintiff must
do more than make a bare assertion of facts which would give the court jurisdiction. (2)
The question whether the plaintiff has shown a prima facie case is not an appropriate test,
at least where the respondent has adduced evidence in opposition. (3) The court cannot,
and should not attempt to, try the issues at the interlocutory stage. (4) Nor does the
expression 'made sufficiently to appear' mean that the court should apply the same
standard of proof as will be appropriate at the trial. For reasons which must have been
special to the situation in *Vitkovice Horni a Hutni Tezirstvo v Korner* but which do not
appear from the report, two of the speeches refer to proof beyond reasonable doubt.
Presumably, in an ordinary case, the proposition implies that the plaintiff need not
establish his case on balance of probability. (5) Leaving aside the speech of Lord Oaksey,

who appears on this particular issue to have been in a minority, the speeches use a variety of terms to express the same concept: 'satisfied', 'a proper one to be heard in our courts', 'a good arguable case', 'a strong argument', a strong case for argument'. These expressions suggest that the plaintiff has to do substantially more than show that the case is merely 'arguable': a word which to my mind at least connotes that, although the claim will not be laughed out of court, the plaintiff will not be justified in feeling any optimism. On the other hand, if I am right on proposition (4), the plaintiff need not go so far as to persuade the judge that he is likely to win.

There is, however, another authority to be taken into account. In *Z Ltd v A* [1982] 1 All ER 556, [1982] QB 558 Kerr LJ laid down a series of guidelines, in which Eveleigh LJ concurred, for the exercise of the Mareva jurisdiction which have been widely acted on in practice. In section 1 of his judgment, Kerr LJ refers on three occasions to the grant of an injunction where the plaintiff is 'likely' to recover judgment. Does this entail that, whatever *Vitkovice v Horni a Hutni Teżirstvo v Korner* [1951] 2 All ER 334, [1951] AC 869 may appear to say, the jurisdiction should not be invoked unless the available evidence points to the conclusion that the plaintiff has a better than even chance of success? I believe not. Kerr LJ was not addressing himself specifically to the present issue. In my judgment, he was doing no more than reiterate that the plaintiff must always demonstrate a likelihood of success, and was not prescribing the degree of likelihood.

In these circumstances, I consider that the right course is to adopt the test of a good arguable case, in the sense of a case which is more than barely capable of serious argument, and yet not necessarily one which the judge believes to have a better than 50% chance of success.

In conclusion, I should add that it is particularly important in the present instance that the court should not be drawn into a premature trial of the action, rather than a preliminary appraisal of the plaintiff's case, for the parties have contracted for a determination by arbitrators, not by the court, and nothing must be done to pre-empt the decision of the agreed tribunal.

Dissipation of assets

It may be useful to start with a series of citations. First, there is the case from which the Mareva jurisdiction derives its name, *Mareva Compania Naviera SA v International Bulkcarriers SA, The Mareva* (1975) [1980] 1 All ER 213 at 215 per Lord Denning MR:

> '[There is jurisdiction to grant an injunction if] there is a danger that the debtor may dispose of his assets so as to defeat [the debt] before judgment.'

In *Rasu Maritima SA v Pertamina Perusahaan Pertambangan Minyak Dan Gas Bumi Negara (Pertamina) and Government of Indonesia (as interveners)* [1977] 3 All ER 324 at 334, [1978] QB 644 at 660–661 Lord Denning MR (approving Kerr J) said:

> '... on being apprised of the proceedings, the defendant is liable to remove his assets, thereby precluding the plaintiff in advance from enjoying the fruits of a judgment which appears irresistible on the evidence before the court. The defendant can then largely ignore the plaintiff's claim in the courts of this country and snap his fingers at any judgment which may be given against him.'

In *Etablissement Esefka International Anstalt v Central Bank of Nigeria* [1979] 1 Lloyd's Rep 445 at 448 Lord Denning MR said:

> '[The jurisdiction exists] where there is danger of the money being taken out of the jurisdiction so that if the plaintiffs succeed they are not likely to get their money.'

Brandon LJ said (at 449):

> '[The jurisdiction exists where] the assets of the defendants are likely to be removed from the jurisdiction so as to avoid payment of any judgment which the plaintiffs might obtain.'

a In *Iraqi Ministry of Defence v Arcepey Shipping Co SA (Gillespie Bros & Co Ltd intervening),
The Angel Bell* [1980] 1 All ER 480 at 485–486, [1981] QB 65 at 71–72 Robert Goff J
rejected a submission that the purpose of the jurisdiction is 'to freeze a foreign defendant's
assets in this country to ensure that there is a fund available in this country from which
the plaintiff will be able to satisfy a judgment'. Robert Goff J went on to say that the
purpose of the jurisdiction was not to rewrite the law of insolvency—

b '. . . but simply to prevent the injustice of a foreign defendant removing his assets
from the jurisdiction which might otherwise have been available to satisfy a
judgment.'

In *Third Chandris Shipping Corp v Unimarine SA, The Pythia, The Angelic Wings, The Genie*
[1979] 2 All ER 972 at 985, [1979] QB 645 at 669 Lord Denning MR said:

c 'The plaintiff should give some grounds for believing that there is a risk of the
assets being removed before the judgment or award is satisfied. The mere fact that
the defendant is abroad is not by itself sufficient. No one would wish any reputable
foreign company to be plagued with a Mareva injunction simply because it has
agreed to London arbitration. But there are some foreign companies whose structure
invites comment. We often see in this court a corporation which is registered in a
country where the company law is so loose that nothing is known about it, where it
d does no work and has no officers and no assets. Nothing can be found out about the
membership, or its control, or its assets, or the charges on them. Judgment cannot
be enforced against it. There is no reciprocal enforcement of judgments. It is
nothing more than a name grasped from the air, as elusive as the Cheshire cat. In
such cases the very fact of incorporation there gives some ground for believing there
is a risk that, if judgment or an award is obtained, it may go unsatisfied . . . Other
e grounds may be shown for believing there is a risk. But some such should be
shown.'

Lawton LJ said ([1979] 2 All ER 972 at 987, [1979] QB 645 at 671–672):

'The mere fact that a defendant having assets within the jurisdiction . . . is a
foreigner or a foreign corporation cannot, in my judgment, by itself justify the
f granting of a Mareva injunction. There must be facts from which the Commercial
Court, like a prudent, sensible commercial man, can properly infer a danger of
default if assets are removed from the jurisdiction . . . [The judges of the Commercial
Court] have special experience of commercial cases and they can be expected to
identify likely debt dodgers as well as, probably better than, most businessmen.
They should not expect to be given proof of previous defaults or specific incidents
g of commercial malpractice. Further, they should remember that affidavits asserting
belief in, or the fear of, likely default have no probative value unless the sources and
grounds thereof are set out . . . In my judgment an affidavit in support of a Mareva
injunction should give enough particulars of the plaintiff's case to enable the court
to assess its strength and should set out what enquiries have been made about the
defendant's business and what information has been revealed, including that relating
h to its size, origins, business domicile, the location of its known assets and the
circumstances in which the dispute has arisen. These facts should enable a
commercial judge to infer whether there is likely to be any real risk of default.
Default is most unlikely if the defendant is a long-established, well-known foreign
corporation or is known to have substantial assets in countries where English
judgments can easily be enforced either under the Foreign Judgments (Reciprocal
j Enforcement) Act 1933 or otherwise. But if nothing can be found out about the
defendant, that by itself may be enough to justify a Mareva injunction.'

In *Montecchi v Shimco (UK) Ltd* [1979] 1 WLR 1180 at 1183–1184 Bridge LJ said:

'. . . the basis of the Mareva injunction is that there has to be a real reason to
apprehend that if the injunction is not made, the intending plaintiff in this country

may be deprived of a remedy against the foreign defendant whom he seeks to sue ... Here, for all we know ... the sellers ... are persons of perfectly sound financial standing ... If those counterclaims are eventually successful, then they will result in judgments ... which will be enforceable in Italy under the procedure provided by the Foreign Judgments (Reciprocal Enforcement) Act 1933 ...'

In *Barclay-Johnson v Yuill* [1980] 3 All ER 190 at 195, [1980] 1 WLR 1259 at 1265 Sir Robert Megarry V-C said:

'[For the jurisdiction to exist] it must appear that there is a danger of default if the assets are removed from the jurisdiction. Even if the risk of removal is great, no Mareva injunction should be granted unless there is also a danger of default.'

In *Prince Abdul Rahman Bin Turki Al Sudairy v Abu-Taha* [1980] 3 All ER 409 at 412, [1980] 1 WLR 1268 at 1273 Lord Denning MR said:

'[An injunction may be granted against a resident of the United Kingdom] if the circumstances are such that there is a danger of his absconding, or a danger of his assets being removed out of the jurisdiction or disposed of within the jurisdiction, or otherwise dealt with so that there is a danger that the plaintiff, if he gets judgment, will not be able to get it satisfied.'

In *Z Ltd v A* [1982] 1 All ER 556 at 561, [1982] QB 558 at 571 Lord Denning MR said:

'The Mareva jurisdiction extends to cases where there is a danger that the assets will be dissipated in this country as well as by removal out of the jurisdiction.'

Kerr LJ said ([1982] 1 All ER 556 at 571–572, [1982] QB 558 at 585–586):

'[It is an abuse to use the jurisdiction] in circumstances where there may be no real danger of the defendant dissipating his assets to make himself "judgment-proof". ... [Relief should only be granted where there are] reasons to believe that the defendant has assets within the jurisdiction to meet the judgment, in whole or in part, but may well take steps designed to ensure that these are no longer available or traceable when judgment is given against him ... the great value of this jurisdiction must not be debased by allowing it to become something which is invoked simply to obtain security for a judgment in advance, and still less as a means of pressurising defendants into settlements.'

These dicta must be approached with some caution, for the law and practice on the grant of Mareva injunctions has not stood still since the jurisdiction was first devised. Thus, I believe that it is no longer either necessary or sufficient (if it ever was) to establish that there is a risk that the assets will be taken abroad: although this will, of course, always be a very material consideration. Moreover, most of the passages quoted come from cases on which this particular point was not in issue. This may account for the apparent discrepancy in the authorities as to the necessity for proof that the defendant will deal with his assets with the object, and not just with the effect, of putting them out of the plaintiff's reach.

Nevertheless, certain themes can be seen to run through the cases. It is not enough for the plaintiff to assert a risk that the assets will be dissipated. He must demonstrate this by solid evidence. This evidence may take a number of different forms. It may consist of direct evidence that the defendant has previously acted in a way which shows that his probity is not to be relied on. Or the plaintiff may show what type of company the defendant is (where it is incorporated, what are its corporate structure and assets, and so on) so as to raise an inference that the company is not to be relied on. Or, again, the plaintiff may be able to found his case on the fact that inquiries about the characteristics of the defendant have led to a blank wall. Precisely what form the evidence may take will depend on the particular circumstances of the case. But the evidence must always be there. Mere proof that the company is incorporated abroad, accompanied by the

allegation that there are no reachable assets in the United Kingdom apart from those
a which it is sought to enjoin, will not be enough.

THE FACTS
The strength of the claim
    I will deal first with the claim concerning boiler tubes, to which the greater part of the
monetary loss is attached. This raises issues of interpretation and of fact.
b   The issue of interpretation arises from the words 'average damages affecting class'. This
curious expression raises several questions. (1) Must the defects actually affect the vessel's
class? Or is the test whether the defects should affect the class? What happens if the
classification surveyor (a) does not know about the defects; (b) does not know about the
defects but should have known about them; (c) did know about them, but failed to
appreciate their significance? (2) What is the extent, if any, of the vendor's duty to
c disclose defects to the surveyor? If he has such a duty at all, does it comprise only the
defects of which he actually knows, or does it embrace all defects of which he should
have known? (3) Does the term extend to all defects, or only to those which are
accidental? (4) If so, is the obligation limited to those accidental defects which are covered
by insurance? If so, does this mean an insurance in ordinary terms (and if so, what are
ordinary terms) or to the terms of the vendor's own particular policy?
d   These are not easy questions. There is authority which deals with some of them. In
Piccinini v Partrederiet Trigon II, The Alfred Trigon [1981] 2 Lloyd's Rep 333 Robert Goff J
held that the warranty related only to those defects which did affect class, or would have
done if known to the surveyor, and which resulted from an accidental cause covered by
insurance in the ordinary form. It is probable, although perhaps not inevitable, that the
arbitrators in the present case will regard themselves as bound by this decision. But the
e losing party may seek leave to appeal; if leave is granted, the judge may be persuaded to
take a different view; and in any event the solution proposed in *The Alfred Trigon* does
not dispose of all the problems raised by the present dispute. I cannot predict the outcome
of all this, and indeed I believe that it would be wrong to try. All one can do is to
approach the issues of fact in the light of *The Alfred Trigon*, but to note that it is not
necessarily the last word on all the points which arise.
f   Accordingly, any assessment of the buyers' prospects of success in the arbitration must
deal with the existence of defects at the time of delivery; their degree; the extent to
which a classification surveyor ought to have known about them; the extent to which
their existence (known or unknown) ought to have affected the vessel's class; the conduct
of the sellers in pointing them out, or not pointing them out, to Germanischer Lloyd;
the cause of the defects, and in particular whether they arose accidentally, or by wear and
g tear; and, if accidentally, whether through a peril insured under a notional insurance
policy, or the sellers' actual insurance policy.
    The following groups of evidence are at present before the court. (1) A history on the
following lines: leakages disclosed by tests alleged (but apparently also denied) to have
been regarded by the buyers as sufficient; repair of the leakages thus disclosed during
February 1983; further leakages at the beginning of March 1983, with more repairs
h done; another leak on 6 March, repaired in the course of the same day; a further leakage
on 7 March, and another on 8 March (the day of delivery) also repaired within the day.
(2) A series of telex messages from the buyers, directed to the head office of Germanischer
Lloyd as well as to the sellers, expressing their apprehensions as to the state of the boiler
tubing, and their forecasts of what would be found if the boilers were opened up in the
way which the buyers asserted was correct. (3) A series of intimations by the sellers that
j the vessel was fully classed. Subsequently, a senior surveyor from the head office of
Germanischer Lloyd, Mr W Stephens, visited the ship and had discussions with the
parties and his society's local non-exclusive surveyor. There is an issue about whether (as
one of the buyers' deponents asserts) Mr Stephens admitted that in the light of
information now available he would wish to carry out repairs, or whether in a telex
message (which is itself said to be ambiguous) he indorsed the views of his local surveyor,

given before delivery, that the ship was fit to be classed. (4) The intervention of a new classification society, in the shape of Det Norske Veritas (DNV). At first sight, it seems strange indeed that a vessel which was to perform only one voyage before being laid up should be favoured with entry in two classification societies. It was, however, explained in argument that DNV were invoked, not because their refusal to accept the vessel as fit for class could in itself retrospectively entail that the vessel was subject to average damage affecting class, but because a strong adverse opinion expressed by the surveyors of one society would be evidence to show that the vessel should not have been classed by Germanischer Lloyd. At all events, a principal surveyor from DNV has carried out ultrasonic measurements of tube thicknesses and recommends the renewal of numerous tubes. His opinion is concurred in by Lieut-Comdr K I Short, an independent surveyor retained by the buyers. On the other hand, there is a report by Mr J C Edon, a surveyor appointed by the sellers, based on an inspection made after delivery of the vessel. This indicates that in Mr Edon's opinion the condition of the tubing was in general acceptable, apart apparently from certain water wall tubes which the surveyor considers could prudently be repaired at the present stage, rather than incur the expense of opening up the boiler again on some subsequent occasion. (5) The buyers speak, at second hand, of reports by the purchasers of a sister ship, sold out of lay-up at about the same time, that there had been serious problems with the boilers after delivery. The sellers, however, depose that there have been no complaints from these purchasers.

What is to be made of this body of evidence? Not very much, in my view. The evidence consists of a mass of contradictory and not always comprehensible technical assertions, unilluminated by oral evidence from persons who will be eventual witnesses at the hearing of the arbitration, such as Mr Mizra (the non-exclusive surveyor of Germanischer Lloyd), Mr Stephens, Mr Haakonsen (the surveyor of DNV), Mr May (the sellers' technical superintendent), Mr Tsakalotos, Mr Schmidt (the manager of the company which performed the pre-delivery repairs), and so on. At first sight one can well feel sceptical about an inference of such widespread defects, based on the spasmodic occurrence of a comparatively small leakage, all repaired before delivery. One could sympathise with the suggestion by the sellers that the buyers, having bought a cheap ship (the price was not greatly above the scrap value) are now seeking to have her converted into a trouble-free ship, at the sellers' expense. Tempting as this approach may be, I do not think it can properly be adopted at the present stage: for there is the evidence of Commander Short and (at second hand) of the DNV surveyors, against whose impartiality no imputation has been made. If they consider that a prudent owner would effect the repairs proposed by DNV (bearing in mind the temperature and pressure at which the boiler operates) I cannot find it proper to dismiss the buyers' assertions as inherently implausible.

As regards the cause of the defects, there is a direct conflict of evidence between the independent experts, whether this was wear and tear, or negligence by the crew in failing to prepare the vessel for lay-up. If the latter opinion prevails at the arbitration, the buyers will plainly have grounds for arguing that the damage was of a type covered by the ordinary hull policy.

The intervention of the DNV surveyor also gives the buyers real grounds for contending that whatever damage exists ought to have been ascertained by the Germanischer Lloyd surveyor, or that it ought to have been pointed out to the surveyor by the sellers. On at least some of the possible meanings of cl 18 (including, I believe, the one favoured by Robert Goff J) this gives the buyers a real case for arguing that there was a breach of contract by the sellers.

There remains the additional claim relating to the tailshaft and stern gland. The buyers have recently come forward with what seems to be quite strong evidence that some actual damage is present. In addition there is a dispute about leakage which is quite impossible to resolve, or indeed in some measure to understand, on the evidence now available. I believe that the buyers have a real claim, in relation to these items of dispute.

The position as regards the likely cost of repairs, and of the time taken to carry them out, is unsatisfactory. The estimates vary by a factor of more than 20. This discrepancy is due to a great extent, but by no means entirely, to the difference of opinion as to what work is called for. On the material available, I feel obliged to hold that the buyers do have a real case for claiming the whole of the amount to which the injunction relates, although, if the repairs are as necessary as they assert, they will presumably carry them out, and thus enable some more accurate quantification to be made.

In all these circumstances I think it right to hold, notwithstanding some initial scepticism, that the buyers have demonstrated a sufficient case to satisfy the first of the requirements for the grant of a Mareva injunction. In reaching this conclusion I have relied solely on cl 18 of the memorandum of agreement. I need therefore say nothing about the claim under cl 19, about which I have reservations, to say the least.

I should mention one further point. In the initial affidavit Mr Nott-Bower asserts that the Germanischer Lloyd surveyor was 'in effect turning a blind eye to what are clearly non-permanent and unsatisfactory repairs to boiler tubing'. This expression conveys to me a much more serious imputation than mere negligence. The conclusions just expressed should not be understood as suggesting that the buyers have substantial grounds to support this imputation, which forms no part of my assessment of the buyers' case.

Risk of dissipation of assets

It is convenient at this stage to mention an issue between counsel as to the way in which the court should approach the buyers' assertion that they need to be protected against the risk of seeing the sellers' assets dissipated before the award becomes enforceable.

For the sellers, it was contended that the court should look first at the evidence led for the buyers on the ex parte hearing, and that if this was sufficient to establish the necessary degree of risk, the inquiry should go no further. The sellers' own evidence could not legitimately be used to reinforce the buyers' case.

For the buyers, criticism was made of the evidence for the sellers, which was said to be incomplete and unsatisfactory, on several important points.

In my judgment, neither of these attitudes is wholly correct. The judge who hears the proceedings inter partes must decide on all the evidence laid before him. The evidence adduced for the defendant will normally be looked at for the purposes of deciding whether it is enough to displace any inferences which might otherwise be drawn from the plaintiff's evidence. But I see no reason in principle why, if the defendant's evidence raises more questions than it answers, and does so in a manner which tends to enhance rather than allay any justifiable apprehension concerning dissipation of assets, the court should be obliged to leave this out of account. On the other hand, the plaintiff has no right to criticise the defendant's evidence, for omissions or obscurities. The defendant is entitled to choose for himself what evidence, if any, he adduces. The less impressive his evidence, the less effective it will be to displace any adverse inferences. But there must be an inference to be displaced, if the injunction is to stand, and comment on the defendant's evidence must not be taken so far that the burden of proof is unconsciously reversed.

So one must start with the evidence for the buyers. I have already set out the relevant passages from Mr Nott-Bower's affidavit. The contents amount to this. A West German company has incurred a large indebtedness. It has recently sold its only two ships. It has no assets in this country apart from the price of the vessel which (the buyers surmise) will immediately be removed from the jurisdiction. The deponent is 'pessimistic' about the buyers honouring an award unless the money is retained within the jurisdiction. Furthermore, the sellers have refused to give an indemnity in respect of further leakages.

I will deal with the last point first. It amounts to a complaint that the sellers have failed to admit liability in advance, in respect of defects not yet known to exist. I see no reason why they should do any such thing, or why their refusal to do so should justify the inference that if they are held liable they will no longer be in funds to pay.

The remainder of the evidence led on the ex parte application was of a familiar kind, and, I must add, of a kind which I believe very often procures the grant of an injunction at the present day. Counsel on behalf of the sellers has, however, drawn attention to certain important omissions from the affidavit. (1) The deponent did not say that the sellers, or companies and persons connected with them, have a history of default on loans or trade debts, that, in the words of Lawton LJ, they are 'debt dodgers'. He did not speak to any bad reputation in the trade. He did not even say that the buyers had tried without success to find out about the sellers' reputation. (2) He did not say, and indeed in the case of a company incorporated in the Federal Republic of Germany, could not say that companies registered there are difficult to track down, or are notoriously fallible in providing assets to meet large adverse judgments. (3) He did not say, and again could not say, that there exists no mechanism for enforcement of awards in the sellers' country of incorporation, for the Federal Republic (unlike the Republic of Liberia, in which the buyers are incorporated) is a party to the New York Convention on the Recognition and Enforcement of Foreign Arbitral Awards (New York, 31 December 1958; TS 20 (1976); Cmnd 6419).

To what extent are these omissions compensated by new material brought forward by the buyers on the inter partes hearing? Apart from some comment on the sellers' evidence, two points are made in an affidavit from the buyers' solicitors.

First, an account is given of an unsuccessful attempt by the buyers to persuade the sellers to put up security in the shape of a guarantee by a substantial company in the group of which the sellers form part. In my judgment, this gets the buyers nowhere, for the argument is circular. If the sellers are worthy people, whose readiness to satisfy an adverse judgment there is no sound reason to impugn, the court should not interfere with the right to employ their assets as they wish. If the case is not one for interference by injunction, the sellers should not be compelled to provide security to avoid an injunction. If they should not be compelled to provide such security, they are merely standing on their rights in refusing it, and no adverse inference can be drawn as to their probity.

The second item of new evidence introduced by the sellers concerns the corporate structure of the sellers. I will return to this shortly.

I now turn to the evidence for the sellers, furnished in an affidavit of Mr Henning Oldendorff, an officer of the sellers' managers. The most relevant part reads:

'(4) I confirm very emphatically:—(1) there is and has never been any intention of dealing with those proceeds so as to avoid any award that may be made against them; (2) the proceeds would probably have been removed from the Citibank account in London for other normal business of the company because they could be put to better use than earning a low rate of interest; (3) the most likely use to which the money would be put is investment in other German companies in the Oldendorff group; (4) there is and has never been any intention of liquidating the company so as to avoid enforcement of any award; (5) if the market improves sufficiently the company may well become shipowners again, although it is to be appreciated that losing nearly $100 million on the price of the 'Niedersachsen' and the 'Schleswig Holstein' has not been a happy experience. I totally reject Mr. Nott-Bower's suggestion that we would "very quickly" remove the money implying that we would act improperly.

(5) I would add that since the company of Messrs. Egon Oldendorff K.G. was formed in 1921 by my father, Herr Egon Oldendorff, to my knowledge, none of the Oldendorff associated companies have ever: (a) defaulted on a loan; (b) failed to honour an arbitration award in whatever jurisdiction; (c) failed to honour a court judgment in any jurisdiction. As a result the Oldendorff Group has an excellent reputation in respect of the above matters in the shipping world.'

The buyers say that this affidavit reinforces their own evidence, and so in part it does. It confirms their assertion that the moneys will be removed from the jurisdiction, unless the injunction is maintained. It goes on to admit that once removed from the United

Kingdom, the funds will not stay with the company, but will be redeployed within the group; and the affidavit does not say that they will necessarily stay in West Germany. The affidavit also shows what is indeed obvious, that the sellers have suffered a grievous financial blow from the fall in the market, which must impair or totally preclude their ability to meet from their own funds any damages which may be awarded.

These are important points, and the sellers could well have done more to answer them. Thus: (1) the sellers have not said anything about the corporate structure of the Oldendorff group, or how the partners in the buyers' limited partnership, referred to in the affidavit of Mr Strong of the buyers' solicitors, fit into the structure as a whole; (2) the sellers have said nothing about the capitalisation of the group. The only information comes from Commander Short's affidavit, which indicates a very modest share capital for the immediate proprietors of the sellers; (3) the sellers have given no information at all about their own activities or finances. They do not even say whether they are still trading; (4) not a single figure is given for the assets, turnover or profits of any company in the Oldendorff group.

These omissions are such that if the sellers had the task of making the court confident the money would be there when called for, I would doubt very much whether they had succeeded. But this is not their task. They have no obligation to disclose their financial affairs, simply to answer a challenge from the buyers which is unsupported by solid evidence. Their reticence does not justify the inference that they have uncomfortable facts to hide. True, they have suffered losses on ships which (like all trading ships) were heavily mortgaged. Yet the sellers are not bankrupt; the mortgages have been redeemed, no doubt with backing from the rest of the group; there is no suggestion that the group as a whole has failed to weather the storm. If the group has absorbed losses of nearly $100m on these two ships, why should the court assume that it will let the company go to the wall for a further loss of less than one-hundredth of this amount? (I should add that, since the buyers were, on their own evidence, ready to accept a corporate guarantee for the amount claimed, they can scarcely be heard to assert that the group is not able, as distinct from willing, to meet the claim).

More than this, however, there is the evidence that the other Oldendorff companies have always paid their debts. There is no evidence the other way. No guilt by association can be attributed to the sellers.

In all these circumstances, I consider that the buyers have failed to prove a degree of risk sufficient to justify the maintenance of the injunction. Having been reminded of the authorities, and after hearing full argument, I am bound to say that I am doubtful whether the ex parte relief should have been granted in the first place. It may well be that current practice has unwittingly crept away from the authorities. If this case should go further, this is a matter on which guidance would, I believe, be welcome to the judges who hear these applications. Be that as it may, I consider that on the evidence now before the court the application to discharge the injunction should be allowed.

Further matters

There are three other questions, canvassed during argument, which require to be mentioned only briefly, in view of the conclusion which I have just expressed.

First, the sellers complained that there was no mention in Mr Nott-Bower's affidavit of the fact that the sellers were members of a long-established group of companies. There is force in this complaint. To the ex parte judge, there was nothing to detract from the impression of a defendant which had once been a two-ship foreign company, and was now a no-ship company, with a substantial claim against it. The picture is now seen to be different. How well informed the buyers were before they launched the proceedings, I do not know, but it is hard to credit that they would do business with a concern of whose financial and corporate background they were wholly ignorant. Plaintiffs who seek Mareva relief will do well to bear in mind that the same obligations of candour apply to these proceedings, as to any other form of ex parte application.

Second, it is contended for the sellers that the present case is an abuse of the Mareva procedure. The matter arose in this way. As I have said, the first ex parte application was made before the sale was completed. The affidavit of Mr Nott-Bower disclosed the intent to apply the injunction to the purchase price. After completion, the application was renewed. At this time, reference was made to *Negocios del Mar v Doric Shipping Corp SA, The Assios* [1979] 1 Lloyd's Rep 331. This was a case in which the vendors of a ship had obtained a Mareva injunction in advance of completion without disclosing their intention to employ it for the retention of the purchase price. The Court of Appeal upheld the decision of Mocatta J, who discharged the injunction on the ground that the court should have been informed of the vendor's intention. This decision was plainly distinguishable in the present instance, since full disclosure was made in Mr Nott-Bower's affidavit. There was, however, another authority on the question, which was not before the court when the ex parte injunction in the present case was granted, namely *Z Ltd v A* [1982] 1 All ER 556, [1982] QB 558. In the course of the judgment, to which I have already referred, Kerr LJ said ([1982] 1 All ER 556 at 571–572, [1982] QB 558 at 585):

'The second, and fortunately much rarer, illustration of what I would regard as an abuse of this procedure, is where it is used as a means of enabling a person to make a payment under a contract or intended contract to someone in circumstances where he regards the demand for the payment as unjustifiable; or where he actually believes, or even knows, that the demand is unlawful; and where he obtains a Mareva injunction ex parte in advance of the payment, which is then immediately served and has the effect of "freezing" the sum paid over. Thus, we were told by counsel for the plaintiff that payments are sometimes made for premiums which are required illegally on the assignment of leases, and which are then "frozen" immediately as soon as the payment has been made. In effect, this amounts to using the injunction as a means of setting a trap for the payee. A reported instance of such a case (though not in a context of alleged illegality) is *The Assios* [1979] 1 Lloyd's Rep 331, where the injunction was set aside because the plaintiff had not disclosed to the court that he intended to use the order for this purpose. However, in my view even the disclosure of the intention should not suffice to obtain the injunction in such cases. If a person is willing to make such a payment, appreciating the implications, the courts should not assist him to safeguard the payment in advance by means of a Mareva injunction.'

I do not know what effect a citation of this judgment, that is, the judgment of Kerr LJ, would have had, if made at the stage of the ex parte application. Quite possibly, I would have acceded to the argument now advanced for the buyers, that Kerr LJ was dealing only with applications made in advance of payment; and I would no doubt have been impressed by the information, furnished on the present hearing, that the plaintiffs in *The Assios* had, notwithstanding the decision of the Court of Appeal, obtained an injunction once the price had been paid.

The matter has now been argued out in full, at the inter partes hearing. I have found it difficult. Counsel for the buyers pointed out, rightly, as it seems to me, that there is no logic in a rule which would prevent a plaintiff from enjoining the disposal of an asset, simply because the asset took the shape of moneys paid to the defendant by the plaintiff himself. Nor would a rule be workable, if it precluded an application for Mareva relief within a reasonable time of the asset having been paid by the plaintiff to the defendant. The only solution, counsel for the buyers contended, is to treat sums paid by the plaintiff on the same footing as any other asset.

While I see the logic of this, it is not compelling. There is something unattractive about the idea of a buyer, who is ostensibly paying the full price of a chattel, preparing himself behind the seller's back to deprive him of part of the price. This gives the buyer the best of both worlds. He is spared the awkward decision whether to reject the res vendita, with the possible commercial loss to himself from not having the chattel, coupled with the risk of an action by the seller for non-acceptance. Instead, he gets the res vendita, avoids an action, and can secure himself for a cross-claim in damages, pursued in his own good time. I am very doubtful whether this is a proper use of the Mareva jurisdiction. On the other hand, how is the judge to identify the cases where relief should be refused? I believe that the answer may, and I emphasise 'may', be that it will normally be an abuse of the procedure for a seller to restrain the dispersal of the purchase price where (a) the claim on which the injunction is founded is itself based on the contract of sale and (b) the court can infer that the seller knows of the facts on which his claim is based before the sale is completed. In the event however, it is not necessary to express a concluded view on this point, since I propose to set aside the injunction on other grounds.

Finally, I should say that if I had been disposed to maintain the injunction, I would have wished to hear submissions on whether the buyers' cross-undertakings in damages should be secured. The buyers are incorporated in Liberia, a state with which the United Kingdom has no arrangements for reciprocal enforcements of judgments. Perhaps they are a wealthy company, with abundant assets in the United Kingdom. So far, they have not said so. Here again, however, it is not necessary to explore the matter, in view of the conclusion which I have reached on the principal issue.

In the result, the application succeeds, and the injunction will be discharged.

Order to discharge injunction. Leave to the buyers to appeal. Injunction to continue in force pending the appeal.

K Mydeen Esq   Barrister.

Interlocutory appeal
The buyers appealed against Mustill J's decision. The sellers served a respondent's notice that the decision to discharge the injunction should be affirmed.

John Griffiths QC and *Bernard Eder* for the buyers.
Timothy Young for the sellers.

Cur adv vult

29 July. The following judgment of the court was delivered.

KERR LJ. This is the judgment of the court on an appeal from a reserved judgment of Mustill J delivered on 10 May 1983 whereby he discharged a Mareva injunction, after a hearing inter partes, which he had himself previously granted on the plaintiffs' application ex parte. In the course of his lengthy judgment the judge referred to many of the authorities concerning the grant or refusal of Mareva injunctions in the context of two questions on which he felt that further guidance was needed. He formulated these questions as follows (see p 402, ante):

'First, what probability of success at the ultimate trial is the plaintiff required to demonstrate, before an injunction can be properly granted or maintained? Second, what type of prejudice must the plaintiff demonstrate, in the shape of a risk of dissipation of assets, and with what degree of conviction must it be shown, before the defendant's assets can properly be detained to await a possible judgment?'

The voluminous evidence was directed to both these aspects, though mainly to the first. We begin by summarising this, which we can do fairly shortly.

The first question
The dispute arose out of a memorandum of agreement dated 24 January 1983 in what is usually known as the Norwegian sale form whereby the plaintiffs (the buyers) agreed

to buy the mv Niedersachsen from the defendants (the sellers) for a total price of $US3,745,000. As provided in the printed form, a deposit of 10% was to be paid by the buyers on signing the contract and the balance on delivery 'without any deductions'. Both payments were to be made to the sellers' account with Citibank, London. The printed clause providing for dry docking and inspection was deleted, and the dispute centres on an additional cl 18 of which the following terms are material:

'Delivery of the vessel where presently anchored off Dubai, without dry-docking, safely afloat . . . with steam raised in both boilers and ready to sail between 14th of February, 1983, and 7th of March, 1983, in sellers' option . . . present class fully maintained, free of recommendations, free of average damages affecting class . . .'

Although the vessel was in class with Germanischer Lloyd, the buyers had grave doubts about the condition of her boilers, since there had been some leakages in February 1983 and further leakages on 6, 7 and 8 March, the day on which the vessel was delivered, all of which were said to have been repaired, but which understandably gave concern to the buyers. There was also some evidence suggesting that there might be damage to the tailshaft and stern gland. The buyers and an independent surveyor who advised them disagreed with the conclusion of the surveyors of Germanischer Lloyd that the vessel had been properly classed, as required by the contract, and there was also some appearance of dissent from this conclusion by a surveyor of Det Norske Veritas, another classification society which was brought in on behalf of the buyers. The sellers and their advisers refuted all these conclusions. The main point at issue is not the condition of the boilers and the other alleged defects as such, but whether these constituted 'average damages affecting class'. The vessel was about seven years old; she was bought as she lay at a price which was said to be not greatly in excess of her scrap value (although this value is also in dispute); and the sellers maintained that the alleged defects were due to wear and tear and not 'average damages affecting class'.

The buyers' first ex parte application for a Mareva injunction was made on 7 March, the day before the vessel's delivery. The judge rightly rejected this as being premature. The buyers then completed the purchase and paid the balance of the price and renewed their application on the following day, asking for an order to freeze the total amount of $3,745,000 in the sellers' account at Citibank. The judge granted this application, but only to the extent of $787,000, the buyers' then estimate of the cost of repairs and of their resulting loss. On 29 and 30 March and 11 April there was then an inter partes hearing on the sellers' application to discharge the injunction, and the judge did so on 10 May for the reasons discussed hereafter. These bear on the second of the two questions posed by him, as set out above, with which we will deal later on in this judgment.

Since the inter partes hearing the buyers have produced further affidavit evidence (without objection from the respondent sellers) describing what the state of the boilers and the tailshaft was in fact found to be after the vessel had been delivered and had sailed to Bahrein and had been opened up for repairs. They say that whereas their original estimate of the cost of repairs and of other losses which they would sustain had been $787,000, their present estimate is $1,300,000. However, the sellers have not had the opportunity of dealing with these allegations, and in the circumstances it is unnecessary to consider them further. There was rightly no application before this court to increase the amount of the injunction beyond the sum of $787,000, and there still remains the hotly disputed issue whether any of the defects were 'average damages affecting class'. The substance of the buyers' appeal is simply that the injunction should not have been discharged pending the hearing of the dispute by arbitration under the auspices of the London Maritime Arbitrators Association, which has been fixed to begin in about eight months.

It is convenient to pause at this point since this is all that needs to be said by way of summarising the evidence on the first of the questions posed by the judge. Having referred to a number of the authorities, he answered this by saying, in effect: 'Have the plaintiffs (the buyers) shown that they have a good arguable case?' He took this test from the judgment of Lord Denning MR in *Rasu Maritima SA v Perusahaan Pertambangan Minyak Dan Gas Bumi Negara (Pertamina)* [1977] 3 All ER 324 at 334, [1978] QB 644 at 661 and pointed out that this test was followed by this court in *Farey-Jones (Insurance) Ltd v IFM Funding GmbH* [1979] CA Transcript 223. Although other, and perhaps slightly stronger, words have been used in other cases, the sellers did not challenge this formulation of the present appeal. We respectfully agree with it, but would add that this aspect of the evidence before the court should not be looked at in isolation when deciding whether or not to exercise the discretion to grant a Mareva injunction. The ultimate basis for this jurisdiction is now to be found in s 37 of the Supreme Court Act 1981. Subsection (1) provides:

'The High Court may by order (whether interlocutory or final) grant an injunction . . . in all cases in which it appears to the court to be just and convenient to do so.'

In the context of Mareva injunctions one must now also have regard to sub-s (3):

'The power of the High Court under subsection (1) to grant an interlocutory injunction restraining a party to any proceedings from removing from the jurisdiction of the High Court, or otherwise dealing with, assets located within that jurisdiction shall be exercisable in cases where that party is, as well as in cases where he is not, domiciled, resident or present within that jurisdiction.'

It follows that the evidence, including the evidence on the second question posed by the judge to which we turn in a moment, must be looked at as a whole. A 'good arguable case' is no doubt the minimum which the plaintiff must show in order to cross what the judge rightly described as the 'threshold' for the exercise of the jurisdiction. But at the end of the day the court must consider the evidence as a whole in deciding whether or not to exercise this statutory jurisdiction.

In the present case the judge weighed the evidence on this aspect and also referred to the decision of Robert Goff J in *Piccinini v Partrederiet Trigon II, The Alfred Trigon* [1981] 2 Lloyd's Rep 333 on the meaning of 'average damages affecting class' and concluded that the buyers had satisfied the test of a good arguable case. This was not challenged on behalf of the sellers on this appeal and we therefore find it unnecessary to say anything further about this aspect.

The second question

We then turn to the second of the questions posed by the judge, and we begin again by summarising the evidence which bears on this. The main evidence for the buyers was provided in an affidavit sworn by a Mr Nott-Bower, a director of Embircos Shipping Agency Ltd who act as the agents in this country for the buyers' managers, Buenamar Cia Naviera SA of Piraeus, Greece, the buyers themselves being a company incorporated in Liberia. He said that the sellers were a West German corporation who were selling their only two vessels, the Niedersachsen and the Schleswig Holstein, the latter being sold elsewhere. In this connection it appeared later in the evidence that both vessels had originally been built on behalf of the sellers at a cost of about $50m each and that they were now being sold at low prices due to the shipping slump, but that the mortgages on both of them had been fully discharged prior to their sale. The material extract from Mr Nott-Bower's affidavit is in para 7, from which the following extracts need to be set out in full:

'I verily believe that if the Plaintiffs take delivery of the ship and pay the whole of the price to the sellers they will have no security for legitimate claims and will thus be effectively prevented from pursuing legitimate claims. The vessel is under steam, her class certificates are in order and a notice of readiness has been issued. Accordingly, the Plaintiffs are effectively put in the position of being obliged to take delivery though knowing that the vessel is defective. The Defendants are a West German corporation who are selling both of their only two vessels. The Defendants have an account with Citibank, London, WC2 i.e. within the jurisdiction of this Honourable Court. The moneys payable under the MOA are to be paid into such account. I verily believe that on closing such moneys as held in such account will be removed very quickly so that the Defendants will have no assets in this country against which the Plaintiff Buyers would be able to enter any award or judgment. I am pessimistic about the prospects of the Defendants honouring any award of judgment unless they are forced to keep sufficient assets in this country. A request was made by a telex dated 4th March 1983 to the sellers that they should undertake to indemnify the buyers in respect of further leakages when steam was raised but such request was ignored . . . Finally, I should mention that it would be the intention of the Plaintiffs not to disclose the existence of any injunction that the Court may make until immediately after closing and delivery of the ship. If the Defendants are notified of the injunction beforehand, the Plaintiffs fear that the Defendants will sell the vessel elsewhere or may seek to assign the proceeds of sale to a third party.'

Before dealing with the sellers' evidence in reply and the buyers' evidence by way of riposte, it is convenient to make a number of comments on this evidence which were also raised in the judgment below and discussed on the appeal before us.

First, Mr Nott-Bower made no reference to the fact that the buyers formed part of the Oldendorff group of companies, who are well known in shipping circles generally. This fact was not disputed, and it was also not seriously disputed that the buyers were perfectly well aware of this when they agreed to buy the vessel; indeed, they subsequently offered to consider the discharge of the injunction by consent against a guarantee from a major company in this group. The judge felt that Mr Nott-Bower's affidavit was open to criticism for not having referred to this fact, and counsel for the buyers rightly accepted this on the present appeal. It is obviously a matter which is relevant to the second question posed by the judge.

Secondly, the buyers adduced no evidence about the sellers (let alone the group) to support Mr Nott-Bower's expression of pessimism about the prospects of the sellers honouring any award or judgment, other than what is stated in the passage quoted above. The reference to the sellers' refusal 'to indemnify the buyers in respect of further leakages when steam was raised' was rightly disregarded by the judge as inappropriate; it would have amounted to an admission of liability in advance in respect of defects which were disputed and which depended in any event on the meaning of 'average damages affecting class'.

Thirdly, there was the fact that the buyers were proposing to use the machinery of a Mareva injunction in order to freeze the price of the vessel as soon as it was paid over, unbeknown to the sellers. In this connection the judge referred to a passage in my judgment in *Z Ltd v A* [1982] 1 All ER 556 at 571–572, [1982] QB 558 at 585, with which Eveleigh LJ agreed ([1982] 1 All ER 556 at 571, [1982] QB 558 at 584) and expressed reservations about this conduct on the part of the buyers even though their intentions in this regard had of course been fully disclosed in Mr Nott-Bower's affidavit. However, given the fact that a plaintiff's intention in this regard is fully disclosed to the court, as it must be, we do not think that it would be desirable to express any views about this aspect. We agree with the judge when he said (at p 412, ante):

'There is something unattractive about the idea of a buyer, who is ostensibly paying the full price of a chattel, preparing himself behind the seller's back to deprive him of part of the price. This gives the buyer the best of both worlds.'

This factor should certainly be borne in mind by the court when it arises, and it may well militate against the exercise of the discretion to grant the injunction in such cases. However, in other cases the circumstances might well be such as to justify a Mareva injunction even in the face of this factor. In our view it would not be appropriate to seek to lay down any guidelines about it.

a Since this was the whole of the evidence which was before the judge when he granted the Mareva injunction ex parte to the extent of $787,000, it is again convenient to pause at this point, in particular since the judge refers to the different problems which arise in the exercise of this jurisdiction at the stage of an application ex parte and at the later stage of an application inter partes to discharge the injunction. In this connection he said (at p 411, ante):

b 'Having been reminded of the authorities, and after hearing full argument, I am bound to say that I am doubtful whether the ex parte relief should have been granted in the first place. It may well be that current practice has unwittingly crept away from the authorities. If this case should go further, this is a matter on which guidance would, I believe, be welcome to the judges who hear these applications.'

c However, in our view this is again not a matter on which this court should, or usefully could, express any general view. Although the buyers' evidence on this aspect is open to the three criticisms mentioned above, the first of which was probably unknown to the judge at that stage, we do not think that it would be useful to seek to lay down any standard of evidence which applicants for Mareva injunctions must satisfy in order to succeed on an ex parte application. Bare assertions that the defendant is likely to put any asset beyond the plaintiff's grasp and is unlikely to honour any judgment or award are *d* clearly not enough by themselves. Something more is required. Viewed from this point of view, the buyers' evidence in the present case can certainly be described as exiguous. In that respect it is very much a borderline case. However, the judge presumably took the view that in all the circumstances there was just enough to justify the limited injunction which he granted, leaving it to the sellers to apply to have it discharged, as happened, and knowing that no real harm would thereby befall them which could not *e* be dealt with by an order as to costs. Accordingly, despite the judge's implied invitation to us to do so, we would not go so far as to say that, in the exercise of his discretion, he was wrong to make the order which he made. However, the exiguousness of the buyers' evidence on this aspect must naturally weigh strongly, as it did with the judge in this case, when the court comes to consider the whole of the evidence on the application inter partes to discharge the injunction.

f We then turn to the remainder of the evidence on this aspect which was before the judge on the sellers' application inter partes to discharge the injunction, as he did. The evidence on behalf of the sellers was contained in a short affidavit by a Mr Henning Oldendorff, and it is necessary to quote all except the last paragraph of this in full:

g '(1) I am a Generalbevollmaechtiguer for Messrs. Egon Oldendorff K.G., who are the managers of Trave Schiffahrtsgesellschaft m.b.h. Und Co. K.G. I thus have a general and complete power to act on behalf of Messrs. Egon Oldendorff K.G. without necessary reference to other Directors or Shareholders of Messrs. Egon Oldendorff.

(2) The contents of this affidavit are true to the best of my knowledge, information and belief, such being obtained from my personal knowledge and *h* experience of the business practice of the Oldendorff Group of Companies and of the circumstances of this case.

(3) I refer to the affidavit of Mr. Nott-Bower and in particular to the allegations in paragraph 7 thereof regarding the prospects of our honouring any award or judgment.

j (4) I confirm very emphatically: (1) there is and has never been any intention of dealing with those proceeds so as to avoid any award that may be made against them; (2) the proceeds would probably have been removed from the Citibank account in London for other normal business of the company because they could be put to better use than earning a low rate of interest; (3) the most likely use to which the money would be put is investment in other German companies in the Oldendorff group; (4) there is and has never been any intention of liquidating the company so as to avoid enforcement of any award; (5) if the market improves sufficiently the company may well become shipowners again, although it is to be appreciated that losing nearly $100 million on the price of the 'Niedersachsen' and the 'Schleswig Holstein' has not been a happy experience. I totally reject Mr. Nott-Bower's suggestion that we would "very quickly" remove the money implying that we would act improperly.

(5) I would add that since the company of Messrs. Egon Oldendorff K.G. was formed in 1921 by my father, Herr Egon Oldendorff, to my knowledge, none of the Oldendorff associated companies have ever: (a) defaulted on a loan; (b) failed to honour an arbitration award in whatever jurisdiction; (c) failed to honour a court judgment in any jurisdiction. As a result the Oldendorff Group has an excellent reputation in respect of the above matters in the shipping world.'

By way of riposte to this there was some further evidence on behalf of the buyers which can be summarised quite briefly. The buyers evidently made no attempt to make any enquiries about the financial resources or standing of the sellers or of the Oldendorff group. In an affidavit by a partner of the firm of solicitors acting for the buyers there is a reference to Embiricos Shipping Agency having made some vague attempts to obtain bank references in respect of the sellers and that these 'had produced little useful information'. It was also stated that on Citibank in London being requested that the sellers should provide 'a corporate guarantee' this had met with a firm refusal. Then there was evidence that the selling company itself was a limited partnership with a share capital of only DM20,000. Finally, there was evidence that when the buyers offered to consider the discharge of the injunction by consent on the basis of a bank guarantee, as already mentioned, or a guarantee from a major company in the group, this was refused; the sellers' solicitors stated in a telex that 'our clients feel very strongly that there is no merit in your clients' claim' and that the sellers would be applying to have the injunction discharged.

That was the evidence before the judge on the hearing inter partes. On this appeal the buyers thought it right to adduce further evidence in the form of two press cuttings from Lloyd's List newspaper, without objection on behalf of the sellers, referring to a dispute in March 1975 between the Oldendorff group and a German shipyard about the possibility of cancelling or varying a contract for the construction of two vessels against the background of the shipping slump. This was designed to cast a blemish on the sellers' reputation. But such disputes have been commonplace and worldwide in the shipping industry over the last decade or so. In our view this adds nothing whatever to the buyers' case.

In the ultimate analysis the issue on this appeal is whether or not this court should interfere with the exercise of the judge's discretion when he decided to discharge the injunction. As to this, we are clearly of the view, for the reasons discussed below, that no case has been made out on behalf of the buyers which would justify us taking this course. Recent decisions of the House of Lords have emphasised the importance of appellate courts resisting the temptation to interfere with the exercise of judicial discretions other than in limited circumstances which do not apply here: see e g *Hadmor Productions Ltd v Hamilton* [1982] 1 All ER 1042, [1983] AC 191 and *Garden Cottage Foods Ltd v Milk Marketing Board* [1983] 2 All ER 770, [1983] 3 WLR 143. We will deal below with the buyers' submissions in this regard. At the same time, since the judge treated this case as one which might provide some guidance, in particular on the second question which he posed, and since this request was echoed in the arguments before us, we think it right to make a number of general comments. However, these are not in any way intended to be exhaustive about the exercise of the discretion concerning Mareva injunctions in general.

(1) Although the discretion ultimately rests on the words of s 37 of the Supreme Court Act 1981 to grant an interlocutory injunction 'in all cases in which it appears to the court to be just and convenient to do so', certain material criteria have already been laid down in a number of well-known authorities, to which regard must be had in the application

of these wide words in relation to Mareva injunctions. We mention this because some of the submissions of counsel for the buyers on this appeal appeared to go much further. Thus, he submitted at one stage of his argument that the fact that the sellers did not assert that they required the frozen sum of $787,000 for the purpose of their trade or to pay their creditors, but merely to invest as they thought best, was in itself a ground for granting the injunction, coupled with the buyers 'good arguable case', because this would do little harm to the sellers, in particular if the buyers' cross-undertaking in damages was supported by security, as was offered on this appeal (though not below). He also submitted that if the sellers wished to have the use of these funds, they could easily provide a bank guarantee instead, in order to secure the buyers. Finally, he submitted, in effect, that the grant of Mareva injunctions should be greatly extended generally, so as to align the practice in this country with what he claimed to be the position in other jurisdictions, of requiring defendants to provide security for claims which appear to the court to be well-founded, unless the defendants show some sufficient reason why this should not be done.

In our view all these submissions go much too far in the light of the authorities and are indeed wholly inconsistent with the origin and development of this jurisdiction. The machinery of the Mareva injunction is extremely useful in appropriate cases. But, as the law stands, this jurisdiction cannot be invoked for the purpose of providing plaintiffs with security for claims, even when these appear likely to succeed (we are speaking generally and not with reference to this case), and even when there is no reason to suppose that an order for an injunction, or the provision of some substitute security by the defendants, would cause any real hardship to the defendant. Counsel for the buyers even went so far as to suggest that unless this jurisdiction were extended along these lines, Mareva injunctions might fall into desuetude. But the tendency is notoriously the other way. In his judgment the judge referred to 'a rapid and sustained increase in the number of applications'; and it is clear that his general concern was that under the present practice Mareva injunctions may well be granted too readily in some cases.

(2) Since the origin of this jurisdiction, the authorities clearly show that in order to obtain a Mareva injunction, a plaintiff must show that he would suffer some prejudice as a result of what the judge referred to in his second question as a 'dissipation of assets' in the event of the injunction being refused. The issue is as to the test which the plaintiff must satisfy. We were told on this appeal that there is a difference of judicial opinion whether the test is, to use Mustill J's words, 'that the defendant will deal with his assets with the object, and not just with the effect, of putting them out of the plaintiff's reach'. To some extent this difference appears to have arisen from a phrase in an obiter passage in my judgment in *Z Ltd v A* [1982] 1 All ER 556 at 572, [1982] QB 558 at 585 that a defendant may 'take steps *designed to* ensure that these [assets] are no longer available or traceable when judgment is given . . .' Thus, we were referred to an unreported judgment of Bingham J in *Home Insurance Co v Administratia Asicurarilor de Stat* (29 July 1983) in which these words were interpreted 'as a requirement that one must show nefarious intent'. However, this interpretation of the emphasised words goes much further than the tenor of the authorities to which we refer below. We also consider that the distinction mentioned by the judge in the present case, which he did not in fact find it necessary to resolve, between 'object' and 'effect', is not the right basis for providing the appropriate test. In our view the test is whether, on the assumption that the plaintiff has shown at least 'a good arguable case', the court concludes, on the whole of the evidence then before it, that the refusal of a Mareva injunction would involve a real risk that a judgment or award in favour of the plaintiff would remain unsatisfied.

The judgment in the present case quotes many passages which have referred to this aspect of the Mareva jurisdiction. We need not repeat these here. In support of the test indicated above we would only quote the following, which should be read in their context, though bearing in mind, as the judge pointed out, that although most of the reported cases have dealt with the removal of assets from the jurisdiction, Mareva injunctions can, and nowadays frequently are, also granted where there is a danger of a dissipation of assets within this country.

(a) *Etablissement Esefka International Anstalt v Central Bank of Nigeria* [1979] 1 Lloyd's Rep 445 at 448 per Lord Denning MR:

'The Mareva injunction is only to be granted where there is a danger of the money being taken out of the jurisdiction so that if the plaintiffs succeed they are not likely to get their money.'

(b) *Third Chandris Shipping Corp v Unimarine SA, The Pythia, The Angelic Wings, The Genie* [1979] 2 All ER 972 at 985, [1979] QB 645 at 669 per Lord Denning MR:

'In such cases the very fact of incorporation there gives some ground for believing there is a risk that, if judgment or an award is obtained, it may go unsatisfied.'

And per Lawton LJ ([1979] 2 All ER 972 at 987, [1979] 1 QB 645 at 671–672):

'There must be facts from which the Commercial Court, like a prudent, sensible commercial man, can properly infer a danger of default if assets are removed from the jurisdiction . . . These facts should enable a commercial judge to infer whether there is likely to be any real risk of default.'

(c) *Montecchi v Shimco (UK) Ltd* [1979] 1 WLR 1180 at 1183 per Bridge LJ:

'. . . the basis of the Mareva injunction is that there has to be a real reason to apprehend that if the injunction is not made, the intending plaintiff in this country may be deprived of a remedy against the foreign defendant whom he seeks to sue.'

(d) *Barclay-Johnson v Yuill* [1980] 3 All ER 190 at 195, [1980] 1 WLR 1259 at 1265 per Sir Robert Megarry VC:

'. . . it must appear that there is a danger of default if the assets are removed from the jurisdiction. Even if the risk of removal is great, no Mareva injunction should be granted unless there is also a danger of default.'

(v) *Prince Abdul Rahman Bin Turki Al Sudairy v Abu-Taha* [1980] 3 All ER 409 at 412, [1980] 1 WLR 1268 at 1273 per Lord Denning MR:

'So I would hold that a Mareva injunction can be granted against a man even though he is based in this country if the circumstances are such that there is a danger of his absconding, or a danger of the assets being removed out of the jurisdiction or disposed of within the jurisdiction, or otherwise dealt with so that there is a danger that the plaintiff, if he gets judgment, will not be able to get it satisfied.'

(3) There is a further problem, concerning the respective evidence of the parties, which is referred to in the judgment and was also discussed in the arguments before us. It can best be dealt with by setting out some inevitably lengthy extracts from the judgment, but these will also serve to show how the judge reached his decision on the exercise of his discretion. We have already said that we see no basis for reviewing his decision, and nothing that we say is intended to imply any disagreement with it. However, we have emphasised certain passages on which we comment below. The first passage is (see p 409, ante):

'For the buyers, criticism was made of the evidence for the sellers, which was said to be incomplete and unsatisfactory, on several important points. In my judgment, neither of these attitudes is wholly correct. The judge who hears the proceedings inter partes must decide on all the evidence laid before him. The evidence adduced for the defendant will normally be looked at for the purposes of deciding whether it is enough to displace any inferences which might otherwise be drawn from the plaintiff's evidence. But I see no reason in principle why, if the defendant's evidence raises more questions than it answers, and does so in a manner which tends to enhance rather than allay any justifiable apprehension concerning dissipation of assets, the court should be obliged to leave this out of account. *On the other hand, the plaintiff has no right to criticise the defendant's evidence, for omissions or obscurities. The*

defendant is entitled to choose for himself what evidence, if any, he adduces. The less
impressive his evidence, the less effective it will be to displace any adverse inferences.
But there must be an inference to be displaced, if the injunction is to stand, and
comment on the defendant's evidence must not be taken so far that the burden of
proof is unconsciously reversed.'

The judge then referred to aspects of the evidence which it is unnecessary to set out
and continued with certain criticisms made on behalf of the sellers of the buyers'
evidence, as follows (at p 410, ante):

'(1) The deponent did not say that the sellers, or companies and persons connected
with them, have a history of default on loans or trade debts, that, in the words of
Lawton LJ, they are "debt dodgers". He did not speak to any bad reputation in the
trade. He did not even say that the buyers had tried without success to find out
about the sellers' reputation. (2) He did not say, and indeed in the case of a company
incorporated in the Federal Republic of Germany, could not say that companies
registered there are difficult to track down, or are notoriously fallible in providing
assets to meet large adverse judgments. (3) He does not say, and again could not say,
that there exists no mechanism for enforcement of awards in the sellers' country of
incorporation, for the Federal Republic (unlike the Republic of Liberia, in which
the buyers are incorporated) is a party to the New York Convention on the
Recognition and Enforcement of Foreign Arbitral Awards (New York, 31 December
1958; TS 20 (1976); Cmnd 6419).'

He then referred in detail to the affidavit of Mr Oldendorff, already quoted, and went
on (at pp 410–411, ante):

'The buyers say that this affidavit reinforces their own evidence, and so in part it
does. It confirms their assertion that the moneys will be removed from the
jurisdiction, unless the injunction is maintained. It goes on to admit that once
removed from the United Kingdom, the funds will not stay with the company, but
will be redeployed within the group; and the affidavit does not say that they will
necessarily stay in West Germany. The affidavit also shows what is indeed obvious,
that the sellers have suffered a grievous financial blow from the fall in the market,
which must impair or totally preclude their ability to meet from their own funds
any damages which may be awarded. These are important points, and the sellers
could well have done more to answer them. Thus: (1) the sellers have not said
anything about the corporate structure of the Oldendorff group, or how the partners
in the buyers' limited partnership, referred to in the affidavit of Mr Strong of the
buyers' solicitors, fit into the structure as a whole; (2) the sellers have said nothing
about the capitalisation of the group. The only information comes from Commander
Short's affidavit, which indicates a very modest share capital for the immediate
proprietors of the sellers; (3) the sellers have given no information at all about their
own activities or finances. They do not even say whether they are still trading; (4)
not a single figure is given for the assets, turnover or profits of any company in the
Oldendorff group. *These omissions are such that if the sellers had the task of making the
court confident the money would be there when called for, I would doubt very much whether
they had succeeded. But this is not their task. They have no obligation to disclose their financial
affairs, simply to answer a challenge from the buyers which is unsupported by solid evidence.*
Their reticence does not justify the inference that they have uncomfortable facts to
hide. True, they have suffered losses on ships which (like all trading ships) were
heavily mortgaged. Yet the sellers are not bankrupt; the mortgages have been
redeemed, no doubt with backing from the rest of the group; there is no suggestion
that the group as a whole has failed to weather the storm. If the group has absorbed
losses of nearly \$100 m on these two ships, why should the court assume that it will
let the company go to the wall for a further loss of less than one-hundredth of this
amount? (I should add that, since the buyers were, on their own evidence, ready to

accept a corporate guarantee for the amount claimed, they can scarcely be heard to assert that the group is not able, as distinct from willing, to meet the claim). More than this, however, there is the evidence that the other Oldendorff companies have always paid their debts. There is no evidence the other way. No guilt by association can be attributed to the sellers. In all these circumstances, I consider that the buyers have failed to prove a degree of risk sufficient to justify the maintenance of the injunction.'

On this appeal counsel for the buyers criticised the passages which we have emphasised and submitted that they showed that the judge had exercised his discretion on a wrong basis. He submitted that these placed the burden of proof exclusively or excessively on the buyers and that this approach is incorrect once the matter comes to be heard inter partes. If the emphasised passages are taken out of their context, we think that there would be substance in this criticism. Thus, while it is obviously up to the sellers what evidence they put before the court, the buyers are equally clearly entitled to comment adversely on any evidence which the sellers may adduce. However, immediately before the first of the emphasised passages, the judgment correctly stated that 'The judge who hears the proceedings inter partes must decide on all the evidence laid before him', and this is clearly what the judge did in this case. Whether the inter partes hearing takes the form of an application by the defendant to discharge the injunction, as is usual in the Commercial Court, or whether, as in the Chancery Division, the injunction is only granted for a limited time and there is then an inter partes hearing with regard to whether or not it should be continued, the judge must consider the whole of the evidence as it then stands in deciding whether to maintain or continue, or to discharge or vary, the order previously made.

On the present appeal we have been mainly concerned with the tests to be applied in answering the two questions posed by the judge. However, other matters may often also have to be borne in mind. The ultimate test for the exercise of the jurisdiction is whether, in all the circumstances, the case is one in which it appears to the court 'to be just and convenient' to grant the injunction: see s 37 of the Supreme Court Act 1981 which we have already set out. Thus, the conduct of the plaintiff may be material, and the rights of any third parties who may be affected by the grant of an injunction may often also have to be borne in mind: see *Galaxia Maritime SA Mineralimportexport, The Eleftherios* [1981] 1 All ER 796, [1982] 1 WLR 539. Further, it must always be remembered that if, or to the extent that, the grant of a Mareva injunction inflicts hardship on the defendant, his legitimate interests must prevail over those of the plaintiff, who seeks to obtain security for a claim which may appear to be well founded but which still remains to be established at the trial. There is no need to repeat here what was said in that connection in *Z Ltd v A* [1982] 1 All ER 556 at 571–572, [1982] QB 558 at 585–586. If the plaintiff is in a position to contend that his claim is not open to doubt, then he must satisfy the requirements of an application for summary judgment under RSC Order 14. But if he applies for a Mareva injunction on the ground that he has 'a good arguable case', then the balance should be weighed as we have indicated above.

In the present case the judge correctly applied the two tests which fell to be considered on the facts, and there is no basis for criticising the conclusion which he reached in exercising his discretion. Accordingly, this appeal must be dismissed.

Appeal dismissed; damages, if any, to be assessed; application for leave to appeal to the House of Lords refused; application that injunction be continued refused.

Solicitors: *Ince & Co* (for the buyers); *Holman Fenwick & Willan* (for the sellers).

Henrietta Steinberg   Barrister.

Allnatt London Properties Ltd v Newton

COURT OF APPEAL, CIVIL DIVISION
SIR JOHN DONALDSON MR, O'CONNOR AND DILLON LJJ
28 OCTOBER 1982

Landlord and tenant – Business premises – Surrender of tenancy – Restriction on agreements purporting to preclude tenant from applying for new tenancy – Purporting to preclude – Lease requiring tenant to offer to surrender lease before he is entitled to consent to assign – Tenant offering to surrender lease and offer accepted by landlord but tenant subsequently withdrawing offer – Landlord suing tenant to enforce agreement – Whether agreement void as 'purporting to preclude' tenant from applying for new tenancy at end of term – Landlord and Tenant Act 1954, s 38(1).

By a lease made in 1972 the landlords demised certain business premises to the tenant for 21 years from 25 March 1972. The lease provided that if the tenant desired to assign the premises he had first to make the landlords 'an offer in writing . . . to surrender the lease with vacant possession . . . in consideration of the payment by the Landlords . . . of a sum representing the net premium value (if any) of the lease for the unexpired residue of the term'. Seven years after the commencement of the lease the tenant wished to assign the premises and approached the landlords for consent to assign. The landlords refused their consent and required the tenant to offer to surrender the lease. By a letter dated 20 December 1979 the tenant offered to surrender the lease 'in accordance with the terms of the lease' and on 9 January 1980 the landlords accepted the offer. Subsequently the tenant withdrew his offer to surrender. The landlords issued a writ against the tenant, seeking (i) a declaration that there was an enforceable contract for the surrender of the lease, (ii) specific performance of the contract and (iii) damages. The tenant submitted that the agreement to surrender was rendered void by s 38(1)[a] of the Landlord and Tenant Act 1954 because Pt II of that Act applied to the tenancy and the agreement purported to preclude the tenant from making an application or request for a new tenancy under Pt II of the Act. The judge refused to grant the relief sought. The landlords appealed.

Held – On the true construction of s 38(1) of the 1954 Act, an agreement purported to preclude a tenant from making an application or request for a new tenancy if the effect of the agreement was in fact to preclude him from doing so, and if it had that effect it was void and ineffective by virtue of s 38(1). It followed that, since the effect of the agreement to surrender would have been to preclude the tenant from applying for a new tenancy under the 1954 Act, the agreement was void and unenforceable. The appeal would accordingly be dismissed (see p 425 *b* to *d* and *g, post*).

Joseph v Joseph [1966] 3 All ER 486 followed.

Decision of Sir Robert Megarry V-C [1981] 2 All ER 290 affirmed.

Notes

For the prohibition against contracting out of Pt II of the Landlord and Tenant Act 1954, see 27 Halsbury's Laws (4th edn) para 477.

For the Landlord and Tenant Act 1954, s 38, see 18 Halsbury's Statutes (3rd edn) 578.

Case referred to in judgments

Joseph v Joseph [1966] 3 All ER 486, [1967] Ch 78, [1966] 3 WLR 631, CA.

Appeal

The plaintiffs, Allnatt London Properties Ltd (the landlords), appealed against the order of Sir Robert Megarry V-C dated 20 November 1980 ([1981] 2 All ER 290) whereby he

---

a   Section 38(1) is set out at p 425 *a b, post*

(i) refused the landlords' claim for a declaration that there existed an enforceable contract for the surrender by the defendant, Ronald James Newton (the tenant), to the landlords of the tenant's lease dated 20 April 1972, of business premises known as Building 665, Pulborough Way, Green Lane, Hounslow, and also specific performance of the contract, and damages in addition to or in lieu of specific performance, and (ii) granted the tenant a declaration that the purported agreement to surrender the term created by the lease dated 20 April 1972 was void by virtue of s 38 of the Landlord and Tenant Act 1954. The facts are set out in the judgment of Dillon LJ.

Derek Wood QC and *J H G Sunnucks* for the landlords.
Paul de la Piquerie for the tenant.

DILLON LJ (delivering the first judgment at the invitation of Sir John Donaldson MR). This is an appeal from the decision of Sir Robert Megarry V-C given on 20 November 1980 ([1981] 2 All ER 290). The appellants, who were the plaintiffs in the action, are the landlords, and the respondent, who is the sole defendant, is the tenant of certain business premises known as Building 665, Pulborough Way, Green Lane, Hounslow, held under a lease of 20 April 1972 for a term of 21 years from 25 March 1972.

Clause 3(21)(b) of the lease contained a covenant by the defendant—

'Not, (subject to the proviso to this clause) to assign underlet or part with the possession or occupation of the demised premises as a whole Provided Always that if at any time and so often as the Tenants shall desire to assign or underlet the demised premises as a whole the Tenants shall make to the Landlord an offer in writing in the terms hereinafter mentioned . . .'

The terms of the offer in writing were to be this:

'. . . shall be in the terms following namely the Tenants shall offer to surrender the Lease with vacant possession and otherwise free from encumbrances on a date three months from the date of the said written offer in consideration of the payment by the Landlords to the Tenants of a sum representing the net premium value (if any) of this Lease for the unexpired residue of the term [such value to be agreed or determined as provided in the clause].'

On 6 December 1979 the tenant's solicitors wrote to the landlords asking for consent to an assignment of the lease to certain gentlemen, enclosing references. The landlords replied saying that they would not consider any application to assign until they had first been offered a surrender as required by the lease. On 20 December 1979 the tenant made the formal offer to surrender the lease in accordance with the terms of the lease. On 9 January 1980 the landlords by their solicitors stated that they were prepared to accept the tenant's offer of surrender in accordance with the terms of the lease. They suggested that the surrender date be 25 March 1980 provided vacant possession could be given by that date and they also made reference to surveyors inspecting the premises and the payment of some rent which had either by then been paid or was shortly thereafter paid.

After certain further correspondence which does not matter, on 6 March 1980 the tenant's solicitors wrote, and on behalf of their client they withdrew, or purported to withdraw, the offer to surrender. The tenant has, we are told, remained in occupation of the premises for business purposes ever since.

The proceedings were brought by the landlords claiming as the primary relief: 'A declaration that there exists an enforceable contract for the surrender by the Defendant to the Plaintiffs of the lease', and specific performance of that contract.

The Vice-Chancellor rejected that claim because he held that the contract relied on, namely the offer of surrender and the acceptance of that offer, fell foul (as these were business premises) of s 38(1) of the Landlord and Tenant Act 1954. That section reads as follows:

a
'Any agreement relating to a tenancy to which this Part of this Act applies (whether contained in the instrument creating the tenancy or not) shall be void (except as provided by subsection (4) of this section) in so far as it purports to preclude the tenant from making an application or request under this Part of this Act or provides for the termination or the surrender of the tenancy in the event of his making such an application or request or for the imposition of any penalty or disability on the tenant in that event.'

b
Subsection (4) does not matter for present purposes because the parties did not so arrange their affairs as to fall within it.

In *Joseph v Joseph* [1966] 3 All ER 486, [1967] Ch 78 the Court of Appeal held that in s 38(1) the expression 'purports to preclude the tenant from making an application or request under this Part of this Act' means 'has the effect of precluding the tenant'. Therefore, in *Joseph v Joseph* an agreement made by tenants for the giving up of possession

c
and surrender of their tenancy at a future date was void and ineffective under the 1954 Act and could not be enforced.

The Vice-Chancellor held that *Joseph v Joseph* entirely covered the present case and precluded specific performance of the agreement relied on by the landlords. In my judgment he was entirely right in that conclusion; *Joseph v Joseph* also binds us with the same result.

d
Counsel for the landlords has argued that the present case is distinguishable from *Joseph v Joseph* because in the present case the offer of surrender of the tenancy was put forward by the tenant himself under no overriding compulsion from the landlords save that it was put forward under the terms of the clause in the lease. It was put forward at a time when the tenant was wanting to assign and so was not himself minded to take personal advantage of the protection of Pt II of the 1954 Act.

e
To a considerable extent those arguments would apply to the facts of *Joseph v Joseph* itself, where the parties entered into an agreement to surrender at a future date obviously not intending themselves, when they made that agreement, to take advantage of the provisions of the 1954 Act. I do not see that any valid distinction can be drawn. The effect of the surrender being enforced will be that nobody can take advantage of the protection of Pt II of the 1954 Act, whereas if the tenant remains in possession (as he has

f
in fact done since he withdrew his offer to surrender) he is in a position to take advantage of that protection; or, alternatively, if he were able to assign the lease, the assignee would be able to take advantage of the protection; both the tenant and the assignee fall within the purpose of the 1954 Act and the lease.

Joseph v Joseph covers this case, and I would dismiss the appeal.

g
O'CONNOR LJ. I agree for the reasons given by Dillion LJ.

SIR JOHN DONALDSON MR. I also agree for the same reasons.

Appeal dismissed. Leave to appeal to the House of Lords refused.

Solicitors: *Marshall Shortland & Co*, Willesden (for the landlords); *Paul Gromett & Co* (for the tenant).

Frances Rustin   Barrister.

Re American Greetings Corp's Application

HOUSE OF LORDS

LORD DIPLOCK, LORD FRASER OF TULLYBELTON, LORD SCARMAN, LORD BRIDGE OF HARWICH AND
LORD BRIGHTMAN

5, 6 DECEMBER 1983, 26 JANUARY 1984

Trade mark – Registered users – Trafficking in trade mark – Application for registration of trade mark and registration of person as registered user – Proprietor not using or proposing to use mark in connection with goods similar to those to be marketed by licensees – Licence agreements including quality control provisions exercisable by proprietor over licensees' goods – Whether grant of proprietor's applications tending to facilitate 'trafficking' in trade mark – Trade Marks Act 1938, s 28(6).

The appellants, an American company, were the proprietors of a trade mark which consisted of the drawing of a fictional character, a little girl, to which they gave the name Holly Hobbie. They used the trade mark extensively on or in relation to greeting cards and a small range of other goods marketed by them in the USA. The drawing and name were popular with the American public, causing the appellants to engage in the USA in the business of licensing the use of the drawing and name (known as 'character merchandising') to merchants who wished to promote their own ranges of goods by using the trade mark in connection with those goods. The appellants wished to extend the character merchandising aspect of their business to the United Kingdom by licensing traders in the United Kingdom to make use of the Holly Hobbie name in relation to the goods of the licensees, being goods in which the appellants did not trade and never had traded. Accordingly, the appellants applied under s 29(1)(b)[a] of the Trade Marks Act 1938 to the registrar of trade marks for registration of the mark in respect of 12 classes of goods which the appellants' licensees wished to market in association with the name. Each application was supported by a registered user agreement with the relevant licensee and also by an application for the registration of the licensee as a registered user under s 28[b] of the 1938 Act. Each agreement contained comprehensive provisions by means of which the appellants were able to exercise control over the quality of the licensee's goods which were to be marketed under the appellants' trade name. The assistant registrar refused to grant the application on the ground that the grant of registered user status would tend to facilitate 'trafficking' in the appellants' mark, contrary to s 28(6) of the 1938 Act. On appeal, the judge and the Court of Appeal upheld his decision. The appellants appealed to the House of Lords.

Held – For the purposes of s 28(6) of the 1938 Act 'trafficking in a trade mark' meant dealing in a trade mark primarily as a commodity in its own right rather than for the purpose of identifying or promoting merchandise in which the proprietor of the mark was interested. If there was no real trade connection between the proprietor of the mark and the licensee of his goods, the registrar was entitled to conclude that the grant of the licence to use the trade mark to promote the licensee's goods amounted to trafficking in the mark. Whether a sufficient trade connection existed was a question of fact and degree in every case, but in any event provision for quality control by the proprietor of the mark

___

a Section 29(1), so far as material, provides: 'No application for the registration of a trade mark in respect of any goods shall be refused, nor shall permission for such registration be withheld, on the ground only that it appears that the applicant does not use or propose to use the trade mark . . . (b) if the application is accompanied by an application for registration of a person as a registered user of the trade mark, and the tribunal is satisfied that the proprietor intends it to be used by that person in relation to those goods and the tribunal is also satisfied that that person will be registered as a registered user thereof immediately after the registration of the trade mark.'

b Section 28, so far as material, is set out at p 429 h j, post

over the goods of the licencee was not in itself sufficient to establish the required

a connection. On the facts, the assistant registrar and the High Court were entitled to take the view that the registration of the licencees as registered users under s 28 would tend to facilitate trafficking in a trade mark. The appeal would accordingly be dismissed (see p 427 *g* to p 428 *b* and *g h* and p 432 *j* to p 433 *g*, post).

John Batt & Co v Dunnett [1899] AC 428 considered.

Decision of the Court of Appeal [1983] 2 All ER 609 affirmed.

b
Notes

For registration of a proposed registered user of a trade mark, see 38 Halsbury's Laws (3rd edn) 587, para 980.

For the Trade Marks Act 1938, ss 28, 29, see 37 Halsbury's Statutes (3rd edn) 913, 916.

c **Cases referred to in opinions**

Batt (John) & Co v Dunnett [1899] AC 428, HL; *affg* sub nom *Re John Batt & Co's Registered Trade Marks, Re Carter's Application* [1898] 2 Ch 432, CA; *affg* [1898] 2 Ch 432.

Bowden Wire Ltd v Bowden Brake Co Ltd (1914) 31 RPC 385, HL.

'*Bostitch*' *Trade Mark* [1963] RPC 183.

d **Appeal**

The applicants, American Greetings Corp, a company incorporated in the State of Ohio, USA, appealed with leave of the Appeal Committee of the House of Lords granted on 7 July 1983 against the decision of the Court of Appeal (Sir John Donaldson MR, Dillon LJ and Sir Denys Buckley) ([1983] 2 All ER 609, [1983] 1 WLR 912) on 28 April 1983 dismissing an appeal by the appellants against the judgment and order of Whitford J

e ([1983] 2 All ER 609, [1983] 1 WLR 269) on 29 October 1982 dismissing an appeal by the appellants from the decision of the assistant registrar of trade marks, Mr D G A Myall (acting for the registrar), dated 2 April 1982, refusing 12 applications by the appellants made pursuant to the Trade Marks Act 1938, to register the trade mark Holly Hobbie in 12 different classes of the register of trade marks, on the ground that the grant of the applications would tend to facilitate trafficking in the trade mark contrary to s 28(6) of

f the 1938 Act. The facts are set out in the opinion of Lord Brightman.

Robin Jacob QC and *Michael Silverleaf* for the appellants.
Gerald Paterson for the registrar of trade marks.

Their Lordships took time for consideration.

g 26 January. The following opinions were delivered.

LORD DIPLOCK. My Lords, I have had the advantage of reading in draft the speech of my noble and learned friend Lord Brightman. I agree with it, and for the reasons he gives I would dismiss this appeal.

h **LORD FRASER OF TULLYBELTON.** My Lords, I have had the advantage of reading in draft the speech of my noble and learned friend Lord Brightman, and I agree with it. Like him, I am quite willing to accept that character merchandising has become a widespread practice in various countries, including the United Kingdom, and that it is perfectly harmless. But it is, in my opinion, reasonably clear that the appellants' proposals

j for exploiting the 'Holly Hobbie' trade mark would facilitate 'trafficking' in the mark, and would indeed themselves constitute trafficking. Parliament has seen fit to legislate against such trafficking in s 28 of the Trade Marks Act 1938, and it is not open to the registrar or the courts to disregard the provisions of that section. They have therefore rightly refused the appellants' application in this case.

I would dismiss the appeal.

LORD SCARMAN. My Lords, I have had the advantage of reading in draft the speech
to be delivered by my noble and learned friend Lord Brightman. For the reasons he gives *a*
I would dismiss the appeal.

LORD BRIDGE OF HARWICH. My Lords, I find myself constrained to agree that
this appeal must be dismissed, but I do so with undisguised reluctance.

There came a point in the argument when the question was posed by my noble and
learned friend Lord Diplock: 'If this is not trafficking in trade marks, what is?' To that *b*
question, despite the valiant efforts of counsel for the appellants, no satisfactory answer
has been forthcoming. Likewise, I can find no ground to quarrel with the meaning
ascribed by my noble and learned friend Lord Brightman to the expression 'trafficking
in a trade mark' as 'dealing in a trade mark primarily as a commodity in its own right
and not primarily for the purpose of identifying or promoting merchandise in which
the proprietor of the mark is interested.' But these considerations lead to the conclusion *c*
that the phrase 'trafficking in a trade mark' in s 28(6) of the Trade Marks Act 1938 and
parallel expressions found in the report of the Goschen committee (see Report of the
Departmental Committee on the Law and Practice Relating to Trade Marks (Cmd 4568
(1934))) which preceded the Act are precisely apt descriptions of the commercial activity
now widely known as 'character merchandising'.

I can well understand that this activity, which I assume was little known, at all events *d*
on this side of the Atlantic, in the 1930s never entered the consideration of the legislators
in 1938 nor of the members of the Goschen committee on whose recommendations they
acted. They were concerned that the public should not be hoodwinked and to this end
set their faces against allowing the reputation for quality attaching to a trade mark to be
used deceptively by a mere purchaser of the right to use the mark.

But character merchandising deceives nobody. Fictional characters capture the *e*
imagination, particularly of children, and can be very successfully exploited in the
marketing of a wide range of goods. No one who buys a Mickey Mouse shirt supposes
that the quality of the shirt owes anything to Walt Disney Productions.

Many marks will, of course, be protected by copyright. But when a mark consists
simply in a name, it will be unprotected. It would seem from examples shown to your
Lordships in the course of the argument that not a few marks in the character *f*
merchandising field have already been accepted by the registrar under s 28 before the
present very large group of applications thrust the trafficking issue to the forefront. I do
not pause to consider whether marks already registered which ought not to have been
will be open to challenge. It will be bad enough, in my view, that the whole field of
character merchandising will now be wide open to piracy. The protection, if any, of the
original inventor of the character will lie in the uncertain remedy of a passing off action. *g*
This situation seems likely to generate a mass of difficult and expensive litigation which
cannot be in the public interest.

In short, though I can find no escape from s 28(6) of the 1938 Act, I do not hesitate to
express my opinion that it has become a complete anachronism and that the sooner it is
repealed the better.

h

LORD BRIGHTMAN. My Lords, this appeal relates to a commercial activity
commonly called 'character merchandising'. The expression is used to signify the
exploitation of a well-known invented name, whereby the author or promoter of the
name licenses or purports to license its use on the goods of traders who have no other
connection with the licensor. If the invented name is a registered trade mark of the
licensor in respect of certain classes of goods, the licensor may wish to protect his position *j*
by obtaining registration of the mark in respect of the goods of the licensee. The question
is whether, on the facts of the case before your Lordships, applications for the registration
of the trade mark 'Holly Hobbie' in respect of the goods of certain licensees were properly
refused by the registrar on the ground that registration would tend to facilitate trafficking
in a trade mark contrary to s 28(6) of the Trade Marks Act 1938.

a   The applicants, American Greetings Corp, who are the appellants, are an American company. They carry on business as designers and producers of greetings cards. Some years ago one of their designers produced a drawing of a child dressed in a pinafore and bonnet to whom the name 'Holly Hobbie' was given. 'Holly Hobbie' captured the imagination of the American public. The drawing and name are extensively used by the appellants on or in connection with greetings cards and a small range of other goods which the appellants manufacture or buy in and market. No difficulty would arise on an

b   application to register the trade mark in regard to those goods.

The appellants however desire to exploit the name 'Holly Hobbie' in a wider field, by licensing other traders to make use of the name in relation to the goods of the licensees, being goods in which the appellants do not and never have traded. The procedure is that after the grant by the appellants of a licence to a trader who wishes to use the name 'Holly Hobbie', the appellants apply to the registrar for the registration of the mark in respect

c   of that class of goods, and for the registration of the licensee as the registered user thereof.

The majority of trade mark applications are made under s 17 of the 1938 Act. Under this section a person claiming to be the propietor of a trade mark 'used or proposed to be used' by him may apply for the registration of the mark in the register of trade marks. Clearly such an application could not be made by the appellants in respect of the goods of the licensees, since the mark is not used or intended to be used by the appellants in

d   relation to such goods. Those goods are produced by or for, and until sale remain the exclusive property of, the licensees. A non-user of a trade mark may, however, apply for registration in the cases specified in s 29(1) of the 1938 Act. Paragraph (a) of that subsection deals with the case of the applicant who wishes to assign the trade mark to a company which is about to be formed, with a view to the use of the mark in relation to that company's goods. Paragraph (b) deals with the case of a licensee. There are three

e   conditions. First, the application by the proprietor of the mark is to be accompanied by an application for the registration of a person (the licensee) as a registered user of the mark. Second, the proprietor must intend the mark to be used by the proposed registered user in relation to the goods in question. Third, the 'tribunal' (presumably the registrar or the court) must be satisfied that the proposed user will in fact be registered as a registered user of the mark immediately after the registration of the mark. The last of

f   these conditions brings s 28 into play. Section 28 is devoted to the subject of registered users. This was a new concept. The section enables a person other than the proprietor of the mark to be registered as a registered user thereof. The section proceeds (sub-s (2)) on the basis (shortly stated) that use of a mark by a registered user thereof shall be deemed to be use by the proprietor thereof. Under sub-s (4) the application for the registration of a person as a registered user must be made jointly by the proprietor and the user, and

g   particulars must be given (a) of the relationship existing or proposed, between the proprietor and the proposed registered user, and (b) showing the degree of control by the propietor over the permitted use which their relationship will confer. Under sub-s (5) if the registrar is satisfied that the use of the mark in relation to the proposed goods by the proposed registered user will not be contrary to the public interest, the registrar may register the proposed registered user as a registered user in respect of the goods in

h   question. There is no problem in the instant case in relation to the requirements of sub-ss (1) to (4), and it is to be assumed for present purposes that no problem arises in regard to the public interest. The stumbling block is sub-s (6). It reads as follows:

> 'The Registrar shall refuse an application under the foregoing provisions of this section if it appears to him that the grant thereof would tend to facilitate trafficking in a trade mark.'

j   Although sub-s (6) in terms makes the registrar the judge of whether the grant of registered user status would tend to facilitate trafficking, sub-s (11) subjects his decision to a right of appeal to the High Court.

The only other part of the 1938 Act to which I need refer is s 68(1). This defines 'trade mark', with an immaterial exception, as a mark—

'used or proposed to be used in relation to goods for the purpose of indicating, or so as to indicate, a connection in the course of trade between the goods and some person having the right either as proprietor or as registered user to use the mark . . .'

I give the definition but I do not myself think that it helps to resolve the central problem in this case, namely the meaning in a trade mark context of the word 'trafficking'. In particular, the definition does not of itself demand any connection in the course of trade between the proprietor of a mark and the registered user thereof.

My Lords, I turn now to the facts of the present case in more detail. The appellants entered into 12 licence agreements relating to 12 classes of goods. Your Lordships were referred to two such agreements, and I assume that they are representative of the other ten. The earlier in time was dated 3 April 1978 and was made between the appellants and Oneida Silversmiths Ltd, an English company. By cl 1 the appellants granted Oneida a non-exclusive licence to use the trade mark 'Holly Hobbie' in the United Kingdom and in Ireland on and in connection with breakfast sets, cutlery and other tableware, so long as such goods were manufactured by Oneida in accordance with standards, specifications and instructions submitted to or approved by the appellants. Under cll 3 and 4 the appellants were given the right to inspect the finished goods and the method of manufacture thereof, to receive samples of the goods and to receive for approval all packages, labels, advertising and other material on which the trade mark appears. The agreement was for two years unless determined earlier by either side. The agreement does not reveal what consideration (if any) was payable for the licence. The other agreement was dated 1 July 1978 and was made between the appellants and General Mills (UK) Ltd, as successors to Chad Valley Co Ltd. By cl 1 the appellants granted to the licensee the exclusive right of using the 'Holly Hobbie' characters, including the associated copyrights and trade marks, on and in connection with the manufacture, sale and distribution of toys etc throughout the world except Canada, Japan and USA. Under cl 2 the appellants undertook to sell to the licensee art reproduction material for use in producing goods and to supply creative art services. Under cl 3 the appellants reserved the right to approve all uses of the 'Holly Hobbie' trade mark on or in connection with the licensee's goods, including advertising, and to approve the nature and quality of the goods associated with the 'Holly Hobbie' trade mark. There were further provisions for access to the licensee's premises, and for samples. The licence was for a term of eight years, with a provision for optional extension for a further 12 years. Clause 5 provided for substantial royalties, with a minimum royalty of $3,000,000 for the first eight years.

The 12 applications related to 12 classes of goods. Their range was immense, including toilet products, tableware, lamp shades, silver boxes, printed matter, furniture, textiles, sleeping bags, slippers, table mats, and toys.

On 2 May 1979 the appellants applied to the registrar for registration of the mark in respect of the different classes of goods under s 29(1)(b) and for registration of the licensees as registered users under s 28. On the wording of s 29, that application was bound to fail if the s 28 application would fail.

The applications came before the assistant registrar of trade marks who gave his written decision on 2 April 1982. At one of the hearings the appellants' agent, Mr Grant, said, in my view correctly, that the appellants were engaged in two sorts of enterprise, as manufacturers and merchants on their own account and 'as licensors in the business of character merchandising'. The assistant registrar examined documentary material produced by the appellants in evidence, including 'A Gallery of Fresh Ideas from American Greetings', the last page of which contained an open invitation to all and sundry to become licensees of the 'Holly Hobbie' mark. The assistant registrar found as follows:

'In my opinion these items show that the applicants' business is really that of providing a marketing advertising service and is saying, in effect, to any manufacturer of any product whatever that, if they like to get on the bandwaggon, they can use the applicants' trade marks. It seems clear that any Tom, Dick or Harry, in any trade a whatever will be given a licence if he applies for one and that the applicants are, in effect, hawking the trade mark around. Mr Grant did not dissent from this as a description of character merchandising, but submitted that this kind of exploitation of a character is legitimate.'

The assistant registrar defined trafficking as 'treating the mark itself as a source of income without any existing reputation attaching to the mark for the [particular class of] goods concerned'. He held that the grant of the applications would tend to facilitate b trafficking in a trade mark. Accordingly, he refused the applications under s 29. On appeal, his decision on the facts and the law was upheld by the High Court (see [1982] 2 All ER 609, [1983] 1 WLR 269). The case then went to the Court of Appeal, which dismissed the appeal (see [1983] 2 All ER 609, [1983] 1 WLR 912). Dillon LJ, delivering the leading judgment, said that 'there must be a trade connection between the proprietor of the mark and the goods of the licensee on which the mark is to be used', and he c rejected the submission that 'the mere inclusion in an agreement of quality control provisions provides automatically a trade connection where otherwise there would be none' (see [1983] 2 All ER 609 at 621, [1983] 1 WLR 912 at 918–919). Sir Denys Buckley agreed with the judgment of Dillon LJ and added that in his opinion—

d ' "trafficking" in s 28(6) extends to any conduct carried out or intended to be carried out in respect of a mark or a proposed mark with a view to commercial gain which is not a bona fide exploitation of that mark in pursuance of the true function of a trade mark, viz its use 'in relation to goods for the purpose of indicating, or so as to indicate, a connection in the course of trade between the goods and some person having the right either as proprietor or as registered user to use the mark.'

(See [1983] 2 All ER 609 at 623, [1983] 1 WLR 912 at 921.) Sir John Donaldson MR e agreed with both judgments.

There is no definition of trafficking in the 1938 Act. It is a word with several shades of meaning, ranging from ordinary reputable buying and selling to unlawful or improper commerce. When one seeks to discover the sense in which the word is used in a trade mark context, the clues are sparse. The starting point is, I think, *Re John Batt & Co's Registered Trade Marks* [1898] 2 Ch 432, decided at the close of the last century. In that f case Romer J directed that certain marks should be expunged from the register on the ground that there had been no bona fide intention to use them. Romer J said (at 436):

'. . . one cannot help seeing the evils that may result from allowing trade-marks to be registered broadcast, if I may use the expression, there being no real intention of using them, or only an intention possibly of using them in respect of a few articles. The inconvenience it occasions, and the cost it occasions, are very large, and g beyond that I cannot help seeing that it would lead in some cases to absolute oppression, and to persons using the position they have got as registered owners of trade-marks (which are not really bonâ fide trade-marks) for the purpose of trafficking in them and using them as a weapon to obtain money from subsequent persons who may want to use bonâ fide trade marks in respect of some classes in h respect of which they find these bogus trade-marks registered.'

There was an unsuccessful appeal to the Court of Appeal (see [1898] 2 Ch 432 at 439), and ultimately to your Lordships' House (see sub nom *John Batt & Co v Dunnett* [1899] AC 428), where Earl of Halsbury LC picked up the same notion of trafficking when he said (at 430):

j 'Here is a gentleman who for seventeen years has been in possession of a trade-mark. There are a variety of circumstances which can be suggested—that it was needed for the purpose of trading under a particular form of mark, and so protecting the trade which he had either begun or intended to begin, or that he was disposed to register any number of trade-marks for the purpose of vending them to others to whom they might appear as pleasant and attractive trade-marks.'

He added that there were 'circumstances which certainly would suggest he was a dealer in trade-marks . . .'

The law clearly did not recognise the entitlement of the owner of a trade mark to deal with it, like a patent, as a commodity in its own right. The same point was highlighted 15 years later in your Lordships' House in *Bowden Wire Ltd v Bowden Brake Co Ltd* (1914) 31 RPC 385, where Earl Loreburn said (at 392):

'The object of the law is to preserve for a trader the reputation he has made for himself, not to help him in disposing of that reputation as of itself a marketable commodity, independent of his goodwill, to some other trader. If that were allowed, the public would be misled, because they might buy something in the belief that it was the make of a man whose reputation they knew, whereas it was the make of someone else . . . In this case the appellants parcelled out the right to use their trade mark as if they had been dealing with a patent.'

The committee appointed in 1933 under the chairmanship of Viscount Goschen, to report whether any and if so what changes in the existing law and practice relating to trade marks was desirable, had this point in mind. The committee, reporting in the following year, recommended a relaxation of some of the restrictions on the assignment of trade marks, and in particular, a facility for a person to register a trade mark to be used only by others under the 'registered user' provisions proposed by the committee (see Report of the Departmental Committee on the Law and Practice Relating to Trade Marks (Cmd 4568)). This recommendation was, however, subject to the proviso (p 8) that 'trafficking in registered trade marks is not thereby facilitated'.

It was against this background that Parliament enacted s 8 of the Trade Marks (Amendment) Act 1937, which (with an immaterial exception) became s 28 of the consolidating Trade Marks Act 1938.

The crucial question, then, is: what is meant by trafficking in a trade mark, a tendency to facilitate which is fatal to an application by the proprietor and the proposed registered user? Or, to put the question more bluntly, if a commercial activity such as that falling to be considered by your Lordships in the instant case is not trafficking in a trade mark, what is?

It is fair to say that the *Batt* case, at first instance, is the only pre-1938 reported case discovered by counsel in which the word 'trafficking' has been used judicially in a trade mark context.

Counsel for the appellants has deployed formidable arguments in support of the appellants' case that sub-s (6) is not fatal to them. It is said, correctly, that a number of famous trade marks are to be found on the register in relation to classes of goods which have no conceivable connection with the goods responsible for the fame of the mark; the use of the name 'Coca-Cola' on T-shirts, for example. But your Lordships do not know the circumstances in which such registrations were allowed, and in particular what weight may have been given to any advantage accruing to the licensor of a free advertisement for his products.

The appellants accept that in the case of the grant of a licence by the proprietor of a mark to another trader to use that mark on the licensee's own goods, there must always be some connection in the course of trade between the proprietor of the mark and the goods to which the mark is to be applied by the licensee, if registration is to be granted, but, the appellants submit, this connection is sufficiently established if the proprietor controls or is able to control the nature and quality of the goods put on the market under the mark. Put shortly, quality control is said to be enough. 'Trafficking', it is submitted, is confined to the sort of situation described by Romer J in *Batt*'s case, where the mark is sought to be registered merely to enable to proprietor to use it as a means of extorting money from another who, on a later occasion, wishes to make bona fide use of the mark. No doubt in a number of cases, eg *'Bostitch' Trade Mark* [1963] RPC 183, a provision for quality control by the licensor over the goods of the licensee has been relevant in establishing a connection in the course of trade between the licensor and such goods.

Such decisions are confined to their own factual circumstances, and I can discern no
general rule that the mere ability to control quality is always to be sufficient to establish
the required connection. In fact, the quality control exercisable in the cases before us, so
far as we have seen examples of the licence agreements, is slight. In the Oneida case it is
confined to a right to inspect and to approve if the appellants so wish. In the case of
General Mills (Chad Valley) agreement, the licensee must submit samples for written
approval prior to use or sale.

For my part, I am quite prepared to accept that character merchandising, in the sense
of the exploitation of the reputation of famous marks by making them available to a
wide variety of products, has become a widespread trading practice on both sides of the
Atlantic. It may well be that it is perfectly harmless and in most cases probably deceives
nobody. These considerations do not, however, help to decide what Parliament intended
by trafficking in trade marks or justify placing a gloss on the meaning to be attributed to
that expression. I do not feel able to agree with the appellants' submission that the
purpose of sub-s (6) was confined to the prevention of trafficking in the *Batt* sense.
Trafficking as stigmatised by Romer J in that case was in effect the stockpiling of trade
marks, without any use or intended use in relation to the goods of the proprietor, with
the intention of turning them to account when other traders wished to make use of the
marks on their own goods. I see no reason for thinking that sub-s (6) was solely directed
against trafficking in that very narrow sense.

My Lords, although as a matter of ordinary English, trafficking in trade marks might
mean the buying and selling of trade marks, it seems obvious that it is to have a more
specialised meaning in a trade mark context. I have no quarrel with the definitions
suggested by the assistant registrar and by Sir Denys Buckley, but perhaps one further
attempt on my part may not be out of place. The courts have to grope for some means of
delineating the forbidden territory, and different modes of expression may help to
indicate boundaries which are not and cannot be marked out with absolute precision. To
my mind, trafficking in a trade mark context conveys the notion of dealing in a trade
mark primarily as a commodity in its own right and not primarily for the purpose of
identifying or promoting merchandise in which the proprietor of the mark is interested.
If there is no real trade connection between the proprietor of the mark and the licensee
or his goods, there is room for the conclusion that the grant of the licence is a trafficking
in the mark. It is a question of fact and degree in every case whether a sufficient trade
connection exists. In my opinion, on the facts of these particular applications, the assistant
registrar and the High Court were entitled to take the view that the registration of the
licensee as a registered user, pursuant to s 28, would tend to facilitate trafficking in a
trade mark.

I would dismiss this appeal.

Appeal dismissed.

Solicitors: *Slaughter & May* (for the appellants); *Treasury Solicitor.*

Mary Rose Plummer   Barrister.

Re Garage Door Associates Ltd

CHANCERY DIVISION
MERVYN DAVIES J
27, 28 JULY 1983

Company – Compulsory winding up – Petition by contributory – Petition for winding up or for relief on ground of unfair prejudice – Dispute about ownership of shares – Petition also alleging unfair prejudice to member – Whether petition should be struck out – Companies Act 1980, s 75.

Although the hearing of a petition to wind up a company presented by a contributory is not the appropriate procedure for the determination of a dispute about the ownership of shares in the company and the petition will be dismissed if the petitioner's case is solely concerned with the determination of such a dispute, if the petition also contains an alternative claim for relief under s 75[a] of the Companies Act 1980, namely that a member's shares be purchased by the company or other members because the affairs of the company have been conducted in a manner unfairly prejudicial to that member, the court may allow the petition to proceed, because in those circumstances the hearing of the petition would not be an improper forum for debate about the true ownership of the shares since the court could deal first with the application under s 75 and then, if appropriate, with the winding-up petition (see p 437 e f h j, post).

Re Bambi Restaurants Ltd [1965] 2 All ER 79 and *Re JN2 Ltd* [1977] 3 All ER 1104 distinguished.

Notes

For presentation of a winding-up petition by a contributory, see 7 Halsbury's Laws (4th edn) para 1006, and for cases on the subject, see 10 Digest (Reissue) 938–939, 5489–5502.

For the Companies Act 1980, s 75, see 50(1) Halsbury's Statutes (3rd edn) 167.

Cases referred to in judgment

Bambi Restaurants Ltd, Re [1965] 2 All ER 79, [1965] 1 WLR 750.
Company, Re a (No 00440 of 1981) (12 March 1982, unreported), Ch D.
Ebrahimi v Westbourne Galleries Ltd [1972] 2 All ER 492, [1973] AC 360, [1972] 2 WLR 1289, HL.
JN2 Ltd, Re [1977] 3 All ER 1104, [1978] 1 WLR 183.
Needham (Leon) Ltd, Re (1966) 110 SJ 652.
Wilsons Automobiles and Coachworks Ltd, Re [1975] CA Transcript 536A.

Motion

On 8 July 1983 Charles Walter Goodwin presented a petition praying (i) that Garage Door Associates Ltd (the company) be wound up by the court pursuant to the Companies

---

a   Section 75, so far as material, provides:
    '(1) Any member of a company may apply to the court by petition for an order under this section on the ground that the affairs of the company are being or have been conducted in a manner which is unfairly prejudicial to the interests of some part of the members (including at least himself) or that any actual or proposed act or omission of the company (including an act or omission on its behalf) is or would be so prejudicial . . .
    (3) If the court is satisfied that a petition under this section is well founded it may make such order as it thinks fit for giving relief in respect of the matters complained of.
    (4) Without prejudice to the generality of subsection (3) above, an order under this section may . . . (d) provide for the purchase of the shares of any members of the company by other members or by the company itself and, in the case of a purchase by the company itself, the reduction of the company's capital accordingly . . .'

Act 1948, or, alternatively, (ii) that an order be made under s 75 of the Companies Act 1980 (a) setting aside the allotment of 799 shares of £1 each in the capital of the company made or purportedly made on 18 September 1980, (b) directing Bryan Alexander Booth and/or Doreen Ann Booth (the respondents to the petition) to purchase from him the £1 share of £1 in the capital of the company registered in the register of members of the company in his name at a price to be determined. By notice of motion dated 19 July 1983 the Booths applied for an order striking out, as an abuse of the process of the court, so much of the petition as related to Mr Goodwin's claim that the company be wound up. The facts are set out in the judgment.

John Brisby for the Booths.
Michael Todd for Mr Goodwin.

MERVYN DAVIES J. This is a motion to strike out in a matter under the Companies Act 1948 and 1980. It relates to a petition presented by Mr Charles Walter Goodwin on 8 July 1983. Mr Goodwin says he is a contributory of Garage Door Associates Ltd. The company is a private company, limited by shares and incorporated on 25 August 1976. It carries on business as automatic laundry proprietors. The authorised share capital is £1,000 in £1 shares. The petition states that 801 shares have been issued and credited as fully paid up. The 801 shares appear in the register of members as belonging to Mr Goodwin as to 1 share, to Mr B A Booth as to 500 shares, and Mrs D A Booth as to 300 shares. Mr and Mrs Booth are respondents to the petition.

The petition states: 'The issue of 799 of the said 801 issued shares in the capital of the Company is a matter of which Your Petitioner complains.' So if 799 shares were disregarded, there would be one share held by Mr Goodwin and one share held by one or other of the Booths.

The Booths are directors of the company. I need not detail the allegations in the petition save to say that it said that the company was, in effect, a joint venture between Mr Goodwin and Mr Booth and that there has been a falling out together with a complaint about the issuing of the 799 shares I have mentioned and, further, Mr Goodwin's exclusion from the business. Mr Goodwin was at one time a director of the company but he resigned on 29 April 1982.

In the prayer Mr Goodwin seeks a winding-up order and, alternatively, under s 75 of the 1980 Act, orders in the following terms:

'(2) That Orders may be made pursuant to Section 75 of The Companies Act 1980, (A). setting aside the allotment of 799 shares of £1 each in the capital of the Company made or purportedly made on or about 18th September 1979; (B) that:— (i) Mr. and/or Mrs. Booth do purchase from Your Petitioner, Charles Walter Goodwin, the £1 Share of £1 in the capital of the Company registered in the Register of Members of the Company in the name of Your Petitioner at a price to be determined in manner hereinafter appearing . . .'

Then there is suggested the manner of valuation. I need read no further from the prayer in the petition.

The notice of motion, dated 19 July 1983, is by the Booths in their capacity as contributories and as respondents to the petition. The Booths seek, so far as now material, an order striking out as an abuse of the process of the court so much of the Goodwin petition as relates to the Goodwin claim that the company be wound up.

The evidence in support of the motion is an affidavit by Mr Booth sworn on 19 July 1983. The affidavit refers not only to the Goodwin petition but also to a petition by the Booths themselves that antedates the Goodwin petition. The Booth petition was presented on 9 June 1983. The relief there sought is s 75 relief. There was also read to me parts of the affidavit of Mr Booth sworn on 14 June 1983 in support of the Booth petition but I do not think I need mention that affidavit further. It relates to matters which will no doubt be examined in detail when the petition comes on for hearing.

In answer to the affidavit in support of the motion, there is an affidavit of Mr John Richard Pratt. He is the solicitor who acts for Mr Goodwin. In para 5 of that affidavit there are these words:

'. . . It is apparent from the Petition herein that the essence of my client's dispute with the company and Mr. and Mrs. Booth is the extent of members' shareholdings in the company and the beneficial ownership thereof. I humbly submit that the Petition herein and Affidavit evidence in support indicate prima facie that the Petitioner and Mr. Booth are each entitled in their own right to one share in the company, that each of them is beneficially entitled thereto and that the issue of further shares in September 1979 to Mr. and Mrs. Booth is at least questionable and at worst, as is submitted by the Petitioner, of no effect. I respectfully submit that any prima facie case supporting the contentions of Mr. and Mrs. Booth is no more substantial than and, indeed, I submit less substantial than, that supporting the contentions of my client Mr. Goodwin.'

Counsel for the Booths said there was a dispute about the ownership of the shareholdings in the company. In that situation, he said, it was not right to allow the petition to proceed so far as winding up is concerned. When there is a dispute about share ownership, it is not right that a dispute should be decided in the course of a winding-up petition, or indeed, he said, in the course of a s 75 petition especially when winding up is claimed as well. I was referred to *Buckley on the Companies Acts* (14th edn, 1981) vol 1, p 530 where there are these words:

'If the petitioner's case depends upon the determination of a question as to the beneficial ownership of shares, the petition will be dismissed, for it is not the appropriate procedure for the determination of such a question.'

In the context of that extract the word 'petition' means a petition to wind up. I was referred to *Re Bambi Restaurants Ltd* [1965] 2 All ER 79, [1965] 1 WLR 750. That is a case concerning a winding-up petition and has no reference to s 210 of the 1948 Act or, of course to s 75 of the 1980 Act. I was also referred to *Re Leon Needham Ltd* (1966) 110 SJ 652. That is a case in which the judge refused to decide a dispute about share ownership on motion, and a petition that was to be heard at the same time was, in consequence, dismissed. The report does not show what relief was being claimed in the petition but, in any event, the case is clearly distinguishable from the case before me because in *Needham* the petitioners had not been registered as shareholders. Here, Mr Goodwin is at present on the register as the registered holder of one share in the company. In *Re JN 2 Ltd* [1977] 3 All ER 1104 at 1108–1109, [1978] 1 WLR 183 at 187–188, Brightman J said this:

'It is, of course, common practice to dismiss a creditor's petition if the debt is bona fide disputed by the company. This seems to me a wholly proper attitude to be adopted by the court. The presentation of a winding-up petition has an immediate effect on the ability of a company to deal with its assets, although capable of mitigation by an appropriate order under s 227 [of the Companies Act 1948]. Frequently in the case of a trading company the presentation of a petition will damage the financial standing of the company. It therefore seems to be obviously correct that the court should not allow a creditor's petition to remain on the file longer than is necessary once the status of the petitioner is in doubt. In my judgment this reasoning applies with even greater force to a petition by a person whose status as a contributory is in dispute. In the case of a disputed creditor's petition, the petitioner has at least an unsatisfied *claim* against the assets of the company. A person asserting that he is a contributory has not, in so asserting, any claim against the company's assets. It makes no difference whatever to the quantum of the company's assets whether the contributory succeeds or fails in his claim to be a shareholder. It therefore seems to me to be all the more important that he should not be permitted to present a petition and thereby interfere with dispositions by the company of its assets and risk damaging the financial standing of the company, so long as his right to be a shareholder of the company is in dispute. That dispute is not between the company and a person claiming against the company, but between a shareholder and a person claiming to be a shareholder. Let that dispute be settled first before the company is brought on to the scene by the resentation of a petition. By being brought on to the scene I mean of course as a substantial party. By dismissing the petition the court is not driving a litigant from the judgment seat, or doing any injustice to him. The court will be merely requiring him to establish his right to present a petition before he is permitted to take a step which has such an immediate and potentially damaging effect on the company. In these circumstances I propose to dismiss the petition.'

There again, the judge was speaking in the context of a petition that sought winding up and not either s 210 or s 75 relief; and, indeed, in *Re JN2 Ltd* the petitioner was not registered as a shareholder.

I was also referred to two unreported cases: one is *Re Wilsons Automobiles and Coachworks Ltd* [1975] CA Transcript 536A, a decision of the Court of Appeal on 16 December 1975. This, again, was a case in which winding up and no other relief was sought on the petition. There is then *Re a company (No 00440 of 1981)* (unreported), a decision of Slade J on 12 March 1982. I do not see that anything in that judgment affords any helpful guidance in this case. As I understand it, the petitioner in that case was not a member of the company within s 26 of the Companies Act 1948.

The authorities that I have mentioned do not seem to me to point to any firm grounds for requiring me to allow the application that is before me. It seems plain that if when a contributory's petition to wind up has been launched there emerges the fact that there is a relevant dispute about the ownership of the shares in the company, then the petition to wind up will be dismissed and the appropriate course is by writ or otherwise to have the dispute about the share ownership settled. The words from *Buckley* that I have read, succinctly express that sentiment. *Re Bambi Restaurants Ltd* [1965] 2 All ER 79, [1965] 1 WLR 750 appears to me to be authority for the same sentiment although perhaps, as counsel for Mr Goodwin submitted, that case ought now to be reviewed in the light of *Ebrahimi v Westbourne Galleries Ltd* [1972] 2 All ER 492, [1973] AC 360. However, I do not think it is necessary for me to take that course here. The position facing me is rather different.

The Goodwin petition does not ask merely for winding up. It asks, in the alternative, for relief under s 75. It should also be borne in mind that Mr Goodwin is a registered holder of his share, with his name on the company register which is prima facie evidence of the fact that he is a contributory (see s 118 of the Companies Act 1948). Accordingly, Mr Goodwin has, at present at any rate, a locus standi to present a petition. Now not only has Mr Goodwin the necessary locus standi, but the petition he presents raises, pursuant to s 75, the question of the validity of the 799 shares that I have mentioned. The Booth petition will no doubt come on for hearing with the Goodwin petition. That Booth petition raises an issue about the beneficial ownership of the sole Goodwin share, alleging that it belongs beneficially to the Booths. Accordingly, when the petitions come on for hearing, the matter of the ownership of all the shares in the company, save the one original Booth share, will be debated. I see no occasion for saying that the hearing of those petitions is an improper forum for any debate about the true ownership of the shareholding. After all, those appear to me to be the very issues that are respectively raised by the petitions.

In these circumstances, I see no grounds for striking out from the Goodwin petition the claim regarding winding up. Surely the right course to take is to allow the petition to proceed. In that way the issue as to share ownership will be settled, and afterwards, if appropriate, the winding-up application can be prosecuted.

Counsel for the Booths has very rightly been anxious to lift the shadow of a prospective winding up from the company. I sympathise, of course, with that view, but counsel for Mr Goodwin has given an undertaking not to advertise his petition and there is in existence s 227 relief granted by Harman J. I would propose to extend that s 227 relief until the hearing of the petition and if counsel for the Booths seeks to have any further protection, I should welcome hearing any observations that he has to make in that regard. For the moment, I accordingly dismiss the notice of motion save for considering any remarks counsel for the Booths may wish to make about protecting the company pending the petition.

Motion dismissed.

Solicitors: *Blyth Dutton* (for the Booths); *Buss Stone & Co*, Tonbridge (for Mr Goodwin).

Jacqueline Metcalfe   Barrister.

Gill & Duffus SA v Berger & Co Inc

HOUSE OF LORDS

LORD DIPLOCK, LORD KEITH OF KINKEL, LORD ROSKILL, LORD BRANDON OF OAKBROOK AND LORD TEMPLEMAN

14 NOVEMBER, 15 DECEMBER 1983

Sale of goods – Cif contract – Sale by sample – Certificate of quality – Conclusive evidence clause – Contract for sale by sample providing that independent inspector's certificate of quality to be final – Goods discharged at port of discharge in two instalments – Sellers obtaining certificate of quality in respect of first instalment only – No certificate obtained in respect of second instalment – Buyers' wrongly rejecting conforming documents tendered by sellers – Sellers electing to treat contract as repudiated – Whether buyers entitled to reject whole consignment because second instalment not conforming with contract description – Whether buyers' right to reject goods for non-conformity surviving sellers' rescission of contract – Sale of Goods Act 1893, s 30(1)(3).

The sellers sold a quantity of 500 tonnes of Argentine bolita beans, 1974 crop, to the buyers under a cif contract which provided that the beans shipped were to conform with a sample submitted to the buyers and sealed by an independent inspector. The contract further provided, by a conclusive evidence clause, that a certificate of quality issued by the inspector at the port of discharge was to be 'final'. Payment for the beans was to be made in cash on presentation of documents by the sellers to the buyers' bank. The consignment was discharged at the port of destination in two instalments of 445 tonnes and 55 tonnes at an interval of 13 days. Shortly after the first instalment of 445 tonnes was discharged the sellers presented shipping documents relating to the whole consignment to the buyers' bank but they were wrongly rejected on the ground that the documents presented did not include a certificate of quality. Instead of treating the buyers' rejection of the documents as a wrongful repudiation of the contract the sellers obtained a certificate of quality from the inspector at the port of discharge in respect of the 445 tonnes then available and re-presented the documents, but they were again rejected by the buyers. The sellers then treated the buyers as being in default and commenced arbitration proceedings in which the board of appeal of a trade association found that the beans shipped did not, according to independent analysis, correspond with the sealed sample held by the inspector and that the buyers were therefore not liable to accept and pay for the beans. On the sellers' appeal, the judge found that the beans had been delivered in two separate consignments and held that the buyers were bound to accept the 445 tonnes because the inspector's certificate was conclusive that that consignment conformed to the contract description but that they were entitled to reject the 55 tonnes because there was no certificate of quality relating to that consignment. The buyers appealed to the Court of Appeal, contending, inter alia, that since the certificate of quality obtained by the sellers was not conclusive in relation to the 55 tonnes which, as the trade association's board of appeal had found, did not conform with the contract description, it followed (i) that, if the 55 tonnes were ignored as not conforming with the contract, the sellers had in effect delivered to the buyers 'a quantity of goods less than [they had] contracted to sell', which entitled the buyers to reject the whole consignment of 500 tonnes under s 30(1)ᵃ of the Sale of Goods Act 1893, or (ii) alternatively, that if the 55 tonnes were taken into account the sellers had delivered to the buyers 'the goods [they had] contracted to sell mixed with goods of a different description not included in the contract', which entitled the buyers to reject the whole consignment of 500 tonnes under s 30(3) of the 1893 Act. The Court of Appeal held that although the conclusive evidence clause prevented the buyers from resiling from the certificate of quality in respect of the 445 tonnes they were nevertheless entitled to rely on s 30(1) and (3) to reject the whole consignment. The sellers appealed to the House of Lords.

Held – The appeal would be allowed for the following reasons—

(1) The refusal of a buyer under a cif contract to pay to the seller, or to a banker nominated in the contract, the purchase price of the contract goods when the seller presented at the place stipulated in the contract shipping documents which, on their face, conformed with the documents required by the contract constituted a fundamental breach of contract which entitled the seller to treat the contract as repudiated and as relieving him of any obligation to continue to perform his own obligations under it. Since the buyers had wrongly rejected the documents presented by the sellers because a certificate of quality was not part of the shipping documents required to be presented by the sellers to obtain payment and since the sellers had, eventually, treated that wrongful rejection of their documents as a repudiation of the contract by the buyers, it followed that the sellers were not thereafter required to deliver any beans at all to the buyers. In those circumstances, the absence of a certificate of quality covering the whole consignment was irrelevant in determining the buyers' liability and the question whether the buyers were entitled to reject the whole consignment under s 30(1) or (3) of the 1893 Act did not arise (see p 443 e to p 444 a and f g, p 446 e f and p 448 c to g, post); dictum of Lord Cairns in *Shepherd v Harrison* (1871) LR 5 HL at 132 applied; *Henry Dean & Sons (Sydney) Ltd v O'Day Pty Ltd* (1927) 39 CLR 330 considered.

(2) On the measure of damages, the buyers were prima facie liable for the difference between the contract price of the whole consignment of 500 tonnes of beans and the market price for which the documents representing the consignment could be sold at the date the repudiation was accepted, but subject to the buyers' right to claim, or set off, damages for any failure by the sellers to perform their own primary obligations, including the obligation to ship beans that conformed with the contract, which were due to be performed before the contract was rescinded, and in that respect the certificate of quality could be relevant in determining whether the sellers had failed to perform their own obligations by being in breach of a warranty as to description or quality. However, the buyers were unable to show any such breach of warranty on the part of the sellers, because the effect of the conclusive evidence clause was that the 445 tonnes conformed with the contract by virtue of the certificate of quality, which also in effect covered the 55 tonnes because there was no suggestion that the 55 tonnes differed in quality from

---

ᵃ Section 30, so far as material, provides:

'(1) Where the seller delivers to the buyer a quantity of goods less than he contracted to sell, the buyer may reject them, but if the buyer accepts the goods so delivered he must pay for them at the contract rate . . .

(3) Where the seller delivers to the buyer the goods he contracted to sell mixed with goods of a different description not included in the contract, the buyer may accept the goods which are in accordance with the contract and reject the rest, or he may reject the whole . . .'

the 445 tonnes. It followed that the buyers were liable in damages to the sellers in respect of the whole consignment of 500 tonnes (see p 442 *j* to p 443 *c*, p 444 *g* to *j*, p 447 *d* to *h* and p 448 *b* to *g*, post).

Per curiam. Where the description of goods agreed to be sold includes a statement as to their quality and provides that a certificate as to quality is to be final, the certificate is in fact final as regards whether the goods correspond with the quality required by the description notwithstanding that the certificate may later be proved to be inaccurate (see p 445 *h j* and p 448 *d* to *g*, post); *Toepfer v Continental Grain Co Ltd* [1974] 1 Lloyd's Rep 11 approved.

Notes

For the buyer's right of rejection under a cif contract, see 41 Halsbury's Laws (4th edn) para 928, and for cases on the subject, see 39 Digest (Repl) 717–722, 2027–2053.

For the Sale of Goods Act 1893, s 30, see 30 Halsbury's Statutes (3rd edn) 26.

As from 1 January 1980 s 30 of the 1893 Act was replaced by s 30 of the Sale of Goods Act 1979.

Cases referred to in opinions

Bowes v Shand (1877) 2 App Cas 455, [1874–80] All ER Rep 174, HL.
Chao (trading as Zung Fu Co) v British Traders and Shippers Ltd [1954] 1 All ER 779, [1954] 2 QB 459, [1954] 2 WLR 365.
Dean (Henry) & Sons (Sydney) Ltd v O'Day Pty Ltd (1927) 39 CLR 330, Aust HC.
Shepherd v Harrison (1871) LR 5 HL 116.
Toepfer v Continental Grain Co Ltd [1974] 1 Lloyd's Rep 11.

Appeal

By an award made by an umpire (Mr K J Arnott) dated 28 December 1977 in favour of Berger & Co Inc, of San Francisco, California, USA (the sellers), in an arbitration held under the rules of the Grain and Feed Trade Association Ltd (GAFTA) between the sellers and Gill & Duffus SA, of Geneva, Switzerland (the buyers), arising out of the sale of 500 tonnes of Argentine bolita beans under a contract dated 22 December 1976 on the terms of GAFTA 41, the umpire awarded that by their failure to take up documents the buyers were in default and should pay the sellers the sums of $US58,899·50 (damages) and $US39,946·45 (storage expenses), plus interest. The buyers appealed to the Board of Appeal of GAFTA, which set aside the umpire's award on 15 April 1980 but stated their opinion in the form of a special case for the opinion of the High Court. By para 52 of their award the question of law posed by the Board of Appeal for the decision of the court was 'whether on the facts found and on the true construction of the contract the buyers are liable to the sellers in damages'. By a supplemental award dated 3 April 1981 the Board of Appeal found that the goods tendered did not correspond with the contractual description. The sellers appealed. On 31 July 1981 Lloyd J ([1982] 1 Lloyd's Rep 101) allowed the appeal in part, holding that the buyers were liable to the sellers in damages in respect of 445 tonnes of beans but not in respect of the balance of 55 tonnes because there was no certificate of quality in respect of the latter. The buyers appealed and the sellers cross-appealed. On 2 March 1983 the Court of Appeal (Sir John Donaldson MR and Slade LJ, Robert Goff LJ dissenting) ([1983] 1 Lloyd's Rep 622) allowed the buyers' appeal and dismissed the cross-appeal, holding that the buyers were not liable in damages to the sellers in relation to either the 445 tonnes or the 55 tonnes of beans. The sellers appealed to the House of Lords with leave of the Court of Appeal. The facts are set out in the opinion of Lord Diplock.

Bernard Rix QC and *Elizabeth Birch* for the sellers.
David Johnson QC and *Peregrine Simon* for the buyers.

Their Lordships took time for consideration.

15 December. The following opinions were delivered.

LORD DIPLOCK. My Lords, the subject matter of this appeal is a single contract dated 22 December 1976 for the sale of a consignment of 500 tonnes of 'Argentine Bolita Beans—1974 Crop' as per sample, cif Le Havre, on the terms of GAFTA 41 subject to certain variations, of which the most material was a provision (the certification clause) that a certificate of quality at port of discharge given by General Superintendence Co Ltd (GSC) of Paris should be final.

At the outset of his judgment in the Court of Appeal Sir John Donaldson MR set out the arbitral and litigious history of this case since 1 April 1977, when the appellants, Berger & Co Inc (the sellers), appointed their arbitrator in a claim against the respondents, Gill & Duffus SA (the buyers), in the dispute that had by then arisen between them and the sellers. By the time judgment had been given by the Court of Appeal that history had extended over nearly six years and had involved proceedings by way of saisie conservatoire in the Tribunal de Commerce at Le Havre, hearings by arbitrators, who disagreed, followed by a hearing by an umpire, who made an award in favour of the sellers, then an appeal to the Board of Appeal of GAFTA culminating in an award in the form of a special case in April 1980 and in a supplemental award in April 1981, in compliance with a remission ordered by the High Court (Mustill J) at a hearing in January of that year (see [1981] 2 Lloyd's Rep 233). The hearing of the special case in the High Court recommenced before a different judge (Lloyd J) in July 1982 (see [1982] 1 Lloyd's Rep 101). He found partly in favour of the buyers and partly in favour of the sellers. From his judgment an appeal to the Court of Appeal was brought (see [1983] 1 Lloyd's Rep 622). They found by a majority (Sir John Donaldson MR and Slade LJ) wholly in favour of the buyers. Robert Goff LJ dissented and would have found wholly in favour of the sellers. In face of this diversity of judicial opinion between judges of great experience in commercial law, the Court of Appeal gave leave to appeal to your Lordships' House. So a claim for damages for an alleged breach of a contract for the sale of goods committed on 30 March 1977 will have taken more than six and a half years in order to obtain final resolution of it. Sir John Donaldson MR rightly described this delay, up to the time of hearing in the Court of Appeal, as deplorable. Now, nearly twelve months later, I would substitute for 'deplorable', a 'disgrace to the judicial system'.

The delay and expense arise from the refusal of the buyers to comply with and the failure of some of the arbitration and judicial authorities to recognise the obligation, freely negotiated and included in the contract between the parties in the interests of speed, certainty and economy, to accept as final the certificate of the expert chosen by the parties to indicate whether the quality of the cargo delivered by the sellers was equal to the quality of the sealed sample furnished by the sellers.

My Lords, I venture to think that by the time the case had reached the Court of Appeal it had managed to acquire a deceptive appearance of complexity which an analysis of the legal nature of the duties of the buyers and sellers under the contract of sale of 22 December 1976 should have shown that it did not possess. Stripped down to its essentials that contract, apart from the certification clause, was on ordinary cif terms.

The contract was set out in a confirmation note dated 22 December 1976 and signed on behalf of the buyers and the sellers. The only provisions of this document which it is necessary to set out are:

> 'We herewith confirm to you the following transaction by our intermediary on the conditions of: GAFTA 41 LONDON ARBITRATION where not contradictory to the terms below . . .
> COMMODITY: ARGENTINE BOLITA BEANS—1974 *Crop*.
> QUALITY: As per sample submitted to buyers and sealed by the General Superintendence Company Ltd., Paris
> QUANTITY: 400 (four-hundred) to 500 (five-hundred) metric tons at seller's option to be declared latest 10/2/1977 . . .

DESTINATION: CIF LE HAVRE/ANTWERP at seller's option preferably Le Havre . . .
a
SHIPMENT: February/March 1977
PAYMENT: Net cash against documents on first presentation through: Banque de Paris et des Pays-Bas, Geneve . . .
SPECIAL CONDITIONS & REMARKS: Quality final at port of discharge as per certificate of General Superintendence Company Ltd., indicating that the quality of the lot is equal to the one of the sealed sample. Charges for sealing of samples at seller's expense.'
b

Under the quantity clause the sellers declared the full 500 tonnes on 3 February 1977, and this quantity was shipped on the Salland from Limon in Costa Rica under a bill of lading dated 28 February. The vessel arrived at Le Havre on 21 March, but for some reason (which does not appear) she left after discharging 9,661 bags containing only 445 tonnes of the consignment, and over-carried the balance of 55 tonnes to Rotterdam, where it was transhipped and brought back to Le Havre in another vessel and was discharged there on 2 April 1977.
c

So much for what happened to the goods themselves. I turn next to what happened to the shipping documents relating to the goods. These documents under ordinary cif terms (incorporated without material alteration in GAFTA 41) comprise: invoice, full set on board bill of lading and policy or certificate of insurance. It is not disputed that shipping documents which satisfied this requirement and covered the whole contract quantity of 500 tonnes were presented at the buyers' bank in Geneva on 22 March 1977 as provided for by the clause of the contract appearing against the rubric 'Payment'. The buyers, however, rejected the documents and refused to pay against presentation on the ground that they did not include 'Certificate of Quality on discharge made out on behalf of all parties by GSC certifying that the goods are of the same quality as the sample sealed by GSC Paris when the business was concluded.'
d

e

My Lords, a certificate by GSC as to the quality of the goods at port of discharge under the certification clause in the contract is not, and is indeed incapable of being, included among shipping documents which a seller is required to tender to his buyer in return for payment of the price under a contract of sale in ordinary cif terms. Although an argument to the contrary was apparently persisted in by the buyers up to the Court of Appeal, its hopelessness has now been recognised and it has not been advanced in the argument for the buyers in your Lordships' House.
f

The sellers did not elect to treat as a wrongful repudiation of the contract the buyers' rejection of the documents as good tender under the contract and their consequent refusal to pay the price on presentation on 22 March. Instead the sellers set about getting from GSC a certificate under the certification clause as to the quality of the 445 tonnes that had been discharged at Le Havre and were all that were available for sampling there.
g

On 29 March 1977 GSC issued a certificate in the following terms:

'CERTIFICATE OF QUALITY AND INSPECTION No 15.944

In pursuance of an order given to us by: BERGER and Company to inspect: Quality of 10.894 bags "BEANS BOLITAS" at time of Discharge by sampling. We hereby certify that we inspected the quality of a parcel designated as: –9.661 Bags "BEANS BOLITAS", No marks   discharged ex m/s "SALLAND" in LE HAVRE on the 21st March 1977. According to the results of the analysis performed on the samples drawn by us on a 10% basis at random, the parcel of beans discharged from m/s "SALLAND" is equal to the samples previously sealed by us and kept in our possession.
h

PARIS, 29th March 1977
j
SOCIETE GENERALE DE SURVEILLANCE S.A.'

The shipping documents were re-presented to the buyers on 30 March together with this certificate, but were again rejected. This time the sellers did treat the buyers' refusal to pay the price on presentation of the documents as a wrongful repudiation of the contract and by telex of 1 April 1977 they elected to treat the contract as rescinded. This had the consequence in law that all primary obligations of the parties under the contract

which had not yet been performed were terminated. This termination did not prejudice
a the right of the party so electing to claim damages from the party in repudiatory breach
for any loss sustained in consequence of the non-performance by the latter of his primary
obligations under the contracts, *future as well as past*. Nor did the termination deprive
the party in repudiatory breach of the right to claim, or to set off, damages for any *past*
non-performance by the other party of that other party's own primary obligations, due
to be performed before the contract was rescinded. In the instant case these latter
b obligations included a primary obligation, to be performed by the sellers at the time of
shipment, and thus before the date of termination of the contract, to ship goods that
were in conformity with the contract, albeit that the right of disposal of the goods was
reserved by the sellers until payment by the buyers for the shipping documents on
presentation.

My Lords, at all relevant times the Sale of Goods Act 1893 was still in force in its
c original terms. The contract of sale was one by sample as well as by description. The
goods, 'Argentina Bolita Beans—1974 Crop', were two-year-old beans and as such were
of a kind prone to contain some admixture of impurities and of defective beans, the
extent of which would be revealed by a sample by reference to which the contract of sale
was made, if such a sample were properly taken so as to be representative of the bulk
shipment.

d Your Lordships in the instant case are thus not dealing with the converse of the
example of conduct that was the subject of Lord Blackburn's well-known aphorism in
Bowes v Shand (1877) 2 App Cas 455 at 480, [1874–80] All ER Rep 174 at 185: '. . . If you
contract to sell peas, you cannot oblige a party to take beans.' Parenthetically, I may add
that in the case of a cif contract it is difficult to see how, without fraud on his part, the
seller could ship beans but nevertheless be in a position to tender shipping documents
e conforming to those called for by a cif contract to sell peas; and nothing that I say is
intended to cover cases of fraud.

In the instant case it has never been contended that the actual shipping documents
tendered by the sellers to the buyers on 22 March 1977 and retendered on 30 March did
not relate to the whole quantity of 500 tonnes or did not on the face of them conform to
the terms of the cif contract of 22 December 1976. That being so it is, in my view, a
f legal characteristic of a cif contract so well established in English law as to be beyond the
realm of controversy that the refusal by the buyer under such a contract to pay to the
seller, or to a banker nominated in the contract if the contract so provides, the purchase
price on presentation at the place stipulated in the contract of shipping documents which
on their face conform to those called for by the contract constitutes a fundamental breach
of contract, which the seller is entitled to elect to treat as rescinding the contract and
g relieving him of any obligation to continue to perform any of his own primary
obligations under it, or, to use the terminology of the Sale of Goods Act 1893, 'to treat
the contract as repudiated'. So far as concerns the instant case the relevant primary
obligation of the sellers of which they were relieved was any further obligation to deliver
to the buyers any of the goods that were the subject matter of the contract.

That a refusal by the buyer to accept the tender of shipping documents which on the
h face of them conform to the requirements of a cif contract and on such acceptance to pay
the contract price amounts to a breach of condition (in the meaning given to that
expression in the Sale of Goods Act 1893) has been taken for granted so universally by
English courts as not to have attracted any subsequent positive exposition worthy of
citation, ever since Lord Cairns put it thus in *Shepherd v Harrison* (1871) LR 5 HL 116 at
132–133, a case where payment was to be by acceptance of a documentary bill of
j exchange:

> 'I hold it to be perfectly clear that when a cargo comes in this way, protected by a
> bill of lading and a bill of exchange, it is the duty of those to whom the bill of lading
> and the bill of exchange are transmitted in a letter, *either "to approbate or to reprobate"*
> *entirely and completely, then and there.*'

Recognition of the principle so stated (to which I have myself supplied the emphasis) is implicit in all judgments dealing with bankers' confirmed credits as a mode of payment including the most recent judgments of this House.

I have not overlooked a case decided in the High Court of Australia in 1927, *Henry Dean & Sons (Sydney) Ltd v O'Day Pty Ltd* 39 CLR 330, to which deprecative reference is made in the current edition of *Benjamin's Sale of Goods* (2nd edn, 1981) para 1717. The case turned largely on a question of pleading which in New South Wales in 1927 followed the system that applied in England before the Supreme Court of Judicature Act 1873. By a majority of three to two (Knox CJ, Higgins and Starke JJ, Isaacs and Powers JJ dissenting), it was held that, when a buyer under a cif contract who was suing the seller for damages for non-delivery of goods which corresponded to the contract description was met by a plea by the seller that, by reason of the buyer's previous non-acceptance of a documentary bill of exchange accompanied by conforming documents, the buyer had failed to prove the essential allegation in his pleading that he was ready and willing to perform the contract at the time when tender of the actual goods that had been shipped under the bill of lading had been made. The two judges in the High Court who formed the minority took the orthodox view that the buyer's refusal to accept the documentary bill on presentation made him unable to establish his readiness and willingness to perform the contract. Of the majority, Knox CJ and Higgins J appear to have held that a cif buyer is entitled to reject conforming shipping documents if it should *subsequently* turn out that the actual goods shipped under the conforming documents did not in fact conform to the contract, a view which, if correct, would destroy the very roots of the system by which international trade, particularly in commodities, is enabled to be financed. Starke J, although he concurred with Knox CJ and Higgins J in the outcome of the action, did not adopt this ratio decidendi. He regarded the case as a special one turning on its particular facts; and I must confess that I have been unable to discover in his judgment any clear statement of some legal principle that he was treating as applicable to those facts.

There was thus no ratio decidendi that commanded the support of a majority of the High Court of Australia. Maybe for this reason, so far as I have been able to ascertain, *Henry Dean & Sons (Sydney) Ltd v O'Day Pty Ltd* has never been regarded as meriting citation in any later case. It has for more than half a century justifiably remained one of those submerged cases which lawyers in general have tacitly accepted as being a total loss, until it was dredged up in the course of the hearing of the instant case in your Lordships' House to provide, in the judgments of Knox CJ and Higgins J, a tabula in naufragio for the buyers. In my opinion what was expressed to be the ratio decidendi of those judgments is not the law of England.

In the instant case the sellers did elect to treat the contract as repudiated on 1 April 1977. They then ceased to be under any contractual obligation to deliver to the buyers any 'Argentine Bolita Beans—1974 Crop'. The buyers on the other hand became liable to the sellers in damages for breach of contract. Prima facie the measure of such damages would be the difference between the contract price of the 500 tonnes of beans that were the subject matter of the contract and the price obtainable on the market for the documents representing the goods at date of the acceptance of the repudiation. Such prima facie measure might, however, fall to be reduced by any sum which the buyers could establish they would have been entitled to set up in diminution of the contract price by reason of a breach of warranty as to description or quality of the goods represented by the shipping documents that had been actually shipped by the sellers if those goods had in fact been delivered to them. In the events that happened the certification clause in the contract is in my opinion relevant only to the measure of damages to which the sellers are entitled. It does not go to the buyers' liability even if they could show that the damages should be nominal only.

The umpire, who had awarded the sellers damages on the basis of the prima facie measure I have mentioned above together with warehousing costs and interest, gave no reason for his award. The Board of Appeal in their award in the form of a special case set out the facts, including those relating to the buyers' refusal to pay the price on tender of the shipping documents and the sellers election to treat the cif contract as thereby repudiated, in meticulous detail. The award stated the question of law for the court in the following terms (which became so familiar before the case stated method of appeal to the High Court was abolished):

'. . . the Question of Law for the decision of the Court is whether on the facts found and on the true construction of the Contract the Buyers are liable to the Sellers in damages.'

This form of question left it open to counsel at the hearing in the High Court to advance whatever arguments in law arising from the facts found that his ingenuity might suggest to him, whether or not a similar argument had been addressed to the Board of Appeal. Accordingly, I do not find it necessary to refer to those parts of the award that record the submissions made to them by the parties or to the board's own reasoning that led them to the conclusion that the buyers were under no liability to the sellers in damages.

My Lords, the fact that the consignment of 500 tonnes was discharged at Le Havre in two instalments of 445 tonnes and 55 tonnes respectively at an interval of 13 days between them owing to over-carriage of the latter quantity to Rotterdam, coupled with the fact that the only certificate of quality obtained from GSC related to the 445 tonnes first delivered, had the unfortunate result that the case was conducted in the High Court before Lloyd J as if, instead of there having been a single contract for the sale of 500 tonnes of Argentine bolita beans cif Le Havre, there had been two separate contracts, one for 445 tonnes and the other for 55 tonnes. In relation to the 445 tonnes the fact that the rescission of the contract on 1 April 1977 necessarily included the remaining 55 tonnes as well appears to have been overlooked, and the matter was argued and dealt with by the judge entirely on the question whether the GSC certificate was conclusive that the 445 tonnes with which it dealt conformed to the contract. He held, on the authority of Toepfer v Continental Grain Co Ltd [1974] 1 Lloyd's Rep 11, that it was and he restored the award of the umpire as respects this part of the shipment.

It appears from the judgment of Lloyd J that a belated allusion to the cif contract for the 55 tonnes having been rescinded, thus obviating the necessity for a GSC certificate for that tonnage, was made by counsel for the sellers, but the judge, not being invited to do otherwise, dealt with this part of the shipment as if it were the subject of a separate contract and appears to have regarded that contract as requiring the sellers to provide the buyers with a GSC certificate of quality relating to all goods delivered thereunder and the buyers as entitled to reject any goods for which such a certificate was not supplied by the sellers.

My Lords, before turning to the fate of the instant case in the Court of Appeal, it is convenient to deal with the conclusiveness of the GSC certificate of quality. Toepfer v Continental Grain Co Ltd was a case of a cif sale of wheat by description alone, viz 'No. 3 hard amber durum wheat of U.S. origin'. The contract contained no provision for a sample, but it incorporated a term: 'Official certificates of inspection to be final as to quality.'

The words used in a contract of sale that refer to the goods agreed to be sold (not being 'specific goods' as defined in s 62 of the Sale of Goods Act 1893) often include words that describe a characteristic as to quality or condition that they possess which distinguishes them from other goods of the same general kind. What Toepfer v Continental Grain Co Ltd decided was that, where the description of the goods agreed to be sold included a statement as to their quality and provided that a certificate as to quality was to be final, the certificate was final as to the correspondence of the goods with that part of the description of them in the contract that referred to their quality (in casu 'No. 3 hard amber') notwithstanding that the certificate was proved to have been inaccurate. The conclusion reached by the Court of Appeal in Toepfer v Continental Grain Co Ltd is, in my opinion, plainly right. My own preferred analysis of the reason why it is consistent with s 13 of the Sale of Goods Act 1893 is that, while 'description' itself is an ordinary English word, the Act contains no definition of what it means when it speaks in that section of a contract for the sale of goods being a sale 'by description'. One must look to the contract as a whole to identify the kind of goods that the seller was agreeing to sell and the buyer to buy. In *Toepfer's* case it was not 'No. 3 hard amber durum wheat' simpliciter but durum wheat of United States origin for which a certificate had been issued by a United States government official stating that its quality was that which is described in the trade as 'No. 3 hard amber'.

Similarly, where, as in the instant case, the sale (to use the words of s 13) is 'by sample as well as by description', characteristics of the goods which would be apparent on reasonable examination of the sample are unlikely to have been intended by the parties to form part of the 'description' by which the goods were sold, even though such characteristics are mentioned in references in the contract to the goods that are its subject matter.

My Lords, the cif contract in the instant case contains provisions opposite the rubrics 'Quality' and 'Special conditions & remarks' respectively, which make the certificate of GSC conclusive as to the conformity of the bulk shipment at port of discharge with the sample that had been submitted to the buyers while the contract was in course of negotiation and had been sealed by GSC. It must have been the intention of the parties that the conclusiveness of the certificate would be limited to those characteristics of the contract goods that would be apparent on reasonable examination of the sample; but there is no suggestion in the instant case of any disconformity between the goods as delivered at Le Havre and the sealed sample in respect of any characteristic which reasonable examination of the sample would not have revealed. Since Lloyd J, and all three members of the Court of Appeal, accepted that such was in law the effect of these provisions of the cif contract, I need say no more about them except to express my respectful concurrence.

I turn now to analyse what it was that went wrong with the case in the Court of Appeal. Here it was recognised that the cif contract was a single contract for a consignment of 500 tonnes. What appears to have been wholly overlooked is that the sellers, on 1 April 1977, had in fact elected, as they were entitled to do, to treat the buyer's rejection of the shipping documents as a repudiatory breach that had brought to an end their primary obligation under the contract to deliver any goods at all to the buyers. No mention of this election on the sellers' part is to be found in any of the judgments. Robert Goff LJ, in his dissenting judgment, does say that on rejection of the documents by the buyers 'the sellers became entitled to bring the contract [sc for the 500 tonnes] to an end' (see [1983] 1 Lloyd's Rep 622 at 635), but there is nothing to indicate that his attention was directed to the fact that the sellers had acted on that entitlement and *had* brought the contract to an end.

My Lords, it is trite law for which I do not find it necessary to refer to any other authority than the judgment of Devlin J in *Chao (trading as Zung Fu Co) v British Traders and Shippers Ltd* [1954] 1 All ER 779 at 795–796, [1954] 2 QB 459 at 487–448 that, when a buyer under a cif contract accepts shipping documents which transfer the property in the goods to him, the property in the goods that he obtains is subject to the condition subsequent that it will revest in the seller if on examination of the goods themselves on arrival the buyer finds them to be not in accordance with the contract in some respect which would entitle him to reject them, and he does in fact reject them. But this is because the cif contract remains on foot; and, being a contract for the sale of goods, the buyer has the right under s 34 of the Sale of Goods Act 1893 to reject the goods themselves for non-conformity with the contract and retains this right until he has had a reasonable opportunity of examining the goods after they have been delivered.

My Lords, it is not necessary in the instant case to consider whether a similar right to reject the goods on delivery is retained by a buyer who, in breach of contract, had refused to accept the shipping documents when duly presented in accordance with the provisions of the contract, and the seller has *not* elected to treat such refusal as a repudiatory breach bringing all further primary obligations on his part under the contract to an end. Delivery of the goods themselves, even for the purpose of examination, to a buyer who is not the holder of the bill of lading would seem to require some agreed amendment to the cif contract of sale; so one would not be concerned only with rights of the buyer arising under the original cif contract. Under the original cif contract a right of the buyer at his election to reject shipping documents and a right at his election to reject the goods themselves on delivery are separate and successive rights. The latter does not become exercisable until the seller has unconditionally appropriated the goods to the contract. Under a cif contract this does not happen until his reservation of the right of disposal of the goods by his withholding from the buyer the shipping documents which represent them is terminated by his transferring the shipping documents to the buyers. In so far as Robert Goff LJ in a passage of his judgment appears to accept the contrary as being a necessary corollary of the principle applied in *Chao* I think, with respect, that he was wrong.

Whatever legal problems might be presented by a situation resulting from a seller's failure to treat the buyer's rejection of conforming shipping documents as bringing the contract to an end, it would, in my view, be contrary to the basic concepts of the law of contract that deal with the different remedies for different categories of breach if a seller of goods who had elected to treat the buyer's breach of a condition of the contract, or a fundamental breach of an innominate term, as bringing to an end his own further primary obligations under the contract (or in the terminology of the Sale of Goods Act 1893 'to treat the contract as repudiated') continued to be under any legal obligation to deliver to the buyer any goods, if the election so to treat the buyer's breach were made before the actual goods had been delivered to him. As already mentioned, if the seller sued the buyer for damages for his failure to pay the price of the goods against tender of conforming shipping documents, the buyer, if he could prove that the seller would not have been able to deliver goods under those shipping documents that conformed with the contract of sale, would be able to displace the prima facie measure of damages by an amount by which the value of the goods was reduced below the contract price by that disconformity; but this goes to a quantum of damages alone.

My Lords, in the Court of Appeal, all 500 tonnes of beans were treated as if they had been tendered by the sellers to the buyers on discharge at Le Havre and there rejected by the buyers. As respects the 445 tonnes, both Sir John Donaldson MR and Slade LJ accepted that the GSC certificate was conclusive and that that quantity conformed with the contract, but as respects the 55 tonnes for which there was no such certificate they accepted the finding of the Board of Appeal of GAFTA (which related to the whole bulk of the 500 tonnes of beans shipped) that those 55 tonnes did not conform to the contract. This, Sir John Donaldson MR reasoned, led to the conclusion that the sellers had delivered to the buyers a quantity of goods conforming to the contract less by 55 tonnes than the quantity they had contracted to sell, thus entitling the buyers to reject the whole 500 tonnes under s 30(1) of the Sale of Goods Act 1893, or alternatively under s 30(3). So, in effect, these two members of the Court of Appeal treated the sellers' obligation to deliver the contract goods to the buyers at Le Havre and the buyers' right to reject them for disconformity with the contract after examination as surviving the sellers' justified determination of the cif contract under which alone any obligation of the sellers to deliver goods to the buyers arose. For reasons previously given I think that this must be erroneous in law.

Robert Goff LJ does not, in his dissenting judgment, analyse the legal effects of the rescission of the cif contract. He goes straight to the question of damages. He treats the case as one in which the sellers are entitled to recover the price payable under the contract on tender of shipping documents unless the buyers can prove that they would have been entitled to reject the goods on delivery at Le Havre. Since, even if there had been no rescission, the certification clause made a GSC certificate conclusive as respects characteristics of the goods that would be apparent on reasonable examination of the sealed sample, the buyers, in order to rely on s 30(1) or (3), would have to prove that, on the balance of probabilities, GSC would not have issued a certificate covering the balance of 55 tonnes that was not available at Le Havre for sampling when GSC's certificate for the 445 tonnes was issued. There is no suggestion in the award of the Board of Appeal of GAFTA that there was any difference in quality between the 445 tonnes and the 55 tonnes. Indeed, the opinion stated in their award that the goods delivered did not conform to the contract is expressly said to apply to the whole bulk of 500 tonnes, so it is evident that the quality of the beans shipped was a matter on which expert opinion may differ. It is to avoid this kind of dispute that parties incorporate conclusive certification clauses in contracts of sale of commodities.

Given the absence of any suggestion of difference in quality between the 55 tonnes and the 445 tons that GSC had certified as equal to the sealed sample by reference to which the cif contract was made, the buyers lacked the finding of fact essential to their defence in part to the sellers' claim in damages that on balance of probabilities GSC would not have issued a similar certificate in respect of the 55 tonnes. It was for this reason that Robert Goff LJ would have found wholly in favour of the sellers and restored the award of the umpire.

For the reasons given in the rather more elaborate analysis of the legal nature of the contracting parties' rights which result from the facts found in the Board of Appeal's award, I agree with the result reached by Robert Goff LJ. I would allow the appeal, answer the question of law posed in the special case in favour of the sellers in respect of the whole 500 tonnes and uphold the alternative award of the Board of Appeal of GAFTA. The buyers must pay the sellers' costs in this House and in all courts below.

LORD KEITH OF KINKEL. My Lords, having had the benefit of reading in advance the speech of my noble and learned friend Lord Diplock, I agree that, for the reasons given by him, the appeal should be disposed of in the manner which he has proposed.

LORD ROSKILL. My Lords, I have had the advantage of reading in draft the speech delivered by my noble and learned friend Lord Diplock. For the reasons he gives I too would allow this appeal and make the other orders proposed by him.

LORD BRANDON OF OAKBROOK. My Lords, I have had the advantage of reading in draft the speech prepared by my noble and learned friend Lord Diplock. I agree with it, and for the reasons which he gives would allow the appeal and make the other orders proposed by him.

LORD TEMPLEMAN. My Lords, for the reasons given by my noble and learned friend Lord Diplock, I too would allow this appeal and make the other orders proposed by him.

Appeal allowed. Award of umpire restored.

Solicitors: *Middleton Potts & Co* (for the sellers); *Richards Butler & Co* (for the buyers).

Mary Rose Plummer   Barrister.

R v Delgado

COURT OF APPEAL, CRIMINAL DIVISION
LORD LANE CJ, SKINNER AND McCOWAN JJ
21 NOVEMBER 1983

Drugs – Controlled drugs – Possession with intent to supply – Supply – Defendant in temporary control of drug for owner with intention of soon returning drug to owner – Whether intention to 'supply' drug to owner – Whether transfer of physical control from one person to another test of 'supplying' – Misuse of Drugs Act 1971, s 5(3).

The appellant was charged on indictment with having a controlled drug, namely cannabis, in his possession with intent to supply it to another contrary to s 5(3)[a] of the Misuse of Drugs Act 1971 (count 1) and with possession of a controlled drug, namely cannabis, contrary to s 5(2) of that Act (count 2). His story was that he had been asked by two friends, who had stolen a bag containing a substantial quantity of cannabis but who had nowhere to keep it for the time being, to keep it for them for a couple of hours and then to deliver the bag to them at a stated time and place and that when he was arrested he was on his way to his friends with the bag to deliver it to them. At first he pleaded not guilty to both charges but at his trial he changed his plea on count 2 to guilty. After giving evidence of his account of the events he submitted that on the basis of his account he had a good defence to count 1 because he had merely been returning the cannabis to his friends to whom it belonged and therefore did not have the necessary intent to 'supply' them with the drug, within s 5(3). The judge ruled that in returning the drug to his friends the appellant was 'supplying' them with the drug within s 5(3) and that, since on his own evidence he had been in possession of the drug with intent to 'supply' in that sense, his evidence amounted to an admission of the offences charged in count 1. Following that ruling the appellant changed his plea on count 1 to guilty and was convicted on both counts. He appealed against his conviction on count 1 contending that the judge's ruling was erroneous in law.

Held – The word 'supply' in the context of s 5(3) of the 1971 Act meant the transfer of physical control of a drug from one person to another and covered a wide range of transactions where such transfer was the common feature. Questions regarding the transfer of ownership or legal possession of a drug were, therefore, irrelevant to the question whether there had been an intent to supply a drug. Since on the appellant's own evidence he had had possession of a substantial quantity of cannabis with the intention of transferring control of it from himself to his two friends at an agreed time and place, it followed that he had had an intent to 'supply' the drug to his friends for the purpose of s 5(3). Accordingly, the judge's ruling had been correct. The appeal would therefore be dismissed (see p 452 *c* to *e*, post).

Notes

For possession of a controlled drug with intent to supply, see 11 Halsbury's Laws (4th edn) para 1093 and 30 ibid para 746, and for cases on the subject, see 15 Digest (Reissue) 1077–1078, 9170–9173.

For the Misuse of Drugs Act 1971, s 5, see 41 Halsbury's Statutes (3rd edn) 884.

Cases referred to in judgment

Holmes v Chief Constable Merseyside Police [1976] Crim LR 125, DC.
R v Aramah (1982) 76 Cr App R 190, CA.

---

a   Section 5(3), so far as material, provides: '. . . it is an offence for a person to have a controlled drug in his possession . . . with intent to supply it to another . . .'

R v Greenfield (Evan) [1983] Crim LR 397, CA.
R v Harris (Janet) [1968] 2 All ER 49, [1968] 1 WLR 769, CA.   **a**

Appeal
On 24 June 1982 in the Crown Court at Inner London Sessions before his Honour Judge West-Russell and a jury the appellant, Winston Delgado, pleaded not guilty to an indictment containing two counts: possession of a controlled drug, namely cannabis, with intent to supply it to another, contrary to s 5(3) of the Misuse of Drugs Act 1971   **b** (count 1), and possession of a controlled drug, ie cannabis, contrary to s 5(2) of that Act (count 2). At his trial the appellant gave evidence that the cannabis which was found in his possession belonged to two friends and that at the time of his arrest he had been on his way to deliver the cannabis to them. He changed his plea on count 2 to guilty and submitted that he had a good defence to count 1 because on his evidence he did not have any intent to 'supply' the drug to his friends. The judge ruled that the returning of the   **c** cannabis to the friends did constitute a 'supply' of the drug to them within s 5(3) and that as, on the appellant's own evidence, he was in possession of the drug with intent to supply as so defined he had no defence to the offence charged in count 1. The appellant then changed his plea on count 1 to guilty. The judge sentenced the appellant to four years' imprisonment on count 1 and to two years' concurrent imprisonment on count 2. The appellant appealed against his conviction and against sentence. The facts are set out in   **d** the judgment of the court.

M A P Hopmeier (assigned by the Registrar of Criminal Appeals) for the appellant.
Linda Stern for the Crown.

SKINNER J delivered the following judgment of the court. On 24 June 1982 at the   **e** Crown Court at Inner London Sessions before his Honour Judge West-Russell the appellant pleaded not guilty to an indictment containing two counts. The first charged him with possession of cannabis with intent to supply to another, contrary to s 5(3) of the Misuse of Drugs Act 1971, and the second charged simple possession of the same amount of cannabis, contrary to s 5(2) of the same Act. Early in the trial he changed his plea from not guilty to guilty on count 2, and subsequently he was sentenced to two   **f** years' imprisonment on that count.

The appellant himself gave evidence at his trial and at the conclusion of his evidence, at the invitation of both counsel, the judge ruled that, accepting the appellant's evidence, he had no defence in law to the charge in count 1. Thereupon, on counsel's advice, the appellant changed his plea to guilty on that count and was sentenced to four years' imprisonment.

He now appeals against his conviction by leave of the full court, though, since the   **g** appeal raises a point of law, leave was strictly unnecessary.

The facts are these. On Sunday 3 January 1982, some time in the later afternoon, the appellant was being driven in a minicab from an address in the East End to Trafalgar Avenue, off the Old Kent Road. He had with him a holdall. Inside the holdall was a carrier bag. The carrier bag contained 6.31 kg of cannabis wrapped in 1 lb packages, the street value of which was estimated to be at least £15,000.

The cab was stopped by a police officer, solely because it was not displaying a vehicle excise licence. Immediately it was stopped, the appellant showed signs of extreme distress and ran away leaving the holdall in the car. He was arrested very shortly afterwards.

Initially he said that he had found the drugs. Subsequently he gave the story which he   **h** repeated to the jury, which was that he was transporting the cannabis for two friends named Rowland and Judah. At the trial he enlarged on this. He said that he had met Rowland and Judah, who were acquaintances, earlier that day at Hackney. They had told him that they had stolen the cannabis. He said they told him that they did not have anywhere to keep it and asked him to keep the bag for a few hours. Later he said they asked him to look after it for them for a couple of hours. He said that he had arranged to

deliver the cannabis to them at 5 o'clock that afternoon in an amusement arcade near
Brockwell Park. He was on his way there when he was arrested. When he was asked
what he was going to get out of it, he said that they told him they would give him a piece
of cannabis for himself to smoke. Pressed about how much he expected, he said it could
have been an ounce. That was the extent of his involvement, so he said, and he was
adamant that he was not concerned with the disposal of the cannabis after he had
redelivered it to Rowland and Judah.

After hearing counsel's submissions the judge ruled that the returning of the drugs to
the 'owners', in other words to Rowland and Judah, was an act of supplying and, since on
the appellant's own evidence he had kept possession with that intent, his evidence
amounted to an admission of the offence. It was at that point that he changed his plea.

Counsel for the appellant now argues that that ruling by the judge was wrong. He
submits that s 5(3) of the 1971 Act was not directed against an offence of this kind. It was
directed solely against the supply to what he describes as third parties, and he seeks to
define the word 'supply' in the relevant subsection as the act of providing drugs to a
person who has no ownership or control over the goods.

He relies on the extended definition of 'possession' afforded by s 37(3) of the 1971 Act,
which reads:

> 'For the purposes of this Act the things which a person has in his possession shall
> be taken to include any thing subject to his control which is in the custody of
> another.'

He says that to supply by passing possession to somebody who already by the statute has
possession involves a totally unrealistic concept. In support of his argument he cited to
us the decision of this court in *R v Greenfield (Evan)* [1983] Crim LR 397, which was
decided on 28 February 1983.

That was a case in which the appellant was looking after drugs for the owner who was
himself a supplier to the ultimate purchasers or consumers. The case was dealt with in
the court below and summed up to the jury by the judge on the basis that the appellant
was an aider and abettor in the possession with intent to supply. This court ruled that the
judge was wrong in the way he put the matter to the jury. Lord Lane CJ giving the
judgment of the court said: 'The real problem in this case is the meaning of the words of
the charge, that is to say the meaning of s 5(3) of the Misuse of Drugs Act 1971'. He went
on to read the particulars of the offence in the indictment and made this comment:

> 'On the assumption that the handing back of the drugs to X, as the judge directed
> the jury, was not a supply, what we have to ask ourselves is whether the intention
> undoubtedly held, if his statements to the police are accepted, by this man, namely
> the intention that these drugs should be supplied by X to another, is a sufficient
> offence in the words of the 1971 Act. It is not an altogether easy point. We have
> come to the conclusion that the intent of somebody else to supply is not enough.
> The words of the Act are plain, that is to say "with intent to supply", which in our
> judgment predicate that it should be the intent on the part of the person who
> possesses to supply, and not the intent of someone other than that who is in
> possession of the drugs to supply. Consequently it follows that whichever way one
> looks at the matter, the judge was not correct in leaving the matter in the way he
> did to the jury. There is no doubt that, had the matter been left simply on the
> question whether this man himself intended to supply, the jury may very well have
> come to the conclusion that that was made out.'

By that last sentence this court was reserving the point which is the subject of argument
in this appeal.

In addition, counsel for the appellant cited to us *R v Harris (Janet)* [1968] 2 All ER 49,
[1968] 1 WLR 769. That was a case where the appellant who was charged with supplying
had merely injected the owner of the drugs with his own drugs. The drugs which were

injected never left the presence of the owner nor, as it was strongly argued, his physical control. This court held that, on those facts, there was no act of supplying.

Counsel for the Crown argues that it is the passing of physical control of the drugs which is the important matter to consider, and that questions of possession and ownership are largely irrelevant. She mentioned, without fully citing to us, a case in which the Divisional Court held that a man who purchases on behalf of a group of people and later distributes the goods among the group is supplying to others within the subsection. However that decision, in *Holmes v Chief Constable Merseyside Police* [1976] Crim LR 125, turned on the definition of 'supplying' under s 37(1) of the 1971 Act, which includes the words 'supplying includes distributing' and therefore it is of little help to us.

Thus we are driven back to considering the word 'supply' in its context. The judge himself relied on the dictionary definition, which is a fairly wide one. This court has been referred to the *Shorter Oxford English Dictionary* which gives a large number of definitions of the word 'supply', but they have a common feature, viz that in the word 'supply' is inherent the furnishing or providing of something which is wanted.

In the judgment of this court, the word 'supply' in s 5(3) of the 1971 Act covers a similarly wide range of transactions. A feature common to all of those transactions is a transfer of physical control of a drug from one person to another. In our judgment questions of the transfer of ownership or legal possession of those drugs are irrelevant to the issue whether or not there was intent to supply.

In the present case on his own evidence the appellant had possession of a substantial quantity of cannabis. His intention was to transfer control of it to his two friends at an agreed time and place. In those circumstances it seems to us that the judge was entirely right in his ruling, and that therefore the argument put forward by counsel for the appellant has no foundation.

In those circumstances the appeal against conviction is dismissed.

The court then heard submissions on the appeal against sentence.

SKINNER J. The appellant also by leave of the single judge appeals against his sentences of four years' imprisonment on the first count of the indictment and two years' imprisonment on the second count to run concurrently.

He is a man of 29, a self-employed tailor with a wife and two children to support. He came to the United Kingdom from Jamaica in 1965. He had four convictions for dishonesty in his early years. The last was in 1972 and this is his first conviction since. He has not served any previous custodial sentence. The social inquiry report which was prepared before the verdicts were known said that he was suitable for community service.

Counsel for the appellant argues that the sentence in this case was too high. While conceding it is within the guidelines which were laid down in the decision in *R v Aramah* (1982) 76 Cr App R 190 by this court, he says that the judge was wrong in thinking that it merited a sentence at the top of the range suggested by this court for offences of this kind. He says that if the appellant had been concerned in the ultimate distribution of the drugs he could not be making that submission, but, since he was not, he suggests the sentence ought to be reduced.

In the judgment of this court the scale of this operation and the appellant's part in it not only rendered an immediate custodial sentence inevitable, but made it right for the judge to impose the sentence he did; it is well within the range suggested for this type of offence in the decision in *R v Aramah*. In those circumstances the appeal against sentence is also dismissed.

Appeals against conviction and sentence dismissed.

17 January 1984. The court refused leave to appeal to the House of Lords but certified, under s 33(2) of the Criminal Appeal Act 1968, that the following point of law of general public

importance was involved in its decision: whether a person who took temporary possession and
a   *control of drugs from and at the request of A 'supplied' those drugs, within the meaning of the*
Misuse of Drugs Act 1971, when he returned the drugs to A.

Solicitors: *D M O'Shea* (for the Crown).

Sophie Craven   Barrister.

b

Secretary of State for Defence and another v Guardian Newspapers Ltd

COURT OF APPEAL, CIVIL DIVISION
c   SIR JOHN DONALDSON MR, GRIFFITHS AND SLADE LJJ
15, 16 DECEMBER 1983

Evidence – Privilege – Press – Newspaper reporter – Source of information – Informant
wrongfully passing Crown's confidential document to defendant newspaper for publication –
Defendant ignorant of identity of informant but document bearing distinguishing marks likely to
d   *lead to identification by Crown – Crown bringing action against defendant for return of document*
for purpose of discovering informant's identity – Whether Crown entitled to order for disclosure
– Whether disclosure necessary in interests of national security – Contempt of Court Act 1981,
s 10.

A memorandum, classified 'secret', was prepared by the Ministry of Defence concerning
e   the handling of publicity relating to the installation of nuclear weapons at a Royal Air
Force base. The original of the document was sent to the Prime Minister and six copies
were circulated to senior members of the government and to the cabinet secretary. A
photostat copy of the memorandum was 'leaked' by an unknown informant to the
defendant newspaper, which subsequently published it. The Crown requested the return
of the photostat copy so that it could attempt to identify the informant from markings
f   made on the document. The defendant claimed that, since the markings would be very
likely to identify the source of the information, it was not required to deliver up the
copy, by virtue of s 10[a] of the Contempt of Court Act 1981, which provided that a person
was not required to 'disclose . . . the source of information contained in a publication for
which he is responsible, unless it be established to the satisfaction of the court that
disclosure is necessary in the interests of justice or national security or for the prevention
g   of disorder or crime'. The Crown issued a writ seeking recovery of the photostat copy
and injunctions restraining the defendant from, inter alia, destroying or defacing it. The
Crown also sought interlocutory relief in the same terms pending trial of the action. The
Crown contended that, since the copy was Crown property and Crown copyright, it was
entitled to its return or, alternatively, to discovery of it so that, in the interests of national
security, it could identify the defaulting Crown servant who had leaked the information
h   to the defendant. The judge held that s 10 of the 1981 Act did not prevent the
enforcement of proprietary rights and that therefore the Crown was entitled to the return
of the copy. The defendant appealed.

Held – On its true construction the effect of s 10 of the 1981 Act was to restrict the
court's inherent jurisdiction relating to the disclosure of documents by permitting the
j   court to order disclosure only where it was necessary in the interests of justice or national
security or for the prevention of disorder or crime. On the facts and irrespective of its
proprietary rights, the Crown was entitled to the return of the document because it had

---

a   Section 10, so far as material, is set out at p 456 *h*, post

satisfied the court that there was a risk to national security unless the informant could be found. That risk lay not in the exposure by the defendant of the contents of the particular *a* document but in the fact that a Crown servant who was in a position to handle material which was classified 'secret' was in breach of his duty of trust. The appeal would accordingly be dismissed (see p 458 *c d* and *f* to *j*, p 459 *j* to p 460 *f*, p 461 *j* to p 462 *g* and p 463 *b* to *d*, post).

Norwich Pharmacal Co v Customs and Excise Comrs [1973] 2 All ER 943 and *British Steel Corp v Granada Television Ltd* [1981] 1 All ER 417 considered.   *b*

Per curiam. It is doubtful whether s 10 of the 1981 Act applies to prevent the enforcement of proprietary rights where recovery of property pursuant to those rights under the general law has the incidental effect of disclosing a source of published information (see p 457 *j*, p 459 *b* to *e* and p 461 *d e*, post).

Per Slade LJ. It is doubtful whether a publisher who is ignorant of a source can resist an order for disclosure merely because it might, and not necessarily will, reveal that *c* source (see p 461 *h j*, post).

Notes

For disclosure of a journalist's sources of information, see 37 Halsbury's Laws (4th edn) para 1070.

For the Contempt of Court Act 1981, s 10, see 51 Halsbury's Statutes (3rd edn) 505.   *d*

Cases referred to in judgments

British Steel Corp v Granada Television Ltd [1981] 1 All ER 417, [1981] AC 1096, [1980] 3 WLR 774, Ch D, CA and HL.
Nichols Advanced Vehicle Systems Inc v Rees [1979] RPC 127.
Norwich Pharmacal Co v Customs and Excise Comrs [1973] 2 All ER 943, [1974] AC 133, *e* [1973] 3 WLR 164, HL.
Warne & Co v Seebohm (1888) 39 Ch D 73.

Case also cited

Ladbroke (Football) Ltd v William Hill (Football) Ltd [1964] 1 All ER 465, [1964] 1 WLR 273, HL.   *f*

Interlocutory appeal

The defendant, Guardian Newspapers Ltd (the Guardian), appealed against the order of Scott J dated 15 December 1983 whereby he ordered it to deliver forthwith to the plaintiffs, the Secretary of State for Defence and Her Majesty's Attorney General, the document published in the Guardian newspaper on 31 October 1983 under the heading *g* 'Heseltine's briefing to Thatcher on cruise timing'. The facts are set out in the judgment of Sir John Donaldson MR.

Lord Rawlinson QC and *Peter Prescott* for the Guardian.
Simon D Brown for the Crown.

h

SIR JOHN DONALDSON MR. This case raises once again the extent to which journalists should be allowed to protect their sources of information. It comes to us on appeal from an order, made on 15 December 1983 by Scott J, which requires the Guardian newspaper to deliver to the Secretary of State for Defence or the Attorney General a document entitled 'Deliveries of Cruise Missiles to RAF Greenham Common— *j* Parliamentary and Public Statements'.

This document was prepared in the Ministry of Defence on or about 20 October 1983. It was classified 'Secret', and only seven copies left that ministry. It appears that the author was the Secretary of State for Defence and the primary addressee was the Prime Minister, but copies were also sent to the Home Secretary, the Foreign Secretary, the Lord President of the Council, the Lord Privy Seal, the Chief Whip and the Secretary of the Cabinet.

Next day the Guardian received a photocopy of one of these copies. No one on the Guardian staff knows whence it came or who delivered it. It simply arrived at the news desk with other material. The editor made various inquiries designed to establish whether or not it was authentic and was satisfied that it was. He also gave considerable thought to whether the national interest would be damaged by its publication. His conclusion was that it would not be, and on 31 October he published it. Next day the Prime Minister was questioned about the document in the House of Commons, but nothing further occurred until 11 November when the Treasury Solicitor wrote to the editor asking him to deliver up the document forthwith.

On 17 November solicitors for the Guardian replied in the following terms:

'Our clients have a document as described in your letter. In the top and bottom right-hand corner of the first page there are certain markings, an attempt to obliterate some of which had been made before the document was delivered anonymously to our clients' offices. On the top left-hand corner of the blank side of the fourth page there appear some faint markings which may reflect those on the front page. The Editor takes the view that these various markings might disclose, or assist in the identification of, the source of the information to The Guardian, although he is unable to decipher them himself and does not know the source. In accordance with the well established convention of journalism, which now has statutory force by virtue of section 10 of the Contempt of Court Act 1981, he is not prepared to take any step which might lead to the disclosure of the source of information published in his newspaper. As the Editor is concerned only to protect his source, I am, without prejudice to any argument as to the property in the document, authorised to hand it to you, with the three areas of marking excised from it. This would provide you with the whole of the text. If that course is not acceptable and you are minded to seek an injunction from the court on the lines mentioned in our telephone conversation on 14th November, will you please note that my firm has instructions to accept service of proceedings. No doubt, if you decide to take that course, you will co-operate with us in arranging a time for the hearing of the application which would be convenient to Counsel on both sides. In the meantime, you may take it that the document will be preserved intact.'

On 21 November the Treasury Solicitor replied that the proposal to deliver up the document with certain parts excised was unacceptable and that proceedings would be begun. This in fact happened on the following day.

In an affidavit filed on behalf of the Secretary of State for the Defence, Mr Richard Hastie-Smith, the principal establishment officer of the ministry, referred to the article in the Guardian for 31 October entitled 'Heseltine's briefing to Thatcher on cruise timing'. He continued as follows:

'Beneath the title of the said article is a description of a document, stated to be marked "Secret" and dated 20th October 1983, which is alleged to have come into the possession of the Defendant. That document is said to be headed "Deliveries of Cruise Missiles to RAF Greenham Common—Parliamentary and Public Statements". If such document is authentic it is the property of the Crown and no authority has been given to pass it to or to disclose it to the Defendant. The copyright in such unpublished document is vested in the Crown and no consent has been given by or on behalf of the Crown to its reproduction or publication by the Defendant. Such document can only have been passed to the Defendant or have come into its possession in breach of a duty of confidentiality owed to the Crown. Only seven copies of the said document were despatched from the Ministry of Defence [and he sets out the addressees]. The fact that a document marked "Secret" addressed by the Secretary of State for Defence to the Prime Minister on the 20th October 1983 which was concerned with a matter of great significance in relation to the defence of the United Kingdom and the North Atlantic Treaty Organisation had, by the 31st October 1983, found its way into the possession of a national newspaper, is of the gravest importance to the continued maintenance of national security. It also represents a threat to the United Kingdom's relations with her allies, who cannot be expected to continue to entrust Her Majesty's Government with secret information which may be liable to unauthorised disclosure, even though its circulation is restricted to the innermost circles of Government. Thus the identity of the person or persons who disclosed or assisted in the disclosure of the above mentioned document to the Defendant must be established in order that national security should be preserved.'

He also in a following paragraph said:

'The Plaintiffs are entitled to receive the document in the state in which it came into the hands of the Defendant and it should not be defaced in any way.'

Mr Peter Preston, the editor of the Guardian, filed an affidavit in reply setting out how the document had come into the possession of the newspaper, what he had done to check its authenticity and the thought which he had given to whether it was proper to publish the document. The affidavit goes on to say that the Guardian would never publish anything which in the editor's opinion would damage national security and to argue that publication in this case did not do so.

Counsel for the Guardian has elaborated this theme, but it is clear to me that Mr Preston has misunderstood the gravamen of the Crown's complaint. Whether or not the editor acted in the public interest in publishing this document is not the issue. The Crown's concern is quite different. It is that a servant of the Crown who handles classified documents has decided for himself whether classified information should be disseminated to the public. If he can do it on this occasion, he may do it on others when the safety of the state will truly be imperilled. The editor will no doubt retort that in such circumstances he would not publish, but the responsibility for deciding what should and should not be published is that of the government of the day and not that of individual civil servants or editors. Furthermore, and this is the Crown's case, friendly foreign states may well be prepared to entrust the government of the day with sensitive information if its security is in the hands of ministers, but will not be prepared to do so if it is in the hands of individual civil servants or editors. It is not the publication of the article which forms the basis of the Crown's complaint, but the fact that a copy got into unauthorised hands.

The case for the Crown before the judge can be stated very simply. The original document was, they said, Crown property and Crown copyright. Any copy of that document was an infringing copy and, by the combined effect of ss 2, 4, 18 and 39 of the Copyright Act 1956, the Crown had the same rights in respect of the copy in the possession of the Guardian as it would have in respect of the original. That being so, it was entitled to an order requiring the Guardian to deliver up the copy.

The Guardian did not challenge these assertions up to the point at which the Crown claimed an order for delivery up. However, it contended that it was entitled to resist such an order in reliance on s 10 of the Contempt of Court Act 1981. This provides, so far as material:

'No court may require a person to disclose . . . the source of information contained in a publication for which he is responsible, unless it be established to the satisfaction of the court that disclosure is necessary in the interests of justice or national security or for the prevention of disorder or crime.'

For the Guardian it was submitted that an order to deliver up the copy document would infringe this section, since, as was virtually admitted, the sole purpose of the Crown's claim was to enable it to trace the source of the Guardian's information.

The judge held that, on its true construction, s 10 of the 1981 Act was not intended to interfere with proprietary rights. The Crown's proprietary rights were not challenged and it followed that it was entitled to the order which it sought. He went on to say that, *a* if it had been necessary for the Crown to rely on the exceptions to s 10, he would have refused to make any order at this stage, leaving it to the Crown to establish by evidence called at the trial of the action that the exceptions applied.

 Both parties now appeal. The Guardian for the first time challenges the Crown's right of property. It also challenges the judge's construction of the effect of s 10 of the 1981 Act. The Crown for its part challenges the judge's view that it cannot rely on the exceptions to s 10 in the absence of a full trial.

b In my judgment this matter can and should be approached from a different point of view. Prior to the enactment of the 1981 Act it was the practice of the courts to have regard to the conscientious objections of priests, doctors, journalists and others to breaching express or implied undertakings of confidentiality. I say 'to have regard to' because the courts had to balance competing public interests. Section 10 of the 1981 Act, within the scope of its application, varied this discretion or practice to the extent that,

c unless the exceptional circumstances were established to its satisfaction, the court was bound to refuse to require any person to disclose the source of information contained in a publication. The section did not, however, remove the court's discretion outside this category.

 In the instant case there is a very high degree of probability that the original document was copied using Crown reproduction facilities and Crown materials. If this is right, the

d copy document in the possession of the Guardian is Crown property. If, contrary to all probability, the original document was removed from Crown premises, copied elsewhere using private apparatus and materials and then returned to Crown premises, the copy was an infringing copy. Prima facie therefore the Crown has all such rights in respect of the copy as it would have in respect of a document which was its own property.

 It is at this point that the Guardian introduces a new argument, which was not put

e before the judge. It is the brainchild of Mr Prescott, who is an expert on copyright law and who has appeared with Lord Rawlinson QC for the Guardian. In his submission quasi ownership of an infringing copy only extends to so much of the document as infringes Crown copyright and the obliterated markings are not necessarily Crown copyright. Accordingly the Crown's right to delivery of the copy document in the possession of the Guardian does not extend to that part of it which contains the obliterated

f markings.

 For my part I can see no grounds for thinking that the original markings which have now been obliterated were not put on the document by a servant of the Crown in the course of his official duties. As such they would be Crown copyright. Furthermore, I am not sure that it is open to the Guardian to take this point on appeal when it failed to take it below. However, even assuming that this point were made good, it would certainly be

g open to the Crown to shift its ground and allege, in the alternative to asserting proprietary rights, that it was entitled to disclosure of the document in order to assist it in identifying the servant of the Crown who, in breach of his fiduciary duty, had copied the original document and supplied that copy to the Guardian (see *Norwich Pharmacal Co v Customs and Excise Comrs* [1973] 2 All ER 943, [1974] AC 133). Accordingly the Crown's claim to proprietary rights is not crucial to its right to the relief claimed, and the only real issue

h and the Guardian's only real defence to the Crown's claim is that which turns on the right of the Guardian to resist disclosure of its sources of information.

 I have considerable sympathy with the judge's construction of s 10 of the 1981 Act. That provides 'No court may require a person to disclose . . . the source of information contained in a publication . . .' It does *not* provide that 'No court may require a person to take any action which may result in the disclosure of the source of information contained

j in a publication'. Prima facie it is directed at the situation in which a court says, 'Tell me your source of information' or 'Give discovery of a document which will reveal the source of your information.' If this is right, the section has no application if the Crown is entitled to rely on proprietary rights, but it would apply if the Crown was asserting a *Norwich Pharmacal* right of discovery.

 However, for present purposes I am content to take a broader view and one which is more favourable to the Guardian. It rightly contends that the Crown has no practical interest in the document, save to the extent that scientific examination of it may reveal *a* or help to reveal who was responsible for making the copy and giving it to the Guardian. If s 10 is intended to cover such a case, the Crown is not entitled to the order which it seeks unless it can bring itself within the exception.

Exactly the same result will be reached if s 10 has no application. The courts will then be free to exercise their traditional discretion based on the principles which have received parliamentary approval in s 10. That they have a discretion whether or not to order the *b* delivery up of personal property is not in doubt. It has always existed at common law and it is confirmed by s 3(3)(*b*) of the Torts (Interference with Goods) Act 1977.

Accordingly, as I see it, the real issue here is whether the s 10 exception or its common law equivalent is made out. The judge took the view that this would raise a triable issue which could not or should not be resolved in interlocutory proceedings. I disagree. Mr Preston in his affidavit and counsel for the Guardian in argument have stressed that the *c* publication of the content of this document has given potential enemies of this country no information which will be of any assistance to them. So be it. That is not the case which the Crown is making. The Crown case is that it has in its employment a servant or servants who have access to classified information and who are prepared, for reasons which seem good to them, to betray the trust which is reposed in them. Whether or not any harm has been done on this occasion, the next may be different. It is no answer to *d* this threat that the editor of the Guardian is a patriotic and responsible citizen. The responsibility for deciding what information shall be treated as classified and what shall be released into the public domain is not his or that of an individual civil servant applying his own criteria. It is that of ministers who are answerable to the nation through Parliament. The maintenance of national security requires that untrustworthy servants in a position to mishandle highly classified documents passing from the Secretary of State *e* for Defence to other ministers shall be identified at the earliest possible moment and removed from their positions. This is blindingly obvious and would not become any less obvious at any trial.

It is therefore quite unnecessary to go into the Crown's allegation that what has happened may well discourage friendly powers from entrusting ministers with sensitive information, although I would have thought that this was only slightly less obvious. *f*

Accordingly it is fully established that the exception to s 10 applies and that this is a case in which, on any view of s 10, the court is free to exercise its discretion. The same result would have been reached if, instead of considering national security, regard was had to the interests of justice or the prevention of crime. The Crown is entitled to discovery as an aid to pursuing its rights against its dishonest servant (see the *Norwich Pharmacal* case and *British Steel Corp v Granada Television Ltd* [1981] 1 All ER 417, [1981] *g* AC 1096). Refusal to order delivery up would wholly frustrate this right and be contrary to the interests of justice. Furthermore, the Crown is threatened with further acts which constitute very serious breaches of the Official Secrets Acts 1911 to 1939 and delivery up of the documents is necessary for the prevention of crime.

I would unhesitatingly dismiss the appeal and affirm the judge's order to deliver up the document for the reasons which I have expressed and which differ from his reasons. *h*

GRIFFITHS LJ. I agree that the Crown is entitled to the order it seeks, but as my reasons for so deciding are different from those of Scott J I will state them shortly.

Before the judge it was not contended that the copyright in the text of the article was not vested in the Secretary of State or in the Crown. No point was taken in the evidence of the Guardian to suggest otherwise, and prima facie the circumstances point towards *j* the copyright covering the entire contents of the document. In the absence of any evidence to the contrary and bearing in mind that the point was never taken before the judge, the argument of counsel for the Guardian has raised no doubt in my mind over the question of the Crown's right to the copyright of this particular document.

But apart from this the circumstances I think also point to the probability that the

photocopy was made on a government machine and on government paper, in which case
the claim can be founded on a right of property in the entire document.

And as a further alternative the Crown could found its claim on its entitlement to see
the document for the purposes of pursuing a claim against its defaulting employee: see
British Steel Corp v Granada Television Ltd [1981] 1 All ER 417 at 459, [1981] AC 1096 at
1174.

The real question to my mind is whether the Guardian has made good its claim to be
protected from an order to hand over the document by s 10 of the Contempt of Court
Act 1981. The Guardian claims that if it is forced to do so it will reveal the source from
which the document came to it. I think it very probably will do so; certainly the Crown
believes it will; it is the only reason why it wants to see the document.

The judge held that s 10 was of no avail to the Guardian because the section could not
be applied to limit proprietary remedies to which an owner of property must under the
general law be entitled. He appears to have limited the operation of the section to a
situation in which there is a direct refusal to name a known source.

I would not construe the section so narrowly. In a situation such as this, where a
plaintiff is claiming a document either because he has the copyright in it or because he
owns the property in it or because he wishes to see it, he has no absolute right to the
document: in each case the court has a discretion whether it should order delivery of the
document to the plaintiff. If the only purpose of claiming the document is to discover
the source that provided the document, I read the opening words of s 10, 'No court may
require a person to disclose', as directing the court not to exercise its discretion in favour
of the plaintiff unless the case falls within one of the exceptions in the second limb of the
section. If it were otherwise, we might arrive at this rather absurd state of affairs. Suppose
a leaked document arrived on the editor's desk with a covering letter saying that the
writer of the letter had obtained the document from a government file and he felt it to
be his duty to disclose the malpractice revealed in the document and he hoped the editor
would publish it, and he signed the letter. If the editor did publish it, the court could not
require the editor to name the writer of the covering letter, nor could the court require
him to produce the covering letter because this would be requiring the editor to disclose
his source, unless of course the government could establish that the case fell within the
second limb of the section. Now suppose that instead of writing a covering letter, because
he had no paper readily to hand, the source wrote exactly the same information on the
back of the document and signed it. If the court ordered the return of the document, it
would in effect have ordered the editor to reveal his source.

The press have always attached the greatest importance to their ability to protect their
sources of information. If they are not able to do so, they believe that many of their
sources would dry up and this would seriously interfere with their effectiveness. It is in
the interests of us all that we should have a truly effective press, and it seems to me that
Parliament by enacting s 10 has clearly recognised the importance that attaches to the
ability of the press to protect their sources. I cannot believe that Parliament could have
intended that whether or not the protection existed should depend on so fortuitous a
circumstance as the existence of a covering letter as opposed to a message on the back of
the document. I can see no harm in giving a wide construction to the opening words of
the section because by the latter part of the section the court is given ample powers to
order the source to be revealed where in the circumstances of a particular case the wider
public interest makes it necessary to do so.

I would therefore construe this section as enjoining the court not to make any order
that will have the result of requiring a person to disclose the source of information unless
it is established to the satisfaction of the court that disclosure is necessary in the interests
of justice or national security or for the prevention of disorder or crime.

Prima facie, therefore, I would have held that the Guardian was entitled to the
protection of s 10.

However, in the particular circumstances of this case I have no doubt that it should be
ordered to hand over the document forthwith because it is in my view clearly established

that it is necessary in the interests of national security that the source from which this document came should be identified.

The facts reveal what is to my mind a very serious state of affairs. Someone in the government service, having access to highly classified material, is untrustworthy. We are dealing with a document emanating from the Ministry of Defence marked 'Secret' with a very restricted high level circulation. To take an unauthorised copy of such a document and put it into circulation is the clearest possible breach of security procedures and, I accept from counsel for the Crown, a breach of the Official Secrets Acts 1911 to 1939. It is true that on this occasion the revelation of the contents of the documents did not damage national security, and the editor of the Guardian behaved, as one would expect of him, in a responsible manner before publishing the document. But that is not the point. The threat to national security lies in the fact that someone, probably in a senior position and with access to highly classified material, cannot be trusted. Nobody knows his motivation for revealing this particular document and nobody knows what other documents of a far more sensitive nature he may be prepared to copy or to whom he may be prepared to show them. So long as he is unidentified he presents a very serious threat to our national security. Whatever security procedures are prescribed, their success depends in large measure on the trustworthiness of those who operate them and have access to classified material. Such people are very carefully vetted and they have to be trusted. I regard it as a matter of urgency that every possible step should be taken to identify this untrustworthy person and to remove him from a position in which he has access to classified material.

I cannot see how any amount of further evidence or cross-examination at a further hearing could alter the present situation one iota. Too much time has already passed: the trail will be growing cold and the culprit taking steps to cover his tracks. There must be no more delay. The document must be handed over immediately.

For these reasons I would dismiss this appeal.

SLADE LJ. I agree. The nature of the order made by Scott J was a mandatory order compelling the Guardian to deliver up the relevant document, made on an interlocutory motion. The first inquiry must therefore be as to the Crown's rights in respect of this document. In my judgment the affidavit sworn on its behalf establishes a strong prima facie right to be treated as the owner of the document by virtue of s 18(1) of the Copyright Act 1956. Counsel for the Guardian has submitted that the Crown's rights of copyright do not extend to that part of the document which is covered by the markings referred to in the Guardian's evidence and that, if the matter proceeds to trial, a process of severance may be required, which would at least prevent the Crown from recovering the part of the document covered by the markings, which is the part it really wants. In this context he referred us to the decision of Stirling J in *Warne & Co v Seebohm* (1888) 39 Ch D 73 and certain dicta of Templeman J in *Nichols Advanced Vehicle Systems Inc v Rees* [1979] RPC 127 at 141. However, the facts of those two cases are far removed from the facts of the present case and I am not yet persuaded that there is any substance in this point, which was not argued before the judge. I therefore proceed on the basis which appears to have been common ground before him that the Crown has established the strong prima facie right to which I have referred.

Section 3 of the Torts (Interference with Goods) Act 1977 would, if the matter proceeded to trial in the ordinary way, give the court a discretion to award damages to the Crown instead of making an order for delivery of the document. But, as the judge pointed out, the intrinsic value of the document is nil and to deprive the Crown of the remedy of delivery up would deprive it of any effective remedy at all. On the basis of the present evidence, I therefore conclude that, if the matter were to proceed to trial, and if s 10 of the Contempt Act 1981 is disregarded, all the probabilities are that the Crown would obtain an order for delivery up of the document intact and in its present state.

I therefore turn to s 10 of the 1981 Act, on which the Guardian's defence to this motion is principally based. It is convenient to repeat the material words of the section:

a
'No court may require a person to disclose . . . the source of information contained in a publication for which he is responsible, unless it be established to the satisfaction of the court that disclosure is necessary in the interests of justice or national security or for the prevention of disorder or crime.'

The Guardian submits, in effect, that Scott J, in making the order which he did make, acted in contravention of the section by requiring it to disclose the source of information contained in a publication for which it is responsible (the publication being the article which appeared in the Guardian newspaper on 31 October 1983) and that the Crown has not established any of the matters which it has to establish to take itself outside the ambit of the section.

b

In at least two significant respects the facts of the present case are very different from those considered by the House of Lords in *British Steel Corp v Granada Television Ltd* [1981] 1 All ER 417, [1981] AC 1096, the decision which was the precursor of s 10 of the 1981 Act. First, it seems that in that case the name of the relevant source was known to Granada Television. Second, the relevant documents had been handed over to the British Steel Corp by the time when the appeal was heard, so that no question of proprietary remedies arose. The order appealed from in that case had been one simply requiring Granada Television to make and serve an affidavit setting forth the relevant name or names.

c

d
For my part, I have some doubts whether s 10 has any relevance at all on the facts of the present case. It is, I think, at least arguable that, as the judge held, Parliament, in enacting s 10, did not intend to interfere with the rights of owners to recover documents or other property to which they have proprietary rights under the general law, even if the delivery of the property in question may have the incidental effect of disclosing a source of published information. A pointer in the opposite direction may be the consideration that an order for delivery up of a document which has no intrinsic value to the person seeking the order, other than as a means of identifying the publisher's source of information, would at least seem to offend the spirit of the section. On the other hand, I think there is some force in the submission made by counsel for the Crown that the type of order for disclosure of sources of information, on which the section is intended to place restrictions, is simply an order which *in terms* directs disclosure by oral evidence or affidavit, such being the type of disclosure under consideration by their Lordships in the *British Steel* case.

e

f

Apart from this point, there is a further reason why I have some doubts whether s 10 has any application on the particular facts of the present case. As the editor of the Guardian says in para 16 of his affidavit: 'The Guardian does not know, and has no means of finding out who the source is.' It is common ground that the reason why the Crown is seeking delivery of the document is that it hopes or expects that it may enable it to identify the source of the leak. The evidence presently before the court, however, does not establish with any certainty at all whether or not the effect of the order sought by the Crown will in fact involve disclosure of the Guardian's source of information. This entirely depends on whether the partially blacked-out markings on the document, as to which the Guardian has put in evidence only limited particulars, will lead the Crown to the source. It is, I think, arguable that a publisher who seeks to pray in aid s 10 of the 1981 Act for the purpose of resisting an order which would otherwise be appropriately made against him must satisfy the court by affirmative evidence that the effect of the order in question, if made, *will* (not just may) compel him to reveal a source of information.

g

h

j
However, it is not necessary to express a conclusion on these two arguable points which seem to me to arise on the construction of s 10 because, in agreement with Sir John Donaldson MR and Griffiths LJ, but respectfully differing from the judge, I am satisfied that any disclosure of a source of the Guardian's information which may be involved in the delivery of the document is necessary in the interests of national security. A substantial part of the affidavit of the editor of the Guardian has been directed to

showing that no issue of national security arises from the publication of the contents of the document. It is common ground that the publication of this particular document does not jeopardise national security. But that is not the relevant point. **a**

The relevant points are, in my opinion, these. On 20 October 1983 seven copies of a document marked 'Secret' (and seven copies only) were dispatched from the Ministry of Defence to the Prime Minister, the Secretary of State for the Home Department, the Secretary of State for Foreign and Commonwealth Affairs, the Lord President of the Council, the Lord Privy Seal, the Chief Whip and the Secretary of the Cabinet. Since the **b** document was marked 'Secret', it must have been obvious to any persons who had access to it that, whatever its contents, it was intended by the writer to be confidential. On the evening of 21 October a photostat copy of this same document was delivered by some unknown person to a national newspaper. As counsel for the Guardian accepted in argument, the person responsible for the leak must have been guilty of a betrayal of trust. While the publication of the particular document in question appears to have **c** involved no risk to national security, we must take judicial knowledge of the fact that many other documents dispatched from the Ministry of Defence to one or more of the seven recipients whom I have mentioned will be of a highly confidential nature and could gravely prejudice the national security if published. If a person who has access to documents passing from the Ministry of Defence to one or more of these recipients was sufficiently untrustworthy and irresponsible to supply the document in question to a **d** national newspaper in the present instance, I see no reason why the Ministry of Defence or this court should be expected to assume that this same person may not betray his trust once again, and on the next occasion by disclosing more sensitive documents, to the jeopardy of the national interest. I therefore accept the submission of counsel for the Crown that national security requires that the identification of the offending persons should be established as soon as possible and correspondingly that the disclosure sought **e** is necessary in the interest of national security.

The Guardian's editor, in his affidavit, suggests that the logical extension of the Crown's argument to this effect is that any newspaper would be compelled to reveal the source of his information, however trivial or domestic, on the ground that the source has demonstrated himself as being capable of leaking official documents and might thereafter be transferred to some more security sensitive post. He suggests that such argument **f** would rapidly render s 10 of the 1981 Act otiose. With respect to him, I disagree. The present case, on its facts, has the special features that the document in question was marked 'Secret', emanated from a naturally and properly security-sensitive ministry and was addressed solely to the seven persons whom I have mentioned. Counsel for the Guardian has observed that further evidence on the national security aspect could be given at the trial. However, I am satisfied that, notwithstanding the fortunately innocuous character of the particular document in question, the very fact of its finding **g** its way to a national newspaper gives rise to special and justifiable anxiety in the context of national security. And this is not to cast any aspersions on the responsibility of the Guardian newspaper itself, whose conduct has not been criticised in any way in this court.

On the particular facts of this case, I would also accept the separate and independent submission of counsel for the Crown that the disclosure sought is necessary in the **h** interests of justice. I cannot see that the Guardian itself is likely to suffer any damage by an order for disclosure. I repeat that this is not a case where it is being asked to disclose the name of a known source. The editor, in his affidavit, says that it seems to him that the Guardian has a duty to do everything it can, acting responsibly, to protect the confidentiality of its unknown sources, because it is in the public interest that people who give information to newspapers should have every protection that a newspaper can **j** provide. I appreciate his concern to protect his newspaper's sources, but the Guardian could scarcely be fairly criticised on the grounds of having failed to take adequate steps to protect the confidentiality of its unknown source when it has strenuously resisted the order sought by the Crown, both here and in the court below. In contrast, it seems to me

that, if the Crown is compelled to wait until the trial before it can obtain the document,
a it, and indeed the national interest, could well suffer irreparable damage through the
further activities of the unknown informant. Thus, on weighing the balance in the
particular circumstances of this case, I think that to confine the Crown to its remedy
against the Guardian and to deny it the opportunity of a remedy against the as yet
unidentified source would be a significant denial of justice (compare the observations of
Lord Wilberforce in the *British Steel* case [1981] 1 All ER 417 at 460, [1981] AC 1096 at
b 1175).

For these reasons, I think that s 10 of the 1981 Act affords no defence to the Guardian
against the present claim and that there is every likelihood that, if this claim were to
proceed to trial, the court would affirm the Crown right to delivery of the document.

It remains to consider whether relief by way of an order for delivery should have been
granted by the court in the exercise of its discretion on an interlocutory motion in
c advance of the trial. In my opinion, the balance of convenience pointed overwhelmingly
in favour of such an immediate order being made. In this connection, I attach importance
not only to what I have said in the context of the interests of national security and justice
but to the need for speedy action if the Crown is to have the best chance of discovering
the identity of the wrongdoer.

For these reasons, albeit for reasons rather different from those relied on by the judge,
d I think he reached the right conclusion and I would agree that this appeal should be
dismissed.

Appeal dismissed. Stay refused. Leave to appeal to the House of Lords granted.

Solicitors: *Lovell White & King* (for the Guardian); *Treasury Solicitor.*

Diana Procter   Barrister.

Secretary of State for Trade and Industry v Booth
The Biche

QUEEN'S BENCH DIVISION
KERR LJ AND WEBSTER J
10, 14 OCTOBER 1983

Shipping – Passengers – Carrying passengers in excess – Ship used for sail training excursions for groups of people – Groups participating in sailing vessel – Whether people in groups 'passengers' – Whether people in groups 'engaged . . . on the business of the ship' – Merchant Shipping Act 1894, s 271 – Merchant Shipping (Safety Convention) Act 1949, s 26(1)(a).

The respondent was the owner and master of a vessel, a yawl, in respect of which there was no certificate as to survey under the Merchant Shipping Act 1894. The respondent used the vessel to take groups of people on 'sail training' excursions for which he made a charge. Throughout the voyages the members of the groups were expected to assist in handling the vessel under sail. On one occasion the group consisted of 29 persons and on another of 25 persons. The Secretary of State laid informations against the respondent that on those two occasions he was the master of the vessel when it proceeded on an excursion with more than 12 passengers on board without there being in force in respect of the vessel a certificate as to survey contrary to s 271[a] of the 1894 Act. The magistrates found that the business of the vessel was to sail on the excursions and that she could not have been operated under sail without the groups' participation. The magistrates dismissed the charge on the ground that the members of the groups were not 'passengers' for the purpose of s 271 of the 1894 Act because they were actively engaged in sailing the vessel throughout the voyage and were therefore 'engaged . . . on the business of the ship' within s 26(1)(a)[b] of the Merchant Shipping (Safety Convention) Act 1949, which defined the expression 'passenger' for the purposes of the 1894 Act as being any person carried in a ship except, inter alios, 'a person . . . engaged in any capacity on board the ship on the business of the ship'. The Secretary of State appealed.

Held – The word 'engaged' in the expression 'engaged . . . on the business of the ship' in s 26(1)(a) of the 1949 Act meant engaged under a contractually binding agreement whereby the person in question was obliged to render services on board in some capacity. Since the members of the groups were not 'engaged . . . on the business of the ship' merely by reason of the fact that during the excursions they were occupied in sailing or participating in the sailing of the vessel, they did not fall within the exception set out in s 26(1)(a) and consequently they were 'passengers'. The appeal would accordingly be allowed and the case would be remitted to the magistrates with a direction to convict (see p 468 j and p 469 a to d and j to p 470 a, post).

Dictum of Vaughan Williams LJ in *The Scarsdale* [1906] P at 114 applied.

Notes

For the requirement of passenger steamer certificates as to survey, see 43 Halsbury's Laws (4th edn) para 813.

For the meaning of 'passenger', see ibid para 801, and for cases on the subject, see 42 Digest (Repl) 1056, 8760–8762.

For the Merchant Shipping Act 1894, s 271, see 31 Halsbury's Statutes (3rd edn) 209.

For the Merchant Shipping (Safety Convention) Act 1949, s 26, see 31 ibid 594.

---

a   Section 271, so far as material, is set out at p 465 *h j*, post
b   Section 26(1), so far as material, is set out at p 466 *b*, post

Cases referred to in judgment

Hanna, The (1866) LR 1 A & E 283.

Minerva, The (1825) 1 Hag Adm 347, 166 ER 123.

Scarsdale, The [1906] P 103, CA; *affd* [1907] AC 373, HL.

Case also cited

Graham v Duncan [1950] 2 All ER 534, [1951] 1 KB 68, DC.

Case stated

The Secretary for Trade and Industry appealed by way of case stated by the justices for the petty sessional division of Poole in the county of Dorset in respect of their adjudication as a magistrates' court sitting at Poole on 20 December 1982 whereby they dismissed two informations preferred by the Secretary of State against the respondent, Charles Hector Booth, alleging that on two occasions (namely 7 July 1982 and 30 July 1982) he had committed an offence under s 271 of the Merchant Shipping Act 1894, as amended, by proceeding to sea or on a voyage or excursion in his ship, the Biche, with more than 12 passengers aboard without there being in force in respect of the ship a certificate of survey as required by Pt III of that Act. The question of law for the opinion of the High Court was whether the persons referred to in the informations were passengers within the meaning of s 26(1) of the Merchant Shipping (Safety Convention) Act 1949 or whether they fell within the class of persons referred to in the exception set out in s 26(1)(a). The facts are set out in the judgment of the court.

John Reeder for the Secretary of State.
The respondent did not appear.

Cur adv vult

14 October. The following judgment of the court was delivered.

KERR LJ. This is the judgment of the court on a case stated at the request of the Secretary of State by the justices for the petty sessional division of Poole in Dorset, in respect of their dismissal of two informations laid against the respondent as master of a yawl known as the Biche, on the ground that the vessel proceeded to sea or on a voyage or excursion with more than 12 passengers on 7 and 30 July 1982 without there being in force a certificate of survey in respect of the vessel, as required by Pt III (ss 267–368) of the Merchant Shipping Act 1894. The respondent was not present or represented before us, although the hearing had been adjourned in order to give him this opportunity.

Both of the informations were laid under the Merchant Shipping Act 1894, s 271, as amended by the Merchant Shipping Act 1964, and the Merchant Shipping Act 1979, s 43(3), Sch 6, Pt VII, para 3. The relevant provisions of s 271, in its amended form, are as follows:

> '(1) Every passenger steamer which carries more than twelve passengers shall be surveyed once at least in each year in the manner provided in this Part of this Act; and no ship (other than a steam ferry boat working in chains) shall proceed to sea or on any voyage or excursion with more than twelve passengers on board, unless there is in force in respect of the ship a certificate as to survey under this Part of this Act, applicable to the voyage or excursion on which the ship is about to proceed, or that voyage or excursion is one in respect of which [the Secretary of State] has exempted the ship from the requirements of this subsection . . .
>
> (3) If a ship proceeds to sea or on any voyage or excursion when it is prohibited from doing so by subsection (1) of this section, the owner and the master of the ship shall be guilty of an offence and liable on conviction on indictment to a fine or on summary conviction to a fine not exceeding one thousand pounds.'

A 'passenger steamer' is now defined by s 17(2) of the Merchant Shipping Act 1964 as including—

'any ship while on or about to proceed on a voyage or excursion in any case where a passenger steamer's certificate is required to be in force in respect of her.'

The informations turn on the meaning of 'passenger' in the context of the facts stated in the case, and the relevant statutory definition is to be found in s 26 of the Merchant Shipping (Safety Convention) Act 1949. The material provision for present purposes is s 26(1)(a), which reads as follows:

'In Part III of the principal Act [which includes s 271] . . . the expression "passengers" means any person carried in a ship, except—(a) a person employed or engaged in any capacity on board the ship on the business of the ship . . .'

There are certain other exceptions from the term 'passenger', and there are also various powers available to the Secretary of State to exempt vessels from these requirements. However, none of these are relevant to the present case.

The facts found in the case stated are set out in para 2 as follows:

'(i) The respondent is the owner of a gaff rigged yawl known as "Biche". The vessel is a ship within the meaning of section 271 of the Merchant Shipping Act, 1894. (ii) The vessel was built in France in 1934 for use in the tunny fishing industry. It is a little under 69 feet in length and 22 feet across its beam. Although it is not unique it is a vessel of distinctive character. (iii) The vessel has been registered in the United Kingdom with General Register and Records Office of Shipping and Seamen since 1973. There is no certificate in force as to survey under Part III of the Merchant Shipping Act, 1894. (iv) Originally built solely for sail the vessel has since been fitted with a Perkins diesel engine. That engine is necessary to enable the vessel to be manoeuvred in the confines of Poole Quay. The vessel has also been equipped with four double berth cabins. Apart from those cabins there is no seating facility for passengers to be seated in the conventional sense. (v) A crew of five or six adults is necessary to handle the vessel under sail. (vi) In recent years the respondent has made the vessel available for a variety of maritime activities including voyages abroad, sailing in local waters, fishing and diving. The vessel is promoted commercially in as much as there is a charge per head for the use of its facilities. Use of the vessel is arranged through Seaways Leisure Venture Club. That organisation has no proprietary interest in the vessel neither is it hired by them. The Club is simply a booking agency. (vii) On the 7th day of July, 1982 "Biche" was alongside the Quay at Poole. On board were the respondent and Mr. Kenneth Parvin who was acting as mate for that particular day. Mr. Parvin had sailed with the respondent on previous occasions in this same capacity. He is the holder of a certificate of competency as a Yachtmaster issued by the Board of Trade in 1974 and is a Royal Yachting Association/National Schools Sailing Association Day-boat Instructor. His services are entirely voluntary, he receives no payment from the respondent. (viii) On this day a party of approximately 27 teenagers, pupils from a local comprehensive school, together with two teachers boarded the vessel for a voyage or excursion. (ix) On the 30th day of July, 1982 "Biche" was again alongside the Quay. On this occasion the respondent was accompanied by Mr. Peter John Ridley. Mr. Ridley is a teacher of nautical studies. He was a seaman for 22 years and holds a Yachtmaster's certificate. He has sailed with the respondent for 5 years. He gives his services voluntarily. (x) On this date a party of some 23 boys aged between 11 and 14 years together with two adult supervisors boarded the vessel for a voyage or excursion. This party was spending a summer camp at Studland near Poole. (xi) Both of these parties had booked their excursions through Seaways Leisure Venture Club; paying the appropriate charges in advance. The forms that were used bore the statement, "I also acknowledge that my presence on board 'Biche' is in the capacity of unpaid crewing participation except where indicated". We are not satisfied that

every member of the parties boarding "Biche" on these two occasions completed the
respective forms. However, if that was not done the booking was made on behalf of
the party by a representative acting as agent for the remainder. Everyone who
joined the vessel on these two dates was aware that they would be expected to assist
in handling the vessel under sail. They were aware of that before the vessel left the
Quay at approximately 10.00 a.m. (xii) The excursion on these two occasions
followed the same formula. The respondent calls it sail training or sail participation.
On each occasion the respondent introduced the party to the vessel and explained
the various functions. The parties were then divided into teams and the vessel put
out into the harbour. Once clear of the Quay the various teams were engaged in
hoisting, setting and trimming the various sails. The vessel is equipped with jib,
foresail, mainsail, mizzen and top sail. Once set the sails have to be continuously
trimmed throughout the day. The vessel sailed out of the harbour and into the open
sea in Poole Bay. The duties on board kept everyone engaged through the day.
When they were not actively engaged they received instructions in basic nautical
principles. The vessel returned to the quay between 5 and 6 p.m. Light refreshments
and souvenirs could be purchased on board. (xiii) It was the intention of the people
on board "Biche" on these two occasions to take part in sailing the vessel. "Biche"
could not have operated under sail without their participation. The business of the
vessel was to sail on an excursion, all those on board being engaged from time to
time throughout the day in operating the vessel for that purpose.'

The case then recites the respective contentions of the parties and discusses the question
whether the burden of proof concerning the applicability of s 26(1)(a) of the 1949 Act
lay on the Secretary of State or on the respondent, with which we find it unnecessary to
deal.

The conclusion of the justices was then stated as follows:

'The persons on board on each occasion were not passengers within the meaning
of Section 271 of the Merchant Shipping Act, 1894 as defined in Section 26 of the
Merchant Shipping (Safety Convention) Act, 1949 because they were actively
engaged in sailing the vessel throughout the voyage and therefore were engaged in
the business of the ship.'

From this conclusion it is apparent that, while the justices rightly took the view that
the youngsters on board on the two occasions could not be regarded as 'employed' on
board the ship within the exception in s 26(1)(a), they were nevertheless of the opinion
that they were 'engaged . . . on board the ship on the business of the ship' within the
terms of that provision. In para 2(xiii) of the case 'the business of the ship' is found to
have been 'to sail on an excursion', and no issue arises on this finding for present purposes.
The issue turns on the word 'engaged'.

From the conclusion of the justices set out above, it is clear that 'engaged' was
interpreted by them to refer merely to the activities of the persons concerned while they
were on board, viz their active participation in the sailing of the vessel. However, on
behalf of the Secretary of State it was submitted to us that the history of the legislation,
as well as a number of authorities, show that this word has a special meaning connoting
a contractually binding agreement by the persons in question to serve on the ship in
some defined capacity, and that it was accordingly not open to the justices to interpret it
in the way in which they did, merely by reference to the activities of those on board.
This material was evidently not before the justices, but in our view it clearly supports the
submission on behalf of the Secretary of State. We therefore deal with it below. However,
it is no part of our function in the present case to attempt to categorise the persons or
activities which may fall to be considered in the context of the words 'engaged in any
capacity on board the ship on the business of the ship'. Thus, on a passenger liner or
cruise ship, there may be all kinds of persons rendering services for the benefit of the
fare-paying passengers, such as freelance lecturers, hairdressers, persons serving in shops
on board etc; and even cross-Channel ferries usually carry duty-free shops. While all such

persons may well fall within the exception, our function in the present case is only to
decide whether the young persons on board this vessel on the two occasions in question   a
can be considered to have been so 'engaged' merely by reason of the fact that, during the
excursion, they were occupied in sailing or participating in the sailing of the vessel.

The earliest authority cited to us was the decision of Lord Stowell in *The Minerva* (1825)
1 Hag Adm 347, 166 ER 123. It appears from the judgment that the relevant statute was
then a 1729 Act which referred to the agreement or contract of seamen or mariners as
one 'for so long a time as he or they shall ship themselves for'. However, in describing   b
the nature of such contracts, Lord Stowell already used the words 'engage' and
'engagement' which subsequently found their way into the legislation in lieu of words
such as 'ship themselves'. He said (1 Hag Adm 347 at 352, 166 ER 123 at 125–126):

> 'Upon the subject of the mariners' contract, I think it is not unfit to premise an
> observation or two, which appear to me not immaterial. The mariners' contract is
> an ancient instrument, necessary to describe the engagement of the contracting   c
> parties, with respect to the only two particular obligations which they have
> contracted, and which alone were necessary to be contracted for. One of them to be
> stipulated on the part of the shipowner—a description of the intended voyage; and
> the other, on the part of the seaman—engaging for the rate of wages which he was
> content to accept for his services on that voyage.'
>
                                                                                              d

The judgment of Dr Lushington in *The Hanna* (1866) LR 1 A & E 283, to which we
turn later, suggests that the first statutory appearance of this term was in the Merchant
Shipping Act 1854, but we can go straight to the consolidating statute, the Merchant
Shipping Act 1894 itself. In its unamended form, s 271 was slightly different, which is
immaterial for present purposes, and the definition of 'passenger' was also different.
Section 267 then provided: e

> '... The expression "passenger" shall include any person carried in a ship other
> than the master and crew, and the owner, his family and servants...'

However, the expression 'employed or engaged' was then already used in the definition
of 'seaman' in s 742, as it still is. This defines a seaman as including 'every person (except
masters and pilots), employed or engaged in any capacity on board any ship.' Apart from   f
the addition of the words 'on the business of the ship', the exception from the term
'passenger' in s 26(1)(a) of the 1949 Act clearly echoes this definition of 'seaman'.
Moreover, the meaning of 'engagement' in a similar context fell to be considered by this
court in *The Scarsdale* [1906] P 103. The case concerned the construction and effect of
s 114(2)(a) of the 1894 Act, which has since been repealed, but it is nevertheless of interest
for present purposes since it shows that the word 'engagement' is a term of art in shipping   g
legislation. Section 114(2) was in the following terms:

> 'The agreement with the crew shall contain as terms thereof the following
> particulars:—(a) Either the nature, and, as far as practicable, the duration of the
> intended voyage or engagement, or the maximum period of the voyage or
> engagement and the places or parts of the world, if any, to which the voyage or   h
> engagement is not to extend...'

It was common ground before us that a statutory 'crew agreement', as it is now called,
was not required for the Biche, since she is under 80 register tons engaged solely on
coastal voyages (see reg 3(a)(ii) of the Merchant Shipping (Crew Agreements, Lists of
Crew and Discharge of Seamen) Regulations 1972, SI 1972/918). However, it is clear
from the judgments in *The Scarsdale* and, in particular, from that of Vaughan Williams   j
LJ, that the word 'engagement' relates to the contractual terms governing the services on
board of the persons in question. Thus, Vaughan Williams LJ said (at 114):

> 'It seems to me that the word "engagement" in both of these alternatives [in
> s 114(2)(a)] covers a time agreement as distinguished from a voyage agreement.

Under the first alternative the agreement has to be for a fixed time; under the second, for the maximum period of time.'

As it seems to us, in the definition of 'passenger' in s 26(1)(a) of the 1949 Act, which is determinative for present purposes, in the exception of 'a person . . . engaged in any capacity on board the ship on the business of the ship', the word 'engaged' must properly be construed against the background of these statutory provisions and authorities. It has a technical meaning relating to the terms of the engagement of the person in question to render services on board in some capacity, and it cannot properly be interpreted to refer merely to his activities while on board and to the question whether or not these happen to have been carried out 'on the business of the ship'. For instance, if a person comes on board as a fare-paying passenger, but renders assistance to the crew during the voyage, he does not thereby cease to be a passenger or become 'engaged on the business of the ship' for the purposes of this provision.

Construed in this way, the youngsters on board on these two occasions were clearly not 'engaged'. Even if one gives effect to the 'acknowledgment' signed by them or accepted on their behalf, as found in para 2(xi) of the case, that 'my presence on board "Biche" is in the capacity of unpaid crewing participation . . .', this clearly did not engage them to anything, since it did not purport to impose any obligation on them, let alone one which was legally binding. They were not 'engaged', and they engaged themselves to nothing. Moreover, on the occasion of the excursion on 30 July 1982 the 23 boys on board are found to have been aged under 16, so that any contract with them to serve on the ship would have been unlawful (see the provisions restricting the employment of children on ships referred to in *Temperley's Merchant Shipping Acts* (7th ed, 1976) paras 1344–1345).

Finally, one should note the exceptive nature of the definition of 'passenger' in s 26(1)(a) of the 1949 Act. The section is drafted so that 'any person carried in a ship' is a 'passenger' unless he or she falls within one of the exceptions, the only relevant one for present purposes being that in para (a). A difficulty which faced Dr Lushington in *The Hanna* (1866) LR 1 A & E 283 has therefore disappeared from the legislation which we now have to consider. That case turned on the definition of 'seamen' in what is now s 742 of the 1894 Act, which we have already quoted. The master, as an act of kindness, had allowed a man to come on board for a voyage from Sweden to England free of charge, but on the basis that 'he was to do what he could' to assist on board, but who was otherwise treated as a passenger. One issue was whether he was a passenger or not, since the presence of a passenger on board would have required the vessel to employ a pilot. Dr Lushington concluded (at 292) that, on the whole, this person could not be regarded as a passenger, but that 'in fact, he was a nondescript'. Under the present form of definition, however, a 'nondescript' classification of the young persons on board on these occasions would involve a contravention of s 271 of the 1894 Act provided, as we think for the reasons already stated, that they do not fall within the exception in para (a). In saying this, we are not intending to indicate any view that they could not properly be regarded as 'passengers' in any event, in particular since a charge was made in respect of each of them (see para 2(vi) of the case). But, whether or not this be so, it is sufficient that they were neither persons 'employed' nor persons 'engaged' within the terms of this exception.

The question of law for the opinion of the court is:

'whether the persons referred to in the informations set out herein were passengers within the meaning of Section 26(1) of the Merchant Shipping (Safety Convention) Act, 1949 or whether they fall within the class of persons referred to in the exception (a) of the said section.'

In our view, the answer to this question is that the persons in question are to be treated as passengers and do not fall within the exception. Accordingly, since the case states all the relevant facts and covers all the relevant law, we consider that this matter should be remitted to the justices with a direction to convict and to impose whatever penalty they consider to be appropriate.

Appeal allowed. Case remitted to the justices with a direction to convict and to impose whatever penalty they considered appropriate.

Solicitors: *Treasury Solicitor.*

Raina Levy   Barrister.

The Abidin Daver

HOUSE OF LORDS
LORD DIPLOCK, LORD EDMUND-DAVIES, LORD KEITH OF KINKEL, LORD BRANDON OF OAKBROOK AND LORD TEMPLEMAN
19, 20 DECEMBER 1983, 26 JANUARY 1984

Practice – Stay of proceedings – Foreign defendant – Action in rem – Action by foreign plaintiffs against defendants' vessel whilst vessel in English port – Grounds for justifying stay of English proceedings – Proceedings pending in foreign court commenced by defendants – Whether existence of foreign proceedings sufficient ground for granting stay of English proceedings – Whether existence of foreign proceedings a factor to be taken into account in weighing balance of convenience.

As a result of a collision in the Bosphorus between the plaintiffs' vessel and the defendants' vessel, the Turkish defendants commenced proceedings in Turkey for damages against the Cuban plaintiffs. Subsequently the plaintiffs served a writ on a sister ship of the defendants' vessel in England and brought an action in rem in the Admiralty Court against the defendants for damages in respect of the collision. The defendants applied for a stay of the proceedings in the Admiralty Court. The judge stayed the proceedings on the grounds that there were in existence other proceedings in the Turkish court, that the litigation between the parties could be more conveniently tried in the Turkish court and that the plaintiffs would not be deprived of any juridical advantage if the proceedings in the English court were stayed, since an undertaking had been offered by the defendants to provide security for any cross-claim that the plaintiffs might decide to make in the Turkish action. The plaintiffs appealed to the Court of Appeal, which allowed the appeal and removed the stay, on the grounds that mere balance of convenience was not a sufficient ground for depriving the plaintiffs of the advantage of pursuing their action in the English courts and the fact that there was a claim by the defendants against the plaintiffs pending in Turkey was not of itself a bar to the plaintiffs bringing their claim in England. The defendants appealed to the House of Lords.

Held – Where a plaintiff wished to pursue his claim in the English courts despite the fact that there was already an action between the plaintiff and the defendant pending in a foreign jurisdiction which was a natural and appropriate forum for the resolution of the dispute between the parties, the court ought to exercise its discretion to stay the English action unless the plaintiff established objectively by cogent evidence that even-handed justice might not be accorded to him in the foreign jurisdiction or that there was some personal or juridical advantage only available to him in the English action and of such importance that it would be unjust to deprive him of that advantage. Although the mere balance of convenience or the mere disadvantage of a multiplicity of suits could not, of themselves, be decisive in tilting the scales, a strong or an overwhelming balance of convenience or a multiplicity of suits involving serious consequences with regard to expense and other matters might easily, and most probably would, tilt the scales. On the balance of convenience, there was an overwhelming case for the English proceedings to a be stayed, since Turkey was the country with which the matter litigated had the closest connection and was also the natural and appropriate forum from the point of view of convenience and expense. Moreover, there was no evidence that in Turkey a counterclaimant in a maritime collision case would be under any disadvantage compared with a plaintiff, or that the plaintiffs would not obtain justice in the Turkish courts. Accordingly, the appeal would be allowed and a stay granted (see p 475 c to e and j to p 476 d and g to j, p 478 f to j, p 479 c to f and h j, p 482 c to h, p 483 a b and g to p 484 b and

b f g, p 485 f to p 486 a and p 487 a to f, post).

The *Atlantic Star* [1973] 2 All ER 175 and *MacShannon v Rockware Glass Ltd* [1978] 1 All ER 625 applied.

The *Tillie Lykes* [1977] 1 Lloyd's Rep 124 explained.

Decision of the Court of Appeal [1983] 3 All ER 46 reversed.

c **Notes**

For general principles governing stay of proceedings, see 8 Halsbury's Laws (4th edn) paras 407, 787–788, and for cases on the subject, see 11 Digest (Reissue) 631–633, 1696–1689.

Cases referred to in opinions

d *Amin Rasheed Shipping Corp v Kuwait Insurance Co, The Al Wahab* [1983] 2 All ER 884, [1983] 3 WLR 241, HL.

Aratra Potato Co Ltd v Egyptian Navigation Co, The El Amria [1981] 2 Lloyd's Rep 119, CA.

Atlantic Star, The, Atlantic Star (owners) v Bona Spes (owners) [1973] 2 All ER 175, [1974] AC 436, [1973] 2 WLR 795, HL; rvsg [1972] 3 All ER 705, [1973] QB 364, [1972] 3 WLR 746, CA.

e *Hyman v Helm* (1883) 24 Ch D 53.

Janera, The [1928] P 55, [1927] All ER Rep 49.

Logan v Bank of Scotland (No 2) [1906] 1 KB 141.

London, The [1931] P 14.

Lucile Bloomfield, The [1964] 1 Lloyd's Rep 324.

McHenry v Lewis (1882) 22 Ch D 397.

f *MacShannon v Rockware Glass Ltd* [1978] 1 All ER 625, [1978] AC 795, [1978] 2 WLR 362, HL.

Madrid, The [1937] 1 All ER 216, [1937] P 40.

Monte Urbasa, The [1953] 1 Lloyd's Rep 587.

Peruvian Guano Co v Bockhwoldt (1883) 23 Ch D 225, [1881–5] All ER Rep 715.

Quo Vadis, The [1951] 1 Lloyd's Rep 425.

g *Soya Margareta, The, Soya Lovisa (cargo owners) v Soya Margareta (owners)* [1960] 2 All ER 756, [1961] 1 WLR 709.

St Pierre v South American Stores (Gath & Chaves) Ltd [1936] 1 KB 382, [1935] All ER Rep 408, CA.

Thornton v Thornton (1886) 11 PD 176, [1881–5] All ER Rep 715.

Tillie Lykes, The [1977] 1 Lloyd's Rep 124.

h **Interlocutory appeal**

The defendants, the Turkish owners of the vessel Abidin Daver, appealed with leave of the Appeal Committee of the House of Lords granted on 7 July 1983 against the decision of the Court of Appeal (Sir John Donaldson MR, Dunn and Purchase LJJ) on 17 May 1983 ([1983] 3 All ER 46, [1983] 1 WLR 884) allowing an appeal by the plaintiffs, the

j Cuban owners of the vessel Las Mercedes, from the judgment of Sheen J given on 4 May 1983, whereby he ordered the plaintiffs' action against the defendants for damages arising out of a collision between the two vessels in the Bosphorus, which was commenced by writ issued on 29 June 1982, to be stayed on an undertaking being given by the defendants to provide security for any cross-claim that the plaintiffs might decide to make in proceedings commenced by the defendants against the plaintiffs on 16 April

1982 in the Sariyer District Court in Turkey arising out of the same cause of action. The facts are set out in the opinion of Lord Diplock.

David Steel QC and *Nigel Teare* for the Turkish owners.
Bernard Rix QC and *Elizabeth Blackburn* for the Cuban owners.

Their Lordships took time for consideration.

26 January. The following opinions were delivered.

LORD DIPLOCK. My Lords, shortly before midnight on 23 March 1982 there was a collision between a Turkish ship, the Abidin Daver, and a Cuban ship, the Las Mercedes. It happened in the Bosphorus just outside the Turkish port of Buyukdere where both vessels had anchored to shelter from high winds and strong currents. The Turkish ship is owned by a Turkish state corporation (the Turkish shipowners). She was on a voyage from Braila in Romania to Iskenderun in Turkey laden with a cargo of petroleum prospecting pipes. The Cuban ship is owned by a Cuban state corporation (the Cuban shipowners). What the voyage was on which she was engaged at the time of the collision does not appear from the evidence before your Lordships. Both vessels sustained damage in the collision.

Although navigation in the Bosphorus by merchant vessels of other nationalities is subject to an international convention (see Convention regarding the Regime of the Straits (Montreux, 20 July 1936; TS 30 (1937); Cmd 5551)), the place where the collision took place is situated in Turkish territorial waters. The Turkish shipowners accordingly took prompt steps in the District Court of Sariyer, the Turkish court which exercises Admiralty jurisdiction in the area in which Buyukdere is situated to have the Cuban ship arrested and to start an action in that court (the Turkish action) against the Cuban shipowners as defendants for damages for negligence in the navigation and management of the Cuban ship. The Cuban ship owners, or their P & I insurers on their behalf, put up security to obtain the release of their ship, but they do not appear to have taken any other active step in the Turkish action. Until 2 July 1982 the Turkish action was proceeding normally in accordance with the Turkish Code of Civil Procedure under which the Cuban shipowners would have been entitled to bring a cross-claim against the Turkish shipowners if they had wished to do so.

The Turkish Code of Civil Procedure was introduced in 1927 as part of the westernisation of Turkish law instituted by Kemal Ataturk. It is based on the civil procedure code of the Swiss canton of Neuchatel of 1922. At the date of the Turkish law reforms this had been the most recently drafted of the procedural codes in use in those European countries which follow the system of the civil law. Consequently, it is one in which the court itself plays a more active investigatory role than does a judge under the English system of civil procedure. The substantive commercial law of Turkey which has been in force since the reforms of the 1920s for similar reasons has its basis in the German Commercial Code of 1895. It is not suggested that as respects collisions at sea Turkish substantive law differs in any relevant respect from English law.

On 2 July 1982, some three months after the commencement of the Turkish action in which they were defendants, the Cuban shipowners took advantage of the presence in an English port of a sister ship of the Abidin Daver to arrest her and commence an action in rem (the English action) against the Turkish shipowners as defendants claiming damages for their negligence in causing the collision at Buyukdere on 23 March 1982, which was the subject of the Turkish action in which the Turkish shipowners were plaintiffs and the Cuban shipowners defendants. Security was duly provided to obtain the release of the sister ship.

It is in proceedings on a motion by the Turkish shipowners to stay the English action that this appeal to your Lordships is brought. Sheen J granted the stay on an undertaking that was offered by the Turkish shipowners to provide security for any cross-claim that

the Cuban shipowners might decide to make in the Turkish action. He regarded the case
a for exercising his discretion in this way as a clear one and refused leave to appeal; but
leave was granted by the Court of Appeal and subsequently the judge's exercise of his
discretion was reversed and the stay removed by a unanimous Court of Appeal (Sir John
Donaldson MR, Dunn and Purchas LJJ) (see [1983] 3 All ER 46, [1983] 1 WLR 884).
Leave to appeal from the Court of Appeal's judgment was granted by this House.

My Lords, it is I hope not unfair to say that the decision of the narrow majority of this
b House in *The Atlantic Star, Atlantic Star (owners) v Bona Spes (owners)* [1973] 2 All ER 175,
[1974] AC 436 was initially accepted with reluctance, particularly by the judges of those
English courts, Admiralty and Commercial, to which foreigners so often voluntarily
resort for resolution of their legal disputes. It was treated at first as having been decided
on its own special facts rather than being of wider import. This is not surprising since it
may not be possible to recognise as such a decision that will turn out to have provided a
c landmark in the development of English law, until time has exposed to view the legal
landscape that lies beyond the decision. Looked at in the perspective of the ten years that
have now elapsed since the decision in *The Atlantic Star*, it has become readily identifiable
not as a mere decision on its own exceptional facts but as a landmark case.

The decisions of English courts during the hundred years between the passing of the
Judicature Acts, the relevant starting point, and the hearing in this House of *The Atlantic*
d *Star* are analysed in some detail in four of the speeches in that case. The effect of those
decisions was the subject of a scathing summary by Lord Reid as follows ([1973] 2 All ER
175 at 180–181, [1974] AC 436 at 453):

> 'They support the general proposition that a foreign plaintiff, who can establish
> jurisdiction against a foreign defendant by any method recognised by English law,
> is entitled to pursue his action in the English courts if he genuinely thinks that that
e > will be to his advantage and is not acting merely vexatiously. Neither the parties
> nor the subject-matter of the action need have any connection with England. There
> may be proceedings on the same subject-matter in a foreign court. It may be a far
> more appropriate forum. The defendant may have to suffer great expense and
> inconvenience in coming here. In the end the decisions of the English and foreign
> courts may conflict. But nevertheless the plaintiff has a right to obtain the decision
f > of an English court. He must not act vexatiously or oppressively or in abuse of the
> process of the English court, but these terms have been narrowly construed.'

After referring to an observation of Lord Denning MR adulatory of the administration
of justice by English courts (see [1972] 3 All ER 705 at 709, [1973] QB 364 at 381–382),
Lord Reid said:

g > 'My Lords, with all respect, that seems to me to recall the good old days, the
> passing of which many may regret, when inhabitants of this island felt an innate
> superiority over those unfortunate enough to belong to other races.'

Or, as Kipling more forthrightly phrased it, 'lesser breeds without the Law'.

The last sentence in Lord Reid's summary of the general proposition to be extracted
h from the previous authorities is derived from the statement of Scott LJ in *St Pierre v South*
American Stores (Gath & Chaves) Ltd [1936] 1 KB 382 at 398, [1935] All ER Rep 408 at 414
as to the applicable rule which is cited in full in the speeches of Lord Morris, Lord
Wilberforce and Lord Kilbrandon. I shall refer to this as 'the 1936 rule'.

The approach adopted by the majority of this House to the re-examination of what
Lord Reid had described as 'the rather insular doctrine' as he had stated it in the passage
j that I have cited, followed the step-by-step technique that is typical of the way in which
principles that have informed the common law of England undergo development by
judicial decision so as to enable justice to be done in the changing circumstances in which
the common law falls to be applied. In *The Atlantic Star* the particular device employed
was to give to the words 'vexatious' and 'oppressive' in the 1936 rule a more flexible or
liberal application than would have accorded with the interpretation that had been placed

on these expressions as terms of legal art in any of the previous authorities or, as Lord Kilbrandon pointed out, would be ascribed to them in ordinary speech. How 'flexible' and how 'liberal' this application was to be it was left to subsequent cases to show.

The next significant pace forward in the step-by-step approach was taken four years later in *MacShannon v Rockware Glass Ltd* [1978] 1 All ER 625, [1978] AC 795. In three of the four reasoned speeches expounding the unanimous decision of this House the continued use of the words 'vexatious' and 'oppressive' in expressing the principles on which the court's discretion to grant a stay of English proceedings was specifically deprecated and abandoned.

MacShannon was not a case where litigation on the same subject matter between the same parties was simultaneously proceeding in any jurisdiction other than England; nor had *The Atlantic Star* been treated as a case in which there was lis alibi pendens between the same parties, although technically the plaintiffs in the English action had taken a precautionary step in the Belgian court to forestall a time bar operating against them in that country if they were to be prevented from proceeding with their action in England.

Accordingly, in *MacShannon's* case, when I ventured to restate the 1936 rule in amended form, I was not concerned to deal with what account should be taken of the existence of lis alibi pendens in exercising a discretion to grant a stay of proceedings brought in England in the capacity of plaintiff by a person who is defendant to an action with the same subject matter which is being actively pursued against him in a foreign court that is unquestionably one of competent jurisdiction. In *St Pierre v South American Stores (Gath & Chaves) Ltd* there was in fact a lis alibi pendens, but this had been brushed aside by Scott LJ and is not referred to in his statement of the rule that until the decision of this House in *The Atlantic Star* had been so often cited and applied with the words 'vexatious' and 'oppressive' being used in their literal sense.

In the interval between the judgments of this House in *The Atlantic Star* and those in *MacShannon's* case the question of the weight, if any, to be given to lis alibi pendens fell to be determined by Brandon J in *The Tillie Lykes* [1977] 1 Lloyd's Rep 124. Founding himself on certain passages in the speech of Lord Wilberforce in *The Atlantic Star* he reached the conclusion which he expressed in the following words (at 126): '. . . the *mere existence* of a multiplicity of proceedings *is not to be taken into account at all* as a disadvantage to the defendant' (my emphasis). He later qualified that categorical statement by acknowledging that there might be exceptional cases where the bringing of the second action in England while the foreign action was proceeding might cause an unusual hardship to a particular defendant; but as a general rule the fact that to permit the England action to be pursued would result in concurrent actions on the same subject matter proceeding in two different jurisdictions could not be sufficient to justify depriving the plaintiff of the advantage to which he was entitled, if an English court of competent jurisdiction could be found, to choose it as the forum in which he preferred to litigate the matter.

My Lords, in the instant case Sheen J was of opinion that the minimal importance attached by Brandon J in *The Tillie Lykes* to the avoidance of concurrent actions between the same parties and about the same subject matter in two different courts of competent jurisdiction was no longer consonant with the general approach to the question of staying proceedings in English courts that had been adopted by this House in *MacShannon's* case. It was because the members of the Court of Appeal took the view that Sheen J's assessment of the effect of the speeches in *MacShannon's* case disclosed an error of law that they felt justified in setting aside the Admiralty judge's exercise of his discretion in favour of staying the English proceedings and in assuming a discretion of their own, which they proceeded to exercise in the opposite way. This conflict of judicial opinion, as it seems to me, makes it incumbent on your Lordships to provide guidance as to the extent to which the existence of lis alibi pendens ought to influence a judge in exercising his discretion whether or not to impose a stay on an action which it is sought to bring in England on the same subject matter by a person who is already a defendant in the foreign action.

Before turning to this topic, however, it may be convenient to draw attention to the

other factors that point to Turkey as the forum in which justice can be done between the
a parties at less inconvenience and expense than in England. Neither of the parties has any
connection with England, nor has the subject matter of the action. The collision took
place in Turkish territorial waters between a Turkish ship manned by a Turkish crew,
who reside in the vicinity of the Bosphorus, and a Cuban ship manned by a Cuban crew
that had been piloted by a local Turkish pilot to the place at which she was brought to
anchor at some time previous to the collision. Surveyors appointed by the Turkish court
b made a report on the collision within a few days of its occurrence and the damage to the
Turkish ship was surveyed after the collision in a Turkish port in the locality. So far as
witnesses on the Turkish side are concerned, the convenience and economy of having the
action tried in the nearby Turkish court of Admiralty jurisdiction as compared with
having it tried in England are all one way; while so far as the convenience of witnesses
on the Cuban side is concerned, there is little to choose between England and Turkey,
c except for a suggestion that the master and first officer of the Cuban ship might be able
(though perhaps unwise) to give their evidence in the English language instead of in
their native tongue, which is Spanish. In my view, as in that of Sheen J, not only was
Turkey the country with which the matter litigated had the closest connections, but also
the natural and appropriate forum from the point of view of convenience and expense
has, from the outset, been and still remains the District Court of Sariyer in Turkey, where
d proceedings were promptly started by the Turkish shipowners against the Cuban
shipowners as defendants and were proceeding with all due dispatch when the writ in
the English action was issued by the Cuban shipowners. I may add that there is no
evidence to suggest that the costs of litigation, as represented by the total amount of court
and lawyers' fees, are greater in Admiralty cases tried in Turkey than they are in similar
cases when they are tried in England. One thing however is self-evident: it must be more
e expensive to litigate about liability for the same collision in two jurisdictions than it
would be to litigate in one alone.

  True it is that, by arresting the sister ship of the Abidin Daver in an Admiralty action
in rem in England, the Cuban shipowners obtained security for their claim in respect of
the collision in the Bosphorus of 23 March 1982. In some cases this may well be a decisive
juridical advantage to be gained by a plaintiff by pursuing an Admiralty action in
f England, rather than in some foreign jurisdiction which would otherwise be more
appropriate but in which security cannot be obtained by arresting the ship involved in
the collision or a sister ship. But security where, as is usual, it has been put up by P & I
insurers is readily transferable from one jurisdiction to another. In the instant case it does
not appear from what source the security to obtain the release of the Turkish sister ship
was provided; but the Turkish shipowners undertook before Sheen J to put up security
g in the District Court of Sariyer for any counterclaim the Cuban shipowners may wish to
pursue in that court. So the advantage of security for the respective claims of the Turkish
and Cuban shipowners arising out of the collision has no effect in tilting the balance in
favour of continuing the English action by the Cuban shipowners.

  My Lords, both Sheen J and the Court of Appeal avowedly refrained from embarking
on a comparison of the quality of justice obtainable in a collision case conducted in a
h Turkish court which adopted a procedural system that is followed in civil law in other
countries and that obtainable in a similar case conducted in an English court under the
common law system of procedure. The Court of Appeal had expressed a similar view in
the judgment of Brandon LJ in *Aratra Potato Co Ltd v Egyptian Navigation Co, The El Amria*
[1981] 2 Lloyd's Rep 119. This House, too, in *Amin Rasheed Shipping Corp v Kuwait
Insurance Co, The Al Wahab* [1983] 2 All ER 884 at 892, [1983] 3 WLR 241 at 251–252,
j has very recently indorsed the view that it is quite inappropriate for English judges to
undertake any such supposed comparison or to allow the exercise of their discretion to
stay an English action to be influenced by it.

  In the same case this House also made it clear that the balancing of advantage and
disadvantage to plaintiff and defendant of permitting litigation to proceed in England
rather than, or as well as, in a foreign forum is to be based on objective standards

supported by evidence. Unlike the rule as it was stated by Lord Reid to have been applied before *The Atlantic Star*, a mere belief, however genuinely held, by a would-be plaintiff   *a* or his legal advisers that it would be to his advantage to pursue an action in the English court rather than to participate in proceedings in what would appear to be the more natural and appropriate forum is insufficient to justify refusal of a stay, unless the belief is supported by objective evidence.

The possibility cannot be excluded that there are still some countries in whose courts there is a risk that justice will not be obtained by a foreign litigant in particular kinds of   *b* suits whether for ideological or political reasons, or because of inexperience or inefficiency of the judiciary or excessive delay in the conduct of the business of the courts, or the unavailability of appropriate remedies. But, where there is already a lis alibi pendens in a foreign jurisdiction which constitutes a natural and appropriate forum for the resolution of the dispute, a plaintiff in an English action, if he wishes to resist a stay on the ground that even-handed justice may not be done to him in that particular foreign jurisdiction,   *c* must assert this candidly and support his allegations with positive and cogent evidence. In the instant case the affidavit filed on behalf of the Cuban shipowners in opposition to the stay contained no cogent evidence of this kind. It confined itself to tenuous innuendoes that Turkish lawyers might prove to be timorous advocates in a suit against a Turkish state-controlled corporation. The contents of this part of the affidavit are most aptly described by quoting the complete couplet of Alexander Pope, of which the first   *d* line when cited on its own is too familar to have escaped banality (see *Epistles and Satires of Horace Imitated, Prologue, Epistle to Dr Arbuthnot*):

> 'Willing to wound, and yet afraid to strike,
> Just hint a fault, and hesitate dislike.'

So I turn to the crucial question of what influence on the exercise of his discretion   *e* whether to grant a stay of the English proceedings or not the judge should have attributed to the fact that at the time the stay was applied for there was already proceeding in a natural and appropriate forum, the District Court of Sariyer, litigation between the same parties about the same subject matter in which the roles of plaintiff and defendant were reversed.

My Lords, the essential change in the attitude of the English courts to pending or   *f* prospective litigation in foreign jurisdictions that has been achieved step by step during the last ten years as a result of the successive decisions of this House in *The Atlantic Star, MacShannon* and *Amid Rasheed* is that judicial chauvinism has been replaced by judicial comity to an extent which I think the time is now ripe to acknowledge frankly is, in the field of law with which this appeal is concerned, indistinguishable from the Scottish legal doctrine of forum non conveniens.   *g*

Where a suit about a particular subject matter between a plaintiff and a defendant is already pending in a foreign court which is a natural and appropriate forum for the resolution of the dispute between them, and the defendant in the foreign suit seeks to institute as plaintiff an action in England about the same matter to which the person who is plaintiff in the foreign suit is made defendant, then the additional inconvenience and expense which must result from allowing two sets of legal proceedings to be pursued   *h* concurrently in two different countries where the same facts will be in issue and the testimony of the same witnesses required can only be justified if the would-be plaintiff can establish objectively by cogent evidence that there is some personal or juridical advantage that would be available to him only in the English action that is of such importance that it would cause injustice to him to deprive him of it.

Quite apart from the additional inconvenience and expense, if the two actions are   *j* allowed to proceed concurrently in the two jurisdictions the courts of the two countries may reach conflicting decisions, a possibility which (pace Sir John Donaldson MR's use of the adjective in the instant case) is far from being merely 'theoretical' in a case of a collision between two ships, where the measure of liability of one ship to the other is dependent on the court's view of the comparative fault of each ship. Since the District a Court of Sariyer would be recognised by the English High Court as a court of competent jurisdiction, any judgment given by it against the Cuban shipowners would be enforceable in England by action; so an unseemly race to be the first to obtain judgment in the jurisdictions in which the Turkish shipowners and the Cuban shipowners respectively are plaintiffs might well ensue; and novel problems relating to estoppel per rem judicatam and issue estoppel, which have not hitherto been examined by any English court, might also arise. Comity demands that such a situation should not be

b permitted to occur as between courts of two civilised and friendly states. It is a recipe for confusion and injustice.

Faced with such a daunting prospect it may well be that a defendant on being refused a stay of the concurrent action brought against him subsequently in England will feel driven to settle on terms more favourable to the other party than he would if the litigation had proceeded in the form of claim and cross-claim in the court of competent

c jurisdiction in which he had already instituted proceedings as plaintiff, or, if attempts at settlement fail, will become a counterclaimant in the English proceedings instead of continuing with his foreign action. The failure of judges in any of the decided cases to embark on an examination of the inevitable inconveniences, expense and injustices that might result if concurrent actions between the same parties arising out of the same collision did in fact continue to be fought out to the bitter end, suggests that those judges

d acted on the assumption that the parties in their own commercial interests would never allow this to happen. The assumption, although probably realistic, has nevertheless remained tacit until it was articulated in the instant case in the judgment of Sir John Donaldson MR where he said ([1983] 3 All ER 46 at 51, [1983] 1 WLR 884 at 892):

e 'If there is any serious inconvenience to the Turkish shipowners in being involved in two sets of proceedings, they have their remedy. They can transfer their claim here where it will be dealt with in the same proceedings as that of the Cubans.'

My Lords, in his judgment in the instant case Sheen J considered that those factors to which I have already referred and which are set out in greater detail in the speech of Lord Brandon pointed ineluctably to the District Court of Sariyer as the forum in which the litigation between the parties arising out of the collision can be much more conveniently

f tried and that the Cuban shipowners would not suffer any juridical disadvantage from trial at Sariyer. In his reserved judgment the judge did not lay particular stress on the increase in inconvenience, expense or the potential confusion which would result from Turkish and English actions being pursued concurrently; but that these considerations were among those that were in his mind as well as those to which he referred expressly is evident from his rejection of the submission that the interpretation placed on *The*

g *Atlantic Star* in *The Tillie Lykes*, if it were understood as suggesting that very little weight should be attached to the fact of there being lis alibi pendens, could survive the ratio decidendi of the speeches in this House in *MacShannon*.

On appeal from this exercise by the judge of his discretion, Sir John Donaldson MR in his judgment, which was extempore, expressed his own opinion that, if one ignored the fact that there was already a Turkish action on foot, the factors in favour of the Turkish

h and the English Courts respectively as the more convenient forum in which to carry on litigation about the collision, among which he included the greater experience of the English Admiralty Court of collision cases, would be fairly evenly balanced. Consequently it would seem, though this is not explicitly spelt out in the judgment, he did not think that the Turkish shipowners as defendants in the English action had satisfied the court that there was another forum to whose jurisdiction they were amenable in which justice

j could be done between them and the Cuban shipowners at substantially less inconvenience or expense. The Turkish shipowners thus, in his opinion, did not satisfy the first and positive condition in the restatement to be found in *MacShannon* of the 1936 rule. Such a balancing of the weight to be attached to different factors in favour of one forum rather than another is of the very essence of discretion, and with the way in which it has been exercised by a judge of first instance an appellate court is not entitled to interfere except on principles that have been so often stated by this House that I need not repeat them here.

The justification for exercising their own discretion in substitution for that of the Admiralty judge and with the opposite result that was relied on by all three members of the Court of Appeal was that Sheen J had erred in law in thinking, as it was inferred he had, that the effect of the speeches in this House in *MacShannon* was that the fact that the Turkish action was in existence and was being actively pursued with due dispatch should be given more than that minimal weight that it had been said in *The Tilly Lykes* ought to be ascribed to the existence of the lis alibi pendens that existed in that case. If this can be correctly classified as a question of law at all, it will be evident from what I have previously said that I think the judge rightly identified the step forward from *The Atlantic Star* that had been taken in *MacShannon*. If, as I think would be more accurate, the question is classified as one of discretion, the judge's exercise of it could only be reversed if it could be credibly said that no reasonable judge who had not misunderstood the evidence before him could have reached the conclusion that the English action ought to be stayed. This, however, was not a ground relied on by the Court of Appeal.

Dunn LJ, with whose judgment as well as that of Sir John Donaldson MR, Purchas LJ expressed his own agreement, considered that the Admiralty judge had also erred in law in failing to treat as a legitimate juridical advantage of which the Cuban shipowners would be deprived if prevented from pursuing their action in England, the fact that they would, as plaintiffs, be in control of the English action whereas in Turkey they would be counterclaiming as defendants. So the second and negative condition of the *MacShannon* restatement of the 1936 rule, as well as the first and positive condition, was not complied with.

My Lords, in my own practice at the Bar, I was not conscious of any handicap to my clients in obtaining justice, even under the English adversarial system, in consequence of their appearing as counterclaimants in an action rather than as plaintiffs. My own practice, it is right to say, did not embrace actions about collisions either at sea or on land; but, when as a Queen's Bench judge, particularly on circuit, I acquired considerable familiarity with actions about collisions on land, it never crossed my mind that the outcome of the action before me could be influenced by which party was plaintiff and which defendant and counterclaimant. But the disadvantages, if any, of being counterclaimant instead of plaintiff in an English Admiralty action are beside the point. The juridical disadvantage to the Cuban shipowners which Dunn LJ was contrasting with the advantage of being plaintiff in the English action is being counterclaimant in the Turkish action; and there is no evidence that in that jurisdiction, where civil law procedure is adopted, a counterclaimant in a maritime collision case labours under any disadvantage compared with a plaintiff, except as regards security. If the lodging of security be a safeguard that is of any significance in an action in a Turkish court against a Turkish state corporation that, according to the Cuban shipowners' writ in the English action, operates a fleet of not less than 58 vessels, this matter is disposed of by the Turkish shipowners' offer to provide in the Turkish action security for the Cuban shipowners' counterclaim. An undertaking to this effect can be embodied in the order granting a stay of the English action.

For all these reasons I would allow the appeal and restore the stay of the English action granted by the Admiralty judge, incorporating in the order the undertaking proffered by the Turkish shipowners to put up security for any counterclaim in the Turkish action that the Cuban shipowners may bring, the amount of the security in default of agreement by the parties to be settled by the Admiralty registrar.

Since preparing this speech I have had the opportunity of reading in draft the speech which will be delivered by my noble and learned friend Lord Brandon, with which, as will become evident, I am in complete agreement.

LORD EDMUND-DAVIES. My Lords, on completing my reading of the relevant material preparatory to hearing this appeal, I wrote the words 'Wasn't he right?' alongside the following passage in the brief reversed judgment of Sheen J:

'I am left in no doubt that the Sariyer Court is clearly a more appropriate forum than this court . . . [Counsel for the plaintiffs] was unable to point to any juridical advantage of which the plaintiffs would be deprived if I grant a stay. [She] submitted that this court has an almost overwhelming advantage of experience of collision actions. It is true that this court has considerable experience of collision actions, but I must not allow myself to be drawn into making comparisons between the ability of this court and the ability of another court in a friendly state to do justice in such cases. Since I have formed the view that the litigation between the parties to this action arising out of the collision can be much more conveniently tried in the District Court of Sariyer and that the plaintiff will not suffer any juridical disadvantage from trial at Sariyer, it follows that justice demands that this action be stayed.'

My Lords, the subsequent hearing of the appeal convinced me that the proper answer to my initial question is an affirmative one. The reasons leading me to that conclusion are those fully expounded in the speeches of my noble and learned friends Lord Diplock and Lord Brandon, both of which I gratefully adopt.

I therefore concur in allowing the appeal and in the order they propose.

LORD KEITH OF KINKEL. My Lords, I agree that this appeal should be allowed for the reasons given in the speech of my noble and learned friend Lord Diplock to which I would add only a few supplementary observations.

In *MacShannon v Rockware Glass Ltd* [1978] 1 All ER 625, [1978] AC 795 I sought to analyse the speeches of Lord Reid and Lord Wilberforce in *The Atlantic Star, Atlantic Star (owners) v Bona Spes (owners)* [1973] 2 All ER 175, [1974] AC 436 and observed that a distinction was to be drawn between a case where England is the natural forum for the plaintiff to bring his action and a case where it is not. By 'the natural forum' I mean that with which the action has the most real and substantial connection. In the present case it is abundantly plain, having regard to the features which are very fully described in the speech of my noble and learned friend Lord Brandon, that Turkey is, and England is not, the natural forum.

I said in *MacShannon's* case [1978] 1 All ER 625 at 645, [1978] AC 625 at 829:

'Where, however, the defendant shows that England is not the natural forum and that if the action were continued there he would be involved in substantial (ie more than de minimis) inconvenience and unnecessary expense, or in some other disadvantages, which would not affect him in the natural forum, he has made out a prima facie case for a stay, and if nothing follows it may properly be granted. The plaintiff may, however, seek to show some reasonable justification for his choice of forum in the shape of advantage to him. If he succeeds it becomes necessary to weigh against each other the advantages to the plaintiff and the disadvantages to the defendant, and a stay will not be granted unless the court concludes that to refuse it would involve injustice to the defendant and no injustice to the plaintiff.'

The last sentence should be read with the insertion of the words 'the grant would involve' before the words 'no injustice to the plaintiff.'

In this case the defendants would, if required to meet the plaintiffs' claim in an English rather than in a Turkish court, plainly be involved in substantial inconvenience and unnecessary expense. The dependence in the Sariyer District Court at Buyukdere in Turkey of the proceedings instituted by the defendants, in which the plaintiffs' claim is capable of being dealt with, has the effect that the inconvenience and expense would be compounded. The plaintiffs have entirely failed to demonstrate any reasonable justification for their choice of the English forum in the shape of a legitimate forensic or personal advantage. It follows that, on a proper application of the principle I have set out, Sheen J correctly concluded that a stay should be granted and that the Court of Appeal wrongly reversed his decision.

LORD BRANDON OF OAKBROOK. My Lords, on 23 March 1982 a collision took place in the Bosphorus off the port of Buyukdere between two ships, the Las Mercedes and the Abidin Daver. The Las Mercedes is a Cuban ship owned by a Cuban state corporation, who are the respondents in this appeal. The Abidin Daver is a Turkish ship owned by a Turkish state corporation, who are the appellants. Each ship blames the other for the collision, and each of the owners claims to be entitled to recover damages for the other in respect of it.

Following the collision, the Turkish owners obtained immediately from the local court, the Sariyer District Court, an order for the detention of the Las Mercedes. On 16 April 1982 the Turkish owners as plaintiffs began proceedings against the Cuban owners as defendants in the same Turkish court, in which they claimed damages in respect of the collision. Turkish lawyers acting for the Cuban owners performed the equivalent of acknowledging service in the Turkish action, so putting their clients in a position to defend that action. The Cuban owners further provided such security for the Turkish owners' claim as enabled the Las Mercedes to be released from detention.

On 29 June 1982 the Cuban owners as plaintiffs began an action in rem in the Admiralty Court in England against the Abidin Daver and 57 sister ships of hers, in which they also claimed damages in respect of the same collision. On 2 July 1982 the Cuban owners served the writ in the English action on the ship Gazi Osman Pasha, one of the sister ships of the Abidin Daver, which was then in a Welsh port, and arrested her there. English lawyers acting for the Turkish owners acknowledged service of the writ and the Turkish owners provided such security for the Cuban owners' claim as enabled the Gazi Osman Pasha to be released from arrest.

On 28 July 1982 the Turkish owners issued a notice of motion in the English action in which they applied for a stay of it, broadly on the ground that both the claim of the Turkish owners and the cross-claim of the Cuban owners should be adjudicated on by the Turkish court, and the Turkish court alone.

Affidavits relating to the application for a stay of the English action were filed by both sides and the motion later came on for hearing before Sheen J on 28 and 29 April 1983. On 4 May 1983 the judge, after delivering a reserved judgment, made an order by which he granted the Turkish owners' application for a stay with costs and refused the Cuban owners leave to appeal.

Subsequently the Cuban owners applied to the Court of Appeal for leave to appeal from the order of Sheen J and to adduce further affidavit evidence in support of their case. The applications were heard and granted by a division of the Court of Appeal consisting of Sir John Donaldson MR, Dunn and Purchas LJJ, which then proceeded to hear the substantive appeal. By an order dated 17 May 1983 the Court of Appeal allowed the Cuban owners' appeal with costs and removed the stay (see [1983] 3 All ER 46, [1983] 1 WLR 884). By a further order dated 25 May 1983 the Court of Appeal refused an application by the Turkish owners to appeal to your Lordships' House. Leave for them to do so was, however, later granted by the Appeal Committee.

My Lords, it is not in dispute that both the Sariyer District Court in Turkey and the Admiralty Court in England are courts of competent jurisdiction to try and determine the question of liability for the collision and to assess the damages payable by the one side or the other. So far as the Admiralty Court in England is concerned, jurisdiction to hear and determine the Cuban owners' claim in an action in rem is conferred on it by ss 20 and 21 of the Supreme Court Act 1981. It does not, however, necessarily follow that, because an English court has jurisdiction to try and determine a particular claim, it is always and in all circumstances obliged to exercise that jurisdiction. On the contrary, so far as the High Court in England (including the Admiralty Court) is concerned, the court has power, even though it has jurisdiction to try and determine a particular action brought before it, to decline to exercise that jurisdiction, and instead to grant a stay of the action, either of its own motion or on the application of any person, whether a party to the action or not. That power to stay is part of the inherent jurisdiction of the High Court, expressly preserved by s 49(3) of the 1981 Act.

The exercise of the High Court's power to grant a stay under that section is a matter for the discretion of the court. Such discretion is not, however, unfettered. On the contrary, it is a discretion which has to be exercised with great caution in accordance with principles which have been established by judicial authority over the years.

My Lords, until two recent decisions of your Lordships' House, the principles governing the exercise of the High Court's power to grant a stay of an action even though it had jurisdiction to try and determine it, were accepted as being those laid down by Scott LJ in *St Pierre v South American Stores (Gath & Chaves) Ltd* [1936] 1 KB 382 at 398, [1935] All ER Rep 408 at 414. In that case Scott LJ, referring to the power to grant a stay under s 41 of the Supreme Court of Judicature (Consolidation) Act 1925 (the predecessor of s 49(3) of the 1981 Act), said:

> 'The true rule about a stay under s. 41, so far as relevant to this case, may I think be stated thus: (1) A mere balance of convenience is not a sufficient ground for depriving a plaintiff of the advantages of prosecuting his action in an English Court if it is otherwise properly brought. The right of access to the King's Court must not be lightly refused. (2) In order to justify a stay two conditions must be satisfied, one positive and the other negative: (a) the defendant must satisfy the Court that the continuance of the action would work an injustice because it would be oppressive or vexatious to him or would be an abuse of the process of the Court in some other way; and (b) the stay must not cause an injustice to the plaintiff. On both the burden of proof is on the defendant. These propositions are, I think, consistent with and supported by the following cases: *McHenry v. Lewis* ((1882) 22 Ch D 397); *Peruvian Guano Co v. Bockhwoldt* ((1883) 23 Ch D 225, [1881–5] All ER Rep 715); *Hyman v. Helm* ((1883) 24 Ch D 531); *Thornton v. Thornton* ((1886) 11 PD 176, [1886–90] All ER Rep 311); and *Logan v. Bank of Scotland (No. 2)* ([1906] 1 KB 141 at 150–151, [1904–7] All ER Rep 438 at 443).

The application of these principles operated in practice in such a way as to make it extremely difficult for a defendant to obtain a stay of an action brought in the High Court in England, otherwise than where the bringing of it was of itself an abuse of the process of the court. The reason for this was that it was extremely difficult for a defendant to satisfy the court that the continuance of the action would work an injustice to him because it would be oppressive or vexatious to him in the opprobrious sense which these epithets were generally regarded as having in the context in which they were used.

It is not now, and was not in the past, infrequent, following a collision between two ships, A and B, for two actions to be brought in respect of it, one by the owners of ship A as plaintiffs against the owners of ship B as defendants in a foreign court of competent jurisdiction, and the other by the owners of ship B as plaintiffs against the owners of ship A as defendants in the Admiralty Court in England, which is, of course, precisely what has happened in the present case. In such cases it also occurred from time to time that the owners of ship A would apply to the Admiralty Court here for a stay of the action before it, on the ground that both claim and cross-claim could and should be decided by the foreign court concerned. The situation until 1973, however, was that such applications were invariably dismissed, the broad ground for refusing a stay being that the bringing and continuance of the action here was not, merely by reason of the co-existence of the action abroad, so oppressive or vexatious to the owners of ship A as to work them an injustice. Reported examples of such cases include *The Janera* [1928] P 55, [1927] All ER Rep 49, *The London* [1931] P 14, *The Madrid* [1937] 1 All ER 216, [1937] P 40, *The Quo Vadis* [1951] 1 Lloyd's Rep 425, *The Monte Urbasa* [1953] 1 Lloyd's Rep 587, *The Lucile Bloomfield* [1964] 1 Lloyd's Rep 324 and *The Soya Margareta, Soya Lovisa (cargo owners) v Soya Margareta (owners)* [1960] 2 All ER 756, [1961] 1 WLR 709. The result in practice therefore was that, although the court in such cases had, and recognised that it had, a discretion to grant or refuse a stay, it invariably exercised such discretion (so far as any reported applications are concerned) in the same way, namely by refusing a stay.

My Lords, I said that this was the situation until 1973. In that year the principles in accordance with which a court should exercise its discretion to stay an action properly brought before it came to be considered for the first time in your Lordships' House in *The Atlantic Star, Atlantic Star (owners) v Bona Spes (owners)* [1973] 2 All ER 175, [1974] AC 436. Some four years later they came to be considered a second time in *MacShannon v Rockware Glass Ltd* [1978] 1 All ER 625, [1978] AC 795.

It would not, I think, serve any useful purpose to go into the facts of these two cases, which differed from each other and from those in the present case, although *The Atlantic Star* had some features analogous to the latter. All that I consider that it is useful to do is to express my view of the combined result of these two decisions, so far as the principles governing the exercise by a court of its discretion to grant or refuse a stay are concerned. That result can, in my opinion, be put into three separate, but interconnected, compartments.

First, the need for an applicant for a stay to satisfy the court that the continuance of the action against him would work him injustice because it would be oppressive or vexatious to him no longer exists. In *The Atlantic Star* it was said that the words 'oppressive' and 'vexatious' were not terms of art and must be given a much broader and much less rigid sense than had been given to them in the past. In *MacShannon v Rockware Glass Ltd* the process in the development of the law which had been begun in *The Atlantic Star* was carried a long step further: it was said that it would be better for the future, in order to avoid confusion, to get rid altogether, in the formulation of the relevant principles, of the words 'oppressive' and 'vexatious', and with them of the opprobrious concepts which their ordinary and natural meaning necessarily evoked.

Second, with these two opprobrious epithets out of the way, the second part of the test laid down by Scott LJ in *St Pierre v South American Stores (Gath & Chaves) Ltd* could be reformulated as follows:

'(2) In order to justify a stay two conditions must be satisfied, one positive and the other negative: (a) the defendant must satisfy the court that there is another forum to whose jurisdiction he is amenable in which justice can be done between the parties at substantially less inconvenience or expense, and (b) the stay must not deprive the plaintiff of a legitimate personal or juridical advantage which would be available to him if he invoked the jurisdiction of the English court.'

The reformulation just cited, which omits significantly, in relation to (b), any reference to burden of proof, is contained in the speech delivered in *MacShannon v Rockware Glass Ltd* [1978] 1 All ER 625 at 630, [1978] AC 795 at 812 by Lord Diplock. I venture to think, however, that it accorded with the opinions of all the other members of the Appellate Committee in that case.

Third, and this concept emerges most clearly from the speech of Lord Wilberforce in *The Atlantic Star*, the exercise of the court's discretion in any particular case necessarily involves the balancing of all the relevant factors on either side, those favouring the grant of a stay on the one hand, and those militating against it on the other. Such balancing may be a difficult process and some cases may be very near the line.

My Lords, as I indicated earlier, the decision whether to allow or refuse an application for the stay of an action, even though the court has jurisdiction to try and determine it, is a discretionary decision for the judge of first instance to whom the application is made. It follows that, where the judge of first instance has exercised his discretion in one way or the other, the grounds on which an appellate court is entitled to interfere with the decision which he has made are of a limited character. It cannot interfere simply because its members consider that they would, if themselves sitting at first instance, have reached a different conclusion. It can only interfere in three cases: (1) where the judge has misdirected himself with regard to the principles in accordance with which his discretion had to be exercised; (2) where the judge, in exercising his discretion, has taken into account matters which he ought not to have done or has failed to take into account matters which he ought to have done; or (3) where his decision is plainly wrong. That being the position, I turn to consider how Sheen J dealt in his judgment with the

application for a stay which was before him in the present case, and, since the Court of
Appeal thought fit to reverse his decision, to see whether any of the three permissible
grounds entitling them to do so are established.

I consider, first, whether the judge directed himself correctly with regard to the
principles in accordance with which he was obliged to exercise his discretion. So far as
this is concerned only an affirmative answer is possible. He began his judgment by
saying:

> 'On this motion counsel for the defendants moves for an order that this action be
> stayed on the ground that there is another forum to whose jurisdiction the
> defendants are amenable, namely the Sariyer District Court at Buyukdere in Turkey,
> in which justice can be done between the parties at substantially less inconvenience
> and expense and that a stay of this action will not deprive the plaintiffs of a legitimate
> or juridical advantage in this court.'

It is clear that the judge derived this passage from the formal grounds for the grant of a
stay set out in the Turkish owners' notice of motion dated 18 July 1982. It is equally clear
that whoever drafted those grounds was seeking to adapt as closely as possible to the
present case the reformulation of the relevant principles in the speech of Lord Diplock in
MacShannon v Rockware Glass Ltd which I cited earlier.

In relation to the first and positive question formulated by Lord Diplock, the judge
went on to say:

> 'The first question which I must answer is whether there is another jurisdiction
> which is clearly more appropriate than England for the trial of the action. The
> defendants must satisfy me of the existence of such other jurisdiction.'

Later in his judgment, after dealing with the first question and answering it in the
affirmative, he said this about the submissions made to him by junior counsel in this
appeal, who appeared as sole counsel for the Cuban owners before him: 'Mrs Blackburn
was unable to point to any juridical advantage of which the plaintiffs will be deprived if
I grant a stay.' In this connection it is necessary to mention that the Turkish owners had
all along offered to provide security for any counterclaim which the Cuban owners might
wish to raise in the Turkish action if a stay of the English action were granted, and your
Lordships were told that this offer still stands. There was accordingly no risk that, if the
Cuban owners were compelled, by a stay of their action here, to bring a counterclaim in
the Turkish court, they would be deprived of adequate security in respect of it.

The passages which I have quoted from the judge's judgment support the view which
I expressed earlier that the question whether the judge directed himself correctly with
regard to the principles according to which he was obliged to exercise his discretion could
only be answered in the affirmative.

I consider, second, whether the judge, in exercising his discretion, took into account
the right matters and not the wrong matters. He began by taking into account the
following numerous matters which he regarded as favouring a stay. First, the collision
occurred in Turkish waters. Second, one of the two ships involved, the Abidin Daver,
was a Turkish ship manned by a Turkish crew resident in Turkey. Third, the Las
Mercedes had been led to her anchorage shortly before the collision by a Turkish pilot
whose evidence was material. Fourth, any members of the crew of the Las Mercedes who
might be required to attend the trial could attend the Turkish court without any more
inconvenience than they would be subjected to by having to come to London. Fifth, if
the case was tried by the Turkish court, the Turkish witnesses would be away from their
homes for a much shorter period, and that for that reason there would be less disruption
caused to their work. Sixth, under the system of justice administered in Turkey, the
Turkish court had appointed a surveyor who had already interviewed relevant witnesses
and prepared a report for the court. Seventh, the litigation had no connection with
England, except for the arrest of one of the sister ships of the Abidin Daver in an English
port.

The judge went on to consider the following further matters put forward by counsel for the Cuban owners as militating against a stay. First, the Cuban witnesses whom it would be necessary to call could speak English but not Turkish. Second, the Cuban owners chose to sue in England because they understood English procedure but might not understand Turkish procedure. And, third, the Cuban owners wished to make progress with the action.

Subject to one point to which I shall refer later, it seems to me that the judge took into account all the right matters and did not take into account any wrong matters.

I consider, third, whether it could be said that the judge's decision was plainly wrong. With regard to this he said, after referring to the first four of the seven factors which he regarded as favouring a stay:

> 'There is thus an overwhelming balance of convenience for the witnesses if the trial takes place in Turkey rather than in London.'

Later, after referring to the matters put forward by counsel for the Cuban owners as militating against a stay, he said:

> 'I have come to the conclusion that I should give very little weight indeed to any of these points. The first and second are balanced by the facts that the defendants' witnesses speak the language of the Turkish court and the defendants understand Turkish procedure. As to the third point, I have no reason to think that the Turkish shipowners do not want to press on with this litigation.'

Finally, in the last paragraph of his judgment, the judge said:

> 'Since I have formed the view that the litigation between the parties to this action arising out of the collision can be much more conveniently tried in the District Court of Sariyer and that the plaintiff will not suffer any juridical disadvantage from trial at Sariyer, it follows that justice demands that this action be stayed.'

I set out earlier the factors on either side which the judge took into account. The assessment of the weight to be given to those factors, and the balancing of the factors on one side against those on the other, were matters entirely for the judge to deal with. On the footing, therefore, that he directed himself correctly with regard to the principles in accordance with which he had to exercise his discretion, and that he took into account the right factors and not the wrong ones, it is, in my opinion, impossible to say that the decision which he reached was plainly wrong. On the contrary, it appears to me to have been plainly right.

My Lords, I now turn to examine the grounds on which the Court of Appeal thought it right to reverse the judge's conclusion. A study of the judgments of Sir John Donaldson MR and Dunn LJ, with both of whom Purchas LJ agreed, shows that they considered that Sheen J had erred in principle in regarding, as he undoubtedly did, the co-existence of the Turkish action as a decisive factor in the exercise of his discretion.

Sir John Donaldson MR said ([1983] 3 All ER 46 at 51, [1983] 1 WLR 884 at 891–892):

> 'Further, I think it is clear that the judge, in balancing the various factors, was giving very full weight, as, indeed, he was entitled to do on the view he took of the law, to the fact that there were already proceedings on foot in Turkey. But I have come to the conclusion that the judge erred in principle . . . It is a factor of which account should be taken, but it is not a factor which, of itself, is of sufficient weight to displace the right of a plaintiff to choose his own forum and, of itself, to create a tilt in the other direction.'

Dunn LJ said ([1983] 3 All ER 46 at 51–52, [1983] 1 WLR 884 at 892):

> 'At the outset of his judgment the judge asked himself the question whether the Turkish court or the English court was the more appropriate forum for the trial of

this action, and held on a balance of convenience that the Turkish court was clearly
the more appropriate. With respect to the judge, that was the wrong question to
ask. *The Atlantic Star* and *MacShannon v Rockware Glass Ltd* . . . show that the English
Court of Admiralty, whose jurisdiction has been invoked in rem, is prima facie the
natural and appropriate forum in which to bring an action of this kind, and is
recognised as such by international convention. A mere balance of convenience is
not a sufficient ground for depriving the plaintiffs of the advantages of pursuing
their action in the Admiralty Court. The fact that there is a claim by the defendants
against the plaintiffs already pending in Turkey is not of itself a bar to the plaintiffs
claiming in this country against the defendants for damages arising out of the same
collision as is being litigated in Turkey . . .'

Both Sir John Donaldson MR and Dunn LJ, in expressing the views which they did,
appear to have placed considerable reliance on an earlier decision made by me when
sitting as a judge of first instance in the Admiralty Court. That case was *The Tillie Lykes*
[1977] 1 Lloyd's Rep 124, and both the members of the Court of Appeal referred to
appear to have regarded my judgment in that case as authority for the proposition that,
in cases of the kind here concerned, little or no importance should be attached to the co-
existence of another action relating to the same subject matter in a foreign court.
The Tillie Lykes was decided after the decision of your Lordships' House in *The Atlantic
Star* but before its later decision in *MacShannon v Rockware Glass Ltd*. In my judgment in
The Tillie Lykes I had directed myself by reference to statements in the speech of Lord
Wilberforce in *The Atlantic Star* [1973] 2 All ER 175 at 194, [1974] AC 436 at 469, in
which he had said that the disadvantage to the defendant, in order that it should be taken
into account at all, must be serious, and in particular that it must involve more than the
mere disadvantage of multiple suits. After considering what I regarded as all the relevant
factors on either side in that case, the facts of which were materially different from those
of the present case, I concluded that there was no sufficiently serious disadvantage to the
defendants, apart from and additional to the mere disadvantage of multiple suits, to
justify a stay of the action against them. I did not purport to lay down any principle of
law at all; I only sought to apply to the particular facts of the case before me the principle
of law laid down by Lord Wilberforce in the passage from his speech in *The Atlantic Star*
to which I have referred.

With great respect to the members of the Court of Appeal in the present case, I think
that they have fallen into error by giving insufficient weight to the epithet 'mere' in the
expressions 'mere balance of convenience' and 'mere disadvantage of multiplicity of
suits', as these expressions, or other expressions similar to them, are used in the authorities.
Mere balance of convenience cannot, of itself, be decisive in tilting the scales; but strong,
and a fortiori overwhelming, balance of convenience may easily, and in most cases
probably will, be so. Similarly, the mere disadvantage of multiplicity of suits cannot of
itself be decisive in tilting the scales; but multiplicity of suits involving serious
consequences with regard to expense or other matters, may well do so. In this connection
it is right to point out that if concurrent actions in respect of the same subject matter
proceed together in two different countries, as seems likely if a stay is refused in the
present case, one or other of two undesirable consequences may follow: first, there may
be two conflicting judgments of the two courts concerned; or, second, there may be an
ugly rush to get one action decided ahead of the other, in order to create a situation of res
judicata or issue estoppel in the latter.

In my judgment the criticism made by the Court of Appeal, that Sheen J erred in
principle in treating the co-existence of the Turkish action as a decisive factor on the facts
of the present case, is not justified. It was not a case of mere balance of convenience: it
was an overwhelming case. It was not a case of mere disadvantage of multiplicity of suits:
it was a case which was liable to cause, if both actions continued, much difficulty and
trouble. On the footing that the Court of Appeal was wrong in holding that the judge

erred in principle in the way that it thought, there was, in my opinion, no valid ground
for its interfering with the exercise of the discretion vested in him as the judge of first *a*
instance.

My Lords, leading counsel who appeared for the Cuban owners before your Lordships
submitted that the judge had failed to take into account a matter which was in evidence
before him, namely that, if the Cuban owners were compelled, by a stay of their action
here, to counterclaim in the Turkish action, the procedure of the Turkish court would
require them to deposit in advance, as security for the costs of the court, a proportion, *b*
probably about 15%, of the amount of their counterclaim. It is only right to say that
there is no reference in the judge's judgment to this matter as a factor to be taken into
account as militating against a stay. In my view, however, there are two reasons why this
circumstance should not be regarded as in any way vitiating his judgment. The first
reason is that, although the judge did not mention this matter in his judgment, it does
not follow that he did not have it in mind and take it into account. The evidence before *c*
him was confined to three affidavits only, and it is unlikely that the judge would have
overlooked anything which appeared in them. The second reason was given by Sir John
Donaldson MR, when he pointed out that the Cuban owners would probably have to
give security for costs under English procedure if their action here were allowed to
continue, so that their liability in respect of security for costs might well be the same, or
something like the same, in the one court as in the other (see [1983] 3 All ER 46 at 49, *d*
[1983] 1 WLR 884 at 889).

My Lords, there are two further matters with which I feel that it is necessary to deal.

The first matter is that the judge expressly declined to enter into any comparison
between the capacities of the Turkish and English courts to try justly and satisfactorily
the dispute between the parties. In doing so he was following observations made by me
when sitting in the Court of Appeal in *Aratra Potato Co Ltd v Egyptian Navigation Co, The* *e*
El Amria [1981] 2 Lloyd's Rep 119 at 126–127, observations which appear to me to accord
with the views of your Lordships' House, as recently expressed by Lord Diplock in *Amin
Rasheed Shipping Corp v Kuwait Insurance Co, The Al Wahab* [1983] 2 All ER 884 at 892,
[1983] 3 WLR 241 at 251–252.

I hope that I shall not be thought discourteous to Sir John Donaldson MR if I say that,
while paying lip service to the avoidance of any comparisons of that kind, his heart was *f*
not really in what he felt obliged to concede. Thus he said ([1983] 3 All ER 46 at 49,
[1983] 1 WLR 884 at 889):

> 'I share entirely the reluctance of Sheen and Brandon JJ to express any view as to
> the relative merits of particular courts. That must be a matter of subjective
> judgment which I, as a judge of an English court, and an ex-Admiralty judge, do
> not feel that I should make. What I think can be said, and I doubt whether it would *g*
> be controverted by anybody, is that the English Admiralty Court has a vast amount
> of international maritime experience in this field going back over the centuries.
> While I do not doubt for one moment that the Turkish courts have long maritime
> experience, I doubt very much whether it is as international or extensive. That is
> not a criticism, and should not be taken as a criticism, of the Turkish courts; it is an
> accident of geography. The English courts are situated on an island off Europe. That *h*
> has led, as a matter of history, to their being involved in far more maritime disputes
> than Turkey or any country similarly situated.'

Sir John Donaldson MR will, I trust, forgive me if I say that, having paid lip service to
the need to avoid comparison between English and foreign courts, he then proceeded to
make just such a comparison. *j*

The second matter arises from certain paragraphs in the affidavit sworn in support of
his clients' case by a solicitor in the distinguished firm of solicitors acting for the Cuban
owners in this case. Paragraphs 13 and 14 of his affidavit are drawn in such a way as to
cast aspersions on the capacity of the Turkish court to try the Turkish action properly,
and on the independence from the executive of any Turkish lawyer acting for the owners

of a foreign ship against the owners of a Turkish ship. No sufficient grounds are given
a for these aspersions, and they should, in my opinion, never have been made.

Having dealt with those two further matters, it only remains for me to say that, for
the reasons which I have given earlier, I would allow the appeal with costs here and
below, and restore the order of Sheen J dated 4 May 1983, save in so far as it refuses the
Cuban owners' application for leave to appeal. I would, however, vary the order in one
respect, by making the stay conditional on the provision by the Turkish owners within
b 28 days of sufficient and satisfactory security for any counterclaim of the Cuban owners
in the Turkish court. If there should be any dispute about the amount or nature of such
security, it should be referred to the Admiralty Registrar for decision.

LORD TEMPLEMAN. My Lords, for the reasons given by my noble and learned
friends Lord Diplock and Lord Brandon, I too would allow this appeal.

c There was ample material from which Sheen J came to the conclusion that the Sariyer
District Court of Turkey is a forum in which justice can be done between the parties at
substantially less inconvenience and expense and that a stay of the English proceedings
will not deprive the Cuban owners of a legitimate personal or jurisdictional advantage
which will be available to the Cuban owners if they invoke the jurisdiction of the English
court. In other cases, where these conditions are not satisfied, English proceedings will
d not be stayed merely because of the dangers and difficulties of concurrent actions. There
is ample scope for a litigant to choose the exercise of the English jurisdiction, of which
Sir John Donaldson MR is justly proud, notwithstanding that proceedings have already
been instituted under a foreign jurisdiction provided that the events which happen prior
to the hearing of an application for a stay of the English proceedings do not demonstrate
that the foreign forum is to be preferred on grounds of convenience and expense. An
e ugly rush to get one action decided ahead of the other is not to be replaced by an ugly
rush to issue proceedings in one country before the issue of proceedings in another. Most
collision cases are collisions between insurance companies. They can by agreement avoid
or put an end to concurrent actions. An insurance company should not endeavour to
insist on choosing a forum by reference to the national flag of the insured vessel or the
nationality of the insured owners in the hope that patriotism will affect the result. In the
f present case, however, Sheen J rightly came to the conclusion that there was no
justification for inflicting English proceedings on the Turkish owners in addition to the
Turkish proceedings.

Appeal allowed.

Solicitors: *Holman Fenwick & Willan* (for the Turkish owners); *Richards Butler & Co* (for
the Cuban owners).

Mary Rose Plummer   Barrister.

R v Immigration Appeal Tribunal and another, ex parte Secretary of State for the Home Department
and other applications

QUEEN'S BENCH DIVISION (CROWN OFFICE LIST)
TAYLOR J
30 JUNE, 11 JULY 1983

Divorce – Foreign decree – Recognition by English court – Overseas divorce – Proceedings in country outside British Isles – Proceedings – Talaq divorce – Talaq pronounced by husband in United Kingdom – Husband a national of Pakistan – Wife resident in Pakistan – Notice of talaq served on Pakistani authorities and wife in accordance with Pakistani law – Talaq not revoked and marriage validly dissolved under Pakistani law – Whether divorce 'obtained by means of . . . proceedings' in Pakistan – Recognition of Divorces and Legal Separations Act 1971, s 2.

A Pakistani Muslim living in England wished to divorce his wife, who was living in Pakistan. He pronounced talaq in England against her, and in accordance with Pakistani law sent written notice that he had done so to her and to the appropriate public authority in Pakistan. The talaq was not revoked and 90 days later the marriage was declared dissolved according to Pakistani law. In subsequent immigration proceedings the question arose whether the talaq divorce should be recognised by the English courts under s 2[a] of the Recognition of Divorces and Legal Separations Act 1971.

Held – The pronouncement of talaq was part of the 'proceedings' by means of which the divorce had been obtained, and accordingly the proceedings had taken place partly in England and partly in Pakistan. Since on its true construction s 2(a) of the 1971 Act afforded recognition only to, inter alia, divorces obtained by 'proceedings' which took place entirely outside the British Isles, it followed that, even though the divorce was effective under Pakistani law, it could not be recognised by the English courts (see p 493 b c f g and j to p 494 f, post).

Dicta of Lord Fraser and of Lord Scarman in *Quazi v Quazi* [1979] 3 All ER at 911, 918 applied.

Per curiam. The words 'other proceedings' in s 2(a) cover the bare pronouncement of talaq in a country where the pronouncement is in itself sufficient to effect a divorce (see p 491 a b and p 493 b c, post); *Zaal v Zaal* (1983) 4 FLR 284 followed; *Sharif v Sharif* (1980) 10 Fam Law 216 and *Chaudhary v Chaudhary* (1983) 13 Fam Law 177 not followed.

Notes

For the recognition of overseas divorces, see 8 Halsbury's Laws (4th edn) paras 484–485, and for cases on the subject, see 11 Digest (Reissue) 564–566, 1270–1279.

For the Recognition of Divorces and Legal Separations Act 1971, ss 2, 3, see 41 Halsbury's Statutes (3rd edn) 219.

Cases referred to in judgment

Chaudhary v Chaudhary (1983) 13 Fam Law 177.
Manzoor v Allah Wasaya PLD 1973 BJ 36.
Quazi v Quazi [1979] 3 All ER 897, [1980] AC 744, [1979] 3 WLR 833, HL.
Qureshi v Qureshi [1971] 1 All ER 325, [1972] Fam 173, [1971] 2 WLR 518.
R v Registrar General of Births, Deaths and Marriages, ex p Minhas [1976] 2 All ER 246, [1977] QB 1, [1976] 2 WLR 473, DC.

---

[a] Section 2, so far as material, is set out at p 490 g, post

Secretary of State for the Home Dept v Nasira Begum (3 July 1981, unreported), IAT.

a *Sharif v Sharif* (1980) 10 Fam Law 216.

Zaal v Zaal (1983) 4 FLR 284.

Applications for judicial review

R v Immigration Appeal Tribunal and anor, ex p Secretary of State for the Home Dept

b The Secretary of State for the Home Department applied, with the leave of McNeill J granted on 26 November 1982, (1) for an order of certiorari to bring up and quash the decision of the Immigration Appeal Tribunal, dated 27 August 1982, whereby the tribunal allowed an appeal by the respondent Seada Bi against the decision of an adjudicator on 8 March 1981 whereby he dismissed her appeal against the refusal of the Secretary of State to grant her indefinite leave to remain in the United Kingdom as the wife of Mohammed Gulzar, and (2) for a declaration that the proceedings whereby

c Mohammed Gulzar purported to dissolve his marriage to Kosir Yasmeen did not constitute an 'overseas divorce' for the purposes of s 2 of the Recognition of Divorces and Legal Separations Act 1971. The facts are set out in the judgment.

R v Secretary of State for the Home Dept, ex p Ghulam Fatima

d Ghulam Fatima applied, with the leave of McNeill J granted on 23 September 1982, for an order of certiorari to bring up and quash the decision of an immigration officer made on 31 July 1982 whereby he refused her leave to enter the United Kingdom. The facts are set out in the judgment.

R v Secretary of State for the Home Dept, ex p Shafeena Bi

e Shafeena Bi applied, with the leave of McCowan J granted on 3 June 1983, for an order of certiorari to bring up and quash (1) the decision of an immigration officer made on 24 February 1983 whereby he refused her leave to enter the United Kingdom, and (2) a decision, dated 26 May 1983, giving directions for her removal to Pakistan. The facts are set out in the judgment.

f *Simon D Brown* for the Secretary of State.

David Latham for the Immigration Appeal Tribunal.

Ghulam Yazdani for the respondent Seada Bi.

Sibghatullah Kadri and *Harjit Grewal* for the applicant Ghulam Fatima.

Owais Kadri for the applicant Shafeena Bi.

g   *Cur adv vult*

11 July. The following judgment was delivered.

TAYLOR J. These three applications for judicial review have been heard together since they all turn on the same point, namely: what is the effect in English law of a talaq

h divorce pronounced in England, but perfected in Pakistan?

In the first application, the Secretary of State for the Home Department applies for judicial review of a determination by the Immigration Appeal Tribunal, dated 27 August 1982, allowing an appeal by Seada Bi from the decision of an adjudicator dismissing her appeal from the refusal of the Secretary of State to grant her indefinite leave to remain in the United Kingdom as wife to Mohammed Gulzar (the sponsor). Although Seada Bi is

j strictly respondent to this application, she was initially an applicant for leave to remain in the United Kingdom and, for convenience, I shall refer to her in this judgment as 'the applicant' on this first application.

In the second application, Ghulam Fatima (the applicant) seeks judicial review of an immigration officer's decision, dated 31 July 1982, refusing her leave to enter the United Kingdom as fiancée of Mohammed Afzal (the sponsor).

In the third application, Shafeena Bi (the applicant) seeks judicial review of an immigration officer's decision, dated 24 February 1983, refusing her leave to enter the United Kingdom as fiancée of Mohammed Zamir (the sponsor) and of directions for her removal from the United Kingdom, dated 26 May 1983.

According to ancient Muslim law, if a husband pronounces talaq three time, that is immediately effective to dissolve a marriage between Muslims. Such a form of talaq has been called 'a bare talaq' as it requires no further steps, not even notification to the wife. It is still recognised as sufficient in some countries, for example Dubai.

However, in 1961, the Muslim Family Laws Ordinance was enacted in Pakistan to prevent the hasty dissolution of marriages by talaq pronounced unilaterally by the husband. Section 7 of the ordinance provides:

'(1) Any man who wishes to divorce his wife shall, as soon as may be after the pronouncement of talaq in any form whatsoever, give the chairman notice in writing of his having done so, and shall supply a copy thereof to the wife.

(2) Whoever contravenes the provisions of subsection (1) shall be punishable with simple imprisonment for a term which may extend to one year or with fine which may extend to 5,000 rupees or with both.

(3) Save as provided in subsection (5), a talaq unless revoked earlier, expressly or otherwise, shall not be effective until the expiration of 90 days from the day on which notice under subsection (1) is delivered to the chairman . . .'

'Chairman' refers to the chairman of the relevant local union council in Pakistan and the ordinance is expressed to apply to Muslim citizens of Pakistan wherever they may be. There are further provisions, which I need not recite, requiring the chairman to set up reconciliation proceedings, but participation by the spouses in such proceedings is not obligatory. It is common ground, therefore, that there are three requirements for a talaq to be effective in Pakistani law: (1) pronouncement of the talaq, either orally or in writing; (2) the giving in writing of notice to the chairman; and (3) the supply of a copy of the notice to the wife. This full talaq procedure is to be contrasted with the 'bare talaq' of the ancient law.

In English law two principles are clear. First, when the full talaq procedure takes place wholly in a country overseas and is effective by the laws of that country, the divorce will be recognised here if either spouse was a national of that country at the relevant time. Authority for that proposition lies in ss 2 and 3 of the Recognition of Divorces and Legal Separations Act 1971 and the decision of the House of Lords in *Quazi v Quazi* [1979] 3 All ER 897, [1980] AC 744.

Section 2 of the 1971 Act, omitting irrelevant words, reads as follows:

'Sections 3 to 5 of this Act shall have effect . . . as respects the recognition in the United Kingdom of the validity of overseas divorces . . . which—(*a*) have been obtained by means of judicial or other proceedings in any country outside the British Isles; and (*b*) are effective under the law of that country.'

Section 3, again omitting the irrelevant words, reads as follows:

'(1) The validity of an overseas divorce or legal separation shall be recognised if, at the date of the institution of the proceedings in the country in which it was obtained . . . (*b*) either spouse was a national of that country . . .'

In *Quazi v Quazi* the husband pronounced talaq in Pakistan and complied with the rest of the procedure there. The only point for decision was whether the full talaq procedure amounted to 'other proceedings' within s 2(*a*) so as to be recognised under s 3. The House of Lords held that it did. Lord Fraser said ([1979] 3 All ER 897 at 911, [1980] AC 744 at 817):

'I express no opinion whether a bare talaq pronounced in some country where, unlike Pakistan, it would be effective without any further procedure, should be recognised under the [1971 Act] as a valid divorce.'

I have been referred to conflicting decisions on this point: two by Wood J (*Sharif v Sharif* (1980) 10 Fam Law 216 and *Chaudhary v Chaudhary* (1983) 13 Fam Law 177) and one by Bush J (*Zaal v Zaal* (1983) 4 FLR 284). Wood J held that the single act of pronouncing a bare talaq, albeit three times, could not be classed as proceedings. Bush J, basing his opinion on the speech of Lord Scarman in *Quazi*, thought it could. It is strictly unnecessary to come to a conclusion on this point in order to decide the present case as I am here concerned with the full talaq procedure and not a bare talaq. But the point does have persuasive relevance, as I shall indicate, and I should therefore say that I prefer the view expressed by Bush J.

The second principle is that, where the full talaq procedure takes place wholly within the British Isles, English law does not recognise it as an effective divorce. In *Qureshi v Qureshi* [1971] 1 All ER 325, [1972] Fam 173 a Muslim husband pronounced talaq in England. His wife was also in England and the talaq was put in writing and the letter sent to her. A copy was sent to the High Commissioner for Pakistan in London, who acted in an equivalent role to the chairman of the relevant union council in Pakistan. It was held that, despite the non-forensic character of that procedure, nothing prevented the divorce, which was effective under Pakinstani law, from being also recognised by English law.

As a direct result of that decision, and to overrule it, Parliament enacted s 16(1) of the Domicile and Matrimonial Proceedings Act 1973, which reads as follows:

'No proceeding in the United Kingdom, the Channel Islands or the Isle of Man shall be regarded as validly dissolving a marriage unless instituted in the courts of law of one of those countries.'

In *Quazi v Quazi* [1979] 3 All ER 897 at 911, [1980] AC 744 at 818 Lord Fraser said of s 16(1) of the 1973 Act:

'That provision seems clearly intended to reverse the decision in *Qureshi v Qureshi* but it would be ineffective for that purpose unless the word "proceeding" applies to the talaq which was the form of divorce in that case. The implication is that a talaq is a proceeding in the sense of the 1973 Act. That Act is in my opinion relevant to the construction of the 1971 Act because it amended the 1971 Act, into which it inserted a substituted s 6, and s 16 of the 1973 Act refers to the substitution. The fact that the word "proceeding" is used in the singular throughout s 16 is not in my opinion of any particular significance. It seems to be used in the same sense as "proceedings" in the plural in the 1971 Act. Thus in sub-s (2) of s 16, which is to apply notwithstanding anything in s 6 of the 1971 Act "as substituted by s 2 of this Act", the word is used in the singular, and in the substituted s 6 in the plural.'

Accordingly, full talaq procedure overseas will be recognised in the United Kingdom; full talaq procedure in the British Isles will not. But what of a transnational procedure, such as occurred in the present applications? The facts may be stated shortly.

In the first application, Seada Bi is a Pakistani national, as is her sponsor, Mohammed Gulzar. He came to the United Kingdom in 1966 and was registered as a citizen of the United Kingdom and Colonies in 1975. Meanwhile, in 1973, on a visit to Pakistan he married his first wife. On 23 February 1978, in England, he pronounced a talaq against her. The talaq was communicated in writing to the wife and to the chairman of the Mangla Mirpur Union Council. The chairman sought to set up reconciliation proceedings. They failed. Ninety days elapsed and the marriage was declared dissolved according to Pakistani law. In November 1978 the applicant arrived in the United Kingdon to marry the sponsor and was given three months' leave to stay. On 31 January 1979 a form of marriage took place between them at Aylesbury Register Office. In February 1979 an application was made for the applicant to have leave to remain indefinitely in the United Kingdom. After inquiries, the Secretary of State was not satisfied that the talaq divorce was effective under English law and, therefore, was not satisfied that the subsequent marriage was valid. On 2 June 1980 leave was therefore refused. An appeal to an adjudicator was dismissed on 8 May 1981. On 21 August 1982 the Immigration Appeal Tribunal allowed the appeal from that adjudication, following their earlier decision in *Secretary of State for the Home Department v Nasira Begum* (3 July 1981, unreported). The Secretary of State now applies for judicial review of that decision. The Immigration Appeal Tribunal has appeared before me by counsel merely to indicate that the tribunal has decided on advice not to seek to support its decision. The question on this application is simply whether or not the talaq divorce was by English law effective to dissolve the sponsor's first marriage.

In the second application the facts very briefly are as follows. The applicant, Ghulam Fatima, is a Pakistani national. She sought entry into the United Kingdom on 31 July 1982 as fiancée of her sponsor. He is also a Pakistani national and was married in January 1968 in Pakistan. In November 1968 he came to the United Kingdom. On 22 May 1978 he pronounced a talaq against his wife and made a statutory declaration that he had done so before a solicitor in Bolton. Copies of that document were sent to the wife and to the chairman of the relevant union council in Pakistan. No reconciliation having been effected and 90 days having elapsed, the marriage was dissolved according to Pakistani law. However, the immigration officer, not being satisfied that the marriage was effectively dissolved according to English law, could not be satisfied that the intended marriage between the applicant and the sponsor could take place within a reasonable time. He therefore refused the applicant entry.

In the third application Shafeena Bi, a Pakistani national, arrived at Heathrow on 24 February 1983 seeking entry as fiancée of her sponsor. The sponsor, also a Pakistani national, had settled in England in 1974, but had been married in 1970 in Pakistan whilst on a visit there. He returned to England alone after the marriage, and his wife stayed in Pakistan. On 17 September 1981 he pronounced a talaq against her and made a statutory declaration that he had done so before a solicitor in Redditch, Worcestershire. Two copies of that declaration were sent to Pakistan, one to the wife and one to the chairman of the relevant local union council. No reconciliation occurred and, after 90 days had elapsed, that divorce was effective under Pakistani law. The immigration officer took the same view as the immigration officer in Ghulam Fatima's case. He therefore refused entry. On 26 May 1983 amended directions were given for the applicant's removal, following a decision by the Secretary of State to remove her.

The question in applications two and three is therefore whether the immigration officer in each case was entitled to take the view that he could not be satisfied that the proposed marriages could take place within a reasonable time.

I have referred to the talaq procedure in each of these cases as 'transnational' because in each the pronouncement of the talaq and the sending of the notice occurred in England, but the reception of the notice by the chairman of the relevant local union council and the remainder of the procedure occurred in Pakistan. The first question is whether these talaq divorces were obtained by proceedings wholly in Pakistan, as contended by the applicants, or by proceedings partly in England and partly in Pakistan. If the former, then the applicants will succeed. If the latter, then a second question arises: do proceedings partly in the British Isles and partly in Pakistan qualify for recognition under ss 2 and 3 of the 1971 Act, or must the proceedings be wholly outside the British Isles?

On the first question, it is conceded by the applicants that the pronouncement of a talaq is a necessary requirement, but their argument is that the pronouncement is not part of the proceedings by which the divorce is obtained. The crucial proceedings, it is said, are the receipt by the chairman of the notice and any proceedings subsequent to that. All of those occurred in Pakistan and without them there could be no divorce. Therefore, the proceedings by which the divorce was obtained were wholly in Pakistan. But, by the same token, there can be no divorce unless initially talaq is pronounced and that occurred in England. Section 7(1) of the 1961 ordinance clearly requires that there should be, first, a pronouncement and then, as soon as may be afterwards, notice to the chairman that it has been done: two separate steps.

It is then argued that the pronouncement is merely the manifestation of a wish to

divorce and is not itself part of any proceedings, which consist entirely of the notice to
the chairman and the steps thereafter. In support of this proposition, I was referred to

a *Manzoor v Allah Wasaya* PLD 1973 BJ 36. After quoting the terms of s 7 of the 1961
ordinance, Aftab Hussain J said (at 39): 'The pronouncement of divorce therefore does
not operate as divorce. It is merely manifestation of wish to divorce.' However, that case
was concerned with an application for a judicial divorce and all the judge was saying was
that in Pakistan a bare talaq does not, without more, achieve divorce. There is nothing

b mutually exclusive about an act being a manifestation of a wish to divorce and being a
step in proceedings. In English law, a divorce petition is a manifestation of a wish to
divorce; it is undoubtedly also part of, and indeed the institution of, divorce proceedings.
Further, if I am correct in preferring the view of Bush J, that a bare talaq (in a country
where that is sufficient) comes within 'other proceedings' in s 2 of the 1971 Act, then the
pronouncements in the present case must amount to more than just a mere wish and

c must be part of the full talaq proceedings.
  This conclusion is supported by passages in the speeches of Lord Fraser and Lord
Scarman in *Quazi v Quazi* [1979] 3 All ER 897 at 911, 918, [1980] AC 744 at 817, 826.
Lord Fraser said:

d '. . . I am of the opinion that the talaq and the notice to the civil judge, a copy of
  which has to be sent to the wife, taken together are "proceedings" within the sense
  of s 2 of the 1971 Act. The proceedings are instituted by the talaq itself, which
  forms part of them. That must be so having regard to the provision in s 3(1) of the
  Act that the tempus inspiciendum for habitual residence and nationality is the date
  of the institution of the proceedings.'

Lord Scarman said:

e 'Under the law of Pakistan, therefore, talaq is the institution of proceedings
  officially recognised as leading to divorce and becomes an effective divorce only
  after the completion of the proceedings and the expiry of a period laid down by
  statute. The proceedings in this case were, therefore, officially recognised, and led to
  a divorce legally effective in Pakistan. Further, the trial judge was correct in holding
  that the effective divorce was obtained *by means* of these proceedings; for without

f them there would have been no effective divorce.' (Lord Scarman's emphasis.)

  I am satisfied that the pronouncement of talaq in England in each of these cases was
part of the proceedings, and indeed the institution of proceedings, by means of which
the divorce was obtained. The proceedings were, therefore, partly in the British Isles and
partly in Pakistan.

g That finding requires me to consider the second question posed: are such proceedings
within the scope of s 2(*a*) of the 1971 Act? The only decision directly on this point, to
which I was referred, was *R v Registrar General of Births, Deaths and Marriages, ex p Minhas*
[1976] 2 All ER 246, [1977] QB 1. There, the facts were similar to those in the present
cases, the only difference being that the husband, after pronouncing talaq and giving
notice while in England, later travelled to Pakistan and attended a hearing set up by the

h relevant chairman. The court held that the divorce could not be recognised as the
proceedings were not outside the British Isles. Unfortunately, the case proceeded on a
misunderstanding of the full talaq procedure. The court thought that, once the talaq was
pronounced in England, the marriage was brought immediately to an end, subject only
to effluxion of 90 days and a power to revoke the talaq during that time. This error was
pointed out by Lord Fraser in *Quazi v Quazi* [1979] 3 All ER 897 at 910, [1980] AC 744

j at 816. Since the court did not consider the truly transnational nature of the proceedings,
I think it best to ignore the decision for the purposes of this judgment, although I believe
on the true facts that it was still correctly decided.
  On behalf of the applicants, it is argued that the divorces were obtained in Pakistan,
since that is where the proceedings culminated. They were effective under Pakistani law
and, therefore, they complied with both limbs of s 2. I cannot accept that argument.

First, it is important to read ss 2 and 3 together. Section 3 confines recognition of the overseas divorces to cases where 'at the date of the institution of the proceedings in the country in which it was obtained . . . (b) either spouse was a national of that country'. The institution of the proceedings being the pronouncement of the talaq, that section clearly contemplates that the pronouncement is to be in the country where the divorce is obtained. Any other construction would involve more than one set of proceedings. But, as I have indicated by citations from *Quazi v Quazi* [1979] 3 All ER 897 esp at 911, [1980] AC 744 esp at 817 per Lord Fraser, with its specific references to s 3, the full talaq procedure is one set of proceedings only.

Again, the requirement in s 2(a) that the overseas divorce be obtained by means of other proceedings in any country outside the British Isles clearly means that the entirety of the proceedings should be in the overseas country. It is not possible to imply the words 'or partly in' after the words 'other proceedings in'.

Finally, I come to the policy of the legislation, taking the two statutes together. No doubt the scheme of the 1971 Act was to give recognition to divorces obtained in overseas proceedings by foreign nationals and recognised by their country. The desirability of effecting that policy was strongly stressed by counsel for the applicants. However, it is equally clear that the object of s 16(1) of the 1973 Act is to deny recognition to divorces obtained by persons within the jurisdiction and, therefore, subject to the laws of the United Kingdom by any proceedings other than in a United Kingdom court. It would clearly be contrary to that policy to give recognition where the proceedings were instituted in England by a pronouncement of talaq and were perfected by post in Pakistan.

For these reasons, I conclude that in the first application the Secretary of State was right and in the second and third applications the immigration officer was right. I appreciate that all the applicants in these cases needed to do to achieve their wish was to go briefly to Pakistan and do as was done in *Quazi v Quazi*. This may seem to render the present decision technical and even hollow. But, in my judgment, the words of the statutes lead plainly and inevitably to this result, which is in accordance with the policy of the legislation that I have outlined.

The first application must therefore be granted. An order of certiorari must go to quash the determination of the Immigration Appeal Tribunal and there will be a declaration as sought. The two other applications must be refused.

Orders accordingly.

Solicitors: *Treasury Solicitor*; *B C Mascarenhas*, Wood Green (for the respondent Seada Bi); *J Esner & Co*, Bolton (for the applicant Ghulam Fatima); *Wakefield & Co*, agents for *Browning & Co*, Redditch (for the applicant Shafeena Bi).

N P Metcalfe Esq   Barrister.

a # Freevale Ltd v Metrostore (Holdings) Ltd and another

CHANCERY DIVISION
DONALD RATTEE QC SITTING AS A DEPUTY JUDGE OF THE HIGH COURT
21 JULY 1983

b *Specific performance – Sale of land – Land belonging to company – Vendor company placed in receivership by debenture holder before completion of contract for sale of land – Whether appointment of receiver destroying purchaser's equitable interest in land under contract for sale – Whether appointment of receiver affording vendor company defence to claim for specific performance of contract.*

c Where a limited company enters into a contract to sell land, thereby conferring on the purchaser an equitable interest in the land, the fact that the vendor company is placed in receivership by a debenture holder of the company prior to completion of the contract does not destroy the purchaser's equitable interest in the land under the contract and substitute for it a mere right to claim damages against the vendor company if the contract d is not completed; instead the vendor company remains liable to complete the contract. Accordingly, the appointment of a receiver does not of itself afford the vendor company a defence to a claim by the purchaser for specific performance of the contract (see p 503 c to g, post).

Pearce v Bastable's Trustee in Bankruptcy [1901] 2 Ch 122 and *Re Bastable, ex p Trustee* [1901] 2 KB 518 applied.

e ## Notes

For specific performance of a contract for the sale of land, see 42 Halsbury's Laws (4th edn) paras 258, 259.

For the effect of appointment of a receiver on a company's contracts, see 7 ibid para f 880.

Cases referred to in judgment

Airlines Airspares Ltd v Handley Page Ltd [1970] 1 All ER 29, [1970] Ch 193, [1970] 2 WLR 163.

Bastable, Re, ex p Trustee [1901] 2 KB 518, CA.

g *Holloway v York* (1877) 25 WR 627.

Lochgelly Iron and Coal Co Ltd v North British Rly Co 1913 1 SLT 405.

Macleod v Alexander Sutherland Ltd 1977 SLT (Notes) 44.

Moore v Paterson (1881) 9 R 337.

Pearce v Bastable's Trustee in Bankruptcy [1901] 2 Ch 122.

Pooley, Re, ex p Rabbidge (1878) 8 Ch D 367, CA.

h *Southern Foundries (1926) Ltd and Federated Foundries Ltd v Shirlaw* [1940] 2 All ER 445, [1940] AC 701, HL.

Stewart v Kennedy (No 1) (1890) 15 App Cas 75, HL.

Appeal

j This was an appeal by the plaintiff, Freevale Ltd, from an order of Master Gowers made on 1 July 1983 refusing to grant the plaintiff's claim against the defendants, Metrostore (Holdings) Ltd and Metrostore (Hayes) Ltd, for an order for specific performance of an agreement dated 4 February 1983 made between the defendants and the plaintiff, to sell the plaintiff three pieces of land at the aggregate price of £300,000, and giving the defendants leave to defend the plaintiff's action for specific performance of the agreement and for damages. The appeal was heard in chambers but judgment was given by Donald Rattee QC in open court. The facts are set out in the judgment.

a

Timothy Lloyd for the plaintiff.
Richard Hacker for the defendants.

DONALD RATTEE QC. I have before me an appeal from Master Gowers from an order he made on 1 July 1983 in which he refused to make an order for specific performance under RSC Ord 86, and instead gave leave to the defendants in the action to defend. The action is one by a company, Freevale Ltd, against two defendant companies, Metrostore (Holdings) Ltd and Metrostore (Hayes) Ltd, and is an action claiming specific performance of an agreement for the sale of land.

b

For present purposes, the material facts are set out in the statement of claim, and those facts as alleged are now admitted by a defence that has been put in on behalf of the defendants, so that there is no dispute between the parties as to the material facts. For present purposes, all I need say about the facts is that, as appears from the statement of claim, there was an agreement in writing of 4 February 1983, made between the two defendants of the one part and the plaintiff of the other, whereby the defendants agreed to sell and the plaintiff to buy three pieces of land at an aggregate price of £300,000.

c

That contract of sale was subject to various special conditions with which I need not be concerned for the purpose of deciding the issue I have to decide on the appeal, because there is no dispute between the parties that that contract would have been an appropriate subject for an order for specific performance at the suit of the plaintiff purchaser were it not for one fact, and one fact alone, and that is that since the date of the contract a receiver has been appointed in respect of the affairs of each of the two defendant companies, appointed out of court by a debenture holder having a debenture from each of the two defendants.

d

e

The master decided that the court would not, or perhaps might not, grant an order for specific performance against a company which is in receivership. Counsel for the plaintiff says that that decision was wrong. He says (and, as I say, I do not think there is any dispute between the parties as to this) that but for this fact of receivership the relevant contract would have been subject to an order for specific performance at the behest of the plaintiff, because, like all other contracts for the sale of land, prima facie damages are not an appropriate or satisfactory or sufficient remedy for breach. Counsel says a fortiori damages are not an adequate remedy for breach of the contract in the present case, where, having regard to the fact of the receivership in relation to both the defendants, there is indeed real doubt as to how valuable, if at all, the right to damages against the defendants would be having regard to their likely financial position.

f

g

Counsel for the defendants, on the other hand, says that, because a receiver has been appointed of each of the defendant companies, the court will not order specific performance of the contract in the action brought by the plaintiff, and for that proposition he relies on two authorities. The first of those is *Airlines Airspares Ltd v Handley Page Ltd* [1970] 1 All ER 29, [1970] Ch 193. The headnote reads as follows, and I think I should read it in full ([1970] Ch 193 at 193–194):

h

'The plaintiffs were the assignees of the benefit of an agreement dated December 23, 1966, and made between K. Ltd. and K. of the first part and the first defendants of the other part, under which the first defendants agreed, inter alia, to pay to K. Ltd. and K. a commission of £500 in respect of every aircraft of a type known as "Jetstream" sold by the first defendants. On October 28, 1968, the first defendants issued a debenture to the bank; and on August 7, 1969, the bank, under the power contained in the debenture, appointed a receiver who was accorded the wide powers conferred on a mortgagee under the Law of Property Act, 1925. The receiver, in order to carry out his duties in the most effective manner, caused the first defendants to create a subsidiary company, A. Ltd., to which the first defendants on August 15, 1969, assigned such parts of their undertaking as represented an economically viable

j

a business namely, their business connected with the "Jetstream" aircraft. The receiver then entered into negotiations for the sale of the shares of A. Ltd., to American interests, and notified K. and the plaintiffs that he could no longer comply with the agreement of December 23, 1966. The plaintiffs sought an injunction to restrain the sale of the shares, and a declaration that they were entitled to the agreed commission. Graham J. granted an ex parte injunction on August 29, 1969, restraining the sale. On a motion to continue the injunction:—*Held*, that where a

b receiver appointed by debenture holders, in realising a company's assets to the best advantage, had made it clear that he did not in any event intend to adopt a contract entered into by the company with a third party, and where the repudiation of the contract would not adversely affect the realisation of those assets, or seriously affect any future trading prospects of the company, the receiver was in a better position as to current contracts than the company itself, and could frustrate the contract in

c circumstances where the company itself would not be entitled to do so. Accordingly, the plaintiffs were not entitled to restrain the receiver from acting in the manner proposed by him of selling the shares of A. Ltd. to American interests, and the injunction granted would be discharged.'

The first thing to note about the facts of that case is that the contract concerned was not one of which the court would, apart from the receivership, grant specific performance.

d That appears clear from the judgment of Graham J (see [1970] 1 All ER 29 at 31, [1970] Ch 193 at 197). After having set out the argument of the parties, Graham J really crystallises the question with which the court was concerned in that case, and gives his answer to it, and he said this ([1970] 1 All ER 29 at 32, [1970] Ch 193 at 198–199):

'That question [and by that he means the question for determination by the court in that case] may be stated as follows. Is a receiver and manager, appointed by

e debenture-holders, in a stronger position, from the legal point of view, than the company itself, in respect of contracts between unsecured creditors and the company? Assuming that the company, on the authority of *Southern Foundries (1926) Ltd v Shirlaw* [1940] 2 All ER 445, [1940] AC 701 cannot put it out of its own power to perform contracts it has entered into, can a receiver in effect do so on its behalf if, at the same time, he has made it clear that he is not going to adopt the

f contract anyway, and if, as is, in my judgment, the case here, the repudiation of the contract will not adversely affect the realisation of the assets or seriously affect the trading prospects of the company in question, if it is able to trade in the future? Counsel, when I asked them, were not able to produce any authority which gave a direct answer to this question, but there is a helpful passage dealing generally with "current contracts" in Buckley on the Companies Acts ((13th edn, 1957) p 224). This

g passage, to my mind, makes it clear that, in the author's view, the answer to the question I have posed above must be "yes". It seems to me that it is common sense that it should be so, since otherwise almost any unsecured creditor would be able to improve his position and prevent the receiver from carrying out, or at any rate carrying out as sensibly and as equitably as possible, the purpose for which he was appointed. I therefore hold that the receiver, within the limitations which I have

h stated above, is in a better position than the company, qua current contracts, and that, in the present case, the receiver, in doing what he has done and is purporting to do, in connection with the transfer of Aircraft's shares, is not doing anything which the plaintiffs are entitled to prevent by this motion.'

In my judgment, that decision of Graham J really affords me no help on the question which is raised by the present case, which is a totally different question. In my judgment,

j the real question raised in the present case is, does the appointment out of court of a receiver in respect of a company vendor of land somehow destroy the equitable interest in the land which was vested in the purchaser prior to the appointment of the receiver by virtue of the subsisting valid contract for its sale and purchase, or does the appointment of a receiver alternatively somehow prevent the court perfecting that equitable interest by making an order for specific performance?

As I say, in my judgment, Graham J's decision in the *Airlines Airspares* case really does not point the way to the correct answer to the question which I have just formulated. In his case, there was no contract for the sale of land whose enforcement the court was considering, and, as I have said, there was no doubt that the contract that the court was considering was not one which would have been subject to an order for specific performance whether or not there had been a receiver on the scene.

The second authority on which counsel for the defendants relies is a Scottish case, *Macleod v Alexander Sutherland Ltd* 1977 SLT (Notes) 44. Inevitably, having regard to the different legal terminology that unfortunately exists between the Scottish and the English jurisdictions, it is not at all points easy to follow the rather abbreviated report that appears in Scots Law Times, but the report is comparatively short and I propose for the purpose of convenience to read it in full. It reads as follows (at 44):

'In 1972 the pursuer sold the defenders an area of ground at Inverness on missives which provided inter alia that the defenders should perform certain specified building and construction work in relation to the ground. The work was never carried out. The pursuer raised an action seeking decree of implement and, failing implement, damages of £10,000.'

I intervene to say, as I understand it, a decree of implement is the equivalent of a decree of specific performance. The report goes on (at 44–45):

'The defenders were a company incorporated under the Companies Act and a receiver was appointed to the company in June 1974 by creditors holding a floating charge secured over the company's entire assets. The receiver accordingly had complete control over the company's assets. The defenders had ceased to trade in the sense that they were no longer carrying on a building business. They did not employ anyone who could carry out the work, nor did they own the necessary materials. They averred that it was impossible for them to perform their obligations to the pursuer. Section 17(4) of The Companies (Floating Charges and Receivers) (Scotland) Act 1972 provides that contracts undertaken by a company prior to the appointment of a receiver continue in force notwithstanding the appointment. Counsel for the pursuers submitted that it was no answer for a company which had undertaken contractual obligations to say that they no longer had the means of performing them. The defenders admitted that they were in breach of contract and were willing that decree should pass against them for payment of damages. The only question remaining at issue was whether the pursuer was entitled to decree of specific implement. In refusing decree of implement and granting decree for payment of damages the Lord Ordinary (Lord Stott) said: "It is plain that the defenders are not in a position to obtemper decree of specific implement through their directors as would normally be the position if the company were not in receivership…"'

Again there is a certain difficulty of terminology, but I understand that that really is equivalent to saying it is plain that the defenders were not in a position to comply with a decree of specific performance through their directors. The Lord Ordinary went on:

'Counsel for the pursuer, however, submitted that the position was fundamentally the same, inasmuch as they would be able to act through the receiver. But, the receiver is not in the position of a director. No doubt he is deemed to be the agent of the company in relation to its property, but his acts are not the acts of the company. They are his own acts, and by s. 17(2) of the Act he incurs personal liability on a contract entered into by him in the performance of his functions. It is true that, as counsel pointed out, he has a right to be indemnified out of the company's property, but whether that right is of practical value may be a question of circumstances and in any event the fact remains that the primary liability rests on the receiver himself. Since ex hypothesi the responsibility for whatever is done in implement of the contract must in fact be done by the receiver it seems to me to be out of the question to pronounce a decree ostensibly against the company, which would in effect result in the receiver either incurring personal liability or in his bearing the responsibility for a contempt of court (whether his own or the company's). That consideration applies with all the greater force when I am asked to pronounce such a decree in an action to which the receiver is not a party. It follows from what I have said that decree in terms of the pursuer's first conclusion should not be granted and the argument for refusing it is reinforced, if one considers the position from the point of view of enforcement. The only sanction suggested by counsel for the pursuer for failure to obtemper such a decree against a limited company would be the imposition of a monetary penalty and counsel was unable to refer to any report of such having been done. That, I think, is why the learned author of Gloag on *Contract* ((2nd edn, 1929) p 659) suggests that an action against a corporate body concluding for the performance of some act which can be performed vicariously is incompetent without an alternative conclusion for damages, and may afford the explanation also for Lord Kinnear's observations in *Lochgelly Iron and Coal Co. Ltd. v. North British Railway Co.* ((1913) 1 SLT 405), where he expressed doubts as to whether a contract with a railway company would support a decree ad factum praestandum. For the purposes of the present case it is unnecessary to affirm so wide a proposition, and counsel for the defenders did not invite me to do so. Specific implement, counsel submitted, referring to *Moore v. Paterson* ((1881) 9 R 337)... was an equitable remedy. It would, I think, be inequitable to grant a decree ad factum praestandum against a company which can act only through the agency of a receiver and which, if the receiver should decline to act, would inevitably be in contempt of court in respect of an omission which they would be powerless to remedy. To pronounce such an order in a case in which the sanction of a monetary penalty would have to be imposed on defenders for a contempt which they have no means of purging except through the intervention of an agent whose actings they had no power to control, would not only be ineffective, but would as it seems to me, be unfair to the defenders and no doubt also to their creditors. The case would appear to be one of those envisaged by Lord Watson in *Stewart v. Kennedy* ((1890) 15 App Cas 75 at 103) in which circumstances have occurred which would "make it inconvenient and unjust to enforce specific performance". "The object of a decree is to enable the pursuer to secure his right, not to punish the defender" (Gloag on *Contract* ((2nd edn, 1929) p 657)).'

The essence of the decision in that Scottish case, in my judgment, appears from the judgment of the Lord Ordinary in the passage where he says:

'Since ex hypothesi the responsibility for whatever is done in implement of the contract must in fact be done by the receiver it seems to me to be out of the question to pronounce a decree ostensibly against the company, which would in effect result in the receiver either incurring personal liability or in his bearing the responsibility for a contempt of court (whether his own or the company's).'

The facts, of course, in that case were that it was no longer physically possible for the company, which had become little more than a shell, it having ceased its business, to have complied with an order for specific performance to carry out the works required by the contract. The works could only have been carried out if the receiver, in exercise of his powers, had entered into some other obligations, contracts, be they what they may, but some other arrangements whereby he or the company could acquire the means with which to perform the company's obligations under the contract, and the Lord Ordinary is saying, as I understand him in that passage I have just reread, that that being so, the decree for specific performance could only have been complied with at the cost of the receiver himself undertaking some personal liability, and that, not surprisingly, the court would not impose.

But those facts take the case, in my judgment, a long way from the problem I have to deal with in the present case. If any order for specific performance is made in the present case, there is no question of the receiver having to incur any personal liability as the only alternative to being in contempt of court. The land the subject of the contract remains in the company. There is no difficulty, prima facie at any rate, in its being conveyed by the company acting through the receiver pursuant to an order for specific performance, if made. Moreover, for that reason, in my judgment, the present case is not (as the Lord Ordinary concluded his case was) one of those described by Lord Watson in *Stewart v Kennedy* (*No 1*) (1890) 15 App Cas 75 at 103 as one in which circumstances have occurred 'which would make it inconvenient and unjust to enforce specific performance'. I see no inconvenience in enforcing specific performance in the present case merely because a receiver has been appointed of the defendant company; neither do I see any injustice in it. In my judgment, the injustice, if anywhere, lies in the defendants' argument that the true position is that the mere appointment of a receiver of the vendor company ipso facto deprives the purchaser of the right he would otherwise have to specific performance of his contract. That seems to me to carry with it more risk at least of injustice than a conclusion that the receiver, or the company with the receiver in control, is not immune from specific performance.

In any event, of course, again the Scottish decision to which I have just referred did not consider, because it did not arise, the question of the effect, if any, of the appointment of a receiver on the equitable interest of a purchaser under a contract of sale entered into by a company before the appointment of a receiver. So, again, I did not for my part find it of any great assistance in answering the question I have to answer.

Much more assistance, in my judgment, is to be derived from two authorities in the sphere of bankruptcy to which I was referred by counsel on behalf of the plaintiff, and, indeed, by counsel on behalf of the defendants. The first of those is *Pearce v Bastable's Trustee in Bankruptcy* [1901] 2 Ch 122, where the headnote reads:

'Specific performance may be enforced against the trustee in bankruptcy of a vendor of property, and, if the property is leasehold, he cannot disclaim the contract without disclaiming the lease.'

In the course of his judgment, Cozens-Hardy J said (at 125):

'It has been contended on his [that is the trustee in bankruptcy's] behalf that the fact of the bankruptcy makes all the difference as regards the liability to specifically perform a contract. In support of that, *Holloway* v. *York* ((1877) 25 WR 627) has been referred to. The effect of that decision is correctly stated in Dart's Vendors and Purchasers ((6th edn, 1888) p 1126)—that is to say, that specific performance cannot be decreed against the trustee in bankruptcy of the purchaser. That decision has no application to a case in which the vendor's trustee in bankruptcy is the defendant. If any authority is needed in support of this finding, it is to be found in *Ex parte Rabbidge* ((1878) 8 Ch D 367 at 370) where James L.J. said: "The result was that, upon the adjudication being made, the legal estate in the property vested in the trustee in the bankruptcy, subject to the equity of the purchaser under the contract. That equity gave him a right to have the property conveyed to him, upon payment of the purchase-money to the person to whom the property belonged." And Cotton L.J. said (at 371): "The trustee in the bankruptcy . . . had vested in him the estate of the bankrupt in the property. He was not in the fullest sense of the word a trustee of the property for the purchaser, because the whole of the purchase-money had not been paid. But he took the legal estate in the property, subject to the equity of the purchaser under the contract, which gave the purchaser the right to say, Convey me the estate on my paying the purchase money." Anything more explicit on this part of the case could not well be imagined. All that the plaintiff asks the trustee to do is to execute the engrossment already approved and assign the property to him, and, the plaintiff disclaiming any right of proof against the bankrupt's estate, an order for such execution, and that the defendant is to pay the costs of the action, must be made.'

I appreciate of course, that the court in that case was concerned with the position of a vendor's trustee in bankruptcy and not the receiver of a vendor company, and I, of course, appreciate that one important difference between those two situations is that the property of the bankrupt in the *Pearce* case, including the property subject to the contract of sale, vested in the trustee in bankruptcy, whereas the defendant company's property in the present case is not vested in the receiver. But none the less, in my judgment, the approach which is adopted there by Cozens-Hardy J to determining the non-effect of bankruptcy on the equitable interest which a purchaser of land from a bankrupt had before the onset of bankruptcy is certainly of assistance in considering the effect or non-effect of the appointment of a receiver of the vendor companies in the present case.

The other bankruptcy authority which arose, in fact, out of the same bankruptcy is in the Court of Appeal and is *Re Bastable* [1901] 2 KB 518, and the headnote there reads:

'The trustee in a bankruptcy cannot, under s. 55 of the Bankruptcy Act, 1883, disclaim a contract entered into by the bankrupt for the sale of a lease unless he also disclaims the lease itself. Sect. 55 was intended to enable the trustee to get rid of an onerous property or contract, and it does not enable him to disclaim a contract merely because it would be more beneficial to the estate that the contract should not be carried out. The trustee cannot by a disclaimer take away from a purchaser of land from the bankrupt the equitable interest which vested in him under his contract.'

It is the latter sentence in the headnote which is obviously particularly relevant in the present case. The decision, so far as material, was that the trustee in bankruptcy of the bankrupt, who had prior to the bankruptcy contracted to sell land, could not by exercising his power of disclaimer destroy the equitable interest in the land of a purchaser under that contract. Now, of course, a receiver, as I say, is in a very different position. He does not have vested in him the property of the company, and perhaps more particularly, in considering the decision in *Re Bastable*, he does not have the power to disclaim. So, of course, the facts considered by the Court of Appeal were different, and the question was different, but none the less, in my judgment, the reasoning explained by Romer LJ in his judgment as to the effect of bankruptcy on the equitable interest of a purchaser from the bankrupt is extremely helpful in the situation with which I am confronted. In fact, the decision of the Court of Appeal was unanimous, but I think for present purposes the most help is to be derived from Romer LJ's judgment, where at the beginning of the judgment he says (at 527–528):

'It is in substance contended on behalf of the trustee [that is the trustee in bankruptcy] that if a vendor of real estate, by contract entered into with a purchaser, becomes bankrupt, the trustee in the bankruptcy of the vendor, without disclaiming the land or the interest in the land which was the subject of the contract, can, by disclaiming the contract alone, put himself in the position of owner of the estate freed altogether from the purchaser's interest in the estate, leaving the purchaser only the remedy of proving in the bankruptcy for any loss he may have suffered by having his contract destroyed.'

Pausing there, of course that is in effect the position in which the defendants say that the purchaser plaintiff company is left in the present case without even the need for any disclaimer. The defendants say the effect of the mere appointment of the receiver is that the plaintiff is left with what may well be a useless remedy in damages. Romer LJ goes on:

'That would, indeed, be a serious contention if it could be maintained, because the result would be, that in every case in which an owner of real estate who had contracted to sell it subsequently became bankrupt, and after the contract of sale and before the bankruptcy the property had increased in value, the trustee in the bankruptcy would be able to deprive the purchaser of all interests in the estate and leave him merely the right to prove in the bankruptcy for any loss he might have incurred by the destruction of his contract, in which case he might possibly receive only an infinitesimal dividend upon the amount of his proof. It cannot, I think, be that such a result was ever intended by the Act.'

Romer LJ was referring to s 55 of the Bankruptcy Act 1883. I would say similarly it is difficult to believe that that result of the appointment of a receiver could ever have been intended by the common law. Romer LJ goes on (at 528–530):

'And indeed when s. 55 is examined, it has, in my view, no such operation or effect. The fallacy of the argument for the appellant lies, I think, in ignoring the nature of the interest of a purchaser of real estate after a contract for its sale has been made between him and the owner of the estate. The purchaser has, then, something more than a pecuniary interest under his contract. He has an equitable interest in the land itself. Fortunately, it is not necessary for us now to investigate what the precise nature of that interest is, but it is an interest in the land—an interest which is assignable, which can be devised, and which, in the event of the purchaser dying intestate, would pass to his heir. That interest in the land would remain whatever might be the effect of a disclaimer by the trustee in the vendor's bankruptcy of the contract for sale. Assume that the contract of sale could be disclaimed by the trustee in the bankruptcy separately and apart from any disclaimer by him of the property the subject of the contract. What, then, would be the effect under s. 55 of such a disclaimer? If the contract is to be regarded separately, apart from the trustee's interest in the land itself, what was the nature of the contract? Regarded separately, it is a contract under which the bankrupt's estate would be entitled to receive the balance of the purchase-money on conveyance of the property to the purchaser. Dealing with it strictly, and assuming that such a contract could be separately disclaimed, what would be the effect of the separate disclaimer? The sole effect would be this. It would prevent the trustee from afterwards insisting that the purchaser was bound to pay to the bankrupt's estate the balance of his purchase-money. I can indeed imagine a case in which the disclaimer might have a further effect. For example, suppose under the contract of sale the vendor had agreed to do some act which would cast expense upon the estate, so that if the trustee had to carry out the contract as a whole he would have to carry it out at the expense of the estate. I have no doubt that in such a case a disclaimer would also free the estate from direct liability to expend that money or to perform the acts which the bankrupt had contracted to do. But in any case the disclaimer of the contract would operate to determine any right of the trustee thereafter to call upon the purchaser to pay any money or to do any other thing to perfect his interest in the land. A disclaimer of a contract under such circumstances under s. 55 cannot operate to destroy a third person's interest in property which existed before the disclaimer. No disclaimer by the trustee could in my opinion take away the equitable interest in the land which the purchaser has acquired under his contract. That interest remains, and the sole effect of the disclaimer of the contract by the trustee would be that the purchaser could say, "I have now this equitable interest in the land, and I am freed from the obligation of tendering or paying the balance of my purchase-money." That being so, what is the position of this purchaser? He has the right to this estate and an equitable interest in it subject to the mortgage, and subject to this—that the trustee has vested in him something in the nature of a legal estate. In a case of that kind it is the common practice of the Bankruptcy Court on the application of a person in that position to say to the trustee in the bankruptcy, "If you have no further interest in the property but an outstanding legal estate, your duty is to convey that estate to the purchaser if you do not disclaim the property." In substance I think that is what the Divisional Court have done. They have, and I think rightly, treated the purchaser's application as one calling upon the trustee either to disclaim the property, or, if he does not disclaim it, then to convey it to the purchaser.'

In my judgment, although, as I say, clearly Romer LJ was considering a different situation and a different question, exactly the same reasoning applies to the question I have to answer. There is no doubt, because there is no dispute, that but for the receivership the contract in the present case would have been subject to an order for specific performance, and that prior to the receivership the plaintiff purchaser had an equitable interest in the property of exactly the same nature as that referred to by Romer LJ.

Romer LJ decided that there was no statutory authority which extended the power of disclaimer of a trustee in bankruptcy to make a disclaimer which had the effect of destroying the equitable interest of the purchaser under the pre-existing contract. Now, the receivers in the present case have no power to disclaim, but that merely goes to destroy, one might say, the part of the problem that faced Romer LJ and the other members of the Court of Appeal in *Re Bastable*. So there is no question in this case of any disclaimer having destroyed the equitable interest of the plaintiff. The highest the defendants can put their case (and, with great fairness, counsel for the defendants tries to put it no higher) is that the mere appointment of the receivers ipso facto somehow destroyed the equitable interest in the land which the plaintiff already had and substituted for it the mere right to damages, a right which may well (it may not) prove cold comfort when the affairs of the defendants are ultimately sorted out by the receivers.

Quite apart from the fact that, as I say, the defendants' argument leads, in my judgment, to a situation of considerable injustice to a purchaser who finds himself at risk of, in effect, losing his contract if before completion the vendor company suffers the appointment of a receiver, quite apart from the fact that it leads to that injustice, in my judgment, the defendants' contention is not supported by any authority which has been referred to before me, and is quite inconsistent, in my judgment, with the nature of the equitable interest of a purchaser of land.

In my judgment, the defendants in this case are in just the same position as the trustee in bankruptcy was in *Re Bastable* to whom Romer LJ referred as 'having no further interest in the property but an outstanding legal estate', subject, of course, to the lien for the unpaid part of the purchase price. That being so, it seems to me quite clear that the court ought to perfect the interests of the purchaser by calling on the companies to transfer that legal estate in perfection of the equitable interest already vested in the plaintiff.

So it follows, in my judgment, that the mere fact of receivership of the defendants affords no defence to a claim for specific performance. I do not overlook the fact that in this appeal I am only concerned with the question of whether leave should be given to the defendants to defend the claim; but the only point, as I say, that is raised as a possible defence is the legal effect of the appointment of a receiver. It is a pure point of law. It has been fully argued before me. I cannot see that anything is to be gained by anybody from some one or other party having to incur the expense of a further trial on the same point of law. In my judgment, the defence that is raised is sufficiently clearly unsustainable that the master should have refused leave to defend, and accordingly I would allow this appeal, and it now becomes necessary to consider the form of the order for specific performance that ought to be made.

Appeal allowed. Leave to appeal.

Solicitors: *Clintons* (for the plaintiff); *Stringer Saul & Justice* (for the defendants).

Hazel Hartman   Barrister.

British Steel Corp v Cleveland Bridge and Engineering Co Ltd

QUEEN'S BENCH DIVISION (COMMERCIAL COURT)

ROBERT GOFF J

6, 9–13, 16–18 NOVEMBER, 21 DECEMBER 1981

Contract – Quantum meruit – Work done in anticipation of contract – No contract concluded – Steel manufacturer negotiating with contractor to make and supply cast-steel products for construction work – Contractor requesting manufacturer to commence production in anticipation of contract being entered into – Manufacturer making and supplying cast-steel products – Parties unable to agree on contractual terms – Whether contractor entitled to value of products on a quantum meruit.

The defendants successfully tendered for the fabrication of steel work in the construction of a building. The design required steel beams to be joined to a steel frame by means of steel nodes. The plaintiffs, who were iron and steel manufacturers, were approached by the defendants to produce a variety of cast-steel nodes for the project. The plaintiffs prepared an estimated price based on incomplete information and sent it to the defendants by telex on 9 February 1979. After further discussions as to the appropriate specifications and technical requirements the defendants sent a letter of intent to the plaintiffs on 21 February which (i) recorded the defendants' intention to enter into a contract with the plaintiffs for the supply of cast-steel nodes at the prices itemised in the telex of 9 February, (ii) proposed that the contract be on the defendants' standard form, which provided for unlimited liability on the part of the plaintiffs in the event of consequential loss due to late delivery, and (iii) requested the plaintiffs to commence work immediately 'pending the preparation and issuing to you of the official form of sub-contract'. The plaintiffs would not have agreed to the defendants' standard form of contract and intended to submit a formal quotation once they had the requisite information. The plaintiffs did not reply to the letter of intent since they expected a formal order to follow shortly and instead they went ahead with the manufacture of the nodes. The defendants then indicated for the first time that they required delivery in a particular sequence. There were further discussions as to the proper specifications to be met in the manufacture but no final agreement was reached. The specifications were then changed extensively by the defendants after the first castings proved to be unsatisfactory. On 16 May the plaintiffs sent the defendants a formal quotation on their standard form, quoting a significantly higher price with delivery dates to be agreed. The defendants rejected the quotation and again changed the specifications. The plaintiffs went ahead with the manufacture and delivery of the nodes and eventually, at a meeting between the parties on 1 August, the parties reached provisional agreement on the basis of the quotation given on 16 May but they were unable to agree on other contract terms such as progress payments and liability for loss arising from late delivery. By 28 December all but one of the nodes had been delivered, delivery of the remaining node being held up until 11 April 1980 due to an industrial dispute at the plaintiffs' plant. The defendants refused to make any interim or final payment for the nodes and instead sent a written claim to the plaintiffs for damages for late delivery or delivery of the nodes out of sequence. The amount claimed far exceeded the quoted price. The plaintiffs thereupon sued for the value of the nodes on a quantum meruit, contending, inter alia, that no binding contract had been entered into. The defendants counterclaimed for damages for breach of contract for late delivery and delivery out of sequence and claimed a right of set-off, contending, inter alia, that a binding contract had been created by the various documents, especially the letter of intent, and by the plaintiffs' conduct in proceeding with the manufacture of the nodes.

Held – A contract could come into existence following a letter of intent, either by the letter forming the basis of an ordinary executory contract under which each party a assumed reciprocal obligations to the other, or under a unilateral contract (ie an 'if' contract) whereby the letter amounted to a standing offer which would result in a binding contract if acted on by the offeree before it lapsed or was validly withdrawn. On the facts, an executory contract had not been created by the plaintiffs acceding to the defendants' request in the letter of intent that they begin work on the nodes pending the issue of a formal sub-contract, since at that stage the parties were still negotiating over material contractual terms such as price and delivery dates and it was therefore impossible

b to say what those terms were. Furthermore, in all the circumstances an 'if' contract had not been created by the plaintiffs carrying out the work, since that work was at that stage being done pending a formal sub-contract, the terms of which were still in a state of negotiation, in particular with regard to the plaintiffs' liability for consequential loss and delay, so that it was impossible to determine the extent of the liability. Instead, the parties had confidently expected a formal contract to be concluded and the letter of intent

c had requested the plaintiffs to commence work, which they had done in order to expedite performance under the anticipated contract. Since the parties had ultimately been unable to reach final agreement on the price or other essential terms, the contract was eventually not entered into and therefore the work performed in anticipation of it was not referable to any contractual terms as to payment or performance. In those circumstances, the defendants were obliged to pay a reasonable sum for the work done pursuant to their

d request. In any event, assuming an 'if' contract had been concluded, the plaintiffs would not have been under a contractual obligation to complete the contract work and a fortiori would not have been under any obligation to complete within a reasonable time. Moreover, even if the plaintiffs had been under a contractual obligation to complete the work within a reasonable time, on the facts, they would not have been in breach of that obligation. Accordingly, the plaintiffs were entitled to succeed on their claim and the

e defendants failed in their counterclaim and set-off (see p 509 j to p 510 f and j to p 511 f and j to p 512 a and e f, post).

Hick v Raymond & Reid [1891–4] All ER Rep 491 applied.

Notes

f For quantum meruit claims, see 9 Halsbury's Laws (4th edn) paras 692–696, and for cases on the subject, see 12 Digest (Reissue) 145–148, 836–850.

For rights to set-off and counterclaim for breach of contract, see 9 Halsbury's Laws (4th edn) para 608.

For unilateral contracts, see ibid paras 206, 239, 248, 252.

Cases referred to in judgment

g *Courtney & Fairbairn Ltd v Tolaini Bros (Hotels) Ltd* [1975] 1 All ER 716, [1975] 1 WLR 297.

Foley v Classique Coaches Ltd [1934] 2 KB 1, [1934] All ER Rep 88, CA.

Hillas (W N) & Co Ltd v Arcos Ltd (1932) 147 LT 503, [1932] All ER Rep 494, HL.

Lacey (William) (Hounslow) Ltd v Davis [1957] 2 All ER 712, [1957] 1 WLR 932.

May & Butcher Ltd v R (1929) [1934] 2 KB 17, [1929] All ER Rep 679, HL.

h *OTM Ltd v Hydranautics* [1981] 2 Lloyd's Rep 211.

Pantland Hick v Raymond & Reid [1893] AC 22, sub nom *Hick v Raymond & Reid* [1891–4] All ER Rep 491, HL.

Sanders & Forster Ltd v A Monk & Co Ltd [1980] CA Transcript 35.

Turriff Construction Ltd v Regalia Knitting Mills Ltd (1971) 222 EG 169.

Action

j By a writ issued on 11 July 1980 the plaintiffs, British Steel Corp (BSC), sued the defendants, Cleveland Bridge and Engineering Co Ltd (CBE) for £229,832·70 being the total price outstanding for 137 cast steel nodes manufactured, sold and delivered to CBE between 12 July 1979 and 11 April 1980. By their points of defence and counterclaim, CBE admitted liability in the sum of £200,853 but claimed a right of set-off in respect of the sum of £867,735·68 which they counterclaimed against BSC as damages for breach of contract. The facts are set out in the judgment.   *a*

Philip Naughton and *John Grace* for BSC.
Richard Seymour for CBE.

Cur adv vult
                                                                                          b

21 December. The following judgment was delivered.

ROBERT GOFF J. In this action the plaintiffs, British Steel Corp (whom I shall refer to as BSC), are claiming from the defendants, Cleveland Bridge and Engineering Co Ltd (whom I shall refer to as CBE), the sum of £229,832·70 as the price of 137 cast-steel   *c* nodes and other related goods sold and delivered to CBE, or alternatively are claiming the like sum on a quantum meruit. In their defence and counterclaim, CBE admit that the goods were sold and delivered to them, and further admit liability in a sum of £200,853; but that admission is subject to a plea of set-off against the sum of £867,735·68 counterclaimed by them on the ground that BSC had, in breach of contract, delivered the nodes too late and out of sequence. Accordingly CBE's net counterclaim is for the   *d* difference between these two sums, viz £666,882·68.

An order was made limiting the hearing before this court to certain specified issues. However, after a short discussion at the beginning of the hearing, it was agreed that the hearing would only be extended by a short time if I dealt with the whole question of liability; and since I felt that it was desirable that I should do so, to avoid a possibly unsatisfactory division of the trial into various issues to be tried by different tribunals, I   *e* acceded to a joint application to try the whole issue of liability, leaving only quantum to be decided later if necessary, probably by an official referee. In point of fact, by the end of the trial on liability, the quantum of BSC's claim had been agreed by the parties to be the sum claimed by them in their statement of claim, viz £229,832·70.

I turn then to the facts of the case. This is a case in which there is no doubt that BSC did in fact manufacture the 137 cast-steel nodes in question at the request of CBE, and   *f* did deliver them to CBE. But, despite protracted negotiations between the parties, no formal contract was ever entered into between them. CBE complained that BSC were late in delivering the nodes, and that the causes of delay were (with one minor exception) all within the control of BSC; they also complained that BSC failed to deliver the nodes in the sequence requested by CBE. In these circumstances, two main areas of dispute developed between the parties. First, was there any binding contract between the parties   *g* at all, under which the nodes were delivered? CBE contended that there was such a contract, which was to be found in certain documents (including a letter of intent issued by CBE dated 21 February 1979) and the conduct of BSC in proceeding with the manufacture of the nodes. BSC's primary contention was that no binding contract was ever entered into, and that they were entitled to be paid a reasonable sum for the nodes on a quantum meruit, a claim sounding not in contract but in quasi contract. The   *h* motives of the parties in putting their cases in these different ways lay primarily in the fact that, unless there was a binding contract between the parties there was no legal basis for CBE's counterclaim for damages in respect of late delivery or delivery out of sequence. So far as delivery was concerned, CBE's submission was that BSC's obligations, under the contract alleged by them to have come into existence, was to deliver the goods in the requested sequence and within a reasonable time.   *j*

The first issue is concerned therefore with an analysis of the legal relationship between the parties. The second issue is whether, if CBE are right in their submission that there was a binding contract as alleged by them, BSC were in breach of that contract in delivering the goods late and out of sequence. This latter issue is concerned primarily with consideration of the various events and difficulties which occurred in production of a the nodes by BSC, and deciding whether, in the light of these events, BSC failed to deliver the goods within a reasonable time as alleged by CBE.

It is right that I should record at this stage that, on the arguments as finally developed before me, BSC abandoned an argument that a binding contract was concluded between the parties, on BSC's standard terms, at a meeting held on 1 August 1979 and also that CBE did not press an argument that there was a contract contained in or evidenced by certain documents. I have no doubt that both parties were right in deciding not to pursue
b these respective arguments.

Having outlined the issues before the court, I shall now proceed to set out the background facts of the case.

The plaintiffs are, as I have said, BSC; but in this case I am concerned with a profit-making division of BSC, the Forges, Foundries and Engineering Group (FFE). The head office of FFE is at their River Don works at Sheffield; in or near Sheffield they have not
c only offices, but also a large foundry and a laboratory. Another medium-sized foundry within FFE is at their Craigneuk works at Motherwell, in Scotland; it is with this foundry that I am chiefly concerned in this case. Craigneuk (as I shall call it), although forming part of FFE, has its own general manager and sales manger, and enters into contracts without reference to the head office of the group in Sheffield.

CBE are a company concerned with steel fabrication. Their works are at Darlington
d and at Port Clarence on Teesside. They form part of the Trafalgar House group of companies.

A company associated with CBE, Cementation (Saudi Arabia) Ltd, in which Trafalgar House hold a substantial shareholding, was concerned in the construction of a bank (known as the Sama Bank) at Dammam in Saudi Arabia. It was intended that CBE should be subcontractors for the fabrication of steel work for the bank. The bank was to be of an
e unusual construction. The main body of the building was to be suspended from four columns, and was to have a steel lattice-work frame. There was a requirement for nodes for use at the centres of the lattice work, providing the points at which diagonal steel beams would join the lattice work on the surface of the building.

[His Lordship then made the following findings of fact. CBE discovered that BSC had been working on the development of cast steel nodes and accordingly contacted BSC.
f Thereafter discussions took place between the parties with a view to a contract being entered into for the manufacture of the cast steel nodes for CBE by BSC. BSC prepared an estimated price based on the incomplete information which was then available to it and on 9 February 1979 sent the following telex to CBE:

g 'STEEL CASTINGS FOR NODES NODE PLATE DRG 773/73 £1225 EACH NODES DRG 773/41 £941 EACH PROPOSED PRICE FOR REMAINING ITEMS £1300 PER TONNE. PRICES WOULD REMAIN FIXED FOR DURATION OF CONTRACT. CONTRACT WILL BE SUPPLIED IN UNMACHINED CONDITION FINISHED TO NORMAL FOUNDRY STANDARDS. MATERIAL, HEAT TREATMENT AND INSPECTION WOULD BE IN ACCORDANCE WITH INFORMATION CONTAINED IN OUR TELEX DATED 29 JAN 79. PATTERN COSTS £6500 LUMP SUM DELIVERY: COMMENCE DELIVERY IN 10 WEEKS FROM RECEIPT OF ORDER AND FINAL DRAWINGS AT A RATE TO BE AGREED.'

h Further discussions on technical aspects and appropriate specifications for the manufacture of the nodes took place between the parties and then on 21 February 1979 CBE sent a letter of intent to BSC which read as follows:

'SAMA BANK — DAMMAM
j We are pleased to advise you that it is the intention of Cleveland Bridge & Engineering Co. Ltd. to enter into a Sub-Contract with your company, for the supply and delivery of the steel castings which form the roof nodes on this project. The price will be as quoted in your telex (Mr. Dorrance to Mr. Roberts) dated 9th February '79 which is as follows: Nodes to drawing No. 773/73 £1225 each Nodes to drawing No. 773/41 £941 each. The price for the remaining items being £1300 per tonne. In addition the pattern costs will be a lump sum of £6500. The form of

Sub-Contract to be entered into will be our standard form of sub-contract for use in conjunction with the I.C.E. General Conditions of Contract, a copy of which is enclosed for your consideration. We also enclose a copy of the Client's fabrication Specification in relation to Structural Steelwork (pages 5A.1 to 5A.37 incl.) which is to be complied with where applicable. However, the specification for the castings will generally be in accordance with the discussions held at the Consultant Engineer's offices on 20th February '79 at which your Mr. Dorrance and other representatives of your company were present. We understand that you are already in possession of a complete set of our node detail drawings and we request that you proceed immediately with the works pending the preparation and issuing to you of the official form of sub-contract.'

In fact BSC were not then in possession of a full set of drawings. BSC did not reply to the letter because a formal order was expected to follow shortly thereafter. BSC would not have agreed to the ICE conditions of contract which provided for unlimited liability for consequential loss arising from late delivery. BSC intended to submit a formal quotation for individual prices once they had a full set of documents from which to make their calculations. In the mean time BSC processed the letter as an order and began preparations for manufacture in order not to delay final deliveries. On 27 February 1979 CBE sent a telex to BSC giving details of test plates which would be required, and also the sequence in which delivery of the nodes was required by CBE. That was the first intimation which BSC had that CBE required the nodes to be delivered in a particular sequence. There were further discussions and negotiations between the parties over the specifications to be met in the manufacture of the nodes and, because little had been agreed, Mr Kain, BSC's works manager, sent the following telex to CBE on 4 April:

'THERE ARE FAR TOO MANY UNRESOLVED QUERIES . . . WE ARE VERY CONCERNED THAT THIS COULD RESULT IN INCREASED COST AND DELAYS AT LATER STAGES DURING MANUFACTURE. WE ARE THEREFORE NOT PREPARED TO PROCEED WITH THIS CONTRACT UNTIL WE HAVE AN AGREED SPECIFICATION COVERING ALL THESE POINTS WHICH HAS BEEN RATIFIED BY CLEVELAND BRIDGE.'

Thereafter there were further discussions between the parties and although a number of matters remained unresolved it was agreed that BSC should go ahead with the manufacture of the first cast. The first experimental nodes cast were not satisfactory and CBE required extensive alterations to the patterns and specifications. The parties met on 15 May and apparently agreed on a further revision of the draft specifications. On 16 May BSC sent CBE a formal quotation on their standard form, quoting a price of £212,100 with the date of delivery to be agreed. This was a substantial increase in the prices quoted in BSC's telex of 9 February and CBE decided that the increased price was unacceptable. As a result BSC offered to reduce the price by 9%. Meanwhile BSC did all it could to make up production time lost by the rejection of the first cast, and to expedite delivery of the nodes. CBE continued to query the reasons for the price increase and again raised questions over the specifications (which had been revised by CBE on a further occasion since 15 May). Further problems were experienced by BSC in the production of suitable nodes but these were eventually overcome. On 6 July at a heated meeting between the parties BSC urged CBE to accept the quotation of 16 May and to place a formal order with them. CBE responded by tabling a contract on its standard form based on the prices contained in BSC's telex of 9 February. This contract was rejected by BSC. Despite the failure to agree on a price or other contract conditions BSC went ahead with the casting and delivery of nodes in stages in an effort to comply with CBE's requirements for delivery. At a meeting between the parties on 1 August 1979 provisional agreement was reached on the price contained in BSC's quotation of 16 May but the parties were unable to agree at that stage on the other contract conditions, especially those relating to consequential damages and a proposed performance bond.

BSC agreed to submit a revised delivery schedule and to attempt to speed up delivery of
a the completed nodes. Further disruption was caused to production by an industrial
dispute and by further technical difficulties. Eventually both of these difficulties were
overcome. Deliveries continued despite a failure to agree the contract terms, especially
the mode of payment, and despite CBE's failure to make any interim payment. By 28
December BSC had delivered all but one of the 137 nodes, the last node being held back
by BSC to ensure that payment would be made by CBE. A steelworkers' dispute began
b on 1 January 1980 which lasted several weeks with the result that the last node was not
delivered to CBE until 11 April 1980. In the meantime CBE refused to make any
payment to BSC until the nodes were on site in Saudi Arabia, on the basis that CBE would
not be paid by the main contractors until that time. That was inconsistent with CBE's
earlier assurances about progress payments. After a stormy meeting between the parties
on 6 February, BSC heard nothing more from CBE about payment, apart from a self-
c exculpatory letter from CBE two days later, until in April 1980 CBE submitted a written
claim to BSC for damages for late delivery, which claim far surpassed BSC's claim for the
price of the goods delivered. CBE's written claim for damages precipitated BSC's own
action for damages commenced by writ on 11 July 1980 in which CBE counterclaimed
and claimed a right of set-off. His Lordship continued:]

Such are the facts of the case. I now turn to the first issue in the case, which is
d concerned with the legal basis for BSC's claim for payment, and in particular whether
there was any binding contract between BSC and CBE and, if so, what were its terms. As
I have already indicated, it is the contention of CBE that there was such a contract;
whereas BSC contends that they are entitled to payment in quasi contract.

As I indicated at the beginning of this judgment, CBE alleged two alternative contracts
in their points of defence and counterclaim; but the first of these alternatives was not
e pursued. Their remaining submission was that the agreement between the parties was
comprised in the request by CBE to BSC, in their letter dated 21 February 1979, that BSC
proceed to manufacture the nodes (viz the request contained in CBE's letter of intent),
the notification by CBE to BSC in their telex dated 27 February 1979 as to the sequence
in which delivery of the nodes was required, and the conduct of BSC in proceeding with
the manufacture of the nodes. As I have also indicated, although BSC allege in their
f pleadings that an agreement was reached between the parties, on BSC's standard
conditions, at the meeting of 1 August 1979, the allegation was rightly abandoned by
BSC in the course of the hearing, and they advanced their claim for payment simply on
the basis of quasi contract.

Now the question whether in a case such as the present any contract has come into
existence must depend on a true construction of the relevant communications which
g have passed between the parties and the effect (if any) of their actions pursuant to those
communications. There can be no hard and fast answer to the question whether a letter
of intent will give rise to a binding agreement: everything must depend on the
circumstances of the particular case. In most cases, where work is done pursuant to a
request contained in a letter of intent, it will not matter whether a contract did or did
not come into existence, because, if the party who has acted on the request is simply
h claiming payment, his claim will usually be based on a quantum meruit, and it will
make no difference whether that claim is contractual or quasi-contractual. Of course, a
quantum meruit claim (like the old actions for money had and received and for money
paid) straddles the boundaries of what we now call contract and restitution, so the mere
framing of a claim as a quantum meruit claim, or a claim for a reasonable sum, does not
assist in classifying the claim as contractual or quasi contractual. But where, as here, one
j party is seeking to claim damages for breach of contract, the question whether any
contract came into existence is of crucial importance.

As a matter of analysis the contract (if any) which may come into existence following
a letter of intent may take one of two forms: either there may be an ordinary executory
contract, under which each party assumes reciprocal obligations to the other; or there

may be what is sometimes called an 'if' contract, ie a contract under which A requests B to carry out a certain performance and promises B that, if he does so, he will receive a certain performance in return, usually remuneration for his performance. The latter transaction is really no more than a standing offer which, if acted on before it lapses or is lawfully withdrawn, will result in a binding contract.

The former type of contract was held to exist by Mr Edgar Fay QC, the offical Referee, in *Turriff Construction Ltd v Regalia Knitting Mills Ltd* (1971) 202 EG 169; and it is the type of contract for which counsel for CBE contended in the present case. Of course, as I have already said, everything must depend on the facts of the particular case; but certainly, on the facts of the present case (and, as I imagine, on the facts of most cases), this must be a very difficult submission to maintain. It is only necessary to look at the terms of CBE's letter of intent in the present case to appreciate the difficulties. In that letter, the request to BSC to proceed immediately with the work was stated to be 'pending the preparation and issuing to you of the official form of sub-contract', being a sub-contract which was plainly in a state of negotiation, not least on the issues of price, delivery dates, and the applicable terms and conditions. In these circumstances, it is very difficult to see how BSC, by starting work, bound themselves to any contractual performance. No doubt it was envisaged by CBE at the time they sent the letter that negotiations had reached an advanced stage, and that a formal contract would soon be signed; but, since the parties were still in a state of negotiation, it is impossible to say with any degree of certainty what the material terms of that contract would be. I find myself quite unable to conclude that, by starting work in these circumstances, BSC bound themselves to complete the work. In the course of argument, I put to counsel for CBE the question whether BSC were free at any time, after starting work, to cease work. His submission was that they were not free to do so, even if negotiations on the terms of the formal contract broke down completely. I find this submission to be so repugnant to common sense and the commercial realities that I am unable to accept it. It is perhaps revealing that, on 4 April 1979, BSC did indeed state that they were not prepared to proceed with the contract until they had an agreed specification, a reaction which, in my judgment, reflected not only the commercial, but also the legal, realities of the situation.

I therefore reject CBE's submission that a binding executory contract came into existence in this case. There remains the question whether, by reason of BSC carrying out work pursuant to the request contained in CBE's letter of intent, there came into existence a contract by virtue of which BSC were entitled to claim reasonable remuneration; ie whether there was an 'if' contract of the kind I have described. In the course of argument, I was attracted by this alternative (really on the basis that, not only was it analytically possible, but also that it could provide a vehicle for certain contractual obligations of BSC concerning their performance, eg implied terms as to the quality of goods supplied by them). But the more I have considered the case, the less attractive I have found this alternative. The real difficulty is to be found in the factual matrix of the transaction, and in particular the fact that the work was being done *pending* a formal sub-contract the terms of which were still in a state of negotiation. It is, of course, a notorious fact that, when a contract is made for the supply of goods on a scale and in circumstances such as the present, it will in all probability be subject to standard terms, usually the standard terms of the supplier. Such standard terms will frequently legislate, not only for the liability of the seller for defects, but also for the damages (if any) for which the seller will be liable in the event not only of defects in the goods but also of late delivery. It is a commonplace that a seller of goods may exclude liability for consequential loss, and may agree liquidated damages for delay. In the present case, an unresolved dispute broke out between the parties on the question whether CBE's or BSC's standard terms were to apply, the former providing no limit to the seller's liability for delay and the latter excluding such liability altogether. Accordingly, when, in a case such as the present, the parties are still in a state of negotiation, it is impossible to predicate what liability (if any) will be assumed by the seller for, eg, defective goods or late delivery, if a formal contract should be entered into. In these circumstances, if the buyer asks the seller to commence work 'pending' the parties entering into a formal contract, it is difficult to

infer from the buyer acting on that request that he is assuming any responsibility for his
performance, except such responsibility as will rest on him under the terms of the
contract which both parties confidently anticipate they will shortly enter into. It would
be an extraordinary result if, by acting on such a request in such circumstances, the buyer
were to assume an unlimited liability for his contractual performance, when he would
never assume such liability under any contract which he entered into.

For these reasons, I reject the solution of the 'if' contract. In my judgment, the true
analysis of the situation is simply this. Both parties confidently expected a formal contract
to eventuate. In these circumstances, to expedite performance under that anticipated
contract, one requested the other to commence the contract work, and the other complied
with that request. If thereafter, as anticipated, a contract was entered into, the work done
as requested will be treated as having been performed under that contract; if, contrary to
their expectation, no contract was entered into, then the performance of the work is not
referable to any contract the terms of which can be ascertained, and the law simply
imposes an obligation on the party who made the request to pay a reasonable sum for
such work as has been done pursuant to that request, such an obligation sounding in
quasi contract or, as we now say, in restitution. Consistently with that solution, the party
making the request may find himself liable to pay for work which he would not have
had to pay for as such if the anticipated contract had come into existence, eg preparatory
work which will, if the contract is made, be allowed for in the price of the finished work
(cf *William Lacey (Hounslow) Ltd v Davis* [1957] 2 All ER 712, [1957] 1 WLR 932). This
solution moreover accords with authority: see the decision in *Lacey v Davis*, the decision
of the Court of Appeal in *Sanders & Forster Ltd v A Monk & Co Ltd* [1980] CA Transcript
35, though that decision rested in part on a concession, and the crisp dictum of Parker J
in *OTM Ltd v Hydranautics* [1981] 2 Lloyd's Rep 211 at 214, when he said of a letter of
intent that 'its only effect would be to enable the defendants to recover on a quantum
meruit for work done pursuant to the direction' contained in the letter. I only wish to
add to this part of my judgment the footnote that, even if I had concluded that in the
circumstances of the present case there was a contract between the parties and that that
contract was of the kind I have described as an 'if' contract, then I would still have
concluded that there was no obligation under that contract on the part of BSC to continue
with or complete the contract work, and therefore no obligation on their part to complete
the work within a reasonable time. However, my conclusion in the present case is that
the parties never entered into any contract at all.

In the course of his argument counsel for BSC submitted that, in a contract of this
kind, the price is always an essential term in the sense that, if it is not agreed, no contract
can come into existence. In support of his contention counsel relied on a dictum of Lord
Denning MR in *Courtney & Fairbairn Ltd v Tolaini Bros (Hotels) Ltd* [1975] 1 All ER 716 at
719, [1975] 1 WLR 297 at 301 to the effect that the price in a building contract is of
fundamental importance. I do not however read Lord Denning MR's dictum as stating
that in every building contract the price is invariably an essential term, particularly as he
expressly referred to the substantial size of the contract then before the court. No doubt
in the vast majority of business transactions, particularly those of substantial size, the
price will indeed be an essential term, but in the final analysis it must be a question of
construction of the particular transaction whether it is so. This is plain from the familiar
trilogy of cases which show that no hard and fast rule can be laid down but that the
question in each case is whether, on a true construction of the relevant transaction, it was
consistent with the intention of the parties that even though no price had been agreed a
reasonable price should be paid (*May & Butcher Ltd v R* (1929) [1934] 2 KB 17, [1929] All
ER Rep 679, *W N Hillas & Co Ltd v Arcos Ltd* (1932) 147 LT 503, [1932] All ER Rep 494
and *Foley v Classique Coaches Ltd* [1934] 2 KB 1, [1934] All ER Rep 88). In the present case,
however, I have no doubt whatsoever that, consistently with the view expressed by Lord
Denning MR in *Courtney & Fairbairn Ltd v Tolaini Bros (Hotels) Ltd*, the price was indeed
an essential term, on which (among other essential terms) no final agreement was ever
reached.

It follows that BSC are entitled to succeed on their claim and that CBE's set-off and counterclaim must fail. But, in case this matter should go further, I propose, having heard the evidence and the submissions of the parties, to express my opinion on the question whether, if BSC were under any obligation to deliver the goods in a reasonable time, they were in breach of that obligation. In this part of my judgment, I do not propose to consider any question of delivery out of sequence; an obligation to deliver in a certain sequence could only have arisen from an express term in a contract between the parties, and I am satisfied that no such express term can possibly be said to have been agreed in the present case; and if any court should hereafter form a different view, the difference between the actual and contractual order of delivery can be ascertained without difficulty.

I turn to the question of delivery within a reasonable time. It was common ground between the parties that the principles I had to apply in this connection were those stated by the House of Lords in *Pantland Hick v Raymond & Reid* [1893] AC 22, [1891–4] All ER Rep 491, viz that the question of what constituted a reasonable time had to be considered in relation to the circumstances which existed at the time when the contractual services were performed, but excluding circumstances which were under the control of the party performing those services. As I understand it, I have first to consider what would, in ordinary circumstances, be a reasonable time for the performance of the relevant services; and I have then to consider to what extent the time for performance by BSC was in fact extended by extraordinary circumstances outside their control.

[His Lordship then considered the evidence and concluded that a reasonable period for the manufacture of the 137 nodes was 55½ weeks and that since such a period would have gone well beyond 11 April 1980 when the last node was in fact delivered it followed that if, contrary to his Lordship's previously expressed opinion, BSC had been bound to complete the work within a reasonable time they would not have been in breach of that obligation. His Lordship continued:]

However, as I have already held, there was in my judgment no obligation on BSC to deliver the nodes within a reasonable time. It follows that BSC are entitled to judgment on their claim in the sum of £229,832·70 and that CBE's set-off and counterclaim must be dismissed.

Judgment for the plaintiffs.

Solicitors: *Lovell White & King* (for BSC); *A Paul Powell*, Darlington (for CBE).

K Mydeen Esq   Barrister.

Gubay v Kington (Inspector of Taxes)

HOUSE OF LORDS
LORD FRASER OF TULLYBELTON, LORD SCARMAN, LORD BRIDGE OF HARWICH, LORD BRANDON OF
OAKBROOK AND LORD BRIGHTMAN
30 NOVEMBER, 1 DECEMBER 1983, 26 JANUARY 1984

Capital gains tax – Disposal of assets – Husband and wife – Married woman living with her husband – Wife not resident in United Kingdom in year of assessment – Husband resident in United Kingdom for part of year of assessment – Husband making gift of shares to wife – Whether husband liable to capital gains tax on gift of shares – Whether husband resident in United Kingdom for year of assessment – Finance Act 1965, s 45(3), Sch 7, para 20 – Income and Corporation Taxes Act 1970, s 42.

On 4 April 1972 the taxpayer's wife left the United Kingdom and took up residence in the Isle of Man. The taxpayer and his wife remained matrimonially united but the taxpayer continued to be resident in the United Kingdom for tax purposes. On 7 July the taxpayer transferred a large holding of shares to his wife by way of gift, which if the wife had been resident in the United Kingdom would not have attracted any liability to capital gains tax. The taxpayer was assessed for capital gains tax on the market value, some £1·4m, of the shares comprised in the gift on the basis that he had made chargeable gains in respect of disposals, including the gift of shares to his wife, made in the 1972–73 tax year. The taxpayer claimed that he was exempt from capital gains tax by virtue of para 20(1)[a] of Sch 7 to the Finance Act 1965 because the shares had been transferred by him to his wife, who was 'a married woman living with her husband' for the purposes of para 20(1). By s 45(3)[b] of the 1965 Act references in para 20 to a married woman living with her husband were to be construed in accordance with 'section 42(1)(2)[c] of the Income and Corporation Taxes Act 1970', which provided, by s 42(2)(a), that where a married woman was living with her husband and 'one of them is, and one of them is not, resident in the United Kingdom for a year of assessment' they were to be assessed for tax as if they were permanently separated, subject to the proviso to s 42(2), which stated that their aggregate liability to tax was not to be increased thereby. The Special Commissioners and, on appeal by the taxpayer, the judge and the Court of Appeal all held that the para 20(1) exemption did not apply. The taxpayer appealed to the House of Lords, contending, inter alia, that if the taxable status of himself and his wife was to be determined according to s 42(2)(a) of the 1970 Act then the whole of s 42(2), including the proviso, applied so that his aggregate liability for capital gains tax was no greater than if he had not been geographically separated from his wife. The Crown contended, inter alia, that the proviso was to be disregarded in determining the taxpayer's tax liability.

Held (Lord Scarman dissenting) – The reference in s 45(3) of the 1965 Act to 'section 42(1)(2)' of the 1970 Act was a reference to the whole of s 42 of the 1970 Act, including the proviso to s 42(2), with the result that, as in the case of liability for income tax, where a husband and wife were separated geographically for the whole or part of a tax year in circumstances which were not likely to be permanent they were not to be liable to a greater aggregate amount of capital gains tax than if they had not been separated. Since the husband would not have been liable to capital gains tax on the transfer of the shares if his wife had been living in the United Kingdom it followed, applying the proviso to s 42(2), that he was not liable merely because at the time of the transfer he was geographically but not matrimonially separated from his wife. The appeal would accordingly be allowed (see p 516 c d and g, p 517 a to g, p 522 c to j, p 523 c, p 527 a to f and p 529 e to h, post).

a   Paragraph 20(1) is set out at p 523 j to p 524 a, post
b   Section 45(3) is set out at p 520 j, post
c   Section 42 is set out at p 521 a to d, post

Per Lord Bridge and Lord Brandon. The expression 'resident in the United Kingdom for a year of assessment' in s 42(2) of the 1970 Act does not necessarily mean resident in the United Kingdom throughout such year, but includes residence for only part of the relevant year (see p 523 *b c* and p 526 *g h*, post).

Decision of the Court of Appeal [1983] 2 All ER 976 reversed.

Notes

For the treatment of disposals between husbands and wives for capital gains tax purposes, see 5 Halsbury's Laws (4th edn) paras 126, 128, 181.

For the Finance Act 1965, s 45, Sch 7, para 20, see 34 Halsbury's Statutes (3rd edn) 916, 961.

For the Income and Corporation Taxes Act 1970, s 42, see 33 ibid 79.

With effect from 6 April 1979, s 45(3) of and para 20 of Sch 7 to the 1965 Act were replaced by ss 155(2) and 44 respectively of the Capital Gains Tax Act 1979.

Cases referred to in opinions

Browning v Duckworth [1935] 1 KB 605.
Stone v Yeovil Corp (1876) 1 CPD 691.

Appeal

Albert Gubay, the taxpayer, appealed against the decision of the Court of Appeal (Sir John Donaldson MR and Dillon LJ, Sir Denys Buckley dissenting) ([1983] 2 All ER 976, [1983] 1 WLR 709) on 15 April 1983 upholding the decision of Vinelott J ([1981] STC 721) on 6 July 1981 dismissing his appeal by way of case stated (set out at [1981] STC 722–730) from the determination of the Commissioners for the Special Purposes of the Income Tax Acts confirming an assessment to capital gains tax for the year 1972–73 in respect of a gift of certain shares by Mr Gubay to his wife. The facts are set out in the opinion of Lord Fraser.

Stewart Bates QC and *Robert Venables* for Mr Gubay.
Andrew Morritt QC and *Robert Carnwath* for the Crown.

Their Lordships took time for consideration.

26 January. The following opinions were delivered.

LORD FRASER OF TULLYBELTON. My Lords, this appeal is concerned with a claim by the Revenue for capital gains tax from the appellant (Mr Gubay) in respect of a gift of shares made by him to his wife. Mr Gubay's liability to the tax depends on whether Mrs Gubay was, at the date of the gift, 'a married woman living with her husband' within the meaning of the provisions of the Finance Act 1965 relating to capital gains tax. If she was, Mr Gubay is not liable for capital gains tax on the gift. If she was not, Mr Gubay is liable for tax on chargeable gains of some £1·4 m in respect of the gift. So far, the Revenue have been successful in upholding the assessment in principle before the Special Commissioners, before Vinelott J ([1981] STC 721) and before the Court of Appeal (Sir John Donaldson MR and Dillon LJ, Sir Denys Buckley dissenting) ([1983] 2 All ER 976, [1983] 1 WLR 709).

Both Mr Gubay and his wife were resident and ordinarily resident in the United Kingdom up to 4 April 1972. On that date Mrs Gubay ceased to be resident or ordinarily resident in the United Kingdom, and she was not so resident at any time during the year of assessment 6 April 1972 to 5 April 1973. She was absent from the United Kingdom throughout that year. Mr Gubay continued to be resident or ordinarily resident in the United Kingdom until 28 October 1972 when he left the United Kingdom and was neither resident nor ordinarily resident here for the remainder of the year of assessment 1972–73. Between 4 April and 28 October 1972 Mrs Gubay lived mainly in the Isle of

Man, where Mr Gubay visited her frequently. At all relevant times Mr and Mrs Gubay were living together in the ordinary sense of that expression. The gift of shares was made on 7 July 1972.

Capital gains tax, of the long-term type with which this appeal is concerned, was introduced by s 19 of the Finance Act 1965. A person is chargeable to the tax in respect of chargeable gains accruing to him in a year of assessment during 'any part of which' he is resident or ordinarily resident in the United Kingdom: see s 20. Mr Gubay, having been resident in the United Kingdom for part of the year of assessment 1972–73, is in principle chargeable in respect of gains accruing during that year. Assets which are disposed of by way of gift are deemed to have been disposed of by the donor for a consideration equal to their market value: see s 22(4)(a). Mr Gubay will therefore be chargeable to tax on the gain which was realised on the disposal of the shares, unless he can rely on the exemption under para 20 of Sch 7 to the 1965 Act in favour of disposals between spouses where the wife is a married woman living with her husband. That paragraph provides as follows:

'(1) If, in any year of assessment, and in the case of a woman who in that year of assessment is a married woman living with her husband, the man disposes of an asset to the wife . . . both shall be treated as if the asset was acquired from the one making the disposal for a consideration of such amount as would secure that on the disposal neither a gain or a loss would accrue to the one making the disposal . . .'

Section 45(3) of the 1965 Act provided as follows:

'References in this Part of this Act to a married woman living with her husband should be construed in accordance with section 361(1)(2) of the Income Tax Act 1952.'

Section 361 of the Income Tax Act 1952 has been repealed and replaced in almost identical terms by s 42 of the Income and Corporation Taxes Act 1970, which was a consolidating Act. Section 42 was the section in force during the tax year 1972–73, but I think it is simpler to refer to s 361 as if it had not been superseded. It was in the following terms:

'(1) A married woman shall be treated for income tax purposes as living with her husband unless either—(a) they are separated under an order of a court of competent jurisdiction or by deed of separation; or (b) they are in fact separated in such circumstances that the separation is likely to be permanent.

(2) Where a married woman is living with her husband and either—(a) one of them is, and one of them is not, resident in the United Kingdom for a year of assessment; or (b) both of them are resident in the United Kingdom for a year of assessment but one of them is, and one of them is not, absent from the United Kingdom throughout that year, the same consequences shall follow for income tax purposes as would have followed if, throughout that year of assessment, they had been in fact separated in such circumstances that the separation was likely to be permanent:

Provided that where this subsection applies and the net aggregate amount of income tax (including surtax) falling to be borne by the husband and the wife for the year is greater than it would have been but for the provisions of this subsection, the [Board] shall cause such relief to be given (by the reduction of such assessments on the husband or the wife or the repayment of such tax paid (by deduction or otherwise) by the husband or the wife as [the Board] may direct) as will reduce the said net aggregate amount by the amount of the excess.'

The only question is whether on 7 July 1972 Mrs Gubay fell under the description of a married woman living with her husband if that expression is construed in accordance with s 361(1)(2) of the 1952 Act. The question can be narrowed down considerably. It is common ground, and is indeed obvious, that neither paragraph of sub-s (1) of s 361 applies because Mr and Mrs Gubay were not separated by order of the court or by deed, nor were they in fact separated permanently or at all. So there is nothing in that subsection to prevent Mrs Gubay being treated as living with her husband in 1972–73. It is also common ground that para (*b*) of sub-s (2) is not applicable because one of the spouses (Mrs Gubay) was not resident in the United Kingdom for the year of assessment 1972–73. The live issue is whether para (*a*) of sub-s (2) of s 361 applies, on the basis that Mr Gubay was, and Mrs Gubay was not, resident in the United Kingdom for the year of assessment 1972–73, and, if it does apply, what consequences follow for the purposes of capital gains tax, having regard to the later provisions of sub-s (2).

In the Court of Appeal Sir Denys Buckley decided in favour of Mr Gubay on the ground that no part of sub-s (2) gives any guidance as to the proper construction of the expression 'a married woman living with her husband'. He therefore treated the reference in s 45(3) of the 1965 Act to sub-s (2) of s 361 of the 1952 Act as mere surplusage. I cannot agree with that course, for two reasons. In the first place Parliament has referred in s 45(3) not merely to s 361 but expressly to 'section 361(1)(2)'. Parliament must therefore have considered that it was possible to obtain guidance as to the construction of the expression from both subsections. The court is therefore, in my opinion, not entitled to dismiss the reference to sub-s (2) as surplusage. Secondly, if we were to treat sub-s (2) as having no bearing on the construction of the expression, we would be giving an unduly limited meaning to the word 'construed' in s 45(3). It is evidently not used there in a very strict sense. Even sub-s (1) of s 361 does not, strictly speaking, deal with construction; it does not provide that the expression married woman living with her husband 'means' so and so, but only, that a married woman shall be 'treated for income tax purposes as' living with her husband unless she is separated in one of the ways there specified. By way of contrast examples of provisions for construction in the strict sense are found in s 45(2) of the 1965 Act which provides in several places that a certain expression 'has the meaning assigned to it' in another section. The word 'construed' should, I think, be read in relation to sub-s (2) in the same rather broad sense as it is in relation to sub-s (1).

Subsection (2) deals with cases which are the opposite of those dealt with in sub-s (1), that is to say with cases where a married woman *is* living with her husband in fact, and it provides that in the circumstances there mentioned 'the same consequences shall follow for income tax purposes' as would have followed if they had been separated. The practical effect of that provision seems to me to be not very different from that of a provision that, in the circumstances mentioned, the woman is to be 'treated for income tax purposes as' separated from her husband. Regarded in that way, sub-s (2) gives just as much guidance on construction as sub-s (1). I am therefore of opinion that, subject always to any effect the proviso to sub-s (2) may have, the effect of the main part of sub-s (2) is that Mrs Gubay is to be treated for income tax purposes, and therefore also for capital gains tax purposes, as not living with her husband for the year 1972–73 because they fall within para (*a*) of s 361(2). Were it not for the proviso, I would therefore agree with the conclusion of Dillon LJ on this point (see [1983] 2 All ER 976 at 982, [1983] 1 WLR 709 at 718).

I turn now to consider the proviso to sub-s (2) of s 361. It has been suggested that the proviso should be disregarded, for one of two reasons. The first reason was that it was said to be excluded by the terms of s 45(3) of the 1965 Act. This argument derives such plausibility as it has from the unusual style in which s 45(3) has been drafted, in respect that it refers to 'section 361(1)(2)'. The omission of 'and' between (1) and (2) is unusual, though not unique (see the Capital Gains Tax Act 1979, s 60(*c*)) but, so far as I can see, it is irrelevant for present purposes. A more substantial point is that s 361 only has two subsections, and it is difficult to see why the draftsman did not simply refer to 'section 361'. A suspicion even rose in the course of argument that '361(1)(2)' might have been a misprint but I am satisfied that that is not so. We have confirmed with the Clerk of the Parliaments that s 45(3) is printed exactly as it was enacted. But it does seem possible that 'section 361(1)(2)' is intended to mean something different from simply 'section 361' and

the suggestion was that it was intended to cut out the proviso to sub-s (2). This view
seems to have commended itself to Sir John Donaldson MR (see [1983] 2 All ER 976 at
984, [1983] 1 WLR 709 at 720) but he did not consider it at any length. I do not think it
can be right. In the first place the proviso is part of sub-s (2). If there were any doubt
about that, the doubt is removed by the terms of the proviso itself which opens with the
words 'provided that, where *this subsection* applies . . .'. Secondly, disregard of the proviso
on this ground seems to me to involve making two highly speculative suppositions: (1)
that Parliament intended to exclude some part of s 361 and (2) that the particular part to
be excluded was the proviso to sub-s (2). I am not aware of any convention of statutory
draftsmanship that would support these speculations and in my view the conclusion is
unwarranted.

The second reason why it is said that the proviso should be excluded is that it does not
give guidance on construing the expression in question. That is literally correct, but I
have already explained why in my view the direction to construe the expression 'in
accordance with section 361(1)(2)' has to be taken in a broad sense. I think its effect is
that s 361 is to apply to capital gains tax as nearly as possible in the same way as it applies
to income tax. That is the same as saying that wherever the section refers to income tax
it is to be read as referring also to capital gains tax. If that is correct then the whole of the
section must apply including the proviso so far as it can be applied, and any benefit that
would be conferred by the proviso for income tax purposes must also be conferred for
capital gains tax purposes. Where sub-s (2) applies, with the consequence that a married
couple are to be treated for tax purposes as separated, the result (apart from the proviso)
may be advantageous to them for capital gains tax purposes in some respects (for example
they may not be limited to one main residence: see s 29(8) of the 1965 Act) and
disadvantageous in other respects, for example in the present case. The effect of the
proviso as originally drafted is that where the subsection would operate to the disadvantage
of the spouses by increasing the amount of income tax payable by them, relief is to be
given to the husband or to the wife so as to cancel out the excess. The effect of s 45(3) is,
in my opinion, that the same relief must be given where the subsection would operate to
their disadvantage in respect of capital gains tax.

Having regard to the views I have expressed it is unnecessary for me to consider the
argument for Mr Gubay which apparently occupied a large part of the time in the Court
of Appeal and turned on the meaning of the expression 'for a year of assessment' in
s 361(2)(a).

For these reasons I would allow this appeal.

I understand that the majority of your Lordships is in favour of allowing the appeal by
upholding Mr Gubay's argument on the proviso, but as that argument was advanced for
the first time when the case reached this House, it would not be right for Mr Gubay to
have full costs of the litigation. On the other hand the difficulty has been caused entirely
by an exceptionally obscure piece of drafting for which Mr Gubay is in no way to blame.
I would suggest that justice could be done by giving Mr Gubay his costs in this House
and making no order for costs to or for either party in the courts below.

LORD SCARMAN. My Lords, Pt III of the Finance Act 1965 introduced into the fiscal
law the capital gains tax as we now know it. The question in this appeal is what meaning
is to be attributed to references in Pt III of that Act to 'a married woman living with her
husband'. Section 45(3) of the 1965 Act purports to answer the question by referring the
questioner to 'section 361(1)(2) of the Income Tax Act 1952'. If the draftsman believed,
as he surely did, that the reference would provide the answer to the question, the progress
of this litigation will have sadly disappointed him. The true meaning of s 45(3) is
obscure: and s 361 of the 1952 Act, in the interpretative role which it was given in 1965,
answers no questions but poses several problems. At the end of the day this little piece of
legislation by reference has given rise to a prolonged and confusing litigation, which
would be laughable if it were not for the serious waste of the time and money of the
taxpayer and the Crown which has been its consequence.

My Lords, I have the misfortune to differ from the rest of your Lordships on the related problems of the construction of these two sections to which the question in the appeal gives rise. Since, as I understand it, the case raises no important question of legal principle, I shall be brief, conscious that my view, however tenaciously I may hold it, is not the law.

The issue arises in respect of a year of assessment (1972–73) which was subsequent to the consolidation of the income tax statutes in 1970 but before the consolidation of the capital gains tax legislation in 1979. Neither consolidation altered the provisions which fall to be construed. To avoid confusion, I will discuss the issue by reference to the Income Tax Act 1952 and Pt III of the Finance Act 1965.

On 7 July 1972 Mr Gubay, the appellant, made a gift of shares to his wife. It is this disposal which gives rise to the claim for tax. Mr Gubay was resident, or ordinarily resident, in the United Kingdom during part of the year of assessment (1972–73) and is, therefore, liable to capital gains tax on the disposal, if it gave rise to a chargeable gain. Mr Gubay submits that it did not, and relies on para 20(1) of Sch 7 to the 1965 Act which provides, so far as material, that if in a year of assessment, and in the case of 'a woman who in that year was a married woman living with her husband', a man disposes of an asset to his wife, the disposal shall be treated as for a consideration of such amount as would secure that neither a gain nor a loss would accrue to him. Put very simply, the effect of the paragraph is that the wife steps into the position of her husband: he is deemed to make no gain or loss: if later she disposes of the asset or part of it, she will be treated for the purposes of the tax as having acquired the asset for the price her husband originally paid for it. No chargeable gain (or loss), therefore, arises on the disposal, but a chargeable gain will arise if later the wife sells the asset or any part of it for more than her husband gave to acquire it.

Mrs Gubay was a married woman living with her husband during the fiscal year 1972–73. Their married life had not then, nor has it since, suffered a break-down. They live a united married life. Though not separated, they were in 1972–73 physically apart for substantial periods of the year. She ceased to be resident in the United Kingdom on 4 April 1972 when she went to live in the Isle of Man: he continued to make his ordinary residence in the United Kingdom until 28 October 1972, after which date he also ceased to reside here. During the months April to October 1972 he paid frequent visits to the Isle of Man where she resided.

If the term 'a married woman living with her husband' means in the context of the 1965 Act what in common speech it says, Mrs Gubay was living with her husband, and para 20(1) of Sch 7 to that Act applies. Mr Gubay would, therefore, succeed, for there would be no chargeable gain. But the term does not have its ordinary meaning in the context of the capital gains tax legislation, for s 45(3) of the 1965 Act provides:

'References in this Part of this Act to a married woman living with her husband should be construed in accordance with section 361(1)(2) of the Income Tax Act 1952.'

Section 45 of the 1965 Act is an interpretation section. Subsection (3) offers guidance, but no definition. Note two points: the term 'a married woman living with her husband' *should* (not 'shall') be construed in accordance with specific provisions of the 1952 Act, and those provisions are specified as '*section 361(1)(2)*' of that Act. The choice of the auxiliary word 'should', which denotes possibility, probability, preference, or desire rather than a mandatory command, reveals, I think, no more than the draftsman's awareness that he was directing that the term 'a married woman living with her husband' when used in Pt III of the 1965 Act should be construed in accordance with a section which was not itself a defining or interpretative provision.

But what the draftsman intended by the words 'in accordance with section 361(1)(2)' of the 1952 Act is wrapped in mystery. That section contains two subsections, (1) and (2), to which a proviso is attached. The proviso qualifies sub-s (2). A reference to s 361 simpliciter would have sufficed. Why did he trouble to specify, therefore, the two subsections? Did he intend to exclude the proviso? But he cannot have so intended, since

the proviso is part of sub-s (2) which he expressly includes, its effect being to limit the
a consequences of the subsection. Or did he, knowing that s 361 was not designed as an
interpretative section, include a reference to the two subsections so as to emphasise that
both 'should' be regarded in construing references in the 1965 Act to a married woman
living with her husband. I was attracted at one stage of the argument by the proposition
that the reference to the two subsections, when a reference to the section simpliciter
would have sufficed, must mean that the proviso should be disregarded. But I am satisfied
b that this will not do: the proviso is part of sub-s (2) which it qualifies.

Section 45(3), therefore, refers us to the whole of s 361, the full terms of which I now
set out:

'(1) A married woman shall be treated for income tax purposes as living with her
husband unless either—(a) they are separated under an order of a court of competent
jurisdiction or by deed of separation; or (b) they are in fact separated in such
c circumstances that the separation is likely to be permanent.

(2) Where a married woman is living with her husband and either—(a) one of
them is, and one of them is not, resident in the United Kingdom for a year of
assessment; or (b) both of them are resident in the United Kingdom for a year of
assessment but one of them is, and one of them is not, absent from the United
Kingdom throughout that year, the same consequences shall follow for income tax
d purposes as would have followed if, throughout that year of assessment, they had
been in fact separated in such circumstances that the separation was likely to be
permanent:

Provided that where this subsection applies and the net aggregate amount of
income tax (including surtax) falling to be borne by the husband and the wife for
the year is greater than it would have been but for the provisions of this subsection,
e the Commissioners of Inland Revenue shall cause such relief to be given (by the
reduction of such assessments on the husband or the wife or the repayment of such
tax paid (by deduction or otherwise) by the husband or the wife as those
Commissioners may direct) as will reduce the said net aggregate amount by the
amount of the excess.'

f Subsection (1) gives the ordinary meaning of a married woman living with her
husband. Standing by itself, it would include Mrs Gubay's situation in the fiscal year
1972–73. Subsection (2) is a very strange provision to be given an interpretative function.
It begins by asserting and assuming what is in issue, 'where a married woman is living
with her husband', and then declares that in certain specified circumstances the same
consequences shall follow for income tax purposes as would have followed if the man
g and wife had in fact separated, the separation being likely to be permanent. Confronted
with the subsection, Sir Denys Buckley in the Court of Appeal could find no guidance in
it as to the construction of the term 'a married woman living with her husband' when
used in the 1965 Act and rejected it as surplusage (see [1983] 2 All ER 976 at 979, 981,
[1983] 1 WLR 709 at 714–715, 717). I have been greatly tempted to follow him. But to
do so would, I think, be flatly to contradict the express reference in s 45(3) to the
h subsection. Parliament intended the courts (and others) to have regard to sub-s (2).

If one does what Parliament has plainly said one should do, I do not doubt that the
subsection, when transplanted into its role of guidance for the purposes of the 1965 Act,
is saying that for capital gains tax purposes there are circumstances, which it sets out, in
which a married woman who is living with her husband is to be treated as one who is
not. It is, however, suggested that this is altogether too subtle an interpretation of the
j words of the subsection. But to my mind it is the suggestion which is too subtle. If the
'same consequences' are to follow as if she were separated, she is to be treated for the
purposes of the subsection as if she were separated.

The circumstances in which she is to be so treated are set out in (a) and (b) of the
subsection. Mrs Gubay falls within (a); for her husband was, but she was not, resident in
the United Kingdom for the year of assessment. Once it is accepted that regard must be
paid to the subsection in construing Pt III of the 1965 Act, it follows from the body of

the subsection that for capital gains purposes Mrs Gubay should be treated as 'separated' from her husband in the year of assessment 1972–73.

But it has been submitted by Mr Gubay (for the first time in this House) that the proviso indicates the contrary: that is to say, it cancels out any guidance towards 'separation' which might be found in the body of the subsection. Like Sir John Donaldson MR in the Court of Appeal, I do not find the proviso any help in construing the capital gains tax legislation. The proviso merely imposes a specific duty on the Revenue to give relief for income tax purposes against a consequence of treating a woman as separated from her husband under (a) or (b) of the subsection. It offers no guidance as to the meaning of 'a married woman living with her husband': on the contrary, it assumes for its purpose that 'the subsection applies'. It accepts without contradiction what the subsection says, namely that a woman who falls within (a) or (b) is to be treated as if she was separated from her husband save in one respect only.

Accordingly, in my view, we must construe para 20(1) of Sch 7 to the 1965 Act as not covering the disposal of shares on 7 July 1972. Mrs Gubay, on the proper construction of the Schedule, was not, for the purposes of the capital gains tax, to be treated as a married woman living with her husband at the relevant time. I would dismiss the appeal.

LORD BRIDGE OF HARWICH. My Lords, until 1972 Mr and Mrs Gubay were both ordinarily resident in the United Kingdom. During the year 1972 both ceased to be so resident, ordinarily or at all, but the effective date of cesser in the wife's case was 4 April, in the husband's 28 October. There was never any kind of rift in their matrimonial relationship and between the two dates mentioned Mr Gubay made frequent visits to his wife, then residing in the Isle of Man. On 7 July 1972 he gave her a block of shares which, had he sold them at their market value, would have realised for him a gain of nearly £1·4 m chargeable to tax under the Finance Act 1965.

Married couples do not enjoy many fiscal advantages over those who live together unmarried, indeed the reverse is normally the case, but at least, as is well known, spouses can ordinarily make gifts of capital assets to each other without incurring any liability to capital gains tax. It must, therefore, I think, have occasioned as much surprise to the officials of the Inland Revenue as to Mr Gubay himself to discover that, as the Revenue contend, he had chosen to make the gift of shares to his wife in circumstances which temporarily deprived him of this immunity. Had he made the gift before 4 April 1972, or after 5 April 1973, there would clearly have been no capital gains tax liability. By making it on 7 July 1972, he was, the Crown says, voluntarily though no doubt unwittingly, making a handsome gift to them as well as to his wife. If the Crown is right, the unfortunate Mr Gubay must feel that he has fallen into a trap for the unwary set for him by the extreme obscurity of the legislative provisions which fall to be applied. The extent of the obscurity is perhaps best illustrated by the fact that the point which the majority of your Lordships find decisive of the appeal was first taken before your Lordships' House, and does not seem to have occurred to the mind of any of the Special Commissioners, the learned judge, the members of the Court of Appeal (except possibly Sir John Donaldson MR), or the learned counsel engaged at any of the three earlier stages of this litigation.

For the purpose of assessing chargeable gains and allowable losses under the 1965 Act, a disposal by way of gift is 'deemed to be for a consideration equal to the market value of the asset': see s 22(4)(a). But by para 20(1) of Sch 7, in the case of 'a married woman living with her husband', the disposal of an asset by one spouse to the other is treated as a 'disposal for a consideration of such amount as would secure that on the disposal neither a gain or a loss would accrue to the one making the disposal.' Section 45(3), as amended by the Income and Corporation Taxes Act 1970, provides:

'References in this Part of this Act to a married woman living with her husband should be construed in accordance with section 42(1)(2) of the Income and Corporation Taxes Act 1970.'

Section 42 of the 1970 Act re-enacts without amendment provisions first enacted by s 34
of the Finance Act 1950 and re-enacted by s 361 of the Income Tax Act 1952. The section
provides:

> '(1) A married woman shall be treated for income tax purposes as living with her
> husband unless—(a) they are separated under an order of a court of competent
> jurisdiction, or by deed of separation, or (b) they are in fact separated in such
> circumstances that the separation is likely to be permanent.
>
> (2) Where a married woman is living with her husband and either—(a) one of
> them is, and one of them is not, resident in the United Kingdom for a year of
> assessment, or (b) both of them are resident in the United Kingdom for a year of
> assessment, but one of them is, and one of them is not, absent from the United
> Kingdom throughout that year, the same consequences shall follow for income tax
> purposes as would have followed if, throughout that year of assessment, they had
> been in fact separated in such circumstances that the separation was likely to be
> permanent:
>
> Provided that, where this subsection applies and the net aggregate amount of
> income tax falling to be borne by the husband and the wife for the year is greater
> than it would have been but for the provisions of this subsection, the Board shall
> cause such relief to be given (by the reduction of such assessments on the husband
> or the wife or the repayment of such tax paid (by deduction or otherwise) by the
> husband or the wife as the Board may direct) as will reduce the said net aggregate
> amount by the amount of the excess.'

The question is whether Mrs Gubay in the year of assessment 1972–73, when Mr
Gubay undoubtedly remained liable to United Kingdom income and capital gains tax,
was or was not 'a married woman living with her husband' construed 'in accordance with
section 42(1)(2) of the 1970 Act'. If she was, the appeal succeeds; if not, it fails.

The first puzzling feature of s 45(3) of the 1965 Act is the omission of the conjunctive
'and' between the references to sub-ss (1) and (2) of s 42 of the 1970 Act. But counsel for
the Crown has drawn our attention to other examples, both in the 1965 Act and in other
revenue statutes, of this style of draftsmanship being used, albeit not consistently. No
doubt we must read the provision as a reference to s 42(1) and (2). But what is the point
of referring by number to the two subsections of a section which has only two? If the
reference were to section 42 simpliciter, there would be no problem at all. Subsection (1)
does, in effect, provide what amounts to a definition, albeit expressed to be 'for income
tax purposes', of the phrase 'a married woman living with her husband'. She is a woman
who is not separated by court order, by deed, or in such circumstances that the separation
is likely to be permanent. Subsection (2), on the other hand, does not purport to add to,
subtract from, or in any way to qualify that definition. On the contrary, as its opening
words show, it is dealing throughout with a woman who is within the definition. What
it provides is that, although she *is* 'a married woman living with her husband', in certain
circumstances certain limited tax consequences are to follow as if she were not. Thus,
apart from the express reference to sub-s (2) in s 45(3) of the 1965 Act, no one would
dream of looking beyond sub-s (1) in construing references in that Act to 'a married
woman living with her husband'.

In the Court of Appeal ([1983] 2 All ER 976, [1983] 1 WLR 709) the first ground of
Sir Denys Buckley's dissenting judgment in favour of Mr Gubay was that it was
impossible to obtain from sub-s (2) any guidance as to the construction of the phrase 'a
married woman living with her husband', and that the court was therefore constrained
to reject the express reference to sub-s (2) as surplusage. I am much impressed by this
view. I find the principle concisely stated by Brett J in *Stone v Yeovil Corp* (1876) 1 CPD
691 at 701, where he said:

> 'It is a canon of construction that, if it be possible, effect must be given to every
> word of an Act of Parliament or other document; but that, if there be a word or a
> phrase therein to which no sensible meaning can be given, it must be eliminated.'

No doubt it is a strong application of this principle to hold that it renders nugatory in a statute not merely a word or a phrase but the express incorporation by reference of a whole subsection. I am far from saying that Sir Denys Buckley was wrong to do so. But the point is a difficult one. In the end I prefer to reach no conclusion on this ground but to proceed on the basis that, however intractable the problem, sub-s (2) must somehow be forced to yield up its arcane meaning as an aid to the construction of the relevant words in the 1965 Act.

A view which may possibly (but not certainly) be implicit in the short passage in the judgment of Sir John Donaldson MR (see [1983] 2 All ER 976 at 984, [1983] 1 WLR 709 at 720) is that the reference to sub-s (2) should be read as a reference only to so much of the subsection as precedes the colon, on the ground that the proviso is printed as a separate paragraph following on, but distinct from, what, on this view, may be regarded as the body of the subsection. The difficulty about this view is that the proviso, as the opening words 'Provided that, where this subsection applies' make clear beyond doubt, is itself part and parcel of the subsection. Hence, this view attributes to the draftsman a degree of incompetence or obscurantism, or both, of which I find it impossible to suppose he could have been guilty.

A very much more subtle argument is advanced by counsel for the Crown in an attempt to extract from sub-s (2) so much of the subsection as the Crown wishes to treat as an aid to construction, but without reference to the tax consequences contemplated by the subsection, subject as those consequences are to the limitation imposed by the proviso, which is fatal to the Crown's contention. According to counsel's argument, to distil from sub-s (2) so much of the language as is relevant to the construction of the words 'a married woman living with her husband' and to exclude the rest, it is necessary to strike out the words 'the same consequences shall follow for income tax purposes as would have followed if', and to substitute the words 'they shall be treated as if'. On the same principle, so runs the argument, the proviso can be disregarded as irrelevant to construction.

Ingenious as this argument undoubtedly is, I cannot accept it. Not only does it require the subsection to be radically rewritten, but it also depends on what I regard as a false antithesis between parts of the subsection which are, and parts of the subsection which are not, capable of giving guidance in construing the words 'a married woman living with her husband' in the capital gains tax legislation. If the subsection can be looked at for that purpose at all, it must be looked at as a whole. Whatever the form of s 42(2) of the 1970 Act and its predecessors, its substance has always been clear. Where a married woman living with her husband is temporarily separated from him in the circumstances contemplated by sub-s (2)(a) or (b), they are to be treated as permanently separated to the extent that separate tax assessment will be to their advantage, but not so as to increase their aggregate liability to tax. In short, the subsection is essentially a relieving, not a taxing, provision. If this provision has to be applied with reference to a married woman living with her husband in construing the capital gains tax legislation, the only sensible meaning which, in my opinion, can be attributed to it, is that it was intended to be applied to a married couple's capital gains tax liability by analogy with its application to their income tax liability. This result can be achieved without doing any violence to the statutory language. All that is necessary is that s 42 of the 1970 Act is to be read into the capital gains tax legislation in its entirety, but with the substitution of the phrase 'capital gains tax purposes' for the phrase 'income tax purposes' wherever the latter occurs. In the result, in a year of assessment to which sub-s (2)(a) or (b) applies, each spouse can profit from separate assessment, eg by realising gains without liability to tax up to the limit of the current statutory exemption, but their aggregate capital gains tax liability cannot exceed what it would have been if there had been no temporary separation.

If any reinforcement of this conclusion in favour of Mr Gubay is needed, I find it it in the time-honoured principle that the subject is not to be taxed except by clear words. At all material times, Mrs Gubay was a married woman living with her husband both in the ordinary meaning of that phrase and in accordance with the definition provided by s 42(1) of the 1970 Act. Her husband's gift of shares to her in 1972 was, therefore, on the

face of it, a disposal governed by para 20(1) of Sch 7 to the 1965 Act, not by s 22(4). If the
a Crown is to make good its claim to charge capital gains tax in respect of that disposal
pursuant to s 22(4), it must show that the incorporation by reference of s 42(2) of the
1970 Act clearly entitles it to do so. I must accept, in deference to my noble and learned
friend Lord Scarman, that the statutory language can arguably be read so as to lead to this
result. I cannot understand, however, how it can possibly be said to do so clearly.

The only issue argued before the Special Commissioners and the judge, and the main
b issue argued in the Court of Appeal, turned on the construction of the words in s 42(2)(a)
of the 1970 Act, 'resident in the United Kingdom for a year of assessment'. On the view
I take this issue ceases to be relevant, but I should add that, in my opinion, the Special
Commissioners, the judge, and the majority of the Court of Appeal reached the right
conclusion on this point for the reasons given in the judgment of Dillon LJ. In this House
we have had the advantage of being referred to *Browning v Duckworth* [1935] 1 KB 605.
c This shows the previous state of the law which s 34(2)(a) of the Finance Act 1950 was
plainly intended to reverse. It entirely supports the conclusion on the point of the Special
Commissioners and the judge, affirmed by the majority of the Court of Appeal.

I would allow the appeal. On the question of costs I concur in the proposal made by
my noble and learned friend Lord Fraser.

d **LORD BRANDON OF OAKBROOK.** My Lords, this appeal concerns a married
couple, Mr and Mrs Gubay, to whom I shall refer collectively as 'the spouses'. More
particularly the appeal concerns the liability of Mr Gubay for capital gains tax for the
year of assessment 1972–73 (the relevant year).

During the relevant year Mrs Gubay was neither resident nor ordinarily resident in
the United Kingdom. Mr Gubay on the other hand was, during part of the relevant year,
e namely from 6 April to 28 October, both resident and ordinarily resident there. Although
the spouses were geographically separated for substantial parts of the relevant year, their
marriage was at all material times a happy one, and, when circumstances permitted, they
lived together in a shared home in either the Isle of Man or New Zealand.

On 7 July in the relevant year Mr Gubay made a gift to Mrs Gubay of 479,638 shares
in Kwik Save Discount Group Ltd (the gift). It is common ground between Mr Gubay
f and the Revenue that, during the relevant year, he became liable for capital gains tax on
£7,650, that being the amount of chargeable gains arising out of transactions other than
the gift. It is contended for the Crown, but disputed by Mr Gubay, that he became liable
for further capital gains tax on chargeable gains of £1,392,315 arising out of the gift,
making a total of chargeable gains of £1,399,965.

Having been assessed for capital gains tax for the relevant year on chargeable gains
g which included those alleged to arise out of the gift, Mr Gubay appealed unsuccessfully
against such assessment, firstly to the Special Commissioners, secondly by case stated to
the High Court (Vinelott J) (see [1981] STC 721) and, thirdly, to the Court of Appeal (Sir
John Donaldson MR, Dillon LJ and Sir Denys Buckley) (see [1983] 2 All ER 976, [1983]
1 WLR 709). The decision of the Court of Appeal was, however, a majority one only,
with Sir Denys Buckley dissenting. The husband now brings a fourth appeal, with the
h leave of the Court of Appeal, to your Lordships' House.

My Lords, liability for capital gains tax is dealt with in Pt III of the Finance Act 1965.
It is not in dispute that, unless Mrs Gubay was, during the relevant year, living with Mr
Gubay within the meaning of that expression in Pt III of the 1965 Act, the further
assessment in respect of the gift was correctly made by the Inland Revenue pursuant to
ss 20(1), 22(1) and 22(4) of that Act.

j The 1965 Act, however, contains a special provision relating to spouses living together
during any particular year of assessment. This provision, which is made applicable by
s 29(9) of the 1965 Act, is to be found in para 20 of Sch 7 to it. That paragraph provides:

'(1) If, in any year of assessment, and in the case of a woman who in that year of
assessment is a married woman living with her husband, the man disposes of an
asset to the wife, or the wife disposes of an asset to the husband, both shall be treated

as if the asset was acquired from the one making the disposal for a consideration of such an amount as would secure that on the disposal neither a gain or a loss would accrue to the one making the disposal . . .'

The effect of this provision, in the case of spouses who are living together during any particular year of assessment, even though both are resident or ordinarily resident in the United Kingdom, is that disposals of assets between the two of them, whether by gift or otherwise, can never give rise to chargeable gains for the purposes of capital gains tax for that year.

If the matter stopped there, it may well be that no problem would arise. The legislature, however, thought it necessary to deal expressly with the meaning to be given, for the purposes of Pt III of the 1965 Act, to the expression 'a married woman living with her husband'. The method adopted by the legislature to achieve this end was to enact s 45(3) of the 1965 Act, which provides:

'References in this part of this Act to a married woman living with her husband should be construed in accordance with section 361(1)(2) of the Income Tax Act 1952.'

Section 361 of the Income Tax Act 1952 has since been repealed and re-enacted in almost identical terms in s 42 of the Income and Corporation Taxes Act 1970. I shall, however, for convenience treat the relevant provisions as being those of s 361 of the 1952 Act.

Section 361 of that Act was in these terms:

'(1) A married woman shall be treated for income tax purposes as living with her husband unless either—(a) they are separated under an order of a court of competent jurisdiction; or (b) they are in fact separated in such circumstances that the separation is likely to be permanent.

(2) Where a married woman is living with her husband and either—(a) one of them is, and one of them is not, resident in the United Kingdom for a year of assessment; or (b) both of them are resident in the United Kingdom for a year of assessment but one of them is, and one of them is not, absent from the United Kingdom throughout that year, the same consequences shall follow for income tax purposes as would have followed if, throughout that year of assessment, they had been in fact separated in such circumstances that the separation was likely to be permanent:

Provided that where this subsection applies and the net aggregate amount of income tax (including surtax) falling to be borne by the husband and the wife for the year is greater than it would have been but for the provisions of this subsection, the Commissioners of Inland Revenue shall cause such relief to be given (by the reduction of such assessments on the husband or the wife or the repayment of such tax paid (by deduction or otherwise) by the husband or the wife as those Commissioners may direct) as will reduce the said net aggregate amount by the amount of the excess.'

There are certain significant features of both s 45(3) of the 1965 Act and s 361 of the 1952 Act to which attention should be drawn. Dealing first with s 45(3) of the 1965 Act, there are the following significant features. Firstly, it is, in form at least, a provision relating, and relating only, to construction; it is not, in form at least, a provision incorporating into and applying to Pt III of the 1965 Act s 361 of the 1952 Act. Secondly, in so far as it is a provision relating to construction, it is concerned, and concerned only, with the meaning to be given to the expression 'a married woman living with her husband' in Pt III of the 1965 Act. Thirdly, it provides that the meaning to be given to that expression in that part of the 1965 Act is to be in accordance with s 361(1)(2) of the 1952 Act. Fourthly, the reference to 'section 361(1)(2)' of the 1952 Act is peculiar in two ways: first, s 361 only has two subsections, namely sub-s (1) and sub-s (2), so that a reference to s 361 simpliciter would, one would have thought, have been sufficient; and,

secondly, the word 'and', which one would have expected to find between '(1)' and '(2)',
is absent.

a   Turning, secondly, to s 361 of the 1952 Act, its significant features are these. Firstly,
the only part of the section which contains or consists of a provision relating to
construction is sub-s (1). That subsection defines the circumstances in which a married
woman will, and those in which she will not, for income tax purposes and during a
particular year of assessment, be treated as living with her husband. Secondly, sub-s (2) is
b   not, either in substance or in form, a provision relating to construction; it is rather a
provision relating to deeming a state of affairs to be other than it actually is, and to the
consequences, for certain specified purposes, of such deeming process. It requires that a
married woman, who is in fact living with her husband within the definition contained
in sub-s (1), should in certain specified circumstances be treated, for income tax purposes
and for a particular year of assessment, as if she were not so living. One of those sets of
c   circumstances is specified in para (a) of sub-s (2) and they are these: when one of two
spouses is, and the other is not, resident in the United Kingdom for a particular year of
assessment. Thirdly, the part of sub-s (2) which deals with the consequences of a married
woman being deemed not to be living with her husband when she is in fact doing so has
two parts: firstly, a part containing the requirement the nature of which I have set out
above; and, secondly, a part containing a proviso of some length imposing a crucial
d   limitation or qualification on the effect of such requirement. These two parts are,
however, not separate, either from each other or from paras (a) and (b) which precede
them. On the contrary, the two parts, along with paras (a) and (b), constitute together
sub-s (2) as a whole.

I have not found it altogether easy to discover, with any degree of certainty, the precise
nature of the argument for the Crown, which has prevailed so far with the Special
e   Commissioners, Vinelott J and the majority in the Court of Appeal. The nature of the
argument, as I believe it to be, is this. The effect of s 45(3) of the 1965 Act, on its true
interpretation, is to incorporate into and apply to Pt III of that Act the whole of s 361 of
the 1952 Act, except the proviso which forms the last part of sub-s (2) of that section; and
further, where there occurs, in the provisions so incorporated and applied, the expression
'for income tax purposes', to substitute for it the different expression 'for capital gains tax
f   purposes'.

The result of giving that effect to s 45(3) of the 1965 Act, so the argument goes, is this.
On the facts of the case the spouses were, during the relevant year, in the situation
specified in s 361(2)(a) of the 1952 Act, in that one of them, Mr Gubay, was, and the
other of them, Mrs Gubay, was not, resident in the United Kingdom for that year. This
was so because the expression 'resident in the United Kingdom for a year of assessment',
g   as used in sub-s (2)(a), did not necessarily mean resident in the United Kingdom
throughout the year of assessment concerned, but included in its meaning resident in
the United Kingdom for only a part of such year. Therefore Mrs Gubay was to be treated,
for capital gains tax purposes for the relevant year, as not living with her husband.
Therefore the exemption from liability to capital gains tax in respect of disposals between
spouses contained in para 20 of Sch 7 to the 1965 Act did not apply to the gift. Therefore
h   the Revenue were right in assessing Mr Gubay to capital gains tax on the chargeable gains
arising out of it.

Sir Denys Buckley was not prepared to accept that s 45(3) of the 1965 Act had the effect
set out above, and he had two alternative reasons for being unwilling to do so. His
primary reason was this. Section 45(3) of the 1965 Act is (as I indicated earlier) a provision
relating, and relating only, to construction. It provides that references in Pt III of the
j   1965 Act to 'a married woman living with her husband' should be construed in
accordance with s 361(1)(2) of the 1952 Act. That can only mean that the expression
concerned must be given the same meaning in Pt III of the 1965 Act as is assigned to it
by s 361(1)(2) of the 1952 Act. The only part of s 361 of that Act, however, which assigns
a meaning to the expression concerned is sub-s (1) of that section. Subsection (2) is not (as
I also indicated earlier) a provision relating to construction at all, but is of quite a different

character. Having regard to these matters, the reference in s 45(3) of the 1965 Act to sub-
s (2), as well as sub-s (1), of s 361 of the 1952 Act is a reference to which no sensible or   *a*
effective meaning can be given, with the consequence that such reference should be
treated as surplusage and wholly disregarded. It is, however, necessarily to be implied
that, when applying the meaning of the expression concerned assigned to it by s 361(1)
of the 1952 Act, there should be substituted for the words 'for income tax purposes',
where they occur in the first two lines of that subsection, the words 'for capital gains tax
purposes'.   *b*

The second alternative reason why Sir Denys Buckley was not prepared to accept the
argument for the Crown with regard to the effect of s 45(3) of the 1965 Act was this.
Even assuming that that argument was correct in principle, the expression 'resident in
the United Kingdom for a year of assessment', as used in s 361(2)(a) of the 1952 Act,
meant resident in the United Kingdom throughout such year, and did not mean resident
in the United Kingdom for only a part of it. Mr Gubay was only resident in the United   *c*
Kingdom from 6 April to 28 October in the relevant year, and therefore the spouses did
not come within s 361(2)(a) of the 1952 Act at all. On that basis, the exemption contained
in para 20 of Sch 7 to the 1965 Act did apply to the gift, and the Revenue were again
wrong in assessing Mr Gubay to capital gains tax on the chargeable gains arising from it.

My Lords, both the argument for the Crown, and that on which Sir Denys Buckley
founded his primary reason for not being prepared to accept it, present difficulties. So   *d*
far as the argument for the Crown is concerned, the main difficulty can be expressed in
this way: that, while s 45(3) by its terms only requires the expression 'a married woman
living with her husband' to be construed in accordance with s 361(1)(2) of the 1952 Act,
the argument for the Crown involves reading s 45(3) as if it said something like this:
'The provisions of s 361 of the Income Tax Act 1952 are to be incorporated into and
applied to Pt III of this Act, as if, firstly, the expression "for capital gains tax purposes"   *e*
were substituted for the expression "for income tax purposes" wherever it occurs, and,
secondly, sub-s (2) of the section did not include the proviso to it.' With regard to the
exclusion of the proviso to subsection (2), it was suggested during the course of the
argument before your Lordships that the legislature, by using the peculiar expression
'section 361(1)(2)', was indicating its intention of referring to both subsections of the
section, but at the same time of excluding the proviso to sub-s (2). This suggestion   *f*
appears to me to be entirely speculative, and my reaction to it is to say that, if the
legislature had intended to convey any such intention, it could easily have used plain
words in which to express it. In fact, however, it chose not to do so.

So far as Sir Denys Buckley's primary argument is concerned, it involves wholly
disregarding the presence of '(2)' after 'section 361(1)' in s 45(3) of the 1965 Act. To do
this would be contrary to the fundamental principle that, whenever it is possible to do   *g*
so, effect should be given to each and every part of a statutory provision.

As regards Sir Denys Buckley's alternative reason for rejecting the argument for the
Crown, which it is only fair to say that he expressed with considerable hesitation, I do
not, with great respect, share his view. In my opinion, the expression 'resident in the
United Kingdom for a year of assessment' does not necessarily mean resident in the
United Kingdom throughout such year, but includes in its meaning resident there for   *h*
only a part of it. In this connection it is, to my mind, significant that in s 361(2)(b) both
the expression 'for a year of assessment' and the expression 'throughout that year' are
used. This indicates what one would expect, namely that, when the legislature meant to
say 'throughout a year' it took care to express its meaning in plain words.

My Lords, as I have indicated earlier, both the argument for the Crown which found
favour below, and that on which Sir Denys Buckley founded his primary reason for   *j*
rejecting it, involve substantial difficulties. It is your Lordships' good fortune, however,
not to be compelled to opt for either the one argument or the other.

This is because counsel for Mr Gubay raised for the first time in your Lordships' House,
with your Lordships' leave, a third view of the effect of s 45(3) of the 1965 Act, which,
while not free of all difficulty, presents less difficulty than either of the two views which
have until now been under consideration, and moreover produces a result which appears

reasonably fair from the point of view of taxation policy. The third view so put forward is that the effect of s 45(3) of the 1965 Act is indeed, as the Crown has contended, to incorporate into and apply to Pt III of that Act sub-s (2), as well as sub-s (1), of s 361 of the 1952 Act, and, for the purposes of such incorporation and application, to substitute the expression 'for capital gains tax purposes' for the expression 'for income tax purposes' wherever the latter occurs, but that such incorporation into an application to Pt III of the 1965 Act of sub-s (2) of s 361 of the 1952 Act extends to the whole of sub-s (2), including the proviso to it.

The result of giving s 45(3) of the 1965 Act this effect does not, as I have already said, get over all the difficulties involved in the other two views. It does not get over the difficulty of treating a provision, which by its terms relates only to construction, as if it were a provision relating to incorporation and application. That difficulty must, I think, be accepted and disregarded. The result does, however, get over two difficulties: firstly, that of wholly disregarding the '(2)' in s 45(3) of the 1965 Act (which Sir Denys Buckley's reasoning requires); and, secondly, that of arbitrarily treating the insertion of '(2)' after 'section 361(1)' as bringing in sub-s (2) but without the proviso, which, if the subsection is given its ordinary and natural meaning, is an integral and fundamental part of it.

As for the third view producing a result which appears reasonably fair and sensible from the point of view of taxation policy, the situation resulting from the third view is that where spouses, while not separated in circumstances which are likely to be permanent, are nevertheless separated geographically for the whole or part of a particular year of assessment, they are not, on account of that geographical separation alone, to be liable to a greater aggregate amount of capital gains tax than if they had not been so separated geographically. In substance the third view has the result that the situation of spouses for capital gains tax purposes is made similar to that which already existed for income tax purposes.

My Lords, I am clearly of the opinion that the third view of the effect of s 45(3) of the 1965 Act which I have just been discussing is the correct one, and, as a consequence of that, that the two different views of that effect previously put forward by the Crown on the one hand and preferred by Sir Denys Buckley on the other, must be rejected.

Since I am of that opinion it follows necessarily that I would allow the appeal and set aside the order of Vinelott J dated 6 July 1981 ([1981] STC 721) and the order of the Court of Appeal dated 15 April 1983 ([1983] 2 All ER 976, [1983] 1 WLR 709). As to costs, I think that, having regard to the history of the case, the Crown should pay the costs of Mr Gubay in this House, but that there should be no order for costs in either of the courts below.

LORD BRIGHTMAN. My Lords, the facts essential to the decision in this case can be stated in a few words. Mrs Gubay ceased to be resident in the United Kingdom at the end of the fiscal year 1971–72. Her husband remained resident in the United Kingdom in the next fiscal year until 28 October 1972. On 7 July that year he made to his wife a gift of shares in regard to which there was an unrealised capital gain. Capital gains tax is claimed on that disposal.

The gift had no tax saving objective. If the gift had been made some three months earlier or nine months later there would have been no arguable claim to tax. The tax, if rightly payable, has properly been described as a windfall to the Exchequer. The liability, if any, was purely adventitious. It would however be wrong to criticise the Crown for claiming this windfall and no one does. The Crown has, in general, no option but to claim such tax as a statute says shall be payable. If the statute is obscure, as is here the case, the Crown has in general no option but to ask the court to interpret it.

The general rule is contained in s 20 of the Finance Act 1965. Subject to exceptions provided by the 1965 Act, a person shall be chargeable to capital gains tax in respect of chargeable gains accruing to him in a year of assessment during any part of which he is resident in the United Kingdom, or during which he is ordinarily resident in the United Kingdom. Mr Gubay was resident and ordinarily resident in the United Kingdom during part of the fiscal year 1972–73. A gift is a disposal which is deemed to take place at

market value. Therefore Mr Gubay is liable to capital gains tax in respect of the gift to
Mrs Gubay unless there is an exception provided by the Act.

An important exception is provided. It is to be found in para 20(1) of Sch 7 to the 1965
Act. The language is convoluted but the meaning is plain. If 'a married woman [is] living
with her husband' and the husband gives an asset to his wife, or vice versa, the disposition
shall be deemed to be made for a consideration which yields neither gain nor loss. The
policy of the 1965 Act is clear. Dispositions between husband and wife, if living together,
are exempt. Their aggregate assets are totally unaffected by the disposition.

The 1965 Act took the precaution of defining what was meant by the conception of 'a
married woman living with her husband'. Some situations would be crystal clear. Others
might give rise to doubt. What amounts to a separation? Must there be an order of the
court? Is a separation pursuant to a deed of separation sufficient? What if there is a de
facto separation, which might be temporary or permanent?

These questions were sought to be answered by s 45(3) of the 1965 Act. Unfortunately
the answer was delphic. Section 45 is an interpretation section in the widest sense. It
states what particular words mean; what particular words include; what particular words
do not include; how particular words shall be construed; and how particular situations
shall be treated. To define when a married woman is living with her husband the
draftsman chose the 'shall be construed' formula by reference to a section in another Act
dealing with a different tax. The clarification, as it was supposed to be, of the simple
conception of a married woman living with her husband, was achieved by the following
provision (as amended):

> '(3) References in this Part of this Act to a married woman living with her
> husband should be construed in accordance with section 42(1)(2) of the Income and
> Corporation Taxes Act 1970.'

This piece of drafting is an oddity. Firstly, the subsection adopts the word 'should'
which can only mean 'ought to', instead of the usual imperative 'shall'. Secondly, when
referring to two subsections in conjunction, the draftsman omits the conjunctive word.
Thirdly, in referring to a section which consists of only two subsections, he refers to the
section by its number and then to the only two subsections by their numbers.

These oddities, however, only give rise to niggling criticisms. The reader will have no
difficulty in substituting 'shall' for 'should'. He will mentally supply the word 'and'
between the two subsection numbers. He will know that he must construe the conception
of a married woman living with her husband in accordance with both subsections of s 42
of the 1970 Act, even if he would have reached the same conclusion had the section
number stood alone. But, if he approaches s 42 with confidence that all will then be
made clear, he will be disappointed because he will find that sub-s (2) of s 42, unlike sub-
s (1) has nothing whatever to do with construction.

Subsection (1) of s 42 of the 1970 Act is indeed a construction provision, as the
marginal note rightly states. It is a definition of the 'shall be treated as' type. It reads as
follows:

> 'A married woman shall be treated for income tax purposes as living with her
> husband unless—(a) they are separated under an order of a court of competent
> jurisdiction, or by deed of separation, or (b) they are in fact separated in such
> circumstances that the separation is likely to be permanent.'

Subsection (2) is not a construction provision. It reads as follows:

> 'Where a married woman is living with her husband and either—(a) one of them
> is, and one of them is not, resident in the United Kingdom for a year of assessment,
> or (b) both of them are resident in the United Kingdom for a year of assessment, but
> one of them is, and one of them is not, absent from the United Kingdom throughout
> that year, the same consequences shall follow for income tax purposes as would have
> followed if, throughout that year of assessment, they had been in fact separated in
> such circumstances that the separation was likely to be permanent:

Provided that, where this subsection applies and the net aggregate of income tax falling to be borne by the husband and the wife for the year is greater than it would have been but for the provisions of this subsection, the Board shall cause such relief to be given (by the reduction of such assessments on the husband or the wife or the repayment of such tax paid (by deduction or otherwise) by the husband or the wife as the Board may direct) as will reduce the said net aggregate amount by the amount of the excess.'

Subsection (2) assumes that a married woman *is* living with her husband. Nothing in sub-s (2) alters that fact. It is the basic assumption on which sub-s (2) proceeds. The subsection then provides that in certain circumstances of geographical separation 'the same consequences shall follow' for income tax purposes as would have followed if, contrary to the fact, the spouses had been separated except that, put shortly, the net aggregate income tax payable by the spouses shall not be increased.

To sum up, the scheme of s 42(1) of the 1970 Act clarifies precisely what is meant by a 'married woman living with her husband'. Subsection (2) provides that, given the existence of that situation, spouses geographically separated are in certain circumstances to enjoy, so far as the aggregate quantum of tax is concerned, the advantages of marital separation without the disadvantages.

The Crown's approach is, in effect, to substitute for 'where a married woman is living with her husband and either' the very opposite, namely 'a married woman shall not be treated as living with her husband if' and to ignore everything else including the proviso. Paragraphs (a) and (b) of sub-s (2) would thereby be converted into an exception to sub-s (1). Or, as the Crown prefers to express it, the words 'the same consequences shall follow for income tax purposes as would have followed if' should be deleted together with the proviso, and there should be substituted 'they shall be treated for capital gains tax purposes as if', again disregarding the proviso.

The taxpayer's approach is to leave sub-s (2) intact but to substitute references to capital gains tax for references to income tax. The effect will be to give to geographically separated spouses possible advantages, eg two tax free allowances, but they will not be penalised for their geographical separation.

My Lords, I choose without hesitation the second approach, for the following reasons. Firstly, it does less violence to s 45(3) of the 1965 Act, which contains no sufficient warrant for ignoring the proviso to sub-s (2) of s 42: the proviso is a part of that subsection. And it involves the minimum alteration to s 42 when its provisions are applied referentially. Secondly, it preserves what seems to me to be the policy of the 1965 Act, namely that disposals between spouses, which ex hypothesi do not realise a gain and which leave the matrimonial assets unaltered, are exempt from capital gains tax. Thirdly, it equates the capital gains tax position with the income tax position, and that seems to me to answer the 'accordance' which s 45(3) of the 1965 Act expressly seeks to achieve. Fourthly, if geographically separated spouses are not to be prejudiced by their separation for income tax purposes, I see no logic in assuming that Parliament intended them to be prejudiced for capital gains tax purposes. All the pointers which I can discern are in favour of the second approach.

For these reasons I would allow the appeal. I am in agreement with your Lordships' proposals as regards costs.

Appeal allowed.

Solicitors: *Rooks Rider & Co*, agents for *Scowcroft & Co*, Douglas, Isle of Man (for Mr Gubay); *Solicitor of Inland Revenue*.

Mary Rose Plummer   Barrister.

Furniss (Inspector of Taxes) v Dawson
and related appeals

HOUSE OF LORDS

LORD FRASER OF TULLYBELTON, LORD SCARMAN, LORD ROSKILL, LORD BRIDGE OF HARWICH AND
LORD BRIGHTMAN

14, 19, 20 DECEMBER 1983, 9 FEBRUARY 1984

*Capital gains tax – Tax avoidance scheme – Tax deferment scheme – Pre-arranged transactions
– Self-cancelling transactions – Scheme designed to avoid or defer capital gains tax liability – Step
in transaction having no commercial or business purpose other than avoidance or deferment of tax
– Whether taxpayer's liability to tax to be determined on basis of all steps in transaction or merely
on basis of ultimate result to taxpayer.*

The taxpayers were the main shareholders in two manufacturing companies, X Ltd and
Y Ltd, which they agreed to sell by an arm's-length transaction to a purchaser for the sum
of £152,000. However, in order to defer the taxpayers' liability to pay capital gains tax
on their share of the purchase price, it was agreed and arranged that the sale would be
accomplished by a scheme whereby a company, G Ltd, would be incorporated in the Isle
of Man, G Ltd would then acquire the taxpayers' shares in X Ltd and Y Ltd for £152,000
by allotting shares in G Ltd to the taxpayers, and G Ltd would then sell the shares in X
Ltd and Y Ltd to the purchaser for a cash payment of £152,000. The scheme was carried
out as planned with the result that the taxpayers ended up as the shareholders of the Isle
of Man company whose only asset was the cash sum of £152,000. The taxpayers were
nevertheless assessed to capital gains tax in respect of the disposal of X Ltd and Y Ltd to
the purchaser, but the taxpayers' appeal against that assessment was upheld by the Special
Commissioners. The Crown appealed on the ground, inter alia, that the effect of the
arrangement was that the taxpayers, rather than G Ltd, had disposed of the shares in X
Ltd and Y Ltd to the purchaser and therefore the taxpayers were liable to capital gains
tax notwithstanding the intervention of G Ltd. The taxpayers contended that G Ltd had
acquired control of X Ltd and Y Ltd and therefore any charge to capital gains tax would
be deferred until such time as the taxpayers disposed of their shares in G Ltd. The judge
dismissed the Crown's appeal, on the ground that the scheme could not be treated as a
nullity for tax purposes because the various steps in the scheme were not self-cancelling
but had enduring legal consequences, such as the fact that G Ltd would continue in
existence and would incur tax liability in respect of the funds held by it and the fact that
the purchaser's right of redress would, if necessary, be against G Ltd rather than against
the taxpayers. The Crown's appeal to the Court of Appeal was dismissed. The Crown
appealed to the House of Lords.

Held – In determining the fiscal consequences of a preplanned tax saving scheme no
distinction was to be made between a series of steps which were followed through by
virtue of an arrangement which fell short of a binding contract and a like series of steps
which were followed through because the participants were contractually bound to take
each step. Accordingly, where a tax avoidance or tax deferment scheme consisted of a
series of prearranged steps, some of which had no commercial purpose other than the
avoidance or deferment of tax, liability to tax was to be determined according to the
substance of the scheme as a whole and its end result, notwithstanding (a) that the
arrangement was non-contractual, or (b) that each particular step had commercial effect
or enduring legal consequences, or (c) that the arrangement was not a self-cancelling
scheme designed to produce neither a loss nor a gain. Applying those principles, since
the intervention of G Ltd had no commercial purpose other than deferment of the
taxpayers' tax liability, the transactions concerning G Ltd were to be disregarded and the

transaction treated simply as the sale of the taxpayers' shares in X Ltd and Y Ltd direct to
the purchaser. On that basis the taxpayers were accordingly liable to capital gains tax.
The Crown's appeal would therefore be allowed (see p 531 *j*, p 532 *b c* and *g* to *j*, p 533 *d*,
p 534 *e* to *g*, p 536 *e* to *g*, p 542 *h* to p 543 *e* and p 544 *a b*, post).
Dictum of Eveleigh LJ in *Floor v Davis (Inspector of Taxes)* [1978] 2 All ER at 1088–
1090, *W T Ramsay Ltd v IRC* [1981] 1 All ER 865 and *IRC v Burmah Oil Co Ltd* [1982] STC
30 applied.
IRC v Duke of Westminster [1935] All ER Rep 259 distinguished.

Notes
For persons chargeable to capital gains tax, see 5 Halsbury's Laws (4th edn) para 115, for
chargeable disposals, see ibid paras 67, 74, and for transfer of shares, see ibid para 57.

Cases referred to in opinions
Edwards (Inspector of Taxes) v Bairstow [1955] 3 All ER 48, [1956] AC 14, [1955] 3 WLR
410, HL.
Eilbeck (Inspector of Taxes) v Rawling [1980] 2 All ER 12; *affd* [1981] 1 All ER 865, [1982]
AC 300, [1981] 2 WLR 449, HL.
Floor v Davis (Inspector of Taxes) [1978] 2 All ER 1079, [1978] Ch 295, [1978] 3 WLR 360,
CA; *affd* [1979] 2 All ER 677, [1980] AC 695, [1979] 2 WLR 830, HL.
Helvering v Gregory (1934) 69 F 2d 809; *affd* (1935) 293 US 465, US SC.
IRC v Burmah Oil Co Ltd [1982] STC 30, HL.
IRC v Duke of Westminster [1936] AC 1, [1935] All ER Rep 259, HL.
Marriott v Oxford and District Co-op Society Ltd [1969] 3 All ER 1126, [1970] 1 QB 186,
[1969] 3 WLR 984, CA.
Ramsay (W T) Ltd v IRC [1981] 1 All ER 865, [1982] AC 300, [1981] 2 WLR 449, HL.

Consolidated appeals
The Crown appealed with leave of the Court of Appeal against the decision of that court
(Oliver, Kerr and Slade LJJ) ([1983] 3 WLR 635) on 27 May 1983 dismissing an appeal by
the Crown from the judgment of Vinelott J ([1982] STC 267) given on 18 December
1981 dismissing an appeal by the Crown by way of case stated (set out at [1982] STC 269–
276) from a decision of the Commissioners for the Special Purposes of the Income Tax
Acts given on 21 January 1976 allowing appeals by the taxpayers, George Edward
Dawson, Douglas Edward Rexford Dawson and Rexford Stuart Dawson, against
assessments to capital gains tax made on the taxpayers in the sums of £57,000, £28,000
and £28,000, respectively, for the year 1971–72. Following the death of the taxpayer G
E Dawson after the Commissioners had given their decision, the appeal was carried on
against his widow, Ella Bertha Dawson, by order of Master Heward dated 13 July 1981.
The facts are set out in the opinion of Lord Brightman.

Peter Millett QC and *Robert Carnwath* for the Crown.
Stephen Oliver QC and *William Massey* for the taxpayers.

Their Lordships took time for consideration.

9 February. The following opinions were delivered.

LORD FRASER OF TULLYBELTON. My Lords, I have had the advantage of
reading in draft the speech prepared by my noble and learned friend Lord Brightman in
these consolidated appeals and I entirely agree with his conclusion and his reasoning. The
facts are fully stated in his speech and I do not repeat them. I wish to add only a few
comments.

The importance of this case is, in my opinion, in enabling your Lordships' House to explain the effect of the decision in *W T Ramsay Ltd v IRC* [1981] 1 All ER 865, [1982] *a* AC 300 and to dispose of what are, I think, the misunderstandings about the scope of that decision which have prevailed in the Court of Appeal. In *Ramsay* the House had to consider an elaborate and entirely artificial scheme for avoiding liability to tax. Viewed as a whole, it was self-cancelling. In the present case the scheme was much simpler, and it was not self-cancelling; on the contrary, it had what Vinelott J described as 'enduring legal consequences' (see [1982] STC 267 at 288). But while the cases differ in that respect, *b* it is not a sufficient ground for distinguishing the present case from *Ramsay*. The true principle of the decision in *Ramsay* was that the fiscal consequences of a preordained series of transactions, intended to operate as such, are generally to be ascertained by considering the result of the series as a whole, and not by dissecting the scheme and considering each individual transaction separately. The principle was stated in the speech of Lord Wilberforce in *Ramsay* [1981] 1 All ER 865 at 871, [1982] AC 300 at 324, *c* especially where his Lordship said:

> 'For the commissioners considering a particular case it is wrong, and an unnecessary self-limitation, to regard themselves as precluded by their own finding that documents or transactions are not "shams" from considering what, as evidenced by the documents themselves or by the manifested intentions of the parties, *the relevant transaction* is. They are not, under the *Duke of Westminster* doctrine [see *IRC* *d* *v Duke of Westminster* [1936] AC 1, [1935] All ER Rep 259] or any other authority, bound to consider individually each separate step in a composite transaction intended to be carried through as a whole' (My emphasis.)

It was by applying that principle that Lord Wilberforce in the next paragraph of his speech in *Ramsay* approved of the approach by Eveleigh LJ to the first stage of the *e* transaction in *Floor v Davis (Inspector of Taxes)* [1978] 2 All ER 1079, [1978] Ch 295. I also attempted to apply the same principle when I expressed the opinion that 'it could in my opinion have been the ground of decision in *Floor v Davis* in accordance with the dissenting opinion of Eveleigh LJ in the Court of Appeal with which I respectfully agree' (see *Ramsay's* case [1981] 1 All ER 865 at 882, [1982] AC 300 at 339). Eveleigh LJ, Lord Wilberforce and I all referred only to the first stage of the transaction in *Floor v Davis*, *f* and we did not rely to any extent on the existence of the second stage, as the Court of Appeal in the present case appear to have thought. The first stage, viewed by itself, was clearly more favourable to the argument for the taxpayer than the two stages taken together: if the argument for the taxpayer failed even at the first stage, that would simply be an additional reason for reaching the decision against him. As it happens, the whole transaction in the present case is very similar to the first stage in *Floor v Davis* (the only *g* material difference being that Greenjacket Investments Ltd has more enduring functions than FNW Electronic Holdings Ltd had in *Floor's* case).

The series of two transactions in the present case was planned as a single scheme, and I am clearly of opinion that it should be viewed as a whole. The relevant transaction, if I may borrow the expression used by Lord Wilberforce, consists of the two transactions or stages taken together. It was a disposal by the taxpayers of the shares in the operating *h* company for cash to Wood Bastow Holdings Ltd.

I would allow the appeals.

LORD SCARMAN. My Lords, I would allow the appeals for the reasons given by my noble and learned friend Lord Brightman. I add a few observations only because I am aware, and the legal profession (and others) must understand, that the law in this area is *j* in an early stage of development. Speeches in your Lordships' House and judgments in the appellate courts of the United Kingdom are concerned more to chart a way forward between principles accepted and not to be rejected than to attempt anything so ambitious as to determine finally the limit beyond which the safe channel of acceptable tax avoidance shelves into the dangerous shallows of unacceptable tax evasion.

The law will develop from case to case. Lord Wilberforce in *W T Ramsay Ltd v IRC*
a [1981] 1 All ER 865 at 872, [1982] AC 300 at 324 referred to 'the emerging principle' of
the law. What has been established with certainty by the House in *Ramsay's* case is that
the determination of what does, and what does not, constitute unacceptable tax evasion
is a subject suited to development by judicial process. The best chart that we have for the
way forward appears to me, with great respect to all engaged on the map-making process,
to be the words of Lord Diplock in *IRC v Burmah Oil Co Ltd* [1982] STC 30 at 32 which
b my noble and learned friend Lord Brightman quotes in his speech. These words leave
space in the law for the principle enunciated by Lord Tomlin in *IRC v Duke of Westminster*
[1936] AC 1 at 19, [1935] All ER Rep 259 at 267 that every man is entitled if he can to
order his affairs so as to diminish the burden of tax. The limits within which this
principle is to operate remain to be probed and determined judicially. Difficult though
the task may be for judges, it is one which is beyond the power of the blunt instrument
c of legislation. Whatever a statute may provide, it has to be interpreted and applied by
the courts; and ultimately it will prove to be in this area of judge-made law that our
elusive journey's end will be found.

LORD ROSKILL. My Lords, I have had the opportunity of reading in draft the
speeches delivered or to be delivered and in common with all your Lordships I have
d reached the clear conclusion that these appeals by the Crown must be allowed and that
the reasoning in the courts below cannot be supported. I respectfully and entirely agree
with the speeches of my noble and learned friends Lord Fraser and Lord Brightman. I
only add to your Lordships' speeches out of respect for all the judges from whom the
House is differing. Repeated perusal of their long and careful judgments has left me with
the impression, which I am comforted to see is shared by my noble and learned friend
e Lord Brightman, that they were seeking a route by which they might confine the
decisions in *W T Ramsay Ltd v IRC* [1981] 1 All ER 865, [1982] AC 300 and *IRC v Burmah
Oil Co Ltd* [1982] STC 30 to cases which were similar on their facts, that is to say where
the transactions under attack were what have been described in argument as 'self-
cancelling'. Those cases apart, what the judges all regarded as the principles long
established by *IRC v Duke of Westminster* [1936] AC 1, [1935] All ER Rep 259 might
f continue to reign supreme and unchallenged. They sought to find support for their
conclusions in the majority judgments in the Court of Appeal in *Floor v Davis (Inspector
of Taxes)* [1978] 2 All ER 1079, [1978] Ch 295 and were not prepared to accept that in
Ramsay's case this House had, at least in principle if not explicitly, approved of the much
discussed dissenting judgment of Eveleigh LJ in the former case. As my noble and
learned friends have pointed out, on any view the relevant statements in those majority
g judgments of Sir John Pennycuick and Buckley LJ were obiter since this House
subsequently decided in favour of the Crown on another point and therefore had no
cause to pronounce on the rival merits of the views expressed on what became known as
'the first issue' (see [1979] 2 All ER 677, [1980] AC 695).

The error, if I may venture to use that word, into which the courts below have fallen
is that they have looked back to 1936 and not forward from 1982. They do not appear to
h have appreciated the true significance of the passages in the speeches in *Ramsay's* case
[1981] 1 All ER 865 at 872–873, 881, [1982] AC 300 at 325–326, 337 of Lord Wilberforce
and Lord Fraser and, even more important, of the warnings in the *Burmah Oil* case [1982]
STC 30 at 32, 39 given by Lord Diplock and Lord Scarman in the passages to which my
noble and learned friend Lord Brightman refers and which I will not repeat. It is perhaps
worth recalling the warning given, albeit in another context by Lord Atkin, who himself
j dissented in the *Duke of Westminster's* case, in *United Australia Ltd v Barclays Bank Ltd*
[1940] 4 All ER 20 at 37, [1941] AC 1 at 29: 'When these ghosts of the past stand in the
path of justice, clanking their mediaeval chains, the proper course for the judge is to pass
through them undeterred.' 1936, a bare half century ago, cannot be described as part of
the Middle Ages but the ghost of the Duke of Westminster and of his transaction, be it
noted a single and not a composite transaction, with his gardener and with other

members of his staff has haunted the administration of this branch of the law for too long. I confess that I had hoped that that ghost might have found quietude with the decisions in *Ramsay* and in *Burmah*. Unhappily it has not. Perhaps the decision of this House in these appeals will now suffice as exorcism.

I would only add, ignoring for the moment that the effect of the *Duke of Westminster's* case was subsequently nullified by statute, that I express no view whether, were that case to arise for decision since 1982, the duke or the Crown would emerge as the ultimate victor.

My Lords, counsel for the taxpayers ultimately found himself constrained to admit that the majority judgments in *Floor v Davis* could not stand alongside the decisions in *Ramsay* and *Burmah*. I think he was entirely right to make this concession. But he sought to distinguish the present cases from *Floor v Davis* on their facts, contending that in these cases Greenjacket Investments Ltd's existence had enduring consequences whereas in *Floor v Davis* Donmarco Ltd, the recipient of the ultimate proceeds of sale, did not. He also submitted that the dissenting judgment of Eveleigh LJ was founded on consideration of stage 2 of the transactions there in question and not only on stage 1. My Lords, with respect, I regard both submissions as untenable. Eveleigh LJ was quite clearly treating the stage 1 transaction as involving a disposal to the ultimate purchaser which itself attracted capital gains tax. There is no relevant reference to stage 2 from beginning to end of his judgment. It was his view which found support in *Ramsay* and rejection of it at the present time would involve rehabilitation of the majority judgments in *Floor v Davis*, which as already pointed out were not and indeed are not now capable of being supported.

My Lords, I think Oliver LJ was also influenced by fears of double taxation were the Crown's submissions to be accepted. In my view the answer to the Lord Justice's fears is provided by my noble and learned friend Lord Brightman in his speech in accordance with the submissions of counsel for the Crown and I have nothing further to add on this part of the case.

In conclusion, therefore, I am convinced that there was a disposal by the Dawsons to Wood Bastow Holdings Ltd in consideration of the payment to be made by Wood Bastow to Greenjacket at the behest of the Dawsons. This disposal is not exempt. Capital gains tax is payable. It is for these reasons as well as for those expressed by my noble and learned friends to whose speeches I have already referred that I would allow these appeals. I would however make no order as to costs in this House.

LORD BRIDGE OF HARWICH. My Lords, I have had the advantage of reading in draft the speech of my noble and learned friend Lord Brightman and I agree with it.

In one sense these appeals can be disposed of on a very short and simple ground. The facts of the present case are, for relevant purposes, indistinguishable from the facts of *Floor v Davis (Inspector of Taxes)* [1978] 2 All ER 1079, [1978] Ch 295, CA; *affd* [1979] 2 All ER 677, [1980] AC 695, HL, limited to the transactions which in that case were referred to throughout as constituting stage 1. *Floor v Davis* was in fact decided in favour of the Crown both in the Court of Appeal and the House of Lords on a ground wholly irrelevant to the present appeal arising from the transactions involved in stage 2, and the stage 1 point was never considered when the case came before this House. Hence the conflicting opinions expressed in the Court of Appeal as to the legal effect of the stage 1 transactions were entirely obiter. The judgment of Eveleigh LJ relating to stage 1 contains no word of reference to stage 2 and the theory that he was influenced in his conclusion as to stage 1 by any of the factors arising at stage 2 is quite untenable. Eveleigh LJ concluded that the transactions involved in stage 1, by themselves, effected a disposal by the taxpayers of their shares to the ultimate purchasers which attracted capital gains tax. That conclusion was unanimously approved, albeit again obiter, by your Lordships' House in *W T Ramsay Ltd v IRC, Eilbeck (Inspector of Taxes) v Rawling* [1981] 1 All ER 865, [1982] AC 300. It inevitably follows that, unless your Lordships are willing to reject that unanimous opinion of the House and reinstate the views on this point of the majority of

the Court of Appeal in *Floor v Davis* (Buckley LJ and Sir John Pennycuick) whose
a reasoning counsel for the taxpayers in the instant case did not feel able to support, the
appeal must succeed.

But in another sense the present appeal marks a further important step, as a matter of
decision rather than mere dictum, in the development of the courts' increasingly critical
approach to the manipulation of financial transactions to the advantage of the taxpayer.
Of course, the judiciary must never lose sight of the basic premise expressed in the
b celebrated dictum of Lord Tomlin in *IRC v Duke of Westminster* [1936] AC 1 at 19, [1935]
All ER Rep 259 at 267, that—

> 'Every man is entitled if he can to order his affairs so as that the tax attaching
> under the appropriate Acts is less than it otherwise would be.'

Just a year earlier Learned Hand J, giving the judgment of the United States Second
c Circuit Court of Appeals in *Helvering v Gregory* (1934) 69 F 2d 809, had said the same
thing in different words:

> 'Anyone may so arrange his affairs that his taxes shall be as low as possible; he is
> not bound to choose that pattern which will best pay the Treasury.'

Yet, while starting from this common principle, the federal courts of the United States
d and the English courts have developed, quite independently of any statutory differences,
very different techniques for the scrutiny of tax avoidance schemes to test their validity.

The extent to which the speeches of the majority in the *Westminster* case still tend to
dominate the thinking in this field of the English judiciary is well shown by the
judgments in the courts below in the instant case (see [1982] STC 267, Ch D; [1983] 3
WLR 635, CA). In particular, the *Westminster* case seems still to be accepted as establishing
e that the only ground on which it can be legitimate to draw a distinction between the
substance and the form of transactions in considering their tax consequences is that the
transactions are shams, in the sense that they are not what, on their face, they purport to
be. The strong dislike expressed by the majority in the *Westminster* case [1936] AC 1 at
19, [1935] All ER Rep 259 at 267 for what Lord Tomlin described as the 'doctrine that
the Court may ignore the legal position and regard what is called "the substance of the
f matter"' is not in the least surprising when one remembers that the only transaction in
question was the duke's covenant in favour of his gardener and the bona fides of that
transaction was never for a moment impugned.

When one moves, however, from a single transaction to a series of interdependent
transactions designed to produce a given result, it is, in my opinion, perfectly legitimate
to draw a distinction between the substance and the form of the composite transaction
g without in any way suggesting that any of the single transactions which make up the
whole are other than genuine. This has been the approach of the United Stated federal
courts enabling them to develop a doctrine whereby the tax consequences of the
composite transaction are dependent on its substance not its form. I shall not attempt to
review the American authorities, nor do I propose a wholesale importation of the
American doctrine in all its ramifications into English law. But I do suggest that the
h distinction between form and substance is one which can usefully be drawn in
determining the tax consequences of composite transactions and one which will help to
free the courts from the shackles which have for so long been thought to be imposed on
them by the *Westminster* case.

I shall attempt no exhaustive exposition of all the criteria by which, for the purpose I
suggest, form and substance are to be distinguished. Once a basic doctrine of form and
j substance is accepted, the drawing of precise boundaries will need to be worked out on a
case by case basis. But I venture to point out what a simple and readily applicable test a
distinction between form and substance would have provided to arrive at the conclusions
already reached in some of the cases of composite transactions decided by your Lordships'
House. It would need no more than a cursory exposition of the avoidance schemes in
Ramsay and *Rawling* to lead any intelligent layman to the conclusion that neither scheme

was designed to achieve any substantial effect in the real world and that the elaborate
steps designed to manufacture a tax deductible loss in each case were purely formal in   *a*
character. If Special or General Commissioners had been directed to approach either case
on the basis that the tax consequences of the interlocking, interdependent and
predetermined transactions were to be judged by reference to the substance not the form
of the composite transaction, I cannot think they would have had any difficulty in
arriving at the right answer.

The facts in *IRC v Burmah Oil Co Ltd* [1982] STC 30 were more complicated but the   *b*
effect of the decision of this House could fairly be summarised by saying that the scheme
adopted by Burmah to convert a bad debt owing to it by a subsidiary company (a non-
deductible loss) into a loss realised on the liquidation of that subsidiary which would be
tax deductible was formal rather than substantial. In the words of Lord Fraser (at 38):

> 'The question in this part of the appeal is whether the present scheme, when
> completely carried out, did or did not result in a loss such as the legislation is dealing   *c*
> with, which I may call for short, a real loss. In my opinion it did not.'

Lord Diplock (at 32) referred to—

> 'a pre-ordained series of transactions (whether or not they include the achievement
> of a legitimate commercial end) into which there are inserted steps that have no
> commercial purpose apart from the avoidance of a liability to tax which in the   *d*
> absence of those particular steps would have been payable.'

This seems to me to be language expressing with perfect precision the concept of steps
which are formal rather than substantial.

The distinction between form and substance in the instant case is still easier to draw.
As my noble and learned friend Lord Brightman has pointed out, if there had been here   *e*
at the outset a tripartite contract between the taxpayers, Greenjacket Investments Ltd
and Wood Bastow Holdings Ltd, the beneficial interest in the taxpayers' shares would
have passed directly to Wood Bastow. The twin purpose of achieving the identical result
by the elaborate and carefully timed scheme fully described in the speech of my noble
and learned friend Lord Brightman was (i) to avoid a direct disposal of the shares to Wood
Bastow and (ii) to ensure that for a scintilla temporis the beneficial interest in the shares   *f*
was held by Greenjacket in order to found Greenjacket's claim to have been in control of
the operating companies for the purposes of para 6(2) of Sch 7 to the Finance Act 1965.
Nothing could be clearer than that these two features of the preordained scheme were
purely formal and had no effect on the substance of the composite transaction.

I would allow the appeals.

LORD BRIGHTMAN. My Lords, the transaction which we are called on to consider   *g*
is not a tax avoidance scheme, but a tax deferment scheme. The scheme has none of the
extravagances of certain tax avoidance schemes which have recently engaged the attention
of the courts, where the taxpayer who has been fortunate enough to realise a capital profit
has gone out into the street and, with the aid of astute advisers, manufactured out of a
string of artificial transactions a supposed loss in order to counteract the profit which he   *h*
has already made. The scheme before your Lordships is a simple and honest scheme
which merely seeks to defer payment of tax until the taxpayer has received into his hands
the gain which he has made.

There are three consolidated appeals. The taxpayers are Mr George Dawson, who has
died since the start of the proceedings and whose estate is represented by his widow, and
his sons Mr Douglas Dawson and Mr Rexford Dawson.

The facts are simple, and were admirably found by the Special Commissioners for the   *j*
purpose of dealing with the only point which was then in issue. They are as follows.

1. Mr George Dawson, together with his wife and two sons, held shares in two
companies (the operating companies) which manufactured clothing. They held all the
shares in one company and most of the shares in the other company. I propose to ignore

this small outside shareholding. Mr Wood was the chairman and managing director of
Wood Bastow Holdings Ltd (Wood Bastow). In September 1971 Mr Dawson and Mr
Wood agreed in principle that Wood Bastow should buy the entire shareholding in the
operating companies.

2. Solicitors were instructed on each side. Further negotiations took place. In particular,
the solicitors acting for Wood Bastow asked for the capital of the operating companies to
be reorganised so as to include the issue of renounceable letters of allotment, in order to
minimise the stamp duty payable by them on the purchase.

3. Acting on advice, the Dawsons decided not to sell directly to Wood Bastow. They
'arranged first to exchange their shares for shares in an investment company to be
incorporated in the Isle of Man. Any sale to [the ultimate purchaser] would, it was
contemplated, be a sale by the Isle of Man company' (see [1982] STC 267 at 270).

4. On 15 November 1971 a meeting took place between the solicitors. At this meeting
the solicitors for Wood Bastow first became aware of the proposal to introduce an Isle of
Man company. They accepted the proposal, subject to certain amendments being made
to the draft documents then in course of preparation. The 20 December was fixed as the
date for completion.

5. On 16 December the following events occurred. (a) A company called Greenjacket
Investments Ltd (Greenjacket) was incorporated in the Isle of Man by Manx solicitors
acting on the instructions of the Dawson solicitors. The subscribers to the memorandum
of association were Mr J E Crellin, a member of the Manx firm of solicitors, and Mr
Moroney, who was articled to them. (b) A meeting of the subscribers took place at which
they and Mr P G Crellin were nominated as the first directors. (c) A first meeting of the
board took place, at which there were produced to the meeting (i) the agreement, which
was then presumably in the form of an unexecuted engrossment or a draft, whereby
Greenjacket would purchase the shares in the operating companies for the sum of
£152,000 which was to be satisfied by the issue of shares in Greenjacket (I will call this
'the first sale agreement') and (ii) a draft agreement for Greenjacket to sell the shares in
the operating companies to Wood Bastow for £152,000 (I will call this 'the second sale
agreement'). (d) At the same board meeting it was resolved (i) that the two sale agreements
be proceeded with, (ii) that the first sale agreement be executed (it was ultimately dated
20 December and exchanged on that date), (iii) that the shares in the operating companies
(with an immaterial exception) be taken in the name of Greenjacket, (iv) that Mr
Moroney be authorised to execute the second sale agreement on behalf of Greenjacket,
and (v) that in anticipation thereof the transfers of the shares in the operating companies
to Wood Bastow (as they would exist after later reorganisation) be executed and held in
escrow, which was then done.

6. On 20 December a meeting for the completion of the sale to Wood Bastow took
place as planned. It was held at the offices of Messrs Browne Jacobson & Roose, the
Dawson solicitors. The following activities took place. (a) Meetings of the boards of the
operating companies and extraordinary general meetings of such companies were held
at which resolutions were passed to reorganise the share capitals of the operating
companies in the manner desired by Wood Bastow. (b) Mr Moroney, who attended
completion, produced the first sale agreement and telephoned the Isle of Man in order to
ascertain that the board of Greenjacket were allotting the consideration shares in that
company to the Dawsons. (c) The boards of the operating companies approved transfers
of the shares therein to Greenjacket. (d) The second sale agreement was exchanged and
the sale completed in consideration of the payment of the purchase money by Wood
Bastow to Greenjacket. (e) The boards of the operating companies approved the transfers
of the shares therein to Wood Bastow.

The board meetings of the operating companies were interrupted on three occasions:
first, to enable extraordinary general meetings to be held to reorganise the share capitals;
second, to enable the first sale agreement to be exchanged between the Dawsons and
Greenjacket; and, third, to enable the second sale agreement to be exchanged. There are
very full minutes of the board meeting of one of the operating companies and similar

minutes exist in the case of the other company. These show that the whole process was
planned and executed with faultless precision. The meetings began at 12.45 pm on 20
December, at which time the shareholdings of the operating companies were still owned
by the Dawsons unaffected by any contract for sale. They ended with the shareholdings
in the ownership of Wood Bastow. The minutes do not disclose when the meeting ended,
but perhaps it was all over in time for lunch.

Section 19 of the Finance Act 1965 charges tax in respect of capital gains accruing to a
person on the disposal of assets. There is no definition of disposal and it scarcely needs
definition. Paragraph 6 of Sch 7 provides certain exceptions in the case of company
amalgamations. One exception applies to shares in a company transferred to another
company which thereby acquires control, in exchange for shares in the transferee
company. In such a case there is deemed to be no disposal of the former shareholding.
The new shareholding and the old shareholding are to be treated as the same asset.

In the instant case Mr George Dawson and his sons were assessed to capital gains tax in
respect of the year 1971–72 in the sums of £57,000, £28,000 and £28,000. The then
argument on the part of the Crown was that Greenjacket did not acquire control of the
operating companies within the meaning of para 6 of Sch 7, because Greenjacket was a
nominee or bare trustee for the Dawsons. If on the other hand, as the taxpayers
contended, Greenjacket did acquire control of the operating companies, any charge to
capital gains tax would, it was contended, be deferred until such time as the taxpayers
disposed of their shareholdings in Greenjacket and thereby realised a chargeable gain. At
this point the one and only question at issue was whether Greenjacket acquired control
of the operating companies within the meaning of the 1965 Act. Indeed, that is in a sense
the only question at issue now, but it falls to be answered in a very different legal context
from that in which it originally fell to be considered.

After a two-day hearing, including the oral evidence of four witnesses, the Special
Commissioners held that Greenjacket had acquired control of the operating companies
within the meaning of the 1965 Act. They therefore held that the first sale agreement
was not a disposal by the Dawsons to Greenjacket for the purposes of capital gains tax,
and the assessments were discharged. The decision was given on 21 January 1976. The
stated case was signed a year later, but for some reason it was over two years before it
reached the High Court. During this long wait there occurred what has been described
as 'a significant change in the approach adopted by this House' towards artificial tax
saving schemes (see *IRC v Burmah Oil Co Ltd* [1982] STC 30 at 32 per Lord Diplock). The
story of this change begins with *Floor v Davis (Inspector of Taxes)* [1978] 2 All ER 1079,
[1978] Ch 295; *affd* [1979] 2 All ER 677, [1980] AC 695. In that case the taxpayer and
others were shareholders in a company, which I shall call 'IDM'. They agreed in principle
to sell their shares to another company, which I shall call 'KDI'. The vendors then decided
to put into effect the following scheme. On 24 February 1974 they caused to be
incorporated a company, which I shall call 'FNW'. On 27 February the vendors agreed to
sell their IDM shares to FNW in consideration of an allotment of shares in FNW. On 28
February FNW agreed to sell the IDM shares to KDI for a cash consideration. This can
conveniently be called stage 1. On 5 April a special resolution was passed to wind up
FNW voluntarily. As a result of a complicated reorganisation of the capital of FNW the
liquidation of FNW had the effect of passing most of its assets, which included the cash
received from KDI, to Donmarco Ltd, a company registered in the Cayman Islands. This
can conveniently be called stage 2. I will first summarise the decision in that case, before
turning in more detail to the judgments. The Court of Appeal held (1) that the taxpayer
could not be regarded as having disposed of his shareholding in IDM to KDI, Eveleigh LJ
dissenting, (2) that FNW acquired control of IDM, so that there was no disposal for capital
gains tax purposes on the sale of the shares by the taxpayer to FNW, but (3) that the
taxpayer had exercised control over the shares in FNW by reason whereof value had
passed out of those shares into the shares in Donmarco, and in consequence the taxpayer
was deemed by virtue of para 15(2) of Sch 7 to have disposed of his shares in FNW and
was taxable accordingly; this paragraph taxes transactions which involve gratuitous
transfers of value derived from assets and is not in point in the instant case.

The leading judgment was delivered by Sir John Pennycuick. The first issue was
a whether the taxpayer made a disposal of his IDM shares to KDI. Before answering this
question he identified the critical transactions as the agreement of 27 February 1969 to
sell the IDM shares to FNW in consideration of the issue of FNW shares, and the sale of
the IDM shares a day later by FNW to KDI. It was, he said, impossible on the plain effect
of the two sale agreements to maintain that the taxpayer had sold his shares to anyone
other than FNW, or that KDI had purchased the shares from anyone other than FNW.
b Buckley LJ similarly held that—

> 'the transactions which together make up stage 1 of the series cannot for the
> present purpose properly be regarded as a disposal by the taxpayer and his sons-in-
> law of their shares in IDM to KDI.'

(See [1978] 2 All ER 1079 at 1090, [1978] Ch 295 at 314.)
c   It will be seen from the full report of the judgments that this conclusion was reached
by both Lords Justices without any reference whatever to the existence of stage 2.
    In his dissenting judgment Eveleigh LJ took the view that the IDM shares were
disposed of by the taxpayer to KDI. The ratio of his decision was as follows ([1978] 2 All
ER 1079 at 1088, [1978] Ch 295 at 312):

> d   'It is clear that right from the beginning the American company [KDI] indicated
> that it would purchase the shares. The only reason for avoiding a direct sale to them
> was the prospect of capital gains tax. In an attempt to avoid paying this, as is frankly
> accepted, the initial transfer to FNW took place. There was however no real
> possibility at any time that the shares would not reach the American company. By
> virtue of their control of FNW the shareholders guaranteed from the moment they
> parted with the legal ownership that the shares would become the property of the
> e   American company. No one could prevent this against their wishes. By virtue of
> the arrangement initially made between them each was under an obligation to the
> other to do nothing to stop the shares arriving in the hands of the American
> company. They controlled the destiny of the shares from beginning to end in
> pursuance of a continuing intention on their part that the shares should be
> f   transferred to KDI.'

    In reaching this conclusion, it will be observed that he also did not refer to or place any
reliance whatever on the existence of stage 2.
    The taxpayer appealed to this House, and naturally opened the appeal by arguing the
only point on which he had failed in the Court of Appeal, namely the applicability of
para 15 of Sch 7. This House decided that point against him, which was sufficient to
g determine the appeal. Counsel for the Crown was not therefore required to address this
House on the issue whether there was a disposal by the taxpayer of the IDM shares to
KDI, and this House had no occasion to express a view.
    The decision of this House in *Floor v Davis* was followed two years later by the decision
in *W T Ramsay Ltd v IRC* [1981] 1 All ER 865, [1982] AC 300. In that case a farming
company had realised a chargeable gain of some £188,000 on the sale of farm land in
h Lincolnshire on which capital gains tax was assessed. In order to mitigate, as it was hoped,
the tax that would otherwise be payable, the taxpayer embarked on a scheme which was
designed to manufacture a paper loss of £175,647 by means of a series of loan and share
transactions. Features of the scheme were as follows. (1) There was no commercial
justification for the scheme. There was no prospect of a profit. In fact there was bound to
be a small loss in the form of the fees and similar expenses which would be payable. (2)
j No step in the scheme was a sham. Every step was genuinely carried through, and was
exactly what it purported to be. (3) There was no binding arrangement that each planned
step would be followed by the next planned step, but it was reasonable to assume that all
the steps would in practice be carried out. (4) The scheme was designed to, and did,
return the taxpayer to the position which he occupied before it began, except for the
payment of the expenses of the scheme. (5) The money needed for the various steps was
lent by a finance house on terms which ensured that the loan came back to the finance

house on completion; the taxpayer's personal outlay was confined to his expenses of the scheme.

The leading speech was that of Lord Wilberforce. He reviewed recent cases, starting with *Floor v Davis*. His comment was as follows ([1981] 1 All ER 865 at 871–872, [1982] AC 300 at 324):

'The key transaction in this scheme was a sale of shares in a company called IDM to one company (FNW) and a resale by that company to a further company (KDL). The majority of the Court of Appeal thought it right to look at each of the sales separately and rejected an argument by the Crown that they could be considered as an integrated transaction. But Eveleigh LJ upheld that argument. He held that the fact that each sale was genuine did not prevent him from regarding each as part of a whole, or oblige him to consider each step in isolation. Nor was he so prevented by the *Duke of Westminster* case [see *IRC v Duke of Westminster* [1936] AC 1, [1935] All ER Rep 259]. Looking at the scheme as a whole, and finding that the taxpayer and his sons-in-law had complete control of the IDM shares until they reached KDI, he was entitled to find that there was a disposal to KDI. When the case reached this House it was decided on a limited argument, and the wider point was not considered. This same approach has commended itself to Templeman LJ and has been expressed by him in impressive reasoning in the Court of Appeal's judgment in *Rawling* [see *Eilbeck (Inspector of Taxes) v Rawling* [1980] 2 All ER 12]. It will be seen from what follows that these judgments, and their emerging principle, commend themselves to me.'

The fact that the court accepted that each step in a transaction was a genuine step producing its intended legal result did not confine the court to considering each step in isolation for the purpose of assessing the fiscal results. Lord Wilberforce said ([1981] 1 All ER 865 at 872, [1982] AC 300 at 325): '. . . viewed as a whole, a composite transaction may produce an effect which brings it within a fiscal provision.' Lord Wilberforce added later ([1981] 1 All ER 865 at 873, [1982] AC 300 at 326):

'To force the courts to adopt, in relation to closely integrated situations, a step by step, dissecting, approach which the parties themselves may have negated would be a denial rather than an affirmation of the true judicial process. In each case the facts must be established; and a legal analysis made; legislation cannot be required or even be desirable to enable the court to arrive at a conclusion which corresponds with the parties' own intentions.'

Lord Fraser delivered a concurring speech, in which he expressed his agreement with the dissenting opinion of Eveleigh LJ in *Floor v Davis* and with the reasoning that led to it. Lord Russell expressed his full agreement with the speeches of Lord Wilberforce and Lord Fraser as did Lord Roskill and Lord Bridge.

Counsel for the taxpayers in this appeal laid emphasis on the fact, which is correct, that in *Ramsay's* case the transactions under attack were, as it was called, 'self-cancelling', which were designed to return and did return the taxpayer to the starting position except for the payment of expenses. Both Lord Wilberforce and Lord Fraser referred expressly to this characteristic. The transactions in the present appeal were not self-cancelling, because Greenjacket was brought into being for an indefinite period, and the consideration money paid by Wood Bastow, which was the foundation of the capital gain, would never reach the hands of the Dawsons, save by way of loan, unless and until Greenjacket was wound up or its capital was reduced.

Following the decision of this House in *Ramsay*, the Revenue early in June 1981 gave notice to the taxpayers under RSC Ord 91, r 4 that it would if necessary contend that the Dawsons had disposed of their shares in the operating companies to Wood Bastow and were liable to capital gains tax accordingly. The appeal came before Vinelott J in mid-July and judgment was reserved. However, before judgment was delivered *IRC v Burmah Oil Co Ltd* [1982] STC 30 was argued and decided in this House. Vinelott J therefore deferred giving judgment until the parties had had an opportunity to consider that case.

Burmah involved another artifical tax avoidance scheme, the details of which are
a irrelevant for present purposes. The importance of the case lies in its reaffirmation of the
Ramsay principle. I read this passage from the speech of Lord Diplock ([1982] STC 30 at
32):

> 'It would be disingenuous to suggest, and dangerous on the part of those who
> advise on elaborate tax-avoidance schemes to assume, that *Ramsay's* case did not
b > mark a significant change in the approach adopted by this House in its judicial role
> to a pre-ordained series of transactions (whether or not they include the achievement
> of a legitimate commercial end) into which there are inserted steps that have no
> commercial purpose apart from the avoidance of a liability to tax which in the
> absence of those particular steps would have been payable. The difference is in
> approach. It does not necessitate the overruling of any earlier decisions of this
> House; but it does involve recognising that Lord Tomlin's oft-quoted dictum in *IRC*
c > *v Duke of Westminster* [1936] AC 1 at 19, [1935] All ER Rep 259 at 267, "Every man
> is entitled if he can to order his affairs so as that the tax attaching under the
> appropriate Acts is less than it otherwise would be", tells us little or nothing as to
> what methods of ordering one's affairs will be recognised by the courts as effective
> to lessen the tax that would attach to them if business transactions were conducted
> in a straightforward way'.
d
The warning was repeated in the speech of Lord Scarman (at 39):

> 'First, it is of the utmost importance that the business community (and others,
> including their advisers) should appreciate, as my noble and learned friend Lord
> Diplock has emphasised, that *Ramsay's* case marks "a significant change in the
> approach adopted by this House in its judicial role" towards tax avoidance schemes.
e > Secondly, it is now crucial when considering any such scheme to take the analysis
> far enough to determine where the profit, gain or loss is really to be found.'

That then was the state of judicial precedent when Vinelott J came to give judgment
in the instant case. He said that the question which he had to decide was how far the new
approach justified or required the proposition for which the Crown contended, that is to
f say the proposition set out in the Ord 91 notice. The gist of his long and careful judgment
is that the principle does not apply, and a transaction cannot be disregarded and treated
as fiscally a nullity if it has 'enduring legal consequences', a phrase which he repeated
several times in his judgment (see [1982] STC 267 at 287, 288). He identified 'the
enduring legal consequences' in the instant case as (i) the fact that Greenjacket owned
beneficially the proceeds of sale of the shares in the operating companies, which were
g brought into Greenjacket's accounts and on the income of which Greenjacket was liable
to tax, and (ii) the fact that Wood Bastow's rights under the second sale agreement were
rights against Greenjacket, whereas it would have had no such rights if the sale had been
by the Dawsons to Wood Bastow. The effect of his judgment was to change Lord
Diplock's formulation from 'a pre-ordained series of transactions . . . into which there are
inserted steps that have no commercial purpose apart from the avoidance of a liability to
h tax' to 'a preordained series of transactions into which there are inserted steps that have
no enduring legal consequences'. That would confine the *Ramsay* principle to so-called
self-cancelling transactions.

The judge's restatement of Lord Diplock's formulation enabled him, as he thought, to
escape from the difficulty imposed by this House's approval of the dissenting judgment
in *Floor v Davis*. FNW was placed in liquidation and its assets distributed; consequently
j its existence had no enduring effect on the rights and obligations of the parties after the
completion of the scheme.

On appeal the leading judgment was delivered by Oliver LJ (see [1983] 3 WLR 635).
He was, I think, greatly influenced by what he conceived to be oppressive double taxation
which would follow if the Crown were right in its submission. His fears were in my
view misconceived. If the Crown's case were correct, there would be a disposal by the
Dawsons to Wood Bastow on which capital gains tax would be payable. There could be

no *additional* capital gains tax on the steps by which that disposal was achieved, namely the sale first to Greenjacket and then by Greenjacket to Wood Bastow, because it is the *a* Crown's case that the fiscal consequences of the introduction of Greenjacket are to be disregarded. The Crown cannot, and does not claim to, have it both ways. There would of course be a charge to capital gains tax when the Dawsons realised their shares in Greenjacket, if a chargeable gain then arose. For that purpose the base cost of the Greenjacket shares allotted to the Dawsons would be the price which they paid for them, namely the value of the shares in the operating companies at the date of the transactions. *b* That element of double taxation exists whenever a shareholder sells at a profit his shares in a company which has itself realised a capital asset at a profit. So I do not see any undesirable element of double taxation involved in the Crown's submission.

Oliver LJ was satisfied that, applying the *Ramsay* principle, he was entitled to reject the Crown's contention provided that the matter was not concluded by this House's approval of the judgment of Eveleigh LJ in the *Floor* case. The question on the appeal, he said, was *c* whether Vinelott J was right to distinguish the *Floor* case. His conclusion was that the judgment of Eveleigh LJ, and therefore this House's indorsement of it, could not properly be read divorced from the background that stage 1 was, and was all along intended to be, followed by stage 2, as a result of which the proceeds of sale became the absolute property of the taxpayers. (I observe in parenthesis that there seems to be no finding in the *Floor* case that the assets of FNW on its liquidation became the absolute property of the *d* taxpayers.) Oliver LJ's approach to the judgment of Eveleigh LJ and to this House's indorsement of it is in my opinion totally untenable. There is no indication whatever that Eveleigh LJ paid the remotest attention to stage 2 at that stage of his judgment, or that the approval of this House proceeded on the basis that the existence of stage 2 was significant or decisive.

Kerr LJ adopted the reasoning and thus the errors of Oliver LJ. *e*

Slade LJ accepted that there was no relevant distinction between the instant case and the *Floor* case, but nevertheless concluded that this House's approval of the dissent of Eveleigh LJ was not intended to bind the court in future cases to the conclusion that, on facts such as were found in stage 1, there had been a disposal by the original vendor to the ultimate purchaser. The references to *Floor*, he said, were 'clearly a convenient mode of illustrating the broader approach to tax avoidance schemes which [their Lordships] *f* were concerned to establish' (see [1983] 3 WLR 635 at 663). Having freed himself from the uncomfortable shackles of judicial precedent, he said that, on the facts, he could not see how there could have failed to be a disposal by the Dawsons to Greenjacket and by Greenjacket to Wood Bastow. He relied particularly on the undisputed fact that the first sale agreement passed the full legal and beneficial title to Greenjacket, and that the second sale agreement passed the full legal and beneficial title to Wood Bastow. *g*

It is difficult to escape the impression that the High Court and the Court of Appeal were determined at all costs to confine the *Ramsay* principle to the sort of self-cancelling arrangement which existed in that case, and to resist what they conceived to be a deplorable inroad into the sacred principles of the *Westminster* case.

My Lords, in my opinion the rationale of the new approach is this. In a preplanned tax saving scheme, no distinction is to be drawn for fiscal purposes, because none exists in *h* reality, between (i) a series of steps which are followed through by virtue of an arrangement which falls short of a binding contract, and (ii) a like series of steps which are followed through because the participants are contractually bound to take each step seriatim. In a contractual case the fiscal consequences will naturally fall to be assessed in the light of the contractually agreed results. For example, equitable interests may pass when the contract for sale is signed. In many cases equity will regard that as done which *j* is contracted to be done. *Ramsay* says that the fiscal result is to be no different if the several steps are preordained rather than precontracted. For example, in the instant case tax will, on the *Ramsay* principle, fall to be assessed on the basis that there was a tripartite contract between the Dawsons, Greenjacket and Wood Bastow under which the Dawsons contracted to transfer their shares in the operating companies to Greenjacket in return for an allotment of shares in Greenjacket, and under which Greenjacket simultaneously contracted to transfer the same shares to Wood Bastow for a sum in cash. Under such a

a tripartite contract the Dawsons would clearly have disposed of the shares in the operating companies in favour of Wood Bastow in consideration of a sum of money paid by Wood Bastow with the concurrence of the Dawsons to Greenjacket. Tax would be assessed, and the base value of the Greenjacket shares calculated, accordingly. *Ramsay* says that this fiscal result cannot be avoided because the preordained series of steps are to be found in an informal arrangement instead of in a binding contract. The day is not saved for the

b taxpayer because the arrangement is unsigned or contains the magic words 'this is not a binding contract'.

The formulation by Lord Diplock in *Burmah* expresses the limitations of the *Ramsay* principle. First, there must be a preordained series of transactions, or, if one likes, one single composite transaction. This composite transaction may or may not include the achievement of a legitimate commercial (ie business) end. The composite transaction

c does, in the instant case: it achieved a sale of the shares in the operating companies by the Dawsons to Wood Bastow. It did not in *Ramsay*. Second, there must be steps inserted which have no commercial (business) *purpose* apart from the avoidance of a liability to tax, not 'no business *effect*'. If those two ingredients exist, the inserted steps are to be disregarded for fiscal purposes. The court must then look at the end result. Precisely how the end result will be taxed will depend on the terms of the taxing statute sought to be

d applied.

In the instant case the inserted step was the introduction of Greenjacket as a buyer from the Dawsons and as a seller to Wood Bastow. That inserted step had no business purpose apart from the deferment of tax, although it had a business effect. If the sale had taken place in 1964 before capital gains tax was introduced, there would have been no Greenjacket.

e The formulation, therefore, involves two findings of fact: first whether there was a preordained series of transactions, ie a single composite transaction; second, whether that transaction contained steps which were inserted without any commercial or business purpose apart from a tax advantage. Those are facts to be found by the commissioners. They may be primary facts or, more probably, inferences to be drawn from the primary facts. If they are inferences, they are nevertheless facts to be found by the commissioners.

f Such inferences of fact cannot be disturbed by the court save on *Edwards (Inspector of Taxes) v Bairstow* [1955] 3 All ER 48, [1956] AC 14 principles.

In *Marriott v Oxford and District Co-op Society Ltd* [1969] 3 All ER 1126 at 1128, [1970] 1 QB 186 at 192 Lord Denning MR said:

'. . . the primary facts were not in dispute. The only question was what was the proper inference from them. That is a question of law with which this court can

g and should interfere.'

Similar observations occur in other reported cases. I agree with the proposition only if it means that an appellate court, whose jurisdiction is limited to questions of law, can and should interfere with an inference of fact drawn by the fact-finding tribunal which cannot be justified by the primary facts. I do not agree with it if it is intended to mean

h that, if the primary facts justify alternative inferences of fact, an appellate court can substitute its own preferred inference for the inference drawn by the fact-finding tribunal. I think this is clear from the tenor of the speeches in this House in *Edwards (Inspector of Taxes) v Bairstow*. The point does not seem to have been the subject matter of explicit pronouncement in any of the reported cases, at least your Lordships have been referred to none, and both propositions have from time to time emerged in judgments

j as a matter of assumption rather than decision. But for my part I have no doubt that the correct approach in this type of case, where inferences have to be drawn, is for the commissioners to determine (infer) from their findings of primary fact the further fact whether there was a single composite transaction in the sense in which I have used that expression, and whether that transaction contains steps which were inserted without any commercial or business purpose apart from a tax advantage, and for the appellate court to interfere with that inference of fact only in a case where it is unsupportable on the basis of the primary facts so found. Accordingly, I respectfully disagree with the judge in the instant case where he expressed the opposite view (see [1982] STC 267 at 287).

The result of correctly applying the *Ramsay* principle to the facts of this case is that there was a disposal by the Dawsons in favour of Wood Bastow in consideration of a sum of money paid with the concurrence of the Dawsons to Greenjacket. Capital gains tax is payable accordingly. I would therefore allow the appeals. I agree that there should be no order for costs in your Lordships' House.

Appeals allowed. No order for costs in the House of Lords.

Solicitors: *Solicitor of Inland Revenue*; *Turner Kenneth Brown*, agents for *Browne Jacobson & Roose*, Nottingham (for the taxpayers).

Mary Rose Plummer   Barrister.

Sevenoaks District Council v Pattullo & Vinson Ltd

COURT OF APPEAL, CIVIL DIVISION
SIR JOHN DONALDSON MR, GRIFFITHS AND SLADE LJJ
16, 25 NOVEMBER 1983

Markets and fairs – Disturbance – Levying of rival market – Market rights conveyed subject to purported reservation of right to hold same-day market within common law distance dealing with same commodities – Whether market rights capable of severance by purported reservation – Whether market held in reliance of reservation properly established.

Markets and fairs – Disturbance – Levying of rival market – Rival market within common law distance – Whether such nuisance actionable without proof of damage.

The vendors, who were the predecessors in title of both the plaintiffs and the defendant, enjoyed rights by virtue of the doctrine of presumed lost grant to hold a market dealing in any commodity on Saturdays and other lawful days in the market place in the manor of Sevenoaks. In 1925 the vendors conveyed to the plaintiffs' predecessor in title all their estate and interest in the market rights excluding, inter alia, the right to sell livestock. At that time the livestock market, which operated on Mondays, was transferred to the cattle market in another part of the manor. Subsequently the vendors' interests which survived the 1925 conveyance were transferred to the defendant's predecessor in title. Thereafter, the plaintiffs operated a general market in the market place on Saturdays and the defendant operated a livestock market in the cattle market on Mondays. In 1981 the defendant started operating a general market on the site of the cattle market on Saturdays and, although that market closed down shortly afterwards, the defendant claimed the right to resume holding a general market on Saturdays in the cattle market. The plaintiffs brought proceedings for a declaration that the defendant was not entitled to hold a general market and an injunction preventing it from doing so. The plaintiffs contended that, since the general market in the cattle market was a rival same-day market within the common law distance of 6⅔ miles from their own general market in the market place, they were entitled to relief without proof of actual damage. The defendant claimed (i) that the 1925 conveyance had severed the original market rights, thus granting (a) to the plaintiffs the right to hold a general market, except for livestock, in the market place on Saturdays and other lawful days and (b) to the defendant the vendors' residual rights to hold a market at any place in the manor on Saturdays and on other lawful days, and (ii) that since the plaintiffs' claim was in nuisance it could not succeed without proof of damage. The judge granted the relief sought, holding (i) that, although it was possible to sever the rights of market, the terms of the 1925 conveyance had not done so, and (ii) that the plaintiffs' claim in damages was actionable without proof of damage. The defendants appealed.

Held – The appeal would be dismissed for the following reasons—

(1) Although the owner of market rights could remove the entire market, or part of the market dealing with particular commodities, from one place to another suitable place in the manor, the owner was not entitled to sever the right of the market itself in order to hold two or more separate same-day markets dealing wholly or in part with the same commodities within the manor at different places. Accordingly the vendors could not by the 1925 conveyance have reserved or retained valid and effective rights to hold a general market on the same day as the plaintiffs' predecessor in title and therefore on its true construction the 1925 conveyance had not severed the right to hold a general market dealing in the same commodities nor had it reserved to the defendant the right to hold a general same-day market concurrently with that of the plaintiffs. The defendant was therefore not entitled to hold such a market (see p 550 g to j, p 551 f to j, p 552 b c, p 553 f and p 554 a to e and h, post); *Curwen v Salkeld* (1803) 3 East 538 and *Wortley v Nottingham Local Board* (1869) 21 LT 582 considered.

(2) Where a market owner claimed relief against the holding of a rival market within the common law distance of $6\frac{2}{3}$ miles, the claim was actionable without proof of damage. It followed that since the defendant had held a general Saturday market in the cattle market within the common law distance of the plaintiffs' market the plaintiffs had established their cause of action even though they had not shown actual or prospective damage (see p 552 j, p 553 f and p 554 f to h, post); *Tamworth BC v Fazeley Town Council* (1978) 77 LGR 238 followed.

Notes

For the nature and creation of a franchise market, see 29 Halsbury's Laws (4th edn) paras 601–608, and for cases on the subject, see 33 Digest (Reissue) 203–208, *1617–1663*.

For the rights and duties of the owner of a market, see 29 Halsbury's Laws (4th edn) para 620, and for cases on the subject, see 33 Digest (Reissue) 208–209, *1664–1666*.

For levying a rival market within the common law distance, see 29 Halsbury's Laws (4th edn) paras 653–658, and for cases on the subject, see 33 Digest (Reissue) 227–228, *1890–1895*.

For the rights of removal of a franchise market, see 29 Halsbury's Laws (4th edn) paras 681–684, and for cases on the subject, see 33 Digest (Reissue) 247–248, *2051–2067*.

Cases referred to in judgments

Armstrong v Sheppard & Short Ltd [1959] 2 All ER 651, [1959] 2 QB 384, [1959] 3 WLR 84, CA.

Curwen v Salkeld (1803) 3 East 538, 102 ER 703.

Miller v Jackson [1977] 3 All ER 338, [1977] QB 966, [1977] 3 WLR 20, CA.

Mosley v Walker (1827) 7 B & C 40, 108 ER 640.

Shelfer v City of London Electric Lighting Co, Meux's Brewery Co v City of London Electric Lighting Co [1895] 1 Ch 287, [1891–4] All ER Rep 838, CA.

Tamworth BC v Fazeley Town Council (1978) 77 LGR 238.

Wortley v Nottingham Local Board (1869) 21 LT 582.

Appeal

The defendant, Pattullo & Vinson Ltd, appealed against the judgment of Mr Donald Rattee QC sitting as a deputy judge of the High Court on 4 February 1983 whereby he granted (i) a declaration that the plaintiffs, Sevenoaks District Council, were entitled to market rights (other than the right to sell livestock or to hold auction sales of any

description) in an ancient market to be held on Saturday in every week in the town of
Sevenoaks in the county of Kent and to the tolls, stallage and other profits appertaining   *a*
to the market and (ii) an injunction that the defendant be restrained from doing (whether
by its directors or by its servants or agents or any of them or otherwise howsoever) the
following acts or any of them, ie holding a market (other than a market limited to the
sale of livestock or an auction sale) in the cattle market site in Hitchen Hatch Lane,
Sevenoaks, Kent on Saturdays or otherwise using or permitting to be used any portion of
its property on the site in such manner as to interfere with or prejudicially affect the   *b*
market rights of the plaintiffs in the ancient market at Sevenoaks, Kent. By a respondent's
notice, the plaintiffs sought that the judgment be upheld on other grounds, namely that
the judge ought to have held that a franchise of market in respect of an area was not
capable of being divided by reference to locations within such area (as opposed to by
reference to commodities to be sold or to market days) so that the parties' common
predecessor in title could not, at the time of their grant in 1925 to the plaintiffs'   *c*
predecessor of the right to hold a general market in the market place in Sevenoaks on
Saturdays and other lawful days, have retained any right to hold a similar market
elsewhere within the manor of Sevenoaks and Knole. The facts are set out in the
judgment of Slade LJ.

Richard Mawrey for the defendant.   *d*
Hazel Williamson for the plaintiffs.

                                                                          Cur adv vult
                                                                                               e
25 November. The following judgments were delivered.

SLADE LJ (giving the first judgment at the invitation of Sir John Donaldson MR). This
is an appeal from an order made on 4 February 1983 at the trial of an action by Mr
Donald Rattee QC, who was sitting as a deputy judge of the Chancery Division. By this
order he declared that the plaintiffs, Sevenoaks District Council—

>   '[are] entitled to market rights (other than the right to sell livestock or to hold   *f*
>   auction sales of any description) in an ancient market to be held on Saturday in
>   every week in the town of Sevenoaks in the County of Kent and to the tolls stallage
>   and other profits to the said market appertaining.'

   The judge further granted an injunction restraining the defendant, Pattullo & Vinson
Ltd, from—

>   'holding a market (other than a market limited to the sale of livestock or an   *g*
>   auction sale) in the Cattle Market site in Hitchen Hatch Lane Sevenoaks aforesaid on
>   Saturdays or otherwise using or permitting to be used any portion of their property
>   on the said site in such manner as to interfere with or prejudicially affect the said
>   market rights of the Plaintiff in the said ancient market at Sevenoaks . . .'

   A market right, whether acquired under the common law or by statute, is a form of   *h*
property, conferring a right to hold a concourse of buyers and sellers to dispose of the
commodities in respect of which the right is given (see 29 Halsbury's Laws (4th edn) para
601). The Crown, by virtue of the royal prerogative, has always had the power to grant
to a subject the right to hold a market and, if such a right depends for its legal existence
on a Crown grant, it is a franchise (see ibid para 603). Since the holder of such a franchise
has a monopoly of market within the relevant area and the justification for this monopoly   *j*
is the public benefit, the Crown's power to grant market rights has always been limited
by the rule that a later grant, if made without the consent of the owner of the rights
conferred by an earlier grant, is void as against him if the courts consider it injuriously
to affect his rights under such earlier grant (see ibid para 605). It has been common
ground before the judge and this court that, because of this limitation, by a long-

a established rule of law, a grantee from the Crown of the right to hold a market in a specific area is entitled to complain of the opening of a new market by another person at any point within 6⅔ miles of the site of the prior market grant. As the judge explained, this distance of 6⅔ miles, within which it was thought appropriate to protect a market owner against competition, was apparently linked in some way to a distance of 20 miles, which it was assumed that a man could walk in a day; but the rationale of this rule requires no investigation for present purposes.

b A market has been held in the market place in the High Street of Sevenoaks (which I shall call 'the market place') from almost time immemorial. In the evidence before the judge there were undisputed references to such markets being held as far back as 1292. He was invited by counsel on both sides to proceed on the assumption that, by virtue of the doctrine of presumed lost grant, the third Baron Sackville, as Lord of the Manor of Sevenoaks and Knole (which I shall call 'the manor'), immediately before the transactions

c to which I am about to refer, was entitled to the widest possible rights to hold a market of any description in Sevenoaks, at least on Saturdays. There appears no reason to doubt the correctness of this assumption.

In 1919 Lord Sackville granted a lease of the right to hold a market in Sevenoaks and of the soil of the market place. Soon after that, the livestock part of this market, which had previously been held from ancient times in the market place, was moved to a site

d known as 'the cattle market', situated at Hitchen Hatch Lane, which is also within the manor. The day of holding such livestock sales was changed from Saturday to Monday. The general non-livestock market continued to be held on Saturdays in the market place. By a conveyance of 7 May 1923 Lord Sackville sold the freehold reversion expectant on the determination of the 1919 lease to Kent and Sussex Farmers Ltd (K & SF).

For present purposes nothing turns on the particular provisions of the 1919 lease and

e the 1923 conveyance. It is common ground that by virtue of these two documents, through an original franchise granted by the Crown, and in the events which had happened, K & SF became entitled to the freehold of the soil of the market place and all the market rights which had previously been vested in Lord Sackville as the lord of the manor, in other words to the widest possible rights to hold a market of any description in Sevenoaks, at least on a Saturday.

f Such was the position when K & SF, on 12 January 1925, executed a conveyance of certain rights in favour of Sevenoaks Urban District Council, the predecessors in title of the plaintiffs. The 1925 conveyance is of cardinal importance in the present case, because it is the foundation of the plaintiffs' claims to a declaration and injunction in the form which the judge gave it.

By the 1925 conveyance the vendors, K & SF, with the concurrence of certain

g mortgagees, conveyed to the Sevenoaks Urban District Council, for a consideration of £450, first, the soil of the market place and, second (I quote from the conveyance):

'. . . all such estate and interest as the Vendors have of and in all those market rights and market to be from time to time held on Saturdays and other lawful days in the said Market Place (but not elsewhere) excluding the right to sell live stock or to hold auction sales of any description.'

h The 1925 conveyance also contained covenants by the vendors for themselves, their successors and assigns that they would not hold any sale by auction in the market place and covenants by the purchasers for themselves, their successors and assigns that they would not give permission to anyone to hold any sale by auction in the market place.

Some two years later by two respective conveyances of 16 March 1927 K & SF, then in

j liquidation, with the concurrence of certain debenture holders and the liquidator, conveyed to Pattullo Higgs & Co Ltd (a) in consideration of £500, the freehold of the site of the cattle market, (b) in consideration of £3,450, the franchise theretofore held and enjoyed by K & SF, and formerly held by their predecessors as part of the manor, comprising the market rights and the markets to be from time to time held on Saturdays and other lawful days in or near Sevenoaks—

'other than and except such market rights as were conveyed by the Vendor Company to the Urban District Council of Sevenoaks by [the 1925 conveyance] . . . but including all such rights as were excluded from such Indenture together with the benefit of the covenants on the part of the said Urban District Council contained in this Indenture . . .'

The particulars of the two 1927 conveyances do not matter, since it is common ground, first, that they operated to convey to Pattullo Higgs & Co Ltd all such rights to hold markets in the manor as K & SF then had power to convey and, second, that any and all such rights have now devolved on the defendant.

Since the date of the 1925 conveyance the Sevenoaks Urban District Council, and more recently the plaintiffs, in reliance on the rights granted by that conveyance, have operated a general market in the market place (or more accurately a part of the market place) on Saturday in each week. The plaintiffs intend to continue operating it and the defendant does not challenge their right to do so.

Since the 1927 conveyances the defendant or its predecessor, in reliance on the rights granted by those conveyances, has continued to operate a livestock market in the cattle market on Monday of each week, which the plaintiffs do not seek to prevent.

The judge also found that (i) since at least 1930 and 'possibly, even, from as early as 1923' the defendant or its predecessors also operated a general market in the cattle market on Mondays, albeit as ancillary to the livestock market, (ii) the defendant in addition now operates a general market in the cattle market on Wednesdays. The plaintiffs do not seek to prevent these activities.

The events that gave rise to the present litigation were these. In August 1981 the defendant started operating on the cattle market on Saturday in each week a new general market which was on a larger scale than that operated by the plaintiffs on Saturday each week in the market place. This new general market did not last very long and was finally closed. As the judge put it:

'There is no suggestion that the defendant's Saturday market on the cattle market did, or in future would, have any adverse effect on the operation of the plaintiffs' Saturday market on the market place.'

However, the defendant still claimed the right to reactivate a general market on Saturdays in the cattle market if it thought fit. The plaintiffs for their part claimed the right to prevent it. Hence the present proceedings, in which the plaintiffs sought what they considered an appropriate declaration and injunction.

In an exceptionally comprehensive and erudite judgment in *Tamworth BC v Fazeley Town Council* (1978) 77 LGR 238 Mr Vivian Price QC sitting as a deputy High Court judge, after a review of all the relevant authorities, decided that there was an irrebuttable presumption that a new market set up to be held on the same day as a franchise market was a nuisance and that the cause of action for nuisance to the franchise market was complete when the franchise owner established that there was a same-day market within the 6⅔ miles distance, unless the new market was licensed by the franchise holder himself or was the subject of a concurrent right of market franchise, either by Crown grant or by statute.

For the purpose of the argument before the judge, counsel for the defendant accepted that the law was correctly stated in the *Tamworth* case and that therefore, if the plaintiffs had taken directly *from the Crown* the right to hold a general market on Saturdays in the market place (there being at the time of such grant no similar market held in the cattle market), the plaintiffs would have been entitled without proof of damage, by an action in nuisance, to restrain the defendant from opening a general market on a Saturday in the cattle market, even though the defendant had done so under a purported grant from the Crown subsequent to the grant to the plaintiffs. The cattle market is much less than 6⅔ miles from the market place.

In the present case, however, neither the plaintiffs nor the defendant derived title through a direct grant from the Crown. This is a case where K & SF (the common

predecessor in title of the plaintiffs and the defendant), which itself had the right to hold
a general market anywhere in Sevenoaks, purported to *sever* its right by granting, to the
plaintiffs, the right to hold a general market in the market place (except for the sale of
livestock) and, to the defendant, its residual rights to hold a market at any place in the
manor. In these circumstances, as appears from the judgment, counsel for the defendant
submitted to the judge in effect that (1) it was possible in law for K & SF, while making a
valid and effective grant to the plaintiffs' predecessor of the right to hold a general market
in the market place, at the same time to make a valid and effective reservation in favour
of themselves and their successors of the right to hold a general market on the same day
anywhere else in Sevenoaks, (2) on the true construction of the 1925 conveyance, K & SF
in fact made such a reservation.

The judge in effect accepted the first of these two propositions (which I will call 'the
defendant's first basic proposition') but rejected the second. He thought that on the true
construction of the 1925 conveyance there had been no such reservation. He considered
that the right at common law for the owner of a market right, without proof of damage,
to bring proceedings for nuisance to restrain a rival market within a 6⅔-mile limit is an
incident of the market right. Consequently, in his view, the grant in the 1925 conveyance
prima facie conferred on the grantee the right to restrain the holding of a rival same-day
general market anywhere within the 6⅔ miles limit by any other person, including the
grantor K & SF (and perhaps a fortiori in the case of K & SF, having regard to the principle
against derogation from grant). He considered that, to rebut this prima facie limitation
on its rights as successor of K & SF by virtue of the 1927 conveyance, the defendant had
to show that the 1925 conveyance on its true construction reserved to K & SF a right to
hold a rival same-day general market, which would override the grantee's prima facie
right to exclusivity. The judge went on to reject the defendant's argument that the
relevant words in the 1925 conveyance, in particular the words 'but not elsewhere',
amounted to an express reservation of this nature. He did not consider that the covenants
regarding the holding of an auction sale in the market place gave any assistance to the
defendant. He concluded:

'I cannot construe the words quoted, or any other words in the 1925 conveyance,
as reserving to the grantor the right to do what otherwise the grant gave the grantee
the right to prevent anyone doing, namely holding a general market within 6⅔
miles of the market place. The words in parenthesis, relied on by [counsel for the
defendant], mean in my judgment no more than they say, namely that the grantee
is not given the right to hold a general market other than in the market place.'

For these reasons, the judge held that the plaintiffs were entitled, without proof of
damage, to complain of the defendant holding a general market on a Saturday in the
cattle market, or anywhere else within 6⅔ miles of the market place. He rejected an
argument that, because there was no suggestion that the plaintiffs would thereby suffer
damage, they should not be granted any injunction restraining the defendant from
resuming the holding of a rival general market on a Saturday. In the result he granted
the plaintiffs relief in the form set out at the beginning of this judgment.

The defendant now appeals from this judgment. The points which it sought to take
by its notice of appeal were in substance three, namely that the judge erred (1) in
construing the 1925 conveyance as not reserving to the grantor the right to hold a
Saturday market of a general nature within the franchise area on a site other than the
market place, (2) in holding that a same-day market is actionable without proof of
damage, (3) in holding that he was bound to grant an injunction or alternatively in the
exercise of his discretion in granting such relief. I will deal with each of these points in
turn.

Quite early in the course of counsel's argument on behalf of the defendant it became
obvious that the construction and effect of the 1925 conveyance must in the first instance
largely depend on the correctness or otherwise of what I have called the defendant's first
basic proposition. Since this court was by no means satisfied that this was necessarily

correct in law, we therefore allowed counsel for the plaintiffs (without opposition from counsel for the defendant) to put in a respondent's notice challenging the correctness of this proposition, even though I think it was not seriously challenged in the court below. The respondent's notice asserts:

'That the learned judge ought to have held that a franchise of market in respect of an area is not capable of being divided by reference to locations within such area (as opposed to by reference to commodities to be sold or to market days) so that the parties' common predecessor in title could not, at the time of its grant in 1925 to the Plaintiff's predecessor of the right to hold a general market in the Market Place in Sevenoaks on Saturdays and other lawful days, have retained any right to hold a similar market elsewhere within the manor.'

Thus, in substance, the submission is that the franchisee of a right of market for a particular locality is not entitled to purport to sever his right by holding in that locality two or more markets, dealing with the same commodities, in different places on the same day.

If this submission is right, it must follow that on no footing can the 1925 conveyance have made an effective reservation entitling the grantor (or its successors) to hold a Saturday market of a general nature within the franchise area on a site other than the market place. For, as counsel for the defendant very properly conceded, the 1925 conveyance could not have operated to confer on the grantor and grantee a totality of rights to hold Saturday markets greater than the grantor itself possessed immediately before the grant.

Counsel for the defendant, however, contended that there is nothing to prevent a franchisee of a right of market for a particular locality from severing his right by holding, in that locality, two or more markets dealing (wholly or in part) with the same commodities on the same day. In this context he referred us to the decision of the Court of Queen's Bench in *Wortley v Nottingham Local Board* (1869) 21 LT 582. In that case Nottingham corporation had a right of market within a manor. The corporation had removed that part of the market which dealt with skins from the market place where the market had been traditionally held to a different locality, which it considered more convenient. The legality of this removal was then challenged. Cockburn CJ rejected this challenge, holding that the corporation was justified in making the transfer. He said (at 584):

'I think it is quite clear that the corporation must be taken to have a right of market anywhere within the manor, and therefore that they could transfer the market from one place to another within such manor, and on the authority of the cases cited this right to transfer a part of the market to another place, so as to suit public convenience, seems to be implied.'

Counsel for the defendant submitted that the phrase 'this right to transfer a part of the market' is in wide general terms and should not be read as confined to a transfer of a particular category of commodities. I cannot accept this submission. It seems to me clear that, in this context, Cockburn CJ was directing his observations solely to a transfer of the last-mentioned nature and that the decision is no authority whatever for the proposition that the owner of a right of market has the right to set up two quite separate markets dealing simultaneously with the same, or partly the same, commodities.

Counsel for the plaintiffs referred us to two more authorities in this context. The first was *Curwen v Salkeld* (1803) 3 East 538 at 544–545, 102 ER 703 at 705, in which Lord Ellenborough CJ held as follows:

'If the lord have a grant of market within a certain place, though he have at one time appointed it in one situation, he may certainly remove its afterwards to another situation within the place named in his grant . . . There is nothing in reason to prevent the lord from changing the place within the precinct of his grant, taking care at the same time to accommodate the public . . . If the lord in the exercise of his right be guilty of any abuse of the franchise, there may be a remedy of another nature. The right of removal however is incident to his grant, if he be not tied down to a particular spot by the terms of it.'

In *Mosley v Walker* (1827) 7 B & C 40, 108 ER 640 the Court of King's Bench held on the evidence that the lord of an ancient market had the right to prevent other persons from selling goods in their private houses situated within the limits of his franchise. In the course of the case, the question arose as to the duties of the lord to provide accommodation for persons from time to time resorting to the market. Bayley J had this to say (7 B & C 40 at 55, 108 ER 640 at 645):

'I take it to be implied in the terms in which a market is granted, that the grantee, if he confine it to particular parts within a town, shall fix it in such parts as will from time to time yield to the public reasonable accommodation.'

The decisions in the *Wortley* case and in *Curwen v Salkeld* are in my opinion authority for the propositions that K & SF, if it had seen fit, would have been entitled (a) to move the entire market from the market place to some other suitable place within the manor, (b) to move a part of the market which dealt with one or more particular commodities to some other suitable place within the manor. The *Wortley* decision thus would, I think, have justified the removal of the livestock part of the market to the cattle market, which took place soon after the 1919 lease.

Counsel for the defendant, however, was able to refer us to no authority which in my opinion came near to showing that K & SF, if it had seen fit, would have been entitled, by virtue of its presumed Crown grant to hold two or more separate general markets, dealing wholly or in part with the same commodities, simultaneously in different places within the manor. On the contrary, the numerous paragraphs from the relevant title in 29 Halsbury's Laws (4th edn) which were read to us by counsel for the plaintiffs and contain much learning on the subject of the rights of market franchisees, to my mind suggest the contrary.

The grant of a right of market by the Crown will affect not only the grantor and the grantee but also the members of the public living in or frequenting the area. Many of the rules which have grown up under the common law for the purpose of regulating the rights and duties of market franchisees have clearly been formulated with the public interest in mind.

If the defendant's contentions in the present context are correct, it must follow, as counsel for the defendant conceded, that the franchisee of a right of market in a particular area would prima facie have the right to conduct at the same time not just two but an unlimited number of general markets in the area, subject to any rights which the Crown might possess to prevent abuse in any particular case. In the absence of any authority which supports this proposition I am unable to accept it.

Accordingly, while I accept that, as was common ground before the judge, K & SF had the widest possible rights to hold *a* general market of any description in the manor, at least on a Saturday, the court cannot in my opinion properly presume that the grant which originally conferred this right entitled the grantee to hold more than one general market on the same day. I might add that our attention has been drawn to no evidence whatever which might suggest that this was in truth the effect of the original grant.

Accordingly, the defendant's first basic proposition is in my judgment ill-founded in law. It must follow that, on any construction of the 1925 conveyance, K & SF did not either reserve or retain valid and effective rights to hold a general market within the manor on the same day as the plaintiffs' predecessor, since such reservation or retention would have been a legal impossibility; the right to hold a general market was not, in my judgment, capable of being severed in this way.

Accordingly, in my opinion, it is not necessary for the plaintiffs to rely on their alternative argument based on the absence of any words in the 1925 conveyance expressly reserving to the grantor the right to hold a same-day general market within 6⅔ miles of the grantee's general market.

Nor is it necessary to consider certain other questions which might have arisen on the construction of the 1925 conveyance, for example the meaning of the phrase 'other *a* lawful days', a matter which was only touched on in the course of argument. We do not have to decide whether a franchise of market is capable in law of being severed by reference to market days, so as to allow the conduct of a market in one place on one day of the week and in another place on another day, since the plaintiffs do not object to the defendant carrying on a general market at the cattle market on days other than Saturdays.

For the reasons already given, it follows that the judge was in my opinion right, in the *b* result, in holding that the plaintiffs have the legal right to object to the defendant's holding a market (other than a market limited to the sale of livestock or an auction sale) in the cattle market on Saturdays.

I now turn to the question of the relief that should be granted, which I think can be dealt with more briefly.

In the *Tamworth* case (1978) 77 LGR 238 at 247 Mr Vivian Price QC quoted a note by *c* Sir Matthew Hale in his commentary to *Fitzherbert's Natura Brevium* (7th edn, 1730). The note read as follows:

'If the market be on the same day it shall be intended a nuisance, but if it be on another day it shall not be so intended and therefore it shall be put in issue whether it be a nuisance or not.' *d*

Mr Price then proceeded to a review of subsequent cases in which this note had been repeated over and over again as being the definitive statement of the rule of law. After this review, he concluded as follows (at 266):

'At the end of the day I have come to the very firm conclusion that the overwhelming preponderance of judicial authority is that the cause of action is complete when the franchise owner establishes that there is a same-day market *e* within the common law distance. In my judgment the statement by Sir Matthew Hale in his commentary to *Fitzherbert's Natura Brevium* is a true statement of the law, subject only to this explanation, that the word "intended" in that statement means that there is an irrebuttable presumption that a new market set up to be held on the same day as the franchise market is a nuisance unless the new market is itself *f* licensed by the franchise market holder or is the subject of a concurrent right of market franchise either by Crown grant or pursuant to statute.'

Counsel for the defendant in his submissions to us did not dispute that there is indeed an overwhelming preponderance of authority supporting the rule as stated by Sir Matthew Hale and explained by Mr Price himself. Nevertheless, he pointed out that the authorities cited to Mr Price were of considerable antiquity and related to different social *g* conditions, and submitted that none of them appear to be technically binding on this court. He pointed out that the protection enjoyed by the market holder stems from the law of nuisance, under which a plaintiff generally has to prove injury or the prospect of injury. In his submission it is anomalous if a market holder can complain of a same-day market, without adducing any evidence as to actual or prospective injury. Since the right of market is a monopoly, he submitted that it would amount to an unreasonable restraint *h* of trade, contrary to public policy, if the court were to intervene to protect such monopoly in a case where a plaintiff does not attempt to prove damage but, on the face of it, merely wishes to prevent the defendant from trading.

I see the force of these submissions and, if the matter were res integra, might well have been attracted by them. Nevertheless, the authorities referred to in the *Tamworth* case are authorities stretching back over many centuries. Even if they are not technically binding *j* on us, in my opinion it is far too late to ask this court to depart from them. The plaintiffs have therefore established their cause of action, even in the absence of proof of any actual or prospective damage.

Finally, counsel for the defendant submitted that if liability has been established, this is a case where an appropriate declaration should be made as to the plaintiffs' rights and, possibly, nominal damages should be awarded, but an injunction should still not be

granted. He referred us to the well-known statement by A L Smith LJ in *Shelfer v City of*
a   *London Electric Lighting Co* [1895] 1 Ch 287 at 322–323, [1891–4] All ER Rep 838 at 848
to the effect that damages in substitution for an injunction may be given in a case where
the injury to the plaintiff's legal rights is small, is capable of being estimated in money
and can be adequately compensated by a money payment, and where it would be
oppressive to the defendant to grant an injunction. He cited the decision of this court in
Armstrong v Sheppard & Short Ltd [1959] 2 All ER 651, [1959] 2 QB 384, where a plaintiff,
b   who had proved the existence of a proprietary right and the infringement of it, was
refused an injunction because the wrong done was trivial, the plaintiff had misled the
defendants and attempted to mislead the court and had suffered no damage.

Though there is no suggestion that the plaintiffs have attempted to mislead anyone in
the present case, counsel for the defendant strongly submitted that the wrong done (if
any) is trivial, that it has caused no damage and that it would be oppressive to the
c   defendant to grant an injunction which would restrict future trading. He also referred us
to the decision of this court in *Miller v Jackson* [1977] 3 All ER 338 at 345, 350–351,
[1977] 1 QB 966 at 982, 988–989 in which both Lord Denning MR and Cumming-Bruce
LJ expressed the view that the court, in exercising its equitable jurisdiction to grant or
refuse an injunction, is under a duty to have regard to the public interest.

The argument based on the public interest, however, seems to me to be somewhat
d   double-edged. If my conclusions so far are right, the plain facts are that the defendant is
claiming the right to hold a general market at the cattle market on Saturdays which it
has no right whatever to hold (whether in relation to the plaintiffs or the public at large)
and that the public must be affected thereby, because the holding of a market must
inevitably involve a restriction, at least to some extent, of the public's rights.

I think there is much force in the judge's observation that—

e   'the very fact that the defendant's activities constitute a nuisance actionable
without proof of damage make this peculiarly a case where damages are not an
appropriate remedy and therefore injunctive relief is.'

Though I would accept, as I infer he did, that he had a residual discretion whether to
grant or withhold an injunction, I do not in all the circumstances think there are any
f   possible grounds for interfering with the exercise of his discretion in granting it.

For all these reasons, I think that the decision of the judge was correct and I would
dismiss this appeal. In conclusion, I would like to express my thanks to counsel on both
sides for their guidance through a recondite and confused branch of the law, which I, for
my part, think might well benefit from attention on the part of the legislature.

g   **SIR JOHN DONALDSON MR.** The result of this appeal depends on the true
construction of the words of the 1925 conveyance:

'. . . such estate and interest as the Vendors have of and in all those market rights
and market to be from time to time held on Saturdays and other lawful days in the
h   said Market Place (but not elsewhere) excluding the right to sell live stock or to hold
auction sales of any description.'

But this in turn depends on what market rights were possessed by the vendors
immediately before the conveyance took effect.

It was accepted both in this court and before the trial judge that the vendors, Kent and
Sussex Farmers Ltd (K & SF) were to be deemed to have enjoyed the most extensive
j   market rights in respect of the Manor of Sevenoaks. Such rights were found by the judge,
without the contrary being seriously argued, to be sufficiently extensive to have enabled
K & SF to grant a purchaser the right to hold a market on the market place, reserving to
themselves the right to hold a similar market on the same day anywhere else in Sevenoaks,
notwithstanding that such a rival market would have infringed the market right granted
to the purchaser but for such reservation. The judge then construed the grant contained
in the conveyance as not containing any such reservation.

For my part, I am not sure that I would have agreed with the construction accepted by the judge, but this is immaterial since I have concluded that his premise as to the extent   *a* of K & SF's right is ill-founded.

If K & SF were able to grant market rights to the purchaser whilst reserving the right to hold a similar market on the same day elsewhere in the manor, it follows that prior to the conveyance their market rights must have enabled them to hold similar markets in more than one place simultaneously. This has never been suggested in any of the authorities, even at a time when markets and market rights were much more important   *b* and better understood than they are today. The furthest that the authorities go is to hold that the proprietor of market rights can transfer *the* market from one place to another within the manor and can transfer part of *the* market, thus producing two dissimilar markets operating simultaneously, e g a general market dealing in everything save skins and cattle and a cattle and skin market: see *Wortley v Nottingham Local Board* (1869) 21 LT 582. In saying this I am not overlooking the suggestion in *Tamworth BC v Fazeley Town*   *c* *Council* (1978) 77 LGR 238 that concurrent market rights may be granted to two separate grantees by the Crown or by statute, but that is not this case.

Against this background, the construction of the conveyance presents no difficulty. K & SF were reserving to themselves the right to establish and maintain a livestock market but, subject thereto and to two other restrictions, were conveying all their market rights to the plaintiffs' predecessor. The two restrictions were that the grantees should only   *d* hold a market in the market place and that there should be no sales by auction. It follows that K & SF thereby deprived themselves of the right to establish or maintain any market, other than a livestock market, and, in the absence of such a market right, were restrained by the common law monopoly restriction inherent in market rights from establishing or maintaining any competitive market.

Two other issues have had to be considered. The first is whether the establishment of   *e* a competing same-day market is actionable without proof of damage. It is true that there is no authority for this proposition which is binding on this court, but there is abundant first instance authority: see the erudite judgment of Mr Vivian Price QC in the *Tamworth* case. For my part I do not think that this court should now hold that so many courts were in error over so long a period. It follows that the fact that the plaintiffs can prove no damage is immaterial, since the competitive market sought to be restrained is a same-   *f* day market.

The second additional issue is whether damages or a declaration of right would be an adequate remedy as an alternative to an injunction. The short answer is that they would not. The defendant has in the past established and maintained and, in the absence of an injunction, intend in the future once again to establish and maintain a market which competes with that of the plaintiffs. Bearing this in mind and the fact that this unlawful   *g* conduct is actionable without proof of damage, I consider that this court has no alternative but to give the plaintiffs injunctive relief. This was the conclusion reached by the judge, albeit by a different route.

I would dismiss the appeal.

GRIFFITHS LJ. I agree that for the reasons given by Sir John Donaldson MR and Slade   *h* LJ this appeal should be dismissed.

Appeal dismissed. Leave to appeal to the House of Lords refused.

Solicitors: *Argles & Court*, Maidstone (for the defendant); *J J Baker*, Sevenoaks (for the plaintiffs).

Diana Procter   Barrister.

a # National Coal Board v Wm Neill & Son (St Helens) Ltd

QUEEN'S BENCH DIVISION

PIERS ASHWORTH QC SITTING AS A DEPUTY JUDGE OF THE HIGH COURT

13, 14, 15, 27 JULY 1983

b *Building contract – Construction – Rules of construction for building contracts – Whether building contracts to be construed differently from other contracts.*

Building contract – Construction – Condition requiring work to be executed according to specification and to satisfaction of employer's engineer – Whether contractor required merely to c *execute work to satisfaction of employer's engineer – Whether contractor additionally required to execute work according to specification – BEAMA RC conditions (1956 edn), cl 4(i).*

Practice – Preliminary point of law – Matters appropriate to be considered as preliminary issues.

d The plaintiffs entered into a contract with the defendants, who were structural engineers, whereby the defendants agreed to dismantle and re-erect, in accordance with the plaintiffs' specification, the conveyors and gantries at the plaintiffs' colliery. The contract incorporated the standard conditions of a trade association (the BEAMA RC conditions (1956 edn)). Clause 4(i) of those conditions provided that 'All Plant to be supplied and all work to be done under the Contract shall be manufactured and executed in the manner set out in the Specification, if any, and to the reasonable satisfaction of the [plaintiffs'] e Engineer . . .' The defendants carried out the work, the plaintiffs' engineer issued a certificate of satisfaction with the work and the plaintiffs paid the defendants. Two years later one of the gantries carrying two of the conveyors collapsed. The plaintiffs alleged that that was due to the defendants' failure to execute the work in accordance with the specification, as required by cl 4(i), and brought an action against them claiming damages for breach of contract. The defendants denied liability, contending that there was a f general rule that such clauses in building contracts were interpreted as imposing merely an obligation to execute the work to the satisfaction of the employer's engineer and not as imposing on the contractor a cumulative obligation to execute the work both in the manner prescribed by the employer and to the satisfaction of his engineer. Accordingly the defendants contended that, once the plaintiffs' engineer had certified his satisfaction with the work, his certificate was conclusive evidence that the work had been carried out g satisfactorily and the plaintiffs were thereafter estopped from complaining of any failure to comply with the specification. The question of the extent of the defendants' obligations under cl 4(i) was ordered to be tried as a preliminary issue.

Held – (1) There was no general rule as to the construction of clauses in building h contracts which required the work required to be done under the contract to be executed according to the employer's specification and to the satisfaction of his engineer. Rather, the general principle of construction of contracts applied to all contracts, whether they were building contracts or not, and in each case the meaning of any clause in a particular contract had to be ascertained by looking at that contract as a whole and giving effect, so far as possible, to every part of it (see p 560 *a b*, p 564 *e f*, p 566 *b*, p 569 *c d* and p 571 *c*, j post); *G H Myers & Co v Brent Cross Service Co* [1933] All ER Rep 9, *Petrofina SA of Brussels v Compagnia Italiana Transporto Olii Minerali of Genoa* (1937) 53 TLR 650 and *Billyack v Leyland Construction Co Ltd* [1968] 1 All ER 783 applied; *Lord Bateman v Thompson* (1875) 2 Hudson's BC (4th edn) 36 considered; *Goodyear v Weymouth and Melcombe Regis Corp* (1865) Har & Ruth 67, *Harvey v Lawrence* (1867) 15 LT 571, *Dunaberg and Witepsk Rly Co (Ltd) v Hopkins Gilkes & Co (Ltd)* (1877) 36 LT 733 and *Newton Abbott Development Co Ltd v*

Stockman Bros (1931) 47 TLR 616 distinguished; *Stratford Borough v J H Ashman Ltd* [1960] NZLR 503 and *Major v Greenfield* [1965] NZLR 1035 not followed.   *a*

(2) On the true construction of cl 4(i) of the BEAMA RC conditions, the defendants were under two obligations, viz to execute the work in the manner set out in the plaintiffs' specification and to execute the work to the reasonable satisfaction of the plaintiffs' engineer (see p 571 *a* to *c* and *e*, post); *Petrofina SA of Brussels v Compagnia Italiana Transporto Olii Minerali of Genoa* (1937) 53 TLR 650 and *Billyack v Leyland Construction Co Ltd* [1968] 1 All ER 783 applied; *Lord Bateman v Thompson* (1875) 2   *b* Hudson's BC (4th edn) 36 not followed.

Observations on what matters are appropriate to be considered as preliminary issues (see p 557 *h* to p 558 *b* and p 573 *d* to *f*, post).

Notes

For the ascertainment and meaning of terms in building contracts, see 4 Halsbury's Laws   *c* (4th edn) paras 1142–1144, and for cases on the subject, see 7 Digest (Reissue) 324–326, 2206–2213.

For stipulations requiring approval of building work, see 4 Halsbury's Laws (4th edn) paras 1194–1199, and for cases on the subject, see 7 Digest (Reissue) 346–347, 383–384, 2276–2283, 2390–2395.

               d

Cases referred to in judgment

Ailsa Craig Fishing Co Ltd v Malvern Fishing Co Ltd [1983] 1 All ER 101, [1983] 1 WLR 964, HL.
Ata Ul Haq v Nairobi City Council (13 February 1959, unreported), PC.
Bateman (Lord) v Thompson (1875) 2 Hudson's BC (4th edn) 36.
Billyack v Leyland Construction Co Ltd [1968] 1 All ER 783, [1968] 1 WLR 471.   *e*
Bruens v Smith 1951 (1) SA 67.
Dunaberg and Witepsk Rly Co (Ltd) v Hopkins Gilkes & Co (Ltd) (1877) 36 LT 733.
East Ham BC v Bernard Sunley & Sons Ltd [1965] 3 All ER 619, [1966] AC 406, [1965] 3 WLR 1096, HL.
Goodyear v Weymouth and Melcombe Regis Corp (1865) Har & Ruth 67.
Hancock v B W Brazier (Anerley) Ltd [1966] 2 All ER 901, [1966] 1 WLR 1317.   *f*
Harvey v Lawrence (1867) 15 LT 571.
Major v Greenfield [1965] NZLR 1035.
Miller v Cannon Hill Estates Ltd [1931] 2 KB 113, [1931] All ER Rep 93, DC.
Myers (G H) & Co v Brent Cross Service Co [1934] 1 KB 46, [1933] All ER Rep 9.
Newton Abbott Development Co Ltd v Stockman Bros (1931) 47 TLR 616.
Petrofina SA of Brussels v Compagnia Italiana Transporto Olii Minerali of Genoa (1937) 53   *g* TLR 650, CA.
Robins v Goddard [1905] 1 KB 294, CA.
Stratford Borough v J H Ashman Ltd [1960] NZLR 503.
Young & Marten Ltd v McManus Childs Ltd [1968] 2 All ER 1169, [1969] 1 AC 454, [1968] 3 WLR 630, HL.

               h

Preliminary issue

The plaintiffs, the National Coal Board, brought an action against the defendants, Wm Neill & Son (St Helens) Ltd, claiming (i) damages for the defendants' breach of a contract, dated 15 January 1968, for the design and/or construction of certain works at Agecroft colliery in the county of Lancaster, and/or (ii) damages for negligence in such design and/   *j* or construction. The plaintiffs alleged, in their reamended statement of claim, that the collapse of a gantry, carrying two conveyors, at the Agecroft colliery on 5 August 1973 was caused by the defendants' breach of the express and implied terms of the contract and by the defendants' negligence. In their further reamended defence, the defendants denied that they were in breach of contract or that they were negligent, pleaded several *a* special defences, and alleged that the collapse of the gantry was solely caused or contributed to by the plaintiffs' negligence. On 2 October 1981 Mr District Registrar Kushner ordered (i) that the following issue raised by the pleadings be tried as a preliminary issue, namely whether the defendants were, under the terms of the contract as pleaded, liable for breach thereof and, if so, whether liability was limited by reason of the contract to £50,000, and (ii) that the issue be settled between the parties and approved by the district registrar. The parties stated the issue as follows: 'Whether upon the facts

b pleaded in Paragraphs 1, 2, 3 and 4 of the re-amended Statement of Claim, the Defences alleged in Paragraphs 2, 2a, 2b, 2c, 3, 3a and 3b of the further re-amended Defence disclose good Defences in law to all the claims pleaded by the Plaintiffs in their re-amended Statement of Claim.' The facts are set out in the judgment.

J J Rowe QC and *Simon Fawcus* for the plaintiffs.

c *E A Machin QC* and *David Clarke QC* for the defendants.

Cur adv vult

27 July. The following judgment was delivered.

d

PIERS ASHWORTH QC. On 15 January 1969 the plaintiffs, the National Coal Board, entered into a contract to carry out structural works at Agecroft colliery, Pendlebury, including the dismantling and re-erection of a number of conveyors and gantries. The contract was made in writing and contained in various documents the plaintiffs' specification, no 1430, dated 3 September 1968, the defendants' tenders dated 1 and 18

e October 1968, the plaintiffs' acceptance dated 15 January 1969, the British Electrical and Allied Manufacturers' Association Ltd conditions of contract, RC version (January 1956 edn), and certain special conditions. The work was completed and paid for by 26 January 1971. That was the end of the defects maintenance period.

On 5 August 1973 sections of the gantry carrying conveyors B and D collapsed, and the plaintiffs allege that that was due to the defendants' breach of contract and negligence.

f The defendants deny breach of contract; they deny negligence; they allege contributory negligence; and they further plead several special defences to which I shall refer later.

On 2 October 1981 Mr District Registrar Kushner made an order that the following issues raised by the pleadings in this action be tried as a preliminary issue, namely whether the defendants were, under the terms of the contract as pleaded, liable for breach thereof and, if so, whether liability is limited by reason of the contract to £50,000. He

g further ordered the issue to be settled by the parties and approved by the district registrar.

Unfortunately, instead of setting out the precise issues to be decided, the parties stated the issues simply by reference to the pleadings, whether on the facts pleaded in paras 1, 2, 3 and 4 of the reamended statement of claim the defences alleged in paras 2, 2A, 2B, 2C, 3, 3A and 3B of the further reamended defence disclosed good defences in law to all the claims pleaded by the plaintiffs in their reamended statement of claim.

h As the hearing of the issues proceeded, it became abundantly clear that some of the matters raised in these paragraphs were not or not exclusively questions of law, and that they depend primarily on issues of fact which cannot be resolved satisfactorily at this stage. As I understand the law, a preliminary issue may well be appropriate where one party says to the other, 'Even if you prove every allegation of fact in your case, nevertheless, as a matter of law you must fail'. It is a great advantage in, for example, the

j case of a building contract, investigation of which may occupy a court for very many weeks. If there is a point of law which may decide the case conclusively one way irrespective of the facts, it is clearly appropriate that the issue on that point of law should be determined before involving the court and the parties in the time and expense of detailed investigation of facts which may never become relevant. That is the position in respect of some of the issues before me. But where a party says, 'If I prove the facts set

out in my pleadings, I must, as a matter of law, succeed', it must be rare, if ever, that such
an issue can properly be decided as a preliminary issue. Even if the court answers the
question of law in favour of that party, it will still have to embark on a full investigation
of the facts with no saving of time and expense. Indeed, the court's ruling on the issue
can only be in the nature of a ruling on a hypothetical case which although adopted in
some jurisdictions is alien to the courts in this country; and that is the position in respect
of at least one of the issues before me.

As the issues were defined by reference to pleadings, I must look, first, at the pleadings.
I have referred to the contract, set out in para 1. By para 2 of the reamended statement of
claim it is pleaded, and this is admitted, that the contract incorporated the BEAMA RC
standard conditions. Reliance is placed on all of them, but certain ones are specifically set
out. Some of these are express conditions and some are implied. The first, (a):

> 'It was an express condition . . . that the Defendants were to carry out all the
> design work required for the project.'

At (b) it is pleaded that—

> 'it was an express condition . . . that arrangement drawings required to be
> submitted for approval by the Engineer should not be departed from in any way
> . . .'

At (c) it is pleaded that—

> 'it was an express condition . . . that all work to be done under the contract should
> be executed in the manner set out in the specification . . .'

There is a quotation from the specification:

> 'The gantry to carry conveyor "B" and conveyor "D" is existing and available at
> Bradford Colliery Landsales Depot. Six sections of existing gantry are to be pieced
> together to form one complete gantry, one end being supported by the Junction
> Tower and the remainder carried by five new trestles from ground level. The
> Contractor is to dismantle this gantry at Bradford Colliery and re-erect at Agecroft
> Colliery and is to include for any modifications required for the new installation.'

It is then pleaded that it was a necessary implication from this requirement—

> 'that the connections between the trestles and the gantry should be so constructed
> as to enable them to withstand normally foreseeable operating pressures.'

By sub-para (d) it is pleaded that—

> 'it was an implied condition that the design and/or construction of the said works
> would be carried out with the competence and care reasonably to be expected of
> structural engineers.'

All of these terms are admitted by para 2 of the further reamended defence, save in a
respect which is no longer material. By para 3 of the reamended statement of claim the
collapse of the gantry is pleaded; and para 4 alleges that that collapse was caused by the
defendants' breach of the express and implied conditions, and by the defendants'
negligence.

There follow particulars of breach of contract and negligence. It is unnecessary for me
to read those. On a perusal of them, some of them appear to relate to omissions of items
included in the specification, and some to bad workmanship. For the purposes of the
issue before me, I must assume that all those allegations are true. It seems to me from
reading the allegations that some of them would probably have been discovered by
reasonable examination by the plaintiffs' engineer, for example the omission of a gusset,
some would not be so discovered, for example defective welding, although counsel for
the plaintiffs contends that none were discoverable by reasonable examination. It is fair
to say that no such allegation was made in the plaintiffs' reply, but, in any event, whether

a   or not the defects were discoverable by reasonable examination must be irrelevant to the issue before me, as I shall show further in this judgment.

By the further reamended defence, para 2 of the reamended statement of claim is admitted, save as set out in para 2(c). It was then pleaded that the effect of cl 25 of the conditions of contract was that at the end of the defects maintenance period the defendants would be under no liability in respect of any defects after the work had been taken over under cl 23. That is, as I have said, at the end of the defects maintenance

b   period on 26 January 1971.

It seemed to me on first reading the pleadings and the contract that this was a clear point of law proper for preliminary issue. However, counsel for the defendants said at the outset that he could not properly advance any case based on cl 25 and he abandoned the issue raised in the original paras 2 and 3 of the defence. Accordingly, I have heard no argument on it and it forms no part of the case before me.

c   By para 2A of the defence, added by amendment, it is pleaded:

'It was further expressly provided by clause 4 of the said B.E.A.M.A. Conditions that the work to be done under the contract should be executed to the reasonable satisfaction of the Engineer.'

By para 2B by reamendment it is pleaded:

d   'It was further expressly provided by clause 18(v) of the said B.E.A.M.A. Conditions (as amended) that except in respect of damage or injury to a person other than the Plaintiffs or to property not belonging to or in the occupation or possession of the Plaintiffs, the liability of the Defendants to the Plaintiffs should in no case exceed £50,000·00.'

e   There is a further paragraph in the defence, para 2C, providing for a further defence, one of the preliminary issues ordered to be tried. Again, counsel for the defendants is not relying on that. I omitted to make a note whether the allegation is abandoned altogether by the plaintiffs or whether counsel for the defendants accepted that it raised questions of facts not proper to a preliminary issue.

By para 3A of the defence it is pleaded:

f   'The said works were carried out to the reasonable satisfaction of the Engineer, who on the 26th January 1971 expressed his reasonable satisfaction by issuing his final certificate authorising the final payment to the Defendants under the contract; in the premises the said certificate is conclusive evidence of the completion of the works in accordance with the contract, and the Plaintiffs are debarred from alleging that the works were not executed in accordance therewith.'

g   By para 3B by further reamendment it is pleaded:

'Further or alternatively the aforesaid expression of satisfaction was a representation made on behalf of the Plaintiffs that the works had been executed in accordance with the contract and the Defendants acted on that representation by leaving the

h   site and by failing to remedy the defects complained of (if any, which is not admitted). In the premises the Plaintiffs are estopped from contending that the works were defective as alleged.'

Accordingly, the issues before me now are the issues contained in paras 2A, 2B, 3A and 3B of the further reamended defence. Those paragraphs give rise to three issues as follows.

1. The extent of the defendants' obligations under the contract. Was it sufficient for

j   them to satisfy the engineer or were they required, in addition, to comply with all the other conditions of the contract? That is the issue which appears in paras 2A and 3A.

2. If the defendants were in breach of contract or negligent, are the damages limited to £50,000? That is para 2B.

3. Are the plaintiffs in any event estopped from alleging defective work? That is para 3B.

The first two issues involve the construction of the contract. I bear in mind the principles of construing a contract. The relevant ones for the purpose of this case are: (1) construction of a contract is a question of law; (2) where the contract is in writing the intention of the parties must be found within the four walls of the contractual documents; it is not legitimate to have regard to extrinsic evidence (there is, of course, no such evidence in this case); (3) a contract must be construed as at the date it was made: it is not legitimate to construe it in the light of what happened years or even days later; (4) the contract must be construed as a whole, and also, so far as practicable, to give effect to every part of it.

I turn to the first issue, the extent of the defendants' obligations. The relevant terms appear in cl 4(i) of the BEAMA conditions:

'All Plant to be supplied and all work to be done under the Contract shall be manufactured and executed in the manner set out in the Specification, if any, and to the reasonable satisfaction of the Engineer . . .'

The specification contains the terms pleaded in the statement of claim. For example, on p 1 of the specification is the term: 'The contractor is to carry out all the design work required for the project.' On p 4: 'The gantry to carry conveyor "B" and conveyor "D" is existing and available at Bradford Colliery Landsdales Depot.' That is the term pleaded in para 2(c). It also contains other terms which are not set out in the statement of claim. For example, on p 6:

'New trestles are to be supplied and erected where required to carry the gantries for the conveyors. These are to be from suitable rolled steel sections and to be complete with all necessary wind bracings, base plates and holding-down bolts.'

Those are not, I believe, gantries which are alleged to have collapsed in this case. On p 7:

'All structural steelwork to be designed to requirements of BS 449. In all cases design materials, methods and workmanship should comply in all respects with requirements of the latest issues of all relevant British Standards Specifications, British Standards Codes of Practice and National Coal Board Specifications.'

I make it clear that whenever I refer in this judgment in the context of the contract to 'compliance with the specification' I include compliance with all the terms and conditions, both those set out which I have set out and all others contained in the contractual documents.

The primary question on the first issue is whether cl 4(i) imposes two independent obligations or only one obligation. Is the obligation to execute the work in the manner set out in the specification and in addition to the reasonable satisfaction of the engineer, or is the obligation merely in executing the works in accordance with specification to complete them to the reasonable satisfaction of the engineer? On the first construction, the obligations are cumulative, and the satisfaction of the engineer has been described in some cases as 'superadded protection for the employer'. On the second construction the satisfaction of the engineer is the overriding requirement as to the sufficiency of the work, so that once the engineer has expressed satisfaction the employer cannot thereafter complain of any failure to comply with the specification.

Where two obligations are set out connected by the conjunction 'and', I would prima facie regard them as independent and cumulative obligations. But counsel for the defendants has presented an impressive argument backed with an imposing list of authorities to the contrary. He has formulated three propositions which he has helpfully set out in writing. His first proposition is:

'Where a construction contract contains a term that a structure is to be erected in a prescribed manner and to the satisfaction of the employer's architect or engineer the contractor fulfils that obligation if on erection the architect or engineer is in fact satisfied even though the structure has not been erected in the prescribed manner.'

His second proposition is:

a
'If the architect or engineer issues a certificate authorising final payment that is conclusive evidence of his satisfaction, whether or not the contract contains terms providing for certification and whether or not, if it does, they provide for such a certificate to have final or conclusive effect as to the sufficiency of the work.'

His third proposition is:

b
'If the contract provides for arbitration, the foregoing principles are unaffected (1) at least in a case where the arbitrator is not given power to open up or review certificates, (2) in any event where the dispute comes before a court and not before an arbitrator.'

The first proposition raises questions of great difficulty which I shall have to consider *c* in detail. I shall deal first with the other two propositions, which I find much easier.

The second proposition. I agree in substance with counsel for the defendants' submission, although for the avoidance of doubt I would insert the word 'unqualified' before 'certificate'. In other words, make it read: 'If the architect or engineer issues an unqualified certificate authorising final payment etc.' The final certificate in this case is clearly an unqualified certificate, and so satisfies counsel's criteria. But although I agree *d* in substance with this proposition I regard it as a proposition of fact rather than of law. No competent or even incompetent architect or engineer would issue a final certificate telling his employer that he could safely pay the contractor in full unless he was satisfied, however incompetently, as to the sufficiency of the work. This is a matter of common sense rather than of law. Accordingly, when I accept that the final certificate is conclusive evidence of satisfaction, I do not mean that it is an irrebuttable presumption in law, but *e* that in practice the architect or engineer would be unable to rebut it.

Counsel for the plaintiffs has directed my attention to the dictionary definitions of 'certify' and urged on me that 'final certificate' should not be taken to mean anything other than expressly stated in it. But this really misses the point. The point is that it is only on the final certificate that the owner releases the retention money, and no owner is going to be prepared to do that unless he or his professional adviser is satisfied that the *f* work has been properly completed. Counsel has not suggested that the engineer was not satisfied to the best of his ability as to the sufficiency of the work executed by the defendants. Accordingly, although I regard this proposition as one of fact, it is not one to which I consider there can be any answer, and accordingly it causes me no difficulty when considering the point of law raised by the first issue.

The third proposition. I have heard much argument on the effect of arbitration clauses. *g* I cannot help feeling that a certain unjustified mystique has been attributed to them. In general an arbitration clause does no more than provide an alternative method of resolving disputes. It is hoped that it is simpler, quicker and cheaper than resorting to a court of law. In building contracts an arbitrator is frequently given additional powers which would not otherwise be open to him and are not open to a judge to exercise. For example, by cl 15 of this contract the contractor is required to proceed with the work in *h* accordance with the instructions of the engineer. By para (b) he is entitled to dispute any such instruction and to refer to arbitration. Were it not for this paragraph, clearly the contractor would have no right to dispute or litigate about any such instruction and, even with para (b), he cannot dispute such an instruction before a court. In this respect, it is right to say the arbitrator has additional powers to a court. But in general, as I have said, arbitration is simply an alternative way of resolving disputes. Accordingly, I agree *j* with counsel for the defendants that the existence of an arbitration clause in a contract should not affect the principles he seeks to establish because arbitration is simply an alternative to an action of law. But the contract must be construed as a whole and the wording in the arbitration clause may assist in the interpretation of other clauses. If, for example, the arbitration clause provides that the arbitrator shall have power to open up and review certificates, it raises a strong presumption that the certificates are not intended

to be conclusive. Such a presumption may be rebutted by a specific provision in the
contract: see *East Ham BC v Bernard Sunley & Sons Ltd* [1965] 3 All ER 619, [1966] AC   *a*
406.

The arbitration clause in this contract, cl 30, contains no such provision entitling the
arbitrator to open up certificates. It is entirely general in its terms:

> '(i) If at any time any question, dispute, or difference shall arise between the
> Owner or the Engineer and the Contractor, either party shall be at liberty to give to   *b*
> the other notice in writing of the existence of such question, dispute, or difference,
> specifying its nature and the point at issue, and requiring that the same be referred
> to Arbitration . . .'

There are then administrative provisions for the appointment of an arbitrator.

Counsel for the plaintiffs submits that the arbitration clause is so general that it is wide
enough to enable the arbitrator to open up certificates and that, therefore, the engineer's   *c*
certificate or, more accurately for the purposes of this argument, his satisfaction to be
implied from the certificate cannot have been intended to be conclusive. However, I
think this is coming perilously close to arguing in circles. I agree that, if the certificate is
not by the terms of the contract made conclusive, cl 30 would entitle the arbitrator to go
behind it. Equally, I think the court could go behind it: see *Robins v Goddard* [1905] 1 KB
294. To this extent I reject proposition 3(2) of counsel for the defendants. But, if it   *d*
appears from a proper construction of the contract that the certificate is intended to be
conclusive, I do not see how the wording of cl 30 can affect this construction. If this claim
had been referred to arbitration and the defendants had taken the same point, the
arbitrator would first have had to decide the issue before me: whether the certificate or
the engineer's satisfaction was conclusive and, if he came to the conclusion that it was
conclusive, he would have had so to rule and to refuse to go behind it.   *e*

Accordingly, I accept the third proposition of counsel for the defendants without the
qualifications he has put in paras (1) and (2). I accept that if the contract provides for
arbitration, the foregoing principles are unaffected, but I add a qualification of my own:
'But the wording of the arbitration clause may assist in the interpretation of other clauses
of the contract, including the certification or satisfaction clauses.' In the present contract
the wording of the arbitration clause, cl 30, is so general as to afford no assistance in the   *f*
interpretation of any of the other clauses. I reject counsel for the plaintiffs' arguments
based on it.

So I come to the first proposition of counsel for the defendants. He has put before me
a line of authority stretching back into last century; indeed all the English authorities in
his favour are in the last century. He makes a strong point that they have stood without
adverse comment and indeed with approval for a century. Counsel for the plaintiffs seeks   *g*
to distinguish all the cases. While I accept that there are distinctions between some of
them, others I find indistinguishable.

The first case in time is *Harvey v Lawrence* (1867) 15 LT 571. In that case a builder
agreed to repair houses according to specification and drawings prepared by the architect.
It was a term of the contract that the work should be done with the best materials
according to the drawings and specifications and to the full satisfaction of the building   *h*
owner or his architect. It was held that the architect's certificate of satisfaction was
conclusive, and that the owner could not produce evidence to show work not done
according to the plans and specifications. Counsel for the plaintiffs may well be right in
submitting that that is not a case of defective work and materials but, as appears from
the argument of the Solicitor General, of variations which the architect was authorised
by the terms of the contract to authorise. If so, the owner was clearly bound by any such   *j*
variations authorised by the architect and the certificate was clearly conclusive on such
matters.

Similarly, *Goodyear v Weymouth and Melcombe Regis Corp* (1865) Har & Ruth 67, which
is referred to in several subsequent authorities, dealt with the question of extras which
again the architect was authorised to authorise.

It may be, therefore, that these are cases which can properly be distinguished and do not afford any assistance to counsel for the defendants. But the same cannot be said of the next one on which he principally relies, *Lord Bateman v Thompson* (1875) 2 Hudson's BC (4th edn) 36. The contractor had contracted to do certain building work in a 'good, substantial and workmanlike manner, but in every event and particular to the satisfaction in all respects of the architect'. There was a clause making the decisions of the architect final and conclusive, but only (so the court found) as against the contractor. Counsel for the plaintiffs submitted in fact this clause should have been construed as making the decision final as against the owner also. Maybe so, but this was not the basis of the court's decision. There was also a proviso (f) to which the court was unable to give any meaning, unless the architect's satisfaction was conclusive. Counsel for the plaintiff seeks to distinguish the present case on that ground, but it is clear from the judgments that the clause I have quoted above was considered by the court of itself to render the architect's satisfaction conclusive.

Lord Coleridge CJ said (at 43):

> 'The question is whether there was any breach of this contract. I am of opinion that even without the proviso [that was proviso (f)] upon the true construction of this contract no action lies. The contractor is to perform the work in a good, substantial and workmanlike manner and with the best materials of their several kinds and to the satisfaction of the architect and Lord Bateman. That, I think, is the true construction of that contract. They are to be good, substantial and workmanlike and to his satisfaction. That is to say, he is to be satisfied that they are good, substantial and workmanlike materials of work. He was so satisfied, and under the terms of this contract both he and his architect—the architect by his certificate, and Lord Bateman by his conduct, as a matter of fact were satisfied within the words of the contract, and accordingly the covenant in this deed was in its terms performed by the defendant, and having been performed by the defendant clearly no action lies upon it. I must say the matter is clear to my own mind upon the construction of the contract, irrespective altogether of the proviso.'

It is therefore clear that Lord Coleridge CJ based his judgment, first, on the words of the contract, which are somewhat similar to those in cl 4(1) in the present contract. He then, second, went on to say that, if there was any doubt about that, proviso (f) confirmed his views.

Grove J came to a similar conclusion (at 46). Similarly also Archibald J.

The case went to the Court of Appeal; the report simply reports that the Court of Appeal heard and dismissed the appeal with costs. Accordingly, we do not know whether the Court of Appeal based its judgment on the first ground in which the Court of Common Pleas decided the matter, namely that the words themselves, joined in that case by the word 'but', imposed only one obligation or whether the Court of Appeal construed the contract as a whole and adopted the second ground adopted by the Court of Common Pleas. So we have only reported the decision of the Court of Common Pleas. Although it was the decision of the full court I do not think it is binding on me. Nevertheless, if it is a decision of general application on a point of law, I should follow it if it could not be distinguished.

Counsel for the plaintiffs seeks to distinguish it in various ways. First, he submits that it was a decision on the whole contract and that proviso (f) was the governing factor. I have already rejected that distinction. Second, he submits that the architect was obviously at fault and, therefore, it was reasonable to absolve the contractor and to leave Lord Bateman to his remedy against the architect. But that is to fall into the trap of construing a contract in the light of subsequent events. The contract must be construed at the time it is made. Third, he submitted that the defects were all obvious, and the architect could have seen them. That appears from the facts set out to be largely true, although one defect had been hidden, so as to prevent the architect from seeing it. But, again, it is really falling into the same trap. Further, there is no suggestion in the judgments in this case or in any of the other cases to which I have been referred that there is any distinction to be drawn between discoverable and undiscoverable defects.

A more substantial distinction is that in *Lord Bateman v Thompson* the contract was what I may call a typical building contract for the erection or substantial alteration of a dwelling house, when all the design, specification and drawings were furnished by the architect, and the work was of a type which was well within the competence of the average general builder, and the architect could reasonably be expected to have at least as much and probably much more expertise than the builder. These are matters which would be known by and in the contemplation of the parties when the contract was entered into, and accordingly might be material matters to take into consideration when interpreting the contract, if I am not bound in law to construe certain words in a certain way. It is right to say, however, that there is no suggestion in *Lord Bateman v Thompson* that this consideration played any part in the judgments in that case. This may not be decisive, and I shall return to the point later.

It was not suggested in argument before me or in any of the other cases to which I have been referred that any material distinction is to be drawn between the use of the word 'but' in *Lord Bateman v Thompson* and the word 'and' in the present case to join the two obligations or the two parts of one obligation if the defendants' contention is right.

I return to the first proposition of counsel for the defendants, which is:

> 'Where a construction contract contains a term that a structure is to be erected in a prescribed manner *and* to the satisfaction of the employer's architect or engineer the contractor as a matter of law fulfils that obligation if on erection the architect or engineer is in fact satisfied . . .'

In a sense the decision in *Lord Bateman v Thompson* is a matter of law because the construction of contracts is a matter of law. Counsel contends that the point established by the judgment in *Lord Bateman v Thompson* is a point of law of general importance.

The question which I have to decide is: did *Lord Bateman v Thompson* lay down a principle of universal application or was it a decision on its own facts?

I have already referred to the general principle of construction, that one must construe contracts as a whole. This was made clear, if it needs to be clear, in *Lord Bateman v Thompson* itself. Grove J said (at 48):

> 'The universal principle is that all parts of a deed must be taken together in order to ascertain its construction.'

Archibald J said (at 50):

> 'As my brother Grove has already pointed out the true mode of construing a document of this kind is to look at all the provisions of it and see how they bear upon each other, and to see what light each part reflects upon the rest.'

It is, therefore, at first sight a little difficult to see how the decision on the meaning of the clause in *Lord Bateman v Thompson* could have been intended to be a decision on the meaning of that clause other than in the context of that contract. Again, it is a matter to which I must return when I have considered the other cases.

Dunaberg and Witepsk Rly Co (Ltd) v Hopkins Gilkes & Co (Ltd) (1877) 36 LT 733 was a case concerning the supply of rails for a railway company. There were various provisions as to inspection and testing the rails, both at the manufacturers' works and after delivery. By cl 12 of the contract it was provided that the entire contract was to be executed in every respect to the satisfaction of the engineer, who should have the power of rejecting any rails he might disapprove of on any grounds whatsoever, and whose decision on any points of doubt or dispute that might arise in reference to the contract should be final. Counsel for the plaintiffs submits that this is simply a case where the engineer's decision is expressed to be final. I agree with counsel for the defendants that on a close analysis the judgment was based not on these concluding words of cl 12 (as no dispute had in fact a been referred to in the engineer) but on the construction of the earlier words in this clause; the judge followed the decision recently given in *Lord Bateman v Thompson*. That was the last English decision directly in his favour to which counsel for the defendants referred. But, as he pointed out, these cases have never been disapproved, and indeed have been referred to with approval or without disapproval in both English and Commonwealth cases, and they have undoubtedly been followed as laying down principles of law in Commonwealth jurisdictions.

b In *Bruens v Smith* 1951 (1) SA 67 Jennett J expressly followed *Lord Bateman v Thompson*. Similarly in the New Zealand case of *Stratford Borough v J H Ashman Ltd* [1960] NZLR 503 at 517, although Cleary J in the Court of Appeal did make it clear that—

c 'It must in every case depend upon the interpretation of the contract as a whole whether, on the one hand, the satisfaction of the architect is to be the over-riding requirement as to the sufficiency of the work even if it does not conform with the specification, or whether, on the other hand, conformity with the specification and the satisfaction of the architect are cumulative requirements.'

But he continued:

d 'Ordinarily, however, as is said in *Hudson on Building Contracts* ((8th edn, 1959) p 217), the former interpretation will prevail in modern building contracts. Even in the absence of express provision that the architect's certificate is to be conclusive, that interpretation is more consistent with the usual contractual provisions empowering the architect to direct or permit deviations from the contract. A builder could not at the same time both conform to the specification and carry out directions from the architect varying the specification. The result then is that e generally the approval of the architect or the engineer, as the case may be, is conclusive as to sufficiency of the work.'

In *Major v Greenfield* [1965] NZLR 1035 at 1061 McCarthy J said:

f 'Some of the conflicts to be found in these and other areas are frankly irreconcilable, and I am satisfied that a way can be found through this jungle only if one keeps steadily in mind the principles of construction of building contracts which were clearly stated in the judgment of this Court delivered by Cleary J. comparatively recently in *Stratford Borough v. J. H. Ashman (N. P.) Ltd*. That judgment emphasises the necessity to decide primarily whether the contract is one where the satisfaction of the architect is to be the overriding requirement as to the sufficiency and quality of the work done, or whether, on the other hand, conformity with the specifications g and the satisfaction of the architect are cumulative requirements. The former interpretation is the one favoured in construing modern building contracts. As a result, even in the absence of express provision that the architect's certificates are to be conclusive, generally those certificates are treated as such. The issue of a formal certificate may not be necessary, "for a certificate is only a mode of expressing the satisfaction". Each case, however, depends finally on its own documents, and the h difficulties in this present case are in great part a product of the uncertainties presented by the documents.'

Undoubtedly these cases do lend support to the submissions of counsel for the defendants, although making it clear that each case depends on its own documents.

Finally, in this line, I refer to the decision of the Judicial Committee of the Privy Council in *Ata Ul Haq v Nairobi City Council* (13 February 1959, unreported). I need refer j only to a passage from the speech of Lord Morris, delivering the opinion of the Judicial Committee:

'Their Lordships consider that the decision in the present case must depend on the construction of its own particular contractual documents and though consideration of the opinions of courts on other words, in other contracts, in other cases is of assistance, the adjudication in this case involves thereafter a return to a study of the contract under review.'

He then referred to *Lord Bateman v Thompson*, without disapproval. He also referred to a case which counsel for the defendants seeks to distinguish, to which I shall subsequently refer, *Newton Abbot Development Co Ltd v Stockman Bros* (1931) 47 TLR 616, also without disapproval. The conclusion I draw from this passage is that Lord Morris treated all these cases as decisions on their own facts, and he re-emphasised that the decision in any case must depend on the construction of its own contractual documents.

Newton Abbot Development Co Ltd v Stockman Bros concerned a building contract under which the defendants agreed to build houses in accordance with plans and specifications and to carry out the work to the satisfaction of the surveyor and sanitary inspector of Newton Abbot Urban District Council. The houses were built, and the council surveyor and sanitary inspector gave certificates of satisfaction, but Roche J held that the clause to build in accordance with the plans and specifications and also the implied term of good workmanship were not subordinate to the provision as to satisfaction of the surveyor and the sanitary inspector, which provision he held gave only a superadded protection to the owner. It is true that there is no reference in the report to *Lord Bateman v Thompson* and the other cases being cited to Roche J, and, further, this is a case where the satisfaction is not to be that of the owner's agent but of an independent third party. This may be a material distinction.

The first reported decision of the Court of Appeal in this country on a similar point is *Petrofina SA of Brussels v Compagnia Italiana Transporto Olii Minerali of Genoa* (1937) 53 TLR 650. It was a case not on a building contract but on a charterparty. The relevant clauses on the charterparty were:

'1. The steamer being tight staunch and strong and every way fitted for the voyage ... 16. The captain is bound to keep the tanks, pipes and pumps of the steamer always clean ... 27. [which was a typed addition to the printed clauses] Steamer to clean for the cargo in question to the satisfaction of the charterers' inspector.'

The same question arose. Was the inspector's satisfaction the overriding requirement or a superadded protection? The Court of Appeal unanimously held that it afforded superadded protection for the charterer.

Lord Wright MR said (at 652–653):

'[Counsel] admits, or it is clear, that clause 1 is an express warranty of seaworthiness in the sense of fitness to carry the stipulated cargo. The words are: "Every way fitted for the voyage." Clause 16 confirms and extends the same warranty, or perhaps rather implies the same obligation which, under clause 1, is made applicable to the initiation of the voyage to the course of the voyage. It says: "The captain is bound to keep the tanks, pipes and pumps of the steamer always clean." It does not matter whether that overlaps clause 1 and then comes on to deal with the later course of the voyage, or whether it is independent of clause 1 and only deals with the later course of the voyage. So far, on this assumption of fact, there can be no question as to the liability of the shipowners. But [counsel for the shipowners] has argued that clause 27 has the effect of excluding this fundamental obligation and substituting for it an obligation merely to clean—that means to clean the holds before loading the cargo in question—to the satisfaction of the charterers' inspector. His argument is that that is a clause which is inserted for the owners' benefit, in this sense, that it cuts down what would otherwise be their general obligation to have the holds fit to receive the cargo at the time when they are loading. I find it impossible to accept that contention. We are dealing with a contract of affreightment, and it is necessary to bear in mind the well-established view which has been so often stated, that if it is sought to effect a reduction of the overriding obligation to provide a seaworthy ship, whether that is express or implied for this purpose does not matter, by other express

terms of the charterparty or contract of affreightment, that result can only be
achieved if perfectly clear, effective, and precise words are used expressly stating that
limitation. I think that the language of clause 27 here is not sufficient. To make it
sufficient I think it would need to be amplified in something like this manner. It
would have to run: "Steamer to clean for the cargo in question to the satisfaction of
the charterers' inspector and if that is done that shall be treated as fulfilment of the
obligations under clauses 1 and 16." Clause 27 does not say so. I think, on the
contrary, it has a much more limited effect. It gives, as I think, an added right to the
charterers. They are entitled before they load the cargo to have an inspection, and to
have a certificate, or whatever the form of the evidence is, that their inspector is
satisfied. But, without express words, the satisfaction of the inspector cannot be
relied on by the owners as a discharge and fulfilment of their obligations. From the
point of view of the charterers this superadded right is something which it is worth
their while to have. It gives them some sort of guarantee against their being involved
in questions such as this, where, unfortunately, notwithstanding inspection, there
had been a failure to provide tanks sufficiently clean and in proper condition.'

Romer LJ said (at 654):

'It is inherent in construction to give effect, where it is possible, to every part of a
written document, none the less because the document happens to be a charterparty.
In the present case, therefore, we must give effect both to clause 16 and to clause 27
of this charterparty, if it be possible. In my opinion, it is possible. In clause 16 the
owner undertakes to keep the tanks, pipes, and pumps of the steamer always clean.
In construing clause 27 you must do so with the knowledge of the fact that by clause
16 that obligation has been undertaken in plain terms by the owner. That being so,
it is plain that the true construction of clause 27 is this—that the owner is saying: "I
have by clause 16 undertaken in plain terms the obligation of keeping the tanks
clean. Not only will I keep the tanks clean but I will keep them clean to the
satisfaction of the charterers' inspector." The result is that the owner can only
discharge his obligations in respect of cleaning under the charterparty by cleaning
the tanks, keeping them clean, and doing so to the satisfaction of the charterers'
inspector. If he keeps them clean, and does not obtain the approval of the charterers'
inspector he has not fulfilled his contract. Nor has he fulfilled his contract if he fails
to keep them clean but the charterers' inspector has expressed his approval of the
state of the tanks.'

That case seems to me to be clear authority against the defendants, unless the case be
distinguished. It cannot make any difference that in that case the relevant terms were in
three separate clauses, whereas here they are in the same clause joined by the word 'and'.

Counsel for the defendants submits that the *Petrofina* case depends on the overriding
nature of the warranty of seaworthiness. But is the warranty of seaworthiness any
different in kind from the warranties expressed or implied in a building contract, or
indeed in any other contract? I should have thought not. The relevant part of the
warranty of seaworthiness in the *Petrofina* case was that the vessel was in every way fitted
for the voyage and would be kept so.

It cannot now be doubted that a similar warranty is implied in contracts for work and
materials. In *G H Myers & Co v Brent Cross Service Co* [1934] 1 KB 46 at 55, [1933] All ER
Rep 9 at 13–14 du Parcq J said:

'. . . the true view is that a person contracting to do work and supply materials
warrants that the materials which he uses will be of good qualify and reasonably fit
for the purpose for which he is using them, unless the circumstances of the contract
are such as to exclude any such warranty.'

That passage was approved by the House of Lords in *Young & Marten Ltd v McManus
Childs Ltd* [1968] 2 All ER 1169, [1969] 1 AC 454. While the reference there is to

materials (which was the point there at issue) I do not doubt that there is a similar warranty as to workmanship.

In the present case there is the express warranty that the work will be executed in the manner set out in the specification. I see no reason why these warranties should be treated any differently from the warranty of seaworthiness in a charterparty. Indeed, it is clear from Romer LJ's judgment, which I have quoted above, that he regarded the fact that the document was a charterparty as adding nothing to the normal principles of construction of a contract.

The final authority on this aspect of the case is *Billyack v Leyland Construction Co Ltd* [1968] 1 All ER 783, [1968] 1 WLR 471, a decision of Edmund Davies LJ sitting as an additional judge of the Queen's Bench Division. The judge held that the cumulative interpretation should be adopted in respect of two obligations joined by the word 'and'. Counsel for the defendants submits that that case can properly be distinguished as the satisfaction was to be that of an independent third party (the building inspector for the local authority) and not of an agent of the owner. Certainly he gains some support from the passage in the judgment in which Edmund Davies LJ said ([1968] 1 All ER 783 at 788, [1968] 1 WLR 471 at 476):

'The main submission advanced on behalf of the defendants is, in the light of the authorities, rather more difficult. Can the plaintiff succeed on the ground that, as I have found, the defendants were in breach of their express undertaking to "build and complete in a workmanlike manner", or are the defendants covered by the fact that, as Mr. Townsend [chief building inspector to the Barnet Urban District Council] testified, they had completed in accordance with the bye-laws and to his satisfaction? The conjunction "and" joins the two parts of cl. 1 of the contract, and there were cited to me a number of authorities to the effect that, where such a conjunction is used, it may well be that in the result the builder is protected if the designated third party expresses his satisfaction with the work done, no matter how badly it was in fact executed. *Lord Bateman v. Thompson* ((1875) 2 Hudson's BC (4th edn) 36) is said to have been such a case, but there, as in many of the other cases cited, the architect or other party whose satisfaction was required was himself appointed by the building owner, who could scarcely be heard to complain once his own appointee had in fact expressed satisfaction with the work. The basic facts of the earlier case of *Harvey v. Lawrence* ((1867) 15 LT 571) appear to be similar in that respect, and this also appears true of several of the cases collected in HUDSON'S BUILDING AND ENGINEERING CONTRACTS ((9th edn, 1965) pp 310–312).'

However, Edmund Davies LJ then turned to consider the effect of the *Petrofina* case, which he said ([1968] 1 All ER 783 at 789, [1968] 1 WLR 471 at 477–478)—

'dealt with a contract of affreightment, but is nevertheless helpful in arriving at a proper conclusion in the present case. There the charterparty contained one clause that the ship was to be in every way fit for the voyage, another that the captain was bound to keep the tanks clean, while cl. 27 provided that the ship was to be clean for the specified cargo to the satisfaction of the charterers' inspector. The inspector in due course expressed himself as satisfied, but in fact the tanks were not clean . . .'

I need not read further from that passage. He sets out the facts, and he there sets out a passage from the judgment of Lord Wright MR. Edmund Davies LJ then went on:

'I apply the ratio decidendi of that case to the present one in this way. In every building contract there are to be implied (in the absence of express words to the contrary) a three-fold undertaking by the builder: (a) that he will do his work in a good and workmanlike manner; (b) that he will supply good and proper materials; and (c) that the house will be reasonably fit for human habitation—see *Miller v. Cannon Hill Estates, Ltd.* ([1931] 2 KB 113, [1931] All ER Rep 93), and *Hancock v. B. W. Brazier (Anerley), Ltd.* ([1966] 2 All ER 901, [1966] 1 WLR 1317). Is there anything expressed in the present contract to exclude any of those terms? Certainly

a
not the undertaking to "complete and build in a workmanlike manner", which in fact expresses one of the terms which would otherwise be implied. Then do the added words serve to exclude them or limit the operation of the express undertaking? In my judgment, they do not. On the contrary, the obligation of the defendants to build in a good and workmanlike manner a house fit for human habitation remained unaffected by the satisfaction ultimately expressed by the local authority regarding the fitness of the house which in due course was built.'

b
I read that passage of Edmund Davies LJ's judgment as showing that he regarded the warranty in a building contract as no different to warranties in any other contract, including a charterparty. And it must be observed that in the *Petrofina* case the satisfaction required was that of the agent of the charterer and not of an independent third party.

Having considered all these authorities, I have come to the conclusion that there is no such rule of law or principle of construction applicable to building contracts or indeed

c
any other contracts as that for which counsel for the defendants contends in his first proposition. Indeed, if there is any rule of law governing the construction of a clause such as this containing two obligations joined by the word 'and' the balance of authority in this country seems to be that the rule is the contrary to that for which counsel contends: see the *Petrofina* case. However, I do not think that there is any particular rule of law relating to the construction of such a clause. The general principles of the

d
construction of a contract apply, and the meaning of any clause must be ascertained from within the particular contract by construing the contract as a whole and giving effect, so far as possible, to every part of it.

Counsel for the plaintiffs submitted that cl 4(i) could be read so as to make the engineer's expression of satisfaction conclusive in respect of defects which the engineer could reasonably discover but not in respect of those which he could not reasonably

e
discover. Indeed at one stage I understood him to be conceding that it did make his satisfaction conclusive in respect of discoverable defects. However, it became clear that this was a misunderstanding. The concession, if it was a concession, came during his argument on the estoppel point.

To construe the clause in this way would not be legitimate construction at all. It would be rewriting the contract. This the court will not do. The clause can only be construed as

f
providing that the engineer's satisfaction will be conclusive in respect of all defects discoverable or undiscoverable or will not be conclusive in respect of any defects, however obvious they may have been to the engineer. Accordingly, I look at the provisions of this contract. I observe that there is no express clause making the certificate or satisfaction of the engineer conclusive. I observe that cl 4(i) appears to impose two obligations: to execute the works according to specification and to execute them to the reasonable

g
satisfaction of the engineer. Further, the later words of cl 4(i) expressly absolve the contractor from liability for certain matters, including the adequacy of any design which the contractor is required by the owner to use. This may suggest that the intention is not to absolve the contractor from responsibility for the adequacy of any design prepared by himself. I observe that many of the clauses give the engineer close control over various aspects of the contract, ie cll 3, 4(i), (iii) and (v), 6, 15, 16, 23 and 25 to mention but some

h
of those on which counsel for the defendants strongly and rightly relies. These are important in the proper construction of this contract. As against this, counsel for the plaintiffs submits that the defendants are part of the Capper Neill Group, and he invites me to take judicial notice that this is a very large, reputable and well-known group of structural engineers. I have no doubt that he is right about that, but unfortunately I cannot recall having heard of them. That is immaterial, because even if I had known of

j
them it would be improper to make judicial use of such knowledge as that would be going outside the four walls of the contract. This may seem a little unfortunate, as it would be absurd for any judge to pretend that he is not aware of the identity of the plaintiffs. However, I can go some way with counsel's submission in so far as the facts are to be found expressly or impliedly in the words of the contract. It was a structural engineering contract and the defendants were to carry out all the design work, as well as

erecting the steelwork to British Standards specifications and codes of practice. It is a
proper inference from this and from the other contractual documents that the defendants
were indeed skilled structural engineers and the plaintiffs relied on them rather more
than would be the case if the plaintiffs' own engineer had carried out the design work. I
have referred to certain parts of the plaintiffs' specification. The contents of the
defendants' tenders are also relevant. An item on the gantries for conveyors B and D
provides:

> 'The existing 6 spans of gantry at . . . Colliery will be dismantled and transported
> to Agecroft where they will be modified to suit the new arrangements. 4 new
> support trestles fabricated from mild steel sections of sufficient strength for the duty
> complete with windbreaks and holding-down bolts would be provided. [And later:]
> The junction tower will be fabricated from rolled steel sections of sufficient strength
> and duty adequately braced and complete with holding-down bolts and washer
> plates.'

Clearly the defendants, as experts, were, as required by the specification, warranting
that the various items designed and erected by them would be of sufficient strength for
their duty. Clause 3 provides for the engineer's approval of the defendants' drawings.
But it would be a strange interpretation of this clause to read it as releasing the defendants
from their express warranties contained in the specifications and tenders. There are many
matters which a reasonably competent engineer would be unable to check, at least
without great difficulty and expense. To check the strength of the structures designed by
the defendants, the engineer would have, in effect, to repeat all the work himself. Once
a work had been completed or indeed during the erection stage it would be virtually
impossible for the engineer to check, for example, the quality of the welding. Inevitably,
it seems to me, the plaintiffs would have to rely to a not insignificant extent on the skill
and expertise of their specialist contractors, and this is amply borne out by perusal of the
contractual documents as a whole.

I have considered the effect of cl 25 (the maintenance period) on cl 4(i). In *Lord Bateman
v Thompson* the alternative reason given by the court for its decision was that if the
architect's satisfaction was not conclusive no meaning could be given to proviso (f). This
proviso is somewhat similar in its effect to cl 25. Does the provision for a maintenance
period (which, of course, is now virtually universal in building contracts) affect the
construction of cl 4(i)? Whichever construction of cl 4(i) is correct, I think that meaning
can be given to the maintenance provisions. I think that the purpose of the maintenance
clause is twofold: (1) it entitles the owner to retain part of the agreed price until the end
of the maintenance period, making it a condition precedent to the contractors' right
to payment of the retention money that he remedies any defects during that period;
and (2) it entitles the contractor to remedy any defect during the maintenance period
himself.

A clause such as this is not specifically enforceable against a contractor. But in the
absence of such a clause the owner would be entitled to employ someone else to remedy
the defects and then claim the cost of the remedial work from the contractor, a course
which almost inevitably would be much more expensive for the contractor than if he is
entitled to remedy the defects himself.

As effect can be given to cl 25, whatever construction of cl 4(i) is adopted, it affords me
no assistance in construing that clause. I express no opinion as to the effect of the fifth
paragraph of cl 25 (which purports to limit the contractor's liability after the works have
been taken over) as no argument has been addressed to me on it, and counsel for the
defendants expressly abandoned any reliance on it.

I have not attempted to set out all the relevant parts of the contractual documents, but
I have read them all and I have them all in mind. I bear in mind all the arguments
addressed to me. I think there is much force in the final submission of counsel for the
defendants on this aspect of the case that it would be businesslike to have a clause

a achieving some finality. But, of course, such a clause could always be expressly set out in a contract, as indeed it is in many of the standard forms with which we are familiar.

In the light of all these matters (to be found within the contract) how should I interpret cl 4(i)? Does it contain two cumulative covenants on the part of the contractor or only one covenant: to execute the works to the satisfaction of the engineer? In my view, it is clearly intended to and does impose two obligations: to execute the works in the manner set out in the specification and also to execute them to the reasonable satisfaction of the

b engineer. I think that as in the *Petrofina* case this superadded right is something which it is worth the owners' while to have, in that it does give them some sort of assurance that they will not find themselves involved in an action such as this. But I can see no reason for interpreting this superadded right as in any way derogating from the contractors' primary obligation to complete the work according to specification.

If it be asked how can such a decision be reconciled with the decision of the Court of

c Common Pleas in *Lord Bateman v Thompson*, I can only answer that each contract must depend on its own terms, construed as a whole. It may well be that, as I have already suggested, a century ago building was a much more straightforward operation requiring no specialist skills other than those ordinarily to be found in the local builder, and that an architect could be expected to have at least as much expertise as the builder in every aspect of the craft. The same may still apply in the case of ordinary simple houses; but

d nowadays in many types of building, including in some cases ordinary houses, specialised methods of construction are involved requiring the services of specialist contractors or sub-contractors and usually several such specialist sub-contractors on any one contract. An architect cannot be expected to be expert in every aspect of specialist trades and has perforce to rely in part on the tradesman's expertise. Whether or not that is a valid distinction, I am left in no doubt as to the correct interpretation of cl 4(i) of this contract.

e Accordingly, I answer the first issue before me in the negative. Paragraphs 2A and 3A of the further reamended defence disclose no defence to the plaintiffs' claim.

The other two issues before me I can deal with much more shortly. The second issue is whether by virtue of cl 18(v) the defendants' liability to the plaintiffs is in any event limited to the sum of £50,000. Clause 18 is headed 'Liability for accidents and damage', but cl 31 provides that the titles of clauses shall not affect the construction of the contract.

f Counsel for the plaintiffs nevertheless invited me to make use of the title to cl 18 to confirm any provisional view I might form of the meaning of cl 18(v), arguing that if the title merely confirmed a view already formed it is not affecting the construction. All I need say is that if I make use of something to confirm, even in the slightest, my views, then I must be allowing this to affect my views. I reject this argument.

Clause 18 contains a motley of provisions circumscribing the parties' responsibilities

g for damage of various kinds. Paragraph (i) concerns the contractors' responsibility for work in progress; para (ii) provides that the contractor shall make good at the owners' expense damage to the works for which the contractor is not responsible; para (iii) provides that the contractor shall indemnify the owner in respect of damage occurring before take-over caused by the contractors' negligence, defective design, work or material; para (iv) contains a similar provision in respect of damage occurring during the

h maintenance period; para (vi) exempts the contractor from liability for and requires the owner to indemnify him in respect of damage caused by the negligence of anyone other than the contractor or his servants or sub-contractors; para (vii) contains provisions concerning the conduct of negotiations and litigation; para (viii) (added by the special conditions) contains provisions as to insurance.

In the middle of these comes para (v). This contains four provisions, three of which

j purport to exempt the contractor from liability and one to limit his liability. The contractor is exempted from liability to the owner (a) for any loss of profit or contracts, (b) except as provided, for any claim made against the owner, (c) for any damage or injury caused by or arising from the acts or omissions of the owner or others, not being the contractors' servants or sub-contractors or save as to damage as provided by cl 19 in

circumstances over which the contractor has no control. Then come the words with
which I am concerned: *a*

'except in respect of damage or injury to a person other than the Owner or to
property not belonging to or in the occupation or possession of the Owner, the
liability of the Contractor to the Owner shall in no case exceed £50,000.'

The original printed words were 'exceed the total value of the Contract' but by the special
conditions those are deleted and 'exceed £50,000' inserted. These words appear to be   *b*
perfectly general. But counsel for the plaintiffs submits that they should be given a
restricted meaning. To what should they be restricted? Clearly they cannot refer to the
other three matters set out in para (v) because in respect of all these the contractor is
totally exempted from liability.

Counsel for the plaintiffs suggests that they should be taken to refer only to the
defendants' negligence and not to breach of contract. Apart from the fact that this seems   *c*
to be the antithesis of the usual argument on the construction of an exemption or
limitation clause, I can see no warrant for any such restriction in the words of the clause.

Counsel for the plaintiffs also suggests that they should be taken not to refer to the
contract works themselves. Again I can see no warrant for such an exclusion, particularly
where there is an express exclusion in respect of property not belonging to or in the
occupation or possession of the owner.   *d*

Finally, counsel for the plaintiffs submits that, if the £50,000 limit does apply to
damage to the works themselves, it applies only to the direct damage and not to the
consequential loss, such as the transport costs claimed in this case. Again I see no warrant
for such a restriction.

The words 'in no case' are as strong as can be imagined. Of course, words such as
'whatsoever' or 'howsoever caused' could have been inserted. But what could they add to   *e*
the strength of the words used? Nothing is nothing, and one cannot add to or subtract
from such a word by adding words of emphasis.

Clauses of limitation of liability have recently been considered by the House of Lords
and contrasted with clauses of exemption in *Ailsa Craig Fishing Co Ltd v Malvern Fishing
Co Ltd* [1983] 1 All ER 101, [1983] 1 WLR 964. But even without the benefit of their
Lordships' speeches, I would have come to the same conclusion, that the last two lines of   *f*
cl 18(v) mean what they say, that in no case (other than the expressly excepted ones) shall
the defendants' liability to the plaintiffs exceed £50,000.

I accordingly answer the second issue in favour of the defendants. Paragraph 2B of
their defence discloses a good defence in law to the plaintiffs' claim in so far as that claim
exceeds £50,000. The defendants' liability in respect of all damage claimed, both direct
and consequential, is limited to the sum of £50,000 in total. This does not, of course, bar   *g*
a claim for interest on this sum of £50,000.

The third issue: estoppel

The defendants contend that by issuing a final certificate the plaintiffs' engineer
represented that the works had been executed in accordance with the contract, and that
the defendants acted on such representation, and that accordingly the plaintiffs are now   *h*
estopped from contending the works were defective as alleged.

It is not sufficient for the defendants to establish that the certificate amounted to a
representation of the engineer's satisfaction. In view of my finding on the first issue, to
be of any assistance to the defendants the certificate would have to amount to a
representation that the works had been completed in accordance with the contract.

I think that it may well do so in some respects. In the light of my finding on the   *j*
construction of cl 4(i), the defendants would be in breach of contract if they in any respect
failed to execute the works in the manner set out in the specification, even if the engineer
expressed his satisfaction and even if the defect was obvious to the engineer, and even if
there was some departure from the specification not amounting to defective
workmanship. I think that the defendants' protection in such events probably does lie in

the field of estoppel. On the other hand, I find it difficult to see how the issue of a final
certificate could amount to a representation as to matters of which the parties know that
the engineer has no knowledge.

Counsel are agreed that the following elements are required to constitute a valid
estoppel by representation: (a) that the alleged representation of the party sought to be
estopped was such as is in law deemed a representation; (b) that the precise representation
relied on was in fact made; (c) that the representation which the party is later sought to
be estopped from making, setting up or attempting to prove contradicts in substance his
original representation according to proper canons of construction; (d) that such original
representation was of a nature to induce and was made with the intention and the result
of inducing the party raising estoppel to alter his position on the faith thereof to his
detriment; and (e) that such original representation was made by the party sought to be
estopped or by some person for whose representation he is deemed in law responsible
and was made to the party setting up the estoppel or to some person in right of whom he
claims.

Counsel for the defendants concedes that to establish element (d) he would have to call
evidence, as that is clearly a question of fact. Questions of fact are also clearly involved in
the other elements. For example, element (b) requires the establishment of the fact that
the precise representation relied on was made. While the issue of the final certificate is
not in dispute, the representation relied on does not appear on the face of it. This is a
matter of inference to be drawn from the certificate and all the circumstances attending
its issue.

The only question of law which seems to me to arise in the third issue is whether the
final certificate is capable as a matter of law of amounting to the representation pleaded.
But even this must depend on the inferences properly to be drawn from it. All I can say
at present is that it is not incapable of amounting to such a representation. However, as
this would leave unanswered the question whether in fact it amounted to the
representation pleaded, as well as all the other questions of fact, I am not prepared to
make any such ruling on the third issue. In my view, this is not the proper subject for a
preliminary issue of law.

I should add out of fairness to Mr District Registrar Kushner, who made the order for
the trial of the preliminary issue, that his order of 2 October 1981 by its terms restricted
the preliminary issue to the first two issues before me. The third issue seems to have
crept in because he then ordered the issue be settled between the parties and approved by
him. Had the parties carried out the spirit of the order and settled the preliminary issue
in clear terms, instead of attempting to define it by reference to pleadings, I doubt
whether this third issue would ever have received the district registrar's approval.

In the event, I decline to determine the issue raised by para 3B of the defence, and
order that it be tried in the action.

Order accordingly.

Solicitors: *J Blackwell*, Stoke-on-Trent (for the plaintiffs); *Sharpe Pritchard & Co*, agents for
Silverbeck & Co, Liverpool (for the defendants).

K Mydeen Esq   Barrister.

R v D

COURT OF APPEAL, CRIMINAL DIVISION
WATKINS LJ, MUSTILL AND SKINNER JJ
27, 28 JUNE, 31 OCTOBER 1983

Criminal law – Kidnapping – Parent – Parent taking away his unmarried child under 18 years – Whether parent committing crime of kidnapping.

   b

Criminal law – Kidnapping – Consent to being taken away – Young child – Child too young to be able to give consent – Whether will of parent to be regarded as will of child – Whether desirable to leave to jury question of consent of child.

Contempt of court – Wardship proceedings – Removal of ward from jurisdiction without leave –   c Proceedings for punishment of contempt – Whether taking ward out of jurisdiction without consent constituting criminal contempt – Whether triable on indictment.

The offence of kidnapping cannot be committed by a parent who takes away his unmarried child who is under the age of majority, ie the age of 18 years. However a parent may be guilty of kidnapping his child if that child has achieved the age of majority   d or has lawfully married under that age, since in either case the child has passed out of the possession of his parents (see p 582 *a b d* and *j* to p 583 *a*, post); *The People (A-G) v Edge* [1943] IR 115, *R v Halle* [1974] 1 All ER 1107 and *R v Austin* [1981] 1 All ER 374 considered.

The fact that a baby or a very young child is unable to give any vestige of proper consent to being taken away is not a compelling reason for regarding the will of the   e child's parent as that of the child (see p 581 *a* to *e*, post); *The People (A-G) v Edge* [1943] IR 115 not followed.

It is highly undesirable to leave to a jury the question of whether a young child has or has not consented to go away with a parent (see p 581 *d e*, post).

Although it is a criminal contempt to take a ward of court out of the jurisdiction without the consent of the court, it is undesirable for such contempt to be tried on   f indictment. Rather, an application for committal should be made pursuant to leave therefor to the Divisional Court of the Queen's Bench Division under RSC Ord 52 either by the person in whose care and custody the ward is, by the Official Solicitor or by the Attorney General. Alternatively, the court whose order has been flouted may act of its own motion under Ord 52, r 5 (see p 579 *e f* and p 583 *g* to *j*, post).

Notes

   g

For the offence of kidnapping, see 11 Halsbury's Laws (4th edn) para 1212, and for cases on the subject, see 15 Digest (Reissue) 1109, 1240, 9312, 10583.

For removing a ward of court from the jurisdiction without consent, see 24 Halsbury's Laws (4th edn) para 579, and for cases on the subject, see 28(2) Digest (Reissue) 919–923, 2277–2313.

For interference with a ward of court as contempt of court, see 9 Halsbury's Laws (4th   h edn) para 36, for punishment for contempt of court, see ibid paras 87–88, 97, and for cases on the subject, see 28(2) Digest (Reissue) 921–922, 2297–2305.

Cases referred to in judgment

Balogh v Crown Court at St Albans [1974] 3 All ER 283, [1975] QB 73, [1974] 3 WLR 314,   j
CA.
Hyde v US (1912) 225 US 347.
People, The (A-G) v Edge [1943] IR 115, Eire SC.
R v Austin [1981] 1 All ER 374, CA.
R v Hale [1974] 1 All ER 1107, [1974] QB 819, [1974] 3 WLR 249, Crown Ct at Bristol.

R v *Nazir* (14 January 1983, unreported), Crown Ct at Snaresbrook.

R v *Tibbits* [1902] 1 KB 77, [1900–3] All ER Rep 896, CCR.

Towne v Eisner (1918) 245 US 418.

Cases also cited

A-G v Butterworth [1962] 3 All ER 326, [1963] 1 QB 696, CA.

Knuller (Publishing, Printing and Promotions) Ltd v DPP [1972] 2 All ER 898, [1973] AC 435, HL.

R v *Jackson* [1891] 1 QB 671, [1891–4] All ER Rep 61, CA.

Appeal against conviction

On 18 May 1982 in the Central Criminal Court before his Honour Judge Lymbery QC and a jury the appellant, D, a New Zealand national, was, on an indictment containing nine counts, convicted of the false imprisonment of his wife Audrey (count 2), contempt of court (counts 4 and 8) and kidnapping his daughter E (count 6). He was acquitted of another count of kidnapping his daughter E (count 1), possession of a prohibited weapon (count 3) and assault occasioning his wife Audrey actual bodily harm (count 5). A count of false imprisonment of his daughter E (count 7) and a count of cruelty to his daughter E (count 9) were ordered to lie on the file. The appellant was sentenced to two years' imprisonment on count 2, to four months' imprisonment on count 4, to fifteen months' imprisonment on count 6 and to six months' imprisonment on count 8, all terms concurrent and suspended for two years. He appealed against his convictions on counts 4, 6 and 8. The facts are set out in the judgment of the court.

Neil Taylor QC and *Peter Ralls* for the appellant
Ann Curnow and *Nicholas Purnell* for the Crown.

Cur adv vult

31 October. The following judgment of the court was delivered.

WATKINS LJ. On 18 May 1982 at the Central Criminal Court before his Honour Judge Lymbery QC and a jury, the appellant, a New Zealander, then 42 years of age, was, in respect of events which took place on 13 and 14 December 1978, convicted of the false imprisonment of his wife Audrey (count 2) and of being in contempt of court, in that by taking E, then two years of age and a ward of court, outside England and Wales and out of the care and control of her mother without the consent of the court, he did an act calculated to interfere with the due administration of justice (count 4). He was acquitted of kidnapping E at that time (count 1). In respect of events which took place on 6 November 1981 he was convicted of a similar offence of contempt of court, E then being a ward and five years of age (count 8), and of kidnapping E in that he stole and unlawfully carried her away against her will (count 6). For these offences he was sentenced to concurrent terms of imprisonment, all suspended for two years, of two years, four months, six months and fifteen months respectively. He appeals against his convictions for contempt of court and of kidnapping only.

The history of this stormy and unhappy family affair begins with the marriage of the appellant to Audrey on 28 July 1973. It was her second marriage. She had a son by her first marriage, which ended in divorce, and a girl, S, born in 1965 and a boy, J, born in 1969 of a long-standing relationship with another man.

In January 1974 the appellant, Audrey, S and J went to live in New Zealand. E was born there on 6 February 1976. In April 1977 S and J returned here to live with their maternal grandparents. In the following September the appellant, Audrey and E came to England ostensibly on a year's holiday. They went to live in a flat in Essex. The marriage was under considerable strain by 10 April 1978 when Audrey applied to the Family Division, by originating summons served on the appellant, to have E made a ward of court and for an order that she have the care and control of her. They separated. She went to a secret address after he had said he would take E to New Zealand.

On 21 July a registrar of the Family Division, by consent, ordered that (1) E continue to be a ward, (2) she remain in the care and control of her mother and (3) a welfare officer's report be prepared with regard to the appellant's application for access. By that time the appellant had returned to New Zealand where, on 21 April, Audrey had commenced proceedings for, inter alia, custody of E.

By the late autumn of 1978 the appellant had made, on his return at about that time to England, careful and devious preparations to take the law into his own hands and to take E, if necessary by force, away from her mother. To assist him in this reprehensible endeavour, he enlisted the assistance of two violent men named Hunter and Aherne.

On 13 December these three men, at about 11.15 pm, when Audrey was watching television, pushed their way into the flat where she had been living with all three children for some time. The appellant had a rope in his hand. Hunter wore a stocking mask and plastic gloves and carried a knife. He unscrewed the door bell. Aherne had a pair of scissors and a knife.

The appellant told Audrey that he had come to take E away. She told the other two men that E was a ward of court. They were as indifferent to that as was the appellant himself. Frightened out of her wits, Audrey woke E and dressed her in the presence of an even more frightened S. The appellant then took her away, she showing no signs of distress as she went. Before leaving the flat, in company with Aherne, the appellant showed Audrey an article which he said was a gas bomb. It was, he said, to be left with Hunter who knew how to activate it and who would, as he did for several hours, remain behind so that the appellant could have a good start on his journey before the police were informed about what was going on. Thus it was that E was taken away from her mother and afterwards by air to New Zealand.

Hunter remained in the flat until 4.30 am the following morning. Audrey telephoned the police when he left. He and Aherne were soon apprehended and at the Crown Court at Chelmsford on 19 March 1979 they were sentenced to concurrent terms of imprisonment of two years for false imprisonment and 12 months for possessing prohibited weapons. A move was made to have the appellant extradited from New Zealand on a charge of false imprisonment, but the application therefore to the Supreme Court was unsuccessful.

Meanwhile, Audrey obtained from Purchas J in the Family Division on 14 December 1978 ex parte orders that E be returned to her forthwith and that the appellant be brought before a judge of the Family Division as soon as possible and an injunction restraining the appellant from, on E's return to her mother, removing the child from her care and control and from taking E out of England and Wales. Subsequently, Audrey went to New Zealand. On 30 January 1979 the Supreme Court there, by consent, awarded her custody of E with liberty to take her back to England and gave the appellant access on terms to be agreed or as ordered by a court in England.

Early in February 1979 Audrey and E returned to England and went to live at an address in Peterborough which was not revealed to the appellant. In October 1981 the question of access remaining unresolved, the appellant came to England, discovered where they were living with S and J, and began to keep a watch on the house.

On 6 November the appellant was let into the house at about 8 am by J. He went upstairs to where E, whom he had not seen for three years, was with her mother. He said he had come to take E away. Audrey, having tried to reason with him, picked her up and, whilst shouting out that she wanted the police informed, carried E out of the house. The appellant followed her, seized E and pushed Audrey into some bushes. By now, neighbours were in the street watching this distressing scene. They saw the appellant rush with E, still in her pyjamas, struggling and screaming into a waiting car which was quickly driven away.

The appellant took E to Eire. Two days later she was reunited with her mother, who had flown there. The appellant was arrested on a warrant issued by Havering Magistrates'

Court, brought back to England and charged with, inter alia, the offences already referred to.

a   On the day following his convictions, Wood J in the Family Division discharged that part of Purchase J's order relating to the appellant's apprehension and ordered that he should not have access to E, who was to remain in her mother's care and control, and that the appellant be restrained from communicating with E and from molesting both her and her mother.

b   The appellant and Audrey are now divorced, as a result of proceedings commenced a considerable time ago which were not concluded sooner owing to difficulties at times in tracing the whereabouts of the appellant.

In the social inquiry report, prepared for the criminal proceedings, the probation officer observed, with much justification, we think:

c   'I realise that this case is one of great complexity. Moreover, it is fraught with the kind of mutual bitterness and emotional conflict more often found in a matrimonial court than in one of criminal jurisdiction.'

Later on, the probation officer went on:

d   'Situations like this are sadly familiar to Probation Officers writing reports for Divorce Courts. Only the very extremes of [the appellant's] behaviour resulting in criminal charges and national publicity make it different from countless other similar cases, whereby the two parties concerned become so locked in battle that eventually neither can or will move sideways . . . In that kind of situation, children become weapons or armoury, as they have so unhappily become in this case.'

e   The Family Division is indeed all too well acquainted with the often appalling consequences of matrimonial strife. It has formidable powers to control the interests of children and to punish those who contemptuously disobey the orders made for the benefit of children, whether or not they be wards of court.

This is a very serious example of the deliberate flouting by a father on two occasions, separated by several years in time, of court orders affecting a ward, but not so serious as to, in our view, prevent the judges of the Family Division, and all other judges of the *f*   High Court for that matter, from sufficiently and properly punishing this appellant for being in contempt for unlawfully and by force taking E away from her mother.

To resort to the criminal court for this purpose is very unusual, if not unique. We were informed that it was done here seeing that the appellant faced anyway the grave criminal charge of false imprisonment, among others, so that all matters could be disposed of once and for all. We shall say later what we think of the wisdom or otherwise *g*   of including in the indictment the so-called common law offences of kidnapping and contempt of court, especially in the light of the facts and the powers and practices of the Family Division and procedures for committal for contempt.

At the trial before the prosecution's case was opened, counsel for the appellant submitted, putting his compendious submissions in very brief and general form, that there is no such offence known to the law as kidnapping in relation to the taking away *h*   by one parent from another of their child, even when that is forcibly done. A father cannot kidnap his own child, he said, so counts 1 and 6 should be quashed. As for the offence of contempt of court, it is, he asserted, unknown, so far as wardship is concerned, for contempt proceedings to be brought in a criminal court for trial by jury. He invited the judge to order that the charges of kidnapping and contempt should not be proceeded with at the trial and that the Attorney General's view whether or not the contempt *j*   charges should be proceeded with later on indictment (assuming but not accepting that, strictly speaking, it is in law permissible to indict for this form of contempt) should be sought.

The judge, in an admirably succinct judgment, answered these submissions in his ruling before he ordered the trial on all counts to proceed. What he said was:

'In my judgment those counts do disclose offences which are known to the common law. And the offence of taking and carrying away a person of any age *a* against that person's will can be committed by a father as well as by a mother or any other person. Having said this, I am far from saying that charges of this nature and in these circumstances are necessarily to be encouraged. Such charges may well be reserved for the more serious cases which go well beyond mere matrimonial conflict and impinge on the public peace and on the public conscience. This leads me to the second submission, which I can take rather more shortly. It has been recognised for *b* some years that the Family Division and the Criminal Division have overlapping jurisdictions. For example, it not infrequently happens that a man who is subject to an injunction not to assault his wife may in its breach be dealt with by the magistrates' court for the assault or by the Family Division. I think, generally speaking, save for the more extreme cases, the question of contempt, of assault and of allied matters in these circumstances may better be dealt with in the Family *c* Division. However, I am clear in my view that such a contempt is a criminal contempt, and that although such proceedings have been rare, a criminal contempt can properly be dealt with on indictment. In this particular case I see no reason to adopt the course proposed by [counsel for the appellant] of adjourning the matter for consideration by the Attorney General, whatever the result of such a course might be. One has to bear in mind here that this is a comparatively serious case of *d* its kind, that although the seizes are clearly domestic in nature, none the less there was violence, there was force, there was use of a prohibited weapon and there was violence in public view.'

The judge's directions on the law of kidnapping have been criticised in this court. It would be appropriate, therefore, to state what they were at this point. He informed the *e* jury that kidnapping was the unlawful stealing and carrying away of any person of any age against that person's will. A father may kidnap his child. The child is a free person under the law just as the father is a free man. A father has parental rights one of which permits him to chastise his child. But, if he goes too far, treats the child too severely, he will be acting unlawfully. He cannot take his child away willy-nilly especially where his rights are affected by a court order or orders. *f*

What the prosecution had to prove to establish the offence was: (1) the appellant had taken and carried E away (that was admitted); (2) this was done against E's will. The jury had to decide whether E, at the age of two or five years, was capable of giving a valid consent to being taken away and, if she was, whether she had given it at either or both of those ages. Had the child, in other words, the capacity to exercise her own will and had she expressed it? If a child of that age could not, in the jury's view, give a valid consent, *g* they had to consider whether the guardian of that child had done so because he was the only person in that circumstance who could. If they were satisfied that the guardian had not (there was no suggestion that the court or the mother had done so) that would also mean they were satisfied that the taking away was against the will of the child. In other words, the guardian's will was the child's will; (3) the carrying away was, to the appellant's knowledge, unlawful. The appellant had no lawful right to deprive either the court or *h* the mother of custody of the child. So the question was: did he think he had? On count 2 he thought he had because he believed E at that time to be an illegal immigrant, so there was an issue to be determined. On count 6, however, this excuse was not raised. So where is the issue on count 6?

The grounds of appeal relating to kidnapping are that the judge erred in law (1) in refusing to quash counts 1 and 6 on the grounds that no criminal offence known to the *j* law was disclosed (at common law, the custody of a minor was vested in the father and he therefore could not kidnap his own child whilst the child was below the age of discretion and/or a minor), (2) in directing the jury that the prosecution had to prove the taking away was against the child's will and that it was a matter of fact for them to decide whether or not the child had such a will and had exercised it, and further that where the

child had not the capacity to consent, then consent could only be given by the child's
guardian, and (3) in directing the jury that the appellant's motive and the history of the
matter was irrelevant.

As to the law of contempt of court, he stated:

> 'What the prosecution has to prove is that E was a ward of court, that [the
> appellant] took E out of the country and there is no dispute about that, and they
> must prove that he took E out of the country knowing he had no right to do so.'

There is, not surprisingly, we think, no complaint about that.

The grounds of appeal with regard to contempt are that the judge erred in law and/or
in exercising his discretion in refusing to adjourn these counts for the Attorney General
to decide whether or not a nolle prosequi should be entered seeing that the customary
forum for contempt proceedings in wardship cases was the Family Division and the
practice of charging contempt on indictment had fallen into disuse since 1902.

If the appellant was properly indicated, or the counts relating to contempt properly
proceeded with and the jury correctly directed on the law, it seems to us that the jury's
verdicts of guilt cannot be faulted. His defence to the contempt committed in 1978 was
that he did not hear Audrey say that E was a ward of court and could not be taken to New
Zealand. He did not realise it was a contempt to take E out of this country. He thought
she was an illegal immigrant whom he had a right, if not the obligation, to take to New
Zealand. Presumably, it was this last-mentioned excuse which brought about his acquittal
of kidnapping. As for the 1981 offences, he admitted all the essential facts.

It is beyond doubt that these convictions are of outstanding importance. This is the
first time in legal history, so we were told, that a father has been convicted of kidnapping
his own child. If the conviction is upheld it will, so counsel for the appellant contends,
create an undesirable precedent which, if followed, will be an impediment to the proper
administration of justice as affecting family matters and an unnecessary burden on juries.
Moreover, to resurrect trial on indictment for contempt is likely to have similar and
unnecessary effects. Contempts for their orders, he says, should be left in the hands of
judges to adjudicate on and where appropriate to punish for. Public policy and interest
is affected by these convictions. Both demand that there should not be unwelcome and
unnecessary extensions of the classes of indictable crime.

In *The People (A-G) v Edge* [1943] IR 115 at 146 Black J defined the word 'kidnapping'
as—

> 'a composite word made up of two colloquial expressions which together denote
> child-snatching . . . but in common parlance it is used to describe the carrying away
> of anybody, child or adult.'

Child snatching by parents is, nowadays, a fairly frequent occurrence, a phenomenon
probably attributable to the high rate of divorce. It is an activity which is not confined to
this country. Some parents, in their endeavours to snatch children, do not acknowledge
the frontiers of other countries as presenting any hindrance to such often quite hazardous
conduct. Whilst it is very properly discountenanced by the courts and the public here,
and often loosely described as kidnapping, it has not, usually at any rate, been thought of
in the context of the commission of the criminal offence of kidnapping or possibly of
any criminal offence unless contempt of court be so regarded.

Yet the offence of kidnapping is centuries old. It has been well recognised as a common
law offence since Elizabethan times, if not before. It has, from time to time, apparently
fallen into disuse, but every now and again it has become a formidable weapon in the
hands of those responsible for the enforcement of the law to punish and to discourage
contemporary forms of the frightful act of the forcible taking away of a person against
his will. In the last decade, certainly, it has often formed a count in indictments alleging
the most savage manifestations of it, the perpetrators of which have been punished very
severely.

It is properly defined as 'the stealing and carrying away, or secreting of any person against that person's will'. There is little modern authority on the offence, which was described as 'the most aggravated species of false imprisonment' (see (1803) 1 East PC 429).

It received a very comprehensive examination, historical and otherwise, by the Eire Supreme Court in *The People (A-G) v Edge* [1943] IR 115, which held that the offence of kidnapping as charged of a boy of 14½ years of age, who consented to being taken against (as was alleged in the indictment) the will of his lawful guardian, one Southgate, was not an offence at common law. The decision hinged on not only the proper definition of kidnapping, but also the age of discretion, a matter dealt with by Gavan Duffy J (at 171):

> 'The common law doctrine is, in effect, that childhood ceases and manhood dawns at 14; consequently, in the absence of statute, there is neither occasion nor reason, from the common law standpoint, to deny to a youth of 14 years, a young man, the capacity and the right to dispose of himself. In my opinion, the age of discretion, with its wide implications, prevailing, as it did, over *patria potestas* on *habeas corpus*, must have been and therefore must be still the test, since, in the absence of statute, there is no other. If that age was the test for discriminating between minors who could and minors who could not consent to abduction, the logic of that test was unassailable, however unreal to us may now appear its factitious foundation, the theory that a boy's conscience and his discernment must both have come to maturity, that is juristic maturity, on the precise eve of his fourteenth birthday. That unhappy term "the age of discretion" recalls two penetrating comments by the late Mr. Justice Holmes of the American Supreme Court:—"It is one of the misfortunes of the law that ideas become encysted in phrases and thereafter for a long time cease to provoke further analysis." [see *Hyde v US* (1912) 225 US 347 at 391] and again:—"A word is not a crystal, transparent and unchanged; it is the skin of a living thought and may vary greatly in color and content according to the circumstances and time in which it is used." [see *Town v Eisner* (1918) 245 US 418 at 425]. But we are not at liberty in this criminal appeal to extend the common law age of discretion to suit our twentieth-century standard.'

He observed:

> 'To carry away or secrete a person against his will is an offence at common law, and no authority is needed for the proposition that a toddling child is in law incapable of the act of the will involved in giving consent; but, in the absence of any law to the contrary, one would, I think, reasonably suppose that a youth in his twenty-first year was in law capable of giving consent; and the question is where precisely, if at all, the common law draws the line. The age of discretion, in my judgment, supplies a clear answer and the only answer.'

Geoghegan J asserted (at 138):

> 'Until the age of discretion has been reached there can be little, if any, doubt that a minor has not the capacity to consent; that consent can be given only by the guardian, and consequently if there is not consent by the guardian the taking away is against the will of the minor.'

In *R v Hale* [1974] 1 All ER 1107, [1974] QB 819 the defendant was committed for trial on an indictment containing a count for kidnapping, the particulars of which offence were that he had unlawfully secreted a girl of 13 years against the will of her parents and lawful guardians. Lawson J quashed the count and held that, in the absence of any allegation that the defendant had secreted the girl by force or fraud or against her will, the particulars disclosed no offence known to the law.

Lawson J did not, in his judgment, venture on the vexed question of the age at which a minor can in law be said to have a will of its own, the age of discretion, in other words.

The judge in the present case, in his ruling on the motion to quash, stated: 'For my part . . . I think it remains questionable whether as a matter of law or of fact a child under

the age of 14 cannot consent.' But seeing that E was at relevant times $2\frac{3}{4}$ and $5\frac{3}{4}$ years, it
a could not, he said, 'realistically be contended' that she 'was capable of giving a valid
consent'.

One of the two foremost questions for this court is whether, in the case of a child who
is taken away from her parent, the will of that parent (assuming the child to have no
will) can be taken to be the will of the child for the purpose of deciding whether this
ingredient of the offence of kidnapping has been established. There is no English
b authority on this subject. It might be said, therefore, that reliance should be placed on
The People v Edge for concluding that a child below the age of discretion, said there to be
14 years, cannot have a will of its own, so its will must be taken to be that of its parents
or of a parent.

Whilst that would be a simple and convenient way of disposing of a difficult problem,
it is not one which attracts itself to us. There are many children of well below that age
who are mentally equipped to understand fully the implications of consenting to, for
c example, leave one parent and go away with the other. To put a parent in peril of being
convicted of kidnapping when a child of, say, 12 years who fully understands what he or
she is doing when consenting to go away with that parent (because an age of discretion
arbitrarily decided on by the court has not been reached) would, in our judgment, be
wholly unjust. Moreover, we are strongly of the view that to leave to a jury the question
d of whether a young child has, or has not, consented to go away with a parent is
undesirable and should not be done.

For one thing, it may, having regard to the age and disposition of the child, prove to
be an impossible task and, for another, it would expose the child to the potentially
harmful ordeal of giving evidence in a criminal trial when inevitably in a highly
emotional state. The fact that children sometimes have to give evidence in sexual cases is
e no warrant for extending the need for this to be done. No judge who has had experience,
in criminal and in family matters, of listening to children's evidence would, we believe,
of his own volition countenance such a thing. The fact that a baby or a child of five years
obviously cannot give any vestige of proper consent to being taken away is not a
compelling reason, in our view, for introducing the notion that the will of a parent shall
be regarded as the will of that child.

f Lest it should be thought that we come to our conclusion with the problems arising
out of matrimonial discord only in mind, we seek to make it clear that we regard our
decision to be of general application. Accordingly, it will affect a person who is not a
parent and who takes away a child.

This should dismay no one for, if the child is under 14 years of age, that person can be
charged with child stealing contrary to s 56 of the Offences against the Persons Act 1861,
g the maximum penalty for which is seven years' imprisonment. If the child or youth is
14 years or over, it is unlikely that any harm would come to it by giving evidence on a
charge of kidnapping and that a jury would find any extraordinary difficulty in evaluating
that evidence.

In this connection, s 20(1) of the Sexual Offences Act 1956 should be borne in mind.
It provides:

h   'It is an offence for a person acting without lawful authority or excuse to take an
        unmarried girl under the age of sixteen out of the possession of her parent or
        guardian against her will.'

The penalty for this offence is a maximum period of imprisonment for two years. Thus,
it is plain, we think, that statute and common law combine effectively to punish those
j who wrongfully interfere with children or youths who are either under or over 14 years
of age.

But, so it may be argued, seeing that a father is not in peril of conviction either under
s 56(1) of the 1861 Act (see *R v Austin* [1981] 1 All ER 374) or in respect of a legitimate
child under s 20(1) of the 1956 Act, he may never be exposed to punishment for taking
away a child from its mother. That is not so. The jurisdiction of judges, as has already

been stated, to punish for disobedience of its orders with regard to children, whether wards of court or not, is extensive and powerful.

Moreover, Parliament deliberately, so it seems to us, by enacting the proviso to s 56 (a section which is similar in terms, although differently constructed, to legislation previously passed on two occasions in the last century, namely in 1814 (54 Geo 3 c 101 (child stealing)) and 1828 (9 Geo 4 c 31 (offences against the person)) intended that neither a father nor a mother should be prosecuted for child stealing.

It is noteworthy, incidentally, having regard to and despite the existence of the offence of kidnapping, that the preamble to the 1814 Act, stated to be an Act for the more effective prevention of child stealing, pronounced:

'Whereas the practice of carrying away young children, by forcible or fraudulent means, from their parents or other persons having the care or charge or custody of them, commonly called child stealing, has of late much prevailed and increased: And whereas no adequate punishment is as yet provided by law in England or Ireland for so heinous an offence . . .'

Clearly Parliament at that time did not regard the offence of kidnapping (for which the punishment can be life imprisonment) as applicable to children 'under the age of ten years'. This age limit was raised to 14 by the 1861 Act.

Our general conclusion is that there is no such offence as the kidnapping of a child who is under the age of 14 years.

The second foremost question is whether a father can, in any circumstances and regardless of a child's age, be guilty of kidnapping. Much able argument was addressed to us on this matter during the course of which the history of parental rights over children, including, until recent times, the superiority of the claim of the father over that of the mother, was traced. Useful and interesting though that was, we see no need to refer to it in this judgment seeing that unquestionably the law does not nowadays regard the rights of the father and mother as affecting their children as other than equal, save to the extent that these may be affected by an order of the court made in wardship or other proceedings.

In Lowe and White *Wards of Court* (1979) p 324 it is stated:

'The problem of the unilateral removal of a child by one parent from another is variously referred to as "child snatching" or "kidnapping". For convenience we have entitled the chapter "Kidnapping" though it should be understood that a parent would not actually be guilty of the crime of kidnapping since he has a prima facie right to the possession of his child.'

It was submitted that this statement, if it be right, contrasts oddly with the decision in *R v Austin*, in which it was held that a parent may be guilty of child stealing, but may not, because of the terms of the proviso, be prosecuted for it.

It is to be noted that it was Parliament, surely mindful of a parent's right to possession of a child, which created the s 56 offence and that it laid down, as one of the essential ingredients of the offence, the taking away of a child by force or fraud. The use of force or fraud is not an essential ingredient of the offence of kidnapping even though the taking has to be against the will of the victim. If Parliament had not declared that, for the purpose of s 56, a parent may be guilty of child stealing, no one could be convicted of aiding and abetting him in stealing. Since the proviso did not include such a person, he or she could be saved neither from prosecution nor from possible conviction for that.

We see nothing incongruous about the statement in *Lowe and White*, with which we entirely agree, and the provisions of s 56 as interpreted in *R v Austin*. We would regard it as odd indeed if Parliament contemplated that a parent could be prosecuted for, and be found guilty of, kidnapping and, although by the same conduct be also guilty of child stealing, be not prosecuted for that.

In our view, the offence of kidnapping, with one exception, is not committed by a parent who snatches a child who is under the age of majority (now 18 years) when a child

becomes, of course, an adult and is no longer possessed by his parents. The exception is
_a_ that, when a child has lawfully married under 18 years, that child too passes out of the
possession of the parents, and the offence of kidnapping may be committed against that
child as it can against a child who has achieved majority. On 14 January 1983 in the
Crown Court at Snaresbrook a man, Mohamed Nazir, was properly convicted on his own
confession, we think, for kidnapping his daughter of 16 years who had married without
his consent (see R v Nazir (unreported)).

_b_ Having regard to the views we have expressed on the common law offence of
kidnapping, we are bound to say that, in our judgment, the judge in the present case
should have quashed the relevant counts in the indictment and that, not having done so,
he misdirected the jury on the law in respect of them. For these reasons, we quash the
conviction for kidnapping.

Turning to the two convictions for contempt of court, it will be recalled that the judge
_c_ was not invited to quash them before the trial commenced, but to adjourn the trial of
the appellant on them to give the Attorney General (to whom the matter should, it was
argued, be referred) an opportunity of deciding whether they should be proceeded with
and the clear contempts dealt with in another way.

The judge declined, in his discretion, to take that course, observing that, whilst
proceeding by indictment for contempt was rarely done, he thought the present case was
_d_ a comparatively serious case having regard to the violence used. He went on to say that
in further matrimonial proceedings, the Family Division would have to deal with what
he called 'the question of purge' meaning, we suppose, that he envisaged some
matrimonial hearing in the court in which the question of whether the appellant had
purged his contempt would have to be dealt with.

There seems to be no doubt that to take a ward of court out of the jurisdiction without
_e_ consent is a criminal contempt. A criminal contempt was, a long time ago, and is still,
according to the opinion of Lawton LJ, expressed obiter in _Balogh v Crown Court at St_
Albans [1974] 3 All ER 283, [1975] QB 73, triable on indictment. However, the last
reported case of trial on indictment for contempt is _R v Tibbits_ [1902] 1 KB 77, [1900–3]
All ER Rep 896, which involved the editor of a newspaper on a charge of conspiring with
the author of certain articles appearing therein to pervert the course of justice. When, if
_f_ ever, a contempt arising out of wardship or other proceedings affecting the custody, care
and control of children has been prosecuted on indictment, we have not been able to
discover.

The customary manner of proceedings in a case of disobedience to the order of a court
which is not committed in the face of the court is by application for committal made
pursuant to leave therefor to the Divisional Court of the Queen's Bench Division under
_g_ RSC Ord 52. In the circumstances of the present case, the application could have been
made by the mother, Audrey, the Official Solicitor or the Attorney General. The court
whose order has been flouted may act of its own motion: see Ord 52, r 5. The court
which makes the committal order may suspend it. The maximum is two years'
imprisonment: see the Contempt of Court Act 1981, s 14(1).

Whilst it appears to be permissible, or was permissible, for a contempt of court in a
_h_ wardship proceeding to be tried on indictment, we think it highly undesirable, in the
light of the remedies now available and having regard to the nature of the proceedings,
that that form of proceeding should be resorted to. For a very long time now, decisions
in all contempt cases have been made by judges who are best equipped to tell whether a
contempt has been committed and may very well be able to do so on affidavit evidence
alone.

_j_ It is not, we think, in the best interests of anyone that a by now almost ancient way of
proceeding should be resurrected, even if it be thought proper to do it 'so that all matters
can be dealt with at once'. That is no sufficient reasons, in our view, for doing that which,
as we have plainly indicated, is now unacceptable.

Thus it is that we must look at the exercise of the judge's discretion which, we
recognise, should not lightly be interfered with. But we think the policy of the law and

the public interest demands that we should do so here for the reasons which we have explained. This was clearly a case in which the judge should have allowed the Attorney General to consider the future of the contempt counts and he having done so, we say further, should have given instructions that they be not proceeded with.

With every respect to the judge, to whose care and industry and clarity of expression in this difficult case we wish to pay tribute, we think he erred in the exercise of his discretion and in the other ways already mentioned.

The convictions for contempt, too, will be quashed.

Appeal allowed. Convictions for contempt of court and kidnapping quashed.

6 December. The court refused leave to appeal to the House of Lords but, on the application of the Crown, certified, under s 33(2) of the Criminal Appeal Act 1968, that the following points of law of general public importance were involved in the decision: (1) whether the common law offence of kidnapping existed in the case of a child victim under the age of 14 years; (2) whether in any circumstances a parent might be convicted of such an offence where the child victim was unmarried and under the age of majority.

26 January 1984. The Appeal Committee of the House of Lords granted a petition by the Crown for leave to appeal.

Solicitors: *Gary Jacobs & Co*, Chadwell Heath (for the appellant); *Director of Public Prosecutions*.

April Weiss   Barrister.

Re Delamere's Settlement Trusts
Kenny and others v Cunningham-Reid and others

COURT OF APPEAL, CIVIL DIVISION
WALLER, SLADE AND ROBERT GOFF LJJ
1, 2, 10 NOVEMBER 1983

Trust and trustee – Accumulation – Income – Power of appointment – Accumulation during minority – Surplus income – Destination of accumulations – Income vested in appointees 'absolutely' – Whether appointee's share falling into estate or back into trust fund if he dies before reaching majority or marrying – Trustee Act 1925, ss 31(2), 69(2).

By a settlement of a trust fund made in 1963 the settlor gave the trustees a power of appointment over the fund to be exercised in favour of a defined class of beneficiaries. In 1971 the trustees executed a revocable deed of appointment which provided that the 'income' of the trust fund was to be held in trust for the settlor's six grandchildren (the appointees) in 'equal shares absolutely'. At the date of the appointment all the grandchildren were minors. Between 1971 and 1980 a substantial amount of income, some £122,000, was accumulated. Since the trust fund was prima facie subject to s 31[a] of the Trustee Act 1925 the question arose whether the £122,000 accumulated during the minorities of the respective appointees formed part of the trust fund pursuant to s 31(2), so that if an appointee died before attaining the age of 18 or marrying his share of the accumulated income would fall back into the general capital of the trust fund and his interest was to that extent defeasible notwithstanding that he had a vested interest in the income, or whether the 1971 appointment showed a sufficient 'contrary intention'

---

a   Section 31, so far as material, is set out at p 588 *d e* and *j* to p 589 *d*, post

a within s 69(2)[b] of the 1925 Act for that Act not to apply to the appointment, with the result that the accumulated income vested in the appointees as and when it accrued and was accordingly held by the trustees indefeasibly for the appointees.

Held – On the true construction of the 1971 appointment the word 'absolutely' was intended to indicate that the vested interests in accrued income given by the appointment to each of the grandchildren was indefeasible in all circumstances. Furthermore, having *b* regard to the age of the appointees at the date of the appointment and the fact that the appointment was not limited in duration, eg to the lifetime of any appointee, it was to be presumed that the trustees regarded with equanimity the possibility that an appointee's share of income might fall into his estate if he died. The effect of the 1971 appointment was, therefore, that income vested in an appointee as and when it accrued and was held by the trustees absolutely and indefeasibly for the appointee. Accordingly, paras (i) and *c* (ii) of s 31(2) of the 1925 Act did not apply to the accumulated income. The appeal would accordingly be allowed (see p 590 *h* to p 591 *j* and p 592 *b* and *e* to *g*, post).

IRC v Bernstein [1961] 1 All ER 320 and dictum of Herring CJ in Re Tompson [1947] VLR at 67 applied.

Re Master's Settlement, Master v Master [1911] 1 Ch 321, Stanley v IRC [1944] 1 All ER 230 and Re Sharp's Settlement Trusts, Ibbotson v Bliss [1972] 3 All ER 151 considered.

d
Notes
For the accumulation of surplus income of property held on trust for a person during infancy, see 24 Halsbury's Laws (4th edn) para 464, and for cases on the subject, see 28(2) Digest (Reissue) 755–756, 873–879.

For the Trustee Act 1925, ss 31, 69, see 38 Halsbury's Statutes (3rd edn) 137, 197.

e
Cases referred to in judgments
IRC v Bernstein [1961] 1 All ER 320, [1961] Ch 399, [1961] 2 WLR 143, CA.
Master's Settlement, Re, Master v Master [1911] 1 Ch 321.
Sharp's Settlement Trusts, Re, Ibbotson v Bliss [1972] 3 All ER 151, [1973] Ch 331, [1972] 3 WLR 765.
f Stanley v IRC [1944] 1 All ER 230, [1944] 1 KB 255, CA.
Tompson, Re [1947] VLR 60.
Turner's Will Trust, Re, District Bank Ltd v Turner [1936] 2 All ER 1435, [1937] Ch 15, CA.

Cases also cited
Buckley's Trusts, Re (1883) 22 Ch D 583.
g Humphreys, Re, Humphreys v Levett [1893] 3 Ch 1, CA.
Inglewood (Lord) v IRC [1983] 1 WLR 366, CA.
Wells, Re, Wells v Wells (1889) 43 Ch D 281.

Appeal
The defendants, Fiona Cunningham-Reid, Duncan Cunningham-Reid, James Beaumont *h* Cunningham-Reid, Mark James Cunningham-Reid, Jane Mary Cunningham-Reid and Charles Ashley Cunningham-Reid, who were beneficiaries under a settlement dated 8 March 1963 made between the settlor, the Hon Ruth Mary Clarisse Delamere, and others, appealed against that part of the judgment of Goulding J dated 15 July 1981 whereby he held that the application of s 31 of the Trustee Act 1925 in respect of the disposal of income of the trusts of the settlement was not excluded by the terms of an *j* appointment made on 19 February 1971 by the plaintiffs, the respondents Thomas Kenny, William Edward Gerald Churcher and Sir Harold Felix Cassel, as trustees of the settlement. The seventh defendant, Noel Robert Cunningham-Reid, was joined as a respondent to represent all the other beneficiaries born and unborn under the settlement. The facts are set out in the judgment of Slade LJ.

---

b   Section 69(2) is set out at p 587 *j*, post

Robert Walker QC for the appellants.
Anthony C Taussig for the trustee respondents.
Christopher McCall for the seventh defendant.

Cur adv vult

10 November. The following judgments were delivered.

SLADE LJ (giving the first judgment at the invitation of Waller LJ). This is an appeal from part of a judgment of Goulding J delivered on 15 July 1981 on an originating summons issued by the trustees of a settlement dated 8 March 1963, made by the Hon Ruth Mary Clarisse Delamere.

On 19 February 1971 the trustees of the settlement, in exercise of a power of appointment thereby conferred on them, executed a revocable deed of appointment (the 1971 apppointment). On 2 October 1980 they executed another deed of appointment (the 1980 appointment). A substantial amount of income arose between the dates of the 1971 appointment and the 1980 appointment which was not distributed but, as one of the trustees put it in an affidavit, was 'accumulated de facto'. As at 31 March 1980 such undistributed income amounted to about £122,000. The substantial issue between the parties is as to the construction of the 1971 appointment and, in particular, whether s 31 of the Trustee Act 1925 applies to it without modification or with modification. If that section applies without modification, it will have had the effect of engrafting on the otherwise absolute interests in accruing income conferred on the appointees by the 1971 appointment a qualifying trust of a special nature, which will have given each of them a title to his or her share of the accumulations if, but only if, he or she attains 18 or marries.

It has been explained to us that considerations relating to capital transfer tax lend added importance to the court's decision on these matters, having regard to the fundamental distinction drawn by the relevant legislation between interests which are 'in possession' and those which are not. However, the court is not asked to decide any Revenue question. The Commissioners of Inland Revenue were informed of the application but did not desire to be joined as defendants. Accordingly, like the judge, I consider that any consequences of the court's decision regarding taxes are not a matter with which it is in any way concerned.

The settlement was one of freehold land and its proceeds. It contained a number of definitions. 'The Beneficiaries' was to mean the present and future children, grandchildren and great-grandchildren of the settlor and eight named individuals. The 'Appointed Class' was to consist of the beneficiaries, together with the issue, husbands, wives, widows and widowers of the beneficiaries. The expression 'Charities' was to mean one named charity. The 'Perpetuity Date' was to be the date 80 years after the date of the settlement or 20 years after the death of the last survivor of the descendants of King George V living at the date of the settlement, whichever should be the shorter period or such earlier date as the trustees should by deed appoint to be such date.

Clause 4(1) of the settlement provided that, subject to certain immaterial provisions—

> 'the Trustees shall stand possessed of the capital and income of the Trust Fund IN TRUST for all or such one or more exclusively of the other or others of the Beneficiaries or the Appointed Class or the Charities or any of them if more than one in such shares and with and subject to such trusts powers and provisions for their respective benefit (including powers of appointment and discretionary trusts of capital and income exercisable from time to time by or at the discretion of the Trustees or any other person or persons) as the Trustees (not being less than three in number) shall by any Deed or Deeds revocable or irrevocable at their absolute discretion appoint.'

Clause 4(2) precluded the making or revocation of any appointment after the perpetuity date.

Clause 5 provided in effect that, subject as aforesaid, the trustees should hold the a income of the trust fund arising before the perpetuity date on discretionary trusts for the benefit of the beneficiaries and the charities.

Clauses 6 and 7 provided that, subject as aforesaid, the trustees should hold the 'capital and income' of the trust fund on trust for such of the grandchildren and great-grandchildren of the settlor as should be living on the perpetuity date, if more than one in such shares as the trustees should on or before the perpetuity date by deed appoint and in default of appointment in equal shares and, subject as aforesaid, on trust for the b charities in equal shares.

By the 1971 appointment the trustees of the settlement executed an appointment of which the operative part was expressed in the following brief terms:

c 'Now this Deed witnesseth that in exercise of the power in that behalf conferred upon the Trustees by the Settlement and of every or any other power them hereunto enabling the Trustees HEREBY APPOINT that the income of the fund subject to the trusts of the Settlement and the income from the investments for the time being representing the same shall be held henceforth UPON TRUST for the Settlor's grandchildren Fiona Cunningham-Reid Duncan Cunningham-Reid James Beau-mont Cunningham-Reid Mark James Cunningham-Reid Jane Mary Cunningham-Reid and Charles Ashley Cunningham-Reid in equal shares absolutely PROVIDED ALWAYS that it shall be lawful for the Trustees at any time or times hereafter before d the Perpetuity Date (as defined by the Settlement) by any deed or deeds to revoke the appointment hereinbefore contained either in whole or in part.'

All the six persons named in the 1971 appointment were grandchildren of the settlor and at the date of its execution were all minors. Fiona had been born on 4 June 1956, Duncan on 14 March 1958, James on 10 November 1965, Mark on 4 October 1962, Jane e on 1 July 1964 and Charles on 25 September 1968. All of them are still living. They are the first six defendants and the appellants in the proceedings. The seventh defendant, Mr Noel Cunningham-Reid, is one of the settlor's two sons and has been joined as a party to represent all the other beneficiaries born or unborn under the settlement. He and the plaintiff trustees are the respondents to this appeal, on which the trustees have taken a neutral stance.

f To complete the history, the trustees on 2 October 1980 executed the 1980 appointment. The broad effect of that deed was to revoke the trusts appointed by the 1971 appointment in relation to four equal sixth part shares of the capital of the trust fund and to appoint new trusts in respect of them and their future income. The appointment, however, contained an unusual condition because it was expressed to have effect if, and only if, no interest in possession, within the meaning of the relevant capital g transfer tax legislation, subsisted in the property appointed at the date of its execution.

The primary question raised by the plaintiff trustees in the originating summons was whether, on the true construction of the 1971 appointment, s 31 of the Trustee Act 1925 applied in whole or in part to the capital of the fund subject to the trusts of the settlement during the period from 19 February 1971 to 1 October 1980, and, if in part, what part.

The principal function of s 31, as counsel on behalf of the appellants pointed out, h appears to be to supply a code of rules governing the disposal of income, especially during a minority, in cases where a settlor or testator has made dispositions of capital and either (a) being an unskilled draftsman, has not thought about income, or (b) being a skilled draftsman, has been content to let the statutory code apply. However, it is important to recognise at the outset that the code embodied in s 31 is included in the 1925 Act as the draftsman's servant, not as his master. For s 69(2) provides that:

j 'The powers conferred by this Act on trustees are in addition to the powers conferred by the instrument, if any, creating the trust, but those powers, unless otherwise stated, apply if and so far only as a contrary intention is not expressed in the instrument, if any, creating the trust, and have effect subject to the terms of that instrument.'

Though, as will be seen, s 31 contains a number of ancillary provisions which are in terms imperative, in addition to the powers properly so-called thereby conferred on *a* trustees, it is common ground that it would suffice to make all or any of the particular provisions of s 31 inapplicable if, on a fair reading of the 1971 appointment, 'one can say that such application would be inconsistent with the purport of the instrument': see *IRC v Bernstein* [1961] 1 All ER 320 at 325, [1961] Ch 399 at 412 per Lord Evershed MR; see also *Re Turner's Will Trusts, District Bank Ltd v Turner* [1936] 2 All ER 1435, [1937] Ch 15. *b*

Before setting out the relevant provisions of s 31, I should mention two further points. First, the section was amended by the Family Law Reform Act 1969, which substituted references to 18 years for references to 21 years, but not so as to affect its application to any interest under an instrument made before 1 January 1970. I shall hereafter refer to s 31 as so amended. Second, it is common ground that the interests of the appointees under the 1971 appointment must be treated as arising under the 1971 appointment, *c* made after 1 January 1970, rather than under the settlement itself, which was made before that date, so that 18 years is the relevant age for all present purposes.

Section 31(1) of the Trustee Act 1925, as so amended, provides:

'Where any property is held by trustees in trust for any person for any interest whatsoever, whether vested or contingent, then, subject to any prior interests or charges affecting that property—(i) during the infancy of any such person, if his *d* interest so long continues, the trustees may, at their sole discretion, pay to his parent or guardian, if any, or otherwise apply for or towards his maintenance, education, or benefit, the whole or such part, if any, of the income of that property as may, in all the circumstances, be reasonable, whether or not there is—(a) any other fund applicable to the same purpose; or (b) any person bound by law to provide for his *e* maintenance or education; and (ii) if such person on attaining the age of eighteen years has not a vested interest in such income, the trustees shall thenceforth pay the income of that property and of any accretion thereto under subsection (2) of this section to him, until he either attains a vested interest therein or dies, or until failure of his interest . . .'

There follows a proviso as to the manner in which the trustees are to decide how much *f* income to apply for maintenance purposes.

Section 31(1) has to be read subject to the qualifying words of s 31(3), which provides that the section applies in the case of a contingent interest only if the limitation or trust carries the intermediate income of the property. Subject to this implicit qualification, s 31, in view of the comprehensive nature of the opening words of the section, is by its terms *capable* of applying where any property is held by trustees in trust for any interest *g* whatsoever. In particular, as Pennycuick V-C observed in *Re Sharp's Settlement Trusts, Ibbotson v Bliss* [1972] 3 All ER 151 at 155–156, [1973] Ch 331 at 339, 'the opening phrase "any interest whatsoever, whether vested or contingent" indisputably comprehends a vested interest subject to defeasance'. Thus, the section, by its terms, is *capable* of applying to the interests of the six appointees under the 1971 appointment, which are agreed to have been vested interests, subject to defeasance by an exercise of the trustees' power to *h* revoke that appointment.

Thus far, s 31 may be said to contain a few surprises. Section 31(2), however, contains provisions which are in some respects materially different from those of its predecessor, s 43 of the Conveyancing and Law of Property Act 1881. It states:

'During the infancy of any such person, if his interest so long continues, the trustees shall accumulate all the residue of that income in the way of compound *j* interest by investing the same and the resulting income thereof from time to time in authorised investments, and shall hold those accumulations as follows:—(i) If any such person—(a) attains the age of eighteen years, or marries under that age, and his interest in such income during his infancy or until his marriage is a vested interest; or (b) on attaining the age of eighteen years or on marriage under that age becomes entitled to the property from which such income arose in fee simple, absolute or determinable, or absolutely, or for an entailed interest; the trustees shall hold the accumulations in trust for such person absolutely, but without prejudice to any provision with respect thereto contained in any settlement by him made under any statutory powers during his infancy, and so that the receipt of such person after marriage, and though still an infant, shall be a good discharge; and (ii) In any other case the trustees shall, notwithstanding that such person had a vested interest in such income, hold the accumulations as an accretion to the capital of the property from which such accumulations arose, and as one fund with such capital for all purposes, and so that, if such property is settled land, such accumulations shall be held upon the same trusts as if the same were capital money arising therefrom; but the trustees may, at any time during the infancy of such person if his interest so long continues, apply those accumulations, or any part thereof, as if they were income arising in the then current year.'

Finally, I should refer to s 31(4), which provides:

'This section applies to a vested annuity in like manner as if the annuity were the income of property held by trustees in trust to pay the income thereof to the annuitant for the same period for which the annuity is payable, save that in any case accumulations made during the infancy of the annuitant shall be held in trust for the annuitant or his personal representatives absolutely.'

The striking feature of sub-s (2) is that, as Lord Greene MR pointed out in *Stanley v IRC* [1944] 1 All ER 230 at 233, [1944] KB 255 at 261, para (ii) thereof has the effect of—

'engrafting upon the vested interest originally conferred on the infant by the settlement or other disposition a qualifying trust of a special nature which confers on the infant a title to the accumulations if, and only if, he attains [the age of majority] or marries.'

The effect of para (ii), where it applies, is thus to defeat the interest (albeit a vested interest) of the infant in the accumulations if he dies before attaining 18 or marrying, and to cause them to rejoin the general capital of the trust property from which they arose. Substantially the question in the present case is whether or not, as the appellants submit, the trustees, by the language of the 1971 appointment, have evinced sufficiently clearly an intention that the title of the infant should *not* be defeasible in this manner and correspondingly that paras (i) and (ii) of s 31(2) of the 1925 Act should not apply to the trusts thereby appointed. It is not in dispute that the provisions relating to maintenance and accumulation of income contained in s 31(1) do not apply to the 1971 appointment, since this subsection, according to its terms, is quite capable of applying to the trust capital of which the income has been dealt with by that appointment and its application would in no way be inconsistent with the purport of that instrument.

Two further points are, I think, clear. First, on any possible footing, Fiona, who attained 18 years in 1974, and Duncan, who attained that age in 1976, were as from such dates (if not before) respectively absolutely and indefeasibly entitled to the accumulations of income made in respect of their interests under the 1971 appointment.

Second, the respective accumulations of income which had been made during the infancy of James, Mark, Jane and Charles in respect of their interests under the 1971 appointment were not subject to the power of revocation reserved to the trustees by that deed. The judge so held and, though that part of his decision has been challenged in a respondent's notice, this challenge is not now pursued. In my judgment it is indisputable that each of the six appointees has a vested interest in his share of income accruing under the 1971 appointment before that appointment is revoked, and that any exercise of such powers cannot divest him of income which has already accrued (see *Re Master's Settlement, Master v Master* [1911] 1 Ch 321).

The judge accepted that under the terms of the 1971 appointment 'read alone, the grandchildren take absolute, outright indefeasible title'. Nevertheless, as he observed, and as counsel emphasised on behalf of the seventh defendant, the mere fact that an instrument may have conferred on an infant a vested interest in the relevant income *a* which has been accumulated is not by itself enough to exclude the provisions of s 31(2) of the Trustee Act 1925. This is made clear by the words in parenthesis near the beginning of para (ii), 'notwithstanding that such person had a vested interest in such income'. If, for example, a settlement, without more, simply directs property to be held in trust for A for life and A is an infant at the date of its execution, there will be nothing to prevent both sub-s (1) and sub-s (2) from applying to the interest appointed, unless *b* there are other provisions in the settlement which show that this is not the intention. Counsel for the respondents drew particular attention to the words 'save that in any case accumulations made during the infancy of the annuitant shall be held in trust for the annuitant or his personal representatives absolutely', which appear at the end of s 31(4). He submitted that these words, read together with the earlier words of this subsection, clearly show Parliament's intention that in the ordinary case, not involving an annuity, *c* where property is held on trust to pay the income thereof to an infant, accumulations of income made during the infancy will not necessarily belong to the infant or his estate.

The judge summarised the principal argument placed before him as relying on the strong force of the word 'absolutely', which appears in the 1971 appointment. As to this point, he said this:

'The word "absolutely" has, of course, different meanings in different contexts. *d* Sometimes it is a word of limitation to show that a capital and not a mere temporary interest is intended. Sometimes it is used to exclude some condition or qualification. There are other meanings too. In the end, and the point must in the end be a short one, I do not consider that the insertion of this word "absolutely" is nearly clear enough to express a contrary intention or to constitute an overriding term of the trust instrument that would exclude sub-s (2) of s 31 by virtue of sub-s (2) of s 69.' *e*

The judge accordingly held that s 31 was not excluded by the terms of the 1971 appointment but that the provisions of sub-ss (1) and (2) were applicable to the trusts declared by it.

I recognise that, as counsel for the respondents submitted, it is for the appellants to show that the 1971 appointment requires the qualification or exclusion of all or any part *f* of s 31, since it is one of general application unless and in so far as a contrary intention appears from the trust instrument. Nevertheless, with the greatest respect to the judge, the principal difficulty which I find in his judgment is that, while stating that the word 'absolutely' has different meanings in different contexts, he gives no express indication as to the meaning which he attaches to the word in the context of the 1971 appointment, and no explanation why the word is there. Counsel for the appellants pointed out the *g* drafting of this deed is unusually terse and emphatic and I think it must be presumed that every single word was intended to have its due force. What then is the proper force to be attributed to the word 'absolutely' (if it is not to be rejected as wholly otiose) when it appears in an appointment of income executed in favour of six named infant appointees? For my part, I can see only one answer to this question, namely that in this context the word was intended to indicate that the vested interests in income given by *h* the appointment to each of the appointees should be indefeasible. As was pointed out by Herring CJ in an Australian case, *Re Tompson* [1947] VLR 60 at 67, the word 'absolutely' is commonly used with regard to vesting as meaning 'indefeasibly'. As counsel for the respondents suggested, it is conceivable that the draftsman of the 1971 appointment used the word merely with the intention of making it clear that the interests of the appointee in accrued income should not be defeasible by a subsequent exercise of the trustees' *j* power of revocation. Nevertheless, to place a restricted interpretation on the word 'absolutely' on this account would be to confine the ambit of the word to less than its natural meaning and to base one's conclusion on mere speculation as to the intention of the parties to the 1971 appointment. Furthermore, it would involve reaching a conclusion which rendered the word 'absolutely' superfluous since, as appears from *Re Master's*

Settlement, even in the absence of the word 'absolutely', an exercise of the trustees' power of revocation could not have affected the destination of income which had already accrued.

The court is, in my opinion, entitled to deduce the intentions of the trustees in making the 1971 appointment only from the words which they, or their draftsman, chose to employ. Furthermore, as I have said, due weight must be given to every word which they chose to employ. Accordingly, I conclude that the force of the word in this context must be to express the intention that the appointees' respective interests in income accruing during the subsistence of the appointment should not be defeasible in any circumstances whatsoever, in other words, as counsel for the appellants put it, they should keep it 'come what may'. I might add that this is the clear force of the word as used in s 31(2)(i) and (4) of the Trustee Act 1925 itself.

However, counsel for the appellants did not base his argument, and I do not base my conclusion, that the 1971 appointment evinced an intention that each of the appointees should keep his share of income 'come what may' solely on the addition of the word 'absolutely'. There are at least two further significant points. First, this was an appointment of income in favour of six infant beneficiaries, of whom the eldest, as the trustees must be taken to have known, was only 12 at the date of the appointment. Second, subject to the existence of the power of revocation, no limit of time was placed on the duration of the income interests thereby appointed; there is no question of such duration being limited to the lifetime of any appointee. The draftsman thus appears to have contemplated with equanimity the possibility that a share of income might fall into the estate of an appointee who died while the appointment was still unrevoked. It appears inherently improbable that the trustees would have intended that, on the one hand, an infant's personal representatives would continue to receive and retain future income, unless and until their right was taken away by revocation, while on the other hand those same personal representatives would, solely by virtue of s 31(2), be deprived of the right to receive accumulations of income accruing during that same infant's lifetime.

Counsel for the respondents in his helpful argument emphasised, and I accept, that, for reasons which I have already given, the very wording of s 31(2) itself shows that it is capable of applying, even though there may be an apparent inconsistency between the provisions of that subsection and the provisions of the relevant trust instrument; I also accept that it cannot be safely assumed that, in using the phraseology which he did, the draftsman of the 1971 appointment specifically had in mind the provisions of s 31(2) or s 69(2) of the 1925 Act at all. Nevertheless, he for his part accepted that in the end the relevant test must be the *Bernstein* test. Though there were cited to us three authorities dealing with the effect of trust documents executed before the novel provisions of s 31(2) were introduced, I have found them of little assistance. When the *Bernstein* test is translated to the facts of the present case the relevant question must, in my opinion, be this: have the appellants shown that the application of paras (i) and (ii) of s 31(2) of the 1925 Act would be inconsistent with the purport of the 1971 appointment? For my part I am satisfied that they have shown that the application of those paragraphs which would have the effect of defeating the interest of an infant appointee in the accumulations made in respect of his interest if he were to die before attaining 18 or marrying would be wholly inconsistent with the purport of this particular instrument. It follows that, while there is no reason why s 31(1) should not apply to the 1971 appointment, paras (i) and (ii) of s 31(2) must be deemed to have been excluded.

For these reasons, I respectfully differ from the judge on this limited point of construction and would allow the appeal. I would substitute for that part of his judgment which declared that the provisions of sub-ss (1) and (2) of s 31 of the 1925 Act are applicable to the trusts declared by the 1971 appointment a declaration that the provisions of the said subsections are applicable to the said trusts subject to the qualification that any accumulations duly made in respect of the share of each appellant under the terms of the 1971 appointment are and at all times have been held in trust for that appellant absolutely and indefeasibly.

I would make one comment in conclusion. The present case well illustrates that the existence of s 31 of the 1925 Act, for all its obvious advantages and uses, could, in one *a* sense, be said to present a potential trap for a draftsman who is anxious to avoid any possible ambiguity in the course of settling a trust document under which infant beneficiaries are or may become beneficially interested in the income of settled property. In many cases the draftsman may be well advised out of caution either expressly to provide that the section is to apply with or without stated modifications or expressly to exclude its application altogether. *b*

WALLER LJ. I entirely agree with the judgment of Slade LJ. However, I briefly express my reasons for differing from the conclusions of the trial judge. Section 31 of the Trustee Act 1925 was enacted in order both to simplify the task of the draftsman of a trust instrument and to fill gaps which he might unwittingly leave in the disposal of the trust income. And in the absence of a contrary intention in the trust instrument sub-s (2) *c* provided in effect that income of a beneficiary up to the age of 18 which was not applied for his maintenance should be accumulated as part of the trust fund so that if he died unmarried before the age of 18 the accumulated income would form part of the trust fund and not vest in his personal representatives. By contrast sub-s (4) provided that in the case of a vested annuity accumulations made during his infancy should belong to him or his personal representatives 'absolutely'. There are no doubt good reasons for *d* making this distinction in the absence of a contrary intention, but the difference between the two subsections does emphasise the necessity of examining the wording of the trust instrument carefully. In this case the deed of appointment is commendably brief in form and I agree with Slade LJ that this circumstance indicates that every word is included for a purpose. Even in the absence of the word 'absolutely' the effect of the 1971 appointment would have been to give the appellants a title to all accrued income defeasible only if he *e* or she died before the age of 18 unmarried. Without the word 'absolutely', however, the construction contended for by the respondents would have taken effect and the income would have been held by the trustees in accordance with the provisions of sub-s (2). One has to ask therefore why the word 'absolutely' was included.

In my opinion there are two features of the deed of appointment which make it clear that the deed must be construed as having been intended to vary the provisions of *f* s 31(2). These two features are that the deed was expressed to be a settlement of income and that it was expressed to be on trust for the appellants in equal shares 'absolutely'. In my opinion that combination leads to the conclusion that the deed was intended to ensure that the income vested in the appointee as and when it became due and in so far as it was not used for maintenance of the appointee was held by the trustees absolutely and indefeasibly for the appointee. *g*

ROBERT GOFF LJ. I agree.

Appeal allowed. Declaration by Goulding J varied. Leave to appeal to the House of Lords refused.

Solicitors: *Withers* (for the appellants); *Travers Smith Braithwaite & Co* (for the respondents).

Sophie Craven   Barrister.

Woodling v Secretary of State for Social Services

HOUSE OF LORDS

LORD DIPLOCK, LORD SCARMAN, LORD ROSKILL, LORD BRIDGE OF HARWICH AND LORD BRANDON OF OAKBROOK

23, 24 JANUARY, 9 FEBRUARY 1984

National insurance – Attendance allowance – Cooking of meals – Entitlement to allowance – Whether preparation of meals for disabled person constituting 'attention . . . in connection with his bodily functions' – Social Security Act 1975, s 35(1)(a).

National insurance – Invalid care allowance – Entitlement – Right to allowance dependent on disabled person being entitled to attendance allowance – Social Security Act 1975, ss 35, 37.

The preparation of meals for a disabled person does not constitute 'attention . . . in connection with his bodily functions' for which a disabled person is entitled to an attendance allowance for the assistance of another person under s 35(1)(a)[a] of the Social Security Act 1975, because the term 'bodily functions' is a restricted and precise term directed primarily to those functions which a fit person normally performs for himself (see p 594 d to f and p 596 b to h, post); R v National Insurance Comr, ex p Secretary of State for Social Services [1981] 2 All ER 738 applied.

The payment of an allowance for the care of an invalid, pursuant to s 37[b] of the 1975 Act, to a person providing care for a disabled person is dependent on the disabled person being entitled to an attendance allowance under s 35 of that Act (or certain analogous provisions); accordingly, s 37 cannot be used to provide an allowance for care, such as the preparation of meals, which is excluded from the scope of s 35 (see p 594 d to f, p 595 g to j and p 596 h, post); dictum of O'Connor LJ in R v National Insurance Comr, ex p Secretary of State for Social Services [1981] 2 All ER at 745 disapproved.

Notes

For attendance allowance, see 33 Halsbury's Laws (4th edn) para 448.

For the Social Security Act 1975, ss 35, 37, see 45 Halsbury's Statutes (3rd edn) 1120, 1123.

Case referred to in opinions

R v National Insurance Comr, ex p Secretary of State for Social Services [1981] 2 All ER 738, [1981] 1 WLR 1017, CA.

Appeal

On 11 May 1982 the delegated medical practitioner for the Attendance Allowance Board decided that the appellant, Mrs Nona Parks Woodling, did not qualify for an attendance allowance under s 35 of the Social Security Act 1975. On 30 July 1982 the appellant applied for leave to appeal to the Social Security Commissioner against the decision. On 2 September 1982 a Social Security Commissioner, Mr D G Rice, refused leave to appeal and confirmed his decision by letter dated 12 November 1982. The appellant applied,

---

a Section 35(1) is set out at p 594 j, post

b Section 37, so far as material, provides:

 '(1) . . . a person shall be entitled to an invalid care allowance for any day on which he is engaged in caring for a severely disabled person if—(a) he is regularly and substantially engaged in caring for that person . . .

 (2) In this section, "severely disabled person" means a person in respect of whom there is payable . . . an attendance allowance . . .'

with leave of McNeill J granted on 16 December 1982, for orders of certiorari to quash
the decisions of the delegated medical practitioner and the Social Security Commissioner
and an order of mandamus directing the delegated medical practitioner to determine the
claim. On 8 July 1983 Woolf J dismissed the application on the ground that the point
raised in the judicial review proceedings was conclusively determined in the respondent's
favour by the decision of the Court of Appeal in *R v National Insurance Comr, ex p Secretary
of State for Social Services* [1981] 2 All ER 738, [1981] 1 WLR 1017, but granted a certificate
under s 12 of the Administration of Justice Act 1969 certifying that a point of law of
general public importance was involved in the decision justifying an appeal to the House
of Lords. On 10 November 1983 the Appeal Committee of the House of Lords granted
the appellant leave to appeal to the House of Lords. The facts are set out in the opinion of
Lord Bridge.

Louis Blom-Cooper QC and *Richard Drabble* for the appellant.
Simon D Brown and *Stephen Aitchison* for the Secretary of State.

Their Lordships took time for consideration.

9 February. The following opinions were delivered.

LORD DIPLOCK. My Lords, I have had the advantage of reading in draft the speech
of my noble and learned friend Lord Bridge. I agree with it, and for the reasons which
he gives I would dismiss this appeal.

LORD SCARMAN. My Lords, I have had the advantage of reading in draft the speech
to be delivered by my noble and learned friend Lord Bridge. I agree with it, and for the
reasons he gives I would dismiss the appeal.

LORD ROSKILL. My Lords, I have had the advantage of reading in draft the speech
of my noble and learned friend Lord Bridge. I agree with it and for the reasons he gives I
would dismiss the appeal.

LORD BRIDGE OF HARWICH. My Lords, this is an appeal which comes by leave
direct to your Lordships' House from a decision of Woolf J refusing to reverse by
prerogative order decisions of the Attendance Allowance Board and the Social Security
Commissioner which had held that the appellant was not in law entitled to an attendance
allowance under s 35 of the Social Security Act 1975. The judge very properly certified
pursuant to s 12 of the Administration of Justice Act 1969 that a point of law of general
public importance was involved in the decision and that that point of law was one in
respect of which he was bound by a decision of the Court of Appeal in previous
proceedings and was fully considered in the judgments given by the Court of Appeal in
those previous proceedings. The case binding on the judge was *R v National Insurance
Comr, ex p Secretary of State for Social Services* [1981] 2 All ER 738, [1981] 1 WLR 1017
and the present appeal is, in effect, an appeal from that decision.
  Section 35(1) of the 1975 Act provides as follows:

> 'A person shall be entitled to an attendance allowance if he satisfies prescribed
> conditions as to residence or presence in Great Britain and either—(a) he is so
> severely disabled physically or mentally that, by day, he requires from another
> person either—(i) frequent attention throughout the day in connection with his
> bodily functions, or (ii) continual supervision throughout the day in order to avoid
> substantial danger to himself or others; or (b) he is so severely disabled physically or
> mentally that, at night, he requires from another person either—(i) prolonged or
> repeated attention during the night in connection with his bodily functions, or (ii)
> continual supervision throughout the night in order to avoid substantial danger to
> himself or others.'

A person requiring attention only by day or only by night receives an attendance
a allowance at one rate, a person requiring attention both by day and by night at a higher
rate.

It is unnecessary for the purpose of deciding this appeal to examine in detail the nature
or extent of the appellant's disability but suffices to say that the sole criticism of the
decision of the delegated medical practitioner (duly discharging the function delegated
to him by the Attendance Allowance Board) was that, in concluding that the appellant
b was not entitled to attention by day under s 35(1)(*a*) (no claim for attention at night
having been made), he erred in law in excluding from consideration the appellant's
requirement of another person's assistance (to use a neutral term) in preparing her meals
as an element of 'attention . . . in connection with her bodily functions'.

The scope of this provision in its context has been a matter of controversy for some
time. The legislation assumed its present form in 1972. The Court of Appeal was told in
c R v National Insurance Comr, ex p Secretary of State for Social Services that until 1979 it was
the universal practice of delegated medical practitioners to exclude cooking from the
relevant 'attention' to be considered under s 35(1)(*a*). Before 1979, in cases in which the
point was not directly in issue, there were some conflicting dicta of different
commissioners. The only decision directly on the point was a decision of Mr
Commissioner Monroe in 1974 (decision CA 60/74), who held that cooking was not
d within the scope of the relevant 'attention' to which the section applied. In 1979,
however, the matter came before the Chief Commissioner, Sir Rawden Temple QC, who
took a different view (decision CA 2/79). He said:

> 'In my opinion "attention . . . in connection with bodily functions" should be
> broadly interpreted, so as to include not only any physical assistance ultimately
> given to enable the disabled person to eat (or drink), but also to include the necessary
e > steps taken by the attendant to prepare the food (or drink) which is to be consumed,
> with or without later physical assistance to do so.'

This was followed a few months later by the decision of Mr Commissioner Griffiths QC
which was later reversed by the Court of Appeal in *R v National Insurance Comr, ex p
Secretary of State for Social Services*.

f   Before proceeding it is well to remove one misapprehension which arose in *R v National
Insurance Comr, ex p Secretary of State for Social Services*. The claimant, Mrs Packer, was
unquestionably entitled to attention at night under s 35(1)(*b*); only her claim to the
higher rate of allowance dependent on her need for attention by day was in issue. She
was in fact looked after entirely by her daughter, who had given up her job and was in
receipt of an invalid care allowance under s 37 of the 1975 Act. Some observations of the
g court suggest that this allowance was intended to and did make good any deficiency left
by the exclusion of domestic work like cooking from the scope of s 35 (see, in particular,
[1981] 2 All ER 738 at 745, [1981] 1 WLR 1017 at 1027 per O'Connor LJ). With respect,
this is a misreading of the statute. The payment of an invalid care allowance under s 37
to the person providing the care is itself dependent on the disabled person being entitled
to an attendance allowance under s 35 or under certain other analogous provisions, which
h need not be considered in detail. Mrs Packer being entitled in any event to a night
attendance allowance, her daughter could claim the full care allowance under s 37 and in
practice no doubt cared for her mother both by day and by night. But, if the present
appellant is not entitled to an attendance allowance at all, there can be no question of a
person remunerated under s 37 doing her cooking or other domestic work. I do not,
however, take the view that the Court of Appeal having misdirected itself on this point
j necessarily invalidates its conclusion.

The point of construction is a short one, a difficult one and, as the history of controversy
about it has shown, a point on which different minds can fairly take different views. It is
largely a matter of impression and does not admit of elaborate argument or analysis.

First, it is clear that the policy underlying s 35 of the 1975 Act stops short of providing
an attendance allowance for all who are incapable of looking after themselves without

some outside help even if that help is frequently required. Very large areas of domestic work in respect of which the disabled are necessarily dependent on others are deliberately excluded. If cooking is the one domestic chore which qualifies, it is, in a sense, the odd ·man out.

Again, it seems a reasonable inference that the policy of the enactment was to provide a financial incentive to encourage families or friends to undertake the difficult and sometimes distasteful task of caring within the home for those who are so severely disabled that they must otherwise become a charge on some public institution.

The language of the section should, I think, be considered as a whole, and such consideration will, I submit, be more likely to reveal the intention than an attempt to analyse each word or phrase separately. The totality of the language to be construed reads:

'A person . . . is so severely disabled physically or mentally that, by day, he requires from another person . . . frequent attention throughout the day in connection with his bodily functions.'

At first blush, this language does not to my mind fit the person whose physical disablement only prevents him from preparing his own meals.

If I have to break down and attempt to analyse the language, I would emphasise three points. First, the disablement must be severe. Second, the phrase 'bodily functions' is a restricted and precise one, narrower than, for example, 'bodily needs'. Third, the phrase 'attention . . . in connection with his bodily functions', which must, I think, be read as a whole, connotes a high degree of physical intimacy between the person giving and the person receiving the attention. I would add that I fully agree with the observations of Dunn LJ in *R v National Insurance Comr, ex p Secretary of State for Social Services* [1981] 2 All ER 738 at 742, [1981] 1 WLR 1017 at 1023.

At the end of the day I doubt if the construction of the relevant words can be more accurately or more concisely expressed than in the passage from the decision of Mr Commissioner Monroe in 1974 (decision CA 60/74), cited by Dunn LJ ([1981] 2 All ER 738 at 744, [1981] 1 WLR 1017 at 1025):

'I consider that the words of the section refer to a person who needs the relevant degree of attention in connection with the performance of his bodily functions and that they are directed primarily to those functions which the fit man normally performs for himself.'

This criterion has the great merit of being clear and easily applied. I would find it very difficult to formulate any alternative criterion which would not give rise to difficulties in practice. This is not an additional reason for construing the section in the restricted rather than the broad sense. It is perhaps an additional ground for satisfaction in reaching the conclusion that the restricted construction is the correct one.

I would dismiss the appeal.

LORD BRANDON OF OAKBROOK. My Lords, I have had the advantage of reading in draft the speech prepared by my noble and learned friend Lord Bridge. I agree with it, and for the reasons which he gives I would dismiss the appeal.

Appeal dismissed.

Solicitors: *Outred & Co,* agents for *Kirk Jackson & Co,* Swinton (for the appellant); *Solicitor to the Department of Health and Social Security.*

Mary Rose Plummer   Barrister.

Cutts v Head and another

COURT OF APPEAL, CIVIL DIVISION

OLIVER AND FOX LJJ

11, 12, 21 OCTOBER, 7 DECEMBER 1983

Compromise – Offer made before hearing – Refusal of offer – Effect of refusal on costs – Offer made in 'without prejudice' letter expressly reserving right to refer to it on question of costs after judgment if offer refused – Whether letter admissible on issue of costs after judgment in action.

An offer of settlement made before the trial of an action and contained in a letter written 'without prejudice' but expressly reserving the right to bring the letter to the notice of the judge on the issue of costs after judgment in the action if the offer is refused is admissible on the question of costs, without the consent of both parties to the action, in all cases where what is in issue is something more than a simple money claim in respect of which a payment into court would be the appropriate way of proceeding. Such a letter should not be used as a substitute for payment into court, where a payment in is appropriate, and if so used should not be treated as carrying the same consequences as a payment in (see p 606 *h j*, p 608 *c d h j*, p 610 *a* to *f* and p 613 *a* and *f g*, post).

Dicta of Cairns LJ in *Calderbank v Calderbank* [1975] 3 All ER at 342 and of Sir Robert Megarry V-C in *Computer Machinery Co Ltd v Drescher* [1983] 3 All ER at 156 applied.

Walker v Wilsher (1889) 23 QBD 335 explained.

Notes

For 'without prejudice' communications, see 17 Halsbury's Laws (4th edn) paras 212–213, and for cases on the subject, see 22 Digest (Reissue) 407–410, 4082–4108.

Cases referred to in judgments

Archital Luxfer Ltd v Henry Boot Construction Ltd [1981] 1 Lloyd's Rep 642.
Calderbank v Calderbank [1975] 3 All ER 333, [1976] Fam 93, [1975] 3 WLR 586, CA.
Computer Machinery Co Ltd v Drescher [1983] 3 All ER 153, [1983] 1 WLR 1379.
D (J), Re [1982] 2 All ER 37, [1982] Ch 237, [1982] 2 WLR 373.
Daintrey, Re, ex p Holt [1893] 2 QB 116, [1891–4] All ER Rep 209, DC.
Hoghton v Hoghton (1852) 15 Beav 278, 51 ER 545.
Jones v Foxall (1852) 15 Beav 388, 51 ER 588.
McDonnell v McDonnell [1977] 1 All ER 766, [1977] 1 WLR 34, CA.
Potter v Potter [1982] 3 All ER 321, [1982] 1 WLR 1255.
Rabin v Mendoza & Co [1954] 1 All ER 247, [1954] 1 WLR 271, CA.
Scott Paper Co v Drayton Paper Works Ltd (1927) 44 RPC 151; *on appeal* 44 RPC 529, CA.
Stotesbury v Turner [1943] KB 370.
Tomlin v Standard Telephones and Cables Ltd [1969] 3 All ER 201, [1969] 1 WLR 1378.
Tramountana Armadora SA v Atlantic Shipping Co SA [1978] 2 All ER 870.
Walker v Wilsher (1889) 23 QBD 335, CA.
Whiffen v Hartwright (1848) 11 Beav 111, 50 ER 759.
Williams v Thomas (1862) 2 Drew & Sm 29, 62 ER 532.

Cases also cited

French (A Martin) (a firm) v Kingswood Hill Ltd [1960] 2 All ER 251, [1961] 1 QB 96, CA.
Jessop (a solicitor), Re [1910] WN 128, CA.
Mason v Mason [1965] 3 All ER 492, [1966] 1 WLR 767, CA.
Millensted v Grosvenor House (Park Lane) Ltd [1937] 1 All ER 736, [1937] 1 KB 717, CA.
Morrish v Morrish (1983) Times, 30 July, [1983] CA Bound Transcript 350.
Quinn v Leathem [1901] AC 495, [1900–3] All ER Rep 1, HL.

Thornton v Swan Hunter (Shipbuilders) Ltd [1971] 3 All ER 1248, [1971] 1 WLR 1759, CA.
Williams v Goose [1897] 1 QB 471, CA.

a

Appeal

The plaintiff, Oliver Alfred Sidney Cutts, appealed with leave of Foster J against the order
of costs made by Foster J on 22 July 1981 at the trial of an action by the plaintiff against
the defendants, Albert Head and George Edward Head, arising out of the plaintiff's right
of access over the defendants' land in which the plaintiff sought certain declarations and
injunctions and damages. By his order the judge ordered, inter alia, that the defendant
Albert Head should pay to the plaintiff one-half of his costs when taxed. The facts are set
out in the judgment of Oliver LJ.

b

Michael Mark for the plaintiff.
James Leckie for the defendant Albert Head.

c

Cur adv vult

7 December. The following judgments were delivered.

OLIVER LJ. This appeal has taken a very unusual course. It is an appeal from an order   *d*
of Foster J made on the trial of the action on 22 July 1981 and it first came before us on
12 October 1983, when we delivered judgment allowing the appeal in part but dismissing
it on the point with which we have been concerned today. The action was one which
concerned the plaintiff's rights of access over the defendant's land to the plaintiff's fishery.
He claimed certain declarations and injunctions and damages and there was a
counterclaim for various negative declarations and for damages for trespass. After a very   *e*
lengthy hearing the judge found generally in the plaintiff's favour, save that he also
found that the defendant had two sustainable claims for damages. He therefore granted
the plaintiff certain injunctions but he also inserted in the order certain declarations
purporting to limit the plaintiff's enjoyment of his rights of access and a mandatory
order on him to carry out certain repairs. He also awarded the plaintiff damages in a sum
which precisely equalled the damages awarded to the defendant so that, in this respect,   *f*
the claim and the counterclaim cancelled out. The defendant did not appeal against this,
but the plaintiff appealed against the imposition of the restrictions placed by the judge
on the exercise of his rights and also against the order to carry out repairs. That was the
substance of the appeal, although there were subsidiary points on costs.

Before the appeal came on, however, the defendant, no doubt on advice, conceded
(and, I think, clearly rightly conceded) that the declarations and order appealed against   *g*
were made without any jurisdiction and that the judge's order must therefore be varied
accordingly. The result of that was that, but for the subsidiary questions on costs, there
would have been nothing left in the appeal. The plaintiff, however, had obtained the
judge's leave to appeal against the order made as regards the costs of the action, and the
notice of appeal also challenged the correctness of the judge's order as regards the costs of
a hearing before him when, as a result of their failure to agree on the form of the order   *h*
to be made, counsel found it necessary to speak to the minutes. Accordingly, the appeal
was brought on on these two points. The parties were anxious to have the appeal heard
without delay and, having been offered a convenient date on which only two Lords
Justices could be available, they agreed to the appeal being heard by a court so constituted,
notwithstanding that the appeal was, in fact, a final appeal.

I do not think that anybody at that stage appreciated the far-reaching importance of   *j*
the point which, in fact, has occupied most of the time taken in hearing the appeal and,
indeed, counsel for the defendant had not originally, I think, thought that it would be
necessary to refer the court to any authority on the point. With hindsight, it can be seen
that it would have been preferable for the appeal to have been heard by a full court of
three, but the general importance of the point at issue did not fully emerge until the

second day of the hearing, by which time it was, for practical purposes, too late to

a interrupt the hearing and start the whole appeal again before a reconstituted court. We, accordingly, proceeded to hear the appeal, which we allowed as regards the costs of speaking to the minutes. No further question arises as to that.

The main part of the argument, however, was taken up with the other point at issue, namely the general costs of the action. The judge evidently took the view that, since the defendant had succeeded in establishing a claim to damages, albeit one which was

b equalled by the plaintiff's claim, the plaintiff, notwithstanding that he had in the main succeeded in the action, ought not to have the whole of his costs against the defendant. He accordingly ordered that the defendant pay to the plaintiff only half of the plaintiff's taxed costs of the action. That, of course, was an exercise of the judge's discretion which it would not ordinarily be easy for an appellant to challenge successfully, but the point at issue in the appeal, which I will elaborate more fully in a few moments, was whether he

c had exercised his discretion on a wrong principle inasmuch as he had declined to look at and take into consideration an offer of compromise made by the plaintiff before the trial, which was contained in a letter written in a form suggested by this court as being appropriate in matrimonial proceedings relating to financial provision. Counsel for the defendant succeeded in persuading us that, whatever may be the appropriate procedure adopted without argument by this court in matrimonial proceedings, we were bound by

d the authority of a powerful decision of this court (consisting of Lord Esher MR, Lindley and Bowen LJJ) to hold that it was not one which was generally available and that the judge was, therefore, right in principle in declining to take the offer into account when determining the question of costs (see *Walker v Wilsher* (1889) 23 QBD 335). We accordingly dismissed the appeal on this point.

After the hearing, however, and before the order was drawn up, two things emerged.

e In the first place, it emerged that the question in issue had in fact been very recently considered by Sir Robert Megarry V-C, in a case to which we had not been referred, but which plainly would have influenced our decision if it had been known to us (see *Computer Machinery Co Ltd v Drescher* [1983] 3 All ER 153, [1983] 1 WLR 1379). Let me make it quite clear that I am not in the least blaming counsel for not drawing this decision to our attention. They could not, any more than could this court, have known

f of it because it was not in fact reported until the issue of the All England Law Reports published on the Friday following our decision. The second thing that emerged, as a result both of counsel's inquiries and of discussion with some of our colleagues more familiar than we are with practice in the Queen's Bench and Family Divisions, was that the use of the Family Division procedure, both in the Queen's Bench and Family Divisions (and, as it now appears, in the Chancery Division) was, in fact, very much more

g widespread than we had supposed and that it has been frequently sanctioned in this court in proceedings other than matrimonial proceedings although, apparently, without any challenge having been offered to it.

As a result of the publication of the report referred to, counsel for the plaintiff was very properly prompted to draw it to the court's attention and to inquire whether the court would require further argument and, in the circumstances, we thought it right to

h direct that the order should not be drawn up until the matter had been restored and consideration given to the question of whether the judgments delivered on 12 October should be withdrawn. As a result, we have now had the benefit of a much fuller argument than we had when the matter was first before us, and out attention has been directed to a number of authorities not previously cited which, it is argued, whilst they do not directly bear on the point in issue, should cause us to re-examine the view which

j we previously formed that we were bound by authority to come to the conclusion that we did. Having heard that fuller argument, we thought it right to direct that the judgments which we delivered on 12 October should, so far as this point is concerned, be withdrawn in any event, and we accordingly reserved judgment.

I turn, therefore, to a rather more detailed consideration of the relevant facts.

The trial, which lasted some 33 days, took place in the summer of 1981 and, as already indicated, resulted in the plaintiff successfully establishing the rights of access which he claimed in the action. At an earlier stage of the matter, that is to say in July 1979, there had been a motion (which in fact came before Fox LJ) the result of which was a consent order under which undertakings were given on the part of the defendant not to obstruct the access claimed by the plaintiff and undertakings were given on the part of the plaintiff with regard to the use of the access, undertakings which limited that use in a manner more favourable to the defendant than he has, in the event, been found to be entitled to demand. On 15 December 1980, with the trial impending, the plaintiff's solicitors wrote to the defendant's solicitors a letter in which they suggested that the action be compromised on terms which they there set out. This letter was headed 'Without Prejudice' and indicated that, after the failure of previous negotiations, their client had 'now instructed that we write without prejudice with further proposals'. It then set out a series of proposals for the settlement of the action and those proposals undoubtedly would in fact have been more beneficial to the defendant than the order which was finally made on the determination of the action. In particular, it suggested that the access as limited by the undertakings in the consent order should continue, that the plaintiff should pay the defendant a sum of £500 in respect of one of his claims to damages and that, subject to this, all other claims to damages on each side should be treated as cancelling each other out. Each side was to pay its own costs.

In effect, the plaintiff was offering to the defendant everything that the defendant got out of the action and, in fact, a little bit more, because, on the total sum of damages, the defendant was being offered £500 more than he actually got out of the action in which, as has been seen, the two sums of damages precisely cancel out. That letter goes on, after the setting out of the terms, as follows:

'Should the above proposals, as a whole, not recommend themselves to your clients, we would respectfully suggest that they give further consideration to those relating to damages. These are put forward to enable the real issue, that of access, to be dealt with more effectively, and in the event of this being unacceptable to your clients, we reserve the right to bring this letter to the notice of the Judge on the issue of costs.'

When, after judgment, the judge came to deal with the question of costs, counsel for the plaintiff sought to refer to this letter for the purpose of showing that, at least from the date at which the offer in the letter could reasonably have been accepted (which he put at 31 December 1980), this expensive action was totally unnecessary, since the defendant could then have got everything to which he was entitled without a contest. If the letter was admissible that argument was, I think, unanswerable. We have heard counsel for the defendant's submissions to the contrary but, speaking for myself, I have no doubt at all that, on that hypothesis, it almost inevitably followed that the plaintiff was entitled to his costs of the action from the date suggested. The judge, however, declined to look at the letter on the ground that, since it was marked 'Without Prejudice', he was precluded from taking it into consideration. It is that refusal which counsel for the plaintiff relies on as showing that the judge erred in principle in exercising his discretion as to costs in the way in which he did. In support of his contention that the correspondence could be referred to, he drew the judge's attention to two decisions of this court in matrimonial cases which have undoubtedly established the admissibility on questions of costs of letters in the form of the letter in this case in matrimonial proceedings concerned with financial provision for parties to and issue of marriage. It seems, however, that neither counsel was able to draw the judge's attention to any reported case in which the point had been dealt with in proceedings of any other type and the judge accepted the submission of counsel for the defendant that the practice was peculiar to the Family Division.

The first case on which counsel for the plaintiff relied was a decision of this court in *Calderbank v Calderbank* [1975] 3 All ER 333, [1976] Fam 93. That was a matrimonial dispute about what provision should be made for the parties under the provisions of ss 23 and 24 of the Matrimonial Causes Act 1973. There was also a summons before the court

a under s 17 of the Married Women's Property Act 1882. In an affidavit which was sworn on 10 August 1974 the wife had offered to transfer to the husband a house which was occupied by the husband's mother, which was then worth about £12,000, in return for his vacating the matrimonial home which she wanted to sell. He had refused the offer on the ground that it was not adequate for his needs. Heilbron J granted a declaration sought by the wife and ordered a lump sum payment of £10,000 for the husband out of

b the proceeds of sale of the matrimonial home. So it will be seen that, in fact, the husband got rather less out of this than he had been offered by the offer of 10 August, which would in fact have been worth £12,000 to him.

The question of costs came before this court and was dealt with in a judgment of Cairns LJ in which he said ([1975] 3 All ER 333 at 342, [1976] Fam 93 at 105):

c 'Before Heilbron J the wife's application for costs was based on a letter which had been written by the wife's solicitors to the husband's solicitors offering something substantially more than £10,000. Heilbron J, despite that letter being drawn to her attention, made no order as to costs. Immediately after the hearing before her it was discovered that that was a "without prejudice" letter and very properly at the opening of this part of the appeal counsel for the wife asked for the court's guidance whether in those circumstances he was entitled to rely on that letter. We formed

d the opinion that he was not. The letter was written without prejudice. The without prejudice bar had not been withdrawn and therefore we took the view that it was a letter which could not be relied on either before the judge at first instance or before this court. Counsel for the wife then indicated the difficulty that a party might be in in proceedings of this kind when he or she was willing to accede to some extent to an application that was made and desired to obtain the advantages that could be

e obtained in an ordinary action for debt or damages by a payment into court, that not being a course which would be appropriate in proceedings of this kind.'

Cairns LJ then went on to consider how that difficulty might be got over and to suggest a formula which might be used in future cases to ensure that negotiations could be conducted without prejudice to the issue at the trial, but yet nevertheless be referred

f to after judgment when the question of costs came to be considered. He said:

'There are various other types of proceedings well known to the court where protection has been able to be afforded to a party who wants to make a compromise of that kind and where payment in is not an appropriate method. One is in proceedings before the Lands Tribunal where the amount of compensation is in issue and where the method that is adopted is that of a sealed offer which is not

g made without prejudice but which remains concealed from the tribunal until the decision on the substantive issue has been made and the offer is then opened when the discussion as to costs takes place. Another example is in the Admiralty Division where there is commonly a dispute between the owners of two vessels that have been in collision as to the apportionment of blame between them. It is common

h practice for an offer to be made by one party to another of a certain apportionment. If that is not accepted no reference is made to that offer in the course of the hearing until it comes to costs, and then if the court's apportionment is as favourable to the party who made the offer as what was offered, or more favourable to him, then costs will be awarded on the same basis as if there had been a payment in. I see no reason why some similar practice should not be adopted in relation to such matrimonial

j proceedings in relation to finances as we have been concerned with. Counsel for the wife drew our attention to a provision in the Matrimonial Causes Rules 1968, SI 1968/219, with reference to damages which were then payable by a co-respondent, provision to the effect that an offer might be made in the form that it was without prejudice to the issue as to damages but reserving the right of the co-respondent to refer to it on the issue of costs. It appears to me that it would be equally appropriate that it should be permissible to make an offer of that kind in such proceedings as we have been dealing with and I think that that would be an appropriate way in which a party who was willing to make a compromise could put it forward. I do not consider that any amendment of the Rules of the Supreme Court is necessary to enable this to be done.'

Now, in fact, the letter in the *Calderbank* case was not in the form suggested by Cairns LJ and, indeed, the court did not take it into consideration. What had happened there was that the without prejudice offer had been repeated as an open offer in the affidavit referred to above and the costs were dealt with on the footing that the husband ought to have accepted that open offer. Thus, Cairns LJ's suggested procedure was dictum only and, as counsel for the defendant has observed, dictum without any argument in opposition. The procedure suggested is obviously a sensible and convenient one in a case where payment into court is not appropriate, and it is not, therefore, surprising to find that practitioners were quick to adopt it. In *McDonnell v McDonnell* [1977] 1 All ER 766, [1977] 1 WLR 34 a letter had been written in the suggested form (it has since become dignified by the title 'a Calderbank letter') and this court, again without any argument on the matter, accepted and indorsed the practice suggested by Cairns LJ.

I do not think that I need refer to that case in any detail. Ormrod LJ said ([1977] 1 All ER 766 at 769, [1977] 1 WLR 34 at 37):

'The important factor which distinguishes this case is the fact that the husband's solicitors took advantage of a recent decision of this court in *Calderbank v Calderbank*. On 16th December 1975, shortly after serving the notice of appeal, they wrote a letter to the wife's solicitors offering to withdraw the appeal altogether if the wife would agree to a modification of Lane J's order in respect of [the house]. In accordance with the procedure suggested in *Calderbank v Calderbank*, they headed the letter "Without Prejudice" but reserved the right to bring it to the attention of the court after judgment on the question of costs.'

Then he considered the significance of the letter and said ([1977] 1 All ER 766 at 770, [1977] 1 WLR 34 at 38):

'Clearly this is a very important consideration in exercising the court's discretion with regard to costs. It would be wrong, in my judgment, to equate an offer of compromise in proceedings such as these precisely to a payment into court. I see no advantage in the court surrendering its discretion in these matters as it has to all intents and purposes done where a payment into court has been made. A *Calderbank v Calderbank* offer should influence but not govern the exercise of the discretion. The question to my mind is whether, on the basis of the facts known to the wife and her advisers and without the advantage of hindsight, she ought reasonably to have accepted the proposals in the letter of 16th December, bearing always in mind the difficulty of making accurate forecasts in cases such as this. On the other hand, parties who are exposed to the full impact of costs need some protection against those who can continue to litigate with impunity under a civil aid certificate.'

Since the first hearing of this appeal a LEXIS search has been carried out, from which it emerges that the procedure has been resorted or referred to in a number of other reported cases, but always in relation to proceedings for financial provision in the Family Division (see, for instance, *Potter v Potter* [1982] 3 All ER 321, [1982] 1 WLR 1255); and counsel for the defendant draws particular attention to Cairns LJ's reference in the *Calderbank* case to the desirability of such a procedure in 'such proceedings as we have been dealing with' as indicating that he, at any rate, never envisaged the suggested procedure as having any wider application. He points out that the current editions of *Cross on Evidence* (5th edn, 1979) and *Phipson on Evidence* (13th edn, 1982) contain no mention of the *Calderbank* case at all, whilst 17 Halsbury's Laws (4th edn) para 213 states the general rule that a without prejudice letter cannot be referred to on a question of costs and then qualifies it by a footnote which suggests that the Calderbank letter is an exception restricted to 'matrimonial proceedings relating to finance'.

a   What counsel for the defendant particularly relies on, however, is the decision of this court in *Walker v Wilsher* (1889) 23 QBD 335. That was an appeal from Huddleston B, who had, on the question of costs, after trial looked at some without prejudice correspondence and made his order accordingly. That was attacked in the Court of Appeal, Lord Esher MR saying (at 336–337):

b   'The letters and the interview were without prejudice, and the question is whether under such circumstances they could be considered in order to determine whether there was good cause or not for depriving the plaintiff of costs. It is, I think, a good rule to say that nothing which is written or said without prejudice should be looked at without the consent of both parties, otherwise the whole object of the limitation would be destroyed. I am, therefore, of opinion that the learned judge should not

c   have taken these matters into consideration . . .'

Lindley LJ was equally uncompromising. He said (at 337):

'What is the meaning of the words "without prejudice"? I think they mean without prejudice to the position of the writer of the letter if the terms he proposes are not accepted. If the terms proposed in the letter are accepted a complete contract

d   is established, and the letter, although written without prejudice, operates to alter the old state of things and to establish a new one. A contract is constituted in respect of which relief by way of damages or specific performance would be given. Supposing that a letter is written without prejudice then, according both to authority and to good sense, the answer also must be treated as made without prejudice.'

e   A little later he said (at 338):

'No doubt there are cases where letters written without prejudice may be taken into consideration, as was done the other day in a case in which a question of laches was raised. The fact that such letters have been written and the dates at which they were written may be regarded, and in so doing the rule to which I have adverted would not be infringed. The facts may, I think, be given in evidence, but the offer

f   made and the mode in which that offer was dealt with—the material matters, that is to say, of the letters—must not be looked at without consent.'

Bowen LJ was equally adamant. He said (at 339):

'The precise question now before us, as to the admissibility of such evidence for the purpose of deciding as to the costs of an action could not have arisen before the

g   Common Law Procedure Act, 1852. Up to then costs at common law always followed the event, and it naturally follows that there is no authority before that time on the point. Then comes the case before Kindersley, V.C., who did precisely what Huddleston, B., has done here [see *Williams v Thomas* (1862) 2 Drew & Sm 29, 62 ER 532]. I think there was a confusion of thought and reasoning in the judgment of the Vice-Chancellor which we ought not to hesitate to point out. The use that the

h   defendant sought in that case to make of the offer which had been made without prejudice was to attract the attention of the Court to the conduct of the plaintiff upon receiving it. In my opinion it would be a bad thing and lead to serious consequences if the Courts allowed the action of litigants, on letters written to them without prejudice, to be given in evidence against them or to be used as material for depriving them of costs. It is most important that the door should not be shut

j   against compromises, as would certainly be the case if letters written without prejudice and suggesting methods of compromise were liable to be read when a question of costs arose. The agreement that the letter is without prejudice ought, I think, to be carried out in its full integrity.'

This, counsel for the defendant submits, is a clear authority, which is binding on this court, for the proposition that 'without prejudice' means 'without prejudice for all purposes' and that a letter once so marked cannot be referred to at any stage of the proceedings without the consent of both parties. Costs are, he submits, as much an issue in the proceedings as is anything else, and indeed the proposed compromise almost invariably relates to the costs of the proceedings as much as to the other matters in issue.

Counsel for the plaintiff accepts that this court is bound by *Walker v Wilsher* so far as it constitutes decision, although he categorises the wide remarks of the court as to the meaning of the words 'without prejudice' as dicta, but he submits that the case establishes no more than this, that where a letter is headed 'without prejudice' simpliciter, and no reservation is made by the writer similar to that made in the *Calderbank* case, it cannot be referred to on the question of costs. That, indeed, was accepted by the court in the *Calderbank* case. *Walker v Wilsher*, he submits, tells us nothing about a letter of the *Calderbank* type which was not there in issue and indeed was not even contemplated in that case.

The answer of counsel for the defendant to this, and it was one which appealed to us when we first heard the matter, is that it is altogether too restricted a construction of the decision in *Walker v Wilsher*.

The court was concerned with the question of whether the contents of a letter headed 'without prejudice' could be looked at at all, and the court decided that it could not, in other words the 'without prejudice' heading cast a veil, not over the date on which the letter was written or over the fact that it was written, but over the whole of the contents, which would, of course, include the purported unilateral reservation of the right to treat the letter as 'with prejudice' in a certain event. If you cannot refer to the letter at all, you cannot refer to and rely on a reservation contained in it, for that is a reservation which is, in terms, repugnant to the expressed nature of the letter itself. He refers particularly to Lord Esher MR's statement that to look at something written without prejudice would be to destroy 'the whole object of the limitation' and to Lindley LJ's clear opinion that 'the offer made and the mode in which that offer was dealt with—the material matters, that is to say, of the letters—must not be looked at without consent'.

Support for counsel for the defendant's view of the matter is, I think, to be gained from dicta in *Re Daintrey, ex p Holt* [1893] 2 QB 116, [1891–4] All ER Rep 209, a decision of a Divisional Court in Bankruptcy. The question at issue there was whether a particular letter could be relied on as an act of bankruptcy. The letter was one sent by a debtor to a creditor at a time when there was no dispute, headed 'without prejudice' and containing an offer of composition but threatening that payment would be suspended unless the offer was accepted. The court, in holding that the letter was admissible, relied on the fact that there was no dispute and no offer of compromise, so that the sender could not destroy the admissibility of the letter as evidence simply by heading the letter 'without prejudice', the protection afforded by that phrase being limited to negotiations for compromise. In giving the judgment of the court, however, Vaughan Williams J went on to observe obiter ([1893] 2 QB 116 at 120, [1891–4] All ER Rep 209 at 212):

> 'Moreover, we think that the rule has no application to a document which, in its nature, may prejudice the person to whom it is addressed. It may be that the words "without prejudice" are intended to mean without prejudice to the writer if the offer is rejected; but, in our opinion, the writer is not entitled to make this reservation in respect of a document which, from its character, may prejudice the person to whom it is addressed if he should reject the offer, and for this reason also we think the judge is entitled to look at the document to determine its character.'

Thus, counsel for the defendant argues, the plaintiff here is not only in a dilemma himself, but he puts the other party in a dilemma, for he says in one breath 'this is without prejudice' and in the next threatens to use the letter to the prejudice of the other if the offer is not accepted. The two stances are contradictory and, if what Vaughan Williams J said in *Re Daintrey, ex p Holt* is right, the recipient of the letter is entitled to write back and say: 'This is not a without prejudice at all. If you want to negotiate

a without prejudice, by all means let us do so, but you cannot have it both ways. If you wish to use your letter prejudicially against me, you must take your courage in both hands and treat the correspondence as open throughout.' If, however, he does not do that but accepts the letter for what its heading suggests it to be (that is a letter protected from disclosure at any stage of the proceedings), then, counsel for the defendant argues, the writer, whatever he says in the letter, cannot unilaterally claim to retract the protection which he himself has attached to it in using a formula which, since at latest 1889, has a

b fixed and well-understood meaning.

This argument was one from which, on the material before us at the first hearing of this appeal, I found it very difficult to escape, although counsel for the defendant had frankly to admit that the *Calderbank* case (which he has to say is contrary to previous authority) had created an anomaly in the Family Division for which it was very difficult to account. However, he took his stand on the 'sacred' nature of 'without prejudice'

c negotiation (see *Hoghton v Hoghton* (1852) 15 Beav 278 at 321, 51 ER 545 at 561 per Romilly MR) and the oft-reiterated statements that such negotiations are, as a matter of public policy, to be protected from disclosure to the court seised of the dispute (see *Stotesbury v Turner* [1943] KB 370 following *Walker v Wilsher*; and see also *Tomlin v Standard Telephones and Cables Ltd* [1969] 3 All ER 201 at 205–206, [1969] 1 WLR 1378 at 1385 per Ormrod J).

d Now, it is certainly the case, and the contrary is not argued, that the use of the words 'without prejudice' as a cover for negotiations and with no reservation of the sort suggested in the *Calderbank* case has today the same consequences as it had in 1889 when *Walker v Wilsher* was decided. Thus, it cannot be contended that the meaning of the expression has changed. The answer to the question whether, accepting that meaning, it is yet open to a party taking advantage of the protection afforded by the use of the formula to qualify its operation must, I think, therefore be sought in an analysis of the

e underlying basis for the protection and the practice of the courts generally in relation to its application. As to this the argument of counsel for the defendant may, I think, be summarised conveniently in three propositions. (1) The protection from disclosure of without prejudice negotiations rests in part on public policy and in part on convention (ie an express or implied agreement that the negotiations shall be so protected). (2) There is no public policy which precludes a conventional modification of the protection to the

f extent suggested in *Calderbank v Calderbank*. (3) The actual practice adopted in all divisions of the High Court shows that this conventional modification has been generally accepted and is recognised by the courts and to that extent at least public policy has been modified.

That the rule rests, at least in part, on public policy is clear from many authorities, and

g the convenient starting point of the inquiry is the nature of the underlying policy. It is that parties should be encouraged so far as possible to settle their disputes without resort to litigation and should not be discouraged by the knowledge that anything that is said in the course of such negotiations (and that includes, of course, as much the failure to reply to an offer as an actual reply) may be used to their prejudice in the course of the proceedings. They should, as it was expressed by Clauson J in *Scott Paper Co v Drayton Paper Works Ltd* (1927) 44 RPC 151 at 157, be encouraged freely and frankly to put their

h cards on the table. If, however, the protection against disclosure rested solely on a public policy to encourage out-of-court settlement of disputes, *Walker v Wilsher* is not readily intelligible, for, although the court, and in particular Bowen LJ, seem to have been prepared to assume that an inability to refer to the correspondence on a question of costs, after judgment, would encourage settlement, it is difficult to see, if one thinks about it

j practically, how that could do so. As a practical matter, a consciousness of a risk as to costs if reasonable offers are refused can only encourage settlement, whilst, on the other hand, it is hard to imagine anything more calculated to encourage obstinacy and unreasonableness than the comfortable knowledge that a litigant can refuse with impunity whatever may be offered to him even if it is as much as or more than everything to which he is entitled in the action. The public policy justification, in truth, essentially rests on the desirability of preventing statements or offers made in the course of negotiations for settlement being brought before the court of trial as admissions on the question of liability.

It was expressed thus by Romilly MR in *Jones v Foxall* (1852) 15 Beav 388 at 396, 51 ER 588 at 591):

'. . . I find that the offers were, in fact, made *without prejudice* to the rights of the parties; and I shall, as far as I am able, in all cases, endeavour to repress a practice which, when I was first acquainted with the profession, was never ventured upon, but which, according to my experience in this place, has become common of late— namely, that of attempting to convert offers of compromise into admissions of acts prejudicial to the person making them. If this were permitted, the effect would be that no attempt to compromise a dispute could ever be made.'

Once, however, the trial of the issues in the action is at an end and the matter of costs comes to be argued, this can have no further application for there are no further issues of fact to be determined on which admissions could be relevant. One is, therefore, compelled to seek some additional basis for the decision in *Walker v Wilsher* and it is, as it seems to me, to be found in an implied agreement imported from the marking of a letter 'without prejudice' that it shall not be referred to at all. This certainly derives some support from the judgment of Bowen LJ, where he says (23 QBD 335 at 339) that 'the agreement that the letter is without prejudice ought, I think, to be carried out in its full integrity', and it accords with the view expressed by Denning LJ in *Rabin v Mendoza & Co* [1954] 1 All ER 247 at 248, [1954] 1 WLR 271 at 273 where he said:

'It is said, however, that apart from legal professional privilege, there is a separate head of privilege on the ground that the documents came into existence on the understanding that they were not to be used to the prejudice of either party. "Without prejudice" does not appear as a head of privilege in the ANNUAL PRACTICE, but in BRAY ON DISCOVERY ((1885) p 308) it is said: "The right to discovery may under very special circumstances be lost by contract as where correspondence passed between the parties' solicitors with a view to an amicable arrangement of the question at issue in the suit on a stipulation that it should not be referred to or used to the defendant's prejudice in case of a failure to come to an arrangement." That proposition is founded on *Whiffen v. Hartwright* ((1848) 11 Beav 111 at 112, 50 ER 759), where LORD LANGDALE, M.R., refused to order the production of letters which passed without prejudice, "observing, that he did not see how the plaintiff could get over this express agreement, though he by no means agreed, that the right of discovery was limited to the use which could be made of it in evidence." LORD LANGDALE, M.R., there affirms the undoubted proposition that·production can be ordered of documents even though they may not be admissible in evidence. Nevertheless, if documents come into being under an express, or, I would add, a tacit, agreement that they should not be used to the prejudice of either party, an order for production will not be made.'

Whatever may have been the position in 1889, it is, I think, clear that there can now no longer be said to be any reason in public policy why, where offers have been made and refused of everything which could be obtained by the proceedings, that fact should not be brought to the court's attention in the argument as to costs. I say that in the light of the matters which are referred to below. If this is right, then is there any logical reason why, in appropriate circumstances, the conventional meaning of the phrase should not be modified so long as this intended modification is clearly expressed and brought to the attention of the recipient? Is there, to put it another way, any policy of the law which prevents a party to litigation from putting forward an offer of correspondence on the footing that it shall be treated as without prejudice on the issue of liability only? Counsel for the plaintiff submits that there clearly is not and he draws attention to numerous examples of closely analogous procedures which have been sanctioned and recognised in

proceedings where no payment into court is appropriate. To begin with, the procedure
a established by the Rules of the Supreme Court since 1933 for payment into court in the
case of actions for debt or damages, where the fact of payment in is withheld from the
court until after liability has been determined, is neither more nor less than a without
prejudice offer of settlement subject to a reservation that the offer will be brought to the
court's attention when the issue of liability has been determined. The only essential
difference is that it is backed up by a deposit with the court of the amount offered. Thus,
b counsel for the plaintiff submits, it is really unarguable that there is any public policy
which prevents exactly the same thing being done, in a case where a money payment is
not, or is not alone, the relief claimed in the proceedings. And one finds that, in fact,
similar procedures have been adopted in many cases where the defendant is not able to
protect his position by a payment in or where a payment in is not appropriate. Perhaps
the most striking example is that of the sealed offer in arbitration proceedings. Counsel
c for the plaintiff has referred us to the decision of Donaldson J in *Tramountana Armadora
SA v Atlantic Shipping Co SA* [1978] 2 All ER 870 esp at 876, where he said:

> 'Although the respondents' offer of settlement has been referred to as an "open
> offer", this is a misnomer. Offers of settlement in arbitral proceedings can be of
> three kinds, namely "without prejudice", "sealed" and "open". A "without prejudice"
> offer can never be referred to by either party at any stage of the proceedings, because
d > it is in the public interest that there should be a procedure whereby the parties can
> discuss their differences freely and frankly and make offers of settlement without
> fear of being embarrassed by these exchanges if, unhappily, they do not lead to a
> settlement. A "sealed offer" is the arbitral equivalent of making a payment into
> court in settlement of the litigation or of particular causes of action in that litigation.
e > Neither the fact, nor the amount, of such a payment into court can be revealed to
> the judge trying the case until he has given judgment on all matters other than
> costs. As it is customary for an award to deal at one and the same time both with the
> parties' claims and with the question of costs, the existence of a sealed offer has to be
> brought to the attention of the arbitrator before he has reached a decision. However,
> it should remain sealed at that stage and it would be wholly improper for the
f > arbitrator to look at it before he has reached a final decision on the matters in dispute
> other than as to costs, or to revise that decision in the light of the terms of the sealed
> offer when he sees them.'

That case is a striking one because the sealed offer there made was in fact preceded by
a correspondence containing the same offer, so that the sealed offer served precisely the
same effect as a *Calderbank* letter. This case was followed and applied by Ralph Gibson J
g in *Archital Luxfer Ltd v Henry Boot Construction Ltd* [1981] 1 Lloyd's Rep 642 at 654–655.

Now, an arbitrator has the same discretion as to costs as a High Court judge (see
Stotesbury v Turner [1943] KB 370) and counsel for the plaintiff asks rhetorically why, if
this procedure is unexceptionable in arbitrations, should it be incapable of application in
proceedings in the High Court. In fact, the 'arbitration letter' or sealed offer dates back at
least to compulsory arbitrations under the Lands Clauses Acts and has been formally
h recognised as appropriate in compensation cases under the Lands Tribunal Rules.

Again, a procedure almost identical to the *Calderbank* letter has, for a considerable
time, been recognised and accepted in Admiralty cases, and our attention has been drawn
to the following passage in McGuffie Fugeman and Gray *Admiralty Practice* (1964)
pp 325–326, paras 717–718:

j > 'Where a claim is for an unliquidated sum, negotiations for settlement are based
> not on tender but on offers to pay. Offers to pay must not be disclosed or pleaded,
> even if the amount offered has been paid into Court [there follows a reference to
> RSC Ord 22, r 7] ... Another form of offer which is often made is directed to
> proportions of blame and not to amounts of money, this being confined to collisions
> and similar actions where proportions of blame are at stake. At the conclusion of

the trial of liability, the offer is brought to the attention of the judge if the offerer has been as successful or more successful than foreshadowed in his offer . . .'   a

Thus, here, the only difference between the offer envisaged and the *Calderbank* letter is that the offer is an open offer not expressed to be without prejudice but one which is, by practice and convention, treated in exactly the same way as if it were so expressed, save when it comes to the question of costs after liability has been established.

Yet another example of a similar procedure, again where payment into court is   b
inappropriate, is to be found in RSC Ord 16, r 10, where a third party or joint tortfeasor makes an offer of contribution to a particular extent. Even if he reserves the right to bring the offer to the attention of the court, he is not permitted to do so until the question of liability has been determined.

Finally, counsel for the plaintiff draws attention to the former provision referred to by Cairns LJ in *Calderbank v Calderbank*, namely that of r 50 of the Matrimonial Causes Rules   c
1968, which empowered a co-respondent in effect to make a *Calderbank* offer in respect of damages on the footing that it would be referred to only on the question of costs.

Now, all this shows, counsel for the plaintiff (and, I am bound to say, I think rightly) submits, that there is no reason in principle why the *Calderbank* procedure should be treated as restricted only to matrimonial proceedings or why it should be held to be ineffective or unavailable when it differs in form only, though not at all in substance,   d
from similar procedures long recognised and accepted in relation to other types of proceedings. If, he argues, the only impediment is what has come to be regarded as the conventional effect of the use of the words 'without prejudice', the result of the practice of all divisions of the court since *Calderbank v Calderbank* has been that that conventional effect is accepted and recognised as modified to the extent that an offeror is, by the express terms of his offer, entitled to reserve his position after the issue of liability has been   e
determined. It is here, I think, that the actual practice of the courts over the years which have elapsed since the *Calderbank* case becomes of importance. It has been brought to our attention that letters in this form have been in frequent use in the Queen's Bench Division in cases where a payment into court would not be appropriate, for instance where what is in issue is not liability but the proportions of contribution to liability (eg in cases where a defence of contributory negligence is raised), and in the Court of Appeal,   f
where what is in issue is whether a judgment for damages in the court below was excessive. Although we have not been referred to any reported case in this court (other than a matrimonial case) where the procedure has been approved, we understand that its use in proceedings other than matrimonial proceedings has, in at least one case in this court, received the approval of Lord Denning MR, and counsel for the plaintiff has been good enough to tell us that inquiry of practitioners in both the Queen's Bench and   g
Chancery Divisions indicates that the procedure is frequently resorted to there. Counsel for the defendant does not quarrel with this, but takes his stand on *Walker v Wilsher* and submits that the mere fact that a procedure has become common when it has been allowed to pass without argument cannot alter the fact that it is contrary to authority.

I do not, for my part, think that that is a conclusive answer for, if the protection of without prejudice correspondence as regards costs rests, as I believe that it does, on the   h
conventional import of the words, a wide and continued practice adopted and recognised, albeit without challenge, in all divisions of the court may show, and, I think does show, that the conventional meaning has become capable of modification where express reservation is made at the time of the offer without infringing the public policy which protects negotiations from disclosure whilst liability is still in issue.

That brings me to the recently reported decision of Sir Robert Megarry V-C in   j
Computer Machinery Co Ltd v Drescher [1983] 3 All ER 153 at 156, [1983] 1 WLR 1379 at 1382–1383. The Vice-Chancellor said:

'For reasons that will appear, I think that I should pause in my recital of the facts in order to say something about these two cases. For a long while it has been settled law that if letters written "without prejudice" do not result in an agreement, they cannot be looked at by the court even on the question of costs, unless both parties consent: see, for example, *Walker v Wilsher* (1889) 23 QBD 335; *Stotesbury v Turner* [1943] KB 370. Thus if in "without prejudice" correspondence a defendant offers less than the plaintiff is claiming but more than the plaintiff ultimately recovers at the trial, the defendant cannot use his offer in support of a contention that the plaintiff should receive no costs for the period subsequent to the offer. If the claim is purely a money claim, this causes no difficulty: the defendant may pay into court under RSC Ord 22 the sum that he is offering, and although knowledge of this will be withheld from the court until both liability and quantum have been decided, the fact of payment in is admissible, and usually highly relevant, in deciding what order for costs should be made. If, however, the claim is not solely a money claim, but some other relief is sought, such as an injunction, there was formerly no comparable procedure. What was needed was some procedure whereby the defendant could make an offer to submit to an injunction, give an undertaking or afford other relief on the footing that the offer would be without prejudice until the case was decided but with prejudice when it came to costs. It was a procedure of this type which was suggested by Cairns LJ in *Calderbank v Calderbank* [1975] 3 All ER 333 at 342, [1976] Fam 93 at 105–106 and was acted on in *McDonnell v McDonnell* [1977] 1 All ER 766 at 770, [1977] 1 WLR 34 at 38. These were both matrimonial appeals from the Family Division, however, and there has been some uncertainty whether the procedure applies to other cases. Thus 17 Halsbury's Laws (4th edn) para 213 cites *Calderbank v Calderbank* for the proposition that "in matrimonial proceedings relating to finance" a party may make this type of offer, and the 1983 cumulative supplement leaves it there. Nor do the cases appear to have been given the prominence which they deserve. Thus leading books which discuss offers made "without prejudice" still leave unamended statements based on *Walker v Wilsher* (1889) 23 QBD 335, without any mention of either *Calderbank* or *McDonnell*: see, for example, *Phipson on Evidence* (13th edn, 1982) p 374; *Cross on Evidence* (5th edn, 1979) p 301. Nor are the cases mentioned in *The Supreme Court Practice 1982*. In my view, the principle in question is one of perfectly general application which is in no way confined to matrimonial cases. Whether an offer is made "without prejudice" or "without prejudice save as to costs", the courts ought to enforce the terms on which the offer was made as tending to encourage compromise and shorten litigation; and the latter form of offer has the added advantage of preventing the offer from being inadmissible on costs, thereby assisting the court towards justice in making the order as to costs. I should say at once that no point on this arises for decision, as the parties have very sensibly acted on this footing. What I have been saying is as obiter as what Cairns LJ said (and Scarman LJ and Sir Gordon Willmer concurred with) in *Calderbank v Calderbank*; but I hope that the attention of the profession (including authors and editors) will be more generally directed to what seems to me to be a valuable procedural process that is too little used.'

That, of course, was dictum, not decision, and, counsel for the defendant submits, suffers from the same defect as *Calderbank v Calderbank* itself, namely that it was dictum pronounced without there being before the court any argument against the proposition.

Nevertheless, it is extremely powerful dictum and, moreover, dictum which embraces a consideration of *Walker v Wilsher*, which is counsel for the defendant's sheet-anchor. It is, of course, not binding on us, but it has, I think, the importance that it further confirms the width of the practice and general acceptance of the permissibility and effectiveness of the qualification on the accepted meaning of the without prejudice formula to which I have referred above.

That practice had, in fact, previously been recognised (although again without contest) in the Chancery Division in *Re D (J)* [1982] 2 All ER 37 at 51, [1982] Ch 237 at 255, where a letter of offer was taken into account on the question of costs. Although it does not appear from the report, counsel for the plaintiff was able to tell us that he had ascertained from counsel engaged in the case that it was, in fact, a *Calderbank* offer.

Although, as I have said, I was originally persuaded by the argument of counsel for the defendant that Foster J was right to reject the letter of offer in this case, the further *a* argument which we have heard and the considerations to which I have adverted above have compelled me to the conclusion that that decision was wrong. I think that it must now be taken to be established that the *Calderbank* formula suggested by Cairns LJ is not restricted to matrimonial proceedings but is available in all cases where what is in issue is something more than a simple money claim in respect of which a payment into court would be the appropriate way of proceeding. I have not, in saying this, overlooked the *b* submission of counsel for the defendant that, whatever may be the position today, Foster J was right to reach the conclusion that he did in 1981, there being before him no suggestion that the practice had spread beyond the Family Division, where, it must be accepted, there are considerations which make such a procedure particularly desirable and appropriate. In my judgment, however, quite apart from the dictum of Sir Robert Megarry V-C, to which reference has been made, the admissibility of the letter with *c* which this appeal is concerned would have been justified at the time of the hearing before the judge if he had had addressed to him the arguments which have been addressed to us. In the circumstances, he should, in my judgment, have admitted the letter and his failure to do so entitles the plaintiff to succeed in this court. I would, therefore, allow the appeal and vary the order as to costs below by providing that the plaintiff should have half his costs of the action up to 31 December 1980 and the whole *d* of his costs thereafter.

I would add only one word of caution. The qualification imposed on the without prejudice nature of the *Calderbank* letter is, as I have held, sufficient to enable it to be taken into account on the question of costs; but it should not be thought that this involves the consequence that such a letter can now be used as a substitute for a payment into court, where a payment into court is appropriate. In the case of the simple money claim, *e* a defendant who wishes to avail himself of the protection afforded by an offer must, in the ordinary way, back his offer with cash by making a payment in and, speaking for myself, I should not, as at present advised, be disposed in such a case to treat a *Calderbank* offer as carrying the same consequences as payment in.

FOX LJ. The issue is whether a letter of 15 December 1980 written by the plaintiff's *f* solicitors to the defendant's solicitors and communicating suggested terms of compromise can, after judgment in the action, be referred to on the question of costs and against the wishes of the defendant. The letter was headed 'Without prejudice'. After stating the proposed terms, the letter added: 'and in the event of this being unacceptable to your clients we reserve the right to bring this letter to the notice of the judge on the question of costs.' Foster J refused to admit the letter. *g*

I start with *Walker v Wilsher* (1889) 23 QBD 335. It was decided in this court in 1889 and its authority has never been questioned. It was a straightforward case of an offer of terms of compromise made 'without prejudice' and with no further qualification. The letters containing the offer were held not to be admissible on the question of costs.

Lord Esher MR said (at 337): *h*

'It is, I think, a good rule to say that nothing which is written or said without prejudice should be looked at without the consent of both parties, otherwise the whole object of the limitation would be destroyed.'

Lindley LJ said (at 337) that the words 'without prejudice' meant 'without prejudice to the position of the writer of the letter if the terms he proposes are not accepted', but *j* that 'according both to authority and good sense, the answer also must be treated as made without prejudice'.

And Bowen LJ said (at 339):

'. . . it would be a bad thing and lead to serious consequences if the Courts allowed the action of litigants, on letters written to them without prejudice, to be given in a evidence against them or to be used as material for depriving them of costs. It is most important that the door should not be shut against compromises, as would certainly be the case if letters written without prejudice and suggesting methods of compromise were liable to be read when a question of costs arose.'

Re Daintrey, ex p Holt [1893] 2 QB 116, [1891–4] All ER Rep 209 was a bankruptcy case in which it was held that a 'without prejudice' letter was admissible as evidence to prove an act of bankruptcy. Vaughan Williams J, giving the judgment of the Divisional
b Court, after observing that the 'without prejudice' rule was a rule adopted to enable disputants 'without prejudice' to engage in discussion for the purpose of arriving at terms of peace, went on to say ([1893] 2 QB 116 at 120, [1891–4] All ER Rep 209 at 212):

c 'Moreover, we think that the rule has no application to a document which, in its nature, may prejudice the person to whom it is addressed. It may be that the words "without prejudice" are intended to mean without prejudice to the writer if the offer is rejected; but, in our opinion, the writer is not entitled to make this reservation in respect of a document which, from its character, may prejudice the person to whom it is addressed if he should reject the offer . . .'

Those cases, I think, emphasise two things. First, that the purpose of the rule is to facilitate a free discussion of compromise proposals by protecting the proposals and
d discussion from disclosure in the proceedings. The ultimate aim appears to be to facilitate compromise.

Second, whilst the ordinary meaning of 'without prejudice' is without prejudice to the position of the offeror if his offer is refused, it is not competent to one party to impose such terms on the other in respect of a document which, by its nature, is capable of being used to the disadvantage of that other. The expression must be read as creating a situation
e of mutuality which enables both sides to take advantage of the 'without prejudice' protection.

The juridical basis of that must, I think, in part derive from an implied agreement between the parties and in part from public policy. As to the former, Bowen LJ in Walker v Wilsher, after the passage which I have already cited to the effect that it is important that the door should not be shut against compromises, went on to say (23 QBD 335 at
f 339): 'The agreement that the letter is without prejudice ought, I think, to be carried out in its full integrity.'

As to public policy it obviously is desirable to facilitate compromise rather than forcing the parties to litigate to the end. But to achieve a compromise one of them has to make an offer. He might be apprehensive that his offer might be used against him if the negotiations failed. So he would make his offer without prejudice to his position if the
g offer was refused. But that was unfair to the other party. It was one-sided. So it was necessary to extend the without prejudice umbrella to cover both parties.

I come then to Calderbank v Calderbank [1975] 3 All ER 333, [1976] Fam 93, the case which has given its name to the 'Calderbank offer' (ie the kind of qualified 'without prejudice' offer with which we are concerned in this case). In fact, one thing that was quite absent from Calderbank v Calderbank was a Calderbank offer. There seem to have
h been two offers in the case as reported. The first was contained in a letter which was an unqualified without prejudice letter. The second was in an affidavit and was an open offer. The proposition that the letter could be referred to on the question of costs was no more capable of argument than the proposition that the affidavit could not. The Court of Appeal rejected the letter and decided the matter on the affidavit. Counsel, however, asked the court for some guidance as to the course to be followed in matrimonial
j proceedings for financial provision when a party decided to accede to some extent to proposals and desired to obtain the advantages that could be obtained in an ordinary action for debt or damages by a payment into court. It was in these circumstances that Cairns LJ, after referring to the Admiralty and Lands Tribunal procedure, said that it would be appropriate for the offer to be made in the form that it was without prejudice as to the issues but reserving the right to refer to it on costs.

This statement was, however, entirely obiter. The question of the effect in law of a *Calderbank* offer was not an issue in the case at all.

The decision of the Court of Appeal in *McDonnell v McDonell* [1977] 1 All ER 766, [1977] 1 WLR 34 takes the matter no further. The court, it is true, accepted an offer in the *Calderbank* form as being valid, but there is nothing to suggest that the matter was in issue or the subject of any argument.

We have not been referred to any case where the precise question with which we are concerned in this case has been an issue between the parties and has been adjudicated on. We must, therefore, consider the matter on principle. The substantial difficulty in the defendant's way can be put thus. Here is a letter headed 'Without prejudice'. *Walker v Wilsher*, an authority binding on the Court of Appeal, determines that, the offer having been refused, such a letter cannot be referred to on the question of costs after the trial. It is said, however, that the letter is not really 'without prejudice' at all in the *Walker v Wilsher* sense; it is only partially so because the plaintiff chose to restrict its operation by the concluding provision about reference to costs. But that gives rise to the question whether the plaintiff was entitled to pick and choose in that way. The rule is concerned with offers. The use of the formula protects both parties from reference to the offer if it is refused. The reason why the words 'without prejudice' had to be given the extended meaning 'without prejudice to the position of either party if the offer is refused' was because the offeror was not entitled to impose one-sided terms which might prejudice the offeree if the offer was rejected. That, I think, is evident from the judgment in *Re Daintrey, ex p Holt* and also from the judgment of Lindley LJ in *Walker v Wilsher*. The qualification that the offeror is to be quite free to refer to the offer on the question of costs so far from being without prejudice, however, may be highly prejudicial to the offeree. Certainly that could be so in a case like the present where we are concerned with the costs of a 33-day action in the High Court. It is said, therefore, that it was not competent to the plaintiff to make an offer in the terms which he did.

When the matter was first before us that approach seemed to me to be correct. We have now, however, had the advantage of much further argument and much more information about the practice in all divisions of the High Court and I think it is necessary to look at the matter afresh.

I will consider first the question of policy. *Walker v Wilsher*, there is no doubt, proceeds on a policy consideration, namely that the compromise of disputes should be facilitated. Now, an offer of compromise in the *Calderbank* form is not, so far as the substantive issues in the action are concerned, an inhibition on compromise. Down to judgment, the proposal for compromise cannot be referred to. The matter only arises on the question of costs after the issues have been decided. As to that, I am not convinced that the reservation as to costs would inhibit a reasonable compromise. If a party is exposed to a risk as to costs if a reasonable offer is refused, he is more rather than less likely to accept the terms and put an end to the litigation. On the other hand, if he can refuse reasonable offers with no additional risk as to costs, it is more rather than less likely to encourage mere stubborn resistance.

Furthermore, the existing practice, both under the Rules of the Supreme Court and other procedures, are difficult to reconcile with the existence of any public policy objection to the *Calderbank* type of offer.

Thus, the procedure under the rules of court for payment into court in cases where a debt or damages are claimed is, in effect, a *Calderbank* procedure, since the fact of the payment into court cannot be referred to until the issue of liability has been determined. It then becomes material on the question of costs. Other examples are the 'sealed offer' in arbitration proceedings (see *Tramountana Armadora SA v Atlantic Shipping Co SA* [1978] 2 All ER 870) and in Lands Tribunal proceedings (referred to by Cairns LJ in *Calderbank v Calderbank*) and also the Admiralty procedure in apportionment disputes in collision cases (also referred to by Cairns LJ in *Calderbank v Calderbank*). The sealed offer is not a new procedure: it seems to date back to practice adopted in compulsory arbitrations under the Lands Clauses Acts.

In the circumstances, I do not think that we would be justified in rejecting *Calderbank*
offers on grounds of public policy. In principle, they are more likely to fulfil than to
frustrate the public policy of facilitating compromises. And we have no reason to suppose
that, in the various jurisdictions to which I have referred where something akin to the
Calderbank offer has been operated over a substantial period, the practice has been found
to be in any way unsatisfactory or that any criticism of it has developed.

There remains, however, the problem of the effect which, on the authority of *Walker
v Wilsher*, attaches to the words 'without prejudice'. That, as I have indicated, derives, in
my view, from two sources: public policy and an implied agreement that the words are
to have a particular effect. The question of public policy I have dealt with. As regards the
conventional basis (ie agreement) that depends on what, by implication, is to be
attributed to the words 'without prejudice'. It appears from what we are now told by
counsel that the practice of making offers in the *Calderbank* form is by no means limited
to the Family Division (where it was adopted after the decision in *Calderbank v Calderbank*)
but is used in both the Queen's Bench and the Chancery Divisions to a considerable
extent. Counsel for the plaintiff, as I understood him, found on inquiry that the practice
in the Chancery Division was now more widespread than he had previously supposed. It
seems also to be in use to some extent in the Court of Appeal where the dispute concerns
the quantum of damages awarded in the court below. It is clear, therefore, that there has,
over the years, developed a substantial body of practice adopting the *Calderbank* form or
something very similar to it. It seems to me that, if the practice is valid, there is no reason
for restricting it to the Family Division (though it was in relation to certain Family
Division proceedings that Cairns LJ recommended it in *Calderbank v Calderbank*).
Logically, it should then be of universal application, as was indeed the view of Sir Robert
Megarry V-C in *Computer Machinery Co Ltd v Drescher* [1983] All ER 153, [1983] 1 WLR
1379.

In the end, I think that the question of what meaning is given to the words 'without
prejudice' is a matter of interpretation which is capable of variation according to usage in
the profession. It seems to me that, no issue of public policy being involved, it would be
wrong to say that the words were given a meaning in 1889 which is immutable ever
after, bearing in mind that the precise question with which we are concerned in this case
did not arise in *Walker v Wilsher* and the court did not deal with it. I think that the wide
body of practice which undoubtedly exists must be treated as indicating that the meaning
to be given to the words is altered if the offer contains the reservation relating to the use
of the offer in relation to costs.

On the further argument which we have now heard I would, for the above reasons,
and contrary to my original view of the matter, allow the appeal and make the order
proposed by Oliver LJ. I should add that I agree with the concluding observations in his
judgment as to attempts to use the *Calderbank* form as a substitute for payment into court
in the case of a simple money claim.

Appeal allowed. Leave to appeal to the House of Lords refused.

Solicitors: *Phillips & Co*, Salisbury (for the plaintiff); *Church Adams Tatham & Co*, agents
for *Wilsons*, Salisbury (for the defendant).

Mary Rose Plummer   Barrister.

South Tottenham Land Securities Ltd v R & A Millett (Shops) Ltd and another

COURT OF APPEAL, CIVIL DIVISION

OLIVER AND O'CONNOR LJJ

23, 24 NOVEMBER 1983

Landlord and tenant – Rent – Review – Retrospective operation – Rent to be paid on usual quarter days – Lease providing for forfeiture of lease if rent 21 days in arrear – Increased rent determined under review clause payable from specified date – Increased rent not determined until after specified date – Whether rent not due and payable until quarter day following award of increased rent – Whether rent due and payable on date of award.

By a lease of premises made in May 1959 the tenant covenanted to pay to the landlords on the usual quarter days the rent of £640 per annum until 25 March 1980 and from then until 25 March 2001 the same rent or such amount, whichever was the greater, as would be agreed between the parties or, in default of agreement, the fair yearly rent for the premises as determined by an independent arbitrator. The lease contained a forfeiture clause which permitted the landlords to re-enter if the rent or any part of it was in arrear for 21 days after becoming due. The parties failed to agree on the rent payable from 25 March 1980 and an arbitrator was appointed to determine the fair yearly rent for the premises. On 31 October 1980 the arbitrator published his award of the fair rent payable from 25 March 1980 at a sum which exceeded the old rent and gave notice to the parties that he had made his award, but the tenant did not receive a copy of the award until early November 1980. As at 26 November 1980 the tenant had not paid the difference between the old rent and the increased rent in respect of the quarters ending on 24 June and 29 September 1980, and the landlords accordingly forfeited the lease on the basis that the increased rent had become due on 31 October when the arbitrator published his award and the tenant was therefore more than 21 days in arrear with part of the rent reserved by the lease. The tenant contended that the landlords had no right to forfeit the lease on 26 November because under the terms of the lease the increased rent was not due and payable until the quarter day following the arbitrator's award, ie not until 29 December 1980, and accordingly there were no arrears of rent on 26 November and the forfeiture was therefore premature and wrongful. The judge held that the increased rent did not become due until the next quarter day following the tenant's receipt of the terms of the award and that accordingly the landlords were not entitled to forfeit the lease. The landlords appealed.

Held – When a new rent was fixed by an arbitrator under a rent review clause after the review date and the lease provided that the rent was to be paid in equal quarterly instalments on the usual quarter days, the new rent became due and payable on the next quarter day following, and not on the date when the award was taken up. Accordingly, the landlords were not entitled to forfeit the lease for non-payment of rent until the period laid down in the lease, ie 21 days, had elapsed after the next quarter day. The appeal would therefore be dismissed (see p 618 *b* to *j* and p 619 *a*, post).

Per curiam. It is desirable that rent review clauses should deal specifically with what is to happen where there is delay in arriving at the new rent beyond the review date (see p 618 *j* and p 619 *a*, post).

Notes

For rent review clauses and their effect, see 27 Halsbury's Laws (4th edn) paras 215, 217.

Cases referred to in judgments

Torminster Properties Ltd v Green [1983] 2 All ER 457, [1983] 1 WLR 676, CA.

United Scientific Holdings Ltd v Burnley BC, Cheapside Land Development Co Ltd v Messels
Service Co [1977] 2 All ER 62, [1978] AC 904, [1977] 2 WLR 806, HL.

Walsh v Lonsdale (1882) 21 Ch D 9, CA.

Interlocutory appeal

The plaintiffs, South Tottenham Land Securities Ltd (the landlords), appealed against the decision of Woolf J on 10 June 1983 whereby he held, inter alia, (i) that the landlords could not recover from the defendants, R & A Millett (Shops) Ltd and Alan Cyril Millett (the tenants), and/or the third parties, Richard James Driscoll, Ian David Stile and Ava Dawn Dobres, rent at the reviewed rate which was due for the quarters ending on 24 June and 29 September 1980 until the quarter day next following the determination by the arbitrator of the new rent for the period 25 March 1980 to 25 March 2001, viz 25 December 1980, and (ii) that the landlords' purported forfeiture of the lease and re-entry on the demised premises on 26 November 1980 was therefore premature and wrongful. The facts are set out in the judgment of O'Connor LJ.

Michael Barnes QC and *Robin Belben* for the landlords.
Romie Tager for the tenants.
The third parties did not appear.

O'CONNOR LJ (delivering the first judgment at the invitation of Oliver LJ). This appeal raises a single point for decision by this court, namely when is a new rent fixed under a rent review clause after the review date due for payment where the lease lays down that the rent is to be paid in equal quarterly instalments on the usual quarter days?

The facts giving rise to the dispute are all agreed. The landlords granted a lease for 99 years on 6 May 1959. The rent reserved was £640 a year payable in equal quarterly instalments on the usual quarter days. The lease contained a rent review clause for review at 21-year intervals during the period of the lease. Therefore, the first review date was 25 March 1980. I will read the relevant clauses in a moment. The parties were unable to agree a new rent and under the terms of the review clause the matter went to arbitration. The arbitrator published his award on 31 October 1980. The lease contained a forfeiture clause which permitted the landlords to forfeit the lease if the rent *due* remained unpaid for 21 days. No rent was paid within 21 days of 31 October and on 26 November the landlords forfeited the lease, by taking possession of the premises, as they were vacant; it was a shop. In due course they brought an action demanding the difference between the old rent, which had been paid for the quarters of June and September 1980, and the new rent which had been fixed by the award of 31 October down to the date of the forfeiture. The tenants complained that the forfeiture was unlawful because no rent under the arbitration award was due until the next quarter day following, namely 25 December. That was the issue. The judge held that the tenants' contention was right and that the arrears of rent (which it is convenient to call them) were not due until the next following quarter day.

I turn to the relevant terms of the lease. Clause 1 provides that the lessee shall pay—

'yearly during the said term and so in proportion for any less time than a year the respective rents following (that is to say) (a) until the Twenty fifth day of March One thousand nine hundred and eighty the rent of Six Hundred and Forty Pounds and (b) from the said Twenty fifth day of March One thousand nine hundred and eighty and until the Twenty fifth day of March Two thousand and one a yearly rent of Six Hundred and Forty Pounds or such amount (whichever be the greater) as may be agreed between the Landlords and the Lessee before the said Twenty fifth day of March One thousand nine hundred and eighty or in the absence of such agreement as may be determined by an arbitrator to be nominated by the President for the time being of the Royal Institution of Chartered Surveyors on the application of the

Landlords made before but not more than two Quarters before the Twenty fifth day
of March One thousand nine hundred and eighty . . .'   *a*

Thereafter similar provisions were made for the review dates at 42 and 63 years. Then
the clause continues:

'and so that in the case of any such arbitration the amount to be determined by
the arbitrator shall be the amount which shall in his opinion represent a fair yearly
rent for the demised premises having regard to rental values then current for   *b*
property let without a premium with vacant possession and to the provisions of this
Lease (other than the rent hereby reserved) to be paid without any deduction (except
for Landlords' Property Tax) by equal quarterly payments on the Twenty fifth day
of March the Twenty fourth day of June the Twenty ninth day of September and
the Twenty fifth day of December in every year the first of such quarterly payments
to be calculated from the Sixth day of May one thousand nine hundred and fifty   *c*
nine and made on the Twenty fourth day of June One thousand nine hundred and
fifty nine.'

The effect of that provision was that the quarterly payments were in arrear.
    Clause 2 of the lease provides:

'THE Lessee for itself and its assigns HEREBY COVENANTS with the Landlords in   *d*
manner following (that is to say):—(1) To pay the said yearly rent hereinbefore
reserved at the times and in the manner at and in which the same is hereinbefore
reserved and made payable without any deduction (except as aforesaid) . . .'

Lastly, cl 4 provides:

'PROVIDED ALWAYS AND IT IS HEREBY AGREED AND DECLARED as follows:—(i) If the   *e*
respective rents hereby reserved or any part thereof shall be in arrear for twenty-one
days after the same shall have become due (whether any formal or legal demand
therefor shall have been made or not) or in the event of any breach of any of the
covenants and stipulations on the part of the Lessee herein contained it shall be
lawful for the Landlords or any person on their behalf at any time thereafter to re-
enter upon the demised premises . . .'   *f*

I need refer to no other terms in the lease. Just as a matter of history, the original
landlords' reversion had been sold to the present landlords and the tenants were sued on
their covenant, although they had assigned the lease to new tenants who held the shop
and were third parties in the proceedings. The shop, as I have said, was empty at the
relevant time.
    So there is the question: when did the arrears of rent, which were ascertained by the   *g*
award on 30 October, become due? The landlords' contention is that those arrears became
due when the award was published. That is only another way of saying: when the new
rent had been ascertained either by agreement or alternatively by award; in the present
case, by award. The tenants submit that, on the true construction of the lease and in
principle, the arrears did not become due until the next quarter day following.
    There is no authority on this point. The only dicta of relevance is to be found in the   *h*
speech of Lord Diplock in *United Scientific Holdings Ltd v Burnley BC* [1977] 2 All ER 62 at
76, [1978] AC 904 at 935. That case was one of two cases which came to the House of
Lords on a different point, namely whether time was of the essence of the contract in
rent review provisions. So this question was entirely subsidiary. There was a further
question which had been decided in the Court of Appeal and was approved of in *United
Scientific*, namely that the arrears of rent were rent, because there had been decisions to   *j*
the contrary in the past. Lord Diplock in a short passage had this to say about it ([1977] 2
All ER 62 at 76, [1978] AC 904 at 934):

'The landlords also sought a declaration that the market rent as determined by
the valuer, if higher than £117,340 per annum, would be recoverable with effect
from 8th April 1975, ie retrospectively to the review date.'

He then dealt with the question whether it was rent. He held that it was and continued ([1977] 2 All ER 62 at 76, [1978] AC 904 at 935):

'My Lords, under the rent review clause in the instant case the market rent as determined in accordance with the provisions of the clause if higher than £117,340 per annum is expressed to be payable "in respect of the second period", viz the seven years starting on 8th April 1975. Until the market rent has been ascertained the landlords can only recover rent at the rate of £117,340 per annum, which corresponds to the minimum rent in *Walsh v Lonsdale* (1882) 21 Ch D 9. It is only when the market rent has been determined and turns out to be higher than £117,340 that the landowner can recover on the rent day following such determination the balance that has been accruing since 8th April 1975. Therein lies the economic advantage to the tenant of delay in the determination of the market rent to which I have previously referred.'

The researches of counsel show that this point was never considered either by the judge or the Court of Appeal. It was not dealt with in argument and there is no reference to it in any of the other speeches of their Lordships. Viscount Dilhorne agreed in these terms ([1977] 2 All ER 62 at 80, [1978] AC 904 at 940):

'I agree with what my noble and learned friend, Lord Diplock, has said with regard to the dates from which the revised rents would be payable and with his observations on the earlier cases.'

But note that that approval does not show that Viscount Dilhorne was considering whether the rent was to be recoverable before the next following quarter day.

So there is the only guidance from the case law. We were referred to a decision of the Court of Appeal in 1983, *Torminster Properties Ltd v Green* [1983] 2 All ER 457, [1983] 1 WLR 676. There again, Stephenson LJ said that the arrears were payable on the next following quarter day, but the reason for that was that there was an express clause in the lease to that effect and I need make no further reference to it (see [1983] 2 All ER 457 at 460, [1983] 1 WLR 676 at 680).

Counsel for the landlords submitted that, as a matter of principle, once the arrears of rent had been ascertained, there is no reason why they should not become due and payable as at that moment, and that, in the circumstance, the landlords were entitled to forfeit the lease in the present case. He submits that, in principle, there is no reason, commercial or in law, for keeping the landlords out of their money, which everybody recognises has got to be paid sooner or later. He submits that in the present case we should so rule.

When I look back at the terms of the lease, in logic, once the new rent has been ascertained, in this case on 31 October, the amount of the arrears had become due on the quarter days of June and September, and the part from September until 31 October could not be due until the December quarter day. The effect of such a decision would be that, immediately the rent was assessed by the arbitrator and his award published, the tenants would be in breach, because in the nature of things they could not have paid the arrears on the dates when they notionally had become due. Counsel for the landlords, quite rightly, does not submit that that can be a proper construction of the lease. So one is left with this situation, that as at 31 October the arrears cannot be treated as a single arrear. The only arrears are the two sums of money which would have been due on 24 June and 29 September.

Now commercially it may be said that there is no reason why the rent should not become due on the date when the award was published. Counsel for the tenants has submitted that this cannot be right, that rent under this lease is agreed to be paid on rent days, namely the quarter days in the year, and that where one has got an assessment in between quarter days, such as happened here, there is good reason for saying that the arrears do not become due until the next quarter day following. He has submitted that there are a number of grounds for saying that that is a better solution, and I may say here and now that it was the solution to which the judge came. He submits that certainty is required and desirable between landlord and tenant under a lease such as this as to when the rent is to be paid, and that, if the lease contains a rent review clause in terms such as we have here, then, in order to give certainty to the relationship between the two parties when rent is to be paid, the court should confine it to payment on quarter days.

Some help in that construction is in fact obtained from the terms of the lease itself. Clause 2(1) provides that the rent is to be paid 'at the times and in the manner at and in which the same is hereinbefore reserved and made payable'. Now, of course, the arrears cannot be paid in the manner laid down by the lease, which is equal quarterly instalments. But some meaning can be given to the times at which the rent is to be payable and the times are the quarter days and no other. So that to that extent one can get from the terms of the lease itself an indication that these arrears should not be due until the next quarter day following.

Counsel for the landlords has submitted that really the clause can have no application to arrears at all, because it is a single clause and we should not divide the times and the manner. In my judgment, that is not a sufficient reason for adopting a time which is only ascertainable on the date when the award is published, where there is an award, rather than a time which is found in the lease itself. It seems to me that it is much better, in cases such as this, that there should be no doubt about when the rent is due. If the parties choose to put into a lease that rent is due on quarter days, then there are good grounds for saying, where arrears arise in this fashion, that they should not be due until the next following quarter day. In my judgment, the judge came to a correct decision on this point.

It is to some extent a choice between two periods, because, of course, I appreciate the submissions that counsel for the landlords has made that as soon as the award is published, or the rent agreed, one has got a date which is certain. The argument which took place in the court below is no longer relevant here as to the date of publication, but I must say something about it. The law is that an award is published when the arbitrator notifies the parties that he has made his award, but they do not know the contents of it until it is taken up and his fee paid. So that in the present case the parties were notified by letter of 30 October that the award was ready, they received the letter on 31 October (that is how the date of publication was fixed) but of course they did not know the contents of it until the award was taken up. The tenant cannot be expected to pay rent the amount of which he does not know. So, therefore, the publication of the award as a fixed day for discharging the obligation is, in my judgment, quite unworkable. One has to allow some reasonable period of time in individual cases as to when it can be said that the tenant has ascertained how much is due. In the nature of things it is very unlikely to be the day when the award is published. That seems to me to be an objection which points strongly to some other date as being a suitable certain date when the rent is due. As I have said, in the present case it does not seem to be possible to say that it was 31 October. We do not know when the actual details of the award reached the landlords. They wrote off on 31 October enclosing the arbitrator's fee. I do not know what the days of the week were in 1980 but they are unlikely to have received it back before 2 November. Therefore, would it be 2 November from which the 21 days ran or would it be 3 November? Or some later date? There are postal delays, there are weekends to be considered. This kind of uncertainty points strongly to looking for some more certain date from which the arrears of rent are to begin. It is, as I have said, sufficiently found, in my judgment, in the lease. I am confident that the judge came to a correct decision and that where you have got a clause such as this then the arrears of rent do not become due and payable until the quarter day next following the ascertainment of the new rent.

Lastly, modern rent review clauses deal with this problem, so that it does not arise: see, for example, the clause in *Torminster Properties Ltd v Green* [1983] 2 All ER 457, [1983] 1 WLR 676. It is desirable that rent review clauses in leases should deal specifically with what is to happen where there is delay in arriving at the new rent beyond the review date.

I would dismiss this appeal.

OLIVER LJ. I agree that the appeal should be dismissed for the reasons given by O'Connor LJ.

Appeal dismissed.

Solicitors: *Slowes* (for the landlords); *Philip Hodges & Co* (for the tenants).

Carolyn Toulmin   Barrister.

R v Ayres

HOUSE OF LORDS

LORD FRASER OF TULLYBELTON, LORD SCARMAN, LORD BRIDGE OF HARWICH, LORD BRANDON OF OAKBROOK AND LORD TEMPLEMAN

31 JANUARY, 1, 16 FEBRUARY 1984

Criminal law – Conspiracy – Conspiracy to obtain money by deception – Accused charged with conspiracy to defraud – Statute creating offence of conspiracy and abolishing common law offence of conspiracy subject to exceptions – Whether offences mutually exclusive – Whether conspiracy to defraud continuing to be common law offence – Whether conspiracy to defraud at common law can be charged when evidence supports a statutory offence – Criminal Law Act 1977, ss 1(1), 5.

The appellant was charged on indictment with conspiracy to defraud an insurance company by falsely claiming that a lorry (insured for £2,500) and its contents (insured for £10,000) had been stolen in transit. At the trial, at the conclusion of the evidence, counsel for the appellant submitted that since the substance of the offence was a conspiracy to obtain money by deception it ought to have been charged under s 1(1)[a] of the Criminal Law Act 1977 and not as a conspiracy to defraud contrary to common law, and that accordingly the indictment was defective. The trial judge rejected that submission and the appellant was convicted. The Court of Appeal upheld his conviction. The appellant appealed to the House of Lords, contending that a conspiracy to defraud at common law could only be charged when the evidence did not support any statutory, substantive conspiracy, having regard to ss 1 and 5[b] of the 1977 Act.

Held – (1) The statutory offence of conspiracy under s 1 of the 1977 Act and the offence of conspiracy to defraud at common law were mutually exclusive; accordingly an offence which amounted to a common law conspiracy to defraud had to be charged as such and not as a statutory conspiracy under s 1, and a conspiracy under s 1 could not be charged as a common law conspiracy. Adopting a purposive approach to construction, the

---

a   Section 1(1) provides: 'Subject to the following provisions of this Part of this Act, if a person agrees with any other person or persons that a course of conduct shall be pursued which will necessarily amount to or involve the commission of any offence or offences by one or more of the parties to the agreement if the agreement is carried out in accordance with their intentions, he is guilty of conspiracy to commit the offence or offences in question.'

b   Section 5, so far as material, provides:

'(1) Subject to the following provisions of this section, the offence of conspiracy at common law is hereby abolished.

(2) Subsection (1) above shall not affect the offence of conspiracy at common law so far as relates to conspiracy to defraud, and section 1 above shall not apply in any case where the agreement in question amounts to a conspiracy to defraud at common law.

(3) Subsection (1) above shall not affect the offence of conspiracy at common law if and in so far as it may be committed by entering into an agreement to engage in conduct which—(a) tends to corrupt public morals or outrages public decency; but (b) would not amount to or involve the commission of an offence if carried out by a single person otherwise than in pursuance of agreement . . .'

preservation of the offence of conspiracy at common law by s 5(2) of the 1977 Act in so
far as it related to conspiracy to defraud was to be construed as limited to an agreement
which, if carried into effect, would not necessarily involve the commission of any
substantive criminal offence by any of the conspirators. Accordingly, since the only
crime alleged against the appellant was an attempt to obtain money from the insurers by
deception, he should have been charged with conspiracy under s 1 of the 1977 Act, and
the indictment was therefore defective (see p 621 *b c*, p 622 *f g*, p 625 *g h*, p 626 *a c d* and
p 627 *g h*, post); *R v Duncalf* [1979] 2 All ER 1116 and *R v Molyneux, R v Farmborough*
(1980) 72 Cr App R 111 applied.

(2) However, the misdescription of the offence as a common law conspiracy had no
practical effect because the judge had given the appropriate direction in relation to the
only offence of which the appellant could be convicted, namely a conspiracy to obtain
money by deception, and the evidence amply proved that offence so that no miscarriage
of justice had occurred. It followed therefore that, applying the proviso to s 2(1) of the
Criminal Appeal Act 1968, the appeal would be dismissed (see p 621 *b c* and p 627 *d to h*,
post).

Per curiam. In cases where the performance of the agreement constituting the
conspiracy would necessarily involve, or has already involved, the commission of one or
more substantive offences by one or more of the conspirators, one or more counts of
conspiracy, as appropriate, should be charged under s 1 of the 1977 Act. Only exceptional
agreements will need to be charged as common law conspiracies to defraud, when either
it is clear that performance of the agreement constituting the conspiracy would not have
involved the commission by any conspirator of any substantive offence or it is uncertain
whether it would do so. In case of doubt, it may be appropriate to include two counts in
the indictment in the alternative. It would then be for the judge to decide how to leave
the case to the jury at the conclusion of the evidence, bearing always in mind that the
crucial issue is whether performance of the agreement constituting the conspiracy would
necessarily involve the commission of a substantive offence by the conspirator. If it
would, it is a s 1 conspiracy; if it would not, it is a common law conspiracy to defraud
(see p 621 *b c*, p 625 *h* to p 626 *a* and p 627 *g h*, post).

Notes

For conspiracy to defraud and indictments in conspiracy, see 11 Halsbury's Laws (4th
edn) paras 61–62, and for cases on the subjects, see 15 Digest (Reissue) 1398–1403,
12236–12297.

For the Criminal Appeal Act 1968, s 2, see 8 Halsbury's Statutes (3rd edn) 690.

For the Criminal Law Act 1977, ss 1, 5, see 47 ibid 145, 151.

As from 27 August 1981, s 1(1) of the 1977 Act was substituted by s 5(1) of the
Criminal Attempts Act 1981.

Cases referred to in opinions

Knuller (Publishing, Printing and Promotions) Ltd v DPP [1972] 2 All ER 898, [1973] AC 435,
[1972] 2 WLR 143, HL.

R v Duncalf [1979] 2 All ER 1116, [1979] 1 WLR 918, CA.

R v McVitie [1960] 2 All ER 498, [1960] 2 QB 483, [1960] 3 WLR 99, CCA.

R v Molyneux, R v Farmborough (1980) 72 Cr App R 111, CA.

R v Quinn [1978] Crim LR 750, Crown Ct at Nottingham.

R v Walters, R v Tovey, R v Padfield (1979) 69 Cr App R 115, CA.

Scott v Comr of Police for the Metropolis [1974] 3 All ER 1032, [1975] AC 819, [1974] 3
WLR 741, HL.

Shaw v DPP [1961] 2 All ER 446, [1962] AC 220, [1961] 2 WLR 897, HL.

Appeal

On 15 October 1982 in the Crown Court at Reading before his Honour Judge Hilliard
and a jury the appellant, David Edward Ayres, was convicted on indictment of conspiracy
to defraud and was sentenced to eight months' imprisonment. He appealed against his

conviction to the Court of Appeal, Criminal Division (O'Connor LJ, Kilner Brown and Popplewell JJ), which dismissed his appeal on 2 December 1983, refused leave to appeal to the House of Lords, but certified, under s 33(2) of the Criminal Appeal Act 1968, on the application of the appellant, that a point of law of general public importance (set out at p 624 *f*, post) was involved in its decision to dismiss the appeal. On 26 January 1984 the Appeal Committee of the House of Lords granted the appellant leave to appeal. The facts are set out in the opinion of Lord Bridge.

Alan Rawley QC and *Christopher Wilson-Smith* for the appellant.
Igor Judge QC and *Julian Baughan* for the Crown.

Their Lordships took time for consideration.

16 February. The following opinions were delivered.

LORD FRASER OF TULLYBELTON. My Lords, I have had the advantage of reading in draft the speech of my noble and learned friend Lord Bridge, and I agree with it. For the reasons given by him I would dismiss this appeal.

LORD SCARMAN. My Lords, I have had the advantage of reading in draft the speech to be delivered by my noble and learned friend Lord Bridge. I agree with it, and for the reasons which he gives I would dismiss the appeal.

LORD BRIDGE OF HARWICH. My Lords, Pt I of the Criminal Law Act 1977 effected a radical amendment of the law of criminal conspiracy. Criminal conspiracies are now of four kinds only. (1) A conspiracy to commit one or more substantive criminal offences contrary to s 1 of the 1977 Act. The maximum penalty for such a conspiracy is the maximum appropriate to the substantive offence or, if more than one, the most serious of the substantive offences involved in the conspiracy: s 3. Proceedings under s 1 in respect of a conspiracy confined to summary offences may not be instituted except by or with the consent of the Director of Public Prosecutions: s 4(1). (2) A conspiracy made an offence as such by some other enactment, eg s 3(*a*) of the Explosive Substances Act 1883, which is expressly excluded from the scope of s 1 of the 1977 Act by s 5(6). (3) A common law conspiracy to defraud: s 5(2). (4) A common law conspiracy to corrupt public morals or outrage public decency: s 5(3). The surviving common law conspiracies are subject to no limit as to penalty and require no statutory consent to the institution of proceedings.

My Lords, in this appeal we are not directly concerned with conspiracies under heads (2) and (4) but only with the relationship between conspiracies under heads (1) and (3). An early conflict of judicial opinion emerged as to where the line of demarcation should be drawn between statutory conspiracies under s 1 of the 1977 Act and common law conspiracies to defraud in relation to a large and important class of conspiracies which, on their face, appear to be capable of falling within either category. It is that conflict which your Lordships must now resolve in this appeal.

If the phrase 'conspiracy to defraud' is given its widest connotation, it must include every conspiracy of which one element is that the execution of the agreement constituting the conspiracy will involve that the victim is defrauded. Those who would ascribe this wide meaning to the phrase in s 5(2) of the 1977 Act have seized on the words of Viscount Dilhorne in *Scott v Comr of Police for the Metropolis* [1974] 3 All ER 1032 at 1039, [1975] AC 819 at 840:

> '. . . in my opinion it is clearly the law that an agreement by two or more by dishonesty to deprive a person of something which is his or to which he is or would be or might be entitled and an agreement between two or more by dishonesty to injure some proprietary right of his, suffices to constitute the offence of conspiracy to defraud.'

It may be important to remember that this 'definition', if such it was, was given in a case where the criminal conspiracy under consideration did *not* involve the commission of any identifiable offence other than conspiracy and that Viscount Dilhorne's objective in using the words quoted seems to have been to emphasise that this did not prevent the agreement in question amounting to a conspiracy to defraud. Indeed, one of the arguments advanced for the appellant and rejected by the House in that case was that deceit was an essential element of a common law conspiracy to defraud. Be that as it may, Viscount Dilhorne's words, if taken as a comprehensive definition of the offence of conspiracy to defraud, inevitably embrace conspiracies to commit a multitude of other specific offences, as, for example, robbery, burglary, theft, obtaining by deception, most offences of forgery, and a formidable list of minor offences created by statute, many of them summary offences only, in which an element of fraud is involved; in short every offence of which the ingredients include (a) dishonesty and (b) either some injury to private proprietary rights or some fraud on the public. This category of offences, of which the examples given above are by no means exhaustive, must cover a very wide band of the entire spectrum of crime. The only other band of comparable importance would seem to be offences against the person.

One school of judicial thought with regard to the construction of ss 1 and 5 of the 1977 Act holds that any conspiracy to commit an offence involving an element of fraud in the sense explained in the foregoing paragraph is properly indicted as a common law conspiracy to defraud. The contrary view is that, whenever the conspiracy, if carried into execution, would involve the commission of a substantive offence, notwithstanding that the offence involves an element of fraud, the offence committed is a statutory conspiracy under s 1 of the 1977 Act and should be indicted as such.

Before turning to the authorities and arguments bearing on this conflict of opinion, it is well to remove one source of misunderstanding. Some judicial dicta on the subject might be understood as suggesting that the choice whether to prosecute for a statutory conspiracy under s 1 of the 1977 Act or for a common law conspiracy to defraud is one dictated by convenience and that in many cases both options may be open. It was indeed argued for the Crown before your Lordships that the two offences are not mutually exclusive. I have no hesitation at the outset in rejecting this argument. Section 5(2) of the 1977 Act, which preserves conspiracy to defraud at common law as an exception to the general abolition of the offence of common law conspiracy by s 5(1) concludes with the words: '. . . and section 1 above shall not apply in any case where the agreement in question amounts to a conspiracy to defraud at common law.' I can see no escape from the stark choice of alternatives which this plain language imposes. According to the true construction of the 1977 Act, an offence which amounts to a common law conspiracy to defraud must be charged as such and not as a statutory conspiracy under s 1. Conversely a s 1 conspiracy cannot be charged as a common law conspiracy to defraud. It is, in my opinion, of considerable importance to bear in mind the implications of the fact that the offences are thus mutually exclusive in approaching the problem of construction.

The controversy first emerged in a ruling of Drake J in *R v Quinn* [1978] Crim LR 750 that a conspiracy to steal was properly charged as a common law conspiracy to defraud. A few months later the issue reached the Court of Appeal (Lord Widgery CJ, Cumming-Bruce LJ and Neill J) in *R v Walters, R v Tovey, R v Padfield* (1979) 69 Cr App R 115. The appellants appealed against a conviction for common law conspiracy to defraud in circumstances in which they had been clearly guilty of conspiracy to steal motor cars and to obtain money by deception by selling them. The point was taken that they could have been properly convicted only under s 1 of the 1977 Act. In giving the judgment of the court, Lord Widgery CJ said (at 118):

'We are not going to lay down any final conclusions about this case. When a new point of this kind has to be developed, it is better if it is developed slowly. We shall look at the circumstances of this case and see how the statutory provisions work out in relation to it.'

He proceeded to show that the elements of a conspiracy to defraud were proved, pointed out that s 5 of the 1977 Act preserves that offence and that proper directions were given to the jury. He concluded (at 119): 'A conviction having been entered, there

a is nothing more for this Court to do in this case on this day.' Referring to the ruling by Drake J in *R v Quinn*, Lord Widgery CJ added:

'. . . faced with this prospect, he took the firm view, which personally I support as at present advised, that it is perfectly proper to regard a conspiracy to steal as something within a conspiracy to defraud, and accordingly, therefore, if truly the

b offence is conspiracy to steal, the indictment is not rendered invalid merely because it charges a conspiracy to defraud. In many ways it must be preferable that the conspiracy to defraud should be regarded as the greater container, as it were, and able to mop up conspiracy to steal if and when that is convenient having regard to the nature of the case.'

Very soon after this decision the point was raised again in the Court of Appeal in *R v*

c *Duncalf* [1979] 2 All ER 1116, [1979] 1 WLR 918, before Roskill, Ormrod LJJ and Watkins J. This was a simple case of a conspiracy to steal where the appellants, who had been indicted and convicted under s 1 of the 1977 Act, argued that they could only properly have been convicted of conspiracy to defraud at common law. The appeal was dismissed. I cannot do justice to the closely reasoned and careful reserved judgment of the court, delivered by Roskill LJ, without quoting from it at some length ([1979] 2 All

d ER 1116 at 1120–1121, [1979] 1 WLR 918 at 922–923):

'It seems to us that the structure of this part of the 1977 Act is a little curious. One might have expected s 5(1) to appear as s 1(1), the common law offence of conspiracy being abolished (subject, of course, to the provisions of s 5(2) and (3)) before the new statutory offence was created by s 1(1). But the draftsman has in his

e wisdom decided otherwise. The Act starts in s 1(1) by defining the new offence of conspiracy, the definition being stated to be subject to the following provisions of this part of the Act. Though the sidenote to s 1(1) is of course no part of the statute, it seems to us plain that the very language of this subsection, coupled with the provisions of s 5(1) abolishing the common law offence of conspiracy (subject, of course, to s 5(2) and (3) and to the remaining subsections of s 5) shows that the

f definition in s 1(1) is and was intended to be an exhaustive definition. If this approach be right, then the presence of s 5(2) and for that matter of s 5(3) must, we think, be regarded as a limited qualification on that abolition and on the creation of that new statutory offence. But with profound respect to those who have taken a different view, it seems to us wrong to allow that qualification to prevail so as largely to emasculate the two main enacting provisions. The qualification should surely be

g read as preserving only that which requires to be preserved in order that a lacuna should not be left in the law. If ss 1(1) and 5(1) had been left standing without the savings in s 5(2) there would have been a lacuna, because a conspiracy to defraud simpliciter could not fall within s 1(1): see *Scott v Comr of Police for the Metropolis* [1974] 3 All ER 1032, [1975] AC 819 and if those two subsections had been left without the parallel saving in s 5(3), the decision in *Shaw v Director of Public*

h *Prosecutions* [1961] 2 All ER 446, [1962] AC 220 later confirmed in *Knuller (Publishing, Printing and Promotions) Ltd v Director of Public Prosecutions* [1972] 2 All ER 898, [1973] AC 435, might have been seemingly reversed in a statute which, though reforming the law of criminal conspiracy, was not concerned with the law relating to obscene publications. Much reliance was placed in argument before us on the penultimate paragraph of the speech of Viscount Dilhorne in *Scott's* case [1974] 3

j All ER 1032 at 1039, [1975] AC 819 at 840: ". . . in my opinion it is clearly the law that an agreement by two or more by dishonesty to deprive a person of something which is his or to which he is or would be or might be entitled and an agreement by two or more by dishonesty to injure some proprietary right of his, suffices to constitute the offence of conspiracy to defraud." It was said that Parliament must have intended to use the phrase "conspiracy to defraud" in s 5(2) in the sense in which Viscount Dilhorne had there defined it, and therefore s 5(2) must be given a meaning wide enough to embrace every conspiracy the objective of which was

dishonestly to injure some proprietary or other right of the victim. If s 5(2) is to be
literally construed, this argument has obvious force. But we do not think it right to
give so strict or literal a construction to the subsection when the effect of so doing
would be so largely to destroy the obvious purpose of this Act, and a sensible
construction can, as we think, be given to both s 5(2) and s 5(3) as preserving the old
law to, but only to, such extent as is necessary to ensure that a lacuna was not left in
the law by s 1(1).'

Roskill LJ concluded:

'It follows that, with great respect, we find ourselves unable to agree with Drake
J's ruling in R v Quinn [1978] Crim LR 750 or with the dictum tentatively approving
that ruling in R v Walters (1979) 69 Cr App R 115.'

One might have thought that this decision would have settled the controversy, but
this appeal and, so their Lordships understand, other cases awaiting decision in the Court
of Appeal which raise the same point show that not to be so.

The instant case was one of a conspiracy to defraud an insurance company by falsely
claiming that a lorry (insured for £2,500) and its contents (insured for £10,000) had
been stolen. Carrying the conspiracy into effect might have involved the commission of
other offences, but it certainly involved an attempt to obtain money from the insurers
by deception and thus, unless excluded by s 5(2), fell fairly and squarely within s 1 of the
1977 Act. The indictment contained a single count of conspiracy to defraud. At the
conclusion of the evidence, defending counsel submitted that the offence ought properly
to have been charged as a conspiracy to obtain money by deception under s 1 of the 1977
Act. This submission was rejected by the trial judge. The appellant was duly convicted.

Giving the judgment of the Court of Appeal (O'Connor LJ, Kilner Brown and
Popplewell JJ) Kilner Brown J said:

'Although the court in Duncalf accepted that Walters was correctly decided, as it
was bound to do, we doubt that the two decisions can stand together. On the clear
wording of s 5(2), we are content to be bound by the decision in Walters and to hold
that the appellant was properly charged with a conspiracy to defraud.'

The court certified as a question involving a point of law of general importance:

'Whether a conspiracy to defraud at common law can only be charged when the
evidence does not support any statutory, substantive conspiracy, having regard to
sections 1 and 5 of the Criminal Law Act 1977 as amended?'

Leave to appeal was refused by the Court of Appeal but granted by your Lordships'
House.

My Lords, the passing of the 1977 Act followed the publication in March 1976 of the
Law Commission's Report on Conspiracy and Criminal Law Reform (Law Com no 76).
It is legitimate to look at that report to ascertain the mischief which the statute was
intended to remedy. To attempt briefly to paraphrase and summarise, without quoting,
I read the report as identifying the defect in the previous law of criminal conspiracy as
arising from the uncertainty as to what might constitute the subject matter of an
agreement amounting to a criminal conspiracy, which, in general terms, could only be
eliminated by restricting criminal conspiracies to agreements to commit substantive
criminal offences. But as a gloss on this main theme, the report recognised that an
unqualified restriction of criminal conspiracies to such agreements might leave gaps in
the law in certain areas, including fraud, which only the retention of the common law
conspiracy offence could cover. This reading of the Law Commission's report seems to
me to lend powerful support to the construction adopted in R v Duncalf of ss 1(1) and 5(2)
of the 1977 Act.

Further considerations point to the same conclusion. Adopting a purposive approach
to construction, it is difficult indeed to suppose that Parliament, whilst limiting the
punishment of conspirators generally to the maximum appropriate to the substantive

offences they had conspired to commit and giving them the added protection of requiring
a approval from the Director of Public Prosecutions to their prosecution if the substantive
offences in question were summary offences, should have intended to deny both these
advantages to any person agreeing to commit a substantive offence involving an element
of fraud, however trivial that offence might be.

It remains to consider whether any light is thrown on the point at issue by comparing
the language of s 5(2) with that of s 5(3). The latter provides:

b   'Subsection (1) above shall not affect the offence of conspiracy at common law if
      and in so far as it may be committed by entering into an agreement to engage in
      conduct which—(*a*) tends to corrupt public morals or outrages public decency; but
      (*b*) would not amount to or involve the commission of an offence if carried out by a
      single person otherwise than in pursuance of an agreement.'

c No comparable limitation to that imposed by sub-s (3)(*b*) applies to the provision that
sub-s (1) (abolishing the offence of conspiracy at common law) 'shall not affect the offence
of conspiracy at common law so far as relates to conspiracy to defraud'.

So far as one can judge from the short report of *R v Quinn*, Drake J seems to have based
his ruling primarily on this distinction in the statutory language applied to the two
common law conspiracy offences preserved by the 1977 Act. I do not, with respect, find
d this convincing. By itself sub-s (3)(*b*) seems fully to support the view that the underlying
policy of Pt I of the 1977 Act was to preserve the offence of conspiracy at common law
only to the extent necessary to avoid leaving a lacuna in the law. The question then arises
why a similar limitation was not imposed expressly on the scope of the preserved
common law offence of conspiracy to defraud. I believe the answer to be this. Agreements
entered into for a fraudulent purpose may take an almost infinite variety of forms. In
e some cases it may be impossible to say of such an agreement whether or not carrying the
agreement into effect would have involved the commission of any substantive offence.
To constitute an offence of conspiracy under s 1 of the 1977 Act, the agreement must
be—

f   'that a course of conduct shall be pursued which will necessarily amount to or
      involve the commission of any offence or offences by one or more of the parties to
      the agreement if the agreement is carried out in accordance with their intentions . . .'

If s 5(2) had imposed on the preserved common law offence of conspiracy to defraud a
restriction in comparable terms to those used in s 5(3)(*b*) this would have left in limbo
those conspiracies to defraud where the evidence left in doubt the question whether the
execution of the agreement would or would not necessarily have involved the commission
g of some substantive offence by one or more of the conspirators.

For these reasons, and for those expressed in the extract quoted above from the
judgment of the court in *R v Duncalf*, with which I respectfully agree, I conclude that the
phrase 'conspiracy to defraud' in s 5(2) of the 1977 Act must be construed as limited to
an agreement which, if carried into effect, would not necessarily involve the commission
of any substantive criminal offence by any of the conspirators. I would accordingly
h answer the certified question in the affirmative.

The effect of this ruling should not, I believe, create undue difficulty for prosecutors
or judges. In the overwhelming majority of conspiracy cases it will be obvious that
performance of the agreement which constitutes the conspiracy would necessarily
involve, and frequently will in fact have already involved, the commission of one or
more substantive offences by one or more of the conspirators. In such cases one or more
j counts of conspiracy, as appropriate, should be charged under s 1 of the 1977 Act. Only
the exceptional fraudulent agreements will need to be charged as common law
conspiracies to defraud, when either it is clear that performance of the agreement
constituting the conspiracy would not have involved the commission by any conspirator
of any substantive offence or it is uncertain whether or not it would do so. In case of
doubt, it may be appropriate to include two counts in the indictment in the alternative.

It would then be for the judge to decide how to leave the case to the jury at the conclusion of the evidence, bearing always in mind that the crucial issue is whether performance of the agreement constituting the conspiracy would necessarily involve the commission of a substantive offence by a conspirator. If it would, it is a s 1 conspiracy. If it would not, it is a common law conspiracy to defraud.

It follows from what I have said that the appellant was convicted on an indictment which did not charge him accurately with the only offence for which he could properly be convicted. The indictment read:

'Statement of Offence: Conspiracy to defraud.

Particulars of Offence: JAMES POVEY WESTBROOK and DAVID EDWARD AYRES, on divers days between the 28th day of August 1981 and the 12th day of November 1981, conspired together and with other persons not before the Court, to defraud such insurance companies or other persons as might, by the provision of false insurance claims or otherwise, thereafter be induced to part with money to the said James Povey Westbrook and David Edward Ayres, by falsely representing that a lorry load of scallops had been stolen while in transit from the premises of the said David Edward Ayres, through the agency of the said James Povey Westbrook, to the order of International Seafoods Limited.'

The relevant provisions of the Indictment Rules 1971, SI 1971/1253, are to be found in rr 5 and 6, but I do not find it necessary to set them out since there can be no doubt that the indictment did not comply with the rules. It follows that there was a material irregularity in the course of the trial which requires under s 2(1) of the Criminal Appeal Act 1968 that the appeal against conviction be allowed unless the proviso to that subsection can be applied on the ground that no actual miscarriage of justice has occurred. I pause to mention in passing that no substitution of a verdict under s 3 would be possible, since there was no other offence of which the jury could on this indictment have found the appellant guilty.

In a number of cases where an irregularity in the form of the indictment has been discussed in relation to the application of the proviso a distinction, treated as of crucial importance, has been drawn between an indictment which is 'a nullity' and one which is merely 'defective'. For my part, I doubt if this classification provides much assistance in answering the question which the proviso poses. If the statement and particulars of the offence in an indictment disclose no criminal offence whatever or charge some offence which has been abolished, in which case the indictment could fairly be described as a nullity, it is obvious that a conviction under that indictment cannot stand. But, if the statement and particulars of offence can be seen fairly to relate to and to be intended to charge a known and subsisting criminal offence but plead it in terms which are inaccurate, incomplete or otherwise imperfect, then the question whether a conviction on that indictment can properly be affirmed under the proviso must depend on whether, in all the circumstances, it can be said with confidence that the particular error in the pleading cannot in any way have prejudiced or embarrassed the defendant.

Your Lordships were referred to a number of authorities on this aspect of the case but I do not think it would serve any useful purpose to embark on a comprehensive view of them and I propose to refer to only two which seem of particular importance in the present context. The foundation of the modern law is the decision of the Court of Criminal Appeal under the Criminal Appeal Act 1907 by a five judge court (Lord Parker CJ, Stable, Donovan, Ashworth and Salmon JJ) in *R v McVitie* [1960] 2 All ER 498, [1960] 2 QB 483. The defendant had been indicted for 'possessing explosives contrary to section 4(1) of the Explosive Substances Act, 1883'. At the arraignment of the defendant this statement of offence was not read out but only the particulars. The particulars of the offence omitted the word 'knowingly' in relation to the alleged possession, knowledge being an essential ingredient of the offence. The court decisively rejected the contention, which appeared to derive some support from earlier decisions, that the defendant had never been arraigned for any offence known to the law so as to preclude the court from upholding his conviction under the proviso. Giving the judgment of the court, Donovan

J expressed the essential principle in the following passage ([1960] 2 All ER 498 at 503, [1960] 2 QB 483 at 497):

'In the present case it is clear that no embarrassment or prejudice was caused to the appellant by the omission of the word "knowingly" from the particulars, or from the arraignment. He had been properly charged in the first place, and properly committed for trial, and the Attorney-General's fiat was in proper form. If the word "knowingly" had been in the particulars and the chairman had said to the jury "You must be satisfied that McVitie knew that there were explosive substances in the paper bag in the car," the chairman would inevitably have gone on to say, as, indeed, he did, "but McVitie admits he had this knowledge." This essential ingredient of the offence was therefore established, despite the omission of the word in question. The present case is, therefore, a clear case where no substantial miscarriage of justice has occurred . . .'

A decision directly in point on the issue raised by the instant case is *R v Molyneux, R v Farmborough* (1980) 72 Cr App R 111, decided by Shaw LJ, Park and Anthony Lincoln JJ. There, as here, the appellant had been convicted of conspiracy to defraud when the true offence proved against him had been conspiracy to rob. On the substantive point, the court there followed *R v Duncalf.* Having decided that the indictment though defective was not a nullity (perfectly correctly), the court went on to examine the circumstances and to decide that the misnomer in the statement of offence in the light of the particulars and the summing up led to the conclusion that there had been no actual miscarriage of justice.

My Lords, in the instant case I reach the same conclusion for essentially similar reasons though without pausing to consider the nullity point. The particulars of offence in this indictment left no one in doubt that the substance of the crime alleged was a conspiracy to obtain money by deception. The judge in summing up gave all appropriate directions in relation to that offence. The co-accused Westbrook having pleaded guilty, the evidence amply proved that offence against the present appellant. The jury in returning a verdict of guilty must have been sure of his guilt of that offence. The judge passed a modest sentence comfortably below the maximum for that offence. The misdescription of the offence in the statement of offence as a common law conspiracy to defraud had in the circumstances not the slightest practical significance. Even the persuasive arguments advanced by counsel on the appellant's behalf on this aspect of the case failed to persuade me that in these circumstances there can possibly have been any actual miscarriage of justice.

I would accordingly dismiss the appeal.

LORD BRANDON OF OAKBROOK. My Lords, I have had the advantage of reading in draft the speech prepared by my noble and learned friend Lord Bridge. Although I did at one time entertain serious doubts on the question of statutory construction raised by the appeal, his reasoning has convinced me that his view on that question, which is, I understand, shared by all the rest of your Lordships, is the correct one. I also agree that this is a case where the proviso to s 2(1) of the Criminal Appeal Act 1968 should be applied, and I would dismiss the appeal on that ground.

LORD TEMPLEMAN. My Lords, for the reasons given by my noble and learned friend Lord Bridge, I would answer the certified question in the affirmative and dismiss the appeal.

Appeal dismissed.

Solicitors: *Hatchett Jones & Kidgell*, agents for *Wolferstans*, Plymouth (for the appellant); *Sharpe Pritchard & Co* (for the Crown).

Mary Rose Plummer   Barrister.

Barclays Bank Ltd and others v TOSG Trust Fund Ltd and others

COURT OF APPEAL, CIVIL DIVISION

OLIVER, KERR AND SLADE LJJ

16, 17, 18, 19, 20, 23, 24, 25 MAY, 12 JULY 1983

Company – Winding up – Proof and ranking of claims – Rule against double proof – Test of whether rule against double proof applies – Application of rule against double proof – Guarantor's right of proof – Company taking out bond against insolvency – Banks paying over money under bonds when company becoming insolvent – Money used to pay creditors in part – Creditors assigning claims to third party – Banks proving for debt under bonds – Third party proving for debt under assignments – Whether both proofs admissible – If only one proof admissible, whether banks or third party having better right of proof.

In 1970 a group of holiday tour operators, which included C Ltd, set up a scheme to alleviate the consequences to holidaymakers and customers of the insolvency of any of their number. The scheme required individual tour operators who were members of the scheme to take out a banker's bond whereby the bank agreed to pay a specified sum to a company (TOSG), formed as part of the scheme, in the event of the operator becoming insolvent and unable to fulfil its obligations to holidaymakers and customers. The purpose of TOSG was to use money paid to it under the bonds to look after and repatriate holidaymakers stranded abroad and to protect customers who had made prepaid bookings from suffering financial loss. Under the terms of the bonds TOSG was entitled to call in the bond moneys from the bank as soon as the operator concerned became insolvent. The bonds contained no restriction on how TOSG expended or disbursed moneys it received but TOSG was required to pay back to the bank any surplus remaining after the claims of customers had been met. In accordance with the scheme C Ltd arranged for a number of banks to enter into bonds on its behalf in return for the payment of commission and the execution of counter-indemnities under which C Ltd agreed to indemnify the banks against any loss which they sustained under the bonds. In 1974 C Ltd could no longer fulfil its obligations to its customers and went into liquidation. The bond moneys were called in from the banks by TOSG which, after rescuing C Ltd's customers who were stranded abroad, then had some £1·268m to reimburse claims by customers who had paid for holidays which C Ltd was no longer able to provide. Since that amount was unlikely to be sufficient to meet all such claims TOSG entered into an agreement with the Air Travel Reserve Fund Agency (a statutory body set up to compensate persons who lost holidays as a result of the collapse of tour operators) whereby TOSG would, to the extent the bond moneys made possible, reimburse customers who were owed money in return for such customers assigning to the agency their right to prove in the liquidation of C Ltd for the full amount of their claim and the agency would then satisfy customers' debts which remained unpaid by TOSG. In accordance with that agreement TOSG expended, and received assignments to the agency of claims amounting to, some £1·268m while the agency satisfied the remaining claims, amounting to some £3·09m. In the ensuing liquidation of C Ltd the banks proved under the counter-indemnities and the agency proved under the assignments for the £1·268m paid out by TOSG. The liquidators took the view that the rule against double proof prevented the banks and the agency from both proving for the £1·268m. The banks sought a declaration that they were entitled to prove for the £1·268m but the judge held that the agency had the better right of proof, on the assumption that the rule against double proof applied, because the banks had in effect guaranteed C Ltd's liabilities to its customers and were therefore subject to the rule that the proof of a surety could not displace the proof of a creditor unless and until the surety fully discharged all his liabilities to the creditor, and therefore C Ltd's customers (and thus the agency) were entitled to prove as creditors for the whole of their debts in priority to the banks (and without giving credit for moneys received from the banks via TOSG) unless and until the whole of their debts were satisfied and, moreover, considerations of broad equity favoured the agency rather than the banks. The banks appealed, contending, inter alia, that they were entitled by subrogation to assume the rights of customers who had been paid out of the bond moneys.

Held – (1) (Per Oliver and Kerr LJJ) There could not be any subrogation between the banks and TOSG because there was no general principle that if money was lent or supplied by one person to another to enable that other to pay off a debt to a creditor the lender was automatically subrogated to the rights of the creditor, and there was no stipulation that TOSG was required to expend the bond moneys in a manner which entitled the banks to stand in TOSG's shoes (see p 638 a to d f g and p 649 f g, post); *Wylie v Carlyon* [1922] 1 Ch 51 and *Paul v Speirway Ltd (in liq)* [1976] 2 All ER 587 applied; *Brocklesby v Temperance Permanent Building Society* [1895] AC 173 explained.

(2) The effect of the bonds and counter-indemnities given by the banks was (i) that a debt due to the banks, provable in the liquidation of C Ltd, arose as soon as TOSG called in and was paid the bond moneys, and (ii) that, although TOSG was under no contractual obligation to the banks regarding the way in which it spent the bond moneys, nevertheless TOSG was required to refund to the banks any bond moneys which were not expended, thereby reducing pro tanto C Ltd's liability under the counter-indemnities. Furthermore, the effect of the payments by TOSG to customers who were owed money by C Ltd was that the customers' rights to prove in the liquidation of C Ltd were limited to the balance, if any, of their debts still outstanding after the payments made to them by TOSG, and the effect of the assignments to the agency was that the agency was in no better position to prove in the liquidation than the customers or TOSG would have been. In those circumstances it followed that—

(a) (per Oliver LJ) the rule against double proof in a liquidation did apply. The test of whether the rule against double proof applied was whether the two competing claims were in substance claims for payment of the same debt twice over, and, furthermore, that was to be determined at the time of payment of the dividend, at which point the question to be asked was whether two dividends were being sought in the winding up for a liability which the debtor would discharge by one payment if it were solvent. Applying that test, if C Ltd had become solvent after the calling in of the bond moneys and had used its own money to discharge the debts due to its customers, then because the bond moneys would have remained unused and C Ltd would have been required to return them to the banks it would at the same time have discharged its liability to the banks and would thus have only made one payment in discharging both liabilities. Furthermore (Kerr LJ concurring), when the rule against double proof was applied the banks had the better right of proof over the agency because, by analogy with the position of a surety, the banks' position vis-à-vis the customers of C Ltd (and therefore the agency as the assignee of the customers) was akin to that of a surety who had guaranteed a fluctuating account (ie the amount owed by C Ltd to its customers) up to a specified limit and who, if he paid up to that limit, was entitled to that extent to stand in the shoes of the creditor (ie C Ltd's customers) and to prove in priority to him. Moreover, on broad equitable principles the banks had the better right of proof, since they were out of pocket to the full nominal amount of their claims whereas the customers (and therefore the agency) were out of pocket to less than their full nominal claims by reason of having received the banks' money (see p 636 a to j, p 637 e to j, p 640 f, p 641 d j to p 642 a, p 643 c to e h j, p 644 f to j, p 648 d e j, p 650 e j, p 651 e g h and p 652 h j, post); *Ex p Rushforth* (1805) 10 Ves 409, *Hobson v Bass* (1871) LR 6 Ch App 792, dictum of Mellish LJ in *Re Oriental Commercial Bank, ex p European Bank* (1871) LR 7 Ch App at 102 and *Gray v Seckham* (1872) LR 7 Ch App 680 applied; *Ellis v Emmanuel* [1874–80] All ER 1081 considered; *The Liverpool (No 2)* [1960] 3 All ER 307 distinguished;

(b) (per Slade LJ) having regard to the particular facts and the substance of the relevant liability and applying the principle that there could only be one dividend for what was in substance the same debt even though there may have been two contracts, the rule against double proof in a liquidation did apply, because if TOSG had itself taken *a* assignments from C Ltd's customers and then sought to prove for the £1·268m it would in substance have been proving for the same debt as the banks. Furthermore (Kerr LJ concurring), applying the rule against double proof, the banks had the better right of proof because the relevant comparison was not between the respective rights of proof of the banks and C Ltd's customers but between the respective rights of proof of the banks and TOSG, and it could not reasonably be inferred that the parties intended at the time *b* the bonding arrangements were made that TOSG would have the right to expend the bond moneys by purchasing assignments of debts from C Ltd's customers which would take priority over, and destroy, the banks' right to prove for the bond moneys in the liquidation of C Ltd, since such an inference was inconsistent with the nature of the bonding arrangements and produced an inequitable result (see p 649 *j*, p 650 *e f*, p 651 *d*, p 653 *b c e* to *j*, p 654 *d e*, p 655 *d* to *f h* to p 656 *c g h*, post); dictum of Mellish LJ in *Re* *c* *Oriental Commercial Bank, ex p European Bank* (1871) LR 7 Ch App at 102 applied;

(c) (per Kerr LJ) the rule against double proof did not apply because the common intention of the parties concerned in setting up the bonding scheme was that the banks were to be able to prove to the full extent of the bond moneys paid over while each customer was to be able to prove only for the balance of his debt still outstanding after the bond moneys had been paid out, and therefore there was no basis for the application *d* of the rule. However, if, the rule did apply then the banks had the better right of proof (see p 645 *h j*, p 647 *d* to *f*, p 648 *j* to 649 *b* and p 651 *a*, post).

(3) Accordingly, the banks had the right to prove in the liquidation of C Ltd for the £1·268m to the exclusion of the agency. The banks' appeal would therefore be allowed (see p 645 *b*, p 650 *g h*, p 651 *a c* and p 656 *h*, post).

Per Oliver LJ. Where money is lent or supplied by one person to another to enable *e* that other to pay off a debt to a creditor the lender has a right to be subrogated to the rights of the creditor only if there is an agreement between the supplier of the money and the payer of the debt that the money is to be used for that purpose or, on equitable principles, if the supplier of the money is deprived of his right of recovery, e g because of the incapacity of the person to whom the money was lent (see p 638 *b c e*, post).

f

Notes

For the rule against double proofs and its application to sureties, see 3 Halsbury's Laws (4th edn) paras 712, 728, and for cases on proofs by sureties against a bankrupt principal debtor, see 4 Digest (Reissue) 303–306, 2691–2720.

Cases referred to in judgments

Birkley v Presgrave (1801) 1 East 220, 102 ER 86.
Brocklesby v Temperance Permanent Building Society [1895] AC 173, HL.
Deering v Bank of Ireland (1886) 12 App Cas 20, HL; *rvsg sub nom Re Killen, a bankrupt* (1885) 15 LR Ir 388, CA Ir.
Dering v Earl of Winchelsea (1787) 1 Cox Eq Cas 318, 29 ER 1184, [1775–1802] All ER *h* Rep 140.
Ellis v Emmanuel (1876) 1 Ex D 157, [1874–80] All ER Rep 1081, CA.
Fenton, Re, ex p Fenton Textile Association Ltd [1931] 1 Ch 85, [1930] All ER Rep 15, CA.
Gray v Seckham (1872) LR 7 Ch App 680, LJJ.
Hobson v Bass (1871) LR 6 Ch App 792, LC.
Hoey, Re, ex p Hoey (1918) 88 LJKB 273, DC.
Liverpool, The, (No 2) [1960] 3 All ER 307, [1963] P 64, [1960] 3 WLR 597, CA; *rsvg* *j* [1960] 1 All ER 465, [1963] P 64, [1960] 2 WLR 541.
Melton, Re, Milk v Towers [1918] 1 Ch 37, [1916–17] All ER Rep 672, CA.
Midland Banking Co v Chambers (1869) LR 4 Ch App 398, LJJ.
Moss, Re, ex p Hallet [1905] 2 KB 307, [1904–7] All ER Rep 713, DC.
Oriental Commercial Bank, Re, ex p European Bank (1871) LR 7 Ch App 99, LJJ.

Paul v Speirway Ltd (in liq) [1976] 2 All ER 587, [1976] Ch 220, [1976] 2 WLR 715.
Rushforth, Ex p (1805) 10 Ves 409, 32 ER 903.
Sass, Re, ex p National Provincial Bank of England [1896] 2 QB 12.
Wylie v Carlyon [1922] 1 Ch 51.

Cases also cited

Daunt, Re, ex p Joint Discount Co (1871) LR 6 Ch App 455, LJJ.
Liggett (B) (Liverpool) Ltd v Barclays Bank Ltd [1928] 1 KB 48, [1927] All ER Rep 451.
Orakpo v Manson Investments Ltd [1977] 3 All ER 1, [1978] AC 95, HL.
Rees, Re, ex p National Provincial Bank of England (1881) 17 Ch D 98, CA.
Wheeldon v Burrows (1879) 12 Ch D 31, [1874–80] All ER Rep 669, CA.

Appeal

The plaintiffs, Barclays Bank Ltd, Lloyds Bank Ltd, National Westminster Bank Ltd and Wintrust Securities Ltd (the banks), appealed against so much of the judgment of Nourse J given on 27 February 1981 and the order made on 26 June 1981 as dismissed the bank's action against the first defendant, TOSG Trust Fund Ltd (TOSG), the twelfth defendant, Air Travel Reserve Fund Agency (the agency), and the thirteenth defendant, Clarksons Holidays Ltd (Clarksons), in which they sought, inter alia, a declaration against those defendants that the banks were entitled to prove in the liquidation of Clarksons to the exclusion of the agency in respect of all bond moneys expended by TOSG in paying creditors of Clarksons, and declared on the agency's counterclaim that the joint liquidators of Clarksons were entitled and bound to admit in full the proof of debt lodged with them by the agency. The facts are set out in the judgment of Oliver LJ.

Peter Millett QC and *J B W McDonnell* for the banks.
William Stubbs QC and *Leslie Kosmin* for TOSG and the agency.
David Oliver for the liquidators of Clarksons.

Cur adv vult

12 July. The following judgments were delivered.

OLIVER LJ. This is an appeal by the plaintiffs against an order of Nourse J made on 26 June 1981 dismissing their action against the first, twelfth and thirteenth defendants, the respondents to this appeal, and declaring on the twelfth defendant's counterclaim that the joint liquidators of the thirteenth defendant, Clarksons Holidays Ltd, were entitled and bound to admit in full the proof of debt lodged with them by the twelfth defendant.

The appeal raises an interesting and unusual question with regard to the applicability and the manner of application of what is known as the rule against double proof in the liquidation of an insolvent estate. The facts are fully set out in the careful judgment of the judge and need only to be summarised here. The thirteenth defendant, to which I will refer as 'Clarksons', was a wholly-owned subsidiary of Court Line Ltd, which, together with its constituent companies, collapsed during the height of the holiday season of the year 1974. Clarksons was one of Court Line's more prominent tour-operating subsidiaries and was at the material time among the market leaders in the package holiday field. For some years prior to the collapse, anxiety had been expressed among tour operators about the effect on the public image of the industry of the failure of operators to provide holidays for which members of the public had made bookings and paid in advance, and in 1969 a group of the more prominent operators (including Clarksons) formed what was known as the Tour Operators Study Group to consider problems confronting the industry, one of which was the absence at that time of any central organisation which could provide guarantees against failure or cessation of business of tour operators. As a result of that group's deliberations, a company limited by guarantee was formed in 1970 and that is the first defendant, TOSG Trust Fund Ltd, to which I will refer as 'TOSG'. The purpose of this company was to be the recipient of moneys contemplated as becoming payable under bonds or similar provision made by the members in the event of a member becoming unable to fulfil its obligations to its customers and to dispense those moneys in such way as might be most expedient to meet the emergency thus created. The principal object of TOSG in cl 3(A) of its memorandum of association was as follows:

'To manage, utilise, employ and expend funds and moneys paid and/or to be paid to the Company under or by virtue of Bonds, Letters of Credit, Policies of Insurance or similar arrangements obtained by members of the Tour Operators Study Group and issued in favour of the Company each being in respect of a Tour Operator Study Group member and/or its tour operator subsidiaries ("the member Group") or otherwise paid to the Company by such members, in generally alleviating the consequences to such member Group's customers of the business failure of the Tour Operators Study Group member or any other member Group Company in respect of whom such funds or moneys are received by the Company and in particular (but without prejudice to the generality of the foregoing) in making arrangements to procure the expeditious return by an appropriate means of transport to their departure point from the United Kingdom or Ireland of persons stranded abroad as a result of such member Group's business failure, in procuring that persons in the course of holidays abroad at the date of such member Group's business failure are enabled to complete their holidays in suitable accommodation and to return to their departure point from the United Kingdom or Ireland by an appropriate means of transport, in making all necessary travel and accommodation arrangements for persons who have purchased from such member Group, and paid in full, for holidays abroad which, as at the date of the member Group's business failure, had not been commenced and in making such payments as the Company may in its absolute discretion think fit to persons who had paid deposits to such member Group in respect of future holidays abroad and who (being customers of the member Group) otherwise suffer financial loss by reason of the member Group's business failure.'

The members of the study group then established a bonding scheme under which they mutually agreed to provide bonds in favour of TOSG in a form acceptable to that company and they entered into an agreement with TOSG regulating the manner in which TOSG could call up the bonds. The bonds were renewed annually and their amount was to be reviewed in each year but in fact remained from 1971 onwards at a figure equivalent to 5% of the relevant tour operator's turnover for the previous year, that figure being assumed (erroneously as it turned out) to be adequate to cover any failure on the worst possible basis.

Pursuant to these arrangements Clarksons, in October 1973, arranged for bonds to a total value of £2·226m to be issued by five banks, the four appellants and Williams & Glyn's Bank Ltd, which was the plaintiff in a separate action heard at the same time as the action in which this appeal arises.

Those bonds were for the following amounts:

Williams & Glyn's Bank	£873,000
Lloyds Bank	£93,000
Wintrust Securities	£260,000
National Westminster Bank	£500,000
Barclays Bank	£500,000

They were all in the same form, were issued to TOSG and provided that the bank concerned undertook to pay the specified sum but subject to a condition that the bond should be void unless during the period of 12 calendar months commencing on 1 October 1973 any one or more of six specified events should occur. I need not enumerate those in detail. They included the event of TOSG notifying the issuing bank that any company in the Clarkson group could not carry out its obligations, the presentation of a winding-up petition and cessation of payment of debts.

I ought, however, to read the final provision of the document, which is in these terms:

'And in consideration of the issue of this Bond the Fund hereby covenants with the Obligor that upon payment of the said sum of £   specified above by the Obligor to the Fund the Fund will undertake in writing with the Obligor that the Fund will repay to the Obligor on demand such part of the said sum as shall not be expended or required by the Fund in the performance and execution of its rights, duties, powers and discretions as set out in the Fund's Memorandum and Articles of Association, and that such Memorandum and Articles will not be altered during the currency of this Bond without the prior written consent of the Obligor (which shall not be unreasonably withheld) first obtained.'

At the same time each of the issuing banks obtained from Clarksons a counter-indemnity. The form of each indemnity was that normally used by the bank concerned. They are not identical and their precise terms do not matter, for it is not in issue that they created an obligation on Clarksons, in the event of the bond being called up, to indemnify the bank against any loss which it might sustain as a result of having executed the bond.

In August 1974 it became plain that the Court Line Group in general and Clarksons in particular were in such severe difficulties that operations could not continue, and on 15 August the Civil Aviation Authority withdrew Clarksons' civil aviation licence. At the same time Clarksons notified TOSG that it had ceased to trade and could no longer carry out its obligations to its customers. On the following day TOSG notified the banks in writing of the fulfilment of the pre-condition to the operation of the bond and called up the bond moneys immediately. These sums were paid to TOSG and Clarksons were notified by the paying banks. On the same day, 16 August, Clarksons presented its own petition for compulsory winding up and on 21 August Clarksons passed a special resolution to wind up voluntarily.

There then followed a hastily mounted rescue operation, the purpose of which was to enable those customers of Clarksons who were already abroad on holiday to complete their holidays and return to the United Kingdom, an operation which involved, of course, payment for hotel bills and for arrangements with air carriers. In this connection TOSG expended in round terms a sum of £956,000, as to which no question arises on this appeal. The question with which the court is now concerned related to the banks' share of a balance of some £1·268m which remained in TOSG's hands and which was ultimately disbursed by TOSG in paying in full, so far as it would go, customers of Clarksons who had paid for holidays but had never had them.

TOSG had, under its memorandum of association, a complete discretion as to the manner in which it set about alleviating the losses of the holidaymakers, and clearly one approach, but by no means the only one, would have been simply to distribute the funds in its hands among all claimants pro rata to their claims, leaving them to prove for any balance unpaid in the liquidation. There were, however, a number of complications and the final determination and settlement of claims in this way might have taken a considerable time. In particular, there were a number of test cases pending, in cases where moneys had been paid to travel agents by customers and were still held by the agents at the time of the collapse, to determine whether the customer was entitled to a refund from the agent or whether the agent was accountable to the liquidator for the moneys held.

In the mean time, there had been a major development in the political scene, for the collapse had caused a major parliamentary stir and the government of the day was under pressure, and indeed was, I think, anxious, to make some permanent provision for safeguarding both the general public in the future and the victims of this particular disaster. Thus in 1975 there was passed the Air Travel Reserve Fund Act 1975 which brought into being an air travel reserve fund, financed initially by government loan but ultimately by contributions from the industry, for the purpose of compensating persons who had lost their holidays as a result of the collapse of tour operators during 1974 and to provide against similar events in the future. The twelfth defendant (to which I will refer as 'the agency') was established to manage and administer the fund.

It will be convenient here to summarise the relevant provisions of the 1975 Act and the regulations made under it. Section 2(1) states the general application of the fund, which is to be applied in making payments to or for the benefit of customers of air travel organisers in respect of losses or liabilities incurred by them in connection with travel contracts. Subsection (3) restricts the losses and liabilities payable under sub-s (1) to those incurred in consequence of the inability of the air travel organiser to meet his commitments under contracts the time for performance of which fell after 1 April 1974. Subsection (6) deals with the position where there is a bonding scheme such as the present by providing that for the purposes of sub-s (3) a loss or liability shall be treated as having been incurred in consequence of the organiser's inability to meet his contractual commitments if, since the booking was made, the bond has become payable. Subsection (7) is important. That provides that where money is available under such a bond (a) no payment shall be made out of the fund until all the money so available has been paid to or for the benefit of the customers in question or any class or description of those customers, and (b) sub-s (1) shall not apply to any loss or liability so far as it has been reimbursed from such bond moneys. Section 3 empowers the Secretary of State to make rules as to the application of the fund (known as 'benefit rules') and those were in fact made in July 1975.

Rule 3(1) and (2) limits the amount of any payment, in effect, to the amount actually paid by the customer, but r 3(7) provides that, where a customer is eligible for a payment from the fund, the agency shall pay him the total amount permissible under the rules. Rule 3(6) is in the following terms:

'Where a customer of an air travel organiser has received any sum in liquidation or bankruptcy proceedings brought against the air travel organiser, being a sum paid in respect of losses or liabilities to which section 2(1) of the Act applies, that sum shall be deducted from any payment out of the Fund which would otherwise have been made to him in accordance with these Rules.'

Finally, r 4 deals with the conditions to be satisfied before payments are made (including, e g, method of submission and establishment of claims) and r 4(4) provides that the agency may, before making a payment, require the customer to assign to the agency any rights which he may have against the air travel organiser, whether in liquidation or bankruptcy or otherwise.

Well before the 1975 Act was passed negotiations had been in train between TOSG and the Department of Trade with a view to agreeing arrangements under which payments to holidaymakers could be expedited, it having been apparent from the inception that the bond moneys were not going to be sufficient to meet all claims in full and that there would be a substantial balance for which the air travel reserve fund would become responsible when the 1975 Act came into force and the regulations made under it were promulgated. Those negotiations contemplated that, rather than waiting for the complete ascertainment and settlement of all claims, TOSG would settled in full as many undisputed claims as could be discharged out of its available resources, leaving the agency to settle the balance. The original suggestion was that TOSG should take assignments of their claims in the liquidation from those customers whose debts were than paid in full, but it was ultimately considered more convenient that all outstanding claims should be dealt with by the agency so that TOSG could conclude entirely its administration of the bond moneys. Accordingly, it was agreed in principle that as each claim was paid by TOSG the customer concerned should be required to execute an assignment of his rights in favour of the agency. This was intended at first to be subject to the agreement of the banks who had put up the bond moneys, but in fact the only bank which was informed of the proposal was Lloyds, who registered a strong objection. Despite this, however, when the 1975 Act received the royal assent and the agency was formed, an agreement along these lines was entered into between TOSG and the agency and it is this that gave rise to the present proceedings. In the result TOSG settled in full claims of customers to

the extent of the moneys in its hands, each cheque sent out being conditional on the
signature and return by the recipient of an assignment of his claims in the liquidation to
the agency. The banks had, at any early stage, proved for the full sum of £2·226m due
to them under Clarksons' counter-indemnity when the bonds were issued and the agency
now proved not only for the sums which it had disbursed in paying out claims of
customers other than those paid out by TOSG but also in respect of the rights assigned by
those customers who had been paid by TOSG.

There is no dispute that the banks are entitled to prove in the liquidation of Clarksons
for that part of the sums paid by them under the bonds which is represented by the
payments made for repatriating customers (£956,000) but it is the liquidators' contention
that the balance of £1·268m paid out to customers and thus reflected in the agency's
proof is subject to the rule against double proof and that one or other of the two sets of
proofs must be reduced accordingly.

At the trial before Nourse J it was common ground that the rule against double proof
applied to the situation with which the court was confronted and the contest was simply
one between the banks on the one hand and TOSG and the agency on the other as to who
had the better right, in these circumstances, to prove for the moneys which had in fact
been applied in or towards discharging the customers' claims. That is, perhaps, a
simplification, because there were other issues of ultra vires and misfeasance which fell
to be decided but are not in issue on the present appeal. So far as this court is concerned,
there is no dispute either that it was intra vires TOSG to deal with the bond moneys in
the way in which it did deal with them (including the procuring of assignments by
customers to the agency) or that the agency was acting intra vires in arranging for and
taking those assignments. There has, however, in this court been raised a further issue
not argued in the court below, because shortly before the hearing of the appeal began the
banks amended their notice of appeal in order to raise the question whether the rule
against double proof applied at all. An application to strike that amendment out was
refused by this court (although on terms as to costs) because, although the point was a
new one, we took the view that, assuming it to be good, it would be inappropriate that
this court should be put in the position, because of a concession in the court below, of
deciding the appeal on a basis which, on that hypothesis, would be wholly wrong in law.
It has thus been argued before us and should logically be dealt with first. It is put by
counsel for the banks in two ways. First, he submits that the correct time for ascertaining
whether the rule is to apply is at the date of the liquidation. This case is not an orthodox
case of principal and surety. It is a case in which there were created as a matter of fact
two quite distinct contracts with the debtor which had no necessary connection at all. As
soon as the collapse occurred the condition of the bonds was fulfilled and the moneys
became payable to TOSG. At that moment Clarksons became subject to a liability under
the counter-indemnity which was quite independent of its liability to its customers. True
the bond moneys or part of them might, in due course, if TOSG chose, be applied in
paying to the customers what was due to them from Clarksons, but they might not. The
whole fund might have to be expended, for instance, in a repatriation exercise. Thus, it
is argued, the two liabilities were quite independent at the inception, and each creditor,
be he bank or customer, can prove for his own debt. The mere fact that some part of the
moneys provided by the banks may subsequently have been applied in paying out the
customer liabilities cannot make the case one of double proof when it was not originally
so. Thus, counsel for the banks submits, the liquidators should entertain proofs both
from the banks and from the agency, even though that will, of course, be highly
prejudicial to the other unsecured creditors.

His alternative formulation results in the banks alone being able to prove because, it is
said, the agency has, so far as its proof rests on the assignments from customers paid out
by TOSG, nothing for which it can prove. That is said to be so for one of two reasons.
First, it is said that immediately the banks' moneys were paid to the customers, the banks
stood, by subrogation, in the shoes of the customers whose debts had been paid so that,
the customers' rights having, eo instanti, passed to the banks, there was nothing on which
the assignments could operate. The second way of putting it is slightly different but the

result is the same. It is said that for TOSG to arrange with the customers to keep the customers' debts alive notwithstanding the receipt by them of an equivalent sum of money was, and was known to the agency to be, contrary to an implied term to be deduced from the bonds and the counter-indemnities taken in conjunction.

I can deal with these submissions quite shortly, for, speaking for myself, I am unable to accept any of them. Counsel for the banks first way of putting his case is, in my judgment, based on two fundamentally wrong assumptions. In the first place, I am unable to accept that the proper time for determining whether or not the rule against double proof is to apply is the date of the liquidation. I accept the submission of counsel for TOSG and the agency that the rule ought more properly to be styled the rule against double dividends, for its object is to absolve the liquidator from paying out two dividends on what is essentially the same debt. That is a matter which very frequently, for instance in the case of principal and surety, cannot be determined until a payment to the creditor is made. No doubt it can be predicted at the commencement of the liquidation that a case for the application of the rule may arise or that it can never arise, but it may well be impossible to determine at that stage whether it will in fact.

Second, it is, as I think, a fallacy to argue, and this is really the basis of the argument of counsel for the banks, that, because overlapping liabilities result from separate and independent contracts with the debtor, that, by itself, is determinative of whether the rule can apply. The test is in my judgment a much broader one which transcends a close jurisprudential analysis of the persons by and to whom the duties are owed. It is simply whether the two competing claims are, in *substance*, claims for payment of the same debt twice over. It will be necessary to look more closely at the substance of the transactions which have given rise to the problems in the context of which claimant has the better right, but for the moment I accept the broad general proposition of counsel for TOSG and the agency that the rule against double proof in respect of two liabilities of an insolvent debtor is going to apply wherever the existence of one liability is dependent on and referable only to the liability to the other and where to allow both liabilities to rank independently for dividend would produce injustice to the other unsecured creditors.

The rule has nothing to say on the question of which of two proving creditors has the better right to claim a dividend in respect of his debt. It bears merely on the question whether both are to be admitted for dividend and stems from the fundamental rule of all insolvency administration that, subject to certain statutory priorities, the debtor's available assets are to be applied pari passu in discharge of the debtor's liabilities. One way of testing the matter is to ask, in relation to any liability for which proof has been lodged, whether it arises as a result of a payment made in discharge or partial discharge of another liability for which a proof has also been lodged. If the answer to that is affirmative, then it is clear that a distortion of the pari passu principle would occur if both proofs are admitted in full. A simpler test, perhaps, is to postulate the question: what would the position be as regards the payment of the liabilities in respect of which proofs have been lodged if the debtor were now solvent?

Counsel for the liquidator gives by way of illustration what I find a compelling example. Suppose that the insolvent debtor has two creditors, one for £40,000 and one for £20,000, the liability to the latter being guaranteed by a third party to the extent of £10,000. The surety is called on to pay and pays, thus giving rise to a liability in the debtor to indemnify him. Now if the debtor were in fact solvent the amount required to be found to satisfy all his liabilities would be £60,000; but, if the surety is admitted to prove for £10,000 alongside the principal creditor's proof for £20,000, the total liabilities in the insolvency will be £70,000. Thus for the purposes of the liquidation the claims of creditors are computed at a figure in excess of the amount required to discharge them, to the prejudice of the remaining creditor for £40,000. The rule is designed to prevent this occurring. This method of testing the position emerges from the judgment of Mellish LJ in *Re Oriental Commercial Bank, ex p European Bank* (1871) LR 7 Ch App 99. There bills of exchange were accepted by the European Bank against an undertaking by the Oriental Bank to provide funds to meet them on maturity. They were then handed to the Oriental Bank as agent for the drawer and indorsed by them and discounted. Both banks became a   insolvent and the Agra Bank, the holder of the bill, in fact recovered the amount of the bills by proving in their respective liquidations. The European Bank then sought to lodge a proof in the insolvency of the Oriental Bank for, in effect, damages for breach of the undertaking by the latter to provide funds to meet the bills. In rejecting that proof Mellish LJ observed (at 102):

b   'It appears to me clearly that it is substantially the same debt: because if all parties had been solvent, whatever sums the *Oriental Commercial Bank* might have paid to the *Agra Bank*, although they would have paid it, no doubt, for the purpose of performing the contract they had entered into by their indorsement, yet, substantially, whatever sums they might have paid to the *Agra Bank* would have gone in reduction of the sum which the *Oriental Commercial Bank* had promised to pay to the *European Bank*. In that case the *Oriental Commercial Bank* could never have been called upon to pay these bills twice over. It would have made no difference

c   that they had entered into two contracts with two separate parties that they would pay the bills . . . It is clear that they would have performed both contracts by paying the bills once . . .'

The true principle, he observed at the end of his judgment (at 103), is 'that there is only to be one dividend in respect of what is in substance the same debt'.

d   Similar reasoning is to be found in the dissenting judgment of Porter MR in Ireland in *Re Killen, a bankrupt* (1885) 15 LR Ir 388 (subsequently approved by the House of Lords sub nom *Deering v Bank of Ireland* (1886) 12 App Cas 20), where the cumulative proofs of the claimant in respect of different obligations arising out the of the same transaction would have resulted in the amount claimed exceeding the amount of the principal debt.

Now, if, as in my judgment these cases show, the true rule is that there are not to be

e   two dividends in respect of what is in substance the same debt, I can see no logical justification for seeking to fix the position at the commencement of the insolvency. One has, as it seems to me, to look at the position at the point at which the dividend is actually about to be paid and to ask the question then whether two payments are being sought for a liability which, if the company were solvent, could be discharged as regards both claimants by one payment.

f   Tested in this way, the instant case is, in my judgment, one where the rule against double proof does apply and the concession made in the court below was, in my opinion, properly made. It is, of course, true that, if one goes back to the inception of the liquidation, there were two quite separate liabilities. Clarksons owed the holidaymakers the amount which they had paid for a consideration which had wholly failed. It was also liable to the banks for the loss sustained as a result of the calling up of the bonds, the

g   amount of which would depend on the extent to which the bond moneys would in fact be required to meet the holidaymakers' claims. If and so far as those claims were discharged from other sources, the bond moneys would not be required to meet them and, on the terms of the bonds, would fall to be refunded to the banks, thus reducing pro tanto the liability of Clarksons on the counter-indemnities. Thus if Clarksons became solvent in the course of the liquidation (if, for instance, inability to meet commitments

h   which resulted in the bonds being called up had been due merely to a temporary liquidity crisis) the discharge by Clarksons of the debts due to its customers would, as in the *Oriental Commercial Bank* case, at the same time discharge the liability to the banks, disregarding any interest and expense factors, since the bond moneys would then be refunded to them. Thus if bond moneys are in fact applied towards the discharge or partial discharge of the customers' debts the allowance of proofs of debt both for the

j   amount of bond moneys and for the full amount of the customers' debts necessarily involves the liabilities on which dividends are to be declared being computed at a figure in excess of the amount required to discharge those liabilities.

I turn, therefore, to the alternative submissions of counsel for the banks, the first of which is based on a right of subrogation which it is submitted arises from the fact that the debts due to the holidaymakers paid off by TOSG were in fact paid with moneys derived from the banks. It is said that *Brocklesby v Temperance Permanent Building Society*

[1895] AC 173 is authority for the proposition that, where A's money is used to pay B's debt, A is subrogated to the rights of the creditor. For my part, I am unable to deduce any such wide principle from that case, which appears to me to rest on a quite different principle, namely that, where a landowner puts another in possession of his title deeds with authority to raise money on them as his agent, he is not entitled to rely on limitations on the authority of the agent which are not brought to the notice of the lender. Indeed, *Wylie v Carlyon* [1922] 1 Ch 51 is, I think, a clear authority against the wide proposition that a right of subrogation stems from the mere fact that B's debt has been discharged with money in fact derived from A. One has to find, in the contract between the supplier of the money and the payer of the debt, some provision that the money is to be applied for that purpose. I can find nothing of this sort in the contract between the banks and TOSG. No doubt the payment of sums due to the holidaymakers was within TOSG's powers and no doubt this was known to the banks, but that is to say no more than that the banks paid the bond moneys to TOSG for whatever purpose TOSG might see fit to use them within its corporate powers, the only stipulation being that any moneys not so applied should be refunded. It was an out and out payment with, for relevant purposes, no reservations of any sort and was, in my judgment, no different in kind from the payment in *Paul v Speirway Ltd (in liq)* [1976] 2 All ER 587, [1976] Ch 220, save that here there was no obligation on TOSG to repay, other than in relation to moneys not required for its corporate purposes. When one comes to consider the position as between Clarksons and the banks, the case is, I think, a fortiori. Here there was an express right to indemnity giving a direct right of recovery to the banks. Leaving aside the insurance cases (which form a category of their own) and cases of express or implied contract, a right of subrogation arises on equitable principles where otherwise the payer might be deprived of any right of recovery, for instance where money has been lent to an infant and used to discharge debts incurred for necessaries or where money has been borrowed ultra vires or has been paid in discharge of a person's debts without his authority, and I am far from convinced, all other considerations apart, that the equitable principle applies where the payer has already a full and independent right of recovery against the debtor. But, whether that be so or not, I can see no such right in the present case, where TOSG was given an entirely free hand with the bond moneys. One can, perhaps, best test the matter in this way. Suppose that no counter-indemnity had been sought or given and disregard altogether Clarksons' insolvency. The banks undertake, for what they no doubt regard as an adequate consideration, to provide moneys to a third party in a certain event. If the event occurs and if some part of the moneys are applied in fact in paying debts of Clarksons, by what title could the banks claim, in effect, a recoupment for which they never stipulated as part of the original consideration? I can see none.

The alternative proposition of counsel for the banks is expressed thus. Where A provides money to B at C's request for the purpose, inter alia, of paying C's creditors and on terms that C will indemnify A, and B in fact applies the money for that purpose, B cannot keep the claims of C's creditors alive for his own benefit to the prejudice of A and C. He must either extinguish those claims or allow A to be subrogated to them. This is, however, a proposition which makes a number of assumptions and begs a number of questions; and, in the ultimate analysis, counsel for the banks was compelled to justify it by reference, not to any general principle of law, but to an implied term in the contract between A and B (the banks and TOSG) that B will do nothing to impede A's right of subrogation so far as the money is used to pay off debts. I find insuperable difficulties in this. In the first place, it assumes the right of subrogation, and for the reasons stated above, I can find none. But, second, I find it impossible to see any material from which such a term can be implied. There was no restriction at all on the use which TOSG might make of the bond moneys save those imposed by TOSG's own corporate constitution. It was certainly within TOSG's power, if it wished to, to buy up debts and apply any proceeds for its corporate purposes. Whence, then, is any such term to be implied? The banks' obligation was to pay in the stated events. TOSG's only express obligation was to repay anything not required for its corporate purposes; and there is simply no material a from which one can infer, as a matter of business efficacy, an undertaking that the corporate powers would only be used in a certain way or would not be used in a particular way.

In my judgment, therefore, the problem has to be approached, as it was by Nourse J in the court below, on the footing that, subject to the operation of the rule against double proof, the assignments to the agency were effective and that the question of which of the two claimants has the better right to prove has to be resolved by the application of
b equitable principles. Nourse J approached this problem in two quite distinct ways. He recognised that the situation with which the liquidators were faced was an unusual one both by reason of the arrangements made between Clarksons and the banks and TOSG, which does not fit precisely within the framework of any of the decided cases, and by reason of the unusual feature that arrangements were made for the express purpose of keeping the claims of creditors alive for the benefit of someone other than the payer after
c they had in fact received 100p in the the pound on the amounts of their respective claims. It was pointed out to him, however, that apart from a few authorities to which I shall have to refer briefly, all the learning on the subject of priority between rival claimants in respect of the same indebtedness is contained in a series of decisions governing the relationship of principal and surety, as, indeed, is not altogether surprising, for that is normally where the contest arises, and he therefore took those cases as
d governing by analogy the instant case. Quite apart from that, however, he approached the case on the basis of what he referred to as the 'broad equity', arrived at by a consideration of which claimant had the better claim having regard to the intentions of the parties as deducible from their contractual rights and duties and the purpose for which those rights and duties were acquired or assumed. Counsel for the banks attacks the judge's conclusion on both grounds. As to the former, he says that if (which he
e challenges) it is right to take the cases of principal and surety as analogous at all, the judge drew the wrong conclusion about the category into which, as a matter of analogy, the instant case fell. As to the latter, counsel for the banks says that there was no material on which the judge was entitled to arrive at the conclusion at which he did arrive, namely that the claim of the agency was to be preferred to that of the banks.

The instant case is not, of course, literally a case of suretyship, for that involves a
f contract between creditor and surety. Here there is, of course, no contract between banks and the holidaymakers or between TOSG and the holidaymakers. There are, however, obvious similarities. The liability of the banks was only to arise if Clarkson failed to fulfil its obligations to its customers; the funds provided by the banks were applicable in alleviating that failure; and the banks were, ultimately, to have recourse to Clarksons for what they had paid. The principal argument in the court below sought,
g however, to avoid this analogy and to apply, as a test of who had the prior right to prove, the question 'who is out of pocket?' That, in essence, rested on The Liverpool (No 2) [1960] 3 All ER 307, [1963] P 64. There are, in fact, a number of cases in which questions of priority have arisen in double proof situations not arising from the discharge by a surety of his obligations under a guarantee. Apart from The Liverpool (No 2), however, they are all cases where, in addition to the principal debt, it has been sought to prove an additional
h and subsidiary liability, either to the principal debtor himself or to a third party (whether or not a surety) to maintain the value of the security or to indemnify against the failure to maintain it (see Re Hoey, ex p Hoey (1918) 88 LJKB 273, Re Killen, a bankrupt (1885) 15 LR Ir 388, Re Moss, ex p Hallet [1905] 2 KB 307, [1904–7] All ER Rep 713). They are useful illustrations of the test previously propounded of whether the proof under consideration will have the effect of computing the amount of the liabilities in an
j insolvent estate beyond the figure which would be required to extinguish the liabilities if the debtor were solvent, but they are otherwise of little help with the problem raised by this appeal. The Liverpool (No 2), however, stands by itself and is prayed in aid by counsel for the banks as providing a guide in the circumstances of the instant case. There the tanker Liverpool, by negligent navigation, sank the coaster Ousel in the port of Liverpool. Liability was admitted, but the Liverpool obtained a decree limiting its liability under the Merchant Shipping Act 1894 and the question arose what claims could

be admitted to prove against the limitation fund. One of the claims against the Liverpool was a claim in tort by the Mersey Docks and Harbour Board for the cost of raising and moving the Ousel in accordance with their statutory duties. The board also had a statutory remedy for the expenses against the Ousel which they exerted to the limited extent permitted by the Merchant Shipping Acts. The Ousel in its proof against the limitation fund included the amount of the board's limited statutory claim against it (in respect of which it had not, at that time, made any payment) and the question before the court was whether this claim could stand having regard to the board's claim, which made no allowance for anything recoverable from this source. At first instance, Lord Merriman P, applying the analogy of the surety cases, regarded the Ousel as being a surety for part of a debt of ascertained amount and held that the board's claim must be pro tanto reduced (see [1960] 1 All ER 465, [1963] P 64). This was reversed on appeal. Harman LJ found the principal and debtor analogy of little help in a case where there was no principal debtor, but applied it to this extent, that the authorities quite clearly established that a surety who has not paid is not permitted to prove for his contingent debt in competition with the principal creditor (see Re Fenton, ex p Fenton Textile Association Ltd [1931] 1 Ch 85, [1930] All ER Rep 15). The salient feature of The Liverpool (No 2) was that the Ousel had not in fact paid anything. Harman LJ expressed it thus ([1960] 3 All ER 307 at 314, [1963] P 64 at 86):

'In our judgment the answer is that the board has priority because it is actually out of pocket by the whole of its claim, whilst the Ousel is not because she has not yet been obliged to pay.'

This, it is argued, is the closest analogy with the instant case. Here the customers have received 100p in the pound on their debts from TOSG using the bank's money. The agency paid nothing for the assignments to it. Thus, if one is to look for the person who is out of pocket, there can be only one answer. The banks having paid must have the prior right of proof.

This argument is perfectly intelligible, and indeed almost unanswerable if one regards the payment of those customers who were paid to TOSG as an entirely separate transaction isolated from any other arrangement made with the agency, but to my mind it ignores the reality. If one is to look for analogies, it is, I think, essential first to analyse what the total effect of the arrangements was and the reasoning behind them. All the cases stress that in relation to the rule against double proofs it is the substance and not the form that is to be regarded (see e g Re Melton, Milk v Towers [1918] 1 Ch 37 at 60, [1916–17] All ER Rep 672 at 683, Re Oriental Commercial Bank (1871) LR 7 Ch App 99). When regard is had to what actually happened in the instant case, it is, I think, entirely clear that the transaction by which TOSG paid a certain number of customers in full cannot be treated as a transaction on its own isolated from the payment by the agency of the claims of the remaining unpaid customers. The fact is that, if one looks at the reality of the position and asks, 'Who is out of pocket?', the answer is that both the banks and the agency are out of pocket and in that situation The Liverpool (No 2) provides no help, since it provides no guidance as to what would have happened if the Ousel had paid either the whole or a part of its liability and the court declined to express any opinion on whether in exerting its claim against the Ousel the board could be compelled to give credit for any part of the sums received as a result of its claims against the Liverpool.

That the reality is as I have described it seems to me inescapable. Under the Air Travel Reserve Fund Act 1975 and the benefit rules the agency was obliged to pay any balance due to customers after taking into account the bond moneys and anything received by way of dividend in the liquidation, but it could not pay anything at all until the bond moneys were exhausted. A year had already passed during which customers were out of their money and since there were still outstanding claims which were the subject of test actions a further lengthy period would have to elapse before anybody could receive anything unless arrangements could be made to expedite payment to those customers whose claims were beyond dispute. It was in these circumstances that TOSG and the

a agency came to the very sensible arrangement that the bond moneys should be expended in full in paying out customers so that the pre-condition for the agency's making payments was satisfied. This could have been done in several ways. TOSG could have made pro rata payments to customers, leaving it to them either to prove for the balance and to bring into account any dividends received when the agency came to make payments in pursuance of its statutory obligation or to assign such rights of proof as they had to the agency against payment to them of any balance not paid out of the bond
b moneys.

In the event, it was an accident of administrative convenience rather than anything else which dictated the manner in which the problem was in fact dealt with. There was no difference in kind between the customers paid by TOSG and those paid by the agency and the reality is that a single class of creditors was receiving payments on account of their debts from both TOSG and the agency, the latter's contribution in the case of those
c customers paid by TOSG being indirectly provided by the assumption by the agency of the full responsibility for paying the others.

It was against this background that the judge felt it appropriate to apply the analogy of the suretyship cases and, in my judgment, he was right to do so. The assignments were mere machinery and what fell to be regarded was in reality a partial payment by TOSG of the totality of the obligation owed by Clarksons to all its customers as a single
d class. The position therefore fell to be tested as between the banks on the one hand, whose money had provided the payments, and the customers as a whole on the other hand, for the assignments could not assign any greater rights than the customers themselves had at the moment when they were paid.

The principles which emerge from the suretyship cases have been helpfully summarised both in the judgment of Nourse J and in the skeleton arguments prepared by counsel for the guidance of this court. The starting position is that a creditor is entitled
e in an insolvency to prove for the whole sum due to him at the date of the liquidation or receiving order without any obligation to give credit for any sum which he has since received from a third party, unless and until he has received 100p in the pound on his debt. That entitlement, however, may fall to be modified by reason of the rule against double proof where the third party is himself a creditor in the insolvency for the sum
f which he has paid, as in the case of a surety. Whether it is or not depends on whether the payment entitles the payer to be subrogated, to the extent of his payment, to the creditor's right and it is in relation to this question that a number of clearly established rules are deducible from the surety cases.

The basic rule is that the proof of a surety cannot displace the proof of the principal creditor unless and until the surety has fully discharged all his liabilities to the creditor.
g A fortiori it cannot do so where no payment has been made and the liability to the surety remains contingent (Re Fenton [1931] 1 Ch 85, [1930] All ER Rep 15). So long as any liabilities of the surety are outstanding the creditor remains entitled to prove for the full amount of the debt due to him at the date of commencement of the winding up or the receiving order and the surety's proof is excluded.

It is here that there has grown up a distinction, which depends on the construction of
h the contract of suretyship and which is not altogether easy to understand, between cases where the surety guarantees part of an ascertained debt and cases where he is held to have guaranteed the whole debt but subject to a limitation of his liability to less amount than the whole. In the former case, the payment of the amount guaranteed entitles the surety to stand, pro tanto, in the creditor's shoes in the insolvency, since he has discharged the whole of his liability to the creditor. In the latter case, so long as any part of the whole
j debt remains outstanding, the surety, although he has paid up to the limit of his financial liability, is treated as not having discharged his liability to the creditor, presumably on the footing that there nevertheless remains an outstanding obligation on him to see that the whole debt is paid. The distinction may seem over-subtle, but it is clearly established by authority: see the judgment of Blackburn J in Ellis v Emmanuel (1876) 1 Ex D 157, [1874–80] All ER Rep 1081, where the authorities are reviewed.

This rule is, however, subject to a qualification. Where the guarantee is of the whole of a fluctuating balance (eg as in the case of a guarantee of the debtor's current account with a bank) with a limit on the liability of the surety, such a guarantee is to be construed as a guarantee of part only of the debt and the surety paying up to the limit of his liability will be entitled to that extent to stand in the creditor's shoes and prove in priority to him (see *Ex p Rushforth* (1805) 10 Ves 409, 32 ER 903, *Gray v Seckham* (1872) LR 7 Ch App 680). The right of the surety in these circumstances to prove in priority to the principal creditor can, however (as it normally is in bank guarantees), be excluded by the express terms of the contract of guarantee. A provision that the guarantee is to be in addition and without prejudice to any other securities held from or on account of the debtor and that it is to be a continuing security notwithstanding any settlement of account is probably sufficient for this purpose (see *Re Sass, ex p National Provincial Bank of England* [1896] 2 QB 12) but at least there must be some express clause in the contract which can fairly be construed as a waiver by the surety of his rights in favour of the principal creditor (contrast *Hobson v Bass* (1871) LR 6 Ch App 792 with *Midland Banking Co v Chambers* (1869) LR 4 Ch App 398). Such a provision will not readily be inferred merely from the form which the transaction takes (see *Gray v Seckham*).

Those being the principles, how are they to be applied by analogy to the instant case? Nourse J regarded the case as one where the proper analogy was that of a guarantor who guarantees the whole of a debt of fixed amount with a limitation on the amount of his liability, so that even after payment of the whole of the surety's liability the creditor remains entitled to prove for the whole sum. The reasoning behind this conclusion was that the object of TOSG was to alleviate the consequences of Clarksons' business failure. TOSG had a discretion about how this was to be done, but one way of carrying out the object was to recoup any shortfall remaining after the customers had received all available dividends in Clarksons' liquidation. Thus, it was argued, since the obligation of the banks was to be answerable for any balance remaining after all moneys available from other sources had been applied in reduction of the debt, the guarantee was a guarantee of the whole debt, subject only to a limitation on the amount which the banks were to pay. This feature of the relationship appears to have convinced the judge that the case of the guarantor of the whole of a fluctuating balance with a limitation on the amount of liability (as in *Hobson v Bass*) was not to be applied and as I understand his reasoning it was this.

The reason why that case is treated differently from the case of the debt of fixed amount is that it is considered inequitable in the creditor, who is at liberty to increase the balance or not, to increase it at the expense of the surety (see *Ellis v Emmanuel* (1876) 1 Ex D 157 at 163–164, [1874–80] All ER Rep 1081 at 1083). Since, the argument runs, it was contemplated that Clarksons would be entitled to take on liabilities to customers without limitation and since in the event of Clarksons' insolvency TOSG *could* apply the bond moneys in discharging any balance remaining after the disappointed customers had received their dividends in the liquidation, there was in fact nothing inequitable in such indebtedness being increased and accordingly the case is to be treated in the same way as the guarantee of the whole of a debt of ascertained amount.

With respect to the judge and to counsel for TOSG and the agency, from whom the argument originated, I find an element of circularity in this reasoning, which really begs the question of priority by starting from an assumption that it must be decided in favour of the customers. Of course, factually and dependent on the order in which events take place, any surety may find himself paying, up to the amount of this liability, any balance remaining due to the creditor after he has received a dividend on the whole of his debt in the insolvency of the principal debtor. But the mere fact that the creditor may have received a dividend on the whole is not determinative at all of how that dividend falls to be treated when it comes to settling the accounts between the creditor and the surety who, ex hypothesi, has not been able to prove because he has not paid (see, for instance, *Gray v Seckham*, where the creditor had received his dividend before calling up the guarantees, and *Hobson v Bass*, where the sureties had paid but had not themselves proved in the bankruptcy).

It is, of course, true that in the instant case the moneys paid by the banks were paid, not to the creditors in the first instance, but to a third party, TOSG, against whom there would be no recourse for dividends received by the customers, but by the same token, the moneys having actually been paid by the banks, they would themselves have a right of proof under their counter-indemnity in the insolvency for the full amount paid, subject only to reduction of that amount by reason of the rule against double proof. As a practical matter, of course, the liquidator, who was faced with proofs both by the banks and by the customers, and knowing that some part of the bond moneys was bound to be paid in discharge of the indebtedness to the customers, would be bound to defer paying dividends on either until the question of double proof had been cleared up and it had been determined who had the better right to prove. Thus, to say that the bond moneys could be used by TOSG in discharging what was due to the customers after they had proved and received dividends in the liquidation begs the question of the extent to which their proofs should be allowed. It cannot itself be prayed in aid as solving the question. Nor can I, for my part, follow why the contemplation that Clarksons should be entitled to incur obligations without limit should take the case out of the ordinary rule. If the arrangements made in this case are to be treated, as I think they are, as analogous to a guarantee by the banks of Clarksons' liabilities to its customers, they appear to me clearly to be analogous to a guarantee of a balance which is going to fluctuate from time to time but subject to a limit on the surety's liability, and exactly the same considerations as apply in that case to prevent the surety's right of proof being prejudiced by the debtor's increasing his indebtedness appear to me to apply here. If that is right, then the question is whether there can be spelt out of the arrangement some express or implied term to the effect that, in the event of the debtor's insolvency, the banks would not prove for the amount which they had paid under their bonds until the customers had been paid in full. Certainly there is no express term to that effect and, speaking for myself, I am unable to find in the documents or the circumstances in which the bonds were given any such implied term. So far as the banks were concerned, their contract with Clarksons was that they would put up the bond moneys in consideration of the agreed fee and of a right of counter-indemnity which clearly contemplated a proof of debt for the moneys paid in the only likely event in which they would become payable. There is simply no room for any such implication here.

So far as TOSG was concerned, the banks simply entered into an obligation to pay over moneys for TOSG's complete disposition in the stated events. In its defence the agency plead an implied term arising under the bonds that TOSG should be entitled to utilise the bond moneys in any transaction authorised by its constitution and that in such event the banks 'would do nothing to hinder any such transaction or to prevent any such transaction from being effectual'. Speaking for myself I find it impossible to see from what material it is sought to make this implication, but in any event, as was pointed out in the course of the argument, such a term does not assist in the present context. It is said that it was within TOSG's powers to procure assignments to the agency of such rights of proof as the customers had but nothing done by the banks in the least interfered with that. To assist the agency it would, I think, be necessary to imply a term that the banks would not, by proving in the liquidation of Clarksons, do anything which might impede in any way the maximum alleviation possible of the customers' losses. By any ordinary test for the implication of contractual terms, this is fanciful.

If, therefore, the analogy of the surety cases is treated as conclusive of the present case, then, in my judgment, the banks are in the position of the surety under the ordinary form of guarantee of a fluctuating account with a limit on the guarantor's liability and no term excluding the equity which ordinarily arises from that relationship. It would follow that as between the banks and the customers, the banks have the prior right of proof and that, that right must prevail against the agency, which cannot be in any better position than its assignors.

There remains, however, the judge's primary ground of decision. He pointed out that a decision of the case did not necessarily rest on which of two categories of suretyship case bore the closer affinity to it. The determinative factor was the application of equitable principles as applied to a true construction of the parties' intentions. He concluded:

'But in the end I do not need to rely on the analogy at all. I agree with [counsel for TOSG and the agency] that the decisive feature of the present case is the trust fund's power to recoup to the customers any shortfall remaining after they had received all available dividends in Clarksons' liquidation. Once you get to that stage it is apparent that it would indeed be most inequitable for the banks to claim, as against the customers, a rateable proportion of any dividends receivable or received by them. This is not a narrow equity but a broad one. And it is a surer basis for decision than any mere analogy.'

It will be observed that in arriving at the broad equity the judge is here relying on precisely the same argument as that which led him to assimilate the banks' position to that of guarantors of the whole of an ascertained indebtedness. In doing so, it seems that he was much influenced by some figures produced by the chairman of the agency, Sir Kenneth Selby, which were designed to contrast the position as it might have been with the position as it actually was. These figures demonstrated that the total amount due to customers was £4,357,677. On the footing that they all proved and assuming a dividend of 12½p in the pound they would receive £544,710. If they were then paid by TOSG the bond moneys actually paid out (£1,267,759), the agency's liability in pursuance of its statutory duties would then have been £2,545,208. What the agency actually paid to customers was £3,089,918. Thus, it was argued, by adopting the method of paying out first against assignments, the agency would have spent more than its statutory liability to the extent it was unable to recover the customers' proofs of debt assigned to it, a sum of £158,470, on the footing that the banks are admitted to prove in priority to the customers paid by them. That figure, of course, includes the share of Williams & Glyn's Bank, which is not an appellant.

As an exercise in arithmetic this, of course, is admirable, but the assertion that the actual method of dealing with the claims involves an expenditure in excess of the agency's liability rests on the same assumption as the proposition which I have already ventured to criticise. The agency was under a statutory liability to make good anything not met from dividends or bond moneys, but the assertion that it would have expended less if it had waited until the customers received their dividends assumes that there is no question of double proof and therefore begs the question of what dividends were in fact available. These figures demonstrate the arithmetic. They do not, in my judgment, demonstrate the equity, and I cannot, for my part, share the judge's view that there is anything inequitable in allowing the banks who have paid real money to recover a dividend on the sums which they have paid and in reducing the proofs of the customers, who have received real money in priority to other creditors, by the amounts which they have in fact received. Leaving aside, for the moment, the suretyship analogy, if the amounts of the customers' claims had been equal to or less than the bond moneys, there could be no question whatever that the banks were entitled to prove for what they had paid. What is there then in the fact that the customers' debts exceed the amount of the bond moneys that displaces the banks claims? It is only the rule against double proof and that brings one back to the suretyship analogy. If one discards that as a guide, one is left with competitive claims between a class of creditors (the banks) who are out of pocket to the full nominal amount of their claims and a class of creditors (the customers) who are in fact out of pocket to an extent less than the full nominal amount of their claims because of their receipt of the banks' money. Unless there can be found in the arrangements under which the money was put up some implied term which precludes the payers from exerting the limited right of recoupment which they were careful to reserve against the debtor when those arrangements were made, I can see no equity which dictates that the customers' claims should be preferred. It is said that it is illogical that the banks should enter into bonds which they knew were designed to alleviate losses to holidaymakers whilst at the same time reserving the right to 'claw back' from the holidaymakers what they might otherwise have got in the liquidation. This I find an emotive description of what seems to me a perfectly commonsense business arrangement and it really comes back to seeking to imply an intention on the part of the banks not simply that the bond money should be used to alleviate the losses of customers in such way as TOSG might think fit but that such losses should be alleviated to the maximum extent possible by eliminating the rights which the banks had reserved against the debtor. I find no material for any such implication and I cannot think that it would have occurred for one moment to any bystander, officious or otherwise, who was present when the arrangements were made. I find myself, therefore, unable to reach the same conclusion as the judge. In my judgment both the suretyship analogy and the broad equity of the position favour the banks' claim as against that of the agency, and I would allow the appeal.

KERR LJ. For convenience I will refer to the parties as 'Clarksons', 'the banks', 'TOSG', 'the holidaymakers', 'the agency' and 'the liquidators'. The issue on this appeal concerns the right to prove in Clarksons' liquidation for part of the 'bond moneys' provided by the four appellant banks to TOSG. The competing claimants for payment of a dividend by the liquidators on the amount of the bond moneys are the four banks and the agency. However, this is to some extent an over-simplification: each of the banks with which this appeal is concerned seeks to prove for the fixed amount of the bond which it has provided, viz Barclays for £500,000, Lloyds for £93,000, National Westminster for £500,000 and Wintrust for £260,000, and the agency is disputing each of these claims to proof. For convenience it may be simpler to treat the total bond moneys as one composite sum. But in analysing the position one must also constantly bear in mind that each of the banks is a separate claimant in respect of the amount of its bond, even though their claims must stand or fall together. Further, although it is convenient to refer to the bond moneys compendiously, the competing claims are in fact confined to the sums paid by TOSG to holidaymakers directly, to the exclusion of the repatriation costs as to which the banks' right to proof is not in dispute.

There are only three possible solutions. (1) The banks are entitled to prove to the exclusion of the agency. (2) The agency is entitled to prove to the exclusion of the banks. (3) The banks and the agency can both prove.

Either of the first two solutions would follow from the application of the so-called rule against double proof, though, in my view, they also fall to be considered independently from this rule. The third solution can only be correct if this rule has no application to the unusual situation in this case.

Before Nourse J the case proceeded on the basis that the rule against double proof was on all sides assumed to apply. He therefore had to choose between the first two solutions, but on this appeal we have to consider all three. To my mind this provides a better approach to seeking the solution which most closely accords with justice and the presumed intention of the parties concerned. The rule against double proof is highly technical in some facets of its application, but ultimately it is based on what the court regards as justice between all the creditors. Exceptionally it may fall to be applied in unforeseeable situations such as *The Liverpool (No 2)* [1960] 3 All ER 307, [1963] P 64, where the priority between competing claims has to be determined without reference to the parties' presumed intentions before the occurrence of the insolvency. Generally, however, it applies in cases in which there is something in the nature of a debtor-creditor-surety situation which precedes the insolvency. In such cases, the solutions at which the courts have arrived, as illustrated by the decisions to which Oliver LJ has referred, have taken account, expressly or tacitly, of what the parties concerned are to be regarded as having intended. It is on this basis that they have generally decided whether or not the rule applies and, if so, with what consequences as regards priorities. I think that this is particularly important in the present case, since its unusual feature is that Clarksons, in conjunction with the banks and TOSG, set up the bonding arrangements with the express intention that they should take effect in the event of Clarksons' possible insolvency for the benefit of a particular class of creditors. I therefore feel that the safest course is to begin by examining the presumed intentions of the various parties at the time when the bonding arrangements were made.

The parties' intentions
The background can be summarised as follows. In order to strengthen their position

as reliable tour operators in the eyes of members of the public who might book holidays with them, Clarksons, together with other major tour operators, wanted to set up a fund whose existence would be publicised and which would be immediately available to these customers in the event of Clarksons becoming insolvent, at least to the extent that they might run into cash-flow difficulties and become unable to meet their commitments to them, as had notoriously happened in a number of other cases. They therefore combined to set up TOSG as a vehicle for the receipt and application of a fund to be available for this purpose outside their possible liquidation. The main objectives of this fund appear from cl 3(A) of TOSG's memorandum of association. These were to 'alleviate' the consequences of any insolvency to the holidaymakers in two main respects, (i) to enable them to complete their holidays and to bring them home more or less as they had planned, and (ii) to refund to them any prepaid deposits, or prepayments made in full, so that these moneys would be available to them for making alternative holiday arrangements. The total amount of the bond moneys to be provided by Clarksons for these purposes was computed on the basis of 5% of their annual turnover, because it was hoped that, by and large, this could be sufficient to cover what might turn out to be Clarksons' maximum exposure in this respect. However, there was no requirement that Clarksons were to take any account of the total amount of the bond moneys in accepting bookings from their customers; and there was also no suggestion that the banks had any knowledge or concern about the relationship between the amounts which, individually and collectively, they agreed to guarantee by issuing the bonds and the amounts which might at any time be required to meet Clarksons' commitments within the objectives of cl 3(A).

There is also no indication, I think, that in issuing the bonds, the banks acted otherwise than individually to the extent of the various amounts which they undertook to pay to TOSG in the event of Clarksons' insolvency. However, this is of no importance, since, apart from whatever commission which may have been agreed with Clarksons for issuing the bonds, each bank required a counter-indemnity for the bond moneys from Clarksons in the usual way. Each such counter-indemnity was to take effect if and when the bonds were called by TOSG. It was common ground that TOSG, as well as the agency, when it came into existence later on, were well aware of the counter-indemnities.

Against this background, one can then ask oneself the first material question concerning the intention of the parties which set up the bonding arrangements: 'In the event of the bonds being called up, due to Clarksons' insolvency, was it envisaged that the banks would be entitled to prove for the amounts of their respective bonds in Clarksons' liquidation?' To this there can only be one answer: 'Yes, obviously, by reason of the counter-indemnities.' The common intention in this regard can be expressed by each bank saying, in effect, with the assent of Clarksons and TOSG: 'In the event of the bonds being called, we will immediately provide cash to TOSG to the extent of our bond. This will be applied by TOSG for the benefit of Clarksons' customers in accordance with TOSG's memorandum of association, and in particular cl 3(A). Any balance which is not needed for these purposes will be refunded to us. To the extent that there is no refund, we will be left with a claim in Clarksons' liquidation under our counter-indemnity.'

Since this was clearly the common intention of the parties concerned in setting up the bonding arrangements, I am bound to say that, right from the outset, I find it difficult to accept that any answer to the complex problems of this case can be correct in so far as it precludes the banks from proving in Clarksons' liquidation to the full extent of their counter-indemnities. Whatever may be the effect of the mysteries of the rule against double proof, to which I turn later, it would be strange indeed if it led to any other result.

I realise, however, that this approach is too simple and that, in ascertaining the parties' intentions, one must go on and pose a further, more complex, question to the parties who set up the bonding scheme, on the following lines: 'But, suppose that the bond moneys, or their residue after paying for the repatriation of stranded holidaymakers, are paid to customers of Clarksons who have paid deposits or prepaid for their holidays in full, but the bond moneys are found to be insufficient to reimburse them in full, what would then be the rights of the holidaymakers?' I think that the instant answer would be: 'Well, of course, they can claim in the liquidation of Clarksons for the balance.' This,

I think, is the right answer from every commonsense point of view, and it ought to be the right answer in law. However, suppose that the questioner then explained the rule against double proof and repeated the question, somewhat on the following lines: 'But, you see, the position is this. The bond moneys have been provided by the banks, at Clarksons' request and expense, to be applied by TOSG, at any rate as to the relevant part, in order to meet the debts owed by Clarksons to the holidaymakers, who will be one class of Clarksons' creditors in the event of Clarksons' insolvency. In a sense, therefore, the banks are in a position of sureties for the holidaymakers. In general, however, to simplify a legal rule called "the rule against double proof", a creditor can claim against the debtor the full amount of his debt, without having to give credit for anything received from a surety until he has had his debt repaid in full; and, in cases where the rule applies, the creditor can generally claim the full amount of his debt against the insolvent debtor to the exclusion of the surety. Alternatively, if there are competing claims by two creditors for what is in substance the same debt, then one must have priority over the other, because it would not be fair to the general body of creditors of the insolvent debtor that two dividends should be paid for what is in substance the same debt. What then?'

The intelligible part of the answer, no doubt after a good deal of head scratching, would in my view have been somewhat as follows: 'Well, I still think the same. I don't see how the banks can in any event be precluded from claiming on their counter-indemnities. They agreed to pay over the bond moneys for the benefit of the holidaymakers in the event of Clarksons becoming insolvent, but only on the basis that they would then be entitled to claim in Clarksons' liquidation under the counter-indemnities. I don't see how they can lose this right. I can see that Clarksons' liquidators should not pay a dividend on the bond moneys both to the banks and the holidaymakers. But the banks have paid out the bond moneys, and the holidaymakers will have received them, all as had been intended. The holidaymakers will find that they are fortunate to get these sums. And, after all, indirectly the bond moneys will have been made available to the holidaymakers by Clarksons themselves. Why, then, having received them with one hand, should the holidaymakers still be able to claim them from Clarksons' liquidators with the other? So, as I say, the banks should be entitled to a dividend on the bond moneys, and the holidaymakers to a dividend on the balance of their debt after giving credit for what they will have received out of the bond moneys. In so far as I understand your rule against double proof, I don't think that it was ever intended to apply here. But, if it does, then the banks must have the better claim.'

Those, I think, would have been the answers of the persons concerned in setting up the bonding arrangements to the problems raised by this case before the advent of the agency and the complications created by the assignments, to which I come later. I shall also have to deal with the inevitably much more sophisticated answers to these problems in the contrary sense given in the judgment of Nourse J and elaborated in the able argument of counsel for TOSG and the agency on this appeal. Meanwhile, however, in considering the presumed intentions of the various parties before Clarksons' insolvency, one should perhaps also bear in mind two other classes of persons in so far as they dealt with Clarksons in the knowledge of the bonding arrangements: the general body of Clarksons' creditors at any time, and in particular the holidaymakers themselves, who may well have made bookings with Clarksons partly in reliance on these arrangements. But, in my view, their answers would have been precisely to the same effect. The reason is that, from the point of view of justice and common sense, I do not see how they could have been different.

The original effect of the bonding arrangements

After giving answers on the foregoing lines, the holidaymakers would no doubt have added: 'Of course, if the law allows us more, then we would like to have it.' In my view, however, these answers were in accordance with the legal position at the stage when the bonds were established. None of the counsel who appeared on this appeal were able to refer us to any case in which an analogous position had been considered. But sometimes, in new situations, the court has to find a just solution which stems simply from the nature of the transaction, the relationship between the parties and their presumed common intention. For instance, the rules concerning rights and obligations of contribution in general average were originally based simply on 'common principles of justice' (see *Birkley v Presgrave* (1801) 1 East 220 at 227, 229, 102 ER 86 at 88, 89), and these rules were then applied by analogy in laying down the principles of contribution between co-sureties (see *Dering v Earl of Winchelsea* (1787) 1 Cox Eq Cas 318 at 322, [1775–1802] All ER Rep 140 at 143). In my view, the same approach applies here.

However, Nourse J reached a diametrically opposite conclusion, though under the constraint of the applicability of the rule against double proof, since the case before him proceeded on this basis. Having dealt with the analogy of the banks' position as sureties, to which I come later, he said:

'But in the end I do not need to rely on the analogy at all. I agree with [counsel for TOSG and the agency] that the decisive feature of the present case is TOSG's power to recoup to the customers any shortfall remaining after they had received all available dividends in Clarksons' liquidation. Once you get to that stage it is apparent that it would indeed be most inequitable for the banks to claim, as against the customers, a rateable proportion of any dividends receivable or received by them. That is not a narrow equity, but a broad one. And it is a surer basis for decision than any mere analogy.'

With the greatest respect, I find myself wholly in disagreement with this for a number of reasons. First, and quite generally, I think that every principle of 'broad equity' points in the directly opposite direction, for the reasons already mentioned. Second, I think that this definition of the 'decisive feature' begs the question. What is meant by 'all available dividends'? Are they the dividends payable after the banks have also proved for the bond moneys? Or is the assumption that the banks will have been excluded from proof? The test appears to me to be circular, since the question is whether or not the banks are entitled to prove. In this connection it must be borne in mind that the banks' prima facie right of proof will have arisen as soon as the bonds were called, so that, even if all the holidaymakers had then also proved at once for their full debts, the liquidators would have been faced with both claims to prove in full, as they are now. I therefore cannot see how this formulation can provide any answer to the problem. Third, I think that its premise in no way corresponds to the realities of what had been intended, and indeed happened. The whole purpose of the bonds was to provide a fund which, on Clarksons' insolvency, would be immediately available to TOSG for the benefit of the holidaymakers. It was never envisaged that the fund would be distributed only after the holidaymakers had proved in the liquidation and it was known what dividends the holidaymakers would receive. I appreciate, of course, that there could in theory have been an immediate partial distribution, with a reserve being held back until after completion of the liquidation. But this possibility seems to be too artificial to provide any sound basis, at any rate for the purpose of raising any 'broad equity'. The common intention, as well as the objects of TOSG, surely envisaged that every penny of the bond moneys should (apart from administrative expenses) be applied, as quickly as possible, to whatever extent was necessary to alleviate the plight of Clarksons' customers. The possibility of a reserve could only have arisen if there had been a surplus. I can see that, on that assumption, the test posed by Nourse J could have arisen, though subject to the reservations which I have already expressed about it, in deciding whether or not to return the surplus to the banks under the terms of the bonds. But where, as in the present case, the fund in fact proves to be insufficient to meet all the needs of the holidaymakers, it seems to me that this test provides no realistic basis in any event for arriving at a just solution of the problem.

It follows that in my view, leaving aside for the moment the advent of the agency and the effect of the assignments, the correct solution, on the basis of the parties' intentions and 'common principles of justice', is that the banks were to be entitled to prove for the full amount of the bonds, and that each holidaymaker was to be entitled to prove for the balance of his debt after giving credit for whatever he or she may have received out of the bond moneys. I formulate my conclusion at this stage in this way, because, but for a the advent of the agency, the available bond moneys would no doubt have been distributed pari passu between the relevant holidaymakers, as had indeed been TOSG's original intention; but this assumption does not affect what I would respectfully regard as the correct solution in principle. Accordingly, when the bonding scheme was set up, it was intended to operate in a way in which there would be no basis for the application of the rule against double proof.

b *The effect of the subsequent events*

However, I must then turn to what in fact happened when the balance of the bond moneys was distributed by TOSG after the repatriation costs had been met. The facts have already been stated by Oliver LJ, and I need not repeat them. The agreement between TOSG and the agency was, if I may respectfully say so, an extremely sensible one, since it enabled the balance of the bond moneys, together with the new funds available to the agency, to be used to compensate all the relevant holidaymakers in full as quickly and conveniently as possible. However, what was the legal effect, if any, of TOSG paying one category of holidaymakers in full, until the bond moneys became exhausted, but subject in each case to taking an assignment in favour of the agency of these holidaymakers' debts, or of their right to prove in Clarksons' liquidation? This category consisted of those who had made prepayments to Clarksons direct, whereas it was thought that those who had made payments to travel agents would have to await the outcome of a test case. Subsequently they, together with those who had not been paid by TOSG out of the bond moneys, had their prepayments reimbursed by the agency in full. During the argument before us it was found convenient in this connection to refer to the holidaymakers paid by TOSG as 'the Browns' and to those paid by the agency as 'the Smiths', and to refer to the general body of both categories as 'the Brown-Smiths'. I will use the same terminology. The issue therefore turns on whether the banks are entitled to prove in Clarksons' liquidation to the extent of the sums paid to 'the Browns' to the exclusion of the agency, or vice versa, or whether the banks and the agency can both claim a dividend on these sums. It is of course not in dispute that the agency can prove in any event in respect of the payments which it made to 'the Smiths'.

I must begin by dealing shortly with two submissions put forward by counsel for the banks. The first was that the banks had a right to be subrogated to 'the Browns' as soon as 'the Browns' were paid out of the moneys provided by the banks, and that the assignments could not destroy this right of subrogation. In the same way as Oliver LJ I cannot accept this submission. Given the existence of the express counter-indemnities, of which both TOSG and the agency were aware at all times, and the unrestricted powers of TOSG, I cannot see any scope for any parallel implication of a right of subrogation to the same effect as the counter-indemnities.

Second, counsel for the banks submitted that, by requiring the assignments in favour of the agency, TOSG was in breach of some term to be implied as between TOSG and the banks, or possibly, as I understood him, in breach of trust to the banks, and that the banks could rely on these breaches against the agency, since it was in the position of an equitable assignee with notice. Again, I think that these submissions go too far. If one regards the agency as representing all 'the Smiths', I can see, as submitted by counsel for TOSG and the agency, that under the terms of the bonds, which incorporated the wide objects of TOSG, TOSG was entitled to do anything which might be of benefit to 'the Smiths'. Even on this assumption, however, there remains the question whether the assignments had the effect of excluding the banks' right of proof under the counter-indemnities or whether the banks and the agency can both prove. In my view the assignments have no effect on the conclusions which I have already expressed, for a number of alternative reasons which all lead to this result.

The first point in this connection is that I cannot accept any of the arguments of counsel for the banks, which in the end he did not strongly maintain, to the effect that the banks and the agency can both prove and receive a dividend in respect of the payments made by TOSG to 'the Browns'. This would be unfair to the general body of Clarksons' creditors and inconsistent with the principle of the rule against double proof, whether or not this rule is strictly applicable in the circumstances of this case.

Second, as it seems to me, since 'the Browns' were paid by TOSG in full, out of the bond moneys which had been specifically arranged to be provided by Clarksons for their *a* benefit in the event of Clarksons' insolvency, 'the Browns' had no right of proof thereafter, and nothing which they could effectively assign to the agency. There were then no debts owed by Clarksons to 'the Browns' which remained to be assigned. Council for TOSG and the agency countered this by submitting that 'the Browns' cannot for this purpose be considered in isolation, but that, having regard to the reasons which underlay the agreement between TOSG and the agency, the division between 'Browns' and 'Smiths' *b* should be ignored, and that the position should be tested by reference to 'the Brown-Smiths' as a whole, as though TOSG had made a partial payment towards the debts of all the relevant holidaymakers pari passu and had then taken assignments from all of them in favour of the agency. I was at first greatly attracted by this argument, but on reflection it seems to me again that it displaces reality in favour of theoretical possibilities, though on this occasion in a different context. Why should the legal effects of the assignments *c* not be judged by reference to what actually happened? Admittedly, the agreement between TOSG and the agency could have been framed differently, and less conveniently, by each party paying all 'the Brown-Smiths' pari passu, and all of them could then have effected assignments in favour of the agency in consideration of the payments made to all of them by TOSG. But, since this did not in fact happen, why should the effect of the assignments fall to be determined on this hypothetical basis? *d*

Third, however, let it be assumed that this is wrong, and that each transaction between TOSG and one of 'the Browns' is to be regarded as valid and effective in the sense that it constituted a purchase of each debt by TOSG in consideration of its assignment to the agency, and not a payment which extinguished the debt. What is the position then?

The first answer in my view is that the assignments would still have no substantial effect, because they would not entitle the agency to prove in Clarksons' liquidation in *e* competition with the banks. For the reasons stated in the judgment of Slade LJ, which I have seen and with which I respectfully agree, the agency cannot, as TOSG's assignee, be in any better position than TOSG itself. However, it cannot possibly have been in the contemplation of any of the parties, when the bonding scheme was set up, that TOSG might be entitled to buy up the debts of the holidaymakers in order to seek to acquire claims in the liquidation which would rank in priority over the claims of the banks *f* under the counter-indemnities. Any such suggestion as to the rights of TOSG would transgress the common intention of the parties to the bonding scheme to an even greater extent than in relation to the rights of the holidaymakers themselves, with which I have dealt at the beginning of this judgment.

Nevertheless, I can see the force of the argument, though to my mind only a technical one, that the correct analysis resulting from the assignments on these assumptions is that *g* they have the effect of bringing the rule against double proof into operation between the agency and the banks. On that basis, however, it seems to me to be clear, for the reasons explained in the judgment of Oliver LJ, that the effect of the rule in the circumstances of this case is that the banks can prove to the exclusion of the agency. Here again I respectfully differ from Nourse J. He said:

> 'In all the circumstances, if the suretyship analogy is to be applied and carried *h* through, the case is clearly one where there was a guarantee of the whole debt, subject to a limitation on the liability of the surety in the amount of the bond moneys.'

In my view, however, there was clearly no guarantee of the whole debt by the banks, either collectively or, as is more relevant, individually. If the language of the authorities *j* concerning the rule against double proof is to be used at all, then each bank guaranteed, to use the word loosely and I think inaccurately, an indeterminate part of an unknown fluctuating balance up to the limit of its bond. With the greatest respect to Nourse J, I cannot begin to see how the terms of the bonds, albeit that they incorporated all the terms of TOSG's memorandum of association, can be regarded as having guaranteed the whole of any debt or debts whatever. I have already set out earlier in this judgment what appears to me to be a clear formulation of the position of the banks in this regard.

Accordingly, even if the rule against double proof is applicable, it follows from the
a analysis of the authorities in the judgment of Oliver LJ that the banks can prove to the
exclusion of the agency.

For all these reasons I would allow this appeal.

SLADE LJ. I agree that this appeal should be allowed. Oliver LJ has stated the facts and
I will not repeat them, save to the extent necessary to explain my own conclusions.

I think that the task of Nourse J was made more difficult by the fact that no argument
b was addressed to him in support of the contention that the rule against double proof has
no application in the present case and that there is accordingly no reason why both the
four plaintiff banks and Air Travel Reserve Fund Agency (the agency) should not prove
in respect of the relevant debts. In this court we have had the assistance of submissions
by counsel for the banks (albeit in the alternative) in support of this contention, and
submissions from counsel for TOSG and the agency and counsel for the liquidators of
c Clarksons in opposition to it. In the end, for reasons which I will state, I have been
convinced that the contention is unsustainable. Nevertheless, a substantial part of the
argument in this court has centred round it and I have found it helpful in finally
identifying what I regard as the important signposts in this jungle of obscure legal
territory.

I have had the advantage of reading in draft the judgments of Oliver and Kerr LJJ.
d Since I agree with their conclusions that the rule against double proof does apply and that
the claim of the banks takes priority to that of the agency, I hope that it will not appear
discourteous if I deal less specifically than they have done with the able and multifarious
arguments which all counsel have addressed to us. I propose to do little more than
explain the route which leads me to these conclusions.

As soon as the banks paid the bond moneys to TOSG on 16 August 1974, they became
e immediately entitled to prove in the liquidation of Clarksons in respect of the full
amounts so paid, by virtue of the counter-indemnities given them by Clarksons. Under
the express provisions of the bonds, they had a right to demand repayment by TOSG of
such part of the bond moneys as should not be expended by TOSG in the performance
and execution of its rights, duties, powers and discretions as set out in TOSG's
memorandum and articles of association. This right, however, was more theoretical than
f substantial, since Clarksons was hopelessly insolvent and there was no real prospect of
TOSG failing to expend the whole of the bond moneys in this manner.

The banks, in my judgment, had a contractual right (arising by necessary implication
from the terms of the bonds) to prevent TOSG from expending the bond moneys
otherwise than in the performance and execution of its rights, duties, powers and
discretions as set out in TOSG's constitution. Subject to this limitation, however, the
g choice was that of TOSG as to how it should spend the bond moneys and the banks could
not, as a matter of contract, complain about such expenditure, even though it would
inevitably prejudice pro tanto the banks' theoretical rights of subsequently obtaining
recoupment by TOSG of unexpended bond moneys.

TOSG, having received the bond moneys, in accordance with the powers given it by
its memorandum, expended some £956,000 in repatriating customers of Clarksons. The
h banks make no complaint about this expenditure. Though it diminished the banks'
theoretical rights of recoupment against TOSG, TOSG were plainly entitled to effect it
and it did not prejudice the banks' right of proof in the liquidation.

The dispute in the present case has arisen because of the arrangements made by TOSG
and the agency in July 1975 for dealing with the residue of the bond moneys held by
TOSG, in respect of the bonds provided by Clarksons. These arrangements have been set
j out more fully by Oliver LJ in his judgment, so I need only refer to their contents quite
briefly.

The agreement of 23 July 1975 (the assignment agreement) made between the agency
and TOSG provided, inter alia, that TOSG would pay out 'non-T.C.' claims (non test-case
claims) in full as soon as reasonably practical, until the bond moneys (less a retention
fund) were exhausted or until all non-TC claims had been paid in full, and that, when
paying any claim, TOSG would obtain an assignment in favour of the agency from the

payee of his right to prove in the liquidation of Clarksons for the full amount of his claim.   *a*

This provision was duly implemented in the manner contemplated by the assignment agreement. TOSG drew cheques amounting to about £1·268m in favour of customers presenting non-TC claims, which were expressed as not to be honoured unless the assignment form on the back had been signed by the payee; and this form effected an assignment to the agency of all the customer's rights to prove in the liquidation of Clarksons in respect of overseas holidays, which proofs he had lodged with the joint   *b* liquidators.

It would have been possible for the agency and TOSG so to arrange matters so that, when TOSG paid over cheques in respect of the claims in question, it did so on the terms that the customers released all their claims in the liquidation, so that such claims were extinguished. However, the arrangements actually made were, instead, clearly intended to have the effect of operating as assignments of the relevant choses in action, consisting   *c* of the customers' rights to prove in the liquidation, and thus to keep the claims alive.

In the court below, it was submitted by the banks, inter alia, that the assignment agreement was ultra vires TOSG, in so far as it provided for the claims in the liquidation of customers who were paid by TOSG to be assigned to the agency. Nourse J, in my opinion, correctly rejected this submission and it has not been pursued in this court. At one stage in the argument before us, counsel for the banks sought to argue that TOSG, in   *d* arranging for the claims of customers who were paid by it to be assigned to the agency, was in breach of an implied term of the contract entered into between TOSG and the banks when the bonding arrangements were concluded. In my opinion, however, this contention is not well founded. I think that, as a matter of contract, the banks could not complain if TOSG used the bond moneys in any manner authorised by TOSG's constitution.   *e*

However, merely because TOSG was acting neither ultra vires nor in breach of contract in arranging these assignments, it does not follow that the assignments had the legal effect of substantially impairing the banks' rights of proof in the liquidation. For that is the effect of the claim of the agency. It boldly asserts not only that, by virtue of the assignments, it has become entitled to prove in the place of the relevant holidaymakers for the £1·268m but that the banks' previously existing rights of proof have in effect pro   *f* tanto been wholly extinguished, because the rule against double proof applies and the agency's proof takes priority to that of the banks.

In considering this claim of the agency, I would begin by making these observations. The agency is itself a body set up by statute under the Air Travel Reserve Fund Act 1975, with the broad intention of mitigating the losses suffered by holidaymakers on account of the inability of air travel organisers to meet their financial commitments. Furthermore,   *g* it has unquestionably done much to assist those disappointed customers of Clarksons who were not repatriated or paid by TOSG. Nevertheless, these points and the identity of the agency as assignee of the relevant rights of proof are, in my opinion, immaterial for present purposes.

On their true legal analysis, in my opinion, the effect of the relevant transactions was that: (a) TOSG purchased for £1·268 m the rights of proof of the respective holidaymakers   *h* in question (whom I will call 'the assigning holidaymakers'); (b) TOSG directed that the respective purchases should be completed by assignments, not to itself but to the agency.

In these circumstances, and I regard this as a point of crucial importance, the agency, in my opinion, stands in the position in which TOSG would now find itself if it had taken the assignments in favour of itself. Though it is common ground that rights of proof are in principle assignable as choses in action, TOSG manifestly could not have   *j* conferred on the agency better rights of proof in respect of the debts of the assigning holidaymakers than it could have obtained for itself. The fact that the assignee happens to be the agency is immaterial.

At this point I find my approach to this case rather different from that of the judge. In the course of his judgment, after saying that the rule against double proof prevented both the banks and the agency from together proving, he said:

a '[Counsel for the banks] accepts that the agency, as the assignee of the customers' rights to prove in the liquidation is in the same position vis-à-vis the banks as the customers themselves would have been. Accordingly, the only question which I have to decide is whether, at the material time, the banks or the customers had the better right of proof. The reduction of the question to that simple form does not mean that the answer is simple.'

b As will appear from what I have already said, I look at the matter rather differently. Though I agree that the rights of proof of TOSG, through which the agency claims, could not have been *better* than those of the assigning holidaymakers through which TOSG would have claimed, I do not think it should be assumed that the rights of TOSG to prove in competition with the banks would necessarily have been as good as those of the assigning holidaymakers. For reasons which will appear, I think it was only the expenditure of moneys by TOSG in purchasing the relevant rights of proof in such *c* manner as to keep the relevant debts of the holidaymakers alive which caused a double proof situation to crystallise. If such purchase had never taken place and the assigning holidaymakers had been left to prove in respect of their own debts, I think it possible that no question of double proof would have arisen as between them and the banks. Accordingly, in my judgment, the relevant inquiry is: what would have been the position of TOSG vis-à-vis the banks in relation to proof if the assignments had been taken by *d* TOSG in favour of itself? Two questions thus fall to be answered. (1) On the footing that the relevant rights of proof had been assigned to TOSG itself, would the rule against double proof have applied so as to prevent TOSG and the banks from proving in competition with one another? (2) If the answer to question (1) is Yes, would TOSG or the banks have had the better right of proof?

As to question (1) above, the true principle of the rule against double proof, stated by *e* Mellish LJ in *Re Oriental Commercial Bank, ex p European Bank* (1871) LR 7 Ch App 99 at 103, is that—

'there is only to be one dividend in respect of what is in substance the same debt, although there may be two separate contracts.'

Earlier in the same passage of his judgment, Mellish LJ had likewise made it plain that *f* the rule is directed against payment of more than one dividend in respect of the same debt, rather than against presentation of more than one proof. In many cases, such as the present, where more than one proof has been presented, one may find what was sometimes described in argument as a 'potential double proof situation', which can only be finally resolved at a later stage, having regard to the facts subsisting at the time when a dividend is about to be paid (for example, having full regard to the arrangements made *g* pursuant to the assignment agreement in the present case). The purpose of the rule is, of course, to ensure pari passu distribution of the assets comprised in the estate of an insolvent in pro rata discharge of his liabilities. The payment of more than one dividend in respect of what is in substance the same debt would give the relevant proving creditors a share of the available assets larger than the share properly attributable to the debt in question.

h Difficulty may well arise in determining whether, in any given case, two proofs are in respect of what is in substance the same debt. Though various broad tests have been canvassed by both Bar and Bench in argument in this case, I have, for my own part, found none of them wholly satisfactory. The question can, I think, only be determined by reference to the particular facts of the case before the court, bearing in mind that it is the substance of the relevant liability, rather than the form, on which attention must be *j* concentrated.

On the facts of the present case, I have come to the clear conclusion that, if TOSG had itself taken assignments of the rights of proof of the assigning holidaymakers and had then sought to prove in respect of the debts of those holidaymakers, it would have been proving for what were in substance the same debts as an equivalent part (£1·268m) in respect of which the banks were proving. The matter may be tested this way. TOSG would unquestionably have been claiming in respect of the debts owed by Clarksons to the assigning holidaymakers. Though in form the banks' claims arise under the counter-indemnities given them by Clarksons in respect of the bond moneys, in substance they are attributable to the debts owed by Clarksons to the assigning holidaymakers, because: (i) it was only the actual expenditure of bond moneys by TOSG which pro tanto finally crystallised the liability of Clarksons to indemnify the banks, because it finally destroyed any possibility of the banks obtaining recoupment from TOSG; (ii) the particular expenditure of bond moneys by TOSG which finally crystallises the liability of Clarksons to indemnify the banks in respect of the £1·268m was expenditure in the purchase of these very same debts owed by Clarksons to the assigning holidaymakers.

In short, in the contingency now under discussion, the joint liquidators would find themselves faced with two competing proofs, namely one at the suit of TOSG in respect of the debts of the assigning holidaymakers and one at the suit of the banks which arose as a result of TOSG purchasing those very same debts. Subject to the rule against double proof, the substantial effect of the purchase of the debts by TOSG was, I think, to increase the provable liabilities of Clarksons by £1·268m because, until that event, it was always possible that the banks would, in due course, recoup this amount from TOSG, and accordingly would not be entitled to receive any dividend in respect of it in the liquidation of Clarksons.

In these circumstances, regarding the matter as one of substance, I find it impossible to say that if TOSG had itself taken assignments of the rights of proof of the assigning holidaymakers and had then sought to prove for the £1·268m, its proof and the banks' proofs for the equivalent amounts would not have been in respect of the same debts. It would not, in my view, have been open to TOSG and the assigning holidaymakers, even with the consent of the banks (which was never obtained), to prejudice the general body of creditors by effecting transactions of this kind.

If this be correct, it can make no difference in the context of the rule against double proof that TOSG in fact directed the assignments to be made in favour of the agency. The rule must still apply for the protection of the general body of creditors, whichever of the banks and the agency is entitled to invoke it, so as to exclude the other.

I now revert to question (2) above. On the hypothesis that TOSG had taken assignments of the relevant debts in favour of itself, who would have been entitled to the better rights of proof as between itself and the banks? The judge considered that the substance of the relationship between Clarksons, its customers, TOSG and the banks was that the banks were sureties for Clarksons' indebtedness to one class of its creditors, namely its holidaymaker customers. He recognised that the interposition of TOSG between the banks and the customers gave rise to a distinction, but thought that it was not one which affected the substance of the relationship. As he put it: 'TSOG was merely a trustee or, if you prefer it, in the broad sense an agent, for the customers.' On the footing that the banks were to be treated as sureties for Clarksons' indebtedness to its customers, he then proceeded to draw certain analogies with the suretyship cases.

As I have already mentioned, the judge regarded the crucial question for decision as being whether at the material time the banks or the holidaymakers had the better right of proof. On this assumption and on the footing that in substance the banks were sureties for Clarksons' indebtedness to the assigning holidaymakers, I recognise that some assistance might fall to be derived from the suretyship cases, by way of analogy.

Nevertheless, for reasons which I have tried to explain, I think that for the purpose of determining priorities in the liquidation, attention must be focused not so much on the relationship between the banks and the holidaymakers as on that between the banks and TOSG. Indeed, I do not think that the banks can be treated as having had any relationship at all with the holidaymakers. When the bonding arrangements were originally made, the banks did, of course, know and contemplate that, if Clarksons' business failed, and the bond moneys became payable to TOSG, TOSG would use them, so far as necessary, to alleviate the consequences to Clarksons' customers of such failure. If, however, at the time when the bonding arrangements had been made, it had been suggested to the banks that, in the event of the liquidation of Clarksons, the banks' rights in the liquidation would have fallen to be determined on the footing that they were sureties for Clarksons' liabilities to its holidaymakers, I think they would have replied, and would have been justified in replying, that their relationship was solely with TOSG and Clarksons. The banks would have appreciated that, if Clarksons went into liquidation and they became obliged to pay the bond moneys to TOSG, TOSG would be entitled to spend them for the benefit of Clarksons' holidaymakers in accordance with its constitution and that they would not be entitled to complain if it did. Nevertheless, the holidaymakers would have had no rights against the banks and would have owed them no duties. The banks themselves would have had no rights against the holidaymakers and owed them no duties. In the event of the banks becoming obliged to pay the bond moneys to TOSG, their relevant rights would have been simply: (a) a right to prevent TOSG from spending the moneys otherwise than in accordance with its constitution; (b) a right to recover from TOSG any of the moneys not expended by it; (c) a right to prove in the liquidation of Clarksons in respect of the debts which arose in the banks' favour under the counter-indemnities, immediately the bond moneys were paid to TOSG, giving credit for any moneys which might thereafter be recouped to them by TOSG. This brief analysis, to my mind, illustrates how far removed from the relationship of creditor, surety and debtor was the relationship of TOSG, the banks and Clarksons at the time when the bonding arrangements were concluded. The suretyship analogy can only give firm guidance in determining the order of priorities of the banks and TOSG (through whom the agency claims) in the liquidation of Clarksons if one identifies TOSG with the holidaymakers and this, in my opinion, is not a justifiable process.

Nevertheless, the many suretyship cases to which we have been referred do, in my opinion, show that, where both principal creditor and surety are seeking to prove in a bankruptcy in respect of what is in substance the same debt, so that a double proof situation arises, the court will seek to determine the priorities of the two supposed rights of proof by reference to the expressed or presumed intentions of the parties, as manifested in the contract by which the surety undertook his liability. In particular, it will not allow a creditor, who is at liberty to increase the balance due from the debtor, to rely on any such increase in such a manner as to prejudice the surety's rights of proof in the bankruptcy of the debtor, where to do so would be inequitable having regard to the expressed or presumed intentions of the parties as so manifested (see, for example, *Ellis v Emmanuel* (1876) 1 Ex D 157 at 163–164, [1874–80] All ER Rep 1081 at 1083 per Blackburn J). To this limited extent, I think that the suretyship cases do afford some guidance by analogy in the present case for the purpose of determining the respective priorities of the rights of proof of the banks and TOSG (through whom the agency claims) in respect of the £1·268m.

I, therefore, revert to a consideration of the expressed and presumed intentions of the banks and TOSG as at the date when the bonding arrangements were concluded. I do not think it is disputed that TOSG, when it entered into these arrangements, was well aware of the counter-indemnities which had been or were to be given by Clarksons to the banks in respect of any moneys that might become payable by the banks to TOSG. These counter-indemnities were, I think, part of the essential background of the bonding arrangements. Since the events on which the moneys were expressed to become payable under the bonds all presupposed that Clarksons would already be in, or on the verge of, an insolvent liquidation, TOSG must have well known that the banks intended to prove in the liquidation of Clarksons in respect of any such moneys. The present contention of the agency seems to me, on analysis, by necessary implication to involve the proposition that TOSG would have been at liberty (a) to expend the entirety of the bond moneys in purchasing debts of disappointed holidaymakers, (b) then to inform the banks that not a penny was repayable to them by TOSG under the bonds, because all the bond moneys had been properly spent, and (c) then to assert that the banks had no rights to prove for anything whatever in the liquidation, since they would be proving in respect of the same debts as TOSG, and TOSG had the prior right of proof.

I would accept propositions (a) and (b) but find myself quite unable to accept proposition (c). I accept that the purchase by TOSG of debts of disappointed holidaymakers would not actually have involved any breach by TOSG of any express or implied contractual term of the arrangements. Nevertheless, the parties to the bonding arrangements cannot, in my opinion, reasonably be supposed to have contemplated, at the date when they were concluded, that TOSG would have the right to expend bond moneys in such manner as to elevate itself into the position of a proving creditor in Clarksons' liquidation, while at the same time finally destroying the subsisting rights of the banks both (i) to obtain any recoupment from TOSG in respect of the bond moneys, and (ii) to prove in the liquidation. Such an inference would, in my opinion, have been inconsistent with the nature of the bonding arrangements and would have produced a thoroughly inequitable result.

Accordingly, I conclude that the double proof rule applies in respect of the £1·268m and that, if TOSG had taken an assignment of the assigning holidaymakers' debts in favour of itself, the banks would have had a better right of proof in respect of this sum. As I have already explained, I think that the agency can be in no better position than TOSG itself would have been. The banks, in my judgment, therefore have the better right of proof.

Nourse J, in reaching the contrary conclusion, relied in part on possible analogies with the reported cases concerned with principal and surety. I have already referred to this point. However, he attached greater importance on the fact that the power of TOSG 'to alleviate the consequences and so forth of Clarksons' business failure clearly enabled TOSG to recoup to the customers any shortfall remaining *after* they had received all available dividends in Clarkson's liquidation'. He concluded that in the end he did not need to rely on the analogy with the cases relating to principal and surety at all. He said:

> 'I agree with [counsel for TOSG and the agency] that the decisive feature of the present case is TOSG's power to recoup to the customers any shortfall remaining after they had received all available dividends in Clarksons' liquidation. Once you get to that stage it is apparent that it would indeed be most inequitable for the banks to claim, as against the customers, a rateable proportion of any dividends receivable or received by them. That is not a narrow equity, but a broad one. And it is a surer basis for decision than any mere analogy.'

With great respect to the judge, I am not able to agree with this reasoning for two reasons. First, the amount of the dividends available to Clarksons' customers in its liquidation must partially depend on the resolution of the very questions which are in issue in the present litigation. I find it difficult to see how in practice TOSG could possibly have awaited the completion of the liquidation of Clarksons before taking such steps as it was entitled and bound to take under its constitution for the relief of Clarksons' holidaymakers. Second, as I have already indicated, I think that, when broader questions of equity fall to be considered, the relevant comparison is not between the respective rights of proof of the banks and of the holidaymakers, but between the respective rights of proof of the banks and TOSG. When the latter comparison is made, for the reasons which I hope will have already appeared, I am of the clear opinion that any broader considerations of equity favour the banks in preference to TOSG and likewise in preference to the agency, which claims through TOSG.

For all these reasons. I would concur in allowing this appeal.

Appeal allowed. Leave to appeal to House of Lords granted on condition that if and to the extent that the liquidators are incurred with costs in the House of Lords the agency will pay the liquidators on an indemnity basis.

Solicitors: *Wilde Sapte* (for the banks); *Norton Rose Botterell & Roche* (for TOSG and the agency); *Stephenson Harwood* (for the liquidators of Clarksons).

Mary Rose Plummer　Barrister.

Bickel and others v Courtenay Investments (Nominees) Ltd

CHANCERY DIVISION
WARNER J
10, 11, 15 NOVEMBER 1983

Sale of land – Leasehold interest – Consent to assignment – Consent to assignment to be obtained 'where necessary' – Necessary – Tenant contracting to sell residue of term of lease – Landlord's consent required under lease – Consent withheld – Tenant seeking rescission of contract – What facts tenant required to prove – National Conditions of Sale (20th edn), condition 11(5).

On the true construction of condition 11(5)[a] of the National Conditions of Sale (20th edn), which provides, inter alia, that where the interest sold is leasehold for the residue of an existing term the sale is subject to the reversioner's licence being obtained 'where necessary', the question whether the reversioner's consent to the assignment is 'necessary' is to be answered by looking only at the lease, because the word 'necessary' in that condition means 'necessary under the lease' and does not invite an inquiry whether at some stage between contract and completion the reversioner has, by his conduct, rendered his consent unnecessary. Accordingly, all that the vendor has to do if he wishes to rescind the contract under condition 11(5) is to prove (1) that under the lease the reversioner's consent to the assignment is necessary, (2) that he has used his best endeavours to obtain it and (3) that the consent cannot be obtained; it is immaterial that the reversioner's refusal of his consent may be unreasonable (see p 660 *a* to *c* and *j* and p 661 *a* to *c*, post).

Lipmans Wallpaper Ltd v Mason & Hodghton Ltd [1968] 1 All ER 1123 applied.

Notes
For contracts for the sale of leasehold interests in land, see 42 Halsbury's Laws (4th edn) para 104.

For the vendor's duty to obtain the reversioner's consent to an assignment of leasehold, see ibid para 250, and for cases on the subject, see 40 Digest (Repl) 311–312, 2564–2569.

For the exercise of the right of rescission, see 42 Halsbury's Laws (4th edn) para 111, and for cases on the subject, see 40 Digest (Repl) 235–241, 1977–2025.

Cases referred to in judgment
Bain v Fothergill (1874) LR 7 HL 158, [1874–80] All ER Rep 83.
Curtis Moffat Ltd v Wheeler [1929] 2 Ch 224.
Lewis & Allenby (1909) Ltd v Pegge [1914] 1 Ch 782.
Lipmans Wallpaper Ltd v Mason & Hodghton Ltd [1968] 1 All ER 1123, [1969] 1 Ch 20, [1968] 2 WLR 881.
Marshall and Salt's Contract, Re [1900] 2 Ch 202.
Treloar v Bigge (1874) LR 9 Exch 151.
White v Hay (1895) 72 LT 281.
Willmott v London Road Car Co Ltd [1910] 2 Ch 525, [1908–10] All ER Rep 908, CA.

Originating summons
By an originating summons dated 1 June 1983 the plaintiffs, James Murray Bickel, Leonard Harry Goldsmith, Harry Ivan Sparks and Denvelle Ralph Orton, being the trustees of the Ancient Order of Foresters Friendly Society, sought (i) a declaration that on the true construction of a contract dated 7 February 1983 for the sale of the residue of a lease of 13–17 Bury Street, London W1 made between the plaintiffs as vendors and the defendant, Courtenay Investments (Nominees) Ltd, as purchaser, and in the events that

---

a   Condition 11(5) is set out at p 658 *f g*, post

had occurred the plaintiffs were entitled under condition 11(5) of the National Conditions of Sale (20th edn) to rescind the contract, and (ii) further or other relief. The facts are set out in the judgment.

Nicholas Huskinson for the plaintiffs.
John Cherryman QC and *George Bompas* for the defendant.

Cur adv vult

15 November. The following judgment was delivered.

WARNER J. This is an originating summons by which the plaintiffs seek a declaration as to the true construction of a condition which forms part of the National Conditions of Sale (20th edn).

The plaintiffs are the present trustees of the Ancient Order of Foresters Friendly Society. The defendant is a company called Courtenay Investments (Nominees) Ltd; it is a wholly-owned subsidiary of Courtenay Investments Ltd, a substantial property company.

The plaintiffs are the owners of a leasehold interest in a property at 13–17 Bury Street, London W1, which is now empty but which was formerly the well-known hotel and restaurant, Quaglino's. The plaintiffs' lease is dated 1 May 1912 and is for a term of 77½ years from 25 March 1912. Quaglino's plc (which I will call 'Quaglino's') is the plaintiffs' tenant, though I am told that its tenancy, as to the precise nature of which there is some doubt, will come to an end next month.

The plaintiffs' lease contains a covenant by the lessee—

'NOT to assign underlet or part with the possession of the demised premises or any part thereof without first obtaining the written consent of the Lessors but such consent shall not be unreasonably withheld in the case of a respectable and responsible tenant . . .'

By a contract dated 7 February 1983 the plaintiffs agreed to sell the residue of their term to the defendant. Completion was to take place on 9 March 1983. The contract incorporated the National Conditions of Sale (20th edn), condition 11(5) of which reads as follows:

'The sale is subject to the reversioner's licence being obtained, where necessary. The purchaser supplying such information and references, if any, as may reasonably be required of him, the vendor will use his best endeavours to obtain such licence and will pay the fee for the same. But if the licence cannot be obtained, the vendor may rescind the contract on the same terms as if the purchaser had persisted in an objection to the title which the vendor was unable to remove.'

What those last few words import, as one sees if one looks at condition 10(2), is that, if the vendor rescinds the contract, he is to 'return the deposit, but without interest, costs of investigating title or other compensation or payment, and the purchaser is to return the abstract and other papers furnished to him'.

At the date of the contract the reversioner was a company called Joseph Rochford & Sons Ltd (I will call it 'Rochfords'). On 8 March 1983, however (that is on the day before the day fixed for completion of the contract between the plaintiffs and the defendant), Rochfords assigned its interest, which was also a leasehold interest, to Quaglino's.

The plaintiffs have put in evidence a bundle of correspondence that passed during the period from 4 January to 19 April 1983 between the solicitors acting for the plaintiffs, for the defendant, for Rochfords and for Quaglino's respectively. The bundle also contains a few other relevant documents, and it is supplemented by a couple of exhibits to an affidavit sworn on behalf of the defendant. I do not propose to go through that evidence in detail. The plaintiffs rely on it as proving, first, that they (or rather their solicitors on their behalf) used their best endeavours to obtain the reversioner's licence to assign and, second, that despite those endeavours the licence could not be obtained.

a Counsel for the defendant disputed that the evidence showed that the plaintiffs had used their best endeavours to obtain the licence. He relied, in doing so, on the fact that the plaintiffs' solicitors did not promptly comply with a request by the defendant's solicitors made in a letter dated 11 March 1983 that they should pass on to Quaglino's solicitors the contents of that letter. It would obviously have been better if the plaintiffs' solicitors had done so. Their omission was, however, after some further correspondence, remedied by the defendant's solicitors themselves when, on 25 March, they wrote direct

b to Quaglino's solicitors making the same points as they had made in their letter of 11 March. It is manifest that the delay in those points being imparted to Quaglino's solicitors made not the slightest difference to the result. Moreover, in my opinion, in deciding whether the plaintiffs' solicitors, on behalf of the plaintiffs, did use their best endeavours to obtain the licence, one has to look at what they did from February to April 1983 as a whole. The fact is that, during that period, they made repeated and strenuous attempts

c to persuade first Rochfords and then Quaglino's to grant the licence. In my judgment there was no breach of the plaintiffs' obligation to use their best endeavours to obtain the licence.

That those endeavours were not successful is not in doubt. Although a representative of Rochfords telephoned the plaintiffs' solicitors on 4 March and said that Rochfords would be granting the licence, Rochfords in fact never did so; and Quaglino's have

d persistently refused to do so.

On 6 April the defendant issued a specially indorsed writ against the plaintiffs and Quaglino's claiming a declaration that Quaglino's had unreasonably withheld consent to the assignment of the property by the plaintiffs to the defendant and that accordingly the plaintiffs were lawfully entitled under their lease to make that assignment. By that writ, the defendant also claimed against the plaintiffs, firstly, three declarations with

e reference to condition 11(5) of the National Conditions of Sale, viz a declaration that the 'reversioner's licence' referred to in that condition was no longer necessary within the meaning of the condition, a declaration that the sale pursuant to the contract of 7 February was no longer subject to any licence being obtained, and a declaration that the plaintiffs were not entitled to rescind the contract, secondly, specific performance of the contract and, thirdly, damages.

f On 1 June the present originating summons was issued by the plaintiffs. By that summons the plaintiffs seek a declaration that, on the true construction of the contract and in the events that have occurred, the plaintiffs are entitled under condition 11(5) to rescind the contract.

On 14 June the master dismissed a summons by the defendant for summary judgment under RSC Ords 14 and 86 in the writ action.

g On 25 July the master dismissed an application by the defendant for consolidation of the proceedings commenced by the plaintiffs' originating summons with those in the defendant's writ action. An appeal against the master's decision on that application was dismissed by Whitford J on 14 October.

Undoubtedly there is a bona fide issue between the parties whether Quaglino's refusal to grant the licence was reasonable or unreasonable. There is also an issue between them

h whether Rochfords' conduct in withholding the licence was reasonable or unreasonable. Counsel for the defendant invited me to hold that, on the evidence before me, Rochfords' conduct was clearly unreasonable. The contention that Rochfords' conduct was unreasonable was not, however, advanced on behalf of the defendant until the hearing before me. It is not advanced in the defendant's writ action and the evidence in the present proceedings is not directed to it.

j Happily, the submissions put forward on behalf of the plaintiffs and of the defendant respectively as to the true construction of condition 11(5) make it unnecessary for me to decide whether either Rochfords' conduct, or Quaglino's, was reasonable or unreasonable. Accordingly, I express no view on that.

It is common ground that whether the plaintiffs are entitled to the declaration they seek depends on the true construction of the first sentence in condition 11(5), and in particular on what is meant by the words 'where necessary' in that sentence.

Counsel for the plaintiffs concedes that, where a lease contains a covenant against assignment without the landlord's consent in the form of the covenant in the present case, that consent becomes unnecessary if the landlord withholds it unreasonably. So much has been accepted law ever since *Treloar v Bigge* (1874) LR 9 Exch 151. Counsel submits, however that on the true construction of condition 11(5) the question whether the landlord's consent is necessary is to be answered by looking only at the lease; 'necessary', he says, in condition 11(5) means necessary under the lease and does not invite an inquiry whether at some stage between contract and completion the landlord has, by his conduct, rendered his consent unnecessary. Accordingly, counsel says, all that the plaintiffs have to prove here is that under the lease the landlord's consent to an assignment is necessary, that they have used their best endeavours to obtain it and that it cannot be obtained. It is neither here nor there that the landlord's refusal of its consent may be unreasonable.

The submission of counsel for the defendant is that 'where necessary' in condition 11(5) means 'where necessary as between landlord and tenant from time to time during the subsistence of the contract', so that, if the landlord's consent ceases to be necessary, because the landlord unreasonably withholds it, the contract ceases to be subject to that consent being obtained. So long, therefore, as it is bona fide in issue between the parties whether the landlord's consent has been reasonably or unreasonably withheld, the plaintiffs have not established their right to rescind.

I think that, in seeking to resolve a question of that kind as to the construction of an express condition in a contract for the sale of land, it is helpful to have in mind what the position would be in the absence of that condition. In its absence, the contract would be unconditional, so that the vendor would be bound to procure the landlord's licence to assign. If he failed to do so before the proper day for completion, he would be in breach of contract and so liable in damages to the purchaser. Those damages would be limited by the rule in *Bain v Fothergill* (1874) LR 7 HL 158, [1874–80] All ER Rep 83 if the vendor had done his best to obtain the landlord's licence. The court would not, however, order specific performance of the contract if there was a doubt whether the landlord's licence was being withheld reasonably or unreasonably: see per Maugham J in *Curtis Moffat Ltd v Wheeler* [1929] 2 Ch 224 at 235–236. *Re Marshall and Salt's Contract* [1900] 2 Ch 202, to which I was referred, is an example of the court refusing specific performance in such circumstances.

I was referred also to *White v Hay* (1895) 72 LT 281 and *Lewis & Allenby (1909) Ltd v Pegge* [1914] 1 Ch 782. In each of those cases, however, the relevant covenant did not contain the word 'unreasonably'. It merely precluded the landlord from withholding his consent if the proposed assignee was a respectable and responsible person, and it was admitted in each case that the proposed assignee was such a person. The question whether the landlord might be withholding his consent unreasonably did not, therefore, arise. The same is true of *Willmott v London Road Car Co Ltd* [1910] 2 Ch 525, [1908–10] All ER Rep 908, to which Maugham J referred in the passage that I have mentioned.

If the construction of condition 11(5) for which counsel for the defendant contends is right, its effect is to alter that position only to the extent of absolving the vendor from liability for damages if the landlord's consent is reasonably withheld and to give the vendor in that event a right to rescind the contract. It does not alter the position where the landlord's consent is unreasonably withheld. Nor does it do anything to solve the problems that arise where there is a doubt whether the landlord is withholding his consent reasonably or unreasonably.

I do not believe that that can have been the intention of the authors of the National Conditions of Sale, or that it is a sensible intention to impute to parties to contracts incorporating those conditions. I find helpful guidance in the judgment of Goff J in *Lipmans Wallpaper Ltd v Mason & Hodghton Ltd* [1968] 1 All ER 1123 at 1129, [1969] 1 Ch 20 at 35, where he indicated that, in his view, condition 11(5), or more exactly its predecessor in the National Conditions of Sale (17th edn), was intended to afford a vendor security and a quick remedy. He held that the vendor was not even bound, before exercising his right to rescind, to give the purchaser an opportunity to approach the

landlord himself. Goff J would certainly not have held that the vendor was bound to
hold his hand until the question whether the landlord was withholding his consent
reasonably or unreasonably was resolved. Counsel for the defendant conceded that, in
most cases, a prudent vendor, or for that matter a prudent purchaser, would not act on
his own view of the answer to that question, but would await a decision of the court.
Counsel referred me to s 53 of the Landlord and Tenant Act 1954, which enables such a
question to be resolved by the county court, however valuable the property in question.
Even in the county court, however, the proceedings might take some weeks or months,
and there would then be the possibility of an appeal. In any case, I agree with counsel for
the plaintiffs that it cannot be a purpose of condition 11(5) to generate litigation. On the
contrary, its main purpose is to afford the vendor a means of escape from litigation and
delay.

I accordingly propose to make the declaration sought by the plaintiffs.

Declaration that plaintiffs entitled to rescind contract.

Solicitors: *Whittington Tilling & Knight* (for the plaintiffs); *Titmuss Sainer & Webb* (for the
defendant).

Vivian Horvath   Barrister.

Universal City Studios Inc and others v Hubbard and others

COURT OF APPEAL, CIVIL DIVISION
CUMMING-BRUCE AND FOX LJJ
16, 17 NOVEMBER, 21 DECEMBER 1983

*Practice – Inspection of property – Property subject matter of action or in respect of which
question arising – Privilege against self-incrimination – Exception to rule against self-incrimination
– Proceedings for infringement of copyright or passing off – Proceedings for apprehended
infringement of copyright or apprehended passing off – Withdrawal of privilege against self-
incrimination – Extent of withdrawal – Whether withdrawal extending to any offence or only to
offences in connection with infringement of copyright or passing off – Supreme Court Act 1981,
s 72(1)(2)(c)(5).*

*Practice – Inspection of property – Property subject matter of action or in respect of which
question arising – Privilege against self-incrimination – Document lawfully seized pursuant to
court order – Document not made use of in court – Whether return of document should be ordered.*

The words 'any offence' in para (b) of the definition of 'related offence' in s 72(5)[a] of the
Supreme Court Act 1981 should be given their plain and ordinary, and not a restricted,
meaning. Accordingly, in proceedings brought to prevent any apprehended infringement
of rights relating to intellectual property or any apprehended passing off, the withdrawal
by s 72(1) and (2)(c) of the 1981 Act of privilege against self-incrimination of a person or
his or her spouse in respect of a 'related offence' has effect with respect to any offence of
any nature which is revealed by the facts on which the plaintiff relies in those proceedings
and is not restricted merely to offences committed by or in the course of the infringement
or passing off to which the proceedings relate or to any offence involving fraud or
dishonesty which is committed in connection with that infringement or passing off (see
p 664 *c* to *f*, post).

Quaere. Whether, in relation to a document which has been lawfully seized pursuant
to an Anton Piller order, the fact that the document has not been made use of in court is,

---

a   Section 72 is set out at p 663 *d* to p 664 *a*, post

by itself, a sufficient reason to order its return on the ground that it may incriminate a
person (see p 664 *j* and p 665 *a b*, post).   *a*
   Decision of Falconer J [1983] 2 All ER 596 affirmed.

Notes
For privilege against incrimination and statutory exceptions thereto, see 13 Halsbury's
Laws (4th edn) para 92, 17 ibid para 240–242 and 37 ibid para 372, and for cases on the
subject, see 18 Digest (Reissue) 19, 149–152, 97–102, 1195–1246, 22 ibid 433–437,   *b*
4310–4346 and 37(2) ibid 482, 2989.
   For the Supreme Court Act 1981, s 72, see 51 Halsbury's Statutes (3rd edn) 1263.

Cases referred to in judgment
Ashburton (Lord) v Page [1913] 2 Ch 469, [1911–13] All ER Rep 708, CA.
Helliwell v Piggott-Sims [1980] FSR 356, CA.   *c*
ITC Film Distributors v Video Exchange Ltd [1982] 2 All ER 241, [1982] Ch 431, [1982] 3
   WLR 125.

Interlocutory appeal
The appellant, Peter Hubbard, who was the first defendant in a copyright action brought
by the plaintiffs, (1) Universal City Studios Inc (suing on behalf of themselves and on   *d*
behalf of and as representing all other members of the Motion Picture Association of
America Inc), (2) WEA Records Ltd, (3) Go Video Ltd, (4) Guild Home Video Ltd, (5)
Home Video Holdings plc, (6) Intervision Video Ltd, (7) Precision Video Ltd, (8) RCA/
Columbia Pictures UK (a firm), (9) Thorn EMI Video Programmes Ltd, (10) VCL Video
Services Ltd, (11) Videomedia Ltd, (12) Videospace Ltd, (13) Embassy Pictures (a firm)
and (14) MGM/UA Entertainment Co, applied for an order (i) that an Anton Piller order   *e*
made by Whitford J on 29 September 1982 be set aside, (ii) that the plaintiffs, by
themselves or their solicitors, return forthwith to those from whom they took them all
documents and other material taken into their possession in the course of execution of
the Anton Piller order and (iii) that the plaintiffs, by themselves or their solicitors, destroy
on oath all copies made by them of any such documents or other material and make no
further use whatsoever of any information contained in such documents or other   *f*
material. In his affidavit in support of the application the first defendant denied an
allegation of the plaintiffs' that he was the leader of a gang which made counterfeit copies
of certain films of which the plaintiffs owned the copyright and stated that the evidence
on which the plaintiffs had relied on their application for the Anton Piller order was
more consistent with involvement by the first defendant in the manufacture and
distribution of pornographic films than with involvement in the counterfeiting trade.   *g*
The first defendant submitted that he was entitled to claim privilege against self-
incrimination because there was a very serious risk that at the hearing of the plaintiffs'
application for interlocutory relief in their copyright action (i) he might incriminate
himself in respect of unlawful activity with regard to pornographic films if he answered
questions about the documents and (ii) that he might be incriminated by the documents
themselves. On 21 January 1983 Falconer J ([1983] 2 All ER 596, [1983] Ch 241)   *h*
dismissed the first defendant's application on the ground that, by virtue of s 72(1) and
(2)(c) of the Supreme Court Act 1981 the first defendant was not in the circumstances
entitled to claim privilege against self-incrimination. The first defendant appealed to the
Court of Appeal with the leave of the judge. By a respondent's notice dated 8 January
1983 the plaintiffs gave notice that they would contend that Falconer J's judgment should
be affirmed because a claim to privilege was no ground for ordering the return to the   *j*
first defendant of the relevant documents or for ordering that no further use be made of
them and in any event a proper claim to privilege arising out of the relevant documents
was not sustainable.

Alastair J D Wilson for the first defendant.
John P Baldwin for the plaintiffs.

At the conclusion of the argument the court announced that it would dismiss the appeal for reasons to be given later.

21 December. The following judgment of the court was delivered.

CUMMING-BRUCE LJ. On 17 November 1983 this court dismissed the appeal from the order made by Falconer J ([1983] 2 All ER 596, [1983] Ch 241) on 21 January 1983 whereby he dismissed the first defendant's motion to set aside the Anton Piller and Mareva order made on 29 September 1982. The court proceeded forthwith to hear another appeal arising out of connected facts and stated that it would later give reasons for dismissal of this appeal.

The appeal raises first a short point of construction of s 72 of the Supreme Court Act 1981, which provided for the withdrawal of privilege against incrimination of a party or spouse in the proceedings and circumstances specified in the section. As we agree with the judge on his construction of the definition of 'related offence' in s 72(5)(*b*) of the 1981 Act, and with the reasons for that construction, we can deal briefly with the submissions made by the first defendant in support of his contention that the judge was wrong.

It is convenient to set out the words of s 72:

'*Withdrawal of privilege against incrimination of self or spouse in certain proceedings.*—
(1) In any proceedings to which this subsection applies a person shall not be excused, by reason that to do so would tend to expose that person, or his or her spouse, to proceedings for a related offence or for the recovery of a related penalty—(*a*) from answering any question put to that person in the first-mentioned proceedings; or (*b*) from complying with any order made in those proceedings.

(2) Subsection (1) applies to the following civil proceedings in the High Court, namely—(*a*) proceedings for infringement of rights pertaining to any intellectual property or for passing off; (*b*) proceedings brought to obtain disclosure of information relating to any infringement of such rights or to any passing off; and (*c*) proceedings brought to prevent any apprehended infringement of such rights or any apprehended passing off.

(3) Subject to subsection (4), no statement or admission made by a person—(*a*) in answering a question put to him in any proceedings to which subsection (1) applies; or (*b*) in complying with any order made in any such proceedings, shall, in proceedings for any related offence or for the recovery of any related penalty, be admissible in evidence against that person or (unless they married after the making of the statement or admission) against the spouse of that person.

(4) Nothing in subsection (3) shall render any statement or admission made by a person as there mentioned inadmissible in evidence against that person in proceedings for perjury or contempt of court.

(5) In this section—"intellectual property" means any patent, trade mark, copyright, registered design, technical or commercial information or other intellectual property; "related offence", in relation to any proceedings to which subsection (1) applies, means—(*a*) in the case of proceedings within subsection (2)(*a*) or (*b*)—(i) any offence committed by or in the course of the infringement or passing off to which those proceedings relate; or (ii) any offence not within sub-paragraph (i) committed in connection with that infringement or passing off, being an offence involving fraud or dishonesty; (*b*) in the case of proceedings within subsection (2)(*c*), any offence revealed by the facts on which the plaintiff relies in those proceedings; "related penalty", in relation to any proceedings to which subsection (1) applies means—(*a*) in the case of proceedings within subsection (2)(*a*) or (*b*), any penalty incurred in respect of anything done or omitted in connection with the infringement or passing off to which those proceedings relate; (*b*) in the case of proceedings within subsection (2)(*c*), any penalty incurred in respect of any act or omission revealed by the facts on which the plaintiff relies in those proceedings.

(6) Any reference in this section to civil proceedings in the High Court of any

description includes a reference to proceedings on appeal arising out of civil proceedings in the High Court of that description.'

The proceedings brought by the plaintiffs were proceedings claiming relief under s 72(2)(*a*), (*b*) and (*c*). The question of construction relates to the meaning and effect of the statutory definition of 'related offence' in para (*b*) of the definition: 'in the case of proceedings within subsection 2(*c*), any offence revealed by the facts on which the plaintiff relies in those proceedings.'

The first defendant makes a bold submission: although the words of the definition specify 'any offence' the plain and ordinary meaning of those words should be restricted to mean only the offences specified in para (*a*) of the definition, so that 'any offence' means only 'any offence of the kind specified in para (*a*)(i) and (ii) of the definition of 'related offence' in sub-s (5)'.

The first answer to this submission is that if the draftsman had intended to achieve this result it would have been the easiest thing in the world to add the necessary words of restriction to the definition in para (*b*). It is however clear that the draftsman expressly distinguished the extent of the privilege in the case of proceedings within sub-s (2)(*a*) or (*b*) from the extent of the privilege in the case of proceedings within sub-s 2(*c*). The restricted construction for which the first defendant contends renders otiose the whole structure of the distinction between paras (*a*) and (*b*) of the definition. The first defendant submits that there should be no difference between the privilege withdrawn in proceedings as described in sub-s (2)(*a*) and (*b*) on the one hand as compared to the privilege withdrawn in proceedings as described in sub-s (2)(*c*). The answer is that Parliament evidently decided that there should be such a distinction, and defined 'related offence' in quite different and much wider terms in the case of proceedings to prevent future torts than in the cases of proceedings in respect of past or present infringements. The policy of Parliament is to be collected from the words of the 1981 Act is that it is only where there is a risk of further damage to a plaintiff that a defendant is denied the right to claim privilege in respect of self-incrimination for offences not committed by or in the course of or in connection with the alleged infringement. If the words are given their plain and ordinary meaning there is no ambiguity in the definition in para (*b*).

The second ground of appeal is that even on the construction of s 72 which the judge decided, and which we affirm, the offences on the grounds of which the first defendant claims privilege was not revealed by any facts on which the plaintiffs rely in the action. This is a misunderstanding of the allegations of facts in the plaintiffs' evidence. The plaintiffs allege that the facts in the documents and the fact of large numbers of plain tapes found in the pirates' den are not only consistent with but point strongly to an intention to carry out future infringements. So those are the facts relied on by the plaintiffs. The offences for which the first defendant claims the privilege against self-incrimination are offences which he, as defendant, says are revealed by the facts relied on by the plaintiffs. We reject this ground of appeal.

Having dismissed the appeal against the order made by Falconer J, it is unnecessary for this court to decide whether the judge was right in the view that he expressed about the consequence of the restricted construction on the plaintiffs' right to continue to withhold the disputed documents from the first defendant. By a respondent's notice the plaintiffs contend that a successful claim for privilege is no ground for ordering the return to the first defendant of the relevant documents, or for ordering that no further use should be made of the relevant documents. The judge stated ([1983] 2 All ER 596 at 606, [1983] Ch 241 at 255):

'In this particular case, of course, the motion by the first defendant to exclude these documents has been brought before they have been made use of in court. I stress that, in coming to that conclusion, Warner J had had cited to him *Helliwell v Piggott-Sims* [1980] FSR 356. I think that, in view of that decision, if I should conclude that the defendant is not barred by the provisions of s 72 of the Supreme Court Act 1981, I should order the return of the documents concerned and make the order that he seeks, this being a case where the defendant has properly brought a   proceedings for the return of the documents in the form of the present application, and that before they have been adduced in any form or shape or any evidence based on them has been put before the court.'

The judge reached this conclusion after considering *Lord Ashburton v Page* [1913] 2 Ch 469, [1911–13] All ER Rep 708, the *Helliwell v Piggot-Sims* case and the judgment of Warner J in *ITC Film Distributors Ltd v Video Exchange Ltd* [1982] 2 All ER 241, [1982] Ch 431. We heard argument on the respondent's notice. We content ourselves with saying

b   that we entertain serious doubt about the correctness of the judge's conclusion on this question. As the judgment of Falconer J has been reported we think it right to express our doubts, although it has not been necessary to decide the question.

Appeal dismissed. Leave to appeal to the House of Lords refused.

c   Solicitors: *Anthony D Samuels*, Esher (for the first defendant); *A E Hamlin & Co* (for the plaintiffs).

Bebe Chua   Barrister.

---

d   # Hamilton v Martell Securities Ltd

CHANCERY DIVISION
VINELOTT J
28 OCTOBER, 14 NOVEMBER 1983

e   *Landlord and tenant – Breach of covenant to repair – Leave to institute proceedings – Proceedings to recover cost of repairs already carried out by landlord – Landlord carrying out repairs and bringing action against tenant to recover cost of repairs – Whether claim for debt due under lease or claim for damages for breach of repairing covenant – Whether leave required to bring action – Leasehold Property (Repairs) Act 1938, s 1.*

f   Where a tenant fails to comply with a repairing covenant in a lease which expressly confers on the landlord the right to enter on the demised premises, carry out the repairs and recover the cost from the tenant, an action by the landlord to recover the cost of the repairs is, having regard to the express terms of the covenant, a claim for a debt due under the lease rather than a claim for damages for breach of the covenant within s 1(1)[a]

g   and (2) of the Leasehold Property (Repairs) Act 1938, and accordingly the landlord does not require leave under s 1(3) to bring the action against the tenant (see p 673 d e and p 674 j, post).

Bader Properties Ltd v Linley Property Investments Ltd (1968) 19 P & CR 620 and *Middlegate Properties Ltd v Gidlow-Jackson* (1977) 34 P & CR 4 applied.

SEDAC Investments Ltd v Tanner [1982] 3 All ER 646 distinguished.

h   *Sidnell v Wilson* [1966] 1 All ER 681 considered.

Swallow Securities Ltd v Brand (1983) 45 P & CR 328 not followed.

Notes

For a landlord's remedies for breach of the tenant's covenant to repair, in particular an action for damages, see 27 Halsbury's Laws (4th edn) paras 301, 302.

j   For the Leasehold Property (Repairs) Act 1938, s 1, see 18 Halsbury's Statutes (3rd edn) 473.

Cases referred to in judgment

Bader Properties Ltd v Linley Property Investments Ltd (1968) 19 P & CR 620.

---

a   Section 1, so far as material, is set out at p 670 *h* to p 671 *b*, post

Middlegate Properties Ltd v Gidlow-Jackson (1977) 34 P & CR 4, CA.
SEDAC Investments Ltd v Tanner [1982] 3 All ER 646, [1982] 1 WLR 1342.
Sidnell v Wilson [1966] 1 All ER 681, [1966] 2 QB 67, [1966] 2 WLR 560, CA.
Skinners' Co v Knight [1891] 2 QB 542, CA.
Swallow Securities Ltd v Brand (1983) 45 P & CR 328.

Cases also cited
Harrison-Broadley v Smith [1964] 1 All ER 867, [1964] 1 WLR 456, CA.
Land Securities plc v Receiver for the Metropolitan Police District [1983] 2 All ER 254, [1983]
1 WLR 439.

Appeal
By an originating summons as amended, dated 8 September 1983, the plaintiff, Sir
Robert Charles Richard Caradoc Hamilton Bt (the lessor) applied for (1) an order giving
him leave under s 1(3) of the Leasehold Property (Repairs) Act 1938 to take proceedings
for damages for breaches of the covenants to repair contained in a lease dated 21 May
1963 made between the lessor and the predecessor in title of the defendant, Martell
Securities Ltd (the lessee), of premises known as Walton Hall, Wellesbourne,
Warwickshire, (2) a direction under s 2 of the 1938 Act that the lessor should have the
benefit of s 146(3) of the Law of Property Act 1925 in relation to the costs and expenses
incurred in reference to the breaches of covenant, (3) an order that the costs of the
application be taxed by the taxing master and paid by the lessee to the lessor and (4) in
the alternative a declaration that the lessor was entitled to claim from the lessee the cost
of the works carried out by the lessor's contractors, Roadrive Ltd, in respect of the works
set out in the schedule to a notice served by the lessor's solicitors on the lessee dated 6 July
1983 without the leave of the court. By an order made on 21 September 1983 Master
Barratt dismissed the lessor's originating summons. The lessor appealed. The facts are set
out in the judgment.

David Neuberger for the lessor.
John Male for the lessee.

Cur adv vult

14 November. The following judgment was delivered.

VINELOTT J. This is an appeal from a decision of Master Barratt who dismissed an
application by Sir Robert Charles Richard Caradoc Hamilton Bt for leave under s 1(3) of
the Leasehold Property (Repairs) Act 1938 to take proceedings for damages for breaches
of covenants to repair contained in a lease granted by the plaintiff to the predecessor in
title of the defendant, Martell Securities Ltd. I shall refer hereafter to the plaintiff as 'the
lessor', and to the defendant and its predecessors in title as 'the lessee'.

The lease, which is dated 21 May 1963, gave the lessor the right, in the event of the
failure of the lessee to carry out works of repair in compliance with a covenant to repair,
to enter the demised premises, carry out the repairs and recover the cost of them from
the lessee. The lessor, having carried out repairs which the lessee had failed to carry out,
applied for leave to take proceedings to recover the cost of them. It seemed, in the light
of the decision of McNeill J in *Swallow Securities Ltd v Brand* (1983) 45 P & CR 328, that
leave was necessary.

However, it was held by Mr Michael Wheeler QC, sitting as a deputy judge of the
High Court, in *SEDAC Investments Ltd v Tanner* [1982] 3 All ER 646, [1982] 1 WLR 1342,
that the court has no jurisdiction under s 1(3) of the 1938 Act to give a lessor leave to
commence proceedings to recover from a lessee damages for breach of a covenant to
repair if at the date of the application the lessor has entered the demised premises and has
remedied the want of repair. In that case, the lessor did not enter the demised premises
and carry out the repairs pursuant to any provision in the lease, and did not seek to

recover the costs as a debt owed to him. The claim was a claim for damages for breach of
the covenant to repair, and fell clearly within s 1(1) of the 1938 Act. However, it was
conceded before Master Barratt that the decision of Michael Wheeler QC was binding on
him and precluded him from giving leave.

The question raised in the notice of appeal is whether that decision is distinguishable,
and if it is not, whether I ought to follow it. However, in this appeal the lessor also seeks
leave to amend his application to include a claim for a declaration that he is entitled to
recover the cost of the works of repair without leave under s 1(3). I gave leave for that
amendment to be made. It was conceded by counsel for the lessee that a decision that the
court has no jurisdiction to grant the lessor leave to commence proceedings for damages
for breach of covenant would not preclude the lessor from subsequently seeking a
declaration that he is entitled to recover the cost of works of repair without leave. Thus,
the only effect of refusing leave would have been to put the lessor to the expense and
delay of instituting fresh proceedings for a declaration in the terms sought. It was not in
dispute that the lessor had given the lessee adequate notice of his intention to apply to
make this amendment.

The difficulty which confronts the lessor is that McNeill J decided in *Swallow Securities
Ltd v Brand* that a provision giving a lessor the right, in the event of the failure of the
lessee to carry out repairs in accordance with a repairing covenant, himself to remedy the
want of repair and to recover the cost from the lessee, is a right to damages within s 1(2)
of the 1938 Act, and that the lessor cannot therefore enforce his claim to recover the cost
without the leave of the court. If *SEDAC Investments* was rightly decided, the court has
no jurisdiction to give leave after the want of repair has been remedied. If both these
decisions are correct, a provision in a lease giving the lessor the right in the event of
failure of the lessee to carry out repairs in compliance with a repairing covenant himself
to remedy the want of repair and to recover the cost of so doing, is of no practical utility.
Indeed, a provision of this kind is worse than useless; it is a trap. For under s 4(1) of the
Defective Premises Act 1972, a lessor who, under the lease, undertakes an obligation to
repair, owes to persons who might reasonably be expected to be affected by defects in the
premises, to see that they are reasonably safe. That duty is extended by sub-s (4) to the
case where, under the lease, the lessor is given the right, expressly or impliedly, to enter
the demised premises and carry out repairs. He is under the same duty as a lessor within
sub-s (1) as from the time when he first is, or by notice or otherwise, can put himself in a
position to exercise the right. A lessor who reserves the right, in the event of the failure
of the lessee to carry out repairs under a repairing covenant, to enter and carry out the
repairs himself, falls prima facie within sub-s (4), at least after he has given, or is in a
position to give, any notice which, under the terms, express or implied in the lease, he is
required to give before he exercises that right. Thus the effect of including such a
provision is to expose the lessor to a potential liability to third parties without giving him
any effective remedy against his lessee.

If, to protect himself from liability, he enters and does the necessary works of repair,
he cannot enforce his claim to recover the cost without the leave of the court and, the
want of repair having been remedied, the court has no jurisdiction to grant him leave.
Further, it must be at least doubtful whether the court would have jurisdiction to give
him leave to commence proceedings to recover the cost of works which he proposes to
carry out but has not yet carried out. In any event, the danger to third parties might be
so pressing that he could not delay the necessary repairs while he made an application for
leave, which might possibly be opposed or taken to appeal.

The result is so startling as to compel a careful reconsideration of these two decisions.
Before turning to them I should, I think, set out in greater detail the terms of the lease of
21 May 1963, the nature of the work carried out by the lessor, and the terms and history
of the relevant legislation.

The lease was made between the lessor and one Christine Nora Foot. She was the
proprietor of a private school and the lease contains a covenant not to use the demised
premises except for the purposes of a fee-paying school. The demised premises comprise

a substantial mansion house called Walton Hall in Warwickshire, with an extensive park and amenity land. The grounds surround a church, not, of course, included in the demise, called St James's Church, Walton.

A road coloured brown on the plan annexed to the lease (which I will call 'the brown road') runs from the church, through the churchyard and on through the park over a bridge, which crosses a large, ornamental lake, to a public road which leads to Walton. Another road, coloured green on another plan annexed to the lease (which I will call 'the green road') runs from the demised premises over other land not comprised in the lease, to another village called Wellesbourne.

The lease is for a term of 99 years from 29 September 1963. The lessee is given the right to use the green road, subject to the payment to the lessor of a proportion of the cost of repairing it. The lessor reserves a right of way for himself, and all members of the public with or without vehicles, over the brown road and the bridge, for the purposes of obtaining access to the church and graveyard.

The lessee's covenants, which are contained in cl 2 of the lease, contain the following provisions:

'(f) THAT the Lessee will pay to the Lessor all costs charges and expenses (including the legal costs and fees payable to a surveyor) which may be incurred by the Lessor in or in contemplation of any proceedings under Sections 146 and 147 of The Law of Property Act 1925 . . . (i) THAT the Lessee will from time to time and at all times during the said term well and substantially repair cleanse maintain amend and keep the said messuage and buildings on the demised premises and all new buildings which may at any time during the said term be erected thereon by the Lessee and all additions made thereto and the fixtures therein and the walls windows fences sewers drains roads bridges and appurtenances thereof with all necessary repairs cleansings and amendments whatsoever . . . (m) THAT it shall be lawful for the Lessor or his Agents twice or oftener in every year of the said term during reasonable hours in school holiday periods (if possible) and upon reasonable notice being given to the Lessee during the daytime with or without workmen and others to enter the said premises to view the state and condition of the same and of all defects and want of reparation then and there found to give and leave at the said premises notice in writing to the Lessee And that the Lessee will within the period of three calendar months after such notice or sooner if requisite repair and make good the same according to such notice and the covenants in that behalf hereinbefore contained (n) THAT if the Lessee shall at any time make default in the performance of any of the covenants hereinbefore contained for or relating to the repair of the said premises it shall be lawful for the Lessor (but without prejudice to the right of re-entry under the clause hereinafter contained) to enter upon the said premises and repair the same at the expense of the Lessee in accordance with the covenants and provisions of this Lease and the expense of such repairs shall be repaid by the Lessee to the Lessor on demand.'

Pausing there, it is common ground that the lessor cannot proceed under para (n) to make good any want of repair unless the lessor has served notice under para (m), and the lessee has failed to comply with it. The default contemplated by para (n) is a failure to make good wants of reparation after being called on to do so.

Then under cl 2, para (w) there is a covenant:

'THAT the Lessee will pay to the Lessor on demand from time to time one-third of the cost of maintaining the road or way shown coloured green on the plan Numbered 2.'

The lessor's covenants are contained in cl 3. Paragraph (C) reads as follows:

'THAT the Lessor will pay to the Lessee one half of the cost of keeping the bridge coloured brown hatched black on the said plan Numbered 1 in good repair and to pay to the Lessee on demand one third of the costs and expenses incurred by the Lessee in keeping the said roads or drives coloured brown on the said plan Numbered 1 in good repair and condition.'

It is a curious feature of the lease that under cl 2(n) the lessor can prima facie recover the whole cost of works of repair to the bridge and brown road carried out by him, whereas he is liable to contribute part of the cost of repair carried out by the lessee, if the lessee performs its obligation under the repairing covenant. It may be that cl 2(n) should be restricted to the recovery of the costs incurred by the lessor other than the proportion he could have been called on to pay if those works had been carried out by the lessee.

In the event, the question has become academic. The lease was assigned by the original lessee to a company called St Vincent School (Walton Hall) Ltd, in 1964. In 1971, that company wished to assign the lease to another company, Walton Hall (Hotels) Ltd, which proposed to use the hall as an hotel.

By a deed dated 7 April 1971 the covenant restricting the use of the demised premises to use as a private school was modified to permit use as an hotel, and the lessee also agreed other variations, including a provision that the lessee's right to use the green road was to be subject to the payment by the lessee of the whole cost of maintaining it, so far as not maintainable at public expense, and it was also provided that the lessor's right to use the brown road and the bridge was to be free of any obligation to contribute to the cost of repairing them.

In 1978 Walton Hall (Hotel) Ltd, with the licence of the lessor, assigned the benefit of the lease to the defendant. It has, I understand, continued to be used as an hotel.

In January 1981 solicitors acting for the lessor wrote to the lessee's solicitors complaining that the brown road was falling into serious disrepair, and asking that remedial work should be put in hand. The response was a claim that a farmer, a tenant of the lessor, used the road more than the guests of the hotel. That, I think, referred to the green road about which complaint had not then been made. Nothing was done to repair either road, and the matter was taken up again by the lessor's solicitors in January 1982. By a letter dated 25 January 1982 to the lessee's accountants, the lessor's solicitors informed them that they proposed to treat the letter of 8 January 1981 as a notice under the lease calling on the lessee to carry out necessary works of repair to the roads and that the lessee having failed to carry out the repairs, the lessor's surveyors had arranged to obtain an estimate of the cost. They enclosed a copy of the estimate obtained, which was from a company called Roadrive Ltd. They offered to delay for 14 days the giving of instructions to Roadrive to carry out the work, so as to give the lessee an opportunity of considering the estimate and of making alternative proposals. They stressed that any proposals would have to be made quickly, as it was essential that the work should be carried out promptly.

Early in February 1982 the lessee's accountants asked the lessor's solicitors to delay giving instructions to Roadrive pending discussions between them. Nothing happened, and on 2 April 1982 the lessor's solicitors wrote to the lessee's accountants to say that the lessor's surveyors would be instructed to put the repairs in hand without delay and that they would look to the lessees for payment of the cost.

No reply was received. The work was not carried out at once, no doubt because the worst of the bad weather was then over.

On 14 September 1982 the lessor's solicitors wrote to say that if the roads suffered another winter they would become impassable, and that work would be put in hand forthwith unless they had heard by return of post that the lessee's had themselves put the work in hand. Again, nothing happened.

On 22 September the lessor's solicitors had second thoughts. They wrote to the lessee's accountants to say they had advised the lessor that he should not instruct contractors to carry out the work but should issue proceedings to compel the lessee to comply with the covenant.

Then on 12 October there was another change of front. The lessor's solicitors wrote to say that the condition of the roads was such that urgent and substantial works were necessary and that they had given instructions to put the work in hand. That was done. The total costs of the works was £14,680, exclusive of VAT, of which £5,718, exclusive of VAT, was attributable to the repairs to the brown road.

The lessor commenced proceedings in which he claimed damages for breach of the covenant to repair the green road, and has obtained summary judgment for damages to be assessed. If the lessor is right in his main contention in this appeal, he was entitled to recover the cost of the repairs and not to unliquidated damages. However, nothing turns on that. No leave was necessary under the 1938 Act to recover the cost of the repairs to the green road for even if the lessee's covenant to pay the cost of repair was a covenant to keep it in repair within the 1938 Act the green road was not part of the demised premises.

Before turning to the legislation, I should observe that in this case the potential liability of the lessor under the Defective Premises Act 1972 is a real and not a theoretical one. The brown road is used by parishioners and a serious want of repair might cause damage to a car using the road, or even injury to an elderly and infirm parishioner going to and from the church on foot.

Section 146 of the Law of Property Act 1925, which re-enacts with amendments provisions of s 14 of the Conveyancing Act 1881, provides:

'(1) A right of re-entry or foreefiture . . . for a breach of any covenant or condition in the lease shall not be enforceable by action or otherwise, unless and until the lessor serves on a lessee a notice—(a) specifying the particular breach complained of; and (b) if the breach is capable of remedy, requiring the lessee to remedy the breach; and (c) in any case, requiring the lessee to make compensation in money for the breach; and the lessee fails, within a reasonable time thereafter, to remedy the breach, if it is capable of remedy, and to make reasonable compensation in money, to the satisfaction of the lessor, for the breach.'

Section 146(2) gives the lessee the right, if proceedings are taken after notice has been given, to apply for relief against forfeiture. I should read s 146(3) in full:

'A lessor shall be entitled to recover as a debt due to him from a lessee, and in addition to damages (if any), all reasonable costs and expenses properly incurred by the lessor in the employment of a solicitor and surveyor or valuer, or otherwise, in reference to any breach giving rise to a right of re-entry or forfeiture which, at the request of the lessee, is waived by the lessor, or from which the lessee is relieved, under the provisions of this Act.'

Subsection 11 provides that s 146 is not to affect the law relating to forfeiture or relief in case of non-payment of rent.

Section 146 did not, of course, affect a lessor's right to claim damages for breach of covenant. That right was first restricted in the case of a breach of covenant to repair by s 18 of the Landlord and Tenant Act 1927, which provides that damages for breach of a covenant to keep or put premises in repair during the currency of a lease, or to leave or put premises in repair at the termination of the lease, are not to exceed the amount of the diminution in value of the reversion resulting from the breach.

Section 1(1) to (3) of the Leasehold Property (Repairs) Act 1938, as amended by s 51 of the Landlord and Tenant Act 1954, provide as follows:

'(1) Where a lessor serves on a lessee under sub-section (1) of section one hundred and forty-six of the Law of Property Act, 1925, a notice that relates to a breach of a covenant or agreement to keep or put in repair during the currency of the lease all or any of the property comprised in the lease, and at the date of the service of the notice three years or more of the terms of the lease remain unexpired, the lessee may within twenty-eight days from that date serve on the lessor a counter-notice to the effect that he claims the benefit of this Act.

(2) A right to damages for a breach of such a covenant as aforesaid shall not be enforceable by action commenced at any time at which three years or more of the

a   term of the lease remain unexpired unless the lessor has served on the lessee not less than one month before the commencement of the action such a notice as is specified in subsection (1) of section one hundred and forty-six of the Law of Property Act, 1925, and where a notice is served under this subsection the lessee may, within twenty-eight days from the date of the service thereof, serve on the lessor a counter-notice to the effect that he claims the benefit of this Act.

b   (3) Where a counter-notice is served by a lessee under this section, then, notwithstanding anything in any enactment or rule of law, no proceedings, by action or otherwise, shall be taken by the lessor for the enforcement of any right of re-entry or forfeiture under any proviso or stipulation in the lease for breach of the covenant or agreement in question, or for damages for breach thereof, otherwise than with the leave of the court.'

c   Subsection (4) provides that a notice under s 146 must include, in conspicuous characters, a statement of the lessee's right to serve a counter-notice.

Then s 1(5) of the 1938 Act reads as follows:

'Leave for the purposes of this section shall not be given unless the lessor proves—(*a*) that the immediate remedying of the breach in question is requisite for preventing substantial diminution in the value of his reversion, or that the value *d*   thereof has been substantially diminished by the breach; (*b*) that the immediate remedying of the breach is required for giving effect in relation to the premises to the purposes of any enactment, or of any byelaw or other provision having effect under an enactment, or for giving effect to any order of a court or requirement of any authority under any enactment or any such byelaw, or other provision as aforesaid; (*c*) in a case in which the lessee is not in occupation of the whole of the *e*   premises, as respects which the covenant or agreement is proposed to be enforced, that the immediate remedying of the breach is required in the interests of the occupier of those premises or of part thereof; (*d*) that the breach can be immediately remedied at an expense that is relatively small in comparison with the much greater expense that would probably be occasioned by postponement of the necessary work; or (*e*) special circumstances which in the opinion of the court, render it just and *f*   equitable that leave should be given.'

Section 2 of the 1938 Act restricts the right of a lessor on whom a counter-notice is served, to recover costs and expenses within s 146(3) of the 1925 Act relating to the breach in respect of which the notice was given unless the lessor has made an application for leave under s 1(3) of the 1938 Act, and s 2 also gives the court power to direct to what extent, if at all, the lessor is to be entitled to recover those costs and expenses.

g   The 1938 Act was originally restricted to leases of residential property of a rateable value of less than £100 a year. That and other restrictions were lifted by, or modified by, the 1954 Act.

The legislative purpose of the 1938 Act, and the mischief against which it was directed, were described by Lord Denning MR in *Sidnell v Wilson* [1966] 1 All ER 681 at 683, [1966] 2 QB 67 at 76, in the following terms:

h   'The Act of 1938 was passed shortly before the war because of a great mischief prevalent at that time. Unscrupulous people used to buy up the reversion of leases and then bring pressure to bear on the tenants by an exaggerated list of dilapidations. The Act of 1938 applied to leases for seven years or more which had three years or more to run. In such cases Parliament enacted that a landlord, when he gave a notice *j*   under s. 146 of the Law of Property Act, 1925, to make good dilapidations, must state on the notice that the tenant was entitled to give a counter-notice.'

In *Swallow Securities Ltd v Brand* (1983) 45 P & CR 328 the tenant covenanted that she would: 'In accordance with the tenants' covenants in that behalf hereinafter contained', make good defects in the repair of the demised premises 'of which notice in writing shall be given by the lessors to the tenant within two calendar months next after the giving of such notice' (see 45 P & CR 328 at 329). Under cl 3(6) of the lease, the tenant also covenanted that in default of performance of the repairing covenants, she would permit the lessor to enter and do work of repairs, and—

> 'repay to the lessors on demand the cost of such repair, decoration, and maintenance or reinstatement, including any solicitor's counsel's and surveyor's costs and fees reasonably incurred by the lessors in respect thereof such costs to be recoverable by the lessors as if the same were rent in arrear.'

(See 45 P & CR 328 at 330.)

The lessor commenced proceedings to recover the cost of repairs which he claimed to have carried out following notice to, and default by, the lessee. The master struck out his statement of claim on the ground that he had not obtained leave under the Leasehold Property (Repairs) Act 1938 to commence proceedings. That decision was affirmed by McNeill J on appeal. McNeill J, after observing that the purpose of s 1 of the 1938 Act was to prevent forfeiture unless notice was given, and the lessee was given the opportunity of serving a counter-notice, or if he gave a counter-notice the leave of the court was obtained, said (at 334):

> 'The effect, and, to my mind, the landlord's intended purpose, of clause 3(6) of this lease was to circumvent those provisions by claiming that the landlord might, without the notice to the tenant required in the event of a breach of the covenant to repair pursuant to clause 3(4) of the lease, enter and do works and charge the tenant with the cost thereof. Further, by stating in clause 3(6) that such cost was recoverable as arrears of rent the landlord could put himself in the position, by relying on arrears of rent, of relieving himself, contrary to the purpose and intention of the Act, of the material obligations, whereas in truth here the forfeiture or claim for possession is founded on a breach of the covenant to repair—a covenant for breach of which, if forfeiture were sought, the procedure under sections 1 and 146 of [the Law of Property Act 1925] would be necessary.'

He gave four reasons for his conclusion that the lessor's claim was in substance a claim for damages for breach of the repairing covenant, in a passage which I think I should read in full (at 334–335):

> 'I consider, first, that clause 3(6) is wholly inconsistent with the purposes of section 1 of the Act of 1938, and section 18(1) of [the Landlord and Tenant Act 1927]; secondly, that I cannot and do not treat as a debt a sum not ascertainable at the time of the contract and ascertainable only as the cost of repairs carried out on the failure of the tenant to do those repairs in breach of covenant and, further, being fixed at the whim of the landlord in agreement with contractors of his choice; thirdly, that the clause removes from the tenant the choice given to her by the lease to carry out the works of repair at her own expense with contractors of her choice; fourthly, that the clause not only removes from the tenant the protection of the notice to do the repairs provided for by clause 3(4) but also deprives her of the option of having the work done by a contractor of her choice at a price agreed by her; and, finally, that in any event the provision that the amount to be charged or added as arrears of rent is to include solicitor's, counsel's and surveyor's reasonable fees offends against the basic principles of debt as recognised over the centuries unless there is to be imported, as I do not think must necessarily be imported for the efficacy of this lease, some provision such as that such fee should be taxed or be subject to such adjudication as to reasonableness as is laid down by some taxing or professional authority.'

McNeill J was not referred to the passage in the judgment of Lord Denning MR in *Sidnell v Wilson* which I have cited. As I understand it, the particular mischief at which, in the opinion of Lord Denning MR, the 1938 Act was directed was that an unscrupulous landlord would buy the reversion of a lease which had little value as a reversion and harass the tenant with schedules of dilapidations not with a view to ensuring that the property was kept in proper repair for the protection of the reversion, but to put pressure on the tenant, who might be a person of limited means, and who might not be in a position to obtain or accustomed to obtaining proper advice as to his liabilities, to the point at which he would accept an offer for the surrender of his lease.

An unscrupulous landlord who takes that course does not need to put his hand into his pocket to carry out the repairs which he seeks to compel the tenant to carry out, and indeed in the case of a long lease, he might have no real interest in ensuring that those repairs are carried out. It is not to my mind obvious that the presumed legislative purpose of countering that mischief should be extended so as to fetter a lessor's right to recover moneys which he has actually spent.

Counsel for the lessee pointed out that an unscrupulous lessor might similarly carry out repairs pursuant to a clause in the terms of cl 3(6) of the lease in the *Swallow Securities* case not because he genuinely wanted the repairs carried out, but in order to put financial pressure on the lessee. He submitted also that it would be inconsistent with the policy to be inferred from s 18 of the 1927 Act that a lessor should be permitted to enforce indirectly a covenant to repair by carrying out the works and recovering the cost in a case where the injury to the reversion consequent on the want of repair is small. It seems to me that the fact that a lessor must initially meet the cost of carrying out the repairs is itself a considerable disincentive. Whether that is so or not, I am not persuaded that this possible abuse justifies the court in treating an action to recover costs actually incurred by a lessor on repairs as if it were an action for damages for breach of a covenant to repair solely on the ground that the provision enabling a lessor to carry out repairs in the event of default by the lessee and to recover the cost is a device to circumvent the provisions of the 1927 and the 1938 Acts.

However, there is a more fundamental objection to the decision of McNeill J. He was not referred to two important decisions, one of Roskill J and the other of the Court of Appeal. The latter was, of course, binding on him.

In *Bader Properties Ltd v Linley Property Investments Ltd* (1968) 19 P & CR 620 the lessor sought to forfeit a lease for breach of a covenant not to underlet. The action for forfeiture was preceded by the service of notice under s 146, which alleged breaches of the covenant not to underlet and of the lessee's covenant to repair. The main issues were whether the lessor had given a licence to underlet and, if it had, whether it had waived the breach. The lessee succeeded on both these points, but there was a further claim.

The lease contained a covenant by the lessee to pay all expenses, including solicitors' costs and surveyors' fees incurred by the lessor incidental to the preparation and service of a notice under s 146 of the Law of Property Act 1925. The lessor had incurred solicitors' and surveyors' charges in connection with the service of the s 146 notice. Roskill J, after referring to s 14 of the 1881 Act, to s 146(3) of the 1925 Act, and to s 2 of the 1938 Act, said (at 642–643):

'Pausing there, such a counter-notice as contemplated by section 2 of the Act of 1938 was served, and no leave was obtained from the court. The plaintiffs here, however, do not seek to recover by virtue of any statutory provision; they seek to recover by virtue of the express covenant in the lease, and that covenant requires the defendants to pay all expenses incurred by the lessor incidental to the preparation and service of the notice. [Counsel for the defendants] sought to argue that that covenant was affected by the legislation to which I have just referred, and that so long as that legislation operated (as it would until nearly the end of the lease, unless, of course, it were meanwhile repealed), it was ineffective. If, however, a statutory provision is to be relied upon as restricting otherwise plain contractual rights, one would expect to find clear provision to that effect in the statute. [Counsel] was unable to point to any such provision. Moreover, having regard to what Fry L.J. said in *Skinners' Company* v. *Knight* ([1891] 2 QB 542 at 545)—that the expenses there in question were not compensation for breach of the covenant—I take the view that, where the parties have expressly covenanted for expenses of this kind to be paid by one to the other, there is nothing in the various statutory provisions to prevent effect being given to that covenant.'

That decision, as it seems to me, is inconsistent with the last of the reasons given by McNeill J for his conclusion that the claim by the lessor in the *Swallow Securities* case was a claim for damages and not a claim to recover a debt due from the lessee, namely that a provision that such an amount be added as arrears of rent offends against the basic principle of debt as recognised over the centuries, unless there is imported some provision for review of the amount claimed. Moreover the decision of Roskill J in *Bader Properties* that the claim to recover the costs and expenses incidental to the s 146 notice was not affected by the 1938 Act, must I think apply a fortiori to the claim in *Swallow Securities* and the claim in the instant case, to recover moneys actually expended by the lessor in making good a want of repair arising by reason of a breach by the lessee of a repairing covenant.

The decision of Roskill J was affirmed by the Court of Appeal in *Middlegate Properties Ltd v Gidlow-Jackson* (1977) 34 P & CR 4. In that case, the lease contained a similar covenant by the lessee to pay the lessors' legal costs and surveyors' fees of and incidental to the service of a s 146 notice.

Megaw LJ, having pointed out that under s 146(3) the lessor was entitled to recover such costs and expenses as a debt due to him from a lessee, referred to the decision of Roskill J in *Bader Properties* and said (at 10):

'The basis of that decision, as I understand it, was that the claim was not to be treated as being a claim for damages for breach of contract but was to be treated as being a claim for debt—money due under the contract. That decision was binding on the judge in the court below, and, as Mr. Gidlow-Jackson has rightly pointed out to this Court, the judge in the court below was bound to follow it but we are not bound to follow it; we are entitled to overrule it. To that extent we are in a different position from that of the judge. If I thought that the decision of Roskill J. was wrong, I should have no hesitation in so holding and giving effect to that view. In my judgment, however, there is no reason to regard that decision of Roskill J. as being wrong. On the contrary, I think that it obtained strong support from the wording of the provision of section 146(3) of the Law of Property Act 1925, to which I called special attention when I read that subsection. In that subsection there is no doubt that the legislature has deliberately treated the expenses incurred in the employment of a solicitor and surveyor in the preparation of a section 146 notice as properly being described as a debt due from a lessee, by contra-distinction from damages for breach of contract. It is perfectly true that that subsection is not dealing with a case where there is an express covenant in the agreement, but I see no reason why the wording expressly used by the statute in relation to a case dealing with statutory provisions should be given a materially different meaning in relation to the words used in an express covenant such as the words used here.'

Lawton LJ expressed the opinion that the word 'damages' connotes a claim not for liquidated sums but for unliquidated ones; Sir David Cairns held (at 11) that s 1(3) of the 1938 Act could not be relied on by the lessee because—

'I agree that it is only applicable in relation to a claim for damages and because this is not a claim for damages (and in forming that opinion I rely particularly, as Megaw LJ has done, on the language of section 146(3) of the Act of 1925) . . .'

That decision is, of course, binding on me and, in my judgment, compels the conclusion in the instant case that the lessor's right to recover the cost of repairs to the brown road is not a right to damages for breach of a covenant to repair, within s 1(1) and (2) of the 1938 Act. As I have said, these decisions, and the decision of the Court of Appeal

in *Sidnell v Wilson*, were not cited to McNeill J. His attention was also not drawn to the
difficulties which later emerged in *SEDAC Investments Ltd v Tanner* [1982] 3 All ER 646,
[1982] 1 WLR 1342 in applying s 1(5) to a case where a want of repair has actually been
remedied by the lessor, nor to the difficulties which, it seems to me, would equally
confront a lessor who sought leave to bring proceedings to recover the cost of carrying
out repairs before he had actually carried them out.

Counsel for the lessor submitted that the decision of Michael Wheeler QC in *SEDAC
Investments* was also wrong. In that case the lease gave the lessor the right to call on the
lessees to remedy a breach of their covenant to repair, and if they failed to do so to enter
and carry out the repairs and recover from the lessees the cost of the repairs. Urgent
repairs became necessary to the front wall, which was in a dangerous state, and putting
passers-by at risk of serious injury. The lessor did not call on the lessees to carry out the
repairs because, apparently, their advisers had overlooked this provision. The facts also
suggest that if they had not overlooked it, the danger to third parties was such that there
would have been insufficient time to operate the machinery of that provision. The lessors
were apparently advised that they would be liable for any injury to third parties (though
it is not clear on what ground they could have been liable before their right to enter and
carry out repairs had accrued) and that the liability might not be covered by their
insurance policy.

They therefore entered and did the necessary work without first calling on the lessees
to do so, and accordingly lost their right to recover the cost of carrying out the repairs
under the provision I have mentioned. Having carried out the repairs, they served notice
under s 146 requiring the lessors to make compensation equal to the cost of the repairs.
The lessees served a counter-notice.

The deputy judge held that he had no jurisdiction under s 1(5) to give the lessors leave
to commence proceedings, the breach of the covenant having been remedied when the
notice was served.

Counsel for the lessor submitted that the deputy judge erred in that he assumed that
at the date of the service of the s 146 notice, the lessee's breach of covenant had been
remedied. He drew a distinction between remedying a breach of a covenant to repair
and remedying a state of disrepair which, if it arises because of a failure by the lessee to
comply with a repairing covenant, itself constitutes the breach of covenant. He submitted
that if a lessor remedies a state of disrepair which the lessee ought to have remedied, the
lessee's breach of covenant becomes thereafter irremediable, and that the lessor can still
serve a s 146 notice notwithstanding that the breach has become irremediable (see
s 146(1)(b)).

I can see force in the distinction drawn by counsel for the lessor between remedying a
state of disrepair and remedying a breach of covenant, but I am not persuaded that the
decision of the deputy judge that the court has no jurisdiction to give leave under s 1(5)
if the state of disrepair has been remedied was wrong. The ground of his decision was
that the use of the present tense in paras (a) and (d) of s 1(5) of the 1938 Act shows that
the legislature contemplated a situation where a state of disrepair has not been remedied
at the time when the application for leave is made.

Paragraph (e), of course, gives the court a wider discretion, but Michael Wheeler QC I
think took the view that, read in the context of the other paragraphs of sub-s (5), para (e)
was not apt or intended to give the court a discretion in a case where a state of repair has
been wholly remedied and the lessor wishes to rely on the lessee's breach of covenant in
allowing that state of disrepair to arise.

The situation which arose in *SEDAC Investments* was, in fact, very unusual and may
well not have been contemplated by the legislature. It is difficult to imagine circumstances
in which a lessor who reserves a right to enter and remedy a state of disrepair arising
from the lessee's breach, would not also have the right, expressly or by necessary
implication, to recover the cost. In so far as he has the right to recover the cost, that right
is wholly outside the ambit of the 1938 Act. Equally a lessor who does not reserve the
right to enter and remedy a want of repair arising from a breach of the lessee's covenants,

and who none the less does so is, in law, a trespasser, and it is not obvious that he would be entitled to recover the moneys he has spent as damages for breach of covenant, or that he could rely on the lessee's breach of covenant in allowing the want of repair to arise as founding a claim for damages or for forfeiture, once he has himself remedied the state of disrepair. However, the point does not arise for decision and I express no concluded opinion on it.

For the reasons I have given, I think this appeal succeeds. As the point on which the lessor has succeeded was not raised until the matter came before this court, I shall make no order as regards the costs before the master. The lessee must pay the lessor's costs of the appeal.

Appeal allowed.

Solicitors: *Bircham & Co* (for the lessor); *Nabarro Nathanson & Co* (for the lessee).

Jacqueline Metcalfe   Barrister.

R v Dunnington

COURT OF APPEAL, CRIMINAL DIVISION
ACKNER LJ, BELDAM J AND SIR JOHN THOMPSON
15, 29 JULY 1983

Criminal law – Attempt – Acts constituting attempt – Aiding and abetting attempt to commit offence – Whether person who aids and abets attempt to commit an offence himself guilty of an offence – Criminal Attempts Act 1981, s 1(1).

Where a person does an act or acts which would amount to aiding and abetting an offence if that offence were completed, he is guilty of an offence under s 1(1)[a] of the Criminal Attempts Act 1981 even if the principal offence amounts only to an attempt (see p 679 *b* to *e*, post).

Notes
For attempts to commit an offence and acts constituting an attempt, see 11 Halsbury's Laws (4th edn) paras 63–64, and for cases on the subject, see 14(1) Digest (Reissue) 106–109, 713–738.

For the Criminal Attempts Act 1981, s 1, see 51 Halsbury's Statutes (3rd edn) 736.

Appeal
Kevin Vincent Dunnington appealed against his conviction in the Crown Court at Teesside before his Honour Judge Hewitt on 3 February 1983 of attempted robbery contrary to s 1 of the Criminal Attempts Act 1981. The facts are set out in the judgment of the court.

Paul E C White (assigned by the Registrar of Criminal Appeals) for the appellant.
Euan Duff for the Crown.

Cur adv vult

29 July. The following judgment of the court was delivered.

BELDAM J. This appeal raises the question whether a person who aids and abets an attempt to commit an offence is guilty of an offence under the provisions of s 1(1) of the Criminal Attempts Act 1981.

---
a   Section 1, so far as material, is set out at p 677 *g, h,* post

The facts from which the appeal arises are as follows. The appellant, who is now 23
years of age, on the afternoon of Friday, 15 October 1982 met two friends of his, Philip
Peterson and Stephen Wayne Ryan. Together they discussed the commission of a robbery
in Hartlepool. The three of them decided that they would go into a shop, threaten the
occupier and take his money. To go to the scene of the robbery and to get away from it,
after it had been committed, it was decided to steal a car. The appellant undertook to
obtain the car and went over to the car park of Asda Stores in Stockton. He there stole a
Morris 1000 car and drove it back to Hartlepool, where he picked up his co-defendants,
Peterson and Ryan. Having driven past the shop a couple of times to see that there were
no customers inside, Peterson and Ryan, wearing waterproof jackets with the hoods up,
were dropped off to go into the shop to commit the robbery. The appellant sat in the car
and waited. The plan misfired when the shopkeeper resisted the attempts of Peterson
and Ryan to steal his money by threats and put the two of them to flight by throwing
milk bottles at them.

Peterson jumped into the car and the appellant drove down the road to pick up Ryan,
who was running down the road ahead of them. After picking up Ryan the appellant
drove into the country, where they got rid of the jackets by which they might have been
identified.

Eventually, all three of them were arrested and charged with attempted robbery. The
offence formed the basis of count 1 of the indictment on which they appeared at the
Crown Court at Teesside on 3 February 1983. The statement of offence was 'attempted
robbery, contrary to s 1 of the Criminal Attempts Act 1981', the particulars of the offence
being that Philip Peterson, Stephen Wayne Ryan and the appellant, on 15 October 1982,
attempted to rob George Selby Boagey of a sum of money.

When first arraigned Peterson and Ryan pleaded guilty to the charge of attempted
robbery and the appellant pleaded not guilty. Before the appellant was put in charge of
the jury, counsel who appeared for him made a submission to the trial judge, his Honour
Judge Hewitt that, on the facts as we have related them and as to which there was no
dispute, the appellant had not been guilty of the offence with which he was charged and,
accordingly, he invited the judge to rule that on those facts he would have to direct the
jury to acquit the appellant on count 1 of the indictment.

After hearing argument, the judge ruled against counsel's submission for the appellant.
At counsel's request count 1 was then put again to the appellant, who pleaded guilty.

It was conceded by the Crown before the judge, as it was before us, that the part played
by the appellant was solely that of aider and abettor of the offence of attempted robbery.
He had been charged as a principal, pursuant to the provisions of s 8 of the Accessories
and Abettors Act 1861, as amended by the Criminal Law Act 1977.

Section 1(1) of the Criminal Attempts Act 1981 provides:

> 'If, with intent to commit an offence to which this section applies, a person does
> an act which is more than merely preparatory to the commission of the offence, he
> is guilty of attempting to commit the offence.'

Subsection (4) states:

> 'This section applies to any offence which, if it were completed, would be triable
> in England and Wales as an indictable offence, other than . . . (b) aiding, abetting,
> counselling, procuring or suborning the commission of an offence . . .'

For the appellant it was argued that s 1(1), when read with sub-s (4) must mean: 'If,
with intent to commit an offence other than aiding, abetting, counselling, procuring or
suborning the commission of an offence, a person does an act which is more than merely
preparatory to the commission of the offence, he is guilty of attempting to commit the
offence.' Although the appellant's acts were more than merely preparatory to the
commission of the offence of aiding and abetting, they were done with intent to aid and
abet the commission of an offence and so were excluded from the operation of sub-s (1)
of s 1.

The judge ruled against the appellant's submission in these words:

'I think that this means the section does not apply to an attempt to aid and abet, and I think, when one looks at it carefully and puts all the words together, that is the clear meaning of it. You cannot attempt to conspire and you cannot attempt to aid and abet, but here the evidence is, which is accepted on the face of it, that the aiding and abetting was completed. He did all that was required for the aiding and abetting. It was the offence that he was aiding and abetting that, fortunately, was not completed, so I think that the Criminal Attempts Act 1981, s 1 does apply.'

Before us the arguments for the parties were expanded. For the appellant it was accepted that the 1981 Act was based on the Criminal Attempts Bill, a draft of which was contained in the Law Commission's Report on Attempt and Impossibility in relation to Attempt, Conspiracy and Incitement (Law Com no 102) and that the intention of the Law Commission was that, whilst it should remain an offence to aid and abet an attempt to commit a crime, it should be made clear that an attempt to aid and abet a crime was not a criminal offence. Nevertheless, on the true construction of the language used in the 1981 Act, because Parliament had chosen to exclude attempts to aid and abet by the particular form of language used in the Act and by reference to the intention of the offender, aiding and abetting an attempt was in fact excluded from the operation of s 1(1) of the Act. Finally, it was urged that a person in the position of the appellant could nevertheless be charged with conspiring to commit robbery.

For the Crown it was argued that the appellant was not charged with attempting to aid and abet, but with aiding and abetting the attempted robbery. He was in fact an aider and abettor and only charged as a principal for procedural reasons. He had completed all the acts necessary for the offence of aiding and abetting Peterson and Ryan in their attempt to rob Mr Boagey. Notwithstanding the language of s 1(4) of the 1981 Act, the appellant could still be charged as a principal under the provisions of the Accessories and Abettors Act 1861. The exception did not apply to acts of aiding and abetting which were completed, and this was borne out by the use in sub-s (4) of the words '. . . which, if it were completed, would be triable . . .'

The 1981 Act closely follows the wording of the draft Bill contained in the report of the Law Commission.

Whilst recourse can be had to that report, in approaching the interpretation of the section for the background to the law as it was and for the legislative intention, it is not proper or desirable that we should use it as a direct statement of what the proposed Bill was to mean or to take the meaning of the section from its commentary or recommendations. We cannot, therefore, take the meaning of the section from the clear indications in para 2.123, or from the recommendations in para 5.1(9), of the Law Commission's report.

It is to be observed at the outset that if the construction contended for by the appellant is correct, then s 1 of the 1981 Act, which was intended to clarify and define the offence of attempting to commit a crime, has relieved of criminal responsibility all accessories or secondary parties in the commission of crimes which are thwarted, because attempts to commit crime at common law are abolished by s 6(2) of the Act. Thus, for example, persons who participate in an unsuccessful crime, by keeping watch for the perpetrators or driving a getaway car (as in the instant case) would be relieved of criminal liability. It can, therefore, be confidently stated that such a result was not the intention of Parliament and we would only give effect to such a construction if the words permitted of no other sensible meaning. We bear in mind, of course, that this is a penal statute and that conduct exempted from its operation must be given a wide rather than a narrow construction where both are equally compatible with the language used.

Approaching the construction of the section in this way we begin by reminding ourselves that, since s 8 of the Accessories and Abettors Act 1861 became law, any person who aided and abetted, counselled or procured the commission of an offence has been liable to be indicted, tried and punished as a principal offender. Accordingly, any person who actually takes part in the commission of an offence by aiding and abetting another to commit it is liable in law as a principal. It has been a moot question whether, in a case

a in which no person actually participates in the commission of an offence, an accused person can be guilty of the separate offence of attempting to aid and abet the commission of that offence.

For over 120 years those whose proximate acts are done with the intention of aiding and abetting actual participators in crime have been tried and indicted as principals rather than as secondary participants. In excepting from the application of s 1(1) the

b offences referred to in s 1(4), the draftsman of the section clearly treated aiding, abetting, counselling, procuring or suborning the commission of an offence as if it were a separate offence.

Therefore, returning to s 1(1), it is clear that the words 'the offence', where they appear in the phrase 'he is guilty of attempting to commit the offence' must be taken to refer to the same offence as is referred to in the phrase earlier in s 1(1), 'with intent to commit an

c offence'. Thus, rephrasing s 1(1), for the purposes of this case, it would, but for the exception, read: 'If, with intent to commit the offence of aiding and abetting an offence, a person does an act which is more than merely preparatory to the offence of aiding and abetting an offence, he is guilty of attempting to commit the offence of aiding and abetting an offence.'

However, so to provide would have created a new offence. Accordingly, to avoid this

d situation, s 1(4) provided, inter alia, that the provisions of s 1 should not apply to aiding, abetting, counselling, procuring or suborning the commission of an offence. Thus, the 1981 Act prevented the creation of the separate offence of attempting to aid and abet the commission of a crime. It did not remove from criminal responsibility the offence of aiding and abetting an attempt to commit a crime.

We therefore conclude that the submission made on behalf of the appellant was rightly

e rejected by the judge and this appeal is, accordingly, dismissed.

Appeal dismissed.

20 February 1984. The Court of Appeal (Eveleigh LJ, Mars-Jones and Beldam JJ) refused leave to appeal to the House of Lords but certified, under s 33(2) of the Criminal Appeal Act 1968, that

f *the following point of law of general public importance was involved in its decision: whether, where a person did an act or acts which would constitute aiding and abetting an offence, if that offence were completed, he was guilty of an offence under the provisions of s 1(1) of the Criminal Attempts Act 1981 if the principal offence amounted only to an attempt.*

Solicitors: *Peter Ross*, Middlesbrough (for the Crown).

g   N P Metcalfe Esq   Barrister.

Practice Direction

SUPREME COURT TAXING OFFICE

h

Costs – Vouching bills of costs – Certificate as evidence of payment of disbursement not exceeding £200.

1. The Practice Direction of 15 April 1976 ([1976] 2 All ER 446), which prescribed a form of certificate to be used as evidence of payment of any disbursement not exceeding £100 (other than a fee to counsel) in the circumstances therein mentioned, is hereby

j amended by the deletion of the figure £100 and the substitution therefor of the figure £200.

2. With the concurrence of the Senior Registrar of the Family Division and the Admiralty Registrar, this direction is to be applied to all costs in the Supreme Court taxed under their respective jurisdictions.

                                            F T HORNE
1 February 1984   Chief Taxing Master.

Champion v Maughan and another   *a*

QUEEN'S BENCH DIVISION
STEPHEN BROWN LJ AND TAYLOR J
8 DECEMBER 1983

Fish – Obstruction to passage of fish – Fixed engine – Prohibition of placing fixed engine in inland   *b*
or tidal waters – Offence – Whether offence of strict liability – Salmon and Freshwater Fisheries
Act 1975, s 6(1)(a).

On its true construction s 6(1)(a)[a] of the Salmon and Freshwater Fisheries Act 1975,
which provides that any person who 'places a fixed engine in any inland or tidal waters',
shall be guilty of an offence, creates an offence of strict liability for which a person may
be convicted without proof that he intended to obstruct the passage of salmon or   *c*
migratory trout (see p 683 *h* to p 684 *c*, post).

Dictum of Lord Lane CJ in *R v West Yorkshire Coroner, ex p Smith* [1982] 3 All ER at
1104 applied.

Watts v Lucas (1871) LR 6 QB 226 distinguished.

Notes   *d*
For offences of strict liability, see 11 Halsbury's Laws (4th edn) para 18.

For placing fixed engines in inland or tidal waters, see 18 ibid para 670, and for cases
on the subject, see 25 Digest (Reissue) 53–55, 543–561.

For the Salmon and Freshwater Fisheries Act 1975, s 6, see 45 Halsbury's Statutes (3rd
edn) 539.   *e*

Cases referred to in judgements
Bank of England v Vagliano Bros [1891] AC 107, [1891–4] All ER Rep 93, HL.
R v West Yorkshire Coroner, ex p Smith [1982] 3 All ER 1098, [1983] QB 335, [1982] 3
    WLR 920, CA.
Sweet v Parsley [1969] 1 All ER 347, [1970] AC 132, [1969] 2 WLR 470, HL.   *f*
Watts v Lucas (1871) LR 6 QB 226.

Case stated
Anthony Stuart Champion appealed by way of a case stated by the justices of the peace
for the county of Northumberland acting in and for the petty sessional division of
Wansbeck in respect of their adjudication as a magistrates' court sitting at Ashington
whereby they dismissed an information preferred by the appellant against the   *g*
respondents, Geoffrey Maughan and Robert Groves, of unlawfully placing a fixed engine
in tidal waters being waters within the area of the Northumbrian Water Authority on 9
November 1981 at Cambois in the county of Northumberland, contrary to s 6(1)(a) of
the Salmon and Freshwater Fisheries Act 1975. The facts are set out in the judgment of
Taylor J.   *h*

Alan Moses for the appellant.
Gerard F Harkins for the respondents.

TAYLOR J (delivering the first judgment at the invitation of Stephen Brown LJ). This
is an appeal by way of case stated by the justices for the petty sessional division of   *j*
Wansbeck in the county of Northumberland sitting at Ashington in respect of their
adjudication as a magistrates' court on 13 January 1983. They had before them an
information which had been preferred by the appellant on 17 February 1982 against the
respondents that they jointly, on 9 November 1981, at Cambois in the county of

---

a   Section 6(1) is set out at p 681 *d*, post

a
Northumberland unlawfully placed a fixed engine in tidal waters contrary to s 6(1)(a) of the Salmon and Freshwater Fisheries Act 1975.

The justices found the following facts, which were agreed between the parties. On 9 November 1981 a water bailiff of the Northumbrian Water Authority was on duty at Cambois beach at 8.45 pm. Three persons, including the respondents, set a net in tidal waters at right angles to the beach, whilst the bailiff was on duty. The net was tied and made stationary in such a way as to be a fixed engine within the definition set out in s 41

b
of the 1975 Act. The net was still in the same position at 6.30 the next morning, and later that morning the respondents hauled the net out of the water. They then left the beach, carrying the net and some sandbags which had been emptied when the net was hauled in. They were in possession of a fish, but it was not a migratory fish, such as is referred to in the 1975 Act. The respondent Groves admitted, after being cautioned, that he was the owner of the net. The respondents asserted that they were fishing for cod.

c
They also admitted placing the net in position on 9 November.

The justices found as a fact that, because salmon and migratory trout swim close to the shore on their passage northwards along the coast to their rivers of origin, a net set in the manner in which the respondents set this net would form an obstruction to the passage of those fish.

The sole issue before the justices, and indeed before this court, is whether s 6(1)(a) of

d
the 1975 Act creates an absolute offence. Section 6(1) is in these terms:

'Any person who—(a) places a fixed engine in any inland or tidal waters; or (b) uses an unauthorised fixed engine for taking or facilitating the taking of salmon or migratory trout or for detaining or obstructing the free passage of salmon or migratory trout in any such waters, shall be guilty of an offence.'

e
The submissions on behalf of the appellant were as follows. First, the words of s 6(1)(a) are plain beyond any possible ambiguity or doubt, and show that an absolute offence is created by the subsection of placing a fixed engine in inland or tidal waters. Second, it is submitted that the section, taken as a whole, clearly distinguishes between a person who places a fixed engine and one who uses a fixed engine which is already in position. That distinction, says counsel for the appellant, is consistent with the general scheme of the

f
1975 Act, and in particular that part of the Act which is designed to prevent obstruction to the free passage of salmon and migratory trout. The section, he says, as to para (a) creates an absolute offence as against a person who places the engine in position, but as to para (b), in relation to anyone who uses an unauthorised fixed engine, there has to be proved, before an offence can be established, the purpose of taking or facilitating the taking of salmon or migratory trout or detaining or obstructing the free passage of those

g
fish.

Counsel for the appellant points to other sections of the 1975 Act where an offence of user requires proof of the prohibited purpose. In particular he refers to s 7, which is concerned with fishing weirs, and s 8, which is concerned with fishing mill dams. He contrasts those sections with, for example, ss 12 and 13 of the 1975 Act, where making structural alterations or obstructions constitutes an offence without proof of any particular

h
purpose.

Next, counsel for the appellant argues that, although the 1975 Act purports to be by its title a consolidating Act, any presumption that it is not intended to alter the previous law must give way to the plain words of the sub-s 6(1). He submits that the court ought not to have regard to previous Acts on this topic or decisions of the courts on previous Acts, because the precise wording of this Act is unambiguous. He argues further that

j
s 6(1)(a) contains a general prohibition, and there are in other parts of the 1975 Act, to which I shall refer later, specific provisions which derogate from that general prohibition.

Finally, in relation to mens rea it is argued on behalf of the appellant that any presumption that mens rea ought to be an implied requirement in any criminal offence is rebutted in the present instance, partly by the clear words of the section and partly by the subject matter of the statute, which is not an essentially criminal statute but one which prohibits certain acts in the public interest under penalty.

On behalf of the respondents counsel argues that s 6(1)(*a*) does not establish an absolute offence. He submits that the qualifying words in para (*b*) which relate to the purpose of taking or facilitating or detaining or obstructing ought to be implied into para (*a*). He draws attention to the general principle that one ought to require proof of mens rea before a criminal offence can be established. He cites the well-known case of *Sweet v Parsley* [1969] 1 All ER 347, [1970] AC 132 in support of the proposition that mens rea is an essential ingredient of every offence unless some reason can be found for holding that it is not necessary, and the court ought not to hold that an offence is an absolute offence unless it appears that that must have been the intention of Parliament. It therefore becomes extremely important and indeed central to this case to look carefully at the section and see what was the intention of Parliament, because if that intention is unambiguously to create an absolute offence then the principle to which counsel for the respondents refers, and in relation to which he cites from *Sweet v Parsley*, would not be persuasive.

Counsel for the respondents further draws attention to previous statutes relating to this topic, which were in different terms. He referred to s 11 of the Salmon Fishery Act 1861, as amended by s 18(2) of the Salmon Fishery Act 1873. The terms of s 11 did not involve any subdivision as between the placing and the user of fixed engines in different subsections, but dealt with the two together in these terms:

'No fixed Engine of any Description shall be placed or used for catching or for the purpose of facilitating the catching of salmon, or detaining or obstructing the free passage of, Salmon in any inland or tidal Waters . . .'

He cited a case which was based on that statute, *Watts v Lucas* (1871) LR 6 QB 226, but of course that decision, which was drawn to the attention of the justices in the present case, was a decision specifically on the wording of the 1861 Act.

The next statute referred to was the Salmon and Freshwater Fisheries Act 1923. The relevant provision is s 11(1), which is in these terms:

'No fixed engine of any description shall be placed or used for taking or facilitating the taking of salmon or migratory trout or for detaining, or obstructing the free passage of, salmon or migratory trout in any inland or tidal waters.'

Again it is to be noted that no subdivision of the section was made by Parliament in dealing with the placing on the one hand and the user on the other. The two are dealt with in conjunction, and they are both qualified by the need for proof that the placing or the using was for the taking or facilitating of the taking of salmon or migratory trout. The section which is in point in the present case is in quite different terms.

Counsel for the respondents points to the unfortunate consequences, as he described them, of a decision that this section is absolute in its terms. He refers to difficulties that would be experienced all over the country by persons who are quite harmlessly wishing to fish for other than salmon or trout; but the draconian effect to which he refers if this section is absolute, and indeed the anomalies in relation to the licensing provisions to which he drew attention in ss 25 and 26 of the 1975 Act, are capable of being mitigated by provisions within the Act itself which enables orders to be made creating exceptions. Section 28(3) of the 1975 Act provides:

'Subject to subsection (4) below, the Minister may by statutory instrument make an order for the general regulation of the salmon, trout, freshwater and eel fisheries within an area defined by the order.'

Schedule 3 to the 1975 Act, which is expressed to be made under s 28, provides by para 1:

'An order may provide . . . (c) for modifying in relation to the fisheries within the area any of the provisions of this Act which relate to the regulation of fisheries, or of any local Act relating to any fishery within the area.'

Indeed, we were told on behalf of the appellant that an order which to some extent does modify the rigour of s 6(1)(*a*) is in force in the Northumbrian Water Authority's area.

Then counsel for the respondents referred to s 20 of the 1975 Act, which deals with
a the obligation on an occupier of any fixed engine to remove the engine and render it
incapable of taking salmon or migratory trout during the close season. He argues from
that that were they then to replace the engine when next fishing was permitted they
would fall foul of the absolute provisions of s 6(1)(*a*).

For my part I accept the argument counsel for the appellant put forward that there is a
distinction between placing an engine and replacing an engine. The latter may be
b permitted either by orders which could be made, as I have indicated, under s 28, or by
reason of ancient practice and privilege, as provided for in s 6(3) of the 1975 Act.

Finally, counsel for the respondents prays in aid the principle that since this Act is
expressed to be a consolidating statute one ought not to conclude that it introduces that
which was not there previously, namely an absolute offence, without proof of mens rea.
So far as that is concerned it is relevant to look at a recent authority in relation to the
c construction of statutes, and in particular of a consolidating statute. The authority which
was drawn to our attention by counsel for the appellant is *R v West Yorkshire Coroner, ex
p Smith* [1982] 3 All ER 1098, [1983] QB 335. That was a case concerned with the
Coroners Act 1887. Lord Lane CJ said ([1982] 3 All ER 1098 at 1102–1103, [1983] QB
335 at 352):

d 'The Coroners Act 1887 is expressed to be a consolidating statute, though, it is fair
to say, one has to look no further than s 6 of the Act (which provides a whole new
method of redress) to realise that consolidation was not the only aim of the statute.
I start off by examining *Bank of England v Vagliano Bros* [1891] AC 107 at 144–145,
[1891–4] All ER Rep 93 at 113, where Lord Herschell said: "I think the proper
course is in the first instance to examine the language of the statute and to ask what
e is its natural meaning, uninfluenced by any considerations derived from the
previous state of the law, and not to start with inquiring how the law previously
stood, and then, assuming that it was probably intended to leave it unaltered, to see
if the words of the enactment will bear an interpretation in conformity with this
view ..." '

f Lord Lane CJ continued his citation from Lord Herschell and then referred to a
number of other authorities on the interpretation of statutes. He said finally on this
matter ([1982] 3 All ER 1098 at 1104, [1983] QB 335 at 354–355):

'Applying those various considerations then to the words of s 3, I am unable to
find any ambiguity or obscurity. I do not think that the words used are fairly
g susceptible of bearing more than one meaning in their context. Consequently it is
not permissible to have regard, in my judgment, to any earlier statutory enactment
as an aid to construction. No aid is required save the words themselves. It should
perhaps be added that the interpretation of s 3 suggested by counsel as amicus would
itself require extensive wording being read into the section, which, on its own,
perhaps provides an argument against such an interpretation being adopted.'

h Applying those observations to the present case, in my judgment the words of s 6(1)(*a*)
of the 1975 Act are plain and unambiguous. They clearly indicate an absolute offence.
Counsel for the respondents very frankly conceded at the beginning of his argument that
it was necessary to import into s 6(1)(*a*) the qualifying words contained in para (*b*). Lord
Lane CJ in the passage that I have just cited indicated that such a need was in itself
j perhaps an argument against such an interpretation being adopted, and I consider that in
the present case the same argument holds good.

Accordingly, for my part I am satisfied that the interpretation of the statute sought to
be placed on it by the appellant is the correct one. This is an absolute section, and I would
therefore answer the question which has been raised by the justices in their stated case in
the affirmative.

The question is:

'. . . whether Section 6(1)(a) creates an absolute offence and is therefore applicable to any person placing any fixed engine in tidal waters, notwithstanding that there is *a* no intention to obstruct the passage of Salmon or migratory Trout.'

I would answer Yes to that question.

STEPHEN BROWN LJ. Section 6(1)(a) of the Salmon and Freshwater Fisheries Act 1975 provides in ten words a very clear prohibition. Any person who 'places a fixed *b* engine in any inland or tidal waters' shall be guilty of an offence. On agreed facts the justices found that the respondents had placed a fixed engine in tidal waters. In my judgment there is no escape, on that finding, from concluding that the information had been proved. This is not a difficult question. It is a question of construction, and it relates to words which are clear and unambiguous.

I agree, therefore, that this appeal should be allowed for the reasons given by Taylor J. *c* The case will be remitted to the justices, with a direction to convict.

Appeal allowed. Case remitted to justices with a direction to convict.

Solicitors: *J Malcolm Ruddick*, Gosforth (for the appellant); *Frank A Hellawell & Co*, Newbiggin-by-the-Sea (for the respondents). *d*

Raina Levy   Barrister.

e

Practice Direction

FAMILY DIVISION

Affidavit – Filing – Practice – Family Division – Time for filing – Cause or matter for which *f* *hearing date fixed – Affidavit or other document to be lodged not less than 14 days before appointed hearing date.*

1. Where in any cause or matter proceeding in the Principal Registry a party wishes to file an affidavit or other document in connection with an application for which a hearing date has been fixed, the affidavit or other document must be lodged in the Principal *g* Registry *not less than 14 clear days* before the appointed hearing date.

2. Where insufficient time remains before the hearing date to lodge the affidavit or other document as required by para 1 above, it should, in the case of an application before the judge, be lodged in room 775 (Summons Clerk, Clerk of the Rules Department) at the Royal Courts of Justice as soon as possible *before* the hearing; where the application is before the registrar, it should be handed to the clerk to that registrar immediately before *h* the hearing. Service should be effected on the opposing party in the normal way.

3. The Practice Direction of 12 January 1981 ([1981] 1 All ER 323, [1981] 1 WLR 106), except para 3, is cancelled.

B P TICKLE *j* Senior Registrar.

7 February 1984

Alltrans Express Ltd v CVA Holdings Ltd

a

COURT OF APPEAL, CIVIL DIVISION

STEPHENSON, GRIFFITHS AND PURCHAS LJJ

10 NOVEMBER 1983

Costs – Appeal to Court of Appeal – Jurisdiction – Trial judge giving leave to appeal – Whether
b *jurisdiction of Court of Appeal restricted to interfering with judge's order on grounds of failure*
to exercise discretion at all or because of unjudicial exercise of discretion – Whether Court of
Appeal entitled to review judge's discretion on usual grounds.

Costs – Order for costs – Discretion – Plaintiff obtaining leave to enter summary judgment against
defendant for damages to be assessed – Judge assessing damages at nominal sum only – No
payment into court by defendant – Whether absence of payment in entitling judge to treat plaintiff
c *as successful party and to award him costs of hearing to assess damages – Whether judge placing*
undue weight on absence of payment in – Whether defendant entitled to costs of hearing to assess
damages – RSC Ord 14.

The plaintiffs brought an action against the defendants claiming damages for breach of
contract. The defendants admitted they were in breach but alleged that the plaintiffs' loss
d had been calculated on the wrong basis. In proceedings under RSC Ord 14 the plaintiffs
were given leave to enter summary judgment against the defendants for damages to be
assessed and the action was ordered to be transferred to an official referee for the
assessment of damages. After a 15-day hearing the official referee held that the plaintiffs
had failed to prove that they had suffered any loss as a result of the defendants' breach of
contract and were only entitled to nominal damages, which he assessed at £2. Because
e the defendants had not paid any money into court and the plaintiffs had obtained
judgment for damages, albeit for only a nominal sum, the official referee took the view
that the plaintiffs were the successful party and ordered that they should recover their
costs of the hearing from the defendants. The official referee granted the defendants
leave to appeal against the order for costs and the defendants did in fact appeal. On the
hearing of the appeal the plaintiffs contended that, although the official referee had given
f leave to appeal, nevertheless the court was restricted to considering whether the official
referee had failed to exercise his discretion at all or, if he had, whether he had taken into
account wholly irrelevant matters.

Held – The defendants' appeal would be allowed for the following reasons—
    (1) On the jurisdiction issue, where the trial judge gave leave to appeal from his order
g for costs the Court of Appeal's jurisdiction was not specifically restricted, and accordingly
it was entitled to review the judge's order on the same grounds as any other exercise of
judicial discretion, namely that the judge had erred in law, that he had taken into account
irrelevant matters or not taken into account relevant matters, or that he was plainly
wrong because he had given the wrong weight to certain factors (see p 689 *e*, p 690 *a* to *d*
and p 692 *f* to p 693 *a* and *h*, post); dictum of Lord Carson in *Donald Campbell & Co Ltd v*
h *Pollak* [1927] All ER Rep at 49 and *Jones v McKie and Mersey Docks and Harbour Board*
[1964] 2 All ER 842 considered.
    (2) On the discretion issue, since the consequence of the summary judgment was that
the plaintiffs were entitled at least to nominal damages the actual issue between the
parties at the hearing to assess damages was whether the plaintiffs were entitled to more
than nominal damages, and the defendants had in fact succeeded on that issue. It followed
j that the official referee was plainly wrong in placing too much weight on the absence of
any payment in when payment in of the nominal sum of £2 would not have been
accepted by the plaintiffs and thus would not have made any difference to the proceedings.
The official referee had accordingly exercised his discretion wrongly in holding that in
the absence of any payment in the award of £2 to the plaintiffs made them the successful
party. The costs of the hearing to assess damages would therefore be awarded to the

defendants (see p 687 *d* to *f*, p 690 *d e* and *h j*, p 691 *b c*, p 692 *b* to *f* and p 693 *a b* and *e* to   *a*
h, post); *Anglo-Cyprian Trade Agencies Ltd v Paphos Wine Industries Ltd* [1951] 1 All ER 873
applied.

Notes
For exercise of court's discretion to award costs, see 37 Halsbury's Laws (4th edn) paras
714–717 and for cases on the subject, see 37(3) Digest (Reissue) 240–244, 4350–4378.
   For appeals as to costs, see 37 Halsbury's Laws (4th edn) para 724 and for cases on the   *b*
subject, see 37(3) Digest (Reissue) 271–275, 4548–4565.

Cases referred to in judgments
Anglo-Cyprian Trade Agencies Ltd v Paphos Wine Industries Ltd [1951] 1 All ER 873.
Baylis Baxter Ltd v Sabath [1958] 2 All ER 209, [1958] 1 WLR 529, CA.
Campbell (Donald) & Co Ltd v Pollak [1927] AC 732, [1927] All ER Rep 1, HL.   *c*
Findlay v Rly Executive [1950] 2 All ER 969, CA.
Hong v A & R Brown Ltd [1948] 1 All ER 185, [1948] 1 KB 515, CA.
Jones v McKie and Mersey Docks and Harbour Board [1964] 2 All ER 842, [1964] 1 WLR
   960, CA.
London Welsh Estates Ltd v Phillip (1931) 100 LJKB 449, DC.
Ritter v Godfrey [1920] 2 KB 47, [1918–19] All ER Rep 714, CA.   *d*
Scherer v Counting Instruments Ltd [1977] FSR 569, CA.
Taylor (K H) Ltd v Wold Farm Foods Ltd [1982] CA Bound Transcript 275.
Wagman v Vare Motors Ltd [1959] 3 All ER 326, [1959] 1 WLR 853, CA.

Appeal
By a writ dated 20 May 1980 the plaintiffs, Alltrans Express Ltd, claimed against the   *e*
defendants, CVA Holdings Ltd, the sum of £82,500 for breach of contract. The
defendants admitted breach of contract but contested the amount of the loss alleged to
arise from the breach. In proceedings by the plaintiffs under RSC Ord 14 Master
Lubbock, on 6 November 1980, ordered, under Ord 14, r 3, that the plaintiffs should be
given leave to enter judgment against the defendants for damages to be assessed and that
the action should be transferred to an official referee for the assessment of damages. On   *f*
11 January 1983 his Honour Judge Hayman sitting as an official referee assessed the
plaintiffs' damages in the nominal sum of £2. Because the defendants had not made any
payment into court the judge treated the plaintiffs as the successful party and ordered
that the defendants should pay the plaintiffs their costs of the hearing to assess damages.
However, he granted the defendants leave to appeal against the order for costs. The
defendants appealed seeking an order that the plaintiffs should pay the defendants their   *g*
costs of the hearing, alternatively that there should be no order for costs. The grounds of
the appeal were that since the judge held that the plaintiffs had failed to prove entitlement
to any damages other than nominal damages in respect of the Ord 14 judgment, the
defendants were the successful party on the issue of damages, and as the judge had made
no criticism of the defendants' conduct, he erred in awarding costs to the unsuccessful
party, namely to the plaintiffs, and in so exercising his discretion acted unfairly without   *h*
materials on which he could so exercise his discretion. The facts are set out in the
judgment of Stephenson LJ.

Martin Collins QC and *Jeremy F J Russell* for the defendants.
Anthony Thompson QC and *Ignatius Fessal* for the plaintiffs.

STEPHENSON LJ. This an appeal against an order of his Honour Judge Hayman,   *j*
sitting as a judge dealing with official referees' business, in respect of costs. The order was
made on 11 January 1983, and from it he gave leave to appeal. The order sets out the fact
that there had been a hearing extending over 15 days, and ends by saying:

   '[I] do hereby assess the plaintiffs' damages in the sum of £2.00 (two pounds)
   And Do Hereby Order that judgment be entered for the plaintiffs for the said sum

of £2.00 (two pounds) with costs to be taxed if not agreed. And I Do Grant the defendants leave to appeal on the question of costs'.

The assessment came about under an order of a master made as long ago as 6 November 1980; that order was—

'that the Plaintiff has leave to enter Judgment for damages to be assessed. 2. The action be transferred to the Official Referee Business for assessment of damages. 3. Liberty to restore.'

No question arises about the costs of the plaintiffs up to the entering of judgment under RSC Ord 14.

The claim related to the sale of shares by the defendant company to the plaintiff company; they were shares in a third company, and happily we are not concerned with the details of that sale. The claim was really a claim for £82,500, based on an undertaking that the defendants had given to make good a loss from the trading of the third company, and presumably because a breach of that agreement was proved or admitted, or taken to be proved, judgment was given against the defendants for damages to be assessed as I have said. The defence was that the loss had been calculated on the wrong basis, but of course it was not open to the defendants to repeat that defence at the hearing for the assessment of damages and, as I have said, after 15 days the judge came to the conclusion that the plaintiffs were not entitled to £82,500 or anything like it, that they had failed to prove that they had suffered any damage as a result of the defendants' breach of contract and that they were therefore entitled to nominal damages, which he assessed at what I think is one of the figures now given for nominal damages, namely forty shillings or two pounds. But the order that he made was that the plaintiffs should have the costs of that expensive battle which, on the face of it, they would appear to have lost.

I think each member of this court, on seeing the order that the judge had made, thought that he had plainly got the matter wrong and that the right order in such a case would be that the plaintiffs should pay the defendants' costs, the defendants being the successful party and not, as the judge apparently thought, the plaintiffs.

The judge, after considering going as far as making no order as to the costs of the assessment of damages, was persuaded by counsel for the plaintiffs that his clients were the successful party and that they should have those costs. The preliminary view which this court took led us to call on counsel for the plaintiffs to make that good without doing more than refer to the arguments submitted, according to the transcript that we have of them, by counsel for the defendants to the judge and in his skeleton argument. When we put to counsel for the plaintiffs in that way that the judge had made the wrong order and one that we could put right, he submitted with great clarity and cogency that we could not do that because we are prevented by statute and by authority from doing it where there is an appeal against an order for costs, which he submitted is in a special position in consequence of the statute and the authorities on it. His submission was that this court can only entertain an appeal on the question of costs either where there has been no exercise of discretion by the judge who makes the order, or where his exercise of his discretion has not been judicial because he has taken into account some wholly irrelevant matter.

Counsel for the plaintiffs took us first to what is now s 18(1)(f) of the Supreme Court Act 1981, which re-enacts a provision which has been the law through the Judicature Act 1925 since the Judicature Act 1873. Section 18(1)(f) provides that no appeal shall lie to the Court of Appeal—

'without the leave of the court or tribunal in question, from any order of the High Court or any other court or tribunal made with the consent of the parties or relating only to costs which are by law left to the discretion of the court or tribunal . . .'

In support of his submission that on the hearing of appeals on costs the appellate court can only consider the two matters to which I have referred, counsel for the plaintiffs

relied first of all on a decision of this court in *Jones v McKie and Mersey Docks and Harbour Board* [1964] 2 All ER 842, [1964] 1 WLR 960. That was a case in which a judge had *a*
deprived one of two successful defendants of their costs because of conduct which he regarded as misconduct and as related to the issues in the action. By a majority, this court refused to interfere with his order. In the course of giving the leading judgment, Willmer LJ referred ([1964] 2 All ER 842 at 844–845, [1964] 1 WLR 960 at 965–966) to a well-known passage in the speech of Viscount Cave LC in *Donald Campbell & Co Ltd v *b*
Pollak* [1927] AC 732 at 811, [1927] All ER Rep 1 at 41 in which he stated that it appeared to him that the true view was substantially that taken by Lord Sterndale MR in a passage which he had cited from *Ritter v Godfrey* [1920] 2 KB 47, [1918–19] All ER Rep 714 and which ends with this sentence:

> 'But when a judge, deliberately intending to exercise his discretionary powers, has acted on facts connected with or leading up to the litigation which had been proved before him or which he has himself observed during the progress of the case, *c*
> then it seems to me that a Court of Appeal, although it may deem his reasons insufficient and may disagree with his conclusion, is prohibited by the statute [ie the then existing predecessor of s 18(1)(*f*)] from entertaining an appeal from it.'

Willmer LJ went on ([1964] 2 All ER 842 at 845, [1964] 1 WLR 960 at 966): *d*

> 'What it comes to, I think, is that in order to justify an appeal as to costs only this court must be able to say that the judge in the court below, however much he may have been purporting to exercise his discretion, has not really exercised his discretion at all. This court can say that, but can say it only, as I see it, if it is satisfied that the judge in the court below has taken into consideration wholly extraneous and irrelevant matters. That, I think, is also substantially in accordance with what *e*
> JENKINS, L.J., said in *Baylis Baxter, Ltd. v. Sabath* ([1958] 2 All ER 209 at 215, [1958] 1 WLR 529 at 536): "The matter as it now stands really comes to this, that in a case of this sort—that is to say in a case in which it is sought to appeal, without leave [and I stress those words] from an order relating solely to costs—such an application should not be entertained, in view of the express terms of s. 31(1)(h) of the Judicature Act, 1925 [that is, the predecessor of s 18(1)(*f*)], unless the circumstances are such that *f*
> this court can say, in effect, 'In this case the learned judge did not in truth exercise his discretion at all'. It is only in a case of that kind that this court has jurisdiction to entertain such an appeal." '

I stress again those words 'such an appeal', which obviously refer back to an appeal without leave.

Then Harman LJ's judgment was also called to our attention. Counsel for the plaintiffs *g*
relied on what he had said at the end of his judgment ([1964] 2 All ER 842 at 847, [1964] 1 WLR 960 at 969):

> 'Once one concludes that this was a case of an exercise of discretion, the matter is at an end so far as this court is concerned. It is only if there was no exercise of discretion at all that we could interfere, and I do not think there was no exercise of *h*
> discretion.'

Those words, if read literally, are, as it seems to me, too wide. They may have been too wide to cover the case with which their Lordships were dealing, if I may respectfully say so, namely a case which was, like both the authorities they cited, a case where leave to appeal either had not been given or had been refused. But in my judgment they certainly do not have any application to the instant case, or to any case where leave has been given *j*
by the judge who made the order as to costs.

Further, counsel for the plaintiffs relied on an unreported recent decision of this court in *K H Taylor Ltd v Wold Farm Foods Ltd* [1982] CA Bound Transcript 275. I need not refer to the facts of that case. Again it was an appeal from a judge dealing with official referees' business in which the court, through the leading judgment of Ormrod LJ,

quoted and followed *Scherer v Counting Instruments Ltd* [1977] FSR 569. In that case,
a which was again a case where leave had not been given, but in fact refused by an official
referee, Buckley LJ said (at 573):

> 'This court can, however, interfere if upon a true view of the facts the judge has
> either not exercised his discretion at all, or has exercised it otherwise than judicially.'

Ormrod LJ went on to point out the difficulties of distinguishing sometimes between a
b wrong exercise of discretion and an unjudicial exercise of discretion, and he ended his
judgment, with which the other two members of the court agreed, by saying:

> 'So we do not get as far as considering whether the judge exercised his discretion
> correctly. For my part I am quite satisfied that he exercised his discretion judicially
> and made an order which he thought was the right order.'

c I could go at greater length into the speeches and the passages in them which have
been relied on: the speeches of Viscount Cave LC and Lord Atkinson in *Campbell v Pollak*,
both of them approving what Lord Sterndale MR had said in *Ritter v Godfrey*, which the
industry of counsel has not been able to identify as a case where no leave was granted.
But I should refer to the last sentence of the speech of Lord Carson in *Campbell v Pollak*
[1927] AC 732 at 826, [1927] All ER Rep 1 at 49, on which counsel for the plaintiff relies:
d
> 'Whilst, therefore, it is, of course, true that a judge ought to exercise his discretion
> judicially, whether he has done so or not is a question which cannot be raised on
> appeal as to costs, unless the judge gives leave as provided by the section.'

If that means, as counsel for the plaintiffs submits, that where leave is given the court can
only consider whether the judge exercised his discretion judicially, and if satisfied that
e he did, must treat his decision as sacrosanct, I respectfully disagree with it as unsupported
by authority and, as I think, inconsistent with authority.

Counsel for the plaintiffs also referred us, in another connection, to *Findlay v Rly
Executive* [1950] 2 All ER 969. In that and other cases this court has had to consider
appeals from judges' orders which departed from the usual practice as regards costs where
there has been a payment in. It may just be worth referring to *Wagman v Vare Motors*
f *Ltd* [1959] 3 All ER 326, [1959] 1 WLR 853, where this court followed its earlier decision
in *Findlay's* case. That was a case in which a judge had awarded exactly the amount paid
in by the defendants and, giving his reasons for making no order as to costs after the date
of a payment into court, had said ([1959] 3 All ER 326 at 330, [1959] 1 WLR 853 at 858–
859):

> 'I take into account the fact that the sum of £575 has been paid into court; I take
g   into account, in (I am certain) my discretion, the fact that I was not, at any material
> time, giving less than that sum and was wondering about another £25 . . .'

He refused leave to appeal against his order.

In the Court of Appeal Morris LJ, with whom Ormerod and Willmer LJJ agreed, said
([1959] 3 All ER 326 at 331–332, [1959] 1 WLR 853 at 860):

h
> 'I propose to approach this case by considering whether, within the words used
> [by Lord Greene MR in *Hong v A & R Brown Ltd* [1948] 1 All ER 185, [1948] 1 KB
> 515] there was a purported exercise of the discretion without any materials on
> which that discretion could be exercised. It seems to me plain in this case that,
> although the learned judge naturally did not know of the payment into court, the real issue
> between the parties ever after Aug. 18, 1958, was whether £575 was or was not the
j   right sum for the plaintiff to receive.'

He there decided that there had been a purported exercise of the judge's discretion
without any materials on which it could properly be exercised. It does not seem to me to
matter much whether you say that there has been no exercise of discretion, or a purported
exercise of discretion on no materials, or on some matter wholly unconnected with the

litigation. In all those circumstances, as I read the authorities, the Court of Appeal is not banned by the statute from considering an appeal, even in a case where leave to appeal has not been granted.

If I have understood the law rightly it follows, in my judgment, that the preliminary point of counsel for the plaintiffs must fail. We have here a case in which the judge has given leave; it is quite true that he has made it plain that he is not giving leave because he thinks that his order is wrong. In giving leave he said as much; but he thought that the defendants should have leave to appeal on the point, because he thought that he might be arrogant in thinking that there might not be some form of argument. Once the door is opened by leave being given, however, it seem to me that this court is in the same position as it is on any appeal against the exercise of the court's discretion. We must be very careful not to interfere with the judge's exercise of the discretion which has been entrusted to him. We can only do so if he has erred in law or in principle, or if he has taken into account some matter which he should not have taken into account or has left out of account some matter which he should have taken into account, or, and this is an extension of the law which is now I think well recognised, if the Court of Appeal is of opinion that his decision is plainly wrong and therefore must have been reached by a faulty assessment of the weights of the different factors which he has had to take into account. There are various ways of putting that, and that may not be a very good one; but it is a category of error which permits, and indeed requires, this court to reverse or alter the judge's exercise of his discretion. In my judgment this is such a case.

But there is also, I think, apparent on the face of the judge's judgment (and we have the benefit of a transcript of the short judgment that he gave in making the order which he did) an error which we can put our finger on, namely that in the circumstances he gave too much weight to the fact that there had been no payment in; in this case a payment in of £2 and no more. I start where I think counsel for the plaintiffs would have me start, with the importance of not interfering with such an order as this. He gave us the illustration of a decision of the Divisional Court in *London Welsh Estates v Phillip* (1931) 100 LJKB 449 refusing to interfere with the order of an official referee which the court itself would probably not have made. I think the judge was right at any rate to consider the fact that there had been no payment into court in this case. Counsel for the plaintiffs said there could have been a payment into court; there could have been (if the damages had been liquidated) a tender before action and a plea of tender; there could have been an offer by letter, and there was not. He pointed out that under RSC Ord 62, r 5 the court 'shall' take into account the fact of a payment into court, and I think it follows from that that one of the matters a court should take into account is the absence of a payment into court. He has also drawn our attention to the fact that here was an interlocutory judgment for damages to be assessed; and until damages are assessed, even if assessed at only £2, there is no judgment which could be registered or enforced abroad, nothing which would entitle or enable the plaintiffs to prove in a liquidation if unfortunately the defendants had gone into liquidation. He says that, if this appeal is allowed and the order for which counsel for the defendants contends is made, a defendant who has made no payment into court would be better off than a defendant who had made an inadequate payment into court or a late payment into court.

These arguments are plausible, but in my judgment they ignore the reality of the position. I think that the weight to be given first of all to an award of nominal damages and second to the absence of any payment into court depends on all the circumstances of the case. That the judge gave great weight to the absence of a payment into court is I think made plain by what we find in the transcript of the discussion as to costs where, giving his decision, he says:

'What was really exercising me was whether to call it a draw by saying no order as to costs. At the end of the day I feel that would be a Solomonian judgment which would not be right in all the circumstances. The procedure for payment into court is there. If that had been considered (it may have been considered and rejected, I do not know) I imagine that out of caution something more than £2 would have been paid into court. No doubt counsel advising the defendants would have considered what sum they think might have been awarded on the alternative basis that the accounts were not going to be upheld by the court. As I say, having felt that a draw order, as it were, might be the fair thing, I do not feel that that is right in the circumstances. In my judgment, the ordinary rule should apply here which is that the plaintiffs have had judgment for damages to be assessed, the damages have been assessed at £2 and the order for costs will follow that event, which will mean the plaintiffs' costs up to and since the Ord 14 [judgment].'

But the event of an award of £2 was not the event at which the plaintiffs were aiming. They were aiming at £82,500, and the mere fact that they ultimately got something, token or nominal damages, does not enable me to regard them as remaining successful plaintiffs.

I find support for that view of the matter in what Devlin J said in *Anglo-Cyprian Trade Agencies Ltd v Paphos Wine Industries Ltd* [1951] 1 All ER 873. The judge had that case before him and quoted fairly extensively from it. It was a different case from this, with its own special facts. The plaintiffs were claiming over £2,000 for defects in wine which they had bought. By amendment at the trial they pleaded in the alternative that they were entitled to £52, and that was what the judge found they were entitled to. In those circumstances he thought that the defendants were really the successful party, not the plaintiffs, and he ordered the plaintiffs to pay the defendants' costs. It was not a case of nominal damages, although it was a case of trivial damages; but he made some carefully considered observations, stricly obiter, but, if I may respectfully say so, they seem to me to have the force of common sense. He said (at 874):

'No doubt, the ordinary rule is that, where a plaintiff has been successful, he ought not to be deprived of his costs, or, at any rate, made to pay the costs of the other side, unless he has been guilty of some sort of misconduct. In applying that rule, however, it is necessary to decide whether the plaintiff really has been successful, and I do not think that a plaintiff who recovers nominal damages ought necessarily to be regarded in the ordinary sense of the word as a "successful" plaintiff. In certain cases he may be, *e.g.*, where part of the object of the action is to establish a legal right, wholly irrespective of whether any substantial remedy is obtained. To that extent a plaintiff who recovers nominal damages may properly be regarded as a successful plaintiff, but it is necessary to examine the facts of each particular case.'

I do not think that counsel for the plaintiffs could contend that the plaintiffs here were interested in establishing a legal right: they had established that already; what they wanted was money. Then Devlin J went on to say (at 875):

'The plaintiffs, therefore, have not established anything which is of the least use to them, and, in my judgment, they are not to be regarded as successful plaintiffs. If the matter stopped there, therefore, I should treat the defendants as having succeeded and award them the costs of the action.'

Then he considered the special position raised by the amendment, and at the end of his judgment he came back to the first point and said (at 876):

'With regard to . . . the question of costs where a plaintiff has recovered merely nominal damages, I wish to make a further observation. Where a defendant thinks that nominal damages may be recovered and pays into court one shilling, or 20s., or 40s. (which the plaintiff, normally, does not take out), and only nominal damages are in fact recovered, the defendant is entitled to his costs. If the contention of counsel for the plantiffs were right, *viz.*, that a plaintiff who has recovered nominal damages has a *prima facie* right to obtain his costs, or, at any rate, not to pay the defendant's costs, it would be putting a premium, so to speak, on what is in the case of a nominal payment into court, hardly more than a mere matter of ritual.

Accordingly, I shall accept the application of the defendants in this case. There will be judgment for the plaintiffs for the sum which I have awarded, but the costs of the action will be paid by the plaintiffs to the defendants.'

That decision has found no place in the notes to RSC Ord 22 in *The Supreme Court Practice*; in my judgment it is time that it did. It is quite true that the case which Devlin J had to decide was not a case of nominal damage, although it is quite clear that he regarded the £52 as trivial damages and in effect as nominal damages. It is also true that the amendment in that case was made at a time which deprived the defendants of the opportunity of making a payment into court. Counsel for the plaintiffs stressed that that was a different case and a case decided only at first instance and one which has not apparently had much influence on the development of the law. All that may be true but, as it seems to me, what Devlin J said is of great weight and does apply very forcibly to the facts of this case. To have paid £2, or possibly £5 or £10, into court in this case would have been very near to a 'ritual' act. It would not have been taken out; the plaintiffs would have gone on with their mouth opened wider for a much larger sum; they did go on, having established a breach of contract, in the hope of getting a large sum of damages for that breach; in pursuit of that object they took up the time of the court and, more important from the point of view of this appeal, put themselves and the defendants to considerable expense over, as I have said, 15 working days; and at the end they came away empty handed, because I cannot think that £2 in the hand disqualifies them from that description.

Who was the successful party? In my judgment there is only one answer to that question, and once the door is opened by leave being given by the judge, as it seems to me this court is bound in accordance with ordinary principles to say that his exercise of his discretion was not unjudicial, but plainly wrong; that he gave much too much weight to the fact that there had been no payment in in a case in which a payment in would have made no difference at all, and that in all the circumstances of the case the right order was plainly the one which, if my Lords agree, I would make in substitution for that of the judge.

For the reasons I have given, I would allow the appeal and order the plaintiffs to pay the costs which the judge has ordered the defendants to pay.

GRIFFITHS LJ. I agree. By statute, costs are placed within the discretion of the trial judge. When a judge has refused leave to appeal from his order as to costs, the powers of the Court of Appeal to entertain an appeal against his order are extremely limited. Either it must be shown that the judge failed to exercise his discretion at all or alternatively, that in exercising his discretion he took account some wholly extraneous circumstance unconnected with the subject matter of the action, which is to be regarded as tantamount to a failure to exercise a judicial discretion: see *Donald Campbell & Co Ltd v Pollak* [1927] AC 732 esp at 812, [1927] All ER Rep 1 esp at 41 per Viscount Cave LC and the judgment of Jenkins LJ in *Baylis Baxter Ltd v Sabath* [1958] 2 All ER 209 at 215, [1958] 1 WLR 529 at 536–537.

When, however, the judge has given leave to appeal, the Court of Appeal is not so severely restrained. In *Findlay v Rly Executive* [1950] 2 All ER 969 at 972 Denning LJ said:

'The learned judge gave leave to appeal on the question of costs, which is generally a matter for his discretion. The effect of giving leave is that the judge invites reconsideration by this court of his decision, and this court enters on a review of it with less hesitation than it would otherwise do.'

In such cases the ordinary rules as to a review of the judge's discretion apply. This court must not be tempted to interfere with the judge's order merely because we would have exercised the discretion differently from the way in which the judge did. Before a court can interfere it must be shown that the judge has either erred in principle in his approach, or has left out of account, or taken into account, some feature that he should, or should not, have considered, or that his decision is wholly wrong, because the court is forced to the conclusion that he has not balanced the various factors fairly in the scale.

With this in mind, I turn to consider the judge's decision in this case. In my view he went wrong in principle. As a general rule a successful party is entitled to his costs, expressed by the lawyer's phrase 'costs follow the event'. Who was the successful party in the issue, or lis, tried by the judge in this case? Undoubtedly it was the defendants. There was never any contest as to the plaintiffs' entitlement to nominal damages for breach of contract; that flowed inevitably from the RSC Ord 14 judgment. The contest between the parties was whether the plaintiffs were entitled to more than nominal damages, and on this, the only issue tried by the judge, the defendants succeeded. But, because the defendants had not paid a nominal sum into court, the judge regarded the plaintiffs as the successful party. This appears clearly from two passages in his short judgment on costs. He said:

> 'Undoubtedly costs are in the discretion of the court; there is no argument about that. That discretion is to be exercised judicially and the general rule is that a successful plaintiff ought not to be deprived of his costs or, at any rate, slightly lower down the ladder, be ordered to pay the costs of the other side . . . In my judgment, the ordinary rule should apply here which is that the plaintiffs have had judgment for damages to be assessed, the damages have been assessed at £2 and the order for costs will follow that event, which will mean the plaintiffs' costs up to and since the Ord 14 [judgment].'

This appears to me to be a fundamentally wrong approach, and to attach far too much weight to the absence of any payment into court. If the defendants had paid £2 into court, there was no prospect whatever of that sum being accepted; it would have merely been what Devlin J referred to in the *Anglo-Cyprian Trade Agencies Ltd v Paphos Wire Industries Ltd* [1951] 1 All ER 873 at 876 as 'hardly more than a . . . matter of ritual'. It would have had no relevance whatever to the lis between the parties, namely whether the plaintiffs were entitled to more than nominal damages. The object of a payment into court is to enable a defendant to make a reasonable offer to settle the lis between the parties and to protect himself in costs if it is not accepted.

In this case, as I have pointed out, there was no lis other than the entitlement of the plaintiffs to more than nominal damages. A payment of nominal damages into court would have been wholly irrelevant to that lis, and in my view the absence of such a payment is no justification for regarding the plaintiffs as the successful party in the proceedings before the judge. The truth is that it was the defendants who were the successful party.

Accordingly, in my view this court is entitled to review the exercise of the discretion and, for the reasons given by Stephenson LJ, I agree that we should exercise the discretion by awarding the costs to the defendants.

PURCHAS LJ. I agree with both judgments that have been delivered by Stephenson and Griffiths LJJ; there is nothing that I can usefully add.

Appeal allowed. Plaintiffs to pay defendants' costs in action from 6 November 1980. Leave to appeal to House of Lords refused.

Solicitors: *Speechly Bircham* (for the defendants); *Joynson-Hicks & Co* (for the plaintiffs).

Diana Brahams   Barrister.

Attorney General of Trinidad and Tobago and another v McLeod

PRIVY COUNCIL

LORD DIPLOCK, LORD ELWYN-JONES, LORD KEITH OF KINKEL, LORD ROSKILL AND LORD TEMPLEMAN

28 NOVEMBER 1983, 11 JANUARY 1984

Trinidad and Tobago – Constitutional law – Entrenched provisions of constitution – Effect of entrenched provisions – Entrenchment by infection – Whether entrenching of specific provisions having effect of impliedly entrenching other provisions – Constitution of the Republic of Trinidad and Tobago 1976, ss 49, 54.

Trinidad and Tobago – Constitutional law – Human rights and freedoms – Right to protection of law – Whether non-compliance with entrenching provisions in constitution amounting to infringement of right to 'protection of the law' – Whether access to courts to challenge validity of statute sufficient 'protection of the law' – Constitution of the Republic of Trinidad and Tobago 1976, ss 4(b), 54.

Under s 54(2)[a] of the Constitution of the Republic of Trinidad and Tobago certain provisions of the Constitution, including s 4[b] thereof, were entrenched against alteration except by a two-thirds majority of each house of parliament in favour of amendment. Likewise, under s 54(3) of the Constitution certain provisions, including s 49(1)[c], were entrenched by requiring a three-quarters majority of the House of Representatives and a two-thirds majority of the Senate before they could be altered. Section 49(1) stated that members of the House of Representatives were required to vacate their seats on the dissolution of parliament, while s 49(2) specified other circumstances, eg resignation or ceasing to be a citizen of Trinidad and Tobago, in which a member was required to vacate his seat. In 1978 parliament purported to enact the Constitution of the Republic of Trinidad and Tobago (Amendment) Act 1978 which purported to amend s 49(2) by providing that a member was also required to vacate his seat if he resigned from or was expelled by his party. The amendment Act was passed by more than two-thirds but less than three-quarters of the House of Representatives. The respondent was a member of the House of Representatives who came under threat of having to vacate his seat when he fell out with the leadership of his party. He issued an originating motion seeking a declaration that the amendment Act was null and void and an injunction restraining the Speaker from declaring that he had resigned from or been expelled by his party, such a declaration being the first step in making a member vacate his seat. The judge dismissed the application but on appeal the Court of Appeal of Trinidad and Tobago granted the declaration sought, on the grounds (i) that since s 49(2) itself modified the entrenched s 49(1) (so that the entrenchment of s 49(1) 'infected' s 49(2)) any amendment of s 49(2) automatically modified s 49(1) and therefore required a three-quarters majority of the House of Representatives to be valid, and (ii) that the passing of a law which was contrary to the entrenched provisions was an infringement of the respondent's right to 'the protection of the law' under s 4(b) of the Constitution. The Attorney General and the Speaker appealed to the Privy Council.

---

a   Section 54, so far as material, is set out at p 697 *d* to *g*, post

b   Section 4, so far as material, provides: 'It is hereby recognised and declared that in Trinidad and Tobago there have existed and shall continue to exist . . . the following fundamental human rights and freedoms, namely . . . (b) the right of the individual to equality before the law and the protection of the law . . .'

c   Section 49, so far as material, is set out at p 696 *b* and p 698 *a* to *c*, post

Held – The Constitution of the Republic of Trinidad and Tobago was drafted according
a to a coherent and logical pattern in which provisions dealing with the constitutional
characteristics of parliament as the organ of the state in which the plenitude of legislative
power was vested were entrenched while provisions dealing with the internal procedure
and qualification of individuals for membership of parliament were not. The provisions
of s 54(2) and (3) were clear and categorical as to those particular sections which were
entrenched and an argument in favour of the implication of the entrenchment of s 49(2)
b by infection from the express entrenchment of s 49(1) was unsustainable. Since s 49(2)
was not expressly entrenched by s 54(2) and (3) it could be validly amended by a simple
majority and therefore the amendment Act which created a further disqualification of
individuals from membership of the House of Representatives did not infringe the
entrenching provisions of the Constitution. Furthermore, even if the amendment Act
had abrogated, abridged or infringed a fundamental right of the respondent which was
c protected by s 4 of the Constitution, it would not thereby have infringed the entrenching
provisions of the Constitution since s 4 was entrenched by s 54(2) which required only a
two-thirds majority of each house in favour of amendment and the amendment Act had
satisfied that requirement. Accordingly, the respondent was not entitled to the
declarations sought and the appeal would therefore be allowed (see p 698 *j* to p 699 *b* and
j to p 700 *c* and p 701 *j*, post).
d   Per curiam. The enactment in Trinidad and Tobago of a law that is void because it is
inconsistent with the Constitution does not deprive anyone of 'the protection of the law'
for the purposes of s 4(*b*) of the Constitution so long as the judicial system affords access
to the courts for the purpose of obtaining a binding declaration that the particular law is
invalid. In such circumstances it is the access to the courts which is 'the protection of the
law' (see p 701 *b* to *d*, post).

e
Notes
For the constitution of Trinidad and Tobago, see 6 Halsbury's Laws (4th edn) para 1009.

Cases referred to in judgment
Chokolingo v A-G of Trinidad and Tobago [1981] 1 All ER 244, [1981] 1 WLR 106, PC.
f *Harrikissoon v A-G of Trinidad and Tobago* [1980] AC 265, [1979] 3 WLR 62, PC.
Hinds v R [1976] 1 All ER 353, [1977] AC 195, [1976] 2 WLR 366, PC.
Maharaj v A-G of Trinidad and Tobago (No 2) [1978] 2 All ER 670, [1979] AC 385, [1978]
2 WLR 902, PC.
Thornhill v A-G of Trinidad and Tobago [1981] AC 61, [1980] 2 WLR 510, PC.

Appeal
g The Attorney General of Trinidad and Tobago and Arnold Thomasos, Speaker of the
House of Representatives, appealed by final leave to appeal granted by the Court of
Appeal of Trinidad and Tobago on 5 April 1982 from a decision of that court (Hyatali CJ,
Kelsick and Cross JJA) on 29 July 1982 allowing an appeal by the respondent, Errol
McLeod, from the judgment of Bernard J on 19 December 1978 ordering that the
respondent was entitled to a declaration that the Constitution of the Republic of Trinidad
h and Tobago (Amendment) Act 1978 was ultra vires the Constitution of the Republic of
Trinidad and Tobago (being the schedule to the Constitution of the Republic of Trinidad
and Tobago Act 1976), null, void and of no effect. The facts are set out in the judgment
of the Board.

Anthony Lester QC and *The Solicitor General of Trinidad and Tobago (Lionel Jones)* for the
j   appellants.
Mr McLeod did not appear.

11 January. The following judgment of the Board was delivered.

LORD DIPLOCK. The question of substantive law in this appeal is whether Act No

15 of 1978, of which the long title is 'An Act to amend the Constitution of the Republic of Trinidad and Tobago Act, 1976' (the amendment Act), is void under s 2 of the *a* Constitution because it was not supported at the final vote thereon by not less than three-quarters of all the members of the House of Representatives (the House).

The respondent, Errol McLeod, contended that a favourable vote of this size in the House was required, by s 54(3) of the Constitution, in order to validate the amendment Act which purported to amend s 49(2) of the Constitution by adding to the four existing paragraphs, which set out circumstances in which a member of the House is required to *b* vacate his seat, a fifth paragraph in the following terms:

'(e) having been a candidate of a party and elected to the House, he resigns from or is expelled by that party.'

The appeal also raises a subsidiary question of procedural law whether Mr McLeod's *c* proper remedy was by originating motion for redress under s 14(1) of the Constitution, for which the procedure was regulated by Ord 55 of the Rules of the Supreme Court of Trinidad and Tobago, or was by the ordinary process of an originating summons for a declaration that the amendment Act was void.

The facts which gave rise to the originating motion can be stated very shortly. Mr McLeod stood for election to the first parliament of the republic as a candidate of the *d* United Labour Front. He was duly elected, but would appear to have fallen out with the party leadership by the spring of 1978. The amendment Act received 27 favourable votes in the House. This in number fell short of three-quarters of the total membership by one vote. It was assented to by the President on 19 April 1978. On 24 April a letter was addressed to Mr McLeod by the General Secretary of the United Labour Front threatening him with disciplinary proceedings by the party. To this Mr McLeod reacted promptly: *e* on 28 April he issued in the High Court an originating motion under s 14(1) of the Constitution seeking a declaration that the amendment Act was null and void, and an order restraining the Speaker of the House from making a declaration that Mr McLeod had resigned from, or had been expelled by, the party as a candidate of which he had been elected. The claim to an injunction was based on s 4 of the Amendment Act. This inserted a new section in the Constitution, s 49A, which provided for such a declaration *f* being made by the Speaker, on his being informed by the leader in the House of the party as a candidate of which the member was elected, of the resignation or expulsion from that party of a member. On the expiration of 14 days from such declaration s 49A obliged the member to vacate his seat unless within that period he instituted legal proceedings to challenge the allegation that he had resigned, or his expulsion.

The proceedings which Mr McLeod instituted by originating motion were heard by *g* Bernard J on 19 December 1978. He dismissed Mr McLeod's application on the ground of substantive law that s 49(2) of the Constitution, that the Amendment Act purported to alter, was not entrenched by s 54(3) of the Constitution. It could thus, under s 59 of the Constitution, be validly passed by a majority of members present and voting in the House and the Senate respectively.

Mr McLeod's appeal from the dismissal of his motion was allowed by the Court of *h* Appeal on 29 July 1981. It granted the declaration that he sought. Shortly after this, however, the parliament of which he was a member was dissolved; and Mr McLeod did not stand for re-election to the new parliament. He ceased to have any further interest in the proceedings that he had started, with the result that although his name appears on the record as respondent Mr McLeod has taken no part in the appeal to this Board for which the appellants, the Attorney General and the Speaker, obtained final leave on 5 *j* April 1982. Their Lordships have thus been deprived of the advantage of hearing any argument adverse to that which was presented on behalf of the appellants, though, so far as the point of substantive law is concerned, this handicap has been mitigated by the three separate closely reasoned judgments of the Court of Appeal in Mr McLeod's favour.

Section 2 of the Constitution of Trinidad and Tobago provides:

'This Constitution is the supreme law of Trinidad and Tobago, and any other law that is inconsistent with this Constitution is void to the extent of the inconsistency.'

Although supreme the Constitution is not immutable. As was pointed out in the majority judgment of the Judicial Committee in *Hinds v R* [1976] 1 All ER 353 at 361, [1977] AC 195 at 214, constitutions on the Westminster model, of which the Constitution of the Republic of Trinidad and Tobago is an example, provide for their future alteration by the people acting through their representatives in the parliament of the state. In constitutions on the Westminster model, this is the institution in which the plenitude of the state's legislative power is vested.

Such is the case in Trinidad and Tobago. Section 54(1) of the Constitution provides expressly that parliament may alter *any* of the provisions of the Constitution. Except as respects those provisions of the Constitution (the entrenched provisions) specified in s 54(2) or (3), an Act of parliament altering a provision of the Constitution and containing, as sub-s (5) requires, an express statement that such is its purpose is valid and effectual if passed in the House of Representatives and the Senate in accordance with ss 59 to 61, that is to say by a simple majority of the members in each House present and voting thereon and assented to by the President.

As respects the entrenched provisions it is convenient to set out s 54(2), (3) and (6) in full (omitting only references to the Trinidad and Tobago Independence Act 1962):

'(2) In so far as it alters—(a) sections 4 to 14, 20(b), 21, 43(1), 53, 58, 67(2), 70, 83, 101 to 108, 110, 113, 116 to 125 and 133 to 137; or (b) section 3 in its application to any of the provisions of this Constitution specified in paragraph (a), a Bill for an Act under this section shall not be passed by Parliament unless at the final vote thereon in each House it is supported by the votes of not less than two-thirds of all the members of each House.

(3) In so far as it alters—(a) this section; (b) sections 22, 23, 24, 26, 28 to 34, 38 to 40, 46 49(1), 51, 55, 61, 63, 64, 68, 69, 71, 72, 87 to 91, 93, 96(4) and (5), 97, 109, 115, 138, 139, or the Second and Third Schedules; (c) section 3 in its application to any of the provisions specified in paragraph (a) or (b) . . . a Bill for an Act under this section shall not be passed by Parliament unless it is supported at the final vote thereon—(i) in the House of Representatives by the votes of not less than three-fourths of all the members of the House; (ii) and in the Senate by the votes of not less than two-thirds of all the members of the Senate.

(6) In this section references to the alteration of any of the provisions of this Constitution . . . include references to repealing it, with or without re-enactments thereof or the making of different provisions in place thereof or the making of provision for any particular case or class of case inconsistent therewith to modifying it and to suspending its operation for any period.'

It is to be noted that whereas s 49(1) is included in the entrenched provisions specified in s 54(3)(b), s 49(2) does not figure among the provisions entrenched by either sub-s (2) or sub-s (3) of s 54. Section 54(1) therefore authorised its alteration by an Act of parliament passed in the same way and by the same majorities in each House as an ordinary law, provided that it stated, as the amendment Act did in its long title, that its purpose was to alter the Constitution.

It was on this simple ground that Bernard J decided the point of substantive law against Mr McLeod. Accordingly, he did not find it necessary to decide the question of procedural law.

The Court of Appeal, founding itself on the wide definition of 'alteration' in s 54(6), held that s 49(2) as it stood before the passing of the amendment Act had the effect of modifying sub-s (1) of that section, which *is* entrenched by s 54(3). Its reasoning was that the amendment Act makes an additional modification to the entrenched sub-s (1) and accordingly, in order to be valid, the Bill for the Act must at the final vote thereon have been supported in the House of Representatives by the votes of not less than three-quarters of the members of the House, and this requirement had not been satisfied.

This makes it necessary for their Lordships to set out the full text of s 49(1) and (2) of the Constitution as these two subsections stood before the amendment Act: *a*

'(1) Every member of the House of Representatives shall vacate his seat in the House at the next dissolution of Parliament after his election.

(2) A member of the House of Representatives shall also vacate his seat in the House where—(a) he resigns it by writing under his hand addressed to the Speaker, or where the office of Speaker is vacant or the Speaker is absent from Trinidad and Tobago, to the Deputy Speaker; (b) he is absent from the sitting of the House for   *b*
such period and in such circumstances as may be prescribed in the rules of procedure of the House; (c) he ceases to be a citizen of Trinidad and Tobago; (d) subject to the provisions of sub-section (3), any circumstances arise that, if he were not a member of the House of Representatives, would cause him to be disqualified for election thereto by virtue of sub-section (1) of section 48 or any law enacted in pursuance of   *c*
sub-section (2) of that section.'

All three members of the Court of Appeal (Hyatali CJ, Kelsick and Cross JJA) found in the language of sub-s (1) an implication which led them to construe it as if it read: 'Each member of the House of Representatives shall *retain* his seat in the House until the next dissolution of Parliament after his election and shall *then* vacate it.'

It was only by adopting this construction of sub-s (1), for which their Lordships, with   *d*
respect, cannot find justification either in the words of s 49 itself or in the framework of that part of the Constitution, ch 4, that deals with parliament, that the Court of Appeal was able to treat sub-s (2) as being, in the words of Kelsick JA, 'in substance a proviso to s 49(1)'.

Their Lordships would start by drawing attention to the irrational consequences that would follow from treating sub-s (2) as entrenched by infection from sub-s (1) despite its   *e*
conspicuous omission from the list of entrenched provisions in s 54(2) and (3). In a total of 60 entrenched provisions listed in s 54(2) and (3), s 49(1) is one of five only in which a part of a section and not the section as a whole has been singled out for entrenchment. How far then does entrenchment by infection from s 49(1) spread beyond s 49(2) itself? Section 49(2)(d) includes, as a ground for requiring a member to vacate his seat, circumstances arising that would cause him to be disqualified for election by virtue of   *f*
s 48(1) or any law enacted in pursuance of s 48(2). No part of s 48 is itself included among the entrenched sections. Furthermore, s 48(1)(g) opens the door to further grounds of disqualification in the future not already specified in paras (a) to (f), since it disqualifies from election to the House of Representatives any person who 'is not qualified to be registered as an elector at a Parliamentary election under any law in force in Trinidad and Tobago'. That takes one to s 51, which deals with qualification of voters. Section 51 is   *g*
entrenched by s 54(3), but it is drafted in the following terms:

'Subject to such disqualifications as Parliament may prescribe, a person shall be qualified to vote at an election of members to serve in the House of Representatives if, and shall not be qualified to vote at such an election unless, he—(a) is a Commonwealth citizen (within the meaning of section 18) of the age of eighteen   *h*
years or upwards; and (b) has such other qualifications regarding residence or registration as may be prescribed.'

'Prescribe' by the definition section, s 3, means 'prescribed by or under an Act of Parliament'. So the introductory words of the section reserve to Parliament power to pass ordinary laws involving no amendment to the Constitution but which create disqualifications to be a member of the House that are additional to those expressly   *j*
referred to in either s 48 or s 51.

In their Lordships' view this is enough to demonstrate that an argument in favour of implication of entrenchment of s 49(2) by infection from the express entrenchment of s 49(1) is unsustainable. On the contrary, the draftsman's selection for entrenchment of specific provisions of ch 4 of the Constitution dealing with parliament, leaving the other

provisions of that chapter susceptible of amendment by an ordinary Act of parliament,
a provided that it contains a statement that such is its purpose, appears to their Lordships
to follow a coherent and logical pattern.

Broadly speaking it is those provisions of the Constitution that deal with the
institutional characteristics of parliament, as the organ of the state in which by s 53 is
vested the plenitude of the legislative power of the sovereign Republic of Trinidad and
Tobago, that are protected by entrenchment; those provisions that deal with the
b qualifications of individuals for membership of either House and with the internal
procedure of either House are not.

Thus, entrenched provisions require that the parliament of Trinidad and Tobago in
which is vested the power to make laws (s 53) including laws altering the Constitution
(s 54) is to be bicameral, consisting of the President and the Senate and the House of
Representatives (ss 39 and 61) presided over by officers called the President of the Senate
c and the Speaker respectively (s 58). The Senate is to consist of 31 members appointed by
a method which ensures to the government of the day a majority of one (s 40). The
House of Representatives is to consist of 36 members (s 46), elected for separate
constituencies (s 70) by popular vote (s 51), the number of members and the boundaries
of constituencies being subject to review on the recommendation of an independent
Elections and Boundaries Commission (ss 71 and 72). There is to be freedom of speech in
d parliament (s 55(1)) but in other respects parliament may determine the powers and
privileges of each House by an ordinary unentrenched law (s 55(2)). Subject to restrictions
as to money Bills and the powers of the Senate in relation to them, Bills may be introduced
in either House (ss 63 and 64), although s 59, which read in conjunction with s 54
provides that Bills shall be passed by the votes of a majority of members present and
voting thereon, is not entrenched. (This would appear to be somewhat anomalous in
e relation to the general pattern of entrenchment of parliament's institutional characteristics.)

As regards the duration of parliament and the requirements when it shall sit,
parliament must hold a session of each House at least once in every year with an interval
not exceeding six months between each session (s 67). Intervals between sessions are the
result of prorogation or dissolution. Prorogation leaves the membership of both Houses
f unchanged; but dissolution terminates the membership of every member of the Senate
(s 43(1)) and of every member of the House of Representatives (s 49(1)). If any of them
wish to be members of the next parliament they must be either reappointed to the Senate
or re-elected to the House of Representatives (s 69). Subject to possible extension in time
of war or in the presence of an emergency, a parliament must not last longer than five
years from the date of its first sitting although it may be dissolved earlier (s 68); and a
g general election of members to the House of Representatives must be held within three
months of the dissolution and fresh appointments to the Senate must be made by the
President as soon as practicable thereafter (s 69).

In contrast to these entrenched provisions, those provisions which deal with the
qualification of individuals to be appointed to and to remain members of the Senate are
unentrenched. These are ss 41, 42 and 43(2) to (6) and s 44, which deals with temporary
h appointments during temporary inability of senators to perform their functions.
Similarly, as regards the qualifications of individuals to be elected to and to remain
members of the House of Representatives, these also are unentrenched. They are ss 47,
48, 49(2) to (6), on which their Lordships have already commented. Consistently with
this pattern, s 52, which confers on the High Court and on the Court of Appeal
jurisdiction to determine questions of disputed membership of either House, is
j unentrenched.

In their Lordships' view, which is in agreement with that expressed by Bernard J, the
words of s 54(2) and (3) are clear and categorical. Of s 49 only sub-s (1) is entrenched;
sub-ss (2) to (6) are not and there is no room for any implication that they are.
Consequently, parliament was empowered by ss 53, 54(1) and 59 of the Constitution to
proceed, by an Act of parliament not supported by the majorities of votes specified in

either sub-s (2) or sub-s (3) of s 54, to add the new para (e) to s 49(2) of the Constitution creating a further ground on which an individual member of the House of Representatives could be required to vacate his seat, or in other words to create an additional disqualification of individuals for membership of the House.

So on the question of substantive law the appellants succeed in their appeal. Even if Mr McLeod had been right in his original submission that the amendment Act had the effect of abrogating, abridging or infringing some fundamental right to which he was entitled under ss 4 and 5 of the Constitution, this could not avail him on the question of substantive law, because ss 4 to 14 of the Constitution are entrenched, not by sub-s (3) but by sub-s (2) of s 54; and, as was pointed out in the judgment of Bernard J, the majority by which the amendment Act was passed in each House satisfied the requirements of the latter subsection.

Strictly speaking, it is not essential for their Lordships to decide on this appeal the question of procedural law whether Mr McLeod's proper remedy, if he had been right on the question of substantive law, would have been by originating summons for a declaration that the amendment Act was void under s 2 of the Constitution and not by originating motion for redress under s 14(1) of the Constitution. Furthermore, as all three members of the Court of Appeal in the instant case remarked, the Rules of the Supreme Court contain provisions which would enable one procedure to be substituted for the other at any stage before judgment, if it should turn out that the wrong procedure had initially been adopted. Nevertheless, Hyatali CJ and Kelsick JA, in their judgments, did express a view as to the meaning of the expression 'protection of the law' in s 4(b) of the Constitution with which their Lordships feel compelled to express their respectful disagreement.

The Judicial Committee has previously had occasion to draw attention to the necessity of vigilance on the part of the Supreme Court to prevent misuse by litigants of the important safeguard of the rights and freedoms enshrined in ss 4 and 5 that is provided by the right to apply to the High Court for redress under s 14. Two specific forms that such misuse may take have previously been dealt with in judgments of the Judicial Committee. In *Harrikissoon v A-G of Trinidad and Tobago* [1980] AC 265 at 268 it was said of the identical section, although differently numbered, s 6 in the 1962 Constitution:

'The notion that whenever there is a failure by an organ of government or a public authority or public officer to comply with the law this necessarily entails the contravention of some human right or fundamental freedom guaranteed to individuals by Chapter I of the Constitution is fallacious. The right to apply to the High Court under section 6 of the Constitution for redress, when any human right or fundamental freedom is or is likely to be contravened, is an important safeguard of those rights and freedoms; but its value will be diminished if it is allowed to be misused as a general substitute for the normal procedures for invoking judicial control of administrative action. In an originating application to the High Court under section 6(1), the mere allegation that a human right or fundamental freedom of the applicant has been or is likely to be contravened is not of itself sufficient to entitle the applicant to invoke the jurisdiction of the court under the subsection if it is apparent that the allegation is frivolous or vexatious or an abuse of the process of the court as being made solely for the purpose of avoiding the necessity of applying in the normal way for the appropriate judicial remedy for unlawful administrative action which involves no contravention of any human right or fundamental freedom.'

In *Chokolingo v A-G of Trinidad and Tobago* [1981] 1 All ER 244, [1981] 1 WLR 106 the Judicial Committee, applying what they had previously said obiter in *Maharaj v A-G of Trinidad and Tobago (No 2)* [1978] 2 All ER 670, [1979] AC 385, held that the procedure for redress under s 6(1) of the 1962 Constitution was not to be used as a means of collateral attack on a judgment of a court of justice of Trinidad and Tobago acting within its jurisdiction, whether original or appellate.

The instant proceedings do not fall into either of the above categories. Since a question of the interpretation of the Constitution was involved, Mr McLeod would have had an appeal to the Judicial Committee as of right under s 109(1)(c) of the Constitution

_a whichever form of procedure he had adopted; nor, since the High Court was the court of competent jurisdiction whichever procedure he adopted, is there any question of collateral attack on a judgment of a court of competent jurisdiction.

In his originating motion however the only infringement of his fundamental rights that Mr McLeod alleged was his right to 'the protection of the law' under s 4(b) of the Constitution. The 'law' of which he claimed to have been deprived of the protection was s 54(3) of the Constitution, which he contended (successfully in the Court of Appeal)

_b prohibited parliament from passing the amendment Act, except by the majorities specified in that subsection. This argument, although it was accepted by Hyatali CJ and Kelsick JA in the Court of Appeal, is in their Lordships' view fallacious. For parliament to purport to make a law that is void under s 2 of the Constitution, because of its inconsistency with the Constitution, deprives no one of the 'protection of the law', so long as the judicial system of Trinidad and Tobago affords a procedure by which any

_c person interested in establishing the invalidity of that purported law can obtain from the courts of justice, in which the plenitude of the judicial power of the state is vested, a declaration of its invalidity that will be binding on the parliament itself and on all persons attempting to act under or enforce the purported law. Access to a court of justice for that purpose is itself 'the protection of the law' to which all individuals are entitled under s 4(b).

_d Their Lordships have been invited by the appellants to supply a comprehensive definition of what is meant by the expression 'the protection of the law' in s 4(b). This is an invitation which their Lordships consider that they must decline in a case in which, owing to the respondent not being represented, they have not had the benefit of adversarial argument. In *Thornhill v A-G of Trinidad and Tobago* [1981] AC 61 at 70, a case in which a person sought redress, under the section that under the 1962 Constitution

_e corresponded to s 14, for having been deprived of access to his legal adviser while under arrest by the police, the Judicial Committee said in relation to ss 1 and 2 of the 1962 Constitution, which are renumbered ss 4 and 5 in the 1976 Constitution:

'Section 2 is directed primarily to curtailing the exercise of the legislative powers of the newly constituted Parliament of Trinidad and Tobago. Save in the exceptional

_f circumstances referred to in section 4 [sc of the 1962 Constitution] or by the exceptional procedure provided for in section 5 [sc of the 1962 Constitution] the Parliament may not pass any law that purports to abrogate, abridge or infringe any of the rights or freedoms recognised and declared in section 1 or to authorise any such abrogation, abridgement or infringement. But section 2 also goes on to give, as particular examples of treatment of an individual by the executive or the judiciary, which would have the effect of infringing those rights, the various kinds of conduct

_g described in paragraphs (a) to (h) of that section. These paragraphs spell out in greater detail (though not necessarily exhaustively) what is included in the expression "due process of law" to which the appellant was entitled under paragraph (a) of section 1 as a condition of his continued detention and "the protection of the law" to which he was entitled under paragraph (b).'

_h In that passage their Lordships took the precaution of incorporating the words in parenthesis 'though not necessarily exhaustively'. An appeal which is undefended does not provide an appropriate occasion to jettison that precaution and to embark on an attempt to provide a more exhaustive definition of what is meant by 'the protection of the law'. The problem of defining what is included in each of the fundamental human rights and freedoms referred to in the lettered paragraphs of ss 4 and 5(1) is best dealt

_j with on a case-to-case basis.

The appeal must be allowed and the order of Bernard J of 9 December 1978 restored. There will be no order as to costs.

Appeal allowed. No order as to costs.

Solicitors: *Charles Russell & Co* (for the appellants).

Mary Rose Plummer   Barrister.

Brooks v J & P Coates (UK) Ltd

a

QUEEN'S BENCH DIVISION AT LEEDS
BOREHAM J
24, 25, 26, 31 JANUARY 1983

Factory – Workroom – Duty to provide ventilation – Plaintiff working in cotton spinning mill –
Plaintiff exposed to dust given off in course of spinning – Plaintiff contracting byssinosis as result
of inhaling cotton dust – Whether defendant employer providing adequate ventilation to render
harmless cotton dust which is injurious to health – Factories Act 1961, s 4.

b

Factory – Removal of dust – All practicable measures to be taken – Obligation where dust likely
to be injurious or offensive or where substantial quantities of dust of any kind – Duty to provide
exhaust appliances – Plaintiff working in cotton spinning mill – Fine cotton dust given off in mill
not considered likely to be source of danger to health – Plaintiff contracting byssinosis as result
of inhaling dust – Whether dust given off of such character and extent as to be likely to be injurious
or offensive to plaintiff – Whether dust given off in substantial quantities – Whether defendant
employer taking all practicable measures to prevent inhalation and accumulation of dust –
Whether employer in breach of statutory duty in failing to provide exhaust appliances – Factories
Act 1961, s 63.

c

d

Limitation of action – Extension of time limit – Ignorance of claim against employer – Plaintiff
leaving cotton mill because of ill health caused by conditions at work – Plaintiff not knowing that
he was suffering from byssinosis as a result of inhaling cotton dust – Plaintiff bringing action for
damages after expiry of limitation period – Whether plaintiff knowing that condition due in whole
or in part to breach of employers' statutory duty at time of leaving employment – Whether
plaintiff statute-barred from bringing action – Whether court should exercise discretion to allow
action to continue – Whether prejudice to plaintiff if denied right to litigate greater than that
suffered by employer if action allowed to continue – Limitation Act 1980, ss 11, 33.

e

The plaintiff worked in the defendants' cotton spinning mill from 1935 until 1965. In
the course of his employment throughout that period the plaintiff was exposed to
substantial quantities of very fine cotton dust given off in the course of spinning, in
particular during the carding process and the weekly brush stripping. Only very fine
cotton of high quality was spun at the defendants' mill and at no time during the
plaintiff's employment was cotton dust in fine cotton mills regarded by experts or the
defendants as a likely source of danger to the health of employees. In 1958 the plaintiff
received treatment for bronchitis and in 1965 he left the defendants' employment
because of his bronchitic condition. In 1979 the plaintiff was diagnosed as suffering from
byssinosis (a bronchial condition caused by inhaling minute particles of dust) which
coupled with the effects of cigarette smoking had caused his bronchitis. In 1980 the
plaintiff brought an action for damages against the defendants for breach of statutory
duty under the Factories Act 1961 and/or negligence. He contended, inter alia, (i) that
the defendants were in breach of s 4[a] of the 1961 Act in failing to ensure that effective
and suitable provision was made for securing and maintaining the adequate ventilation
of the premises in which he had been employed and for rendering harmless cotton dust
which was injurious to health, and (ii) since even the fine cotton dust given off in the
premises was (a) of such character and extent or (b) in such substantial quantities as to be
likely to be injurious or offensive to the plaintiff, the defendants by failing to take all
practicable measures to protect him against inhaling the dust and to prevent its
accumulating, and in particular by failing to provide or maintain exhaust appliances as
near as possible to the point of origin of the dust, were accordingly in breach of s 63(1)[b]

f

g

h

j

---

a   Section 4 is set out at p 717 *f*, post
b   Section 63(1), so far as material, is set out at p 718 *b*, post

of the 1961 Act. The defendants contended (1) that the plaintiff's claim was barred by
virtue of s 11[c] of the Limitation Act 1980, since the plaintiff was suffering from byssinosis
a in 1965 when, even though he may have been unaware that what he was suffering from
was byssinosis, he nevertheless knew that his condition was due wholly or partly to the
acts or omissions of the defendants on which he relied to bring his action, (ii) that the
court ought not to exercise its discretion under s 33[d] of the 1980 Act to extend the
limitation period, and (iii) that, although the defendants knew that cotton dust could
cause byssinosis, the plaintiff was never exposed to any quantity of dust which was likely
b to be harmful to him, and further, at the time of the plaintiff's employment at the mill
there was no reason to believe that dust in a fine cotton mill was likely to be injurious to
persons employed there.

Held – (1) Since in 1965 the plaintiff knew or ought reasonably to have had knowledge
that his condition was due in whole or in part to the acts or omissions on which he relied
c to bring his action, the action was prima facie barred by virtue of s 11 of the 1980 Act.
However, despite the long delay, the plaintiff was not blameworthy and although there
was real prejudice to the defendants by reason of the delay nevertheless, applying the test
of where would the greater prejudice fall, the prejudice suffered by the plaintiff if he was
denied the right to litigate his claim substantially outweighed the prejudice which would
be suffered by the defendants if the action was allowed to continue. Accordingly, the
d court would exercise its discretion under s 33 of the 1980 Act to allow the action to
proceed (see p 712 h j, p 713 c and p 714 b to d, post).
(2) The defendants were in breach of their statutory duty for the following reasons—
(a) they had failed to carry out their duty under s 4 of the 1961 Act to render harmless
as far as practicable such dust as might be injurious to health. Although the defendants
knew that cotton dust could cause byssinosis and therefore ought to have known that it
e might be dangerous to the plaintiff's health, they had failed to provide adequate
ventilation of the room where the plaintiff worked until 1963 although it was practicable
to do so much earlier (see p 717 j to p 718 a and j, post);
(b) although it was not established that the defendants knew or ought to have known
that cotton dust in a fine cotton mill was likely to be injurious to their employees, the
f dust given off was in sufficient quantities to be offensive to the plaintiff and was present
in substantial quantities. On the facts, the defendants had failed to take all practicable
measures to protect the plaintiff from inhaling the dust or to prevent the dust
accumulating or to fit an exhaust appliance, and accordingly they were in breach of s 63
of the 1961 Act (see p 718 f to j, post).
(3) It followed that the defendants were liable in damages to the plaintiff, but taking
into account the fact that the plaintiff's condition was probably 50% attributable to his
g cigarette smoking the damages would be reduced accordingly (see p 718 j to p 719 b and
f g, post).
Per curiam. (1) On the true construction of s 63 of the 1961 Act, the term 'all
practicable measures' which are required to be taken to protect persons employed in a
factory against, inter alia, the inhalation and accumulation of dust means precautions
h which can be taken without practical difficulty (see p 718 g h, post).
(2) Although s 1[e] of the 1961 Act is mandatory in its terms and imposes an absolute
duty to keep a factory clean, what is considered a clean state is variable and depends on
the processes carried out in the factory (see p 717 e f, post).

Notes
j For qualified statutory obligations imposed by safety legislation, see 20 Halsbury's Laws
(4th edn) para 553.

---

c   Section 11, so far as material, is set out at p 712 b c, post
d   Section 33, so far as material, is set out at p 712 j, post
e   Section 1, so far as material, is set out at p 717 e, post

For ventilation of factory workrooms, see ibid para 616, and for cases on the subject, see 26 Digest (Reissue) 380–381, 2681–2683.

For the duty to protect against dust and fumes in factories, see 20 Halsbury's Laws (4th edn) paras 640–666, and for cases on the subject, see 26 Digest (Reissue) 383–386, 2697–2705.

For the court's power to override limitation periods, see 28 Halsbury's Laws (4th edn) para 694.

For the Factories Act 1961, ss 1, 4, 63, see 13 Halsbury's Statutes (3rd edn) 404, 408, 465.

For the Limitation Act 1980, ss 11, 33, see 50(1) ibid 1262, 1286.

Case referred to in judgment

Graham v Co-op Wholesale Society Ltd [1957] 1 All ER 654, [1957] 1 WLR 511.

Cases also cited

Lea v Armitage Shanks Ltd (19 July 1977, unreported) QBD.
McGhee v National Coal Board [1972] 3 All ER 1008, [1973] 1 WLR 1, HL.
Smith v Central Asbestos Co Ltd [1972] 2 All ER 1135, [1973] AC 518, HL.

Action

By a writ issued on 19 November 1980 the plaintiff, Thomas Brooks, claimed against the defendants, J & P Coates (UK) Ltd, damages for personal injuries, namely byssinosis contracted as a result of his employment with the defendants at their premises at Eagley Mill, Bolton, Lancashire between 1935 and 1965. The facts are set out in the judgment.

Richard Clegg QC and *J J Rowe QC* for the plaintiff.
Christopher Rose QC, Janet Smith and *Philip Hinchliffe* for the defendants.

BOREHAM J. In this action the plaintiff claims damages for personal injury caused, so he alleges, by long exposure to cotton dust during the course of his employment by the defendants, J & P Coates Ltd, at their Eagley Mill at Bolton. The injury of which he complains is the disease known as byssinosis which is a bronchial condition caused by inhaling minute particles of cotton dust. The plaintiff's employment by the defendants spanned a period that began in 1935 and finished in 1965 when the plaintiff was 45 years of age, with the exception of a five-year gap during which the plaintiff served with the army during the war.

It is impossible, it is conceded on all sides, to date the precise onset of byssinosis, but the plaintiff contends that it is due to the defendants' breaches of statutory and common law duties over a long period prior to 1965. The defendants deny liability to the plaintiff, but the issues have been narrowed by a number of admissions made on behalf of the defendants by counsel. It will be necessary to deal with those admissions at a later stage. It is sufficient at this stage to point out that the defendants deny first of all that the plaintiff suffers from byssinosis; second, they deny that he was overexposed to a quantity of dust that was liable to be harmful (and when I speak of dust in the course of this judgment it at all times means cotton dust) and third, they contend that the plaintiff's claim is barred by the provisions of the Limitation Act 1980 and thus they are not liable.

The facts I find are these: the plaintiff is now aged 62. As I have already indicated, he entered the defendants' employ at their Eagley Mill in 1935. In order to understand the work that he did, the conditions in which he did it and the nature of his complaints it is necessary to describe some of the processes in a little detail and to describe too the machinery and the effects that these machines had when in production.

Raw cotton was brought to the mill in bales. It was graded according to the length of fibre or staple and according to its cleanliness. Cottons with the shortest fibres are used

for spinning what are called in the trade 'coarse counts'. They give off much dust in the
course of their spinning. At the other end of the scale the raw cotton with the longest
a staples which give off less dust in the course of spinning are used for what I will call 'fine
counts'. It is now apparently accepted that although in total the dust given off by high
grade fine staple cottons is less, they give off more very fine dust. In each grade, of course,
there are or were varying qualities, quality being judged, as I understand it, by the
cleanliness of the raw cotton and the quantity of debris or trash, as it is called, which is
b present in it. At their Eagley Mills, the defendants processed at all times fine Egyptian or
Sudanese long staple cotton of high quality and of a high state of cleanliness. I accept the
evidence of Mr Isherwood, called on behalf of the defendants, that the quality control
exercised by their purchasing representatives was of a high standard, with the result that
the quantity of dust given off during the processing was substantially lower than in most
other mills.

c   The first room at the mills and the arrival point of the bales of cotton at Eagley was
called the opening and blowing room. There the bales were opened and the cotton was
cleaned of as much trash as possible by being put through a series of beaters and cleaners.
It was then taken in the form of what is called a lap to the card room next door. A lap is,
in layman's terms at any rate, a cylinder of raw cotton which is put onto a spindle from
which it is fed into a carding machine or carding engine to be carded. In essence, the
d carding process consists of drawing out and combing the fibres into parallel lines, to
remove as much of the remaining impurities as is possible and to make the fibres into
what I would describe as a thickish rope which is called a web. The web is then processed
further in the carding room via the draw frames, speed frames and combers into a thread
which is wound onto bobbins. From the card room the thread is taken to the spinning
room and to other departments. It is unnecessary to follow its progress any further
because the plaintiff's work was confined to those first two rooms and in particular to the
e carding room.

       The carding process is carried out on what is called, as I have said, a carding machine
or carding engine. It is known as a revolving flat carding engine and I should say that, as
I understand it, flat does not refer to the shape of the engine, it refers to one of the
essential parts of its mechanism. It seems to me that a detailed explanation or description
f of the carding engine is unnecessary and indeed would be tedious. It is sufficient to say
that, in essence, it comprises, three rotating cylinders which when viewed from the side
of the machine are placed side by side. First there is what is called the taker-in or licker-
in, which revolves in a clockwise direction and under which the lap is fed to the main
cylinder. The cylinder revolves in the opposite direction, anti-clockwise, so that now the
cotton passes over the top of the cylinder above which are the revolving flats on a chain.
g Thus the cotton passes between the top of the cylinder and the underside of the flats.
Thirdly, there is what is called the doffer. How it got its name no one has explained and
it does not matter, it is known as the doffer: it rotates in a clockwise direction so that the
cotton now passes underneath it and onto what is called the coilerhead where it is wound
into a coil. In the course of that journey the cotton is subjected to pressure at three
particular points: first at the taker-in, next at the flats and finally at the doffer and it is
h pressure which causes the release or giving-off of most of what is called the fly and the
dust. The fly comprises the larger particles, mostly pieces of broken fibre. Some particles
of the dust are very small indeed and are invisible to the naked eye except perhaps in a
shaft of bright sunlight. The smallest particles of all, those which are measured as being
of under 5 microns, are those which are respirable by human beings and which are in
some way responsible for byssinosis. I say 'in some way' deliberately, because the medical
j evidence is that, although there is no doubt that small particles of cotton dust inhaled by
human beings may cause byssinosis, the precise process, whether it is chemical, whether
it is associated with allergy or otherwise, is apparently unknown at the moment to
medical science, but being very small and being very light, those very small particles
may very well be suspended in the warm atmosphere of the card room for an appreciable
amount of time. The heaviest concentration of those very fine particles is produced at
the flats.

The amount of fly and dust given off would depend in the main on three factors. First, the type of cotton: the shorter-fibred cotton used in the spinning of coarse counts gives off the greatest volume of fly and dust and the long staple cotton used in the spinning of fine counts produces far less dust. On the other hand, the evidence is that the fine long staple Egyptian cottons, and they were the cottons being spun at the material times by the defendants, give off greater quantities of very fine dust. The second factor is the quality of the cotton, namely its cleanliness and freedom from trash; the third factor is the speed of operation of the carding machines. As I have said, the defendants at all times used fine long staple Egyptian or Sudanese cotton of high quality. Until 1963 or early in 1964 the carding machines operated at a slow speed processing between five and seven pounds of raw cotton per machine per hour. In 1963 or perhaps early in 1964, it hardly matters, semi-high-speed machines were introduced. These processed something of the order of 20 to 22 pounds of raw cotton per hour. In 1967 the process was further speeded up by the introduction of tandem carding machines which processed approximately 35 pounds of raw cotton per hour. Those are the only figures put before the court which indicate the speed or give any indication of the speed at which the carding machines worked. None of those figures has been translated into, for instance, revolutions per minute of the cylinders to which I have referred. It follows therefore that my understanding of speed is a somewhat rough and ready understanding based on that information alone.

Now, in addition to the dust and the fly which was released in the ordinary course of the carding process, additional dust and fly was produced by a periodic and necessary cleaning operation. It was known as brush stripping and was performed on each machine once a week. It was necessary in order to prevent the brush becoming so clogged that it became ineffective. This was work done by the stripper and grinder in the card room. Each stripper and grinder was responsible for about 19 machines prior to 1964 and the operation of brush stripping took about two minutes per machine. There were something of the order of 180 machines in all and that operation of brush stripping was performed on all the machines by the various strippers and grinders in the card room between Monday and Thursday of each week.

I return now to consider the plaintiff's part in these processes. As I have said, he commenced his work in 1935 when he cannot have been more than about 15 years of age. He was given a medical examination by the mill doctor and that was the only medical examination he received at the defendants' hands throughout his employment. He started work in no 1 mill as a lap carrier carrying the laps from the blowing room to the next door carding room. After 12 months he moved to no 2 mill as a card tenter whose duties, which have not been entirely revealed to me in the course of this trial, included the clearing of dust and fly from the doffer cover every hour or so. In 1938 he returned to no 1 mill and there he remained until 1940 when he joined the army, and in the course of those two years he was employed as an apprentice stripper and grinder. In the context of the events as a whole, it seems to me that this period of employment between 1935 and 1940 is of comparatively little significance. When the plaintiff was demobilised from the army in 1945, he was pronounced medically A1, the top grade. There has been no challenge to that assessment, there being no reason to believe that it was not a true assessment of his physical condition. So he returned to the defendants and, after a short spell as a lap carrier, he worked in the card room at no 2 mill as a stripper and grinder until that mill closed in 1963. He then transferred to similar duties in no 1 mill until 1965 when he left the defendants' employment because of the state of his health.

During the last two years he had experienced breathlessness when he was going uphill to his home. Since 1958 his medical records reveal that he had seen his general practitioner on a number of occasions and on some occasions that practitioner had diagnosed that he, the plaintiff, was suffering from bronchitis associated with cigarette smoking. The plaintiff had throughout this period been what is called a moderate smoker, smoking something of the order of 10 to 20 cigarettes a day. When he left the a   defendants' employment in 1965 he took employment as a gardener for the next nine or ten years, I think probably ten years, and during that period of ten years he described himself as quite well able to do his gardening work. He could take his time of course and he suffered no marked breathlessness. In 1975 he left gardening for the better pay of a school caretaker and there ensued during the course of that employment further trouble with his chest. He developed bronchitis in December 1975, that is, very soon after taking on his caretaker duties and again in April 1976. As a result of the latter diagnosis he was

b   sent to see a consultant physician, Dr Mitchell, who was a specialist in the diagnosis and treatment of tuberculosis. Dr Mitchell diagnosed, as the general practitioner had diagnosed, that the plaintiff was suffering from bronchitis and like the general practitioner, not surprisingly, he advised the plaintiff to give up his cigarette smoking. There are before the court two letters written by Dr Mitchell to the plaintiff's general practitioner, both in June 1976. The first letter acknowledges the general practitioner's

c   letter referring the plaintiff to him and makes it clear that general practitioner's letter has spoken of recurrent attacks of coughing and breathlessness over the last two or three years, that is, from about 1973 or 1974 and it speaks of a morning cough and wheeziness and shortness of breath especially on exertion and it asserts that X-rays taken in 1975 indicated that his chest was normal. Seven days later after another X-ray had been taken, the physician reported that the plain X-ray of his chest 'looks a little emphysematic and

d   the other tests showed that the bellow function of his lungs was substantially below average for his age and his size'. Part of that was accounted for by some generalised obstruction of his small tubes and, as I have said, Dr Mitchell diagnosed bronchitis and emphysema and advised the giving-up of cigarettes.

     During the course of his employment as a school caretaker there were further attacks of what were diagnosed as bronchitis which led to his being off work for some three

e   months at the end of 1976, another period of five weeks at the end of 1977/beginning of 1978 and for a period of six weeks between April and June 1978.

     Then in the summer of 1979 the plaintiff was with a friend who had worked in quarries and who, as a result of that work, had contracted the now well-known disease called silicosis. His friend noticed that the plaintiff was coughing or had a cough very much like his own. He, by reason of his silicosis, had had a pension for about ten years

f   and he advised the plaintiff that he ought to apply for a pension for his bronchial condition and so in August of that year the plaintiff did. On 22 October 1979 he was examined by a medical board on behalf of the Department of Health and Social Services. The board certified that he was suffering from byssinosis and assessed his disability at that time as of the order of 40%. The result of this was that the plaintiff left his employment as a caretaker at the end of 1979. As a further result he saw a solicitor in

g   mid-1980 and thereafter proceedings were commenced.

     After those proceedings had started he was examined by three consultant physicians, all of whom have given evidence before this court. The first to examine him was Dr Charles Pickering who was a consultant thoracic physician at the University of Manchester School of Medicine at Wythenshawe Hospital. He is a man of experience and standing. The history that was given by the plaintiff is important for reasons which will emerge.

h   He told Dr Pickering that he had retired from the cotton industry in 1965 as a result of respiratory symptoms which had been present for some three or four years. At the time of his departure he was breathless on exertion and he had symptoms of coughing and wheeziness. These complaints or those symptoms had been most severe on the first day of each working week, they had improved through the remainder of the week and over the subsequent weekend. When he was away on holiday there was a further improvement

j   with again, as occurred weekly, an exacerbation of symptoms on the first day that he was back at work. Then on leaving the cotton industry and taking up his work as a gardener his symptoms improved considerably and he was able to work the normal 40-hour week. Dr Pickering discovered that over the past five years or so, that is during the late seventies and very early eighties, there had been a gradual increase in what the doctor called his symptomatology with increasing shortness of breath and a cough productive of moderate

quantities of sputum. I have said enough, I think, of the history as given by the plaintiff.
Particular notice is to be taken, according to the doctor, of the first of those symptoms of   *a*
breathlessness, coughs and wheezing which were most severe on Monday of each week,
improving during the working week and over the weekend and improving still more
over holiday periods. This symptom is known apparently, and I know it now, as the
Monday symptom. Secondly, it has been particularly observed that there was a substantial
improvement in those ten years after his departure from the cotton industry between
1965 and 1975. Thirdly, Dr Pickering, by reason of the cough-producing sputum, came   *b*
to the conclusion that there was here a smoking-related condition which accounted for a
very considerable proportion of such disability as he was suffering. Dr Pickering describes
the plaintiff as one of those minority of persons who are susceptible to cigarette smoke
and who incur damage to their lungs thereby.

The doctor carried out a number of tests. It is unnecessary to go into them in detail.
They confirmed what had previously been said as to this plaintiff's lung capacity, what is   *c*
called his vital capacity. The doctor came to the conclusion, and I quote—

> 'in the course of his employment [the plaintiff] has developed work-related
> respiratory symptoms. These symptoms were of a character and periodicity entirely
> consistent with a diagnosis of byssinosis and I would assess the level of his disability
> at present as being in the region of 40%.'   *d*

I repeat, because it needs to be emphasised, that in coming to the conclusion that there
was a 40% disability, the smoking-related condition to which reference has already been
made was included.

All that was in June 1981. At the end of April 1982 the plaintiff was seen by Dr
Stretton who is a consultant physician at the Manchester Royal Infirmary. Dr Stretton is
familiar with the cotton spinning industry in Manchester and with the disease known as   *e*
byssinosis. He too was careful in the history that he took from the plaintiff. He described
the plaintiff's occupation and I need not repeat that. I quote from the report of Dr
Stretton which is before me (as, I should have said, is the report of Dr Pickering). Dr
Stretton described the plaintiff as being a stripper and grinder in the card room; he
continued thus:

> 'He was apparently alright away from work at weekends and on holiday but on   *f*
> the first day back at work he was troubled by the stress and breathlessness and a
> productive cough. He had similar symptoms on other days but as the week
> progressed they were less intolerable. [The plaintiff] gave up his job and found
> himself employment as a gardener and during that time his health was much better
> and he was troubled little by coughs and breathlessness. Some years later he took a
> job as a school caretaker and began to suffer frequent chest infections possibly   *g*
> acquired by contact with schoolchildren and he had frequent absences from work
> due to the productive cough and breathlessness. In 1980 he was declared unfit for
> work.'

Now there is the history that was given to Dr Stretton by this plaintiff. Dr Stretton too
carried out lung function tests of the same kind as those carried out by Dr Pickering and   *h*
to the same effect and with the same results. Dr Stretton's conclusion was this: 'The
history of the onset and evolution of [the plaintiff's] chest symptoms is diagnostic of
byssinosis. He is now severely disabled . . .', and it is unnecessary for me to read further.
There too, it is to be observed, in the history given by the plaintiff was what I can now
call the Monday symptom.

Then in mid-1982 the plaintiff was examined by Professor Schilling. He is   *j*
acknowledged as an expert in the field with which this case is concerned. He has
examined many sufferers from byssinosis, visited many mills and he has written articles
on the prevalence and effect of dust in mills. His report is not before me. There is
nothing sinister in that: the fact is that he was asked by the defendants to examine the
plaintiff and no doubt his report was sent to them. In this action he was called by

a the plaintiff and thus his evidence was given more fully in the witness box and is not to be gleaned from any report. The history again was a matter on which Professor Schilling concentrated and he was told this by the plaintiff: when he was aged about 43, which would be in about 1962, he began to notice that he was short of breath when he took the dog for a walk. That condition was worst on Mondays but it improved during the week and was best at the weekends. Professor Schilling also observed that during the period that the plaintiff was employed as a gardener there was an improvement in his condition

b but then he was told that it was because of his shortness of breath that the plaintiff then had to take a lighter job as a caretaker. I interpose here to say I do not accept that as the truth; the plaintiff told the court in the witness box that he left gardening for a better paid job and I am left in no doubt that that is the true reason and he was not accurate when he spoke to Professor Schilling on that particular point. The professor took his smoking history and he too concluded that in 1965 the plaintiff had been suffering from

c byssinosis which was then moderately disabling in its effect. He thought that at the time he examined him, the plaintiff was quite severely disabled.

There then is the common diagnosis of three distinguished and experienced physicians. There is no medical evidence given before this court to the contrary. Nevertheless, counsel on behalf of the defendants has challenged that diagnosis. He submitted in short that the symptoms and the condition of which the plaintiff has complained are

d attributable to cigarette smoking. It is a bold challenge as counsel, not surprisingly, recognises. It is not, on the other hand, a presumptuous challenge. It is based on the following propositions which are agreed by all the doctors. First, that there are no clinical signs and there is no radiological evidence which can support a diagnosis of byssinosis, in other words, X-rays will show nothing. Second, in consequence, the diagnosis depends entirely on the history given by the patient and in that history the Monday symptom is

e vital and by vital I mean, as I understand the doctors to mean, that without it there can be no diagnosis of byssinosis.

Counsel for the defendants does not lack respect for the doctors' standing or their ability. He makes no challenge to the diagnosis if the history given is right, but his argument is that the history given by the plaintiff to those three eminent gentlemen was not correct. He bases that contention on the following: first, that any general practitioner

f worth his salt and practising in an area such as Bolton would be alive to the possibility of byssinosis and yet no such diagnosis was made by the general practitioner between 1938 and 1978. Moreover, it is urged, such general practitioners in such localities would have the knowledge that would enable them to make proper inquiries to elicit the essential history from the patient and yet there is no history of the Monday symptoms ever being mentioned to the general practitioner throughout those long years. Second, no such

g history, that is, no mention of the Monday symptom was given to Dr Mitchell, the consultant physician, in 1976. Third, it was apparently not given to a Dr Oelbaum who, I understand, is another consultant physician who examined the plaintiff in 1980. I have not seen Dr Oelbaum nor have I seen any report of his, but his notes have been seen by Professor Schilling and it is from Professor Schilling that one gleans, and I accept, that there was no mention made to Dr Oelbaum, in the history that he obtained from the

h plaintiff, of the Monday symptom. Counsel for the defendants emphasises, as is the fact, that none of the three consultants whose evidence was given before the court had seen the general practitioner's notes or Dr Mitchell's letters or diagnosis before they made their own diagnoses. I should add in this context that having had that brought to their attention, each one of them says that he accepts what the plaintiff has told him and that the general practitioner's notes and Dr Mitchell's letters do not in any way affect their

j diagnoses.

To add weight to the argument and to his submission that the history given by the plaintiff to those three doctors ought not to be accepted, counsel for the defendants relies on two further matters and they are matters of relevance, indeed of cogency, in this particular context. First, it is accepted that the incidence of byssinosis amongst workers in the blowing and card rooms in mills producing fine counts of cotton is much lower than in those mills producing medium or coarse counts. There is no doubt, says counsel, and I accept that at all material times the defendants were producing fine counts from high quality cotton. In support of that, counsel relies on an article by Professor Schilling which appeared in the Lancet, I think in 1956 or thereabouts, in which amongst other matters, there are set out two tables. The first is headed 'The Prevalence of Byssinosis in male Card Room and Blowing Room Workers aged 40 to 59 according to the type of cotton spun', and I take the two extremes as sufficient for the present purposes. The number of people in those age groups working in fine count mills was 51, of whom 33 were found to be normal and 18 affected in some way by byssinosis. I should say that there is no means of dividing the blow room workers from the card room workers in this table. On the other hand, out of 75 working in coarse count mills, only 23 were normal and a total of 52 were affected by byssinosis. The second table relates, as it is headed, to 'The Prevalence of Byssinosis in Card Room workers' (and note the difference) 'of all ages in fine and coarse mills'; and the sexes here are separated, but I think there is little significance in that. Of the men in the fine mills only 5% were found to have byssinosis whereas 51% in the coarse mills had that disease. Moreover, those who, in the fine mills, had it had been exposed to cotton dust for a substantially longer period than had those in the coarse mills.

In evidence Professor Schilling said, and I accept his evidence, that byssinosis was not a problem in fine count mills in 1956. Those percentages would seem to confirm that view. Moreover, as late as 1972, I think it was, in a report which again is in one of the very large bundles of documents before the court, a report of the Medical Services Division on a survey of respiratory diseases in cotton operatives, one sentence is material: '. . . in the whole survey byssinosis was found in all parts of the factories visited including the Ring Rooms and the Winding Rooms. No cases were found, however, in fine cotton mills.' Counsel for the defendants contends, not without reason, that one is entitled to draw the conclusion that it is very unlikely, to say the least, that the plaintiff would have contracted byssinosis in the fine cotton mill.

The second matter on which he relies is very closely connected. It is this: the defendants themselves have no experience of anyone, other than the plaintiff, who has been engaged solely in fine count mills, contracting byssinosis. Indeed, I think it is fair to say that although they have access to records to the contrary, the plaintiff is unique in the experience of the three doctors whose evidence I have heard.

Those are the arguments put forward on behalf of the defendants in support of the contention that I should not accept as accurate the history given by the plaintiff in that essential regard to those three doctors. These are cogent arguments and they have been attractively, as always, put before the court.

However, I do not in the circumstances, feel able to accept them. I say that for these reasons: first of all, it is plain, as the doctors emphasise, that whether or not a history is accurately given by a patient or whether or not symptoms are accurately described by a patient will depend at least to some extent, and probably, in my judgment, to a large extent, on the investigation undertaken and the questions asked by the doctors concerned. For instance, in Dr Mitchell's letter of June 1976, he speaks only of complaints of constant breathlessness over the previous three years. There is not even a mention of the plaintiff working in a cotton mill for 25 years. One can imagine that a busy general practitioner finds it very difficult to find the time for detailed investigation of the kind which is inevitably undertaken by consultants. Second, I have seen this plaintiff. I have been aware of the importance of the history that he gave or is alleged to have given and with that in mind I have come to the conclusion that he has proved himself to be in this court a substantially honest witness. He has described to the court the Monday symptom, as it is called, and he has given his reasons why it was not mentioned to his own general practitioner. I quote from my own note of his evidence. He said:

'I saw my general practitioner quite often. I made no complaint to him of the tightness of my chest on Monday morning but I had it, I just didn't give it a thought. All the grinders had tightness on the Monday morning.'

a It was suggested to him that over the past three years, understandably since this action has been afoot, he has been talked at, talked to and himself has talked about byssinosis on a great number of occasions and it is suggested that he has thus learned of this crucial symptom and has now convinced himself wrongly, but nevertheless honestly, that he had the Monday symptom. That too, is a matter to which I have given anxious consideration but I do not accept it as an explanation for the plaintiff's evidence and I accept his evidence as that of a substantially honest and truthful witness.

b Third, whilst it is true to say that the plaintiff is unique in the defendants' experience and indeed in the personal experience of all the three medical experts and whilst I accept that the defendants were producing fine counts from high quality cotton, there is no doubt in my judgment, first, that even in fine count mills byssinosis did occur, though the numbers were small. It may be, of course, that those who had byssinosis and are shown in those tables which I have referred to, were working in mills where the quality of the raw cotton was lower than that used by the defendants. One has to bear that
c possibility in mind. Equally, of course, it may be that they were working in mills where contrary to the defendants' practice all the stripping was done under a vacuum hood or some vacuum process. These are matters of conjecture: I merely make the points to indicate that I am alive to the danger of pressing figures and percentages too far.

Second, the plaintiff was exposed not only to the dust that was given off during the
d operation of the carding machines, but during the week he was exposed to that from brush stripping between Monday and Thursday and from the hand cleaning of floors, machines and overhead fixtures. Finally I accept from the plaintiff, and indeed there is really little room for dispute, that he felt better after he left the mill in 1965 and indeed as his medical history indicates he was, in fact, better. There was no complaint during those ten years of bronchial trouble until he took up caretaking when there was a re-
e emergence of symptoms of acute bronchitis which might well be attributable to his contact with children. Dr Pickering regards this as a significant aspect. Whilst, of course, it is not of itself diagnostic, it is in his judgment a significant matter. I accept Dr Pickering's judgment in this matter and I adopt it as my own.

In these circumstances, I conclude that the plaintiff was, as the doctors have diagnosed, in 1965 suffering from byssinosis coupled with the effects of cigarette smoking. Byssinosis
f itself was at that time a chronic and irreversible disability. As to the apportionment between the two, namely byssinosis and the effect of cigarettes, Dr Pickering first took the view that the apportionment between the two, that is, apportionment of his disability between the two, was and I use his words, 'as an educated guess of the order of 40 to 50%'; but on a little pressure from counsel for the defendants he revised that estimate and took the view that at least half of his current disability is due to smoking. Professor
g Schilling gives somewhat similar evidence, but he arrives at the conclusion that probably byssinosis is the greater cause of disability though it is clear from his manner as well as from his evidence that the matters are fairly evenly balanced. I think in those circumstances if I accept, as I do, that their contribution is substantially equal then that is as near as I should be able to get.

Before turning to the question of the defendants' alleged breaches of duty, it is
h convenient to deal with the defendants' contention that the plaintiff's claim is now barred by the terms of s 11 of the Limitation Act 1980 and that I ought not to exercise the discretion which is given under s 33 of the 1980 Act to allow the action to proceed. Many of the facts that are material to the consideration of those issues I have already dealt with and that is why I think it convenient to deal with this matter at this stage. It is necessary only to pick up a few of the strands and continue with the chronology. As I have said, in
j 1965 the plaintiff left the defendants' employment on his doctor's advice. His doctor's advice was to get away from the cotton dust and get employment in the open air and that is what he did. I have found that at that time the plaintiff was indeed suffering from byssinosis though it had not then been diagnosed and he had not heard of that particular disease. There followed, it will be recalled, ten years' employment as a gardener and finally three or four interrupted years as a school caretaker and then in November 1979 came the assessment of the medical panel that he was suffering from byssinosis.

To continue, in March 1980 he took the advice of a solicitor; in mid-1980 he was examined by Dr Oelbaum; the letter before action was sent on 8 August 1980, and the writ was issued on 19 September 1980; it was served on 2 February of the following year. It is not disputed that thereafter the pleadings and all the interlocutory matters were dealt with expeditiously, so that by October 1982 the action was listed for trial. Counsel for the plaintiff contends that by the combined effects of ss 11 and 14 the period of limitation did not commence until well after 20 September 1977; in other words, the writ was issued in time.

It is helpful to remind myself of the provisions of s 11. The relevant provisions are sub-ss (3) and (4), which provide:

'(3) An action to which this section applies shall not be brought after the expiration of the period applicable in accordance with subsection (4)...'
(4) ... the period applicable is three years from ... (b) the date of knowledge ... of the person injured.'

Section 14 defines date of knowledge for the purposes of s 11. Section 14(1) provides:

'In [section 11] references to a person's date of knowledge are references to the date on which he first had knowledge of the following facts—(a) that the injury in question was significant [I pause to say that I am left in no doubt that the plaintiff knew in 1965 that any injury that he had sustained was significant]; and (b) that the injury was attributable in whole or in part to the act or omission which is alleged to constitute negligence, nuisance or breach of duty ...'

Paragraph (b), of course, is a very important paragraph. As it is read, and as it stands, alone it seems to have a subjective connotation: what matters is what the plaintiff knew. But it must be read with s 14(3), which is in these terms:

'For the purposes of this section a person's knowledge includes knowledge which he might reasonably have been expected to acquire—(a) from facts observable or ascertainable by him; or (b) from facts ascertainable by him with the help of medical or other appropriate expert advice which it is reasonable for him to seek ...'

There is, of course, now introduced by sub-s (3) an objective test. Paragraph (c) of sub-s (1) refers to 'the identity of the defendant'. There is no doubt that the plaintiff knew in 1965 the identity of any prospective defendant. Subsection (1) ends: 'and knowledge that any acts or omissions did or did not, as a matter of law, involve negligence, nuisance or breach of duty is irrelevant'.

Counsel for the defendants says that in 1965, having regard to my findings, the plaintiff had, in fact, grade 3 byssinosis; he may not have known the name but the symptoms were serious, his doctor had told him to leave the cotton dust and as he himself said in evidence: 'I left because of the dust and I was getting out of breath going home, I thought the dust was affecting me.' In these circumstances, I am satisfied that in 1965 the plaintiff knew that the condition of his chest was due in whole or in part to acts or omissions on which he now relies. In any event, if he did not have the actual knowledge, I am satisfied (and I quote from s 14(3)) that he ought reasonably to have had the requisite knowledge 'from the facts observable or ascertainable by him'. It follows, therefore, that the plaintiff is not within s 11 and if this action is to proceed, it can only do so if it is equitable for me to exercise discretion under s 33 in the plaintiff's favour. So I turn to s 33. Subsection (1) provides:

'If it appears to the court that it would be equitable to allow an action to proceed having regard to the degree to which—(a) the provisions of sections 11 or 12 of this Act prejudice the plaintiff ... and (b) any decision of the court under this subsection would prejudice the defendants ... the court may direct that those provisions shall not apply to the action ...'

Thus, a balance has to be struck, at the end, between the degree of prejudice to the
a plaintiff and the defendants respectively according to the way in which I exercise my
discretion. Recent authority provides that that discretion is wide and unfettered though,
of course, it must be exercised judicially. Subsection (2) does not apply. Subsection (3) is
important. It provides, in effect, that in applying sub-s (1) the court shall have regard to
all the circumstances of the case and in particular to the six matters that are there set out.
The first is the length of and reasons for the delay on the part of the plaintiff. Here the
b delay is 15 years. There has been expedition thereafter but the delay until the issue of the
writ was long. The reason, I infer, is that the plaintiff did not realise that he had or might
have a cause of action. That, of course, is irrelevant for the purposes of s 14, as that section
expressly so provides, but it is not irrelevant, in my judgment, for the purposes of para
(*a*) of s 33(3). The plaintiff had never heard of anyone having a claim, certainly no one in
his mill, and indeed I am told that it was not until 1976 that such a claim was settled.
c The plaintiff's is the first claim to come before the court and in those circumstances
although one must face the fact of long delay, I find the plaintiff's attitude entirely
reasonable in the circumstances and not blameworthy.

Paragraph (*b*) of s 33(3) is the most important paragraph and I shall come back to that;
I shall deal with the other paragraphs quite shortly first. Paragraph (*c*) relates to the
conduct of the defendants. There is nothing here that can be said adverse to the
d defendant's conduct in this action or prior to its commencement. They must have done
everything that was incumbent on them and indeed probably more, otherwise the
proceedings could never have been ready for trial within such a comparatively short
period of time in such a comparatively difficult matter. There can be no criticism of the
defendants. Paragraph (*d*) in my judgment does not really apply. Paragraph (*e*) concerns
the extent to which the plaintiff acted promptly and reasonably once he knew whether
e or not he might have a cause of action (I paraphrase). Here again, as I have said already
and repetition is unnecesary, there has been commendable expedition once the plaintiff
came to realise that he might have a cause of action and there is no reason to criticise him
on that count. Paragraph (*f*) in my judgment really does not arise: the plaintiff had had
an abundance of medical advice over the years and I say no more about it. So I return to
para (*b*). It relates to the extent to which, having regard to the delay, the evidence adduced
f or likely to be adduced by the plaintiff or the defendants is or is likely to be less cogent
than if the action had been brought within the time allowed by s 11. The effect of delay
on the cogency of the evidence on both sides is not difficult to imagine, indeed it has
been manifest during the hearing. There were times when the plaintiff protested, in
answer to his own counsel's questions, that he could not recall, it was too long ago. I have
sympathy with him. And there were others of the witnesses who reacted, understandably,
g in the same way. Counsel contends on behalf of the plaintiff that in these courts we never
do have fresh recollections in actions of personal injury. I suppose that depends on how
one defines fresh recollections but it is not an argument which appeals to me in the
circumstances of this case. Here, whatever the norm, recollection has had to be stretched
well beyond that norm.

So I turn to consider the effects of the delay on the evidence relating to the question of
h liability. First, it is true to say on the plaintiff's behalf that we are investigating here a
system of work rather than a particular incident and, of course, it is a truism that general
conditions may be comparatively readily recalled even after a long period of time. The
recollection of the sequence of events comprising a single incident is much more difficult
to recapture from the memory. On the other hand, the no 2 mill where the plaintiff
spent most of his working time was closed in 1963, the no 1 mill to which he transferred
j for a couple of years was closed in 1972, the records have gone and, not surprisingly, the
workforce has dispersed. Moreover, this is not one of those cases where in general terms
the defendants have been alerted to the conditions of employment or to an investigation
into the conditions of employment in their mills; this claim by the plaintiff is unique in
the defendants' experience. Thus, they are not dealing with matters that have had to be
recalled or subjected to expert evidence in other proceedings and the like. Second, in this

case the medical diagnosis depends entirely on the history of symptoms given by the
plaintiff and the effect of delay on the cogency of his evidence is manifest. But that is a   *a*
disadvantage to the plaintiff. He must prove his case. If he has to do it either by
manufacturing evidence or giving evidence that is open to the criticism that it is not
reliable, then he fails. Moreover, in the circumstances of this case, it seems to me that the
defendants have probably been less embarrassed than they might have been so far as the
medical aspect is concerned. I say that because the general practitioners' notes are
available and intact for the whole of the relevant period and the family doctor who was   *b*
concerned in 1965 has been available and has given evidence. On balance, therefore,
whilst I accept that there is some real prejudice to the defendants because they are
recalling conditions even 15 to 20 years ago, and that cannot be easy, I am satisfied that it
has been possible for both sides to present a clear enough picture for a fair trial to be had.

With that finding, I turn to the initial and crucial question posed by s 33(1): where
will the greater prejudice fall? On the defendants if I disapply s 11 or on the plaintiff if I   *c*
refuse to disapply it? As to this, I am left in no doubt that the greater prejudice would be
suffered by the plaintiff if I refused to disapply s 11. If the plaintiff succeeds he has a very
substantial claim and the prejudice that would be involved by the denial to him of a
chance to litigate that claim fully, substantially outweighs, in my judgment, such
prejudice as the defendants have suffered by reason of the delay and which I have already
attempted to define. In those circumstances, I have come to the conclusion that it would   *d*
be equitable for me to allow this action to proceed and to disapply the provisions of s 11.

I return to the question of liability. There can be no doubt that the plaintiff's condition
has been caused by his employment: byssinosis comes only from cotton dust and it is
only in the defendants' mills that the plaintiff has been exposed. But the crucial question
remains, whether it has been caused by any breach of duty on the defendants' part. What
then were the relevant circumstances? Throughout the period of the plaintiff's   *e*
employment to 1963, the defendants were spinning high quality fine cottons and their
carding machines were operating at slow speed. Nevertheless, the evidence of the plaintiff
and his witnesses, which I accept in broad terms, although I think that there is some
exaggeration, is that substantial quantities of fly and dust were given off, firstly in the
process of carding and secondly at the weekly brush stripping, and that it permeated the
atmosphere and settled on the walls, floors, machinery and the overhead fittings such as   *f*
electric light fittings, pipes etc. There are no figures showing the amount of dust in the
atmosphere during the relevant period. Mr Brownsett of the Shirley Institute, who has
specialised in problems of dust and their solution or mitigation throughout the whole of
his working life, carried out a number of tests in fine count mills in 1961. The effect of
those tests I can state quite shortly: in the high count mills, the concentration of dust or
the dust load, as he calls it, was 1·6 mg per cubic metre of air at its lowest and about   *g*
3½ mg in the same quantity of air at its highest. I should say at once that those tests did
not involve the defendants' premises and they cannot in my judgment be related to the
defendants' mills, because there is no evidence that the conditions in those mills which
were tested were in any way similar to the conditions or sufficiently similar to the
conditions in the defendants' mills. Indeed, there is no evidence of any relationship
between the figures that I have given and the conditions in the mills that were tested and   *h*
no way of knowing what quality of cotton they were spinning, albeit that they were fine
counts. I have no way of knowing what type of carding and other machinery they had
and to what extent if at all it was provided with dust extraction appliances. I merely
mention these figures to indicate that I have not overlooked them. I find them of no
value in the current circumstances.

In 1967 Mr Brownsett carried out tests in the defendants' mills showing that there   *j*
were levels of concentration, or dust loads, to use his words, above those which were, he
says, generally recognised as the safety standard, namely 1 mg per cubic foot. But Mr
Brownsett, an honest and objective specialist so far as dust is concerned, accepts that he is
unable to relate these 1967 figures back to 1964 or to any period between 1946 and 1963.
In 1967, for instance, we know that there were much faster machines in operation. In

1967 those machines had dust extraction appliances and there was some air-conditioning.
a Mr Brownsett complained of the maintenance of those systems, but be that as it may, the systems were very different indeed. I accept his evidence that it is impossible from his figures to work back. Thus it is that, as I have said at the outset, there are no figures here showing the dust loads in the atmosphere during the relevant period.

I am left, therefore, to judge the situation from the impressions given by the witnesses, in addition to which there is some slight indication of the concentrations that were about
b from the frequency that cleaning had to be done. For instance, the doffer cover which was very near one of the main pressure points had to be cleaned every hour, during which period it collected something between a quarter and a half an inch of fly and dust, most of it, no doubt, fly. What proportion of dust there was in that quarter to half an inch no one can say. It is accepted, and I accept, that the window fans got rid of a fair amount of the dust in the atmosphere up to 1963 but, says the plaintiff and his witnesses,
c a substantial quantity of dust remained. Mr Isherwood, now a managing director of the parent company, Paton & Baldwin, and a man with long experience in the cotton-spinning industry, says that during the relevant period the card room floor was swept twice a day. Again what was swept up was predominantly fly, but there was some dust. The machine sides and frames were cleaned once a day and the overhead fitments, pipes, electric light fittings etc were cleaned once a week on a Friday and then according to the
d plaintiff the atmosphere was cloudy, 'it was pretty thick'.

I am left with the impression from all this evidence that a substantial quantity of dust was given off in the carding process and in the weekly brush cleaning and I have no doubt that some of that was recirculated when it was swept up or brushed from the floor, the machines or other fitments. That being so, the plaintiff contends that the defendants were in breach of their duty to take appropriate measures to reduce the dust in the
e atmosphere. They knew, says the plaintiff, that it was a hazard in that they knew that cotton dust could cause byssinosis; one of the admissions made by counsel on behalf of the defendants is to admit that the defendants knew that. The plaintiff's case continues that the defendants were in breach of their duty in that they failed to heed many of the recommendations made or to use many of the facilities or appliances made available to reduce dust levels in the atmosphere of their mill.

f There is no doubt that the problem of dust has been the subject of a great deal of discussion and many recommendations over the years, in particular by those who advise the cotton industry: this is manifest in the mass of literature which is before me. It is a relief to me and I hope to those interested in this judgment that it is unnecessary to review that literature in any great detail; it is helpful, however, to look at some of the more important parts.

g I start with a report of the factory inspectors in 1909. In that report it is observed first, that there is a serious dust problem when it comes to stripping. As I understand it, the report is there referring to something much greater than the weekly brush stripping to which I have made more than one reference in the course of this judgment. It is referring to stripping as a whole which was done several times a day. It is accepted that most of the daily stripping in the plaintiff's mill was vacuum stripping. In order that this report may
h be put into context, where it refers to 'the strippers', and I paraphrase, 'being surrounded by a cloud of dust' that is not a reference to the weekly brush stripping to which I have referred. At all events, here way back in 1909 were the factory inspectors alerted to the problem of dust in cotton card rooms. In 1924 in a further report by the factory inspectorate, one finds a reference to the need for improved methods of cleaning machinery, pipes and floors. I quote a small passage:

j '. . . the existing method of cleaning machinery, pipes, floors, by means of ordinary brushes has a very important bearing on this subject. Quantities of dust are disturbed, which either settles somewhere else, to be again disturbed in due course, or is held in suspension in the air. The official members of the Committee were very much impressed with this feature of the subject, and are strongly of opinion that cleaning on more up-to-date lines would very materially improve conditions . . .'   *a*

The advantages of vacuum cleaning in a large mill were emphasised. No doubt that was a great innovation in 1924. In 1932 (and we are still some years away from the relevant dates) in, I think, the first report of the departmental committee on dust in card rooms in the cotton industry, there is again reference to the dust given off in stripping cards by hand and at the end of that report a number of recommendations are to be found. Again it is unnecessary for me to go through them all, but reference to some would, I think, be   *b*
helpful. For instance 'at p 601':

'When a so-called "vacuum" stripper is used to strip the cylinder and doffer, it is in some cases necessary to use a stripping brush from time to time. When this is done the brush should be provided with a cover which should be connected to an exhaust [that the defendants, as they accept, have never done].'   *c*

Then in recommendation no 7: 'The general ventilation of a card room should be preferably by means of a downward draught, so as to keep the finer particles below breathing level.' Number 8 recommends that—

'All operatives engaged in the removal of dust and/or dirt from underneath the carding engines, etc should be provided with an efficient type of respirator and there   *d*
should be medical examinations from time to time.'

In the course of the perusual of this documentary evidence, whilst it is clear that the proposals for the removal of dust from floors etc and in the course of stripping are firm, the much more intractable problem was the removal of as much dust as possible from source. In 1946 the Advisory Committee on dust in card rooms observed that the   *e*
removal of dust from the cards in the course of operation was the subject of experiment and in 1957 those experiments bore fruit. The third interim report recommends the Shirley Power Point System (SPPS for short) for removing dust in the course of the operation of the carding machine. Mr Brownsett still thinks this is the best appliance to be put on the market, but there are differences of opinion about that and I am not going to resolve them. The fact is that this report appeared at a time when the industry was in   *f*
one of its recessions and many owners were not able to take up the recommendation to fit this system. In 1960 an alternative, I think it was called the Selrow system, was put forward as a practical alternative to the SPPS and a report emphasises the need for the use of some vacuum system for stripping.

So it is that the plaintiff contends first that throughout the whole period of his employment the stripping should have been done under some sort of vaccum head. As I   *g*
have said, much of the stripping was done with a vacuum appliance three times a day, but the weekly brush stripping, which was a dirty process, was not, and the defendants admit that it was not. Secondly, the plaintiff says that all the cleaning of the floors, machines, fixtures etc should have been done by vacuum methods. It never was and the defendants admit that it never was. Thirdly, the general atmosphere would and should have been improved by the installation of air-conditioning. This was not done until 1963   *h*
when the faster machines were installed. The defendants admit that it was not done until 1963. Fourthly, the defendants could, and they should, have provided the SPPS extraction system soon after 1957 in order to extract as much dust as possible at source. That was not done; no system was installed until 1963 and the defendants admit that that was so.

I pause at that stage simply to say this. The defendants' position in 1957, when the SPPS was recommended by the committee, was that, whilst they were aware of that   *j*
recommendation and they were aware of the Selrow alternative recommended in 1960, they were themselves carrying out their own experiments and had been doing so since 1952 at an experimental plant at Paisley in Scotland and they were still not satisfied with the results, in other words, they were trying and trying hard. Moreover, the defendants took the view that, with the large number of slow machines in the card room, they did

a not have the room to provide the extraction equipment and still leave adequate working space for their workpeople: they had to balance the requirement of the Factories Acts and common law that proper workplaces should be provided. Finally, the defendants saw no reason for the over-hasty provision of the SPPS for the reasons that I have given, namely the slow speed of production and the fineness and high quality of the cotton. They did install extraction equipment in 1963 when the faster machines were used and then they used what I think is called the Atmospheric Control Co's device coupled with air-

b conditioning. Mr Brownsett still says that it is not as good as the SPPS! That is a matter of opinion, and it is a matter on which I am not in a position to pronounce. I have no doubt that the defendants were doing what they thought at that time was their best and I do not criticise their ultimate choice. Nor do I believe there to be grounds for such criticism. On the other hand, even after 1963, the sweeping and cleaning up and the weekly brush-stripping were still done without any vacuum appliance. Finally the

c plaintiff contends that in accordance with those recommendations which I have recently referred to, he should have been supplied with a respirator. The defendants further admit that he was not.

The defendants have sought helpfully, and in my judgment reasonably and responsibly, to narrow the issues because they admit that, throughout the relevant period, they did not do all that was practicable to protect the plaintiff from cotton dust. Their submission

d on this aspect of the matter, put shortly, is that the plaintiff never was exposed to a quantity of dust which was likely to be harmful to him.

The plaintiff relies, firstly, on s 1 of the Factories Act 1961. I quote the essential part: '(1) Every factory shall be kept in a clean state and free from effluvia arising from any drain, sanitary convenience or nuisance . . .' It occurs to me first that that is an absolute duty, it is mandatory in its terms, and second that what is a clean state must be a variable

e for it must, in my judgment, depend on the process carried on in the factory. As Professor Schilling says, if you want absolute cleanliness then you stop spinning cotton; that cannot be the intention. Finally, I doubt very much if s 1 relates to dust which is produced in the course of the process carried on in the factory.

Next the plaintiff relies on s 4 of the 1961 Act which provides under the sub-heading 'Ventilation':

f
> 'Effective and suitable provision shall be made for securing and maintaining by the circulation of fresh air in each workroom the adequate ventilation of the room, and for rendering harmless, so far as practicable, all such fumes, dust and other impurities generated in the course of any process or work carried on in the factory as may be injurious to health.'

g Put broadly, that section, in my judgment, relates to the securing of effective ventilation by the circulation of fresh air. It does not, in my view, enjoin the fitting of exhaust appliances to extract dust at source; if authority is wanted for that proposition I am content to rely on the judgment of Devlin J in *Graham v Co-op Wholesale Society* [1957] 1 All ER 654, [1957] 1 WLR 511.

The section imposes a qualified duty, namely a duty to render harmless, so far as

h practicable, such dust as may be injurious to health. There has been a difference of opinion whether or not it is necessary for the plaintiff to show that the defendants knew or at least ought to have known that there was a risk to health; in this case a risk from the dust generated in the course of any process or work carried out in the factory. I prefer the view that the defendants, if they are to be liable in this regard, must be shown to have known or it must be shown that they ought to have known of the danger, namely

j that the dust might be injurious to health, otherwise how are they to judge what is practicable? However that may be, the defendants knew, it is one of their admissions, that cotton dust could cause byssinosis. They installed some ventilation in the form of fans in four of the windows but these did not provide adequate ventilation. The room was not adequately ventilated until 1963 when the air-conditioning was installed but by that time the plaintiff's symptoms were already manifest. It is not suggested that it was not practicable to install air-conditioning much earlier. In my judgment, therefore, the defendants were in breach of s 4 of the 1961 Act.

Finally the plaintiff relies on s 63 of the 1961 Act, which reads, omitting irrelevant words:

> '(1) In every factory in which, in connection with any process carried on, there is given off any dust . . . of such a character and to such extent as to be likely to be injurious or offensive to the persons employed, or any substantial quantity of dust of any kind, all practicable measures shall be taken to protect the persons employed against inhalation of the dust . . . and to prevent its accumulating in any workroom, and in particular, where the nature of the process makes it practicable, exhaust appliances shall be provided and maintained, as near as possible to the point of origin of the dust . . . so as to prevent its entering the air of any workroom . . .'

It is accepted that s 63 applies to dust given off in any process (1) to such an extent as to be likely to be injurious or offensive to the persons employed, or (2) in any substantial quantity. The plaintiff contends that the defendants knew or should have known that dust, even in the fine count mills, was given off to an extent which was likely to be injurious. He relied particularly on the article by Professor Schilling in the Lancet in 1956 to which I have made reference. There is no evidence that that report, which was in a medical journal, was available to the defendants or, in fact, was known to them. Mr Isherwood denies that it was. Moreover, as I have already indicated, in his evidence Professor Schilling said that in fine count mills dust was not a problem, it was not regarded as a source of danger in 1956. It is relevant too, in my judgment, to observe that Mr Brownsett, whose keenness to solve the problems of dust surely cannot be bettered and who has made a study of dust and its problems all his working life, did not think it necessary to turn his attention to fine mills prior to 1961. Finally, even as late as 1971, it appeared in the report to which reference has already been made that no case of byssinosis had been found in fine cotton mills.

Thus, in my judgment, during the relevant time there is really insufficient evidence that the defendants ought to have considered the dust in this fine count mill as likely to be injurious to the persons employed there. But that is not the end of the matter. The question remains, if it was not injurious to their health was it offensive to them, or to take the second leg, was it given off in a substantial quantity? In my judgment there is no doubt that the quantity of dust was sufficient to be offensive to people working in that mill and certainly was sufficient to be regarded, to use the words of the 1961 Act, as being in substantial quantity. It follows, therefore, that it was the defendants' duty under s 63 of that Act (1) to take all practicable measures to protect the persons employed from inhaling dust, (2) to take all practicable measures to prevent the dust accumulating, and (3), and I quote, 'where the nature of the process makes it practicable', to provide exhaust-carrying appliances as near as possible to the point of origin of the dust so as to prevent it entering the air of any workroom. I take practicable in this context to mean a precaution which could be taken or undertaken without practical difficulty.

In these circumstances I am left in no doubt of the following, first, that the defendants did fail to take all practicable measures to protect the plaintiff from inhaling dust. For instance, they could, and the conditions being what they were, they should, in my judgment, have provided him with a respirator, if all else failed. It is accepted that they did not. It is further accepted, as I understand it, that there was a suitable respirator available. Second, I am left in no doubt that the defendants failed to prevent accumulations of dust by failing to brush strip under a vacuum hood and by failing to clean the machines etc by some vacuum process. Finally, I am left in no doubt that at the end of the 1950s it was practicable for the defendants to fit an exhaust appliance of the kind that I have referred to in the course of this judgment. In those circumstances I find the defendants in breach of s 63 as well as in breach of s 4. There is no doubt that there is a causal connection between the breaches and the injury sustained by the plaintiff and there I find the defendants liable.

So I turn to the question of quantum. The history of the progress of the plaintiff's
a condition has already been dealt with in the main and I want to avoid repetition. He is
now described by the doctors, whose evidence I accept, as being seriously disabled,
though I emphasise that his disability is substantially attributable to the bronchitis which
is due to his cigarette smoking. The plaintiff's own unchallenged evidence as to his
condition is that he suffers from breathlessness and tiredness, he can walk a fair distance
but after about every 200 yards or so he has to stop for a rest. He finds himself breathless
b when he rises in the morning. He uses a spray then and about every four hours during
the day. He is still only 62 but he has to pause from time to time even while he is
dressing. He says that even between putting on his two socks he has to have a bit of a
rest; I accept that. He becomes breathless and tired when he is having a wash or a bath.
He is unable to give the attention that he would like or that he used to give to his
comparatively modest garden. He has given it over, wisely, if I may be allowed to say so,
c to shrubs now and I have no doubt that it will be as interesting and as attractive a garden
as any other could be, but it may not be the way that he wants to do it. He has to do it
that way in order to save labour. If he goes to the public house he has to leave if the
atmosphere gets rather smoky. Clearly the enjoyment of life for him has been
substantially reduced. Happily, the disease known as byssinosis from which he suffers
does not carry with it the added risk of cancer. Happily too in the light of all the medical
d evidence, I find that there is no reason to believe that his expectation of life has been
reduced.

Counsel for the plaintiff in order to assist me to a decision in this, the first contested
case of byssinosis, has helpfully provided a number of cases relating to awards in other
cases of lung disease. They are helpful; I am grateful for them, but as counsel will
understand, they are helpful only as general guides and then only provided it is borne in
e mind, first, that many of them show a degree of disability which is greater than that of
the plaintiff; second, in almost every case in counsel's schedule there was a risk of cancer
and that risk is absent here; and, third, in the present case there is the fact that 50% of the
plaintiff's current disability is not attributable to any breach of the defendants' duty but
to the plaintiff's cigarette smoking. Nevertheless, byssinosis is a seriously disabling
condition and even if he were only half as disabled as he is, which is one way of looking
f at the apportionment between cigarette smoking and byssinosis, then he would still be
quite substantially disabled. Moreover, I must bear in mind that the plaintiff has borne
the effects of this disease now for some 17 years. I have not found it an easy task, I do not
suggest that I have found the touchstone. I must do the best that I can in somewhat novel
circumstances to reach a fair figure to compensate this plaintiff by way of general
damages for pain, suffering, loss of amenity, enjoyment of life past, present and future.
g Having given the matter anxious consideration, I have come to the conclusion that an
appropriate figure is the sum of £14,000. There is an agreed figure for special damages
of £8,688·26.

Judgment for the plaintiff for £22,688·26 damages plus interest and costs.

Solicitors: *John Pickering*, Oldham (for the plaintiff); *Grundy Kershaws*, Manchester (for
the defendants).

John M Collins Esq   Barrister.

Practice Direction

CHANCERY DIVISION

Practice – Summary judgment – Chancery Division – Applications to be made by summons – Summons to be returnable before judge in chambers – Documents required – RSC Ords 14, 86.

Practice – Chancery Division – Interlocutory applications – Applications to be made by summons to master.

Practice – Chambers proceedings – Appeal from master – Grounds of appeal not required in notice of appeal.

Practice – Parties – Change of name – Notice to be filed and copies served on other parties – New name to be substituted in title.

1. *Applications for judgment under RSC Ord 14 or Ord 86*

(a) Any application for judgment under RSC Ord 14 must, by r 2(1), be made by summons; and the same applies to applications for judgment under RSC Ord 86: see r 2(1). Such applications will not be heard on motion save in exceptional circumstances.

(b) Where such an application includes an application for an injunction, it usually has to be adjourned to a judge because in most cases the master cannot grant an injunction. In order to simplify the procedure and save costs, as from 1 May 1984 the summons in such cases should be made returnable before the judge in chambers instead of the master. The return date to be inserted in the summons will be a Monday which (i) for Ord 14 is at least ten clear days (r 2(3)) after the date when the summons will be served, and (ii) for Ord 86 is at least four clear days (r 2(3)) after the date when the summons will be served. The summons should be issued in Chancery Chambers (room 157), and the following documents must be lodged: two copies of the summons; the affidavit in support, together with any exhibits; and a certificate of counsel as to the estimated length of the hearing.

2. *Interlocutory procedural applications*

All interlocutory procedural applications (eg to strike out a pleading) should be made by summons to a master. They should not be made by motion unless there is a sufficient degree of urgency or other good reason which justifies proceeding by way of motion.

3. *Appeals from masters*

In a notice of appeal from a decision of a master it is no longer necessary to state the grounds of appeal. Paragraph 7 of the Practice Direction of 30 December 1982 ([1983] 1 All ER 131, [1983] 1 WLR 4) is varied accordingly.

4. *Change of name*

If after proceedings have been commenced there is a change of name by a party (as on the marriage of a woman), that party must promptly file a written notice of the change of name in Chancery Chambers or the appropriate Chancery district registry, and serve a copy on every other party. When the notice has been filed, the new name must be substituted in the title of the proceedings, followed by the former name (prefaced by the word 'formerly') in brackets. The action number, including the letter, will remain unchanged.

By direction of the Vice-Chancellor.

EDMUND HEWARD
Chief Master.

16 February 1984

Clough Mill Ltd v Martin

CHANCERY DIVISION AT MANCHESTER

HIS HONOUR JUDGE O'DONOGHUE SITTING AS A JUDGE OF THE HIGH COURT

28, 29, 30 JUNE, 11 JULY, 17 AUGUST 1983

Sale of goods – Passing of property – Vendor retaining property in goods – Goods supplied to company on credit terms – Clause reserving vendor's title to goods until goods paid for – Company becoming insolvent before goods paid for – Receiver appointed by debenture holders – Effect of reservation of title clause – Whether clause giving rise to 'charge created by . . . company' in favour of vendor – Whether receiver a 'creditor' of company – Whether charge void against receiver for non-registration – Companies Act 1948, s 95(1).

The plaintiff agreed to supply yarn on credit terms to a company which intended to use it for the manufacture of fabrics. The contract provided that the risk in the goods was to pass to the company on delivery but stipulated, by cl 12, (i) that 'the ownership' of the yarn was to remain with the plaintiff, who reserved the right to dispose of the yarn until it had been paid in full in accordance with the terms of the contract or until such time as the company sold the yarn to its customers by way of bona fide sale, (ii) that if payment became overdue in whole or in part the plaintiff could recover or resell the yarn and enter the company's premises for that purpose, (iii) that payment would become immediately due on the commencement of any act or proceeding in which the company's solvency was involved, and (iv) that if any of the yarn was incorporated in, or used as material for, other goods before such payment 'the property in the whole of such goods shall be and remain with [the plaintiff] until such payment has been made or the other goods shall have been sold . . . and all [the plaintiff's] rights . . . in [the] yarn shall extend to those other goods'. The company became insolvent before it had paid for or used all the yarn. The plaintiff therefore notified the receiver appointed by the company's debenture holders that it wished to repossess the unused yarn in the exercise of its rights under cl 12. However, the receiver refused to recognise that the plaintiff had any rights under cl 12 because, he claimed, cl 12 was a 'charge created by [the] company' in favour of the plaintiff to secure payment of the purchase price of the yarn and as such was void under s 95(1)ᵃ of the Companies Act 1948 for non-registration. The receiver accordingly permitted the company to use the yarn without paying the plaintiff, which thereupon brought an action against the receiver claiming damages for wrongfully depriving it of possession of the yarn and converting the yarn to his own use. The plaintiff contended (i) that since the parties had agreed, as shown by cl 12, that the plaintiff was to retain the legal title to the yarn until payment had been made in full the company had no title to the yarn and could not create a charge over it, and (ii) that even if a charge had been created it was only void under s 95 as against the liquidator or a creditor and not as against the receiver.

Held – (1) In construing a retention of title clause, such as cl 12 of the parties' contract, the court had to establish its true effect by looking at the purpose for which the clause had been inserted in the contract. Since the sole purpose of cl 12 was to provide security

---

a   Section 95, so far as material, provides:

   '(1) . . . every charge created . . . by a company . . . being a charge to which this section applies shall, so far as any security on the company's property or undertaking is conferred thereby, be void against the liquidator and any creditor of the company, unless the prescribed particulars of the charge together with the instrument, if any, by which the charge is created or evidenced, are delivered to or received by the registrar of companies for registration . . .

   (2) This section applies to the following charges . . . (c) a charge created or evidenced by an instrument which, if executed by an individual would require registration as a bill of sale . . . (f) a floating charge on the undertaking or property of the company . . .'

for the payment of the purchase price and since the rights conferred on the plaintiff by the clause were for that limited purpose only, the contract took effect as a contract for the sale of goods whereby the property in the goods passed to the company on delivery and a charge over the yarn was created by the company in favour of the plaintiff by way of security for the payment of the purchase price. It followed that a 'charge' had been 'created by [the] company' which was registrable under s 95(1) of the 1948 Act (see p 726 *h j*, p 729 *c f g*, p 730 *b* to *e* and *h j* and p 731 *a* and *g* to p 733 *a*, post); *Re Bond Worth Ltd* [1979] 3 All ER 919 applied; *McEntire v Crossley Bros Ltd* [1895–9] All ER Rep 829 and *Aluminium Industrie Vaassen BV v Romalpa Aluminium Ltd* [1976] 2 All ER 552 distinguished; *Borden (UK) Ltd v Scottish Timber Products Ltd* [1979] 3 All ER 961 considered.

(2) For the purposes of s 95 of the 1948 Act a 'creditor' meant a secured creditor, and therefore, since the receiver held the yarn for the benefit of the debenture holders who had appointed him and who, in turn, were 'creditors' of the company, it followed that cl 12 was void as against the receiver for non-registration under s 95 when he chose to treat the clause as void against the creditors whom he represented. Accordingly, the plaintiff's claim against the receiver for damages failed (see p 733 *a* to *d*, post).

Notes
For retention of title clauses in contracts for the sale of goods, see 41 Halsbury's Laws (4th edn) paras 707, 731.

For the Companies Act 1948, s 95, see 5 Halsbury's Statutes (3rd edn) 189.

Cases referred to in judgment
Aluminium Industrie Vaassen BV v Romalpa Aluminium Ltd [1976] 2 All ER 552, [1976] 1 WLR 676, CA.

Bond Worth Ltd, Re [1979] 3 All ER 919, [1980] Ch 228, [1979] 3 WLR 699.

Borden (UK) Ltd v Scottish Timber Products Ltd [1979] 3 All ER 961, [1981] Ch 25, [1979] 3 WLR 672, CA.

Connolly Bros Ltd Re, (No 2), Wood v The Company [1912] 2 Ch 25, CA.

Inglefield (George) Ltd, Re [1933] Ch 1, [1932] All ER Rep 244, CA.

McEntire v Crossley Bros Ltd [1895] AC 457, [1895–9] All ER Rep 829, HL.

Action
The plaintiff, Clough Mill Ltd, brought an action against the defendant, Geoffrey Martin (whom the debenture holders of Heatherdale Fabrics Ltd had appointed as the receiver of the company) claiming damages for wrongfully depriving them of possession of certain yarn and converting it to his own use. The facts are set out in the judgment.

James Bonney for the plaintiff.
W A Blackburne for the defendant.

Cur adv vult

17 August. The following judgment was delivered.

HIS HONOUR JUDGE O'DONOGHUE. The plaintiff company carries on business as a spinner of coloured and fancy yarn. In the months of December 1979 and January and March 1980 it entered into four contracts with Heatherdale Fabrics Ltd (the buyer) to sell quantities of yarn to the buyer. The buyer has at all material times carried on the business of a manufacturer of fabrics and it is common ground that the plaintiff sold the yarn to it knowing that it was to be used in this manufacturing process. Details of each of these four contracts are set forth in para 4 of the statement of claim. It is agreed that each of these contracts incorporated 'conditions of contract' printed on the reverse of a standard form of 'yarn contract' used by the plaintiff. I shall refer to the relevant provisions of these conditions in due course.

On 11 March 1980 the defendant was appointed the receiver of the buyer under the terms of a debenture dated 12 September 1975 granted by the buyer in favour of Lloyds Bank Ltd.

On that date the buyer still owed to the plaintiff some part of the purchase price in respect of each of the four contracts, as set forth in para 7 of the statement of claim.

On that date also the buyer still retained in its premises a total of 375 kg of unused yarn so supplied and unpaid for, the precise amounts and value of which are set forth in para 8 of the statement of claim.

On 12 June 1981 the buyer entered into a creditors' voluntary winding up, its total liabilities amounting to a figure in excess of £900,000 and a deficiency against moneys owed to unsecured creditors in excess of £500,000.

The present claim by the plaintiff company against the defendant as receiver is based on the following additional facts. (1) On 11 March 1980, following the appointment of the defendant as receiver, the plaintiff wrote to the receiver a letter stating that the plaintiff wished to repossess the unused yarn then on the premises of the buyer and asking for the receiver to arrange a time for the plaintiff to collect the goods. (2) By a letter dated 13 March 1980, the receiver wrote to all the creditors of the buyer stating, inter alia, that he had been appointed receiver of the assets of this buyer, but that the buyer was unable to pay accounts which were owing at the date of his appointment and that the company would for the present moment continue to trade. (3) By a letter dated 19 March 1980, the plaintiff's solicitors wrote a further letter to the receiver referring to the standard conditions of contract and alleging that under those conditions the ownership of the yarn remained in the plaintiff until payment in full had been made, and requesting the receiver to stop using the unused yarn in the manufacturing process of the buyer and requiring the immediate assurance of the receiver that the plaintiff would be permitted to collect the yarn from the premises of the buyer. (4) By a telex dated 20 March 1980 the solicitors acting for the receiver replied as follows:

'. . . your client's retention of title clause is invalid (inter alia) for non-registration under section 95 of the Companies Act 1948, and therefore 1. The Receiver will continue to use the goods supplied by your clients 2. He will refuse you admission to collect any unused yarn 3. We are instructed to accept service of any proceedings on his behalf . . .'

Thereafter (or thereby) battle lines were drawn.

The receiver has since allowed the buyer to use the yarn in its manufacturing process, but has not paid the balance of the purchase price owed at the date of his appointment.

In the present action the plaintiff alleges that the receiver converted the unused yarn and claims damages for such conversion.

The receiver contends that the rights of retention and other rights afforded to the plaintiff as seller under the conditions of contract amounted to charges by the buyer in favour of the plaintiff to secure payment of the unpaid purchase price, which charges fall within s 95 of the Companies Act 1948, and that such charges never having been registered have always been void against the receiver under the provisions of the section.

Accordingly, it is necessary to consider the relevant terms of the printed 'Conditions of Contract' in each case.

As I have already mentioned, these conditions are printed on the reverse of the form of yarn contract used by the plaintiff company.

No form of yarn contract has been produced in respect of the contract first mentioned in para 4 of the claim, but the yarn contracts for the remaining three contracts have been exhibited. The defendant accepts that each of the four contracts was made subject to the standard conditions as modified by the provisions on the front of the yarn contract in the relevant case.

So far as is material, the conditions of contract provide as follows.

Condition 1 defines, inter alia, 'the Seller' as the plaintiff company and 'the material' as the material to which the document relates.

Condition 10 is headed 'Overdue payments and cancellation' and provides, inter alia, as follows:

'(a) The price payable for the material shall be net and payment shall be made within the period stated overleaf . . . (d) For the purposes of this condition, time of payment shall be of the essence of the contract. (e) The Buyer shall not be entitled to withhold or set-off payment for material delivered for any reason whatsoever.'

Condition 11 is headed 'Passing of Risk and Insurance' and provides as follows:

'The risk in the material shall pass to the Buyer when the Seller delivers the material . . . to the Buyer . . . and the Seller shall have no responsibility in respect of the safety of the material thereafter and accordingly the Buyer shall insure the material thereafter against such risks (if any) as it thinks appropriate.'

Condition 12 is perhaps the most important for the purposes of this action. It is headed 'Passing of Title' and provides as follows:

'However the ownership of the material shall remain with the Seller, which reserves the right to dispose of the material until payment in full for all the material have been received by it in accordance with the terms of this contract or until such time as the Buyer sells the material to its customers by way of bona-fide sale at full market value. If such payment is overdue in whole or in part the Seller may (without prejudice to any of its other rights) recover or re-sell the material or any of it and may enter upon the Buyer's premises . . . for that purpose. Such payments shall become due immediately upon the commencement of any act or proceeding in which the Buyer's solvency is involved. If any of the material is incorporated in or used as material for other goods before such payment the property in the whole of such goods shall be and remain with the Seller until such payment has been made, or the other goods shall have been sold as aforesaid, and all the Seller's rights hereunder in the material shall extend to those other goods.'

Condition 12 is the 'retention of title clause' to which the defendant's solicitors were referring in their telex dated 20 March 1980.

The arguments in the present case are in essence of short compass. The plaintiff claims that 'the ownership' of the disputed yarn remained in it until the buyer had paid for it in full and that accordingly the plaintiff was entitled to reclaim such yarn in specie after delivery of its letter dated 11 March 1980, but that the defendant chose wrongfully to refuse to allow it to do so and later used the yarn without paying for it.

The defendant claims that, on the true construction of the bargain as a whole and of the conditions of contract in particular, the purpose of the plaintiff as seller in retaining any property in the yarn was exclusively as a security for the payment of the purchase price and no more (if necessary, by recourse to the yarn itself), and that as a consequence the provisions of condition 12 can only properly and sensibly be construed as creating a form of security over the yarn for the unpaid purchase price and for no other purpose, and that this amounted to a 'charge' on the yarn which should have been registered under the provisions of s 95 of the Companies Act 1948 and not having been so registered was void as against and did not bind the receiver, who was acting for the secured creditors of the buyer.

Counsel for the plaintiff submitted that his case was in essence based on the following simple propositions: (1) that the relevant yarn which had been delivered by the plaintiff to the buyer was not fully paid for; (2) that some part of the yarn remained unmixed on 11 March 1980 when the request to repossess was made; (3) that such request was wrongfully refused.

Counsel for the plaintiff went on to submit that each contract was a contract for sale of goods within the meaning of the Sale of Goods Act 1893 and the Sale of Goods Act 1979, and that s 19 of the 1979 Act (and of the earlier Act) covers a case such as the present and enables a seller of specific goods to reserve the right of disposal of the goods until certain conditions had been fulfilled.

He argued that condition 12 clearly provides in each contract that 'the *ownership* of the material shall remain with the Seller . . . until he has paid in full.' He conceded that condition 12 entitled the buyer to *use* the yarn, but submitted that this did not and could not affect 'the ownership' of any yarn for the time being remaining unused.

Counsel for the plaintiff submitted that, as a matter of construction, condition 12 clearly provided that the transfer of the property in the yarn was only to take place at some future time (when the seller was paid in full) and that accordingly the contract was 'an agreement to sell' as defined by s 2(5) of the 1979 Act.

The plaintiff claims, therefore, that, since it has reserved to itself 'the ownership' of the yarn, no property in such yarn (at any rate in the yarn which still remained unused on the factory floor) passed to the buyer until it had been paid for in full.

Counsel for the plaintiff referred to the decision of the House of Lords in *McEntire v Crossley Bros Ltd* [1895] AC 457, [1895–9] All ER Rep 829 as an example of a case where the court held that on the true construction of an agreement the property in a steam engine never passed to a lessee but remained with the lessors and that the transaction was therefore not within the provisions of the Bills of Sale Act 1878.

Counsel for the plaintiff then referred me to the more recent decision in *Aluminium Industrie Vaassen BV v Romalpa Aluminium Ltd* [1976] 2 All ER 552, [1976] 1 WLR 676 and said that he drew comfort from the fact that in that case the defendant purchaser admitted that cl 13 of that contract clearly provided that no property in the relevant aluminium foil was to pass to it until the foil had been fully paid for and that it remained a bailee of the foil until all debts were paid.

Counsel for the plaintiff also referred to the subsequent decisions of *Re Bond Worth* [1979] 3 All ER 919, [1980] 1 Ch 229 and *Borden (UK) Ltd v Scottish Timber Products Ltd* [1979] 3 All ER 961, [1981] Ch 25 and summarised his submissions in the following manner: (1) that each of the four contracts in the present case was a contract for sale of goods in which the parties could (and did) agree by condition 12 that the plaintiff should retain the legal property in and the right of disposal of the material sold until it had been paid in full, and that that provision did not amount to a mortgage or charge on the goods redeemable on the buyer paying the balance of the price owed; (2) that there should be implied into each contract permission to the buyer, prior to payment in full of the purchase price, to deal with the material for the purpose of manufacture and/or of sale, but subject to the right of the plaintiff seller reserved in condition 12 to recover and resell any material unsold and to enter the premises of the buyer for that purpose once the price had become overdue and unpaid in whole or in part; (3) that condition 12 also contained express provisions by which goods into which the material sold had become incorporated should become vested in the plaintiff seller; (4) that the material specified in para 8 of the statement of claim (which had not been used in manufacture and had not been sold) clearly remained the subject of the original right of retention of ownership so that, when the receiver refused to give up possession and later used the material in subsequent manufacturing processes, he was guilty of conversion, for which the plaintiff is entitled to claim the value of the yarn so converted, namely £1,190·34; (5) that no charge can have been 'created' by the buyer over the material which had not been paid for for the purposes of s 95 of the Companies Act 1948 since the provisions of condition 12 prevented the buyer from ever enjoying any property in that material until it had been paid for in full; (6) that even if such a charge had been created, it would not be void under s 95 against the defendant since he is a receiver (and a fortiori the agent of the company) and is therefore neither a liquidator nor a creditor of the company within the meaning of that section; (7) that he drew comfort from the *Romalpa* decision because it was there conceded that the property in the unused foil remained in the seller, which was entitled to claim it back again, and because it was there conceded that the relationship of the seller and buyer was that of a bailor and bailee for the purposes of tracing, and in particular that the judgments did proceed on the basis that the property in the unused foil which had been sold had been retained by the plaintiff seller up to the very moment of such sale; (8) that he drew comfort from the *Borden* decision and in particular from (a) that part of the judgment of Bridge LJ ([1979] 3 All ER 961 at 971, [1981] Ch 25 at 42) referring to the 'elaborate, and presumably effective, example of . . . a stipulation' by which a seller of material acquires rights over a finished product in the *Romalpa* case, (b) that part of the judgment of Templeman LJ ([1979] 3 All ER 961 at 973, [1981] Ch 25 at 44) in which he held that the seller could retain property in the resin at least until it was incorporated in the chipboard, when it ceased to exist and (c) that part of the judgment of Buckley LJ ([1979] 3 All ER 961 at 974, [1981] Ch 25 at 45) in which he held that under the terms of the conditions in that case the legal property in the resin initially remained in the seller; (9) that he distinguished the *Bond Worth* case from the present case because in that case only the 'equitable and beneficial' ownership had been retained; finally, (10) that it could not be right to say that, every time a contract for sale of goods provides that property in those goods is not to pass until the price has been paid in full, such an arrangement constitutes a charge, and that there is no compelling reason why it should create a charge, as distinct from an express retention of title, which the parties are entitled to agree under s 19 of the Sale of Goods Acts 1893 and 1979.

Counsel for the defendant receiver summarised his 'key' submissions in the following outline form: (1) that as a matter of construction condition 12 created a 'charge' on the yarn supplied (for as long as it was not fully paid for *and* remained identifiable as yarn) to secure payment to the plaintiff seller for the unpaid purchase price; (2) that this charge was 'created' by the buyer and did not arise by operation of law; (3) that this charge was registrable under s 95(2)(c) or (f) of the Companies Act 1948; (4) that since this charge was not so registered it is void against the liquidator of the buyer and against any creditor of the buyer; (5) that 'creditor' for the purposes of that section means a secured creditor, ie a creditor who has acquired a proprietory right to an interest in the subject matter of the unregistered charge; (6) that the defendant receiver held the unused yarn as receiver for the benefit of debenture holders who appointed him (according to their respective priorities) and subject thereto for the liquidator on behalf of the other secured and the unsecured creditors of the buyer; and (7) that the debenture holders who appointed the receiver are (and were at all material times, even before the resolution to wind up) creditors of the buyer within the meaning of s 95.

Counsel for the defendant submitted generally that, since these key submissions were all made on the basis that any attempt by the seller to retain property in the yarn was made exclusively as a security for the payment of the purchase price and that as a result the buyer was only, in effect, creating a charge over the yarn in favour of the seller, he would seek to argue before the appropriate tribunal that the admission made in the *Romalpa* case with regard to the unsold foil (which had not been used in a manufacturing process) may have been wrongly made.

Counsel then elaborated on his key submissions in a succinct and helpful manner, which I do not need to set forth in detail.

Of his key submissions, by far the most important in my judgment is the first, with regard to the meaning and effect of condition 12 of the contract.

Thus counsel for the plaintiff points to the first sentence of condition 12, which provides:

'. . . the ownership of the material shall remain with the Seller . . . until payment in full for all the material [has] been received by it . . .'

and seeks to construe these words literally and on their own. It seems, however, to me that one ought to consider these words in the context of the whole contract and endeavour to ascertain what meaning and effect can properly be ascribed to them in such context.

Prima facie (apart from condition 12) these four contracts are simply contracts for the sale of goods in which the plaintiff sells yarn to the buyer knowing that the buyer intends to use such yarn in its normal manufacturing process before it has paid for the yarn (and maybe even before such payment has become due). So it would appear that, if the parties really intended that the plaintiff should retain (what I may term) 'absolute' ownership in the yarn until payment in full, it would follow that the plaintiff could repossess the yarn at any time prior to payment in full even though to do so would frustrate the purpose of the sale and delivery.

The plaintiff, however, concedes that its right to repossess only arises on default of payment. If this is correct, then it would seem to follow that until such default actually occurs 'the ownership' retained by it is something less than absolute ownership. This being so, I find it somewhat difficult to distinguish the words 'the ownership' in the present context from the words 'equitable and beneficial ownership' used in *Re Bond Worth*. Thus I find it difficult in the case of chattels (as distinct from real property) to understand the precise significance of the distinction between 'legal' ownership on the one hand and 'equitable and beneficial' ownership on the other, particularly in a context such as the present where yarn is being delivered in the knowledge that it is to be used in a manufacturing process.

The concession made by the plaintiff in the present case that its right to repossess the yarn only arises on default of payment by the buyer suggests strongly that the prime purpose of condition 12 in the present case (as was the purpose of condition 13 in the *Romalpa* case) is to ensure that the seller eventually receives the purchase price and no more, if necessary by recourse to the yarn itself.

This being so, I am much attracted to the argument that this right of recourse to the yarn being a limited right can most sensibly be achieved by conferring on the seller some form of charge on the yarn supplied as security for the outstanding purchase price.

Moreover, the fourth sentence of condition 12 provides:

> 'If any of the material is incorporated in or used as material for other goods before such payment the property in the whole of such goods shall be and shall *remain* with the Seller until such payment has been made . . . and all the Seller's rights hereunder in the material shall extend to those other goods . . .'

In my judgment, it would be a misuse of the word 'remain' to say that the *whole* of such manufactured goods shall *remain* in the seller when it is clearly envisaged that the yarn may only be one constituent of the whole, and that the whole may well comprise other materials which were never at any time within the ownership of the seller.

I note that Buckley LJ, in his judgment in the *Borden* case [1979] 3 All ER 961 at 974, [1981] Ch 25 at 46, expressed the view that is was impossible for the plaintiffs to 'reserve' any property in the manufactured chipboard because they never had any property in it; and it would seem to follow in my judgment that in the present case the most which the fourth sentence of condition 12 could achieve is to create some form of charge in favour of the plaintiff over the newly manufactured goods of the buyer for the limited purpose of securing payment for the purchase price of the original yarn, some of which had been incorporated in such goods. If that is the position in relation to the fourth sentence of condition 12, what reason can there be for treating the first sentence of condition 12 in any different way? (I shall refer further to this aspect of this matter later.)

Moreover, I observe that condition 12 does not contain any provision with regard to the proceeds of sale received by the buyer when he comes to sell the manufactured goods (or, indeed, the yarn itself, if sold to its customers by way of bona fide sale at full market value).

If the plaintiff had retained full and absolute ownership of the yarn up to the point of such resale, one would perhaps have expected that the agreement would have contained some provision with regard to the proceeds of resale or claims which the buyer might have against his buyer as appear in cl 13 of the *Romalpa* case. The absence of such a provision is not in itself of prime importance in construing condition 12 of the present case, but it may well be a factor to be taken into account in construing the condition in its context.

I have considered *McEntire v Crossley* [1895] AC 457, [1895–9] All ER Rep 829, on which counsel for the plaintiff sought to rely, and I consider that that case is distinguishable from the present case on a number of grounds, including the fact that the parties had therein deliberately chosen to create a relationship of lessor and lessee and had chosen to treat the arrangement as one of lease and not of sale until the moment when the consideration had been paid in full. More particularly, the subject matter of that transaction was a steam engine, which was intended to remain unchanged at all material times, and there was no element (as there is in the present case and as there was in *Re Bond Worth* and in *Borden (UK) Ltd v Scottish Timber Products Ltd*) of the sale of material which both parties knew would be used in a manufacturing process.

Thus I note with interest that Lord Herschell LC in his judgment in *McEntire v Crossley Bros Ltd* [1895] AC 457 at 463, [1895–9] All ER Rep 829 at 832 stated clearly:

'. . . and if the appellants could have pointed here to *any* provision in this deed inconsistent with the intention that the property should remain in the vendors, I think they might very likely have succeeded . . .' (My emphasis.)

And Lord Watson in his judgment stated ([1895] AC 457 at 467–468, [1895–9] All ER Rep 829 at 834):

'If there be one point on the face of this contract clearer than another, it is, that the intention of the parties was that the seller should not part with his dominium over the thing which he was selling, and that its property should not become vested in the purchaser until the last farthing of the price was paid. If there had been in the deed language which shewed that the parties were using those expressions inadvertently, or that they had entered into other stipulations which were in substance contrary to the expressed intention, the case would have been otherwise. They might, for instance, have given power to the purchaser to exercise a right which implied *his* dominium before the contractual term for the passing of the property arrived. But there is no case of that kind here.' (My emphasis.)

It would seem clear that Lord Watson was envisaging in the instance he mentioned a right given to the purchaser (such as the right to incorporate the yarn in a manufacturing process which we have in the present case) from which it could properly be inferred that some property in the goods had passed to the purchaser even though the document states that it was not to pass.

I have also considered with interest *Aluminium Industrie Vaassen BV v Romalpa Aluminium Ltd* [1976] 2 All ER 552, [1976] 1 WLR 676, on which counsel for the plaintiff also seeks to rely. I note in particular that in that case (despite a slightly misleading headnote in the Weekly Law Reports) there is no mention in the body of the report that the defendant company had gone into liquidation, and it is clear that the provisions of s 95 of the Companies Act 1948 were never argued as such.

It was unnecessary in that case to consider whether or not a charge had been created, since the defendant buyer was content to concede that it held unsold foil as a bailee. The principal question in the case was whether or not the fiduciary relationship which had thus been conceded to exist prior to sale of the foil by the buyer to third parties continued to exist after such sale so as to entitle the plaintiffs to trace the proceeds of the sub-sale and to recover them.

Moreover, it is clear that condition 13 in the *Romalpa* case contained the most explicit provisions as to storage of the foil apart from the ôther goods of the buyer, if the seller required it so to do.

Slade J in *Re Bond Worth Ltd* [1979] 3 All ER 919 at 951, [1980] Ch 228 at 263 referred to the admission by the buyer in the *Romalpa* case that it was nothing more than a bailee of the foil whilst it remained in its possession as being 'a concession of crucial importance, the like of which has not of course been made here . . .' Such a concession has certainly not been made by the defendant receiver in the present case.

In the present case (as in *Re Bond Worth* and in the *Borden* case) the yarn had been delivered by the seller knowing that such goods were intended for use by the buyer in its normal manufacturing processes before the yarn would be paid for in full, and, as counsel for the defendant in the course of his submissions commented, it is perhaps somewhat ironic that the party in the *Romalpa* case which chose to submit that cl 13 of that agreement was intended to provide a security for the plaintiffs against the risks of non-payment was counsel acting for the plaintiffs as sellers (see [1976] 1 WLR 676 at 688, in

a   the first full paragraph of which page the reference to the 'defendants' as sellers must clearly be a misprint; cf [1976] 2 All ER 552 at 562).

Accordingly, it seems to me that the *Romalpa* case may properly be distinguished from the present case, firstly, in that in the *Romalpa* case (as distinct from the present case and from *Re Bond Worth* and the *Borden* case) there was no evidence that the foil was intended

b   to be used in any manufacturing process, so that there was nothing in that case to suggest that the buyer was anything more than a mere bailee as was conceded by the buyer, and, secondly that in the present case (unlike the *Romalpa* case) there was no duty to store the yarn separately from other goods and there was no duty to account for the proceeds of sale of manufactured goods when ultimately sold.

In my judgment the circumstances in *Re Bond Worth* appear to be much closer to the present case than those in the *Romalpa* case.

c   Those circumstances are summarised by Slade J (see [1979] 3 All ER 919 at 936, [1980] Ch 228 at 245–246) and bear a striking similarity to those of the present case, inter alia, in so far as in both cases (1) the contracts are 'absolute contracts for sale of goods', (2) the risk is expected to pass to the buyer on delivery, (3) the retention of title by the seller is manifestly not intended to confer on or to reserve to the seller *all* the rights which would

d   be enjoyed by a sui juris person having sole beneficial title to the property such as the right to call for delivery of the goods so long as the buyer was not in default under its payments, (4) the buyer was to be at liberty to use the goods for the purpose of its manufacture before payment had been made in full, (5) that if the goods should become constituents of or be converted into other products the retention of title clause should pass to such other products, (6) the buyer was to be at liberty to sell all or any part of the

e   goods and to transfer property therein to a purchaser, which in itself goes far beyond the provisions of s 25 of the Sale of Goods Act 1979.

It seems to me that the principal distinction between the contract in *Re Bond Worth* and the contract in the present case is that in the former case the seller was expressed to retain the 'equitable and beneficial ownership' although the legal ownership presumably did pass, whereas in the present case condition 12 purports to reserve to the plaintiff seller

f   simply 'the ownership' in the yarn.

But what does 'the ownership' mean in such circumstances? Is it wholly different from the 'equitable and beneficial ownership' referred to in *Re Bond Worth*?

In this regard I am much attracted to the submission made by counsel for the defendant that, in any case where a seller of chattels purports to hold back either the bare legal ownership or the equitable and beneficial ownership in such chattels until he has paid for them in full, it is the *purpose* for which such retention is made which is critical;

g   and if it is clear that the purpose was by way of *security* for the payment of the unpaid purchase price then the transaction as a whole should be construed as a charge. This is the approach taken by Slade J in *Re Bond Worth* [1979] 3 All ER 919 at 939, [1980] Ch 228 at 248 when he said:

> 'In my judgment any contract which, by way of security for the payment of a
h   > debt, confers an interest in property defeasible or destructible on payment of such
> debt . . . must necessarily be regarded as creating a mortgage or charge as the case
> may be.'

Moreover, when Slade J then went on to consider the characteristics of a mortgage or charge as summarised by Romer LJ in the earlier case of *Re George Inglefield Ltd* [1933]

j   Ch 1, [1932] All ER Rep 244, Slade J found that all the characteristics were present in the *Bond Worth* case and in particular the intention of the parties that if the seller exercised its right of retention and sold the goods for an amount more than sufficient to pay the outstanding debt the buyer would surely be entitled to receive the surplus (and if sold for less than the debt the seller would still be entitled to recover the balance from the buyer). In my judgment, these elements are all clearly present in the present case.

Slade J suggested that the relevant questions were first whether or not the retention of title clause operated to confer on the seller rights by way of charge (and if so in what manner) and he expressed the view that those were the only rights which that clause could have conferred on the seller in that case. Later, he considered the argument advanced by the seller that if any such charge had been created by the retention of title clause such a charge was created by the seller in favour of itself by way of exception and not by the buyer: (see [1979] 3 All ER 919 at 940, 942, [1980] Ch 228 at 250, 252).

He distinguished *Re Connolly Bros Ltd (No 2)* [1912] 2 Ch 25, on which such argument had been based, and expressed the view that on the transfer of legal property in land or chattels an express or implied *grant back* in favour of the original grantor is required to create such a mortgage or charge, saying ([1979] 3 All ER 919 at 943, [1980] Ch 228 at 253):

'If the court is satisfied that both parties to a transaction of sale have contracted that the vendor shall have defined rights by way of mortgage or charge over the subject-matter of this sale, no doubt it will be prepared to imply the necessary grant back of such rights by the purchaser . . .'

Later, in deciding the meaning and effect of the retention of title clause in *Re Bond Worth*, Slade J put the matter as follows ([1979] 3 All ER 919 at 945, [1980] Ch 228 at 256):

'Applying similar reasoning [to that of Lord Herschell LC in *McEntire v Crossley Bros Ltd* [1895] AC 457 at 466, [1895–9] All ER Rep 829 at 833], I conclude that the proper manner of construing the retention of title clause, together with all the other relevant provisions of the contracts of sale read as a whole, is to regard them as effecting a sale in which the entire property in the Acrilan passes to Bond Worth [the buyer] followed by a security eo instanti given back by Bond Worth to the vendor, Monsanto. In my judgment, therefore, Bond Worth rather than Monsanto must be regarded as the creator of the relevant charge in relation to the first category of charged assets. A fortiori it must be so regarded in relation to the second, third and fourth categories, since the third and fourth categories, at least, might include or represent (inter alia) property for which Monsanto had never at any time been the owner (e g materials belonging to Bond Worth, other than Acrilan, with which Acrilan had to be mixed). Charges over these categories could not possibly have been created except by grant made by Bond Worth. This, in my judgment, would be a powerful reason in itself for concluding that Bond Worth should be treated as having been the grantor and creator of the charges over *all* the categories of assets comprised in the retention of title clause if, contrary to my view, it had been theoretically possible for charges on the first and second categories to have been created without the need for any express or implied grant by Bond Worth.' (Slade J's emphasis.)

Finally, I note than Slade J, in dealing with the *Romalpa* case in general terms concluded that that decision only provided very limited assistance or guidance on the facts of the case then before him (see [1979] 3 All ER 919 at 952, [1980] Ch 228 at 264).

Having considered all the circumstances of the present case in relation to those considered by Slade J in *Re Bond Worth*, I have arrived at the same view in relation to the present case.

So I turn finally to the decision in *Borden (UK) Ltd v Scottish Timber Products Ltd* [1979] 3 All ER 961, [1981] Ch 25. Condition 2 of the contract in that case provided that, although the risk was to pass to the buyer immediately, the 'property' in the goods was only to pass when the goods (the subject of that contract and of all other contracts between the parties) had been paid for in full. So it would seem that there is no substantial difference between the wording of condition 2 in that case and of condition 12 in the present case.

In considering the situation where resin had been delivered to the buyer for use in its

manufacturing process in circumstances where the seller had no right to call for its return
a or to object to its use in the manufacture of chipboard, Bridge LJ said ([1979] 3 All ER
961 at 965–966, [1981] Ch 25 at 35):

> '... it seems to me quite impossible to say that this was a contract of bailment.
> The contract was essentially one of sale and purchase, subject only to the reservation
> of title clause, whatever its effect may have been. Now what was the effect of that
> clause? Looked at in principle, and independent of authority, I find it difficult to see
> **b** how the clause was apt to create any fiduciary relationship. I am much attracted by
> the view which was canvassed in argument that the effect of condition 2 was such
> that the beneficial interest in the resin passed to the buyers, who were to be entirely
> free to use it for their own purposes in the manufacture of chipboard, and that all
> that was retained by the sellers was the bare legal title to the resin so long as the resin
> existed, held as security for the unpaid price ...'

c
Pausing there, I must say, with respect, that I am much attracted to that view in the
circumstances of this present case, substituting yarn for resin and fabrics for chipboard,
although I realise that the yarn may not lose its physical identity in quite the same
manner as the resin would seem to do.

Later, in considering the *Romalpa* case, Bridge LJ pointed out certain clear distinctions
d between the two cases and added ([1979] 3 All ER 961 at 968, [1981] Ch 25 at 38):

> 'But to my mind the most important distinction is that the essence of the decision
> in *Romalpa* was that on the facts found or admitted Romalpa were selling the
> plaintiffs' material, the aluminium foil, as agents for the plaintiffs. It seems to me
> quite impossible to say here that in using the plaintiffs' resin in their own
> manufacturing process to manufacture their own chipboard the buyers could
> **e** possibly be described as acting in any sense as agent for the sellers.'

Similarly, I find it difficult to see how in the present case the buyer could be said to be
acting as agent of the plaintiff (or as bailee only, or, indeed, in any other fiduciary
capacity) when it accepted delivery of yarn which both parties knew would be used by
the buyer in its manufacturing process possibly even before it was paid for.
f I also draw some comfort in that view from the judgment of Templeman LJ, when he
said ([1979] 3 All ER 961 at 972–973, [1981] Ch 25 at 44):

> 'On behalf of the sellers it was submitted that the retention of title condition,
> which reserved to the sellers the property in the resin, imposed on the buyers
> fiduciary duties and enables the sellers to trace the resin through all its
> transformations. In my judgment, when resin was sold and delivered the property
> **g** in the resin could be retained by the sellers, and was retained, only as security for
> the payment of the purchase price and other debts incurred, and to be incurred, by
> the buyers to the sellers in respect of supplies of resin. If the buyers repudiated one
> contract the sellers could accept that repudiation and recover possession of the resin.
> If the sellers did not accept repudiation, or if the buyers failed to make payment due
> under any other contract, the sellers could enforce their security by selling the resin,
> **h** for which purpose they had reserved the title to themselves. When resin was sold
> and delivered, the buyers admittedly took possession subject to the title and right of
> the sellers; but the buyers did not receive the resin in any fiduciary capacity, but for
> themselves as purchasers. They could not sell and make title to the resin, because
> the title had been retained by the sellers. But the buyers were free to employ the
> resin in the manufacture of chipboard. When the resin was incorporated in the
> **j** chipboard, the resin ceased to exist, the sellers' title to the resin became meaningless
> and the sellers' security vanished. There was no provision in the contract for the
> buyers to provide substituted or additional security. The chipboard belonged to the
> buyers.'

In the present case, it will be remembered, the fourth sentence of condition 12 clearly did attempt to create an interest in the manufactured goods in favour of the plaintiff, which in my judgment would amount to creating a charge over such manufactured goods in favour of the plaintiff.

    a

In arriving at this view, I am again comforted by the views expressed by Templeman LJ ([1979] 3 All ER 961 at 973, [1981] Ch 25 at 44–45):

> 'For good measure, it seems to me that if the sellers have any interest or share in chipboard or proceeds of sale of chipboard, or property representing proceeds of sale of chipboard, they fall foul of s 95 of the Companies Act 1948. Any such interest or share must have been agreed to be granted by the buyers when they bought and accepted delivery of resin on the terms of the retention of title condition. Any such interest or share must have been created by the buyers when they employed the resin in the manufacture of chipboard. Any such interest or share must have been agreed to be granted and must have been created as security and only as security for the payment of the debts incurred and to be incurred by the buyers to the sellers in respect of the supply of resin. Those debts were charged on the interest or share granted and created by the buyers. If tracing is permissible, the charge attached to the chipboard, when chipboard was manufactured, then attached to the proceeds of sale when the chipboard was sold, and finally attached to any property representing those proceeds of sale of chipboard. If the buyers created a charge on chipboard, such a charge is void against the liquidators and creditors of the buyers under s 95 ... We were much pressed with the *Romalpa* case, in which buyers were entitled to sell goods supplied by unpaid sellers, but only as agents for the sellers, who retained the property in the goods pending payment. On the construction of a contract described by Roskill LJ in refusing leave to appeal to the House of Lords as 'a rather simple contract, not altogether happily expressed in the English language, but [which] could not govern any other case', the court implied an obligation on the buyers to account as bailees and held that the sellers were entitled to trace the proceeds of sale. Section 95 was not argued; it does not appear whether the buyers were in liquidation, and in any event the argument was probably not put forward because the retention of title in the sellers' goods was thought not to be the creation of a charge by the buyers. In the present case the buyers did not manufacture or sell chipboard, or perform any other function as agents for the sellers, and any charge on the buyers' chipboard and other property of the buyers must necessarily have been created by the buyers and be void.'

    b

    c

    d

    e

    f

But the prime question still remains whether the first and second sentences of condition 12 can be read independently of the fourth sentence so as to effect a simple retention of title different from the charge on the manufactured goods so clearly created by the fourth sentence.

    g

In my judgment, the approach which was urged by counsel for the defendant, that in construing a provision such as the present retention of title clause it is the purpose of such retention which is the crucial factor, is the correct approach. It follows that, if the court is satisfied that this purpose was by way of security for the payment of unpaid purchase moneys, then the transaction as a whole should be construed as a charge. As I have already said, this is the approach taken by Slade J in *Re Bond Worth* [1979] 3 All ER 919 at 939, [1980] Ch 228 at 248.

    h

When I listened to counsel for the plaintiff in his persuasive opening of his case when he put his case fairly and squarely on all fours with the *Romalpa* case, I was initially attracted to it. But having had my mind directed most carefully to the judgment of Slade J in *Re Bond Worth* and to the judgments in the *Borden* case, I have formed the view that as a matter of construction it would not be proper to treat the first sentence of condition 12 in total isolation from the remainder of condition 12, or indeed to read the first sentence in isolation from the commercial purpose of the various agreements for the sale of yarn which the parties chose to enter into. In my judgment, the present case may be

    j

a   readily distinguished from the *Romalpa* case on its facts, and is for all practical purposes more closely allied to the facts and circumstances in *Re Bond Worth*.

Having formed that view on the question of construction of condition 12, I have no hesitation in accepting the other submissions made by counsel for the defendant, which may perhaps be summarised (perhaps inelegantly) as follows: that the charge so created was registrable under s 95 of the Companies Act 1948 and being unregistered is void against the liquidator and any creditor of the buyer; that 'creditor' of the buyer for the

b   purposes of s 95 means a secured creditor; that the defendant receiver held the yarn as receiver for the benefit of the debenture holders who had appointed him and who must in turn have been 'creditors' of the buyer within the meaning of s 95. It follows, in my judgment, that the plaintiff seller, having failed to register its rights under the provisions of condition 12 as a charge in accordance with requirements of s 95 of the Companies Act 1948, is not now entitled to complain if the receiver has chosen to treat those

c   provisions as void against the creditors whom he represents. Accordingly, it must follow, in my judgment, that the present claim by the plaintiff seller for damages against the receiver must fail.

I must say that I am greatly indebted to both counsel for the careful and helpful manner in which they argued their respective cases.

d   *Action dismissed.*

Solicitors: *Foysters*, Blackburn (for the plaintiff); *Saffman & Co*, Leeds (for the defendant).

M Denise Chorlton   Barrister.

e
Kuwait Minister of Public Works v Sir Frederick Snow & Partners (a firm) and others

f
HOUSE OF LORDS
LORD FRASER OF TULLYBELTON, LORD BRIDGE OF HARWICH, LORD BRANDON OF OAKBROOK AND LORD TEMPLEMAN
6, 7 FEBRUARY, I MARCH 1984

Arbitration – Award – Enforcement – Foreign award – Enforceability – Whether to be enforceable award must post-date foreign state becoming a party to convention – Arbitration Act 1975, s 3.

g   On the ordinary and natural meaning of s 7(1)[a] of the Arbitration Act 1975 the question whether a state 'is a party to the New York Convention' is to be determined by reference to the time of proceedings for the enforcement under that Act of an arbitration award rather than by reference to the date of the award itself. It follows that an arbitration award made in the territory of a foreign state is enforceable in the United Kingdom as a

h   'Convention award' under s 3[b] of the 1975 Act if the state in which the award was made is a party to the convention at the date when proceedings to enforce the award begin, even if it was not a party at the date when the award was made (see p 734 d e, p 736 h j, p 737 b to e and p 739 e to g, post).

Decision of the Court of Appeal [1983] 2 All ER 754 affirmed.

Notes

j   For arbitration awards, see 2 Halsbury's Laws (4th edn) paras 634–635, and for cases on the subject, see 3 Digest (Reissue) 303–305, 2040–2044.

For the Arbitration Act 1975, ss 3, 7, see 45 Halsbury's Statutes (3rd edn) 35, 36.

a   Section 7(1), so far as material, is set out at p 736 *e f*, post
b   Section 3, so far as material, is set out at p 735 *j*, post

Appeal

The defendants, Sir Frederick Snow & Partners (a firm), George Frederick Brian Scruby   *a*
and Arthur Henry Brown, appealed, with leave of the Appeal Committee of the House
of Lords granted on 28 July 1983, against the decision of the Court of Appeal (Stephenson,
Kerr and Fox LJJ) ([1983] 2 All ER 754, [1983] 1 WLR 818) on 17 March 1983 allowing
an appeal of the respondent plaintiff, the Minister of Public Works of the State of Kuwait,
from part of the judgment of Mocatta J ([1981] 1 Lloyd's Rep 656) dated 19 February
1981 in proceedings by the respondent against the appellants to enforce an arbitration   *b*
award made in Kuwait on 15 September 1973 whereby he held that the award relied on
by the respondent was not a 'Convention award' for the purposes of the Arbitration Act
1975. The facts are set out in the opinion of Lord Brandon.

Desmond Wright QC and *Nicholas Dennys* for the appellants.
Bernard Rix QC and *J Tracy Kelly* for the respondent.   *c*

Their Lordships took time for consideration.

1 March. The following opinions were delivered.

LORD FRASER OF TULLYBELTON. My Lords, I have had the advantage of   *d*
reading in draft the speech by my noble and learned friend Lord Brandon, and I agree
with it. For the reasons given by him I would dismiss this appeal.

LORD BRIDGE OF HARWICH. My Lords, For the reasons given in the speech of
my noble and learned friend Lord Brandon, with which I agree, I would dismiss this
appeal.   *e*

LORD BRANDON OF OAKBROOK. My Lords, this appeal raises a short point of
construction with regard to the meaning and effect of the expression 'Convention award',
as used in those provisions of the Arbitration Act 1975 which relate to the enforcement
in the United Kingdom of foreign arbitral awards.

The award with regard to which the question which I have stated arises is an award   *f*
made by a Kuwaiti arbitrator in Kuwait on 15 September 1973 in respect of disputes
arising out of a contract made as long ago as 1958 and relating to the construction of an
international airport in Kuwait. The parties to the contract were, on the one side, the
government of the State of Kuwait and, on the other side, a British firm of civil
engineering consultants, then known as Frederick S Snow & Partners. The award
required the payment by Frederick S Snow & Partners to the government of the State of
Kuwait of a sum which, with interest up to 1979 only, amounted to well over £3·5m.   *g*
Proceedings to enforce the award in England were only begun on 23 March 1979, and it
is those proceedings that the point of construction referred to above arises for decision.

The history of the dispute between the parties, and of the long and convoluted
proceedings which eventually followed, is fully set out in the judgment of Kerr LJ in the
Court of Appeal (Stephenson, Fox and Kerr LJJ) ([1983] 2 All ER 754, [1983] 1 WLR   *h*
818), to which reference can be made if necessary. That being so, I do not think that it
would serve any useful purpose for me to repeat that history here.

As the matter now stands before your Lordships, the only effective parties to the
proceedings are George Frederick Brian Scruby and Arthur Henry Brown, the second and
third appellants respectively, to whom I shall refer collectively as 'the appellants', and his
Excellency the Minister of Public Works of the government of the State of Kuwait, who   *j*
is the respondent. Further, the only question for decision is whether the respondent is
entitled to enforce the award referred to earlier (the award) against the appellants as a
Convention award under the enforcement provisions of the 1975 Act. In this connection
it is common ground now (although it was not so earlier) that, if the award is a
Convention award under the 1975 Act, the appellants are the only persons against whom,

a subject to defences under that Act on which they would wish to rely, the award can be enforced under it.

Mocatta J at first instance ([1981] 1 Lloyd's Rep 656) decided that the award was not a Convention award for the purposes of the 1975 Act, and could not therefore be enforced by the respondent against the appellants under it. The Court of Appeal unanimously reached the opposite conclusion and reversed the judgment of Mocatta J in this respect. The appellants now bring a further appeal, with the leave of the Appeal Committee, to your Lordships' House.

b My Lords, the long title of the 1975 Act is 'An Act to give effect to the New York Convention on the Recognition and Enforcement of Foreign Arbitral Awards'. The New York Convention there referred to (the convention) (TS 20 (1976); Cmnd 6419) came into being on 10 June 1958. On 23 December 1975 the United Kingdom became a party to the convention, and the 1975 Act giving effect to it, which had been passed on 25 February 1975, was brought into force. On 27 July 1978 Kuwait became a party to the convention, and on 12 April 1979 an Order in Council, declaring that Kuwait, together with a large number of other states, was a party to the convention, came into operation.

c It will be seen, therefore, that on 15 September 1973, when the award was made, Kuwait had not yet become a party to the convention; but that by 23 March 1979, when the present proceedings to enforce the award were begun, Kuwait had done so.

d The case for the appellants is that a foreign arbitral award can only qualify as a convention award for the purposes of the 1975 Act if the state in which it was made was already a party to the convention at the date of the award. Accordingly, the award was not a convention award, and could not be enforced by the respondent against the appellants under that Act. The case for the respondent on the other hand is that it is sufficient for a foreign arbitral award to qualify as a convention award under the 1975 Act if the state in which it was made has become a party to the convention by the date when proceedings to enforce the award are begun, even though it was not such a party at the date when the award was made. Accordingly, the award was a convention award for the purposes of the 1975 Act and was enforceable by the respondent against the appellants under that Act. The question which of these cases should prevail depends on the true construction of the relevant provisions of the 1975 Act.

f My Lords, the 1975 Act is divided, in form though not in express terms, into three parts, each with a different cross-heading. The first part of the Act, consisting of s 1 only, has the cross-heading 'Effect of arbitration agreement on court proceedings', and deals with the staying of actions, other than domestic actions as later defined, in cases where the parties to such actions have agreed to refer the subject matter of them to arbitration. The second part of the Act, consisting of ss 2 to 6, has the cross-heading 'Enforcement of Convention awards', which, subject to the later definition of the expression 'Convention award', summarises the scope of those sections. The third part of the Act, consisting of ss 7 and 8, has the cross-heading 'General'. Section 7(1) deals with matters of interpretation.

In relation to the question raised by this appeal the following provisions of the 1975 Act are relevant:

h *'Enforcement of Convention awards*

2. Sections 3 to 6 of this Act shall have effect with respect to the enforcement of Convention awards; and where a Convention award would, but for this section, be also a foreign award within the meaning of Part II of the Arbitration Act 1950, that Part shall not apply to it.

3.—(1) A Convention award shall, subject to the following provisions of this Act, be enforceable—(a) In England and Wales, either by action or in the same manner as the award of an arbitrator is enforceable by virtue of section 26 of the Arbitration Act 1950 . . .

4. The party seeking to enforce a Convention award must produce—(a) the duly authenticated original award or a duly certified copy of it; and (b) the original arbitration agreement or a duly certified copy of it; and (c) where the award or

agreement is in a foreign language, a translation of it certified by an official or sworn translator or by a diplomatic or consular agent.

5.—(1) Enforcement of a Convention award shall not be refused except in the cases mentioned in this section.

(2) Enforcement of a Convention award may be refused if the person against whom it is invoked proves—(a) that a party to the arbitration agreement was (under the law applicable to him) under some incapacity; or (b) that the arbitration agreement was not valid under the law to which the parties subjected it or, failing any indication thereon, under the law of the country where the award was made; or (c) that he was not given proper notice of the appointment of the arbitrator or of the arbitration proceedings or was otherwise unable to present his case; or (d) (subject to subsection (4) of this section) that the award deals with a difference not contemplated by or not falling within the terms of the submission to arbitration or contains decisions on matters beyond the scope of the submission to arbitration; or (e) that the composition of the arbitral authority or the arbitral procedure was not in accordance with the agreement of the parties or, failing such agreement, with the law of the country where the arbitration took place; or (f) that the award has not yet become binding on the parties, or has been set aside or suspended by a competent authority of the country in which, or under the law of which, it was made.

(3) Enforcement of a Convention award may also be refused if the award is in respect of a matter which is not capable of settlement by arbitration, or if it would be contrary to public policy to enforce the award . . .

6. Nothing in this Act shall prejudice any right to enforce . . . an award otherwise than under this Act or Part II of the Arbitration Act 1950.

General

7.—(1) In this Act . . . "Convention award" means an award made in pursuance of an arbitration agreement in the territory of a State, other than the United Kingdom, which is a party to the New York Convention; and "the New York Convention" means the Convention on the Recognition and Enforcement of Foreign Arbitral Awards adopted by the United Nations Conference on International Commercial Arbitration on 10th June 1958.

(2) If Her Majesty by Order in Council declares that any State specified in the Order is a party to the New York Convention the Order shall, while in force, be conclusive evidence that that State is a party to that Convention . . .'

The dispute between the parties to the appeal was, as might have been expected, concentrated on the definition of the expression 'Convention award' contained in s 7(1) of the 1975 Act. Further, since the award plainly came within the first part of the definition as 'an award made in pursuance of an arbitration agreement in the territory of a State, other than the United Kingdom', the dispute was narrowed down further to the meaning to be given to the last part of the definition, namely 'which is a party to the New York Convention'. For the appellants it was contended that this phrase, although it used the present tense in the word 'is', related back to the time when the award was made. For the respondent it was contended that the phrase, by using the present tense in the word 'is', plainly referred to the time of enforcement, that is to say to the time when proceedings for enforcement under s 3(1)(a) were begun.

In order to see which of these two contentions is to be preferred, it is helpful to transpose the definition of the expression 'Convention award' contained in s 7(1) bodily into ss 2 and 3. If that is done, the relevant parts of those sections read:

'**2.** Sections 3 to 6 of this Act shall have effect with respect to the enforcement of awards made in pursuance of an arbitration agreement in the territory of a State, other than the United Kingdom, which is a party to the New York Convention . . .

3.—(1) An award made in pursuance of an arbitration agreement in the territory of a State, other than the United Kingdom, which is a party to the New York

Convention shall, subject to the following provisions of this Act, be enforceable—
(a) in England and Wales, either by action or in the same manner as the award of an
arbitrator is enforceable by virtue of section 26 of the Arbitration Act 1950 . . .'

Sections 2 and 3, being in the second part of the Act, which has the cross-heading
'Enforcement of Convention awards', are dealing, firstly, with the right to enforce foreign
arbitral awards and, secondly, with the procedure by which that right of enforcement
can be exercised. In that context it appears to me to be plain, when the definition of
'Convention award' contained in s 7(1) has been transposed bodily into ss 2 and 3, as has
been done above, that the use of the present tense in the word 'is' in the phrase 'which is
a party to the New York Convention' must, as a matter of the ordinary and natural
interpretation of the words used, mean that the phrase relates to the time of enforcement
and not to any other time. In particular, if it had been the intention of the legislature
that the phrase should relate to the date of the award, then the draftsman would surely
have used words which made that intention clear such as 'which is and was at the date of
the award a party to the New York Convention'. It is my opinion, therefore, that the
meaning of the expression 'Convention award' contended for by the respondent,
according as it does with the ordinary and natural interpretation of the words used in the
context of ss 2 to 6, is the correct one; and that the meaning of that expression contended
for by the appellants, requiring as it does the insertion by implication into the phrase
'which is a party to the New York Convention', after the word 'is', the additional words
'and was at the date of the award', or some other words to the like effect, cannot be
supported.

My Lords, counsel for the appellants put in the forefront of his argument against
construing the expression 'Convention award' in the way that I have indicated that I
think it should be construed what can conveniently be described as the retrospectivity
point. His argument was that courts had always refused to give statutes retrospective
effect unless they contained clear words which showed that such effect was intended,
that, if the phrase 'which is a party to the New York Convention' were to be interpreted
as relating to the time of enforcement of an award rather than the time of its making,
the result would be to give the 1975 Act retrospective effect, and that there were in this
case no plain words in the Act showing that such effect was intended. The way in which
he contended that the Act would, on the assumption made, have retrospective effect was
this. An award made in a foreign state which was not a party to the convention at the
time of its making would not be enforceable in the United Kingdom under the 1975 Act
unless and until that foreign state subsequently became a party to the convention. On
that happening, however, an award which could not previously have been so enforceable
would, immediately and ipso facto, become so.

While this argument appears on first presentation to be of considerable force, there
are, I think, two answers to it which show that it is not well founded. The first answer is
that the presumption against interpreting a statute as having retrospective effect is based
on the assumption that, if retrospective effect were to be given to it, the result would be
to deprive persons of accrued rights or defences. In the present case I am not persuaded
that to give the 1975 Act retrospective effect in the sense which has been discussed would
deprive anybody either of an accrued right or of an accrued defence. On the footing that
awards made in a foreign state before that state became a party to the convention are not
convention awards for the purposes of the 1975 Act, and cannot therefore be enforced
under it, the result is simply that a person wishing to enforce such an award in the United
Kingdom would be obliged to bring an action on it at common law, the right to do this
being expressly preserved by s 6 of the 1975 Act. It cannot therefore be said that, if the
construction of the 1975 Act which I prefer is correct, the result is to make an award,
which could not previously have been enforced against a person at all, newly enforceable
against him under the 1975 Act. On the contrary, the award could always have been
enforced against him by one form of procedure, and the only result is that it subsequently
becomes enforceable against him by a second and alternative form of procedure.

Counsel for the appellants pressed strongly an argument that a wider range of defences would be available to a defendant in an action to enforce an award at common law than would be available to him in enforcement proceedings under the 1975 Act, and that, because of this, the result of giving a retrospective effect to that Act would be to deprive a defendant of defences which would otherwise have been available to him. In my view, however, there is no legal basis for this argument. I set out earlier in full the provisions of s 5(2) and (3) of the 1975 Act. These provisions afford a wide range of defences to a person against whom an award is sought to be enforced under that Act. Moreover, although counsel for the appellants was asked by your Lordships on more than one occasion to give an example of a defence which would be available to a defendant to a common law action on an award, but would not be available to him in enforcement proceedings in respect of the same award under the 1975 Act, he was quite unable to do so. The true position, in my view, is that the statutory defences contained in s 5(2) and (3) of the 1975 Act cover the whole field of the defences which would be available in a common law action. Summing up, therefore, I would say that, in so far as the construction of the 1975 Act which I prefer involves giving retrospective effect to that Act, such effect does not take away any accrued rights or defences, and is therefore free from the objections to it which would exist if it did so.

The second answer to the retrospectivity point is this. If there is, contrary to the views which I have expressed above, any valid objection to giving the 1975 Act the kind of retrospective effect which has been discussed, then on a proper construction of the phrase 'which is a party to the New York Convention', as used in the definition of 'Convention award' in s 7(1) of the 1975 Act, the legislature has, in my view, shown in clear terms its intention to give the Act that retrospective effect.

On both these grounds, therefore, I am of the opinion that the argument based on retrospectivity fails and should be rejected.

My Lords, while I am content to decide the question raised by this appeal solely on what I consider to be the correct meaning of the expression 'Convention award' as defined in s 7(1) of the 1975 Act, it appears to me that that construction gains added support from the terms of s 7(2), which I also set out in full at an earlier stage. That subsection contemplates that the normal way in which a party, who seeks to enforce a foreign arbitral award under the 1975 Act, will prove that the state in which the award was made is a party to the convention is by producing an Order in Council of the kind there authorised. It is clear from the wording of s 7(2) that the only matter which an Order in Council made under it can declare is that one or more foreign states specified in the order are, as at the date of the order, a party to the convention. If the phrase 'which is a party to the New York Convention', as used in the definition of the expression 'Convention award' contained in s 7(1) of the 1975 Act, were to be construed in the way contended for by the appellants, one would expect that s 7(2) would authorise Orders in Council which not only declared that one or more foreign states were parties to the convention, but also stated the dates on which they became such parties.

There remains one further point with which I think that I ought to deal. It has long been established that, if a provision in a domestic Act giving effect to the adherence by the United Kingdom to an international convention is ambiguous, a United Kingdom court is entitled to refer to the text of the convention concerned in order to obtain assistance, if it can, in resolving the ambiguity. In the present case I do not consider, as I hope that I have made it clear, that the definition of the expression 'Convention award' contained in s 7(1) of the 1975 Act is ambiguous. If that is wrong, however, and the definition is ambiguous, it is permissible to refer to the text of the New York Convention in order to obtain assistance in resolving the ambiguity. Such assistance is, in my view, to be found in art VII, para 2, of that convention, which provides:

'2. The Geneva Protocol on Arbitration Clauses of 1923 and the Geneva Convention on the Execution of Foreign Arbitral Awards of 1927 shall cease to have effect between Contracting States on their becoming bound and to the extent that they become bound, by this Convention.'

The Geneva Protocol of 1923 (TS 4 (1925); Cmd 2312) and the Geneva Convention of 1927 (TS 28 (1930); Cmd 3655) there referred to were earlier international treaties dealing with the recognition of foreign arbitration agreements and the enforcement of foreign arbitral awards respectively. The United Kingdom was a party to both treaties and gave effect to the first by the Arbitration Clauses (Protocol) Act 1924, and to the second by the Arbitration (Foreign Awards) Act 1930, both of which were repealed by, and substantially re-enacted in, the Arbitration Act 1950.

The effect of art VII(2) of the New York Convention is that, on two or more states which were parties to the Geneva treaties of 1923 and 1927 becoming parties to the New York Convention, and thereby becoming bound by its provisions, the two earlier treaties shall no longer apply as between such states. If the expression 'Convention award' in the 1975 Act is construed in the way contended for by the appellants, the result of art VII(2) would be to produce a grave lacuna in the reciprocal recognition and enforcement of arbitral awards as between many states. The existence of this lacuna can be illustrated in this way. Suppose that before 1975 states A and B were both parties to the Geneva Convention of 1927: in that case awards made in state A could be enforced pursuant to that treaty in state B and vice versa. Suppose next that in 1975 both states A and B became parties to the New York Convention. Then, on the appellants' construction of the expression 'Convention award', an award made in state A in, say, 1970 could not be enforced as a convention award in state B because, at the time when such award was made, state A was not yet a party to the New York Convention. At the same time, by reason of art VII(2), of the New York Convention, the award made in state A could not be enforced in state B under the Geneva Convention of 1927 because that treaty would, on states A and B becoming parties to the New York Convention in 1975, have ceased to have effect as between them. The existence of this lacuna, as between the United Kingdom and other states who were previously parties to the Geneva Convention of 1927 and have since become parties to the New York Convention, cannot have been intended by the legislature when it passed the 1975 Act. These considerations strongly reinforce the view that the construction of the expression 'Convention award' in the 1975 Act contended for by the appellants is wrong, and the construction contended for by the respondent is right.

My Lords, for the reasons which I have given, I am of the opinion that the decision of the Court of Appeal was right, and that the appeal should accordingly be dismissed with costs.

LORD TEMPLEMAN. My Lords, for the reasons given by my noble and learned friend Lord Brandon I would dismiss this appeal.

Appeal dismissed.

Solicitors: *Blakeney's* (for the appellants); *Charles Russell & Co* (for the respondent).

Mary Rose Plummer   Barrister.

R v Courtie

a

HOUSE OF LORDS

LORD DIPLOCK, LORD FRASER OF TULLYBELTON, LORD SCARMAN, LORD ROSKILL AND LORD BRIDGE OF HARWICH

25 JANUARY, 1 MARCH 1984

b

Criminal law – Buggery – Maximum punishment varying according to factual ingredients present – Whether more than one offence created – Sexual Offences Act 1956, s 12(1) – Sexual Offences Act 1967, ss 1, 3.

On the true construction of the statutory provisions, more than one offence is created by s 12(1)[a] of the Sexual Offences Act 1956 (in so far as it makes it an offence for a man to commit buggery with another man) when read with ss 1[b] and 3[c] of the Sexual Offences Act 1967 (which respectively decriminalise buggery when committed in private by two consenting males aged 21 or over and provide for different maximum penalties according to the factual ingredients of the case, namely consent or the lack of it and the respective ages of the accused and the other man). Accordingly, where a man is guilty of buggery contrary to s 12(1) of the 1956 Act, the maximum penalty which may be imposed in any particular case will depend on which of the factual ingredients of the offence have been established beyond reasonable doubt to the satisfaction of the jury (see p 743 *j* to p 744 *a* and *g* to p 745 *a* and 746 *c d* and *g* to *j*, post).

c

d

Where it is uncertain whether a particular factual ingredient of the offence of buggery existed, charges which include allegations of factual ingredients which attract different maximum penalties should be put into separate counts on the indictment to simplify the task of the judge when he sums up to the jury and that of the jury in understanding what alternatives are open to them when they retire to deliberate on their verdict (see p 746 *f* to *j*, post).

e

Notes

For the offence of buggery, see 11 Halsbury's Laws (4th edn) para 1031, and for cases on the subject, see 15 Digest (Reissue) 1049–1050, 9029–9051.

For the Sexual Offences Act 1956, s 12, see 8 Halsbury's Statutes (3rd edn) 423.

For the Sexual Offences Act 1967, ss 1, 3, see ibid 577, 578.

f

Cases referred to in opinions

R v Miller [1983] 1 All ER 978, [1983] AC 161, [1983] 2 WLR 539, HL.

Verrier v DPP [1966] 3 All ER 568, [1967] 2 AC 195, [1966] 3 WLR 924, HL.

Woolmington v DPP [1935] AC 462, [1935] All ER Rep 1, HL.

g

Appeal

On 12 October 1982 in the Crown Court at York before his Honour Judge Bennett QC and two lay justices, the appellant, Thomas Courtie, pleaded guilty to an indictment containing one count of buggery contrary to s 12(1) of the Sexual Offences Act 1956 committed with a male person aged 19 years. The court sentenced the appellant to three years' imprisonment. The appellant appealed against sentence and on 24 May 1983 the Court of Appeal, Criminal Division (Watkins LJ, Heilbron J and Sir John Thompson) dismissed the appeal. On 29 July 1983 the Court of Appeal refused an application by the appellant for leave to appeal to the House of Lords but certified, under s 33(2) of the

h

j

---

a   Section 12(1) provides: 'It is felony for a person to commit buggery with another or with an animal.'

b   Section 1, so far as material, is set out at p 743 *f* to *h*, post

c   Section 3, so far as material, is set out at p 744 *d* to *f*, post

a   Criminal Appeal Act 1968, that a point of law of general public importance (set out at p 746 *c*, post) was involved in the decision to dismiss the appeal. The facts are set out in the opinion of Lord Diplock.

Barry Mortimer QC and *D Peter Hunt* for the appellant.
Harry Ognall QC and *Robert Andrews* for the Crown.

b   Their Lordships took time for consideration.

1 March. The following opinions were delivered.

LORD DIPLOCK. My Lords, this case comes before your Lordships in the guise of an appeal against sentence only. This is a subject matter which seldom involves a certifiable question of law of general importance such as would qualify it for the grant of leave to

c   appeal to the House of Lords. I cannot, myself, recall any criminal appeal confined to sentence only having come before this House since I started to sit here in 1968, although shortly before that a solitary example had been provided in *Verrier v DPP* [1966] 3 All ER 568, [1967] 2 AC 195. In truth, however, the instant appeal raises two questions involving basic principles of English criminal law, one substantive, the other procedural.

d   The substantive principle is that to which in *Woolmington v DPP* [1935] AC 462 at 481, [1935] All ER Rep 1 at 8, in a speech which bears indicia of collaborative authorship, Viscount Sankey LC applied the metaphor of 'the one golden thread that is always to be seen throughout the web of English criminal law'. The principle so referred to is that an accused person cannot be convicted of any offence with which he is charged unless it has been established by the prosecution that each one of the factual ingredients which are included in the legal definition of that specific offence was present in the case that has

e   been brought against him by the prosecution.

One way in which the prosecution may establish that all the factual ingredients of the specific offence with which the accused person is charged did exist is by the accused, on his arraignment, entering an informed and unequivocal plea of guilty to the charge set out in an indictment which complies with s 3 of the Indictments Act 1915 in that it

f   contains a statement of the specific offence with which the accused is charged together with such particulars as may be necessary for giving reasonable information as to the nature of the charge.

In the absence of such an informed and unequivocal plea of guilty by the accused, the prosecution, if it is to obtain the accused's conviction for the specific offence charged, must prove to the satisfaction (beyond reasonable doubt) of the person or persons in whom is vested the function of trying facts, that each and every factual ingredient of that

g   offence existed in the case of the accused. The factual ingredients of every criminal offence, whether it be statutory or an offence at common law, consist of the conduct of the accused and his state of mind at the time of that conduct. Heedful of the recent admonition contained in my speech in *R v Miller* [1983] 1 All ER 978 at 980, [1983] 2 AC 161 at 174, with which the other members of the Appellate Committee concurred, I

h   use the expressions conduct and state of mind in preference to speaking of actus reus and mens rea.

It marks no snapping of Viscount Sankey LC's golden thread that s 6 of the Criminal Law Act 1967 should permit the accused (either on a plea or on a verdict of guilty) to be convicted of a lesser offence than the specific offence charged, if the allegations in the indictment contained in the charge of the specific offence amount to or include all the factual ingredients of the lesser offence. This is not substantive English criminal law: it

j   is procedural only. It deals with the form of indictments and how charges of specific offences contained in them may be framed and, if so framed, are to be understood.

It is a procedural principle of a different order that is raised in the instant appeal. It is one that is basic to English criminal law, viz that, if there has not been an informed and unequivocal plea of guilty, the question whether any particular factual ingredient of the specific offence charged (or of any lesser offence of which he might be convicted on that indictment) was present in the case against an accused person falls to be determined by those persons, and by those persons alone, in whom, under English criminal procedure, there is vested the function of finding whether or not the factual ingredients necessary to constitute the offence have been proved to their satisfaction. Who those persons are in any particular case depends on the mode of trial, ie summarily or an indictment; but in the instant case your Lordships are concerned only with a prosecution on indictment, and where such is the mode of trial those persons are the jury. An accused person who has been arraigned on indictment is entitled to avail himself of the chance of obtaining from a jury a verdict of not guilty of the specific offence with which he has been charged and of any lesser offence, if there be one, of which he might lawfully be convicted on that indictment, if the jury regard themselves as being left in reasonable doubt whether the existence of any single one of the factual ingredients of the specific offence charged or of the lesser offence has been proved to their satisfaction. Such is an accused person's right notwithstanding that the jury's verdict of not guilty will not disclose which of what may have been several necessary factual ingredients of the offence the jury regarded the prosecution as having failed to prove beyond reasonable doubt.

I should mention in precautionary parenthesis, although it is not a matter that is involved in the instant appeal, that the function of the jury as triers of fact to the exclusion of the judge in a trial on indictment is limited to finding facts that are brought to their attention by admissible evidence, all questions as to the credibility and weight to be attached to such admissible evidence being for the jury alone. What evidence is admissible, however, is a question of law and accordingly the function of determining it is vested in the judge to the exclusion of the jury, even though this may involve, as in the cases of dispute as to the voluntary character of confessions, determination by the judge and not the jury of questions of credibility and weight to be attached to evidence of fact directed to the collateral issue of admissibility.

It lies within the power of Parliament to modify or exclude by statute either or both of these basic principles of English criminal law and to do so either generally or in relation to particular offences; but, as was said by this House in R v Miller [1983] 1 All ER 978 at 980, [1983] 2 AC 161 at 174, where it is contended that particular provisions of a statute do have that effect—

> 'Those particular provisions will fall to be construed in the light of general principles of English criminal law so well established that it is the practice of parliamentary draftsmen to leave them unexpressed in criminal statutes, on the confident assumption that a court of law will treat those principles as intended by Parliament to be applicable to the particular offence unless expressly modified or excluded.'

Such facts of the instant case as have made it necessary for your Lordships to consider, in an appeal against sentence only, the two basic principles of English criminal law, one substantive and the other procedural, to which I have referred, can be stated briefly. They are set out in somewhat greater detail in the judgment of the Court of Appeal.

The appellant was arraigned in the Crown Court at York, before a circuit judge sitting with two justices, on an indictment containing a single count in which the statement of offence and particulars of offence were as follows:

'STATEMENT OF OFFENCE

BUGGERY, contrary to Section 12(1) of the Sexual Offences Act 1956

PARTICULARS OF OFFENCE

THOMAS COURTIE, on the 6th day of February 1982, committed buggery with [the complainant], a male person under the age of twenty one years, namely of the age of nineteen years.'

To that indictment the appellant pleaded guilty. In order to appreciate what were the
legal consequences of such a plea it is necessary to analyse the wording of the indictment
in the light of the relevant legislation.

The statement of offence refers only to s 12(1) of the Sexual Offences Act 1956. Like
its predecessor, s 61 of the Offences against the Person Act 1861, this section makes
statutory the previously existing common law offence of buggery without incorporating
any definition of its essential factual ingredients. All that the 1956 Act does in addition
as respect the offence of buggery which is relevant to the instant appeal is to prescribe in
para 3 of Sch 2 as the maximum penalty for the common law offence imprisonment for
life. The conduct that was the necessary ingredient of buggery at common law was the
penetration by the male human sexual organ of the anus of another human being or an
animal. It was thus an offence which necessarily involved the participation of a male
human being (described in the 1956 Act as a 'man' regardless of whether or not he had
reached the age of majority), but it could be committed by the active participant with
another man, with a female human being (described in that Act as a 'woman' regardless
of her age) or with an animal; and when committed with another human being with his
or her consent both the active and the passive participant in the act were guilty of the
offence.

So far as it deals with buggery committed with a woman or animal, s 12(1) of the 1956
Act remains unchanged; but so far as it deals with buggery committed with another
man its effect has been profoundly modified by the Sexual Offences Act 1967, while para
3 of Sch 2 of the 1956 Act, which lays down imprisonment for life as the maximum
penalty for buggery whatever the circumstances in which and the man with whom
buggery was committed, has been extensively amended by the 1967 Act.

I have referred to s 12(1) of the 1956 Act as being modified rather than as being
amended, for s 1 of the 1967 Act does not bring about the profound changes that it made
in the previously existing law relating to buggery committed with another man, by
altering or adding to the wording of s 12(1) of the 1956 Act. It leaves the wording of that
section unaltered and the section itself unrepealed.

The provisions of the 1967 Act which are most relevant to the instant case are to be
found in ss 1 and 3. Section 1(1), (2), (6) and (7) call for citation in full:

'(1) Notwithstanding any statutory or common law provision, but subject to the
provisions of the next following section, a homosexual act in private shall not be an
offence provided that the parties consent thereto and have attained the age of
twenty-one years.

(2) An Act which would otherwise be treated for the purposes of this Act as being
done in private shall not be so treated if done—(a) when more than two persons
take part or are present; or (b) in a lavatory to which the public have or are permitted
to have access, whether on payment or otherwise . . .

(6) It is hereby declared that where in any proceedings it is charged that a
homosexual act is an offence the prosecutor shall have the burden of proving that
the act was done otherwise than in private or otherwise than with the consent of the
parties or that any of the parties had not attained the age of twenty-one years.

(7) For the purposes of this section a man shall be treated as doing a homosexual
act if, and only if, he commits buggery with another man or commits an act of gross
indecency with another man or is a party to the commission by a man of such an
act.'

It was argued by counsel for the Crown before your Lordships' House that the only
legal effect of sub-s (1) was to leave the crime of buggery committed with a man intact,
but to provide the accused person with a defence if certain conditions were fulfilled, viz
(i) that the act of buggery with a man was committed in private, (ii) that the man with
whom it was committed had attained the age of 21 (whom for brevity I will refer to as
an 'adult') and (iii) that such adult had consented to the act. But this contention as to the
limited effect of sub-s (1) is, in my view, irreconcilable with the provisions of sub-s (6)

which place on the prosecution the burden of proving each one of those three factual ingredients, the existence of any one or more of which converts into a criminal offence conduct which would otherwise not amount to one.

From the fact that the statutory definition of a criminal offence involves the existence of at least one of several necessary factual ingredients which differ from one another, it need not always follow that as many different statutory offences are created as there are necessary factual ingredients that are alternative to one another. The Theft Act 1968 provides several examples of single statutory offences of which there can be alternative factual ingredients, while at common law this has been the case with buggery itself, which could be committed with a man *or* a woman *or* an animal. But, in the case of the 1967 Act, s 3 provides for different maximum punishments according to which one or more of the alternative factual ingredients, the existence of one at least of which is made necessary by s 1(1) in order to amount to an offence, has been established by the prosecution. Indeed, s 3 goes further: by sub-s (1) it provides for different maximum punishments according to whether, in cases where any one or more of the factual ingredients made necessary by s 1(1) exists, the man with whom buggery is committed is over or under the age of 16 years. Section 3(1), so far as is relevant to the instant case, provides:

'(1) The maximum punishment which may be imposed on conviction on indictment of a man for buggery with another man of or over the age of sixteen shall, instead of being imprisonment for life as prescribed by paragraph 3 of Schedule 2 to the Act of 1956, be—(a) imprisonment for a term of ten years except where the other man consented thereto; and (b) in the said excepted case, imprisonment for a term of five years if the accused is of or over the age of twenty-one and the other man is under that age, but otherwise two years . . .'

The corresponding amendments to para 3(a) of Sch 2 to the 1956 Act are made by s 3(3) and (4) of the 1967 Act, as follows:

'(3) References in this section to a person's age, in relation to any offence, are references to his age at the time of the commission of the offence.

(4) Accordingly the said Schedule 2 shall be amended as follows:—(a) in paragraph 3(a) for the word "Life" there shall be substituted the words "If with a boy under the age of sixteen or with a woman or an animal, life; otherwise the relevant punishment prescribed by section 3 of the Sexual Offences Act 1967" . . .'

My Lords, the effect of this is that the 1967 Act creates a number of specific offences for which the maximum punishment prescribed varies on a descending scale from imprisonment for life (the life-offence), through imprisonment for ten years (the ten-year offence), imprisonment for five years (the five-year offence) down to imprisonment for two years (the two-year offence), according to the existence or absence of particular factual ingredients.

Thus buggery with a boy under the age of 16 is a life-offence, whether committed in private or public and with or without the boy's consent. Buggery with a man aged 16 years or over *without his consent* is a ten-year offence whether committed in private or in public; but it becomes a five-year offence if the accused is an adult and the other party is 16 to 20 years old and consented to the act. If the accused himself is not yet an adult the offence with a consenting 16 to 20 year old is reduced to a two-year offence. Buggery committed otherwise than in private between adults both of whom consent to it is a two-year offence on the part of each of them.

My Lords, where it is provided by a statute that an accused person's liability to have inflicted on him a maximum punishment which, if the prosecution is successful in establishing the existence in his case of a particular factual ingredient, is greater than the maximum punishment that could be inflicted on him if the existence of that particular factual ingredient were not established, it seems to me to be plain beyond argument that Parliament has thereby created two distinct offences, whether the statute by which they

a
are created does so by using language which treats them as being different species of a single genus of offence or by using language which treats them as separate offences unrelated to one another. It is the former method that is adopted by the draftsman of ss 1 and 3 of the 1967 Act. A foretaste of this method may be found in s 10 of, and para 14(a) of Sch 2 to, the 1956 Act itself. The statement of offence in the instant case may therefore just pass muster, provided that it is supplemented by adequate particulars of offence which give to the appellant reasonable information which of the particular

b
species of offences falling within the genus buggery was the offence with which he was charged.

This brings me to the particulars of offence in the instant case. Although I have already quoted them, their importance to the disposition of the instant appeal justifies setting them out again here:

c
'THOMAS COURTIE, on the 6th day of February 1982, committed buggery with [the complainant], a male person under the age of twenty one years, namely of the age of nineteen years.'

So the only factual ingredients of the offence committed by the appellant that are alleged are (1) that he committed buggery with another man, (2) that the other man was

d
aged between 16 and 20 years. There is no allegation that the other man did not consent; so the only factual ingredients of the offence that the appellant was charged with having committed were the ingredients necessary for a five-year offence. There was no mention of the additional factual ingredient, absence of consent by the other man, which it would have been necessary for the prosecution to establish in order to convert the five-year offence into the ten-year offence. It follows that the only offence that the prosecution established by the appellant's plea of guilty to this indictment was that he had committed

e
a five-year offence.

Since the sentence passed on the appellant by the judge was three years and thus within the five-year maximum, this appeal would never have come before your Lordships were it not for the way in which the appellant's case was dealt with by the judge after the appellant had pleaded guilty. When counsel for the Crown was recounting to the judge

f
the prosecution's version of the facts of the case against the appellant, which included statements indicating that the other man, so far from consenting voluntarily to being buggered by the appellant, was forced to submit to it by terrifying violence used against him by the appellant, a lengthy argument between counsel for the appellant and counsel for the Crown ensued. Towards the end of this argument counsel for the Crown asked the judge whether he intended to treat the indictment as disclosing only the five-year offence. On the judge's intimating that he did, counsel for the Crown sought leave to

g
add another count to the indictment containing an additional allegation of absence of consent, but this application was refused by the judge. This was a matter that clearly lay within his discretion. Had he acceded to the application and the appellant had pleaded not guilty to the additional count, the charge against him on that count would have had to be tried by a jury and the question whether on the evidence called before them the prosecution had established beyond reasonable doubt that the other man had *not*

h
consented to being buggered by the appellant would be a question for determination by the jury, to the exclusion of the judge.

Having refused the application to add the additional count, however, the judge on the following day announced that he (and the two justices of the peace who were sitting on the Bench with him) would themselves try the question of fact whether or not the other man had consented to what the appellant did to him. This they proceeded to do, and

j
themselves to hear evidence on this issue. It is apparent from the remarks addressed to the appellant by the judge when sentencing him that, as a result of the evidence then adduced before them, the judge and the justices sitting with him had determined that there had been no consent by the other man and that the appellant was being sentenced on the basis that he had indeed committed the ten-year offence.

My Lords, in taking on himself (and the two justices) the function of deciding that there existed in the case against the appellant a necessary factual ingredient of the ten- *a* year offence for which he was sentenced, although the appellant had never admitted the existence of that factual ingredient by his plea of guilty on arraignment to a lesser five-year offence which did not require the existence of that factual ingredient, the judge was acting contrary to the second basic principle of English criminal law to which I referred at the outset of this speech. The question whether the other man had consented or not was one of fact and if, in a trial on indictment, it was disputed it was a question to be *b* determined by the jury on admissible evidence adduced before them and not to be determined by anyone else.

The Court of Appeal took the contrary view to that which I have developed. They certified as the point of law of general public importance involved in their decision:

'Does section 12(1) of the Sexual Offences Act 1956, by reason of the provisions of section 3(1) of the Sexual Offences Act 1967, contain more than one offence?' *c*

To that question for the reasons that I have discussed I would give the answer Yes, although I would substitute for the reference to s 3(1) of the Sexual Offences Act 1967 a reference to ss 1 and 3.

It follows that, having been sentenced on the basis that he had committed a ten-year offence, whereas he should have been sentenced for a five-year offence only, the appellant's *d* appeal against sentence must be allowed. For the sentence of three years' imprisonment pronounced on him from which he has by now been released on parole, there should be substituted a sentence that will result in his period of parole being terminated forthwith together with any liability to be recalled to imprisonment.

I would only add that what went wrong in the instant case could have been avoided in one or other of two ways. It would have been possible under s 6 of the Criminal Law Act *e* 1967 to have included in the particulars of offence in the indictment against the appellant the allegation that the buggery was committed without the complainant's consent thus charging a ten-year offence. The issue of consent would then have been left for the decision by the jury and if they found that absence of consent had not been proved by the prosecution to their satisfaction they could have convicted the appellant of the lesser five-year offence. But what, in my view, is much the more suitable way is to put into *f* separate counts in an indictment charges which include allegations of factual ingredients which attract different maximum punishments, as counsel for the Crown had vainly, although belatedly, sought to do in the instant case. This simplifies the task of the judge when he sums up to the jury, and that of the jury in understanding what alternatives are open to them when they retire to deliberate on their verdict.

g

LORD FRASER OF TULLYBELTON. My Lords I have had the advantage of reading in draft the speech of my noble and learned friend Lord Diplock, and I agree with it. For the reasons given by him I would allow this appeal against sentence, and substitute the sentence proposed by him.

h

LORD SCARMAN. My Lords, I have had the advantage of reading in draft the speech of my noble and learned friend Lord Diplock. I agree with it and for the reasons which he gives I would allow the appeal.

LORD ROSKILL. My Lords, I have had the advantage of reading in draft the speech of my noble and learned friend Lord Diplock. I agree with it and for the reasons he gives *j* I would allow the appeal.

LORD BRIDGE OF HARWICH. My Lords, for the reasons given in the speech of my noble and learned friend Lord Diplock, with which I agree, I would allow this appeal.

a *Appeal allowed. Order of Court of Appeal, Criminal Division of 29 July 1983 set aside and cause remitted to that court with a direction that for the sentence of three years' imprisonment there be substituted a sentence resulting in the appellant's period of parole being terminated forthwith together with any liability to be recalled to imprisonment. Certified question answered by a declaration that s 12(1) of the Sexual Offences Act 1956, by reason of the provisions of ss 1 and 3 of the Sexual Offences Act 1967, contains more than one offence. Costs of appellant and the Crown in House of Lords and Court of Appeal to be paid out of central funds.*

b Solicitors: *Lee Bolton & Lee*, agents for *Max Gold & Co*, Hull (for the appellant); *Sharpe Pritchard & Co*, agents for *Leslie M Bell*, Hull (for the Crown).

Mary Rose Plummer   Barrister.

c # R v Taaffe

HOUSE OF LORDS
LORD FRASER OF TULLYBELTON, LORD SCARMAN, LORD ROSKILL, LORD BRIDGE OF HARWICH AND
LORD BRIGHTMAN
d 7 DECEMBER 1983, 1 MARCH 1984

Customs and excise – Importation of prohibited goods – Knowingly concerned in fraudulent evasion of prohibition or restriction – Knowingly – Importation of drugs – Controlled drug – Defendant carrying controlled drug in mistaken belief that it was currency – Defendant mistakenly believing importation of currency prohibited – Whether defendant 'knowingly' concerned with e *fraudulent evasion of prohibition on importation of controlled drug – Customs and Excise Management Act 1979, s 170(2).*

The respondent smuggled a controlled drug into the United Kingdom intending fraudulently to evade a prohibition on importation, but he mistakenly believed the goods to be currency and not drugs and that the importation of currency was prohibited.
f He was charged under s 170(2)[a] of the Customs and Excise Management Act 1979 with being knowingly concerned in the fraudulent evasion of the prohibition on the importation of a controlled drug imposed by s 3(1) of the Misuse of Drugs Act 1971. At his trial the judge ruled that even on the respondent's version of events he was obliged to direct the jury to convict the respondent because the respondent believed he was importing prohibited goods even though he did not know the precise nature of the
g goods. The respondent was convicted. He appealed against his conviction to the Court of Appeal, which allowed his appeal and quashed his conviction on the ground that the requisite mens rea for an offence under s 170(2) was actual knowledge and since the defendant believed that the substance he was importing was currency, the importation of which was not a criminal offence, his mistake of law did not convert the importation into a criminal offence. The Crown appealed to the House of Lords.

h **Held** – When the state of an accused person's mind and his knowledge were ingredients of the offence with which he was charged, he had to be judged on the facts as he believed them to be. Accordingly, since the respondent mistakenly believed that by clandestinely importing currency he was committing an offence, his mistake of law could not convert his actions into the criminal offence of being 'knowingly concerned' in the importation
j of a controlled drug within s 170(2) of the 1979 Act since he had had no guilty mind in

---

a   Section 170(2), so far as material, provides: '. . . if any person is, in relation to any goods, in any way knowingly concerned in any fraudulent evasion or attempt at evasion . . . (b) of any prohibition or restriction for the time being in force with respect to the goods under or by virtue of any enactment . . . he shall be guilty of an offence under this section and may be detained.'

respect of that offence. It followed therefore that the appeal would be dismissed (see p 748 *h j*, p 749 *e g h* and p 750 *a* to *c*, post).

R v Hussain [1969] 2 All ER 1117 approved.

R v Hennessey (Timothy) (1978) 68 Cr App R 419 doubted.

Decision of the Court of Appeal [1983] 2 All ER 625 affirmed.

Notes

For the requirement of mens rea, see 11 Halsbury's Laws (4th edn) paras 4, 10–11, and for cases on the subject, see 14(1) Digest (Reissue) 17–23, 36–64.

For the importation of controlled drugs and assisting in offences abroad, see 30 Halsbury's Laws (4th edn) para 745 and 11 ibid para 1098, and for cases on the subject, see 15 Digest (Reissue) 1085–1086, 9186–9193.

For the Misuse of Drugs Act 1971, s 3, see 41 Halsbury's Statutes (3rd edn) 882.

For the Customs and Excise Management Act 1979, s 170, see 49 ibid 443.

Cases referred to in opinions

R v Courtie [1984] 1 All ER 740, HL.

R v Hennessey (Timothy) (1978) 68 Cr App R 419, CA.

R v Hussain [1969] 2 All ER 1117, [1969] 2 QB 567, [1969] 3 WLR 134, CA.

Appeal

The Crown appealed with leave of the Appeal Committee of the House of Lords granted on 7 July 1983 against the decision of the Court of Appeal, Criminal Division (Lord Lane CJ, McCowan and Nolan JJ) ([1983] 2 All ER 625, [1983] 1 WLR 627) on 14 April 1983 allowing an appeal by the respondent, Paul Desmond Patrick Taaffe, against his conviction on 18 November 1982 in the Crown Court at Gravesend before Mr Recorder D J Griffiths of being knowingly concerned in the fraudulent evasion contrary to s 170(2) of the Customs and Excise Management Act 1979 of the prohibition on the importation of a controlled drug imposed by s 3(1) of the Misuse of Drugs Act 1971, to which offence the respondent had pleaded guilty following a ruling by the recorder that the agreed facts did not afford a defence to the charge. The Court of Appeal had refused the Crown leave to appeal to the House of Lords but on 29 April 1983 certified, under s 33(2) of the Criminal Appeal Act 1968, that a point of law of general public importance (set out at p 749 *a*, post) was involved in the decision. The facts are set out in the opinion of Lord Scarman.

Anthony Arlidge QC and *Christopher Aylwin* for the Crown.
Lord Rawlinson QC and *Roy Roebuck* for the respondent.

Their Lordships took time for consideration.

1 March. The following opinions were delivered.

LORD FRASER OF TULLYBELTON. My Lords, I have had the advantage of reading in draft the speech of my noble and learned friend Lord Scarman, and I agree with it. For the reasons given by him I would answer the certified question in the negative and dismiss the appeal.

LORD SCARMAN. My Lords, the certified question in this appeal by the Crown from the decision of the Court of Appeal quashing the respondent's conviction in the Crown Court at Gravesend neatly summarises the assumed facts on which the recorder ruled that, even if they were proved to the satisfaction of a jury, the respondent would not be entitled to be acquitted. The question is in these terms:

'When a defendant is charged with an offence, contrary to section 170(2) of the Customs and Excise Management Act 1979, of being knowingly concerned in the fraudulent evasion of the prohibition on the importation of a controlled drug—Does the defendant commit the offence where he: (a) imports prohibited drugs into the United Kingdom; (b) intends fraudulently to evade a prohibition on importation; but (c) mistakenly believes the goods to be money and not drugs; and (d) mistakenly believes that money is the subject of a prohibition against importation.'

In effect, the recorder answered the question in the affirmative and the Court of Appeal in the negative.

There was no trial, for the respondent changed his plea to guilty after the recorder's ruling. On his appeal against conviction, the judgment of the Court of Appeal was delivered by Lord Lane CJ. The judgment recites the history of the case and the assumptions on which a decision had to be taken (see [1983] 2 All ER 625, [1983] 1 WLR 627). It is unnecessary to burden the House with a repetition of what is there so clearly set forth.

Lord Lane CJ construed the subsection under which the respondent was charged as creating an offence not of absolute liability but as one of which an essential ingredient is a guilty mind. To be 'knowingly concerned' meant, in his judgment, knowledge not only of the existence of a smuggling operation but also that the substance being smuggled into the country was one the importation of which was prohibited by statute. The respondent thought he was concerned in a smuggling operation but believed that the substance was currency. The importation of currency is not subject to any prohibition. Lord Lane CJ concluded ([1983] 2 All ER 625 at 628, [1983] 1 WLR 627 at 631):

'He [the respondent] is to be judged against the facts that he believed them to be. Had this indeed been currency and not cannabis, no offence would have been committed.'

Lord Lane CJ went on to ask this question:

'Does it make any difference that the [respondent] thought wrongly that by clandestinely importing currency he was committing an offence?'

The Crown submitted that it did. The court rejected the submission: the respondent's mistake of law could not convert the importation of currency into a criminal offence; and importing currency is what it had to be assumed that the respondent believed he was doing.

My Lords, I find the reasoning of Lord Lane CJ compelling. I agree with his construction of s 170(2) of the 1979 Act; and the principle that a man must be judged on the facts as he believes them to be is an accepted principle of the criminal law when the state of a man's mind and his knowledge are ingredients of the offence with which he is charged.

I also agree with Lord Lane CJ that this case differs on its facts from R v Hussain [1969] 2 All ER 1117, [1969] 2 QB 567 and R v Hennessey (Timothy) (1978) 68 Cr App R 419. While there can be no doubt that R v Hussain was correctly decided, it may be that R v Hennessey will have to be reconsidered in the light of the House's decision today in R v Courtie [1984] 1 All ER 740. For the court in R v Hennessey appears to have paid no regard to the effect of s 26 of the Misuse of Drugs Act 1971 on s 304 of the Customs and Excise Act 1952. According to the principle enunciated in R v Courtie, it would seem likely that these two sections (now consolidated into s 170 of the 1979 Act) have substituted several offences, where the prohibited goods are controlled drugs and other prohibited imports, for the one offence in relation to all prohibited imports which existed before the Misuse of Drugs Act 1971 was enacted. But the point does not arise and I therefore express no concluded opinion whether the decision in R v Hennessey can stand with that of the House in R v Courtie.

For the reasons given by Lord Lane CJ in the Court of Appeal, with whose judgment I fully agree, I would answer the certified question in the negative and dismiss the appeal.

LORD ROSKILL. My Lords, I have had the advantage of reading in draft the speech of my noble and learned friend Lord Scarman. I agree with it and for the reasons he gives I would dismiss the appeal.

LORD BRIDGE OF HARWICH. My Lords, for the reasons given in the speech of my noble and learned friend Lord Scarman, with which I agree, I would dismiss the appeal.

LORD BRIGHTMAN. My Lords, I agree.

Appeal dismissed.

Solicitors: *Solicitor for the Customs and Excise*; *Fanshaw Porter & Hazlehurst*, Birkenhead (for the respondent).

Mary Rose Plummer   Barrister.

Practice Direction

CHANCERY DIVISION

Practice – Chancery Division – Interlocutory applications – Causes or matters outside London.

1. The Practice Direction of 13 October 1983 ([1983] 3 All ER 544, [1983] 1 WLR 1211) extended the existing procedure for interlocutory applications in the northern area to interlocutory applications in cases proceeding in the Birmingham, Bristol and Cardiff registries. As from 1 March 1984 that procedure will extend to Chancery interlocutory applications not only in those registries but also in any other registry in the areas of the circuits within which the Birmingham, Bristol and Cardiff registries are situate. For convenience, the Practice Direction, which in other respects is unchanged, is set out below in its amended form; and as from 1 March 1984 this will replace the Practice Direction of 13 October 1983.

2. Where a Chancery cause or matter is proceeding in a district registry, any interlocutory application to a judge should normally be made or adjourned to the judge exercising Chancery jurisdiction in the area of the circuit within which that registry is situate. This includes appeals from the district registrar, and to these RSC Ord 58, r 4 applies. Any such application issues out of the district registry. This procedure was established in 1972 for Chancery cases in the northern area (see paras 3 to 5 of the Practice Direction of 10 December 1971 ([1972] 1 All ER 103, [1972] 1 WLR 1)), and it applies equally to Chancery cases proceeding in any district registry in the area of the circuits in which the Chancery district registries of Birmingham, Bristol and Cardiff are situate.

3. If it is impracticable or inexpedient to follow this procedure, and the court so directs, or if the parties so agree, the application may instead be made to a Chancery judge in London. In these exceptional cases the application is issued out of room 157 at the Royal Courts of Justice.

4. As from 1 March 1983 the Practice Direction of 13 October 1983 ([1983] 3 All ER 544, [1983] 1 WLR 1211) is hereby revoked.

By direction of the Vice-Chancellor.

16 February 1984

EDMUND HEWARD
Chief Master.

Dimbleby & Sons Ltd v National Union of Journalists

HOUSE OF LORDS

LORD DIPLOCK, LORD FRASER OF TULLYBELTON, LORD SCARMAN, LORD BRIDGE OF HARWICH AND LORD BRANDON OF OAKBROOK

1, 2 FEBRUARY, 1 MARCH 1984

Trade dispute – Acts done in contemplation or furtherance of trade dispute – In contemplation or furtherance of – Secondary action in furtherance of dispute – Validity of secondary action – Contract for supply of goods or services between employer who is party to dispute and employer to whom secondary action relates – Goods or services supplied to associated company of employer who was party to dispute – Union action aimed at disrupting supply of goods or services to associated company – Whether secondary action by union immune from action in tort – Trade Union and Labour Relations Act 1974, s 13(2) – Employment Act 1980, s 17(3).

The appellant journalists' union was engaged in a long-standing trade dispute with a newspaper publishing company (TBF Ltd) whose newspapers were printed by an associated company (TBF Printers) using non-union labour. TBF Ltd and TBF Printers had parallel shareholdings and were controlled by the same parent company. The union had blacked TBF Ltd in the course of the dispute and instructed its members to refuse to work for or to supply copy to TBF Ltd. The respondent company published a number of local newspapers which were printed by an associated company. When publication of those newspapers was stopped by a strike the respondents entered into a contract with TBF Printers to print their newspapers. The appellant union instructed those of its members who were journalists employed by the respondents to refuse to supply copy to the respondents for printing by TBF Printers on the grounds that its associated company, TBF Ltd, had been blacked. The journalists complied with that instruction under the threat of expulsion from the union. The respondents then suspended the journalists and issued a writ seeking injunctions restraining the union from (i) inducing its members to breach their contracts of employment with the respondents and (ii) interfering with the respondents' contracts with their advertisers and with TBF Printers. The respondents also sought interlocutory relief in similar terms. The judge granted the interlocutory injunctions sought. The union appealed, contending, inter alia, that it was immune, under s 13(1)[a] of the Trade Union and Labour Relations Act 1974, from action in tort by the respondents because its actions were taken 'in contemplation or furtherance of a trade dispute' between it and the respondents or between it and TBF Ltd. In particular, the union contended that the dispute concerning the respondents' journalists was a dispute between workers and their employer relating wholly or mainly to terms and conditions of employment and was therefore a 'trade dispute' within s 29(1)(a)[b] of the 1974 Act. The

---

respondents contended that any immunity from action which the union might otherwise
have enjoyed by virtue of s 13(1) had been removed by s 17ᶜ of the Employment Act
1980 because the union's action amounted to unlawful secondary action since the
contract which the union was seeking to disrupt was not a contract for the supply of
goods or services 'between an employer who is a party to the dispute [ie TBF Ltd] and the
employer under the contract of employment to which the secondary action relates [ie
the respondents]', within s 17(3)(a). The Court of Appeal dismissed the appeal. The union
appealed to the House of Lords, contending, inter alia, that the dispute concerning the
respondents' journalists was also a dispute relating to the 'allocation of work or the duties
of employment as between workers or groups of workers' and was therefore a trade
dispute within s 29(1)(c) of the 1974 1974 Act.

Held – The appeal would be dismissed for the following reasons—

(1) The admitted breach of their contracts of employment by the respondents'
journalists in refusing to provide copy for the respondents' newspapers could not in itself
be a trade dispute about the terms and conditions of their employment, within s 29(1)(a)
of the 1974 Act (see p 756 j to p 757 d and p 759 e to h, post).

(2) Having regard to the definitions of 'trade dispute' and 'worker' in s 29(1) and (6) of
the 1974 Act, only a demarcation dispute between workers or groups of workers
employed by the same employer could give rise to a trade dispute over the 'allocation of
work or the duties of employment as between workers or groups of workers' for the
purposes of s 29(1)(c) and therefore it was not open to the union to argue that the
allocation of work as between the respondents' associated company and TBF Printers
could give rise to a trade dispute within s 29(1)(c) (see p 757 e to g and p 759 e to h, post).

(3) Although there was an admitted trade dispute between the union and TBF Ltd
and therefore the union's actions were taken in contemplation or furtherance of a trade
dispute within s 13 of the 1974 Act, the evidence showed that the union's action in
inducing the respondents' journalists to breach their contracts of employment would
amount to interference with the contract between the respondents and TBF Printers
(unless it could be shown that the respondents could withdraw from that contract at any
time) and the contracts between the respondents and their advertisers (which would
undoubtedly be broken if the respondents did not publish their newspapers). The union's
actions therefore amounted to unlawfully interfering with contracts which were not
contracts of employment and therefore s 17 of the 1980 Act applied to remove the
immunity from action to which the union would otherwise have been entitled under
s 13 (see p 757 g to p 758 b and p 759 e to h, post).

(4) Having regard to the fact that under s 17(7) of the 1980 Act (applying s 30(5)ᵈ of
the 1974 Act) TBF Printers were an 'associated employer' of TBF Ltd for the purposes of
s 17(4) (which legalised certain secondary action directed against an associated employer
of an employer who was a party to the dispute), it was not open to the union to argue
that TBF Printers as an associated company of TBF Ltd were, for the purposes of s 17(3),
an employer who was a party to the suit (see p 758 e to p 759 a and e to h, post).

(5) In all the circumstances therefore there were no grounds for concluding that the
unions would succeed in establishing a good defence at the trial and accordingly there

---

c   Section 17, so far as material, provides:
     '(1) Nothing in section 13 of the 1974 Act shall prevent an act from being actionable in tort on
  a ground specified in subsection (1)(a) or (b) of that section in any case where—(a) the contrtact
  concerned is not a contract of employment, and (b) one of the facts relied upon for the purpose of
  establishing liability is that there has been secondary action which is not action satisfying the
  requirements of subsection (3)... below ...
     (3) Secondary action satisfies the requirements of this subsection if—(a) the purpose or principal
  purpose of the secondary action was directly to prevent or disrupt the supply during the dispute of
  goods or services between an employer who is a party to the dispute and the employer under the
  contract of employment to which the secondary action relates ...'
d   Section 30(5), so far as material, is set out at p 758 g, post

a   were no grounds for interfering with the judge's exercise of his discretion to grant the injunctions sought by the respondents (see p 759 *c* to *h*, post).

Decision of the Court of Appeal [1984] 1 All ER 117 affirmed.

Notes

For legal liability for secondary industrial action, see 47 Halsbury's Laws (4th edn) para 575.

b   For the Trade Union and Labour Relations Act 1974, ss 13, 29, 30, see 44 Halsbury's Statutes (3rd edn) 1769, 1779, 1781, and for s 13(1) of that Act (as substituted by the Trade Union and Labour Relations (Amendment) Act 1976, s 3(2)), see 46 ibid 1941.

For the Employment Act 1980, s 17, see 50(2) ibid 2635.

Cases referred to in opinions

c   *American Cyanamid Co v Ethicon Ltd* [1975] 1 All ER 504, [1975] AC 396, [1975] 2 WLR 316, HL.

Hadmor Productions Ltd v Hamilton [1982] 1 All ER 1042, [1983] 1 AC 191, [1982] 2 WLR 322, HL.

Merkur Island Shipping Corp v Laughton [1983] 2 All ER 189, [1983] 2 AC 570, [1983] 2 WLR 778, HL.

d   *NWL Ltd v Woods, NWL Ltd v Nelson* [1979] 3 All ER 614, [1979] 1 WLR 1294, HL.

Salomon v Salomon & Co Ltd [1897] AC 22, [1895–9] All ER Rep 33, HL.

Interlocutory appeal

The National Union of Journalists (the NUJ) appealed against the judgment of the Court of Appeal (Sir John Donaldson MR, Griffiths and Stephen Brown LJJ) ([1984] 1 All ER

e   117, [1984] 1 WLR 67) on 6 December 1983 dismissing the NUJ's appeal against the judgment and order of Sir Neil Lawson sitting as a judge of the High Court on 18 November 1983 whereby he granted the respondents, Dimbleby & Sons Ltd (Dimbleby), interlocutory injunctions (i) restraining the NUJ whether by itself, its officers, servants or agents from issuing instructions to or otherwise encouraging journalists employed by Dimbleby from refusing to assist or participate in the production of copy and material

f   for publication in the Richmond and Twickenham Times, the Brentford, Chiswick and Isleworth Times, the Barnes, Sheen and Mortlake Times and the Teddington and Hampton Times, and (ii) requiring the NUJ to withdraw such instructions or encouragement already given. The facts are set out in the opinion of Lord Diplock.

J Melville Williams QC and *John Hendy* for the NUJ.

g   *Stephen Silber* and *Ali Malek* for Dimbleby.

Their Lordships took time for consideration.

1 March. The following opinions were delivered.

h   **LORD DIPLOCK.** My Lords, this is an appeal against a judgment of the Court of Appeal (Sir John Donaldson MR, Griffiths and Stephen Brown LJJ) ([1984] 1 All ER 117, [1984] 1 WLR 67) refusing to set aside an interlocutory injunction against the appellant trade union, the National Union of Journalists (the NUJ), that had been granted on 18 November 1983 by Sir Neil Lawson sitting as a High Court judge a few months after his retirement from the High Court Bench.

j   The action in which the interlocutory injunction was granted was brought by the respondent company (Dimbleby), who are publishers of several local weekly newspapers (the Dimbleby newspapers) circulating in suburban areas to the west of London. The cause of action alleged in the writ issued against the NUJ was the common law tort of inducing or procuring breaches of or interference with the performance of contracts (the advertising contracts) between Dimbleby and a number of advertisers in the Dimbleby newspapers, and of a contract between Dimbleby and a printing company in Nottingham, TBF (Printers) Ltd (TBF Printers), for the printing of the Dimbleby newspapers by TBF Printers. The method of inducement or procurement alleged to have been adopted by the NUJ was instructing, under threat of disciplinary sanctions, 13 journalists employed by Dimbleby who were members of the NUJ (the NUJ journalists) to break their contracts of employment with Dimbleby by refusing to supply copy and material for publication in the Dimbleby newspapers. The relief claimed in the writ was damages for the common law torts alleged and injunctions to restrain the NUJ from continuing to commit them.

By notice of motion on 25 October 1983 Dimbleby applied for interlocutory injunctions (1) to restrain the NUJ from continuing to instruct or otherwise encourage the NUJ journalists to refuse to assist or participate in the production of copy or other material for publication in the Dimbleby newspapers and (2) to withdraw forthwith any such instructions or encouragement already given.

In the exercise of his discretion the judge granted interlocutory injunctions to this effect on 18 November 1983; and on an appeal from this interlocutory order the exercise of his discretion in this manner was upheld by the Court of Appeal. It was because this was the first action to reach this House in which, as a result of the withdrawal of immunity of trade unions from actions in tort that was effected by ss 15 to 17 of the Employment Act 1982, damages and injunctions, both interlocutory and final, were sought against a trade union itself and not merely personally against one or more of its individual office-holders that an Appeal Committee of this House gave the NUJ leave to appeal here despite the fact that this is only an interlocutory appeal.

My Lords, this case is not one in which there is before this House, or was before the Court of Appeal, any evidence that had not been before the judge when he granted the injunctions; so, as was pointed out in *Hadmor Productions Ltd v Hamilton* [1982] 1 All ER 1042 at 1046, [1983] 1 AC 191 at 220, the function of your Lordships in this appeal, initially at any rate, is one of review only. You may set aside the judge's exercise of his discretion on the ground that it was based on a misunderstanding of the law or of the evidence before him, or because even though no error of law or fact can be identified the judge's decision to grant the injunctions was so aberrant that it must be set aside on the ground that no reasonable judge regardful of his duty to act judicially could have reached it.

The general principles to be applied by a judge in deciding whether or not to grant an interlocutory injunction were laid down by this House in *American Cyanamid Co v Ethicon Ltd* [1975] 1 All ER 504, [1975] AC 396. It is enough to quote a few sentences from the unanimous opinion of the House ([1975] 1 All ER 504 at 510, [1975] AC 396 at 407):

'The use of such expressions as "a probability", "a prima facie case", or "a strong prima facie case" in the context of the exercise of a discretionary power to grant an interlocutory injunction leads to confusion as to the object sought to be achieved by this form of temporary relief. The court no doubt must be satisfied that the claim is not frivolous or vexatious; in other words, that there is a serious question to be tried. It is no part of the court's function at this stage of the litigation to try to resolve conflicts of evidence on affidavit as to facts on which the claims of either part may ultimately depend nor to decide difficult questions of law which call for detailed argument and mature consideration. These are matters to be dealt with at the trial.'

To the first of the sentences from *American Cyanamid v Ethicon* that I have cited, a statutory modification was made by s 17(2) of the Trade Union and Labour Relations Act 1974, which was added to that section by para 6 of Pt III of Sch 16 to the Employment Protection Act 1975. In effect this subsection provides that, in exercising its discretionary power to grant an interlocutory injunction in an action to which it would be a defence that the acts complained of were done in contemplation or furtherance of a trade dispute, the court shall take into consideration the likelihood of such defence succeeding at the trial.

Section 17(2) of the 1974 Act remains in force although the definition of what
constitutes a trade dispute has been much narrowed by s 18 of the Employment Act
1982. It applies to interlocutory injunctions against trade unions now that their
immunity from a suit in tort has been removed by ss 15 to 17 of the 1982 Act; and it
applies in cases in which the plaintiff claims that the acts of the trade union that are
complained of constitute 'secondary action' that is rendered actionable by s 17 of the
Employment Act 1980 notwithstanding that such secondary action is taken in
contemplation or furtherance of a trade dispute.

These changes in the law, which have been made by the 1980 and 1982 Acts, took
place after the decision of this House in *NWL Ltd v Woods* [1979] 3 All ER 614, [1979] 1
WLR 1294, where there is a passage which refers to what were the practical realities in
an action brought by a plaintiff against an individual office-holder of a trade union who
had been acting on his trade union's behalf. These practical realities, I said, were—

'(1) that the real dispute is not between the employer and the nominal defendant
but between the employer and the trade union that is threatening industrial action,
(2) that the threat of "blacking" or other industrial action is being used as a
bargaining counter in negotiations either existing or anticipated to obtain agreement
by the employer to do whatever it is the union requires of him, (3) that it is the
nature of industrial action that it can be promoted effectively only so long as it is
possible to strike while the iron is still hot; once postponed it is unlikely that it can
be revived, and (4) that, in consequence of these three characteristics, the grant or
refusal of an interlocutory injunction generally disposes finally of the action; in
practice actions of this type seldom if ever come to actual trial.'

(See [1979] 3 All ER 614 at 624, [1979] 1 WLR 1294 at 1305.)

As a result of the passing of the 1980 and 1982 Acts, however, what in 1979 were
practical realities no longer apply in 1983 to a suit against a trade union claiming damages
for an injunction to restrain it from a secondary action which is actionable. If the suit
succeeds, the trade union will be liable not only in damages up to a substantial maximum
(£125,000 in the case of the NUJ), but also for costs without any maximum limit, and to
unlimited fines or sequestration of its assets if, by breaching an injunction, it should
commit contempt of court.

In the paragraph of my speech in *NWL Ltd v Woods* which precedes the reference to
the practical realities, I had pointed out that, if the plaintiff continued the action to a
successful conclusion, it was unlikely that damages on the scale that the plaintiff would
have sustained would be likely to prove recoverable from the individual defendant or
defendants who alone, at that time, could be made defendants to the suit. That was what
lay at the root of the 'reality' that I numbered (4). At so early a stage in the action as that
at which an injunction is generally sought (as it was in the instant case), there is no reason
for a judge to exercise his discretion on the assumption that the case will never proceed
to trial and final judgment where the defendant is the trade union itself and not a mere
individual office-holder in it.

The statutory requirement of s 17(2) of the 1974 Act that in exercising his discretion
whether or not to grant an interlocutory injunction the judge shall have regard to the
likelihood of the defendants succeeding in establishing a defence under s 13, s 14(2) or
s 15 of the 1974 Act on the ground that the acts complained of were done in
contemplation of a trade dispute applies, as I have already mentioned, also (since the 1980
Act) to any issue between the plaintiff and the defendant whether the acts complained of
were excluded from the protection of s 13 of the 1974 Act by the provisions of s 17 of
the 1980 Act relating to actionable secondary action. What is meant by 'have regard to
the likelihood' was explained by Lord Fraser in *NWL Ltd v Woods* [1979] 3 All ER 614 at
627, [1979] 1 WLR 1294 at 1309. As respects all other issues raised by way of defence to
the action the criterion to be applied in order to make recourse to the balance of
convenience necessary is the ordinary criterion laid down in *American Cyanamid v Ethicon
Ltd*: is there a serious question to be tried?

My Lords, the facts which had given rise to the issue of the writ and the simultaneous application for an interlocutory injunction in the instant case, as they appeared from the *a* affidavit evidence that had been adduced before the judge, are recounted in the judgment of Griffiths LJ to which reference can be made (see [1984] 1 All ER 117 at 119ff, [1984] 1 WLR 67 at 70ff). To indicate what were the various points taken on behalf of the NUJ in an attempt to persuade your Lordships that the judge had exercised his discretion wrongly, I need do no more than mention the facts disclosed by the affidavit evidence in very summary form.   *b*

The Dimbleby newspapers were printed not by Dimbleby themselves but by an associated company, an arrangement which your Lordships were informed is common in the case of publishers of provincial newspapers. The associated company, Dimbleby Printers Ltd, had been, and apparently still are, engaged in a trade dispute with a powerful trade union that enforces a 'closed shop' in nearly all establishments engaged in the printing trade, the National Graphical Association (the NGA). As a result of this trade *c* dispute there was a strike by members of the NGA employed by Dimbleby Printers Ltd which stopped the Dimbleby newspapers from appearing after 19 August 1983. In order to resume publication of the Dimbleby newspapers, Dimbleby had to find an alternative printer for their newspapers who did not employ members of the NGA. It found one in TBF Printers, which was an associated company of T Bailey Forman Ltd, the publishers of the Nottingham Evening Post, with whom the NUJ has been engaged in a trade *d* dispute which started in 1979 and is still continuing. The two companies have parallel shareholding and are controlled by the same (third) company.

In the first week of October 1983 Dimbleby entered into an oral contract with TBF Printers for the provision by Dimbleby to TBF Printers of copy for the Dimbleby newspapers and the printing of the necessary quantities of those newspapers by TBF Printers. On learning of this the NUJ, which apparently at that stage did not know that *e* TBF Printers was a different company from T Bailey Forman Ltd, with which it was in long-standing dispute, instructed the NUJ journalists employed by Dimbleby to refuse to provide copy to Dimbleby for printing by TBF Printers. With this instruction, given on 10 October 1983, the NUJ journalists complied. They refused to provide copy to their employer, Dimbleby, as their contracts of employment required them to do. As a result of that refusal, which they persisted in, they were suspended from their employment *f* and so remain.

My Lords, since this is only an interlocutory appeal and from the evidence given at the trial there may emerge a picture of the facts of the case different from that which is disclosed by the affidavits and documents that were before the judge, I shall confine myself (1) to mentioning the main grounds on which it was contended by the NUJ that there was a likelihood that its defence that its acts which were the subject of the suit were *g* done in contemplation or furtherance of a trade dispute and that the balance of convenience lay in favour of refusing the injunction sought and (2) to giving a brief indication of the reasons why, in my opinion, on the evidence as it stands at present, none of these contentions is likely to succeed.

I start with the simplest argument advanced on behalf of the NUJ. This was that the NUJ journalists' refusal, on the instructions of the NUJ, to provide copy to Dimbleby *h* constituted in itself a trade dispute between workers and their employer as to the terms and conditions of their employment, within the meaning of s 29(1)(a) of the 1974 Act, as amended by s 18 of the 1982 Act. The simplicity of this argument lies in the fact that it obviates the necessity of entering into the legislative maze created by s 17 of the 1980 Act through which this House was constrained to thread its way in *Merkur Island Shipping Corp v Laughton* [1983] 2 All ER 189, [1983] 2 AC 570. Section 17(2) would exclude from *j* the definition of 'secondary action' any inducement of the NUJ journalists to break or interfere with their contracts of employment by Dimbleby, and this would prevent any resulting breach or interference with the performance of any contract between Dimbleby and a third party from giving rise to an action in tort.

There was, however, in the evidence before the judge no vestige of any claim by the

NUJ itself or by the NUJ journalists that their current contracts of employment by
Dimbleby (and it is only their *current* contracts that can be relevant to this argument)
contained a term entitling them to refuse to comply with instructions given to them by
Dimbleby to provide copy of the kind that they were employed to obtain, if they received
instructions to the contrary from the NUJ. Indeed, it passes beyond the bounds of
credibility that any responsible newspaper proprietor would agree to such a term in
contracts of employment with his journalists. The evidence that was before the judge
makes it perfectly clear that the NUJ journalists acknowledged that by refusing to provide
copy for the Dimbleby newspapers so long as they were to be printed by TBF Printers
they were breaking their contracts, albeit they were doing so reluctantly on the
instructions, enforceable by disciplinary sanctions, that had been given to them by the
NUJ. But for the fact that, contrary to the unanimous opinion of the Court of Appeal,
the judge himself appears to have thought that there was a trade dispute between
Dimbleby and the NUJ as to the terms and conditions of employment by Dimbleby of
the NUJ journalists, I should not myself have thought that on this issue the evidence
before the judge raised any arguable question to be tried; but, having regard (as s 17(2)
of the 1974 Act commands me) to the likelihood of the NUJ's succeeding in this particular
defence at the trial, I agree with the Court of Appeal that the likelihood is minimal.

Your Lordships were also invited to consider an alternative ground on which it was
submitted that there existed a trade dispute between Dimbleby and the NUJ, viz the
'allocation of work or the duties of employment as between workers or groups of workers'
within the meaning of s 29(1)(c) of the 1974 Act, the allocation sought to be relied on
being the allocation between workers employed by Dimbleby Printers Ltd (not Dimbleby
themselves) and workers employed by TBF Printers.

This contention does not appear to have been advanced on behalf of the NUJ before
either the judge or the Court of Appeal. Even if an argument to this effect could have
been advanced with any degree of plausibility before the amendment of s 29 of the 1974
Act by s 18 of the 1982 Act, all vestige of plausibility is removed by the amended
definitions of 'trade dispute' and 'worker' found in sub-ss (1) and (6) respectively. The
effect of sub-s (1) is to redefine 'trade dispute' as a dispute between workers and their
employer wholly 'or mainly related to' one or more of the matters listed in s 29(1).
Subsection (6), so far as relevant, provides '"worker", in relation to a trade dispute with
an employer, means—(a) a worker employed by that employer . . .' So allocation of work
or duties of employment between workers or groups of workers as a possible subject of a
trade dispute is now limited to demarcation issues between workers or groups of workers
employed by the same employer. The likelihood of the NUJ succeeding in this particular
defence is, in my view, nil.

It is not now disputed that in October 1983 when the NUJ journalists refused to
provide copy to be printed by T Bailey Forman Ltd there was still in existence a trade
dispute between the NUJ and T Bailey Forman Ltd. This has the consequence that it
becomes necessary to apply the four-stage process of examination of the facts in evidence
before the judge which, according to the analysis of the section by this House in *Merkur
Island Shipping Corp v Laughton*, is called for by s 17 of the 1980 Act.

On the issues that are involved in this four-stage process, the first contention for the
NUJ was that the evidence before the judge did not disclose that a failure by Dimbleby
to provide copy to be printed by TBF Printers would constitute a breach of any primary
obligation of Dimbleby to TBF Printers under the oral printing contract. It is the fact
that the particulars of the primary obligations of each party under that contract which
are deposed to in the affidavits before the judge are scanty; but, since the avowed
intention of the NUJ was to prevent the printing contract from being performed at all,
the likelihood of the NUJ's succeeding at the trial on its argument on this issue is, in my
view, small unless at the trial further evidence can be adduced to show that the printing
contract was not a synallagmatic contract at all but a mere unilateral or 'if' contract
without any obligations on the part of Dimbleby as to its duration. In any event, there
was sufficient evidence before the judge of contracts between Dimbleby and various

advertisers under which Dimbleby undertook primary obligations to publish advertisements in particular positions in consecutive weekly issues of Dimbleby newspapers *a*
extending long beyond October 1983 which would be broken if the NUJ journalists
refused to provide the necessary copy for such issues. Neither the printing contract nor
the advertising contracts were contracts of employment; and I do not think that the
evidence before the judge discloses any perceptible likelihood of a defence by the NUJ on
this ground turning out to be successful at the trial of the action.

Little time needs to be spent on the argument on behalf of the NUJ, which is purely *b*
one of statutory construction, that TBF Printers, although a separate corporate entity
from T Bailey Forman Ltd, was nevertheless a party to the trade dispute between the NUJ
and the latter company.

My Lords, the reason why English statutory law, and that of all other trading countries,
has long permitted the creation of corporations as artificial persons distinct from their
individual shareholders and from that of any other corporation even though the *c*
shareholders of both corporations are identical is to enable business to be undertaken
with limited financial liability in the event of the business proving to be a failure. The
'corporate veil' in the case of companies incorporated under the Companies Acts is drawn
by statute and it can be pierced by some other statute if such other statute so provides;
but, in view of its raison d'être and its consistent recognition by the courts since *Salomon
v Salomon & Co Ltd* [1897] AC 22, [1895–9] All ER Rep 33, one would expect that any *d*
parliamentary intention to pierce the corporate veil would be expressed in clear and
unequivocal language. I do not wholly exclude the possibility that even in the absence of
express words stating that in specified circumstances one company, although separately
incorporated, is to be treated as sharing the same legal personality of another, a purposive
construction of the statute may nevertheless lead inexorably to the conclusion that such
must have been the intention of Parliament. It was argued for the NUJ in the instant case *e*
that, because TBF Printers and T Bailey Forman Ltd were operating companies with
identical shareholding and were companies of which a single holding company had
control, TBF Printers as well as T Bailey Forman Ltd were 'an employer who is a party to
the dispute' between the NUJ and T Bailey Forman Ltd within the meaning of that
phrase where it is used in s 17(3) of the 1980 Act.

My Lords, this seems to me to be a quite impossible construction to put on the phrase *f*
'an employer who is a party to the dispute' in the context in which it appears in sub-s (3).
This subsection is followed immediately by sub-s (4), which deals with secondary action
against an 'associated employer'. By sub-s (7) the definition of the expression 'associated
employer' in s 30(5) of the 1974 Act is adopted for the purposes of s 17 of the 1980 Act.
That definition provides:

> '. . . any two employers are to be treated as associated if one is a company of which *g*
> the other (directly or indirectly) has control, or if both are companies of which a
> third person (directly or indirectly) has control; and in this Act "associated employer"
> shall be construed accordingly.'

TBF Printers are thus an associated employer of T Bailey Forman Ltd. Section 17(4),
read in conjunction with s 17(1)(b), legalises a particular kind of secondary action if it is *h*
directed against an 'associated employer of an employer who is a party to the dispute',
although it would be unlawful if it were directed against any other person. If one were
to accept the construction of s 17(3) of the 1980 Act for which the NUJ contends, s 17(4)
would be entirely otiose; and, if an associated employer were ipso facto an employer who
is a party to the suit, the phrase in sub-s (4) which I have quoted would make nonsense.

In the passage that I have already cited from *American Cyanamid Co v Ethicon Ltd* it was *j*
said that it was no part of the court's function on an application for an interlocutory
injunction to decide difficult questions of law which call for detailed argument and
mature consideration. The argument that as a matter of statutory construction TBF
Printers as an associated company of T Bailey Forman Ltd were 'an employer who is a
party to the dispute' within the meaning of s 17(3) of the 1980 Act does not raise a

question of law which falls within this category. It is, in my view, one which your
a Lordships are justified in disposing of here and now by saying that it is unsustainable.
The same applies to the argument that Dimbleby were estopped from denying that
the printing contract was entered into with T Bailey Forman Ltd because, as is alleged by
the NUJ, when Mr Dimbleby first told the NUJ that he had made arrangements for the
printing of the Dimbleby newspapers in Nottingham, he left them with the impression
that the contract under which this was to be done was a contract with T Bailey Forman
b Ltd. Any misapprehension under which the NUJ may have originally laboured, however,
as to which company was the party to the printing contract had been removed before the
date when the interlocutory injunctions were granted; so no estoppel, even if there
might have been one previously, could still be relied on then. At the most, estoppel
might go to damages recoverable at the trial for the period before the NUJ discovered the
mistake under which it had been labouring if it proves that the mistake was induced by
c a representation by Dimbleby.

My Lords, finally on the question whether an appellate court would be entitled to
interfere with the way in which the judge exercised his discretion, I have already referred
to what was said on this topic in *Hadmor Productions Ltd v Hamilton*. I cannot discern in
the judge's judgment any misunderstanding of the evidence before him and, although,
like the Court of Appeal, I think the judge misunderstood the law in thinking that there
d was any trade dispute in existence between Dimbleby and the NUJ or the NUJ journalists
at the time when the NUJ is alleged to have induced the journalists to break their current
contracts with Dimbleby, the only consequence of correcting this error of law is to make
the case in favour of the grant of the interlocutory injunctions stronger rather than
weaker.

In my opinion no ground has been shown that would have entitled the Court of
e Appeal or would entitle your Lordships to interfere with the exercise by the judge of his
discretion. I would dismiss the appeal with costs.

LORD FRASER OF TULLYBELTON. My Lords, I have had the advantage of
reading in draft the speech of my noble and learned friend Lord Diplock and I agree with
it. For the reasons given by him, I too would dismiss the appeal.
f

LORD SCARMAN. My Lords, I have had the advantage of reading in draft the speech
delivered by my noble and learned friend Lord Diplock. I agree with it and for the
reasons he gives I would dismiss the appeal with costs.

LORD BRIDGE OF HARWICH. My Lords, for the reasons given in the speech of
g my noble and learned friend Lord Diplock, with which I agree, I would dismiss this
appeal.

LORD BRANDON OF OAKBROOK. My Lords, I have had the advantage of
reading in draft the speech prepared by my noble and learned friend Lord Diplock. I
agree with it and for the reasons which he gives I would dismiss the appeal.
h

Appeal dismissed.

Solicitors: *Bindman & Partners* (for the NUJ); *Cameron Markby* (for Dimbleby).

Mary Rose Plummer   Barrister.

Williams & Glyn's Bank plc v Astro Dinamico Cia Naviera SA and another

HOUSE OF LORDS

LORD FRASER OF TULLYBELTON, LORD EDMUND-DAVIES, LORD BRIDGE OF HARWICH, LORD BRANDON OF OAKBROOK AND LORD TEMPLEMAN

8 FEBRUARY, I MARCH 1984

Practice – Stay of proceedings – Foreign defendant – Jurisdiction – Foreign defendant simultaneously disputing jurisdiction of court and applying for stay of proceedings pending outcome of proceedings abroad – Whether application to stay amounting to submission by defendant to jurisdiction of court – Whether court having jurisdiction to consider application to stay before considering question of jurisdiction to deal with merits – Whether court ought first to consider application to stay if decision on jurisdiction can only be reached by deciding issue which is subject of foreign proceedings.

Where a foreign defendant disputes the jurisdiction of the court and at the same time applies for a stay of proceedings pending the outcome of proceedings abroad, the application to stay the proceedings does not amount to a submission to the jurisdiction of the court. Furthermore, the court has jurisdiction in those circumstances to consider the application to stay the proceedings before considering the question of jurisdiction to deal with the merits, and it ought first to consider the application to stay if a decision on jurisdiction can only be reached by deciding the issue which is the subject of the foreign proceedings (see p 763 d to j, p 764 h j and p 765 d to g, post).

Dictum of Denning LJ in *Re Dulles's Settlement Trusts, Dulles v Vidler* [1951] 2 All ER at 72, approved.

Notes

For stay of proceedings generally, see 37 Halsbury's Laws (4th edn) paras 437–439, and for cases on the subject, see 37(3) Digest (Reissue) 53–56, 3247–3258.

Cases referred to in opinions

Dulles's Settlement Trusts, Re, Dulles v Vidler [1951] 2 All ER 69, [1951] Ch 842, CA.
Pitchers Ltd v Plaza (Queensbury) Ltd [1940] 1 All ER 151, CA.
Rein v Stein (1892) 66 LT 469; affd [1892] 1 QB 753, CA.
Wilkinson v Barking Corp [1948] 1 All ER 564, [1948] 1 KB 721, CA.

Interlocutory appeal

The plaintiffs, Williams & Glyn's Bank plc, appealed, with leave of the Appeal Committee of the House of Lords granted on 28 July 1983, from the judgment of the Court of Appeal (Stephenson and Robert Goff LJJ) ([1983] 2 Lloyd's Rep 485) dated 18 May 1983 allowing the appeal of the respondent defendants, Astro Dinamico Cia Naviera SA and Georgian Shipping Enterprises SA, against part of the order of Bingham J dated 2 November 1982 made pursuant to RSC Ord 12, r 8(5) giving directions for the disposal of the summons dated 1 June 1982 issued by the respondents whereby the judge ordered, inter alia, that the application for a stay of proceedings be heard and ruled on, if necessary, after the court had determined the question of whether it had jurisdiction. The facts are set out in the opinion of Lord Fraser.

Edward Evans-Lombe QC and *John Bertin* for the appellants.
Michael Tugendhat for the respondents.

Their Lordships took time for consideration.   .

1 March. The following opinions were delivered.

LORD FRASER OF TULLYBELTON. My Lords, the appellants, Williams & Glyn's Bank, are suing the respondent companies, which are both registered in Panama but are owned and managed in Greece. The respondents have made an application under RSC Ord 12, r 8 disputing the jurisdiction of the English courts. They have also, simultaneously, applied for a stay of the action on grounds which may be summarised in one or other or both of the brocards forum non conveniens and lis alibi pendens. The respondents say that the issues which will determine the decision on jurisdiction, and to a large extent also the decision on the merits, are already raised in proceedings in the courts in Greece and that it is more appropriate and convenient for the dispute to be decided in Greece. The only question before the House at this stage is whether the English court should consider the question of jurisdiction first or the question of the stay first. Bingham J decided that the first question to be decided was whether the English court has jurisdiction. The Court of Appeal (Stephenson and Robert Goff LJJ) on 18 May 1983 reversed his decision and ordered that the question of whether or not to grant a stay should be decided first. Against that decision the appellants have appealed to your Lordships' House.

The factual background, so far as directly material to the present question, is as follows. In accordance with an agreement dated 12 October 1976 the appellants lent the sum of $US10m to a Greek company called Ulysses Shipping Agency Ltd which was one of their customers. The loan was secured by, inter alia, two guarantees, one from each of the respondent companies. Each guarantee was backed by a mortgage of a ship belonging to the company. The guarantees and mortgages were expressed to be executed on behalf of the respondents by a Mr Nicholas Vlassopulos. His authority to do so was vouched by documents which were expressed to be powers of attorney signed by an officer of each of the respondent companies and extracts of minutes of meetings of directors and shareholders of each of the respondent companies certified by the same officer.

In 1982, as the loan to Ulysses had not been repaid, the appellants sought to enforce their security and they demanded repayment from, inter alia, the respondents. In March 1982 by a writ and points of claim the appellants claimed payment from the respondents. The loan agreement to Ulysses and the guarantees are all expressed to be governed by English law. The mortgages are both expressed to be governed by Greek law. The basis on which jurisdiction over the respondents is asserted is that the respondents have expressly submitted to the jurisdiction of the English courts by a clause in the guarantees. Each guarantee includes a clause (cl 7) to the following effect:

'THIS GUARANTEE shall be governed and construed in all respects in accordance with the laws of England in relation to all claims hereunder. The guarantor irrevocably submits to the jurisdiction of the English courts and any legal process or demand or notice may be made or served on the Guarantor at the registered office in England for the time being of N. & J. Vlassopulos Ltd . . .'

Service of the writ in the action was duly effected at the specified office. In reply the respondents contended that the guarantees and mortgages were invalid on various grounds. One ground was that they were gratuitous alienations of the respondents' property, and as such were ultra vires the respondents' officers and the respondents themselves. Another ground was that the guarantees and mortgages had been executed without any authority whatever, that the power of attorney was invalid and that the meeting at which it was said to have been authorised never took place. In short the defence is that the power of attorney and the minutes were fraudulent. If the latter ground is well-founded the guarantees, including of course cl 7, on which the jurisdiction of the English courts depends, are null and void, and the English courts have no jurisdiction.

As I mentioned earlier the respondents have started proceedings in Greece. The appellants have a branch office there and are therefore subject to the jurisdiction of the

Greek courts. We were informed that criminal proceedings against some of the persons involved had also been started in Greece, but it is not clear whether these proceedings are similar to a private prosecution in England and I do not regard the criminal proceedings as having any bearing on the present question. It appears that the Greek civil proceedings raise questions very similar to those in issue in the English proceedings; in particular they seek declarations that the guarantees are void and of no effect by reason of the fact that they had been entered into without authority and for fraudulent purposes.

In these circumstances the appellants on 24 March 1982 issued their writ in England relying for jurisdiction on cl 7 in each of the guarantees. The respondents wish to dispute the jurisdiction and they accordingly followed the procedure laid down in RSC Ord 12. They acknowledged service of the writ; such acknowledgment does not constitute a waiver of an irregularity in the writ: see Ord 12, r 7. Then they took out a summons giving notice of their intention to dispute the jurisdiction in accordance with Ord 12, r 8(1). Their notice was dated 1 June 1982 and was in two parts. The first part applied for—

'(1) an order setting aside the Writ issued on 24th March 1982 or service of the said Writ on the [respondents], and/or
(2) an order declaring that the said Writ had not been duly served on the [respondents], and/or
(3) such other relief as may be appropriate on the grounds that the contracts purportedly made on behalf of the [respondents] which are the subject of this action were signed without authority and pursuant to a conspiracy to defraud the [respondents] between the signatory thereof Mr Vlassopulos and [the officer who signed the power of attorney].'

The second part of the summons was in the following terms:

'(4) alternatively an order that all further proceedings herein be stayed on the ground that: (i) in November 1981 the [respondents] commenced proceedings in the Court of Piraeus Greece to whose jurisdiction the [appellants] have submitted and that court will determine the issues arising in the [appellants'] claim herein; (ii) the subject matter of the proceedings has little connection with England; (iii) neither of the [respondents] is English nor resident in England; and (iv) it is more appropriate and convenient for the dispute to be decided in Greece.'

The appellants had applied for an order under Ord 14 but this was refused by Staughton J on 12 July 1982. At that stage the matter came before Bingham J on 2 November 1982. He was invited to decide, in the light of the respondents' summons, whether the court ought first to decide the question of a stay or the question of jurisdiction. In the ordinary case there can be little doubt that the question of jurisdiction would fall to be decided first; logically the court must decide whether it has jurisdiction before it can go on to consider any other question in the action. But the peculiarity of this case is that a decision on jurisdiction could only be reached by deciding whether the guarantees were valid or not and thus in effect deciding the issue which is at the heart of the action. A decision on that issue would turn largely on disputed questions of fact which are likely to be strenuously contested, and the investigation of which would inevitably take a considerable time.

The primary contention on behalf of the appellants is that the court has no power to give priority to hearing the respondents' application for a stay over their objection to the jurisdiction. This was said to be the effect of Ord 12, r 8. If that rule were the only source of the court's power in this matter, there would be considerable force in this submission. Rule 8(1), which sets out the various forms of order on this subject for which a defendant may apply, evidently contemplates an order which immediately decides the issue. Paragraph (h) although wide in its terms ('such other relief as may be appropriate') must be read in its context and is not appropriate to include an order to stay. Similarly, r 8(5) seems to contemplate that the court will either dispose of the matter in dispute immediately or give directions for its disposal: for example by making an order allowing cross-examination of witnesses, as the judge did in this case. But the powers of the court are not limited to those derived from r 8. It has also the much wider and more general power conferred, or preserved, by the Supreme Court Act 1981, s 49(3), which provides:

'Nothing in this Act shall affect the power of the Court of Appeal or the High Court to stay any proceedings before it, where it thinks fit to do so, either of its own motion or on the application of any person, whether or not a party to the proceedings.'

That subsection recognises the wide powers of the court, including power to stay proceedings 'of its own motion', but the argument for the appellants involves saying that the court has no power, even of its own motion, to stay an action in which its jurisdiction is disputed. That seems to me an extravagant proposition which could only be made to appear plausible by drawing a technical distinction between staying an action and adjourning it. For example, it can hardly be doubted that the court has power to adjourn a hearing on a question of disputed jurisdiction until a vital witness can be available. If so, I can see no reason in principle why it cannot stay the proceedings to await the outcome of proceedings in Greece. I do not think that a technical distinction can sensibly be drawn between adjourning for the former purpose and staying for the latter purpose. Accordingly I reject this contention.

It was further contended on behalf of the appellants that the respondents either had waived any objection to the jurisdiction because they had taken a step in the action by applying for a stay, or that they would waive any objection if they persisted with their application in priority to disputing the jurisdiction. My Lords, it would surely be quite unrealistic to say that the respondents had waived their objection to the jurisdiction by applying for a stay as an alternative in the very summons in which they applied for an order giving effect to their objection to the jurisdiction. That summons makes it abundantly clear that they are objecting, and the fact that they ask for a decision on their objection to be postponed until the outcome of the Greek proceedings is known is not in any way inconsistent with maintaining their objection. I can see no reason in principle or common sense why the respondents should not be entitled to say: 'We object to the jurisdiction of the English courts, but we ask for the proceedings necessary to decide that and the other issues to be stayed pending the decision of the proceedings in Greece.' The argument to the contrary which was accepted by Bingham J was that, if the court were to entertain the application for a stay, it would be assuming that it had jurisdiction to entertain the action. With the greatest respect to the judge, I agree with Robert Goff LJ in the Court of Appeal that that view is mistaken. The fallacy is in confusing two different kinds of jurisdiction: the first is jurisdiction to decide the action on its merits, and the second is jurisdiction to decide whether the court has jurisdiction of the former kind. The distinction was explained in *Wilkinson v Barking Corp* [1948] 1 All ER 564 at 567, [1948] 1 KB 721 at 725 by Asquith LJ, who said:

'The argument we are here rejecting seems to be based on a confusion between two distinct kinds of jurisdiction. The Supreme Court may by statute lack jurisdiction to deal with a particular matter—in this case, matters including superannuation claims under s 8 of the Act of 1937. It has, however, jurisdiction to decide whether or not it has jurisdiction to deal with such matters, and by entering an unconditional appearance, a litigant submits to the former jurisdiction (which exists), but not to the latter (which does not).'

By entertaining the application for a stay in this case, the court would be assuming (rightly) that it has jurisdiction to decide whether or not it has jurisdiction to deal with the merits, but would not be making any assumption about its jurisdiction to deal with the merits.

Counsel for the appellants referred to some cases as authorities for his proposition that the respondents, by merely applying for a stay, had taken a step in the proceedings which necessarily involved waiving their objection to the jurisdiction. Several of the cases arose under the Arbitration Act 1889, s 4 and they are not helpful in considering the present *a* issue. But in one of the arbitration cases, *Pitchers Ltd v Plaza (Queensbury) Ltd* [1940] 1 All ER 151 at 156, Goddard LJ made an observation on facts, hypothetical in that case, which come very close to the actual facts in the present case. He said:

'For myself, I am not at all satisfied that, if the defendant filed an affidavit in answer to an application for judgment under R.S.C., Ord. 14, although he may raise *b* the arbitration clause, it may not be said that he has taken a step in the action *unless at the same time* he has taken out a summons to stay the action. Of course, if he has taken out a summons to stay the action which comes on (as, in the ordinary course, it would) at the same time as the summons for judgment, and the master refuses the application to stay, and says, "On the plaintiff's summons, I give judgment;" I should say that there could be no doubt that, in appealing against both the refusal of the master to stay and the order giving leave to sign judgment, the defendant is *c* not taking a step in the action. He has done what he can, by taking out the summons to stay, to get the action referred.' (Emphasis mine.)

A case which was concerned with waiver of the right to object to the jurisdiction of the court also contains observations adverse to the appellants' contention. The case is *Rein v Stein* (1892) 66 LT 469 at 471, where Cave J in the Divisional Court said: *d*

'It seems to me that, in order to establish a waiver, you must show that the party alleged to have waived his objection has taken some step which is only necessary or only useful if the objection has been actually waived, or if the objection has never been entertained at all.'

Applying that to the present case, the stay is not *only* useful if the objection to jurisdiction *e* has been waived, because one principal purpose of the stay would be to postpone the inquiry into the questions on which jurisdiction depends until the outcome of the Greek proceedings is known. In *Re Dulles's Settlement Trusts, Dulles v Vidler* [1951] 2 All ER 69, [1951] 1 Ch 842 the question was whether a father, who was an American resident outside England, had submitted to the jurisdiction of the English courts in a dispute about payment of maintenance to his child in England. He had been represented by *f* counsel in the English court, who argued that he was not subject to their jurisdiction. Denning LJ said ([1951] 2 All ER 69 at 72, [1951] 1 Ch 842 at 850):

'I cannot see how anyone can fairly say that a man has voluntarily submitted to the jurisdiction of a court when he has all the time been vigorously protesting that it has no jurisdiction. If he does nothing and lets judgment go against him in default of appearance, he clearly does not submit to the jurisdiction. What difference in *g* principle does it make, if he does not merely do nothing, but actually goes to the court and protests that it has no jurisdiction? I can see no distinction at all.'

That observation seems very apposite in the present case, where the respondents have from the beginning been vigorously protesting that the English courts have no jurisdiction over them. The fact that they have simultaneously asked for a stay is, in the *h* unusual circumstances of this case, in no way inconsistent with that protest.

For these reasons I am of opinion that the Court of Appeal rightly held that the judge had erred in law when he decided that the application for a stay necessarily implied acceptance of the jurisdiction. If that is right, the decision whether to deal first with the question of jurisdiction or with the application for a stay was one for the exercise of the judge's discretion. The judge appears to have regarded himself as exercising a discretion, *j* but with all respect that seems to me to be wrong: if he had been right in his view as to the necessary effect of dealing first with the application for a stay, he was obliged to decide, as he did, to deal with jurisdiction first. Even if his decision was made in the exercise of his discretion, it was made on an erroneous view of the law, and the Court of Appeal therefore had to exercise their own discretion on a correct view of the law. That they have done, and their decision that the application for a stay be considered first cannot in my view be said to be unreasonable. Indeed I consider it was plainly right. It is unnecessary for me to repeat at length the reasoning of Robert Goff LJ who gave the leading judgment in the Court of Appeal. It is enough to say that his view was that a decision on the application for a stay could probably be reached by the court after a hearing lasting not more than one day, whereas a decision on the question of jurisdiction would take much longer and would involve considerable inquiry into the facts. It is relevant to notice that Bingham J had ordered that cross-examination of the deponents to affidavits was to be allowed. Difficult questions of foreign law will also arise, and these may involve both Greek law and Panamanian law as the defendant companies are registered in Panama. Many of the same questions will be raised in the proceedings in Greece. Accordingly there are obvious arguments of convenience and economy in time and money in favour of deferring a decision on jurisdiction until the Greek proceedings have been concluded.

I must emphasise that, in what I said in the last paragraph, I am doing no more than indicating why the application for a stay should be considered first. I am far from indicating any view, even of the most tentative character, whether the decision should be in favour of granting a stay or not. That decision will be for the judge after hearing argument, and nothing that is said in your Lordships' House at the present stage of proceedings should influence his decision in any way.

I would dismiss the appeal and affirm the order of the Court of Appeal.

LORD EDMUND-DAVIES. My Lords, having had the advantage of reading in draft the speech prepared by my noble and learned friend Lord Fraser, I restrict myself to saying that I respectfully agree with it and with the reasons he gives for dismissing this appeal.

LORD BRIDGE OF HARWICH. My Lords, for the reasons given in the speech of my noble and learned friend Lord Fraser, with which I agree, I would dismiss this appeal.

LORD BRANDON OF OAKBROOK. My Lords, I have had the advantage of reading in draft the speech prepared by my noble and learned friend Lord Fraser. I agree with it and for the reasons which he gives I would dismiss the appeal.

LORD TEMPLEMAN. My Lords, for the reasons given by my noble and learned friend Lord Fraser I would dismiss this appeal.

Appeal dismissed.

Solicitors: *Constant & Constant* (for the appellants); *Allen & Overy* (for the respondents).

Mary Rose Plummer   Barrister.

R v Central Criminal Court, ex parte Boulding

QUEEN'S BENCH DIVISION

WATKINS LJ AND TAYLOR J

12 DECEMBER 1983

Crown Court – Binding over – Powers of court – Terms of order – Opportunity to make representations against order – Severity of order – Court binding over convicted defendant for two years on terms that he entered into recognisance in substantial sum – Court not giving defendant's counsel opportunity to make representations against order – Whether natural justice requiring court to give defendant or his counsel opportunity to make representations against order – Whether order invalid as being in terrorem.

The applicant, who held strong views on the manufacture of furs, was convicted by a magistrates' court of using insulting words and behaviour outside the premises of a fur-manufacturing company. The magistrates fined the applicant £10 and ordered him to pay the costs of the hearing. The applicant appealed against the conviction to the Crown Court, which, on rehearing the case, convicted the applicant and, in addition to upholding the magistrates' fine of £10 and the order for costs, imposed an order binding over the applicant for two years to keep the peace and be of good behaviour on terms that he entered into a recognisance in the sum of £500 with the alternative of three months' imprisonment. The order was imposed with the applicant's consent but without any enquiry into his means and without giving his counsel an opportunity to make representations against it. The applicant applied for an order of certiorari to quash the binding-over order on the ground that it was made in excess of the court's jurisdiction, was unduly harsh and oppressive, and was contrary to the rules of natural justice because the applicant's counsel had not been given an opportunity to make representations before the order was imposed.

Held – Where the Crown Court intended to impose a binding-over order on a convicted defendant requiring him to enter into a recognisance in a substantial sum, natural justice required the court to give the defendant or his legal representative an opportunity to make representations against the imposition of such an order, and also required the court to inquire into the defendant's means before imposing such an order. That was so irrespective of the seriousness of the defendant's conduct and the possibility of repetition of the conduct. Furthermore, a binding-over order ought not to be in such terms that it acted in terrorem of the defendant by, for example, effectively inhibiting his right to free speech within the law. Since the Crown Court had not given the applicant's counsel an opportunity to make representations and had not inquired into the applicant's means before imposing the binding-over order, the court had acted in breach of the rules of natural justice and certiorari would be ordered to quash the order (see p 769 *d* to *j*, post).

Dictum of Lord Widgery CJ in *R v Woking Justices, ex p Gossage* [1973] 2 All ER at 623 considered.

Notes

For recognisances to keep the peace, see 11 Halsbury's Laws (4th edn) paras 521–522.

Cases referred to in judgment

R v Woking Justices, ex p Gossage [1973] 2 All ER 621, [1973] QB 448, [1973] 2 WLR 529, DC.

Sheldon v Bromfield Justices [1964] 2 All ER 131, [1964] 2 QB 573, [1964] 2 WLR 1066, DC.

Cases also cited

a   *Lansbury v Riley* [1914] 3 KB 229, [1911–13] All ER Rep 1059, DC.
Metropolitan Properties Co (FGC) Ltd v Lannon [1968] 3 All ER 304, [1969] 1 QB 577, CA.
R v Crown Court at St Albans, ex p Cinnamond [1981] 1 All ER 802, [1981] QB 480, DC.
R v Sharp, R v Johnson [1957] 1 All ER 577, [1957] 1 QB 522, CCA.
Veater v G [1981] 2 All ER 304, [1981] 1 WLR 567, DC.

b   **Application for judicial review**

Stephen Boulding applied, with leave of Mann J granted on 3 May 1983, for an order of certiorari to bring up and quash the order made by his Honour Judge Buzzard and two magistrates at the Central Criminal Court on 19 January 1983 binding the applicant over for two years to keep the peace in the sum of £500. The facts are set out in the judgment of Watkins LJ.

c   *Ann Wallace* for the applicant.
John Laws for the respondent.

WATKINS LJ. Stephen Boulding is a bus driver employed by London Transport. He
d   is a married man of 34 years of age. He moves for judicial review of an order of binding over imposed on him at the Central Criminal Court.

The circumstances which brought him to that situation were that at the Mansion House, before the City magistrates, he was convicted of using insulting words and behaviour contrary to s 35(13) of the City of London Police Act 1839, as amended. He was thereupon fined the sum of £10 and ordered to pay the costs of the hearing. From
e   that conviction he appealed to the Crown Court. On 19 January 1983 he faced his Honour Judge Buzzard and two magistrates, who conducted (as is usual on an appeal from magistrates) a rehearing of the case.

The applicant is a man with very strong views about the manufacture of furs. He makes those views plain to those who are engaged in that commercial enterprise. On 16 July 1982 he was doing that when police officers felt it necessary to take him into custody.
f   The evidence which the police officers gave to the magistrates and subsequently to the Central Criminal Court can be summarised in this way. The applicant went to the premises of the Hudson's Bay fur company and shouted at persons employed there: 'Murderers; fur trade out.' He made threats. He stated that their trade was 'evil', and that they should not be in the fur trade. As a result of that manifestation of his views, a large crowd assembled, most of whom were engaged in the fur trade and who had become
g   very angry at what he was saying. They jeered at him. Some raised their fists. He was asked to be quiet by the police officers. He refused and said: 'You've got no right; you're the bastard who'll end up in court.'

When the applicant was in the police car, being taken to the police station, he became very excited and said to the police officers: 'We have only just started, sunshine; there's 20 more like me.' They told him to calm down, but his only response to that was: 'You're
h   as bad as those murderers: you support them.'

In giving evidence on his own behalf, he admitted that he had used the word 'murderers' to two employees of the Hudson's Bay company. He admitted that he used a megaphone in order to make his views more widely known.

He was again convicted at the Central Criminal Court where the judge took a rather more severe view than the magistrates at the Mansion House of his conduct. He and the
j   magistrates sitting with him not only kept in being the fine imposed by the City magistrates and the order for costs made below, but ordered him to pay the costs of the appeal and in addition, without inviting any comment whatsoever beforehand from counsel who was, on that occasion, appearing for the applicant, they bound him over for two years to keep the peace and be of good behaviour, and ordered him to enter into a recognisance in the sum of £500, with the alternative of three months' imprisonment.

The applicant, on being asked to do so, consented to being bound over. Whether he consented to that in respect of all those terms, or merely to being bound over, the material before us does not reveal. But I am prepared to assume that he was fully appraised of the terms before he gave his consent. At all events, he signed the necessary recognisance after being bound over and before leaving the court.

The grounds in support of the motion for judicial review relate exclusively to the binding-over order. They are contained in a document the contents of which I summarise as follows. It is contended that the binding-over order was in excess of the court's jurisdiction. Alternatively it was unduly harsh and oppressive. It was in any event, it is said, an abuse of the process of the court and, therefore, an invalid order. It is further said that the rules of natural justice were not obeyed, seeing that it was made without providing an opportunity for representations to be made against the imposition of it on the applicant's behalf. Finally, it is contended by counsel for the applicant that there was an appearance of bias in the manner in which the order was imposed.

Counsel for the applicant derives support for that last contention from words used by the judge when he said:

> 'Democracy is a delicate plant which has flowered with difficulty at different times and places in the history of mankind. Civilisation can exist without democracy and has done for most of recorded history, but it cannot exist without the rule of law. Some minorities believe that they have a divine right to use lawful and unlawful means to impose what they believe is right. In that respect they are no different from the adherents of Hitler. We are here to see that the law is obeyed whatever the motives of those who disobey it.'

It is convenient, I think, to dispose of that contention by expressing my view of it at this stage. The judge may have been wiser and spoken a little more temperately if he had avoided any reference to Hitler. But that apart, I can see nothing whatsoever objectionable in what he said. I cannot think that any right-thinking person, sitting in court, listening to the judge, could sensibly have come to the conclusion that he was in any way biased against the applicant.

At the heart, as I see it, of the motion to review the decision to bind over the applicant, is this. It is wrong, so it is submitted, for the court to bind over a person, albeit he is a convicted person, without first of all giving him an opportunity to make representations about the intention of the court to make such an order. Furthermore, it is wrong for no opportunity to be given to a defendant, or to the person representing him, to make submissions as to the size of the recognisance which the court is minded to cause the defendant to enter into. This is in relation not only to the size of the recognisance in financial terms, but also to the length of the term of imprisonment declared.

In this connection we have been referred to what was said by Lord Widgery CJ in *R v Woking Justices, ex p Gossage* [1973] 2 All ER 621, [1973] QB 448. That was a case in which an applicant was bound over to keep the peace for 24 months in his own recognisance of £100. It is unnecessary to say anything about the facts. I turn immediately to the concluding observations of Lord Widgery CJ ([1973] 2 All ER 621 at 623, [1973] QB 448 at 451):

> 'I think from the extracts from Lord Parker CJ's judgment [in *Sheldon v Bromfield Justices* [1964] 2 All ER 131 at 133, 134, [1964] 2 QB 573 at 577, 578] that I have read, Lord Parker CJ would have taken the same view; but, be that as it may, it seems to me to be putting it far too high in the case of an acquitted defendant to say that it is a breach of the rules of natural justice not to give him an indication of the prospective binding-over before the binding-over is imposed. That is not to say that it would not be wise, and indeed courteous in these cases for justices to give such a warning; there certainly would be absolutely no harm in a case like the present if the justices, returning to court, had announced they were going to acquit, but had immediately said "We are however contemplating a binding-over; what have you

got to say?" I think it would be at least courteous and perhaps wise that that should
be done, but I am unable to elevate the principle to the height at which it can be
said that a failure to give such a warning is a breach of the rules of natural justice.'

It must be noted that Lord Widgery CJ was there referring to a situation in which it
was proposed to bind over an acquitted defendant. Counsel for the respondent, for whose
valuable submissions I wish to express gratitude, contends that, in the case of a convicted
defendant, the observations of Lord Widgery CJ would have very much greater force and
thus bind this court.

I appreciate, of course, that Lord Widgery CJ firmly declined to acknowledge that a
failure by a court to give a defendant an opportunity to be heard prior to the making of
a binding-over order constituted a breach of the rules of natural justice. But I do not
regard him as having said that there are no circumstances in which a part of a binding-
over order can be said to be so severe that the court is bound in justice, before imposing
that part of the order on a defendant, to give him the opportunity to make representations
about that part.

The present case is a very good example, so it seems to me, of a case in which a
defendant's means and other personal circumstances should have been inquired into and
representations allowed in respect of them. Without such an inquiry and further
assistance from him, or his counsel, I cannot see how the court could alight on a proper,
just and suitable sum of recognisance. The question is therefore not whether there was a
failure to act with due caution and to be sensitive to the need to allow the defendant to
be heard but whether that failure amounts to a breach of the rules of natural justice.

In my judgment it does. It is one thing to impose a small or trivial sum of money as a
recognisance without inquiring and so on; it is quite another to impose, without
inquiring into the means of a defendant, a relatively large sum. To impose such a sum
might work a very great injustice on a defendant, no matter how serious the conduct
which has brought about his conviction is regarded and the possibility of his repeating
that conduct in the future. A binding over must not be in such terms contemplated as
effectively to inhibit a convicted person from exercising his right to free speech within
the law. In other words it must not appear to be in terrorem.

This court has been given information which the court below had not, namely
information about the means of the applicant. He was, and very likely still is, a bus
driver. At that time, he earned £140 gross per week. His wife was working, earning
£130 gross per week, but she either has or is soon to give up work because of pregnancy.
They had between them £400 in savings. If those facts had been known to the court
below, I question very seriously whether it would have imposed so high a figure as £500
as the recognisance that the applicant was called on to enter into.

In my judgment, although a court may say, without giving a defendant the
opportunity to be heard on the matter: 'We intend to bind you over'; what it may not
do, unless it is going to impose as a recognisance a trivial sum, is to impose a sum which
is markedly larger than that in comparative terms without looking at the means of the
defendant and giving him, or his counsel or solicitor, an opportunity for making
representations.

In that respect, I think the rules of natural justice do demand that the court conducts
itself as I have indicated. Since the court here did not do that, I would allow this
application and quash the order.

TAYLOR J. I agree.

Application granted. Binding-over order quashed.

Solicitors: *Mackenzie Patten & Co*, Southall (for the applicant); *Treasury Solicitor*.

April Weiss   Barrister.

R v Newcastle-upon-Tyne Justices, ex parte Hindle
Hindle v Thynne

QUEEN'S BENCH DIVISION

ROBERT GOFF LJ AND FORBES J

11, 12 JULY, 8 AUGUST 1983

Road traffic – Driving while unfit to drive through drink or drugs – Burden of proof – Consumption of alcohol after ceasing to drive but before breath test – Evidence before court that defendant had consumed alcohol after ceasing to drive but before breath test – Whether prosecution under burden to negative such evidence – Road Traffic Act 1972, s 6.

Magistrates – Information – Abuse of process – Two informations arising out of same incident – Second information laid in general terms – Second information capable of being consistent or inconsistent with first information – Prosecution failing to give further particulars of second information – Whether second information should be dismissed as abuse of process of court.

On 17 March 1982 a police constable found the defendant's unattended car after it had collided with a wall. Shortly afterwards the defendant arrived and admitted having been the driver of the car. The constable, who subsequently gave evidence that the defendant was dishevelled and smelt of alcohol, asked him to provide a specimen of breath. The defendant told the constable that he had had a drink since the accident and that it was only two minutes since he had had that drink. The constable waited a further 20 minutes and then took a specimen of the defendant's breath which proved positive. The defendant was arrested and taken to a police station, where he provided a specimen of blood, subsequent analysis of which showed the defendant to have had a blood-alcohol concentration above the prescribed limit. During the course of questioning at the police station, the defendant denied having had the drink after the accident in order to frustrate the breath test procedure. On 30 June a summons was issued alleging that the defendant had driven with excess alcohol in his blood contrary to s 6(1)[a] of the Road Traffic Act 1972 (the breathalyser summons). On 17 August the defendant appeared before justices and pleaded not guilty. The matter was adjourned for hearing on 28 September, which was 11 days after the expiry of the six-month period permitted by s 127(1)[b] of the Magistrates' Courts Act 1980. On 24 August a summons was issued alleging that the defendant had obstructed a police officer in the execution of his duty, but no particulars of the offence charged were given. Since it appeared that the breathalyser summons proceeded on the basis that the defendant had not consumed alcohol after ceasing to drive, and therefore implied that he had lied to the constable when he said that he had done so, the defendant's solicitor sought further particulars to discover whether the obstruction summons proceeded on the basis that the defendant had lied to the constable (which would have been consistent with the breathalyser summons) or on the basis that the defendant had deliberately consumed alcohol after the accident in order to frustrate the breathalyser test (which would have been inconsistent with the breathalyser

---

a   Section 6(1) provides: 'If a person drives or attempts to drive a motor vehicle on a road or other public place, having consumed alcohol in such a quantity that the proportion thereof in his blood, as ascertained from a laboratory test for which he subsequently provides a specimen under section 9 of this Act, exceeds the prescribed limit at the time he provides the specimen, he shall be guilty of an offence.'

b   Section 127(1), so far as material, provides: 'Except as otherwise expressly provided . . . a magistrates' court shall not try an information or hear a complaint unless the information was laid, or the complaint made, within 6 months from the time when the offence was committed, or the matter of complaint arose.'

summons). The prosecution did not provide any further particulars. When the defendant

a appeared before the justices on 28 September he pleaded not guilty to the obstruction summons and the hearing of both summonses was adjourned to 5 November, and by consent it was arranged that, in order to avoid prejudice to the defendant, the two summonses would be heard by differently constituted benches of magistrates. On 5 November the justices acceded to a prosecution application to adjourn the obstruction summons until after the hearing of the breathalyser summons and rejected a defence

b application to dismiss the obstruction summons as an abuse of the process of the court. The hearing of the breathalyser summons then proceeded before another bench of magistrates. The hearing was not completed on that day and was adjourned to 17 January 1983, when the justices accepted a submission by the defendant that there was no case to answer, on the grounds that there was evidence before the court that the defendant had consumed alcohol after ceasing to drive and before giving a specimen of breath, which rendered the subsequent breath test inadmissible, and that the prosecution had failed to

c discharge the burden of proving the admissibility of the blood test and accordingly had failed to establish a prima facie case. The justices dismissed the breathalyser summons. The prosecution appealed by way of case stated. The defendant sought judicial review of the decision of the justices on 5 November 1982 not to dismiss the obstruction summons as an abuse of the process of the court.

d

Held – (1) Where, on a charge of driving a motor vehicle with a blood-alcohol concentration above the prescribed limit contrary to s 6(1) of the 1972 Act, evidence was placed before the court to show that the accused had consumed alcohol after ceasing to drive but before taking the test, the prosecution had then to discharge the burden which rested on them to negative that fact. In such circumstances if the court concluded that

e the accused might have so consumed alcohol it was bound to acquit him. On the facts, the only matters on which the justices could have relied as constituting such evidence were (a) the defendant's statement to the police constable that he had had a drink after the accident, which was an entirely self-serving statement, (b) the questions asked by the police constable of the defendant and the answers thereto, and (c) the justices' conclusion that the defendant had had both the time and the opportunity to consume alcohol after

f the accident. None of those matters, however, could constitute sufficient evidence raising the issue whether the defendant had consumed alcohol after ceasing to drive, and accordingly there was no basis for the justices' acceptance of the defendant's submission that the prosecution had failed to establish their case. In all the circumstances, however, no order would be made on the case stated (see p 776 *f* to *h*, p 777 *e* to *j* and p 778 *c* to *j*, post); dicta of Lord Goddard CJ in *R v Lobell* [1957] 1 All ER at 736, of Lord Goddard CJ in *R v McPherson* (1957) 41 Cr App R at 215–216, *Practice Note* [1962] 1 All ER 448 and

g dictum of Lord Parker CJ in *R v Durrant* [1969] 3 All ER at 1359 applied.

(2) Because the information was laid and the obstruction summons issued in the general terms that the defendant had wilfully obstructed a constable in the execution of his duty, which charge was in the circumstances ambiguous in that it could be read as referring to one or other of two inconsistent offences, and because the prosecution had

h failed to give the requisite particulars when asked to do so, the obstruction summons was prejudicial and embarrassing to the defendant, and if permitted would have allowed the prosecution to postpone, until after the expiry of the six-month limitation period laid down by s 127(1) of the 1980 Act, their decision whether to prosecute for a particular offence. If the decision had been properly taken before the expiry of the six-month period the prosecution would have had no difficulty in providing the defendant with the

j particulars he had requested. Furthermore, the defendant had suffered prejudice in consequence of the manner in which the prosecution had proceeded, because he was deprived of the opportunity of making any further submission to the court as to the manner in which the two summonses should be proceeded with. If the prosecution had stated that their case was that the defendant had lied to the police, the defendant could have asked for both summonses, being consistent, to be dealt with by the same bench of magistrates, whereas, if the prosecution's case was that the defendant had deliberately

consumed alcohol after the accident to frustrate the breath test procedure, the defendant
could have objected to the prosecution proceeding with two inconsistent summonses. It   *a*
followed that, since the hearing of the summons under s 6(1) of the 1972 Act had already
commenced, the prejudice to the defendant was irretrievable, and the course pursued by
the prosecution in respect of the summons alleging obstruction amounted to an abuse of
the process of the court. An order of prohibition would therefore issue, prohibiting the
justices from proceeding further with the hearing of the obstruction summons (see p 781
d to *j* and p 782 *a* to *j*, post); *R v Brentford Justices, ex p Wong* [1981] 1 All ER 884 applied;   *b*
R v Dolan (1975) 62 Cr App R 36 and *R v Smythe* (1980) 72 Cr App R 8 distinguished.

Notes

For driving a vehicle with excess alcohol concentration and procedure and evidence on
offences relating to drink, see 40 Halsbury's Laws (4th edn) paras 486–496.

For the duty of a magistrates' court to determine whether there is a case to answer, see   *c*
29 ibid para 363.

For the giving of sufficient particulars in an information, see ibid para 319, and for
cases on the subject, see 33 Digest (Reissue) 119–121, 776–783.

For the Road Traffic Act 1972, s 6, see 42 Halsbury's Statutes (3rd edn) 1648.

For the Magistrates' Courts Act 1980, s 127, see 50(2) ibid 1552.

As from 6 May 1983 s 6 of the 1972 Act was substituted by s 25(3) of and Sch 8 to the   *d*
Transport Act 1981.

Cases referred to in judgment

Practice Note [1962] 1 All ER 448, [1962] 1 WLR 227, DC.
R v Alyson [1976] RTR 15, CA.
R v Brentford Justices, ex p Wong [1981] 1 All ER 884, [1981] QB 445, [1981] 2 WLR 203,   *e*
    DC.
R v Dolan (1975) 62 Cr App R 36, CA.
R v Durrant [1969] 3 All ER 1357, [1970] 1 WLR 29, CA.
R v Lobell [1957] 1 All ER 734, [1957] 1 QB 547, [1957] 2 WLR 524, CCA.
R v McPherson (1957) 41 Cr App R 213, CA.   *f*
R v Smythe (1980) 72 Cr App R 8, CA.
Rowlands v Hamilton [1971] 1 All ER 1089, [1971] 1 WLR 647, HL.
Woolmington v DPP [1935] AC 462, [1935] All ER Rep 1, HL.

Cases also cited

R v Lennard [1973] 2 All ER 831, [1973] 1 WLR 483, CA.   *g*
R v St Albans Crown Court, ex p Cinnamond [1981] 1 All ER 802, [1981] QB 480, DC.
R v Tottenham Justices, ex p Joshi [1982] 2 All ER 507, [1982] 1 WLR 631, DC.
Rendell v Hooper [1970] 2 All ER 72, [1970] 1 WLR 747, DC.
Thornley v Clegg [1982] RTR 405, DC.

Applications for judicial review and case stated   *h*

R v Newcastle-upon-Tyne Justices, ex p Hindle

Clive Miller Hindle applied with the leave of Stephen Brown J granted on 24 January
1983, for (i) an order of prohibition prohibiting the justices sitting at Newcastle-upon-
Tyne from hearing a trial on a summons issued on 24 August 1982 following an
information laid on the same date alleging that on 17 March 1982 the applicant wilfully   *j*
obstructed a constable of the Northumbria Police in the execution of his duty and (ii) an
order of mandamus directing the justices to dismiss the summons as an abuse of the
process of the court and as being grossly prejudicial to the applicant. The applicant also
applied, with the leave of Mann J granted on 22 April 1983, for an order of mandamus
directing the Newcastle-upon-Tyne justices sitting at Gosforth on 17 January 1982 to
make an order for costs against the prosecution and in favour of the applicant in respect

of the dismissal by the justices of a summons alleging an offence under s 6 of the Road
Traffic Act 1972 on a finding that there was no case to answer. The facts are set out in the
judgment of the court.

Thynne v Hindle

Chief Superintendent Ian Thynne of the Northumbria Police appealed by way of a case
stated by the justices for the petty sessional division of the city of Newcastle-upon-Tyne
on 17 January 1982 in respect of their adjudication as a magistrates' court sitting at
Gosforth whereby, on the hearing of a summons preferred by the appellant against Clive
Miller Hindle that on 17 March 1982 he drove a motor vehicle having consumed alcohol
in such quantity that the proportion of alcohol in his blood exceeded the prescribed limit
contrary to s 6 of the Road Traffic Act 1972, the justices accepted a submission by the
defendant that the prosecution had failed to discharge the burden of proving the
admissibility of a blood test and, accordingly, failed to establish a prima facie case. The
facts are set out in the judgment of the court.

Patrick Cosgrove for Mr Hindle.
Duncan Matheson for the prosecution.

Cur adv vult

8 August. The following judgment of the court was delivered.

ROBERT GOFF LJ. There are before the court three related matters, which arise out
of two decisions of different benches of justices sitting at Newcastle-upon-Tyne. The first
is an appeal by way of case stated, the appellant being Chief Superintendent Thynne and
the respondent Clive Miller Hindle, who is a practising solicitor. This appeal is against a
decision of one bench of justices to dismiss an information preferred against the
respondent by the appellant, charging him with the offence of driving a motor vehicle
having consumed alcohol in such quantity that the proportion in his blood, as ascertained
from a laboratory test for which he provided a specimen, exceeded the prescribed limit,
contrary to s 6 of the Road Traffic Act 1972. The justices dismissed the summons when
they accepted a submission made by counsel for the respondent at the close of the
prosecution case that there was no case to answer.

The other two matters are applications for judicial review, brought by leave of the
single judge. The first of these is directed towards an order of the same bench of
magistrates under which, following the dismissal of the above information, they declined
to make any order of costs against the prosecution in favour of the defendant, Mr Hindle.
He now applies for an order of mandamus requiring the justices to make such an order.

The second is directed to an order by a different bench of magistrates under which
they refused to dismiss another information laid against Mr Hindle, charging him with
obstructing a police officer in the execution of his duty. This information, as will appear
later, arose out of the same events as the first. The justices were asked to dismiss the
second information as being an abuse of the process of the court. They declined to do so
and the applicant, Mr Hindle, now seeks an order of mandamus requiring the justices to
dismiss the summons on those grounds.

The events in question occurred in Newcastle-upon-Tyne on the evening of 17 March
1982. A police officer, Pc Lamb, found a BMW car (which in fact belonged to Mr Hindle)
unattended, having come into collision with a brick wall. Shortly afterwards, Mr Hindle
arrived at the scene of the accident. He admitted being the driver of the car. The evidence
of Pc Lamb was that Mr Hindle was dishevelled and smelt of alcohol; and, when the
officer said that he wished him to provide a specimen of breath, Mr Hindle replied: 'I
have just had a drink down the road when I contacted my wife, and had it not been for
the fact that I wanted to collect some files in my car I would not have returned.'

In response to an inquiry by the officer, Mr Hindle said that it had been about two
minutes since his last drink. The officer waited a further 20 minutes and then took a

specimen of his breath which proved positive. Later that evening the remainder of the breathalyser procedure was followed, the specimens again proved positive, subsequent analysis showing that a blood specimen contained 101 mg of alcohol in 100 ml of blood. At the police station a series of questions was addressed to Mr Hindle by Pc Lamb. A written copy of these questions and the answers given by Mr Hindle was before the justices.

They culminated in the following exchange:

'Q. Will you tell me briefly what you drank at the pub? A. Yes. I had a double brandy before the phone call and a brandy after the phone call.

Q. Do you wish to make a statement under caution regarding this matter? A. I'm happy with the answers I have given you.

Q. Can I just ask you why you took a drink when you knew that you may be required to provide a specimen of breath after having been involved in an accident? A. Well, to be quite frank, as you may have realised when you spoke to me it didn't even occur to me that you would wish to take a specimen of breath. If it had occurred to me I must be honest and state that I'm not sure that I would have returned to the car.

Q. Had you had a drink prior to the accident? A. I'd had very little to drink prior to the accident.

Q. I put it to you that you had a drink after the accident in an effort to conceal the fact that you had a drink prior to the accident. A. That's absolutely untrue. I could have gone home or anywhere else quite easily if I'd wanted to conceal anything.'

The justices concluded that the officer satisfied himself that Mr Hindle had consumed alcohol since the accident.

On 30 June 1982 a summons was issued alleging that Mr Hindle had driven with excess alcohol in his blood. On 17 August Mr Hindle appeared before the justices. He pleaded not guilty to the charge, and the matter was put back for hearing on 28 September. It is to be observed that 28 September was 11 days after the expiry of six months from the date of the offence in question, viz 17 March 1982.

On 24 August 1982 a summons was issued alleging that Mr Hindle had obstructed a police officer in the execution of his duty. On 28 September the matter came on before the justices. Mr Hindle applied for it to be transferred to a different bench of magistrates on the ground that, as a solicitor in local practice, he would be known to the justices. His application was refused. Mr Hindle pleaded not guilty to the obstruction summons. The hearing of both summonses was put back to 5 November. By consent it was arranged that (to avoid prejudice to Mr Hindle) the two summonses would be heard by differently constituted benches of magistrates.

On 5 November 1982 the prosecution applied for the obstruction summons to be adjourned until after the hearing of the breathalyser summons. The defence opposed this application, and in their turn applied for an order that the obstruction summons be dismissed as an abuse of the process of the court. The bench of magistrates dealing with that matter acceded to the prosecution's application, and rejected the defence application. This latter decision is the subject matter of Mr Hindle's second application for judicial review before this court. The hearing of the breathalyser summons then proceeded before the other bench of magistrates. Because of the other applications there was a late start. The hearing was not completed that day. It was adjourned until 17 January 1983. On that occasion the justices upheld the defence submission of no case to answer and rejected a defence application for an order for costs against the prosecution. These decisions are the subject matter of the prosecution's appeal by way of case stated, and Mr Hindle's first application for judicial review, now before this court.

We turn first to the case stated. After the material facts had been briefly set out, the case continued as follows:

'In accordance with rule 81 of the Magistrates' Courts' Rules, 1981 (SI 1981/552) a   ... the question upon which the opinion of the High Court is sought is whether there was evidence on which the court could come to its decision, in particular concerning the finding of fact set out at paragraph x above. A short statement of the evidence supporting that statement of fact is set out below.'

The finding of fact in para (x) above was that: 'The officer satisfied himself that Hindle had consumed alcohol since the accident.' After the passage we have just quoted there followed a short statement of the evidence, which comprised evidence of the discovery

b   of the accident by the police, the subsequent arrival of Mr Hindle at the scene of the accident, the conversation which then took place between Pc Lamb and Mr Hindle, the carrying out of the breathalyser procedure, and the last part of the interview between Pc Lamb and Mr Hindle, which we have already quoted in full.

The magistrates then set out the rival contentions of the parties on the defence submission of no case to answer. The contentions of the prosecution were summarised

c   in para 3 of the case stated as follows:

'The Appellant contended that as the proper statutory procedure had been followed, the prosecution had established a case which could only be rebutted by evidence given by the Respondent that he had consumed alcohol after ceasing to drive. It was not open to the Respondent to rely solely on the claims that he had

d   consumed alcohol after ceasing to drive, which he made in reply to questions put to him by a police officer, but was a matter that had to be supported by evidence which could be properly tested by the Court. There was a case to answer and the Court were asked to rule accordingly.'

The contentions of the defence were then set out in para 4 of the case stated:

e   '(1) That the burden of proof remains upon the Prosecution throughout. It does not transfer to the Defence at any time. (2) To prove its case the Prosecution were required to prove that the Appellant had not had an alcoholic drink after the accident and before the blood test was taken. (3) The burden of proof was analogous to that in a case of "self-defence", where the burden remained with the Prosecution to prove the absence of self-defence. (4) To require the Defendant to give evidence

f   was the equivalent to transferring the burden of proof to the Defence. (5) The Prosecution called no evidence to discharge their burden as set out in (2) supra, notwithstanding that they had established the identity of the public house at which the Appellant asserted he had consumed liquor. (6) Such evidence as was called by the Prosecution was to the contrary, and was predicated upon the presumption that the Appellant had had such a drink, in particular:—(i) the Appellant had had ample

g   opportunity to have such a drink; (ii) his observed actions were entirely consistent with his having had such a drink; (iii) there was nothing inconsistent with his having had such a drink; (iv) the investigating officer had acted throughout on the basis that the Appellant had consumed such a drink; (v) at the first opportunity, and as soon as it became relevant, the Appellant asserted that he had had a drink. (7) In the premises, the Prosecution failed to establish a prima facie case.'

h   The justices then expressed the following opinion in para 6 of the case stated:

'i) Evidence indicating that alcohol had been consumed after the accident was introduced by the prosecution in examination in chief. ii) The arresting officer did not appreciate the significance of a driver consuming alcohol after ceasing to drive as a result of an accident and before giving a specimen of blood for analysis. iii) The

j   defendant had both the time and opportunity to consume alcohol after the accident. iv) The consumption of alcohol after the defendant ceased to drive and before the breathalyser test rendered the subsequent blood test inadmissible. v) The prosecution failed to discharge the burden of proving the admissibility of the blood test and, accordingly, failed to establish a prima facie case. We dismissed the case without calling upon the defence, but without making any order as to costs.'

The justices then posed this question for the opinion of the court (para 7 of the case stated):

'Whether a defendant who claims that he had consumed alcohol after he had been involved in a road traffic accident and before being required to take a breath test under section 8(2) of the Road Traffic Act 1972 must in any event support that claim by giving evidence to the court.'

We have to say that we are unhappy about the abstract form of this question. If read literally, it can only be answered in the negative. It is certainly possible to conceive of a case where evidence is extracted from prosecution witnesses in cross-examination, or from a defence witness other than the defendant, that the defendant has consumed alcohol after ceasing to drive before being required to take a breath test, in which event it may be unnecessary for the defendant himself to give evidence. But, as is foreshadowed by the first question posed by the justices (viz whether there was evidence on which they could come to their decision, in particular concerning their finding of fact in para (x) of the case) and was recognised in argument before us, the justices must have been seeking, in their second question, the opinion of the court on the question whether, on the facts of the case before them, it was necessary for evidence on that issue to be called on behalf of the defence, which presumably would be the evidence of Mr Hindle himself. We read the question in that sense, and we shall so treat it for the purposes of this case.

It appears from the case that the justices accepted the defence submission on the basis that there was evidence that alcohol had been consumed by Mr Hindle after ceasing to drive and before the breath test and that, if that was so, there could be no conviction under s 6 of the 1972 Act: see *R v Alyson* [1976] RTR 15, in which the Court of Appeal applied the decision of the House of Lords in *Rowlands v Hamilton* [1971] 1 All ER 1089, [1971] 1 WLR 647. However in *R v Durrant* [1969] 3 All ER 1357 at 1359, [1970] 1 WLR 29 at 32, a decision of the Court of Appeal which was approved in *Rowlands v Hamilton*, it was made plain by Lord Parker CJ, who delivered the judgment of the court, that the prosecution did not have to negative at the outset the possibility that the accused had consumed alcohol between the time when he ceased to drive and the time of the test. It was, said Lord Parker CJ, 'one of those cases where the defence must raise the point, but at the end of the day it will be for the prosecution to show that the story could not be true'. So the question arises: did the defence 'raise the point' before the justices in the present case?

It is obvious that the point was being taken before the justices on behalf of Mr Hindle, in the sense that the cross-examination of the prosecution witnesses, and in particular of Pc Lamb, was directed towards it. But that, in our judgment, is not enough. For the point to be raised, so that the prosecution has to discharge the burden of negativing it, it must in our judgment have been raised by evidence. This appears from the judgment of Lord Goddard CJ in *R v Lobell* [1957] 1 All ER 734 at 736, 1 QB 547 at 551, where he had this to say in relation to the comparable matter of self-defence in cases of homicide and wounding:

'If an issue relating to self-defence is to be left to the jury there must be some evidence from which a jury would be entitled to find that issue in favour of the accused, and ordinarily, no doubt, such evidence would be given by the defence. But there is a difference between leading evidence which would enable a jury to find an issue in favour of a defendant and in putting the onus on him. The truth is that the jury must come to a verdict on the whole of the evidence that has been laid before them. If, on a consideration of all the evidence, the jury are left in doubt whether the killing or wounding may not have been in self-defence the proper verdict would be not guilty. A convenient way of directing the jury is to tell them that the burden of establishing guilt is on the prosecution but that they must also consider the evidence for the defence which may have one of three results: it may convince them of the innocence of the accused, or it may cause them to doubt, in which case the defendant is entitled to an acquittal, or it may, and sometimes does, strengthen the case for the prosecution. It is, perhaps, a fine distinction to say that before a jury can find a particular issue in favour of an accused person he must give some evidence on which it can be found but, none the less, the onus remains on the prosecution. What it really amounts to is that if, in the result, the jury are left in doubt where the truth lies the verdict should be not guilty, and this is as true of an issue as to self-defence as it is to one of provocation, though of course the latter plea goes only to a mitigation of the offence.'

This passage was quoted by Lord Goddard CJ himself when delivering the judgment of the Court of Criminal Appeal in *R v McPherson* (1957) 41 Cr App R 213 at 215–216, a case of provocation. He said:

'The cases have left the matter in some difficulty, though perhaps not in doubt. We know that since WOOLMINGTON v. DIRECTOR OF PUBLIC PROSECUTIONS ([1935] AC 462, [1935] All ER Rep 1) the onus in a murder case is on the prosecution throughout, that is to say, the prosecution must prove that the prisoner killed the victim with malice aforethought. There are cases in which the prosecution open facts which of themselves would show provocation, and then it would be clearly for the prosecution to destroy those facts or prove other facts which would show a jury that there was not provocation in the case to reduce the offence from murder to manslaughter. But in the great majority of cases in which provocation is relied on as reducing the case to manslaughter, it is the prisoner who brings evidence to show that he was provoked, and that he acted under the influence of that provocation.'

In our judgment, the position was the same under s 6 of the Road Traffic Act 1972. If evidence was placed before the court (nearly always by the defence, but possibly through witnesses called by the prosecution) to show that the accused consumed alcohol after ceasing to drive but before the test, then the prosecution had to discharge the burden which rested on them to negative that fact. In such circumstances if, at the end of the day, the tribunal concluded that the accused might have so consumed alcohol, then they had to acquit him.

Turning to the case before us, the only matters on which the justices could have relied as constituting such evidence were (1) Mr Hindle's statement to Pc Lamb that he had had a drink after the accident, which was of course an entirely self-serving statement, and (2) the questions asked by Pc Lamb of Mr Hindle, and the answers which he gave to those questions, which we have already set out in this judgment. On the basis of that evidence, the justices concluded that Pc Lamb 'satisfied himself that Hindle had consumed alcohol since the accident'. That can only mean, on the evidence, that Pc Lamb, when he asked his questions of Mr Hindle, believed his assertion and accepted that he had consumed alcohol since the accident. There is also the conclusion of the justices that Mr Hindle had both the time and the opportunity to consume alcohol after the accident, but that can of itself have been of no probative value.

In our judgment, none of these matters, whether taken individually or collectively, could constitute evidence which raised the issue that Mr Hindle had consumed alcohol after ceasing to drive. Indeed, in the absence of special circumstances, it is difficult to see how there could be such evidence, unless the accused himself gave evidence of the fact, or some other person gave evidence who had seen him consuming alcohol at the relevant time. Certainly, in our judgment, neither Mr Hindle's statement to Pc Lamb, nor the latter's acceptance of it, nor the fact that Mr Hindle had the time and the opportunity to consume alcohol, could constitute the necessary evidence. These are simply matters which no doubt could have been relied on by the defence, had the evidential basis been laid before the court.

In a Practice Note dated 9 February 1962 ([1962] 1 All ER 448, [1962] 1 WLR 227) Lord Parker CJ (sitting in this court with Ashworth and Fenton Atkinson JJ) set out for the benefit of magistrates considerations which should as a matter of practice guide them when submissions were made of no case to answer. He said:

> 'A submission that there is no case to answer may properly be made and upheld: *a*
> (a) when there has been no evidence to prove an essential element in the alleged
> offence; (b) when the evidence adduced by the prosecution has been so discredited
> as a result of cross-examination or is so manifestly unreliable that no reasonable
> tribunal could safely convict on it. Apart from these two situations a tribunal should
> not in general be called on to reach a decision as to conviction or acquittal until the
> whole of the evidence which either side wishes to tender has been placed before it.   *b*
> If, however, a submission is made that there is no case to answer, the decision should
> depend not so much on whether the adjudicating tribunal (if compelled to do so)
> would at that stage convict or acquit but on whether the evidence is such that a
> reasonable tribunal might convict. If a reasonable tribunal might convict on the
> evidence so far laid before it, there is a case to answer.'

c

Having regard to the terms of this Practice Direction, there was in our judgment no
basis for the justices' acceptance of the defence submission in the present case. On the
evidence before the justices at the time of the submission, the point had simply not been
raised. We have little doubt that, since they concluded that Pc Lamb had accepted that
Mr Hindle had consumed alcohol after the accident, and since it had been made plain to
them by Mr Hindle's counsel that his case was that he had indeed done so, the justices   *d*
could see no point in the trial going on. But their actual conclusion appears to have been
based on the opinion formed by them that 'Evidence indicating that alcohol had been
consumed after the accident was introduced by the prosecution in the examination in
chief' (see para 6(i) of the case stated), which in our judgment cannot be correct, for the
reasons we have given; indeed it was probably based on the assumption that Pc Lamb's
evidence of what Mr Hindle told him constituted evidence of the truth of that statement.   *e*

It follows that, in our judgment, the first question posed by the justices (viz whether
there was evidence on which the justices could come to their decision) should be
answered in the negative; and, reading the second question as asking whether, on the
facts of the case before the justices, it was necessary for evidence on the issue of drinking
after the accident to be called on behalf of the defence, we would answer that question in
the affirmative.   *f*

There remains the question of the order which this court should now make in relation
to this matter, having regard to our answers to the two questions posed in the case. We
were told by counsel for Mr Hindle (who appeared before the justices below) that Mr
Hindle, if called to give evidence at the hearing of the breathalyser summons, would
without doubt have stated that he had had a drink after the accident. Having regard to
what has transpired on the hearing of these matters before this court, it appears that the   *g*
prosecution do not suggest that Mr Hindle told a lie to Pc Lamb when he stated at the
time that he had had a drink after the accident. Their case, as was made plain for the first
time by counsel for the prosecution at the start of the hearing before this court on 11
July, is rather that Mr Hindle deliberately consumed alcohol after the accident in order
to lay the basis for a defence under s 6 of the 1972 Act. It is plain from the reaction of the
justices to the defence submission of no case to answer that, if Mr Hindle gave evidence   *h*
before them that he had had a drink after the accident, they would without doubt acquit
him of the offence with which he was charged under the breathalyser summons. In these
circumstances, although we are of the opinion that the justices should not, on the
evidence before them, have accepted the defence submission of no case to answer,
nevertheless it would be otiose now to remit this matter to the justices for a further
hearing just to go through the formality of Mr Hindle standing up and saying yet again   *j*
that he had had a drink after the accident. In all the circumstances, therefore, apart from
answering the two questions in the manner we have indicated, we shall make no further
order on the case stated, save such order, if any, as to costs as may be appropriate after
hearing counsel for both parties.

In the light of our answers to the questions in the case stated, Mr Hindle's application for judicial review of the justices' refusal to make an order of costs in his favour on the breathalyser summons does not now arise.

We turn to the second application for judicial review, which relates to the justices' refusal to dismiss the information charging Mr Hindle with obstructing a police officer in the execution of his duty.

As we have already recorded, following an information which had been laid on 24 August 1982, a summons was issued on that date, the charge being that Mr Hindle 'did wilfully obstruct a constable of the Northumbria Police in the execution of his duty'. No other particulars were given of the offence charged. The information had been laid only three weeks before the expiry of the six-month period specified in s 127 of the Magistrates' Courts Act 1980. It has since been alleged that a number of attempts were made by Mr Hindle's solicitor to seek particulars of the charge; this was however denied by Mr Cooper, the solicitor acting for the prosecution. It was accepted by him, however, that on 14 October 1982 a letter had been written by Mr Hindle's solicitor to the prosecution solicitor, in which the following request was made:

'We would also be obliged if you would specify the basis on which our client is alleged to have obstructed the police, and also would you please identify the police officer.'

The point which was troubling Mr Hindle's solicitor was this. The charge under s 6 of the 1972 Act was apparently being advanced on the basis that Mr Hindle did not consume alcohol after ceasing to drive, and therefore implied that Mr Hindle did not tell the truth when he stated to the police that he had done so. Mr Hindle's solicitor was therefore concerned to know whether the charge of obstructing a police officer in the execution of his duty was being made on the basis that Mr Hindle had lied to the police when making their inquiries or whether it was being made on the basis that Mr Hindle had deliberately taken a drink after the accident with a view to frustrating the breathalyser test.

However, no particulars appear to have been provided by the prosecution in response to the letter dated 14 October. Both summonses were due to be heard on 5 November, by consent before different benches of magistrates. On that occasion, the prosecution applied for the obstruction summons to be adjourned until after the hearing of the breathalyser summons. This application the defence opposed, and they applied for the obstruction summons to be dismissed as an abuse of the process of the court. The justices acceded to the prosecution's application, and dismissed the defence application. It is the latter decision of the justices of which Mr Hindle now seeks judicial review.

There is an unfortunate conflict of evidence between Mr Hindle's solicitor and the prosecuting solicitor as to what transpired before the justices on that occasion. The account of the defence, which was confirmed on affidavit, is succinctly set out in the grounds on which they seek relief as follows:

'13. On the 5th day of November 1982 the Prosecution applied to have the "obstruction" summons adjourned until a later date. The Defence opposed and counter-applied to have the summons dismissed as an abuse of the process, relying, inter alia, upon the case of Regina -versus- Brentford Justices ex parte Wong ([1981] 1 All ER 884, [1981] QB 445), and the provisions of Section 104 of the Magistrates Court Act 1952.

14. In the ensuing submissions the Prosecution admitted that the "obstruction" summons had been drafted in that way to allow for two distinct interpretations, as follows:—(i) That the Applicant had had an alcoholic drink after the accident and, as a result, had obstructed any constable of the Northumbria Police who might have come along in the execution of his duty, as any such constable may wish to commence the breathyliser [sic] procedure; (ii) that the Applicant had not had an alcoholic drink after the accident and, as a result, had obstructed P.C. Lamb in the execution of his duty by lying to him in saying that he had had a drink.

15. Further, The Prosecution admitted that it had not decided on what basis it intended to proceed, if at all, on the "obstruction" summons until after it had heard *a* the Defence run by the Applicant in the trial upon the "breathyliser"[sic] summons. The "breathyliser"[sic] summons was adjourned until 17th day of January 1983 for trial.

16. Upon being invited by the Defence to elect the basis upon which it wished to proceed on the "obstruction" summons, in which case the Defence would withdraw its application to dismiss, the Prosecution refused so to do.' *b*

On that basis, it was submitted that there had been an abuse of the process of the court because (a) the prosecution were alleging two distinct and mutually exclusive offences in the same information and summons, (b) the prosecution thereby had not determined within the period established by s 104 of the Magistrates' Courts Act 1952 the particulars of the offence of which they were alleging the applicant was guilty and so had not made a firm decision to prosecute on any particular basis, and (c) in the premises, the *c* prosecution had laid an information, not with a firm view to prosecute, but with a view to inhibit the defence of the applicant on the breathalyser summons.

Further, it was submitted that there had been a denial of natural justice in that 'After a minimum of ten months after the matters alleged, the Applicant still does not know the case he is being asked to meet on the "obstruction" summons'. It was therefore alleged that the justices acted in excess of their jurisdiction in refusing to dismiss the *d* obstruction summons and would act further in excess of their jurisdiction if they were to proceed to hear a trial on that summons.

The account of the prosecuting solicitor, as set out in his affidavit, was however that the basis of the defence application to have the obstruction summons dismissed as an abuse of process was that the prosecution were required to make up their minds whether or not they were alleging that Mr Hindle had had a drink after the accident, and that *e* accordingly they could not proceed both with the breathalyser summons and the obstruction summons. At no stage were the prosecution required by the court to elect the basis on which they wished to proceed on the obstruction summons, nor was any indication given as to terms on which the defendant would withdraw his application to have the obstruction summons dismissed as being an abuse of process. The matters being discussed and argued before the court were the validity of proceedings for obstruction as *f* an alternative to the proceedings for driving a motor vehicle having consumed excess alcohol, not on the basis specified in para 14 of the grounds of relief, because the application before the justices was to dismiss the obstruction summons as being an abuse of process as an alternative to the breathalyser summons.

This evidence was however disputed by the applicant's solicitor (Mr Hindle's solicitor) in a further affidavit, to which he exhibited the contemporaneous note taken by him at *g* the time when counsel appeared before the justices on 5 November 1982.

It appears to us that there was room for misunderstanding between those representing Mr Hindle and the prosecuting solicitor on 5 November. Our reasons for thinking so are as follows. When the prosecution laid the information for obstruction on 24 August, they were faced with the imminent expiry of the six-month time limit for the laying of any such information and the fact that, although they considered that they could properly *h* assert that Mr Hindle had obstructed a police officer in the execution of his duty, they felt uncertain whether such obstruction had taken the form of deliberately frustrating the breathalyser procedure by consuming alcohol after the accident, or of untruthfully telling the police that he had so consumed alcohol. So they laid the information, and the summons was issued, in general terms. Faced with such a summons, the only thing which those acting for Mr Hindle could do was to seek particulars. If particulars had *j* been given, the prosecution would have had to come down from the fence. Had they then asserted that their case was that Mr Hindle had lied to the police, such a case would have been consistent with the breathalyser summons, which could only succeed if Mr Hindle had not had a drink after ceasing to drive. But, if they asserted that Mr Hindle had deliberately had a drink after the accident in order to frustrate the breathalyser procedure, the two summonses would have been inconsistent, and particulars in that

a form could have provoked an attack by the defence on the basis that the prosecution could not properly launch two inconsistent sets of criminal proceedings at the same time. In a sense, therefore, the defence, by seeking particulars of the obstruction summons, were laying the ground for an attack on the two summonses as being inconsistent. It is scarcely surprising therefore that, while the initial attack by the defence took the form of a complaint that the obstruction summons, unparticularised, was prejudicial and

b embarrassing, the prosecution saw it as an attack on the two summonses being advanced at the same time.

Be that as it may, having studied the contemporaneous note, we are satisfied that the burden of counsel's complaint before the justices on behalf of Mr Hindle was that the obstruction summons itself was open to the two alternative interpretations which we have already referred to, which were explained to the justices, and that it was therefore

c prejudicial and embarrassing. It must, moreover, have been at least implicit in the submission then being made that the burden of Mr Hindle's complaint was that the facts of the offence had not been stated with sufficient particularity; so that, if particulars had been given, the sting would have been drawn from the specific complaint then being made.

In these circumstances it appears to us that the situation was most unsatisfactory. Mr

d Hindle was entitled to be given such particulars of the offence as were necessary to give reasonable information of the nature of the charge (see r 100 of the Magistrates' Courts Rules 1981, SI 1981/552). Furthermore, as was established by this court in *R v Brentford Justices, ex p Wong* [1981] 1 All ER 884 at 887, [1981] QB 445 at 450 per Donaldson LJ: '. . . it is open to justices to conclude that it is an abuse of the process of the court for a prosecutor to lay an information when he has not reached a decision to prosecute.' No

e doubt the prosecution acted in perfectly good faith in the present case, but by laying a charge which was ambiguous in the sense that it could be read as referring to one or other of two inconsistent offences, and by failing to give the requisite particulars when asked to do so, the effect was that the prosecution were preserving an opportunity to advance their case on the basis of either of these two offences under the one summons when it came on for hearing. In our judgment, this is at least as objectionable a course as

f the laying of an information where no decision has been taken to prosecute, for, if permitted, it would allow a prosecution to postpone, until after the expiry of the six-month period, their decision whether to prosecute for a particular offence. If the decision had been properly taken before the expiry of the six-month period, there should have been no difficulty in formulating the particulars requested. Furthermore, Mr Hindle suffered prejudice in consequence of the manner in which the prosecution proceeded,

g for he was deprived of the opportunity of making any further submission to the court as to the manner in which the two summonses should be proceeded with. If the prosecution had stated that their case was that Mr Hindle had lied to the police, he could sensibly have asked for both summonses, being consistent, to be dealt with at the same time by the same bench of magistrates. If, on the other hand, the prosecution's case was that Mr Hindle had deliberately consumed alcohol after the accident to frustrate the breathalyser

h procedure, it would have been open to the defence to object to the prosecution proceeding with two inconsistent summonses. Since the hearing of the breathalyser summons has already commenced, that prejudice is, in our view, irretrievable.

It was suggested to us by counsel for the prosecution that there was nothing wrong in the prosecution proceeding with the two inconsistent summonses, ie (1) the breathalyser summons and (2) the obstruction summons on the basis of deliberately drinking after

j ceasing to drive. This we cannot accept. It is true that, in for example the case of alternative charges of theft and handling, it may be proper to initiate a prosecution on the basis that the accused stole or alternatively handled certain goods (see *R v Dolan* (1975) 62 Cr App R 36 and *R v Smythe* (1980) 72 Cr App R 8). Of course, a man who handles goods will generally also have stolen them. However, a man cannot be convicted of handling goods by reason of his having been the original thief of those goods, having regard to the definition of the offence of handling in s 22(1) of the Theft Act 1968. Even so, a prosecutor may, without impropriety or inconsistency, allege on the basis of certain facts that the accused was guilty of theft as the original thief of the goods but that, if not, he was guilty of handling the goods. In the present case, however, the two summonses were mutually exclusive in the sense that, since the breathalyser summonses proceeded on the basis that the analyst's certificate showed conclusively the amount of alcohol in Mr Hindle's blood at a time before he ceased to drive, and, since (as we now know) the obstruction summons proceeded on the basis that Mr Hindle deliberately consumed alcohol after ceasing to drive and before the relevant specimen was taken, neither summons could be pursued without necessarily relying on facts which were diametrically opposed to the facts giving rise to the offence alleged in the other; and we do not see how a prosecutor could properly lay concurrent informations which were in this sense inconsistent, because he could not at the same time state that the accused had committed, or was suspected of having committed, each offence (see s 1 of the Magistrates' Courts Act 1980).

In all the circumstances we are satisfied that, objectively considered, the course pursued by the prosecution in respect of the obstruction summons did indeed amount to an abuse of the process of the court. We adopt the words used by Donaldson LJ in *R v Brentford Justices, ex p Wong* [1981] 1 All ER 884 at 887, [1981] QB 445 at 450 when he said:

'It is perhaps hard on the prosecutor to characterise that as an abuse of the process of the court because I am sure there was no intention by the prosecutor to abuse the process of the court.'

In our judgment, however, this manner of proceeding did amount to an abuse of process, and it appears therefore that the justices erred in not recognising it as such.

The question now arises as to the form of order which the court should make. In *R v Brentford Justices, ex p Wong*, where the justices thought that they had no discretionary power not to hear the case, this court remitted the case to them to give them an opportunity to reconsider the matter in the light of the court's holding that they did have such a power. In the present case, however, quite apart from our decision that there was an abuse of process by the prosecution and that Mr Hindle has in consequence been irretrievably prejudiced, it would in our judgment be wrong to remit the matter to the justices for reconsideration. For the position now is that on the first day of the hearing before this court, on 11 July, the prosecution, through their counsel, stated that the offence charged in the obstruction summons was deliberately consuming alcohol after ceasing to drive. It follows that it now appears that the obstruction summons, issued on 24 August, is a summons wholly inconsistent with the breathalyser summons, the hearing of which began on 5 November without the defence having an opportunity then to object that the two summonses were inconsistent. This being so, it cannot be right, in our judgment, to allow the obstruction summons to be proceeded with. In all the circumstances of the case, we consider that the proper order of this court is an order of prohibition, prohibiting the justices from proceeding further with the hearing of the obstruction summons.

Orders accordingly. Both parties' costs to be paid out of central funds.

Solicitors: *Swinburn G Wilson & Son*, Newcastle-upon-Tyne (for Mr Hindle); *Collyer-Bristow*, agents for *D E Brown*, Newcastle-upon-Tyne (for the prosecution).

N P Metcalfe Esq   Barrister.

Practice Direction

FAMILY DIVISION

Practice – Family Division – Estimated length of hearing – Notice of estimate.

1. Recent experience has shown that in some cases the estimated length of hearing of Family Division summonses and applications for hearing before a judge at the Royal Courts of Justice has been inaccurate, with a resultant waste of time for all concerned with litigation and a needless increase in costs. In order to remedy this situation the following procedure will apply with effect from the date of this registrar's direction.

2. On the issue of a summons or application (including restoring an adjourned summons or application or one referred to a judge) which is expected to last in excess of one day, the form of notice of estimate, duly completed, must be lodged with the Clerk of the Rules. The form should be signed by counsel, if already instructed, or by the solicitor acting for the party.

3. A copy of the completed notice must be served at once on every other party. On receipt by the solicitor he, or counsel if instructed, must consider the estimate and if he disagrees with it adopt the procedure in para 6 as soon as possible.

4. A copy of the completed notice or any revised notice must be included in every set of instructions or brief sent to counsel.

5. It is the continuing responsibility of all solicitors and counsel when dealing with the case to consider whether or not the latest estimate recorded on the notice is accurate.

6. If any solicitor or counsel considers that the estimate needs revising either way a copy of the notice of estimate should be made, completed at box 5 with the proposed revised estimate and served on the other parties and the Clerk of the Rules. The revised estimate should, whenever possible, be agreed with all other parties and signed jointly before being sent to the Clerk of the Rules. In the event of disagreement reference should be made to the Clerk of the Rules.

7. If an additional summons or a cross-summons is issued returnable on the same date, a separate notice of estimate should only be filed if the latest estimate is affected.

8. If within seven days of the date fixed for hearing it becomes apparent that the estimate requires revision, the Clerk of the Rules should be notified at once by telephone.

9. This registrar's direction does not apply to a party acting in person, but if the respondent(s) is represented by counsel or solicitor and he estimates that the matter will last in excess of one day he must immediately complete a notice of estimate and send it to the Clerk of the Rules.

10. The procedure relating to registrar's hearings, at the Divorce Registry, Somerset House, is not affected by this direction.

11. Copies of the form of notice of estimate, D208 are available from the Clerk of the Rules Department at the Royal Courts of Justice and room G39 of the Divorce Registry in Somerset House.

B P Tickle
Senior Registrar.

1 March 1984

[An appendix to the direction, which is not set out herein, sets out the form of notice of estimate.]

Practice Direction

a

FAMILY DIVISION

Practice – Family Division – Counsel's fees – Interlocutory fees – Scale of fees to be allowed on taxation.

The Senior Registrar of the Family Division, in consultation with the Senate of the Inns of Court and the Bar, has decided that the scale of fees set out hereafter would be proper to be allowed on taxation in respect of instructions and briefs delivered on or after 1 March 1984.

b

It is emphasised that the list is intended only to be a guide as to the broad range of fees applicable to the average 'weight' of each item of work, and higher or lower fees may be allowed in appropriate cases.

c

The items in the list are those most frequently found in the most common kind of case, but the list itself is not exhaustive. For example, it will be observed that brief fee relating to contested suits or to ancillary relief have not been dealt with, since it is considered that conditions vary too much for them to be included in a scale.

The Senior Registrar confirms his predecessor's view that, when, in circumstances which merit it, counsel gives an oral opinion in the course of a conference, his fees therefor may be substituted for the routine conference fee. The taxing officer will require to be satisfied that it was appropriate to have dealt with the matter orally. It should not be assumed that, as a matter of course, the fee given for such an oral opinion will be the same fee as for one in writing.

d

Each fee, except a conference fee, is intended to cover any necessary perusal of papers in connection with the item. Counsel should indorse on his brief the time taken for preparation and for conference.

e

Answer (plain denial)	£10
Answer (with no cross-charge)	£20
Answer (with cross-charge)	£35–£50
Request for particulars	£15
Particulars	£15–£55
Reply (plain denial)	£10
Reply (other than a plain denial)	£20–£40
Advice on evidence	£25–£80
Opinion (comprehensive)	£35–£70
Opinion (limited)	£20–£35
Notice of appeal or counter-notice	£25–£40
*Affidavit (main)	£28–£75
*Affidavit (minor supporting)	£10–£25
Questionnaire (request or answer)	£15–£65
Brief—registrar (procedural)	£30–£50
Brief—judge (ex parte injunction)	£35–£45
Brief—judge (injunction)	£40–£160
Brief—judge (uncontested application in chambers)	£30–£45
Consultation (Queen's Counsel)	£30 (first half hour) £15 thereafter
Conference (junior counsel)	£15 (first half hour) £12 thereafter

f

g

h

j

* If drafted with other affidavits an omnibus fee may be allowed.

6 March 1984

R v Heston-Francois

COURT OF APPEAL, CRIMINAL DIVISION

WATKINS LJ, MICHAEL DAVIES AND FRENCH JJ

20, 21 OCTOBER 1983, 31 JANUARY 1984

Criminal law – Trial – Stay of proceedings – Oppressive conduct by prosecution – Conduct alleged to amount to abuse of process of court – Whether judge under duty to try issue before arraignment and to stay proceedings if abuse of process found.

Where, on an application by a defendant before arraignment, the defendant alleges that the prosecution have been guilty, either by reason of the activities of the police or by other means, of oppressive conduct said to constitute an abuse of the court's process (eg improperly obtaining evidence, tampering with evidence or seizing the defendant's documents prepared for his defence), the trial judge is under no general duty to conduct a pre-trial inquiry on that issue, either by the hearing of evidence or on agreed facts, and then, in the event of finding such abuse, to exercise a discretion whether to stay proceedings on the indictment. Such conduct by the prosecution falls to be dealt with in the trial itself, either by judicial control on the admissibility of evidence or by the judicial power to direct (usually at the close of the prosecution's case) a verdict of not guilty or by the jury taking account of it in evaluating the evidence before them (see p 793 *a* to *d*, post).

R v Bow Street Magistrates, ex p Mackeson (1982) 75 Cr App R 24 distinguished.

Connelly v DPP [1964] 2 All ER 401, *R v Riebold* [1965] 1 All ER 653 and *DPP v Humphrys* [1976] 2 All ER 497 considered.

Notes

For staying the trial of an indictment, see 11 Halsbury's Laws (4th edn) para 216.

Cases referred to in judgment

Connelly v DPP [1964] 2 All ER 401, [1964] AC 1254, [1964] 2 WLR 1145, HL.
DPP v Humphrys [1976] 2 All ER 497, [1977] AC 1, [1976] 2 WLR 857, HL.
R v Bow Street Magistrates, ex p Mackeson (1982) 75 Cr App R 24, DC.
R v D [1984] All ER 574, [1984] 2 WLR 112, CA.
R v Hartley [1978] 2 NZLR 199, NZ CA.
R v Riebold [1965] 1 All ER 653, [1967] 1 WLR 674, Assizes.

Appeal

On 23 February 1982 in the Crown Court at Inner London Sessions before his Honour Judge Shindler QC and a jury the appellant, Michael Heston-Francois, was convicted of two counts of burglary and one count of handling stolen property to which he was sentenced to concurrent terms of 5 years' imprisonment on each count of burglary and 18 months' imprisonment on the count of handling stolen property. On 24 February 1982 in the same court, following his committal thereto under s 38 of the Magistrates' Courts Act 1980 on his pleading guilty on 22 July 1981 in the Camberwell Green Magistrates' Court, the appellant was sentenced to concurrent terms of 18 months' imprisonment on each of two charges of handling stolen property and to 12 months' imprisonment on another charge of handling stolen property, those sentences to be concurrent with the sentences passed on 23 February. On 30 March 1983 Mann J refused the appellant leave to appeal against conviction and sentence. The appellant renewed his application to the Court of Appeal, which granted him leave to appeal. The facts are set out in the judgment of the court.

Louis Blom-Cooper QC and *Harjit Grewal* (neither of whom appeared below) for the appellant.

C J Crespi for the Crown.

Cur adv vult

31 January. The following judgment of the court was delivered.

WATKINS LJ. On 23 February 1982 in the Crown Court at Inner London Sessions before his Honour Judge Shindler QC and a jury the appellant was convicted after a long trial of two offences of burglary and one of handling stolen property. He was thereupon sentenced to concurrent terms of 5 years', 5 years' and 18 months' imprisonment respectively. On the following day the same court sentenced him to concurrent terms of 18 months', 18 months' and 12 months' imprisonment respectively for three offences of handling stolen property on which, following a plea of guilty, a magistrates' court had committed him for sentence. These sentences were ordered to run concurrently with those passed on the indictment.

The appellant is now 49 years of age. He has a very bad criminal record. He is a resourceful, intelligent and persistent man, who has submitted massive submissions on over 500 sheets of foolscap paper in support of his application for leave to appeal. He has also applied to call numerous witnesses at the hearing. The single judge examined with very great care the appellant's applications. Providing cogently expressed reasons therefor, he refused them. However, on the appellant's renewal of his application to this court, the appellant was granted leave to appeal primarily on the ground that, according to him, there had been, prior to his trial, conduct by police officers which amounted to an abuse of the process of the court. This is alleged to have arisen from the seizure by the police, between committal and trial, from the appellant's home of a large quantity of documents and tape recordings, amongst which were papers specifically prepared for his defence. His application to call witnesses here was refused.

Mr Blom-Cooper QC, who did not appear in the court below, has appeared for the appellant in this court and confined his argument on behalf of the appellant to two grounds of appeal, namely that relating to an alleged abuse of the process of the court and a further allegation to the effect that the prosecution failed to disclose to the jury in respect of one of the burglaries relevant evidence in relation to a footprint impression which had been found in dust at the scene of the crime.

In 1979 the appellant, who for several years previously seems to have led a law-abiding and useful life, was employed as a security guard at a number of buildings in Clerkenwell, some of which had been converted into small units let as workshops to manufacturing jewellers. The main door of one of these premises, namely Pennybank Chambers, was secured during working hours by a Yale lock, to which each unit holder had keys, and by a Chubb security lock, which was used at night and on Sundays. There were three holders of keys to the Chubb lock, of whom the appellant was one.

During a weekend early in December 1979 a unit at Pennybank Chambers, which was let to Michael John Disdale, was broken into (burglary 1). A large quantity of jewellery, precious metals and stones belonging to him were stolen. Police inquiries failed to reveal the identity of the burglar or burglars. The appellant made a statement to the police and to a Mr Shane, one of the other key holders who was the manager of the premises, which had the effect of casting away any suspicion of implication in the burglary which may otherwise have fallen on him, despite the fact that no signs were discovered of a forcible opening of the main door.

Towards the end of April 1980 there was another burglary (burglary 2) at Pennybank Chambers. This time a unit let to Pierre Luigi Biagotti was broken into. A quantity of jewellery, precious metals and stones, a brief case, a welding hammer, a screw driver and a pair of pliers belonging to him were stolen. Yet again, no signs were discovered of force having been applied to open the main door. So it was thought that these two burglaries must have been committed with at least the assistance of someone responsible for the safety of the premises in one way or another. This time suspicion did fall on the appellant. He was questioned very closely about both burglaries. He resolutely denied being involved in either of them. A fellow employee of the appellant, one Colin Gayton, was also questioned about burglary 2. After some prevarication, he confessed to that crime as well as to another burglary (burglary 3) at the premises and, in a written statement, asserted that burglary 2 had been committed by himself and the appellant, who was the instigator of it. Gayton did not give evidence at the trial, but he was convicted of burglaries 2 and 3. The appellant was tried for burglary 3, but was acquitted and, accordingly, we are not concerned with it in this appeal. Gayton was placed on probation for two years.

On 30 April 1980 the appellant's flat, which had been let to him by his employers, was searched by the police in the presence of the appellant and Gayton, who by then were both under arrest. In the course of the search, the police found jewellers' equipment, acid for testing precious metals and trade magazines. The appellant said that he was interested in these materials as a hobby. In a basement, to which the appellant admitted he possessed the only key, the police found a camping gas burner bearing traces of precious alloys. Hidden on a rafter there were two watch cases which Gayton pointed out. The smaller of these watch cases was, in August 1980, identified by Disdale as part of the property stolen from his unit in burglary 1. At the same place a buckle and a lump of gold were found. The appellant said these had belonged to his estranged wife and the buckle was part of the strap of the smaller watch. The lump of gold was the result of his attempt to melt down his wife's jewellery. For this purpose, he had used a different burner. He suggested that the shiny traces on the burner, which was taken away by the police, might be rust. He could offer no explanation for the presence of the watches and other things on the beam.

Gayton also pointed to a hole in the basement wall which was concealed by a black wooden flap, hinged to the brickwork. Inside the police found in an envelope a driving licence, an insurance certificate and an MOT test certificate. These had been lost by one John Robertson in July 1979. The appellant admitted having amended the address on the licence, but denied having traced the signature of Robertson. He also said that a lot of other people used the basement. These were the stolen documents of which the appellant was convicted of dishonestly handling.

Following the search of the flat and basement, the appellant and Gayton were taken to the basement of the premises which had been burgled, where tools, footwear, gloves and protective clothing were found, of which a boiler suit, a left shoe, a crowbar, a claw hammer and a heavy hammer were connected by scientific evidence with burglary 2. When he was asked about the claw hammer and crowbar, the appellant made no reply. When asked if he owned the heavy hammer, he said he knew nothing about it and was not saying anything until he had seen his solicitor. He denied ownership of various other articles, whereupon Gayton said: 'Come on Mick, don't muck them about. You know they're yours same as the rest of the stuff here.' To this, the appellant responded: 'You say what you want, Colin, I'm not saying anything more.'

The appellant was interviewed by the police on at least six occasions. He made no admissions. He did not challenge the evidence given by the police about those interviews, save as to inconsequential matters, but maintained nevertheless that he had been subjected by the police to threats and serious violence.

Briefly stated, his defence to burglary 1, as explained by him to the jury, was that, while he was inspecting the premises in the early hours of Monday morning, he smelt something burning. He thought there might be a fire so he telephoned Mr Disdale, among others, and the fire brigade. Before anyone including the police came to his assistance, he came across the burglars. One of them threatened him with a sawn-off shotgun and ordered him into a side room. While there he heard shouts and then a number of footsteps running away. He recognised the voice of a man who was, according to him, employed at one of the units.

As for burglary 2, he maintained that he had been one of a large number of guests at a party given to celebrate his mother's birthday. During the course of that evening and the early hours of the following morning, he made two short visits to the premises to check that all was well. All seemed to him to be well. After his second visit he was telephoned and informed that the alarm at the premises had gone off. He went immediately to inquire into what had happened and telephoned for the police, who soon, on this fresh inquiry, formed the view, as we have already stated, that the burglaries had been carried out with assistance from someone intimately concerned with the premises.

There is no doubt whatsoever that Gayton's confession was largely instrumental in causing the police to arrest the appellant. But, since this could not be used as evidence against him at the trial, the evidence relied on was circumstantial. It included matters already referred to and, among other things, the fact that the proceeds of burglary 2 were found in other workshop premises which up to then had not been in use, but of which the appellant was also the security guard. He was also one of several key holders of those other premises. The other key holders, who included Mr Shane, were excluded from complicity both in the burglary and in the secreting of the proceeds of it in those premises.

The appellant gave the jury a detailed account of his movements on all relevant occasions. He was supported in a number of respects by witnesses called on his behalf. He and they were obviously disbelieved. Furthermore, the jury rejected the appellant's intricate explanation for his proclaimed innocent possession of John Robertson's driving licence and other papers.

It is unnecessary to say anything more of the evidence of the burglaries, save to relate in outline the circumstances arising out of the existence of a footprint in an area of dust at Pennybank Chambers after the commission of burglary 2. There was no doubt that the appellant's shoes were taken from him for the purpose of attempting to match one of them with the footprint.

Nevertheless, at the trial one of the police officers, Det Sgt French, involved in the inquiries into burglary 2, denied in cross-examination any knowledge of the existence of the footprint as, so it is said, did another officer named Watts. Consequently, in summing up, the judge directed the jury that an issue existed as to who between the appellant and, in particular, French had told the truth whether a footprint had been made by someone and had been seen by the police.

Unfortunately, as we know, but the judge did not through the failure of the prosecution to inform him, two other officers who had given evidence, namely Det Sgt Kelly and Det Con Mills, were aware of the existence of the footprint. They had not been asked a single question about it by the prosecution or defence, although they had made a comparison of the footprint and the shoes belonging to the appellant's brother. So an issue affecting credibility only (the footprint was certainly not made by the appellant), which did not in fact exist, entered the jury's consideration.

The appellant alleges that the prosecution's duty was to correct, during the progress of the summing up, the erroneous but understandable view which the judge had formed as to the existence of this issue, by telling him of the knowledge of Mills and Kelly. This duty was clearly not performed. We asked counsel for the Crown, who prosecuted in the court below, to provide an explanation for this omission. He did so to our complete satisfaction. Apparently, seeing that none of the appellant's shoes matched the footprint, its existence was regarded as an irrelevance. It was not evidence against the appellant and no mention of it was made in the depositions of Mills and Kelly. These officers were not in court during the summing up and counsel for the Crown was unaware of their knowledge of the footprint. He learned of it only as a result of inquiries he made in order to provide the explanation which this court had demanded of him.

Whilst we can well understand how the appellant's suspicions that the prosecution behaved unfairly and unscrupulously arose, now that we know how this unfortunate lapse occurred we, without hesitation, acquit the prosecution of behaving in any way improperly. The question is: did the fact that this issue of credibility was left to the jury, and may have been resolved by them in favour of the prosecution, so prejudice the appellant as to make his conviction unsafe or unsatisfactory?

In our judgment, having regard to the many issues raised in the course of the trial, most if not all of which went to, among other things, credibility, we find it impossible to believe that the jury were in any degree influenced into convicting the appellant by the existence of this issue, no matter how (if at all) they resolved it.

Counsel for the appellant, in making his succinct submissions on this ground of appeal, described it as a makeweight to the matter on which he was really placing reliance and to which we now turn our attention.

In July 1981 the appellant was on bail awaiting trial. Police officers at Brixton began to keep a watch on his activities because they had reason to believe that he was committing criminal offences. That belief was well founded. On 8 July he was arrested and he confessed to dishonestly handling two stolen cars and to dishonestly handling a stolen test certificate. Hence his committal for sentence by justices to the Crown Court at Inner London Sessions and the imposition on him of a total sentence of 18 months' imprisonment, as stated at the outset of this judgment.

He was arrested at his home by Brixton police officers, who had a warrant to search the appellant's home for stolen jewellery. They took away with them a number of files belonging to the appellant and some tapes on which there were recordings. These documents and recordings had been prepared for use in his defence to the burglary charges.

At the trial the appellant alleged that Kelly and Mills had conspired with Brixton police to have him arrested on trumped-up charges, so that his documents could be seized and shown to them. They would then, he said, be able to adapt their evidence to frustrate his defence.

In order to see this serious allegation in its proper context and to reveal the role of Kelly and Mills in an incident which was responsible for occupying the time of the court for a number of days, we quote from the summing up where these matters are vividly and accurately explained:

'As far as the seizure of the [appellant's] files and documents is concerned in July 1981, neither police officer, Sgt Kelly nor Det Con Mills, has ever denied or made a secret of seeing those very many files and documents when informed by the Brixton police that they were there at the police station. They reported it to their superiors, it was reported to the solicitor for the Metropolitan Police and they reported it to the [appellant's] solicitors that they had seen the files. You may think that, if they were thoroughly dishonest police officers, they would have kept that to themselves and if they meant to get some advantage out of that, they would not have. There was absolutely no need for them to do that. That is one way of testing it. They have never made any secret of it. According to them, on instructions from their superiors, they went along on an afternoon in July 1981 to Brixton station, I think between 2 and 4.30 or thereabouts, having received information from the Brixton police that documents had been seized. You remember the evidence: they told you that they were looking for a specific document or documents that referred to a particular aspect of the case. They were pressed on that . . . The allegation was that witnesses for the prosecution were likely to be interfered with. "That is why we went through those papers to find out, look for a document to see whether it would give us a clue and that is why the name 'Disdale'," he told you, "was all important to me at that time." You remember, Mr Disdale could not be found for a long time. There is no suggestion that they found anything to suggest that [the appellant] had, in fact, interfered with any witness, you must appreciate that . . . As for adapting their evidence having looked through those files, members of the jury, you will remember, will you not, that the evidence in this case, including the statements of the two police officers, Sgt Kelly and Det Con Mills, were served on the defence before 1 September 1980. No question of adapting their evidence in any shape or form as far as that is concerned. You remember how this went through in the magistrates' court. In the magistrates' court you can have a full hearing, because the magistrate has got to decide whether there is a case to answer to send up to the Crown Court fit for a jury.'

Before arraignment in the Crown Court at Inner London Sessions, application was made on behalf of both the appellant and Gayton to stay the proceedings for the reason that defence documents had been seen by prosecution witnesses. This constituted, it was said, an abuse of the court's process. Accordingly, at the conclusion of lengthy submissions, the judge was invited to order a stay, which would have the effect of preventing a trial from taking place. He declined to make that order.

Counsel for the appellant contends that the judge, for a number of reasons, was in error in making that decision. He very helpfully provided us in advance of the hearing of this appeal with his 'Heads of Argument', from which, being a model of clarity and brevity, we quote verbatim. They were stated by him as follows:

'PRELIMINARY SUBMISSION.

On an application by the defence to stay criminal proceedings, on the grounds that there has been an abuse of the process of the Court, the trial judge must determine the issue before arraignment, either on agreed facts or after hearing evidence. Judge Shindler Q.C. wrongly ruled on the preliminary issue without having heard all the relevant evidence. Moreover, if submission 1 below is correct, the learned judge misdirected himself on the law . . .

MAIN SUBMISSIONS

1. The court always possesses an inherent jurisdiction to stay criminal proceedings at any time, on the ground that there has been an abuse of the process of the court, which is not limited to the proceedings in and about the courtroom but extends to the whole criminal process, from criminal investigation to conviction . . . 2. Legally privileged documents found by a prosecuting authority cannot be removed from the possession of their owner or his legal representatives without their consent, unless the prosecuting authority can demonstrate to the court that it reasonably suspected that the documents contained evidence of the commission of crime . . . 3. The seizure and removal, without consent, of documents that on the face of them have been brought into existence by an accused (or his legal representative) for the purpose of preparing his defence in criminal proceedings for which he has already been committed for trial is to go behind the accused's right to silence, and is, therefore, an abuse of the process of the Court. 4. Even if (contrary to the submissions above) the seizure and removal of legally privileged documents by a prosecuting authority is lawful, the use of the contents of the documents for the purpose of conducting the prosecution is an abuse of the process of the court. The burden is upon the prosecuting authority to satisfy the court that no such use has in fact been made of the contents of such documents.'

The problem posed to us involves the power of the court not only to control the procedures of a trial, but also to decide whether a trial shall take place at all. Lord Devlin said in *Connelly v DPP* [1964] 2 All ER 401 at 483, [1964] AC 1254 at 1347: '. . . a general power, taking various specific forms, to prevent unfairness to the accused has always been a part of the English criminal law . . .'

In some instances, this power is exercised by the Crown Court judge. For example, where a plea of autrefois acquit or autrefois convict is successfully established, or where the indictment is incurably defective, or a nolle prosequi has been entered, the judge will quash the indictment. Where the bringing of criminal proceedings is itself oppressive, justices may be restrained by judicial review from embarking on committal proceedings. This course was adopted in *R v Bow Street Magistrates, ex p Mackeson* (1982) 75 Cr App R 24, where the Divisional Court concluded that improper use had been made of a deportation order in a foreign country in order to circumvent extradition proceedings.

a In *R v Riebold* [1965] 1 All ER 653, [1967] 1 WLR 674 the judge of first instance refused leave to proceed on an indictment in the following circumstances. The indictment charged conspiracy and also a very large number of substantive offences, being the overt acts performed by the conspirators in pursuance of the conspiracy. The Crown elected to proceed on the conspiracy count. When, following verdicts of guilty, the convictions on the conspiracy count had been quashed, the Crown was refused leave to proceed on the substantive counts. This, no doubt, was an example of the exercise by the judge of the
b 'residual discretion to prevent anything which savours of abuse of process' (see per Lord Reid in *Connelly's* case [1964] 2 All ER 401 at 406, [1964] AC 1254 at 1296).

Where there has been oppressive conduct savouring of abuse of process, it seems clear that the Court of Appeal, Criminal Division may quash a conviction on the ground that it is 'unsatisfactory' or 'unsafe' (see s 2(1)(a) of the Criminal Appeal Act 1968).

The foregoing are examples of the various specific forms by which the courts exercise
c their inherent jurisdiction, the existence of which is not in doubt, to prevent unfairness to an accused. The question here is, however, whether a trial judge has a duty, on the application of a defendant before arraignment, to try an issue by the hearing of evidence or on agreed facts whether or not the prosecution has been guilty, by the activities of police officers or by other means, of oppressive conduct said to constitute an abuse of the court's process and then, on so finding, to exercise a discretion whether or not to stay
d proceedings on the indictment.

The fact that no such duty has, it would seem, ever been successfully asserted hitherto is not conclusive against its existence. Lord Salmon said in *DPP v Humphrys* [1976] 2 All ER 497 at 527–528, [1977] AC 1 at 46:

e 'I respectfully agree with my noble and learned friend, Viscount Dilhorne, that a judge has not and should not appear to have any responsibility for the institution of prosecutions; nor has he any power to refuse to allow a prosecution to proceed merely because he considers that, as a matter of policy, it ought not to have been brought. It is only if the prosecution amounts to an abuse of the process of the court and is oppressive and vexatious that the judge has the power to intervene.'

See also per Lord Edmund-Davies in *DPP v Humphrys* [1976] 2 All ER 497 at 535, [1977]
f AC 1 at 55:

'While judges should pause long before staying proceedings which on their face are perfectly regular, it would indeed be bad for justice if in such fortunately rare cases as *R v Riebold* their hands were tied and they were obliged to allow the further trial to proceed.'

g The dangers inherent in the exercise by a trial judge of a general duty to stop a prosecution in limine because it conflicts with his own sense of fairness is well illustrated by *DPP v Connelly* itself. When Connelly's conviction of murder on the first trial had been quashed, an indictment against him for robbery arising out of the same incident came before John Stephenson J, when autrefois acquit was advanced as a plea in bar. A jury was empanelled for the purpose of adjudicating on that plea. The judge directed the
h jury that the plea had not been established and they returned a verdict accordingly. He further held that the only discretion he had in the circumstances was to express an opinion as to the propriety of the Crown's proceeding with the robbery indictment. He expressed the opinion that this would be wrong but, the Crown insisting on proceeding, he said he could not stop the trial (see [1964] AC 1254 at 1259). Had the judge stayed the proceeding on the indictment, a criminal, whom the Court of Appeal and the House of
j Lords subsequently held to have been rightly convicted on the second indictment, would have gone free.

It is easy to foresee that the performance of such a duty in a case such as that before us would present difficult procedural problems, for example (i) of defining the issues claimed to exist, which may be very complex, (ii) of providing for representation of persons whose conduct is impugned, (iii) of ensuring that the persons affected are sufficiently aware of the case they have to meet. Whilst these problems may be overcome, the issues referred to are best left, we think, to be dealt with during the course of the trial and, if necessary, later by the Court of Appeal. The Court of Appeal will have the advantage, one of which we have had the benefit in this case, of assessing whether the defendant has suffered any actual prejudice in the course of the trial.

The exercise of any such duty and discretion as is contended for could have other and more unfortunate consequences. No appeal would lie from the decision of the trial judge, save possibly on an Attorney General's reference, with the disadvantage, inter alia, that there would be no opportunity for appellate courts to establish uniformity of approach in such cases. It would seem to be undesirable to say the least save in exceptional circumstances (as to which in respect of criminal contempt, see *R v D* [1984] 1 All ER 574, [1984] 2 WLR 112) for a trial judge to exercise a power unchallengable by the prosecution, to stay proceedings which are apparently regular both in form and in substance.

In the present case, the application to Judge Shindler to stay proceedings on the indictment was founded on the premise that, as has already been stated, police officers had improperly obtained possession of the appellant's files and tapes and other police officers had perused them for the purpose of the pending trial. The only substantial consequence of that perusal, on which counsel for the appellant relied, was that the prosecution thereby had advance knowledge of the names of the witnesses whom the appellant intended to call at his trial. In argument before us, counsel for the appellant conceded that he could not show that any use was made at the trial of any information contained in the files.

We are satisfied, from a close perusal of the transcript of the summing up and from reading the 500 pages of grounds of appeal prepared by the appellant and those drafted by counsel, that, had there been any basis for an assertion that use had indeed been made at the trial of the appellant's files or tapes, we should have found it, or have had it brought to our notice by or on behalf of the appellant. It was alleged that police officers approached a potential witness for the defence, a man called Hattley, 'seeking', in counsel's words, 'to interfere with the defence'. But counsel later conceded that Hattley had been unaffected by any approach of that kind and gave the evidence he was from the outset apparently prepared to give.

However, counsel for the appellant submits considerations of that kind are irrelevant. They arise from hindsight. If the judge, as he should have done, had conducted a kind of pre-trial inquiry, the trial may never have started, in which event they would not have arisen. The seizure of legally privileged documents, as was done here, is enough to bring into being his duty to inquire before the trial and to exercise the discretion to stay inevitably, says counsel, in favour of the appellant. That not having been done, this court should declare the trial a nullity and quash the convictions appealed against. It is not this court's concern, he went on to say, that the appellant was not in fact, as was conceded, prejudiced by what happened to his documents.

Counsel for the Crown countered those arguments by submitting that to hold such an inquiry would have far-reaching implications. It is important, he said, that criminal courts are not used to discipline the police. Victims of crime and the public at large have an interest in prosecutions going on. Here, there was a proper committal. The right to silence, which he agrees is an important fundamental right (it was much referred to by counsel for the appellant), is properly to be preserved by the discretion of a judge to exclude evidence. Evidence, including a confession improperly obtained, may be and sometimes is declared to be admissible, the weight to be given to it being left to the jury. A pre-trial inquiry such as the appellant contends the judge in this case was under a duty to embark on would itself be open to abuse by unscrupulous and dishonest accused persons. The criminal trial sytem would be placed in jeopardy. The facts of the present case demonstrated the importance of, among other things, discovering during the trial whether alleged misconduct by the police had had any effect on the evidence and any likely bearing on the result. It had had none. In *Mackeson's* case, much relied on by counsel for the appellant, there was no reference in the judgment to the principle sought

a to be established here.

We were much impressed by the submissions of counsel for the Crown. They accord with our view that there is no general duty laid on a judge to conduct a pre-trial inquiry on the application of an accused and, thereafter, to exercise a discretion whether or not he should stay the proceedings.

As we have said, the court's inherent jurisdiction to stay proceedings is not in doubt.

b There is high authority for its existence, as was acknowledged in *R v Hartley* [1978] 2 NZLR 199. There is equally no doubt, in our opinion, that this jurisdiction, the whole scope of which does not arise for examination by us, does not include an obligation to hold a pre-trial inquiry, designed to bring about a stay of proceedings, into such allegations as the improper obtaining of evidence, tampering with evidence and seizure of a defendant's documents prepared for his defence. However reprehensible conduct of

c this kind may be, it is not, at least in circumstances such as the present, an abuse or, in another word, a misuse of the court's process. It is conduct which, in these circumstances, falls to be dealt with in the trial itself by judicial control on admissibility of evidence, the judicial power to direct a verdict of not guilty, usually at the close of the prosecution's case, or by the jury taking account of it in evaluating the evidence before them.

We do not consider that the trial judge erred in any way in refusing to hold a pre-trial

d inquiry. We can find no reason to suppose that the verdict in this case was either unsafe or unsatisfactory.

The unlawful and unjustified seizure of a defendant's documents prepared for his defence should not, of course, occur. Any activity of this kind, apart altogether from its possible implications on the conduct of a trial, is deserving of censure and probably the activation of the police disciplinary code. Whilst we do not feel able to say, on the

e material before us, that the police officers' conduct in this case was of that order, we do feel it right to say that police officers must regard documents, albeit that they are lawfully seized from a defendant following arrest and committal for trial, with great caution, lest they contain matters for which a defendant is entitled to claim the protection of privilege so that his right to silence be not destroyed.

For these reasons, this appeal is dismissed.

f

Appeal dismissed.

The court refused leave to appeal to the House of Lords but certified, under s 22(2) of the Criminal Appeal Act 1968, that the following point of law of general public importance was involved in the decision: whether, where the seizure and removal of legally privileged documents, relevant to a criminal prosecution, by a police officer from the possession of a defendant without his consent was alleged to constitute an abuse of the process of the court, the duty of the trial judge to prevent unfairness to the defendant included (1) a duty to conduct a pre-trial inquiry on the application of the defendant and (2) on a finding of such abuse to exercise a discretion whether or not the proceedings should be stayed.

15 March. The Appeal Committee of the House of Lords (Lord Diplock, Lord Keith of Kinkel and Lord Templeman) dismissed a petition by the appellant for leave to appeal.

Solicitors: *Mackenzie Patten & Co* (for the appellant); *D M O'Shea* (for the Crown).

N P Metcalfe Esq   Barrister.

R v Bromley Licensing Justices, ex parte Bromley Licensed Victuallers' Association

a

QUEEN'S BENCH DIVISION (CROWN OFFICE LIST)
WOOLF J
8 DECEMBER 1983

b

Licensing – Occasional permission – Persons entitled to object to grant of occasional permission – Whether only police may object – Whether trade association such as licensed victuallers' association entitled to object – Licensing (Occasional Permissions) Act 1983, s 1(1).

Licensing – Occasional permission – Grant – Period of permission – Number of permissions required – Occasional permission sought for series of periods on successive days – Performances by operatic society on successive nights – Total time for which permission sought not exceeding 24 hours – Whether separate permissions required for each period – Licensing (Occasional Permissions) Act 1983, s 1(1).

c

A trade association similar to a licensed victuallers' association, as well as the police, is entitled to oppose an application made to licensing justices by an organisation not carried on for private gain for the grant under s 1(1)ᵃ of the Licensing (Occasional Permissions) Act 1983 of an occasional permission to sell intoxicating liquor at a function connected with such an organisation's activities. However, licensing justices have a discretion in appropriate cases to refuse to entertain a trade association's objection if, having heard the nature of the objection and the facts relied on by the association, they conclude that no useful purpose would be served by hearing the objection (see p 797 *g* to *j*, post).

d

e

The power given to licensing justices by s 1(1) of the 1983 Act to grant an occasional permission to sell intoxicating liquor 'during a period not exceeding twenty-four hours' is limited, in respect to the period for which the occasional permission is sought, to one continuous period of 24 hours; where application is made for a series of periods on successive dates, eg an application by an operatic society to sell alcohol at performances on successive nights, then, even though the total period for which the occasional permission is sought does not exceed 24 hours, separate permissions for each period are required (see p 798 *d*, post).

f

Notes

For occasional licences, see 26 Halsbury's Laws (4th edn) paras 19–20, and for cases on the subject, see 30 Digest (Reissue) 85–87, 642–650.

g

Case referred to in judgment

R v Bow Street Stipendiary Magistrate, ex p Comr of Police of the Metropolis [1983] 2 All ER 915.

h

Application for judicial review

Bromley Licensed Victuallers' Association applied, with the leave of Webster J granted on 26 October 1983, for declarations (1) that the decision of the Bromley Licensing Justices sitting at Bromley Magistrates' Court on 23 September 1983 to refuse to hear objections other than from the police on the hearing of an application for the grant of an occasional permission under the Licensing (Occasional Permissions) Act 1983 made by the Biggin Hill Light Operatic Society was wrong in law and (2) that the justices' decision to grant one permission only enabling the society to sell intoxicating liquor at

j

---

a   Section 1(1) is set out at p 795 *h*, post

performances given by it on four consecutive evenings was wrong in law. The facts are
set out in the judgment.

Vivian Robinson for the association.
The justices did not appear.

WOOLF J. This is an application by the Bromley Licensed Victuallers' Association for
judicial review in respect of a decision by the Bromley Licensing Justices sitting in
Bromley on 23 September 1983. The justices are not represented before the court but
very helpfully and properly they have filed before the court an affidavit explaining their
decision which is under attack.

Counsel for the association, who has if I may say so very clearly and skilfully put
forward before the court the arguments on behalf of the association, has dealt with the
difficulties which faced the justices and, in particular, has dealt with the arguments
contained in the affidavit of the justices. As counsel for the association, who has some
considerable experience in this field, indicated that the points involved were ones of
general importance in regard to licensing I considered whether it was necessary for me
to seek the assistance of an amicus, but having heard counsel's arguments I am satisfied I
can deal with the points which are raised without the benefit which could be obtained
from an amicus.

The background to the application is as follows. The Licensing (Occasional Permissions)
Act 1983 enables eligible organisations, which are organisations not carried on for
purposes of private gain, to apply to licensing justices for occasional permissions. The
Biggin Hill Light Operatic Society, by their treasurer, Mr Powell, applied for such a
permission in respect of performances which the society were to hold on four successive
nights at a local school which they hoped would be attended by some 120 people each
evening. During each performance it was naturally desired that they should have the
facility for selling alcoholic liquor.

When the matter came before the licensing justices the association wished to appear
and oppose the grant of occasional permissions. The justices declined to hear the
association. They took the view that only the police were entitled to make objection.
They also, in relation to the four performances, granted one permission. It is the
contention of the association that instead of one permission being granted it was necessary
for four separate permissions to be granted. That is a matter of some significance because,
as will be apparent when I refer to the relevant statutory provision, the number of
permissions which can be granted to organisations such as the operatic society is strictly
limited.

The justices were acting under the Licensing (Occasional Permissions) Act 1983. That
Act, as its preamble makes clear, is an Act to empower licensing justices to grant to
representatives of organisations not carried on for private gain occasional permissions
authorising the sale of intoxicating liquor at functions connected with the activities of
such organisations. The power to grant permissions is contained in s 1(1), which is in
these terms:

> 'Licensing justices may, if satisfied as to the matters mentioned in subsection (2)
> below, grant to an officer of an eligible organisation or of a branch of such an
> organisation a permission (referred to in this Act as an occasional permission)
> authorising him to sell intoxicating liquor during a period not exceeding twenty
> four hours at a function held by the organisation or branch in connection with the
> organisation's activities.'

Subsection (2) sets out the matters on which the licensing justices must be satisfied
before they grant such a permission. They are:

> '(a) that the officer is a fit and proper person to sell intoxicating liquor and is
> resident in their licensing district; (b) that the place where the function is to be held

will be a suitable place for intoxicating liquor to be sold and is situated in that district; and (c) that the sale of intoxicating liquor at the function is not likely to *a* result in disturbance or annoyance being caused to residents in the neighbourhood of that place, or in any disorderly conduct.'

Subsection (4) provides:

'Not more than four occasional permissions may be granted in a licensing district in any period of twelve months in respect of functions held by the same organisation *b* or branch.'

There is a restriction with regard to the sale of intoxicating liquor on Sundays and then there is a definition of 'eligible organisation' contained in sub-s (6).

Section 2 deals with the application for occasional permissions. Subsection (1) requires that it shall be in writing and contain various details with relation to the application. Subsection (2) requires that the application shall be served on the licensing justices not *c* less than one month before the date of the function in respect of which the application is made. The fact that a month's notice, which is a substantial period of time, is required is not without significance. Under sub-s (3) of s 2, the clerk, on receipt of the application, has to send a copy to the police.

Subsection (5) says that in addition to the clerk sending to the applicant notice of the date, time and place of the session he has to show, in the list he keeps under para 6 of Sch *d* 2, the name and address of the applicant, the nature of the application and the place where the function in question is to be held. That subsection links up with the ordinary applications for justices' licences in relation to which the clerk for each licensing session has to keep a list of persons applying for ordinary justices' licences.

Prior to the passing of the 1983 Act, activities of the sort which were being conducted by the society were catered for under s 180 of the Licensing Act 1964, as amended. That *e* section provided in sub-s (1):

'Justices of the peace may, on the application of the holder of a justices' on-licence, grant him a licence (in this Act referred to as an "occasional licence") authorising the sale by him of any intoxicating liquor to which his justices' on-licence extends at such place other than the premises in respect of which his justices' on-licence was *f* granted, during such period not exceeding three weeks at one time, and between such hours, as may be specified in the occasional licence . . .'

When the terms of s 180 of the 1964 Act are compared with the provisions of the 1983 Act the object of the 1983 Act becomes clearly apparent. It is designed to assist those carrying on activities such as were being carried on by the society by dispensing with the *g* cumbersome procedure for having to arrange for a licence holder to apply for an occasional licence in respect of an activity which was taking place in connection with some charitable or similar function.

It is well known to those who practice in the licensing field that associations similar to the applicants in this matter regularly attend before licensing justices to oppose the grant of new licences. They do so largely to protect the interests of the existing trade, but this *h* is accepted and has been recognised for many years because it is appreciated that, although the motivation for the association attending and opposing the grant of such licences is largely one of self-interest, they assist the justices to perform their function by bringing before the justices material which would perhaps not otherwise have been brought to their notice, although the police can also perform a similar function. Sometimes the association is in a much better position than the police to put relevant material before the *j* justices.

It is the contention of counsel for the association that in relation to occasional permissions the intent of the legislation is that there should be no departure from the ordinary practice in relation to the grant of justices' licences. Of course, the occasions on which associations are going to think it worth while going to the expense of opposing

occasional permissions one would hope would be rare. However, clearly there can be
circumstances where they would wish to do so as indicated in this present matter.
In support of their decision the justices, in their affidavit, set out three separate
arguments. The first is that the 1983 Act obviously followed the precedent established
by s 180 of the 1964 Act in relation to occasional licences and does not provide for any
form of public or private notice to individuals or bodies or organisations which might be
interested in opposing other than the police. What is said by the justices in that paragraph
of their affidavit is absolutely right with regard to s 180 of the 1964 Act but is not
accurate with regard to the 1983 Act because, instead of following the precedent of s 180,
in fact the 1983 Act expressly followed the precedent provided by the main and principal
Act in requiring the matters to be listed in the list by the clerk, with the result that
anyone can inspect that list. The clerk has notice for at least a month and clearly it was
intended by Parliament that in addition to the police other persons should be informed.
It seems to me that prima facie there would not have been that requirement if it had not
been intended that others apart from the police were entitled to object; indeed, contrary
to the view of the justices, the contrast in language between s 180 of the 1964 Act and
that of the 1983 Act indicates to me that there was a different approach by Parliament
from that under s 180.

The second paragraph set out in the affidavit as supporting the justices' decision is in
these terms:

> 'The purported objection of the Association was based upon trade protection
> principles and we were informed that no objection was taken either to the Society
> or the applicant or to the nature of the function which prompted the application.'

No doubt the justices may be right in the inference they draw as to the nature of the
motivation of the association. However, as I have sought to indicate, even though that
may be the motivation, the association could still play a useful function and, as I have
indicated in my reference to the 1983 Act s 1(2) sets out three matters in respect of which
the justices have to be satisfied. Those are certainly matters on which the association
might have brought to the attention of the justices relevant considerations. The justices
have a general discretion apart from those three matters and again it is right to say that
the association could bring to the attention of the justices relevant information of which
they would not otherwise be aware.

The third matter is:

> 'Our duties and obligations under section 1(2) of the Act could be properly and
> adequately performed by receiving evidence from the applicant and by questioning
> him as to his character, experience and mode of operation of the bar.'

I have no doubt that in the vast majority of cases that is absolutely right, but if
Parliament intended objectors, apart from the police, to have the right of objection then
the mere fact that the justices feel they could perform their function in that way is no
answer. I would only add this. It is very difficult to anticipate whether or not a particular
objection is going to be helpful. It would be wrong for justices to prejudge that matter
without having full details of the nature of the objection. I therefore consider that the
justices were wrong in taking the view that they did, but as a matter of law and principle
they were not required to hear the association.

I do not want what I have said to be misinterpreted. The licensing justices remain
masters of their own procedure except in so far as there is a specific statutory provision
which controls the way they exercise their functions. Justices must retain a discretion in
appropriate cases to make it clear that a particular form of objection is of no advantage or
help to them and is wasting their time. If, in those circumstances, having ascertained the
nature of the objection and learning the facts relied on, they come to the conclusion that
they do not wish to hear more, then I apprehend this court would certainly not seek to
interfere with justices who, being anxious to proceed with other applications, deal quite
shortly with objections which are wasting their time. The justices have very heavy

commitments today and I would not want it to be thought by anything I have said in this judgment that I was suggesting that the justices were required to hear out long and extended objections by trade associations in relation to occasional permissions which, under the provisions of the 1983 Act which I have already read, are confined to four in a year and obviously are not matters which should be required to take up a substantial part of the time of licensing justices.

Turning to the second point in support of their contention that they were entitled to grant a single permission in respect of four performances, the justices clearly took the view that this was a single function. Speaking for myself, I have grave reservations whether, using the word 'function' in its ordinary meaning, it is apt to cover performances of four separate nights in a school hall. I do not propose to decide that matter because in my view it is not necessary for me to do so having regard to my view of the subsection as a whole.

The justices not only regarded this as a single function, but thought they were entitled to grant one permission because the periods during which the bar would be open would not exceed, in total, 24 hours. The argument of counsel for the association advanced to the contrary was that the words 'a period not exceeding twenty-four hours' meant that the power to grant a permission was limited to one continuous period and if that one continuous period exceeded 24 hours it would contravene the 1983 Act. But so would a permission which covered a series of periods contravene the provisions of the Act even though their total did not exceed 24 hours. It seems to me clear on the language that what is meant is that there should be able to be granted a permission for one continuous period not exceeding 24 hours.

Here the justices were required to grant four separate permissions. I can well understand why the justices would be reluctant to adopt that interpretation: it would mean that in that particular school there could only be four performances where these permissions could be granted, so the granting of these permissions would mean that during the rest of the year, if there was to be alcohol sold, it could not be sold under the 1983 Act but would have to be sold under an occasional licence.

Although that is an undesirable consequence of my interpretation, I still adopt that interpretation and draw attention to the fact that s 180 of the 1964 Act quite clearly enables occasional licences to be for a period not exceeding three weeks. Thus, if you have a function which extends, and I accept that it can in appropriate circumstances extend, up to a period of three weeks there can be one occasional licence for that.

As Glidewell J said in *R v Bow Street Stipendiary Magistrate, ex p Comr of Police of the Metropolis* [1983] 2 All ER 915 at 917: 'The event or function, it is clear, may take place only on one day or may extend over a number of days, that matters not.' However, although it may extend over a number of days it must still be a single function.

If, under the 1983 Act, you were able to grant a permission for the sale of intoxicating liquor, on different dates, as long as the total time did not exceed 24 hours, you could have a situation where on 48 occasions a single permission would apply and that would mean that you could have a permission under the 1983 Act where you could not have an occasional licence under s 180 of the 1964 Act. Clearly the power under the 1983 Act is intended to be more limited than the power under s 180, and it seems to me, therefore, that the interpretation of counsel for the association not only accords with the actual words used but also accords with the intent and spirit of the provisions.

I would just add one more word with regard to this. I was, although this was not a matter relied on by the justices, for a time concerned about the fact that s 1(3)(c) of the 1983 Act says 'the hours between which such liquor may be so sold and the date (or dates) on which those hours fall [must be set out in the permission]'. The reference to 'dates' might suggest that you could have different periods. However, with regard to that, counsel for the association pointed out that you could have a period of less than 24 hours that extended over two days and I agree with him that that is the probable explanation of the use of the word 'dates' in s 1(3)(c).

a It follows that I have come to the conclusion that the justices were also wrong in this matter in granting the permission in the terms which they did. What they should have done, if they were prepared to do so, was to grant four separate permissions. Accordingly, in this case I would be prepared to grant relief.

However, the society have already taken advantage of the permission which was granted, the society being no doubt in ignorance of the difficulties created by the course taken by the justices. They no doubt were able to enjoy alcoholic refreshment on each
b performance. It would therefore be quite pointless for me now to grant any relief. The judgment which I have given I hope clarifies the law, and, subject to counsel for the association seeking to persuade me to do otherwise, I propose, having given this judgment, to make no order.

No order.

c
Solicitors: *Lickfolds Wiley & Powles* (for the association).

Dilys Tausz   Barrister.

d
R v Secretary of State for the Home Department and others, ex parte Tarrant and another
R v Wormwood Scrubs Prison Board of Visitors, ex parte Anderson and others

e
QUEEN'S BENCH DIVISION
KERR LJ AND WEBSTER J
13, 14, 17, 18 OCTOBER, 8 NOVEMBER 1983

f
Natural justice – Prison board of visitors – Exercise of disciplinary powers – Request by prisoner for legal representation or assistance of friend or adviser – Whether prisoner entitled as of right to legal representation or assistance of friend or adviser at disciplinary hearing before board – Whether board having discretion to allow legal representation or assistance of friend or adviser – What matters should be taken into consideration in exercising discretion – Prison Act 1952, s 47(2) – Prison Rules 1964, r 49(2).

g
The applicants were convicted prisoners who were charged with grave or especially grave offences against prison discipline, namely assault or attempted assault on a prison officer, contrary to r 51 of the Prison Rules 1964, or mutiny, contrary to r 52. At the respective inquiries by prison boards of visitors into the charges each applicant requested legal representation while two of the applicants also requested the assistance of a friend or
h adviser at the hearing. The board of visitors refused the requests in each case. The applicants applied for judicial review, inter alia, by way of certiorari on the grounds (a) that a prisoner was entitled as of right to legal representation or to the assistance of a friend or adviser, and (b) alternatively, the boards had a discretion in the matter and ought to have exercised that discretion by allowing legal representation.

j
Held – (1) Although a prisoner appearing before a board of visitors on a disciplinary charge was not entitled as of right to have legal representation or the assistance of a friend or adviser, as a matter of natural justice a board of visitors had a discretion to allow such representation or assistance at any hearing before it under the common law rule that a prisoner retained all civil rights not taken away from him expressly or by necessary

implication, since (a) the power of a board of visitors to control its own procedure was not limited by common law or by statute and therefore a board had an unfettered *a* discretion to allow legal representation or assistance from a friend or adviser, (b) the exercise of such a discretion would sometimes be necessary in order to comply with the requirements under s 47(2)ᵃ of the Prison Act 1952 and r 49(2)ᵇ of the 1964 rules that a prisoner charged with a disciplinary offence be given a proper and full opportunity of presenting his case, and (c) neither the disciplinary structure under the 1964 rules, the procedure of boards of visitors, nor the practical consequences that could follow from *b* boards having such a discretion impliedly detracted from the existence of such a discretion (see p 805 *b*, p 806 *h*, p 807 *a* to *c*, p 811 *d h*, p 812 *a b f*, p 813 *a b d* and *g* to p 814 *e*, p 815 *b c*, p 823 *b* and *j* to p 824 *a* and *h* to p 825 *f* and *j* and p 826 *c d*, post); dictum of Lord Denning MR in *Enderby Town Football Club Ltd v Football Association Ltd* [1971] 1 All ER at 218, *Fraser v Mudge* [1975] 3 All ER 78, dictum of Lord Denning MR in *Maynard v Osmond* [1977] 1 All ER at 79 and *Raymond v Honey* [1982] 1 All ER 756 *c* applied; dicta of Lord Tenterden CJ in *Collier v Hicks* (1831) 2 B & Ad at 669, 671 and *McKenzie v McKenzie* [1970] 3 All ER 1034 distinguished; *R v Pentridge Prison Visiting Justice, ex p Walker* [1975] VR 883 and *R v Hull Prison Board of Visitors, ex p St Germain* [1979] 1 All ER 701 considered.

(2) In regard to the applicants who were charged with mutiny under r 52, no board of visitors properly directing itself could reasonably have refused the applicants' request for *d* legal representation, having regard to the complicated nature of the charge, the need to comply with s 47(2) and r 49(2) and the gravity of the consequences if the charge was proved. In regard to the applicants who were charged with assaulting a prison officer, their requests for legal representation or for assistance from a friend or adviser ought to have been considered on the merits. Since in each case the board had totally failed to exercise its discretion it followed that there had been a breach of natural justice and *e* certiorari would be ordered (see p 815 *g h*, p 818 *b*, p 821 *d j*, p 822 *d* to p 823 *c* and p 826 *e* to *h*, post).

Per curiam. When exercising the discretion to allow legal representation or the assistance of a friend or adviser, a board of visitors should first bear in mind the overriding obligation under r 49(2) of the 1964 rules to ensure that a prisoner is given 'a full opportunity . . . of presenting his . . . case', and should also take into account, inter alia, *f* (1) the seriousness of the charge and the potential penalty, (2) whether any points of law are likely to arise, (3) a prisoner's capacity to present his own case, (4) procedural difficulties arising from the fact that a prisoner awaiting adjudication before a board is normally kept apart from other prisoners and may therefore be inhibited in the preparation of his defence, and the difficulty for some prisoners of cross-examining witnesses, particularly expert witnesses, (5) the need for reasonable speed in making an *g* adjudication, and (6) the need for fairness as between prisoners or as between prisoners and prison officers (see p 816 *f* to p 817 *f*, p 823 *b* and p 825 *d e*, post).

Notes
For offences against prison discipline, see 37 Halsbury's Laws (4th edn) paras 1169–1173, and for cases on the subject, see 37(3) Digest (Reissue) 394–396, 5272–5275. *h*

For the Prison Act 1952, s 47, see 25 Halsbury's Statutes (3rd edn) 851.

For the Prison Rules 1964, rr 49, 51, 52, see 18 Halsbury's Statutory Instruments (4th reissue) 21, 22, 23.

Cases referred to in judgments
Campbell and Fell v UK (1982) 5 EHRR 207.
Collier v Hicks (1831) 2 B & Ad 663, 109 ER 1290. *j*
Enderby Town Football Club Ltd v Football Association Ltd [1971] 1 All ER 215, [1971] Ch 591, [1970] 3 WLR 1021, CA.

---

a   Section 47(2) is set out at p 804 *f*, post
b   Rule 49(2) is set out at p 804 *g*, post

Engel v The Netherlands (No 1) (1976) 1 EHRR 647.

Engel v The Netherlands (No 2) (1976) 1 EHRR 706.

Fraser v Mudge [1975] 3 All ER 78, [1975] 1 WLR 1132, CA.

General Medical Council v Spackman [1943] 2 All ER 337, [1943] AC 627, HL.

McKenzie v McKenzie [1970] 3 All ER 1034, [1971] P 33, [1970] 3 WLR 472, CA.

Maynard v Osmond [1977] 1 All ER 64, [1977] QB 240, [1976] 3 WLR 711, CA.

Pergamon Press Ltd, Re [1970] 3 All ER 535, [1971] Ch 388, [1970] 3 WLR 792, CA.

Pett v Greyhound Racing Association Ltd [1968] 2 All ER 545, [1969] 1 QB 125, [1968] 2 WLR 1471, CA.

Pett v Greyhound Racing Association Ltd (No 2) [1969] 2 All ER 221, [1970] 1 QB 46, [1969] 2 WLR 1228.

R v Blundeston Prison Board of Visitors, ex p Fox-Taylor [1982] 1 All ER 646, DC.

R v Derby Justices, ex p Kooner [1970] 3 All ER 399, [1971] 1 QB 147, [1970] 3 WLR 598, DC.

R v Grant, Davis, Riley and Topley [1957] 2 All ER 694, [1957] 1 WLR 906, C-MAC.

R v Hull Prison Board of Visitors, ex p St Germain [1979] 1 All ER 701, [1979] QB 425, [1979] 2 WLR 42, CA.

R v Hull Prison Board of Visitors, ex p St Germain (No 2) [1979] 3 All ER 545, [1979] 1 WLR 1401, DC.

R v Pentridge Prison Visiting Justice, ex p Walker [1975] VR 883.

Raymond v Honey [1982] 1 All ER 756, [1983] 1 AC 1, [1982] 2 WLR 465, HL.

Russell v Duke of Norfolk [1949] 1 All ER 109, CA.

University of Ceylon v Fernando [1960] 1 All ER 631, [1960] 1 WLR 223, PC.

Wiseman v Borneman [1969] 3 All ER 275, [1971] AC 297, [1969] 3 WLR 706, HL.

Cases also cited

A-G v BBC [1980] 3 All ER 161, [1981] AC 303, HL.

Ashby v White (1704) 14 State Tr 695, HL.

Board of Education v Rice [1911] AC 179, [1911–13] All ER Rep 36, HL.

Byrne v Kinematograph Renters Society Ltd [1958] 2 All ER 579, [1958] 1 WLR 762.

De Verteuil v Knaggs [1918] AC 557, PC.

Dyson v A-G [1912] 1 Ch 158, CA.

John v Rees [1969] 2 All ER 274, [1970] Ch 345.

Osgood v Nelson (1872) LR 5 HL 636, HL.

Pan-American World Airways Inc v Dept of Trade [1976] 1 Lloyd's Rep 257, CA.

R v Gartree Prison Board of Visitors, ex p Mealy (1981) Times, 14 November.

R v Highpoint Prison Board of Visitors, ex p McConkey (1982) Times, 23 September.

R v Secretary of State for the Environment, ex p Brent London BC [1983] 3 All ER 321, [1982] QB 593, DC.

R v Secretary of State for the Home Dept, ex p Bhajan Singh [1975] 2 All ER 1081, [1976] 1 QB 198, CA.

Waddington v Miah [1974] 2 All ER 377, [1974] 1 WLR 683, HL.

Ward v James [1965] 1 All ER 563, [1966] 1 QB 273, CA.

Waugh v British Rlys Board [1979] 2 All ER 1169, [1980] AC 521, HL.

Applications for judicial review

James Tarrant, Roy Derek Leyland, Thomas Tangney, Christopher Clark and James Anderson, all convicted prisoners, each applied with the leave of a judge for, inter alia, orders of certiorari to quash awards made against them by a prison board of visitors inquiring into prison disciplinary charges or the decision by the board of visitors to proceed with adjudications into such charges, on the ground that the boards were in breach of natural justice in refusing the applicants' requests for legal representation at the hearings or for the assistance of a friend or adviser. In the case of the applicant Tarrant, the respondents were the Secretary of State for the Home Department and the board of visitors of Albany prison, in the case of the applicant Leyland, the respondents

were the board of visitors of Albany prison, and in the case of the applicants Tangney, Clark and Anderson, the respondents were the board of visitors of Wormwood Scrubs   *a*
prison. The facts are set out in the judgment of Webster J.

Stephen Sedley QC and *Edward Fitzgerald* for Tangney, Clark and Anderson.
Edward Fitzgerald for Tarrant.
Andrew Collins and *Nigel Seed* for Leyland.
Simon D Brown for the boards of visitors.   *b*
The Secretary of State did not appear.

Cur adv vult

8 November. The following judgments were delivered.

WEBSTER J (giving the first judgment at the invitation of Kerr LJ). These are five   *c*
applications by convicted prisoners for judicial review, each applicant seeking to quash a
decision of a prison board of visitors on various grounds, all five of them also asking for
injunctions or declarations or both. The respondents to two of the applications are the
board of visitors of Albany prison, and to the other three the respondents are the board
of visitors of Wormwood Scrubs prison.

There is one ground which is common to each application, namely that the applicant,   *d*
at the hearing by the board of visitors of a disciplinary charge against him, was refused
legal representation. Two applicants also rely on the board's refusal to allow a friend or
adviser to be present with him at the hearing and one on its refusal to allow him to
consult a solicitor before the hearing. In four out of the five cases the applicant complains
of other decisions of the board of visitors in question which he claims to be unlawful.
The short facts giving rise to each of the applications are as follows.   *e*

The applicant Tarrant. On 20 May 1983 he was serving a sentence of 16 years'
imprisonment at Albany prison. On that date, although he had already lost some
remission, he was still entitled to 4½ years' remission. Having been charged with mutiny
together with others on 20 May 1983, on 21 July he appeared before a panel of the board
of visitors of Albany prison. On 21 July the hearing was adjourned after the evidence
against him had been given. It was to have resumed in August; but, as a result of leave   *f*
given by Popplewell J on 12 August to make the present application, the hearing has
been further adjourned pending the decision of this court.

The applicant Leyland. On 20 May 1983 he was serving a sentence of 8½ years at Albany
prison. He has also been charged with mutiny on that date, together with others,
including Tarrant. The first hearing of that charge by a panel of the board of visitors of
the prison on 20 July 1983 was adjourned because of the absence of prosecution witnesses.   *g*
On 22 July the board found the charge proved and awarded a loss of 400 days' remission
and 56 days' stoppage of earnings. The latter part of that order was suspended by an order
of Mann J with effect from 7 September 1983.

The applicant Tangney. On 24 June 1983 he was serving a sentence of life imprisonment
at Wormwood Scrubs. He has been charged with seven disciplinary offences, including
an assault on a prison officer, on that date. Those charges were heard by a panel of the   *h*
board of visitors of Wormwood Scrubs prison on 6, 25 and 26 July 1983. On that last
date the charges were found to have been proved and he was awarded 112 days' loss of
privileges and loss of associated work. That award was suspended with effect from 12
September when Mann J gave this applicant leave to make this application.

The applicant Clark. On 16 June 1983 he was serving a sentence of life imprisonment
at Wormwood Scrubs. He has been charged with four disciplinary offences, including   *j*
abusive and threatening language, and attempting to assault a prison officer, on that date.
On 12 August those offences were found to have been proved and he was awarded 77
days cellular confinement and exclusion from associated labour by a panel of the board
of visitors of Wormwood Scrubs prison. That award has been suspended with effect from
19 September by an order of McCullough J.

The applicant Anderson. On 16 June 1983 he was serving a sentence of life imprisonment

a at Wormwood Scrubs. He has been charged with four disciplinary offences on that date, including assaulting a prison officer. The hearing of those charges by a panel of the board of visitors of Wormwood Scrubs prison was adjourned part-heard on 30 August 1983.

All five applicants were kept in seclusion from the date when they were first charged. All five applicants requested legal representation and were refused it by the board in question. The applicants Tangney and Anderson also requested, and were refused, the

b presence of a friend or adviser.

Judicial review

The decisions of boards of visitors when adjudicating on charges of offences against discipline have been subject to judicial review since the decision of the Court of Appeal

c in *R v Hull Prison Board of Visitors, ex p St Germain* [1979] 1 All ER 701, [1979] QB 425.

Boards of visitors, disciplinary offences and hearings

There have been boards of visitors since the Prison Act 1898 when they were established for non-local prisons. Local prisons already had visiting committees elected

d by the magistrates of quarter sessions. After quarter sessions were abolished by the Courts Act 1971, boards of visitors were appointed for local prisons. There are now about 115 boards. Boards have two functions. They have an administrative, sometimes described as a pastoral, function which includes the duty to hear complaints made to them by prisoners (see s 6(3) of the Prison Act 1952 and r 95(1) of the Prison Rules 1964, SI 1964/ 388). Their second function is to adjudicate on charges of offences against discipline in

e the exercise of their disciplinary powers under the 1952 Act.

There are three categories of offences against discipline provided by the 1964 rules, as amended by the Prison (Amendment) Rules 1974, SI 1974/713.

The first category consists of about 15 offences in respect of which the prison governor has power to make one or more of a number of 'awards', which include forfeiture of remission of sentence for a period not exceeding 14 days: see rr 47 and 50.

f The second category of offences, described in the marginal heading to r 51 as 'Graver offences', consists of:

'(*a*) escaping or attempting to escape from prison or from legal custody, (*b*) assaulting an officer, or (*c*) doing gross personal violence to any person not being an officer . . .'

g By r 51, where a prisoner is charged with any of those offences, the governor hears the charge first but, unless he dismisses the charge, he—

'shall . . . forthwith inform the Secretary of State and shall, unless otherwise directed by him, refer the charge to the board of visitors.'

He may also under r 51 refer to the board of visitors a prisoner charged with any

h serious or repeated offence against discipline (not being an offence to which r 52 applies) for which the awards the governor can make seem insufficient. If the board find an offence under r 51 proved, the awards which they have power to make include exclusion from associated work, stoppage of earnings, and cellular confinement, in each case for a period not exceeding 56 days, and forfeiture of remission for a period not exceeding 180 days. Rule 51(5) gives to the Secretary of State a power to require any charge to which

j r 51 applies to be referred to him, instead of to the board of visitors, in which case an officer of the Secretary of State inquires into the charge and, if he finds the offence proved, has power to make one or more of the awards which the board have power to make.

The third category of offences, namely those created by r 52, are described in the marginal heading to that rule as 'Especially grave offences'. Those offences are: '(*a*)

mutiny or incitement to mutiny; or (b) doing gross personal violence to an officer . . .'
Where a prisoner is charged with one of those offences, the governor must forthwith
inform the Secretary of State and must refer the charge to the board of visitors unless
otherwise directed by the Secretary of State. The powers of the board, if they find the
offence proved, include the power to make one or more of the awards listed in r 51(4)
'. . . so however that, if they make an award of forfeiture of remission, the period forfeited
may exceed 180 days'.

The following procedural provisions are relevant to these applications. Rule 48
provides:

> '(1) Where a prisoner is to be charged with an offence against discipline, the
> charge shall be laid as soon as possible.
>
> (2) A prisoner who is to be charged with an offence against discipline may be kept
> apart from other prisoners pending adjudication.
>
> (3) Every charge shall be inquired into, in the first instance, by the governor.
>
> (4) Every charge shall be first inquired into not later, save in exceptional
> circumstances, than the next day, not being a Sunday or public holiday, after it is
> laid.'

Rule 49(1) provides:

> 'Where a prisoner is charged with an offence against discipline, he shall be
> informed of the charge as soon as possible and, in any case, before the time when it
> is inquired into by the governor.'

Where a board of visitors adjudicates on an offence under r 51, the panel must consist
of not more than five nor fewer than two members of the board. Where, however, a
board adjudicates on an offence under r 52, the panel must consist of not more than five
nor fewer than three members, at least two being justices of the peace.

Finally, but most pertinently to the present applications, s 47(2) of the Prison Act 1952
provides:

> 'Rules made under this section shall make provision for ensuring that a person
> who is charged with any offence under the rules shall be given a proper opportunity
> of presenting his case.'

That requirement is carried into effect by the provisions of r 49(2) of the 1964 rules,
which provides:

> 'At any inquiry into a charge against a prisoner he shall be given a full opportunity
> of hearing what is alleged against him and of presenting his own case.'

Finally I refer to two matters of practice or procedure. Rule 49(1), as has been seen,
requires a prisoner to be informed of a charge as soon as possible and, in any case, before
it is inquired into by the governor. And r 48(3) provides that every charge be inquired
into, in the first instance, by the governor. Although it appears to be the practice, where
a charge is referred to the board of visitors, to inform the prisoner again of that charge,
and although, it appears, the detail of the charge may on that occasion be amended, it
seems that the prisoner will have been aware of the charge against him, which the board
of visitors hears, at least in substance since before he first appeared on that charge before
the governor.

As to the timing of hearings, it was common ground at the hearing of the applications
that a charge can come before a board of visitors within a matter of days of its having
been laid. On the other hand, the periods intervening between the date of the alleged
offence and the first hearing by the board in the cases of these applicants varied from
between about 14 days in the case of Tangney to about two months in the cases of
Leyland and Tarrant, a period which was probably partly attributable to the number of
prisoners involved and to their dispersal, after the alleged offences, to other prisons.

The right to legal representation

a   I shall first consider the contention made on behalf of each applicant, except Leyland, that there is an entitlement, as of right, to have legal representation at a hearing before the board of visitors, leaving until later the contention that a board has a discretion to grant legal representation and the contentions relating to the presence of a prisoner's friend or adviser at the hearing.

It seems to me that, as a result of the decision of the Court of Appeal in *Fraser v Mudge*
b   [1975] 3 All ER 78, [1975] 1 WLR 1132, this court is bound to decide that a prisoner is not entitled, as of right, to be legally represented before a board of visitors.

The plaintiff in that case was a prisoner serving a long term of imprisonment who had been charged with an offence under r 51. That charge was due to be heard by the board of visitors at Bristol prison at 2.15 pm on 12 June 1975. But before the hearing a writ was issued on the plaintiff's behalf claiming, inter alia, an injunction to restrain the board
c   from inquiring into the charge until he was represented by a solicitor and counsel of his choice. Chapman J refused to grant an injunction and the Court of Appeal dismissed the plaintiff's ex parte appeal against that refusal. Counsel who appears on these applications for the applicants Tangney, Clark and Anderson appeared for the plaintiff in that case.

Because, on these applications, he and counsel for the applicant Tarrant have asked us to distinguish that decision from the facts of these applications, it is necessary to cite parts
d   of the short judgments given in the case. Lord Denning MR said ([1975] 1 WLR 1132 at 1133–1134; cf [1975] 3 All ER 78 at 79):

'We all know that, when a man is brought up before his commanding officer for a breach of discipline, whether in the armed forces or in ships at sea, it never has been the practice to allow legal representation. It is of the first importance that the cases should be decided quickly. If legal representation were allowed, it would mean
e   considerable delay. So also with breaches of prison discipline. They must be heard and decided speedily. Those who hear the cases must, of course, act fairly. They must let the man know the charge and give him a proper opportunity of presenting his case. But that can be done and is done without the matter being held up for legal representation. I do not think we ought to alter the existing practice. We ought not to create a precedent such as to suggest that an individual is entitled to legal
f   representation. There is no real arguable case in support of this application and I would reject it.'

Roskill LJ said ([1975] 3 All ER 78 and 80, [1975] 1 WLR 1132 at 1134):

'One looks to see what are the broad principles underlying these rules [the Prison Rules 1964]. They are to maintain discipline in prison by proper, swift and speedy
g   decision, whether by the governor or the visitors; and it seems to me that the requirements of natural justice do not make it necessary that a person against whom disciplinary proceedings are pending should as of right be entitled to be represented by solicitors or counsel or both.'

Counsel for Tangney, Clark and Anderson submits that this court is not bound to
h   follow that decision because its ratio decidendi is inconsistent with the ratio decidendi in *Ex p St Germain* [1979] 1 All ER 701, [1979] QB 435. He submits that the ratio decidendi in *Fraser v Mudge* was that in considering the application of the rules of natural justice to disciplinary hearings at a prison, the same rules apply to the governor as to the board of visitors; whereas, he submits, the Court of Appeal in *Ex p St Germain* distinguished between them.

j   But in my view there is no inconsistency between the two decisions, for two reasons. In the first place, in *Ex p St Germain* the decision was much broader than that in *Fraser v Mudge*: it was simply that certiorari would lie against the board of visitors, whereas the decision in *Fraser v Mudge* was, specifically, that there was no right to legal representation before the board. But secondly, and in my view conclusively, it does not seem to me that the Court of Appeal as a whole in *Ex p St Germain* distinguished between the governor and the visitors. Megaw LJ certainly did so. He said ([1979] 1 All ER 701 at 711, [1979] QB 425 at 447–448):

'To my mind, contrary to the submission put forward by the board of visitors in their respondents' notice, while the board of visitors have numerous other functions connected with the administration of the prison, their function in acting as a judicial tribunal in adjudicating on charges of offences against discipline, and in making awards consequent on findings of guilt, is properly regarded as a separate and independent function, different in character from their other functions. It is materially different, in my judgment, from the functions of the governor in dealing with alleged offences against discipline. While the governor hears charges and makes awards, his position in so doing corresponds to that of the commanding officer in military discipline or the schoolmaster in school discipline. His powers of summary discipline are not only of a limited and summary nature but they are also intimately connected with his functions of day-to-day administration. To my mind, both good sense and the practical requirements of public policy make it undesirable that his exercise of that part of his administrative duties should be made subject to certiorari. But the same does not apply to the adjudications and awards of boards of visitors who, to quote from the alternative submission on this part of the case of counsel for five of the applicants, "are enjoined to mete out punishment only after a formalised enquiry and/or hearing".'

But Shaw LJ appears to me not, at least conclusively, to have made the same distinction. He said ([1979] 1 All ER 701 at 717–718, [1979] QB 425 at 456):

'I do not for my part find it easy, if at all possible, to distinguish between disciplinary proceedings conducted by a board of visitors and those carried out by a prison governor. In each case the subject-matter may be the same; the relevant fundamental regulations are common to both forms of proceedings. The powers of a governor as to the award he can make (which really means the punishment he can impose) are more restricted than those of a board of visitors in a corresponding situation; but the essential nature of the proceedings as defined by the Prison Rules is the same. So, in nature if not in degree, are the consequences to a prisoner.'

Waller LJ simply said that he would reserve a final decision on whether or not certiorari would lie against the governor of a prison until the question arose (see [1979] 1 All ER 701 at 719, [1979] QB 425 at 458).

In my view, therefore, there is no inconsistency between the decision in *Fraser v Mudge* and that in *Ex p St Germain*.

Counsel for Tarrant, I take it, would seek to distinguish *Fraser v Mudge* from the facts of his client's application on the ground that his client is charged with an offence under r 52 whereas that case was concerned with an offence under r 51. In my view, in the light of the passages from the judgment which I have quoted, it would not be open for this court to distinguish Tarrant's application on that ground.

In my view, therefore, this court is bound by the authority of *Fraser v Mudge* to decide that none of the applicants were entitled, as of right, to be legally represented at their hearing before their board of visitors.

Have the board a discretion to allow legal representation?

Consideration of this question starts from a principle which is common ground, namely that—

'under English law, a convicted prisoner, in spite of his imprisonment, retains all civil rights which are not taken away expressly or by necessary implication . . .'

(See *Raymond v Honey* [1982] 1 All ER 756 at 759, [1983] 1 AC 1 at 10, 14 per Lord Wilberforce and Lord Bridge.)

But the common ground ends there; for counsel for the respondent boards submits
_a_ that the effect of *Fraser v Mudge* is that, the court in that case having decided that a
prisoner has no entitlement to legal representation as of right, that principle is of no
relevance to these applications. For my part, I reject that submission. It does not follow
from the decision that a prisoner has no entitlement to legal representation as of right,
that the board before which he appears has no discretion to grant him legal representation;
and, if it has such a discretion, then he has the right that the board should, in this case,
_b_ exercise that discretion and exercise it fairly and properly. In my view, therefore, the
principle enunciated by Lord Wilberforce and Lord Bridge in *Raymond v Honey* applies
to this case. In short, therefore, two questions fall to be answered: first, has the board in
principle, at common law, such a discretion? Second, is such a discretion taken away
expressly or by necessary implication?

The argument in support of the existence of such discretion begins with the principle,
_c_ which is not challenged, that subject to any overriding or inconsistent statutory provisions
a board, like any other tribunal, is master of its own procedure.

The next question, therefore, is whether there is any rule or decision of common law
which limits that power in relation to legal representation: specifically, whether at
common law a board prima facie has, or prima facie does not have, a discretion to grant
it.

_d_ In the course of argument the court was referred to a large number of authorities
which, it was suggested, supported the proposition that such a discretion exists. Speaking
for myself, having re-examined each of them, only a handful of them go to this question.
The majority go rather to the question of how tribunals should exercise their duty to
hear an issue fairly or to the application of such a duty to hearings by boards of visitors in
relation to questions other than the discretion to allow legal representation.

_e_ I turn, then, to those authorities which, in my view, are relevant to the immediate
question. In *Pett v Greyhound Racing Association Ltd* [1968] 2 All ER 545, [1969] 1 QB 125
(which I shall call 'Pett (No 1)') a trainer of greyhounds, who held a licence to train from
the Greyhound Racing Association, sought a declaration that he was entitled to be
represented by counsel at a disciplinary inquiry conducted by track stewards, there being
nothing in the rules of the association providing for the procedure to be followed at such
_f_ an inquiry. Cusack J, in chambers, granted an interlocutory injunction to the trainer,
and the Court of Appeal dismissed the association's appeal against that decision. The
Court of Appeal in their judgments dealt only with the question whether it was arguable
that the trainer was entitled, as of right, to legal representation; no member of the court
considered the question whether, without such entitlement, there was none the less a
discretion in the stewards or the association to allow it to him. I mention this decision
_g_ primarily because it is the chronological starting point of the relevant line of decisions
and because of the decision of Lyell J at the substantive hearing of the case; but it is
convenient at this stage to quote one passage from the judgment of Lord Denning MR
which is material, not to the existence of the discretion, but to considerations which go
to the exercise of it, if it exists. Lord Denning MR said ([1968] 2 All ER 545 at 549,
[1969] 1 QB 125 at 132):

_h_ 'It is not every man who has the ability to defend himself on his own. He cannot
bring out the points in his own favour or the weaknesses in the other side. He may
be tongue-tied or nervous, confused or wanting in intelligence. He cannot examine
or cross-examine witnesses. We see it every day. A magistrate says to a man: "You
can ask any questions you like"; whereupon the man immediately starts to make a
speech. If justice is to be done, he ought to have the help of someone to speak for
_j_ him; and who better than a lawyer who has been trained for the task? I should have
thought, therefore, that when a man's reputation or livelihood is at stake, he not
only has a right to speak by his own mouth. He also has a right to speak by counsel
or solicitor.'

Despite that interlocutory decision, in *Pett v Greyhound Racing Associated Ltd (No 2)*

[1969] 2 All ER 221, [1970] 1 QB 46 Lyell J decided that the defendant association had not acted contrary to the rules of natural justice in refusing to allow the plaintiff to be legally represented at the inquiry: the plaintiff had no right to be legally represented. He came to that conclusion because, in his view, there were two conflicting authorities, one the dicta of the Court of Appeal in *Pett (No 1)* and the other a decision of the Privy Council in *University of Ceylon v Fernando* [1960] 1 All ER 631, [1960] 1 WLR 223, not cited to the Court of Appeal in *Pett (No 1)*, neither of which were binding on him. He took the view that the two were irreconcilable and that he had no alternative but to choose between them and, after long and anxious consideration, he preferred the view of the Privy Council (see [1969] 2 All ER 221 at 231, [1970] 1 QB 46 at 66). The point taken in *Fernando's* case was that a university student, accused of having cheated in an examination, was not given an opportunity to question the 'essential witness' against him. The university statutes included a clause which was silent as to the procedure to be followed by the vice-chancellor in satisfying himself of the truth or falsity of such an accusation. Lyell J cited the following passage from the opinion of their Lordships, given by Lord Jenkins ([1960] 1 All ER 631 at 639, [1960] 1 WLR 223 at 233):

'So far as the plaintiff is concerned, it appears to their Lordships that he must be taken to have agreed, when he became a member of the university, to be bound by statutes of the university, including cl. 8, and, in the event of cl. 8 being put in operation against him could not insist on the adoption by the vice-chancellor of any particular procedure beyond what the clause expressly or by necessary implication requires. In the absence of any express requirement, he is thrown back on the necessary implication that the vice-chancellor's procedure will be such as to satisfy the requirements indicated in [certain authorities] to which their Lordships have just referred, and thus to comply with those elementary and essential principles of "fairness" which must, as a matter of necessary implication, be treated as applicable in the discharge of the vice-chancellor's admittedly quasi-judicial functions under cl. 8, or, in other words, with the principles of natural justice.'

Lyell J, having quoted that paragraph, concluded ([1969] 2 All ER 221 at 231, [1970] 1 QB 46 at 66):

'I find it difficult to say that legal representation before a tribunal is an elementary feature of the fair dispensation of justice. It seems to me that it arises only in a society which has reached some degree of sophistication in its affairs.'

So far as I can see, Lyell J, like the Court of Appeal in *Pett (No 1)* before him, considered only the plaintiff's right to legal representation: he did not consider the tribunal's discretion to allow him to have it. Quite apart from that, the decision, which in any event is of course only of persuasive authority, is distinguishable from the present case, since in that case both the trainer and the student had, or were to be deemed to have, voluntarily accepted the procedure in question, whereas it cannot be said that the applicants in this case have voluntarily accepted any procedure.

In *R v Derby Justices, ex p Kooner* [1970] 3 All ER 399, [1971] 1 QB 147 the justices had ordered that on committal proceedings legal aid be given for the applicants, who were charged with murder and other offences, to be represented by a solicitor only. Section 74 of the Criminal Justice Act 1967 provided:

'(1) ... legal aid ... shall be taken, subject to the following provisions of this section, as consisting of representation by a solicitor and counsel ...

(2) Notwithstanding anything in the last foregoing subsection legal aid ordered to be given for the purposes of any proceedings before a magistrates' court shall not include representation by counsel except in the case of any indictable offence where the court is of opinion that, because of circumstances which make the case unusually grave or difficult, representation by both counsel and solicitor would be desirable.'

a Lord Parker CJ, having recited those provisions, said that in the first instance there was a complete discretion in the justices whether or not to grant legal aid at all, subject to limitations imposed by s 75 which are not material for present purposes. He continued ([1970] 3 All ER 399 at 401, [1971] 1 QB 147 at 150):

'The second question is whether that legal aid should include representation by counsel. That depends on whether in the opinion of the magistrates' court such a course is desirable having regard to circumstances making the case unusually grave *b* or difficult. In my opinion a case of alleged murder, though not necessarily difficult, is undoubtedly grave, and no good reasons appear in the present case why representation by counsel is not desirable. Indeed, as I have already pointed out, when it comes to a trial there is a specific provision that it shall include counsel. I think that in the case of committal proceedings for alleged murder it should be recognised as a rule of practice that legal aid should include representation by *c* counsel. Accordingly in my judgment an order of mandamus should issue.'

John Stephenson and Cooke JJ agreed.

The facts of that case are in many ways a long way from the facts of the present case; but the two cases have in common similar expressions: 'unusually grave' cases in s 74(2) of the 1967 Act and 'Especially grave offences', the marginal heading to r 52 of the 1964 *d* rules.

Clear authority for the existence of such a discretion, in principle, in the case of an ordinary domestic tribunal is to be found in a dictum of Lord Denning MR in the later case of *Enderby Town Football Club Ltd v Football Association Ltd* [1971] 1 All ER 215 at 218, [1971] 1 Ch 591 at 605, where, distinguishing for the first time in this line of cases between 'right' and 'discretion', he said:

e 'The case thus raises this important point: Is a party who is charged before a domestic tribunal entitled *as of right* to be legally represented? Much depends on what the rules say about it. When the rules say nothing, then the party has no absolute right to be legally represented. It is a matter for the *discretion* of the tribunal. They are masters of their own procedure: and, if they, in the proper exercise of their discretion, decline to allow legal representation, the courts will not interfere. Such *f* was held in the old days in a case about magistrates: see *Collier v Hicks* (1831) 2 B & Ad 663, 109 ER 1290. It is the position today in the tribunals under the Tribunals and Inquiries (Evidence) Act 1921. I think the same should apply to domestic tribunals, and for this reason: In many cases it may be a good thing for the proceedings of a domestic tribunal to be conducted informally without legal representation. Justice can often be done in them better by a good layman than by a *g* bad lawyer. This is especially so in activities like football and other sports, where no points of law are likely to arise, and it is all part of the proper regulation of the game. But I would emphasise that the discretion must be properly exercised. The tribunal must not fetter its discretion by rigid bonds. A domestic tribunal is not at liberty to lay down an absolute rule: "We will *never* allow anyone to have a lawyer to appear for him." The tribunal must be ready, in a proper case, to allow it.' (Lord Denning *h* MR's emphasis.)

In *R v Pentridge Prison Visiting Justice, ex p Walker* [1975] VR 883 Harris J, sitting in the Supreme Court of Victoria, decided, in a decision of much greater relevance than the *Enderby* case though of less authority, that a prisoner appearing before a visiting justice had no right to demand to be represented by a legal practitioner but that the justice had *j* a discretion to permit him legal representation unless that discretion was inconsistent with some express statutory provision. Counsel for the boards points out that the proceedings in question differed from those in this case in that the hearing was before a visiting justice and the proceedings were on oath; and that the existence of the discretion was conceded. *R v Pentridge Prison Visiting Justice* was heard between 3 and 5 June 1975 and was decided on 24 June. Meanwhile the Court of Appeal had decided *Fraser v Mudge*

on 12 June 1975. It is understandable in these circumstances that neither case is referred
to in the other.

In my view the decision in *Fraser v Mudge* is not to be regarded as a decision relevant
to the present question, namely whether the tribunal has a discretion to allow legal
representation. It concluded, as I have said, for the purposes of this court the question
whether a prisoner is entitled, as of right, to legal representation. But, save for one
reference in the recital of the facts to the fact that the clerk to the board of visitors would
not advise the board 'either to allow legal representation or to adjourn the enquiry' (see
[1975] 3 All ER 78 at 79, [1975] 1 WLR 1132 at 1133), there is no consideration
whatsoever, that I can see, of the question whether a board has a discretion to grant legal
representation, and Mr Stephen Sedley QC, who appeared for the plaintiff in the case,
tells us that that point was not raised. That absence of reference to the question of
discretion is to be contrasted with the distinction made by Lord Denning MR between
'right' and 'discretion' in the *Enderby Town Football* case and in *Maynard v Osmond* [1977]
1 All ER 64, [1977] QB 240.

The final case in this line of authority is *Maynard v Osmond* in which the Court of
Appeal held that Parliament, by r 8(3) and (6) of the Police (Discipline) Regulations 1965,
SI 1965/543, which applied to disciplinary charges against junior police officers, had not
conferred either a right to legal representation or a discretion in the disciplinary tribunal
to permit it. *Fraser v Mudge* was cited in argument, but not referred to in the judgments.
Counsel for the boards relies on this authority in support of his contention that boards of
visitors have no such discretion either. It is necessary, therefore, to consider the judgments
in that case. Lord Denning MR said ([1977] 1 All ER 64 at 79, [1977] QB 240 at 252):

> 'On principle, if a man is charged with a serious offence which may have grave
> consequences for him, he should be entitled to have a qualified lawyer to defend
> him. Such has been agreed by the government of this country when it adhered to
> the European Convention on Human Rights. But also, by analogy, it should be the
> same in most cases when he is charged with a disciplinary offence before a
> disciplinary tribunal, at any rate when the offence is one which may result in his
> dismissal from the force or other body to which he belongs; or the loss of his
> livelihood; or, worse still, may ruin his character for ever. I gave the reason in *Pett v
> Greyhound Racing Association Ltd* [1968] 2 All ER 545 at 549, [1969] 1 QB 125 at 132:
> "If justice is to be done, he ought to have the help of some one to speak for him; and
> who better than a lawyer who has been trained for the task?" He should, therefore,
> be entitled to have a lawyer if he wants one. But, even if he should not be entitled
> *as of right*, I should have thought that as a general rule the tribunal should have a
> *discretion* in the matter. Legal representation should not be forbidden altogether.
> The tribunal should have a discretion to permit him to have a lawyer if they think
> it would assist. They are the masters of their own procedure and, unless clearly
> forbidden, should have a discretion to permit it.' (Lord Denning MR's emphasis.)

It will be seen from Lord Denning MR's emphasis that he was making the distinction,
which he made in the *Enderby Town Football* case but did not make in *Fraser v Mudge*,
between the plaintiff's entitlement as of right, and the tribunal's discretion. But later he
said ([1977] 1 All ER 64 at 79, [1977] QB 240 at 253):

> 'As a matter of construction, it seems to me that the regulations require a police
> officer to be represented by a member of the police force. He cannot be represented
> by a lawyer.'

Lord Denning MR then went on to give his reasons for that conclusion and continued
([1977] 1 All ER 64 at 80, [1977] QB 240 at 253):

> 'Apart from these points of construction, it seems to me that in these disciplinary
> proceedings, fairness can be obtained without legal representation.'

Orr LJ said ([1977] 1 All ER 64 at 82, [1977] QB 240 at 255):

a   '. . . I find it impossible to construe the regulations as conferring either a right to
        legal representation or a discretion in the tribunal to allow it . . .'

Finally, Waller LJ said ([1977] 1 All ER 64 at 84–85, [1977] QB 240 at 259):

        'Is there a discretion in the chief constable? It was argued by counsel for the
        plaintiff that the plaintiff was entitled to legal representation as of right or at the
b   least that he had a prima facie right. Therefore, if the regulations took away the
        right there would be a residuary discretion in the tribunal to allow legal
        representation in a particular case . . . Whatever may be the rights of an individual
        when private persons seek to set up tribunals controlling the rights of that individual,
        and there may be arguments both ways in such cases, I am of the opinion that
        disciplinary proceedings in disciplined forces such as the armed services and the
c   police are in a different category.'

        Although it is not entirely clear whether Waller LJ came to that conclusion as a matter
of the construction of reg 8, it is in my view clear that Lord Denning MR and Orr LJ
concluded that there was no discretion as a matter of construction of that regulation, and
not as a matter of common law.

d   In the light of these authorities I conclude that there is no rule or decision of common
law which limits the power of a board of visitors to be master of their own proceedings
so as to deprive them of a discretion, which must be inherent in that power, to permit
legal representation.
        The next question which arises, therefore, is whether that discretion, and the applicants'
right to have it properly exercised, has been 'taken away expressly or by necessary
e   implication', to adopt the words of Lord Wilberforce and Lord Bridge. On behalf of the
applicants it is contended that there is nothing to take it away.
        Counsel for the boards, while not, as I understand him, contending that those rights
have been expressly taken away, submits that they have been taken away, or are to be
deemed to have been taken away, by necessary implication. Before considering that
submission, however, it is right to record his concession that a board of visitors does have
f   a discretion to permit an interpreter when the presence of an interpreter is necessary to
enable the prisoner to be given a full opportunity of hearing what is alleged against him
and of presenting his own case.
        I hope that I do no injustice to the arguments of counsel for the boards if I summarise
them as follows. Firstly he submits that the boards, being masters of their own procedure,
have been free to regulate that procedure since they were established and, in particular,
g   to decide not to permit legal representation; that they have never permitted legal
representation; and that therefore any right on the part of a prisoner to require them to
exercise a discretion to grant legal representation has been lost by what counsel describes
as 'ancient and long-established usage'. But he does not seek to prove any custom or usage
in the proper sense nor, indeed, to prove any practice or any past decision of any board,
let alone of 115 different boards. For my part I have to conclude that this particular
h   submission is misconceived.
        Secondly he submits that the discretion is to be regarded as having been taken away by
necessary implication because it is inconsistent with the disciplinary structure, and he
makes, I think, two particular points in this connection. The first point is in reliance on
r 37 of the 1964 rules which (without the amendment introduced in 1972 which is not
material to this point) provides:

j   '(1) The legal adviser of a prisoner in any legal proceedings, civil or criminal, to
            which the prisoner is a party shall be afforded reasonable facilities for interviewing
            him in connection with those proceedings, and may do so out of hearing but in
            sight of an officer.
            (2) A prisoner's legal adviser may, with the leave of the Secretary of State,

interview the prisoner in connection with any other legal business in the sight and
hearing of an officer.'

　　His argument, although not expressed precisely in this way, is that, by application of
the maxim expressio unius exclusio alterius, the rules, by expressly including the right
of a legal adviser to interview a prisoner, must be taken by implication to exclude the
right of a legal adviser to represent him. But in my view r 37 is to be read in its particular
context which is under a general heading, above r 33, of 'Letters and visits generally';
and in my view the right to legal representation is not taken away by necessary
implication from r 37.

　　His second point is that, in his submission, hearings by boards of visitors are more
inquisitorial than adversarial in form and he cites, in support of that contention, part of
para 5.100 of the Report of the Committee of Inquiry into United Kingdom Prison
Services (Cmnd 7673 (1979)) (the 'May report') and in particular that—

> '. . . an adjudication [of a board] was essentially a forum for dealing with internal
> disciplinary matters in which the adjudicating panel had an inquisitorial function
> as opposed to simply weighing the evidence advanced by both sides as in court
> proceedings.'

　　For my part I fully accept that, even at a disciplinary inquiry, a board has functions
which are additional to the necessity of resolving an issue between a reporting officer and
the prisoner; for instance it may be part of the board's proper function, in the course of
such a hearing, to inquire into the surrounding circumstances of the alleged offence so as
to provide themselves with information for the purpose of carrying out their
administrative or pastoral functions. Counsel for the boards submits that for a board
which lacks the assistance of a legally qualified clerk, which is not bound by the technical
rules of evidence and before which no evidence is given on oath, it would be inappropriate
to introduce a lawyer to represent one side only. In my view the disadvantages which
may accrue from the introduction of a lawyer to represent one side only are matters
which a board can properly take into account when exercising the discretion whether or
not to permit a prisoner to have legal representation; but in my view the issue between
the reporting officer and the prisoner is of an adversarial nature and, in any event, the
procedure as a whole is not one which leads me to the conclusion that there is any
implication, let alone any necessary implication, to be drawn from it that a board should
have no discretion to allow legal representation before it.

　　Just as many of the applicants' arguments in support of the existence of a discretion
went, in my view, to the way in which the discretion should be exercised rather than to
its existence, so too, in my view, does the third argument of counsel for the boards
against its existence. None the less, it is convenient to deal with it at this stage. He
prefaces this argument by citing a passage from the judgment of Sachs LJ in *Re Pergamon
Press Ltd* [1970] 3 All ER 535 at 542, [1971] 1 Ch 388 at 403:

> 'In the application of the concept of fair play, there must be real flexibility, so that
> very different situations may be met without producing procedures unsuitable to
> the object in hand. That need for flexibility has been emphasised in a number of
> authoritative passages in the judgments cited to this court. In the forefront was that
> of Tucker LJ in *Russell v Duke of Norfolk* [1949] 1 All ER 109 at 118, and the general
> effect of his views has been once again echoed recently by Lord Guest, Lord Donovan
> and Lord Wilberforce in *Wiseman v Borneman* [1969] 3 All ER 275 at 280, 283, 288,
> [1971] AC 297 at 311, 314, 320. It is only too easy to frame a precise set of rules
> which may appear impeccable on paper and which may yet unduly hamper,
> lengthen and, indeed, perhaps even frustrate (see per Lord Reid in *Wiseman v
> Borneman* [1969] 3 All ER 275 at 277, [1971] AC 297 at 308) the activities of those
> engaged in investigating or otherwise dealing with matters that fall within their
> proper sphere. In each case careful regard must be had to the scope of the proceeding,

the source of its jurisdiction . . . the way in which it normally falls to be conducted and its objective.'

Applying those considerations, counsel for the boards submits that if one board is to be given the discretion to grant legal representation then it follows that all boards must have it, and that if all boards are to have it the result will produce innumerable logistical difficulties, unfairness as between prisoners, and delay.

In my view each of those objections, if relevant at all, goes not to the existence of the discretion but to the way in which it should be applied, if it exists. None the less I will deal with them at this stage.

The logistical difficulties which he contemplates are as follows. Many prisoners would apply for legal representation before many boards. It would be necessary for them to apply at some preliminary hearing, for which no provision is made, or at the first hearing and, were they to apply at the first hearing and be granted legal representation, then an adjournment would be necessary. It is unlikely that there would be any uniformity with regard to the granting of legal representation amongst 115 boards comprising about 100 members; and each of those boards would have great difficulty in deciding how to exercise their discretion. The exercise of the discretion adversely to a prisoner would often lead to that decision being challenged.

For my part I can see little force in any of these objections. It was common ground that there are approximately 3,000 adjudications by boards of visitors each year, that is to say, at a very crude average, about 30 adjudications each year by each board. Once a recognised practice has been evolved, it does not seem to me likely that large numbers of prisoners will apply for legal representation in excess of those to whom it is granted. It seems to me that procedures could easily be devised for avoiding the necessity of adjourning first hearings. I do not see any great likelihood of there being any wide divergence between decisions of various boards. In any event, where the objection is one which goes to administrative convenience, I refer, with respect, to the comment of Geoffrey Lane LJ in *R v Hull Prison Board of Visitors, ex p St Germain (No 2)* [1979] 3 All ER 545 at 550, [1979] 1 WLR 1401 at 1406 where, dealing with the question whether a discretion to allow a witness to be called could be validly exercised where considerable administrative inconvenience would be caused were that to be done, he said:

'But mere administrative difficulties, simpliciter, are not in our view enough. Convenience and justice are often not on speaking terms (see per Lord Atkin in *General Medical Council v Spackman* [1943] 2 All ER 337 at 341, [1943] AC 627 at 638.'

Counsel's second objection is that to give a board such a discretion would produce unfairness, a sense of grievance, and therefore the risk of indiscipline amongst prisoners because no legal aid would be available for legal representation granted to them so that some, though entitled to it in the exercise of the board's discretion, would not be able to afford it and would therefore have to go without. But this inequality of resources has always been a factor in legal proceedings when legal aid has not been available or where it is still not available. Until September of this year, for instance, it has not been available for appeals to mental health review tribunals which involve hearings having many features similar to hearings before boards of visitors. They take place in institutions, sometimes closed institutions; no evidence is given on oath; the technical rules of evidence do not apply; yet legal representation has been allowed to appellants without the medical officer who puts the case against him having any representation. And it is reasonable to infer that not all appellants would have had the resources to enable them to pay for legal representation. In any event facilities are available, in some places and in certain circumstances, for free legal representation. For my part, therefore, although this, also, is a factor which in my view a board is entitled to take into account as part of the background to the exercise of its discretion, it does not affect the existence of that discretion.

I make the same comment on the third and last objection of counsel for the boards under this heading, namely that to give or allow boards such a discretion will introduce unnecessary delay into a process which is intended to be swift. He quotes, in this context, a sentence from para 5.102 of the May report:

'. . . to provide legal representation and legal aid could only introduce unwarranted cost and delays where continuing uncertainty can quickly affect the mood of staff and inmates in volatile institutions.'

But in my view that objection must be seen against the period which elapsed in the cases of the applicants Tarrant and Leyland. Even if, which would not necessarily follow, grant of legal representation would extend periods of that kind by about a month, it does not seem to me that that factor can possibly be sufficient to lead to the implication that the discretion does not exist, although it may be relevant to the exercise of it.

I conclude, therefore, that there is in my view nothing which takes away expressly or by necessary implication the discretion of a board of visitors to grant legal representation or, therefore, the right on the part of the prisoner to require the board to exercise it.

If the boards have such a discretion, I do not, for my part, see any reason for distinguishing, as a matter of principle, between a hearing of an offence under r 51 and of an offence under r 52, that is to say I see no reason for deciding that a board has a discretion under r 52 but does not have one under r 51. The differences between the effect and implications of those two rules will have been seen from the provisions to which I referred at the beginning of this judgment. But there is nothing, in any of the reasoning which has led me to the conclusion that a board of visitors has the discretion, which leads also to the conclusion that there is any difference between those two rules which affects the existence, as distinct from the exercise, of that discretion. Accordingly in my view every board of visitors has a discretion to grant legal representation at any hearing before it.

In the light of this conclusion it does not seem to me to be necessary to deal with the arguments advanced in reliance on art 6 of the European Convention on Human Rights (the Convention for the Protection of Human Rights and Fundamental Freedoms (Rome, 4 November 1950; TS 71 (1953); Cmd 8969)), the decision of the European Court of Human Rights in *Engel v The Netherlands (No 1)* (1976) 1 EHRR 647, or the opinion of the European Commission of Human Rights on the applications in *Campbell and Fell v UK* (1982) 5 EHRR 207.

Right to a friend or adviser

The submission that a prisoner is entitled to have the assistance of a friend or adviser is founded on the two authorities of *Collier v Hicks* (1831) 2 B & Ad 663, 109 ER 1290 and *McKenzie v McKenzie* [1970] 3 All ER 1034, [1971] P 33. The point at issue in *Collier v Hicks* was whether an attorney was entitled as of right, without the justices' permission, to act as an advocate to a party in proceedings before them. The court held that he was not. But Lord Tenterden CJ said (2 B & Ad 663 at 669, 109 ER 1290 at 1292):

'Any person, whether he be a professional man or not, may attend as a friend of either party, may take notes, may quietly make suggestions, and give advice . . .'

Parke J said (2 B & Ad 663 at 671–672, 109 ER 1290 at 1293):

'All may be present, and either of the parties may have a professional assistant to confer and consult with, but not to interfere in the course of the proceedings.'

These, strictly, obiter dicta were approved by the Court of Appeal in *McKenzie v McKenzie*, which decided that a party to the trial of a divorce suit is entitled to have a friend present in court beside him to assist him in the manner described by Lord Tenterden CJ.

a But in my view these authorities cannot be applied to hearings before boards of visitors. A magistrates' court, and the court in which a divorce trial is taking place, is a public court to which all have access; and if a member of the public gives assistance to a party without interfering in the course of the proceedings he does no more than assert his right as a member of the public to come into court and associate with a party to those proceedings. But hearings before boards of visitors are not public hearings at all, and no one has the right to attend them without the invitation or permission of the board of

b visitors. For my part, therefore, I take the view that a prisoner is not entitled, as of right, to require the board to allow him to be assisted by a friend or adviser.

Friend or adviser: discretion

But the process of reasoning which leadings me to conclude that the board has a discretion to allow legal representation to a prisoner leads equally to the conclusion that

c it has a discretion to allow a prisoner to be assisted by a friend or adviser. If, however, someone has been allowed to attend the hearing to assist the prisoner in the manner described by Lord Tenterden CJ, and if, without the permission of the visitors, he interferes or participates in the proceedings, then the visitors would be entitled to require him to leave.

d

Was any discretion exercised?

It is common ground that in none of the five cases, in each of which the applicant asked to be allowed to be legally represented, did the board consider whether, in the circumstances, it ought to grant the request; nor, in the two cases in which the applicant asked for the assistance of a friend or adviser at the hearing (Tangney and Anderson) did

e the board in either case consider whether they should grant that request. Each board took the view that the applicant had no right to legal representation or assistance and that it had no power to grant it. That attitude is illustrated by the chairman of the board which heard Leyland's application. When Leyland said that he was entitled to a legal representative and that he would like one present, the chairman said:

f   '. . . there is no rule that we have to follow, or can follow, which gives you any right to legal representation. May be there will be one day but at the moment the rules of the prison are such that you are not able to be legally represented.'

It is not suggested that the chairman was referring to any specific rule. It is simply common ground that all boards have taken the view that neither representation nor assistance of any kind can be allowed.

g It follows that in none of the five cases did the board exercise, one way or the other, its discretion whether or not to allow legal representation; nor did the board in the cases of Tangney and Anderson exercise a discretion whether or not to allow the presence of a friend or adviser.

In the light of that conclusion this court has a discretion to quash the awards in the three cases where the hearing was concluded, namely the cases of Leyland, Tangney and

h Clark. It also has a discretion to quash the decision by the boards hearing the charges against Tarrant and Anderson to proceed with their adjudication. I will consider how, in my view, this court should exercise that discretion, and its discretion to make other consequential orders, at the conclusion of this judgment.

j

Proper exercise of a board's discretion

It is contended, on behalf of each of the applicants, that each board, having a discretion to grant legal representation, ought to have granted it because, it is contended, no board properly directing itself could reasonably exercise that discretion in any other way. It is necessary, therefore, to consider the arguments which have been advanced which go to that question and to the more general question of the considerations which any board ought to take into account in exercising this discretion.

All those arguments rely, as a starting point, on the dictum of Lord Denning MR in *Pett (No 1)* [1968] 2 All ER 545 at 549, [1969] 1 QB 125 at 132. I will, in a moment, list a number of factors which should be taken into account and which, if properly taken into account, the applicants submit should inevitably lead to a decision to grant legal representation to them. Before embarking on that list, however, I will deal with one matter, which in argument featured at the head of it but which can now, for reasons which I will explain, be put on one side. I refer to the question of the standard proof to be applied by the boards.

Boards are provided with what seems to me, judging particularly by those parts of it to which we have been referred, a very useful and comprehensive guide entitled 'Procedure for the conduct of an adjudication by a Board of Visitors' published by the Prison Department of the Home Office in April 1977 and reprinted in November 1978, which I shall refer to as 'the guide'. Though otherwise comprehensive, that guide makes no reference to the standard of proof; nor is there any reference to it in the internal regulations (which I shall call 'the standing orders') published by the Prison Department of the Home Office in June 1981 or in a Home Office publication published in April 1981 entitled 'Boards of Visitors Adjudications and Related Areas', described to us as a training document. The point was argued, as it seems to me with some force, that the standard of proof to be applied is central and critical to a board's adjudication and that, if it is not accepted that the criminal standard of proof applies, a prisoner cannot have a fair hearing unless a lawyer can argue the point on his behalf. Before us, however, counsel for the boards conceded, rightly in my view, that the standard of proof to be applied is a criminal one and, although he does not appear on behalf of the Secretary of State for Home Affairs, I have no doubt that he would not have made that concession without the Home Office's approval. It seems reasonable to infer, therefore, that for the future, either by an amendment to the guide or in some other way, boards will be advised to apply the criminal standard of proof. Although still material to decisions already made by these, and perhaps other, boards, this point should not be of any relevance in the future.

As it seems to me, the following are considerations which every board should take into account when exercising its discretion whether to allow legal representation or to allow the assistance of a friend or adviser. (This list is not, of course, intended to be comprehensive: particular cases may throw up other particular matters.)

1. The seriousness of the charge and of the potential penalty.

2. Whether any points of law are likely to arise. There is of course a duty to ensure that the prisoner understands the charge, a duty which is reflected in the guide (p 12, para 11): 'Ask the accused whether he understands the charge(s) and explain anything to him about which he is in any doubt.' But the clerks who sit with boards are not legally qualified and there may be cases where a legal point arises with which the prisoner, without legal representation, cannot properly deal. A charge of mutiny, which I consider later in this judgment, is at least potentially in this category for the reasons which I will give. It was also suggested in argument that difficult questions of intent might arise; but for my part, looking at the list of disciplinary offences and the way in which those offences are described, it seems to me unlikely that such questions will arise, except very rarely, other than in charges of mutiny.

3. The capacity of a particular prisoner to present his own case. In 'Justice in Prison', a report of a committe of Justice of which Sir Brian McKenna was the chairman and which was before the court, the following passage is quoted (in para 117, p 57) from a report by the Home Office research unit based on an experiment of interviewing a number of prisoners before and after adjudication of their cases:

'Some of the prisoners were poorly educated and not very intelligent. Furthermore, a few spoke poor English and a few appeared to have psychiatric problems. Unless they are given considerable assistance, it is unrealistic to expect such men to prepare an adequate written statement or to present their case effectively.'

(See Smith, Austin and Ditchfield, 'Board of Visitors Adjudications', Research Unit paper 3, Home Office (1981) p 31.) As I have said, counsel for the boards does not suggest that a board has no right to admit an interpreter and there must be some cases where this is necesary. I have no doubt, moreover, that in very many cases, where assistance is necessary, the chairman of the board is capable of doing it so as to ensure the fair hearing to which the prisoner is entitled. But the standing orders, and the guide, provide for the giving of an opportunity to a prisoner to make a written reply to the charge; and an illiterate prisoner could not make use of that opportunity without some assistance. Similarly, a board might not always be satisfied that a mentally subnormal prisoner could be assured of a full opportunity of presenting his own case merely by the assistance of the chairman of the board.

4 Procedural difficulties. An affidavit has been sworn, in support of three of the applicants, by Mr Ivan Henry, who is a member of a board of visitors, a magistrate and a legal executive. He points out that a prisoner awaiting adjudication is normally kept apart from other prisoners under r 48(2) of the 1964 rules pending the adjudication and that this may inhibit the preparation of his defence. He points out that without the capacity to interview potential witnesses, prisoners are often unable to satisfy boards of visitors that it is reasonable to call a witness and that, where a prisoner asks questions through a chairman, there is frequently no effective presentation of a case or effective cross-examination or testing of the evidence. I will consider in more detail the questions of calling witnesses and cross-examination later in this judgment. But in my view a board, when considering the exercise of its discretion, should taken into account any special difficulties of the kind I have mentioned and should particularly bear in mind the difficulty which some prisoners might have in cross-examining a witness, particularly a witness giving evidence of an expert nature, at short notice without previously having seen that witness's evidence.

5. The need for reasonable speed in making their adjudication, which is clearly an important consideration.

6. The need for fairness as between prisoners and as between prisoners and prison officers.

In my view, all these are matters which a board should take into account in deciding whether to allow legal representation, or the assistance of a friend or adviser, bearing in mind the overriding obligation to ensure that a prisoner 'be given a full opportunity of hearing what is alleged against him and of presenting his own case' (r 49(2)).

Should legal representation be allowed or should it have been allowed in these cases?
    The applicants Tarrant and Leyland. The charge against Tarrant was that—

'At about 11.35 am on 20.5.83 at B3 landing you committed an offence under paragraph 1 of Rule 47. Mutinies or incites another prisoner to munity; i.e. at about 11.35 hrs on 20.5.83 you mutinied in that armed with a broom handle you told Officers Jones and Spurling to leave the landing. You then in the company of [four other prisoners] started to smash the stairwell screening around B2 landing.'

The charge against Leyland was in the same terms down to and including the words 'mutinies or incites another prisoner to mutiny', continuing:

'i.e. at about 11.30 hrs on 20.5.83 you mutinied in that, in the company of [six other prisoners] you smashed cell windows and stairwell screening on B2 landing.'

There is agreement between counsel for the boards and counsel for Leyland that mutiny means 'an offence which deals with collective insubordination, collective defiance or disregard of authority or refusal to obey authority': see per Lord Goddard CJ in *R v Grant, Davis, Riley and Topley* [1957] 2 All ER 694 at 696, [1957] 1 WLR 906 at 908. At

Tarrant's hearing the word was not explained to him, although at Leyland's hearing the chairwoman said: '. . . the definition of mutiny is a concerted act of indiscipline involving more than one person relating to the overthrow or supplanting of constituted authority.' It seems to me that in most, if not all, charges of mutiny, and certainly in these two cases, questions are bound to arise whether collective action was intended to be collective, i e whether it was concerted or not, and as to the distinction between mere disobedience of a particular order on the one hand and disregard or defiance of authority on the other.

In my judgment, where such questions arise or are likely to arise, no board of visitors, properly directing itself, could reasonably decide not to allow the prisoner legal representation. If this decision is to have the result that charges of mutiny will more frequently be referred to the criminal courts in some other form I, personally, would not regard that result as a matter of regret.

The applicants Tangney, Clark and Anderson

The charges against Tangney and Anderson each included one charge of an assault on a prison officer under r 51 of the 1964 rules. Each of them were, therefore, exposed to the risk of 'an award' of forfeiture of remission for a period not exceeding 180 days, or more, if, as counsel for the boards contends but which is challenged on behalf of the applicants, a board has power to make consecutive awards, a point on which I need express no view. For my part, I do not think that it can possibly be said that any reasonable board properly directing itself would be bound to grant legal representation or (in the case of Tangney and Anderson who applied for it) would be bound to have allowed the presence of an adviser. I would, therefore, leave the matter to be decided by any board before which it may come, if it does so.

Other issues

Tarrant. His hearing is part heard, and he asks for a declaration that the board of visitors that has heard his case so far should disqualify itself. Counsel for the boards does not resist such a declaration and it will accordingly be made.

Leyland. Five grounds of relief, none of which I have yet considered, are relied on on his behalf.

1. The first ground is that there was no evidence to substantiate the charge of mutiny. As the award in his case must be quashed in any event for the reasons which I will give, it does not seem to me necessary or desirable to express a view on this point.

2. The charge which was referred to the board alleged the commission of the offence on B1 landing but the charge which was tried was changed to B2 landing. The board did not have jurisdiction to try the charge since it had not properly been referred to it. In my view there is no substance in this point. The transcript of proceedings shows that Leyland accepted that the original charge referred to B1 landing because of a clerical error, and I have no doubt that the charge was properly before the board and that they had jurisdiction to hear it.

3. 'No adequate explanation of the offence was given nor was the applicant given sufficient time or particulars to enable him properly to understand what was alleged against him or to prepare his case.' As I have already said, the chairwoman explained the meaning of mutiny to Leyland; but she did not explain to him what was meant by a 'concerted act of indiscipline' and, if regard is had only to the transcript, it would seem that Leyland received no adequate explanation of the offence. Nonetheless he himself referred to 'the riot', to 'the intervention squad' and to 'the barricades', and his defence was simply that he was not participating in 'the riot'. In these circumstances it seems to me very unlikely that, in the event, any injustice was done in failing fully to explain the charge to him. Having defined mutiny for him the chairwoman asked Leyland whether he had had time to reply to the charge and to prepare his defence. Leyland said, 'No', but the chairwoman replied, 'You have had time'. Despite the fact that Leyland received the charge in its first (incorrect) form on 23 June 1983, the charge in its amended and final

form was dated 22 July, the day before the hearing before the board; and in these circumstances, in my view, the chairwoman ought to have investigated the matter sufficiently so as to enable the board to be satisfied that Leyland had had sufficient time and particulars to enable him properly to understand what was alleged against him and to prepare his case. But she did not do so.

4. The applicant was prevented by the chairwoman from cross-examining to the extent necessary to enable him to present his case properly. This point arises in the following circumstances. Officer Harries had given evidence that he saw Leyland at about 11.30 am through a hole which had been made. Leyland wished to pursue with this officer a suggestion that another prisoner had been charged with making that hole at 11.55 am so that, if that charge was accurately laid, Officer Harries could not have seen him, Leyland, at 11.30. After Officer Harries had given his evidence and Leyland had asked him a few questions, he asked: 'How is it that you saw me through that hole at 11.30 when you have already said that Banks made the hole at 11.55? You could not have seen me through the hole. It would not have been there at half-past eleven.' The chairwoman, without allowing Officer Harries to answer the question, herself interposed and said; 'There is no evidence here that anything happened at 11.55. Mr Harries has said "At about 11.30 hours".' She therefore herself took over the question after discussion with Leyland and said: 'To summarise that question, Mr Harries, was the hole there when you saw Leyland in that area?' But that question, of course, was not the question which Leyland himself had wished to put. A short time later, after Leyland had asked Officer Harries whether he had seen any people with masks on, the chairwoman said: 'I think we have gone far enough with Mr Harries. He gave his evidence and you have had an opportunity to question him on his evidence.' Leyland replied: 'I have further questions. This is very important to me, and seeing as this man is the one that is charging me I would like to put a few more points.' After further discussion, the chairwoman said: 'You may ask him questions on what Mr Harries has told this board, and you, I think, have done that. If you want a repeat of that I will give it to you, and if they are pertinent to what is said we will allow the questions.' A little later Leyland said to her: 'What I want to know is, was there anybody else with me other than the six mentioned on my charge sheet?' The chairwoman replied: 'I think Mr Harries has answered that question in the number that he saw.' Although there were some further limited questions which Leyland was allowed to put, for my part, it seems to me that the chairwoman was not allowing him a fair opportunity to question the officer. There was no reason whatsoever why he should not have been allowed to question the officer about the circumstances in which the other prisoner had been charged with having made the hole at 11.55. Paragraph 14(2) of the guide reads: 'If the accused in any way abuses the opportunity to question the officer directly the chairman may insist on questions being put through him.' I have no doubt that that guidance is sound; but I have equally no doubt that if a prisoner is to receive a full opportunity of hearing what is alleged against him and of presenting his case, he must be allowed to ask his own questions unless he abuses that right, which in my view, Leyland was not doing on this occasion.

5. The applicant was not permitted to call all relevant witnesses whom he wished to call. Geoffrey Lane LJ considered this question in *R v Hull Prison Board of Visitors, ex p St Germain (No 2)* [1979] 3 All ER 545 at 550, [1979] 1 WLR 1401 at 1406:

> 'There was some suggestion that the chairman should have no discretion to disallow the calling of a witness whose attendance is requested by the prisoner. This suggestion was largely withdrawn in the course of argument and we do not think it had any validity. Those who appear before the board of visitors on charges are, ex hypothesi, those who are serving sentences in prison. Many such offenders might well seek to render the adjudications by the board quite impossible if they had the same liberty to conduct their own defences as they would have in an ordinary criminal trial. In our judgment the chairman's discretion is necessary as part of a

proper procedure for dealing with alleged offences against discipline by prisoners. However, that discretion has to be exercised reasonably, in good faith and on proper grounds. It would clearly be wrong if, as has been alleged in one instance before us, the basis for refusal to allow a prisoner to call witnesses was that the chairman considered that there was ample evidence against the accused. It would equally be an improper exercise of the discretion if the refusal was based on an erroneous understanding of the prisoner's defence, for example, that an alibi did not cover the material time or day, whereas in truth and in fact it did. A more serious question was raised whether the discretion could be validly exercised where it was based on considerable administrative inconvenience being caused if the request to call a witness or witnesses was permitted. Clearly in the proper exercise of his discretion a chairman may limit the number of witnesses, either on the basis that he has good reason for considering that the total number sought to be called is an attempt by the prisoner to render the hearing of the charge virtually impracticable or where quite simply it would be quite unnecessary to call so many witnesses to establish the point at issue. But mere administrative difficulties, simpliciter, are not in our view enough.'

The guide at para 18 reads:

'If the accused asks to call witnesses, whether named in advance . . . or during the hearing, ask him to say what he thinks their evidence will show or prove. Unless the adjudicating panel is satisfied (after any submission from the accused) that the witnesses will not be able to give useful evidence, they should be called.'

That paragraph is, clearly, quite unobjectionable.

At his first hearing on 20 July, Leyland, who had written down the names of eight witnesses whom he might wish to call, was asked by the chairwoman whether he had changed his mind about them and he replied that he had not. Then followed this exchange:

'*Chairwoman.* We will find out whether they are going to be helpful to this case. 9441 McGhee, what can he tell us? *Leyland.* Being, as he is, charged with me, I am supposed to have done that with him. If I was with him from a distance of only feet away, right, and Mr Harries was 50 feet away, if I was with McGhee smashing up he would have seen me, wouldn't he? Right? So I want all those people I was charged with to come in to say whether in actual fact they saw me at any time during that riot, or whether I was smashing up or what.
Chairwoman. The next one is 4989 Bennett. Which part of the charge would Bennett help with? *Leyland.* The same part.
Chairwoman. Perez, who is here. *Leyland.* Yes.
Chairwoman. Austin, Baldock, Tarrant, Banks, Scales. We may well feel that in order for you to support your defence you may not need every one of those. It may be you consider that one or two, or three, may be, who are more easily available, would be able to support your defence without calling the ones who are not available for good reasons. *Leyland.* Yes, but the way I see it, it is a serious charge.
Chairwoman. It is a very serious charge. *Leyland.* And I am liable to lose all my remission for this so I want as many witnesses as possible for my defence as regards whether I was actually there doing that or not.'

Shortly after, the hearing was adjourned. On 22 July when it was resumed, Leyland asked to be allowed to call three witnesses. He wanted to call Banks to corroborate his evidence, which was in issue, that he had a beard at the material time. The chairwoman asked whether Banks was available and being told that he had been returned to another prison said to Leyland: 'You have heard that answer.' Leyland asked to call Scales also, inter alia, to prove that he, Leyland, was wearing a beard. Finally he asked to call Perez, *a* who had been charged with him and was supposed to have been in his company to confirm whether he, Leyland, actually was in his company at any time smashing anything. In answer to the chairwoman's question he said that Perez could also give evidence about his beard. Then followed this exchange:

> 'Chairwoman. The panel do not feel they need three prisoners to say whether they saw you had a beard so we are satisfied to call Perez if he is still here. Leyland. Can I make a point? Banks can confirm about this hole, and when it was supposed to have
b been made, and it is very important because if the hole was not there at 11.30 I could not have been seen through the hole.
> Chairwoman. I have already told you that the panel are not, and have not, during this adjudication accepted any definite times. All times mentioned have been "about" and "roughly".'

c The matter concluded with the chairwoman allowing only Perez to be called.

It may be that the panel, by the time that request was made, had concluded (as could in fact well be the case) that there was nothing in Leyland's point about the hole and that he had been properly identified. But in my view they should not have reached any such conclusion without hearing witnesses whom Leyland wished to call to substantiate his evidence on those issues; and in my view the board was in breach of its duty to give
d Leyland a full opportunity of presenting his case when they allowed only Perez to give evidence on his behalf.

Tangney. He also relies on the ground that the board placed an unlawful limit on the number of witnesses he could call. The facts are as follows. He said that he wanted to call six witnesses, who were witnesses to the offence. The chairwoman immediately replied that the board would allow three inmate witnesses. The first was called, but said that he
e was not at the scene. The second was called and he gave evidence about it, and the third was called and said that he could not see the scene. Tangney commented that he should not have called him and then asked: 'Can I have replacement witnesses?' The chairwoman replied: 'I don't think so. You have already named your witnesses.' He was, however, allowed to call one more witness but that witness also, when called, said he was not even in the prison on the day in question and did not, therefore, witness the events. Tangney
f then said to the chairwoman: 'As I've had no contact with witnesses I'd still like to call another two or three and Mr Furness [a prison officer].' Mr Furness, but no other witness, was called; and Tangney said that he would like it placed on record that it was very unfair that he was not allowed to call other witnesses.

In the event, therefore, he was able to call only the prisoner who had witnessed the events in which he, Tangney, was alleged to have been involved. He had called three
g witnesses who, as it turned out, did not witness those events, or said that they did not do so; and it should have been apparent to the board that Tangney had been kept apart from other prisoners under r 48(2) of the 1964 rules, that he might, as he said was the case, not have had any contact with any of them and that it might therefore be necessary for him to call a number of witnesses before finding more than one who had witnessed the scene. In these circumstances I do not see how the board could have been satisfied that none of
h the other witnesses whom Tangney wished to call would be able to give useful evidence should they be called; nor, applying Geoffrey Lane LJ's test in *Ex p St Germain (No 2)*, do I see how they could have concluded that Tangney's wish to call more evidence was an attempt to render the hearing impracticable or that it was unnecessary to call so many witnesses to establish the point at issue. In my judgment, therefore, the board failed to exercise its discretion properly in this respect.

j *Clark.* He also relies on the ground that his board placed an unlawful limit on the number of witnesses to be called. The facts were as follows. It was the applicant's defence to the charges in respect of which he had pleaded not guilty that he had not been present where the offences were alleged to have taken place, but that he had been elsewhere at the time. Before the first hearing on 12 August, the applicant had indicated that he proposed to call nine witnesses, all of whom were inmates of the prison at the date of the offence, in his defence. At the commencement of the hearing on 12 August, the applicant asked for an adjournment because four of those witnesses had been moved to another prison and were not available to give evidence. The chairwoman asked him what those four would contribute that the other five could not. The applicant replied that they were part of his defence that he was not at the scene of the offence. The chairwoman asked him if they could 'give' more than the other five who were available. The applicant replied that the four could help him give a stronger defence but that they were all to give the same evidence. The board considered the applicant's application for an adjournment and, because they considered that the four additional witnesses would not add to the evidence of the five who were available, they refused to adjourn.

Counsel for Clark submits that the decision to refuse to allow the four further witnesses failed to take into account the possibility that those four, or some of them, might be more credible than the five witnesses available. Counsel for the board submits that a prisoner cannot be entitled to call an unlimited number of witnesses in the hope that sooner or later one of them will turn out to be a 'good' witness.

As Geoffrey Lane LJ made clear in *Ex p St Germain (No 2)*, a prisoner cannot use his right to call witnesses in an attempt to render the hearing of the charge virtually impracticable; but it seems to me that, whether or not the board would have been entitled, having heard the first five witnesses, to refuse to allow the other four (a matter about which I have some doubt), they were not entitled to take that view at least until they had heard those five. Having heard those five, if they accepted their evidence they could, quite properly, be satisfied that the further four would not be able to give useful evidence. If, however, having heard those five, they did not believe them, or they were left in doubt about whether or not to accept their evidence then, as it seems to me, they could not, without more, have been satisfied that the other four would not be able to give useful evidence unless they made some assumptions such that either the case charged was made out (which would have been a premature decision) or that those other witnesses would be unreliable (an assumption which they would not be entitled to make). In my view, therefore, this board also failed to exercise its discretion properly in this regard.

Should any decisions of the boards of visitors be quashed?

In my view the awards in the case of Leyland, Tangney and Clark and the decision in the case of Tarrant and Anderson to continue the proceedings without legal representation must each be quashed. In my view failure to consider the exercise of the discretion, which existed, to allow legal representation was in all cases a substantial infringement of the applicants' rights, whether or not, if the discretion had been exercised, it would have been exercised in the applicants' favour. In the case of Tarrant and Leyland, the decision must also, in my view, be quashed because in those cases, for the reasons that I have given, any reasonable tribunal, properly exercising their discretion, would, in my judgment, have allowed those applicants to have legal representation. That conclusion would not be affected by the fact that in the future boards will know what standard of proof to apply, because in the cases of those two applicants the complicated nature of the charges and the gravity of the consequences that could follow if the charges were to be proved are of themselves, in my view, sufficient to necessitate the granting of legal representation.

The orders

I prefer not to formulate the orders or declarations which are to be made consequential on this judgment until counsel have heard it and have made submissions about its effect.

KERR LJ. I agree that the applications of Tangney, Clark and Leyland to quash the adjudications of the boards of visitors on them must be granted, and that the applications

of Tarrant and Anderson also succeed to the extent that the part-heard adjudications on
them cannot proceed. In all these cases it will be open to hold fresh adjudications on the
applicants on these charges by differently constituted boards of visitors, but only after
due consideration by these boards of the applicants' requests for legal or other
representation in accordance with our judgments on these applications. In the same way
as Webster J, I have not formed any view whether it is appropriate, in addition, to make
any of the declarations asked for in these cases, and I would like to hear counsel on these
matters when they have had an opportunity of considering our judgments.

In reaching these conclusions I am in agreement with the judgment of Webster J, and
I only add some remarks of my own because of the importance of the issues concerning
the legal representation of prisoners charged with disciplinary offences under the Prison
Rules 1964, SI 1964/388, before boards of visitors.

It is clear from the voluminous material before us that until now it has been taken for
granted that there is an inflexible rule (using the word in a loose sense) that prisoners
cannot and will not have any form of representation or assistance when facing such
charges. Counsel for the boards sought to rely on the long standing acceptance of this
state of affairs as something which should in itself lead to the rejection of the arguments
on behalf of the applicants. He relied, understandably faintly, on the reference by Parke
J to regulation by 'ancient usage' in Collier v Hicks (1831) 2 B & Ad 663 at 672, 109 ER
1290 at 1293, but it is clear that no question of any legally binding custom or usage can
be invoked in the present context. In effect, counsel for the boards submitted that because
something has always been taken for granted it must be correct as a matter of law. In
former times he might have relied on the adjective 'novel' as sufficient to carry the
conclusion that no question as to any rights concerning legal representation is now
capable of being raised. But I cannot accept any argument on these lines as being
determinative, or even persuasive, to any extent whatever, particularly in the light of the
far-reaching development of the principles of our administrative law during recent
decades. In this connection it must be remembered that it was only as the result of the
unanimous decision of the Court of Appeal in R v Hull Prison Board of Visitors, ex p St
Germain [1979] 1 All ER 701, [1979] QB 425 that the jurisdiction of judicial review has
been established in relation to proceedings before boards of visitors, and that it is this
jurisdiction which provides the foundation for the present applicants. It should also be
noted that the subsequent proceedings in that case, in R v Hull Prison Board of Visitors, ex
p St Germain (No 2) [1979] 3 All ER 545, [1979] 1 WLR 1401, resulted in the quashing of
six of the seven adjudications on the ground of non-compliance with the principles of
natural justice.

It is in the context of the principles of natural justice that the issues concerning the
legal representation of prisoners charged before boards of visitors now arise for
determination. For the moment I leave aside the question of some lesser kind of assistance
in the form of an adviser or 'McKenzieman': see McKenzie v McKenzie [1970] 3 All ER
1034, [1971] P 33. The issues concerning legal representation on such charges can be
formulated as follows. (1) Does a prisoner have an absolute right to be granted legal
representation whenever this is requested by him? (2) If not, is there an absolute bar
against granting such requests, or is there a discretion whether to grant them or not?
I therefore deal with these questions in turn.

An absolute right

I agree that in this court the first of these questions must in any event be answered in
the negative, because the decision of the Court of Appeal in Fraser v Mudge [1975] 3 All
ER 78, [1975] 1 WLR 1132 is directly in point and binding on us. I cannot accept any of
the arguments to the contrary, and I think that counsel representing Leyland was entirely
right to concede this. Furthermore, quite apart from what was said in Fraser v Mudge by
Lord Denning MR and Roskill LJ, it cannot for one moment be accepted on the
authorities that in all proceedings, whether of an adversarial or inquisitorial character,

with potentially grave consequences for the persons concerned, the principles of natural justice impose any obligation on the tribunal or body in question to allow legal representation automatically on request. In many cases this would not only be unnecessary but indeed counter-productive: see *Collier v Hicks* (1831) 2 B & Ad 663, 109 ER 1290, *Enderby Town Football Club Ltd v Football Association Ltd* [1971] 1 All ER 215 at 218, 221, [1971] Ch 591 at 605, 609 per Lord Denning MR (in the passage which Webster J has already cited), Fenton Atkinson and Cairns LJJ as well as *Maynard v Osmond* [1977] 1 All ER 64 at 79, 82, 84–85, [1977] QB 240 at 252, 255, 259 per Lord Denning MR, Orr and Waller LJJ.

It was submitted that the report of the European Commission of Human Rights in *Campbell and Fell v UK* (1982) 5 EHRR 207 should lead us to a different conclusion. This report was based on art 6 of the European Convention on Human Rights (TS 71 (1953); Cmd 8969) dealing with 'the determination . . . of any criminal charge', whereas the jurisdiction of the Court of Appeal in *Ex p St Germain* was based on the classification of the charges as 'disciplinary' and of the appeal as not arising in a 'criminal cause or matter'. Paragraph 3 of art 6 provides:

'Everyone charged with a criminal offence has the following minimum rights . . . (c) to defend himself in person or through legal assistance of his own choosing or, if he has not sufficient means to pay for legal assistance, to be given it free when the interests of justice so require.'

The report of the majority of the commission was to the effect that prisoners charged with 'especially grave offences' under r 52 of the Prison Rules 1964, SI 1964/388, which in those cases also included mutiny, were entitled to invoke this provision. It is clear, however, that this court cannot accept any argument based solely on this report, since we are bound by the settled jurisprudence of our law to which I have already referred. Her Majesty's government has not accepted the conclusions of the majority of the members of the commission; the case has been argued before the European Court of Human Rights and the judgment is now pending. However, in relation to Tarrant and Leyland, who were also charged with mutiny under r 52, our conclusion on the present applications leads to the same result in practice, though for different reasons, as the application of art 6(3)(c) of the convention with the exception of a right to legal aid, which is regulated by statute. In this connection it may be helpful to record that it was common ground before us that legal aid is not available for the representation of prisoners before boards of visitors in any circumstances, but that the green form scheme, covering legal advice up to a cost of £40, would in principle be available in appropriate cases. The position under the convention may arise for consideration by the Home Secretary and possibly by Parliament when the pending judgment of the court has been given, and it may be that this will also take the outcome of the present applications into account.

A right to the exercise of a discretion

I therefore turn to the second question, whether there is an absolute bar to the grant of legal representation or whether there is a discretion in boards of visitors to grant such requests. As it seems to me, under our law, including the principles of natural justice, there cannot be any answer to this question other than that boards of visitors have a discretion to grant requests for legal representation in appropriate cases. This must be so for at least two reasons. First, since there is no statutory provision to the contrary, boards of visitors are masters of their own procedures and are entitled to decide for themselves whether or not to grant such requests. In the same way as any other tribunal or body inquiring into any charges against anyone, they have an unfettered right to decide whom they will hear on behalf of the persons charged.

Second, the grant of legal representation, when this is requested, must in some cases necessarily follow from s 47(2) of the Prison Act 1952 and r 49(2) of the Prison Rules

1964. Both of these provide, in effect, that a prisoner charged with any offence under the
a rules must be given a proper and full opportunity of presenting his case. Suppose then
that in a particular instance a board of visitors is of the view that this requirement can
only be complied with if the prisoner is legally represented, or even that the board is
doubtful whether this objective can be attained without legal representation. How, then,
could the board refuse such a request? Such situations are by no means necessarily
fanciful. The evidence before us shows that such views may well be held by the members
b of boards, in a number of cases, who are at present constrained by the 'rule' that legal
representation is simply out of the question. Moreover, while the principles of natural
justice are of course primarily designed for the protection of persons against whom
charges of some kind are made, they must also operate for the benefit of tribunals or
bodies who have the task of investigating the charges and deciding on the consequences
for the persons charged. They must be entitled to conduct their proceedings on the basis
c of what they consider to be appropriate, according to justice as they see it.

Given that there is a discretion to grant requests for legal representation when boards
of visitors consider it appropriate to do so, what then are the rights of prisoners who
make such requests? The answer, in my view, is that they have the right to a proper
consideration of such requests on their merits by each board to whom such a request is
made.

d It does not follow, however, that such requests will necessarily be granted, except that
they must always be granted if, in the view of the board, the circumstances are such that
legal representation is or may be required in order to comply with the prisoner's rights
under r 49(2). In order to reach a conclusion whether or not to grant any such request, I
agree that boards should take account of the considerations which have been listed by
Webster J in his judgment, together with any other circumstances which they may
e regard as material in any individual case.

Before returning to the applications in the present case I would mention two other
general matters.

First, although counsel for the boards understandably disclaimed reliance on any
'floodgates' argument if boards of visitors have a discretion to grant legal representation,
the possibility that the consequences might assume 'floodgate' proportions inevitably
f played a part in his submissions, and he relied on considerations of public policy in
support of these. Speaking for myself, I do not accept that there will be such consequences;
nor that their possible advent can properly affect our decision. As regards the latter point,
I would respectfully echo mutatis mutandis what Waller LJ said in *Ex p St Germain* [1979]
1 All ER 701 at 725, [1979] QB 425 at 465–466 in the context of the availability of
judicial review of the decisions of boards of visitors. He said:

g 'I realise that when dealing with prisoners living in a prison world there is the
risk of a number of unmeritorious applications for judicial review. This is a risk
which must always be accepted so long as there is a possibility of a meritorious
application . . . The fact that there are no precedents for such applications is a
possible indication that there will not be a flood of applications. But even if there
h were, that would not be a ground for refusing the remedy, because there might in a
particular case be a possibility of real injustice.'

As regards the first point, the likelihood of a flood of applications, I doubt very much
whether this will materialise or that the number of applications will lead to great logistic
difficulties in practice. Really unmeritorious applications are not likely to be numerous,
j since these would merely be seen as liable to have an adverse effect on the boards
concerned. The Prison Department of the Home Office has already produced guidelines
(in the so-called 'Green Book', April 1977, reprinted in November 1978) for the 'Procedure
for the Conduct of an Adjudication by a Board of Visitors'. We were referred to many
passages of this publication, but, with the exception of the question of the standard of

proof, to which Webster J has referred in his judgment, no criticism of any kind of any of its contents was made on behalf of any of the applicants in these cases. If our judgments on these applications stand, it would be open to the Home Office to incorporate guidelines dealing with the appropriate procedures for any requests for legal representation which may be made hereafter, so as to ensure uniformity and to minimise any consequential delay; and also as to how such requests should be approached by individual boards in individual cases on the basis of our judgments on these applications. If this course is adopted, it will equally dispose of another argument advanced by counsel for the boards, somewhat in terrorem, that the right to grant requests for legal representation in appropriate cases is likely to result in a great variety of differing decisions. In all these respects, possibly with the assistance of the courts in one or two early cases, I would envisage that a settled and acceptable pattern would soon emerge, as so frequently happens in relation to innovations which, at first sight, appear unacceptable and impracticable.

The second matter concerns the question of a prisoner having the assistance of an adviser, 'a McKenzieman' (see *McKenzie v McKenzie* [1970] 3 All ER 1034, [1971] P 33). For myself, I would not exclude this in cases where (i) the prisoner asks for this form of assistance, (ii) it appears to the board appropriate to grant it, and (iii) the request relates to a suitable person who is readily available and willing to assist, namely not a fellow prisoner, but, for instance, a probation officer, social worker or clergyman acquainted with the prisoner. I can well imagine that requests may frequently be made for such assistance rather than for legal representation.

The result concerning the present applications

In all five applications, requests for legal representation, and, in three of them, for an adviser, were made and rejected by the boards as a matter of course, without any consideration of their merits. Although we were not told so expressly, I infer that legal representation, or advice from someone who might have been suitable, would have been available if the requests had been granted. I agree with Webster J that on the facts of the cases of Tarrant and Leyland, who were charged with mutiny under r 52, a proper exercise of the board's discretion would necessarily have led to their requests for legal representation being granted. I also agree that in relation to Tangney, Clark and Anderson their requests deserved to be considered on their merits, without expressing any view as to the conclusion which would be appropriate. I therefore consider that there was a breach of the principles of natural justice in relation to all five applicants due to the summary rejection of their requests and that the adjudications on them must be quashed with the consequences to which I have referred at the beginning of this judgment.

Other issues raised by some of the applicants

Although it follows from our decision that these do not affect the outcome, I agree in all respects with the judgment of Webster J so far as the other grounds for these applications are concerned. I would only add this. It is certainly true that proceedings before boards of visitors are to some extent 'inquisitorial' in their nature, as well as having the 'adversary' character to which we are accustomed in proceedings against persons generally, whether they be ciminal, disciplinary or of whatever nature: see *R v Blundeston Prison Board of Visitors, ex p Fox-Taylor* [1982] 1 All ER 646 at 648 per Phillips J. In my view such classifications have little significance and may well be misleading; thus, I have not heard it suggested that they have any bearing on questions concerning legal representation of, or other assistance to, the persons charged. In the context of the functions of prison boards of visitors it must also be said that one cannot feel anything but admiration for the work which they undertake and the greatest sympathy for the extent to which their patience must often be tried when they have to carry out adjudications such as those in the present case. But if any classification of the procedure *a* on adjudications by them is to be made, it should be borne in mind that the term 'accusatorial' is also sometimes used in this context. I feel bound to say that this was the word which crossed my mind on reading some parts of the notes of the proceedings to which Webster J has referred.

We will hear counsel on the appropriate orders to be made on these applications when counsel have had time to consider our judgments.

b *Orders of certiorari granted.*

Solicitors: *B M Birnberg & Co* (for Tangney, Clark, Anderson and Tarrant); *Gamlens*, agents for *George E Baker & Co*, Guildford (for Leyland); *Treasury Solicitor.*

N P Metcalfe Esq   Barrister.

c

Practice Direction

d

FAMILY DIVISION

Child – Welfare – Welfare report – Report of court welfare officer – Confidentiality of report – Notice to be indorsed on all reports.

e The following wording must be boldly indorsed on all court welfare officers' reports filed in Family Division proceedings and on all copies which are supplied to the parties or their solicitors:

f 'This report has been prepared for the court and should be treated as confidential. It must not be shown nor its contents revealed to any person other than a party or a legal adviser to such a party. Such legal adviser may make use of the report in connection with an application for legal aid.'

The registrar's directions dated 7 June 1973 (unreported) and 8 February 1982 ([1982] 1 All ER 512, [1982] 1 WLR 234) are hereby cancelled.

g Issued with the concurrence of the Lord Chancellor.

B P TICKLE
Senior Registrar.

24 February 1984

Jenkins v Lombard North Central plc   *a*

QUEEN'S BENCH DIVISION
ROBERT GOFF LJ AND FORBES J
25, 26, 29 JULY 1983

Consumer protection – Consumer credit – Advertising – Seeking business – Advertisement *b*
indicating willingness of advertiser to provide credit – Form and content of advertisement – Car
dealer – Price sticker on car displaying name and logo of well-known finance company – Whether
sticker 'indicating' that company willing to provide credit – Consumer Credit Act 1974, ss 43(1),
167(2) – Consumer Credit (Advertisements) Regulations 1980.

The defendant company, which provided a wide range of financial services (including
the granting of credit facilities) to the public on a nation-wide scale, supplied a car dealer *c*
with stickers to be placed on cars offered for sale. The stickers displayed on the right-
hand side the price of the car in bold print, and on the left-hand side the company's name
and logo in smaller print. The prosecutor preferred three informations against the
company alleging that each sticker constituted an advertisement 'indicating', within the
meaning of s 43(1)*[a]* of the Consumer Credit Act 1974, that the company was willing to
provide credit facilities for the purchase of the car and therefore, in failing to comply *d*
with the requirements of the Consumer Credit (Advertisements) Regulations 1980
governing such advertisements, the company had committed an offence under s 167(2)*[b]*
of the 1974 Act. The informations were dismissed on the ground that the stickers did
not 'indicate' the company's willingness to provide credit. The prosecutor appealed,
contending that, in view of the company's widespread reputation for providing credit
facilities, an ordinary person would interpret the stickers as indicating that the company *e*
was willing to provide that service in respect of the cars on which the stickers were
placed.

Held – On the true construction of s 43(1) of the 1974 Act an advertiser 'indicated' that
he was willing to provide credit only if he stated in some way as a fact, rather than merely
suggested, that he was willing to do so. Since the company's stickers did not state as a fact *f*
that the company would provide credit for the purchase of cars on which the stickers
were placed the company had not committed an offence under s 167(2). The appeal
would therefore be dismissed (see p 834 g to p 835 a and c to f, post).
Maurice Binks (Turf Accountants) Ltd v Huss [1971] 1 All ER 104 applied.

Notes   *g*
For the control of advertising under the Consumer Credit Act 1974, see 22 Halsbury's
Laws (4th edn) paras 55–56.
For the Consumer Credit Act 1974, ss 43, 167, see 44 Halsbury's Statutes (3rd edn)
782, 869.
For the Consumer Credit (Advertisements) Regulations 1980, see 14 Halsbury's
Statutory Instruments (4th reissue) 324.   *h*

Cases referred to in judgment
Binks (Maurice) (Turf Accountants) Ltd v Huss [1971] 1 All ER 104, [1971] 1 WLR 52, DC.
Doble v David Greig Ltd [1972] 2 All ER 195, [1972] 1 WLR 703, DC.
Hanlon v Law Society [1980] 2 All ER 199, [1981] AC 124, [1980] 2 WLR 756, HL.
Jackson v Hall [1980] 1 All ER 177, [1980] AC 854, [1980] 2 WLR 118, HL.   *j*

---

a Section 43(1) is set out at p 829 j, post
b Section 167(2), so far as material, provides: 'A person who contravenes any regulations made under
section 44 . . . commits an offence.'

Case stated

a Paul Christopher Jenkins appealed by way of case stated against the decision of F D L Loy Esq, a stipendiary magistrate for Leeds, given on 30 July 1982, whereby the magistrate dismissed three informations preferred by the appellant against the respondents, Lombard North Central plc, alleging that, in respect of three separate cars at the premises of Ripon Motors Ltd, Horsforth, Leeds, the respondents had indicated a willingness to provide credit for the purchase of the relevant car, in contravention of the Consumer Credit
b (Advertisements) Regulations 1980, SI 1980/54, being regulations made under s 44 of the Consumer Credit Act 1974, contrary to s 167(2) of that Act. The facts are set out in the judgment of Robert Goff LJ.

Anthony Scrivener QC, Anthony Purnell and *Julien Hooper* for the appellant.
Richard Yorke QC and *Charles Falconer* for the respondents.

c
                                                                  Cur adv vult

29 July. The following judgments were delivered.

d **ROBERT GOFF LJ.** There is before the court an appeal by way of case stated by Paul Christopher Jenkins, who represents the Director General of Fair Trading, against a decision of Mr Loy, a stipendiary magistrate for Leeds, whereby he dismissed three informations preferred by the appellant against the respondents, Lombard North Central plc, alleging that, in respect of three separate cars at the premises of Ripon Motors Ltd, Horsforth, Leeds, the respondents had indicated a willingness to provide credit for the
e purchase of the relevant car, in contravention of the Consumer Credit (Advertisements) Regulations 1980, SI 1980/54, being regulations made under s 44 of the Consumer Credit Act 1974.

It will perhaps be convenient if I refer first to the relevant provisions of the Consumer Credit Act 1974. Counsel for the appellant took us briefly through the Act in order to demonstrate the breadth of its scope. He certainly revealed an Act of extraordinary length
f and complexity, which must raise very considerable problems for those officials whose task it is to see that it is enforced and for those citizens, whether corporate or individual, who are affected by its terms and seek conscientiously to abide by them. An example of the latter is found in the respondents. They came into existence by the amalgamation of two finance companies. They are a subsidiary of the National Westminster Bank and have been in existence as such since October 1971. They provide a wide range of financial
g services to the public on a national scale, including the taking of deposits, banking facilities, raising funds on the money market, the granting of credit facilities and the granting of leasing facilities to persons, whether corporate or individuals, who wish to use the item leased for the purpose of their business. In relation to consumer transactions for the purchase of motor cars arranged through introductions made by motor dealers, the respondents invariably provided credit by means of conditional sale agreements.

h I come then to the Consumer Credit Act 1974. The sections of the Act with which this case is immediately concerned are ss 43 and 44. These are to be found in Pt IV of the Act, entitled 'Seeking Business', the first part of which is headed 'Advertising' and consists of ss 43 to 47. Sections 43 and 44 provide:

'**43.**—(1) This Part applies to any advertisement, published for the purposes of a
j business carried on by the advertiser, indicating that he is willing—(a) to provide credit, or (b) to enter into an agreement for the bailment or (in Scotland) the hiring of goods by him.

(2) An advertisement does not fall within subsection (1) if the advertiser does not carry on—(a) a consumer credit business or consumer hire business, or (b) a business in the course of which he provides credit to individuals secured on land, or (c) a

business which comprises or relates to unregulated agreements where—(i) the proper law of the agreement is the law of a country outside the United Kingdom, and (ii) if the proper law of the agreement were the law of a part of the United Kingdom it would be a regulated agreement.

(3) An advertisement does not fall within subsection (1)(a) if it indicates—(a) that the credit must exceed £5,000, and that no security is required, or the security is to consist of property other than land, or (b) that the credit is available only to a body corporate.

(4) An advertisement does not fall within subsection (1)(b) if it indicates that the advertiser is not willing to enter into a consumer hire agreement.

(5) The Secretary of State may by order provide that this Part shall not apply to other advertisements of a description specified in the order.

44.—(1) The Secretary of State shall make regulations as to the form and content of advertisements to which this Part applies, and the regulations shall contain such provisions as appear to him appropriate with a view to ensuring that, having regard to its subject-matter and the amount of detail included in it, an advertisement conveys a fair and reasonably comprehensive indication of the nature of the credit or hire facilities offered by the advertiser and of their true cost to persons using them.

(2) Regulations under subsection (1) may in particular—(a) require specified information to be included in the prescribed manner in advertisements, and other specified material to be excluded; (b) contain requirements to ensure that specified information is clearly brought to the attention of persons to whom advertisements are directed, and that one part of an advertisement is not given insufficient or excessive prominence compared with another.'

The allegations against the respondents in the three informations laid against them by the appellant were that, in the case of each of the three cars at the premises of Ripon Motors Ltd, an advertisement published for the purposes of a business carried on by the advertiser (the respondents) indicated that the respondents were willing to provide credit, and that since none of the advertisements fell within any of the exceptions in sub-ss (2), (3), (4) and (5) of s 43, each was caught by s 43(1), with the result that Pt IV of the Act applied to each of them. Furthermore, since none of the advertisements complied with the regulations made by the Secretary of State, pursuant to s 44, ie the Consumer Credit (Advertisements) Regulations 1980, there was an offence committed by the respondents in respect of each advertisement.

The advertisements complained of were the subject matter of photographs conveniently annexed to the case by the magistrate. Each took the form of a price display, ie a long notice or sticker, about two or three feet in length and about six inches in height, white in colour, but trimmed with blue. These were obviously intended to be used, and were in each case being used, by Ripon Motors Ltd to be placed on cars for sale by them, stating the asking cash price for the cars. Each price display was divided vertically by a blue line, leaving a larger part on the right (nearly three-quarters of the length) for stating the asking cash price for the car, which was entered in each case in prominent black figures. In the remaining, smaller part, on the left, there appeared in black, smaller print first the word 'Lombard', underneath that word in smaller print the words 'North Central', and underneath again, in very small print, the word 'Limited' and second, to the left of that name, the 'logo' of that company, which appears to consist of a stylised form of the symbol of the '£' sterling. In the case of one of the three advertisements complained of, but not of the other two, the printed words 'cash price' appeared also above the price placed on the price display. Each of the three advertisements was displayed on a car for sale at the premises of Ripon Motors Ltd.

We were told by counsel, and we have no doubt that this was correct, that the respondents had not the slightest intention of contravening the Consumer Credit Act 1974 and that everything had been done by them under legal advice, with the intention

of acting in accordance with the provisions of the Act. However, having regard to the
a nature and complexity of the regulations made by the Secretary of State under s 44, it
was very difficult for the respondents to comply with them in certain respects. Thus, the
most relevant regulation for present purposes, reg 6 (to which counsel for the appellant
referred us) presupposes that the advertiser has specified an occupation of his in the
advertisement; the respondents, not being back-street moneylenders, but a substantial
finance company offering a wide range of facilities, which change from time to time,
b considered that they would experience considerable difficulty, and indeed embarrassment,
if they attempted to describe an occupation of theirs in an advertisement. Faced with
difficulties of this kind, the respondents sought to concentrate on what in the case stated
is called 'corporate advertising', ie reminding the public of the existence of the company
by advertising its name without referring to any specific service. That the respondents
were indeed attempting to comply with the provisions of the Act, and with the
c regulations made under s 44, was demonstrated by a 'Dealers' Guide', attached to the case,
in which the respondents explained to dealers with whom they carried on business how
to use, inter alia, the price displays, which are the subject of the present proceedings. In
their dealers' guide a passage relating to the respondents' price displays was as follows:

> 'PRICE DISPLAYS. Whilst little change is necessary we do require you to affix "cash
> price" onto your existing windscreen price panels and price stands. "Cash price"
d stickers will be provided. If you have any of our very early price indicators which
> include the words "Yours with a little help from" these must be removed and
> destroyed by October 6th and our representatives will replace them. No information
> whatsoever relating to Lombard's credit terms must be placed on goods displaying
> our cash price panels and except for our brochures, no other point of sale material
> from Lombard can be displayed. So before October 6th you must withdraw and
e destroy all other Lombard promotional displays.'

In relation to brochures supplied by them to dealers, the Dealers' Guide states:

> 'BROCHURES. All our brochures have been redesigned to comply with the
> Regulations and present stocks must be destroyed. If brochures are displayed in
> your showroom they must be away from the goods. If they are placed on or very
f near to goods showing a cash price, you will also have to display an APR and comply
> with other complicated requirements of the Regulations.'

Then, in relation to other advertising, it states:

> 'OTHER ADVERTISING. If you wish to produce your own advertising offering credit
> terms either for use in the showroom or in the press we strongly advise that you
g seek independent legal advice because you will be required to comply with the
> Regulations which are extremely complex. Also, if any of your advertising includes
> our name you must let us see it for our approval before it is used. We cannot
> emphasize too strongly that if any advertisement or publicity referring to credit is
> in breach of the Act both you and Lombard could be found to be criminally liable.
h If you have any doubts, talk to our representatives who will help wherever they can.'

Against this background, I turn to the specific complaints in this case. The magistrate
made the following findings regarding the business of the respondents in para 2.3 of the
case, which reads as follows:

> 'I accepted the evidence of the Respondent's witness Kenneth Warriner that the
j Respondent employed two main methods of advertising. The first was service
> advertising i.e. describing a particular service provided e.g. credit, leasing, deposit
> taking. The second was corporate advertising i.e. bringing to the attention of the
> public the existence of the company by advertising its name without referring to
> any specific or particular service. Prior to the date on which the Regulations came
> into force (6th October, 1980) the Respondent pursued a policy of service advertising

in car dealers' showrooms, of the sort shown in annex 4, with stands and windscreen stickers intended to display the cash price of the vehicles similar to those described *a* above but with the addition of the words "yours with a little help from Lombard". These had been withdrawn by the 6th October, 1980 as the Respondent accepted that such wording would indicate a willingness on the part of the Respondent to provide credit for the vehicles to which they were attached, causing infringement of the Consumer Credit (Advertisements) Regulations 1980 and the Respondent had accordingly notified motor dealers with whom it had an association to destroy *b* all such forms of advertising. The only stickers and stands which the Respondents have permitted to be used in their dealers' showrooms after the 6th October 1980 are those of the sort which form the subject matter of this prosecution. The purpose of these stands and stickers was to fulfil the dealers' need for a method of displaying the price and to keep the Respondent's name in the public eye (i.e. corporate advertising). It was the practice of the Respondent to circulate all its dealers with a *c* pamphlet entitled "Dealer Guide" which is annex 7 hereto. This pamphlet described the new form of advertising to be used in the future.'

Thus, having set out the issue in the case before him, which was whether the price displays and each of them constituted an 'advertisement . . . indicating that' the respondents were 'willing . . . to provide credit', he set out the various contentions of the appellant and the respondents. *d*

The appellant had contended, inter alia, that in determining the meaning and import of an advertisement, regard can properly be had to the reputation of the advertiser as well as to the effects of any previous advertising by him, and that the advertisements complained of were conveying the following information to a customer (para 4(e) of the case): *e*

'(i) that he has the option of paying a cash price to acquire the particular vehicle, which would not involve Lombard North Central in any way; (ii) alternatively he may consider Lombard North Central Limited which is a well-known finance company, and the acquisition of vehicles on credit terms is widespread in the motor trade; (iii) that one of the services known to be offered by Lombard North Central Limited is credit for the acquisition of motor vehicles; (iv) that the main purpose in *f* Lombard North Central Limited's displaying its name in such a format is to indicate that it would be willing to provide credit to a suitable customer who required credit to acquire the particular vehicle to which the sticker was attached.'

Therefore, submitted the appellant, the advertisements did indicate that the advertiser was willing to provide 'cash' (sic; this must be a misprint in the case stated for 'credit'). *g*

The contentions for the respondents included, in particular, submissions that (i) the word 'indicating' in s 43(1) of the 1974 Act meant in some way stating that the advertiser was willing to provide credit, but that, if there was any ambiguity, the subsection, being penal, should be construed in favour of the respondents, and (ii) whether or not the advertisements were indications of willingness to provide credit must depend solely on an examination of the advertisements themselves in their physical context and not by *h* reference to any extrinsic material, in particular the reputation of the advertiser. On the facts of the case, it was submitted that the advertisements did not indicate that the respondents were willing to provide credit. Reliance was placed on two authorities, which were cited to the magistrate, viz *Maurice Binks (Turf Accountants) Ltd v Huss* [1971] 1 All ER 104, [1971] 1 WLR 52 and *Doble v David Greig Ltd* [1972] 2 All ER 195, [1972] 1 WLR 703. *j*

Having heard these rival submissions, the magistrate formed the opinion that none of the three advertisements constituted an indication published by the respondents that they were willing to provide credit on the three cars within the meaning of s 43(1) of the 1974 Act and, accordingly, on 30 July 1982 he dismissed each information. He then posed this question for the opinion of the court:

a
'Whether the cash price sticker published by the Respondent and attached to the motor vehicle referred to in the charges constituted an "advertisement" published for the purpose of a business carried on by the Respondent indicating that the Respondent was willing to provide credit within the meaning of Section 43(1) of the Act.'

b
In the course of his opening, counsel for the appellant referred us to reg 6 of the Consumer Credit (Advertisements) Regulations 1980 made under s 44 of the 1974 Act. That regulation provides:

c
'*Simple credit advertisements.* The requirements of this regulation are—(a) that the only indication in the advertisement that the advertiser is willing to provide credit is an indication that he carries on a business within paragraphs (a) to (c) of section 43(2) of the Act in the form of his name and a statement either of an occupation of his or of the general nature of such an occupation; and (b) that the advertisement does not specify the cash price, or other price, of any goods, services, land or other things.'

d
By virtue of reg 5, an advertisement complying with reg 6 is an advertisement complying with the regulations. Counsel for the appellant referred us to this regulation to demonstrate the circumstances in which the respondents could, if they had wished, publish an advertisement which complied with the regulations; though while so doing, he warned us that counsel for the respondents would be submitting that it would not be legitimate to refer to the regulations for the purpose of construing the 1974 Act. The reference to this regulation however prompted the court to inquire whether an advertisement, for example on a hoarding by a roadside or by a railway line, which

e
simply contained a prominent display of the respondents' name and logo, would be caught by s 43 and, if so, whether such an advertisement would be within the requirements of reg 6. Counsel for the appellant's response was to submit that such an advertisement, having regard to the public reputation of the respondents, would be caught by s 43 because the appropriate test was whether an ordinary person would take the advertisement as an indication that the advertiser was willing to provide credit, and

f
in considering the reaction of the ordinary person, account should be taken of the widespread knowledge of members of the public of the reputation of the respondents as providers of credit facilities. He also submitted that such an advertisement was not protected by reg 6 because one of the two criteria specified in the regulation was missing, viz a statement of occupation of the advertiser. The court expressed some surprise at both these submissions. It was put to counsel for the appellant that perhaps some distinction

g
should be drawn between information derived by members of the public from the advertisement on the one hand, and the reputation of the advertiser on the other, so that, in the example of a simple advertisement of the respondents' name and logo on a roadside hoarding, all the advertisement would do would be to remind those who read it of the existence of the respondents. It was further put to him that the form taken by reg 6 reflected a reading by the Secretary of State of s 43(1) that an advertisement was not

h
caught by the subsection when the advertisement itself contained no statement that the advertiser was willing to provide credit. Counsel for the appellant's response was belatedly to join forces with counsel for the respondents and submit that we could not look at the regulations to construe the Act: a submission with which the court felt an instinctive sympathy, later to be fortified by reference to *Jackson v Hall* [1980] 1 All ER 177, [1980] AC 854 (though cf *Hanlon v Law Society* [1980] 2 All ER 199 at 218, [1981] AC 124 at

j
193–194 per Lord Lowry). Even so, our perhaps illegitimate foray into the regulations left me with a feeling that the Secretary of State did indeed share the view which we formed, on a reading of s 43(1), that the advertisement itself must indicate that the advertiser is willing to provide credit, so that, in the example of the simple advertisement of the respondents' name and logo on a hoarding by the roadside, the advertisement would not be caught by s 43(1), however much members of the public who read the

advertisement might, through their knowledge of the respondents' reputation, connect their name with the provision of credit facilities. Later in his reply, counsel for the *a* appellant accepted that such an advertisement would not be caught by the subsection.

Furthermore, I am unhappy about the test proposed by counsel for the appellant whether an advertisement indicates that the advertiser is willing to provide credit, viz whether an ordinary person would take the advertisement as an indication that the advertiser is willing to grant credit. My unhappiness derives not only from the fact that the reaction of the ordinary reader may find its origin not in what is indicated in the *b* advertisement, but in some other source of information (which is no doubt why the word 'ordinary' has been introduced into counsel for the appellant's test), but also because the test seems to impose a gloss on the word 'indicating' as used in s 43(1).

In this connection counsel for the respondents submitted that it was wrong, when construing the section, to depart in this way from the words of the section. Here, he relied on the decision of this court in *Maurice Binks (Turf Accountants) Ltd v Huss* [1971] 1 *c* All ER 104, [1971] 1 WLR 52. In that case justices had convicted the appellants of an offence under s 10(5) of the Betting, Gaming and Lotteries Act 1963, on the ground that the prominent display of the appellants' name over premises in Duke Street, Darlington, constituted an advertisement indicating that the particular premises were a licensed betting office. The Divisional Court allowed the appeal. Ashworth J, who delivered the judgment of the court, said ([1971] 1 All ER 104 at 107–108, [1971] 1 WLR 52 at 57– *d* 58):

> 'That disposes of two of counsel for the appellants' points and one now comes to the one that is of substance which is to the effect that whatever else the sign is, it is not an advertisement indicating, under s 10(5)(*a*), that any particular premises are a licensed betting office. It is perfectly true to say that there is nothing whatever on the sign of itself expressly to indicate that the premises are a licensed betting office. *e* It is only by an extended use of the word "indicating" that any substance can be found in the case put forward by the prosecution. Counsel for the respondent has called the court's attention to the fact that in the Concise Oxford Dictionary two meanings are given to the word "indicate". The first meaning is one which clearly in this case does him no good at all, a meaning which is: "Point out, make known, show." But he refers to the secondary meaning, which is: "Suggest, call for; state *f* briefly; be a sign of, betoken." He says that this sign at least suggests that the premises to which it is affixed are a licensed betting office. If I may say so, that is a plausible argument, attractively presented, but it is without any foundation whatever ... "Indicating" in my view in the subsection means "showing". It involves the first of the two meanings put forward by counsel for the respondent, and it is to be noted that in s 10(5) the word is used twice, in para (*a*) "indicating that any particular *g* premises are a licensed betting office", secondly in para (*b*) "indicating where any such office may be found", and in para (*c*) although the word is not used, the expression is "drawing attention to the availability of, or to the facilities afforded to persons resorting to, such offices". In my judgment the use of the word "indicating" in paras (*a*) and (*b*) is a use which is within the first meaning; it is not a case of "suggesting", and I am confirmed in that approach to the matter by the fact that the *h* subsection and the paragraph use these words "indicating that any particular premises are a licensed betting office". It involves to my mind the proposition that the sign must be, so to speak, a statement of fact, and in this case there is nothing on the sign to state as a fact that the premises to which the sign is attached are a licensed betting office. To avoid misunderstanding let me say at once, it could suggest to people passing along Duke Street, Darlington, that this may be a place where they *j* can make a bet for cash, but what is penalised in s 10(5) is an advertisement indicating not that the premises may be, but that they are, a licensed betting office.'

That this is the proper construction to place on the word 'indicating' in s 43(1) of the Consumer Credit Act 1974 is, in my judgment, supported by the use of the word 'indicates' in two other places in the section: in sub-ss (3) and (4), which I have already quoted in this judgment and each of which must mean that the advertisement will not fall within the subsection if it 'indicates' certain specified matters, in the sense that it states those matters.

We have therefore to ask ourselves the question whether any of the three advertisements complained of state that the respondents were willing to grant credit terms.

The case for the appellant was that each of the three advertisements did so, in relation to the particular car on which it was placed. No doubt it is right that the advertisement must be construed sensibly in its context, and it may well be that some members of the public, who happen to be aware of the business of the respondents, might think that the placing of a price display in this form on a vehicle at a garage 'suggested' that the respondents might be willing to give credit in respect of the vehicle in question. This could lead such a person to inquire within the garage whether credit facilities were in fact available. If he did so, he would presumably be given a copy of the brochure furnished by the respondents to the garage, as to which it is not suggested that it did not comply with the requirements of the Consumer Credit Act 1974.

As Ashworth J pointed out in *Maurice Binks (Turf Accountants) Ltd v Huss*, a suggestion is not enough, a fortiori where the suggestion is derived in part from the knowledge of the advertisers' business, obtained not from the advertisement itself. I ask myself, like Ashworth J, whether the sign constituted a statement of the relevant fact, in the present case, that the advertiser was willing to provide credit in respect of the car on which the sign was placed. Construing the sign in its context, I answer that question in the present case in the same manner as Ashworth J did in *Maurice Binks (Turf Accountants) Ltd v Huss*, by saying that there is nothing on the relevant sign to state as a fact the matter of which complaint is made.

In the end the point, which is essentially one of construction of the 1974 Act, is a short one. I find myself in complete agreement with the opinion formed by the magistrate. I would answer the question posed by him in the negative, and would therefore dismiss the appeal.

FORBES J. I agree.

Appeal dismissed.

9 August. *The court refused leave to appeal to the House of Lords but certified, under s 1(2) of the Administration of Justice Act 1960, that the following point of law of general public importance was involved in the decision: whether on a proper construction of the word 'indicating' in s 43(1) of the Consumer Credit Act 1974 it was necessary for the advertisement in question itself to state as a fact or otherwise show that the advertiser was willing to provide credit or whether surrounding circumstances could be taken into account and if so whether the surrounding circumstances could include the public reputation of the advertiser.*

10 November. *The Appeal Committee of the House of Lords (Lord Diplock, Lord Fraser and Lord Brandon) dismissed a petition by the appellant for leave to appeal.*

Solicitors: *Treasury Solicitor ; Wilde Sapte* (for the respondents).

N P Metcalfe Esq   Barrister.

Showboat Entertainment Centre Ltd v Owens

EMPLOYMENT APPEAL TRIBUNAL

BROWNE-WILKINSON J, MR J P M BELL AND MR R THOMAS

10, 28 OCTOBER 1983

Race relations – Unlawful discrimination – Discrimination against complainant personally – Less favourable treatment – Manager instructed not to admit black people to amusement centre – Manager dismissed for refusing to obey instruction – Whether manager discriminated against personally on racial grounds – Race Relations Act 1976, ss 1(1)(a), 4(2)(c).

In October 1980 the applicant, who was white, was employed as the manager of an amusement centre operated by the respondents. In April 1981 he was dismissed from the respondents' employment. He complained to an industrial tribunal, alleging that he had been dismissed because of his refusal to carry out a racially discriminatory instruction by the respondents to exclude young black people from the amusement centre. The industrial tribunal held that the respondents' conduct amounted to unlawful discrimination against the applicant under s 4(2)(c)[a] of the Race Relations Act 1976. The respondents appealed, contending that a person was unlawfully discriminated against on racial grounds under s 1(1)(a)[b] of the 1976 Act only where the conduct complained of related to the race of the complainant, that therefore it was not open to a person to complain of unfair treatment suffered by him because of another person's race and that since the applicant had not been discriminated against on the grounds of his own race he had not been unlawfully discriminated against under s 4(2)(c).

Held – Section 1(1)(a) of the 1976 Act covered all cases of discrimination on racial grounds regardless of whether the racial characteristics in question were those of the person treated less favourably or of some other person. The only question in each case was whether the unfavourable treatment suffered by the complainant was caused by racial considerations. It followed that where an employee was dismissed for refusing to carry out racially discriminatory instructions of any sort from his employer he was unlawfully discriminated against by the employer. Accordingly the appeal would be dismissed (see p 839 e to h, p 840 e and g to p 841 a and p 842 b c g h, post).

Zarczynska v Levy [1979] 1 All ER 814 followed.

Race Relations Board v Applin [1974] 2 All ER 73 considered.

Notes

For the meaning of unlawful discrimination, see 4 Halsbury's Laws (4th edn) para 1035.

For the Race Relations Act 1976, ss 1, 4, see 46 Halsbury's Statutes (3rd edn) 395, 398.

Cases referred to in judgment

Race Relations Board v Applin [1974] 2 All ER 73, [1975] AC 259, [1974] 2 WLR 541, HL; affg [1973] 2 All ER 1190, [1973] QB 815, [1973] 2 WLR 895, CA.

Race Relations Board v Charter [1973] 1 All ER 512, [1973] AC 868, [1973] 2 WLR 299, HL.

Zarczynska v Levy [1979] 1 All ER 814, [1979] 1 WLR 125, EAT.

Appeal

Showboat Entertainment Centre Ltd appealed against the decision of an industrial tribunal (chairman Mr A L Gordon) sitting at Shrewsbury on 23 November 1982

---

a   Section 4(2), so far as material, is set out at p 837 j, post

b   Section 1(1), so far as material, is set out at p 837 h, post

whereby it upheld a complaint brought by the applicant, Gwilym Owens, under s 54 of
a   the Race Relations Act 1976 that Showboat had unlawfully discriminated against him on
racial grounds under s 4(2)(c) of the 1976 Act, and awarded Mr Owens compensation in
the sum of £1,350. The facts are set out in the judgment of the appeal tribunal.

R J Harvey QC and A E C Thompson for Showboat.
Benet Hytner QC and Nigel Gilmour for Mr Owens.

b
                                                                        Cur adv vult

28 October. The following judgment was delivered.

BROWNE-WILKINSON J. Mr Owens complained to an industrial tribunal that he
c   had been unlawfully discriminated against by his employers, Showboat Entertainment
Centre Ltd (Showboat), contrary to s 4(2)(c) of the Race Relations Act 1976. The industrial
tribunal upheld his complaint and awarded him compensation of £1,350. Showboat
appeal against that decision.

The reasons given by the industrial tribunal for their decision are very lengthy and
intricate. For the purposes of this judgment the relevant facts can be summarised very
d   shortly. Mr Owens is a white man. He was employed by Showboat as manager of an
amusement centre (operated by Showboat) from 23 October 1980 to 23 April 1981,
when he was dismissed. Since he had been employed for less than the qualifying period
of 52 weeks, he had no right to complain that he had been unfairly dismissed under the
Employment Protection (Consolidation) Act 1978. However he alleged, and the industrial
tribunal held, that he had been dismissed because of his refusal to carry out a racially
e   discriminatory instruction from Showboat to exclude young blacks from the amusement
centre. The industrial tribunal held, with some reluctance, that it was bound by the
decision of this appeal tribunal in Zarczynska v Levy [1979] 1 All ER 814, [1979] 1 WLR
125 to hold that such conduct amounted to unlawful discrimination against Mr Owens.

On this appeal Showboat challenge the correctness of the decision in the Levy case.
They also allege that certain findings of the industrial tribunal were wrong either as
f   being based on some misdirection in law or on the grounds that they were perverse. By
agreement, we have heard argument first on the question whether the Levy case is rightly
decided and ought to be followed. This judgment deals only with that question.

In essence, the question raised by this appeal is whether, for the purposes of the 1976
Act, A can unlawfully discriminate against B on the ground of C's race. To answer that
question it is necessary to look at the 1976 Act in some detail. In outline, the structure of
g   the Act is as follows. Part I defines what constitutes 'discrimination'. Discrimination may
consist either of racial discrimination or victimisation. For present purposes it is only
necessary to consider racial discrimination: it was not submitted that there had been
discrimination by victimisation of Mr Owens. Section 1(1)(a) provides as follows:

'A person discriminates against another in any circumstances relevant for the
h   purposes of any provision of this Act if—(a) on racial grounds he treats that other
less favourably than he treats or would treat other persons . . .'

Then Pts II and III of the 1976 Act render unlawful certain acts of discrimination in
the employment field and other fields. We are only directly concerned with Pt II of the
Act, s 4(2)(c) of which provides as follows:

j   'It is unlawful for a person, in the case of a person employed by him at an
establishment in Great Britain, to discriminate against that employee . . . (c) by
dismissing him, or subjecting him to any other detriment.'

Part IV is headed 'Other Unlawful Acts' and includes s 30 which provides as follows:

'It is unlawful for a person—(a) who has authority over another person . . . to instruct him to do any act which is unlawful by virtue of Part II or III, or procure or attempt to procure the doing by him of any such act.'

Part VIII of the Act deals with enforcement. Section 53(1) provides as follows:

'Except as provided by this Act no proceedings, whether civil or criminal, shall lie against any person in respect of an act by reason that the act is unlawful by virtue of a provision of this Act.'

Then s 54(1)(a) provides:

'A complaint by any person ("the complainant") that another person ("the respondent")—(a) has committed an act of discrimination against the complainant which is unlawful by virtue of Part II . . . may be presented to an industrial tribunal.'

Section 63(1) provides as follows:

'Proceedings in respect of a contravention of section 29, 30 or 31 shall be brought only by the Commission in accordance with the following provisions of this section.'

Broadly, the effect of these provisions is as follows. The racially discriminatory instructions given by Showboat to Mr Owens were unlawful by virtue of s 30. But under s 63 only the Commission for Racial Equality has the right to bring proceedings based on such illegality. Mr Owens can only bring a complaint if he brings himself within s 54(1)(a) by showing that there has been unlawful discrimination 'against' him. Therefore the question is whether the racially discriminatory instruction not to admit blacks (which constituted discrimination 'against' the blacks excluded) can also be regarded as discrimination 'against' Mr Owens.

In the *Levy* case the circumstances were broadly the same as in the present case: an employee who had not got the necessary qualifying period to complain of unfair dismissal was dismissed because of her refusal to obey an instruction not to serve black customers. This appeal tribunal held that she had been unlawfully discriminated against, contrary to s 4(2)(c) of the 1976 Act. It is plain that one of the determinant reasons for the decision was that any other view would have produced the result that an employee who was dismissed for refusal to obey a racially discriminatory, and therefore unlawful, order would have no redress; the remedy available to the Commission for Racial Equality under ss 30 and 63 was of no value to such an employee. Against that background, in reliance on certain dicta in the Court of Appeal, this appeal tribunal felt able to depart from what they apparently thought was the literal meaning of the words in the 1976 Act and hold that there had been unlawful discrimination against the employee.

In argument, counsel for Mr Owens, whilst supporting the actual decision in the *Levy* case, has not sought to rely on the reasoning in the judgment. In summary, counsel's submissions were as follows. The ordinary canons of construction have to be applied in this case, ie if the words of the 1976 Act are plain, effect must be given to them; but if they are susceptible of two possible meanings that meaning should be adopted which gives effect to the intention of the legislature if such intention can be discerned. He submits that the words in s 1(1)(a) 'on racial grounds' are clear and cover any case where the race (whether of the complainant or of a third party) was an effective cause of the detriment suffered by the complainant. In particular, he submits, there is no room for impliedly limiting the general words of s 1(1)(a) so as to read them as referring only to the racial characteristics of the complainant. Alternatively, he submits that, if there are two possible meanings of the words 'on racial grounds', we should adopt the meaning which gives effect to the intendment of Parliament, and Parliament cannot have intended that an employee, faced with an unlawful racialist order, would have to choose between complying with such an unlawful order (thereby himself committing an unlawful act) or disobeying the order thereby jeopardising his job without any possibility of compensation for its loss. Counsel for Mr Owens further submits that the existence of s 30 and of the Commission for Racial Equality's right to complain of a breach of it is not a   inconsistent with Mr Owens having a separate right to complain of the employers' unlawful instructions.

Counsel for Showboat does not suggest any different approach to the construction of the statute. But in his submission it is clear when the statute is looked at as a whole that, for discrimination on racial grounds to be 'against' a complainant, the grounds must relate to the race of the complainant and not of others. He relies on the fact that s 30 comes in Pt IV of the 1976 Act which is headed 'Other Unlawful Acts'; he submits that

b   the use of the word 'Other' shows that the giving of a racialist instruction would not, apart from s 30, be an unlawful act. Moreover, he submits that Pt IV of the 1976 Act is dealing with matters which are preparatory to, and therefore predate, any act which is rendered unlawful by Pts II and III and it is for this reason that they are dealt with separately. He submits that, to the extent that it is legitimate to have regard to the intendment of Parliament, it is not possible to find an intendment to give every employee

c   suffering as a result of racially deplorable conduct by the employer an individual right to complain: certain remedies are given to the Commission for Racial Equality alone. Moreover, Mr Owens's inability to complain of what has been done is due to the requirement of the 52-week qualifying period for the purposes of unfair dismissal, a requirement which in practice leaves many employees without redress for grossly unfair dismissals in areas other than racial discrimination. Finally, he submits that even if it is

d   possible to say that there could be discrimination against Mr Owens by reason of discrimination related to another's race, s 1 still requires one to compare the employers' treatment of Mr Owens with the treatment they would have given to another manager who also refused to obey the instructions. It is plain that such other manager would also have been dismissed. Therefore, says counsel for Showboat, there is no relevant discrimination.

e   We have not found this an easy case to decide and our minds have changed from time to time during the course of the argument. But in the end we accept that the argument of counsel for Mr Owens is correct. In our judgment the words of s 1(1)(a) are capable of two possible meanings, the one reflecting the broad approach of counsel for Mr Owens and the other the narrower approach of counsel for Showboat. It is plain that the person 'against' whom there has been discrimination is the person who is being treated less

f   favourably by the discriminator, i e the words 'that other' in para (a) refer back to 'another' in the phrase 'a person discriminates against another' at the beginning of the subsection. Therefore the only question is whether Mr Owens was treated less favourably 'on racial grounds'. Certainly the main thrust of the legislation is to give protection to those discriminated against on the grounds of their own racial characteristics. But the words 'on racial grounds' are perfectly capable in their ordinary sense of covering any reason for

g   an action based on race, whether it be the race of the person affected by the action or of others.

We do not find that any of the arguments of counsel for Showboat compel us to give the words a narrow meaning. The fact that the giving of racialist instructions is dealt with separately in s 30 in a part of the Act headed 'Other Unlawful Acts' is in our judgment explicable without requiring the words 'on racial grounds' to be given a

h   narrow meaning. The mere giving of racialist instructions is not, on any view, rendered unlawful by the earlier provisions of the Act. Parts II and III of the 1976 Act only render discrimination unlawful to the extent that such discrimination has been manifested in the various ways specifically mentioned in Pts II and III. Therefore, apart from s 30, the mere giving of the instruction unaccompanied by any action pursuant to such an instruction which falls within Pt II or Pt III would not be rendered unlawful by Pt II or

j   Pt III of the Act. Therefore, s 30 by making unlawful the giving of the instruction itself is creating another unlawful act, namely the mere giving of the instruction. Moreover, there is nothing manifestly absurd in giving the Commission for Racial Equality the right to take proceedings to stop the giving of such instructions (if necessary by means of an application for an injunction under s 63(4)) at the same time as giving a right of individual redress to someone who has actually suffered as a result of such instruction.

We do not accept the submission of counsel for Showboat that Pt IV (including s 30) is dealing only with matters which are preparatory to (and predate) any actual act of discrimination. Although s 29 (dealing with advertisements) and s 31 (dealing with inducement to commit unlawful acts) relate to acts predating any discrimination rendered unlawful by Pts II and III, s 28 is dealing with discriminatory practices which may concurrently give rise to individual claims under Pts II and III. Moreover, ss 32 and 33 create vicarious liability concurrent with the liability of the prime wrongdoer. We can see no pattern indicating that Pt IV as a whole deals only with matters which predate discrimination rendered unlawful by Pts II and III.

At this stage we should note a point not relied on by counsel for Showboat but which has caused us some hesitation. Section 1 of the 1976 Act deals with direct discrimination in sub-s (1)(a) and indirect discrimination in sub-s (1)(b). It seems to us clear that in relation to indirect discrimination under sub-s (1)(b) the discrimination must relate to the race of the person against whom it is exercised. Thus, the requirement or condition is applied to 'that other'; it is the racial group of 'that other' whose ability to comply with the requirement has to be considered; it is detriment to 'that other' which has to be shown. Throughout the section, the words 'that other' relate back to the person who at the beginning of the section is the person against whom there has been discrimination. It seemed to us that if, for the purposes of indirect discrimination, the racial characteristics of the complainant were the only relevant ones, it might be argued that the same must also be true in relation to direct discrimination under s 1(1)(a). However, counsel for Showboat did not take up the suggestion and, in relation to this case, counsel for Mr Owens provided the answer. He said that if, for example, an employee refused to carry out an indirectly discriminatory recruitment policy on the grounds that it was racially discriminatory and was dismissed for such refusal, his dismissal would be 'on racial grounds' within s 1(1)(a) notwithstanding that his refusal was a refusal to be a party to indirect discrimination within s 1(1)(b).

We can therefore see nothing in the wording of the 1976 Act which makes it clear that the words 'on racial grounds' cover only the race of the complainant. As we have said, it seems to us that on the words of the Act alone it is open to give the words either a narrow or a broad construction. In *Race Relations Board v Charter* [1973] 1 All ER 512 at 516, [1973] AC 868 at 887 Lord Reid said (of the 1968 Act):

'I would infer from the [1968] Act as a whole that the legislature thought all discrimination on racial grounds to be deplorable but thought it unwise or impracticable to attempt to apply legal sanctions in situations of a purely private character.'

We are not here dealing with matters of a purely private character. Moreover Parliament, by s 30, has shown that the giving of instructions to discriminate on racial grounds was conduct of a kind within its intendment. The only question is whether Parliament's intentions stopped short of giving a remedy to somebody to whom such instructions were given. We find it impossible to believe that Parliament intended that a person dismissed for refusing to obey an unlawful discriminatory instruction should be without a remedy. It places an employee in an impossible position if he has to choose between being party to an illegality and losing his job. It seems to us that Parliament must have intended such an employee to be protected so far as possible from the consequences of doing his lawful duty by refusing to obey such an instruction. We do not consider that the 52-week qualifying period thought by Parliament to be appropriate in relation to other cases of unfair dismissal would be thought to be appropriate in cases of racial discrimination to which no such time limit is attached. Nor do we think that the existence of the Commission for Racial Equality's right to enforce s 30 affects our view: there is no reason why the individual's right to complain of the wrong done to him and the Commission for Racial Equality's right to stop unlawful action generally by injunction should not coexist.

We therefore conclude that s 1(1)(a) covers all cases of discrimination on racial grounds whether the racial characteristics in question are those of the person treated less favourably or of some other person. The only question in each case is whether the unfavourable treatment afforded to the claimant was caused by racial considerations.

We, like the appeal tribunal in the *Levy* case, gain considerable support from certain remarks made in the Court of Appeal in *Race Relations Board v Applin* [1973] 2 All ER 1190, [1973] 1 QB 815. That case was concerned with incitement by Mr Applin to stop foster parents taking in coloured children placed with them by the local authority. The case turned on whether a refusal by such foster parents to take coloured children would have been unlawful under ss 1 and 2 of the Race Relations Act 1968. Section 1 of the 1968 Act provided as follows:

'For the purposes of this Act a person discriminates against another if on the ground of colour, race or ethnic or national origins he treats that other, in any situation to which section 2 . . . applies, less favourably than he treats or would treat other persons . . .'

It was argued that by refusing to take coloured children the foster parents would have discriminated against the coloured children themselves or alternatively against the local authority who sought to place such children with foster parents. The Court of Appeal held that such conduct would have amounted to discrimination against the children themselves. But Lord Denning MR said that they would also have discriminated against the local authority. Counsel had put to the Court of Appeal the example of two white women who were refused entrance to a public house if accompanied by coloured men. After quoting s 1 of the 1968 Act, Lord Denning MR said ([1973] 2 All ER 1190 at 1196, [1973] 1 QB 815 at 828):

'That definition of discrimination is wide enough to cover the case of the two women. They are treated less favourably than other women on the ground of colour. Similarly in this case, [the foster parents] would discriminate against the local authorities on the ground of colour if they said: "We will take white children only".'

Stephenson LJ said ([1973] 2 All ER 1190 at 1199, [1973] 1 QB 815 at 831):

'The persons who seek to obtain or use the services which the [foster parents] are concerned with providing are the three local authorities who send them children to board and foster. The persons who obtain and use them are the foster children boarded out with the [foster parents]. If the position is as simple as that and that is a complete account of it, then it is necessary to decide (what counsel for the first defendant has conceded) that A can discriminate against B on the ground of C's colour, race or ethnic or national origin. If that were necessary I would so decide in agreement with Lord Denning MR.'

The *Applin* case went to the House of Lords (see [1974] 2 All ER 73, [1975] AC 259). Only Lord Simon in the House of Lords dealt with this particular point. He said this ([1974] 2 All ER 73 at 92, [1975] AC 259 at 289):

'Moreover, I respectfully agree with Lord Denning MR ([1973] 2 All ER 1190 at 1196, [1973] QB 815 at 828) that by insisting on white children only the [foster parents] would be, within the statutory definition, discriminating against the local authorities themselves on the ground of colour. It is inadmissible to read s 1(1) as if it read "on the ground of *his* colour". Not only would this involve reading into the subsection a word which is not there; it would also mean that some conduct which is plainly within the "mischief" would escape—for example, discriminating against a white woman on the ground that she had married a coloured man. It would therefore, in my view, be discrimination if the [foster parents] had treated local authorities seeking boarding-out facilities for coloured children less favourably than they *would* treat local authorities who either had no coloured children in care or who proffered none for boarding-out.' (Lord Simon's emphasis.)

Although there are substantial differences between the 1968 Act and the 1976 Act which normally render it dangerous to treat authorities on the earlier Act as helpful on the later Act, in this instance the definition of discrimination in the two Acts is very similar. Although it seems to have been conceded in the Court of Appeal that A could discriminate against B on the ground of C's colour, that concession was approved. Moreover it does not appear that the same concession was made in the House of Lords. Therefore, although we are not bound by the dicta, they are in our view persuasive authority for holding that A can discriminate against B on the ground of C's colour. Once this point is reached, there seems to be no stopping point short of holding that any discriminatory treatment caused by racial considerations is capable of falling within s 1 of the 1976 Act.

Finally, we must deal with the submission of counsel for Showboat that, in deciding whether or not Showboat discriminated against Mr Owens, one has to compare how Showboat treated Mr Owens with the way in which Showboat would have treated another manager who also refused to carry out the unlawful racialist instructions. Counsel for Showboat says that is to compare like with like. In our judgment, this submission is misconceived. Although one has to compare like with like, in judging whether there has been discrimination you have to compare the treatment actually meted out with the treatment which would have been afforded to a man having all the same characteristics as the complainant except his race or his attitude to race. Only by excluding matters of race can you discover whether the differential treatment was on racial grounds. Thus, the correct comparison in this case would be between Mr Owens and another manager who did not refuse to obey the unlawful racialist instructions.

Counsel for Showboat relied in support of his argument on a dictum of Lord Salmon in *Race Relations Board v Applin* [1974] 2 All ER 73 at 96, [1975] AC 259 at 294 where he said this:

'Even if local authorities may be regarded as a section of the public and as seeking to obtain facilities or services for themselves, I doubt whether the [foster parents], if they refused to foster coloured children in the care of those local authorities, would be discriminating against them unless it could be shown that they were willing to foster coloured children in the care of other local authorities. It is, however, unnecessary to express a concluded view on this point . . .'

In our judgment, this dictum, far from supporting the submission of counsel for Showboat, is against it. Lord Salmon is saying that you have to ask whether the foster parents would have adopted a different attitude to different local authorities, comparing their refusal of coloured children from one local authority with their acceptance of such children from another local authority. You do not assume that the person with whom the comparison is made has the same racial characteristics or attitude to racial conduct as the complainant.

We therefore agree with the decision in the *Levy* case (although for rather different reasons) and hold that on the facts as found by the industrial tribunal the industrial tribunal were right in law in holding that Mr Owens had been unlawfully discriminated against. Unless the parties wish to test this decision in the Court of Appeal, the appeal must be restored for further hearing on the other points raised by the notice of appeal.

Order accordingly. Leave to appeal to the Court of Appeal granted.

Solicitors: *Henry S Charles*, Loughborough (for Showboat); *Cuff Roberts North Kirk*, Liverpool (for Mr Owens).

K Mydeen Esq   Barrister.

Chilvers v Rayner

QUEEN'S BENCH DIVISION
ROBERT GOFF LJ AND FORBES J
4, 5, 29 JULY 1983

Hallmarking – Unhallmarked articles – Prohibited descriptions of unhallmarked articles – Offence to supply unhallmarked article to which description indicating it is made of precious metal is applied – Whether an offence of strict liability – Hallmarking Act 1973, s 1(1)(b).

It is an offence of strict liability to supply or offer to supply an unhallmarked article to which is applied a description indicating that it is wholly or partly made of gold, silver or platinum, contrary to s 1(1)(b)[a] of the Hallmarking Act 1973, and accordingly the prosecution does not have to prove mens rea on the part of the accused (see p 847 c to f, post).

Dicta of Lord Reid in *Warner v Metropolitan Police Comr* [1968] 2 All ER at 360 and of Lord Diplock in *Sweet v Parsley* [1969] 1 All ER at 362 applied.

Notes

For offences of strict liability, see 11 Halsbury's Laws (4th edn) para 18.

For the hallmarking of precious metals, see 9 ibid para 1406.

For the Hallmarking Act 1973, s 1, see 43 Halsbury's Statutes (3rd edn) 1769.

Cases referred to in judgments

Clode v Barnes [1974] 1 All ER 1166, [1974] 1 WLR 544, DC.

Lim Chin Aik v R [1963] 1 All ER 223, [1963] AC 160, [1963] 2 WLR 42, PC.

Macnab v Alexanders of Greenock Ltd 1971 SLT 121.

R v Tolson (1889) 23 QBD 168, [1886–90] All ER Rep 26, CCR.

Sweet v Parsley [1969] 1 All ER 347, [1970] AC 132, [1969] 2 WLR 470, HL.

Warner v Metropolitan Police Comr [1968] 2 All ER 356, [1969] 2 AC 256, [1968] 2 WLR 1303, HL.

Case stated

Alan Chilvers appealed by way of case stated by the justices for the county of Surrey, acting in and for the petty sessional division of Guildford, in respect of their adjudication on 3 November 1982 as a magistrates' court sitting at the Law Courts, Guildford, whereby, on an information preferred by the respondent trading standards officer, Albert John Rayner, they convicted him of an offence under s 1(1)(b) of the Hallmarking Act 1973 and fined him £200. The facts are set out in the judgment of Robert Goff LJ.

Andrew Collins for the appellant.
Andrew Phillips for the respondent.

Cur adv vult

29 July. The following judgments were delivered.

ROBERT GOFF LJ. There is before the court an appeal by way of case stated from a decision of justices sitting at Guildford, under which they found the appellant guilty of an offence contrary to the Hallmarking Act 1973.

An information had been preferred against the appellant by the respondent, a trading standards officer, that he, in the course of trade as a dealer in jewellery and precious metals, supplied to Pia Theresia Hauselmann an unhallmarked article, namely an 18 carat Russian gold bangle, to which the description 'gold' was applied, contrary to s 1(1)(b)

---

a   Section 1(1) is set out at p 844 e, post

of the Hallmarking Act 1973. That charge was found to be proved and the appellant was
fined £200 and ordered to pay a sum towards the prosecution costs. The case raises the
question whether the offence created by s 1(1)(*b*) of the 1973 Act is an absolute offence.

The facts of the case, as found by the justices, are as follows. On 12 January 1982 Mrs
Hauselmann purchased a Russian bangle from Orlando Jewellers, 1 Sydenham Road,
Guildford, of which the appellant was the proprietor. The bangle was accurately described
as 18 carat gold. It was offered at £671·77; that price was reduced by 40% as being part
of a 'sale', and was further reduced to £363 in consideration of payment of £300 in cash
and £63 by credit card. The appellant had purchased the bangle in 1979 from Celine
Collection, with whom he had traded for some time, for £160. The bangle bore some
markings, but was not hallmarked. The assay office to which the appellant sent items for
hallmarking had not received this bangle to hallmark. On these facts, the justices
concluded that the appellant had supplied an unhallmarked article to which the
description 'gold' was applied.

Before the justices, the appellant contended that the prosecution had not established
the essential ingredient of mens rea, whereupon the prosecution contended that the
section did not require any proof of mental state on the part of the appellant. The justices
formed the opinion that it was not necessary for the prosecution to prove mens rea and
so found the case proved.

The question posed by the justices for the opinion of the court is:

'Whether the offence created by s 1(1)(*b*) of the Hallmarking Act 1973 is an
absolute offence so that the prosecution does not have to prove mens rea.'

I turn next to the Hallmarking Act 1973. Section 1(1) provides as follows:

'Subject to the provisions of this Act, any person who, in the course of a trade or
business—(*a*) applies to an unhallmarked article a description indicating that it is
wholly or partly made of gold, silver or platinum, or (*b*) supplies, or offers to supply,
an unhallmarked article to which such a description is applied, shall be guilty of an
offence.'

By sub-s (2) it is provided that sub-s (1) shall not apply to a description which is
permitted by Pt I of Sch 1 to the Act and, by sub-s (3) it is provided that sub-s (1) shall not
apply to an article within Pt II of Sch 1. Part I of Sch 1 sets out a list of permissible
descriptions, e g 'plated' or 'rolled' gold. Part II sets out a list of exempted articles, such as,
for example, '1. An article which is intended for despatch to a destination outside the
United Kingdom'.

It is striking that s 1(1) of the 1973 Act follows very closely the wording of s 1(1) of the
Trade Descriptions Act 1968, to which indeed reference is made in other subsections of
s 1 of the 1973 Act. Section 1(1) of the Trade Descriptions Act 1968 has been held to
create an offence of absolute liability, subject to the statutory defences, in particular the
defence set out in s 24 of the Act: see *Clode v Barnes* [1974] 1 All ER 1166, [1974] 1 WLR
544 and *Macnab v Alexanders of Greenock Ltd* 1971 SLT 121.

There is no equivalent of s 24 in the Hallmarking Act 1973. However, there are certain
provisions of that Act creating other offences which expressly require knowledge on the
part of the accused as an ingredient of the offence. Thus, s 4(4) provides that a person
who knowingly makes a false statement in furnishing any information to an assay office,
for the purposes of s 4(2) (ie for the purposes of showing the assay office to its satisfaction
that the relevant article was made in the United Kingdom, with a view to its being
hallmarked) shall be guilty of an offence.

Section 6, which is concerned with counterfeiting, creates a number of offences, each
of which requires a specified intent on the part of the accused, or knowledge or belief by
him, that the relevant object is counterfeit. It is of particular interest that s 6(1)(*c*) provides
that any person who 'utters any counterfeit of a die or any article bearing a counterfeit of
a mark . . . shall be guilty of an offence . . .' and that s 6(3) provides:

'For the purposes of subsection (1) . . . a person utters any counterfeit die or article bearing a counterfeit of a mark if, knowing or believing the die or mark, as the case may be, to be a counterfeit, he supplies, offers to supply, or delivers the die or article.'

Here, the actus reus is very similar to that prohibited by s 1(1)(b). Yet here, unlike s 1(1)(b), knowledge or belief on the part of the accused that the die or mark is counterfeit is expressly made an ingredient of the offence.

Section 7(6) is also striking. It provides as follows:

'It shall be an offence for any person knowingly or any dealer to supply or offer to supply any article bearing any mark of the character of a hallmark and which under subsection (1) of this section may, if the article is in the possession of an assay office, be cancelled, obliterated or defaced, unless the article has been first submitted to an assay office to enable them at their discretion so to cancel, obliterate or deface that mark.'

In this subsection a distinction is therefore drawn between a dealer and other persons and whereas, in the case of other persons, knowledge on their part is an ingredient of the offence created by the subsection, no knowledge is required where the accused is 'a dealer'.

Having regard to these provisions of the Act, it came as no surprise that counsel for the appellant did not seek to argue that mens rea in the form of knowledge of the facts rendering the act an offence under s 1(1) was an ingredient of such an offence. Founding his argument on the speech of Lord Diplock in *Sweet v Parsley* [1969] 1 All ER 347 at 361–362, [1970] AC 132 at 163, he submitted that what had to be proved was the absence of belief, held honestly and on reasonable grounds, that the article was hallmarked. In his submission, it was not enough for the accused to escape conviction that he should have believed the article was hallmarked: he must have believed it to be so on reasonable grounds. So, he submitted, if there was absence of the relevant knowledge on the part of the accused, only if that absence of knowledge was attributable to his carelessness would he be convicted.

However, this submission faces the immediate difficulty that it is very difficult to reconcile with the provisions of paras 3(1), 5 and 6 of Sch 3 to the 1973 Act. They provide as follows:

'3.—(1) Where an offence under this Act which has been committed by a body corporate is proved to have been committed with the consent and connivance of, or to be attributable to any neglect on the part of, any director, manager, secretary or other similar officer of the body corporate, or any person who was purporting to act in any such capacity, he as well as the body corporate shall be guilty of that offence and shall be liable to be proceeded against and punished accordingly . . .

5. In proceedings for an offence under this Act committed by the publication of an advertisement it shall be a defence for the person charged to prove that he is a person whose business it is to publish or arrange for the publication of advertisements and that he received the advertisement for publication in the ordinary course of business and did not know and had no reason to suspect that its publication would amount to an offence under this Act.

6. In any proceedings for an offence under section 1 of this Act, it shall be a defence for the person charged to prove that—(a) in reliance on information supplied by another person, he believed that the article concerned was one which was exempt from hallmarking by virtue of Part II of Schedule I to this Act; and (b) that he could not with reasonable diligence have ascertained that it was not such an article.'

In these paragraphs, liability to conviction is therefore made to depend respectively on 'neglect', or having 'no reason to suspect' that the facts would amount to an offence, or that the accused 'could not with reasonable diligence have ascertained' that the article was not exempt. It is noteworthy that para 6 is expressly directed to offences under s 1. These provisions would appear to be otiose if counsel for the appellant's submission is correct.

While referring to Sch 3, it is of some interest to note also para 4, which provides as follows:

'Where the commission by any person of an offence under this Act is due to the act or default of some other person that other person shall be guilty of the offence, and a person may be charged with and convicted of the offence by virtue of this paragraph whether or not proceedings are taken against the first-mentioned person.'

This paragraph is in terms identical to s 23 of the Trade Descriptions Act 1968. Likewise, para 5 is in terms identical to s 25 of the 1968 Act. Section 1(1) of that Act has been held to create an offence which is absolute, subject to the statutory defences. It is difficult not to conclude that the same construction should, in the circumstances, be placed on the very similar words of s 1(1) of the 1973 Act. It is obvious that the important statutory defence contained in s 24 of the 1968 Act has been advisedly omitted from the 1973 Act, especially as the provisions of the neighbouring ss 23 and 25 of the 1968 Act are mirrored in paras 4 and 5 of Sch 3 to the 1973 Act. This conclusion is moreover entirely consistent with the nature of the offence created by s 1(1) of the 1973 Act.

In *Warner v Metropolitan Police Comr* [1968] 2 All ER 356 at 360, [1969] 2 AC 256 at 271–272 Lord Reid referred to the 'long line of cases in which it has been held with regard to less serious offences that absence of mens rea was no defence'. He continued:

'Typical examples are offences under public health, licensing and industrial legislation. If a person sets up as say a butcher, a publican, or a manufacturer and exposes unsound meat for sale, or sells drink to a drunk man or certain parts of his factory are unsafe, it is no defence that he could not by the exercise of reasonable care have known or discovered that the meat was unsound, or that the man was drunk or that his premises were unsafe. He must take the risk and when it is found that the statutory prohibition or requirement has been infringed he must pay the penalty. This may well seem unjust, but it is a comparatively minor injustice, and there is good reason for it as affording some protection to his customers or servants or to the public at large. Although this man might be able to show that he did his best, a more skilful or diligent man in his position might have done better, and when we are dealing with minor penalties which do not involve the disgrace of criminality it may be in the public interest to have a hard and fast rule. Strictly speaking there ought perhaps to be a defence that the defect was truly latent so that no one could have discovered it. But the law has not developed in that way, and one can see the difficulty if such a defence were allowed in a summary prosecution. These are only quasi-criminal offences and it does not really offend the ordinary man's sense of justice that moral guilt is not of the essence of the offences.'

Again, in *Sweet v Parsley* [1969] 1 All ER 347 at 362, [1972] AC 132 at 163, immediately after the very passage on which counsel for the appellant relied in support of his submission (where Lord Diplock set out the principle in *R v Tolson* (1889) 23 QBD 168, [1886–90] All ER Rep 26), Lord Diplock said:

'Where penal provisions are of general application to the conduct of ordinary citizens in the course of their everyday life the presumption is that the standard of care required of them in informing themselves of facts which would make their conduct unlawful, is that of the familiar common law duty of care. But where the subject-matter of a statute is the regulation of a particular activity involving potential danger to public health, safety or morals, in which citizens have a choice whether they participate or not, the court may feel driven to infer an intention of Parliament to impose, by penal sanctions, a higher duty of care on those who choose to

_a_ participate and to place on them an obligation to take whatever measures may be
necessary to prevent the prohibited act, without regard to those considerations of
cost or business practicability which play a part in the determination of what would
be required of them in order to fulfil the ordinary common law duty of care. But
such an inference is not lightly to be drawn, nor is there any room for it unless there
is something that the person on whom the obligation is imposed can do directly or
indirectly, by supervision or inspection, by improvement of his business methods
_b_ or by exhorting those whom he may be expected to influence or control, which will
promote observance of the obligation (see _Lim Chin Aik_ v. _Reginam_ ([1963] 1 All ER
223 at 228, [1963] AC 160 at 174).'

In my judgment, the offence created by s 1(1) of the 1973 Act falls within the category
of offences so described by Lord Reid and Lord Diplock. It is not a truly criminal offence,
but an offence of a quasi-criminal character. True, an offence relating to hallmarking
_c_ does not fall precisely within the description 'offences under public health, licensing and
industrial legislation', or within the description 'involving danger to public health, safety
or morals'. But I do not understand either Lord Reid or Lord Diplock to have been giving
a complete list of the relevant offences, which must, in my judgment, having regard to
the authorities, extend to include such matters as trade descriptions, although in such
cases the absolute offence is of course subject to any statutory defences set out in the
_d_ relevant Act of Parliament. Furthermore, in accordance with the passage in the advice of
the Privy Council in _Lim Chin Aik v R_, referred to by Lord Diplock in _Sweet v Parsley_, it
cannot be said that there is nothing which a person on whom the relevant obligations
under the 1973 Act are imposed can do, in any of the manners indicated by Lord Diplock,
which will promote the observance of the obligation.

For these reasons, I am satisfied that the offence under s 1(1) of the 1973 Act is, like the
_e_ offence created by s 1(1) of the Trade Descriptions Act 1968, an absolute offence. I find
myself in agreement with the opinion expressed by the justices in the case stated and I
would answer the question posed for our decision in the affirmative and dismiss the
appeal.

_f_ **FORBES J.** I agree.

_Appeal dismissed. The court refused leave to appeal to the House of Lords but certified, under
s 1(2) of the Administration of Justice Act 1960, that the following point of law of general public
importance was involved in the decision: whether it was necessary for any mental state to be
established in order that a person might be convicted of an offence under s 1(1)(b) of the
Hallmarking Act 1973._

_24 November. The Appeal Committee of the House of Lords (Lord Keith of Kinkel, Lord Roskill
and Lord Brandon of Oakbrook) dismissed a petition by the appellant for leave to appeal._

Solicitors: _Barry Lewis_, Guildford (for the appellant); _F A Stone_, Kingston-upon-Thames
(for the respondent).

N P Metcalfe Esq   Barrister.

Practice Direction

SUPREME COURT TAXING OFFICE

Practice – Queen's Bench Division – Counsel's fees – Interlocutory fees – Accident cases – Scale of fees to be allowed on taxation.

The list of counsel's fees which was last increased in October 1981 has been the subject of discussion between the Chief Taxing Master and the Senate of the Inns of Court and the Bar. A list of the new fees relating to such cases, which will come into operation in respect of instructions and briefs delivered on or after 1 March 1984, is set out below. The fees in the list will be proper to be allowed on taxation in the normal run of such cases where the item has been dealt with fully. Save in the case of conference fees, each fee is intended to cover any necessary perusal of papers in connection with the item. A lower fee may be appropriate where the item has not been dealt with comprehensively or was unusually simple, or where more than one item has been dealt with simultaneously. If a higher fee has been agreed it will need to be justified on taxation, as indeed will any fee which is claimed whether included in the list or not.

	Personal injury cases	Running down cases
Statement of claim	£35	£25
Defence without counterclaim	£30	£20
Defence (plain admission)	£10	£10
Particulars—request	£15	£15
answers	£18	£18
Reply with or without defence to counterclaim	£20	£18
Third party notice (not to stand as statement of claim)	£20	£20
Interrogatories and answers	£30	£30
Advice on evidence	£40	£40
Opinion (including opinion on appeal)	£30	£30
Opinion on liability	£35	£35
Opinion on quantum	£35	£35
Opinion on liability and quantum	£50	£50
Opinion on liability, quantum and evidence	£90	£90
Notice of appeal to Court of Appeal and counter-notice	£35	£35
Brief on summons before master	£30	£30

Conference fees
Queen's Counsel   £30 for first half hour, £15 for each succeeding half hour
Junior counsel   £15 for first half hour, £12 for each succeeding half hour

F T HORNE

1 March 1984   Chief Taxing Master.

Stokes (Inspector of Taxes) v Costain Property Investments Ltd

COURT OF APPEAL, CIVIL DIVISION

WALLER, FOX AND ROBERT GOFF LJJ

25 JANUARY, 17 FEBRUARY 1984

Income tax – Capital allowances – Machinery or plant – Ownership of machinery or plant – Machinery or plant belonging to taxpayer in consequence of expenditure – Belong – Machinery or plant installed by tenant becoming landlord's fixtures – Whether machinery or plant belonging to tenant – Finance Act 1971, s 41(1).

The taxpayer company installed lifts and central heating equipment in buildings at two sites at which it had undertaken development work. At neither site was the taxpayer the freeholder of the land, but, when the development was completed, it became entitled to a lease or an underlease of both sites. It was common ground that on installation the lifts and central heating equipment, admitted to be machinery or plant, became landlord's fixtures. The taxpayer claimed that the lifts and central heating equipment installed in the buildings belonged to it for the purposes of s 41(1)(b)[a] of the Finance Act 1971 and that accordingly the expenditure incurred thereon qualified for a first-year allowance. The inspector of taxes rejected the claim on the ground that machinery or plant which had become landlord's fixtures could not properly be said to 'belong' to a tenant, within s 41(1)(b). The General Commissioners upheld the taxpayer's claim. On appeal by the Crown, the judge reversed the commissioners' determination, holding that because at the material times the taxpayer was only a leaseholder the lifts and central heating equipment did not belong to it. The taxpayer appealed.

Held – The word 'belonging' in s 41(1)(b) of the 1971 Act could not be satisfied by any lesser interest than absolute ownership, and accordingly it was not an apt use of language to say that landlord's fixtures belonged to the leaseholder. It followed that the lifts and central heating equipment which on installation by the taxpayer became part of the landlord's fixtures could not be said to 'belong' to the taxpayer within s 41(1)(b). The appeal would therefore be dismissed (see p 854 a to j and p 855 c e and h to p 856 c and h, post).

Decision of Harman J [1983] 2 All ER 681 affirmed.

Notes

For first-year allowances, see 23 Halsbury's Laws (4th edn) para 426.

For expenditure met directly or indirectly by a person other than the taxpayer, see ibid paras 389, 1298.

For the Finance Act 1971, s 41, see 41 Halsbury's Statutes (3rd edn) 1459.

Cases referred to in judgments

IRC v George Guthrie & Son 1952 SC 402.

Union Cold Storage Co Ltd v Simpson (Inspector of Taxes) [1939] 2 All ER 94, [1939] 2 KB 440, CA; *rvsg* [1938] 4 All ER 673.

Cases also cited

Ben-Odeco Ltd v Powlson (Inspector of Taxes) [1978] 2 All ER 1111, [1978] 1 WLR 1093, HL.

Lupton (Inspector of Taxes) v Cadogan Gardens Developments Ltd, Carlton Tower Ltd v Moore (Inspector of Taxes), Carlton Tower Ltd v IRC [1971] 3 All ER 460, CA.

---

a   Section 41(1) is set out at p 852 d e,

Ramsay (W T) Ltd v IRC, Eilbeck (Inspector of Taxes) v Rawling [1981] 1 All ER 865, [1982]
AC 300, HL.
Rank Xerox Ltd v Lane (Inspector of Taxes)[1979] 3 All ER 657, [1981] AC 269, HL.
Sargaison (Inspector of Taxes) v Roberts [1969] 3 All ER 1072, [1969] 1 WLR 951.
Smith's Settlement Trusts, Re, Executor Trustee and Agency Co of South Australia Ltd v IRC
[1951] 1 All ER 146, [1951] Ch 360.

Appeal
Costain Property Investments Ltd (the taxpayer company) appealed against the decision
of Harman J ([1983] 2 All ER 681, [1983] 1 WLR 907), dated 28 March 1983 allowing an
appeal by the inspector of taxes by way of case stated (set out at [1983] 2 All ER 682–686)
from the determination of the Commissioners for the General Purposes of the Income
Tax for the division of Second East Brixton that plant and machinery, which on
installation became landlord's fixtures, belonged to the taxpayer company as leaseholder
within the meaning of s 41(1) of the Finance Act 1971. The facts are set out in the
judgment of Fox LJ.

D C Potter QC and *Andrew Thornhill* for the taxpayer company.
Robert Carnwath for the Crown.

Cur adv vult

17 February. The following judgments were delivered.

FOX LJ (delivering the first judgment at the invitation of Waller LJ). This is an appeal
by Costain Property Investments Ltd (the taxpayer company) from a decision of Harman
J ([1983] 2 All ER 681, [1983] 1 WLR 907) reversing determinations of the General
Commissioners that the taxpayer company is entitled to capital allowances in respect of
certain plant and machinery. Put very shortly, the issue arises in this way. The allowances
are not available if the plant and machinery did not 'belong' to the taxpayer company at
the relevant time. At that time the plant and machinery were landlord's fixtures in
buildings leased to the taxpayer company on long leases. The question is whether, on the
true construction of the Finance Act 1971, it can be said that the items did 'belong' to the
taxpayer company at the time.

The case is concerned with two pieces of land. The first is at Maidenhead. By an
agreement dated 19 April 1973 between the borough of Maidenhead (the corporation),
Richard Costain Ltd (Costain) and the taxpayer company (which was at all times the
wholly-owned subsidiary of Costain), the taxpayer company agreed to develop the site as
shops, offices and flats in accordance with agreed plans. On satisfactory completion of the
development, the corporation agreed to grant the taxpayer company a lease of the
development for 99 years at a specified rent.

In December 1973, as part of the financing arrangements, Costain and the taxpayer
company entered into an agreement with a bank (Fleming) under which the taxpayer
company undertook to complete the development and Fleming undertook to pay the
cost to a specified sum. The taxpayer company undertook to procure the grant of the
lease of the development to Fleming and Fleming agreed to grant an underlease of the
development to the taxpayer company for 99 years less 10 days.

The development was duly completed and on 15 September 1975 the corporation
granted the head lease of 99 years to Fleming. Fleming, in turn, on 16 September 1975
granted the underlease to the taxpayer company. On 10 October 1975 the taxpayer
company sublet part of the development to Costain and subsequently sublet the
remainder to various tenants.

Included in the cost of the development was expenditure of about £465,000 on plant
a and machinery consisting principally of lifts and central heating equipment. A question
whether the cost of these items was 'incurred' by the taxpayer company having regard to
the financing arrangements with Fleming was determined by the judge in favour of the
taxpayer company and there is no appeal from that.

It is not in dispute that the lifts and other items of plant and machinery form part of
the freehold (ie are landlord's fixtures).

b The other piece of land is at Kennington. By an agreement in February 1974 a charity
agreed to grant to the taxpayer company a 99-year lease of this land on terms that the
taxpayer company would first, at its own expense, erect an office block and church hall
on the land according to approved plans. The construction was completed on 30 October
1975. The cost included expenditure of £50,905 on plant and machinery. On 29
December 1975 the charity granted the head lease to the taxpayer company in pursuance
c of the agreement. On the same day the taxpayer company underlet the whole
development for a term of 25 years. On 30 December 1976 the taxpayer company
assigned the headlease to a friendly society for £388,600. The society was, by the
assignment, required to grant an underlease back to the taxpayer company for a term of
99 years less 3 days. This was done on 30 December 1976.

At this point it will be convenient if I refer to the legislative history of the relevant
d statutes.

Customs and Inland Revenue Act 1878, s 12

This authorised the commissioners to allow such deductions as they thought just and
reasonable—

e   'as representing the diminished value by reason of wear and tear during the year
of any machinery or plant used for the purposes of the concern, and belonging to
the person or company by whom the concern is carried on; and for the purpose of
this provision, where machinery or plant is let to the person or company by whom
the concern is carried on upon such terms that the person or company is bound to
maintain the machinery or plant, and deliver over the same in good condition at the
f   end of the term of the lease, such machinery or plant shall be deemed to belong to
such person or company . . .'

And there was a further provision in the section giving relief to the lessor where the
machinery or plant was let on terms that the burden of maintenance and restoration fell
on him; this provision contained no requirement as to 'belonging'.

g *Income Tax Act 1918*

The provisions of the 1878 Act were substantially re-enacted in Sch D, Cases I and II, r
6(1), (2) and (5).

Income Tax Act 1945

Section 15: this introduced the initial allowances where 'a person carrying on a trade
h incurs capital expenditure on the provision of machinery or plant for the purposes of the
trade'. There was no requirement about 'belonging'. Section 20: this recasts the relief to
lessors in respect of wear and tear originally granted by the 1878 Act but, again, did not
introduce any requirement as to 'belonging'.

Income Tax Act 1952

Section 279 (initial allowances), s 280 (wear and tear or annual allowance) and s 298
(lessors) consolidated the previous provisions. In 1952 the First Division of the Court of
Session decided *IRC v George Guthrie & Son* 1952 SC 402. It was held that the initial
allowance could be claimed by a trader who had paid for machinery but never received
delivery because the vendor sold it to another customer. That decision, in effect, was
reversed by the Finance Act 1957, s 16.

Finance Act 1957

Section 16 provided that the initial allowance should not be made in respect of *a* expenditure on plant or machinery unless in consequence of the trader incurring it the machinery or plant 'belongs to him at some time during his basis period for that year of assessment'.

Capital Allowances Act 1968   *b*

This is a consolidation as follows. (1) *Initial allowance.* Section 18 consolidated the 1945 and 1952 provisions as amended by the 1957 Act. Thus the 'belonging' requirement was retained. (2) *Wear and tear allowance.* Section 19 re-enacted the provisions of the 1952 Act (which derived from the 1878 Act). The 'belonging' requirement was retained. (3) *Lessors.* Section 42 re-enacted s 298 of the 1952 Act. There is no requirement about 'belonging'.   *c*

Finance Act 1971

That brings me to the Finance Act 1971, with which this case is concerned. It introduces new provisions in respect of machinery and plant allowance.

The 'first year allowances' (the initial allowances) are dealt with by s 41(1) in the *d* following terms:

> 'Subject to the provisions of this Chapter, where—(a) a person carrying on a trade incurs capital expenditure on the provision of machinery or plant for the purposes of the trade, and (b) in consequence of his incurring the expenditure, the machinery or plant belongs to him at some time during the chargeable period related to the incurring of the expenditure, there shall be made to him for that period an allowance (in this Chapter referred to as "a first-year allowance") which shall be of an amount determined in accordance with section 42 below.'

Section 44 authorises writing down allowances. Section 44(1) provides:

> 'Subject to the provisions of this Chapter, where—(a) a person carrying on a trade *f* has incurred capital expenditure on the provision of machinery or plant for the purposes of the trade, and (b) in consequence of his incurring the expenditure, the machinery or plant belongs, or has belonged, to him, and (c) the machinery or plant is or has been in use for the purposes of the trade, allowances and charges shall be made to and on him in accordance with the following provisions of this section.'

Section 46 forms, with ss 44 and 47, a group of sections which are cross-headed 'Application to machinery and plant on hire purchase etc or lease and to activities other than trades'.

Section 46 provides as follows:

> '(1) Where machinery or plant is first let by any person otherwise than in the *h* course of a trade, then, whether or not it is used for the purposes of a trade carried on by the lessee—(a) the capital expenditure incurred by the lessor in providing the machinery or plant shall be treated for the purposes of this Chapter as having been incurred in providing it for the purposes of a trade begun to be carried on by him, separately from any other trade which he may carry on, at the commencement of the letting, and (b) the machinery or plant shall be treated for the purposes of this *j* Chapter as being used for the purposes of the trade from the time when the trade is treated as begun until the time when the lessor permanently ceases to let it otherwise than in the course of a trade, and then as permanently ceasing to be so used: Provided that this subsection shall not apply to machinery or plant let for use in a dwelling house.'

a
(2) Where a lessee incurs capital expenditure on the provision for the purposes of a trade carried on by him of machinery or plant which he is required to provide under the terms of the lease, the machinery or plant shall be treated for the purposes of this Chapter as belonging to him for so long as it continues to be used for the purposes of the trade; but, as from the determination of the lease, section 44(5) above shall have effect as if the capital expenditure on providing the machinery or plant had been incurred by the lessor and not by the lessee.'

b
The taxpayer company has claimed first-year allowances in respect of its expenditure on the plant and machinery comprised in the two developments. The total expenditure claimed was:

Accounting period ended 31 December 1975	£79,994
Accounting period ended 31 December 1976	£427,195.

c
The General Commissioners allowed the taxpayer company's appeal and held that, notwithstanding that the taxpayer company was, in the case of each piece of land, entitled to a long lease, the plant and machinery 'belonged' to the taxpayer company within the meaning of ss 41(1) and 44(1) of the 1971 Act 'in any commonsense view', and that accordingly the taxpayer company was entitled to the allowances claimed (see [1983] 2 All ER 681 at 685).

d
On appeal to the High Court, Harman J reversed that determination on the ground that, at the material times, the taxpayer company being only a leaseholder, the machinery and plant did not 'belong' to the taxpayer company. An argument that in relation to the Maidenhead land the taxpayer company did not 'incur' the expenditure was rejected by Harman J and is not pursued. It is not contended that the taxpayer company was, at any relevant time for the purposes of this appeal, the absolute owner of the machinery or plant in question.

e
The taxpayer company's case is as follows.

Maidenhead land

The taxpayer company is, it is contended, entitled to the first-year allowance for the accounting periods 1975 and 1976 because it satisfied the provisions of ss 46(1) and 41(1) of the 1971 Act, in that: (i) the taxpayer company incurred capital expenditure on providing the machinery and plant; (ii) the machinery and plant were first let by the underleases of parts of the buildings; that letting was otherwise than in the course of a trade; (iii) consequently, s 46(1) of the 1971 Act deemed the capital expenditure to have been incurred for the purposes of a notional trade carried on by the taxpayer company at the commencement of the letting (the appeal, as I understand the position, is concerned with first-year allowances only); (iv) the taxpayer company, by reason of the underlease granted to it on 16 September 1975, was the absolute beneficial owner of a term of years in the land, machinery and plant; (v) on the true construction of s 41(1), the machinery and plant accordingly 'belonged' to the taxpayer company at the relevant times; (vi) 'belong' is not a technical word and must be construed in a businesslike and commonsense way; it includes assets comprised in property in which a taxpayer owns a term of years absolute in possession, particularly where the term is likely to extend beyond the possible life of the machinery or plant.

Kennington land

Substantially the same case is advanced by the taxpayer company save that the first letting occurred in 1976. At that date the taxpayer company owned a 99-year lease less 3 days.

The first three of the taxpayer company's propositions, which I have listed, are correct. But, although the taxpayer company's claim derives from s 46(1), the provisions of s 41(1) remain to be satisfied. Section 41(1)(b) imposes the requirement that 'the machinery or plant belongs to him at some time during the chargeable period'.

The requirement of 'belonging' first appears in the legislation on this subject in s 12 of the 1878 Act. In that section it is difficult to suppose that the word 'belonging' can have been intended to mean anything other than absolute ownership. The section permits a deduction in respect of the diminished value by reason of wear and tear during the year of the plant or machinery. If that relief was to be available to the lessee, it would mean, in many cases, that although part (perhaps a large part) of the loss by way of diminished value would fall on the freeholder it would be the lessee who got the tax benefit. That this was not the intention of the legislature is evident from the immediately following provision, which is to the effect that where the machinery or plant is let to the person by whom the concern is carried on on terms that the person is bound to maintain the machinery or plant and deliver it up in good condition at the end of the lease the same shall 'be deemed to belong' to such person. This latter provision is obviously intended to confer a benefit on the lessee to which he will not otherwise have been entitled. It cannot, therefore, have been contemplated that a lessee would come within the first part of the section.

Initial allowances were introduced by the Finance Act 1945. Under s 15(1) the claimant only had to show that he carried on a trade and incurred capital expenditure for the purposes of the trade; there was no requirement about 'belonging'. Under the provisions of s 15 the taxpayer company in the present case would have succeeded.

But, for whatever reason (it may or may not have been the decision in *IRC v George Guthrie & Son* 1952 SC 402), the law was altered by the Finance Act 1957, which excluded the initial allowance unless, in consequence of the incurring of the expenditure by the claimant, the machinery or plant 'belongs to him at some time during his basis period for that year of assessment'.

I return to s 41(1) of the 1971 Act. Did the machinery and plant in question 'belong' to the taxpayer company at some time during the relevant chargeable period? The only ground for saying that it did is that the taxpayer company held a lease, of 99 years or thereabouts, of the property of which the plant and machinery formed part during the relevant period. It was contended below that the requirement of 'belonging' was satisfied by the right to possession of the property in question, but that argument was not advanced before us. I agree that 'belong' and 'belonging' are not terms of art. They are ordinary English words. It seems to me that, in ordinary usage, they would not be satisfied by limited interests. For example, I do not think one would say that a chattel 'belongs to X' if he merely had the right to use it for five years. Nor do I think it is an apt use of language to say that landlord's fixtures 'belong' to the leaseholder. He cannot remove them from the building. He cannot dispose of them except as part of the hereditament and subject to the provisions of the lease and for the term of the lease.

In *Union Cold Storage Co Ltd v Simpson (Inspector of Taxes)* [1939] 2 All ER 94, [1939] 2 KB 440 (which did not raise the present point) Clauson LJ thought it was obvious that plant did not belong to a taxpayer who held a 21-year lease of premises which included the plant, and du Parcq LJ agreed with him (see [1939] 2 All ER 94 at 102, 105, [1939] 2 KB 440 at 455, 461). Macnaghten J in the High Court seems to have regarded 'belonging' in para (1) of r 6 of Cases I and II of the 1918 Act as meaning ownership (see [1938] 4 All ER 673 at 675). Further, for the reasons which I have indicated, I do not think that the draftsman of the 1878 Act can have regarded a lessee as satisfying the word 'belong'.

In so far as one is left in doubt about the matter, I think that it is resolved and the point is concluded by the provisions of s 46(2) of the 1971 Act. That provision is to the effect that a lessee is to be 'treated' as a person to whom machinery or plant belongs but only if he is required to provide the plant or machinery under the terms of the lease. It is common ground that the taxpayer company is not itself within the provision. The importance of the provision is that it is inconsistent with the view that machinery or plant comprised in a term 'belong' to the lessee. Thus, if the taxpayer company's contention is right, s 46(2) is otiose. The machinery or plant would, on the taxpayer company's construction, belong to the lessee as a matter of fact and there would be no need to 'treat' it as belonging to him.

It is said on behalf of the taxpayer company that s 46(2) is dealing with a lease of
a chattels only and is not concerned with a lease of land. I do not accept that. The subsection
is drawn in comprehensive terms and I see no justification for restricting it to a lease of
chattels. I cannot imagine that the subsection would have been drawn in its present form
if the draftsman was intending such a limitation. Further, the idea of a simple lease of
chattels where the lessee is required to provide the chattels is an odd one.

I might add that the draftsman had very much in mind the difference between the
b position of a lessee and an absolute owner. Thus, in the case of a lease, special provision is
necessary to determine how a balancing adjustment is to be made under s 44(5). It is
necessary because at the end of the term the machinery and plant will revert to the lessor,
and it is he (and not the lessee) who will realise the disposal value. Accordingly, provision
needs to be made to bring it into account. The final provision of s 46(2) does that.

In the circumstances, I can only conclude that the machinery and plant comprised in a
c lease as landlord's fixtures do not 'belong' to the lessee, and that accordingly this appeal
should be dismissed. I cannot, however, regard the state of the law as satisfactory. The
purpose of the statutory provisions is evidently to encourage investment in machinery
and plant. In this case very large sums were expended on such investment but, under the
enactment as it stands, nobody will receive the tax allowance in respect of it. The
freeholder will not because the freeholder did not incur the expenditure and is not
d carrying on the trade. And the taxpayer company will not because the items did not
belong to it. The Crown is unable to suggest any policy reason why a person in the
position of the taxpayer company should be refused relief. It is to be hoped that the
ambit of the legislation in this respect will be reconsidered.

ROBERT GOFF LJ. I agree. The point in the case is a short one. It is concerned with
e the meaning of the word 'belongs' in s 41(1)(b) of the Finance Act 1971: in relation to the
present case, it is whether the machinery or plant (here, lift and central heating
equipment) incorporated into leasehold premises, of which the taxpayer company is the
lessee under a lease for nearly 99 years, *belonged* to the taxpayer company, within the
meaning of that word as used (in the present tense) in s 41(1)(b) as such lessee during the
relevant chargeable period.

f Counsel for the taxpayer company submitted that it did. He submitted that the
taxpayer company as leaseholder owned a legal estate, viz a term of years absolute in
possession, in the building, including the machinery and plant incorporated into it. Both
in legal terms and in commonsense terms, therefore, the machinery or plant could be
described as belonging to the taxpayer company. It made no difference that the freeholder
could also be described as a person to whom the machinery or plant belonged, because
g only one person could obtain the capital allowance. Furthermore, this construction was
supported by the policy underlying the provision of allowances under Ch I of Pt III of the
Finance Act 1971, which was to encourage investment; it would be inconsistent with
that policy that no capital allowance should be payable to the taxpayer company in the
circumstances of this case.

I must confess to feeling some sympathy with the submission that to deny the taxpayer
h company a capital allowance would be inconsistent with the policy of this chapter of the
1971 Act. But I feel bound to say that, on a true construction of the 1971 Act, a lessee of
a building in which machinery or plant is incorporated as a landlord's fixture is not a
person to whom such machinery or plant belongs, unless it is provided in the 1971 Act
that he should be treated as such. This is made plain beyond doubt by s 46(2) of the 1971
Act, which provides that, where a lessee for the purposes of a trade carried on by him
j incurs capital expenditure on machinery or plant which he is required to provide under
the terms of the lease, the machinery or plant *shall be treated* for the purposes of the
chapter as belonging to him. If the argument of counsel for the taxpayer company is
right, that provision would prima facie be pure surplusage. Counsel tried to escape from
that conclusion by submitting that the function of s 46(2) was to provide only for the
case of lessees of chattels, who could not otherwise be regarded as persons to whom the

relevant chattels belonged. But that construction is, in my judgment, unacceptable. It would be very strange if Parliament introduced this particular provision solely to deal *a* with leases of chattels; and, referring as it does simply to 'a lessee', it does not look as though it was intended to operate in so restricted a manner. Furthermore, no explanation can be given why a lessee of a chattel should only be able to obtain a capital allowance when he is required to provide the machinery or plant under the terms of the lease, whereas (on the submission put by counsel for the taxpayer company) a lessee of land suffers from no such restriction. The conclusion is, in my judgment, inescapable that a *b* lessee of land in which machinery or plant has been incorporated as a landlord's fixture is not, on a true construction of the 1971 Act, a person to whom such machinery or plant belongs.

This conclusion is consistent with the legislative history. I refer in particular to s 12 of the Customs and Inland Revenue Act 1878, which is the legislative ancestor of s 46(2), and which is the section in which, for the first time, the word 'belonging' appears to have *c* been used in this legislation. The section was concerned with an allowance for depreciation of machinery or plant. Under the section, the allowance was only available in respect of machinery or plant used for the purposes of the relevant concern and 'belonging' to the person or company by whom the concern was carried on; however, wherever machinery or plant was let to the person or company by whom the concern was carried on on such terms that the person or company was bound to maintain the *d* machinery or plant, and deliver it over in good condition at the end of the lease, such machinery or plant was *deemed* to *belong* to such person or company. In the context of an allowance for depreciation, it is understandable that the allowance for depreciation should only be available to the owner of the machinery or plant, or to a lessor subject to such obligations. Why it was thought right by the legislature to use in that section (or indeed thereafter) the expression 'belonging to' rather than 'owned by' nobody could explain; *e* but it is plain that that is what is meant, and that the reference to a person or company to whom machinery or plant is let must embrace not only lessees of chattels but also lessees of buildings in which the machinery or plant is incorporated. It seems that the present legislation still betrays the influence of this section, notwithstanding the development of capital allowances, and in particular the introduction of initial allowances, with the new policy of encouraging investment as opposed to simply permitting a just allowance for *f* depreciation. It is, I suspect, because the legislature has failed to take full account of the change in policy that persons such as the taxpayer company in the present case are excluded from an entitlement to a capital allowance.

Finally, the construction of the 1971 Act which I favour is consistent with the views expressed obiter in *Union Cold Storage Co Ltd v Simpson (Inspector of Taxes)* [1938] 4 All ER 673 at 678–679; [1939] 2 All ER 94 at 96, 102, [1939] 2 KB 440 at 448, 455–456, both *g* by Macnaghten J at first instance and by Scott and Clauson LJJ in the Court of Appeal on rr 6(1) and (2) under Sch D, Cases I and II, of the Income Tax Act 1918.

For these reasons, I agree that the appeal should be dismissed.

WALLER LJ. I also agree.

h

Appeal dismissed. Leave to appeal to the House of Lords refused.

Solicitors: *Solicitor of Inland Revenue*; *Peter Nicoll* (for the taxpayer company).

Clare Mainprice   Barrister.

Sanders Lead Co Inc v Entores Metal Brokers Ltd

COURT OF APPEAL, CIVIL DIVISION

STEPHENSON AND KERR LJJ

17, 18, 24 NOVEMBER 1983

Practice – Parties – Adding persons as parties – Jurisdiction – Addition of person with only commercial interest in outcome of proceedings – Interest of creditor of party to action – Whether Mareva creditor of a party having sufficient interest to be joined as party to action – Whether necessary to have interest directly related to subject matter of proceedings – RSC Ord 15, r 6(2)(b)(ii).

Injunction – Interlocutory – Danger that defendant may transfer assets out of jurisdiction – Effect of injunction – Whether Mareva creditor having sufficient interest in outcome of proceedings between third party and debtor to be joined as party to proceedings – RSC Ord 15, r 6(2)(b)(ii).

The plaintiffs brought an action against the defendants claiming payment of the purchase price of a quantity of lead. The defendants, while not disputing their purchase of the lead, claimed that the purchase had been made from a subsidiary of the plaintiffs and that the purchase price was owed to the subsidiary instead of the plaintiffs. The defendants set up a special account in which they held the amount owing pending resolution of the dispute. By an unconnected contract the subsidiary agreed to purchase a quantity of lead from the applicants and when the subsidiary breached the terms of that contract the applicants brought an action for damages against the subsidiary and obtained a Mareva injunction over all the assets of the subsidiary within the jurisdiction. The injunction specifically referred to the moneys held by the defendants in their special account. The plaintiffs applied to be, and were, joined as defendants in the action between the applicants and the subsidiary which had given rise to the Mareva injunction. That action was ordered to be tried at the same time as the action between the plaintiffs and the defendants. The applicants then applied under RSC Ord 15, r 6(2)(b)(ii)[a] to be joined as defendants in the action between the plaintiffs and the defendants, on the ground that there existed between the applicants and a 'party to the cause or matter . . . a question or issue arising out of or relating to or connected with [the] relief or remedy claimed in the cause or matter' which it was just and convenient to determine at the same time. The judge ordered the applicants to be joined as defendants in the action, on the basis that they would suffer immediate and direct financial harm if the defendants allowed the action to go by default since ownership of the defendants' debt would thus be decided in a way which defeated the applicants' claim. The plaintiffs appealed against the order.

Held – A person had to have an interest directly related to the subject matter of an action before he was entitled to intervene in the action under RSC Ord 15, r 6(2)(b)(ii). A mere commercial interest in the outcome of the action, divorced from its subject matter, such as the interest of a creditor of one of the parties, was not sufficient to entitle a person to intervene. Since the question whether the defendants' debt was owed to the plaintiffs or the subsidiary was not in issue between any of those parties and the applicants and since the Mareva injunction had not conferred on the applicants any proprietary interest in, or charge over, the moneys in the defendants' special account the applicants were not entitled to intervene in the action between the plaintiffs and the defendants. The judge had therefore had no jurisdiction to order the applicants to be joined as defendants in the action. In any event, even if he had had jurisdiction he ought to have exercised his discretion by refusing to allow the applicants to be joined, because it was only in the most exceptional circumstances that a Mareva creditor ought to be permitted to intervene in

---

[a] Rule 6(2), so far as material, is set out at p 862 c d, post

an action where his interest in the outcome related solely to the fate of his injunction. The plaintiffs' appeal would therefore be allowed (see p 858 *h*, p 860 *d e*, p 862 *e* and *g* to *a* p 863 *j*, p 864 *d* to *f* and p 865 *a* to *d*, post).

Notes

For injunctions restraining a defendant from removing assets out of the jurisdiction, see 24 Halsbury's Laws (4th edn) para 1018 and 37 ibid para 362, and for cases on the subject, see 28(2) Digest (Reissue) 1091–1094, 918–960.   *b*

Cases referred to in judgments

Bekhor (A J) & Co Ltd v Bilton [1981] 2 All ER 565, [1981] QB 923, [1981] 2 WLR 601, CA.
Gore v Van Der Lann (Liverpool Corp intervening) [1967] 1 All ER 360, [1967] 2 QB 31, [1967] 2 WLR 358, CA.
Gurtner v Circuit [1968] 1 All ER 328, [1968] 2 QB 587, [1968] 2 WLR 668, CA.
Iraqi Ministry of Defence v Arcepey Shipping Co SA (Gillespie Bros & Co Ltd intervening), The *c* *Angel Bell* [1980] 1 All ER 480, [1981] QB 65, [1980] 2 WLR 488.
Rexnord Inc v Rollerchain Distributors Ltd [1979] FSR 119.
Spelling Goldberg Productions Inc v BPC Publishing Ltd [1981] RPC 280, CA.
Tetra Molectric Ltd v Japan Imports Ltd (Win Lighter Corp intervening) [1976] RPC 541, CA.
White v London Transport Executive [1971] 3 All ER 1, [1971] 2 QB 721, [1971] 3 WLR 169, CA.   *d*

Interlocutory appeal

The plaintiffs, Sanders Lead Co Inc (SLC), appealed against the order made by Bingham J on 22 October 1983 whereby the judge ordered that the applicants, Metal Traders (UK) Ltd (Metal), be joined as defendants in an action brought by SLC against the defendants, Entores Metal Brokers Ltd (Entores), by writ dated 26 January 1983. The facts are set out *e* in the judgment of Kerr LJ.

M G Tugendhat for SLC.
Christopher Moger for Entores.
Jonathan Hirst for Metal.

f

At the conclusion of argument the court announced that SLC's appeal would be allowed for reasons to be given later.

24 November. The following judgments were delivered.

KERR LJ (giving the first judgment at the invitation of Stephenson LJ). I will refer to *g* the plaintiffs as 'SLC' and to the defendants as 'Entores'. This is an appeal by SLC from an order made by Bingham J on 20 October 1983 ordering another party, Metal Traders (UK) Ltd (to whom I will refer as 'Metal'), to be added as defendants to this action pursuant to RSC Ord 15, r 6. Since the action is fixed for 28 November 1983, the appeal was expedited and we heard counsel for all three parties on 17 and 18 November. We then announced that the appeal would be allowed for reasons to be given as soon as *h* possible. My reasons for allowing this appeal are accordingly set out below.

The case is very unusual and of some general importance on the question whether an alleged creditor who has obtained a Mareva injunction should be allowed to intervene in an action with which he is in no way concerned, other than that the outcome of the action is liable, to put it generally for the moment, to destroy the effectiveness of the injunction.   *j*

The background is complex and requires to be explained in some detail. In February and August 1982 certain contracts for the purchase and sale of quantities of lead were concluded between Metal and a company called Sanders Lead International Inc, a subsidiary of SLC, to which I will refer as 'SLI'. The contracts called for performance in November 1982 and January to March 1983 respectively. Metal contend that SLI have

committed serious breaches of these contracts and are claiming about $US1,482,000 by
a way of damages against SLI. SLI have denied liability and have also denied that the
contracts are subject to arbitration under the rules of the London Metal Exchange. In the
latter connection it should be mentioned that, since SLI (as well as SLC) are incorporated
in Alabama, USA, SLI have purported to rely on the law of Alabama as entitling them to
revoke a submission to arbitration in London, even though there appears to be no doubt
that the contracts in question were subject to English law. I mention this because it is
b part of the background which explains the unremitting, and in the circumstances
perhaps understandable, efforts by Metal to obtain, and maintain, some security for their
claims against SLI. For present purposes, however, this court is not otherwise concerned
with the arbitration claims by Metal against SLI, and cannot take any account of whatever
may be the merits of Metal's position in relation to these claims.

   In these circumstances Metal cast around, as they frankly admit, to see whether they
c could find any asset of SLI within the jurisdiction of the English courts. Their inquiries
led them to Entores, who informed Metal that Entores had purchased 500 tons of lead
from SLI at a price of $223,197, and that this sum was, or would shortly be, owing by
Entores to SLI. On hearing this, Metal issued an originating summons against SLI for a
Mareva injunction which, in its ultimate form, comprised all assets of SLI within the
jurisdiction of the English courts and the whole of the debt owed by Entores. Metal had
d persuaded Entores to pay the amount of $223,197 into a special account, and the
application for a Mareva injunction referred specifically to the moneys standing in that
account. I will refer to the originating summons between Metal and SLI for convenience
as 'the Mareva proceedings'.

   I must next say something about the purchase contract made by Entores. Although it
is clear that Entores genuinely believe that this was made with SLI, as has been deposed
e on affidavit on behalf of Entores and as they informed Metal in good faith, it is in fact
doubtful whether this contract was made with SLI or with SLC. In the present action
SLC are suing Entores for the price of $223,197 on the ground that SLC and not SLI were
the sellers to Entores, which Entores deny. The doubts as to the identity of the sellers
arise from the fact that both companies carry on business from the same address in
Alabama, that a Mr Wiley Sanders is the president of SLI, that a Mr George Sanders is the
f senior vice-president of sales for both SLC and SLI, and that both appear to have been
concerned in the making of this contract. The contract was made partly by telephone
and partly by telegrams or telexes, and the fact that all of these were addressed to SLC
and not to SLI at their common address may not be conclusive as to the identity of the
sellers. Moreover, SLC appears to be the producing company and SLI, at any rate in
relation to international sales such as the one in the present instance, the marketing
g company, with possible fiscal reasons for this set-up. It is also common ground that all
previous contracts between Entores and the Sanders group were made with SLI and that
they have never previously made a contract with SLC. Some of the information (or
allegations) concerning SLC and SLI emanates from Metal, a subsidiary of Metal Traders
Inc of New York, who have some knowledge of the organisation of the Sanders group
and feel that they have strong reasons for believing that the sellers to Entores were SLI
h and not SLC. However, these are all matters which will or may require investigation in
the present action by SLC against Entores.

   I then turn to the history of the Mareva proceedings and of the present action, which
has been very unusual. As already mentioned, Metal sought a Mareva injunction against
any assets of SLI within the jurisdiction, with particular reference to the moneys in the
special account set up by Entores, representing the price which Entores contend to be
j due to SLI. This injunction was initially granted by Lloyd J to a limited extent on 13
January 1983, and was then increased by him on 20 January to comprise all SLI's assets
within the jurisdiction and the whole of the sum of $223,197 in this account. We have
heard no argument on the question whether a Mareva injunction in this form should or
should not have been granted, and for the present purposes I assume that it was validly
granted without in any way seeking to indicate any view to the contrary. However, in

relation to the next stage of the proceedings it is necessary to bear in mind the nature and effect of a Mareva injunction in relation to the moneys standing in this account.

What happened was that, virtually simultaneously, SLC issued two proceedings. On 25 January they applied to be joined as defendants to the Mareva proceedings between Metal and SLI and for the discharge of the Mareva injunction so far as concerned the moneys standing in the special account set up by Entores. Secondly, on 26 January they issued their writ in the present action against Entores to recover the price of the lead which SLC contend that they, and not SLI, had sold to Entores. I will deal first with the position concerning the Mareva proceedings.

Affidavits were filed on behalf of SLC and Metal in support of the discharge and maintenance of the Mareva injunction respectively. These, and a later affidavit sworn on behalf of Entores, show that the position adopted by all the parties, no doubt for tactical reasons, involved a misconception and misstatements about the legal status of the moneys in the special account. So far as SLC are concerned, this is at once apparent from their summons asking that the Mareva injunction be discharged 'on the grounds that the assets referred to in the said Order are the property of Sanders Lead Co and not the defendants', ie SLI. On the other side, the affidavits on behalf of Metal and Entores equally erroneously treated the effect of the Mareva injunction as having created a charge in favour of Metal over the moneys standing in the special account. The fallacy in the position taken up by SLC is virtually self-evident. The moneys in the special account belong to Entores and not to SLI, let alone SLC. They were merely moneys which Entores had earmarked for the purpose of paying the debt which in their view was due to SLI. So far as the position of Metal and Entores is concerned, it is settled law that, although the moneys standing in the special account were expressly mentioned in the terms of the Mareva injunction obtained by Metal against SLI, this created no charge or any proprietary interest of any kind in favour of Metal over these moneys (see *Iraqi Ministry of Defence v Arcepey Shipping Co SA (Gillespie Bros & Co Ltd intervening), The Angel Bell* [1980] 1 All ER 480, [1981] QB 65 per Robert Goff J, as approved by this court in *A J Bekhor & Co Ltd v Bilton* [1981] 2 All ER 565, [1981] QB 923). As it seems to me, this misapprehension of the legal position has given rise to some of the problems with which this appeal is concerned.

SLC's application to be joined as a defendant to the Mareva proceedings and for the discharge of the injunction came before Leggatt J on 31 January 1983. There is some difference of recollection as to what took place in the course of this hearing, which (as is sometimes inevitable in interlocutory proceedings in the Commercial Court) may have been conducted under some pressure of time. According to counsel who has appeared on behalf of SLC throughout, he himself not only realised, but also then made it clear, that the application by SLC for the discharge of the injunction was hopeless and that it could not proceed. On the side of Metal, as we were informed by counsel who appeared for them on this appeal but had not represented them previously, it was not appreciated that counsel for SLC was, in effect, throwing in his hand entirely in relation to SLC's application for the discharge of the injunction. Moreover, it is clear that neither SLC's application to be joined as defendants to the Mareva proceedings nor their application for the discharge of the injunction have ever been withdrawn. Indeed, the order made by Leggatt J on 31 January allowed SLC's application to be joined as additional defendants to the Mareva proceedings, and he adjourned generally their application for the discharge of the injunction. The reason, no doubt, was that neither of these orders was opposed by Metal. From what we were told it appears that Leggatt J was informed that SLC had by then issued their writ against Entores in the present action, and that he also made it clear, in my view quite rightly, that there could in any event be no basis for resolving any of the conflicting contentions in this case through the means of the Mareva proceedings. If the order for the joinder of SLC to these proceedings had been opposed by Metal (or Entores) and fully argued, I feel sure that Leggatt J would not have permitted SLC to be joined as additional defendants. SLC have no locus standi in the Mareva proceedings, and there is no issue in the Mareva proceedings which is fit to be tried.

At this point the conspicuous absence of SLI throughout all these proceedings should

be noted. The reasons are no doubt obvious. SLI have instructed no solicitors in this
a country and are clearly anxious to do nothing which might bring them within reach of
the English courts. Counsel for SLC only appeared on behalf of SLC. However, as
between SLC and SLI the only proper party to apply for the discharge of the Mareva
injunction would of course have been SLI and not SLC.

I then turn to the subsequent history of the present action. As already mentioned, SLC
had issued their writ against Entores on 26 January 1983. Entores, who are of course in
b something of a cross-fire position, then applied by a summons dated 9 February for
various alternative forms of relief designed to ease their position, with a view to Metal
'making the running' against SLC. These included an application to allow Entores to
interplead. However, interpleader as between SLC and SLI was clearly hopeless, since
SLI, for obvious reasons, have never claimed against Entores that SLI were the sellers, and
that the price of $223,197 was accordingly due to SLI. In effect, Entores therefore applied
c for interpleader relief as between SLC and Metal. It was in connection with this
application, as I have already mentioned, that it was asserted in an affidavit on behalf of
Entores, clearly quite wrongly, that the Mareva injunction created a charge in favour of
Metal over the moneys standing in the special account. Alternatively, Entores asked for
a stay of the action, or for consolidation of the Mareva proceedings with the action, or
alternatively for an order that the Mareva proceedings and the action be tried at the same
d time. This summons came before Bingham J on 25 February 1983. The order which he
ultimately made was that the Mareva proceedings and the present action should be tried
together, and no one appealed against this order. In his later judgment, which is the
subject matter of the present appeal, Bingham J said in regard to this earlier order:

'The precise considerations for my order on 25 February I cannot recall and did
not detail in my judgment. I admit that it may not have been a very good order to
e have made. However, I consider that probably what was in my mind was that it was
desirable for the issue as to the contracting party in [the present action] to be resolved
at a hearing where Metal Traders could also be heard.'

I will revert to this observation again later. The order, as such, was clearly unusual, since
it implied that there could be a trial as between Metal and SLC in the Mareva proceedings
f on issues which were based on misconceptions on all sides. Moreover, trials on affidavit,
and whether with or without cross-examination of the deponents, in Mareva proceedings
should in my view be discouraged, unless they relate to a specific asset over which claims
to proprietary rights can properly be asserted, or where a third party can properly claim
to have some locus standi for applying for a variation or discharge of the injunction.
However, Bingham J was faced with a most unusual position and with the difficulty that
g all parties concerned were ad idem to the extent of the legal misconceptions to which I
have already referred. It is therefore not surprising that he made an unusual order. From
this it now follows that counsel and solicitors representing Metal will in fact be in court
during the trial of the present action between SLC and Entores, albeit in relation to SLC's
misconceived, but unwithdrawn, application against Metal in the Mareva proceedings
for the discharge of the Mareva injunction. This is also a matter to which I refer again
h below.

I then come finally to the last step in the history of the present action from which this
appeal arises. (There have also been other applications, both in the action and in the
Mareva proceedings, to which it is unnecessary to refer.) As already mentioned, in about
June 1983 the present action between SLC and Entores was fixed for 28 November. On
3 October Metal then issued a summons in the action asking (a) that they be joined as
j defendants to the action together with Entores, and (b) for extensive further discovery to
be given by SLC. The further discovery related to the status and respective positions of
SLC and SLI as the producing and marketing companies within the Sanders group, and
to their previous international sale contracts, for the purpose of finding material to
substantiate the contention, which Metal would like to advance in the action, that the
sellers to Entores were SLI and not SLC. This summons again came before Bingham J on

22 October 1983. In the event, due to pressure of time, the whole of the argument was concerned with issue (a), whether Metal could, and properly should, be joined as defendants to the present action together with Entores. Bingham J clearly felt that the application presented difficult problems, both as to his jurisdiction and as to the exercise of his discretion. In the end, however, he ordered that Metal should be joined as defendants to the present action, but no order was made on Metal's application for discovery. His judgment was not reserved and was also clearly given under pressure of time.

SLC are now appealing against the order for the joinder of Metal as additional defendants. The issues which arise for decision by this court are whether there was jurisdiction to make this order and, if so, whether there is any basis for interfering with the discretion exercised by Bingham J in making it.

Both of these question turn on RSC Ord 15, r 6(2)(b)(ii), which is in the following terms:

'At any stage of the proceedings in any cause or matter the Court may on such terms as it thinks just and either of its own motion or on application . . . (b) order any of the following persons to be added as a party, namely . . . (ii) any person between whom and any party to the cause or matter there may exist a question or issue arising out of or relating to or connected with any relief or remedy claimed in the cause or matter which in the opinion of the Court it would be just and convenient to determine as between him and that party as well as between the parties to the cause or matter . . .'

I have come to the clear conclusion, though not without some hesitation, that the judge had no jurisdiction to order the joinder of Metal under this provision. The main passage in his judgment dealing with this question is as follows:

'The matter was well argued and the issue is by no means an easy one. However, I think the proper way to approach it is to have regard to the very wide language of the rule and to ask the question: if [the present action] went by default so far as Entores were concerned, would the intervener applicant suffer an immediate and direct financial harm such that it would be unfair not to allow them a forensic opportunity to avoid that result at the trial? If I conclude Yes, that would resolve the question of jurisdiction.'

The judge then answered this question in the affirmative on the ground that, if SLC were to succeed in the present action, 'Metal Traders would suffer immediate and direct financial harm, the result being that the ownership of the chose in action would be decided in a way defeating Metal Trader's claim' in the Mareva proceedings.

I am sure that when Bingham J referred to 'the ownership of the chose in action' he was referring to the debt owed by Entores either to SLC or to SLI, and not to the moneys in the special account as such. I have already dealt with this aspect. Nevertheless, in my view the approach which he adopted is much wider than the rule permits. Although the judge added, 'This is not to say that every creditor could say they had an issue,' his formulation would go virtually as far as this, at any rate in relation to every alleged creditor holding a Mareva injunction which would be affected by the outcome of an action in which such creditor otherwise has no interest whatever. The question which falls to be answered is: what is the question, or issue, between Metal on the one hand and SLC or Entores or both on the other, arising out of, or relating to or connected with, SLC's claim for the price of the lead purchased by Entores? In my view there is no such question or issue within the terms and proper application of Ord 15, r 6(2)(b)(ii). Whether Entores owe the price of the lead to SLC or to SLI is not an issue between any of them and Metal. It is true that Metal would suffer 'immediate and direct financial harm' if SLC win the action, but only because Metal are an alleged creditor of SLI, whose assets within the jurisdiction will in that event not include the moneys in the special account set up by Entores. But Metal have no proprietary interest in, or charge over, these moneys, and in a   my view it would make no difference even if they had such an interest, because the moneys themselves are not the subject matter of SLC's claim, which is merely for payment of an alleged debt. Metal would still only be in the same position as any alleged creditor of, or a person having some other financial interest in, one of the parties to an action with which they have no other concern. Indeed, in the present case Metal's financial interest relates to SLI, who are not even a party to the action; but this also makes no difference.

b   In my view the rule requires some interest in the would-be intervener which is in some way directly related to the subject matter of the action. A mere commercial interest in its outcome, divorced from the subject matter of the action, is not enough. It may well be impossible, and would in any event be undesirable, to attempt to categorise the situations in which the interests of would-be interveners are sufficient to satisfy the requirements of the rule. The authorities show that the existence of a cause of action

c   between the intervener and one of the parties is not a necessary prerequisite for this purpose. But they also go no further than to show that there must be some direct interest in the subject matter, such as an alleged infringement of a patent, trade mark or copyright with which the intervener is concerned (see *Tetra Molectric Ltd v Japan Imports Ltd (Win Lighter Corp intervening)* [1976] RPC 541 and *Rexnord Inc v Rollerchain Distributors Ltd* [1979] FSR 119), though even in such cases the interest of the intervener must raise an

d   existing issue and not merely a contingent one (see *Spelling Goldberg Productions Inc v BPC Publishing Ltd* [1981] RPC 280). Another illustration is provided by cases where the intervener can show that he will in some way be compelled to 'foot the bill', depending on the outcome of the action (see *Gurtner v Circuit* [1968] 1 All ER 328 at 331, [1968] 2 QB 587 at 595), though I bear in mind that the wording of Ord 15, r 6(2) was then much narrower than it is now. However, as counsel for Metal rightly conceded, no case has

e   gone so far as to allow intervention by someone who is only a creditor, or alleged creditor, with no more than a creditor's commercial interest in the outcome of the action, and in my view it makes no difference whatever that the creditor in question is one who has obtained a Mareva injunction whose fate may in some way depend on the outcome.

In his lucid and forceful submissions, which I found most helpful, counsel for Metal also argued that the present case is different from the position of 'creditor-interveners'

f   generally, because in this case an issue was raised against Metal by SLC themselves, when SLC applied for the discharge of the Mareva injunction. He also submitted that the sole purpose of SLC in bringing the action against Entores was to defeat Metal's Mareva injunction against SLI, though this presupposes that SLC were not in fact the sellers, which obviously begs the whole question. But in my view none of this makes any difference to Metal's position under Ord 15, r 6(2)(*b*)(ii). The issue raised by SLC against

g   Metal, apart from being misconceived, was raised in the Mareva proceedings. The fact that it was raised there has nothing to do with the subject matter of the present action as such. I therefore conclude that Bingham J had no jurisdiction to make the order which is under appeal.

However, even if I should be wrong on the question of jurisdiction, I would in any event allow this appeal on the question of discretion. If an alleged creditor who has

h   obtained a Mareva injunction could ever be permitted to intervene in an action where his interest in the outcome relates solely to the fate of his injunction, then this could only be so in the most exceptional circumstances. Such exceptional circumstances might exist where there is an allegation of collusion between the parties to the action in order to defeat the injunction. But even in such cases I think that the intervener's appropriate remedy would be to apply for a stay of the action, which is in some cases possible even

j   though he is not a party: see s 49(3) of the Supreme Court Act 1981 and *Gore v Van Der Lann (Liverpool Corp intervening)* [1967] 1 All ER 360 at 368, [1967] 2 QB 31 at 45 per Salmon LJ. However, I can see no exceptional circumstances whatever in the present case. There was obviously no collusion against Metal; on the contrary, Entores's co-operation with Metal was directed to the maintenance, and not the destruction, of Metal's Mareva injunction. All the judge said, bearing directly on the question of discretion, was:

'One crucial consideration is the position of Entores. If there were every reason to suppose Entores would fight as full-bloodedly as a defendant concerned to avoid liability it would be a powerful argument against the intervener application. However, this is not quite the position here. Entores wished to drop out and interplead. They expressed their neutrality. Their reason for welcoming joinder is to avoid them bearing the brunt of the battle. They would prefer to let Metal Traders get on with the battle.'

But in my view this does not give a full picture of the position. Metal have gone so far as to agree to indemnify Entores in respect of their costs of fighting the action against SLC. This is an important point which was not mentioned by Bingham J in his judgment. Entores are represented by experienced solicitors and counsel, and, although they have no direct financial interest in the outcome of the action, there is no reason to think that they will not contest it fully and properly. They have told Metal, and stated on affidavit, that they believe that their purchase contract was made with SLI and not SLC, and in their defence they have fully and properly raised this issue. The position at the trial will therefore be similar to that described by Lord Denning MR in refusing joinder of the Motor Insurers' Bureau under the old rule in *White v London Transport Executive* [1971] 3 All ER 1 at 4, [1971] 2 QB 721 at 727. Moreover, I agree with counsel for SLC that to allow Metal to be joined in this action would be to accord them rights similar to those available to judgment creditors in relation to garnishee proceedings (see RSC Ord 49, r 6), and that this would constitute a dangerous precedent even if (contrary to my view) the necessary jurisdiction is provided by Ord 15, r 6(2)(b)(ii).

The only aspect of Entores's resistance to SLC's claim in the present action of which Metal have made some criticism is that, in relation to the discovery to be given by SLC, Entores have not cast their net as widely as Metal would wish to do by their own summons for discovery, which I have already mentioned, and which in my judgment cannot now be pursued by Metal. I express no views about the merits of this request for discovery, particularly when it comes so late, other than to say that counsel for Metal did convince me that in the special circumstances of this case it may not have constituted as unwarrantable a 'fishing expedition' as I had thought at first. But, whatever may be its merits in relation to the issues in the action, it cannot provide any ground for allowing Metal to become a party to the action.

Nevertheless, as the result of the unusual, and in my view incorrect, orders which allowed SLC to become a party to the Mareva proceedings and for these proceedings to be heard at the same time as the action, the position in fact is that Metal will be represented by solicitors and counsel during the hearing of the action, as already mentioned.

This brings me to the question as to the extent, if any, to which Metal may be entitled to play some part at the hearing of the action. This will be entirely a matter for the discretion of the judge who tries the action, whoever he may be. He will no doubt bear in mind the earlier passage from the judgment of Bingham J which I have set out. Furthermore, I have no doubt that, particularly in an action in the Commercial Court, the judge will not allow himself to be deflected in any way, by attempts to rely on procedural technicalities, from his task of ascertaining who, as between SLC and SLI, were in fact the sellers to Entores. That, and that alone, will be the purpose of the action. If it should be found necessary, in his view, to accede to some further application for discovery, or even to an adjournment, I am sure that he will not hesitate to consider such applications if they are necessary in order to arrive at the truth. The background material on which Metal would wish to rely, if they could, owing to their closer knowledge of the affairs of the Sanders group, has now been brought to the notice of the court, in the sense that it is referred to in the documents which we have had to consider on this appeal. All this material is available to Entores, and SLC, their legal advisers and witnesses have had full warning of it. In these circumstances I have no doubt that the real issues in the unusual situation of this case will not be allowed to go by default in any way.

However, for all the foregoing reasons I have no hesitation in concluding that this appeal must be allowed, as we have already announced, with an order that Metal must pay the costs of SLC and Entores both here and below. In saying this, I should like to express my great appreciation of the clarity and helpfulness of the submissions of counsel who appeared on this appeal, particularly since they had to conduct it again under some pressure of time.

STEPHENSON LJ. I agree with all that Kerr LJ has said.

Like him, I find it easier to decide that the judge was wrong in the exercise of his discretion, if he had a discretion, than to decide that he was wrong in holding that he had jurisdiction. My doubt on the latter point would not arise, or would at any rate be more easily stifled, if SLC had not intervened in the Mareva proceedings, misconceived though their intervention was. For I find some difficulty in denying that the question or issue whether Entores owed the price of lead bought and sold to SLC or SLI is not only connected with the remedy claimed in the present action by SLC against Entores, but also exists between SLC and Metal by reason of SLC having raised it in the Mareva proceedings between Metal and SLI.

It would, however, be wrong to allow a person who is not a party to an action to confer on the court a jurisdiction which it does not and should not have; and it would be right to allow the appeal for the reasons given by Kerr LJ.

Appeal allowed.

Solicitors: *Simmons & Simmons* (for SLC); *Smiles & Co* (for Entores); *Middleton Potts & Co* (for Metal).

Diana Brahams   Barrister.

P v W   *a*

FAMILY DIVISION
WOOD AND BOOTH JJ
19 OCTOBER, 14 DECEMBER 1983

Minor – Custody – Access – Enforcement of order – Order of magistrates' court – Jurisdiction of   *b*
justices to enforce access order by imposing monetary penalty or by committal to prison –
Guardianship of Minors Act 1971, s 9 – Domestic Proceedings and Magistrates' Courts Act
1978, s 8 – Magistrates' Courts Act 1980, s 63(3).

Minor – Custody – Access – Enforcement of order – Proceedings for contempt – When such
proceedings should be instituted – What must be proved in such proceedings – What details should
be included in summons – Magistrates' Courts Act 1980, s 63(3).   *c*

Magistrates have jurisdiction under s 63(3)*a* of the Magistrates' Courts Act 1980 to deal
with any alleged breach of an order for access made under s 9*b* of the Guardianship of
Minors Act 1971 or s 8*c* of the Domestic Proceedings and Magistrates' Courts Act 1978.
However, before an alleged breach of an order for access can be punished under s 63(3)   *d*
of the 1980 Act as a contempt of court, it must be shown that the breach was deliberate,
and where a court is dealing with problems of access every other course should be
attempted before issuing proceedings for contempt. Such proceedings should be regarded
as a weapon of last resort. Furthermore, a summons issued under s 63 of the 1980 Act
should give clear details of the alleged breach of the order (eg by specifying, whenever
possible, the date, approximate time and place of the alleged breach) so that the   *e*
respondent to the summons may know precisely what is alleged against him (see p 867 c
d, p 870 g h, p 871 b c and p 872 j, post).
    Re K (a minor) (access order: breach) [1977] 2 All ER 737 applied.
    Quaere. Whether a magistrates' court has power, under s 63(3) of the 1980 Act, to
punish a person who has acted in breach of its order but who has remedied the breach
before a summons has been issued (see p 867 c d and p 872 c d f g, post).   *f*

Notes
For the enforcement of orders made in domestic proceedings by magistrates, see 13
Halsbury's Laws (4th edn) para 1337, and for cases on the subject, see 27(2) Digest
(Reissue) 1002–1007, 8056–8076.
    For the Guardianship of Minors Act 1971, s 9, see 41 Halsbury's Statutes (3rd edn) 766.   *g*
    For the Domestic Proceedings and Magistrates' Courts Act 1978, s 8, see 48 ibid 746.
    For the Magistrates' Courts Act 1980, s 63, see 50(2) ibid 1495.

Cases referred to in judgment
B(B) v B(M) [1969] 1 All ER 891, [1969] P 103, [1969] 2 WLR 862.
K (a minor) (access order: breach), Re [1977] 2 All ER 737, [1977] 1 WLR 533, DC.   *h*

Appeal
On 28 February 1983 the father of a young child issued a summons alleging that the
child's mother had consistently disobeyed an order made by the Old Street Magistrates'
Court on 28 May 1982 granting him access to the child, and requiring her to show cause   *j*
why she should not be committed to prison or ordered to pay a fine pursuant to s 63 of

---

a   Section 63(3), so far as material, is set out at p 869 b c, post
b   Section 9, so far as material, is set out at p 869 e, post
c   Section 8, so far as material, is set out at p 869 f, post

the Magistrates' Courts Act 1980. On 15 April 1983 the Old Street Magistrates' Court
a found that she had failed to comply with the order for access but made no order against
her under s 63 of the 1980 Act. She appealed against their decision, contending, inter
alia, that they had no jurisdiction to deal with an alleged breach of an order for access.
The facts are set out in the judgment of Wood J.

Frances Webber for the mother.
b *Kay Halkyard* for the father.

Cur adv vult

14 December. The following judgment was delivered.

c

WOOD J. Before I give my judgment, I would like to make it clear that this case has
been incorrectly listed. I am sitting here as a Divisional Court, notionally with Booth J,
who is on circuit. She has read my draft judgment and has authorised me to say that she
agrees with it.

This is an appeal by notice of motion against the decision of justices sitting at the Old
d Street Magistrates' Court on 15 April 1983. The appellant before us is the mother and the
respondent is the father of a little girl, R, who was born on 27 October 1978.

On 15 April the justices were considering an application by the respondent father to
commit the mother for breach of an order granting access to him. On 18 May 1979 the
father had been granted access once each week for two hours. On 18 July 1980 he had
applied to commit the appellant but this had been refused and the access had been
e increased from two hours to four hours, once per week. On 1 May 1981 the respondent
had applied for staying weekend access and this had been refused. Finally, on 28 May
1982 the order which was the subject matter of the present complaint was made, and I
quote:

'that the complainant [the father] had the right of access to the minor, [R], once a
f   week on Saturdays between 11.00 am and 7.00 pm, at the home of [the father's
brother] at Newington Green.'

It is common ground that subsequently the meeting place was changed to that of the
mother's parents. All these orders were made under the provisions of the Guardianship
of Minors Act 1971 and the Guardianship Act 1973.

The history of the matter, over which there is virtually no dispute, continues thus.
g The father changed his address in May 1982 and the mother did not know where to find
him. The access, as I have said, took place at the grandparents' address and the father did
not know the mother's address, as she had been given leave by the justices not to disclose
it to him. Access continued until Christmas 1982, but on occasions the father did not
choose to avail himself of the opportunities to see his daughter. On 20 December 1982
the father went to the grandparents' home taking with him a present for R, but found
h the house empty. The grandparents had moved and he did not know of the move and
did not know the new address. He approached his own solicitors who were in touch with
the mother's solicitors on the telephone shortly before Christmas. The mother's solicitors
did not know precisely where their client was, but on 5 January 1983 the mother went
to see her own solicitors, to whom she had been trying to speak over the Christmas
period. The little girl, R, had been ill and had been in hospital for a day over the
j Christmas break suffering from measles and convulsions.

On 5 January 1983 the mother's solicitors wrote to the father's solicitors as follows:

'We refer to your telephone call to us before Christmas and would inform you
that our client did apparently try to contact us over the Christmas period, when our
office was either closed or the writer was on leave. We confirm that her parents have

moved from the address where your client was collecting [R] for access. Also we understand that the child was ill before Christmas and was admitted to hospital for a short period. We further understand that your client himself has moved, and we would be grateful if you would let us have his current address, so that our client can contact him whenever necessary or in situations such as this in the future. Our client is willing to disclose her address, providing your client will give a written undertaking that he will only call at her address for the purposes of access as directed by the court. We are instructed that he was in the habit of calling sometimes two or three times a week at the grandparents' home, pestering them generally and often being abusive. Our client wishes to make it clear that she is not prepared to tolerate this sort of behaviour and she will take immediate action should it ever occur in the future.'

The letter goes on further to complain that he does not always arrive and that he has not been paying proper sums by way of maintenance, which were in arrears.

There was a reply from the father's solicitors dated 18 January which did not include the undertaking required and on 20 January the mother's solicitors indicated that they were not prepared to disclose her address without the written undertaking, but that—

'Subject to the above our client is very willing to allow access to commence this Saturday. She is prepared to make arrangements so that somebody else can be at her home when your client collects [R] at 11.00 a.m.'

Nothing further was heard from the father who, acting in person, issued the summons under s 63 of the Magistrates' Courts Act 1980 on 28 February. Access was in fact resumed on 26 March 1983 and there were three periods of access prior to the hearing on 15 April.

The father's case is that the mother was in breach of the order of 28 May 1982 for some three weeks from 20 December 1982 until 5 January 1983. The summons of 28 February 1983 required the mother to attend court to answer an information—

'That on 28th May 1982 the Old Street Magistrates' Court made an order under section 10(1) of the Guardianship of Minors Act 1971 granting access to the informant, [the father], as parent to his daughter, [R], and that you have consistently disobeyed that order in that you have declined to allow such access and that accordingly you show cause why you should not be committed to prison or be ordered to pay a fine pursuant to section 63 of the Magistrates' Courts Act 1980.'

The justices heard evidence from the father and the mother, and gave short reasons, which I set out in full:

'We are satisfied (1) that access normally took place at ... the home of [the mother's] parents; (2) that [the father] was a difficult and highly strung person; (3) that access could be an occasion of dispute and abuse between the parties, and that [the father] was largely the source of this trouble; (4) that [the mother] and her family were antagonistic to [the father], not without reason; (5) that the premises [of the mother's parents] were vacated in or about Christmas 1982, thus making it impossible for [the father] to obtain access to the child at that address; (6) that [the mother] did not before that date nor thereafter within a reasonable time tell [the father] at what premises access to [R] could be continued. We were, therefore, satisfied that [the mother] had by her act and default but not wilfully disobeyed the order of 28th May 1982 to afford [the father] access to [R] on Saturdays. We consider the overall merits and justice of the case did not require the imposition of a penalty or a committal to custody, and we accordingly made no order pursuant to section 63 of the Magistrates' Courts Act 1980.'

The first point raised was on jurisdiction. We were told that the question whether an alleged breach of an order for access fell to be dealt with under s 63 had never been the

subject of full argument before the Divisional Court. In *Re K (a minor)* [1977] 2 All ER
a 737, [1977] 1 WLR 533 Baker P had expressed the view that it did, with which view
Latey J had agreed, but it was stressed by them that their view had been taken without
full argument. We therefore invited counsel in the present case to argue the issue fully
and granted a short adjournment for that purpose.

I turn first to s 63 of the 1980 Act itself, the relevant parts of which read as follows:

b '. . . (3) Where any person disobeys an order of a magistrates' court made under
an Act passed after 31st December 1879 to do anything other than the payment of
money . . . the court may—(a) order him to pay a sum not exceeding £50 for every
day during which he is in default or a sum not exceeding £1,000; or (b) commit
him to custody until he has remedied his default or for a period not exceeding 2
months; but a person who is ordered to pay a sum for every day during which he is
in default or who is committed to custody until he has remedied his default shall
c not by virtue of this section be ordered to pay more than £1,000 or be committed
for more than 2 months in all for doing . . . the same thing contrary to the order
(without prejudice to the operation of this section in relation to any subsequent
default) . . .'

An order for access is an order other than an order for payment of money which
d requires to be obeyed and therefore would seem to fall within that section.

It is, however, argued by counsel for the appellant mother that this is not so. Counsel
looks first at s 9(1) of the Guardianship of Minors Act 1971, under which the present
order was made, and which reads:

'The court may, on the application of the mother or father of a minor (who may
apply without next friend), make such order regarding—(a) the custody of the
e minor; and (b) the right of access to the minor of his mother or father, as the court
thinks fit having regard to the welfare of the minor and to the conduct and wishes
of the mother and father.'

She points out that a distinction is made between custody and access, and that the
phrase used is 'the right of access'. The same distinction is to be found in s 8(2) of the
f Domestic Proceedings and Magistrates' Court Act 1978, the relevant parts of which read:

'On an application for an order . . . the court . . . shall have power to make such
order regarding—(a) the legal custody of any child of the family who is under the
age of eighteen, and (b) access to any such child by either of the parties to the
marriage or any other person who is a parent of that child, as the court thinks fit.'

g This distinction is said to be maintained in the enforcement sections of each Act.
Section 13(1) of the 1971 Act, as amended by the Guardianship Act 1973, the Domestic
Proceedings and Magistrates' Courts Act 1978 and the Magistrates' Courts Act 1980,
reads:

'Where an order made by a magistrates' court under this Act contains a provision
committing to any person the actual custody of any minor, a copy of the order may
h be served on any person in whose actual custody the minor may for the time being
be, and thereupon the provision may, without prejudice to any other remedy open
to the person given the custody, be enforced under section 63(3) of the Magistrates'
Court Act 1980 as if it were an order of the court requiring the person so served to
give up the minor to the person given the custody.'

j Very similar wording is to be found in s 33 of the 1978 Act. Each enforcement section
refers only to an order for custody.

Counsel for the mother submits that the reason why the enforcement provisions are
required is that a custody order is merely declaratory, and therefore the order to deliver
up needs to be inserted. She also lays stress on the words 'as if it were an order of the
court requiring the person so served to give up the minor . . .' It is also right to note that

when making a custody order, or care and control order within the family and wardship jurisdictions, it is very common for a judge to add an order giving details of the date, time and place for the handing over of a child. The argument continues that an order for access is also merely declaratory and although not expressly excluded is pointedly absent from the enforcement sections and that therefore s 63 of the 1980 Act does not apply to an order for access.

It is conceded that if one looks at the plain wording of s 63 then disobedience of an order for access would seem to fall within it, but counsel for the mother submits that the inclusion of the enforcement sections together with their wording should lead the court to the opposite conclusion.

Counsel for the father gladly accepted the concession made on the natural and ordinary meaning of the words in s 63, and answered the remainder of the submission in one of two ways. First, she submitted that a custody order was not merely declaratory but implied an obligation to hand over a child, that the enforcement provision was inserted in order to make the position abundantly clear and to emphasise the obligation in those difficult cases where at the date of the making of an order the child was in the possession of the person against whom that order had been made. The enforcement provisions were said to be ex abundanti cautela. Second, she argued that if a custody order is merely declaratory and needed the support of an enforcement section, nevertheless an order for access was clearly an order which not only gave rights to parties but also obligations. She relied on these words in the judgment of Baker P in *Re K* [1977] 2 All ER 737 at 740, [1977] 1 WLR 533 at 536:

'But it does seem to me, and again I emphasise that I am saying this without having a full argument on the matter, that an access order is an order to do something other than the payment of money. True in this case, and in many cases, the actual order is that "the respondent shall have following rights of access", and that I think follows closely on the wording of the Guardianship of Minors Act 1971, s 10(1), ". . . such order regarding . . . the right of access to the minor . . .", but in the ultimate analysis, and I think this is clearer from the wording of the access provision of the Children Act 1975, s 34(1) ". . . requiring access to the child to be given to the applicant"; an order for access is an order that something shall be done. It is an order that the custodial parent shall permit, shall give, shall allow, access to the other parent and of course the reciprocal way of looking at it is that it is an order that the other parent shall have the right to see, shall visit, shall have the child, shall be able to take the child, so my opinion is that an access order can be enforced under s 54(3) of the [Magistrates' Courts Act 1952]. Whether it is wise to do it of course is a very different matter . . .'

Having heard full argument I am content to accept and follow the conclusion reached by the court in *Re K* and by inference by the court in *B v B* [1969] 1 All ER 891 at 903, [1969] P 103 at 117–118, which was that justices have jurisdiction under the provisions of s 63 to deal with any alleged breach of an order for access made under the provisions of s 9 of the 1971 Act or s 8 of the 1978 Act. It seems to me to matter not whether the correct view is that a custody order is or is not merely declaratory.

On a careful reading of each enforcement section it is clear that the time at which the draftsman is looking is that immediately after the making of the original order. For the purposes of enforcement at a later time it would seem right that the justices should have their powers under s 63(3) of the 1980 Act both in respect of custody and access orders. Any other view would provide endless opportunity for niceties of argument. So much for jurisdiction.

The appellant mother's case on the facts can be put under three headings. First, it is submitted that, in their findings that the mother had acted in default but not 'wilfully disobeyed' the order of 28 May 1982, the justices had erred in that the disobedience must be a wilful disobedience. Second, it is said first that the summons did not adequately identify the contempt alleged, and in any event on the evidence there was no contempt.

Third, it is said that in any event the alleged breach of the access order had been remedied
a prior to the issue of the summons on 28 February 1983 and that on the authority of *B v B*
the contempt had to be one which was continuing at least at the date of the issue of the
summons if not at the date of the hearing.

I look at these matters in that order. A contempt of court is a very serious matter
which involves the element of 'fault' and where the liberty of the subject is at stake.
There are a number of authorities, to which I do not intend to refer, but I am quite
b satisfied that any failure to obey an order of the court must be wilful, a deliberate
intention. The act or omission must be carried out with the knowledge of the obligation
to do or to refrain from doing something. The summons itself should, in my judgment,
give clear details of the alleged breach. It is in most cases possible to give particulars of
date, time or approximate time, and place of the alleged breach, and this should be set
forth so that the respondent to the summons is quite clear what is alleged against him or
c her. In the High Court an originating summons is issued supported by an affidavit and
that affidavit must make clear the precise allegations which are made against the
respondent. The summons in this case, in my judgment, was too vague, and counsel for
the mother is justified in her criticism of it.

Looking at the evidence as a whole, it is plain that the mother did what she could over
the Christmas period to meet the problems with which she was faced. She did not know
d the father's address; she tried to get in touch with her solicitors and she did succeed in
communicating with them early in January 1983. The child was in hospital for a day,
suffering from measles, and obviously required particular care and attention. The
Christmas break and festivities intervened, and the only criticism that might be made is
that she failed to notify her own solicitors of the proposed change of address of the
grandparents. There was an offer of a resumption of access early in the New Year and
e access was in fact resumed in March; it could have been resumed much earlier. Looking
at the whole of the facts I am not satisfied that there was any real fault in the mother on
which an allegation could be based of disobedience of the order for access. Not only,
therefore, did the justices err in the direction which they gave themselves on the nature
of the disobedience but also on the facts as a whole. In my judgment the mother must
succeed on both these points.

f The last submission made by counsel for the mother has caused me some anxious
thought. Section 63 of the Magistrates' Courts Act 1980 had its origins in s 54(3) of the
Magistrates' Courts Act 1952. That section was considered by a Divisional Court of this
Division consisting of Simon P and Baker J in *B v B* [1969] 1 All ER 891, [1969] P 103. It
seems from the report that the amendment made to s 54(3) of the 1952 Act by s 41(1),
and Sch 4 to, of the Criminal Justice Act 1961 may not have been brought to their
g attention. It was a case in which a father had failed to return his two children to their
mother at the end of an access period. The justices made an order under s 54(3) of the
1952 Act committing the father to prison for two months for contempt of court. They
suspended that order for a period of 12 months. A number of other points arose for
consideration in the case and Simon P, having dealt with them, came to consider the
power of the justices (a) to suspend the sentence of 12 months and (b) to commit to
h prison for two months. Simon P said ([1969] 1 All ER 891 at 899–900, [1969] P 103 at
113–114):

> 'In my view, therefore, the justices had no power to suspend any sentence of
imprisonment which they may have imposed. Their purported suspension for one
year was a nullity. The only portion of this part of their order which could have any
j effect was, therefore, the order for committal for two months. I turn, then, to
consider whether they had any power to make such an order. It is now accepted that
the High Court has power to commit for a definite as well as for an indefinite period.
The justices have only the power that is given to them by s. 54(3) of the Act of 1952.
This is a penal provision and therefore must be construed strictly. What the justices
could have done was to commit the father to custody until he had remedied his

default, such imprisonment not to exceed two months. They had no power, in my view, to commit him to prison for two months. If they wished to invoke the section, the proper order would have been to commit the father to prison until he caused [the elder child] to be handed over to the mother at a specified time and place, such imprisonment not to exceed two months (or such lesser period as might appear to be justified). In my view, therefore, the father is entitled to succeed on this part of the appeal, and the order of the justices purporting to send him to prison for two months, suspended for twelve months, must be set aside for two reasons: first, they had no power to suspend the sentence; and secondly, they had no power to impose a sentence of imprisonment for two months.'

In that case the breach of the order was a continuing one and counsel for the mother therefore submits that the alleged contempt must have been a continuing breach at least to the date of the summons for the justices to have any power to impose penalties under s 63 of the 1980 Act.

If this be correct, then a magistrates' court would have no power to punish a breach of its order once remedied, nor would there be any sanction for a person who committed a series of contempts which were in themselves isolated incidents or contempts which were remedied within a short time. Such contempts could well occur when a person was in breach of an order under s 16 of the Domestic Proceedings and Magistrates' Courts Act 1978, e g to refrain from molestation, or from visiting or entering a matrimonial home.

Looking once again at s 63 of the 1980 Act, I note the wording defining the powers of the court. It is worth repeating:

'. . . (3) . . . the court may—(a) order him to pay a sum not exceeding £50 for every day during which he is in default *or* a sum not exceeding £1,000; or (b) commit him to custody until he has remedied his default *or* for a period not exceeding 2 months . . .' (My emphasis.)

In each of paras (a) and (b) the powers of the court are set out in the alternative. The first part of each phrase gives a power to fine or to commit to prison, in para (a) 'for every day during which he is in default' and in para (b) 'until he has remedied his default'. The second part of each phrase gives power to fine up to £1,000 or to commit for a period not exceeding two months.

It would seem possible to argue that the first part of each phrase makes provision for a continuing disobedience and the second half provides for a punishment in respect of a past contempt. This possible construction would meet the problems which I have posed above under s 16 of the 1978 Act. It is, however, unnecessary to reach any conclusion on this point in the present case and this appeal must be allowed for the other reasons which I have given. The respondent father himself issued the summons to commit in the present case and, as I have indicated, he had no justification for so doing.

In looking at *Re K* [1977] 2 All ER 737 at 740, [1977] 1 WLR 533 at 536–537, I notice that Latey J stressed the importance of access when he said:

'. . . save in comparatively rare and exceptional cases, where a marriage has broken down it really is of the first importance in the interests of the children that they should have, and know that they have, the love and support of both parents; and they can only know that, especially if they are very young, if they have real and regular contact with the non-custodial parent.'

After the break-up of a family or of a personal relationship in which children are involved, a court is dealing not only with emotions which need to be smoothed and controlled, but also with the problems of re-establishing relationships between adults and between adults and children. Such situations need firm but understanding treatment. I only wish to stress that when dealing with problems of access every other course should be considered or attempted before issuing proceedings for contempt. These should be regarded as the weapon of last resort.

a   Finally, I would just like to emphasise that nowhere in this judgment do I seek to criticise the justices in the present case, who were dealing with a difficult problem and a complex point of law.

It follows, therefore, that the appeal must be allowed, and the order of the justices be varied so that the summons is dismissed. There will be no order as to costs, save legal aid taxation.

b   *Appeal allowed; order of justices varied.*

Solicitors: *Clinton Davis & Co* (for the mother); *Hallewell & Co* (for the father).

Bebe Chua   Barrister.

c

Practice Direction

d   SUPREME COURT TAXING OFFICE

Costs – Taxation – Time limit – Application for taxation out of time – Notice of intention to proceed to be given – Objection to extension of time to be raised as preliminary point on substantive hearing of taxation – Legal aid taxation – Legal Aid Act 1974, Sch 2 – RSC Ord 3, r 6, Ord 62,
e   *rr 7(5), 21(3)(4) – Legal Aid (General) Regulations 1980, reg 104.*

1. Parties wishing to begin proceedings for the taxation of any costs are reminded of the time limits imposed by RSC Ord 62, r 21(3) and (4).

2. When proceedings for taxation have not been commenced before the expiration of one whole year from the date when the judgment or order directing taxation was entered
f   or perfected or from the date of any other provision or event entitling a party to apply for taxation, the party seeking the taxation is required to give to every other party interested in the taxation not less than one month's notice of his intention to proceed pursuant to RSC Ord 3, r 6 (see *Pamplin v Frazer* (1983) 127 SJ 786).

3. When such proceedings are commenced after the expiration of the prescribed time limits then, whether or not a notice to proceed is required, no formal application for an extension of time need be made on taking the reference. In such a case, unless any other
g   party interested in the taxation makes a prior application, the question of an extension of time may be raised as a preliminary point on the substantive hearing of the taxation.

4. When a notice of intention to proceed is required but has not been given, and in any other appropriate case, any party interested in the taxation may make an application either before or as a preliminary point at the substantive hearing under the provisions of
h   RSC Ord 62, r 7(5). In all such cases the application or the taxation as the case may be must be referred to a taxing master.

5. If any application is made pursuant to this direction before the reference has been taken to a taxing officer, the application shall be referred to the sittings master.

6. When the only taxation required is pursuant to Sch 2 to the Legal Aid Act 1974, no application is required on taking a reference out of time. In any case where he considers it appropriate so to do, the taxing officer will, of his own motion, serve notice on the
j   party entitled to the taxation under the provisions of reg 104 of the Legal Aid (General) Regulations 1980, SI 1980/1894.

F T HORNE
Chief Taxing Master.

9 February 1984

Westwood v Secretary of State for Employment

HOUSE OF LORDS

LORD DIPLOCK, LORD KEITH OF KINKEL, LORD BRIDGE OF HARWICH, LORD BRANDON OF
OAKBROOK AND LORD BRIGHTMAN

13, 14, 15 FEBRUARY, 15 MARCH 1984

*Contract – Damages for breach – Wrongful dismissal – Employee dismissed without receiving
notice or payment in lieu following employers' insolvency – Employee receiving social security
benefits – Employee receiving payment from Secretary of State out of Redundancy Fund –
Whether Secretary of State entitled to deduct benefits from payment – Whether employee under
duty to mitigate loss – Employment Protection (Consolidation) Act 1978, ss 49(1), 50, 51,
122(1)(3), Sch 3.*

The respondent's employers became insolvent and as a result the respondent was
dismissed without receiving the 12 weeks' notice to which he was entitled under s 49(1)(c)
of the Employment Protection (Consolidation) Act 1978 or any payment in lieu thereof.
The respondent remained unemployed for more than 15 months and claimed and
received unemployment benefit and earnings-related supplement for the maximum
periods of entitlement of twelve months and six months respectively. After the expiry
of his entitlement to unemployment benefit he received supplementary benefit. The
Secretary of State for Employment paid the respondent out of the Redundancy Fund,
pursuant to s 122 of the 1978 Act, the sum of £525·21, which represented the amount
he would have earned during the 12 weeks' period of notice less the aggregate of
unemployment benefit and earnings-related supplement which he had received for that
period. A complaint by the respondent to an industrial tribunal that the Secretary of
State was not entitled to make the deduction was rejected. The Employment Appeal
Tribunal allowed an appeal by the respondent, holding that the benefits received were in
principle deductible in mitigation of damages for loss of earnings flowing from the
wrongful dismissal but that in the circumstances no deduction should be made because
the benefit the respondent had received from those payments was to be set off against the
loss of entitlement to unemployment benefit and earnings-related supplement which he
would have received twelve and six months later respectively had he not been obliged to
claim them prematurely by his employer's failure to give him notice. The Secretary of
State appealed to the Court of Appeal, which dismissed the appeal on the ground that an
employee who was entitled under the 1978 Act to a minimum statutory period of notice
for his contract of employment to be terminated had a statutory right to be paid the full
amount due during the period of notice calculated in accordance with s 50 of and Sch 3
to the 1978 Act and that that right was not subject to any deduction by reference to a
common law duty on the part of the employee to mitigate his damage. The Secretary of
State appealed to the House of Lords.

Held – An employee who was dismissed without the minimum statutory notice to
which he was entitled under s 49 of the 1978 Act could recover damages for breach of
contract under s 51 of that Act, but he was under a duty to mitigate those damages and
for that purpose unemployment benefit was to be taken into account. However, a
plaintiff who had suffered damage was only required to account by way of mitigation for
the net gain accruing to him of a kind properly to be taken into account and which he
would not have received but for the tort or breach of contract giving rise to his damage.
On the facts, the net gain to the respondent in benefits received was not the actual benefit
he received during the 12 weeks' notice period but the lesser sum he received as
supplementary benefit after the premature expiration of the unemployment benefit and
earnings-related supplement period occasioned by his wrongful dismissal. The order of

a   the Employment Appeal Tribunal was therefore correct and the appeal would be allowed
to that extent (see p 875 h and p 878 b to d and h to p 879 b e and h to p 880 b and f g, post).
Parsons v BNM Laboratories Ltd [1963] 2 All ER 658 applied.

Notes
For an employee's rights on his employer's insolvency, see 16 Halsbury's Laws (4th edn)
para 786:31.

b   For the duty to mitigate loss flowing from a breach of contract, see 9 ibid paras 552,
554 and 12 ibid para 1193, and for cases on the subject, see 17 Digest (Reissue) 124–130,
242–274.
For deductions from an award of damages for benefits received or receivable, see 12
Halsbury's Laws (4th edn) para 1152.
For the Employment Protection (Consolidation) Act 1978, ss 49, 50, 51, 122, Sch 3, see
c   48 Halsbury's Statutes (3rd edn) 499, 500, 501, 577, 622.

Cases referred to in opinions
Parry v Cleaver [1969] 1 All ER 555, [1970] AC 1, [1969] 2 WLR 821, HL.
Parsons v BNM Laboratories Ltd [1963] 2 All ER 658, [1964] 1 QB 95, [1963] 2 WLR 1273,
CA.
d   *Secretary of State for Employment v Wilson* [1978] 3 All ER 137, [1978] 1 WLR 568, EAT.

Appeal
The Secretary of State for Employment appealed with leave of the Court of Appeal
against the decision of that court (Eveleigh, O'Connor and Purchas LJJ) ([1983] 3 WLR
730) on 28 June 1983 dismissing an appeal by the appellant from the decision of the
e   Employment Appeal Tribunal (Browne-Wilkinson J, Mr R V Cooper and Mr E A Webb)
([1982] ICR 534) given on 20 May 1982 and an order dated 7 December 1982 allowing
an appeal by the respondent, Walter Westwood, from the decision of an industrial
tribunal (Mr J H Morrish, Mr C J Maloney and Mrs R Study) sitting at Leeds dated 16
November 1981 whereby the tribunal dismissed the respondent's application made
under ss 122 and 124 of the Employment Protection (Consolidation) Act 1978 for a
f   payment out of the Redundancy Fund. The facts are set out in the opinion of Lord
Bridge.

Peter Scott QC and *Peter Goldsmith* for the appellant.
Stephen Sedley QC and *Robert Allen* for the respondent.

g   Their Lordships took time for consideration.

15 March. The following opinions were delivered.

LORD DIPLOCK. My Lords, I have had the advantage of reading in draft the speech
of my noble and learned friend Lord Bridge. I agree with it, and for the reasons which
h   he gives I would allow this appeal.

LORD KEITH OF KINKEL. My Lords, I have had the benefit of reading in advance
the speech to be delivered by my noble and learned friend Lord Bridge. I agree that, for
the reasons given by him, this appeal should be allowed.

j   **LORD BRIDGE OF HARWICH.** My Lords, on 9 May 1980 the respondent's
employers became insolvent and in consequence the respondent was dismissed without
notice. Having been continuously employed for 12 years or more the respondent was
entitled by virtue of s 49(1)(c) of the Employment Protection (Consolidation) Act 1978
to not less than 12 weeks' notice. The wrongful dismissal being attributable to the
employers' insolvency, the employers' liability to the employee in respect thereof is

imposed on the Secretary of State by s 122(1) and (3)(*b*) of the 1978 Act, to be met out of the Redundancy Fund, with a right over, for what it is worth, against the insolvent   *a*
employers under s 125(1). The liability of the Secretary of State cannot exceed that of the insolvent employers.

The respondent remained unemployed for more than 15 months. He received unemployment benefit and earnings-related supplement for the maximum periods of entitlement (approximately twelve months and six months respectively). After the expiry of his entitlement to unemployment benefit he received supplementary benefit.   *b*

On 3 February 1981 the Secretary of State paid the respondent £525·21. This represented the amount he would have earned during the 12 weeks' period of notice (£1,052·76) less the aggregate of unemployment benefit and earnings-related supplement which he in fact received in the same period. In due course the respondent complained to an industrial tribunal, pursuant to s 124, that he was entitled to recover the balance on the ground that the benefits received had been wrongly deducted. The tribunal rejected   *c*
this complaint.

The respondent appealed to the Employment Appeal Tribunal (see [1982] ICR 534). Put shortly the effect of their judgment was that the benefits received were, in principle, deductible in mitigation of damages for loss of earnings flowing from a wrongful dismissal, following *Secretary of State for Employment v Wilson* [1978] 3 All ER 137, [1978] 1 WLR 568 and *Parsons v BNM Laboratories Ltd* [1963] 2 All ER 658, [1964] 1 QB 95.   *d*
However, in consequence of the premature termination of his employment, the respondent, in mitigating his damages suffered during the 12 weeks' notice period, had been obliged to claim prematurely the unemployment benefit and earnings-related supplement to which he had only a limited entitlement. Having remained unemployed beyond the period of his entitlement to both these types of benefit, his ultimate position was that he had in the period of approximately fifteen months following the wrongful   *e*
dismissal received less than he would have done if he had been given due notice, been paid by his employers during the first 12 weeks and then received his unemployment benefit and earnings-related supplement for the full periods of entitlement. In effect this loss was the difference between the aggregate of unemployment benefit and earnings-related supplement paid during the first 12 weeks of unemployment and the supplementary benefit paid during the first 12 weeks after the unemployment benefit   *f*
period expired. The parties agreed this figure in the sum of £212·67 and the Employment Appeal Tribunal ultimately ordered that this sum be paid by the Secretary of State to the respondent.

The Secretary of State appealed to the Court of Appeal and the respondent renewed, by way of a respondent's notice, his contention that he was entitled to recover from the Secretary of State the full amount he would have been able to earn during the notice   *g*
period without deducting any benefits received by him.

The judgments of the Court of Appeal (Eveleigh, O'Connor and Purchas LJJ) ([1983] 3 WLR 730), as I understand them, proceed on the basis that an employee entitled under the 1978 Act to a minimum statutory period of notice to terminate his contract of employment, whether or not he is given that notice, has a statutory right to be paid the full amount due during the period of notice calculated in accordance with the provisions   *h*
of s 50 and Sch 3 and that this statutory right is not subject to any deduction by reference to a common law duty on the part of the employee to mitigate his damage.

The formal order of the Court of Appeal dismisses the appeal by the Secretary of State but makes no adjustment to the sum ordered by the Employment Appeal Tribunal to be paid to the respondent (which the logic of the judgments would seem to require to be increased to cover the full difference between the sum already paid and the amount the   *j*
respondent would have earned during the 12 weeks' notice period calculated in accordance with s 50 and Sch 3) unless, as I presume, this was intended to be covered by a clause in the order reserving liberty to apply. The Court of Appeal gave to the Secretary of State leave to appeal to your Lordships' House on his undertaking not to disturb the Court of Appeal's order as to costs in favour of the respondent and to pay the respondent's costs in this House in any event.

a   The issues arising for decision in the appeal are: (1) is an employee dismissed without notice or with less than the minimum notice required by s 49 of the 1978 Act under any duty to mitigate the damage he suffers from loss of earnings? (2) if yes, is unemployment benefit (including earnings-related supplement) to be taken into account in mitigation? (3) if questions (1) and (2) are answered affirmatively, what, if any is the effect on the damages recoverable if the employee claims unemployment benefit and earnings-related supplement during the statutory period of notice, so that his limited rights thereto are
b   exhausted before he is again employed?

   The provisions of ss 49 to 51 of and Sch 3 to the 1978 Act reproduce with detailed amendments provisions first enacted by ss 1 to 3 of and Sch 2 to the Contracts of Employment Act 1963. The detailed amendments were effected successively by the Contracts of Employment Act 1972 and the Employment Protection Act 1975. The principal provision of s 49 is to require minimum periods of notice to be given by an
c   employer to determine a contract of employment according to the length of the employee's period of continuous employment. These minima have been raised by the amendments referred to, but the basic principle by which this provision operates has remained unchanged since 1963.

   Section 50 of and Sch 3 to the 1978 Act reproduce, again with minor amendments, the provisions first enacted by s 2 of and Sch 2 to the Contracts of Employment Act 1963 for
d   calculating an employer's liability to pay the employee during the minimum period of notice required by the statute. Different formulae, modified by the Employment Protection Act 1975 in minor detail, apply to employments for which there are normal working hours and to employments for which there are no normal working hours. Special provisions apply if the employee is, during the notice period, granted leave at his own request or goes on strike. Schedule 3 contains provisions relating to sickness and
e   industrial benefit first introduced by the 1972 Act. The schedule makes no provision, because none is needed, for the case where the employee continues to perform his contractual work and receive his contractual pay during the period of notice. The evident primary purpose of the schedule is to prevent the employer denying the employee, provided he is willing to work, the benefit of the statutory notice period by denying or curtailing his opportunity to work. By para 7(1) of Sch 3 (reproducing verbatim in para
f   6(1) of Sch 2 to the Contracts of Employment Act 1963) it is provided:

   'If, during the period of notice, the employer breaks the contract of employment, payments received under this Schedule in respect of the part of the period after the breach shall go towards mitigating the damages recoverable by the employee for loss of earnings in that part of the period of notice.'

g   Finally s 51 of the 1978 Act reproduces exactly the effect of s 3 of the Contracts of Employment Act 1963 as follows:

   'If an employer fails to give the notice required by section 49, the rights conferred by section 50 (with Schedule 3) shall be taken into account in assessing his liability for breach of the contract.'

h   As a commentary on the effect of these provisions I cannot do better than adopt the language of Phillips J, giving the judgment of the Employment Appeal Tribunal in *Secretary of State for Employment v Wilson* [1978] 3 All ER 137 at 140, [1978] 1 WLR 568 at 572, a case decided under the Contracts of Employment Act 1972, as amended by the Employment Protection Act 1975. He said:

j   'These provisions, and the scheme of the 1972 Act generally, suggest to us that the intention of the Act is to incorporate into the contract of employment the statutory terms laid down by the Act, and that an employee who wished to enforce them would sue on his contract of employment as statutorily amended, and not on the statute. A contrary view is possible, but the matter seems to us to be put beyond doubt by s 3 which deals specifically, according to the side note, with the "Measure of damages in proceedings against employers". It provides: "If an employer fails to give the notice required by section 1 of this Act, the rights conferred by section 2 of this Act (with Schedule 2 to this Act) shall be taken into account in assessing his *a* liability for breach of the contract." This section plainly assumes that if an employer fails to give the notice required by s 1 the remedy for the employee is to proceed by way of a claim for damages for breach of contract and that in those proceedings when quantifying his loss the rights conferred by s 2 (in this case to be paid during the period of notice) will be taken into account. If this is right, and if the employee's remedy is of that kind, it seems to us that it must follow that the amount of damages *b* falls to be reduced by earnings of the employee during the period of notice.'

Even without reference to the sidenote to s 3 (now s 51 of the 1978 Act), which may not strictly be available as an aid to construction, the conclusion is, to my mind, clear that a claim for failure to give notice under s 51 is a claim for wrongful dismissal, the only 'breach of contract' which the section can possibly have in contemplation, and that the liability of the employer for that breach of contract is a liability in damages, calculated *c* with regard to the amount the dismissed employee could have earned in accordance with his rights conferred by s 50 and Sch 3 if he had been given due notice, but subject to the duty of mitigation.

Giving the leading judgment in the Court of Appeal, Eveleigh LJ, having set out the principal provisions of ss 49, 50, 51 and 122 of and Sch 3 to the 1978 Act, said ([1983] 3 WLR 730 at 735): *d*

'The above provisions are those which are directly relevant to the present claim. However, the Act forms a comprehensive code governing the relationship between employer and employee and contains many sections in which the employer is under a liability to make a payment of some kind. The issue in the present case is whether the liability with which we are concerned is basically contractual or whether it is *e* statutory, creating rights for the employee which are his by virtue of his status and not by virtue of contract. To answer this question it is necessary to look at the Act as a whole.'

It is here that I must respectfully part company with him. The 1978 Act was a pure consolidation. In so far as it reproduced the relevant provisions of the Contracts of *f* Employment Act 1972, as amended by the Employment Protection Act 1975, it cannot have changed their meaning. Nor, as it seems to me, can the Employment Protection Act 1975 itself, which only amended the Contracts of Employment Act 1972 in very minor respects, conceivably have been intended to effect a radical change in the nature of the rights derived from the provisions now found in ss 49 to 51 of and Sch 3 to the 1978 Act.

Eveleigh LJ relied on provisions of the 1978 Act found in Pts II and III, which derive *g* from the Employment Protection Act 1975, and in Pt V, which derive from the Industrial Relations Act 1971, as amended by the Trade Union and Labour Relations Act 1974. In my respectful opinion, these are all quite irrelevant to the construction of ss 49 to 51 and Sch 3.

I would therefore hold, contrary to the view of the Court of Appeal, that an employee dismissed without the minimum statutory notice to which he is entitled under s 49 may *h* recover damages for breach of contract under s 51 but is under a duty to mitigate those damages.

The question whether unemployment benefit is to be deducted in mitigation of the damages due to a plaintiff wrongfully dismissed is authoritatively settled for the Court of Appeal by the decision in *Parsons v BNM Laboratories Ltd* [1963] 2 All ER 658, [1964] 1 QB 95, where it was held by Sellers, Harman and Pearson LJJ that the benefits were *j* deductible. It was suggested in argument before your Lordships that that decision could not stand with the reasoning of your Lordships' House in *Parry v Cleaver* [1969] 1 All ER 555, [1970] AC 1, but I have found no clear statement of principle in the speeches of their Lordships in that case which is applicable to the question which your Lordships now have to decide. *Parsons's* case having stood and been acted on for 20 years, your

Lordships should, I submit, hesitate to overrule it unless clearly persuaded that it was wrongly decided. For my part I am not so persuaded.

First, as a matter of causation, it is clear that the loss of earnings and the receipt of benefit both flow from the same cause; indeed the whole purpose of the compulsory scheme which makes unemployment benefit available to all those who lose their employment is to provide the unemployed man with a substitute for earnings. Second, if the benefits are not deducted, the dismissed employee during the period of notice to which he was entitled recovers double compensation. Are there any countervailing considerations which would promote a sense of injustice that the unemployment benefits should inure to the advantage of the employer who is the contract breaker? The two categories of receipt by the victim of a tort or a breach of contract which provide the classic examples of sums not falling to be deducted from the damages he may claim are the fruits of private insurance or of private benevolence. The reasons for thes exclusions are obvious. I do not see any analogy at all between the generosity of private subscribers to a fund for the victims of some disaster who also have claims for damages against a tortfeasor, and the state providing subventions for the needy out of funds which, in one way or another, have been subscribed compulsorily by various classes of citizens. The concept of public benevolence provided by the state is one I find difficult to comprehend. But there is a more respectable argument for the view that unemployment benefit is the fruit of insurance to which employers and employees and the state have all contributed in different proportions. This is superficially plausible, because unemployment benefit is paid out of a fund known as the National Insurance Fund. But it is to be observed that less than 10% of the fund is expended on unemployment benefit (the lion's share goes to provide retirement pensions) and, more significantly, that the payments which sustain the fund, by whatever name called, are made by way of compulsory levies of citizens in different circumstances, and to some extent on the general body of taxpayers, so that they may properly be regarded as much more closely analogous to a tax than to a contractual premium payable under an insurance policy. My Lords, these considerations lead me to the conclusion that *Parsons*'s case was rightly decided. I fear that all I have done is to express at much greater length what was said so much more neatly and concisely by Pearson LJ in *Parsons*'s case [1963] 2 All ER 658 at 684, [1964] 1 QB 95 at 143–144:

> 'Is the plaintiff's receipt of unemployment benefit a matter too remote to be taken into consideration in ascertaining his net loss resulting from the wrongful dismissal? The common-sense answer is that of course it is not too remote. It is not "completely collateral". The dismissal caused the plaintiff to become unemployed, and therefore entitled, as a matter of general right under the system of state insurance and not by virtue of any private insurance policy of his own, to receive unemployment benefit. The effect of the dismissal was not to deprive him of all income but to reduce his income by substituting unemployment benefit for his salary. It would be unrealistic to disregard the unemployment benefit, because to do so would confer on the plaintiff, to the extent of £59 2s. 6d., a fortuitous windfall in addition to compensation.'

What was the effect, if any, on the respondent's entitlement to damages against his former employers of his receipt of unemployment benefit and earnings-related supplement 12 weeks earlier than if he had received the notice to which he was entitled, and, since he remained unemployed, the consequent exhaustion of his rights to both those benefits 12 weeks earlier than otherwise would have been the case? I was at first inclined to think that the damages must be assessed exclusively by what he lost in earnings, less what he received in benefit, during the 12 weeks' notice period and that any later diminution of benefits attributable to continuing unemployment was too remote to be taken into account. On further reflection I have reached the conclusion that this is not the right approach to the question. A plaintiff who has suffered damage need only account by way of mitigation for the *net* gain accruing to him, of a kind properly to be taken into account, and which he would not have received but for the tort or breach of contract giving rise to his damage. Thus typically, a wrongfully dismissed employee will be able to set off against any earnings in a new job to be deducted from his damages *a* the reasonable expenses of travelling and advertising incurred in obtaining that new job. So here I think that the right way in which the question should be formulated is: against the lost earnings caused by the respondent's dismissal without notice, what was, in the events which happened, the net gain to the respondent in benefits received? The answer to this question is not the actual benefits received during the 12 weeks' notice period, but the lesser sum received as supplementary benefit after the premature expiry of the *b* unemployment benefit and earnings-related supplements periods occasioned by the wrongful dismissal. This is the answer given by the Employment Appeal Tribunal, whose order required the Secretary of State to make up the difference between the benefits deducted in calculating the original payment by the Secretary of State and the supplementary benefit received in the first 12 weeks after the unemployment benefit period expired, an amount agreed, as mentioned earlier, in the sum of £212·67.   *c*

This result is unlikely to cause practical difficulty when the wrongfully dismissed employee is claiming in the courts against a solvent employer. By the time the action is heard, the necessary facts are likely to be known, or, if necessary, an adjournment can be sought. We were much pressed in argument with the practical difficulties to which this result would give rise in a case where the insolvent employer's liability falls to be met by the Secretary of State under s 122(3)(*b*) of the 1978 Act. The Secretary of State, it is said, *d* will normally pay promptly, within, say, six months, of the dismissal. At that stage he will properly deduct the full amount of the unemployment benefit received by the employee during the notice period. What happens if after a further six months the employee is still unemployed, the unemployment benefit period expires and supplementary benefit at the lower rate is paid instead? It seems to me that the practical answer is that any further sum then accruing due to the employee in accordance with *e* the principles indicated in this opinion, if not paid voluntarily by the Secretary of State, could properly be the subject of a claim to an industrial tribunal under s 124 and, if the claim was out of time, there would be an unanswerable claim for an extension under the provisions of the section.

I would allow the appeal to the extent necessary to restore the order of the Employment Appeal Tribunal dated 7 December 1982.   *f*

LORD BRANDON OF OAKBROOK. My Lords, I have had the advantage of reading in draft the speech prepared by my noble and learned friend Lord Bridge. I agree with it, and for the reasons which he gives I would allow the appeal to the extent proposed by him.

g

LORD BRIGHTMAN. My Lords, I agree with the speech of my noble and learned friend Lord Bridge, and would allow this appeal.

Appeal allowed.

Solicitors: *Treasury Solicitor*; *Leonard Ross & Craig*, agents for *Pearlman Grazin & Co*, Leeds (for the respondent).

Mary Rose Plummer   Barrister.

a # Thompson and others v Smiths Shiprepairers (North Shields) Ltd
and other actions

b QUEEN'S BENCH DIVISION AT NEWCASTLE-UPON-TYNE
MUSTILL J
5–9, 12–16, 19–23, 27, 28 SEPTEMBER, 3–6 OCTOBER, 14 NOVEMBER 1983

Master and servant – Duty of master – Safety of employees – Common law duty to protect employee from foreseeable risk of danger to health – Noise – Danger to hearing – Noise in
c *shipbuilding and shiprepairing yards – Failure to provide protection against noise – Failure to investigate effect of noise levels in yards – Test of liability – Whether liability to be determined according to practice in industry as a whole.*

Master and servant – Liability of master – Negligence – Apportionment of liability – Apportionment between period when employer in breach of duty and period when not in breach –
d *Employees' hearing progressively impaired by stages because of exposure to noise in course of employment – Noise in shipbuilding yards – Employer failing to provide protection to employees – Common practice throughout industry not to provide protection when damage initially caused – Employer later in breach of duty of care in not providing protection – Whether employer's liability to be apportioned between period when employer in breach of duty and period when not in breach.*

e The plaintiffs were employed as labourers or fitters in shipbuilding and shiprepairing yards over a long period, stretching from the 1940s (or earlier) to the 1970s. During their employment in the yards the plaintiffs were exposed to excessive noise which by stages progressively impaired their hearing. At all material times the employers knew that noise levels in the yards exposed their workforce to the risk of hearing loss but failed to
f provide the workforce with any protection against noise until the early 1970s. Up until 1963 there was no official guidance or effective expert advice on the problem of industrial noise and the employers' inertia and indifference to the problem was in line with common practice throughout the industry, which at that time treated industrial noise as an inescapable feature of the industry. In 1963 the Ministry of Labour issued a pamphlet on industrial noise and thereafter expert advice and adequate and reasonable protective
g devices were available to the employers. In 1980 and 1981 the plaintiffs brought actions against their employers claiming damages for negligence in failing to provide protection against noise in the yards or to investigate and take advice on noise levels and thus causing the plaintiffs' hearing to be impaired. Although it was impossible to quantify precisely when particular degrees of damage had been caused to the plaintiffs, the evidence clearly established that a substantial part of the damage had occurred before 1963 and that after
h 1963 the plaintiffs' exposure to noise in the yards had merely aggravated the existing damage and accelerated the progress of the plaintiffs towards hearing disability and handicap. The employers admitted that the plaintiffs had suffered impairment of hearing resulting from exposure to noise in the yards but contended that their failure to provide protection amounted to actionable negligence only in respect of the latter part of the plaintiffs' employment and that therefore they were only liable for the damage which
j was caused to the plaintiffs during that part of their employment.

Held – (1) The test to be applied in determining the point of time at which an employer's failure to provide protection against industrial noise constituted actionable negligence was what would have been done at any particular time by a reasonable and prudent employer who was properly but not extraordinarily solicitous for his workers'

safety in the light of what he knew or ought to have known at the time. Accordingly, an
employer was not negligent if at any given time he followed a recognised practice which   *a*
had been followed throughout the industry as a whole for a substantial period, even
though that practice may not have been without mishap, and at that particular time the
consequences of a particular type of risk were regarded as an inescapable feature of the
industry. Furthermore, the question of whether an employer was negligent in failing to
take the initiative in seeking out knowledge about facts which were not obvious was to
be judged according to the practice at the time in the industry. In all the circumstances,   *b*
the employers' failure to provide protection against noise in the yards did not constitute
actionable negligence before 1963, although thereafter it did (see p 888 *h* to p 889 *f* and
p 894 *j* to p 895 *b d e* and *h*, post); *Morris v West Hartlepool Steam Navigation Co Ltd* [1956]
1 All ER 385 and dictum of Swanwick J in *Stokes v GKN (Bolts and Nuts) Ltd* [1968] 1 WLR
at 1783 applied.

(2) Where an employer failed to provide his employee with protection against   *c*
exposure to industrial noise which caused the employee to suffer progressive impairment
of his hearing by stages and where that failure was not a breach of the employer's duty of
care at the time the damage was initially caused to the employee but became a breach of
duty at a later stage, the employer was only liable for that part of the damage which
occurred to the employee during the period when the employer was in breach of duty.
It followed that the plaintiffs could not recover the whole of their loss from their   *d*
employers but were only entitled to recover compensation for the additional detriment
they had suffered during the period when the employers were in breach of duty.
However, in apportioning the plaintiffs' loss and the damages to which they were entitled
the court would make allowances in the plaintiffs' favour to take account of the
uncertainties involved in making such an apportionment (see p 906 *c* to *g*, p 908 *a* to *g*,
p 909 *e* to *j*, p 910 *c d*, p 915 *a* to *h* and p 916 *b* to *d* and *h* to p 917 *a*, post); *Dingle v*   *e*
Associated Newspapers Ltd [1961] 1 All ER 897 and *McGhee v National Coal Board* [1972] 3
All ER 1008 considered.

Notes
For an employer's common law duty of care, see 16 Halsbury's Laws (4th edn) para 715,
and for the standard of care in negligence generally, see 34 ibid 10.   *f*
    For apportionment of damages for negligence, see 12 ibid para 1210.

Cases referred to in judgment
Baker v Willoughby [1969] 3 All ER 1528, [1970] AC 467, [1970] 2 WLR 50, HL.
Balfour v William Beardmore & Co Ltd 1956 SLT 205.
Bank View Mill Ltd v Nelson Corp and Fryer & Co (Nelson) Ltd [1942] 2 All ER 477; *rvsd*   *g*
    [1943] 1 All ER 299, CA.
Berry v Stone Manganese and Marine Ltd [1972] 1 Lloyd's Rep 182.
Bonnington Castings Ltd v Wardlaw [1956] 1 All ER 615, [1956] AC 613, [1956] 2 WLR
    707, HL.
Cartwright v GKN Sankey Ltd [1972] 2 Lloyd's Rep 242; *rvsd* (1973) 14 KIR 349, CA.
Clarkson v Modern Foundries Ltd [1958] 1 All ER 33, [1957] 1 WLR 1210.   *h*
Crookall v Vickers-Armstrong Ltd [1955] 2 All ER 12, [1955] 1 WLR 659.
Dingle v Associated Newspapers Ltd [1961] 1 All ER 897, [1961] 2 QB 162, [1961] 2 WLR
    523, CA.
Fazel v Cape Insulation Ltd (6 April 1982, unreported), QBD at Manchester.
Heal v Garringtons Ltd (26 May 1981, unreported), QBD.
Heslop v Metalock (Britain) Ltd (24 November 1981, unreported), QBD.   *j*
Jobling v Associated Dairies Ltd [1981] 2 All ER 752, [1982] AC 794, [1981] 3 WLR 155,
    HL.
Long v Thiessen & Laliberte (1968) 65 WWR (NS) 577.
McGhee v National Coal Board [1972] 3 All ER 1008, [1973] 1 WLR 1, HL.
Moeliker v A Reyrolle & Co Ltd [1977] 1 All ER 9, [1977] 1 WLR 132, CA.

a   *Morris v West Hartlepool Steam Navigation Co Ltd* [1956] 1 All ER 385, [1956] AC 552, [1956] 1 WLR 177, HL.

Nicholson v Atlas Steel Foundry and Engineering Co Ltd [1957] 1 All ER 776, [1957] 1 WLR 613, HL.

Robinson v British Rail Engineering Ltd (18 June 1981, unreported), QBD; *affd* [1982] CA Bound Transcript 438.

Smith v British Rail Engineering Ltd [1980] CA Transcript 532.

b   *Smith v Manchester Corp* (1974) 17 KIR 1, CA.

Stevenson v Buchanan & Brock Pty Ltd [1971] VR 503.

Stokes v GKN (Bolts and Nuts) Ltd [1968] 1 WLR 1776.

Wallhead v Ruston & Hornsby Ltd (1973) 14 KIR 285.

Cases also cited

c   *Brooks v J & P Coates (UK) Ltd* [1984] 1 All ER 702.

Carragher v Singer Manufacturing Co Ltd 1974 SLT 28.

Cartledge v E Jopling & Sons Ltd [1963] 1 All ER 341, [1963] AC 758, HL.

Cavanagh v Ulster Weaving Co Ltd [1959] 2 All ER 745, [1960] AC 145, HL.

Clark v MacLennan [1983] 1 All ER 416.

Firman v Ellis [1978] 2 All ER 851, [1978] QB 886, CA.

d   *McIntyre v Doulton & Co Ltd* (22 March 1978, unreported), QBD.

Nimmo v Alexander Cowan & Sons Ltd [1967] 3 All ER 187, [1968] AC 107, HL.

Thompson v Brown [1981] 2 All ER 296, [1981] 1 WLR 744, HL.

Consolidated actions

By writs issued in 1981 and 1982, Albert Edward Thompson, David Mason Gray and
e   James William Nicholson, each of whom at the material time was a labourer in a ship
repair yard, brought actions (the group A actions) against their employer, Smiths
Shiprepairers (North Shields) Ltd (Smiths), claiming damages for industrial deafness
alleged to have been caused by Smith's negligence and/or breach of statutory duty in
failing to protect the plaintiffs from exposure to excessive noise at work; and William
Blacklock, Robert Waggott and John Alexander Mitchell, each of whom at the material
f   time was a fitter in a shipbuilding yard, brought similar actions (the group B actions)
against their respective employers, Swan Hunter Shipbuilders Ltd (Swan Hunter) in the
case of Mr Blacklock and Mr Waggott, and Vickers Armstrong Ltd (Vickers) and Swan
Hunter in the case of Mr Mitchell. On 28 January 1983 Mustill J ordered that all six
actions should be consolidated and should proceed together with three more similar
actions (the group C actions) brought by Joseph Hutchinson, Eric Doughty and John
g   McQuillan against Austin & Pickersgill Ltd, that the nine actions should be divided into
the three groups A, B and C and that the actions in each group should be tried together
and each group of actions should be tried consecutively. In the event, Mustill J tried the
group A and B actions but postponed trial of the group C actions. The facts are set out in
the judgment.

h   *Christopher Rose QC, Anthony Temple* and *Oliver Ticciati* for the group A plaintiffs.
Richard Clegg QC, John Hoggett and *Roger Farley* for the group B plaintiffs.
Brian Appleby QC, L D Lawton QC, William Woodward and *Peter Bowers* for Smiths and
Swan Hunter.
Christopher Holland QC and *Stuart Brown* for Vickers.

j   *Cur adv vult*

14 November. The following judgment was delivered.

MUSTILL J. It has been known for at least 150 years that persons working in conditions
of excessive noise are liable to suffer deafness. In 1886 Thomas Barr delivered a paper

which described many of the most important features of what is now called noise-
induced hearing loss. Since the beginning of this century, and probably long before,   *a*
shipyards have been recognised as noisy places, where workers have tended to become
deaf. Everyone knew this, but nobody did anything about it. Apathy and fatalism
prevailed amongst workers, employers, trades unions and legislators alike. Deafness was
treated as an inescapable fact of shipyard life. Not until the early 1970s was any effective
and systematic provision made for the protection of persons employed in shipbuilding
and ship repair yards. In consequence, there are now thousands of people still alive whose   *b*
work has caused them to become hard of hearing. The present plaintiffs are amongst
them.

Until 1975 there was no statutory provision for persons suffering from industrial
deafness. In that year, the complaint became a prescribed disease, for the purposes of the
National Insurance (Industrial Injuries) Act 1965, so that in principle industrial injury
benefit would be payable. The conditions for benefit were, however, very stringent, and   *c*
persons such as the plaintiffs, who are not very deaf, did not qualify for payment.
Accordingly, the idea was conceived of suing the employer at common law, with the aim
of recovering damages even in those cases where the loss of hearing was comparatively
slight. The response was so widespread that the legal processes were in danger of being
swamped by the flood of claims: more than 20,000 of them. Accordingly, a number of
cases have been selected, differing as to identity of employer, type of work, length of   *d*
service, degree of deafness, and so on, with the intention of establishing a set of criteria
which would be applicable to the broad majority of claims, without the need to bring
every single claim to trial. Three distinct groups of three actions were selected. In the
event only the actions in groups A and B were heard, and are now for judgment. The
actions in group C remain for decision on some future occasion. The parties in groups A
and B are as follows: *e*

GROUP A

Plaintiff	Defendant
Mr Albert Edward Thompson	Smiths Shiprepairers (North Shields) Ltd
Mr David Mason Gray	Smiths Shiprepairers (North Shields) Ltd
Mr James William Nicholson	Smiths Shiprepairers (North Shields) Ltd

f

GROUP B   *g*

Plaintiff	Defendant
Mr William Blacklock	Swan Hunter Shipbuilders Ltd
Mr Robert Waggott	Swan Hunter Shipbuilders Ltd
Mr John Alexander Mitchell	Vickers Armstrong Ltd and Swan Hunter Shipbuilders Ltd

h

The plaintiffs in group A were all employed at the material time as labourers in ship
repair yards. The plaintiffs in group B were fitters in shipbuilding yards. All are admitted
to have suffered impairment of hearing as a result of excessive noise, or as a result of
excessive noise combined with the effects of ageing.

The actions within each group were tried together. The two groups were tried
consecutively. The issues in all six actions were to a great extent the same, and some of   *j*
the counsel, solicitors and expert witnesses took part in the trial of both groups. The legal
representation was not however the same throughout, nor was the factual and expert
evidence common to the two groups, save to the extent that some of the expert evidence
given in group A was specifically adopted for the purposes of group B. This might have
been a source of difficulty, since the parties to the group A actions were entitled to insist,

a and did insist, that the decisions in their actions should be arrived at by reference exclusively on the evidence given in the trial of group A, and without modification in the light of evidence adduced in the subsequent trial of group B, to which they were not parties. It would not have been practical, within the allotted time, to write and deliver a judgment in the group A cases before embarking on the trial of group B. Accordingly, in order to safeguard the position of the group A plaintiffs, I arrived at and formulated (without making public) a series of findings on the central issues of fact in group A. If it

b had subsequently appeared that the development of the issues in group B was such as might lead to materially different conclusions, I would have thought it appropriate to adjourn the hearing so as to deliver judgment in group A before completing the trial of group B. In the event, this did not become necessary. The shape of the issues in group B proved to be the same as in group A, and the expert evidence in group B, although in some respects more elaborate, did not materially affect the weight which I had given to

c the kindred evidence in group A, and in almost all instances served merely to expand or illustrate what had previously been said.

In these circumstances, it is appropriate to deal with the central issues of fact in a single judgment, distinguishing between the groups only where this is necessary to reflect the special positions of the individual parties.

d *The issues*

The following issues arose for decision.

A *Breach of duty at common law* (1) According to what principles should the defendants' liability at common law be adjudged? (2) What steps did the various defendants take to protect the plaintiffs from exposure to excessive noise whilst in their employment, and when were these steps taken? (3) Were these steps which could and

e should have been, but were not taken by the defendants; and, if so, when should they have been taken?

B *Breach of statutory duty* (1) Did s 26 of the Factories Act 1937, and s 29 of the Factories Act 1961 create duties which are material to the present actions? (2) If so, were the defendants in breach of these duties?

C *What is the present state of the plaintiffs' hearing capacity?*

f D *Causation* (1) Were the deficiencies in each plaintiff's hearing caused in whole or in part by any breach of duty by the respective defendants? (2) If so, in the case of each plaintiff, what, if any, part of such deficiency is proved to have been caused by exposure to excessive noise whilst the relevant defendant (or, in the case of action 1982 M no 937, the relevant defendants) was in breach of its duty under statute or at common law?

E *Damages* (1) What is the correct measure of damages for any pain, suffering and

g loss of amenity proved to have been caused to each plaintiff by a breach of duty? (Except in the case of action 1981 G no 2086 there is no claim for special damages). (2) Should any, and if so what, award be made to reflect a diminution in each plaintiff's prospects in the labour market?

F *Limitation of actions* (1) Are any of the plaintiff's claims prima facie time-barred by ss 11 and 14 of the Limitation Act 1980? (2) If so, should the court exercise its discretion

h to exclude the time limit, under s 33 of the 1980 Act?

Issues of contributory negligence were raised on the pleadings, but these were abandoned at the trial by all three defendants.

Noise and the human ear

j This case is concerned with sound which is heard by the human ear. Other methods of experiencing sound are not material. Wave-like agitations of the atmospheric air are collected by the outer ear; conducted by the middle ear; and experienced by the inner ear, where minute hairs are set in motion. This motion is translated into neural impulses which create in the brain the subjective impression of hearing. The pitch of a pure tone of sound is determined by the frequency of the wave motion which conveys it. The greater the frequency, the higher the pitch of the tone. Each doubling of frequency raises the pitch by one octave.

The basic unit of frequency is one cycle per second or one Hertz. For present purposes, however, it is more convenient to express frequencies in terms of kilohertz (kHz).

Very few sounds experienced in everyday life consist of a single pure tone. Almost always, sounds are composed of a complex mixture of frequencies across a wide range. Frequency between roughly 0.05 to 20 kHz can be perceived by the human ear. Those frequencies which are essential to the comprehension of speech lie in the band between 0.25 and 4 kHz.

A reference to the 'loudness' of a sound may have two meanings. First, it may signify the subjective impression gained by the hearer as the result of the processing of the sound by the mechanical and neurological apparatus of the ear and the brain. Second, it may mean the actual intensity with which the sound waves strike the organ of hearing. These two types of loudness are related, but only indirectly. The perceived loudness of the sound is dependent not only on its intensity but also on its frequency, on the relationship between the sound in question and other sounds being heard at the same time, and on the characteristics of the individual who is hearing the sound. Very broadly speaking, the human ear reacts logarithmically to sound, so that a perceived increase in intensity will fall far short of the actual increase in intensity. It is possible to make measurements of perceived hearing loss, but these are not sufficiently precise to be useful in a case such as the present.

On the other hand, it is possible to measure with tolerable accuracy the objective intensity of a sound at a particular point in space. The method adopted is to assume an arbitrary reference level of intensity, roughly equivalent to a sound which is just audible to the human ear, and to express the measured intensity in terms of a ratio between the intensity and the reference intensity. The human ear is capable of accommodating an immense range of noise intensities. For example, the sound of a pneumatic drill at 20 feet is about 1,000m times as intense as a sound which is barely audible. To express the ratio directly in these terms would be clumsy, and accordingly the scale is shortened by adopting a logarithmic set of units, so that every increase in intensity of 10db reflects an increase in intensity by a factor of 10. Thus a sound measured at 20 db is 10 times as intense as a sound of 10 db. A sound of 30 db is 100 times as intense as a sound of 10 db, and so on. The same principle works in reverse. Reducing a sound intensity from 100 to 70 db entails that it is reduced not to seven-tenths, but to one-thousandth, of its former value. Even an apparently trivial reduction of 3 db amounts to a halving of the intensity.

In a case such as the present, which is primarily concerned with the effects of continuous high noise levels, rather than with percussive noise, the measurement of noise intensity at one particular place and at one particular time is not sufficient. The sound to which the worker is actually exposed may be intermittent, or of varying intensity. Accordingly, means have been developed of arriving at an equivalent continuous sound level, denoted by the symbol Leq. This is the notional sound level which, in the course of an eight-hour period, would cause the same A-weighted sound energy to be recorded as that due to the actual sound over the actual working day. (I refer to A-weighting at a later stage.)

Unlike the eye, the ear has no means of protecting itself against intense sensations. The logarithmic responses of the ear enable it to accommodate large increases in intensity, but beyond a certain level, the fine hairs, put into agitation by the incoming vibrations, suffer degradation and ultimate destruction. This process is irreversible. Hearing loss caused by excessive noise does not improve spontaneously after the exposure has ceased, and there is no known cure.

The construction of the ear is such that it responds particularly well to frequencies lying between 1 and 4 kHz. Accordingly, it is the parts of the hearing mechanism which deal with frequencies in this band which suffer particular damage from excessive noise: and these are the frequencies which lie within the range of normal speech. This effect

can be seen when an audiogram is made of the patient's hearing losses. The technique is
a to present the patient with pure tones at different frequencies (of which the most
important for present purposes are 0.5, 1, 2, 4 and 6 and 8 kHz) and to measure the level
of intensity at which he first begins to perceive the tone. Where the results are depicted
in the shape of a graph which plots hearing loss against frequency, a marked dip in
hearing capacity can be seen to occur at 1 kHz (or sometimes 2 kHz) with a low point at
4 kHz often accompanied by a recovery at 8 kHz. This cliff-shaped or V-shaped graph is
b a prime diagnostic feature of noise-induced hearing loss.

Since, for the reasons just indicated, the principal risk of deafness from continuous
excessive noise is associated mainly with sound lying within the 1–4 kHz frequency
band, measurements of the total intensity at all frequencies or the intensity at any single
frequency, are likely to be misleading when the extent of the risk is assessed. Accordingly,
instruments are manufactured which give differential weight to the measured sound
c levels, so as to give a figure reflecting a notional response of a human ear. Figures which
have been adjusted in this manner are described as 'A-weighted', and are expressed as
units 'dbA'.

The impact of excessive noise is not the only cause of hearing loss. There is an ageing
process, known as presbyacusis, which entails the progressive loss of the upper frequencies.
The audiogram of a person suffering from this kind of hearing loss will display a slope,
d but the profile is of a different shape from the cliff or notch typical of noise-induced
deafness.

Quantification of hearing loss

e Expressions such as 'deafness, hearing loss and damage to hearing' are convenient
enough for general discussion, but are not sufficiently precise when it comes to assessing
the harm done to the individual's organs of hearing, the extent to which this harm was
brought about by an actionable breach of duty, and the monetary amount which is
appropriate to compensate him for the wrongdoing. Accordingly, I shall adopt the
following terminology proposed in a document referred to at the trial as 'the Blue Book'
f approved by the Councils of the British Association of Otolaryngologists and the British
Society of Audiology (although apparently not by the membership as a whole).

Hearing Impairment   This is a loss or abnormality of function of the hearing system.

Disability   This is any lack or restriction (resulting from an impairment) or ability to
receive everyday sounds, in either a quiet or noisy background, in the manner or within
the range considered normal for human hearing.

g *Handicap*   This is the disadvantage for a given individual resulting from the
impairment or disability that restricts the activities that would be expected for that
individual (taking account of age, sex and social, cultural, economic, psychological,
medical and environmental factors).

The quantification of the consequences of excessive noise proceeds in very different
ways, according to which of these three types of damage is under consideration. Hearing
h impairment cannot be measured directly by scrutinising the deterioration of the hearing
organs. An objective quantification can, however, be made by means of pure-tone
audiometry. The results of audiometric tests, when plotted as an audiogram, are an
important guide to diagnosis, in conjunction with clinical examination. They do not
however provide an immediate measure of disability, and still less of a handicap.
Attempts to make direct measurements of disability have not so far achieved great
j success. Accordingly, where schemes have been established for compensating large
numbers of sufferers from hearing loss, the technique has been to make use of an average
of hearing losses at selected frequencies, the average loss in decibels being set against a
conventional scale of disability expressed either in percentages or numbered classes. The
question whether any compensation at all is payable, and if so what the amount should

be, is then determined by the patient's rating according to the percentage or class derived from the scale.

Since the degree of impairment suffered by the individual patient very often differs markedly from one frequency to another, the choice of frequencies from which the average is taken may have an important effect on the patient's classification. Opinions have differed on the choice. In the United States, which was first in the field, the average was taken at 0.5, 1 and 2 kHz. Some experts felt, however, that this could lead to injustice, for the higher frequencies are usually lost first, so that measurements at the lower frequencies might underrate the impairment of someone whose hearing loss was in the early stages. Accordingly, a system known as the Coles–Worgan scheme was devised which took account of the loss at 4 kHz, as well as at the three lower frequencies. This system is interesting, because the assessment of disability involves not only the audiometric testing but also the clinical comparison of the subjects' apparent disability with a series of standard descriptions. The combination of these two methods leads to the subject being assigned to one of ten classes of increasing severity, each class being given a brief label, such as 'slight' or 'moderate'. These descriptions and labels are useful when it comes to the assessment of damages because they enable the court to set the disabilities of these particular plaintiffs against those of others who have previously received awards, whilst always bearing in mind that disability and handicap, unlike hearing loss, are not capable of direct quantification. Accordingly, I have incorporated them in this judgment, in the shape of Annex A.

The two selections of frequencies previously mentioned are not the only ones to have found favour. For example, averages are widely taken in the United Kingdom at 1, 2 and 3 kHz, and the scheme of compensation administered by the Department of Health and Social Security makes use of such averages, the qualification for the receipt of any payment at all being a binaural hearing loss of at least 50 db. Recently, opinions have been expressed in favour of averages at 1, 2 and 4 kHz, and these form the basis of a scheme set out in the Blue Book.

In the course of the hearing, use was made of the Coles–Worgan scheme, and of averages at 1, 2 and 3 kHz and 1, 2 and 4 kHz. It is unnecessary to decide whether one method is better than another. They all point in the same direction, provided note is taken that where the losses are comparatively small, the average at 1, 2 and 4 kHz is likely to display a larger impairment than assessments made on the other bases.

Breach of duty at common law

The plaintiffs allege that the defendants were negligent in the following respects: (i) in failing to recognise the existence of high levels of noise in their shipyards, and the fact that such noise created a risk of irreversible damage to hearing; (ii) in failing to provide any or sufficient ear protection devices, or to give the necessary advice and encouragement for the wearing of such devices as were provided; (iii) in failing to investigate and take advice on the noise levels in their yards; (iv) in failing to reduce the noise created by work in their yards; (v) in failing to organise the layout and timing of the work so as to minimise the effect of noise. In the first instance I will concentrate on items (i) and (ii), since these are by far the most substantial.

There was general agreement that the principles to be applied when weighing up allegations of this kind are correctly set out in the following passage from the judgment of Swanwick J in *Stokes v GKN (Bolts and Nuts) Ltd* [1968] 1 WLR 1776 at 1783:

'From these authorities I deduce the principles, that the overall test is still the conduct of the reasonable and prudent employer, taking positive thought for the safety of his workers in the light of what he knows or ought to know; where there is a recognised and general practice which has been followed for a substantial period in similar circumstances without mishap, he is entitled to follow it, unless in the light of common sense or newer knowledge, it is clearly bad; but, where there is developing knowledge, he must keep reasonably abreast of it and not be too slow to apply it; and where he has in fact greater than average knowledge of the risks, he may be thereby obliged to take more than the average or standard precautions. He must weigh up the risk in terms of the likelihood of injury occurring and the potential consequences if it does; and he must balance against this the probable effectiveness of the precautions that can be taken to meet it and the expense and inconvenience they involve. If he is found to have fallen below the standard to be properly expected of a reasonable and prudent employer in these respects, he is negligent.'

I shall direct myself in accordance with this succinct and helpful statement of the law, and will make only one additional comment. In the passage just cited, Swanwick J drew a distinction between a recognised practice followed without mishap, and one which in the light of common sense or increased knowledge is clearly bad. The distinction is indeed valid and sufficient for many cases. The two categories are not, however, exhaustive, as the present actions demonstrate. The practice of leaving employees unprotected against excessive noise had never been followed 'without mishap'. Yet even the plaintiffs have not suggested that it was 'clearly bad', in the sense of creating a potential liability in negligence, at any time before the mid-1930s. Between the two extremes is a type of risk which is regarded at any given time (although not necessarily later) as an inescapable feature of the industry. The employer is not liable for the consequences of such risks, although subsequent changes in social awareness, or improvements in knowledge and technology, may transfer the risk into the category of those against which the employer can and should take care. It is unnecessary, and perhaps impossible, to give a comprehensive formula for identifying the line between the acceptable and the unacceptable. Nevertheless, the line does exist, and was clearly recognised in *Morris v West Hartlepool Steam Navigation Co Ltd* [1956] 1 All ER 385, [1956] AC 552. The speeches in that case show, not that one employer is exonerated simply by proving that other employers are just as negligent, but that the standard of what is negligent is influenced, although not decisively, by the practice in the industry as a whole. In my judgment, this principle applies not only where the breach of duty is said to consist of a failure to take precautions known to be available as a means of combating a known danger, but also where the omission involves an absence of initiative in seeking out knowledge of facts which are not in themselves obvious. The employer must keep up to date, but the court must be slow to blame him for not ploughing a lone furrow.

I now turn to the facts. The inquiry must start with the knowledge of the defendants. Little time need be taken over this. Actual knowledge can be proved directly in the case of Smiths with effect from 1963, when they received a copy of the Ministry of Labour publication entitled 'Noise and the Worker' (Safety, Health and Welfare New Series Booklet no 25). It is, however, quite clear that actual knowledge can properly be inferred in the case of all the defendants from a date much earlier than this. It is true that the deleterious effects of noise were slow to attract public interest, and that attention has been concentrated much more on the environmental effects, rather than on the risk undergone by the worker. It could well be said that it was only from the mid-1950s that the problem of industrial noise began to gain general recognition. We are not here concerned, however, with general recognition. What matters is the knowledge of these particular employers, who were conducting a notoriously noisy trade.

When Thomas Barr published his masterly paper on an 'Inquiry into the Effects of Loud Sound upon the Hearing of Boilermakers and Others working in Noisy Surroundings' in the Proceedings of the Glasgow Philosophical Society in 1886, the fact that noisy work led to deafness had been known for many years. Barr's paper identified the essentials of the problem: the prevalence of the condition amongst riveters, caulkers, platers and 'holders-on'; the loss of the higher frequencies; the rapid onset of the condition; and the need to use protective devices such as cotton wool or rubber plugs, particularly in the early stages of employment. This work should have been the foundation of a sustained course of study. It was not, with the result that only recently have doctors and scientists begun to explain the mechanism and development of noise-induced hearing loss. An employer who took an interest in the subject might, for most of the twentieth century, have had to be content with published material which was *a* incomplete and in some instances misleading. But those employers who were engaged in shipbuilding and shiprepair had no need for published material. With one exception, the whole of the oral evidence and the voluminous written material very properly collected and adduced at the trial point to the same conclusion, namely that everyone in these industries took the existence of the problem for granted. The sole exception consists of the evidence given by two plaintiffs in Group B, who stated that they had not realised *b* that noise was making themselves or their workmates deaf. I suspect that this evidence was coloured by the witnesses' awareness of the issues on limitation. At all events I reject the evidence, and find that at all material times the defendants knew that the noise levels in their yards were such as to expose their workmen to a risk of hearing loss.

The next step is to consider what means the defendants took to combat this risk. Here we come to a striking feature of the case. Not one witness has been called from any of *c* the three defendants to explain what if any consideration they gave to the problem, what decisions were taken, and for what reason. The defendants were not obliged to account for their choice of witnesses and did not do so. Plainly, the further back into history the inquiry is taken, the more difficult it is to find anyone with personal knowledge of the individual employer's processes of thought. But such persons must exist in respect of more recent times, and the omission to call them has ruled out any possibility of a finding *d* that the defendants specifically addressed themselves to the question, and took a decision which was reasonable at the time, even if appearing mistaken in retrospect. On the other hand, I do not think it legitimate to draw inferences adverse to the defendants from the complete absence of factual evidence on their side, and in particular to infer that at some date in the past the management considered the problem and cynically decided to do nothing about it. It would be proper, before drawing such an inference, to test it against *e* the contemporary documents, and this is no longer possible because, with a few exceptions, none prior to the 1970s remain in existence. It is not the defendants' fault that the case is so old, and it would be unfair to assume against them that the missing documents would have revealed something damaging. This being so, I consider that the right course is to proceed on the basis that, until such dates as the existing documents begin to provide concrete information, the defendants simply shared in the indifference *f* and inertia which characterised the industry as a whole.

I therefore turn to the documents disclosed by each of the defendants. So far as concerns Smiths, these suggest that for some time before 1971 (it is impossible to say for how long) cotton wool had been available on issue from the ambulance room. The three relevant plaintiffs gave evidence, which I accept, that they had worn cotton wool (at least for the time) but this was on their own initiative. There seems to have been an experiment *g* with the use of earplugs (in the Swan Hunter group, of which Smiths had become part, if not in Smiths themselves), but this came to an end in October 1973 on the advice of the factory doctor, who considered them a potential source of damage and infection. Of more lasting worth was the introduction of Billesholm wool (see below) on some date before October 1971 (see the minutes of the defendants' safety committee meeting on 14 October 1972; the wording suggests that this was quite a recent innovation). In addition, *h* on the initiative of a trades union representative the company began to consider the provision of ear muffs for men in particularly noisy occupations. The management at first turned the suggestion down, and it was not until two years later, in November 1973, that muffs were made available in the ambulance room, initially on a restricted basis. Of the three plaintiffs, Mr Thompson and Mr Gray applied for muffs (the latter as a result of seeing a poster) in April 1974 and 1973 respectively, and thereafter continued to wear *j* them. Mr Nicholson asked for muffs on two or three occasions, but was told that they were for the men actually using the caulking, chipping and rivetting machines. None were issued to him, before he retired in 1979. There is no evidence that any of these men were offered, or asked for, Billesholm wool.

So far as concerns Swan Hunter, it appears that Billesholm wool was available some time before March 1972. During that month it was recognised that caulkers would

a require a greater degree of protection, and trials were made of the liquid seal and the solid foam types of ear muff. By the middle of 1973 muffs were on general issue to caulkers, and were also available to those working in the vicinity. Of the plaintiffs in Group B, Mr Blacklock and Mr Gray each asked for and received muffs at about that time, and thereafter wore them when they were in noisy surroundings. For some reason, Mr Mitchell did not receive ear muffs until 1979, when he applied for a pair on the

b advice of his shop steward.

The position as regards Vickers cannot now be clearly ascertained. A small group of papers has survived relating to inquiries made by the management of the Barrow yard during 1962 and 1963. (This was not Mr Mitchell's principal place of employment with Vickers.) Quotations were invited and received during 1962 for Amplivox Supersonex ear defenders (a type of plug). At about the same time, Vickers received a letter and

c pamphlet advertising the merits of Billesholm wool. During 1964 the works doctor was in correspondence with Amplivox, to obtain a quotation for a recording audiometer. There is no indication that orders were placed for these items during the remaining period of Mr Mitchell's service with Vickers, and I am satisfied from his evidence that he was given no form of protection by Vickers, except on an isolated occasion when he took part in the sea trials of a naval vessel.

d Having thus described what the defendants did do, the next step is to consider what they could have done to provide ear protection. The position may be summarised as follows.

For at least 100 years men in the shipbuilding and boiler-making trades have been putting cotton wool in their ears. It is probable that the purpose was more to reduce the unpleasant sensation of noise, rather than to prevent the onset of deafness. By the early

e years of this century, writers were suggesting the use of plugs made from rubber, vulcanite, 'clay fibre', plasticine or cobblers' wax mixed with cotton wool, and so on. The attenuating properties of these devices would have been variable. Some of them are quite good, for example the mixture of cotton wool and wax which is still on sale in chemists' shops today. Any of them would have been better than nothing. One or two passing references in the literature claim that these substances were employed by boilermakers,

f but it must be doubtful whether they achieved any widespread amount of use.

The 1914–18 war did, however, stimulate the production of a specially designed hearing protector, in the shape of the Mallock–Armstrong ear defender. This provided an average attenuation of 16 db. If worn continuously this would undoubtedly have saved many men in the shipbuilding industry from loss of hearing. It was, however, uncomfortable and difficult to retain. Whether in fact it was ever used to any great

g extent in industry must be highly questionable.

Between the two world wars a few devices, such as the 'Aurotechtor', the Soundex Vulcanite plug, and the Luxton ear stop appear to have been in commercial production. Whether they achieved any wide circulation in industry is now impossible to say.

The 1939–45 war provided an important stimulus for research in the armed forces (notably the Royal Air Force), not only into the physiology of noise-induced deafness, but

h also into ways in which the human ear might be protected. The investigations covered two species of protector which are material to the present case. First, there were two types of earplugs. Amongst these, the most important was the V-51R earplug. This was an efficient device, since it gave a mean attenuation over seven frequencies of 24 db, and considerably better at the important 2 and 4 kHz octaves. It was comparatively comfortable to wear, and in an unpublished Royal Air Force report by Air Vice-Marshal

j Dixon and Squadron Leader (subsequently Professor) Hinchcliffe, produced in 1954 it was described as the 'preferred insert defender'. The V-51R appears to have been introduced to the English commercial market in about 1951.

The other type of protector examined by the Royal Air Force researchers was a novelty: namely the ear muff. At first, muffs were rather primitive. The Nosonic Mk 1 ear muffs had an average protection of 14.2 db, although with a much better performance in the upper frequency ranges. The Nosonic Mk 2 was more effective, with an average attenuation of 21.8 db. It was, however, distinctly uncomfortable to wear, since the sponge rubber ear pieces had had to be gripped tightly by means of a headband if they were to give proper protection. Subsequently, by about 1958, liquid seal ear muffs were developed and marketed. These were easier to wear, but they tended to leak.

It will be seen from this summary that there was an interval of several years between the moment when the defendants could have taken steps to furnish ear protection, and the time when this was in fact made available to their employees. The defendants say that when assessing their culpability for hearing losses sustained during the period, account should be taken of more than one factor.

First, it is contended that the defendants were not unique in their lack of precaution for their employees' welfare. So far as concerns the shipbuilding industry, the defendants cannot be said (on the evidence as tendered at the trial) to have been any more remiss than others similarly placed. There were traces in the material put before the court that one shipyard may in later years have taken some steps to reduce the incidence of noise. Quite apart from the fact that this was not in an admissible form, the information was far too imprecise to justify a finding adverse to these defendants.

Again, looking beyond the shipbuilding industry to the life of the nation as a whole, the defendants can fairly point out that virtually everyone who might have been expected to concern themselves with the problem of occupational deafness in fact paid very little attention to it. (i) Legislative intervention in the field of industrial noise has been late and fragmentary. The Factories Acts have never specifically referred to noise. Only two sets of regulations (in the woodworking industry, and in relation to the cabs of agricultural tractors) have demanded protection for the ears of workers. The shipbuilding industry is governed by stringent regulations, yet these have nothing to say about noise. In the field of compensation, as distinct from prevention, it was not until 1975 that industrial deafness became a prescribed disease, nearly twenty years after the enactment of the legislation which made such prescription possible. This is in sharp contrast to the position in the United States, where such deafness has been the subject of federal and state workmen's compensation legislation for several decades. (ii) Discussion in Parliament was almost non-existent during the period under consideration. Occasionally a question would be asked, eliciting neutral answers: such as those given in 1953 and 1967 to the effect that research was in progress. The few debates were largely concerned with the environmental effects of noise. (iii) Commissions of inquiry paid little and belated attention to the topic. It is understandable that the report of the Geddes committee on shipbuilding (Shipbuilding Inquiry Committee 1965–1966 Report (March 1966) (Cmnd 2937)) made only fleeting reference to noise, since the inquiry was concerned with ways to make the industry more competitive. Much more striking is the fact that when the Wilson committee was set up to report on the problem of noise (Noise, Final Report (July 1963) (Cmnd 2056)) its terms of reference were not originally conceived to embrace the effect of noise on the worker, and it was on the committee's own initiative that the subject was investigated and made the subject of Ch 13 (Occupational Exposure to High Levels of Noise). (iv) The representatives of the workers seem to have given the matter a low priority. In 1932 a forward-looking doctor addressed a meeting in Plymouth on the problems of noise in the dockyard, and distributed samples of earplugs. The lecture was summarised in the annual report of the Trades Union Congress. Yet when a member of Parliament asked in the House of Commons 28 years later, whether representations had been made by organisations of workers, he was told that they had not. Whatever activity there may have been on the part of the unions before and after this date seems to have been concerned more with procuring the prescription of deafness as an industrial disease, rather than forcing the employers to prevent it from happening. It is perhaps also relevant to note that those concerned with advising sufferers from industrial deafness were, for one reason or another, slow to appreciate the possibility that the employers might be regarded as sufficiently blameworthy to have incurred liability at common law: for the first action claiming damages in negligence was not heard until 1969, six years after the publication of 'Noise and the Worker' (Safety, Health and Welfare New Series Booklet no 25), which explained the problem, and some of the steps which might be taken to overcome it, in the clearest possible way. (v) Evidence as to the attitude of the employers' organisations is incomplete, but it does appear that they paid little attention to the topic until galvanised by the publication in 1972 of the Department of Employment's code of practice for reducing the exposure of employed persons to noise (prepared by the Industrial Health Advisory Committee's sub-committee on noise, presided over by C H Sisson). It is perhaps characteristic that when a conference was held in Newcastle-upon-Tyne on safety in the shipbuilding and shiprepair industries none of the speakers made any reference to noise. (vi) The inspectorate of factories, which is the guardian of the public interest on questions of safety in reference to individual places of work showed no great concern about noise. In the absence of legislation it could not have gone further than exhortation, but it did not even go so far, during the period now under consideration. Six years after the publication of the Wilson report, the annual report of HM Chief Inspector of Factories for 1969 (Cmnd 4461) stated that the inspectorate had been giving increasing thought to the subject. Only in 1968 were a few inspectors given instruction on noise measurement, and issued with the necessary instruments. It is plain that this was regarded as a first and tentative step towards a programme of noise control.

Viewed with hindsight, this seems a depressing history of apathy and neglect. There must be a reason for it. One suggestion by the defendants adopted the following passage from the foreword to the Department of Employment's 1972 code of practice:

> 'The general solution to this problem, which is a complex one, has been hampered more by ignorance than neglect. Until the pioneer work of Professor Burns and Dr. Robinson was published in March, 1970, we lacked the necessary scientific knowledge of the precise levels of noise, and of the duration of exposure to them, which can cause damage.'

It is not for the court to say whether this is a sufficient explanation for the previous absence of authoritative official guidance on the levels at which noise exposure becomes dangerous, or the ways in which noise levels can be accurately measured and corrected, and on the ways of forecasting the protection given by various kinds of ear defender. For my part, I find it hard to see how a lack of exact knowledge could justify the general lack of concern by those directly concerned, in the existence of the problem and the need to do something about it. In any event, this is not the point. Even if accurate information was not available, the defendants knew the nature of the risk. Means were available to minimise it. The only question is whether the defendants should have been sufficiently aware in general terms that solutions existed, and should have made use of them, even in the absence of precise knowledge of their value. I return to this later.

Other and more convincing explanations have been suggested for the lack of urgency. In human terms, deafness is an underrated affliction. The hardships imposed by blindness are there for all the sighted to see. More imagination is needed to picture the isolation, frustration and fatigue endured by those who cannot hear. Hardness of hearing can be sometimes as much a matter for derision, as for sympathy.

Furthermore, it is realistic, not insensitive, to acknowledge that the handicaps suffered by these plaintiffs are less striking than those of other victims of industrial life. Excessive noise does not kill, or shorten the expectation of life. It does not lead to paralysis, mutilation or scarring. There is no pain, although in some instances a distressing tinnitus may be an additional symptom. At the levels with which we are concerned, exposure for the whole of a working lifetime does not bring about total deafness, or anything approaching it. The symptoms do not render the sufferer unfit for further work in the industry: indeed, more than one writer has pointed out the unpleasant paradox that a worker made deaf by excessive noise is better able to endure the discomfort of such noise than a person with unimpaired hearing. All in all, the consequence of a noise-induced hearing loss goes no further than a real, but not total, diminution in the opportunity to enjoy life to the full.

This feature is particularly important in the context of an industry where the possibility of serious injury and even death is ever present, and where hardihood is taken for granted. It does not form an excuse for neglect, but it is part of the perspective against which to adjudge the culpability of omissions taking place ten, twenty or thirty years ago.

I now turn to the next group of facts relevant to the issue of negligence, namely those concerning the employer's means of knowing what appliances were available to minimise the effect of noise. It is plain that great pains have been taken to comb the literature for references to protection. The fruits have been, comparatively speaking, modest. Some of the references come from publications (eg 'Annals of Otolaryngology', 1944 (US)) of which even a specialist might excusably have been ignorant. Others would be accessible to a specialist, but not to an industrialist or his works doctor. One must be careful, when considering documents culled for the purpose of a trial, and studied by reference to a single isolated issue, not to forget that they once formed part of a flood of print on numerous aspects of industrial life, in which many items were bound to be overlooked. However conscientious the employer, he cannot read every textbook and periodical, attend every exhibition and conference, on every technical issue which might arise in the course of his business; nor can he necessarily be expected to grasp the importance of every single item which he comes across. Thus, if a works doctor regularly reads the Lancet from cover to cover he would have seen the modest announcement of the V-51R earplug in the edition of 28 April 1951, but it would in my view be unrealistic to hold that all shipbuilders and repairers were thereafter on notice of the existence of plastic earplugs whose manufacturers claimed an attenuation of 30 db.

Nevertheless, references to protective devices in a wide variety of printed sources became more common during the 1950s, and the safety and medical officers of factories and yards might well, from those sources alone, have been able to recognise that ear muffs and protective inserts were on the market; so they could set about tracking them down, and deciding whether they were worth the considerable effort which would have been required to have them put into use.

More important than this, however, was the availability of expert advice. I am satisfied on the evidence that there were organisations, commercial and otherwise, which if approached by an enterprising medical officer, could and would have put him in touch with methods of ear protection, and would have given advice on their efficacy. Certainly from 1962 onwards the advice ought to have embraced, and there is no reason to doubt that it would have embraced Billesholm wool and varieties of liquid seal ear muffs.

The question has, however, been raised whether if the defendants had ordered protectors the men would have consented to wear them. This argument has no relevance to any date later than about 1973, for we know that the plaintiffs did thereafter wear whatever ear protection was offered to them. It is, however, a factor to be taken into account in respect of earlier years, for workers (and, importantly, their union representatives) were much less aware than latterly of the usefulness and desirability of wearing protective devices of any kind. A shipyard employer who had tried in (say) 1951 to blaze a trail by urging or compelling his men to wear such devices might well have taken some considerable time to win them over. Furthermore, account must be taken of the fact that some of the earlier devices, even if providing useful attenuation, were neither easy to retain nor comfortable to wear. For example, the Mallock–Armstrong protector was not designed, and not suitable, for continuous wear. In my judgment the same applies, though to a much lesser extent, to the V-51R earplug. Perhaps this could have been worn successfully throughout a 12-hour shift. Nobody tried, in the shipbuilding industry, and the evidence on its use elsewhere is thin. But I believe that it would have been hard indeed to bring it into general use much before the dates when more comfortable devices were available to give a satisfactory degree of protection.

In the light of all these factors, one must answer this question. From what date would a reasonable employer, with proper but not extraordinary solicitude for the welfare of his workers, have identified the problem of excessive noise in his yard, recognised that it a was capable of solution, found a possible solution, weighed up the potential advantage and disadvantages of that solution, decided to adopt it, acquired a supply of the protectors, set in train the programme of education necessary to persuade the men and their representatives that the system was useful and not potentially deleterious, experimented with the system, and finally put it into full effect? This question is not capable of an accurate answer, and indeed none is needed, as will appear when the scientific aspects of the case are considered.

b   Various years were selected as rough markers, for the purpose of argument. I reject without hesitation the notion that the date lay somewhere in the years immediately preceding and following the 1939–45 war. It was not until 1951, with the inconspicuous entry of the V-51R into the United Kingdom market, that even a really enlightened employer would have started to ask himself whether something could be done. Even then, I consider that it pitches the standard of care too high to say that an employer

c would have been negligent, from that date, in failing to find, decide on, and put into effect a system of using the protectors then available. At the other extreme, I consider that the choice of a date as late as 1973 cannot be sustained. The problem, and the existence of different ways in which it might have been combated, had been well known for years; there had been devices which were both reasonably effective, and reasonably easy to wear; and if the employers did not know precisely what they were they would

d have had no difficulty in finding out.

        All this being so, I conclude that the year 1963 marked the dividing line between a reasonable (if not consciously adopted) policy of following the same line of inaction as other employers in the trade, and a failure to be sufficiently alert and active to measure up to the standards laid down in the reported cases. After the publication of 'Noise and the Worker' there was no excuse for ignorance. Given the availability of Billesholm wool

e and reasonably effective ear muffs, there was no lack of a remedy. From that point, the defendants, by offering their employees nothing, were in breach of duty at common law.

        Having reached this conclusion, it is unnecessary to deal at length with the other grounds on which negligence is alleged. Failure to investigate the level of noise could not as a separate complaint found liability on a date earlier than the one determined by the considerations which I have already mentioned. As regards reduction in noise levels by

f methods of suppression at source, I am not satisfied on the evidence (a) that such methods were practicable, except perhaps as regards ventilation fans, (b) that if adopted in respect of fans, the general noise levels endured by these plaintiffs would have been affected at all, or if they had been affected, by what amounts and over what periods of time, or (c) that such methods were sufficiently current before 1963 to justify the finding of a breach of duty before that date. Similarly, as regards reorganisation of layout and timing, I

g would have required full and explicit evidence from persons experienced in the production side of shipbuilding before I could find that even today the defendants are being negligent in failing to take such measures, still less that they ought to have been taken twenty or thirty years ago. No such evidence was adduced at the trial. The allegation must be rejected.

        Accordingly I shall approach the remaining issues in the actions on the footing that

h the defendants were in breach of their duties on and from a date in the year 1963 which I do not intend precisely to specify.

Apportionment: the expert evidence

        The next question is this. On the assumptions that (a) from 1963 the defendants were

j causing damage to the plaintiffs' organs of hearing by an actionable breach of duty, and (b) the plaintiffs had already suffered some degree of damage from excessive noise which did not amount to a breach of duty, how (if at all) should the sums awarded to the plaintiffs reflect the existence of these two varieties of noise-induced hearing loss? Should the hearing loss be apportioned pro rata as between the periods of actionable and non-actionable exposure? Or should it be apportioned on some other basis? Or should it not

be apportioned at all, but instead allocated entirely to the period during which the
defendants were in breach?

In order to make this part of the case intelligible it is necessary to say something about
a set of 'Tables for the Estimation of Noise-Induced Hearing Loss' by D W Robinson and
M S Shipton (the NPL tables), which constituted the National Physical Laboratory
Acoustics Report Ac61 (2nd edn), 1977. These had their origin in a ministerial mandate
for research under the auspices of the National Physical Laboratory and the Medical
Research Council, designed to produce information relevant to a decision on the
'prescription' of noise-induced deafness. The field-work was carried out on subjects
screened as otologically normal, who had been exposed to various periods of excessive
noise. The data were then subjected to statistical analysis by W Burns and D W Robinson,
whose results were published in 1970 as Hearing and Noise in Industry (HMSO). The
essence of the Burns and Robinson research was a formula designed to express a relation
between (a) noise level and the time of exposure and (b) the noise-induced hearing loss at
various frequencies to be expected in various percentages of the exposed population.
Subsequently, in 1977 the arithmetical consequences of the Burns–Robinson formula,
with certain refinements, were embodied in the NPL tables. Essentially, the tables fall
into three parts: (i) tables 1 to 3 permit the calculation of a 'noise immission level' from a
combination of the Leq at various times, and the period or periods of exposure (the noise
immission level may be regarded as the total 'noise dose' whether continuous or
intermittent, received by the subject, over a given period); (ii) table 4 gives the corrections
for age-related loss at various frequencies; (iii) tables 5 and 6 predict the percentiles of the
population which will suffer a given hearing loss from a given noise dose.

Some features of the NPL tables must be noted. First, the formula was based on a cross-
sectional, not a serial survey. This was not a case of each subject being tested again and
again after successive periods of exposure. Instead, most if not all of the subjects were
tested once only, the subjects being chosen from people with varying periods of exposure.
A 'longitudinal' survey would be attractive, but apparently none exists, at least on any
significant scale.

Second, that part of the fomula relating the total noise dose to the noise levels over a
period of time is logarithmic in shape. The fruits of the 'equal energy' hypothesis, this
formula entails that after the first year, if the noise level is constant, the increase in the
noise dose is purely a function of the time of exposure. This produces the consequence,
distinctly odd to the layman's eye, that in the second year the addition to the noise dose
(ie noise immission level) will always be 3 db, in the third year it will be 1·8 db and so
on. This will be so whether the noise level in the first and subsequent years is (say) 80 db,
or the vastly greater intensity of (say) 120 db. Thus, unless the noise level increases after
the initial years (a case with which we are not concerned here) the graph of noise dose,
according to the Burns–Robinson formulation, will always rise very rapidly in the first
year, much less rapidly in the second year, more slowly still in the third year, and so on
until it has slowed right down by about the tenth year. Since the noise dose plays a major
part in the formula (item 2.1 in the introduction to the NPL tables) which gives the
prediction of anticipated hearing loss, the graph of hearing loss against time will also
show the features of rapid increase in the early years, followed by tailing-off. (There is
another non-linear feature in the formula, which also entails that hearing loss does not
vary directly with time, but it is unnecessary to enter into this.)

One particular feature of the relationship between hearing impairment and duration
of exposure is that the shape of the curve varies from frequency to frequency, so that,
although the feature of a rapid initial rise in impairment is present throughout the
frequency range, it is much more marked at 3 and 4 kHz than at 1 and 2 kHz. A series
of curves have been plotted together, in the defendants' schedule 8, and this document
gives a useful picture of the differential effect of excessive noise at the various frequencies.

A third aspect of the NPL tables is that they reflect an empirical formula. The work of
Burns and Robinson proceeded by the selection (using skill and intuition) of a formula
with a shape which seemed likely to fit the experimental data, and then adjusting the
constants until the best possible fit was obtained. This is a highly respectable scientific

method, but it is of importance to note that the formula does not purport to be derived
logically from the physical properties of sound and the human ear.

   Finally, as the preface to the NPL tables makes clear, they are designed to apply only to
the given statistical distribution of hearing levels in a noise-exposed population. As the
authors say, 'prediction for the individual remains impossible'.

   Against this background, it is now possible to summarise the rival contentions of the
parties. It is convenient to begin with the *defendants'* case which proceeds by the following
stages: (1) measure each plaintiff's hearing loss at various frequencies, and produce an
average of the losses at 1, 2 and 3 kHz; (2) correct the average by deducting the predicted
hearing loss due to age alone (from table 4); (3) estimate the noise intensities to which
the plaintiff would have been exposed over various periods of time, in the various jobs
which he did whilst employed by the defendants; (4) from these estimates compute a
total noise dose over the period of this employment (tables 1 to 3); (5) consult table 6 in
order to see into what percentile of the population depicted by the tables the plaintiff
would have to be put, in order to make his age-corrected hearing loss fit with his total
noise dose. The assignment of a percentile in this way eliminates any potential error in
the subsequent stages of the exercise due to the fact that the plaintiff's hearing
characteristics may deviate from the norm; (6) thenceforth using only those parts of the
tables which relate to the percentile thus assigned, look back along the tables, so as to
tabulate the hearing loss at the end of each year, right back to the outset of his
employment. As one would expect, the hearing losses at the outset are much greater
than those in later years. Taking Mr Gray as an example, the noise-induced hearing loss
was 24·1 db in 1936 (after one year of service); 32 db by 1938; 34·7 db by 1950; 37·7 db
by 1963; 38·7 db by 1968 and 39·2 db by 1973. Of his total hearing loss expressed in
decibels, only about one-eighth occurred in the last 25 years of his employment; (7)
repeat the process, this time employing for all periods after the relevant date the
attenuations which would have been gained by diligent use of the best available
protectors. This produces a trivial improvement in hearing level: between 0·8 and 4 db,
varying according to the circumstances of the individual case; (8) thus, it can be seen that
whatever the effect may have been on younger men, the breach made no appreciable
difference to the present situation of the plaintiffs.

   Accordingly, say the defendants, an apportionment is possible, but yields a nil recovery.

   The *plaintiffs'* response is on the following lines. (1) The NPL tables cannot be relied on
to yield results which are valid for all populations. Other workers have produced data
which show that the curve of hearing loss is much nearer to a straight line, particularly
at 1 and 2 kHz, than the Burns–Robinson report would predict. (2) Even if the NPL
tables are acceptable in their proper sphere, the use which the defendants have made of
them is wholly illegitimate, because it ignores the fact that they are intended to predict
the reaction of groups, not single individuals, to noise. (3) Inspection of the results for
the individual plaintiffs at different frequencies shows how dangerous it is to predict
individual results from statistical analysis. (4) Even if the exercise were acceptable in
theory, it is useless in practice, since the figures for the noise intensities experienced by
the plaintiffs at different times are no more than guesswork. If they are wrong, the total
noise dose is wrong, and this means that the plaintiff is put in the wrong percentile.
Moreover, the noise doses at intervening times are also wrong. This means that the whole
reconstruction of each plaintiff's history is totally unreliable. (5) It follows that the
method of apportionment proposed by the defendants is unworkable. They have
suggested no other method, and none exists. This being so, the court should follow
McGhee v National Coal Board [1972] 3 All ER 1008, [1973] 1 WLR 1 and award damages
on the assumption that the proved noise-induced hearing loss is in its entirety attributable
to the defendants' breach of duty. (6) Even if the graph of impairment tails off with time,
the graph of *disability* does not. The relationship is more linear. Thus, if an apportionment
is to be made, it should be on a straight-line basis. Adopting this approach, a substantial
hearing loss can be assigned to the period of the defendants' breach of duty; certainly
enough to be the subject of an award in damages.

   To these contentions, the *defendants* reply thus. (1) Although the tables cannot be used for prediction in the individual case, the exercise of looking back along the history of noise loss, in the light of a percentile attributed by reference to a measured hearing loss does not involve prediction, and is unobjectionable. (2) *McGhee's* case applies only to a situation where apportionment is wholly impossible. In the present case, although complete accuracy cannot be arrived at, it would be unjust to throw on the defendants a liability for the major part of a disability, which was inflicted at a time when the defendants were not in breach. (3) There is no theoretical or experimental support for the propositions that the progression of disability is linear, and that the apportionment should be on a straight-line basis.

These arguments were supported by evidence, and by a considerable body of documents, in the shape of calculations, graphs and extracts from the literature. Before assessing the evidence, two comments must be made on it.

First, the evidence came forward in a way which impeded methodical assessment of the technical issues. Interlocutory orders had required the substance of the experts' evidence to be disclosed well in advance of the trial. Reports were indeed exchanged, albeit too late. But they did not contain more than a preliminary sketch of the evidence. Throughout the trial, the witnesses produced copies of pages extracted from learned works, and schedules or tables produced overnight, often in manuscript. These would be put to the witnesses in cross-examination, often with little forewarning, so that they could not properly deal with them at the time. On occasion, a riposte would be produced at a later stage of the trial, or on the trial of a later group of actions.

The court would, I believe, have been justified in holding the parties to the orders for the disclosure of expert evidence in advance, and in declining to admit this new material. Certainly, this would greatly have shortened the hearing. In the event, however, I decided not to adopt such a strict approach. Although these are not test cases, in the sense of anyone having agreed to be bound by the outcome, it is certainly the hope of all concerned that they will at least provide some pointers towards the resolution of similar disputes by agreement. Settlements in other cases would be hampered if the present trial had gone to judgment in the absence of what the experts believed to be material evidence. The evidence was therefore admitted, but it did not emerge in a way which enabled the experts to give of their best.

Second, the court had the benefit of evidence from three acknowledged experts in the field: Dr R R A Coles, Professor R Hinchcliffe and Professor D W Robinson. In some cases, a judge will prefer the evidence of one expert witness, because he is more authoritative, lucid, or resourceful than the expert called by the other wide. This is not such a case. All three gentlemen were impressive, in their different ways. The views expressed hereafter are founded on the reasoning which was brought forward, and the materials adduced to support it, rather than any choice of preference amongst the witnesses. I mention this in particular because it seemed to me that from time to time a shadow was cast by the defendants over the objectivity of Dr Coles's evidence. That there are strong differences of opinion outside the courtroom as to some of the scientific issues here discussed is quite plain, and there were clear echoes of these differences in the course of the trial. But I am quite satisfied that Dr Coles's evidence was not thereby put out of balance. I have carefully considered the criticisms made of his evidence, and so far as they are relied on to suggest that Dr Coles had forsaken the role of independent expert for that of advocate, I reject them.

I now turn to the issues raised by the arguments which I have summarised. Since the NPL tables lie at the heart of the dispute, it is convenient to begin with the plaintiffs' contention that quite apart from any complaints about the use of the tables for apportionment of hearing loss, they cannot even be relied on as an accurate statistical representation of how a sample of the population is likely to react to excessive noise. This part of the case has a curious history. Both counsel for the group A plaintiffs and counsel for the group B plaintiffs explicitly disclaimed any attack on the validity of the tables as such. In the event, however, Dr Coles found himself quite unable to refrain from embarking on such an attack. This undoubtedly took the defendants by surprise, and in an ordinary case the complete exclusion of the evidence might well have been justified. On this occasion, however, I felt that all the controversies should be thoroughly aired, and in the event the defendants were able to bring forward materials to counter the attack, without suffering any real disadvantage.

At the heart of Dr Coles's criticism was the failure of the Burns–Robinson formula to predict the experimental results contained in various published works: notably, an article by W Taylor et al entitled 'Study on Noise and Hearing in Jute Weaving' (July 1965) 38 Journal of the Acoustical Society of America 113–120, an article by R L Kell entitled 'Hearing Loss in Female Jute Weavers' (1975) 18 Annals of Occupational Hygiene 97–109 and an article by Mrs W Passchier-Vermeer in *Occupational Hearing Loss* (ed D W Robinson, 1971) 15–33. The first two articles represented the fruits of successive studies of female jute weavers in Dundee who had been exposed to constant high levels of noise for long periods of time. The work of Mrs Passchier-Vermeer was to collate the data published from a number of sources throughout the world. The results undoubtedly diverged from those given by the Burns–Robinson formula (see figures 2 to 5 in Kell's paper). By comparison with the other data, Burns–Robinson predicts lower rates of impairment. Moreover, at 2 kHz (although not at 4 kHz) there is a marked difference in the shape of the curves. The relationship is much more nearly linear in the case of the other data than the one given by Burns–Robinson. In addition, Dr Coles maintains that the audiograms of the present plaintiffs show a poor fit with the results predicted by Burns–Robinson.

To this, Professor Hinchcliffe replies that the audiograms are really quite a good fit. The defendants point out that the Dundee jute weavers were a homogeneous population, exposed to continuous noise of the same characteristics, and that their measured losses might not be representative of the populations and noise types and levels with which we are concerned here, and that conversely the data collated by Passchier-Vermeer may be collected from too broad a geographical base to be a useful guide in the present instance. Finally, the defendants say that binaural averages of the various plaintiffs taken together do tend to show the results grouping round the Burns–Robinson median figures, so that this trial is in itself a small-scale vindication of the formula. To this, Dr Coles replies that this is only what one would expect: the more there is averaging, the smoother the results.

The evidence given at the trial is plainly the reflection of a wider controversy, which is currently unresolved. For practical reasons, proceedings in court cannot possibly yield a clear and complete solution. I cannot go further than to state the following conclusions. (1) The NPL tables cannot be rejected outright. They are the only comprehensive sources of data currently available. Even Dr Coles recommends their use for diagnostic purposes. Professor Robinson spoke on their behalf, and no criticisms were made of the methods used by his colleagues to obtain their results. The plaintiffs have put forward nothing to replace them. It was not, I believe, suggested that Taylor, Kell and Passchier-Vermeer were more reliable, merely that their results were different; and in any event a choice could not be made without a much closer scrutiny of the merits and demerits of the rival work than is possible in the framework of a trial where none of the rival authors have been heard. I think it right to approach the case on the basis that the picture given by the NPL tables is broadly reliable, whilst recognising (in company with their authors) that they are not the last word on the subject. (2) In one particular respect, the tables must be used with special caution, namely by recognising that there may be room for doubt as to the progression at some of the lower frequencies, notably at 2 kHz. (3) Accordingly, any attempt at apportionment should assume that, taking the population as a whole, the greater part of the hearing impairment will take place in the earlier years, say the first ten, but that the progression will be slower (and if the sources relied on by the plaintiffs are correct, much slower) at the lower frequencies, so that the characteristic notched shape of the audiogram will in course of time broaden out towards the left-hand (lower frequency) side of the graph. This later loss may have a disproportionate effect, so far as speech comprehension is concerned, where the subject has already lost the upper frequencies which otherwise would have enabled recognition of the consonants. I believe these conclusions to be in broad agreement with the conclusions of the various workers in this field whose results are briefly set out in W J Sulkowski *Industrial Noise Pollution and Hearing Impairment* (1980) (TT 76–54047).

I now turn to the plaintiffs' contention that even if, when properly used, the NPL tables are tolerably reliable, it is impossible to employ them as a means of apportioning impairment in terms of time. This was advanced on three broad fronts.

First, it was asserted that the tables could not be used for 'retrospection', ie an exercise which involved looking back along the course of the individual's history of hearing loss, starting with the measured hearing loss at the present time. Since the foreword to the tables makes it clear that they are not intended for use to predict individual hearing losses, how can they properly be used in the opposite direction? I do not accept this argument, at least when it is carried to the extent of rejecting the retrospection argument in its entirely. When used prospectively, three facts are known or assumed: the subject's initial hearing loss (nil), the continuous noise immission level, and the duration of the exposure. These facts are not enough to enable a precise prediction of the course of the subject's hearing loss in the future, and of the impairment at which he will arrive at the end of the period of exposure. This is so because of the very wide variation in the amount of the loss, as represented by the figures attributable to the different percentiles, resulting from the variations in the susceptibilities of the various subjects. But the position is crucially different where retrospection is in issue. Here, there is an additional known fact, namely the actual hearing loss at the end of the period. By permitting the subject's assignment to a percentile, this enables a much more reliable view to be formed of his losses in the past: not completely reliable, for the reasons which I shall state, but nevertheless not entirely speculative.

Perhaps an analogy is legitimate. A bunch of ribbons is attached at one end of the top of a flag-staff, and allowed to stream out in a strong breeze. They will follow the same general configuration, but the ends of the ribbons will not all be in the same place, nor will the ribbons follow the same path. Now imagine the further ends of the ribbons held together. The ribbons will still flutter individually, but their individual shapes will be much closer to one another. So also here. If the upper end of a person's hearing loss curve is anchored by the known hearing loss at the end of the period, there will still be scope for uncertainty, in the light of the variables which I shall mention, as to the exact path which the curve has followed. Nevertheless the possible courses of hearing loss, for the individual, will have a much closer resemblance to each other, than if the ends of the curves floated entirely free.

I am much fortified in the view that there is nothing fundamentally unsound in the use of the NPL tables for retrospection by the evidence of Professor Robinson. He willingly accepted that the formula had not been devised for this purpose, and that its use in this way had not occurred to him until these disputes had brought it into prominence. Nevertheless, he could see nothing wrong with it. Professor Robinson was an impressive witness, moderate in the expression of his views, and with no personal axe to grind. He was co-author of the work on which the tables were founded. If he regards retrospection as permissible, the court should be very slow to differ.

I now turn to the second ground of criticism, namely that whatever the merits of retrospection for groups of subjects, the tables cannot properly be used for this purpose in the individual case. This is an altogether more substantial objection. Retrospection can only yield an accurate view of the course of hearing loss, if (a) the amplitude and consistency or otherwise of the noise immission levels are precisely known, (b) the present hearing loss is accurately known even on an average basis, (c) the subject can fairly be assumed to have susceptibilities which correspond at all frequencies with the percentiles assigned by the use of averages over several frequencies, (d) the subject can be assumed to have susceptibilities which vary with time and exposure (if at all) only in accordance with the norm, and (e) the effect of ageing on the plaintiff corresponded with the assumptions underlying the NPL tables. The plaintiffs contend that none of these conditions is shown to be fulfilled here.

As regards condition (a), the proper assessment of the noise immission levels is important, for two reasons. (i) The successive immission levels go to make up the total noise dose which, when compared with the actual hearing loss, yields the percentile into which the subject should be assigned. The choice of percentile has an important effect on the distribution of hearing loss over the period of exposure. For subjects in the upper percentiles (less sensitive persons) the rapid initial rise, followed by an early flattening will be less conspicuous than in the case of subjects in the lower percentiles. (ii) For obvious reasons, the question whether the original noise immission level is maintained throughout or subsequently falls away with an improvement in working conditions, will also affect the relationship between hearing loss and time.

The combined effect of these two factors may be of real significance, when apportionment is in issue. This is well demonstrated by the document which forms Annex B to this judgment (formerly a part of the defendants' schedule 10). This shows the course of hearing loss of Mr Mitchell first tabulated (as option A) on the assumption of those immission levels for which the defendants finally argued, viz successive Leq's of 102, 97, 97 and 93 db, falling as the years progressed, and a similar tabulation made on the assumption (option B) that the Leq remained at 102 db throughout. These calculations were made solely for the purposes of illustration, but they are nevertheless instructive. For example, according to option A, 50% of hearing loss (averaged over 1, 2 and 3 kHz) could have taken place by the end of the sixth year; on the constant noise level assumed by option B, the same loss could not have been achieved until the thirteenth year. Again, by the year 1963, under option A, 94% of the impairment could already have occurred, whereas there would have been only 76% under option B. Thus the exercise in retrospection cannot be relied on as accurate, unless the calculation starts with noise immission figures which are equally reliable. As I shall later suggest, no such figures exist.

Next, there is the possibility of error in the measurement of current hearing impairment which underlies assumption (b) above. Certainly, the figures now before the court for each plaintiff are close enough for it not to matter which is chosen at the stage when quantum of damages is assessed. Nevertheless, there is a margin of error (perhaps 10 db at most), which has some bearing on the assignment to percentile, and hence to the distribution of the impairment over the period of exposure.

Probably of more significance is assumption (c) above, namely that the susceptibility of the individual plaintiff corresponds with the norm at all frequencies. This must be highly suspect. The use of averages conceals the possibility of wide variations in susceptibility from ear to ear, and from frequency to frequency: and hence inaccuracies in the answer to the question whether for any given ear or frequency, the plaintiff suffered a particular degree of impairment earlier or later than would be predicted by following the path laid down by the figures given in the NPL tables for the percentile to which the use of averages had assigned him. Even where averages are not employed, and figures for each frequency are taken from the plaintiffs' audiograms, the assignment to percentiles varies widely from frequency to frequency, and from ear to ear: as witness the calculations set out in the plaintiffs' schedules 12 and 14.

Next, there is assumption (d). If an individual's measured impairment cannot be reconciled with the answer predicted by applying the NPL tables to the total noise dose, they can be made to fit by assigning him to a percentile more or less distant from the median: ie by saying that his organs of hearing are more or less susceptible to noise damage than the norm. For many purposes this is perfectly legitimate. But is it legitimate for the retrospection? May it not be the case that susceptibility varies not only from individual to individual, but also from time to time in the same individual? The answer to that question is unknown. Whether in fact such a variation exists, and if so how it progresses, is at present uncertain. An article by Dr Coles in 1963 suggested that susceptibility falls as exposure progresses. But he no longer adheres to this view. A table in *Burns and Robinson* p 174 shows variations with no clear pattern: but the periods of exposure were only a few years. I doubt whether much can be derived from this limited material.

Finally, the retrospection exercise assumes that the plaintiffs correspond with the NPL norms as regard the effect of ageing. There is some evidence to suggest that this assumption cannot be taken for granted (exhibit E to Dr Coles's proof of evidence in the group B actions), and also that at least in some instances the effects of excessive noise and ageing may not be fully additive (W J Sulkowski p 166).

Plainly all these possible sources of imprecision, when taken together amply justify the warning against the use of statistical data in individual cases, which are to be found in the introduction to the NPL tables, the Draft International Standard and the British Standard of 1976.

Equally plainly they are sufficient to destroy any pretensions of accuracy in the defendants' various 'Course of Hearing Loss' calculations. Whatever claims may have been made at the outset, I believe that by the end of the trial of group B they were no longer being relied on except by way of illustration. But does this justify the plaintiffs' assertion that the retrospection exercise should be jettisoned altogether? I will leave this question for the time being, to discuss the problem of the actual noise levels, returning to it at a later stage.

The identification of the noise immission levels to which the plaintiffs were subject is important for two reasons. First, because it is relevant to an argument that even if the defendants had provided protection at the time when, if the conclusion indicated above is correct, it should have been provided, the devices then available would not have afforded complete protection, so that not all the damage suffered by the plaintiffs after that time was attributable to the breach. Second, because the noise immission level has an important influence on the course of hearing loss.

The first point need not be considered at length. Billesholm down gives a mean attenuation of about 21 db, with a much better performance in the important 4 kHz frequency band. The ear muffs available in 1963 would have yielded a markedly better result. I am quite satisfied on the evidence that, even allowing for the difficulties of assessing the noise levels, and recognising that protectors may not function as efficiently when worn at work as in ideal laboratory conditions, the noise immission levels cannot have been so high that if the workers had used the wool continuously, and the muffs in exceptionally noisy conditions, there would still have been a residue of noise over the maximum safe level to bring about further noise induced deteriorations in the plaintiffs' hearing after the year 1963.

The second question raises altogether more difficult problems. It is hard enough to form a reliable estimate of the noise conditions prevailing today, without having to carry the exercise backwards in time some forty years or more. Yet the exercise has to be done, not only for the obvious reason that if the noise level has been lower in more recent years, the damage to hearing is also likely to have been less, but also because the ascertainment of the total noise dose is an element in determining the subject's sensitivity, and hence in determining the general trend of his deterioration (because the higher the percentile, the greater the amount of damage suffered in later years).

The evidence on this important topic was extremely thin. There must be persons, still in management or retired, who could have given evidence about it, yet the defendants called no witnesses of fact. Similarly, one would expect that the plaintiffs' trade unions would have access to men with long experience in the trade, who could provide some concrete information; but none gave evidence. The plaintiffs did their best to help, but although I regard their evidence as truthful (save in the case of two of them, to the limited extent which I have indicated) it was not to my mind completely reliable, the more so because some of the plaintiffs tended to agree rather readily with the question most recently asked. By the end of the trial I was unable to form any clear view about whether, and if so to what extent, the gradual replacement of rivetting by the processes loosely described as caulking has reduced the overall noise exposures of persons not directly working in those trades. Nor indeed was there even any agreement on when that replacement had taken place. In all the circumstances I am not prepared to go further than to say that the levels of noise to which these plaintiffs were exposed did not become worse with the passage of time.

Evidence about the noise levels prevailing in the more recent past comes from three
a sources. First, there were direct measurements of Leq for particular workers throughout
a working day. At intervals throughout the 1970s readings were made of noise levels in
the Swan Hunter yards. These are conveniently summarised in the plaintiffs' sch 13.
Unfortunately, these are of little direct help, in the absence of any witness to explain
exactly how they were taken. Perhaps some of them were obtained by using personal
dose meters, but some undoubtedly were not, and I believe that they do no more than
b confirm in very general terms the kind of noise levels likely to be encountered on
occasions during days which may or may not have been typical, by persons engaged in
various trades. Rather more useful were measurements made by expert witnesses during
inspections at Smiths and Swan Hunter between November 1982 and March 1983 using
meters which gave readings of continuous Leq, but even these were not as a rule
maintained for long enough to give a picture of the working day as a whole.
c On 17 February 1983 there was a full day's reading taken by Mr T P B Hallam at Swan
Hunter, during the fitting out of the Ark Royal. This yielded a figure of 86·8 db.
Unfortunately this reading does not justify any general conclusion, for it is clear that the
inspection happened to be made on a quiet day; and indeed it is obvious that the figure
cannot be representative of conditions day in day out for the past decades, or otherwise
the plaintiffs would not have suffered their known hearing losses.
d A second way of arriving at the noise levels would be to start with measurements of
the intensities experienced by workers using particular types of tool, or working at given
distances from others who were using particular tools, or were just positioned in the
general noise environment of the yard. Assumptions could then be made about the
lengths of time during a working day for which the subject would have been exposed to
noise during the day, so that a figure could be arrived at for a typical working day. Much
e care was devoted by the expert witnesses on both sides to computations of this nature.
These could not however form any but the most general guide, unless they were founded
on reliable assumptions, and in my judgment they were not. Even in relation to a single
day, there was no evidence which I felt able to treat as accurate about the way in which
the day was divided up. Moreover, in shipyard work (unlike the case of, say, Kell's jute
workers) the idea of a typical day is misleading. Shipbuilding work is cyclic, with a noisy
f period of construction, followed by a less noisy fitting out, and followed again by shorter,
but more noisy, trials. Ship repairing has less clearly marked phases, but the noise
involved in relation to any particular ship would depend on the repairs which needed to
be done. Moreover, even within the phases, the workers' exposure would vary from day
to day. These fitters and labourers were peripatetic, and the intensities to which they
were exposed would depend, not only on the length of time during which they were
g using particular tools, but also on the localities where they were using them, and on the
activities and proximities of other workers using noisy tools. This being so, all the
calculations were open to serious objection, and counsel for both plaintiffs and defendants
were able to land some damaging blows in cross-examination.
This is quite plainly insufficient material on which to base any precise finding as to the
noise immission levels to which the plaintiffs were subject. Fortunately, no such finding
h is required for the purposes of this section, since I have already rejected the retrospection
exercise as a means of arriving at an accurate reconstruction of the plaintiffs' hearing
losses throughout their years of service. What one does need to know is whether the
immission levels were as high as the plaintiffs' experts contended: for if this were so the
result would be to assign the plaintiffs (or at least those in group B) to very high
percentiles of susceptibility, and hence enable them to say that a greater proportion of
j the hearing loss than would be the case with a median susceptibility would have taken
place during the later years. In my opinion, the evidence does make it possible to form a
view on this. My conclusion is that the Leqs, taken as a whole, were very substantially
below the 115 db for which the plaintiffs contended. In case it should become material,
I would if necessary be willing to find that the immission levels for the plaintiffs, day to
day and year to year, were of the order of 100–105 db. But I need not go this far. For
present purposes, it is sufficient to find that the Leqs were at such a level as to justify the

assumption that the plaintiffs' noise impairment curves lay close enough to the median curves to allow an exercise such as those performed for option B (in the defendants' schedule 10) to give a very general representation of the kind of way in which the hearing losses progessed over the years.

Finally, there is the need to establish the relationship between impairment and disability, so that the latter can be used as one of the ways of assessing hardship, in the course of fixing an appropriate measure of damages. This is another controversial area, in which the information is less than complete, although the position will no doubt improve when Professor Robinson has completed a study on which he is now embarked. Certainly, on the material now available there would be no justification for translating the retrospection exercise, which is concerned with hearing impairment, directly into a measurement of disability, and still less of handicap, for as the Draft International Standard points out—

> 'The definition of hearing handicap depends upon the quality of speech intelligibility desired, the average level of background noise, and with respect to the relative importance of the various frequencies, perhaps even on the language.'

There is indeed some evidence that disability increases slowly at first, under constant noise exposure, and thereafter accelerates (see the articles by R G Habib and R Hinchcliffe 'Subjective Magnitude of Auditory Impairment' (1978) 17 Audiology 68–76; S Prasansuk and R Hinchcliffe 'Subjective Magnitude of Auditory Handicap in Thailand' (1978) 61 Journal of the Medical Association of Thailand 452–457; V Priede and R R A Coles 'Speech Audiometry' (1976) Journal of Laryngology and Otology 1086). On the other hand, as Professor Hinchcliffe points out, his own data show this feature only for impairments greater than 40 db; below that figure, the relationship between impairment and handicap is more nearly linear (see Coles, proof in group B, exhibit B). One may also have recourse to the comparisons between the audiometric results for the plaintiffs in the present actions, with their apparent degrees of handicap (and to similar comparisons in respect of previous reported and unreported cases) which seem to show quite convincingly that the two are no more than broadly related. The data in W J Sulkowski p 57 suggest a similar conclusion.

In addition to the rather scant experimental evidence, there is the qualitative argument that when many decibels have been lost, the remainder are the more precious; or, to put it another way that if the upper frequencies have disappeared at an early stage, the later loss of the lower frequencies have a disproportionate effect on speech discrimination.

In the end, I have come to the conclusion that when forming a picture of the way in which each plaintiff's disability and handicap have progressed over the years, real weight must be given to a relationship between impairment and disability/handicap which works in the opposite direction to that between time and impairment: so that there is more enhancement of disability/handicap in the later years than the NPL curves at 4 kHz would allow. But I am not prepared to go so far as accepting that the two cancel one another out, and produce a straight-line relationship between time and disability. The solution proposed in the Blue Book seems a practical and economical basis on which to administer schemes involving large numbers of claims. But although in one sense these actions are test cases, the object of this judgment is not to devise a scheme which can readily be put into practice. I have to decide the disputes according to the evidence. The validity of the Blue Book system has been put in issue, and I am bound to hold that neither the straight line method, nor any other simple solution which could be offered in its place, has been established by the material now before the court.

Before leaving this part of the case, it is necessary to mention one possible short cut to an answer on apportionment. Hearing impairment can take place for a substantial time before it manifests itself in disability. If one could know the number of decibels at which this happens, and if one could also know on what date each plaintiff's deafness became apparent, this would precisely establish a point on the impairment curve, which would enable a better judgment to be made as to the level of impairment in 1963.

Unfortunately, this inquiry is fruitless, for a number of reasons. There seems to be no
general agreement even for an average of the level of impairment at which hearing loss
becomes perceived: some put it at 20 db, others higher. Quite apart from this, it is
acknowledged that there are wide variations from one individual to another. Younger
people are more likely than their elders to notice a given hearing loss. The nature of the
subject's social and working life may determine when the onset is first recognised.
Sometimes, recognition will take place, not because a particular level has been reached,
but because an event happens which chances to draw the attention of the sufferer, or
those around him. Add to all this the perfectly understandable fact that the plaintiffs
were not in my judgment able to remember with anything like the accuracy which
would be required for a calculation just when their hearing loss began, and it is to my
mind plain that no help can be derived from this source.

Apportionment: the law

Before proceeding to a conclusion on the legitimacy of the apportionment exercise, it
is necessary to decide by what principle of law the questions should be adjudged.

The full and helpful submissions of counsel involved a discussion of several reported
and unreported decisions. As a preliminary review, it is in my judgment useful to
consider what one might expect the position to be if the matter were approached entirely
by reference to first principles and common sense.

The starting point for any inquiry into the measure of damages is the principle that
the court should so far as possible endeavour to restore the plaintiff to the position in
which he would have found himself but for the defendant's wrongful act. The
impracticability of giving full effect to this principle must be recognised at every stage of
the process. Money can never properly compensate a loss which consists of social
impairment rather than financial deprivation. Quantification of damages for personal
injury involves the use of conventional measures, the adoption of which at once makes
nonsense of any attempts at mathematical accuracy. In a field where the subject matter
is people, not contracts, bank balances and abstract rights, the recognition that certain
results are unacceptable in human terms must rightly lead to alternative solutions which
cannot be easily rationalised. Complete logical rigour cannot be attained.

Nevertheless, it is instructive at least to begin by adopting the primary rule to which I
have referred, and seeing whether it yields sensible results. The first step is to consider
the case of a worker, whose hearing has been impaired by excessive noise wrongfully
suffered whilst in the service of successive employers A and B. The basic principle
suggests that A should be liable in full, but not more than in full, for the impairment
existing when the worker leaves his employment. Ideally, this should be assessed by
reference to the damage suffered by the structure of his organs of hearing. But this
cannot directly be measured, so it is quantified in terms of the decibel hearing loss, and
the inquiry can be focussed by asking what would be the result if the worker had issued
a writ immediately on leaving A's employment, and brought the matter very speedily to
trial. Again, however, one cannot move directly from decibels to money. The
intermediate step is the ascertainment of symptoms: for it is the symptoms which are
the immediate cause of loss. It is, however, essential to recognise that symptoms are of
two kinds. First, those (if any) which the plaintiff has already suffered and is suffering at
the date of trial. Second, those symptoms which, because of damage to bodily structure
suffered through breach, are definitely going to happen, or may happen, at a future date.
A familiar example of the second category is the osteoarthritis which, the expert witnesses
agree, will probably appear within the next five years as the result of damage to a knee,
although the joint is for the time being free from symptoms. In the present context,
such symptoms take the shape of (i) the earlier onset of presbyacusis which will be
suffered by anyone whose 'non-disability' reservoir of hearing impairment has been
drawn on by excessive noise, and (ii) the further handicap which may be suffered by the
plaintiff if he undergoes further exposure to excessive noise. A proper award of damages
against employer A will recognise the existence of both current and potential symptoms.

What of employer B? Principle and common sense demand a recognition of the fact that he has 'taken over' the plaintiff in a condition where his organs of hearing are already damaged, and where he is already subject to actual and potential symptoms. It would be an injustice to employer B to make him liable for damage already done before he had any connection with the plaintiff. His liability, first principles suggest, should be limited to compensation for (a) the perpetuation and amplification of the handicaps already being suffered at the moment when the employment changed hands, and (b) the bringing to fruit in the shape of current hardship those symptoms which had previously been no more than potential

If this reasoning is followed, the result should be that the recoveries against A and B will amount in total to the award which would have been made if the damage had all been caused by the wrongs of a single employer, and, equally, that the assessment of such an award could form at least the starting point of any quantification of the individual liability of employers A and B.

Next, one must consider how this approach can be applied to a case where either (a) there are two successive employers, of whom only the second is at fault, or (b) there is a single employer, who had been guilty of an actionable fault only from a date after the employment began. Logic suggests that the analysis should be the same. Employer B has, once again, 'inherited' a workman whose hearing is already damaged by events with which that employer has had no connection, or at least no connection which makes him liable in law. The fact that, so far as the worker is concerned, the prior events unfortunately give him no cause of action against anyone should not affect the principles on which he recovers from employer B. Justice looks to the interests of both parties, not to those of the plaintiff alone.

This solution presupposes a division of responsibility between A and B, or (in the case of the second example) between non-blameworthy and blameworthy sources of noise. How precise must this division be, before it can found an apportionment in law? What happens if the apportionment is insufficiently precise? To the latter question, general principle supplies only a guarded answer. In strict logic, the plaintiff should fail for want of proof that the breach has caused the damage. Yet this seems *too* strict, for the plaintiff has proved some loss; perhaps it should all be attributed to the fault, simply as a matter of policy.

The answer to the first question seems less difficult. The degree of accuracy demanded should be commensurate with the degree of accuracy possible, in the light of existing knowledge, and with the degree of accuracy involved in the remainder of the exercise which leads to the computation of damages. It is senseless to demand the utmost accuracy at one stage of a calculation, which involves the broadest assumptions at another stage, and the application of conventional measures of recovery at yet another. I return to this point later.

It must now be considered whether this proposed solution accords with the reported cases. At least at first sight, it is supported by a handful of decisions, none of them binding on this court: viz *Crookall v Vickers-Armstrong Ltd* [1955] 2 All ER 12, [1955] 1 WLR 659, *Balfour v William Beardmore & Co Ltd* 1956 SLT 205, *Long v Thiessen & Laliberte* (1968) 65 WWR (NS) 577, *Stevenson v Buchanan & Brock Pty Ltd* [1971] VR 503 (assessment under a statutory scheme), *Berry v Stone Manganese and Marine Ltd* [1972] 1 Lloyd's Rep 182, *Wallhead v Ruston & Hornsby Ltd* (1973) 14 KIR 285, *Cartwright v GKN Sankey Ltd* [1972] 2 Lloyd's Rep 242, *Heal v Garringtons* (26 May 1981, unreported). See also *Fazel v Cape Insulation* (6 April 1982, unreported). Only *Clarkson v Modern Foundries Ltd* [1958] 1 All ER 33, [1957] 1 WLR 1210 appears to point the other way, and even this could perhaps be distinguished on the facts. Furthermore, the propositions set out above are reinforced by the statements of principle (admittedly uttered in a different context) of Lord Reid and Lord Pearson in *Baker v Willoughby* [1969] 3 All ER 1528 at 1533–1534, 1534–1535, [1970] AC 467 at 493–494, 495 and also that of Lord Keith in *Jobling v Associated Dairies Ltd* [1981] 2 All ER 752 at 764, [1982] AC 794 at 815, who said:

a
'... it would clearly be unjust to reduce the damages awarded for the first tort because of the occurrence of the second tort, damages for which are to be assessed on the basis that the plaintiff is already partially incapacitated ... In the event that damages against two successive tortfeasors fall to be assessed at the same time, it would be highly unreasonable if the aggregate of both awards were less than the total loss suffered by the plaintiff. The computation should start from an assessment of that total loss. The award against the second tortfeasor cannot in fairness to him
b
fail to recognise that the plaintiff whom he injured was already to some extent incapacitated.'

In contradiction to the propositions stated above, the plaintiffs address a number of arguments, which may be arranged under four headings.

First, the plaintiffs rely on the principle of law stated by Devlin LJ in *Dingle v Associated Newspapers Ltd* [1961] 1 All ER 897 at 916, [1961] 2 QB 162 at 188–189 in the following
c
terms:

'Where injury has been done to the plaintiff and the injury is indivisible, any tortfeasor whose act has been a proximate cause of the injury must compensate for the whole of it. As between the plaintiff and the defendant it is immaterial that there are others whose acts also have been a cause of the injury and it does not matter
d
whether those others have or have not a good defence. These factors would be relevant in a claim between tortfeasors for contribution, but the plaintiff is not concerned with that; he can obtain judgment for total compensation from anyone whose act has been a cause of his injury.'

In the case of Mr Mitchell, the plaintiff seeks to apply this principle directly, so as to hold both Vickers and Swan Hunter liable in full. In the other actions, it is applied by analogy
e
so as to attribute entire responsbility for the damage to the employer whose breach of duty has contributed to the hearing impairment now suffered by the plaintiffs.

For the purposes of the present discussion I am prepared to assume, without being wholly convinced, that the principle stated by Devlin LJ can be transferred to a situation where the contributions to the damages are made, not by the acts of different persons, but by the faulty and non-faulty acts of the same person. Even on this assumption,
f
however, it is evident that the principle will apply only if the various acts contribute to what can fairly be regarded as the same item of damage. That this is so is made plain not only by the way in which the principle is formulated by Devlin LJ, but also in a passage which follows the one just quoted ([1961] 1 All ER 897 at 916, [1961] 2 QB 162 at 189):

'If four men, acting severally and not in concert, strike the plaintiff one after
g
another and as a result of his injuries he suffers shock and is detained in hospital and loses a month's wages, each wrongdoer is liable to compensate for the whole loss of earnings. If there were four distinct physical injuries, each man would be liable only for the consequences peculiar to the injury he inflicted, but in the example I have given the loss of earnings is one injury caused in part by all four defendants. It is essential for this purpose that the loss should be one and indivisible; whether it is so
h
or not is a matter of fact and not a matter of law.'

Can it be said here that each plaintiff is suffering from an injury which is one and indivisible? Undoubtedly in one sense it can: for the plaintiff is hard of hearing, a disability which cannot now be severed into component parts, in the same way as one might distinguish between the individual items which go to make up a condition
j
described as 'multiple injuries'. Nor indeed, if one looks behind the disability and handicap to the measured impairment, is it possible to regard the impairment as divisible, as if by saying that a hearing loss of 60 db can be treated as two losses, each of 30 db. But this is not the end of the story. Even the measured impairment is only a symptom of the deteriorated condition of the organs of hearing. This condition is not the direct product

of a group of acts, not necessarily simultaneous, but all converging to bring about one occurrence of damage. Rather, it is the culmination of a progression, the individual *a* stages of which were each brought about by the separate acts of the persons sued, or (as the case may be) the separate non-faulty and faulty acts of the only defendant. In my judgment, the principle stated by Devlin LJ does not apply to this kind of case. Moreover, even if it could be regarded as apposite where the successive deteriorations and their respective causes cannot on the evidence be distinguished, it does not in my opinion demand the conclusion that where the court *knows* that the initial stage of the damage *b* was caused by A (and not B) and that the latter stage was caused by B (and not A), it is obliged in law to proceed (contrary to the true facts) on the assumption that the faults of each had caused the whole damage. So also in the case where it is *known* that when the faulty acts of the employer began, the plaintiff's hearing had already suffered damage.

Thus, I do not find in the plaintiffs' first argument any reason to discard the propositions stated above. Before parting with this argument, I should mention that reliance was *c* placed on the decision and dicta of Stable J in *Bank View Mill Ltd v Nelson Corp and Fryer & Co (Nelson) Ltd* [1942] 2 All ER 477. For my part I do not consider that these help to solve the present problem, the more so since the statement (at 483) would appear to justify the conclusion that if the respective contributions were indistinguishable, the outcome would be a recovery of 50% not 100%, a conclusion for which, if I correctly understood them, counsel for the plaintiffs did not seriously contend. *d*

The second argument advanced by the plaintiffs is differently expressed, but may in essence be no more than a variant of the first. It is to this effect, that where it is proved that a wrongful act has made a material contribution to the plaintiff's injury, the law regards this as a sufficient discharge of the plaintiff's burden of proof on causation to render the defendant liable for the injury in full: and that since the effect of the defendants' wrongful acts was to cause a more than negligible injury to the organs of *e* hearing, the question of apportionment does not arise. That the first part of this argument is well founded cannot be doubted: see *Bonnington Castings Ltd v Wardlaw* [1956] 1 All ER 615, [1956] AC 613 and *Nicholson v Atlas Steel Foundry and Engineering Co Ltd* [1957] 1 All ER 776, [1957] 1 WLR 613. It is a pragmatic rule, designed to avoid the unjust conclusion that a plaintiff who cannot establish the precise degree to which the wrongful act has contributed to the loss must fail entirely for want of proof. These decisions are of *f* the highest authority, but they cannot properly be extended to a case where this particular injustice is not in prospect, and where it is known that events which are not a breach of duty by the defendant are the entire cause of the first stage of the damage, and that events which do constitute a breach of duty are a cause (although not in the present case the sole cause, having regard to the ageing factor) of the subsequent aggravation of that damage.

The third of the plaintiffs' arguents is founded on the decision of the House of Lords *g* in *McGhee v National Coal Board* [1972] 3 All ER 1008, [1973] 1 WLR 1. The facts were as follows. The pursuer was sent by his employers to empty some brick kilns, where working conditions were hot and dusty. The employers did not provide adequate washing facilities, with the result that the plaintiff had to cycle home from work, still caked in sweat and grime. He thereupon contracted dermatitis. It was found as a fact that the need to cycle home with brick dust adhering to his skin (which the court had *h* held to be a breach of duty) had materially added to the risk that he might develop the disease, but in the current state of medical knowledge the evidence could not go so far as to prove that if the appellant had been able to wash off the dust, he would not have contracted the disease. On these facts, the House of Lords held that the pursuer was entitled to recover in full for the consequences of the dermatitis. This decision rightly received detailed examination in the course of counsel's submissions, as a result of which *j* I can deal with the matter quite briefly. I believe that the essence of the decision was as follows. (1) The sole issue in dispute by the time the case reached the House of Lords was whether the plaintiff had sufficiently proved a causal connection between the breach of duty and his loss. If, as the courts below had held, he had not proved this, then his claim must entirely fail. If he had proved it, then the claim would succeed in full. The question of apportionment did not arise. (2) The plaintiff was faced with two obstacles: (a) he could not prove to what extent the breach had contributed to the disease, and (b) he could not even prove that was a cause at all, in the sense of being an event without which the disease would not have been contracted. (3) The first obstacle was overcome by recourse to the principle exemplified in *Bonnington's* case [1956] 1 All ER 615, [1956] AC 613 and *Nicholson's* case [1957] 1 All ER 776, [1957] 1 WLR 613, namely that where there are two or more causes concurrent in effect, if not necessarily in time, any contribution by the defendants' wrongdoing greater than de minimis is sufficient to establish causation. To this extent *McGhee* adds nothing to the existing law. (4) Where *McGhee* did break new ground was in the solution to the plaintiffs' second problem. The 'evidential gap' created by the absence of proof that the breach was at the very least a causa sine qua non was bridged by treating the proof that the breach had increased the risk of the disease as if it were proof that the breach had actually caused the disease. This device was a fiction, as Lord Wilberforce pointed out (see [1972] 3 All ER 1008 at 1013, [1973] 1 WLR 1 at 7), but it was one which had to be adopted in the interests of justice, to prevent the plaintiff from losing his claim through failure to prove what, in the current state of medical knowledge, he had no means of proving.

If this is a correct analysis of the decision, it seems to me that it can have no bearing on the present dispute. We are not here concerned with excessive noise creating merely a risk of damge, but with a causal connection between noise and injury which is a proved fact. There is no evidential gap, and no need for any presumption or fiction.

Moreover, *McGhee* was quite a different case on the facts. The decision would have been in point if the plaintiff had already contracted dermatitis as a result of contact with dust, to an extent impossible to define with precision, before the time came when the employer should have provided him with washing facilities. But these were not the facts, and I find nothing in the speeches to suggest what answer their Lordships would have given to the question now in dispute.

Accordingly, I reject the submission that *McGhee* demands a recovery for the full amount of impairment in the present case. Any other conclusion would accord ill with the real shape of the issues. A strange feature of this trial has been the reversal of the parties' usual roles. In the ordinary case, the plaintiff sets out to identify the damage which was caused by the defendant's breach; the defendant, as his primary line of defence, contends that no part of the damage of which the plaintiff complains was in fact caused by the breach, so that the claim entirely fails. It must be very unusual indeed to find it happening, as happened here, that the plaintiff urges by evidence and argument that it is impossible for him to prove a causal connection between the breach and any identifiable part of the damage. In effect, these plaintiffs are trying to prove causation in the general, and disprove it in the particular, at the same time. I cannot think it legitimate for a plaintiff to assert an evidential gap, and then use the *McGhee* principle to bridge it by a device which enables him to recover in full for a loss, part of which is known to have occurred before the wrongful conduct began.

Finally, considerations of policy were advanced in support of the plaintiffs' case, on the following lines. If the authorities so far cited do not enable the plaintiffs to recover, then some new law must be made. Here we have damage which was undeniably caused (except in the case of Mr Mitchell) by the acts and omissions of only one employer. Some of those acts and omissions were wrongful. The reason why precise quantification is impossible lies in the very fact that the employers had failed to protect their workmen by taking audiograms at the proper time. In such circumstances, fairness demands that the plaintiffs should be entitled to recover their loss in full.

Whilst I sympathise with this contention, I cannot accept it. The defendants as well as the plaintiffs are entitled to a just result. If we know (and we do know, for by the end of the case it was no longer seriously in dispute) that a substantial part of the impairment took place before the defendants were in breach, why in fairness should they be made to pay for it? The fact that precise quantification is impossible should not alter the position. The whole exercise of assessing damages is shot through with imprecision. Even the measurements of the plaintiffs' hearing loss contain a substantial margin of error. The use of an average involves an over-simplification, and the choice of frequencies for the average materially affects the apparent outcome of the measurements. The translation of impairment into disability is arbitrary. The translation of disability into handicap requires a purely judgmental assessment by the court of the effect which the disability has had on the circumstances of the individual plaintiff. The last stage of the process, which requires the assessed handicap to be turned into an award of damages, again requires the court, as a matter of judgment, to place the plaintiff at the correct point on a scale of possible monetary awards, accommodating all ranges of deafness from the very worst to the very least, a scale which is itself arbitrary by its very nature.

Thus, whatever the position might be if the court were to find itself unable to make any findings at all on the issue of causation and was accordingly being faced with a choice between awarding for the defendants in full, or for the plaintiff in full, or on some wholly arbitrary basis such as an award of 50%, I see no reason why the present impossibility of making a precise apportionment of impairment and disability in terms of time, should in justice lead to the result that the defendants are adjudged liable to pay in full, when it is known that only part of the damage was their fault. What justice does demand, to my mind, is that the court should make the best estimate which it can, in the light of the evidence, making the fullest allowances in favour of the plaintiffs for the uncertainties known to be involved in any apportionment. In the end, notwithstanding all the care lavished on it by the scientists and by counsel I believe that this has to be regarded as a jury question, and I propose to approach it as such.

Before leaving this part of the case, I should mention one further ground on which it could be argued that the whole of the damage should be attributed to the period during which the defendants were in breach: namely that the purpose of an award is to compensate the plaintiff for the hardship which he has suffered, and (it could be said in the present case) all the hardship manifested itself during the period of breach. If sound, this argument would provide a welcome means of circumventing the difficult problems to which this trial has given rise. In my view it is not sound, notwithstanding that it was adopted in *Heslop v Metalock (Britain) Ltd* (24 November 1981, unreported). The submissions and evidence tendered in that case were much less elaborate than those brought forward here, and the decision gave insufficient weight to the considerations that (a) the purpose of the award is to compensate for the damage to hearing organs, and not simply for the symptoms resulting from it, and (b) the employer (as at the moment of first breach) 'inherited' a potential plaintiff whose hearing was already substantially impaired. Neither leading counsel for the plaintiffs was, by the end of the trial, disposed to embrace this argument with any warmth, and I no longer believe it to be correct.

The individual plaintiffs

I now turn to the facts relative to the individual plaintiffs. In narrative form, they are as follows.

Mr A E Thompson

Mr Thompson is 62 years of age. He was employed by Smiths from 1936 until 1983 (when he was made redundant), with an interval between 1941 and 1946 on account of war service. He worked until about 1966 on a piece gang attached to the paint shop, in the course of which he used a pneumatic scaling tool for about one quarter of his time. The balance of the time was spent in painting and doing other jobs. Others used chipping, scaling and caulking tools in the vicinity, and there was also rivetting nearby until this came to an end.

Since before the war Mr Thompson had used cotton wool in his ears on his own initiative, mostly to keep the dust from penetrating the eardrums. He found that it did make some difference to the amount of unpleasant noise. He was never issued with

earplugs. In 1973 he saw posters which gave warning about noise, and he went to get ear
muffs. Thereafter he wore them whenever there was noise.

Recent pure-tone audiograms give average hearing losses (depending on the ear chosen
and the frequencies chosen to make up the average) between 52 and 57 db. The losses in
each ear at 4 kHz were 70 db. Mr Thompson fell into Disability Group V, designated
'moderate', on the Coles–Worgan scale.

He was provided with a hearing-aid in 1980. For about the last 16 years Mr Thompson
has suffered from a continuous buzzing sound in his ears; it does not cause him any
anxiety or difficulty in sleeping; and indeed it does not affect his life.

The onset of the deafness appears to have been noticed in about 1956. Without a
hearing-aid, Mr Thompson could hardly make out a conversation if he was not face to
face with the other person. He had difficulty in hearing the door bell, or the television
set it if was not turned up. He also had difficulties in the more noisy conditions of
working mens' clubs. He would have to sit next to the telephone in order to hear it.

Mr Thompson wears the hearing-aid all day. He has no trouble in hearing the phone
when wearing his aid; and there was very little evidence that he suffered trouble of any
other kind.

During his evidence, Mr Thompson wore his hearing-aid in the ear which was nearest
to counsel. He missed very little of what was said. I would have described him as slightly
hard of hearing, when wearing his aid. I did not have the opportunity to observe him
when he was not wearing the aid.

Applying scales of disability to the result of the audiograms yields disability assessments
ranging between 45 and 51%. This seems rather to over-state the loss of amenity actually
suffered by Mr Thompson, probably because, like the other plaintiffs in group A, he has
been very successful in coming to terms with his disability.

Mr D M Gray

Mr Gray is 63 years of age. He was employed by Smiths from 1935 until 1983 (when
he became redundant) except for an interval between 1941 and 1946 on war service.

Mr Gray was employed throughout as a general labourer. His jobs included the
cleaning of tanks, scaling with a scaler and chipper, and using other pneumatic tools to
clear away marine growth.

Before the war he first began to wear cotton wool on his own initiative. He began to
wear muffs in 1973 when he went to ask for them from the ambulance room.

Mr Gray's average hearing losses range between 57 and 68 db. At 4 kHZ the losses are
70 and 85 db in the two ears. He falls into Disability Group V (moderate) on the Coles–
Worgan scale.

Mr Gray was issued with a hearing-aid in 1981. About six years after he first noticed
deficiencies in his hearing, Mr Gray observed a buzzing which happened most of the
time, and sounded like wind gushing through his ears. It was more noticeable in a quiet
place. It is an irritation, but not a source of anxiety. It does not cause him any difficulty
in sleeping.

Without the hearing-aid, he has difficulty in hearing someone speaking with a low
tone, and in making out the conversation if people are speaking in groups. He cannot
hear the telephone or the door bell without the hearing-aid, and he needs to have the
television volume turned up too high for other people's comfort.

(It is convenient at this point to mention that there is a sameness about the kind of
complaint put forward by each of the plaintiffs in the two groups which, to my mind, is
derived not only from the fact that they are suffering from the same medical condition,
but also from the method adopted to 'process' the vast quantity of claims which underlie
the present action. This is not to say that the plaintiffs were consciously exaggerating
their symptoms. On the contrary, and this is particularly so of the group A plaintiffs, I
have formed the impression that they were if anything tending to play them down. Nor
do I in the least suggest that the plaintiffs were improperly coached to give answers

contrary to the true facts. Inevitably, some kind of standardised format would have to be adopted in order to elicit the facts from such a large number of men in a reasonably economical way. Nevertheless, when assessing the loss of amenity by reference to complaints about ringing door bells, noisy working men's clubs and so on, it is necessary to recognise that their descriptions of their condition might not have sounded quite the same if given without any previous examination.)

Mr Gray finds that the hearing-aid has helped a great deal. For example, he can now hear the telephone. But there are still problems of vibration if there is too much surrounding noise.

Mr Gray was wearing his hearing-aid (on the ear opposite to counsel) when he gave evidence. He occasionally experienced difficulty in hearing. I formed the impression that his hearing was a little worse than that of Mr Thompson. I did not have the opportunity to observe him when he was not wearing his aid. In general, I have formed the impression that he was the most seriously affected of all the six plaintiffs. This was in general agreement with the results of the audiograms.

Mr J W Nicholson

Mr Nicholson is 69 years of age. He worked for Smiths continuously from 1928 or 1929 until he retired in 1979. For the first year or two he worked as a rivet catcher. Then he worked on cleaning tanks (a quiet job) and then as a stager for two or three years. Finally, he began as a waterman before the war and continued right through until he retired. The job itself was comparatively quiet, but he could be near someone who was caulking and cleaning up for a welder.

About 25 years ago he began to wear cotton wool on his own initiative, on account of the noise. He noticed muffs being worn in 1973 or 1974, and inquired after them at the ambulance room, but was told that they were only for men who were actually using the caulking or chipping or rivetting machines. Accordingly, he never wore them.

Mr Nicholson's measured average hearing losses ranged from 27 to 42 db. The impairment at 4 kHz is 60 db in each ear. He falls into Disability Group II, designated 'very slight', on the Coles–Worgan scale.

Mr Nicholson was issued with a hearing-aid in 1982, but was advised that for the moment he should only wear it when watching television. He speaks of an occasional buzzing noise, lasting a matter of seconds 'like the sound of the fridge'. This does not really bother him. He first noticed impairment of hearing about 25 years ago, and it has gradually got worse. Even now, it is no great problem. He has difficulties if he is on a bus or is in the bar of a club and there are people talking: he cannot quite hear what they are saying. He also has to turn up the television set, if he is not wearing his aid. But for the purposes of ordinary conversation he can manage perfectly well.

Mr Nicholson was not wearing a hearing-aid whilst he gave evidence. He appeared to have no difficulty in appreciating what was being said in court. Indeed, without advance knowledge, I doubt whether I would have realised that he was suffering from any hearing impairment, beyond that which is not infrequently found in men of his age. On any view of the matter, Mr Nicholson's degree of impairment is much less than that of Mr Thompson and Mr Gray: a fact which is in accord with the figures revealed by the audiograms.

Mr W Blacklock

Mr Blacklock is 59 years of age. After working for two years in a bicycle shop he joined Vickers as an apprentice when 16 years old. He was employed in various yards as a fitter until 1953, when he joined Swan Hunter. He remained there, apart from intervals of three months and eighteen months elsewhere, until his retirement in 1983.

Mr Blacklock wore ear muffs from 1973 onwards, whenever the surroundings were noisy. He never saw any Billesholm wool.

His audiograms showed average hearing losses between 20 and 42 db. The losses at
4 kHz were 65 and 70 db. Mr Blacklock falls into the Disability Group II (ie 'very slight')
on the Coles–Worgan scale.

Mr Blacklock does not wear a hearing-aid. He noticed in about 1978 that he had a
buzzing noise in his ear. It has been going on longer, in more recent years. It is most
noticeable when conditions are very quiet. The condition was not serious enough for Mr
Blacklock to mention it spontaneously to the specialists who interviewed him, nor was it
referred to when his claim was put forward in 1982.

He first began to notice something wrong with his hearing in about 1976, when his
wife drew attention to the fact that he kept asking her to repeat what she had said. He
could not hear the telephone when it was in the passage way, and he had to have the
television set turned up. There was also difficulty in hearing conversation when he was
in a group at the social club. Mr Blacklock's evidence suggested a loss of amenity rather
greater than would be expected from the results of his audiogram. This may well be
because Mr Blacklock, like the other plaintiffs in group B, has not yet succeeded in
coming to terms with his disability as well as have the plaintiffs in group A.

I formed the impression, when Mr Blacklock gave evidence, that if I had not already
known the results of his audiograms, I would have not noticed that he was hard of
hearing.

Mr R Waggott

Mr Waggott is 55 years of age. He began as an apprentice in the Neptune yard in 1944,
and with an interval of three months of non-noisy occupation with a company in
London, he has been with Swan Hunter ever since. Since the end of his apprenticeship
he has been an on-board engine room fitter, with the exception of the time between 1951
and 1957, when he was a deck fitter. The noisy tools which he himself used were the
hand hammer and the grinder.

He began to wear ear muffs in about 1972 or 1973, when he saw that other fitters had
them, and they said that muffs were available. He had put them on at periods of noise,
and did not wear them continuously. Before this, he had brought some cotton wool from
home, for about a year before getting ear muffs.

His audiograms reveal average losses ranging from 23 to 30 db. At 4 kHz the losses
are 50 db in each ear. He falls into Disability Group I, namely 'just significant' on the
Coles–Worgan scale.

Mr Waggott noticed, about four to five years ago, a slight ringing in his ears at times:
perhaps two or three times a week. It was only a source of irritation, and was not
important enough to mention unless he was directly asked.

He places the time at which he first noticed impairment of hearing at about ten to
twelve years ago. Here again, his wife had commented on the fact that she had to repeat
things. There were the usual problems of hearing door bells and telephone bells from
other rooms. So also with the difficulties of carrying on conversation at the club, or
listening to the comedians there.

Mr J A Mitchell

Mr Mitchell is 61 years old. After a short time working in an office, he commenced in
1938 as an apprentice fitter with Parsons Marine at Wallsend. When he had served his
time, he went to other employers and then into the army, where he served in the Royal
Electrical and Mechanical Engineers. No substantial amount of noise was involved. He
then went to work for Vickers in 1949, and continued there until 1969 when Swan
Hunter took over the Vickers' interests in the Walker Yard. He was an engine room fitter
throughout, until he took an office job in 1980. This happened because he became
subject to eye trouble, which has substantially deprived him of the sight in one eye.

Mr Mitchell was never provided with earplugs or earmuffs at Vickers. At some time
during the 1960s he was briefly given a set of earplugs whilst he went on the trials of a

frigate. Perhaps the earplugs came from Naval sources, but in any event he never used them again. He started to use ear muffs when he began to work on the Ark Royal, having *a* been told by the shop steward to get them. Previously, he had known that ear protectors were available in the yard, but he did not think that they were much use. Nobody seemed to bother at all.

Some few years ago Mr Mitchell began to notice a sound in his ear, varying from a buzz to a screech. He would hear it perhaps two or three times a week, principally when things were quiet. It does not affect him badly, and he tried to forget it.   *b*

It is very hard to be sure when Mr Mitchell first noticed his deafness. Perhaps it was in about 1970, when he went to his doctor (as he did on several occasions) to have his ears syringed. I need not repeat the details of his problems with the interference in his social life, since mostly they are on the same lines as those of the other witnesses. There is, however, this additional fact that he enjoys music of virtually every kind except modern popular music, and has found his enjoyment of it to be substantially reduced. (For future *c* reference, I should say that of all the six plaintiffs who gave evidence, Mr Mitchell is the one who impressed me most as giving a fair and realistic account of the handicap produced by his hearing impairment).

The audiograms show Mr Mitchell as having average impairments ranging between 17 and 35 db. His losses at 4 kHz are 70 and 65 db. He falls into Disability Group II (very slight) on the Coles–Worgan scale.   *d*

Breach of statutory duty: limitation

Before proceeding to express my conclusions I must deal with two additional issues. These would have been important, if my views had been other than they are, but in the event they have no bearing on the outcome of the actions. Since this judgment is already very long, I will deal with these issues very summarily.   *e*

First, by way of alternative to their claim at common law, the plaintiffs asserted a breach of the Factories Acts, and in particular a breach of s 29(1) of the Factories Act 1961. This cause of action could not have arisen before 1959, when the employer's duty was expanded to include the safety of the employee's place of work. Since I have fixed the year 1963 as the date when the common law duty was first broken, the claim under the statute adds virtually nothing to the liability already established. This being so, I will *f* do no more than say that I do not regard the facts as establishing a breach of the duty under s 29(1).

Second, the defendants have asserted that the claims are all statute-barred by virtue of the Limitation Act 1980. I accept the argument to this extent, that I find that the date of knowledge, for the purposes of ss 11 and 14 of the Act was, in the case of each plaintiff, more than three years before the date on which the writ was issued. This does however, *g* leave me with a discretion under s 33. The relevant principles are established by the cases cited in argument. I have taken them all into account, and need not burden this judgment by stating a list of them. In addition I have, of course, taken into account the factors specifically identified in s 33(3) of the Act. If I had been disposed to decide the case in favour of the plaintiffs by giving effect to their argument on *McGhee*, on the basis that the noise environment in former years cannot be accurately reconstructed, I would *h* have given serious study to the question whether the defendants would have been in a better position if the writs had been issued more promptly. Even on this basis I doubt whether I would have exercised the discretion against the plaintiffs, for I believed their evidence that although they were aware of a compensation scheme which the boilermakers' union had negotiated, it did not occur to them, or apparently to the representatives of their own unions (none of whom were called as witnesses) that they *j* might have a cause of action against their employers, until the present cascade of writs began to be issued. In the event, however, the matter seems to me plain. The plaintiffs have valid claims, albeit small. Any prejudice caused by the delay since the accrual of their continuing cause of action (and I am not convinced that there has been any great prejudice) has damaged them just as much as the defendants. I do not consider that the

interests of justice would be properly serviced by holding the claims to be statute-barred
a and accordingly I exercise my discretion in favour of the plaintiffs.

Conclusions
    I now proceed at last to draw together these conclusions of law and fact.
    First, I must consider whether the apportionment exercise is legitimate at all, or
b whether the attempt to ascertain the handicap attributable to that part of each plaintiff's
employment, which lay between periods where the defendants were not in fault (for
want of knowledge) and were not in fault again (because they supplied the requisite
protection) would involve such a blind guess that it should not be attempted, but should
rather yield to a presumption that all the loss was caused whilst the defendants were in
breach. It will, I believe, have already become apparent that in my judgment the exercise
c should not be rejected. The undeniable imperfections and inaccuracies of the process
need no further emphasis. I acknowledge them all. Nevertheless, a clear picture emerges.
To my mind it is absolutely plain that (i) for all plaintiffs, the greater part of the damage
at the upper frequencies was done before the breach began, (ii) the loss of the lower
frequencies at this time was less, but still really substantial, and (iii) the handicap
attributable to the breach was rather greater than the hearing loss curves and tables would
d suggest, particularly in the case of the group A plaintiffs, whose impairment was already
serious enough for any further impairment to be important. I believe that justice can
properly be served by giving effect to these findings, however rough and ready the result.
    Next, it must be decided how the process should be carried out. One possibility is to
assign to each plaintiff the figure which would have been awarded as damages if the
whole of the hearing loss had been attributable to the defendants' breach, and then to
e apply a fraction or percentage representing the court's view of the part which was in fact
so attributable. I believe that this is an entirely proper approach where the disability
proceeds by clearly identifiable stages, and where the damages appropriate to stage A
may be derived by subtracting from the notional total recovery, the damages attaching
to stage B. I believe, however, that this may be misleading in a case such as the present,
as it gives to the calculation a spurious air of accuracy and might suggest that the chosen
f percentages are based directly on the defendants' computer print-outs, or similar
materials.
    In my judgment it is better to go straight to the heart of the problem, by saying that
when the breaches began the plaintiffs were persons whose hearing impairments might
(in some cases) have caused some unacknowledged disability, but little or no handicap,
that these plaintiffs would, as the effects of age progressed, have found themselves
g becoming subject to patent disability and handicap, that at the time of the breach they
were already in a condition where any further exposure to noise would accelerate their
progress towards disability and handicap, and that the further exposure during the period
of breach did have just this effect. In blunter terms, the plaintiffs are people who in
1963 were already going to be hard of hearing in later life, and the breach merely served
to accelerate and enhance the progress. A monetary value should then be directly assigned
h to this additional detriment. Finally, an eye should be cast on the general level of damages
appropriate where liability is established for the whole of the hearing loss, to make sure
that the sums awarded for a part of the impairment are not seriously out of proportion.
    Pausing for a moment to consider this last stage of the process, I should mention an
argument advanced by counsel on behalf of Vickers, to the effect that the middle range
of the current tariff of damages for deafness is pitched too high, by reference to the sums
j awarded for injuries to limbs and other organs. There may be force in this, as there may
also be force in the comment that at the top end of the scale the sums awarded for total
or near-total deafness are too low, and do not recognise the great distress which the
affliction can bring about; so that in essence the scale of awards is too compressed in the
middle. This argument will be available to counsel for Vickers, if the case proceeds to
another court, but I cannot give effect to it here. This court is bound, in practice if not in

theory, by the levels established by the Court of Appeal in *Smith v British Rail Engineering Ltd* [1980] CA Transcript 532 and *Robinson v British Rail Engineering Ltd* [1982] CA Bound Transcript 438. In particular, I think it right to take note of the opinion, expressed by the majority of the Court of Appeal in the latter case, that the awards at first instance in *Robinson v British Rail Engineering Ltd* (18 June 1981, unreported) and *Heslop v Metalock (Britain) Ltd* (24 November 1981, unreported) were rather too high. (When using these cases as a yardstick the ages of the subjects must be borne in mind. The older men will tend to have suffered a more prolonged handicap, but it should not be forgotten that their current impairment is likely to contain a greater element attributable solely to ageing.)

Applying these principles to the present claims, one finds that the plaintiffs had all had substantial periods of exposure to noise before the breaches began in 1963, that the breaches continued for 10 years, or in some cases 16 years, that thereafter there was no significant exposure to noise although the ageing process was continuing. At the end of it all, two plaintiffs have suffered a moderate hearing loss, but can manage very well with hearing-aids. The remainder are much less seriously damaged, so much so that an award on the basis of full liability would be unlikely to exceed the county court limit of jurisdiction. Plainly, the awards for the aggravation of impairment and acceleration of hardship due to the breaches cannot be large.

Treating the matter as a jury question and giving no further reasons beyond saying that I have borne in mind (a) the general configuration of the median curves of the NPL tables, (b) the fact that the effect in terms of disability and hardship of losing a given number of decibels depends on how many have already been lost, and (c) the manifold uncertainties affecting the process of quantification, I make the following awards:

GROUP A

Mr Thompson:	£1,350
Mr Gray:	£1,250 plus £295 as special damages for the cost of his hearing aid. (No separate argument was addressed on apportionment in relation to the latter item.)
Mr Nicholson:	£850

GROUP B

Mr Blacklock:	£850
Mr Waggott:	£600
Mr Mitchell:	£250 (in relation to his claim against Vickers) and £650 (in relation to his claim against Swan Hunter)

I hold that there are no grounds on which to make any additional awards of damages to reflect the kind of prospective loss which was the subject of decisions such as *Smith v Manchester Corp* (1974) 17 KIR 1 and *Moeliker v A Reyrolle & Co* [1977] 1 All ER 9, [1977] 1 WLR 132.

It may be said that these are small awards, even for men who are not very deaf. So they are, considering that the impairment of the plaintiffs' hearing comes from a working lifetime of exposure to excessive noise. It is, however, essential to remember what these actions are about. The court is not here to set up and administer a scheme which would provide these men with a complete indemnity for their loss of hearing, whoever their employers might have been, and irrespective of whether and to what degree those employers were at fault. If it is felt that the existing provisions for industrial injury benefits in the field of deafness are too ungenerous, the remedy must lie elsewhere. Here, the court is faced with six actions claiming damages for negligence. The plaintiffs have chosen to allege that their employers were in breach of their duty at common law to take reasonable care on their behalf, and that their employers' wrongful failure to take such care has caused them to suffer damage. Having made these allegations they must prove

them. They have succeeded only in part. In an action at law, justice looks to the interest
of both sides, and although it may seem harsh that these men should have no ampler
remedy, it would be unjust to the defendants to hold them liable for more than the
proven consequences of their default.

I cannot leave this case without two acknowledgments. First, to the skill and industry
of counsel, whose closing addresses illuminated and clarified a series of difficult factual
and legal issues. Second, to Mr Francis Lythgoe, formerly District Registrar at the
Newcastle-upon-Tyne District Registry, on whose initiative the possibility of bringing
these actions to trial in advance of all the others was first canvassed, and whose energetic
conduct of the interlocutory proceedings did much to facilitate their being brought to
trial within a commendably short time.

Judgment for the plaintiffs accordingly.

Solicitors: *Marrons Livingston & Co*, Newcastle-upon-Tyne (for the group A plaintiffs);
Brian Thompson & Partners, Newcastle-upon-Tyne (for the group B plaintiffs); *Linsley &
Mortimer*, Newcastle-upon-Tyne (for Smiths and Swan Hunter); *A V Hammond & Co*,
Bradford (for Vickers).

John M Collins Esq   Barrister.

ANNEX A

THE COLES–WORGAN CLASSIFICATION

Description of the handicaps associated with the auditory handicap groups

Group O   No significant auditory handicap
Group I   The hearing is not sufficiently impaired to affect the perception of speech,
except for a slight (additional to normal) difficulty in noisy backgrounds
Groups II and III   Slight (II) to moderate (III) difficulty whenever listening to faint
speech, but would usually understand normal speech. Would also have distinctly greater
difficulty when trying to understand speech against a background of noise
Groups IV and V   Frequent difficulty with normal speech and would sometimes (IV)
or often (V) have to ask people to 'speak up' in order to hear them, even in face-to-face
conversation. Great (IV) or very great (V) difficulty in a background of noise
Group VI   Marked difficulties in communication since he would sometimes be unable
to clearly understand even loud speech. In noise he would find it impossible to distinguish
speech
Groups VII and VIII   Would only understand shouted or amplified speech, and then
only moderately well (VII) or poorly (VIII)
Group IX   Minimal speech intelligibility even with well-amplified speech
Group X   Virtually totally deaf with respect to understanding of speech

Note   In Groups II to IX some benefit could potentially be gained from a suitable
hearing aid

DISABILITY RATINGS

Sensorineural hearing level averaged over 500–1000–2000 Hz (binaural assessment) db	Sensorineural hearing level at 4000 Hz (binaural) db	Auditory handicap group	Brief description of handicap	Suggested disability rating %
up to 25	up to 25	O	not significant	0
up to 25	over 25, up to 50	I	just significant	5
up to 25	over 55	II	very slight	10
over 25, up to 30	n/a	II	very slight	10
over 30, up to 40	n/a	III	slight	20
over 40, up to 50	n/a	IV	mild	35
over 50, up to 60	n/a	V	moderate	50
over 60, up to 70	n/a	VI	marked	65
over 70, up to 80	n/a	VII	fairly severe	80
over 80, up to 90	n/a	VIII	very severe	90
over 90, up to 100	n/a	IX	extremely severe	95
over 100	n/a	X	total	100

ANNEX B

PERCENTAGE GROWTH NIHL
to nearest whole number

John Mitchell

Year	Option 'A' %	Option 'B' %	Year	Option 'A' %	Option 'B' %
1938	0	0	1958	87	67
1940	16	4	1960	92	72
1942	33	18	1963	94	76
1944	45	29	1965	95	81
1946	54	37	1970	98	89
1948	54	37	1972	99	91
1950	62	45	1973	99	93
1951	66	48	1974	99	94
1952	70	51	1976	100	97
1954	76	57	1979		100
1956	81	61			

Option 'A' is based on Mr Acton's assessments
Option 'B' assumes a constant Leq of 102 db(A) until hearing protection was provided

Practice Direction

SUPREME COURT TAXING OFFICE

Legal aid – Taxation of costs – Agreement as to costs – Proceedings to which assisted person a party – Assessment of costs by Law Society – Procedure – Legal Aid Act 1974, Sch 2 – Legal Aid (General) Regulations 1980, reg 100A.

1. Regulation 100A of the Legal Aid (General) Regulations 1980, SI 1980/1894 (amended with effect from 1 November 1983 by the Legal Aid (General) (Amendment No 2) Regulations 1983, SI 1983/1483) provides:

'(1) Where in any proceedings to which an assisted person, or a former assisted person, is a party and which have been brought to an end by a judgment decree or final order, there has been an agreement in respect of the costs to be paid by any other party to the assisted person, or former assisted person, which that person's solicitor and counsel (if any) is willing to accept in full satisfaction of the work done, the amount of the costs shall be submitted to the appropriate area committee which shall, in accordance with Schedule 2 to the [Legal Aid Act 1974], fix the amount of costs by assessment made without a taxation . . .'

The regulation further provides that the area committee may if it thinks fit request the appropriate taxing officer to fix the amount of costs by assessment made without a taxation.

If such request is made by the area committee to the Supreme Court Taxing Office or Admiralty Registrar the appropriate taxing officer will (i) in the normal course, assess the costs without requiring the attendance of the solicitor, (ii) if he considers it necessary, require production of such papers and vouchers as he thinks fit and/or require the solicitor to attend for further explanation, (iii) issue a certificate of assessment of the costs.

2. The Practice Direction of 10 May 1972 ([1972] 2 All ER 624, [1972] 1 WLR 783) is cancelled.

F T HORNE
Chief Taxing Master.

13 March 1984

R v Secretary of State for the Home Department, ex parte Anderson

a

QUEEN'S BENCH DIVISION
ROBERT GOFF LJ AND MANN J
1, 2, 21 DECEMBER 1983

b

Prison – Access to legal adviser – Access to discuss commencement of proceedings – Proposed civil proceedings against prison officer for assault – Proposed proceedings arising out of prison treatment – Governor refusing visit by legal adviser to discuss proposed litigation – Visit contrary to simultaneous ventilation rule in prison standing orders which requires prisoner to lodge written complaint with governor before discussing complaint with legal adviser – Whether simultaneous ventilation rule ultra vires – Whether rule impeding prisoner's right of access to courts – Whether unimpeded access to solicitor part of right of access to courts – Prison Act 1952, s 47(1) – Prison Rules 1964, rr 33(1), 34, 47(12).

c

By s 47(1)[a] of the Prison Act 1952 the Secretary of State was empowered to make 'rules for the regulation and management of prisons . . . and for the . . . discipline and control of persons required to be detained therein'. Pursuant to that power the Secretary of State made the Prison Rules 1964, which provided (a) by r 33(1)[b], that the Secretary of State could impose restrictions on a prisoner's communications with other persons, (b) by r 34[c], that a prisoner was not entitled to communicate with any person in connection with legal business except with the leave of the Secretary of State, and (c) by r 47(12)[d], that it was a disciplinary offence for a prisoner to make a false and malicious allegation against a prison officer. Pursuant to r 33 the Secretary of State made standing orders for prisons which provided that a prisoner was entitled to be visited by his legal adviser except where the purpose of the visit was to discuss 'complaints about prison treatment which the inmate has not yet raised through the prescribed [complaints] procedure'. The standing orders further stated (by the so-called 'simultaneous ventilation rule') that as soon as a complaint about prison treatment had been made through the prescribed complaints procedure it could be the subject of a visit by the prisoner's legal adviser. The applicant was a prisoner who wanted his solicitor to visit him to advise him about commencing civil proceedings against a prison officer for an assault arising out of a disturbance at the prison. The applicant had not made a written complaint to the prison governor about the assault and accordingly permission for the visit was refused by the prison authorities, who took the view that the prisoner was not entitled to be visited by his solicitor until he had made a written complaint about the assault to the prison governor. The refusal to allow the visit was confirmed by the Home Office. The applicant applied for judicial review of the decisions of the prison authorities and the Home Office seeking, inter alia, declarations that the simultaneous ventilation rule was ultra vires and that the applicant was entitled to visits from his solicitor without first having to make a written complaint to the prison governor about the assault.

d

e

f

g

Held – The simultaneous ventilation rule embodied in the standing orders relating to prisons went beyond the mere regulation of the circumstances in which a prisoner could have access to his legal adviser and instead constituted an impediment to a prisoner's right of access to the courts, since unimpeded access to a solicitor for the purpose of obtaining advice and assistance in connection with the initiation of civil proceedings was

h

j

---

a   Section 47(1) is set out at p 922 *h*, post
b   Rule 33 is set out at p 923 *a* to *d*, post
c   Rule 34, so far as material, is set out at p 923 *d*, post
d   Rule 47(12) provides: 'A prisoner shall be guilty of an offence against discipline if he . . . (12) makes any false and malicious allegation against an officer . . .'

a inseparable from the right of access to the courts themselves, and the prerequisite of making a written complaint to the prison governor before being allowed access to a solicitor impeded that right of access because it exposed the prisoner to the possibility of being charged under r 47(12) of the 1964 rules with making a false and malicious allegation against a prison officer. The simultaneous ventilation rule was therefore ultra vires s 47(1) of the 1952 Act and r 33 of the 1964 rules and the declarations sought would accordingly be granted (see p 928 *c* to p 929 *a c d* and *h*, post).

b   *Golder v UK* (1975) 1 EHRR 524 and *Raymond v Honey* [1982] 1 All ER 756 applied.

Notes

For prisoners' access to legal advice and assistance, see 37 Halsbury's Laws (4th edn) paras 1178, 1179, and for cases on the subject, see 37(3) Digest (Reissue) 409, *5361, 5365–7*.

For the Prison Act 1952, s 47, see 25 Halsbury's Statutes (3rd edn) 851.

c For the Prison Rules 1964, rr 33, 34, 47, see 18 Halsbury's Statutory Instruments (4th reissue) 17, 21.

Cases referred to in judgment

Golder v UK (1975) 1 EHRR 524.
Raymond v Honey [1982] 1 All ER 756, [1983] 1 AC 1, [1982] 2 WLR 465, HL.
d *Silver v UK* (1980) 3 EHRR 475.

Cases also cited

A-G v BBC [1980] 3 All ER 161, [1981] AC 303, HL.
A-G v Butterworth [1962] 3 All ER 326, [1963] 1 QB 696, CA.
A-G v Times Newspapers Ltd [1973] 3 All ER 54, [1974] AC 273, HL.
e *Pan-American World Airways Inc v Dept of Trade* [1976] 1 Lloyd's Rep 257, CA.
R v Board of Visitors of Highpoint Prison, ex p McConkey (1982) Times, 23 September.
R v Secretary of State for Home Dept, ex p Bhajan Singh [1975] 2 All ER 1081, [1976] QB 198, DC and CA.
Silver v UK (1983) 5 EHRR 347.
Solosky v R (1980) 105 DLR (3d) 745.
f *Waugh v British Rlys Board* [1979] 2 All ER 1169, [1980] AC 521, HL.

Application for judicial review

James Anderson applied, with the leave of Woolf J granted on 25 July 1983, for judicial review of (1) a decision of the assistant governor of Wormwood Scrubs prison, Mr Bolter, made on 13 July 1983 refusing the applicant's legal adviser permission to visit the
g applicant on 14 July 1983 to give legal advice and (2) a decision of a Home Office official made on 20 July 1983 confirming the assistant governor's decision. The relief sought was (1) a mandatory injunction ordering the governor of Wormwood Scrubs prison and his servants or agents and other Crown servants under his control to permit the applicant to be interviewed immediately by his legal adviser for the purpose of taking instructions and being given legal advice out of earshot of a prison officer and (2) declarations that the
h applicant was entitled to be interviewed in connection with the matter that had given rise to his request for legal advice, that the applicant was entitled to conduct an interview out of earshot of a prison officer, that prison department standing order 5A(34), in so far as it prohibited visits by a legal adviser to advise on prisoners' complaints about prison treatment prior to the lodging of an internal complaint with the prison authorities, was unlawful and ultra vires, and that the applicant was entitled to correspond with his
j solicitor in connection with the proposed litigation without first lodging a complaint through the internal disciplinary procedures. The respondent was the Secretary of State for the Home Department. The facts are set out in the judgment of the court.

Edward Fitzgerald for the applicant.
Simon D Brown for the respondent.

Cur adv vult

21 December. The following judgment of the court was delivered.

ROBERT GOFF LJ. There is before the court an application by James Anderson for judicial review. The applicant is at present serving a term of imprisonment in Wormwood Scrubs prison. His application, which is brought by leave of the single judge, is for relief in various forms, the purpose of which is to enable him to see a solicitor with a view to her advising him and receiving instructions without his first having to comply with a certain requirement of the standing orders for prisons issued by the Home Office; and the basic issue in the case before us is whether the relevant provisions of the standing orders are ultra vires.

The background of the matter is as follows. On 16 June 1983 there appears to have been some form of disturbance in Wormwood Scrubs prison. We are not concerned to consider precisely what happened on that occasion, although it appears to have resulted in a physical confrontation between prison officers and a number of inmates. Following this disturbance, the applicant was charged with six offences against prison discipline; these have been referred by the governor of the prison to the board of visitors for trial.

Miss Akester, who is an articled clerk with the firm of solicitors of Messrs B M Birnberg & Co, received a request to advise the applicant in connection with the possible commencement of legal proceedings on his behalf. This request appears to have been received by her from another firm of solicitors, which acted for the applicant in relation to criminal proceedings. The proposed proceedings, in respect of which she was informed that the applicant required advice, were civil proceedings alleging assault by one or more prison officers, arising, as we understand it, out of the disturbance which occurred at the prison on 16 June 1983.

Miss Akester made an appointment to see the applicant on 14 July. However, on 13 July she was telephoned by an assistant governor of the prison, Mr Bolter. He stated (as we now know correctly) that the applicant was intending to make allegations about the conduct of prison officers; and he told Miss Akester that the applicant was not entitled to consult a solicitor about the matter unless he had previously initiated an internal complaint, as required by standing orders. This he had not done.

So the interview between Miss Akester and the applicant, arranged for 14 July, did not take place. On 15 July Miss Akester wrote to the governor of the prison renewing her request for access to the applicant. On the following day, she was informed by the prison authorities that her letter had been passed on to the Home Office. Subsequently the Home Office informed her that it did not wish to interfere with Mr Bolter's advice and that it believed his interpretation of the standing orders to be correct. As a result the interview has not taken place, although there have since been four interviews between the applicant and Miss Akester (on one occasion accompanied by counsel instructed by her firm) in connection with the present application, in July, August and September 1983. We have been told that the applicant has not been 'advised directly' on the proposed civil action, and that no steps have yet been taken on his behalf to initiate it.

It will, we think, be helpful if at this stage we set out the relevant provisions of the standing orders, together with the legislative background. We begin with the Prison Act 1952. Section 47(1) of that Act provides as follows:

'The Secretary of State may make rules for the regulation and management of prisons, remand centres, detention centres and Borstal institutions respectively, and for the classification, treatment, employment, discipline and control of persons required to be detained therein.'

Pursuant to the power contained in that section the Secretary of State made certain rules known as the Prison Rules 1964, SI 1964/388. We propose to set out the text of certain parts of rr 33 to 37A of these rules. (Rule 37A was a subsequent addition, the first three paragraphs of that rule being added by SI 1972/1860, and the last paragraph by SI 1976/503.)

Rules 33 to 37A comprise those rules which fall under the heading 'Letters and visits'.

Rule 33, which is headed 'Letters and visits generally', and para (3) of which was amended
by SI 1974/713, reads as follows:

> '(1) The Secretary of State may, with a view to securing discipline and good order
> or the prevention of crime or in the interests of any persons, impose restrictions,
> either generally or in a particular case, upon the communications to be permitted
> between a prisoner and other persons.
>
> (2) Except as provided by statute or these Rules, a prisoner shall not be permitted
> to communicate with any outside person, or that person with him, without the
> leave of the Secretary of State.
>
> (3) Except as provided by these Rules, every letter or communication to or from
> a prisoner may be read or examined by the governor or an officer deputed by him,
> and the governor may, at his discretion, stop any letter or communication on the
> ground that its contents are objectionable or that it is of inordinate length.
>
> (4) Every visit to a prisoner shall take place within the sight of an officer, unless
> the Secretary of State otherwise directs.
>
> (5) Except as provided by these Rules, every visit to a prisoner shall take place
> within the hearing of an officer, unless the Secretary of State otherwise directs.
>
> (6) The Secretary of State may give directions, generally or in relation to any visit
> or class of visits, concerning the days and times when prisoners may be visited.'

Of r 34, which is headed 'Personal letters and visits', we think we need only set out para
(8), which reads:

> 'A prisoner shall not be entitled under this Rule to communicate with any person
> in connection with any legal or other business, or with any person other than a
> relative or friend, except with the leave of the Secretary of State.'

We omit rr 35 and 36 (headed respectively 'Police interviews' and 'Securing release') but
we propose to set out the full text of r 37, and also paras (1) and (4) of r 37A. They provide
as follows:

> **37.**—(1) The legal adviser of a prisoner in any legal proceedings, civil or criminal,
> to which the prisoner is a party shall be afforded reasonable facilities for interviewing
> him in connection with those proceedings, and may do so out of hearing but in the
> sight of an officer.
>
> (2) A prisoner's legal adviser may, with the leave of the Secretary of State,
> interview the prisoner in connection with any other legal business in the sight and
> hearing of an officer.
>
> **37A.**—(1) A prisoner who is a party to any legal proceedings may correspond
> with his legal adviser in connection with the proceedings and unless the Governor
> has reason to suppose that any such correspondence contains matter not relating to
> the proceedings it shall not be read or stopped under Rule 33(3) of these Rules . . .
>
> (4) Subject to any directions of the Secretary of State, a prisoner may correspond
> with a solicitor for the purpose of obtaining legal advice concerning any cause of
> action in relation to which the prisoner may become a party to civil proceedings or
> for the purposes of instructing the solicitor to issue such proceedings.'

Pursuant to his powers under r 33, the Secretary of State has issued standing order 5
entitled 'Communications'. Part A of the standing order is concerned with visits, and
Part B with correspondence. We are concerned with order 5A(34), which is entitled 'Visits
by Legal Advisers', and (by reference) with order 5B(34), entitled 'General Correspondence',
and in particular with para (j) of that order. Order 5A(34) provides as follows:

> 'VISITS BY LEGAL ADVISERS.
>
> Inmates may be visited by legal advisers acting in their professional capacity.
> Visiting orders need not be surrendered. All visits between inmates and legal
> advisers should be in the sight of a prison officer. An inmate who is a party to legal
> proceedings is entitled under Rule 37(1) to a visit with his legal adviser out of the

hearing of a prison officer to discuss those proceedings. Other visits with a legal adviser acting in his professional capacity should also be allowed out of hearing *a* provided the subject to be discussed is disclosed to the governor in advance and does not offend against the restrictions on correspondence with legal advisers set out in Order 5B 34. Visits by members of the legal profession as a friend or relative of an inmate are subject to the general rules on domestic visits. (See also Order 5F 7 and SO 8A 5).'

b

It will be observed that one of the requirements imposed by that order in respect of certain visits by legal advisers is that the subject to be discussed does not offend against the restrictions on correspondence set out in order 5B(34). That order provides (so far as is relevant) as follows:

'GENERAL CORRESPONDENCE.

Correspondence covered by Order 5B 33(e), "general correspondence", may not *c* contain the following . . . j. Complaints about prison treatment which the inmate has not yet raised through the prescribed procedures unless the complaints are about a matter already decided at region headquarters or the complaints are about a matter which does not require investigation or on which no corrective or remedial action is possible, such as complaints of a general nature about conditions, e g about overcrowding or poor facilities, which are basically descriptive of the conditions the *d* inmate is experiencing and his feelings about them. As soon as a complaint about prison treatment has been made through the prescribed procedures it may be mentioned in correspondence. The prescribed procedures are: i. with respect to an adjudication, by petition to the Secretary of State; ii. with respect to an allegation of misconduct or impropriety by a member of staff, in writing to the governor, or by petition to the Secretary of State; iii. in relation to any other matter, by petition to *e* the Secretary of State or by application to the Board of Visitors or by application to a visiting officer of the Secretary of State. Statements about prison treatment are not treated as complaints when they are matters of fact, e g that an inmate has suffered injury, or that he has been punished for an offence against prison discipline, or that he is in the process of making a complaint through the proper channels . . .'

f

It will at once be apparent that, in acting as he did, Mr Bolter (with the subsequent approval of the Home Office) was invoking order 5A(34). He was referring to the provision of that order that—

'Other visits with a legal adviser acting in his professional capacity should also be allowed out of hearing providing the subject to be discussed is disclosed to the governor in advance and does not offend against the restrictions on correspondence *g* with legal advisers set out in Order 5B 34.'

Here, the subject to be discussed between the applicant and his legal adviser was an alleged assault on the applicant by a prison officer. No complaint had been made by the applicant in respect of such assault through the prescribed procedure, the appropriate procedure in such a case being a complaint in writing to the governor. It was for this *h* reason that the prison authorities, as Mr Bolter told Miss Akester, decided that the interview arranged between her and the applicant for 14 July should not take place. At the heart of the applicant's present application for judicial review lies a challenge to the vires of the provision of order 5A(34) which (by reference to order 5B(34)(j)) imposes the restriction so invoked by the prison authorities.

For the sake of completeness, we propose to record the fact that under r 47(12) of the *j* Prison Rules 1964 a false and malicious allegation by an inmate of a prison against a member of the staff is a disciplinary offence. So, if a prisoner makes a complaint against a member of the staff, he may expose himself to a charge of having committed such an offence. We were told that because of this it is the practice in prisons in this country, where a prisoner has indicated a desire to make a complaint against a member of the staff, that he should be supplied with a document warning him of the provision before he pursues the matter any further. There was in evidence before us a copy of the form of document so used (in fact, one used in Pentonville prison), which reads as follows:

> 'Having indicated that you wish to make a complaint against a member of staff, the following warning is administered, not to put pressure upon you, but to make sure you understand your position. If you believe a member of staff has behaved improperly you are right to report the matter and if you can show that what you say is true, you have nothing to fear. On the other hand a false and malicious allegation by an inmate against a member of staff is a disciplinary offence. An allegation is false and malicious if the allegation is untrue, and you make it knowing it to be untrue or without caring whether it is true or not. Do you understand that? It is for you to decide whether you wish to pursue your complaint. If you do, your complaint will be fully investigated and you will not have another opportunity to withdraw it. It will be up to you to show that what you say is true or at least that you have good reasons for believing it to be true. If the investigation appears to show that your allegation is false and that you either knew it was false or did not care whether it was true or false, you may be charged with making a false and malicious allegation against an officer. If on reflection you wish to withdraw your complaint, you may do so and that will be the end of the matter. If having considered the matter you wish to continue you: (i) MUST MAKE A FULL WRITTEN STATEMENT OF YOUR COMPLAINT. (ii) MAY ADD ANY FURTHER RELEVANT INFORMATION TO THE WRITTEN STATEMENT YOU HAVE ALREADY MADE. (iii) MUST GIVE THE NAME OF ANY PERSONS WHO YOU WISH TO GIVE EVIDENCE.'

It is plain that underlying this case there is a problem of the relationship between the internal investigation within a prison of a matter giving rise to an allegation by an inmate against a member of the prison staff and the right of an inmate to pursue his complaint by a civil action against a member of the staff in the ordinary courts. Until comparatively recently the standing orders issued by the Home Office embodied the principle of the prior ventilation rule, viz that such allegations must *first* be pursued and investigated within the prison system. However, following the decision of the European Commission of Human Rights in *Silver v UK* (1980) 3 EHRR 475, the prior ventilation rule was abandoned, and there was substituted for it the simultaneous ventilation rule, now embodied in orders 5A(34) and 5B(34)(j). As we have seen, these orders impose a restriction on visits by a legal adviser, acting in a professional capacity, to an inmate who is not party to legal proceedings, namely that the subject matter of the visit should not be a complaint about prison treatment which the inmate has not yet raised through the prescribed procedure; in the present case, in writing to the governor.

It is right to observe that a simultaneous ventilation rule was briefly discussed in the judgment of the Commission in *Silver v UK* (1980) 3 EHRR 475. The British government had sought to justify the prior ventilation rule on the ground that it was—

> 'necessary, having regard to the ordinary and reasonable requirements of imprisonment, to enable prison authorities to provide an immediate remedy, where warranted, and to maintain staff morale by preventing, or limiting, wild allegations against prison officers.'

(See 3 EHRR 475 at 502, para 300.)

The Commission, while accepting that 'the ordinary and reasonable requirements of imprisonment justify a system of internal inquiry into prisoners' complaints about their treatment or conditions in prison', nevertheless did not consider that this justified a prior ventilation rule. The Commission continued:

> 'The Commission is of the opinion that the need to provide an immediate remedy would be equally satisfied by a simultaneous ventilation rule. As to limiting wild allegations against prison staff, the Commission notes that even if the internal inquiry finds against the prisoner he may still then make his allegations to his

Member of Parliament. Persons against whom such allegations are made have the
ordinary protection of the civil law of defamation, and prison officers have a further *a*
protection in that it is a disciplinary offence for a prisoner to make false and
malicious allegations against them. A conviction for this offence by the board of
visitors may entail serious sanctions such as loss of remission of sentence.'

(See 3 EHRR 475 at 502–503, paras 301–302.)

Hence, no doubt, the introduction of the simultaneous ventilation rule, in place of the *b*
prior ventilation rule, in the present standing orders. However, the submission of counsel
for the applicant before us was that the simultaneous ventilation rule, though less
objectionable than the prior ventilation rule, suffers from the same defect, in that it
imposes a fetter on an inmate's right of access to the courts of this country. In summary,
counsel's submissions were as follows.

(1) A prisoner remains invested with all civil rights which are not taken away expressly
or by necessary implication (see *Raymond v Honey* [1982] 1 All ER 756 at 759, [1983] 1 *c*
AC 1 at 10 per Lord Wilberforce).

(2) At the forefront of those civil rights is the right of unimpeded access to the courts;
and the right of access to a solicitor to obtain advice and assistance with regard to the
initiation of civil proceedings is inseparable from the right of access to the courts
themselves. In this connection, counsel for the applicant referred us in particular to art
6(1) of the Convention for the Protection of Human Rights and Fundamental Freedoms *d*
(Rome, 4 November 1950; TS 71 (1953); Cmd 8969), as interpreted by the European
Court of Human Rights in *Golder v UK* (1975) 1 EHRR 524.

(3) A citizen's right of unimpeded access to the courts can only be taken away by
express enactment (see *Raymond v Honey* [1982] 1 All ER 756 at 762, [1983] 1 AC 1 at 14
per Lord Bridge). Section 47 of the Prison Act 1952 is insufficient to authorise hindrance *e*
or interference with so basic a right as the right of unimpeded access to the courts (see
[1982] 1 All ER 756 at 760, [1983] 1 AC 1 at 12–13 per Lord Wilberforce). Accordingly,
the regulations made thereunder, ie the Prison Rules 1964, must either be interpreted
accordingly, or, in so far as they purport to authorise action which does amount to an
impediment to such access, they must be regarded as ultra vires (see [1982] 1 All ER 756
at 760, 762, [1983] 1 AC 1 at 13, 15 per Lord Wilberforce and Lord Bridge).

(4) The simultaneous ventilation rule amounts to such an impediment. It does so *f*
because, by requiring an inmate to make his complaint in the prescribed form (here, in
writing to the governor), it exposes him to the possibility of being charged with making
a false and malicious allegation against a member of the prison staff; and the mere threat
of this occurring could be sufficient to deter an inmate from making a complaint in a
controversial situation, in which event he would not be free to obtain the assistance of a
solicitor in pursuing his complaint in the civil courts. *g*

(5) Accordingly, the withholding of leave for a legal adviser to visit and interview an
inmate because of failure to comply with the simultaneous ventilation rule is
unauthorised by any provision of the Prison Rules (in particular by r 33) which must be
read as not permitting any contrary construction.

Counsel for the respondents submitted that there was no absolute principle that any *h*
impediment to an inmate's right of access to his solicitor was ultra vires. The question
was one of balance. The greater the deprivation of civil rights and the degree of
interference with the due course of justice, the greater the need for a clearly intra vires
provision to justify the restriction and the more reluctant will the courts be to construe
the rule-making process to permit the restriction. Furthermore, he submitted, a crucial
distinction must be drawn between a regulation which impedes an inmate's right of *j*
access to the courts, and one which regulates the circumstances in which an inmate may
have access to a solicitor. Whereas the former is, on the principles stated by the House of
Lords in *Raymond v Honey* [1982] 1 All ER 756, [1983] 1 AC 1, not permissible, the latter
is within the powers conferred on the Secretary of State by s 47(1) of the Prison Act 1952
to make rules for, inter alia, the regulation and management of prisons, and discipline
and control of persons required to be detained therein. In publishing standing orders

regulating the circumstances in which an inmate may have access to a solicitor, the
a   Secretary of State was fully entitled to take into account, in the interests of the good
administration of prisons and indeed of all inmates in prisons, the benefits flowing from
the prompt investigation within prisons of complaints against members of the prison
staff. These advantages were summarised in Mr Bolter's affidavit as follows:

'7 ... It is fundamental to the good order and discipline of a prison that
complaints about prison treatment are communicated to the Governor as soon as
b   they arise and that an investigation can be made and appropriate action taken as
soon as possible. In this respect it would be most unsatisfactory if complaints about
prison treatment were being aired outside prison before the prison authorities had
had a chance to investigate and remedy the matters complained of. Malpractices in
a closed institution can affect the lives of all those who have to live and work in the
institution. It is, therefore, of the greatest benefit to them that complaints about the
c   running of such institutions should be speedily investigated and resolved.
8. It is particularly important that complaints against members of staff should be
speedily investigated. If a prisoner makes an allegation against an officer which on
investigation seems well founded, it may be necessary to suspend an officer from
duty. On the other hand a prisoner might make an allegation against an officer
which on investigation seems to be false and malicious. By virtue of Prison Rule
d   47(12) it is a disciplinary offence to make a false and malicious allegation against an
officer. It would be difficult to bring such a charge if the prisoner had not made his
allegation in prison.'

In considering the rival submissions of the parties, we have the benefit of guidance
from the House of Lords in Raymond v Honey [1982] 1 All ER 756, [1983] 1 AC 1, to
e   which we have already referred. In that case the respondent, Raymond, was an inmate of
Albany prison, of which the appellant was the governor. The respondent, who was
engaged in legal proceedings, wrote a letter to his solicitors from prison which the
appellant, having reason to believe that it contained material not related to those
proceedings, caused to be opened and read (pursuant to his powers under rr 33 and 37A
of the Prison Rules 1964). He found that it contained an allegation against an assistant
f   governor that he had caused a book of the respondent's to be lost or to disappear, and he
therefore stopped the letter. Thereafter the respondent prepared an application to the
High Court for leave to apply for an order of committal of the appellant for contempt of
court, together with supporting documents. The appellant stopped this application on
the ground that it included an allegation against a prison officer and that, under the
Prison Rules as they then stood, it could not be forwarded because the prior ventilation
g   rule had not been complied with. The respondent pursued his application for an order
of committal of the appellant for contempt of court, both in respect of stopping the letter
and of stopping the application. The Divisional Court, while dismissing the application
in respect of the letter, held that the appellant had been in contempt of court in stopping
the application. Both parties appealed to the House of Lords, which affirmed the decision
of the Divisional Court on both points. On the appellant's appeal, it was held by the
h   House of Lords that under English law a convicted prisoner, in spite of his imprisonment,
retains all civil rights which are not taken away expressly or by necessary implication;
and that there is nothing in the Prison Act 1952 which confers power to make regulations
which would deny, or interfere with, the right of a prisoner to have unimpeded access to
a court. Section 47 was insufficient to authorise hindrance or interference with so basic a
right; and the regulations contained in the Prison Rules must be interpreted accordingly
j   (see [1982] 1 All ER 756 at 759–760, [1983] 1 AC 1 at 10, 12–13 per Lord Wilberforce)
or, in so far as they did hinder or interfere with that right, they were ultra vires (see
[1982] 1 All ER 756 at 762, [1983] 1 AC 1 at 14–15 per Lord Bridge).
From this it follows that, if the simultaneous ventilation rule in orders 5A(34) and
5B(34) constitutes an impediment to the right of inmates of prisons, like other citizens,
to have access to the courts, it too must be ultra vires. We have therefore to consider
whether it constitutes such an impediment.

It is in this context that we have to consider the submission of counsel for the respondents that the simultaneous ventilation rule does no more than regulate the *a* circumstances in which inmates of prisons may have access to solicitors. We, for our part, accept that it is proper, and indeed inevitable, that some regulations must exist for that purpose. We can see a good example of such a regulation in order 5A(34) itself, which provides that 'Other visits with a legal adviser . . . should also be allowed out of hearing provided the subject to be discussed *is disclosed to the Governor in advance* . . .' (our emphasis). Such disclosure is necessary to enable the governor to satisfy himself that the *b* visitor is the legal adviser of the inmate acting in his professional capacity; and counsel for the applicant, in the present case, disclaimed any intention to criticise order 5A(34) in this respect. But does the simultaneous ventilation rule fall within the same category? No doubt the purposes underlying the simultaneous ventilation rule are, as explained in Mr Bolter's affidavit, entirely understandable; and it may appear at first sight somewhat strange that an inmate should be enabled to institute legal proceedings against a prison *c* officer for, eg an assault, without at the same time making a formal internal complaint against the prison officer to the prison authorities. But we have come to the conclusion that the simultaneous ventilation rule does go beyond regulating the circumstances in which an inmate may have access to his solicitor, and does constitute an impediment to the inmate's right of access to the courts. As such it must, in our judgment, be ultra vires.

On the principles stated by the House of Lords in *Raymond v Honey*, there is no room *d* for the type of balancing operation proposed by counsel for the respondents. If any restriction goes beyond the scope of regulating the circumstances in which visits of legal advisers to inmates may take place, and so constitutes an impediment to the right of access to the courts, it is on the authority of that case unauthorised by the Prison Rules 1964, or indeed by s 47(1) of the Prison Act 1952.

We approach the matter as follows. First of all, we accept the submission of counsel *e* for the applicant that unimpeded access to a solicitor for the purpose of receiving advice and assistance in connection with the possible institution of civil proceedings in the courts forms an inseparable part of the right of access to the courts themselves (see the decision of the European Court of Human Rights in *Golder v UK* [1975] 1 EHRR 524, the case which prompted the addition of para (4) to r 37A of the Prison Rules 1964). There must indeed be few prisoners who possess the knowledge and skill of the *f* respondent in *Raymond v Honey*, so as to be able themselves to identify and draft the relevant initiating process and prepare the necessary supporting documents.

Secondly, in our judgment the simultaneous ventilation rule constitutes an impediment to the right of access to a solicitor, because it requires the inmate to do something unnecessary for the purpose of enabling him to see his solicitor, and which otherwise he could not be required to do. No inmate can be compelled to make an internal complaint *g* against a member of the prison staff, and it is possible to envisage circumstances of a controversial nature in which an inmate may hesitate to make an internal complaint for fear that he may be accused of committing the disciplinary offence of making a false and malicious allegation against a member of the prison staff, an offence which, if found proved against him, may result in his suffering punishment in the form of loss of privileges or loss of remission. As it seems to us, a requirement that an inmate should *h* make such a complaint as a *prerequisite* of his having access to his solicitor, however desirable it may be in the interests of good administration, goes beyond the regulation of the circumstances in which such access may take place, and does indeed constitute an impediment to his right of access to the civil courts.

As we can see from *Raymond v Honey* itself, an inmate can initiate civil proceedings without making any formal complaint, simply by dispatching the necessary documents *j* to the court by post. Such a communication cannot be stopped by the governor, and is not therefore, under the standing orders, subject to the simultaneous ventilation rule (see order 5B(33)(a)). It must, we consider, be inherent in the logic of the decision of the House of Lords in *Raymond v Honey* that an inmate's right of access to a solicitor for the purposes of obtaining advice and assistance with a view to instituting proceedings should

be unimpeded, in the same way as his right to initiate proceedings by dispatching the
necessary documents for that purpose by post is unimpeded.

It follows that we accept, in substance, the submission of counsel on behalf of the
applicant. We turn next, therefore, to the form of the relief which we consider to be
appropriate in the circumstances.

The relief sought by the applicant is as follows. (1) A mandatory injunction ordering
the governor of Wormwood Scrubs prison and his servants or agents and other Crown
servants under his control to permit his legal adviser to interview the applicant
immediately for the purpose of taking instructions and giving legal advice out of hearing
of a prison officer. (2) An order of mandamus directing the Secretary of State to grant
his legal adviser leave to interview the applicant out of hearing of a prison officer. (3) A
declaration that the applicant is entitled to be interviewed by his legal adviser in
connection with such matter as has given rise to his request for legal advice. (4) A
declaration that the applicant is entitled to an interview out of the hearing of a prison
officer. (5) A declaration that standing order 5A(34), in so far as it prohibits visits by a
legal adviser to advise on prisoners' complaints about prison treatment prior to the
lodging of an internal complaint with the prison authorities, is ultra vires. (6) A
declaration that the applicant is entitled to correspond with his solicitors in connection
with the proposed litigation without first lodging a complaint through the internal
disciplinary procedures.

Of these proposed heads of relief, we are prepared to make declarations reflecting the
substance of paras (5) and (6), there being no material distinction between visits and
correspondence for present purposes. We can see no virtue in making, in addition, a
declaration in terms of para (3). So far as the declaration in para (4) is concerned, we can
see no need for any such declaration. Under r 33(5) of the Prison Rules 1964, it is
provided that 'Except as provided by these rules, every visit to a prisoner shall take place
within the hearing of an officer, unless the Secretary of State otherwise directs'. Pursuant
to that rule, it is provided in order 5A(34) that the relevant visit shall be out of hearing,
provided that the subject to be discussed is disclosed to the governor in advance and
provided that the simultaneous ventilation rule is complied with. It is common ground
that if the latter requirement is removed, the visit should not take place in the hearing of
an officer, so no declaration is required. We only suggest that those responsible for
amendment of the Prison Rules may wish to reconsider r 37(2), since it appears in part to
be inconsistent with r 33(5) and with order 5A(34).

Finally we have considered whether any mandatory order should be made, as asked
for in para (1). We have come to the conclusion that no such order is required. The
opposition of the prison authorities and the Home Office to the interview between the
applicant and his solicitor has been based entirely on the applicant's failure to comply
with the simultaneous ventilation rule as provided in the standing orders. We think it
sufficient, in these circumstances, to declare the relevant provisions of the standing orders
to be ultra vires. It follows that we shall confine the relief granted by us to declarations
under paras (5) and (6). We shall hear any submissions which counsel may wish to make
about the precise form which these declarations should take.

Declarations accordingly.

Solicitors: *B M Birnberg & Co* (for the applicant); *Treasury Solicitor.*

Raina Levy   Barrister.

Rimmer v Liverpool City Council　　　　*a*

COURT OF APPEAL, CIVIL DIVISION
STEPHENSON, GRIFFITHS AND PURCHAS LJJ
8, 10 NOVEMBER, 6 DECEMBER 1983

Negligence – Landlord's liability – Landlord also designer and builder of premises – Liability of　*b*
defendant as landlord and/or designer and builder – Council designing and building flats
containing panel of thin and easily breakable glass – Tenant of flat breaking glass and injuring
hand – Whether council owing duty of care to tenant as landlord and/or as builder and designer.

The plaintiff was the tenant of a council flat which had been designed and built by the
council. An internal wall of a narrow passage in the flat leading from the lounge to the
kitchen contained a panel of thin breakable glass which was unprotected by a sill or other　*c*
means. At the start of his tenancy the plaintiff complained about the glass panel to the
council's housing department because of the possible danger to his young son but was
told that the panel was a standard installation and could not be changed. Some time later,
while walking near the glass panel, the plaintiff tripped or stumbled, put out his hand to
save himself and in doing so put his hand through the panel thereby sustaining injury.　*d*
He brought an action against the council in negligence, alleging that the council was in
breach of the duty of care which it owed as landlord to the plaintiff as tenant in letting a
flat to the plaintiff which contained a dangerous feature, namely the glass panel. The
trial judge found for the plaintiff. The council appealed.

Held – Although a bare landlord of unfurnished premises did not owe any duty of care
to a tenant in regard to the state of the premises when they were let, a landlord who also　*e*
designed or built the premises owed, in his capacity of designer or builder, a duty of care
to all persons (not just the tenant) who might reasonably be expected to be affected by
the design or construction of the premises, the duty being to take reasonable care to see
that such persons would not suffer injury as the result of faults in the design or
construction of the premises. Since the council had designed and built the flat, it owed,　*f*
as designer and builder, a duty of care to the plaintiff and, on the facts, was in breach of
that duty. The fact that the plaintiff knew that the glass panel was dangerous did not
exonerate the council from liability, because the plaintiff had not been free to remove or
avoid the danger by altering the panel or leaving the flat. The council's appeal would
therefore be dismissed (see p 933 *b* and *g* to *j*, p 938 *a* to *h*, p 939 *j* and p 940 *a b*, post).

Dicta of Evershed MR in *Denny v Supplies and Transport Co Ltd* [1950] 2 KB at 382, of
Denning LJ in *Greene v Chelsea BC* [1954] 2 All ER at 325, of Denning LJ in *Slater v Clay*　*g*
Cross Co Ltd [1956] 2 All ER at 628, of Denning LJ in *Riden v A C Billings & Sons Ltd*
[1956] 3 All ER at 364, of Lord Wilberforce and of Lord Salmon in *Anns v Merton London*
Borough [1977] 2 All ER at 504, 512 and *Batty v Metropolitan Property Realizations Ltd*
[1978] 2 All ER 445 applied.

Cavalier v Pope [1906] AC 428 distinguished.　　　　　　　　　　　　　　　　*h*

Notes
For a landlord's duty of care to his tenant, see 34 Halsbury's Laws (4th edn) para 31–33.

Cases referred to in judgment
Anns v Merton London Borough [1977] 2 All ER 492, [1978] AC 728, [1977] 2 WLR 1024,　*j*
　HL.
Batty v Metropolitan Property Realizations Ltd [1978] 2 All ER 445, [1978] QB 554, [1978]
　2 WLR 500, CA.
Bottomley v Bannister [1932] 1 KB 458, [1931] All ER Rep 99, CA.
Cameron v Young [1908] AC 176, HL.

Cartledge v E Jopling & Sons Ltd [1963] 1 All ER 341, [1963] AC 758, [1963] 2 WLR 210, HL.

Cavalier v Pope [1906] AC 428, HL.

Clay v A J Crump & Sons Ltd [1963] 3 All ER 687, [1964] 1 QB 533, [1963] 3 WLR 866, CA.

Clayton v Woodman & Son (Builders) Ltd [1962] 2 All ER 33, [1962] 1 WLR 585, CA.

Davis v Foots [1939] 4 All ER 4, [1940] 1 KB 116, CA.

Denny v Supplies and Transport Co Ltd [1950] 2 KB 374, CA.

Donoghue (or M'Alister) v Stevenson [1932] AC 562, [1932] All ER Rep 1, HL.

Dutton v Bognor Regis United Building Co Ltd [1972] 1 All ER 462, sub nom *Dutton v Bognor Regis UDC* [1972] 1 QB 373, [1972] 2 WLR 299, CA.

Gallagher v N McDowell Ltd [1961] NI 26.

Greene v Chelsea BC [1954] 2 All ER 318, [1954] 2 QB 127, [1954] 3 WLR 12, CA.

Junior Books Ltd v Veitchi Co Ltd [1982] 3 All ER 201, [1983] 1 AC 520, [1983] 3 WLR 477, HL.

Pirelli General Cable Works Ltd v Oscar Faber & Partners Ltd [1983] 1 All ER 65, [1983] 2 AC 1, [1983] 2 WLR 6, HL.

Riden v A C Billings & Sons Ltd [1956] 3 All ER 357, [1957] 1 QB 46, [1956] 3 WLR 704, CA; *affd* [1957] 3 All ER 1, [1958] AC 240, [1957] 3 WLR 496, HL.

Robbins v Jones (1863) 15 CBNS 221, [1861–73] All ER Rep 544, 143 ER 768.

Siney v Dublin Corp [1980] IR 400.

Slater v Clay Cross Co Ltd [1956] 2 All ER 625, [1956] 2 QB 264, [1956] 3 WLR 232, CA.

Smith v Marrable (1843) 11 M & W 5, 152 ER 693.

Voli v Inglewood Shire Council (1963) 110 CLR 74, Aust HC.

Wilson v Finch Hatton (1877) 2 Ex D 336

Appeal

The defendant, Liverpool City Council, appealed against the judgment of his Honour Judge Nance sitting as a judge of the High Court on 6 May 1982 whereby he gave judgment for the plaintiff, John Rimmer, for £2,500 agreed damages on the plaintiff's claim against the council for negligence and/or breach of statutory duty. The facts are set out in the judgment of the court.

Christopher Rose QC and *J F Appleton* for the council.
Michael Morland QC and *D M Harris* for the plaintiff.

Cur adv vult

6 December. The following judgment of the court was delivered.

STEPHENSON LJ. This appeal arises out of an accident which was thus described by his Honour Judge Nance in giving judgment for the plaintiff on 6 May 1982:

'At about 9.30 in the evening of 28 December 1975 the plaintiff was making his way from the lounge to the kitchen. He was carrying a cup and saucer. The floor was somewhat encumbered by toys and the little boy, who was still playing possibly with a moving toy. The plaintiff at a point near to the lounge door stumbled or tripped because of, or because of his endeavours to avoid, some obstruction on the floor. He fell forward.'

He put out his left hand to try to save or help himself and with quite considerable force put his hand through a glass panel in front of him, thereby sustaining quite substantial injuries to his left hand and wrist. For that injury he claimed from the defendant council and received from the judge damages which were agreed at £2,500 with interest.

The place where the accident occurred was a flat which the plaintiff had taken from the council on a weekly tenancy in May 1974. The flat was one of a block of 24 in *a* Boundary Street East, Liverpool, built by the council, through their direct works department, in 1959 to the same design in all material respects. The design and construction included the glass panel which cut the plaintiff's hand. That was a panel of glass which was translucent, not transparent, forming part of an internal wall directly opposite the lounge or living room door at a height of 2 ft above the floor of a corridor or passage 2 ft 10 in wide. So the glass across the passage was no more than 2 ft 10 in from *b* the living room door. It was there to give light to the passage. It was 4 ft 3 in high and 2 ft wide; and it was only ⅛ in or 3 mm thick.

The original project architect in the council's architects' department at one stage specified Georgian wired glass for this feature, that is wired glass ¼ in (6 mm) thick. But in 1959 at some stage the architect in charge altered the requirement to pattern glass ⅛ in (3 mm) thick, and at the time of the trial those flats which were available for inspection *c* had these original thin glass panels.

The plaintiff gave evidence, which the judge accepted, that at the start of his tenancy he complained to a technical officer with the council's housing department of the danger to his five-year-old son of the glass because of its thinness, but was told it was standard and nothing could be done about it. That officer gave evidence neither recalling nor disputing the plaintiff's evidence, but stating that he had never heard of any complaint *d* by any other tenant of these 24 flats about this glass feature or of any other such accident as the plaintiff's.

The judge considered first the danger and then the duty, and we shall do the same. He said:

> 'I now consider whether the installation of thinner glass brought about a dangerous or more dangerous condition with a reasonably foreseeable risk of injury *e* or greater injury and whether, if so, the council ought to be adjudged to be at fault for creating or at the time of the letting to the plaintiff, allowing to continue that danger or greater danger and accepting such risk or greater risk. If appropriate I shall then have to consider the problem whether there was a duty owed to the plaintiff in this regard. To me it is an elementary proposition of common sense that *f* easily breakable glass presents a risk of some, possibly serious, injury if a braking hand penetrates the glass. I do not need an expert to tell me that and it is no surprise that all the experts are agreed that there is an inherent risk of injury if glass is so broken. That does not mean that it is always wrong to use such glass for a window or screen in any building work. One must balance many factors.'

He then went on to consider the position of the glass, the cost, the professional advice *g* available in 1959, the British Standards Institution's codes of practice and the evidence of the plaintiff's experts.

He concluded that the 1959 architect had no code of practice to guide him on the safety of glass but none the less—

> 'in 1959 there was a foreseeable risk that someone might stumble and put his *h* hand against this glass and break it. I reach this conclusion with the assistance of the expert evidence but also because it seems to me that the narrow corridor, the juxtaposition of lounge door and glass, the lowness of the glass, the lack of any protective sill or any other protective device made the risk obvious, and one which could so easily have been reduced by adopting the idea of the original design architect for ¼ in (6 mm) Georgian wired glass. I so consider that whoever changed *j* the design, a servant of the council, was at fault.'

He went on to look at the 1974 position when the council let the flat to the plaintiff and concluded that an intelligent reading of the 1966 and 1972 codes of practice would have called to the minds of the architects' department the risk of danger to anyone stumbling against this glass 'unprotected as it was and low as it was, and thin as it was';

a the department were not relieved from reconsidering the position in the light of after gained information; the council were at fault in letting to the plaintiff 'a flat which they ought to have known contained this foreseeably dangerous and easily substituted glass'.

These findings were challenged in the notice of appeal and more faintly in the argument of counsel for the council. But they seem to us soundly based on the facts and the evidence by a judge who carefully balanced all the relevant factors, and they are therefore beyond challenge in this court. If there was a duty of care it was broken. The

b real issue raised by this appeal is not negligence but duty. Was there a duty of care?

On this question of the council's duty to the plaintiff we have heard interesting and attractive arguments on both sides, and have been taken to a number of well-known authorities, as was the judge. The duty for which the plaintiff argued and which the judge imposed was a duty at common law. It was not alleged that there was any contractual liability. A statutory liability had been pleaded under ss 1 and 3 of the

c Defective Premises Act 1972, which came into force on 1 January 1974 (see s 7(2)). But any claim under s 1 was barred by s 1(5), by which any cause of action the plaintiff had under the section was deemed to have accrued in 1959, when the building was completed; s 3 does not create a duty but preserves any existing duty of care in relation to work which 'is done', which does not naturally mean 'has been done', before the 1972 Act came into force, like the construction of this glass panel, from abatement by subsequent

d disposal of the premises such as a letting (see s 6(1)). Section 4, which the judge treated as having been alleged, though it was not pleaded, was abandoned before trial because the duty it imposes on a landlord is only a duty to take reasonable care to see that the premises let are reasonably safe from personal injury (or from damage to property) caused by a failure to carry out an obligation to maintain or repair the premises (see s 4(3)), and there was no such failure here. There was apparently no such obligation, and certainly no want

e of repair.

We shall have to refer to that 1972 Act again, but the judge was right to consider that the only duty which could be owed to the plaintiff by the council was a duty of care at common law. He was able to hold that there was such a duty, which he formulated in this conclusion:

f 'I have reached the conclusion that the law today is that a landlord must apply his mind before letting to a tenant to the question of whether the premises may be considered to be reasonably safe. He must have in contemplation the reasonable use of the premises by the proposed tenant, his family and his visitors. In contract he may make exclusion clauses. That does not apply here. In my judgment, therefore, there was and is a legal duty on a landlord to take reasonable steps to ensure that the premises are reasonably safe. For the reasons I have set out I hold that this landlord,

g the council, failed in their duty in 1959 or, at the latest, 1974. Therefore there is liability to the plaintiff.'

Counsel for the plaintiff seeks to support that formulation. We have come to the conclusion that it was not open to the judge, and is not open to any court below the highest, to say that that is the law, however desirable that it should be, but that counsel

h for the plaintiff is right in his alternative and less ambitious submission that there was a legal duty on *these* landlords to take reasonable care to see that this flat was reasonably safe for the plaintiff because they were both the designers and the builders of this flat, and they failed in their duty by designing and constructing a dangerous feature in this glass panel.

In 1906 the House of Lords held that the wife of a tenant, to whom a landlord had let

j a dilapidated house unfurnished, had no right of action against the landlord for injuries caused by her falling through the dangerous floor; she knew of the danger and she was not a party to the agreement to repair the floor which the landlord's agent had made with her husband: see *Cavalier v Pope* [1906] AC 428. Two years later the wife and family of a tenant who all contracted typhoid fever from insanitary drains in a house in Scotland were equally unsuccessful; the tenant had a claim on a contractual obligation to repair

implied by the law of Scotland, and it was settled; but the House applied the principle
common to the laws of Scotland and of England which *Cavalier v Pope* had applied to *a*
defeat the claim of his wife and family: see *Cameron v Young* [1908] AC 176.

The question raised by this appeal is whether the authority of *Cavalier v Pope* binds
this court to hold the council immune from liability to the plaintiff, or whether it does
not, either because it is inconsistent with later decisions of the House of Lords, which
was (we think) the judge's view, or because it can be distinguished from this case, which
is our own view.   *b*

Cavalier v Pope is not without its followers, and not without its critics. It has been
applied by this court in *Bottomley v Bannister* [1932] 1 KB 458, [1931] All ER Rep 99 and
again in *Davis v Foots* [1939] 4 All ER 4, [1940] 1 KB 116. In *Bottomley's* case the court
granted immunity to builders who had sold to a purchaser a house newly built with a
gas boiler which was dangerous unless the flow of gas was properly regulated. It was not
properly regulated and the purchaser and his wife, occupying the house as tenants at will, *c*
were fatally poisoned by the gas. In *Davis's* case the tenant of a flat, let by the couple who
had previously lived there, sued them for the death of her husband from gas poisoning
from a pipe left open by the landlords' son when he moved a gas fire; the court upheld
the landlords' appeal and took away the damages which the judge had awarded the
widow.

Between these two decisions the House of Lords had decided *M'Alister (or Donoghue) v* *d*
Stevenson [1932] AC 562, [1932] All ER Rep 1, which du Parcq LJ held could not be
applied to Mrs Davis's case because she had a reasonable opportunity for examining a
plainly apparent defect as soon as the gas was turned on. The long line of cases in which
Donoghue v Stevenson has been considered and applied ends, as far as this appeal is
concerned, with *Anns v Merton London Borough* [1977] 2 All ER 492, [1978] AC 728, in
which both *Cavalier v Pope* and *Bottomley v Bannister* were also considered.   *e*

The immunity which protected Pope from Mrs Cavalier's claim rested on the long-
established principle stated by Erle CJ in a judgment (written according to Scrutton LJ
by Willes J) in *Robbins v Jones* (1863) 15 CBNS 221 at 240, [1861–73] All ER Rep 544 at
547:

> 'A landlord who lets a house in a dangerous state, is not liable to the tenant's
> customers or guests for accidents happening during the term; for, fraud apart, there *f*
> is no law against letting a tumbledown house; and the tenant's remedy is upon his
> contract, if any.'

Common sense refused to extend the immunity to those who let furnished houses in
a defective condition: see *Smith v Marrable* (1843) 11 M & W 6, 152 ER 693, *Wilson v*
Finch Hatton (1877) 2 Ex D 336. But the Court of Appeal felt bound to maintain it in *g*
favour of a landlord or vendor 'even if he has constructed the defects himself or is aware
of their existence': see *Bottomley v Bannister* [1932] 1 KB 458 at 468, [1931] All ER Rep 99
at 102 per Scrutton LJ.

In *Donoghue v Stevenson* [1932] AC 562 at 577–578, [1932] All ER Rep 1 at 10 Lord
Buckmaster buttressed his dissent from the decision of the majority of their Lordships in
favour of making the manufacturer of a defective article liable to any persons so closely *h*
and directly affected by his acts or omissions that he might reasonably have them in
contemplation as being so affected by asking:

> 'If such a duty exists, it seems to me it must cover the construction of every
> article, and I cannot see any reason why it should not apply to the construction of a
> house. If one step, why not fifty? Yet if a house be, as it sometimes is, negligently *j*
> built, and in consequence of that negligence the ceiling falls and injures the occupier
> or any one else, no action against the builder exists according to the English law,
> although I believe such a right did exist according to the laws of Babylon.'

Yet Lord Atkin referred to *Cavalier v Pope* and *Bottomley v Bannister* without disapproval
and Lord Macmillan distinguished *Cavalier v Pope* and *Cameron v Young* (in which he had

been engaged as counsel) by putting them 'in a different chapter of the law' (see [1932]
a AC 562 at 597–598, 609, [1932] All ER Rep 1 at 19, 25).

In *Greene v Chelsea BC* [1954] 2 All ER 318, [1954] 2 QB 127 the Court of Appeal
refused to extend the *Cavalier v Pope* immunity to a requisitioning case where the
council's licensee had been injured by a defective ceiling. Denning LJ there said ([1954]
2 QB 127 at 138; cf [1954] 2 All ER 318 at 324):

b 'During the nineteenth century there was a doctrine current in the law which I
will call the "privity-of-contract" doctrine. In those days it was thought that if the
defendant became connected with the matter because of a contract he had made,
then his obligations were to be measured by the contract and nothing else. He owed,
it was said, no duty of care to anyone who was not a party to the contract. This
doctrine received its quietus by the decision of the House of Lords in *Donoghue v.*
Stevenson, but it has been asserted again before us today. We must, I think, firmly
c resist the revival of this out-worn fallacy. *Cavalier v. Pope* is a relic of it which must
be kept in a close confinement. This is not a landlord and tenant case.'

We respectfully agree that *Cavalier v Pope* must be kept in close confinement.

In *Dutton v Bognor Regis United Building Co Ltd* [1972] 1 All ER 462, [1972] 1 QB 373
the Court of Appeal upheld a judgment against the defendant council at the suit of a
d plaintiff who had bought a house built with defective foundations from the first
purchaser and had suffered financial loss. By a majority the court extended the *Donoghue*
v Stevenson neighbour principle to cover her claim against the council, she having settled
her claim against the builder-owner on advice that as the law stood a claim in negligence
against him could not succeed. Stamp LJ considered that it was not open to this court to
question the true effect of *Cavalier v Pope* and *Bottomley v Bannister* (see [1972] 1 All ER
462 at 489, [1972] 1 QB 373 at 414); Sachs LJ said that *Bottomley v Bannister* had now to
e be looked at in the light of what was decided in *Donoghue v Stevenson*, and *Cavalier v Pope*
was distinguishable because the landlord did not there create the dangerous state of affairs
and the defect was obvious (see [1972] 1 All ER 462 at 479, [1972] 1 QB 373 at 401–402).
Lord Denning MR, however, stated that *Bottomley v Bannister* was no longer authority
and '*Cavalier v Pope* has gone too. It was reversed by the Occupiers' Liability Act 1957,
f s 4(1)' (see [1972] 1 All ER 462 at 472, [1972] 1 QB 373 at 394).

We gratefully accept what Sachs LJ said, but we must respectfully dissent from what
Lord Denning MR said about *Cavalier v Pope*. Section 4(1) of the 1957 Act, and s 4(1) of
the Defective Premises Act 1972 which replaced and extended it, imposed a liability only
on landlords who are under an obligation to repair or maintain the tenants' premises and
only for defects in maintenance and repair. Section 4(1) of the 1957 Act limited a
g landlord's liability to default in carrying out his obligation for maintenance or repair;
s 4(1) of the 1972 Act, while it extends the ambit of the duty to all persons who might
reasonably be expected to be affected by defects in the state of the premises, retains the
limitation by defining defects in s 4(3) as those arising from an act or omission which
constitutes a failure by the landlord to carry out his obligation for maintenance or repair.
Neither of these sections imposed on a landlord any duty in respect of the state of a
h tenant's premises at the date of letting.

How do these statutory duties affect *Cavalier v Pope*? The House of Lords there decided
two things. (1) A landlord can let an unfurnished house which is in a dangerous state;
and that means that, if the tenant had been injured by a danger known to the landlord
but not to him, he could not have recovered damages for any breach of duty, in contract
or in tort, unless there was a special term imposing not merely a contractual duty to
j maintain and repair but a warranty of fitness for safe habitation. The tenant (Mr Cavalier)
had a special contract and was not himself injured, but the House began their
consideration of his wife's case by approving *Robbins v Jones* (1863) 15 CBNS 221, [1861–
73] All ER Rep 544. (2) A stranger to the contract of tenancy was owed no duty; so the
tenant's wife who was injured lost her action against the landlord. Landlords, and not
only landlords but owners who did not let but sold their land and buildings, were

immune from liability not only to strangers to their contracts of sale or letting but to the parties to those contracts themselves. For contractual duties were regarded as excluding delictual duties and a contractual relationship determined completely the rights and obligations of the related parties, as well as the rights of third parties.

There are enactments which improve the position of some tenants against some landlords by the statutory implication of covenants to keep in repair (see s 32 of the Housing Act 1961), and, more important, though not applicable to the tenant with whom this appeal is concerned, by implying a condition that the house is at the commencement of the tenancy, and an undertaking that it will be left by the landlord during the tenancy, fit for human habitation (see s 6 of the Housing Act 1957). It is also now the law, authoritatively stated by Lord Macmillan in *Donoghue v Stevenson* [1932] AC 562 at 610, [1932] All ER Rep 1 at 25, that one person may owe another a common law duty of care coexisting with a contractual duty and a contractual relationship does not necessarily exclude a relationship of proximity giving rise to the duty formulated in that case. It is unnecessary to go into the important effects that this coexistence of duties may have on the measure of damages and the period of limitation. Suffice it to note for the purpose of this appeal that this development of the law has been applied by this court to lessees of a house built on land without proper support and consequently unfit for habitation so as to enable them to recover damages for financial loss both from the builders of the house for their negligence and from the developers of the land, who employed the builders and let the house, for their negligence as well as for their breach of contract: see *Batty v Metropolitan Property Realizations Ltd* [1978] 2 All ER 445, [1978] QB 554, a case relied on by the judge and approved by the House of Lords in *Junior Books Ltd v Veitchi Co Ltd* [1982] 3 All ER 301, [1983] 1 AC 520.

Batty's case was a case of economic loss, but it cannot be argued that the tenants would have been any less successful if they had suffered personal injury. The court was applying the decision of the House of Lords in *Anns v Merton London Borough* [1977] 2 All ER 492, [1978] AC 728, which considered a local authority's liability to lessees of flats for the negligence of one of its officers in inspecting inadequate foundations of the block containing the flats, and held that the local authority did owe the lessees a duty of care, as had been rightly decided in *Dutton's* case. In the course of the appeal the House had to consider the position of the builder. Lord Wilberforce, with whose speech Lord Diplock, Lord Simon and Lord Russell agreed, said ([1977] 2 All ER 492 at 504, [1978] AC 728 at 758–759):

'I agree with the majority in the Court of Appeal in thinking that it would be unreasonable to impose liability in respect of defective foundations on the council, if the builder, whose primary fault it was, should be immune from liability. So it is necessary to consider this point, although it does not directly arise in the present appeal. If there was at one time a supposed rule that the doctrine of *Donoghue v Stevenson* did not apply to realty, there is no doubt under modern authority that a builder of defective premises may be liable in negligence to persons who thereby suffer injury: see *Gallagher v N McDowell Ltd* [1961] NI 26, per Lord MacDermott CJ, a case of personal injury. Similar decisions have been given in regard to architects (*Clayton v Woodman & Son (Builders) Ltd* [1962] 2 All ER 33, [1962] 1 WLR 585, *Clay v A J Crump & Sons Ltd* [1963] 3 All ER 687, [1964] 1 QB 533). *Gallagher's* case expressly leaves open the question whether the immunity against action of builder-owners, established by older authorities (e g *Bottomley v Bannister* [1932] 1 KB 458, [1931] All ER Rep 99) still survives. That immunity, as I understand it, rests partly on a distinction being made between chattels and real property, partly on the principle of "caveat emptor" or, in the case where the owner leases the property, on the proposition that (fraud apart) there is no law against letting a "tumbledown house" (*Robbins v Jones* (1863) 15 CBNS 221 at 240, [1861–73] All ER Rep 544 at 547, per Erle CJ). But leaving aside such cases as arise between contracting parties, when the terms of the contract have to be considered (see *Voli v Inglewood Shire Council*

(1963) 110 CLR 74 at 85, per Windeyer J), I am unable to understand why this principle or proposition should prevent recovery in a suitable case by a person, who has subsequently acquired the house, on the principle of *Donoghue v Stevenson*: the same rules should apply to all careless acts of a builder: whether he happens also to own the land or not. I agree generally with the conclusions of Lord Denning MR on this point (*Dutton's* case [1972] 1 All ER 462 at 471–472, [1972] 1 QB 373 at 392–394).'

Lord Wilberforce there does two things. First, he approves the decision of the Court of Appeal in Northern Ireland that a builder may be liable to those injured by his negligence in building, and thereby confirms Lord Buckmaster's fear that English law would in this respect have to conform to the laws of Babylon. Second, he answers the open question whether the immunity of builder owners still survives in the negative: the builder owner is no more immune from the consequences of careless building than is the builder who is not the owner. Lord Salmon was of the same opinion. He said ([1977] 2 All ER 492 at 511–512, [1978] AC 728 at 767–768):

'I recognise that it would be unjust if, in the circumstances of this case, the whole burden should fall on the council whilst the contractor who negligently put in the faulty foundations remained free from liability. It has, however, been decided in *Gallagher v N McDowell Ltd* that a building contractor owes a duty of care to the lawful user of a house and that accordingly the contractor is liable for any damage caused to a lawful user by the contractor's negligence in constructing the house. I agree with that decision for the reasons given by Lord MacDermott CJ in delivering the leading judgment in the Northern Ireland Court of Appeal. I also adopt what Lord Denning MR said on this topic in *Dutton's* case [1972] 1 All ER 462 at 471–472, [1972] 1 QB 373 at 393: "The distinction between chattels and real property is quite unsustainable [in relation to the principles laid down in *Donoghue v Stevenson*]. If the manufacturer of an article is liable to a person injured by his negligence, so should the builder of a house be liable." The contrary view seems to me to be entirely irreconcilable with logic or common sense. The instant case differs from *Gallagher's* case in that the contractors were also the owners of the land on which they built the block of maisonettes. In *Bottomley v Bannister* [1932] 1 KB 458 at 468, [1931] All ER Rep 99 at 102 (decided just before *Donoghue v Stevenson*) Scrutton LJ said: "Now it is at present well established English law that, in the absence of express contract, a landlord of an unfurnished house is not liable to his tenant, or a vendor of real estate to his purchaser, for defects in the house or land rendering it dangerous or unfit for occupation, even if he has constructed the defects himself or is aware of their existence." I certainly do not agree with the words in that passage "even if he has constructed the defects himself". The immunity of a landlord who sells or lets his house which is dangerous or unfit for habitation is deeply entrenched in our law. I cannot, however, accept the proposition that a contractor who has negligently built a dangerous house can escape liability to pay damages for negligence to anyone who, eg falls through a shoddily constructed floor and is seriously injured, just because the contractor happens to have been the owner of the land on which the house stands. If a similar accident had happened next door in a house which the contractor had also negligently built on someone else's land, he would not be immune from liability. This does not make any sense. In each case the contractor would be sued for his negligence as a contractor and not in his capacity as a landowner: the fact that he had owned one plot of land and not the other would be wholly irrelevant. I would hold that in each case he would be liable to pay damages for negligence. To the extent that *Bottomley v Bannister* differs from this proposition it should, in my view, be overruled. *Cavalier v Pope* [1963] 2 All ER 575, [1964] AC 465 is so far away from the present case that I express no opinion about it.'

From the middle of the last passage we extract Lord Salmon's opinion that a landlord of an unfurnished house may be liable to his tenant for defects rendering it dangerous if he has constructed them himself.   *a*

If that is the law, this appeal fails. We think the decision of this court in *Batty v Metropolitan Property Realizations Ltd* [1978] 2 All ER 445, [1978] QB 554 confirms that it is the law. The landowner who designs or builds a house or flat is no more immune from personal responsibility for faults of construction than a building contractor, or from personal responsibility for faults of design than an architect, simply because he has disposed of his house or flat by selling or letting it. The council through their architects'   *b*
department designed, and through their direct works department built, the plaintiff's flat with its dangerous glass panel. They owed him, not as tenant but, like his wife or his child, as a person who might reasonably be expected to be affected by the provision of the glass panel in the flat, a duty to take such care as was reasonable in all the circumstances to see that he was reasonably safe from personal injury caused by the glass panel. They knew the thickness of the glass, and on the judge's finding they ought to have known   *c*
that, placed where it was, it was dangerous to the occupants of the flat. The plaintiff himself considered it dangerous; but, even if he had the right (which we doubt), he certainly was under no duty to protect or remove it, and he had been told it was standard and nothing could be done about it.

In those circumstances his knowledge that the glass was dangerously thin cannot exonerate the council. 'Knowledge or opportunity for inspection, per se and without   *d*
regard to any consequences they may have in the circumstances, cannot be conclusive against the plaintiff', said Evershed MR, with the agreement of Jenkins LJ, in *Denny v Supplies and Transport Co Ltd* [1950] 2 KB 374 at 382; and this court there held that stevedores, who had stowed timber so badly that a wharfingers' employee was injured in the course of unloading it, were liable to him on the principle of *Donoghue v Stevenson* [1932] AC 562, [1932] All ER Rep 1, notwithstanding the fact that at the start of the   *e*
unloading he had drawn attention to the bad loading and had thereafter continued to unload because there was no practical alternative. That knowledge of a danger was only a bar to a person injured by the danger being owed a duty of care by the person who created the danger where the injured person was really and truly free to act on his knowledge was a principle stated in this court by Denning LJ in several appeals concerning persons on or near dangerous premises: see *Greene v Chelsea BC* [1954] 2 All   *f*
ER 318 at 325, [1954] 2 QB 127 at 139, *Slater v Clay Cross Co Ltd* [1956] 2 All ER 625 at 628, [1956] 2 QB 264 at 271, *Riden v A C Billings & Son Ltd* [1956] 3 All ER 357 at 364, [1957] 1 QB 46 at 59. His opinion was recognised in s 2(4) of the Occupiers' Liability Act 1957 and approved by the House of Lords when the last case went to appeal (see [1957] 3 All ER 1 esp at 14–15, [1958] AC 240 esp at 265–266 per Lord Somerville).

From these authorities we take the law to be that an opportunity for inspection of a   *g*
dangerous defect, even if successfully taken by A who is injured by it, will not destroy his proximity to B who created the danger, or exonerate B from liability to A, unless A was free to remove or avoid the danger in the sense that it was reasonable to expect him not to do so, and unreasonable for him to run the risk of being injured by the danger. It was not reasonable or practical for the plaintiff to leave the flat or to alter the glass panel. He remained in law the council's neighbour, although he had complained that the glass was   *h*
too thin.

We reach our decision without treating *Cavalier v Pope* [1906] AC 428 as overruled, for Pope did not design or construct the floor through which Mrs Cavalier fell. He was not a builder-owner, but what may be called a bare landlord, or a landowner as such: see *Gallagher v N McDowell Ltd* [1961] NI 26 at 38 per Lord MacDermott LCJ. Counsel for Mr and Mrs Anns submitted to the House that it was not necessary to overrule *Cavalier v*   *j*
Pope (see [1978] AC 728 at 744); and their Lordships refrained from doing so, and left for another day the immunity of a bare landlord, too closely confined to avail the council but too deeply entrenched in our law for any court below the highest to disturb or destroy it.

We have not investigated the statutory powers under which the council built these flats; but the decision of the Supreme Court in Eire in *Siney v Dublin Corp* [1980] IR 400 suggests that the council's position as housing authority might provide another reason for making them liable to the plaintiff in negligence, even though they are not liable in contract.

We were pressed by counsel for the council with several objections to the council's liability. One was that in holding them liable we should be putting into effect the recommendation of the Law Commission's Report on the Civil Liability of Vendors and Lessors for Defective Premises (Law Com no 40), which was embodied in cl 3 of their Draft Defective Premises Bill (p 38) but not in the 1972 Act, which adopted their other recommendations. That clause imposed a duty to neighbours on the *Donoghue v Stevenson* principle on—

'a person who disposes of premises, knowing at the material time or at any time thereafter while he retains possession of the premises that there are defects in the state of his premises.'

But that clause carried out the commission's recommendations about dangerous defects not created by the vendor or lessor (pp 16–19) and this appeal is concerned with dangerous defects created by the vendor or lessor (pp 13–16), which was, perhaps imperfectly, provided for by cl 1 (p 28) now substantially reproduced in s 1 of the 1972 Act.

Another objection was that causes of action arising at common law from the same defect in a dwelling but resulting in different kinds of injury and damage would accrue at different times for the purposes of the Limitation Acts. A breach of the statutory duty to build dwellings properly, which is imposed by s 1 on 'a person taking on work for or in connection with the provision of a dwelling', gives rise to a cause of action which is deemed by s 1(5) to accrue 'at the time when the dwelling was completed', and that is so whether the breach causes personal injury and consequential loss or physical damage to property resulting in personal injury or economic loss. (The wide words describing the person who owes the duty might cover the builder-owner, but it has not been contended for the council that, if they do, they exclude the common law duty which the judge imposed. Indeed it could not be contended in the face of s 6(2) of the 1972 Act, which provides that 'any duty imposed by or enforceable by virtue of any provision of this Act is in addition to any duty a person may owe apart from that provision'.) If, however, a builder-owner owes a common law duty, breaches of it in faulty design and construction will constitute causes of action which accrue, where the damage caused by the negligent design or construction results in economic or financial loss, at the date when the damage came into existence, whether discoverable then or only later (see *Pirelli General Cable Works Ltd v Oscar Faber & Partners Ltd* [1983] 1 All ER 65, [1983] 2 AC 1), but where the damage results in personal injury, at the date when the injury causes damage, which, except in cases where the damage is done by the insidious onset of a progressive disease (see *Cartledge v E Jopling & Sons Ltd* [1963] 1 All ER 341, [1963] AC 758), may be many years later, as in the present case. It might indeed have been the end of this century before anybody put his hand through one of these glass panels. But defects in design and construction are in most cases likely to cause discoverable injury or damage to persons on the property within a reasonable time after the building has been completed, and we do not foresee a spate of actions too late to be tried fairly for builder-owners.

A third objection was the cost to local authorities and the council in particular: the expense of replacing all these panels with thicker glass would be very great. But, if the flats are dangerous as they are, the money would be well spent in making them safe.

In our judgment, the judge formulated the duty too widely so as to include the bare landlord as well as the builder owner. It may be that to impose a duty on all landowners who let or sell their land and dwellings, whether or not they are their own designers or builders, would be so great a change in the law as to require legislation. But, in our judgment, this court can and should hold, following *Batty v Metropolitan Property Realizations Ltd* [1978] 2 All ER 445, [1978] QB 554 and distinguishing *Cavalier v Pope* [1906] AC 428, that the council, as their own architect and builder, owed the plaintiff a duty to take reasonable care in designing and constructing the flat to see that it was reasonably safe when they let it to him. They failed in that duty. We accordingly dismiss the appeal.

Appeal dismissed.

Solicitors: *W I Murray*, Liverpool (for the council); *S Cornforth*, Liverpool (for the plaintiff).

Diana Brahams   Barrister.

Practice Direction

SUPREME COURT TAXING OFFICE

Costs – Taxation – Procedure – Postal facilities – Acknowledgment of receipt of papers.

Solicitors who wish to make use of the existing postal facilities and who require an acknowledgment of the receipt of papers must enclose with the papers a list either written on a stamped addressed postcard or else sent with a stamped and addressed envelope. No responsibility will be accepted for documents alleged to have been sent unless an acknowledgment is produced.

F T Horne

27 February 1984   Chief Taxing Master.

a
R v Crown Court at Swindon, ex parte Pawittar Singh

QUEEN'S BENCH DIVISION
STEPHEN BROWN LJ AND TAYLOR J
6 DECEMBER 1983

b

Crown Court – Binding over – Powers of court – Person who or whose case is before the court – Victim of offence of inflicting grievous bodily harm in court to give evidence for Crown – Defendant in case agreeing to be bound over and victim never called as witness – Court binding over victim as well as defendant – Whether victim a 'person who or whose case is before the court' – Whether court having jurisdiction to make binding over order – Whether court should bind over victim of c *grievous bodily harm – Justices of the Peace Act 1968, s 1(7).*

A defendant was brought before the Crown Court charged on indictment with inflicting grievous bodily harm on the applicant. The applicant, who was not the complainant in the magistrates' court, was present in the Crown Court because the Crown required him to give evidence in the case. The defendant agreed to be bound over to keep the peace,
d whereupon the Crown decided not to offer any evidence against him and accordingly the applicant was never called on to give evidence. None the less, the Crown Court, purporting to act under s 1(7)[a] of the Justices of the Peace Act 1968, also bound over the applicant to keep the peace on the basis that he was 'a person who or whose case is before the court' within s 1(7). The applicant applied for an order of certiorari to quash the binding-over order made against him, on the ground that the court had no jurisdiction
e to make it.

Held – Since the applicant was not the complainant in the case and had not attained or assumed the role of a witness in the case before the Crown Court he was not 'a person who or whose case is before the court' within s 1(7) of the 1968 Act. Accordingly, the Crown Court had lacked jurisdiction to make the binding-over order against him. It
f followed that certiorari would go to quash the order (see p 943 *b c* and *e*, post).
Sheldon v Bromfield Justices [1964] 2 All ER 131 distinguished.
Per curiam. A binding-over order should only be made where there is evidence before the court which indicates the likelihood that the peace will not be kept. Moreover, where a defendant is charged with inflicting grievous bodily harm on another person, it will be rare for that other person to be bound over (see p 943 *c* to *e*, post).

g
Notes
For binding over under statute, see 11 Halsbury's Laws (4th edn) para 522.
For the Justices of the Peace Act 1968, s 1, see 21 Halsbury's Statutes (3rd edn) 394.

Cases referred to in judgment
h *R v Crown Court at St Albans, ex p Cinnamond* [1981] 1 All ER 802, [1981] QB 480, [1981] 2 WLR 681, DC.
Sheldon v Bromfield Justices [1964] 2 All ER 131, [1964] 2 QB 573, [1964] 2 WLR 1066, DC.

Case also cited
j *R v Aubrey-Fletcher, ex p Thomson* [1969] 2 All ER 846, [1969] 1 WLR 872, DC.

Application for judicial review
Pawittar Singh applied, with the leave of Glidewell J granted on 19 May 1983, for an

_____
a   Section 1(7) is set out at p 42 *g h*, post

order of certiorari to quash an order made in the Crown Court at Swindon before Mr
Recorder G E Moriarty QC on 18 March 1983 binding over the applicant to keep the *a*
peace. The facts are set out in the judgment of Stephen Brown LJ.

Roland Watt for the applicant.
The respondent did not appear.

 b

STEPHEN BROWN LJ. This is an application for judicial review, pursuant to leave
granted by Glidewell J. The applicant seeks an order of certiorari to remove into this
court and to quash an order made by the Crown Court at Swindon on 18 March 1983
ordering that he be bound over to keep the peace in the sum of £250.

The facts giving rise to the order of the Crown Court may be shortly stated. Before the
court, on 17 March 1983, was one Andrew Lawrence Wallace, who was charged on an *c*
indictment with an offence of inflicting grievous bodily harm, contrary to s 20 of the
Offences against the Person Act 1861. He was charged with assaulting the applicant on
12 November 1982.

The applicant was present at the Crown Court on 17 March 1983, in the capacity of
answering the requirement that he should give evidence as a witness on behalf of the
Crown. He was in the capacity of what one may colloquially call 'the complainant', *d*
although in these proceedings he was not a party because the prosecution was brought
by the Crown. The witness statements before the court indicate that the applicant had
sustained a severe injury to his face and eye, which is shown in the photograph which
was exhibited before the court and which has been exhibited before this court as part of
the documents supporting this application.

The injury was alleged to have been inflicted by Mr Wallace, who, as a result of the *e*
force that he used, sustained a fracture of his hand. It appears that counsel for the Crown
offered no evidence against Mr Wallace on Mr Wallace being willing to submit to an
order of the court binding him over to keep the peace. The court then also required that
the applicant should be bound over to keep the peace. The applicant objected to that
course being taken and, as a result, the matter was adjourned to the next day, 18 March,
when counsel, who has appeared before this court today, made submissions to the court *f*
that it would be an excess of jurisdiction for the court to make such an order in respect
of the applicant and, in any event, it was a course which should not be taken in the
circumstances. However, those submissions were not accepted by the recorder who was
sitting at the Crown Court. He proceeded to make the order which is the subject of this
application. The court purported to make an order under the provisions of s 1(7) of the
Justices of the Peace Act 1968. That subsection provides: *g*

> 'It is hereby declared that any court of record having a criminal jurisdiction has,
> as ancillary to that jurisdiction, the power to bind over to keep the peace, and power
> to bind over to be of good behaviour, a person who or whose case is before the court,
> by requiring him to enter into his own recognisances or to find sureties or both, and
> committing him to prison if he does not comply.' *h*

Counsel for the applicant submitted to this court that the applicant was not a person
whose case was before the court on 18 March 1983. He was present at the court because
he was required by the Crown to be a witness. He was not the person who had laid the
complaint in the magistrates' court. He was not even a person who was a witness at the
time. The order was made, no evidence having been called, because the Crown decided *j*
to offer no evidence against Mr Wallace, who was the defendant in the proceedings.

Counsel for the applicant submitted that, although it is plain on the authorities (he
referred in particular to *Sheldon v Bromfield Justices* [1964] 2 All ER 131, [1964] 2 QB 573)
that a witness is a person before the court for the purposes of the relevant section, none
the less no evidence was adduced in this case and, as no evidence had been given by the

applicant, he was not a person before the court. Accordingly, it was submitted that the recorder had no jurisdiction to make the order.

Counsel made a subsidiary alternative submission that, if he was wrong about the point of jurisdiction, none the less the making of the order was so unreasonable as to constitute an excess of jurisdiction, which would be subject to the remedy of an order of certiorari. For my part, I have no doubt that counsel's primary submission succeeds. The applicant, in my judgment, was not a person who or whose case was before the court within the meaning of s 1(7) of the 1968 Act. He had not attained or assumed the role of a witness since no evidence was called. He was not, as I have already stated, a complainant in any technical sense. These were proceedings brought by the Crown and his presence at the court was in order that he should be a witness if and when he was called. Accordingly, on the ground of jurisdiction, this application succeeds and the order for certiorari will go.

I wish to say a further word about the procedure of binding over a witness in a case such as this. In my judgment, it is a serious step to take and should only be taken where facts are proved by evidence before the court which indicate the likelihood that the peace will not be kept. Such cases may occur, but it seems to me that they will be exceedingly rare. Certainly, it must be rare in cases where the Crown has decided to prosecute a particular person on indictment, for an offence of inflicting grievous bodily harm on another person, for that other person to be bound over. None the less, it is clear that there may be jurisdiction, but care must be taken to see that the requirements of the 1968 Act are fulfilled so far as jurisdiction is concerned. I would not wish to express a view in this case on the subsidiary submission of counsel for the applicant, which is based on a very different case, that of *R v Crown Court at St Albans, ex p Cinnamond* [1981] 1 All ER 802, [1981] QB 480. That case related to the length of a period of disqualification imposed in respect of road traffic offences. The circumstances seem to me to be entirely different and do not assist me in considering this particular situation.

TAYLOR J. I agree.

Certiorari granted.

Solicitors: *Watkins Pulleyn & Ellison*, agents for *Andrews Hepworth & Co*, Swindon (for the applicant).

Dilys Tausz   Barrister.

Practice Direction

FAMILY DIVISION

Legal aid – Taxation of costs – Agreement as to costs – Proceedings to which assisted person a party – Assessment of costs by Law Society – Matrimonial causes – Procedure – Legal Aid Act 1974, Sch 2 – Legal Aid (General) Regulations 1980, reg 100A.

The Legal Aid (General) Regulations 1980, SI 1980/1894, were amended with effect from 1 November 1983 by inserting a new regulation, reg 100A (see SI 1983/1483).

Where, in proceedings which have been brought to an end by a judgment, decree or final order, there has been agreement about the costs to be paid to the assisted person, or former assisted person, which that person's solicitor and counsel (if any) is willing to accept in full satisfaction of the work done, the amount of the costs is to be submitted to the appropriate area committee, which shall, in accordance with Sch 2 to the Legal Aid Act 1974, fix the costs by assessment without taxation. The area committee may if it thinks fit request the appropriate taxing officer to fix the amount of costs by assessment made without a taxation. The new regulation also enables any solicitor or counsel who is dissatisfied with any decision on an assessment made by the area committee to make written representations to the Council of the Law Society. The council is empowered to allow such costs as appear to it to be the amount which would have been allowed had the costs been taxed under Sch 2 to the 1974 Act.

If the area committee requests the taxing officer to fix the amount of costs, the taxing officer will assess them, normally without the attendance of the solicitor, although if he considers it necessary he may require the solicitor to attend for further explanation. Similarly he may additionally or alternatively require the solicitor to supply all necessary papers, documents and details to support the bill including (a) correspondence and attendance notes, (b) cases to and opinions of counsel, (c) counsel's fee note, (d) experts' reports and accounts. No taxing fee will be payable.

The taxing officer will issue his certificate of assessment of the costs which the solicitor shall produce to the legal aid area committee for payment of his costs and counsel's fees (if any) in accordance with Sch 2 to the 1974 Act.

A similar practice should be followed in matrimonial causes proceeding in divorce county courts and district registries of the High Court.

The registrar's direction of 25 October 1972 ([1972] 3 All ER 911, [1972] 1 WLR 1472) is cancelled.

Issued with the concurrence of the Lord Chancellor.

9 March 1984

B P TICKLE
Senior Registrar.

Palmer and another v Southend-on-Sea Borough Council

COURT OF APPEAL, CIVIL DIVISION

DUNN AND MAY LJJ

30 NOVEMBER, 1 DECEMBER 1983, 19 JANUARY 1984

Industrial tribunal – Procedure – Complaint of unfair dismissal – Presentation of complaint to tribunal – Time limit for presentation of complaint – Not reasonably practicable for complaint to be presented within prescribed period – Relevant considerations – Employee pursuing employer's domestic appeals procedure – Whether 'reasonably practicable' for employee to present complaint while appeal pending under domestic procedure – Employment Protection (Consolidation) Act 1978, s 67(2).

Where an employee whose employment is terminated does not present a complaint of unfair dismissal to an industrial tribunal until after the end of the three-month period prescribed by s 67(2)[a] of the Employment Protection (Consolidation) Act 1978 the fact that he is pursuing an appeal against his dismissal under the employer's domestic appeals procedure is not by itself sufficient reason for the industrial tribunal to decide that 'it was not reasonably practicable' for the employee's complaint to be presented within the prescribed period and that the employee should be allowed to present his complaint outside the prescribed period. On the true construction of s 67(2), although the test of whether it 'was not reasonably practicable' for an employee to present a complaint is not limited to whether the employee was not reasonably capable physically of presenting the complaint, it is not sufficient for an employee to show merely that it was not reasonable for him to file the complaint. The correct approach in applying s 67(2) is whether in all the circumstances, including the fact of pending proceedings (if any) under the employer's domestic procedure, it was reasonably feasible for the employee to present his complaint within the limitation period. That is a question of fact and the Employment Appeal Tribunal ought not to inquire into the correctness of the industrial tribunal's decision on that question unless the industrial tribunal's decision is perverse (see p 954 *j* to p 955 *f* and p 956 *b*, post); *Singh v Post Office* [1973] ICR 437 applied; dictum of Browne-Wilkinson J in *Bodha (Vishnudut) v Hampshire Area Health Authority* [1982] ICR at 205 approved; *Dedman v British Building and Engineering Appliances Ltd* [1974] 1 All ER 520, *Porter v Bandridge Ltd* [1978] 1 WLR 1145 and *Wall's Meat Co Ltd v Khan* [1979] ICR 52 considered; dictum of Kilner Brown J in *Crown Agents for Overseas Governments and Administration v Lawal* [1979] ICR at 109 disapproved.

Observations on the considerations to be taken into account by an industrial tribunal in considering whether it was reasonably practicable for an employee to present his complaint within the prescribed period (see p 955 *f* to *j*, post).

Notes

For the time for presenting a complaint of unfair dismissal, see 16 Halsbury's Laws (4th edn) para 637.

For the Employment Protection (Consolidation) Act 1978, s 67, see 48 Halsbury's Statutes (3rd edn) 518.

Cases referred to in judgment

Bodha (Vishnudut) v Hampshire Area Health Authority [1982] ICR 200, EAT.

---

a Section 67(2) is set out at p 946 *h*, post

Crown Agents for Overseas Governments and Administration v Lawal [1979] ICR 103, EAT.
Dedman v British Building and Engineering Appliances Ltd [1974] 1 All ER 520, [1974] 1 *a*
    WLR 171, CA.
House of Clydesdale v Foy (J L) [1976] IRLR 391, EAT.
MacDonald v South Cambridgeshire RDC [1973] ICR 611, NIRC.
Marshall v Gotham & Co Ltd [1954] 1 All ER 937, [1954] AC 360, [1954] 2 WLR 812, HL.
Porter v Bandridge Ltd [1978] 1 WLR 1145, CA.
Singh v Post Office [1973] ICR 437, NIRC.   *b*
Times Newspapers Ltd v O'Regan [1977] IRLR 101, EAT.
Wall's Meat Co Ltd v Khan [1979] ICR 52, CA.

Interlocutory appeal
Peter Alfred Palmer and Rodney Saunders appealed against the judgment of the
Employment Appeal Tribunal (Neill J, Mr G A Peers and Ms Pat Smith) given on 23 *c*
March 1983 dismissing their appeals from the decision of an industrial tribunal (chairman
Mr M S Hunter-Jones) sitting at London North on 19 July 1982 that it was reasonably
practicable for the appellants to have presented their complaints of unfair dismissal by
the respondents, Southend-on-Sea Borough Council, within the time limit laid down in
s 67(2) of the Employment Protection (Consolidation) Act 1978. The facts are set out in
the judgment of the court.   *d*

Steven Whitaker for the appellants.
Mervyn Roberts for the respondents.

Cur adv vult
                                                                                       e
19 January. The following judgment of the court was delivered.

MAY LJ. This is an appeal from a judgment of the Employment Appeal Tribunal of 23
March 1983. The appeal tribunal then had before it two associated appeals by the present
appellants against the decision of an industrial tribunal held at London North on 19 July
1982. This is one more in the line of cases concerned with the time limit imposed by the *f*
relevant legislation for presenting complaints of unfair dismissal to an industrial tribunal.
    The present statutory provisions are contained in s 67 of the Employment Protection
(Consolidation) Act 1978, although it will be necessary later in this judgment to refer to
the earlier similar legislation. For the present, the relevant provisions of s 67 are as
follows:

> '(1) A complaint may be presented to an industrial tribunal against an employer *g*
> by any person (in this Part referred to as the complainant) that he was unfairly
> dismissed by the employer.
>   (2) Subject to subsection (4), an industrial tribunal shall not consider a complaint
> under this section unless it is presented to the tribunal before the end of the period
> of three months beginning with the effective date of termination or within such
> further period as the tribunal considers reasonable in a case where it is satisfied that *h*
> it was not reasonably practicable for the complaint to be presented before the end of
> the period of three months . . .'

At the material time both these appellants had been employed by the respondents at
Southend airport for substantial periods approaching 25 years. In the summer of 1980 it
was suggested that both men had been involved in the theft of fuel at the airport. On *j*
2 September a letter was written by Mr Clarke, the director of engineering and planning
services of the borough council, to each of these appellants to the effect that the council
had heard that the two men had been charged by the police for this alleged offence and
would be appearing in court in due course. The letter went on to say that pending the

outcome of the proceedings they would be suspended on half pay. The second paragraph of each letter was in the following terms:

> 'In the event that you are adjudged to be not blameworthy your suspension will be lifted and you will be entitled to re-imbursement of lost pay. On the other hand, a conviction by a Court will establish gross misconduct which could lead to instant dismissal.'

Early in April 1981 the two men appeared before the Crown Court and were convicted of theft. On 8 April 1981 Mr Clarke wrote to them again. His letter said:

> 'I have been informed that in the Crown Court you were found guilty of the theft of a quantity of petrol which was the property of the Council. In these circumstances I consider that gross misconduct has been clearly established and, accordingly, your Contract of Employment is terminated forthwith.'

He then informed the appellants of their right of appeal to the appeals committee of the council within the period provided. That right of appeal was exercised and the matter came before the appeals committee on 22 April, that is a fortnight after Mr Clarke's letter. On the following day Mr Laws, the chief executive officer and town clerk of Southend-on-Sea Borough Council, wrote as follows:

> 'I write formally to confirm the decision intimated verbally at yesterday's hearing, which was that the Appeals Committee have upheld the decisions of the Chief Officers in dismissing Messrs. Saunders and Palmer for gross misconduct. The Committee did, however, indicate that in the event of an appeal to a higher Court against the Crown Court's decision being decided in favour of your members, they would (without any promise as to the outcome of such consideration) be prepared to look at the matter again.'

That letter was sent by Mr Laws to Mr Taylor, who was the officer of the trade union who had been acting on behalf of the present appellants.

No further action was then taken in the matter by way of application to an industrial tribunal, nor did the two men seek to exercise any further right of appeal internally, though we understand that the machinery did provide for an appeal to a regional body.

On 19 February 1982 the appellants' convictions for theft were quashed by the Court of Appeal, Criminal Division. Following this, Mr Taylor wrote to the respondents on 19 February 1982 drawing their attention to the fact that the convictions had been quashed and asking for the appellants' reinstatement. On 25 March solicitors acting for the appellants in their turn wrote to the respondents and their letter ended:

> 'Our clients appealed against your decision of the 8th April, 1981 to dismiss them for gross misconduct and this was heard by the Appeals Committee of the Council. We understand that this appeal was dismissed but our clients were told that the final decision would not be made until the hearing of the appeal against their conviction. As the Appeal has now been heard and as the convictions have been removed we can see no obstacle to re-instatement and we await hearing from you in respect of this matter as soon as possible.'

On 1 April 1982 Mr Laws replied. He referred to the letter of 25 March and in the second paragraph of his letter said:

> 'The Personnel Committee at its recent meeting gave further consideration to this matter including your representation on behalf of your clients, but after a very full discussion felt unable to accede to the request you made regarding re-instatement or compensation.'

The appeals committee, it appears, is a sub-committee of the personnel committee of the council.

On 28 April 1982 these appellants filed originating applications alleging wrongful dismissal by the respondents at the central office of industrial tribunals. As these *a* applications were filed over a year after the effective date of determination of the appellants' employment by the respondents, as defined by s 55(4) of the 1978 Act, it was necessary to give consideration to the question of the statutory time limit under s 67(2). It was in these circumstances that the two applications came before the industrial tribunal at London North by way of a preliminary hearing on 19 July 1982. The question for the tribunal, as it recognised, was whether it could be satisfied that it had not been reasonably *b* practicable for the appellants' complaints to be presented within the relevant three-month period. The appellants' argument before the industrial tribunal was that on the proper construction of the chief executive's letter of 23 April 1981 the respondents' domestic appeals procedure had not been exhausted; that in the event (as occurred) of a favourable decision in the Court of Appeal they would have the right to ask for a review; and that it was a reasonable course of action not to make a complaint to an industrial *c* tribunal and thus prejudice the appellants' domestic appeals before the Court of Appeal had announced its decision. In support of this argument counsel referred the tribunal to certain dicta of Kilner Brown J in *Crown Agents for Overseas Governments and Administration v Lawal* [1979] ICR 103 at 109, which we shall have to consider later in this judgment.

One member of the industrial tribunal was satisfied that it had not been reasonably practicable for the appellants' complaints to be presented within the prescribed time. He *d* accepted the interpretation of the letter of 23 April 1981 contended for by counsel for the appellants. His experience was that in such cases it was normal practice for trades unions, as was the fact in the instant case, to advise their members not to present a complaint to an industrial tribunal, since that might prejudice the internal appeal.

The majority of the industrial tribunal, however, was not so satisfied. They thought that the first paragraph of the letter of 23 April 1981 made the situation quite clear; the *e* internal appeal had been dismissed; the appeal procedure had been exhausted (unless the employees decided to go on to the next stage, which was an appeal to the Herts and Essex Regional Committee); it had been unwise for the appellants to rely on the limited hope contained in the second paragraph of the letter of 23 April as making it 'not reasonably practicable' to present their complaints to the tribunal before the decision of the Court of Appeal. In the view of the majority it was not only practicable but it would have been a *f* very sensible course of action for a dismissed employee, such as one of the appellants, confident of his innocence, to have presented a complaint, drawn the attention of the industrial tribunal to the letter of 23 April 1981 and requested a postponement until the Court of Appeal had reached a decision. The decision of the majority of the tribunal continued in this way:

g

'If, of course, the applicants or their adviser had thought that in default of a postponement the applications would be bound to fail, that would not have been something that would make it "not reasonably practicable" to present the complaint. It could be argued that the presentation was not reasonably practicable if a premature presentation would have been likely to prejudice the internal appeal.'

h

The majority of the tribunal then went on to find as a fact that the respondents' internal appeal procedure had been exhausted in April 1981 and that it was thus unnecessary to express any concluded view on the argument to which they had just referred, namely that a presentation would not have been reasonably practicable if a premature one would have been likely to prejudice the internal appeal procedure.

On the question posed by the statute itself to the tribunal, the majority concluded that *j* it was not satisfied that it had not been reasonably practicable for the complaints to have been presented within the prescribed period of three months and therefore dismissed the applications.

It was the appellants' appeal from that decision to the Employment Appeal Tribunal

which was considered on 23 March 1983 and is now the subject of this further appeal to
us.

The argument for the appellants before the appeal tribunal was, in effect, the same as
that before the industrial tribunal. The appeal tribunal considered first the conclusion of
the majority of the industrial tribunal that the effect of the respondents' letter of 23 April
1981 was that the appellants' internal appeals had been dismissed and finally disposed of.
They held that that finding by the majority below had not been perverse.

Secondly, having considered a number of earlier authorities, the appeal tribunal agreed
with the decision of another division of the tribunal, presided over by the then president,
in *Bodha (Vishudut) v Hampshire Area Health Authority* [1982] ICR 200 that the words
'reasonably practicable' in s 67(2) meant reasonably capable of being done and not merely
reasonable. Adopting that construction of the relevant subsection the appeal tribunal
held that the majority of the industrial tribunal had come to the right conclusion on the
facts of this particular case, namely that it *was* reasonably practicable for the complaints
to have been presented within the prescribed period of three months. The Employment
Appeal Tribunal accordingly dismissed the appellants' appeal and it is from that dismissal
that this appeal now comes before us.

There have been a substantial number of decisions on this section and its predecessors
both in the Employment Appeal Tribunal and this court which in our respectful view
are not easy to reconcile. We think that this is so for a number of reasons. First, the use
of the word 'practicable' or of the words 'reasonably practicable' is not really apt in this
particular context. In its ordinary English meaning 'practicable' is effectively the
equivalent of 'able to be done'. It will have to be a somewhat special factual situation in
which an employee is not within the time limited able to fill in and take to his relevant
industrial tribunal office the usual and prescribed form of originating application
complaining that he has been unfairly dismissed.

On the other hand, if the relevant section is so construed it is a strict limitation
provision and a number of the reported cases have been ones where it has been well
arguable that to apply the section in its full strictness would be likely to produce clear
injustice. One need only take as an example cases such as the instant one, where an
employee has been dismissed summarily as the result of a criminal conviction. It is very
difficult in those circumstances, if not impossible, to contend that he has been unfairly
dismissed. Thus it might well be thought that there was little to be gained by filing an
originating application at that time. Nevertheless any appeal by the convicted employee
is likely to take substantially longer than the three months provided for by the section.
If, in the event, such an appeal succeeds and the possibility of making a complaint of
unfair dismissal then becomes apparent, the disgruntled employee will of course
immediately find himself time-barred.

Nevertheless, there is the contrary argument, in which we think there is considerable
force, that it is desirable to decide these disputes between employers and employees as
quickly as possible after the dismissal and to remember that the procedure at industrial
tribunal hearings is intended to be as informal as practicable. To achieve such a reasonably
prompt and informal turnover, Parliament may well have considered it necessary to have
a relatively short limitation period which will apply in the majority of these cases.

The argument for the appellants before us was, first, that as the result of the earlier
decisions of this court s 67(2) must be liberally construed. In effect this means that in a
given case one has to ask whether it would have been reasonable to have done what
could, as a matter of physical practicability, have been done. In the instant case, the
argument continued, whilst the criminal proceedings were still pending and whilst, on
what it was contended was the true construction of the letter of 23 April, the respondents'
internal appeals procedure had not been exhausted, it could not be said that it would
have been reasonable to have presented a complaint at least until a reasonable time after
the determination of the criminal appeal. The appellants thought, so it was submitted,
that if the criminal appeals succeeded they would be reinstated. If they failed, there

would be no point in going to an industrial tribunal at all. Further they had been advised
by their trade union that as the door had been left open in the internal appeals procedure,   *a*
it would be unwise possibly to prejudice their position vis-à-vis the respondents by filing
a complaint of unfair dismissal, which it was obvious that at that stage could not succeed.

In these circumstances, although from the point of view of physical practicability it
would have been possible to have filed originating applications within the three-month
period, it would have been purposeless and unreasonable to have done so, and thus the
appeal should be allowed and the view of the minority of the industrial tribunal upheld.   *b*

Further, and as part of the appellants' general argument, counsel contended that the
finding by the majority of the industrial tribunal at the end of para 15 of their decision
that the respondents' internal appeal procedure had been exhausted in April 1981 had
been perverse.

In reply counsel for the respondents submitted that what is reasonably practicable
within s 67(2) is a question of fact for the tribunal and thus an appellate court should   *c*
only interfere either when there was no evidence to support such a finding of fact, or
alternatively if thereafter the tribunal clearly applies to their findings of fact a construction
of s 67(2) different from that held by this court to be the correct one.

Second, the fact that an employee is still going through the employer's appeal
procedure is not a matter to be treated specially. Parliament had not taken up the
suggestion that it should be so treated expressed at the end of the judgments of the   *d*
National Industrial Relations Court in *Singh v Post Office* [1973] ICR 437 at 440 and
MacDonald v South Cambridgeshire RDC [1973] ICR 611 at 615, and thus the court should
not do so of its own motion.

The series of decisions on the point with which this appeal is concerned starts with the
two to which we have just referred. In both of them the relevant time limit was
contained in r 2(1)(a) in the schedule to the Industrial Tribunals (Industrial Relations,   *e*
etc) Regulations 1972, SI 1972/38. That provided for only a four-week period 'unless the
tribunal is satisfied that in the circumstances it was not practicable for the complaint to
be presented before the end of that period'. In *Singh*'s case the employee was still invoking
the Post Office domestic appeals procedure when he presented a complaint of unfair
dismissal to the industrial tribunal, but he did so more than four weeks after his dismissal.
Apart from the fact that he was still involved in the internal disputes procedure, there   *f*
was no reason why he could not have made his complaint within the time limit. The
National Industrial Relations Court upheld the decision of the industrial tribunal that
the employee complainant was out of time. After referring to the argument based on
convenience to the effect that a complaint of unfair dismissal should be deferred until
after the employer's domestic appeals procedure had been completed, Brightman J,
giving the judgment of the court, said ([1973] ICR 437 at 440):   *g*

> 'On the other hand, the wording of the regulation is strong. The four weeks' time
> limit is required to be observed, unless the tribunal are satisfied in the circumstances
> that it was not practicable for it to be observed. This involves a test of feasibility, not
> a test of desirability or convenience or anything of that sort. In the circumstances of
> this present case it cannot in our view be asserted that it was not feasible for the   *h*
> employee to present his complaint while the appeals procedure was still current,
> because he in fact did so.'

MacDonald v South Cambridgeshire RDC was principally concerned with the then
statutory definition of the employee's 'effective date of termination' but in the same
general context. At the end of the judgment of the court, after it had held that on its
finding of what had been the effective date of termination the employee had failed to   *j*
make his complaint within the four-week limitation period, Griffiths J said in giving the
judgment of the court ([1973] ICR 611 at 615):

> 'We are not, however, without sympathy for the dilemma in which the employee's

a solicitor found himself when he was consulted on September 23. He could, of course, as the tribunal pointed out, have made an application forthwith to the tribunal alleging unfair dismissal and asking the tribunal to delay the hearing of that application until the domestic appeal had been determined. We nevertheless understand his reluctance to advise this course whilst at the same time pursuing a domestic appeal, for it might be interpreted as pre-judging the outcome of the domestic appeal. We accept Mr. Tyrell's submission that every encouragement

b should be given to follow domestic procedures before having resort to industrial tribunals, and we hope that as a result of this case consideration will be given to the advisability of an amendment to the Act of 1971 to provide that time shall not run against an employee until he has exhausted his rights under the domestic procedures of his employers. In the meantime, employees and their advisers must be alert to preserve their rights by complying with the time limits provided by the Act of

c 1971.'

We then turn to the first decision of the Court of Appeal on the point in *Dedman v British Building and Engineering Appliances Ltd* [1974] 1 All ER 520, [1974] 1 WLR 171. In that case solicitors consulted by the dismissed employee within four weeks of this dismissal did not tell him that he had to present his complaint within that time and he in fact presented it after the expiry of that period. The industrial tribunal, the National

d Industrial Relations Court and the Court of Appeal all held that the employee was statute-barred. Lord Denning MR emphasised the strictness of the time limit and the fact that it went to the jurisdiction of the industrial tribunal so that unless the employee could bring himself within what he described as the 'escape clause' the tribunal had no power to extend the relevant time. He then drew attention to the difference of approach to the escape clause between the Industrial Court sitting in Scotland and that sitting in England.

e The former construed the word 'practicable' in its strict literal sense; the latter construed it more liberally in favour of the employee. His judgment then continued ([1974] 1 All ER 520 at 525, [1974] 1 WLR 171 at 176):

'This difference must be resolved. In my opinion the words "not practicable" should be given a liberal interpretation in favour of the man. My reason is because
f a strict construction would give rise to much injustice which Parliament cannot have intended.'

Lord Denning MR then gave and discussed a number of examples of such injustice and went on to consider the position of an employee who goes to skilled advisers and they make a mistake. He then summarised his conclusions in that case in this way ([1974] 1 All ER 520 at 526, [1974] 1 WLR 171 at 177):

g
'Summing up, I would suggest that in every case the tribunal should enquire into the circumstances and ask themselves whether the man or his advisers were at fault in allowing the four weeks to pass by without presenting the complaint. If he was not at fault, nor his advisers—so that he had just cause or excuse for not presenting his complaint within the four weeks—then it was "not practicable" for him to
h present it within that time. The court has then a discretion to allow it to be presented out of time, if it thinks it right to do so. But, if he was at fault, or if his advisers were at fault, in allowing the four weeks to slip by, he must take the consequences. By exercising reasonable diligence, the complaint could and should have been presented in time.'

j The judgment of Stamp LJ was based on the strict literal construction of the phrase in the rule. He said ([1974] 1 All ER 520 at 527, [1974] 1 WLR 171 at 178):

'In my judgment the fact that he did not know the necessary application had to be made within four weeks of his dismissal is wholly irrelevant to the question whether it was practicable or "not practicable" for the complaint to be presented before that period had expired. If, as the fact is, there was nothing to discourage, impede, or prevent him presenting the complaint at some time during the four *a* weeks how can it be said that it was not practicable for him to do so! Suppose there was another man in precisely the same position as Mr Dedman, with the same knowledge of his right, the same lack of knowledge of the time limit, who did in fact present his complaint in the course of the third week, how could it be said that it was not practicable for Mr. Dedman to have done so!'

b

In his judgment Scarman LJ agreed with Lord Denning MR on the point of construction. He said ([1974] 1 All ER 520 at 528, [1974] 1 WLR 171 at 179):

> 'The word "practicable" is an ordinary English word of great flexibility: it takes its meaning from its context. But, whenever used, it is a call for the exercise of common sense, a warning that sound judgment will be impossible without *c* compromise.'

The majority view in *Dedman*'s case, therefore, was that the relevant phrase should not be construed in its strict literal sense, but liberally or flexibly. Respectfully, however, whilst this approach is easy to state, we do not think that it is at all easy to apply in practice.

d

By the time that the Employment Appeal Tribunal came to decide *Times Newspapers Ltd v O'Regan* [1977] IRLR 101 the relevant provisions of the 1972 regulations had been replaced by para 21(4) of Sch 1 to the Trade Union and Labour Relations Act 1974. As a result the limitation period had become three months instead of four weeks and the material phrase had become 'not reasonably practicable'. These statutory provisions have been re-enacted in the subsequent legislation and are now those in s 67(2) of the 1978 *e* consolidation Act with which we are directly concerned. In the *Times Newspapers* case the Employment Appeal Tribunal held that despite the changes in the statutory provisions it should still continue to apply the guidance to be derived from the majority judgments in *Dedman*'s case.

We were then referred to the Court of Appeal decision in *Porter v Bandridge Ltd* [1978] 1 WLR 1145. In that case the employee was charged in May 1976 with theft from his *f* employers and was dismissed. He consulted solicitors. At the trial of the criminal charge in March 1977 the prosecution offered no evidence and he was acquitted. Early in April 1977 the employee presented a complaint of unfair dismissal to an industrial tribunal, which held that it was not satisfied that it had not been reasonably practicable for the complaint to be presented within three months of the dismissal. The Employment Appeal Tribunal dismissed the employee's appeal. This court in its turn dismissed the *g* employee's further appeal by a majority. Waller LJ, with whose judgment Stephenson LJ agreed, held, first, that the liberal construction of the statutory provisions approved in *Dedman*'s case should still be applied; but second, that even so the industrial tribunal's view of the facts was correct; nevertheless, third, that at least the Court of Appeal should be very reluctant to interfere in a matter of industrial employment law in which both the industrial tribunal and the appeal tribunal had unanimously come to the same *h* conclusion. In his dissenting judgment Ormrod LJ felt himself compelled to take a different view of the facts of the case, particularly on the question whether the applicant knew at material times of the existence of his remedy, and thus held the industrial tribunal to have misdirected itself in law.

The next Court of Appeal decision was in *Wall's Meat Co Ltd v Khan* [1979] ICR 52. In that case the employee thought that his claim for unfair dismissal was proceeding before *j* the same tribunal as was in fact dealing with his claim for unemployment benefit, and thus let the three months pass. The industrial tribunal to which eventually, after consulting solicitors, his complaint of unfair dismissal was presented, found that it had not been reasonable practicable for him to have presented his complaint within time and

a assumed jurisdiction. The employers' successive appeals to the Employment Appeal Tribunal and then the Court of Appeal were dismissed. All three members of the latter court thought that the decision whether or not it had been reasonably practicable for a complainant to present his application within the statutory three months was primarily a question of fact for the industrial tribunal. In his judgment Lord Denning MR expressed the view that where a dismissed employee allowed the limitation period to pass merely because he was waiting for the result of pending criminal proceedings against **b** him, this was not an acceptable reason for saying that it was not 'reasonably practicable' to present his claim within time. His judgment continued (at 56):

> 'I would venture to take the simple test given by the majority in *Dedman's* case ([1974] ICR 53 at 61). It is simply to ask this question: Had the man just cause or excuse for not presenting his complaint within the prescribed time? Ignorance of **c** his rights—or ignorance of the time limit—is not just cause or excuse, unless it appears that he or his advisers could not reasonably be expected to have been aware of them. If he or his advisers could reasonably have been so expected, it was his or their fault, and he must take the consequences. That was the view adopted by the Employment Appeal Tribunal in Scotland in *House of Clydesdale Ltd.* v. *Foy* ([1976] IRLR 391) and in England in *Times Newspapers Ltd.* v. *O'Regan* ([1977] IRLR 101)— **d** decisions with which I agree. The present case is not one where the man was ignorant of his rights or of the time limit. He was aware of them, but he thought quite naturally that his claim was already lodged and was being processed before the appropriate tribunal.'

Shaw LJ said (at 57):
e

> 'It seems to me axiomatic that what is or is not reasonably practicable is in essence a question of fact. The question falls to be resolved by finding what the facts are and forming an opinion as to their effect having regard to the ordinary experience of human affairs. The test is empirical and involves no legal concept. Practical common sense is the keynote and legalistic footnotes may have no better result than to **f** introduce a lawyer's complications into what should be a layman's pristine province. These considerations prompt me to express the emphatic view that the proper forum to decide such questions is the industrial tribunal, and that their decision should prevail unless it is plainly perverse or oppressive. Section 88 of the Employment Protection Act 1975 provides for appeal to the appeal tribunal only on questions of law.'
g

Shaw LJ then agreed with the view that had been expressed in *Dedman's* case that the material words should be given a liberal interpretation in favour of the employee. He went on to hold that the first essential condition that must obtain in order for it to be reasonably practicable to present a complaint in due time is that the complainant knows that he has a present claim. However once a dismissed employee is aware of his right to **h** make a claim, then mere ignorance of the time limit does not, ipso facto, prevent its presentation within the prescribed period from being reasonably practicable. His judgment concluded by reiterating that the resolution of the question of what is reasonably practicable does not depend on legal refinements or some subtle nuance of the law. It must be the product of the ad hoc good sense of an industrial tribunal rather than of legal principles expounded in a court of law.
j The general approach to the statutory phrase suggested by Brandon LJ was this (at 60–61):

> 'The performance of an act, in this case the presentation of a complaint, is not reasonably practicable if there is some impediment which reasonably prevents, or

interferes with, or inhibits, such performance. The impediment may be physical, for instance the illness of the complainant or a postal strike; or the impediment may *a* be mental, namely, the state of mind of the complainant in the form of ignorance of, or mistaken belief with regard to, essential matters. Such states of mind can, however, only be regarded as impediments making it not reasonably practicable to present a complaint within the period of three months, if the ignorance on the one hand, or the mistaken belief on the other, is itself reasonable. Either state of mind will, further, not be reasonable if it arises from the fault of the complainant in not *b* making such inquiries as he should reasonably in all the circumstances have made, or from the fault of his solicitors or other professional advisers in not giving him such information as they should reasonably in all the circumstances have given him.'

In its turn his judgment ended (at 63) by repeating that the questions which arise in *c* these cases—

'are primarily matters of fact for the decision of the industrial tribunal trying the particular case, and that appeals on such questions, involving as they often do the dressing up of questions of fact so as to have the appearance of questions of law, are, in general, undesirable and to be discouraged.' *d*

In an obiter dictum in the judgment of the Employment Appeal Tribunal in *Crown Agents for Overseas Governments and Administration v Lawal* [1979] ICR 103 at 109 to which we have already referred, Kilner Brown J said:

'Merely as a statement of general principle, it would seem to us that in cases where *e* a person is going through a conciliation process, or is taking up a domestic appeal procedure, whether it be on discipline, or whether it be for medical reasons, that common sense would indicate that while he is going through something which involves him and his employer directly, he should be able to say, "It is not reasonably practicable for me to lodge my application within the three months." This is the view not only of this particular division of the appeal tribunal but we have taken *f* steps to canvass the views of other members, including other judicial members. The view of the appeal tribunal as a whole is that normally, though by no means always, it would be open to say in the case of a person who is going through an appeal process and loses, that not only does the date go back to the original date of dismissal but that the applicant so caught by the effluxion of time should be able to satisfy an industrial tribunal that he is entitled to the benefit of what is usually called the *g* "escape" clause.'

However in *Bodha v Hampshire Area Health Authority* [1982] ICR 200 at 205 another division of the appeal tribunal presided over by Browne-Wilkinson J disagreed in these terms:

'Despite the reference to there having been consultation with other members of *h* his appeal tribunal, the fact that both the argument and the judgment were concluded on the same date shows that such consultation was obviously not very widespread. For the reasons we have given, we do not think we should follow that dictum having had the matter fully argued before us. There may be cases where the special facts (additional to the bare fact that there is an internal appeal pending) may persuade an industrial tribunal, as a question of fact, that it was not reasonably *j* practicable to complain to the industrial tribunal within the time limit. But we do not think that the mere fact of a pending internal appeal, by itself, is sufficient to justify a finding of fact that it was not "reasonably practicable" to present a complaint to the industrial tribunal.'

a In the light of the passages from earlier judgments of this court which we have quoted in this judgment, we respectfully prefer the views on the effect of a pending internal appeal on the question whether it has been reasonably practicable to present a complaint within the time limit expressed by the Employment Appeal tribunal in *Bodha's* case to those expressed in the *Crown Agents* decision.

However, in *Bodha's* case the Employment Appeal Tribunal also said (at 204):

b 'The statutory test remains one of practicability. The statutory words still require the industrial tribunal to have regard to what *could* be done albeit approaching what is practicable in a common-sense way. The statutory test is not satisfied just because it was reasonable not to do what could be done . . . Reasonably practicable means "reasonably capable of being done" not "reasonable".'

c If, in this dictum, Browne-Wilkinson J was intending to limit the meaning of the phrase 'reasonably practicable' to that which is reasonably capable *physically* of being done, then on the authorities to which we have referred this we think would be too restrictive a construction.

In the end, most of the decided cases have been decisions on their own particular facts and must be regarded as such. However we think that one can say that to construe the *d* words 'reasonably practicable' as the equivalent of 'reasonable' is to take a view too favourable to the employee. On the other hand 'reasonably practicable' means more than merely what is reasonably capable physically of being done, different, for instance, from its construction in the context of the legislation relating to factories: cf *Marshall v Gotham & Co Ltd* [1954] 1 All ER 937, [1954] AC 360. In the context in which the words are used in the 1978 consolidation Act, however, ineptly as we think, they mean something *e* between these two. Perhaps to read the word 'practicable' as the equivalent of 'feasible' as Brightman J did in *Singh's* case and to ask colloquially and untrammelled by too much legal logic, 'Was it reasonably feasible to present the complaint to the industrial tribunal within the relevant three months?' is the best approach to the correct application of the relevant subsection.

What, however, is abundantly clear on all the authorities is that the answer to the *f* relevant question is pre-eminently an issue of fact for the industrial tribunal and that it is seldom that an appeal from its decision will lie. Dependent on the circumstances of the particular case, an industrial tribunal may wish to consider the manner in which and reason for which the employee was dismissed, including the extent to which, if at all, the employer's conciliatory appeals machinery has been used. It will no doubt investigate what was the substantial cause of the employee's failure to comply with the statutory *g* time limit; whether he had been physically prevented from complying with the limitation period, for instance by illness or a postal strike, or something similar. It may be relevant for the industrial tribunal to investigate whether at the time when he was dismissed, and if not then when thereafter, he knew that he had the right to complain that he had been unfairly dismissed; in some cases the tribunal may have to consider whether there has been any misrepresentation about any relevant matter by the employer *h* to the employee. It will frequently be necessary for it to know whether the employee was being advised at any material time and, if so, by whom; of the extent of the advisers' knowledge of the facts of the employee's case; and of the nature of any advice which they may have given to him. In any event it will probably be relevant in most cases for the industrial tribunal to ask itself whether there has been any substantial fault on the part of the employee or his adviser which has led to the failure to comply with the statutory *j* time limit. Any list of possible relevant considerations, however, cannot be exhaustive and, as we have stressed, at the end of the day the matter is one of fact for the industrial tribunal taking all the circumstances of the given case into account.

Returning to the present appeal, we do not think that the majority of the industrial tribunal misunderstood the factual question which they had to decide, nor that in

deciding it they applied any test or principle wrong in law. The majority's finding at the
end of para 15 of their decision, that the internal appeal procedure had been exhausted *a*
in April 1981, cannot be said to have been perverse. In our opinion this ought to have
been sufficient for the Employment Appeal Tribunal to dismiss the appeal to them. We
feel that it was unnecessary, and indeed respectfully incorrect in law for the appeal
tribunal to have gone on, as they did, to consider whether the industrial tribunal's
ultimate conclusion on the facts found by it was or was not correct. Even if the appeal
tribunal might themselves have reached a different conclusion on those facts, this *b*
mattered not: the conclusion was one for the industrial tribunal.

In these circumstances, though on grounds not entirely those relied on by the
Employment Appeal Tribunal, we think that the employees' appeal to it from the
industrial tribunal rightly failed and that their appeal to this court must consequently
also fail.

c

Appeal dismissed. Leave to appeal to the House of Lords refused.

Solicitors: *L Bingham & Co* (for the appellants); *F G Laws*, Southend-on-Sea (for the
respondents).

Diana Procter   Barrister.

d

R v Secretary of State for the Environment, *e*
ex parte Hackney London Borough Council
and another

COURT OF APPEAL, CIVIL DIVISION   *f*
SIR JOHN DONALDSON MR, DUNN AND BROWNE-WILKINSON LJJ
16, 17, 18, 19, 31 JANUARY 1984

*Rates – Rate support grant – Reduction – Statutory discretion of Secretary of State to reduce
grant – Secretary of State notifying local authority of amounts to be paid and dates on which
payment to be made – Secretary of State subsequently making decision to reduce amounts and
notifying local authority accordingly – Decision quashed on local authority's application for* *g*
*judicial review – Local authority requesting payments in accordance with original notification –
Secretary of State refusing and withholding payment pending second decision – Whether local
authority entitled to payment in accordance with original notification – Whether Secretary of
State entitled to defer payment pending second decision – Local Government Act 1974, s 2(2) –
Local Government, Planning and Land Act 1980, ss 48, 49, 50 – Rate Support Grant Regulations*
1979, reg 5. *h*

*Rates – Rate support grant – Reduction – Statutory discretion of Secretary of State to reduce
grant pending introduction of new legislation – Secretary of State making decision pursuant to
transitional provisions to reduce local authority rate support grant – Decision quashed on local
authority's application for judicial review – Secretary of State making second decision after end
of year to which transitional provisions applying – Validity of second decision – Local Government,* *j*
Planning and Land Act 1980, ss 48, 49, 50.

*Estoppel – Issue estoppel – Judicial review – Whether doctrine of issue estoppel appropriate in
applications for judicial review.*

a The Secretary of State for the Environment was required by the Local Government Act 1974 to make annual rate support grants to local authorities in England and Wales in accordance with the Rate Support Grant Regulations 1979. Section 2(2)^a of the 1974 Act authorised payment of rate support grants 'at such times as the Secretary of State may with the consent of the Treasury determine', while reg 5(1)^b of the 1979 regulations required the Secretary of State to estimate, on the best information available to him, and notify each local authority of the amounts to be paid to it for the year by way of rate

b support grant. Regulation 5(1) also empowered the Secretary of State to 'make and notify to the authority such further estimates of the said amounts, taking into account information not previously available, as he may think fit'. In November 1980 the Local Government, Planning and Land Act 1980 received the royal assent. That Act introduced a new system for the distribution of rate support grants in 1981–82. Sections 48 to 50 of the 1980 Act took effect immediately and provided transitional measures for the year

c 1980–81 whereby the Secretary of State was empowered to reduce the rate support grant payable to an authority under the 1974 Act if the authority's expenditure in that year exceeded a specified level. However, the Secretary of State could not exercise his power to reduce the amount of rate support grant payable to an authority for the year 1980–81 until the House of Commons approved a 'multipliers order' made by the Secretary of State specifying, in accordance with ss 49(4)^c and 50(2)^d of the 1980 Act, the principles

d for determining the multipliers to be used for calculating the amount of the reduction of the rate support grant. On 16 December 1980 a rate support grant increase order, specifying the notional uniform rate for 1980–81, and a rate support grant multipliers order were laid before the House of Commons. By a letter dated 6 January 1981 the Secretary of State notified the applicant local authority that, subject to possible reductions made by the Secretary of State pursuant to his powers under ss 48 to 50 of the 1980 Act,

e specified amounts of rate support grant would be paid to it on certain dates in 1981. On 15 January 1981 the multipliers order and the increase order were approved by the House of Commons. On 26 January the Secretary of State made a decision under ss 48 to 50 to reduce the rate support grant payable to the applicant authority for the year 1980–81 and notified the authority on 6 February of the reduced amounts and the dates on which they would be paid. The authority applied to the Divisional Court for an order of

f certiorari to quash the Secretary of State's decision of 26 January on the grounds, inter alia, (i) that the multipliers order was ultra vires and of no effect because it did not specify 'the principles on which the multipliers were to be determined' in accordance with ss 49(4) and 50(2) but merely prescribed how the multipliers were to be ascertained, and was unreasonable and capricious in effect, and (ii) that the Secretary of State had not lawfully exercised the discretion conferred on him by ss 48 to 50 because he had refused

g to hear representations from the authority after the 1980 Act had been passed and before he exercised his discretion but had instead acted on the basis of a policy formulated prior to the enactment of the Act, with the result that he had fettered his discretion and was in breach of the rules of natural justice by not acting fairly. The Divisional Court held that the multipliers order was valid and effective from 15 January 1981 and was not unreasonable in its effect but nevertheless quashed the Secretary of State's decision of 26

h January 1981 on the ground that after being given power under the 1980 Act but before making his decision the Secretary of State had refused to listen to any representations

---

a   Section 2(2) is set out at p 967 d e, post

b   Regulation 5(1) is set out at p 969 j to p 970 a, post

j   *c*   Section 49(4) provides: 'The principles on which multipliers are determined under this section shall be specified in an order made by statutory instrument by the Secretary of State.'

d   Section 50(2), so far as material, provides: 'The Secretary of State shall carry out the variation [of the needs element of rate support grant], in relation to any authority, by multiplying the additional amount of needs element payable . . . by a multiplier determined on principles specified in an order made by statutory instrument by the Secretary of State.'

which the applicant authority and the other authorities affected desired to make. The
authority then requested the Secretary of State to pay the amounts set out in his letter of   *a*
6 January 1981. The Secretary of State refused and continued to withhold payment. On
19 February 1982 the Secretary of State purported to make a second decision in the same
terms as his decision of 26 January 1981 reducing the rate support grant payable to the
authority for the year 1980–81. The authority applied for judicial review of the Secretary
of State's decision of 19 February 1982, contending that it was entitled as of right to
payment of rate support grant in accordance with the letter of 6 January 1981 because   *b*
such entitlement had been conclusively decided by the Divisional Court in the previous
proceedings so as to raise an issue estoppel against the Secretary of State. The Divisional
Court dismissed the application. The authority appealed, contending (i) that the Secretary
of State was estopped by the Divisional Court's first decision from denying that the
authority was entitled to the full amount of rate support grant and (ii) that on the true
construction of s 2(2) of the 1974 Act and s 48(1)*e* of the 1980 Act, which provided that   *c*
the rate support grant was 'payable to a local authority for the year 1980–81', the Secretary
of State was under a duty to pay the grant to the authority in the amounts and on the
dates set out in his letter of 6 January 1981. The authority further sought leave to argue
that the multipliers order was itself invalid on the grounds that it did not show the
principles on which the determination of the multiplier was to be made as required by
ss 49(4) and 50(2) of the 1980 Act, and that in any event, even if the multipliers order   *d*
was valid, the Secretary of State had not exercised his powers consistently with the
principles of that order.

Held – The appeal would be dismissed for the following reasons—

(1) The Secretary of State was not under a duty to pay the amounts on the dates set out
in his letter of 6 January 1981 because (per Sir John Donaldson MR and Dunn LJ)   *e*
although s 2(2) of the 1974 Act entitled a local authority to receive the full rate support
grant, it nevertheless authorised the Secretary of State, subject to Treasury consent, to
make payments of particular amounts on particular dates in the exercise of his discretion,
and in the exercise of that discretion, provided he exercised it bona fide, the Secretary of
State was entitled to defer payment of rate support grant until he had made his second
decision, and (per Browne-Wilkinson LJ) the Secretary of State's letter of 6 February 1981   *f*
was to be treated as a revised estimate, made under reg 5(1) of the 1979 regulations, of
the rate support grant payable to the authority which superseded the earlier estimate
notified in the letter of 6 January 1981 and although the 6 February estimate later proved
to be erroneous the 6 January estimate once superseded became spent and could not be
revived (see p 963 *h* to p 964 *a*, p 965 *a*, p 967 *g* to p 968 *a*, p 969 *d* and p 970 *d* to *h*, post).

(2) On its true construction s 48(1) of the 1980 Act did not limit the power to reduce   *g*
the rate support grant 'payable' to a local authority for the year 1980–81 by requiring the
power to be used before the end of that year; instead, s 48(1) merely required the power
to be used in respect of the year 1980–81. Accordingly, the Secretary of State's second
decision on 19 February 1982 was clearly valid and it followed that he was entitled to
withhold the payment of rate support grant (see p 962 *e* and *j* to p 963 *a*, p 965 *a*, p 969 *b*
to *e* and p 970 *h*, post).   *h*

(3) Issue estoppel did not arise because the question whether the authority was entitled
to payment immediately on the Secretary of State's decision of 6 January 1981 being
quashed was not in issue in the first proceedings before the Divisional Court, since the
decision in those proceedings was concerned solely with the then existing entitlement of
the authority and not with when the authority was entitled to be paid. Furthermore it
was not inconsistent to hold that payment could be postponed until after the 'entitlement'   *j*
had been extinguished by the second decision. In any event, although the court had an
inherent discretion in the interests of finality not to allow a particular issue which had
already been litigated to be reopened, it was doubtful whether the doctrine of issue

---

e   Section 48(1), so far as material, is set out at p 969 *a*, post

estoppel could be relied on in an application for judicial review. In such proceedings the
court was not finally determining the validity of a tribunal's order as between the parties,
but was deciding whether there had been an excess of jurisdiction (see p 964 *j* to p 965 *b*,
p 968 *e f*, p 969 *d e* and p 970 *h*, post).

(4) The application for leave to argue that the multipliers order was invalid would be
refused because it would be inconsistent with the principles of judicial review to allow a
party to challenge the validity of a statutory instrument which had been approved by
Parliament more than three years previously and acted on ever since (see p 964 *g*, p 965 *b*,
p 968 *h*, p 969 *d e* and p 970 *h*, post).

Decision of the Divisional Court of the Queen's Bench Division [1983] 3 All ER 358
affirmed.

Notes

For rate support grants, see 28 Halsbury's Laws (4th edn) paras 1262–1271.

For issue estoppel, see 16 ibid paras 1530–1533, and for cases on the subject, see 21
Digest (Reissue) 37–106, 232–727.

For judicial review generally, see 37 Halsbury's Laws (4th edn) paras 567–583.

For the Local Government Act 1974, s 2, see 4 Halsbury's Statutes (3rd edn) 641.

For the Local Government, Planning and Land Act 1980, ss 48, 49, 50, see 50(2) ibid
1345, 1346.

Cases referred to in judgments

Associated Provincial Picture Houses Ltd v Wednesbury Corp [1947] 2 All ER 680, [1948] 1
KB 223, CA.
Calvin v Carr [1979] 2 All ER 440, [1980] AC 574, [1979] 2 WLR 755, PC.
Hoffman-La Roche (F) & Co AG v Secretary of State for Trade and Industry [1974] 2 All ER
1128, [1975] AC 295, [1974] 3 WLR 104, HL.
Lake v Lake [1955] 2 All ER 538, [1955] P 336, [1955] 3 WLR 145, CA.
Livingstone v Westminster Corp [1904] 2 KB 109.
R v Secretary of State for the Environment, ex p Brent London BC [1983] 3 All ER 321, [1982]
QB 593, [1982] 2 WLR 693, DC.
Rootkin v Kent CC [1981] 2 All ER 227, [1981] 1 WLR 1186, CA.

Cases also cited

Carl-Zeiss-Stiftung v Rayner & Keeler Ltd (No 2) [1966] 2 All ER 536, [1967] 1 AC 853, HL.
DPP v Humphrys [1976] 2 All ER 497, [1977] AC 1, HL.
Hoystead v Taxation Comr [1926] AC 155, [1925] All ER Rep 56, PC.
Mills v Cooper [1967] 2 All ER 100, [1967] 2 QB 459, DC.
R v Hartington Middle Quarter (Inhabitants) (1855) 4 E & B 780, 119 ER 288.
War Damage Act 1943, Re, Re 56 Denton Road, Twickenham, Middlesex [1952] 2 All ER
799, [1953] Ch 51.

Appeal

Camden London Borough Council (Camden) appealed to the Court of Appeal against the
decision of the Divisional Court of the Queen's Bench Division (May LJ and McNeill J)
([1983] 3 All ER 358, [1983] 1 WLR 524) on 28 January 1983 whereby it dismissed, inter
alia, (i) an application by Camden for judicial review of a decision of the Secretary of State
for the Environment as evidenced by a letter dated 19 February 1982 from the
Department of Environment to Camden, and (ii) an application to amend the relief
sought and the grounds to include a challenge to the vires of the Rate Support Grant
(Principles for Multipliers) Order 1980. The facts are set out in the judgment of Dunn
LJ.

Roger Henderson QC and *Charles George* for Camden.
Robert Alexander QC, Simon D Brown and *Paul Walker* for the Secretary of State.

DUNN LJ (giving the first judgment at the invitation of Sir John Donaldson MR). This is an appeal by Camden London Borough Council (Camden) from the judgment of the Divisional Court (May LJ and McNeill J) ([1983] 3 All ER 358, [1983] 1 WLR 524) whereby on 28 January 1983 the court dismissed Camden's application for judicial review of decisions of the Secretary of State for the Environment purportedly made in accordance with the provisions of the Local Government Act 1974 and the Local Government Planning and Land Act 1980, and in particular of a decision notified to Camden by letter dated 19 February 1982, whereby the Secretary of State withheld and/or reduced the amount of rate support grant payable to Camden in respect of the year 1980–81.

The application has a long history and complicated background, and I gratefully adopt the account of the rate support grant system and of the background of events set out in the judgment of the Divisional Court in *R v Secretary of State for the Environment, ex p Brent London BC* [1983] 3 All ER 321 at 324–343, [1982] 1 QB 593 at 609–633 (the *Brent* case), and the findings of the Divisional Court on that application, the provisions of ss 1(1), 2(2) and 3 of the 1974 Act and reg 5 of the Rate Support Grant Regulations 1979, SI 1979/1514, and the subsequent events set out in the judgment of the Divisional Court in the present application (see [1983] 3 All ER 358 at 359–362, [1983] 1 WLR 524 at 529–533).

In order that this judgment should be comprehensible, it is however convenient to set out certain dates which are relevant to the decision of the Secretary of State in respect of the year 1980–81. This was the year to which the transitional provisions contained in ss 48 to 50 of the 1980 Act applied. The year ran from 1 April to 31 March, and the year beginning 1 April 1981 was appointed as 'the commencing year' for the new system of block grants introduced by the 1980 Act.

In November 1979 the government published a white paper *The Government's Expenditure Plans 1980–81* (Cmnd 7746) setting out its proposals for legislation for the introduction of the new block grant system, and for transitional arrangements for the year 1980–81. Thereafter the following events took place.

16 November 1979: white paper proposals discussed at a meeting of the Consultative Council on Local Government Finance.

28 November: rate support grant order together with the 1979 regulations and report for the year 1980–81 were laid before Parliament pursuant to the provisions of the 1974 Act.

9 January 1980: the Department of Environment wrote to, inter alios, Camden notifying it of the estimates of individual payments and the dates of such payments of rate support grants for the year 1980–81.

16 January: debate in the House of Commons on rate support grants report and order for 1980–81.

17 January: Rate Support Grant Order 1979, SI 1980/57 took effect.

1 April: 1979 regulations came into force.

18 November: royal assent to 1980 Act introducing the new system of the block grants and transitional provisions.

16 December: Rate Support Grant (Increase) (No 2) Order 1980, SI 1980/2049, made pursuant to the 1974 Act. Report on that order and the Rate Support Grant (Principles of Multipliers) Order 1980, SI 1980/2047 (the multipliers order), made pursuant to the 1980 Act all laid before Parliament.

6 January 1981: the Department of Environment wrote to, inter alios, Camden notifying it of revised calculations of estimated payments of rate support grant for 1980–81. Paragraph 4 of the letter stated 'The adjustments referred to in this letter take no account of' the multipliers order.

14 January: Rate Support Grant (Increase) (No 2) Order 1980 and multipliers order both approved by Parliament.

15 January: above orders took effect.

a 26 January: Secretary of State's decision to implement the transitional arrangements under the 1980 Act.

6 February: the Department of Environment wrote to Camden notifying it of reductions in the needs element of rate support grant for 1980–81 in the approximate sum of £5m pursuant to the transitional arrangements (the first decision).

March: the amounts withheld under the transitional arrangements were distributed to other authorities.

b 1 April: block grant system came into effect.

21 October: Divisional Court quashed the first decision on the ground that the Secretary of State had refused after obtaining his power under the 1980 Act and before making his decision to listen to any new representations which the applicants desired to make. The court added ([1983] 3 All ER 321 at 357, [1982] QB 593 at 647):

c
> 'It will of course be open to the Secretary of State after considering the applicants' representations, now fully documented, to reach any decision he considers right, and which is within the terms of the 1980 Act and the multipliers order.'

It was accepted in the Divisional Court and in this court that that observation was obiter, and not binding on any subsequent court.

d 9 November: the Department of Environment wrote to Camden inviting further representations, which were duly made in subsequent correspondence.

26 November: the Department of Environment wrote to Camden refusing to pay the moneys withheld pursuant to the first decision.

2 December: the time limited for appealing from the order of the Divisional Court expired.

e 4 February 1982: application by Camden for judicial review of the Secretary of State's decision to withhold payments as communicated by his letter of 26 November 1981.

19 February: the Department of Environment wrote to Camden notifying it that the rate support grant for 1980–81 would be abated in accordance with the multipliers order unless Camden was able to show that its expenditure fell within the terms of certain waivers, which Camden was unable to do (the second decision).

f 28 January 1983: the Divisional Court dismissed Camden's application for judicial review on the grounds that under the terms of the 1974 Act the Secretary of State was empowered to decide when and in what amounts instalments of rate support grant were to be paid, and that in the absence of lack of bona fides (which was not alleged) the Secretary of State had power to defer payments of amounts to which the applicants would otherwise have been entitled until he decided, after hearing any further representations, *g* whether to exercise his transitional powers to reduce the amounts of rate support grant for the year 1980–81 (see [1983] 3 All ER 358, [1983] 1 WLR 524). The court also decided that the judgment in the previous proceedings in the Divisional Court did not raise an issue estoppel against the Secretary of State, and that in any event issue estoppel could not be raised in applications for judicial review under RSC Ord 53.

In this court the argument of counsel for Camden depended essentially on the *h* following submissions. The letters of 9 January 1980 and 6 January 1981 evidenced determinations by the Secretary of State pursuant to s 2(2) of the 1974 Act of the amounts of the payments to be made to Camden in respect of rate support grant for the year 1980–81 and of the dates on which both amounts were to be paid. Subject to the provisions of the 1980 Act and of the multipliers order those amounts and dates could not be varied save by regulations made pursuant to s 10 of the 1974 Act, and the *j* regulations in fact made were inappropriate to cover the reductions in rate support grant made under the 1980 Act. Accordingly, the Secretary of State was under a duty to make payments of the amounts and on the dates set out in the two letters, and Camden had a corresponding right to receive those amounts on those dates. Counsel for Camden accepted that the Secretary of State could, by a valid exercise of his powers under the

1980 Act, have reduced those amounts but not retrospectively. In other words, he could withhold any amount unpaid at the date he made his decision, but could not recoup any sums already paid. In particular any decision under the 1980 Act must, on a purposive construction of the Act and the multipliers order, be validly made before the end of the transitional year, ie 31 March 1981. Counsel for Camden submitted accordingly that if the first decision had been valid the Secretary of State could have reduced the amounts of the payments falling due between the date of the decision and 31 March, but was bound to pay all amounts due down to that date in full. But since the first decision had been held to be invalid, and the Secretary of State relied only on the second decision made after the end of the transitional year, and at a time when the block grants scheme had come into effect, the second decision was not effective to reduce the amounts set out in the two letters.

The first part of the submissions depended on the construction of the 1974 Act, in particular s 2(2), and the second part of the submission depended on the meaning of the phrase 'payable to a local authority for the year 1980–81' in s 48 of the 1980 Act. Counsel for Camden submitted that the word 'payable' in its ordinary and natural meaning meant 'to be paid' and was looking to the future. The meaning of the word 'payable' accepted by the Divisional Court, that in its context it was descriptive and not strictly temporal and that the phrase in question meant 'in respect of' the year 1980–81, was an unnatural use of the word 'payable', and not justified in what was in effect a penal provision which should be construed in favour of the subject.

Counsel for the Secretary of State submitted that the first question arising for decision was whether or not the second decision was valid. He submitted, and I accept, that it plainly was. There is nothing in the 1980 Act or in the multipliers order to indicate that the power to reduce rate support grants must be exercised within the transitional year. On the contrary, the whole scheme of the 1974 Act is that the final amount of rate support grant may not be ascertained and conclusively determined until after the end of the relevant year. Payments and adjustments of rate support grants are commonly made after year end. The 1980 Act did not become law until over seven months of the transitional year had elapsed, and it is inconceivable that Parliament should have intended that the power to reduce was to be exercised during the year, having regard to the purposes of the transitional provisions. I adopt in relation to the second decision what was said by the Divisional Court in the *Brent* case [1983] 3 All ER 321 at 346, [1982] QB 593 at 636 in relation to the first decision:

'Here the order clearly relates to its prescribed purposes: to act against those who over-budget or overspend. At that stage it is not to encourage them to make reductions. The year 1980–81 in respect of which the Secretary of State is given power to reduce the amount of rate support grant payable commences in April 1980 and the Act came into force in November 1980. At a time when the power was given, January 1981, it was then far too late for the overspenders to take any decisive action. It is common knowledge that it is not possible to take action at short notice which makes any substantial reduction in the expenditure budgeted for the immediate or near future, especially so in the case of local government. That was the reason for the earlier warning or exhortations in 1979 and the advance notice by the Secretary of State of the nature of the powers which he would seek and how he would exercise them. The purpose of s 48 is, to our mind, quite clear. It is to give power to take action against those whose uniform rate, or adjusted uniform rate, exceed their notional uniform rate. This must have been patently obvious to Parliament when the Bill was debated and to the House of Commons when the multipliers order was laid, and subsequently considered and approved on 14 January.'

Further I accept the construction of s 48 of the 1980 Act adopted by the Divisional

Court in the present application that the words 'payable to a local authority for the year 1980–81' means payable in respect of the year 1980–81.

Counsel for the Secretary of State went on to submit that the Secretary of State was under no duty to pay the amounts referred to in the letter of 6 January 1981 after the first decision had been quashed. That decision was valid until it was quashed (see *F Hoffman-La Roche & Co AG v Secretary of State for Trade and Industry* [1974] 2 All ER 1128 at 1153–1154, [1975] AC 295 at 365 per Lord Diplock and *Calvin v Carr* [1979] 2 All ER 440 at 445–446, [1980] AC 574 at 589–590 per Lord Wilberforce). Its subsequent quashing did not have the effect of placing on the Secretary of State a duty to pay the amounts set out in the letter of 6 January 1981. Such a duty could only be extracted from the relevant legislation itself. Counsel for the Secretary of State relied on the construction placed by the Divisional Court on s 2(2) of the 1974 Act ([1983] 3 All ER 358 at 363–364, [1983] 1 WLR 524 at 534–535):

'Nevertheless we think that in general s 2(2) of the 1974 Act gives the Secretary of State and the Treasury the final say, subject to general legal principles, about when and in what amounts instalments of grants are paid. We do not think that the word "determine" in s 2(2) connotes the type of formal decision for which counsel for the applicants contended. We have no doubt that if the Secretary of State refused or delayed making rate support grants to local authorities under what is now s 53(8) of the 1980 Act for no good reason, so as to frustrate the purpose of this part of the legislation, then this court could intervene by way of judicial review and grant whatever relief was required. However, we do not think that any "determination" of when and in what instalments a grant is to be paid is immutable.'

He submitted that throughout the 1974 Act and the regulations the Secretary of State was empowered to make estimates which were subject to variations and was given a discretion as to the amounts to be paid on any particular date. He was not required to make and did not make any formal irrevocable determination of any amount to be paid on any particular date. In making the payments he did he was doing no more than exercise a statutory discretion: see *Rootkin v Kent CC* [1981] 2 All ER 227 at 233, [1981] 1 WLR 1186 at 1195 per Lawton LJ:

'It is the law that if a citizen is entitled to payment in certain circumstances and a local authority is given the duty of deciding whether the circumstances exist and if they do exist of making the payment, then there is a determination which the local authority cannot rescind. That was established in *Livingstone v Westminster Corpn* [1904] 2 KB 109. But that line of authority does not apply in my judgment to a case where the citizen has no right to a determination on certain facts being established, but only to the benefit of the exercise of a discretion by the local authority.'

Counsel for the Secretary of State submitted that the decisions of the Secretary of State to reduce the amount of rate support grants constituted a discretionary recalculation of his estimate of rate support grant for 1980–81 and that reg 5 of the 1979 regulations provided machinery for such recalculation.

I accept the construction of s 2(2) of the 1974 Act adopted by the Divisional Court. I do not think that the letter of 6 January 1981 placed on the Secretary of State any duty to pay the amounts on the dates there specified, or that Camden had any right to receive those amounts on those dates. No doubt in the ordinary course of good administration they would have been paid, but for the provisions of the 1980 Act. But it has rightly not been suggested that in the exercise of his discretion the Secretary of State was wrong to withhold the payments pending a decision under the 1980 Act. What is said is that he had no power to do so. I do not agree. There is nothing in s 2(2) to prevent the Secretary of State from withholding payment after the court had quashed his first decision until, after reconsideration, he had made his second decision. Once the Secretary of State had made his second decision, s 10 of the 1974 Act and reg 5 of the 1979 regulations provided appropriate machinery for recalculating the estimates of the reduced amounts of rate support grant. No conclusive calculation for the year 1980–81 had been made at any   *a* time before the second decision.

So much for the principal question argued on the appeal. In the course of the argument counsel for Camden applied for leave to argue that the multipliers order was itself invalid on the grounds that it did not show the principles on which the determination of multiplier was to be made in conformity with ss 49(4) and 50(2) of the 1980 Act, and that in any event the exercise of his powers by the Secretary of State was not consistent   *b* with the principles of the multipliers order properly construed. This point was decided against Camden by the Divisional Court in the *Brent* case [1983] 3 All ER 321, [1982] QB 593. In an interlocutory decision we refused the application of counsel for Camden without giving reasons. His argument in support of it may be summarised as follows. Following the decision in *Lake v Lake* [1955] 2 All ER 538, [1955] P 336, Camden had no right of appeal against the finding as to the validity of the multipliers order, because a   *c* finding that the order was invalid would not have affected the form of the court order made in the *Brent* case. Camden had succeeded in that case on the basis that the decision of the Secretary of State in the exercise of his powers under the multipliers order was contrary to natural justice. Assuming, contrary to the principal argument of counsel for Camden, that issue estoppel did not apply to proceedings for judicial review, as held by the Divisional Court in the instant case, then the first opportunity which Camden had to   *d* argue the validity of the multipliers order in this court was in this present appeal, and it would be unjust that it should not be given that opportunity.

This is a new point raised for the first time in this court. After this present application was made, Camden applied to a differently constituted Court of Appeal for leave to appeal out of time against the decision in the *Brent* case that the multipliers order was valid. The application was refused, and it was never suggested in the course of argument   *e* that Camden had no right of appeal. On the contrary, it was accepted by both parties that it had. The decision not to appeal within the time limit was a quite deliberate one taken by Camden on advice.

I am not persuaded that the decision in *Lake v Lake* leads to the conclusion that Camden had no right of appeal in the *Brent* case against the decision of the Divisional Court as to the validity of the multipliers order. It is true that the statutory jurisdiction of this court   *f* is confined to appeals against judgments or orders. In *Lake v Lake* the court could not have varied the form of order made in the court below even if it had found in favour of the appellant on the question at issue. That is not the situation here. The form of order made by the Divisional Court could have been varied on appeal if Camden had succeeded in arguing that the multipliers order was invalid. But in any event I do not think that it would be consistent with the principles of judicial review to allow a party to challenge   *g* the validity of a statutory order which was approved by Parliament over three years ago and has been acted on ever since.

The final ground of appeal was that the Secretary of State was estopped from denying that as at the date of the present application for judicial review Camden was entitled to receive the full amounts of rate support grant on the dates set out in the letters of 9 January 1980 and 6 January 1981. The passages in the judgment in the *Brent* case relied   *h* on as raising an issue estoppel are set out in the judgment of the Divisional Court under appeal and the argument in support (see [1983] 3 All ER 358 at 364–365, [1983] 1 WLR 524 at 535–536). The Divisional Court rejected the argument for the reasons given which I adopt (see [1983] 3 All ER 358 at 365–367, [1983] 1 WLR 524 at 537). In my judgment no issue estoppel arose in the present case.

Although not necessary for my decision I also incline to the view that the Divisional   *j* Court was right to hold that the doctrine of issue estoppel cannot be relied on in applications for judicial review, although the court has an inherent jurisdiction as a matter of discretion in the interests of finality not to allow a particular issue which has already been litigated to be reopened. This depends on the special nature of judicial

review under RSC Ord 53, which makes it different both from ordinary civil litigation
inter partes and from criminal proceedings. Like the Divisional Court, I adopt the passage
from Professor H W R Wade *Administrative Law* (5th edn, 1982) p 246 set out in the
judgment of the Divisional Court (see [1983] 3 All ER 358 at 367, [1983] 1 WLR 524 at
539).

For the above reasons I would dismiss the appeal.

SIR JOHN DONALDSON MR. This appeal concerns the duty of the Secretary of
State in relation to the payment of rate support grant for the financial year 1980–81. The
rate support grant is payable under provisions contained in the Local Government Act
1974. They were summarised in the judgment of the Divisional Court in *R v Secretary of
State for the Environment, ex p Brent London BC and others* [1983] 3 All ER 321, [1982] QB
593, the 'others' including Camden London Borough Council (Camden).

At the stage at which the *Brent* case came before the Divisional Court, the Secretary of
State had decided, in the exercise of powers conferred on him by ss 49 and 50 of the Local
Government, Planning and Land Act 1980 and by the Rate Support Grant (Principles for
Multipliers) Order 1980, SI 1980/2047 (the multipliers order), to reduce the rate support
grant which would otherwise have been payable to local authorities whose rate borne
expenditure exceeded a certain level and to distribute the amount so gained to other local
authorities. The applicants sought four different forms of relief by way of judicial review,
namely: (1) the quashing of the Secretary of State's decision; (2) a declaration that the
multipliers order did not constitute a decision to reduce or vary the amount of the rate
support grant; (3) a declaration that the multipliers order was ultra vires and of no effect;
(4) a declaration of the rights of the parties in lieu of an injunction—

> 'restraining the Secretary of State for the Environment from causing the amount
> of Rate Support Grant otherwise payable to the applicants ... to be reduced or varied
> otherwise than pursuant to a decision according to law and in any event not before
> any order under section 49(4) or section 50(5) of the said Act has effect.'

The order of the court (Ackner LJ and Phillips J), after reciting these claims for relief,
confined itself to quashing the Secretary of State's decision. However, the reasoned
judgment explained why the decision was quashed and the other conclusions of the court
in the following terms ([1983] 3 All ER 321 at 357, [1982] QB 593 at 646–647):

> '(1) The multipliers order is valid. (2) The Secretary of State did not misdirect
> himself as to his powers under ss 48 to 50 of the 1980 Act. (3) The Secretary of
> State's decision to reduce the rate support grants of each of the applicants was a
> decision which, subject to (4) below, the Secretary of State was entitled to reach. (4)
> The Secretary of State did not validly exercise his discretionary powers because, after
> obtaining them and before making his decision to reduce the rate support grants,
> he refused to listen to any new representations which the applicants desired to make.
> (5) The Secretary of State's decision must be quashed. It will of course be open to the
> Secretary of State after considering the applicants' representations, now fully
> documented, to reach any decision he considers right, and which is within the terms
> of the 1980 Act and the multipliers order.'

The decision referred to had been made on 26 January 1981 and it purported to reduce
the amount of rate support grant payable to Camden by over £5m. As a matter of
machinery, effect was given to this by reducing the instalments of rate support grant
which had been notified to Camden as being payable on 9, 16 and 23 February and 9, 16
and 23 March 1981. The order quashing this decision was made on 21 October 1981.
Thereafter the Secretary of State engaged in the appropriate consultative processes and on
19 February 1982 made a fresh decision which again purported to reduce the rate support
grant payable to Camden by the same amount.

Once the decision of 26 January 1981 was quashed, Camden pressed for payment of that part of the rate support grant which had been withheld. Getting no satisfactory response, Camden on 10 February 1982 launched the present proceedings which, in effect, claimed payment of those moneys together with interest. When Camden learnt of the decision of 19 February it widened the scope of its application by seeking to quash that decision. A Divisional Court consisting of May LJ and McNeill J ([1983] 3 All ER 358, [1983] 1 WLR 524) dismissed that application and Camden now appeal.

There can be no doubt that the Secretary of State is under a duty to pay every local authority the full amount of the rate support grant which is due to it under the various rate support grant orders. However, that amount is not fixed definitively at the beginning of the financial year concerned. Rate support grant is based on what may be described as 'formulae' and the values to be attached to the different elements are unlikely to be known with complete accuracy until later in the financial year or indeed after it has ended. The statutory scheme takes account of this fact and rate support grant is initially paid on the basis of estimates.

In the case of the year 1980–81, the rate support grant was payable pursuant to the Rate Support Grant Regulations 1979, SI 1979/1514, and reg 5 required the Secretary of State to estimate and notify to each local authority the amounts of the constituent elements of the rate support grant which would become payable for the year and, so soon as he had sufficient information for the purpose, to make a conclusive calculation of the amounts payable, again notifying the various local authorities.

Quite apart from delays and difficulties in evaluating the different factors which bear on the total amount of rate support grant payable to each local authority, it usually happens that the original rate support grant order has to be supplemented by a further order increasing the amount of rate support grant to take account of unforeseen increases in the level of prices, costs and remuneration. Power to do so is conferred on the Secretary of State by s 4 of the Local Government Act 1974. In the case of the year 1980–81 it was exercised by the Rate Support Grant (Increase) (No 2) Order 1980, SI 1980/2649, which came into force on 15 January 1981.

So far as 1980–81 was concerned, the matter was further complicated by the enactment of the Local Government, Planning and Land Act 1980. Sections 48 to 50 of that Act gave the Secretary of State power to reduce the rate support grant payable to what had been referred to as 'high spending' local authorities. The power was discretionary in nature, but if he decided to exercise it he had to make certain reports to Parliament and also to specify certain multipliers in a statutory instrument. If all this was done, the effect was to reduce the resources and needs elements of the rate support grant payable to some local authorities. Since the total available amount of rate support grants is distributed amongst local authorities in accordance with provisions which, inter alia, take account of their relative needs and resources, the effect of reducing the needs and resources claims of some authorities was to increase the amount of rate support grants payable to other authorities.

In January 1980 the Secretary of State wrote to all local authorities telling them that instalments of rate support grants would be payable at weekly intervals on specified dates between April 1980 and March 1981. He also gave them his estimate of how much would be payable and specified the proportion of the total which he proposed to pay on each date.

On 6 January 1981 he wrote to local authorities, including Camden, with revised estimates of the amount of rate support grant. These took account of information received during the previous year and also of the Rate Support Grant (Increase) (No 2) Order 1980. The revised estimate showed an increase in rate support grants and the Secretary of State informed local authorities by how much the payments on account of rate support grants to be made on and after 9 February 1981 would be adjusted to take account of this increase. However, the letter warned Camden that the adjusted figures took no account of the effect of the Rate Support Grant (Principles for Multipliers) Order 1980 and, by implication, of the effect of the decision which the Secretary of State was minded to make pursuant to his powers under ss 48 and 50 of the 1980 Act reducing the rate support grant payable to Camden.

That decision (the first decision) was reached on 26 January 1981 and on 6 February 1981 the Secretary of State informed Camden of the amount of the reduced instalments of rate support grant which would be paid on six dates in February and March 1981.

Camden claims that since the first decision was quashed, they were entitled to be paid the larger instalments notified in the letter of 6 January, whereas they have only received the reduced sums notified in that of 6 February. It is at this point that it is important to remember the nature of these proceedings. Camden has applied for judicial review. Accordingly it has to show that the Secretary of State was under a duty to pay these larger instalments on the dates notified in the letter of 6 January or at least when the first decision was quashed and in any event before 10 February 1982 when these proceedings were begun. Alternatively, in so far as the Secretary of State had a discretion whether to pay the increased amounts, Camden must show that no reasonable Secretary of State could have refrained from paying them before 10 February 1982.

It is at this point that Camden is faced with problems. There is undoubtedly a duty to pay each local authority the full amount of the rate support grant which ultimately is due to it, but nowhere in the 1974 Act, the 1980 Act or in any regulations is it provided by what instalments, of what amounts and on what dates it shall be paid. Camden seeks to overcome this problem by reference to s 2(2) of the 1974 Act, which provides:

'Subject to the following provisions of this section, payments in respect of the elements of rate support grant shall be made to a local authority at such times as the Secretary of State may with the consent of the Treasury determine, and shall be made in aid of the revenues of the authority generally; and the provisions of Schedule 2 to this Act shall have effect with respect to the determination of the amounts payable to any local authority in respect of those elements for any year.'

Camden then submits that the Secretary of State having by his letter of 6 January 'determined', with the consent of the Treasury, to pay the sums notified by that letter on the specified dates was under a duty to do so. In answer to the obvious retort that the sums notified in that letter were expressed to be subject to the effect of the multipliers order and of decisions under the 1980 Act to reduce its rate support grant, Camden submits that, since the decision was quashed, no account need be taken of this qualification.

I agree with the Divisional Court in considering that this involves a complete misconstruction of s 2(2) of the 1974 Act. In my judgment the subsection authorises the Secretary of State, subject to Treasury consent, to make payments of such amounts and on such dates as he sees fit in the exercise of his discretion, provided that ultimately he pays the whole rate support grant due. In order to succeed, Camden must therefore show that the Secretary of State has erred, in a *Wednesbury* sense, in the exercise of his discretion (see *Associated Provincial Picture Houses Ltd v Wednesbury Corp* [1947] 2 All ER 680, [1948] 1 KB 223). This Camden cannot do.

It is common ground that, as a matter of good administration, payments on account of rate support grant have to be made at frequent intervals and that local authorities should, so far as practicable, be given advance notification of what will be the amount of each instalment. Rate support grant was in fact paid at frequent intervals and on the dates notified.

The complaint is simply that the Secretary of State paid the amounts notified in the letter of 6 February 1981 and not the higher amounts notified in that of 6 January. For my part I do not see why the Secretary of State, in appropriate circumstances, should not amend a notification of the amount which he intends to pay. However, the letter of 6 February 1981 did not amend the notification contained in the letter of 6 January 1981, which in terms contemplated that what would actually be paid would be a lower sum by virtue of the decision of 26 January which was then in contemplation. The letter of 6 February simply defined that reduction.

A variant of this complaint was the submission that, once the Secretary of State knew that his decision of 26 January was invalid, he should have paid the £5m which would have become payable to Camden at some time in the absence of a reduction in its rate support grant pursuant to a valid decision under the 1980 Act. This might be correct were it not for the fact that the Secretary of State was contemplating making and did later make a second decision to the same effect. I do not see why the Secretary of State in the exercise of his discretion should not have refrained from making a supplementary payment to Camden until he had decided whether or not to reach such a decision.

Camden also advanced an argument based on issue estoppel. In the *Brent* case [1983] 3 All ER 321 at 354–355, 356, [1982] QB 593 at 643, 645 the court referred to the Rate Support Grant (Increase) (No 2) Order 1980 and said:

'Thus on [15 January 1981] all the applicants were entitled to receive the rate support grant provided by the Rate Support Grant Order 1979 as thus increased . . . Thus the decision (made on 26 January 1981) to reduce the applicants' rate support grants adversely affected not merely an expectation but a right to substantial sums of money . . . Moreover, having regard to the applicants' accrued right to the support grant, he would not be properly discharging his duty of fairness.'

Camden submitted that, in the face of this finding, the Secretary of State could not be heard to argue that there was no right to payment of the £5m once the first decision had been quashed.

In my judgment this contention fails for at least two reasons. First, whether or not Camden was entitled to payment immediately on the first decision being quashed was not in issue in the *Brent* case, there being no claim for a mandatory order or declaration concerning the time of payment. Second, the finding was concerned solely with the then existing entitlement of Camden and not with *when* Camden was entitled to be paid. It is in no way inconsistent with that judgment to hold that payment could properly be postponed until after the 'entitlement' had been extinguished by the second decision under the 1980 Act. Furthermore, I share the doubts expressed by May LJ and McNeill J as to the applicability of issue estoppel in judicial review proceedings.

There remains only the effect of the second decision itself. If this can be effectively attacked, Camden is indeed entitled to receive the additional £5m, although the question of when it has to be paid might still be open to argument. That decision was attacked on two grounds. First it was said that the multipliers order, which formed an essential basis of the second decision, was invalid. Second it was said that the 1980 Act did not authorise any such decision after the end of the 1980–81 financial year.

The validity of the multipliers order was in issue in the *Brent* case and it was held to be valid. Although Camden succeeded in the sense that it obtained an order quashing the first decision, it failed to obtain a declaration that the multipliers order was invalid and could have appealed that part of the court's decision. In fact it sought leave to appeal and failed in its application. In these circumstance, in the exercise of our discretion, we refused to allow this point to be reargued and I do not find it necessary to decide whether Camden was not in any event estopped from arguing it. These being judicial review proceedings, I am inclined to think that it was not.

The second ground of argument, namely that the 1980 Act powers could only be used during the year 1980–81, is based on the following considerations. (a) In a report to Parliament (see HC Paper (1979-80) no 280, paras 42, 46) the Secretary of State said that the new (1980) legislation was intended to provide for transitional arrangements between the pre-existing system and the new block grant system to be introduced for 1981–82 and that—

'These powers are intended to be available only for the interim period until the *a*   block grant system comes into effect in 1981/82. As soon as the new grant system is introduced, the transitional arrangements will be repealed.'

(b) Section 48(1) of the 1980 Act provides that 'The Secretary of State may reduce the amount of rate support grant payable to a local authority for the year 1980–81 . . .' It is submitted that this means that the grant can only be reduced by action taken before the end of that year.

b   I do not accept this construction of s 48(1). I regard the subsection as conferring a power to reduce the grant payable *for* or *in respect of* the year 1980–81 but not as indicating any limitation on when the power can be used. It contains no such words of limitation and rate support grant is subject to adjustment in other respects long after the financial year has ended. The report to Parliament is consistent with this view.

c   In the light of these conclusions, it is unnecessary to decide whether, if the Secretary of State ought to have paid the increased instalment of rate support grant in February and March 1981, he could have recovered the amount of the increase once the second decision had been made, but I have no doubt that he could have done so under reg 5(4) of the Rate Support Grant Regulations 1979 by deduction from any balance of the rate support grant still payable in respect of the year 1980–81 or from the rate support grant payable in respect of any subsequent year or by demand for repayment.

d   I would dismiss the appeal.

BROWNE-WILKINSON LJ. I agree that this appeal should be dismissed. I agree with the judgments of both Sir John Donaldson MR and Dunn LJ that the second decision of the Secretary of State to reduce the amount of the rate support grant was valid and that no issue estoppel arises in this case. I add my own views only on the question *e*   whether, pending the making of the second decision of the Secretary of State on 19 February 1982, Camden was legally entitled to be paid the rate support grant without reduction.

To succeed, Camden must show that at some date there was an obligation, legally enforceable against the Secretary of State, that it should be paid a sum of money which was not in fact paid. For this purpose Camden submits that s 2(2) of the Local Government *f*   Act 1974 imposes a legal obligation to pay the estimated amount of the rate support grant on dates which had been determined. Then, says Camden, the letter of 6 January 1981 and the annexed schedule showed that specific sums of money were to be paid on specified dates in respect of the rate support grant. Therefore, it is said, there was a legal obligation to pay the amount so specified on the dates specified. Camden submits that, although the amounts notified as being payable were altered by the letter of 6 February 1981, such letter was sent pursuant to the invalid first decision of the Secretary of State to *g*   reduce the rate support grant and that accordingly the purported change in the instalments of rate support grant payable were equally invalid. Thus, says Camden, its right to payment of the sums specified in the letter of 6 January 1981 remained in force.

The Divisional Court held that this argument failed at its very foundations since s 2(2) of the 1974 Act imposes no legal obligation on the Secretary of State to pay any sum on any particular date. I have some doubts whether that is correct. However, it is unnecessary *h*   for me to reach any concluded view on the point since I reach the same conclusion by a different route.

The scheme of the 1974 Act and the Rate Support Grant Regulations 1979, SI 1979/1514, seems to me to be as follows. Under s 1 of the 1974 Act the Secretary of State fixes the estimated aggregate amount of rate support grant. Then, under s 2 of the Act, he divides this estimated aggregate amount into the three elements: the needs element, the *j*   domestic element and the resources element. Regulation 5(1) of the 1979 regulations provides as follows:

'The Secretary of State shall, upon the best information available to him, estimate and notify to each local authority the amounts of the constituent elements of rate support grant which will become payable to the authority for the year; and he will make and notify to the authority such further estimates of the said amounts, taking into account information not previously available, as he may think fit.'

Accordingly, the Secretary of State is bound to notify each local authority of the estimated aggregate amount of each element payable to that authority in respect of the year in question. It is to be noted that the amounts to be notified are estimates and that such estimates can be revised. I will assume in Camden's favour that, under s 2(2) of the 1974 Act if a time or times for payment have been decided and notified by the Secretary of State, thereupon there would come into being a legal obligation on the Secretary of State to pay the estimated sums notified under reg 5 on the dates determined.

On 6 January 1981 the Secretary of State pursuant to reg 5(1) notified Camden of the increased amounts to be paid pursuant to the Rate Support Grant (Increase) (No 2) Order 1980, SI 1980/2049, and specified dates on which the instalments were to be payable. On 26 January 1981 he made his first decision to reduce the amount of the rate support grant payable to Camden pursuant to the transitional provisions in the 1980 Act. Then on 6 February 1981 he notified Camden of the revised estimated amounts which were to be paid on 9, 16 and 23 February and March 1981.

The letter of 6 February was in my judgment a revised estimate of the amount of the rate support grant notified by the Secretary of State pursuant to reg 5. Counsel for Camden contended that there was no power to notify such revised estimate consequential on a reduction made under the transitional provisions of the Local Government, Planning and Land Act 1980. He submitted that reg 5 only covered revised estimates resulting from information supplied by the local authorities. I do not so construe reg 5(1): it is a general power to make revised estimates as the Secretary of State 'may think fit' provided that he takes into account information not previously available. On 6 February 1981 such information included the reduction in the amount of the rate support grant pursuant to the first decision. Any other conclusion would lead to the result that Parliament had enacted the transitional provisions in the 1980 Act without providing any machinery whereby the estimated amounts payable under ss 1 and 2 of the 1974 Act could be adjusted to reflect a reduction order made under the 1980 Act.

In my judgment the notification in the letter of February 1981 of the estimated amounts payable superseded the earlier notification of 6 January 1981. It is impossible to have two conflicting notifications under reg 5 in force simultaneously. I do not accept the submission of counsel for Camden that, because the first decision of the Secretary of State to reduce the rate support grants was subsequently declared invalid, the letter of 6 February 1981 is to be treated as of no effect. True, the estimate notified by the letter of 6 February subsequently proved to be erroneous. But in my judgment that does not mean that it was not a revised estimate of the amounts payable under para 5(1), at least during the period between 6 February and the decision of the Divisional Court declaring the first decision of the Secretary of State to be invalid. Therefore the estimate of 6 February superseded the estimate of 6 January, which became spent once and for all. The estimate in the letter of 6 January could not be revived even if the letter of 6 February was subsequently held to be invalid.

For these reasons in my judgment Camden cannot show that at any time it was entitled to be paid the estimated sums notified in the letter of 6 January or any sum other than that specified in the letter of 6 February 1981. Its claim therefore fails.

Appeal dismissed. Leave to appeal to the House of Lords refused.

Solicitors: *F Nickson* (for Camden); *Treasury Solicitor.*

Diana Procter   Barrister.

R v Bagshaw and others

COURT OF APPEAL, CRIMINAL DIVISION
O'CONNOR LJ, KILNER BROWN AND POPPLEWELL JJ
8, 9, 10 NOVEMBER, 2 DECEMBER 1983

Criminal evidence – Corroboration – Direction to jury – Mental patient with criminal conviction detained in special hospital – Patient sole witness for prosecution – Whether full warning to be given to jury of danger of acting on patient's uncorroborated evidence.

Patients who are detained under the Mental Health Act 1959 in a special hospital after conviction of an offence are not a special category of suspect witnesses whose evidence requires the judge to warn the jury that it is dangerous to convict if their evidence is uncorroborated. However, if such a patient satisfies to a very high degree the criteria which make the uncorroborated evidence of certain categories of witnesses suspect, the judge ought to warn the jury that it is dangerous to convict on the patient's uncorroborated evidence (see p 977 c to e, post).

Dicta of Lord Diplock in *DPP v Hester* [1972] 3 All ER at 1076 and of Lord Hailsham LC in *DPP v Kilbourne* [1973] 1 All ER at 446–447 considered.

Notes

For corroboration in criminal proceedings, see 11 Halsbury's Laws (4th edn) paras 453–457, and for cases on the subject, see 14(2) Digest (Reissue) 618–621, 5026–5078.

For the Mental Health Act 1959, see 25 Halsbury's Statutes (3rd edn) 42.

As from 30 September 1983 (subject to certain exceptions and transitional provisions) the 1959 Act was replaced by the Mental Health Act 1983.

Cases referred to in judgment

Arthurs v A-G for Northern Ireland (1970) 55 Cr App R 161, HL (NI).
DPP v Hester [1972] 3 All ER 1056, [1973] AC 296, [1972] 3 WLR 910, HL.
DPP v Kilbourne [1973] 1 All ER 440, [1973] AC 729, [1973] 2 WLR 254, HL.
People, The (A-G) v Dominic Casey (No 2) [1963] IR 33.
R v Holland, R v Smith [1983] Crim LR 545, CA.
R v Prater [1960] 1 All ER 298, [1960] 2 QB 464, [1960] 2 WLR 343, CCA.
R v Price [1968] 2 All ER 282, [1969] 1 QB 541, [1968] 2 WLR 1397, CA.
R v Riley (1979) 70 Cr App R 1, CA.
R v Russell (1968) 52 Cr App R 147, CA.
R v Williams [1956] Crim LR 833, CCA.

Cases also cited

Davies v DPP [1954] 1 All ER 507, [1954] AC 378, HL.
R v Bone [1968] 2 All ER 644, [1968] 1 WLR 983, CA.
R v Mackenney, R v Pinfold (1981) 76 Cr App R 271, CA.

Applications for leave to appeal

On 11 May 1982, in the Crown Court at Nottingham before his Honour Judge Hopkin and a jury, the appellants, Robert Keith Bagshaw, Brian Holmes and Allen John Starkey, were convicted on various counts of a joint indictment of ill-treating certain patients, contrary to s 126 of the Mental Health Act 1959. The appellant Bagshaw was sentenced to three months' imprisonment, suspended for eighteen months, and the appellants Holmes and Starkey were each sentenced to concurrent terms of nine months' imprisonment, suspended for two years. Each of them applied for leave to appeal against

conviction. With the consent of counsel, the court treated the hearing of the applications
as the hearing of the appeals. The facts are set out in the judgment of the court.   *a*

Barry Mortimer QC and *Aidan S Marron* for the appellants.
Jeremy Roberts QC and *Richard Dixon* for the Crown.

At the conclusion of the arguments the court announced that the appeals against
conviction would be allowed for reasons to be given later.   *b*

2 December. The following judgment of the court was delivered.

O'CONNOR LJ. On 10 November we granted leave to appeal to these three applicants.
With the consent of counsel we treated the hearing of the applications as the hearing of
the appeals, and allowed their appeals against conviction. We now give our reasons for so   *c*
doing.

At all material times the appellants were nurses at Rampton Hospital, which is a secure
hospital catering for patients suffering from varying degrees of mental disorder. Most,
but not all, are also subject to orders of the court under the Mental Health Act 1959 made
following conviction for crimes of various kinds including homicide.

In April 1979 a television programme about Rampton was screened. It was a piece of   *d*
investigative journalism which alleged widespread ill-treatment of the patients by the
nursing staff. As a result of this programme, a police inquiry into allegations was
initiated, the television company handing over a dossier of some 800 complaints from
patients and ex-patients. In due course some 20 nurses were charged with various offences
of ill-treating patients contrary to s 126 of the 1959 Act and suspended from duty. The
charges against these men have resulted in no less than 14 trials at the Nottingham   *e*
Crown Court of which in only 5 were any defendants convicted.

The present case is concerned with nurses and patients in Dolphin Ward. That ward is
a secure ward housing some 35 to 40 patients suffering from severe mental disorder and
dangerous in the sense that they may do violence to others or themselves. Each patient is
allocated to one of the senior doctors who acts as his responsible medical officer. The
ward is visited daily by junior medical staff. The nursing in the ward is organised on a   *f*
shift basis; five or six nurses on duty and a charge nurse being in charge of the shift.
Apart from the nurses on duty and the doctors, there are many visitors to the ward who
are key holders, for example, the senior nursing officers with responsibilities for more
than one ward, ministers of religion, social workers and maintenance men.

To say that these patients are difficult to nurse is an understatement of the problems
with which the nurses have to contend every day. Among the patients are those suffering   *g*
from epilepsy, schizophrenia, paranoia and psychopathic disorder. They are cunning,
untruthful and suffer from hallucinations. The nurses have to watch for and try and
anticipate outbursts of uncontrolled aggressive violence. Sometimes they are too late and
must move in to rescue a patient or one of their own number from attack. Violent
aggressive patients have to be removed to seclusion and medicated. As a part of the
therapy, a system of forfeits and rewards has to be operated. In the nature of things,   *h*
many patients object to the forfeit part of the therapy. A nursing record is maintained
for each patient and any injury to a patient has to be reported and recorded. Patients who
have had to be restrained and placed in seclusion may quite honestly believe that they
have been ill-treated and bear a grudge against a nurse or nurses, and later make false
accusations of acts of ill-treatment.

The prosecution case against the appellants on each and every count in the indictment   *j*
depended entirely on the uncorroborated evidence of a single patient. When the hearing
started in this court the appellants, in their grounds of appeal, made no complaint
whatsoever about the summing up, but submitted that the verdicts were unsafe or
unsatisfactory on the grounds: (i) that the three complainants on whose evidence the

a   verdicts of guilty depended were men of proven unreliability, who, according to the
     medical evidence for the prosecution, might easily invent the incidents to which they
     spoke and put them forward with conviction; (ii) that their evidence on at least some
     counts was contradictory and confused; (iii) that the events, the subject matter of the
     counts, happened long ago; (iv) that on at least some of the counts, supporting evidence
     might have been expected from other patients: none was forthcoming; (v) that the jury
     reached inconsistent verdicts.

b   During the hearing we gave leave to the appellants to amend their grounds by raising
     a further ground, namely to question the adequacy of the judge's direction to the jury on
     the way in which they were to treat the evidence of the complainants. We should like to
     say at once that the judge's summing up is a masterpiece of lucidity and fairness. He gave
     an impeccable direction to the jury that they should treat the evidence of the complainants
     with the greatest caution. The question is whether these witnesses were such that a full
c   warning was required, namely that it was dangerous to convict on their unsupported
     evidence. Before we consider the adequacy of the direction we must look, as shortly as
     we may, at the alleged offences and the persons involved.
         The first four counts in the indictment, three against the appellant Holmes, and one
     against the appellant Starkey, depended on the evidence of the complainant, Errol
     Roberts. Errol Roberts was sentenced to borstal training for burglary at the Crown Court
d   at Gloucester in November 1972. While on remand he had tried to hang himself and
     had broken up his cell. His stay at Feltham borstal was stormy. He refused to work, and
     spent his time howling, banging, smashing up his room and pilfering. He had
     hallucinations, visual and auditory, and said that he could turn people into animals. His
     condition deteriorated and he became so disturbed that in March 1974 he was transferred
     to Rampton under s 72 of the 1959 Act. His stay in Rampton was no less stormy. The
e   records repeatedly refer to attacks on staff, great violence and the necessity for seclusion.
     He attempted to strangle a fellow patient. He made flagrant homosexual advances to
     patients, which were ill received. He was idle, cunning and needed constant supervision.
     He continued to suffer from hallucinations. Dr Perera said that the diagnosis of
     psychopathic disorder may have been mistaken and that he was, in truth, a schizophrenic
     suffering from paranoia and hallucinations. From late 1980 he improved, and in 1981
f   he was discharged. He gave evidence in April 1982.
         The appellant Holmes joined the nursing staff at Rampton as a student nurse in 1970.
     After three years he gained the necessary qualifications to be a staff nurse, and at all
     material times he was a staff nurse. He was promoted to a charge nurse in 1980, and on
     the face of it, his record is one of dedicated service to the patients. The appellant Starkey
     went to Rampton as a student nurse in 1973. After three years he qualified as a staff
g   nurse. He, too, was a staff nurse at all material times.
         Count 1 against Holmes alleged as particulars of the offence that on a day unknown
     between April 1977 and March 1979 he ill-treated Roberts by punching him on the jaw.
     Roberts gave evidence of an occasion when he said that he was wrongly accused of
     masturbating in the television room; given the extra labour of scrubbing the floor and
     that while he was so engaged, Holmes came by and gratuitously punched him. The
h   nursing record showed that in September 1977 he had indeed been found masturbating
     in the television room and given extra work to do, but Holmes flatly denied punching
     him. At one stage in cross-examination Roberts said that he was not sure whether this
     incident had even occurred. But later, in answer to the judge, he said that he was sure.
     The jury convicted.
         The particulars of count 2 against Holmes were that on a day unknown between April
j   and July 1978 he ill-treated Roberts by beating him in the charge nurse's office. Roberts
     said that he was wrongly accused by a nurse named Elliot of spying on staff in the
     lavatory through the spyhole, that Elliot took him to the billiard room and together with
     another nurse, named Blackburn, gave him a beating and took him down to the charge
     nurse's office where Holmes was to be found, and that Holmes punched him for good

measure. The defence isolated two days in June and July of 1978 when all these nurses were on duty together. Holmes gave evidence that he remembered such an incident, but flatly denied that he had punched Roberts. The jury acquitted.

Count 3 alleged that Holmes had ill-treated Roberts between April 1977 and March 1979 by hitting him on the head with a billiard cue. Roberts tried to give evidence in support of this count alleging that Holmes and other nurses playing snooker hit him on the head with a billiard cue. However, during his evidence-in-chief it became apparent that he was acting as scorer and all that was happening was that he might have been tapped on the shoulder to mark up the score. The judge directed a verdict of not guilty.

Count 4 against Starkey alleged that between March 1977 and March 1979 he ill-treated Roberts by punching him about the body. Roberts gave evidence that when the patients lined up in order to be searched before going to bed, Starkey was in the habit of punching both him and other patients in the belly. He said that he was treated like a punch-bag. Starkey accepted that the patients had to be frisked at this stage, but denied punching the complainant Roberts or any other patient. This was a count where the defence suggested that supporting evidence might be expected. Although at least two patients, Hutchinson and Morten gave evidence, no supporting evidence was forthcoming. The jury convicted.

The complainant Trevor Watson was sentenced in 1974 to four years' imprisonment for robbery and malicious wounding. Later that year he was transferred to Rampton under s 72 of the 1959 Act. Watson is an epileptic who suffered numerous fits. He was a very strong man and very violent. He was described as a paranoid skilful liar who would go to any lengths to accuse staff. He suffered from hallucinations, he made false accusations and later admitted their falsity.

Count 5 against Holmes alleged that between March 1977 and March 1979 he ill-treated Watson by punching him, sometimes on the jaw, sometimes on the body. Watson alleged that for no reason whatever Holmes would, from time to time, punch him when they met in the corridor or elsewhere in the ward. He alleged that on one occasion he was struck with such violence that his lip was cut and left a scar which he had shown to the police. His record showed numerous minor injuries received on the playing field and one injury of a cut lip sustained in an epileptic fit. Watson declared that this was a cover up by Holmes to account for having split his lip by punching him. Unfortunately, the record showed that this incident occurred three months after Holmes had left Dolphin Ward. Holmes denied the allegations. The jury convicted.

Count 6 alleged that Holmes ill-treated Watson by threatening to place him in seclusion for an improper reason, namely for sending a letter to the National Council for Civil Liberties. Watson alleged that after he emerged from a period in seclusion he had written a letter to the National Council for Civil Liberties, that Holmes asked him what he was going to do with it and that, when Watson said that he proposed to post it, Holmes had forced him to destroy it under threat of returning him to seclusion. Holmes denied the incident flatly. The jury convicted.

The complainant Philip Theodorou pleaded guilty to manslaughter on the ground of diminished responsibility at the Central Criminal Court in 1975 and came to Rampton under a court order. This man also was a violent, aggressive patient. He had a history of epilepsy. He suffered emotional paranoid outbursts, made false complaints and had to be placed in seclusion on a number of occasions.

Count 7 against Starkey alleged that he ill-treated Theodorou by punching him about the body. This again was a dormitory line-up allegation, and was denied by Starkey. The jury convicted.

Count 8 alleged that Starkey ill-treated Theodorou by putting his arm round his neck and threatening to kill him. Theodorou alleged that this incident occurred in the dormitory and that Starkey came over to him, held him by the neck and half strangled him saying that he would kill him and bury him in a field. Starkey denied the allegation. The jury acquitted.

Count 9 was another allegation against Starkey that he ill-treated Theodorou by
punching him in the stomach. The evidence of Theodorou was very confused on this
count. He talked about a joint attack by Blackburn and Starkey, and that Starkey had
kicked him when he was on the floor. The judge directed a verdict of not guilty.

The appellant Bagshaw went to Rampton in 1971 as a student nurse. He did not
achieve the qualifications of Holmes, but qualified as a state enrolled nurse in 1975. He
was attached to a shift in Dolphin Ward from July 1977 until January 1980.

Count 10 alleged that Starkey and Bagshaw ill-treated Theodorou by striking him on
the face on 15 January 1979. This incident is said to have been begun by the charge
nurse, Frow, coming to the dormitory, seizing Theodorou by the hair, dragging him
down the corridor and placing him in a side room in seclusion. According to Theodorou,
Bagshaw, Starkey and Holmes came into the room and he, Theodorou, threatened to
report Bagshaw and Starkey to the Home Office, whereupon each of them slapped him
on the face. The earlier part of this incident was spoken to by the witnesses Morten and
Hutchinson. There was, of course, no support for the allegations against Starkey and
Bagshaw. The jury convicted.

The last count with which we are concerned against Holmes alleged that he ill-treated
Theodorou in January 1979 by making improper threats to him as to what would happen
if he reported certain matters to his family. This count again arose out of the incident on
15 January, and the particulars speak for themselves. Holmes denied the allegation. The
jury convicted.

This short review of the case is, we hope, enough to show that these convictions,
resulting from the uncorroborated evidence of men such as the three complainants, must
give rise to great anxiety in this court. At the same time, we must and do bear in mind
that the purpose of s 126 of the 1959 Act is to protect patients in mental hospitals, and
that men like these three complainants may well be the kind of patient most in need of
protection.

It is against this background that we have to consider the direction given by the judge
how the jury should treat the evidence of the complainants in this case. We must set out
the direction given by the judge in full. He said:

'Now let us turn to consider the complainants in this case, Roberts, Watson,
Theodorou and Kirby [Kirby was a complainant in a count against Starkey on which
the jury were unable to reach agreement.] The first point we know about all four is
that they have all been convicted of serious criminal offences, and even if that were
all, I should have to tell you that you would have to look at their evidence very
carefully, and the fact that they have been convicted of serious criminal offences
would be sufficient to affect their credibility. But the matter does not rest there
because of course at the time they were all persons who were mentally ill, and they
were all persons who were mentally ill at the time they made these allegations
against these three defendants. Now then I must caution you, ladies and gentlemen,
that before you act on their evidence you must approach it with the very greatest
caution and you must examine it with the very greatest care. You ask why? I will
tell you. First of all, at the time that these events are alleged to have happened, all of
them were mentally ill. Secondly, they had all been convicted of serious offences.
Thirdly, all at times were deluded, but it is quite clear from the medical evidence,
you may think, that, even if a person is deluded, he could honestly believe those
delusions and appear convincing to you because he is able to give a detailed account
of that delusion. Fourthly, they may well be acting from motives of resentment or
revenge. And fifthly, this type of allegation is very easy to make but it is very
difficult to refute. The power of lying unfortunately as a human being, members of
the jury, is unlimited, and how much more is it unlimited in somebody (a) who is a
convicted criminal, (b) may be motivated by resentment, revenge or by something
that we do not even know of? Therefore, before acting on their evidence, you must

exercise, as I say, the very greatest degree of caution and you must examine their evidence with the very greatest care. Let me tell you this, there is absolutely no support at all for what they say, but on the other hand it is for you to say, having seen them, having seen each one examined and cross-examined in this court, whether you are sure that they are telling the truth. If you are sure that one or all of them are telling the truth then of course you may act on that evidence. If, taking into account the warnings which I have given you, which are not something may I say, ladies and gentlemen, thought up by the judge for the purposes of this case, but are warnings that judges have given to juries for years, not in cases of this nature because cases of this nature are rare, but in cases where you have complainants of this sort ... if, bearing in mind the warnings I have given you, which are based on the courts' experience over the years, none the less bearing those warnings in mind, if you are sure that these complainants are telling the truth then of course you may act on their evidence. If you are sure that they are telling you the truth, then you may find convictions on their evidence although it stands alone and unsupported. It is entirely up to you. You may think that possibly a good way of approaching this was suggested by counsel for the Crown. First, say to yourselves, "Am I sure that the witness is an honest witness?" If you are sure he is an honest witness then go on to say to yourselves, "He may be honest but am I sure he is accurate?" It is only when you are sure of those two matters that you should consider acting on his evidence.'

It will be seen that the judge did not warn the jury that it was dangerous to convict on the uncorroborated evidence of these complainants. Ought there to have been such a direction? A convenient summary of the need for corroboration in English law is found in the speech of Lord Hailsham LC in *DPP v Kilbourne* [1973] 1 All ER 440 at 446–447, [1973] AC 729 at 739–741. After dealing with the statutory requirements, the Lord Chancellor continued ([1973] 1 All ER 440 at 447, [1973] AC 729 at 740):

'But side by side with the statutory exceptions is the rule of practice now under discussion by which judges have in fact warned juries in certain classes of case that it is dangerous to found a conviction on the evidence of particular witnesses or classes of witness unless that evidence is corroborated in a material particular implicating the accused, or confirming the disputed items in the case. The earlier of these classes to be recognised was probably the evidence of accomplices "approving" for the Crown, no doubt, partly because at that time the accused could not give evidence on his own behalf and was therefore peculiarly vulnerable to invented allegations by persons guilty of the same offence. By now the recognised categories also include children who given evidence under oath, the alleged victims, whether adults or children, in cases of sexual assault, and persons of admittedly bad character. I do not regard these categories as closed. A judge is almost certainly wise to give a similar warning about the evidence of any principal witness for the Crown where the witness can reasonably be suggested to have some purpose of his own to serve in giving false evidence (cf *R v Prater* [1960] 1 All ER 298, [1960] 2 QB 464 and *R v Russell* (1968) 52 Cr App R 147). The Supreme Court of the Republic of Ireland has apparently decided that at least in some cases of disputed identity a similar warning is necessary (*People v Dominic Casey (No 2)* [1963] IR 33 at 39–40). This question may still be open here (cf *R v Williams* [1956] Crim LR 833 and *Arthurs v A-G for Northern Ireland* (1970) 55 Cr App R 161 at 169).'

We have in mind, without setting them out, passages from the speeches in *DPP v Hester* [1972] 3 All ER 1056 at 1059–1060, 1072–1073, [1973] AC 296 at 309, 324–325 per Lord Morris and Lord Diplock. The correct approach to the problem was stated by Lord Diplock in *DPP v Hester* [1972] 3 All ER 1056 at 1076, [1973] AC 296 at 328, where he said:

a   'My Lords, if a summing-up is to perform its proper function in a criminal trial by jury it should not contain a general disquisition on the law of corroboration couched in lawyer's language but should be tailored to the particular circumstances of the case. It would be highly dangerous to suppose that there is any such thing as a model summing-up appropriate to all cases of this kind. No doubt if there is unsupported evidence on oath of a child complainant fit to be left to the jury, the judge should tell them that it is open to them to convict on her evidence alone,

b   although he should remind them forcibly of the danger of doing so. But there is no need for him to tell them of what kind of evidence *could* amount to corroboration of her story, if in fact there is none at all.'

The only other matter of law is that it is well established that no set form of words are required so long as it is made clear to the jury that it is dangerous to convict on the

c   unsupported evidence of the witness.

Patients in hospital under the 1959 Act are not a category like accomplices or complainants in sexual cases, nor would we wish to make them into an additional category. Patients detained in a special hospital after conviction for an offence or offences, even if they are not a category, may well fulfil to a very high degree the criteria which justify the requirement of the full warning in respect of witnesses within accepted categories. It seems to us that in such cases nothing short of the full warning that it is

d   dangerous to convict on the uncorroborated evidence of the witness will suffice.

The cases recognise that there is a difference between a warning that the jury should approach the evidence of a witness with caution and a warning that it is dangerous to convict. Indeed, the difference is obvious (see *R v Price* [1968] 2 All ER 282, [1969] 1 QB 541, *R v Riley* (1979) 70 Cr App R 1 and *R v Holland, R v Smith* [1983] Crim LR 545).

e   We are in no doubt that the three complainants in the present case were shown to be persons in respect of whom the full warning was essential. It follows that in our view these convictions are unsafe and must be quashed.

We would only add that the first ground of appeal, if it stood alone, might or might not suffice. We say that because we are conscious that in practice it would mean that the protection afforded to patients by s 126 of the 1959 Act would be cut down to a large

f   extent. It would be tantamount to saying that a conviction based on the uncorroborated evidence of such a complainant could not be safe. That would be to step outside the common law and usurp the function of Parliament.

Appeals allowed. Convictions quashed.

The court refused leave to appeal to the House of Lords but certified, under s 33(2) of the Criminal Appeal Act 1968, that the following point of law of general public importance was involved in the decision: whether, in a case where the evidence for the Crown was solely that of a witness who was not in one of the accepted categories of suspect witnesses, but who, by reason of his particular mental condition and criminal connection, fulfilled the same criteria, it was necessary for the judge to warn the jury that it was dangerous to convict on his uncorroborated evidence.

Solicitors: *Tracey Barlow Furniss & Co*, Worksop (for the appellants); *Director of Public Prosecutions*.

N P Metcalfe Esq   Barrister.

Patel and another v Ali and another

a

CHANCERY DIVISION
GOULDING J
17, 18 JANUARY 1984

Specific performance – Sale of land – Refusal of specific performance – Hardship – Hardship to *b* *defendant – Unforeseen change in defendant's circumstances subsequent to date of contract – Unavoidable delay in completing contract not due to either party's fault – Defendant a young married woman with three young children contracting bone cancer resulting in amputation of leg subsequent to date of contract – Defendant becoming dependent on assistance from family and friends living in neighbourhood of house contracted to be sold – Removal to another home elsewhere likely to deprive her of that assistance – Whether hardship entitling court to refuse specific* *c* *performance of contract.*

In July 1979 the defendant and her co-owner of a house which they occupied entered into a contract to sell the house to the plaintiffs. At that date the defendant, a married Pakistani woman aged 23 who spoke little English and who had one young child, was in good health. The completion date under the contract was in August 1979. Performance of the contract was subject to a long delay which was not the fault of either party to the *d* contract. In May 1979 the defendant's husband had been adjudicated bankrupt and within a week of the contract for the sale of the house being signed his trustee in bankruptcy had obtained an injunction restraining completion of the sale, but by July 1980 the defendant was released from an undertaking which prevented her completing the contract. By that date the defendant was found to have bone cancer and she had to have a leg amputated. On 11 August 1980 the plaintiffs issued a writ seeking specific *e* performance of the contract. At the end of August 1980 the defendant gave birth to her second child, and in August 1983, she had a third child. Because of her physical disability and her inability to speak much English the defendant relied on assistance from friends and relations who lived very near to the house contracted to be sold to keep her home going and to care for her children. In September 1983 the court made an order for specific performance of the contract. The defendant appealed against that order. She *f* submitted that, because of the hardship she would suffer if she had to leave the house and move to a neighbourhood where she would be deprived of the daily assistance from her friends and relations, specific performance of the contract should be refused and the plaintiffs should be left to their remedy in damages for breach of the contract.

Held – Although a person of full capacity who contracted to buy or sell immovable *g* property took the risk of hardship to himself and his dependants, whether arising from existing facts or unexpectedly supervening in the interval before completion, the court could, in the exercise of its discretion in a proper case, refuse specific performance of such a contract on the ground of hardship suffered by the defendant subsequent to the date of the contract, even if the hardship was not caused by the plaintiff and did not relate to the subject matter of the contract. On the facts, it would inflict hardship amounting to *h* injustice on the defendant to order specific performance of the contract since that would have the effect of asking her to do what she had never bargained for, viz to complete the sale after more than four years and after all the unforeseeable changes that had taken place during that period. Moreover, after the long period of delay (for which neither party was to blame) it would be just to leave the plaintiffs to their remedy in damages. Accordingly, the court would order that, provided the defendant paid into court by a *j* specified date, or otherwise secured for the plaintiffs' benefit, a fixed sum of money, the order for specific performance would be discharged and an inquiry would be ordered into the damage suffered by the plaintiffs by reason of the breach of the contract (see p 982 *a* to *f* and p 983 *a b*, post).

a *City of London v Nash* (1747) 3 Atk 512, *Webb v Direct London and Portsmouth Rly Co* (1852) 1 De GM & G 521, dictum of James LJ in *Tamplin v James* [1874–80] All ER Rep at 562 and *Sobey v Sainsbury* [1913] 2 Ch 513 considered.

Notes

For hardship as a defence to a claim for specific performance, see 44 Halsbury's Laws (4th edn) paras 472–477, and for cases on the subject, see 44 Digest (Repl) 51–56, 371–414.

b

Cases referred to in judgment

Gall v Mitchell (1924) 35 CLR 222, Aust HC.
Holliday (a bankrupt), Re, ex p the trustee of the bankrupt v The bankrupt [1980] 3 All ER 385, [1981] Ch 405, [1981] 2 WLR 996, CA.
c *London (City) v Nash* (1747) 3 Atk 512, 26 ER 1095, LC.
Sobey v Sainsbury [1913] 2 Ch 513.
Tamplin v James (1880) 15 Ch D 215, [1874–80] All ER Rep 560, CA.
Webb v Direct London and Portsmouth Rly Co (1852) 1 De GM & G 521, 42 ER 654, LJJ.

Cases also cited

d *Burrow v Scammell* (1881) 19 Ch D 175.
Nicholas v Ingram [1958] NZLR 972.
Norton v Angus (1926) 38 CLR 523.
Price v Strange [1977] 3 All ER 371, [1978] Ch 337, CA.

e **Appeal**

The defendant, Suriya Ali (otherwise Surrya Ali), appealed from the decision of Master Barratt given on 19 September 1983 ordering specific performance of a contract for the sale by the defendant and Nazir Ahmed (otherwise Nazir Ahmad) of a house known as 136 Sheaveshill Avenue, London NW9 to the plaintiffs, Dine Shkumar Nigindas Patel and Jaymal Nigindas Patel. The appeal was heard in chambers but judgment was given
f by Goulding J in open court. The facts are set out in the judgment.

Michael Briggs for the defendant.
Jonathan Simpkiss for the plaintiffs.
Mr Ahmed did not appear.

g **GOULDING J.** On 19 September 1983 the vacation master, on an application under RSC Ord 86, ordered the specific performance of a contract dated 31 July 1979 for the sale by the defendants to the plaintiffs in this action of a suburban dwelling house known as 136 Sheaveshill Avenue, Kingsbury, London NW9. I have now to decide an appeal from that order. The notice of appeal, dated 26 September 1983, is expressed to be on behalf of both defendants, but counsel who appeared before me represented only the
h first-named defendant, to whom I shall henceforth refer as 'the defendant', and the second-named defendant has not appeared on the appeal. The grounds of appeal are entirely personal to the defendant and do not directly concern her co-defendant.

Counsel on both sides, desiring to avoid further delay and expense to their clients, have agreed that I should treat this appeal as the trial of the action and finally dispose of it on the affidavit evidence before me. To reach that result the plaintiffs agree that I may treat
j as evidence, subject of course to due consideration of their weight, unsworn statements by medical men and by officers of the social services department and the housing department of the local authority, the London Borough of Barnet, in whose area the property lies, such statements being identified by and exhibited to an affidavit of a legal executive employed by the defendant's solicitors.

The circumstances of the case are unusual and it has caused me some anxiety. The argument for the defendant, as it has been eloquently presented on paper and by her counsel, necessarily arouses so much sympathy that I felt for a long time that any exercise of discretionary jurisdiction in her favour would probably be unfair to her opponents, just because of the force of such sympathy.

The material facts are not in dispute and can be shortly stated. In 1979 the defendant was living in the property with her husband, Mr Ali. They occupied it as their matrimonial home. Another couple, Mr and Mrs Nazir Ahmed, were also living in the house. Mr Ahmed is the second defendant to the action. The property was freehold and was registered in the name of Mr Ahmed and the defendant, who claim to be not only legally but beneficially entitled thereto. On 31 July 1979 the contract was entered into between both defendants as vendors and the plaintiffs, Mr and Mrs Patel, as purchasers. The price was £24,000, and the contractual completion date 28 August 1979.

The performance of the contract has been subject (and this is a circumstance which, to my mind, is of the greatest importance in the case) to a quite extraordinary delay, for which neither side on this appeal has sought to blame the other. The causes of the delay have not been explored in detail in the evidence, but it appears that a great deal of it can be put down to two difficulties. In the first place, the trustee in bankruptcy of Mr Ali has made claim to a beneficial interest in the property. Mr Ali had been adjudicated bankrupt on 9 May 1979, in pursuance of a petition presented late in the previous year, and within a week of the signature of the contract his trustee obtained an ex parte injunction restraining the completion of the sale. The ensuing litigation in the bankruptcy court culminated in an order of Fox J made on 21 July 1980. The judge released the defendant from undertakings, and Mr Ahmed from an injunction, preventing completion of the sale on the footing that the trustee in bankruptcy would prosecute his claim against the proceeds of sale. The second cause of delay, so it is said, was a succession of difficulties experienced by the plaintiffs in effecting service of proceedings on Mr Ahmed, who has returned to Pakistan. The writ in this action was issued on 11 August 1980, the application for summary judgment not until 4 July 1983.

Meanwhile, the circumstances of the defendant had changed disastrously. At the date of the contract she had one child who was still a baby, and, so far as she knew, she was in good health. She was about 23 years old. She spoke and still speaks, in the words of her solicitor's affidavit, 'virtually no English at all'. In the summer of 1980 she was found to have a bone cancer in her right thigh. On 24 July 1980, that is three days after the order of Fox J in the bankruptcy proceedings, her right leg was amputated at the hip joint. She was then in an advanced state of pregnancy and gave birth to her second child on 31 August. In the spring of 1981 her husband went to prison and remained there until mid-summer 1982. After his release she became pregnant again and her child was born in August 1983.

The defendant has been fitted with an artificial leg. She is able to walk about the house and dress herself, but not to do shopping, and she needs help with household duties and with the children. She is greatly dependent on friends and relations to enable her to keep her home going and to look after her children, especially on her sister who, I was told, lives only a few doors away, and on a friendly neighbour, Mrs Dhillon.

It is in these circumstances that the defendant asks the court to refuse specific performance of the contract and to leave the plaintiffs to their remedy in damages. Her advisers recognise that the court must be satisfied that the legal remedy will be effective, and there is evidence that sympathetic persons in the Muslim community in which she lives are willing to put up money for that purpose.

That the hardship to the defendant of enforced removal from the property would be great is, on the evidence, beyond doubt. Any accommodation which the local authority could immediately provide for the defendant is likely to deprive her of the daily assistance on which she relies, or at least greatly to diminish it. The move would necessarily cause much more severe disturbance to the lives of the children, now aged five years, three

years and five months, than a family removal does in ordinary cases, and might even
make it impossible for the defendant to keep them with her, handicapped as she is by
her physical disability.

The hardship which would be caused to the plaintiffs if specific performance were
refused and adequate pecuniary compensation were available is not, so far as the evidence
reveals, greater than what is necessarily involved in being disappointed of the purchase
after so long a delay. Since the contractual date for completion in 1979 the plaintiffs have
lived in accommodation rented from their local authority, the London Borough of
Barnet.

It is not in dispute that, like other equitable relief, the specific performance of contracts
is a discretionary remedy, but, in the ordinary case of a sale of land or buildings, the court
normally grants it as of course and withholds it only on proof of special facts. The
textbooks and reported decisions have long recognised hardship as one ground on which,
in a proper case, a purchaser or vendor may be refused specific performance and be left
to his right to damages for breach of contract at law. The difficulty is to determine within
what limits hardship to a defendant can properly be said to justify this exercise of judicial
discretion. There is no doubt that, in the majority of cases, the hardship which moves
the court to refuse specific performance is either a hardship existing at the date of the
contract or a hardship due in some way to the plaintiff. In the present case, neither of
those conditions being satisfied, the plaintiffs rely strongly on that principle or practice,
which is stated in varying terms in all the well-known textbooks. It is sufficient for me
to cite a passage from *Fry on Specific Performance* (6th edn, 1921) p 199, paras 417–418:

'It is a well-established doctrine that the Court will not enforce the specific
performance of a contract, the result of which would be to impose great hardship
on either of the parties to it; and this although the party seeking specific performance
may be free from the least impropriety of conduct. The question of the hardship of
a contract is generally to be judged of at the time at which it is entered into: if it be
then fair and just and not productive of hardship, it will be immaterial that it may,
by the force of subsequent circumstances or change of events, have become less
beneficial to one party, except where these subsequent events have been in some
way due to the party who seeks the performance of the contract. For whatever
contingencies may attach to a contract, or be involved in the performance of either
part, have been taken upon themselves by the parties to it. It has been determined
that the reasonableness of a contract is to be judged of at the time it is entered into,
and not by the light of subsequent events, and we have already seen that the same
principle applies in considering the fairness of a contract.'

However, the principle so stated cannot be erected into a fixed limitation of the court's
equitable jurisdiction. It is recognised, both by Fry LJ's book and in the argument of
counsel for the plaintiffs in the present action, that the court has sometimes refused
specific performance because of a change of circumstances supervening after the making
of the contract and not in any way attributable to the plaintiff.

One such case is *City of London v Nash* (1747) 3 Atk 512, 26 ER 1095, where Lord
Hardwicke LC refused specific performance of a contract which required the demolition
of houses and building of new ones, because he thought that the demolition would be a
public loss and no benefit to the plaintiffs, who would be sufficiently compensated by
damages at law. This seems a strong case, because the difficulties were due to breaches of
contract by the defendant himself. The report shows, however, that the Lord Chancellor
was also influenced by laches on the part of the city (see 3 Atk 512 at 517, 26 ER 1095 at
1098). Another relevant case is *Webb v Direct London and Portsmouth Rly Co* (1852) 1 De
GM & G 521, 42 ER 654, where the Lords Justices refused specifically to enforce a
purchase of land by the company after it had abandoned its proposed enterprise of
constructing a railway from Epsom to Portsmouth. Similar in principle are the cases
where the court has refused injunctions to compel specific performance of restrictive

covenants by reason of a change in the character of the neighbourhood, even where the plaintiff and his predecessors in title have in no way contributed thereto: see *Sobey v Sainsbury* [1913] 2 Ch 513 at 529. Thus, I am satisfied that the court's discretion is wide enough, in an otherwise proper case, to refuse specific performance on the ground of hardship subsequent to the contract and not caused by the plaintiff.

Another limitation suggested by counsel for the plaintiffs was that, in the reported cases, as he said, hardship successfully relied on has always related to the subject matter of the contract and has not been just a personal hardship of the defendant. Certainly, mere pecuniary difficulties, whether of purchaser or of vendor, afford no excuse from performance of a contract. In a wider sense than that, I do not think the suggested universal proposition can be sustained. In *Webb's* case the hardship in no way affected the title to the property or its physical condition. It was a hardship to the railway company to be compelled to pay for land it could never use, just as it is a hardship to the defendant here to be compelled to convey a house she cannot now well do without.

The important and true principle, in my view, is that only in extraordinary and persuasive circumstances can hardship supply an excuse for resisting performance of a contract for the sale of immovable property. A person of full capacity who sells or buys a house takes the risk of hardship to himself and his dependants, whether arising from existing facts or unexpectedly supervening in the interval before completion. This is where, to my mind, great importance attaches to the immense delay in the present case, not attributable to the defendant's conduct. Even after issue of the writ, she could not complete, if she had wanted to, without the concurrence of the absent Mr Ahmed. Thus, in a sense, she can say she is being asked to do what she never bargained for, namely to complete the sale after more than four years, after all the unforeseeable changes that such a period entails. I think that in this way she can fairly assert that specific performance would inflict on her 'a hardship amounting to injustice' to use the phrase employed by James LJ, in a different but comparable context, in *Tamplin v James* (1880) 15 ChD 215 at 221, [1874–80] All ER Rep 560 at 562. Equitable relief may, in my view, be refused because of an unforeseen change of circumstances not amounting to legal frustration, just as it may on the ground of mistake insufficient to avoid a contract at law.

In the end, I am satisfied that it is within the court's discretion to accede to the defendant's prayer if satisfied that it is just to do so. And, on the whole, looking at the position of both sides after the long unpredictable delay for which neither seeks to make the other responsible, I am of opinion that it *is* just to leave the plaintiffs to their remedy in damages if that can indeed be effective.

I have come to this conclusion without taking into account the welfare of the defendant's children except as involved in her own personal hardship. I much doubt whether, even in the present atmosphere of opinion on which her counsel dwelt in his address, the interests of the children are material in their own right, though he did derive some support from the obiter observations of Isaacs J in the High Court of Australia in *Gall v Mitchell* (1924) 35 CLR 222 at 230, where he said:

> 'Hardships of third persons entirely unconnected with the property are immaterial. But I do not think that rule excludes the case of third persons so connected with the defendant that, by reason of some legal or moral duty which he owes them, it would be "highly unreasonable" for the Court actively to prevent the defendant from discharging his duty. The circumstances of such a case might, in my opinion, be properly weighed for the purpose of determining the discretion of the Court.'

On the other hand, I am not persuaded by the suggestion of counsel for the plaintiffs that the refusal of specific performance may not be of value to the defendant because of the still undetermined claim of her husband's trustee in bankruptcy. It seems not unlikely that, if she can succeed in keeping possession of the house here, she may also keep it in the bankruptcy court, at any rate for a period of some years, even if the trustee's claim is well founded: cf *Re Holliday (a bankrupt)* [1980] 3 All ER 385, [1981] Ch 405.

I will hear counsel on the precise form of order. What I have in mind is this. The order
a will recite the parties' agreement to treat the hearing of the appeal as the trial of the
action as between the plaintiffs and the defendant. I will direct that, if within a specified
period (I suggest on or before 29 February 1984) a certain sum is paid into court to the
credit of the action, or otherwise secured to the satisfaction of the plaintiffs, then the
master's order will be discharged. Instead, an inquiry will be ordered what damage the
plaintiffs have suffered by reason of the two defendants' breach of contract and the first
b defendant (whom I have been calling the defendant) will be ordered to pay the amount
found due on the inquiry and the plaintiffs' taxed costs of the action, including this
appeal, the costs of the inquiry being reserved. I have heard argument regarding the sum
to be paid in, and I fix it at £10,000. If the money is not provided by the date specified,
the appeal is to stand dismissed with costs. In either event, there will be a legal aid
taxation of the costs (so far as not previously dealt with) of those parties who have been
c legally aided incurred during the respective periods when they have been so aided. I
perceive that the order may confer a benefit on Mr Ahmed, though absent from the
appeal, but that seems to me inevitable in the circumstances.

Order accordingly.

d Solicitors: *Ralph Haring & Co*, Hampstead (for the defendant); *Gerard Hales & Co*, Ealing
(for the plaintiffs).

Evelyn M C Budd   Barrister.

e

f

R v Governor of Durham Prison,
ex parte Singh

QUEEN'S BENCH DIVISION (CROWN OFFICE LIST)
WOOLF J
13 DECEMBER 1983

g

*Immigration – Deportation – Detention pending deportation – Extent of Secretary of State's
power to detain person subject to deportation order – Immigration Act 1971, Sch 3, para 2(3).*

h When a deportation order has been made in respect of a person, the Secretary of State's
power under the Immigration Act 1971, Sch 3, para 2(3)[a], to detain that person until his
removal from the United Kingdom is subject to the following limitations: (i) the power
may only be used for the purpose of detaining the individual concerned pending his
removal from the United Kingdom, (ii) the power is limited to a period which is
reasonably necessary for that purpose, and (iii) the Secretary of State must exercise all

j _____

   a Paragraph 2(3), so far as material, provides: 'Where a deportation order is in force against any
       person, he may be detained under the authority of the Secretary of State pending his removal or
       departure from the United Kingdom (and if already detained . . . when the order is made, shall
       continue to be detained unless the Secretary of State directs otherwise).'

reasonable expedition to ensure that steps are taken to secure the person's removal from the United Kingdom within a reasonable time. The Secretary of State should not exercise *a* the power at all if it appears to him that he is not going to be able, within a reasonable time, to operate the machinery provided under the 1971 Act for the removal of the person who is to be deported (see p 985 *d* to *g*, post).

Notes

For detention pending deportation, see 4 Halsbury's Laws (4th edn), para 1015, and for *b* cases on the subject, see 2 Digest (Reissue) 205, 1169.

For the Immigration Act 1971, Sch 3, para 2, see 41 Halsbury's Statutes (3rd edn) 77.

Cases referred to in judgment

R v Governor of Richmond Remand Centre, ex p Ashgar [1971] 1 WLR 129, DC. *c* *Singh (Sital), Re* (8 July 1975, unreported), DC.

Case also cited

R v Governor of Brixton Prison, ex p Sarno [1916] 2 KB 742, DC.

Motion *d*

The applicant, Hardial Singh, who was detained in HM Prison at Durham pending his deportation from the United Kingdom pursuant to a deportation order made by the Secretary of State for the Home Department on 16 June 1983, applied for an order directing the issue of a writ of habeas corpus ad subjiciendum to the governor of the prison to secure the applicant's release. The facts are set out in the judgment. *e*

Terry Munyard for the applicant.
Andrew Collins for the respondent.

f

WOOLF J. This is an application for habeas corpus by Mr Hardial Singh which, in my view, raises an issue of considerable importance as to how long it is proper for the Home Secretary lawfully to detain an individual in prison pending their removal from this country, pursuant to the deportation machinery.

The applicant is an Indian national who was born in India on 19 December 1957. He entered this country on 14 December 1977, just before his twentieth birthday. He was *g* given indefinite leave to remain in the United Kingdom and there is no suggestion whatsoever that he did otherwise than enter this country lawfully, and there is no suggestion that he has not been lawfully in this country since 1977.

However, he committed two offences of a criminal nature which brought him before the courts, one of burglary, which was dealt with in 1980, and a further offence of burglary which was dealt with in 1982. In relation to the second offence he was sentenced *h* to 12 months' imprisonment. In addition, the earlier sentence of imprisonment which had been imposed on him, but suspended, was brought into force, the consequence being that he had to serve a total of two years' imprisonment. In the ordinary way, because prior to his being dealt with for the second offence he had been in custody, he would have been released on 20 May 1983.

However, in January 1983, while serving at an open prison, he had a visit from *j* immigration officers and he says that he then realised, although there had been no recommendation for deportation by the court, that he might be deported. He became distressed and he absconded from prison. He was arrested two weeks later and he then lost remission in consequence of his escaping from prison. His new date of release was

a   12 August 1983. He was, in fact, due to be granted parole on 20 July 1983 and if it had
not been for the action taken by the Home Office he would have been released from
Durham Prison on that date. In fact, he is still at Durham Prison and he is being held in
Durham Prison in conditions which he finds distressing. He is sharing a cell with two
others. He is treated in the same way as a prisoner on remand is treated. He therefore
does not take part in any work activities and remains locked in a cell for 23 hours a day.
The reason why he is being detained is that on 4 March 1983 the Secretary of State made

b   a decision to make a deportation order in respect of the applicant on the ground that the
Secretary of State deemed his deportation to be conducive to the public good. The reason
for the Secretary of State taking that view was, undoubtedly, the convictions to which I
have made reference.

The applicant accepts that the Secretary of State perfectly properly came to that
conclusion. He had a right of appeal, which right of appeal expired on 18 March, but he

c   did not exercise that right of appeal. Having made a decision to deport the applicant, the
next stage in the machinery is the making of a deportation order. That was done and the
deportation order was served on the applicant on 16 June 1983, while he was still serving
his prison sentence.

Under Sch 3 to the Immigration Act 1971 the Secretary of State has the power to detain
an individual who is the subject of a decision to make a deportation order, under para

d   2(2) of the schedule, pending the making of the deportation order. That power requires
the person to be detained under para 2(3) after the making of a deportation order and
pending the removal of the person from the United Kingdom.

Since 20 July 1983 the applicant has been detained under the power contained in para
2(3) of Sch 3 to the Immigration Act 1971. Although the power which is given to the
Secretary of State in para 2 to detain individuals is not subject to any express limitation

e   of time, I am quite satisfied that it is subject to limitations. First of all, it can only
authorise detention if the individual is being detained in one case pending the making
of a deportation order and, in the other case, pending his removal. It cannot be used for
any other purpose. Second, as the power is given in order to enable the machinery of
deportation to be carried out, I regard the power of detention as being impliedly limited
to a period which is reasonably necessary for that purpose. The period which is reasonable

f   will depend on the circumstances of the particular case. What is more, if there is a
situation where it is apparent to the Secretary of State that he is not going to be able to
operate the machinery provided in the Act for removing persons who are intended to be
deported within a reasonable period, it seems to me that it would be wrong for the
Secretary of State to seek to exercise his power of detention.

In addition, I would regard it as implicit that the Secretary of State should exercise all

g   reasonable expedition to ensure that the steps are taken which will be necessary to ensure
the removal of the individual within a reasonable time. In this connection I have been
referred to two authorities which give some assistance. The first is *R v Governor of
Richmond Remand Centre, ex p Asghar* [1971] 1 WLR 129. The facts of that case are really
of no assistance but, in the course of giving judgment, Lord Parker CJ said (at 132):

h   'The matter in my judgment does not end there, because, even if I were wrong in
that, and valid directions were given, the question remains whether, pursuant to
paragraph 4(1), the applicants continued thereafter, that is after the directions, to be
held pending removal in pursuance of such directions. It quite clearly contemplates,
of course, that there will be some interval of time between the giving of the
directions and their implementation, and for that period of time there is authority

j   to detain. But when one turns to the facts of this case, the reality of the position is
that the applicants were being detained pending the trial at the Central Criminal
Court at which they were required to give evidence. Accordingly on that second
ground I think that detention was not justified. Mr Slynn [counsel for the
respondent] has argued very forcibly that of course the period contemplated that

may elapse between the giving of the directions and the actual removal must be a reasonable period. He says here that in all the circumstances it was reasonable for the Secretary of State to require the detention of these two men pending the completion of the trial at the Central Criminal Court. Much as I wish I could accede to that argument, it does seem to me that while a reasonable time is contemplated between the giving of the directions and the final removal, that is a reasonable time necessary to effect the physical removal, the truth of the matter is that the Home Office naturally desires to do nothing which will interfere with the trial. One sympathises with this object, but of course it can be achieved, by giving these applicants conditional permits. There are obvious practical reasons why this course is not adopted, because as experience has shown, nothing may ever be seen of the applicants again.'

The other case, which is unreported, *Re Sital Singh* (8 July 1975) was another decision of the Divisional Court. The judgment of the court in that case was given by Milmo J. It concerned a suspected illegal entrant. The Secretary of State had authorised the removal of that illegal entrant on 24 April 1975. The matter came before the court on 8 July 1975, some 2½ months later. The applicant had, however, been in custody since 17 March, 3½ months prior to the decision of the court. In giving judgment the judge said:

'The court is satisfied that everything that can be reasonably done by the Secretary of State for Home Affairs to urge the Indian High Commission to produce a travel document has been done and is being done.'

In those circumstances the court said:

'It may be that a case will arise when the detention awaiting deportation is excessive, and when that case does arise, it will be considered. But in the judgment of this court the present case falls far short of that mark.'

The only other feature that I would draw attention to of that case is that the court was informed by counsel that a communication had been received from the High Commission saying that a reply to the application for a travel document relating to the applicant would be received within the next ten days.

Counsel for the applicant submits that the facts of this case are very different from that case. First of all, I accept that there is a real distinction between the *Sital Singh* case and this case in that there the applicant was an illegal entrant who should never have been in this country at all. That cannot be said of the present applicant. In addition, it is submitted that in that case the court was satisfied that everything that can be reasonably done by the Secretary of State had been done. I am bound to say that in this case I am not so satisfied. The Home Office have filed evidence which refers, first of all, to the interview which took place on 24 January 1983. It is said he then claimed that his passport was in the custody of the Leicester police, but that was untrue. Inquiries were made at various addresses in Bradford but the passport was not discovered.

The matter then goes straight to 7 September 1983 where the deponent, on behalf of the Home Office, points out that the Durham police reported they were having difficulties in obtaining a travel document for the applicant, and therefore could not proceed with the deportation at that time. I know not the precise nature of those difficulties, but I anticipate they are the usual difficulties, because the Indian High Commission were unable to make documents available.

From 7 September we go straight to 17 October. It is recorded that, on 17 October, the Durham police reported that the Indian High Commission were making inquiries in relation to establishing the applicant's identity. No travel document was forthcoming at that time.

On 24 October, so far as I am aware, there took place the first communication directly between the Home Office and the Indian High Commission. There was a telephone call

on that day with regard to travel documentation. The Home Office were asked by the
a High Commission to give further information concerning the district of birth of the
applicant. I am told this request was conveyed to the Durham police, but I am not told
whether or not the Durham police complied with that request.

On 10 November the only letter was written by the Home Office to the High
Commission. It concerned not only the applicant, but a few other persons in a similar
predicament. It read:

b

> 'I understand that a number of requests have been made to officials in the High
> Commission by the police and officers in our Deportation Machinery Group for the
> requisite documentation but so far without success. These three men have been
> detained well beyond the normal period and we are anxious to avoid any further
> untoward delay in their departure, especially since they all express a wish to return
c > to India as soon as possible.'

There has been no reply to that letter and, apart from the fact I was told by counsel on
behalf of the Home Office that there was an inquiry made yesterday of the Indian High
Commission, apparently nothing has occurred since, either in the way of an inquiry by
the Home Office, or any action or activity on the part of the Indian High Commission.
d   The applicant had been taking what steps he could to achieve a satisfactory resolution
of his problem. He is quite prepared to return to India. He has been in touch with a
member of Parliament who has been in touch with the Minister of State. The Minister
of State answered a letter from that member of Parliament, dated 11 October, by a letter
dated 2 November. It was pointed out in the letter by the minister that he did not feel
justified in authorising Mr Singh's release from detention pending his removal to India.
e The minister said, having regard to his convictions and the fact he had absconded, that
he took the view that this was not a case where, if the applicant were released, he would
surrender at a later stage.

Counsel for the Home Office points out the difficulties that the Home Office are
under. If they sought to remove this man then the probabilities are that he would not be
accepted in India, or by any other country, so he would merely be returned to this
f country and if this country did not accept him on his return, he would pass to and fro,
back and forth. Counsel for the respondent has also pointed out the problem of trying to
achieve a more expeditious result from the Indian High Commission.

I fully recognise and appreciate these difficulties, but it does seem to me that on the
limited material which is before me the Home Office have not taken the action they
should have taken and neither have they taken that action sufficiently promptly.
g   The question of deporting this man has clearly been under consideration at least since
January 1983. Apparently, no direct action was taken by the Home Office until October
1983. The matter was left in the hands of the Durham police since October. It does seem
that more activity could have taken place, particularly bearing in mind that the applicant's
solicitors had made it abundantly clear that if no action was taken they were proposing
to apply to this court. What is more, there is the disturbing fact that the applicant had
h become distressed by his continuing detention and had made an attempt to take his own
life.

If the matter ended there, for my part, I would regard this as a case where this applicant
was now entitled to a writ of habeas corpus, or an order for his release. I would take the
view that the implicit limitations imposed on the power of detention contained in the
Act had not been complied with. However, I am told by counsel for the respondent that
j the affidavit of the applicant was only received by the Home office yesterday, that their
evidence had to be prepared with great expedition for this hearing and that further
material might be able to be put before this court, in particular as to what is the position
in relation to the documentation which has been requested from the Indian High
Commission. He asked for the matter, therefore, to be further adjourned for seven days.

I am not prepared to grant an adjournment for seven days but, with some hesitation, I am prepared to grant an adjournment until Friday.

In taking that course, I have in mind that if it is shown to this court that the applicant is due to be removed within a very short time indeed, then it would be proper for him to remain in detention for that short time. But, if, when the matter comes before me on Friday, there is no intimation given to me on behalf of the Home Office that he will be so removed, this is a case where he should be released unless, having taken advantage of the adjournment, the Home Office are in a position to put before the court evidence which reveals a wholly different situation from that indicated by the evidence which is at present before me.

Therefore, in those circumstances, I grant that limited adjournment, taking the view that a very short additional period of further detention will not result in such an injustice to the applicant as requires me to refuse the Home Office an opportunity to file further evidence, bearing in mind that they can reasonably say that the late service on them has not given them proper time to put their case in order.

Order accordingly.

Solicitors: *Helen Carr*, Bradford (for the applicant); *Treasury Solicitor* (for the respondent).

Raina Levy   Barrister.

Attorney General's Reference (No 2 of 1983)

COURT OF APPEAL, CRIMINAL DIVISION
LORD LANE CJ, McCOWAN AND LEGGATT JJ
30 JANUARY, 3 FEBRUARY 1984

Explosives – Offence – Making or possessing explosive substance – Defence of lawful purpose – Making petrol bomb – Whether defence of lawful purpose available where defendant's object in making or possessing substance is self-defence against apprehended imminent attack – Explosive Substances Act 1883, s 4(1).

Criminal law – Self-defence – Premeditated acts – Whether self-defence limited to spontaneous responses to actual violence – Whether self-defence encompassing premeditated acts done in anticipation of violence.

Acts of self-defence which may be relied on as a valid defence to a criminal charge are not limited to spontaneous acts done in response to actual violence. Accordingly, if a person who is found to be in possession of a petrol bomb is charged under s 4(1)[a] of the Explosive Substances Act 1883 with making, possessing or having under his control an explosive substance, it is a good defence, by way of showing that he possessed the explosive substance 'for a lawful purpose' within s 4(1), for the accused to show on the balance of probabilities that his purpose in possessing the explosive substance was to protect himself or his family or property by way of self-defence against an imminent and apprehended

---

[a] Section 4(1), so far as material, is set out at p 990 *j* to p 991 *a*, post

attack (such as might occur in a riot) by means which he believed to be no more than
a reasonably necessary to meet the attack (see p 993 *f* to *j*, post); *R v Fegan* [1972] NI 80
applied; *Grieve v Macleod* 1967 JC 32 and *Evans v Hughes* [1972] 3 All ER 412 considered.

Although a person may make a petrol bomb with the lawful object of protection
against imminent apprehended attack, if he remains in possession of the bomb after the
threat of the apprehended attack has passed, his object in making the bomb may cease to
be lawful. Furthermore, only very rarely will the circumstances be such that the
b manufacture or possession of a petrol bomb will be for a lawful purpose (see p 993 *g h*,
post).

Notes

For self-defence, defence of others and defence of property as justification, see 11
Halsbury's Laws (4th edn) paras 1217–1218, and for cases on the subject, see 15 Digest
c (Reissue) 1189–1192, 10196–10233.

For possessing or making explosive substances, see 11 Halsbury's Laws (4th edn) para
1208, and for cases on the subject, see 15 Digest (Reissue) 1453, 12841–12844.

For the Explosive Substances Act 1883, s 4, see 8 Halsbury's Statutes (3rd edn) 221.

Cases referred to in judgment

Evans v Hughes [1972] 3 All ER 412, [1972] 1 WLR 1452, DC.
d *Evans v Wright* [1964] Crim LR 466, DC.
Grieve v Macleod 1967 JC 32.
Palmer v R [1971] 1 All ER 1077, [1971] AC 814, [1971] 2 WLR 831.
R v Cousins [1982] 2 All ER 115, [1982] QB 526, [1982] 2 WLR 621, CA.
R v Fegan [1972] NI 80, CCA (NI).

Cases also cited

e *R v Bourne* [1938] 3 All ER 615, [1939] 1 KB 687, CCA.
R v Jura [1954] 1 All ER 696, [1954] 1 QB 503, CCA.
Taylor v Mucklow [1973] Crim LR 750, DC.
Winkle v Wiltshire [1951] 1 All ER 479, [1951] 1 KB 684, DC.

Reference

f The Attorney General referred, under s 36 of the Criminal Justice Act 1972, the following
point of law to the Court of Appeal, Criminal Division for its opinion: whether the
defence of self-defence was available to a defendant charged with offences under s 4 of
the Explosive Substances Act 1883 and s 64 of the Offences against the Person Act 1861.
The facts are set out in the opinion of the court.

g *Michael Hill QC* and *Nicholas Purnell* for the Attorney General.
Anthony Scrivener QC and *Daniel Serota* as amici curiae.
The defendant did not appear.

Cur adv vult

h 3 February. The following opinion of the court was delivered.

LORD LANE CJ. The question referred by Her Majesty's Attorney General to this
court for consideration is as follows:

'Whether the defence of self-defence is available to a defendant charged with
j offences under Section 4 of the Explosive Substances Act 1883 and Section 64 of the
Offences Against the Person Act 1861.'

The defendant appeared before the Crown Court on 13 October 1982 facing an
indictment containing four counts. Counts 2 and 4 were withdrawn from the jury's
consideration during the course of the trial and the jury returned verdicts of not guilty
on counts 1 and 3.

Counsel for the Attorney General concedes before this court that he cannot succeed on his contention with regard to s 64 of the Offences against the Person Act 1861 (count 3). Consequently the issues are confined to a consideration of the charge under s 4 of the Explosive Substances Act 1883.

The charge laid under that section reads as follows:

'[The defendant] on the 13th day of July 1981 made a certain explosive substance to wit, a petrol bomb, in such circumstances as to give rise to a reasonable suspicion that he had not made it for a lawful object.'

The case arose in the following way. The defendant is a man of good character aged 40 at the material time. He owned a shop in an area where on two nights during July 1981 there was extensive rioting. Some 300 police officers had been engaged in trying with only limited success to restore order against a barrage of stones and petrol bombs. Shops were damaged and looted.

On the night of 11–12 July 1981, £600 worth of damage was done to the defendant's shop and £400 worth of his goods were looted. The defendant remained in his shop without sleep and in fear of attack from 1.30 am on 12 July to the morning of 14 July. He was justifiably in fear that he and his property might be the subject of further attack. So much so, he had had his shop boarded up and protected by fire resistant paint. He had bought 22 fire extinguishers at a cost of some £200. On 13 July he equipped himself with three containers of sulphuric acid (the subject of count 3) intending, if necessary, to spray any attacker therewith. On the same day he made ten petrol bombs and placed them on the upstairs landing of the shop. These bombs were conceded to be explosive substances. In the event the expected attack never materialised.

When questioned by the police some five months later, the defendant gave a full account of his actions, which he confirmed in evidence before the Crown Court. He described his state of mind and intentions as follows:

'My intentions were to use them purely to protect my premises should any rioters come to my shop. I thought I would be able to throw a petrol bomb from my office window onto the pavement to keep them away from my shop. I had no intention to injure anyone but to use purely as a last resort to keep them away from my shop.'

Later he said this:

'Such was my state of mind, at the height of the rioting, I even considered using acid which we keep on the premises for filling batteries, as a first line of defence . . . which I would have used to spray the acid in a fine spray which from personal experience causes irritation to the skin and smarting of the eyes, but would not cause any serious damage.'

There was very little, if any, dispute between the parties as to the facts of the case.

On the first day of the trial, counsel for the Crown submitted that self-defence was not available as a defence to any of the counts in the indictment. The judge ruled against that submission. With regard to count 1 the basis of his decision was that it must be open to a defendant to say 'my lawful object is self-defence'.

It is conceded by counsel for the Attorney General that the judge summed up the case to the jury in a clear and concise way. We would like to echo that concession and add that the direction to the jury was a model of simplicity, clarity and brevity. The judge dealt correctly with the ingredients of each of the counts and gave to the jury an accurate and illustrated direction as to self-defence. Counsel for the Attorney General submits that the judge erred in ruling that the defendant was entitled to rely on self-defence.

Section 4(1) of the 1883 Act provides:

'Any person who makes or knowingly has in his possession or under his control any explosive substance, under such circumstances as to give rise to a reasonable suspicion that he is not making it or does not have it in his possession or under his

control for a lawful object, shall, unless he can show that he made it or had it in his
a possession or under his control for a lawful object, be guilty of [an offence] . . .'

Counsel for the Crown argued at the trial that self-defence did not provide a valid
defence to this defendant on this charge because such a plea is available only to justify
actual violence by a defendant. Counsel for the Attorney General contends that it does
not exist as a justification for preliminary and premeditated acts anticipatory of an act of
b violence by the defendant in the absence of any express statutory provision therefor.

It was common ground that by virtue of ss 3, 4 and 39 of the Explosives Act 1875, the
manufacture and storage of other explosives, as well as gun powder, are prohibited except
under licence. The petrol bombs which this defendant made were, as already mentioned,
admitted for present purposes to constitute 'explosive substances' within the meaning of
the 1883 Act.

c Counsel for the Attorney General submits that to allow a man to justify in advance his
own act of violence for which he has prepared runs wholly contrary to the principle and
thinking behind legitimate self-defence and legitimate defence of property. Both are
defences which the law allows to actual violence by a defendant, and both are based on
the principle that a man may be justified in extremis in taking spontaneous steps to
defend himself, others of his family and his property against actual or mistakenly
d perceived violent attack.

It was argued that, if a plea of self-defence is allowed to s 4 of the 1883 Act, the effect
would be that a man could write his own immunity for unlawful acts done in preparation
for violence to be used by him in the future. Rather than that, goes on the argument, in
these circumstances a man should protect himself by calling on the police or by
barricading his premises or guarding them alone or with others, but not with petrol
e bombs.

The researches of counsel have turned up only one case directly in point. In *R v Fegan*
[1972] NI 80 the defendant was a Roman Catholic man married to a Protestant. On that
account he had been subjected to threats and beatings. He had moved to a different area
without avail and had thereupon equipped himself with a revolver and ammunition. He
described how he bought the gun for his own protection and, if need be, for the
f protection of his house and family.

Having been charged and convicted under s 4 of the 1883 Act, he appealed to the
Northern Ireland Court of Criminal Appeal on the ground that the trial judge did not
direct the jury that if the defendant showed on balance of probabilities that he had the
weapon for a lawful object, he was entitled to be acquitted of the statutory offences of
possessing a pistol without a firearm certificate and possessing ammunition.

g The court held that, assuming that the defendant could have shown that his possession
of the revolver and ammunition was with a lawful object, the summing up was defective.
The principal question of law for the court was whether that assumption was sound.
Delivering the judgment of the court Lord MacDermott LCJ said (at 87):

'Where, as here, a firearm is possessed without certificate, permit or other
authority . . . the possession is unlawful and will usually constitute an offence. But
h does that mean that a firearm so possessed cannot at the same time be possessed for
a lawful object? The absence of a certificate, permit or other authority may well be
evidence relevant to the question of the existence or non-existence of a lawful object,
but we do not think such absence of authority is in law necessarily incompatible
with the firearm concerned being possessed for a lawful object.'

j The court emphasised the need, in ascertaining whether an object is lawful, to
distinguish between possession and purpose. Moreover, possession for a lawful object
must be construed as meaning possession for a lawful object only without there being
also an unlawful object.

There followed the following passage (at 87–88), on the correctness of which the
present reference turns:

'Possession of a firearm for the purpose of protecting the possessor or his wife or family from acts of violence, *may* be possession for a lawful object. But the lawfulness of such a purpose cannot be founded on a mere fancy, or on some aggressive motive. The threatened danger must be reasonably and genuinely anticipated, must appear reasonably imminent, and must be of a nature which could not reasonably be met by more pacific means. A lawful object in this particular field therefore falls within a strictly limited category and cannot be such as to justify going beyond what the law may allow in meeting the situation of danger which the possessor of the firearms reasonably and genuinely apprehends.' (Lord MacDermott LCJ's emphasis.)

The court held that it was open to the jury to conclude 'that the appellant genuinely and reasonably feared for the life and safety of himself or his family and held the pistol for use if necessary as a protection against this danger'. The appeal was therefore allowed.

Counsel for the Attorney General did not seek to distinguish that case on the facts, and rightly so. He nevertheless submitted that possession of a firearm for purposes of self-defence is incompatible with possession for a lawful object. Pointing to the classic exposition of self-defence in *Palmer v R* [1971] 1 All ER 1077 at 1088, [1971] AC 814 at 831–832, he argued that what lies behind the concept is spontaneous reaction, by contrast with anticipatory acts such as have exercised the courts in the context of the Prevention of Crime Act 1953, s 1(1). That subsection provides that:

'Any person who without lawful authority or reasonable excuse, the proof whereof shall lie on him, has with him in any public place any offensive weapon shall be guilty of an offence . . .'

In this context the following cases are relevant: *Evans v Wright* [1964] Crim LR 466, *Grieve v Macleod* 1967 JC 32 and *Evans v Hughes* [1972] 3 All ER 412, [1972] 1 WLR 1452. In the last of those cases, after referring to the first two, the Divisional Court said ([1972] 3 All ER 412 at 415, [1972] 1 WLR 1452 at 1455):

'. . . it may be a reasonable excuse for the carrying of an offensive weapon that the carrier is in anticipation of imminent attack and is carrying it for his own personal defence . . .'

and stressed that—

'the threat for which this defence is required must be an imminent particular threat affecting the particular circumstances in which the weapon was carried.'

Counsel for the Attorney General contends that it was deemed necessary in the Act to provide a 'reasonable excuse' defence which would not have been necessary if the approach to self-defence found in *R v Fegan* as anticipatory justification was good law. In aid of this argument he also invoked *R v Cousins* [1982] 2 All ER 115, [1982] QB 526, in which this court held that the trial judge had erred in failing to leave to the jury the question whether the defendant had 'lawful excuse' for a threat to kill, within the meaning of s 16 of the Offences against the Person Act 1861. According to counsel cases of this kind show how the courts have had to grapple with the extent to which particular statutory answers are to be allowed to provide excuses for preparation to meet anticipated or feared violence. In his submission the concept of 'lawful object' could not avail the defendant in the present case because he could not show his object to have been wholly and exclusively lawful.

In our judgment, approaching a priori the words 'lawful object', it might well seem open to a defendant to say, 'My lawful object is self-defence.' The defendant in this case said that his intentions were to use the petrol bombs purely to protect his premises should any rioters come to his shop. It was accordingly open to the jury to find that the defendant had made them for the reasonable protection of himself and his property against this danger. The fact that in manufacturing and storing the petrol bombs the defendant committed offences under the 1875 Act did not necessarily involve that when

a he made them his object in doing so was not lawful. The means by which he sought to fulfil that object were unlawful, but the fact that he could never without committing offences reach the point where he used them in self-defence did not render his object in making them for that purpose unlawful. The object or purpose or end for which the petrol bombs were made was not itself rendered unlawful by the fact that it could not be fulfilled except by unlawful means. The fact that the commission of other offences was

b unavoidable did not result in any of them becoming one of the defendant's objects.

The court respectfully agrees with the conclusion of the Court of Criminal Appeal of Northern Ireland that 'possession of a firearm for the purpose of protecting the possessor from acts of violence *may* be possession for a lawful object'. Whether it is so or not must be determined in any given case by the jury in the light of directions such as the trial judge here gave.

c In the judge's summing up the threatened danger was assumed, as was the defendant's anticipation of it. Also assumed, no doubt on the basis of the evidence led, was the imminence of the danger. What the judge on the facts of the case before him left to the jury was the reasonableness of the means adopted for the repulsion of raiders. He did that in comprehensive and, as we have remarked, in well-illustrated terms.

Consistent with the decision in *R v Fegan* [1972] NI 80, though not cited to the court

d in Northern Ireland, were the decisions of the Divisional Court in *Evans v Hughes* and of the High Court of Justiciary in *Grieve v Macleod*. In a parallel series of cases (decided under the Prevention of Crime Act 1953), those courts decided that the question of reasonableness of excuse for possession of an offensive weapon must be considered in relation to the 'immediately prevailing circumstances'. It may be a reasonable excuse that the carrier is in anticipation of imminent attack and is carrying the weapon for his own

e personal defence. Those cases point to a similar conclusion to that reached by the court in *R v Fegan*.

In our judgment a defendant is not left in the paradoxical position of being able to justify acts carried out in self-defence but not acts immediately preparatory to it. There is no warrant for the submission on behalf of the Attorney General that acts of self-defence will only avail a defendant when they have been done spontaneously. There is

f no question of a person in danger of attack 'writing his own immunity' for violent future acts of his. He is not confined for his remedy to calling in the police or boarding up his premises.

He may still arm himself for his own protection, if the exigency arises, although in so doing he may commit other offences. That he may be guilty of other offences will avoid the risk of anarchy contemplated by the reference. It is also to be noted that although a

g person may 'make' a petrol bomb with a lawful object, nevertheless, if he remains in possession of it after the threat has passed which made his object lawful, it may cease to be so. It will only be very rarely that circumstances will exist where the manufacture or possession of petrol bombs can be for a lawful object.

For these reasons the point of law referred by Her Majesty's Attorney General for the consideration of this court is answered by saying: the defence of lawful object is available

h to a defendant against whom a charge under s 4 of the 1883 Act has been preferred, if he can satisfy the jury on the balance of probabilities that his object was to protect himself or his family or his property against imminent apprehended attack and to do so by means which he believed were no more than reasonably necessary to meet the force used by the attackers.

Opinion accordingly.

Solicitors: *Director of Public Prosecutions; Treasury Solicitor.*

N P Metcalfe Esq   Barrister.

Westminster City Council v Select Management Ltd

QUEEN'S BENCH DIVISION (CROWN OFFICE LIST)
TAYLOR J
19, 20 DECEMBER 1983

Health and safety at work – Non-domestic premises – Statutory duty of persons having control of such premises – Duty owed to persons who are not their employees but who use non-domestic premises made available to them as place of work etc – Person having control of block of flats – Whether lifts and electrical installations serving common parts of block are 'non-domestic premises' – Whether lifts and electrical installations 'made available as place of work' etc to persons repairing and maintaining them – Whether person having control of block of flats owing statutory duty to such persons – Health and Safety at Work etc Act 1974, ss 4, 53(1).

On the true construction of ss 4[a] and 53(1)[b] of the Health and Safety at Work etc Act 1974, premises which are not in the exclusive occupation of the occupants of a private dwelling, such as lifts and electrical installations serving the common parts of a block of flats, are 'non-domestic premises' for the purposes of s 4 and are, within the meaning of s 4(1)(b), 'made available . . . as a place of work or as a place where . . . plant . . . [is] provided' for the use of persons who come to repair and maintain the premises. Accordingly, the person who has 'control' of such premises for the purposes of s 4 owes to persons who are not his employees a duty under s 4(2) to ensure, so far as reasonably practicable, that those premises are 'safe and without risks to health' (see p 996 c d g and j, post).

Notes

For improvement notices, see 20 Halsbury's Laws (4th edn) para 473.

For the Health and Safety at Work etc Act 1974, ss 4, 53, see 44 Halsbury's Statutes (3rd edn) 1090, 1136.

Appeal

The Westminster City Council appealed against the decision of an industrial tribunal sitting at London (Central) (chairman Lady E Mitchell) on 28 January 1983 and registered on 9 March 1983, whereby the tribunal allowed appeals by the respondents, Select Management Ltd, against three improvement notices, served on them by the council, relating to the common parts of a block of flats at 6 Hall Road, London NW8, which the respondents owned. The facts are set out in the judgment.

James Goudie for the council.
Richard Nussey for the respondents.

Cur adv vult

20 December. The following judgment was delivered.

TAYLOR J. This is an appeal by the Westminster City Council against the decision of an industrial tribunal held at London and entered in the register on 9 March 1983. The tribunal allowed appeals by the respondents, Select Management Ltd, against three improvement notices served on them by the council, as the enforcement authority, under s 21 of the Health and Safety at Work etc Act 1974. The notices related to the common parts of a block of flats managed by the respondents at 6 Hall Road, London NW8, and alleged that the respondents had contravened s 4 of the Act. Two of the

---

a   Section 4 is set out at p 995 b to f, post
b   Section 53(1), so far as material, is set out at p 995 g h, post

notices, dated 20 September 1982, related to lifts nos 1 and 2 at the block of flats. The
a third notice, dated 5 October 1982, related to the electrical installation serving the
common parts of the flats. All three notices required the respondents to remedy the
alleged contraventions by carrying out work specified in the schedules which were
attached.

The only issue before the industrial tribunal, and it remains the only issue on this
appeal, was whether s 4 of the 1974 Act applied to the respondents in respect of any part
b of this block of flats. By a majority the tribunal held that it did not and, accordingly, the
council had no power to serve the improvement notices.

Section 4 of the 1974 Act reads as follows:

'(1) This section has effect for imposing on persons duties in relation to those
who—(*a*) are not their employees; but (*b*) use non-domestic premises made available
to them as a place of work or as a place where they may use plant or substances
c provided for their use there, and applies to premises so made available and other
non-domestic premises used in connection with them.

(2) It shall be the duty of each person who has, to any extent, control of premises
to which this section applies or of the means of access thereto or egress therefrom or
of any plant or substance in such premises to take such measures as it is reasonable
for a person in his position to take to ensure, so far as is reasonably practicable, that
d the premises, all means of access thereto or egress therefrom available for use by
persons using the premises, and any plant or substance in the premises or, as the case
may be, provided for use there, is or are safe and without risks to health.

(3) Where a person has, by virtue of any contract or tenancy, an obligation of any
extent in relation to—(*a*) the maintenance or repair of any premises to which this
section applies or any means of access thereto or egress therefrom; or (*b*) the safety
e of or the absence of risks to health arising from plant or substances in any such
premises; that person shall be treated, for the purposes of subsection (2) above, as
being a person who has control of the matters to which his obligation extends.

(4) Any reference in this section to a person having control of any premises or
matter is a reference to a person having control of the premises or matter in
connection with the carrying on by him of a trade, business or other undertaking
f (whether for profit or not).'

There is no doubt that the respondents had control of the blocks of flats in connection
with the carrying on by them of a trade, business or other undertaking within sub-ss (2)
and (4). The crucial question is whether, under sub-s (1)(*b*), the lifts and electrical
installation were non-domestic premises made available to persons who were not the
g employees of the respondents as a place of work or as a place where they might use plant
or substances provided for their use there.

Section 53(1) defines non-domestic premises obliquely in contrast to domestic premises.
The definition is as follows:

'"domestic premises" means premises occupied as a private dwelling (including
any garden, yard, garage, outhouse or other appurtenance of such premises which is
h not used in common by the occupants of more than one such dwelling), and "non-
domestic premises" shall be construed accordingly.'

On behalf of the council it was argued that while each flat in the block is a private
dwelling and therefore domestic premises, any staircases, lifts and electrical installations
are not. They are therefore to be regarded as non-domestic premises. Even if a lift or
j electrical installation is an appurtenance of a private dwelling, within the bracketed
words of the definition, it would, the council says, still be non-domestic premises because
it is used in common by occupants of more than one dwelling. When men came to
inspect or repair either the lifts or the electrical installation, they would, so the council
contends, be using non-domestic premises made available to them as a place of work.
Accordingly, all the requirements of s 4(1) would be satisfied and the duty under s 4(2)
therefore attaches to the respondents.

Counsel for the council contended that this was in accordance with the scheme of the Act. The aim is to secure the health and safety of persons at work, whether their work *a* happens to be in a fixed place at their employer's premises or in a succession of places on the premises of others. Again, s 1(3) of the Act shows it to be aimed at risks attributable to the manner of conducting an undertaking, the plant used for the purposes of the undertaking, and the condition of the premises so used.

On behalf of the respondents it was argued that neither the lifts nor the electrical installation nor, indeed, any part of the block of flats could properly be described as non- *b* domestic premises. The word 'appurtenances' should be construed ejusdem generis with garden, yard, garage and outhouse. All of those lie outside the fabric of the main building and the internal lift is not of the same genus.

How then did a lift or common staircase fall to be described, since domestic premises means premises occupied as a private dwelling? Counsel for the respondents was driven to contend that the common lift or staircase was, in some way, part of a private dwelling *c* and, indeed, part of each private dwelling in the block of flats. I cannot accept that argument. The wording of the definition may not be the most felicitous, especially in relation to a block of flats. However, I am satisfied that any premises which are not in the exclusive occupation of the occupants of one private dwelling are non-domestic premises. Therefore, the common lifts in this block and the electrical installation serving the common parts are non-domestic premises. *d*

An argument which found favour with the majority of the tribunal was again addressed to this court: that it is artificial to regard the common parts of the block as non-domestic interstices of domestic premises. But this is to substitute for the specific definition of domestic premises in s 53(1) a looser definition encompassing the whole block or building as primarily residential and, therefore, domestic premises as a single indivisible unit. Premises, as defined in s 53(1), includes any place. Someone who enters *e* a common foyer has, therefore, entered on premises, but not domestic premises as defined, since the foyer cannot be a private dwelling. The foyer is, therefore, non-domestic premises and likewise in the case of the lifts and electrical installation.

The second argument of counsel for the respondents was based on the wording of s 4(1)(b). That refers to those who use non-domestic premises made available to them as a place of work. He contended that those words apply to persons who work on some *f* process within the premises and not to those who come to maintain and repair the very fabric of the premises itself. Since the only persons who work on the lifts and electrical installation are repair and maintenance men, counsel for the respondents contended that this limb of s 4 shows the section to be inapplicable to these premises.

In my judgment, there is no reason why the words of s 4(1)(b) should not apply both to persons working at a process on the premises and those working, albeit occasionally, *g* on repair and maintenance there. Indeed, it would be anomalous if they did not. To take an example raised during argument, a commercial garage is undoubtedly non-domestic premises. Why should s 4 impose on those controlling the garage duties in relation to incoming workmen engaged on car repair, but not in relation to incomers cleaning windows or repairing a hydraulic lift? Moreover, there is the second limb of s 4(1)(b) which says: '. . . use non-domestic premises made available to them as a place of work *or* *h* *as a place where they may use plant or substances provided for their use there.*' A lift is within the definition of plant under s 53(1), so when a visitor to the block of flats makes use of the lift which is provided for his use there, he is a person in relation to whom duties are imposed on the controllers of the premises. In my judgment, the council is right in asserting that s 4 does apply to the common parts of this block of flats which are, by definition, non-domestic premises. *j*

It was urged on me that as the Act contains penal sanctions in regard to breaches of various provisions, including s 4, I should construe the section in favour of the respondents if the words are capable of more than one interpretation. I have that principle well in mind, but I have reached the conclusion that the words of the statute are unambiguous a and clear and that the construction contended for by the council is right. Accordingly, the appeal must be allowed and the improvement notices must stand.

Appeal allowed.

Solicitors: *T F Neville* (for the council); *Penningtons* (for the respondents).

b April Weiss   Barrister.

c

Brice and others v Brown and others

d QUEEN'S BENCH DIVISION
STUART-SMITH J
4, 5, 6, 7, 8, 13 JULY 1983

Damages – Personal injury – Nervous shock – Entitlement to recover damages for nervous shock
– Matters to be established by plaintiff – Reasonable foreseeability of consequence of tortfeasor's
e *breach of duty of care – Liability for direct consequences of breach of duty – Whether material*
that tortfeasor could not reasonably foresee precise injury sustained by plaintiff – Whether
material that plaintiff having underlying personality disorder.

The plaintiff was a 42-year-old woman who had had a hysterical personality disorder
since early childhood. However, signs and symptoms of that disorder manifested
f themselves only at infrequent intervals and at a relatively moderate level so that she was
able to lead a happy and socially accepted life. The plaintiff was married with three
children and although there were occasional serious eruptions in the marital relationship
and periods when the plaintiff suffered from depression and bouts of psychosomatic
complaints she was on the whole able to cope and enjoy life and her family. In 1980 the
plaintiff and a daughter were passengers in a taxi which was involved in a collision with
g an oncoming bus. The plaintiff sustained relatively minor injuries but the daughter was
badly cut on the forehead and seemed at the time to have suffered alarming injuries
although she made a relatively rapid recovery. Shortly after the incident the plaintiff
became very moody and unable to sleep and neglected the cooking and the housework.
Thereafter the plaintiff's mental state became much worse. She attempted suicide on a
number of occasions and her behaviour became unsocial and bizarre in the extreme,
h with the result that she was admitted to hospital under the Mental Health Act 1959 on
three occasions. In 1981 the plaintiff brought an action against the defendants, the
respective owners and drivers of the taxi and the bus, claiming, inter alia, damages for
her condition and for the cost of her future care. The plaintiff submitted that the stress
caused to her vulnerable personality by the accident had resulted in a severe mental
illness which had seriously disabled her. The plaintiff further contended that, although
j the extent of her mental disorder might not have been foreseeable, the nervous shock
suffered by her was a reasonably foreseeable consequence of the accident. The defendants
denied liability, contending that, for a tortfeasor to be held liable for nervous shock
consequent on his tort, the precise nature and extent of that nervous shock had to have
been foreseeable by him.

Held – In an action against a tortfeasor for damages for nervous shock (ie mental injury or psychiatric illness as opposed, on the one hand, to grief and sorrow and, on the other, *a* to physical or organic injury), once the plaintiff had established (a) that the circumstances of the tort caused or materially contributed to the nervous shock and (b) that the nervous shock suffered by the plaintiff (who was, for this purpose, to be assumed to be a person of normal disposition and phlegm) had been reasonably foreseeable by the tortfeasor as a natural and probable consequence of the breach of his duty of care, the plaintiff was entitled to damages for nervous shock and such of its direct consequences as were not *b* dissimilar in type or kind, whether initially reasonably foreseeable or not. It was immaterial that the tortfeasor could not have foreseen the precise mental or psychological process that led to the kind or type of injury sustained by the plaintiff, and likewise, where the plaintiff had an underlying personality disorder, it was immaterial that a completely normal person would not have suffered the consequences actually suffered by the plaintiff. It followed that, on the facts, the plaintiff was entitled to damages for her *c* condition and there would be judgment for her accordingly (see p 1006 *h* to p 1007 *a* and *d* to *f* and p 1008 *j*, post).

Dicta of Lord Parker CJ in *Smith v Leech Brain & Co Ltd* [1961] 3 All ER at 1162 and of Lord Wilberforce, of Lord Russell and of Lord Bridge in *McLoughlin v O'Brian* [1982] 2 All ER at 301, 309, 311–312 applied.

Hay (or Bourhill) v Young [1942] 2 All ER 396 distinguished.   *d*

Notes

For liability for nervous shock, see 34 Halsbury's Laws (4th edn) para 8, and for cases on the subject, see 17 Digest (Reissue) 145–147, 377–392.

For remoteness of damage, see 12 Halsbury's Laws (4th edn) para 1128, and for cases *e* on the subject, see 36(1) Digest (Reissue) 62–65, 306–307, 224–237, 1232–1236.

Cases referred to in judgment

Hay (or Bourhill) v Young [1942] 2 All ER 396, [1943] AC 92, HL.
Hinz v Berry [1970] 1 All ER 1074, [1970] 2 QB 40, [1970] 2 WLR 684, CA.   *f*
McLoughlin v O'Brian [1982] 2 All ER 298, [1983] 1 AC 410, [1982] 2 WLR 982, HL.
Smith v Leech Brain & Co Ltd [1961] 3 All ER 1159, [1962] 2 QB 405, [1962] 2 WLR 148.

Action

By a writ issued on 19 August 1981 and indorsed with a statement of claim, amended on *g* 17 May 1983 pursuant to the order of Master Bickford-Smith dated 10 May 1983, the first plaintiff, Sheila Teresa Brice, a patient suing by her husband and next friend, Peter Frank Brice, the second plaintiff, Susan Brice, an infant suing by her father and next friend Peter Frank Brice, and the third plaintiff, Peter Frank Brice, brought an action against the first defendant, Clive Alan Brown, the second defendants, Marigold Dry Cleaners Ltd (trading as Panshanger Taxis), the third defendant, Colin Anthony *h* Armstrong, and the fourth defendants, London Country Bus Services Ltd, claiming, for the first and second plaintiffs, damages for pain, injuries and loss and damage, and, for the third plaintiff, damages for the loss of the society and the services of the first plaintiff and for trouble, inconvenience and expense, and loss and damage, arising out of a collision between a Ford Cortina taxi owned by the second defendants and driven by their servant or agent the first defendant and in which the first and second plaintiffs were *j* passengers, and a Leyland omnibus owned by the fourth defendants and driven in the opposite direction by their servant or agent the third defendant along Knightsfield, Welwyn Garden City in the county of Hertford on 2 February 1980, the collision alleged to have been caused by the negligence of the first and third defendants or one or other of *a* them as servants or agents of the second and fourth defendants respectively. The facts are set out in the judgment.

Christopher Holland QC and *Michael Gettleson* for the plaintiffs.
Jonathan Woods for the first and second defendants.
Julien Hooper for the third and fourth defendants.

b   *Cur adv vult*

13 July. The following judgment was delivered.

STUART-SMITH J. On 2 February 1980 the plaintiff, Mrs Brice, was involved in a collision between a taxi, in which she was travelling as a passenger with her daughter Susan, and a bus. The taxi was driven by the first defendant and owned by the second *c* defendant. The bus was owned by the fourth defendant and driven by the third defendant. The plaintiff sustained relatively trivial physical injuries. Her daughter was quite seriously injured, and I dealt with her case before the trial of this action. There is no doubt now that the plaintiff suffers a severe mental illness, and she is severely disabled by it. There is no dispute between the parties that that illness is a genuine one. The plaintiff's case is that it has resulted from the accident, from stress caused by that accident *d* to her vulnerable personality, it being a hysterical reaction to that accident. The defendants, on the other hand, say that it is unconnected with the accident, either that it is an endogenous depression or that it is a hysterical reaction, possibly brought on initially by the accident but now superseded by the endogenous depression.

The plaintiff's claim therefore is for general damages and for the costs of care for her, because she at the moment cannot look after herself. The plaintiff's husband also claims *e* for loss of consortium of his wife and loss of her services. The plaintiff herself did not give evidence: she was unfit to do so. It is necessary to look at her history so far as it is known. The history is gained from what she has told doctors from time to time over the years supplemented by the evidence of her husband.

She was born on 2 August 1937 and was one of 12 children. Four brothers died in infancy. She herself was involved in the death of one of these children. He had apparently *f* been put to bed in a cot or bed and tied down by his parents so that he should not fall out of it. She, then aged about ten, took pity on him, released his ties and tried to take him out but unfortunately dropped him and he sustained a head injury. The death certificate in relation to that child shows death through bronchial pneumonia, but that may well have resulted from the injuries he sustained. Shortly after that incident her parents appear to have separated, and she was taken into care and looked after in a convent. It *g* was a restricted and highly disciplined community. She remained there until 15, when she went into domestic service, being described as a relatively immature person. After some two or three years there she joined the Women's Royal Army Corps and seems to have been relatively happy and did well as a cook. She met her husband in the course of her service and they became engaged. She in fact became married while she was still in the army but she shortly afterwards left. She obtained a good report on her discharge.

h After her marriage in June 1957 she bore three children: George, born in January 1959; Julie, born in January 1964; and Susan, who was involved in the accident, in March 1971. There is no doubt that the marriage went through some turbulent patches. The information in relation to this comes mainly from the general practitioner's notes, Dr Green, and also from the plaintiff's husband himself. In 1962 there was an incident of domestic violence followed by a consultation with a psychiatrist by the plaintiff, and she *j* appears to have been recommended Lardil which was an antidepressant. In 1967 she sustained a fractured pelvis in a road accident, but she appears to have recovered from that. In September 1967 there is also a note in the general practitioner's notes that she alleged that she had been beaten up by her husband. In 1968 the general practitioner's notes record that she was complaining of having been depressed for ten years on and off.

In 1971 she was prescribed Valium, and in 1974 the notes again indicate an incident of some violence when she claimed that her buttocks had been bruised following a row. It is possible that following that event she left her husband for a short time. In 1975 she told her general practitioner that her marriage had broken up. She left home for a period between January and March, which was probably about six weeks. She took the two girls with her. There was one other occasion, probably in 1966, when she left home for a short time following what the plaintiff's husband described as an accidental occasion when he injured her. At times she has told the doctors that before the accident she had sexual relations with three or four men other than her husband, the last of those being only some months before the accident. How reliable that information is is not clear.

Despite these considerable difficulties the husband described their life together, particularly in the year or so before the accident, as happy. Julie, the daughter, described the relationship as being a very close and happy one between her mother and father, although they had a few ups and downs. I think there is no doubt that the husband and wife tended to go their own ways so far as their enjoyments were concerned. The plaintiff's husband was a hard worker, and in his off time he tended to go fishing or to the pub. His wife was more concerned with the home. She watched a lot of television and was more interested in the children. But in the two years or so before the accident they seem to have discovered mutual interests in music and also in painting, and to some extent that brought both husband and wife together. The picture that emerges is of a woman who had a difficult childhood, subject to considerable trauma, who might well be vulnerable to stress. In womanhood she managed on the whole to cope. She suffered from bouts of psychosomatic complaints, occasional serious eruptions in the marital relationship, and in my judgment the evidence is consistent with her having a hysterical personality disorder derived from traumatic events in childhood but able on the whole to cope. In particular she was a competent mother who cared for the children and brought them up well. She was close to them and did a number of things with them. She was an averagely competent housewife and cook, if anything being over house-proud. She gave considerable assistance to her husband in his business as a carpet cleaner, because by her answering the telephone, giving estimates and making appointments he was able to devote his whole time to those activities. She suffered from occasional depression, but on the whole she enjoyed life and her family.

The accident, as I have indicated, occurred on 2 February 1980 when she and her daughter were returning from the shops by taxi. The taxi, according to the plaintiff's account as recorded in two statements which were put in under the Civil Evidence Act 1968, had been driving a good deal too fast. They came to a road called Knightsfield, where a vehicle was parked on the nearside. The taxi pulled out to overtake it when coming in the opposite direction round the bend was a bus. According to the plaintiff's account the accident must have been a frightening one because she could see that the collision was going to take place with the oncoming bus. In due course it did take place. She attempted to cover her daughter and protect her from injury, but unhappily Susan sustained a most alarming laceration of the forehead. She now has a 10-cm scar running from the eye up into the hairline, and it is perhaps difficult from that to realise quite how alarming that injury must have seemed at the time. The husband, who saw her in hospital, thought that she had lost the whole of her scalp because the skin contracted upwards over the head. She was bleeding and obviously in great distress.

In February (the exact date is not known) the plaintiff wrote a letter to her solicitors giving a graphic description of the accident, of her fears at the time and of her concern and apprehension about Susan. It is not necessary to read it, but it speaks eloquently of her fear and panic at the time. It also describes her state of physical shock at the time and refers to a trivial injury to her hand.

Following the accident both Susan and the plaintiff were taken to hospital. Susan was detained for two or three nights. The plaintiff spent the first night in hospital and visited her until she came out. In fact Susan made a relatively rapid recovery. The plaintiff's husband described the situation following the accident in these terms. He said the child recovered very quickly: 'Within a few days all the stress had gone out. We relaxed, or at least I did. I think she was still in a state of shock. [That is referring to the plaintiff.] She did not sleep, certainly. Within a week she was complaining of heart pains and dizziness.' He said that he dismissed that as being of no significance.

On 8 February 1980 she consulted a partner of the general practitioner's practice and was prescribed an analgesic, presumably for the chest pain of which she was complaining. According to the plaintiff's husband, in the weeks that followed his wife did not seem to sleep at all. At that time his brother-in-law was staying and she spent the night talking to him, and so far as he could see she never slept at all, although plainly she must have done. After two to three weeks he described her, and it is confirmed by Julie, as being very moody and very snappy. According to the husband, at the end of February they went to the general practitioner to get some better tablets for sleeping. They previously used Panadol but they were having no effect. There is no record of that visit, but I have no reason to doubt the husband's evidence about it. They appear to have had very little effect on the position. He described her at that time, that is to say at about the end of February, as suffering from tiredness, loss of energy, very snappy and she neglected the housework and the cooking. Both the husband and the daughter say that she was complaining of being frightened about the accident and she could not get it out of her mind. She told Julie that she kept seeing the bus coming in slow motion.

On 1 April 1980 she again consulted a partner in the general practitioner's practice who recorded a reactive depression to a road traffic accident. He prescribed anti-depressants and a sedative. He does not record what she actually said, but it is quite clear from that note that she must have related her symptoms to the road traffic accident.

The family went for a holiday in Italy shortly after this time but it was not a success. On 28 April she again consulted her general practitioner and different drugs were prescribed. She went again on 2 May. It is quite clear that by this time her condition had reached a somewhat worrying state. She describes seeing or dreaming about evil spirits. She thought she was dying, and she believed she had got cancer. She was prescribed Mogadon for sleeping and anti-depressants. By this time her husband described her condition as very bad. She appears to have thought that both her husband and Julie were trying to poison her. On 29 May she attempted suicide by drinking a bottle of wine after she had taken a large quantity of tablets. There is no reason to suppose that that was anything other than a genuine attempt to take her life. She was admitted to hospital, the Queen Elizabeth II hospital, and the in-patient note which seems to have been taken at that time records under 'History from the patient':

> 'It all started following the car accident. The patient felt sorry about the daughter getting hurt. She became worried that the daughter would suffer after effects of injury and this kept her getting depressed. Insomnia with loss of appetite and interest, tearful on and off.'

Then it goes on to describe the holiday in Italy which was not a success, and she believed that her husband was trying to kill her.

Thereafter the hospital notes indicate violent changes of mood and bizarre behaviour on the part of the plaintiff. The hospital seems to have diagnosed a depressive illness, seemingly brought about by the accident. Towards the end of her stay there she was allowed home at the weekends. On 22 June another serious attempt at suicide was made. She was returned to hospital. There appears to have been a further attempt on 30 June. Early in July she was found in a compromising position with a male patient. It seems that she had sexual relations with him. This got back to the plaintiff's husband, who was extremely angry both with her and with the hospital. She appears to have made another, probably this time half-hearted, attempt at suicide, and on 10 July to the evident relief of the hospital she discharged herself. I think they were thankful to get rid of a troublesome patient.

Over the next few months she continued to behave in a most bizarre way. She wandered off for sometimes weeks at a time and sometimes days. She probably behaved like a prostitute in London and elsewhere. She slept rough in the woods and did not take any proper food. The hospital were reluctant to take her back. She was rejected at home for her unsocial behaviour and because her husband, understandably I think, thought that she was some sort of moral danger to the girls. On 14 September she was again admitted to the Queen Elizabeth II hospital pursuant to s 136 of the Mental Health Act 1959, having been found in a destitute state. She remained there until 29 October. The picture again presented by the notes is one of changing moods but on the whole, isolated, sullen, unco-operative, secretive and not taking drugs. The plaintiff's husband described her as being unrepentant, aggressive and like a nasty spoilt child. On the final night of her stay there she disappeared, apparently hiding on the sixth floor of the hospital. She was discharged the next day, once again the hospital being clearly relieved to get rid of a troublesome patient.

Shortly before her admission on the second occasion to the Queen Elizabeth II hospital the plaintiff's husband met a divorced lady, Mrs Clay. She had three children. The two eldest were grown up. She was living with the youngest one in a council house. An attachment began to form between them and increasingly from that time onwards Mrs Clay came to the house to help out with the housework and to help look after Susan. Mrs Clay, who gave evidence, is a sensible, understanding and forebearing lady. About this time, possibly a little earlier, Julie left to go and live at her boyfriend's house with his family. She had been very close to her mother. She described their relationship as being like sisters. After leaving school at Easter she had looked after her mother and the house for some months until August, when she got a job. She found life in the house absolutely intolerable. Since then she has become married to her boyfriend.

On her discharge from the Queen Elizabeth II hospital on the second occasion the plaintiff lived at home. Her husband described her as awful. He said: 'The intensity of crying and screaming got worse; I could not bear it.' On 10 November he came home to find the house in darkness. The plaintiff was in the hall. She had pulled out the main cable where the electricity comes into the junction box in an attempt to kill herself. He found her shaking and she would not let him near her. She was admitted to Hillend hospital following that, under s 29 of the Mental Health Act 1959. Again her history was taken from the patient and she appears to have related her symptoms to the accident. Her behaviour in hospital as recorded in the hospital notes continued to be bizarre. She was convinced that she was suffering from venereal disease. She certainly had some infection in the genital region but it does not appear to have been venereal disease. The hospital appears to have diagnosed recurrent depression in a neurotic personality following the road traffic accident. She was allowed home over Christmas 1980. The plaintiff and her husband were in the house alone. He said that the time was absolutely miserable. She was crying and tearing her clothes and scratching her chest. In fact she must have been somewhat variable because in the hospital notes her husband is said to have described her as better at some stage. In any event she was discharged from Hillend hospital early in January 1981, and since that time she has lived at home. There have been two subsequent occasions when there were short admissions to hospital when she had been found wandering on a railway line, probably contemplating suicide, although not having made any attempt to do so.

Since January 1981 her condition has to some extent stabilised though her behaviour remains highly abnormal. Her present state is described by her husband. She spends most of her time in one room. She covers the window with a blanket, and even in the extremely hot weather which we have been experiencing recently she does not open the window and she stays in there, the room being like an oven. In the winter time she is in there nearly all the time. In the summer she will go out for walks in the fields. She goes uninvited into the neighbours' gardens and is often most inappropriately dressed, wearing either a bra and knickers or in hot weather one or two hot jerseys. She is unable to cook or wash her own clothes. She can now take a bath and does bath herself, but until a   comparatively recently she had to be bathed, and her husband described it in a graphic phrase, 'like bathing a cat'. She has peculiar habits in relation to her toilet. She apparently was reluctant to use the W C and would urinate on the floor. Her husband could not understand this until Dr Green suggested that a bucket should be provided, and she now for the most part uses the bucket. She does not do it on the floor. She lives largely on biscuits. She very rarely eats with the family and she takes food which they leave out for her. She pleads with people in a pathetic way to cut off her head and kill her. She wrings

b   her hands and appears to be miserable a great deal of the time. She seems to want to play with children and continues to do bizarre and inappropriate things like untying the laces of her son-in-law's shoes; but there is no doubt that there has been some improvement. She is no longer vicious or aggressive. She is slightly less reluctant to mix with the family, and she seems to be making some response at last to overtures of affection. But there is no doubt that at the moment she is severely deranged. She needs supervision. She cannot

c   be left alone for long. She has caused damage with matches. She is inclined to leave the cooker on. She breaks up the children's things and Susan's room and the plaintiff's husband's and Mrs Clay's room have to be locked to keep her out. She has to be cooked for, tidied after, shopped for and have her clothes washed.

        The plaintiff's case in summary is this: that she had pre-existing the accident a personality disorder probably stemming from her traumatic childhood. That disorder

d   was relatively well managed so that some signs and symptoms remained latent. Others appeared at infrequent intervals and at a relatively moderate level so that she was able to lead a happy and socially acceptable life, particularly in the last few years before the accident. The accident, so it is said, applied a stress to a vulnerable aspect of her personality so as to aggravate and make patent the underlying disorder, producing with increasing intensity signs and symptoms of a hysterical personality disorder; that in the six months

e   following the accident her resultant behaviour was markedly variable reflecting possibly the inner struggle with her personality disorder, but thereafter the disorder was effectively uncontrolled so that she was driven away from the world into childhood and seeks to drive away the world by anti-social behaviour. With the passage of time and increased patience and understanding by those who look after her and love her there has been some slight improvement, but the prognosis is very uncertain.

f   That case was supported by the evidence of Dr Connell, a consultant psychiatrist, and Dr Green, the patient's general practitioner. The first and second defendants by their counsel submit that the plaintiff has not proved that her condition was caused by the accident, or, alternatively, if immediately after the accident she suffered a condition attributable to it, that condition at some time changed and became what is known as an endogenous depression and was not attributable to it. The third and fourth defendants,

g   whose case was supported by the evidence of Dr Granville Grossman, another consultant psychiatrist, is different and it is now that she is suffering from an endogenous depression which is totally unrelated to the accident. But it has to be noted that Dr Granville Grossman has changed his mind on two occasions in relation to the plaintiff's condition. Originally in August 1982 following his first interview with her he shared in substance the views of Dr Connell and Dr Green, although it is somewhat differently expressed in

h   his report. He then appears to have seen the Queen Elizabeth II hospital notes and the notes from the general practitioner, and it was his conclusion following that examination, but without seeing the plaintiff again, that she was either deliberately or hysterically exaggerating her symptoms. There is no basis whatever for the conclusion that she was deliberately exaggerating her symptoms, and so far as I can see there never has been any basis for such a conclusion. Dr Granville Grossman does not suggest now that that is the

j   case. In my judgment it was a serious clinical error of judgment on the part of Dr Granville Grossman ever to have thought that she could have been simulating these symptoms deliberately.

        Finally, and this is based on a chance meeting with the plaintiff at an examination which was arranged, he has come to the conclusion that she is suffering from an endogenous depression unconnected with the accident that came on after the accident coincidental with it and totally unconnected with it. The reasons for this conclusion appear to be first of all that she is no longer exhibiting bizarre characteristics such as might be found in a hysterical personality. For my part I find her conduct in relation to the toilet, her inappropriate behaviour in walking round the neighbourhood in bra and knickers, her behaviour playing with children and being like a child bizarre characteristics. Dr Granville Grossman tended to dismiss these features of the case as being of no importance. Of course if his theory is right they are inconsistent with it if they are of any significance. Moreover, it is quite clear that in the past, as Dr Granville Grossman accepts, and indeed it was the basis of his original diagnosis, she did manifest some extremely bizarre behaviour: the suicides, especially the attempt at electrocution, the promiscuous behaviour, the wandering off and matters of that sort. All those features led Dr Granville Grossman to his original diagnosis that there was a gross hysterical overlay. Dr Granville Grossman did not suggest, and there is no evidence to support a conclusion from the doctors, that the plaintiff's underlying condition has in fact changed at some time since the accident. For my part I find the submission made on behalf of the first and second defendants that initially she suffered a hysterical personality disorder but that it has subsequently at some undefined time changed to an endogenous depression in the highest degree improbable.

Secondly, Dr Granville Grossman relied on the fact that the plaintiff was suffering from a number of delusions which he said were characteristic of endogenous depression. For example, that she was suffering from cancer, but an examination of the general practitioner's notes indicate that she had had fears of suffering from cancer before the accident; and the delusion that she was suffering from venereal disease. There is no doubt that she did have some condition, although it may not have been venereal disease, at the time which I have indicated. Dr Granville Grossman also indicated that her present almost consistent miserable state was only consistent with an endogenous depression. Thirdly, he appears to have relied for his conclusion on the gap in time between the accident and the onset of symptoms. It was my impression that Dr Granville Grossman's view was to a large extent based on the belief that there was no reliable evidence of any symptoms being reported before April 1980, and that appears to have been based on the notes indicating the first visit to the general practitioner in which the road traffic accident is referred to. I am satisfied that in fact she sustained shock at the time, that she suffered from insomnia, that within two to three weeks at the most she manifested uncharacteristic neglect of her household duties, became snappy and moody during the day but with periods of lovingness at night. She also was experiencing or claimed to be experiencing pains in the chest, and whether or not those pains were initially organically based there is no evidence, but she appears to have been complaining of them still when she was admitted to hospital and they are referred to in October 1980 in the hospital notes. I do not find it surprising in the context of her history that she did not go earlier to see her general practitioner about the effects of this accident, or at any rate there is no record of her having attributed her complaints towards it.

If one looks at the characteristics that Dr Granville Grossman said that he would have expected if this was a hysterical reaction to the stress of the accident, it is possible to say that all those characteristics are present. First of all, he said that he would have expected to find intense concern for the child and, secondly, hostility to the taxi driver. It may be a matter of degree and interpretation, but it seems to me that that is a possible interpretation of what the plaintiff was saying in the letter in February to her solicitors. I think strains of the same thing come through in the in-patient notes. Thirdly, he said he would have expected her to suffer from lack of sleep. There is clear evidence that that is what she did suffer from. Fourthly, that she would suffer from loss of appetite; it is true that there is no direct evidence about that, but in the notes which I have read in relation to the history she gave to the hospital there is a reference to loss of appetite. Fifthly, he said that he would have expected to find concentration on the accident by her. All the records of her accounts of her symptoms at a time when she was able to give them to the doctors appear to refer her symptoms to the accident. Moreover, in the evidence which I

have already referred to, the family say that she was constantly referring to the accident
and the fact that she could not get it out of her mind.

In so far as there is a choice between the evidence of Dr Granville Grossman and that
of Dr Connell and Dr Green I much prefer the views of the latter. I was much impressed
by Dr Green. He had the great advantage of knowing the patient for a period well before
this accident and has seen much of her since. He is clearly a thoughtful and intelligent
man; he is not a trained psychiatrist, but like many general practitioners has much
experience of psychiatric problems. He brings to the problem of diagnosis great concern
for his patient, an inquiring mind and a great deal of common sense. His diagnosis was
supported by Dr Connell and it was again supported by Dr Granville Grossman's original
view. I do not think there was really any justification for Dr Granville Grossman
changing his mind about that. It follows that I reject the suggestion or contention put
forward by counsel for the first and second defendants that there has been some change
in her condition so that she is now suffering from an endogenous depression.

Counsel for the first and second defendants contends that as a matter of law the
plaintiff cannot recover even on those findings. He submits that the expression 'nervous
shock' is out of date, and that before the plaintiff can succeed she must prove first that
she sustained a psychiatric illness and second that that illness was reasonably foreseeable
by the defendants. He contends that, unlike the condition which the plaintiff in *Hinz v
Bury* [1970] 1 All ER 1074, [1970] 2 QB 40 suffered, which was a reactive depression
(although it is not so described in the report), a hysterical personality disorder is not a
psychiatric illness, and that so far from being reasonably foreseeable such a case as this
had never been experienced by the two experienced psychiatrists, and therefore it could
not have been foreseen by the defendants. Both psychiatrists described it as a unique case
and one that could not have occurred in a normal person. He relies firstly on the speech
of Lord Wright in *Hay (or Bourhill) v Young* [1942] 2 All ER 396 at 405–406, [1943] AC
92 at 110:

> 'What is now being considered is the question of liability, and this, I think, in a
> question whether there is a duty owing to members of the public who come within
> the ambit of the act, must generally depend on a normal standard of susceptibility.
> This, it may be said, is somewhat vague. That is true; but definition involves
> limitation, which it is desirable to avoid further than is necessary in a principle of
> law like negligence, which is widely ranging and is still in the stage of development.
> It is here, as elsewhere, a question of what the hypothetical reasonable man, viewing
> the position, I suppose *ex post facto*, would say it was proper to foresee. What danger
> of particular infirmity that would include must depend on all the circumstances;
> but generally, I think, a reasonably normal condition, if medical evidence is capable
> of defining it, would be the standard. The test of the plaintiff's extraordinary
> susceptibility, if unknown to the defendant, would in effect make the defendant an
> insurer.'

He submits that, if the plaintiff's condition is due to her underlying personality
disorder and the results of stress on it resulting in the unique and bizarre breakdown, she
did not have a normal standard of susceptibility and that a hypothetical reasonable man
could not foresee that the psychiatric results would eventuate.

Secondly, he relies on the speech of Lord Bridge in *McLoughlin v O'Brian* [1982] 2 All
ER 298 at 311–312, [1983] 1 AC 410 at 431–432:

> 'The basic difficulty of the subject arises from the fact that the crucial answers to
> the questions which it raises lie in the difficult field of psychiatric medicine. The
> common law gives no damages for emotional stress which any normal person
> experiences when someone he loves is killed or injured. Anxiety and depression are
> normal human emotions. Yet an anxiety neurosis or a reactive depression may be
> recognisable psychiatric illnesses, with or without psychosomatic symptoms. So, the
> first hurdle which a plaintiff claiming damages of the kind in question must

surmount is to establish that he is suffering, not merely grief, distress or any other normal emotion, but a positive psychiatric illness. That is here not in issue. A plaintiff must then establish the necessary chain of causation in fact between his psychiatric illness and the death or injury of one or more third parties negligently caused by the defendant. Here again, this is not in dispute in the instant case. But, when causation in fact is in issue, it must no doubt be determined by the judge on the basis of the evidence of psychiatrists. Then, here comes the all important question. Given the fact of the plaintiff's psychiatric illness caused by the defendant's negligence in killing or physically injuring another, was the chain of causation from the one event to the other, considered ex post facto in the light of all that has happened, "reasonably foreseeable" by the "reasonable man"? A moment's thought will show that the answer to that question depends on what knowledge is to be attributed to the hypothetical reasonable man of the operation of cause and effect in psychiatric medicine. There are at least two theoretically possible approaches. The first is that the judge should receive the evidence of psychiatrists as to the degree of probability that the particular cause would produce the particular effect, and apply to that the appropriate legal test of reasonable foreseeability as the criterion of the defendant's duty of care. The second is that the judge, relying on his own opinion of the operation of cause and effect in psychiatric medicine, as fairly representative of that of the educated layman, should treat himself as the reasonable man and form his own view from the primary facts whether the proven chain of cause and effect was reasonably foreseeable.'

He then went on to consider that question.

Lord Wilberforce dealt with the question of the expression 'nervous shock'. He said ([1982] 2 All ER 298 at 301, [1983] 1 AC 410 at 418):

'Although we continue to use the hallowed expression "nervous shock", English law, and common understanding, have moved some distance since recognition was given to this symptom as a basis for liability. Whatever is unknown about the mind-body relationship (and the area of ignorance seems to expand with that of knowledge), it is now accepted by medical science that recognisable and severe physical damage to the human body and system may be caused by the impact, through the senses, of external events on the mind. There may thus be produced what is as identifiable an illness as any that may be caused by direct physical impact. It is safe to say that this, in general terms, is understood by the ordinary man or woman who is hypothesised by the courts in situations where claims for negligence are made. Although in the only case which has reached this House (*Hay (or Bourhill) v Young* [1942] 2 All ER 396, [1943] AC 92) a claim for damages in respect of "nervous shock" was rejected on its facts, the House gave clear recognition to the legitimacy, in principle, of claims of that character.'

Nevertheless all their Lordships in that case continued to use the phrase 'nervous shock', albeit in inverted commas. I think it is a convenient phrase to describe mental injury or psychiatric illness to distinguish it from, on the one hand, grief and sorrow and, on the other, physical or organic injury. The psychiatric illness does not have to have any particular label or term of art applied to it. Used in the sense which I have indicated the plaintiff has in my judgment to establish three things: firstly, that the circumstances of the accident caused or materially contributed to the nervous shock; secondly, that the nervous shock was reasonably foreseeable by the tortfeasor as a natural and probable consequence of the breach of his duty of care. For this purpose the plaintiff is assumed to be a person of normal disposition and phlegm (see per Lord Russell in *McLoughlin v O'Brian* [1982] 2 All ER 298 at 309, [1983] 1 AC 410 at 429). This would exclude the pursuer in *Hay (or Bourhill) v Young* as a person who faints at the sight of a road accident no matter who is involved. And, thirdly, that once the first two matters are established the plaintiff is entitled to compensation for nervous shock and such of its direct consequences as were not dissimilar in type or kind, whether or no the same were initially reasonably to be foreseen. Such has been the rule in relation to physical injuries for many years. I can see no reason in principle why mental injury should be in a different category: see *Smith v Leech Brain & Co Ltd* [1961] 3 All ER 1159 at 1162, [1962] 2 QB 405 at 415 per Lord Parker CJ, where he said:

'The test is not whether these defendants could reasonably have foreseen that a burn would cause cancer and that Mr. Smith would die. The question is whether these defendants could reasonably foresee the type of injury which he suffered, namely, the burn. What, in the particular case, is the amount of damage which he suffers as a result of that burn, depends on the characteristics and constitution of the victim.'

Taken literally the passage from the speech of Lord Bridge to which I have referred may seem to give support for the contention of counsel for the first and second defendants that the tortfeasor must foresee the precise nature and extent of the psychiatric illness that the accident causes, but that was not the relevant problem that the House of Lords were considering in *McLoughlin v O'Brian* and I do not think for a moment that Lord Bridge intended to apply a different rule to psychiatric as opposed to physical injury or to impugn the long line of authorities of the so-called 'eggshell skull' cases or the principle in *Smith v Leech Brain & Co Ltd*.

Applying those principles to this case I have already held that the circumstances of the accident caused or materially contributed to the plaintiff's condition. Secondly, in my judgment the tortfeasor could reasonably foresee that nervous shock in the sense to which I have referred would result to a mother of a normally robust constitution in the circumstances which occurred. She was actually present in the vehicle, saw the impending disaster and was confronted with a child who appeared disastrously injured. Finally, the kind and type of injury which she has in fact sustained is the same as that which could reasonably have been foreseen. The fact that the tortfeasor could not foresee the precise name the psychiatrists were to put on the condition or the precise mental or psychological process that led to that result is immaterial. So is the fact that a completely normal person would not have suffered the consequences that the plaintiff in fact suffered. In my judgment the plaintiff is entitled to recover in law.

I turn then to the question of assessment of general damages. The plaintiff's life is clearly one of considerable misery. She leads a totally abnormal existence. She wants to be a child and she is conscious that she is not, and that gives rise to a conflict in her personality. She is isolated and cut off from those she has loved and who love her and from the community. The first question is: how long will this condition last? Since it is not organically based it cannot be said with certainty that it will last indefinitely. The prognosis is very guarded. Neither Dr Connell nor Dr Green thought that any treatment was relevant to her condition. The hope was that her personality would be rebuilt. It may be possible, but there is no certainty about it. Secondly, it is relevant to bear in mind that she had a vulnerable or fragile personality which might have resulted in the same consequences in any event. But if Dr Connell and Dr Green are right the relevant stress which had to be applied to her was probably something which touched off the trauma in her childhood. It was therefore something which was probably related to her own child, namely Susan, and since Susan is now 12 that condition or that state of affairs would not have lasted indefinitely, and therefore the relevant trauma would have to have occurred probably in the next four years or so. In my judgment the chances of a major breakdown of this sort occurring had the accident not taken place are relatively remote. There were of course chances of minor and relatively temporary troubles occurring from time to time as they had done in the past. That chance was relatively high. It is reasonable to describe the plaintiff's pre-existing life as by no means a bed of roses. Nevertheless, the condition which she now suffers is in my judgment a serious one and calls for a substantial award of damages. I assess the general damages in the sum of £22,500.

Secondly, in so far as the plaintiff is concerned there falls to be considered the cost of care. This falls into two parts, namely pre-trial and for the future. Apart from the first two or three weeks and for periods in hospital and when she was absent she has needed *a* to be cared for since the accident. The plaintiff's claim is based on 25 hours a week at £2 per hour. That cost, £2 an hour, is agreed as being the present rate for a nursing auxillary or some such person, and it is quite clear that no paid help could really be obtained for less than that. I take the figure of £6,500 as being the appropriate cost or the appropriate sum to award for pre-trial care of the plaintiff. For the future the problem is difficult. There are a number of imponderable factors. How long will she need it, whether she *b* might have had the onset of a similar condition in any event, how long the present arrangement which exists in the house will last, and whether if it does not she will be involved in considerably greater expense of having a housekeeper to look after her or going into a paying institution or possibly of her having to be admitted and cared for under the national health service. There is finally the possibility that she may make a successful attempt at suicide. Some of these factors tend to reduce, others tend to increase *c* the appropriate figure.

I start with the proposition that if this condition were to be permanent and there were no diminution in her expectation of life I would take a multiplier of 15 years for a woman of 46. But that figure has to be discounted to reflect the factors to which I have referred. In my judgment the appropriate multiplier is one of 10. I take £2,600 as the multiplicand and that produces a figure of £26,000 for the future cost of care. In addition *d* there are special damages of £45. Counsel for the plaintiffs submitted that she had lost her earning capacity. She had not worked for many years apart from assisting her husband in the house, and it is quite clear that she would not be likely to look for work at least until Susan had grown up and left school. Even then because of the frequency of her psychosomatic troubles it seems to me unlikely that she would have had a high earning capacity. Nevertheless there is to my mind some loss of earning capacity, but it *e* must be assessed at a low sum. I award the sum of £1,000 under that head.

I turn then to the claim of the plaintiff's husband. Although the action for loss of consortium and services has now been abolished by s 2 of the Administration of Justice Act 1982, it survives in relation to those causes of action which accrued before 1 January 1983. I assess the loss of consortium in the sum of £500. The loss of services falls again into two periods, pre-trial and post-trial. Apart from the first few weeks after the accident *f* the plaintiff's husband has been totally deprived of the services of his wife as a cook, housekeeper, assistant in his work and someone to look after Susan. I bear in mind that in awarding £50 a week in respect of the plaintiff's claim for care I must be careful not to duplicate the compensation. But in my judgment the very minimum damage that can be placed on these services is £20 a week, especially since the likelihood is that an element of board and lodging is involved for anyone providing those services. For the *g* period from the accident to date I award £3,250. For the future counsel for the plaintiffs would be content to confine his claim to the period during which Susan will still need the presence of a woman about the house. The need for such a person has been clearly demonstrated, not only by the problems that Susan has already experienced but by her evident dependence on Mrs Clay. I think that this is likely to continue for about five years, and I take a multiplier of 3½ on a multiplicand of £1,040 a year, producing a figure *h* of £3,640. In addition to that there is a sum of £80 travelling expenses which it seems to me should be appropriately awarded to the plaintiff's husband when he went to visit his wife in hospital.

In the result there will be judgment for the plaintiff in the sum of £56,045 and for the plaintiff's husband in the sum of £7,470.

j

Judgment for the plaintiffs.

Solicitors: *Ross Williams* (for the plaintiffs); *Stevensons* (for the first and second defendants); *Gascoin & Co* (for the third and fourth defendants).

K Mydeen Esq   Barrister.

Ali v Secretary of State for the Home Department

COURT OF APPEAL, CIVIL DIVISION

SIR JOHN DONALDSON MR, FOX AND STEPHEN BROWN LJJ

21 FEBRUARY, 1 MARCH 1984

Court of Appeal – Evidence – Further evidence – Principles on which received – Application for judicial review – Applicant seeking order of certiorari to quash decision of immigration officer – Judge refusing application and applicant appealing – Applicant seeking to adduce fresh evidence before Court of Appeal – Evidence available at hearing before trial judge – Whether fresh evidence should be admitted in appeal.

Immigration – Detention – Illegal entrant – Burden of proof that entry illegal – Immigration officials refusing entry clearance certificate because not accepting identity of applicant – Applicant successfully appealing to adjudicator – Applicant obtaining indefinite leave to enter United Kingdom – Secretary of State obtaining further evidence casting doubt on applicant's identity – Whether burden of proof on Secretary of State to show that on balance of probabilities that applicant an illegal entrant – Whether further evidence obtained after adjudicator's decision showing that fraud practised on adjudicator.

The applicant was a citizen of Bangladesh. In 1973 the applicant's father, C, applied for entry clearance certificates for his wife and children, including the applicant. As a result of certain information and doubts that C was the father of the children, the applications were rejected. In March 1977 after the matter was fully investigated an adjudicator held that he was satisfied that C was in fact the father of the children and he allowed the appeal. The applicant was accordingly permitted to enter the United Kingdom. In 1983, as a result of further investigations, the Home Office decided that the applicant was not C's son and ordered his detention as an illegal entrant. The applicant applied for an order of judicial review. The Divisional Court found that, on the evidence which had come into existence since the adjudicator's decision, the Home Office had established that the applicant was not C's son and accordingly was an illegal entrant. The applicant appealed to the Court of Appeal and sought leave to adduce further evidence to support his case that he was C's son.

Held – (1) Applying the principle that there should be finality in litigation, the Court of Appeal would refuse to allow fresh evidence to be adduced on an appeal from a decision of the Divisional Court on an application for judicial review unless the wider interests of justice required the fresh evidence to be admitted. It was an abuse of the process of the Court of Appeal to use an appeal as a means of retrying the originating application on different and better evidence, since the Court of Appeal was limited to deciding whether the Divisional Court's decision was right on the available evidence before it, unless there was new evidence which could not have been made available to the Divisional Court by the exercise of reasonable diligence or unless there was some other exceptional circumstance which justified the admission and consideration of the new evidence by the Court of Appeal. Since the fresh evidence had been clearly available and should have been placed before the Divisional Court, the evidence would not be admitted on appeal (see p 1014 c d f g and p 1017 d to g, post); *Ladd v Marshall* [1954] 3 All ER 745 and *Re Tarling* [1979] 1 All ER 981 applied.

(2) The onus was on the Secretary of State to prove to the satisfaction of the court that, on the balance of probabilities, the applicant was an illegal entrant. The degree of probability was proportionate to the gravity of the issue and, since the issue before the

court involved the liberty of the subject, the degree of probability required was therefore high. Furthermore, the decision of the adjudicator, reached after an investigation on oral *a* testimony, was not merely an element to be taken into account by the Divisional Court together with the new information resulting from the Home Office's investigations which had come into existence after that date; instead, the Divisional Court had in effect to determine whether that new information showed that a fraud had been practised on the adjudicator or was such that it undermined the adjudicator's decision. On the facts and on the balance of probabilities, it had not been established that a fraud had been *b* practised on the adjudicator. The appeal would therefore be allowed (see p 1011 c, p 1014 j to p 1015 e, p 1016 f to j and p 1017 c d and f, post); *Khawaja v Secretary of State for the Home Dept* [1983] 1 All ER 765 applied.

Cases referred to in judgments

Khawaja v Secretary of State for the Home Dept [1983] 1 All ER 765, [1984] AC 74, [1983] 2 *c* WLR 321, HL.
Ladd v Marshall [1954] 3 All ER 745, [1954] 1 WLR 1489, CA.
R v Secretary of State for the Environment, ex p Hackney London BC [1983] 3 All ER 358, [1983] 1 WLR 524, DC; affd [1984] 1 All ER 956, CA.
R v Secretary of State for the Home Dept, ex p Hussain [1978] 2 All ER 423, [1978] 1 WLR 700, CA. *d*
R v Secretary of State for the Home Dept, ex p Miah (1983) Times, 19 July.
Tarling, Re [1979] 1 All ER 981, [1979] 1 WLR 1417, DC.

Case also cited

Leeder v Ellis [1952] 2 All ER 814, [1953] AC 52, PC.

Notes

For the power of the Court of Appeal to receive further evidence on questions of fact, see *e* 37 Halsbury's Laws (4th edn) para 693, and for cases on the subject, see 37(3) Digest (Reissue) 183–191, 3963–3998.
    For judicial review generally, see 37 ibid paras 567–583.
    For illegal entry, see 4 Halsbury's Laws (4th edn) paras 976, 1027, and for detention of persons liable to be removed from the United Kingdom, see ibid para 1009. *f*

Appeal

The applicant, Momin Ali, appealed against the decision of Webster J, hearing the Crown Office list, on 5 October 1983 whereby the judge dismissed an application for judicial review by way of an order for certiorari to bring up and quash the decision of an immigration officer dated 23 January 1983 that the applicant was an illegal entrant. The *g* facts are set out in the judgment of Sir John Donaldson MR.

Sakhawat Husain for the applicant.
John Laws for the Secretary of State.

Cur adv vult *h*

1 March. The following judgments were delivered.

SIR JOHN DONALDSON MR. Momin Ali, son of Cherag Ali, and Fozlu, son of Roquib Ali, are both citizens of Bangladesh. The applicant says that he is Momin. The Secretary of State says that he is Fozlu. If he is Momin, he has permission to stay in this *j* country. If he is Fozlu, he is an illegal immigrant.
    Personation is a continual problem for the immigration authorities and it is much more of a problem when the immigrants come from a country without fully developed personal records. Immigration officers wrestle with the problem both at home and

a abroad and there is a system of appeals to specialist adjudicators, who have unrivalled experience. It is unfortunate that the instant application has arisen in circumstances in which the applicant has no right of appeal to an adjudicator, who would be better equipped to resolve the issues than is a court. It is even more unfortunate that this is not an isolated application.

b Ever since the decision in *R v Secretary of State for the Home Dept, ex p Hussain* [1978] 2 All ER 423, [1978] 1 WLR 700, immigration cases concerning illegal immigrants have formed a material part of the Crown Office list, but so long as the duty of the court was only to consider whether the decision was based on reasonable grounds, the task was manageable. However, in *Khawaja v Secretary of State for the Home Dept* [1983] 1 All ER 765, [1984] AC 74 the House of Lords redefined the supervisory duty of the court in three crucial respects. First, the issue ceased to be whether the Secretary of State had reasonable grounds for his decision and became whether his decision on illegality was *c* justified. Second, the burden of justification was held to lie on the Secretary of State. Third, the standard of proof was held to be commensurate with the seriousness of an issue involving personal liberty.

This is bound to result in a very considerable increase in the number of applications to the Divisional Court at a time when that court is already very fully occupied and it is for consideration whether it would not be more sensible and more efficient to arrange that *d* they be heard by specialist adjudicators.

This dispute as to the applicant's identity is of long standing. In October 1973 application was made to the British High Commission in Dacca for entry clearance certificates for Mr Cherag Ali, his wife and children, including Momin Ali. Mr Cherag Ali was successful on the basis that he was a returning resident. The applications of the others were adjourned because of allegations by an informant and, after further inquiries *e* and the receipt of further allegations from the informant, all the applications were rejected. The basis for the rejection seems to have been doubts whether Mr Cherag Ali was the husband of the lady said to be his wife and whether he was the father of the children, including the present applicant.

There was an appeal to an adjudicator, who in March 1977 allowed the appeal and directed the issue of entry certificates. The applicant was then aged 21. It is clear from *f* the adjudicator's decision that the matter was very fully and carefully investigated. The adjudicator correctly directed himself that the burden of proof lay on Mr Cherag Ali and those who claimed to be his relations to satisfy him that they were indeed his wife and children. The adjudicator recorded that they had discharged this burden.

On the strength of this decision, the applicant was permitted to enter this country without limitation on the duration of his stay. The Home Office now say that they had *g* grave doubts about the correctness of that decision, but did not appeal. The plain fact is that they could not appeal, because the adjudicator made no error of law and they had to have further evidence before they could bypass the adjudicator's decision. All went well for two years, but then the Home Office was informed, by what was called a 'police informant', that the applicant was not the son of Cherag Ali as he claimed, but really a nephew, Fozlu, son of Roquib Ali. I do not know anything about the source of the *h* information, the circumstantial details supplied or the apparent reliability of the source, but it is reasonably clear that this was the same allegation as had earlier been made and investigated and rejected by the adjudicator, who had been told, and may well have accepted, that there were many people of Mr Cherag Ali's village who were jealous of the progress which his family had made.

For whatever reason, in June 1979 the Home Office decided to take the matter further *j* and the applicant was detained briefly and interviewed by an immigration officer, who also interviewed Mr Cherag Ali. It emerged that the applicant had not been living with Mr Cherag Ali for the past six months, because Mr Cherag Ali disapproved of his drinking habits. Nevertheless, Mr Cherag Ali was able to produce the applicant's passport. The immigration officer doubted whether Mr Cherag Ali's wife was old enough to be the mother of the applicant, but the matter which really aroused his suspicions was the fact that the applicant did not know the name of the baby who had been born nine *a* months before and who must have been in the same house with him for three months. I share the immigration officer's surprise, but since it is common ground that the applicant was living in the house with the baby for three months, I would have expected him to know the baby's name whether or not it was his brother.

The applicant was released after a few hours and later his passport was returned to him. He thought, not unreasonably, that the incident was closed. In this he was gravely *b* mistaken.

The following year the applicant visited Bagladesh and at about the same time the British High Commission, on instructions from the Home Office, mounted what can only be described as an 'expedition' to the applicant's home village of Holimpur. There were no less than four entry clearance officers involved, travelling in two Land Rovers. For the last three miles they had to walk and cross two rivers, one by boat and the other *c* by way of what is described as 'a rather precarious bamboo bridge'. It is clear that the local inhabitants regarded them with hostility and at one stage they had to beat a strategic retreat. They were armed with photographs of the applicant and of two other people who were, or claimed to be, sons of Mr Cherag Ali and therefore brothers of the applicant, if he was who he claimed to be. However, it seems probably that the photograph of the applicant was one which had been taken eight years before, when he was 16. What they *d* may not have anticipated was that they would meet the applicant, but this is what happened.

Just outside the village the applicant came from the direction of the bazaar and introduced himself. He asked whether they were making inquiries in connection with his family and, on being told that this was so, invited them to visit Mr Cherag Ali's compound. Two officers went with him and two went to other compounds. *e*

The two who went to the Cherag Ali compound seemed to have concentrated on determining whether the applicant was staying there and disbelieved him when he said that he was. The basis of their disbelief was that he did not seem to have any spare clothes, other than a shirt, and had no washing things. He also had some women's clothing in a suitcase which bore someone else's name and which he said that he had borrowed. The clothing was said to be gifts which he had brought with him. So far as *f* identification was concerned, one villager in this compound identified the applicant as Fozlu, but the rest said that he was Momin. The report relies heavily on this identification as Fozlu and dismisses the contrary identifications with the words, 'The rest of the family all agreed the sponsor's story as naturally they would'.

The officers who went to other compounds had to rely on their photographs and it is fair to say that there were several identifications of the old photograph of Momin as *g* being Fozlu.

The officers clearly had difficulty in getting answers to their questions, but whether this was a sign of hostility to their invasion of the village or whether, as they thought, it was due to a briefing by or on behalf of the applicant may be a matter for conjecture. It may, of course, have been partly one and partly the other. What is, I think, clear is that the entry clearance officers did not go to the village with an open mind. They clearly *h* believed their informants and were going there in order to establish that the applicant was Fozlu and not Momin. This approach is understandable. The Dacca entry clearance officers probably had always thought that the claims of Mr Cherag Ali to be the father of the applicant were fraudulent, but they had been overruled by an adjudicator in London, who was not as familiar with local conditions.

On the strength of this report, the interview with the applicant in June 1979 when he *j* did not know the name of the baby, and the fact that there had been many statements made to the Home Office between 1974 and 1979 that the applicant was not the son of Mr Cherag Ali, the Home Office then decided that the applicant was an illegal immigrant and authorised his detention. However, he could not be traced until 27 January 1983

when he was arrested. The matter was somewhat complicated by the fact that, when
arrested, the applicant told the immigration officers that he had married a United
Kingdom resident in April 1982, by whom he had a son. The suggestion seems to be that
this marriage was effected in order to provide a second line of defence to any attempt to
deport him, but, if so, it suffered from a number of defects, not least the fact that there
was some evidence that one or other or both parties of the marriage may thereby have
been committing bigamy.

The applicant was released on bail when he applied for judicial review and his
application was heard by Webster J on 5 October 1983. The judge dismissed his
application and he was rearrested. He is now in custody and we have to determine his
appeal.

The judge founded his decision on two matters. The first was the results achieved by
the 'expedition', saying that if the applicant had in fact been the son of Mr Cherag Ali he
would have been residing in the village to which he belonged and that it was clear that
he was not so residing. The second matter was his ignorance of the baby's name.
Somewhat surprisingly the only evidence filed in support of the application was an
affidavit by Mr Cherag Ali asserting that the applicant was indeed his son and relying on
the decision of the adjudicator. This led the judge to say:

'Counsel for the Secretary of State also relied, with a very slight emphasis, on the
fact that no evidence has been adduced on this application by the applicant in order
to rebut the inferences drawn from the evidence adduced on behalf of the Secretary
of State. Again, for my part, I do not place much reliance on that. Of course, it is the
case that the only evidence that I have before me and the only evidence that the
various immigration officers had before them that the applicant was an illegal
entrant was the evidence relied on by the Secretary of State. I say that with one
qualification. At all material times, there has been available to the immigration
authorities and to the Secretary of State, a decision of an adjudicator, which is dated
14 March 1977. That decision arose in these circumstances. In October 1973, Cherag
Ali, the applicant's sponsor, applied for an entry clearance certificate in Dacca to
enable his wife and five of his purported children, including this applicant, to join
him in this country. That certificate was refused and the wife and the five children
appealed to the adjudicator against that refusal. The adjudicator allowed that appeal.
He gave his determination and reasons at some length when he did so. Counsel for
the applicant places reliance on that decision and on the reasons for it. However,
although it is right that that decision should not be disregarded, none the less the
evidence to which the immigration officer, the Secretary of State and I have had
primary regard is the evidence which has come into existence since that date. Taking
into account that evidence, I am satisfied that the Secretary of State has established
from the material before him, which is now before me, to a high degree of
probablility, that the applicant was not Momin Ali, the son of Cherag Ali, as he
purported to be when he entered this country in 1977 and again in 1980, but was
Fozlu Ali, the son of Roquib Ali. Accordingly, he was an illegal entrant when he
entered on both these occasions.'

On the hearing of this appeal, the applicant sought to supplement the evidence
available to the judge by his own affidavit offering a full explanation of events when he
met the entry clearance officers in Bangladesh, by an affidavit from the applicant's sister
and by no less than ten other affidavits which one way or another support his case. His
solicitor, in a further affidavit, explained that the reason why none of this evidence was
placed before the judge was that 'It was felt that the case of the applicant was strong
enough and that the evidence now adduced was not necessary'.

This at once raised the question of whether this court, in hearing an appeal from the
Divisional Court in a claim for judicial review, should apply the principles set out in the

judgments in *Ladd v Marshall* [1954] 3 All ER 745 at 748, [1954] 1 WLR 1489 at 1491. They are, per Denning LJ, that—

> 'first, it must be shown that the evidence could not have been obtained with reasonable diligence for use at the trial: second, the evidence must be such that, if given, it would probably have an important influence on the result of the case, although it need not be decisive: third, the evidence must be such as is presumably to be believed, or in other words, it must be apparently credible, although it need not be incontrovertible.'

We refused to allow the evidence to be admitted. In my judgment the evidence met the second and third criteria, but manifestly did not meet the first. Just as I think that the doctrine of issue estoppel has, as such, no place in public law and judicial review (see *R v Secretary of State, ex p Hackney London BC* [1983] 3 All ER 358, [1983] 1 WLR 524, *affd* [1984] 1 All ER 956, CA), so I think that the decision in *Ladd v Marshall* has, as such, no place in that context. However I think that the principles which underlie issue estoppel and the decision in *Ladd v Marshall*, namely that there must be finality in litigation, are applicable, subject always to the discretion of the court to depart from them if the wider interests of justice so require. In expressing this conclusion, I find myself in complete agreement, mutatis mutandis, with the judgment of the Divisional Court, given by Gibson J, in *Re Tarling* [1979] 1 All ER 981 at 987, [1979] 1 WLR 147 at 1422–1423, when he said:

> 'Firstly, it is clear to the court that an applicant for habeas corpus is required to put forward on his initial application the whole of the case which is then fairly available to him. He is not free to advance an application on one ground, and to keep back a separate ground of application as a basis for a second or renewed application to the court. The true doctrine of estoppel known as res judicata does not apply to the decision of this court on an application for habeas corpus . . . There is, however, a wider sense in which the doctrine of res judicata may be applicable, whereby it becomes an abuse of process to raise in subsequent proceedings matters which could, and therefore should, have been litigated in earlier proceedings . . .'

This fresh evidence was clearly available and should have been placed before Webster J. It is not the function of this court, as an appellate court, to retry an originating application on different and better evidence. We are concerned to decide whether the trial judge's decision was right on the materials available to him, unless the new evidence could not have been made available to him by the exercise of reasonable diligence or there is some other exceptional circumstance which justifies its admission and consideration by this court. That is not this case.

I return, therefore, to a consideration of the judge's judgment on the basis of the materials available to him. In *R v Secretary of State for the Home Dept, ex p Miah* (1983) Times, 13 July, Woolf J was also confronted with a situation in which the main issue had been considered by an adjudicator. He said:

> 'Having regard to the fact that the matter has previously been before the adjudicator, who has considered the merits and heard evidence on oath, it seems to me only right that in considering all the evidence now in the way directed by the House of Lords, I should primarily devote my attention to the material which has come to the knowledge of and is available to the Home Office now, which was not available to the Home Office when they appeared before the adjudicator. Having regard largely to that evidence, considered against the background of their previous evidence, I have to come to a conclusion, in effect, whether or not I am satisfied that a fraud was practised on the adjudicator. I certainly have to consider whether the evidence which is now available is such that it undermines that decision of the adjudicator.'

In my judgment this approach is right and it is not the one adopted by the judge. The standard of proof required by the House of Lords where there has been no previous adjudication is that appropriate to an allegation of a serious character and one involving the liberty of the subject. Here an even higher standard is required, because the starting point is a binding decision of an appropriate tribunal in favour of the applicant. That decision may not render the issue of his status res judicata, but it comes very close to it. If it is to be reversed, the Home Office must prove fraud to a standard appropriate to such an allegation.

The judge's approach was to examine the evidence and then add in the decision of the adjudicator as something in the nature of a makeweight. This seems to me to be wholly wrong.

I would accept that the evidence adduced by the Home Office, coupled with the failure by the applicant to produce significant rebutting evidence (he did not himself file any affidavit) gives rise to serious doubts. But doubts are one thing. Finding fraud is quite another. The evidence about the name of the baby is trivial once it is accepted that the applicant lived in the same household. The evidence from Bangladesh is more substantial, but we only have the report of the entry clearance officers who, in my view, were not inquiring, so much as seeking confirmation for a preconceived view. Furthermore, the cross-currents of a population, some of whom were suspicious of the entry clearance officers and some of whom were probably antipathetic to the Cherag Ali family, are likely to muddy the river of truth at the best of times and what emerged seems to me to be quite insufficient to find fraud on the part of an applicant who, on the face of a decision that he was genuine, has come to this country in 1977 and settled here for seven years.

I would allow the appeal and quash the decision of the Secretary of State.

FOX LJ. Cherag Ali came to the United Kingdom in 1963 or thereabouts. In 1973 application was made to the British High Commission, Dacca, for entry certificates to the United Kingdom to enable six persons, namely Sofia Katun and Momin, Nojib, Rahman and Shobib Ali and Salema Katun, to join Cherag Ali here. The application was on the basis that Sofia was the wife of Cherag and that the others were his children. Momin Ali is the present applicant. That application was refused because the Secretary of State was not satisfied that the six applicants were related to Cherag. In particular it appears from para 3 of the affidavit of Mr Mould, one of the immigration officers, filed on the present application, that the entry clearance officer had received information that, inter alia, the present applicant was not Cherag's son. The six applicants then appealed to the adjudicator.

The adjudicator gave a very full written decision in March 1977. The adjudicator, on the third page of his decision, refers to letters 'which suggested that some of the applicants were imposters'.

Cherag gave evidence before the adjudicator for four hours and was cross-examined. Accepting that the burden of proof was on the applicants, the adjudicator nevertheless found that, on the balance of probabilities, the burden was discharged and that the appellants were the persons they claimed to be. He therefore directed entry certificates be issued. All the applicants were duly granted leave in July 1977 to enter the United Kingdom for an indefinite period.

In 1979 the Home Office received information from 'a police informant' that Momin, the present applicant, and his brother Nojib were not the sons of Cherag but were nephews. The Secretary of State's case is that the applicant is the son of Roquib Ali. We do not know, in any further detail, the nature of the information so supplied. However, in consequence of that information, the Home Office instituted further inquiries. These were, as to part, in England and part in Bangladesh.

In England it was ascertained that the applicant was no longer living with Cherag.

That was in June 1979; he had ceased to live with Cherag about six months earlier. It appears that the applicant did not know the name of the baby born to Cherag three   *a* months before the applicant's departure from Cherag's home.

In 1980 the applicant visited Bangladesh. At the same time the British High Commission instructed four entry clearance officers to visit Holimpur, which was the applicant's village, and make enquiries about his identity.

On arrival at the village the four officers split into two groups. One group visited Cherag's compound. The applicant went with them. He was asked if he slept there and   *b* he said he did. He produced a suitcase to prove it. The suitcase bore the name of another person (who, he said, had lent it to him) and which contained women's clothing which he said he had bought as gifts. When asked where his own clothes were he produced one shirt and said the rest were at the laundry. In the house was a man named Ilias Ali. When asked who was Fozlu, son of Roquib Ali, he pointed to the applicant. However, the report of the entry officer says: 'The rest of the family all agreed the sponsor's [Cherag's]   *c* story as naturally they would.'

The other group of two entry officers visited another compound. In relation to the identification of photographs by this group the following occurred according to the officer's report. (i) Waris Ali identified a photograph of the applicant as being Fozlu, the son of Roquib Ali. (ii) Moskondor Ali identified the photograph as being Fozlu, but said he was the son of Cherag. (iii) Shawkat Ali did not recognise Momin's photograph.   *d* Subsequently he asked to see the photograph again and identified Momin as the son of Cherag because he saw him in Cherag's house in the United Kingdom. (iv) Haris Ali identified the applicant's photograph as Fozlu, son of Roquib Ali. (v) Moh'd Abdul, a member of the Union Council, identified a photograph of the applicant as that of a son of Roquib Ali (name unknown) of the village of Debarachak, which is a village in his district as also is Holimpur. (vi) Abdul Aziz could not recognise a photograph of the   *e* applicant. (vii) Monhor Noquib could not identify a photograph of the applicant but said he was not a son of Cherag.

Since we refused leave to the applicant to file further evidence on the hearing of this appeal, the only evidence filed on his behalf is the affidavit in support of the application for judicial review. That affidavit was, however, sworn by Cherag who deposes that the applicant is his son by Sofia.   *f*

The onus is on the Secretary of State to prove to the satisfaction of the court that, on the balance of probabilities, the applicant is an illegal entrant. The degree of probability is proportionate to the gravity of the issue and, since the present issue involves the liberty of the subject, the degree of probability required is high (see *Khawaja v Secretary of State for the Home Dept* [1983] 1 All ER 765, [1984] AC 74).

The judge, in considering the proper approach to the case said that, while the decision   *g* of the adjudicator should not be disregarded, nevertheless the evidence to which the immigration officer, the Secretary of State and he himself had primary regard was the evidence that had come into existence since that date. I do not feel able to agree with that. I think it attaches insufficient importance to the decision of the adjudicator reached after an investigation on oral testimony. In my opinion the adjudicator's decision is not merely an element to be taken into account together with the new evidence. It is of more   *h* fundamental importance than that. Of course, all the evidence must be considered but I agree with the view expressed by Woolf J in *R v Secretary of State for the Home Dept, ex p Miah* (1983) Times, 19 July that, in such a case, the court has to come to a conclusion, in effect, whether or not it is satisfied that a fraud was practised on the adjudicator. He cannot have been innocently misled.

In approaching these problems, it is necessary to be clear as to the function of the four   *j* entry clearance officers who visited Cherag's village. That they were engaged on an honest search for facts I do not doubt. But they were sent on behalf of one party to what was likely to become, if it was not already, an active dispute. They were not engaged on an independent judicial inquiry. That is not a criticism of them at all but it needs to be

kept in mind when, for example, one considers their statement that 'the rest of family all
a agreed the sponsor's story as naturally they would'.

Looking at the whole of the facts, it seems to me that there are substantial indications
both ways. Some of the villagers identified the applicant's photograph as that of Fozlu.
One could not recognise the photograph of the applicant. On the other hand, some
members of Cherag's family supported Cherag's case. And two villagers identifed the
photograph as a son of Cherag. Then there is Cherag himself. He, at least, knows the
b truth. He gave evidence for four hours before the adjudicator and was subjected to what
the adjudicator described as 'testing' cross-examination. The adjudicator, at the end of it
all, said that he found nothing sufficient to say that Cherag's evidence on the whole was
not credible. Further, Cherag in the present proceedings has sworn that the applicant is
his son.

The evidence that the applicant could not state the name of the baby (which is odd on
c any view of the case since he was living in the house for three months after the child was
born) and the episode of the suitcase do not seem to me to take the matter much further.

At the end, I am not satisfied on the balance of probabilities, and to the high standard
which the nature of the case requires, that the adjudicator was deceived. It is possible
that he was, but I am left in doubt about it since the Secretary of State's evidence on this
application is not tested by cross-examination and, in any event, is not all one way. I
d would allow the appeal accordingly.

As to the principles applicable to the admission of further evidence in such cases as
this, I agree with Sir John Donaldson MR. But accepting the existence of a wider
discretion in the court to admit fresh evidence on this appeal than exists in ordinary civil
litigation, I see no reason to exercise it in favour of the applicant here. The court is
exercising appellate jurisdiction from the decision of the judge. It is not a jurisdiction to
e rehear the whole case on new evidence. The evidence now sought to be adduced could
perfectly well have been placed before the judge.

STEPHEN BROWN LJ. I have had the advantage of reading the judgments of Sir
John Donaldson MR and of Fox LJ. I agree that the appeal should be allowed for the
f reasons which they give. I also agree that the further evidence sought to be admitted on
behalf of the appellant should not be admitted. The issue in the present case was entirely
one of fact and in my judgment the principles underlying the decision in *Ladd v Marshall*
[1954] 3 All ER 745, [1954] 1 WLR 1489 should apply.

Appeal allowed.
g

Solicitors: *B C Mascarenhas*, Wood Green (for the applicant); *Treasury Solicitor*.

Frances Rustin   Barrister.

Sidaway v Bethlem Royal Hospital Governors and others

COURT OF APPEAL, CIVIL DIVISION

SIR JOHN DONALDSON MR, DUNN AND BROWNE-WILKINSON LJJ

8, 9, 10, 13, 14, 23 FEBRUARY 1984

Medical practitioner – Negligence – Test of liability – Risk of misfortune inherent in treatment proposed by doctor – Doctor's duty to warn of inherent risk of misfortune – Operation to relieve persistent pain in neck resulting in serious disablement of patient – Doctor warning patient of material risks but not of all risks inherent in operation – Whether standard of care required of doctor in giving advice before operation the same as that normally required of medical practitioner in course of diagnosis and treatment – Whether higher standard requiring full disclosure to patient of all details and risks before operation.

The plaintiff was advised by a surgeon employed by the defendant hospital governors to have an operation on her spinal cord to relieve persistent pain in her neck and shoulders. Prior to the operation the surgeon told the plaintiff of the possibility of disturbing a nerve root and the consequences of doing so, but he did not mention the possibility of danger to the spinal cord. The plaintiff consented to the operation, which in the event resulted in the plaintiff being severely disabled. She brought an action against, inter alios, the hospital governors for damages for personal injury, contending that the surgeon had been in breach of the duty of care he owed the plaintiff because he had failed to warn her of all the possible risks inherent in the operation, so that the plaintiff had not been in a position to give an 'informed consent' to the operation. At the trial there was expert evidence that there was approximately a 1% to 2% risk of damage to the nerve roots and a lesser risk of damage to the spinal cord. The trial judge dismissed the plaintiff's action and the plaintiff appealed.

Held – When advising a patient about a proposed course of treatment a doctor was under a general duty to disclose, or withhold, such information as was reasonable in all the circumstances to enable the patient to make a rational choice whether to agree to or refuse the proposed treatment. The standard of care which the doctor was required to exercise in discharging his duty to inform the patient of risks inherent in the treatment was the same as that required of the doctor in his diagnosis and treatment, namely to act in accordance with a practice rightly accepted by a body of skilled and experienced medical men. It followed that the doctrine of informed consent, based on full disclosure of all the facts to the patient, was not the appropriate test in English law, since the relevant circumstances determining the ambit of the duty of disclosure included the patient's age, whether the patient was of sound mind, the patient's true wishes and whether the patient's rational choice would be impaired if certain information were not withheld from him. Since the expert evidence showed that it was in accordance with accepted medical practice not to give a specific warning of the risk of spinal cord damage occurring in the operation performed on the plaintiff because the risk of such damage was too remote, the judge had been right to dismiss the plaintiff's claim. The plaintiff's appeal would therefore be dismissed (see p 1026 f to p 1027 a and e to j, p 1028 b to j, p 1029 c and j to p 1030 j, p 1031 b, p 1032 c d and f to p 1033 a and d to g, p 1034 f to j and p 1035 a to p 1036 b, post).

Bolam v Friern Hospital Management Committee [1957] 2 All ER 118 applied.

Canterbury v Spence (1972) 464 F 2d 772 and *Reibl v Hughes* (1980) 114 DLR (3d) 1 not followed.

Per Browne-Wilkinson LJ. In general a doctor is not under a duty to inform a patient of the ordinary risks normally attendant on an operation (see p 1034 j, post).

Notes

For the standard of care required of doctors, see 34 Halsbury's Laws (4th edn) para 12, and for cases on the subject, see 33 Digest (Reissue) 262–288, 2162–2330.

Cases referred to in judgments

a   *Billage v Southee* (1852) 9 Hare 534, 68 ER 623.

Bolam v Friern Hospital Management Committee [1957] 2 All ER 118, [1957] 1 WLR 582.

Canterbury v Spence (1972) 464 F 2d 772, US App DC; *cert denied* 409 US 1064.

Cavanagh v Ulster Weaving Co Ltd [1959] 2 All ER 745, [1960] AC 145, [1959] 3 WLR 262, HL.

Chatterton v Gerson [1981] 1 All ER 257, [1981] QB 432, [1981] 3 WLR 1003.

b   *Greaves & Co (Contractors) Ltd v Baynham Meikle Partners* [1975] 3 All ER 99, [1975] 1 WLR 1095, CA.

Hedley Byrne & Co Ltd v Heller & Partners Ltd [1963] 2 All ER 575, [1964] AC 465, [1963] 3 WLR 101, HL.

Hills v Potter [1983] 3 All ER 716.

Hopp v Lepp (1980) 112 DLR (3d) 67, Can SC.

c   *Hunter v Hanley* 1955 SLT 213.

Maynard v West Midlands Regional Health Authority (1983) Times, 9 May, HL.

Morris v West Hartlepool Steam Navigation Co Ltd [1956] 1 All ER 385, [1956] AC 552, [1956] 1 WLR 177, HL.

Mutual Life and Citizens' Assurance Co Ltd v Evatt [1971] 1 All ER 150, [1971] AC 793, [1971] 2 WLR 23, PC.

d   *Nocton v Lord Ashburton* [1914] AC 932, [1914–15] All ER Rep 45, HL.

R v Clarence (1888) 22 QBD 23, [1886–90] All ER Rep 133, CCR.

R v Flattery (1877) 2 QBD 410, CCR.

Reibl v Hughes (1980) 114 DLR (3d) 1, Can SC.

Saif Ali v Sydney Mitchell & Co (a firm), P (third party) [1978] 3 All ER 1033, [1980] AC 198, [1978] 3 WLR 849, HL.

e   *Whitehouse v Jordon* [1981] 1 All ER 267, [1981] 1 WLR 246, HL.

Cases also cited

Bly v Rhoads (1976) 222 SE 2d 783.

Clarke v Adams (1950) 94 SJ 599.

Cobbs v Grant (1972) 8 Cal 3d 229, Calif SC.

f   *Gillick v West Norfolk and Wisbech Area Health Authority* [1984] 1 All ER 365, [1983] 3 WLR 859.

Hatcher v Black (1954) Times, 2 July.

Huguenin v Baseley (1807) 14 Ves 273, [1803–13] All ER Rep 1, LC.

Kenny v Lockwood [1932] 1 DLR 507.

Letany v Cooper [1964] 2 All ER 929, [1965] 1 QB 232.

g   *Lindsey CC v Marshall* [1936] 2 All ER 1076, [1937] AC 97.

Richter v Estate Hammann 1976 (3) SA 226 (CPD).

Schloendorff v Society of New York Hospital (1914) 211 NY.

Smith v Auckland Hospital Board [1965] NZLR 191.

Appeal

h   The plaintiff, Amy Doris Sidaway, appealed against the decision of Skinner J on 19 February 1982 dismissing the plaintiff's action against the first defendants, the Board of Governors of the Bethlem Royal and Maudsley Hospitals, and the second defendants, Coutts & Co and Mrs Valda Helen Falconer, the executors of the estate of Murray Falconer deceased, for damages for personal injury suffered by the plaintiff as a result of an operation carried out on the plaintiff by Mr Murray Falconer while employed by the first *j*   defendants. The facts are set out in the judgment of Sir John Donaldson MR.

Leslie Joseph QC and *Gerald Rabie* for the plaintiff.
Adrian Whitfield QC and *Nicola Davies* for the defendants.

Cur adv vult

23 February. The following judgments were delivered.

SIR JOHN DONALDSON MR. Medicine is not now, and never has been, an exact science. Despite the exercise of the greatest skill, things can go wrong. They went wrong in the case of Mrs Sidaway. She underwent an operation for the relief of pain and ended up severely disabled. The issue in this appeal is not whether anything could have been done to avoid this result. It is whether she should have been more fully informed of the risks before she agreed to the operation. Skinner J held that had the plaintiff been more fully informed she would not have agreed to undergo the operation. But he also held that she was told as much as any patient would have been told by many responsible skilled and experienced neuro-surgeons. This, in his judgment, was all that in law she was entitled to expect and he dismissed her claim.

The plaintiff's medical problems began in 1958 when she injured an elbow and, as a result, suffered persistent pain. She underwent an operation on the elbow and it was immobilised in plaster. This was successful in relieving the pain in her elbow, but she then began to experience pain in her neck and right shoulder. This was treated by a number of conservative procedures, but without success. She was then referred to Mr Falconer, who was a neuro-surgeon at the Maudsley Hospital. He correctly diagnosed that the cause of the pain was a narrowing of the spinal column between the fifth and sixth vertebrae. He therefore decided to remove the disc between these vertebrae and to fuse them by a bone graft.

This operation, which took place in December 1960, was successful, although it was two years before the pain disappeared. The plaintiff described Mr Falconer as 'a man of very, very few words'. She was to be given a myelogram as an aid to diagnosis, but had to ask the nursing staff what was involved. And neither Mr Falconer, nor anyone else, told her that she was to have a bone graft. This she only discovered when she came round from the anaesthetic. However, as I say, the operation was a success and the plaintiff, who was seen by Mr Falconer annually between 1960 and 1970, remained free from pain. This continued until 1973, when the pain recurred. At the same time the plaintiff received a letter from Mr Falconer asking her how she was getting on. Bearing in mind that the plaintiff was not a private patient, it is a great tribute to Mr Falconer's compassion and interest that he wrote as he did. In reply the plaintiff wrote reporting that she was experiencing 'pain in the right arm and shoulder, the same pain as I have experienced before, also the left forearm'.

Mr Falconer replied by inviting her to attend his out-patient clinic. He decided to do another myelogram, but, for a variety of reasons, she was not admitted to hospital for this purpose until 11 October 1974. By then the pain was worse. Mr Falconer decided to do a further operation and the plaintiff remained in hospital as an in-patient until this was done on 29 October. The nature of the operation and the risks involved are described in the following passage from Skinner J's judgment:

'The operation consisted of a laminectomy of the fourth cervical vertebra and a facetectomy or foraminectomy of the disc space between the fourth and fifth cervical vertebrae. [The object of this exercise is to widen the space between the vertebrae through which the nerves emerge.] A laminectomy is an excision of the posterior arch of the vertebrae. It gives the surgeon access to the foramen or channel through which nerves travel from the spine laterally. Randomly placed in the foramina, running alongside the nerves, are small blood vessels known as the radicular arteries. These supply blood to the cord and are extremely vulnerable because of (a) their size and (b) the unpredictable nature of their siting. In one foramen, there may be one, two or more radicular arteries. Their rupture or blockage may cause damage to the cord by depriving it temporarily or permanently of its blood supply at the relevant level. In the operation Mr Falconer freed the fourth cervical nerve root by removing the facets, or small bony protuberances, from the fourth vertebra and used a dental drill to free the nerve within the foramen... Mr Falconer was working at times *a* within three millimetres of the spinal cord. What is more, the operation involved exposing the cord and interfering with the nerve roots. It is common ground between all the distinguished neuro-surgeons who have given evidence before me that this procedure involves specific risks of damage above those common to and inherent in any operation under general anaesthetic ... The specific risks in the procedure, according to Mr Uttley, who was called for the plaintiff, are (a) damage to the spinal cord by direct contact or indirectly by damage to the radicular arteries

b and (b) damage to the nerve roots. The possible effects of such damage, he said, covered the whole spectrum from pins and needles to paraplegia. He put the degree of risk at between 1% and 2%. Mr Schurr, a consultant colleague of Mr Falconer for many years and his successor as director of the unit, did not dissent from this figure, though he disliked its expression in percentage terms. He considered the danger of damage to the root or cord in the hands of a good surgeon as between 1% and 2%: a

c rare occurrence but a material risk. Mr Polkey, now a consultant in the unit, and Professor Logue accepted that the risk was a material one but emphasised that it was not a single risk. The risk of spinal cord damage by itself was, in their opinion, less than 1%.'

The judge's conclusion as to the risks involved is contained in the following passage from

d his judgment:

'In my judgment, the operation which the plaintiff underwent carried an inherent risk that, even if the surgeon exercised proper care and skill, the spinal cord might be damaged causing weakness or paralysis from the C4/5 level and that the nerve root might be damaged causing pain and/or weakness along the path of the nerve.

e The risk was a material one, best expressed to a layman as a 1% to 2% risk of ill effects ranging from the mild to the catastrophic.'

However, I think it is common ground that the risk of damage to the spinal column is much less than that of risk to the root of a nerve. On the other hand, the consequences of damage to the spinal column are very much more serious. Whereas damage to the root

f of a nerve may produce localised numbness, damage to the spinal cord can produce paralysis. In the case of the plaintiff, whatever went wrong has produced a severe impairment of movement on her right side and some ill effects on the left. Her loss has been assessed in monetary terms at £67,000.

There was considerable difficulty in deciding what information the plaintiff was given before she agreed to the operation, because it is no doubt difficult for her to remember,

g and Mr Falconer died in 1977. However, there is no challenge to the judge's conclusion that (a) Mr Falconer did not tell the plaintiff that this was an operation of choice or an 'elective operation', meaning thereby that it could be postponed or even refused at the price of enduring pain and possibly increasing pain meanwhile, and (b) while Mr Falconer told the plaintiff of the possibility of disturbing a nerve root and of the consequences of doing so, he did not refer to the danger of damage to the spinal cord.

h The judge also held (a) that in refraining from drawing the plaintiff's attention to these two very important factors, Mr Falconer 'was following a practice which, in 1974, would have been accepted as proper by a responsible body of skilled and experienced neuro-surgeons', and (b) that Mr Falconer 'did not make a full disclosure to the plaintiff of all the risks involved in the operation she was about to undergo so that she was in a position to make a fully informed decision whether to agree to it'.

j In dismissing the plaintiff's claim the judge directed himself in the way in which McNair J directed the jury in *Bolam v Friern Hospital Management Committee* [1957] 2 All ER 118, [1957] 1 WLR 582. He declined an invitation to redefine or develop the law on the lines which appealed to the Supreme Court of Canada in *Reibl v Hughes* (1980) 114 DLR (3d) 1 at 13. The issue in this appeal is whether he was right and, if he was not, (a) what is the correct self-direction? and (b) what is the effect on the plaintiff's claim?

Bolam v Friern Hospital Management Committee

Mr Bolam was a voluntary patient in a mental hospital and, during the course of being   *a*
administered electro-convulsive therapy, he suffered bilateral 'stove in' fractures of the
acetabula. He made three allegations against the hospital, namely (1) that they failed to
administer a relaxant drug before treating him, (2) that, not having administered such a
drug, they failed to ensure sufficient manual restraint and (3) that they failed to warn
him of the risks involved in the treatment. The first two complaints relate to medical
treatment. The third relates to the right of a patient to agree or to refuse to agree to   *b*
treatment advised by his doctors. McNair J directed the jury in these terms ([1957] 2 All
ER 118 at 121–122, [1957] 1 WLR 582 at 586–588):

> 'Before I turn to that, I must tell you what in law we mean by "negligence". In
> the ordinary case which does not involve any special skill, negligence in law means
> this: Some failure to do some act which a reasonable man in the circumstances   *c*
> would do, or doing some act which a reasonable man in the circumstances would
> not do; and if that failure or doing of that act results in injury, then there is a cause
> of action. How do you test whether this act or failure is negligent? In an ordinary
> case it is generally said, that you judge by the action of the man in the street. He is
> the ordinary man. In one case it has been said that you judge it by the conduct of
> the man on the top of a Clapham omnibus. He is the ordinary man. But where you   *d*
> get a situation which involves the use of some special skill or competence, then the
> test whether there has been negligence or not is not the test of the man on the top
> of a Clapham omnibus, because he has not got this special skill. The test is the
> standard of the ordinary skilled man exercising and professing to have that special
> skill. A man need not possess the highest expert skill at the risk of being found
> negligent. It is well-established law that it is sufficient if he exercises the ordinary   *e*
> skill of an ordinary competent man exercising that particular art. I do not think that
> I quarrel much with any of the submissions in law which have been put before you
> by counsel. Counsel for the plaintiff put it in this way, that in the case of a medical
> man negligence means failure to act in accordance with the standards of reasonably
> competent medical men at the time. That is a perfectly accurate statement, as long
> as it is remembered that there may be one or more perfectly proper standards; and   *f*
> if a medical man conforms with one of those proper standards then he is not
> negligent. Counsel for the plaintiff was also right, in my judgment, in saying that a
> mere personal belief that a particular technique is best is no defence unless that
> belief is based on reasonable grounds. That again is unexceptionable. But the
> emphasis which is laid by counsel for the defendants is on this aspect of negligence:
> He submitted to you that the real question on which you have to make up your   *g*
> mind on each of the three major points to be considered is whether the defendants,
> in acting in the way they did, were acting in accordance with a practice of competent
> respected professional opinion. Counsel for the defendants submitted that if you are
> satisfied that they were acting in accordance with a practice of a competent body of
> professional opinion, then it would be wrong for you to hold that negligence was
> established. I referred, before I started these observations, to a statement which is   *h*
> contained in a recent Scottish case, *Hunter* v. *Hanley* (1955 SLT 213 at 217), which
> dealt with medical matters, where the Lord President (LORD CLYDE) said this: "In
> the realm of diagnosis and treatment there is ample scope for genuine difference of
> opinion, and one man clearly is not negligent merely because his conclusion differs
> from that of other professional men, nor because he has displayed less skill or
> knowledge than others would have shown. The true test for establishing negligence   *j*
> in diagnosis or treatment on the part of a doctor is whether he has been proved to
> be guilty of such failure as no doctor of ordinary skill would be guilty of if acting
> with ordinary care." If that statement of the true test is qualified by the words "in
> all the circumstances", counsel for the plaintiff would not seek to say that that
> expression of opinion does not accord with English law. It is just a question of

a

b

c

expression. I myself would prefer to put it this way: A doctor is not guilty of negligence if he has acted in accordance with a practice accepted as proper by a responsible body of medical men skilled in that particular art. I do not think there is much difference in sense. It is just a different way of expressing the same thought. Putting it the other way round, a man is not negligent, if he is acting in accordance with such a practice, merely because there is a body of opinion that takes a contrary view. At the same time, that does not mean that a medical man can obstinately and pig-headedly carry on with some old technique if it has been proved to be contrary to what is really substantially the whole of informed medical opinion. Otherwise you might get men today saying: "I don't believe in anaesthetics. I don't believe in antiseptics. I am going to continue to do my surgery in the way it was done in the eighteenth century". That clearly would be wrong. Before I deal with the details of the case, it is right to say this, that it is not essential for you to decide which of two practices is the better practice, as long as you accept that what [the defendant consultant psychiatrist] did was in accordance with a practice accepted by responsible persons . . .'

The *Bolam* direction was considered and approved by the House of Lords in *Whitehouse v Jordan* [1981] 1 All ER 267, [1981] 1 WLR 246 and in *Maynard v West Midlands Regional Health Authority* (1983) Times, 9 May. In *Maynard's* case Lord Scarman delivered a speech with which the other members of the House agreed. He said:

d

e

f

g

h

j

'The only other question of law in the appeal is as to the nature of the duty owed by a doctor to his patient. The most recent authoritative formulation is that by Lord Edmund-Davies in the *Whitehouse* case [1981] 1 All ER 276 at 277, [1981] 1 WLR 246 at 258. Quoting from the judgment of McNair J in *Bolam v Friern Hospital Management Committee* he said that "'The test is the standard of the ordinary skilled man exercising and professing to have that special skill.' If a surgeon fails to measure up to that standard in *any* respect ('clinical judgment' or otherwise), he has been negligent . . ."[Lord Edmund-Davies's emphasis.] The present case may be classified as one of clinical judgment. Two distinguished consultants, a physician and a surgeon experienced in the treatment of chest diseases, formed a judgment as to what was, in their opinion, in the best interests of their patient. They recognised that tuberculosis was the most likely diagnosis. But, in their opinion, there was an unusual factor, viz swollen glands in the mediastinum unaccompanied by any evidence of lesion in the lungs. Hodgkin's disease, carcinoma and sarcoidosis were, therefore, possibilities. The danger they thought was Hodgkin's disease; though unlikely, it was, if present, a killer (as treatment was understood in 1970) unless remedial steps were taken in its early stage. They therefore decided on mediastinoscopy, an operative procedure which would provide them with a biopsy from the swollen gland which could be subjected to immediate microscopic examination. It is said that the evidence of tuberculosis was so strong that it was unreasonable and wrong to defer diagnosis and to put their patient to the risks of the operation. The case against them is not mistake or carelessness in performing the operation, which it is admitted was properly carried out, but an error of judgment in requiring the operation to be undertaken. A case which is based on an allegation that a fully considered decision of two consultants in the field of their special skill was negligent clearly presents certain difficulties of proof. It is not enough to show that there is a body of competent professional opinion which considers that theirs was a wrong decision, if there also exists a body of professional opinion, equally competent, which supports the decision as reasonable in the circumstances. It is not enough to show that subsequent events show that the operation need never have been performed, if at the time the decision to operate was taken it was reasonable in the sense that a responsible body of medical opinion would have accepted it as proper. I do not think that the words of the Lord President (Clyde) in *Hunter v Hanley* 1955 SLT 213 at 217 can be bettered [and then Lord

Scarman quoted that part of the judgment of the Lord President which was cited by McNair J in the passage from *Bolam v Friern Hospital Management Committee* that I *a* have quoted. Lord Scarman continued:] I would only add that a doctor who professes to exercise a special skill must exercise the ordinary skill of his speciality. Differences of opinion and practice exist, and will always exist, in the medical as in other professions. There is seldom any one answer exclusive of all others to problems of professional judgment. A court may prefer one body of opinion to the other; but that is no basis for a conclusion of negligence.' *b*

In the instant appeal it is accepted, as it must be, that this is the law in relation to complaints of negligence in diagnosis and treatment, the topics with which *Whitehouse* and *Maynard* were concerned. However, it is submitted that there has been no consideration or approval by this court or by the House of Lords of the *Bolam* direction in the context of a duty to inform the patient of the risks inherent in the treatment proposed *c* to be carried out. In my judgment this is correct, although, if there is no valid distinction, the *Bolam* direction must also be applied to this other aspect of the doctor/patient relationship. It was so applied by Bristow J in *Chatterton v Gerson* [1981] 1 All ER 257, [1981] QB 432 and by Hirst J in *Hills v Potter* [1983] 3 All ER 716.

United States law *d*

It is a feature common to both the law of England and of all the United States that, subject to certain immaterial exceptions, the consent of the patient is required to surgical procedures. In the absence of consent, the surgeon commits an assault and is liable for damages for trespass to the person. However, in some of the United States this has been taken further and it has been held that what is required in order to avoid a charge of assault or a liability for trespass to the person is a consent based on knowledge of all the *e* facts relevant to the formation of an intelligent and informed consent.

The leading authority is probably *Canterbury v Spence* (1972) 464 F 2d 772. The starting point of the decision is expressed (at 780) to be—

'the concept, fundamental in American jurisprudence, that "[e]very human being of adult years and sound mind has a right to determine what shall be done with his *f* own body. . . ." True consent to what happens to one's self is the informed exercise of a choice, and that entails an opportunity to evaluate knowledgeably the options available and the risks attendant upon each. The average patient has little or no understanding of the medical arts, and ordinarily has only his physician to whom he can look for enlightenment with which to reach an intelligent decision. From these almost axiomatic considerations springs the need, and in turn the requirement, *g* of a reasonable divulgence by physician to patient to make such a decision possible.'

The court then considered what was the extent of the duty of disclosure and concluded (at 784) that it should be—

'a standard set by law for physicians rather than one which physicians may or *h* may not impose upon themselves.'

The standard adopted was a duty to disclose all 'material' risk inherent in the proposed treatment, and what was material was to be judged by a 'prudent patient' test (at 787):

'[a] risk is thus material when a reasonable person, in what the physician knows or should know to be the patient's position, would be likely to attach significance to *j* the risk or cluster of risks in deciding whether or not to forego the proposed therapy.'

The court then concluded that where a doctor failed to make the appropriate disclosure a patient could either treat the consent as a nullity and sue for battery (trespass to the person) or treat the non-disclosure as negligence. The periods of limitation applicable to these courses of action are different and so are the measures of damage.

Canadian law

a   In *Hopp v Lepp* (1980) 112 DLR (3d) 67 the Alberta Court of Appeal had reversed the trial judge's finding that the doctor had given the patient sufficient information before obtaining his consent to the surgical procedures. It had then proceeded to give judgment for the patient on the basis that there was no true consent and that he was entitled to damages for battery or assault. The Supreme Court of Canada restored the trial judge's finding as to the sufficiency of the disclosure and, accordingly, did not have to consider

b   whether, if the disclosure had not been sufficient, there would have been such a liability. The duty of disclosure was defined in the following terms (at 81):

'In summary, the decided cases appear to indicate that, in obtaining the consent of a patient for the performance upon him of a surgical operation, a surgeon, generally, should answer any specific questions posed by the patient as to the risks involved and should, without being questioned, disclose to him the nature of the

c   proposed operation, its gravity, any material risks and any special or unusual risks attendant upon the performance of the operation. However, having said that, it should be added that the scope of the duty of disclosure and whether or not it has been breached are matters which must be decided in relation to the circumstances of each particular case.'

d   In *Reibl v Hughes* (1980) 114 DLR (3d) 1 at 10–11 the Supreme Court of Canada rejected the concept that an uninformed consent to surgical procedures is not a true consent, Laskin CJC saying:

'In situations where the allegation is that attendant risks which should have been disclosed were not communicated to the patient and yet the surgery or other medical treatment carried out was that to which the plaintiff consented (there being no

e   negligence basis of liability for the recommended surgery or treatment to deal with the patient's condition), I do not understand how it can be said that the consent was vitiated by the failure of disclosure so as to make the surgery or other treatment an unprivileged, inconsented [sic] to and intentional invasion of the patient's bodily integrity. I can appreciate the temptation to say that the genuineness of consent to

f   medical treatment depends on proper disclosure of the risks which it entails, but in my view, unless there has been misrepresentation or fraud to secure consent to the treatment, a failure to disclose the attendant risks, however serious, should go to negligence rather than to battery. Although such a failure relates to an informed choice of submitting to or refusing recommended and appropriate treatment, it arises as the breach of an anterior duty of due care, comparable in legal obligation to the duty of due care in carrying out the particular treatment to which the patient

g   has consented. It is not a test of the validity of the consent.'

The Supreme Court of Canada followed its own decision on the duty of disclosure in *Hopp v Lepp*, but Laskin CJC elaborated on the standard to be applied (at 12–13):

'I think the Ontario Court of Appeal went too far, when dealing with the standard

h   of disclosure of risks, in saying . . . that "the manner in which the nature and degree of risk is explained to a particular patient is better left to the judgment of the doctor in dealing with the man before him". Of course, it can be tested by expert medical evidence but that too is not determinative. The patient may have expressed certain concerns to the doctor and the latter is obliged to meet them in a reasonable way. What the doctor knows or should know that the particular patient deems relevant

j   to a decision whether to undergo prescribed treatment goes equally to his duty of disclosure as do the material risks recognized as a matter of required medical knowledge. It is important to examine this issue in greater detail. The Ontario Court of Appeal appears to have adopted a professional medical standard, not only for determining what are the material risks that should be disclosed but also, and concurrently, for determining whether there has been a breach of the duty of disclosure. This was also the approach of the trial Judge, notwithstanding that on the facts he found against the defendant. (Indeed, the trial Judge seems also to have *a* overstated the duty of disclosure. The Court of Appeal, in contrast, seems to have understated it. Generally, the failure to mention statistics should not affect the duty to inform nor be a factor in deciding whether the duty has been breached.) To allow expert medical evidence to determine what risks are material and, hence, should be disclosed and, correlatively, what risks are not material is to hand over to the medical profession the entire question of the scope of the duty of disclosure, including the *b* question whether there has been a breach of that duty. Expert medical evidence is, of course, relevant to findings as to the risks that reside in or are a result of recommended surgery or other treatment. It will also have a bearing on their materiality but this is not a question that is to be concluded on the basis of the expert medical evidence alone. The issue under consideration is a different issue from that involved where the question is whether the doctor carried out his professional *c* activities by applicable professional standards. What is under consideration here is the patient's right to know what risks are involved in undergoing or foregoing certain surgery or other treatment. The materiality of non-disclosure of certain risks to an informed decision is a matter for the trier of fact, a matter on which there would, in all likelihood, be medical evidence but also other evidence, including evidence from the patient or from members of his family. It is, of course, possible *d* that a particular patient may waive aside any question of risks and be quite prepared to submit to the surgery or treatment, whatever they be. Such a situation presents no difficulty. Again, it may be the case that a particular patient may, because of emotional factors, be unable to cope with facts relevant to recommended surgery or treatment and the doctor may, in such a case, be justified in withholding or generalizing information as to which he would otherwise be required to be more *e* specific.'

English law

Consent

I am wholly satisfied that as a matter of English law a consent is not vitiated by a failure on the part of the doctor to give the patient sufficient information before the *f* consent is given. It is only if the consent is obtained by fraud or by misrepresentation of the nature of what is to be done that it can be said that an apparent consent is not a true consent. This is the position in the criminal law (see *R v Clarence* (1888) 22 QBD 23 at 43, [1886–90] All ER Rep 133 at 144) and the cause of action based on trespass to the person is closely analogous. I should add that the contrary was not argued on this appeal.

g

The duty of disclosure

In the context of medical diagnosis and treatment, the law is content to adopt the standard of the ordinary skilled medical man exercising and professing to have that special skill, because the courts are rightly satisfied that the medical profession as a whole is working and will continue to work to the standards which the law requires. It may be that the same is true of the duty of disclosure, but I do not regard this as self-evident. Let *h* me say at once that this is not intended to be a criticism of the medical profession. Its members are dedicated to saving life and maintaining health. A doctor's duty of care, as the profession would readily concede, involves him in evaluating risks and weighing advantages and disadvantages before recommending a particular type of treatment. But, having decided what to recommend, there must be a natural and, up to a point, praiseworthy desire that this advice shall be accepted and a strong temptation not to say *j* anything to the patient which might lead to its rejection and so frustrate the doctor's prime object, which is to maintain and improve the patient's health.

Once it is conceded, as of course it is, that a patient who is of sound mind, sufficient age and capable of exercising a choice is entitled to grant or withhold consent to treatment as he sees fit, the relationship of doctor and patient must carry with it some duty to give

information to the patient which will enable him, if so minded, to reach a rational
a decision. The problem is how to define the duty and, having defined it, how to determine
whether the duty has been discharged.

In the present appeal, counsel for the plaintiff submits that there is a duty to disclose
the general nature of the treatment or procedure, the prospects of success or failure in
achieving the purpose, any inherent material risks or risks of substance and whether or
not the procedure is one of necessity or one of choice. He further submits that the
b materiality of any risk depends on its foreseeability, the expected frequency of occurrence
and the potential gravity of the consequences and that that materiality is to be judged by
the court, rather than doctors, and by objective standards. In partial support of this
submission, he draws attention to the fact that in *Chatterton v Gerson* [1981] 1 All ER 257
at 266, [1981] QB 432 at 444 Bristow J, although applying the *Bolam* test, did appear to
be applying a test which was independent of current professional practice when he said:

c   'In my judgment there is no obligation on the doctor to canvass with the patient
anything other than the inherent implications of the particular operation he intends
to carry out. He is certainly under no obligation to say that if he operates
incompetently he will do damage. The fundamental assumption is that he knows
his job and will do it properly. But he ought to warn of what may happen by
misfortune however well the operation is done, if there is a real risk of a misfortune
d   inherent in the procedure, as there was in the surgery to the carotid artery in the
Canadian case of *Reibl v Hughes*. In what he says any good doctor has to take into
account the personality of the patient, the likelihood of the misfortune, and what in
the way of warning is for the particular patient's welfare.'

At one stage in his submissions, counsel for the plaintiff argued that the disclosure of
e information is not an exercise of technical or professional expertise by the doctor. This I
am quite unable to accept. What information should be disclosed and how and when it
should be disclosed is very much a matter for professional judgment, to be exercised in
the context of the doctor's relationship with a particular patient in particular
circumstances. It is for this reason that I would reject the American formulation of the
duty by reference to a 'prudent patient' test. No doubt it is valid if the doctor happens to
f be treating that happy abstraction, the 'prudent patient', but I suspect that he is a fairly
rare bird and I have no doubt that his removal to the courts from his natural habitat,
which would, I assume, be a seat or hand rail on the Clapham omnibus, would do
nothing for patients or medicine, although it might do a great deal for lawyers and
litigation.

I think that it is a mistake, and not in accordance with the traditional way in which
g the common law is developed, to formulate different aspects of the duty of care with
precision. It is the general duty which matters. Precision comes when the general duty
is applied to a particular situation. The general duty of a doctor to disclose information
to his patient, as I would formulate it, is to take such action by way of giving or
withholding information as is reasonable in all the circumstances of which the doctor
knows or ought to know, including the patient's true wishes, with a view to placing the
h patient in a position to make a rational choice whether or not to accept the doctor's
recommendation. I refer to the withholding of information as well as to giving it because
I recognise that there are cases in which the imparting of too much information may
well hinder rather than assist the patient to make a rational choice. I also refer expressly
to the patient's *true* wishes because, while I recognise that the patient has an overriding
right to as little or as much information as he wishes and can absorb, it by no means
j follows that the expression of a wish for full information either generally or specifically
represents the reality of the patient's state of mind.

One has only to state the duty in this way for it to be apparent that its performance
involves professional expertise. It follows that whether or not a particular doctor has or
has not fallen below the requisite standard of care must be tested in the first instance by
reference to the way in which other doctors discharge their duty, ie the *Bolam* test.

However, I accept the view expressed by Laskin CJC that the definition of the duty of care is not to be handed over to the medical or any other profession. The definition of the duty of care is a matter for the law and the courts. They cannot stand idly by if the profession, by an excess of paternalism, denies its patients a real choice. In a word, the law will not permit the medical profession to play God.

Thus, while I accept the *Bolam* test as the primary test of liability for failing to disclose sufficient information to the patient to enable that patient to exercise his right of choice whether or not to accept the advice proffered by his doctor, I do so subject to an important caveat. This is that the profession, or that section of it which is relied on by the defendant doctor as setting the requisite standard of care, is discharging the duty of disclosure as I have defined it. This, incidentally, accords with the approach of Parliament, which, in s 1(5) of the Congenital Disability (Civil Liability) Act 1976, enacted that—

> 'The defendant is not answerable . . . if he took reasonable care having *due regard* to then received professional opinion applicable . . . but this does not mean that he is answerable only because he departed from received opinion.'

'Due regard' involves an exercise of judgment, inter alia, whether 'received professional opinion' is engaged in the same exercise as the law. This qualification is analogous to that which has been asserted in the context of treating a trade practice as evidencing the proper standard of care in *Cavanagh v Ulster Weaving Co Ltd* [1959] 2 All ER 745, [1960] AC 145 and in *Morris v West Hartlepool Steam Navigation Co Ltd* [1956] 1 All ER 385, [1956] AC 552 and would be equally infrequently relevant. In my judgment Skinner J was right to reject the approach of Professor Logue, which was not to refer to small risks if he thought that, in his hands, they were trivial. While it is true that he did so on the basis that none of the other medical witnesses adopted the same approach, I think that, in an appropriate case, a judge would be entitled to reject a unanimous medical view if he were satisfied that it was manifestly wrong and that the doctors must have been misdirecting themselves as to their duty in law.

Another way of expressing my view of the test is to add just one qualifying word (which I have emphasised) to the law as Skinner J summarised it, so that it would read:

> 'The duty is fulfilled if the doctor acts in accordance with a practice *rightly* accepted as proper by a body of skilled and experienced medical men.'

Applying that test to the facts found by the judge, it is clear that Mr Falconer acted in accordance with a practice accepted as proper by a body of skilled and experienced medical men. The only question is whether it was a proper practice. For my part, I cannot understand, let alone accept, the criticism that Mr Falconer failed to inform the plaintiff that what he proposed was an 'elective operation'. This may be a useful category in terms of medical priorities and medical administration. But it is meaningless to a patient. All operations are elective: the patient always has a choice. What the patient needs to have placed fairly before him or her are the alternatives. This seems to have been done. Nor can I accept the criticism that, while telling the plaintiff of the possibility of disturbing a nerve root and of the consequences of doing so, Mr Falconer did not refer to the danger of damage to the spinal cord. It is a rare patient who wants to know what may go wrong in terms of what part of his body may be accidentally damaged. What the average patient wants to know is what is the likelihood of something going wrong and, if it does, what will be the consequences for him. As I understand the evidence and the judge's findings based on that evidence, Mr Falconer regarded the possibility of there being damage to a nerve root as sufficiently real to inform the plaintiff of the possible consequences, but he regarded the possibility of spinal cord damage as too remote to form any part of the basis of a judgment by the plaintiff on whether or not she should agree to accept the treatment recommended by him. The fact that in the event he was proved wrong does not prove that he was negligent. His peers took the same view and, for my part, I cannot conclude on the evidence that they were wrong.

For these reasons I would dismiss the appeal.

DUNN LJ. The question of law which arises for decision in this appeal is whether, in
a order to prove negligence against a doctor or surgeon in respect of a failure to warn a
patient of the risks of a particular treatment or operation, the plaintiff must prove that
the doctor had fallen below a standard of practice recognised as proper by a competent
body of medical opinion or whether the doctor is bound to warn the patient of any risk
which, on the medical evidence, is material to the decision of the patient to undergo the
treatment, unless the doctor can prove that such disclosure would be detrimental to the
b patient or is impracticable, as where the patient is unconscious.

I deal first, as preliminary questions, with two arguments developed by counsel for the
plaintiff which form the basis of the decision in the United States case of *Canterbury v
Spence* (1972) 464 F 2d 772, which was the genesis of the subsequent American and
Canadian cases, notably the decision of the Supreme Court of Canada in *Reibl v Hughes*
(1980) 114 DLR (3d) 1, and led to the transatlantic doctrine of 'informed consent'.

c The first argument was that unless the patient's consent to the operation was a fully
informed consent the performance of the operation would constitute a battery on the
patient by the surgeon. This is not the law of England. If there is consent to the nature
of the act, then there is no trespass to the person. So in *R v Clarence* (1888) 22 QBD 23,
[1886–90] All ER Rep 133 a conviction of rape was quashed where the woman did not
know that the prisoner was suffering from a venereal disease which he communicated to
d her. If she had known, she would not have consented to sexual intercourse, but as she
had consented to the act of sexual intercourse, even though without knowledge of the
probable risk of infection, there was no rape. On the other hand, in *R v Flattery* (1877) 2
QBD 410, where a doctor had had sexual intercourse with a patient under pretence of
performing a surgical operation, his conviction of rape was upheld because the patient
had only consented to an operation and not to the act of sexual intercourse. As Bristow J
e said in *Chatterton v Gerson* [1981] 1 All ER 257 at 265, [1981] QB 432 at 443: '. . . once
the patient is informed in broad terms of the nature of the procedure which is intended,
and gives her consent, that consent is real . . .', so that it affords a defence to a battery.

The second argument was that a doctor stood in a fiduciary relationship to his patient
and was, on the principles laid down in *Nocton v Lord Ashburton* [1914] AC 932, [1914–
15] All ER Rep 45, under a duty to disclose all material facts to his patient. The doctrine
f of fiduciary relationships has been developed in equity so as to raise a presumption of
undue influence where there has been a disposition of property from one person to or for
the benefit of another, and that other stands in a special relationship of confidentiality
towards the person making the disposition. So in *Billage v Southee* (1852) 9 Hare 534, 68
ER 623 an excessive medical account was set aside on terms that the doctor was entitled
to no more than reasonable remuneration, since the doctor was in a confidential
g relationship with his patient, and the excess was presumed to have been an abuse of that
relationship. But this doctrine has been confined to cases involving the disposition of
property, and has never been applied to the nature of the duty which lies on a doctor in
the performance of his professional treatment of his patient. In any event, I do not find
it helpful in considering the duty of the doctor to his patient to draw analogies, which
are in any case ill-founded, from other branches of the law which have developed in
h different circumstances and for different reasons.

Taking a strict view of the principle of stare decisis there is no English decision binding
on this court which compels us to answer the question posed in this appeal one way or
the other. I therefore approach the case on principle, although there are persuasive
indications in some of the authorities. It is incontrovertible that a doctor owes a duty of
care to his patient. Like all professional men (because he falls into no special category: see
j *Whitehouse v Jordan* [1981] 1 All ER 267 at 276, [1981] 1 WLR 246 at 258 per Lord
Edmund-Davies) he is bound to use the standard of care of the ordinary skilled man
exercising and professing to have a special skill, in his case medicine or surgery (see
Greaves & Co (Contractors) Ltd v Baynham Meikle & Partners [1975] 3 All ER 99, [1975] 1
WLR 1095). His functions include diagnosis, advice and treatment. In the realm of
diagnosis and treatment the true test for establishing negligence is whether the doctor

has been proved to be guilty of such failure as no doctor of ordinary skill would be guilty of if acting with ordinary care (see *Hunter v Hanley* 1955 SLT 213 at 217 per the Lord President (Clyde) and *Maynard v West Midlands Regional Health Authority* (1983) Times, 9 May per Lord Scarman). In the realm of advice the standards of his profession are also to be applied (see *Saif Ali v Sydney Mitchell & Co (a firm), P (third party)* [1978] 3 All ER 1033 at 1043, 1051, [1980] AC 198 at 220, 231 per Lord Diplock and Lord Salmon).

In giving advice the professional man will normally refer to the advantages and disadvantages of the course which he recommends. I can see no difference in principle between referring to the disadvantages of a particular course of action, or in the case of a doctor of a particular treatment, and warning of the risks of such treatment. Indeed, as a matter of evidence, I foresee practical difficulties in distinguishing between advice and warning. And, since his advice as to the advantages of a particular treatment is to be judged in accordance with the standards of his profession, in my judgment his advice as to the disadvantages, including any warning or lack of warning of the risks, should be subject to the same standard. There is nothing in the authorities to support a different view. On the contrary, no distinction was made in *Bolam v Friern Hospital Management Committee* [1957] 2 All ER 118, [1957] 1 WLR 582 between diagnosis and treatment on the one hand and warning of the risks involved in the treatment on the other. The same standard was applied throughout, and, although the approval of the House of Lords to the case has been limited in terms to diagnosis and treatment, it has never been suggested by their Lordships that the wrong test was applied in relation to the alleged failure to warn.

It is superficially attractive to say, 'Once it is established by medical evidence that there is a material risk in the treatment, then the doctor is under a duty to warn his patient of that risk unless he can show that the patient would be likely to suffer a detriment outweighing the disclosure of the risk.' I do not believe, however, that there is a separate and distinct duty to warn ancillary to the doctor's general duty of care. It is accepted by the appellant that whether or not there is a material risk in the proposed treatment is a matter of expert evidence. But, as the argument before us showed, that question is itself not usually susceptible of a definite answer because each doctor is dealing with his own individual patient whom he is under a duty to treat to the best of his skill and judgment. Whether the risk is 'material' will itself depend on the condition, personality and circumstances of the patient. Doctors after all treat patients and not diseases. The nature and extent of the warning, and the decision whether there is to be a warning at all, is so closely linked to the medical prospect of the risk that it forms part of the overall clinical judgment of the doctor as to the preferred treatment for the patient. This clinical judgment can only be tested by applying the standards of the profession, and it would be extremely difficult to separate and distinguish between the different facets of the judgment made by the doctor. In my judgment the court should not interfere unless the clinical judgment of the doctor taken as a whole falls below the generally accepted standards of the profession.

Accordingly, in my judgment McNair J was right in *Bolam v Friern Barnet Hospital Management Committee* to direct the jury that, in determining whether or not the plaintiff was entitled to succeed on his allegation of failure to warn, the material consideration was whether or not the defendants, in not warning him of the risks involved in the treatment, had fallen below a standard of practice recognised as proper by a competent body of professional opinion. The doctrine of 'informed consent' forms no part of English law.

I confess that I reach this conclusion with no regret. The evidence in this case showed that a contrary result would be damaging to the relationship of trust and confidence between doctor and patient, and might well have an adverse effect on the practice of medicine. It is doubtful whether it would be of any significant benefit to patients, most of whom prefer to put themselves unreservedly in the hands of their doctors. This is not in my view 'paternalism', to repeat an evocative word used in argument. It is simply an

a
acceptance of the doctor/patient relationship as it has developed in this country. The principal effect of accepting the proposition advanced by the plaintiff would be likely to be an increase in the number of claims for professional negligence against doctors. This would be likely to have an adverse effect on the general standard of medical care, since doctors would inevitably be concerned to safeguard themselves against such claims, rather than to concentrate on their primary duty of treating their patients.

I would dismiss the appeal.

b
BROWNE-WILKINSON LJ. The primary facts of this case are set out in the judgment of Sir John Donaldson MR and I will not repeat them.

In order to succeed on this appeal, the plaintiff must show that the judge misdirected himself in holding that no case had been established in negligence against Mr Falconer since, in making only limited disclosure of the special risks of the operation, Mr Falconer had acted 'in accordance with a practice accepted as proper by a body of skilled and

c
experienced medical men'. Counsel for the plaintiff submits that in relation to disclosure of special risks (as opposed to diagnosis and treatment) the decision whether or not a proper disclosure has been made does not fall to be determined solely by the practice of the medical profession.

Counsel for the plaintiff rests his case firmly on negligence and nothing else. But, at

d
least in opening the appeal, he relied heavily on decisions in certain states of the United States of America and in the Supreme Court of Canada. Those cases establish in those jurisdictions the doctrine of so-called 'informed consent'. In order to face the real problems raised by this appeal, it is necessary first to consider whether that transatlantic doctrine is consistent with the law of England and should be applied in English courts.

Cases of this sort can be approached in two different ways. First, it can be said that the

e
operation constituted a trespass to the person of the patient since, in the absence of full knowledge of the risks, the patient has not validly consented to the operation. Second, it can be said that (although there was a valid consent to the operation) the doctor was in breach of a duty of care in failing to give sufficient information of the risks to the plaintiff. It is, in my judgment, clear that the genesis of the transatlantic doctrine of informed consent lies in the first of these approaches.

f
As I understand the development of the doctrine, it starts from the proposition that it is for the patient, not the doctor, to determine what happens to the patient's body. Then the transatlantic cases rely heavily on certain equitable doctrines. It is said that a doctor is in a fiduciary position vis-à-vis his patient: see *Canterbury v Spence* (1972) 161 F 2d 772 at 782; *Hopp v Lepp* (1980) 112 DLR (3d) 67 at 75 (and the reliance on *Nocton v Lord Ashburton* [1914] AC 932, [1914–15] All ER Rep 45). From this premise, two consequences

g
are said to flow. First, as a fiduciary the doctor is under a special duty to make full disclosure; second, without such full disclosure there can be no valid 'consent': see *Canterbury v Spence* (at 780, 782), *Hopp v Lepp*, *Reibl v Hughes* (1980) 114 DLR (3d) 1 at 5 (which treats the duty of disclosure as established by *Hopp v Lepp*). The next stage in the reasoning is that, in the absence of an informed and therefore valid consent, the doctor has no defence to a claim in trespass: see *Canterbury v Spence* (at 780, 782), *Hopp v Lepp* (at

h
70). Finally, the need of an informed consent having been established in the context of the law of trespass, the duty to make the necessary disclosure for that purpose is treated as giving rise in the context of negligence to a duty of care to make the same disclosure: see *Canterbury v Spence* (esp at 793), *Reibl v Hughes* (at 5, 9–11).

Although the law of the United States and Canada has the same equitable and common law roots as our own, the present-day law in the different jurisdictions is not necessarily

j
the same. Therefore I am in no way criticising the transatlantic decisions when I say that the reasoning behind those decisions does not accord with the present law of England.

Equity imposes on certain people fiduciary obligations in relation to the property of their clients or patients. Normally these fiduciary duties take the form that the fiduciary is accountable for any profit made by him from his fiduciary position or from gifts made to him by the client or patient unless he can show that such profit was made with the fully informed consent of the client or patient. Thus a solicitor must not make a personal   *a* profit by the use of information or property belonging to a client except with the fully informed consent of the client. Again, certain relationships (eg solicitor and client, doctor and patient) give rise to a presumption in equity that a gift from the client or patient to the solicitor or doctor was procured by undue influence and the fiduciary is not allowed to retain such a gift unless he can show that the client or patient fully intended to make it in the full knowledge of all relevant circumstances. In this context of dealings with   *b* property, equity has developed a concept that a fiduciary cannot get rid of his fiduciary duties without the informed consent of the client or patient. But I am not aware of any other type of case where English law provides that an apparently valid consent is invalid solely on the grounds of lack of knowledge of the surrounding circumstances or the consequences of giving such consent.

In my judgment there is no ground in English law for extending this limited doctrine   *c* of informed consent outside the field of property rights in which it is established. The doctrine is in each case based on the principle that the person said to be in a fiduciary position may have abused his position of trust to make a personal profit for himself. That principle has no application to the present type of case where there is no suggestion that the doctor is abusing his position for the purpose of making a personal profit.

The only example of the extension of fiduciary duties to other fields is the decision of   *d* the House of Lords in *Hedley Byrne & Co Ltd v Heller & Partners Ltd* [1963] 2 All ER 575, [1964] AC 465, which extended the scope of the decision in *Nocton v Lord Ashburton* [1914] AC 932, [1914–15] All ER Rep 45. *Nocton v Lord Ashburton* itself was a case where a solicitor had negligently failed to give an accurate statement of the position of his client, as a result of which the client had agreed to a transaction from which the solicitor personally profited. It was therefore a case within the strict confines of the traditional   *e* equitable doctrine. In *Hedley Byrne v Heller* the House of Lords extended the law, by extrapolation from *Nocton v Lord Ashburton*, to hold that there might be other relationships giving rise to a duty of care not to make negligent statements. But there is nothing in the speeches in the House of Lords in *Hedley Byrne v Heller* to suggest that their Lordships were doing more than finding the duty of care in such relationships. There is nothing to suggest that the House of Lords were applying the doctrine of fully informed consent to   *f* such liability in negligence.

I can therefore find nothing in English law to justify a conclusion that, in relation to a consent to trespass to the person, the fact that the consent is being given to someone in a fiduciary relationship vis-à-vis property requires the consent to be held invalid unless given with full information. Nor can I see any policy reason to make such an extension. The concept that carrying out an operation constitutes a battery to the plaintiff does not   *g* accord with common sense. Moreover, I note that in *Reibl v Hughes* the Canadian Supreme Court, while adhering to the doctrine of informed consent in relation to the law of negligence, held that, even in the absence of informed consent, there was no cause of action in trespass to the person.

The position therefore in English law is this. The plaintiff in fact consented to the operation actually performed. This consent provides a complete answer to any claim in   *h* trespass since, whether or not she was fully informed of the risks attendant on the operation, the doctrine of informed consent is not part of the law of England. Moreover, since the doctrine of informed consent is the basis on which the transatlantic cases have built their definition of the duty to warn, the transatlantic definition of the extent of that duty is not applicable in the United Kingdom. It follows that the emphasis in the transatlantic cases on the aboslute right of the plaintiff to determine whether or not to   *j* have the operation only after receiving full disclosure of the risks is not relevant in English law, whether the cause of action be founded in trespass or in negligence. Liability in negligence depends on the duty of care to be observed by the defendant; it does not depend on the 'rights' of the plaintiff, other than the plaintiff's right not to be negligently injured. I therefore receive no assistance from the transatlantic cases in the determination of this appeal.

Turning to the cause of action in negligence, I accept the submission of counsel for the defendants that it is important to distinguish between the duty of care and the performance of that duty. As to the duty of care itself, the decisions at first instance have uniformly applied to the question of adequate warning the same test as that applied in relation to diagnosis and treatment, namely: did the doctor act 'in accordance with a practice accepted as proper by a responsible body of medical men skilled in that particular art'? (see *Bolam v Friern Hospital Management Committee* [1957] 2 All ER 118 at 112, [1957] 1 WLR 582 at 587). In the *Bolam* case the claim was based not only on negligent treatment but also on negligent failure to give adequate warning. The same test was applied to both aspects of the claim. The *Bolam* test has been approved by the House of Lords in *Whitehouse v Jordan* [1981] 1 All ER 267, [1981] 1 WLR 248 and *Maynard v West Midland Regional Health Authority* (1983) Times, 9 May. But those cases were concerned solely with diagnosis and treatment and not with warnings. I do not reagrd them as deciding the point before us. It is necessary therefore to approach the matter free of authority binding on this court.

I start by considering the general duty of care which the law would impose on anyone who in the course of business has undertaken to give advice, whether or not he held himself out as possessing any special professional or other skill. Such a person would owe a duty of care: see *Hedley Byrne v Heller* and *Mutual Life and Citizens' Assurance Co Ltd v Evatt* [1971] 1 All ER 150, [1971] AC 793. In my judgment, in the absence of special circumstances, such a person would owe a duty to disclose any unusual and material risks of which he knows or ought to know and which will be run if the advice he tenders is adopted. In my judgment the assumption of the role of adviser, whether or not such advice involves any special skill or judgment, carries with it the duty to disclose material and unusual risks. Take for example a hotel brochure which represents to guests of the hotel that there is sea swimming but fails to point out that there are sharks in the sea. It seems to me plain that the failure to disclose the risk of sharks would be a breach of an obvious duty of care.

If there is such a general duty of care, irrespective of any special skill, is the test to be different if the giver of the advice holds himself out as possessing some professional or other special skill? I can see no reason why the duty of care in such a case should be any lower than the general duty of care, although the determination of the question whether the duty has been performed may give rise to special problems. A man who holds himself out as possessing special skills assumes a higher, not a lower, duty of care. If this were not the case it would theoretically be open to a profession to adopt a practice which exempted its members from a duty which the law imposes on the rest of society. As counsel for the plaintiff submitted, guidance can be obtained from considering the position of other skilled advisers. Take for example the case of a consulting engineer who advises his client to erect a particular type of structure, knowing that there is an unusual and material risk attached to such structure but having himself formed the reasonable view that the benefits of such structure outweigh such risk. In my judgment his duty of care would extend to warning the client of the material risk since it is for the client, not the adviser, to decide whether to take such risk. Once it was established that there was such a risk and the engineer either knew or, in the exercise of reasonable professional skill, ought to have known of such risk, it would be for the court to decide whether the risk was a material one and whether adequate disclosure had been made. The existence of the risk would have to be proved by expert professional evidence and the question whether the engineer ought to have known of it would be judged by the standard of the reasonable engineer. But the duty to disclose the risk and the answer to the question whether there had been an adequate disclosure would be determined by the general law, not by the standard of the profession.

In my judgment therefore the justification for treating a doctor as being under a duty to disclose different from that applicable in other cases cannot be found simply in the fact that in relation to the diagnosis and treatment of patients he is exercising a   *a* professional skill. The justification (if any) must be found in factors peculiar to the medical profession which demonstrate that the general rule applicable to other professions is inappropriate in that case. Are there such factors?

There are a number of factors which undoubtedly distinguish the doctor's position from that of any other professional man in relation to the disclosure of unusual but material risks. Two are fundamental. First, in general terms the patient goes to the   *b* doctor to be cured and the overriding concern of the doctor is to use his professional skill to effect a cure. Second, the process of treatment depends to a substantial extent on the relationship between doctor and patient, in particular on the confidence of the patient in the doctor. If the disclosure of the risks results in prejudicing the ability of the doctor to cure and the confidence of the patient in the doctor, the existence of a duty to disclose such risks would positively militate against the main purpose of the relationship, a factor   *c* not present in relation to disclosure of risks by any other professional adviser.

There are undoubtedly cases where the emotional state of the patient is such that disclosure of the full risks of any proposed course of treatment would be medically harmful to the patient. To require a doctor to disclose such risks in such circumstances would run counter to his main functions. Again, the relationship of trust and confidence between doctor and patient may be severely shaken by a formal communication of risks;   *d* there can in practice be no clear-cut line between the tendering of advice as to the possible courses of treatment and their respective benefits and the warnings of danger attendant on such treatment. Some patients may not want to be told of the risks, and to thrust the information on them might damage the relationship with the doctor. These matters point to a conflict between a general duty to disclose risks and the achievement of the purpose of the relationship.   *e*

Moreover, the materiality of any particular risk must in the ordinary case depend on the relationship between the object to be achieved by the operation and the nature of the risk involved. If there is a $\frac{1}{2}\%$ risk of total paralysis, that might well be a material risk in the context of an operation designed to get rid of a minor discomfort but not in the context of an operation required to avoid death. The decision as to the materiality of a risk does not depend simply on the difference between an elective operation and an   *f* essential operation: it depends on the balancing of benefits and risks.

These factors persuade me that there are good grounds for holding that in relation to doctors the duty to disclose risks should be approached on a different basis from that applicable to ordinary professional men. But I am not satisfied that it is right to say that the law imposes on doctors no duty to disclose. I start from the basic proposition that in the ordinary case it is for the patient, not for the doctor, to decide whether he wishes to   *g* run the risk of an operation. The doctor knows that the patient will be relying on his advice in taking that decision and most people want to know the material risks in taking a particular course of action before they take it. One would therefore expect the doctor to be under a duty to give to the patient the information relevant to the decision he has to take. I do not think that the practical considerations which I have mentioned require the complete elimination of a general duty of care on doctors to warn of special risks. For   *h* myself I would hold that in general the doctor is under a duty to take such steps to ensure that the patient has such information relating to the benefits and material risks of the operation as is reasonable in all the circumstances. Such formulation of the duty, while establishing the general right of the patient to the information necessary to make his decision, takes account of many of the special circumstances I have mentioned. In particular there would be no duty to disclose risks if the doctor reasonably considered   *j* that such disclosure would be medically harmful to the particular patient or if the patient had clearly indicated that he did not want to know of the risks. It is of course obvious that the doctor is not under any duty to give information as to the ordinary risks normally attendant on any operation.

I have so far only considered the formulation of the duty, if any. But of equal practical importance is the proof of the performance of the duty by the doctor. If the duty is as I have formulated it above, the crucial question will be whether the steps in fact taken are in all the circumstances reasonable. This, being a matter of professional judgment and the balancing of risks against benefits, must essentially be determined by reference to the practices of the profession, ie according to the *Bolam* test. Thus the decision whether the risk is material and the adequacy of the disclosure will fall to be determined by reference to the accepted practices of the medical profession and not, as in the ordinary case of the professional man, by the court applying its own standards.

In short, there is only one practical distinction between the view I favour and the *Bolam* case. All questions of disclosure will be decided by reference to the practice of the profession save that an omission to disclose risks could not be justified solely by reference to a practice of the profession which does not rely on the circumstances of the particular patient. For example, in the present case one of the experts said:

> 'But, if you raise this problem at all, when it is really remote, you are going to create a great deal of anxiety in the patient and they may postpone it or forgo it altogether and, if we do this to, say, 150 patients, in 149 you have created anxieties which prove to be entirely unnecessary, and the question is really whether this is justified for just one individual who may suffer a calamity. I think one has to weigh up those points and I decide, anyhow, myself, if the risks are as small as this, that this is the right way to manage it.'

Unless this passage can be taken as demonstrating that the doctor did not regard the risk as a material one, his approach provides no good reason for withholding information from the patient. It is the existence of this view in parts of the medical profession (ie that the benefits to 149 patients outweigh their duty to the one who suffers and that it is for the doctor and not the patient to decide) which in my view makes it important that the law should establish that there is a prima facie duty to inform.

It is inevitable that in considering this case one is acutely aware of the policy problems which it raises. In particular, I have been very conscious of the need to ensure that the duty of care imposed by the law is not such as to inhibit the proper function of the medical profession in caring for the sick by exposing doctors to the threat of legal proceedings in which their actions will be judged with hindsight, not by reference to the standards of those skilled in the art, but by judges or juries. It is for this reason that I am not prepared to adopt the much stricter rules as to disclosure laid down in the transatlantic cases which involve an objective judgment both as to the materiality of the risk and the adequacy of the disclosure. It is common knowledge that such rules have led to a large number of claims against doctors based on failure to warn; in consequence, a number of states in the USA have introduced legislation to modify the doctrine of informed consent. But in my judgment if the law is established on the basis that I have set out above no such consequences should enure in this country. Given the basic acceptance that it is for the patient to decide whether to have the operation, there will be no need for the doctor to 'look over his shoulder' for fear of legal claims. His conduct will continue to be judged in accordance with the standards of his profession.

Applying those principles to the present case, the doctors who gave evidence were agreed that the combined risk of nerve root damage and spinal cord damage was material. They agreed that in the case of an elective operation the patient should be given warning of such risks. The plaintiff was indeed warned of some risk but not specifically of the risk of spinal cord damage. The medical evidence does not establish what was the degree of risk of cord damage in isolation; but two of the experts said that the risk of cord damage was less than that of nerve root damage (ie necessarily less than 1%). Two of the doctors said that they would not specifically warn of cord damage. Mr Polkey plainly took the view that he would not warn of the danger of cord damage as opposed to nerve root damage because he thought that the risk was too remote to require mention. There was therefore evidence, which the judge accepted, that it was in accordance with an accepted medical practice not to warn specifically of cord damage because the risk of such damage was too remote. The position therefore is that Mr Falconer gave warning of the risk which, according to an accepted professional practice, was the only material risk. Mr Falconer therefore performed his duty of care, even if it is formulated in the way I have suggested above.

For these reasons, I too would dismiss the appeal.

Appeal dismissed. Leave to appeal to the House of Lords granted.

Solicitors: *Armstrong & Co*, Forest Hill (for the plaintiff); *Le Brasseur & Bury* (for the defendants).

Frances Rustin   Barrister.

Freeman v Home Office

COURT OF APPEAL, CIVIL DIVISION
SIR JOHN DONALDSON MR, FOX AND STEPHEN BROWN LJJ
22, 23 FEBRUARY, 7 MARCH 1984

Medical practitioner – Trespass to the person – Consent to medical treatment – Prison – Prison medical officer administering drug to prisoner – Prisoner contending that drug administered by force without his consent – Whether prisoner's consent required to be informed consent.

In 1973, while serving a term of life imprisonment, the plaintiff had administered to him certain drugs. In 1979 the plaintiff brought an action against the Home Office claiming damages for trespass to the person, on the grounds that a medical officer employed by the prison authorities, together with other prison officers, had administered the drugs to him by force against his consent. He contended (i) that the drugs prescribed by the medical officer were not for the relief of any recognisable mental illness or disorder but were purely to control him, and that a prisoner could not, in law, give consent to treatment by a prison medical officer where the medical officer was not acting in his capacity as a doctor but as a disciplinarian, and (ii) that for a patient's consent to be operative in law it had to be informed, ie the patient had to be told (a) what he was suffering from, (b) what was the precise nature of the treatment being proposed and (c) what, if any, were the adverse effects and risks involved in the treatment. The judge found that the plaintiff had consented to the administration of the drugs and he accordingly dismissed the action. The plaintiff appealed.

Held – Since the doctrine of informed consent formed no part of English law, the sole issue was whether on the facts the plaintiff had consented to the administration of the drugs and on that issue the trial judge had found that the plaintiff had so consented.

a Furthermore, the judge was right to hold that in the circumstances the plaintiff was not incapable in law of giving his consent to the treatment by the prison medical officer. The appeal would accordingly be dismissed (see p 1043 d to f and h j, p 1044 d e and p 1045 b and e to h, post).

Sidaway v Bethlem Royal Hospital Governors [1984] 1 All ER 1018 applied.
Dictum of Scott LJ in Bowater v Rowley Regis BC [1944] 1 All ER at 465 considered.
Decision of McCowan J [1983] 3 All ER 589 affirmed.

b

Notes
For trespass to the person, see 38 Halsbury's Laws (3rd edn) 760, para 1251, and for cases on the subject, see 46 Digest (Repl) 415–429, 581–740.
For prison officers, see 37 Halsbury's Laws (4th edn) para 1116.

c

Cases referred to in judgments
Bowater v Rowley Regis BC [1944] 1 All ER 465, [1944] KB 476, CA.
Kaimowitz v Michigan Dept of Mental Health (1973) 42 USLW 101, 2063, Cir Ct, Wayne Cty, Mich.
M'Alister (or Donoghue) v Stevenson [1932] AC 562, [1932] All ER Rep 1, HL.
d Sidaway v Bethlem Royal Hospital Governors [1984] 1 All ER 1018, CA.

Cases also cited
Raymond v Honey [1982] 1 All ER 756, [1983] 1 AC 1, HL.
Reibl v Hughes (1980) 114 DLR (3d) 1, Can SC.

e

Appeal
The plaintiff, David Freeman, appealed against the judgment of McCowan J ([1983] 3 All ER 589, [1984] 2 WLR 130) dated 19 May 1983 whereby he dismissed the plaintiff's action against the defendants, the Home Office, for damages for, inter alia, trespass to the person by the administration of certain drugs by or under the direction of Dr Cedric f Melville Xavier, the servant or agent of the defendants and/or certain prison officers at HM Prison Wakefield being also servants or agents of the defendants, between September 1972 and December 1972 against the plaintiff's will and/or without his consent. The facts are set out in the judgment of Stephen Brown LJ.

Louis Blom-Cooper QC and Judith Beale for the plaintiff.
g John Laws for the defendants.

Cur adv vult

7 March. The following judgments were delivered.

h

STEPHEN BROWN LJ (giving the first judgment at the invitation of Sir John Donaldson MR). This is an appeal by the plaintiff from the judgment of McCowan J ([1983] 3 All ER 589, [1984] 2 WLR 130) of 19 May 1983 whereby the judge dismissed his claim for damages against the Home Office (the defendants) and ordered that judgment should be entered for the defendants. The plaintiff is and was at all material j times a prisoner serving a life sentence imposed on him on 30 July 1970 at the Central Criminal Court following conviction for a number of offences of indecent assault and buggery and certain other offences.

By a writ issued on the 15 October 1979 and served on 17 October 1979 the plaintiff claimed damages from the defendants for alleged—

'Assault and/or battery and/or trespass to the person by the administration to him of certain drugs, namely Stelazin and/or Modecate and/or Serenace ("the drugs") by or under the direction of [Dr. Xavier], the servant or agent of the defendants and/or certain prison officers at H.M. Prison Wakefield ("the Prison") ... between ... September 1972 and ... December 1972 against the plaintiff's will and/or without his consent.'

Secondly, he claimed for 'negligence in administering the drugs to him as aforesaid'. By their defence the defendants denied trespass to the person and negligence, and alleged that at all material times the plaintiff expressly consented to the administration of each of the said drugs and that no drug was administered without his consent. .

The defence also pleaded the Limitation Act, and an application was made by the defendants for an order that the plaintiff's claim should be dismissed or stayed on the grounds that it was statute-barred. They further alleged that they were prejudiced in the conduct of the action by reason of the plaintiff's delay, in particular because the doctor named in the writ and statement of claim, Dr Xavier, had died on 1 October 1977. The plaintiff invoked the power conferred on the court under s 2D of the Limitation Act 1975 now s 33 of the Limitation Act 1980) and on 23 January 1981 Taylor J rejected the defendant's application. On appeal to the Court of Appeal the court allowed the defendants' appeal, holding that having regard to the death of Dr Xavier it would not be equitable to allow the plaintiff to pursue his claim in negligence and that claim was struck out of the writ. However, the Court of Appeal held that it would be equitable to permit him to pursue his claim in respect of the alleged trespass to the person, since it appeared from his affidavit that he was not alleging that the doctor was present when prison officers allegedly forcibly injected him.

The case before McCowan J proceeded, therefore, on the claim laid in trespass against the person and not in negligence. In November 1970 the plaintiff had been transferred to Wakefield Prison. His evidence was that in July 1972 Dr Xavier, a consultant psychiatrist, came to Wakefield Prison as one of a team of five medical officers at the prison under the principal medical officer, Dr Pendry Williams, and took over the psychiatric care of the plaintiff. The plaintiff was in the highest security category 'A' and consistently protested his innocence of all the charges of which he was convicted. Whilst in prison he suffered from bouts of depression; he attempted suicide on a number of occasions. Some of the attempts were considered to have been genuine and some considered to have been gestures.

In February 1972 Wakefield Prison had considered the possibility of transferring the plaintiff to Broadmoor Special Hospital under the provisions of s 72 of the Mental Health Act 1959. He was examined by a consultant psychiatrist, Dr McQuaid of Broadmoor Hospital, who reported that he obviously had a very severe personality disorder but doubted whether he was susceptible to treatment and accordingly did not consider him suitable for transfer to Broadmoor. Thereafter the plaintiff was moved from the prison hospital in Wakefield to the ordinary wing where he behaved in a disruptive way, smashing a television set amongst other things. A prison officer is said to have found him attempting to hang himself with his vest and shirt, although the plaintiff denied that that in fact occurred.

The medical records before the judge showed that on 25 February 1972 he was examined by the principal medical officer, Dr Pendry Williams, who noted that he was not chronically depressed at interview:

'... He is evasive and not very truthful. Says he smashed up the T.V. normally used for general viewing on a landing, as he was annoyed with a prisoner opening his cell door, and saw this as a means of getting into hospital. States he attacked television with a chair after repeated blows. Says set was quickly replaced thereafter. A man of moods, who behaves as a spoilt child. Little time for feelings of fellow inmates or society at large. Abnormality is of personality and character ...'

It is relevant to note that the records before the court showed that from February 1971
a on the recommendation of the senior medical officer, Dr Knox, the plaintiff had been
under the care of a visiting consultant psychotherapist, Dr Goddard. In December 1971
Dr Goddard had prescribed electro-convulsive therapy for the plaintiff but the plaintiff
had not accepted this and it was not carried out. It was after this that the attempt to have
him transferred to Broadmoor was made.

In July 1972 Dr Xavier took over the psychiatric care of the plaintiff. The first record
b in the plaintiff's case papers of Dr Xavier having dealt with him appears on 3 August
1972. On 10 August 1972 Dr Xavier is recorded as having prescribed Stelazin to be taken
orally. The plaintiff refused to take it. There are also entries in the case papers relating to
17, 24 and 30 August 1972 which record that the plaintiff refused oral medication
prescribed by Dr Xavier.

On 31 August 1972 Dr Xavier is recorded as having prescribed Stelazin again. The
c records show that the plaintiff refused to take the Stelazin and on 31 August 1972 there
is an entry by a prison officer, Mr Copley, to the effect that the plaintiff 'states he does not
want anything to do with Dr. Xavier'.

The case papers show that on 1 September 1972 the plaintiff still refused to take
medication orally and on that day Dr Xavier is recorded as having prescribed Serenace to
be injected intra-muscularly and the plaintiff was injected on that day. It is not disputed
d that injections of Serenace were also given on 2 and 3 of September 1972. The plaintiff's
claim was that these injections were administered by force against his will. Subsequently,
on 3 November, 20 November and 4 December 1972, he was injected with Modecate
prescribed by Dr Xavier. Again the plaintiff's contention was that these injections were
administered against his will and were administered by force.

The plaintiff's evidence was that he first remembered meeting Dr Xavier on 10 August
e 1972 for two minutes or so in the chief hospital officer's room at the prison and that Dr
Xavier asked him to try his mixture, saying, 'It will make a new man of you.' The
plaintiff said that he replied, 'No, I don't want it. I feel better. I don't need the drugs,' and
that that was all that happened on that occasion. He then saw Dr Xavier each week whilst
he was attending the workshop and again he was asked by the doctor if he would have
his mixture, and that each time he refused.

f On 31 August 1972 he had a brief meeting with Dr Xavier when he was again asked
to accept his mixture. On no occasion did the doctor tell him what the mixture was and
he did not ask him. The plaintiff said that he told the doctor that he wanted nothing to
do with him or his treatment.

On 1 September 1972 the plaintiff said that he was working normally in the workshop
between 10.00 am and 11.00 am when he was called out by an officer and taken back to
g the prison hospital and to his cell. He said he was not told why and he did not ask and
then he was locked in his cell. He told the court:

'A few minutes after, at least four or five prison hospital officers unlocked my cell
and came in. No doctor was present. I particularly remember the officer holding
the syringe, a Mr Clark, the younger of the two officers called Clark. Mr Copley
h may have been present. I can't remember the identity of any of the others. They
were with me no more than five minutes, if that. The officers entered. Mr Clark
was holding the syringe with the needle upwards. With his other arm he held a wad
of cotton wool over the needle. There was a strong smell of surgical spirit. Clark
said "Drop your trousers and lie down". I said "I don't want any drugs". One of
them said "It's on doctor's orders. You can have it the easy way or the hard way". I
j continued to protest and put my back to the wall and said "I'm not having it". At
least four or five men seized me and manhandled me to the bed. They held me
down and wrenched my trousers off. I threshed about on the bed and shouted.
Clark said "If you don't keep still, when this needle goes in it could snap off in your
arse and be very painful". I was terrified. When I felt the needle going in my

buttocks I stopped struggling. I surmise it was my left buttock from the position of my bed. They continued to hold me down until the needle was withdrawn. Then they released me and went out of the cell. Nothing more was said to me. I was left locked in. I cannot remember which officer next unlocked my cell. I said nothing to him. I knew it was dinner time. In the afternoon I went to the workshop. I became very ill and returned to the hospital. I became very agitated and had a pain in my head. I felt very debilitated.'

He gave a full account of the injections on the two succeeding days and also alleged that he was injected on 4 September, although there was no record in the case papers of such an event. Thereafter oral administrations of drugs were prescribed and given, but the plaintiff said that he spat out all the drugs, retaining them in his mouth until he was able to do so.

The judge also heard the evidence of one of the prison hospital officers, Clifford Copley. He gave evidence to the effect that he did not remember an occasion when he gave the plaintiff an injection, but he said, 'It's quite possible that I did,' adding:

'On no occasion can I remember forcing the drug on him or being with others when that was done. I do not remember him ever complaining to me that he had been forcibly injected. If he had made a complaint of forcible injection, I would have put it in the occurrence book and reported it to the doctor in charge.'

He also said under cross-examination on behalf of the plaintiff that if a prisoner was going to be difficult the senior medical officer would have to be informed and he would come up:

'If a prisoner objected, we would not just go ahead and inject him, we would call the medical officer. The prisoner can refuse. If he is struggling, he does not want it. If the man refused the injection, we would tell the MO, and if he said we had to give it none the less, we would give it using the minimum force.'

But, he said, 'I do not remember ever using force in any case, not just in the case of Mr Freeman'; and he concluded by saying that—

'if it had ever happened that a doctor had insisted on our injecting a prisoner, despite the fact that he refused it, and we would have had to do it with minimum force, there would have been an entry to that effect in the occurrence book.'

The judge said that having seen Mr Copley he impressed him as an honest and decent prison officer, and the judge went on to say:

'I accept his evidence, including that part of it dealing with where the oral drugs were usually given. I do not accept the plaintiff's evidence that he never swallowed the Stelazine or Tryptizol.'

The plaintiff had said that he always spat out the drugs which he was given orally.

The judge heard evidence from other prison officers and at the conclusion of his review of their evidence he said:

'I see no reason to doubt the truth of the evidence given by those prison officers. I accept that they were completely unaware of any absence of consent to the injections on the part of the plaintiff. I prefer their account.'

He also rejected the plaintiff's evidence that he had complained of forcible injections to Dr Knox and to a Mr Grave:

'Having seen the plaintiff and heard his evidence, I would not have been satisfied on his evidence alone of the truth of these allegations.'

The judge in fact rejected the plaintiff's evidence; he did not believe it and said so in

straightforward terms. After a careful and thorough review of the evidence, the judge
said:

> 'There is in fact no evidence that the plaintiff's capacity to consent was overborne
> or inhibited in any way. He gave no such evidence. He does not suggest for a
> moment that he was not man enough to say "No" and, had that been his evidence,
> having seen him I would not have believed him. On the contrary, his evidence is
> that he said "No" to the drugs in plain terms, and no lack of information or fear of
> the consequences would have persuaded him to say "Yes" had he not been overborne
> by physical force. There is, moreover, no evidence from any other source that he
> was overborne by the prison situation. He refused electro-convulsive therapy and
> that was respected; he refused to have a tooth out and that was respected. I am
> satisfied that if this man had not been consenting, it would have been necessary for
> him physically to be held down and injected by superior force. I have no doubt that
> did not happen. Therefore I conclude that he consented.'

The judge therefore made a clear finding of fact that the plaintiff had in fact consented
to the injections of the drugs on the material occasions.

Before this court counsel on behalf of the plaintiff accepts that the judge totally rejected
the plaintiff's evidence and he does not seek to challenge the judge's decision so to do. He
says that he accepts that the plaintiff must be taken to have 'permitted' the injections and
argues that none the less the judge was wrong to conclude that the plaintiff in fact
consented to the treatment. He states that in support of his submission he relies
exclusively on the documentation contained in the hospital case papers and the hospital
occurrence book which are before the court. He invites the court to note the indorsement
on the cover for the hospital case papers which reads 'Not to have any tranquillisers or
sedatives unless referred S.M.O. 2.2.71'. Counsel for the plaintiff laid special stress on a
memorandum written by Dr Xavier to the assistant governor of B wing on 5 October
1972. That memorandum related to the plaintiff and began:

> 'This man has continued to improve upon a mixture which he now takes
> voluntarily and admits that he feels better. His general demeanour has improved
> and I notice that he talks with the other inmates in the prison. He has lost his state
> of tension, together with being cantankerous and querulous.'

The submission is made that the phrase 'which he now takes voluntarily' should be
accorded a special meaning indicating that previously he had not been accepting the
drugs voluntarily. Counsel for the plaintiff complains that the judge was wrong in failing
to draw that inference. He refers also to a memorandum of Dr Xavier of 14 March 1977
made in answer to inquiries with regard to a parliamentary question asked about this
plaintiff's case. It includes a reference to the drugs which were prescribed; and in
connection with that matter a passage reads:

> 'Stelazine 10 mg. 10 August 1972—prescribed and refused. This was reduced to
> 2·5 mg twice a day on 31 August 1972 and he refused. Later he agreed. Serenace—
> intramuscularly daily because of his obvious hostility and cantankerous behaviour.
> Stelazine 5 mg. twice a day—accepted on 7 September 1972 till 14 September 1972.
> Re-prescribed on 12 October 1972 till 2 November 1972.'

On the second page of this memorandum the doctor wrote:

> 'It will be noted with the passing of the months, while in Wakefield, the amount
> of medication administered has gradually subsided. Also it is of interest to know
> that electro convulsive therapy had been advocated but not given due to inmate's
> refusal. At no time were drugs administered to inmate without his consent. If
> inmate asked for a drug to be discontinued this was done. Personally, I do not
> advocate the use of drugs and prefer to leave the inmate to the regime and

management within the prison system ... In conclusion may I please draw the attention of the authorities to the libellous statement made by inmate on my integrity as a medical officer ...'

The judge said:

'There can be no doubt in my mind that Dr Xavier knew that the plaintiff was reluctant to have these drugs and that for some time Dr Xavier did not succeed in persuading him to have them, but it does not follow that he never did. There is reason to think that the plaintiff's views and reactions tended to be erratic.'

Counsel for the plaintiff submits that not only should the judge have inferred the absence of consent by reference to the documentary evidence but, furthermore, that it is impossible within the prison context as between a prisoner and a prison medical officer for free and voluntary consent to exist, at least, he added, in the absence of any written consent form. The prison medical officer is not merely a doctor, he is, submits counsel for the plaintiff, a prison officer within the meaning of the Prison Rules 1964 and accordingly is a person who can influence a prisoner's life and his prospects of release on licence. There must inevitably be an atmosphere of constraint on an inmate in such circumstances. He cited the well-known passage from the judgment of Scott LJ in *Bowater v Rowley Regis BC* [1944] 1 All ER 465, [1944] 1 KB 476 at 479:

'In regard to the doctrine *volenti non fit injuria*, I would add one reflection of a general kind. That general maxim has to be applied with especially careful regard to the varying facts of human affairs and human nature in any particular case, just because it is concerned with the intangible factors of mind and will. For the purpose of the rule, if it be a rule, a man cannot be said to be truly "willing," unless he is in a position to choose freely; and freedom of choice predicates, not only full knowledge of the circumstances upon which the exercise of choice is conditioned, in order that he may be able to choose wisely, but the absence from his mind of any feeling of constraint, in order that nothing shall interfere with the freedom of his will.'

He also cited the unreported American case of *Kaimowitz v Michigan Dept of Mental Health* (1973) 42 USLW 101, 2063, the decision of a circuit court in the County of Michigan in 1973 which is the subject of a learned article (in Brooks *Law, Psychiatry and the Mental Health System* (1974) p 902). The judgment appears in the course of the article. The case concerned an inmate of a state hospital who had been committed to that institution as a criminal sexual psychopath and had signed what was termed an 'informed consent form' to become an experimental subject for experimental surgery and he later withdrew his consent. The court had to consider the nature of a legally adequate 'informed consent'. Although counsel for the plaintiff recognised that having regard to recent authority 'informed consent' as such does not apply to the law of this country, he nevertheless placed reliance on a passage of the judgment (see p 914 of the article):

'We turn now to the third element of an informed consent, that of voluntariness. It is obvious that the most important thing to a large number of involuntarily detained mental patients incarcerated for an unknown length of time, is freedom. The Nuremberg standards require that the experimental subjects be so situated as to exercise free power of choice without the intervention of any element of force, fraud, deceit, duress, overreaching, or other ulterior form of constraint or coercion. It is impossible for an involuntarily detained mental patient to be free of ulterior forms of restraint or coercion when his very release from the institution may depend upon his cooperating with the institutional authorities and giving consent to experimental surgery.'

And (at p 915):

a

    'Involuntarily confined mental patients live in an inherently coercive institutional environment. Indirect and subtle psychological coercion has profound effect upon the patient population. Involuntarily confined patients cannot reason as equals with the doctors and administrators over whether they should undergo psychosurgery. They are not able to voluntarily give informed consent because of the inherent inequality of their position.'

b

Counsel for the plaintiff seeks to apply those considerations and that reasoning to the position of the plaintiff in this present case, and he argues that in fact a valid free and voluntary consent cannot be given by a person such as the plaintiff, who is in prison, to a prison medical officer who is an officer of the prison having a disciplinary role in relation to him. Counsel for the plaintiff also drew the court's attention to the statutory provisions

c

of the Mental Health Act 1983 which relate to detained and voluntary patients. The provisions are to be found in ss 57 and 58 of the Act and relate to the question of consent and impose certain statutory safeguards which have to be fulfilled. He submits that a prisoner like the plaintiff is in a similar situation and accordingly that the court should bear in mind such safeguards in considering whether consent is established.

    It was the intention of counsel for the plaintiff to argue additionally that even if

d

(contrary to his submission) a prisoner can give a legally valid consent to treatment by a prison medical officer, such consent must be 'informed consent'. Having regard to the decision of this court in *Sidaway v Bethlem Royal Hospital Governors* [1984] 1 All ER 1018, it is not open to him to argue that 'informed consent' is a consideration which can be entertained by the courts of this country. Nevertheless, he submitted to the court that in psychiatric treatment the test of consent should be that which is required by ss 57 and 58

e

of the Mental Health Act 1983.

    Although the circumstances and the facts giving rise to the allegations made in this action afford an opportunity for interesting matters of principle and policy to be raised and considered, nevertheless I find myself in complete agreement with the trial judge that the sole issue raised at the trial, that is to say whether the plaintiff had consented to the administration of the drugs injected into his body, was essentially one of fact. The

f

judge considered with care all the evidence, both oral and documentary, and it is clear from his careful judgment that he took into account the various submissions which counsel for the plaintiff made as to the nature and effect of the documentary evidence and the setting in which the events occurred. The judge said ([1983] 3 All ER 589 at 597, [1984] 2 WLR 130 at 145):

g

    'The right approach, in my judgment, is to say that where, in a prison setting, a doctor has the power to influence a prisoner's situation and prospects a court must be alive to the risk that what may appear, on the face of it, to be a real consent is not in fact so. I have borne that in mind throughout the case.'

Essentially, however, the matter is one of fact. The judge made the positive finding that the plaintiff consented. He rejected the submission of counsel for the plaintiff that the

h

plaintiff was entitled to judgment because he was incapable in law of giving his consent to the treatment by Dr Xavier in question. In my judgment he was right so to do. There was ample evidence to justify his finding of fact and accordingly the decision to which he came. It is not for this court to consider and decide this appeal on the basis of an alternative and hypothetical set of facts and circumstances.

    I would dismiss this appeal.

j

SIR JOHN DONALDSON MR. In *M'Alister (or Donoghue) v Stevenson* [1932] AC 562, [1932] All ER Rep 1 the plaintiff claimed damages on the basis that a ginger beer bottle contained a snail. Professional folklore has it that there never was a snail, but under Scottish procedure it was still possible to decide what would have been the rights and liabilities of the parties if there had been a snail. That this was immensely valuable cannot be denied, because this decision provides the foundation stone for the modern law of negligence. For better or for worse, it is rare for it to be possible in an English court to decide what would be the rights and liabilities of the parties on the basis of assumed facts. The instant appeal is not such a case. The facts have been found and we know that there was no 'snail'.

Undeterred by this obstacle, counsel appearing for the plaintiff has sought to argue that (a) his client never in fact consented to being injected (factual absence of consent), (b) his client, being a prisoner serving a life sentence, could not as a matter of law consent to such treatment (legal inability to consent), and (c) even if he could consent in fact and in law, such a consent was no defence to a claim for damages for trespass to the person unless, before he consented, he had been told (i) what he was suffering from, (ii) what was the precise nature of the treatment prescribed, and (iii) what, if any, were the side effects and risks involved in that treatment (uninformed consent). It may be convenient to deal with these contentions in reverse order.

Uninformed consent

This appeal was overtaken by a decision of a differently constituted division of this court, which held that the American doctrine of 'informed consent' has no place in the law of England: see *Sidaway v Bethlem Royal Hospital Governors* [1984] 1 All ER 1018. If there was real consent to the treatment, it mattered not whether the doctor was in breach of his duty to give the patient the appropriate information before that consent was given. Real consent provides a complete defence to a claim based on the tort of trespass to the person. Consent would not be real if procured by fraud or misrepresentation but, subject to this and subject to the patient having been informed in broad terms of the nature of the treatment, consent in fact amounts to consent in law.

This point may be open to argument if the decision in *Sidaway* is reversed by the House of Lords, but not otherwise.

Legal inability to consent

Counsel for the plaintiff submitted that such were the pressures of prison life and discipline that a prisoner could not, as a matter of law, give an effective consent to treatment in any circumstances. This is a somewhat surprising proposition since it would mean that, in the absence of statutory authority, no prison medical officer could ever treat a prisoner. The answer of counsel for the plaintiff was in part that outside medical officers could be brought in, but I am not persuaded that this would reduce the pressures, whatever they may be.

In support of this proposition, we were referred to the judgment of Scott LJ in *Bowater v Rowley Regis BC* [1944] 1 All ER 465, [1944] 1 KB 476 at 479. Scott LJ there said:

'In regard to the doctrine *volenti non fit injuria*, I would add one reflection of a general kind. That general maxim has to be applied with especially careful regard to the varying facts of human affairs and human nature in any particular case, just because it is concerned with the intangible factors of mind and will. For the purpose of the rule, if it be a rule, a man cannot be said to be truly "willing," unless he is in a position to choose freely; and freedom of choice predicates, not only full knowledge of the circumstances upon which the exercise of choice is conditioned, in order that he may be able to choose wisely, but the absence from his mind of any feeling of constraint, in order that nothing shall interfere with the freedom of his will.'

The maxim volenti non fit injuria can be roughly translated as 'You cannot claim damages if you have asked for it', and 'it' is something which is and remains a tort. The maxim, where it applies, provides a bar to enforcing a cause of action. It does not negative the cause of action itself. This is a wholly different concept from consent which, in this context, deprives the act of its tortious character. Volenti would be a defence in the *a* unlikely scenario of a patient being held not to have in fact consented to treatment, but having by his conduct caused the doctor to believe that he had consented.

The judge expressed his view on this aspect of the argument by saying ([1983] 3 All ER 589 at 597, [1984] 2 WLR 130 at 145):

> 'The right approach, in my judgment, is to say that where, in a prison setting, a doctor has the power to influence a prisoner's situation and prospects a court must be alive to the risk that what may appear, on the face of it, to be a real consent is not
b in fact so.'

I would accept that as a wholly accurate statement of the law. The judge said that he had borne this in mind throughout the case. The sole question is therefore whether, on the evidence, there was a real consent.

c *Factual absence of consent*

The case of counsel for the plaintiff was that he was forcibly restrained from resisting the administration of the injections by no less than four or five prison officers. It was *not* that, due to the constraints of prison life and discipline, his will to refuse the injections was overborne and what appeared to be consent was in reality merely submission. The judge rejected this allegation of forcible restraint. He saw and heard the plaintiff give
d evidence at length and concluded that if he had not been consenting, it would have been necessary for him physically to be held down and injected by superior force. He had no doubt that this did not happen and he therefore concluded that the plaintiff consented.

There was ample evidence to support this conclusion, the plaintiff having on at least two occasions refused to accept treatment. Counsel for the plaintiff accepts the finding that there was no physical restraint and the judge's rejection of the plaintiff's evidence.
e However, he says, 'Ignore my client's evidence. Treat it as if it had never been given. You are then left only with documentary evidence and this evidence, viewed in isolation, enables me to argue that my client never consented and his failure to resist or protest must be interpreted as submission rather than consent.' Only counsel for the plaintiff could have made such a submission attractive and even he could not make it remotely plausible. This simply was not the plaintiff's complaint. His complaint was that far from
f submitting or giving any appearance of consent, his resistance was physically overborne. If he had suggested that the facts were otherwise and that he had submitted rather than consented to the treatment, this allegation could have been investigated and the plaintiff could have been cross-examined about it. But it was not.

For these reasons I would dismiss the appeal.

g **FOX LJ.** I have had the advantage of reading in draft the judgments of Sir John Donaldson MR and Stephen Brown LJ. I agree that the appeal should be dismissed for the reasons which they give.

Appeal dismissed. No order for costs. Leave to appeal to the House of Lords refused.

h Solicitors: *Bindman & Partners* (for the plaintiff); *Treasury Solicitor.*

Frances Rustin   Barrister.

Wings Ltd v Ellis

a

QUEEN'S BENCH DIVISION
ROBERT GOFF LJ AND MANN J
22, 23 NOVEMBER, 2 DECEMBER 1983

Trade description – False or misleading statement as to services etc – Making a statement – When b
offence committed – Statement contained in defendant's travel brochure – Defendant unaware
that statement false at date of publication – Defendant subsequently learning of falsity – Steps
taken to rectify mistake before statement read by complainant – Whether steps taken reasonable –
Whether offence committed – Trade Descriptions Act 1968, s 14(1)(a).

Trade description – False or misleading statement as to services etc – Statement made recklessly
– Statement made in travel company's brochure – Falsity of statement not known to persons c
directing company's mind and will – Whether offence committed by company – Trade Descriptions
Act 1968, s 14(1)(b).

The appellant, a holiday tour operator, published a brochure which gave details of the
holidays it would have available for the 1981–82 winter season, and which mistakenly
indicated that certain hotel accommodation in Sri Lanka was air-conditioned. In May d
1981 the appellant discovered the mistake. It instructed all its staff to amend their
brochures and instructed its sales agents to inform travel agents and customers of the
error when initial telephone bookings were made. It also prepared a letter for sending to
customers who had already booked holidays. In January 1982 W booked a holiday with
the appellant in Sri Lanka, but neither the appellant nor the travel agent informed him
that the hotel was not air-conditioned. On his return home after the holiday W e
complained to the appellant and to a trading standards officer. Informations were laid
against the appellant alleging that in the course of a trade or business it made a statement
which it knew to be false as to the nature of the accommodation, contrary to s 14(1)(a)[a]
of the Trade Descriptions Act 1968 and that in the course of a trade or business it
recklessly made a statement which was false as to the nature of the accommodation
contrary to s 14(1)(b) of the 1968 Act. The appellant was convicted by the magistrates. f
On appeal by way of case stated,

Held – The appeal would be allowed and the convictions quashed for the following
reasons—
(1) An offence under s 14(1)(a) of the 1968 Act was a result-crime and the specified
state of mind required for a person to be guilty of an offence under that subsection could g
exist at a moment of omission subsequent to the act of publication of the statement but
prior to the occurrence of the result (ie the statement being read, heard or seen by the
person to whom it was communicated). However, to constitute the offence it had to be
shown that the defendant had omitted to take an available opportunity to counteract the
effect of publication and the opportunity was one which, in the circumstances, it would
have been reasonable to expect him to take and which, if taken, could have prevented h
the result. Since, in all the circumstances, the appellant had done all that could reasonably
have been expected of it in order to neutralise the error in the brochure once it had been
discovered, there was no evidence on which a reasonable and properly instructed bench
of magistrates could have convicted the appellant under s 14(1)(a) (see p 1052 d to
p 1053 a and p 1054 b c, post); *R v Thomson Holidays Ltd* [1974] 1 All ER 823 and *R v*
Miller [1983] 1 All ER 978 applied. j
(2) It was established law that the commission of an offence under the 1968 Act
required a specific intent and that a corporate defendant could not be guilty unless the

---
a Section 14(1) is set out at p 1049 *f g*, post

a requisite intent was a state of mind of one or more of the natural persons who constituted the defendant's directing mind and will. Since, on the facts, there was no evidence of recklessness on the part of any of the natural persons who constituted the appellant's directing mind and will, there was no evidence on which a reasonable and properly instructed bench of magistrates could convict the appellant under s 14(1)(b) of the 1968 Act (see p 1053 b and h to p 1054 c post); *Tesco Supermarkets Ltd v Nattrass* [1971] 2 All ER 127 applied.

b **Notes**

For standard of recklessness required under s 14 of the Trade Descriptions Act 1968, see 11 Halsbury's Laws (4th edn) para 14.

For the Trade Descriptions Act 1968, s 14, see 37 Halsbury's Statutes (3rd edn) 959.

Cases referred to in judgment

c *Bolton (H L) (Engineering) Co Ltd v T J Graham & Sons Ltd* [1956] 3 All ER 624, [1957] 1 QB 159, [1956] 3 WLR 804.

Coupe v Guyett [1973] 2 All ER 1058, [1973] 1 WLR 669, DC.

MFI Warehouses Ltd v Nattrass [1973] 1 All ER 762, [1973] 1 WLR 307, DC.

R v Miller [1983] 1 All ER 978, [1983] 2 AC 161, [1983] 2 WLR 539, HL.

R v Thomson Holidays Ltd [1974] 1 All ER 823, [1974] QB 592, [1974] 2 WLR 371, CA.

d *Tesco Supermarkets Ltd v Nattrass* [1971] 2 All ER 127, [1972] AC 153, [1971] 2 WLR 1166, HL.

Case stated

Wings Ltd appealed by way of case stated by the justices for the City of Plymouth in respect of their adjudication as a magistrates' court sitting at St Andrew Street, Plymouth, e on 17 January 1983, whereby, on informations preferred by the respondent, David Kenneth Ellis, they convicted the appellant (i) of an offence under s 14(1)(a)(ii) of the Trade Descriptions Act 1968 and (ii) of an offence under s 14(1)(b)(ii) of that Act, and fined the appellant £500 in respect of each offence. The facts are set out in the judgment of the court.

f *James Price* for the appellant.

Nicholas Nardecchia for the respondent.

Cur adv vult

2 December. The following judgment of the court was delivered.

g **MANN J.** There is before the court an appeal by way of case stated by the justices of the City of Plymouth in respect of their adjudication as a magistrates' court on 17 January 1983.

On 9 August 1982 informations were laid by the respondent alleging that the appellant, on 13 January 1982—

h '(i) did in the course of a trade or business, make a statement which [the appellant] knew to be false as to the nature of the accommodation at the Seashells Hotel, Negombo, Sri Lanka, namely the statement "AC" contained in the description of the said hotel on page eight of [the appellant's] brochure, namely "Wings faraway holiday Winter Oct 1981–Apr 1982" indicating that the bedrooms at the said hotel were air conditioned, whereas in fact they were not. Contrary to Section 14(1)(a)(ii) of the Trade Descriptions Act 1968. (ii) did in the course of a trade or business, j recklessly make a statement which was false as to the nature of the accommodation at the Seashells Hotel, Negombo, Sri Lanka, namely the photograph titled "Bedroom at Seashells Hotel" on page eight of [the appellant's] brochure, namely "Wings faraway holidays Winter Oct 1981–Apr 1982" the said photograph being likely to be taken as an indication that the bedrooms of the said hotel were air conditioned whereas this was not the case as the photograph was not of any bedroom at the Seashells Hotel. Contrary to Section 14(1)(b)(ii) of the Trade Descriptions Act 1968.'

The justices found the following facts:

'(a) A Mr. Wade who lives in Callington, Cornwall booked a holiday in Sri Lanka for himself and his wife, with the Appellant through A.A. Travel Services Limited, who are travel agents, on the 13th January 1982, commencing on 3rd March 1982. The Wings brochure from which he selected the holiday indicated that the hotel rooms were air conditioned by use of the code letters AC. A photograph in the brochure indicated to Mr. Wade that the room was of a sealed type because there was no indication of ceiling fans, mosquito nets or other forms of outside ventilation. (b) On arrival at the hotel, Mr. Wade found that the hotel was not air conditioned, ventilation being by means of lattice work over the windows and overhead fans. Mosquito nets were also necessary because of the insects and creatures which were able to enter the room. This caused discomfort to Mr. Wade and his wife. (c) On his return to this country Mr. Wade complained to the Appellant and to the Trading Standards Department. (d) In the first charge, the Appellant knew of the error that "AC" was false in May 1981. On discovering the error the Appellant sent a memorandum dated 1st June 1981 to all their staff instructing them to amend their own brochures. A letter was prepared for sending to clients who had already booked holidays, but this was not sent to Mr. Wade who did not receive one. He could only be contacted via the travel agents. The memorandum also instructed sales agents to inform travel agents and customers of the error when initial telephone booking were made. (e) Mr. Wade was never informed of the lack of air conditioning either by the travel agent or by the Appellant, although the travel agent might well have known. The Appellant was reckless in printing the wrong hotel room photograph. The Appellant admitted that the wrong photograph had been inserted. The photograph in the brochure was approved as being correct by the contracts manager. The mistake could only be detected by someone with personal knowledge of the hotel, the contracts manager being the person most likely to know, he having visited the hotel two or three times before the brochure was issued.'

On those findings, we comment only that it is not surprising that a letter was not sent to Mr Wade, in that he did not book his holiday until seven or eight months after the discovery of the error.

The justice's opinion is expressed as follows:

'We were of the opinion that a statement is made when it is published and both offences were committed by the use of the code letters "AC" and the printing of the wrong bedroom photograph in the brochure which was read by Mr. Wade before booking his holiday, and upon which he relied absolutely. We found that the Appellant recklessly made the statement concerning the wrong hotel bedroom, on the ground that no adequate checking was ever carried out to ensure that it was the right photograph.'

The justices appended a copy of the notes of evidence to the case.

The issues before the justices raised difficult questions of law. They have asked the opinion of this court on the following questions:

'1. Whether the two facts (a) that the Appellant's customer Mr. Wade read the brochure containing the statement "AC" on the 13th January 1982 and (b) that employees of the Appellant discovered that the said statement was false before that date in about May 1981, by themselves suffice to support a conviction of the Appellant under Section 14(1)(a) [of the Trade Descriptions Act 1968] of knowingly making a false statement, regardless of any other evidence, or of evidence that Mr.

a   Wade's travel agent in common with all other persons inquiring about or booking
     at the Seashells Hotel were told that it was not air conditioned.
         2. Whether there was evidence on which the court could make the finding of
     fact made by it that the Appellant knew the statement "AC" to be false.
         3. Whether to secure a conviction under Section 14(1)(a) it was necessary for the
     prosecution to prove guilt, or guilty knowledge, on the part of a director or a
     controlling manager of the Appellant who represents the directing mind and will
b   of the company and controls what it does.
         4. Whether on the true construction of Section 14(1)(a) the offence thereby
     created involves some dishonesty.
         5. Whether a reasonable bench of magistrates could decide that the photograph
     titled "Bedroom at Seashells Hotel" was likely to be taken as an indication that the
     bedrooms of the said hotel were air conditioned.
c   6. Whether the conviction under Section 14(1)(b)(ii) can be supported in the
     absence of any finding of fact that the said photograph was likely to be taken as an
     indication that the bedrooms of the said hotel were air conditioned, and whether
     there was evidence on which the court could make such a finding.'

     For convenience, we have divided the next question into two parts:

d   '7. Whether to secure a conviction under Section 14(1)(b) it was necessary for the
     prosecution to prove recklessness [a] on the part of a director or a controlling
     manager of the Appellant who represents the directing mind and will of the
     company and controls what it does, or [b] on the part of an employee of the
     Appellant responsible for the publication of the said brochure.
         8. Whether there was evidence on which the court could make the finding of
e   fact made by it that the Appellant was reckless.'

         As will have appeared, the appellant answered two informations, each alleging a
     separate offence. The first related to the statement 'AC' and the second related to the
     statement which was the photograph of the bedroom. The first was laid under s 14(1)(a)
     of the Trade Descriptions Act 1968, whilst the second was laid under s 14(1)(b). The
f   appellant was convicted of both offences. Section 14(1) provides:

         'It shall be an offence for any person in the course of any trade or business—(a) to
         make a statement which he knows to be false; or (b) recklessly to make a statement
         which is false; as to any of the following matters, that is to say,—(i) the provision in
         the course of any trade or business of any services, accommodation or facilities; (ii)
         the nature of any services, accommodation or facilities provided in the course of any
g   trade or business; (iii) the time at which, manner in which or persons by whom any
         services, accommodation or facilities are so provided; (iv) the examination, approval
         or evaluation by any person of any services, accommodation or facilities so provided;
         or (v) the location or amenities of any accommodation so provided.'

         The propriety of a conviction under s 14(1)(a) suggests the following questions: (a) if
h   the appellant did not know (as it did not) that the false statement 'AC' had been published
     in the brochure, could it, on the facts, be guilty of making a statement which it knew to
     be false when it subsequently discovered, before Mr Wade read it, that the statement had
     been published; and (b) if the defendant is a body corporate, must the knowledge of
     falsity be that of a natural person who is amongst those natural persons who constitute
     the directing mind and will of the company?
j   The propriety of a conviction under s 14(1)(b) suggests the following questions: (a) if
     the defendant is a body corporate, must the recklessness be that of a natural person who
     is amongst those natural persons who constitute the directing mind and will of the
     company; (b) did the statement which was a photograph indicate that the bedroom is air
     conditioned, ie was the statement to that extent false; and (c) was there evidence to

support a conclusion that the statement was made recklessly, in the sense of being made
without regard to its truth or falsity? We shall deal separately with each conviction. *a*

Section 14(1)(a)

If, for the purposes of this offence a statement is made when it is published or uttered,
the only moment at which knowledge of falsity could exist would be the moment of
publication or utterance. Accordingly, if this hypothesis is correct, the appellant would *b*
have been entitled to an acquittal because there was no evidence that anyone within the
company knew that the statement 'AC' had been made when the brochure was published.
(There was evidence that the statement may have been a typographical error.) That the
error was discovered after publication (as it was on some day before 1 June 1981) would
have been irrelevant.

We are, however, compelled to take a different view because of the decision of the *c*
Court of Appeal, Criminal Division in *R v Thomson Holidays Ltd* [1974] 1 All ER 823,
[1974] QB 592. The submissions of counsel for the appellant, to which we wish to pay
tribute, were mounted by reference to the decision.

In that case, the defendant, having previously been convicted of recklessly making a
false statement in a brochure, was arraigned on three counts, charging it with recklessly
making the same false statement in the same brochure, albeit at the instance of three *d*
new complainants. The defendant pleaded autrefois convict, but the trial judge ruled
that the plea was invalid. The defendant's argument on appeal was that there was only
one act of making and that that act was publication of the brochure containing the
statement. The argument was rejected and Lawton LJ, delivering the judgment of the
court, said ([1974] 1 All ER 823 at 827–828, [1974] QB 592 at 597):

  e

'We do not accept that construction. The words used in s 14(1)(b) must, of course,
be given their ordinary meaning; but they must be construed in their context in an
Act which was intended by means of new statutory provisions to prohibit
"misdescriptions of goods, services, accommodation and facilities provided in the
course of trade." See the long title. It was an Act for the protection of members of
the public generally, and it specifically provided that every local weights and *f*
measures authority should have the duty of enforcing its provisions within their
own area (see s 26) and have special powers to do so (see ss 27 and 28). The general
scheme of the Act seems to envisage protection for individual members of the
public. In our judgment, when the phrases "in the course of any trade or business"
and "recklessly to make a statement which is false" are construed in their context,
the factor of communication must be considered. The words "in the course of trade *g*
or business" connote dealings between people—and the object of the Act is to
prohibit certain kinds of misdescription in the course of dealings between people.
Further anyone who in the course of any trade or business makes a statement does
so to people: there would be no point in making it unless there was someone to
whom it could have some effect. It follows in our judgment that a statement is
made when it is communicated to someone. When that will be will depend on the *h*
facts of each case. A travel firm which employed door-to-door salesmen to peddle
misleading information about package holidays might make a false statement at
every house at which they called; another such firm, putting out misleading
information in a television advertisement, would make the statement at the time of
the broadcast which would probably be seen by millions of people. Now the
appellants put into circulation amongst the public two million copies of a brochure *j*
each of which contained false statements intended by them to be read by, and to
influence, one or more readers. The brochures were intended to do what a door-to-
door salesman would do, namely give information about holidays; but with the
printed word the information would be given when the brochures were read. In

a
our judgment this is when the false statements were made, and they were made to each reader.'

This passage requires the ingredients of an offence under s 14 of the 1968 Act to be: (a) the defendant must have voluntarily published or uttered the statement in the course of a trade or business; (b) the statement must be false; (c) the defendant must have one of the requisite states of mind (ie knowledge of falsity or recklessness); and (d) a person for whom the statement is intended must have read, seen or heard it.

b
If this statement of ingredients is correct, then the offence is incomplete until a reading is proved. The reading in this case was a reading by Mr Wade on 13 January 1982, which was, therefore, the date of the offence alleged. It was a date after that on which persons in the appellant's organisation came to know that the false statement was in the brochure which had been voluntarily published. The respondent argued that knowledge coincident with the moment of reading was sufficient and that that moment was the only relevant

c
moment. We cannot agree. The act of reading is a chance event in relation to the state of a defendant's mind. Moreover, it is nonsensical that a defendant should be not guilty if, at the moment of publication, he knew the statement to be false, but, by the moment of reading, he had been (wrongly) persuaded of its truth. We reject the moment of reading as the moment at which the requisite state of mind must exist.

To reject the moment of publication as the moment at which the state of mind could

d
exist would be an absurdity. There is no reason why a person who publishes a statement which, at the moment of publication, he knows to be false should not be guilty of an offence. That, as we have said, is not this case. The question here is whether the moment of publication is the only moment at which the state of mind can exist. This case is one where a defendant voluntarily publishes a brochure containing a false statement, without knowing that it did so, but who discovers that it did before the complainant read it. The

e
circumstance directs us to *R v Miller* [1983] 1 All ER 978, [1983] 2 AC 161.

In *R v Miller* the House of Lords had before it a case of arson. That crime is a result-crime, in that it is not complete unless and until the conduct of the defendant has caused the specified result (see [1983] 1 All ER 978 at 980, [1983] 2 AC 161 at 174–175 per Lord Diplock). The certified question before the House was ([1983] 1 All ER 978 at 979, [1983] 2 AC 161 at 174):

f
'Whether the actus reus of the offence of arson is present when a Defendant accidentally starts a fire and thereafter, intending to destroy or damage property belonging to another or being reckless as to whether any such property would be destroyed or damaged, fails to take any steps to extinguish the fire or prevent damage to such property by that fire?'

g
The question was answered Yes. Lord Diplock, with whose speech the other members of the House agreed, said ([1983] 1 All ER 978 at 981, [1983] 2 AC 161 at 175–176):

'Since arson is a result-crime the period [from immediately before the moment of ignition to the completion of the damage to the property by the fire] may be considerable, and during it the conduct of the accused that is causative of the result

h
may consist not only of his doing physical acts which cause the fire to start or spread but also of his failing to take measures that lie within his power to counteract the danger that he has himself created. And if his conduct, active or passive, varies in the course of the period, so may his state of mind at the time of each piece of conduct. If, at the time of any particular piece of conduct by the accused that is causative of the result, the state of mind that actuates his conduct falls within the description of one or other of the states of mind that are made a necessary ingredient

j
of the offence of arson by s 1(1) of the Criminal Damage Act 1971 (ie intending to damage property belonging to another or being reckless whether such property would be damaged), I know of no principle of English criminal law that would prevent his being guilty of the offence created by that subsection. Likewise I see no

rational ground for excluding from conduct capable of giving rise to criminal liability conduct which consists of failing to take measures that lie within one's *a* power to counteract a danger that one has oneself created, if at the time of such conduct one's state of mind is such as constitutes a necessary ingredient of the offence.'

Amongst the circumstances where the defendant omits 'to take measures that lie within [his] power to counteract a danger that [he himself has] created' are those where *b* the omission is accompanied by the intent that the danger 'should fructify in actual damage', and those where he refrains 'either because he has not given any thought to the possibility of there being . . . risk [of damage to another's property] or because, although he has recognised there was some risk involved, he has none the less decided to take that risk' (see [1983] 1 All ER 978 at 981–982, [1983] 2 AC 161 at 176, 178). In each of those circumstances the defendant is guilty of arson. *c*

We read the speech of Lord Diplock as applicable to all result-crimes, so there is no reason why we should distinguish between members of the category. Thus, in any result-crime, if the result is caused both by the initial act of the defendant and by his subsequent omission, then the requisite state of mind may exist either at the moment of the initial act or at the moment of the omission. It is important to remember that Lord Diplock said that the omission must be an omission 'to take measures that lie within one's power *d* to counteract a danger that one has oneself created. It must follow, in our judgment, that a subsequent omission will not be causative of the result unless the omitted opportunity that was available to the defendant was one which, in the circumstances, it would have been reasonable to expect him to take and was one which, if taken, could have prevented the result.

In summary, our understanding of the principle applicable to a result-crime, as derived *e* from the speech of Lord Diplock, is that a court has to look for causative conduct, which can include a failure to counteract following on an initial act, and the coexistence with that conduct of a requisite state of mind.

Is an offence under s 14 of the 1968 Act a result-crime? We accept that it is. The initial act is the publication and the relevant result is that of a particular person reading the statement, for until that occurs the offence is incomplete (see *R v Thomson Holidays Ltd* *f* [1974] 1 All ER 823, [1974] QB 592). The act of reading is a voluntary act by the person concerned and is thus one over the occurrence of which the defendant has no control. But the particular reader does what was intended by the publisher, and there is, in our judgment, a sufficient nexus between cause (publication) and effect (reading).

As an offence under s 14 of the 1968 Act is a result-crime, we accept that the specified state of mind could exist at a moment of omission, subsequent to the act of publication, *g* but prior to the occurrence of the result. It could, however, so exist only if there was an omission to take an available opportunity which was one which, in the circumstances, it would have been reasonable to expect it to take and which, if taken, could have prevented the result, ie the reading by Mr Wade of the statement 'AC'.

On the evidence before the justices, we cannot see how any reasonable and properly instructed bench could conclude that there was such an omission. Prior to booking a *h* holiday through his agent, Mr Wade was a person unknown to the appellant. A quarter of a million copies of the brochure containing the statement 'AC' had been printed and a large number were distributed. Total recall was impossible of achievement and even to attempt it would have involved the suspension of the October 1981 to April 1982 Faraway programme, thus depriving the public of a choice and imposing a very substantial commercial loss on the appellant. The publication of a correction slip would *j* have been futile, for the identity of all of those needing correction was unknown. We do not rehearse what the appellant actually did. Suffice to say, in our judgment, it immediately did all that could reasonably have been expected in order to neutralise the error once it had been discovered.

For the reasons which we have given, the appeal in regard to the conviction under
a s 14(1)(*a*) must be allowed and the conviction quashed. The question of who must possess
a knowledge of falsity does not arise.

Section 14(1)(b)

The appellant is a limited company and it is established that, where the commission of
an offence under the 1968 Act requires a specific intent, then a corporate defendant is not
b guilty unless the requisite intent was a state of mind of one or more of those natural
persons who constitute the directing mind and will of the company. Lord Widgery CJ
described such persons as 'the ruling officers' in *Coupe v Guyett* [1973] 2 All ER 1058 at
1063, [1973] 1 WLR 669 at 675. These persons were described in *Tesco Supermarkets Ltd
v Nattrass* [1971] 2 All ER 127 at 132, [1972] AC 153 at 171 by Lord Reid in the following
terms:

c   'Normally the board of directors, the managing director and perhaps other
        superior officers of a company carry out the functions of management and speak
        and act as the company. Their subordinates do not. They carry out orders from
        above and it can make no difference that they are given some measure of discretion.
        But the board of directors may delegate some part of their functions of management
        giving to their delegate full discretion to act independently of instructions from
d   them. I see no difficulty in holding that they have thereby put such a delegate in
        their place so that within the scope of the delegation he can act as the company.'

Viscount Dilhorne said ([1971] 2 All ER 127 at 145–146, [1972] AC 153 at 187):

        'Following this, Denning LJ in *H L Bolton (Engineering) Co Ltd v T J Graham & Sons
        Ltd* [1957] 1 QB 159 at 172; cf [1956] 3 All ER 624 at 630 said: "A company may in
e   many ways be likened to a human body. It has a brain and nerve centre which
        controls what it does. It also has hands which hold the tools and act in accordance
        with directions from the centre. Some of the people in the company are mere
        servants and agents who are nothing more than hands to do the work and cannot be
        said to represent the mind or will. Others are directors and managers who represent
        the directing mind and will of the company, and control what it does. The state of
f   mind of these managers is the state of mind of the company and is treated by the
        law as such." If, when Denning LJ referred to directors and managers representing
        the directing mind and will of the company, he meant, as I think he did, those who
        constitute the directing mind and will, I agree with his approach.'

Lord Diplock said ([1971] 2 All ER 127 at 155, [1972] AC 153 at 199–200):

g   'In my view, therefore, the question: what natural persons are to be treated in law
        as being the company for the purpose of acts done in the course of its business,
        including the taking of precautions and the exercise or due diligence to avoid the
        commission of a criminal offence, is to be found by identifying those natural persons
        who by the memorandum and articles of association or as a result of action taken by
        the directors, or by the company in general meeting pursuant to the articles, are
h   entrusted with the exercise of the powers of the company.'

Although the descriptions vary, the concept is clear. A company cannot be guilty of
an offence unless the specified state of mind was a state of mind of a person who is or
forms part of the directing mind and will of the company. As to the personal liability of
such persons, see s 20 of the 1968 Act.
j   Was there evidence on which a reasonable bench of justices, properly instructed, could
be sure that there was recklessness by such a person in the present case?
        'Recklessness' means failing to have regard to the truth or falsity of the statement (see
MFI Warehouses Ltd v Nattrass [1973] 1 All ER 762 at 768, [1973] 1 WLR 307 at 313).
We can find nothing in the evidence which suggests that a person ruling the company

was privy to the selection of the photograph. In particular, we reject the respondent's suggestion that Michael Stephen-Jones, who approved the photograph and who variously *a* called himself a 'long haul development manager' and 'the contracts manager', could be inferred to be a member of the relevant class. The most that could be said for the respondent is that the members of this class, although establishing a system, failed to establish a system which would have prevented the mistake which occurred. That failure cannot, in our judgment, constitute 'recklessness'. There may be cases where the system is such that he who establishes it could not be said to be having regard to the truth or *b* falsity of what emerged from it, but that is not this case.

For the reasons which we have given, the appeal in regard to the conviction under s 14(1)(b) must be allowed and the conviction quashed.

We answer questions 1, 7(b) and 8 No and question 7(a) Yes. Questions 2, 3, 5 and 6 do not arise; whilst as to question 4 we can answer only that the offence is one of making a statement which he who makes it knows to be false. *c*

Appeal allowed. Convictions quashed.

The court refused leave to appeal to the House of Lords but certified, under s 1(2) of the Administration of Justice Act 1960, that the following point of law of general public importance was involved in the decision: whether a defendant may properly be convicted of an offence under *d* *s 14(1)(a) of the Trade Descriptions Act 1968 where he had no knowledge of the falsity of the statement at the time of its publication but knew of the falsity at the time when the statement was read by the complainant.*

1 March. The Appeal Committee of the House of Lords granted the respondent leave to appeal.

Solicitors: *Knapp-Fishers* (for the appellant); *J E Coyne*, Plymouth (for the respondent). *e*

Dilys Tausz   Barrister.

Holgate-Mohammed v Duke   *f*

HOUSE OF LORDS
LORD DIPLOCK, LORD KEITH OF KINKEL, LORD BRIDGE OF HARWICH, LORD BRANDON OF OAKBROOK AND LORD BRIGHTMAN
15, 16 FEBRUARY, 29 MARCH 1984

g

Arrest – Arrest without warrant – Reasonable cause – Exercise of power of arrest – Constable arresting suspect in belief that confession more likely if suspect subjected to stress and pressure of arrest – Whether proper exercise of power of arrest – Whether constable properly exercising discretion – Whether belief that suspect might confess if arrested an extraneous consideration in exercise of discretion to arrest – Criminal Law Act 1967, s 2(4).

h

The appellant was a lodger in a house from which some jewellery was stolen. Some months later the owner of the jewellery recognised it in the window of a jeweller's shop and informed the police. The jeweller's description of the person who sold the jewellery to him was thought by the owner of the jewellery to fit the appellant. From that, a detective constable investigating the owner's complaint considered that he had reasonable cause for suspecting that the appellant had stolen the jewellery, but also considered that *j* the jeweller's evidence alone would not be sufficient to convict the appellant. He therefore decided to arrest the appellant in the belief that she would be more likely to confess to the theft if she was arrested and taken to a police station for questioning than if she was merely questioned in her home. The constable accordingly exercised his power under

s 2(4)[a] of the Criminal Law Act 1967 to arrest the appellant without a warrant. She was
a then taken to a police station and interrogated. No evidence was obtained linking her
with the crime, and she was released about six hours later. The appellant brought an
action against the chief constable claiming damages for false imprisonment. The judge
awarded the plaintiff £1,000 damages on the ground that there had been a false
imprisonment because the arresting officer's sole reason for arresting the plaintiff under
s 2(4) rather than interviewing her under caution was that he thought she would be
b more likely to confess if she was subjected to the greater stress and pressure involved in
an arrest and deprivation of liberty. The Court of Appeal allowed an appeal by the chief
constable, on the ground that where a constable had reasonable cause for suspecting that
a person had committed an arrestable offence he could exercise the power of arrest under
s 2(4) and use the period of detention to establish whether his suspicions were justified
and also to seek further material evidence, rather than having to make all practicable
c inquiries before exercising the power of arrest. The appellant appealed to the House of
Lords.

Held – In exercising his power of arrest under s 2(4) of the 1967 Act a police constable
was exercising an executive discretion which could only be questioned under the well-
established principles applicable to the exercise of such a discretion. For the purpose of
d applying those principles, a belief held in good faith by the constable that there was a
greater likelihood that a suspect would respond truthfully to questions about a crime if
he was questioned under arrest at a police station than if he was questioned at his own
home was not an extraneous consideration and he was therefore entitled to take that
belief into account when deciding whether to make the arrest. Since there were no
grounds for believing that the arresting officer had not exercised his discretion properly,
e he had therefore not acted unlawfully when arresting the plaintiff. The appeal would
accordingly be dismissed (see p 1057 *e* to *j* and p 1059 *j* to p 1060 *d*, post).
Associated Provincial Picture Houses Ltd v Wednesbury Corp [1947] 2 All ER 680 applied.
Decision of Court of Appeal sub nom *Mohammed-Holgate v Duke* [1983] 3 All ER 526
affirmed.

f **Notes**
For the exercise by a constable of the power to arrest without warrant, see 11 Halsbury's
Laws (4th edn) para 111, and for cases on the subject, see 14(1) Digest (Reissue) 196–198,
1399–1433.
For the Criminal Law Act 1967, s 2, see 8 Halsbury's Statutes (3rd edn) 553.

Cases referred to in opinions
g *Associated Provincial Picture Houses Ltd v Wednesbury Corp* [1947] 2 All ER 680, [1948] 1
KB 223, CA.
Christie v Leachinsky [1947] 1 All ER 567, [1947] AC 573, HL.
R v Turnbull [1976] 3 All ER 549, [1977] QB 224, [1976] 3 WLR 445, CA.
Shaaban Bin Hussien v Chong Fook Kam [1969] 3 All ER 1626, [1970] AC 942, [1970] 2
WLR 441, PC.
h *Wiltshire v Barrett* [1965] 2 All ER 271, [1966] 1 QB 312, [1965] 2 WLR 1195, CA.

Appeal
Mariam Holgate-Mohammed appealed with the leave of the Appeal Committee of the
House of Lords granted on 8 December 1983 against the decision of the Court of Appeal
(Sir John Arnold P and Latey J) sub nom *Mohammed-Holgate v Duke* [1983] 3 All ER 526,
j [1984] QB 209 given on 13 July 1983 allowing the appeal of the respondent, John Duke,
the Chief Constable of Hampshire, against the decision of his Honour Judge Inskip QC
in the Portsmouth County Court on 20 December 1982 whereby the judge awarded the

---

a   Section 2(4), is set out at p 1056 *e*, post

appellant £1,000 damages in her action against the respondent for false imprisonment. The facts are set out in the opinion of Lord Diplock.

a

Alan Tyrrell QC and *Robin W Belben* for the appellant.
Barry Mortimer QC and *Robert Beecroft* for the respondent.

Their Lordships took time for consideration.

b

29 March. The following opinions were delivered.

LORD DIPLOCK. My Lords, this appeal is in a civil action for false imprisonment brought by the appellant, Mrs Holgate-Mohammed, against the Chief Constable of Hampshire and arising out of her arrest without warrant at her home on 8 May 1980 by an officer of the Hampshire Constabulary, Det Con Offin, and her subsequent detention *c* in custody at Southsea police station for a period of about six hours, after which time she was released on police bail under s 38(2) of the Magistrates' Courts Act 1952 (now s 43(3) of the Magistrates' Courts Act 1980). She was later informed by the police that she need not surrender to her bail as no further proceedings would be taken against her.

Your Lordships are not concerned with rights of arrest at common law for it is not disputed that an arrestable offence had been committed, and what Det Con Offin was *d* purporting to exercise was the statutory power of arrest without warrant conferred on him by s 2(4) and (6) of the Criminal Law Act 1967. Subsection (6) confers a right of entry on premises by a constable for the purpose of exercising the power of arrest conferred on him by sub-s (4), which reads as follows:

> 'Where a constable, with reasonable cause, suspects that an arrestable offence has been committed, he may arrest without warrant anyone whom he, with reasonable *e* cause, suspects to be guilty of the offence.'

The word 'arrest' in s 2 is a term of art. First, it should be noted that arrest is a continuing act: it starts with the arrester taking a person into his custody (sc by action or words restraining him from moving anywhere beyond the arrester's control), and it continues until the person so restrained is either released from custody or, having been *f* brought before a magistrate, is remanded in custody by the magistrate's judicial act. In practice, since the creation of organised police forces during the course of the nineteenth century an arrested person, on being taken into custody by a constable, is brought to a police station and it is there that he is detained until he is either brought before a magistrate or released, whether unconditionally or on police bail. In modern conditions any other way of dealing with an arrested person once he has been taken into custody *g* would be impracticable; and s 43 of the 1980 Act, providing for grant of bail by the police, is drafted on the assumption that this is what will be done.

Strictly speaking, the arrester may change from time to time during a continuous period of custody since the arrester is the person who at any particular time is preventing the arrested person from removing himself from custody; but, although this may be important in a case where the initial arrest has been made by a person who is not a *h* constable (a 'citizen's arrest'), it is without practical significance in the common case of arrest by a constable and detention in police custody at a police station, since s 48(1) of the Police Act 1964 makes the chief constable of the police area vicariously liable for torts committed by members of the force that he commands in the performance or purported performance of their duties as constables.

Second, it should be noted that the mere act of taking a person into custody does not *j* constitute an 'arrest' unless that person knows, either at the time when he is first taken into custody or as soon thereafter as it is reasonably practicable to inform him, on what charge or on suspicion of what crime he is being arrested: see *Christie v Leachinsky* [1947] 1 All ER 567, [1947] AC 573. In the instant case, however, there is no suggestion that the

a appellant, when she was arrested at her home by Det Con Offin, was not fully informed by him of the offence, burglary of jewellery at a house at which she was residing in December 1979, which he suspected her of having committed. Very shortly after the burglary some of the jewellery had been sold to a jeweller in Portsmouth; but it was not until more than four months later, at the end of April 1980, that the victim of the burglary recognised her jewellery in the shop window and informed the police of this. The jeweller's description of the vendor was thought by the victim to resemble that of
b her former lodger, the appellant, and she so informed Det Con Offin, who had accompanied her to the jeweller's shop.

Section 2(4) of the 1967 Act makes it a condition precedent to a constable's having any power lawfully to arrest a person without warrant that he should have reasonable cause to suspect that person to be guilty of the arrestable offence in respect of which the arrest is being made. Whether he had reasonable cause is a question of fact for the court to
c determine. The county court judge by whom the appellant's action for false imprisonment was heard at first instance and who had the advantage of hearing and seeing the witnesses held that Det Con Offin did have reasonable cause for suspecting her to be guilty of the crime of burglary. The Court of Appeal, which had the advantage of examining either a transcript or a note of the oral evidence, came to the same conclusion. Your Lordships have enjoyed neither of these advantages. The only facts that are available to this House
d are such fragments as can be garnered from the judgments below. Your Lordships are thus faced on this issue with concurrent findings of fact with which there is no material that could possibly justify interference.

There are likewise concurrent findings of fact of the courts below that the duration of the appellant's detention at Southsea police station was, in the circumstances of which your Lordships are not fully apprised, not unreasonable. With the findings on this issue,
e too, this House in my view is in no position to interfere.

So the condition precedent to Det Con Offin's power to take the appellant into custody and the power of the other constables at Southsea police station to detain her in custody was fulfilled; and, since the wording of the subsection under which he acted is 'may arrest without warrant', this left him with an executive discretion whether to arrest her or not. Since this is an executive discretion expressly conferred by statute on a public officer, the
f constable making the arrest, the lawfulness of the way in which he has exercised it in a particular case cannot be questioned in any court of law except on those principles laid down by Lord Greene MR in *Associated Provincial Picture Houses Ltd v Wednesbury Corp* [1947] 2 All ER 680, [1948] 1 KB 223, that have become too familiar to call for repetitious citation. The *Wednesbury* principles, as they are usually referred to, are applicable to determining the lawfulness of the exercise of the statutory discretion of a constable under
g s 2(4) of the 1967 Act, not only in proceedings for judicial review but also for the purpose of founding a cause of action at common law for damages for that species of trespass to the person known as false imprisonment, for which the action in the instant case is brought.

The first of the *Wednesbury* principles is that the discretion must be exercised in good faith. The county court judge expressly found that Det Con Offin in effecting the initial
h arrest acted in good faith. He thought that he was making a proper use of his power of arrest. So his exercise of that power by arresting the appellant was lawful unless it can be shown to have been 'unreasonable' under *Wednesbury* principles, of which the principle that is germane to the instant case is 'he [sc the exerciser of the discretion] must exclude from his consideration matters which are irrelevant to what he has to consider'.

As Lord Devlin, speaking for the Judicial Committee of the Privy Council in *Shaaban*
j *Bin Hussien v Chong Fook Kam* [1969] 3 All ER 1626 at 1630, [1970] AC 942 at 948, said:

'Suspicion in its ordinary meaning is a state of conjecture or surmise where proof is lacking; "I suspect but I cannot prove". Suspicion arises at or near the starting point of an investigation of which the obtaining of prima facie proof is the end.

When such proof has been obtained, the police case is complete; it is ready for trial
and passes on to its next stage.'   *a*

ie bringing the suspect before a magistrates' court on a charge of a criminal offence.
   The other side of the same coin is where the investigation, although diligently pursued,
fails to produce prima facie proof which, as Lord Devlin also pointed out (see [1969] 3
All ER 1626 at 1631, [1970] AC 942 at 949), must be in the form of evidence that would
be admissible in a court of law. When the police have reached the conclusion that prima   *b*
facie proof of the arrested person's guilt is unlikely to be discovered by further inquiries
of him or of other potential witnesses, it is their duty to release him from custody
unconditionally: see *Wiltshire v Barrett* [1965] 2 All ER 271, [1966] 1 QB 312.
   Det Con Offin and, no doubt, those other officers of the Hampshire police who had
been concerned in the inquiries into the burglary that had been committed in December
1979 were well aware that their case against the appellant depended on whether the   *c*
jeweller would be able to identify, on an identification parade, a customer whom he had
seen only once, and that for a comparatively brief period five months before, and whether
he would be able to justify his identification in such a manner as would instil in a jury
that high degree of confidence in his not having been mistaken that is called for by the
guidance given in *R v Turnbull* [1976] 3 All ER 549, [1977] QB 224. Det Con Offin and
his fellow police officers concerned in the inquiries thought (with obvious justification)   *d*
that, even if the jeweller were to succeed in picking out the appellant on a properly
conducted identification parade, such evidence would be too weak to justify convicting
her of committing the crime of burglary in December 1979. In these circumstances, if
she had in fact committed the offence of which there were reasonable grounds at the
time of her arrest for suspecting her to be guilty, the only kind of admissible evidence
probative of her guilt that would be likely to be procurable would be a confession   *e*
obtained from the appellant herself.
   Det Con Offin thought that she would be more likely to confess to what he had
reasonable cause to believe to be the truth if she were arrested and taken for questioning
to the police station. In other words, the reason why Det Con Offin arrested her was that
he held the honest opinion that the police inquiries were more likely to be fruitful in
clearing up the case if the appellant was compelled to go to the police station to be   *f*
questioned there. It is relevant to add that officers who had been concerned, as Det Con
Offin had not, in the original investigations in December 1979 would have been available,
and there would have been facilities for recording any statements that the appellant
decided to make.
   The county court judge, however, described Det Con Offin's reason for making the
arrest in somewhat emotive phraseology (for which I have myself supplied the emphasis)   *g*
as being 'to subject her to the *greater stress and pressure* involved in arrest and deprivation
of liberty in the belief that if she was going to confess she was more likely to do so in a
state of arrest'. Yet, despite his use of the expressions 'stress' and 'pressure', the judge went
on to find that the questioning to which the appellant was subjected at the police station
was conducted with complete propriety. 'There was not,' he said, 'any suggestion of
verbal bullying at the police station or anything approaching it.' Indeed, it would appear   *h*
that the appellant's solicitor, who had been sent for at her request, was present for part of
the time at least and made no complaint of the arrest or the nature of the questioning or
the length of time for which she was being detained.
   So, applying *Wednesbury* principles, the question of law to be decided by your
Lordships may be identified as this: was it a matter that Det Con Offin should have
excluded from his consideration, as irrelevant to the exercise of his statutory power of   *j*
arrest, that there was a greater likelihood (as he believed) that the appellant would
respond truthfully to questions about her connection with or knowledge of the burglary,
if she were questioned under arrest at the police station, than if, without arresting her,
questions were put to her by Det Con Offin at her own home from which she could

a   peremptorily order him to depart at any moment, since his right of entry under s 2(6) of
the Criminal Law Act 1967 was dependent on his intention to arrest her?

My Lords, there is inevitably the potentiality of conflict between the public interest in
preserving the liberty of the individual and the public interest in the detection of crime
and the bringing to justice of those who commit it. The members of the organised police
forces of the country have, since the mid-nineteenth century, been charged with the duty
of taking the first steps to promote the latter public interest by inquiring into suspected
b   offences with a view to identifying the perpetrators of them and of obtaining sufficient
evidence admissible in a court of law against the persons they suspect of being the
perpetrators as would justify charging them with the relevant offence before a magistrates'
court with a view to their committal for trial for it.

The compromise which English common and statutory law has evolved for the
accommodation of the two rival public interests while these first steps are being taken by
c   the police is twofold.

(1) No person may be arrested without warrant (ie without the intervention of a
judicial process) unless the constable arresting him has reasonable cause to suspect him to
be guilty of an arrestable offence; and arrest, as is emphasised in the Judges' Rules
themselves, is the only means by which a person can be compelled against his will to
come to or remain in any police station.

d   (2) A suspect so arrested and detained in custody must be brought before a magistrates'
court as soon as practicable, generally within 24 hours, otherwise, save in a serious case,
he must be released on bail (see ss 43(1) and (4) of the Magistrates' Courts Act 1980).

That arrest for the purpose of using the period of detention to dispel or confirm the
reasonable suspicion by questioning the suspect or seeking further evidence with his
assistance was said by the Royal Commission on Criminal Procedure in England and
e   Wales (Cmnd 8092) in 1981, at para 3.66 'to be well established as one of the primary
purposes of detention upon arrest'. That is a fact that will be within the knowledge of
those of your Lordships with judicial experience of trying criminal cases, even as long
ago as I last did so, more than 20 years before the Royal Commission's report. It is a
practice which has been given implicit recognition in r 1 of successive editions of the
Judges' Rules (see Practice Note [1964] 1 All ER 237, [1964] 1 WLR 152) since they were
f   first issued in 1912. Furthermore, parliamentary recognition that making inquiries of a
suspect in order to dispel or confirm the reasonable suspicion is a legitimate cause for
arrest and detention at a police station was implicit in s 38(2) of the Magistrates' Courts
Act 1952 (which is now reproduced in s 43(3) of the Magistrates' Courts Act 1980, with
immaterial amendments consequent on the passing of the Bail Act 1976). That
subsection, so far as is relevant for present purposes, reads:

g   'Where, on a person's being taken into custody for an offence without a warrant,
it appears to any such officer as aforesaid [sc a police officer not below the rank of
inspector, or the police officer in charge of the police station to which the person is brought]
that the inquiry into the case cannot be completed forthwith, he may grant him
bail in accordance with the Bail Act 1976 subject to a duty to appear at such a police
station and at such a time as the officer appoints unless he previously receives a
h   notice in writing from the officer in charge of that police station that his attendance
is not required . . .'

So whether or not to arrest the appellant and bring her to the police station in order to
facilitate the inquiry into the case of the December burglary was a decision that it lay
within the discretion of Det Con Offin to take.

j   In my opinion the error of law made by the county court judge in the instant case was
that, having found that Det Con Offin had reasonable cause for suspecting the appellant
to be guilty of the burglary committed in December 1979 to which he rightly applied
an objective test of reasonableness, the judge failed to recognise that the lawfulness of the
arrest and detention based on that suspicion did not depend on the judge's own view

whether the arrest was reasonable or not, but on whether Det Con Offin's action in arresting her was an exercise of discretion that was ultra vires under *Wednesbury* principles because he took into consideration an irrelevant matter. For the reasons that I have given and in agreement with the Court of Appeal, I do not think that in the circumstances Det Con Offin or any other police officers of the Hampshire Constabulary acted unlawfully in the way in which they exercised their discretion.

I would dismiss this appeal.

LORD KEITH OF KINKEL. My Lords, I have had the benefit of reading in draft the speech of my noble and learned friend Lord Diplock. I agree with it, and for the reasons he gives I too would dismiss the appeal.

LORD BRIDGE OF HARWICH. My Lords, for the reasons given in the speech of my noble and learned friend Lord Diplock, with which I agree, I would dismiss this appeal.

LORD BRANDON OF OAKBROOK. My Lords, I have had the advantage of reading in draft the speech prepared by my noble and learned friend Lord Diplock. I agree with it, and for the reasons which he gives I would dismiss the appeal.

LORD BRIGHTMAN. My Lords, I would dismiss this appeal for the reasons given by my noble and learned friend Lord Diplock.

Appeal dismissed.

Solicitors: *Lovell Son & Pitfield*, agents for *H F E Mathews*, Portsmouth (for the appellant); *Theodore Goddard & Co*, agents for *R A Leyland*, Winchester (for the respondent).

Mary Rose Plummer   Barrister.

Barclays Bank Ltd and others v TOSG Trust Fund Ltd and others

HOUSE OF LORDS

LORD DIPLOCK, LORD KEITH OF KINKEL, LORD BRANDON OF OAKBROOK, LORD BRIGHTMAN AND LORD TEMPLEMAN

20, 21, 22 FEBRUARY, 29 MARCH 1984

Company – Winding up – Proof and ranking of claims – Rule against double proof – Company taking out bank bond against insolvency – Banks paying over money under bonds when company becoming insolvent – Money used to pay creditors in part – Creditors assigning claims to third party – Banks proving for debt under bonds – Third party proving for debt under assignments – Whether both proofs admissible – Whether banks or third party having better right of proof if only one proof admissible.

In 1970 a group of holiday tour operators, which included C Ltd, set up a scheme to alleviate the consequences to holidaymakers and customers of the insolvency of any of their number. The scheme required individual tour operators who were members of the scheme to take out a banker's bond whereby the bank agreed to pay a specified sum to a company (TOSG), formed as part of the scheme, in the event of the operator becoming insolvent and unable to fulfil its obligations to holidaymakers and customers. The purpose of TOSG was to use money paid to it under the bonds to look after and repatriate holidaymakers stranded abroad and to protect customers who had made prepaid bookings

from suffering financial loss. Under the terms of the bonds TOSG was entitled to call in the bond moneys from the bank as soon as the operator concerned became insolvent and
a TOSG was required to pay back to the bank any surplus remaining after the claims of customers had been met. In accordance with the scheme C Ltd arranged for a number of banks to enter into bonds on its behalf in return for the payment of commission and the execution of counter-indemnities under which C Ltd agreed to indemnify the banks against any loss which they sustained under the bonds. In 1974 C Ltd could no longer fulfil its obligations to its customers and went into liquidation. The bond moneys were
b called in from the banks by TOSG which, after rescuing C Ltd's customers who were stranded abroad, then had some £1·268m to reimburse claims by customers who had paid for holidays which C Ltd was no longer able to provide. Since that amount was unlikely to be sufficient to meet all such claims TOSG entered into an agreement with the Air Travel Reserve Fund Agency (a statutory body set up to compensate persons who lost holidays as a result of the collapse of tour operators) whereby TOSG would, to the
c extent the bond moneys made possible, reimburse customers who were owed money in return for such customers assigning to the agency their right to prove in the liquidation of C Ltd for the full amount of their claim and the agency would then satisfy customers' debts which remained unpaid by TOSG. In accordance with that agreement TOSG expended, and received assignments to the agency of claims amounting to, some
d £1·268m while the agency satisfied the remaining claims. In the ensuing liquidation of C Ltd the banks proved under the counter-indemnities and the agency proved under the assignments for the £1·268m paid out by TOSG. The liquidators took the view that the rule against double proof prevented the banks and the agency from both proving for the £1·268m. The banks sought a declaration that they were entitled to prove for the £1·268m but the judge held that the agency had the better right of proof because the banks had in effect guaranteed C Ltd's liabilities to its customers and were therefore
e subject to the rule that the proof of a surety could not displace the proof of a creditor unless and until the surety fully discharged all his liabilities to the creditor, and therefore C Ltd's customers (and thus the agency) were entitled to prove as creditors for the whole of their debts in priority to the banks (and without giving credit for moneys received from the banks via TOSG) unless and until the whole of their debts were satisfied. On appeal by the banks the Court of Appeal allowed the appeal, holding that the rule against
f double proof did not apply or if it did the banks had the better right of proof. The agency appealed to the House of Lords.

Held – On the true construction of the bonds and counter-indemnities the only reason for, and consequence of, a payment made by TOSG to a customer of C Ltd was the discharge of C Ltd's indebtedness to that customer. The customer's claim against C Ltd
g was thereafter extinguished and there was then vested in the banks (who had provided the money by which the customer was paid) an indisputable claim against C Ltd for that money under the indemnity. That was so regardless of whether a customer's claim was satisfied in full or only in part by TOSG. The arrangement between TOSG and the agency, which was not consented to by the banks, could not affect that situation and any
h assignment by a customer to the agency was worthless because the customer, having been paid, then had nothing to assign to the agency. Since the payment by TOSG had reduced the customers' debts by £1·268m and increased the banks' debts by a like amount the banks were entitled to prove in the liquidation of C Ltd for that amount to the exclusion of the agency. The agency's appeal would therefore be dismissed (see p 1062 *d* to *g*, p 1063 *d* to *g*, p 1065 *g* to *j*, p 1066 *f* to *h* and p 1067 *h* to p 1068 *a* and *d* to
j p 1069 *a*, post).

Decision of the Court of Appeal [1984] 1 All ER 628 affirmed.

Notes

For the rule against double proofs and its application to sureties, see 3 Halsbury's Laws (4th edn) paras 712, 728, and for cases on proofs by sureties against a bankrupt principal debtor, see 4 Digest (Reissue) 303–306, 2691–2720.

Appeal

The Air Travel Reserve Fund Agency (the agency) appealed against the judgment of the
Court of Appeal (Oliver, Kerr and Slade LJJ) ([1984] 1 All ER 628, [1984] 2 WLR 49)
given on 12 July 1983 allowing the appeal of the plaintiffs, Barclays Bank Ltd, Lloyds
Bank Ltd, National Westminster Bank Ltd and Wintrust Securities Ltd (the banks),
against the judgment of Nourse J ([1984] BCLC 1) given on 27 February 1981 dismissing
the banks' action against, inter alia, TOSG Trust Fund Ltd (TOSG), the agency and
Clarksons Holidays Ltd (Clarksons) in which the banks sought, inter alia, a declaration
that the banks were entitled to prove in the liquidation of Clarksons to the exclusion of
the agency in respect of all bond moneys expended by TOSG in paying creditors of
Clarksons. On a counterclaim by the agency the judge made a declaration that the joint
liquidators of Clarksons were entitled and bound to admit in full the proof of debt lodged
with them by the agency. Clarksons appeared in the appeal as second respondent. TOSG
took no part in the appeal. The facts are set out in the opinion of Lord Templeman.

Leonard Hoffmann QC and *Leslie Kosmin* for the agency.
Peter Millett QC and *J B W McDonnell* for the banks.
David Oliver for Clarksons.

Their Lordships took time for consideration.

29 March. The following opinions were delivered.

LORD DIPLOCK. My Lords, I have had the advantage of reading in draft the speeches
of my noble and learned friends Lord Brightman and Lord Templeman. I agree with
them and for the reasons which they give I would dismiss this appeal.

LORD KEITH OF KINKEL. My Lords, I have had the benefit of reading in draft the
speeches to be delivered by my noble and learned friends Lord Brightman and Lord
Templeman. I agree with them, and for the reasons they give would dismiss this appeal.

LORD BRANDON OF OAKBROOK. My Lords, I have had the advantage of
reading in draft the speeches prepared by my noble and learned friends Lord Brightman
and Lord Templeman. I agree with both speeches, and for the reasons given in them I
would dismiss the appeal.

LORD BRIGHTMAN. My Lords, I agree with the speech to be delivered by my noble
and learned friend Lord Templeman.

The issue can be stated briefly. Barclays Bank Ltd (I take the one bank as a convenient
example) has a right of action against Clarksons Holidays Ltd, which is stayed by reason
of a compulsory winding-up order, and therefore a prima facie right of proof in Clarksons'
liquidation, by reason of the indemnity given to it by Clarksons for good consideration.
What, if anything, has happened to deprive Barclays of that right of action and that right
of proof?

TOSG Trust Fund Ltd (TOSG) was established in 1970 as a company limited by
guarantee primarily to utilise money received from a tour operator's bond in alleviating
the consequences to tourists of the insolvency of that tour operator. TOSG had no power
under its constitution to pay anything to its members. It was nothing more than a
receptacle for money received on account of tour operators' bonds with machinery for
distribution of such money among tourists who might be damnified by the failure of a
tour operator. On 1 October 1973 Barclays executed a bond obliging it to pay £500,000
to TOSG in the event of Clarksons' failure. Simultaneously, Clarksons executed a counter-
indemnity in favour of Barclays obliging it to indemnify Barclays against all payments
under the bond. On 15 August 1974 Clarksons failed. On the following day Barclays
paid £500,000 to TOSG in performance of its obligation under the bond. Thereupon

Clarksons became indebted to Barclays in the like sum under the counter-indemnity. On
a 16 August Clarksons was commenced to be wound up. The first operation conducted by
TOSG was to spend about £956,000 out of the bond moneys received from Barclays and
others in repatriating some 34,000 stranded tourists. The right of Barclays to prove under
its counter-indemnity in the liquidation of Clarksons for a due proportion of its £500,000
in respect of the aggregate expenditure of £956,000 is not questioned, and rightly so
because there can be no answer to that claim. TOSG retained the rest of the bond moneys
b in hand pending a decision when and how to alleviate, pursuant to its memorandum of
association, the remaining consequences to tourists of Clarksons' failure, that is to say,
tours paid for but lost. On 15 November 1974 Barclays lodged a proof in the liquidation
for £500,000. On 23 July 1975 TOSG entered into an agreement with the twelfth
appellant, the Air Travel Reserve Fund Agency (the agency), to pay out in full a certain
description of tourists' claims until the bond moneys were exhausted, and to obtain (I
c add, for what it might be worth) 'an assignment in favour of the agency from the payee
of his right to prove in the liquidation of Clarksons . . . for the full amount of his claim'.
That agreement was made without the consent of Barclays, and therefore could not
conceivably have any direct effect on Barclays' right of action (stayed by the compulsory
order) and proof pursuant to the counter-indemnity. The selected class of tourists was
then paid off and the funds of TOSG exhausted. Each recipient put his signature to a
d form of assignment, which was expressed to transfer to the agency all the recipient's
rights against Clarksons in respect of overseas holidays in accordance with his proof as
lodged with the joint liquidators.
  If a sum of money is paid to a creditor in an insolvency by reference to his claim, the
money will usually be paid with the object of effecting one of three purposes: one
purpose might be to extinguish the debt either wholly or pro tanto; a second purpose
e might be to constitute consideration for the purchase of the debt by the payer so that the
payer becomes beneficially entitled to any dividend in the liquidation; a third purpose
might be the due performance by a surety of his obligation to the creditor under a
contract of suretyship.
  The last of these purposes cannot have been the reason for the payment in the instant
case, because there was no contract of suretyship between TOSG and the tourists. The
f second of these purposes cannot have been the reason for the payment, because it was
never the function of TOSG to buy up the debts of tourist-creditors for the benefit of
third parties, such as the agency or anybody else. Consistently with the objects of TOSG
the only possible reason for, and consequence of, a payment made by TOSG to a tourist-
creditor was the discharge of Clarksons' indebtedness to such creditor. No arrangement
between TOSG and the agency could affect that situation. The assignment was therefore
g worthless because there was nothing to assign. Accordingly, I can see no possible
impediment, on the ground of double proof or anything else, which can preclude
Barclays' right to claim in the liquidation under the counter-indemnity.
  For these short reasons I would dismiss this appeal.

LORD TEMPLEMAN. My Lords, the sole question in this appeal is whether when
h the defendants, TOSG Trust Fund Ltd (TOSG), out of £2,226,000 provided by the
respondent banks at the request of the respondent, Clarksons Holidays Ltd (Clarksons),
paid £1,268,000 to Clarksons' customers, the claims of those customers against Clarksons
for breach of contract were reduced by £1,268,000 or were assigned to the appellant, the
Air Travel Reserve Fund Agency (the agency).
  The relevant evidence consists of two undisputed documents entered into by Clarksons
j and the banks before the agency came into existence.
  Clarksons was a tour operator which contracted to provide, and accepted advance
payments in respect of, holidays abroad. Clarksons was a member of the Tour Operators
Study Group formed to solve the problems which arose on the business failure of a tour
operator. The group incorporated TOSG, whose object, as set out in cl 3(A) of its
memorandum of association, as applied to Clarksons, was:

'To manage, utilise, employ and expend funds and moneys paid . . . under or by virtue of Bonds, Letters of Credit, Policies of Insurance or similar arrangements obtained by [Clarksons] and issued in favour of [TOSG] . . . in generally alleviating the consequences to [Clarksons'] customers of the business failure of [Clarksons] and in particular (but without prejudice to the generality of the foregoing) in making arrangements to procure the expeditious return . . . of persons stranded abroad as a result of [Clarksons'] business failure, in procuring that persons in the course of holidays abroad at the date of [Clarksons'] business failure are enabled to complete their holidays . . . in making all necessary travel and accommodation arrangements for persons who have purchased from [Clarksons], and paid in full, for holidays abroad which . . . had not been commenced and in making such payments as [TOSG] may in its absolute discretion think fit to persons who had paid deposits to [Clarksons] in respect of future holidays abroad or who (being customers of [Clarksons]) otherwise suffer financial loss by reason of [Clarksons'] business failure.'

By the Civil Aviation Act 1971 and reg 3 of the Civil Aviation (Air Travel Organisers' Licensing) Regulations 1972, SI 1972/223, Clarksons could not act as an air travel organiser without a licence from the Civil Aviation Authority. That authority could only grant a licence if satisfied that the resources of Clarksons and the financial arrangements made by Clarksons were adequate for discharging Clarksons' actual and potential obligations in respect of the activities in which Clarksons was engaged. The Civil Aviation Authority licensed Clarksons to carry on business as an air travel tour operator subject to Clarksons obtaining bonds providing for the payment of the aggregate sum of £2,225,850 in the form prescribed by the authority and subject to Clarksons not making available accommodation for the carriage of more than 2,040,000 passengers on 2,040,000 journeys.

The respondent banks offered to enter into the requisite bonds for sums amounting in the aggregate to £2,226,000. Each bank knew that Clarksons could not carry on business without bonds totalling £2,226,000 but each bank made independent arrangements with Clarksons to provide a specified sum. For example, by a letter dated 24 September 1973 Barclays Bank wrote to Clarksons enclosing a bond for £500,000 executed by Barclays and a counter-indemnity for execution by Clarksons. The letter informed Clarksons that the account of Clarksons with Barclays had been debited with £5,000, the agreed commission at the rate of 1% per annum on the issue of the bond, and informed Clarksons that the overdraft on Clarksons' accounts with Barclays would continue to attract interest at 2% above Barclays' bank rate, then 11%. By the counter-indemnity, which was executed by Clarksons on 25 September 1973, Clarksons requested and authorised Barclays to give the bond to TOSG and undertook and agreed—

'To indemnify you [Barclays] from and against all payments actions proceedings damages costs claims demands expenses or losses which you may make suffer incur or sustain by reason or on account of you having executed the Bond or otherwise in the premises howsoever.'

Barclays was authorised to debit Clarksons' account with Barclays with £500,000 if and as soon as Barclays made payment under the bond. Thus interest would run against Clarksons as soon as Barclays paid up on the bond. The bond, which was dated 1 October 1973, provided that Barclays was 'held and firmly bound unto [TOSG] in the sum of £500,000 . . .' The bond was declared to be 'void unless during the period of 12 calendar months commencing 1st October, 1973' Clarksons should incur a business failure, if, for example, 'a Petition shall be presented to the Court for the compulsory winding up of [Clarksons]. . . .' In consideration of the issue of the bond, TOSG—

'hereby covenants with [Barclays] that upon payment of the said sum of £500,000 . . . [TOSG] will undertake . . . [to] repay to [Barclays] on demand such part of the said sum as shall not be expended or required by [TOSG] in the performance and execution of its rights, duties, powers and discretions as set out in [TOSG's] a Memorandum and Articles of Association, and that such Memorandum and Articles of Association will not be altered during the currency of this Bond without the prior written consent of [Barclays] (which shall not be unreasonably withheld) first obtained.'

Thus Barclays agreed to advance £500,000 to be employed in alleviating the consequences to Clarksons' customers of Clarksons' business failure. The money was to
b be paid to TOSG and TOSG was not to alter its constitution. These provisions ensured that Barclays' £500,000 would be employed in or towards the costs and expenses of meeting Clarksons' liabilities to some or all of its customers and for no other purpose. TOSG agreed to account to Barclays for any part of the £500,000 which was not expended or required for Clarksons' customers. Clarksons agreed to indemnify Barclays. Barclays accepted no contractual obligation towards the customers of Clarksons. Barclays did not
c warrant to TOSG or anyone else that Barclays' bond plus any other assets available to pay Clarksons' customers would be sufficient to meet all the claims of Clarksons' customers in full. Barclays did not agree that their right to reimbursement under Clarksons' indemnity should be subordinated to any claim by any unpaid customer. Barclays agreed to pay £500,000 and Clarksons agreed to repay.

Similar bonds and indemnities were entered into by and with each of the other
d respondent banks for different sums which, with Barclays' bond, amounted to £2,226,000. The differences between the arrangements by Clarksons with Barclays and the arrangements made between Clarksons and the other respondent banks are not relevant to these proceedings.

On 15 August 1974 Clarksons suffered a business failure. On 16 August TOSG required the banks to pay, and the banks did pay, the aggregate sum of £2,226,000 secured by the bonds. On the same day Clarksons presented its own winding-up petition on the grounds
e of insolvency, and on 7 October 1974 Clarksons was ordered to be wound up. The banks' right to repayment from Clarksons under the indemnities thereupon became a right to prove in the liquidation. TOSG disbursed £958,000 out of the moneys provided by the banks under the bonds, and it is conceded that the banks can prove for this sum. TOSG expended the remaining £1,268,000 out of the aggregate sum of £2,226,000 paid under
f the bonds in reimbursing in full, so far as the moneys would go, deposits and advance payments made by Clarksons' customers who never, in the event, enjoyed the holidays for which they had paid. The banks' claim to prove under their indemnities for this sum of £1,268,000 is disputed by the appellant agency, which, in the circumstances which I shall shortly narrate, claim to be assignees of the right to prove for £1,268,000.

The rights of the banks to prove in the liquidation of Clarksons for £1,268,000 depend
g on the true construction and effect of the bonds and indemnities which were entered into in 1973 before the agency came into existence. The rights of the banks under the arrangements they made with Clarksons could not be modified or ignored without their consent.

There are four possible constructions of the bonds and the indemnities read with the memorandum of association of TOSG. Three of those constructions blush with
h implausibility. Firstly, the payment by TOSG of £1,268,000 to the customers might not affect the rights of those customers to prove in the liquidation of Clarksons for damages for breach of contract amounting to £1,268,000. Secondly, the payment by TOSG might entitle TOSG to assert a claim to prove in the liquidation of Clarksons and to distribute any dividend received by TOSG between other customers of Clarksons. Thirdly, the payment by TOSG might effect an assignment of the customers' claims to the banks.
j Fourthly, the payment by TOSG might extinguish the claims of the customers by the amounts received.

As to the first possibility, the terms of the bond executed by Barclays are not apt to shower gifts on customers selected by TOSG. Neither Clarksons nor Barclays could properly make any such gifts. A customer whose claim against Clarksons for breach of contract amounted to £1,000 and who accepted £1,000 from TOSG out of Barclays'

£500,000 could not thereafter assert a claim against Clarksons or prove in the liquidation of Clarksons for that £1,000. If he was paid and accepted £500, he could only prove for the balance of £500.

As to the second possibility, the terms of the bond and the memorandum of association are not apt to vest in TOSG anything other than the right to receive £500,000 from Barclays and the irrecoverable duty to employ that sum in alleviating the financial consequences to Clarksons' customers of the business failure of Clarksons. If TOSG did not employ the whole of Barclays' £500,000 for authorised purposes, the balance was to be refunded to Barclays.

It was submitted that Barclays had agreed to limit its rights to any balance remaining in the hands of TOSG, and that Barclays had agreed that the right of a customer owed £1,000 to prove for that sum should, on payment by TOSG, pass to TOSG so that TOSG could prove for £1,000 and distribute the dividend to any customer who had not been paid. It was submitted that Barclays must have intended and must be taken to have agreed that its claims against Clarksons should be subordinated to the claims of all Clarksons' customers, so that Barclays could receive no dividend in respect of its £500,000 under its indemnity unless and until all Clarksons' customers had recovered all their financial losses from TOSG and Clarksons' liquidators. It is quite impossible to spell out of the bond any obligation by Barclays other than the obligation which Barclays discharged of paying £500,000 to TOSG. The indemnity made it quite clear that as between the banks and Clarksons payment by Barclays under the bond created an immediate liability enforceable against Clarksons for repayment of the sum of £500,000, less any moneys which might in the event be repaid by TOSG. Barclays did not confer on TOSG the right to prove in the liquidation for £1,000 if TOSG paid a customer £1,000 out of Barclays' money. Clarksons did not agree and Clarksons could not lawfully agree to repay Barclays £1,000 and at the same time confer or allow to be conferred on TOSG the right to prove for £1,000. If £1,000 of Barclays' money was paid by TOSG to a customer, then Clarksons only relevant liability was to pay £1,000 to Barclays under the indemnity.

As to the third possibility, payment by TOSG to a customer could not assign the claim of that customer to Barclays because the terms of the bond did not provide for an assignment, which was unnecessary in view of the indemnity.

In my view, on the true and simple construction of the bond and the indemnity, when TOSG paid £1,000 of Barclays' money to a customer whose claim against Clarksons amounted to £1,000, the claim of that customer against Clarksons was extinguished and there became vested in Barclays an indisputable claim against Clarksons for £1,000 under the indemnity. If TOSG paid £200 to a customer whose claim was £1,000, then the customer could thereafter only claim and prove for the balance of £800 and Barclays could claim and prove under its indemnity for £200. By the indemnity Clarksons agreed to repay to the banks every penny that the banks paid under the bond and that TOSG paid to the customers.

In the event TOSG extinguished claims of Clarksons' customers to the extent of £1,286,000 and the banks became entitled to prove for £1,286,000 under their indemnities.

By the Air Travel Reserve Fund Act 1975, the Air Travel Reserve Fund Agency was incorporated and a fund was created to be financed by air travel operators and supported by way of loans from the government. By s 2(6)(b) of the 1975 Act the agency's fund became applicable to meet the losses of any customer if at the time of booking there was in force 'any bond or other security provided or procured by the air travel organiser for the protection of his customers . . .' By s 2(7) the agency was not to pay out of the fund until any bond moneys had been expended (see s 2(7)(a)) and the customer was not to recover from the agency's fund any losses or liabilities 'in so far as the customer has been reimbursed in respect thereof from any money paid under the bond . . .' (see s 2(7)(b)).

Before TOSG distributed the sum of £1,286,000 to Clarksons' customers, the agency came into existence and certain arrangements were made between TOSG and the agency a   which, it is said, found a claim by the agency to prove for £1,286,000 in the liquidation of Clarksons.

The Air Travel Reserve Fund Agency Benefit Rules, made under powers conferred by the 1975 Act, expressly provided for the agency to pay the losses incurred by a customer of Clarksons in consequence of Clarksons' business failure, and authorised the agency before making any payment to require the customer to assign to the agency 'any rights he may have against' Clarksons in the liquidation (see r 4(4)).

b   By an agreement (the assignment agreement) dated 23 July 1975 and made between TOSG and the agency, but to which the banks were not parties, it was agreed that TOSG would, subject to the retention of certain reserves and expenses, employ all the moneys remaining in the hands of TOSG and applicable for the purpose of alleviating the consequences of the business failure of Clarksons in repaying in full, so far as the moneys would go, deposits and advance payments made by Clarksons' customers who never, in the event, enjoyed the holidays for which they had paid. The agency agreed to pay the

c   claims of all Clarksons' customers remaining outstanding after the moneys available to TOSG to reimburse Clarksons' customers were exhausted. TOSG agreed that before paying any customer of Clarksons TOSG 'will obtain an assignment in favour of the Agency from the payee of his right to prove in the liquidation of Clarksons ... for the full amount of his Claim'. TOSG paid £1,286,000, part of the aggregate sum of

d   £2,226,000 provided by the banks pursuant to their bonds, to Clarksons' customers. Each customer who received part of the sum of £1,286,000 lodged a claim with the joint liquidators of Clarksons, and assigned in writing to the agency 'all my ... rights against [Clarksons] under my ... claim against [Clarksons] in respect of overseas holidays which I ... have lodged with the Joint Liquidators'.

The banks claim to prove for £1,286,000, part of the sum of £2,226,000, pursuant to

e   the indemnities given by Clarksons. The agency claims to prove for £1,286,000 on the grounds that the assignments to the agency by the customers who received £1,286,000 from TOSG were effective to vest in the agency the right to prove for that sum.

A number of arguments have been put forward on behalf of the agency at different stages of these proceedings.

It was argued as a matter of construction that the only right of the banks was to recover

f   from TOSG any moneys (in the event none) which were not paid out by TOSG to the customers. I have already rejected this argument. The right of the banks under the bonds to claim from TOSG any moneys which TOSG did not expend is supplementary to and not inconsistent with the right of the banks under the indemnities to claim from Clarksons any moneys which TOSG did expend. The trial judge was persuaded that TOSG could—

g   'recoup to the customers any shortfall remaining after they had received all available dividends in Clarksons' liquidation. Once you get to that stage it is apparent that it would indeed be most inequitable for the banks to claim, as against the customers, a rateable proportion of any dividends receivable or received by them. That is not a narrow equity, but a broad one.'

h   (See [1984] BCLC 1 at 15.)

But equity, broad or narrow, does not overlook the distinction between a debt and a dividend on a debt, nor does it enable TOSG to ignore or modify the legal rights of the banks under the bonds and the indemnities. Under those documents the banks paid and TOSG distributed £1,286,000 and the banks became entitled to dividends on £1,286,000. The customers received £1,286,000 from TOSG and ceased to be entitled to dividends

j   on £1,286,000. If the customers had received dividends in respect of their claims of £1,286,000 before TOSG distributed that sum, or by mistake after that distribution, then those dividends could not be paid to TOSG and employed in discharging further debts of the same or other customers and could not be paid to the agency or retained by the customers but must be handed over by the customers to the banks or by the customers to TOSG and by TOSG to the banks. In practice, no difficulty arises. The liquidators will pay the dividends on £1,286,000 to the banks because the banks provided that sum pursuant to the bonds in discharge of the liabilities of Clarksons to its customers, and because the banks became entitled to be indemnified by Clarksons pursuant to the indemnities. The liquidators will pay to the agency dividends on the sums which the agency provided in discharging further liabilities of Clarksons to its customers.

It was suggested that Clarksons and the banks intended to make the maximum possible provision for Clarksons' customers and to preclude the banks from proving in the liquidation of Clarksons unless or until all the customers were repaid in full. This suggestion would require there to be read into the documents provisions which do not exist. Then it was suggested that it was inequitable for the banks to claim any dividends until the customers had been paid in full. This suggestion transposes responsibility for the customers. The tour operators, including Clarksons, were responsible for the bonding scheme. The government was responsible for the licensing scheme. When the bonding scheme and the licensing scheme, which had been widely publicised, were found unexpectedly to be inadequate protection, the operators and the government very properly accepted responsibility to the customers for the shortfall. The banks had only accepted responsibility for the payment of £2,226,000 and on terms that Clarksons would indemnify the banks. The fact that a bank may suffer less anguish if it loses £1,000,000 than an individual customer who loses £1,000 does not justify the intervention of equity to improve the contractual rights of the customers and to defeat the contractual rights of the banks.

It was argued that the payment by TOSG of £1,286,000 to the customers entitled TOSG to the benefit of the customers' claims for that sum and to direct those customers to assign the benefit of their claims to the agency. But it appears from the unalterable provisions of the memorandum of association of TOSG that TOSG was only an authorised agent for the distribution to the customers of moneys provided by the bonds. The memorandum and the bonds conferred on TOSG the right to select the individual customers and to determine how the losses of those customers were to be alleviated by the employment of the bond moneys.

It was argued below, with a wealth of erudition, that the proofs submitted by the banks and the agency in respect of £1,286,000 paid by TOSG to the customers were double proofs of the same debt and that the priority between those double proofs fell to be determined by equitable rules. In my view there were two mutually exclusive debts, namely the debt which Clarksons owed the customers under their contracts and the debt which Clarksons owed the banks under their indemnities. Payment by TOSG reduced the customers' debts by £1,286,000 and increased the banks' debt by the like sum. The customers could not assign to the agency the right to prove for debts which had been discharged. There is no double proof. The proof submitted by the agency must be rejected.

The agency argued that the banks were in a position analogous to the position of a surety who has paid part of a debt and cannot prove in the insolvency of the debtor until the creditor has been paid in full. But the rights and liabilities of a surety depend on the true construction of the obligations which the surety assumes. The banks assumed no liability save the liability to pay TOSG £2,226,000 to be employed in paying customers. The banks fully met their obligations. I can discern no legal or equitable principle or analogy which would enable the customers who were paid by TOSG to assign their former claims to or for the benfit of the customers who, through no fault of the banks, could not be paid by TOSG.

In a final variation, the agency argued that Clarksons' liability to its customers constituted a principal debt and Clarksons' liability to the banks constituted a secondary debt and that a secondary debt could not be paid until the primary debt had been discharged. In my opinion there were no primary or secondary debts, whatever those expressions may mean. The customers were owed £1,286,000 and have been paid. The banks are owed £1,286,000 and have not been paid.

The Court of Appeal also reached the conclusion that the banks could prove for *a*   £1,286,000 and the agency could not. For the reasons I have endeavoured to express I would dismiss this present appeal with costs. By agreement between the agency and the liquidators of Clarksons, the costs of the liquidators are payable on an indemnity basis.

Appeal dismissed.

b   Solicitors: *Slaughter & May* (for the agency); *Wilde Sapte* (for the banks); *Stephenson Harwood* (for Clarksons).

Mary Rose Plummer   Barrister.

c

Peacock v Peacock

FAMILY DIVISION AT BRISTOL

d   BOOTH J

12 JANUARY 1983

Divorce – Maintenance – Order – Refusal of order – Maintenance pending suit – Applicant receiving supplementary benefit – Order for maintenance not taking applicant outside limit of entitlement to supplementary benefit – Whether order should be refused because order will not

e   *benefit applicant – Whether court bound by Department of Health and Social Security's assessment of respondent's financial obligations to applicant.*

Where a party to a divorce suit applies for an order of maintenance pending suit and interim periodical payments for the children of the marriage, the divorce registrar is not entitled to refuse to make the order solely on the ground that it will not benefit the

f   applicant because it will not take the applicant outside the limit of his or her entitlement to supplementary benefit. The quantum of any order is to be assessed according to what is reasonable in all the circumstances, having regard to the respondent's income, needs and obligations, both present and future, although the court may also take into account the fact that the applicant is receiving supplementary benefit. Furthermore, in making its order, the court is not bound by the assessment made by the Department of Health

g   and Social Security of the respondent's financial obligations to the applicant and accordingly the court may assess as the appropriate order for financial relief pending suit an amount which differs from the figure assessed by the department (see p 1071 *c* to *h*, post).

Notes

h   For maintenance pending suit, see 13 Halsbury's Laws (4th edn) paras 791–797, and for cases on the subject, see 27(2) Digest (Reissue) 651–668, 4877–5072.

Case cited
Stockford v Stockford (1981) 3 FLR 58, CA.

j   **Appeal**
The wife, the petitioner in a divorce suit, appealed from the decision of Mr Registrar Bolton, made in the Bristol Divorce Registry on 2 December 1982, refusing to make an order pending suit for her maintenance and for periodical payments for the two children of the marriage, on the ground that having regard to the husband's income no order which could be made would benefit the wife because it would not take her outside her

entitlement to supplementary benefit. The appeal was heard and judgment given in chambers. The case is reported by permission of Booth J. The facts are set out in the judgment.

Mr D R F Burrows, solicitor, for the wife.
Michael Roach for the husband.

BOOTH J. This is an appeal by the wife, who is the petitioner in the suit, from the refusal by Mr Registrar Bolton on 2 December 1982 to make a maintenance pending suit order for herself and a periodical payments order in respect of the two children of the marriage. It raises an interesting point of law on which I am asked to rule and on which I agree that there is no reported authority.

The facts of the matter are these. The husband and wife were married on 8 July 1967, and they have two children, both girls, now aged respectively 14 and 12. On 6 July 1982 the wife filed a petition under the provisions of s 1(2)(b) of the Matrimonial Causes Act 1973. At that time both parties were living together in the former matrimonial home, but in November 1982 the husband left the house where the wife and the two children have continued to live together.

The proceedings are not defended, and a date has been fixed, 9 February 1983, for the pronouncement of a decree nisi of divorce, the registrar's certificate having already been given.

On 30 July 1982 the wife applied for financial relief and sought maintenance pending suit for herself and periodical payments for the children. Affidavits were sworn by the wife on 29th July and by the husband on 19 October; but events have overtaken the facts set out in those affidavits. However, the financial postion of each party can be very briefly stated.

The wife's financial position in a nutshell is that she is almost wholly dependent on supplementary benefit and the allowances which she receives in respect of the two children. She has a very small earned income of about £5 a week as a child minder; that is not referred to in her affidavit and is a very recent development. She continues to live in the matrimonial home. She receives from the Department of Health and Social Security a single person's supplementary benefit allowance in respect of herself and in respect of each child, and in relation to the mortgage on that property some £420 a year is paid by the department.

The husband is employed as a workshop foreman for a transport firm. When he swore his affidavit he was earning somewhat more than he is at the present time because, no doubt in the present employment situation, he has had to take a reduction in his income. It is now agreed that his gross income is £107 per week which, after national insurance and tax has been paid, leaves him a net income of £81·90 a week.

He is presently living in his father's home, which he is able to do by paying his father a fairly nominal amount in respect of food and lodging of £20 a week. This provides him with a roof over his head and one meal a day, and he has travelling expenses of some £10 a week. He is also paying premiums on endowment policies which are collateral securities for the mortgage on the home, amounting to £7·20 a week.

The Department of Health and Social Security has assessed the husband's obligations in respect of his wife and children and the mortgage of the matrimonial home at a figure of £20 a week. This the husband is paying to the department by way of a voluntary payment and from which, of course, he gets no tax benefit. So he is in the position of being interested, as is the wife, in obtaining an order from the court which will at any rate give him the benefit of some tax relief, which the assessment of the Department of Health and Social Security does not.

I have not seen any written reasons of the registrar but I am told that his refusal to make an order in this matter was on the ground that no order that he could make, on the husband's income, would bring the wife and children outside the bracket of entitlement for supplementary benefit, and therefore he saw no point, as I understand it, in making the order. It is against that approach that the wife appeals.

a   Mr Burrows on the wife's behalf accepts that no order that this court could make against this husband is going to benefit the wife. The only benefit will be to the taxpayers through the Department of Health and Social Security. The department itself is not urging the wife to make an application, but I am told that it is a matter of concern to practitioners generally that there is a divergence of view whether, in circumstances such as these, an order should be made by the court where it concerns only maintenance pending suit and interim periodical payments for the children, so that it is an order

b   which is not expected to subsist for very long. The question is whether the court should disregard the position with regard to supplementary benefit, and on an application by a wife (or, indeed, by a husband) should make orders on the figures following the usual course of assessment.

There is no authority precisely on this point; but it seems to me, and indeed both Mr Burrows for the wife and counsel for the husband agree, that the principles on which the

c   court has to act with regard to supplementary benefit must be the same for applications for maintenance pending suit and interim periodical payments as they are for what are called final orders, that is full periodical payments' orders either for a spouse or for children. It seems to me that there is no reason in principle why the court should have a different approach with regard to the former than it does to the latter. It is established law, as I understand it, that the fact that the wife is receiving supplementary benefit and

d   any order that the court can make will not assist her or place her outside the supplementary benefit bracket is, in the main, not a relevant matter to which the court should have regard. The fact that the wife is receiving supplementary benefit may be taken into account in assessing maintenance pending suit, or, indeed, the periodical payments. It is a matter for the court to have regard to in its discretion. But the general principle is that the quantum of any order should be assessed, in circumstances such as

e   these, on what the husband on his income can reasonably afford to pay, having regard to his needs and to his obligations, and of course in cases which concern maintenance after a decree, having regard to all matters to which the court must have regard under s 25 of the 1973 Act.

In my judgment if the registrar merely took the approach that any order that he could make would not benefit the wife and therefore there was no point in making the order,

f   that was an incorrect approach.

A further point in this matter is that the husband himself is entitled to ask the court for appropriate orders, and to ask the court to assess the amount he should pay. The court is not bound by the assessment of the Department of Health and Social Security, and I do not think that the husband is necessarily bound by any such assessment. He has got the right to come to court and to ask the court to make its own assessment, which it will

g   probably do on a much broader principle, as in fact is the situation in this case. The court has a duty to make an order which is reasonable in all the circumstances, and to take into account all the needs and obligations of the husband, and, as counsel has argued on his behalf today, to take into account his future liabilities and problems in setting himself up as he has recently left the matrimonial home. The figure that the court may think proper to order may not be that at which the Department of Health and Social Security

h   assesses as the husband's obligations. Therefore, it seems to me that not only the wife but also the husband is entitled to ask the court for a proper assessment. But nothing I have said is to be taken in any way to encourage fruitless litigation in maintenance pending suit and interim periodical payments applications where there can be no real benefit to either party from any court order.

I have come to the conclusion that that certainly is not the case in this matter. The

j   husband will have a benefit by reason of a court order inasmuch as he will get tax relief, and therefore it is proper for the court to assess how much he should pay towards his wife and his children. It is immaterial to look at the wife's financial position any further.

The husband's situation has been approached in this way. He has a net income of £81·90 a week. His counsel has asked me to deduct from that the board and lodging monies that he pays to his father of £20 a week, and his travelling expenses of £10 a week, together with the premiums for the insurance policies of £7·20 a week. They are all actual commitments which the husband has to honour. Counsel for the husband also asked me to take into account the fact that were he dependent on supplementary benefits the husband would receive a single man's allowance assessed at £25·70 per week. He says that this amount also should be deducted from his net income because that is a sum of money assessed as a basic subsistence allowance which any single man requires of necessity to keep himself, over and above the moneys he pays for board and lodging. If all these sums are deducted from the net income of £81·90 a week it leaves the husband with about £20 a week in fact in his hands. Counsel for the husband argues that, whereas the Department of Health and Social Security in all probability took that sum of £20 as being the proper amount that the husband should pay for the wife and the two children (and which he is paying by way of voluntary allowance), it does not take into account the fact that this husband, who has recently left the matrimonial home, has other expenses. In particular he is in the throes of looking for a future home for himself. He has found a flat into which he hopes to move in the next few weeks, but that will cost him by way of rent some £35 a week. Then he will have all the additional expenses of running a home for himself which might reasonably be expected in the case of a husband who has had to leave the family home. Therefore, counsel for the husband says, it is really not a fair assessment to take from the husband the full balance of £20 a week, leaving him at only subsistence standard with the subsistence allowance of £25·70 per week with which to look after himself. That, he says, is far too small for the husband and the amount, he says, that the wife and children should have by way of global figure is not more than £15 per week.

Mr Burrows on behalf of the wife has taken somewhat different an approach. It is a broad approach. The husband is now making a voluntary allowance of £20 a week. If that is grossed up, and on the basis that the Department of Health and Social Security will continue to pay the mortgage interest in respect of the matrimonial home, that will come to a figure of about £28 a week. As the husband is now paying £20 net out of his own pocket and has been doing so for some weeks, it would be proper to take that amount of £28 gross as being the global figure to be divided between the wife and the two children. So, in fact, the figures are little different between the husband and the wife. It is agreed that the order that I make will have to subsist for some three to four months before all the financial matters can be finally resolved by the court.

In my view I have to take a broad approach and I have to look closely at the needs of this husband in the difficult position in which he finds himself now. He has not only the difficulties that any man must have when he is faced with a reduced income but also the difficulties that he has as a single man now living by himself and about to set up in a new home. I think the approach of counsel for the husband in the circumstances of this case is the correct one. I think that the correct global figure for the present time is £15 a week, which for the purpose of the order should be divided equally between the wife and the two children, giving a maintenance pending suit order of £5 a week in respect of the wife and interim periodical payments in respect of the two children of £5 each a week. That is not to say, of course, that that is in any way a guideline for the future when all the financial matters are resolved between these two spouses, but it seems to me to be a proper figure for the husband to pay for the matter of three to four months before that final situation can be achieved.

That is the order I propose to make. I will allow the appeal and order maintenance pending suit for the wife of £5 a week and interim periodical payments to each of the two children of £5 a week.

Order accordingly.

Solicitors: *E J Watson Cox & Counsell*, Bristol (for the wife); *Roberts & Co*, Bristol (for the husband).

Bebe Chua   Barrister.

a
Pickles and another v Insurance Brokers Registration Council

QUEEN'S BENCH DIVISION
WATKINS LJ AND McCULLOUGH J
1, 2 NOVEMBER 1983

b

Insurance – Broker – Registration – Application for registration – Application on ground that applicant has 'carried on' business as an insurance broker for prescribed period – Whether applicant required to have adequate practical experience in work of an insurance broker – Insurance Brokers (Registration) Act 1977, s 3(1)(c)–(g).

c
Insurance – Broker – Registration – Application for registration – Refusal of application – Appeal – Powers of court – RSC Ord 55, r 3(1).

For a person to have 'carried on' or to have been employed by a person 'carrying on' the business of an insurance broker for the requisite period for the purposes of s 3(1)(c), (d), (e), (f) or (g)[a] of the Insurance Brokers (Registration) Act 1977 so as to entitle him to
d registration as an insurance broker he must satisfy the Insurance Brokers Registration Council that for not less than that period he has carried on business as an insurance broker or been employed by a person so carrying on business to an extent which has provided him with adequate practical experience in the work of an insurance broker (see p 1078 c d and j to p 1079 d and h, post).

Since an appeal from a decision of the Insurance Brokers Registration Council is, by
e virtue of RSC Ord 55, r 3(1), by way of rehearing, the court may draw such inferences and make such decisions as it thinks appropriate (see p 1079 f to h, post).

Notes
For registration of insurance brokers and qualifications for registration, see 25 Halsbury's Laws (4th edn) paras 891–892.
f   For the Insurance Brokers (Registration) Act 1977, s 3, see 47 Halsbury's Statutes (3rd edn) 354.

Case cited
Town Investments Ltd v Dept of the Environment [1977] 1 All ER 813, [1978] AC 359, HL.

g ## Appeals
John David Pickles and Mary Patricia Pickles (the applicants) appealed against the refusal of the Insurance Brokers Registration Council on 28 June 1983 to register them as insurance brokers under the Insurance Brokers (Registration) Act 1977. The facts are set out in the judgment of McCullough J.

h *T B Hegarty* for the applicants.
Duncan Matheson for the council.

McCULLOUGH J (delivering the first judgment at the invitation of Watkins LJ). Mr and Mrs Pickles appeal against a refusal of the Insurance Brokers Registration Council to register their names in the register of insurance brokers. This is only the second case of
j its kind to come before this court.
Before 1977 anyone could lawfully describe himself as an insurance broker, and no professional body existed to secure the maintenance of professional standards on the part of those who so described themselves. In 1977 there was passed the Insurance Brokers (Registration) Act 1977. Its long title reads as follows:

---

a   Section 3(1) is set out at p 1075 a to d, post

'An Act to provide for the registration of insurance brokers and for the regulation
of their professional standards; and for purposes connected therewith.'

It was brought into effect in stages between 1 December 1977 and 1 December 1981.

By s 1 the Insurance Brokers Registration Council was set up. It was charged with the
general function of carrying out the powers and duties conferred on it by the Act. By s 2
the council was charged with the duty to establish and maintain a register of insurance
brokers, ie all those who were entitled under the Act to be registered. Section 3 laid
down the qualifications which individuals must possess for registration. I shall return to
this section in detail.

Section 11(1) obliged the council to make rules requiring registered insurance brokers
to ensure that their businesses have working capital of a prescribed minimum amount,
that the value of their business assets should exceed the limit of their liabilities by a
prescribed minimum amount and that the number of insurance companies with which
they place insurance business, and the amount of insurance business which they place
with each insurance company, is such as to prevent their businesses from becoming
unduly dependent on any particular insurance company. Rules were duly made: see the
Insurance Brokers Registration Council (Accounts and Business Requirements) Rules
Approval Order 1979, SI 1979/489.

Section 5 reads as follows:

'(1) Before refusing an application for registration under section 3 of this Act . . .
the Council shall give the person by whom . . . the application was made an
opportunity of appearing before and being heard by a committee of the Council.

(2) Where the Council refuse any such application, the Council shall, if so required
by the person by whom . . . the application was made within seven days from
notification of the decision, serve on that person . . . a statement of the reasons
therefor.

(3) A person . . . whose application is so refused may within twenty-eight days
from—(a) notification of the decision, or (b) if a statement of reasons has been
required under subsection (2) above, service of the statement, appeal against the
refusal to the Court.

(4) The Council may appear as respondent on any such appeal and for the purpose
of enabling directions to be given as to the costs of any such appeal the Council shall
be deemed to be a party thereto, whether they appear on the hearing of the appeal
or not.

(5) On the hearing of any such appeal the Court may make such order as it thinks
fit and its order shall be final.'

Other sections, to which I need not refer in detail, concern the approval of educational
institutions and qualifications, the supervision of such institutions and qualifying
examinations, the making of further rules relating to bank accounts, the holding of
money, the keeping of accounting records, the preparation and submission to the council
of balance sheets and profit and loss accounts, the drawing up of a code of conduct, the
making of rules for the provision of indemnity against losses from claims in connection
with businesses and the setting up of an investigating committee for preliminary
investigation of allegations and complaints against registered insurance brokers, and the
setting up of a disciplinary committee.

The aim, clearly, is that in time registered insurance brokers will enjoy the reputation
and standing of people who conduct their calling by professional standards. Accordingly
the description 'insurance broker' is only to be used by those whose names are on the
register, and if anyone not so registered uses the expression he commits a criminal
offence: see s 22 of the 1977 Act, which came into operation on 1 December 1981.

The principal issue in this appeal concerns the construction of s 3(1)(c) of the 1977 Act.
In order to deal sufficiently with the submissions made on each side, it is necessary for
me to read the whole of s 3(1) and (2):

'(1) Subject to subsection (2) below and to section 16 of this Act, a person shall be entitled to be registered in the register if he satisfies the Council—(a) that he holds a qualification approved by the Council under section 6 of this Act, being a qualification granted to him after receiving instruction from an institution so approved; or (b) that he holds a qualification recognised by the Council for the purposes of this paragraph, being a qualification granted outside the United Kingdom; or (c) that he has carried on business as an insurance broker, or as a whole-time agent acting for two or more insurance companies in relation to insurance business, for a period of not less than five years; or (d) that he holds a qualification recognised by the Council for the purposes of this paragraph and has carried on business as mentioned in paragraph (c) above for a period of not less than three years; or (e) that he has been employed by a person carrying on business as mentioned in paragraph (c) above, or by an insurance company, for a period of not less than five years; or (f) that he holds a qualification recognised by the Council for the purposes of this paragraph and has been employed by a person carrying on business as mentioned in paragraph (c) above, or by an insurance company, for a period of not less than three years; or (g) that he has knowledge and practical experience of insurance business which is comparable to that of a person who has carried on business as an insurance broker for a period of five years; or (h) that he holds a qualification recognised by the Council for the purposes of this paragraph and has knowledge and practical experience of insurance business which is comparable to that of a person who has carried on business as an insurance broker for a period of three years.

(2) A person shall not be entitled to be registered in the register by virtue of subsection (1) above unless he also satisfies the Council—(a) as to his character and suitability to be a registered insurance broker; and (b) in a case falling within paragraph (a), (b), (e) or (f) of subsection (1) above, that he has had adequate practical experience in the work of an insurance broker; and (c) if he is carrying on business as an insurance broker at the time when the application is made, that he is complying with the requirements of rules under section 11(1) of this Act.'

Before considering the rival submissions advanced on each side I should set out such of the facts of the case as are relevant.

Mr and Mrs Pickles are business partners. On 17 June 1976 they signed an agreement that they should become partners in the business of estate agents, surveyors, valuers and insurance brokers previously carried on by Mr Pickles alone. This was to be carried on at two addresses, one in Rochdale under the name of John D Pickles & Co (the name under which Mr Pickles alone had previously carried on business since 1970) and one in Oldham under the name of Frank Crossland & Co. The firm's letterhead described the firm as 'Incorporated valuers, estate agents, insurance brokers, commercial property consultants, rating and compensation surveyors'.

On 4 July 1981 Mr Pickles completed an application for registration of his name (ie his own name and not that of his firm). This was in the form required by rules made for the purpose under s 8. In Pt II of the form, at para 3, against 'recognised insurance qualification', 'place of qualification' and 'date of qualification' he put blanks. In para 4 'other qualifications' he put 'Fellow of the Incorporated Society of Valuers and Auctioneers. Fellow of the Rating and Valuation Association'. In para 5 'particulars relating to that business disclosed in Part I section J' (which was the business of John Pickles & Co at the Oldham address), sub-para (i) 'nature of business', he wrote 'Insurance Brokers, Valuers, Estate Agents, Rating and Compensation Surveyors, Commercial Property Consultants'. He stated that he was a partner, that the business had commenced on 4 July 1970 and, under sub-para (vii), entitled 'the nature of the duties undertaken', he put 'see 5(i) Full Time'.

One notes that the order in which the various activities of the business were listed differed from that in the letter heading.

In Pt V he gave details of his career and occupation. I need only refer to the later entries. 'July 1970 to date' (for John Pickles & Co) under the heading 'Position held and nature of duties' he wrote: 'Partner, Life General & Motor Insurance brokerage. General practice estate agency. Valuation, Sales, Lettings, Management of residential, commercial and industrial property including rating and compensation purchase work.' Below that, from 'July 1978 to date', he put the name of another firm, also with an address in Rochdale, and 'Managing Director. Property dealing and investment management'.

Mrs Pickles's application of the same date was in similar terms. The business was described in the same way as in her husband's application. Under 'nature of duties undertaken', she also said 'see 5(i) Full-Time'. In relation to her career and occupation, I need only read: 'April 1976–Date, John Pickles & Company, Partner, Life General and Motor Insurance brokerage. General practice estate agency.' Then from July 1978 to date there is the name of another firm and 'Company Secretary, Property dealings, investment management'.

The council noted that the applicants' business described a number of different occupations and that no indication had been given by either applicant as to how much of his or her time was spent in each of the different occupations. Anxious to learn what personal knowledge and experience each applicant had of the business of an insurance broker, the council on 18 February 1982 sent to each applicant a letter, in broadly similar terms.

The letter to Mr Pickles contained this passage:

'I have been instructed to enquire further as to the percentage of your time spent broking insurance matters on a day by day basis for John Pickles and Company since 1970. If this has varied at all over the years, please indicate this in as much detail as possible.'

The letter to Mrs Pickles included this passage:

'I have been instructed to enquire further as to the nature of your duties with John Pickles & Co since 1970 and the percentage of your time spent broking insurance matters for that Company.'

On 2 March Mr Pickles replied on behalf of both applicants. His letter contained this paragraph:

'We cannot quite understand the reason for the question which you now ask. We are not full-time insurance brokers as you can see from our letterheading. We do not know that there is anything in the Registration requirements which states that we must be full-time insurance brokers in order to be registered as insurance brokers under the Act and we would therefore be pleased if you would let us know why you need this further information.'

The council replied on 25 March 1982. The letter contained this passage:

'I would advise you that the Council must satisfy itself that each applicant can demonstrate his or her entitlement to registration under one or more of the sub-paragraphs of Section 3 of the Act. In order to achieve this, the Council must know exactly how much practical experience of insurance broking each applicant has and if this is not apparent from the application form, the Council makes further enquiries of the applicant in order that this point may be clarified. As your own business is also concerned with valuation and estate agency work, the Council merely wish to be advised as to how much of your own time is spent broking insurance matters for your business as opposed to your activities on the estate agency side.'

On 6 April both applicants replied in a long letter which it is not necessary for me to read in full. A great deal of it contained assertions of their competence, something about which the council had not, so far as I can see, ever sought further information. Its inquiry

had been directed solely to each individual's experience. The letter contained these
sentences:

> 'Upon checking our accounts we see that our annual premium income at the
> present moment stands at approximately £50,000 per annum not including life
> assurance commission which probably now reached something in the order of
> £1,500 per annum. Obviously since our business started in 1970 the amount of
> insurance business which we do has grown very considerably but so too has the
> income from other parts of our business. It is hard to assess exactly how much time
> in each week is spent broking insurance but we would say that approximately one-
> fifth of the time is actually spent broking. We are not merely motor insurance
> brokers but handle numerous household and business insurances of every kind. We
> have approximately 400 very satisfied clients.'

The general effect of that letter was that one-fifth or thereabouts of the firm's time was
spent broking insurance. The letter did not say how much of Mr Pickles's time was so
spent, nor did it say how much of Mrs Pickles's time was so spent; yet the question had
been directed to them as individuals, and it was as individuals that they sought
registration.

That being the position, the council was minded to refuse each of the applications
because neither applicant had put before it material which satisfied the council that he or
she had been carrying on business *as an insurance broker* for at least five years.

Having regard to the requirements of s 5(1), which I have read, a letter was written on
4 June to Mr Pickles and on 7 June to Mrs Pickles. Each contained identical passages as
follows:

> 'I am instructed to advise you that the Council is at present minded to refuse your
> application. Before making any decision, however, the Council have asked me to
> notify you that you may elect to appear before and be heard by a Committee of the
> Council ... Section 3 of the Act requires you to satisfy the Council of your
> entitlement to be registered and the Committee will seek such additional
> information from you to enable the members of the Committee to make a decision
> in relation to your application. Apart from clarifying any matters which may arise
> from the Statement originally made to the Council and subsequent information
> supplied by way of correspondence, the Committee will be enquiring into your
> personal knowledge and practical experience directly related to the handling of
> insurance business and, where relevant, your experience as an intermediary acting
> between insurer and insured.'

On 9 July the applicants replied by their solicitors. There was then an exchange of
correspondence in which the applicants' solicitors took the stance that the council was
obliged to register the applications under s 3(1)(c) and had no right to inquire into their
personal experience of insurance business.

During the correspondence, which there is no need to recite, the council again stressed
that it was concerned to know what was each individual's practical experience of
insurance broking.

No further information was provided by either applicant. The opportunity to appear
before the council was not taken up and on 28 February 1983 the council decided that
the applicants had not satisfied it that the requirements of s 3 had been fully met.
Accordingly, both applications were refused and each applicant now appeals to this court
against that refusal.

It is common ground that each applicant has complied with the requirements of the
rules made under s 11(1), that each applicant is of good character and that, save on the
question of the adequacy of his or her personal practical experience of insurance broking,
each is suitable to be registered as an insurance broker. The argument turns on the extent
to which adequate practical experience of insurance broking is a necessary criterion for
registration.

Counsel for the applicants contends that the council misconceived the powers and duties conferred on it by s 3 and that it embarked on a wide-ranging inquiry into the experience and competence of each applicant when it was not entitled to do so. In my judgment, as a simple matter of construction of the letters written by the council, it was not inquiring into the applicants' competence. It was, however, plainly inquiring into their individual practical experience of insurance broking. Counsel accepts that a limited inquiry of this nature is called for, but he contends that, on a proper construction of s 3, such an inquiry should be carried no further than is necessary to show that each applicant has indeed been carrying on the business of insurance broking for at least five years. He further submits that on the material before the council no conclusion was possible other than that each applicant had been doing so. Accordingly the notice of motion recited that an order was to be sought from this court that the names be registered. Alternatively he submits that, if the court felt unable to go so far, it should quash the refusals to register, remit the matters to the council and direct it to reconsider the applications in the light of what counsel contends is the correct view of the construction of s 3(1)(c) of the 1977 Act.

Counsel appearing for the council submits that in a s 3(1)(c) application, just as much as in an application under any other paragraph of s 3(1), an applicant must satisfy the council that he has adequate practical experience of the work of insurance broking. If that is right then, of course, the council must be the judge of the adequacy of that experience.

Counsel for the applicants seeks to support his construction of s 3(1)(c) with three arguments. First, he says that, having regard to the large number of persons using the description 'insurance broker' before the 1977 Act came into force, it must be taken to have been the intention of Parliament that all those that had been doing so for at least five years should automatically be entitled to registration; otherwise what he called 'the established rights' of those persons would be taken away. I cannot accept this argument. Whatever be the correct construction of s 3(1)(c), it is a construction which must apply to applications from those who claim to have been carrying on business as insurance brokers for five years before s 3 of the Act came into force, and which must also apply to applications from those who in, say, ten years' time claim to have carried on such business for five years by that time. I can see nothing which suggests that Parliament intended that those practising at the time the 1977 Act came into force should be treated more favourably than those who only began to practise thereafter.

Second, he relies on the fact that s 3(1)(c) provides for two alternatives, one of which is that the applicant has carried on business as an insurance broker for five years. The other is that he has carried on business as a whole-time agent acting for two or more insurance companies in relation to insurance business for five years. He contrasts the phrase 'whole-time agent' with the phrase 'insurance broker'. This indicates, so he submits, that there is no need to have been a 'whole-time insurance broker'.

Third, he relies on s 3(2)(b), which requires the applicant to satisfy the council that he has adequate practical experience of the work of an insurance broker only in the cases set out in paras (a), (b), (e) and (f) and not in the cases set out in paras (c), (d), (g) and (h). The omission of a reference to paras (g) and (h) in s 3(2) is explained by the fact that practical experience is referred to in paras (g) and (h) themselves but, so he contends, the omission of any reference to it in paras (c) and (d) must have been deliberate. If that is correct then it means that para (c) is satisfied by an applicant who has carried on business as an insurance broker for five years but who has not, in so doing, acquired what the council would regard as 'adequate practical experience in the work of an insurance broker'.

In my judgment, this is hardly the effect which one would expect to find in a section which elsewhere stresses the need for 'adequate practical experience'. I am quite unable to read the section in this way. Reading s 3 as a whole, I have no doubt that, when Parliament referred to a person who has carried on business as an insurance broker for not less than five years, it was intending to refer to someone who had carried on that business to an extent which provided him with adequate practical experience of the

business of an insurance broker. I can see no other reason for the omission of any
reference to 'adequate practical experience' in paras (c) and (d) and the inclusion of such
reference, by one provision or another, in each of the other six paragraphs.

The same indication, I believe, comes from a reference to a 'whole-time agent' in para
(c). A part-time agent was not to qualify, nor was a whole-time agent who had only acted
for one company. I infer that such persons were excluded because they were not thought
to have the necessary degree of practical experience of the business of an insurance
broker.

Although the matter does not arise for decision in this case, it may be helpful to say
that, in my view, whenever the phrase 'carried on [or 'carrying on' or 'has carried on']
business as an insurance broker' appears in s 3, it refers to the carrying on of that business
to the extent which I have indicated. Any other construction would leave open the
possibility, which Parliament could not, I believe, have intended, that whereas an
applicant under para (e) had to demonstrate that his five years' employment had given
him 'adequate practical experience', an applicant under para (g) would be entitled to
registration even though his knowledge and practical experience were inadequate, for it
might only be comparable with that of a person who had carried on business as an
insurance broker for five years but not to such an extent as to give him adequate practical
experience in the work of an insurance broker.

The construction which I believe to be correct accords, in my view, with the general
purpose of the 1977 Act as revealed in the different sections and in its long title. I detect
no error of law in the approach which the council adopted in considering these
applications.

The applicants were not informed of the reasons for the refusal of the council to
register their names. Had they asked they would have been given them, but they did
not. We do have, however, an affidavit from Mr Fryer, the registrar and secretary of the
council, which makes clear, not only that the council properly addressed its mind to the
need for the applicants to satisfy it that they had 'adequate practical experience in the
work of an insurance broker', but also that, on the material before it, the council was not
so satisfied. In so deciding the council was acting as a body of professional men making a
judgment on a matter affecting the standards of their own profession, and their views are
therefore entitled to considerable respect in this court.

The appeal to this court is by way of rehearing: see RSC Ord 55, r 3(1). Our approach
should be that adopted in the Civil Division of the Court of Appeal: we can draw such
inferences and make such decisions as we think are appropriate. Adopting that approach
I can find no basis on which the decisions of the council on these two applications should
be overturned.

I should add only this. Even if I had felt able to accept the submissions of counsel for
the applicants on the law, I would not for myself have thought it right to order the
registration of these applicants. I would have favoured remitting the case to the council
with the direction that it reconsider the applications in the light of the law as this court
has declared it. But, in the event, this has not arisen and I would, for these reasons,
dismiss these appeals.

WATKINS LJ. I agree.

Appeal dismissed.

Solicitors: *A S Coupe & Co*, Rochdale (for the applicants); *Stanleys & Simpson North* (for the
council).

April Weiss   Barrister.

R v Lee

COURT OF APPEAL, CRIMINAL DIVISION
ACKNER LJ, GLIDEWELL AND LEGGATT JJ
21 NOVEMBER 1983

Criminal law – Court of Appeal – Jurisdiction – Appeal against conviction – Ground of appeal – Plea of guilty – Unequivocal plea – Defendant fit to plead and intending to plead guilty after receiving expert advice – Whether unequivocal plea depriving Court of Appeal of jurisdiction to hear appeal against conviction – Criminal Appeal Act 1968, s 2(1)(a).

Criminal law – Appeal – Fresh evidence – Admission – Admission following conviction on unequivocal plea of guilty – Evidence not previously heard by a court merely because of plea of guilty – Circumstances in which court will receive such fresh evidence – Criminal Appeal Act 1968, s 23(1).

Criminal law – Appeal – Fresh evidence – Admission – Fresh evidence necessarily to be admissible evidence – Criminal Appeal Act 1968, s 23(1).

Where a defendant has been convicted on his own plea of guilty the court is not deprived of its jurisdiction under s 2(1)(a)[a] of the Criminal Appeal Act 1968 to allow an appeal against conviction, even though the defendant was fit to plead, knew what he was doing, intended to make the pleas that he did and pleaded without equivocation after receiving expert advice, provided that the court is satisfied that under all the circumstances of the case the conviction is unsafe or unsatisfactory (see p 1084 h, post); R v Shannon [1974] 2 All ER 1009 considered; dictum of Avory J in R v Forde [1923] All ER Rep at 479 not followed.

Where a defendant has been convicted on his own unequivocal plea of guilty, it will only be on very rare occasions that the court will consider it necessary or expedient in the interests of justice to allow evidence which, because of the plea of guilty, has not been heard by a court to be received under the general discretionary power given to the court by s 23(1)[b] of the 1968 Act (see p 1084 j, and p 1085 c to e and p 1086 b c, post); dicta of Lord Diplock and of Lord Kilbrandon in *Stafford v DPP* [1973] 3 All ER at 767, 769 and R v Lattimore (1975) 62 Cr App R 53 applied.

Where fresh evidence is received by the court under s 23(1) of the 1968 Act it must necessarily be admissible evidence (see p 1085 b c, post); R v Dallas [1971] Crim LR 90 and dictum of Scarman LJ in R v Lattimore (1975) 62 Cr App R at 56 followed.

Notes

For appeals against conviction following a plea of guilty, see 11 Halsbury's Laws (4th edn) para 611, and for cases on the subject, see 14(2) Digest (Reissue) 754, 6277–6285.

For the admission of fresh evidence on appeal against conviction, see 11 Halsbury's Laws (4th edn) para 642, and for cases on the subject, see 14(2) Digest (Reissue) 778–786, 6577–6695.

For the Criminal Appeal Act 1968, ss 2, 23, see 8 Halsbury's Statutes (3rd edn) 690, 706.

Cases referred to in judgment

R v Dallas [1971] Crim LR 90, CA.
R v Forde [1923] 2 KB 400, [1923] All ER Rep 477, CCA.
R v Lattimore (1975) 62 Cr App R 53, CA.

---

a   Section 2(1), so far as material, is set out at p 1084 b, post
b   Section 23(1) is set out at p 1084 j to p 1085 a, post

R v Olivo [1942] 2 All ER 494, CCA.

a *R v Shannon* [1974] 2 All ER 1009, [1975] AC 717, [1974] 3 WLR 155, HL.

Stafford v DPP, Luvaglio v DPP [1973] 3 All ER 762, [1974] AC 878, [1973] 3 WLR 719, HL.

Ruling

b During the course of an application for leave to appeal against his conviction on a plea of guilty in the Crown Court at Leeds before Tudor Evans J on 20 January 1981, the applicant, Bruce George Peter Lee, sought the ruling of the Court of Appeal on whether, notwithstanding his plea of guilty, the court had jurisdiction to hear the application and on whether, if the court had such jurisdiction, it could receive certain fresh evidence. The facts are set out in the judgment of the court.

c *Harry Ognall QC* and *Peter Heppel* for the applicant.
Gerald Coles QC and *David Wagstaff* for the Crown.

ACKNER LJ. On 20 January 1981 in the Crown Court at Leeds before Tudor Evans J the applicant pleaded guilty to 11 indictments.

d The first indictment, in numerical sequence, was indictment no 810041. The counts to which he pleaded guilty were as follows: count 1, arson; that was at 12 Selby Street and the date was 4 December 1979; count 2, manslaughter of Charles Hastie; count 3, manslaughter of Paul Hastie; and Count 4, manslaughter of Peter Hastie. All those manslaughter pleas, and the others to which we shall refer, were by reason of diminished responsibility.

e It was following his oral and written confessions to the arson to which I have just referred that he admitted, both orally and in writing, ten other arson or arson-related matters and they became the subject matter of the following ten indictments which are both in numerical order and in date order of their occurrence. Indictment no 810042; count 2, arson; that was at 70 Askew Avenue on 23 June 1973; count 3, manslaughter of Richard Ellerington. Indictment no 810043: arson at 33 Glasgow Street; that was on 12 October 1973; count 3, manslaughter of Arthur Smythe. Indictment no 810044: count 2, arson of the clothing of David Brewer; that was in premises known as Humber Buildings on 19 October 1973; count 3, manslaughter of David Brewer. Indictment no 810045: count 2, arson of 7 Minnie's Terrace on 23 December 1974; count 3, manslaughter of Elizabeth Rokahr. Indictment no 810046: count 2, arson of 9 Gorthorpe on 3 June 1976, count 3, manslaughter of Andrew Edwards. Indictment no 810047: g arson of 43 West Dock Avenue on 2 January 1977; count 3, manslaughter of Katrina Thacker. Indictment no 810048: count 2, arson at Wensley Lodge on 5 January 1977; counts 3 to 13, manslaughter of 11 named men. Indictment no 810049: count 2, arson at 4 Belgrave Terrace on 27 April 1977; count 3, manslaughter of Deborah Gold; count 4, manslaughter of Mark Jordan. Indictment no 810050: count 2, arson at 2 Brentwood Villas on 6 January 1978; counts 3 to 6, manslaughter of Mrs Christine Dickson and her h three sons. Indictment no 810051: arson at 407 Troutbeck House on 22 June 1979.

The applicant was ordered to be detained, without limit of time, at Park Lane Hospital under ss 60 and 65 of the Mental Health Act 1959.

Despite the extensive confessions made by the applicant, it was not anticipated that he would plead guilty. In fact, the case had been listed for a pre-trial review on 19 January 1981. The applicant, however, instructed his counsel that he wished to plead guilty. He j had, of course, the great advantage of the services of extremely experienced leading counsel, Mr Harry Ognall QC, and junior counsel, both of whom appear before us today.

Counsel saw the judge in his chambers on 19 January, the day before the pleas were taken. We have, at the instance of the applicant, the benefit of a transcript of what took place. Counsel expressed the view to the judge that his present instructions caused him anxiety and disquiet. He said that it was difficult to get instructions from the applicant, who had shifted his ground as to guilt, the present change being about the fourth change of instructions. Counsel pointed out that one of the factors causing anxiety was the conclusion of a public inquiry into the cause of one fire, the Wensley Lodge fire of 1977, that it was accidental.

However, all the reporting psychiatrists agreed that the applicant was fit to plead. When the case was called on, the pleas were made clearly and consistently and were quite properly accepted by the judge.

On 9 June 1982, long out of time, an application was made for leave to appeal. This application was supported by provisional grounds of appeal settled by junior counsel. As to the failure to seek leave to appeal in time, the following reasons were given:

'(1) That before and at the time of his trial and for a considerable period thereafter, the Applicant was confused, in a state of shock and had little appreciation of his situation. He found it difficult to relate to his legal advisers or to give full and proper instructions in respect of his defence; (2) The Applicant felt that his oral and written confessions constituted a considerable body of evidence against him and it was not until the results of enquiries made by the Sunday Times . . . were made known to him (March 1982) did he feel that there was any prospect of successfully persuading any Court of his innocence or any hope of a successful application for leave to appeal.'

It was then acknowledged in those provisional grounds of appeal that the grounds of appeal which then followed fell within no recognised category of grounds of appeal. In summary, they were as follows. (1) The applicant was of low intelligence and of a deprived and institutionalised background; his pleas of guilty were prompted 'not by any acknowledgment of his guilt but out of motives of a desire for notoriety and publicity'. (2) His legal advisers had grave doubts whether on a trial or series thereof the prosecution could prove his criminal responsibility, and specific reference was made to the Wensley Lodge fire. (3) The value of the whole of the confessions as evidence against the applicant was 'flawed with the same central doubt as to the motive which prompted them as attaches to the validity of his pleas'. (4) By reason of inquiries made by the Sunday Times, there were now grounds for believing 'in respect of most if not all of the deaths the subject of the several indictments, the Applicant has untainted alibis'. An example was given in relation to the fire at 50 Humber Buildings, Madeley Street on 19 October 1973.

On 29 October 1982 the applicant swore an affidavit in which he said, inter alia:

'3. That it had been my intention to plead not guilty to all charges on all indictments and to the best of my knowledge and belief preparations were being made for my defence at trial. The indictments against me were due to be listed for "pre-trial review" before the Honourable Mr. Justice Tudor Evans on the 19th January 1981 at Leeds.

4. That by the 19th January 1981 some seven months had elapsed since my arrest. I had been interviewed at great length on many occasions by the Police and had been examined and interviewed on more occasions than I can remember by medical men and by representatives from my instructing solicitors.

5. That it was and still is my case that I had been badgered into admitting the offences and each of them by a prolonged and remorseless interrogation by Detective Superintendent Sagar. Throughout the various interviews he kept suggesting to me ways in which I could have started the various fires. I was extremely drunk when arrested and during the course of my first interviews (in respect of the "Hastie" fire—Indictment 11) [I interpose there to say that that is Selby Street] I was feeling very unwell. I admitted that offence in order to obtain respite from the pressure of the interrogation and having made one admission I thought there was little point in failing to admit anything else that was put to me: it seemed to me that the Police would not accept any denials and it was easier for me simply to accede to their suggestions rather than to refute them.

6. That, as a consequence, when my case was due for pre-trial review I felt depressed at the enormity of my situation and I was feeling the strain of the previous seven months and had lost the will to fight. I felt that I could not face a trial—or series of trials—and was very much influenced by that fact that shortly before my first Crown Court appearance Dr. Sasieni had told me that there would be a place specially waiting for me at a special hospital in Liverpool if I pleaded guilty to manslaughter on the basis of diminished responsibility. At this time this prospect seemed more attractive than further periods on remand facing murder charges. I, therefore, on the 19th January 1981 decided to plead guilty and on this day informed my legal advisers of my intention. I must emphasise that up until this day my legal advisers had no reason to believe other than that I intended to plead not guilty to all charges. I acknowledge that I was prevailed upon by both my counsel and my solicitor to reconsider this decision but my mind was made up and therefore the case was heard as a plea of guilty on the following day.

7. That it took over six months thereafter for me to regain my composure and reflect upon my position. I now realise that the course I insisted upon following (namely pleading guilty) was wrong.

8. That I hereby declare that I had nothing to do with any of the deaths or fires the subject of the various indictments. I would respectfully plead for a chance to stand my trial in respect of them.

9. That at this time I cannot give any details of any alibi in respect of any of the fires save that at 12 Selby Street (indictment 11). I maintain that I was home during the night of the fire. I understand that investigations have revealed that I have an alibi in respect of the fire at 50 Humber Buildings (indictment 3) and that investigations may reveal that I may have an alibi in respect of 7 Minnie's Terrace (indictment 4) and 9 Gorthorpe, Orchard Park Estate (indictment 5) in that at the time of these last two fires I was living at Brook Cottages, Driffield and that it may well have been difficult—if not impossible—for me to have travelled to Hull to start these fires without being missed.

10. That I can only respectfully repeat and emphasise that my pleas of guilty were tendered not because they represented the truth but because I felt so overborne by the pressure of events generally that I felt that I could not take any more.'

There are a number of points which can be made by contrasting this affidavit with the provisional grounds of appeal to which we have referred, but for the purpose of this ruling there is no need to do that.

The applicant has, at the direction of the court, sworn a further affidavit dealing with each of the 11 fires and, in particular, the confessions which he made to the police. In reperfected grounds of appeal it is submitted, inter alia, that:

'. . . the applicant's pleas of guilty were ill considered and were significantly out of accord with the evidence which if the court grants leave will be called on behalf of the applicant at the hearing of the application and/or the appeal . . . In the circumstances in the absence of the alleged confessions there was no evidence in respect of any count on any indictment upon which a jury could safely convict and in the context of this case and the state of mind of this applicant and the evidence which the applicant would seek to adduce, the validity of these confessions is called seriously into question . . .'

The reperfected grounds of appeal then go on to deal with the various fires. As regards evidence, apart from that of the applicant, notice was given of some eleven witnesses for whom leave to call is to be sought, including an expert, Mr Bland, who has reported on each of the fires.

After the articles appeared in the Sunday Times, an inquiry into the offences and into their investigations was conducted by officers led by Mr Brooke, Assistant Chief Constable of South Wales. Extensive bundles of many hundreds of pages have been submitted by the Director of Public Prosecutions, for whom they were prepared by the investigating team from South Wales. Many of these documents in these bundles are referred to by Mr Bland when dealing fire by fire with the charges of arson.

Moreover, the Crown has conducted the unusual, but most helpful course in this unique case, of putting in written submissions in order to summarise some of the prosecution arguments and to provide a working index to the many bundles of documents.

We now come to the court's jurisdiction. Section 2(1)(*a*) of the Criminal Appeal Act 1968 provides as follows:

> 'Except as provided by this Act, the Court of Appeal shall allow an appeal against conviction if they think—(*a*) that the verdict of the jury should be set aside on the ground that under all the circumstances of the case it is unsafe or unsatisfactory . . . and in any other case shall dismiss the appeal . . .'

As originally drafted, s 2(1)(*a*) was confined to the 'verdict of the jury'. The word 'conviction' was substituted by s 44 of the Criminal Law Act 1977 following the decision of the House of Lords in *R v Shannon* [1974] 2 All ER 1009, [1975] AC 717, where the court drew attention to the failure to give the court power to intervene where the accused had pleaded guilty.

It is relevant to refer to the speech of Lord Salmon, where he said ([1974] 2 All ER 1009 at 1050, [1975] AC 717 at 773):

> 'The 1968 Act was, I think, intended to extend the powers conferred by the Criminal Appeal Act 1907. It was certainly not intended to diminish them. Section 4(1) of the 1907 Act, amongst other things required the Court of Criminal Appeal to allow an appeal (subject to the proviso) if they thought "that on any ground there was a miscarriage of justice".'

Similar views were expressed by Viscount Dilhorne (see [1974] 2 All ER 1009 at 1036, [1975] AC 717 at 757).

At an earlier passage in his speech (see [1974] 2 All ER 1009 at 1036, [1975] AC 717 at 756) Viscount Dilhorne quoted from the judgment of Avory J in *R v Forde* [1923] 2 KB 400 at 403, [1923] All ER Rep 477 at 479, a decision of the Court of Criminal Appeal:

> 'A plea of Guilty having been recorded, this Court can only entertain an appeal against conviction if it appears (1.) that the appellant did not appreciate the nature of the charge or did not intend to admit he was guilty of it, or (2.) that upon the admitted facts he could not in law have been convicted of the offence charged.'

Viscount Dilhorne concluded, however, that the appeal in that case had nevertheless been entertained on the ground provided in s 4(1) of the Criminal Appeal Act 1907, viz 'that there had been a miscarriage of justice'. Avory J's observation could not, therefore, be taken as an all-embracing one. In any event, it was not a decision on the new power given to the Court of Appeal under the 1968 Act and it is not binding on us.

The fact that the applicant was fit to plead, knew what he was doing, intended to make the pleas he did, pleaded guilty without equivocation after receiving expert advice, although factors highly relevant to whether the convictions on any of them were either unsafe or unsatisfactory, cannot of themselves deprive the court of the jurisdiction to hear the applications.

Fresh evidence. It is well established that s 23 of the 1968 Act contains two different powers. Under sub-s (2) a duty is imposed on the court to receive further evidence if the conditions of that subsection are met. Subsection (1), however, gives a general discretionary power to the court: see *R v Lattimore* (1975) 62 Cr App R 53.

It is essentially on this subsection that the applications are based. Section 23(1) provides:

> 'For purposes of this Part of this Act the Court of Appeal may, if they think it necessary or expedient in the interests of justice—(*a*) order the production of any

a   document, exhibit or other thing connected with the proceedings, the production
of which appears to them necessary for the determination of the case; (*b*) order any
witness who would have been a compellable witness in the proceedings from which
the appeal lies to attend for examination and be examined before the Court, whether
or not he was called in those proceedings; and (*c*) subject to subsection (3) below,
receive the evidence, if tendered, of any witness.'

b   It is to be noted that Scarman LJ, in giving the judgment of the court in *R v Lattimore*
said (at 56): 'It is also inconceivable that the Court would receive inadmissible evidence:
for the Court must act according to law.'

This was also the view of the court in *R v Dallas* [1971] Crim LR 90, where the
commentary makes the telling observation: 'If it were otherwise the rules of evidence
would be stultified through the tendering on appeal by convicted persons of evidence
c   which had been rejected as inadmissible at the trial.'

Thus, the question we have to answer is: is it necessary or expedient in the interests of
justice that we should allow, in a case where no evidence at all was called before a jury,
evidence which would or could have been called if the applicant had, by pleading not
guilty, caused the trial to take place? Superadded to the applications to call that evidence
are, of course, applications to call evidence which has since the convictions become
d   available. Obviously the answer to this question must depend on the particular
circumstances of the case.

The decision which we are now making is not intended to provide any general
precedent. Indeed, it is our view that the occasions on which this court will allow
evidence to be called, after there has been an unequivocal plea of guilty, will be very rare.
We regard this case, as indeed do both counsel, as wholly exceptional, if not unique.

e   However, we have read the Sunday Times articles, they being part of the voluminous
material put before us. We can well appreciate the public concern that those articles
must have occasioned, not only on the ground that in respect of some of the arsons it was
alleged that they could not have been committed by the applicant, but, much more
serious and sinister, because of the allegations made as to how his confessions had been
obtained and how it had been sought to corroborate his accounts.

f   We are satisfied that, in the wholly unusual circumstances of these applications, it is
necessary and expedient in the interests of justice that we should, at this stage, hear
relevant and admissible evidence called by both the applicant and the Crown whether
the convictions on the first indictment were either unsafe or unsatisfactory. As stated
above, this indictment related to the most recent arson alleged, 12 Selby Street, on 4
December 1979.

g   We adopt this course because, if, as is contended in the grounds of appeal, the judge
should have ordered pleas of not guilty to be entered to all the indictments, then it is
undoubtedly the case that the Crown would have elected to proceed on this very
indictment. It is, of course, well settled that each indictment, as opposed to each count in
the indictment, must be tried separately, the most recent authority being *R v Olivo* [1942]
2 All ER 494.

h   In the light of our decision on the Selby fire, we will hear submissions as to the other
ten indictments. We should however make this observation, about this court's function
in these circumstances. We have set out the relevant terms of s 2 of the 1968 Act.

In *Stafford v DPP* [1973] 3 All ER 762 at 769, [1974] AC 878 at 912 Lord Kilbrandon
said:

j   'The setting aside of a conviction depends on what the appellate court thinks of
it—that is what the Act says. If it were necessary to expand the question which a
member of the court, whose thoughts are in question, must put to himself, it may
be, "Have I a reasonable doubt, or perhaps even a lurking doubt, that this conviction
may be unsafe or unsatisfactory? If I have I must quash. If I have not, I have no
power to do so".'

To quote the words of Lord Diplock ([1973] 3 All ER 762 at 767, [1974] AC 878 at 906), but inserting the word 'conviction' in place of 'the verdict of the jury':

> 'I agree with [Viscount Dilhorne, Lord Cross and Lord Kilbrandon] that the statute under which this appeal is brought to this House requires each of us to ask himself the question: under all the circumstances of the case as it now stands in the light of the additional evidence, am I myself satisfied that the [conviction] was safe and satisfactory?'

Thus, in hearing and making our decision in due course on the evidence called before us, which evidence, because of the plea of guilty, has not hitherto been heard by a court, we are not seeking to usurp the functions of a jury; we are carrying out our statutory obligations of either allowing the appeal (assuming, of course, we give leave), because we think that the conviction was either unsafe or unsatisfactory, or, if we do not so think, of dismissing it.

Ruling accordingly.

Solicitors: *Philip Hamer & Co*, Hull (for the applicant); *Director of Public Prosecutions.*

N P Metcalfe Esq   Barrister.

Douglas-Scott v Scorgie

COURT OF APPEAL, CIVIL DIVISION
WATKINS AND SLADE LJJ
19 JANUARY 1984

Landlord and tenant – Implied covenant to repair – Short lease of dwelling house – Duty of landlord to keep in repair structure and exterior of dwelling house – Demised premises consisting of top floor flat in building – Whether roof immediately above flat capable of being part of 'structure' or 'exterior' of flat – Housing Act 1961, s 32(1)(a).

Where the subject of a lease is the top floor flat in a building, the roof above the top floor flat is capable of being part of 'the structure and exterior' of the dwelling comprising the flat, within s 32(1)(a)[a] of the Housing Act 1961, regardless of whether the roof forms part of the premises demised, and if, on the particular facts and having regard to the ordinary use of words, the roof can be regarded as part of the 'structure' or 'exterior' of the flat considered as a separate dwelling the landlord is then under an obligation by virtue of s 32(1)(a) to keep the roof in repair (see p 1090 b c f to h and p 1091 e f, post).
Campden Hill Towers Ltd v Gardner [1977] 1 All ER 739 applied.

Notes
For a landlord's implied obligations to repair, see 27 Halsbury's Laws (4th edn) paras 139, 267, and for cases on the subject, see 31(2) Digest (Reissue) 597–605, 4863–4928.
For the Housing Act 1961, s 32, see 16 Halsbury's Statutes (3rd edn) 351.

---

[a] Section 32(1), so far as material, is set out at p 1088 c d, post

Cases referred to in the judgment

a *Campden Hill Towers Ltd v Gardner* [1977] 1 All ER 739, [1977] QB 823, [1977] 2 WLR 159, CA.

Cockburn v Smith [1924] 2 KB 119, [1924] All ER Rep 59, CA.

Appeal and application for leave to appeal

The plaintiff, Kay Douglas-Scott, the tenant of the top floor flat of a building known as
b 47 Crawford Street, London W 1, brought two actions in the Bloomsbury and Marylebone
County Court against the defendant, Dudley Scorgie, the landlord, claiming damages for
breach of the landlord's covenant implied by s 32(1) of the Housing Act 1961, to keep in
repair the structure and exterior of a dwelling house, by reason of the defendant's failure
to keep in repair the roof immediately above the plaintiff's flat. On 21 May 1982 Mr
Recorder S Goldstein dismissed the actions on a preliminary point of law taken by the
c defendant that s 32 did not extend to the roof, and he also refused the plaintiff's
application to amend her particulars of the claims to plead breach of the defendant's
obligations at common law. The plaintiff appealed against the recorder's order dismissing
the actions and applied for leave to appeal against his refusal to give her leave to amend
her pleadings. The facts are set out in the judgment of Slade LJ.

d *John Hamilton* for the plaintiff.
Francis Phillimore for the defendant.

SLADE LJ (delivering the first judgment at the invitation of Watkins LJ). The appellant
in this appeal is Miss Kay Douglas-Scott. She has been a tenant of the respondent, Mr
Dudley Scorgie, of the third floor flat, 47 Crawford Street, London W 1, the third floor
e being the top floor of the building in which the flat is situated. Two actions were
instituted by Miss Douglas-Scott, as plaintiff, in the Bloomsbury and Marylebone County
Court against Mr Scorgie, as defendant, in 1976 and 1979, seeking damages against him
substantially on the ground that he had failed to keep in repair the roof of the building
over the flat in breach of his alleged implied obligations under s 32 of the Housing Act
1961. The actions took a shockingly long time to come to trial but eventually, by an
f order made in that court on 21 May 1982, Mr Recorder S Goldstein refused an application
by the plaintiff to amend her particulars of claim in the two actions, and dismissed both
of them. He dismissed the actions without hearing evidence, in response to a preliminary
point of law taken on behalf of the defendant, this being that the obligations of repair
imposed on the defendant as landlord by s 32 of the 1961 Act cannot extend to the roof
of the premises. The application to amend, which he refused, was an application by the
g plaintiff for leave to amend her pleadings, in effect by pleading a breach of the defendant's
obligations at common law as opposed to statute.

There are now before the court, first, an application by the plaintiff for leave to appeal
from the refusal of the recorder to give her leave to amend her pleadings; and second, an
appeal from his order dismissing the two actions.

I shall deal with the substantive appeal first. The question arising on it may, I think,
h be summarised thus: was the recorder right to hold as a matter of law, without hearing
evidence, that the obligations of repair imposed on the defendant as landlord by s 32 of
the 1961 Act cannot extend to the roof of the premises?

The original tenancy agreement was dated 28 February 1967 and was made between
the defendant as landlord and the plaintiff as tenant. Clause 1, so far as it is material,
j provided:

'THE Landlord shall let and the Tenant shall take—ALL that suite of rooms or flat
consisting of one room kitchen and bathroom on the 3rd floor forming part of the
messuage or buildings known as 47 Crawford Street W.1. Together with the use of
the entrance hall and lift (if any) Staircase outer door and vestibule of the said
buildings in common with the other tenants and occupiers thereof And together

with the fixtures furniture and effects now in and upon the premises hereby agreed to be demised and more particularly specified in the Inventory thereof signed by the parties hereto For the term of 7 months from the 1st day of March 1967 [and then the clause goes on to specify the rent].'

By cl 2(3) the tenant agreed to keep the interior of the premises in repair. Clause 6 provided:

'THIS Agreement shall take effect subject to the provisions of Section 32 of the Housing Act 1961 if applicable to the tenancy hereby created.'

The original term of seven months under the tenancy agreement has of course long since expired. I understand that the plaintiff now holds as statutory tenant on the terms of the agreement so far as applicable to the statutory tenancy.

At this point it will be convenient to read the relevant provisions of s 32 of the 1961 Act. Subsection (1), so far as material, provides as follows:

'In any lease of a dwelling-house, being a lease to which this section applies, there shall be implied a covenant by the lessor—(a) to keep in repair the structure and exterior of the dwelling-house (including drains, gutters and external pipes) . . .'

Section 32(5) provides, inter alia:

'"Lease of a dwelling-house" means a lease whereby a building or part of a building is let wholly or mainly as a private dwelling, and "the dwelling-house" means that building or part of a building.'

Section 33(1) provides that s 32 of the Act applies to any lease of a dwelling house granted after the passing of the Act, being a lease for a term of less than seven years. Pausing here, there is, I think, no doubt that s 32 applies in general terms to the tenancy of this flat, and that, having regard to the definitions which I have quoted, the flat itself is 'the dwelling-house' for the purpose of applying the provisions of s 32. The contrary has not been argued.

The plaintiff claims that the roof of the premises, 47 Crawford Street, is part of the 'structure' or 'exterior' of that dwelling house within the meaning of s 32(1)(a). The recorder held that it was not. The plaintiff challenges his decision on this point. More narrowly stated, this is the substantive issue now before this court.

It is perhaps convenient to begin by considering whether the roof of the premises, 47 Crawford Street, actually forms part of the premises let to the plaintiff. This point can be dealt with very shortly. In this context we have been referred to the decision of this court in *Cockburn v Smith* [1924] 2 KB 119 esp at 128, 134, [1924] All ER Rep 59 esp at 62, 65 per Bankes and Sargant LJJ. In the face of this decision counsel on behalf of the plaintiff has not attempted to argue that the roof actually forms part of the demised premises in the present case. Since this point has not been argued before us, I will proceed on the assumption that this concession is a correct one.

However, the mere fact that the roof does not, in conveyancing terms, form part of the demised premises by no means concludes the matter, as is shown by the recent decision of this court in *Campden Hill Towers Ltd v Gardner* [1977] 1 All ER 739, [1977] QB 823. That case concerned an underlease of a third floor flat comprised in a block of flats, not on the top floor of the building in question. The county court judge had taken the view that in applying the provisions of s 32(1) of the 1961 Act to a flat comprised in a block of flats, the whole shell of the building had to be regarded as the exterior of the dwelling house. The Court of Appeal rejected this very broad construction of para (a) of s 32(1). On the other hand, it likewise rejected a very narrow construction submitted on behalf of the landlords to the effect that para (a) cannot apply to anything, with the exception of drains, gutters and external pipes, which is not a part of the property

demised. Megaw LJ, in the course of delivering the judgment of the court, said this
a ([1977] 1 All ER 739 at 745, [1977] QB 823 at 834):

> 'We do not accept the lessors' contention insofar as it would limit "the structure
> and exterior of the dwelling-house" to that which, in the conveyancing meaning, is
> included in the particular terms of the demise in the lease. Anything which, in the
> ordinary use of words, would be regarded as part of the structure, or of the exterior,
> *b*   of the particular "dwelling-house", regarded as a separate part of the building, would
> be within the scope of para (*a*). Thus, the exclusion by the words of cl 2 of the
> underlease of "any part of the outside walls" would not have the effect of taking
> outside the operation of para (*a*) that which, in the ordinary use of language, would
> be regarded as the exterior wall of the flat—an essential integral part of the flat, as a
> dwelling-house; that part of the outside wall of the block of flats which constitutes a
> *c*   wall of the flat. The paragraph applies to the outside wall or walls of the flat; the
> outside of inner party walls of the flat; the outer sides of horizontal divisions
> between flat 20 and flats above and below; the structural framework and beams
> directly supporting floors, ceilings and walls of the flat. We do not accept the lessees'
> contention so far as it goes further.'

d   Having cited this passage in his judgment in the present case, the recorder then
proceeded immediately to accept the argument of counsel who then, as now, was
appearing on behalf of the defendant, in the following passage as recorded in the note of
his judgment:

> '[Counsel for the defendant] goes on to argue that there is only one possible
> *e*   interpretation of the words of Megaw LJ. If the roof was part of the demise there
> would be no problem. [Counsel for the defendant] says the roof is expressly excluded
> from the agreement. The roof is an external part of the building, not subject to the
> provisions of s 32. What are you left with? One is left with the definition of the
> operation of s 32 as given by Megaw LJ. It seems to me that I am totally bound by
> Megaw LJ's words in that judgment and I am happy so to be bound since it tells me
> *f*   the extent of the obligations under s 32. They do not include, regrettably as far as
> the plaintiff is concerned, the roof. [Counsel for the defendant] says, and sensibly,
> that it does not mean to say the landlord has no obligations as far as his dealings
> with the roof are concerned but they do not happen to be the obligations mentioned
> by s 32 of the Housing Act 1961, and I agree. It seems therefore that [counsel for
> the defendant's] preliminary point is well founded. I have a certain amount of
> *g*   sympathy with those who have pleaded the plaintiff's case, but the particulars of
> claim as drafted show no cause of action. Unless I hear an application to amend and
> allow it the consequences are that the actions fail.'

The recorder then proceeded to hear an application for leave to amend. He dismissed
that and the actions as well.
h   Counsel for the defendant has told us that, in the course of counsel's addresses to the
recorder, he was given some information as to the factual position in regard to the roof.
Counsel for the defendant clearly considered that the case proceeded before the recorder
on an agreed basis in regard to the relevant facts. However, I think that no agreement of
this nature has been established to an extent that this court can safely proceed on it.
There is no such agreement recorded in any of the documentation before us and none is
j   referred to in the judgment of the recorder.
    The recorder himself appears to have regarded the passage which I have cited from the
Campden Hill Towers case [1977] 1 All ER 739 at 745, [1977] QB 823 at 834, which he
himself cited, as authority for the proposition that a roof above the top floor flat of
premises can *never* form part of the structure and exterior of a dwelling house in relation

to that top floor flat, within the meaning of para (*a*) of s 32(1), unless the roof actually forms part of the demise. For my part, I think this involves a misunderstanding of what Megaw LJ said. In my opinion, for present purposes the crucial sentence in Megaw LJ's judgment in the *Campden Hill Towers* case is this:

> 'Anything which, in the ordinary use of words, would be regarded as part of the structure, or of the exterior, of the particular "dwelling-house" regarded as a separate part of the building, would be within the scope of para (*a*).'

Following this guidance given by the Court of Appeal, the crucial question to which the recorder should have directed his mind was, in my opinion, whether the roof of the premises would, in the ordinary use of words, be regarded as a part of the structure or of the exterior of the plaintiff's top floor flat, when that flat is regarded as a separate part of the building, 47 Crawford Street. If on the evidence the proper answer to this question is in the affirmative, I can see no reason why the roof should not fall within the scope of para (*a*).

It is true that in his judgment Megaw LJ, having enunciated the relevant test, proceeded to enumerate a number of particular items to which, on the particular facts of that case, para (*a*) would apply, that is to say—

> 'the outside wall or walls of the flat; the outside of inner party walls of the flat; the outer sides of horizontal divisions between Flat 20 and flats above and below; the structural framework and beams directly supporting floors, ceilings and walls of the flat.'

(See [1977] 1 All ER 739 at 745, [1977] QB 823 at 834.)

This enumeration thus did not include the roof of the building in that case. The recorder, as I read his judgment, appears to have attached much importance to this omission. However he apparently did not appreciate that there was one obvious reason for it, and one crucial distinction between the facts of that case and the facts of this. The flat in question in the *Campden Hill Towers* case was not a top floor flat. Presumably, therefore, in the ordinary use of words there would have been no question of the roof in that case being regarded as a part of the structure or of the exterior of that particular flat, viewed as a separate part of the building. It seems to me that quite different considerations may apply where the subject of a tenancy is a top floor flat. I can see no reason in principle why the roof above such a flat should not be capable in some circumstances of falling within the scope of para (*a*).

To take the simplest case by way of example, if the ceiling and roof of a particular top floor dwelling all formed part of one flat, inseparable, structural unit, it would seem to me prima facie that in the ordinary use of words, the roof and ceiling would be regarded as part of the structure or exterior of that dwelling, as much as its outside walls, inner party walls and so forth. On the other hand, I do not think one can go so far as to say that the roof, or part of the roof, which lies above *any* so-called top floor flat necessarily will fall within the definition in para (*a*) of the subsection. Borderline cases for example, might arise where one found a void space or an uninhabited loft between the flat and the roof. Everything must depend on the particular facts of the case.

In the present case we have been told that the roof of the plaintiff's flat is not a flat roof, that it has a valley gutter and that there is a gap between the roof and the ceiling of the flat, though I think none of these matters is yet formally in evidence. These points, if they are agreed or are supported by proper evidence, may conceivably provide some ammunition for the defendant when he seeks to argue that the roof of these particular premises cannot, in the ordinary use of words, be regarded as part of the structure, or of the exterior, of this particular top floor flat, and thus does not fall within para (*a*) of s 32(1). On the other hand, the plaintiff will no doubt argue that, notwithstanding these points, the roof is still an 'essential integral part of the flat', viewed as a separate dwelling house, to echo the words of Megaw LJ.

In my judgment the recorder plainly erred in dealing with this matter as a preliminary
a question of law in the absence of evidence, or in the absence of clearly agreed facts and in
holding, in effect as a matter of law and without regard to the evidence, that the plaintiff's
claim based on s 32(1)(*a*), as pleaded, was on the face of it demurrable. For the reasons
which I have tried to explain, the mere fact that the roof does not actually form part of
the demised premises by no means concludes the matter. I therefore think that the
recorder erred in accepting the preliminary point advanced by the defendant's counsel
b and in dismissing the action without proceeding to a full hearing with proper evidence.

Regretfully, therefore, because it will inevitably put the parties, or the legal aid fund,
to considerable further expense and delay, I would set aside the recorder's orders in both
actions and direct a new trial of both of them before another judge. The parties will of
course be free to adduce before him such relevant evidence as they may be advised, or
formally to agree the relevant facts sufficiently specifically to enable him to reach his
c decision. In the light of that evidence, or those facts, the judge hearing the case will, in
my opinion, have to follow the guidelines given by this court in the *Campden Towers* case
and, in so far as they are not agreed, to make the necessary findings of fact in regard to
this particular building.

With regard to the plaintiff's application for leave to appeal from the recorder's refusal
to grant her leave to amend her pleadings, I would give her such leave. On the appeal on
d this point, I would simply remit her application for leave to amend to be dealt with by
the judge who conducts the new trial. For my part, I would not wish to fetter his
discretion in dealing with that application for leave to amend when it comes before him,
by expressing any opinion as to its merits or otherwise. He will, I think, have to deal
with it in the circumstances as they exist when he hears the case, though no doubt he
will take into account any submissions which may be based on the long past history of
e this unfortunate matter.

WATKINS LJ. I agree. As Slade LJ has explained, this matter has been troublesome in
many respects. It has involved a great deal of expense, which is being borne by the legal
f aid fund, in other words, by the public. But a point of considerable importance to
landlords and tenants is involved, which requires clarification so far as roofs of buildings
within which there are a number of flats are concerned, and especially with regard to the
top flat, or flats, within such a building.

Like Slade LJ, I believe it to be the proper function of the judge who tries this matter
on a rehearing to determine such application as is made to him on behalf of the plaintiff
g for leave to amend the particulars of claim. I did at one stage during the argument
express the view that I would be unlikely to grant that application; however, following
that observation it is right to say that counsel for the plaintiff informed me that there
was in his possession an affidavit made by the plaintiff which purports to provide an
explanation for the delay which has been occasioned in bringing about a hearing of her
claim. That affidavit was not shown to this court. Accordingly, I should not like it to be
h said, in the absence of seeing the contents of that affidavit, that I have formed any
concluded view as to how I would deal with the application. That leaves the circuit judge
who is directed to take this rehearing absolutely free to determine the matter as he sees
the justice of it.

The order of this court is that the appeal be allowed and that the substantive matter be
referred back to the Bloomsbury and Marylebone County Court for rehearing. The
j rehearing must be conducted by one of the circuit judges sitting regularly at that court.

I think it is necessary to add that, regardless of what is said in the affidavit as an
explanation for the delay, it is incumbent on all those connected with this matter, and on
the court at Bloomsbury, to ensure as far as is possible that the rehearing takes place
without any further delay.

Application for leave to appeal granted. Appeal allowed. Action remitted to Bloomsbury and Marylebone County Court for rehearing by a circuit judge sitting regularly at that court, the rehearing to take place without further delay.

Solicitors: *Rubinstein Callingham* (for the plaintiff); *Mackrell & Co* (for the defendant).

Sophie Craven   Barrister.

McGregor (Inspector of Taxes) v Randall
McGregor (Inspector of Taxes) v Gillett

CHANCERY DIVISION
SCOTT J
9 FEBRUARY 1984

Income tax – Emoluments from office or employment – Receipt 'from' employment – Payment in return for variation of service contract – Lump sum payment – Payment made to compensate employee for loss of commission – Whether payment emolument from employment – Income and Corporation Taxes Act 1970, ss 181, 183.

The taxpayers were the directors of a company, their service contracts with which entitled them to salary and profit commission. In 1978 the company became a wholly-owned subsidiary of a Swedish corporation, the policy of which was to pay its executives a salary only. Accordingly in 1979 the company's board resolved to secure a variation of the taxpayers' service contracts by removing the provision for payment of commission on profits. To compensate the taxpayers for that change the company increased their salaries and paid them £6,000 each. The Revenue assessed the taxpayers to income tax on the £6,000 under Sch E by virtue of ss 181[a] and 183[b] of the Income and Corporation Taxes Act 1970, claiming that the payments were a profit of their employment. The taxpayers appealed, contending that the payments were compensation for giving up a contractual right, and, being payments in lieu of damages for breach of contract, were not taxable. The General Commissioners decided that the payments were of a capital nature taking on the character of damages and that ss 181 and 183 did not apply. The Crown appealed.

Held – Where an employee was entitled under the terms of his employment to periodic salary or commission and he accepted a lump sum in lieu of all or part of such salary or commission, the lump sum was taxable as an emolument from his office or employment under s 181 of the 1970 Act. The terms of the agreement showed that the £6,000 was paid as compensation for the variation in the terms of the taxpayers' contracts of employment, which continued thereafter on the same terms as before subject to that variation. Accordingly the payments were emoluments from the taxpayers' employments and were taxable under Sch E. The appeals would therefore be allowed (see p 1097 j, p 1098 c to h and p 1099 b to h, post).

---

a Section 181, so far as material, is set out at p 1098 *a b*, post
b Section 183, so far as material, is set out at p 1098 *b c*, post

a *Cameron v Prendergast (Inspector of Taxes)* [1940] 2 All ER 35, dicta of Viscount Simon LC in *Tilley v Wales (Inspector of Taxes)* [1943] 1 All ER at 283 and of Evershed MR in *Henley v Murray (Inspector of Taxes)* [1950] 1 All ER at 908–909 applied.
Bolam (Inspector of Taxes) v Muller (1947) 28 TC 471 followed.

Notes

b For voluntary payments to a holder of an office or employment, see 23 Halsbury's Laws (4th edn) para 644, and for cases on the subject, see 28(1) Digest (Reissue) 323–331, *1148–1193*.

For sums received under a service contract, see 23 Halsbury's Laws (4th edn) para 681, and for cases on the subject, see 28(1) Digest (Reissue) 335–337, *1211–1218*.

For the Income and Corporation Taxes Act 1970, ss 181, 183, see 33 Halsbury's Statutes (3rd edn) 255, 260.

c

Cases referred to in judgment

Bolam (Inspector of Taxes) v Muller (1947) 28 TC 471.
Cameron v Prendergast (Inspector of Taxes) [1940] 2 All ER 35, [1940] AC 549, HL.
Dewhurst v Hunter (Inspector of Taxes) (1932) 146 LT 510, [1932] All ER Rep 753, HL.
Du Cros v Ryall (Inspector of Taxes) (1935) 19 TC 444.
d *Henley v Murray (Inspector of Taxes)* [1950] 1 All ER 908, 31 TC 351, CA.
Tilley v Wales (Inspector of Taxes) [1943] 1 All ER 280, [1943] AC 386, HL.

Cases also cited

Bird (Inspector of Taxes) v Martland, Bird (Inspector of Taxes) v Allen [1982] STC 603.
Duff (Inspector of Taxes) v Barlow (1941) 23 TC 633.
e *Holland (Inspector of Taxes) v Geoghegan* [1972] 3 All ER 333, [1972] 1 WLR 1473.
IRC v Williams's Exors [1943] 1 All ER 318, CA; *affd* [1944] 1 All ER 381n, HL.

Cases stated

McGregor (Inspector of Taxes) v Randall

f 1. At a meeting of the Commissioners for the General Purposes of the Income Tax for the division of King's Lynn (Norfolk) held on 25 August 1982 at Vancouver House, King's Lynn, Norfolk, Derek Alfred John Randall appealed against an assessment to tax under Sch E for the year 1979–80 in the sum of £6,000.

2. The question for determination was whether the sum of £6,000 mentioned above was liable to income tax under Sch E by virtue of s 181 of the Income and Corporation *g* Taxes Act 1970.

3. At the same time the commissioners heard an appeal by Christopher John Gurney Gillett against an assessment to tax under Sch E for the year 1979–80 also in the sum of £6,000. The commissioners were informed by the parties that the facts and their respective contentions in respect of both appeals would be identical for all material purposes.

h [Paragraph 4 listed the documents admitted before the commissioners.]

5. The following facts were admitted before the commissioners. (a) Mr Randall and Mr Gillett (the taxpayers) had been directors of the Miln Marsters Group Ltd (the company) for many years and still were directors. (b) They had service agreements with the company which entitled them to a salary and profit commission. (c) The company became a wholly-owned subsidiary of Hilleshög AB, a Swedish company, in the summer *j* of 1978. (d) It was the policy of the Swedish company to remunerate its executives by way of a fixed salary only. (e) At a meeting of a committee of the board of the company on 20 April 1979 it was resolved in respect of three directors of the company (including each of the taxpayers) as follows: (i) to offer the taxpayers £6,000 each and Mr Day £3,000 to secure a variation of their service agreements by removing the provision for

payment of profit commission; (ii) that the salaries of the three directors be (a) from 1 January 1979 Mr Randall £25,000 per annum, Mr Gillett £18,000 per annum and Mr Day £11,000 per annum (b) from 1 May 1979 Mr Randall £28,000 per annum, Mr Gillett £20,160 per annum and Mr Day £12,000 per annum. The full terms of the resolutions of the board were set out in the minutes of the meetings annexed to the documents admitted before the commissioners. (f) In pursuance of the resolutions the company secretary wrote to each of the taxpayers in the terms of the letter dated 24 April 1979 admitted before the commissioners. (g) On the foot of each of the letters the taxpayers indorsed their agreement to the offer in the terms therein set out. (h) The remuneration of the taxpayers had been as follows:

Year to		Randall £	Gillett £
31.5.75	Salary	9,184	6,900
	Commission	1,783	1,782
		10,967	8,682
31.5.76	Salary	15,000	8,604
	Commission	2,920	2,920
		17,920	11,524
31.5.77	Salary	15,000	8,604
	Commission	4,714	4,714
		19,714	13,318
31.5.78	Salary	15,000	8,604
	Commission	4,590	4,590
		19,590	13,194
Period to			
30.4.79	Salary	17,086	11,019
	Compensation	6,000	6,000
30.4.80	Salary	28,000	20,160
Period to			
31.12.80 (8 months)	Salary	22,400	16,128
Year to			
31.12.81	Salary	35,728	25,724

6. It was contended on behalf of the taxpayers that: (a) the sum of £6,000 which had been included in the Sch E assessment raised on the taxpayers as a chargeable emolument was not so chargeable under the provisions of s 181(1) of the Income and Corporation Taxes Act 1970 but was a payment to which s 187(2) of that Act applied and was exempt from tax under the provisions of s 188(3) of the Act; (b) the sum of £6,000 which had been offered to each of the taxpayers at the board meeting of the company on 20 April 1979 was a payment in exchange for the taxpayers' agreement to the variation of their service agreements to remove payment of commission on profits from their remuneration; (c) the payment accordingly was not a sum received by the taxpayers for past, present or future services as directors of the company but was compensation in return for giving up a contractual right; (d) the company could not cancel unilaterally the taxpayers' rights to payment of commission on profits under their contracts of

service; were they to do so, they would have been open to proceedings for damages for
a breach of contract and for constructive dismissal; on the authority of *Du Cros v Ryall*
(*Inspector of Taxes*) (1935) 19 TC 444 damages received for breach of contract were not
chargeable to tax; (e) the instigation for the change in the contractual terms of
employment derived from the company and not from the taxpayers; that was as a
consequence of the change of ownership of the company and in order to comply with
the overall policy of the new owning group; (f) moreover, if the taxpayers had gone on
b enjoying commission in addition to salary, there was a substantial likelihood that the
taxpayer Randall would have been receiving a higher rate of remuneration than the
chairman of the parent group, because, the company being a market leader for a new
Australian sugar beet seed, the company's profits therefore would be potentially higher
in the next five years; (g) the amount of compensation paid was substantially less than
any commission which would have been payable to the taxpayers had there been no
c change in their terms of employment; the increased salary which was awarded to each of
the taxpayers in respect of the years subsequent to that in which their right to commission
was removed demonstrated that it was that increase in salary which was the consideration
for future services and that the compensation was in consideration of the taxpayers
having given up their contractual rights. (h) moneys paid to obtain a release from a
contingent liability under contracts of employment were not remuneration for services
d rendered or to be rendered under that contract and were therefore not received 'from the
contract of employment' (see *Dewhurst v Hunter* (*Inspector of Taxes*) (1932) 146 LT 510,
[1932] All ER Rep 753); the payments to the taxpayers in the case before the
commissioners came within that description; a lump sum payment by a company to a
director as compensation for relinquishing a right to receive remuneration was not
chargeable to income tax (see *Duff* (*Inspector of Taxes*) *v Barlow* (1941) 23 TC 633);
e accordingly the payments made in the case before the commissioners were not so
chargeable; whilst it had been held that moneys received by employees consequent on
the termination of their right to retain the proceeds from the sale of salvage were
assessable for income tax (see *Holland* (*Inspector of Taxes*) *v Geoghegan* [1972] 3 All ER 333,
[1972] 1 WLR 1473), in that case the payments had been made as an inducement for
striking employees to return to work and therefore clearly for future services; the case
f was not therefore authority to determine the matter before the commissioners against
the taxpayers; further, the rights were not part of their contracts of employment but
were given to them by the council which enabled the employees to derive income not
from their employers but the outside world; (i) the payment was not one made to either
taxpayer as an inducement not to resign from his employment and to continue to
provide services to the company and was not therefore governed by the authority of
g *Cameron v Prendergast* (*Inspector of Taxes*) [1940] 2 All ER 35, [1940] AC 549; (j) whilst it
was accepted that on the authority of *Tilley v Wales* (*Inspector of Taxes*) [1943] 1 All ER
280, [1943] AC 386 a sum paid as compensation for the reduction in a director's salary
was assessable for income tax, any payment in respect of compensation for loss of pension
rights was similar to compensation for the loss of commission and therefore, within the
authority of that case, the payment for loss of commission was not taxable; in the
h taxpayers' case there was no reduction in salary; in *Tilley v Wales* the directors gave up a
proportion of fixed salary whereas in the taxpayers' case the rights given up were to
unquantified and unquantifiable sums, the payment of which was in any event only
contingent on the company's profits; the payments made to the taxpayers were not
related to services actually rendered by the directors but to the company's profits; (k)
whilst *Bolam* (*Inspector of Taxes*) *v Muller* (1947) 28 TC 471 appeared to be authority for
j the proposition that a payment of a lump sum to a director in consideration of his
surrendering a right under his service agreement to receive commission on the
distributed profits of the company was properly assessable to income tax, in that case the
instigation for the change had stemmed from the director and not from the company
and moreover in the case of the taxpayers before the commissioners the commission

would depend on the amount of group profits over which they had no control (as opposed to the director concerned in *Bolam v Muller* who had a voice in the amount of profits distributed by his company).

7. It was contended on behalf of the Crown that: (a) the sums of £6,000 were chargeable to tax under Sch E by virtue of ss 181(1) and 183(1) of the Income and Corporation Taxes Act 1970 as a profit of the taxpayers' employment, it being immaterial that the payment was made in the form of a lump sum; (b) accordingly the assessments were rightly made and should be confirmed.

8. The following authorities were referred to: *Bolam (Inspector of Taxes) v Muller* (1947) 28 TC 471, *Cameron v Prendergast (Inspector of Taxes)* [1940] 2 All ER 35, [1940] AC 549, *Du Cros v Ryall (Inspector of Taxes)* (1935) 19 TC 444, *Duff (Inspector of Taxes) v Barlow* (1941) 23 TC 633, *Henley v Murray (Inspector of Taxes)* [1950] 1 All ER 908, *Dewhurst v Hunter (Inspector of Taxes)* (1932) 146 LT 510, [1932] All ER Rep 753, *Holland (Inspector of Taxes) v Geoghegan* [1972] 3 All ER 333, [1972] 1 WLR 1473, *Tilley v Wales (Inspector of Taxes)* [1943] 1 All ER 280, [1943] AC 386.

9. The commissioners were of the opinion that, at the time of the agreement recorded in the letter of 24 April 1979, the company (having become part of a larger concern, Hilleshög AB Ltd) was obliged to conform with the policy of that concern and therefore found it necessary unilaterally to change the conditions of employment of the taxpayers by cancelling their entitlement to commission. The commissioners were of the opinion that the amount of compensation paid to the taxpayers in pursuance of the agreement was so low in relation to the amount of commission earned and likely to be earned that it could not properly be regarded as a payment to secure their future services without such entitlement to commission and that the real compensation for their agreeing to continue to serve the company as directors whilst foregoing the commission was to be found in the increased salary which they each earned thereafter. The commissioners were therefore of the opinion that the 'compensation' was a sum paid by the company in lieu of the damages which would have been recoverable had they unilaterally broken the contracts of employment and was accepted and received by the taxpayers as such. The payments accordingly in the commissioners' view were of a capital nature taking on the character of damages and were in their view not income chargeable to income tax under Sch E pursuant to the provisions of ss 181 and 183 of the Income and Corporation Taxes Act 1970.

10. That being so, whilst the payment to Mr Randall was clearly one to which the provisions of s 187 of that Act applied, it was not chargeable to tax by virtue of the provisions of s 183(3), the amount being less than £10,000.

11. The commissioners therefore allowed the appeals in each case and discharged the assessment.

12. Immediately on being informed of the determination of the appeal, the Crown declared dissatisfaction therewith as being erroneous in point of law, and on 3 September 1982 required the commissioners to state a case for the opinion of the High Court pursuant to s 56 of the Taxes Management Act 1970.

13. The question of law for the opinion of the court was whether on the evidence before the commissioners the sum of £6,000 was chargeable to tax under s 181 of the Income and Corporation Taxes Act 1970.

McGregor (Inspector of Taxes) v Gillett

Christopher John Gurney Gillett appealed against an assessment to tax under Sch E for the year 1979–80 in the sum of £6,000. The appeal was heard together with that of Derek Alfred John Randall. The facts relating to the appeal, the issues involved and the determination of the commissioners were identical to those in the appeal of Mr Randall.

Robert Carnwath for the Crown.
Mr Gillett appeared in person.
Mr Randall did not appear.

SCOTT J. There are two cases before me today, both arising out of the same facts. The taxpayers in the two cases are Mr Randall and Mr Gillett. Neither has been represented before me; Mr Gillett, however, has appeared in person. The relevant primary facts are not in dispute, and I can take them from para 5 of the case stated in respect of Mr Randall:

'The following facts were admitted before [the commissioners]: (a) The taxpayers have been directors of the Miln Marsters Group for many years and still are directors. (b) They had service agreements with the Company which entitled them to a salary and profit commission. (c) The [company] became a wholly owned subsidiary of Hilleshog AB, a Swedish Company, in the summer of 1978. (d) It was the policy of the Swedish company to remunerate its Executives by way of a fixed salary only. (e) At a meeting of a Committee of the Board of the [company] on 20 April 1979 it was resolved in respect of 3 directors of the Company (including each of the [taxpayers]) as follows:—(i) to offer Messrs Randall and Gillett £6000 each and Day £3000 to secure a variation of their service agreements by removing the provision for payment of profit commission. (ii) that the salaries of the 3 directors be:—i. from 1 January 1979—Randall £25,000 per annum, Gillett £18,000 per annum and Day £11,000 per annum; ii. from 1 May 1979 Randall £28,000 per annum, Gillett £20,160 per annum and Day £12,000 per annum. The full terms of the resolutions of the Board are set out in the minutes of the said meeting . . .'

I think I need not refer to the terms of those minutes, which are sufficiently summarised in what I have read. Paragraph 5 continues:

'(f) In pursuance of the said resolutions the Company Secretary wrote to each of the [taxpayers] in the terms of the letters [dated 24 April 1979 admitted before the commissioners]. (g) On the foot of each of the said letters the [taxpayers] endorsed their agreement to the said offer in the terms therein set out.'

The terms of those letters and the terms of the indorsements are, in my view, highly important. I will, therefore, read those in full. The letter, which bore the date 24 April 1979, from the company to Mr Randall is in these terms:

'Dear Sir,
As you know, the Company is now a wholly-owned subsidiary of Hilleshög A.B. and, as you are also aware, it is the policy of Hilleshög that its directors and executives and those of its subsidiaries are remunerated on the basis of a fixed annual salary and that it is therefore contrary to this policy that the terms of your service contract with the Company entitle you to annual commission on the consolidated profit of the Company. In order to bring your terms of service into compliance with Hilleshög's group policy, we are prepared to pay you £6,000 in order to obtain your agreement to the cancellation of future commission entitlement with effect from 1st June, 1978. If you accept this offer, please would you sign the acceptance form on the enclosed duplicate copy of this letter and return it to the Company Secretary at the above address so that it is received there by the 30th April, 1979, being the Company's year-end date.'

And then at the foot of this letter there is the indorsement, signed by Mr Randall in acceptance of the proposal. The indorsement is in these terms:

'I agree to the cancellation of all future commission entitlement with effect from 1st June 1978 and agree to accept £6,000 in full and final compensation therefore on the terms set out above.'

The £6,000 was thereby accepted by Mr Randall as compensation for the cancellation of all future commission entitlement which would otherwise have arisen under the terms of his employment by the company. The sums of £6,000 to each of the taxpayers were accordingly paid. I need not trouble with the position regarding Mr Day, because there is no tax appeal so far as he is concerned. Each of the taxpayers was assessed to tax under

Sch E for the year 1979–80 on that sum of £6,000. The General Commissioners, on appeal by the respective taxpayers, discharged that assessment; the Crown now appeals *a* by way of case stated. The question of law expressed in the case is whether, on the evidence I have referred to, the sums of £6,000 were chargeable to tax under s 181 of the Income and Corporation Taxes Act 1970. Section 181 provides that '... Tax under this Schedule shall be charged in respect of any office or employment on emoluments therefrom ...' The question is, therefore, whether the £6,000 is an emolument from Mr Randall's office or employment. The question in regard to Mr Gillett is obviously *b* exactly the same. In this judgment I shall refer to Mr Randall; the references will apply mutatis mutandis to Mr Gillett.

Section 183(1) of the Act defines emoluments as including 'all salaries, fees, wages, perquisites and profits whatsoever'. There is, therefore, no doubt that the £6,000 is an emolument. Is it, however, an emolument from his, and again I quote from s 181, 'office or employment'? *c*

In my judgment, there is overwhelming authority for the proposition that, where an employee is entitled, under the terms of his employment, to periodic salary or commission and he accepts a lump sum in lieu of all or part of such salary or commission, then the lump sum is taxable under s 181 (see *Henley v Murray (Inspector of Taxes)* [1950] 1 All ER 908, *Cameron v Prendergast (Inspector of Taxes)* [1940] 2 All ER 35, [1940] AC 549 and *Tilley v Wales (Inspector of Taxes)* [1943] 1 All ER 280 at 283, [1943] AC 386 at *d* 393 per Viscount Simon LC). This proposition is, in my judgment, enough to conclude the case in favour of the Crown. In their letter of 24 April 1979, the employers offered to pay Mr Randall £6,000 and I quote: '... in order to obtain your agreement to the cancellation of future commission entitlement with effect from 1st June, 1978.' Mr Randall accepted that sum in full and final compensation for that cancellation. The nature of the agreement between Mr Randall and his employers is set out in the letter *e* and Mr Randall's indorsement thereon. The proposition I have referred to plainly, in my judgment, applies.

Counsel for the Crown relied particularly on *Bolam (Inspector of Taxes) v Muller* (1947) 28 TC 471. In that case the taxpayer was employed on a fixed salary and commission basis. By an agreement made on 30 September 1942 the taxpayer received a capital sum of £1,250 in compensation for surrendering his right to commission as from 1 November *f* 1940, subject thereto his employment continuing on the same terms as before. Atkinson J held that the £1,250 was taxable. He said (at 475):

'It seems to me so plain. It is obvious, of course, that the bonuses he would have received if they had been paid under the agreement would have been profits from his employment, and the mere fact that they agree on another form of remuneration *g* does not alter its character.'

In my judgment the facts of that case are indistinguishable from those of the present. *Bolam v Muller* was a case where, as here, the employee's employment was intended to continue on the same terms as before, as varied by the particular agreement.

On the other side of the coin there are cases where a sum is paid to an employee as compensation for loss of his employment. Such sums are not taxable under s 181 of the *h* 1970 Act. The distinction is pointed out by Evershed MR in *Henley v Murray (Inspector of Taxes)* (1950) 31 TC 351 at 362–363; cf [1950] 1 All ER 908 at 908–909, where he said:

'It is quite clear I think that bargains of this kind may take at any rate one of two forms. A man who has a contract in respect of which he is entitled to periodic remuneration may say, "Well, I will take now a lump sum instead of the periodic *j* remuneration in the future, and though I will continue to serve under my contract, I shall not be expected to do quite as much work", or he may even say, "I shall not be expected to do any work at all." If that were the form of the arrangement in this case, I think it would be true to say that the lump sum which was paid was profits which became payable under his contract, and that it was paid to him by virtue of his office or employment . . . But there is another class of case where the bargain is, as it seems to me, of an essentially different character, for in the second class of case the contract itself goes altogether and some sum becomes payable for the consideration of the total abandonment of all the contractual rights which the other party had under the contract.'

In the present case, the employment of Mr Randall was intended to, and did, continue, but it was to continue on varied terms. The extent of the variation appears from the letter of 24 April 1979 with the indorsement thereon. There was to be a fixed annual salary which, as one may see from the terms of the board resolution, was to be at an increased rate of £25,000 with effect from 1 January 1979, and then £28,000 with effect from 1 May 1979, and secondly there was to be the cancellation of the commission with effect from 1 June 1978. The £6,000 may have been trivial in amount by comparison with the anticipated commission. The increased salary may also have been regarded by the parties as part compensation for loss of the commission. But there is, in my judgment, no factual justification for the inference drawn by the commissioners, expressed in para 9 of the case stated, that the £6,000—

'was a sum paid by the company in lieu of the damages which would have been recoverable had they unilaterally broken the contracts of employment, and was accepted and received by the [taxpayers] as such.'

That inference contradicts the expressed indorsements signed by each of the taxpayers, and is also inconsistent with the taxpayers' own case. In para 6(b) of the case stated, the taxpayers' contention on this point is set out in these terms:

'The sum of £6000 which had been offered to each of the [taxpayers] at the Board Meeting of their employing Company on the 20th April 1979 was a payment in exchange for the [taxpayers'] agreement to the variation of their Service Agreements to remove payment of commission on profits from their remuneration.'

The contention, so expressed, brings the case, in my judgment, clearly within the proposition to which I referred earlier in this judgment. None of the cases relied on by the taxpayers before the commissioners, and to which I have been very properly referred by counsel for the Crown, seem to assist the taxpayers. *Dewhurst v Hunter (Inspector of Taxes)* [1932] All ER Rep 753 was a decision reached on the facts of the case and has been distinguished on that basis in subsequent cases. Those facts, to my mind, do not permit any useful comparison with the facts of the present case.

In *Du Cros v Ryall (Inspector of Taxes)* (1935) 19 TC 444 and in the *Tilley* case the sums in question were paid for loss of rights which would or could not be enjoyed while the employment was current. The comparison sought to be drawn in the taxpayers' arguments, as set out in the cases stated, between the loss of pension rights and the loss of contractual remuneration during the currency of employment seems to me to be misconceived. Accordingly, I conclude the sums of £6,000 are taxable under s 181 of the Income and Corporation Taxes Act 1970.

Appeals allowed.

Solicitors: *Solicitor of Inland Revenue.*

Clare Mainprice   Barrister.

Gardner v Moore and others

HOUSE OF LORDS

LORD HAILSHAM OF ST MARYLEBONE LC, LORD DIPLOCK, LORD KEITH OF KINKEL, LORD BRANDON OF OAKBROOK AND LORD TEMPLEMAN

28 FEBRUARY, 5 APRIL 1984

Motor insurance – Rights of third parties against insurers – Motor Insurers' Bureau – Liability in respect of intentional criminal act – Road Traffic Act 1972, s 145(3).

The plaintiff suffered serious injuries when the first defendant deliberately drove his motor vehicle at the plaintiff and hit him. The first defendant was subsequently sentenced to three years' imprisonment for wounding the plaintiff with intent to cause him grievous bodily harm. At the time of the offence the first defendant was not insured against third party risks as required by Pt VI (ss 143–158) of the Road Traffic Act 1972. The plaintiff brought an action against the first defendant claiming damages for personal injuries and against the second defendants, the Motor Insurers' Bureau, seeking a declaration that, by virtue of an agreement between the bureau and the Secretary of State that the bureau would compensate victims of uninsured drivers who were unable to satisfy a judgment in favour of the victim, they were liable to indemnify the plaintiff against any unsatisfied judgment the plaintiff might obtain against the first defendant. The trial judge awarded the plaintiff £15,526·35 damages and made a declaration against the bureau in the terms sought. The bureau appealed direct to the House of Lords, contending that under the general principle of insurance law that a person was not entitled to profit from his own iniquity Pt VI of the 1972 Act could not be construed as requiring a person who used a motor vehicle to insure himself against liability incurred by him in respect of bodily injury which was intentionally and criminally inflicted by him on another person.

Held – On its true construction s 145(3)[a] of the 1972 Act required a motorist to take out a policy of insurance indemnifying him against 'any liability', however arising, incurred by him in respect of the death of or bodily injury to any person 'caused by, or arising out of the use of, a vehicle on a road'. The plaintiff's injuries were so caused and accordingly if his judgment against the first defendant remained unsatisfied the Motor Insurers' Bureau were liable to indemnify the plaintiff. The doctrine of public policy that a person was not entitled to profit from his own wrongdoing did not apply in the circumstances, since the satisfaction of the first defendant's liability to the plaintiff was incidental to the main purpose of the agreement between the bureau and the Secretary of State, which was the protection of innocent third parties. The bureau's appeal would therefore be dismissed (see p 1104 b c, p 1106 a b and p 1107 b to e and h to p 1108 b, post).

Hardy v Motor Insurers' Bureau [1964] 2 All ER 742 approved.

Notes

For the liability of the Motor Insurers' Bureau in respect of intentional criminal acts, see 25 Halsbury's Laws (4th edn) para 787, and for a case on the subject, see 29 Digest (Reissue) 624, 5421.

For the Road Traffic Act 1972, Pt VI, see 42 Halsbury's Statutes (3rd edn) 1786.

Cases referred to in opinions

Amicable Society v Boland (1830) 4 Bli NS 194, [1824–34] All ER Rep 570, 5 ER 70, HL.
Bell v Carstairs (1811) 14 East 374, 104 ER 646.

---

a   Section 145(3), so far as material, is set out at p 1104 a, post

Beresford v Royal Insurance Co Ltd [1938] 2 All ER 602, [1938] AC 586, HL; *affg* [1937] 2
a   All ER 243, [1937] 2 KB 197, CA.
Burrows v Rhodes [1899] 1 QB 816, [1895–9] All ER Rep 117.
Cleaver v Mutual Reserve Fund Life Association [1892] 1 QB 147, [1891–4] All ER Rep 335,
      CA.
Crippen's Estate, Re [1911] P 108, [1911–13] All ER Rep 207.
Hardy v Motor Insurers' Bureau [1964] 2 All ER 742, [1964] 2 QB 745, [1964] 3 WLR 433,
b   CA.
Haseldine v Hosken [1933] 1 KB 822, [1933] All ER Rep 335, CA.
James v British General Insurance Co Ltd [1927] 2 KB 311, [1927] All ER Rep 442.
Mixnam's Properties Ltd v Chertsey UDC [1964] 2 All ER 627, [1965] AC 735, [1964] 2
      WLR 1210, HL; *affg* [1963] 2 All ER 787, [1964] 1 QB 214, [1963] 3 WLR 38, CA.
Tinline v White Cross Insurance Association Ltd [1921] 3 KB 327.

c
Appeal

By a writ issued on 27 May 1981 the plaintiff, Alan Gardner, claimed damages for
personal injuries caused to the plaintiff by the negligence and/or breach of duty of the
first defendant, Alan Moore, arising out of an incident on or about 21 March 1981. By
an order of Mr District Registrar P H Berkson in chambers dated 12 October 1981 the
d   Motor Insurers' Bureau were added as second defendants. On 28 July 1983 Caulfield J in
the Queen's Bench Division at Liverpool ordered that the first defendant should pay the
plaintiff £15,526·35 damages, interest thereon and costs, and further directed that
judgment should be entered for the plaintiff against the second defendant for a declaration
and declared that the second defendant was liable to indemnify the plaintiff in respect of
the judgment against the first defendant. The second defendants appealed against the
e   judgment direct to the House of Lords pursuant to a certificate under s 12 of the
Administration of Justice Act 1969 that a point of law of general public importance was
involved in the decision and that that point of law was one in respect of which the judge
was bound by a decision of the Court of Appeal in previous proceedings, viz *Hardy v
Motor Insurers' Bureau* [1964] 2 All ER 742, [1964] 2 QB 745, and was fully considered in
the judgments given by the Court of Appeal in those previous proceedings. Leave to
f   appeal was granted by the Appeal Committee of the House of Lords on 24 October 1983.
The first defendant took no part in the proceedings before the House of Lords. The facts
are set out in the opinion of Lord Hailsham LC.

Piers Ashworth QC and *Charles James* for the appellants.
Andrew Rankin QC and *R A Fordham* for the respondent.

g
Their Lordships took time for consideration.

5 April. The following opinions were delivered.

LORD HAILSHAM OF ST MARYLEBONE LC. My Lords,

h
Judgment appealed from

This is an appeal by the Motor Insurers' Bureau (second defendants) using the so-called
'leap frogging' procedure from a judgment of Caulfield J given on 28 July 1983 whereby
it was adjudged that the first defendant should pay to the plaintiff £15,526·35 damages
and interest and the costs of the action and that judgment should be entered against the
j   second defendants for a declaration to the effect that the second defendants are liable to
indemnify the plaintiff in respect of the judgment against the first defendant.

The facts and course of proceedings

The proceedings arise from the personal injuries which the plaintiff sustained on 22
March 1981 as the result of being run down by a motor vehicle driven by the first

defendant. From first to last the first defendant has played no part in the proceedings and has never disputed his liability to the plaintiff. No question arises as to the quantum of damages.

The injuries sustained by the plaintiff were caused by the intentionally criminal act of the first defendant, who deliberately drove his vehicle onto the pavement where the plaintiff was walking and intentionally ran him down. There is no dispute about this. On 24 July 1981 in the Crown Court at Liverpool the first defendant pleaded guilty to a charge under s 18 of the Offences against the Person Act 1861 of wounding the plaintiff with intent to cause him grievous bodily harm, and was sentenced by his Honour Judge Temple QC to serve a term of imprisonment of three years.

At the time of the collision the first defendant was not insured by any relevant policy of insurance under Pt VI of the Road Traffic Act 1972. The writ was issued on 27 May 1981 against the first defendant, and the present appellants were added by order dated 12 October 1981 of Mr District Registrar P H Berkson in chambers and the statement of claim amended accordingly so as to include the claim against which the present appellants now appeal that the present appellants were bound to indemnify the plaintiff by virtue of the current agreement (that dated 22 November 1972) between the appellants and the Secretary of State for the Environment.

At the hearing before Caulfield J it was not disputed that the judge was bound by the decision of the Court of Appeal in *Hardy v Motor Insurers' Bureau* [1964] 2 All ER 742, [1964] 2 QB 745, and the judge gave judgment for the plaintiff accordingly with a certificate pursuant to s 12 of the Administration of Justice Act 1969 and for leave to present a petition to your Lordships' House. Leave to appeal was subsequently granted by the Appeal Committee of your Lordships' House.

The question for appeal

The sole question for decision by the House is accordingly whether *Hardy v Motor Insurers' Bureau* was correctly decided. This depends primarily on the true construction of the agreement relating to uninsured drivers of 22 November 1972 between the appellants and the Secretary of State for the Environment (the MIB agreement), Pt VI of the Road Traffic Act 1972 and the proper application of any relevant rule of law or public policy arising from the fact that the actions alleged against the first defendant were not caused by negligence or recklessness but by his deliberate act amounting to an offence under s 18 of the Offences against the Person Act 1861.

Before proceeding further it is perhaps relevant to point out the function of the MIB agreement and the sister and similar agreement of the same date between the same parties relating to untraced drivers. Part VI of the Road Traffic Act 1972 is designed to protect the innocent third party from the inability to pay of a driver who incurs liability by causing him death or personal injuries. This it does partly (ss 143 and 145) by imposing an obligation on all drivers to insure against third party liability under sanction of the criminal law, and partly by conferring on a successful plaintiff a right of direct recourse in the civil courts against the judgment debtors' insurers if he is insured in the manner prescribed (eg ss 148 and 149). This by itself leaves a gap in the protection afforded to the innocent third party by Pt VI since a guilty driver may be either uninsured altogether or untraceable so that it is not known whether he is insured or not and if so by whom. It is to fill this gap that the two agreements between the MIB and the Secretary of State for the Environment have been voluntarily entered into. Their foundations in jurisprudence are better not questioned any more than were the demises of John Doe and the behaviour of Richard Roe in the old ejectment actions.

The relevant material

By cl 1 of the MIB agreement (the definition clause) it is provided:

'In this Agreement ... "relevant liability" means a liability in respect of which a policy of insurance must insure a person in order to comply with Part VI of the Road Traffic Act 1972.'

The sole question for decision in this appeal accordingly depends on the answer to the question whether the events which happened constitute a 'relevant liability' within the meaning of the definition clause of the MIB agreement.

That this is in fact the only issue appears from cl 2 of the MIB agreement, which is in the following terms:

'SATISFACTION OF CLAIMS BY M.I.B.

2. If judgment in respect of any relevant liability is obtained against any person or persons in any Court in Great Britain whether or not such a person or persons be in fact covered by a contract of insurance and any such judgment is not satisfied in full within seven days from the date upon which the person or persons in whose favour the judgment was given became entitled to enforce it then M.I.B. will, subject to the provisions of Clauses 4, 5 and 6 hereof, pay or satisfy or cause to be paid or satisfied to or to the satisfaction of the person or persons in whose favour the judgment was given any sum payable or remaining payable thereunder in respect of the relevant liability including any sum awarded by the Court in respect of interest on that sum and any taxed costs or any costs awarded by the Court without taxation (or such proportion thereof as is attributable to the relevant liability) whatever may be the cause of the failure of the judgment debtor to satisfy the judgment.'

Clauses 4, 5 and 6 of the agreement, to which cl 2 is subject, need not be cited at length. Clause 4 provides that nothing in the agreement shall prevent the recovery by the insurers or MIB (as the case may be) against the assured or any other person. Clauses 5 and 6 provide for various conditions precedent to and exemptions from any liability on the part of MIB which admittedly have no application to the instant appeal.

In order to decide the appeal it is accordingly necessary to look at the provisions of Pt VI of the Road Traffic Act 1972. This was a consolidation Act passed some eight years after *Hardy*'s case which was decided under the earlier consolidation Act of 1960. The 1972 Act was thus passed in the light of *Hardy*'s case and without any attempt to amend the law as therein it was stated to be. Some argument was based on the legislative history underlying the 1972 Act, principally the Road Traffic Act 1930 (which may be read with the Third Parties (Rights against Insurers) Act 1930), and the amending Acts of 1934 and (after the 1960 consolidation Act) 1971. In my opinion, however, except as a matter of history these previous Acts do not affect my judgment as to the construction of the present consolidating Act of 1972, except that it may be noted in passing, again as a matter of history, that the long title of the Road Traffic Act 1930, referring in effect to Pt II of that Act (provision against third party risks), ss 35 and 36 of which correspond to ss 143 and 145 of the 1972 Act, describes the purpose as 'to make provision for the protection of third parties against risks arising out of the use of motor vehicles . . .' This corresponds with the description of Pt VI of the 1972 Act: 'Third-Party Liabilities. Compulsory insurance or security against third-party risks.'

In my opinion the two vital provisions of the 1972 Act are respectively s 143(1) and s 145(1) to (3). These respectively read as follows and are taken, so far as material, verbatim from the 1930 Act. Section 143(1) reads:

'Subject to the provisions of this Part of this Act, it shall not be lawful for a person to use, or to cause or permit any other person to use, a motor vehicle on a road unless there is in force in relation to the use of the vehicle by that person or that other person, as the case may be, such a policy of insurance or such a security in respect of third-party risks as complies with the requirements of this Part of this Act; and if a person acts in contravention of this section he shall be guilty of an offence.'

Section 145(1) to (3) provides:

'(1) In order to comply with the requirements of this Part of this Act, a policy of insurance must satisfy the following conditions.

(2) The policy must be issued by an authorised insurer, that is to say, a person or body of persons carrying on motor vehicle insurance business in Great Britain.

(3) Subject to subsection (4) below, the policy—(a) must insure such person, persons or classes of persons as may be specified in the policy in respect of any liability which may be incurred by him or them in respect of the death of or bodily injury to any person caused by, or arising out of, the use of the vehicle on a road . . .'

For my present purpose the remaining provisions of s 145 are irrelevant.

It follows, therefore, so far, that in order to constitute a 'relevant liability' within the meaning of the MIB agreement the judgment which has been obtained against the first defendant must have been a judgment payable in respect of a liability incurred by the first defendant for damages for personal injury 'caused by or arising out of the use of' the first defendant's vehicle on the road. At this stage, I find it irresistible to quote the words used by Diplock LJ in *Hardy v Motor Insurers' Bureau* [1964] 2 All ER 742 at 750, [1964] 2 QB 745 at 766:

'Thus, the only issue before the learned county court judge was whether the liability of Phillips to pay damages for the personal injuries he caused to the plaintiff by his criminal act was a liability against which Phillips was required to be insured by s. 201 and s. 203 of the Road Traffic Act, 1960. Those sections require every person who uses a vehicle on a road to take out a policy of insurance indemnifying him (s. 203(3)(a)) "in respect of any liability which may be incurred by him . . . in respect of the death of or bodily injury to any person caused by, or arising out of, the use of the vehicle on a road." The injuries which the plaintiff sustained were caused by, or arose out of, Phillips' use of his motor van on a road. Phillips' liability to the plaintiff falls within the ordinary meaning of the very simple words used in the statute. Why should some other meaning be ascribed to them? It is true that there may be cases in which it is apparent from the context, the subject-matter or the disclosed policy of a statute, that Parliament must have intended general expressions which it has used to be understood in a narrower sense than that which they would ordinarily bear. *Mixnam's Properties, Ltd.* v. *Chertsey U.D.C.* ([1963] 2 All ER 787, [1964] 1 QB 214), which was confirmed in a judgment . . . of the House of Lords (see [1964] 2 All ER 627, [1965] AC 735) is the most recent example of such a case. But what is there in the context, the subject-matter or the disclosed policy of Part 6 of the Road Traffic Act, 1960, which compels the conclusion that, notwithstanding that the liability which Phillips incurred to the plaintiff falls within the ordinary meaning of the words of s. 203 which I have quoted, those words are, nevertheless, to be understood as excluding it?'

The appellants' contention

Before I come to deal with the remaining provisions of the 1972 Act and, in particular ss 148 and 149 which I believe shed some light on the questions to be considered, I believe it to be desirable to set out now the nature of the appellants' contention and the way in which it is contended to influence the result of the present appeal. In brief, the appellants invoke what is alleged to be a general principle of insurance law, indeed, as I understand it, of the general law of contract. That there is such a general principle I do not doubt. It is, in substance, that a person (or those that stand in the shoes of such a person) may not stand to gain an advantage arising from the consequences of his own iniquity. I do not know that this gains (or loses) much by turning it into Latin and saying, 'Ex turpi causa non oritur actio.' Nor do I believe that much is gained by attempting a distinction between a contract the sole purpose of which is to gain an illicit advantage under the rule (which must be an illegal contract) and one which covers a variety of possibility of events, some or one of which might infringe the rule, and thus give rise to an unenforceable obligation under an otherwise enforceable contract. In support of the general proposition, which is not, I believe, in doubt, the appellants cited *Bell v Carstairs* (1811) 14 East 374 at 394, 104 ER 646 at 653, *Amicable Society v Boland*

(1830) 4 Bli NS 194, [1824–34] All ER Rep 570, *Burrows v Rhodes* [1899] 1 QB 816 at 828,
[1895–9] All ER Rep 117 at 124, *Tinline v White Cross Insurance Association Ltd* [1921] 3
a KB 327, *James v British General Insurance Co Ltd* [1927] 2 KB 311, [1927] All ER Rep 442,
Haseldine v Hosken [1933] 1 KB 822, [1933] All ER Rep 1 (a champertous agreement by a
solicitor) and *Beresford v Royal Insurance Co Ltd* [1937] 2 All ER 243, [1937] 2 KB 197,
CA; *affd* [1938] 2 All ER 602, [1938] AC 586, HL. They might, no doubt have added *Re
Crippen's Estate* [1911] P 108, [1911–13] All ER Rep 207 (on a slightly different line of
b authority). Reference was also made to the doubts in the Porter report (see Report of the
Committee on the Law of Defamation (Cmd 7536)), which gave rise to the insertion of
s 11 in the Defamation Act 1952.

    But the doctrine has its limits. The real contrast is really between *Cleaver v Mutual
Reserve Fund Life Association* [1892] 1 QB 147, [1891–4] All ER Rep 335 and *Beresford's*
case, where it seems to me that the limits of the public policy doctrine are fairly clearly
c defined. As Lord Esher MR said in *Cleaver* [1892] 1 QB 147 at 153, [1891–4] All ER Rep
335 at 338: '. . . this doctrine ought not to be stretched beyond what is necessary for the
protection of the public . . .' In the words of Fry LJ ([1892] 1 QB 147 at 160, [1891–4] All
ER Rep 335 at 342): '[The doctrine] appears to me to throw no impediment in the way
of a suit by those who claim with clean hands themselves and as assigns of the innocent
insured.' Lopes LJ was to the same effect.

d *The decision in Hardy v Motor Insurers' Bureau*
    All these cases were fully considered in *Hardy's* case; cf [1964] 2 QB 745 at 752 per
Diplock LJ in argument; see also [1964] 2 All ER 742 at 746–747, [1964] 2 QB 745 at
760–761 per Lord Denning MR, in a passage which seems to me to summarise admirably
the reasoning under scrutiny in the present appeal:

e   'This rule is not rested on an implied exception in the policy of insurance. It is
    based on the broad rule of public policy that no person can claim indemnity or
    reparation for his own wilful and culpable crime. He is under a disability precluding
    him from imposing a claim. This difference is important, because if the policy of
    insurance should come, by assignment or otherwise, into the hands of a person who
    is not affected by the disability, then such a person can enforce the policy according
f   to its terms; see *Cleaver v. Mutual Reserve Fund Life Association*, and *Beresford v. Royal
    Insurance Co., Ltd.* Apply that principle here. The policy of insurance, which a
    motorist is required by statute to take out, must cover any liability which may be
    incurred by him arising out of the use of the vehicle by him. It must, I think, be
    wide enough to cover, in general terms, any use by him of the vehicle, be it an
    innocent use or a criminal use, or be it a murderous use or a playful use. A policy so
g   taken out by him is good altogether according to its terms. Of course, if the motorist
    intended from the beginning to make a criminal use of the vehicle—intended to
    run down people with it or to drive it recklessly and dangerously—and the insurers
    knew that that was his intention, the policy would be bad in its inception. No one
    can stipulate for iniquity. But that is never the intention with which such a policy
    is taken out. At any rate no insurer is ever party to it. So the policy is good in its
h   inception. The question only arises when the motorist afterwards makes a criminal
    use of the vehicle. The consequences are then these: if the motorist is guilty of a
    crime involving a wicked and deliberate intent, and he is made to pay damages to
    an injured person, he is not himself entitled to recover on the policy. But if he does
    not pay the damages, then the injured third party can recover against the insurers
    under s. 207 of the Road Traffic Act, 1960; for it is a liability which the motorist,
    under the statute, was required to cover. The injured third party is not affected by
j   the disability which attached to the motorist himself. So, here, the liability of
    Phillips to the plaintiff was a liability which Phillips was required to cover by a
    policy of insurance, even though it arose out of his wilful and culpable criminal act.
    If Phillips had been insured, he himself would be disabled from recovering from
    the insurers. But the injured third party would not be disabled from recovering

from them. Seeing that he was not insured, the defendants must treat the case as if he were. They must pay the injured third party, even though Phillips was guilty of felony. I would, therefore, dismiss the appeal.'

See also, to the same effect, Pearson and Diplock LJJ ([1964] 2 All ER 742 at 749, 750–751, [1964] 2 QB 745 at 765, 767). It seems to me that the outcome of the general principle invoked by the appellants is that whereas it may be invoked against the wrongdoer it cannot be invoked against an innocent third party whose claim is not through that of the wrongdoer. The case is also well summed up by Diplock LJ ([1964] 2 All ER 742 at 751, [1964] 2 QB 745 at 767–768):

'From this, which, in my view, is the correct formulation of the rule, two consequences follow: (i) The court's refusal to assert the right is exercisable only against the person (including anyone who is regarded in law as the successor of that person, such as a personal representative or trustee in bankruptcy) who has committed the anti-social act out of which the right would, in the absence of the rule, arise; it is not exercisable against any other person in whom the right arising out of the contract is vested. Thus, in *Cleaver v. Mutual Reserve Fund Life Association*, the contract of insurance on the life of Mr. Maybrick was enforceable by his executors although the right arising out of the statutory trust in favour of his murderer, Mrs. Maybrick, under s. 11 of the Married Women's Property Act, 1882, was unenforceable, and, since enforceability is the badge of a trust, the court held that the statutory trust had come to an end. (ii) The court's refusal to assert a right, even against the person who has committed the anti-social act, will depend not only on the nature of the anti-social act but also on the nature of the right asserted. The court has to weigh the gravity of the anti-social act and the extent to which it will be encouraged by enforcing the right sought to be asserted against the social harm which will be caused if the right is not enforced. Thus, although before the Law Reform (Married Women and Tortfeasors) Act, 1935, the court refused to enforce any right of contribution between joint tortfeasors even where the joint tort was negligence, the rights of the assured under contracts of insurance against loss caused by his own negligence were enforced at the suit of the assured notwithstanding that the negligence was criminal; see *Tinline v. White Cross Insurance Association, Ltd.* and *James v. British General Insurance Co., Ltd.* How, then, does the rule affect a contract of insurance to pay a sum of money, whether by way of indemnity or otherwise, on the occurrence of an event which may or may not be caused by the anti-social act of the assured? First, the rule has no effect on the construction of the contract. It deals with enforceability of rights arising out of the contract. One first construes the contract to see what the parties agreed; see *Beresford v. Royal Insurance Co., Ltd.* The rule does not alter that. Secondly, the contract so construed is not unlawful. It is capable of giving rise to legally enforceable rights if, apart from the rule, the rights of the assured are capable of becoming vested in a third party other than one who is regarded in law as the successor of the assured, such as the personal representative (*Beresford v. Royal Insurance Co., Ltd.*) or his trustee in bankruptcy (*Amicable Society v. Bolland*). I agree, with respect, with LORD ATKIN's opinion expressed in *Beresford's* case ([1938] 2 All ER 602 at 607, [1938] AC 586 at 600), that an assignee for value before the occurrence of the event would not be prevented from enforcing the contract notwithstanding that the event was caused by the anti-social act of the original assured.'

The effect of the later sections in Pt VI of the Road Traffic Act 1972

This leads me to point to the light shed on the policy of the 1972 Act by ss 148 and 149. It is true, of course, that these sections were grafted onto ss 143 and 145 (which, to the extent cited above, were copied from the 1930 Act) but without any apparent belief in the mind of the legislature that the scion was incompatible with the stock. The appellants sought to invoke the doctrine that, since the words of ss 143 and 145 of the *a* 1972 Act were borrowed from the earlier Act which admittedly did not contain the equivalent of ss 148 and 149, they should be read without them. I do not altogether accept this, but, if I did, I would regard the argument as two-edged, since, as I have already pointed out, the words of ss 143 and 145 are sufficiently wide in their literal meaning to dispose of the case in a sense adverse to the appellants. But with the two additional sections the purposive construction becomes even clearer. Section 149 in particular imposes on the insurer for the benefit of an innocent third party an obligation

b to recompense him for the liability incurred by an uninsured third party in respect of a liability for which he should have been insured under ss 143 and 145. The MIB agreements impose on the appellants an obligation to underwrite this liability so far as regards uninsured or untraceable tortfeasors. The two agreements were intended precisely to protect the innocent third party either because the insurer did not choose or was not able to discharge his liability under s 149 or because the wrongdoer was not

c covered by a relevant policy of insurance at all (which is the present appeal) or was untraceable. To invoke, as the appellants now do, the well-known doctrine of public policy that a man may not profit by the consequences of his own wrongdoing seems to me to stand the principle of public policy on its head. There are no socially desirable consequences flowing from its application in the sense contended for by the appellants. On the contrary, all the pointers in ss 143 and 145 read alone, or in ss 143 and 145 as read

d in conjunction with ss 148 and 149, seem to me to point exactly in the opposite direction. The construction of the MIB agreement contended for by the appellant is contrary to the grammatical sense of the agreement, read, as it must be read, in the context of the statute, and the construction of the statute contended for by the appellants is contrary both to its manifest grammatical meaning and to the policy illustrated by its more mature articulation.

e
Two extraneous matters

There are two matters which I feel inclined to add, simply to show that they are irrelevant. We were invited by the appellants to examine the actual terms of policies and certificates issued by existing insurance companies, with a view to ascertaining the meaning of the word 'accident' in the description of the risk thereby insured. I am not

f sure that we were right to examine these. I assume we were. But either they cover the risks required to be insured against by ss 143 and 145 of the Road Traffic Act 1972 and applied by the certificates or they do not. If they do, well and good. If they do not, the certificates would amount to a misrepresentation of the risks covered by the policies. In neither case can they affect the construction either of the statute or of the MIB agreement.

The second document which we were invited to examine was the Criminal Injuries Compensation Scheme, which expressly covers the use of a motor vehicle as a weapon.

g Indeed, para 13 of the defence delivered by the appellants expressly contended 'that the plaintiffs claim should be brought under the Criminal Injuries Compensation Scheme'. I do not myself understand why. The two remedies are not necessarily mutually exclusive alternatives and were not designed to be so. The Criminal Injuries Compensation Scheme is itself markedly less advantageous to the claimant than the MIB agreement, and since

h the MIB agreement and road traffic legislation came into being long before the Criminal Injuries Compensation Scheme was introduced I cannot see that the scheme can be used as an aid to their construction.

In the event, the appeal fails and must be dismissed with costs.

j **LORD DIPLOCK.** My Lords, I have had the advantage of reading in draft the speech of my noble and learned friend the Lord Chancellor. I agree with it, and for the reasons which he gives I would dismiss this appeal.

LORD KEITH OF KINKEL. My Lords, for the reasons given in the speech of my noble and learned friend on the Woolsack, I too would dismiss the appeal.

LORD BRANDON OF OAKBROOK. My Lords, I have had the advantage of reading in draft the speech prepared by my noble and learned friend the Lord Chancellor. *a* I agree with it, and for the reasons which he gives I would dismiss the appeal.

LORD TEMPLEMAN. My Lords, for the reasons given by my noble and learned friend the Lord Chancellor, I would dismiss the appeal.

Appeal dismissed.

b

Solicitors: *L Bingham & Co*, agents for *Davis Campbell & Co*, Liverpool (for the appellants); *Hextall Erskine & Co*, agents for *E Rex Makin & Co*, Liverpool (for the respondent).

Mary Rose Plummer　　Barrister.

c

Re Trafford's Settlement

Moore and another v Inland Revenue Commissioners

d

CHANCERY DIVISION
PETER GIBSON J
15, 16 FEBRUARY 1984

Capital transfer tax – Interest in possession – Settlement – Discretionary trust – Settlement *e* *providing for trustees to hold income of trust funds on protective trusts during life of settlor and to pay or apply income for benefit of settlor and his wife and children in their discretion – Settlor dying unmarried and without children – Whether settlement conferring on settlor a determinable life interest in trust funds – Whether settlor as sole member of class of beneficiaries not closed until his death having absolute entitlement to income as it accrued – Trustee Act 1925, s 33(1).*

f

By cl 2(a) of a settlement made in 1951 the settlor directed the trustees to 'hold the income of the Trust Funds during the life of the Settlor upon protective trusts and . . . pay or apply the same to or for the benefit of the settlor and of any wife whom he may marry and the child or children or issue of the settlor . . . or any of them as the Trustees shall in their absolute discretion think fit'. Clause 4 of the settlement provided that the trustees should not exercise certain powers without the settlor's consent in writing *g* 'during the continuance of the protective trust hereby declared in his favour'. The settlor died in June 1978. He never married and never had any children. In 1983 the Revenue determined that the value of the funds subject to the settlement fell to be included in the settlor's estate for the purposes of capital transfer tax. The trustees appealed, seeking a declaration that the trust funds did not fall to be included in the settlor's estate. It was common ground between the parties that the appeal turned on the question whether the *h* settlor had been beneficially entitled to an interest in possession in the trust funds immediately before his death. The Crown contended that he had been so entitled, on the grounds (i) that, by virtue of s 33[a] of the Trustee Act 1925, cl 2(a) was to be construed as conferring on the settlor a determinable life interest in the trust funds or, alternatively, (ii) that the settlor had been entitled as of right to the income as it accrued, there being no fact known to the trustees which would justify them withholding the income from *j* him. The trustees contended (i) that cl 2(a) did not state that the protective trust was for the benefit of the settlor but created an immediate discretionary trust of income during the life of the settlor which was inconsistent with a determinable life interest to be succeeded by a discretionary trust on a forfeiture as provided by s 33(1) of the 1925 Act

---

a Section 33, so far as material, is set out at p 1111 *d* to *j*, post

and (ii) that since the class of beneficiaries, of which the settlor was the sole member, was
a   capable of increase until his death the trustees were not bound to distribute income to
the settlor as it accrued and consequently the settlor could not be said to have an interest
in possession in the trust fund.

Held – (1) On its true construction cl 2(a) of the settlement created not a protective trust
in favour of a principal beneficiary but an immediate discretionary trust in favour of a
b   class of beneficiaries, and accordingly s 33 of the 1925 Act did not apply (see p 1111 *j* to
p 1112 *d* and p 1113 *a b*, post).

(2) Where the income accruing to the trustees of a discretionary trust was in favour of
a class of beneficiaries which was not closed, the sole member of that class for the time
being could not claim an immediate entitlement to that income as long as there existed
a possibility that another member of the class could come into existence before a
reasonable time for the distribution of the accrued income had elapsed, and on the facts
c   the settlor's entitlement to income under the trust was subject to such a possibility (see
p 1113 *b* to *g*, p 1114 *d* to *f* and p 1115 *a* to *d*, post); *Re Weir's Settlement, MacPherson v
IRC* [1970] 1 All ER 297 applied; *Re Nelson, Norris v Nelson* (1918) [1928] Ch 920
distinguished.

(3) It followed therefore that immediately before his death the settlor had had no
interest in possession in the trust funds and accordingly the trust funds did not fall to be
d   included in his estate for the purposes of capital transfer tax. The court would make a
declaration accordingly (see p 1115 *d* and *j*, post).

Notes

For the meaning of interest in possession, see 19 Halsbury's Laws (4th edn) para 636, and
for cases on the subject, see 26 Digest (Reissue) 17–19, 66–70.
e   For the Trustee Act 1925, s 33, see 38 Halsbury's Statutes (3rd edn) 146.

Cases referred to in judgment

Gourju, Re, Starling v Custodian of Enemy Property [1942] 2 All ER 605, [1943] Ch 24.
Locker's Settlement Trusts, Re, Meacham v Sachs [1978] 1 All ER 216, [1977] 1 WLR 1323.
McPhail v Doulton [1970] 2 All ER 228, [1971] AC 424, [1970] 2 WLR 1110, HL.
f   *Nelson, Re, Norris v Nelson* (1918) [1928] Ch 920, CA.
Pearson v IRC [1980] 2 All ER 479, [1981] AC 753, [1980] 2 WLR 872, HL.
Smith, Re, Public Trustee v Aspinall [1928] Ch 915, [1928] All ER Rep 520.
Weir's Settlement, Re, MacPherson v IRC [1970] 1 All ER 297, [1971] Ch 145, [1969] 3
WLR 860, CA.

g   **Case also cited**

Gulbenkian's Settlement Trust, Re, Whishaw v Stephens [1968] 3 All ER 785, [1970] AC 508,
HL.

Adjourned summons

By a settlement made on 15 June 1951 between John L Trafford and others the trustees
h   were directed to hold the income of the trust fund during the life of the settlor on
protective trusts and to pay or apply the income to or for the benefit of the settlor and
any wife whom he might marry or any of them as the trustees in their absolute discretion
thought fit. The settlor died on 7 June 1978. By a notice of determination made on 30
August 1983 the Inland Revenue Commissioners determined that the value of the funds
subject to the settlement fell to be included in the settlor's estate for capital transfer tax
j   purposes. The trustees, Dinah Anne Moore and Timothy William Osborne, appealed
against the notice and by an originating summons dated 6 October 1983 sought a
declaration from the court that the value of the funds did not fall to be included in the
estate of the settlor. The facts are set out in the judgment.

Donald Rattee QC and *Simon Taube* for the trustees.
Christopher McCall for the Crown.

PETER GIBSON J. This is an appeal by the trustees of a settlement made on 15 June 1951 by the late Mr John Trafford (the settlor) against a capital transfer tax determination made on 30 August 1983 by the Commissioners of Inland Revenue. The settlor died on 7 June 1978. The commissioners determined that the value of the funds subject to that settlement fell to be included in the settlor's estate for capital transfer tax purposes. By the originating summons before me the trustees seek a declaration that the value of those funds does not fall to be so included.

The settlor was born on 5 March 1924. By his settlement he settled certain securities which, together with any additions thereto and the property for the time being representing the same, were called 'the trust funds'. Clause 2(a) of the settlement is in the following form:

'The Trustees shall hold the income of the Trust Funds during the life of the Settlor upon protective trusts and shall pay or apply the same to or for the benefit of the settlor and of any wife whom he may marry and the child or children or issue of the settlor by any wife whom he may marry or any of them as the Trustees shall in their absolute discretion think fit.'

Clause 2(b) reads as follows:

'After the death of the settlor the Trustees shall hold such proportion of the income of the Trust Funds as the settlor shall by any deed or deeds revocable or irrevocable or by Will or Codicil appoint upon protective trusts for the benefit of any wife whom he may leave him surviving during her life or for any lesser period.'

Subject thereto the trust funds were to be held on such trusts for the children and remoter issue of the settlor as he should appoint with a default trust for such of the children as survived him and attained 21 or married under that age, and the settlor reserved a general power of appointment to himself which he could exercise by deed or will in the event of there being no child or issue attaining a vested interest.

By cl 3, so far as material, the statutory power of advancement was expressed to be exercisable by the trustees with the consent only of the settlor during his lifetime. By cl 4 certain additional powers were conferred on the trustees. I need read only part of cl 4(b):

'The following powers shall be exercisable from time to time and at any time by the Trustees Provided that they shall not be exercised without the consent in writing of the settlor during the continuance of the protective trust hereby declared in his favour or if any part of the income of the Trust Funds shall have been irrevocably appointed by the settlor to any wife of the settlor without the consent in writing of such wife prior to the determination of the protective trust arising in her favour by virtue of such appointment.'

There was then an immaterial qualification; and then two powers to which the clause applied, that is to say to raise and pay capital, were specified. I need not read further from that settlement.

By a declaration of trust dated 18 December 1953 the settlor declared that certain property was to be held on trust for sale and that the net proceeds of sale were to be held on the same trusts as the settlement. The declaration of trust was revocable, but the power of revocation was released by a deed dated 18 March 1954. By a deed of release and appointment dated 29 September 1977 the settlor released the power in cl 2(b) of the settlement to appoint in favour of a surviving wife; and he exercised his general power by giving to his cousin, Mr Nicholas Moore, what amounted to a general power subject only to the necessity to obtain the consent of the trustees to the exercise of such power as exercised by deed. There is a default trust for Mr Moore if he attains 60. Mr Moore is 37. The settlor never married and never had any children.

It is common ground between counsel for the trustees and counsel for the Crown that this appeal turns on the question whether the settlor was beneficially entitled to an

interest in possession in the funds the subject of the settlement immediately before his
_a_ death. If he was, then under para 3(1) of Sch 5 to the Finance Act 1975 he must be treated
as having been beneficially entitled to the property in which his interest subsisted. That
has the consequence that the funds are treated as forming part of his estate (see s 23(1) of
the 1975 Act) and that on his death tax is charged as if immediately before his death he
had made a transfer of value, the value transferred being equal to the value of his estate
(see s 22(1)). The trustees say that the settlor was not beneficially entitled to an interest in
_b_ possession; the Crown claims that he was. I am told that if the trustees are right in their
contention some capital transfer tax is payable on the settlor's death in respect of the
funds comprised in the settlement, but that if the Crown is right a substantial additional
amount of tax is payable.

Two issues have been debated before me. First, on the true construction of cl 2(a) of
the settlement, (a) did the settlor have a determinable life interest which was never
_c_ determined until his death, as counsel for the Crown contends, or (b) was the settlor only
interested as an object of the discretionary trust of income contained in cl 2(a), as counsel
for the trustees contends? If the answer is in sense (a), counsel for the trustees accepts that
the settlor had an interest in possession and the Crown succeeds. But, second, if the
answer is in sense (b), did the settlor nevertheless have an interest in possession by virtue
of being the only object of the discretionary trust of income? Counsel for the Crown
_d_ contends that he had such an interest; counsel for the trustees argues for the contrary.

Central to the first issue is the applicability of s 33 of the Trustee Act 1925, in relation
to cl 2(a), and it is convenient to read sub-s (1) of that section at the outset:

'Where any income, including an annuity or other periodical income payment, is
directed to be held on protective trusts for the benefit of any person (in this section
called "the principal beneficiary") for the period of his life or for any less period,
_e_ then, during that period (in this section called "the trust period") the said income
shall, without prejudice to any prior interest, be held on the following trusts,
namely:—(i) Upon trust for the principal beneficiary during the trust period or
until he, whether before or after the termination of any prior interest, does or
attempts to do or suffers any act or thing, or until any event happens, other than an
advance under any statutory or express power, whereby, if the said income were
_f_ payable during the trust period to the principal beneficiary absolutely during that
period, he would be deprived of the right to receive the same or any part thereof, in
any of which cases, as well as on the termination of the trust period, whichever first
happens, this trust of the said income shall fail or determine; (ii) If the trust aforesaid
fails or determines during the subsistence of the trust period, then, during the
residue of that period, the said income shall be held upon trust for the application
_g_ thereof for the maintenance or support, or otherwise for the benefit, of all or any
one or more exclusively of the other or others of the following persons (that is to
say)—(a) the principal beneficiary and his or her wife or husband, if any, and his or
her children or more remote issue, if any; or (b) if there is no wife or husband or
issue of the principal beneficiary in existence, the principal beneficiary and the
persons who would, if he were actually dead, be entitled to the trust property or the
_h_ income thereof or to the annuity fund, if any, or arrears of the annuity, as the case
may be; as the trustees in their absolute discretion, without being liable to account
for the exercise of such discretion, think fit.'

Subsection (2) of that section reads, so far as material: 'This section . . . has effect subject
to any variation of the implied trusts aforesaid contained in the instrument creating the
_j_ trust.'

Counsel for the trustees submits that there is no room for the application of s 33 for
two reasons. First, the wording needed to import the provisions of s 33(1) is not present
as cl 2(a) does not state that there is a principal beneficiary. With this can be contrasted
cl 2(b), which correctly uses language which makes s 33(1) applicable, thereby showing
that the draftsman of the settlement was well aware of how to apply the statutory

provisions. Second, cl 2(a) created an immediate discretionary trust of income during the life of the settlor, and that is inconsistent with a determinable life interest succeeded by a discretionary trust only on a forfeiture, as provided by s 33(1).

Counsel for the trustees submits that the words 'upon protective trusts' are merely descriptive, the trusts being designed to protect the settlor, then a young man of only 27 and, I should add, evidently possessed of a sizeable fortune, as can be seen from the list of securities which he settled. The reason for the settlor avoiding the use of wording such as would create a protective trust to which s 33 applies can, says counsel for the trustees, be found in the rule that a gift over by a settlor of his own property on bankruptcy is void against his trustee in bankruptcy. Counsel for the trustees was able, by a citation of the editions current in 1951 of Prideaux's *Precedents in Conveyancing* (23rd edn, 1937) vol 3, p 126, 16 *Forms and Precedents* (3rd edn) pp 561, 615 and *Wolstenholme and Cherry's Conveyancing Statutes* (12th edn, 1932) vol 2, p 1323, to show that a settlor to protect his own income against loss under a future bankruptcy was advised to create an immediate discretionary trust. Finally, counsel for the trustees submits that, if s 33(1) were applicable, the immediate discretionary trust of cl 2(a) must be taken to be a variation of s 33(1), and, by s 33(2), s 33(1) takes effect subject to that variation.

Valiantly though counsel for the Crown tried to rebut those submissions, I can see no answer to them. Counsel for the Crown submitted that, on the true construction of the settlement as a whole, cl 2(a) must be construed as conferring on the settlor a determinable life interest by reference to s 33, and that, subject to the variation that instead of the discretionary trust of income that would arise on a forfeiture in favour of the classes of beneficiaries specified in s 33(1)(ii)(a) and (b) respectively, the settlor had limited the beneficiaries to the single class specified in cl 2(a).

Counsel for the Crown frankly acknowledged that in that construction it is necessary to read into cl 2(a) two separate sets of words. First, after the words, 'The Trustees shall hold the income of the Trust Funds during the life of the Settlor upon protective trusts' must be read in the words 'for his benefit'. This, says counsel for the Crown, is in accord with the description in cl 4(b) of that trust: 'the protective trust hereby declared in his favour', that is to say in the settlor's favour. I see force in that submission taken in isolation, but it must be considered against the other indications in the settlement. The second set of words which counsel for the Crown would read into cl 2(a) is wording such as one finds at the start of s 33(1)(ii): 'If the trust aforesaid fails or determines during [the life of the settlor]'; and this he would read in before the words 'shall pay or apply'. In other words, instead of the immediate discretionary trust contained in cl 2(a) if read literally, a condition precedent has to be inserted postponing the operation of the trust. That does considerable violence to the clause as it now stands, and in my judgment cannot be justified unless otherwise it can be clearly demonstrated that that was the settlor's intention.

Counsel for the Crown relies on the contrast between the words which one finds in cl 3, 'with the consent only of the settlor during his lifetime', and the words in cl 4(b), 'without the consent in writing of the settlor during the continuance of the protective trust hereby declared in his favour'; and he submits that the latter form of wording can only be explained as indicating that the period referred to may be less than the settlor's lifetime. He submits that it means the same as the words found later in cl 4(b) referring to the necessity for the consent in writing of a wife of the settlor, to whom an irrevocable appointment under cl 2(b) is made, prior to the determination of the protective trust arising in her favour. But counsel for the Crown was not able to offer any explanation of the difference in wording between the two parts of cl 4(b). Certainly the reference to the period for the settlor's consent was unnecessarily elaborate as a reference to during his lifetime, but in relation to the wife and her determinable life interest the draftsman has correctly referred to 'determination', and the different language for the husband seems to me to be a pointer to the fact that the settlor did not have an interest of the same character as the wife. The fact of such different language in the same clause seems to me to be a slightly stronger pointer than the contrast in language between cll 3 and 4(b).

a In summary, I am left in no doubt that it is impossible to read into cl 2(a) the words for which counsel for the Crown contends. I accept that the reference to protective trusts in that clause as well as the reference in cl 4(b) to the protective trust declared in favour of the settlor are descriptions of the trusts intended to protect the settlor in relation to the income of the property settled by him during the lifetime of the settlor. Consequently, in my judgment the trust in cl 2(a) took effect as an immediate discretionary trust and subsisted as such until the settlor's death.

b I turn, then, to the second issue. In the light of the decision of the House of Lords in *Pearson v IRC* [1980] 2 All ER 479, [1981] AC 753, the expression 'interest in possession' connotes a present right of present enjoyment ([1980] 2 All ER 479 at 487, [1981] AC 753 at 775 per Viscount Dilhorne) or, to put together various expressions used by Lord Keith ([1980] 2 All ER 479 at 495, [1981] AC 753 at 786), an immediate entitlement, which for the time being is absolute, to income as it accrues. I do not see any material distinction between the two formulations.

c The settlor was from the date of the settlement to the date of his death the sole beneficiary in existence under the discretionary trust. Until his death there was always the possibility that the class of beneficiaries might increase were he to marry. Nevertheless, in the events that happened he alone was entitled to the income, and had the trustees sought to apply income for his benefit in some way other than by paying it to him he would have been able to require payment to himself or as he should direct. Subject only to the question of the effect on that entitlement of a possible increase in the class and to any right of the trustees consequently to withhold income from the settlor, that much is, I think, common ground as being the effect of *Re Nelson, Norris v Nelson* [1928] Ch 920, a 1918 decision of the Court of Appeal which was reported following the decision in *Re Smith, Public Trustee v Aspinall* [1928] Ch 915, [1928] All ER Rep 520.

e Counsel for the trustees submits that the possibility of an increase in the class of beneficiaries had the effect that the settlor did not immediately before his death have a present right to present enjoyment of the income or an immediate absolute entitlement to the income as it accrued, because, he said, the trustees were not bound to distribute the income to the settlor immediately. The settlor was one object of the discretionary trust the class of beneficiaries of which, up to his death, was capable of increase. The trustees would have been justified in withholding income at least for a while with a view to considering whether a further beneficiary might come into existence and fall to be considered, notwithstanding that such beneficiary was not living or ascertained at the time when the income accrued or was received. For this he relies on the decision of the Court of Appeal in *Re Weir's Settlement, MacPherson v IRC* [1970] 1 All ER 297, [1971] Ch 145. In that case there was a discretionary trust of income for, in the events that happened, a class consisting of two members, a husband and his wife. At all times the whole income was paid to the wife. On the husband's death, the wife was left as the sole surviving member of the class of discretionary objects, and that class was no longer capable of increase. Estate duty was claimed by the Crown under s 2(1)(b), and alternatively s 1, of the Finance Act 1894.

h The judgment of the Court of Appeal, consisting of Harman, Russell and Megaw LJJ, was delivered by Russell LJ. In it they examined the rights of a sole object under a discretionary trust, and it is on their views of those rights as a matter of the law of trusts that counsel for the trustees chiefly relies. Russell LJ referred to the wife becoming entitled to receive the income after her husband's death, not by virtue of being a tenant for life but by virtue of being the sole object of the discretionary trust (see [1970] 1 All ER 297 at 302, [1971] Ch 145 at 167). Though counsel for the Crown placed reliance on this reference to the wife's entitlement to receive income, it is of course a statement as to the position of a sole object of a closed class. Counsel for the trustees, rightly in my view, accepts that in such a case for capital transfer tax purposes the sole object will have an interest in possession. But that is not this case because the class was not closed.

Russell LJ referred to the hypothetical case of a discretionary trust of income for the children for the time being living of A, B and C, and said that in such a case—

'a sole object for the time being would not necessarily be entitled as such to insist on payment over of every penny come to the hands of the trustees; the trustees on learning of an imminent addition to the class of objects, eg a child of an impoverished C, would be entitled to keep income in hand with a view to applying it for the benefit of C's child.'

(See [1970] 1 All ER 297 at 302, [1971] Ch 145 at 167.)

Russell LJ then said that those considerations showed that in a real sense the one discretionary trust remained though but one object was living.

Those remarks show that in the judgment of the Court of Appeal a beneficiary who comes into existence or is ascertained after income has been received by the trustees may nevertheless have that income paid to him or applied for his benefit. It is not for me to cast doubt on the correctness of that proposition; suffice it to say that its correctness was not challenged by counsel for the Crown. Further, in *Re Locker's Settlement, Meacham v Sachs* [1978] 1 All ER 216 at 220, [1977] 1 WLR 1323 at 1327 Goulding J, although holding that beneficiaries, made additional members of a class of objects of a discretionary trust of income after a reasonable period had elapsed since the receipt of certain income, should not benefit from that stale income, nevertheless was prepared to give effect to that proposition in the declaration that he was prepared to make.

Counsel for the trustees submits that once it is accepted that income as it is received will not necessarily belong to the sole discretionary object for the time being, as is the case where a future member of the class of objects may yet come into existence, it cannot be postulated that that object has an immediate absolute right to the income as it accrues. Counsel for the Crown seeks to counter that in this way. First, he submits that, as Simonds J held in *Re Gourju, Starling v Custodian of Enemy Property* [1942] 2 All ER 605, [1943] Ch 24, the obligation of the trustees under a discretionary trust of income is to apply the trust income as and when they receive it, with such necessary limitations on absolute obligation as the practical necessities of the case demand. Trustees are not entitled, regardless of the needs of the beneficiaries, to retain income where there is a discretionary trust to pay or apply that income. That proposition I accept.

Second, he submits that the settlor was entitled as of right to the income in the absence of there being any facts known to the trustees which would justify withholding the income from him, and he submits that in the present case there is no evidence that the trustees did know of any such facts. He says that if the trustees failed to pay him any income the settlor would have been entitled to go to the court, as Lord Wilberforce indicated in *McPhail v Doulton* [1970] 2 All ER 228 at 247, [1971] AC 424 at 456–457, to obtain a direction that the trustees distribute that income to him. Counsel for the Crown based himself on *Re Nelson*, which he said was a case of an open-ended class of beneficiaries under a discretionary trust of income who nevertheless were treated by the Court of Appeal as having an entitlement to all the income; a fortiori, says counsel for the Crown, where there is a single beneficiary in an open-ended class.

If that were the decision in *Re Nelson* then there would be an inconsistency between that decision and that in the *Weir* case. That would be surprising in view of the fact that *Re Smith* (following which, as I have said, *Re Nelson* was reported) was cited in the *Weir* case. But I am not satisfied that there is any such inconsistency. In *Re Nelson* there was a class of discretionary objects consisting of a man, his wife and his children. There was in fact only one child of the man and his wife, and that child had attained 21. The man, his wife and the child had assigned, by way of mortgage, their interest. The question for the court was whether, notwithstanding the mortgage, the income ought to be withheld from the mortgagee and applied for the benefit of the man, his wife and the child. Not surprisingly, the court answered that question in the mortgagee's favour on the footing that all the persons entitled to the benefit of the trust had disposed of their interest in the income. It may well be, having regard to the age of the child, that the wife was beyond the age of childbearing and that the class was closed. In any event, no question such as was considered by the Court of Appeal in the *Weir* case as to the entitlement of a future beneficiary in respect of income already in the hands of the trustees was considered in *Re Nelson*.

a Attracted though I have been to the common sense of the Crown's argument on the particular facts of this case that the settlor was in reality the only beneficiary, I am nevertheless persuaded by counsel for the trustees that that argument is, in the light of the *Weir* case, wrong. When income is received by the trustees of a discretionary trust of income, the sole object of a class which is not yet closed cannot in my judgment claim an immediate entitlement to that income. It is always possible that before a reasonable time for the distribution of that income has elapsed another object will come into existence or

b be ascertained and have a claim to be considered as a potential recipient of the benefit of that income. So long as that possibility exists, the sole object's entitlement is subject to the possibility that the income will be properly diverted by the trustees to the future object once he comes into existence or is ascertained. Indeed, in strictness the entitlement of the sole object is only an entitlement that the trustees should consider whether to pay income to him. In respect of income already received it may be possible to say that such an entitlement has arisen, but for present purposes I must consider the position

c immediately before the death of the settlor not in relation to income previously received by the trustees but in relation to the settlor's rights to income then or thereafter accruing. Such income as it accrued was subject to the possibility that it could properly be withheld by the trustees from the settlor and diverted to a future beneficiary, unlikely though the possibility of such beneficiary coming into existence or being ascertained undoubtedly

d was in the present case. On that footing the settlor did not immediately before his death have an interest in possession.

Although in general the courts will not look at any anomalies to which a particular construction of a fiscal statute gives rise, I do not think in this case that I should ignore the remarkable and unsatisfactory results that would obtain if the Crown were correct. In the *Weir* case the Court of Appeal placed reliance on the fact that, on the Crown's

e contention in that case, there would be a series of passings for estate duty as an open-ended class of beneficiaries dropped to one or increased to two from time to time. Counsel for the Crown accepts that in the present case there would similarly be charges to capital transfer tax in those events as interests in possession came into existence or terminated as a result of the class dropping to one or increasing to two.

The matter does not stop there. If the right of the trustees to withhold income from a

f sole object depends on the particular circumstances known to the trustees, there could be further changes as the position known to the trustees changed from time to time. For example, whilst the settlor in the present case was known to the trustees not to have any intention to marry, on the Crown's contention he would have an interest in possession. However, if he then became engaged, so that his fiancée was potentially a beneficiary and as such might have a claim to be considered when the marriage occurred as a recipient of benefit from income already received, and the fact of that engagement was known to the

g trustees, then the settlor would cease to have an interest in possession. If the engagement were known to have been broken off with no other engagement in view, the interest in possession would revive. It is highly unsatisfactory that the position should vary according to the state of the knowledge of the trustees.

Counsel for the Crown rightly points out that other examples can be given in the

h capital transfer tax legislation of strange consequences which flow from an indisputable construction of particular statutory provisions. He submitted that such anomalies ought not to affect the court's decision. Nevertheless, the results of the Crown's arguments seem to me to be so bizarre that at the very least I can derive comfort therefrom in reaching the conclusion which I have reached.

For those reasons, in my judgment the settlor did not have an interest in possession in

j the funds the subject of the settlement, and I propose so to declare. In conclusion I should like to express my gratitude to counsel on both sides for their highly skilled assistance.

Declaration accordingly.

Solicitors: *Wiggin & Co*, Cheltenham (for the trustees); *Solicitor of Inland Revenue*.

Clare Mainprice   Barrister.

Banin v MacKinlay (Inspector of Taxes)

CHANCERY DIVISION

HARMAN J

8 FEBRUARY 1984

Income tax – Appeal – Hearing – Natural justice – Duty to hear parties – Appeal to Special Commissioners – Taxpayer in person – Taxpayer not attending hearing – Taxpayer seeking to conduct hearing by presenting written argument – Taxpayer sending documents to commissioners – Commissioners refusing to read or admit documents – Whether breach of rules of natural justice – Whether commissioners exercising discretion to admit documents properly – Whether privilege to plead before commissioners by writing extending to litigants in person – Taxes Management Act 1970, s 50(5).

The inspector of taxes raised assessments on the taxpayer for the years 1975–76 to 1981–82 and the taxpayer's appeals against them were listed for hearing before the Special Commissioners on a Monday. On the Friday before that date a bundle of documents marked 'Pleadings and Affidavits' was handed in to the commissioners on the taxpayer's behalf. The taxpayer did not attend the hearing and his representative, an employee of his accountant, stated that he was not familiar with the case and had attended solely in order to read a statement by the taxpayer to the commissioners and to note their decision. The Special Commissioners refused to admit the taxpayer's statement, and decided the appeals solely on the evidence and arguments put forward by the Crown. The taxpayer appealed, contending (i) that, although the procedure at the hearing before the commissioners was regulated by s 50[a] of the Taxes Management Act 1970, the commissioners were subject to the rules of natural justice and in particular the rule that they should hear both sides, and that that rule entitled a litigant to put his case before the court in any form he pleased, whether by writing, film, tape recording or any other method, (ii) that the privilege granted to lawyers by s 50(5) of the 1970 Act, by which they might plead in writing, extended to litigants in person and (iii) that the commissioners had had a discretion to look at the 'pleading' (the affidavit being admittedly inadmissible) and in refusing to do so they had failed to exercise their discretion properly.

Held – There was no rule of natural justice which entitled a litigant to conduct his case in any manner he chose nor was there one which entitled a litigant in person to conduct his case in writing without attending court. Section 50(5) of the 1970 Act conferred a special privilege on the legal profession which did not extend to litigants in person. The commissioners had no reason to believe that the 'pleading' contained arguments and not averments of fact which were inadmissible. In all the circumstances, the taxpayer had not demonstrated any error which would justify the court in overturning the commissioners' decision and accordingly the appeal would be dismissed (see p 1124 *d* to p 1125 *a f g* and *j* to p 1126 *b*, post).

Notes

For a person's right to be heard, see 1 Halsbury's Laws (4th edn) paras 74–77, and for cases on the subject, see 1(1) Digest (Reissue) 200–201, 1172–1176.

For the procedure on appeals to the commissioners, see 23 Halsbury's Laws (4th edn) paras 1607–1617, and for cases on the subject, see 28(1) Digest (Reissue) 555–562, 2024–2059.

For the Taxes Management Act 1970, s 50, see 34 Halsbury's Statutes (3rd edn) 1296.

---

a   Section 50, so far as material, is set out at p 1124 *c*, post

Case referred to in judgment

a *Caldicott v Varty (Inspector of Taxes)* [1976] 3 All ER 329.

Cases also cited

Forth Investments Ltd v IRC [1976] STC 399.
Hawkins v Fuller (Inspector of Taxes) [1982] STC 468.

b **Case stated**

1. At a meeting of the Commissioners for the Special Purposes of the Income Tax Acts held on 25 October 1982 Mayer Menahem Banin (the taxpayer) appealed against the following assessments to income tax and National Insurance Contributions Class 4 (NIC):

Year	Income as manufacturing jeweller	Income from property	NIC
	£	£	£
1975–76	3,000 (further)		
1976–77	12,000	2,000	3,300
1977–78	12,000	100	3,750
1978–79	15,000	200	4,250
1979–80	10,000	500	4,750
1980–81	15,000	1,000	5,650
1981–82	20,000	1,000	6,850

2. Shortly stated the questions for the commissioners' decision were: (1) for 1975–76 to 1978–79 inclusive what the amounts were of the profits or losses made by the taxpayer as manufacturing jeweller in the years ended 30 April 1974, 1975, 1976 and 1977, which respectively formed the bases of assessment for those years; (2) whether or not a balancing charge under s 44(3) of the Finance Act 1971 was due for 1978–79; (3) whether a certificate should be granted under s 70(3) of the Taxes Management Act 1970 that tax charged by the assessment for 1975–76 carried interest under s 88 of that Act; (4) whether, for all the remaining appeals, notices under s 51(1)(*b*) of the 1970 Act should be granted.

3. No oral evidence was adduced before the commissioners, except to the extent that information supplied orally by Mr MacKinlay, the district inspector, who presented his case before the commissioners, might be said to constitute evidence.

[Paragraph 4 listed the documents proved or admitted before the commissioners.]

5. On Friday, 22 October 1982 Sugarwhite Halle Davis & Co (the accountants) delivered to the office of the Special Commissioners a bundle of documents which consisted of, or included, a document described as 'Pleadings and Affidavit' made by the taxpayer. The clerk to the commissioners telephoned Mr Davis of the accountants to tell him that, in accordance with their practice, the commissioners would not look at the documents before the hearing convened for Monday, 25 October, and urged him to see that the taxpayer was represented at the meeting by someone prepared to open the case on his behalf. Mr Davis told the clerk to the commissioners that the taxpayer had no money and was 'on social security'. Mr Davis did not himself attend the appeal meeting, but sent Mr De Silva, a member of his staff. Mr De Silva knew nothing of the case other than what he had learned from a partial reading of the taxpayer's statement, and attended the hearing merely with a view to read that statement to the commissioners and to note the outcome of the appeals, not to argue the taxpayer's case. Mr De Silva was unable to tell the commissioners why the taxpayer had not come himself to the hearing to give evidence, but referred to the statement which, he said, mentioned that the taxpayer was inarticulate and unable to speak well.

6. No postponement of the hearing had been sought. The taxpayer's failure to attend the hearing, a failure for which no satisfactory explanation was offered, meant that he could not be examined on any evidence which he might offer, whether written or oral. The commissioners therefore decided not to admit his statement. They proceeded on the

footing that they would hear the inspector and reach their determination on the basis of any acceptable evidence which the inspector might put before them.

7. As a result of such evidence as was adduced before the commissioners, the following facts were found to be proved or admitted.

7.1 The taxpayer was a manufacturer of jewellery from 1 May 1969 until some time in the year prior to the hearing; he traded as 'C & M Banin'. Initially he had been in business at 22 Cross Street, London EC1 and latterly at 1 Albemarle Way, London EC1.

7.2 Accounts for the business were submitted for several accounting periods up to and including the year to 30 April 1977. The main assessment for 1975–76 should have been based on the accounts for the year to 30 April 1974. An estimated assessment in the sum of £8,000 had been made for 1975–76, and was not appealed against. The accounts, which were prepared by the accountants, were undated, and were not submitted until the following year. They showed a net profit of £10,760. The tax computation showed the net chargeable income, after deducting capital allowances of £2,765, as £7,995. The £2,765 represented 100% initial allowances on plant and machinery. The balance sheet showed drawings of £5,900. For 1976–77 an estimated assessment was made in the sum of £12,000. That assessment was appealed against and in support of the appeal accounts were submitted for the year to 30 April 1975, together with accounts for the previous year. The trading and profit and loss account showed a net profit of £11,362 before charging depreciation of £906. The tax computation showed the net chargeable income, after deducting capital allowances totalling £4,247, as £7,115. The balance sheet showed drawings of £4,645 and capital introduced of £9,000. For 1977–78 an estimated assessment was made in the sum of £12,000. The accounts submitted by the accountants (on 17 April 1979) for the accounting period to 30 April 1976 consisted only of a trading and profit and loss account, which showed a loss of £4,768. There was no balance sheet. For 1978–79 an estimated assessment was made in the sum of £15,000. The accounts for the year to 30 April 1977 (submitted on 17 April 1979) again consisted only of a trading and profit and loss account and showed a loss of £4,001. In the year to 30 April 1977, which formed the basis for the 1978–79 assessment, machinery was disposed of for £2,600. The accounts for the last three years included a report by the accountants that the accounts had been prepared from the books, records (or documents), vouchers, information and explanations of the proprietor and were certified to be in accordance therewith. The certificate for the first year's accounts did not include a reference to the proprietor's explanations. The deduction of £270 for rent in the 1974 accounts was replaced by a deduction of £1,395 for rent and rates in the following year (£1,216 in 1976 and £2,781 in 1977). There was no deduction for wages in the 1974 accounts, but there were deductions of £1,950 in 1975, £4,996 in 1976 and £8,357 in 1977. In all four years a figure appeared for 'Purchases and Subcontracting': £38,624 in the year to 30 April 1974, £61,121 in 1975, £56,285 in 1976 and £131,071 in 1977.

7.3 On 29 April 1977 the inspector queried the figure in the 1975 balance sheet of £9,000 for capital introduced. On 6 July the accountants stated that 'The capital introduced was from [the taxpayer's] family from abroad and was remitted through his bank'. On 19 August the inspector sought more detailed information. On 30 November the accountants stated that their information was that £9,000 came from members of the taxpayer and the taxpayer's wife's families in Israel as the result of a 'whip round', and that their families had assisted the taxpayer and his wife continually over the last few years in their difficulties which had 'been exacerbated by the "fiasco" of the property position'. The inspector pressed for documentary evidence. The documents proved or admitted included a copy of a letter dated 6 June 1978 from Midland Bank Ltd to C & M Banin which stated: 'We confirm that the credit for £9,000·00 paid into your account on 21 August 1974 was a cheque on Bank Leumi (UK) Ltd. Bow Bells House, London drawn by Bank Leumi le-Israel Banking Services Centre.' On 17 April 1979 the accountants sent a copy of a manuscript document in Hebrew, dated 3 April 1979 which, they said, came from the taxpayer's brother and 'loosely summarised' confirmed that the families of the taxpayer and the taxpayer's wife had from time to time assisted the taxpayer with small a amounts and in 1974, as a result of a special effort, a large amount of money was collected which was remitted to London by cheque to enable the taxpayer's business to continue. The letter went on to say:

b '. . . our client reiterates that he has received financial assistance from time to time from his family but unfortunately so far has been unable to find any documentation among his own papers. He has asked us to point out that members of his family from time to time visit this country and therefore the help received is often by way of cash and in the circumstances no records were maintained. It must be remembered that this assistance is given within a family and is not some commercial transaction.'

The taxpayer was invited several times to attend the tax office with his accountants to give evidence of his financial relationship with his wife's and his own family in Israel, but had not done so. In his income tax return for 1965–66 the taxpayer claimed c dependent relative relief in respect of weekly payments of £2 to his father (born in 1889) who lived with his daughter, the taxpayer's sister, in Israel. In his tax return for 1966–67 the taxpayer claimed relief for weekly payments of £80. A declaration made by the taxpayer's father in Israel on 4 September 1965 stated that the taxpayer sent his father 'Through the bank & personal' £95 a year. The discrepancy between the amounts claimed for the two years coupled with the declaration made by the taxpayer's father led d the commissioners to infer that the claim in the 1966–67 form arose from a misreading of the claim form, and was intended to be a claim for £80 in total. At the time when the two returns were made by the taxpayer (30 April 1965 and 6 July 1966 respectively) he was not in business on his own account but employed by a firm in Kirby Street, London EC1. The relief was not claimed in 1967–68 as the taxpayer wished to relinquish it in favour of another.

e 7.4 The Revenue were not dissatisfied only with the explanations given about the £9,000 capital introduced in the year to 30 April 1975. It was felt that there were other unsatisfactory features in the accounts submitted. One such feature was the absence of balance sheets for the years ended 30 April 1976 and 1977; none were prepared. In a letter dated 13 February 1980 the accountants wrote:

f 'Since only Trading and Profit and Loss Accounts were prepared, therefore much of the information regarding the Balance Sheet items was not extracted. The trading figures were obtained by direct reference to Day Books, V.A.T. Returns, etc., and therefore . . . no adjustments were made for trade debtors and creditors.'

The inspector was also concerned about the figures for drawings. In relation to the 1974 g and 1975 accounts the accountants were asked in a letter dated 29 April 1977 for 'an analysis for each year distinguishing cheque items from cash and non-recurring expenditure from ordinary private personal living expenses', and to state how the taxpayer recorded the cash drawings. The accountants replied that £5,393 of the 1974 drawings (£5,900 in total) were from the bank and the balance in cash, and that £3,468 of the 1975 drawings (£4,645 in total) were from the bank and the balance in cash. They h added: 'No formal record of drawings was maintained but in the preparation of the accounts a cash account was prepared and the balance of this account was taken to drawings.' On 19 August 1977 the inspector pressed for an analysis of the sums of £5,393 and £3,468. On 30 November 1977 the accountants stated that the drawings 'were ascertained by extracting all items of expenditure which were identifiable as being business expenditure and the balance was taken to drawings'. The drawings for the years j ended 30 April 1976 and 1977 were not extracted by the accountants. The accounts contained estimated sums for travelling expenses and for lighting and heating. The inspector queried the increase in turnover from £42,402 in the year to 30 April 1974 to £64,255 in the following year and the increase from £44,572 in the year to 30 April 1976 (a drop from the previous year) to £143,167 in the year to 30 April 1977. No clear explanation was given for the first increase. The second increase resulted from an

expansion and a change in the pattern of operation, using internal staff instead of, as
before, sub-contracting most of the manufacturing processes. The increase in wages in   *a*
the year to 30 April 1977 reflected this.

7.5 Apart from matters relating to the accounts of the business, the correspondence
between the Inland Revenue and the accountants (not all of which was before the
commissioners) contained references to property owned by the taxpayer and to
commitments of his in respect of bank and building society loans and loan interest and
life assurance premiums. The taxpayer had owned a flat at 22 Carlton Mansions, acquired   *b*
in 1971, which had proved difficult to sell. In September 1975 he had bought a property
at 140 Franklin Gardens for £32,000, of which £22,000 was financed by the Royal
Insurance Co, £5,500 was still outstanding to the vendor at 6 July 1977 and £4,000 (the
inspector said) had been provided from the taxpayer's own resources. The commissioners
inferred from the reference in the accountants' letter dated 30 November 1977 to the
property position (quoted in para 7.3) and from the further statement by the accountants   *c*
in the same letter that they understood that one of the properties of which the taxpayer
was 'seeking to divest himself would by now have been sold were it not for the advent of
squatters' that the taxpayer had invested in property. The inspector mentioned a house
at 50 Elmcroft Crescent, London NW11 which was first let in 1975–76.

7.6 The latest letter in the documents proved or admitted was from the Revenue to
the accountants and was dated 24 November 1981. In it the Revenue view was clearly set   *d*
out. The letter mentioned the lack of response to repeated requests to interview the
taxpayer and the intention to list the open appeals for 1976–77 to 1980–81 for hearing
before the General Commissioners (who subsequently relinquished their jurisdiction).
The accountants were asked what witnesses they intended to call in addition to the
taxpayer and what documentary evidence they intended to present apart from the
relevant accounts. A list of the figures in which it was proposed to ask the commissioners   *e*
to determine the appeals for 1976–77 to 1978–79 was enclosed, with an explanation of
how they had been arrived at. The Revenue had prepared an analysis of personal income
and expenditure of the taxpayer in the years ended 30 April 1974 and 30 April 1975,
based on documents and information supplied by the accountants. Two items in the
analysis were estimated figures: for Class 2 NIC and expenses for living and for running
a car. Setting the income figures for each year against the outgoings (including the two   *f*
estimated items) the analysis suggested a minimum deficiency of income to meet
personal expenditure, in the first year of £1,436 and in the second year of £3,267. The
inspector then dealing with the matter took the view that the deficiency for 1976–77
represented business takings not reflected in the taxpayer's accounts, and she made, on
the same day as the letter was written, a further assessment for 1975–76 in the sum of
£3,000, to make good tax lost to the Crown as a result of the taxpayer's fraud, wilful   *g*
default or neglect. The inspector's view was that 'the alleged understatement of profits
would be likely to have occurred consistently'. In the absence of information enabling
her to quantify the extent to which it might have occurred in the years ended 30 April
1976 and 1977, she took the base figure of £3,000 (the deficiency of £3,267 for the year
ended 5 April 1975 rounded down) and scaled it forward for inflation using the consumer
price index factors for calendar years. A schedule of the computation resulting from the   *h*
exercise, which otherwise adopted the figures in the accounts, was enclosed. The inspector
invited the accountants to indicate which figures in the analysis they did not accept,
giving alternative figures and supporting evidence or information with a view to
establishing the analysis as an 'agreed document'. She invited the accountants to give
reasons for claiming that a balancing charge was not due for 1978–79 on account of the
machinery sold and indicated her intention of asking for precepts to be issued for   *j*
accounts for the two years ended 5 April 1981 in respect of income from property. She
also set out her views of the capital of £9,000 introduced in the year to 30 April 1975
and the reasons for dissatisfaction with the evidence offered in relation to it. Her view
was that the £9,000 represented business profits not reflected in the taxpayer's accounts,
accumulated partly in the year ended 30 April 1975 and partly in earlier years.

a
8. As the commissioners had already indicated (see paras 5 and 6 above), no submissions were made on behalf of the taxpayer.

9. The inspector's submissions were summarised as follows.

9.1 The main doubt about the introduction of the capital of £9,000 was the inadequate evidence as to its source. The letters dated 17 April from the accountants to the Revenue referred to in para 7.3 were at best no more than hearsay evidence. The taxpayer had consistently refused to attend the tax office to provide further information. The absence
b of satisfactory records in respect of a transfer of money, for which permission would almost certainly have had to be obtained under Israeli law, had not been explained. If the taxpayer's relatives in Israel were sufficiently wealthy to give him £9,000 in 1974, he would scarcely have needed to maintain his father in 1965–66 and 1966–67, the years for which he claimed dependent relative relief in respect of his father.

9.2 The statement of incomings and outgoings included estimates for living and car
c expenses of £1,500 in the first year and £2,000 in the second year. Those were not extravagant figures yet even so they suggested that there was no money at all available for the taxpayer to live on.

9.3 The estimated assessment of £8,000 for 1975–76 was not appealed against. The further assessment of £3,000 was for 1975–76, the year when the capital of £9,000 was introduced into the business. It was reasonable to assume that there was some under-
d recording of receipts in the year to 5 April 1974 and that £9,000 had somehow been saved from, but not put through the accounts of, the business, possibly over a number of years. The replies received from the accountants in answer to queries about the way in which the accounts had been drawn up indicated that the accounts were prepared from incomplete records.

9.4 The explanation about drawings in the letter from the accountants dated 30
e November 1977 (see para 7.4) suggested the possibility that cash sales had been overlooked. There were no balance sheets for the years ended 30 April 1976 and 1977, and so no subsequent adjustment for debtors (£2,739) and creditors (£14,517) recorded in the 30 April 1975 balance sheet and no records subsequent thereto of drawings from the business.

9.5 In the absence of a more satisfactory explanation it was for the taxpayer to displace
f the assessments from 1976–77 onwards. The assessments should be determined in the figures suggested by the Revenue, including the balancing charge of £2,600 for 1978–79, full initial allowances having been given for machinery previously acquired.

9.6 Notices under s 51(1)(b) of the Taxes Management Act 1970 should be given in respect of 1979–80, 1980–81 and 1981–82, in relation to income under Sch D, Case I and in relation also to income under Sch A.

g
9.7 An interest certificate under s 88 of the 1970 Act in respect of the further assessment for 1975–76 should be granted. On the basis of the figures put forward by the inspector (in the letter dated 24 November 1981: see para 7.6), and having regard to the inadequacy of the explanations put forward on behalf of the taxpayer, it was open to the commissioners to find that the taxpayer had been guilty of wilful default but, since the further assessment for 1975–76 was made in time, it would be sufficient for the
h purposes of an interest certificate to find neglect. The figures prepared by the inspector were sufficient evidence that there had been omissions of income (see *Amis v Colls (Inspector of Taxes)* (1960) 39 TC 148 at 161–162).

10. The commissioners took the view that the taxpayer's accountants had been made sufficiently aware, both from the extended correspondence with the Revenue and in particular from the letter of 24 November 1981 (see para 7.6), of the case that had to be
j met. It appeared to the commissioners that the taxpayer was content to leave the handling of the matters in issue to the accountants. The accountants, on being told of the desirability of sending a representative to the appeal meeting, complied in form only, Mr De Silva being empowered only to read (should the commissioners admit it) the taxpayer's statement and to note the commissioners' decision. The commissioners dealt with the matters before them in the manner set out in para 11.

11. The commissioners decided as follows:

'1975/76   *a*
We decided, upon the facts found by us [paragraph 7], and on the authority of
Amis v Colls), that the Inspector had made out a *prima facie* case that there had been
omissions from the accounts for the year to 30 April 1974 which formed the basis
of assessment for the year 1975/76. In the absence of representations before us on
behalf of the [taxpayer] that there was no *prima facie* case to answer, it was open to
us to find that there had been wilful default or neglect. ([The inspector] did not   *b*
contend that there had been fraud.) As the further assessment for 1975/76, being
made on 24 November 1981, was in time, it was not necessary for us to do more
than find neglect. We did find that there was neglect.
We confirmed the assessment under Case I in the sum of £3,000.

1976/77, 1977/78 and 1978/79   *c*
Upon the facts found by us, and in the absence of any representations before us
on behalf of the [taxpayer], or any response by the Accountants to the figures put
before them in the Inspector's letter of 24 November 1981, we determined these
assessments in accordance with the Inspector's figures, as follows:—

	Case I	Schedule A
		d
1976/77	Increased from £12,000 to £14,562	Reduced to nil
1977/78	Reduced from £12,000 to nil. Losses £818	Confirmed in the sum of £100
1978/79	Reduced from £15,000 to £3,221 (which included a balancing charge of £2,600)	Confirmed in the sum of £200

e
We determined the Class 4 National Insurance Contributions in accordance with
the determinations of income.

Interest Certificate
We granted a certificate under Section 70(3) Taxes Management Act 1970 that
the tax charged by the further assessment for 1975/76 carries interest.   *f*

Section 51
We refused to give a notice under Section 51(1)(*b*) Taxes Management Act 1970;
we agreed to give a notice under Section 51(1)(*a*) requiring the delivery of particulars
sufficient to enable the Inspector to determine the chargeable income of the
[taxpayer] in respect of each of the years 1979/80, 1980/81 and 1981/82, and   *g*
postponed the hearing of those appeals sine die for hearing in due course, should
that be necessary, before any two Commissioners.
(Our Clerk has since been informed by the Inland Revenue that it is considered
that the notice has been complied with.)'

12. Immediately after the determination of the assessments in respect of the years   *h*
1975–76 to 1978–79 the commissioners invited Mr De Silva to express dissatisfaction on
behalf of the taxpayer, which (but only after the desirability of doing so in order to
preserve the taxpayer's right to appeal against the determinations had been explained to
him) he did. On 28 October 1982 the accountants, on behalf of the taxpayer, required
the commissioners to state a case for the opinion of the court pursuant to the Taxes
Management Act 1970, s 56.   *j*
13. The questions of law for the opinion of the court were: (1) whether the
commissioners' decision not to admit the document submitted on behalf of the taxpayer
and described as 'Pleadings and Affidavit' was correct; (2) whether, given the
commissioner's finding that the inspector had made out a prima facie case that there had
been omissions from the accounts which formed the basis of the further assessment for

1975–76, and in the absence of any representations on behalf of the taxpayer, it was open
a to the commissioners (a) to confirm the further assessment for 1975–76 and (b) to grant
a certificate under s 70(3) of the 1970 Act in respect of the tax charged by that assessment;
(3) whether it was correct, given the findings of fact, for the commissioners to increase
the assessment for 1976–77.

b *C W Koenigsberger* for the taxpayer.
Robert Carnwath for the Crown.

HARMAN J. This purports to be an appeal by case stated against a decision of the
Special Commissioners given at their meeting held on 25 October 1982. It is most unlike
all ordinary revenue cases stated in that it depends on no issue of substantive revenue
c law, nor on any interpretation of facts found by the Special Commissioners. The
submissions put by counsel for the taxpayer are that the conduct of the hearing before
the Special Commissioners was erroneous in point of law, so that no proper hearing took
place at all. Effectively he is not concerned with the detail of the case or with the possible
arguments of law arising on it: he simply submits that his client never had a proper
hearing at all. One of the oddities is that in fact that was not the position adopted by the
d taxpayer at the hearing because a 'hearing' is one of the things he did not want. The
taxpayer wished to have a rehearsal of arguments in writing, and not a hearing. The
taxpayer is apparently in difficult circumstances and claims (there is no admissible
evidence about it) that he is unable to afford proper representation by skilled people to
present his arguments for him.

The matter arose as follows. There had been a very long history of failure to supply
e documents, failure to answer questions, failure to produce accounts and so on, leading
eventually to a long and detailed letter from the relevant inspector of taxes to accountants
acting for the taxpayer, dated 24 November 1981. No response was received to that letter,
and eventually these appeals were listed for hearing some eleven months later. The
Friday before the Monday on which the appeals were due for hearing, a bundle of
documents marked 'Pleadings and Affidavits' was handed in to the commissioners.
f Counsel for the taxpayer has conducted this case, in my view correctly, on the proposition
that the affidavit part of the documents was plainly inadmissible and improper, and the
commissioners were right not to look at it.

The Monday following, a person called Mr De Silva came to the hearing. The
accountant who had been advising the taxpayer did not himself attend. Mr De Silva is
described as a member of the accountants' staff, and appears to have been a fairly low-
g grade employee. He apparently told the Special Commissioners that he knew nothing of
the case other than what he had learned from a partial reading of the taxpayer's statement
(that appears to be a reference to a statement of, presumably, facts) and that he had
attended merely to read the statement and to note the outcome. He gave no explanation
of why the taxpayer lacked the common courtesy to come or to send any letter to the
commissioners explaining why he could not come. Mr De Silva stated (it must have been
h a matter of evidence, and what the foundation of fact was is unknown) that the taxpayer
was 'inarticulate and unable to speak well'. Whether he had a stutter, a distinct cockney
accent, or what, is not explained. No postponement of the hearing was sought.

Faced with this situation, a situation in which a very long process had gone on,
culminating in a long and detailed letter 11 months earlier setting out the full Revenue
case, so that every opportunity to meet it had been given, followed by the delivery of
j documents described as 'Pleadings and Affidavits' coupled with an unexplained refusal to
attend, the commissioners were in difficulty as to what they should do. It is plain that
the commissioners are a body constituted under statute. Their procedure, it is common
ground between counsel for the Crown and counsel for the taxpayer, is regulated by s 50
of the Taxes Management Act 1970, supplemented to some degree by further sections of
that Act which are not material for present purposes. Section 50 contains in it sub-s (5),

and I was handed by way of exposition of the argument put by counsel for the Crown an interesting memorandum showing the history of s 50(5).   *a*

It starts, amusingly, by having been exactly the opposite of what it is today. In 1880, the prohibition was enacted in s 57(9) of the Taxes Management Act 1880, which provided:

> 'No barrister, solicitor, attorney, or any person practising the law [I suppose the last phrase refers to special pleaders in equity] shall be allowed to plead before the said Commissioners on such appeal for the appellant . . . either vivâ voce or by writing.'   *b*

Thus, the total exclusion of lawyers was the then rule. Gradually that was transformed, and the words 'vivâ voce' were turned into 'orally', so that today, in s 50(5) of the Taxes Management Act 1970, it reads:

> 'Upon any appeal the Commissioners shall [it is mandatory] permit any barrister or solicitor to plead before them . . . either orally or in writing, and shall hear any accountant . . .'   *c*

that is to say a qualified accountant. It is notable that there is a distinction drawn between the privilege thereby conferred on the legal profession as a whole to plead either orally or in writing, and on accountants, who are required to be heard but in respect of whom no reference to writing is made.   *d*

The basic submission put by counsel for the taxpayer is that s 50, although it is the procedural section, is subject to and supplemented by the rules of natural justice. With that counsel for the Crown does not quarrel. Counsel for the taxpayer goes on to assert that it is a rule of natural justice that every person may put before the body deciding his cause his arguments in any such form as he pleases: by film, by tape recording, by writing   *e* or by any sort of method. In my judgment, there is no such rule of natural justice. The rule of natural justice that will apply is that well-known and basic proposition, audi alteram partem: each side has a right to be heard. Without placing too much stress on the word 'heard', or on the word 'hear' in s 50(5), it seems to me that the whole concept of the common law has at all times been for 'hearings', that is how cases in court and, of course, tribunals are commonly described, to be conducted by oral argument. There are,   *f* of course, qualifications to that. In the House of Lords, litigants have for generations been required to put in a printed case, which is an elaborate written document. None the less, the argument before the House of Lords is conducted orally. In the courts many documents in writing are placed before the court, but the hearing is conducted orally. In my judgment, if a litigant in person wishes to conduct a hearing before the court, he cannot simply put his arguments in writing and refuse to come; he must attend the   *g* hearing and present the arguments.

Of course litigants may well be allowed to supplement their arguments, which they may be afraid they have expressed badly or which they may wish to clarify because they are inarticulate, by summarising them in writing and putting down the points, even developing them in writing, and handing them in, saying, 'There is the basis of my argument; will you, the tribunal, read it?' But that is a very different thing from the   *h* proposition that there is a basic right to conduct your case in any such manner as you choose, and, in particular, to conduct your case in writing without your own attendance. In my judgment there is no such right, and there is no entitlement as a matter of natural justice to present cases in writing. I therefore reject the taxpayer's first argument.

His second argument was that to refuse to allow argument to be presented in writing was contrary to the express statutory provision in s 50(5). In my judgment that is to   *j* reverse the whole nature of s 50(5), which confers a special privilege on the legal profession, granted, I suppose, because it was hoped that their pieces of paper would be relevant and adequately expressed, a hope which I fear is too often not realised. None the less, it is a privilege granted, and it is drawn by express contrast to what is allowed to accountants. In my view it is completely inconsistent with the proposition that all

a litigants have a right to present their cases in writing and that this subsection is some extension to the legal profession of that right. This is a special privilege granted, and it carries no wider or more general right.

The taxpayer's third argument was that the Special Commissioners here had a discretion to look at this bundle of documents which they failed to exercise properly. It is, as I have said, accepted by the Crown, and I have myself accepted in this judgment, that there is a power, not a duty, to allow documentary argument, documentary **b** summaries and so on, to be put in. Indeed, the little summary of the history of s 50(5) put in before me here is exactly such a matter, and one knows very well that in heavy cases a summary of their main points is frequently put in, in writing, by counsel. The discretion thus exists, and is shown to have been exercised by Special Commissioners in a case which counsel for the taxpayer cited to me: *Caldicott v Varty (Inspector of Taxes)* [1976] 3 All ER 329 at 331, where it appears, from para 7 of the case, that 'The taxpayer **c** was not present or represented at the hearing before' the commissioners in that matter and that 'The following written representations by the taxpayer were read by the Crown's representative', obviously by agreement with the Crown. There is thus a discretion, and it is indeed on occasion exercised in favour of the admission of written documents even if the taxpayer is not there.

The difficulty here is: on what grounds am I, as a matter of law, to say that the **d** commissioners, who considered the matter and who set out in para 6 of the case stated their decision not to admit the document, erred in law? What did they fail to take into account which they should have taken into account, or what principle of law did they not consider? Counsel for the taxpayer submits that it must in every case be that you should read the document which you are asked to exercise your discretion to admit before you decide whether or not to admit it. In my judgment that is to seek to put the **e** cart before the horse. The question is: should you admit it? If you do, then you read it. And the reasons why you should admit it will be properly urged in a letter or in some other form of representation, or by an employee, in this case Mr De Silva, who attended on this occasion and who could have been instructed to submit that matter.

But here the commissioners were faced with no explanations but with a document described as 'Pleadings and Affidavits'. It is conceded so far as the affidavit part is **f** concerned that they rightly should not have looked at it, because it would have been an attempt to give evidence which would not have been lawful evidence within the appropriate provisions in the Taxes Management Act 1970. It would have struck me, as it would strike many lawyers, that a document described as 'Pleadings and Affidavits' would probably contain in the pleadings part averments of fact and in the affidavit part evidence to support those facts. That is how any practising lawyer would take those **g** words. Counsel for the taxpayer points out to me, in my view correctly, that s 50(5) itself, in using the word 'plead', as it does, plainly uses it in the form of 'argue', which is a perfectly proper use of the English language; and he says that the Special Commissioners should have understood that this bundle called 'Pleadings and Affidavits' may have consisted in part of argument and in part of evidence, and they should have read the argument while not reading the evidence.

h It is quite plain that no such proposition was advanced to the Special Commissioners, and it is in my view uncertain whether they in fact ever considered that it may have contained argument on questions of law or on inferences which were properly to be drawn from the primary facts before the Special Commissioners. The great probability is, in my view, that it would not have contained any such thing. The whole history of this matter, which in my view the Special Commissioners were entitled to bear in mind **j** in considering the exercise of their discretion, shows a long history of delay and of failure to provide documents and suchlike, and no suggestion of reasoned argument based on propositions of law or on inferences to be drawn which contradicted the Crown's main contention.

It seems to me that the commissioners were placed in a difficult and unenviable state, with a document which is admittedly now partly if not wholly inadmissible and

irregular, and that in looking at the document and considering the history they were
entitled to come to the conclusion, and no error of law is demonstrated in their so doing,   *a*
that they would not admit the bundle into the hearing. It seems to me that they acted in
a way in which I confess I think I would have been likely to act, and certainly not in a
way which demonstrates any error which I, sitting here, could possibly correct. In my
judgment, therefore, there is no substantive point raised on the hearing before the Special
Commissioners, and this appeal must be dismissed.

   b

Appeal dismissed with costs. Order for costs not to be enforced without leave of the court.

Solicitors: *Kean & Kean*, Hampstead (for the taxpayer); *Solicitor of Inland Revenue*.

Clare Mainprice   Barrister.

   c

The Andria

COURT OF APPEAL, CIVIL DIVISION
WALLER, SLADE AND ROBERT GOFF LJJ
8, 10 NOVEMBER, 19 DECEMBER 1983

   d

*Admiralty – Jurisdiction – Action in rem – Arrest of ship – Plaintiff invoking jurisdiction to obtain
security for award in arbitration proceedings – Plaintiff swearing affidavit in ex parte application
for arrest – Affidavit not disclosing existence of arbitration proceedings or that arbitration being*   *e*
*actively pursued – Warrant for arrest issued – Whether Admiralty Court having jurisdiction to
arrest ship where plaintiff's purpose is to obtain security in arbitration proceedings – Whether
court should exercise discretion to arrest ship where plaintiff's purpose is to obtain security in
arbitration proceedings – Whether court should refuse to exercise jurisdiction if plaintiff's affidavit
fails to disclose material fact of arbitration proceedings – Administration of Justice Act 1956,
s 1(1) – RSC Ord 75, r 5(1).*

   f

In September 1979 the plaintiffs, who were the owners of cargo lately laden on the
defendants' only ship, issued a writ in rem in the Admiralty Court claiming damages
against the defendants for breach of the contract of carriage of the cargo. The plaintiffs
did not serve the writ, although they renewed it a year later. In April 1981 the parties
reached agreement to arbitrate. Since at that time the defendants were not aware of the
action in rem the arbitration agreement did not provide for stay of the action.   *g*
Furthermore, the arbitration agreement did not require the defendants to provide
security for payment of any award made against them in the arbitration, and nor did the
defendants respond to inquiries by the plaintiffs seeking such security. Consequently the
plaintiffs had no security for any award they might obtain in the arbitration. The parties
actively pursued the arbitration. In July 1981 the defendants sold the ship, which was   *h*
their only asset. When the ship entered English waters in August 1981 the plaintiffs
applied ex parte in the Admiralty Court to serve on the ship their writ in the action in
rem and also applied for the arrest of the ship, their purpose being to obtain security for
their claim in the arbitration proceedings. The plaintiffs swore an affidavit in support of
the warrant of arrest, in which they failed to disclose the arbitration agreement of April
1981 or that the parties were actively pursuing arbitration. On the basis of that affidavit   *j*
the plaintiffs obtained a warrant and the ship was arrested. The defendants' protection
and indemnity club furnished an undertaking to the plaintiffs that the club would pay
any sum awarded to the plaintiffs in the arbitration in return for the ship's release from
arrest. The ship was then released from arrest. The plaintiffs informed the defendants
that they did not intend to proceed with the action in rem unless it proved necessary in

order to maintain or enforce security in the arbitration. The defendants applied to the
_a_ Admiralty Court for an order discharging the undertaking given to procure the ship's
release and a declaration that the court had no jurisdiction to arrest the ship, because the
Admiralty jurisdiction in rem under s 1(1)(g)^a of the Administration of Justice Act 1956
to hear and determine a claim for damage to goods carried in a ship, and the jurisdiction
under RSC Ord 75, r 5(1)^b to arrest the ship against which the action was brought, could
not be invoked for the purpose of obtaining security for an award in arbitration
_b_ proceedings. The judge granted the order and made the declaration sought. The plaintiffs
appealed.

Held – (1) Where a plaintiff filed and issued a writ in an action in rem which was
indorsed with a claim which fell within s 1(1) of the 1956 Act and also filed an affidavit
for the purpose of the arrest of the ship against which the action was brought, that was
_c_ sufficient to found the Admiralty Court's jurisdiction to arrest the ship pursuant to the
power contained in RSC Ord 75, r 5(1). The plaintiff's purpose in invoking the Admiralty
jurisdiction was irrelevant to the existence of the jurisdiction, and therefore even though
that purpose was simply to obtain security in arbitration proceedings the Admiralty
Court had jurisdiction to arrest the relevant ship. Accordingly, the judge had erred in
making the declaration sought by the defendants (see p 1133 e to p 1134 c, post); _The Cap_
d Bon [1967] 1 Lloyd's Rep 543 and _The Maritime Trader_ [1981] 2 Lloyd's Rep 153 not
followed.
    (2) However, exercise of the power of arrest under RSC Ord 75, r 5(1) was discretionary,
not mandatory, and could therefore be affected by the manner in which or the purpose
for which the plaintiff invoked the Admiralty jurisdiction. Since the Admiralty Court's
purpose in exercising its power of arrest under Ord 75, r 5(1) was to provide security in a
_e_ plaintiff's action in rem, it followed that where a plaintiff invoked the Admiralty
jursidiction to arrest a ship simply to obtain security in other proceedings, such as an
arbitration, the court would exercise its discretion by refusing to issue a warrant of arrest.
Furthermore, on an ex parte application for the arrest of a ship a plaintiff was under a
duty to make full disclosure to the court of all the material facts. The plaintiffs' failure to
disclose in their affidavit that arbitration proceedings were being actively pursued and
_f_ that their purpose in invoking the jurisdiction was to obtain security for an award in
those proceedings was a failure to disclose material facts that amounted to vexatious
conduct and an abuse of the court's process. It followed that the judge was right to
discharge the undertaking given to secure the ship's release from arrest and the appeal
from the judge's order would therefore be dismissed (see p 1134 _b f g_ and p 1135 _a_ to p
1136 _c_, post); _The Rena K_ [1979] 1 All ER 397 distinguished.

_g_ **Notes**
For the jurisdiction in rem, see 1 Halsbury's Laws (4th edn) para 311, and for cases on the
subject, see 1(1) Digest (Reissue) 219–223, 1240–1251.
    For the Administration of Justice Act 1956, s 1, see 1 Halsbury's Statutes (3rd edn) 21.
    Section 1 of the 1956 Act was replaced by s 20 of the Supreme Court Act 1981.
_h_   As from a day to be appointed s 26 of the Civil Jurisdiction and Judgments Act 1982
will enable the court on staying or dismissing Admiralty proceedings on the ground,
inter alia, that the dispute should be submitted to arbitration to retain an arrested ship
(or any bail or security given instead) as security for the satisfaction of any award given
in the arbitration.

_j_ **Cases referred to in judgment**
Cap Bon, The [1967] 1 Lloyd's Rep 543.
Dalglish v Jarvis (1850) 2 Mac & G 231, 42 ER 89.

_a_   Section 1(1) so far as material, is set out at p 1132 _j_, post
_b_   Rule 5(1) is set out at p 1133 _h_, post

Golden Trader, The, Danemar Scheepvaart Maatshappij BV v Golden Trader (owners) [1974]
  2 All ER 686, [1975] QB 348, [1974] 3 WLR 16.   *a*
Hagen, The [1908] P 189, [1908–10] All ER Rep 21, CA.
Maritime Trader, The [1981] 2 Lloyd's Rep 153.
Negocios del Mar SA v Doric Shipping Corp SA, The Assios [1979] 1 Lloyd's Rep 331, CA.
R v Kensington Income Tax Comrs, ex p Princess de Polignac [1917] 1 KB 486, CA.
Rena K, The [1979] 1 All ER 397, [1979] QB 377, [1978] 3 WLR 431.

                                                                                                    b
Cases also cited
Banco, The, Monte Ulia (owners) *v Banco* (owners) [1971] 1 All ER 524, [1971] P 137, CA.
Berny, The, Berny (cargo owners) *v Berny* (owners) [1978] 1 All ER 1065, [1979] QB 80.
Cooper v Williams [1963] 2 All ER 282, [1963] 2 QB 567, CA.
Monica S, The, Monica Smith (cargo owners) *v Monica Smith* (now *Monica S* (owners)) [1967] 3
  All ER 740, [1968] P 741.   *c*
Moschanthy, The [1971] 1 Lloyd's Rep 37.
St Anna, The [1983] 2 All ER 691, [1983] 1 WLR 895.

Appeal
The plaintiffs, the owners of cargo lately laden on board the ship Andria, since renamed
the Vasso, appealed from the order of Sheen J made on 23 June 1982 in the appellants'   *d*
action in rem against the respondents as the owners of the Andria claiming damages for
breach of contract and/or duty in the carriage of the appellants' cargo on board the
Andria, whereby on a motion in the action by the respondents Sheen J ordered (1) that
the respondents were entitled to a declaration that the Admiralty Court's jurisdiction
under s 1(1) of the Administration of Justice Act 1956 could not be invoked by the
service on 28 August 1981 of the writ in the action in rem on the vessel when she was in   *e*
port at Ipswich and her consequent arrest, (2) that the service of the writ on, and the
arrest of, the vessel, should be set aside, and (3) that a guarantee or security given on
behalf of the respondents to procure the vessel's release from arrest should be discharged.
The facts are set out in the judgment of the court.

Roger Buckley QC and *Hilary Heilbron* for the appellants.   *f*
Julian Flaux for the respondents.

                                                                                    Cur adv vult

19 December. The following judgment of the court was delivered.
                                                                                                    g

ROBERT GOFF LJ. There is before the court an appeal by the appellants from an
order by Sheen J, under which he ordered that a letter of undertaking given by the
United Kingdom Mutual Steam Ship Assurance Association (Bermuda) Ltd (which I shall
refer to as 'the club'), which had been given in order to procure the release of the ship
Vasso from arrest by the appellants, should be discharged.   *h*
    The Vasso was formerly called the Andria. The appellants have a claim against the
respondents for damage suffered by goods carried on board the Andria, then in the
ownership of the respondents, under a bill of lading dated 1 February 1979. The goods
in question consisted of a cargo of calcium ammonium nitrate in bulk, carried from
Lisbon to Antwerp in February 1979; the appellants allege that during the voyage the
cargo was water-damaged or contaminated by rust and pieces of wood. The ship was a   *j*
chartered ship, and the charterparty contained an arbitration clause. After the appellants'
claim was made, there was a dispute whether the arbitration clause was incorporated into
the bill of lading, the appellants contending that it was and the respondents that it was
not; as a result of recent authority, it is now common ground that it was not so
incorporated.

a However, it was necessary for the appellants to protect their position, having regard to the one-year time limit in the Hague Rules which applied to the bill of lading contract. So the appellants' solicitors caused proceedings to be commenced within that period against the respondents in Greece and also in this country; there were two writs issued in this country, one in an action in rem in the Admiralty Court and the other in an ordinary action in personam in the Commercial Court. The writ in the Admiralty action was issued on 28 September 1979. A year later it was renewed.

b Negotiations took place between the solicitors acting for the parties in this country with a view to entering into an ad hoc arbitration agreement. The negotiations were contained (primarily at least) in letters and telexes passing between the solicitors. Agreement was reached on 24 April 1981; the agreement to arbitrate was expressed to be subject to the appellants discontinuing their proceedings in Greece, which they did. There was no term requiring discontinuance of the proceedings in this country, of which c the repondents knew nothing because neither of the writs had been served. Nor was the ad hoc arbitration agreement made conditional on the provision of security by the respondents to secure payment of any award made against them. The parties then appointed their arbitrators. On 3 July 1981 the appellants' solicitors wrote to the respondents' solicitors proposing an order for directions in the normal form. So the arbitration was being actively pursued, in the usual way.

d Meanwhile, in about July 1981, the respondents had sold the Andria to other shipowners. She was renamed the Vasso. In August 1981, under her new ownership, she entered English waters; she was due to call at Ipswich in late August. The appellants had been keeping a watch on her movements through Lloyd's intelligence department. It appeared to them that they had an opportunity of obtaining security for their claim, by serving the Admiralty writ on the ship and arresting her.

e For the appellants, security for the claim was important. The respondents were a one-ship company; if they sold the ship, they could well dispose of the proceeds and so be unable to meet the appellants' claim. The appellants' solicitors had inquired of the respondents' solicitors, in October 1980, whether, if there was to be an agreement to arbitrate in London, the respondents would put up security; but they received no response to this inquiry. As we have recorded, the ad hoc arbitration agreement was not f made conditional on the provision of security by the respondents. So there was no security for any award made in the arbitration. Then in July 1981 the respondents disposed of their only asset, the ship. To the appellants it must have appeared, in August, that the arrest of the ship at Ipswich provided their only chance of ensuring that an arbitration award against the respondents would be of any value. The mere fact that the respondents had sold the ship was not of itself a bar to serving the Admiralty writ on her g and arresting her because, since the appellants had prudently issued the Admiralty writ while the ship was in the respondents' ownership, and had subsequently renewed it, the Admiralty Court's jurisdiction could be invoked by an action in rem against the ship which was, when the action was brought (ie when the writ was issued), beneficially owned as respects all the shares in her by the respondents (see s 3(4) of the Administration of Justice Act 1956).

h On 27 August 1981 the appellants' solicitors sent a telex message to the respondents' solicitors. They referred to their inquiry about security in October 1980 and continued:

'It has come to our attention that the vessel (now the "Vasso") is currently at Ipswich and our clients have instructed us to renew our request for security. We must therefore request your confirmation by 4 pm today that the club are prepared to provide their undertaking in standard Clyde/Miller wording in the amount of j DM 330,000 plus interest and costs, failing which our instructions are to seek arrest of the vessel. By way of explanation we should add that an in rem writ was issued in 1979 and subsequently renewed and that in support of application for security we would rely on the decision in the "Rena K" ([1978] 1 Lloyd's Rep 345).'

On the following day, 28 August, the respondents' solicitors replied by telex as follows:

'Thanks your telex yesterday contents of which noted. We have taken our clients' instructions and comment as follows:—1. Our clients have disposed of the beneficial interest which they had in the above vessel and have no interest at all in the "Vasso" to which you refer in your telex. 2. The club does not have an entry for the "Vasso" and is therefore not in a position to put up security. 3. We note that a writ was issued in 1979. Since then, our respective clients have agreed that the matters in issue between them should be referred to arbitration in London, and our clients do not accept that you are entitled to take any action against any asset of theirs.'

So, on that day, the appellants' solicitors took steps to arrest the Vasso at Ipswich. An affidavit was sworn on the same day to lead the warrant of arrest. It was in the normal form; but it made no mention of the fact that the parties had in April 1981, after the claim had arisen, entered into an ad hoc arbitration agreement, or that that arbitration was being actively pursued. On the following day, 29 August, a warrant for the arrest having been issued, the writ was served on the Vasso at Ipswich and she was arrested.

As a result of the arrest of the ship, steps were taken to secure her release from arrest by means of a protection and indemnity club (P & I club) undertaking. These negotiations appear to have taken place at first on the telephone, between the parties' solicitors. Then, on 1 September, the respondents' solicitors telexed the appellants' solicitors as follows:

'We refer to our telcon this morning in which we asked for your confirmation that, if a letter of undertaking was to be given by our clients' P and I Club in respect of the claim you mention in your telex of 27th August, you would agree to the incorporation into the said letter of undertaking a provision to the effect that such undertaking would be discharged and cancelled if the English High Court of Justice was to stay the present proceedings unconditionally. Please may we have your confirmation of this so that we may obtain our clients' further instructions.'

The appellants' solicitors replied by telex on the same day as follows:

'Thank you for your telex this morning. Our clients will accept security without prejudice to your right to apply to High Court of Justice for a stay of proceedings and for an order that the said security should be released. We suggest that you send us a draft amendment to the standard Clydes/Millers undertaking.'

On the next day, 2 September, the club furnished its written undertaking to the appellants' solicitors. It provided:

'In consideration of your consenting to the release from arrest and/or refraining from taking action resulting in the arrest of the "vasso" . . . we hereby undertake to pay to your solicitors on your behalf on demand such sums as may be awarded to you in arbitration in London or on appeal therefrom or as may be agreed to be recoverable [from the respondents in respect of the appellants' claim, interest and costs, up to a maximum of DM 500,000].'

The guarantee contained the following express term:

'We undertake that we will, within 14 days of the receipt from you or your solicitors of a request so to do, instruct solicitors to accept on behalf of [the respondents] service of proceedings brought by you in the English High Court of Justice and to enter appearance thereto, without prejudice, however, to any application which may be made to the court for a stay of the proceedings, and/or for an order that the security comprised herein be released.'

The ship was then released from arrest. On 4 September 1981 the appellants' solicitors wrote to the respondents' solicitors as follows:

'We refer to our recent exchanges about this case. As we indicated to you previously, the purpose of the arrest of the "vasso" was to obtain security for our clients' claim in Arbitration, in accordance with the decision in the "Rena K". It is

a
not our clients' intention to proceed further with the High Court action except insofar as this may prove to be necessary for the purpose of maintaining or enforcing the security. Accordingly we are now enclosing by way of service the Points of Claim in the Arbitration. We should be grateful if you would acknowledge receipt in due course. We look forward to receiving your clients' Points of Defence.'

b
With the ship's release from arrest, the immediate urgency went out of the matter, which then took its leisurely course. On 10 March 1982 the respondents issued a notice of motion, asking for the following relief:

c
'(1) ... a declaration that the Admiralty jurisdiction of the said Court under section 1(1) of the Administration of Justice Act 1956 should not have been and cannot be invoked by an action in rem against the vessel ANDRIA now renamed VASSO and, accordingly, that the said vessel ought not to have been arrested at Ipswich in or about September 1981, on the grounds that the claim of the above-named Plaintiffs in respect of which they sought security by way of such arrest has been submitted to arbitration pursuant to an agreement between the parties made in or about April 1981; AND (2) ... an order that the guarantee and/or security up to the amount of DM 500,000 given by the United Kingdom Mutual Steam Ship Assurance Association (Bermuda) Limited on 2nd September 1981 in order to procure the release from arrest of the said vessel ANDRIA now renamed VASSO should be discharged and that the proceedings herein should be stayed on the grounds that the claim in respect of which the Plaintiffs sought security by way of such arrest has been submitted to arbitration; AND (3) for an Order that the costs of this application be paid by the Plaintiffs in any event.'

d

e
The motion was supported by an affidavit sworn by a member of the respondents' solicitors on 17 June 1982. He set out the history of the matter and exhibited certain documents. His affidavit concluded:

f
'In the circumstances, whatever the reason was for the issue of the Writ in rem on 28 September 1979 and its subsequent extension, it is clear from the fact that an arbitration agreement was made in April 1981 and Arbitrators appointed, that the present proceedings were only continued by way of arresting the vessel for the purpose of obtaining security for the claim in arbitration. It was not intended by the Plaintiffs to continue those proceedings in order that this Honourable Court should decide the merits of the Plaintiffs' claim. That is confirmed by the fact that on 7 September 1981, only five days after the P & I Club letter was put up subsequent to the vessel's release from arrest, the Plaintiffs served their Points of Claim in the arbitration. In my respectful submission, this Honourable Court has no power to arrest a vessel solely for the purposes of providing a party with security for a claim in an arbitration as in the present case. Accordingly, I ask for a declaration and/or an Order as set out in the Notice of Motion.'

g

h
On 22 June 1982 a member of the appellants' solicitors swore an affidavit in reply. He set out the history of the matter as seen from his clients' point of view. He concluded with the following paragraph:

'The Defendants are a Company incorporated in Panama. Following the sale of the "ANDRIA" the Defendants have, so far as the Plaintiffs are aware, no assets which would be available for the enforcement of any arbitration award. The Plaintiffs therefore fear that, if the security herein is released unconditionally and if they then obtain an award in respect of the full amount of their Claim, the Defendants might well be unable to satisfy it, even if all available steps to enforce the award were taken. I therefore respectfully request that this Honourable Court should refuse to make the Order sought by the Defendants or should alternatively Order that the security should only be released on terms that the Defendants provide alternative security for payment of any award in the Arbitration.'

j

The matter came on for hearing before Sheen J on 23 June. He held that the appellants' only purpose in arresting the Vasso was to obtain security for the satisfaction of whatever *a* award might ultimately be made by the arbitrators. He held that the appellants invoked the jurisdiction of the Admiralty Court on 28 August 1981, when the writ in rem was served on the ship; on that date, therefore, they did so with the purpose of obtaining security. The appellants did not therefore purport to invoke the jurisdiction of the court for the purpose of hearing and determining any claim. Accordingly, on the basis of his own decision in *The Maritime Trader* [1981] 2 Lloyd's Rep 153, in which he followed *b* earlier decisions of Brandon J in *The Cap Bon* [1967] 1 Lloyd's Rep 543 and *The Rena K* [1979] 1 All ER 397, [1979] QB 377, the court had no jurisdiction to arrest the ship on 28 August 1981. He therefore made the declaration sought by the respondents, and ordered that the club's letter of undertaking be discharged.

From that order, the appellants appealed to this court. Their principal ground of appeal was that the judge erred in law in holding that the court had no jurisdiction to *c* arrest the ship; and it was submitted by counsel for the appellants that, in so far as it was decided otherwise in *The Cap Bon* (which was followed by the judge in the present case), that case was wrongly decided.

The Cap Bon was concerned with a claim by charterers against shipowners under a charterparty containing an arbitration clause. The ship was chartered to carry potatoes from Alexandria to this country; and, while she was being discharged at Liverpool, the *d* charterers commenced an action in rem against her for a cargo damage claim, and the writ was served on her and she was arrested. The shipowners then entered an appearance and a bail bond was provided to obtain the ship's release, the bail bond purporting to provide security for any sum adjudged against the shipowners in the action or in any arbitration proceedings. Nearly three months later, the shipowners commenced arbitration proceedings against the charterers for demurrage; the charterers then *e* appointed their arbitrator both in respect of their cargo damage claim and in respect of the shipowners' demurrage claim. The shipowners subsequently asked the charterers for a statement of claim in the action. The charterers' answer was that the dispute fell within the arbitration clause, that the purpose of the action was to obtain security and that, although they would consent to the action being stayed, they would resist an application for the dismissal of the action. The shipowners then applied for an order that, unless the *f* charterers served a statement of claim by a certain date, the action should be dismissed. Brandon J, reversing the district registrar, granted the order for which the shipowners asked, and also ordered that, in the event of the action being so dismissed, the bail should be released.

The underlying reason for Brandon J's decision was that the charterers had in that case brought two sets of proceedings for their cargo damage claim, that to bring two sets of *g* proceedings for the same claim was prima facie vexatious, and that, when a party does so, the court can compel him to elect whether to go on with the one set of proceedings or the other. The effect of Brandon J's decision was to compel the charterers to make that election. But, in the course of his judgment, he expressed the opinion that the charterers had sought to invoke the Admiralty jurisdiction not to obtain the hearing and determination of a claim but for the purpose of obtaining security for an award in *h* arbitration proceedings, and that an Admiralty court had no jurisdiction to arrest ships or to keep ships under arrest for that purpose. He referred to s 1(1) of the Administration of Justice Act 1956, which provides:

> 'The Admiralty jurisdiction of the High Court shall be as follows, that is to say, jurisdiction to hear and determine any of the following questions or claims [there *j* then follows a series of claims in lettered paragraphs, including] ... (g) any claim for loss of or damage to goods carried in a ship ...'

Next, having referred to s 3(4) of the 1956 Act, Brandon J said ([1967] 1 Lloyd's Rep 543 at 547):

'Sect. 3(4) provides that the Admiralty jurisdiction may be invoked by an action *in rem*, and the jurisdiction referred to is the jurisdiction to hear and determine various types of claim as set out in Sect. 1(1). It is to be inferred from that that the object of the process *in rem* is to provide security for a plaintiff in respect of any judgment which he may obtain as the result of the hearing and determination of a claim. That is the purpose of proceeding *in rem* and, subject to the point I made, that it covers also payment of a sum due under a settlement in an action, it is the sole purpose of such process. It seems to me that in the present case the plaintiffs have sought to invoke the Admiralty jurisdiction of the Court *in rem* for a wholly different purpose, or at any rate seek now to maintain that process for a wholly different purpose. The different purpose is not security for the payment of a judgment of the Court or security for the payment of a sum due under the settlement of an action in the Court, but security for the payment of an award in an arbitration conducted pursuant to Clause 33 of the charter-party. In my view the Admiralty Court has no jurisdiction to arrest ships or to keep ships under arrest for that purpose; it only has jurisdiction to arrest ships and keep ships under arrest for the purpose of providing security for a judgment of the Court. Bail in an Admiralty action *in rem* represents the *res*, and it follows, in my view, that the Admiralty Court has no jurisdiction to require bail as a condition of release, or to maintain that bail, for the collateral purpose to which I have referred.'

He was later to follow his decision in *The Cap Bon* in *The Golden Trader, Danemar Scheepvaart Maatschappij v Golden Trader (owners)* [1974] 2 All ER 686 at 692–693, [1975] QB 348 at 355–356 and (after reconsideration) in *The Rena K* [1979] 1 All ER 397 at 413, [1979] QB 377 at 402.

While we entertain the greatest respect for any opinion expressed by Lord Brandon, we find ourselves unable to agree with his view that the court has no *jurisdiction* to arrest a ship, or to maintain an arrest, where the purpose of the plaintiff is simply to obtain security for an award in arbitration proceedings. We are ourselves unable to conceive of a case where the jurisdiction of the court depends on the purpose of the plaintiff in invoking the court's jurisdiction. Generally speaking, the word 'jurisdiction' simply expresses a power of the court: in cases such as the present, the power of the court to 'hear and determine', ie to adjudicate on, certain types of claim. These types of claim are set out in the lettered paragraphs of what used to be s 1(1) of the Administration of Justice Act 1956 (now s 20(2) of the Supreme Court Act 1981); and, as appears from s 3(4) of the 1956 Act (now s 21(4) of the 1981 Act) that jurisdiction may be invoked by an action in rem in the case of some, though not all, of those types of claim. Of course, where the court's jurisdiction may be invoked by an action in rem, the court must have the power to arrest; the provisions regulating the invocation and exercise of that power are to be found in RSC Ord 75, rr 5 ff, in particular r 5 (concerned with the warrant of arrest) and r 13 (concerned with release of property under arrest). Order 75, r 5(1), provides:

'After a writ has been issued in an action in rem a warrant in Form No. 3 in Appendix B for the arrest of the property against which the action or any counterclaim in the action is brought may, subject to the provisions of this rule, be issued at the instance of the plaintiff or of the defendant, as the case may be.'

This rule reflects the simple fact that, subject to the filing of the necessary praecipe and affidavit, the only prerequisite to the court's jurisdiction to issue a warrant for arrest is that a writ must have been issued in an action in rem. So, provided that a writ is issued on which there is indorsed a claim falling within one of those lettered paragraphs of s 1(1) of the 1956 Act (now s 20(2) of the 1981 Act) which are specified in s 3(4) of the 1956 Act (now s 21(4) of the 1981 Act) as justifying the invocation of the Admiralty jurisdiction by an action in rem, the court, in our judgment, has *jurisdiction* to issue a

warrant for the arrest of the relevant ship, and to execute that warrant, the exercise of
that jurisdiction being regulated by the relevant rules in Ord 75.

In our judgment, the purpose of the plaintiff in invoking the Admiralty jurisdiction
cannot affect the existence of the jurisdiction. The jurisdiction is simply there. The court
has the power to arrest. But the exercise of the power is, as Ord 75, r 5(1) shows, not
mandatory; the court may decline to exercise it. Furthermore, under r 13(4) of Ord 75,
the court has a discretionary power to order the release of property under arrest. The
court's decision whether to exercise either of those powers may be affected by the manner
in which, or the purpose for which, the plaintiff has proceeded. These are matters to
which we will return in a moment.

It follows that we are, with respect, unable to agree with the opinion expressed by
Brandon J that an Admiralty court has no jurisdiction to arrest, or to maintain an arrest
of, a ship when the purpose of the plaintiff is simply to obtain security for an award in
arbitration proceedings; and it also follows that, in the present case, the judge erred in
following that opinion, and in making the declaration sought by the respondents.
However, the matter does not stop there. For the real point at issue between the parties
in the present case is whether the club should or should not be released from its letter of
undertaking. We have therefore to consider whether, on the basis that the court did have
jurisdiction to arrest the ship in the present case, we should interfere with the judge's
order that the club's letter of undertaking should be discharged.

We are concerned in this case with a letter of undertaking given to secure the release
of a ship from arrest, when that arrest was obtained by a party as security for a claim
which he was actively pursuing in arbitration proceedings. We have to consider the
propriety of an arrest obtained in such circumstances; and we think it right to approach
that question in the context of the general principles governing the relationship between
proceedings in arbitration and actions (in particular, actions in rem) in court.

The mere fact that the dispute between the parties falls within the scope of an
arbitration agreement entered into between them does not of itself generally preclude
one of them from bringing an action. Accordingly, the mere existence of an arbitration
agreement will not of itself prevent a party from issuing a writ, or serving the writ and
(in the case of an action in rem) procuring the arrest of the ship, or otherwise proceeding
with the action. But the arbitration agreement can, of course, have certain consequences.
For example, if an action is begun, the other party may apply for a stay of proceedings.
Generally speaking, the court's power to grant a stay in such a case is discretionary;
though of course in cases falling within s 1 of the Arbitration Act 1975 the court is bound
to grant a stay. Again, if a party actively pursues proceedings in respect of the same claim
both in the court and in arbitration, his so proceeding may be regarded as vexatious and
an abuse of the process of the court; if so, the court may, in the exercise of its inherent
power, require him to elect in which forum he will pursue his claim: see *The Cap Bon*
[1967] 1 Lloyd's Rep 543.

Next, let it be supposed that, before the court has granted a stay of proceedings under
the Arbitration Acts, the plaintiff has obtained security by the arrest of a ship in an action
in rem. If the stay is granted in the exercise of its discretionary power under s 4 of the
Arbitration Act 1950, the court may require, as a condition of granting a stay, that
alternative security should be made available to secure an award made in the arbitration
proceedings see *The Golden Trader* [1974] 2 All ER 686, [1975] QB 348. If a mandatory
stay is granted under s 1 of the Arbitration Act 1975, no such term can be imposed. But
it has been held by Brandon J that, where it is shown by the plaintiff that an arbitration
award in his favour is unlikely to be satisfied by the defendant, the security available in
the action in rem may be ordered to stand so that, if the plaintiff may have thereafter to
pursue the action in rem (possibly using an unsatisfied arbitration award for the purpose
of an issue estoppel) the security will remain available in that action: see *The Rena K*
[1979] 1 All ER 397, [1979] QB 377. (We have not had to consider the principle in that
case, and we have not heard argument on the point; however, we proceed on the basis
that that principle is sound.)

However, on the law as it stands at present, the court's jurisdiction to arrest a ship in
an action in rem should not be exercised for the purpose of providing security for an
award which may be made in arbitration proceedings. That is simply because the purpose
of the exercise of the jurisdiction is to provide security in respect of the action in rem,
and not to provide security in some other proceedings, eg arbitration proceedings. The
time may well come when the law on this point may be changed: see s 26 of the Civil
Jurisdiction and Judgments Act 1982, which has however not yet been brought into
force. But that is not yet the law. It follows that, if a plaintiff invokes the jurisdiction of
the court to obtain the arrest of a ship as security for an award in arbitration proceedings,
the court should not issue a warrant of arrest. Of course, if the plaintiff fails to reveal that
arbitration proceedings are being actively pursued and that his purpose is to obtain
security for an award in those proceedings, the court may inadvisedly issue a warrant.
But for a plaintiff so to proceed may be vexatious and an abuse of the process of the court.
Not only has he failed to disclose material facts to the court on an ex parte application,
but he has actively pursued proceedings in court at the same time as actively pursuing
arbitration proceedings, which is (unless the plaintiff is seeking, on appropriate evidence,
security in the action on the principle in *The Rena K*) vexatious. If so, the court may, on
learning of the material facts, order the release of the ship from arrest, and may order the
discharge of any security provided consequent on the arrest.

In the present case, we see precisely such an abuse of process. The affidavit sworn to
lead the warrant of arrest was in the usual form. But nothing was said in it about the
facts that, after the dispute had arisen, the parties had entered into an ad hoc arbitration
agreement with the plain intention that the dispute should be dealt with by arbitration,
and that the parties were, at the time when the affidavit was sworn, actively pursuing
proceedings under that arbitration agreement. Yet on those facts, in the absence of any
evidence justifying an arrest of the ship as security in the action under the principle in
The Rena K, it would have been apparent that the arrest was being sought to obtain
security for an arbitration award; and, on the law as it stands at present, a ship should not
be arrested for that purpose. Though we do not for one moment suggest any bad faith
on the part of the deponent, the fact is that the affidavit sworn to lead the warrant of
arrest failed to disclose facts which were material to the issue of the warrant; and, as a
result of that non-disclosure, the warrant was issued and thereafter the ship was arrested
and the club undertaking given to procure the release of the ship from arrest. The form
of the club undertaking confirms all too clearly the fact that the purpose of the appellants
was (despite reference to *The Rena K* in certain documents) to obtain security for an award
in arbitration proceedings. It follows, in our judgment, that the invocation by the
appellants of the court's jurisdiction to arrest the ship amounted in the circumstances of
the case to an abuse of the process of the court and that the club's letter of undertaking
must be discharged.

Counsel for the appellants submitted that, on the facts at the time, they were entitled
to have the ship arrested on the principle in *The Rena K*, because the respondents, having
disposed of their only asset, would in all probability have no means to satisfy any
arbitration award. Of course, the principle in *The Rena K* could not justify obtaining
security for an arbitration award as such; and so this submission did not provide any basis
for justifying the obtaining of security in the form of the club's letter of undertaking.
The thrust of the argument of counsel for the appellants must have been that, if the court
was minded to order that the club's letter of undertaking should be discharged, it should
only do so on the terms that fresh security should be provided, on *The Rena K* principle,
to secure a judgment in the action. But the difficulty with this submission is that,
although the facts may have been there to support the obtaining of security in the action
on *The Rena K* principle, they were not deposed to in the affidavit sworn to lead the
warrant of arrest, which in due course led to the club giving its letter of undertaking. It
is axiomatic that in ex parte proceedings there should be full and frank disclosure to the
court of facts known to the applicant, and that failure to make such disclosure may result
in the discharge of any order made on the ex parte application, even though the facts

were such that, with full disclosure, an order would have been justified (see *R v Kensington Income Tax Comrs, ex p Princess de Polignac* [1917] 1 KB 486). Examples of this principle are to be found in the case of ex parte injunctions (*Dalglish v Jarvis* (1850) 2 Mac & G 231, 42 ER 89), ex parte orders made for service of proceedings out of the jurisdiction under RSC Ord 11 (*The Hagen* [1908] P 189 at 201, [1908–10] All ER Rep 21 at 26 per Farwell LJ) and Mareva injunctions (*Negocios del Mar SA v Doric Shipping Corp SA, The Assios* [1979] 1 Lloyd's Rep 331). In our judgment, exactly the same applies in the case of an ex parte application for the arrest of a ship where, as here, there has not been full disclosure of the material facts to the court.

Accordingly, the court having in the present case issued the warrant of arrest on the basis of an affidavit which failed to disclose material facts, the appropriate course was to make an unconditional order for the discharge of the security obtained by reason of the arrest. For these reasons, although we shall (for the reasons we have given) set aside the declaration made by the judge, we shall dismiss the appeal from his order that the letter of undertaking be discharged.

In conclusion, there are certain observations which we wish to make. First, during the course of the argument before this court, there was some discussion of the possibility that the appropriate course of the respondents, in the circumstances of the present case, would be to apply for a stay of the action in rem; and indeed we gave them leave to amend their respondent's notice for this purpose. However, we now consider that the appropriate way of dealing with the matter is to order simply that the letter of undertaking should be discharged, for the reasons we have given. A stay of proceedings is unnecessary for this purpose.

Second, we wish to observe that technical problems of the kind which have fallen for consideration in this case, and which fell for consideration in *The Rena K*, would very largely disappear if s 26 of the Civil Jurisdiction and Judgments Act 1982 were to be brought into force.

Declaration set aside. Appeal against order dismissed.

Solicitors: *Clyde & Co* (for the appellants); *Richards Butler & Co* (for the respondents).

Sophie Craven   Barrister.

End of Volume 1